THE FOURTEENTH MENTAL MEASUREMENTS YEARBOOK

EARLIER PUBLICATIONS IN THIS SERIES

THE FOURTEENTH MENTAL MEASUREMENTS YEARBOOK

BARBARA S. PLAKE and JAMES C. IMPARA

Editors

LINDA L. MURPHY
Managing Editor

The Buros Institute of Mental Measurements
The University of Nebraska-Lincoln
Lincoln, Nebraska

2001
Distributed by The University of Nebraska Press

Note to Users

TABLE OF CONTENTS

INTRODUCTION

This publication of *The Fourteenth Mental Measurements Yearbook* (*14th MMY*) is the Buros Institute's first publication in the new millennium. Ushering in the new century has brought some important changes to the *Mental Measurements Yearbook* series. As always, the volume contains candidly critical reviews of commercially available tests that are new or have been revised since the publication of the last *Yearbook*. However, two changes should be noted. There is now an additional criterion for tests to meet in order to receive a review and we are discontinuing test references.

Previously, to be reviewed in the *Yearbook*, a test had to be (a) commercially available, (b) new or revised since last reviewed in the *MMY* series, and (c) published in the English language. There was no criterion related to the availability of technical documentation. Starting with the *14th MMY*, in order to be reviewed in the *Yearbook* series, a test must meet the previous criteria, *and* in addition, have at least some documentation about its development and/or technical properties.

In previous volumes in the *MMY* series, test references were selected by Buros Institute staff who searched through hundreds of professional journals. Because of the availability of online search features that allow users to do independent reference searches, it was our decision to discontinue providing such references in the *MMY* series.

THE FOURTEENTH MENTAL MEASUREMENTS YEARBOOK

The *14th MMY* contains reviews of tests that are new or significantly revised since the publication of the *13th MMY* in 1998. Reviews, descriptions, and references associated with many older tests can be located in other Buros publications: previous *MMY*s and *Tests in Print V*.

Content. The contents of the *14th MMY* include: (a) a bibliography of 430 commercially available tests, new or revised, published as separates for use with English-speaking subjects; (b) 802 critical test reviews by well-qualified professional people who were selected by the editors on the basis of their expertise in measurement and, often, the content of the test being reviewed; (c) a test title index with appropriate cross-references; (d) a classified subject index; (e) a publishers directory and index, including publisher addresses and other contact information with test listings by publisher; (f) a name index including the names of authors of all tests, reviews, or references included in this *MMY*; (g) an index of acronyms for easy reference when a test acronym, not the full title, is known; and (h) a score index to refer readers to tests featuring particular scores of interest to them.

As noted above, in order for tests to be reviewed in this and future *Yearbooks*, they must meet an additional criterion related to the availability of documentation about test development or technical properties. Therefore, not all tests submitted for review are reviewed in this volume. In order to make users aware of the availability of these tests, albeit without supporting documentation, a listing of tests (including name of publisher) received but not reviewed is included in the Appendix. The Appendix also includes a list of tests that meet review criteria but that were received too late for review in this volume. These tests (plus additional tests received in the coming months) will be reviewed in *The Fifteenth Mental Measurements Yearbook*.

Organization. The volume is organized like an encyclopedia, with tests being ordered alphabetically by title. If the title of a test is known, the reader can locate the test immediately without having to consult the Index of Titles.

The page headings reflect the encyclopedic organization. The page heading of the left-hand page cites the number and title of the first test listed on that page, and the page heading of the right-hand page cites the number and title of the last test listed on that page. All numbers presented in the various indexes are test numbers, not page numbers. Page numbers are important only for the Table of Contents and are located at the bottom of each page.

TESTS AND REVIEWS

The *14th MMY* contains descriptive information on 430 tests as well as 802 test reviews by 461 different authors. Statistics on the number and percentage of tests in each of 18 major classifications are contained in Table 1.

The percentage of new and revised or supplemented tests according to major classifications are contained in Table 2. Overall, 296 of the tests included in the *14th MMY* are new and have not been listed in a previous *MMY* although many descriptions were included in *Tests in Print V* (*TIP V*; 1999). The Index of Titles can be consulted to determine if a test is new or revised.

Test Selection. A new policy for selecting tests for review is effective for this *14th MMY*. The new policy for selecting tests for review requires at least minimal information be available regarding test development. The requirement that tests have such minimal information does not

TABLE 2
NEW AND REVISED OR SUPPLEMENTED TESTS BY MAJOR CLASSIFICATION

Classification	Number of Tests	Percentage New	Revised
Achievement	15	53.3	46.7
Behavior Assessment	37	73.0	27.0
Developmental	26	42.3	57.7
Education	14	57.1	42.9
English and Language	34	58.8	41.2
Fine Arts	0	0.0	0.0
Foreign Languages	1	100.0	0.0
Intelligence and General Aptitude	26	50.0	50.0
Mathematics	5	80.0	20.0
Miscellaneous	39	76.9	23.1
Neuropsychological	35	88.6	11.4
Personality	98	73.5	26.5
Reading	15	26.7	73.3
Science	1	100.0	0.0
Sensory-Motor	12	75.0	25.0
Social Studies	0	0.0	0.0
Speech and Hearing	14	71.4	28.6
Vocations	58	81.0	19.0
Total	430	68.8	31.2

assure the quality of the test, it simply provides reviewers with a minimum basis for critically evaluating the quality of the test. We select our reviewers carefully and let them and well-informed readers decide for themselves about the quality of the tests. Some new or revised tests are not included because they were received too late to undergo the review process and still permit timely publication, or because some reviewers did not meet their commitment to review the test. A list of these tests is included in the Appendix and every effort will be made to have them reviewed for *The Fifteenth Mental Measurements Yearbook*.

There are some new or revised tests for which there will be no reviews although these tests are described in *Tests in Print V*. The absence of reviews occurred for a variety of reasons including: We could not identify qualified reviewers, the test materials were incomplete so reviews were not possible, the tests were sufficiently obscure that reviews were deemed unnecessary, the publisher advised us the test is now out-of-print before reviews were completed, or the test did not meet our criterion for documentation. Descriptions of all these tests still in print were published in *TIP V*.

TABLE 1
TESTS BY MAJOR CLASSIFICATIONS

Classification	Number	Percentage
Personality	98	22.8
Vocations	58	13.5
Miscellaneous	39	9.1
Behavior Assessment	37	8.6
Neuropsychological	35	8.1
English and Language	34	7.9
Developmental	26	6.0
Intelligence and General Aptitude	26	6.0
Achievement	15	3.5
Reading	15	3.5
Education	14	3.3
Speech and Hearing	14	3.3
Sensory-Motor	12	2.8
Mathematics	5	1.2
Foreign Languages	1	.2
Science	1	.2
Fine Arts	0	.0
Social Studies	0	.0
Total	430	100.0

Reviewer Selection. The selection of reviewers was done with great care. The objective was to secure measurement and subject specialists who represent a variety of different viewpoints. It was also important to find individuals who would write critical reviews competently, judiciously, fairly, and in a timely manner. Reviewers were identified by means of extensive searches of the professional literature, attendance at professional meetings, and recommendations from leaders in various professional fields. Perusal of reviews in this volume will also reveal that reviewers work in and represent a cross-section of the places in which tests are taught and used: universities, public schools, businesses, and community agencies. These reviewers represent an outstanding array of professional talent, and their contributions are obviously of primary importance in making this *Yearbook* a valuable resource. A list of the individuals reviewing in this volume is included at the beginning of the Index section.

Readers of test reviews in the *14th MMY* are encouraged to exercise an active, analytical, and evaluative perspective in reading the reviews. Just as one would evaluate a test, the readers should evaluate critically the reviewer's comments about the test. The reviewers selected are competent professionals in their respective fields, but it is inevitable that their reviews also reflect their individual perspectives. *The Mental Measurements Yearbooks* are intended to stimulate critical thinking about the selection of the best available test for a given purpose, not the passive acceptance of reviewer judgment. Active, evaluative reading is the key to the most effective use of the professional expertise offered in each of the reviews.

INDEXES

As mentioned above, the *14th MMY* includes six indexes invaluable as aids to effective use: (a) Index of Titles, (b) Index of Acronyms, (c) Classified Subject Index, (d) Publishers Directory and Index, (e) Index of Names, and (f) Score Index. Additional comment on these indexes is presented below.

Index of Titles. Because the organization of the *14th MMY* is encyclopedic in nature, with the tests ordered alphabetically by title throughout the volume, the test title index does not have to be consulted to find a test if the title is known. However, the title index has some features that make it useful beyond its function as a complete title listing. First, it includes cross-reference information useful for tests with superseded or alternative titles or tests commonly (and sometimes inaccurately) known by multiple titles. Second, it identifies tests that are new or revised. Third, it may cue the user to other tests with similar titles that may be useful. Titles for the 94 tests not reviewed because of insufficient technical documentation are included in the Index of Titles. It is important to keep in mind that the numbers in this index, like those for all *MMY* indexes, are test numbers and not page numbers.

Because no *MMY* includes reviews of all tests currently in print, a particular test of interest may not be reviewed in this volume. To learn if a commercially published test has been reviewed in this or an earlier volume of the *MMY*, users may access the Buros page on the World Wide Web (www.unl.edu/buros). In addition to other information about Buros products or services, there is a "Test Review Locator" that will indicate if a test has been reviewed and the *MMY* in which the review can be found. As an alternative, *Tests in Print V* can be consulted. This volume provides a cross-reference to reviews of still-in-print tests in the *MMY* series.

Index of Acronyms. Some tests seem to be better known by their acronyms than by their full titles. The Index of Acronyms can help in these instances; it refers the reader to the full title of the test and to the relevant descriptive information and reviews.

Classified Subject Index. The Classified Subject Index classifies all tests listed in the *14th MMY* into 18 major categories: Achievement, Behavior Assessment, Developmental, Education, English and Language, Fine Arts, Foreign Languages, Intelligence and General Aptitude, Mathematics, Miscellaneous, Neuropsychological, Personality, Reading, Science, Sensory-Motor, Social Studies, Speech and Hearing, and Vocations. Each test entry in this index includes test title, population for which the test is intended, and test number. The Classified Subject Index is of great help to readers who seek a listing of tests in given subject areas. The Classified Subject Index represents a starting point for readers who know their area of interest but do not know how to further focus that interest in order to identify the best test(s) for their particular purposes.

Publishers Directory and Index. The Publishers Directory and Index includes the names and addresses of the publishers of all tests included in the *14th MMY* plus a listing of test numbers for each individual publisher. Also included are the telephone and FAX numbers and email and Web addresses for those publishers who responded to our request for this information. This index can be particularly useful in obtaining addresses for specimen sets or catalogs after the test reviews have been read and evaluated. It can also be useful when a reader knows the publisher of a certain test but is uncertain about the test title, or when a reader is interested in the range of tests published by a given publisher.

Index of Names. The Index of Names provides a comprehensive list of names, indicating authorship of a test, test review, or reviewer's reference.

Score Index. The Score Index is an index to all scores generated by the tests in the *14th MMY*. Test titles are sometimes misleading or ambiguous, and test content may be difficult to define with precision. But test scores often represent operational definitions of the variables the test author is trying to measure, and as such they can define test purpose and content more adequately than other descriptive information. A search for a particular test is most often a search for a test that measures some specific variable(s). Test scores and their associated labels can often be the best definitions of the variable(s) of interest. The Score Index is a detailed subject index based on the most critical operational features of any test—the scores and their associated labels.

Lists of Tests Not Reviewed (Appendix). These lists identify tests that were not reviewed either because they did not meet our review criteria or because their reviews were still in progress at the time we went to press. The 94 tests not reviewed because they did not meet our criterion for sufficient technical documentation are numbered and presented in the same format used for the preceding tests that were reviewed. However, only the test title and publisher name are provided. Other descriptive information for these tests may be found in *Tests in Print V*. No descriptive information is provided for the 157 tests listed that will be reviewed for the *15th MMY*. Some of these instruments are described in *Tests in Print V* but most were not yet available when *TIP V* was published.

See the Buros web page for information about electronic or FAX access to these reviews prior to the publication of the *15th MMY*.

HOW TO USE THIS YEARBOOK

A reference work like *The Fourteenth Mental Measurements Yearbook* can be of far greater benefit to a reader if some time is taken to become familiar with what it has to offer and how it might be used most effectively to obtain the information wanted.

Step 1: Read the Introduction to the *14th MMY* in its entirety.

Step 2: Become familiar with the six indexes and particularly with the instructions preceding each index listing.

Step 3: Use the book by looking up needed information. This step is simple if one keeps in mind the following possibilities:

1. Go directly to the test entry using the alphabetical page headings if you know the title of the test.

2. Consult the Index of Titles for possible variants of the title or consult the appropriate subject area of the Classified Subject Index for other possible leads or for similar or related tests in the same area, if you do not know, cannot find, or are unsure of the title of a test. (Other uses for both of these indexes were described earlier.)

3. Consult the Index of Names if you know the author of a test but not the title or publisher. Look up the author's titles until you find the test you want.

4. Consult the Publishers Directory and Index if you know the test publisher but not the title or author. Look up the publisher's titles until you find the test you want.

5. Consult the Score Index and locate the test or tests that include the score variable of interest if you are looking for a test that yields a particular kind of score, but have no knowledge of which test that might be.

6. If after following the above steps you are not able to find a review of the test you want, consult the lists of tests that are not reviewed (Appendix) either because they did not meet our selection criteria or the reviews were not completed in time for publication in this volume. In addition, you can look in *TIP V* or visit the Buros web page (www.unl.edu/buros) and use the test locator service to identify the *MMY* that

contains the description and any available reviews of the test of interest.

7. Once you have found the test or tests you are looking for, read the descriptive entries for these tests carefully so that you can take advantage of the information provided. A description of the information provided in these test entries is presented later in this section.

8. Read the test reviews carefully and analytically, as suggested above. The information and evaluations contained in these reviews are meant to assist test consumers in making well-informed decisions about the choice and applications of tests.

9. Once you have read the descriptive information and test reviews, you may want to order a specimen set for a particular test so that you can examine it firsthand. The Publishers Directory and Index has the address information needed to obtain specimen sets or catalogs.

Making Effective Use of the Test Entries. The test entries include extensive information. For each test, descriptive information is presented in the following order:

a) TITLES. Test titles are printed in boldface type. Secondary or series titles are set off from main titles by a colon.

b) PURPOSE. For each test there is a brief, clear statement describing the purpose of the test. Often these statements are quotations from the test manual.

c) POPULATION. This describes the groups for which the test is intended. The grade, chronological age, semester range, or employment category is usually given. For example, "Grades 1.5–2.5, 2–3, 4–12, 13–17" means that there are four test booklets: a booklet for the middle of first grade through the middle of the second grade, a booklet for the beginning of the second grade through the end of third grade, a booklet for grades 4 through 12 inclusive, and a booklet for undergraduate and graduate students in colleges and universities.

d) PUBLICATION DATE. The inclusive range of publication dates for the various forms, accessories, and editions of a test is reported.

e) ACRONYM. When a test is often referred to by an acronym, the acronym is given in the test entry immediately following the publication date.

f) SCORES. The number of part scores is presented along with their titles or descriptions of what they are intended to represent or measure.

g) ADMINISTRATION. Individual or group administration is indicated. A test is considered a group test unless it may be administered only individually.

h) FORMS, PARTS, AND LEVELS. All available forms, parts, and levels are listed.

i) MANUAL. Notation is made if no manual is available. All other manual information is included under Price Data.

j) RESTRICTED DISTRIBUTION. This is noted only for tests that are put on a special market by the publisher. Educational and psychological restrictions are not noted (unless a special training course is required for use).

k) PRICE DATA. Price information is reported for test packages (usually 20 to 35 tests), answer sheets, all other accessories, and specimen sets. The statement "$17.50 per 35 tests" means that all accessories are included unless otherwise indicated by the reporting of separate prices for accessories. The statement also means 35 tests of one level, one edition, or one part unless stated otherwise. Because test prices can change very quickly, the year that the listed test prices were obtained is also given. Foreign currency is assigned the appropriate symbol. When prices are given in foreign dollars, a qualifying symbol is added (e.g., A$16.50 refers to 16 dollars and 50 cents in Australian currency). Along with cost, the publication date and number of pages on which print occurs is reported for manuals and technical reports (e.g., '93, 102 pages). All types of machine-scorable answer sheets available for use with a specific test are also reported in the descriptive entry. Scoring and reporting services provided by publishers are reported along with information on costs. In a few cases, special computerized scoring and interpretation services are noted at the end of the price information.

l) FOREIGN LANGUAGE AND OTHER SPECIAL EDITIONS. This section concerns foreign language editions published by the same publisher who sells the English-language edition. It also indicates special editions (e.g., Braille, large type) available from the same or a different publisher.

m) TIME. The number of minutes of actual working time allowed examinees and the approximate length of time needed for administering a test are reported whenever obtainable. The latter figure is always enclosed in parentheses. Thus,

"50(60) minutes" indicates that the examinees are allowed 50 minutes of working time and that a total of 60 minutes is needed to administer the test. A time of "40–50 minutes" indicates an untimed test that takes approximately 45 minutes to administer, or—in a few instances—a test so timed that working time and administration time are very difficult to disentangle. When the time necessary to administer a test is not reported or suggested in the test materials but has been obtained from a catalog or through correspondence with the test publisher or author, the time is enclosed in brackets.

n) COMMENTS. Some entries contain special notations, such as: "for research use only"; "revision of the ABC Test"; "tests administered monthly at centers throughout the United States"; "subtests available as separates"; and "verbal creativity." A statement such as "verbal creativity" is intended to further describe what the test claims to measure. Some of the test entries include factual statements that imply criticism of the test, such as "1990 test identical with test copyrighted 1980."

o) AUTHOR. For most tests, all authors are reported. In the case of tests that appear in a new form each year, only authors of the most recent forms are listed. Names are reported exactly as printed on test booklets. Names of editors generally are not reported.

p) PUBLISHER. The name of the publisher or distributor is reported for each test. Foreign publishers are identified by listing the country in brackets immediately following the name of the publisher. The Publishers Directory and Index must be consulted for a publisher's address and other contact information.

q) FOREIGN ADAPTATIONS. Revisions and adaptations of tests for foreign use are listed in a separate paragraph following the original edition.

r) SUBLISTINGS. Levels, editions, subtests, or parts of a test available in separate booklets are sometimes presented as sublistings with titles set in small capitals. Sub-sublistings are indented and titles are set in italic type.

s) CROSS REFERENCES. For tests that have been listed previously in a Buros Institute publication, a test entry includes—if relevant—a final item containing cross references to the reviews, excerpts, and references for that test in those volumes. In the cross references, "T5:467" refers to test 467 in *Tests in Print V*, "11:121" refers to test 121 in *The Eleventh Mental Measurements Yearbook*, "8:1023" refers to test 1023 in *The Eighth Mental Measurements Yearbook*, "T3:144" refers to test 144 in *Tests in Print III*, "7:637" refers to test 637 in *The Seventh Mental Measurements Yearbook*, "P:262" refers to test 262 in *Personality Tests and Reviews*, "2:1427" refers to test 1427 in *The 1940 Yearbook*, and "1:1110" refers to test 1110 in *The 1938 Yearbook*. In the case of batteries and programs, the paragraph also includes cross references—from the battery to the separately listed subtests and vice versa—to entries in this volume and to entries and reviews in earlier *Yearbooks*. Test numbers not preceded by a colon refer to tests in this *Yearbook*; for example, "see 45" refers to test 45 in this *Yearbook*.

ACKNOWLEDGMENTS

The publication of *the 14th Mental Measurements Yearbook* could not have been accomplished without the contributions of many individuals. The editors acknowledge gratefully the talent, expertise, and dedication of all those who have assisted in the publication process.

Linda Murphy, Managing Editor, is a critical member of the Buros team. In addition to her strong work ethic, she provides a historical base and a knowledge level that keeps us from making many errors we might make without her wise counsel. She makes our job as editors much more palatable than it would otherwise be. Nor would the publication of this volume be possible without the efforts of Robert Spies, Associate Director, Gary Anderson, Editorial Assistant, and Rosemary Sieck, Clerical Assistant. As always, their efforts go far beyond that required as part of normal job responsibilities. Janice Nelsen (former Institute Secretary) and Rasma Strautkalns (current Institute Secretary) are also recognized for their important contributions to the success of our efforts. We appreciate all the efforts of these permanent staff, each of whom contributes more than their share to the development and production of all of the Buros Institute's products.

This volume would not exist without the substantial efforts of the test reviewers. We are very grateful to the many reviewers who have prepared test reviews for the Buros Institute. The willingness of these reviewers to take time from their busy professional schedules to share their expertise in the form of thoughtful test reviews is appreciated. *The Mental Measurements Yearbook* would not exist were it not for their efforts.

The work of many graduate students helps make possible the quality of this volume. Their efforts have included writing test descriptions, fact checking reviews, looking for test references, and innumerable other tasks. We thank Rene Ayers, Ouyang Bo, Marta Coleman, Christine Gibbon, Jorge Gonzalez, Wei Huang, Jessica Jonson, Sean Kitaoka, Gary Loya, Heidi Paa, and Elisabeth Sundermeier for their assistance.

Appreciation is also extended to our National and Departmental Advisory Committees for their willingness to assist in the operation of the Buros Institute and for their thought-provoking suggestions for improving the *MMY* series and other publications of the Buros Institute of Mental Measurements. During the period in which this volume was prepared the National Advisory Committee has included Gary Melton, Anthony Nitko, Charles Peterson, Lawrence Rudner, Paul Sackett, and Frank Schmidt.

The Buros Institute is part of the Department of Educational Psychology of the University of Nebraska-Lincoln and we have benefited from the many departmental colleagues who have contributed to this work. We are also grateful for the contribution of the University of Nebraska Press, which provides expert consultation and serves as distributor of the *MMY* series.

SUMMARY

The *MMY* series is a valuable resource for people interested in studying or using tests. Once the process of using the series is understood, a reader can gain rapid access to a wealth of information. Our hope is that with the publication of the *14th MMY,* test authors and publishers will consider carefully the comments made by the reviewers and continue to refine and perfect their assessment products.

Barbara S. Plake
James C. Impara
March 2001

Tests and Reviews

[1]

ACCESS—A Comprehensive Custody Evaluation Standard System.

Purpose: Constructed as a "total system for conducting child custody evaluations."

Population: Children, parents, and others involved in child custody evaluations.

Publication Date: 1997.

Administration: Individual.

Price Data, 1997: $495 per complete kit including Bricklin Perceptual Scales Comprehensive Starting Kit with 3.5-inch unlimited use computer scoring profile, Perception-of-Relationships Test Comprehensive Starting Kit with 3.5-inch unlimited use computer scoring profile, Parent Awareness Skills Survey Comprehensive Starting Kit; Parent Perception-of-Child Profile Comprehensive Starting Kit, Custody Evaluation Questionnaires Kit, Custody Evaluation Interview Kit, Custody Evaluation Observation Kit, and Custody Evaluation Aggregation and Administration Kit.

Time: Administration time not reported.

Comments: Ratings by parents, children, teachers, and health/mental health professionals.

Authors: Barry Bricklin and Gail Elliot.

Publisher: Village Publishing.

a) BRICKLIN PERCEPTUAL SCALES.
Comments: See T5:334.

b) PERCEPTION-OF-RELATIONSHIPS TEST.
Comments: See T5:1917.

c) PARENT AWARENESS SKILLS SURVEY.
Comments: See T5:1879.

d) PARENT PERCEPTION OF CHILD PROFILE.
Comments: See T5:1886.

e) CUSTODY EVALUATION QUESTIONNAIRES KIT.
Purpose: "Designed to gather self-report data ... in every single area that are considered important in model custody statutes."

Population: Children, parents, grandparents, and collateral informants involved in a custody evaluation.

Scores: No scores, ratings only.

Forms, 6: Parent Self-Report Questionnaire, "Would" Questionnaire, Child Data Questionnaire, Child Self-Report Questionnaire, Child's Access to Parental Strengths Questionnaire, Child's Sexual Abuse Questionnaire.

f) CUSTODY EVALUATION INTERVIEW KIT.
Purpose: Designed for conducting custody evaluation interviews.

Population: Professionals conducting custody evaluation interviews.

Scores: No scores, structured interviews only.

Forms, 5: Parent Interview, Physician Interview, Teacher Interview, Mental Health Professional Interview, Corroborative Source Interview.

g) CUSTODY EVALUATION OBSERVATION KIT.
Purpose: Constructed to "discriminate among the different ways, positive and negative, a child responds to parental communications."

Population: Professionals conducting custody evaluations.

Scores: No scores, ratings by observers.

Forms, 2: Adult Observation Form, Child Observation Form.

h) CUSTODY EVALUATION AGGREGATION AND ADMINISTRATION KIT.
Purpose: "Designed to aggregate the enormous amount of information gathered" in custody evaluations.

Population: Professionals conducting custody evaluations.

Scores: No scores.

Comments: Also includes phone logs, critical targets forms, and model contracts.

Review of ACCESS—A Comprehensive Custody Evaluation Standard System by MARK W. ROBERTS, Professor of Psychology, Idaho State University, Pocatello, ID:

Bricklin and his associates have developed a complicated, sequenced evaluation system to assist family law courts in determining the primary custodial parent who would serve the best interests of the child. The ACCESS system consists of several different measurement methods: questionnaires (6), structured interviews (5), an observation system, and standardized tests (4). The user is guided by the ACCESS Manual, manuals for each of the four tests, an ACCESS Critical Targets Form that synthesizes information from the many sources, and an 18-step ACCESS Aggregation Booklet that structures a sequential, decision-making strategy to arrive at a recommendation for the primary custodial parent and a custody plan.

The two basic measurements used by ACCESS are the Bricklin Perceptual Scales (BPS; T5:334) and the Perception-Of-Relationships Test (PORT; T5: 1917). The BPS is administered orally to children age 6 and older. The child rates each parent on a numberless dimension from "Very Well" to "Not So Well" for 32 different parenting functions. The BPS has been reviewed previously by Hagin (1992) and by Schaffer (1992). The BPS does not appear to have changed in quality since those reviews. Neither of the previous reviewers nor this reviewer believe the psychometric foundation of the BPS is sufficient for use, other than as an aid to clinical judgment. There are no reliability data nor standard errors of measurements for the four BPS Scales. In the manual of one of the newer ACCESS tests (PASS, Supplement #9, p. 10), Bricklin mentions an unpublished dissertation in which 20 volunteer subjects displayed a one-week test-retest reliability of .84 on the BPS, but provides no other details. BPS validity data are limited to agreement ratios regarding the "Parent Of Choice." Clearly, to validate a test-recommended Parent Of Choice, one would need data demonstrating that child adjustment was better when the BPS-identified Parent Of Choice was awarded primary custody. Such research is possible, but has not been implemented.

The PORT is a seven-item projective test based on drawings of self and family members. Children, ages 3 and above, are asked to draw pictures of each parent (Task 1), draw themselves into pictures including parents (Tasks II, III, IV, & V), indicate a preferred parental house for a storybook animal (Task VI), and report on the dreams about father/mother of a storybook animal and indicate which dream is "nicer" (Task VII). Port administration is well standardized and objectively scored. Relative location of the child to each parent, expressed preferences, and relative drawing equality for each parent yield a Parent Of Choice for each Task. The parent with the most preferences is the PORT Parent Of Choice.

The PORT manual (p. 40) discusses the intent of the author to sample a child's "gut feeling" and "psychological disposition" toward each parent (Task I), the degree of psychological "closeness" (Tasks II-V), and both "conscious" (Task VI) and "wish-oriented" (Task VII) desires regarding parents. No item development plan or theoretical model is provided beyond these remarks. The manual reports test-retest reliability (administration interval = 4 to 8 months) for three samples of subjects ($n = 8$; $n = 6$; $n = 10$) in terms of the number of subjects who "shifted" the final Parent Of Choice (only 2 of 24 shifted). No reliability coefficient nor standard error are reported for the PORT total score. Validity data are offered in terms of percent agreement between PORT and other methods of determining the Parent Of Choice (BPS, judicial decision, and mental health professional judgments). Agreements ranged from 83% to 95% across six samples. No effort was made to validate PORT scores on child adjustment measurements. Therefore, the reliability and validity of scores from PORT do not appear to be adequately established.

The author suggests two additional uses of PORT for which no evidence is provided: (a) detecting physical or sexual abuse (manual, pp. 43–47); and (b) determining which parent is to be recommended for primary custody when there is a discrepancy between the BPS and PORT Parent Of Choice. The author contends that PORT data can be subdivided into PORT C components ("originating at more conscious layers") and PORT U components ("originating at less conscious layers"). Basically, PORT C items are the revealed parent preferences of the storybook animals (Tasks VI & VII), whereas the remaining items plus dream content are considered PORT U items. Some age variation is suggested (ACCESS manual, pp. 35–36). The author's division of PORT items lacks a theoretical or empirical basis.

The ACCESS system relies on the BPS and PORT. All other measurements play supportive roles or are combined subjectively to address "critical targets." Specifically, when the BPS and PORT converge (ACCESS Step 5), reported to occur from 83% to 90% (in two samples), ACCESS instructs the examiner to "cross-validate" (ACCESS Step 8) the provisional primary custodial parent against two additional measurements: the Parent Awareness Skills Survey (PASS; T5:1879) and the Parent Perception of Child Profile (PPCP; T5:1886). ACCESS Step 8, however, asserts that whenever both PORT and BPS indicate the same Parent Of Choice, PASS and PPCP will always confirm the data yielded by BPS and PORT. If true, it would appear that the "cross-validation" is actually unnecessary.

The other "cross-validation" tool for BPS and PORT is the Parent Perception of Child Profile (PPCP) (ACCESS Step 4). Items from 13 areas of child function (e.g., interpersonal relations, school history, etc.; see T5:1886) are presented orally or can be self-administered (e.g., "How often does your child go on overnight visits with friends?"; "How often does your child have temper tantrums?"; etc.). Presumably, the parent who is genuinely interested and involved with the child will be able to accurately recall a detailed set of information about the child's history and current behavioral patterns. Each of 121 items calls for an open-ended verbal (or written, if self-administered) response or a rating on one of several scales. To be useful for ACCESS, reliable informants other than the parents must be enlisted to provide corroborative information (e.g., a school teacher). Parent responses are compared to informant responses for "Accuracy" and "Scope of Knowledge." PPCP data are also synthesized subjectively across all 121 items to score three macro dimensions: "Depth of Knowledge" (a 3-point scale ranging from "many details" to "some details" to "no details"), "Emotional Tone" (a 3-point scale ranging from "positive" to "neutral" to "negative"), and "Value/Philosophy" (a 3-point scale ranging from "encouraging self-esteem & initiative" to "neutral" to "constrictive"). In addition, an "Irritability Scale" is administered, based on 5-point rating scales of 21 dysfunctional/deviant child behaviors. From the Irritability Scale the

clinician gleans "Areas Needing Improvement." Finally, 39 items are presented a second time on a "Recall Test." The author contends that, "parents who seek custody of a child for reasons other than genuine interest" (PPCP Manual, p. 5) will be less likely to recall their previous answers. On ACCESS Step 4 the two parents are compared on the various PPCP dimensions to yield an overall Parent of Choice.

If the BPS and PORT converge and are "cross-validated" by PASS and PPCP, the ACCESS user is told to skip to Step 15 and use the "Critical Targets Form" before arriving at a final judgment and a custody plan. The Critical Targets Form is a system for subjectively synthesizing prescribed sources of information to yield a brief written summary for each of 40 targets. For example, the examiner is instructed to synthesize BPS, PORT, PASS, and Observations (described below) to consider, "The degree to which each parent is aware of the importance of communicating to the child in words and actions understandable to the child." ACCESS Step 15 articulates strategies for using the 16 "Other Critical Targets" to construct an overall custody plan. In particular, examiners are instructed to further subjectively synthesize the "Other Critical Target" information on four variables: Credibility, Mother-Relevance, Father-Relevance, and/or Difference and Parent Favored. As usual in ACCESS, there is no empirical demonstration of interjudge reliability for synthesizing information from the many sources to the Critical Targets Form, nor the further synthesis to the four ACCESS Step 15 variables.

In order to complete ACCESS Step 15, the user brings to bear some of the remaining measurements of the ACCESS system. The Custody Evaluation Questionnaires Kit includes six questionnaires. Three are parent self-report devices that the ACCESS Manual recommends be mailed for self-administration in the home, but could be used as "interview guides": Child Data (By Parent), Child's Access to Parental Strength Data (CAPS Form), and Parent Self-Report Data. Items call for open-ended written responses to general topics concerning the child, the parent, or the mother-father relationship. Some questions reflect themes and actual items from the BPS and the PPCP. The three parent questionnaires appear to be clinical tools, possibly assisting in the custody plan or used as evidence for convergence with

BPS or PPCP information. No psychometric properties are explicated.

The three remaining questionnaires are structured child interviews. ACCESS recommends using the Child Self-Report Data and the Would Questionnaire as the final step in data collection and incorporating the findings into the Critical Targets Form. The Child Self-Report Data includes 67 items evoking child beliefs about the parents (several are BPS items). The Would Questionnaire is a 12-item sentence-completion projective test. Each item begins with a situation (e.g., "The teacher sends a note home saying that your work is poor and you might fail your grade"). The child then completes the sentence, "My mother would ...," followed by, "My father would ...." No psychometric foundation is presented for either measurement. The last of the six questionnaires, the Child Sexual Abuse Questionnaire, is a structured interview to be used as a component of a child abuse investigation. The instrument has no direct relevance to ACCESS.

The Custody Evaluation Interview Kit includes five structured interviews designed for teachers, physicians, parents, mental health professionals, and a generic informant. All are similar to the PPCP and could fill the role of providing the corroborative information needed to complete PPCP Accuracy and Scope of Knowledge Scales. Again, these appear to be clinical tools, used in ACCESS at Step 15 when completing the Critical Targets Form.

The ACCESS Family Interaction Observation system is described in the ACCESS Manual as a method to detect "nurturant and useful" parenting thought to occur if the parent "honors the child's symbol systems and information processing strategies" (p. 16). Games and puzzles are suggested interaction formats, but the examiner can apply wide latitude, based on child developmental level. Children are observed with both parents and then with each parent individually. Interactions are coded in terms of person, initiating/responding, speaking/listening/acting, and positive/negative (regarding emotional tone or behavioral self-sufficiency). In addition, eight parent actions are labeled on the coding sheet (e.g., "Communicates warmth and love"). It is actually quite a complicated system, and not at all well explained in the manual. Bricklin references his book (1995, chapter 2) for more details. Nevertheless, glaring

problems are manifest. None of the codes are given adequate operational definitions; how the data are aggregated is not specified (frequencies, probabilities?); no time limits are mentioned; the location and behavior of the observer is not discussed; and most importantly, no evidence of interobserver reliability for specific codes or behavioral composites is mentioned. Bricklin's hypothesis that "nurturant and useful" parents do so via synchronicity with the child's "symbol system and information processing strategies" is a fascinating, but a very global and unsubstantiated perspective.

In summation, the ACCESS system constructed by Bricklin and associates over the past several decades is a fascinating clinical tool that begs for an adequate psychometric foundation. As currently described, ACCESS does not meet minimum standards for test construction, reliability, or validity. The ACCESS system is very expensive and very time-consuming. ACCESS is not recommended for use. A practitioner performing custody evaluations might consider recent reviews on the status of psychological tests in the field (Brodzinsky, 1993) and current utilization practices (Ackerman & Ackerman, 1997). The only competing test this reviewer is aware of is the Ackerman-Schoendorf Scales for Parent Evaluation of Custody, reviewed by Arditti (1995) and by Melton (1995) in the *Mental Measurements Yearbook*. Ackerman's system appears to follow more traditional test development and reliability strategies than Bricklin's, but suffers from the same validation problems. Namely, custody researchers have yet to demonstrate that measurement-based decisions regarding the primary custodial parent enhance subsequent child adjustment.

REVIEWER'S REFERENCES

Hagin, R. A. (1992). [Review of the Bricklin Perceptual Scales]. In J. J. Kramer & J. C. Conoley (Eds.), *The eleventh mental measurements yearbook* (pp. 117–118). Lincoln, NE: Buros Institute of Mental Measurements.

Shaffer, M. B. (1992). [Review of the Bricklin Perceptual Scales]. In J. J. Kramer & J. C. Conoley (Eds.), *The eleventh mental measurements yearbook* (pp. 118–119). Lincoln, NE: Buros Institute of Mental Measurements.

Brodzinsky, D. M. (1993). On the use and misuse of psychological testing in child custody evaluations. *Professional psychology: Research and practice, 24*, 213–219.

Arditti, J. A. (1995). [Review of the Ackerman-Schoendorf Scales for Parent Evaluation of Custody]. In J. C. Conoley & J. C. Impara (Eds.), *The twelfth mental measurements yearbook* (pp. 20–22). Lincoln, NE: Buros Institute of Mental Measurements.

Bricklin, B. (1995). *The custody evaluation handbook: Research-based applications and solutions.* New York: Brunner/Mazel.

Melton, G. B. (1995). [Review of the Ackerman-Schoendorf Scales for Parent Evaluation of Custody]. In J. C. Conoley & J. C. Impara (Eds.), *The twelfth mental measurements yearbook* (pp. 22–23). Lincoln, NE: Buros Institute of Mental Measurements.

Ackerman, M. J., & Ackerman, M. C. (1997). Custody evaluation practices: A survey of experienced professional (revisited). *Professional psychology: Research and practice, 28*, 137–145.

[2]
ACDI—Corrections Version and Corrections Version II.

Purpose: "Designed for troubled youth screening and assessment."

Population: Troubled youth between the ages of 12 and 18 years in juvenile probation, parole, and corrections programs.

Publication Dates: 1988-1995.

Acronym: ACDI.

Administration: Group.

Price Data: Available from publisher.

Time: (15–25) minutes.

Comments: Both computer version and paper-pencil format are scored on IBM-PC compatibles.

Author: Risk & Needs Assessment, Inc.

Publisher: Risk & Needs Assessment, Inc.

a) VERSION I.

Scores, 5: Truthfulness, Alcohol, Drug, Adjustment, Distress.

b) VERSION II.

Scores, 6: Truthfulness, Alcohol, Drug, Adjustment, Distress, Violence.

Review of the ACDI—Corrections Version and Corrections Version II by CAROL COLLINS, Family Counseling and Research Center, Caldwell, ID:

The ACDI—Corrections Version is a 104-question self-report instrument designed to measure adolescents' level of risk or propensity toward problems of alcohol or drug use; problematic adjustment at home, at school, and with authority and peers; and experiences of anxiety or depression. The ACDI—Corrections Version II adds a violence scale that measures the use of physical force to injure, damage, or destroy. It identifies the level of danger of the youth's harming self or others. Version II consists of 143 questions. Completion time is 25 to 30 minutes. Both tests also have a Truthfulness Scale that measures the respondent's level of truthfulness while taking the test.

ADMINISTRATION AND SCORING. Respondents are presented a survey of 104 questions (143 for Version II) that can be administered either by paper and pencil or on the computer. All questions are answered as "True" or "False." If the pencil-and-paper version is used, the individual answers must be entered into the computer to generate scores. Once they are entered, scores are interpreted and available to the evaluator within 5 minutes. A thorough orientation and training manual gives instructions to the interviewer for both pencil-and-paper and computer versions.

Space is available on the assessment form to enter subjective observations of the evaluator and to enter the evaluator's recommendations for treatment. Publishers caution that results should be considered in conjunction with any significant observations made by the evaluator. They acknowledge that treatment recommendations made as a result of ACDI testing can have life and death implications.

Percentile scores are given on each of the individual measures. Each scale score is classified in terms of the range of risk it represents. Risk range is identified as "Low Risk," "Medium Risk," "Problem Risk," and "Severe Problem Risk."

NORMING INFORMATION. Detailed norming information and research history are provided with the test, which has been standardized on juvenile probationers. It has also been standardized on a state-by-state basis. Several summaries of specific studies are included with the test package.

Based on research identifying significant gender differences on two of the scales, gender-specific norms have been established for the Truthfulness scale and the Violence scale. Publishers are careful to note that gender differences may vary depending on the geographical area.

One of the strong features of the test is the ongoing research program that allows annual updates to their norming information database. Each filled test diskette must be returned to the publisher before another can be purchased. This provides continual input to be added to their database and contributes to the ongoing improvement of the test.

RELIABILITY. In summary of scientific findings, the publishers state that "reliability refers to consistency of results regardless of who uses the instrument. ACDI results are objective, verifiable and reproducible" (manual, p. 6). Statistical data provided support the internal consistency of the ACDI.

VALIDITY. Extensive research is cited summarizing validity studies of the ACDI. In validity studies, each of the scales is treated separately. Studies indicate a high correlation of scores from the ACDI and results from the Minnesota Multiphasic Personality Inventory (MMPI). Concurrent validity was examined by comparing scores from ACDI scales with comparable scales on the MMPI.

SUMMARY. The Adolescent Chemical Dependency Inventory (ACDI) Corrections and ACDI-II can be useful to evaluators attempting to determine the level of risk or propensity for problems of adolescents in the areas specified by the scales. It should be considered a tool to aid the evaluator, who must consider test results in conjunction with his or her subjective observations and professional judgment. A possible danger is that an evaluator who has many respondents to assess may use the test in an assembly-line fashion, taking the test scores at face value, without adding his or her own experiential wisdom and without considering significant information provided by the respondent. Test publishers caution evaluators to consider the grave consequences of their recommendations.

With these cautions in mind, the ACDI is a convenient, easy-to-take test that provides immediate scoring results. This reviewer believes the ACDI is a satisfactory and useful instrument for the purpose for which it is designed.

Review of the ACDI—Corrections Version and Corrections Version II by MARK POPE, Associate Professor, Division of Counseling, University of Missouri–St. Louis, St. Louis, MO:

The Adolescent Chemical Dependency Inventory-Corrections Version II (ACDI-CV2) is a 143-item self-report behavioral inventory published in 1994 and designed as a risk and needs assessment for 12–18-year-olds who have been mandated to one of the following types of programs: juvenile probation and parole, court-related services, and corrections program. Two other versions of this instrument still exist and are available, but the CV2 revision is specifically designed for "juvenile courts and probation departments desiring to know how violence prone the juvenile offender is" ("Scientific Findings," p. 10).

Risk and needs assessment for juvenile offenders help judges, probation and parole officers, corrections officers, case managers, juvenile offender counselors, or social workers plan and recommend the overall treatment program for individual juvenile offenders. For example, if a juvenile offender scores in the "problem" range (70-90 percentile) on the "Drugs" subscale, part of the treatment plan might be to have regular drug screen testing and to attend regular individual and group drug abuse counseling sessions.

This type of inventory has the potential to decrease the waste and inefficiency in nonindividualized treatment planning. By accurately identifying problem areas for the individual juvenile offender, a treatment plan that works on the real risk factors for this particular juvenile offender and actually may, therefore, decrease rates of recidivism.

The materials for the ACDI-CV2 include: a test booklet, an answer sheet, an orientation and training manual, a computer operating guide, a scoring quick reference sheet, an inventory of scientific findings, and a report on the use of the inventory by the Missouri Division of Youth Services.

The reusable test booklet is a four-page (11-inch x 17-inch bifold) with black ink on a light blue, heavyweight paper. The instructions are clear and are printed on the left half-page of page 1 along with the copyright line at the bottom. Items are segmented into two sections with specific instructions for completing each section at the beginning of each section. The first 130 items are included in Section 1 and are generally simple and straightforward. Five specific items are much more complex and confusing and would not be easily understood by a juvenile offender population.

The last 13 items are included in Section 2 and are referred to in the "orientation and training manual" as the structured interview. The individual responses to each of these 13 items are simply printed directly on the computer-generated narrative report with no other interpretation. These items can be used as an important interpretive device as they ask questions about the juvenile offender's perception of his or her situation or needs. Comparisons between these responses and the subscale scores can offer important data about the young offender where perceptions and subscale scores either differ or are similar.

The answer sheet is printed in black ink on a light blue 20 pound paper on one side of an 8 1/2-inch x 11-inch sheet. General demographic items are included at the top of the answer sheet (name, age, sex, education [highest grade], ethnicity [race], and date). Of these items the prompt for the ethnicity item is "ETHNICITY (RACE): ____," which may be confusing to the test taker. A better formulation would be "ETHNICITY/RACE: ____" so that more accurate data may be gathered.

Directly following the demographic items is a box containing 13 specific juvenile offender items that query specific frequency data on age at first arrest, number of felony convictions, number of drug-related arrests, etc. The 130 items in the first section require the respondent to place an "X" under "T" for true or "F" for false for each item. Each of the 130 items is clearly marked on the answer sheet followed by two blank underscores for the juvenile offender's response.

It is important to note that no hand or manual scoring is provided for the ACDI-CV2. All scoring is done via an IBM-compatible personal computer. Even where respondents have completed the paper-and-pencil version, the data must be entered manually, as the materials are not designed to allow for data entry through scanning.

The bottom part of the answer sheet is devoted to the inventory item responses. Section 1 item responses are placed in a box on the left side of that area with Section 2 responses separated into another box on the right.

The response formats for each of the two sections appear to be more appropriate for a computer screen than for paper-and-pencil response formats. Although this may aid manual data entry using the answer sheet, there are better formats for paper-and-pencil administration. Further, there are no row line breaks in the five 26-item columns. This format is visually difficult and leads to errors in responding to items.

The narrative report is generated immediately upon completion of the inventory and consists of a four-page report. The first page of the narrative is a profile report with the percentile scores on each of the six subscales numerically and graphically displayed. The graphical display of the percentile scores is segmented into four sections: low risk, medium, problem, and max, which leaves little error or variability in interpretation of the scores. At the bottom of the profile report, headed by "Additional Information Provided by Client," are the juvenile offender's responses to the 13 specific juvenile offender items that query frequency data on age at first arrest, number of felony convictions, number of drug-related arrests, etc. The header is important as this data might be misunderstood as an objective factual report of verified data.

The next two pages of the report provide a narrative interpretation of the six subscale percentile scores along with a blank section for observations and comments, staff member signature, and

date. The final page of the report identifies "significant items"—items that are "unusual responses and direct admissions" (p. v) along with the specific item responses to each of the 143 items on the inventory.

Six subscales are used to provide feedback to the administrators regarding the response patterns of the individual offender. The subscales include: Truthfulness (a validity scale), Alcohol, Adjustment, Drugs, Distress (anxiety and depression), and Violence. The subscales were rationally derived using an eight-person committee: three psychologists and five juvenile corrections counselors, and then analyzed for final selection using item-whole coefficients. The ACDI-CV2 also provides normative data by gender for two subscales—Alcohol and Distress. According to the authors, "it is important to note that these gender differences may vary according to geographical area" (p. 3), and so they suggest that local users of the instrument collect their own local norms.

An important innovation in the computer scoring of this inventory is truth-corrected scores. Using the individual's scores on the Truthfulness scale (identifies attempts to fake or underreport problems and concerns), when scoring the completed answer sheet the computer identifies and adds back into each scale score the amount of error variance associated with that particular person's untruthfulness, resulting in these truth-corrected scores, similar to the correction factor loading in the MMPI.

Even though the "orientation and training manual" declares that the subscales have some relationship to other similar recognized objective measures, the authors do not report in that manual the specific similar scales nor the strength of the correlation. These data are found in another publication, "ACDI: An Inventory of Scientific Findings." In that publication, the data presented are limited to two studies (1989, 1990) correlating Minnesota Multiphasic Personality Inventory (MMPI) scores (unspecified version) with the original ACDI. This is a strength of the instrument. These comparisons are delivering evidence of a type of criterion-related validity called concurrent validity. Unfortunately, these studies are not cited anywhere in any professional journal, nor attributed to any other researcher; therefore, it can only be assumed that they must have only been published in this particular place, by unknown authors.

The reported relationships between the MMPI and the ACDI are moderate. In the 1989 study, they range from .53 to .61 and, in the 1990 study, from .39 to .53. Both are in acceptable ranges and show that, although there is some relationship between scores on the MMPI and ACDI, there is not so much as to make the scales exactly the same.

As to issues of psychometric reliability, the authors of this instrument report measures of within-scale, inter-item reliability over a period of years from 1989 to 1996 ranging from .73 to .89. It is important to note that even though the authors do mention the test-retest form of reliability, they do not provide any data on such measures. This instrument is not a measure of personality where we look for measures of stability. It is instead a behavioral measure, where we expect and hope for changes, especially with a population such as juvenile offenders. Measures of stability such as test-retest reliability are much less important here. This instrument could have usefulness as an outcome evaluation measure in these circumstances.

The authors also report use of the instrument with non-Caucasian juvenile offenders and female juveniles along with substantial amounts of demographic data. This is another strength of the instrument; however, no analysis has been done with any other cultural or sexual group regarding any performance differences between groups.

SUMMARY. Overall, the ACDI-CV2 is a strong entry into the new substance abuse inventory market. It has carved a strong niche for itself in the juvenile offender market where counselors, probation and parole officers, and judges alike have been asking for instruments with strong evidence of psychometric quality. This instrument fulfills its objectives.

[3]
Achievement Motivation Profile.

Purpose: "Designed to be a measure of a student's motivation to achieve" and related personality characteristics.
Population: Ages 14 and older in high school, junior college, and college.
Publication Dates: 1995–1996.
Acronym: AMP.
Scores, 18: Response style (Inconsistent Responding, Self-Enhancing, Self-Critical), Motivation for Achievement (Achiever, Motivation, Competitiveness, Goal Orientation), Inner Resources (Relaxed Style, Happiness, Patience, Self-Confidence), Interpersonal Strengths (Assertiveness, Personal Diplomacy, Extroversion, Cooperativeness), Work Habits (Planning and Organization, Initiative, Team Player).
Administration: Group.
Price Data, 1999: $99.50 per complete kit including 20 AutoScore™ forms, manual ('96, 93 pages), 2 WPS Test Report prepaid mail-in answer sheets for computer scoring and interpretation, and 2-use disk for on-site computer scoring and interpretation and 2 PC answer sheets; $32.50 per 25 AutoScore™ forms; $47.50 per manual; $11.50 each for 1–9 AMP mail-in answer sheets; $9.90 each for 10+ AMP mail-in answer sheets; $190 per 25-use microcomputer disk (PC with Microsoft Windows); $15 per 100 microcomputer answer sheets; $9.50 per fax service scoring.
Time: (20–30) minutes.
Authors: Jotham G. Friedland, Sander I. Marcus, and Harvey P. Mandel.
Publisher: Western Psychological Services.

Review of the Achievement Motivation Profile by STEVEN V. OWEN, Senior Biostatistician, Department of Preventive Medicine and Community Health, University of Texas Medical Branch, Galveston, TX:

The Achievement Motivation Profile (hereafter, AMP) is a 140-item, self-report survey that primarily assesses achievement motivation. The purposes of the survey are to discover possible reasons for school underachievement and to assist in counseling underachieving students. An implicit assumption of the AMP is that certain personality characteristics have causal influence on achievement; if we can pinpoint faulty characteristics, then an intervention may be developed to address the deficiencies. There is no acknowledgement that the causal functions may actually be reversed, that is, poor school achievement may influence achievement motivation. Mandel, Friedland, and Marcus are careful in the manual to say that the AMP should not be used as the sole assessment tool for evaluating underachievement.

The AMP is said to be based on the developmental theory of academic work performance (Erikson). Except for the use of general psychodynamic language, though, little of Erikson's theory is evident in the instrument or the Achievement Motivation Profile manual. The AMP is aimed at students from 9th grade (at least of age 14) through college, and this range covers two of Erikson's developmental stages. From Erikson's (1963) descriptions, these two stages seem to have different interpretations and implications for achievement motivation, but nothing in the AMP acknowledges such differences. The scoring protocol, norms, and suggestions for student counseling do not speak to the two stages.

The AMP's 140 item stems are short, self-descriptive statements, and total test time is about 20–30 minutes. Respondents use a 5-point response scale with endpoints of "Always True" and "Always False." The word "Always" would seem to steer respondents away from the endpoints and thus reduce score variability. Although the authors refer to the response scale as a "Likert scale," they give no rationale for avoiding the usual "Strongly Agree" to "Strongly Disagree" scaling.

Hand scoring the AMP is tedious and somewhat complex. The survey's publisher also offers scoring services. Fortunately, the AMP has a computer program available for scoring and report writing. Scores from a student's answer sheet may be transferred to a computer version of the AMP, and scoring accomplished rapidly and accurately. A program option also allows a student to take the AMP. Computer-assisted testing is easy, rapid, and intuitive. The computerized report format, which may be printed directly, is a listing and bar graph of respondent T-scores.

The AMP's 140 items generate a total of 24 scores. Three scores refer to response style: Inconsistent Responding, Self-Enhancing, and Self-Critical. The Inconsistent Responding score is derived from examining 15 pairs of similar items. When a respondent varies by more than a point on an item pair, it is counted as an instance of inconsistency. The Self-Enhancing and Self-Critical scores come from the same 12 items that suggest socially desirable responses (e.g., "I work hard"). When a respondent gives too many "Always True" or "Always False" endorsements, the summary scores will show up as inflated Self-Enhancing or Self-Critical depictions. In that case, the test authors recommend caution in interpreting the remaining scale scores.

Six scores are calculated that reflect "informal" career interest areas: Realistic, Investigative, Artistic, Social, Enterprising, and Conventional. The test authors acknowledge that these brief scales are only suggestive and should be used with other assessments to assist in career counseling.

The focus of the AMP is contained in four general areas comprising 15 subscales. The practitioner familiar with Eriksonian developmental theory will see that these areas and subscores do sound contemporary, but they do not reflect Erikson's writings. The scale arrangement is as follows: (1) Motivation for Achievement, with subscales (a) Achiever, (b) Motivation, (c) Competitiveness, (d) Goal Orientation; (2) Inner Resources, with subscales (a) Relaxed Style, (b) Happiness, (c) Patience, (d) Self-Confidence; (3) Interpersonal Strengths, with subscales (a) Assertiveness, (b) Personal Diplomacy, (c) Extroversion, (d) Cooperativeness; (4) Work Habits, with subscales (a) Planning and Organization, (b) Initiative, (c) Team Player.

The subscales contain between 5 and 15 items, but the items are not always unique to a particular subscale. Of the 140 items, 58 are used in two or more of the 24 subscales. One item shows up on 7 subscales. When items are appointed to more than one subscale, the constructs indicated by the scales are confounded, and the correlations among subscales are thereby inflated. The problem strikes at the heart of construct validity evidence, because discriminant and convergent evidence is based on correlations that are partly an artifact of multiply used items. The problem also affects reliability estimates of subscales, which become nonindependent because of shared items.

The assignment of items to six of the 15 primary subscales was based mainly on clinical judgment and the assignment to another six subscales was based on empirical data, such as interitem correlations and validity coefficients. Nothing is said about how the remaining three subscales came to be. The grouping of subscales into their general areas was based on factor analysis (not further detailed) and authors' judgment. Most of the item assignments appear to fit the parent construct.

Other validity evidence comes in the form of correlations between AMP subscale scores and public and private high school teachers' ratings of students on the same dimensions. These validity coefficients range from .03 to .65 (manual, pp. 61–62), with a median correlation of only .30. Perhaps most surprising are the low coefficients for readily observable behaviors, such as Competitiveness (.13) and Extroversion (.37 and .17).

A known groups analysis compared high school "overachievers," "achievers," and "underachievers" on the core AMP subscales plus two of the response style scales. Only four of the subscales were able to distinguish all three groups; two subscales showed differences between overachievers and underachievers, and the remaining 11 scales could not discriminate among any groups.

Additional construct validity evidence comes from convergent and discriminant validity coefficients with the Edwards Personal Preference Scale and the 16-PF. Here, the test authors overstate the meaning of some validity coefficients, bringing forward values as small as .21 and .34 to show convergent evidence between similar constructs. Weak coefficients, such as .05 between AMP Relaxed Style, and 16-PF Warm and Easygoing, are overlooked.

There are a few more impressive validity coefficients between AMP scores and the Eysenck Personality Inventory scores and the State-Trait Anxiety Inventory. But the sample of only 37 university physical education students limits the generalizability of these coefficients. Still more coefficients (153) are produced between AMP scores and Symptom Checklist-90 scores from a small sample of high school students, and between AMP scores and scores from the Multiscore Depression Inventory (176 coefficients) for another high school group. Instead of making a priori predictions about the correlational patterns, though, the authors present a welter of coefficients from such personality measures, search for confirming coefficients, and often overlook disconfirming data.

Internal consistency estimates of the 15 core AMP scales, calculated from the entire normative sample (N = 1,738), range from .58 to .84, with a median coefficient of .75. Stability estimates were calculated for a high school subsample (n = 122) over a 60-day interval; they ranged from .61 to .89, with a median coefficient of .83.

Standard errors of measurement, long suggested in various versions of the *Standards for Educational and Psychological Testing*, are not reported. Users would have to calculate for themselves standard errors, and from them, confidence intervals around scores for groups or for individuals.

Norm tables are given that compare American and Canadian students (grade levels unstated), male and female students (grade levels unstated), different grade divisions (high school, junior college, and college students), and Black, Hispanic, and White students (grade levels unstated). The tables are quite limited in that they only report AMP subscale means and standard deviations for each subgroup. Also, some subgroups are small (e.g., 29 Black students; 14 Hispanic students). Less than 13% of the normative group came from 4-year college students.

Mandel et al. (the test authors) offer a detailed series of six case studies of unsatisfactory school achievement based on real student histories. No evidence is offered that interventions derived from AMP score patterns actually improved school performance. Test results beyond the AMP are also discussed, but Mandel et al. sometimes discuss them in casual language that offers little insight about school performance. Intervention recommendations sometimes focus on improving school achievement, but in other cases, speculative suggestions are made: "[A]n exploration of the sources of his sadness was recommended ... to enable him to again achieve in school" (manual, p. 35).

SUMMARY. The theoretical orientation and constructs of the AMP will appeal to clinicians and counselors who have a psychodynamic bent. Interventions developed on the basis of AMP data appear to be largely a matter of faith that the AMP is a useful diagnostic tool. Practitioners with less enthusiasm for psychodynamic theory will likely be unimpressed with the personality detail provided by the AMP, and may wish to design achievement interventions without this complex assessment tool. In any case, the collection and patterns of psychometric evidence for the AMP is not as convincing as Mandel et al. suggest. At the very least, the tool needs a refined scoring protocol to remove items that are assigned to two or more constructs simultaneously. It also would profit from a larger and more diverse normative sample; this in turn would allow multigroup confirmatory factor analysis to address questions about the AMP's dimensionality.

REVIEWER'S REFERENCE

Erikson, E. (1963). *Childhood and society* (2nd ed.). New York: W. W. Norton.

Review of the Achievement Motivation Profile by JAY R. STEWART, Assistant Professor and Director, Rehabilitation Counseling Program, Bowling Green State University, Bowling Green, OH:

GENERAL DESCRIPTION. The Achievement Motivation Profile (AMP) is a self-report instrument designed to aid education professionals and mental health clinicians, including psychologists and counselors, in assessing students' motivation to achieve and related personality characteristics. The AMP consists of 140 self-descriptive statements. The student responds to each statement by agreeing or disagreeing with the veracity of the statement on a 5-point Likert scale, ranging from *always true* to *always false*. The responses produce 15 scale scores and three validity measures.

The scale scores are grouped into four main areas. The Achiever, Motivation, Competitiveness, and Goal Motivation scales comprise the Motivation for Achievement scale score. The Relaxed Style, Happiness, Patience, and Self-Confidence scales produce the Inner Resources scale. Assertiveness, Personal Diplomacy, Extroversion, and Cooperativeness constitute the Interpersonal Strengths scale. Finally, the Planning and Organization, Initiative, and Team Player scales make up the Work Habits scale. Three validity measures are also produced: (a) Inconsistent Responding, (b) Self-Enhancing, and (c) Self-Critical.

THEORETICAL MODEL AND TEST DEVELOPMENT. Mandel and Marcus (1988) articulated the theoretical and pragmatic foundation for the AMP in their analysis of research results on underachievement, presentation of their developmental theory model, and their approach to differential diagnosis of individuals who are underachievers. From their research review, Mandel and Marcus concluded that a number of interacting factors resulted in a student's underachievement. They also believed that because everyone progressed through a number of developmental stages (each with its own potential for a particular psychopathology), therapists should be aware of both the student's personality structure and developmental stage. The authors also stated that the central feature of the model was that behavior is motivated. Additionally, the personality structure is, according to the authors, meaningfully organized with a core set of issues or needs. Thus, personality factors are arranged in an interactive matrix with core issues, which define the central motivating factors. Certain core issues are associated with each stage of personality development. As the individual progresses through the successive stages of development, the core issues change. The core issues involved conflicts to be resolved so that the personality structure matures. The AMP is based on the assumption that the individual's self-perception and self-presentation are critical to understanding his or her motivations and behaviors. The AMP was designed to assist in the identification of motivational and personality contributors to underachievement.

AMP items were developed to address issues relating to perception of self and others, work and achievement, and personal expectations. Potential AMP items were first administered to students and working adults in academic and career counseling settings and compared with a comprehensive set of objective data on each respondent. The scales were developed through grouping similar appearing items and then refining and validating the groupings through statistical analysis.

STANDARDIZATION. The AMP was standardized in the United States and Canada on 1,738 students, 14 years or older, in high school, junior college, or university settings. Fifty-five percent of the students were female and 10% of the students were ethnic minorities. Because the authors felt that there were only relatively minor differences among subgroups of students as to ethnic group, gender, and country of residence, the AMP norms were based on the entire sample.

RELIABILITY. Reliability data were gathered for the AMP scales. The AMP scales produced the range of alpha scores from .58 to .84 with a median of .75. A test-retest period of 60 days for 122 Canadian high school students yielded reliability estimates ranging from .61 to .89 on the AMP scales.

VALIDITY. The AMP concurrent and discriminant validities have been investigated. Mandel and Gavin (1991) found the Motivation for Achievement scale to correlate significantly with high school students' overall grade-point averages. A number of AMP scales discriminated significantly among students who were identified as falling in one of the following groups: (a) academic problems, (b) conduct disorders, (c) overanxious, or (d) both anxious and depressed (Mahy, in press). Additionally, their skills differentiated between achievers and underachievers (Mandel & Marcus, 1988).

INSTRUMENT ADMINISTRATION AND INTERPRETATION. The AMP can be administered either in paper-and-pencil or computer format. Most individuals can complete the test items in 20 to 30 minutes. It also can be either hand or computer scored. Computer scoring produces scale scores and discussion of each scale score, meaning of scale score combinations (profiles), and recommendations, including student counseling and performance improvement strategies. The authors encouraged test administrators to ensure students respond to all items; the AMP should not be scored if 15 or more items are missing or double-marked.

The scoring involves several steps in the hand-scored version. First, the raw scale scores are totaled, then the results are entered on the AMP Profile Form. The Profile Form produces a set of profiles for the four main scale areas and Response Style scores. *T*-scores and percentiles are listed in a column next to the profile scores and can be determined through visual inspection of the AMP Profile Form. The authors advise that the results should be combined with other sources of data, particularly for academic remediation.

SUMMARY. The AMP can be a valuable tool in assessing students who show indications of academic underachievement. The wording of the test items is sufficiently simple to allow most students to complete the assessment tool accurately. Additionally, the test prompts the clinician to investigate a wide range of factors that may contribute to student underachievement. However, there are some important issues to consider before using the test. First, the authors have not provided standardized scores for specific ethnic populations. This is unfortunate because of the evidence indicating that students from minority populations are most at risk for academic underachieving. Second, although the test is easy to take, it is difficult to score by hand. It is suggested that clinicians who intend to use the test often should consider computer scoring. Third, because academic underachievement can result from a combination of student choice, medical status, and mental disorders such as depression, clinicians are advised to continue investigating other potential problem areas even after the AMP provides valuable information on factors contributing to underachievement. Finally, the cure for underachievement is inevitably related to school personnel. It would be helpful if the manual would provide more direction for translating scale scores into general and specific school-based, teacher and tutor interventions. The goal for the AMP, to increase student performance, may be the most important goal that America has for its student population in this century. For this reason, it appears that continued research on the instrument's usefulness and application is essential.

REVIEWER'S REFERENCES

Mandel, H. P., & Marcus, S. I. (1988). *The psychology of under achievement: Differential diagnosis and differential treatment.* In I. B. Wiley (Series Ed.), *Wiley series on personality processes.* New York: John Wiley & Sons.

Mandel, H. P., & Gavin, D. (1991). *Correlations between MAI scales and both intelligence and academic performance in a high school sample.* Unpublished study, Institute on Achievement and Motivation, York University, Toronto.

Mahy, A. (in press). *Validation of MAI using semi-structured interviews to diagnose types of high school underachievers.* Master's thesis, Department of Psychology, York University, Toronto.

[4]
Adaptive Behavior Evaluation Scale, Revised.

Purpose: Designed to assist in "making diagnostic, placement, and programming decisions for mentally retarded and emotionally disturbed/behaviorally disordered children and adolescents."

Population: Ages 5-0 to 18-0.

Publication Dates: 1983–1995.

Acronym: ABES.

Scores, 10: Communication, Self-Care, Home Living, Social, Community Use, Self-Direction, Health and Safety, Functional Academics, Leisure, Work.

Administration: Individual.

Forms, 2: Adaptive Behavior Evaluation Scale, School Version; Adaptive Behavior Evaluation Scale, Home Version.

Price Data, 1999: $146 per complete kit including school ('95, 73 pages) and home ('95, 66 pages) versions of technical manuals, Adaptive Behavior Intervention manual ('95, 316 pages), and 50 each school and home versions rating forms; $12.50 per technical manual (school or home); $31 per 50 rating forms (school, home in English or home in Spanish); $24 per Adaptive Behavior Intervention manual; $35 per scoring disk (IBM or Macintosh); $149 per computerized Adaptive Behavior Intervention manual (IBM).

Time: (15–20) minutes.

Author: Stephen B. McCarney.

Publisher: Hawthorne Educational Services, Inc.

Cross References: For reviews by Mary Ross Moran and Harvey N. Switzky of an earlier edition, see 12:14.

Review of the Adaptive Behavior Evaluation Scale, Revised by JOHN H. KRANZLER, Professor of Educational Psychology, College of Education, University of Florida, Gainesville, FL:

TEST CONVERAGE AND USE. The Adaptive Behavior Evaluation Scale, Revised (ABES) is a norm-referenced rating scale designed to measure the adaptive skills of children and youth between 5 and 18 years of age. The ABES was revised to measure the 10 areas of adaptive skills as defined by the American Association of Mental Retardation (AAMR): Communication Skills, Self-Care, Home Living, Social, Community Use, Self-Direction, Health and Safety, Functional Academics, Leisure, and Work. The ABES is intended to be used by school personnel as a measure of general and specific adaptive skills to: "(a) screen for adaptive skills problems; (b) provide an adaptive skill measure for any referred student; (c) provide information that may contribute to the diagnosis of mental retardation; (d) develop goals and objectives for identified problem areas; (e) identify instructional activities for identified problem areas; [and] (f) document entry points, progress which occurs as a result of interventions, and identify exit points from special service delivery, if appropriate" (manual, p. 7). Home and School versions of the ABES are available. The complete set of materials includes two technical manuals, rating forms, and an intervention manual for the adaptive skills measured by the ABES. The manual lists possible goals and objectives for each adaptive skill area and may be used to develop individualized education plans (IEP).

TEST ADMINISTRATION AND SCORE REPORTING. The ABES is relatively easy to administer and score and takes about 15–20 minutes to complete. Instructions for completing and scoring are detailed and easy to follow. The ABES may be completed by parents/guardians, by classroom teachers, or by other school personnel (e.g., aides, counselors), provided that they have adequate familiarity with the student. "Familiarity" is defined in terms of general knowledge of the student, not in terms of length of time known. The author states that "no established length of time is necessary to observe or work with a child or youth before rating the child or youth" (manual, p. 27). The ABES may be used in an interview format if parents need assistance in completing the form for any reason.

The Home and School versions of the ABES consist of the same set of 104 items, with approximately 10 items per adaptive skill area. The person completing the scale must rate the child or youth on each item using the following scale: 5—Demonstrates the behavior or skill at all times (consistently); 4—Demonstrates the behavior or skill most of the time; 3—Demonstrates the behavior or skill inconsistently; 2—Is developing the behavior or skill; 1—Does not demonstrate the behavior or skill; 0—Is not developmentally appropriate for the student's age group. All 104 items must be completed using this rating scale, even when the rater has not had opportunity to observe a particular skill or behavior. Given that the demands on adaptive skills in home and school environments tend to differ, it seems reasonable to assume that at least some parents and educators will have an incomplete understanding of a student's adaptive skills. On the School version, when the person completing the scale has not observed a particular item, the rater is advised to consult another educator who may have knowledge about a student's ability to perform that skill or behavior. The manuals do not indicate what one should do when an educator with that knowledge cannot be found. No advice for addressing this potential problem on the ABES is given on the Home version.

On both Home and School versions, subscale scaled scores and percentile ranks are available for each of the 10 adaptive skills areas defined by the AAMR. These scaled scores are derived from separate norming samples and can be used to construct a profile of adaptive skills. An Adaptive Skills Quotient (ASQ) ($M = 100$, $SD = 15$), interpreted as a general measure of adaptive behavior, is also available on the ABES.

STANDARDIZATION AND NORMS. The standardization samples for the Home and School versions of the ABES consist of 4,740 and 7,124 subjects between the ages of 5 and 18 years. Subjects were selected from public and private schools in approximately 25 states in all four major geographic regions. School systems were randomly selected from the major geographic regions of the United States. Personnel in the participating school systems were responsible for randomly selecting parents and teachers at each grade level to rate students, who were in turn responsible for randomly selecting students and for returning completed forms. A table is presented in each manual describing the norming sample by sex, race, residence, geographic region, father's occupation, and mother's occupation. The percentage of students with disabilities in each standardization sample is not reported, despite the fact that school systems were encouraged to identify students with disabilities. The variables reported for both versions of the ABES compare fairly well with the *Statistical Abstract of the United States, 1992,* except for the underrepresentation of racial/ethnic minorities and students from the Northeast region. Whites from the North Central region are markedly overrepresented in the standardization samples of both versions of the ABES.

For the School version, norms tables are provided at 1-year intervals for boys and girls from 5 through 18 years. For the Home version, norms tables are provided at 1-year intervals for boys from 5 to 16 years and at a 2-year interval from 17 to 18; and for girls at 1-year intervals from 5 to 13 years and at a 2-year interval from 14 to 15 and 16 to 18. No rationale is given for combining ages at these levels. Norms tables for the total sample are not included, nor are supplemental norms for special populations (e.g., children and youth with mental disabilities) on either version. Descriptive statistics across items or subscales by gender and age also are not presented. Although information on the distribution of scores is lacking, they are reported in the manuals to be skewed, thereby raising the issue of the appropriateness of using normalized standard scores on the ABES.

RELIABILITY AND VALIDITY. The reliability of scores from the ABES appears to be adequate. Test-retest reliability was evaluated for 109 students on the School version and 83 students on the Home version over a 30-day interval. Stability coefficients exceeded .75 for boys and girls for the following age groups: 5–7, 8–10, 11–13, 14–16, and 17–18. Although these coefficients are acceptable, they are based on small samples (8–10 participants per age group). Interrater reliability was evaluated with 57 pairs of educators on the School version and 60 pairs of parents/guardians on the Home version. Interrater reliability coefficients ranged from .77 to .84 on the School version across age, and from .75 to .86 on the Home version. Though acceptable, these coefficients are also based on small samples (4–5 pairs of raters per age level). Estimates of internal consistency reliability of the ABES are good. Cronbach's alphas are reported for each of the 10 subscales and for the total score on each version. The alpha for total scores was .95 for each version, and ranged from .82 to .95 across subscales on the Home version and from .86 to .97 on the School version.

Several aspects of validity are reported for the ABES. Content-oriented evidence of construct validity is provided in each manual. The conceptual framework for the ABES is clear and based on the prevailing definition of adaptive skills by the AAMR. The initial pool of items was developed by educational diagnosticians and special education personnel who work with mentally disabled students. The initial pool of items was then examined by a similar group of experts and subjected to field trials. Given the omission of descriptive statistics by age in the manuals, age differentiation validity cannot be evaluated. Item-total score correlations and principal components analyses (with varimax rotation) were used to examine the factor structure of the ABES. All but one item on the ABES correlated with the total score above .30. Results of the principal components analyses do not support the factor structure of the ABES, however. Only three factors were found to underlie individual differences in adaptive skills on both versions. These results, therefore, do not support combining items into 10 subscales. Intra-individual analysis of a student's profile of adaptive skills, therefore, is not recommended. Hierarchical factor analysis also was not conducted to examine the appropriateness of combining subscales into one general score. These results suggest that the ABES lacks structural fidelity, because the scored aspects of the ABES (i.e., subscale scores and ASQ) are not consistent with the definition of adaptive skills upon which it is based.

Criterion-related evidence of validity was examined by correlating subscale scores and the ASQ with scores on other widely used measures of adaptive skills (e.g., Vineland Adaptive Behavior Scales, Adaptive Behavior Inventory for Children). The pattern of correlations between scores on both versions of the ABES and these external criteria was both rational and consistent with construct theory. Significant differences between groups of children and youth with mental disabilities and nonidentified subjects also were found in the expected direction on both versions of the ABES. No empirical evidence was presented to support the use of the ABES with other groups (e.g., behaviorally disturbed children and youth), despite the fact that it is intended for use with these students. Moreover, items on the ABES were not analyzed for possible test bias across racial/ethnic minority groups.

SUMMARY. The Adaptive Behavior Evaluation Scale—Revised (ABES) is a norm-referenced rating scale developed to measure the general and specific adaptive skills of children and youth between the ages of 5 and 18 years. Home and School versions of the ABES are available. The ABES is relatively easy to administer and score and can be completed in roughly 15–20 minutes. Scaled scores and percentile ranks are available for 10 adaptive skills areas as well as for general adaptive behavior. Norms for the ABES are somewhat representative of the United States populations, but racial/ethnic minority groups and students from the Northeast region are underrepresented in both standardization samples. Reliability of the ABES is satisfactory, but examinations of test-retest and interrater reliability were based on small samples across age levels. The construct validity evidence for the ABES is questionable, given the absence of factor analytic support for the 10 subscale scores and the ASQ. Ipsative (i.e., intraindividual) analysis of a student's subscale scores is not recommended. Evidence supporting the use of the ABES with emotionally disturbed children and youth also was not reported, nor were analyses of possible test bias with racial/ethnic or other groups. The ABES should be used with caution until further research has been conducted.

Review of the Adaptive Behavior Evaluation Scale, Revised by MARK D. SHRIVER, Assistant Professor of Pediatrics, and MERILEE McCURDY, Pediatric Psychology Intern, Munroe-Meyer Institute for Genetics and Rehabilitation, University of Nebraska Medical Center, Omaha, NE:

The Adaptive Behavior Evaluation Scale, Revised includes a Home Version and a School Version and was developed to incorporate the 1992 changes in the American Association for Mental Retardation's (AAMR) definition of Mental Retardation. AAMR and this instrument identify 10 areas of adaptive skills including: Communication, Self-Care, Home Living, Social, Community Use, Self-Direction, Health and Safety, Functional Academics, Leisure, and Work. The Home Version and the School Version of the Adaptive Behavior Evaluation Scale, Revised (hereafter called ABES-H-R and ABES-S-R) are intended to screen and measure adaptive skills, assist with diagnosis of mental retardation, develop Individual Education Plan (IEP) goals, and monitor child progress. This instrument is intended to assess "adaptive skills with any student experiencing academic or behavioral difficulties regardless of the severity or suspected handicapping condition" (technical manual, p. 5). Unless otherwise noted, the comments below are relevant to both the ABES-H-R and ABES-S-R.

TEST ADMINISTRATION AND SCORING. The ABES-R is appropriate for children ages 5 through 18 years. Teachers and parents respond to 104 items regarding the extent to which the child demonstrates the skill reflected by the item. Quantifiers for each item range from a rating of "1" for "does not demonstrate the behavior or skill" to "5" for "demonstrates the behavior or skill at all times (consistently)." Items can also be rated as a "0" for "not developmentally appropriate for the student's age group"; however, this may be difficult for a parent or teacher to determine with limited knowledge of child development.

Guidelines for rating the child are provided on the rating form. A profile sheet for scoring is attached as part of the rating form. A separate scoring sheet is needed, however, for transferring scores and computing subscale and total scale scores. Total raw scores are computed for each of the 10 subscales. The subscales have a range from 8 items (for Self-Care) to 29 items (for Social). Many items contribute to the raw score of more than one scale. Raw scores for each subscale are computed into standard scores. These standard scores are added together and computed into an Adaptive Skills Quotient. The Adaptive Skills quotient has a mean of 100 with a standard deviation of 15. The subscale standard scores have means of 10 and standard deviations of 3. Percentile scores are also provided.

The Adaptive Behavior Intervention Manual (ABIM) is also provided to assist with the development of the IEP by including goals and objectives corresponding to each item on the scale. Possible interventions are provided in the ABIM relative to each item. It is encouraging to see test developers attempt to link assessment with intervention and progress monitoring.

DEVELOPMENT OF THE ABES-R. In Fall of 1993, 43 diagnosticians and special education personnel were asked to recommend adaptive skills necessary for success in the 10 adaptive skill areas recommended by AAMR. No other information regarding the diagnosticians and special education personnel is provided. Hundreds of items were collapsed and combined by the authors to form 128 items. These items were returned to the 43 diagnosticians and special education personnel for further revision resulting in an item pool of 110 items. These items were then assigned to one or more of the 10 adaptive behavior skill areas based on face validity. Field testing of items took place in 14 school districts in Missouri. Results of the field testing are not further described, but this may be how the item pool was reduced from 110 items to 104.

NORMATIVE SAMPLE. The normative sample for the ABES-S-R consisted of 7,124 students from 24 states in the four major geographical regions of the United States; however, the Northeast and South regions appear to be underrepresented. Almost half of the sample is derived from the North Central region of the U.S. Other characteristics include sex, race, residence, and parents' occupation. Caucasian students appear to be slightly overrepresented whereas Hispanic students appear underrepresented. Likewise urban/suburban students are underrepresented and rural students are overrepresented. Sample sizes are presented for each age level and range from 99 (age 18) to 861 (age 9) with most over 400. Children with disabilities are reportedly included in the normative sample, although no information is presented about them.

The normative sample for the ABES-H-R consisted of 4,740 children from 26 states in the four major geographic regions of the United States, however, the Northeast and West are underrepresented, whereas almost half of the sample comes from the North Central region. Other characteristics presented include sex, race, residence, and parent's occupation. Caucasian students are overrepresented and African American and Hispanic students are underrepresented. Likewise, urban/suburban students are underrepresented and rural students are over represented. Sample sizes are presented for each age level and range from 189 to 668 for ages to 14 years. Sample sizes for ages 15 years through 18 years dwindle considerably and range from 15 (age 18) to 62 (age 15). These sample sizes are too small for adequate normative comparison.

RELIABILITY. Cronbach's coefficient alpha was used to calculate internal consistency for each version's subscales and total scale. The ABES-H-R coefficient alpha values ranged from .82 to .95 on the subscales and equaled .95 for the total scale. The ABES-S-R coefficient alpha values ranged from .86 to .97 for the subscales and equaled .95 for the total scale.

Test-retest reliability was assessed on 83 students over a 30-day period and ranged from .76 to .95 for the subscales on the ABES-H-R. Test-retest reliability for the ABES-S-R included 109 subjects over a 30-day period and ranged from .75 to .92. Test-retest reliability for the total score is not provided.

Interrater reliability for the ABES-H-R was calculated by two parents or guardians rating the adaptive behavior of 60 children. The correlations ranged from .75 to .86 with an average of .82. For the ABES-S-R, this involved 57 sets of two educators rating 71 student's behavior. The inteerrater reliability estimates ranged from .77 to .84 with an average of .82.

VALIDITY. Content validity evidence is based on the development of the ABES-R according to the AAMR's current definition of adaptive behavior skills. Development and standardization of the ABES-R is described above. In addition, item analysis examined response distributions and correlations of items within subscales. A point biserial correlation technique was used to examine the discriminating power of items. Item/total score correlations are reported to be above the minimum level of acceptance of .30 for the ABES-H-R and ABES-S-R.

Criterion-related validity evidence is provided by correlations of scores from the ABES-H-R with those from the Adaptive Behavior Inventory for Children (ABIC) and the Vineland Behavior Evaluation Scale—Interview Edition (VABS-IE). Correlations ranged from .586 to .911 ($n = 47$) with the ABC and ranged from .208 to .882 ($n = 31$) for the VABS-IE. The samples for the studies consisted of children ages 5 to 12 with a previous diagnosis of mental retardation.

The ABES-S-R was correlated with the Adaptive Behavior Inventory for Children (ABIC), Vineland Adaptive Behavior Scales—Classroom Edition (VABS-CE), and the Adaptive Behavior Inventory (ABI). Correlations ranged from .518 to .926 with the ABIC ($n = 51$), from .213 to .831 for the VABS-CE ($n = 39$), and from .503 to .922 ($n = 47$) for the ABI. Students for the first two studies ranged from 5 to 12 years of age, and for the third study, ranged from 5 to 18 years of age.

Construct validity was examined by factor analysis, diagnostic validity, subscale interrelationships, and item validity. It appears that there is "one overwhelming factor that dominates the scale" (p. 17, ABES-H-R and ABES-S-R). Additional factor analysis results indicate that both versions of the ABES-R support these overlying factors. It does not appear that factor analysis confirmed the composition of the 10 adaptive behavior areas.

Diagnostic validity is examined by rating students with previously diagnosed mental retardation in the moderate or severe range using the ABES-H-R or ABES-S-R. For both scales, mean subscale scores ranged from 4 to 7 or one to two standard deviations below the mean.

SUMMARY. The authors appear to have responded well to concerns or questions raised in earlier reviews of the ABES. The current measure appears to represent almost a complete overhaul of the earlier editions and it is positive that the developers have attempted to link the measure with the AAMR adaptive skill areas. In addition, the availability of an intervention manual may assist educators in linking adaptive behavior assessment with intervention and progress monitoring. The normative samples should be more representative of the national population and sample sizes are small at the upper age levels of the ABES-H-R. The reliability evidence presented is strongest for the total score obtained from both versions of the ABES-R, although stability evidence is still needed. It appears that the factor analysis may best support the construct validity of the total score rather than the subscale scores. Additional evidence for content validity, criterion-related validity, and construct validity is needed before recommending the use of this test in place of other commonly used measures such as the Vineland Adaptive Behavior Scales (Sparrow, Balla, Cicchetti, & Doll, 1985; T5: 2813) or the AAMR Adaptive Behavior Scales (Lambert, Nihira, & Leland, 1993; Nihira, Leland, & Lambert, 1993; T5:1 and T5:2).

REVIEWER'S REFERENCES

Lambert, N., Nihira, K., & Leland, H. (1993). ABS-S:2 AAMR Adaptive Behavior Scale—School, Second Edition. Austin, TX: PRO-ED.

Nihira, K., Leland, H., & Lambert, N. (1993). ABS-RC:2 AAMR Adaptive Behavior Scale—Residential and Community, Second Edition. Austin, TX: PRO-ED.

Sparrow, S. S., Balla, D. A., Cicchetti, D. V., & Doll, E. A. (1985). Vineland Adaptive Behavior Scales. Circle Pines, MN: American Guidance Service.

[5]
AD/HD Comprehensive Teacher's Rating Scale, Second Edition [1998 Revision].

Purpose: "Designed to help identify attention disorder, with or without hyperactivity."

Population: Grades K–Adult.

Publication Dates: 1986–2000.

Acronym: ACTeRS.

Administration: Individual.

Editions, 2: Paper-and-pencil; microcomputer.

Price Data, 2001: $47 per Teacher and Parent Form examiner's kit including manual (2000, 31 pages) and 50 rating/profile forms; $32 per 50 rating/profile forms; $175 per microcomputer version for 100 administrations including manual, IBM-PC only; $100 per microcomputer version for 50 administrations including manual, IBM-PC only; $15 per introductory kit including manual, sample Parent rating/profile Form, sample Teacher rating/profile Form, sample Self-Report Form, and annotated bibliography of research; $15 per manual.

Time: [5–15] minutes.

Comments: IBM-PC necessary for administration of microcomputer edition; parent forms available in Spanish.

Authors: Rina K. Ullmann, Esther K. Sleator, Robert L. Sprague, and MetriTech staff.

Publisher: MetriTech, Inc.

a) ACTeRS TEACHER FORM.

Population: Grades K–8.

Scores, 4: Attention, Hyperactivity, Social Skills, Oppositional Behavior.

Price Data: $47 including manual and 50 forms; $32 per 50 forms.

Time: Untimed.

b) ACTeRS PARENT FORM.

Scores, 5: Attention, Hyperactivity, Social Skills, Oppositional Behavior, Early Childhood.

Price Data: $47 including manual and 50 forms; $32 per 50 forms.

Time: Untimed.

c) ACTeRS SELF-REPORT.

Population: Adolescence through adulthood.

Scores, 3: Attention, Hyperactivity/Impulsivity, Social Adjustment.

Price Data: $51 including manual and 50 forms; $37 per 50 forms.

Time: Untimed [10–15 minutes].

Cross References: For reviews by Robert J. Miller and Judy Oehler-Stinnett of an earlier edition, see 12:15 (2 references); see also T4:89 (1 reference); for reviews by Ellen H. Bacon and Ayres G. D'Costa of an earlier edition, see 11:7 (2 references).

Review of the AD/HD Comprehensive Teacher's Rating Scale, Second Edition [1998 Revi-

sion] by CEDERICK O. LINDSKOG, Professor, and JANET V. SMITH, Associate Professor, Department of Psychology and Counseling, Pittsburg State University, Pittsburg, KS:

The title ACTeRS is an abbreviation for AD/HD Comprehensive Teachers Rating Scale. The instrument was originally a teacher's rating scale, and underwent revision in 1990. The currently reviewed version carries the same name (ACTeRS), but now has three forms, a Teacher Form, a Parent Form, and a Self-Report Form. The Teacher and Parent Forms were included in the 1997 version of the manual. A representative of the publisher indicated by telephone that all three forms will be included in the next printing of the manual, which is at press as of this date. These ACTeRS products, according to the manual, "were designed with three goals: (1) to put appropriate emphasis on attention; (2) to be useful to clinicians for diagnosis of ADD and monitoring of treatment effects; and (3) to reveal individual differences in the behavior of children who manifest a deficit in attention, both before and during treatment" (p. 1). The Teacher Form (TF) and Parent Form (PF) are similar in structure and content. Each has a Likert-type scale (1 = *almost never* to 5 = *almost always*) to rate behavioral descriptors. The forms share four categories of 4 to 7 items. Those categories are Attention, Hyperactivity, Social Skills, and Oppositional Behavior. The PF has a fifth category called Early Childhood. The TF has a total of 24 items in the four categories, and the PF has 25 items in five. The manual designates the TF as the primary instrument, and clearly states that the role of the PF is to "improve diagnostic accuracy by providing a second, objective evaluation" (p. 1).

Raw scores are converted into percentile ranks on the charts printed on the protocol. Normalized T scores are available in the manual for those who wish to use a standard score. Norms are gender specific. Administration and scoring are very easily accomplished, with little room for error. Item pools for both forms were obtained by defensible methods including reviews and expert opinion. The item pools were narrowed utilizing various factor analyses until most items loaded on one factor only.

TEACHER FORM. The current version of the TF was reviewed in the *Twelfth Mental Measurements Yearbook* (Miller, 1995; Oehler-Stinnett,

1995). It was restandardized beginning in 1989, and the norms were expanded from K–5 to K–8. The current sample was 2,362 students. Approximately 150 students from each grade from K–5 were included in order to confirm data from the original standardization. The bulk of the students in the current standardization were in Grade 6 (N = 518), Grade 7 (N = 448), and Grade 8 (N = 493). No additional information was provided in the manual with regard to other standardization sample characteristics such as gender (although a footnote in the manual led the reviewer to conclude the sample was equivalent numbers of boys and girls), national geographic distribution, urban/rural, ethnicity, or parent education (or socioeconomic status). This lack of information precludes the interpretation of these scores for purposes of initial diagnostics due to significant risk of bias error.

Reliability for scores from the TF was reported by using three approaches: internal consistency, test-retest, and interjudge. The internal consistency is impressive. The initial standardization group and the 1989 group showed .92 to .97 across the four areas measured by the Teacher Form. The test-retest is somewhat less impressive, with correlations of .78 to .82 (N = 80 boys and girls) across the four areas. These data are somewhat flawed in that there was no report of time elapsed between the tests, and the number of subjects is few. The interjudge correlations range from .51 to .73, indicating that although the items are consistent, use of them may not be, which supports the use of multiple informants. The manual is very brief in discussion of reliability issues.

The manual fails to adequately address some basic validity issues. The manual provides impressive data on factor loadings of the items, which may be evidence for construct validity; however, there is no explicit discussion of evidence supporting validity for the TF of this instrument. Some evidence is presented to indicate that the instrument differentiates between AD/HD and LD children, but the data are presented as differences between percentile ranks instead of a more discriminating statistic utilizing a standard score. It is not apparent from the data available whether or not the differences are statistically significant.

PARENT FORM. The authors state that the child must show a deficit in Attention before a diagnosis can be made. They state that for a child who scores "at or below the 10th percentile, no matter what the other scores, one can confidently feel that the diagnosis of AD/HD is legitimate" (manual, p. 17). There is no rationale for score cutoffs. This reviewer is not convinced that a Teacher Form of unclear reliability and validity with an Attention subscale of six items is possessed of sufficient power to make that discrimination.

The Parent Form presents impressive internal consistency as a reliability measure. The first group was an undifferentiated group of boys and girls, both AD/HD diagnosed and nondiagnosed. The range of ratios across the five areas was from .78 (Early Childhood) to .96 (Attention). Another study of nondiagnosed boys and girls (N = 108) revealed generally lower figures (.80 to .89), probably due to restriction in variability of the sample, according to the manual. Again, the manual did not address other measures of reliability for the Parent Form.

The section of the manual devoted to the Parent Form states that "The validity ... rests in part on the relationship between its scales and those of the Teacher Form" (manual, p. 14). Because the PF consists predominantly of items paralleling the TF, one would expect a significant relationship to exist, similar to the situation with the Wechsler Intelligence Scale for Children— Revised (WISC-R) and the Wechsler Intelligence Scale for Children—Third Edition (WISC-III), which have a high level of common items. Furthermore, because the TF section of the manual lacks discussion of validity, linking it to another form of the instrument does not provide sufficient evidence to support claims of validity. The PF does, however, present data indicating the instrument differentiates well between AD/HD diagnosed and nondiagnosed children. In addition, there was an attempt to link the PF items to the TF items presumably to make parallel the percentile scores of the two forms. As is the case with the TF, there are T score equivalents in the manual for those wishing to convert the percentile ranks to standard scores, with separate norms for boys and girls.

SELF-REPORT FORM. The Self-Report Form consists of 10 items each to assess adults in the areas of Attention and Social Adjustment, and 15 items to address Hyperactivity, for a total of 35 items. The raw scores for each area are converted to gender neutral percentile ranks. As is the case with the other scales, a chart is in the manual to convert the percentiles into T scores.

There were few data speaking to the standardization of 1,012 cases. The reliability figures are based on a sample of 990 adult men and women, 10% diagnosed AD/HD, with no further descriptions given. The internal consistency for this sample was mediocre. The values were .88 Total, .82 for Attention, .86 for Hyperactivity/ Impulsivity, and .70 for Social Adjustment. Perhaps the low percentage of diagnosed cases again led to a restriction of score variability, which lowered the internal consistency scores.

The Self-Report Form was normed on adults, yet the manual indicates that the instrument's validity rests in part on its relationship to the TFK and the PF, which are clearly normed and standardized on children in Grades K–8. The manual does not use the term face validity, but obviously it is intended, as the only apparent relationship between these forms is item similarity. There are no statistical data provided or implied. As was the case with the PF, this Self-Report does a good job of discriminating between diagnosed and nondiagnosed individuals.

SUMMARY. The ACTeRS has evolved from a single Teacher Form to include a parent rating and a self-rating. It is easy to use, score, and interpret. The TF and PF apply to children in Grades K–8, and the Self-Report applies to adults. On all the forms, the items seem to be well selected, and on the PF and Self-Report, they discriminate well between diagnosed and nondiagnosed populations. There are a number of barriers to recommending the use of this instrument to diagnose AD/HD. First is the lack of norming data as specified above. Next is the lack of statistically significant evidence to support validity and insufficient evidence of reliability for any of these forms. This instrument may have use in screening or activities such as monitoring treatment effects, but cannot be recommended for use in any phase of diagnostics. The high level of internal consistency establishes the potential of this instrument if data were provided for the norming, standardization, reliability, and validity as noted above.

To assess AD/HD from a DSM-IV diagnostic approach, the Attention Deficit Disorders Evaluation Scale (ADDES; 28) is a better choice. In considering the emerging evidence of AD/HD complexity and literature on comorbidity, it is prudent to recommend a multidimensional instrument such as the Achenbach Child Behavior Checklist (T5:451), or the Behavior Assessment System for Children (40), either of which is more likely to detect evidence of commonly comorbid conditions such as a Learning Disability, Oppositional Defiant Disorder, Conduct Disorder, Obsessive-Compulsive Disorder, or Depression.

REVIEWER'S REFERENCES

Miller, R. J. (1995). [Review of the ADD-H: Comprehensive Teacher's Rating Scale, Second Edition.] In J. C. Conoley & J. C. Impara (Eds.), *The twelfth mental measurements yearbook* (pp. 38–40). Lincoln, NE: Buros Institute of Mental Measurements.
Oehler-Stinnett, J. (1995). [Review of the ADD-H: Comprehensive Teacher's Rating Scale, Second Edition.] In J. C. Conoley & J. C. Impara (Eds.), *The twelfth mental measurements yearbook* (pp. 40–42). Lincoln, NE: Buros Institute of Mental Measurements.

Review of the AD/HD Comprehensive Teacher's Rating Scale, Second Edition [1998 Revision] by EVERETT V. SMITH, JR., Assistant Professor of Educational Psychology, University of Illinois, Chicago, IL:

The AD/HD Comprehensive Teacher's Rating Scale (ACTeRS) is a simple and short rating scale instrument used for the diagnosis and monitoring of treatment of attention deficit disorder (ADD). Several additions to this version of the ACTeRS include extending the scale's utility to include a Parent form (K–8), a Self-report form (adolescence through adulthood), the availability of the Parent form in Spanish, and the addition of a new subscale—Early Childhood—found in the Parent form. The availability of the Parent form is especially relevant given that the DSM-IV states that some symptoms must be present in more than one setting in order to make a diagnosis.

The Teacher form consists of 24 items grouped by subscale with separate profiles for boys and girls. The directions require the teacher to compare the child's behavior with that of his or her classmates and record the evaluation on a 5-point frequency scale with the endpoints labeled *Almost Never* and *Almost Always*. A potential problem with this 5-point scale is that it leaves the teacher in the position of interpreting the meaning of the second, third, and fourth rating points. If a teacher perceives the midpoint as average and rates a child as average on all items, the child would have percentile scores in the "problem direction" on the profile charts. A better-defined rating scale may be advantageous.

The Parent form consists of 25 items grouped by subscale, again with separate profiles for boys and girls. The majority of the items are identical to

those on the Teacher form but include examples in order to help parents assess their child's behavior. Another distinction from the Teacher form is the inclusion of an Early Childhood subscale. This subscale is to be used in conjunction with teacher and parent ratings as additional diagnostic information. The response format is identical to the Teacher form, as are the potential problems mentioned previously.

The Self-report form consists of 35 nongrouped items measuring Attention, Hyperactivity/Impulsivity, and Social Adjustment. A 5-point rating scale with labels of *Strongly Disagree*, *Disagree*, *Uncertain*, *Agree*, and *Strongly Agree* help define the meaning of each rating point.

The Teacher and Parent forms are also available in the microcomputer version. Although the microcomputer version was not included for evaluation, the manual does an excellent job detailing the options available to the potential user. A strength of the microcomputer version is the ability to encrypt information to protect privacy. A limitation is the lack of a Windows version.

SCORING. Scoring for all three pencil-and-paper forms is conducted in the traditional summative rating scale technique in which points are assigned according to the ratings circled and then summed for the items comprising each of the subscales to arrive at scale scores.

INTERPRETATION. For the Teacher and Parent forms, the scale scores for each subscale are circled on the appropriate gender-specific profile. From these profiles, percentile ranks are available. The authors recommend that a child receiving a percentile at or below the 10th percentile on the Attention subscale, regardless of other scores, be diagnosed as ADD. Scoring above the 10th and below the 25th percentile results in a handicapped rating and should only be considered ADD if other subscales confirm the diagnosis.

For the other subscales, scores at or below the 25th percentile should be considered a major deficit, from the 25th to the 40th percentile a moderate problem, from the 40th to the 50th percentile a mild problem and above the 50th percentile no problem. The manual provides only limited empirical evidence for the clinical validity of the proposed cutscores. However, the manual stresses that the profile of scores should be used in conjunction with everything else that is known regarding a child's behavior to make an informed decision about treatment and diagnosis. T scores with a mean of 50 and standard deviation of 10 are available in the manual.

The Self-report form also uses percentile interpretations, but does not provide separate profiles for males and females. No additional information concerning reliability, validity, the norming procedure, etc., for this form was provided.

DEVELOPMENT AND NORMING. The Teacher form was developed from a 43-item behavior scale administered to a norm group of 1,339 children across the elementary grades (K through 5). The final 24 items were chosen through the use of factor analysis. In 1989, the norms were extended through the eighth grade. This restandardization is based on 2,362 students rated by 84 teachers. A factor analysis replicated the results found in the original standardization. The manual does not fully explain the norming procedure or the normative sample (geographic region, ethnicity, SES, etc.). Without this information it may be difficult to ascertain whether the ACTeRS is appropriate for a given setting.

The Parent form was developed based on group interviews with parents of children with attention disorders. From these interviews, the 24 items of the Teacher form were retained and an additional 9 items developed. A factor analysis based on parent ratings of 892 children (478 diagnosed with ADHD) resulted in the retention of 25 items for the final Parent form. The Parent form was equated with the Teacher form so that percentile ranks on each form would "reflect comparable degrees of adequacy" (manual, p. 14). This process was done for all subscales except for the Early Childhood subscale, for which comparable items on both forms do not exist. Andrich's Rasch rating scale model (Andrich, 1978) was used to conduct the equating. The use of such methods is commendable. Unfortunately, the results of the equating process are not provided. Therefore, the comparability of the percentiles across forms is questionable. Additional information concerning the fit of the items to the model on the Parent form needs to be provided.

RELIABILITY. Reliability for the Teacher form is reported as internal consistency, test-retest, and interrater estimates. The authors report interrater reliability for 124 children each rated by two teachers. Simple correlations were .61 for the Attention subscale, .73 for Hyperactivity, .51 for Social Skills, and .59 for Oppositional. These reported levels of interrater reliability are not sufficiently high to warrant use as a diagnostic tool. Test-retest coefficients based on a sample of 80 boys and girls ranged from .78 to .82. The length of time between administrations was not provided. For the initial sample of 1,339 children in Grades K–5 internal consistency estimates are all in the .90s, which is quite good considering the number of items per subscale is fairly small (five to seven items). For the restandardization sample the internal consistency estimates again were quite good, ranging from .92 to .97.

For the Parent form, two samples are used to provide internal consistency estimates. The first sample consists of 240 ADHD diagnosed and 281 nondiagnosed children for estimating internal consistency for the Attention, Hyperactivity, Social Skills, and Oppositional subscales. For the Early Childhood subscale 261 children were used, "most" of whom had an ADHD diagnosis. The reason for the fluctuating sample sizes is not provided. Reliability estimates ranged from .78 to .96. The second sample was based on 108 nondiagnosed children. All estimates were in the .80s, ranging from .81 to .89. Noticeably lacking are test-retest estimates.

VALIDITY. Several studies using the Teacher form are presented for evidence of validity. One study differentiated an ADD-H group (n = 85) from a learning disabled group (n = 124). These differences are reported in terms of mean percentile rankings on the four subscales. Mean percentile ranks for the LD group were statistically higher (less problematic) than those of ADD-H students. Another study demonstrated that mean scores on Attention and Hyperactivity of attention disorder students (n = 23), LD students (n = 23), and a control group (n = 31) were statistically different, with the attention disorder students having the lowest percentiles ranks and the controls the highest.

Studies have also used the Teacher form to monitor the behavior of ADHD students in response to medication. Scores on Attention and Hyperactivity improved as students were placed on increased medication; improvements on the Social Skills and Oppositional subscales were smaller. Based on this research, the manual claims the ACTeRS may be useful for monitoring the effects of intervention. However, the relatively few items on each subscale may limit the sensitivity of the instrument to detect change.

For the parent form an item-level discriminant function analysis was conducted to evaluate each item's ability to differentiate ADHD diagnosed children from nondiagnosed children. No information was presented to evaluate the results of this analysis. A series of univariate tests demonstrated statistically significant group mean differences between 256 children with an attention disorder diagnosis and 221 controls on all five subscales. A more appropriate multivariate technique such as MANOVA with follow-up testing would provide more information regarding the nature of group differences.

SUMMARY. The ACTeRS is easy to administer, score, and interpret. This reviewer encourages additional reliability and validity studies using the Teacher and Parent forms before using these instruments for diagnostic purposes or for monitoring the effects of treatment. Details concerning the development of the Self-report form needs to be included.

REVIEWER'S REFERENCE

Andrich, D. (1978). A binomial latent trait model for the study of Likert-type attitude questionnaires. *British Journal of Mathematical and Statistical Psychology, 31,* 84–98.

[6]
Adjustment Scales for Children and Adolescents.

Purpose: "Designed to assess through teacher observation behavior pathology in youths."
Population: Ages 5–17.
Publication Dates: 1993–1994.
Acronym: ASCA.
Scores, 10: Overactivity, Underactivity, Attention-Deficit Hyperactive, Solitary Aggressive-Provocative, Solitary Aggressive-Impulsive, Oppositional Defiant, Diffident, Avoidant, Delinquent, Lethargic-Hypoactive.
Administration: Individual.
Price Data, 1995: $74.95 per complete kit including 25 male and 25 female self-scoring forms and profiles and manual ('94, 68 pages); $20.56 per 25 self-scoring forms and profiles (specify male or female); $34.95 per manual.
Time: (10–20) minutes.
Comments: Behavior checklist to be completed by a teacher about a student; scored by a psychologist or assessment specialist.
Authors: Paul A. McDermott, Neville C. Marston, and Denis H. Stott.
Publisher: Ed & Psych Associates.
Cross References: See T5:69 (1 reference).

Review of the Adjustment Scales for Children and Adolescents by GARY L. CANIVEZ, Associate Professor of Psychology, Eastern Illinois University, Charleston, IL:

The Adjustment Scales for Children and Adolescents (ASCA) is an objective behavior rating instrument completed by the student's classroom teacher and designed for use with all noninstitutionalized youths ages 5 through 17 (Grades K–12). The ASCA was based on psychologists' preferences for objective definitions of youth psychopathology and advantages of unobtrusive observations. In contrast to instruments that require teachers to estimate the general frequency or severity of problem behaviors and infer pathology from those ratings, the ASCA uniquely assesses psychopathology based on problem behaviors that occur in multiple situations within the school environment and in general norms (McDermott, 1994). In addition to the core and supplemental syndromes, the ASCA provides two global (broad band) or overall adjustment scales (Overactivity and Underactivity), which correspond to the second order factors that emerged. These global scales are similar to the externalizing (conduct problem) and internalizing (withdrawal) dimensions frequently found in the literature on childhood psychopathology (Quay, 1986) and the majority of child psychopathology measures.

The ASCA has excellent normative characteristics. It was standardized on 1,400 (700 male, 700 female) noninstitutionalized children ages 5 through 17 (Grades K–12) and very closely matches the United States Census estimates for race/ethnicity, parent education (primary social class index), national region, and community size as well as U.S. Department of Education estimates for various disabilities and giftedness. Standardization data were collected by The Psychological Corporation and the ASCA was conormed with the Differential Abilities Scales (DAS; Elliot, 1990) for 1,260 youths. The ASCA sample ranged from 55 to 145 on the DAS, and the means and standard deviations for all intellectual and achievement areas closely approximated 100 and 15, respectively (McDermott, 1993, 1994).

Reliability estimates are generally acceptable and typical of better measures of child and adolescent psychopathology. Internal consistency estimates for the total standardization sample ranged from .67 to .86 for the six core syndromes and two supplementary syndromes and equaled .92 for the Overactivity scale and .82 for the Underactivity scale. Test-retest reliabilities over a 30-school-day interval (n = 40) ranged from .66 to .91 for the six core syndromes and two supplemental syndromes and equaled .75 for the Overactivity scale and .79 for the Underactivity scale. Interobserver reliabilities (n = 22) ranged from .65 to .85 for the six core syndromes and two supplemental syndromes and equaled .75 for the Overactivity scale and .79 for the Underactivity scale. Mean differences across time and between the two observers for the six core syndromes and two global adjustment scales were not significant and indicated consistent levels of stability and agreement.

Initial validity studies summarized in the ASCA manual and published elsewhere (McDermott, 1993; McDermott et al., 1995) provide broad support of the first and second order factor structure, convergent and divergent validity, and discriminant validity. Studies examining convergent and divergent validity of the ASCA with the Conners' Teacher Rating Scale (CTRS; Trites, Blouin, & Laprade, 1982) and the Child Behavior Checklist (CBCL; Achenbach & Edelbrock, 1983) showed significant positive correlations among similar dimensions and low, nonsignificant correlations among dissimilar dimensions. Correlations between the ASCA and the DAS, although statistically significant because of the large sample size, were low, accounting for no more than 5% shared variance for any cognitive or academic variable, also supporting the ASCA's divergent validity (McDermott, 1994, 1995). Additional research has indicated the ASCA is excellent in discriminating students classified as socially or emotionally disturbed (SED) from normal, learning disabled, speech/language disabled, and gifted youths (McDermott, 1993, 1994; McDermott et al., 1995).

The ASCA rating form is completed by the student's teacher after having observed the student for a minimum of 40 school days to provide adequate opportunity to view the student in multiple situations. The ASCA takes about 10 to 20 minutes to complete and the directions are clearly presented. Although there are male and female versions of the ASCA rating form, each rating form is identical in content with the exception of gender referents. According to McDermott (1994) the ASCA should be scored by a psychologist or other assessment specialist. The scoring key for the ASCA self-scoring rating form is printed on the reverse side of the back page and the examiner need only unfold the form to expose the key. This allows the examiner to score the six core syndromes, two supplementary syndromes, and two overall adjustment scales by observing which distinct symbols are marked/shaded and summing like symbols. Syndrome raw scores are transferred to the back page of the ASCA rating form allowing the examiner to plot a profile and record T scores and percentiles, which are easily obtained from the Appendix of the ASCA manual. T scores were reportedly "normalized" to equate the core, supplemental, and global syndromes so identical T scores indicate equal rarity (percentiles) (McDermott, 1994). ASCA score distributions are positively skewed, a common feature of scales assessing psychopathology (McDermott, 1993; Kamphaus & Frick, 1996). Extensive clinical use of the ASCA indicates that due to occasional subtle imperfections in the printing process, examiners should check the alignment of the rating form and scoring key to verify correct alignment to ensure scoring accuracy.

McDermott (1993, 1994) presents three methods of interpretation for the ASCA: Cut-Score, Syndromic Profile, and Discriminant Classification interpretation. The Cut-Score approach is a univariate approach; the Syndromic Profile and Discriminant Classification approaches are multivariate classification methods. The ASCA manual presents detailed instructions and rationale for the application of each of these methods as well as appropriate limitations and cautions. Additional guidance in interpretation integrating forthcoming validity studies should be incorporated in future editions of the ASCA manual.

Both the Syndromic Profile Interpretation and Discriminant Classification Interpretation methods are dependent on multiple mathematical calculations for accurate classification. In the case of Syndromic Profile Interpretation an examiner could compare the youth's profile to as many as 22 different profile types yielding 22 generalized distance scores (GDS) and the probability of calculation errors increases with each GDS produced. Examiners utilizing the ASCA should be extremely careful in their calculations to be sure results and classifications are accurate or utilize computerized methods now available (Canivez, 1998; Watkins, 1996).

An advantage of the ASCA's large, representative national sample is that it allows for estimation of prevalence or base rates of various problem behaviors and psychopathologies and investigation of demographic variability with respect to differential prevalence in the population. Such studies are now available for the ASCA (McDermott, 1996; McDermott & Schaefer, 1996; McDermott & Spencer, 1997) and are useful for interpreting results.

SUMMARY. The ASCA is a new, nationally normed objective behavior rating scale completed by a student's classroom teacher. Nearly all behaviors presented are directly observable by a teacher; however, some are unlikely to be observed by teachers and would likely be dependent on reports from others (viz., delinquent activities outside of school). Reliability data presented in the ASCA manual are generally acceptable and initial validity studies provide support for the ASCA. Due to the dichotomous nature of ASCA items, internal consistency estimates may be somewhat lower than instruments that require raters to estimate frequency or intensity of behaviors (items) on a 3–5-point continuum. Additional independent investigations utilizing larger samples are needed to verify and extend the preliminary psychometric data reported in the ASCA manual. Although Native American and Asian American students were included proportionally in the standardization sample, little is presently known about the psychometric characteristics of the ASCA with these specific groups and should be the focus of future research. Future validity studies will help to determine whether the factor structure and syndrome types for large representative samples of these students are consistent with those obtained with the standardization sample. The large nationally representative standardization sample, multisituational assessment, and multivariate test interpretations through syndromic profile and discriminant classification analyses are noteworthy strengths of the ASCA. As the ASCA is a teacher report behavior rating scale it should not be, nor is it intended to be, the only method used in assessing child psychopathology, as other sources of information about other environments where the child interacts are also important. This reviewer's appraisal of the ASCA based on clinical use is very positive. It is easy to administer, score, and interpret, and provides relevant data. Teachers reported having enjoyed being able to endorse positive behaviors and not just rating negative or problematic behaviors. Teachers also reported that completion of the ASCA rating form was easy, demanded minimal amounts of time, and did not require them to estimate "how much or how often" behaviors were demonstrated. Most importantly, teachers found ASCA results relevant to child behaviors and situations they encounter in school environments. Cut score and syndromic profile interpretation descriptions in clinical cases resulted in both teachers and parents positively endorsing the accuracy of the ASCA (social validity). If future psychometric research is as positive as that presently conducted, the ASCA should become one of the most popular and cost effective behavior rating instruments available.

REVIEWER'S REFERENCES

Stott, D. H. (1966). *The social adjustment of children.* London: University of London Press.

Stott, D. H., Marston, N. C., & Neill, S. J. (1975). *Taxonomy of behaviour disturbance.* London: University of London Press.

Trites, R. L., Blouin, A. G. A., & Laprade, K. (1982). Factor analysis of the Conners Teacher Rating Scale based on a large normative sample. *Journal of Consulting and Clinical Psychology, 50,* 615–623.

Achenbach, T. M., & Edelbrock, C. (1983). *Manual for the Child Behavior Checklist and Revised Child Behavior Profile.* Burlington, VT: University of Vermont.

Quay, H. C. (1986). Classification. In H. C. Quay & J. S. Werry (Eds.), *Psychopathological disorders of childhood* (3rd ed., pp. 1–34). New York: Wiley.

Elliot, C. D. (1990). *Differential Ability Scales: Introductory and technical handbook.* San Antonio: Psychological Corporation.

McDermott, P. A. (1993). National standardization of uniform multisituational measures of child and adolescent behavior pathology. *Psychological Assessment, 5,* 413–424.

McDermott, P. A. (1994). *National profiles in youth psychopathology: Manual of Adjustment Scales for Children and Adolescents.* Philadelphia, PA: Edumetric and Clinical Science.

McDermott, P. A. (1995). Sex, race, class, and other demographics as explanations for children's ability and adjustment: A national appraisal. *Journal of School Psychology, 33,* 75–91.

McDermott, P. A., Watkins, M. W., Sichel, A. F., Weber, E. M., Keenan, J. T., Holland, A. M., & Leigh, N. M. (1995). The accuracy of new national scales for detecting emotional disturbance in children and adolescents. *Journal of Special Education, 29,* 337–354.

McDermott, P. A., & Weiss, R. V. (1995). A normative typology of healthy, subclinical, and clinical behavior styles among American children and adolescents. *Psychological Assessment, 7,* 162–170.

Kamphaus, R. W., & Frick, P. J. (1996). *Clinical assessment of child and adolescent personality and behavior.* Boston, MA: Allyn and Bacon.

McDermott, P. A. (1996). A nationwide study of developmental and gender prevalence for psychopathology in childhood and adolescence. *Journal of Abnormal Child Psychology, 24,* 53–66.

McDermott, P. A., & Schaefer, B. A. (1996). A demographic survey of rare and common behaviors among American students. *Journal of Clinical Child Psychology, 25,* 352–362.

Watkins, M. W. (1996). *ASCA Calculator* (Computer Software]. State College, PA: Author.

McDermott, P. A., & Spencer, M. B. (1997). Racial and social class prevalence of psychopathology among school-age youth in the United States. *Youth and Society, 28,* 387–414.

Canivez, G. L. (1998). Automated syndromic profile and discriminant classification analyses for the Adjustment Scales for Children and Adolescents (ASCA). *Behavior Research Methods, Instruments, and Computers, 30,* 732–734.

Review of the Adjustment Scales for Children and Adolescents by RICHARD V. SCHOWENGERDT, Assistant Professor of Psychology and Counseling, Pittsburg State University, Pittsburg, KS, and School Psychologist, Olathe, KS:

The Adjustment Scales for Children and Adolescents (ASCA) is a behavioral rating scale that assesses the degree of adjustment in children aged 5 to 17 years. The ASCA is completed by a classroom teacher who has known the student a minimum of 40 school days. The format of the ASCA is unique from that of other empirically based scales. It contains 156 discrete descriptions of behavior grouped into the broad categories of *Relationship with Teacher, Coping with School Work, Games and Play, Relationships with Other Students, Unsocialized Behavior, and Other Behaviors that Cause Concern.* When responding, teachers are instructed to check as many behaviors under these categories as they observe in the target student.

The ASCA contains 96 scorable items that key on the situational aspects of appropriate or deviant behavior for familiar classroom activities. The ASCA focuses on behaviors that are generalizable across age, gender, and ethnicity. The ASCA seeks to provide a more definitive diagnosis that leads more directly to intervention than behavior checklists that identify behavior by degree and intensity, such as the Child Behavior Checklist (CBCL; T5:451). The ASCA yields T-scores for six core behavioral syndromes, overactivity and underactivity, and two supplementary syndromes. Attention Deficit Hyperactive, Solitary Aggressive (Provocative), Solitary Aggressive (Impulsive), Oppositional Defiant, Diffident, and Avoidant are the core syndromes. Overactivity is scored by combining the Attention-Deficit, Solitary Aggressive (Provocative), Solitary Aggressive (Impulsive), and Oppositional Defiant syndromes. Underactivity is based on interpretation of the Diffident and Avoidant syndromes. The ASCA offers suggestions for cutscore interpretation of the scales that are consistent with other empirically based scales of rating behavior. Interpretation of the Overactivity and Underactivity scales is less straightforward as the user must examine the T-score pattern of the component core syndrome for correct interpretation.

The ASCA also offers syndromic profile interpretation that is based on the T-score distribution for the 1,400-student sample for the six core syndromes. Fourteen major syndrome types and eight clinical subtypes are described using age, gender, socioeconomic status, cognitive ability, achievement, and handicapping condition as variables. A complicated "best fit" method is described

for the user to obtain the correct profile interpretation for the student being rated. The difficulty of matching obtained scores to syndrome and the fact that no evidence of reliability or validity is presented for these derived syndromes argues against using this interpretive method to make behavioral predictions for students.

A discriminant classification interpretation that allows the profile of any youth to be measured for its likeness to normal or disturbed youth populations is presented. Examples for calculation are given but caution is advised due to the lack of uniform definition inherent across groups of children labeled as handicapped. This interpretation is the most demanding of all interpretations of the ASCA and may be irrelevant given the concern with inconsistent population variables.

TEST DEVELOPMENT, RELIABILITY, AND VALIDITY. The ASCA was heavily influenced by the British and Canadian versions of the Bristol Social Adjustment Guides, the American edition of the Learning Behaviors Scale, and the Study of Children's Learning Behaviors. Behavioral descriptions in the language of teachers (reducing the need for inference about psychological processes) were developed by interviewing teachers. Item selection and retention was based on field trials and review by expert analysts. The ASCA syndromes were derived using factor analytic methods common in test development. The core syndromes were confirmed factorially on an oversample of 1,034 students who were not part of the standardization sample. The Lethargic Syndrome could not be generalized to students older than 11 years and Delinquent could not be applied to preadolescent girls, thus becoming Supplementary Syndromes that could not be generalized across the entire 5- to 17-year age range.

Although claiming generalizability for all youth ages 5 to 17, the ASCA manual reports significant analysis of variance effects for sex and age, which are unexplained. Reliability estimates for the replicability of the syndromes were adequate. Interrater agreement was based on 22 children in one state. Test-retest reliability was based on a one-month interval study with 40 adolescent females who were white and nonhandicapped. Coefficients for interrater reliability ranged from .65 to .85 and .66 to .91 for test-retest reliability for only the core syndromes.

No reliability estimates are reported for the supplementary syndromes. Reliability is crucial to appropriate test development. The ASCA has not demonstrated temporal reliability for the psychopathologic sample it purports to measure. The fact alone argues against use of the ASCA for classification of students.

Convergent and divergent validity were examined using established scales of behavior pathology. The ASCA manual reports correlatational studies with the Conners' Teacher Rating Scale (CTRS; 1982 version) and the Child Behavior Checklist. As one would expect, the ASCA Overactivity Syndrome correlates highest with the Conners' hyperactivity factor. Other strong positive correlations are seen between Solitary Aggressive (both provocative and impulsive) and Conners' Conduct Problem. The ASCA manual claims finer variations than the CTRS for classifying youth, but this is arguable. The correlations for the ASCA and Child Behavior Checklist are less strong and the manual reports only the highest correlations claiming lack of space for all correlations computed. The ASCA does not report correlations between scores from the Attention-Deficit Hyperactive Syndrome and the CBCL Attention factor. The CBCL has strong factorial validity and the ASCA partial correlations as presented do not make a strong case for convergent validity with the CBCL. Appropriate levels of sensitivity and specificity, both .81, are reported for the ASCA for identifying subpopulations in the normative sample.

NORMING—STANDARDIZATION PROCEDURES. The ASCA was normed on a sample of 1,400 youths equally divided by gender with 108 subjects at each year and grade level for ages 5 to 17 and grades kindergarten to 12. The sample includes students with perceptual, speech, motor, intellectual, or sensory handicaps. The sample was constructed according to gender, age, grade level, national region, community size, ethnicity, parent education level, family structure, and handicapping condition. The sample is closely aligned across these variables to the 1990 census. The school sites and states included are not specified in the manual and should be reported. The ASCA is commended for giving careful attention to developing a representative national sample that includes children with handicaps.

UTILITY. The ASCA is easily readable in language that is familiar to teachers. It should be completed in 10–20 minutes and the instructions to the teacher are clear. There are two forms of the ASCA differing only in gender pronouns as requested by teachers in the development of the ASCA.

Scoring the protocol is relatively straightforward and similar to other behavior rating scales. The use of T-scores to interpret student pathology is familiar to intended users. Applying other recommended interpretations of the ASCA is questionable.

The ASCA provides only one perspective of youth behavior whereas the demands in education are for multiple sources of information on troubled students. A better choice for users desiring behavioral assessment is the Behavior Assessment System for Children (BASC; 40). The BASC is well normed, psychometrically sound, and employs multiple informants. Given the inadequately estimated reliability of the ASCA, as well as previously stated concerns, it might best be used as a screening or preassessment measure to help teachers refine their concerns about student behavior.

SUMMARY. The Adjustment Scales for Children and Adolescents is a well-normed, factorially developed scale that attempts to classify psychopathology and appropriate adjustment in school-aged youth. The ASCA introduces multisituation variables in an attempt to refine the measurement of pathology. The ASCA is user friendly to the teachers who complete it. The ASCA has inadequate estimates of reliability and limited evidence of validity and cannot be recommended for use as a classification instrument. The ASCA has potential to make a unique contribution to behavioral assessment if these problems can be corrected.

[7]
Adolescent Apperception Cards.

Purpose: "Intended to suggest themes and evoke narratives that include ... family, sibling, and peer relationships; abuse and neglect."
Population: Ages 12–19.
Publication Date: 1993.
Acronym: AAC.
Scores: No scores.
Administration: Individual.
Forms, 2: Black, White.

Price Data, 1999: $95 per kit including Adolescent Apperception Cards (Black and White versions included); $49 per cards (specify version).
Time: [45–60] minutes.
Comments: Publisher recommends (a) training and experience in projective testing and in working with adolescents, and (b) that the test be used as one component of a comprehensive battery of measures.
Author: Leigh Silverton; illustrated by Laurie Harden.
Publisher: Western Psychological Services.

Review of the Adolescent Apperception Cards by DAVID M. KAPLAN, Professor and Director of the Graduate Program in Counseling, Alfred University, Alfred, NY, and MOLLY L. VANDUSER, Alfred, NY:

The Adolescent Apperception Cards (AAC) is a projective test designed to assess relationship and family problems in 12–19-year-olds. There are two versions, one designed for white subjects and one designed for black subjects. Each version consists of 11 cards, with four from each set having separate pictures for males and females.

Each card is supposed to pull for a specific set of themes, (e.g., parental neglect, sexual abuse, domestic violence, paternal discipline, or sexual attitudes). The subject is shown each card (presumably white subjects are shown the white version and black subjects are shown the black version) and instructed to make up a story about each picture represented by the card. The evaluator is then instructed to interpret the resulting stories in terms of character description, theme, plot, resolution, story content, and methods of discourse.

The manual is sparse, consisting of only five pages. A second serious shortcoming of the AAC manual is the lack of theoretical rationale. Although there are many statements made about the theme for each card, little is stated about why that should be so. Because no theoretical framework is offered to support the development of any of the pictures, the evaluator is left with the message, "Trust us, we know what each card pulls for."

Another serious, if not fatal, shortcoming of the AAC is the total absence of any psychometric data to support the reliability or validity of the instrument. This is inconsistent with the *Code of Fair Testing Practices in Education* (Joint Committee on Testing Practices, 1988) which states that test developers "provide information that will help users gather evidence to show that the test is meeting its intended purpose(s)."

Because of the above deficiencies, the AAC cannot be recommended at this time.

REVIEWER'S REFERENCE

Joint Committee on Testing Practices. (1988). *Code of fair testing practices in education.* Washington, DC: Author.

Review of the Adolescent Apperception Cards by JODY L. SWARTZ-KULSTAD, Assistant Professor of Counselor Education, University of Wisconsin—Superior, Superior, WI:

The Adolescent Apperception Cards (AAC) is a projective storytelling measure designed to be a noninvasive, nonthreatening adjunct to the clinical assessment process. Conceptually modeled after the Thematic Apperception Test (TAT; Murray, 1943), the AAC provides 11 stimulus cards designed to elicit the framework an adolescent (aged 12–19) "uses to interpret interpersonal sequences, the kinds of emotional responses an individual is likely to experience, the way an individual perceives behavior of others, and an individual's characteristic way of construing interpersonal relationships" (manual, p. 1). Specific interpersonal relationships include family relationships (parental, sibling, or sibling-figures) and peer relationships.

THEORETICAL FOUNDATION. Though the AAC is based on the theoretical work of Murray (1943), more recent work by Bruner (1990) and Singer (1990) related to narrative discourse provides a better understanding of the rationale for this assessment. Narrative discourse suggests that people create stories based on their experience and that story schemas provide a glimpse into how individuals construct meaning out of their environment. According to the administration manual, schemas are viewed as resulting from the individual's personality and experience. As with other storytelling measures, the stimulus card is intentionally ambiguous; the respondent must use his or her imagination and internal resources to construct meaning, in the form of a story, based on the content of each picture. Singer (1990) suggested that each story schema follows a hierarchical pattern beginning with a setting, then a theme, a plot, and finally a resolution.

CLINICAL THEMES. In addition to common developmental issues of adolescence, the AAC cards are designed to evoke themes related to neglect, physical and sexual abuse, peer rejection, and substance abuse. For example, Card 11 may elicit themes of parental concern, drug abuse, and sexual abuse, whereas Card 2M/2F may suggest themes related to aloneness, neglect, and ability to use personal resources.

TEST MATERIALS, ADMINISTRATION, AND SCORING. The AAC provides 15 stimulus cards, 4 of which have separate male/female versions. Two versions of the AAC are available, one with Euro-American characters and one with African-American characters (referred to by the author as the White and Black versions). The manual included in the materials describes principles of use, general framework for interpretation, guidelines for administration and interpretation, and diagnostic considerations. However, information about selection of the scenes and whether the themes associated with the scenes actually distinguish between individuals with or without those concerns is not provided.

According to the manual, with no normative base, the AAC must only be used by professionals with training and experience in both projective techniques and working with adolescents, or by individuals who are being supervised by a professional with such training and experience. It would seem, though, that with the AAC focus on family issues, a general understanding of family systems theories would be essential, as would a sensitivity to cultural differences in conceiving reality, family relations, and social interactions.

Before administering the AAC, the user should insure that a projective technique will indeed provide a useful adjunct to the assessment and treatment process. The AAC should be used only if it is determined that if can provide information relevant to the particular assessment questions relevant to the client. Additionally, it is important to ascertain that rapport with the client has been sufficiently established. Once the specific clinical issues are identified, cards relevant to the themes of interest are selected—all 11 may be used for a comprehensive assessment. Although not mentioned by the author, it would seem that the more information available, the more confident the clinician can be in his or her overall interpretation.

Ample time should be reserved for the assessment session, approximately an hour. The session itself is a give and take, with the clinician providing encouragement and praise as the client responds to the cards. The clinician reads a specified introduction that discusses what is needed to evaluate the response. When clients do not provide all elements (i.e., a general description of the scene, the previous event(s), the outcome, or the thoughts or feelings of the characters), they should be prompted for the information. All client responses must be recorded verbatim and, if a written record is kept, all clinician prompts might be recorded as well. Additionally, if desired, the clinician can assess cognitive flexibility or ability to engage in propositional reasoning by asking if the client can think of another end to the story. At most, information obtained must be viewed as tentative hypotheses; without a formal inquiry phase, information from the assessment process could well be misinterpreted. Clearly, clinicians should be warned against differential praise/encouragement for responses; how the clinician responds may well influence the way that the individual responds, skewing the results and "planting" ideas that have no substance.

INTERPRETATION. Caution must be exercised in interpreting the AAC. This is not a measure that can be interpreted in isolation. At a minimum, the client's age and family situation must be known; the more information that is available, the better able the clinician is to provide a thorough understanding of the client's responses. The AAC is interpreted according to the hierarchical structure mentioned previously—including setting, theme, plot, and resolution. In addition to the four structural elements, story content provides clues to client dynamics and can assist in the interpretation of the responses. Specific information that can be gleaned from analyzing story content includes the interplay of affects (emotional states of main characters, other characters), styles of relating among the characters, and causality. According to the manual, causality is "examined at many levels … consideration must be given to the events that are described and to how the main character, through his or her specific plans, arrived at the outcome" (manual, p. 4). Finally, how the client tells the story should be taken into consideration.

PSYCHOMETRIC PROPERTIES. No information on reliability and validity is available. This is a serious consideration in using the AAC; conclusions drawn must be viewed as tentative and backed up by other standard assessment methods.

Although some suggest that projective measures should not be held to the same standards as objective tests, at a minimum some evidence of interrater agreement should be provided.

SUMMARY. Following on the footsteps of the TAT, the AAC provides an intriguing way to explore family and peer relationship themes for an adolescent population. The strength of the AAC lies in its potential as a tool to engender an understanding of the subjective reality of the individual. Adolescents present a unique clinical population, often torn between family and peers and limited by difficulties within either psychosocial domain. Information from the AAC can provide a window into the individual client's particular situation. It is limited, however, by lack of any psychometric information. Although not wholly defensible, the author does state the AAC is not expected to stand alone and its interpretive value lies in its use with a comprehensive battery of other assessments. Clearly, this is a statement that must be heeded if the AAC is to be used as part of any assessment process.

REVIEWER'S REFERENCES
Murray, H. (1943). Thematic Apperception Test. Cambridge, MA: Harvard University Press.
Bruner, J. (1990). Acts of meaning. Cambridge, MA: Harvard University Press.
Singer, M. (1990). The psychology of language: An introduction to sentence and discourse processes. Hillsdale, NJ: Lawrence Erlbaum Associates.

[8]
Adolescent Dissociative Experiences Scale.
Purpose: Designed as a "screening measure for pathological dissociation during adolescence."
Population: Ages 11–17.
Publication Date: 1996.
Acronym: A-DES.
Scores, 5: Dissociative Amnesia, Absorption and Imaginative Involvement, Depersonalization and Derealization, Passive Influence, Total.
Administration: Individual or group.
Price Data, 1998: $12 per test.
Time: (10–15) minutes.
Comments: A 30-item self-report measure, derived from the Dissociative Experiences Scale (original adult version) (T5:846).
Authors: Judith Armstrong, Frank Putnam, and Eve Carlson.
Publisher: The Sidran Foundation.

Review of the Adolescent Dissociative Experiences Scale by ROSEMARY FLANAGAN, Adjunct Associate Professor of Psychology, St. John's University, Jamaica, NY:

The Adolescent Dissociative Experiences Scale (A-DES) is an instrument in preliminary stages of development, with the information on development, validation, and the psychometric properties of the scale available in journal articles. The manual was not made readily available for review. The author suggested that dissertations using the A-DES be examined. [The scale is a public domain document that can be reproduced for research or practice, without author permission, according to Armstrong, Putnam, Carlson, Libero, and Smith (1992). However, The Sidran Foundation serves as distributor and does charge a small fee for the instrument and manual.]

A dissociative symptom is defined as a "disruption in the usually integrated functions of consciousness, memory, identity or perception of the environment" (American Psychiatric Association, 1994, p. 477). Dissociative symptoms are common to a number of psychiatric disorders, including the dissociative disorders, borderline personality disorder, eating disorders, and post-traumatic stress disorder, yet these symptoms also appear in nonclinical populations. A measure for adults, the Dissociative Experiences Scale (DES; Bernstein & Putnam, 1986), has reportedly demonstrated utility in the evaluation of dissociative states and their relationship to trauma (van Ijzendoorn & Schuengel, 1996), and suicidality and self-mutilation (Demitrack, Putnam, Brewerton, Brandt, & Gold, 1990). Similarly, the Child Dissociative Checklist (CDC; Putnam, Helmers, & Tricket, 1993) has been helpful in assessing dissociation in traumatized and maltreated children. Neither measure was found to be suitable for assessing adolescents may present multiple difficulties. Difficulty differentiating genuine pathology from typical adolescent functioning underscores the need for a measure such as the A-DES.

Subsumed under the global construct of dissociation, are items reflecting Dissociative Amnesia (Items 2, 5, 8, 12, 15, 22, 27), Absorption and Imaginative Involvement (Items 1, 7, 10, 18, 24, 28), Passive Influence (Items 4, 14, 16, 19, 23), and Derealization/Depersonalization (Items 3, 6, 9, 11, 13, 17, 20, 21, 25, 26, 29, 30). This conceptualization is consistent with the results of a taxometric analysis of dissociative experience (Waller, Putnam, & Carlson, 1996) that indicated that those aspects of dissociation are likely to differentiate pathological from nonpathological dissociative states in adults. The array of items and variables appears helpful for distinguishing between dissociation that may be secondary to trauma or psychopathology as compared to dissociation that is part of adolescent identity formation. The items have face validity and are similar to those in the DES.

Inspection of the 30 items indicates that there are items that clearly assess pathological states, items that may reflect pathology, and items that assess what is, in all likelihood, typical adolescent behavior. For example: "I get so wrapped up in my toys or stuffed animals that they seem alive," "My relationships with my family and friends change suddenly and I don't know why," or "I feel like there are different people inside of me." Items are rated on an 11-point scale, along a continuum of 0 = *never* and 10 = *always*, making differentiation between normal and pathological symptoms more likely. Scores are obtained by averaging individual item scores; the range of possible scores is 0–10.

For a sample of normal adolescents (Smith & Carlson, 1996), divided into three age groups (12–13, 14–15, 16–17 years) containing 18–22 youth, preliminary norms and psychometric properties were developed. The adolescents were obtained from regular education classes in a Midwest school. Seventy-eight percent were Caucasian, the remaining 22% described themselves as Native Americans, Hispanics, African-American, Asian, and "Other"; 62% were male. For purposes of developing norms, a college student sample (N = 46) from a Midwest college were administered both the A-DES and the Dissociative Experiences Scale (DES, Bernstein & Putnam, 1986), which is believed to be more appropriate for this age group. Reviews offer mixed options of its development and psychometric properties (Juni, 1995; Waller, 1995).

The total mean A-DES score for the three adolescent age groups was 2.24 ± 1.4 (range = 2.14–2.33); this same value for the college students was .78 ± .95. Mean subscale differences were observed. Amnesia, Absorption, Depersonalization/Derealization, and Passive Influence were 2.37, 2.46, 1.87, and 2.75 for the adolescent sample, and 1.38, 2.02, 1.10, and 1.71, for the college sample, respectively. College student scores on the A-DES and DES demonstrated a moderate relationship (r = .77). Even though these data are promising, larger samples are needed to determine whether the within-sample variability can be reduced. Over a 2-week interval, stability for the adolescent sample was acceptable (r = .77). Cronbach's alpha for the total scale was .92, which is acceptable, with subscale values ranging from .64–.83. Split-half reliability, using the Spearman-Brown formula, was .94. The authors indicated that the items were divided into conceptually similar halves. These data were not available for inspection, and the method of judging was not specified. The relationship between stability and internal consistency is within acceptable guidelines (Nunnally & Bernstein, 1994).

Further examination of psychometric properties (Armstrong, Putnam, Carlson, Libero, & Smith, 1997) was conducted for a clinical sample of 102 participants. Approximately 75% were inpatients, and the remaining youth were either outpatients, or were attending a day-treatment program/school. The sample was generally balanced in regard to gender and the number of youth in each of three age cohorts (12–13, 14–15, 16–17 years); 80% of the youth were Caucasian. Participants belonged to one of seven groups (dissociative disorders, psychotic disorders, impulse control disorders, substance abuse disorders, nonpsychiatric, affective disorders, oppositional defiant disorders, other), based on their DSM-IV (American Psychiatric Association, 1994) chart diagnoses.

Internal consistency was equally high using the Spearman-Brown formula and Cronbach's alpha (.92 and .93, respectively). Coefficient alpha for the subscales was .72, .73, .82, and .85. These higher values may reflect the greater homogeneity of the clinical groups as compared to the normal youth tested previously. Preliminary evidence of criterion validity was demonstrated by comparing the means for the groups, which revealed significant differences. Post-hoc analysis using Tukey's HSD test indicates that the dissociative disorders group was significantly different from all groups except those with psychotic disorders. The mean score for the dissociative group was 4.8 ± 1.1; the authors recommend that total scores greater than 3.7 merit further evaluation. Comparison of the normal group to the dissociative disorders group revealed significant differences on all subscales. Partially collapsing the data indicated that the dissociative disorders group was significantly different from the general psychiatric group, but not different from the psychotic disorders group. No age effects were demonstrated. Significant differences were found between those who reported a history of physical and sexual abuse compared to those who reported no abuse; this finding was replicated (Keck-Seeley, 1998).

There are methodological limitations, despite encouraging findings. A broader geographic base and larger numbers of participants should be sampled. There was no matching across groups, and the control group was a convenience sample. The regrouping of the data and the sampling techniques violate the assumptions of the statistical tests used, limiting the utility of the conclusions. Use of chart diagnoses is problematic in research because these may change over the course of treatment. It is encouraging, however, that the internal consistency of the total score is high across studies and populations, and is ample for clinical decision making (Kaplan & Sacuzzo, 1997). Construct validity needs to be more clearly established.

SUMMARY. Although a promising measure, the stage of development of the A-DES is too preliminary for use in endeavors other than research. The scale may be helpful to highly experienced clinicians who frequently encounter youth experiencing dissociative states; the measure is not sufficiently refined for general clinical practice in settings such as schools. The A-DES could be very useful in schools because such problems are seen infrequently, yet the school psychologist may be the first mental health professional involved with a particular case.

REVIEWER'S REFERENCES

Bernstein, E. M., & Putnam, F. W. (1986). Development, reliability, and validity of a dissociation scale. *Journal of Nervous and Mental Disease, 174,* 727–735.

Demitrack, M. A., Putnam, F. W., Brewerton, T. D., Brandt, H. A., & Gold, P. W. (1990). Relation of clinical variables to dissociative phenomena in eating disorders. *American Journal of Psychiatry, 147,* 1184–1188.

Putnam, F. W., Helmers, K., & Trickett, P. K. (1993). Development, reliability and validity of a child dissociation scale. *Child Abuse and Neglect, 17,* 731–741.

American Psychiatric Association. (1994). *Diagnostic and statistical manual of mental disorders* (4th ed.). Washington, DC: Author.

Nunnally, J. C., & Bernstein, I. H. (1994). *Psychometric theory* (3rd ed.). NY: McGraw-Hill.

Juni, S. (1995). [Review of the Dissociative Experiences Scale.] In J. C. Conoley & J. C. Impara (Eds.), *The twelfth mental measurements yearbook* (pp. 314–317). Lincoln, NE: Buros Institute of Mental Measurements.

Waller, N. G. (1995). [Review of the Dissociative Experiences Scale.] In J. C. Conoley & J. C. Impara (Eds.), *The twelfth mental measurements yearbook* (pp. 317–319). Lincoln, NE: Buros Institute of Mental Measurements.

Smith, S. R., & Carlson, E. B. (1996). Reliability and validity of the Adolescent Dissociative Experiences Scale. *Dissociation, 9,* 125–129.

Van Ijzendoorn, M. H., & Schuengel, C. (1996). The measurement of dissociation in normal and clinical populations: Meta-analytic validation of the Dissociative Experiences Scale. *Clinical Psychology Review, 16,* 365–382.

Waller, N. G., Putnam, F. W., & Carlson, E. B. (1996). Types of dissociation and dissociative types: A taxometric analysis of dissociative experiences. *Psychological Methods, 1,* 300–321.

Armstrong, J. G., Putnam, F. W., Carlson, E. B., Libero, D. Z., & Smith, S. R. (1997). Development and validation of a measure of adolescent dissociation: The Adolescent Dissociative Experiences Scale. *Journal of Nervous and Mental Disease, 185,* 491–495.

Kaplan, R. M., & Saccuzzo, D. P. (1997). *Psychological testing: Principles, applications, and issues* (4th ed.). Pacific Grove, CA: Brooks-Cole.

Keck-Seeley, S. M. (1998). Preliminary validation of the Adolescent Dissociative Experiences Scale (PTSD, Sexual Abuse). Unpublished doctoral dissertation. Akron, OH: University of Akron.

Review of the Adolescent Dissociative Experiences Scale by RAMASAMY MANIKAM, Clinical Faculty, University of Maryland School of Medicine, Baltimore, MD:

The Adolescent Dissociative Experiences Scale (A-DES) is a 30-item self-report measure for children aged 11–17. This measure is derived from the Dissociative Experiences Scale (original adult version; T5:846). The broad spectrum of dissociative experience can be identified for further in-depth understanding by scoring four subscales that include (a) Dissociative Amnesia, (b) Absorption and Imaginative Involvement, (c) Depersonalization and Derealization, and (d) Passive Influence. A score of 4.8 (standard deviation of 1.1) is given as the mean for dissociative adolescents. The authors recommend further evaluation for dissociative disorder diagnosis on all scores above 3.7.

Subjects mark the frequency of their experiences on a scale from 0 to 10; with 0 meaning "never" had such experiences and 10 meaning "always" having such experiences. The readability level is reported at 5.2 (using the Flesch-Kincaid method) and 5.4 (using the Coleman-Liau method) (Smith & Carlson, 1996).

AUTHOR'S BASIS AND PURPOSE OF SELECTING ITEMS. The authors are experienced in the study of dissociative phenomena in adolescents and thus have drawn the items from their clinical experience and the theoretical underpinnings of dissociative symptoms. A need existed to capture the unique experiences adolescents undergo, which are dissimilar to those of children and adults. This instrument is a first step towards fulfilling that need.

ADEQUACY OF DIRECTIONS AND TRAINING REQUIRED TO ADMINISTER. The directions needed are few and straightforward and do not require much training for the assessment portion of the scale. However, one must be knowledgeable and have the training and experience to interpret, diagnose, and use the information obtained for any research or treatment planning.

COMMENTS REGARDING DESIGN OF TEST. The test is designed to capture the "as if" feeling and experience suggestive of out-of-body and -world experiences of adolescents. Items in the scale have good face validity.

VALIDATION. In norming the scale, the authors used nonclinical junior and high school students, nonclinical college students, and patients in a health facility. Test-retest reliability was conducted using a subsample (14–15-year-old high school students, $N = 22$) of the total sample, after a 2-week interval. A correlation coefficient of .77 was obtained. Internal consistency using the split-half method is .94. As evidence of concurrent validity, the A-DES compared to that of the DES; a high correlation was found ($r = .77$) in a group of college students.

OTHER EMPIRICAL EVIDENCE INDICATING WHAT THE TEST MEASURES. The scale has strong parallels in theory and construct from the child and adult versions that are strongly supportive of the concept and validity of scores from this instrument.

Generalizability of the results from this scale should be guarded. The validation sample is largely Caucasian (over 70%) whereas the samples from other minority populations are rather small (range from 3%–5%). Moreover, the scale failed to distinguish the psychotic group from the dissociative disordered group (Armstrong, Putnam, Carlson, Libero, & Smith, 1997).

COMMENTS REGARDING ADEQUACY OF TECHNICAL PROPERTIES FOR PARTICULAR PURPOSES. The A-DES as a screening tool for dissociative symptoms is a measure that has merit. It can help identify individuals or groups with dissociative experiences due to trauma, physical and sexual abuse, and other "as if" bodily experiences. This scale can further aid clinicians in sub-typing pathological reports in adolescents.

GENERAL EVALUATION. Dissociative experiences occur at all ages. The types of life activities and experiences and therefore the nature and severity of dissociative phenomena differ among children, adolescents, and adults. Instruments are available to measure dissociative experiences in children and adults. The A-DES fills the existing gap in the adolescent population and can aid in defining adolescent diagnosis with greater precision.

The A-DES is a brief instrument. It is easy to administer and does not require more than 30 minutes. Directions are appropriately given to not include experiences when under the influence of alcohol or drugs. However, it is not clear if individuals should exclude similar experiences occurring during fatigue, sleep and sensory deprivation, as well as hypnogogic and hypnopompic hallucinations. If so, adding this to the directions would free the examiner from depending on memory.

SUMMARY. The A-DES can be a useful screening instrument. The scores may provide useful information when included as part of a comprehensive assessment battery. Adolescents falling within the significant range of scores should be further evaluated with a more in-depth interview and/or testing.

A-DES is too new to have complete validation studies. Sensitivity studies of the A-DES will require a great deal more research.

Dissociative experiences are common occurrences of other mental disorders including depression, obsessive personality type, anxiety, and schizophrenia. These should be classified under the major category rather than as a separate disorder.

REVIEWER'S REFERENCES

Smith, S. R., & Carlson, E. B. (1996). Reliability and validity of the Adolescent Dissociative Experiences Scale. *Dissociation, 9*, 125–129.
Armstrong, J. G., Putnam, F. W., Carlson, E. B., Libero, D. Z., & Smith, S. R. (1997). Development and validation of a measure of adolescent dissociation: The Adolescent Dissociative Experiences Scale. *Journal of Nervous and Mental Disease, 185*, 491–495.

[9]
Adolescent Psychopathology Scale.

Purpose: Designed to "evaluate symptoms of psychological disorders and distress in adolescents … measures psychopathology, personality, and social-emotional problems and competencies."
Population: Ages 12–19.
Publication Date: 1998.
Acronym: APS.
Scores: 40 scales in 4 domains: Clinical Disorders Domain (Attention-Deficit/Hyperactivity Disorder, Conduct Disorder, Oppositional-Defiant Disorder, Adjustment Disorder, Substance Abuse Disorder, Anorexia Nervosa, Bulimia Nervosa, Sleep Disorder, Somatization Disorder, Panic Disorder, Obsessive-Compulsive Disorder, Generalized Anxiety Disorder, Social Phobia, Separation Anxiety Disorder, Posttraumatic Stress Disorder, Major Depression, Dysthymic Disorder, Mania, Depersonalization Disorder, Schizophrenia); Personality Disorder Domain (Avoidant, Obsessive-Compulsive, Borderline, Schizotypal, Paranoid); Psychosocial Problem Content Domain (Self-Concept, Psycho-social Substance Use Difficulties, Introversion, Alienation-Boredom, Anger, Aggression, Interpersonal Problems, Emotional Lability, Disorientation, Suicide, Social Adaptation; Response Style Indicators (Lie,

Consistency, Infrequency, Critical Item Endorsement); Factor Scales (Internalizing Disorder Factor, Externalizing Disorder Factor, Personality Disorder Factor).
Administration: Individual or group.
Price Data: Available from publisher.
Time: (45–60) minutes.
Comments: A 346-item self-report scale; developed to be consistent with the DSM-IV disorders; test form is entitled Adolescent Mental Health Questionnaire; software for computerized (Windows) scoring program included.
Author: William M. Reynolds.
Publisher: Psychological Assessment Resources, Inc.

Review of the Adolescent Psychopathology Scale by TIMOTHY R. KONOLD, Assistant Professor of Education, University of Virginia, Charlottesville, VA:

The Adolescent Psychopathology Scale (APS) represents an ambitious effort to measure 40 dimensions of adolescent psychopathology, 25 of which are reflections from the DSM-IV. The 40 scales are organized according to clinical disorders (20 scales), personality disorders (5 scales), psychosocial problems (11 scales), and response style indicators (4 scales). In addition, three broad factor scores (i.e., Internalizing, Externalizing, and Personality) can also be obtained by combining various scales. The manual indicates that the 346 items that comprise the APS were written on a third grade reading level and can be completed by most adolescents within 45–60 minutes. The APS is intended for use with adolescents ranging in age from 12 to 19 years. The standardization sample comprised a respectable size for an initiative of this magnitude (N = 1,827) and standardization was in accordance with 1990 U.S. Census data on the variables of gender, ethnicity, and age.

The APS manuals are very well written and provide a good deal of background research that serves to remind clinicians of the complex issues involved in measuring adolescent psychopathology. Scoring is facilitated through a computer program that allows users to choose between several normative groups for individual score comparisons. Norms are provided by gender, age, and gender by age. However, the manual encourages use of the total standardization sample when making normative comparisons. The program utilizes a missing data function that allows users to obtain scale scores when up to 20% of the data for that scale are missing. In addition, a clinical report is produced that provides various summary tables and a graphic profile.

The reliability and validity for scores from the APS were investigated through multiple studies. These studies were often carried out on both the standardization sample and a clinical group. In some instances, studies were further conducted on meaningful subgroups (e.g., gender and adolescent age). For the most part, the majority of scales demonstrated favorable internal consistency estimates for the standardization sample, as well as across gender, age, and a clinical sample. For example, when the combined standardization and clinical samples were considered, the majority of the 36 nonresponse style scales demonstrate values of .80 or greater. Similarly, only 6 of the 36 nonresponse style scales failed to demonstrate test-retest estimates of .80 or greater.

The construct validity of the APS was investigated, in part, through a series of principal component analyses designed to substantiate the aforementioned structure of the scale. These analyses supported the internalizing externalizing dimensions forecasted by the author. Principal component item analyses within each of the scales also revealed relatively similar factor structures for clinical and nonclinical groups. Often, however, the importance of these scale-specific factors varied as a function of the group under investigation. That is, although items tended to hang together in the same manner for these two groups, the dominant factor often varied as a function of the group under investigation. As a result, the amount of variance accounted for by the subfactors was not necessarily consistent for the clinical and nonclinical groups. Thus, although the manual explicitly cautions against interpretations beyond the scale scores, these results suggest that the importance of some scale specific items may vary as a function of whether the adolescent has a disorder or not.

Relationships between the APS and existing measures of psychopathology were investigated to address the issue of concurrent validity. Discriminant validity was investigated using correlations between measure of IQ and social desirability, and contrasted groups validity was explored through score comparisons between adolescents comprising the standardization and clinical samples. These latter comparisons were conducted on each of the 40 scales comprising the APS with both age and gender serving as covariates. Results of these studies lend support to the validity of the instrument's uses. The author appropriately qualifies findings, when needed, to avoid overstating the results and describes the implications of each study. Despite the encouraging evidence of validity that is provided, users would benefit from a greater understanding of the scale's sensitivity and specificity for distinguishing between adolescents with and without known psychopathologies.

SUMMARY. The APS is likely the only measure of its kind that provides clinicians with multiple measures of psychopathology directed specifically at adolescents. The manuals provide a great deal of information pertaining to the theoretical basis for the scale as well as empirical evidence to support many of the author's claims, with few exceptions.

Review of the Adolescent Psychopathology Scale by WAYNE C. PIERSEL, Licensed Psychologist, Heartspring, Wichita, KS:

The Adolescent Psychopathology Scale (APS) is a new assessment instrument designed to evaluate the symptoms of psychological disorders and distress in adolescents ranging in age from 12 to 19. The APS is intended to evaluate the severity of symptoms associated with internalizing and externalizing disorders along with other interpersonal and emotional problems relevant to adolescents. The author asserts that the APS is intended to be consistent with the diagnostic categories contained in the DSM-IV. As such, the APS is a broad measure of adolescent psychopathology, personality, and socioemotional problems. The test provides scores on 40 scales that measure 20 clinical disorders, 5 personality disorders, 11 psychosocial problem content areas, and 4 response styles. As such this instrument is an ambitious undertaking.

The APS is based on the conceptual distinction of externalizing versus internalizing expressions, symptoms, or problems (Achenbach & McConaughy, 1992). The goal of the APS is to assess presence and severity of symptoms or behaviors associated with disorders listed in DSM-IV. The author states that the APS is not intended to provide for a formal diagnosis of various disorders.

The format of the APS inventory is unique in several ways. First, different reference time frames are used for the various sections such as: (a) in the past 6 months, (b) in the past year, (c) in the past month, and (d) in general. The number of response options ranges from two to five depending on the item. The differing time frames theoretically permit identification of symptoms that are presently acute as well as identification of symptoms that have occurred during some longer time frame or that have occurred in the past and are not currently present. The range of responses from two to five permits respondents to answer yes/no questions as well as questions more suited to severity ratings.

PSYCHOMETRIC CHARACTERISTICS. The standardization sample consisted of 1,827 participants ranging in age from 12 to 19. The various ethnic groups in the sample were not proportionally represented. Hispanics were underrepresented. Caucasians comprised over two thirds of the sample. The breakdown of the clinical sample (506 participants) revealed that conduct disorder (24%) and substance abuse (21%) comprised slightly less than half of the sample. A number of the disorders for which symptoms are being assessed by the APS were not represented or adequately represented in the clinical sample.

Extensive information is provided to address validity concerns. Data are presented on criterion-related and contrasted groups validity. The author presents concurrent validity data by comparing the APS with the Minnesota Multiphasic Personality Inventory (MMPI), various measures of anxiety and depression, and social desirability. They also present data comparing the standardization sample with the clinical sample. The data presented do provide initial support for the construct validity of the APS scales. However, the author did not conduct convergent-discriminant analysis using the multitrait, multimethod analysis (Campbell & Fiske, 1959). A multitrait, multimethod analysis would more firmly confirm or disconfirm the convergent and discriminant validity of the APS. The only discriminant validity evidence presented involves comparison of the APS scales with a measure of social desirability and a measure of cognitive ability. The data do indicate generally nonsignificant correlations with ability and low to moderate correlations with social desirability. There is no attempt to systematically examine the convergent and discriminant validity of the clinical, personality, or psychosocial scales. Given that all the validity data were self-report, the issue of method variance remains unresolved. Further, the intercorrelations among the different diagnostic categories were moderately high and statistically significant. The author did not address the theoretical issue of the validity and independence of the various constructs underlying the diagnostic categories.

THE MANUAL. The Administration and Interpretation Manual is very well organized and written. The initial chapter presents an excellent introduction to the assessment of problem behavior and an excellent overview of the current state of the field of adolescent psychopathology. The second chapter presents a readable description of the APS and the various scales. The number of items per clinical scale ranges from a high of 29 for major depression to a low of 6 for obsessive, compulsive disorder. In addition to the clinical scales, the APS contains four response style indicator scales. The Lie scale contains 10 items, the Consistency Response scale contains 25 items, the Infrequency scale contains 26 items, and the Critical item scale contains 63 items. The entire instrument contains 346 items. In addition to the various clinical scores, the APS also provides an Internalizing Factor score, an Externalizing Factor score, and a personality disorder score.

SHORTCOMINGS. Although the manual does contain a clinical sample, many of the disorders purported to be measured by the APS are not adequately represented in the clinical sample. The manual does not address the special considerations and issues that are present with self-report inventories. No attempt is made to relate the APS to various rating scales completed by observers such as parents and teachers. There is no discussion of the validity concerning the various diagnostic categories.

OVERALL IMPRESSION. The APS represents a welcome addition to the limited pool of standardized assessment instruments available to assess problem behavior in adolescents. The APS is refreshing in being designed for the adolescent population rather than being an instrument that was modified from an instrument that was originally designed for adults. The APS was specifically designed for the adolescent population. The inclusion of a separate clinical sample is a welcome innovation even though the clinical sample is limited for many diagnostic categories. The validity data are among the most complete encountered by this reviewer. This reviewer gives a qualified recommendation to the APS. It clearly represents an advancement for the assessment of adolescents who are experiencing significant life difficulties.

REVIEWER'S REFERENCES

Campbell, D. T., & Fiske, D. W. (1959). Convergent and discriminant validation by the multitrait-multimethod matrix. *Psychological Bulletin, 56*, 81–105.
Achenbach, T. M., & McConaughy, S. H. (1992). Taxonomy of internalizing disorders in childhood and adolescence. In W. M. Reynolds (Ed.), *Internalizing disorders in children and adolescents* (pp. 19–60). New York: Wiley.

[10]
Adult Attention Deficit Disorders Evaluation Scale.

Purpose: Designed to provide a measure of inattention and hyperactivity-impulsivity in adults.
Population: Adults.
Publication Dates: 1996–1997.
Acronym: A-ADDES.
Scores, 3: Inattentive, Hyperactive-Impulsive, Total Percentile Rank.
Administration: Individual.
Price Data, 1999: $146.50 per complete kit including 50 self-report rating forms, 50 Home Version rating forms, 50 Work Version rating forms, Self-Report technical manual ('96, 43 pages), Home Version technical manual ('96, 41 pages), Work Version technical manual ('96, 40 pages), and Adult Attention Deficit Disorders Intervention manual ('97, 183 pages); $31 per 50 rating forms (specify Self-Report, Home Version, or Work Version); $20 per 50 ADDES/DSM-IV forms; $12.50 per technical manual (specify Self-Report, Home Version, or Work Version); $16 per Adult Attention Deficit Disorders Intervention manual; $2 per Comparing the Technical Aspects of Adult Attention-Deficit/Hyperactivity Disorder Rating Scales review.
Time: Untimed.
Comments: Behavioral rating system with three forms: Home, Work, and Self-Report; may be completed in one sitting or over a period of days.
Authors: Stephen B. McCarney, Paul D. Anderson, and Michele T. Jackson (manual).
Publisher: Hawthorne Educational Services, Inc.
  a) HOME VERSION.
  Comments: To be completed by a spouse or other close relative/friend who observes daily behavior in the home; best when used in conjunction with Work and Self-Report versions.
  b) WORK VERSION.
  Comments: To be completed by an employer, supervisor, or fellow employee who can closely observe the subject's work behaviors; best when used in conjunction with Work and Self-Report versions.

Review of the Adult Attention Deficit Disorders Evaluation Scale by HELEN KITCHENS, Associate Professor, Troy State University—Montgomery, Montgomery, AL:

The Adult Attention Deficit Disorders Evaluation Scale (A-ADDES) was developed to determine the existence of Attention-Deficit/Hyperactivity Disorder (ADHD) in adults. According to the technical manual, as many as "2 to 5 million adults" (p. 4) may have ADHD and the majority have not been identified or treated. The A-ADDES was designed to document characteristics of ADHD as set forth in the *Diagnostic and Statistical Manual of Mental Disorders, Fourth Edition* (American Psychiatric Association, 1994).

There are three versions of the A-ADDES to assess the characteristics of inattention and hyperactivity-impulsivity: One version assesses the client's perspective and two additional versions solicit information from employers, supervisors, co-workers, and spouse or other relatives (A-ADDES—Work, Home, and Self-Report Versions). The Self-Report Version is composed of 58 items, the Home Version has 46, and the Work Version has 54. The Work and Home Versions assess the same basic behaviors, but are phrased so that they reflect activities that occur in those particular settings. The Self-Report Version assesses general behaviors (i.e., I lose track of what I am doing), and also addresses particular settings (i.e., I am disorganized at work). Each version can be completed in approximately 15 minutes. For each statement there is a quantifier that ranges from *do not engage in the behavior* (0) to occurs *one to several times per month* (1), *per week* (2), *per day* (3), or *per hour* (4).

All versions of the A-ADDES are easily scored by hand. Raw scores are summed for each subscale and converted to standard scores using the conversion tables that, for the Self-Report Version, are normed to 9 age groups for males and 13 age groups for females. The standardization group for the A-ADDES Home Version provides eight age-sex groups for normative comparison, and the Work Version provides 7 age groups for males and 8 age groups for females. Standard scores are summed and converted to an overall percentile score. The subscale standard scores and the percentile are recorded on the Profile. Standard scores have a mean of 10 and a standard deviation of 3. Standard scores between 7 and 13 are considered average, whereas standard scores in the range of 6 to 4 represent *a significant need for attention,* and those in the range of 3 to 90 represent *an extreme need for attention.*

Normative data for the Self-Report Version was based on 2,249 adults, ages 18.0 to 71 years in 45 states representing all major geographic regions of the United States. The Work Version was normed on 1,867 adults, ages 18.0 to 65+ years in 43 states, and the Home Version was normed on 2,003 adults, ages 18.0 to 65+ in 44 states. The standardization sample came from white collar, blue collar, and service and farm occupations and education level ranged from high school dropouts to college graduates.

Scores from the Self-Report, Home, and Work Versions show good evidence of reliability. The Home and Work Versions have estimates of subscale reliability using test-retest, internal consistency, and interrater reliability. The Self-Report Version has estimates of test-retest reliability and internal consistency reliability. Test-retest correlations over 30 calendar days ranged from .77 to .78 for the Self-Report Version, .72 to .80 for the Home Version, and .80 to .84 for the Work Version. Internal consistency reliability was .98 for the Self-Report and Work Versions, and .97 for the Home Version. Interrater reliability coefficients ranged from .61 to .73 for all age levels for the Work Version, and from .38 to .62 for all age levels for the Home Version. The standard error of measurement is reported for each age-sex group on all three versions.

Evidence of content and construct validity is reported for all three versions of the A-ADDES. Diagnostic validity is reported for the Home and Self-Report Versions. Support for content validity of each version is based on a thorough review of the literature and input from a total of 464 psychiatrists and psychologists to establish the item pool.

Construct validity was examined by factor analysis using principal components analysis. Two major areas of behavior were identified and further examined by varimax rotation analysis. Though each subscale loaded primarily on the appropriate factor, there is some overlap on both factors. Factor analysis of the subscales using the principal components method revealed that the Inattention subscale is made up of two main axes representing organization skills and task management on the first axis and predominately listening skills on the second axis. The two main axes that make up the Hyperactive-Impulsive subscale are impulsive behavior and hyperactive behavior.

Diagnostic validity for the Home and Self-Report Versions was investigated by using a random sample from the normative group. These persons were compared with a corresponding group diagnosed as having ADHD. The mean total subscale scores of the ADHD group were significantly lower than were those of the randomly selected non-ADHD group.

Three separate technical manuals provide information on reliability, validity, administration, scoring, and interpretation for each version of the A-ADDES. Additionally, there are appendices that provide tables for converting raw scores to subscale standard scores, and subscale standard scores to percentile scores. The interpretation section includes step-by-step information on how to develop goals and objectives from the rating scale items. Interventions appropriate in facilitating client improvement can be found in the *Adult Attention Deficit Disorders Intervention Manual* that is purchased separately.

SUMMARY. The A-ADDES is a useful tool to be used in conjunction with other information in identifying behaviors related to inattention and impulsivity-hyperactivity. The brevity of all three versions makes them appealing to the individual being assessed as well as those in the home and workplace who are asked to provide input. Information gleaned from others (work and home) with knowledge of the client's behavior is particularly helpful for those individuals who lack insight into their own behavior.

One aspect of the technical manuals that could be improved is the combination of the three technical manuals into one with sections for each version. This would facilitate ease of use, and help with redundancy of some of the information.

Particularly important for clinicians is the provision for writing goals and objectives from scale items. Though the *Adult Attention Deficit Disorders Intervention Manual* must be purchased separately, it supplies a plethora of ideas for the client and clinician to explore in order to develop a program of behavioral interventions.

REVIEWER'S REFERENCE

American Psychiatric Association. (1994). *Diagnostic and statistical manual of mental disorders* (4th ed.). Washington, DC: Author.

Review of the Adult Attention Deficit Disorders Evaluation Scale by JAMES C. REED, Chief Psychologist, St. Luke's Hospital, New Bedford, MA:

The Attention-Deficit/Hyperactivity Disorder on adults is defined in the American Psychiatric Association's *Diagnostic and Statistical Manual of Mental Disorders, 4th Edition* (1994). For the diagnosis of ADHD to be made, its existence must be present in at least two settings (e.g., at home and at school or at work). Hyperactive-impulsive or inattentive symptoms must also be present before age 7 years, although the diagnosis may occur later.

The three forms or parts of the Adult Attention Deficit Disorders Evaluation Scale (A-ADDES) may be viewed as the operational definition of the APA's construct of ADHD. For each of the three scales the items are based on DSM-IV criteria, and the items for each of the three scales were developed with the input of over 400 psychiatrists and psychologists who were working with Attention Deficit/Hyperactivity Disorder adults. The authors report that the A-ADDES may be used to "(a) Screen for characteristics of Attention Deficit/Hyperactivity Disorder; (b) Provide a measure of Attention-Deficit/Hyperactivity Disorder behavior for any adult experiencing hyperactive, impulsive, or attention difficulties; (c) Provide information which may contribute to the diagnostic process for Attention-Deficit/Hyperactivity Disorder; (d) Develop program goals and objectives; and (e) Identify intervention activities for Attention-Deficit/Hyperactivity Disorder" (manual, p. 5). The test is also accompanied by a 183-page manual containing suggestions, check lists, contracts, reminder lists, etc., which may be used in intervention and behavior modification programs.

The scoring system for each scale is the same. Each item is scored on a 5-point scale according to the frequency of the behavior identified or described: 0 - *Does not engage in the behavior,* 1 - *One to several times per month,* 2 - *One to several times per week,* 3 - *One to several times per day,* and 4 - *One to several times per hour.* For each scale all scores are converted to *T*-scores, which are converted to percentile ranks. Each form has two subscales: Inattentive and Hyperactive Impulses. The existence of the subscales was empirically confirmed by factor analysis. For each of the scales the normative data were gathered between June 1995 and June 1996. The validity evidence for the scales is primarily content validity based on DSM-IV criteria. The technical psychometric data for each scale are presented in the corresponding manual, and they meet commonly accepted standards for psychometric criteria.

What follows is a brief presentation of selected information that is unique to the particular scale. Additional psychometric information and descriptions of the normative samples are presented for each of the scales in the relevant manual.

Self-Report Version: Fifty-eight items are to be completed by the patient with 15 minutes to complete. It need not be completed in a single setting. *Normative Sample:* 2,204 subjects from 45 states from 18 years through 71+ years. *Test-Retest Reliability Estimates:* Inattention: .78, Hyperactive/Impulsive: .77, Total Scale: .97 (38 adults with a 30-day interval).

Work Version: A 54-item scale to be completed by an employer, supervisor, or co-worker who is familiar with the patient and has observed him or her on a regular basis with a measure of consistency and over time (manual, p. 18). Fifteen minutes completion time. *Normative Sample:* 1,867 subjects from 43 states from 18 years through 65+ years. *Test-Retest Reliability:* Inattention: .80, Hyperactive/Impulse: .84, Total Scale: .83 (52 adults with a 30-day interval).

Home Version: Forty-six items requiring 15 minutes to complete by a person with primary observational opportunities (e.g., a spouse, significant other, roommate, or person who interacts with the subject in the home environment; manual, p. 23). *Normative Sample:* 2,003 subjects from 44 states from 18 years through 65+ years. *Test-Retest Reliability Estimates:* Inattention: .80, Hyperactive/Impulsive: .72. *Total Scale:* .76 (36 adults with a 30-day interval).

The authors have done a particularly thorough job in presenting relevant data such as the gender of the normative sample, the number of subjects in each standardization group, the geographic area of the norm sample, occupation, education, residence, etc. One who uses the test could determine whether or not the patient being evaluated was representative of the norm group. ADHD in either adults or children is a diagnosis primarily based on history. For the diagnosis to be made in an adult, there must be evidence that the symptoms were present at age 7 or earlier. The A-ADDES does not provide this information. Furthermore, for the diagnosis to be made, the behavior of concern cannot be explained by another clinical disorder (e.g., mental retardation, schizophrenia, conduct disorder, etc.). These points are made in the test manual. In short, the diagnosis of ADHD cannot be made on the basis of the A-ADDES alone.

A strength of the A-ADDES is that it includes ratings from the work setting and the home setting in addition to the self-rating. The clinician not only has the opportunity to evaluate the accuracy of the patient's self-perception and the reality of his or her complaints but also to determine how pervasive is the patient's distractible behavior (i.e., are the patient's behaviors a problem of self-perception or do they have an adverse impact on the environment of either the home, work, or both?). Obviously for the scales to be maximally useful, both the Home scale and the Work scale must be filled out by observers who know the patient and who are trustworthy. These factors may or may not be under the clinician's control. Of course, the authors of the test are not responsible for the skill of the clinician.

A brief word about the intervention manual. It contains page after page of suggestions that may prove helpful in the behavioral management of the ADHD patient. For example (manual, p. 81): Gets overexcited #1. Play easy listening music when you are overexcited. #3. Exercise regularly to relieve tension and stress. #15. Avoid situations where you may become overexcited (e.g., bars, nightclubs, athletic events, concerts, etc.), and so on. The suggestions may be appropriate, but how does one get the patient to comply? The value of the manual will depend on the skill of the therapist.

SUMMARY. The A-ADDES provides a component of information that may be useful in the differential diagnosis of ADHD Syndrome. The test instructions are clear. It is easy to score. The test items satisfactorily reflect DSM-IV criteria. The information pertaining to reliability, the factor structure of the test, the characteristics of the normative sample, and other related psychometric information are satisfactorily presented in the manual. The diagnosis of Adult Attention Disorder is not an easy one to make and, in my opinion, it is too frequently used as a wastebasket label. The authors of the test give appropriate warnings. Clinicians who are interested in the diagnosis and the treatment of the population for whom this test is intended should give careful consideration to the use of these scales.

REVIEWER'S REFERENCE
American Psychiatric Association. (1994). *Diagnostic and statistical manual of mental disorders* (4th ed.). Washington, DC: Author.

[11]
Adult Language Assessment Scales.

Purpose: "Designed to provide complete information about language proficiency of adults who speak English as a Second or Foreign Language."

Population: Adults.

Publication Date: 1991.

Acronym: A-LAS®.

Scores, 10: Listening (Conversations, Same/Different, Total), Speaking (Vocabulary, Making Sentences, Newscast, Sounds, Total), Pronunciation, Total.

Administration: Individual.

Forms, 2: A, B.

Price Data, 1993: $110.25 per complete kit (Form A) including oral administration manual (28 pages) (Forms A and B), oral scoring and interpretation manual (53 pages) (Forms A and B), cue picture book (Form A), audiocassette for the oral language component (Form A), audiocassette for the additional pronunciation section (Form A), audiocassette holder, and 50 answer booklets (Form A); $73.50 per augmentation kit (Form B including cue picture book (Form B), audiocassette for oral language component (Form B), audiocassette for pronunciation section (Form B), and 50 answer booklets (Form B); $60.20 per 25 reading and mathematics booklets (specify level and Form); $41 per 50 writing booklets (specify Form); $23 per 50 reading and mathematics answer sheets (specify level); $28.50 per 50 oral answer booklets (specify form); $25 per 50 oral profile sheets (specify form); $14 per 50 oral and reading, writing, and mathematics profile sheets (specify form); $16.25 per extra administration and scoring manual (specify level and form); $17 per oral administration manual; $19.25 per oral scoring and interpretation manual; $11.55 per technical report; $24.95 per cue picture book (specify form); $14.20 per audiocassette (specify form and story).

Time: (25–30) minutes.

Comments: Includes equivalent forms, A and B.

Authors: Sharon E. Duncan and Edward A. DeAvila.

Publisher: CTB/McGraw-Hill.

Review of the Adult Language Assessment Scales by ROGER A. RICHARDS, Consultant, Office of Certification and Credentialing, Massachusetts Department of Education, Malden, MA:

There may be evidence to support the use of the Adult Language Assessment Scales—Oral (A-LAS-O), but if so, the authors and publisher appear to be keeping it to themselves. It is not possible to evaluate the A-LAS-O because almost no information is given about its psychometric properties.

MAJOR DEFICIENCIES. The rationale for the test, for example, is dealt with in 16 lines of print. Test development is summarized, within a section on Test Content, in one sentence: "The content of Forms A and B was strongly guided by the results of more than 15 years of field use and research within the LAS testing system" (Oral Scoring and Interpretation Manual, p. 2). In neither the administration nor the scoring and interpretation manual do we find a discussion of validity. The closest we come is a statement buried in a section labeled "Distribution of scores": "The distribution of scores for the monolingual speakers was extremely limited and concentrated in the upper quarter of scores for the total population. On the other hand, the distribution for the ESL or EFL speakers ranged from very low to very high, as expected" (Oral Scoring and Interpretation Manual, p. 48). And the only reference to reliability is an instruction to test administrators to obtain 90% agreement on practice ratings on two sections of the test before embarking on official scoring.

PURPOSES. The purposes of the test are somewhat obscure. We are told that the A-LAS-O "is designed to provide complete information about adult language proficiency" (Oral Scoring and Interpretation Manual, p. 1). There is no substantiation for this claim. It is further stated that "A-LAS-O is intended for use as a screening device with adults who speak English as a Second or Foreign Language … test results provide standard score, identification levels, and placement categories. These results may be used to assist in identification of those in need of language services and placement into appropriate programs" (Oral Scoring and Interpretation Manual, p. 1). No guidance is provided on how to use test scores in this identification process. The answer form lists five testing purposes: "Hire, Placement, Psychological Services, Program Evaluation, and Personnel Services." That a single instrument can be useful for all of these functions seems dubious, particularly when no suggestions are offered on how to apply test results to any of the identified functions.

FORMS. The test may be given in either the Short (Parts 1–4) or Long (Parts 1–6) Form. The two sections are designated the Oral Language Component (Parts 1–4) and the Pronunciation

Component (Parts 5 and 6). The underlying rationale is unclear, for the labeling suggests that pronunciation is something other than oral language. Two forms of each version are available.

PARTS. In Part 1, which measures Vocabulary, the subject is asked to identify 20 nouns and 10 verbs from drawings. A tape provides 10 adjectives, for each of which an antonym is required.

Part 2, Conversations, presents a recorded dialogue followed by 10 questions about the dialogue. The validity of this section is questionable for two reasons: First, the conversations are fairly long and the questions fairly detailed, the result being that an individual's score may reflect memory as well as language facility; and second, the yes-no format and the limited number of questions introduces a significant guessing factor.

In Part 3, Making Sentences, the examinee is asked to describe in a complete sentence the action suggested by each of five drawings. Each sentence is rated 3, 2, 1, or 0.

Part 4, Newscast, requires summarizing a recorded hypothetical news broadcast. The administrator is directed to write down the respondent's summary verbatim. Unless the administrator knows shorthand, this requirement may be cumbersome and may seriously restrict the examinee's fluency.

Part 5, Same or Different, consists of 34 pairs of similar-sounding words; the task is to indicate whether the two words are the same or different. In each form only 6 of the 34 pairs are the same.

Part 6, Sounds in Words, asks the person being tested to repeat 35 words or phrases presented on tape. Although the items range from a single word to as many as 6 words, each is scored only for the one phoneme underlined in the answer booklet.

TESTING MATERIALS. The testing materials are of good quality. Instructions for administering the various parts are clear and adequate. The drawings are generally unambiguous. Form A contains a couple of items that might be difficult for an urban population: a bale of hay and a tractor, and Form B requires the identification of a hatchet. Directions for scoring are exemplary, with a wealth of sample responses and explanations of the assigned ratings.

The quality of the tapes is excellent. Although the pace is a bit fast for the intended audience, the voices are pleasing, the intonations are natural, the enunciation is clear, and the quality of the recording is professional. The content of the conversations and newscasts is appropriate and likely to engage the interest of those being tested.

SCORING. Conversion tables make a seemingly complicated scoring system quite manageable (Oral Scoring and Interpretation Manual, pp. 39, 41). There is a curious inconsistency in the distribution of points among parts for the Short Form and Long Form. To make sure that total scores equal the magical 100 points, the Long Form borrows half the points for Parts 1 and 2 to use for Part 5 and 6, the result being that Parts 3 and 4 yield 1.5 times the points for Parts 1 and 2 on the Short Form but 3 times on the Long Form. A very brief section labeled "Subscale weighting procedures" sheds no light on this issue (Oral Scoring and Interpretation Manual, p. 48). However, without knowing the standard deviations of the various parts, conclusions about the weighting are not possible.

The section on interpretation of total scores consists of a table showing the scores (bands of 20 points, conveniently enough) that correspond to five levels: fluent, high intermediate, low intermediate, high beginner, and low beginner. It would be helpful to have information on the distribution of scores among various populations, but no such data are given. Also useful would be comparisons of ratings assigned through some other means of assessment with scores yielded by the A-LAS-O.

In a discussion of standard error of measurement, the authors discuss "gray-area bandwidths" (Oral Scoring and Interpretation Manual, p. 42). They suggest that to assign appropriate levels for borderline scores, the examiner should consider other sources of information about the test-taker's language skills. They provide an observation rating sheet to assist in the process. The use of data outside the test to assign ratings to test results is unusual, to say the least. One wonders why we could not simply use the observation form in the first place.

CONCLUSION. If a potential user is willing to have blind faith in the author's 15 years of experience that apparently informed the development of the test, this instrument might be useful. The most striking feature of the A-LAS-O is the contrast between the relative sophistication of the testing materials and the limited treatment, if any, of psychometric considerations. The latter makes it impossible to endorse the test.

Review of the Adult Language Assessment Scales by WAYNE H. SLATER, Associate Professor, Department of Curriculum and Instruction, University of Maryland, College Park, MD:

The Adult Language Assessment Scales (A-LAS®) was constructed to provide comprehensive data about the language proficiency of adults who speak English as a Second Language (ESL) or English as a Foreign Language (EFL). Consisting of two parts, the Oral Language component (Short Form) measures comprehension, vocabulary, and language production. The Pronunciation component measures pronunciation and oral discrimination. The authors explicitly state that the A-LAS is not an achievement test, because it only measures achievement in course content that is focused on the development of listening and speaking abilities. Keeping this limitation in mind, the test generates identification levels and standard scores. The authors contend that these results may be used to identify students who require language assistance and placement in special programs. Because the A-LAS package includes equivalent forms, A and B, it offers the user the opportunity to measure language growth over time. After the user determines specific goals for an assessment, either the A-LAS Long Form (Oral Language and Pronunciation component), the A-LAS Short Form (Oral Language component), or the Pronunciation component alone may be used. The Language Assessment Scales (LAS) significantly influenced the content and development of the A-LAS with one of the results being the A-LAS's use of a convergent approach to assessment of oral proficiency. That is, the total oral score is derived from performance across the linguistic categories—phonemes, morphemes, and syntax. It also uses diverse measurement procedures, content areas, and scoring procedures. Unfortunately, the authors fail to provide the potential user with the requisite theoretical underpinnings to support their rationale. Just as important, the A-LAS subscales are not timed. The Short Form of the instrument requires 15–20 minutes and the Long Form, 25–30 minutes, depending on the proficiency of the individual.

Consisting of four parts, the Oral Language component includes Part 1: Vocabulary, which contains three sections: Nouns, Verbs, and Adjectives. The Nouns section assesses the ability to produce a label for an illustrated object selected from four domains (body parts, farm and ranch, office/small business, and food services). The Verbs section assesses the ability to construct the present progressive (-ing) form of a correct verb form to describe the action illustrated in the cues (pictures); and the Adjectives section assesses the ability to produce the antonym of 10 high frequency adjectives used in instructional or employment environments. A low score on Part 1 suggests a lack of sufficient immersion in oral English vocabulary and/or usage and serves as a predictor of difficulty in adult education or employment communication as well as in reading, writing, and mathematics. The purpose of Part 2: Conversations is to assess oral comprehension. It consists of dialog prompts and 10 yes-no questions. It measures receptive language and focuses on the ability to understand and comprehend what is heard in informal conversation. The individual is asked to respond to questions based on factual information presented in the prompt that is prerecorded on a cassette and illustrated in the *Cue Picture Book*. A low score in this section suggests that an individual may have difficulty in understanding conversations, discussions, and lectures. Alternate prompts are available for this section. The purpose of Part 3: Making Sentences is to determine the ability of individuals to generate a complete descriptive sentence. The task consists of five picture prompts. Finally, the individual listens to a newscast that is illustrated with four drawings. Then the individual is asked to retell the events of the newscast in his or her own words. Scores on this task provide a metric indicating the degree of proficiency of an individual in producing an oral narrative. One alternate prompt is available.

Consisting of two parts, the Pronunciation component assesses individuals' competency on specific phonemes (sounds) determined to cause major difficulty for individuals acquiring English as a Second (ESL) or Foreign Language (EFL). In Part 5: Same or Different, the individual is assessed for auditory discrimination using minimal-pair test items. This approach is a modification of Wepman's Auditory Discrimination Test (T5:2870). A low score in this section suggests that the individual may have difficulty understanding decoding words and sentences in instructional or work environments. In Part 6: Sounds in Words, individuals are assessed for phoneme production. This section includes target phonemes embedded in words, phrases, and short sentences, in initial, medial, and final positions as appropriate. The target phoneme is underlined in each test item. The individual listens to and repeats each word, phrase, or sentence prerecorded on a cassette tape. Individuals identified as low scorers in this section may have difficulty making themselves understood in an instructional or employment setting. The authors strongly recommend the use of the prerecorded cassettes for Part 1: Vocabulary (Adjectives), Part 2: Conversations, Part 4: Newscast, Part 5: Same or Different, and Part 6: Sounds in Words to ensure that the test is standardized for each individual.

As mentioned earlier, the A-LAS consists of both Oral Language and Pronunciation components. All subscales of both components except Parts 3: Making Sentences and 4: Newscast are scored simultaneously by the test administrator. Individual responses to Parts 3 and 4 are specific to each individual and thus require holistic scoring by trained personnel. In order to maintain high levels of validity and reliability, the authors have constructed a reliability exercise that test administrators must complete and attain a reliability level of 90% agreement.

A Total Score and Identification Level may be derived from the Oral Language section alone (Short Form of the test), the Pronunciation component alone, or from the two sections combined (Long Form of the test). The authors discuss the notion of gray-area scores, the reliability of scores near cutoff or criterion levels. This potential problem results from proficiency categories determined on the basis of pre-established, cutoff scores. Because the probability of error is highest at or near these cutoff scores, potential misclassifications must be considered. To reduce this probability, the authors apply the standard error of measurement (*SEM*) to create a bandwidth to be used as a gray area to identify individuals for whom classification errors are most probable. If an individual's total score falls in the gray-area bandwidth, the test administrator is told to consider the placement as provisional until additional data are collected. The A-LAS Observation Form may also be used to address this issue. The authors make the claim that their studies have shown that when observational data are used in

concert with A-LAS test results, placement errors are reduced by as much as 50%.

The authors provide a fairly comprehensible Oral Administration Manual and an Oral Scoring and Interpretation Manual for the A-LAS. The Oral Administration Manual addresses such topics as Preparation by the Administrator, Using the Cassettes, Testing Cautions, and Calculating Short Form, Pronunciation, and Long Form Raw Scores. The Oral Scoring and Interpretation Manual includes extensive information on topics such as Scoring, Gray-Area Scores and Standard Error of Measurement, Interpretation (Proficiency Level and Category), Placement (A-LAS Performance Profile), Interpretation of Pronunciation Total Score, the A-LAS Observation Form, and numerous Rating Samples.

At the same time, the authors need to seriously consider updating and further developing their overview and rationale for the A-LAS with current theory and rigorous research in this line of inquiry. In addition, technical information, such as norms, normative procedures, score reliability, validity of test results, references, and normative tables are not reported for the A-LAS in either test manual, and these are serious omissions (Anastasi & Urbina, 1997).

SUMMARY. To conclude, this reviewer has serious reservations about recommending the use of the Adult Language Assessment Scales (A-LAS) as a screening device with adults who speak English as a Second (ESL) or Foreign Language (EFL). In carefully constructed pilot studies, results from the A-LAS might be useful for the preliminary identification of those in need of language services and placement into appropriate programs. However, any placement derived from this test should be considered highly tentative until the examiner confirms or disconfirms the suggested placement with additional formal and informal assessments that are supported by strong validity and reliability data.

REVIEWER'S REFERENCE

Anastasi, A., & Urbina, S. (1997). *Psychological testing* (7th ed.). Upper Saddle River, NJ: Prentice-Hall.

[12]
Adult Personality Inventory [Revised].

Purpose: Designed as a "tool for analyzing and reporting differences in personality, interpersonal style, and career preferences."
Population: Ages 16–adult.
Publication Dates: 1982–1996.

Acronym: API.

Scores, 25: Personality Scores (Extroverted, Adjusted, Tough-Minded, Independent, Disciplined, Creative, Enterprising); Interpersonal Style Scores (Caring, Adapting, Withdrawn, Submissive, Uncaring, Non-Conforming, Sociable, Assertive); Career/Lifestyle Scores (Practical, Scientific, Aesthetic, Social, Competitive, Structured); Validity Scores (Good Impression, Bad Impression, Infrequency, Uncertainty).

Administration: Group or individual.

Time: (45–60) minutes.

Comments: Self-report; computer scored and interpreted.

Author: Samuel E. Krug.

Publisher: MetriTech, Inc.

a) API NARRATIVE REPORTS.

Purpose: "Oriented to the test taker, provides users with scores, extensive interpretive information in narrative form, and a series of questions that guide the reader toward a practical application of assessment data."

Price Data, 1999: $49 per Narrative Report kit including Interpretive and Technical Guide ('96, 53 pages), processing of 5 reports, 2 reusable test booklets, and 5 answer sheets; $48.75 per 5 reports; $89.50 per 10 reports; $196.25 per 25 reports; $337.50 per 50 reports; $16.50 per manual; $16 per 10 reusable test booklets.

b) API/PC.

Purpose: "Administers, scores, and generates immediate test results for the same 21 scales and validity checks as the API Narrative Report."

Price Data: $54 per API/PC Introductory kit including manual ('96, 21 pages), and 5-report demo disk; $18 per manual; $105 per 10 administrations disk; $237.50 per 25 administrations disk; $400 per 50 administrations disk; [off-line assessment support materials: $16 per 10 reusable test booklets; $14 per 50 answer sheets; $20 per 50 scannable answer sheets; $36 per 50 decision model worksheets].

Comments: Supports both on-line or off-line testing; IBM version only (5.25-inch HD or 3.5-inch DD); optional 189-item short version requires 25–35 minutes for administration.

c) API/CAREER PROFILE.

Purpose: Oriented to the test administrator and compares the individual test taker with Occupational Decision Models and user created models.

Forms, 2: Form E "includes expanded descriptions of the 6 career/lifestyle factors;" Form M offers "automatic comparisons of the individual test taker to each of the decision models."

Price Data: $59 per API/Career Profile Introductory Kit (Form E or M) including API/Career Profile manual (n.d., 71 pages), and 5-report demo

disk; $120 per 10 administrations disk; $275 per 25 administrations disk; $475 per 50 administrations disk; $20 per manual.

Comments: Supports both on-line or off-line testing; IBM version only; optional 189-item short version requires 25–35 minutes for administration.

d) API-UTIL PROGRAM.

Purpose: Designed to convert API data records to ASCII files and "correctly formatted" ASCII files to API data records.

Price Data: $48 per program.

e) APISTORE PROGRAM.

Purpose: Designed for high-volume users to store API data from multiple diskettes in one convenient location.

Price Data: $250 per program.

Cross References: For a review by Rik Carl D'Amato of an earlier edition, see 12:20; see also T4:106 (4 references); for a review by Brian Bolton of an earlier edition, see 9:54.

Review of the Adult Personality Inventory [Revised] by KEVIN LANNING, Associate Professor of Psychology, Honors College of Florida Atlantic University, Jupiter, FL:

The Adult Personality Inventory (API) is a 324-item omnibus measure of personality, interpersonal style, and fit with occupational themes. The API is intended for persons 16 years of age and older, with items that require no more than a fourth-grade reading level, and can be administered in group as well as individual settings. The API takes approximately one hour to complete, although the manual reports that testing time is reduced by half when the measure is administered by computer.

The API may be considered as a direct descendant of the venerable Sixteen Personality Factor Questionnaire (16PF: Cattell, Eber, & Tatsuoka, 1970; T5: 2417). The API items were selected from an initial pool of 564 items designed to measure Cattell's 16 core constructs (D'Amato, 1995; Krug, 1995). These were reduced on the basis of factor analyses of items characterizing each of these constructs, then augmented in order to sample from four domains of item content identified by Werner and Pervin (1986). These domains include the cognitive (e.g., beliefs) and affective (emotions) domains, preferences, and behavioral activities. The majority of the API items are measures in the cognitive domain, with the remainder of items sampled roughly equally from the other three domains (Krug, 1995).

Cognitive items of the API include not only statements of belief, but also items that measure cognitive ability (e.g., 927 - 838 = ?). The inclusion of ability items is an unusual feature of the API, one that has been carried forward from the 16PF, and that does not characterize competing measures such as the California Psychological Inventory (T5:372), the Eysenck Personality Questionnaire (T5:999), or the Revised NEO Personality Inventory (T5: 2218). On the API, unlike the 16PF, the ability items are presented in a separate section of the test, and sample systematically from the quantitative as well as verbal and analytic domains.

This "compartmentalizing" of the ability items has the effect of making the API more user-friendly than the 16PF. The user-friendliness is also manifest in the use of a consistent, simplified response format for the API items, and, most importantly, in the scales themselves. The end user of the API does not receive scores on Cattell's 16 primary factors. Instead, the API provides scores on three classes of measures, including personal characteristics, interpersonal style, and career/lifestyle factors. These measures, though derived from equations based on the 16PF, are likely to have greater relevance in many applied settings than the 16PF scales (Bolton, 1991). Unfortunately, the equations used to compute the API scales are not provided in the test materials, nor is the API hand-scorable.

The personal characteristic scales of the API include measures labeled Extroverted, Adjusted, Tough-Minded, Independent, Disciplined, Creative, and Enterprising. The first five of these correspond to the second-order factors scored on the current version of the 16PF. These five measures are argued to map onto the familiar five-factor model (Krug, 1995), although the particulars of this mapping are not given in the API materials. The latter two measures appear to have been rationally constructed, though informed from empirical studies of creativity and need for achievement, respectively.

The interpersonal style scales are intended as measures of the interpersonal circle. Proceeding clockwise around this circle, the eight scales are labeled Caring, Adapting, Withdrawn, Submissive, Uncaring, Nonconforming, Sociable, and Assertive. Correlations among these measures reveal a close fit with the expected circumplex structure, with strong negative correlations for opposing measures (e.g., caring-uncaring), more modest correlations for oblique and adjacent scales (caring-adapting), and near-zero correlations for ostensibly orthogonal measures. Unfortunately, although the internal structure of the interpersonal scales is attractive, relations between these scales and the API personal characteristics scales are problematic. For example, Wiggins (Wiggins & Trapnell, 1997) has argued that the interpersonal circle represents the Extraverted-Agreeable plan of the five-factor model, but in the API the interpersonal measures are most strongly correlated with the personal characteristics Adjusted and Independent. Further, the Adjusted measure is most highly correlated with Caring and (inversely) Submissive; the Independent measure is related to Sociable vs. Withdrawn. This counterintuitive pattern of correlations may be attributable to idiosyncrasies in the naming of API scales or to a real divergence between the API and the constructs of the interpersonal circumplex. Unfortunately, neither the manuals nor the empirical literature illuminate this.

The career/lifestyle factors are labeled Practical, Scientific, Aesthetic, Social, Competitive, and Structured. These are based on an earlier study of the 16PF, in which discriminant function analysis was used to isolate personality characteristics associated with different occupations. Six of the dimensions that differentiated these occupational groups were retained from this analysis and projected onto the API (Ahadi, 1991). These six API career dimensions appear similar to Holland's occupational themes. The career factors should be considered as complements to the measures of personal characteristics and interpersonal style. In some cases, scales in different domains (e.g., Independent-Scientific) are correlated very highly, indeed at or near the limits of their reliabilities. Such high correlations are to be expected in a multilevel instrument such as the API, and serve to remind the user that the domains of personality, interpersonal behavior, and career/lifestyle should not be considered independent.

In addition to three domains of content, the API includes four validity scales: Good Impression, Bad Impression, Infrequency, and Uncertainty. The first two of these were empirically developed; the first three are used in calculating scores on the content scales of the instrument.

That is, in the event the respondent attains an above-average score on a validity scale, the content scales are adjusted based on correlations between the validity and the content scales.

Previous reviews of the API have criticized the manual for the lack of technical information (Bolton, 1985; D'Amato, 1995). That lack has been addressed, thought not altogether remedied, by the publication of a new Interpretive and Technical Guide. Although the Guide does not include some of the information that was available in the earlier test manual (such as a joint factor analysis of the 16PF and API), it does include the full 25 x 25 matrix of correlations among the API scales. These correlations, based on a large sample (N = 1,477), were not provided in the earlier manual. Although the demographic make-up of this sample is not provided, the Guide does provide descriptive statistics relating the API scales to gender and age, as well as some data concerning Black-White differences on the test.

The primary evidence for validity presented in the Guide is a description of correlations between the API and other self-report measures of personality. Unfortunately, these correlations are based on a sample of only 80 individuals, and the actual magnitude of the correlations is not given. More extensive evidence is provided concerning the reliabilities of the API scales, including test-retest statistics on a small sample and internal consistencies from two separate studies. These internal consistencies are generally high, particularly for the personal characteristic (median alpha = .81) and interpersonal style (.80) scales. The Guide also provides evidence concerning the comparability of the standard 324-item version of the API with a 189-item short version of the test. The scales appear similar though not identical in the two forms of the test, with a median correlation between long and short versions of approximately .91, and alphas typically .06 lower for the short-form scales.

A software package, AKPI/Career Profile is of potential use in vocational and occupational settings. The manual for this software includes projected API profiles for individuals in 38 different occupations. In a 1991 study, Ahadi represented 37 of these occupations as three-letter, ipsative codes based on the API career factors. These API codes were then compared to the three-letter Holland codes for the same occupa-

tions. For the 37 occupations, 23 showed at least "reasonably close" congruence between the API and Holland codes. Congruence was generally better for occupations requiring less than a college education, and was lowest for occupations such as Biologist, School Superintendent, and Physician.

A "decision model" feature is incorporated into the API/Career Profile and the API/PC, a second software package. The decision model consists of a series of 64 paired comparisons, in which decision makers are asked which of two test characteristics is more valuable for a particular situation. This process leads users to a more careful consideration of their criterion or ideal, and provides a model against which actual protocols can be compared. Users of the Career Profile software have the option of an automated comparison of protocols against occupational models as well. But until there is more evidence concerning the criterion-related validity of the API, these decision models should be used with caution (Drummond, 1987).

SUMMARY. The API is a potentially rich, multilevel personality inventory, one that provides measures of constructs that will be of interest to test users in a wide range of settings. Further, the API scales are highly internally consistent, suggesting a univocality of meaning of the measures. Unfortunately, evidence that directly links API scales scores to other measures, to observer ratings, and to behavior-based criteria remains insufficient. It is hoped that the next few years will see additional research into the properties of the API, and that this test will begin to fulfill its promise.

REVIEWER'S REFERENCES

Cattell, R. B., Eber, H. W., & Tatsuoka, M. M. (1970). *Handbook for the 16PF.* Champaign, IL: Institute for Personality and Ability Testing.

Bolton, B. (1985). [Review of the Adult Personality Inventory.] In J. V. Mitchell, Jr. (Ed.), *The ninth mental measurements yearbook* (pp. 55–56). Lincoln, NE: Buros Institute of Mental Measurements.

Werner, P. D., & Pervin, L. A. (1986). The content of personality inventory items. *Journal of Personality and Social Psychology, 51,* 622–628.

Drummond, R. J. (1987). [Review of the Adult Personality Inventory.] In D. J. Keyser & R. C. Sweetland (Eds.), *Test critiques: Volume VI* (pp. 21–25). Kansas City, MO: Test Corporation of America.

Ahadi, S. A. (1991). The use of API career factors as Holland occupational types. *Educational and Psychological Measurement, 51,* 167–173.

Bolton, B. (1991). Comments on "The Adult Personality Inventory." *Journal of Counseling & Development, 69,* 272–273.

D'Amato, R. C. (1995). [Review of the Adult Personality Inventory.] In J. C. Conoley & J. C. Impara (Eds.), *The twelfth mental measurements yearbook* (pp. 52–54). Lincoln, NE: Buros Institute of Mental Measurements.

Krug, S. E. (1995). Career assessment and the Adult Personality Inventory. *Journal of Career Assessment, 3,* 176–187.

Wiggins, J. S., & Trapnell, P. D. (1997). Personality structure: The return of the Big Five. In R. Hogan, J. Johnson, & S. Briggs (Eds.), *Handbook of personality psychology* (pp. 737–765). San Diego: Academic Press.

[13]
Adult Rating of Oral English.

Purpose: "Designed to assess the oral English language skills of secondary and adult students" who speak English as a second language.

Population: Adult and secondary students in vocational education and employment training programs.

Publication Date: 1995.

Acronym: AROE.

Scores, 15: Pronunciation, Grammar, General Vocabulary, Vocational Vocabulary, Building Blocks Subscore; Listener and Speaker scores for Conversation, Instructions, Explanations, Clarification/Verification; Discourse Subscore; Mean Proficiency Score; Total Score.

Administration: Individual.

Price Data, 1997: $75 per training kit including 5 user's handbooks (43 pages) and 25 matrix scoring sheets; $20 per set of 25 matrix scoring sheets; $15 per user's handbook; $10 per technical manual (16 pages); $15 per supplementary video explaining use and purpose.

Time: Untimed.

Comments: A rating scale completed by teachers about individual students' skills; supplementary video explaining use and purpose is available.

Authors: Annette M. Zehler and Patricia A. DiCerbo.

Publisher: Development Associates, Inc.

Review of the Adult Rating of Oral English by ROGER A. RICHARDS, Consultant, Office of Certification and Credentialing, Massachusetts Department of Education, Malden, MA, and Adjunct Professor of Communication, Bunker Hill Community College, Boston, MA:

The Adult Rating of Oral English (AROE) is a scoring matrix for recording teachers' assessments of the English-language skills of adults "within vocational education and employment training programs" (User's Handbook, p. 7). By guiding the teacher through the elements of oral language, it provides a uniform approach to evaluating different individuals by insuring that consistent criteria are applied to all and by eliminating the risk that one or more factors may receive disproportionate weighting in the total assessment.

The rater is required to judge 11 elements of a subject's linguistic proficiency and to assign a score of 0 to 5 to each according to which descriptor is most applicable. The proficiency levels for pronunciation are typical:

Level 0. No ability.

Level 1. Speech is very difficult to understand; repetition is always needed.

Level 2. Speech is difficult to understand; repetition is often needed.

Level 3. Speech is sometimes difficult to understand; repetition is sometimes needed.

Level 4. Speech is seldom difficult to understand; repetition is only occasionally needed.

Level 5. Speech is close to (or the same as) that of a native speaker.

The sum of the ratings for Pronunciation, Grammar, General Vocabulary, and Vocational Vocabulary yields a Building Blocks Score; similarly, rating for Conversation as a Listener, Conversation as a Speaker, Instructions as a Listener, Instructions as a Speaker, Explanations as a Listener, Explanations as a Speaker, and Clarification/Verification are summed to obtain a Discourse score. The total score equals the Building Blocks plus the Discourse score.

The method of administration is described as follows:

> No testing sessions with the students are necessary in using the AROE. The AROE essentially asks teachers to do what you are already doing, that is, to observe your students' skills in English and to make judgments about those skills …. The AROE ratings are based on the teacher's observations of the student's use of English across the variety of situations and topics encountered in the classroom. (User's Handbook, pp. 8–9)

Despite some external trappings that may confuse the uninitiated, the AROE is neither standardized nor a test. (Neither is it an "Adult Rating," whatever that might be; rather, it is a rating of adults' oral English.) There is no uniform content to which all test takers are required to respond, there is no uniform method of administration, there are no objective criteria for determining scores, and there are no norms or other guides to the interpretation of results.

Making the fine distinctions called for would be possible only in a situation in which the teacher knows the students extremely well and has had extensive opportunity to observe their English in a variety of contexts. Even then, differentiating among instructions, explanations, and clarification/verification, for example, must be very difficult. The authors claim that "teachers report feeling comfortable in rating after about 15–30 hours of working with their students" (User's Handbook, p. 9).

A claim of face validity is based on reactions of teachers and other vocational program staff who have reportedly found the instrument useful. As evidence of concurrent/criterion-related validity, the authors offer correlations in the range of .65 to .70 between the AROE and the Basic English Skills Test (BEST) Short Form ($n = 22$) and between the AROE and the Bilingual Vocational Oral Proficiency Test (BVOPT) ($n = 69$). The rationale for such comparison is not clear because the BEST and BVOPT are vehicles for determining language proficiency whereas the AROE is merely a form for recording subjectively assigned judgments of proficiency.

The discussion of reliability provides measures of internal consistency and comparisons of independent ratings assigned by pairs of raters. Concerning the former, the authors state, "Since the AROE components are designed to measure oral language proficiency, items should positively correlate with each other" (Technical Manual, p. 9). The measures of internal consistency all fall within the range of .89 to .99. That being the case, we have to ask, what is the point of determining component scores if they match each other so closely? If each of the scores measures a discrete aspect of oral language, should we not expect lower intercorrelations?

The interrater reliability of the AROE is not impressive. For the 11 component scores, correlation coefficients range from -.12 to .95 for samples of between 9 and 63 students. For the total of nine samples ($N = 197$ for Building Blocks and $N = 284$ for Discourse), the intercorrelations are all in the .70s. These relatively low correlations are hardly surprising. The authors sum up a major flaw of the AROE in acknowledging that:

> The level of agreement between raters varied across sites and teachers but was generally moderately high to high. Variation could be partially accounted for by rater differences in terms of educational background and instructional time with student. (Technical Manual, p. 9)

The AROE does not yield new information about its subjects' performance. It simply provides a format for recording teacher evaluations of performance. It may be helpful in assisting teachers to make more systematic assessments of their students, but a locally developed rating scale could probably prove just as useful and less costly.

Review of the Adult Rating of Oral English by GERALD TINDAL, Professor, Behavioral Research and Teaching, University of Oregon, Eugene, OR:

The Adult Rating of Oral English (AROE) provides qualitative information on the oral proficiency of adult learners of English as a second language. "The focus is on those oral English language skills that are particularly important within on-the-job situations" (p. 7). The ratings are based on teacher observations in classroom situations and topics, with various matrices provided for ensuring the reflections are pertinent to work settings. Both the matrix and video training package were developed with funds from the U.S. Department of Education, Office of Vocational and Adult Education. The instrument is composed of two parts, a Building Blocks matrix and a Discourse matrix, to help define areas of strength and weakness, track progress, and guide placement decisions. The entire instrument is packaged with a User's Handbook, a scoring sheet, a summary information sheet, a training plan, and a technical manual.

The teacher rates the student on each proficiency by selecting one of six levels of proficiency (generally, in all the scales, 0 reflects no ability and 5 reflects the ability of a native English speaker). Three steps are provided for actually rating a student, with the teachers first directed to think back over the past 2–3 weeks in which they have observed the student using English, second to review the rating descriptions, and third to "select the description that best matches the student's most consistent level of performance over the past 2–3 weeks" (p. 9). The authors recommend using the instrument whenever the teacher is comfortable making such decisions (usually after 15–30 hours of working with students).

The manual is divided into sections that organize the two matrices. In the Building Blocks matrix, four basic components of oral proficiency are considered: Pronunciation, Grammar, General Vocabulary, and Vocational Vocabulary. In the Discourse matrix, seven components are included to determine how well the examinee is able to use the Building Blocks in actual communication: Conversation as a Listener, Conversation as a Speaker, Instructions as a Listener, Instructions as a Speaker, Explanations as a Listener, Explanations as a Speaker, and Clarification/Verification.

These two matrices provide, therefore, a total of 11 constructs on which to rate proficiency, each of them organized into two opposing pages. In each of these ratings, the examiner is directed to think about "why is it important?" and "what should I look for when rating the construct?" A final section is provided for each construct that raises "issues in rating" (p. 15).

Within each rating level, general descriptions, not specific skills, are listed to help the rater make a selection. For example, in the Building Blocks matrix of Grammar, the examiner is provided one scale that moves from a 0 (No ability) to a 1 ("uses only very few basic forms and structures; errors make all speech very difficult to understand") to a 3 ("uses a range of forms and structures; errors make some speech difficult to understand") to a 5 ("uses forms and structures at a level close to [or the same as] that of a native speaker") (p. 14). And, as an example in the Dicourse matrix for Conversation, the examiner is directed to use the 0–5 scale for making judgments of the student on two related scales: as a listener and as a speaker. The scale guides the examiner with descriptions of understanding and speaking from the low to the high end: with isolated words and phrases, then in the context of everyday topics, next within a context of less familiar topics [with some difficulty or easily], and finally in the context of a native speaker.

In the manual, the examiner is provided guidelines for rating and steps to follow, and then directions for scoring the AROE to determine the student's Total Score and Mean proficiency Level. The Total Score is the sum of all ratings in the Building Blocks and Discourse matrices whereas the Mean Proficiency is simply the average for all components that have been rated. A final section provides several ways the AROE can be used and guides the examiner in how to handle difficult situations (working with shy individuals, students who repeat classes, students with no literacy, etc.). The manual is extremely well organized, designed, and easy to use.

TECHNICAL ADEQUACY OF THE AROE. The AROE was developed by reviewing the vocational curricula and related research, assessing vocational program needs, constructing a pilot instrument, and field-testing it. The two matrices arose from the review of the literature, which then was expanded into a needs assessment of 35 individuals working in 22 vocational education and employment programs serving adult English language learners. Again, the two matrices were further articulated. With its construction and pilot testing, the following procedures have been described in a technical manual. First, discussion sessions were held to define the context for administration (teacher observation within authentic classroom situations using a reflective judgment that requires little time). Second, 12 sites were identified through the National Center for Research in Vocational Education (NCRVE). In this pilot testing, three workshops were held and then a video-training session was conducted.

Summary of technical data includes the following:

1. Ninety four percent of the respondents agreed or strongly agreed that the AROE was a useful measure of language proficiency and that it included the essential indicators of oral proficiency in vocational education and employment training programs.

2. On two other measures of language ability, it correlated about .70 with the Basic English Skills Test (BEST) and .66 with the Bilingual Vocational Oral Proficiency Test.

3. Reliability was investigated by measuring both internal consistency (which ranged from .89 to .99) and rater agreement (median of approximately .80).

4. Item statistics were displayed for all 11 components with four different sites, generally reflecting similar results in three of the four sites.

SUMMARY. This instrument has been very carefully developed and organized. It provides a very useful tool for vocational educators to use with students for whom English is a second language. The essential elements of oral language are well differentiated, easily obtained, and highly useful in the classroom context. As the authors indicate, the instrument can help teachers make many useful decisions about diagnostics, progress, and placement. The manuals and materials are very well organized and professionally published. The technical data are clear and support the use of this instrument in the context described by the authors. In future editions of the test, it might be useful to include factor analysis for documenting the dependence or independence of the traits and student change scores to document the sensitivity of the scale for tracking progress.

[14]

Ages and Stages Questionnaires.

Purpose: Designed to identify infants and young children who show potential developmental problems.

Population: Ages 4–48 months.

Publication Date: 1995.

Acronym: ASQ.

Scores, 5: Communication, Gross Motor, Fine Motor, Problem Solving, Personal-Social.

Administration: Group.

Price Data, 1997: $135 per complete system including 11 reproducible questionnaires, 11 reproducible, age-appropriate scoring sheets, and user's guide (165 pages).

Time: (10–30) minutes.

Comments: "A parent-completed, child-monitoring system."

Authors: Jane Squires, LaWanda Potter, and Diane Bricker.

Publisher: Paul H. Brookes Publishing Co., Inc.

Review of the Ages and Stages Questionnaires by DOROTHY M. SINGLETON, Associate Professor of Education, Winston-Salem State University, Winston-Salem, NC:

The Ages and Stages Questionnaires (ASQ): A Parent-Completed, Child-Monitoring System is a series of 11 questionnaires designed to identify infants and young children who show potential developmental problems or disabilities. The questionnaires are designed to be completed by parents along with trained professionals, if needed, with children at 4-month intervals (e.g., 4, 8, 12, 16, 20, 24, 30, ... 48 months of age, with optional questionnaires available at 6 and 18 months). The parent involvement of this system meets the mandates of PL 99-457 and PL 102-119. The early detection of developmental problems with children is the goal of this assessment. The Ages and Stages Questionnaires were developed to address the effectiveness of early intervention for children who are considered as being at-risk for developmental problems. The questionnaires are divided into five different areas: Communication, Gross Motor, Fine Motor, Problem Solving, and Personal-Social. Each questionnaire contains 30 questions. Each question of the different questionnaires is answered by checking *yes, sometimes,* or *not yet,* and if indicated, by explaining the response.

The questionnaires consist of 5–6 pages, with very clear directions on the front page. There are ASQ Information Summary pages after each questionnaire. The questionnaires have also been translated into Spanish. Cutoff scores are identified for each area of the questionnaire. Cutoff points are used as markers to separate young children who require referral and assessment from those who do not.

The cutoff points are used in order to have the best balance between the underreferrals and the overreferrals. The guidebook provides information on the sensitivity, true positive, false positive, and overreferral and underreferral rates when the cutoff points are adjusted. Use of the area total divided by the number of items answered to get a final score, based on what is age appropriate may deflate or inflate scores. This would not be in the best interest of children because it could lead to inappropriate identification of needs for young children.

The authors caution against the improper use of the questionnaires. Although there is flexibility with the ASQ system, parents must not assess their children by using a single screening to identify a delay. There must be consistency in the process in order to identify all problem areas.

The normative sample identified by the authors is based on information given by parents regarding individual child development according to age. The sample size was large enough to develop stable estimates with this age group. Subjects from the normative sample were infants and young children who met the following criteria: (a) no previous history of developmental or serious health problems as reported by parents, (b) birth at full term (greater than 37 weeks), and (c) no assignment to a Neonatal Intensive Care Unit (NICU). No demographic information is included in this analysis, which could influence the reliability of the data.

It is clear that reliability and validity evidence are prevalent in the Ages and Stages Questionnaires (ASQ): A Parent-Completed, Child-Monitoring System. The reliability studies consist of internal consistency analyses (relationship between developmental areas and overall scores); correlational analyses (all correlations were significant at $p < .0001$); and Cronbach's coefficient alpha (was calculated for all five areas). Test-retest reliability (2- to 3-week interval), interobserver reliability, and standard error of measurement are reported.

The authors point out that the relative operating characteristics (ROC) analyses, determination of screening cutoff points, and studies on concurrent validity provide validation information about the ASQ system. These validation procedures are considered to be appropriate. The relative operating characteristic analyses were employed to provide a single value measure of accuracy, which is reported as the area of a curve. The area of the entire graph can vary between .50 and 1.0 for perfect discrimination. The application of the ROC to the ASQ system was to establish whether cutoff points based on the risk group, the nonrisk group, or a combined group were most accurate.

The authors should be aware of P.L.-99-457's Individual Family Support Plan (IFSP) and its implications for long-term objectives every 6 months, rather than annually. The IFSP for infants and toddlers and their families must have a statement of the child's present levels of development. This statement must include present levels of physical development, cognitive development, language and speech development, psychosocial development, and self-help skills. Any organization adopting this program should be aware of the law, also.

SUMMARY. The Ages and Stages Questionnaires: A Parent Completed, Child-Monitoring System is designed to detect potential developmental problems or disabilities of infants and young children. These questionnaires should be used properly and consistently with the identified population of children.

Review of the Ages and Stages Questionnaires by RHONDA H. SOLOMON, Psychologist, Los Angeles Unified School District, Los Angeles, CA:

The Ages and Stages Questionnaires (ASQ): A Parent-Completed, Child-Monitoring System is an effective and affordable method of determining which infants and young children require further evaluation. It was previously called the Infant/Child Monitoring Questionnaires. The ASQ relies most heavily on parent participation, which is a sound constructive approach. Parents know a great deal about their children, and with the assistance of these structured and easy-to-read questionnaires they are able to share this information with child development professionals, such a psychologists, language-speech pathologists, and child development specialists. The questionnaires are aimed at a fourth to sixth grade reading level, and have corresponding illustrations to many of the assessed items. The protocol is broken into various

month intervals that can be plotted on a card. The questionnaire can be mailed to a parent or they can come to a location and have the information collected through interview.

The ASQ meets many of the guidelines put out by the National Center for Clinical Programs for Zero to Three, per the manual. The instrument is a developmental screening that can take place on a developmental basis. The instrument is based on sound child development and assessment principles. Many of the items have age equivalence scores that have been compared to the Revised Gesell Schedules and the Bayley Scales of Infant Development.

This is the second revision of this questionnaire, and with each revision comes the improvement of a working document screening tool. The ASQ fulfills a need for quality screening instruments that can gather data quickly and accurately, on infants and young children. The protocols are available in both English and Spanish, and are color-coded for easy reference. All the material may be photocopied. This offers a well-documented savings on the frequent reordering of copyrighted materials. The authors encourage the user to copy all the information in the course of a service provision to families. The information can be gathered numerous ways, including: mailed to parents within the home; completed with the assistance of a nurse or by a social worker on a home visit or during a telephone interview; completed by parents at a medical clinic prior to a well-child check-up; or completed by the child's regular caregiver at a childcare center.

The comprehensive manual offers much in the way of tables and figures, and even a detailed index. The manual provides various high-risk criteria for screening inclusion. The screening program was developed in response to an outcry for assistance in following numerous low income/high risk infants. Parental consent forms, demographic information sheets, and demographic information update sheets are included. Information designed to be used in determining the need for follow-up is also provided, as are remedial activity suggestions.

The deficits with the ASQ are within its technical report and information gathering methods. It is not listed as one of the Infant and Preschool Screening Tests that is recommended by the National Center for Clinical Infant Programs. The demographic characteristic of the standardization population is the Infant/Child Monitoring Project in Oregon. Some additional programs in Youngstown, Ohio and at the University of Hawaii have supplied data through their projects. The sex of the child was collected, although the ethnicity, family income, and education level of parents was not always collected. Results of statistical analyses are provided in the manual, although much of the information was not present. The ASQ also has a high level of false positives and false negatives. At some age levels, the false positives can be as high as 18.67%, with false negatives as high as 48.98%. The results from the ASQ have to be reviewed by a trained child development professional, psychologist, or similar professional to lessen the high rate of over- and underidentification. The ASQ is available as an inexpensive resource, but at this time there continue to be screening tests that offer more consistent scores but take longer to administer and are substantially more expensive in testing equipment and personnel. These screening assessment tools include: The Early Screening Inventory (ESI; 135) and The Birth to Three Developmental Scale.

SUMMARY. The information collected by the ASQ appears to be valid, although the results should be interpreted and used with caution. Remember, the ASQ is only one portion of a screening assessment.

[15]
Alcohol Use Disorders Identification Test.

Purpose: A screening procedure "to identify persons whose alcohol consumption has become hazardous or harmful to their health."
Population: Adults.
Publication Date: 1992.
Acronym: AUDIT.
Scores, 2: Core, Clinical.
Administration: Individual or group.
Price Data, 1996: Test and manual (33 pages) are free; $75 per training module.
Time: [2] minutes.
Comments: Developed by World Health Organization and validated on primary care patients in six countries; available in English, Japanese, Spanish, Norwegian, and Romanian.
Authors: Thomas F. Babor, Juan Ramon de la Fuente, John Saunders, and Marcus Grant.
Publisher: World Health Organization [Switzerland]; also available from Thomas F. Babor.
Cross References: See T5:135 (6 references).

Review of the Alcohol Use Disorders Identification Test by PHILIP ASH, Director, Ash, Blackstone and Cates, Blacksburg, VA:

The Alcohol Use Disorders Identification Test (AUDIT) (Allen & Columbus, 1995, pp. 260-261) was developed in a six-country (Australia, Bulgaria, Kenya, Mexico, Norway, USA) World Health Organization collaborative project to design a screening instrument to identify people whose alcohol consumption has become hazardous and harmful to their health. It should be noted that this is the first instrument of its kind to be derived on the basis of a cross-national study (Babor, de la Fuente, Saunders, & Grant, 1992).

Screening with the AUDIT provides data useful in deciding about treatment alternatives such as brief intervention with heavy drinkers or specialized treatment for more seriously ill patients. The AUDIT package includes the AUDIT Core and an optional Clinical Screening Procedure. This procedure includes two questions about traumatic injury (e.g., "Have you injured your head since your eighteenth birthday?"), five on clinical evaluation (e.g., presence of hand tremor), and a blood test (Serum GGT). Although the Clinical Screening Procedure does not refer directly to problems with alcohol, it may elicit relevant information where patients are defensive toward alcohol-specific questions.

To develop the AUDIT Core, a 150-item assessment schedule was administered to subjects ($N = 1888$) attending representative primary health care facilities in the participating countries. A 10-item self-report questionnaire (the AUDIT) was selected to cover the domains of alcohol consumption, drinking behavior, and alcohol-related problems. It may be paper-and-pencil self-administered or administered in an interview in 2 minutes. Questions 1–3 measure quantitative alcohol consumption, 4–6 drinking behavior, 7–8 adverse reactions, and 9–10 alcohol-related problems. Responses to each question are scored from 0 to 4, for a maximum possible AUDIT score of 40. Among those diagnosed as having hazardous or harmful alcohol use, 92% had an AUDIT score of 8 or more, and 94% of those with nonhazardous consumption had a score of less than 8 (Saunders, Aasland, Babor, de la Fuente, & Grant, 1993).

According to the authors' research report (Saunders et al., 1993, p. 799), the differences between the AUDIT and most other existing questionnaires include the following: (a) it tries to identify problem drinkers at the "less severe end of the spectrum" rather than those with established dependence or alcoholism; (b) it emphasizes hazardous consumption and frequency of intoxication rather than drinking behavior itself and its consequences; and (c) it refers to alcohol experiences in the past year as well as over the patient's lifetime, improving relevance to current drinking status, and it does not require the test-taker to identify himself or herself as a problem drinker. Two questions (9–10) have 3 responses (scored 0, 2, 4). The remaining questions (1–8) have 4-choice responses based upon frequency (from, e.g., "never," "1 or 2" to, e.g., "daily or almost daily," "10 or more"). They yield item scores from 0 (lowest frequency choice) to 4 (highest frequency choice). The authors anticipated that using specific frequency continua will reduce underreporting of adverse effects.

The manual (Babor et al., 1992) is a 28-page document that introduces the AUDIT by discussing the advantages of screening for alcohol problems, the developmental history of the AUDIT, applications of the AUDIT to the early identification of alcohol-related problems, and the scoring and interpretation of the AUDIT. The authors point out that although alcohol screening tests have most often been used to identify who *may probably* be alcohol abusers (case finding), the AUDIT is directed at screening known drinkers to deal with their problems and treatment approaches. The AUDIT is claimed to be the first screening test specifically for use in primary care cases. The seven text chapters of the manual are followed by a list of references and six appendices covering research guidelines, validity evidence in the AUDIT, etc., including a copy of the AUDIT.

Extensive research has been undertaken on the reliability, validity, and other psychometric characteristics of the AUDIT. Both test-retest and internal consistency measures (Fleming, Barry, & MacDonald, 1991) have shown satisfactory reliability. High intrascale reliabilities (alpha coefficient mean values of .93 and .81) were found among the drinking patients' drinking behavior and adverse psychological reactions domains (Saunders et al., 1993, pp. 794–795).

Concurrent, construct, and discriminant validities of the AUDIT were assessed by Bohn, Babor, and Kranzler (1995, p. 425ff). Significant concurrent validities were found against other alcoholism measures such as the MAST (Michigan Alcohol Screening Test) and the MacAndrews scales ($r = .31$ to $r = .887$). Coefficients for the AUDIT Core were consistently higher than for the AUDIT Clinical. Construct validities for five risk factors, four drinking consequences, and three drinking attitudes showed significant correlations ($r = .27$ to $r = .88$) for 11 of the 12 measures for AUDIT Core for male subjects ($n = 107$), but fewer significant correlations for AUDIT Core for female subjects ($n = 91$), or for either sex for AUDIT Clinical scores. An analysis of discriminant validity found a significant difference between nondrinkers and harmful drinkers, but no significant gender or gender x drinker group difference. Similar validity evidence was reported by Babor et al. (1992, p. 21).

SUMMARY. Overall, the AUDIT is a useful device for discriminating between alcoholics and medical patients and in the early detection of hazardous or harmful drinking, and is more successful than the Michigan Alcohol Screening Test (MAST; 232) in discriminating hazardous drinkers from nonhazardous drinkers. A well-written manual and substantial published supporting research commend the instrument for serious consideration in the assessment of people with difficult alcohol problems. Its multinational origins and translations also commend it as a device for conducting cross-cultural alcoholism studies.

REVIEWER'S REFERENCES

Fleming, M. F., Barry, K. L., & MacDonald, R. (1991). The Alcohol Use Disorders Identification Test (AUDIT) in a college sample. *International Journal of the Addictions, 26,* 1173–1185.

Babor, T. F., de la Fuente, J. R., Saunders, J., & Grant, M. (1992). *Programme on Substance Abuse: AUDIT—The Alcohol Use Disorders Test: Guidelines for Use in Primary Health Care* (an update of WHO Document No. WHO/MNH/DAT/89.4 under the same title) [Switzerland]: World Health Organization.

Saunders, J. B., Aasland, O. G., Babor, T. F., de la Fuente, J. R., & Grant, M. (1993). Development of the Alcohol Use Disorders Identification Test (AUDIT): WHO collaborative project on early detection of persons with harmful alcohol consumption—II. *Addiction, 88,* 791–804.

Allen, J. P., & Columbus, M. (Eds.) (1995). *Assessing alcohol problems: A guide for clinicians and researchers.* Washington, DC: National Institute on Alcohol Abuse and Alcoholism.

Bohn, M. J., Babor, T. F., & Kranzler, H. R. (1995). The Alcohol Use Disorders Identification Test (AUDIT): Validation of a screening instrument for use in medical settings. *Journal of Studies on Alcohol, 58*(4), 423–432.

Review of the Alcohol Use Disorders Identification Test by HERBERT BISCHOFF, Licensed Psychologist, Psychology Resources, Anchorage, AK:

The Alcohol Use Disorders Identification Test (AUDIT) is a screening procedure produced by a multicultural collaboration of six nations under the sponsorship of the World Health Organization (WHO). The AUDIT is intended to be used primarily by health care providers to detect harmful or hazardous drinking habits. The AUDIT is not a diagnostic tool, and the authors are clear about its limitations and intended uses. The AUDIT is made up of two components. The first part is a core 10-item questionnaire that addresses drinking patterns including indications of "hazardous alcohol consumption, evidence of dependence symptoms, and harmful alcohol consumption." The second part, which is administered only in cases of a "positive" on the first part, is a clinical screening instrument of eight items covering trauma history, clinical examination, and a blood test.

The intended use of the AUDIT is to detect, or more appropriately screen, persons who may be engaging in dangerous drinking habits, referred to as either harmful, hazardous, or evident of dependence. Referring to the ICD-10 the authors define harmful drinking as, "a pattern of use which is already causing damage to health." Hazardous drinking refers to "an established pattern of use carrying with it a high risk of future damage to health, physical or mental, but which has not yet resulted in significant medical or psychiatric ill effects." Evidence of dependence is defined by symptoms, patterns of behaviors, and debilitating social and occupational consequences of long-term alcohol dependence, as described in the DSM-IV and ICD-10.

The AUDIT has also been found to have high levels of concurrent and construct validity. There have been numerous studies on the efficacy of using the AUDIT screening instrument, and it has been established as providing reliable and valid scores of harmful and hazardous drinking patterns with high levels of accuracy in detecting dependence in multinational and widely varied populations (Bohn, Babor, & Kranzler 1995; MacKenzie, Langa & Brown, 1996; Saunders, Aasland, Babor, de la Fuente, & Grant, 1993). Scores from the AUDIT have been found to be highly reliable in identifying persons who currently demonstrate the above patterns of behavior.

The AUDIT appears to be a highly useable, quickly administered, and cost efficient tool for health care providers to use in the course of various types of clinical interviews. During the short time the AUDIT has been available, it has proven itself when compared to more traditional methods, such as the Michigan Alcohol Screening Test (MAST), TWEAK, and the MMPI's (Minnesota Multiphasic Personality Inventory) MacAndrew Alcoholism scale. Overall, the AUDIT may be an even more reliable indicator of problem drinking patterns with certain populations, such as ethnic minorities and the long-term unemployed (Cherpitel & Clark, 1995; Claussen & Aasland, 1993; Luckie, White, Miller, & Icenogle, 1995).

There are, however, some limitations with the AUDIT and its manual. These include information on how the cutoff point was determined, how results vary from population to population, and how the 10 items were chosen. The information is covered in supplemental material provided by the test authors in the forms of varying research projects that have demonstrated the AUDIT to provide highly reliable and valid scores and to be a useful instrument. Another concern with the test manual is the lack of normative data; nor is there an explanation of how various cultures view harmful or hazardous drinking. This may leave the test administrator confused about the validity of scores from the AUDIT when there are no apparent considerations devoted to the importance of context, other than suggested ideal situations when administering the test. For instance, it is assumed a drink containing 10g of alcohol is the typical quantity per drink cross-culturally. Yet, there is no consideration given to how drinking is viewed culturally, or to the effects of perceived social desirability on the respondents' level of self-reporting. Moreover, there is no discussion on how possibly to control for these potential effects.

SUMMARY. In summation, the AUDIT appears to be an easily administered screening tool that provides reliable scores for health care providers to ascertain if an individual is engaging in potentially damaging drinking patterns. The AUDIT's limitations include limited diagnostic utility and problems with the testing manual. It appears to be a useful tool for health care providers to facilitate treatment or interventions for persons already suffering the effects of alcohol misuse or those soon to be suffering the damaging effects of long-term harmful alcohol consumption.

REVIEWER'S REFERENCES

Claussen, B., & Aasland, O. G. (1993). The Alcohol Use Disorders Identification Test (AUDIT) in a routine health examination of long-term unemployed. *Addiction, 88*(3), 363–368.

Saunders, J. B., Aasland, O. G., Babor, T. F., de la Fuente, J. R., & Grant, M. (1993). Development of the Alcohol Use Disorders Identification Test (AUDIT): WHO collaborative project on early detection of persons with harmful alcohol consumption—II. *Addiction, 88*, 791–804.

Bohn, M. J., Babor, T. F., & Kranzler, H. R. (1995). The Alcohol Use Disorders Identification Test (AUDIT): Validation of a screening instrument for use in medical settings. *Journal of Studies on Alcohol, 56*(4), 423–432.

Cherpitel, C. J., & Clark, W. B. (1995). Ethnic differences in performance of screening instruments for identifying harmful drinking and alcohol dependence in the emergency room. *Alcoholism Clinical and Experimental Research, 19*(3), 628–634.

Luckie, L. F., White, R. E., Miller, W. R., & Icenogle, M. V. (1995). Prevalence of estimates of alcohol problems in a Veterans Administration outpatient population: AUDIT vs. MAST. *Journal of Clinical Psychology, 51*(3), 422–425.

MacKenzie, D. M., Langa, A., & Brown, T. M. (1996). Identifying hazardous or harmful alcohol use in medical admissions: A comparison of AUDIT, CAGE, and Brief MAST. *Alcohol and Alcoholism, 31*(6), 591–599.

[16]
Analyzing the Communication Environment.

Purpose: "An inventory of ways to encourage communication in functional activities."
Population: Preschool to adolescent children with severe disabilities.
Publication Date: 1993.
Acronym: ACE.
Scores: Total score only.
Administration: Individual.
Price Data, 1999: $99 per complete kit including 90-minutes VHS videotape and softbound instructor's guide (85 pages); $79 per videotape; $26.50 per manual.
Time: Administration time not reported.
Authors: Charity Rowland and Philip Schweigert.
Publisher: Communication Skill Builders—A Division of The Psychological Corporation.

Review of Analyzing the Communication Environment by PAT MIRENDA, Associate Professor, University of British Columbia, Vancouver, British Columbia, Canada:

It is important to note from the outset that this is not a measurement tool that is used to measure peoples' abilities, skills, or understandings. Rather, Analyzing the Communication Environment (ACE) is an inventory designed to analyze the communication value of specific classroom environments and activities in which children with severe communication impairments participate. Such impairments may include dual sensory impairments, mental retardation, and autism, among others. The inventory is intended for use by teachers and speech-language pathologists who support such children across the age range, especially in school settings. The complete ACE kit consists of an administration manual, the inventory, and a videotape illustrating each of the inventory items with children from the target population.

The ACE is completed through observations of a specific child in environments of concern (e.g., classrooms) over several days. The authors suggest that the ACE be used to assess many activities in which the child participates across the day. For each activity, the assessor observes the child on at least two occasions and evaluates the extent to which the child's communication is supported and encouraged along six dimensions: (a) the activity itself, (b) the students' communication system, (c) the adult interaction that occurs, (d) the group dynamics, (e) the materials used, and (f) the specific opportunities provided for communication. Responses are recorded on an inventory form that can be used subsequently to plan interventions that will increase the communication value of the activity. In the end, the ACE results in a profile depicting the strengths and weaknesses of the communication environment, rather than of the child.

The inventory is uniquely designed to address the primary concerns articulated by researchers and professionals who support individuals with severe communication impairments in schools: a potential lack of adequate and meaningful communication opportunities. Without such opportunities, children with little or no speech are likely to have difficulty learning to use one or more augmentative or alternative modes of communication (Beukelman & Mirenda, 1998). The ACE is the only published resource that focuses specifically on assessment of communication opportunities as one component of a holistic communication intervention.

Although the inventory is not complicated to use, it is deceptively sophisticated with regard to the individual items it comprises. Rather than attempting to provide detailed written explanations for each item, the authors have (wisely) chosen to illustrate each on videotape. Although this no doubt increases the assessor's accuracy when rating, it also demands that assessors take the time to watch the videotape (which is 91 minutes long) prior to using the ACE for the first time. Although some assessors may not need this level of orientation, many do; however, the time required may discourage use of the tape, even when such training is needed. It is important to emphasize that the videotape is considered to be an integral part of the assessment system, and should be viewed by all assessors prior to using the inventory for the first time.

The ACE was constructed on the basis of the authors' lengthy and well-respected research records in this area, and after consultation with teachers, students, and speech-language pathologists involved with the target population. Unfortunately, little information is provided in the manual with regard to the specific consultative and other processes that were used to determine the exact items used to evaluate each dimension on the inventory. However, the authors have published psychometric data about the ACE in other sources. For example, Rowland and Schweigert (1993) had three independent raters score 23 videotapes of target activities that were approximately 15 minutes in length. Across all items, the mean interobserver agreement was 92%. Specifically, the interobserver agreement for the six dimensions of the ACE were as follows: activity: 94%; students' communication system: 91%; adult interaction: 91%; group dynamics: 90%; materials: 92%; and specific opportunities for communication: 95%.

Validity of the ACE was assessed by comparing it with the rate of communicative behavior of participants, to examine how well it predicts the amount of communication actually produced by a child while engaged in the observed activity. Rowland and Schweigert (1993) described the procedures used in this regard in some detail across 11 children with dual sensory impairments (ages 3–18). The mean kappa coefficient across participants was .86, indicating a high correlation between ACE ratings and child communicative acts.

SUMMARY. The ACE is a potentially useful instrument for identifying the strengths and weaknesses of communication environments such as classrooms. It also contains specific suggestions for remediating deficiencies identified by each item on the inventory, all of which are based on the empirical literature in the areas of speech-language pathology, education, and augmentative/alternative communication. Indeed, this is perhaps the primary strength of the ACE: It not only encourages objective evaluation of communication opportunities, but also provides support to the assessor to make positive changes in this regard.

REVIEWER'S REFERENCES

Rowland, C., & Schweigert, P. (1993). Analyzing the communication environment to increase functional communication. *Journal of the Association for Persons with Severe Handicaps, 18,* 161–176.

Beukelman, D. R., & Mirenda, P. (1998). *Augmentative and alternative communication: Management of severe communication disorders in children and adults* (2nd ed.). Baltimore: Paul H. Brookes.

Review of Analyzing the Communication Environment by SHEILA PRATT, Assistant Professor of Communication Science & Disorders, University of Pittsburgh, Pittsburgh, PA:

Analyzing the Communication Environment (ACE) consists of an observational checklist of 52 statements and was developed to evaluate the extent to which educational or training environments inhibit or facilitate communication in students with severe disabilities associated with limited communication skills. The inventory is divided into six categories: the activity, the student's communication system, adult interactions, group dynamics, materials, and opportunities for communication.

The ACE manual provides a general rationale for the inventory, specific rationale for each statement, a brief description of administration procedures, and suggestions for effecting change relative to each statement. The authors also suggest that the inventory can be used to document when efforts to modify communicative environments are implemented and to record when desired behavioral changes are achieved. As such, the construct validity of the inventory is rooted in the therapeutic framework endorsed by the authors. The basic assumption underlying the ACE is that the social and physical characteristics of the environment limit the communication effectiveness of students who are severely disabled and nonverbal, and that these characteristics, and not necessarily the child, should be the focus of change.

The procedure for administering the inventory is described briefly in the main text of the manual although an accompanying training tape and attached viewer's guide elucidate the process more fully. However, the instructions for using the training materials are vague as is the criterion for an acceptable level of training. The administration procedures consist of an observer viewing a student and teacher or speech-language pathologist (SLP) while performing a target activity. The type of activity is not specified although in some cases it can involve a group of students. The task of the observer is to proceed through the inventory and determine whether certain behaviors and conditions are present. The activity can be viewed online or from videotape and the observer can be the teacher/SL or an independent observer. It should be noted, however, that the validation and reliability studies conducted on the inventory were performed only from videotape and the independence of the observers was not specified (Rowland & Schweigert, 1993). When assessing the activity it should be viewed from start to finish in order to include the transitions in and out of the activity. The observation also should occur on at least two different occasions to determine consistency of the environment and behaviors. Once the inventory is completed the observer determines which categories or sections of the inventory have a restricted number of statements checked. The teacher/SLP then can focus on the items in these sections for change. The proportion of relevant statements checked also can be calculated but there is no means to compare the results to any population sample or severity level, so the resulting proportions have limited additional application.

Although the rationale for the inventory, as well as supporting references can be found in the ACE manual, a complete description of the development of the inventory and the psychometric properties of the inventory is lacking. This leaves the impression that the inventory is largely an informal assessment tool.

A more comprehensive justification and description of the inventory, along with its development and psychometric characteristics can be found in Rowland and Schweigert (1993). The inventory was an outgrowth of an intervention program that was an attempt to increase the spontaneity and frequency of communication of a group of 11 children with dual sensory impairments by modifying the communicative environment. The children were developmentally delayed, nonverbal, and ranged in age from 3 to 18 years. The teachers and SLPs working with the children initially developed the inventory categories and items. The inventory was assessed first by the teachers and clinicians and then by independent observers and outside experts. Multiple revisions were made to improve the interobserver reliability, validity, and sensitivity of the instrument. The inventory was then field-tested on a second group of 11 students (ages 3–12 years) who had a range of multiple impairments associated with severe developmental delay and limited communicative function. The size of both groups of children was small and the groups differed in type of impairment, but given the severity of their communication disabilities, the inventory likely is appropriate for the intended population.

During the field-testing, the activities of the second group of students were videotaped bimonthly over the course of a year. A sample of 23 sessions was quasi-randomly selected and evaluated with the ACE by three trained observers. The scope of the training of the observers and their independence from the activities, children, and the test development were not clear. One observer evaluated the entire sessions, whereas a second observer assessed the first half of the sessions and the other observer assessed the second half of the sessions. All of the children were represented in at least two sessions: one early and one later recording. The overall average interobserver agreement was 92% with percent agreement ranging from 71% to 100% for individual items and from 90% to 95% across categories. Agreement also was consistent across sessions, averaging 94%. The interobserver agreement was high for this type of inventory but the limited number of observers calls to question whether similar levels would be maintained for a larger number of independent observers. Intraobserver agreement also was assessed to determine the stability of the observers' judgments over time. It too was high with the average agreement ranging from 92% to 94% for the three observers.

As indicated above, the goal of the inventory is to assess communication environment in an effort to determine whether certain conditions inhibit effective communication behaviors. Therefore, one measure of predictive validity provided by Rowland and Schweigert (1993) was to compare the results of the inventory to the rate of intentional communication behaviors produced by the children. The argument for making this comparison was that environments conducive to communication should result in more communication behaviors by students. Kappa coefficients were calculated for each child per each session and resulted in a favorable mean coefficient of .86. Additional measures of predictive validity, such as relating modifications of activities and corresponding changes in communication behaviors to changes on the ACE were not presented.

Factors not addressed in either the Rowland and Schweigert (1993) publication or the ACE manual were whether the items on the inventory capture the spectrum of activities commonly associated with and important to this population, and the extent to which the inventory is biased by the instructional framework endorsed by the authors. Moreover, the authors provide no documentation on whether the use of the ACE is effective as a framework for teachers and SLPs from which to effect change in the classroom. Although the statements in the inventory appear to be logical, measures of their relative sensitivity and applicability were not described.

SUMMARY. The ACE is an observational checklist that was developed to assess the physical and social environment of a specific group of children for whom few assessment tools are available: children with severe delays and limited oral skills. It is an unusual assessment tool in that it focuses on the communication environment and not exclusively on the communication skills of the child. Based on somewhat restricted documentation, the ACE appears to be appropriate for its intended population and likely valid for its intended purpose. There also is evidence that the inventory can be used reliably. What is not well documented is its potential impact on intervention and improvements in the communication behaviors of the target population.

REVIEWER'S REFERENCE

Rowland, C., & Schweigert, P. (1993). Analyzing the communication environment to increase functional communication. *Journal of the Association for Persons with Severe Handicaps, 18,* 161–176.

[17]
The Apraxia Profile: A Descriptive Assessment Tool for Children.

Purpose: Designed to identify and describe the apraxic component present in a child with speech intelligibility deficits.
Population: Ages 3–13.
Publication Date: 1997.
Scores: 11 ratings: Oral Motor Exam (Automatic Oral Movements, Volitional Oral Movements-Nonverbal, Volitional Oral Movements-Verbal); Diadochokinesis; Words; Phrases and Sentences; Connected Speech Sample; Observations; Apraxic Characteristics Checklist; Listener Response; Communicative Impact.
Administration: Individual.
Forms, 2: Preschool Profile, School-Age Profile.
Price Data: Not available.
Time: Administration time not reported.
Author: Lori A. Hickman.
Publisher: Communication Skill Builders—A Division of The Psychological Corporation.
[Editor's Note: The publisher advised in February 2001 that this test is now out of print.]

Review of The Apraxia Profile: A Descriptive Assessment Tool for Children by THOMAS W. GUYETTE, Associate Professor, Marquette University, Milwaukee, WI:

The purpose of The Apraxia Profile is "to help you identify and describe the apraxic characteristics present in a child with speech intelligibility deficits" (manual, p. 2). The test targets "children 3 to 13 years of age who have normal hearing but compromised intelligibility and/or reduced verbal output" (manual, p. 3). It is reported that the test can be administered and the data interpreted in 40 to 55 minutes. There are two test forms; one for preschool-age children and one for school-age children.

The Apraxia Profile is composed of five sections. In the first section, entitled "Oral Motor Exam," the examiner evaluates the child's automatic oral movements, volitional oral movements (both verbal and nonverbal), and diadochokinetic rates. Each of these subsections is scored by summing up the number of successful attempts at the task. In Section 2, "Words," the child is asked to repeat single words while the examiner scores each word for articulation errors. Section 3, "Phrases and Sentences," involves having the child repeat rhymes one sentence at a time, count from 1 to 10, and repeat short sentences. In this section the examiner is instructed to vary the rate, pitch, intonation, and volume and the child is instructed to say the sentences "just like I say them." The subsection on prosody is the only subsection in Section 3 that is scored. In Section 4, "Connected Speech Sample," the examiner records 25 utterances and analyzes these for mean length of utterance and intelligibility. In Section 5, "Apraxia Characteristics Checklist," the examiner (using information obtained during the previous testing) is instructed to check each of a list of 50 apraxia characteristics that apply to the child being evaluated. After administering the five sections, the data are transferred to a summary page.

The Apraxia Profile does not meet a number of important psychometric standards. For example, the manual does not have a literature review. The section entitled "Overview" is brief. There is no discussion of a theory of apraxia and the author does not organize the "profile" around a theoretical model. There is no information on how the test was developed and/or how the test items were selected.

The author did not collect normative data for any of the subtests in the profile. Some data are included to help interpret the diadochokinetic rates subtest; however, these data were collected previously and published by other authors. For the four other subtests, there are no normative data to help the user interpret the test scores. This lack of data makes it difficult to interpret an individual's scores on these items. It seems incongruous to calculate scores for each of the subtests but have no idea how to interpret a particular subtest score. The speech pathologist would want to know how a child with a functional articulation disorder would score on theses subtests as compared with how a child with a diagnosis of apraxia of speech would score. Without this information, a speech pathologist would be unable to interpret these test results.

No reliability information is provided. This is problematic because many of the judgments the examiner is asked to make lack the rigorous criteria needed to obtain reliable judgments. For example, it would likely be difficult to obtain reliable judgments of whether the patient maintains the necessary velum strength during repeated "ah ah ah." Reliability problems are also likely with the prosody judgments (i.e., judging whether the child repeats a sentence with the same rate, pitch, intonation, and volume as the examiner). Aside from the issue of judgment reliability, it would also be important to know if the test has adequate test-retest reliability.

There is no empirical information on the validity of The Apraxia Profile. This would be a serious problem for any testing instrument but the problem is magnified when you consider that developmental apraxia of speech is a controversial diagnosis to begin with. Aside from the lack of empirical data, there is no clear attempt to establish the content validity of the test. For example, the Apraxia Characteristics Checklist is an important part of the Profile. The author states that "researchers and clinicians have indicated [that the characteristics on the checklist] are associated with DVA" (manual, p. 29). She also states that "The first ten items on the checklist are those characteristics considered to be most indicative of DVA" (manual, p. 29). However, these statements are not supported through citation of any research that supports the author's claim.

SUMMARY. This profile lacks basic psychometric information. For example, there are no normative data (excepting the previously published diadochokinetic rate data) that would allow the test user to determine how his or her patient's

score differs from either a normal or impaired population. There are no reliability data, which is especially important because many of the test items involve difficult judgments. There are no validity data, which also is problematic because of the controversial nature of this diagnosis. Overall, I would not recommend this test.

Review of The Apraxia Profile: A Descriptive Assessment Tool for Children by AIMÉE LANGLOIS, Professor, Department of Child Development, Humboldt State University, Arcata, CA:

SYNOPSIS. The Apraxia Profile: A Descriptive Assessment Tool for Children is purported to help speech-language pathologists make a differential diagnosis of developmental apraxia of speech in 3- to 13-year-old children. In addition, it is intended to help clinicians plan intervention, document change(s) over time, and explain error patterns in children's apraxic speech to their teachers and parents. Each Profile assesses a child's ability to control movements of the oral structures during four tasks: an oral motor exam, repetition of words, repetition of phrases and sentences, and connected speech. These comprise the first four sections of the Profile. In a fifth section the examiner completes an "Apraxia Characteristics Checklist" on the basis of the child's tested performance and information from other sources such as an interview with parents. The last section is a "Summary Page" where the examiner enters scores, notes his/her observations, provides conclusions, and identifies intervention priorities.

Instructions are given for administering and scoring a child's performance on each task in the first four sections of the Profile as well as for completing the Apraxia Characteristics Checklist and the summary page. The profile takes about half an hour to administer and 15 to 20 minutes to interpret. The instructions are summarized on the Profile and detailed in the manual that accompanies it. The manual also has a chapter titled "Interpretation," which parallels the Profile and includes guidelines for interpreting each section. Four appendices, including case studies, and a reference list complete the manual.

CRITIQUE. The author provides an excellent rationale for the design of the Apraxia Profile; the population for which it is intended is identified and its purposes clearly delineated. However, this test has many omissions that preclude its use for establishing a differential diagnosis and planning treatment. These omissions are discussed below on the basis of criteria delineated by Rudner (1994), Swisher (1988), and McCauley and Swisher (1984).

DEFINITION OF THE STANDARDIZATION SAMPLE. The manual provides no evidence that the Profile was standardized on children with developmental verbal apraxia (DVA), the population for which it is intended. However, the author specifies that the children who are tested with the instrument be between 3 and 13 years of age, have normal hearing, and show "compromised intelligibility and/or reduced verbal output" (manual, p. 3); these terms are not defined operationally nor are they used to describe a standardization sample. Except for a child's diadochokinesis scores, which are compared to norms established in separate 1972 and 1987 studies, it appears that criteria for performance and diagnosis are derived from the author's 13 years of practice as a speech-language pathologist. Without a normative sample it is impossible to determine whether and how a particular child compares to other children with and without DVA; furthermore, the establishment of a differential diagnosis becomes suspect.

RELIABILITY. The manual does not provide evidence that reliability testing was conducted to determine either the stability of test scores over time or that obtained by different examiners. Given its stated purpose that the Profile allows clinicians to document baseline measures and changes in these over time, the absence of test-retest reliability seriously weakens such documentation. Therefore, it is not possible to determine with any certainty if changes in Profile scores for a child diagnosed with DVA are due to growth, regression, or results of intervention (typical factors related to change), or to sources of measurement error such as fatigue, nervousness, and guessing.

The lack of test-retest reliability evidence is compounded by the absence of information on interrater reliability. The instructions for administration and scoring of the Profile require subjective judgments (e.g., "vary the rate [slow, normal, fast] as you present each sentence," "are the child's responses to the single-syllable slower than normal?") and are thus open to interpretation and systematic error. In this case, the absence of interrater reliability has two major problems. First,

the degree to which a child with DVA would receive similar scores, diagnosis, and priorities for treatment from different clinicians is not known; this is a situation children and their parents cannot well afford. Second, it is impossible to determine to what extent clinicians rate the children they test in ways that lower or increase their scores, thus bringing into question the validity of the resultant diagnosis.

VALIDITY. The author selected items and activities for testing DVA on the basis of a review of the literature in the field. However, there is no evidence that quantitative methods were used to study and control item difficulty and validity. Given that the Profile is to be used with children from 3 to 13 years of age, attention to item difficulty is especially needed. Furthermore, because the profile is designed to help clinicians make a differential diagnosis, plan intervention, and document changes, the absence of predictive validity seriously weakens the outcome(s) and recommendation(s) made on the basis of Profile scores. Finally, the delineation of a child's articulation errors on the basis of phoneme position in words has dubious construct validity because this overlooks the effects of co-articulation.

TEST ADMINISTRATION. The administration process is described in some detail in terms of needed materials and what to do with or say to a child; however, most instructions are so subjective that examiners are likely to be unsure of or carry out and interpret the procedures in various ways. For example, on all tasks for which children are required either to imitate the examiner or repeat what he or she has said, it is not stated whether a second or third presentation of the same item is possible or prohibited, thus leaving the choice to the clinician. When it comes to scoring, most items also leave too much room for interpretation; terms such as "excess" saliva, "adequate" tongue movement, and responses "slower than normal" that are seen throughout the Profile are not defined operationally and thus leave the clinician to decide what is excessive, adequate, or normal. This problem is compounded by the absence of evidence of interrater reliability.

QUALIFICATIONS OF TEST ADMINISTRATOR. It appears that the Apraxia Profile is designed for use by speech-language pathologists; however, the qualifications of these professionals are not specified either in terms of years or types of experience with children. Without this information and in the absence of interrater reliability estimates, the value of test results obtained for any child is dubious.

SUMMARY. The Apraxia Profile could be used as a guide but not as a test in the assessment of children suspected of presenting DVA. The absence of norms, the lack of reliability and validity data, and the subjectivity of its administration and scoring procedures seriously undermine the Profile's usefulness as a means of establishing a differential diagnosis and documenting patient change. However, the organization of the score sheet provides a framework for gathering and presenting data that are routinely obtained during oral motor examinations. As such, and on the basis of its numerous omissions, the Profile could and should only be used as a guideline for assessment and as part of a complete test battery to determine the diagnosis of DVA. The Profile's secondary title as "a descriptive assessment tool" supports this conclusion.

REVIEWER'S REFERENCES

McCauley, R. J. & Swisher, L. (1984). Psychometric review of language and articulation tests for preschool children. *Journal of Speech and Hearing Disorders*, *49*(1), 34–42.

Swisher, L. (1988, Spring). Measurement as a dangerous activity. *HEARSAY*, 6–9.

Rudner, L. M. (1994, April). *Questions to ask when evaluating tests.* ERIC/AE Digest. (Report No. TM024537). Washington, DC: ERIC Clearinghouse on Measurements and Evaluation. (ERIC Document and Reproduction Services No. ED385607)

[18]
Aprenda®: La prueba de logros en español—Segunda edición.

Purpose: Designed to measure the academic achievement of Spanish-speaking students.
Publication Dates: 1990–1998.
Acronym: Aprenda 2.
Administration: Group.
Price Data, 1999: $28.25 per multiple-choice assessment kit (Preprimer–Advanced) including test booklet and directions for administering ('97, 68 pages), practice test and directions, answer document, and reviewer's edition; $14.50 per 25 practice tests and directions (Preprimer–Intermediate 3); $4.25 per single copy directions for administering practice tests (Preprimer–Intermediate 3); $11.25 per directions for administering (Preprimer–Advanced); $84 per 25 reusable test booklets (Intermediate 1–Advanced); $35.25 each per overlay keys for scoring machine-scorable answer documents (Intermediate 1–Advanced); $23.50 each per response keys (Preprimer-Advanced); $102.75 per 25 machine-scorable test booklets (Preprimer-Primary 3); $65.25 per 100 type 1 machine-scorable an-

swer documents (Intermediate 1–Advanced); $5.25 per package of 25 markers/rulers (Preprimer–Advanced); $53 per technical manual ('98, 331 pages); $58.75 per spring or fall multilevel norms book (all levels); $17.75 per 25 preview for parents (Preprimer–Advanced, in Spanish); $17.75 per 25 understanding test results (Preprimer–Advanced); $18.75 per compendium of instructional objectives (all levels); $27.75 per guide for classroom planning (all levels); $9.75 per open-ended assessment kit per level across Reading, Mathematics, and Writing (Primary 1–Advanced) including one open-ended directions for administering ('97, 68 pages), and reviewer's edition; $23 per 25 open-ended test booklets for Reading, Mathematics, and Writing (Primary 1–Advanced); $26.75 per single copy scoring guides for open-ended assessments for Reading, Mathematics (Primary 1–Advanced); $7.25 per single copy open-ended directions for administering Reading, Mathematics, Writing (Primary 1–Advanced); $19.25 per single copy manual for Interpreting Writing (Primary 1–Advanced); Information on optional score/reporting services, package services and electronic services can be obtained by contacting the publisher.
Foreign Language Edition: Test booklets written in Spanish; content mirrors Stanford Achievement Test Series (Stanford 9; T5:2484).
Authors: Harcourt Brace Educational Measurement.
Publishers: Harcourt Brace Educational Measurement.

a) PREPRIMER (PREPRIMARIO).
Population: Grades K.5–1.5.
Scores, 6: Sounds and Letters, Word Reading, Sentence Reading, Total Reading, Mathematics, Listening to Words and Stories.
Time: (140) minutes.
b) PRIMARY 1 (PRIMARIO 1).
Population: Grades 1.5–2.5
Scores, 11: 8 multiple-choice scores (Word Reading, Reading Comprehension, Total Reading, Mathematics: Problem Solving, Mathematics: Procedures, Total Mathematics, Language, Listening), and 3 open-ended scores (Reading, Mathematics, Writing).
Time: (265) minutes.
c) PRIMARY 2 (PRIMARIO 2).
Population: Grades 2.5–3.5.
Scores, 11: 8 multiple-choice scores (Reading Vocabulary, Reading Comprehension, Total Reading, Mathematics: Problem Solving, Mathematics: Procedures, Total Mathematics, Language, Listening), and 3 open-ended scores (Reading, Mathematics, Writing).
Time: (260) minutes.
d) PRIMARY 3 (PRIMARIO 3).
Population: Grades 3.5–4.5.

Scores, 11: 8 multiple-choice scores (Reading Vocabulary, Reading Comprehension, Total Reading, Mathematics: Problem Solving, Mathematics: Procedures, Total Mathematics, Language, Listening), and 3 open-ended scores (Reading, Mathematics, Writing).

Time: (280) minutes.

e) INTERMEDIATE 1 (INTERMEDIO 1).

Population: Grades 4.5–5.5.

Scores, 12: 9 multiple-choice scores (Reading Vocabulary, Reading Comprehension, Total Reading, Mathematics: Problem Solving, Mathematics: Procedures, Total Mathematics, Language, Listening, English), and 3 open-ended scores (Reading, Mathematics, Writing).

Time: (320) minutes.

f) INTERMEDIATE 2 (INTERMEDIO 2).

Population: Grades 5.5–6.5.

Scores, 12: 9 multiple-choice scores (Reading Vocabulary, Reading Comprehension, Total Reading, Mathematics: Problem Solving, Mathematics: Procedures, Total Mathematics, Language, Listening, English), and 3 open-ended scores (Reading, Mathematics, Writing).

Time: (330) minutes.

g) INTERMEDIATE 3 (INTERMEDIO 3).

Population: Grades 6.5–8.9.

Scores, 12: 9 multiple-choice scores (Reading Vocabulary, Reading Comprehension, Total Reading, Mathematics: Problem Solving, Mathematics: Procedures, Total Mathematics, Language, Listening, English), and 3 open-ended scores (Reading, Mathematics, Writing).

Time: (330) minutes.

h) ADVANCED (AVANZADO).

Population: Grades 9.0–12.9.

Scores, 9: 6 multiple-choice scores (Reading Vocabulary, Reading Comprehension, Total Reading, Mathematics, Language, English), and 3 open-ended scores (Reading, Mathematics, Writing).

Time: (265) minutes.

Cross References: For reviews by Maria Medina-Diaz and Salvador Hector Ochoa of an earlier edition, see 13:12.

Review of Aprenda®: La prueba de logros en español—Segunda edición by JOSEPH O. PREWITT DIAZ, School Psychologist, Chester, PA:

Aprenda®: La prueba de logros en español—Segunda edición (Aprenda 2) is designed to measure the achievement of bilingual students (Spanish/English) in reading, language arts, and mathematics. The Aprenda 2 was designed to reflect the Stanford Achievement Test Series (Ninth edition; T5:2484). The test consists of eight levels: a Preprimer level, three Primary levels covering from Grade 1 to Grade 4, three Intermediate levels covering Grades 4 through 8, and an Advanced level covering Grades 9–12. Test items are multiple-choice and provide 3-, 4-, or 5-response options. The test can also be administered in an open-ended form. Answers are recorded in the test booklets using machine-scorable bubbles.

Reading comprehension and grammar are emphasized in the reading subtests; computation and practical applications are emphasized in the mathematics sections. Test instructions are available in English and Spanish. Test administrators should be fluent Spanish speakers. Designations of "below average," "average," and "above average" are presented next to each skill so that strong and weak areas are immediately apparent (technical manual, p. 32). Criterion-referenced scores are available in four levels: "superior performance," "solid academic performance," "partial mastery," and "less than partial mastery." Group reports are also available.

The second edition was an attempt to provide a test that aligned more to current curriculum trends (technical manual, p. 8). The rationale was that Aprenda 2 would determine how Spanish-speaking children in bilingual education programs have acquired concepts and skills necessary in the educational environment. This edition updates the normative information in order to make comparisons more valid, and updates the information available about testing. Finally, the publisher revised the look of the test to make it more relevant to Spanish-speaking students.

The development of the test took into consideration the content of current editions of major textbooks written in Spanish. The authors claim that they have also considered the most recent state and district school curricula and educational objectives in bilingual and ESL programs. The authors reviewed four commercially made curriculum series in reading and language arts, four in mathematics, and three English-as-a-Second Language curriculums. They also list a curriculum unit for first through sixth grades produced by the Secretary of Public Education in Mexico, and a mathematics curriculum prepared by the Secretary of Education of Puerto Rico. The local curriculum units include three curriculum series prepared by the Texas Education Agency and three curriculum series prepared by the Secretary of Education of Mexico.

Items were sent to Spanish-speaking curriculum specialists in each content area for external review. Items were developed and reviewed for content, style, and appropriateness for measuring the stated objective, as well as for ethnic, socioeconomic, cultural, regional, and gender bias (technical manual, p. 10). Four sets of specialists participated in the development of the test: Spanish-speaking content experts, Spanish editors, measurement specialists, and bilingual and ESL teachers.

The tryout of items was performed throughout the United States, Mexico, and Puerto Rico (technical manual, p. 14). In the United States, Spanish bilingual programs from 23 states participated in the national item tryout program. The majority of these bilingual programs were in the southwest. To determine the linguistic applicability of the items, several experts on the language and culture of Puerto Rico, Cuba, Dominican Republic, Central and South America, and Mexico examined the items for linguistic applicability.

The Mantel-Haenszel procedures were used to analyze and to compare between male and female to identify potentially problematic items. The authors should have considered level of lingualism of children, language used in the classroom, time of language use, and type of program.

A National Research Program took place during the fall and spring of 1996. The technical manual reports that a total of 21,000 students from 160 schools participated in the spring standardization. In the fall standardization approximately 25,000 students participated.

The Kuder-Richardson procedures were utilized to estimate internal consistency reliability of the items in the test. The reliability coefficients for all grades for subtests in the national school population (spring standardization) ranged from .80 to .95. The reliability coefficients for all grades in the Spanish-speaking population (spring standardization) ranged from .71 to .93. The coefficient for the national school population ranged from .80 to .97. The coefficient for the Spanish-speaking population ranged from .74 to .97. The interrater reliability estimates for the writing assessment program for the national school population ranged from .79 to .86. The interrater reliability estimates for the writing assessment program for the Spanish-speaking school population ranged from .73 to .86.

Three sources of validity evidence (content, criterion-related, and construct) were gathered. Content validity analyses attempted to relate test items to the curriculum for which it was based. To support criterion-related validity, correlations between corresponding subtest and totals for Aprenda 2 and Aprenda 1 were sought. These correlations ranged between .54 to .91. Further evidence for construct validity is presented in the form of correlations between corresponding subtests at adjacent levels. These correlations ranged from .36 to .89.

SUMMARY. Constructing a test in the United States that measures the academic achievement of Spanish-speaking students in bilingual education programs is a major challenge. This test mirrors the Stanford Achievement Test, Ninth Edition. The authors went to great lengths to involve experts to address language, curriculum, and programs. Existing commercially developed curriculums in the United States were examined. Aprenda 2 appears to be a psychometrically sound instrument for a district using one of the commercially produced materials used to develop the test, and for bilingual education programs in the state of Texas.

The problem with this test is that the test constructor assumes that bilingual education programs teach a similar content throughout the United States. This test may not apply for children in sheltered English, or in transitional bilingual programs using a curriculum other than the ones used to develop the items for this test. In addition, the authors claim that the items in this test are valid for *all* Central and South America. This is a misrepresentation of the test. The contextual uses of language in those countries and the local and regional meanings are very different. This test would provide inaccurate information in school districts that do not offer instruction in English and Spanish. This test should be used with caution in Puerto Rico and Mexico. The norms for this test were based on Spanish-speaking populations in the United States. There is no evidence that norms for Puerto Rico or Mexico were developed.

The authors make assumptions that statistical manipulation can be made of all the variables present in the population for which the test was developed. Some variables that were not controlled include diverse education strategies and time of instruction in Spanish and English. In the case of Mexico and Puerto Rico, there is no discussion of the characteristics of the population, the educational systems, and the time and language used for instruction and in everyday life interaction.

Review of Aprenda®: La prueba de logros en español—Segunda edición by MARIA PRENDES LINTEL, Psychologist, The Wellness Center, Lincoln, NE, and FRANCISCA ESTEBAN PETERSON, School Psychologist, Lincoln Public Schools, Lincoln, NE:

Aprenda®: La prueba de logros en español—Segunda edición is designed to measure Spanish-speaking students' school achievement in reading, language arts, and mathematics. In addition, it provides information upon which decisions for improving instruction can be made. The Second Edition of the Aprenda battery (Aprenda 2) provides updated content intended to reflect the current national "consensus" curriculum and modern educational trends. This test was developed on the premise that Spanish-speaking students in bilingual programs have acquired the concepts and skills necessary to succeed in the academic environment and can demonstrate their achievement on a test that targets these concepts and skills in their native language. The first Aprenda (Aprenda 1) appeared in 1990 and the authors indicate the new edition was prompted by "(1) the significant changes that had occurred in the school curriculum for Spanish-speaking students; (2) the need for updating the norms and interpretive materials; and (3) the need to provide for the continuous assessment of achievement in the basic skill areas for students from kindergarten through grade 12 whose primary language of instruction is Spanish" (technical manual, p. 8).

Aprenda 2 was designed to be consistent with the content and processes measured by the Stanford Achievement Test Series, Ninth Edition (Stanford 9; T5:2484). Further, the development process, according to the authors, included careful analyses of the most recent editions of the major Spanish textbook series in the basic subject areas, and the most recent state and district school curricula and educational objectives in bilingual and ESL programs.

This review will identify concerns as well as strengths of the Aprenda 2. With regard to strengths, sound procedures and efforts were utilized throughout the test development process. Special efforts were made to select the most appropriate items, particularly in terms of the breadth of specialists who are reported to have reviewed the items. The authors indicate that the items were reviewed by (a) Spanish-speaking content experts who focused primarily on the correctness of item content; (b) Spanish editors who attended to the appropriate wording and grammatical structure of the items; (c) measurement specialists who concentrated on the application of good item-writing techniques; and (d) bilingual and ESL teachers who participated in the local and national try-out programs. Moreover, bilingual and ESL teachers representing school districts from around the country were brought to a one-week standard-setting meeting.

Aprenda 2 is not a translation of the Stanford 9, even though it was designed to be parallel in content. Test questions and passages were developed entirely in Spanish (except Matematicas: Procedimientos). This feature continues to be a strength of the Aprenda batteries, both 1 and 2. Translating items can be problematic because item translation may change the difficulty level of an item. In addition, generating the items in Spanish provides an opportunity for items actually to reflect both the language and the culture of the population for which the instrument was intended. Instructions in Spanish are clear, concise, grammatically correct and, for the most part, with the appropriate register for each grade level.

Although the country of origin of the authors who wrote the open-ended assessment reading stories is not diverse enough, the content of the stories is of high interest and the themes are likely to be within the experience of a high number of students. Pictures also help close some of the gaps.

During the tryout program, items were field-tested through the United States, in Mexico, and in Puerto Rico. School districts in the U.S. were sampled based on the 1990 U.S. Census data indicating schools with bilingual populations. Stratification variables included country of origin and geographic region. A total of approximately 15,000 participated in the tryout program, including Spanish bilingual programs from 23 states. More than 6,000 students from Mexico and Puerto Rico participated in the tryout program. In addition, there were sufficient numbers of students at each grade level for the tryout and standardization programs. Each tryout booklet was administered to nearly 200 students per grade in April and May of 1995.

Regarding the standardization populations that participated in the spring and fall 1996, approximately 21,000 students from 160 school districts participated in the spring standardization and approximately 25,000 participated in the fall standardization with 10,000 students participating in the equating programs (equating of levels and equating to the first edition of Aprenda).

Changes in the field of educational achievement testing are reflected in the use of both multiple-choice and open-ended assessments as well as the inclusion of new types of assessments involving student-generated, handwritten responses that are hand-scored. In addition, attempts to balance cognitive levels of test items are also reported. Users may decide if the battery includes sufficient items emphasizing basic understanding and thinking skills.

Scaled scores, percentile ranks, stanines, normal curve equivalents, grade equivalents, achievement/ability comparisons, content and process cluster performance categories, p-values, performance standards, and performance indicators are clearly reported. Because different types of scores have different properties, the authors have included brief yet strong explanations of the uses and limitations of each score scale both in general and specifically for the Aprenda 2. Likely misinterpretations of scores are also explicitly forwarned.

Another strength of Aprenda 2 is the availability of practice tests. Practice tests for students taking the Preprimer through the Intermediate 3 levels are available.

Good scoring rubrics for reading comprehension and writing assessment are included. The scoring guides include general procedures for scoring as well as pointers, steps in the scoring process, and sample student responses. These features make scoring easier and more standardized. Scoring from the publisher is also available.

TECHNICAL INFORMATION ON TEST SCORES. The technical manual includes extensive technical information for users. Evidence is provided in support of criterion-related validity, construct validity, and content validity. Evidence is particularly strong in terms of content validity.

Furthermore, the authors add an excellent statement and information to help users determine the validity of the Aprenda 2 for their particular setting: "validity can be evaluated through careful examination of the test content, which is presented in the Aprenda 2 *Compendium of Instructional Objectives*. Comparison of the content of Aprenda 2 with the instructional objectives of a school's curriculum will provide evidence of the validity of Aprenda for use in that school" (technical manual, p. 37).

Reliability issues are also addressed. Reliability information is detailed for multiple-choice and open-ended items for the spring and fall Spanish-speaking and the national populations. Interrater reliability coefficients are addressed for the Writing Assessment Program, an important issue pertaining to the accuracy and consistency of the hand scorers. Intercorrelations among Aprenda 2 subtests and Naglieri Nonverbal Ability Tests are also included. Other important information for users such as completion rate and p-values are also presented.

The availability of an ESL portion could be viewed as either a strength or a concern. Users are urged to determine whether the Aprenda 2 is sufficiently aligned with the curriculum used in their ESL program. As with the Spanish version, the issue becomes particularly important if student performance contributes to high stakes decisions.

A number of concerns need to be raised. These concerns are identified below.

Although reflecting the content and processes of the Stanford 9 and using various major Spanish textbook series and materials from United States and Mexico can be considered strengths of this battery, these features can also be considered problematic. In educational achievement testing, the lack of alignment with curriculum may bear on questions of content-related test bias. The technical manual indicates that most of the curricula consulted were from Texas or Mexico. In addition, the Mexican curricula were heavily representative of the elementary school grades (first through sixth grades).

Regarding appropriateness of items, according to the authors, each item was reviewed and edited for content, style, and appropriateness for measuring the stated objective. Ethnic, socioeconomic, cultural, regional, and gender bias were also considered. Review of language similarities and differences for the various Hispanic populations in the United States was given special attention. The items were carefully checked for readability and vocabulary by comparing them with Spanish-language instructional materials at appropriate grade levels. Despite the authors' efforts, some regional differences among Spanish-speaking individuals' word usage are still apparent. Unless specifically taught, the following are examples of terms that can be problematic: "nudo central" to describe the middle development of the story and "reescribir" to indicate "rewrite" (Writing Assessment Program Directions for Administering Primario 1/2, pp. 7–8); "cuatro" as the name of a stringed instrument in the story "Rosario y el Conjunto Puerto Rico" (Reading Open-Ended Scoring Guide, p. 120). Serious bias may result from lack of clarity in test instructions and/or scoring rubrics that tend to credit responses more typical of one group than another.

According to the authors, readability and vocabulary were compared with Spanish language instructional materials at appropriate grade level. However, it is not easy to pinpoint from the manual which specific materials were used and what these reading levels are. It is unlikely that the materials consulted, such as the major Spanish textbook series in the basic subject areas, and the most recent state and district school curricula and educational objectives in bilingual and ESL programs, all have reading levels consistent with each other. This is probably even more unlikely when we take into account that some of these materials are from Mexico. Unless reading levels are clearly stated for content areas, users may not be able to tell whether they are measuring reading skills or actual content knowledge base.

Because test content should be chosen to ensure the intended inferences from test scores are equally valid for members of different groups of test takers, it was disappointing to have the authors report that country of origin and geographic region were the stratification variables for the tryout sample, and then see limited cultural/linguistic backgrounds included in the Advisory Panel membership. Most members of the panel were Mexican (eight), Cuba and the Dominican Republic were represented by two members, Puerto Rico by two, Central America by two more, and all of South America by two members. One panel member represented Spain.

In the same vein, the stories used for the seven levels of the Aprenda 2 open-ended assessment in reading also demonstrate a limited variety of backgrounds. Of the seven readings, two are by authors listed from Argentina, two from Puerto Rico, one from Bolivia, one from Chile, and one from Spain.

Selected statistical procedures were used to identify items that did not fit predetermined psychometric specification with respect to group performance. Prior to the selection of items for the final form of Aprenda 2, all items from the tryout were analyzed according to the Mantel-Haenszel procedures, and comparisons were made between males and females. (Because all students taking Aprenda were of Hispanic origin, there was no need, according to the authors, to make comparisons based on ethnicity.) The authors' lack of need to use differential functioning analysis based on ethnicity is hard to reconcile with their recognition that Spanish-speaking populations are not homogeneous. This issue should be carefully considered by users.

Although the percentage of total U.S. Spanish-speaking school enrollment by geographic region and country of origin does closely match the percentage of students who participated in the standardization program, there are several issues that need clarification. First is the use of the "Bilingual/ESL" label to describe 74.7% to 82.3% of the students listed under Special Services (Programs). It is confusing to see students who most likely have been taught in vastly different ways and have been exposed to vastly different curricula listed together under one label. Second is the lack of allusion to bilingual or more specifically Spanish CALP (Cognitive/Academic Language Proficiency) levels. The Aprenda's premise "is that students in bilingual programs have acquired the concepts and skills necessary to succeed in the academic environment and can demonstrate their achievement on a test that targets these concepts and skills in their native language" (technical manual, p. 8). And the goal is "to provide continuous assessment of achievement in the basic skill areas for students from kindergarten through grade 12 whose primary language of instruction is Spanish" (technical manual, p. 8), yet Spanish proficiency levels of the students are not reported. Although the authors did address some comparability of samples ("All students took the Naglieri

Nonverbal Ability Test, First Edition [NNAT], which ensured comparability of the samples in terms of measured non-verbal ability across all levels of the battery" (technical manual, p. 23), the lack of specific information regarding Spanish CALP levels across all levels of the battery is a serious omission. Because the Aprenda is in Spanish, different levels of Spanish proficiency most certainly would affect student scores. Users should be aware that unless they know the Spanish CALP of their students and that of the students who participated in the standardization sample, they may be measuring Spanish language proficiency instead of achievement in the areas of reading, math, and/or language arts.

Efforts were also made to include Spanish-speaking students with special conditions such as emotionally disturbed, learning disabled, mentally handicapped, hearing impaired, visually impaired, and other. Percentages, however, are small (ranging from .1% to .9%), and more importantly, no information is included regarding adaptation used to assess these students. Information regarding accommodations is a major issue all school districts face. Without this information, districts are left on their own to make such decisions, and interpretation of results may be seriously compromised.

Users are also advised to consider the fact that from Grade K.1 through 6.1 there are six Aprenda 2 levels available. Only one level is available for Grades 6.8 through 8.8 (Intermediate 3) and one more for Grades 8.8 through 13.1 (Advanced) (Table 6, p. 23).

Finally, the length of the test may be an issue to consider, particularly for younger students. For example, in this reviewer's opinion, 40 minutes of writing for students assessed with the Primary 1/2 Writing Assessment Program may be excessive.

SUMMARY. In general, when considering an assessment instrument, users should be informed consumers and should carefully consider the population for which the test is intended, the skills it is intended to measure, and the manner and contexts in which the scores are to be used. No assessment instrument is valid for all purposes and for all individuals. Users are reminded that the Aprenda 2 is primarily designed to measure "Spanish-speaking students' school achievement in reading, language arts, and mathematics, and provides information upon which decisions for improving

instruction can be made" (technical manual, p. 7). Furthermore, because there are several areas of concern (reading levels used for language arts and mathematics, ESL/bilingual program students grouped together, lack of information regarding accommodations for students with disabilities, consulted curricula most representative of Texas and Mexico, limited number of levels available at the higher grades) and serious unanswered questions regarding the Spanish proficiency of the students who were included in the standardization sample, users are cautioned regarding making comparisons with their target population. Valuable information may be gleaned from the Compendium of Instructional Objectives as well as from the open-ended student performance and even from the obtained statistical data, as long as interpretation is consistent with the available evidence provided by the authors. The authors should be commended for their efforts and encouraged to address the concerns in their Aprenda 3.

[19]
Arithmetic Skills Assessment Test.

Purpose: "Designed to quickly determine the approximate mathematical abilities of students with unknown math skills."
Population: High school and adults.
Publication Dates: 1993–1995.
Scores, 3: Whole Numbers, Fractions/Mixed Numbers, Decimals.
Administration: Group.
Price Data, 1993: $89 per computer application including 2 diskettes, 2 back-ups, management, and documentation.
Time: (15) minutes.
Comments: Computerized, self-administered; available in Macintosh Version, Apple II Version, Windows Version, and MS-DOS Version.
Author: Howard Behrns.
Publisher: Educational Activities, Inc.

Review of the Arithmetic Skills Assessment Test by MICHAEL B. BUNCH, Vice President, Measurement Incorporated, Durham, NC:

OVERVIEW. The Arithmetic Skills Assessment Test is designed to provide a quick assessment of the mathematics achievement levels of high school age examinees of unknown mathematical ability. The content covered is limited to the four basic operations (addition, subtraction, multiplication, and division) within three general areas (whole numbers, fractions and mixed numbers, and decimals). The computerized version begins with a difficult item and then bases presentation of further items on the examinee's last response. It is possible to complete the test with as few as 14 responses, assuming all 14 are correct.

DEVELOPMENT. Test items were developed around 119 skills. These 119 skills stem from the application of the four operations within the three domains. The publisher provides no rationale for the selection of these particular skills. They are not correlated to any standard set (e.g., those promulgated by the National Council of Teachers of Mathematics). They do represent a reasonable breakdown of fundamental mathematical skills.

PSYCHOMETRIC PROPERTIES. The publisher provides no evidence of psychometric properties. Although the ordering of items by difficulty suggests that some data analysis has been performed, no item difficulty values are given in the manual.

EASE OF USE. The program that administers and scores the test is quite easy to install and run. Directions are clear and easy to follow. Beyond those two points, there are several drawbacks. First, the program submitted for review is in DOS, although Windows and Macintosh versions exist. The reviewed program was written or last updated in 1991, which is several generations ago in terms of computer program development. Second, the on-screen images are extremely crude, as one might expect from a program of that vintage. Third, although the examinee is able to navigate to a small degree, there is no way to correct an error on screen. For example, when entering the components of a mixed-number response, the examinee first enters the whole number, tabs to the next box, enters the numerator, tabs to the next box, and enters the denominator. If the examinee needs to go back to the whole number or the numerator to correct a mistake or miskeyed entry, there is no way to do so. Fourth, the class management portion of the program has some severe limitations. The floppy disk version has a limit of 100 files. Even when using the hard drive or network version of the program, the user is advised to delete files from time to time "to maintain the speed and ease of use of the program" (Instructions, p. 6).

SUMMARY. Although the items of the Arithmetic Skills Assessment Test do possess face validity as reasonable measures of the 119 skills related to the addition, subtraction, multiplication, and division of whole numbers, fractions, and decimals, the publisher offers no empirical evidence of their utility. The scores, although seemingly meaningful, are not supported by any documentation of their meaningfulness. The computerized version of the test sent for review has the very tired look of a remnant of a bygone era. Teachers or school administrators interested in determining as quickly as possible the mathematical skills of a new student or group of students would be well advised to seek a different product to help them.

Review of the Arithmetic Skills Assessment Test by KEVIN D. CREHAN, Associate Professor of Educational Psychology, University of Nevada, Las Vegas, Las Vegas, NV:

The Arithmetic Skills Assessment Test (ASAT) is a computer-administered individualized exercise designed to provide a quick comprehensive assessment of arithmetic computation achievement. The ASAT is intended to provide quick (30 to 60 minutes) assessment of approximate mathematical strengths and weaknesses especially suited to adult education settings with limited and/or erratic time schedules. The test has three sections, whole numbers, fractions, and decimals. Each of the three sections is divided into four subsections based on the arithmetic operations of addition, subtraction, multiplication, and division. The resulting 12 area tests are further composed of a varying number of skills measured (6 to 14) based on the complexity of the arithmetic operation involved. A resulting total of 119 skill measures are included in the test. It appears that there are two items per skill or 238 items in total. A teacher-accessible management system maintains records of student performances by alphabetical class lists. Each record displays the results for the student on each of the 119 skills tested as passed, failed, missed (incorrect on first attempt and correct on second attempt), or quit (student opted to exit the test). A grade level estimate for each area and an overall grade level estimate are provided. This latter estimate is the same as the lowest grade level attained for any of the 12 area tests. Class lists may be modified or deleted by individual student record or by the entire class. The management system allows storage of data for up to 10 teachers and up to six classes per teacher.

ADMINISTRATION. Following student login, the computer administration begins with the presentation of an item measuring the most difficult skill tested in the first area, which is addition of whole numbers. In this case the skill measured is addition of three addends of three digits with regrouping. The student works the problem with paper and pencil and enters an answer on the keyboard. If correct, the student is then presented the most difficult item in the next area. If correct answers continue, the student would complete the test by correctly responding to an item measuring the most difficult skill in each of the 12 areas and have a record of total mastery for the arithmetic skills measured by the ASAT. If the student's answer is incorrect, the student is presented an item at a lower skill level within the area. If incorrect answers continue through the lowest skill level, the student is advanced to the most difficult item in the next area. Hitting the space bar can skip an item, a response that appears to be treated the same as an incorrect answer by the program. That is, when an item is skipped, the next item is at a lower skill level within the area or the highest skill level on the next area. The student is not given feedback on success or failure when responding to an item. The student may quit the test and begin again at the same point at a later time. Once the test is completed, the student's record must be deleted before retaking the test.

TECHNICAL. No information on item development or selection is presented. However, the items are clearly representative of arithmetic computations for each of the 119 indicated skills. There is no mention of evidence related to reliability or validity.

OBSERVATIONS AND RECOMMENDATIONS. The ASAT offers a convenient option for the individual measurement and recording of the results on the arithmetic skills tested. It does not provide immediate feedback to the student or diagnostic information to the teacher. Computer programs, such as this one, can relatively easily accomplish remedies for both of these omissions. The computer can recognize answers that are representative of common errors and misconceptions in computation and provide both the student and teacher with corrective statements.

The program allows movement through the 12 test areas in only one direction. It might be desirable if the student were allowed to move around among the 12 areas at will. Additionally, the program always begins measurement in each area with an item measuring the most difficult skill, regardless of the student's previous performance. It would also make sense to modify the program to take previous performance into consideration in the determination of the initial skill level tested in each area.

SUMMARY. The ASAT may be useful as a quick computer assessment of arithmetic computation skill. However, the computer program has limited flexibility and does not take full advantage of its potential for usefulness.

[20]
Ashland Interest Assessment.

Purpose: "A career interest inventory for individuals with restricted abilities developed in response to a need for a career measure to accommodate individuals with barriers to employment due to educational, physical, emotional, cognitive, or psychiatric conditions."
Population: Adults and adolescents.
Publication Date: 1997.
Acronym: AIA.
Scores: 12 scales: Arts and Crafts, Sales, Clerical, Protective Service, Food Service, Personal Service, Health Care, General Service, Plant or Animal Care, Construction, Transportation, Mechanical.
Administration: Group.
Price Data, 1999: $52 per examination kit including manual ('97, 94 pages), 10 hand-scorable question and answer booklets, 10 profile sheets, 10 scoring sheets, one set of templates, and one machine-scorable question and answer booklet for an extended report; $26 per test manual; $16–$18 (depending on volume) per 25 hand-scorable question and answer booklets; $16–$19 (depending on volume) per 25 response sheets (including 25 scoring sheets and 25 profile sheets); $21 per set of templates; $54–$59 (depending on volume) per 10 machine-scorable question and answer documents for extended reports; $99 per software package including disks, software manual for Windows, test manual, and 10 coupons for computer report.
Time: (35) minutes.
Foreign Language Edition: Hand-scorable and machine-scorable question and answer booklets and extended reports available in French.
Comments: Scored by self, publisher, or computer.
Authors: Douglas N. Jackson and Connie W. Marshall.
Publisher: Sigma Assessment Systems, Inc.

Review of the Ashland Interest Assessment by RICHARD J. McCOWAN, Professor Emeritus and

Director, Research and Evaluation, Center for De-velopment of Human Services, State College at Buf-falo, Buffalo, NY, and SHEILA C. McCOWAN, Doctoral Candidate of Counseling Psychology, State University of New York at Buffalo, Buffalo, NY:

The Ashland Interest Assessment (AIA) is a career interest measure for adults with employ-ment limitations due to educational, physical, emotional, cognitive, or psychiatric conditions such as learning disabilities, developmental disabilities, brain injuries, or chronic psychiatric problems. It can be used with high school dropouts, people on public assistance with limited job experience, or adults with limited proficiency in the English language.

TEST CONSTRUCTION. The AIA con-tains 144 forced-choice items consisting of two statements that describe work-related activities. It is a group-administered test with a completion time of 20 to 90 minutes (average 35 minutes) for the designated population. Items are printed in larger type and are written at a third grade reading level. Respondents select which of two activities would be more interesting (e.g., "Wash floors. Show watches to customers.").

The instrument has 12 scales with 24 items representing each scale. The scale names are broad and easy to understand and include Arts and Crafts, Personal Service, Food Service, Clerical, Sales, General Service, Protective Service, Health Care, Mechanical, Construction, Plant or Animal Care, and Transportation. Items describe tasks asso-ciated with entry level jobs such as sales, health care, clerical, security, and general work roles that involve maintenance or personal services.

The AIA differs from general vocational interest assessments such as the Strong Interest Inventory (T5:1790) and the Career Directions Inventory (T5:406) in three major ways. These instruments were developed using norms from a Canadian population with characteristics that lim-ited employment. The inventory is linguistically less demanding and appropriate for people who are interested in immediate employment, rather than post-secondary education.

The authors used advanced item selection methods and scale construction strategies to pre-pare the inventory. They developed constructs using the research literature in vocational interests and experiences. Scales were specified using the Career Directions Inventory and the Jackson Vo-cational Interest Survey, but a new pool of items was prepared to address the content appropriate for the target population.

VALIDITY. Validity evidence was gathered in four phases. During Phase 1, a preliminary version using a single-item format was adminis-tered to a representative population of 115 males and 86 female respondents. This process deter-mined whether respondents "like" the item and if each item was a good representative of its target scale. The item efficiency index (IEI) (Neill & Jackson, 1976) measured how well each item cor-related with its own scale compared with other scales. An item was rejected if it had an extremely high or low endorsement rate, less than a 95% response rate, a low efficiency index, or a higher irrelevant scale correlation relative to the target scale correlation. Mean IEI correlations and irrelevant item correlations were used to assess the effectiveness of each scale. Scale intercorrelations were used to determine if the scales were orthogonal.

During Phase 2, single and forced-choice versions were administered to 86 and 103 indi-viduals, respectively. Item and scale analyses were completed for both versions. The forced-choice format was utilized to reduce response bias and maximize variance by pairing items with similar endorsement popularities.

During Phase 3, 88 individuals completed the assessment including 38 males and 50 females ranging in age from 16 to 50 years. Scale analyses revealed substantial item correlations ranging from .41 to .58. Cronbach alpha reliability evidence for each scale ranged from .79 to .91. The national standardization was completed in Phase 4 based on responses from 1,498 Canadians including 739 males and 759 females. Separate factor analyses were completed for males and females using the Basic Interest scale intercorrelation matrix from the normative sample.

RELIABILITY. Cronbach alpha reliability estimates were calculated for each of the Basic Interest scales on the normative sample across and between groups (combined and separate sex groups). Coefficients ranged from .72 (General Service) to .90 (Construction) for the combined group, from .69 (General Service) to .88 (Con-struction) for the male group, and from .73 (Gen-eral Service) to .87 (Health Care and Construc-tion) for the female group. These coefficients indicate consistency of measurement across scales.

SCORING AND REPORTS. A mail-in scoring service provides computerized basic and extended reports. Sample reports are available from the publisher. Demonstration versions are available on the company's interest site.

The AIA can be easily scored by hand using a plastic template or by computer using software available from the publisher. Users purchase Windows software for a registration fee that includes a test manual, software manual, installation disks, 10 scoring coupons, and unlimited telephone support. The software runs under Windows 3.1, 95, or 98 and requires a minimum configuration of a 486 computer (IBM compatible) with 8 MB memory. The software can only be installed on one computer, but it can be accessed by multiple computers on a network.

The interface has two main windows: a respondent window that lists people who have taken the test and an output window that lists all generated reports. The software is usage controlled. After it is registered, the company provides a password that initializes a protected counter on the hard drive. Attempts to move or adjust the counter render it invalid. The counter tracks the number of coupons purchased. Coupons are required to generate reports. When new reports are generated, the number of coupons used depends on the complexity of the report. When coupons are used up, new reports cannot be generated until more coupons are purchased.

CONCLUSION. The AIA is a well-designed, statistically sound instrument appropriate to use with individuals with backgrounds that limit employment. Norms established with a Canadian population should be comparable for United States clients. The manual is clearly written and provides detailed information describing the procedures used to develop, validate, and norm the test. Strong evidence was presented for construct validity. It is a relevant, easy-to-use tool that provides beneficial information for clients and counselors. It meets a current, socially significant need by providing an instrument appropriate for clients who are difficult to place in jobs.

REVIEWER'S REFERENCE

Neill, J. A., & Jackson, D. N. (1976). Minimum redundancy item analysis. *Educational and Psychological Measurement, 36,* 123–134.

Review of the Ashland Interest Assessment by MARY ROZNOWSKI, Associate Professor of Psychology, Ohio State University, Columbus, OH:

The Ashland Interest Assessment (AIA) is an inventory of career interests, especially designed to be appropriate for persons facing a variety of barriers to regular employment. The "language level, content, and potential career options" (manual, p. 1) of the AIA were chosen to address conditions that restrict a person's ability to make use of other inventories. Restricted abilities refer to any educational, physical, emotional, cognitive, or psychiatric conditions that may impact a person. Limited linguistic demands are made on respondents by the AIA and thus the measure holds a unique niche among interest inventories.

The AIA contains 12 Basic Interest scales with 24 items representing each scale. A forced-choice format is used. The respondent selects Item A or B as the activity he or she is most interested in performing. Examples of AIA Basic Interest scales are: sales, clerical, and protective services.

The measure is useful for educational and career exploration counseling and decision making as well as for conducting research. The AIA can be used for individuals intending to secure vocational placements that do not necessarily require a high school diploma.

Its stated aim is "to provide information that is useful for discovering the types of careers that coincide with a person's vocational interests" (manual, p. 3). It is important to note that the AIA is not intended to predict future job *performance*. Thus, the user is warned to keep in mind the distinction between probable satisfaction with a career versus probable performance levels. The AIA has not been evaluated for personnel selection. It is solely usable for determining the career interests of individuals with handicapping conditions.

Users are advised to look at high and low Basic Interest scale scores. The overall configuration of the profile compared to various occupational groups is also useful for those interested in using the measure. Each AIA scale is a relatively homogeneous set of occupationally relevant activities. High scores indicate interests similar to those in a particular occupational group such as carpenters, and not an interest in carpentry, per se.

Advanced item selection methods and scale construction strategies were employed in the development of the AIA. Summary statistics and percentile equivalents of raw scores, based on fairly large samples, are given in the test manual and are useful.

Carefully elaborated item selection and use objectives along with a flowchart of AIA test construction/item selection are given in the manual. The flowcharts are very well done and indicate that great care went into test construction. Item evaluation was carried out according to several statistical/measurement indices. Response bias and item readability were also evaluated. *P*-values, item-scale correlations, and item efficiency indices were used in selection. Factor analysis of previous vocational interest measures provided the initial Basic Interest scales for the AIA. Extensive and careful examination of initial data collected yielded the scales. Instead of using job titles, items include statements of activities that are common to job incumbents.

A second stage of test construction involved the careful development of a forced-choice test format. Items/stems were paired using an algorithm designed to identify the most "similar items in terms of endorsement popularities (p-values) while constraining the number of times items from the same two scales were paired" (manual, p. 45).

Item correlations were reported as "substantial" but were between .41 and .58. These values are much lower than what would be desirable, however. Sample sizes could also have been larger. Alpha reliability estimates were quite high for the scales, which is a plus.

Finally, a large group of individuals were tested in order to obtain normative data. This was fairly well done and the data are useful.

Principal components analysis was carried out. However, it is unclear why this was done. Validity data are unfortunately largely missing. Factor (principal components) analysis data are included, but those are clearly not sufficient in a validation sense.

SUMMARY. The developers of the Ashland Interest Assessment have done a commendable job with this measure. However, additional work is needed before confidence can be placed in the validity of scores from the assessment inventory.

[21]
ASSESS Expert Assessment System Version 5.X.

Purpose: "Designed to measure characteristics related to good decision making and effective job performance in professional and managerial jobs."

Population: Potential employees and candidates for promotion in professional, managerial, and sales positions.

Publication Date: 1997.

Scores: Updated and shortened versions of the Guilford Zimmerman Temperament Survey (GZTS) and Dynamic Factors Opinion Survey (DFOS) provide normative results on 23 characteristics grouped in 5 dimensions: Thinking Style, Workstyle, Motivational Characteristics, Emotional Style and Interpersonal Style; Intellectual Ability Tests: 7 possible scores: Watson-Glaser Critical Thinking, Raven's Standard Progressive Matrices (Abstract Reasoning), Thurstone Test of Mental Alertness, Arithmetic Reasoning, Employee Aptitude Survey 1 (EAS1)—Verbal Comprehension, EAS2—Numerical Ability, EAS7—Verbal Reasoning; Battery.

Administration: Group or individual.

Price Data, 1998: $995 per one-time purchase of the initial HASP key preloaded with units for 5 administrations, ASSESS software, user's guide (85 pages), technical manual (83 pages), 1 reusable personality survey booklet, 5 personality survey answer sheets, 1 Raven test booklet, 5 Raven answer sheets, 1 Watson-Glaser appraisal booklet, 5 Watson-Glaser answer sheets, 5 Thurstone self-scoring tests, scoring keys, samples of additional ability tests; report costs vary from $42.50 to $125 depending on report type and volume; additional consulting services available to customize the report.

Time: Administration time varies for each test.

Comments: Detailed narrative reports provide profile level interpretation of personality and ability scores in comparison with a professional database; graphic profile results allow for additional comparison to specific subgroups; selection reports include interview and reference probes; developmental reports include specific developmental suggestions; career manager reports provide job search and job fit suggestions; onsite scoring; administration via paper, PC, or internet.

Authors: Bigby/Havis & Associates, Inc.

Publisher: Bigby/Havis & Associates, Inc.

Review of the ASSESS Expert Assessment System Version 5.X by PETER F. MERENDA, Professor Emeritus of Psychology and Statistics, University of Rhode Island, Kingston, RI:

The ASSESS Expert System (Version 5.X) with a copyright and release date of 1997 appears to be the fourth successive form of the instrument dating back to 1970. In the technical manual, reference is made to the 1970, 1986, and the 1996 systems. In introducing the system, the authors, David G. Bigby et al., associates of the publisher, Bigby, Havis & Associates, Inc. (BHA), a management consulting firm, state that the system comprises "a battery of standard ability tests and personality inventories" (technical manual, p. 1). This initial statement appearing on the first page of the technical manual is incorrect and, therefore, misleading. The system is rather a collection of seven ability tests plus an inventory yielding six personality profiles. In order to qualify as a *battery* of tests and inventories they must be a set of assessment instruments "standardized on the same population so that norm-referenced scores on the several tests can be compared or used in combination for decision making" (see Glossary, p. 89, AERA, APA, & NCME, 1985).

In the Introduction section in the technical manual, it goes on to say that "ASSESS is an expert system designed to model the judgments of psychologists in the interpretation of an assessment battery and in the writing of reports based on these judgments" (p. 1). It is claimed that ASSESS is an expert computer program that stimulates judgments of experts based on evaluation and interpretation of the test scores and relates them to personnel decisions regarding hiring, promotion, placement, and development of employees.

There are seven intellectual ability tests included in the first part of ASSESS. These are (a) Watson-Glaser Critical Thinking Appraisal, Form S, 1994; (b) Raven's Standard Progressive Matrices, 1958; (c) Thurstone Test of Mental Alertness, 1952; (d) Arithmetic Reasoning Test, 1983; (e) Employee Aptitude Verbal Comprehension Test, 1984, 1956; and (f) Employee Aptitude Verbal Reasoning Test, 1984–1956. The ASSESS Personality Survey consists of the Guilford-Zimmerman Temperament Survey (GZTS), 1976, and the Dynamic Factors Opinion Survey (DFOS), 1944, redeveloped in shortened form of the AS-SESS Personality Battery. Nowhere in the technical manual does it say that the collection of tests was ever standardized and normed on a new sample representative of the population serviced by the management consulting firm, Bigby, Havis, & Associates, Inc.

However, in Section 5 of the technical manual, some attempts to renorm the ASSESS Personality Survey and the intellectual abilities tests are mentioned. Percentile scores are presented for 16 personality dimensions: Watson-Glaser, Raven's, Thurstone, and EAS-1, 2 & 7, and the Arithmetic Test. It is stated that these percentile equivalents of raw scores are based on

an unspecified and undescribed "professional norm group" (p. 49) of an unknown size. Adherence to Standards 4.1–4.9 (pp. 33–34, AERA, APA, & NCME, 1985) is therefore, woefully lacking. This fact is coupled with the more important fact that the psychometric properties of the ASSESS as a "battery" are alleged to have been demonstrated as sound (see Sections 1, 2, 3, and 10, AERA, APA, & NCME, 1985). It raises doubts regarding the validity and usefulness of the Template Normative Information.

EVIDENCES OF PSYCHOMETRIC PROPERTIES OF ASSESS. In critiquing assessment instruments, test reviewers carefully read the technical manual seeking to establish that documented evidences of sound psychometric properties actually do exist. This was the first procedure followed by this reviewer. The principal properties are those presented as *primary* ones in the test *Standards* (AERA, APA, & NCME, 1985) relating to Validity, Reliability and Errors of Measurement, Test Development and Revision, Scaling, Norming, Score Comparability and Equating, and General Principles of Test Use. From this standpoint, the review initially focused on the publisher's claim that the ASSESS Expert System, Version 5.X was developed as a battery. Unfortunately, no such evidence was disclosed in the technical manual.

In Section 2, Intellectual Ability Tests, the seven separate tests are identified and data are reported in tables attesting to the validity of the individual instruments. No reliability studies are cited. And those validity studies that are cited are the ones that were conducted by the authors and their contemporaries dating from 1963 to 1986. It is noted that neither in the text of the technical manual nor in the Bibliography (Section 6) is a single member of the ASSESS 5.0 Team referenced as an author or co-author of a published research study on the psychometric properties of the ability tests in the ASSESS, individually, or in combination.

In Section 3, The ASSESS Personality Survey, as is true in Section 2, the tabled data are those attributed primarily to the authors of two early personality inventories (GZTS and DFOS) and their contemporaries dating from 1958–1974. However, unlike the individual ability tests, the development of the ASSESS 5.0 Personality Battery by the BHA team is reported. This was accomplished by selecting items from the GZTS and DFOS surveys to "create a shortened and improved personality survey." Separate forms of the revised personality survey were produced, varying from 480 to 350 items. But, the developmental research, especially the required statistical analyses and factor analysis method and procedures employed are not reported (see Merenda, 1997). Internal consistency coefficients for the 16 personality Survey Scales are reported. Two points need to be made regarding this information: (a) It is misleading to label it as a *Reliability* table. Coefficient alphas are compared between the short scales and the original scales; (b) except for three scales with coefficients in the .80s the remaining ones are considered *borderline* (.70s), or unacceptable (.60s and .50s). The Cronbach alpha is a measure of internal consistency (homogeneity of items). However, in the construction or reconstruction of assessment instruments, the developers are expected to follow this phase or analysis by investigating the stability, over time (test-retest), or equivalence of forms (alternate forms). Standard 2.6 (AERA, APA, & NCME, 1985, p. 21) cautions the researcher not to substitute internal analysis for the latter.

In Section 4, Criterion-Related Validation Research, in-house validation research is reported. Eight studies are briefly described and validity data are reported. However, because none of these studies has been published in an appropriate refereed professional journal, it is incumbent upon the authors of the technical manual to provide in the manual the details of the studies (rationale, procedures, methodology, and results) that are required in prepublication manuscripts and articles.

The ASSESS Expert System 5.X is accompanied by another manual, the User's Guide, the contents of which provide the user with information about the assessment system and directions on operating the computer-driven system that produces psychological evaluations. These specific steps produce reports (Screening, Selection, Development, or Career Manager) for use in rendering a variety of personnel decisions in business and industry. The reports are based largely on the scoring, evaluation, and interpretation by a staff psychologist of the tests in the system that have been administered to clients. The software is designed to have the administration of the personality survey done by paper and pencil or by computer—on a PC. The ability tests not only must be administered by paper and pencil format, but also must be hand scored.

For a technical review and critique of educational and psychological assessment instruments, it is only the technical manual that is thoroughly reviewed. This is so because the soundness of the psychometric properties of the instruments included in the assessment system may be evaluated by what is reported or omitted—in that manual. Hence, this review has been made primarily by studying the contents of the technical manual.

SUMMARY. The ASSESS Expert System (Version 5.X) purports to "measure characteristics related to good decision making and effective job performance in professional and managerial jobs" (user's guide, pp. 2–3). How well the system accomplishes this is, in the judgment of this reviewer, highly questionable. The reasons for this conclusion are:

1. The combination of the ability tests and personality survey is promoted as an assessment battery, which it does not appear to be. In reality it appears to be a collection of several tests that cannot legitimately and psychometrically yield meaningful profiles.

2. The required empirical evidences of Validity, Reliability, and Errors of Measurement, and Norming of the collection of tests and inventory have not been reported and documented as a battery in the technical manual and/or in the published professional literature.

3. The proper factor analysis and multivariate analyses of such a complex assessment system have either not been performed or have yet to be reported to and evaluated by the psychology community.

On one hand, the authors and publisher are to be commended for the voluminous normative data they have collected and analyzed over the years, and which underlie the confidential ASSESS Screening Reports to clients. On the other hand, they can be faulted for not conducting—or at least not publishing in the professional literature—classification and predictive validity studies attesting to the usefulness of the reports. In this regard, it is the judgment of this reviewer that the principals and the staff psychologists have failed to fulfill their obligations to the psychology community by not submitting their internal (in-house) developmental research studies and validity studies to refereed journals.

It is possible—or even likely—that some of the criticisms can be counteracted by the authors who may still have information and data that are currently not presented in the authors who may still have information and data that are currently not presented in the content of the technical manual. Hence, it is recommended that the authors and publisher revise the manual to provide the potential user with a greater assurance of the psychometric soundness of the system. It is further recommended and strongly advised that the authors continue their research efforts and publish their results in respected referred journals (e.g., the APA's *Journal of Applied Psychology*). A final word of caution to potential and prospective users of the system: CAVEAT EMPTOR.

REVIEWER'S REFERENCES

American Educational Research Association, American Psychological Association, & National Council on Measurement in Education. (1985). *Standards for educational and psychological testing.* Washington, DC: APA, Inc.

Merenda, P. F. (1997). A guide to the proper use of factor analysis in the conduct and reporting of research: Pitfalls to avoid. *Measurement and Evaluation in Counseling and Development, 30,* 156–164.

Review of the ASSESS Expert Assessment System Version 5.X by STEPHEN OLEJNIK, Professor of Educational Psychology, University of Georgia, Athens, GA:

The user's manual and the technical report for the ASSESS Expert Assessment System Version 5.X are well written and clearly state the purpose, usage, and limitations of the system of tests and reports that are available. The system is very flexible with administration using a computer or a paper-and-pencil format possible. A potential limitation with this system is the total amount of time needed to complete the entire test battery. Some tests have no time limit, so the total amount of time needed to complete all measures can only be approximated. Based on the user's manual guidelines, a total of 3 hours of actual test time is needed for the complete battery of tests. The administration of the entire test battery, however, is not necessary. Users may limit the number of ability measures taken but must include the entire personality survey, which by itself requires approximately one hour (a little less if completed by computer).

Four types of reports can be generated that are intended to assist in personnel decision making in the following areas: applicant screening, employee selection, professional development, and career management. Each report includes a graphical summary of the respondent's performance on the measures taken relative to normative samples and a summary of the respondent's strengths and weaknesses. In addition, the latter three reports provide an in-depth analysis as well as suggestions appropriate for the specific purpose of the report. For example, the selection report provides suggestions for interview questions and the development report provides suggestions to the professional on what he or she may try to do to ameliorate his or her weaknesses.

Scores are reported in percentile ranks relative to a population of professionals (managers of projects rather than people) and 24 specific managerial positions. For each attribute a score outside the 25th to 75th percentile range is identified as either an individual strength or weakness. Two problems exist with the current information provided on the normative data. First, no information is provided on how the normative data were obtained. A description (e.g., experience levels, gender, educational levels) of the participants in each normative group and when and how they were recruited would have been useful. Second, for most of the specific managerial positions, the sample sizes are very small. Over 65% of the normative samples for the specific positions had a sample size less than 200 with a median sample size of 141. The generic professional category, however, is based on a sample of 1,204 respondents. Confidence in the interpretation of the scores will vary depending on the size of the normative group. Estimates of intellectual ability are based on the performance on seven tests focusing on verbal, arithmetic, and reasoning skills. Reliability estimates for these measures are not provided. Some data are available to support the validity of the ability measures. Correlations between the seven ASSESS ability measures and alternative ability measures are given for all tests. Some of these correlations, however, are based on samples of high school students rather than an adult population. In addition, correlations between job performance and some measures of ability are reported. These correlations, although statistically significant at the .05 level, are fairly low. Additional information on sample sizes, score variability, and descriptions of the samples on which the estimates were obtained would have been useful.

The personality survey provides scores on 23 attributes grouped into five broad categories. These attributes are derived from 16 scales based on responses to 351 dichotomous items selected and revised form the Guilford-Zimmerman Temperament Survey (GZTS) and Dynamic Factors Opinion Survey (DFOS). Coefficient alpha is provided for each of the 16 scales and ranges between .57 (Self-Reliance) to .85 (Detail Interest) with an average alpha coefficient equaling .72. Reliability estimates for individual attributes, however, are not reported. Some scales are used for more than one attribute. No other estimates of reliability are provided.

Two types of validity data are reported. First, factor analytic and correlational studies on the original GZTS and DFOS are provided. Because the ASSESS Personality Survey is based on a subset of revised items from both instruments, this earlier work provides little support for the current instrument. Additional factor analytic and correlational studies are needed for the new instrument.

Second, three studies are presented, each examining the extent to which a success profile index based on the ASSESS correlates with performance ratings. In all three studies statistically significant correlations are reported. There are two problems with these data. First, the development of the success profile index is vague. A subset of ASSESS scales were selected and used to develop a success index. But the specific scales selected are not identified and a rationale is not provided for the specific score ranges used as the criteria to define success. Second, although these studies are well intentioned, the results are not meaningful because in actual practice a success profile index is not used or encouraged. An analysis of personality profiles of successful and unsuccessful professionals (disciminant analysis) would be more meaningful.

An adverse impact analysis for two of the studies is also reported. Differences between males and females and differences between majority and minority respondents on the success profile index were examined. No statistically significant differences were observed.

SUMMARY. Overall, the battery of measures provided in the ASSESS Expert Assessment System Version 5.X can provide some useful information relevant to personnel decision making with regard to hiring, promoting, and developing individuals in the managerial workforce. Additional studies, however, are needed to strengthen the evidence supporting the interpretation of the scores. Specifically, much larger samples are needed to generate norms for specific positions, reliability estimates for the ability and personality attributes should be obtained, and appropriate validation of the profile scores are needed. With the current data available, users of this system should be very cautious when interpreting the observed scores.

[22]
Assessing and Teaching Phonological Knowledge.

Purpose: Designed to assess children's reading readiness and diagnose a child's reading difficulty.
Population: Young children.
Publication Date: 1998.
Scores: 5 ratings: Acquiring Implicit Awareness of Sound Patterns in Words; Segmenting Words into Sounds; Sound Blending, Manipulating Sounds Within Words; Phonemic Recoding: Bridging to Written Words.
Administration: Individual.
Forms, 3: Screening Checklist, Parental Referral Form, Profile Sheet.
Price Data, 1998: $89 per starter set including manual (144 pages), record book, checklist, and task sheets; $49 per manual; $20 per record book; $16 per checklist; $10 per task sheets.
Time: Administration time not reported.
Author: John Munro.
Publisher: ACER Press, Australian Council for Educational Research, Ltd. [Australia].

Review of Assessing and Teaching Phonological Knowledge by REBECCA McCAULEY, Associate Professor, Communication Sciences, University of Vermont, Burlington, VT:

TEST STRUCTURE. This measure was designed to be used by teachers and educational diagnosticians for the assessment of individual children to determine the child's progress in the development of the phonological knowledge prerequisite to reading. Further, the author also notes that it was to determine "whether reading and spelling difficulties may be due to delayed or immature development of phonological knowledge" (manual, p. ix). Ages for which the measure is to be used are not specified directly, but it appears to have been developed for use with children in the early school years.

Documentation for the measure begins with a brief, but thoughtful review of some of the extensive literature now available on the varieties of implicit and explicit knowledge of a language's sound structure that support children's development of literacy. In particular, the introduction sets the stage for the types of tasks assessing rhyming, alliteration, word segmentation, sound blending, sound manipulation, and letter-sound knowledge. As the author convincingly asserts, this framework is consistent with current, widely accepted conceptualizations of the targeted content area (Yopp, 1988).

ADMINISTRATION AND SCORING. The manual includes detailed discussions of the procedures to be used for task administration. The measurement process begins with a screening procedure involving a screening checklist, parent referral form, and profile sheet. The profile sheet is the most thorough of the three components and is completed by the examiner who observes the child in "naturalistic classroom situations" (manual, p. 26). Based on those observations, the examiner rates the frequency of between 4 to 10 behaviors in four areas: oral communication, word pronunciation, reading aloud, and spelling. Performance is used to determine whether the more in-depth measure is used at all and, if used, whether it is used in its entirety.

The measure itself consists of the five sets of tasks: Task 1, Acquiring awareness of sound patterns in words (viz., rhyming, and alliteration); Task 2, Segmenting words into component parts (e.g., onsets and rimes, syllables, sounds); Task 3, Sound blending (viz., onset and rime; sound sequences); Task 4, Manipulating sounds within words (viz., deletion, substitution, segmentation of longer words into sounds); and Task 5, Phonemic re-coding of written symbols into sounds (viz., demonstrating knowledge of letter names, pronunciation of letter clusters and longer sequences of letters). The inclusion of these varied tasks makes it stand out as a relatively comprehensive measure of phonemic or phonological awareness.

Each task includes up to four practice items followed by a very small number of assessment items at each level within the task. For example, for Task 1.1—Recognizing rhyming words, the child is first given one practice item in which he is shown a row of four pictures and asked to repeat all of the names, then only the names that rhyme. Then, the child is given three actual items consisting of four words composed of three, four, and five segments. The line drawings used to elicit responses and other materials associated with the measure are attractive and likely to appeal to examiners and tested children. Criteria for the numerical scoring of items within subsections are quite clear; however, guidelines for interpretation of total task performance—though sometimes extensive—are qualitative in nature and appear susceptible to considerable examiner variability.

The booklet containing the measure ends with an extensive discussion of teaching methods tailored to address each of the measurement tasks. Although this feature undoubtedly adds to the attractiveness of this publication for the potential purchaser, it is not clear that this adds to its value from a measurement perspective.

TECHNICAL QUALITIES. No empirical support is provided for the use of the measure for any purpose. This is quite unfortunate given the theoretical promise of the measure. Specifically, no data of any kind are provided concerning validity or reliability. Even the detailed discussion of item writing and selection, which is often used to help support content validity, is missing. Norms, which would be important for the identification of delay—one of the stated purposes of the measure—are also absent.

SUMMARY. Despite a strong rationale, detailed delineation of test administration procedures, and an attractive format, this measure lacks most of the qualities associated with either a norm-referenced or criterion-referenced standardized measure. Thus, its value for clinical or educational decision making is severely limited until additional data are collected. Among more reasonable alternatives are a screening measure authored by Torgesen & Bryant (1994) and a somewhat more in-depth measure authored by Sawyer (1987). Although both of these measures are substantially reduced in scope from the one reviewed here, their more extensive documentation of reliability and validity make them more acceptable choices at this time.

REVIEWER'S REFERENCES

Sawyer, D. J. (1987). Test of Awareness of Language Segments. Frederick, MD: San Antonio, TX: PRO-ED, Inc.
Yopp, H. K. (1988). The validity and reliability of phonemic awareness tests. *Reading Research Quarterly, 23*, 2, 159–177.
Torgesen, J. K., & Bryant, B. R. (1994). Test of Phonological Awareness. San Antonio, TX: PRO-ED, Inc.

Review of Assessing and Teaching Phonological Knowledge by STEVEN A. STAHL, Professor of Reading Education, The University of Georgia, Athens, GA:

In spite of the recent research attending to the importance of phonological awareness for early reading, there are few published measures of this ability. It would seem that Assessing and Teaching Phonological Knowledge would have a niche. Unfortunately, this measure contains several serious flaws that reduce its utility.

As viewed by the author of this measure, phonological awareness is a developmental construct. This test uses five tasks, each with subtasks, to represent a developmental sequence, beginning with tasks measuring the child's implicit awareness of sound patterns (rhyme and alliteration), proceeding to segmenting words into sounds, sound blending, manipulating sounds in words, and finally bridging from phonological tasks to written words. Roughly this scheme seems to work, but there are problems. Research seems to show that partial segmentation is easier than blending, but full segmentation (included here with partial segmentation) is more difficult (e.g., Stahl & Murray, 1994; Yopp, 1988).

Each of these tasks (implicit awareness, etc.) is broken down into between 2 and 5 subtasks, or a total of 18 subtasks. Here is the problem. The author wants to represent the richness of phonological awareness behavior, but is constrained by the attention span of target children. Although there are no norms given, one assumes this test is intended for 4- to 7-year-olds. Because of the need for a quick test, most of the subtasks have only three to six items. The tasks themselves seem appropriate for the age level and would likely be engaging. However, no data are provided on reliability, but with such few items, subtask reliability is likely to be unacceptable. The five tasks taken as a whole have more items, but because they use many different formats, they are also not likely to be very reliable. There are no data provided on concurrent validity with other measures of phonological awareness, nor is any evidence provided regarding predictive validity of scores from other measures of early reading.

In addition, there is a section on teaching phonological awareness. There are useful activities here, perhaps more useful than the assessment portion of the book.

SUMMARY. In short, Assessing and Teaching Phonological Knowledge may be useful as a quick screening device, but needs to be followed up by a more reliable measure for diagnosis. For a standardized, formal measure, one might look at the Test of Phonological Awareness (Torgesen & Bryant, 1994; T5:2708) or the subtests of some of the new achievement batteries, such as the Woodcock-Johnson Tests of Achievement—III. There are a number of useful measures in articles by Stahl and Murray (1994) and Yopp (1988). These measures all have their own limitations. There is continuing work done on how best to measure phonological awareness and it is hoped this work will lead to psychometrically sound measures.

REVIEWER'S REFERENCES
Yopp, H. K. (1988). The validity and reliability of phonemic awareness tests. *Reading Research Quarterly, 23*, 159–177.
Stahl, S. A., & Murray, B. A. (1994). Defining phonological awareness and its relationship to early reading. *Journal of Educational Psychology, 86*, 221–234.
Torgesen, J. K., & Bryant, B. (1994). Test of Phonological Awareness. Austin, TX: PRO-ED.

[23]
Assessing Motivation to Communicate.

Purpose: Designed to assess communication apprehension and willingness to communicate.
Population: Postsecondary students.
Publication Date: 1994.
Acronym: AMTC.
Scores, 5: Group Discussions, Meetings, Interpersonal Conversations, Public Speaking, Total.
Administration: Group.
Price Data: Available from publisher.
Time: Administration time not reported.
Comments: Instrument consists of two assessment tools (The Personal Report of Communication Apprehension and The Willingness to Communicate) administered on a Macintosh computer, Operating System 7.0 or higher.
Author: Speech Communication Association.
Publisher: National Communication Association.

Review of Assessing Motivation to Communicate by RIC BROWN, Associate Vice President, Research, Graduate and Extended Programs, California State University, Sacramento, Sacramento, CA:

The Assessing Motivation to Communicate (AMTC) is a computerized assessment tool formatted for the Macintosh (version 7.0 or higher), using HyperCard version 2.1 or higher. The AMTC is referred to as an affective domain assessment, diagnosing two dimensions of self-reported communication: the Personal Report of Communication Apprehension (PCRA-24) and Willingness to Communicate (WTC). The manual includes text and a series of computer screen print outs (those seen by the test taker) with explanatory notes. The intended audiences for the scales are reported to be college students (for advising), teachers/instructors (for content and pedagogy), and administrators (for placement and program efficacy).

The manual consists of 30 pages with 20 articles appended. The articles include theoretical underpinnings for communication competence, communication apprehension, and interjection approaches to communication. In addition, several articles present data pertaining to reliability and validity of scores from the two scales.

The 24-item PCRA-24 specifically addresses communication apprehension along four dimensions: speaking in public, speaking in groups, speaking in meetings, and speaking in dyads. Respondents are to mark each statement regarding their feelings with respect to communication on a 5-point scale from *strongly agree* to *strongly disagree* (e.g., fear of giving a speech). In addition to a total score, a subscore on each of the speaking contexts can be obtained. Evidence is reported in one of the appended articles regarding reliability and content validity of the total score of the scale. No reliability data were presented with respect to the four subscores.

The Willingness to Communicate scale (WTC) is a 20-item instrument. The scale is reported to measure an individual's predisposition towards approaching or avoiding initiation to communicate. Respondents are asked to respond to each item using a 0 to 100 scale, indicating the percentage of time they would choose to communicate (e.g., talk with their physician). A total score can be obtained, as well as seven subscores. An article appended to the manual presents reliability data for the total score and appropriately notes lower reliability for the subscores with only three to four items. The article also presents data to support validity in terms of content and the construct being measured. Although some data are presented with respect to scores from other cultures, there is no report of studies of cross-cultural validation (Brown, 2000). However, appropriate cultural limitations are noted.

The manual also presents information on file management for those who have taken the test on the computer. In addition, there are tables presenting score ranges (norms, in a sense) so respondents can be categorized in terms of their communication skill level (e.g., high communication apprehension, low willingness to communicate, etc.).

SUMMARY. In general, the total scores on the PCRA-24 and the WTC have sufficient psychometric properties to be useful in the context for which they are intended. It would have been useful had the manual presented a summary of the reliability and validity data for the two instruments. The inclusion of articles would then have added to the manual presentation itself.

However, one serious limitation is noted with respect to the medium of delivery. Although the manual (1994) provides a rationale for the use of a computerized assessment tool, citing several national "trends," the technology is quite old. The current availability of Macintosh in the version 8.6 and 9.0 range indicates that the 7.0 version is very dated. Even though current Macintosh computers will likely read the disk containing the assessments, technologies have come a long way in the past 6 years. Thus, advantages of computerized assessment could be regained if a nonplatform-specific upgrade of instrument delivery (web or Java base) could be completed.

REVIEWER'S REFERENCES
American Educational Research Association, American Psychological Association, & National Council on Measurement in Education (Joint Committee). (1985). *Standards for educational and psychological testing.* Washington, DC: APA.
Brown, R. (2000). Measuring the construct of locus of control in an international setting. *Phi Beta Delta International Review, X,* 165–173.

Review of Assessing Motivation to Communicate by CLAUDIA R. WRIGHT, Professor, Educational Psychology, California State University, Long Beach, Long Beach, CA:

Assessing Motivation to Communicate (AMTC) is a computerized assessment made up of two instruments that provide affective measures of oral communication competency: (a) the 24-item version of the Personal Report of Communication Apprehension (PRCA-24; McCroskey, 1970) and (b) the Willingness to Communicate Scale (WTC; McCroskey & Richmond, 1987). The PRCA-24 is a self-report anxiety measure comprising four communication situations (group discussions, meetings, interpersonal conversations, and public speaking) and yielding four subscores and a total score. The 20-item WTC was developed to assess one's predisposition to either approach or avoid communication in 12 different situations. Eight scores are generated including a total score, four context scores that parallel those in the PRCA-24 (Public Speaking, Meetings, Groups, and Interpersonal), and three receiver scores (Stranger, Acquaintance, and Friend). Three general purposes for the AMTC include diagnosing communication apprehension to inform student academic advisement, placement decisions, and the modification of curricula and instruction to support learning. Selected studies provide modest, indirect support for these purposes.

TESTING MATERIALS, ADMINISTRATION, AND SCORING. The AMTC requires access to an Apple Macintosh (Operating System 7.0 or higher), HyperCard Version 2.1 or higher, and a compatible printer. A HyperCard-formatted disc includes an introduction, testing instructions, and the two instruments stored in separate files. A packet of materials offers a draft form of a technical manual that provides detailed directions for administering the computerized tests, retrieving scores from the program, cautions for program use, and contact numbers if problems are encountered. Information for interpreting scores is limited to a table of cutoff scores for "high" and "low" WTC classifications. For the teacher who wishes to use the tests in conjunction with instruction, a lecture guide is included with suggested course materials to support class discussions. Copies of selected articles dealing with the reliability and validity of PRCA-24 and WTC test scores offer some of the psychometric information that is required to make judgments about the two tests; however, one must sift through this collection to retrieve relevant test-related statistics.

The AMTC program loads on a single computer eliminating the option of group administration unless several computers are designated for this purpose. Each test, which can be taken at different times by the respondent, is self-administered and takes approximately 5 to 10 minutes to complete including set-up time. The total time for the administration of the two tests is estimated at 15 minutes.

Each test is computer scored and a set of scores displayed; the data may be retrieved for an individual respondent or a group of respondents. The PRCA-24 employs a 5-point Likert-type response formatted scale and yields four formula-derived scores. Each of the four subgroup scores (group discussions, meetings, and interpersonal communications) ranges from 6 to 30; with total scores ranging from 24 to 120. For communicating in each respective situation, the higher the score the more anxious is the respondent.

The WTC is made up of 20 items reflecting communication situations, 8 of which are "fillers" and not included in the final score computation. The respondent provides an estimate of the percentage of time that he or she would choose to communicate in each situation. An average percentage is computed for each of the four three-item context subscores and for each of the three four-item receiver subscores. The WTC total score is the average of the three receiver subscores. To aid in the interpretation of the eight WTC scores, the fact sheet provides a table of "norms," which lists "high" and "low" cutoff scores and the means for each category. The normative data were obtained from a sample of 1,641 college students in West Virginia.

RELIABILITY. In a review of several articles provided by the publisher, coefficient alpha reliability estimates reported for total PRCA-24 scores ranged from .93 to .97. For a set of scores on the public speaking subset of PRCA-24 items, reliability estimates ranged from .79 to .88 for two test administrations. No other reliability information was found.

The internal-consistency reliability estimate for WTC total scores was .93 ($N = 1,641$) with ranges of .86 to .95 attributed to other studies. Reliability estimates reported for the four context scores ranged from .60 to .83 and from .70 to .91 for the three receiver subscores (McCroskey, 1992). For a subsample of 174 respondents, a stability estimate for the total WTC scores was .79 (and .86 when corrected for attenuation). Internal-consistency estimates for the same sample were .92 and .91 for each of the two test administrations.

VALIDITY. Concurrent validity coefficients were reported between PRCA-24 scores and a measure of assertiveness assessed by scores on the Rathus Assertiveness Schedule (RAS) (Rathus, 1973). The coefficients obtained between scores on the RAS and PRCA-24 were .70 for total scores and .52, .60, .56, and .61 for public speaking, meetings, groups, and interpersonal, respectively.

The content of the WTC scores was derived by crossing four types of context with three types of receivers common in communication situations, yielding 12 items. A factor analysis supported the unidimensionality of scale scores; no factorial-related support was provided for the subscore scales. A construct validity coefficient of .41 was obtained between WTC total scores and scores on the Verbal Activity Scales (VAS) (McCroskey,

1977), a test designed to measure shyness or talking frequency. For the same sample, a correlation of -.52 was observed between WTC and PRCA-24 total scores. Correlations between WTC total scores and measures of other constructs were .22 with self-esteem, -.29 with introversion, and .59 with self-perceived communication competence; however, no information as provided regarding sample characteristics or the measures employed. In a study designed to assess predictive validity, a sample of college students classified as having either a "high "or "low" predisposition to communicate based on WTC scores, were observed for level of interactions during thee classroom sessions. As hypothesized, the "high" group participated more in class than did the "low" group. In a second study, WTC scores were used to predict (a) initial agreement to attend a setting where communication would be required, (b) actual attendance, and (c) if the respondent failed to attend, his or her resistance to participation. Findings supported the hypotheses that "high" WTC scorers would be more likely (a) to agree to attend, (b) actually attend, and (c) exhibit less resistance toward participating on follow-up (all $p<.001$).

SUMMARY. The AMTC provides for the assessment of two affective aspects of oral communication including anxiety about communicating in certain situations and the tendency to approach or avoid such situations. Although reliability and validity information for both PRCA-24 and WTC scores were reported, no statistics were provided for data obtained under computerized testing conditions. The differences between scores obtained under group administration and individualized computer testing conditions are relevant and should be included for consideration. A well-organized technical manual is needed that compiles relevant psychometric information for both the PRCA-24 and the WTC. Finally, cross-cultural WTC data were noted in McCroskey (1992) with lower test scores from Sweden, Australia, Finland, Estonia, and Micronesia compared with U.S. samples. The Micronesian sample registered the lowest scores suggesting possible cultural differences. More current reliability and validity information is needed for the two measures that reflect the cultural and language diversity typically found in U.S. schools.

REVIEWER'S REFERENCES

McCroskey, J. C. (1970). Measures of communication-bound anxiety. *Speech Monographs, 37,* 269–277.

Rathus, S. A. (1973). A 30-item schedule for assessing assertive behavior. *Behavior Therapy, 4,* 398–406.

McCroskey, J. C. (1977). *Quiet children and the classroom teacher.* Falls Church, VA: Speech Communication Association.

McCroskey, J. C., & Richmond, V. P. (1987). Willingness to communicate. In J. C. McCroskey & J. A. Dally (Eds.), *Personality and interpersonal communication* (pp. 129–156). Newbury Park, CA: Sage.

McCroskey, J. C. (1992). Reliability and validity of the Willingness to Communicate Scale. *Communication Quarterly, 40*(1), 16–25.

[24]
Assessing Your Team: Seven Measures of Team Success.

Purpose: Intended to give insight and understanding in assessing a team.
Population: Teams.
Publication Date: 1994.
Scores, 7: Purpose, Role, Strategy, Processes, People, Feedback, Interfaces.
Administration: Group.
Price Data, 1997: $24.95 per package including Team Leader's manual (38 pages) and Team Member's manual (31 pages); $9.95 per Team Member's manual.
Time: [.5] day.
Authors: Dick Richards and Susan Smyth.
Publisher: Jossey-Bass Pfeiffer.

Review of Assessing Your Team: Seven Measures of Team Success by PETER F. MERENDA, Professor Emeritus of Psychology and Statistics, University of Rhode Island, Kingston, RI:

Seven scores on the assessment for assessing team well-being are proposed, and each member of the team completes the form. The form consists of 28 statement alleged to measure team "well being."

The first four statements relate to the team's purpose. Statements 5–8 relate to the role enacted by the members to achieve the purpose; 9–12 to the strategy employed by the members in guiding their day-to-day activities; 13–16 to the process to be used; 17–20 to the expertise and knowledge of the people who comprise the team regarding how to implement the strategy being employed; 21–24 to solicitation of feedback from key stakeholders; 25–28 to managing critical relationships with outsiders—interfaces. Each statement is responded to by each member of a team on a 6-point Likert-type rating scale ranging from *strongly disagree* (1) to *strongly agree* (6). The assessment form is presented in the Team Member's manual. The form is self-scoring.

Also included in the manual is a Team Well-Being Feedback Form on which each individual team member lists the ratings given to each of the 28 statements. This form is sent to the person who is collecting the team's data.

Included further in the manual is a bibliography labeled as Resources, which is classified according to the seven steps in the assessment. There are 54 listings under Resources. All but 4 are internal reports by the publisher, Pfeiffer & Company. Notably absent are references to research with the instrument and publications in the appropriate refereed journals. This is considered by this reviewer to be a serious omission to test critiques and psychometricians in general. Hence, in the absence of a technical manual accompanying the two Assessing Your Team manuals, this reviewer sought to find the information supporting the sound psychometric properties of the assessment instrument in the Team Leader's Manual. Unfortunately, he did not. In that manual, only very brief, unsupported claims are made about Reliability, Item Discrimination, Differences Between Area Averages, and Validity. Therefore, this reviewer's comments are being made according to the requirements for assessment instruments published for operational use (AERA, APA, & NCME, 1985) as they relate to both what is and what is not contained in that manual.

It is stated early in the *Standards for Educational and Psychological Testing* (AERA, APA, & NCME, 1985) that "Tests and testing programs should be developed on a sound scientific basis" (Standard 3.1). Seven Measures of Team Success provide no empirical evidence that this standard has been met. The authors and/or their collaborators either have not conducted the necessary developmental research to attain sound psychometric properties or they have not published their findings in the required appropriate professional journals.

Before proceeding to comment specifically on what the authors claim in the Team Leader's manual, it is considered important for the benefit of potential users to excerpt portions of the three standards in Section 5, Test Publication: Technical Manuals and User's Guides (AERA, APA, & NCME, 1985).

Standard 5.1. "A technical manual should be available to prospective test users at the time a test is published or released for operational use."

Standard 5.3. "Technical manuals should cite a balanced and representative set of studies regarding general and specific test uses. The cited studies, except published work, and propriety studies, should be made available on request to the prospective test user by the publisher."

Standard 5.7. "Promotional material for a test should be accurate. Publishers should avoid using advertising techniques that suggest that a test can accomplish more than is supported by its research base."

This third standard (5.7) is included in the review because on the back cover of the Team Leader's manual, it is announced: "At last, an assessment process especially for work teams!" It goes on to say, "Here's the essential 'first step' for creating a successful continuous-improvement program for a team. Assessing Your Team provides a model for assessing the well-being of a team, offering seven functions that should be continually monitored to *ensure* that the team is functioning properly," (italics added).

In the Leader's Manual, it is merely stated that two studies had been conducted to show that the assessment is psychometrically sound. Brief, incomplete, and questionable data are reported only for the second study. Reliability (split-half) is claimed to be "as high as .96." However, no statistical tables or other pertinent data describing a scientific empirical study are reported to support this claim. In addition, the split-half method is not considered to be an appropriate estimate of the reliability of scores—especially for seven subscales. Rather, the method is one that may provide a reliability estimate based on a measure of internal consistency of the items comprising the test or subscales. A more appropriate estimate of reliability would be test-retest and for internal consistency, Cronbach's alpha for 6-point scales.

For item discrimination it is simply stated that the 28 items discriminate positively between high-scoring and low-scoring examinees. No further details are given, nor are data shown. For differences between area averages it is stated that a rank test was performed to test the differences among the seven subscales, but the use of the simple rank test is not defended. More seriously, it is claimed that the differences were all *significant*. Because this claim is based on $p < .01$, at most it may be concluded that *statistical* significance merely had been shown. To claim that the differences are actually *significant* additional evidence of importance or meaningfulness of the results (such as a power analysis) would be needed.

As for validity, it is claimed that "Formal validity is high" (Leader's manual, p. 26) without producing the required details and tabled data.

Again the error is made in confusing the distinction between *significant* and *statistically significant*. To say that "significant" correlations were obtained gives no indication of how low the correlation coefficients could have been. No sample sizes are given. For sample sizes of 100 or more the standard error of r is about .10 so a coefficient of only .20 would be judged to be statistically significant, but then r is only .04.

SUMMARY. Assessing Your Team is, as stated by the authors in both of the manuals that accompany the assessment, "a series of six steps for assessing a team's well-being." However, it does not qualify as an assessment in accordance with psychometric definition and requirements. Hence, it should not be promoted and marketed as such a device. The authors and publisher are hereby urged to correct such an impression for the benefit and welfare of potential users.

REVIEWER'S REFERENCE

American Educational Research Association, American Psychological Association, & National Council of Measurement in Education. (1985). *Standards for educational and psychological testing.* Washington, DC: APA, Inc.

[25]
Assessment of Adaptive Areas.

Purpose: Designed to identify deficits in 10 adaptive skill areas of mental retardation.
Population: Ages 3–60+ years.
Publication Date: 1996.
Acronym: AAA.
Scores: Communication, Self-Care, Home-Living, Social, Community Use, Self-Direction, Health and Safety, Functional Academics, Leisure, Work.
Administration: Individual.
Price Data, 2000: $98 per complete kit including examiner's manual (143 pages) and 25 Profile/Examiner Record Booklets; $46 per examiner's manual; $54 per 25 Profile/Examiner Record Booklets.
Time: (30) minutes.
Comments: The AAA is a system of reassigning the items from the Adaptive Behavior Scale—Residential and Community: Second Edition (T5:1) and the Adaptive Behavior Scale—School: Second Edition (T5:2) into the 10 adaptive skill areas delineated by the American Association on Mental Retardation.
Authors: Brian R. Bryant, Ronald L. Taylor, and Diane Pedrotty Rivera.
Publisher: PRO-ED.

Review of the Assessment of Adaptive Areas by JACK A. CUMMINGS, Professor and Chair, Department of Counseling and Educational Psychology, Indiana University, Bloomington, IN:

Bryant, Taylor, and Rivera outline four purposes for the Assessment of Adaptive Areas (AAA): identifying individuals with mental retardation; determining adaptive strengths and weaknesses; documenting progress in adaptive behavior domains; and conducting research. Using the AAA to identify individuals with significant deficits in their adaptive behavior functioning is described as the primary purpose of the scale. As the AAA yields scores for the 10 American Association for Mental Retardation (AAMR) adaptive behavior domains, the authors suggest that examiners may find clinical utility in the intraindividual differences observed relative to an individual's scores. These data would in turn be a "first step in planning an appropriate individualized program" (examiner's manual, p. 3).

STANDARDIZATION. The AAA represents a method for interpretation of selected items from the AAMR Adaptive Behavior Scale—Residential and Community: Second Edition (T5:1; Nihira, Leland, & Lambert, 1993) and the AAMR Adaptive Behavior Scale—School: Second Edition (T5:2; Lambert, Nihira, & Leland, 1993). The AAA uses items on these two versions of the AAMR Adaptive Behavior Scales to generate scores that correspond to the 10 adaptive behavior domains outlined in the 1992 AAMR definition of mental retardation. The AAA does not have a standardization sample that is independent of the AAMR Adaptive Behavior Scales. This means the quality of the AAA rests on the adequacy of the standardization procedures employed in the construction of the AAMR Adaptive Behavior Scales.

Both *Thirteenth Mental Measurements Yearbook* reviewers (Carey, 1998; Harrison, 1998) had praise for the standardization sample of the AAMR Adaptive Behavior Scale—Residential and Community, Second Edition. They noted the sample is generally representative of the country at large. Carey (1998) observed that for the AAMR Adaptive Behavior Scale, whites and African Americans are adequately represented. However, Carey (1998) notes for Asians there is underrepresentation with 0.8% in the sample relative to 5.2% in the United States. Harrison (1998) pointed out that 80% of those sampled lived in either small community facilities or large residential facilities. Only 20% of the sample lived either independently or with parents. This means the sample favors individuals who need "relatively significant amounts of professional support" (Harrison, 1998, p. 3). Despite these caveats, both Carey (1998) and Harrison (1998) recommend the use of the 1993 Residential and Community version of the Adaptive Behavior Scale.

Likewise for the School version of the AAMR Adaptive Behavior Scale, the recent *Thirteenth Mental Measurements Yearbook* reviewers (Harrington, 1998; Stinnett, 1998) were favorably impressed with the standardization sample. Stinnett (1998, p. 10) noted that the standardization sample "was of good size and diversity to be suited for most applications." Stinnett (1998) observed that the standardization sample of the AAMR Adaptive Behavior Scale—School, Second Edition does not include individuals with mental retardation who have IQs in the range from 71–75. He underscored the importance of the omission by citing Gresham, MacMillan, and Siperstein (1995) who point out that individuals with IQs from 71 to 75 outnumber those with IQs from 55 to 70 (2.8% of the population vs. 2.5%). The problem is that the larger of the two groups of people with MR was not represented in the sample. Stinnett does not view the problem as a serious flaw, but cautions the user to recognize the discrepancy between the 1992 AAMR definition of mental retardation with 75 as the upper limit and the one used by the AAMR Adaptive Behavior Scales with 70 as the upper limit.

SCORING. The manual provides an example with appropriate sections of AAMR Adaptive Behavior Scale protocol with the corresponding sections of the AAA. The combination of the example and organization of the AAA protocol make scoring lucid.

RELIABILITY. The median internal consistency coefficients reported for the mental retardation sample range from .89 to .98. These reliability estimates result in low standard errors of measurement for the 10 domains. The stability of the AAA domain scores was assessed by six teachers who rated five students each, and then 2 weeks later repeated the rating of each student. The stability coefficients ranged from .78 to .94 with the median falling at .83. These data suggest scores from the scale are reliable and stable.

VALIDITY. Bryant et al. reported that the three test authors and 12 experts in mental retardation and assessment sorted AAMR Adaptive Behavior Scale items into the 10 adaptive behavior domains. Item weighting in a domain score was determined by the percentage of agreement on an item's assignment to the domain. This contrasts with a more conventional approach to test construction wherein the authors would begin with a table of specifications and write items to fill cells. A more complete content analysis would have asked expert judges to consider the pool of items for each domain and determine if those items adequately captured the domain, specifying whether important items were missing. For instance, in the AAMR descriptions of adaptive skills areas (examiner's manual, p. 137), the Social domain is described as "Skills related to social exchanges with other individuals, including initiating, interacting, and terminating interaction with others." Given this definition, the task of the content validity judge would be to assess the degree to which the items covered the Social domain. A review of the AAA social items reveals an item that addresses initiation of group social activities, but no items relative to initiating or terminating an interaction with an individual.

With respect to construct validity, Bryant et al. presented a table of median scores by age level and domain area. As expected, the median scores rise as age increases and therefore support the developmental nature of the AAA. Two tables with intercorrelations of the domain scores are provided for the non-mental-retardation and retardation samples. Unfortunately, the intercorrelations are not broken down by age group. Given that age growth slopes of domains vary, the intercorrelations would be expected to change with age. The presentation in the AAA manual did not include factor analytic findings. Previous factor analytic research with adaptive behavior scales (Harrison, 1987; McGrew & Bruininks, 1989) would predict the likelihood of extracting 10 factors from the AAA items to be low. For instance, Harrison's review revealed the number of factors extracted from various adaptive behavior scales to range from 2 to 7. McGrew and Bruininks (1989) noted that 2 factors were most often extracted for the previous version of the AAMD Adaptive Behavior Scale.

INTERPRETATION. As noted above, the primary purpose of the AAA is the identification of individuals with mental retardation. The authors recommend the use of standard scores ($M = 10$, $sd = 3$) in the interpretation of the domains.

Unfortunately, they fail to specify whether one should use the norms for the "non-mental retardation sample" or the "mental retardation sample." Descriptive ratings (Average, 8–12; Below Average, 6–7; Poor, 4–5; and Very Poor, 1–3) are provided for the standard scores. Unanswered questions include the following: What score or rating should be used to judge deficit adaptive behavior functioning in a given domain? What is the implication for identification of an individual when a subset of scores is in the Average range with the others in Very Poor range? Are certain domains more critical to the identification of an individual with mental retardation? Although age-equivalent scores are provided, examiners are cautioned not to use them because they can be misleading.

As one of the purposes of the AAA was to provide ipsative comparisons of an individual's performance across the 10 adaptive behavior domains, suggestions should be given on how one determines whether performance in one area is reliably higher than the individual's general level of adaptive behavior functioning. Bryant et al. appropriately pointed out that there are differences in reliabilities associated with each scale. The Communication domain with a reliability of .94 would have a relatively narrower band of fluctuation due to error than would the Home-Living domain with a reliability of .76. Without suggestions as to how to determine reliable strengths and weaknesses, it is likely that users will make errors. For example, one might conclude a strength or weakness existed when, in fact, the profile of scores showed expected variation based on the reliability of the scales.

CONCLUSION AND SUMMARY. The AAA is a partial solution to the problem of incompatibility between adaptive behavior measures and the domains specified in the AAMR definition of mental retardation. The introduction of the AAMR definition has been controversial (Luckasson, Schalock, Snell, & Spitalnik, 1996; MacMillan, Siperstein, & Gresham, 1996; Smith, 1994). Researchers (Borthwick-Duffy, 1993; MacMillan, Gresham, & Siperstein, 1993; Vig & Jedrysek, 1996) have questioned the defensibility of 10 separate domains of adaptive behavior. Factor analytic approaches often have yielded relatively distinct abilities, but none have produced findings that support the 10 AAMR adaptive behavior domains. This results in a thorny situation for the practitioner faced with decisions on the presence or absence of mental retardation. If one embraces the 1992 AAMR definition, the item categorizations and resulting domain scores provided by the AAA are an improvement over a clinician's intuitive sorting of items into the 10 AAMR adaptive behavior domains.

REVIEWER'S REFERENCES

Harrison, P. L. (1987). Research with adaptive behavior scales. Journal of Special Education, 21, 37–68.

McGrew, K. & Bruininks, R. (1989). The factor structure of adaptive behavior. School Psychology Review, 18, 64–81.

McGrew, K. & Bruininks, R. (1990). Defining adaptive and maladaptive behavior within a model of personal competence. School Psychology Review, 19, 53–73.

Borthwick-Duffy, S. (1993). Review of mental retardation: Definition, classification, and systems of support (9th ed.). American Journal on Mental Retardation, 98, 541–544.

Lambert, N., Nihira, K., & Leland, H. (1993). AAMR Adaptive Behavior Scale—School: Second Edition. Austin, TX: PRO-ED.

MacMillan, D. L., Gresham, F. M., & Siperstein, G. N. (1993). Conceptual and psychometric concerns about the AAMR definition of mental retardation. American Journal on Mental Retardation, 98, 325–335.

Nihira, K., Leland, H., & Lambert, N. (1993). AAMR Adaptive Behavior Scale—Residential and Community: Second Edition. Austin, TX: PRO-ED.

Smith, J. D. (1994). The revised AAMR definition of mental retardation: The MRDD position. Education and Training in Mental Retardation and Developmental Disabilities, 29, 179–183.

Gresham, F. M., MacMillan, D. L., & Siperstein, G. N. (1995). Critical analysis of the 1992 AAMR definition: Implications for school psychology. School Psychology Quarterly, 10, 1–19.

Luckasson, R., Schalock, R. L., Snell, M. E., & Spitalnik, D. M. (1996). The 1992 AAMR definition and preschool children: Response from the Committee on Terminology and Classification. Mental Retardation, 34, 247–253.

MacMillan, D. L., Siperstein, G. N., & Gresham, F. M. (1996). A challenge to the viability of mild mental retardation as a diagnostic category. Exceptional Children, 62, 356–371.

Vig, S., & Jedrysek, E. (1996). Application of the 1992 AAMR definition: Issues for preschool children. Mental Retardation, 34, 244–246.

Carey, K. T. (1998). [Review of the AAMR Adaptive Behavior Scale—Residential and Community, Second Edition]. In J. C. Impara & B. S. Plake (Eds.), The thirteenth mental measurements yearbook (pp. 1–3). Lincoln, NE: Buros Institute of Mental Measurements.

Harrington, R. G. (1998). [Review of the AAMR Adaptive Behavior Scale—School, Second Edition]. In J. C. Impara & B. S. Plake (Eds.), The thirteenth mental measurements yearbook (pp. 5–9). Lincoln, NE: Buros Institute of Mental Measurements.

Harrison, P. L. (1998). [Review of the AAMR Adaptive Behavior Scale—Residential and Community, Second Edition]. In J. C. Impara & B. S. Plake (Eds.), The thirteenth mental measurements yearbook (pp. 3–5). Lincoln, NE: Buros Institute of Mental Measurements.

Stinnett, T. A. (1998). [Review of the AAMR Adaptive Behavior Scale—School, Second Edition]. In J. C. Impara & B. S. Plake (Eds.), The thirteenth mental measurements yearbook (pp. 9–14). Lincoln, NE: Buros Institute of Mental Measurements.

Review of the Assessment of Adaptive Areas by MARK D. SHRIVER, *Assistant Professor of Pediatrics and* MERILEE McCURDY, *Pediatric Psychology Intern, Munroe-Meyer Institute for Genetics and Rehabilitation, University of Nebraska Medical Center, Omaha, NE:*

The Assessment of Adaptive Areas (AAA), a scoring system that recategorizes the items of the AAMR Adaptive Behavior Scale—Residential and Community, Second Edition (ABS-RC2; Nihira, & Leland, 1993; T5:1) and the AAMR Adaptive Behavior Scale—School, Second Edition (ABS-S2; Lambert, Nihira, & Leland, 1993; T5:2) generates scores for each of the 10 adaptive skill areas identified by the American Association for Mental Retardation (AAMR) as being critical in assessing mental retardation (examiner's manual, p. 2). Subsequently, the AAA has four stated purposes that correspond to the purposes espoused for the ABS-RC2 and the ABS-S2: (a) to identify people who are significantly below their peers in adaptive functioning, (b) to identify adaptive strengths and weaknesses, (c) to monitor progress, and (d) to serve as a measure of adaptive functioning for research purposes.

Although the AAA is meant primarily as a procedural step in obtaining adaptive behavior scores following administration of the ABS-RC2 or ABS-S2, the outcomes of the AAA differ from the outcomes of the ABS-RC2 and ABS-S2. The reliability and validity of the outcomes of the AAA, therefore, will be evaluated relative to the stated purposes of the AAA presented above. For reviews of the ABS-RC2 and ABS-S2, please see Carey (1998), Harrison (1998), Harrington (1998), and Stinnett (1998).

DEVELOPMENT OF THE AAA. As noted above, the AAA was developed to be more consistent with the AAMR's diagnostic criteria for mental retardation that include three components: (a) intellectual functioning of 75 or below, (b) onset before age 18 years, and (c) significant disabilities in two or more adaptive areas. The 10 adaptive areas described by AAMR are Communication, Self-Care, Home-Living, Social, Community Use, Self-Direction, Health and Safety, Functional Academics, Leisure, and Work.

The AAA was developed by reassigning items from the ABS-RC2 and ABS-S2 to each of these 10 areas. Reassignment was conducted by "12 experts in mental retardation" (manual, p. 50) plus the authors of the AAA. Each expert assigned items from the ABS-RC2 and ABS-S2 to one or more of the 10 AAMR adaptive behavior areas. Each item from the ABS-RC2 and ABS-S2 was worth 5 points and could be assigned to 5 of 10 areas (1 point for each area), 4 of 10 (i.e., 2 points for 1 area and 1 point for each of 3 areas), 3 of 10 (i.e., 2 and 2 and 1), 2 of 10 (i.e., 3 points and 2 points), or all 5 points for that item could be awarded to one area. Percentages were generated for each item within each area by dividing the total ratings by the number of points assigned. Scoring weights (see scoring below) were assigned by giving a 3 if the percentage was 75 or greater, a 2 if

the percentage was between 50 and 74, and a 1 if the percentage was between 25 and 49.

Point-biserial correlation was calculated to evaluate an item's discriminating power. Median item discrimination correlations ranged from .24 to .50 for a nonmental-retardation sample and .53 to .67 for a mental-retardation sample. As a whole, these numbers suggest good item discrimination for their respective areas.

SCORING. Scoring of the AAA takes place after administration and scoring of the ABS-RC2 or the ABS-S2 is completed. Items from the ABS are transferred to the AAA. As described above, the items on the AAA are weighted on a 1–3 scale. These items are summed into the 10 adaptive skill areas for the corresponding ABS-S2 or ABS-RC2 protocol. Standard scores, percentiles, and age equivalent scores may be computed. Standard scores for each of the areas have a mean of 10 and a standard deviation of 3. Practice scoring is recommended to minimize errors and practice protocols are available.

NORMATIVE SAMPLE. The AAA relies upon the same normative sample as used in the ABS-RC2 and the ABS-S2. It appears the scores from the original normative samples for these two measures were reassigned and calculated anew for the AAA. The ABS-RC2 sample is composed of 4,103 individuals 18 years to 60+ years old with a previous diagnosis of mental retardation. Approximately 61% of the sample had a standard score below 50 o an intellectual measure. Approximately 39% of the sample had a standard score between 50 to 70 and none of the sample has a standard score between 70 and 75. The sample is overrepresented on the lower end of the normal curve for individuals diagnosed with mental retardation. The sample appears to be representative of national population with and without mental retardation for ethnicity and geographic region.

The ABS-S2 is composed of two normative samples. One sample consists of 2,074 children 3 years to 21 years with a previous diagnosis of mental retardation. Again, the sample appears to be overrepresented for children with lower standard scores on intelligence measures, as 60% of the sample had an intelligence test standard score below 50. Forty percent of the sample had a standard score on an intelligence measure between 50 and 70, and none of the sample had a standard score between 70 and 75. The sample is largely representative of the national population in terms of ethnicity and geographic region. The sample sizes for each year between ages 3 and 8 are less than 100.

The second sample consists of 1,245 children between the ages of 3 and 18 years who do not have a diagnosis of mental retardation. Again, sample sizes are largely representative of the national population in terms of ethnicity and geographic region and gender. Except for ages 8 and 10, the sample sizes for each of the age groups are less than 100.

For diagnostic purposes, it may be difficult to interpret scores on the AAA using the ABS-RC2 normative sample as an average score would indicate that the individual evaluated was functioning within an average range compared to individuals with mental retardation. The degree to which the individual being evaluated differed from a normative group representative of the population at large is not possible to determine. The same difficulty with diagnostic interpretation would occur on the AAA using the ABS-S2 mental retardation normative sample.

RELIABILITY. Internal consistency was examined using coefficient alpha across all subjects from the normative sample. Median correlations for the mental-retardation samples are .875 to .98 and for non-mental-retardation samples .76 to .94. The correlations across all the areas are generally high. Likewise, examination of the standard error of measurement (*SEM*) across all the areas indicates that the *SEM*s are typically low.

Evidence for test-retest reliability is minimal. Six teachers rated five students without mental retardation and than repeated their ratings of these students 2 weeks later. No information about the teachers or the students is provided. Correlations between ratings ranged from .78 to .94 across areas. These are moderate correlations across a relatively short time span. There is a need for more evidence regarding the stability of results over time.

No information is presented in the manual regarding interscorer reliability. This is important, especially because the authors recommend that mastery of the test scoring system does take practice.

VALIDITY. Evidence for content validity relies largely on the development of the measure as described above. Except for the item discrimination analysis, no other empirical evidence for content validity is presented.

Concurrent validity evidence is provided by examining correlations between the AAA areas and the Vineland Adaptive Behavior Scales composite score (VABS). It is not clear which VABS form was used (i.e., Classroom, Interview). Other than number of participants (63), no information is provided about the study sample. Correlations ranged from .16 to .62.

In a second study, the authors developed an "informal scale" of adaptive behavior and 32 evaluators completed this scale and the ABS-RC2/AAA on 32 students. No information about the evaluators or students is presented. Correlations between the informal scale and AAA scores range from .43 to .77. However, it is difficult to determine the meaning of this information as there is no psychometric information provided about the informal scale developed by the authors. More information about these studies, as well as additional evidence for criterion-related validity is needed.

Evidence for construct validity is provided through examination of age differentiation of the adaptive area scales raw scores, intercorrelations of the AAA area scores, relationship to mental ability tests, group differentiation, and item validity. In summary, raw scores generally increased with age within most of the adaptive behavior areas. The sample with mental retardation was less likely to evidence increases in raw scores. There did appear to be a decline in some of the area raw scores after the age of 18 years.

Correlations between area scores ranged from .36 to .80 for the non-mental-retardation sample and between .48 and .87 for the mental-retardation sample.

Intelligence test scores from the standardization samples were correlated with the AAA area scores. Tests examined were the Stanford-Binet Intelligence Scale, Leiter International Performance Scale, Slosson Intelligence Test, and the Wechsler Adult Intelligence Scale—Revised. The correlations presented are moderate, and are generally highest for the Wechsler Intelligence Scale for Children—Revised (WISC-R) (.35 to .84). Also, these intelligence tests are currently out-dated editions, and it is unknown how the AAA may correlate with intelligence tests currently in use.

Evidence for group differentiation is provided by examination of differences in mean raw scores between the sample with mental retardation and the sample without mental retardation. The sample with mental retardation had lower raw scores than the sample without mental retardation. Finally, the item discrimination correlations described above in the development of the measure are referred to gain as evidence for construct validity.

SUMMARY. Because the AAA is based on results from the ABS-RC2 and ABS-S2, any concerns regarding the reliability and validity of scores from them will affect the technical qualities of the AAA. For that reason, potential users of the AAA will need to thoroughly familiarize themselves regarding the strengths and weaknesses of the ABS-RC2 and ABS-S2. The authors of the AAA make the case, however, that the outcomes of the AAA differ from other assessment measures, so it is necessary for them to present evidence regarding the reliability and validity of the AAA outcomes. More evidence is needed to demonstrate the reliability and validity of this measure.

The AAA represents another time-consuming step in the assessment of adaptive behavior, and therefore the authors should demonstrate the diagnostic and/or treatment utility of completing this step. Currently, education and psychiatric diagnoses for mental retardation do not rely upon the AAMR definition of mental retardation. It is questionable if this scoring method contributes anything to assessment practice at this time. In addition, other measures, such as the Adaptive Behavior Evaluation Scale—Revised (McCarney, 1995; 4) provide scores using the AAMR adaptive behavior areas without additional scoring steps. It appears that continued use of the more commonly used measures of adaptive behavior, such as the ABS-RC2 and ABS-S2 or the Vineland Adaptive Behavior Scales (Sparrow, Balla, Cicchetti, & Doll, 1985; T5:2813) is still the most effective and efficient practice for assessing adaptive behavior.

REVIEWERS' REFERENCES

Sparrow, S. S., Balla, D. A., Cicchetti, D. V., & Doll, E. A. (1985). Vineland Adaptive Behavior Scales. Circle Pines, MN: American Guidance Service.
Lambert, N., Nihira, K., & Leland, H. (1993). AAMR Adaptive Behavior Scale—School, Second Edition. Austin, TX: PRO-ED.
Nihira, K., Leland, H., & Lambert, N. (1993). AAMR Adaptive Behavior Scale—Residential and Community, Second Edition. Austin, TX: PRO-ED.
McCarney, S. B. (1995). The Adaptive Behavior Scale—Revised. Columbia, MO: Hawthorne Educational Services, Inc.
Carey, K. T. (1998). [Review of the AAMR Adaptive Behavior Scale—Residential and Community, Second Edition.] In J. C. Impara & B. S. Plake (Eds.), *The thirteenth mental measurements yearbook* (pp. 1–3). Lincoln, NE: Buros Institute of Mental Measurements.
Harrington, R. G. (1998). [Review of the AAMR Adaptive Behavior Scale—School, Second Edition.] In J. C. Impara & B. S. Plake (Eds.), *The thirteenth mental measurements yearbook* (pp. 5–9). Lincoln, NE: Buros Institute of Mental Measurements.
Harrison, P. L. (1998). [Review of the AAMR Adaptive Behavior Scale—Residential and Community, Second Edition.] In J. C. Impara & B. S. Plake (Eds.), *The thirteenth mental measurements yearbook* (pp. 3–5). Lincoln, NE: Buros Institute of Mental Measurements.
Stinnett, T. A. (1998). [Review of the AAMR Adaptive Behavior Scale—School, Second Edition.] In J. C. Impara & B. S. Plake (Eds.), *The thirteenth mental measurements yearbook* (pp. 9–14). Lincoln, NE: Buros Institute of Mental Measurements.

[26]

Assessment of Parenting Skills: Infant and Preschooler.

Purpose: Designed to "evaluate the parenting skills of parents of children between birth and five years of age."

Population: Parents of children between birth and five years of age.

Publication Date: 1998.

Acronym: APSIP.

Scores, 13: Discipline, Fears (Stranger Anxiety, Mobility Fears, Separation Fears, Nightmares and Night Terrors, Fears of Real Events, Abstract Fears, Doctors and Dentists), Tantrums, Crying, Individual Differences and Temperament, Daily Routine, Parental Strengths and Weaknesses.

Administration: Individual.

Price Data, 1998: $109 per complete kit including 6 APSIP booklets, 6 summary sheets, and manual (21 pages); $79 per 6 APSIP booklets; $39 per instruction manual.

Time: Administration time not reported.

Author: Gail Elliot.

Publisher: Village Publishing.

Review of Assessment of Parenting Skills: Infant and Preschooler by T. STEUART WATSON, Professor of Counselor Education/Educational Psychology, Mississippi State University, Starkville, MS:

Calling the Assessment of Parenting Skills: Infant and Preschooler (APSIP) a test or including the word "Assessment" in the title is, at the very least, a misnomer and probably false advertising. There is absolutely nothing about this instrument that qualifies it as a test or assessment device. There are no objective scoring criteria, no reliability or validity data, no criterion- or norm-referenced comparison data, and no reliable or valid standard interpretive guidelines. Actually, this "assessment" instrument would be more accurately labeled as a structured interview for parents.

The kit contains six APSIP booklets and one examiner's manual. The first page of the manual is nothing more than an advertisement for a variety of custody evaluation tests and materials available from the publisher. According to the manual, the purpose of the test is to "evaluate the parenting skills of parents of children between birth and five years of age" (p. ii). Although never stated explicitly, the test appears to be specifically designed to assist clinicians in comparing the relative skills of parents involved in child custody proceedings. If this is indeed the case, a clinician would need an objective criterion against which each parent's responses could be compared. As it currently stands, the clinician is left without any formal criteria to judge or compare the adequacy of responses.

Given that the supposed purpose of the test is to "evaluate" parenting skills, one would logically assume that there are some criteria upon which to judge such skills. This is not the case with the APSIP. The scoring guidelines are nothing more than a listing of 14 different parenting issues/child behaviors (e.g., Discipline, Stranger Anxiety, Abstract Fears, Tantrums, Parental Strengths and Weaknesses) and their corresponding question numbers from the booklet. The author then goes into fairly lengthy detail describing the most appropriate types of parental responses depending upon the developmental level and unique needs of the target child. Most of the author's examples of appropriate parental responding are reasonable, grounded in empirical research, and involve an ample dose of common sense. The problem, however, is the lack of an objective system with which to compare parental responses to those given in the book and/or some type of objective scoring system to rate the appropriateness of the responses. Without any type of evaluative guide, the clinician must rely on his or her own judgment when deciding whether or not a parental response to a stimulus item is appropriate; a skill that does not require the materials in this kit.

The manual contains cursory directions for either evaluator- or self-administration of the instrument. There are very few guidelines presented for self-administration of the test. For example, what reading level is required to complete the instrument, how much time should be provided, what behaviors should the examiner observe while the respondent is completing the instrument, and how much follow-up questioning is permitted by the clinician? These and similar questions need to be addressed before recommending that the instrument be self-administered.

The APSIP booklet (i.e., structured interview form) contains questions regarding personal/ social development, discipline, daily routine, health history, developmental history, school history, fears, communication style, and parental strengths and weaknesses; areas that most skilled clinicians address during parent interviews without benefit of these materials. There is an Irritability Scale that is, perhaps, the most useful section of the test. Specific child behaviors are presented and the respondent indicates, on a scale of 0 (*would not annoy me at all*) to 4 (*angry enough to yell and hit*), how they would respond to the behavior. The examiner can then derive a Total Score on this scale. Because the test is used to compare one parent's responses to the other parent's responses, the two total scores can, theoretically, be compared. However, this is never stated and the clinician, due to the lack of psychometric data, has no reliable or valid means to interpret score differences. More useful to the clinician, however, are the parental responses to the specific behaviors, which may allow some subjective judgment as to the typical parent-child interaction across a variety of behaviors.

There is also a special section devoted to questions regarding twins. It is admirable that the author recognizes the inherent difficulty of parenting two children the same age. In the manual, there is a corresponding section for "scoring" responses to the items regarding parenting twins. It is worth mentioning again that, although the author uses the term "scoring" throughout the manual, there is no scoring as such involved. This allusion to scoring is not only confusing to an examiner becoming acquainted with the materials but misleading as well.

The last page of the booklet contains a "Bricklin Perceptual Scales: Child Perception of Parents Series" Scoring Summary sheet. The applicability of this scoring summary to the APSIP is unknown. In fact, the scoring summary is part of the Bricklin Perceptual Scales (T5:322), another instrument published by the same publisher. Inclusion of this page in the booklet is extremely confusing and certainly seems out of place.

In addition to the multitude of problems associated with this instrument, it is completely self-report and the clinician must rely on the integrity of the respondent to provide truthful answers. This may hardly be the case with parents who are in child custody litigation. Inclusion of a scale or questions to detect deception and other types of misleading responses would be especially appropriate for this type of instrument.

SUMMARY. It is improbable that a clinician would need to purchase this assessment instrument for the purpose as stated in the manual. Perhaps a novice clinician wishing to conduct structured interviews with parents may find the booklet of some assistance, but probably not. There is nothing in the test kit that characterizes this as an "assessment" instrument and the questions contained in the booklet are not substantially different from those used by a well-trained clinician during most standard interviews with parents.

[27]
Attention Deficit Disorders Evaluation Scale, Second Edition.

Purpose: "Designed to provide a measure of inattention and hyperactivity-impulsivity."
Publication Dates: 1989–1995.
Acronym: ADDES.
Scores, 3: Inattentive, Hyperactive-Impulsive, Percentile Total.
Administration: Individual.
Price Data, 1999: $206 per complete kit; $26 per 50 pre-referral documentation forms; $12.50 per manual (School Version ['95, 44 pages] or Home Version ['95, 42 pages]); $31 per 50 School rating forms; $31 per 50 Home rating forms; $20 per 50 ADDES/DSM-IV forms; $149 per computerized manual; $35 per computerized QuickScore.
Authors: Stephen B. McCarney (test and manuals) and Angela Marie Bauer (Parent's Guide to Attention-Deficit Disorders manual).
Publisher: Hawthorne Educational Services, Inc.
  a) ADDES—HOME VERSION.
  Population: Ages 3–20 years.
  Time: [12-15] minutes.
  Comments: Child is rated by a parent/caregiver.
  b) ADDES—SCHOOL VERSION.
  Population: Ages 4–19 years.
  Time: (15–20) minutes.
  Comments: Student is rated by an educator.
Cross References: For reviews by Deborah Collins and Stephen Olejnik of an earlier edition, see 12:38 (1 reference).

Review of the Attention Deficit Disorders Evaluation Scale, Second Edition by HUGH W. GLENN, Educational Consultant, Kohut Psychiatric Medical Group, San Bernardino, CA:

Contrary to the claim of the author of the Attention Deficit Evaluation Scale that it is "the only behavior rating scale commercially available … [that corresponds to] the criteria for the American Psychiatric Association's definition of Attention-Deficit/Hyperactivity Disorder" (technical manual, p. 6), both the Behavior Assessment System for Children: Monitor for ADHD (also reviewed in this volume; 33) and the Attention Deficit Disorders Evaluation Scale, draw heavily upon defining behaviors for ADHD as found in the *Diagnostic and Statistical Manual of Mental Disorders* (4th ed.) (DSM-IV; American Psychiatric Association, 1994).

The two versions of the Attention Deficit Disorder Evaluation Scale, the Home Version (46 items) and the School Version (60 items), include several identical items (Does not listen to or follow verbal directions" and "Does not listen to what others are saying") and numerous highly similar items ("Is easily distracted by other activities in the classroom" and "Is easily distracted by other things happening in the home"). There is little doubt, however, that the scales include only a few mutually exclusive factors; that is, both scales rate a few factors repeatedly. For example, the following items on the School Version likely refer to a single factor, the child's not fulfilling the teacher's expectations for following directions: "Does not listen to or follow directions," "Needs oral questions and directions frequently repeated," "Does not remain on task," and "Fails to follow necessary steps in math problems." Even items associated with hyperactivity-impulsivity may well refer to the same factor: "Makes unnecessary comments or noises in the classroom," "Leaves seat without permission," and "Fails to follow a routine."

Using a variety of phrases, many items on both scales rate impulsivity repeatedly. From the School Version: "Grabs things away from others," "Makes unnecessary comments or noises," "Interrupts the teacher," and "Interrupts other students." From the Home Version: "Intrudes on others," "Does not wait his/her turn in activities," and "Has accidents which are the result of impulsive or careless behavior."

Some scale items lack clarity; for example, "Does not read or follow written directions." The rater is directed to record a "0" if the child "Does not engage in this behavior." Should the child who can read but does not receive the same score? And what score should be given to a child who can or does read but does not often attend to written directions?

Scale items do not always make sense or refer to behaviors found among normal children. How can children who master the spoken language of their linguistic communities on their own and before they enter school have deficits in short-term memory? The short-term deficits this clinician has observed have occurred only when children required to complete nonsense tasks, such as to repeat a series of numbers backwards or to pronounce nonsense syllables. The child who "Forgets," "Climbs on things," and "Bothers others while they are trying to play" seems normal to this reviewer.

Of particular concern are the many items on the School Version related to language learning and reading that also appear as intervention goals in The Attention Deficit Intervention Manual. "Omits, adds, or substitutes words when writing" are natural parts of the writing and reading process.

The 400+ pages in each of the teacher and parent Intervention Manuals suggest classroom and home teachings related to the most common characteristics of ADHD, as found in the DSM-IV. Indeed, these manuals constitute an intervention smorgasbord: More than 6,000 interventions (*dos* and *don't*s) are recommended for parents; and more than 5,000 are suggested for teachers. In neither case, however, is the parent or teacher provided any basis for ranking the importance of a specific behavior to address nor guided in the selection of the most appropriate interventions for a specific behavior.

Flawed learning principles underlie many of the home and classroom interventions presented in the manuals. For example, the goal of Behavior 66 for the teacher is to improve the child's short-term memory. In fact, the capacity of short-term memory in humans is limited (Miller, 1956). Trying to increase a child's short-term memory is futile, as is attempting to teach a monkey to fly. Neither could children learn to speak a language if they lacked auditory memory, the focus of Behavior 63 interventions. If children lacked visual memory, they could not distinguish dogs from cats or Fords from Hondas. The child diagnosed with an auditory memory problem is the same child who has no difficulty remembering baseball "stats" reported on yesterday's evening news, although the same child may not recall a list of nonsense words.

The vast majority of children who will be rated by these scales will have a history of reading failure; many will be nonfluent spellers. They are children who have received intensive instruction in word recognition (word attack), which includes phonic rules and structural analysis skills. The many hours of teaching word skills and practicing word drills have not significantly increased their reading or spelling achievement. The reading and spelling interventions recommended in the Intervention Manuals, however, offer only more of this same pedagogy that seldom helps children with learning difficulties to improve language fluency.

SUMMARY. Clinicians, parents, and teachers guided by learning principles based upon behaviorist psychology will embrace the Attention Deficit Disorders Evaluation Scale and use many of the thousands of interventions found in the Intervention Manuals. Professionals guided by learning principles based upon cognitive psychology, however, will likely look elsewhere for diagnostic and instructional tools.

The DSM-IV states that as many as 5% of school-age children may have an Attention-Deficit/Hyperactivity Disorder. No specific physical features, however, have ever been associated with this condition, and according to DSM-IV (American Psychiatric Association, 1994), "There are no laboratory tests that have been established as diagnostic in the clinical assessment [of this disorder]" (p. 81). Thus the majority of academic deficits among children and adolescents, attributed to ADHD by conventional wisdom, cannot be directly attributable to any mental, neurological, or physiological difference, disorder, or dysfunction.

Understanding how humans perceive the world, comprehend in general, and learn language in particular (Smith, 1994) offers nonpareil insights for identifying important teaching goals and using psychologically and linguistically sound instructional strategies to increase academic performance and improve home and school behavior.

REVIEWER'S REFERENCES

Miller, G. A. (1956). The magic number seven, plus or minus two: Some limitation on our capacity for processing information. *Psychological Review, 63*, 81–92.

American Psychiatric Association. (1994). *Diagnostic and statistical manual of mental disorders* (4th ed.). Washington, DC: APA.

Smith, F. (1994). *Understanding reading: A psycholinguistic analysis of reading and learning to read* (5th ed.). Hillsdale, NJ: Lawrence Erlbaum Associates.

Review of the Attention Deficit Disorders Evaluation Scale, Second Edition by BEVERLY M. KLECKER, Assistant Professor, Department of

Administration, Counseling, and Educational Studies, College of Education, Eastern Kentucky University, Richmond, KY:

DESCRIPTION. The Attention Deficit Disorders Evaluation Scale (ADDES), Second Edition, was developed to aid in the diagnosis of Attention-Deficit/Hyperactivity Disordered (ADHD) children and adolescents. This second edition was revised to measure the three dimensions of ADHD defined by the American Psychiatric Association's *Diagnostic and Statistical Manual, 4th Edition* (DSM-IV; American Psychiatric Association, 1994). These three are (a) Predominantly Inattentive Type, (b) Predominantly Hyperactive-Impulsive Type, and (c) Combined Type.

A diagnosis of ADHD requires that the symptoms be persistent for at least 6 months and that the symptoms be present in two or more situations (American Psychiatric Association, 1994). Two versions of the test are provided, ADDES-Home (60 items) and ADDES-School (46 items). An observer, parent, or educator familiar with the child rates each item on a 5-point scale. The descriptors for the scale points are frequency referenced and range from *does not engage in the behavior* (0), to *occurs one to several times per month* (1), *week* (2), *day* (3), or *hour* (4).

SAMPLES FOR TEST VALIDATION AND NORMING. For the ADDES-School Version, normative data were gathered from 5,795 students, aged 4.0 to 19 years from 137 public school systems in 30 states. The normative sample for the ADDES-Home Version consisted of 2,415 children and youth aged 3 to 20 years from 23 states. Both normative samples were reflective of national population demographics by sex, race, residence, geographic area, father's occupation, and mother's occupation. Ten age-sex standardization groups were developed for each of the tests. Both normative samples include attention-deficit and nonattention-deficit participants.

RELIABILITY. Three measures of reliability are described: test-retest, interrater, and internal consistency. Test-retest (30-day interval between tests) correlations are presented by norm group (10 for each instrument). Reliabilities range from .88 to .97 for the School version and .88 to .93 for the Home version. These reliabilities are satisfactory and are indicative of the stability of the scales.

Two hundred and thirty-seven pairs of educators rated one or more of the 462 students randomly selected from the standardization sample. Pearson Product Moment correlation coefficients for pairs of raters range from .81 to .90 for age levels. One hundred seventy-two pairs of parents were used to measure interrater reliability for the Home version. Pearson Product Moment correlation coefficients for this group range from .80 to .84. Interrater reliability coefficients are presented by age group.

KR-20 measures of internal consistency for both the Inattentive and Hyperactive-Impulsive subscales (for both the Home and School versions of the instruments) exceed .90. It is surprising to find KR-20 values for internal consistency here; no further explanation of how the rating scales were dichotomized for this analysis is presented in the manual. Cronbach's alpha would be the appropriate internal consistency reliability measure for these rating scale data (0–4).

The presentation of the standard error of measurement by subgroup by norm group indicates an attention to detail that is not consistent with the description of how the *SEM* should be used to interpret raw scores. It is troublesome to this reviewer that the Profile Sheet provides a blank for the standard error of measurement but does not encourage the scorer to take the *essential* step of creating a band around the raw score that will indicate a 68% probability of capturing the true measure of Inattentive, or Hyperactive-Impulsive. Leaving the raw score uncorrected and then translating it into a single standard score implies a level of measurement that is not possible. This could be corrected easily and would ensure the ethical reporting of test scores (National Council on Measurement in Education, 1995).

VALIDITY. The content validity question for this test is, "Do the items describe ADHD as defined by the American Psychiatric Association's *Diagnostic and Statistical Manual of Mental Disorders, 4th Edition* (DSM-IV)?" Items were reviewed and refined by 82 private and educational diagnosticians. The items were then field tested with a fairly large sample ($N = 152$) of teachers for the School version, and an unspecified number of parents randomly selected from 12 school districts in Missouri for the Home version. The test manual identifies items in each version of the test that have face validity when compared with the APA's 18 criteria for ADHD.

Factor analysis was used to confirm empirically the two theoretical subscales, Inattentive and Hyperactive-Impulsive. The author offered further proof for construct validity through statistical evidence of the instruments' ability to discriminate between ADHD and non-ADHD participants. Evidence of criterion validity (concurrent) was presented by reporting statistically significant correlations with both Conners' Teacher Rating Scale and the Conners' Parent Rating Scale.

TEST ADMINISTRATION. The instructions for administering the test are clear with the time required (15–20 minutes) delineated. The instructions for hand scoring are straightforward. Norm tables separated by sex and age are provided for easy, specific reference.

SUMMARY. The Attention Deficit Disorders Evaluation Scale, Second Edition has good psychometric properties. Large samples were used to develop the test and convenient norm groups of ample size are provided for reference. Directions for administering and scoring are clear. A provision for including the standard error of measurement to create a band around the raw score should be included for ethical score reporting. There is an additional caution. The APA's DSM-IV definition of ADHD clearly states that the diagnostic behavior pattern must be observed over a period of at least 6 months and in two or more settings. To adequately diagnose ADHD in children, (a) the two versions *must* be used together to obtain measures from both school and home (the author does not make this clear), and (b) the tests must be repeated at an interval greater than 6 months. The "frequency scale" does not measure this "consistency across time" dimension.

The Parent's Guide and Intervention Manual offered with the tests are too fragmented to be either readable or useful. In several instances the solution suggested merely restates the problem with a "don't do it" caveat. The supplementals would be far more helpful with age-specific scenarios and practical examples. With minor changes, this test could be a very useful screening instrument for Attention Deficit/Hyperactivity Disorder.

REVIEWER'S REFERENCES

American Psychiatric Association. (1994). *Diagnostic and statistical manual of mental disorders* (4th ed.). Washington, DC: APA.
National Council on Measurement in Education. (1995). *Code of professional responsibilities in educational measurement.* Washington, DC: NCME.

[28]
Attention Deficit Disorders Evaluation Scale: Secondary-Age Student.

Purpose: "Designed to provide a measure of those characteristics of Attention-Deficit/Hyperactivity Disorder."
Population: Ages 11.5–19.
Publication Dates: 1996.
Acronym: ADDES-S.
Scores, 3: Inattentive, Hyperactive/Impulsive, Total Percentile Rank.
Administration: Group.
Forms, 3: Home, School, DSM-IV.
Price Data, 1999: $160.50 per complete kit including 50 Pre-Referral Attention Deficit Checklists, 50 Intervention Strategies documentation forms, 50 School Version rating forms, 50 Home Version rating forms, 50 ADDES/DSM-IV forms, School Version technical manual, Home Version technical manual, Attention Deficit Disorders Intervention Manual: Secondary-Age Student, and Parent's Guide; $26 per 50 Pre-Referral Attention Deficit Checklists; $26 per 50 intervention Strategies documentation forms; $31 per 50 rating forms (specify School Version or Home Version); $20 per 50 ADDES/DSM-IV forms; $12.50 per technical manual (specify School Version or Home Version); $26 per Attention Deficit Disorders Intervention Manual: Secondary-Age Student; $19 per Parent's Guide; $35 per computerized Quick Score (IBM or Mac); $149 per computerized (IBM only) Parent's Guide to Attention Deficit Disorders.
Time: (15–20) minutes.
Comments: Ratings by parents/guardians and/or teachers.
Author: Stephen B. McCarney.
Publisher: Hawthorne Educational Services, Inc.

Review of the Attention Deficit Disorders Evaluation Scale: Secondary-Age Student by HELEN KITCHENS, Associate Professor, Troy State University—Montgomery, Montgomery, AL:

The Attention Deficit Disorders Evaluation Scale: Secondary-Age Student (ADDES-S) was developed to measure the existence of Attention-Deficit/Hyperactivity Disorders (ADHD) in the secondary-age student. The technical manual reported the prevalence of ADHD "as occurring in 3 to 5 percent of school-aged children with the disorder occurring more frequently in males" (p. 4). The ADDES-S was designed to document characteristics of ADHD (inattention and hyperactivity-impulsivity) as set forth in the *Diagnostic and Statistical Manual of Mental Disorders, Fourth Edition.*

Two versions of the ADDES-S assess the characteristics of inattention and hyperactivity-impulsivity: One version solicits observational information from teachers and others in the school setting with primary observational opportunities (ADDES—Secondary-Age Student Version) and the second version solicits observational information from parents (ADDES—Home Version). The Secondary-Age Student version is composed of 60 items, and the Home version has 46 items. The Secondary-Age Student and Home Versions assess the same basic behaviors, but are phrased so that they reflect activities that occur in those particular settings. Each version can be completed in approximately 15 to 20 minutes. For each statement on the ADDES-S there is a scale that ranges from *does not engage in the behavior* (0) to *occurs one to several times per month* (1), *per week* (2), or *per hour* (4).

All versions of the ADDES-S are easily scored by hand. Raw scores are summed for each subscale and converted to standard scores using the conversion tables which for the Secondary-Age Student Version, are normed on 10 age-sex groups ranging from 11.5 years to 19 years. The standardization group for the ADDES Home Version provides 10 age-sex groups ranging from 3.0 years to 20.0 years for normative comparison. Standard scores are summed and converted to an overall percentile score. The subscale standard scores and the percentile are recorded on the Profile. Standard scores have a mean of 10 and a standard deviation of 3. Standard scores between 7 and 13 are considered average. Standard scores at 6 or below or above 13 are more than one standard deviation from the mean. Subscale standard scores below 4 are two or more standard deviations from the mean and are considered to indicate a *serious level of concern.*

Normative data for the Secondary-Age Student Version are based on 1,280 students from 92 school systems, representing 19 states. Nine hundred and one teachers rated the students. The Home Version is normed on 2,415 children and youth from 23 states with 3,932 parents or guardians rating their children.

The Secondary-Age Student and Home Versions have good evidence of reliability. The Secondary-Age Student and Home Versions have estimates of subscale reliability using test-retest, internal consistency, and interrater reliability. Test-retest correlations over 30 calendar days ranged from .89 to .96 for the Secondary-Age Student Version, and .88 to .93 for the Home Version. Internal consistency reliability was .98 for each of the subscales and .99 for the entire scale on the Secondary-Age Student Version, and .96 for each of the subscales and .98 for the entire scale for the Home Version. Interrater reliability coefficients ranged from .82 to .91 for all age levels for the Secondary-Age Student Version, and from .80 to .84 for all age levels for the Home Version. The standard error of measurement is reported for each age-sex group on both Versions.

Content, construct, diagnostic, and concurrent validity evidence is reported for both versions of the ADDES. Support for content validity of each version is based on a thorough review of the literature and input from 82 private and educational diagnosticians and special education personnel to establish the item pool. For the Home Version, parents of Attention-Deficit/Hyperactivity Disordered children were also asked for their input.

Construct validity was examined by factor analysis using principal components analysis and varimax rotation. On the ADDES-S Version, the Inattention subscale's primary subfactor is made up of questions regarding difficulty in concentration and following directions, the second subfactor is related to academic study habits, and the third relates to written assignments. The Hyperactive-Impulsive subscale did not break into identifiable subfactors indicating that this scale represents a single factor. For the ADDES—Home Version, the Inattentive subscale's primary subfactor relates to concentration and following directions and other subfactors relate to academic study habits, concentration, and memory. The Hyperactive-Impulsive scale breaks down into hyperactivity (physical elements such as running and climbing, and restlessness) and impulsiveness.

Diagnostic validity for the Secondary-Age Student and Home Versions was considered by using results from a random sample from the normative group. Scores for these persons were compared with those from a corresponding group diagnosed as having ADHD. The mean total subscale scores of the ADHD group were much lower than were the results for the randomly selected non-ADHD group. Raw score mean differences between the two groups were significant at the .001 level for all subscales and the percentile score.

Subscale scores from the Secondary Age-Student Version were correlated with subscales on the Conners' Teacher Rating Scale-28, the Attention Deficit Hyperactivity Disorder Test (ADHDT) and Child Behavior Checklist—Teacher Report Form. All three comparisons yielded coefficients exceeding the .001 level of significance and ranged from .417 to .801 for comparisons with the Conners' Teacher Rating Scale-28, from .76 to .93 for the ADHDT, and from .511 to .872 for subscales on the Child Behavior Checklist—Teacher Report Form, which measured the same behavior as the ADDES-S.

Subscale scores from the Home Version were correlated with subscales from the Conners' Parent Rating Scale-48, the Conners' Parent Rating Scale-93, the Children's Attention and Adjustment Survey—Home Form, and the Child Behavior Checklist. All four comparisons yielded coefficients exceeding the .01 level of significance for subscales measuring similar constructs.

Two separate technical manuals provide information on reliability, validity, administration, scoring, and interpretation for each version of the ADDES. Additionally, there are appendices that provide tables for converting raw scores to subscale standard scores, and subscale standard scores to percentile scores. The interpretation section includes step-by-step information on how to develop goals and objectives from the rating scale items. Interventions appropriate in facilitating client improvement can be found in *The Attention Deficit Disorders Intervention Manual* and *The Parent's Guide to Attention Deficit Disorders*. Particularly important for clinicians is the provision for writing goals and objectives from scale items. Though *The Attention Deficit Disorders Intervention Manual* and *The Parent's Guide to Attention Deficit Disorders* must be purchased separately, they supply wonderful ideas for the parent and clinician to explore in order to develop a program of behavioral intervention.

The ADDES-S is a useful tool to be used in conjunction with other information in identifying behaviors related to inattention and impulsivity-hyperactivity. The brevity of both versions makes them appealing to both parents or guardians and educators and other school personnel who are asked to provide input. However, it is doubtful that clinicians or school systems would choose to purchase the ADDES-S as an instrument to measure inattention and impulsivity-hyperactivity considering that there is so little difference between it and the Attention Deficit Disorders Evaluation Scale (27). Based on information from Hawthorne Educational Services, Inc., the ADDES-S was created because secondary educators had expressed dissatisfaction with including younger children in the standardization sample. No items were changed between the ADDES and the ADDES-S though one quantifier (*1 to several times a day*) was omitted on the ADDES-S. As Hawthorne made only one change in the instrument, and the representation of adolescents in the group is about the same, why would clinicians or school systems buy this scale covering only adolescents when they can use the ADDES, which covers a much broader age range (3 to 18)? With school budgets being extremely tight, and clinicians also being mindful of their bottom line, it is likely that the ADDES-S will receive little use. Hawthorne is to be commended, however, for their responsiveness to concerns expressed by secondary school educators.

Review of the Attention Deficit Disorders Evaluation Scale: Secondary-Age Student by JOSEPH G. LAW, JR., Associate Professor of Behavioral Studies and Educational Technology, University of South Alabama, Mobile, AL:

The Attention Deficit Disorders Evaluation Scale: Secondary-Age Student (ADDES-S) contains 60 items that are designed to measure behaviors associated with the DSM-IV diagnostic category of attention-deficit/hyperactivity disorder (ADHD). Teachers are asked to rate a student's behavior on a 4-point scale ranging from *Does not engage in the behavior* to *One to several times per hour*. Raw scores are converted to standard scores and percentiles and plotted on a profile sheet. There are separate subscales for Inattentiveness, Hyperactivity-Impulsivity, and a Total score. The 43-page manual contains an introduction, reliability and validity data, and instructions for administering, scoring, and interpretation. There is a one-page list of references and a brief discussion of ADHD criteria.

The ADDES-S follows closely the publication of the ADDES (McCarney, 1989; 27). The first edition (ages 4.5—18 years) contained 60 items on the School version and was normed on 4,876 students who were rated by 1,567 teachers. The ADDES-S covers a more restricted age range

(11.5 to 19 years) and was normed on 1,280 students who were rated by 901 teachers. Students included those with and without ADHD diagnoses. There is also a new Home version of the ADDES (McCarney, 1995), which is not covered by this review as well as the *Attention Deficit Disorders Intervention Manual* (McCarney, 1994), which is designed to assist adults working with ADHD children and adolescents.

There is much to commend in the ADDES-S. The manual is well organized and easy to use. Administration and scoring instructions are clear and concise. There is a helpful chart that assists the user in comparing individual items to specific DSM-IV criteria for ADHD. The manual also contains a brief discussion of the limitations of the instrument and an outline for comprehensive assessment of ADHD. One positive feature has been removal of the Attention Deficit Disorders title from the top of the teacher rating sheet. It is now simply labeled as the Secondary-Age Student Rating Form. This is less likely to overtly bias or offend teachers who complete the form or others who may see the protocol in a file or on a teacher's desk. The individual items appear to be shorter, more clearly written, and less likely to evoke biased reporting from teachers. Another positive feature is that the norms are listed separately by age and sex.

The manual reports a study of 121 students retested at 30-day intervals. The test-retest reliability estimates for the Inattentive subscale ranged from .90 to .96; .89 to .93 for the Hyperactive-Impulsive subscale; and .90 to .94 for the Total. For a group of 154 students the interrater reliability coefficient was reported as ranging from .82 to .91. Validity data include correlations with instruments such as the Conners-28, with ranges from .42 to .80. The construct validity of the ADDES-S was evaluated using a principal components factor analysis with varimax rotation. The author found three factors on the Inattentive subscale that were described as items focusing on difficulty concentrating and following directions, academic study habits, and problems with written assignments. The Hyperactive-Impulsive subscale appeared to comprise only one factor.

The author has provided a helpful form to assist in verifying ADHD characteristics. The horizontal axis of the form lists the DSM-IV categories for ADHD and the columns list the ADDES-S School and Home version item numbers, which correspond to the diagnostic categories. One limitation is that no such form is available to assist in identifying the three factors of the Inattentive subscale derived from the factor analysis reported in the manual. A further possible concern is the high correlation (.95) between the Inattentive and Hyperactivity-Impulsivity subscales. An earlier review of the ADDES (Collins, 1995) recommended an oblique rotation factor analysis because of the high correlation among the original three subscales, but the author reports performing a varimax rotation instead for the current instrument.

Generally speaking, the norms are representative of the U.S. population. However, students ages 15 to 18 years appear to be underrepresented. For example, 584 males were rated for the ages 11, 12, 13, and 14 years. For the 4-year period of 15 to 18 years there were only 112 students. Thus, 84% of the male norms covered the earlier ages (11–14 years) whereas only 16% covered the later adolescent ages of 15 to 18 years. Females seem to be similarly underrepresented in the older age groups. Conceptually, the need for an ADHD rating scale for the adolescent age range is a very good idea. We would expect to see different manifestations of ADHD in infants, toddlers, primary, and secondary age children. However, with the limited number of students over 15 years of age in the norm group clinicians may wish to supplement this scale with other sources of information for late adolescents. The author's recommendation of a comprehensive approach to assessment is certainly appropriate.

SUMMARY. The Attention Deficit Disorders Evaluation Scale: Secondary-Age Student is a brief, user-friendly rating instrument with good levels of score reliability and promising validity data reported in the manual. This rating instrument will enable clinicians and educators to gather a wealth of descriptive and quantitative data on the behavior of secondary-age students. It will assist in identifying and intervening on behalf of students with ADHD. Future research on the use of this instrument needs to focus on its sensitivity to academic and medical treatment approaches as well as the rate of false positives and negatives.

REVIEWER'S REFERENCES

McCarney, S. B. (1989). Attention Deficit Disorders Evaluation Scale School Version. Columbia, MO: Hawthorne Educational Services, Inc.

Collins, D. (1995). [Review of the Attention Deficit Disorders Evaluation Scale.] In J. C. Conoley & J. C. Impara (Eds.), *The twelfth mental measurements yearbook* (pp. 94–96). Lincoln, NE: Buros Institute of Mental Measurements.

McCarney, S. B. (1995). Attention Deficit Disorders Evaluation Scale Home Version (2nd ed.). Columbia, MO: Hawthorne Educational Services, Inc.

[29]
Attention-Deficit Scales for Adults.

Purpose: Designed as an objective measure of attention deficit in adults.

Population: Adults.

Publication Date: 1996.

Acronym: ADSA.

Scores, 11: Attention-Focus/Concentration, Interpersonal, Behavior-Disorganized Activity, Coordination, Academic Theme, Emotive, Consistency/Long Term, Childhood, Negative-Social, Internal Consistency, Total.

Administration: Individual.

Price Data, 1997: $55 per complete kit including manual (30 pages), and 25 instrument/scoring/profile sets; $25 per 25 additional sets; $30 per manual.

Time: Untimed.

Comments: A 54-item, Likert-scale questionnaire to be administered in a clinical setting; self-report.

Authors: Santo James Triolo and Kevin Richard Murphy.

Publisher: Brunner/Mazel, Inc.

Review of the Attention-Deficit Scales for Adults by JOSEPH G. LAW, JR., Associate Professor of Behavioral Studies and Educational Technology, University of South Alabama, Mobile, AL:

The Attention-Deficit Scales for Adults (ADSA) is a 54-item self-report designed to assess symptoms of attention-deficit/hyperactivity disorder (ADHD) in adults. Each respondent describes his or her behavior on each item as "Never," "Seldom," "Sometimes," "Often," and "Always." The responses are easily scored by tearing off the cover sheet and filling in boxes for the nine subscales and the total column. Raw scores are then plotted on a separate profile sheet and transformed into standard scores with a mean of 50 and a standard deviation of 10. The profile sheet also displays scores as percentile ranks. The subscales include an internal consistency measure and total scores as well as nine clinical subscales labeled as: Attention-Focus/Concentration, Interpersonal, Behavior-Disorganized Activity, Coordination, Academic-Theme, Emotive, Consistency/Long-Term, Childhood, and Negative-Social. The names and item content of each subscale were developed to reflect the authors' concern about the multiple effects of ADHD on the lives of adults.

The ADSA was normed on 306 adults, but the authors failed to specify in the manual the age range of their sample. It was indicated that all members of the norm group were 17 years of age or older, had IQs of 80 or higher, no childhood history of attention or hyperactivity problems, no history of alcohol or drug abuse, and no felony convictions. The reported rationale was to duplicate the average population as much as possible. The mean age was reported as 33.95 years (SD = 11.6), but no upper age limit or further breakdown by age was evident in the manual. As a test subject diverges in age from 33 years the clinician will have difficulty in determining how appropriate the norms are for that person. This may be an important limitation. This is unfortunate because the manual contains a wealth of useful information on the norm group that should assist the user in applying the test in clinical use.

The 30-page manual reports internal consistency statistics on the ADSA. Cronbach's alpha for the 54 items is .8912 with a split-half correlation of .812. Cronbach's alpha for the nine subscales ranged from .0196 for the Childhood subscale to .8215 for the Emotive subscale. The Academic Theme subscale has an alpha of only -.1124. Although they may provide some useful information, Childhood and Academic Theme only have 2 items per subscale, hence their low reliability. Unfortunately, there were no reported test-retest reliability statistics. Validity information is limited, but promising. In a validation study with 87 subjects diagnosed as having ADHD, the mean total score was 45 points higher than that of the 306-person normative group.

The manual contains the results of a stepwise discriminant analysis predicting group membership of the nine ADSA subscales. Four subscales were identified by the step-wise procedure: Consistency/Long-Term, Attention-Focus/Concentration, Behavior-Disorganized Activity, and Negative-Social. These four subscales had the discriminant power to identify correctly 90.8% of the norm group as non-ADHD and incorrectly classified 9.2% as ADHD. For the 87 clinical subjects reported above, 82% were correctly placed in the ADHD category and 18% were erroneously placed in the normal (non-ADHD) category. Even though these four subscales have the greatest discriminating power, the other subscales may assist the clinician by providing clues into the clients' perceptions of their symptoms. A review of individual item responses on scales such as Emotive, Academic Theme, and Interpersonal may give additional insight. The short length of the ADSA facilitates such a process.

The authors provide six case studies with accompanying profiles to illustrate the use of the ADSA in identifying ADHD in adults. These are well written and helpful in assisting the test user to incorporate the results into a comprehensive diagnostic approach. Unfortunately, on the first two profiles the names of the subscales are not listed, making interpretation difficult for the novice. There are a few small problems with the ADSA manual. For example, as noted earlier, there is no evident report on the upper age limit of the 306-person norm group. A clinical validation study reports 87 subjects in one table and 89 subjects on another page. It is not clear from the manual if these are two different groups or the result of a typographical error. The mean IQ of 111 for the norm group is higher than the national average. The geographical representation of the normative subjects was heavily weighted to the northeastern and southeastern regions of the United States.

SUMMARY. This is a brief and easily administered rating scale with potential use as part of a comprehensive adult evaluation. It draws attention to the need for a broad-based process in assessing adults. The authors stress the importance of using the ADSA as part of a process that includes ruling out physical abnormalities, carrying out clinical and collateral interviews, and other procedures. Future research will be needed on the validity and reliability of scores from the ADSA. Studies of the test-retest reliability of this scale as well as its sensitivity to the effects of various treatment approaches are recommended. Because of the lack of ADHD-specific scales for adults, the potential utility of this instrument for the study of ADHD in adults far outweighs its limitations. Practicing clinicians are encouraged to include it in their assessment procedures and to begin gathering data for further research on the topic of adult ADHD.

Review of the Attention-Deficit Scales for Adults by JAMES C. REED, Chief Psychologist, St. Luke's Hospital, New Bedford, MA:

The 54 items that comprise the Attention-Deficit Scales for Adults (ADSA) pertain to the syndrome of Attention-Deficit/Hyperactivity Disorder (AD/HD). The respondent is asked to check one of five categories for each item: Never, Seldom, Sometimes, Often, or Always. Most of the items are worded so that marking "Always" indicates a significant AD/HD-related problem. There are, however, 11 items where the scoring is reversed (i.e., "Never" indicates significant problems, and "Always" suggests no AD/HD-related problems). For example, Item 14 reads, "I finish the home projects I start." The marking of "Never" would suggest problems, and marking "Always" suggests no AD/HD problems.

A total score is obtained but nine content subscales can also be scored. The scores can be converted to T scores (mean of 50 and standard deviation of 10) and percentile ranks. The T scores can be plotted on an "MMPI-like" format and a graphic representation of the profile can be made. "The subscales are named and numbered as follows: (I) Attention-Focus/Concentration; (II) Interpersonal; (III) Behavior-Disorganized Activity; (IV) Coordination; (V) Academic Theme; (VI) Emotive; (VII) Consistency/Long Term; (VIII) Childhood; and (IX) Negative-Social" (manual, p. 1). Each scale has items that are unique to it, but it also has items that are shared or overlap with other scales. To illustrate: Subscale I, Attention-Focus/Concentration, has nine items that are unique, one item it shares with Scale VI (Emotive), and two items it shares with Scale VII (Consistency/Long Term). The scale items are based on content validity (e.g., Items 2 and 5 are unique to Scale I, and they are "I tend to daydream" and "I have trouble putting my thoughts down on paper"). Items 10 and 37 appears on both Scale I and VII. They are "Tasks which need persistence frustrate me" and "I need to be reminded of my daily schedule/duties or appointments." The total number of items per scale is variable. Scale V has two items—1 unique and 1 shared with Scale VIII. Scale III has 23 items—11 unique, 3 shared with Scale VI, 7 shared with Scale VII, and 1 with Scale IX. For the Total Scale, a split-half (odd versus even) reliability coefficient was .81, Cronbach alpha was .89. However, as might be anticipated, there was wide variability in the alpha coefficients among the subscales. Four coefficients varied from .71 to .82, three were between .46 and .57, and the remaining two were .02 and .11. The normative sample consisted of 306 persons (139 females and 167 males) who met the following criteria: (a) 17 years or older; (b) No childhood history of problems with attention or hyperactivity; (c) An IQ of 80 or above as estimated by the Shipley Institute of Living Scale (1940); (d) No reported history of drug and/or alcohol abuse; and (e) No reported history of a felony conviction (manual, p. 3). Descriptive characteristics with respect to marital status, ethnicity, Hollingshead Index of Social Position, etc., are given in the manual. The majority of the subjects came from the northeastern and southeastern region of the United States. States included were Georgia, Florida, Massachusetts, Alabama, New York, and New Hampshire (manual, p. 3).

There were 97 clinical subjects previously diagnosed as having AD/HD who participated in an effort to validate the scales. For Total Score, the mean for the clinical group exceeded the norm group's mean by 45 points, a highly significant difference. For each of the scales the mean for the clinical group was higher than the mean for the normative group, but the significance of the differences was not reported. A discriminate analysis showed that 91% of the normative group were accurately classified, and 82% of the clinical group were accurately classified. The authors state "that the ADSA can be a very useful instrument to help identify adults with AD/HD. This is especially so considering that over 88% of cases were classified correctly by the combined scores of only four subscales, without the aid of history, diagnostic interview, collateral findings, and other diagnostic techniques/procedures" (manual, p. 9). ADSA also has a consistency check. There are four pairs of items that ask almost the same question with a variation in wording. Data presented indicate "that intrasubject consistency can be assumed" (manual, p. 6).

GENERAL COMMENTS. There are some limitations that the potential user should consider. First, the usefulness of the ADSA is limited by the geographical restrictions of the normative sample. The subjects were primarily from the northeast and southeast, and whether or not the findings would hold for another geographical area is open to question. Second, although the items on this scale refer to behaviors associated with AD/HD, it is a stretch to assume that nine reliable subscales can be derived from 54 items, particularly when

there are so few items on some of the scale (2 on Scale V and 3 on Scale IV). Furthermore, four of the scales have alpha coefficients of .5 or lower, and these are unacceptably low. Third, the reported classification rate for the ADSA is high, but whether this rate would hold with cross validation is another question. It is one problem to distinguish between members of a well-screened normal group and patients in an accurately diagnosed clinical group. There is an additional problem in clinical practice, which is not only to differentiate an AD/HD patient from normal, but also to make the differential diagnosis between AD/HD and, say, conduct disorder, schizophrenia, mental retardation, etc. If one were to administer the ADSA to these last named clinical samples, how many of each would score in the range indicative of AD/HD? The problem is one of test sensitivity as well as test specificity.

SUMMARY. The ASDA scale shows promise. It is in need of further research. The research should be directed toward obtaining a more representative normative sample, a validation of the subscales, and a more definitive evaluation of its sensitivity. In its present form, the ADSA has not been as thoroughly developed as the Adult Attention Deficit Disorders Evaluation Scale (McCarney & Anders, 1996; 27), and the clinician might want to consider this scale as an alternative.

REVIEWER'S REFERENCE

McCarney, S. B., & Anderson, P. D. (1996). Adult Attention Deficit Disorders Evaluation Scale. Columbia, MO: Hawthorne Educational Services, Inc.

[30]
Attention-Deficit/Hyperactivity Disorder Test.

Purpose: Designed to "contribute to the diagnosis of students with Attention-Deficit/Hyperactivity Disorder."
Population: Ages 3–23.
Publication Date: 1995.
Acronym: ADHDT.
Scores: 3 subtests (Hyperactivity, Impulsivity, Inattention), plus ADHD Quotient.
Administration: Individual.
Price Data, 1999: $79 per complete kit including manual (46 pages) and 50 summary/response forms in storage box; $39 per 50 summary/response forms; $42 per manual.
Time: (5–10) minutes.
Comments: Ratings by teacher, teacher's aide, or parent.

Author: James E. Gilliam.
Publisher: PRO-ED.

Review of the Attention-Deficit/Hyperactivity Disorder Test by ROBERT J. MILLER, Professor of Special Education, Minnesota State University, Mankato, Mankato, MN:

The Attention-Deficit/Hyperactivity Disorder Test (ADHDT) is a short, concise, standardized, and norm-referenced test instrument designed to contribute to the diagnosis of persons with Attention-Deficit/Hyperactivity Disorder (ADHD). The manual suggests the ADHDT was designed with five purposes including "(a) to identify persons with ADHD, (b) to assess persons referred for behavioral problems, (c) to document progress in the problem areas as a consequence of special intervention programs, (d) to target goals for change and intervention on the student's individualized education program (IEP), and (e) to measure ADHD in research projects" (manual, p. 5). The ADHDT is designed for use either at home or at school by teachers, other professionals, or parents. This test should be completed by an individual who is very knowledgeable of the subject's behavior. The amount of time necessary to administer this behavioral checklist is approximately 5 to 10 minutes in most cases.

The instrument consists of 36 items that comprise behaviors and characteristics of persons with ADHD. Each of the 36 items is gender neutral and consists of a simple statement or phrase of from one to seven words. The person rating the behavior of the subject is to read each short phrase and rate the subject's behavior on a 3-point Likert-type scale ranging from a rating of 0 = *Not a Problem*, 1 = *Mild Problem*, and 2 = *Severe Problem*. The 36 items are arranged in three subtests including: Hyperactivity (13 items), Impulsivity (10 items), and Inattention (13 items). A profile of the subject is created by converting raw scores to standard scores and percentiles for each of the three subtests as well as an overall ADHD Quotient for the subject. In the case of the subtests, the mean standard score has been set at 10 with a standard deviation at 3. For the overall ADHD Quotient, the mean is 100 with a standard deviation of 15.

Total size of the sample of subjects in the standardization group was 2,696. Of this number, 1,279 were previously diagnosed with ADHD,

876 had other handicapping conditions, and 541 were persons without disabilities. Although data from the subjects without ADHD were used in validation studies, they were not included in the norms reported in the test manual. As a result, this test was normed on a nationally represented sample of persons with ADHD including 1,279 subjects from 47 states and Canada. Information pertaining to the norm sample was adequate and demonstrated a good representation of persons of varying ethnicity (Native America 2%, Hispanic 9%, Asian 5%, African-American 13%, and Other, Everyone Else 72%) as well as good geographic representation (Northeast 17%, North Central 21%, South 38%, and West 25%). Males were overrepresented compared to females in the norm sample on a ratio of 4 to 1. However, this discrepancy may well be reflective of the overrepresentation of males to females with ADHD (Nussbaum & Bigler, 1990).

The normative study included the results from teachers (N = 638), as well as parents (N = 391) completing the ADHDT. Even though the normative sample includes children and young adults ages 3 through 23, a closer examination of this sample of subjects with ADHD reveals an underrepresentation of some age groups including age 3 or less (N = 8), age 19 (N = 6), age 20 (N = 3), age 21 (N = 6), age 22 (N = 2), and age 23 (N = 4). This underrepresentation of subjects (less than 1% of the normative sample), particularly at the upper range of the norm sample (age 19–23) makes it difficult to gauge whether the population to which the instrument is normed is reflective of any larger population. Secondary aged students (ages 14–23) represented less than 24% of the total norm sample.

The reliability coefficients for the ADHDT are presented in table format using internal consistency and test-retest estimates. For internal consistency estimates, coefficient alphas were computed for all of the subtests of the ADHDT using a subset of 754 of the subjects with ADHD from the normative sample. Alpha reliability coefficients for males and females ranged from .91 to .97. Data were presented by age group including Hyperactivity (subtest) age group 3–7 as well as age group 8–23; Impulsivity (subtest) age group 3–23; Inattention (subtest) age group 3–23; and ADHD Quotient age group 3–23. Data from the normative sample were also used to calculate coefficient alphas by the rater's role: teacher, parent, psychologist/diagnostician, and spouse. Alpha coefficients for these raters ranged from .93 to .97 for teachers, .89 to .96 for parents, .92 to .97 for psychologist/diagnosticians, and .94 to .98 for spouses. Standard errors of measurement for these raters were appropriately low.

The test-retest studies were included in the manual as evidence of reliability. The first study was administered to a sample of 21 subjects (13 males, 8 females, mean age 10-4). The subjects were rated by their teachers at 2-week intervals. Reliability coefficients for this test-retest ranged from .85 to .92. A second study was performed utilizing the ratings given by college students enrolled in teacher education classes in a special education department. Twenty-one undergraduate students majoring in special education rated 15 male and 6 female students with whom they were working as part of their training. Twelve of the subjects had been diagnosed as having ADHD, 4 as emotionally disturbed, and 5 as learning disabled. No information was presented regarding the age of the subjects in this sample. The college students rated their subjects using a one-week interval. Reliability coefficients for this test-retest ranged from .85 to .94. More test-retest data are needed to enhance the evidence of test-retest reliability provided in the current manual. The total sample on which the test-retest reliability is discussed in the test manual is based on a sample of 42 subjects and this sample size is inadequate. No information is provided regarding the grade level distribution of the sample in these studies.

The discussion of test validity provided by the test manual is substantial. The test manual addresses the content validity, the criterion-related validity, and the construct validity of the instrument. The design of test items was derived from the DSM-IV description of ADHD. They were organized into the three categories of impairments specified in the DSM-IV including hyperactivity, impulsivity, and inattention. Item discrimination and item difficulty analyses were conducted to examine the validity of the test items. Item analysis was achieved on 935 cases selected from the normative sample. The test manual suggests that these cases were selected because these were cases that had complete data (all 36 items answered). Based on this analysis, the following median coefficients were obtained in the item-to-total correlations for the ADHDT: Hyperactivity, .71; Impulsivity, .72; and Inattention, .69. These data support the content validity of the ADHDT.

To examine the criterion-related validity of the ADHDT, the authors compared the scores of subjects on the ADHDT to the scores of the subjects on seven other tests used to diagnose ADHD or behavior concerns. In general, the correlations between the ADHDT and each of these instruments strongly support the validity of the ADHDT as an effective instrument for evaluating behavior problems and ADHD.

The ADHDT was designed to discriminate persons with ADHD from persons who do not have ADHD as well as persons with other types of behavioral problems. To address the validity of this important construct of the instrument, a sample of 551 individuals were randomly drawn for the standardization group. Of these, 352 had been diagnosed by school districts as having ADHD, and 178 were diagnosed as not having ADHD but rather as having a variety of other diagnoses including mental retardation, emotional disabilities, or learning disabilities. Statistically significant differences were found between the groups on each subtest as well as the overall ADHD Quotient score. These results would indicate that the ADHDT can be used to discriminate between persons with and without ADHD. The discussion of validity of the instrument found in the test manual is adequate.

SUMMARY. In conclusion, the ADHDT is a well-designed instrument and a valuable tool for the diagnosis of ADHD. It is easy to administer, easy to score, and easy to interpret. The ADHDT may well be the only norm-referenced and standardized instrument that is normed entirely on persons with ADHD. This norm reference group makes the instrument unique and important. These accolades are tempered with two concerns. First, the limited number of subjects utilized in the test-retest studies included in the test manual do not fully demonstrate the consistency of the scores over time. Second, the norm sample needs to be expanded to include a larger sample of secondary-aged students with ADHD. It is the hope of this reviewer that these limitations will be addressed in future editions of this very interesting instrument.

REVIEWER'S REFERENCE

Nussbaum, N., & Bigler, E. (1990). *Identification and treatment of attention deficit disorder.* Austin, TX: PRO-ED.

Review of the Attention-Deficit/Hyperactivity Disorder Test by ANTHONY W. PAOLITTO, Assistant Professor, School Psychology Program, Ohio State University, Columbus, OH:

The most apparent of the stated goals of the Attention-Deficit/Hyperactivity Disorder Test (ADHDT) are identifying individuals with Attention-Deficit/Hyperactivity Disorder (ADHD) and assessment of referred behavior problems. The author further states that the instrument can be useful in documenting the effects of intervention programs; targeting goals for change and intervention on individualized education programs; and for use as an instrument for research.

The ADHDT is a rating scale with a total of 36 behavioral item "stems" to which a rater responds by circling one of three choices corresponding to each behavioral descriptor: "0" if behaviors are not a problem; "1" if a mild problem; "2" if a severe problem. The items on the ADHDT are grouped into three subtests (Hyperactivity, Impulsivity, and Inattention) that can purportedly be utilized for interpretations individually or along with the total score. (These are the "behavior problems" to which the author is referring in the goals above.)

Guidelines for completing the ADHDT record form are clear and direct; examples are provided, and the rating form itself is well laid out and clean. The ADHDT is hand scored, with the summated raw score ratings for each of the three subtests transferred to standard scores. The sum of these three standard scores can then be converted to an overall test score the author refers to as the "ADHD Quotient." Both administration and scoring of an individual student can usually be completed in 15–20 minutes. The scale can be utilized by parents, teachers, psychologists, or other professionals who observe a particular child being rated. Although it could be assumed that a certain degree of familiarity or classroom exposure with the student being rated is necessary, this is not specifically stated in the manual. This relates to an area of potential confusion relative to subjective interpretation of the rating instructions on the ADHDT Record Form: Neither the form nor the manual specifies the time period upon which the ratings are to be based. Thus, a child who has exhibited variable behaviors with regard to a particular stem might be rated either by the rater's subjective summation of the student's behavior over time, or by their most recent impressions. Therefore, different raters evaluating the same child could produce discrepant findings, not dependent upon the behavior being observed.

The item stems for the ADHDT are derived from the DSM-IV diagnostic criteria for ADHD. The author purports that the clear relationship between the ADHDT items and the DSM-IV criteria enhances the rationale for use of the ADHDT. However, the connection to the actual DSM-IV diagnostic criteria is not clearly established. Even though each of the DSM-IV criteria provide concise, operationally defined descriptors of behavior (e.g., "often fidgets with hands or feet or squirms in seat"), ADHDT item stems are shorter, more general or nebulous descriptors of behavior, usually only one to three words in length (e.g., "fidgets"), which can apply to more behavioral events. This consequently can result in lessened diagnostic accuracy and possible overidentification of the target population. Furthermore, DSM-IV criteria consider three classifications of behavior: ADHD Predominantly Inattentive Type, ADHD Predominantly Hyperactive-Impulsive Type, and ADHD Combined Type. The ADHDT's primary interpretive score, the ADHD Quotient, comprises the sum of the three subtests that contribute near equally to the quotient. The ADHD quotient thus does not reflect or support the DSM-IV criteria that allow for specific classification by either of the predominant types (e.g., even obtaining the maximum raw score points on the ADHDT Inattention Subtest could result in an overall "Below Average" ADHDT Quotient).

There is a further issue regarding the ADHD Quotient relating to the ADHDT's contradictory conceptualization of ADHD in general. ADHD should be regarded as a multifaceted clinical diagnosis that is identified by qualified clinicians utilizing a variety of methods and sources of information. Although the author acknowledges this in various places in the manual (p. 13), he at other times suggests or clearly states the contrary (e.g., "the ADHDT can be used with confidence ... to identify persons with ADHD," manual, p. 5). In addition to the use of the quotient, the accompanying "Interpretation Guide" on the front of the Record Form that links the quotient to the "Probability of ADHD" also offers potential to misrepresent findings from the scale. A further inconsistency is a section on the back of the Record Form that lists nonscored "Key Questions." These questions are consistent with those that should be considered in the decision-making process of evaluating ADHD, and should be more operationally integrated within the ADHDT being at least as important as the ratings themselves.

The manual appropriately cautions that test developers use care in demonstrating that their normative sample is representative of the target group for which the instrument is intended (in this case ADHD). Unfortunately, it is this part of the development of the ADHDT that leaves the most unanswered questions and raises the most concern in recommending its use. The author reports the ADHDT was normed on a sample of 1,279 children and young adults with a diagnosis of ADHD. Teacher ratings were obtained from a random computer selection of teachers selected from a marketed mailing list who reported teaching children with ADHD and other disabilities and were asked to rate their ADHD students. No information is provided regarding procedures the teachers were to use to select these students. Neither is there any information regarding what criteria were to have been used to identify ADHD or steps taken to ensure the diagnostic validity of the ADHD sample. Given the wide variety of diagnostic procedures in ADHD identification, its frequency in being assessed outside the school, and related problems in overidentification and misdiagnosis, the establishment of a properly identified sample is critical before standardizing any instrument geared toward specific clinical populations. Unfortunately, the manual provides no evidence to validate that the actual ADHD subjects used in the normative sample are different from any other subjects. The author appears content to have relied on the self-report of a child's teacher or parent to establish a child's ADHD status. The same evidence is also lacking regarding students with other handicapping conditions (learning disabilities, emotional disturbance, mental retardation) that were used in ADHDT validity studies.

Furthermore, many ADHD individuals routinely take stimulant medication to improve their ability to focus and attend, manifesting in improved classroom behavior. Although the demographics reported for the normative sample do report the percentage who were on medication (59%), there is no indication if students were on this medication (or not, as is usually the practice)

when observed for the normative rating. Obviously, the answer to this question greatly impacts the results of this standardization regardless of the samples' validity, especially if the norm group includes students who were on medication, who could present themselves to raters with fewer observable ADHD behaviors.

Estimates of internal consistency were computed using Cronbach's alpha. Reliability estimates for the behavior subtests ranged from .91 to .94 with the ADHDT Quotient obtaining a reliability estimate of .96 for females and .97 for males. Stability coefficients for teacher ratings were computed after a 2-week interval. Although the reliabilities are more than adequate (.85–.92), the sample is too small ($N = 21$) for results to be meaningful.

For reasons previously mentioned, the shortened item stems of the ADHDT do not "seem to capture the essence of ADHD" (manual, p. 23) as the author contends, raising some questions regarding content validity. Several analyses are presented supporting construct validity with moderate to high coefficients reported; however, small samples or limited descriptions of these comparisons are provided. Likewise, criterion-related validity evidence is reported with several comprehensive behavior-rating scales, all with at least moderate relationships. However, all results must be weighed against the previously mentioned shortcomings with the lack of documentation for the subjects used for the standardization sample.

SUMMARY. Perhaps the least attractive attribute of the ADHDT is the calculation and use of the ADHD Quotient as the interpretive score for the instrument (e.g., "if the subject's ADHD Quotient is 90 or above, the person probably has ADHD," (manual, p. 14). ADHD is a clinical diagnosis derived by multiple methods, clinical insight and judgment in conjunction with empirically validated diagnostic criteria, not a set of behaviors that should be summarized by a single score of one rating scale. Although the ADHDT presents itself as an instrument to be used with confidence in identifying or contributing to the diagnosis of ADHD, the lack of clinical validation pertaining to the standardization sample makes the ADHDT a difficult instrument to recommend as part of an ADHD assessment protocol. Likewise, at least equal caution applies in making any interpretations from the individual subtests (i.e., "behavior problems") and even using ADHDT as a screening device should be done conservatively. The easy use of the instrument regarding administration and scoring may allow it to be used as the author recommends for documenting the effects of intervention programs over time and targeting goals for change on individualized education plans. For those desiring to include a rating scale as part of their ADHD evaluation process directly utilizing the DSM-IV diagnostic criteria, the prudent test user should investigate the ADHD Rating Scale-IV (DuPaul, Power, Anastopoulos, & Reid, 1998).

REVIEWER'S REFERENCE

DuPaul, G. J., Power, T. J., Anastopoulos, A. D., & Reid, R. (1998). ADHD Rating Scale-IV. New York: Guilford.

[31]
The Attentional and Interpersonal Style Inventory.

Purpose: "Developed to measure the critical concentration and interpersonal determinants of performance."
Population: Adults and adolescents.
Publication Dates: 1993–1996.
Acronym: TAIS.
Scores: 18 scales: Attentional (Broad External Awareness, External Distractibility, Conceptual/Analytical, Internal Distractibility, Narrow/Focused, Reduced Flexibility), Interpersonal (Information Processing, Orientation Toward Rules and Risk/Impulse Control, Need for Control, Self Esteem, Physical Competitiveness, Decision Making Speed, Extroversion, Introversion, Expression of Ideas, Expression of Criticism, Expression of Support, Self Critical).
Administration: Individual or group.
Price Data: Certification and test pricing available from publisher.
Time: [20–25] minutes.
Comments: Can be administered via pencil and paper, computer, or the internet.
Author: Robert M. Nideffer.
Publisher: Enhanced Performance Systems, Inc.
Cross References: See T5:226 (2 references).

Review of The Attentional and Interpersonal Style Inventory by PHILLIP L. ACKERMAN, Professor of Psychology, Georgia Institute of Technology, Atlanta, GA:

The Attentional and Interpersonal Style Inventory (TAIS) is a 144-item self-report inventory that purports to measure both personality traits (e.g., Extroversion) and cognitive styles (e.g., Narrow/Focused). According to the publisher, the TAIS may be used in a variety of different ways,

including selection, training/development, and individual counseling. There are two manuals, the first "Predicting Human Behavior" (PHB) provides a description of many studies that have used the TAIS, and also provides a readable description of psychometric and theoretical issues concerning validity, reliability, and interpretation. The second manual, "Taking Care of Business" (TCB), is a self-discovery and development booklet that explains the constructs underlying the test, profile interpretation for the client, interpretations of the different designated personal styles, and provides a series of suggestions for the client and "coach" for "all areas of you life, business, family, sports, [and] education" (p. vi). According to this booklet, "the TAIS was originally designed to be used as a counseling tool, not for selection" and it can be used to address "an individual's relative strengths and weaknesses" (p. 36). Thus, the general approach is intrapersonal—the respondent is told to compare his/her own strengths and weaknesses.

RELIABILITY/VALIDITY. It is difficult to get an overall assessment of the reliability and validity of scores from the TAIS. Part of the problem is a disassociation between the counseling purposes for the TAIS in the TCB manual, and the kinds of reliability and validity data reported in the PHB manual. The PHB manual reports group contrasts (e.g., gender differences, scores before and after some treatment, comparisons between successful and unsuccessful athletes, scores of inventory administration under different instructed response sets, contrasts between police and psychiatric patients and between athletes in different countries). Two studies of test-retest reliability are reported, with somewhat disappointing results. One study of 90 introductory psychology students revealed scale retest reliabilities ranging from .60 to .93 over 2 weeks, whereas the other study of 228 athletes over a year test-retest interval yielded a range of reliabilities from .44 to .69, both in the apparent absence of any treatment intervention. Numerous studies were reported to provide validation data, including item and scale analyses, analyses of gender differences, age differences, correlations with an intelligence test, correlations with MMPI scales, correlations with indexes of marital satisfaction, and so on. Although the individual studies reported in the manual are interesting, there does not seem to be sufficient aggregation to provide summaries of the underlying scale constructs in order to place the scales into a larger nomological network.

NORMS. The PHB manual does not provide a comprehensive set of norms, per se. Instead, the manual reports a series of unconnected profile pattern descriptions for a number of different samples (e.g., athletes, police). No attempts are made to integrate these norms, and so it is not readily possible to evaluate the results of an individual respondent's scores using information from the manual. However, there is a database maintained by the publisher that is used to provide profile interpretations, on the basis of a comparison between the respondent and a larger comparison group (e.g., "business executives").

ADMINISTRATION/INTERPRETATION. Respondents complete items by responding with a frequency "Never" to "Always" scale for the widely arrayed statements about feelings, thoughts, interests, needs, and actions. The inventory is returned to the publisher for scoring and interpretive profile results. The respondent receives both a listing of the scores (*T*-Scores) on the basic scales, as well as a combined narrative report of the individual's scores and a series of observations and recommendations about the individual's attentional and interpersonal styles. One major shortcoming is the lack of evidence supporting differential interpretations of correlated scales. The narrative report provides a definition of each of the underlying constructs. An amalgamation of relevant cartoons and famous quotations then provides a series of observations and recommendations, such as "Learn to laugh at yourself" and "You need to learn to listen." The narrative report can be used in conjunction with the TCB manual to map out a strategy for personal development to improve on the noted areas of weaknesses.

SUMMARY. The TAIS appears to be formulated on some well-validated personality constructs, and several others that have received much less support. The value of the TAIS appears to be mainly in the context of counseling assessment and personal development, although there are few data reported that support the notion that these personality traits or personal styles are malleable in the context of self-discovery, training, or counseling. The data reported in the manual are too incomplete to allow direct application at group levels, such as in selection or training—in that it is not clear, a priori, how one group should differ from another, or how a group profile should appear before and after some intervention. Therefore, the use of the TAIS for broader applications may not be warranted without local validation. The modest scale reliabilities may be a continuing concern for use of the measure.

Review of The Attentional and Interpersonal Style Inventory by EUGENE V. AIDMAN, Lecturer in Psychology, School of Behavioural & Social Sciences & Humanities, University of Ballarat, Victoria, Australia:

According to the test developer, the Attentional and Interpersonal Style Inventory (TAIS) is a 144-item questionnaire intended "to measure those concentration skills which are critical determinants of performance" (Predicting Human Behavior manual, p. 25). In fact, of the 17 scales measured by the TAIS, 6 are purported to reflect attentional processes, 2 are designed to assess behavioral and cognitive control, and 9 subscales describe interpersonal style. The TAIS was originally developed for use with athletic populations but it is asserted to have a broader scope of application. The TAIS has been in circulation for over 20 years and seems to have certain intuitive appeal. However, its psychometric qualities remain very difficult to evaluate. Manuals provided by the publisher contain excellent marketing material aimed at business executives, attempting to educate them—as well as the general public—in general principles of reliability and validity, but failing to provide critical detail of the test developer's own validation studies that would be sufficient for peer review. Relevant reliability and validity data are scarce and presented in a series of assertions although evidence necessary to support these assertions is largely untraceable. In particular, no internal consistency data are available, apart from average item-subscale correlations presented without any description of the sample(s) on which they were obtained. Retest reliability is claimed to range between .6 and .93 over a 2-week period but the references point to either an untraceable publication (Wolfe & Nideffer) or to the manual itself (which does not describe the details of the retest study). Another retest study cites stability coefficients ranging between .44 and .69 over a 12-month period, but refers to a manuscript submitted for publication in 1989. This reviewer's direct enquiry with the test author uncovered a more recent publication with identical title (Bond & Nideffer, 1992) but, sadly, it mentions no reliability data at all. Whether the data were ever published and peer reviewed remains unknown.

Construct validity is claimed to have been evidenced by a number of predictable sex differences and age-related trends in attentional and interpersonal scale scores obtained by members of elite athletic squads at the Australian Institute of Sport (Bond & Nideffer, 1992). The interpretation of these important findings as evidencing construct validity is less than convincing, and their fundamental implications for the differential norming of the instrument are completely overlooked. In addition, the results raise questions on analytical grounds: Using a series of 17 separate ANOVAs on nonindependent TAIS subscales—instead of a single MANOVA with subsequent univariate comparisons contingent on multivariate significance—is bound to have inflated Type I error.

Further evidence of validity is derived from a number of discriminant function analyses attempting to discriminate between diverse subject groups (i.e., police, business executives, psychiatric patients) and certain athletic subgroups. For example, TAIS scale scores were able to discriminate representatives of team sports from both closed-skill and open-skill individual sports, accurately classifying between 41.5% and 57.1% of actual group membership (this accuracy marginally exceeds the value of 33.3% attainable by chance).

Correlations of TAIS subscales with selected measures of anxiety and two clinical scales (Depression and Mania) from the Minnesota Multiphasic Personality Inventory (MMPI) are presented as evidence of both construct and concurrent validity. Unfortunately, the data are reported with insufficient detail (referenced to unpublished conference papers), which makes associations between the TAIS and the MMPI difficult to evaluate.

One of the more promising indicators of the instrument's predictive validity was found in the correlations between two of the TAIS aggregate factor scores and expert (coach's) ratings of athletic performance in the sport of diving. Despite a very small sample size ($N = 15$) the results are quite meaningful and compelling: Impulsivity was highly negatively correlated and Performance Anxiety was moderately negatively correlated with performance ratings. What remains unclear, however,

particularly in light of these interesting findings, is how appropriate is the TAIS as a measure of impulsivity and performance anxiety.

Correlations of TAIS subscales with academic achievement and Wechsler Adult Intelligence Scale (WAIS) derived measures of intelligence are interpreted as further confirming criterion validity of the TAIS. However, this interpretation, coupled with a consistent lack of detail and number of general conceptual errors in presenting validation data, limits the extent to which the results can be generalized. The most notable of such errors is treating associations between the TAIS and anxiety as evidence of construct validity and associations between the TAIS and MMPI-derived depression as evidence of criterion-oriented validity.

The instrument's normative data are completely missing in the documentation provided by the publisher. The manual refers to "standard norms" several times but the t-test data comparing these unspecified norms with descriptive statistics obtained from various athletic samples and groups of police recruits and officers, are meaningless and confusing.

SUMMARY. The overall impression is that psychometric soundness of the TAIS, as currently documented, cannot be established. The manuals provided by the publisher are overloaded with marketing materials inappropriate for technical documentation, yet lacking critical technical detail necessary for peer review. Multiple inaccuracies in referencing make the original research very difficult—if not impossible—to trace. A close examination of the references reveals that, despite its two decades in circulation, the TAIS has had a very limited exposure to serious peer review. At the same time, its psychometric soundness has been repeatedly questioned in the literature—in terms of its factorial structure and its content and construct validity (cf. Summers, Miller, & Ford, 1991; Ford & Summers, 1992). It must therefore be concluded that the TAIS, in its current form, cannot be recommended for use as a proven instrument, unless more rigorous validation research is forthcoming.

REVIEWER'S REFERENCES

Summers, J. L., Miller, K., & Ford, S. K. (1991). Attentional style and basketball performance. *Journal of Sport and Exercise Psychology, 13*, 239–253.

Bond, J. W., & Nideffer, R. M. (1992). Attentional and interpersonal characteristics of elite Australian athletes. *Excel, 8*, 101–110.

Ford, S. K., & Summers, J. L. (1992). The factorial validity of the TAIS attentional-style subscales. *Journal of Sport and Exercise Psychology, 14*, 283–297.

[32]
BarOn Emotional Quotient Inventory.

Purpose: Designed to measure emotional intelligence.

Population: Ages 16 and older.

Publication Date: 1997.

Acronym: BarOn EQ-i.

Scores: 21 content scores: Composite Scale Scores (Total EQ, Intrapersonal EQ, Interpersonal EQ, Adaptability EQ, Stress Management EQ, General Mood EQ), Intrapersonal Subscale Scores (Self-Regard, Emotional Self-Awareness, Assertiveness, Independence, Self-Actualization), Interpersonal Subscale Scores (Empathy, Social Responsibility, Interpersonal Relationship), Adaptability Subscale Scores (Reality Testing, Flexibility, Problem Solving), Stress Management Subscale Scores (Stress Tolerance, Impulse Control), General Mood Subscale Scores (Optimism, Happiness), plus 4 validity indicators (Omission Rate, Inconsistency, Positive Impression, Negative Impression).

Administration: Individual or group.

Price Data, 1999: $10 per summary report; $20 per development report; $36 per group report (volume discounts available); $6 per 3 item booklets (volume discounts available); $42 per mail-in preview package including item booklet, development report, and user's manual; $59.95 per user's set including user's manual, administrator's guide, and facilitator's guide; $24.95 per user's manual; $7.95 per administrator's guide; $39.95 per facilitator's guide; $39.95 per technical manual (234 pages).

Foreign Language Editions: Translations available in Afrikaans, Chinese, Czech, Dutch, French-Canadian, Korean, German, Hebrew, Norwegian, Russian, Spanish (South American), Swedish, Danish, Finnish, French (Euro), Hindi, Indonesian, Italian, Japanese, Portuguese, Slovakian, and Slovene.

Time: (30–40) minutes.

Comments: Paper-and-pencil and computer administrations available.

Author: Reuven Bar-On.

Publisher: Multi-Health Systems, Inc.

Review of the BarOn Emotional Quotient Inventory by ANDREW A. COX, Professor of Counseling and Psychology, Troy State University, Phenix City, AL:

The BarOn Emotional Quotient Inventory is designed to assess the construct of emotional intelligence. This concept refers to capabilities, competencies, and skills required to cope with environmental demands and pressures. Emotional intelligence is an aspect of Wechsler's nonintellective factors of intelligence (Wechsler, 1958) and Gardner's (1983) multiple intelligences.

Sternberg (1997) and Salovey and Mayer (1990) further elaborate that emotional intelligence involves the ability to monitor and discriminate feelings and emotions of self and others, and use this information to guide thinking and actions (Salovey & Mayer, 1990, p. 189).

The test's author suggests that emotional intelligence is multifactorial in nature. The factorial components of emotional intelligence are measured through the instrument's subscales. There are 15 factorial components described for the construct. Each component is composed of sub-components.

The inventory consists of 133 items and can be used with test takers 16 years of age or older with at least a sixth grade reading level as estimated with the Flesch formula. Test items were initially drawn from mental health professionals and review of the mental health literature. Final item selection was attained through item analysis procedures. Test takers respond to a 5-point Likert scale as follows: 1—*Very seldom or not true of me*; 2—*Seldom true of me*; 3—*Sometimes true of me*; 4—*Often true of me*; and 5—*Very often true of me or true of me*. Responses are placed on a scannable answer sheet to be returned to the test publisher for scoring. Computer software is available to administer and score the inventory. Though the technical manual and user's manual describe handscorable answer-profile sheets, these materials are not available at this time [February 1999]. The handscorable version will also have fewer items than the currently available measure. Three types of interpretative reports are provided by the publisher. These reports are easy to read and interpret.

Scores are provided for four validity scales, five composite scales, 15 subscales, and a total quotient. Scores are reported as standard scores relative to the test taker's age and gender with a mean of 100 and standard deviation of 15. Interpretative guidelines for scores are adequately described within the technical manual. Higher scores are thought to be more indicative of success in coping with environmental demands whereas low scores represent problematic coping skills.

The test publisher provides several resources useful to test users. These include a technical manual, user's manual, administrator's guide, and facilitator's resource manual. Test manuals and materials are well written and provide detailed information regarding test administration, scoring, and interpretation. Related resources authored by Goleman (1995, 1998) would augment test use.

The instrument has an international normative base with initial normative data from South Africa, Israel, Argentina, Nigeria, India, and Germany. The test was normed on a North American sample of 3,831 individuals, age 15 to over age 60, in the United States and Canada. Characteristics of the North American sample are adequate relative to gender, ethnic origin, age, educational level, and geographic distribution. Age and gender differences within the normative sample resulted in the development of age- and gender-specific norms for use with the instrument.

The instrument's technical characteristics are extensively described within the technical manual. Reported internal consistency and test-retest reliability estimates appear to be adequate. The instrument has an average internal consistency coefficient of .76. Internal consistency reliability estimates were conducted on several international samples as well as the North American sample. Test-retest reliability procedures were provided for South African samples only. Average test-retest coefficients are .85 and .75 for 1- to 4-month time periods.

Test validation included content, factor, construct, criterion-related, and predictive procedures. Validation data are described in both tabular and narrative form within the technical manual. The instrument's validity appears to be generally adequate. However, some of the validation procedures do not include North American samples, which would be a weakness for this instrument. Predictive validation studies are reported for various groups of individuals. Though promising, additional predictive validation for populations representing various categories of psychopathology is necessary. The technical manual indicates that research is currently in progress to develop profiles that include vocational and psychopathology groups. Preliminary profiles are presented with a sample of business leaders, unemployed individuals, financial services employees, and psychologists. This line of research is promising and would assist in further documenting the instrument's predictive validation as well as clinical utility.

As the construct of emotional intelligence is fairly new, construct validation for the instrument was critical. North American samples were included in validation studies using the Sixteen

Personality Factor Questionnaire (16PF), Personality Assessment Inventory, Symptom Checklist 90, Zung Self-Rating Scale of Depression, and Short Acculturation Scale. Discriminant, convergent, and divergent construct-related validation studies are cited. These studies suggest adequate construct validation.

Though the manual indicates that the inventory can be used in a variety of business, medical, treatment, or educational settings, the test's author recommends that the instrument be used as part of a comprehensive evaluation. The measure would appear to be of limited value when used in isolation in clinical settings, particularly where individual selection, placement, or prediction of behavior are important clinical decisions. There are few instruments available that measure the construct of emotional intelligence. More research is necessary to delineate the implications of emotional intelligence to human behavior and development. The instrument would serve a useful role in this research activity.

Though only three outcome-based studies are reported for the instrument involving treatment impact, the measure may serve a useful role in outcome assessment within clinical settings. The practitioner should use the inventory in conjunction with more traditional measures of clinical outcome such as depression, anxiety, behavior change, etc. The instrument appears to have limited utility with clinical populations that manifest severe pathology. It would be useful with populations that are reasonably healthy from an emotional perspective but seek clinical services at various life-change transition periods or with adjustment-related disorders. In treatment situations, the instrument would serve a useful role in identifying patient strengths.

SUMMARY. The Emotional Quotient Inventory appears to be an excellent measure of the emotional intelligence concept. Technical characteristics are generally adequate. A representative North American normative sample is provided along with international normative samples that would be useful for cross-cultural clinical activity. Normative, validation, scoring, and interpretation information are well presented in test materials and resources. The addition of hand-scoring procedures currently under development will enhance clinical usage. A weakness of the instrument appears to be relative to the emotional intelligence construct itself. In this era of interest in specific clinical outcomes, the instrument would have limited clinical utility unless used in conjunction with other more specific problem- or adjustment-oriented clinical measures. The test's descriptive materials relate an ambitious research agenda. These studies will further enhance the inventory's clinical use.

REVIEWER'S REFERENCES

Wechsler, D. (1958). *The measurement and appraisal of adult intelligence* (4th ed.). Baltimore: Williams & Wilkins.
Gardner, H. (1983). *Frames of mind: The theory of multiple intelligences.* New York: Basic Books.
Salovey, P., & Mayer, J. D. (1990). Emotional intelligence. *Imagination, Cognition, and Personality, 9,* 185–211.
Goleman, D. (1995). *Emotional intelligence.* New York: Bantam.
Sternberg, R. J. (1997). The concept of intelligence and its role in lifelong learning and success. *American Psychologist, 52,* 1030–1037.
Goleman, D. (1998). *Working with emotional intelligence.* New York: Bantam.

Review of the BarOn Emotional Quotient Inventory by ROBERT M. GUION, Distinguished University Professor Emeritus, Bowling Green State University, Bowling Green, OH:

Psychological well-being requires more than the cognitive abilities called intelligence, and more than passive "adjustment" to events in one's environment; it generally seems to require interpersonal abilities, coping abilities, and others not typically considered a part of intelligence. The Emotional Quotient Inventory (EQ-i) was developed to measure a set of such abilities in work and educational environments, in medical and research settings, and other situations where it can augment ordinary mental ability testing (or perhaps stand alone) to describe or predict effectiveness of functioning for individuals or groups.

The EQ-i developed from Bar-On's professional clinical experience and reading. Generalizations drawn from personal experience do not always hold up well under empirical scrutiny. This inventory is an exception. It was not, despite statements in the manual, developed by raw empiricism, nor is it grounded in systematic theory; indeed, it is described as "theoretically eclectic." Nevertheless, the research data base is extensive and tends to support the initial concepts.

The underlying concept of emotional intelligence differs from but is analogous to conventional ideas of cognitive intelligence. It is "an array of noncognitive capabilities, competencies, and skills that influence one's ability to succeed in coping with environmental demands and pressures" (manual, p. 14). The definition is too broad to be fully satisfying; it could include dexterity,

coordination, stamina, and other "noncognitive capabilities" not invoked in developing either the concept or the instrument. Nevertheless, it clearly sets the concept in the realm of abilities rather than more traditional and more amorphous notions of personality traits. Despite the definition, the author wisely avoids dwelling too much on the inevitably murky boundaries between cognitive and noncognitive abilities. For example, one scale—Problem Solving—is defined in terms of such cognitive processes as problem identification, search for relevant information, generating multiple possible solutions (sometimes called divergent problem solving), and deciding among them. Nevertheless, the items comprising the scale seem to refer to preferences and habitual responses to problem situations—generalizable respondent characteristics that go beyond the ordinary idea of cognition in problem solving. That is as it should be; both cognitive and motivational influences combine to influence the effectiveness of things people do.

The author espouses a hierarchical view of intelligence, whether cognitive or emotional. In both aspects of intelligence, a variety of very specific factors combine to produce more general group factors, and these in turn combine to form a still more general factor. In the present inventory, 15 relatively specific factors combine into 5 group factors, and these in turn combine to form a general factor called an emotional quotient. The term is unfortunate; the abilities and skills it taps are not what people (including psychologists) generally consider emotional, and the danger of reification of an EQ, as has happened with IQ, is very real.

The inventory has 133 items and a 5-point response scale for each, ranging from "Not True of Me" to "True of Me." A Flesch count places the English language version at about a sixth grade reading level. The manual describes inventory development in useful detail, and it helps psychometric evaluation by giving highlights of many studies and thorough data analyses (but more detailed reports are cited). Individual scales are brief—as few as 7 items and not more than 11—so most of them have unimpressive but adequate alpha reliability (estimated in three North American samples and in samples from six other countries). Sample sizes are good, ranging from 168 in a German sample to 3,831 in a nonmilitary North American sample. Scale alpha coefficients across samples ranged from .59 to .90; average alphas (the method of averaging was not described) ranged from .69 to .86. Retest reliabilities were obtained in small South African samples. With a one-month time lapse; these were in the .80s for most scales. With 4 months, they dropped generally to the .70s. Of course, the concept of trait constancy familiar in similar studies of cognitive intelligence is less likely to apply to these abilities.

Validity data are grouped to satisfy any idea of validity readers might hold; nearly any adjective anyone has ever placed before *validity*, from face validity to divergent validity, is covered. Nevertheless, a wealth of data supports the inferences of validity, relatively little of it gives reason for questioning. Exploratory and confirmatory factor analyses, and even a relevant path analysis, provided partial support; however, the exploratory analyses gave a best-fit solution for 13 factors (not 15), and subsequent confirmatory analyses was limited to questions raised by it. Other evidence consisted of appropriate correlations with other measures and the absence of inappropriate ones. Much of the validity discussion could be dropped, especially concerning content and face validity. Face validity means little, and content validity was discussed with no definition of domain boundaries.

Administration of the inventory is not complex. An administrator's manual is available, but the technical manual is probably sufficient to administer the English version. There are also Hebrew, Afrikaans, and other versions, and they may pose problems in administration—but I doubt it.

Scoring is another matter. At present the completed inventories must be sent to the publisher for scoring and for reports. Hand scoring might be possible, but the time requirement to develop a key and do the actual scoring for 15 basic scales, 4 validity scales, and the various composites seems excessive. A special, abridged version of the inventory may be available using the publisher's "QuikScore™" answer sheet. That version deletes about half of the items, so it allows only the overall EQ, the five composite scores, and one of the basic 15. No information is offered about the equivalence of these scores and the corresponding scores based on the full item set.

That omission illustrates my major criticism of the EQ-i and its technical manual: Despite much empirical information, assertions are too often made without supporting data. There is a computer version, and the question of score equiva-

lence is not addressed for it, either. It is asserted that, if more than seven items are skipped (i.e., no response), the overall score should be considered invalid, but no data are offered to support this particular cut point. And so on.

SUMMARY. Nevertheless, my overall evaluation of this inventory is favorable. It has been developed carefully, much research has been done, and the research program is a continuing one. It appears to fill a gap by measuring constructs not often measured or rarely measured well. It is surely worth serious attention as an example of things test developers should address in developing and evaluating their instruments.

[33]
BASC Monitor for ADHD.

Purpose: Designed to survey the primary symptoms of ADHD in a format suited to repeated assessments in order to see relationships between treatments and symptoms over time.

Population: Ages 4–18.

Publication Date: 1998.

Acronym: BASC Monitor for ADHD.

Forms, 2: Teacher Monitor Ratings, Parent Monitor Ratings.

Scores: 4 scales: Attention Problems, Hyperactivity, Internalizing Problems, Adaptive Skills; plus Student Observation System (13 adaptive and maladaptive behavior categories).

Administration: Group.

Price Data, 2001: $99.95 per hand-scoring set including 25 Teacher Monitor rating forms, 25 Parent Monitor rating forms, scoring templates, and manual (112 pages); $23.95 per 25 Teacher Monitor rating forms or 25 Parent Monitor rating forms; $29.95 per 25 Student Observation System forms; $199.95 per single-user complete software kit including 25 Teacher Monitor rating forms, 25 Parent Monitor rating forms, manual, and software disks (network version also available).

Time: (5) minutes.

Comments: Instrument is designed to supplement the BASC (40) or to be used independently; questionnaires are completed by parents and teachers; Parent Monitor Ratings form available in Spanish; BASC Monitor software available for Windows 95 or Windows NT, single-user or network versions.

Authors: Randy W. Kamphaus and Cecil R. Reynolds.

Publisher: American Guidance Service, Inc.

Review of the BASC Monitor for ADHD by HUGH W. GLENN, Educational Consultant, Kohut Psychiatric Medical Group, San Bernardino, CA:

The authors of the BASC Monitor for ADHD assume that ADHD is best diagnosed and treated by identifying its primary symptoms as listed in DSM-IV and implementing intervention strategies to eliminate or lessen their intensity or frequency. In addition to the Teacher and Parent Monitor Forms, which consist of behaviors and conditions, the Student Observation System (SOS) provides a tool for clinicians to rate and evaluate student classroom behavior.

Approximately half of the 5-minute, 47-item Teacher Monitor Rating form (46 items on the Parent Monitor Rating form) use the same phrases found in DSM-IV that characterize ADHD. The remaining half consists of an "expanded range of Attention Problems and Hyperactive symptoms" (manual, p. 2). Many items assessed, however, lack any direct relationship to attention problems or to hyperactive symptoms (e.g., "Is sad," "Is creative," "Has lots of ideas," and "Is a good sport"). And many behaviors listed in DSM-IV and corresponding items on the BASC Monitor for ADHD are obviously not mutually exclusive: "Listens to directions," "Talks constantly," "Has a short attention span," and "Easily distracted from classwork" may well point to the same underlying factor, not to different ones. Furthermore, many behaviors listed on the BASC Monitor for ADHD lack any direct relationship with the descriptions of abnormal behavior listed in DSM-IV. The four behaviors cited previously also occur from boredom; for example, when normal children try to read or to do something they already know or do not understand. According to learning theorist and psycholinguist Frank Smith (1994), "Children will not attend to anything they know already ... [and] children exhibit the same symptoms of boredom ... because they cannot make sense of what they are expected to do" (p. 90). Too often classroom instruction and activities do not make sense to the child, which results in boredom, inattention, or hyperactivity. In short, when children do not comprehend, inattention and other behaviors associated with ADHD are observed frequently in normal children and adolescents.

The manual includes extensive data to support the validity and reliability of scores from the BASC Monitor. This reviewer, however, is troubled by the ambiguity of many items on the rating forms. Do a teacher and a parent assess the same behavior when rating "Listens to directions"?

Is assessing a child's attention while listening to directions from the teacher during a mathematics lesson measuring the same factor as when rating a child's attention while a parent provides directions for completing a household chore?

Perhaps the most serious limitation of the BASC Monitor for ADHD is its focus on behavioral symptoms but ignoring their sources. This clinician has evaluated and directed the academic instruction of several thousand children and adolescents diagnosed as, and often medicated for, ADHD. Their symptoms lessened markedly or disappeared altogether within a few months after twice-a-week instructional sessions by clinicians focused upon making sure that each lesson or activity made sense to the student.

The usefulness and validity of scores from the BASC Monitor for ADHD could be greatly improved if the behaviors assessed and reassessed were unambiguously defined and rated within the same context. Instead of assessing the ambiguous "Listens to directions," "Listens to directions during a mathematics lesson" could be rated. "Makes careless error" could refer to errors in judgment, mathematics, or miscues heard during oral reading. Accurately measuring the effectiveness of intervention strategies requires that the same (or highly similar) behaviors or conditions be assessed and reassessed; for example, "Makes careless errors in adding or subtracting whole numbers."

SUMMARY. The use of the BASDC Monitor for ADHD, and particularly its accompanying software, will depend upon whether clinicians believe that when teachers or parents administer this 5-minute instrument, enough insights about children and adolescents diagnosed with ADHD will be revealed for identifying and evaluating intervention strategies. In fact, the BASC Monitor for ADHD diagnoses nothing. According to the test's authors, elevated scores on either the teacher or parent scale signal only the "*possibility* [emphasis added] of ADHD" (manual, p. 2).

REVIEWER'S REFERENCE

Smith, F. (1994). *Understanding reading: A psycholinguistic analysis of reading and learning to read* (5th ed.). Hillsdale, NJ: Lawrence Erlbaum.

Review of the BASC Monitor for ADHD by KEVIN M. JONES, Assistant Professor, University of Cincinnati, Cincinnati, OH:

The BASC Monitor consists of two brief rating scales, one for teachers and one for parents, that survey symptoms related to Attention Deficit/Hyperactivity Disorder (ADHD), internalizing problems, and adaptive skills. These instruments provide repeated assessment of the severity of these symptoms for children aged 4 to 18 years. Information in the manual also is provided for the Student Observation System (SOS), which is a brief, structured observation of both adaptive and maladaptive classroom behavior. These complementary sources of data provide a means by which professionals can systematically record children's progress, an especially useful service when monitoring the effects of psychoeducational and/or pharmacological treatments.

The Teacher Monitor Ratings (TMR) and Parent Monitor Ratings (PMR) consist of 47 and 46 descriptors of behavior, respectively, rated by the respondent on a 4-point scale, ranging from *Never* to *Almost Always*. Although computer software is available, these forms are easily scored by hand, using acrylic scoring templates. Raw scores are translated into corresponding T scores ($m = 50$, $SD = 10$) and percentile ranks for the following four scales. The Attention Problems scale consists of 8 items intended to measure the ability to sustain performance. The Hyperactivity scale consists of 10 items that seem to measure overactivity and impulsivity. The Internalizing Problems (10 items) scale signals the presence of general internalizing symptoms, such as sadness, worrying, or somatization. The Adaptive Skills scale consists of 10 items that sample social skills, leadership, and adaptability. Remaining items include descriptors, such as "Talks too much," that do not load on these four factors but were included in the TMR and PMR because they complete the diagnostic criteria for ADHD included in the DSM-IV (American Psychiatric Association, 1994).

Development of the TMR and PMR consisted primarily of selecting items from the more comprehensive standardization edition of the Behavior Assessment System for Children (BASC) Teacher Rating Scales and Parent Rating Scales (40; Reynolds & Kamphaus, 1992). Technical properties of the TMR and PMR (norms, reliability, validity) were derived or evaluated from previous work with the BASC. Normative data are available for boys, girls, or a combined set across five age groups, and were constructed based on an adequate and representative sample of the U.S. population. Internal consistencies across age groups

are generally high, ranging from .78 to .93 for the TMR, and .67 to .83 for the PMR. Given its purported use as a repeated measure, test-retest reliability is especially important. Based on pairs of ratings obtained from the same teacher or parent over a 2- to 8-week interval, test-retest reliability is generally adequate, ranging from .72 to .93 for the TMR scales, and .57 to .90 for the PMR scales. Much evidence for the validity of the two instruments is presented in the manual. The TMR and PMR are useful, for example, in discriminating subtypes of ADHD. Correlations between the scales of these two instruments and those of other popular rating systems, as well as intercorrelations among the four TMR and PMR scales, are generally in the expected range. A curious exception is the BASC Monitor's Adaptive Skills scale, which appears to be closely related to the Attention Problems scale.

The BASC Monitor advances our current assessment technology in many important ways. First, a systematic method is provided for monitoring whether, consistent with the DSM-IV criteria for ADHD, a particular symptom profile is evident for at least 6 months. Second, the TMR, PMR, and SOS represent a logical link between assessment and treatment because measurement is relatively consistent across baseline and treatment phases. Finally, separating attention and hyperactive-impulsive domains, and including internalizing problems and adaptive skills, provides information not obtained from other currently used monitoring systems, such as the Conners Abbreviated Teacher Rating Scale (Conners, 1973) and the ADHD Rating Scale (DuPaul, Power, Anastopoulos, & Reid, 1998).

There are a few limitations that may warrant more attention in the manual. First, although the SOS "best advances the goal of the BASC Monitor for ADHD" the necessary observation materials are not included in the test package. Presumably, these must be obtained from purchase of the BASC. Second, interpreting treatment effects in terms of statistically significant difference (i.e., pre-post) scores is risky and inconsistent with the basic assumptions of repeated measurement. At the very least, a discussion of internal validity threats (e.g., history) and consideration of within-phase trends seems warranted. Finally, the manual describes no controlled evaluations of the BASC Monitor components in the manner in which they were intended, as a repeated measure of child progress. Further work is needed to determine whether the TMR, PMR, and SOS are sensitive to curricular or pharmacological intervention, and to assess the relationship between changes in adult perceptions and actual child behavior.

SUMMARY. The authors have successfully composed the most sophisticated system available for monitoring problems related to ADHD. Use of the BASC Monitor as described in the manual will provide valuable data needed to make informed treatment decisions.

REVIEWER'S REFERENCES

Conners, C. K. (1973). Rating scales for use in drug studies with children. Pharmacotherapy of children [Special issue]. *Psychopharmacology Bulletin*, 24–84.

Reynolds, C. R., & Kamphaus, R. W. (1992). *Behavior assessment system for children manual*. Circle Pines, MN: American Guidance Service, Inc.

American Psychiatric Association. (1994). *Diagnostic and statistical manual of mental disorders* (4th ed.). Washington, DC: Author.

DuPaul, G. J., Power, T. J., Anastopoulos, A. D., & Reid, R. (1998). *ADHD Rating Scale—IV: Checklists, norms, and clinical interpretation*. New York: The Guilford Press.

[34]

Basic Reading Inventory, Seventh Edition.

Purpose: Designed to assess students' skills to provide them with appropriate reading materials.

Population: Pre-primer through grade 12, grades 3–12.

Publication Dates: 1978–1997.

Scores, 12 to 13: 4 reading scores (Independent, Instructional, Frustration, Listening) for each of 3 subtests (Word Recognition in Isolation, Word Recognition in Context, Comprehension), Reading Rate (Optional).

Administration: Individual.

Levels, 2: Pre-primer to grade 12, grades 3–12.

Forms, 5: A, B, C, LN, LE.

Price Data: Available from publisher.

Time: Administration time not reported.

Comments: Administered and scored by educators; considered to be an "informal test, intended to help teachers gain insight about students' reading abilities.

Author: Jerry L. Johns.

Publisher: Kendall/Hunt Publishing Company.

Cross References: See T5:257 (4 references); for reviews by Jerrilyn V. Andrews and Robert T. Williams of the fifth edition, see 12:43 (3 references); see also T4:255 (4 references); for a review by Gus Plessas of the second edition, see 9:119.

Review of the Basic Reading Inventory, Seventh Edition by MICHAEL HARWELL, Professor, Research Methodology, University of Minnesota—Twin Cities, Minneapolis, MN:

Reviewing the Basic Reading Inventory (BRI) is a little like reviewing the music of The Grateful Dead—either you are a diehard fan and immune to any criticism of the music, or, alternatively, you simply cannot understand the attraction. So it is with the BRI, an instrument intended to assess the oral reading, silent reading, and listening comprehension of K–12 students. It is administered by teachers, reading specialists, and special educators who wish to identify a student's Independent, Instructional, Frustration, and Listening levels for each of three subtests (Word Recognition in Isolation, Word Recognition in Context, Comprehension) plus their reading rate. The instrument comes in five forms (oral reading measure, silent reading measure, listening measure, narrative passages, expository passages). The manual is long (399 pp.) but is well written and has benefited from reorganization.

That this instrument has been severely criticized in previous *MMY* reviews is as easily documented as the unwillingness of the author to incorporate changes that respond to quantitatively oriented criticisms. What are readers to make of an instrument that has never provided reliability or validity information and probably never will? Of an instrument for which previous reviews in the *MMY* are negative yet is in its seventh edition with an established place in the reading literature? Of an instrument for which the newest edition expands the student pool from K–8 to K–12 with virtually no empirical evidence supporting this expansion? Readers should probably conclude that the BRI is going to remain a popular tool for assessing reading skills, that future editions will not incorporate the quantitatively oriented suggestions of reviewers, and that the BRI will continue to be criticized in future *MMY* reviews.

William's (1995) review of the fifth edition of the BRI succinctly characterized the two prevailing views of this instrument by noting that "The Basic Reading Inventory seems confused about whether it wants to be a quantitative tool to categorize a reader's performance in traditional terms or a qualitative tool to describe a reader's interaction with written language" (p. 109). Those who view the BRI as a quantitative tool expect to see normative evidence and reliability and validity documentation in the manual but find none; those who view the BRI as a qualitative tool are apparently pleased with its clinical properties and are not bothered by the absence of traditional psychometric information.

The quantitatively oriented criticisms of this instrument center on the use of BRI scores to assess students' skills in a normative fashion without any accompanying evidence that scores from such assessments are reliable and valid. It is clear from the manual that certain BRI scores are likely to result in an instructional intervention. For example, the fact that a student scoring low (as defined by the BRI user) on the Independent and Instructional components of the Comprehension subtest would be a candidate for some kind of instructional intervention implies a normative framework. The author seems content to allow this normative framework to be based on the experiences of BRI users rather than empirical norms.

A related criticism is the absence of any information about the typical consequences for students who are given the BRI. How do BRI scores typically affect the academic standing or direction of students? Is a student who scores low on some part of the BRI then given a standardized reading test, or are low BRI scores sufficient to trigger reading interventions? How different are the consequences of using the BRI for younger versus older students? Even acknowledging the qualitative nature of this instrument, it seems likely that difficulties with the BRI increase with older students. For example, it is one thing for a teacher to use the BRI to help to pinpoint what they believe are reading difficulties of a student in the first grade and prescribe an appropriate intervention; it is quite another thing for a teacher to use the BRI in a similar fashion with an 11th grader. The use of the BRI to assess an older student's reading skills, and, if necessary, to prescribe an appropriate intervention may fit the description of a so-called high stakes test in some settings. Many in the measurement community believe that instruments used in this way require the strongest possible validity and reliability evidence, yet the BRI provides none.

SUMMARY. The Basic Reading Inventory continues to resist providing quantitatively oriented information such as norms, reliability, and validity evidence. Those who are familiar with the Basic Reading Inventory and are pleased with its qualitative character are likely to continue to use it and to remain immune from criticism of this instrument. Those who believe that an instrument that is used to characterize a student as showing more or less skill or knowledge on something needs to provide norms, reliability, and validity information will continue to be mystified by the attraction of the Basic Reading Inventory.

REVIEWER'S REFERENCE

Williams, R. T. (1995). [Review of the Basic Reading Inventory, Fifth Edition]. In J. C. Conoley & J. C. Impara (Eds.), *The twelfth mental measurements yearbook* (pp. 108–109). Lincoln, NE: Buros Institute of Mental Measurements.

Review of the Basic Reading Inventory, Seventh Edition by STEVEN A. STAHL, Professor of Reading Education, The University of Georgia, Athens, GA:

The Basic Reading Inventory (BRI) is a carefully constructed, well-developed informal reading inventory. It is in its seventh edition and shows evidence of being continually improved and informed by advances in research and practice.

The basic part of the BRI consists of three forms of word lists and passages. The word lists range from preprimer to 12th grade and the passages range from preprimer to Grade 8. Form A is intended for oral reading, Form B for silent reading, and Form C as an optional form for retesting. In addition, there are two sets of longer passages, one narrative and one expository, to counter the criticisms of earlier informal reading inventories that their passages were too short. The longer passages go from Grade 3 to Grade 12. There is also a set of early literacy assessments, designed for a detailed analysis of the reading of children who fail to read at a primer level. These assessments include a measure of alphabet knowledge, a measure of writing, a measure of literacy knowledge, several wordless picture books, a picture story, measures of phonological awareness, as well as additional word lists and preprimer stories. Finally, the BRI manual contains procedures for eliciting and evaluating miscues. The supporting materials contain a detailed account of how to give the BRI, how to interpret the results, how to use the results for instruction, and essays on the history of informal reading inventories and the life of Emmett A. Betts, who developed the notion of instructional, independent, and frustration levels. The added items are probably useful, but the overall effect of the 380 pages can be overwhelming.

The administration instructions seem to be comprehensive and simply written, so that a teacher should be able to administer a BRI with little difficulty. A videotape is available separately from the publisher demonstrating administration techniques as well. The material on scoring and interpretation also seems to be teacher-friendly and easy to follow.

Because an informal reading inventory does not go through a process of item development, as a standardized test might, one must evaluate the construction of the test itself. Content validity was demonstrated through careful development. The word lists were chosen to be representative of words taken from two word compendia, the EDL Core Vocabularies and the Basic Skills Word list, and checked against the Living Word Vocabulary. All of these lists date back to the 1980s. I know of no more current appropriate source of words. Usually words on lists in informal reading inventories tend to reflect the passages. The sampling from graded word lists makes this measure more reflective of children's word recognition abilities.

Passages in Forms A, B, and C were revised from earlier editions. All passages were evaluated by "one or more readability formulas" (manual, p. 105). In addition, the author solicited reactions from users across the United States and Canada. The long narrative and expository passages were developed afresh for this edition. They were field tested on over 350 students apiece, but there are no details given about the nature of the field testing and how the data were analyzed and used.

There is little evidence available about the formal properties of the test. Johns (the test author) argues that, because the BRI is informal, conventional reliability information is meaningless. However, given the detailed instruction on administration, one can be reasonably sure that the BRI will be administered in the same way by nearly all examiners. Helgren-Lempesis and Mangrum (1986) used an earlier version of the BRI with fourth graders and found an alternate form reliability of .72 for the second edition of the BRI. Bristow, Pikulski, and Pelosi (1983) used an earlier version of BRI with children in Grades 2, 4, and 6 and found the second edition to have a .89 correlation with the Metropolitan Achievement Test (MAT) and .75 with the child's book placement in the classroom. They also found that the BRI and the Metropolitan produced estimates of the child's reading level within +/- 1 grade level 89% of the time. These results may not relate to the current edition's properties. Stahl, McCartney, and Montero (in press) used the BRI with first graders and found concurrent correlations of .49

to .54 with subtests of the Iowa Test of Basic Skills (ITBS). Although these are low, for first graders the BRI and the ITBS may be measuring very different abilities. Because first graders read aloud nearly all of the time, an oral measure, such as the BRI, may be a better reflection of children's abilities than a silent reading measure, such as the ITBS or MAT. The BRI has also been used to evaluate Cunningham, Hall, and DeFee's (1991, 1998) reading program.

SUMMARY. The BRI is carefully developed, with clear directions for administration, scoring, and interpretation. Because informal reading inventories, such as the BRI, stress their validity, rather than reliability, the best test of the appropriateness of such a measure may be personal judgment of the appropriateness of the content and the ease of use.

REVIEWER'S REFERENCES
Bristow, P. S., Pikulski, J. J., & Pelosi, P. L. (1983). A comparison of five estimates of reading instructional level. *The Reading Teacher, 37,* 273–279.
Helgren-Lempesis, V. A., & Mangrum, C. T., II. (1986). An analysis of alternate form reliability of five commercially-prepared informal reading inventories. *Reading Research Quarterly, 21,* 209–215.
Cunningham, P. M., Hall, D. P., & Defee, M. (1991). Non-ability grouped, multilevel instruction: a year in a first grade classroom. *The Reading Teacher, 44,* 566–571.
Cunningham, P. M., Hall, D. P., & Defee, M. (1998). Nonability-grouped, multimethod instruction: Eight years later. *The Reading Teacher, 51,* 652–664.
Stahl, S. A., McCartney, A. A., & Monterro, M. K. (in press). *Reading first: An extensive examination of intensive phonics instruction. CIERA Report.* Ann Arbor, MI: Center for the Improvement of Early Reading Instruction.

[35]
Basic School Skills Inventory, Third Edition.

Purpose: Designed to locate children who are at-risk for school failure, who need more in-depth assessment, and who should be referred for additional study.
Population: Ages 4-0 to 8-11.
Publication Dates: 1975–1998.
Acronym: BSSI-3.
Scores, 7: Spoken Language, Reading, Writing, Mathematics, Classroom Behavior, Daily Living Skills, Overall Skill Level.
Administration: Individual.
Price Data, 2001: $86 per complete kit including examiner's manual ('98, 77 pages), and 25 profile/response forms; $49 per examiner's manual; $39 per 25 profile/response forms.
Time: (5–8) minutes.
Comments: Replaces the Basic School Skills Inventory—Diagnostic (T4:256).
Authors: Donald D. Hammill, James E. Leigh, Nils A. Pearson, and Taddy Maddox.
Publisher: PRO-ED.
Cross References: See T5:258 and T4:256 (1 reference); for a review by William J. Webster of the Basic School Skills Inventory—Diagnostic, see 9:120;

for reviews by Byron R. Egeland and Lawrence M. Kasdon of an earlier edition, see 8:424 (2 references).

Review of the Basic School Skills Inventory, Third Edition by R. W. KAMPHAUS, Professor, Department of Educational Psychology, The University of Georgia, Athens, GA:

The premise of the Basic School Skills Inventory, Third Edition (BSSI-3) is atypical in that it is not a direct measure of student academic competencies for ages 4 through 8. The BSSI-3 takes the more unusual approach of using teacher ratings of academic competencies to assess "readiness." Consequently, the BSSI-3 is not an academic readiness test per se but, rather, it is a rating scale that attempts to systematically, and in a standardized way, quantify teacher opinion regarding children's academic competencies in prekindergarten, kindergarten, and the early elementary grades. Rather than being viewed as just another readiness test, the BSSI-3 is more accurately viewed as a method for assessing teacher judgments of child readiness. The BSSI-3 attempts to do that which teachers have always done: gauge a child's readiness using teacher opinion.

As cited in the BSSI-3 manual there is some evidence to suggest that this methodology is useful. Perhaps of greatest importance is the fact that a rating of this nature is based upon the opinion of a teacher who has known the child for some extended period of time. In direct contrast, test performance is susceptible to validity threats that may occur only at the time of testing. If teachers are able to rate academic achievement well then the BSSI-3 results should be very useful. The authors describe their rationale for the utility of the BSSI-3 approach as follows:

> The BSSI-3 provides educators with a means of tapping their ability to judge students' readiness in spoken language, academic skills, behavioral characteristics, or daily living skills with a norm-referenced rating scale. (manual, p. 3)

Evidence of content validity for the BSSI-3 rests on the expertise of classroom teachers. In fact, the original item pool was based on surveys of 50 teachers conducted in the Philadelphia schools in the early 1970s. The item pool has changed considerably since that time based on feedback from reviewers among other factors. The manual provides good detailed descriptions and opera-

tional definitions of the items, their objectives, and mastery criteria. Presumably teachers may use knowledge of the mastery criteria to rate the items. It is doubtful that the typical teacher will read and adequately memorize the mastery criteria prior to completing the scale. The detailed item descriptions are better used to gauge content validity. On one hand, the authors are to be lauded for providing a rationale for inclusion of each item in a scale as suggested by Standard 1.6 of the *Standards for Educational and Psychological Testing* (AERA, APA, & NCME, 1999). In direct contrast, they do not give detailed descriptions of the methods for item selection for the current version nor do they give the qualifications of the item selection team (or expert judges) as required in Standard 1.7.

The BSSI-3 is elegantly simple to administer and score. It would be helpful, however, to have the rating scale categories included at the top of each column where teachers place their ratings so that teachers do not have to continually refer back to the rating scale until they have memorized it adequately.

The normative sample for the BSSI-3 is relatively small but fairly demographically representative of the U.S. population of school children. Reliability coefficients are notably high for both scales and composites.

The authors do address several important validity issues and they include a separate chapter on bias. In fact, item bias was systematically evaluated. Their results suggest that little item bias is present in the scale but they did not use this or any other technique to eliminate or modify items to reduce bias further. In addition, although reliability coefficients are reported separately for ethnic groups (and shown to be uniformly high) evidence of slope or intercept bias or judgmental bias or unfairness reviews were apparently not conducted.

Given that the primary intent of the BSSI-3 is to identify children with academic problems, the analyses of the scales' ability to do so are inadequate. A single paragraph in the manual is devoted to this topic. An analysis of sensitivity (ability to identify true positives) and specificity (ability to identify false negatives) should have been presented. The manual merely reports the low mean total score of 72 for a sample of 42 children with developmental delays without comparison to another clinical sample (e.g., children who are at-risk).

SUMMARY. The BSSI-3 should not be referred to as a "test" per se. The BSSI-3 is, in fact, a rating scale. Consequently, the important user question is not whether to use the BSSI-3 for testing young children to determine readiness and screen for developmental delays, but whether one wishes to quantify teachers' qualitative judgments of readiness. If a user wishes to quantify teacher judgments then the BSSI-3 is a potentially good option that deserves a local tryout. If adopted, the test user should make special efforts to articulate the relationship between BSSI-3 content and local curricular objectives, conduct a judgmental bias review using local personnel, and collect criterion data (e.g., academic achievement outcomes) to determine the sensitivity and specificity of the scale.

REVIEWER'S REFERENCE

American Educational Research Association, American Psychological Association, & National Council on Measurement in Education. (1999). *Standards for educational and psychological testing.* Washington, DC: American Educational Research Association.

Review of the Basic School Skills Inventory, Third Edition by LEAH M. NELLIS, Assistant Professor of Educational Psychology, Northern Arizona University, Flagstaff, AZ:

The Basic School Skill Inventory, Third Edition (BSSI-3) is based upon the previous Basic School Skills Inventory that was composed of a diagnostic and screening form. The conceptual framework of the BSSI-3 is grounded in the premise that classroom teachers should assume a primary role in the assessment of a child's performance and that the assessment of school readiness should reflect the skills and abilities needed to engage in the various activities and tasks in which children engage in the school environment. According to the manual, the inventory was designed to be utilized by classroom teachers to gain information about a child's development of the basic skills considered critical for school success including Spoken Language, Reading, Writing, Mathematics, Classroom Behavior, and Daily Living Skills. The scale was designed for use in the prereferral process to identify children in need of special services. Reference is also made to using the scale for the purposes of diagnosis and special education eligibility.

The item content for the original Basic School Skills Inventory was generated by teachers of kindergarten and first grade of the skills characteristic of children "ready" or "not ready" for school. This skill listing served as the basis for the items of the BSSI-3. The manual reports that a large number of items were administered to groups of children with subsequent item analysis resulting in items being deleted due to being too easy or too difficult for the children. More details of item development and analysis should be included in the manual. Likewise, information about item gradients and subtest floor and ceiling are lacking. A review of the items composing each scale suggests that certain subtests (i.e., Writing and Mathematics) begin at a more advanced level; thus, possibly resulting in the scale being less appropriate for younger children.

The manual states that classroom teachers can complete the ratings and/or administration but that an individual should receive formal training in assessment prior to interpreting the results. In addition, ratings are to be made based upon the teacher's judgment regarding the child's skills in comparison to normally developing, same-age children. Items are scored on a 4-point Likert scale and can be rated 0 (does not perform), 1 (beginning to perform), 2 (performs most of the time), or 3 (performance indicates mastery). A description of item mastery is included for each item; however, the criterion is very subjective on some items with the standards being that of the individual test user or teacher. Further, some items require direct assessment or suggest direct observation if the rater does not have sufficient knowledge. This counters one of the advantages of teacher ratings as purported by the authors. Specifically, items based on direct assessment are not in agreement with the premise of assessment being based on one's extensive knowledge gained over the course of time. This limitation could be addressed by providing a category for raters to endorse when sufficient knowledge is not available.

Standard scores, percentiles, age equivalents, and an overall skill level standard score are available within the normative data. The BSSI-3 was standardized with 757 children residing in 12 states. Data were collected between April and June in 1994 and 1995 and in the fall of 1997. Such collection times may impact the interpretation of ratings completed during other months of the school year given that the manifestation of "readiness skills" varies over the course of an academic year.

The manual reports the technical data regarding reliability and validity and makes claims of high internal reliability (.91), little or no bias among subgroups, high test-retest reliability (.99) (2-week interval), and acceptable interscorer reliability (.96). However, this reviewer is not convinced that the results support the use of the BSSI-3. For example, the authors utilize internal reliability coefficients as evidence that the scale accurately describes a student's ability to achieve in the regular classroom. Further, confidence intervals are established using a standard error of measurement for internal consistency coefficients. In addition, evidence of interscorer reliability was established by having two individual (publishing company staff members) independently score completed protocols. Thus, information was provided regarding the consistency of adhering to scoring procedures. Evidence of consistency across raters in assessing skills and completing the ratings on the BSSI-3 should also have been provided. Test-retest reliability was examined utilizing a limited sample of 49 children selected from one location in the Midwest.

The manual also presented evidence of concurrent validity based upon correlating selected subtests of the BSSI-3 with additional measures of language development, self-help, and social tests, as well as measures of general knowledge. However, such studies were based upon a group of 42 preschool children receiving special services, bringing into question the generalizability of the results. Further, the manual claims that the BSSI-3 has discriminant validity based upon a sample of 42 children with developmental delays achieving an average overall quotient approximately 2 standard deviations below the mean.

SUMMARY. The BSSI-3 was developed to measure an important aspect of a child's development. In addition, the value of teacher ratings is undisputed. However, there appear to be inconsistencies between the stated purpose/goal of the instrument and what the scale actually measures. The manual is lacking information that would assist the test user in making sound judgments regarding the use of the scale. In addition, the reliability and validity evidence of the scale appears questionable given the methodology utilized and the conclusions reached. Although the premise underlying the BSSI-3 is justified, test users should exercise caution in using the scale as a norm-referenced tool in the process of determining educational diagnoses and eligibility for services.

[36]

Battery for Health Improvement.

Purpose: "Designed to identify factors that may interfere with a patient's normal course of recovery from a physical injury."

Population: Patients 18–65 who are being evaluated or treated for an injury.

Publication Date: 1996.

Acronym: BHI.

Scores, 14: Psychological Factors (Depression, Anxiety, Hostility, Borderline, Symptom Dependency, Chronic Maladjustment, Substance Abuse, Perseverance), Environmental Factors (Family Dysfunction, Job Dissatisfaction, Doctor Dissatisfaction), Physical Factors (Somatic Complaints, Pain Complaints, Muscular Bracing).

Administration: Group.

Price Data, 2000: $90 per preview package including manual (109 pages) and answer sheets with test items for three assessments (specify MICROTEST Q or mail-in scoring); $108 per hand scoring starter kit including manual, 10 test booklets, 50 answer sheets, 50 worksheets, and 50 profile forms; $26 per hand scoring test booklets, $18 per 25 MICROTEST Q answer sheets; $20 per MICROTEST Q interpretive report; $22 per mail-in interpretive report; $9.50 per MICROTEST Q profile report; $11.50 per mail-in profile report; $27 per manual; $54 per optional audio-cassette; many items available in both English and Hispanic.

Time: (25–40) minutes.

Authors: Daniel Bruns and John Mark Disorbio with contributions by Julia Copeland Disorbio.

Publisher: NCS (Minnetonka).

Review of the Battery for Health Improvement by GREGORY J. BOYLE, Professor of Psychology, Bond University, Gold Coast, Queensland, and Visiting Professor, Department of Psychiatry, University of Queensland, Royal Brisbane Hospital, Hesston, Australia:

The Battery for Health Improvement (BHI) is a multidimensional, 202-item pencil-and-paper questionnaire intended for the psychological assessment of physically injured patients, important in the management of chronic medical conditions. The BHI assesses psychomedical (including DSM-IV Axis III) disorders including reactive, psycho-physiological, somatoform, and endogenous disorders, and provides an assessment of chronic pain, coincident with many medical conditions. The BHI measures eight psychological constructs (Depression, Anxiety, Hostility, Borderline, Symptom Deficiency, Chronic Maladjustment, Substance Abuse, and Perseverance), three environmental problem areas (Family Dysfunction, Job, and Doctor Dissatisfaction), and three physical factors (Somatic and Pain Complaints, as well as Muscular Bracing). Pain is measured in 10 body areas, whereas symptoms are measured in 9 category areas. Items are based on the theory of psychomedical disorders, and assigned to scales in each content domain. Inappropriate applications are identified in the BHI manual.

Separate community and patient normative samples enable comparison between individual patients and patient norms, and assessment of discriminative validity. However, aside from matching U.S. Census demographics, no indication is provided in the BHI manual of precisely how the normative samples were chosen, or participation rates, making it difficult to assess possible sampling bias. Furthermore, normative sample sizes were a little small (250 and 527 patients; 241 and 725 community individuals) within the somewhat restricted 18–65 year range. However, it should be noted that some BHI constructs (e.g., Job Dissatisfaction) do not apply well either to adolescents or retired patients.

Short-term stability coefficients (mean retest interval of only 6.7 days) range from .88 to .98. No comparison of immediate retest (dependability) versus longer term stability is provided in the BHI manual, so that the reliability of the BHI scales remains somewhat uncertain. With regard to item homogeneity, Cronbach's alpha coefficients range from .74 to .92 ($M = .85$), suggesting narrow breadth of measurement, with possibly some redundant items (cf. Boyle, 1991).

Moderate concurrent/convergent validity correlations with related instruments (MMPI-2, MCMI-III, Minnesota Satisfaction Questionnaire, McGill Pain Questionnaire, and the Pain Location Test) provide some evidence of validity of the separate BHI scales. However, the construct validity of the separate scales remains uncertain. For example, no factor analytic evidence is provided in the test manual to support the proposed scale structure of the BHI instrument. A brief five-item validity scale comprising rarely endorsed items serves as a crude validity index only. The more important issue of motivational distortion (covering inconsistent responding, faking good, faking bad, response sets, etc.) is not addressed. Consequently, determination of invalid profiles is diffi-

cult without further development of validity scales. Some external/predictive validity studies have been undertaken (e.g., Bruns & Disorbio, 1998; Disorbio, 1998), providing empirical support for the utility of the BHI instrument.

Differing numbers of items across the BHI scales is problematic, spuriously causing discrepancies in measurement variance, and making simple comparison of scale scores difficult. In addition, a number of scales have overlapping items, thereby inflating scale intercorrelations. A separate pain scale (comprising 10 items) allows assessment of chronic pain, and relevant norms are provided for different types of pain patients. Nevertheless, the word "pain" appears in no fewer than five of the "non-pain" BHI items, potentially confounding interpretation (cf. Fernandez & Boyle, 1995), although clinically there is a diagnostic overlap between diagnoses of pain disorder and somatization. Furthermore, the BHI does not differentiate between state and trait measures of psychological constructs such as Depression, Anxiety, and Hostility (cf. Boyle, 1985), nor is any information provided in the test manual regarding item-response characteristics (cf. Boyle, 1987).

The BHI structure is organized into three distinct groupings, called "factors" (Psychological, Environmental, and Physical). To verify these groupings, an iterative maximum-likelihood factor analysis of the combined patient and community interscale correlations (provided in the BHI manual) was undertaken. In accord with the hypothetical organization, three factors were extracted and rotated to direct simple structure. Because most psychological variables and all three environmental variables comprised a single factor, and in line with the Scree test, a separate four-factor solution was extracted. Factor 1 loaded highly on five of the psychological variables—Borderline, Hostility, Anxiety, Perseverance, Depression, and an environmental variable—Family Dysfunction. Factor 2 loaded on the three physical variables—Somatic Complaints, Pain Complaints, and Muscular Bracing. Factor 3 loaded on Substance Abuse and Chronic Maladjustment, and Factor 4 loaded on Doctor Dissatisfaction, Symptom Dependency, and Job Dissatisfaction. Evidently, the hypothetical grouping of the BHI is not entirely supported.

On the positive side, the BHI includes contemporary items, and avoids colloquial or slang expressions. Items considered potentially biased (on gender, ethnic, economic, religious, or other grounds) were excluded. Although the BHI manual is relatively informative, further details need to be included regarding psychometric issues. An upgraded Microtest Q version 4.1.2, and an improved BHI interpretive report have recently been released and include some new features.

Nevertheless, further research into the properties of the BHI is recommended, especially evidence of construct and factor analytic validity. Development of cross-cultural norms would greatly facilitate use of the BHI in countries other than the U.S.A., although this may be premature before refinements of the present instrument are undertaken.

SUMMARY. Compared with other psychological instruments, the BHI appears to make a unique contribution to the measurement of psychomedical disorders, allowing treatment to address *both* the medical and psychological components. The BHI has the advantage of enabling comparison of psychological disorders among medical patients using normative data for specific medical conditions. Behavioral health intervention—which requires collaboration between physicians and psychologists—might be facilitated by the appropriate use of the BHI instrument. The assumption underlying construction of the BHI—namely that psychological assessment and intervention plays an important role in the treatment of medical conditions and chronic pain—seems soundly based. Nevertheless, further research is needed to refine the structure and psychometric properties of the BHI instrument.

REVIEWER'S REFERENCES

Boyle, G. J. (1985). Self-report measures of depression: Some psychometric considerations. *British Journal of Clinical Psychology, 24,* 45–59.

Boyle, G. J. (1991). Does item homogeneity indicate internal consistency or item redundancy in psychometric scales? *Personality and Individual Differences, 12,* 291–294.

Boyle, G. J. (1987). Review of the (1985) "Standards for educational and psychological testing: AERA, APA and NCME." *Australian Journal of Psychology, 39,* 235–237.

Fernandez, E., & Boyle, G. J. (1995). *Evaluation of the language of pain as indexed in the McGill Pain Questionnaire.* Paper presented at the 30th Annual Conference of the Australian Psychological Society, Perth, Australia.

Bruns, D., & Disorbio, J. M. (1998). *Violent ideation in medical patients in four insurance systems.* Paper presented at the 106th Annual Convention of the American Psychological Association, San Francisco.

Disorbio, J. M., & Bruns, D. (1998). *Psychological profiles of rehabilitation patients reporting childhood sexual abuse.* Paper presented at the 106th Annual Convention of the American Psychological Association, San Francisco.

Review of the Battery for Health Improvement by EPHREM FERNANDEZ, Associate Professor of Clinical Psychology, Southern Methodist University, Dallas, TX:

One reminder that appears throughout the Battery for Health Improvement (BHI) is that it avoids the risk of overpathologizing those who have been injured. To achieve this, the authors of the BHI normed it on patients who were in actual treatment for some kind of physical injury or injury-related pain (except for asthma, heart attack, stroke, and arthritis not due to injury). The product was a "battery" of 15 scales comprising 202 items for assessing potential psychological, environmental, and physical interferences in the recovery of such patients. In addition, 10 critical items assess dangerousness and physical/sexual abuse and six items (left unscored) pertain to issues of ongoing research interest.

The authors began with more than 1,000 items generated on the basis of their clinical experience and theorizing about what they call psychomedical disorders—better known as functional or psychophysiological disorders. From this, a 600-item pool was obtained and administered to a subset of 250 patients and 527 nonpatients during the development phase of the test. A final set of 202 items was administered to a remaining sample of patients and nonpatients. In addition, the patient group was administered either the MMPI or a battery comprising other collateral tests.

All items were assigned to scales based on a priori notions of how well the item represented the content of the scale in question. The final set of 202 items was selected also on the basis of item-to-scale correlations, and how well items differentiated patients from community subjects.

The choice of clinical scales is purportedly based on the authors' theory of psychomedical disorders that is outlined over four pages in the Appendix. As it stands, the scales are open to a lot of debate. If the fundamental rule is to sample the domain of problems that influence recovery from injury, then several other variables are worth considering, litigation status being among the foremost. Others include social support, outlook (pessimism and catastrophizing), disease conviction, self-efficacy, adherence, therapeutic alliance, and the perceived credibility of treatment. The relevance of these variables is already supported by a huge body of research.

The Pain Complaints scale offers a good idea of the intensity and distribution of pain across multiple areas of the body. However, the Muscular Bracing scale is limited to tensing and guarding of the body in reacting to injury and stress. This should be expanded to include other behaviors such as distortions of posture and gait, facial expressions, and vocalization. Such behaviors can become maladaptive as in chronic pain syndrome. Therefore, assessing them could be a useful prognostic aid, allowing better prediction of recovery from injury.

The Validity scale assesses overendorsement of unusual and uncommon features. However, most of the items are so bizarre and specific (e.g., "I am allergic to the glass found in jars," "I am unusually sensitive to gravity," "I am probably the only person who has ever lived") that they are unlikely to be endorsed. Consequently, it is difficult for a profile to be rendered invalid even though there may be other grounds for invalidation. There is also no scale to assess underendorsement, denial, or "faking good."

The Depression scale captures many cognitions characteristic of depression but purposely ignores some of the classic symptoms such as appetite/weight change and anhedonia. What is measured is not clinical depression but general feelings of inadequacy and hopelessness. The Anxiety scale (ANX) is also cognitive in emphasis and omits some of the physiological reactions. The Hostility scale, as the authors acknowledge, really combines items about cynicism and anger. In assessing depression, anxiety, and anger, the BHI indeed focuses on the primary affective triad found among those with chronic pain and illness (Fernandez, Clark, & Rudick-Davis, 1998). However, three concerns arise. One is that several items are not scale-specific but relate to more than one affect. For example, Item 16 on the ANX scale, "Sometimes, little things bother me for days" could just as easily pertain to anger; Item 20 on the ANX scale, "I am more sensitive to criticism than most people" is also highly related to depression. This may boost the intercorrelations among the three scales beyond a level that reflects natural comorbidity among these three affects. Secondly, it is hard to discern how much of each affect is due to the injury versus other extraneous factors when the items have been worded without any reference to injury. Related to this is a third problem that each scale confounds both situational and dispositional causes of affect.

Psychometrically, the BHI has excellent test-retest stability over a week, correlations ranging from .88 to .98. Internal consistency is also high, the alphas ranging from .75 to .92 for patients and .74 to .92 for community subjects. Interscale correlations are high among the Depression, Anxiety, and Hostility scales, and this is to be expected due to the high comorbidity within this affective triad; however, as already suggested, this could also be the result of item overlap. For 11 of the items across the BHI, the overlap was by design, supposedly to reflect clinical reality. This might account for the elevated intercorrelations between such scales as substance abuse and chronic maladjustment. But the vast majority of scales are significantly correlated, too, and some of these are inexplicable except as artifacts of item construction.

Correlations between the BHI and other collateral instruments administered concurrently were significant for the most part. However, the choice of collateral instrument may be questioned in some instances. For example, the Beck Depression Inventory (Beck, Steer, & Brown, 1996; 37) or Hamilton Depression Inventory (Reynolds & Koback, 1995; T5:1166) would be better than the Minnesota Multiphasic Personality Inventory (MMPI) as a standard against which to validate the depression scale of the BHI. The authors have used MMPI clinical scales to validate the BHI scales of hostility and anxiety, too. Not only are there alternative collateral instruments but the issue of how relevant the MMPI is to a pain/injury population as opposed to a psychiatric population has to be faced (Turk & Fernandez, 1995). The choice of the McGill Pain Questionnaire (MPQ) as a validator of the BHI Pain Complaints scale is fine because the dependent measures were restricted to intensity and location of pain; however, there have been growing doubts about the classification of MPQ pain descriptors (Fernandez & Towery, 1996; Towery & Fernandez, 1996), which question the reliance on subscales of the MPQ. Finally, the Muscular Bracing scale was not concurrently validated but justified on the basis of clinical judgment. This is surprising especially because there are time-honored methods available for assessment of pain/illness behaviors (e.g., the UAB Pain Behavior Scale [Richards, Nepomuceno, Riles, & Suer, 1982]).

Given that the BHI is primarily a prognostic rather than diagnostic instrument, users might be interested in how well scores actually predict recovery from injury or response to treatment. Unfortunately, no data are offered on predictive validity of the test. Neither is there information on the incremental utility of the test. This is an inescapable issue in light of several existing instruments with the same objectives as the BHI (e.g., the PPS, Block, 1996).

Scoring of the BHI is simple and can be done by hand, on computer, or by mail-in. The Automated Interpretive Report includes a summary report for the patient to read. Versatility is also a feature of the reports that can be generated as separate versions tailored to the clinician and test-taker, respectively. Additionally, a progress report graphically illustrates the patient's BHI scale scores over time.

SUMMARY. The BHI is appropriately normed on patients in treatment for physical injury or injury-related pain. Reliability coefficients are good but the issue of validity remains to be established. First of all, the scales and assignment of items to scales seem to have been done a priori; this should be corroborated with factor analyses. Concurrent validity needs to be ascertained in relation to other instruments of the same genre, and the question of predictive validity (specifically, whether BHI scores relate to treatment outcome) needs to be addressed.

REVIEWER'S REFERENCES

Richards, J. S., Nepomuceno, C., Riles, M., & Suer, Z. (1982). Assessing pain behavior: The UAB Pain Behavior Scale. *Pain, 14,* 393–398.
Reynolds, W. M., & Kobak, K. A. (1995). *Hamilton Depression Inventory.* Odessa, FL: Psychological Assessment Resources.
Turk, D. C., & Fernandez, E. (1995). Personality assessment and the Minnesota Multiphasic Personality Inventory in chronic pain. *Pain Forum, 4,* 104–107.
Beck, A. T., Steer, R. A., & Brown, G. K. (1996). Beck Depression Inventory—II. San Antonio, TX: The Psychological Corporation.
Block, A. R. (1996). *Presurgical psychological screening in chronic pain syndromes: A guide for the behavioral health practitioner.* Mahwah, NJ: Lawrence Erlbaum & Associates.
Fernandez, E., & Towery, S. (1996). A parsimonious set of verbal descriptors of pain sensation derived from the McGill Pain Questionnaire. *Pain, 66,* 31–37.
Towery, S., & Fernandez, E. (1996). Reclassification and rescaling of McGill Pain Questionnaire verbal descriptors of pain sensation: A replication. *The Clinical Journal of Pain, 12,* 270–276.
Fernandez, E., Clark, T. S., & Rudick-Davis, D. (1998). A framework for conceptualization and assessment of affective disturbance in pain. In A. R. Block, E. F. Kremer, & E. Fernandez (Eds.), *Handbook of pain syndromes: Biopsychosocial perspectives* (pp. 123–147). Mahwah, NJ: Lawrence Erlbaum & Associates.

[37]

Beck Depression Inventory—II.

Purpose: "Developed for the assessment of symptoms corresponding to criteria for diagnosing depressive disorders listed in the ... DSM IV."

Population: Ages 13 and over.

Publication Dates: 1961–1996.

Acronym: BDI-II.

Scores: Total score only.

Administration: Group or individual.

Price Data, 1999: $57 per complete kit including manual ('96, 38 pages) and 25 recording forms; $27 per manual; $29.50 per 25 recording forms; $112 per 100 recording forms; $29.50 per 25 Spanish recording forms; $112 per 100 Spanish recording forms.

Foreign Language Edition: Available in Spanish.

Time: (5–10) minutes.

Comments: Hand-scored or computer-based administration, scoring, and interpretation available; "revision of BDI based upon new information about depression."

Authors: Aaron T. Beck, Robert A. Steer, and Gregory K. Brown.

Publisher: The Psychological Corporation.

Cross References: See T5:272 (384 references); for reviews by Janet F. Carlson and Niels G. Waller, see 13:31 (1026 references); see also T4:268 (660 references); for reviews by Collie W. Conoley and Norman D. Sundberg of an earlier edition, see 11:31 (286 references).

Review of the Beck Depression Inventory-II by PAUL A. ARBISI, Minneapolis VA Medical Center, Assistant Professor Department of Psychiatry and Assistant Clinical Professor Department of Psychology, University of Minnesota, Minneapolis, MN:

After over 35 years of nearly universal use, the Beck Depression Inventory (BDI) has undergone a major revision. The revised version of the Beck, the BDI-II, represents a significant improvement over the original instrument across all aspects of the instrument including content, psychometric validity, and external validity. The BDI was an effective measure of depressed mood that repeatedly demonstrated utility as evidenced by its widespread use in the clinic as well as by the frequent use of the BDI as a dependent measure in outcome studies of psychotherapy and antidepressant treatment (Piotrowski & Keller, 1989; Piotrowski & Lubin, 1990). The BDI-II should supplant the BDI and readily gain acceptance by surpassing its predecessor in use.

Despite the demonstrated utility of the Beck, times had changed and the diagnostic context within which the instrument was developed had altered considerably over the years (Beck, Ward, Mendelson, Mock, & Erbaugh, 1961). Further, psychometrically, the BDI had some problems with certain items failing to discriminate adequately across the range of depression and other items showing gender bias (Santor, Ramsay, & Zuroff, 1994). Hence the time had come for a conceptual reassessment and psychometrically informed revision of the instrument. Indeed, a mid-course correction had occurred in 1987 as evidenced by the BDI-IA, a version that included rewording of 15 out of the 21 items (Beck & Steer, 1987). This version did not address the limited scope of depressive symptoms of the BDI nor the failure of the BDI to adhere to contemporary diagnostic criteria for depression as codified in the DSM-III. Further, consumers appeared to vote with their feet because, since the publication of the BDI-IA, the original Beck had been cited far more frequently in the literature than the BDI-IA. Therefore, the time had arrived for a major overhaul of the classic BDI and a retooling of the content to reflect diagnostic sensibilities of the 1990s.

In the main, the BDI-II accomplishes these goals and represents a highly successful revamping of a reliable standard. The BDI-II retains the 21-item format with four options under each item, ranging from not present (0) to severe (3). Relative to the BDI-IA, all but three items were altered in some way on the BDI-II. Items dropped from the BDI include body image change, work difficulty, weight loss, and somatic preoccupation. To replace the four lost items, the BDI-II includes the following new items: agitation, worthlessness, loss of energy, and concentration difficulty. The current item content includes: (a) sadness, (b) pessimism, (c) past failure, (d) loss of pleasure, (e) guilty feelings, (f) punishment feelings, (g) self-dislike, (h) self-criticalness, (i) suicidal thoughts or wishes, (j) crying, (k) agitation, (l) loss of interest, (m) indecisiveness, (n) worthlessness, (o) loss of energy, (p) changes in sleeping pattern, (q) irritability, (r) changes in appetite, (s) concentration difficulty, (t) tiredness or fatigue, and (u) loss of interest in sex. To further reflect DSM-IV diagnostic criteria for depression, both increases and decreases in appetite are assessed in the same item and both hypersomnia and hyposomnia are assessed in another item. And rather than the 1-week time period rated on the BDI, the BDI-II, consistent with DSM-IV, asks for ratings over the past 2 weeks.

The BDI-II retains the advantage of the BDI in its ease of administration (5–10 minutes) and the rather straightforward interpretive guidelines presented in the manual. At the same time, the advantage of a self-report instrument such as the BDI-II may also be a disadvantage. That is, there are no validity indicators contained on the BDI or the BDI-II and the ease of administration

of a self-report lends itself to the deliberate tailoring of self-report and distortion of the results. Those of us engaged in clinical practice are often faced with clients who alter their presentation to forward a personal agenda that may not be shared with the clinician. The manual obliquely mentions this problem in an ambivalent and somewhat avoidant fashion. Under the heading, "Memory and Response Sets," the manual blithely discounts the potential problem of a distorted response set by attributing extreme elevation on the BDI-II to "extreme negative thinking" which "may be a central cognitive symptom of severe depression rather than a response set per se because patients with milder depression should show variation in their response ratings" (manual, p. 9). On the other hand, later in the manual, we are told that, "In evaluating BDI-II scores, practitioners should keep in mind that all self-report inventories are subject to response bias" (p. 12). The latter is sound advice and should be highlighted under the heading of response bias.

The manual is well written and provides the reader with significant information regarding norms, factor structure, and notably, nonparametric item-option characteristic curves for each item. Indeed the latter inclusion incorporates the latest in item response theory, which appears to have guided the retention and deletion of items from the BDI (Santor et al., 1994).

Generally the psychometric properties of the BDI-II are quite sound. Coefficient alpha estimates of reliability for the BDI-II with outpatients was .92 and was .93 for the nonclinical sample. Corrected item-total correlation for the outpatient sample ranged from .39 (loss of interest in sex) to .70 (loss of pleasure), for the nonclinical college sample the lowest item-total correlation was .27 (loss of interest in sex) and the highest (.74 (self-dislike). The test-retest reliability coefficient across the period of a week was quite high at .93. The inclusion in the manual of item-option characteristic curves for each BDI-II item is of noted significance. Examination of these curves reveals that, for the most part, the ordinal position of the item options is appropriately assigned for 17 of the 21 items. However, the items addressing punishment feelings, suicidal thought or wishes, agitation, and loss of interest in sex did not display the anticipated rank order indicating ordinal increase in severity of depression across item options. Additionally, although improved over the BDI, Item

10 (crying) Option 3 does not clearly express a more severe level of depression than Option 2 (see Santor et al., 1994). Over all, however, the option choices within each item appear to function as intended across the severity dimension of depression.

The suggested guidelines and cut scores for the interpretation of the BDI-II and placement of individual scores into a range of depression severity are purported to have good sensitivity and moderate specificity, but test parameters such as positive and negative predictive power are not reported (i.e., given score X on the BDI-II, what is the probability that the individual meets criteria for a Major Depressive Disorder, of moderate severity?). According to the manual, the BDI-II was developed as a screening instrument for major depression and, accordingly, cut scores were derived through the use of receiver operating characteristic curves to maximize sensitivity. Of the 127 outpatients used to derive the cut scores, 57 met criteria for either single-episode or recurrent major depression. The relatively high base rate (45%) for major depression is a bit unrealistic for nonpsychiatric settings and will likely serve to inflate the test parameters. Cross validation of the cut scores on different samples with lower base rates of major depression is warranted due to the fact that a different base rate of major depression may result in a significant change in the proportion of correct decisions based on the suggested cut score (Meehl & Rosen, 1955). Consequently, until the suggested cut scores are cross validated in those populations, caution should be exercised when using the BDI-II as a screen in nonpsychiatric populations where the base rate for major depression may be substantially lower.

Concurrent validity evidence appears solid with the BDI-II demonstrating a moderately high correlation with the Hamilton Psychiatric Rating Scale for Depression—Revised ($r = .71$) in psychiatric outpatients. Of importance to the discriminative validity of the instrument was the relatively moderate correlation between the BDI-II and the Hamilton Rating Scale for Anxiety—Revised ($r = .47$). The manual reports mean BDI-II scores for various groups of psychiatric outpatients by diagnosis. As expected, outpatients had higher scores than college students. Further, individuals with mood disorders had higher scores than those individuals diagnosed with anxiety and adjustment disorders.

The BDI-II is a stronger instrument than the BDI with respect to its factor structure. A two-factor (Somatic-Affective and Cognitive) solution accounted for the majority of the common variance in both an outpatient psychiatric sample and a much smaller nonclinical college sample. Factor Analysis of the BDI-II in a larger nonclinical sample of college students resulted in Cognitive-Affective and Somatic-Vegetative main factors essentially replicating the findings presented in the manual and providing strong evidence for the overall stability of the factor structure across samples (Dozois, Dobson, & Ahnberg, 1998). Unfortunately several of the items such as sadness and crying shifted factor loadings depending upon the type of sample (clinical vs. nonclinical).

SUMMARY. The BDI-II represents a highly successful revision of an acknowledged standard in the measurement of depressed mood. The revision has improved upon the original by updating the items to reflect contemporary diagnostic criteria for depression and utilizing state-of-the-art psychometric techniques to improve the discriminative properties of the instrument. This degree of improvement is no small feat and the BDI-II deserves to replace the BDI as the single most widely used clinically administered instrument for the assessment of depression.

REVIEWER'S REFERENCES
Meehl, P. E., & Rosen, A. (1955). Antecedent probability and the efficiency of psychometric signs, patterns, or cutting scores. *Psychological Bulletin, 52,* 194–216.
Beck, A. T., Ward, C. H., Mendelson, M., Mock, J., & Erbaugh, J. (1961). An inventory for measuring depression. *Archives of General Psychiatry, 4,* 561–571.
Beck, A. T., & Steer, R. A. (1987). *Beck Depression Inventory manual.* San Antonio, TX: The Psychological Corporation.
Piotrowski, C., & Keller, J. W. (1989). Psychological testing in outpatient mental health facilities: A national study. *Professional Psychology: Research and Practice, 20,* 423–425.
Piotrowski, C., & Lubin, B. (1990). Assessment practices of health psychologists; Survey of APA Division 38 clinicians. *Professional Psychology: Research and Practice, 21,* 99–106.
Santor, D. A., Ramsay, J. O., & Zuroff, D. C. (1994). Nonparametric item analyses of the Beck Depression Inventory: Evaluating gender item bias and response option weights. *Psychological Assessment, 6,* 255–270.
Dozois, D. J. A., Dobson, K. S., & Ahnberg, J. L. (1998). A psychometric evaluation of the Beck Depression Inventory-II. *Psychological Assessment, 10,* 83–89.

Review of the Beck Depression Inventory-II by RICHARD F. FARMER, Associate Professor of Psychology, Idaho State University, Pocatello, ID:

The Beck Depression Inventory-II (BDI-II) is the most recent version of a widely used self-report measure of depression severity. Designed for persons 13 years of age and older, the BDI-II represents a significant revision of the original instrument published almost 40 years ago (BDI-I; Beck, Ward, Mendelson, Mock, & Erbaugh, 1961) as well as the subsequent amended version copyrighted in 1978 (BDI-IA; Beck, Rush, Shaw, &

Emery, 1979; Beck & Steer, 1987, 1993). Previous editions of the BDI have considerable support for their effectiveness as measures of depression (for reviews, see Beck & Beamesderfer, 1974; Beck, Steer & Garbin, 1988; and Steer, Beck, & Garrison, 1986).

Items found in these earlier versions, many of which were retained in modified form for the BDI-II, were clinically derived and neutral with respect to a particular theory of depression. Like previous versions, the BDI-II contains 21 items, each of which assesses a different symptom or attitude by asking the examinee to consider a group of graded statements that are weighted from 0 to 3 based on intuitively derived levels of severity. If the examinee feels that more than one statement within a group applies, he or she is instructed to circle the highest weighting among the applicable statements. A total score is derived by summing weights corresponding to the statements endorsed over the 21 items. The test authors provide empirically informed cut scores (derived from receiver operating characteristic [ROC] curve methodology) for indexing the severity of depression based on responses from outpatients with a diagnosed episode of major depression (cutoff scores to index the severity of dysphoria for college samples are suggested by Dozois, Dobson, & Ahnberg, 1998).

The BDI-II can usually be completed within 5 to 10 minutes. In addition to providing guidelines for the oral administration of the test, the manual cautions the user against using the BDI-II as a diagnostic instrument and appropriately recommends that interpretations of test scores should only be undertaken by qualified professionals. Although the manual does not report the reading level associated with the test items, previous research on the BDI-IA suggested that items were written at about the sixth-grade level (Berndt, Schwartz, & Kaiser, 1983).

A number of changes appear in the BDI-II, perhaps the most significant of which is the modification of test directions and item content to be more consistent with the major depressive episode concept as defined in the *Diagnostic and Statistical Manual of Mental Disorders—Fourth Edition* (DSM-IV; American Psychiatric Association, 1994). Whereas the BDI-I and BDI-IA assessed symptoms experienced at the present time and during the past week, respectively, the BDI-II instructs the examinee to respond in terms of how he or she has "been feeling during the *past two weeks, including today*" (manual, p. 8, emphasis in original) so as to be consistent with the DSM-IV time period for the assessment of major depression. Similarly, new items included in the BDI-II address psychomotor agitation, concentration difficulties, sense of worthlessness, and loss of energy so as to make the BDI-II item set more consistent with DSM-IV criteria. Items that appeared in the BDI-I and BDI-IA that were dropped in the second edition were those that assessed weight loss, body image change, somatic preoccupation, and work difficulty. All but three of the items from the BDI-IA retained for inclusion in the BDI-II were reworded in some way. Items that assess changes in sleep patterns and appetite now address both increases and decreases in these areas.

Two samples were retained to evaluate the psychometric characteristics of the BDI-II: (a) a clinical sample (*n* = 500; 63% female; 91% White) who sought outpatient therapy at one of four outpatient clinics on the U.S. east coast (two of which were located in urban areas, two in suburban areas), and (b) a convenience sample of Canadian college students (*n* = 120; 56% women; described as "predominantly White"). The average ages of the clinical and student samples were, respectively, 37.2 (*SD* = 15.91; range = 13–86) and 19.58 (*SD* = 1.84).

Reliability of the BDI was evaluated with multiple methods. Internal consistency was assessed using corrected item-total correlations (ranges: .39 to .70 for outpatients; .27 to .74 for students) and coefficient alpha (.92 for outpatients; .93 for students). Test-retest reliability was assessed over a 1-week interval among a small subsample of 26 outpatients from one clinic site (*r* = .93). There was no significant change in scores noted among this outpatient sample between the two testing occasions, a finding that is different from those often obtained with college students who, when tested repeatedly with earlier versions of the BDI, were often observed to have lower scores on subsequent testing occasions (e.g., Hatzenbuehler, Parpal, & Matthews, 1983).

Following the method of Santor, Ramsay, and Zuroff (1994), the test authors also examined the item-option characteristic curves for each of the 21 BDI-II items as endorsed by the 500 outpatients. As noted in a previous review of the

BDI (1993 Revised) by Waller (1998), the use of this method to evaluate item performance represents a new standard in test revision. Consistent with findings for depressed outpatients obtained by Santor et al. (1994) on the BDI-IA, most of the BDI-II items performed well as evidenced by the individual item-option curves. All items were reported to display monotonic relationships with the underlying dimension of depression severity. A minority of items were somewhat problematic, however, when the degree of correspondence between estimated and a priori weights associated with item response options was evaluated. For example, on Item 11 (agitation), the response option weighted a value of 1 was more likely to be endorsed than the option weighted 3 across all levels of depression, including depression in the moderate and severe ranges. In general, though, response option weights of the BDI-II items did a good job of discriminating across estimated levels of depression severity. Unfortunately, the manual does not provide detailed discussion of item-option characteristic curves and their interpretation.

The validity of the BDI-II was evaluated with outpatient subsamples of various sizes. When administered on the same occasion, the correlation between the BDI-II and BDI-IA was quite high ($n = 101$, $r = .93$), suggesting that these measures yield similar patterns of scores, even though the BDI-II, on average, produced equated scores that were about 3 points higher. In support of its convergent validity, the BDI-II displayed moderately high correlations with the Beck Hopelessness Scale ($n = 158$, $r = .68$) and the Revised Hamilton Psychiatric Rating Scale for Depression (HRSD-R; $n = 87$, $r = .71$). The correlation between the BDI-II and the Revised Hamilton Anxiety Rating Scale ($n = 87$, $r = .47$) was significantly less than that for the BDI-II and HRSD-R, which was cited as evidence of the BDI-II's discriminant validity. The BDI-II, however, did share a moderately high correlation with the Beck Anxiety Inventory ($n = 297$; $r = .60$), a finding consistent with past research on the strong association between self-reported anxiety and depression (e.g., Kendall & Watson, 1989). Additional research published since the manual's release (Steer, Ball, Ranieri, & Beck, 1997) also indicates that the BDI-II shares higher correlations with the SCL-90-R Depression subscale ($r = .89$) than with the SCL-90-R Anxiety subscale ($r = .71$),

although the latter correlation is still substantial. Other data presented in the test manual indicated that of the 500 outpatients, those diagnosed with mood disorders ($n = 264$) had higher BDI-II scores than those diagnosed with anxiety ($n = 88$), adjustment ($n = 80$), or other ($n = 68$) disorders. The test authors also cite evidence of validity by separate factor analyses performed on the BDI-II item set for outpatients and students. However, findings from these analyses, which were different in some significant respects, are questionable evidence of the measure's validity as the test was apparently not developed to assess specific dimensions of depression. Factor analytic studies of the BDI have historically produced inconsistent findings (Beck et al., 1988), and preliminary research on the BDI-II suggests some variations in factor structure within both clinical and student samples (Dozois et al., 1998; Steer & Clark, 1997; Steer, Kumar, Ranieri, & Beck, 1998). Furthermore, one of the authors of the BDI-II (Steer & Clark, 1997) has recently advised that the measure not be scored as separate subscales.

SUMMARY. The BDI-II is presented as a user-friendly self-report measure of depression severity. Strengths of the BDI-II include the very strong empirical foundation on which it was built, namely almost 40 years of research that demonstrates the effectiveness of earlier versions. In the development of the BDI-II, innovative methods were employed to determine optimum cut scores (ROC curves) and evaluate item performance and weighting (item-option curves). The present edition demonstrates very good reliability and impressive test item characteristics. Preliminary evidence of the BDI-II's validity in clinical samples is also encouraging. Despite the many impressive features of this measure, one may wonder why the test developers were not even more thorough in their presentation of the development of the BDI-II and more rigorous in the evaluation of its effectiveness. The test manual is too concise, and often omits important details involving the test development process. The clinical sample used to generate cut scores and evaluate the psychometric properties of the measure seems unrepresentative in many respects (e.g., racial make-up, patient setting, geographic distribution), and other aspects of this sample (e.g., education level, family income) go unmentioned. The student sample is relatively small and, unfortunately, drawn from a single university. Opportunities to address important questions regarding the measure were also missed, such as whether the BDI-II effectively assesses or screens the DSM-IV concept of major depression, and the extent to which it may accomplish this better than earlier versions. This seems to be a particularly important question given that the BDI was originally developed as a measure of the depressive syndrome, not as a screening measure for a nosologic category (Kendall, Hollon, Beck, Hammen, & Ingram, 1987), a distinction that appears to have become somewhat blurred in this most recent edition. Also, not reported in the manual are analyses to examine possible sex biases among the BDI-II item set. Santor et al. (1994) reported that the BDI-IA items were relatively free of sex bias, and given the omission of the most sex-biased item in the BDI-IA (body image change) from the BDI-II, it is possible that this most recent edition may contain even less bias. Similarly absent in the manual is any report on the item-option characteristic curves for nonclinical samples. Santor et al. (1994) reported that for most of the BDI-IA items, response option weights were less discriminating across the range of depression severity among their college sample relative to their clinical sample, an anticipated finding given that students would be less likely to endorse response options hypothesized to be consistent with more severe forms of depression. Also, given that previous editions of the BDI have shown inconsistent associations with social undesirability (e.g., Tanaka-Matsumi & Kameoka, 1986), an opportunity was missed to evaluate the extent to which the BDI-II measures something different than this response set. Despite these relative weaknesses in the development and presentation of the BDI-II, existent evidence suggests that the BDI-II is just as sound if not more so than its earlier versions.

REVIEWER'S REFERENCES

Beck, A. T., Ward, C. H., Mendelson, M., Mock, J., & Erbaugh, J. (1961). An inventory for measuring depression. *Archives of General Psychiatry, 4,* 561–571.

Beck, A. T., & Beamesderfer, A. (1974). Assessment of depression: The Depression Inventory. In P. Pichot & R. Oliver-Martin (Eds.), *Psychological measurements in psychopharmacology: Modern problems in pharmacopsychiatry* (vol. 7, pp. 151–169). Basel: Karger.

Beck, A. T., Rush, A. J., Shaw, B. F., & Emery, G. (1979). *Cognitive therapy of depression.* New York: Guilford.

Berndt, D. J., Schwartz, S., & Kaiser, C. F. (1983). Readability of self-report depression inventories. *Journal of Consulting and Clinical Psychology, 51,* 627–628.

Hatzenbuehler, L. C., Parpal, M., & Matthews, L. (1983). Classifying college students as depressed or nondepressed using the Beck Depression Inventory: An empirical analysis. *Journal of Consulting and Clinical Psychology, 51,* 360–366.

Steer, R. A., Beck, A. T., & Garrison, B. (1986). Applications of the Beck Depression Inventory. In N. Sartorius & T. A. Ban (Eds.), *Assessment of depression* (pp. 123–142). New York: Springer-Verlag.

Tanaka-Matsumi, J., & Kameoka, V. A. (1986). Reliabilities and concurrent validities of popular self-report measures of depression, anxiety, and social desirability. *Journal of Consulting and Clinical Psychology, 54,* 328–333.

Beck, A. T., & Steer, R. A. (1987). *Beck Depression Inventory manual.* San Antonio, TX: The Psychological Corporation.

Kendall, P. C., Hollon, S. D., Beck, A. T., Hammen, C. L., & Ingram, R. E. (1987). Issues and recommendations regarding the use of the Beck Depression Inventory. *Cognitive Therapy and Research, 11,* 289–299.

Beck, A. T., Steer, R. A., & Garbin, M. G. (1988). Psychometric properties of the Beck Depression Inventory: Twenty-five years of evaluation. *Clinical Psychology Review, 8,* 77–100.

Kendall, P. C., & Watson, D. (Eds.). (1989). *Anxiety and depression: Distinctive and overlapping features.* San Diego, CA: Academic Press.

Beck, A. T., & Steer, R. A. (1993). *Beck Depression Inventory manual.* San Antonio, TX: Psychological Corporation.

American Psychiatric Association. (1994). *Diagnostic and statistical manual of mental disorders* (4th ed.). Washington, DC: Author.

Santor, D. A., Ramsay, J. O., & Zuroff, D. C. (1994). Nonparametric item analyses of the Beck Depression Inventory: Evaluating gender item bias and response option weights. *Psychological Assessment, 6,* 255–270.

Steer, R. A., Ball, R., Ranieri, W. F., & Beck, A. T. (1997). Further evidence for the construct validity of the Beck Depression Inventory—II with psychiatric outpatients. *Psychological Reports, 80,* 443–446.

Steer, R. A., & Clark, D. A. (1997). Psychometric characteristics of the Beck Depression Inventory—II with college students. *Measurement and Evaluation in Counseling and Development, 30,* 128–136.

Dozois, D. J. A., Dobson, K. S., & Ahnberg, J. L. (1998). A psychometric evaluation of the Beck Depression Inventory—II. *Psychological Assessment, 10,* 83–89.

Steer, R. A., Kumar, G., Ranieri, W. F., & Beck, A. T. (1998). Use of the Beck Depression Inventory—II with adolescent psychiatric outpatients. *Journal of Psychopathology and Behavioral Assessment, 20,* 127–137.

Waller, N. G. (1998). [Review of the Beck Depression Inventory—1993 Revised]. In J. C. Impara & B. S. Plake (Eds.), *The thirteenth mental measurements yearbook* (pp. 120–121). Lincoln, NE: The Buros Institute of Mental Measurements.

[38]
Bedside Evaluation of Dysphagia.

Purpose: Designed to assess swallowing abilities and the factors that may influence those abilities.

Population: Adults neurologically impaired.

Publication Date: 1995.

Acronym: BED.

Scores, 13: Behavioral Characteristics, Cognition and Communication Screening (Cognition, Receptive Language, Expressive Language/Speech Production), Oral Motor Examination (Lips, Tongue, Soft Palate, Cheeks, Mandible, Larynx), Oral-Pharyngeal Dysphagia Symptoms Assessment (Oral State, Pharyngeal State, Additional Observations).

Administration: Individual.

Price Data, 1998: $35 per 25 evaluation forms; $45.50 per manual (56 pages) and 25 evaluation forms.

Time: (15–45) minutes.

Author: Edward Hardy.

Publisher: Imaginart International, Inc.

Review of the Bedside Evaluation of Dysphagia by CARLOS INCHAURRALDE, Professor of Linguistics and Psychologist, University of Zaragoza, Zaragoza, Spain:

The Bedside Evaluation of Dysphagia (BED) provides a comprehensive format for the possible diagnosis of dysphagia in a patient by the speech-language pathologist. It has the form of a checklist in which information is collected about behavior, cognition, and communication abilities, and oral-motor capacity. It is claimed to have been developed mainly for use with neurologically impaired adults—the most suitable candidates being patients with right and left CVA, Parkinson's Disease, traumatic brain injury, and dementia.

The manual gives little information about test development: It was developed "following the author's extensive experience with adult patients in a variety of settings" (p. 1), and it used as an initial basis the protocol that appears in Hardy and Robinson (1993). There is no information at all about reliability, validity, or norms, which should be part of any psychometric or clinical instrument of this kind. On the other hand, there are very clear instructions as to how to collect the information in all the sections of the BED. The manual clearly states the procedure and the alternative responses from the patient, with clear specifications as to what may be considered either "within normal limits" or "impaired." At the end of the evaluation form there is a summary report section, in which the observations are summarized and recommendations are made according to the data collected.

The lack of reliability information is a problem with this test. Interscorer reliability would be extremely important here because there are no scores and most of the BED is based on dichotomous judgments, which may be made differently by different evaluators. Proper evaluation of the suitability of the BED would involve knowing whether it can be used reliably by different examiners. Validity is not clearly addressed either. Content validity relies on the protocol that was used as a basis at the development stage, but there are no data available about item analysis, correlations among the different sections, or correlations with other similar instruments.

The main strength of the BED is its detailed assessment of all the factors relevant for the determination of possibly dysphagia. Thus, it is a good checklist for the trained speech-language pathologist to find out about problems in swallowing that may require further exploration. However, there is no scoring that might help to determine the seriousness of the impairment. The recommendations can range from additional examination by other means to compensatory and rehabilitation strategies. This relies on the subjective judgment of the examiner, which may be questionable because the BED's main weakness is its lack of adequate technical information. As has already been mentioned, it has no information about reliability and validity, which makes it unsuitable as the only source of information.

SUMMARY. The BED is a good exploratory checklist for detecting symptoms of dysphagia, and should be useful for the knowledgeable speech-language therapist. It has very detailed instructions, from which interscorer reliability might, in theory, benefit. However, because there are no clear data about development, validity, and reliability, we should be cautious when using this instrument, especially while filling in the recommendations section of the form. The BED is useful for organizing our observations about the patient, but it cannot help us in making judgments other than those suggested by our previous experience.

REVIEWER'S REFERENCE

Hardy, E., & Robinson, N. (1993). *Swallowing Disorders Treatment manual.* Bisbee, AZ: Imaginart.

Review of the Bedside Evaluation of Dysphagia by STEVEN B. LEDER, Professor of Surgery, Yale University School of Medicine, New Haven, CT:

The Bedside Evaluation of Dysphagia (BED) attempts to evaluate basic cognition and communication skills and oral motor functioning prior to beginning a dysphagia evaluation. This information is then used to determine oral feeding status, diet consistency, compensatory strategies, and rehabilitation techniques for the dysphagic patient. An accompanying response form closely parallels the text and allows for recording of data in a clear and concise manner. The specific categories assessed are Cognition and Communication Screening, Oral-Motor Assessment, Oral-Pharyngeal Dysphagia Symptoms Assessment, Summary, and Recommendations. The text also provides a box entitled Clinical Implications for each category in which the author presents clinical insights, caveats, or recommendations for further diagnostic testing or referral to other professionals.

Although a lot of information is collected during a BED, it is unclear how all the information relates to the goal of diagnosing dysphagia. For example, under Clinical Insights in the Cognition and Communication Screening categories the author focuses on their importance in later swallowing intervention strategies. It is unclear how counting 1–10 or saying the days of the week relate to the purpose of the BED (i.e., the diagnosis of dysphagia). How are tasks such as these important during actual oral-pharyngeal dysphagia testing? Many individuals seen for dysphagia testing are demented or disoriented but can be tested reliably and, with proper supervision, can begin an oral diet.

Much time is devoted to direct oral-motor examination of the lips, tongue, soft palate, cheeks, and mandible, with inferred motor functioning of the larynx. The swallow reflex, however, is very robust and although performing non-swallowing-related maneuvers are helpful in assessing motor function with the goal of correlation with swallowing success, no sensitivity or specificity data related to motor assessment are provided to show their predictive value for swallowing success or failure. For example, many individuals with altered oral, pharyngeal, and laryngeal anatomy and physiology due to stroke or head and neck cancer swallow successfully. It is not, therefore, what structures are impaired or removed that is of importance, but rather the functioning of the remaining structures during the act of swallowing that is of primary importance for swallowing success.

Subjectivity is inherent to the scoring of many subsets. For example, the adjectives "Good, Fair, Poor, Diminished, Hypersensitive, Strong, Weak, Mildly, Moderately, and Severely" are used throughout the BED. No correlation statistics for inter- or intraexaminer agreement were reported nor are correlations with outcome variables to determine if these adjectives actually correspond to the degree of physical abnormality they are attempting to describe. Further, it is not known if the various subsets and items within each subset are hierarchical or of equal importance in predicting dysphagia (e.g., does ability to lateralize the jaw impact on swallowing success to a greater degree than tongue sensitivity and, if so, which of the six discrete areas examined on the tongue is most important?).

Although the BED makes good clinical sense and some of the suggestions are correct on face value, a significant drawback is that no corroborating data are provided to substantiate any of the bedside testing methods, feeding recommendations, or rehabilitative strategies suggested. No objective dysphagia testing (e.g., modified barium swallow or fiberoptic endoscopic evaluation of swallowing) was reported in either the same or similar populations of dysphagic individuals to

support the efficacy of any of the results or recommendations from the BED.

Finally, another significant drawback is that the final judgment of whether to recommend an objective, instrumental dysphagia assessment is purely subjective. In addition to the rather broad (poor posture/positioning), vague (abnormal voluntary cough, change in vocal quality, and impaired secretion management), incorrect (impaired palatal gag reflex), or impossible to test at bedside (impaired laryngeal evaluation) variables stated as sufficient in and of themselves to make a referral for an instrumental assessment, other even broader variables recommended to generate a referral were any pharyngeal stage abnormalities or documented history of aspiration pneumonia. (Indeed, if the latter was present during history taking there would be no need to proceed further with a BED.)

SUMMARY. In conclusion, the BED incorporates many clinical variables that should be assessed prior to performing an instrumental dysphagia assessment. The response form provides a clear way to record this data. Before the BED can be relied upon, however, to provide adequate sensitivity and specificity in diagnosing oral-pharyngeal dysphagia, making appropriate feeding recommendations and intervention strategies, and referring for objective instrumental dysphagia diagnostics, both more corroborative data based on objective dysphagia testing and appropriate test construct and content validity are needed.

[39]

Bedside Evaluation Screening Test, Second Edition.

Purpose: "Designed to assess and quantify language disorders in adults resulting from aphasia."
Population: Patients with language deficits.
Publication Dates: 1987–1998.
Acronym: BEST-2.
Scores, 8: Conversational Expression, Naming Objects, Describing Objects, Repeating Sentences, Pointing to Objects, Pointing to Parts of a Picture, Reading, Total.
Administration: Individual.
Price Data, 1999: $129 per complete kit including examiner's manual ('98, 49 pages), picture book, 25 record forms, and 25 profile/summary sheets; $39 per examiner's manual; $44 per picture book; $39 per 25 record forms; $13 per 25 profile/summary sheets.
Time: (20–30) minutes.
Comments: Replaces the Bedside Evaluation and Screening Test of Aphasia (T4:272).

Authors: Joyce Fitch West, Elaine S. Sands, and Deborah Ross-Swain.
Publisher: PRO-ED.
Cross References: For a review by Malcolm R. McNeil of an earlier edition, see 11:34.

Review of the Bedside Evaluation Screening Test, Second Edition by PAMILLA MORALES, Senior Lecturer, Bolton Institute, Bolton, Lancashire, England:

The Bedside Evaluation Screening Test, Second Edition (BEST-2) was developed as an initial aphasia test to assess quickly and to quantify language deficits in patients who may not be physically able to respond to a full aphasia assessment battery. This test is a revision from the original BEST published in 1987, which contained magnetized objects. The authors opted for pictures in a wire-bound self-standing book, which is easier to manipulate, increased the efficiency of the testing procedure, and reduced the risk of lost objects. The test items remain unchanged apart from a "bar scene" that was replaced with an ice cream vendor scene. The BEST-2 was then field tested and revalidated with the above changes.

The BEST-2 is designed for first language English-speaking adult patients and can be administered and scored within 30 minutes. Its strength as a screening instrument is its flexibility in presentation, with the minimal criterion that the patient be able to sit up in bed and maintain eye contact with the examiner. The BEST-2 is compact and self-contained and is less burdensome than most instruments of this type and design.

The instrument consists of seven subtests with each subtest having the possibility of 30 raw score points. Low scores on the subtests indicate severe impairment, whereas high scores indicate less to no impairment. Raw scores can be changed to standard scores using the tables in the manual. Each individual subtest standard score and/or the sum of the seven standard scores can be assigned a degree of impairment. The test measures conversational expression, naming common objects, simple descriptive and comparative abilities, repetition, auditory comprehension of simple and complex commands, and reading. The instrument has been utilized with individuals from acute medical wards, intermediate care wards, speech and hearing clinics in hospitals and universities, nursing homes, and patient homes.

The scoring system is easy and well explained. The test is designed so that the level of test item difficulty corresponds to a numerical score reflecting severity of involvement. There are four basic levels—A being the most difficult, C representing the easiest item, and D being an error or fail. Each level has two possible scores, which are determined by a quick correct response, with the exception of D, which is scored as 0 (e.g., Level A is assigned 6 and 5). With any delay in response (15 seconds or more) the lower number is scored. The instrument does not make use of basals or ceilings; scores are circled and then added for each subtest, which is then entered into the space provided in the record booklet.

The manual is well organized and provides an excellent rationale and overview for the test, as well as a detailed review of the history of aphasia-testing literature. The name of the test is a bit misleading as it is strictly an aphasia test and it is difficult to determine what a bedside evaluation test would encompass.

Items for the instrument were derived from published studies on aphasia. Secondly, a panel of three speech-language pathologists with practical and theoretical expertise in the area of speech and language skill deficits associated with aphasia were asked to assess the instrument for content validity. Each professional reviewed the items of the BEST-2 subtests and then rated them from 1 (not appropriate) to 4 (highly appropriate). The ratings were then averaged for each subtest and ranged from 3.17–4.00.

The instrument was standardized on a sample of 164 individuals who experienced language impairment as a result of aphasia. Subjects were included only if radiographic evidence diagnosed a left-hemisphere lesion resulting in aphasia. The test was also administered to 30 normal control subjects with no history of cerebrovascular accidents, dementia, hypertension, or any other neurological disorder. All subjects were between the ages of 21 and 95, with a mean age of 70.53. Cronbach's coefficient alphas were computed for two age intervals for the entire norming sample: individuals younger than 75 years of age and individuals 75 years or older. All alphas were between .88–.99.

Standard scores for the subtests and the quotient were intercorrelated for the two age groups. The results were between .52–.94, indicating that the subtests for both groups measure language skills and that they form an aphasia composite score. A factor analysis was also conducted in which all items loaded on one factor, which accounted for 98% of the variance. Standard errors of measurement were calculated for the subtests and the overall aphasia score for the two age groups in the norming sample. For the subtests, these ranged from .30–.85. The overall aphasia score/quotient was 3.00 for under 75 years and 2.60 for 75 years and older. The manual stated that an item discrimination analysis was performed but these numbers were not reported in the manual; instead, they provided median item discrimination coefficients, which were between .74–.96.

Eight *t*-tests, one for each of the subtests and the total test, were conducted with the results indicating that overall, the group with aphasia scored one standard deviation lower than the group with no neurological damage, indicating that the instrument is able to differentiate between groups.

SUMMARY. This instrument accomplishes its basic goal of being an aphasia-screening test with good reliability and validity. It is efficient, easy to transport, and quick to administer and score. Directions are clear and self-explanatory in the record booklet. The pictures are large and distinct, utilizing everyday items such as buttons, keys, nails, and stamps. The subtests are able to identify problem areas and estimate the severity of the patient's overall aphasia. In general, clinicians will find this to be a very useful screening test. The instrument's major limitation is that it is for English speakers only and the scores may be suspect if used with culturally diverse populations.

Review of the Bedside Evaluation Screening Test, Second Edition by CAROLYN MITCHELL-PERSON, Associate Professor of Communication Disorders, Southern University, Baton Rouge, LA:

The Bedside Evaluation Screening Test, Second Edition (BEST-2) is a revision of the original Bedside Evaluation Screening Test (BEST) published in 1987. The purpose of the instrument is to identify and quantify language deficits, assist in establishing treatment goals, and measure and document progress in adults with aphasia (manual, p. v). The battery is designed to provide clinicians with a profile of a patient's language residuals in each communicative modality on a continuum of severity that ranges from no

impairment to severe impairment. Additionally, it is designed as a screening test for English-speaking adult patients in the early stages of recovery from aphasia when they may not be physically able to respond to a full aphasia assessment battery. The rationale for the development and use of the BEST-2 is discussed within an historical context of aphasia testing, commercially available tests of aphasia, the test environment, and the need for bedside testing or screening. The BEST-2 is recommended for use by examiners who have some formal training in assessment. Basic testing procedures are provided for examiners in an effort to assure reliable test administration.

BEST-2 overall objectives are to: (a) determine aphasia type, (b) determine the degree to which aphasia is present, (c) profile the patient's language residuals, and (d) provide a quantitative measure of aphasia severity. The minimal criterion for administration is that the patient be able to sit up in bed and maintain eye contact with the examiner (manual, p. 1).

According to McNeil (1992), the main advantages of the first edition of the BEST over other aphasia tests included: (a) ease of physical manipulation of objects achieved through a magnetic board and objects, (b) the test's portability, (c) the ease of test administration with instructions contained on the test form itself, (d) the "relatively 'culture free'" test items, and (e) rapid administration time (maximum 20 minutes). The authors of the BEST-2 have discontinued the magnetized board with objects and have opted for pictures of the same objects. Other than the switch to pictures, the common household items used are the same in both editions (button, candle, key, nail, stamp). The items are not described as "culture free." The authors state that they have transformed the "bar scene" item in the original test into a scene with an ice cream vendor. A detailed discussion of the rationale for the development and use of the BEST-2 further delineates other main advantages: (a) readily usable for the acute patient, (b) compact and self-contained, (c) 20–minute administration time, (d) meaningful measure of patient's aphasia, (e) translation of scores into severity levels, and (f) subtest sampling of linguistic functioning in speaking, comprehending, and reading. The writing subtests have been eliminated and no detailed discussion of the rationale for the elimination was given.

CONTENT VALIDITY. Authors provide clear statements of the universe of skills represented by the test in their rationale of the BEST-2 subtests. The seven subtests are: Subtest 1—Conversational Expression, Subtest II—Naming Objects, Subtest III—Describing Objects, Subtest IV—Repeating Sentences, Subtest V—Pointing to Objects, Subtest VI—Pointing to Parts of a Picture, and Subtest VII—Reading. The question format is used in five of the seven subtests. Conversational expression is assessed in response to questions. The patient's ability to name objects in the confrontational naming format is based on answering questions. Questions are used to assess the patient's ability to use language to describe objects. The patient is expected to point to parts of pictures in response to questions. In contrast to using question formats in assessment, open-ended stimuli can be used very effectively with verbal adults to elicit conversational responses (Peterson, 1981). The rationale of the BEST-2 authors for using questions is that "it is important to ask the patient questions, and to standardize them by using the same questions with all patients so that responses can be compared" (manual, p. 30). In the reading exercises the patient is asked to read at the sentence, word, and/or paragraph level.

The expert panel used in content validation consisted of three professionals involved in evaluation, rehabilitation, and research of individuals who experience aphasia. The process used to elicit their judgments was subtest rating. The panel was instructed to rate the subtest items for assessing language skills in aphasia as *not appropriate* (1), *somewhat appropriate* (2), *appropriate* (3), or *highly appropriate* (4). The means were as follows: Subtest I, 3.83; Subtest II, 3.67; Subtest III, 3.33; Subtest IV, 3.60; Subtest V, 3.17; Subtest VI, 3.67; and Subtest VII, 4.00. The ratings indicated that six of the subtests were appropriate for measuring language skill deficits in aphasia with the exception of Subtest VII, which was rated as being highly appropriate.

When important decisions are made based on test scores, it is critical to avoid bias, which may unfairly influence examinees' scores (Hambleton & Rodgers, 1998). The Code of Fair Testing Practices in Education (1988) mandates test developers to identify and eliminate biased instruments. There is no evidence that reviews were conducted during the test development and validation process to minimize possible bias resulting from cultural and linguistic diversity, gender, area of residence, or geographic area. The pictures of the common household objects appear free of bias. The pictures of the ice cream vendor appear relatively free of bias with the exception of the overrepresentation of male characters in all scenes.

CONSTRUCT VALIDITY. There are three steps that are generally followed to identify the extent to which a test measures a theoretical construct or trait (construct validity). First, several constructs thought to account for test performance are identified. Second, tentative assumptions are generated that are based on the identified constructs. Third, the tentative assumptions are verified by logical or empirical methods. The BEST-2 authors developed a conceptual framework by identifying four constructs: (a) a test of aphasia should differentiate between individuals experiencing aphasia and those without, (b) the dimensions of the test should correlate with one another and with the total test, (c) one factor should emerge from a factor analysis that measures language skills, and (d) significant correlation between items of each subtest and the total score of the subtest should be identified. There is no discussion of how the basic constructs assumed to underlie the BEST-2 were related to testable questions or tentative assumptions; however, statistically significant evidence is given to support group differentiation and subtests and total test interrelationships. To investigate the group differences, eight *t*-tests were performed. Overall, the groups with aphasia scored about one standard deviation lower than the control group (those without). All subtest and total test intercorrelational coefficients were shown to be statistically significant.

TEST ADMINISTRATION AND SCORING. Test instructions, time limits, use of stimulus materials, testing sequence, and scoring information and procedures are provided in the BEST-2 Record Booklet.

The BEST-2 yields raw scores, percentiles, and standard scores; instructions are provided for the calculation, proper use, and interpretation of the scores. Tables are provided to convert raw scores to standard scores and percentiles for patients younger than 75 years and those 75 years of age and older. Additionally, a table is provided to convert sums of standard scores to BEST-2 quotients and percentiles.

It is stated on the BEST-2 Profile/Summary Sheet that the BEST-2 provides a screening for aphasia in English-speaking adult patients and can be used to determine the type and severity of aphasia. It is implied but not stated that the subtests are designed to assess the impact of aphasia on either language comprehension and/or production in terms of spontaneous speech, labeling, identification, descriptive behavior, speech production ability, and reading (manual, pp. 30–32). In the rationale the authors describe several types of aphasia. There are no clear definitive statements about which type classification system the BEST-2 results support. It appears as though the authors differentiate aphasia types as fluent and nonfluent. The BEST-2 does not yield a score that determines the type of aphasia. The subtest standard scores and/or the sum of the standard scores for the quotient are said to determine the severity of aphasia. The examiner must draw conclusions based on the Severity Rating Profile. For example, a patient may demonstrate severe impairments in labeling (production) and identification (comprehension). In reality, aphasia is manifested differently in every client, and the lines separating one type from another are not clearly defined (Brookshire, 1992).

The authors caution examiners about interpreting the test results. They state that the BEST-2 is not an exhaustive measure of language skill ability in aphasia. When viewed in the context of an individual assessment, the BEST-2 should answer most questions regarding the nature and extent of language deficits for a particular individual (manual, p. 19).

RELIABILITY. Fundamental to the evaluation of the BEST-2 is the degree to which test scores are free from various sources of error and are consistent from one occasion to another. Sources of measurement error, situational error, and subject error will always contribute to an individual's score and impact the reliability of the test. Different types of reliability estimates were used in the BEST-2 to estimate the contributions of different sources of measurement error. Of primary interest were the estimates of internal consistency that accounted for error due to content sampling. Internal consistency reliability was computed using Cronbach's alphas for subtests, quotients, and age intervals for the entire norming sample. All alphas exceeded .90 and appear to indicate the scores from the BEST-2 are highly reliable. A discussion of the rationale for using Cronbach's alphas was provided as well as clear and distinct tables and illustrations.

The amount of test error due to examiner scoring differences is examined. The results of scoring were correlated indicating all coefficients as .99. The sizes of these coefficients appear to support the test's scorer reliability.

TEST DEVELOPMENT AND NORMING. The BEST-2 was standardized on 164 adults from 10 states between 21 and 95 years of age who experienced language impairment as a result of aphasia. The primary diagnosis was cerebrovascular accident. Other diagnoses included closed head injuries, open head injuries, and left hemisphere cerebral tumors. The data collection took place from December 1995 to June 1996. It might be argued that a sample of 164 is small; however, the sample is reported to be representative of aphasic cases relative to gender, area of residents (city-rural), geographic area, and ethnicity as described in aphasia literature relative to demographic information (manual, p. 23). The BEST-2 was also administered to 30 normal control subjects with no history of cerebrovascular accidents, dementia, hypertension, Alzheimer's Disease, or cognitive, learning, or other neurological disorders.

The specific subject demographics described are age, English as the primary language, gender, and primary diagnosis of left hemisphere lesion. Even though the ethnic background is stated as being representative of aphasic cases described in aphasic literature, no specific description of ethnolinguistic diversity is provided. Additionally, no description is provided of the area of residence. The majority of the 30 control subjects resided in Austin, Texas. There is no discussion of specific demographics or comparison of the cultural and linguistic diversity of the 164 subjects and the 30 control subjects.

Two types of normative statistics are described and discussed. Specifically discussed are standard scores for the subtests and the quotient and percentiles. The distributions for standard scores and the quotients were chosen because of wide use and familiarity. Normative tables are shown for patients under 75 years and those 75 years and older. The total number in each category is not indicated; therefore, it could not be determined if the number of subjects was large enough to develop sufficient estimates in each category.

SUMMARY. The BEST-2 is designed as a screening tool for aphasia. In the review of the original BEST by McNeil (1992), several weaknesses were cited such as the lack of test reliability, validity, and theoretical context. In the revised version the authors addressed those weaknesses. The internal consistency for the BEST-2 was determined using the coefficient alpha technique. The coefficients all exceeded .90. Validity is supported by demonstrating that groups of individuals who demonstrate aphasia and those with no neurologic damage are differentiated. There is no evidence that the authors were sensitive to the demographic characteristics of individuals to whom the BEST-2 might be administered. There is no documentation of steps taken during test development, validation, and standardization to evaluate subtest items for bias due to gender, culture, ethnicity, religion, or class. For example, according to Peters-Johnson and Taylor (1986), rates of cerebrovascular accident (primary diagnosis of the normative sample) are high among Latino Americans and African Americans suggesting that aphasia might be frequently occurring within these groups. It would appear reasonable to assume that the BEST-2 might be used with these groups as a screening tool. Using measures normed on White populations to assess non-White people and not considering the implications of the use of measures with clients from various racial and cultural groups are common misuses of assessments (Sedlacek & Kim, 1995). The BEST-2 is recommended to be used as a screening tool to identify and quantify language comprehension and production residuals in patients demonstrating aphasia, to assist in establishing treatment goals with patients, and to measure and document progress in patients with aphasia. The claim that the BEST-2 clearly identifies the type of aphasia is not substantiated. The BEST-2 should be used with patients who have demographic characteristics similar to the normative sample.

REVIEWER'S REFERENCES

Peterson, C. W. (1981). *Conversation starters for speech-language pathology.* Danville, IL: Interstate Printers & Publishers.
Peters-Johnson, C. A., & Taylor, O. L. (1986). Speech, language and hearing disorders in Black populations. In O. L. Taylor (Ed.), *Nature of communication disorders in culturally and linguistically diverse populations* (pp. 157–179). San Diego: College-Hill Press.
Joint Committee on Testing Practice (1988). *Code of fair testing practices in education.* Washington, DC: National Council on Measurement in Education.
Brookshire, R. H. (1992). *An introduction to neurogenic communication disorders* (4th ed.). St. Louis: Mosby-Year Book.
McNeil, M. R. (1992). [Review of The Bedside Evaluation and Screening Test of Aphasia.] In J. J. Kramer & J. C. Conoley (Eds.), *The eleventh mental measurements yearbook* (pp. 86–89). Lincoln, NE: Buros Institute of Mental Measurements.
Hambleton, R., & Rodgers, J. (1995). *Item bias review.* (ERIC Document No. 398241)
Sedlacek, W. E., & Kim, S. H. (1995). *Multicultural assessment.* (ERIC Document No. 391112)

[40]
Behavior Assessment System for Children [Revised].

Purpose: Designed "to aid in the identification and differential diagnosis of emotional/behavior disorders in children and adolescents."
Population: Ages 2 1/2–18.
Publication Dates: 1992–1998.
Acronym: BASC.
Administration: Individual.
Forms, 10: Teacher Rating Scale—Preschool, Teacher Rating Scale—Child, Teacher Rating Scale—Adolescent, Parent Rating Scale—Preschool, Parent Rating Scale—Child, Parent Rating Scale—Adolescent, Self-Report of Personality—Child, Self-Report of Personality—Adolescent, Structured Developmental History, Student Observation System.
Price Data, 1999: $74.95 per starter set including manual, one sample each of the hand-scored forms for all levels of the Teacher Rating Scale, Parent Rating Scale, and Self-Report of Personality, the Structured Developmental History, and the Student Observation Scale; $225.95 per IBM Enhanced ASSIST software (unlimited use).
Comments: Subtests available as separates.
Authors: Cecil R. Reynolds and Randy W. Kamphaus.
Publisher: American Guidance Service, Inc.

a) TEACHER RATING SCALES.
Price Data: $25.95 per 25 hand-scored forms; $16.95 per 25 computer-scored forms.
Time: (10–20) minutes.
1) *Teacher Rating Scales—Preschool.*
Population: Ages 2 1/2–5.
Scores, 11: Externalizing Problems (Aggression, Hyperactivity), Internalizing Problems (Anxiety, Depression, Somatization), Attention Problems, Atypicality, Withdrawal, Adaptive Skills (Adaptability, Social Skills), Behavioral Symptoms Index.
2) *Teacher Rating Scales—Child.*
Population: Ages 6–11.
Scores, 19: Externalizing Problems (Aggression, Hyperactivity, Conduct Problems), Internalizing Problems (Anxiety, Depression, Somatization), School Problems (Attention Problems, Learning Problems), Atypicality, Withdrawal, Adaptive Skill (Adaptability, Leadership, Social Skills, Study Skills), Behavioral Symptoms Index.
3) *Teacher Rating Scales—Adolescent.*
Population: Ages 12–18.

Scores, 18: Externalizing Problems (Aggression, Hyperactivity, Conduct Problems), Internalizing Problems (Anxiety, Depression, Somatization), School Problems (Attention Problems, Learning Problems), Atypicality, Withdrawal, Adaptive Skills (Leadership, Social Skills, Study Skills), Behavioral Symptoms Index.

b) PARENT RATING SCALES.

Price Data: $25.95 per 25 hand-scored forms; $16.95 per 25 computer-scored forms.

Time: (10–20) minutes.

1) *Parent Rating Scales—Preschool.*

Population: Ages 2 1/2–5.

Scores, 14: Same as *a-1* above.

2) *Parent Rating Scales—Child.*

Population: Ages 6–11.

Scores, 16: Externalizing Problems (Aggression, Hyperactivity, Conduct Problems), Internalizing Problems (Anxiety, Depression, Somatization), Attention Problems, Atypicality, Withdrawal, Adaptive Skills (Adaptability, Leadership, Social Skills), Behavioral Symptoms Index.

3) *Parent Rating Scales—Adolescent.*

Population: Ages 12–18.

Scores, 15: Externalizing Problems (Aggression, Hyperactivity, Conduct Problems), Internalizing Problems (Anxiety, Depression, Somatization), Attention Problems, Atypicality, Withdrawal, Adaptive Skills (Leadership. Social Skills), Behavioral Symptom Index.

c) SELF-REPORT OF PERSONALITY.

Price Data: $25.95 per 25 hand-scored forms; $16.95 per 25 computer-scored forms.

Time: (20–30) minutes.

1) *Self-Report of Personality—Child.*

Population: Ages 8–11.

Scores, 16: Clinical Maladjustment (Anxiety, Atypicality, Locus of Control, Social Stress), School Maladjustment (Attitude to School, Attitude to Teachers), Depression, Sense of Inadequacy, Personal Adjustment (Relations with Parents, Interpersonal Relations, Self-Esteem, Self-Reliance), Emotional Symptoms Index.

2) *Self-Report of Personality—Adolescent.*

Population: Ages 12–18.

Scores, 18: Clinical Maladjustment (Anxiety, Atypicality, Locus of Control, Social Stress, Somatization), School Maladjustment (Attitude to School, Attitude to Teachers, Sensation Seeking), Depression, Sense of Inadequacy, Personal Adjustment (Relations with Parents, Interpersonal Relations, Self-Esteem, Self-Reliance), Emotional Symptoms Index.

d) STRUCTURED DEVELOPMENTAL HISTORY.

Price Data: $33.95 per 25 history forms.

e) STUDENT OBSERVATION SYSTEM.

Price Data: $28.95 per 25 observation forms.

Time: [20] minutes.

Cross References: See T5:280 (6 references); for reviews by Jonathon Sandoval and by Joseph C. Witt and Kevin M. Jones, see 13:34 (4 reference).

Review of the Behavior Assessment System for Children [Revised] by JAMES CLYDE DiPERNA, Assistant Professor, School Psychology Program, Lehigh University, Bethlehem, PA:

The Behavior Assessment System for Children (BASC) is a multi-method, multi-informant assessment battery including the Teacher Rating Scales (TRS), Parent Rating Scales (PRS), Self-Report of Personality (SRP), Structured Developmental History (SDH), and Student Observation System (SOS). Originally published in 1992, comprehensive reviews of the BASC appeared in the *Thirteenth Mental Measurements Yearbook* (see Sandoval, 1998; Witt & Jones, 1998). An updated version of the BASC was published in 1998, including additional preschool norms for children ages 2-6 to 3-11. As such, the current review focuses primarily on the preschool forms of the PRS and TRS and concludes with a brief review of the Spanish PRS. (The remainder of the BASC appears to be unchanged from the version reviewed in the last *MMY*.)

DESCRIPTION. Items for the preschool forms of the TRS and BRS were selected based on expert review of the BASC items for school-aged children. The preschool TRS includes 109 items, and time of completion is estimated to be 10–20 minutes. The preschool PRS includes an additional 22 items (131 total), so completion time is expected to be longer for this form. Items on both forms are concise, reflect observable behaviors, and utilize a 4-point frequency rating ranging from *Never* to *Almost Always*. Both forms yield 4 composite scores (Internalizing problems, Externalizing problems, Adaptive Skills, and the Behavioral Symptoms Index) and 10 scale scores (Aggression, Hyperactivity, Anxiety, Depression, Somatization, Attention Problems, Atypicality, Withdrawal, Adaptability, and Social Skills). Norms based on the general population are available by gender (male, female, combined) and age; however, the age ranges are different across the

TRS (2-6 to 3-11, 4-0 to 5-11) and PRS (2-6 to 2-11, 3-0 to 3-ll, 4-0 to 5-11). Clinical norms are provided for older preschool students (ages 4–5) on both forms.

STANDARDIZATION SAMPLE. It is important to note the standardization samples for the preschool TRS and PRS are composed of two distinct cohorts collected at two different points in time. The first cohort (ages 4-0 to 5-11) was collected from 1988 to 1991 during the standardization of the original BASC. The second cohort (ages 2-6 to 3-11) was collected several years later (1997–1998). Although norms and data analyses were conducted separately for these two cohorts, it is unclear if the standardization data for the 4–5-year-old cohort is still representative of the current preschool population given that it was collected over 10 years ago.

Aside from this potential limitation, the standardization samples for both forms are large and accurately reflect most demographic characteristics of the preschool population (based on census projections at the time of standardization). Specifically, gender, race, and mother's level of education (PRS only) are representative of the general population at each age level and for each form. The one demographic characteristic that the PRS and TRS samples fail to adequately approximate is geographic location, with children from the Northeast significantly underrepresented and children from the South significantly overrepresented across all age ranges and forms.

The clinical norm samples for both the TRS and PRS (ages 4–5 only) appropriately include a larger percentage of males (71%) than females (29%). Racial composition for the TRS clinical sample included an adequate percentage of minorities, but minorities were underrepresented in the PRS sample. A larger percentage of clinical participants came from the South and West than from other areas of North America.

In sum, the samples for the PRS and TRS are representative of the preschool population estimates from the early 1990s; however, it is unclear at this time how well the BASC preschool sample represents the U.S. preschool population at the turn of the century.

RELIABILITY. The internal consistency coefficients for the TRS are generally high for the composites across both the younger (.88–.95) and older preschool age groups (.90–.96). Coefficients

for the scales are somewhat lower ranging from .71 to .92 for the younger age group and .78 to .90 for the older age group. A similar pattern emerges across the composites and scales for the clinical sample as well. Specifically, composite reliabilities range from .82 to .94 and scale reliabilities range from .66 to .91.

The authors also provide test-retest and interrater reliability estimates for the older preschool age group. Test-retest correlations (2-month maximum between administrations) generally are high at both the composite (.90–.95) and scale level (.82–.95). Two types of interrater reliability (between teachers) also are reported. The first were based on a small number of teacher pairs each rating a large number of students. Interrater coefficients for these ratings are exceptionally high, ranging from .80 to .91 for the composites, and .60 to .92 for the scales. The second estimates were based on a large number of teacher pairs, each rating a small number of students. These coefficients were consistent with interrater reliability estimates for other behavior rating scales, ranging from .47 to .76 for the composites and .29 to .70 for the scales.

Overall reliability evidence for the use of the TRS with older preschool children (ages 4 to 5) is adequate for the normal population. Internal consistency evidence for use of the TRS with younger preschool children (ages 2-6 to 3-11) also is adequate; however, the lack of test-retest and interrater reliability evidence is a significant limitation. Similarly, internal consistency evidence for the clinical population is acceptable for all but two scales (Anxiety and Somatization), but no evidence of interrater or test-retest reliability is provided for the clinical population.

For the PRS, internal consistency coefficients were calculated across three age groups (2-6 to 2-11, 3-0 to 3-11, 4-0 to 5-11). For the composites, internal consistency coefficients are adequate across all three groups, ranging from .80 to .92. Internal consistency coefficients are somewhat lower for the oldest (.69–.86) and middle (.68–.83) age groups and considerably lower for the youngest age group (.59–.84). For the clinical sample, internal consistency is adequate with composite coefficients ranging from .84 to .94 and scale coefficients ranging from .72 to .91.

The authors provide interrater reliability estimates for two age groups only, combining the youngest two age groups into one. Interrater reliability estimates (between parents) are similar for the composites and scales across both age groups, ranging from .35 to .72. As with the TRS, test-retest correlations (1-month maximum between administrations) only were provided for the older preschool sample. These correlations are high (.85–.90) for the composites and slightly lower (.72–.91) for the scales.

Internal consistency reliability evidence for the use of the PRS with an older preschool sample (ages 4 to 5) is adequate for the normal population. Internal consistency evidence for use of the PRS with children ages 3-1 to 3-11 is minimally acceptable, and evidence for use of the PRS with the youngest preschool sample (ages 2-6 to 2-11) is low. Interrater reliability evidence is appropriate, but test-retest evidence is only provided for the oldest age group. Finally, internal consistency evidence for the clinical sample is acceptable, but no evidence of interrater or test-retest reliability is provided for this population.

VALIDITY.

Evidence of Internal Structure. Separate analyses were conducted to explore the internal structure of the TRS across the younger and older preschool samples. For the older sample, Covariance Structure Analysis (CSA) was used to determine the underlying structure of the constructs measured by the TRS. Although the initial 3-factor model proposed by the BASC authors did not demonstrate good fit with the standardization data, a revised 3-factor model (Externalizing, Internalizing, Adaptive) demonstrated acceptable fit. Separate exploratory factor analyses using the Principal Axis Factoring method supported a 3-factor model for the TRS as well.

To explore the internal structure of the TRS with younger children, the authors compared correlations among TRS scales across the younger and older preschool populations. Statistically significant differences were found across the correlation matrices for the two samples for the TRS; however, factor loadings for the final 3-factor model were very similar across both age groups. Thus, the authors concluded a 3-factor model was appropriate for the younger population as well.

A similar procedure was used to evaluate the internal structure of the PRS across the older and younger preschool age groups. As with the TRS, the authors concluded that a 3-factor model was supported for both age ranges. Overall, the internal structure evidence for both the TRS and PRS is strong across both preschool age ranges.

Evidence based on Relationships with Other Variables. Only one study was conducted exploring relationships between scores on the TRS and another measure of behavior. This study included a diverse sample of 92 students (ages 4–5 only) who were rated using both the TRS and the Conners' Teacher Rating Scale. Correlations between the instruments indicated a pattern of primarily low to moderate relationships, with a few high correlations occurring between scales measuring similar constructs (e.g., hyperactivity).

Two separate correlational studies were conducted for the PRS. The first included a primarily Caucasian sample of 30 children (ages 4–5) who were rated using the PRS and Child Behavior Checklist. Correlations primarily fell in the moderate range, with the highest correlations occurring between similar scales. The second study included a primarily Hispanic sample of 39 children who were rated using the PRS and the Personality Inventory for Children—Revised. Correlations between the two instruments fell in the low to moderate range; however, some of the low relationships were found between scales purportedly measuring similar constructs (e.g., somatic concerns).

Overall, the evidence to support the use of the PRS and TRS based on relationships with other variables is limited for the preschool form. At best, this evidence is minimally acceptable to support the use of these instruments for children ages 4 to 5. It is important to note, however, that *no evidence* is provided for children ages 2-6 to 3-11 for either form. This significant limitation raises questions about the appropriateness of using these instruments with children of this age until such evidence is provided.

CONCLUSION. The purpose of the BASC, as described by the authors, is to "facilitate the differential diagnosis and educational classification of a variety of emotional and behavioral disorders of children and to aid in the design of treatment plans" (manual, p. 1). As evidenced by the appropriate lack of clinical norms for the 2-6 to 3-11 age range, it is questionable whether practitioners truly can (or should) be attempting to diagnose emotional or behavioral *disorders* in the preschool population. The latter purpose of aiding in treatment planning, however, is more appropriate for the preschool population. The evidence provided to support the use of the TRS and PRS for problem identification is minimally sufficient for children ages 4–5 and could benefit from additional validity studies exploring relationships with other measures and/or criteria. The evidence provided in the manual to support the use of the TRS and PRS for children ages 2-6 to 3-11, however, is insufficient to recommend its use at the present time. Although internal consistency and structure evidence is adequate for this age range, more reliability and validity evidence is necessary.

PRS SPANISH FORM. Although the PRS Spanish form was available at the time of the last *MMY* review, the revised manual includes a new appendix with a brief (1-page) description of the development of the Spanish form. Based on this description, it is apparent that the authors went to great lengths to ensure that the BASC was accurately translated into a common form of the Spanish language. Despite these efforts, *no data* are provided in the manual regarding the reliability and validity of the PRS Spanish Form for the intended examinee population. As documented in the most recent *Standards for Educational and Psychological Testing* (AERA, APA, & NCME, 1999), it is insufficient to translate a test into another language without comparing the psychometric properties of the translated test to the properties of the original instrument. Given the lack of such data, the Spanish PRS currently should not be used to provide norm-referenced scores. At best, this instrument should be used as a descriptive information-gathering tool until an evaluation of its psychometric properties has been completed.

REVIEWER'S REFERENCES

Sandoval, J. (1998). [Review of the Behavior Assessment System for Children.] In J. C. Impara & B. S. Plake (Eds.), *The thirteenth mental measurements yearbook* (pp. 128–131). Lincoln, NE: Buros Institute of Mental Measurements.

Witt, J. C., & Jones, K. M. (1998). [Review of the Behavior Assessment System for Children.] In J. C. Impara & B. S. Plake (Eds.), *The thirteenth mental measurements yearbook* (pp. 131–133). Lincoln, NE: Buros Institute of Mental Measurements.

American Educational Research Association, American Psychological Association, & National Council on Measurement in Education. (1999). *Standards for educational and psychological testing.* Washington, DC: American Educational Research Association.

Review of the Behavior Assessment System for Children [Revised (Preschool Edition)] by ROBERT SPIES, Associate Director, Buros Institute of Mental Measurements, University of Nebraska—Lincoln, Lincoln, NE, and CHRISTINA FINLEY JONES, *School Psychologist, Battle Ground School District, Battle Ground, WA:*

DESCRIPTION. The Behavior Assessment System for Children (BASC) has been designed as a comprehensive series of evaluative measures to assist practitioners developing educational interventions and differential diagnoses of children and adolescents with suspected behavioral problems. Using all of this test's component parts, the BASC affords a view that is multidimensional (i.e., externalizing, internalizing, and adaptive behaviors), multinformant (i.e., parent, teacher, older children), and multimethod (i.e., rating scales, developmental history, direct observation). Originally introduced in 1992 for ages 4 through 18, support for the BASC has increased steadily in terms both of research and of acceptance by professionals working in schools and clinical settings. After the initial publication of the BASC manual, the test authors elected to revise the age range of the instrument to include children age 2 years 6 months to 3 years 11 months who potentially could be served by early childhood education programs. The primary focus of this review will address the current test revision for the preschool age group. Readers seeking a comprehensive review of the BASC for older children and adolescents are directed to the previous *Mental Measurements Yearbook* (13:34).

TEST DEVELOPMENT AND STANDARDIZATION. The development of the BASC for preschool children below the age of 4 followed the careful procedures outlined in the earlier edition. Of the five components of the BASC, however, only the Preschool Parent Rating Scale (PRS-P) and the Teacher Rating Scale (TRS-P) required additional data gathering. Changes were determined unnecessary to the structured developmental history (SDH), the direct observation protocol (SOS), and the self-report of personality (SRP), which exists only for children age 8 and over.

The test authors decided the BASC item content already created for children ages 4–5 was appropriate for children as young as 2 years 6 months. Rather than attempt to define a "clinical" level for this youngest group, however, only a set of general norm groups was constructed. The process of norming this new sample of children included amassing data from 41 regionally representative locations across the United States. A total of 678 teacher ratings and 637 parent ratings were secured. Samples were weighted to correspond to recent U.S. population trends in areas of race/ethnicity and mother's education. Because of the expectation that behaviors would be highly variable over the entire 18-month age range of this new sample, results were separated into three 6-month intervals. With the exception of Hyperactivity and Anxiety on the PRS, however, no substantial differences were noted between these three intervals and the prior preschool data secured on 4–5-year olds.

RELIABILITY. Estimates of internal consistency and interrater reliability for the PRS-P and TRS-P generally revealed similar but marginally lower scores when compared to those previously reported with the BASC for age 4 through 5. Internal consistency composites for the TRS-P (i.e., Externalizing and Internalizing Problems, Adaptive and Behavioral Skills) were very high, with scale scores in the upper .80s to middle .90s. As expected, the individual scales of the TRS-P that make up these composites were less strong and only Aggression, Attention Problems, Hyperactivity, and Social Skills were consistently in the higher ranges needed for confident decision making.

No test-retest or interrater reliabilities were reported for the TRS-P for the under-4-year age group. Low to moderate levels of interrater agreement (.29 to .76) that were recorded on the TRS-P for the 4–5-year age group would imply that teachers have difficulty reaching diagnostic consensus on the same student, especially in the area of internalizing and externalizing behaviors.

Estimates of internal consistency for the PRS-P composites (.79 to .94) were somewhat lower than the TRS-P, particularly in the areas of Internalizing Problems and Adaptive Skill. PRS-P interrater reliabilities were compiled by correlating a sample of 67 children's PBS-P scores from their mothers' and fathers' ratings. The resulting interrater reliability estimates yielded modest median correlation values of .59, although this was a slight improvement from the .46 median correlation previously reported for ages 4–5. For ages 4–5, statistical comparisons of the same student using the TRS-P and PRS-P generally were in the low range. Various explanations were given for these low correlations including the situational nature of particular behaviors and individual differences in rater's perceptions.

As a result, users of the TRS-P and PRS-P (particularly at the younger ages) must be alert to respondent variability with these instruments, and the complications these reliability estimates pose for building an accurate behavioral profile of the target child. Due to the limitations in these reliability estimates, practitioners are advised to select the most dependable raters possible and to pool results when more than one individual has adequate knowledge of the child's behavior.

VALIDITY. The validity evidence presented in the BASC manual for the 4–5-year age group rests primarily upon confirmatory factor analysis of its theoretical model, on correlation studies with similar tests used to assess behavior, and on correlation matrices between the TRS-P and PRS-P. In the revised BASC edition for the under-4-year age group, however, only one type of construct validity evidence was presented. Factor analysis was used to compare the previous TRS-P and PRS-P rating scales for 4–5-year-old children to the new data acquired with children age 2 years 6 months to 3 years 11 months. The intercorrelation matrices suggested similar factor structures for both groups on the PRS-P. Although a statistical analysis of the TRS-P indicated differences between the two age groups, these differences were minimal except for the Adaptive Skills and Attention Problems scales.

Other evidence offered to support the validity of the TRS-P and PRS-P at the 4–5-year age levels included comparing BASC scales to other behavioral assessment instruments. Correlations with the Child Behavior Checklist (CBC) were particularly high in matching composite areas (middle .70s) and in most externalizing behaviors but were in the low to moderate range for internalizing and adaptive behaviors. Other tests typically used to assess children at this age level (i.e., the Conners' Teacher Rating Scales and the Personality Inventory for Children) also produced lower correlation levels overall between both composites and individual scales. Low correlations between the BASC and these tests may suggest the measurement of different dimensions of behavior. Correlation studies designed to examine respondent agreement with the same student using both the TRS-P and the PRS-P were in the low range, with composite scores from -.08 (Internalizing Problems) to .43 (Adaptive Skills). Although these scores improve at older age levels, little agreement might be expected between teachers and parents of preschool children age 4–5 years.

Validity data also were presented in the BASC manual supporting the use of the TRS-P and PRS-P in making clinical classification decisions, but no delineation was made between age groups of children involved. Due to the ages at which children typically receive clinical diagnoses, we suspect that the vast majority of these data refer to children in age groups older than preschool.

COMMENTARY. The authors of the BASC have developed an instrument that represents a notable advance in the behavioral assessment of children and adolescents. From the careful development of theoretical constructs reflecting current theory and research to the creation of caution indexes measuring rater response patterns, the BASC provides a variety of tools to assist practitioners with multidimensional assessment. These strengths are most apparent for older children and adolescents. The advantages of the preschool edition of the BASC are less numerous. This is not a reflection of inadequate test development, but it is important to stress the dangers of using diagnostic labels for children of preschool age. The assessment of preschool children's behavior traditionally has presented serious measurement difficulties for test developers. Variability in behaviors due to developmental changes are the rule rather than the exception at this age, and the reliability estimates and validity evidence supporting the preschool BASC reflect this inconstancy.

For practitioners contemplating the weighty and pervasive label of emotional or behavioral disorder for a preschool child, it is essential to gather additional assessment data to support any diagnosis for preschool children. A complete functional assessment would be a necessary complement to any BASC results (O'Neill, Horner, Albin, Storey, & Sprague, 1990). Failure to secure these data may create the label of pathology for a child who is responding consistently to environmental demands.

For high frequency behaviors, direct observation is vital for determining antecedent relationships. However, the momentary-time sampling techniques featured by the Student Observation System of the BASC are less compelling than more sophisticated sequential analysis techniques (e.g., Sharpe & Lounsberry, 1997). In addition, a review of current child developmental theory (e.g.,

Scarr, 1997) may assist practitioners with their assessment and with recommendations for altering environmental contingencies. Using the TRS-P and PRS-P longitudinally to document the developmental course of the student's behavioral problems may be very helpful for the same reason.

The computer software available for the BASC is very useful for interpreting results, but users are advised to exercise caution. With the preschool version, for example, no clinical data exist for children under the age of 4 despite computer-generated reports suggesting otherwise.

SUMMARY. The assessment and diagnosis of emotional and behavioral disabilities at the preschool age level is fraught with complication. Although ample evidence is presented in the manual for the use of this instrument with older children and adolescents, much less support exists for the adequacy of the preschool versions of the Teacher Rating Scales (TRS-P) and the Parent Rating Scales (PRS-P). Practitioners tempted to focus exclusively on these components in order to complete the diagnosis of preschool children are reminded that this instrument is designed to be multimethod and that clinical norms do not exist below age 4. Given the limited reliability and validity support found at the preschool level, the BASC must be used with caution and in conjunction with a full range of alternative assessment techniques.

REVIEWER'S REFERENCES

O'Neill, R., Horner, R. H., Albin, R. W., Storey, K., & Sprague, J. R. (1990). *Functional analysis of problem behavior: A practical assessment guide*. Pacific Grove, CA: Brooks/Cole.

Scarr, S. (1997). The development of individual differences in intelligence and personality. In H. W. Reece & M. D. Franzen (Eds.), *Biological and neuropsychological mechanisms: Life-span developmental psychology* (pp. 1–22). Mahwah, NJ: Lawrence Erlbaum Associates, Inc.

Sharpe, T. & Lounsbery, M. (1997). The effects of a sequential behavior analysis protocol on the teaching practices of undergraduate trainees. *School Psychology Quarterly, 12*, 327–343.

[41]

Behavior Dimensions Scale.

Purpose: Designed to categorize and document existing behavior patterns into recognized areas of behavior disorders to assist in making diagnostic, placement, and programming decisions.

Population: Ages 3–19.

Publication Date: 1995.

Acronym: BDS.

Scores, 7: Inattentive, Hyperactive-Impulsive, Oppositional Defiant, Conduct, Avoidant Personality, Anxiety, Depression.

Administration: Individual.

Price Data, 1999: $148 per complete kit including School Version (59 pages) and Home Version (55

pages) manuals, 50 rating forms (School and Home), intervention manual (323 pages), and computerized scoring disk (IBM); $12.50 per manual (School or Home); $31 per 50 rating forms (School or Home); $31 per 50 Home Version Spanish rating forms; $26 per intervention manual; $35 per computerized scoring disk (IBM).

Time: (20–25) minutes.

Author: Stephen B. McCarney.

Publisher: Hawthorne Educational Services, Inc.

Review of the Behavior Dimensions Scale by KEVIN M. JONES, Assistant Professor, University of Cincinnati, Cincinnati, IL:

The Behavior Dimensions Scale (BDS) consists of two rating scales, one for teachers and one for parents, that survey childhood and adolescent symptoms related to seven DSM-IV (American Psychiatric Association, 1994) disorders: Attention-Deficit/Hyperactivity Disorder (Inattentive or Hyperactive-Impulsive Types), Oppositional Defiant Disorder, Conduct Disorder, Avoidant Personality Disorder, Generalized Anxiety Disorder, and Major Depressive Episode. Beyond providing diagnostic information, the BDS is accompanied by an intervention manual (McCarney & McCain, 1995) that aids in translating factor scores into individualized treatment goals and objectives, with a host of prescriptive intervention recommendations provided.

The BDS School Version and BDS Home Version consist of 99 and 108 items, respectively. Informants provide frequency ratings ranging from *Does Not Engage in the Behavior* (0) to *One to Several Times Per Hour* (4) to assess the severity of symptoms for children aged 3 to 19 years. Raw scores for the seven subscales are easily translated into corresponding subscale standard scores ($m = 10$, $SD = 3$) and percentile ranks. Unlike a majority of informant rating scales, problem areas are indicated by lower subscale standard scores. Ten separate normative tables are provided (boys versus girls across five age groups) that are adequate and representative of the U.S. population. Impressive reliability data include test-retest (administration interval of 30 days) reliability coefficients above .75 on School Version, .78 on Home Version across subscales and age groups, and interrater reliability between two parents or two teachers ranging from .77 to .82. Surprisingly, there are no data assessing interrater reliability between the parent and teacher versions.

An original feature of the BDS is that symptoms are rated in terms of their absolute frequency (e.g., "one to several times per hour"). This strategy is clearly viewed as a strength by the authors, but its unique contribution is unclear for several reasons. First, despite alternative wording, criterion-related studies indicate generally high agreement between BDS subscales and those of other commonly used measures that incorporate more subjective impressions of deviance (e.g., "sometimes," "often"). Second, the wording of many items, such as "has unexcused absences" or "stays out at night despite parental prohibition" may preclude the use of the full range of quantifiers. Finally, absolute frequency ignores other dimensions of behavior, such as duration and intensity. For example, it seems confusing that "using a weapon in a fight" and "making inappropriate comments to others" contribute equally to the Conduct subscale if they are each assigned a "1" (i.e., occur one time per month).

The BDS standardization efforts represented a difficult attempt to preserve a *categorical* model of pathology (DSM-IV; APA, 1994) within a *dimensional* scale. A categorical model is based on the notion that psychopathology is either present or absent, yet the BDS defines the disorder in terms of distance from the population mean. A categorical model also asserts that syndromes are mutually exclusive, yet there is little evidence in the manual that the BDS yields more than a single general index of global dysfunction.

The latter issue is an important one, particularly for a system that purports to provide differential diagnosis and treatment planning. Nine of 21 (43%) of the intercorrelation coefficients between dissimilar subscales on the School Version exceed .70, suggesting a substantial amount of shared variance. Most subscales have multiple items that load on at least two factors, and there are several items that appear on more than one subscale. As evidence of diagnostic validity, subscale standard scores for six populations representing the BDS clinical categories were compared to those of a nonreferred population. Although mean scores across all subscales were lower for the total clinical group, there is no evidence that BDS scores effectively differentiated various clinical populations (i.e., Conduct Disorder versus Avoidant Personality Disorder). Therefore, the most useful level of interpretation may be the total score, as a general screening for behavior disorders.

The utility of the interventions manual is also questionable, primarily because treatment strategies are based on the topography of the behavior, rather than its function. The lists of treatment recommendations for 99 behaviors are approached like an essay test, wherein the ambiguity and sheer number of strategies insure that one or two of them will seem prognostic. Providing positive feedback, acknowledgement, and praise are included for nearly every category.

SUMMARY. Users will find the BDS easy to administer, score, and translate into a written treatment plan. Differential diagnosis and effective intervention, however, will require a more sophisticated assessment model such as the Behavior Assessment System for Children (Reynolds & Kamphaus, 1992; 40) and a functional assessment of problem behaviors.

REVIEWER'S REFERENCES

Reynolds, C. R., & Kamphaus, R. W. (1992). *Behavior Assessment System for Children manual.* Circle Pines, MN: American Guidance Service.
American Psychiatric Association. (1994). *Diagnostic and statistical manual of mental disorders* (4ᵗʰ ed.). Washington, DC: Author.
McCarney, S. B., & McCain, B. R. (1995). *The Behavior Dimensions Intervention manual.* Columbia, MO: Hawthorne Educational Services, Inc.

Review of the Behavior Dimensions Scale by BEVERLY M. KLECKER, *Assistant Professor, Department of Administration, Counseling, and Educational Studies, College of Education, Eastern Kentucky University, Richmond, KY:*

DESCRIPTION. The Behavior Dimensions Scale (BDS) was developed to aid in the diagnosis, placement, and planning for children and adolescents demonstrating significant behavior problems that interfere with their success in the school and home environment. The scale consists of the School Version (99 items) and Home Version (108 items). Each of the subscales is purported to be associated with one of six of the behavior disorders referenced in the American Psychiatric Association's *Diagnostic and Statistical Manual, 4ᵗʰ Edition* (DSM-IV, 1994). These disorders are (a) Attention-Deficit/Hyperactivity Disorder, (b) Oppositional Defiant Disorder, (c) Conduct Disorder, (d) Avoidant Personality Disorder, (e) Generalized Anxiety Disorder, and (f) Major Depressive Episode.

A diagnosis of each of these disorders requires that the symptoms be persistent for at least 6 months and that the symptoms be present in two or more situations (American Psychiatric Association, 1994). The Behavior Dimensions Scale consists of items describing behavior and a 5-point item

rating scale. An educator (School Version) or parent or guardian (Home Version) familiar with the child rates how well each item describes the child's behavior. The descriptors for the scale points are frequency referenced and range from *does not engage in the behavior* (0), to occurs *one to several times per month* (1), *week* (2), *day* (3), or *hour* (4).

SAMPLES FOR TEST VALIDATION AND NORMING. The sample used for standardization was 7,383 children and adolescents distributed evenly across age levels from 5 to 19 years. Demographic characteristics of the standardization sample reflected national statistics of sex, residence, race, geographic area, and occupation of parents. The author states that the standardization sample contained children with no diagnosed disorder and children diagnosed with one of the six disorders identified. This dichotomous grouping of children into nondiagnosed and diagnosed has no further breakdown of how many of the diagnosed children had each of the six disorders. Thus, the reviewer could assume that there may be as few as one in each of the diagnosed categories. This lack of description is troublesome because the scale is being offered to differentiate among the six disorders rather than between "normal" and "disordered" children. The description of the normative sample is incomplete and, perhaps, misleading.

RELIABILITY. The author reported that the test-retest reliabilities (30-day interval) for each of the six subscales were all greater than .76. These measures of stability are within acceptable ranges. Interrater reliabilities for both the School Version (between educators) and Home Version (between parents) were reported as being above .90 for both scales. As the two versions of the BDS contain different numbers of items and different item content, it is not possible to calculate an interrater reliability across environments for the same child. This measure of consistency would be helpful as the DSM-IV descriptions of the disorders require that the behavior be observed in at least two different settings. The author reports that Cronbach's coefficient alpha reliability (internal consistency) for the total scale score was .98.

VALIDITY. Content validity was investigated by creating items from DSM-IV behavior descriptions of the six behavior disorders. Criterion validity is reported (concurrent) by statistically significant correlations between the BDS and the

Child Behavior Checklist, Revised Behavior Problem Checklist, and the Burks' Behavior Rating Scale.

The author states that the construct validity of the test suggests strong diagnostic validity. However, the evidence that the author presents for the construct validity of this test is seriously flawed. Nine of the scale interventions are .72 or above indicating that the subscales are measuring the same construct. The factor analysis described was clearly contraindicated. Gorsuch (1983) stated:

> *Varimax is inappropriate if the theoretical expectation suggests a general factor may occur* [boldface in the original]. To apply varimax, for example, to items of a test with high internal consistency is inappropriate because high internal consistency means there is a general factor underlying most of the items in the test. (p. 185)

Cronbach's coefficient alpha for the total scale was .98; this is strong evidence that the scale is unidimensional. Forcing subscales through an inappropriate use of orthogonal rotation should not be used as evidence for construct validity.

SUMMARY. No credible empirical evidence is presented for the construct validity of this test. The subscales are highly correlated and the measure of internal consistency is .98. Further, no evidence has been provided that the test can discriminate either between children with one of the disorders or between disordered and nondisordered children (this would require sufficient, well-described, samples of children diagnosed with each of the six disorders). There are tests and observation instruments that can be used to diagnose the six disorders described in this review. This reviewer suggests that the reader seek out these individual diagnostic tests through the Buros website and publications. The diagnosis of any of these disorders requires more than a single "point-in-time" evaluation; the DSM-IV states that disordered behavior must be observed for 6 months or longer.

REVIEWER'S REFERENCES

Gorsuch, R. L. (1983). *Factor analysis* (2ⁿᵈ ed.). Hillsdale, NJ: Lawrence Erlbaum Associates.
    American Psychiatric Association. (1994). *Diagnostic and statistical manual of mental disorders* (4ᵗʰ ed.). Washington, DC: Author.

[42]
Behavioral and Emotional Rating Scale: A Strength-Based Approach to Assessment.

Purpose: "Designed to assess the behavioral and emotional strengths of children."
Population: Ages 5-0 to 18-11.

Publication Date: 1998.
Acronym: BERS.
Scores, 6: 5 subscales: Interpersonal Strength, Family Involvement, Intrapersonal Strength, School Functioning, Affective Strength, plus Strength Quotient.
Administration: Individual.
Price Data, 1999: $79 per complete kit; $42 per examiner's manual (60 pages); $39 per 50 summary/response forms.
Time: (10) minutes.
Comments: Normed for two separate groups: Children not identified with emotional or behavioral disorders and children diagnosed with emotional or behavioral disorders.
Authors: Michael H. Epstein and Jennifer M. Sharma.
Publisher: PRO-ED.

Review of the Behavioral and Emotional Rating Scale: A Strength-Based Approach to Assessment by BETH DOLL, Associate Professor of Educational Psychology, University of Nebraska-Lincoln, Lincoln, NE:

The Behavioral and Emotional Rating Scale (BERS) provides a strength-based assessment of students between the ages of 5 and 18. It is particularly intended for the evaluation of students suspected of having emotional or behavioral disabilities. Each of the scale's 52 items describes positive features of a child's interpersonal or emotional behavior, making it an especially useful tool for planning strength-based interventions, documenting student improvement, and showing positive impacts of programs. This focus on competence is a welcome departure from the typical practice of assessment via counting behavioral deficits and emotional problems. Moreover, the scale evidences strong psychometric properties that make it a promising tool for assessment for planning and intervention. Unfortunately, despite the authors' firm commitment to strength-based evaluation, their suggested applications of the BERS are often framed within deficit-based decisions about the nature and extent of a child's emotional or behavioral disability. This use of a strength-based measure to make deficit decisions will be confusing to unsophisticated users. Additionally, using the scale in this manner depends upon the unproven premise that the lack of strength is functionally equivalent to the presence of disorder.

The BERS was carefully developed through a series of empirical investigations. An item pool was first identified by a thorough review of the research, and was then confirmed by surveying over 200 professionals for opinions and additional items. These were then subjected to item discrimination and factor analytic studies to evaluate item intelligibility, utility, and structure. Standardization of the BERS was based upon an excellent nationally representative sample of over 2,000 children, with a second standardization conducted on a similarly representative sample of 861 students with behavior or emotional disabilities. Subsequent evaluations assessed the accuracy of the scale's scores in differentiating between students with and without emotional disabilities. Unfortunately, the manual provides no reference to publication of the BERS research in refereed journals, and the description of the research provided in the manual is not sufficiently complete to judge its methodological soundness. For example, norms are collapsed across age groups to yield standardized scores, such that the ratings of 5-year-olds and 18-year-olds are interpreted relative to the same reference group. This would only be appropriate if the normative group yielded no significant age-based differences in scores, but the manual provides no evidence that this was the case. Thus, the adequacy of the empirical foundation of the scale is difficult to assess. [Editors' Note: Subsequent to the publication of the manual, several referred publications based on the BERS appeared in print.]

One glaring shortcoming in the development of the BERS was the authors' failure to define a conceptual model of behavioral and emotional strengths to guide the scale development. Instead, the scale's item content was based on prior research conducted primarily within a literature and profession ruled by deficit-oriented paradigms; and its five subscales were empirically derived using an exploratory factor analysis. The degree to which these dimensions truly represent a comprehensive set of emotional and behavioral strengths has not been fully tested. This dependence on an empirical structure also raises dilemmas for scale interpretation, because it forces users to reply on a face-analysis of the subscales' labels and item content to determine what individual scores mean.

The technical sophistication of the BERS development is in stark contrast to the manual's promised ease of use by diverse professionals. To make the scale interpretable by even psychometrically naive users, the manual provides a largely accurate but simplified explanation of such technical features as reliability, standard error of measurement, and validity. In a couple of key points, however, this simplification was unsuccessful and even dangerously misleading. One example is the scale's use of a standard score called a "Strength Quotient" to represent the sum of all subscale scores. Its name inaccurately suggests that the score is a quotient, namely the product of dividing performance by age. In fact, interpretation of these scores does not differ across developmental levels. Moreover, the term "Strength Quotient" implies that the score matches the reliability and validity of established intelligence tests, a standard that is rarely evident in emotional or behavioral measures.

Preliminary research reported in the manual suggests that the technical properties of the BERS are excellent. Both within subscales and across the full scale, the BERS demonstrates very strong internal consistency reliability with alpha statistics falling between .85 and .95 for most scales. Moreover, the manual describes a study of 59 students showing good test-retest reliability across 2-week intervals and a second study of nine teachers (96 students) showing interrater reliability for teachers. It would be premature to suggest that reliability has been fully established given the small size of the studies and the lack of replication, but those early results are promising.

The validity of scores from the BERS is also promising. A beginning step towards documenting conceptual validity is seen in the manual's articulate and comprehensive rationale differentiating strength-based assessment from the far-more-common deficit-based evaluation of behavior problems and social deficits. Isolated studies conducted by the authors showed respectable correlations between the BERS and other prominent social and behavioral rating scales, both deficit- and strength-based. An investigation reported in the manual also describes encouraging evidence of the scale's power in discriminating between students with and without emotional or behavioral disabilities.

SUMMARY. Once its development is complete, the Behavioral and Emotional Rating Scale has the potential to reframe affective assessment to represent strengths rather than deficits. This will be an important contribution to the knowledge base around evaluation and planning for children's affective needs. Still, several additional steps are required before the BERS can fulfill that role: The research underlying the measure needs to be peer refereed, and references to its publication should be included in the manual. The factor analysis underlying the scale needs to be verified through replication on independent samples, and a conceptual model is needed to describe the meaning of the scale and its subscale. Evidence needs to be presented to support the scale's use of a single set of norms for all age levels. Finally, further examination of the reliability of scores from the scale and validity evidence needs to be conducted on independent samples and with large numbers of independent users. Until this work is done, the BERS should be used cautiously in both practice and research.

Review of the Behavioral and Emotional Rating Scale: A Strength-Based Approach to Assessment by D. JOE OLMI, Associate Professor, Department of Psychology, The University of Southern Mississippi, Hattiesburg, MS:

As opposed to approaching assessment from a deficit perspective, the Behavioral and Emotional Rating Scale (BERS) is designed to identify behavioral and emotional strengths of children ages 5 to 18. As stated by the authors, the BERS has several uses including (a) IEP development, (b) treatment planning, (c) treatment/intervention evaluation, (d) program/agency evaluation, and (e) research. The BERS consists of 52 items that are to be responded to on a scale of 3 (*very much like the child*) to 0 (*not at all like the child*) across five subscales (Interpersonal Strengths, Family Involvement, Intrapersonal Strengths, School Functioning, and Affective Strength). The instrument also includes a section of eight open-ended questions related to hobbies, sports, preferred school subjects and teachers, and so on, and is designed to be responded to by parents, professionals, or others who are acquainted with the behavior of the referred child. The BERS is intended to identify emotional and behavior skills and competencies that result in appropriate functioning and coping in social and academic settings.

The test kit is relatively simple, containing summary/response forms and an examiner's manual that explains the rationale behind the instrument, a brief description, administration/scoring procedures, interpretation, and normative and psychometric aspects of the BERS. Examiner qualifications are few, and with minimal training, the BERS can be administered by classroom teachers, psychologists, social workers, or other professional personnel. The examiner's manual is rather straightforward, well organized, and reader friendly. The summary/response form is easy to follow with identifying profile, and results information appearing on the front page. The 52 items are contained within the form, with the eight open-ended questions and a brief section for interpretation and recommendations contained on the backside. The open-ended questions are self-explanatory. It should take approximately 10 minutes for a rater to respond to all items of the BERS.

Scoring is fairly simple. As suggested earlier, each of the 52 items is scored along a scale of 3 to 0. Raw scores are totaled for each subscale. Upon completion, each subscale raw score is entered on the front of the summary/response form and converted to percentile ranks and standard scores using tables included in the back of the examiner's manual. Tables for children with emotional or behavioral disorders are included. Subscale standard scores range from 1–20 with a mean of 10 and standard deviation of 3. There is an error in the examiner's manual with regard to calculation of the BERS Strength Quotient where it is stated that, "It [BERS Strength Quotient] is computed by summing the raw scores of the subscales and then converting that sum into a quotient" (p. 19). In fact, the sum of subscale standard scores, not the subscale raw scores, is calculated and converted into the BERS Strength Quotient using another table in the rear of the manual.

With regard to norming, data were gathered for two subject samples (children with emotional and behavioral disorders [EBD] and children without [NEBD]) between 1994 and 1996. The NEBD sample consisted of 2,176 children between ages 5-0 and 18-11 according to characteristics similar to percentage breakdowns of school-age populations in the 1990 U.S. Census. The EBD sample was composed of 861 students in the same age range. Given the great variation of eligibility and assessment standards for Emotional Disturbance, Emotional Disordered, Behavioral Disordered, and all other disability and terminology variations that exist across the nation, there was no indication of how the authors dealt with this variability in the norming process. That information is critical to this reviewer. Furthermore, the normative data would suggest undersampling of females and Hispanics and oversampling of rural and African Americans in the EBD group.

Internal consistency reliabilities, using Cronbach's coefficient alpha method, were acceptable for all subscales and Strength Quotients across age groups. Test-retest (administration interval is 1–2 weeks) and interrater reliabilities ranged from .82 to .99 for the subscales and Strength Quotient.

Content validity was examined through literature review, examination of items of frequently used behavior checklists, and expert review. Item discrimination and factor analysis procedures resulted in the present form of the BERS. Concurrent validity was investigated by comparing the BERS to the Walker-McConnell Scale of Social Competence and School Adjustment-Adolescent Version, the Self-Perception Profile for Children, and the Teacher Report Form of the Achenbach Child Behavior Checklist. Although these are adequate scales in their own right, rationale for their selection was not fully indicated in the manual. All data were collected on small subsamples from schools in Illinois. Correlation coefficient levels are adequate. The presentation on construct validity that was offered in the BERS manual was less than adequate.

SUMMARY. Although the authors attempted to develop an assessment instrument with a strength-based approach, the BERS appears to be nothing new in approach or content. Although it has adequate psychometric properties, there are more comprehensive measures on the market that this reviewer would suggest including the Multidimensional Self Concept Scale (Bracken, 1991), the Assessment of Interpersonal Relations (Bracken, 1993), and the Behavior Assessment System for Children (Reynolds & Kamphaus, 1992).

REVIEWER'S REFERENCES

Bracken, B. A. (1992). Multidimensional Self Concept Scale. San Antonio, TX: PRO-ED.
Reynolds, C. R., & Kamphaus, R. W. (1992). Behavioral Assessment System for Children. Circle Pines, MN: American Guidance Service, Inc.
Bracken, B. A. (1993). Assessment of Interpersonal Relations. San Antonio, TX: PRO-ED.

[43]
Behavioural Assessment of the Dysexecutive Syndrome.

Purpose: "A test battery aimed at predicting everyday problems arising from the Dysexecutive Syndrome."
Population: Ages 16 and above.
Publication Date: 1996.
Acronym: BADS.
Scores, 7: Rule Shift Card, Action Program, Key Search, Temporal Judgement, Zoo Map, Modified Six Elements, Total.
Administration: Individual.
Price Data: Available from publisher.
Time: Administration time not reported; some subtests timed.
Comments: Subtest scores "may be used individually, although validation studies have indicated that the overall battery score is the most sensitive predictor of executive problems"; useful with brain-injured and schizophrenic patients for identifying general or specific deficits in executive functions; supplemental information about patients can be gathered using the self-rating and caregiver rating forms included in the test kit.
Authors: Barbara A. Wilson, Nick Alderman, Paul W. Burgess, Hazel Elmslie, and Jonathan J. Evans.
Publisher: Thames Valley Test Company Ltd. [England].

Review of the Behavioural Assessment of the Dysexecutive Syndrome by RIK CARL D'AMATO, Professor and Director, Programs in School Psychology, the Neuropsychology Laboratory, and the Center for Collaborative Research in Education (CCoRE), and M. Lucille Harrison Professor of Excellence, Division of Professional Psychology, University of Northern Colorado, Greeley, CO:

The Behavioural Assessment of the Dysexecutive Syndrome (BADS) is a test designed to predict problems in living arising from the Dysexecutive Syndrome (DES), frontal lobe impairment, or executive function disorders. The authors report the measure is appropriate for evaluating attention problems, distractibility, social inappropriateness, perseveration difficulties, and problem-solving deficits with this constellation of impairments (Lezak, 1995). It appears that a great deal of confusion exists about the DES given its complexity and diagnostic difficulties. With this in mind, the authors have presented this measure as an *ecologically* valid and clinically useful tool to assist in the diagnosis of the DES (Wilson, 1993).

The authors have provided a brief review of other measures in the field and argue that most measures, like the Wisconsin Cart Sorting Test, focus on a specific (and myopic) sample of behavior (i.e., problem solving with cards), and do not require life-related complex organization abilities covering a long period of time. From the authors' view the only exceptions to this are the Multiple Errands Test and the Six Elements Test. The authors based the development of the BADS on revisions and expansions of these measures as well as on clinical practice, theory, and related research.

A brief but somewhat straightforward 24-page BADS manual offers historical information, a description of the tests, standardization information, administration directions, scoring information, and references. Although the test seems appropriate for neuropsychologists and related service personnel, the manual presents no qualifications that are required to use this battery.

Administration of the test battery requires a stopwatch, a tape recorder, colored pens, a pencil, eraser, the protocol, additional paper, water, and the test and manual. Most of these materials can be organized in the thin plastic case that comes with the test but the size of the case is not sufficient to store all materials. Consequently, the portability of the measure must be questioned. It should be noted that some of these materials are unique and not readily available in all settings (e.g., water, tape recorder).

The BADS consists of six tests that can be combined to provide a total profile standardized score. Like other neuropsychological tests, the BADS offers these six components as individualized tests and *not* subtests. Still, it would seem that these tests may be better conceptualized as subtests than tests themselves. No statistical information is available concerning the factor structure of the six component tests. A questionnaire is also included with the battery.

RULE SHIFT CARDS TEST. This measure uses 21 spiral-bound nonpicture playing cards and evaluates the patient's ability to follow rules and shift from one rule to another. Initially, patients are asked to respond "yes" to a red card and "no" to a black card. This rule is prominently displayed on a large laminated sheet placed in full view of the patient. Later the rule is changed, but also prominently displayed, and patients are asked to respond "yes" if the card turned over was the same color as the previously displayed card, and "no" if the previous card was a different color. Purportedly, this test is one of the easier activities and is used to boost morale, evaluate the patient's ability to shift rules, follow directions, and change mental sets without perseveration.

ACTION PROGRAM TEST. A fascinating and novel apparatus (partially filled with water) is placed in front of the patient and the patient is provided with a variety of equipment. The patient is to remove the cork from a plastic tube using the available equipment. The examiner evaluates the patient's ability to follow the *five* novel steps that are needed to remove the cork. This problem-solving test is extremely unique, interesting, and practical, requiring physical manipulation of a variety of materials. However, it is not easy to set up, and the use of water makes it difficult to handle and administer.

KEY SEARCH TEST. On this test patients receive paper with an empty square on the sheet and a dot below the square. Patients are told that they have lost their keys in a large field. They start on the dot and diagram how they would search the field. Information is provided in the manual concerning how examiners should respond to a variety of questions or problem situations. This task is seen as another *real-life* activity, which seems debatable. Scoring is rather complex, with the manual providing scoring directions that need to be closely studied. Some of the scoring examples were not easy to follow. This test is intended to measure planning and self-monitoring.

TEMPORAL JUDGEMENT TEST. The patient is asked four questions related to how long certain activities take in real life. On this test, some of the questions are worded in an odd fashion and the norms provided do not seem relevant to life in North America. In fact, an informal evaluation of some of these tasks showed 75% of the questions on this test to be wrong for North America. [Editor's Note: This test is published in England. The publisher recommends to all American buyers of the test that they not administer the Temporal Judgement Test because of its British cultural content.]

ZOO MAP TEST. On this test individuals indicate the path they would take on a map when visiting a zoo. A variety of different colored pencils are used to indicate the order of the route taken and certain rules are provided to the patient. Scoring is complex and the frequent exchange of the colored pencils was clumsy. A less difficult second trial is given to evaluate performance under high and low structured conditions. This test is seen as measuring the ability of patients to follow directions, profit from feedback, and problem solve.

MODIFIED SIX ELEMENTS TEST. This measure has the patient dictate, complete arithmetic problems and name pictures. Each of these three tasks is broken down into two components for a total of six elements. The patient is given 10 minutes to complete the test and must switch between tasks during the time period. The test does not focus on the patient's overall performance but on his or her ability to manage the diverse elements of the tasks under time constraints. This test measures the patient's ability to plan, organize, and monitor behavior.

THE DYSEXECUTIVE QUESTIONNAIRE (DEX). A 20-item questionnaire is provided to help gather information about the many difficulties associated with DES. The four broad areas of (a) emotional personality changes, (b) motivational changes, (c) behavioral changes, and (d) cognitive changes were sampled. The questionnaire comes in two versions, one for the individual patient to fill out and the other for a close relative or caregiver to complete. The availability of two questions developed for different respondents is a commendable feature of the test.

Both questionnaires, as well as some of the directions on the tests, have a distinctly British flavor and would need to be modified for use in the U.S. Very limited information is offered in interpreting any of the test scores or in how to compare scores on tests with the DEX scores.

The authors utilized a sample of 216 neurologically healthy subjects to norm the test initially. To assure a mix of intellectual abilities, subjects were placed into three intellectual ability groups—below average (scores of 89 or below), average (scores of 90–109), and above average (scores of 110 and above), based on scores from the National Adult Reading Test (NART). This first step in the normative process was problematic because subjects were placed in IQ groups based on reading scores/premorbid intelligence scores, *not* on "typical" IQ scores. Although reading is certainly a component of intelligence, it is not synonymous (D'Amato, Gray, & Dean, 1988). Equally disturbing is the fact that many neuropsychologically reading-impaired subjects may have been placed in the lowest IQ group when in reality they may have displayed a high IQ in concert with a reading problem (Gaddes & Edgell, 1994). Subjects were then collapsed into age groups of 16–31, 32–47, 48–63, and 64 and above—with about equal numbers of males and females in all groups. The authors attempted to avoid volunteer bias, and sought a balance between age, occupation, and gender. The control subjects ranged from 16 to 87 years old with a mean age of 46.6 (SD = 19.8). The test covers a wide age range with a limited number of subjects in each group. A great deal of the

typical normative information (level of SES, occupation, race) presented in most test manuals is missing and this renders the norms of the measure questionable at best. A validation study with 78 patients with neuropsychological problems between the ages of 16 and 76 was then conducted. Information concerning this group is also inadequate.

The authors report an interrater reliability study with 25 of the control subjects. In essence, one examiner tested these subjects with another watching, and highly reliable scores were reported. However, it is odd to have two examiners present at one time with one watching the other. Test-retest reliability was evaluated with 25 of the normal controls being retested 6–12 months after initial testing. The authors argued convincingly that test-retest reliability is difficult with a novel measure of frontal lobe functions but additional information would prove helpful.

Validity of the measure was determined by comparing the *normal* control group to the group of patients with neuropsychological disorders and the displayed scores were significantly different. Information from schizophrenic subjects is also reported (Wilson, Evans, Emslie, Alderman, & Burgess, 1998). Additional correlations were presented between all six tests of the BADS, the NART, and between Wechsler Adult Intelligence Scale—Revised (WAIS-R) Full Scale scores (when available) and age. The DEX was also factor analyzed and comparisons were made between other's ratings on the DEX and the factor scores. Obviously, a unique feature of this measure is the use of the DEX both individually and by others.

Even though these statistical analyses offered new and interesting information concerning the BADS and how its subcomponents relate to itself and between groups, validity with *other measures* was never established. Although this is typical of many neuropsychological tests (Lezak, 1995) it is especially problematic for a new test, with unique tasks, measuring a specialized syndrome. The BADS does have some face validity—and may be a truly valid measure of the DEX—but only future research can answer that question. Because the authors have stressed the ecological nature of the instrument they may want to compare test scores to real-life functioning as well as to other recognized neurpsychological measures (Wilson, 1993).

SUMMARY. The BADS is a new and interesting "ecological" measure of the DES that purportedly relates to patients' real-life functioning. It is composed of novel tasks and is more comprehensive than some of the measures typically used. Nonetheless, its empirical foundation is questionable due to difficulties in the areas of norms, reliability, validity, and its relation to real-life functioning. Additional studies are needed before it can be recommended for general clinical use—but for research purposes the measure seems promising.

REVIEWER'S REFERENCES

D'Amato, R. C., Gray, J. W., & Dean, R. S. (1988). A comparison between intelligence and neuropsychological functioning. *Journal of School Psychology, 26,* 283–292.

Wilson, B. A. (1993). Ecological validity of neuropsychological assessment: Do neuropsychological indexes predict performance in everyday activities? *Applied & Preventive Psychology, 2,* 209–215.

Gaddes, W. H., & Edgell, D. (1994). *Learning disabilities and brain function: A neuropsychological approach* (3rd ed.). New York: Springer-Verlag.

Lezak, M. D. (1995). *Neuropsychological Assessment* (3rd ed.). New York: Oxford Press.

Wilson, B. A., Evans, J. J., Emslie, H., Alderman, N., & Burgess, P. (1998). The development of an ecologically valid test for assessing patients with a Dysexecutive syndrome. *Neuropsychological Rehabilitation, 8,* 213–229.

Review of the Behavioural Assessment of the Dysexecutive Syndrome by SANDRA D. HAYNES, Assistant Professor, Department of Human Services, The Metropolitan State College of Denver, Denver, CO:

The Behavioural Assessment of the Dysexecutive Syndrome (BADS) is designed to assess "everyday problems arising from the Dysexecutive Syndrome (DES)" (manual, p. 4.). DES emanates from frontal lobe damage and includes such symptoms as decreased attention, increased distractibility, impulsivity, perseveration, difficulty with complicated or new tasks, difficulty using feedback, and behaving inappropriately in social situations. These deficits are analogous to a decrease in executive functioning. Thus, the BADS is designed for persons with suspected frontal lobe injury or other persons with these symptoms.

The inspiration for the BADS originated from the belief that existing assessment tools were limited by brevity and single task orientation. The authors reasoned, therefore, that existing tests did not adequately simulate life where competing demands over extended periods of time tend to be the norm and set out to develop a measure that would more closely imitate life.

The BADS consists of six subtests and a 20-item questionnaire. The manual contains a clear explanation of the object of each subtest and instructions for appropriate and standardized administration procedures. The Rule Shifts Card Test, as the name implies, tests one's ability to shift from one rule to another and to keep track of sequencing information. The Action Program Test is a measure of one's ability to develop a plan of action and solve a problem. The Key Search Test, influenced by a subtest in the Stanford-Binet Intelligence Scale, measures one's ability to search efficiently for a missing object. This subtest is similar to another, the Zoo Map Test, that is designed to test ability to plan a route according to certain rules. The Temporal Judgement Test assesses ability to estimate time to complete a task such as inflating a party balloon. The Modified Six Elements subtest measures the ability to plan, organize, and monitor behavior when faced with different, competing tasks. Finally, the Dysexecutive Questionnaire (DEX) is a 20-item questionnaire in two versions, patient and familiar other, designed "to sample the range of problems commonly associated with the Dysexecutive Syndrome" (manual, p. 7) in the areas of emotion, motivation, behavior, and cognition. The DEX is not a true subtest of the BADS in that it is not used in the calculation of a total profile score. The DEX is used for gathering and comparing information between objective test scores and subjective evaluations by the patient and between subjective evaluations by the patient and a familiar other.

Raw scores are converted into a profile score for each subtest, which is relatively easy to calculate. The profile scores from each subtest are then combined with simple addition. This total profile score is then converted into a standardized score allowing for classification into a performance category ranging from impaired to very superior.

Samples for test validation and norming were small but appear adequate for initial estimates. The authors were careful to select individuals with a wide range of measured intelligence. They included approximately equal numbers of individuals in general and with regard to gender and age in comparison groups. They were also careful to sample without bias as to social economic status and volunteer characteristics. Likewise, the overall patient group was large enough for initial general comparisons. Subgroup categories, however, were inadequate to determine specific group differences and, to the authors' credit, no inferences were made regarding specific groups. However, although the description provided to the Buros Institute of Mental Measurements stated that the BADS should be useful with persons with schizophrenia, the manual does not contain a reference to this group nor did any patients in the patient group have this malady. How groups of persons with potential dysexecutive syndrome arising from different etiologies perform on the BADS is an important area for future study.

Reliability estimates were computed using interrater reliability and test-retest reliability. Results from the former method demonstrate a high degree of consistency among raters lending credence to the notion of easy, consistent scoring of the subtests of the BADS. Test-retest reliability (6-month interval) measures indicated a tendency for normal subjects to perform slightly better on second testing than the first. The authors speculate that this is due to the lack of novelty on second testing. They further surmise that these results may be different with persons who have attentional and memory difficulties and admit that further research is necessary. No other reliability measures were used as they would not be appropriate given the small number of test items and the timed nature of some subtests.

Overall, validity was measured by comparing scores on the subtests between control and patient subjects and scores on the subtests to ratings on the DEX. It was clear that the BADS accurately discriminated between the two groups and that subtest scores accurately reflected subjective measures of impairment.

Content validity was assessed via literature review and construct validity was assessed by comparing the BADS to other tests measuring related content, including the Wechsler Adult Intelligence Scales—Revised, and the National Adult Reading Test IQ equivalent scores. Although in test design the authors mention several tests similar in purpose (e.g., the Wisconsin Card Sort Test), they do not use these for validity estimates. Further study using such tests could help clarify the validity findings of the BADS and help to determine the relative importance and utility of the BADS as compared to other such tests.

Two further improvements could be made. The first involves defining the target population of the BADS. A paragraph in the manual explicitly describing appropriate populations, including age ranges, for test use would be useful. As is, one must search norming data or scoring tables to find appropriate age ranges. Additionally, and perhaps more importantly, more study on how the BADS

discriminates among persons with varying severity of impairment would be highly useful. It is unclear whether all subjects in the patient group had severe damage as a result of various brain injuries or if they had varying degrees of severity of damage. Therefore, whether the BADS discriminates among such groups is unclear as is whether the BADS is useful for detecting mild impairment in DES as well as more severe impairments. The utility of this assessment tool in diverse settings (e.g., out-patient vs. in-patient settings) cannot be adequately determined without such information. Secondly, further review or revision of the description of the Temporal Judgement subtest should be considered. The instructions for the test ask the subject "to estimate how long it takes to do four things." One of the questions does not fit this criteria but rather asks how long an animal is expected to live. Another question, regarding a dental check-up, is unclear. Informal evaluation revealed that persons consistently queried whether a "routine check-up" involved cleaning too. There are no instructions as to how to deal with such a question. The two remaining questions, regarding window cleaning and blowing up a balloon, have correct answer estimates that appear in one instance far too brief and in the other overblown. These two questions also do not seem to be as "commonplace" as the test description suggests. The last three criticisms may be due to cultural differences that need further exploration prior to widespread use in countries other than England. [Editor's Note: A representative of the publisher advises: All American buyers of the complete battery are recommended by us *not* to administer the Temporal Judgement Test because of its British cultural content. We point out to each customer that until American norms based on questions suitable to American citizens are collected they might like to leave out this item and prorate on the other five of the six subtests.]

SUMMARY. Test development was accomplished via sound rationale. Certain modifications could help make the BADS a more viable assessment instrument.

[44]
Belbin Team-Roles Self-Perception Inventory.
Purpose: Designed to determine which contributions each team member can make best.

Population: Teams.
Publication Date: 1994.
Scores: 9 Profiles: Plant, Coordinator, Resource Investigator, Monitor Evaluator, Implementer, Team Worker, Completer-Finisher, Specialist, Shaper.
Administration: Group.
Price Data, 1996: $149 per package including Management Teams book (190 pages), Team Roles at Work book (158 pages), Team-Roles Package for 5-person team, and software (IBM); $24.95 per Management Teams book; $34.95 per Team Roles at Work book; $29.95 per team report; $9.95 per individual unit; $3.95 per observer unit.
Time: [1 day].
Author: Meredith Belbin.
Publisher: Jossey-Bass/Pfeiffer.

Review of the Belbin Team-Roles Self-Perception Inventory by KEITH HATTRUP, Associate Professor of Psychology, San Diego State University, San Diego, CA:

The Belbin Team-Roles Self-Perception Inventory is a paper-and-pencil measure designed to identify respondents' interpersonal and problem-solving styles in small, task-oriented groups or teams. In particular, the measure is designed to identify examinees' profiles of strengths and weaknesses with respect to nine Team Roles. The Inventory includes 10 self-report items in each of seven sections. Within each section, examinees indicate their agreement with each item by distributing 10 points across the 10 items. This provides ipsative scoring of the nine Team Roles: Plant, Coordinator, Resource Investigator, Monitor Evaluator, Implementer, Team Worker, Completer-Finisher, Specialist, and Shaper. The Inventory is not timed and can be administered to groups, although specific guidelines about test administration are not provided in the manual.

Research on the development of the instrument is summarized in the manual and in two books written by the test author: *Management Teams: Why They Succeed or Fail* (1981), and *Team Roles at Work* (1981). Unfortunately, none of these sources provides information relevant to score reliability or item analysis. Evidence of the reliability of scores would contribute to a better understanding of the potential sources of error in observed scores on the measure. A separate Observer Assessment instrument is provided to allow an evaluation of agreement between self and other perceptions.

The test manual and the two books provide lengthy discussions of the program of research that led to the development of the instrument. These sources note that research studies of the performance of groups on complex problems led to the identification of nine distinct ways of contributing to group activities that were later labeled as the Team Roles. Some of the team roles were identified with the assistance of profiles of scores on both published and unpublished measures of cognitive ability and personality. The other roles are identified through observations of behavior in group activities. It might be argued, therefore, that an attempt was made to develop a content valid measure of behavioral styles in groups. The thorough descriptions provided about the nine team roles and their distinct behavioral manifestations contribute to the detailed understanding of the constructs needed to support the test's content validity. However, there is insufficient information about the process used in developing test items and in judging their relevance to the focal constructs to support strong arguments about the content validity of the measure. The population of examinees for whom this test is most appropriate is also not clearly specified.

There is no evidence provided of the criterion-related validity of the measure. Although the nine criterion groups were initially formed on the basis of behavioral observations and profiles of scores on other marker tests, no evidence is provided of relationships between scores on the Self-Perception Inventory and membership in the criterion groups or other independent measures of the team roles. The lack of criterion-related validity of the measure in identifying examinees' best team roles is one of the most significant weaknesses of the measure.

Construct validity of the inventory is supported mainly by the program of studies summarized in the manual and two books. These sources note that studies conducted by the authors found that teams formed in an effort to achieve a balance of team roles performed better than teams that did not have the correct balance of members' roles. It is also reported that teams aware of their members' team roles outperformed teams that were unaware, presumably because the former teams were able to adapt better to the strengths and weaknesses of individual team members. These findings suggest that knowledge of examinees' best and worst team roles may lead to accurate predictions about the behavior of teams. However, the research summarized in these sources is not described in sufficient detail to ascertain whether the findings described ware replicable or generalizable. There are no citations to studies published in scholarly journals or books, and there is no information about the specific design of the studies summarized in the manual and two books. The sources also fail to indicate whether the key findings reported about team roles were based on roles identified through the use of the Self-Perception Inventory or some other method. There is a significant need for independent empirical validation and assessment of the measure. At present, there is simply not enough information available to support inferences about the reliability and validity of the measure.

The ipsative nature of the items in the inventory has advantages and disadvantages. On one hand, examinees are encouraged to rank items in each section in terms of their self-descriptiveness, thereby increasing the likelihood that a clear pattern of strengths and weaknesses will emerge for an examinee across the nine team roles. On the other hand, the items are probably more difficult to complete than simple Likert-type response scales for the average examinee. In addition, ipsative scoring prevents between-examinee comparisons on the individual team roles. The ability to compare examinees on a single team role would facilitate personnel selection decisions.

The test manual does not provide normative data on the measure. A table of norms is provided in *Management Teams: Why They Succeed or Fail* based on a sample of 78 respondents who were "a cross-section of managers from various functions and industries" (p. 158). Unfortunately, it is unclear whether these norms are representative of all managers, or just the average of a diverse sample of managers. It is also unclear from the available information whether these norms apply across genders, experience levels, ages, and organization levels.

Scoring of the measure is done with a computer program provided with the test. Reports are provided that indicate the rank-order of team roles, and the implications of the team role profile for interactions with other team members. The Inventory is part of a team building and management package that provides a great deal of advice and insight about the behavior of individuals in teams. Although very little of the information provided is based on clearly documented empirical findings, the insights should prove beneficial in helping organization members think through some of the issues involved in team-based work. The automated computer scoring of the instrument prevents test users from developing their own local norms and conducting research on the measure, however.

SUMMARY. The Belbin Team-Roles Self-Perception Inventory is part of a comprehensive team building and management package designed to identify team members' strengths and weaknesses in small, task-oriented groups. The program of research that led to the development of the instrument provides some support for the construct validity of the Inventory. However, much more detailed information about the reliability, criterion-related validity, and norms for the measure is needed to guide test users in selecting this test and interpreting scores. Until additional psychometric evidence is made available, the measure can only be recommended for applications in which psychometric issues are secondary, such as in facilitating discussion and understanding of possible behavioral patterns and problems in teams. Additional research, either by test users or the test authors, is needed to support the use of the Inventory for personnel decision making, including the assignment of individuals to teams.

Review of the Belbin Team-Roles Self-Perception Inventory by KRISTIN O. PRIEN, Assistant Professor of Management, Christian Brothers University, Memphis, TN, and ERICH P. PRIEN, Professor of Industrial Psychology (Retired) and President, Performance Management Press, Memphis, TN:

Organizations in the 1990s are devoting a good deal of time and extensive resources to implementing and developing work teams, with the goal of increasing organizational effectiveness. Thus, an instrument designed to provide feedback and useful information to individuals on how they function in a team setting would be quite valuable to both organizations and to team members. However, the Team-Roles Self-Perception Inventory is not that instrument.

The User's Guide accompanying the package, as well as Belbin's two books, *Management Teams: Why They Succeed or Fail* and *Team Roles at Work*, are by the author's admission, completely atheoretical. There is no indication that Belbin has made use of the ample prior research on work teams (e.g., Bettenhausen, 1991; Cohen & Bailey, 1997), the role of personality in teams (see Barry & Stewart, 1997), or team member roles (Bales,

1958). Moreover, Belbin's research suffers from a lack of rigor. In neither the user's guide nor the two accompanying books is there any empirical evidence establishing the connection between team composition and team effectiveness. The team roles as described by Belbin are logically worked out and do not conflict with what we know about teams and team processes, but stronger theoretical backing and empirical evidence for Belbin's model would be an appropriate addition to user documentation.

The setting in which the Team-Roles Self-Perception Inventory was developed was a management training center in which the majority of the participants were white males. This presents several problems. First, management teams are only one type of team. Different teams—self-managed teams, project teams, interdisciplinary teams, work crews—have different compositions and different requirements (Sundstrom, De Meuse, & Futrell, 1990) and it is questionable whether or not research based on only one type of team can be generalized to other teams. Moreover, these other types of teams are more likely to be found in the work setting. Also, there is evidence that gender, race, age, and national culture play an important role in team or group functioning. Again, it is questionable whether or not results based on a sample of white males will generalize to the diverse teams actually found in organizations.

Lack of rigor is again a problem in understanding and interpreting the eight team roles described in the inventory. In the development of the inventory, Belbin used the Watson-Glaser Critical Thinking Appraisal and the 16PF to differentiate among personality types and the roles that each personality type plays within a team. However, there is no specific information on how test scores were used to assign individuals to roles. Role assignments appear to have been made by a combination of observed behaviors and generalized characterizations based on test scores (e.g., "clever" vs. "dull"). Overall, there is little evidence provided to support the construct validity of the eight team roles.

The Belbin Team-Roles Self-Perception Inventory includes a self-report measure of team-related behaviors as well as an observer's assessment of the team member in an adjective checklist form. For the self-report measure, there is no evidence as to how these behaviors were chosen as being representative of the various team roles. The observer assessment suffers from a more serious problem, which is that it requires the observer to characterize the team member rather than to simply report observed behaviors. The characterization uses a 3-point scale: no check mark, check mark ("descriptive"), and double check mark ("very descriptive"). There are no definitions or anchors provided for the adjectives, the lack of which would more than likely result in very low interrater reliability. Neither scale addresses the team member's actual cognitive ability, although that is used as one of the two criteria for assigning roles to members in the original research.

Interpreting the results of the Belbin Team-Roles Self-Perception inventory is problematic because the normative data are based on a sample of 500 management team members. Scale reliabilities and validities (both internal consistency and, for the observer assessment, interrater) are not provided. At a minimum, this information should be provided. Furthermore, the instrument would be more useful if the normative data were not limited to white males and were available for different types of teams.

SUMMARY. There is certainly a need for materials that can be used in organizational team building and team development activities. However, the Belbin Team-Roles Self-Perception inventory does not meet that need. The material provided does not give evidence of the theoretical soundness or the construct validity of the various team roles. In addition, it is very questionable as to whether or not the results generalize past management teams to the project teams, self-directed teams, and work crews that make up the majority of teams in organizations.

REVIEWER'S REFERENCES
Bales, R. F. (1958). Task roles and social roles in problem solving groups. In E. E. Maccoby, T. M. Newcomb, and E. L. Hartley (Eds.), *Readings in social psychology* (3rd ed.) (pp. 437–446). New York: Holt, Rinehart, & Winston.
Sundstrom, E., De Meuse, K. P., & Futrell, D. (1990). Work teams: Applications and effectiveness. *American Psychologist, 45*, 120–133.
Bettenhausen, K. L. (1991). Five years of groups research: What we've learned and what needs to be addressed. *Journal of Management, 17*, 345–381.
Barry, B., & Stewart, G. L. (1997). Composition, process, and performance in self-managed groups: The role of personality. *Journal of Applied Psychology, 82*(1), 62–78.
Cohen, S. G., & Bailey, D. E. (1997). What makes teams work: Group effectiveness research from the shop floor to the executive suite. *Journal of Management, 23*(3), 239–290.

[45]

Bell Object Relations and Reality Testing Inventory.

Purpose: Designed to assess "dimensions of object relations and reality testing ego functioning."

Population: Ages 18 and older.
Publication Date: 1995.
Acronym: BORRTI.
Scores, 8: Object Relations (Alienation, Insecure Attachment, Egocentricity, Social Incompetence); Reality Testing (Reality Distortion, Uncertainty of Perception, Hallucinations and Delusions); Inconsistent Responding; plus two validity indexes: FREQ, INFREQ.
Administration: Group.
Price Data, 1999: $99.50 per complete kit including 2 prepaid Full Form mail-in answer sheets, 2-use clinical disk, 2 Full Form PC answer sheets, and manual; $47.50 per manual; $17.50 per Full Form mail-in answer sheet; $16.50 per Form O mail-in answer sheet; $205 per 20-use clinical disk (Full Form or Form O; PC with Microsoft Windows) including interpretive report; $64.50 per 20-use clinical disk for scoring only; $15 per 100 PC answer sheets (specify Full Form or Form O); $10.50 per FAX Scoring service for Full Form; $9.50 per FAX Scoring Service for Form O.
Time: (15–20) minutes.
Comments: Form O including only items measuring object relations also available.
Author: Morris D. Bell.
Publisher: Western Psychological Services.
Cross References: See T5:297 (2 references).

Review of the Bell Object Relations and Reality Testing Inventory by GLEN FOX, Clinical Occupational Psychologist, Occupational Psychology Services, Sevenoaks, Kent, England:

The Bell Object Relations and Reality Testing Inventory (BORRTI) is a self-administered paper-and-pencil inventory consisting of 90 descriptive statements that the respondent marks as "true" or "false" according to his or her "most recent experience" (manual, p. 3). Scoring yields four Object Relations subscales: Alienation, Insecure Attachment, Egocentricity, and Social Incompetence; and three Reality Testing subscales: Reality Distortion, Uncertainty of Perception, and Hallucination and Delusions. The Object Relations Scales (four subscales) and Reality Testing Scales (three subscales) are each represented by 45 items, and no item was scored for more than one of the seven subscales.

The BORRTI can be computer scored, using either a pre-purchased disk or the bureau scoring service. Scoring and Interpretation are also available by fax. The object Relations items can be administered separately.

INTENDED USERS. The author recommends that the test should be used in the field of psychopathology, in order to measure dimensions of psychological change experienced by patients who were undergoing a course of psychotherapy and were suffering from schizophrenia or related disorders. The printed report describes the test as "designed to help identify patients with disturbed ego functioning including those with personality disorders or clinically relevant reality testing deficits" (manual, p. 57).

Although the manual mentions that some practitioners have made extended use of the test in nonclinical settings, the publishers do not claim that it has application outside clinical groups, in areas such as organizational or management development.

STANDARDIZATION. No norm tables are supplied with the manual, and all technical data relating to scores are supplied in T scores. These were derived from a nonclinical population of 934 students and "high functioning, community active adults" (manual, p. 30). The assumption has been made that scores deviating substantially from those obtained by the standardization sample should be regarded as potentially at risk. Clinical subjects were not included in the sample in the appropriate proportions, and this may exaggerate the differences between their performance and that of the sample mean. It is difficult, therefore, to assess differences between high and low scores because (a) there is likely to be a very restricted range of those suffering from the problems identified by the instrument within the norm group, and (b) without access to raw scores there is no way of determining whether the instrument is skewed or normally distributed. There is no indication given in the manual as to which questions relate to which scales, except for the Frequency/Infrequency scale and the Inconsistent Response item pairs. No item analyses are presented.

RELIABILITY. The internal consistency estimates for scores from the instrument are within acceptable limits, ranging from .9 on Alienation to .78 on Egocentricity. Cronbach's alpha and split-half figures are given, on a sample of 336. Test-retest figures show that the stability across time is a little less good, ranging from .58 (Social Incompetence) to .78 (Reality Distortion) on a sample of 42 across a 26-week time period. Higher test-retest figures are given, ranging from .9 on Egocentricity to .58 on Social Incompetence, but as these come from a sample of only 8, it is difficult to rely satisfactorily on them. These figures would give a standard error of measurement between 6.5 and 4.58 in T scores, the preferred scaling employed by the test.

CONSTRUCT VALIDITY. There is considerable prima facie evidence for good construct validity in the Object Relations Scales, showing the expected correlations with all the appropriate scales of the Eysenck Personality Questionnaire. Significant correlations with appropriate scales of the Minnesota Multiphasic Personality Inventory (MMPI), Positive and Negative Syndrome Scale (PANSS), and SCL-90-R also appear for all the BORRTI scales.

DISCRIMINANT VALIDITY. It should be noted that any differences quoted in the manual between criterion groups to show the discriminant validity of the instrument should at least exceed the standard error of measurement. In fact, out of 35 quoted significant mean differences (in T scores) between various clinical and nonclinical groups, about one-third fall below the size of the standard error of the relevant scale. Again, without t-test data or discriminant function analysis data it is hard to evaluate the discriminant validity of the test.

GUIDANCE RELATING TO USE. The manual makes it clear that the instrument is to be used in clinical situations only by trained and practicing clinicians. There is a helpful chapter on how to use the instrument with clinical subjects, including a number of case studies, and a detailed description of the meaning of and appropriate treatment for high scorers on each scale. There is a table of external correlates for all seven scales, showing the relationship of each to major scales on other well-known clinical instruments.

FAIRNESS. The manual claims no significant differences exist in relation to age or gender. No data are presented in respect of ethnic differences. The analyses relating to gender and age were performed on 326 psychiatric patients.

SUMMARY. The inventory would appear appropriate for use with clinical populations although it would be preferable to be able to base this conclusion on a representative norm group rather than on a wholly nonclinical one.

Review of the Bell Object Relations and Reality Testing Inventory by STEVEN I. PFEIFFER, Adjunct Professor of Psychology and Education, and Executive Director, Duke University Talent Identification Program, Durham, NC:

The Bell Object Relations and Reality Testing Inventory (BORRTI) is a self-administered paper-and-pencil questionnaire consisting of 90 descriptive statements that the respondent endorses as "true" or "false." The BORRTI is not intended as a comprehensive measure of personality, but rather is designed to assess two specific aspects of ego functions—object relations and reality testing. The work of Bellak, Hurvich, and Gediman (1973) on ego functions provides the primary conceptual foundation for the BORRTI.

The BORRTI yields four Object Relations (OR) subscales (Alienation, Insecure Attachment, Egocentricity, and Social Incompetence) and three Reality Testing (RT) subscales (Reality Distortion, Uncertainty of Perception, and Hallucinations and Delusions). The OR and RT scales each consist of 45 items. The instrument is intended for ages 18 and above, with items requiring a sixth-grade reading ability level. Hand scoring is not available due to the complexity of factor score calculations. The test user has the option of either employing a computer-scoring system (using an IBM-compatible microcomputer disk) or mail-in/FAX scoring service provided by the test publisher.

As mentioned above, Bellak et al.'s (1973) influential work on ego functions guided the development of the BORRTI. However, the author of the BORRTI, Dr. Morris Bell, decided to avoid many of the pitfalls of Bellak's earlier work by not using a multipoint scaling and restricting his scale to only 2 of the 12 ego functions measured by Bellak. These were judicious decisions that have made the BORRTI a better psychological instrument.

For each of the seven subscales a diagnostic cutoff score, which corresponds to a standardized T-score of 60 or more, was derived from norms based on 934 nonclinical samples. In addition to each of the OR and RT subscales, scales are available to assess deliberate response distortion used to "faking good" and "faking bad," inconsistent responding, and two validity indexes evaluate the respondent's consistency of responses to frequently and infrequently selected statements. Interpretation of a protocol is based on profile analysis focusing on elevated single and multiple subscale scores.

The BORRTI was developed and standardized in a sound and carefully articulated fashion. The instrument has quite good internal consistency (Cronbach's alpha ranging from .78 to .90), and adequate test-retest reliability (ranging from a high of .90 on the Egocentricity subscale over a 4-week period to low of .58 on Reality Distortion and Uncertainty of Perception over a 4-week and 13-week period) and classification stability. The author is to be commended for providing in the manual substantial empirical support for the validity of the score interpretations from the BORRTI. The BORRTI shows evidence of discriminant validity (e.g., in differentiating among seven clinical groups), predictive accuracy (e.g., 74% "hit rate" [tau statistic of .47] for correctly identifying among four Axis I disorders for the OR scores), and adequate correlations with other clinical rating scales (e.g., Brief Psychiatric Rating Scale, Global Assessment Scale, SCL-90-R, Millon Clinical Multiaxial Inventory [MCMI], and Minnesota Multiphasic Personality Inventory [MMPI]). Relatedly, the manual provides a listing of over 50 published research reports using the BORRTI.

The BORRTI has three noteworthy weaknesses. First, although the standardization group from which the normalized T-scores are derived consists of a nonclinical population, it appears that the sample may not be representative of the entire U.S. population, but rather reflects a middle-class to upper-middle-class sample of unspecified educational level, ethnicity, or racial background. Second, although the normalized T-scores are derived from a nonclinical population, tests of response bias and the validity scales were developed exclusively with clinical samples. Third, and perhaps most telling, are the directions on the Record Form, which instruct the respondent to "respond (to each item) according to your most recent experience." The manual explains, "the ambiguity of the term 'most recent experience' allows for individual interpretation, usually based on the person's own sense of the most recent period of consistent internal experience" (p. 5). The psychometric problems here are twofold: One is not sure what internal time frame the standardization group may have employed, and one can, at best, only guess what internal time frame any given patient may be using.

The BORRTI is a well-conceived and valuable self-rating measure of the ego functions of object relations and reality testing. The test is easy to administer and complete, enjoys strong evidence of reliability and validity, and has a thorough manual, which includes well-written case examples to help the user understand test interpretation. Computer scoring yields not only a comprehensive analysis of a patient's OR and RT, but also a diagnosis and quite helpful treatment recommendations.

REVIEWER'S REFERENCE

Bellak, L., Hurvich, M., & Gediman, H. K. (1973). *Ego functions in schizophrenics, neurotics and normals: A systematic study of conceptual, diagnostic, and therapeutic aspects.* New York: John Wiley & Sons.

[46]
Bilingual Verbal Ability Tests.

Purpose: "Provides a measure of overall verbal ability, and an unique combination of cognitive/academic language abilities for bilingual individuals."
Population: Ages 5 and over.
Publication Date: 1998.
Acronym: BVAT.
Scores, 5: Bilingual Verbal Ability, English Language Proficiency, Picture Vocabulary, Oral Vocabulary, Verbal Analogies.
Administration: Individual.
Price Data, 2001: $159.50 per English test kit (specify Windows or Macintosh); $248 per Spanish test kit (specify Windows or Macintosh); $64 per language test (specify Arabic, Chinese simplified, Chinese Traditional, French, German, Haitian-Creole, Hindi, Hmong, Italian, Japanese, Korean, Polish, Portuguese, Russian, Spanish, Turkish, Vietnamese); $28.50 per 25 test records (available in previously listed languages); $655.50 per complete kit including test easel book with English subtests, 16 sets of tests—1 of each language (note: Hmong test pages are available as an upgrade only and are not included in the complete BVAT kit), storage container, software, manual (1998, 110 pages), multipack of 25 forms—11 Spanish, 7 of the 7-language form, 2 of the French/Russian form, and 1 each of the 6 remaining languages; $65 per training video kit.
Time: (20–30) minutes.
Comments: Yields an aptitude measure that can be used in conjunction with the WJ-R Tests of Achievement (T5:2901); an optional training video with administration procedures is available.
Authors: Ana F. Muñoz-Sandoval, Jim Cummins, Criselda G. Alvarado, and Mary L. Ruef.
Publisher: Riverside Publishing.

Review of the Bilingual Verbal Ability Tests by ALAN GARFINKEL, Professor of Spanish and Education, Purdue University, Department of Foreign Languages and Literatures, West Lafayette, IN:

Any demographic examination of placement statistics for special education will reveal a disproportionate placement of language minority students in classes for those whose verbal skills are abnormally low. Some teachers have long supposed that monolingual English assessment instruments make it impossible to know whether a given child's problem is only a question of linguistic development or one of a genuine deficit in the proficiencies that lie beneath external linguistic features. It might be possible to use a nonverbal instrument to place students, but that would provide only a partial assessment. There are other, similarly unsatisfactory ways to determine placement. However, the Bilingual Verbal Ability Tests (BVAT) represent a genuine departure from the usual by using measures in the home language of students to supplement those made in English.

The Bilingual Verbal Ability Tests are based on three tests whose origin is in the Woodcock-Johnson—Revised Tests of Cognitive Ability (Woodcock & Johnson, 1989a). Test 1 of the BVAT is one of Picture Vocabulary in which learners are asked to name familiar and unfamiliar objects. Test 2 is one of Oral Vocabulary in which learners are asked to name synonyms and antonyms of selected items. The last of the three assesses the ability to comprehend and verbally complete a logical word relationship. All three are in English. Then, the items in the tests that were answered incorrectly in the English version are repeated in the learner's home language. The score of the English test is next adjusted to credit items answered incorrectly in English and correctly in the home language. The test has been translated into 16 home languages selected on the basis of advice provided by Waggoner (1993). There are more than 16 language minority groups in American schools, but those selected are surely the ones most frequently encountered, and the BVAT publisher has established a procedure for adding new languages. Instructions and a training protocol for assistants and volunteers from the various language minority groups are provided. This reviewer is proficient in Spanish and was pleased to note that the translation permits the use of Puerto Rican and Mexican vocabulary items. Moreover, one item was listed as "not translatable" (and thus, not counted) because an attempt at translating it would have created confusions that would have yielded less rather than more evaluative information. This exclusion was sensitive and astute.

The BVAT Comprehensive Manual reports that norms for the BVAT were extracted from a larger range of scores gathered for norming the tests on which the BVAT is based, the Woodcock-Johnson—Revised Tests of Cognitive Ability. The manual further indicates that values calculated for reliability were determined by the split-half procedure. Reliability at a wide range of levels was estimated to be in the high .80s (median for all ages: .96, N = 5,596). The Spanish was standardized with a sample of 542 at a median level of .84 for all 12 grade levels. All 16 language translations were refined and standardized by a consensus procedure after field testing by bilingual assessment professionals. The manual presents an appropriate case for test reliability.

Concurrent validity studies presented in the manual show high levels of correlation with other language proficiency instruments administered at various levels. Content validity is particularly well presented in an examination of the translation protocol, whith assures that dialectal variations are given attention and that untranslatable items are left out of consideration. One comfortably concurs with the manual's indication that the BVAT may be used with confidence in a variety of educational and noneducational settings (manual, p. 86).

Test administration procedures are made very clear. There is a step-by-step description of testing procedures accompanied by a training video that gives the prospective user the feeling of being well introduced to the tests.

Test scoring and reporting are also exceptionally efficient. Software for Macintosh or Windows platforms is provided and the software makes it possible to automatically report BVAT scores in conjunction with the Woodcock-Johnson—Revised Tests of Achievement (Woodcock & Johnson, 1989b). This provides "a system for evaluating the presence and significance of aptitude/achievement discrepancies and for evaluating the contribution from a subject's current level of English language proficiency to any measured discrepancy" (manual, p. 1).

Throughout the test description there is constant evidence of sensitivity to issues of culture and bias. The essential nature of the test is dedicated to unbiased placement of learners in or out of special education classes for the very reason that other tests do not separate verbal ability from English language proficiency and special education classes have disproportionate numbers of language minority children in them. The BVAT seems to have potential for resolving that problem.

One problem that remains open to further thought is the disproportionate number of African American children in special education courses. If minority language groups are misplaced for lack of appreciation of the role of English language proficiency alone in placement decisions, what causes the same result for racial minorities? Could home language be an explanation? Could a specialized BVAT be developed to more clearly analyze that problem, too? Even if not, more widespread use is likely to tell us whether the BVAT is successful in its original goal of making the inclusion of language minority children in special education classes more proportional. The BVAT is a logical concept. It is deserving of greater use and longitudinal study to make a final determination.

SUMMARY. The BVAT addresses the disproportionate placement of language minority children into special education classes by testing them in their home languages. Because of its sensitivity to sociolinguistic issues, the BVAT is recommended for increasingly widespread use and the resulting collection of longitudinal data.

REVIEWER'S REFERENCES

Woodcock, R. W., & Johnson, M. B. (1989a). Woodcock-Johnson—Revised Tests of Cognitive Ability. Itasca, IL: The Riverside Publishing Company.

Woodcock, R. W., & Johnson, M. B. (1989b). Woodcock-Johnson—Revised Tests of Achievement. Itasca, IL: The Riverside Publishing Company.

Waggoner, D. (1993). The growth of multilingualism and the need for bilingual education: What do we know so far? *Bilingual Research Journal, 17*, 1–12.

Review of the Bilingual Verbal Ability Tests by CHARLES W. STANSFIELD, *President, Second Language Testing, Inc., N. Bethesda, MD:*

PURPOSE AND DESIGN. The Bilingual Verbal Ability Tests (BVAT) are designed to be used in bilingual education, program placement and planning, clinical assessment of cognitive development, and research. According to the well-written test manual, the BVAT was designed to "take account of the realities of bilinguals' language development by assessing the linguistic and conceptual knowledge that students possess regardless of language source (p. 11)." The authors claim it can be used independently as a language proficiency measure or in conjunction with the Woodcock-Johnson—Revised Tests of Achievement (WF-R; T5:2901). If used in conjunction with the WJ-R, the two tests can identify aptitude/achievement discrepancies.

The BVAT is based on three subtests of the Woodcock Language Proficiency Battery—Revised (T5:2902), which, in turn, were drawn from the Woodcock-Johnson—Revised Tests of Cognitive Ability (WJ-R COG). These subtests are Picture Vocabulary, Oral Vocabulary, and Verbal Analogies. Each of these subtests is limited to an assessment of the examinee's vocabulary. Pronunciation, morphology, syntax, and other components of language use are not assessed on the BVAT.

ADMINISTRATION. The examiner administers the English version first. Items that are missed in English are then administered in the student's native language. This produces a score for English and a score for bilingual verbal ability (BVA). The latter is considered a global index of the examinee's overall aptitude or cognitive academic language proficiency (Cummins, 1984). In the picture Vocabulary subtest, the examinee names words represented by drawings in an easel book, after they are pointed to by the examiner. In Oral Vocabulary, the examinee gives either a synonym or antonym of a word stated by the examiner. In Verbal Analogies, the examinee completes a second pair of words, based on analogy with an initial pair of words uttered by the examiner. The format is A is to B as C is to ___. The examiner discontinues the test if an examinee misses six or eight items in a row, depending on the subtest.

NON-ENGLISH VERSIONS. The 16 non-English versions of the BVAT were developed by having translators or educators translate the words in the English version to other languages. (Unlike the English version, the foreign language versions do not use colored drawings.) The translated words were reviewed by educators or translators and revised when the lead translator agreed with the reviewers' comments. The authors call this consensus translation. Some words did not function as desired when translated, because the translated word has additional meanings in the target language. Such words were deleted from the test, with the result that the non-English versions are on average one or two items shorter than the English version.

SCORING AND INTERPRETATION. A computer program called the Scoring and Reporting Program for the BVAT can be used to score and generate interpretive score reports for the BVAT. The program uses the background information and item responses collected on each student's Test Record to produce scores and the narrative interpretation. There are scores for English language proficiency (based on the number right in English) and for bilingual verbal ability (BVA), based on the number right in both languages. The latter is considered a global index of the examinee's overall aptitude or cognitive academic language proficiency. If scores are also available for the WJ-R, the program will use them to compare the student's aptitude (bilingual verbal ability) with achievement as indicated on the WJ-R. The program uses the correlation between the WJ-R and the BVAT to determine if the student's level of achievement is higher or lower than expected for students at the same level of bilingual verbal ability. If a student's BVA score is higher than the English language proficiency score, and a significant aptitude/achievement discrepancy exists, the program will attribute this discrepancy to limited English proficiency.

SAMPLES FOR TEST VALIDATION AND NORMING. Norming for the English language portion of the BVAT is based on a subset of the data used to standardize the WJ-R COG. The nationally representative sample is composed of 5,602 subjects between the ages of 5 and 90, including a group representing college/university students. The subpopulation for which the BVAT seems most applicable, students in Grades K–12, consists of 3,213 test takers. Bilingual ability was not considered a factor in selecting subjects for the BVAT norming sample. Therefore, the norms can be considered to represent BVAT performance for a monolingual English-speaking population.

RELIABILITY. Subtest reliabilities are reported by age based on split-half analyses of the norming sample and corrected for length by the Spearman-Brown formula. The median reliability for each test is as follows: Picture Vocabulary (.89), Oral Vocabulary (.90), and Verbal Analogies (.90). The median reliability (.96) of the English Language Proficiency (ELP) score (the total of the three subtests administered in English) is quite high. These reliability data are based on the norming sample of English speakers. The only reliability index reported for bilingual verbal ability among bilinguals is .84. This index represents parallel form reliability for a bilingual Hispanic sample.

CRITERION-RELATED VALIDITY. Five small-scale concurrent validity studies are reported, some of which included bilingual students. Again, most of these studies report correlations for the BVAT ELP score, rather than the BVA score.

However, the correlations are quite good. A correlation with the Pre-LAS of .91 was obtained for 70 kindergarten children. A correlation with the Language Assessment Scales (LAS; DeAvila & Duncan, 1987) of .86 was obtained for over 100 second grade students. In general, these studies seem to show that the BVAT ELP score correlates in the high .80s with measures of English language proficiency. Correlations with other verbal measures and with achievement test scores are in the mid .80s. BVAT correlations with aptitude measures are lower. Furthermore, all of the language proficiency, language development, and achievement measures included in these studies tend to correlate slightly lower with each other than with the BVAT. These correlations support the educational relevance and validity of the BVAT.

CONCLUSIONS. The BVAT is a welcome addition to the assessment field, especially to those seeking a means of providing equitable assessment and educational opportunities for English language learners. The authors of the BVAT have developed an assessment package that provides educators with information regarding the test taker's linguistic and cognitive abilities in English and his or her home language. The package can be easily adopted and implemented.

Some cautions, however, are in order. The BVAT is so well designed in terms of its administration and scoring procedures that it might easily become a panacea for a problem that requires more complex solutions. Because validity is a function not only of what a test measures but how that information is used, it seems important to heed the authors' own advice and not extend the BVAT beyond its intended use: "When combined with behavioral observations, work samples, and other pertinent information, results from the BVAT will assist in making appropriate decisions regarding placement of a student" (manual, p. 5).

Secondly, it would be good to see reliability and validity studies that focus on the BVA score and draw from the bilingual population for which the BVAT is designed.

Of the three tasks on the BVAT, only the first, Picture Vocabulary, is a pure measure of language skill. The second and third tasks combine language skill and cognitive ability (verbal aptitude). As a result, the BVAT is not truly a measure of language proficiency in any language. Because of this, it is most useful with examinees whose non-English home language is other than Spanish. For Spanish-speaking students, other more direct measures of language proficiency, such as the LAS and the IDEA Oral Language Proficiency Test (Ballard, Tighe, & Dalton, 1991; 171) are widely available in parallel Spanish and English versions, and may provide a more valid assessment of language skills. On the other hand, the BVAT does provide an interesting and unique assessment of student abilities that is useful for determining the overall level of cognitive and lexical development of any bilingual individual.

REVIEWER'S REFERENCES

Cummins, J. (1984). *Bilingualism and special education: Issues in assessment and pedagogy*. San Diego, CA: College Hill Press.

DeAvila, E. A., & Duncan, S. E. (1987). Language Assessment Scales. Monterey, CA: CTB/McGraw Hill.

Ballard, W. S., Tighe, P. L., & Dalton, E. F. (1991). IDEA Oral Language Proficiency Test. Brea, CA: Ballard & Tighe.

[47]
The Booklet Category Test, Second Edition.

Purpose: Designed to "measure concept formation and abstract reasoning."
Population: Ages 15 and older.
Publication Dates: 1979–1997.
Acronym: BCT.
Scores: Total score only.
Administration: Individual.
Price Data, 2000: $339 per complete kit including manual ('97, 62 pages), stimulus plates, and 25 response forms; $37 per manual; $35 per 25 response forms.
Time: (30–60) minutes.
Authors: Nick A. DeFilippis and Elizabeth McCampbell.
Publisher: Psychological Assessment Resources, Inc.
Cross References: See T5:326 (10 references) and T4:315 (4 references); for reviews by Raymond S. Dean and Thomas A. Hammeke of an earlier edition, see 9:156.

Review of The Booklet Category Test, Second Edition by CAROLYN M. CALLAHAN, Professor of Educational Leadership, Foundations and Policy, Curry School of Education, University of Virginia, Charlottesville, VA:

The Booklet Category Test (BCT) is a modified version of the Category Test (CT) developed by Ward Halstead (Halstead & Settlage, 1943). Both the original Category Test and the Booklet Category Test are individually administered measures designed to distinguish neurologically impaired (brain damaged) from non-neurologically impaired (normal) adult patients. Classification is based on scores derived from the examinee's ability to discern organizing principles in seven sets of geometric tasks using feedback following the response to each item. The underlying assumption is that the ability of an individual to alter hypotheses in the process of concept formation based on feedback is an indicator of level of functioning. The original form of the test required considerable investment in equipment and time for administration. The current format includes the same items, but uses a more portable, easel format.

The manual provides very clear instructions for administration, scoring, and determination of *T*-scores for examinees under normal conditions. Clear guidelines are provided for classification of functioning level. However, instructions for early termination of subtests and subsequent interpretation of results leave considerable room for interpretation. The items are clear and the materials are of durable quality.

Estimates of, and judgements about, the reliability and validity of the BCT are largely dependent on tenuous assumptions made by the authors that the Category Test and the Booklet Category Test are interchangeable instruments. Although data on the stability of the CT for both normal and brain-damaged patients is provided, the only evidence presented for the BCT is a stability estimate (8 weeks) of .84 on normal patients only. Evidence of validity relies exclusively on extensive research supporting use of the CT to identify patients with general neurological dysfunction. Although the research on the CT provides support for diagnosis of general brain dysfunction, data from only two studies are used to justify the equivalence of the tests. That evidence is limited to correlations between the CT and BCT in two studies ($r = .91$ for normal patients in one study and .80 for alcoholic patients in that same study; $r = .76$ in a study of patients with organic brain syndrome, schizophrenic without brain damage, and patients diagnosed with personality disorders). The authors indicate that future versions of the test manual will provide a review of the body of literature on the test, but they fail to provide such information contemporaneously because of difficulty arising from the fact that "authors … do not cite the use of this test specifically in their research" (p. 1). Given 20 years since the first publication of this form of the test, one would expect more extensive documentation of the ecological and construct validity of the instrument.

The norms are grouped by age, education, and gender in response to evidence cited by the authors that neuropsychological performance is greatly influenced by these variables. Although the authors note that the instrument has been standardized and normed on adolescents and adult 15 years and older, norms are provided only for individuals 20 years old or older. Extensive information is provided on the derivation of the normative tables; however, the BCT norms are "adapted from" data gathered on the Category Test rather than the BCT. The procedures for adaptation are not described. Although the authors refer to existing data regarding the comparability of CT and BCT scores, they fail to provide the evidence of equivalence of scores or citations that would lead one to those sources. Data provided in one study suggest a significant correlation, but the same data also depict notable differences between mean scores on the slide and booklet form. It is unclear whether these differences have been accounted for in the norms provided.

SUMMARY. Even though the reduced equipment costs and portability of this adaptation of the Category Test are positive features of the BCT, the supporting documentation does not warrant substitution of the BCT for the CT. Further evidence of reliability, greater attention to establishment of either concurrent or independent construct and ecological validity of the instrument, and specifically derived normative tables are needed before this instrument can be substituted in clinical assessments.

REVIEWER'S REFERENCE

Halstead, W. C., & Settlage, P. H. (1943). Grouping behavior of normal persons and of persons with lesions of the brain. *Archives of Neurology and Psychiatry, 49,* 489–503.

Review of The Booklet Category Test, Second Edition by DAVID C. S. RICHARD, Clinical Coordinator, Assistant Professor, Psychology, Southwest Missouri State University, Springfield, MO:

The second edition of The Booklet Category Test (BCT) is based on Halstead's Category Test (Halstead & Settlage, 1943) and is primarily designed to study cortical functioning, concept formation, and abstract reasoning in patients with brain damage. The BCT is one of several adaptations of the original Category Test (see Adams & Trenton, 1981; Hartlage & Levitt, 1983; Kimura,

1981; Wetzell & Boll, 1987; and Wood & Strider, 1980; all cited in the BCT Professional Manual). The test is designed for adults, ages 15 to 80.

DESCRIPTION. The BCT is easily administered in an easel format (as opposed to the rear projection system used in the original Category Test) and typically takes between 30 and 60 minutes to administer. However, administration with severely brain-damaged individuals may take quite a bit longer. Each of the seven BCT subtests requires the participant to infer an implicit rule and apply the rule to succeeding items. For every item there are four response options numbered 1 through 4. The participant is to say the number that makes sense given the item's content and the pattern that has emerged on previous items. For example, the first item in a subtest might be one triangle so the correct answer would be "1." The next item might be three triangles so the correct answer would be "3." The examiner provides feedback by telling the participant whether or not their choice was correct. As the test continues, both the stimuli and the implicit rules become more challenging.

The seven BCT subtests range in length from 8 to 40 items. Subtest raw scores are the sums of errors on the subtest and are scaled against norm group by gender, education, and age. The base normative sample was composed of 378 participants who completed the BCT, the Halstead-Reitan, and the Wechsler Adult Intelligence Scale (WAIS). The sample was disproportionately male in nature (64.6% male versus 35.4% female).

Overall, the manual is well written and empirically based. The authors provide a very useful review of studies relevant to the original Category Test and The Booklet Category Test. A classification system is provided in the manual that is of some interpretive use. The BCT has been shown to be a reliable test in both normal and impaired populations. The administration and scoring manual reports several studies conducted by the manual authors, DeFilippis and McCampbell, that appear to demonstrate satisfactory test-retest (administration interval = approximately 3 weeks) reliability in both normal participants ($r = .913$) and alcoholic patients ($r = .804$, p. 29 in the manual). Given that the BCT is largely a visual-spatial task, and the fact that visual-spatial tasks are often prone to practice effects, these stability coefficients are impressive. In general, other researchers have found similarly acceptable levels of reliability in both normals and psychiatric patients. Short forms of the BCT have also been developed with some success (see MacInnes, McFadden, & Golden [1983] for a report).

Based on factor studies of the BCT reported by Choca, Laastch, Wetzel, and Agresti (1993), and cited in the BCT Professional Manual, the BCT appears to be largely a measure of fluid intelligence, visual-spatial skills, and nonverbal reasoning. In their study, BCT raw scores were significantly negatively correlated with Digit Span and Block Design scores on the WAIS-R. However, the BCT's relationship with the Wisconsin Card Sort Test has been modest at best (see Donders & Kirsch, 1991). Other studies have found that poor scores on the BCT are associated with rigid thinking and impaired interpersonal relationships (Schafer, Birchler, & Fals-Stewart, 1994), poorer recovery from brain injury, and different forms of perseveration (Schutz & Gorman, 1995). Lazak (1995) describes the original Category Test as the most sensitive measure of brain damage in the Halstead Battery (p. 610).

However, not much is reported in the way of diagnostic efficiency and criterion-related validity. DeFilippis and McCampbell report (in the BCT Professional Manual) a false positive rate of impairment in approximately 14.4% of normal subjects using a demographically corrected T-score classification system. They later report a false negative rate of 7% (p. 30) for alcoholic patients. Thus, somewhere around 21% of normal patients may be inappropriately classified when using the BCT. Needless to say, a misclassification rate of this magnitude, although comparing favorably to the original Category Test, is not especially comforting.

Even though a considerable amount of research has been conducted on the BCT, additional research is needed in the following areas. First, more criterion-related validity studies are needed. Very little information is provided in the manual as to what scores on the BCT actually predict. For example, contemporary studies regarding the BCT's relationship with recovery rates from traumatic brain injury, stroke, disease, and so on would be especially useful. Shortcomings in this area probably stem from the evolution of the test's use. Originally conceived of as a diagnostic test, imaging techniques are now far more sensitive in identifying and localizing brain damage than the BCT

or any current neuropsychological test. Thus, using the BCT as a process measure of recovery was not its original purpose.

Second, and relatedly, the authors should consider creating recovery norms. For example, norms could be created using time since injury or diagnosis as the critical variable. This would encourage using the BCT as a process instrument, not just a diagnostic tool, and would help neuropsychologists monitor patient recovery.

Third, I was unable to find any studies that addressed the incremental validity of the BCT. Given that the test takes at least 30 to 60 minutes to administer, one might question how much additional information is provided above and beyond scores typically gained in a neuropsychological evaluation (e.g., the WAIS-III Full Scale IQ, Performance IQ, and Performance subtests). For example, the BCT tasks are not entirely dissimilar to those provided on the WAIS-III Matrix Reasoning subtest. An interesting study would be to have one or more neuropsychologists rate behavioral functioning in both impaired and normal subjects, administer the BCT and WAIS-III Performance subtests to all subjects, and then regress WAIS-III and BCT scores on ratings to determine whether the BCT is a significant contributor.

In order to shorten administration, the test developers should think about changing the way the raw scores are calculated. Using error scores means that every item must be administered. However, adapting the test so that raw scores are tallies of correct responses, and items are ordered in degree of item difficulty, would mean that some subtests could be shortened using standard discontinuation rules. Lazak (1995) notes that the test takes too long in many circumstances, especially with brain-injured patients. For high functioning patients, the test becomes tedious and boring.

A more complete discussion of those factors that contribute to BCT performance is also needed. For example, the manual authors report that the BCT is largely a test of visual-spatial skills, fluid intelligence, and nonverbal reasoning. Error scores on the BCT correlate negatively, and significantly, with the Block Design and Digit Symbol subtests of the Wechsler Scales (Choca, Laatsch, Wetzel, & Agresti, 1993) and Lansdell and Donnelly (1977) reported the Category Test correlated highest with Block Design and Picture Arrangement. Although the visual-spatial and nonverbal reasoning components are obvious, less studied has been the effect of processing speed and attention. After all, the test requires that individuals be able to attend to items and apply conceptual rules across items. Impaired short-term memory and/or attention would certainly compromise performance on the BCT. However, it is possible that an individual with poor short-term memory or attention may retain adequate conceptualization and abstraction abilities, as might be the case with highly educated individuals suffering from the early stages of dementia. An interesting study might be to examine individuals known to have attentional and/or learning problems (e.g., learning disabled, ADHD) but no known visual-spatial deficits to see the effect on BCT error scores.

SUMMARY. Overall, the Category Test has a long and distinguished history in neuropsychological assessment. The booklet version is certainly an administrative improvement on the original version. However, more comprehensive criterion-related and incremental validity work is needed.

REVIEWER'S REFERENCES

Halstead, W. C., & Settlage, P. H. (1943). Grouping behavior of normal persons and of persons with lesions of the brain. *Archives of Neurology and Psychiatry, 49,* 489–503.

Lansdell, H., & Donnelly, E. F. (1977). Factor analysis of the Wechsler Adult Intelligence Scale subtessts and the Halstead-Reitan Category and Tapping tests. *Journal of Consulting and Clinical Psychology, 45,* 412–416.

Wood, W. D., & Strider, M. A. (1980). Comparison of two methods of administering the Halstead Category Test. *Journal of Clinical Psychology, 36,* 476–477.

Adams, R. L., & Trenton, S. L. (1981). Development of a paper-and-pen form of the Halstead Category Test. *Journal of Consulting and Clinical Psychology, 49,* 298–299.

Kimura, S. D. (1981). A card form of the Reitan-modified Halstead Category Test. *Journal of Consulting and Clinical Psychology, 49,* 145–146.

Hartlage, L. C., & Levitt, R. A. (1983). *Self-administered Category Test.* Unpublished manuscript.

MacInnes, W. E., McFadden, J. M., & Golden, C. J. (1983). A short-portable version of the Halstead Category Test. *International Journal of Neuroscience, 18,* 41–44.

Wetzell, L., & Boll, T. (1987). Short Category Test: Booklet Format. Los Angeles: Western Psychological Services.

Donders, J., & Kirsch, N. (1991). Nature and implications of selective impairment on the Booklet Category Test and Wisconsin Card Sorting Test. *The Clinical Neuropsychologist, 5,* 78–82.

Choca, J. P., Laastch, L., Wetzel, L., & Agresti, A. (1993, August). *The Halstead Category Test: A fifty year perspective.* Paper presented at the annual meeting of the American Psychological Association, Toronto, Canada.

Schafer, J., Birchler, M., & Fals-Stewart, W. (1994). Cognitive, affective, and marital functioning of recovering male polysubstance abusers. *Neuropsychology, 8,* 100–109.

Lezak, M. D. (1995). *Neuropsychological assessment* (3rd ed.). New York: Oxford University Press.

Schutz, L. E., & Gorman, P. (1995, November). *Process subscales for the Halstead Category Test.* Poster session presented at the annual meeting of the National Academy of Neuropsychology, Orlando, FL.

[48]

Bracken Basic Concept Scale—Revised.

Purpose: Designed to measure relevant educational concepts and receptive language skills.

Population: Ages 2 1/2 to 8.

Publication Dates: 1984–1998.

Acronym: BBCS-R.

Scores, 11: Colors, Letters, Numbers/Counting, Sizes, Comparisons, Shapes, Direction/Position, Self-/Social Awareness, Texture/Material, Quantity, and Time/Sequence.

Administration: Individual.

Price Data, 1999: $200 per complete program including examiner's manual ('98, 223 pages), stimulus manual (276 pages), 25 diagnostic scale record forms, and one screening test; $50 per examiner's manual; $165 per diagnostic scale stimulus manual; $15 per 15 English record forms; $45 per 50 English record forms; $15 per 15 Spanish record forms; $45 per 50 Spanish record forms.

Time: (30) minutes.

Comments: May be used diagnostically or as a screening test by scoring the first six subtests called the School Readiness Composite (SRC); may be used for norm-referenced, criterion referenced, or curriculum-based assessments.

Author: Bruce A. Bracken.

Publisher: The Psychological Corporation.

Cross References: See T5:331 (6 references) and T4:319 (4 references); for reviews by Timothy L. Turco and James E. Ysseldyke of an earlier edition, see 10:33.

Review of the Bracken Basic Concept Scale—Revised by LEAH M. NELLIS, Assistant Professor of Educational Psychology, Northern Arizona University, Flagstaff, AZ:

The Bracken Basic Concept Scale—Revised (BBCS-R) is a recent revision of a widely used instrument in the assessment of young children. Like its predecessor, the BBCS-R is a developmentally sensitive measure of basic concept acquisition and receptive language skills. The manual notes that the primary goal of the revision process was to update the norms and stimulus materials of the BBCS. Specifically, a larger (8.5 by 11-inch) stimulus manual featuring colored artwork with tabbed dividers separating subtests, an expanded examiner's manual, and a carrying case are features that were added to make the instrument more "user-friendly." In addition, the record form was enlarged and expanded to allow for subtest analysis. Fifty additional concepts were added to the BBCS-R to enhance the range of ability assessed resulting in a total of 308 items across 11 subtests. Subtests were rearranged so that the Sizes subtest became a part of the School Readiness Composite (SRC) and the Social/Emotional subtest was renamed Self-/Social Awareness. The wording of item stems was revised to be consistent across subtests. An additional new feature is a Spanish adaptation.

Intended purposes of the BBCS-R include assessment of school readiness, receptive language development, screening for possible developmental delay, learning difficulties, giftedness, and program evaluation. The Spanish Edition is only to be used as a criterion-referenced or curriculum-based measure due to the sample size ($n = 193$) being too small for derivation of normative data.

The 50 additional items added to the BBCS-R were identified in order to increase the number of both easy and difficult items and more completely represent the domain of basic concepts. Tryout testing and bias review were conducted and described adequately in the manual. The BBCS-R was standardized with 1,100 children, aged 2.6–7.11 years. The manual lists demographic characteristics of the sample and provides evidence of good representation. Criteria for inclusion in the sample were age and the ability to complete the testing without modifications; thus, children were not excluded from the sample on the basis of receiving special education or gifted/talented services. Approximately 6% of the sample had been classified as either gifted/talented or special education eligible; therefore, the sample is not representative of children developing normally.

The BBCS-R Spanish Edition is based on item translation and expert review. Many items were adapted as compared to being directly translated and entail features such as vocabulary choices on some items to reflect variations among countries of origin and/or area in which one resides. Research using the Spanish Edition was conducted using a sample of 193 subjects and provided evidence of being reliable and valid as a criterion-referenced tool.

The administration procedures of the BBCS-R are similar to those of the original BBCS. No verbal responses are required and children can indicate their responses through pointing, vocalizing, eye gaze, or eye blink. New features include trial items, a consistent item stem, and a simplified procedure for establishing a basal. Special testing and scoring procedures are identified for children with color blindness. Raw scores on Subsets 1–6 form the SRC and are used to determine the starting point on remaining subtests. Basals are established by administering items from the start point forward until three consecutive passes have

been made. This differs from the BBCS, which required reverse administration from the start point to establish the basal. Normative data include scaled scores, standard scores, confidence intervals, percentiles, and concept age equivalents. The manual includes the data needed to conduct ipsative interpretations of a child's performance.

The manual includes much information regarding the technical characteristics of the scale and, for the most part, the instrument is technically sound. Internal consistency reliabilities were reported for each age group as well as the overall average. Internal consistency coefficients for subtests ranged from .85 to .98, from .78 to .97 for the SRC, and from .96 to .99 for the Total Test. Test-retest reliability data are reported for a sample of 114 children selected "almost equally" from the 3-, 5-, and 7-year age groups of the standardization sample. The children took the test on two occasions 7–14 days apart. Coefficients ranged from a low of .78 (Quantity and Time/Sequence) to a high of .88 (School Readiness Composite), with a median reliability coefficient of .81. Test-retest reliability for the total test was reported as .94.

Concurrent validity of the BBCS-R was evaluated by studying the relationship between the revised scale and the original BBCS. Based upon a limited sample of 54 total children drawn from two age groups (4 and 6 years), correlation coefficients ranged from a low of .55 (Texture/Material) to a high of .81 (SRC) for subtests and .89 for the Total Test score. The manual does not address the lower correlation for the Texture/material subtest. Although this may be due to item changes in the revision process, it is not clear from the information provided. The SRC and Total Test scores were reported to correlate strongly with the Wechsler Preschool and Primary Scale of Intelligence—Revised (WPPSI-R) Verbal, Performance, and Full Scale IQ (.85, .76, and .88, and .82, .72, and .85, respectively). The correlations between the SRC and Total Test scores and the Differential Ability Scales (DAS) Verbal Cluster, Nonverbal Cluster, and General Conceptual Ability (GCA) were also strong (.69, .72, and .79, and .74, .80, .88, respectively). The manual also reports evidence that the BBCS-R is a powerful predictor of academic growth. Two discriminant analyses ($n = 36$ and $n = 37$) were reported to provide evidence of construct validity involving language disorder and developmental delay groups. Although the BBCS-R appears useful in discriminating between such groups and groups of normally developing children, the number of children either not classified or misclassified also suggests the need for additional assessment.

The utility of an instrument designed to identify those with possible developmental delay or giftedness in part depends on the test's ability to assess those at the upper and lower extremes of the distribution. Information regarding the instrument's ceiling and floor is thoroughly outlined in the manual. Data indicate that the instrument has excellent to very good floor and ceiling at all age groups except 7-0 to 7-11, which has a limited ceiling. Thus, the BBCS-R would not be appropriate in the identification of advanced 7-year-olds.

SUMMARY. The BBCS-R is a well-developed, psychometrically sound instrument that will likely continue to serve a solid role in the assessment of young children. The revised stimulus manual, examiner's manual, and record form undoubtedly make the scale easier to use and more appealing to children. The psychometric soundness of the instrument supports its use as a cognitive screener and measure of basic concept development; however, test users are encouraged to include additional assessment measures and tools when classification is a goal. The BBCS-R also serves a valuable role in curriculum-based assessment given the importance of children's concept acquisition in future educational experiences.

Review of the Bracken Basic Concept Scale—Revised by RHONDA H. SOLOMON, Psychologist, Los Angeles Unified School District, Los Angeles, CA:

The Bracken Basic Concept Scale—Revised (BBCS-R) is a comprehensive measure of educational concepts and receptive language development of children of preschool, kindergarten, and first grade age. The test is sensitive to developmentally sequenced skill acquisition, with individualized test administration. It has many uses as a screening and an assessment tool. The advantages of using the BBCS-R are many, with few disadvantages.

The BBCS-R, as the manual emphasizes, was originally developed with the goal of creating the most comprehensive measure of basic concept development available. The information was then compiled, and later divided into 11 distinct conceptual domains. Six of the domains (Colors, Letters, Numbers/Counting, Sizes, Comparisons, Shapes) were grouped together to form the School Readiness Composite. The other five domains (Direction/Position, Self-/Social Awareness, Texture/Material, Quantity, and Time/Sequence) were meant to stand on their own. A composite for the Total Test and for the School Readiness Composite (SRC) can be obtained. The Screening and Assessment Tool is available with English or Spanish Edition record forms.

The norm-referenced interpretation allows the examiner to compare a child's conceptual knowledge with that of a similarly aged peer. The Total Test score is reported to be the most reliable and the most valid representation of a child's overall conceptual development. The BBCS-R offers extensive scoring information. An examiner can easily calculate a standard score, a confidence interval, a percentile rank, a normative classification, and a concept age equivalent for each of the composites, and a scaled score for each of the subtests. The scoring is based on a normal curve, with a mean of 100 and standard error of 15. Total Test scores 85–115 are considered within the average development, with scores above 115 representing accelerated development, and scores below 85 representing delayed development.

The BBCS-R can be used as a speech-language assessment instrument, a cognitive screening, a curriculum-based assessment, a school readiness screening, or a clinical and educational research tool. It does not require expressive language, so it can be used with a variety of language-delayed and cognitively impaired children. The test can be used from screening, through diagnosis, and placement decision making. It was standardized on more than 1,100 children, who receptively and expressively spoke English, and were able to take the test without accommodations or modifications. The children and their families were matched on gender, race, region, parental education, and handicapping conditions with the general population. Four percent of the standardization sample were classified as having a special need, which included: attention deficit disorder (ADD), attention deficit with hyperactivity disorder (ADHD), autism, developmental delay, learning disability, other health impairment, or speech/language delay or disorder. An additional 1.7% of the sample was composed of children receiving gifted and talented services. Students who were to require modification of the testing procedures were excluded. The Spanish Edition had a sample size of only 193. The test can be used by a variety of examiners. Many of these BBCS-R users include psychologists, speech-language pathologists, early childhood educators, licensed professional counselors, child development specialists, educational diagnosticians, teachers, graduate assistants, and doctoral students.

The BBCS-R manual, a most comprehensively detailed, useful, and organized guide, offers much in the way of explanation and self-critique. The revised manual continues to offer theoretical and conceptual bases; development and standardization of both the English and the Spanish Edition; administration and scoring of both the English and the Spanish Edition; interpretation and uses in remediation; and technical characteristics. The manual has numerous appendices, figures, and tables.

The BBCS-R some technical deficits. The first is that the administration takes approximately 30 minutes, but can take upwards of an hour. This is a considerably long time for a child who has not entered the structure of a school day, and who may also have developmental and/or language deficits. The manual states that most children of ages 2-6 to 7-11 years can remain on task for upwards of an hour. This is only the case if the child is within the normal range of skill expectancy. Another deficit is the lack of information in the minority standardization sample regarding parents' years of education. Thirdly, children with color blindness are not to be administered the Colors subtest. Instead, an expectancy table is included as a method of estimating their performance in this area. The problem with this is that the test does not have a built-in method of determining if a child is color blind.

SUMMARY. Overall, the BBCS-R presents as a bigger and better version of the BBCS with an improved manual and testing format. The manual and the test are larger, with full-color pictures. The children and adults in the pictures are balanced in terms of race/ethnicity. The Sizes subtest became part of the SRC, with more items added to each subtest, and some better placed in other subtest domains. The Social/Emotional subtest became the more appropriately named Self-/Social Awareness subtest. The achievement of a basal

score was somewhat simplified with illustrations. This test continues to be one of the most comprehensive means of determining a preschooler, kindergartner, or first-grader's level. The BBCS-R is a sound method of providing a link with assessment and the formation of remedial education interventions. The test is easy to administer and score, and provides a wealth of information.

[49]
Braille Assessment Inventory.

Purpose: Designed to assist educators "in determining whether Braille instruction is an appropriate intervention for students ... who are blind or visually impaired" in order to become more efficient learners as a result of using Braille as their primary reading mode.
Population: Ages 6–18.
Publication Date: 1996.
Acronym: BAI.
Scores, 5: Object Recognition, Visual Orientation, Tactual Orientation, Functional Considerations, Total.
Administration: Individual.
Price Data, 1999: $43.50 per complete kit including technical manual (28 pages) and 50 record forms; $12.50 per technical manual; $31 per 50 record forms.
Time: Untimed.
Authors: Michael N. Sharpe, Donna McNear, and Kevin S. McGrew.
Publisher: Hawthorne Educational Services, Inc.

Review of the Braille Assessment Inventory by JOHN MacDONALD, School Psychologist, North Kitsap School District, Kingston, WA:

The Braille Assessment Inventory (BAI) is a 42-item checklist to assist in deciding whether Braille instruction is appropriate for students ages 6 to 18 who are blind or visually impaired. Norms are conveniently presented on the front of the protocol. Instructions state that only those with observational experience of the student's skills and visual capacities should rate the student. Ratings should be completed in a single sitting. It would seem ideal that the BAI be completed by IEP team members.

INSTRUMENT DEVELOPMENT. Items were developed through a review of expert recommendations for indicators of the appropriateness of Braille instruction. The resulting scale was sent to 600 members of the Association for the Education and Rehabilitation of the Blind and Visually Impaired. Respondents rated each item as (1) *Not at all indicating the need for Braille instruction,* (2) *May or May not indicate a need,* or (3) *Extremely characteristic of the need for Braille instruction.* Respondents also suggested deletion, editing, and addition of indicators. Of the 600 surveys sent, 218 (36%) were returned.

NORMS. Based on field-testing, a revised 48-item rating form was sent to 300 professionals to complete the inventory for 309 individuals who were blind or visually impaired and 67 with no identified disabilities. The norms are based on the 309 individuals. Demographics for this group are presented with a comparison "U.S. Population" data—it appears to be individuals with visual disabilities. The BAI norm group is similar to the U.S. population on ethnicity, family SES, and rural-suburban-urban domicile, with more males (56% vs. 49%), more persons with Mental Retardation (22% vs. 13%), and more persons with physical, health, and hearing impairments (16%, 10%, and 5% vs. 1% for each). No information about the ages of persons in the normative group is provided. The authors state that the scale is based on *functional* norms rather than developmental norms, and that age norms are irrelevant. This reviewer wonders if the utility of teaching a student to read Braille or print will vary by the age of the student.

SUBSCALES. Interitem correlations were subjected to a principal components analysis with varimax rotation. This resulted in five factors accounting for 50% of the variance in total scores. Two of the factors were combined into one subscale (Functional Considerations) because each had too few items and the items had unacceptably low reliabilities. Functional Considerations (FC) is used to compute the total BAI rating, but does not exist as a separate interpretive subscale. Three factors, Object Recognition (OR), Visual Orientation (VO), and Tactual Orientation (TO), are interpretive and are used to compute the total BAI rating. OR consists of items related to the student's ability to visually recognize objects. VO refers to the student's preference for and ability to use vision in learning. TO refers to the student's preference for an ability to use tactile sense in learning. Items on each scale were sequenced according to item difficulty using Rasch modeling.

TOTAL SCALE. Items on the OR, VO, TO, and FC scales are summed to obtain the BAI total score. A panel of experts on blindness and visual impairment reviewed comprehensive information about "all" norming subjects, but this num-

ber was lower (264) than the total number of B/VI subjects in the norming study (309). The experts classified subjects into "Braille" (N = 77), "Print" (N = 167), and "Uncertain" groups (N = 20), independently of the BAI data. The 264 subjects were then classified by the BAI ratings into similar groups, with boundaries for each of the three groups being the 25th and 75th percentile for the expertly defined groups (e.g., total BAI scores of 71 to 79 for the "Braille" groups, 82 to 93 for the "Uncertain" group, and 94 to 103 for the "Print" group). These scores were set to allow for a higher number of false positives (8%) than false negatives (0%) for Braille instruction.

RELIABILITY. Coefficient alphas are reported for each of the three subscales: both OR and VO at .91, and TO at .92. Item-subscale total correlations are also reported, ranging from .45 to .88 for OR, .66 to .91 for VO, and .54 to .91 for TO with most correlations above .80.

VALIDITY. Intercorrelations among the BAI subscales are high: .90 for OR and VO, -.90 for VO and TO, and -.50 for TO and OR. This suggests that OR and VO are essentially measuring the same construct. Exploratory factor analysis also supports viewing the BAI as measuring a single construct. A classification analysis based on experts rating the norming subjects' characteristics independently of BAI ratings supported the diagnostic validity of the BAI—there were 8% false positives and 0% false negatives with regard to Braille instruction. But the diagnostic validity is based on using the same sample to evaluate diagnostic validity as was used in generating cut scores. This inflates validity estimates. Best practice is to test diagnostic validity on an independent sample. A second reason why the reported diagnostic validity may be overoptimistic is due to ignoring the "Uncertain" category. If "Uncertain" is included in false negative estimates, there were 8% false positives, but 10% false negatives.

SUMMARY. As a way of summarizing information available to the IEP team this assessment may be useful. To the extent BAI ratings are used by the team to make decisions, the predictive validity of BAI ratings is critical. The ideal study would be to randomly assign students predicted by BAI ratings to benefit from Braille instruction to print or Braille instruction, do the same for those predicted to benefit from print instruction, and compare reading skills (Print or Braille) at a later developmental stage. The ethical and technical problems of such a study are obvious. The BAI may have high discriminant validity, but it is impossible to tell from the technical manual. Methods used to document content validity are excellent. The ratings appear to be highly reliable, and items seem to be measuring a single construct.

Review of the Braille Assessment Inventory by ROBERT G. MORWOOD, *Professor of Education, and Assistant Director, Point Loma Nazarene University, Pasadena, CA:*

The Braille Assessment Inventory (BAI) was developed as an empirically based scale designed for use by special educators in making decisions associated with the use of the most expeditious mode of teaching reading to visually impaired or blind students. In the manual, the authors state the purpose of the scale is "to provide practitioners and others involved in the [literacy instruction] decision-making process with a means of assessing whether Braille should be used to help an individual attain literacy" (manual, p. 4). The instrument is similar to a checklist that itemizes important factors to consider when making decisions for appropriate delivery approaches for reading instruction. The BAI is a summary profile that measures an attribute. In this case, that attribute is the likelihood that the individual will become a more efficient learner as a result of using Braille as their primary reading mode. The checklist includes a list of indicators to determine the appropriateness of Braille instruction and its impact on the instructional process. The instrument also looks at the characteristics of someone who uses Braille as their primary reading mode. According to the authors, the BAI can provide "objective information about the prerequisite skills and abilities that are necessary to indicate whether Braille instruction has the potential to facilitate an individual's opportunity for learning" (manual, p. 5). It contains a list of important factors related to the decision-making process used as an aid in assessing whether visual reading or Braille should be used to help students attain literacy. The checklist is conceptualized as a Likert rating scale.

The BAI is a 42-item rating scale that yields a composite score composed of three primary subscale areas and a fourth subscale that is included in the final scoring: Object Recognition, Visual Orientation, Tactual Orientation, and Func-

tional Considerations. All four subscales are combined to yield a total BAI score. Each item is scored based on the following criteria: score 1 = *Not at all a Characteristic*, score 2 = *May or May Not Be a Characteristic*, score 3 = *Extremely Characteristic*. The rater then follows a simple three-step process to score the results for interpretation.

BAI information leads to a profile of a set of characteristics that are considered to be reflective of the students who possess the attribute of interest. The instrument is grouped into a series of logical subscale areas related to the instructional process.

The BAI is a checklist that can assist in providing objective information which, combined with the clinical skill of the practitioner, can contribute to the decision-making process. The scoring requires subjectivity on the part of the evaluator and, therefore, a thorough knowledge of blind and partially sighted students and their educational needs may be a significant asset in completing the instrument. The BAI should be used in combination with other standardized instruments and interpreted by appropriately trained clinicians.

The norms for the BAI are developed as functional norms that are based on the extent to which the total score accurately predicted the student's need for Braille instruction. The classifications for all norming subjects were one of three areas (i.e., needing either "Braille Instruction," "Print Instruction," or "Uncertain"). When the distribution of BAI total scores was compared to the classification of a panel of experts it was noted that the BAI total score accurately classified most of the norming subjects, producing an overall classification agreement of 76%.

The reliability estimates for the BAI were obtained through alpha coefficients and standardized item alphas for all subscale areas. Using these methods, the coefficients were above the .90 level.

With regard to classification accuracy, the constructors of the BAI indicate that the instrument is "likely to yield accurate results in most situations where a decision must be made regarding reading mode. This assertion, however, is only valid when the BAI Total Score is used in the classification process and the entire scale has been administered" (manual, p. 17). They further caution the interpreter in drawing premature conclusions and assert that raters must be aware that the BAI Total Score will be the most reliable and valid means from which to base reading mode decisions. A rating guide has been included in the manual to assist the rater in administering the instrument as well as insuring that the BAI ratings are recorded in a reliable manner.

SUMMARY. The BAI manual cautions "that no single instrument will ever be capable of providing teachers with a definitive means of making what are by nature complex and difficult decisions. While the BAI will certainly be helpful in delineating critical factors regarding reading mode, interpreting its results must be consistent with other types of supporting information and appropriate to the long-range academic, functional, and social needs of the student" (p. 21). The test constructor reminds the user that they should not allow a single "score" to drive the decision-making process. This is especially true in cases where conflicting evidence exists and additional efforts are needed to further investigate other hypotheses by using other types of assessments or clinical observation strategies.

The BAI record form seems to be straightforward and clear with good instructions. The use of the BAI should help practitioners in developing appropriate reading mode delivery systems for blind or visually impaired students.

[50]
Brief Neuropsychological Cognitive Examination.

Purpose: Constructed as "an assessment of the severity and nature of cognitive impairment" for psychiatric and neurological patients.
Population: Ages 18 and older.
Publication Date: 1997.
Acronym: BNCE.
Scores, 4: Validity Index, Part I, Part II, Total.
Administration: Individual.
Price Data, 1999: $110 per complete kit including manual (58 pages), stimulus booklet, 20 response booklets, and 20 administration and scoring forms; $32.50 per 20 response booklets; $19.50 per 20 administration and scoring forms; $27 per stimulus booklet; $46 per manual.
Time: (30) minutes.
Author: Joseph Tonkonogy.
Publisher: Western Psychological Services.

Review of the Brief Neuropsychological Cognitive Examination by EUGENE V. AIDMAN, Lecturer in Psychology, School of Behavioural & Social Sciences & Humanities, University of Ballarat, Victoria, Australia:

The Brief Neuropsychological Cognitive Examination (BNCE) is designed for time-efficient assessment of major cognitive functions typically targeted by other neuropsychological instruments. It is intended for preliminary clinical evaluation of patients with both primarily psychiatric disorders and brain injury, as well as other forms of neurological impairment. The BNCE is purported to be sensitive to manifestations of disorders of visual gnosis, language, praxis, memory, and executive functions.

The key characteristic of the BNCE setting it apart from other neuropsychological screening instruments is that it is intended to be sensitive to mild cognitive impairment. Part I includes simple "Orientation," "Presidential Memory" (the choice of U.S. Presidents' names for this conventional memory screener is culturally limiting), "Naming," "Comprehension," and "Constructive Practice" subtests. Part II extends to more complex tasks in its "Shifting," "Incomplete Pictures," "Similarities," "Attention," and "Working Memory" subtests, which are intended to be particularly sensitive to mild cognitive impairment. The BNCE is thus promising to complement other neuropsychological screeners such as screening Tests for the Luria-Nebraska neuropsychological Battery (T5:2334), rather than competing with them.

Although BNCE items are largely derived from A. R. Luria's neuropsychological assessment procedures, originally developed for patients with localized brain lesions, the only two BNCE item trials used to determine the final composition of the test were conducted with psychiatric samples ($N = 48$ and $N = 51$). The inclusion of visual tracking tasks in the Attention subtest, even though conceptually reasonable, raises a number of empirical questions. Given that the original Schulte method is heavily modified and the respective reference is secondary and quite dated, the performance of the new tasks requires more justification. This is particularly important for the bidirectional tracking task in BNCE Item 46, which is based on Gorbov's (1964) major modification of the Schulte method (c/f. Aidman, 1989, 1996) but significantly deviates from it. The possible impact of these deviations is not addressed in the manual.

RELIABILITY. Sadly, no internal consistency data are available for any of the BNCE subtests. Nor is it clear whether or not subtests A through J were treated as items in computing internal consistency estimates for the BNCE Total, Part I and Part II scores. These omissions are regrettable (the author will have had all the necessary data to avoid them) and in stark contrast with a complete and quite adequate report on retest reliabilities.

VALIDITY. The entire validation data appear to have been derived from a single, previously unpublished study involving what the author calls "the clinical reference sample" (N = 212). This, coupled with conceptual errors in presenting validation data, limits the extent to which the results can be generalized. The most notable of such errors is the definition of discriminant validity and the resulting misconstruction of the last technical section of the manual. Labeled "Discriminant Validity," the section in fact reports an interesting criterion validation study. The study employed MRI and CT scan data, patients' levels of independence, and a number of established clinical diagnoses within the above-mentioned clinical reference sample as concurrent validation criteria. Sadly, the study's methodology is not reported in detail sufficient to fully evaluate it. It is clear, however, that the brain imaging data were both underutilized and underreported: The precision of separate 5-point expert ratings of cortical atrophy, ventricular enlargement, and white matter changes was never used. Further, the reporting of these results is incomplete and potentially misleading.

More importantly, the key differential diagnosis question—if and how the BNCE discriminates between different groups of neurological and psychiatric patients with similar degrees of cognitive impairment—requires much more attention than the manual affords. The reported vast differences in BNCE scores between "Mood Disorders," "Schizophrenia," and "Neurological Only" groups are hopelessly confounded by the fact that the latter group's cognitive impairment is simply much more severe! Discriminant function data in the three classification accuracy analyses are much more promising but reported with conceptual inaccuracies. Random selection of subsamples from the actual sample for discriminant function analysis is hardly acceptable and severely limiting the generalizability of the results. The potentially fundamental implications of these data for the BNCE's interpretation as a differential diagnostic tool are never addressed.

Construct validity is evidenced by correlations between scores on the BNCE subtest and total scores with Wechsler Adult Intelligence Scale—Revised (WAIS-R), Wechsler Memory Scale, Trail Making Test, Verbal Fluency, the Boston Naming Test, and the Mini Mental Status Examination (MMSE), ranging from .25 through .71 for composite scores, and -.04 through .64 for subtests, on samples ranging from N = 31 through N = 85. The BNCE has also shown better accuracy than the MMSE in identifying mild cognitive impairment in patients diagnosed with schizophrenia (N = 29) and patients with psychiatric symptoms secondary to a known neurological disorder (N = 26).

SUMMARY. Overall, the BNCE is a promising instrument, particularly with its novel method of detecting mild cognitive impairment, through the distinction between Part I (conventional information processing) and Part II (new and incomplete information processing) scores. However, whether or not the BNCE lives up to its promise remains to be seen. This will largely depend on the extent and quality of psychometric validation data that are yet to be produced for this test. The manual admits that the BNCE's validation is at its preliminary stage. As it stands now, the BNCE reliability data are incomplete (lacking subtests' internal consistency data), validity data are limited (the analysis is less than adequate and partially misconstrued, predictive validity not addressed at all), standardization and normative data are never discussed, and the cutoff scores for the test's key measure—levels of cognitive impairment (mild/ severe)—remain empirically unsubstantiated. However, in the light of the common psychometric difficulties with neuropsychological screening instruments, and the particular historical idiosyncracy of A. R. Luria's clinical method to any form of quantification or standardization, the BNCE in its current form could be cautiously welcomed as a first iteration towards a psychometrically complete instrument, provided that more rigorous validation research is forthcoming.

REVIEWER'S REFERENCES

Gorbov, F. D. (1964). On the operator's distraction tolerance. In *Engineering psychology* [in Russian]. Moscow: Academy of Science.

Aidman, E. V. (1989). The Schulte-Gorbov test of contrast colour tables: A pencil-and-paper modification. In *Psychodiagnostic practicum: Directory and manuals for general tests* (pp. 52–55) [in Russian]. Moscow State University Press.

Aidman, E. V. (1996). Using attention tables for mental exercising. In E. Aidman, J. Armstrong, L. Singer, & G. Singer (Eds.), *Jogging the brain: Mental exercise program for daily use* (pp. 26–30). Bandoora, Melbourne: LaTrobe University Press.

Review of the Brief Neuropsychological Cognitive Examination by SHEILA MEHTA, Associate Professor of Psychology, Auburn University at Montgomery, Montgomery, AL:

PURPOSE AND NATURE OF TEST. The Brief Neuropsychological Cognitive Examination (BNCE) is an individually administered test that provides a short, standardized assessment of the major cognitive functions of neuropsychiatric patients. There are three purposes for using the BNCE: diagnostic neuropsychological evaluation, follow-up assessment, and screening to identify those areas of cognitive functioning that require a more detailed neuropsychological evaluation. The BNCE assesses the major cognitive functions usually targeted by neuropsychological testing, including disorders of memory, gnosis, praxis, language, orientation, attention, and executive functions. The BNCE can be used to help determine whether the source of cognitive impairment is a primary psychiatric disorder or a neurological disease that has psychiatric manifestations. It can also be used to monitor the course of impairment in both types of disorders or the course of improvement during treatment. It can also be useful when evaluating the functional status of patients in terms of their ability to live independently. Validation of the BNCE against MRI and Head CT results enhances its value in identifying not only the presence and degree of various types of cognitive impairment, but also its relation to the etiology and underlying brain pathology. Patterns of cognitive profiles and subtest scores can help differentiate among specific disorders and stages of progression.

Advantages of the BNCE are: It is short; it is easy to use; it is sensitive to mild cognitive impairments that are usually missed by other brief cognitive screening tests; it provides a more thorough assessment of cognitive abnormalities than do most screening devices; and its items are simple enough to use with nonliterate people, although the examinee must be able to read numbers from 1 to 12. A major advantage of the BNCE is that a quantified comparison can be made of revealed abnormalities. The test should not be administered to individuals who have severe visual impairment, visual agnosia, bilateral hand weakness or paralysis, who are in acute psychotic states, who cannot concentrate on the test's instructions, or who have prominent language disorders that cause

an inability to understand the oral instructions and visual material of the test.

The test is divided into two parts. Each part consists of five subtests. Part I subtests are "related to the more conventional types of information processing" (manual, p. 3). These subtests are: Orientation, Presidential Memory, Naming, Comprehension, and Constructive Praxis. Part II subtests involve "processing of novel, incomplete, and less conventional types of information—the kind of processing required for the successful performance of executive functions" (manual, p. 3). These subtests are Shifting Set, Incomplete Pictures, Similarities, Attention, and Working Memory. The test provides a validity score, a total score, separate scores for Part I and Part II, and individual scores for the 10 subtests.

PRACTICAL EVALUATION. Testing materials include a manual, a stimulus booklet, an administration and scoring form, and a response booklet. The manual is excellent in that it provides thorough information on administering and scoring the test, interpreting the scores (including eight interesting case examples), development of the BNCE, and its psychometric properties. The materials are attractive, durable, and easy to use. The directions are clear and the test is simple to administer and score. With a bit of practice, the test can be scored as it is administered. But despite its ease, its developer warns that the BNCE "should only be administered by a trained professional who has the skill to assess an individual's ability to exercise the effort needed to complete the test and to understand both the oral instructions presented by the examiner and the visual material presented in the subtests" (manual, p. 4). The content of the test items is unlikely to offend anyone, especially with the required instructions that warn the test taker that some of the requests may seem "a little odd or silly," thereby avoiding problems with rapport.

Technical Evaluation.

NORMS. People without cognitive impairment usually obtain perfect or near-perfect scores on the BNCE, so the standardization sample is a clinical reference sample. It is composed of 212 individuals, wherein women and Blacks appear to be underrepresented. The size of this sample is small and the subgroup norms, naturally, are even smaller. Moreover, there is no indication that it is a representative clinical sample. The sample included individuals with mood disorder, schizophrenia, substance abuse problems, neurological conditions, mental retardation, atypical psychosis, and AIDS-related dementia. The manual contains a table with mean and standard deviation BNCE scores. No percentiles are available. The manual contains a table of average scores for men and women. The effect size for the difference between men and women was tested and found not to indicate a meaningful difference. Ethnic comparisons were not possible with this small sample size. Meaningful age differences were found and a table in the manual shows average BNCE scores for various age groups.

RELIABILITY. Reliability of the BNCE appears to be good, but again, based on studies with small numbers of participants. Three types of reliability estimates are reported in the manual: test-retest, interrater, and internal consistency. Consistency over a 24-hour period was found to be .95, and over 1–2 weeks was .88 for the Total Score, with the subtest reliabilities ranging from .64 to .97, with a median of .83. Consistency between two examiners was assessed for 20 administrations and the interrater reliability for the Total score was .97. Internal consistency of the BNCE scales was estimated by Cronbach's alpha for both the clinical reference sample and the patients in the test-retest reliability study. Internal consistency estimates for the Total score were .88 and .90; for the Part I score .81 and .86; and for Part II scores .79 and .79.

VALIDITY. Based on the studies reported in the manual, again with small numbers of participants, the BNCE appears to produce scores that are valid for their intended purpose. Evidence for construct validity of the BNCE comes from data showing correlations among the BNCE scores. The correlations among the subtests range from .22 to .65 (median = .43). The correlations are low enough to suggest that each subtest assesses a relatively independent aspect of cognitive functioning but high enough to suggest that they tap related aspects of a broad construct. Further evidence of construct validity comes from data showing correlations between the BNCE and nine other measure of cognitive functioning, such as the Wechlser Memory Scale and the Mini Mental Status Examination. These correlations range from .31 to .71. These correlations are not high but none of the other instruments measure all of the same aspects of cognitive functioning identified for the BNCE.

The important aspect regarding the validity of scores from the BNCE is how well scores reflect degree of impairment and whether they can discriminate among individuals with no known cognitive impairment, those with cognitive impairment related to a psychiatric disorder, and those with impairment related to a known neurological condition. In one study designed to assess the first question, MRI and CT findings were conducted on patients with psychiatric symptoms secondary to a known neurological disorder and patients with schizophrenia and no other known neurological condition. The BNCE scores were directly related to lesion severity for the neurological patients. Unfortunately, the number of participants was small, 23. In studies designed to answer whether the instrument can discriminate between psychiatric and neurological patients, the BNCE performed impressively. The instrument correctly differentiated between neurological and psychiatric patients with *mild* cognitive impairment in 100% of the cases, and between patients with *moderate* to *severe* impairment in 82% of the cases. The BNCE also correctly differentiated between schizophrenic patients and patients with atypical psychosis related to an identifiable neurological lesion in 94% of the cases, demonstrating that the BNCE is useful in discriminating between neurological conditions that mimic psychiatric ones and the actual psychiatric conditions they mimic. Further evidence of concurrent validity comes from a study of correlations between BNCE scores and functional status of neurological and schizophrenic patients, which were .68 and .61, respectively. Another study showed that BNCE scores are related to independent living status. Again, the number of participants in all these studies was small.

CONCLUSION. Because the studies conducted using the BNCE have small numbers of participants, one must reserve judgement about the certainty of the usefulness of this new instrument. However, the available evidence is promising and suggests that the instrument is effective for evaluating the presence and severity of cognitive impairment, the type of functioning that may be impaired, the likely functional status of the patient, and whether the impairment is likely to be related to an identifiable neurological condition

Of course, the BNCE will not substitute for full neurological testing, but what it can do is impressive for a brief test, fills a gap in the existing available instruments, and is the best of its kind.

[51]
BRIGANCE® Diagnostic Comprehensive Inventory of Basic Skills, Revised.

Purpose: Designed for diagnostic and classroom assessment in basic reading skills, reading comprehension, math calculation, math reasoning, written language, listening comprehension, and information-processing.
Population: Ages 5–13.
Publication Dates: 1976–1999.
Acronym: CIBS-R.
Scores: 154 scores in 8 areas: Readiness, Speech, Listening, Research and Study Skills, Reading, Spelling, Writing, Math.
Administration: Individual and group.
Forms, 2: Form A (pretesting), Form B (posttesting).
Price Data, 1998: $179 per Inventory tests with standardization and validation manual ('99, 143 pages) (U.S. or Canadian versions); $149 per inventory only tests (U.S. or Canadian versions); $35 per 10 student record books; $329 per 100 student record books; $14 per class record book; $22 per 10 student profile test booklets; $40 per manual; $70 per 120 readiness or Grades 1–6 scoring sheets; $20 per 30 readiness of Grades 1–6 scoring sheets; conversion software available on CD-ROM.
Time: Specific time limits are listed for some normed/standardized tests.
Comments: "Criterion-referenced"; normed/standardized option for key tests; computer data program available.
Authors: Albert H. Brigance and Frances Page Glascoe (standardization and validation manual).
Publisher: Curriculum Associates, Inc.
Cross References: See T5:340 (1 reference); for reviews by Craig N. Mills and Mark E. Swerdlik of an earlier edition, see 9:162.

Review of the BRIGANCE Diagnostic Comprehensive Inventory of Basic Skills, Revised by GREGORY J. CIZEK, Associate Professor of Educational Measurement and Evaluation, University of North Carolina, Chapel Hill, NC:

The BRIGANCE Diagnostic Comprehensive Inventory of Basic Skills—Revised (CIBS-R) is a revision of a previous version (the CIBS) published in 1983. The primary purpose of the CIBS-R has remained the same, however: to provide detailed objectives-referenced information on fundamental school-based skills for children be-

tween the ages of 5 and 13. This age range makes the CIBS-R useful for gathering information as part of a screening process for students entering kindergarten and as an assessment of skill acquisition in elementary and middle grades. The total program consists of 154 assessments in eight areas, covering Readiness, Speech, Listening, Reading, Spelling, Writing, Research and Study Skills, and Mathematics. The CIBS-R targets contexts in which information about individual student's strengths and weaknesses in these eight areas is desired, and contexts such as planning individualized educational programs (IEP) or referring younger students for gifted/talented educational programs.

A secondary purpose distinguishes the CIBS-R from its predecessor. Namely, the new edition also permits users to make norm-referenced interpretations of student performance. Much of the developmental work for the latest version was conducted to gather the information necessary to support norm-referenced interpretations. Additionally, for some areas, alternate forms have been created to permit pre- and posttesting of skill development.

MATERIALS. The materials supplied with the CIBS-R include a 40-page record book for each student, to be used in monitoring individual student progress across the skill areas. A teacher's record book provides a place to assemble information for all students in a class. A "Standardization and Validation Manual" (Glascoe, 1999) provides technical information. The heart of the program is a 3-inch thick binder that contains all of the assessments. The binder is designed to be placed on a table between an examiner and a student. The pages in the binder contain prompts for the student on one side, and information for the test administrator on the other. The manual recommends that a small pile of books or similar prop may be necessary to raise the spine of the binder so that older students cannot see the information intended to be viewed by the administrator.

ADMINISTRATION, SCORING, AND REPORTING. The CIBS-R assessments are administered individually in any order. General administration directions state that specialized training is not required, and that paraprofessionals could, with appropriate supervision, conduct the assessment. An informal approach to administration is recommended for most instances in which objectives-referenced information is sought. However, users are cautioned to strictly follow administration instructions when norm-referenced scores will be derived.

Actual administration of the test consists of determining lower- and upper-bound functional levels, called *basals* and *ceilings*. In most circumstances, it is recommended that testing begin by administering assessments two grade levels below a student's current grade level in order to establish the basal level—a point at which the student answers all or nearly all items correctly. Testing then continues until the ceiling is reached—a point at which the student answers a series of items incorrectly. A student's responses are entered on the record sheet by placing circles, underlining, triangles, and slash marks to indicate correctness of the student's response and probable mastery level. Overall, the process of determining basal and ceiling levels and recording student responses seems cumbersome and unnecessarily susceptible to error. In addition to the need to recall and transfer correct scoring marks into the record book, the examiner must also keep in mind the basal and ceiling demarcations, which vary from assessment to assessment. For example, for some assessments there is no basal level, for others the level ranges from 3 to 10 consecutive correct responses. Similarly, ceilings range from 2 to 10 in a row incorrect responses, or a requirement to administer all items. No information is provided to validate the use of the basal and ceiling cutoffs.

Administration time varies by level of the student and by the number of assessments administered to a student. It is estimated that the Readiness assessment takes approximately 75 minutes per student; the assessments for Grades 1–6 require 45–60 minutes per student. Considering that this is an individual assessment, the necessity for recruiting qualified paraprofessional or other assistance is obvious.

A listing of skills mastered is the primary objectives-referenced information obtained from the CIBS-R. Norm-referenced scores consist of percentiles, age and grade equivalent scores, instructional ranges, and quotients (scales with a mean of 100 and standard deviation of 15). A software program is available on CD for converting raw scores to the various derived scores.

The technical manual for the CIBS-R recommends that information about a student's per-

formance provided to teachers and parents should consist of "written or oral reports that are practical and useful" and should include "recommendations for specific interventions, instructional materials, and so forth" (Glascoe, 1999, p. 22). Two examples of this reporting are included in the manual. One example shows a norm-referenced report with instructional ranges, percentile ranks, and quotients for several areas. The other is a model of a narrative description of a student's performance, developed by the test administrator, that summarizes the skill levels and adds commentary on behavioral observations. The model narrative is nearly four pages in length, and is thorough in its explanation of results and recommendations for remediation strategies and materials. On the one hand, it is encouraging to see this type of narrative synthesis included as truly useful information that parents and teacher receive following administration of a standardized test. On the other hand, there are at least two causes for serious concern related to this information. First, the behavioral and other information summarized in the report could only come from the person who actually administered the CIBS-R. Thus, this type of reporting would be precluded in situations where a teaching assistant conducted the administration, as such a person would ordinarily lack the training necessary to develop the narrative. Second, and more importantly, the conclusions in the model report seem to go way beyond the data collected by the assessment. For example, the model includes conclusions about the student's self-esteem, effort, "strategies necessary for school success," work rate, and so on. Because this narrative information might likely be more salient to parents and teachers than the quantitative scores, it is essential that it be based on more careful measures of those behaviors.

NORMS. The norm sample for the CIBS-R consisted of 1,121 students recruited from six U.S. cities in four geographical regions. Within each city, one or two schools were identified that had roughly one-third of their students in each of three (high, medium, and low) SES strata, with the lowest stratum defined as participation in federal free or reduced lunch programs. Within schools, two classrooms per grade were selected and students of parents who consented to participate were included. The manual does not described how these cities or classrooms were identified, although the characteristics of the norming sample appear to be roughly comparable with national demographics in terms of gender, race/ethnicity, region, community type, and SES. Administration conditions for the norm group appear to mirror the conditions under which the CIBS-R would be administered in practice.

VALIDITY. A reviewer of the 1983 edition of the CIBS observed that "no validity data are reported" (Mills, 1985, p. 213). That omission has been addressed in the CIBS-R, though the validity evidence provided is still inadequate. For example, in an objectives-referenced instrument, content validity evidence would seem to be of utmost importance. For some CIBS-R tests (called validated assessments), the test binder provides references to textbook series and grade levels in which the skill is normally encountered; references to scholarly references are also occasionally provided. For other tests, content validity information is not included. Overall, the level of content validity evidence provided falls short of "abundant" as claimed in the technical manual.

In terms of relationships with other criterion measures, the CIBS-R shows expected correlations with norm-referenced tests such as the Iowa Tests of Basic Skills, the Stanford Achievement Test, and the California Achievement Test. A separate table shows that the CIBS-R Readiness assessment is a reasonable strong predictor of future performance on the second grade form of the Stanford, although this evidence is based on an undescribed sample of 109 kindergarten students.

Some construct validity evidence is also provided, although it does not always confirm the intended use of the test. A table of CIBS-R intercorrelations is provided; these all are fairly high and positive. However, scores on the listening vocabulary comprehension grade placement test correlated equally well with scores on reading, math, and written expression composites; spelling grade-placement test scores correlate more strongly with the math composite than with reading comprehension. Other correlations reveal that scores on the CIBS-R are related to age and grade level, with higher scores associated with advanced age and grade; scores on the CIBS also correlate moderately to fairly strongly with Wechsler Intelligence Scale for Children—Third Edition (WISC-III) full scale IQ scores. Based on the preponderance of the construct validity evidence provided, a reasonable case could be made that the CIBS-R functions nearly as effectively as a measure of general cognitive ability as it does as a measure of discrete skill mastery.

Finally, a few key concepts related to validity are not presented well in the supporting documentation for the CIBS-R. For example, features described in the test binder note that many of the assessments have been "validated" and that term is used repeatedly where "standardized" or "normed" would be correct. In another place, the technical manual defines *discriminant validity* in an unusual way as "the ability of a test to identify strengths or weaknesses in development, academics, and so forth" (p. 33).

RELIABILITY. Information on reliability for the CIBS-R begins with a helpful text box that highlights definitions of key terms used to describe reliability. These definitions are clear and should help most users to interpret the indices presented.

Several types of reliability information are reported. Test-retest correlations were calculated on scores gathered 2 weeks apart from a sample of 41 students across Grades K–6. The results were not reported separately by grade level, but based on the total group. With few exceptions, these correlations all exceeded .80. Test-retest correlations are reported separately by level for a timed reading comprehension test, with a median value of .97 (although the manual fails to mention the spurious effect of speededness on these reliability estimates). Test-retest correlations are also reported separately for the Readiness assessment; these values are all in the .90s for composite areas of major interest such as mathematics, writing, and reading.

Following relevant professional guidelines, internal consistency estimates and corresponding standard errors of measurement (*SEMs*) are also provided. These are given separately for ages 6 through 12. The values reported seem reasonable for a test of this type. However, users may not be familiar with the unusual statistic selected for reporting internal consistency (Guttman's lambda). Users should also be cautioned about the inaccurate definition of standard errors which, it is claimed, can be "added to and subtracted from each student's raw score in order to provide a theoretical, error-free indicator of true performance" (manual, p. 35). Additionally, the suggested interpretations of the lower *SEM* as the student's independent skill level and the upper *SEM* as a failure level are unsupported.

SUMMARY. The CIBS-R can be used as it is primarily intended: as an objectives-referenced tool for documenting elementary and middle school students' mastery of specific skills. The CIBS-R is an improvement over its previous edition. The revision demonstrates greater attention to validity, and users can now derive norm-referenced scores.

If test development and validation is an ongoing process, the CIBS-R still has some way to go, however, on both the norm- and objectives-referenced paths. To foster more valid objectives-referenced interpretations, additional information must be provided on the rationale for including the skills that are assessed by the CIBS-R; some evidence should be provided to support the mastery/nonmastery cutoffs; and items should be developed that more clearly differentiate between the constructs assessed. For more defensible norm-referenced interpretations, additional information on the norm group and separate information for age and grade levels would be desirable. The materials should be revised to make them easier to work with and more technically accurate, and some attention might be directed toward understanding how the assessment functions for students who are not native speakers of English.

Until further developmental work remedies some of these concerns, the CIBS-R is probably best used as an adjunct information-gathering tool. It is possible that the CIBS-R attempts to do too much by attempting to satisfy the needs of those interested in both objectives- and norm-referenced assessment. Currently, numerous high-quality norm-referenced measures exist that have much more to commend them. For example, users interested in a group-administered norm-referenced test would do well to choose an achievement battery such as the Iowa Tests of Basic Skills (T5: 1318). Users interested in an individually administered instrument can select from tests such as the Woodcock-Johnson Psycho-Educational Battery—Revised (T5: 2901). As these and other achievement batteries evolve to provide more objectives-based information, future refinements of the CIBS-R might productively enhance the objectives-based and diagnostic features that are the foundation of that test.

REVIEWER'S REFERENCES

Mills, C. R. (1985) [Review of the Comprehensive Inventory of Basic Skills.] In J. V. Mitchell, Jr. (Ed.), *The ninth mental measurements yearbook* (pp. 212–215). Lincoln, NE: Buros Institute of Mental Measurements.

Glascoe, F. P. (1999). *Standardization and validation manual for the Brigance Comprehensive Inventory of Basic Skills—Revised*. North Billerica, MA: Curriculum Associates.

Review of the BRIGANCE Diagnostic Comprehensive Inventory of Basic Skills—Revised by MARY J. McLELLAN, Associate Professor, Northern Arizona University, Flagstaff, AZ:

Any one who has worked in schools with the special education population has probably had experience with the BRIGANCE Comprehensive Inventory of Basic Skills (CIBS). Originally published in 1976, this curriculum-based academic achievement tool was revised in 1983. The other Brigance scales are the Inventory of Early Development (T5:2213), Inventory of Basic Skills (T5:342), Inventory of Essential Skills (T5:343), Life Skills Inventory (53), and Employability Skills Inventory (52). The Brigance Screens are a series of instruments that have also been widely used by professionals working with the preschool population. Arthur Brigance began a national study in 1997 to revise and update the skill sequences of the CIBS. The newly revised instrument was published in 1999. Frances Page Glascoe authored the Standardization and Validation Manual, which now accompanies the CIBS-R. Curriculum Associates, Inc. has maintained the publication of all the Brigance products.

Craig Mills and Mark Swerdlik reviewed the CIBS in the *Ninth Mental Measurements Yearbook* (9:162). Their reviews were quite comprehensive and generally positive, with cautions regarding the utility of the results. They cautioned test consumers that the test was to be used to assess skill acquisition and not to make normative comparisons. This review will focus on the changes instituted to provide the BRIGANCE Comprehensive Inventory of Basic Skills—Revised (CIBS-R).

The CIBS-R has important changes that need to be noted. The most profound addition from the previous edition is the derivation of standard scores in the areas of basic reading skills, reading comprehension, math calculation, math reasoning, written language, and listening comprehension. Frances Page Glascoe from Vanderbilt University completed the standardization and validation process. The information related to the process is included in the Standardization and Validation Manual. Dr. Glascoe carefully describes the procedures for completing the standardization sample and the methods used to obtain the standardized scores. Although the final statistics match the demographic characteristics of the 1997 U.S. Census, the method of obtaining participants was somewhat unique when compared to traditional standardization procedures. Six school sites were used and in each site one or two schools were selected. The teachers of two classrooms per grade level solicited participation from students. The teachers at the selected schools assessed their own students with 26% of the sample being collected in the fall, 29% in the winter, and 45% in the spring. Teachers are typically the people who administer the CIBS-R and this was the justification for teachers administering the test to their own students. The test-retest reliability and interrater reliability were gathered based on a sample of 41 students who were administered the test by their teacher and then by an educational diagnostician 2 weeks later. The correlation scores range between .70 to .98 and were deemed satisfactory by the author to support adequate reliability. Alternate forms reliability was calculated based on selected subtests and also was judged to be adequate. The correlations reported were within the satisfactory range. The *SEM*s were calculated and are utilized to define the instructional range for students for the standardized version. When administered as a criterion-referenced measure, the instructional range is defined by the basal and ceiling items. Dr. Glascoe reported that validity evidence for scores from the instrument was satisfactory based on concurrent validation with widely used tests of achievement and intelligence.

For the standardized version of the test, the scores are based on a mean of 100 and a standard deviation of 15. This information transfers easily into the most widely used instruments and aids in the calculation of discrepancy formulas when appropriate. Percentile, grade equivalent, and instructional ranges are also provided in the norm tables. To obtain an age equivalent the test giver must go to another table for a conversion. The calculation of the instructional range is found in chapter 2 of the manual and is based on the raw score plus and minus the *SEM*. Then the conversion of these scores is made from the grade equivalent table.

Three supplemental composite scores can be calculated as part of the standardized scoring section. These three composite scores are purported to relate to information processing in the areas of math, writing, and reading. All three composite scores are based on production rates and appear to have been named for user appeal rather than actual

utility. Test users are strongly encouraged to use caution when judging the validity of these three composites.

SUMMARY. The CIBS-R is a good revision of a standard curriculum-based instrument that is widely used by teachers for assessment of their students. This test certainly provides one of the most extensive selections of items of achievement batteries available. Teachers and practitioners are availed with a huge range of items with which to track their student's progress. The addition of derived standard scores in the key areas of achievement marks a major addition to the measure. The first attempt at adding normative properties to this curriculum-based measure has limitations, but is worth consideration. The standardized scoring can be completed with the reproducible scoring sheets located at the back of the Standardization and Validation Manual. The administration directions for the standardized version of the test and the curriculum-based version are different and the authors chose to include the standardized directions in boxes on the necessary pages. The reviewer questions why the directions could not be the same for both versions. Continued use of the criterion-referenced application of this measure is strongly recommended, but the standardized version should be used with caution when determining eligibility of students for special education services.

[52]

BRIGANCE® Diagnostic Employability Skills Inventory.

Purpose: Designed to assess employability and basic skills in the "context of job-seeking or employment situations."

Population: Prospective job-applicants.

Publication Date: 1995.

Scores: 8 skills: Reading Grade-Placement Assessments; Career Awareness and Self-Understanding; Job-Seeking Skills and Knowledge; Rating Scales; Reading Skills; Speaking and Listening Skills; Pre-Employment Writing; Math and Concepts.

Administration: Group.

Price Data, 1998: $89.95 per manual (233 pages); $24.95 per 10 Learner Record Books; $229 per 100 Learner Record Books; $12.95 per Program Record Book.

Time: Administration time varies.

Author: Albert H. Brigance.

Publisher: Curriculum Associates, Inc.

Review of the BRIGANCE® Diagnostic Employability Skills Inventory by JoELLEN V. CARLSON, Measurement and Training Consultant, Washington, DC:

This inventory is one of a series in the BRIGANCE® System. It is designed for use primarily in special or alternative education and school-to-work programs for learners with special needs, such as disabilities or limited English proficiency, who are working toward basic, entry-level employability. It is not proposed to assess mastery of skills required for specific jobs or careers.

The manual states that the inventory assesses "the major skills viewed as prerequisites to employability" (p. vii). There is, however, no discussion of the qualifications of those making this judgment and little of the process by which it was determined. Many of the assessments in the inventory purport to test the skills shown in the Comprehensive Adult Student Assessment System (CASAS; T5:645) and the Secretary's Commission on Achieving Necessary Skills (SCANS) compilation.

The content of the inventory is based on pre-employment and employment-related situations. All reading, listening, and speaking skills are presented in the context of specific areas, such as the job application, the job interview, pay and benefits, and life skills included in the BRIGANCE® Diagnostic Life Skills Inventory (53). Content includes calendar and time concepts, simple measurements, money concepts, common signs in looking for employment, information signs, safety signs, directions obtained from common employment forms, an application for a social security card, simple employment applications, complex employment applications, and other job-related situations, such as completing a job résumé outline. The Rating Scales are self-evaluated and intended to aid the learner in becoming more aware of traits, behaviors, attitudes, or skills he or she might strive to develop for better workplace adjustment.

According to the author, the instrument was developed in response to users' requests that the Life Skills and Vocational Skills sections of the BRIGANCE® Diagnostic Inventory of Essential Skills (T5:343; published in 1981) be published separately. Unfortunately, the information provided about the development of this inventory is insufficient upon which to base judgment of content validity. An appendix provides a brief history, citing reliance on responses and critiques from users of the Inventory of Essential Skills and other BRIGANCE® inventories, review of publications, and the author's knowledge and experience. A few field test locations are named and the personnel are thanked for their ideas, recommendations, and constructive criticism; no other description of their involvement is given. Empirical information is absent.

Rather than a score, this instrument yields a skill-by-skill inventory. It is recommended primarily as a screening tool to refer a student for additional assessment and/or instruction and, secondarily, as a tool to group learners for instruction. Each skill area begins with a statement of purposes, instructions on how to use the Learner Record Book if applicable, and an overview of the assessment methods. Throughout the materials, the person being assessed is referred to as "the learner," reinforcing the intent and focus on use in instruction. All sections have guides and directions for using the results as an educational tool. Sample instructional objectives and detailed task/skills breakdowns are included in each section.

A Quick Screen is included to help determine whether the assessments in the inventory are appropriate for a particular learner. The inventory is untimed, with instructions to allow as much time as the learner needs or to quit as judgment dictates. Most of the tasks lend themselves to either an oral or a written response.

The manual is thorough and well organized, and its format appears to be efficient and easy to use. The instructor page presents specific directions for administering, a copy of the learner page (where appropriate), background testing notes, what the instructor should say, and teaching objectives. The manual states that administering the inventory does not require special training, and specifically states that tutors and aides can administer the inventory. Sometimes alternative approaches are suggested for presenting the tasks or obtaining responses. For example, it is suggested that, when presenting a full page of words to learners with limited reading ability, the administrator should ask them to read the words they know rather than going word by word.

Instructions to "Identify or Hypothesize Reasons for Errors" (manual, p. ix) are included as one step of the assessment. It also encourages the administrator to select/adapt and add items as needed to get a variety of indicators of the learner's skill. The manual also encourages rephrasing directions when needed and even suggests demonstrating the type of response expected. The author encourages the use of multiple assessments and emphasizes using all data available in making judgments about the learner. There is also admonition to check to be sure that a learner who can perform certain skills during the assessment can apply those skills to daily activities.

SUMMARY. The manual mentions no technical data at all and does not explain why no data are included. Despite the lack of empirical information, this instrument seems to have a degree of face validity and appears to be a potentially useful tool for teachers in planning curricular objectives and instructional approaches. Given the impressive scope, detail, apparent efficiency, and potential utility of this instrument, a program of psychometric research should certainly be undertaken. Information about the instrument's objectivity, reliability, and validity—particularly documentation of content validity and investigation of concurrent and predictive validity—are essential to broaden its utility.

Review of the BRIGANCE® Diagnostic Employability Skills Inventory by WILLIAM C. TIRRE, Senior Research Psychologist, Air Force Research Laboratory, Brooks Air Force Base, TX:

TEST COVERAGE AND USE. The BRIGANCE® Diagnostic Employability Skills Inventory (BDESI) is intended to be used as a criterion-referenced set of assessments for evaluating the reading, writing, speaking, listening, comprehending, and computing skills that are needed for employment. Examinees most likely will be participants in adult basic education, English as a second language programs, vocational education, and various programs focusing on job training and placement.

TEST CONSTRUCTION AND NORMS. As with many criterion-referenced tests, the BDESI does not have published norms, but they are needed nonetheless (Shaycroft, 1979). Items in the BDESI have the appearance of being scaled by grade equivalence, but no mention is made of the procedures followed in either domain specification, item selection, or in setting standards of competence. For a criterion-referenced test with this intended use, it is especially important that the testing

procedures and items be extensively pilot-tested and refined for use with special populations. Although it appears that the BDESI has been developed over a decade of experience, it is impossible to tell from the information given the extent to which the BDESI has been administered to appropriately composed samples of the target populations.

RELIABILITY. The test developer does not report reliability coefficients for the BDESI. Reliability estimation is as important for criterion-referenced tests as it is for norm-referenced tests. Shaycroft (1979) argued that classical test theory should be applied to criterion-referenced tests.

VALIDITY. Content validity (or content representativeness) is a primary concern for a criterion-referenced test and, unfortunately, the test developer did not describe how the content for the test was specified or how the items were created. But content validity is not the only concern, and it is meaningful to gather construct and criterion-related validity evidence for criterion-referenced tests as well (Hambleton, 1984). Here again, the test developer does not report any evidence for the validity of the BDESI. When construct validity is assessed, the question is: What do test scores mean? What person variables explain variation in test scores? To approach this question intelligently, the test developer must have a theory that identifies hypotheses about test responses. Given the anecdotes the test developer uses to illustrate the appropriate use and interpretation of the test, it would appear that at least the beginning of a theory exists. This theory must be documented and tested empirically.

This next point might have been addressed under reliability just as appropriately. The internal consistency of some of the BDESI's subtests might be questioned (i.e., it is likely the internal consistency is low and that one construct does not dominate some subtests). A case in point is the Motor Coordination rating scale. In this scale the student is evaluated on 20 "motor-coordination skills" including the following (my terms): physical strength, stamina, flexibility/mobility, work speed, familiarity with tools, driving skills, work accuracy, and dependability. Each of these items is likely to be important in an assessment of a person's employability, at least for some job categories; but it does not appear that these items actually comprise a unidimensional scale.

Criterion-related validity for a criterion-referenced test can be assessed in much the same way as it is for a norm-referenced test (Hambleton, 1984). One approach to validating the BDESI's claim to assess and train employability skills would be to compare two reference groups (i.e., program graduates [masters of the employability skills] and program entrants who are just beginning the training program). The groups could be compared on a work sample test and/or on employability assessments made by a sample of human resources professionals unaware of the candidates' graduation status.

TEST ADMINISTRATION. The test developer did a superior job in giving explicit directions to the test administrator. The BDESI appears to be easily administered by an adult educator or similarly trained professional. Directions to the test user do not stress rigid adherence to a standardized testing procedure—allowances are made to accommodate the wide range of individuals one is likely to encounter.

TEST REPORTING. A 30-page "Learner Record Book" is provided that allows the test user to document progress. Skills for which mastery is demonstrated can be circled in different colors for each evaluation and learning objectives to be mastered by the next evaluation can be underlined. Quantitative scores are not reported because the intent is to indicate what skills the learner has mastered and what skills need to be addressed in training. This is something of a philosophical difference, but I think it would be useful to provide percentile scores where the comparison group is the adult education student population at program entry, program departure, and regular intervals in between. Grade equivalent scores should be avoided. But perhaps the training programs where the BDESI might be used are too diverse in composition for meaningful normative groups. The Learner Record Book provides a lot of detail, but I think it also would be useful to have a one- or two-page report that graphically depicts progress.

TEST AND ITEM BIAS. The test developer sidesteps the testing bias issues by reminding the reader that the intended use of the test was not to provide a score that could be used for comparison with a specific population. The skills assessed in the inventory appear to be selected for their relevance to employment, and so if the inventory is biased, one might argue that so is the typical employment setting.

SUMMARY. As an instructional tool in adult education, employability skills training, and similar programs, the BDESI might be quite useful. I would still like to see more documentation on its construction, especially details on domain specification and validation of the skill hierarchy implicit in the instrument. Evidence of psychometric quality for scores from the BDESI leaves a lot to be desired. Criterion-referenced tests need to provide evidence of validity and reliability, but the test developer has not reported any empirical work on either. Test administration should be easy enough to accomplish, but test reporting could be improved by having a two-page report that graphically depicts progress.

REVIEWER'S REFERENCES

Shaycroft, M. F. (1979). *Handbook of criterion-referenced testing: Development, evaluation, and use.* New York: Garland STPM Press.
Hambleton, R. K. (1984). Validating the test scores. In R. A. Berk (Ed.), *A guide to criterion-referenced test construction* (pp. 199–230). Baltimore, MD: The Johns Hopkins University Press.

[53]

BRIGANCE® Diagnostic Life Skills Inventory.

Purpose: Designed to evaluate "listening, speaking, reading, writing, comprehending, and computing skills within the context of everyday situations."

Population: Grades 2–8.

Publication Date: 1994.

Scores: 9 skills: Speaking and Listening Skills, Functional Writing Skills, Words on Common Signs and Warning Labels, Telephone Skills, Money and Finance, Food, Clothing, Health, Travel and Transportation.

Administration: Group.

Price Data, 1998: $89.95 per manual (239 pages); $24.95 per 10 Learner Record Books; $229 per 100 Learner Record Books; $12.95 per Program Record Book.

Time: Administration time varies.

Author: Albert H. Brigance.

Publisher: Curriculum Associates, Inc.

Cross References: See T5:344 (1 reference).

Review of the BRIGANCE® Diagnostic Life Skills Inventory by CLEBORNE D. MADDUX, Professor of Educational Psychology and Information Technology in Education, University of Nevada, Reno, NV, and RHODA CUMMINGS, Professor of Educational Psychology and Human Growth and Development, University of Nevada, Reno, NV:

The BRIGANCE Diagnostic Life Skills Inventory is a criterion-referenced instrument designed to evaluate skills taught in a life-skills curriculum including those involved in listening, speaking, reading, writing, comprehending, and computing. (The items relating to the computing skill involve arithmetic calculations, rather than expertise in the use of computers.) According to the manual, the instrument was developed in response to requests from educators in the field that items relating to life skills in another inventory by the same author be published separately.

The instrument is organized into nine separate sections (called *assessments*) of basic life skills. Because the BRIGANCE Diagnostic Life Skills Inventory is criterion-referenced, it yields no overall or subtest scores. Each item is recorded as either mastered or not mastered.

An additional, optional assessment consists of five rating scales to help assess more subjective speaking skills, listening skills, health practices and attitudes, self-concept, and auto safety skills. The manual states that the primary purpose of these rating scales is to help identify and formulate instructional objectives, and that no formal scoring is needed for this purpose. However, the manual goes on to suggest that if scores for the rating scales are desired, they may be computed using the following scale: Much Improvement Needed = 0, Could be Improved = 3, Acceptable = 4, and Very Good = 5. This would be a highly questionable procedure, however, because the manual provides no rationale for this unusual scaling and no psychometric evidence of any kind.

Items range in difficulty from Grades 2 to 8 and responses may be oral or written, at the discretion of the examiner. If administered individually, the manual states that the instrument can be administered in 10 to 20 minutes, whereas group administration (an option for all areas except Speaking and Listening Skills) may decrease the total time needed. The manual suggests that the instrument can be administered to students in a variety of programs, including adult basic education, English as a second language, secondary special education, and family literacy programs. According to the manual, the instrument can be used to determine baseline learning skills prior to intervention or on a pretest/posttest basis to assess growth. Further, it is designed to provide information about curriculum needs for individuals and assistance in selecting appropriate individual learning goals.

The instructions for examiners are extremely well written, clear, and complete, and include suggested verbatim scripts. However, in keeping with the spirit of criterion-referenced assessment, the manual emphasizes that the administration procedures as well as specific content can be modified according to instructor and learner needs.

The assessments are easy to administer and the system for recording and scoring responses is easy to use and well thought out. The instrument comes bound in a three-ring binder that includes (a) introductory material, (b) a Quick-Screen inventory, and (c) specific administration instructions and student plates for each assessment.

The Quick-Screen is a brief inventory containing items similar to, but different from those in the full inventory. The Quick-Screen is designed to give the examiner a preliminary indication of (a) whether or not the inventory will be useful with an individual learner, (b) a learner's competency level in the various life skills areas, and (c) which assessment should be used with a given learner as a starting point. The Quick-Screen is of little value, not only because no psychometric data are presented, but also because there is no explanation for why the authors chose to include items from only five of the nine sections included in the full inventory. Then too, items seem to jump too quickly from easy to very difficult skills with little or no transition.

The binder also contains a reference section and various appendices. The appendices include useful information about how to use the results of the inventory in individual special education program planning. However, this information should be updated to reflect recent reauthorizations of special education law, including the change of name to the Individuals with Disabilities Education Act, and the recent requirement for individual transition plans (ITPs).

The inventory also includes a Learner Record Book and a Program Record Book. The Learner Record Book is for use with individuals, whereas the Program Record Book is for use with groups of students who have been assessed with the inventory.

The manual states that the Learner Record Book can be used to: "1. Track the progress of an individual learner; 2. Communicate information in a conference; 3. Communicate learner data to other personnel" (p. x). Specifically, the Learner

Record Book provides a simple, creative, and efficient system of color codes to make easy identification, across repeated administrations, of those skills that were mastered, and those that have been assessed and set as objectives for the future. The manual does an excellent job of explaining this system and providing examples.

The Program Record Book is optional and includes another simple recording system to identify skills mastered and skills for future teaching and mastery.

The main shortcoming of this inventory is its lack of acceptable psychometric data. Reliability and validity concerns are not addressed, and the manual states only that the instrument was developed after considering suggestions from the field, research reports, and experience of the author in constructing other assessment instruments.

A critical issue in criterion-referenced instruments is content validity. Yet, this is never mentioned, and the user has no way to assess whether or not items included are truly representative of the specified skill.

Reliability is also never mentioned. Thus, there is no way to assess test-retest reliability or interscorer reliability. These omissions are especially serious because the manual stresses the usefulness of the inventory on a pretest/posttest basis, and because it also stresses that no special training is needed to administer the inventory.

SUMMARY. The BRIGANCE Diagnostic Life Skills Inventory is a criterion-referenced instrument designed to assess skills in listening, speaking, reading, writing, comprehending, and computing (arithmetic calculation). The inventory is easy to administer, and the various recording devices are simple and useful. It is unfortunate that the test developers chose not to include any psychometric information. No reliability or validity data are presented. Until this omission is rectified, the inventory will remain an interesting but highly experimental instrument with unknown psychometric properties.

Review of the BRIGANCE® Diagnostic Life Skills Inventory by JAMES A. WOLLACK, Assistant Scientist, Department of Testing & Evaluation, University of Wisconsin—Madison, Madison, WI:

The Brigance Diagnostic Life Skills Inventory (B-LSI) is an extremely flexible and comprehensive tool for assessing the basic skills that people use routinely to function in society. The B-LSI, which may be administered either individually or in groups, is intended to be administered to people in eighth grade through adulthood. The items range in difficulty from second grade level through eighth grade level, although the contexts of the items are appropriate for the older audience for whom the test is designed. The manual suggests using the B-LSI in a variety of educational programs, including adult basic education, English as a second language (ESL), secondary special education, vocational education, and family literacy.

The B-LSI measures nine different general skills: Speaking and Listening, Functional Writing, Words on Common Signs and Warning Labels, Telephone Skills, Money and Finance, Food, Clothing, Health, and Travel and Transportation. Within each skill, there are several other components. Where appropriate, components are also broken down into very specific objectives. The B-LSI has five rating scales assessing speaking skills, listening skills, health practices and attitudes, self-concept, and auto safety. It also provides a useful quick screen.

There is no particular order to the B-LSI. Test users are advised to pick and choose the particular content areas that they wish to assess and the order in which they want to assess them. Test users may spend as little or as much time assessing an individual or group as is appropriate, but it is unlikely that one would elect to administer the entire battery of skills to any one person or group of persons.

Test users are given a great deal of latitude in administering the B-LSI. Not only do they pick and choose the specific content areas to assess, but the user also has a lot of flexibility in determining whether to administer the inventory individually or in a group, whether to collect oral or written responses, when to discontinue the assessment, how much time to devote to a particular assessment, and, perhaps most importantly, whether to ask follow-up questions to determine the extent of the examinee's comprehension. As an example of a typical question, examinees taking the Warning and Safety Signs assessment are shown a picture with a variety of signs in context (e.g., the word "Ambulance" appears on the side of an ambulance and "Emergency Exit" appears above a door) and a variety of signs not in context (i.e., just the name of the sign). The standardized directions instruct the test user to say the name of one of the signs aloud, and have the examinee locate that sign. At the test user's discretion, he or she may ask follow-up questions such as "What does this sign mean?" "Where would you see these words?" or "What action should be taken when it is seen?" but it is not required for credit. Because one's adaptive functioning depends heavily on one's understanding of a situation, not just recognition of the situation, the comprehension follow-up questions should most certainly be used to get an accurate sense of the examinee's skills. However, these follow-up questions will probably limit one's ability to administer these assessments to groups and will likely increase the necessary testing time. It is also unfortunate that no standards exist for determining the appropriateness of the responses to these questions.

The strength of the B-LSI definitely lies in the breadth of skills and the comprehensiveness of the components within these skills, although the test user would benefit by having the difficulty level (e.g., grade level) of each component identified. The items appear to cover the important content, are clear, and are well presented. The items nicely assess knowledge both in and out of context, and the difficulty range of items seems appropriate for the target audience. The B-LSI also provides a very nice format for recording information. The Learner Record Book allows the test user to carefully keep track of the different skills assessed, including whether they have been mastered or not and how much progress has been made between assessments, and identify sets of individual objectives that will be targeted for instruction prior to the next assessment. This information should be very useful for writing an Individualized Education Plan (IEP). The optional Program Record Book allows the teacher to compile data for an entire class of students. In this book, all 265 individual objectives, grouped by skill and component, are listed across the top of the pages. Each examinee is listed in a separate row down the page. Instructors use an easy symbolic notation to represent, for each student, whether skills have been assessed and set as an objective, introduced but not achieved, achieved, or not assessed. After these data are entered, this format provides the instructor an easy way to quickly identify groups of students with similar profiles, so that the instructor may design curricular units that are tailored to those students' needs.

Although the B-LSI does appear to be a potentially very useful test for special education, ESL, and vocational education teachers, it is not without its weaknesses. The most noticeable shortcoming is that there are no data provided to help the user gauge a student's overall level of skill. The test is marketed as a criterion-referenced test, so complete normative data may not be appropriate. Still, it is important to note that evidence of a significant delay in adaptive skills is necessary to obtain a classification of a cognitive disability. Therefore, if a school psychologist needs to administer a norm-referenced life skills assessment instrument for a special education diagnosis, it might be difficult to justify the added expense and time required to also administer the criterion-referenced B-LSI. It would also be very useful to see information on the difficulty or importance of various components and objectives for different subpopulations. Also, as the B-LSI is currently designed, it is only possible to generate a score for an objective (and items within the objective), but not for the component or scale. Instead, the user is asked to look at the pattern of objectives and make a determination of whether or not the component is sufficiently well understood. Similarly, users must look at the pattern across components and make a subjective decision as to whether the skill is mastered. If a teacher decides that a student has several areas of weakness, there are no mechanisms in place for determining which constitute the most problematic deficiencies. Scoring tips to help teachers make these sorts of decisions would be most welcome. A final weakness is that the manual contains no information on reliability, validity, or scale construction. At the very least, data on the treatment utility of the B-LSI should certainly be included.

At the end of the inventory, five rating scales are provided to collect information on traits/behaviors that are not easy to assess objectively. On these scales, each of 20 items is rated on a 4-point scale: much improvement needed, could be improved, acceptable, or very good. Although the manual discourages creating a composite score, it does say that, if a score is needed, the weights of 0, 3, 4, 5, respectively, may be applied to the four categories above. This weighting is quite unconventional and no justification, statistical or pedagogical, is provided. These rating scales are designed to be completed by either a well-informed rater or by the target individual, yet many of the questions cannot be answered well by raters, and others are clearly written with an external rater in mind. As examples, on the Listening Skills Rating Scale, the rater is in a poor position to judge whether the target individual "pushes worries, fears, and problems away while listening," but the target individual is in a poor position to judge whether he or she "appears interested in what the speaker is saying" (manual, p. 200). Also, to get the scoring to come out in the right direction, many of the items are phrased in the negative. Negatively phrased questions are often confusing, especially for use as a self-evaluation with students with cognitive deficiencies. Finally, because these are rating scales measuring unobservable constructs, it is important that good data be provided as to the reliability and validity of these scales, but no such data are provided. Without the requisite psychometric data, it is difficult to recommend using these rating scales for anything more than research purposes.

At the time of this review, there were no published articles on the B-LSI in the educational or psychological literature. As a result, there is some work yet to be done to establish that teachers can accurately interpret a student's profile and identify those areas most in need of remediation.

SUMMARY. The B-LSI appears to be a useful tool for assessing life skills and developing IEPs for students with disabilities. It is performance based, and so can provide users with rich information about the specific skills that have and have not been mastered. It is a very complete and well-conceived battery, appears easy and quick to administer, and offers users a great deal of flexibility. It is a worthy rival to the adaptive behavior inventories currently available.

[54]
Brown Attention-Deficit Disorder Scales.

Purpose: Designed to "elicit cognitive and affective indications of Attention-Deficit Disorder."
Publication Date: 1996.
Acronym: Brown ADD Scales.
Scores, 6: Organizing and Activating to Work, Sustaining Attention and Concentration, Sustaining Energy and Effort, Managing Affective Interference, Utilizing "Working Memory" and Assessing Recall, Total.
Administration: Individual or group.
Price Data, 2000: $94.50 per starter kit including manual (112 pages), 1 Treatment Monitoring Worksheet, 5 Adolescent Ready Score Answer Documents, 5 Adult Ready Score Answer Documents, 5 Adolescent Brown ADD Diagnostic Forms, and 5 Adult Brown ADD Diagnostic Forms; $34 per 25 Adolescent Ready Score Answer Documents; $34 per 25 Adult Ready Score Answer Documents; $16 per 10 Adolescent Brown ADD Diagnostic Forms; $17 per 10 Adult Brown ADD Diagnostic Forms; $67.50 per manual.
Time: (15–30) minutes.
Author: Thomas E. Brown.
Publisher: The Psychological Corporation.
  a) ADOLESCENT SCALE.
  Population: Ages 12 to 18.
  b) ADULT SCALE.
  Population: Ages 18 and over.

Review of the Brown Attention-Deficit Disorder Scales by NADEEN L. KAUFMAN, Lecturer, Clinical Faculty, Yale University School of Medicine, and ALAN S. KAUFMAN, Clinical Professor of Psychology, Yale University School of Medicine, New Haven, CT:

The Brown Attention-Deficit Disorder Scales (Brown ADD Scales) is composed of two "Ready-Score," 40-item, self-report scales (one for adolescents, ages 12–18 years, and one for adults, ages 18 and older) that are similar to each other, differing primarily in the wording—but not the intent—of a number of items. The adolescent form is geared for students, and is oriented toward school ["Has difficulty memorizing (e.g., vocabulary, math facts, names, dates)"], whereas the adult form is more generic or job-oriented ["Has difficulty memorizing (e.g., names, dates, information at work)"]. Occasionally, the wording is more difficult in the adult form (e.g., the words "setting priorities" are included in an "adult" item about bogging down when presented with many things to do, but are excluded from the adolescent version of the item). Nonetheless, a majority of items (22 out of 40) are identical in both forms, and many others differ by a word or two.

The Brown ADD Scales are intended for use with adolescents and adults known or suspected of having symptoms of Attention-Deficit Disorders (ADDs), with or without impulsivity and hyperactivity. Although the DSM-IV (American Psychiatric Association, 1994) lists criteria for assessing Inattention, Hyperactivity, and Impulsivity to diagnose Attention-Deficit Hyperactivity Disorder (ADHD), the Brown ADD Scales focus exclusively on the Inattention criteria, even tapping a range of symptoms beyond these criteria, "to assess for additional cognitive and affective impairments often associates with ADDs" (manual, p. 1). The Brown ADD Scales are clearly created in the image of the author's own clinical (and not necessarily mainstream) model of ADD and ADHD which relates to his focus on Inattention; he virtually excludes the Hyperactivity and Impulsivity symptoms that are intuitively associated with impulse inhibition. Indeed, one of the seven conceptual assumptions on which the Brown ADD Scales rest is, "Hyperactivity/impulsivity is not an essential element in ADDs" (manual, p. 8).

Brown lists three uses for his scales, which may be administered "by a wide range of professionals with graduate training in psychological assessment" (manual, p. 12): (a) the preliminary screening of individuals suspected of having an attention-deficit disorder; (b) as one part of a more comprehensive battery for assessing attention-deficit disorders; and (c) as an instrument for monitoring treatment effectiveness for people with ADDs who are receiving medications or other interventions. However, his emphasis on the screening role of his scales and its usefulness as only a piece of a larger picture is occasionally compromised by statements that imply that scores on his scales can be nearly definitive for a diagnosis: "scores of 50 or more strongly suggest an ADD diagnosis for adolescents and adults" (p. 1). In addition, the graph for interpreting scores on the total scale converts "high" scores to the category "ADD highly probable."

ADMINISTRATION AND SCORING. The two 40-item Ready Score forms, one for adolescents and one for adults, may be administered orally or in written (self-administered) format. For adolescents, oral inquiry is preferred, ideally with one or both parents present, such that student and parent are both queried (though scores are supposed to be kept for each respondent, it is the student's responses that yield the scores). Parents are included, according to the author, to allow each person to offer a different perspective plus more data, to curb exaggerations, and to allow each participant to gain appreciation of others' perspectives. Not stated by the author are the potential problems that might occur for adolescents in the presence of their parents, namely the loss of confidentiality, feeling inhibited about saying unpopular things, being entirely truthful, and

so forth; similarly, parents may be more truthful and less inhibited if they are questioned privately, especially because teen relationships may be tenuous. At the least, examiners should have some type of clinical or counseling experience to buttress their requisite assessment experience to deal with subtle confrontations, hostility, or lack of appropriate participation by one or more family members. Apart from possible problems in the interactions between parent and teen, the adolescent Ready Score form is easy to administer. The adult form, likewise, is easy to administer in either an oral or written form. Adults have the option of bringing a close friend, spouse, or parent to the oral evaluation (in which case the same joint procedures described for adolescents are used), but the potential conflicts are minimized because the referred adult has control over the situation.

The Brown ADD Scales yield a total score plus subscores in the following clusters: (a) organizing and activating for work (resulting from chronic problems with a high threshold for arousal or high anxiety); (b) sustaining attention and concentration (either receptive, when listening, or actively, when engaged in an activity such as reading); (c) sustaining energy and effort (inconsistent energy or sustained effort due to laziness, sluggishness, or lack of vigilance); (d) managing affective interference (moods that affect social interactions, related to irritability, frustration, and anger); and (e) utilizing "working memory" and accessing recall (forgetting to bring a needed item or to do a necessary task, misplacing things).

Each of the 40 items on the adolescent or adult scale is scored on a 4-point scale. Students or adults are asked to listen to each item (or read each item) and indicate if that item has been a problem for them over the past 6 months. If it is "never" a problem, the score is 0. Problems once a week or less are scored 1; twice a week = 2; almost every day = 3. Two lines of 0–3 scores are provided for each of the 40 items to enable the examiner to record the referred person's responses (top row) and the collateral Informant's responses (bottom row). To obtain scores, examiners must tear off the perforated edge of the answer sheet, transfer all item scores to the appropriate column for each cluster, add two subtotals per cluster to get the cluster raw scores (which requires careful attention to a confusing array of "connecting" lines), and transfer cluster and total scores to a graph that permits conversion of raw scores to T scores (an optional step). On the graph, total scores are also converted to a category (e.g., "ADD probable but not certain"). Although it is logical (because of the range of scores possible for each) that it is total raw score, and not total T score, that is categorized, the instructions do not tell examiners that important fact; misinterpretations are quite feasible. In addition, the extensive transferring of item and cluster scores, and the possible confusion when summing subtotals, encourages clerical errors. A better designed answer sheet would have allowed the responses to be recorded in their pertinent column, thereby avoiding the transferring. The use of T scores is both confusing and puzzling. The manual includes extensive interpretive information, but it is the raw scores, and not the T scores, that are interpreted. Although examiners are instructed to convert raw scores to T scores as an optional step, the metrics of this presumably standardized score are not provided. One thing is evident from the conversion table, however: The mean of 50 and standard deviation of 10 that are routinely applied to T scores were not used for the Brown ADD Scale; T scores for Brown's scales range from ≤ 50 to 100+ with a midpoint of about 75.

On the positive side, the items written for both adolescents and adults are stated in an empathic tone; no test items are phrased to sound negative or judgmental. Therefore, the items are likely to elicit pertinent commentary or complaints from the client and will help form a "connection" with the examiner.

In addition to the 40-item scales, the Brown ADD Scales include booklets known as Diagnostic Forms to aid in a multifaceted assessment of Attention-Deficit Disorders. The 15-page forms, one targeted for adolescents and the other for adults, includes five pages with written questions followed by blank lines for writing responses as a means of summarizing the client's clinical history; one page for copying over the scores on the 40-item scale; one page for determining multi-rater agreement on the DSM-IV criteria for ADHD, including Hyperactivity and Impulsivity; as well as additional pages to allow screening for co-morbid disorders, for recording an array of scores derived from Wechsler's (1981, 1991) IQ scales (the manual discusses interpretation of the Brown ADD Scales in the context of scores obtained on the Wechsler Intelligence Scale for Children—Third Edition

[WISC-III] and Wechsler Adult Intelligence Scale—Revised [WAIS-R]), and for integrating all data and information into a diagnostic format. These forms are likely to be useful for novice examiners who have limited experience and will be able to benefit from the extreme structure built into the forms. Experienced examiners, who have already developed their own interviewing, assessment, and diagnostic strategies, may find the forms confining and of little practical value, especially if their orientation is even moderately different from Brown's approach.

PSYCHOMETRIC PROPERTIES. The Brown ADD Scales report total scores, cluster scores, and categories for those assessed by this instrument, but do not present data for an actual standardization sample of adolescents or adults. Instead, several research samples, clinical and nonclinical within both the adolescent and adult age ranges, are described. When subsamples were combined, the nonclinical samples numbered 190 adolescents and 143 adults; the clinical ADD samples (composed of individuals both with and without Hyperactivity in approximately equal numbers) totaled 191 adolescents and 142 adults. Within the adolescent and adult samples, the clinical and nonclinical samples were reasonably matched on gender, age, socioeconomic status (SES), and ethnic background, permitting meaningful comparisons for determining the diagnostic validity of the scales. However, the nonclinical samples, which provided the basis for interpreting scores yielded by the Brown ADD Scales, do not match U.S. Census data on these key background variables. The percentages for White, Hispanics, and African-Americans seem to be similar to U.S. Census proportions (no Census data are provided), but the sample is decidedly of higher SES than the nation as a whole, and does not report data for geographic region or community size. The gender distribution reveals a proportion of 87 males to 13 females within the adolescent nonclinical population compared to a very different ratio of 44 males to 56 females among the nonclinical adult sample. The former proportion may reflect the fact that many more males than females are referred for possible ADD, but that does not alter the fact that such a disproportion of males to females makes the sample highly undesirable as a reference group. Furthermore, the nonclinical samples are too small to be appropriate standardization samples. This concern ranks as the largest drawback of the scales.

Comparison of the clinical and nonclinical samples reveals exceptional discriminant validity for the five clusters and the total score for both adolescents and adults. Total raw scores averaged about 72 for the adolescent clinical sample compared to 39 for the nonclinical sample. For adults, the respective values were about 78 and 31 (*SD* = 16), for a discrepancy of nearly 2 *SD*s. These are impressive results, and they maintained for all five scales. Whereas discrimination between the clinical and nonclinical samples offers some evidence of the construct validity of the Brown ADD Scales, in general, construct validity evidence is meager. Item-total correlations are presented as a kind of evidence of construct validity, and these coefficients are generally good, but no evidence is offered (other than the face validity of the items) to support the separate identify of the five clusters or to validate the construct that each purports to measure.

Evidence of concurrent validity is offered by examining relationships of the Brown ADD Scales to the Wechsler scales (WISC-III or WAIS-R, depending on the person's age). Brown demonstrated that adolescents and adults with ADD scored substantially lower on the triad of subtests associated with attention-concentration than on the Verbal or Spatial triads. If, indeed, the three component tasks measured attention-concentration for the ADD samples (or working memory, or freedom from distractibility, other interpretations commonly assigned to the trio of subtests; see Kaufman, 1994), then the Brown/Wechsler data do offer good evidence of the concurrent validity of the Brown ADD Scales.

Coefficient alpha reliability coefficients for the total scale were .92–.93 for the two nonclinical samples, .90 for the adolescent clinical sample, and .86 for the adult clinical sample. These values are acceptable. However, the values of .95–.96 reported in the manual by Brown for the combined clinical and nonclinical samples are bogus and should not be interpreted. The distributions of scores described in the discriminant validity studies are clearly bimodal, preventing meaningful interpretation of either reliability or validity data for combined samples. Unfortunately, the only values presented for the five clusters are for the combined sample. Therefore, the values of .70 to .89 for adolescents and .79 to .92 for adults should

not be interpreted; they are spuriously high to an unknown degree. The test-retest stability, fortunately, was obtained on 75 nonclinical adolescents over a 2-week interval and the resultant coefficient of .87 indicates excellent stability. Unfortunately, coefficients are not reported for the five clusters; mean scores on the two testings are not reported, preventing any understanding of practice effects; and no stability data were obtained for the adult form.

OVERALL EVALUATION. One of the key strengths of the Brown ADD Scales is the author himself, who is an astute, experienced clinician whose in-depth knowledge of ADD, his empathy for families affected by it, and his enthusiasm for the topic are all quite evident by reading the manual. Brown's approach, however, is more clinical than research based. He has written extensively on ADD, but apparently has not conducted an abundance of published research on ADD to support his conception of the disorder. The research that he cites in support of his theoretical approach (manual, pp. 9–11) seems tangential and limited in scope.

Yet he has developed an instrument for adolescents and adults, with the latter group being underserved and often ignored. His development of truly an adult-oriented scale reflects a very nice contribution to the ADD field. So, too, is the manual for the scales. Though it is occasionally disorganized (it is not always easy to know where to find pertinent information), it is written in a reader-friendly style that explains important concepts in a straightforward manner. Brown avoids technical language and jargon and presents material in a consistently commonsense manner, from the assumptions he makes as a foundation for his approach and his scales to the impressive amount of interpretive material (including useful case studies) that fill the manual. He offers concrete suggestions, such as when giving feedback to clients, and gives many clear examples. In addition, he offers the reader numerous cautions about ADD diagnosis and makes suggestions of supplementary measures to use to assess areas not covered by the Brown ADD Scales. The examiner who is inexperienced with ADD will learn much from giving the scales to a client and from reading the manual, and will conceivably use the results of the screening scales to refer the client to an expert, if need be. One caution concerns the considerable claims made for the use of the scales for monitoring treatment: Research documentation is sorely needed to determine its utility for this important purpose.

SUMMARY. The Brown ADD Scales provide screening scales for measuring inattention and symptoms associated with inattention, and are targeted for adolescents and adults; they make an especially important contribution to adult assessment because that group is often ignored in the diagnosis and treatment of ADD. The test items are worded empathetically and should elicit meaningful responses from referred clients. The scales are administered to the client, even though a parent or collateral informant is also advised to provide responses to the questions (especially for adolescents). It is good to have the client's perceptions as part of the diagnostic process, but it is a negative of the scales that only the client's responses are assigned scores. Administration is easy, but scoring is more complex than necessary and may lead to clerical errors. Evidence of discriminant validity is excellent, internal consistency reliability is good for the total score, but statistics provided did not permit evaluation of the reliability of the five clusters. In addition, there is meager construct validity evidence for the five clusters. The biggest shortcomings of the Brown ADD Scales are the lack of a large, representative normative sample for adolescents or adults, and the limited research base in support of the author's model. The biggest positives are the author's clinical expertise and the informative, easy-to-read test manual. On balance, the instrument should be quite useful for ADD diagnosis if used appropriately as a screening tool or as part of a comprehensive battery; its role for monitoring treatment (including the effects of administering the same scale several times) needs to be demonstrated with empirical research.

REVIEWER'S REFERENCES

Wechsler, D. (1981) *Manual for the Wechsler Adult Intelligence Scale—Revised (WAIS-R)*. San Antonio, TX: The Psychological Corporation.

Wechsler, D. (1991). *Manual for the Wechsler Intelligence Scale for Children: Third edition*. San Antonio, TX: The Psychological Corporation.

American Psychiatric Association. (1994). *Diagnostic and statistical manual of mental disorders* (4th ed.). Washington, DC: Author.

Kaufman, A. S. (1994). *Intelligent testing with the WISC-III*. New York: Wiley.

Review of the Brown Attention-Deficit Disorder Scales by E. JEAN NEWMAN, Assistant Professor of Educational Psychology, University of South Alabama, Mobile, AL:

The Brown Attention-Deficit Disorder Scales consist of a self-report assessment for adolescents (ages 12–18) and adults. The 40-item instruments are designed to be used for initial screening, as part of the comprehensive diagnosis process and as an assessment (in repeated administrations) of ongoing treatment.

The author suggests that a professional read the questions to the subject, asking for self-ratings and examples. In the case of adolescents, the author suggests that one or both parents be present and offer their assessment to items after the subject offers his or her self-score. The instrument is designed to easily record the self-report scores, as well as the "collateral" scores, with instructions for separate scoring and interpretation. Administrator skill level requirements are defined as "a wide range of professionals with graduate training in psychological assessment" (manual, p. 12). Scoring is made simple by design of the instrument, and clear instructions are offered in the training manual.

A preliminary test was developed within the clinical practice of the author. A pilot test consisted of a 40-item instrument administered to 40 students aged 12 years to college age, and an additional unspecified number of adults, all of whom had been referred for attention and/or achievement problems, and all of whom met criteria for Attention Deficit Without Hyperactivity in the *Diagnostic and Statistical Manual of Mental Disorders,* Third Edition (DSM-III). The scores were compared with those of 40 "nonclinical adolescents and adults" (manual, p. 31). No description was offered related to sampling methodology. Likewise, no description of any modification of the original instrument was found. Because the pilot instrument contained 40 items, as did the published instrument, it can only be surmised that no changes in item content were made.

Subsequently, there were two phases of data collection in each age group. The adolescent version was administered to 76 subjects (ages 12–18) in Phase I and 134 in Phase II, who had been referred to a clinical psychologist for academic underachievement. The scores were compared with a matched sample of 75 (Phase I) and 115 (Phase II) nonclinical students, randomly selected from one junior and one senior high school.

The adult scale was formed, during this second phase, by rewording items on the adolescent scale. This rephrased scale was administered to 50 adults in Phase I and 123 in Phase II, who had sought treatment for ADD-like symptoms, and who met DSM-III criteria for Attention Deficit Disorder With or Without Hyperactivity. A comparison group of nonclinical adults was tested for comparison, recruited from "two work settings and one civic organization" (manual, p. 32). Although there was a "Phase 1" and "Phase 2," no evidence of revision or editing between phases was reported.

Demographic data indicate equivalent numbers for each two-age span in the adolescent group in both the clinical and nonclinical groups. Eighty-seven percent of the nonclinical sample were male, and 80% of the clinical sample; 13% of the nonclinical and 21% of the clinical sample were female. Seventy-one percent of the nonclinical were white, and 74% of the clinical; 17% of the nonclinical were African American, and 15% of the clinical; 13% of the nonclinical were Hispanic, and 11% of the clinical. Among the clinical, 40% fell within the normal IQ range, and 60% in the above average range. Therefore, this instrument should only be used with subjects who have a measured IQ score in the average or above average range.

Among the adults tested, 44% of the nonclinical group and 61% of the clinical group (total $n = 245$) were male; 56% of the nonclinical and 39% of the clinical group were female. Other demographic data were relatively similar to data from the adolescent sample. Scores on the adolescent scale tended to increase significantly with age. However, when age regressed against scores from the instrument, it was reported that the ADD diagnosis accounted for difference more than did age.

Although the 40 items on the scale include symptoms from the diagnostic checklist of the DSM-IV, the author clearly states that the instrument is based on a broader, dimensional model. Therefore, an unspecified number of the 40 items were constructed based on the author's own theoretical model. The author further divided the items into five clusters used for diagnosis, although these clusters are not analogous to categories contained in the DSM-IV. The ranges of within-cluster consistency ranged from .57 to .80. The correlation between clusters ranges from .68 to .86. Five professionals in the area of Attention Deficit Disorders diagnosis also reviewed the instruments. Using Kappa scores, interrater reliability was .85.

The author assessed concurrent validity using subtest scores from the appropriate Wechsler Intelligence Scales (WISC-R, WISC III, and WAIS); measures of attention, short-term memory, concentration, and processing speed were assessed using Arithmetic, Digit Span, Symbol Search, and Coding/Digit Symbol. The reader is referred to the manual for specific descriptions of analysis, where similarities are shown between self-reported ADD-related deficits and deficits on IQ subtest comparisons.

Significant differences were found, among all ages, between clinical and nonclinical subjects, supporting the ability of the Brown Scales to discriminate between ADD and non-ADD subjects. In addition to the assessment instruments and manual, the complete kit contains a diagnostic form for both adolescents and adults. Sections include a Clinical History Protocol, Scoring Summary of the instrument, a Multirater Evaluation Form to parallel the DSM-IV, a Screener for Comorbid Disorders, an Examiner's Worksheet for IQ Test Data, a Summary of Wechsler Scores relevant to ADD Diagnosis, and an Overall Summary of Diagnostic Data form. Although these forms represent the basic standard now acceptable for diagnosis, the format and explanations provide an excellent summative tool for thorough assessment and evaluation.

SUMMARY. The Brown ADD Scales provide a unique assessment in targeting the adolescent and adult population. Its unique emphasis on those with above-average intelligence provides detailed theoretical and psychometric means for assessing this subgroup. Statistical analyses provide adequate support for psychometric properties assessed thus far. Therefore, the instrument may be appropriately recommended for initial screening and possible assessment of ongoing treatment for the two target populations. However, the instrument is based on the author's theoretical model, which is not fully congruent with currently acceptable diagnostic standards as represented in the DSM-IV. Both the symptom characteristics and the diagnosis (ADD, rather than AD/HD) suggest problematic concern for practitioners, therapists, school systems, and insurance companies, all of whom perceive the model presented in the DSM as currently standard. Therefore, for diagnostic purposes, the instrument may not be recommended currently.

Review of the Brown Attention-Deficit Disorder Scales by JUDY OEHLER-STINNETT, Associ-

ate *Professor of Applied Behavioral Studies, Oklahoma State University, Stillwater, OK:*

NEED FOR INSTRUMENT. The Brown Attention-Deficit Disorder Scales (Brown ADD Scales) are designed to measure "symptoms of Attention-Deficit Disorders" in adolescents ages 12–18 and in adults 18 years and older. Its intended purposes are to screen for ADD in areas such as cognitive and affective impairment as well as in attention, to be utilized as part of a comprehensive measurement, and for treatment monitoring. Compared to the numerous behavior rating scales for children, there is a need for a scale such as the Brown ADD Scales for the adolescent and adult age groups. Additionally, the Brown ADD Scales is unique in that it is a self-report measure asking clients directly about the difficulties they encounter in daily living. Another strength of the Brown ADD Scales is the inclusion of a diagnostic form that guides practitioners in utilizing the scale as part of a comprehensive assessment, including test results, DSM-IV criteria, screener for comorbid disorders, and summary of Wechsler information in data interpretation. Thus, rather than simply saying, "don't use this test alone," specific written information utilizing the Brown ADD Scales within the context of a multifactored assessment is provided with the test itself.

THEORETICAL/RATIONAL TEST DEVELOPMENT. The Brown ADD Scales is based on the author's theoretical model derived from an extensive review of the theoretical literature of Attention Deficit Disorder (ADD) and symptoms described by clinical clients. Five clusters capture the dimensions of this theory: Organizing and Activating to Work, Sustaining Attention and Concentration, Sustaining Energy and Effort, Managing Affective Interference, and Utilizing "Working Memory" and Accessing Recall. As such, it is one of the few measures that captures the cognitive and motivational components of functioning that might contribute to problems in everyday living experienced by adolescents and adults with ADD. These important dimensions have been further described by Russell Barkley as critical in the understanding of ADD/ADHD.

STATISTICAL TEST DEVELOPMENT/ PSYCHOMETRIC PROPERTIES. Initial development of the Brown ADD Scales included administering the initial item pool (the number of initial items was not reported) to clinical clients

(number also not reported). Refinement of the scale to 40 items was completed; item analysis and selection processes were not described. Item alphas for clusters (subscales) and the total score are reported. Item-cluster alphas ranged from .70 to .89 for the adolescent scale and .79 to .92 for the adult scale. Items with very low item-cluster alphas remain in the scale (rs range from .18 to .76 for the adolescent scale and from .26 to .84 for the adult scale). The total alphas lend stronger support for the scales; the total alpha for the adolescent version was .95 and for the adult version, .96. Cluster intercorrelations range from .57 for Managing Affective Interference with Memory/Recall to .80 for Organization/Activation with Sustaining Energy and Effort. Although internal consistency data are useful aspects of test development for construct validity as well as for reliability, it is unfortunate that further statistical analyses substantiating the theoretical model of the scale were not conducted. Because of this, the suggestion that a profile analysis should be conducted with clusters is not warranted by the data presented.

The 40 items were administered to samples of adolescents and adults in order to demonstrate group differences. In two studies, the adolescent and adult versions discriminated clinical (ADHD) from nonclinical groups; however, studies utilizing the scale with other diagnostic groups or those with comorbid disorders are not reported. Sensitivity and specificity data for development of diagnostic cutoff scores are reported, presumably based on the clinical diagnosis from the practitioner from whom the clinical sample was obtained. Cutoff score recommendations are reported as yielding false negative rates for the adolescent scale at 10% and false positive rates at 22%. For the adult scale, the false negative rate is reported as 4% and the false positive rate at 6%. Appropriately, in this section users are admonished to use these for screening purposes only.

The adolescent version was evaluated for monitoring of medication treatment effects. Brown ADD Scales scores improved, as did GPA, for adolescents on stimulant medication. This is an important step in use of a clinical scale in working with persons with ADHD. However, as with several other scales developed in clinic settings, the Brown ADD Scales assume that demonstrating group differences and treatment effects are sufficient for test development and neglect critical aspects of construct validity and test norming.

Frequency of agreement of the Brown ADD Scales with a Bannatyne interpretation of the Wechsler scales is reported as concurrent validity. Correlations with other rating scales or self-report measures are not reported. The manual encourages practitioners to have the client as well as a collateral (e.g., parent for the adolescent scale) complete the rating. In the validity section, a correlation of .84 is reported for a self-report versus parent rating.

NORMATIVE INFORMATION. Adolescent norms are based on the initial samples gathered from one private-practice psychologist for the clinical sample (*n* = 191) and from two schools for the nonclinical sample (*n* = 190). The adult norms are based on two samples from a private practice psychologist for the clinical sample (*n* = 142) and from work/civic settings for the nonclinical sample (*n* = 143). There is a much greater number of males than females in the clinical samples. Demographic information such as age, socioeconomic status, race/ethnicity, and IQ level are reported as being basically representative of the U.S. Census; however, with such a small and limited sample, norms are inadequate for national application. There is no description of how standard scores were derived; thus, it is unclear whether these are based on the clinical, nonclinical, or the total sample of each level of the test. Norms utilizing the parent rating for the adolescent scale would be useful. The adolescent norms are based solely on adolescent self-report rather than a combination of self-report with parent input.

Test-retest reliability for a 2-week interval is reported as .87 for a sample of 75 adolescents, which is acceptable. No test-retest reliability is reported for the adult version. Confidence intervals based on normative data adjusted for regression to the mean and test reliability are reported for use in treatment monitoring.

ADMINISTRATION/SCORING/INTERPRETATION. Instructions for administration include having the adolescent and at least one parent respond to oral inquiry. For the adult form, a collateral person is optional and the test can be completed orally or in writing. Scoring is based on self-report regardless of the method of administration. Raw scores are converted to *t*-scores on the ready-score protocol. Cutoff scores are coded on a threshold continuum. There are also directions for completing the treatment monitoring form that includes sections for pre- and posttreatment ratings. Detailed descriptions on utilizing the diagnostic form information are also provided; this includes history, comorbid disorder, and DSM-IV screening, and reviewing IQ data.

A separate interpretation section is provided. A detailed description of the behaviors associated with each cluster is provided for interpretation purposes. However, until further psychometric work is complete, use of these interpretations should be limited to an informal symptom checklist.

SUMMARY AND RECOMMENDATIONS. Upon first reading, the Brown ADD Scales is an exciting scale because it is based on state-of-the-art models of ADHD that go beyond DSM diagnoses. However, this reviewer is looking forward to the Psychological Corporation's continuing work in examining and documenting the technical quality of this instrument. As the new child version is developed, it is hoped that basic psychometric steps will be implemented as well.

[55]
Burns Brief Inventory of Communication and Cognition.

Purpose: Designed to "assist in determining which of a client's cognitive or communication skills are impaired as a result of a neurological lesion or other disease process, and to assist in selecting appropriate treatment targets and functional treatment goals."
Population: Adults with neurological impairment.
Publication Date: 1997.
Acronym: Burns Inventory.
Scores: Left Hemisphere Inventory: 16 scores in 5 domains: Auditory Comprehension (Yes/No Questions, Comprehension of Words and Sentences, Comprehension of Paragraphs), Verbal Expression (Automatic Speech, Verbal Repetition, Responsive Naming-Nouns, Responsive Naming-Verbs, Confrontation Naming), Reading (Oral Reading of Words and Sentences, Reading Comprehension of Words and Sentences, Reading Comprehension of Functional Paragraphs), Writing (Writing to Dictation, Functional Writing), Numerical Reasoning (Time, Money, Calculation); Right Hemisphere Inventory: 12 scores in 3 domains: Scanning and Tracking (Functional Scanning and Tracking, Scanning and Tracking of Single Words), Visuo-Spatial Skills (Functional Spatial Distribution of Attention, Spatial Distribution of Attention, Recognition of Familiar Faces, Gestalt Perception, Visuo-Spatial Construction-Clock, Visuo-Spatial Organization for Writ-

ing), Prosody and Abstract Language (Spontaneous Expressive Prosody, Receptive Prosody, Inferences, Metaphorical Language); Complex Neuropathology Inventory: 15 scores in 4 domains: Orientation to Factual Memory (Orientation to Person/Place/Time, Factual Current and Remote Memory), Auditory Attention and Memory (Auditory Attention/Vigilance, Immediate Auditory Recall of Digits, Immediate Auditory Recall of Digits with Distractions, Immediate Auditory Recall of Functional Information); Visual Perception (Color Recognition, Picture Matching, Word Matching); Visual Attention and Memory (Functional Short-Term Recognition, Short-Term Recognition of Pictures, Short-Term Recognition of Words, Divided Visual Attention, Delayed Recognition of Pictures, Delayed Recognition of Words).

Administration: Individual.

Forms, 3: Inventories: Left Hemisphere Inventory, Right Hemisphere Inventory, Complex Neuropathology Inventory.

Price Data, 1999: $156.50 per complete kit; $21 per 15 Right Hemisphere record forms; $21 per 15 Complex Neuropathology record forms; $26.50 per 15 Left Hemisphere record forms; $47.50 per stimulus plates; $51.50 per examiner's manual (116 pages); $5.50 per 3-minute audiocassette.

Time: (30) minutes per inventory.

Comments: For use by speech pathologists; each inventory can be used separately or all three can be used as a battery.

Author: Martha S. Burns.

Publisher: The Psychological Corporation.

Review of the Burns Brief Inventory of Communication and Cognition by JOAN C. BALLARD, Clinical Neuropsychologist, Assistant Professor of Psychology, State University of New York College at Geneseo, Geneseo, NY:

The Burns Brief Inventory of Communication and Cognition (Burns Inventory) is intended for use by speech-language pathologists. Its stated purposes are (a) to determine which cognitive or communications skills are impaired in patients with known neurological lesions or disease, and (b) to help develop appropriate treatment goals. The author cites demands of managed care as the impetus for the test's development, emphasizing clinical needs for "a more efficient, cost effective assessment tool for adults with neurological impairment" (manual, p. 1). The author also notes that "clinical experience" historically played an important role in assessment and intervention, but emphasizes "the reality that inexperienced and experienced clinicians alike ... are being asked to

make clinical judgments faster, without extensive testing" (manual, preface).

To address these needs, the Burns Inventory includes three sets of materials comprising the "Left Hemisphere Inventory" (LH), the "Right Hemisphere Inventory" (RH), and the "Complex Neuropathology Inventory" (CN). It is important to note that the inventory titles refer to the patient groups for which each is intended. Specifically, the LH Inventory is intended for patients whose lesions are known to be left-sided, the RH Inventory for patients with right-sided lesions, and the CN Inventory for individuals with closed head injury or presumed dementing diseases. The Burns Inventory is NOT intended to make differential diagnoses of right versus left, or focal versus diffuse brain lesions. Although stated in the manual, this caveat is not emphasized, and "inexperienced" users may be confused about appropriate test uses.

Each inventory is divided into cognitive domains, and further subdivided into five-item "task sets." Scores for each task set are marked on a profile grid on the record form cover. In this criterion-referenced test, scores falling within the "target range" (shaded area on the grid) indicate "moderate impairment" on a specific skill and are used by the clinician to select treatment goals. A "goal bank" of treatment objectives is provided for each task set.

Evaluation of the manual and test materials on the Burns Inventory raises concerns about appropriateness of subject samples, test development rationale and processes, psychometric characteristics of the test, clarity of administration/scoring procedures, and recommended uses of test results. The first concern focuses on samples used in pilot and validity studies. The initial items were piloted by one examiner using a small number ($N = 15$) of individuals with no known neurological impairment. Although the stated purpose of this first pilot study was to determine whether normal subjects could respond correctly to each item, no information is provided on how many items met this criterion. Item revisions are not described. The second pilot employed three speech pathologists as examiners and 11 adult neurological patients as subjects. This small sample included 7 females, a wide age range, and a predominance of patients with left-sided lesions. Feedback from examiners led to undisclosed revisions.

The sample for the validity study of the final version of the test is somewhat more representative, but important information is missing. A total of 333 patients were tested by 78 examiners in 27 states. Patients were categorized with left cerebrovascular accident (LCVA), right cerebrovascular accident (RCVA), or closed head injury (CHI) only if they had no other medical or neurological conditions. However, the category of Alzheimer's/Dementia (AD/DM) included a variety of drug-related, psychiatric, neurological, and medical conditions, raising questions about group homogeneity. The number of patients in each category was not stated explicitly, but was deduced from tables. Most patients were within one year post-onset. The 108 LCVA patients and 85 RCVA patients were relatively evenly distributed among age ranges of 30–54, 55–69, and 70–80. However, the vast majority of the 55 AD/DM patients were aged 70–80, and the 85 CHI patients were considerably younger (with most under 30 and none over 69). Gender, race/ethnicity, geographic region, and education level were presented separately, with no indication of how evenly these characteristics were distributed across diagnostic categories.

The second concern centers on the lack of clarity about the test development process. A rationale for each task set is provided as evidence of content validity, but the method by which items within task sets were initially selected or written is not given. No information is provided on criteria for revising or deleting items at each stage of pilot testing. Neither expert ratings of item content nor item discriminability indices are provided. These statistics are particularly important given questionable organization or content of some task sets. For example, the "Functional Scanning and Tracking" task set could be used to assess left neglect in RCVA patients. However, none of the five items require scanning of the far left quarter of the stimulus. As another example, the "short-term" and the "delayed" recognition of pictures and words are separated by only one task (less than 5 minutes). The intervening "Divided Visual Attention" task, a modified Stroop paradigm, uses printed words that may serve as interference for the delayed word recognition task. In addition, the Stroop task is reversed from the usual order, with the patient asked to name colors of mismatched color-words first and to read the words (ignoring the ink color) second. The rationale for these departures from procedures of well-established tests is not given.

Two methods were used to identify "target treatment ranges" for each task set. First, a standard-setting panel of 18 experienced speech-language pathologists developed profiles of expected performance levels for patients at the lower and upper end of the "moderately impaired" continuum. Discrepancies between profiles were resolved through discussion. These ranges are shown as shaded areas on profile grids. The second method employed ratings made by examiners after testing to divide patients in the validity study into severity levels. Midpoints between means for "moderately impaired" patients and for categories above and below this group were used as cutoffs for target treatment ranges. These ranges are indicated on the report forms by diagonal lines on the profile grids (///). Although the treatment ranges established through these two methods overlapped substantially, the CHI and AD/DM subgroups produced significantly different ranges on the CN inventory. The manual does not discuss possible reasons for these differences (which could include the age differences of the two subgroups). In addition, the manual does not describe which subgroup is indicated by the use of directional diagonal lines (/// and \\\) on the profile grid. Finally, the manual does not address the lack of independence between the clinician's ratings of severity and the patient's test performance.

A third concern with the Burns Inventory involves its psychometric characteristics. Interrater reliability for three subjectively scored task sets was adequate. Internal consistency appears adequate to good for the task sets and cognitive domains, ranging from .74 to .97. Test-retest reliabilities at 2- to 7-day intervals were adequate, with only 6 of 58 task sets and cognitive domains below .70 (most on the RH Inventory). However, the number of subjects involved in each estimate is not given. Furthermore, it is unclear whether all subjects were included in each estimate or whether only subjects from the relevant diagnostic category were used in calculating reliability estimates for the LH, RH, and CN Inventories.

Validity data provided in the manual are inadequate. Content validity is evidenced only by stated rationales for each task set. Factor analysis yielded five factors, three of which included task sets from two or three inventories, raising questions (unaddressed in the manual) about construct validity and about the appropriateness of using only one inventory with a given patient. Concurrent validity evidence for scores from the Burns Inventory with other measures of the cognitive skills is not provided, based on the questionable argument that "because the purpose of the Burns Inventory is not to diagnose the type or severity of disorders, or to determine whether or not an individual is disordered, comparing performance on the Burns inventory with performance on other measures of communication or cognition will not assure validity of the instrument" (manual, p. 98). The only evidence offered for concurrent validity is the overlap in the target ranges identified by the standard-setting panel and by validity study data. Unfortunately, significant differences between the CHI and the AD/DM subgroups suggest that the CN inventory lacks such validity. Furthermore, although patients in the validity study completed all three inventories, no information on discriminant validity is provided. Given that each inventory was designed for use with a specific group of neurological patients, it would be helpful to know whether these patient groups produced predictable differences in performance across the three inventories.

A fourth concern regards information about administration and scoring. Record forms are relatively well designed and easy to use. Each includes a helpful checklist of medical history. Unfortunately, the administration/scoring chapter in the manual adds little information beyond that on the record forms. In fact, the few directions included in the manual, but not on the record forms, could easily be added to the forms. The guidelines for scoring items that are answered with help from the examiner often include the phrase, "Use your clinical judgment." This recommendation is surprising given the author's earlier statements about the usefulness of the Burns Inventory even for "inexperienced" clinicians. For some tasks, important procedural directions are missing. For example, the patient probably should not view the examiner's face during the "Receptive Prosody" task set, but this procedure is not stated. For other task sets, the scoring key provides space to record whether or not the item is repeated, even though the directions prohibit the examiner from doing so.

Each inventory also includes a set of "preinventory" tasks in the form of observational checklists. However, the manual includes no definitions, examples, or criteria on which to base observations, and there are no directions in the manual for how to interpret or use the results of the observations. If the purpose of the "pre-inventory" task is to determine the appropriateness of using the full inventory, then this purpose should be stated and guidelines for doing so should be provided. In addition, it may be most useful for the clinician to use all three of the "pre-inventory" tasks prior to choosing the full inventory(s) to be administered.

The description in the test manual of the theory behind the instrument may also be confusing, at least to clinicians without substantial training in neuroanatomy. The author presents an adaptation of Mesulam's (1985) model of brain organization as the theoretical basis for the test. Although interesting to students of functional neuroanatomy, this portion of the manual is too brief and too laden with cognitive psychology constructs to be of much use to the average test user. The presentation of cognitive tasks as left or right hemisphere tasks is somewhat oversimplified. For example, the manual states that "many experts agree" that vigilance (sustained attention) is a right hemisphere task, but gives no citations to back up this statement.

Finally, the recommended uses of the test raise additional concerns. The manual recommends choosing treatment goals for skill areas identified as moderately impaired on the basis of a five-item task set. Such a small sample of behavior is best considered a screening instrument, yet no guidelines are given for deciding when to pursue more in-depth testing of skill areas. In addition, the manual suggests that the clinician may use only one inventory, based on the location of known brain lesions, for any given patient. This view of patients as falling nearly into categories is unrealistic. Furthermore, information about relatively intact cognitive skills is often as important in treatment planning as is information about impairment. The goal of saving time (and money) should not be preeminent in planning assessment strategies.

SUMMARY. The Burns Inventory is a newly developed test that may eventually prove useful for screening, but that needs substantial field-testing and revision. In the next edition of the test, it will be most helpful to see estimates of concurrent validity with other measures of the same cognitive skills, estimates of discriminant validity of the Left and Right Hemisphere Inventories, and greater clarity in the procedures used to obtain these estimates. The manual can be improved by adding operational definitions for behavioral observations, including more evidence of item content validity, reducing the degree of "clinical judgment" required for scoring and administration, and emphasizing the need for in-depth testing of skills identified as impaired.

REVIEWER'S REFERENCE

Mesulam, M. (1985). Patterns in behavioral neuroanatomy: Association areas, the limbic system, and hemispheric specialization. In M. Mesulam (Ed.), *Principles of behavioral neurology* (pp. 1–70). Philadelphia: F. A. Davis.

Review of the Burns Brief Inventory of Communication and Cognition by RICHARD I. FREDERICK, Staff Psychologist, U.S. Medical Center for Federal Prisoners, Springfield, MO:

The Burns Brief Inventory of Communication and Cognition (Burns Inventory) was developed to accommodate the limited time speech pathologists have to assess impairments in cognitive or communication skills and to develop treatment goals for individual with impairments. A general assumption of the Burns Inventory is that clinicians will have information about the location of brain lesions or will have general knowledge about the nature, location, and extent of brain damage. The Burns Inventory is not intended to be a diagnostic tool and the author strongly discourages its use for differential diagnosis. The test is intended for clients for whom the diagnosis is reasonably clear from the medical workup.

The test has three parts, each established to assess the extent of impairments that typically result from damage in the left hemisphere, the right hemisphere, or from complex neuropathologies (e.g., multiple lesions, closed head traumas, or dementing processes).

The Left Hemisphere Inventory is designed to assess receptive and expressive oral and written language skills typically impaired after focal lesions to the left perisylvian regions. The tasks on the left hemisphere Inventory are organized into five sections: Auditory Comprehension, Verbal Expression, Reading, Writing, and Numerical Reasoning.

The Right Hemisphere Inventory is designed to assess attention, visuo-spatial perception and construction, and communicative skills commonly affected by focal lesions in the right cerebral hemisphere. The Right Hemisphere Inventory contains three sections: Scanning and Tracking, Visuo-Spatial Skills, and Prosody and Abstract Language.

The Complex Neuropathology Inventory is designed to assess attention and memory components of cognition associated with deep, diffuse cerebral lesions. The task sets for the Complex Neuropathology Inventory, therefore, are organized into four sections: Orientation and Factual Memory, Auditory Attention and Memory, Visual Perception, and Visual Attention and Memory.

The separation of test items into these categories speeds the assessment process, a primary goal of the instrument. Each part of the Burns Inventory can be administered in about 30 minutes. The author has emphasized speed and efficiency. The administration time can be speeded up if the client performs well on "predictor tasks." Based on the client's satisfactory performance on these tasks, the administrator can forego administration of more difficult items within a scale. The assessment process leads directly to scripted goals that are tied directly to measured impairment and are joined together to formulate a treatment plan.

Administration is straightforward, simple, and easy to learn. Instructions are clear, Each test has its own record form, in which test instructions are included. Unfortunately, most of the text is uncomfortably small and will prove a challenge for the myopic. Test materials are sturdy, but would have benefited from stiffer cardstock. The test is not intended for nonnative speakers of English. An analysis of potential bias was not reported; however, the author clearly restricted the domain of test questions to specific assessment of potential impairments in each of the three categories of brain damage.

The author provides a detailed, research-based explanation of the purpose and rationale of each item and its placement within the battery. A content analysis was provided by 77 speech pathologists and one psychologist, who evaluated by questionnaire the appropriateness of the content, case of administration, and clarity of auditory and visual stimuli. Final selection of test items was based on these inputs.

The author established two separate scoring ranges for identifying moderate and severe impairment. The first range of scores was established through "standard setting," a criterion-referenced process in which experts predicted how individuals with certain lesion locations would perform on each test item. Eighteen speech pathologists experienced in assessing and treating individuals with neurological disease were recruited to participate in a standard setting panel for the Burns Inventory. They established profiles for two types of clients. The first profile represented the individual who "just qualifies as moderately impaired" along a continuum from mildly impaired to severely impaired. The second profile represented the client who "just qualifies as severely impaired," just severe enough not to be classified as moderately impaired. After the panel members completed their ratings for all three inventories, the data were compiled into graphs with each panel member's ratings plotted. Agreement was established as 70%–90% agreement about placement of scores.

The second range of scores was established by a primary validity study of the population for which the test is intended. The study included 278 patients between the ages of 18 and 80 who were diagnosed with right or left cerebral vascular accidents or closed head injuries. Individuals were selected if they had no additional or previous medical conditions that could result in further neurological complications. Additionally, 55 individuals with Alzheimer's disease or dementia were included in the validity study. The selection of individuals appropriately matches the geographic, educational, and ethnic spectrum of the United States. Coincident to testing, clinician examiners rated the severity of impairment as normal, mild deficit, moderate deficit, or severe deficit in the categories contained within each of the three test batteries. Following testing, an overall rating of impairment was established as the most severe rating in any category. Mean test scores for individuals within each category established the second range of scores.

The ranges established by the standard setting panel are broader than the ranges defined by the standardization data. In a few instances, the validity study data revealed that individuals with moderate level impairment performed either higher or lower than predicted by the standard setting panel. The author recommended use of the narrow ranges to prioritize intervention goals and use of the broad ranges assists clinicians in identifying a larger number of possible target treatments.

A principal components analysis with varimax rotation suggested a five-factor solution, of expressive language, visuo-spatial integrity, abstract language concepts, visual attention and memory, and expressive prosody.

Reliability was assessed by a test-retest method. Fifty-nine patients from the primary validity study were retested within one week. Stability coefficients for test items were consistently high. Interrater reliability coefficients for tasks that are scored subject to interpretation were also consistently high.

SUMMARY. The Burns Inventory delivers on all its promises. It is not a neuropsychological instrument designed for differential diagnosis. It is a rapidly administered inventory that quickly identifies symptoms and problems that are amenable to treatment and ties those findings to specific treatment goals. Clinicians who need to produce efficient, objective, and measurable treatment plans for individuals with documented brain injuries will find the Burns Inventory to be a valuable testing tool.

[56]

Burns/Roe Informal Reading Inventory: Preprimer to Twelfth Grade, Fifth Edition.

Purpose: Provides information about the reading skills, abilities, and needs of individual students in order to plan an appropriate program of reading instruction.
Population: Beginning readers–grade 12.
Publication Dates: 1985–1999.
Acronym: IRI.
Scores, 2: Word Recognition, Comprehension.
Administration: Individual.
Levels, 14: Preprimer, Primer, First Reader, Second Grade, Third Grade, Fourth Grade, Fifth Grade, Sixth Grade, Seventh Grade, Eighth Grade, Ninth Grade, Tenth Grade, Eleventh Grade, Twelfth Grade.
Price Data: Available from publisher.
Time: (40–50) minutes.
Authors: Betty D. Roe and Paul C. Burns.
Publisher: Houghton Mifflin.
Cross References: See T5:357 (1 reference) and T4:343; for reviews by Carolyn Colvin Murphy and Roger H. Bruning and by Edward S. Shapiro of an earlier edition, see 10:37.

Review of the Burns/Roe Informal Reading Inventory: Preprimer to Twelfth Grade, Fifth Edition by FELICE J. GREEN, Professor of Education, University of North Alabama, Florence, AL:

The Burns/Roe Informal Reading Inventory: Preprimer to Twelfth Grade, Fifth Edition (IRI) is designed to determine the independent, instructional, frustration, and listening levels of students reading from the Preprimer to the 12th grade level. The listening test can indicate students' reading potential, or capacity to improve reading skills. The rest of the IRI provides information about specific strengths and weaknesses in both reading comprehension and word recognition skills, which enables teachers to plan appropriate reading programs for their students. The inventory is also useful for resource rooms and reading clinics, as well as in the training of preservice teachers in methods courses.

Scores obtained from administering the Burns/Roe Informal Reading Inventory, like other informal reading inventories, are not standardized, or do not yield normed scores. The examinee is evaluated using preestablished standards, and results are reported in grade equivalents.

The passages in this IRI, which include both fiction and nonfiction selections, are well written. Although the passages appear to be on the stated reading levels, passages PP and P are longer than those in many informal reading inventories.

The test writers have included notes to the examiner at the end of passages that include proper nouns—most are people's names—telling the examiner not to count these words as miscue pronunciations. The notes instruct the examiner to pronounce the words for the examinee. This is very good, but there is one thing missing. Many examiners will have trouble pronouncing international names of people CORRECTLY; therefore, phonetic respellings should be provided for all of the names. (One pronunciation is provided in an introductory statement.) One of the positive aspects of the IRI is that it DOES include stories about people from diverse backgrounds.

There are 8 comprehension questions at the end of Passages PP through 2, and there are 10 questions at the end of Levels 3 through 12. There are ample higher order questions at each level, which is not always the case with such tests. Beginning with the PP level, there are inference and cause/effect questions. Other types of questions used to check comprehension at all levels are main idea, detail, sequence, and vocabulary. Teachers can do an analysis of the types of questions missed most frequently to help them decide which comprehension skills need to be taught to individual students.

Directions for administering and scoring the IRI are clearly written and are accompanied by examples. There should be no confusion about administering and scoring the inventory if directions and examples are studied carefully, although some practice for the novice may be necessary.

There are four forms of the IRI, which is good for examiners who wish to measure silent and oral reading at each level. Combining oral and silent reading results yields more diagnostic information than either one alone, if the examiner has the time to administer both, and there are two tests for pretesting and two for posttesting.

Another positive aspect of the Burns/Roe Informal Reading Inventory is that it provides several alternative suggestions for using the IRI other than the traditional uses and methods for administering. One such suggestion is that of retelling the reading selections, rather than asking the questions at the end of each passage. A detailed discussion of the use of retelling is included, along with a Free Recall Processing Checklist to use, if this method of checking comprehension is chosen.

An alternate method is also given for asking young readers the Main Idea question when the questions at the end of the selections are used. It is pointed out that young readers may not understand the concept of "main idea"; therefore, they will not be able to answer the question, "What is the main idea of this story?" The novice examiner may not know to reword, or how to reword the question, in order to get the desired response from a young reader.

In addition to testing word recognition and comprehension skills, the IRI can be used to determine the reading rate of a student. Explicit directions are given for obtaining the reading rate.

Excellent forms are provided for tabulating and reporting the results of the IRI. The Worksheet for Qualitative Analysis of Uncorrected Miscues in Context enables the examiner to fill in the three sections of the Summary Form. The three sections of the Summary Form are Miscue Analysis of Phonic and Structural Analysis Skills, the Summary of Strengths and Weaknesses in Word Recognition, and the Summary of Strengths and Weaknesses in Comprehension. These forms facilitate the examiner in analyzing results of the IRI and making the proper educational decisions for their students.

SUMMARY. The Burns/Roe Informal Reading Inventory is an excellent tool for detecting reading strengths and weaknesses of students. It is one of the better IRIs available.

Review of the Burns/Roe Informal Reading Inventory: Preprimer to Twelfth Grade, Fifth Edition by TIMOTHY SHANAHAN, Professor of Urban Education, University of Illinois at Chicago, Chicago, IL:

The idea of the informal reading inventory (IRI) is quite simple. Some texts are harder to read than others, and it is difficult to teach students well from materials that are too hard or too easy. An efficient way of finding out which texts would be best for teaching would be to observe children while they try to read from various books. The IRI is a set of assessment procedures that does just that. For much of the century it was thought that teachers needed to construct their own IRIs on the basis of the materials from which they taught.

Test makers eventually challenged this notion by publishing IRIs that were not linked to particular instructional materials, and studies have shown that reasonable predictions can be made on the basis of commercial IRIs, except at the first grade level. Because of their ease of use, commercial IRIs have grown in popularity over the years. The Burns/Roe Informal Reading Inventory, now in its fifth edition, is among the most popular of these.

The Burns/Roe Informal Reading Inventory (IRI) is an individually administered test that is used to determine a child's frustration, instructional, and independent reading levels, and to identify specific strengths and weaknesses in word recognition, reading rate, oral reading, and reading comprehension. Classroom teachers and reading specialists can use this inventory to discern children's instructional needs, and this IRI is often used in the professional training of teachers. The test can be given in about 40–50 minutes by an experienced administrator. The authors usually provide clear directions for administration and interpretation—including a helpful case study, though the explanatory material could be better organized. The inclusion of previews, a case study, and frequently asked questions lead to repetition and make it difficult to locate specific information.

An IRI is an array of word lists and passages selected to represent varied difficulty levels, and a loose set of qualitative and quantitative observational procedures for interpreting children's performances with these materials. Unlike standardized assessments, the directions are recommendations rather than rules. As these authors point out, informal tests are "not bound by formal directions, defined time limits, or a restricted set of materials or procedures" (manual, p. 1). The purpose is to make good instructional decisions, and users should experiment with the instrument to make the best predictions possible. The authors are usually supportive of such informal use—often, though not always, pointing out alternatives or explaining the reasoning behind their own choices.

The Burns/Roe IRI includes a word recognition test (two forms) and a passage reading test (four forms). The word recognition test includes 14 word lists (Preprimer, Primer, and Grades 1–12). There are 20 words in each list, which should be sufficient to support reliability, though no reliability statistics are provided. These lists are used to determine word recognition skills in isolation from context. The word lists appear to be appropriately difficult for the levels they represent. No data on the equivalence of the two forms are provided. The authors offer no explanation of why they have included word lists through the 12th grade level, a nontraditional approach. It seems doubtful that the higher level lists would reveal much about students' knowledge of sight vocabulary or phonics. It seems that test users could skip these levels of the word test with little loss of information.

The passage reading test includes 14 reading passages at the same levels as the word lists. These passages range in length from 53–237 words, and each is accompanied by a list of 8–10 comprehension questions. The passages are used to evaluate students' oral and silent reading and listening comprehension. The readability levels of the passages have been tested by formula (Spache or Fry), but there has been no systematic attempt to represent the range of reading demands. For example, some IRIs have narrative and expository test forms, so that both literary and content reading abilities can be examined. This test, however, includes mainly stories or factual narratives, even at the senior high school levels. Only 11 of the 56 passages are expository, no expository tests are used through the first six levels of the test, and there is no systematic representation of content or text type. This is a definite weakness for a test that will often be used with older students.

The oral reading procedures are similar to those of most IRIs, with a couple of notable exceptions. Burns and Roe recommend not counting self-corrections for level setting, but do count repetitions—including those made to self-correct. IRI makers have long disagreed about how to handle repetitions, so I won't quibble with their decision. However, their rationale for doing this is weak—a study by Ekwall (1974) that used contradictory evaluative criteria. Most IRIs use Betts' level-setting criteria. The Burns/Roe IRI, however, uses Powell's criteria at Grades 1 and 2. The difference of accuracy required for instructional level (99% vs. 85%) is considerable and the Powell criteria have not been widely accepted in the field. Unfortunately, there is no explanation for this choice, and the directions for administering it are unclear. Are these criteria for use with first and second grade passages or children? This IRI, in spite of all of its mostly sound advice on the interpretation of oral reading, fails to offer any suggestions for dealing with dialect, an especially important issue for those working with racial and linguistic minorities.

The comprehension questions emphasize recall of main ideas, sequence, details, cause and effect, inferences, and vocabulary. The test encourages analysis of error types, though studies of this topic show no clear differences due to question type. The manual indicates that "teachers should be careful to avoid drawing conclusions from extremely limited samples" (manual, p. 5). They go on to suggest the value of noticing that a student erred 9 of 10 times with a particular question type. The problem with this is that comprehension patterns are rarely this stark, and few students would ever be asked to answer 10 questions of the same type on this test.

SUMMARY. The Burns/Roe Informal Reading Inventory is a practical means for determining reading levels and instructional needs for elementary and secondary students. It provides a useful collection of word lists and carefully graded reading passages for evaluating students' oral and silent reading and comprehension, including some helpful guidance for evaluating students' silent reading speed. The manual is confusing at times, and the authors offer little explanation for several of their recommendations or claims. No evidence is provided concerning any of the psychometric properties of the test such as reliability or concurrent validity, though various design features suggest that these are probably sound. Most of the passages used in this test are stories, so it is questionable how informative this test will be to most secondary school teachers.

REVIEWER'S REFERENCE

Ekwall, E. E. (1976). Should repetitions be counted as errors? *The Reading Teacher, 29,* 365-367.

[57]
Butcher Treatment Planning Inventory.

Purpose: Designed to provide psychotherapists with "relevant personality and symptomatic information early in the treatment process."

Population: Adults in therapy.
Publication Date: 1998.
Acronym: BTPI
Administration: Individual or group.
Price Data, 1999: $118 per starter kit including manual (236 pages), 10 full form reusable question booklets, 25 full form answer/profile sheets, scoring templates, 1 free sample symptom monitoring form reusable question booklet, 1 free sample symptom monitoring ready score answer document; $60 per symptom monitoring supplement hand scoring kit including 10 reusable question booklets and 25 ready score answer booklets; $16 per 10 full form question booklets; $11 per 10 symptom monitoring form reusable question booklets; $25.50 per 25 full form answer sheets; $13 per 25 symptom monitoring answer sheets; $53.50 per 25 symptom monitoring ready score answer documents; $53.50 per manual; $32 per full form scoring templates.
Comments: Normed on ages 18 and over; hand- or computer-scored; paper-and-pencil or computerized administration; computer-generated interpretive reports available.
Author: James N. Butcher.
Publisher: The Psychological Corporation.

a) FULL FORM.
Scores, 16: Validity Scales (Inconsistent Responding, Overly Virtuous Self-Views, Exaggerated Problem Presentation, Closed-Mindedness), Treatment Issues Scales (Problems in Relationship Formation, Somatization of Conflict, Low Expectation of Benefit, Self-Oriented/Narcissism, Perceived Lack of Environmental Support), Current Symptom Scales (Depression, Anxiety, Anger-Out, Anger-In, Unusual Thinking), General Pathology Composite, Treatment Difficulty Composite.
Time: [30] minutes.
b) SYMPTOM MONITORING FORM.
Scores: Includes only Current Symptom Scales from *a* above.
Time: [12] minutes.
c) TREATMENT PROCESS/SYMPTOM FORM.
Scores: Includes only Treatment Issues Scales and Current Symptom Scales from *a* above.
Time: Administration time not reported.
d) TREATMENT ISSUES FORM.
Scores: Includes only Validity Scales and Treatment Issues Scales from *a* above.
Time: Administration time not reported.

Review of the Butcher Treatment Planning Inventory by WILLIAM E. HANSON, Assistant Professor, Department of Educational Psychology, University of Nebraska—Lincoln, Lincoln, NE:

The Butcher Treatment Planning Inventory (BTPI) is a norm-referenced, self-report instrument composed of 210 true-false statements. According to promotional materials, it is designed to assess client characteristics that may facilitate and/or interfere with treatment progress. It is based on the premise that, by identifying clinically meaningful personality characteristics (e.g., a client's attitude toward treatment), as well as a client's "emotional status" (manual, p. xiii), pretreatment planning—and ultimately treatment outcomes—can be improved. In this review, I will comment on three aspects of the BTPI, namely, its development and recommended uses, the adequacy of its norming and scoring procedures, and the overall reliability and validity of its scale scores.

DEVELOPMENT AND RECOMMENDED USES. From the outset, the author attempted to build validity into the instrument. Initially, for example, he defined carefully the constructs of interest, of which there are 14. The 14 constructs, referred to as "process portraits," and the associated BTPI scales, in parentheses, are Consistency of Self-Description (INC), Honesty of Self-Description (VIR), Credible Reporting of Symptoms (EXA), Closed-Mindedness (CLM), Problems in Relationship Formation (REL), Somatization of Conflict (SOM), Low Expectation of Therapeutic Benefit (EXP), Self-Oriented Behavior or Narcissism (NAR), Perceived Lack of Environmental Support (ENV), Presence of Depressed Mood (DEP), Presence of Disabling Anxiety (ANX), Intense Anger Expression or Lack of Anger Control (A-O), Pathological Anger Turned Inward (A-I), and Unusual Thinking or Bizarre Beliefs (PSY). Test items were then developed, using a combination of rational and empirical methods, to measure each of the 14 constructs. In the end, four validity scales (INC, VIR, EXA, and CLM) and 10 clinical scales (REL, SOM, EXP, NAR, ENV, DEP, ANX, A-O, A-I, and PSY) were included in the instrument, each based on 15 to 61 (occasionally) overlapping items. Two composite scales, General Pathology Composite (GPC) and Treatment Difficulty Composite (TDC), were also included to "help the practitioner judge whether a change in symptom expression between two test administrations can provide an appropriate and reliable estimate of changed self-perception" (manual, p. 16). The inclusion of these two scales is a distinguishing feature of the BTPI and will likely prove useful to prospective test users.

Four forms of the instrument are available for use: the Full Form, which includes all 16 scales; a Symptom Monitoring Form, which includes five of the clinical scales (DEP, ANX, A-O, A-I, and PSY); a Treatment Process/Symptom Form, which includes all 10 of the clinical scales; and a Treatment Issues Form, which includes the four validity scales and five of the clinical scales (REL, SOM, EXP, NAR, and ENV). The four forms are not interchangeable; each form is intended for slightly different purposes and has slightly different administration requirements. The Symptom Monitoring and Treatment Process/Symptom Forms, for example, are intended for "symptom tracking" and for detecting potentially problematic personality variables/symptom tracking, respectively. They should be used only if the test user is confident that the client is cooperative, engaged actively in the therapeutic process, and committed to changing his or her life situation. Test users are therefore advised to select BTPI forms carefully, depending on their immediate needs and on the client being assessed.

The author states that the BTPI "can be effectively used at several points during psychological treatment to provide the therapist with information on the client's 'workability' in therapy and to document the progress or lack of progress in reducing disabling symptoms" (manual, p. 10). Other recommended uses include: pre- and posttreatment assessment; case management evaluation; program evaluation; and, as its namesake suggests, treatment planning. Sample questions a test user might hope to answer about a client include, among others: What is the client's motivation for treatment at this time? How open is the client, both in terms of disclosing personal information and in receiving self-relevant feedback? Does the client possess any interpersonal qualities that might interfere with the development of a therapeutic alliance? Potential uses aside, an important practical question still remains: With whom should the BTPI be used? To answer this question, one must consider the adequacy of the instrument's norming procedures. Its scoring procedures will also be discussed briefly in the next section.

NORMING AND SCORING PROCEDURES. Normative information is available for three separate samples: an adult nonclient, or "normal," standardization sample; a college sample; and an adult client, or "clinical," sample. The standardization sample consists of 800 geographically diverse U.S. community-dwelling adults (400 men and 400 women) who volunteered to complete the BTPI, in addition to 11 other assessment-related instruments/questionnaires. Unfortunately, the manual does not report how these individuals were identified and/or recruited to participate in the norming study. Attrition rates are also not reported. Nevertheless, the sample matches closely 1993 and 1995 U.S. Census data and is generally representative of U.S. adults in terms of sex, age, education, and employment/ occupational status. Although adult African American and Hispanic/Latino(a) group members are represented adequately, it is unclear whether members of two other culturally distinct American racial-ethnic minority groups (i.e., Asian American and Native American) are represented adequately. Presumably, members of these two groups are included in the "other" category, but specific percentages are not reported. It is also unclear how, if at all, race-ethnicity affects/relates to BTPI scale scores, as this information is likewise not reported.

The college sample consists of 379 University of Minnesota students (173 men and 206 women) who were enrolled in an introductory psychology course. No other demographic characteristics of this sample are reported. The clinical sample consists of 460 therapist-identified adult outpatient clients (189 men and 271 women) who were in the process of receiving psychological treatment. In contrast to the standardization sample, the college and clinical samples are not representative of U.S. adults. Women, educated individuals (i.e., >2 years of college), and Caucasians, for example, are overrepresented in the clinical sample, and men and racial-ethnic minority group members are underrepresented. The availability of "special norms" for college and clinical samples is, in this case, a double-edged sword. On one hand, it allows test users to make scale score comparisons between hypothetically similar populations. On the other hand, given that the samples are less representative, such comparisons may, at best, be premature and, at worst, be inappropriate.

In any event, to answer the question raised earlier, it appears that the BTPI can be used with adult Caucasian, African American, and Hispanic/ Latino(a) clients across a variety of educational and socioeconomic levels, provided that they are at least 18 years of age and, according to the author,

have at least a 6th-grade reading ability (J. N. Butcher, personal communication, April 18, 1999). However, its use with Asian American, Native American, and U.S. immigrant clients, as well as with clients who have "special needs" (e.g., visually impaired) is equivocal.

Administration and scoring guidelines, discussed in chapter 2 of the manual, are relatively straightforward and easy to understand. BTPI Full and Symptom Monitoring Forms can be administered by hand or by computer. They can also be scored by hand, using a set of transparent templates, or by computer, using scoring software supplied by the publisher. The Treatment Process/Symptom and Treatment Issues Forms, however, can be administered and scored only by computer. Computer-based BTPI profiles and interpretive reports are available for all four forms of the instrument.

To facilitate interpretation, raw scores are converted to linear T-scores, with a mean of 50 and a standard deviation of 10. As noted earlier, test users are advised to use the male and female norms developed for the standardization sample. Although it may prove useful to plot simultaneously the college or clinical (i.e., "Mental Health Context") norms onto a profile sheet, these norms should probably not be used in isolation.

In contrast to the administration and scoring guidelines, the interpretation guidelines are rather complex and difficult to understand. The manual is not particularly clear, for example, about what constitutes an elevated score. Indeed, recommended cut-scores appear to vary across BTPI scales. For some scales (e.g., VIR, EXP), T-scores greater than 55 are considered "high" and, for other scales (e.g., EXA), T-scores greater than 70 are considered "high." Moreover, no interpretative information is provided for "low" scores. Test users are advised to exercise caution in interpreting scale scores and to familiarize themselves with the manual, which, incidentally, deserves special comment.

The manual is over 200 pages long and contains 83 tables, 11 figures, three case illustrations, seven appendixes, and 112 references. Though well written and informative, it is somewhat cumbersome to read. Sifting through the vast amount of information will prove challenging to even the most experienced test users. At a minimum, it would be helpful to have summary tables of individual BTPI scale score interpretations, similar to those presented in other manuals written by the author (e.g., Butcher, Dahlstrom, Graham, Tellegen, & Kaemmer, 1989).

RELIABILITY AND VALIDITY. Reliability estimates of BTPI Full Form scale scores vary considerably. Estimates of internal consistency, for example, range from "unacceptable" (<.70; 38%) to "fair" (.70–.79; 27%) to "good" (.80–.89; 31%) to "excellent" (>.89; 4%; cf. Cicchetti, 1994). Of note, the INC scale, a measure of consistent/inconsistent responding, is not included above, because "the item pairs are heterogeneous and would not be expected to have a psychometric relationship to one another" (manual, p. 53). Split-half reliability estimates are uniformly higher across samples (standardization, college, clinical) and sexes (female, male, combined). Internal consistency and split-half estimates of the Symptom Monitoring, Treatment Process/Symptom, and Treatment Issues Forms are not reported.

Test-retest reliability estimates of BTPI Full Form scale scores range from .55 (INC)–.93 (EXA; standardization sample) to .69 (INC)–.97 (EXA; college sample), with a median test-retest reliability coefficient of .89. Test-retest reliability estimates of the Full Form with the Symptom Monitoring and Treatment Process/Symptom Forms range from .71 (A-I)–.88 (PSY; standardization sample) to .65 (EXP)–.93 (SOM; standardization sample), respectively, with a median test-retest reliability coefficient of .84. Test-retest information is not reported for the clinical sample or for the Treatment Issues Form. These estimates may, however, be spuriously high due to brief time intervals between test administrations (e.g., *Mdn* test-retest intervals: 7 days for the standardization sample, 30 minutes for the college sample). Appropriately, the author urges test users to consider these figures upper-bound estimates of reliability. Standard error of measurement (*SEM*), a common method of estimating the reliability of a given individual's test/scale score, is not reported for any of the scales. This is an especially noteworthy omission—one that should be corrected in future editions of the manual.

Preliminary evidence of content, criterion-related, and construct validity of BTPI scale scores is provided in the manual (by sample). Evidence of content validity is documented more-or-less satisfactorily. It should be noted, however, that expert judges were not involved in the development or rating of any of the test items, which would have

added to the content validity of the instrument's test items/scale scores.

Evidence of criterion-related validity, in particular concurrent validity, is demonstrated by reporting correlations between BTPI scale scores and therapist ratings of client behaviors/symptoms. The author states that "clients with high BTPI scale scores were considered by therapists to manifest the symptomatic and treatment problems defined by the content of the scales" (manual, p. 101). It is unclear, however, whether or not the therapists had access to the clients' test results prior to completing their ratings. If they did, then this may have "contaminated" the data and may have artificially inflated the obtained correlation coefficients. Evidence of predictive validity of BTPI scale scores is still needed.

Evidence of construct validity, in particular convergent validity, is demonstrated by reporting correlations between BTPI scale scores and 10 well-established tests/scales that measure similar constructs. Reported correlation coefficients are sufficiently high across samples and are generally in the expected direction. Evidence of discriminant validity, however, is less compelling across samples. Of note, BTPI scale scores are highly interrelated, with nearly half (44%) of the total sample interscale correlation coefficients at or above .50. Factor analyses of the instrument have resulted in a four- or seven-factor solution, depending on whether the scales or the individual test items are studied.

Obviously, more validation research is needed. It will be particularly important, for example, to demonstrate the incremental and treatment validity of the BTPI scale scores. On page 18 of the manual, the author states:

> The scales provide convenient summaries of important problem areas and can serve as an effective vehicle for giving personality and therapy-related feedback to the client. The information the client was provided through self-assessment can affect the course of therapy by aiding in the treatment planning and by altering the change process itself.

The extent to which the BTPI is, in fact, shown to (a) aid in treatment planning, a special case of incremental validity; and (b) alter the change process, a special case of treatment validity, will likely play a major role in determining the instrument's fate.

SUMMARY. Overall, the BTPI is an intriguing new assessment instrument. Its emphasis on treatment planning and on measuring *nonspe-*

cific therapeutic factors (e.g., a client's attitude toward treatment) makes it unique among available assessment instruments. Its true merits, however, are largely undetermined. Recommendations for its use in clinical practice (cf. Ben-Porath, 1997) are, at this point, based mostly on potential rather than on demonstrated usefulness/performance. Regardless, Anastasi (1992) aptly reminds users that tests are merely tools and that "whether any tool is an instrument of good or harm depends on how the tool is used" (p. 610). If used responsibly, the BTPI has, in my opinion, the "potential" to do clients, and for that matter therapists, more good than harm.

REVIEWER'S REFERENCES

Butcher, J. N., Dahlstrom, W. G., Graham, J. R., Tellegen, A., & Kaemmer, B. (1989). *Minnesota Multiphasic Personality Inventory-2 (MMPI-2): Manual for administration and scoring.* Minneapolis, MN: University of Minnesota Press.

Anastasi, A. (1992). What counselors should know about the use and interpretation of psychological tests. *Journal of Counseling and Development, 70,* 610–615.

Cicchetti, D. V. (1994). Guidelines, criteria, and rules of thumb for evaluating normed and standardized assessment instruments in psychology. *Psychological Assessment, 6,* 284–290.

Ben-Porath, Y. S. (1997). Use of personality assessment instruments in empirically guided treatment planning. *Psychological Assessment, 9,* 361–367.

Review of the Butcher Treatment Planning Inventory by SAMUEL JUNI, Professor, Department of Applied Psychology, New York University, New York, NY:

The underlying issue encountered when evaluating the Butcher Treatment Planning Inventory (BTPI) is a methodological one: If we truly rely on self-report, then why bother with scaling procedures at all—we might as well just ask the respondent straightforwardly about any issues. We can inquire directly whether the person feels depressed, confused, or other questions. It is arguable that the respondent may not understand certain clinical terminology, or may have an idiosyncratic interpretation of clinical terms. It is not clear, however, just what such new instruments add over the standard DSM diagnostic procedures (e.g., SADS questionnaire; T5:2305). "The BTPI is … based on the idea that if you want to know something about a client, you ask and he or she will share it" (manual, p. xiii). This absolute statement is hardly convincing. What if the client is unaware of a problem, or is unwilling to share it? Attempting to assert a broad base for the instrument, the author describes it as atheoretical, although it is admittedly closest to the cognitive-behavioral orientation. The author argues that although the approach is behavioral, it focuses on "non-specific" or common factors in psychotherapy.

Although the descriptions can be incorporated into dynamic approaches, the self-reports are not quite symptom related, but deal with clinical labels and general behaviors as well. Alas, the behavioral limitations in questioning preclude dynamic elaboration because of omissions that cannot be corrected. It is noteworthy that the manual veers into presenting the instrument as relevant to personality change efforts. However, the behavioral orientation leads one to expect that symptoms, rather than personality, be the circumscribed focus of this instrument.

The validation section is difficult to read due to acronyms that are used for the scales. The document would be much enhanced if the scale names were spelled out.

The instrument features instructions for plotting scores on a graph, where the Validity Scales, Treatment Issues, and Current Symptoms are all connected in a continuous regression line. Although this parallels the Minnesota Multiphasic Personality Inventory (MMPI), it comes with no interpretive framework. In addition, the linkage of the line across validity and clinical scales is difficult to interpret, and not explained by the manual.

Part of the manual is a manifesto on psychotherapy philosophy. The instrument reflects this philosophy. The instrument is presented within the context of "assessment therapy," the approach that sees feedback as promoting behavioral change. Paradoxically, in describing the scale construction, the author details the manner in which process variables in assessment were isolated from the treatment process. Applications of the overall inventory are highlighted to include pretreatment assessment as well as progress during therapy. I would add, as well, posttreatment assessment.

In the normative study, volunteers were paid $25 to $35 dollars for their time. The variations of these payments are not explained. The median test-retest interval was 7 days. It would be instructive to know the range as well. Test-retest correlations are reported as mostly being in the range of .80 or above. In fact, only 8 of the 16 uncorrected correlations are equal to or greater than .80, of which two are actually composite scores for which reliability would be expected to be artifactually inflated. Test-retest reliability for the college student sample used an interval of 30 minutes. The authors recognize the shortness of this period, but still argue for the relevance of the results. In terms of accepted psychometric practice, one would be hard put to construe any meaning from such short retest periods.

The extensive field study validation with outpatients was conducted by asking therapists to identify clients who might be willing to participate. Clearly, this is a preselected group of clients. More questionable is the fact that BTPI results were returned to the therapists, who were then asked to complete progress notes 3 months later. The threat of a self-fulfilling prophecy effect looms large here, for it is feasible that therapists' inputs in the progress notes were influenced by the BTPI report in the client file, and can thus hardly be taken as validating those very reports. In addition, the qualitative ratings of therapists after 3 months do not have clear reliability or validity in terms of how they were collapsed in the presentation in the manual.

The validity and reliability studies support the legitimacy of the instrument. There are, nonetheless, shortcomings in the detailed Process Portraits—shortcomings that are understandable given the scope and robustness of the inventory. In addition, there are occasional item anomalies that detract from the readability and reliability of the assessment. These are outlined below.

PROCESS PORTRAIT SHORTCOMINGS.

Consistency of Self-Description: This scale isolates clients who are *unable* or *unwilling* to present themselves consistently, who may therefore have difficulty in treatment if their cooperation is needed. One can argue with the "unable" criterion because therapeutic methods do exist to deal with resistance.

Honesty of Self-Description: The independence of this portrait from the former is perplexing. What use would consistency be to the psychotherapy without honesty?

Credible Reporting of Symptoms: Here, again, it is not at all clear how credibility differs from honesty.

Closed-Mindedness: This factor includes both the lack of sharing and the lack of listening to feedback. It also parallels the incongruous heterogeneity of the Consistency of Self-Description factor, in that it encompasses both unwillingness and inability to engage in these behaviors. It would seem that even from a strict behavioral point of view, these disparate tendencies would have differential therapy implications, rendering their amalgamation problematical.

Problems in Relationship Formation: This factor is described succinctly, but its implications insofar of transference are studiously avoided.

Self-Oriented Behavior or Narcissism: This factor is described as centering on the feeling that one need not alter one's behavior to suit others. A rather marginal aspect of narcissism is then added to the scale definition—the feeling that one does not receive all the attention one deserves from others. This addition deviates from the phenomenological factor description and is clearly limited to the psychodynamic view that is underrepresented in this instrument.

Two factors are described that are functionally equivalent: Presence of Depressed Mood and Pathological Anger Turned Inward. Behaviorally, the latter cannot be observed and is the dynamic explanation of the former.

Validity Scale: Similar item pairs are used to determine consistency of response. An example is "I really like to try out new and different things" and "I usually like to try out different ways of doing things." The slight variations in wording are not explained. Why not just repeat the item twice, as is done in other tests for validity (e.g., MMPI)?

It is curious that Close-Mindedness is included in the Validity Scale cluster. Especially in view of the definition of Close-Mindedness as featuring unwillingness to listen to feedback, it appears that it includes elements that are not at all related to validity. Being open to new ideas should have no effect on the validity of self-presentation.

Included in the Treatment Issue Scale is Somatization of Conflict. This scale purportedly measures a "tendency to avoid dealing with conflict through the development of somatic symptoms" (manual, p. 11). In fact, most of the items simply deal with the presence of bodily complaints. The facet of conflict avoidance is interpretative in nature, and psychodynamic in orientation. This orientation is not representative of the self-report that this inventory focuses upon, and is especially inconsistent with the cognitive behavioral stance with which it most identifies.

It would appear that Problems in Relationship Formation is used both as a screen for therapy appropriateness and an index of change in psychotherapy as the process evolves.

Perceived Lack of Environmental Support: The author clearly is focused on the perception of the client. It would appear that as a Treatment

Issue scale, the items would be more productive if they focused on the actual rather than perceived aspects of support, for it is the former that are most crucial for a client's perseverance in behavioral change programs.

It is not clear why the author needs to create new scales for anxiety, anger, and unusual thinking, rather than resorting to well-validated scales in the literature (e.g., MMPI [T5:1697], Manifest Anxiety Scale [T5:2214], or various scales of aggression).

Unusual Thinking: The definition includes a reference to "malignant thinking." This is an unusual term, and is quite unexpected in a behaviorally based nosological work.

The author also lists addenda of item groups (which are not scales per se) dealing with specific item content for special problems such as suicidality, drug abuse, violence, and abusive relationships. It is not clear why these clusters were not established psychometrically as bona fide scales and are left to perusal instead of quantification.

The relevance of the Somatization Scale is marginal. This scale deals with the tendency to get sick in times of distress. It seems not to have much impact on conceptualizing a problem.

The manual discusses resistance to therapy when therapy is initiated at the behest of another. The Narcissism scale is meant to measure the tendency of clients to be so self-oriented that they think they are in no need of change. Apparently, the author is implicitly taking sides in secondary referrals, assuming that the client must need changing if a referral is made. Is it not feasible that the referral source is incorrect, and that the client is correct when she or he insists that no change is necessary? In addition, the manual links Narcissism to low self-esteem. It is not at all clear how the two are linked conceptually, as this seems a psychodynamic theoretical linkage, rather than one based on phenomenology of self-report.

In interpreting the Depression Scale, the author deviates most noticeably from his avowed intent of reflecting responses noninterpretively. High numbers of responses about feeling tired and lacking motivation are seen as indicative of suicidal contemplation. The author seems to have fallen into the personality analysis trap he had painted away into a corner. According to the self-report commitment, suicidality should be best assessed by direct suicidal items, not by multiple responses to depressive items that have no manifest relationship to suicide.

The Aggression Inward Scale is interpreted almost projectively, contingent on a psychodynamic personality approach. Overtly, the items reflect self-blame. Psychodynamically, this can be seen as Turning Against the Self, presuming that the original aggression is not directed anywhere intrinsically, but rather is being redirected defensively by the respondent. Again, this violates the avowed self-report rationale of the inventory.

It is noteworthy that the inventory chooses anger as an affective divide, differentiating between those who turn anger inward and those who turn anger outward. Being closely related to the psychodynamic defensive mode, one can question why a parallel divide was not demarcated for positive affect as well. Is it not just as reasonable to differentiate between those who turn positive love feelings inward and those who turn them outward?

INC and EXP show low alpha coefficients that the manual reports as "not unexpected" (p. 54). The rationales given for this demurral are equivocal, however. INC consists of item pairs that are similar, with the scaling looking for inconsistencies across pairs. Although it is true that the items are not expected to relate, one could compute "matching scores" for each pair, and then use the scores in a test of internal consistency. The EXP scale is described as being inherently lacking in internal consistency because there are various disparate reasons why clients do not seek treatment. The logic here is quite weak—if the reasons are disparate enough to make the scale internally inconsistent, then the rationale of considering the items as one scale score is invalid as well.

The Therapy Experience Survey asks respondents if they ever thought of speaking to a psychologist or psychiatrist about problems. One wonders why social workers are ignored in this item because they do provide a major portion of psychotherapy in this country.

In the factor analysis, Defensiveness is defined by the Overly Virtuous Self-View Scale. The psychodynamic interpretation here is surprising for an instrument that attempts to be phenomenological and descriptive. Similarly, Somatization of Conflict is a scale name one would expect in a psychodynamic theoretical instrument. Which conflict theory is referenced here is unclear because the items deal with bodily symptoms with nary a mention of conflict. Dynamically, furthermore, one could just as well invoke alternate constructs such as guilt or depression. There is an implicit message here, as well, that the respondent is somaticizing and not really sick. The basis of this assumption is not evident at all.

The Inconsistency Scale is described as suggesting that items were responded to randomly. It thus comes as a surprise to the reader to find this scale included in a larger factor of Cynicism and Uncooperativeness, where clear intent of misinformation is attributed to the respondent.

The Exaggerated Problem Presentation Scale shows anomalous gender differentials. For the college sample males, the scale seems associated with increased mental health problems. Yet, women generally produce higher scores on this scale than do men. There is an apparent inconsistency here that admittedly falls beyond the scope of the manual, but is perplexing nonetheless.

The description of Close-Mindedness in the manual is multifaceted and confusing. At times, high scorers are described as aloof; at other times, they are described as being controlling in relationships. Overall, it is not clear whether such individuals are closed "minded" or have a closed communication style. There seems to be no particular personality theory that would justify uniting such attributes into one construct.

The Perceived Lack of Environmental Support Scale centers entirely on client's beliefs. Such beliefs are seen as relevant to therapy outcome. It is remarkable that the manual does not consider the possibility that such beliefs may, in fact, reflect the reality of the environmental situations of some clients.

ITEM ANOMALIES.

Inconsistent Responding features sets of paired items where response consistency would be expected. It also includes one triad of similar items: "1. I can usually make my mind up with great ease; 71. I don't usually take much time to think over problems before I decide something; 99. I find that I can usually make up my mind with great ease." This triad is then used in the scale by computing one "hit" for 1 vs. 71 and one "hit" for 1 vs. 99. This loads the response for 1 doubly into the scale. Furthermore, it is not clear why 71 vs. 99 was not used instead.

Occasionally, two ideas are combined in one item, making item intent unclear. Consider Item

9: "I get so upset with myself at times for giving in to people that I want to hurt myself"; or Item 24: "I sometimes have thoughts of hitting or injuring someone else to get back at them." Why subsume the problem of subservience to others with suicidality, or the notion of aggression with that of revenge?

Some items have qualifications of "these days" (e.g. 5, 11), "now" (e.g., 22), or "recently" (e.g., 34); some refer to the past (e.g., 13, 21), and others have no limiting time referent. In some items, tenses are actually mixed. Consider Item 8: "I frequently get annoyed over things people have said to me." No rationale is given to these tense differentials in the manual.

Some items are limited to specific demographics, leaving those outside these demographics with no rational means of responding. Consider Item 67, which refers to irritability on the job due to pressure. The response of an unemployed person surely would introduce unreliability into the relevant scales.

Occasional items do not refer to the respondent at all, but rather to the truth versus falsehood of an abstraction. Consider Item 90 referring to the assertion that most problems could be solved by using horoscopes and astrology charts, Item 178 about the effects of vitamins on mental health, or Item 200 referring to the advisability of keeping feelings to oneself.

The Anger-Inward scale includes some items that do not seem relevant to this construct. Consider, for example, Item 187: "I have many regrets over things I have done wrong to others." Where is the anger component in this assertion?

SUMMARY. The inventory is impressive in its scope and its psychometric integrity, despite anomalies in factor definitions, specific validation iniquities, and item construction shortcomings. Its theoretical foundation and perspective are distinctly behavioral and, as such, its applicability to other diagnostic perspectives is curtailed. The use of the inventory in assessment and treatment planning is justified, although its utility over and above standard DSM interview-based diagnosis has not been convincingly demonstrated.

[58]

California Computerized Assessment Package.

Purpose: Designed as a "standardized assessment of reaction time and speed of information processing."

Population: Ages 21–58.
Publication Dates: 1986–1998.
Acronym: CalCAP.
Scores, 7: Simple Reaction Time, Choice Reaction Time for Single Digits, Serial Pattern Matching, Lexical Discrimination, Visual Selective Attention, Response Reversal and Rapid Visual Scanning, Form Discrimination.
Administration: Group.
Forms, 2: Standard, Abbreviated.
Price Data, 1998: $495 per complete kit including manual ('96, 80 pages), standard battery and abbreviated battery; $10 per demonstration program; $15 per manual.
Time: (20–25) minutes.
Foreign Language Editions: Danish, Flemish, French, German, Norwegian, and Spanish editions available.
Comments: IBM AT or compatible, 512K RAM, color display or active color matrix laptop, and MS-DOS 3.1 or greater required.
Author: Eric N. Miller.
Publisher: Norland Software.

Review of the California Computerized Assessment Package by HOWARD A. LLOYD, Neuropsychologist, Hawaii State Hospital, Kaneohe, HI:

The California Computerized Assessment Package (CalCAP) is a computerized assessment tool modeled after the Continuous Performance Task (CPT). There are multiple versions of the Continuous Performance Task, all of which measure sustained attention and reaction time. The CalCAP improves on most standard versions of the CPT by including reaction time tasks that require lexical discrimination, selective visual attention, visual scanning, and form discrimination. The manual provides adequate descriptions of each of the seven tasks that comprise the standard, full-length administration of this test. An abbreviated form of the CalCAP can also be administered. Unlike many psychological tests, the CalCAP is available in multiple languages, for which the author and publishers should be praised.

The CalCAP manual provides a good description of the test and administration procedures. The reference card facilitates ease of administration by eliminating the need to refer to the manual for basic information on starting and running the program. A considerable amount of information regarding how the computer files are organized and how this data can be stored and managed is also included. This is at times technical material and may be of limited interest or usefulness for many users of this test. The manual also provides basic interpretive guidelines that are consistent with the implied intended use of the CalCAP as a screening tool for identification of neuropsychological impairment. Unfortunately, the author does not clearly specify the intended use of this test, and it is left to the examiner to determine how the test should be used. This is of concern particularly because in the introduction section of the manual the author indicates that the CalCAP was designed to "assess a number of cognitive domains, including speed of processing (reaction time), language skills, visual scanning, form discrimination, recognition memory, and divided attention" (p. 1), whereas later in the manual the author indicates that the "cognitive functions assessed by the CalCAP program are best described as timed psychomotor skills requiring focused and sustained attention" (p. 17). Such lack of clarity regarding the intended use of the CalCAP makes it vulnerable to misuse as a more complete neuropsychological instrument than the author seems to have intended. The CalCAP appears to be best used as a screening tool to identify patients in need of further evaluation using traditional neuropsychological tests, and as a measure of focused, sustained, and divided attention.

The CalCAP was normed on a group of 641 men ranging in ages from 21 to 58 years, with a mean education of 16 years. These normative data are reported for the entire sample and for age- and education-stratified groups. The vast majority of the normative subjects were Caucasian (93%), and minority subjects were underrepresented. This raises some concerns about the usefulness of the CalCAP with non-Caucasian individuals. It is also unfortunate that a sample of women was not included. The author does present normative data from an independent group of researchers indicating that there is no difference between the performance of men and women on the CalCAP, though the sample size for this study was relatively small. Supplemental norms gathered by other independent researchers for third, fourth, fifth, and sixth grade children are also reported in the manual. It is also unfortunate that normative data are not available for native speakers of the various languages in which the CalCAP is available.

The psychometric properties of the CalCAP are well within acceptable ranges. The internal consistency reliability coefficients for simple and choice reaction time were high (.77–.95) supporting the consistency with which the CalCAP measures reaction time. The 6-month test-retest coefficients for the CalCAP are more variable (.20–.68), reflecting the impact of state-dependent factors on this reaction time measure (e.g., fatigue). However, it should be noted that the lowest test-retest coefficients were for the Simple Reaction Time measures (.20–.29), and that the Choice Reaction Time test-retest reliability coefficients were more respectable (.43–.68). It is notable that the 6-month test-retest reliability for the CalCAP Choice Reaction Time measures was consistent with the 6-month test-retest reliability of several conventional neuropsychological tests (.47–.77).

The validity evidence for scores from the CalCAP was gathered by correlating performance on the CalCAP with performance on several conventional and commonly used neuropsychological tests (Digit Span, Symbol Digit Substitution, Rey Auditory Verbal Learning Test, Verbal Fluency, Trails A&B, and Grooved Pegboard). These correlations were, however, rather low (.02–.37). It is unfortunate that the author did not attempt a similar comparison between the CalCAP and other computer-administered reaction time measures (e.g., VIGIL, TOVA, Connors CPT). Such a comparison would have been a more appropriate means of assessing construct validity.

SUMMARY. In summary, as stated in the manual, "the skills measured by the CalCAP are best described as timed psychomotor skills requiring focused and sustained attention" (p. 17). This task is a good screening measure for neuropsychological dysfunction, with the emphasis on screening. Major limitations are associated with limited normative information on minorities, women, older adults, and children. As noted above, it is also unfortunate that the CalCAP has not been compared with other computerized measures of reaction time and focused and sustained attention. The strengths of the CalCAP include its relative ease of administration and interpretation, availability of versions in multiple languages, and its usefulness for repeated testing as might be necessary in research or rehabilitation settings.

Review of the California Computerized Assessment Package by GORAN WESTERGREN, Chief Psychologist, and INGELA WESTERGREN, Neu- ropsychologist and Licensed Psychologist, Department of Clinical Psychology, State Hospital, Halmstad, Sweden:

The California Computerized Assessment Package (CalCAP) is, as the name suggests, a computer-based test developed in the tradition of experimental cognitive laboratories and is modeled on the Continuous Performance Task, a measure of sustained attention and reaction time. Because of this, the test can be administered by technical level personnel and the computer controls the presentation of complex stimuli to the subject. These features reduce variability in test administration.

In its standard design (10 Simple and Choice reaction time measurements), CalCAP gives a broad assessment of a number of the patient's cognitive functions. The functions assessed by the CalCAP program are chiefly described as timed psychomotor skills requiring focused or sustained attention.

Scores from the CalCAP also demonstrate high levels of construct validity compared to traditional neuropsychological tests that measure motor speed and attention (Trail-Making, Grooved Pegboard), verbal memory (Rey Auditory Verbal Learning Task), memory span (Wechsler Adult Intelligence Scale—Revised Digit Span), and verbal fluency.

The computer automatically records subject performance and produces a report in seconds, using age- and education-specific norms derived from 641 men ranging in ages from 21–58 years (with a mean education of 16 years). The final scores are available immediately in tabular and graphical formats. The response measurements are presented as mean and median reaction times as well as total numbers of true and false positive responses. In addition, by using Signal detection theory, the CalCAP offers measurements of the subject's ability to discriminate between the true signal and character items and the degree to which the subject deviates from the optimal likelihood ratio.

In the manual there is also access to normative data for third to sixth grade children, although in limited populations. There are also some normative data for comparison of scores for men and women. There are no statistically significant differences between men and women after adjusting for differences in age and education.

There are no norm data for the foreign language editions (Danish, Flemish, French, German, Norwegian, and Spanish) but there is really no reason to believe that the data from English-speaking environments should not be directly applicable.

From the reliability point of view it is naturally a strength in the CalCAP that the stimulus material is presented under strictly controlled forms and that the responses are measured with the same precision. The constructor of the test believes that the measurements can be used to assess slowed cognition, focused and divided attention, sustained attention, and rapid visual scanning and that this is ideal for longitudinal assessment of cognitive changes due to disease, medications, and cognitive rehabilitation. The test battery is said to have relevance for studies of clinical groups such as multiple sclerosis, hyperbaric nitrogen narcosis, HIV infection, dementia, drug abuse, and traumatic brain injury. This applies to the qualified clinical and research level. However, at a more "everyday" clinic level, a lot of work is required to translate these measurements into terms and functions that are more directly understood by nonpsychologists.

The graphical interface seems a little aged with its DOS environment and ought to be converted to Windows immediately. With this conversion the whole test would be clearer and the administration would be significantly easier. With the fast developments in the IT field there is naturally a problem with computer-based tests because the graphical construction must continually be updated in order for the test not to appear out-of-date. The test's outward appearance could affect the patient negatively. Due to the current graphical design of the CalCAP, however well thought, the assessment appears to be out-of-date or still at a prototype stage.

SUMMARY. The CalCAP is a broad, cognitive based, reaction time test of most interest for research work and for the advanced clinic. The CalCAP would need to be adapted for the Windows environment to satisfy the normal clinician.

[59]

California Q-Sort (Revised Adult Set).

Purpose: Designed as "a systematic way of comparing different [intra-individual] personalities with one another."
Population: Adults.
Publication Dates: 1961–1990.
Acronym: CAQ-90.
Scores: Ratings in 9 categories ranging from most uncharacteristic to most characteristic.
Administration: Individual.

Price Data, 1998: $25 per sampler set including instructions ('90, 5 pages), sorting guide ('90, 4 pages), and 100 cards.
Time: (30–40) minutes.
Comments: For an adaptation for children, see The California Child Q-Set (T5:365).
Author: Jack Block.
Publisher: Mind Garden, Inc.
Cross References: See T5:373 (43 references) and T4:362 (20 references), T3:356 (1 reference); for reviews by Allen L. Edwards and David T. Lykken and excerpted reviews by Samuel J. Beck and John E. Exner, Jr., see 6:72 (2 references); see also P:28 (1 reference).

Review of the California Q-Sort (Revised Adult Set) by GEORGE DOMINO, Professor of Psychology, University of Arizona, Tucson, AZ:

The California Q-Sort (Revised Adult Set) (CQ-Set) had its beginnings in the early 1950s as a way of codifying personality descriptions of subjects, such as Air Force officers, who were being assessed at the Institute of Personality Assessment and Research (IPAR) of the University of California, Berkeley. In these studies, individuals typically chosen because of leadership or achievement (e.g., creative architects, writers, medical school students, women mathematicians, etc.) were invited to come to IPAR in small groups to be assessed with a variety of instruments and procedures. After each assessment, the staff needed to describe each examinee in a variety of ways, including standardized procedures. Out of this context there evolved two major techniques: the Adjective Check List and the CQ-Set.

The CQ-Set thus has been used, and continues to be used, in dozens of studies not only from IPAR and its "sister" Institute of Human Development, but also by other researchers. There are of course many Q sets now available, but the CQ-Set is by far the best known and most widely utilized.

The CQ-Set consists of 100 descriptive statements such as "responds to and appreciates humor," "interested in members of the opposite sex," that are presumed to provide a comprehensive description of an individual's personality. The sorter, usually but not necessarily a trained individual in the area of mental health and/or personality assessment, describes the subject (who could be the sorter, but is usually a different person) by sorting the 100 statements into nine categories, ranging from most to least *salient*. A fixed number of statements are sorted into each category, following a quasinormal distribution. No scores are obtained. The distribution of statements simply represents a description of a particular individual using a standardized set of items, and a standardized distribution. Nevertheless, an amazing number of statistical analyses can be undertaken, and these are clearly discussed in Jack Block's monograph [reprinted in 1978 by Consulting Psychologists Press, Inc.] on the Q-sort method.

So much for background information. The current CQ-Set is a "revised" edition. A comparison of the 100 original statements with their revised version indicates that although all 100 items were retained, a number of them show revised wording. For example, Item #2 was originally: "Is a genuinely dependable and responsible person"; now the item reads "is dependable and responsible." Item #17 originally read "behaves in a sympathetic or considerate manner"; the "or" now reads "and." Thus, most if not all the changes appear to be minor, cosmetic, and perhaps unnecessary. According to the publisher, the revisions were made to "adapt the language for sorting by lay users."

The revised version is now called the CAQ-90; the 90 refers to the year of copyright and is somewhat misleading in that a user may well look for a 90-item set. Anyone ordering this receives four pages of instructions, five pages of sorting guide, and the 100 statements. The instructions are simple, clear, and can be found as well in Jack Block's monograph. The sorting guide consists of two duplicate sets (why two?) where the sorter can record the card numbers for each pile in a quasinormal table, and then copy these onto a record sheet. Actually, the first table is not needed because one can directly fill out the record sheet. In addition, if one is going to compare two or more Q-sorts, for example to calculate a correlation coefficient, there are better layouts that can be used to minimize transcriptions of pile values. The 100 statements are printed on standard two-sided pages, so that the user would first need to reproduce. The materials that accompany the CAQ-90 have no discussion of psychometric issues such as reliability and validity, nor of the key issues relevant to the CQ-Set, such as content validity, issues of social desirability, interrater agreement, etc. Jack Block's monograph has the information, but it is sadly outdated, and does not provide the user with current citations. Repeated attempts to obtain a copy of the monograph from the publisher failed until a photocopied version was provided.

SUMMARY. I feel rather saddened, like seeing an old friend in shabby clothing. The CQ-Set can be extremely useful and should be introduced to a whole new generation of researchers and practitioners who may not be familiar with this technique. But simply rewording some items is not the way to do it.

REVIEWER'S REFERENCE

Block, J. (1961). *The Q-Sort method in personality assessment and psychiatric research.* Springfield, IL: Charles C. Thomas.

[60]
Campbell-Hallam Team Development Survey.

Purpose: "Designed to give teams standardized feedback on their strengths and weaknesses."

Population: Members of intact working teams.

Publication Date: 1994.

Acronym: TDS.

Scores, 19: Resources (Time and Staffing, Information, Material Resources, Organizational Support, Skills, Commitment), Efficiency (Mission Clarity, Team Coordination, Team Unity, Individual Goals, Empowerment), Improvement (Team Assessment, Innovation, Feedback, Rewards, Leadership), Success (Satisfaction, Performance, Overall Index).

Administration: Group.

Forms, 2: Observer, Member.

Price Data, 1999: $180 per preview package including 10 individual survey booklets, team report, individual report for each team member, manual (216 pages), administrator's guide (15 pages), and facilitator's guide (16 pages); $15 per individual survey and report; $10 per 10 observer survey forms; $60 per team report including scoring of one team report, narrative summary profile, miniature profile, and item response summary; $35 plus $10 per item per supplemental items summary reports; $30 per manual; $10 per administrator's guide; $20 per facilitator's guide; $50 per set of manual, administrator's guide, and facilitator's guide.

Time: (20–25) minutes.

Authors: Glenn Hallam and David Campbell.

Publisher: NCS (Minnetonka).

Cross References: See T5:379 (1 reference).

Review of the Campbell-Hallam Team Development Survey by FREDERICK T. L. LEONG, Professor of Psychology, The Ohio State University at Columbus, Columbus, OH:

The factors that influence work groups and how they can function more effectively has been a longstanding interest in the field of Industrial/Organizational Psychology (see Dunnette, 1976).

However, during the last decade, increased attention has been paid to the importance of teams and team work in organizations from both organizational scientists and practicing managers (e.g., Parker, 1990; Katzenbach & Smith, 1993). The Team Development Survey (TDS) is a recently developed measure of team performance and functioning that fits with this trend. The Team Development Survey purports to measure the strengths and weaknesses of a team as perceived by members of that team. There are 18 scales with the Team Development Survey with measured dimensions such as organization support, mission clarity, team unity, and satisfaction.

The Team Development Survey (TDS) was developed using a combined rational and empirical strategy. The TDS was initially developed based on conceptual and theoretical grounds to measure the various dimensions that are relevant to assessing team performance and functioning. Next, the Team Development Survey was revised empirically through an evaluation of the items and the various psychometric properties to refine and improve the scale until it more closely captured the underlying theoretical conceptual scheme. In combining the rational and empirical approaches to instrument development, the TDS is able to take advantage of the strengths of both approaches.

In general, the TDS has acceptable psychometric properties. For example, the internal consistency is quite adequate with a median Cronbach's alpha of .69 (ranges from .61 to .95). Test/retest stability (17-day interval on average) was also quite good with a median correlation of .80 (ranges from .69–.90). Empirical evidence for the construct validity of the TDS, although not extensive, is adequate. The authors have sought to evaluate the construct validity of the Team Development Survey by comparing the perceptions of the team members with the results of their own individual perceptions. The assumption is that if the TDS is measuring team performance and functioning accurately, then most of the individual team members will perceive the TDS results as consistent with their own perceptions. In other words, it should be found that when asked individually the team members are agreeing that the Team Development Survey results are consistent with their own individual perceptions of how the team is performing. The authors did this by calculating the correlations between the average team scores and the average observer's scores, and they also calculated correlations between the average team scale scores and the performance assessed by observer's team leader and the members as a way of assessing criterion-related validity. Therefore, there seems to be some evidence of the construct and criterion-related validity of scores from the Team Development Survey.

The advantage of the Team Development Survey is that it is a standardized form of assessing team performance that provides feedback to team members and team leaders as to the various dimensions of team functioning and relative strengths and weaknesses. The Team Development Survey also has the advantage of allowing individual members to find out discrepancies between their own individual perceptions and the overall team perceptions of the various dimensions. In addition, the Team Development Survey has normative scores for use in establishing a comparative standing with regards to each team's functioning.

Whereas the TDS is a rigorously developed measure of team performance and functioning, there are a couple of problems with the current version. First, authors of the TDS provided only a partial assessment of the criterion-related validity of the measure. Although the established relationships between the TDS scores and observer scores is one aspect of criterion-related validity, also needed are direct links to outcomes. For example, a more important type of criterion-related validity study would be to demonstrate that TDS scores are actually significantly related to organizational outcomes such as productivity. Theoretically, those teams that have more resources and higher levels of efficiencies (e.g., mission clarity, team unity, and empowerment) should be more productive than those teams with less resources and lower levels of efficiencies as measured by the TDS. In other words, team performance should be meaningfully related to various aspects of work performance. This type of criterion-related validity is still lacking for the TDS and should be collected in future studies.

Second, there are problems with the measurement of a high level phenomenon like team performance. In general, most psychological tests measure phenomena at the individual level of analysis such as a person's level of self-esteem, self-efficacy, or various temperamental characteristics. Whenever psychologists attempt to measure higher level phenomena such as organizational climate and so on, the complexity and challenges are therefore multiplied. This is the same with any attempts to measure team performance and functioning. As indicated by James and Jones (1974) in research with organizational climate there is a potential methodological problem in trying to assess higher level phenomena such as organizational climate by simply summing the responses of all the members of an organization. The same problem pertains here with regards to assessing team performance by summing individual team members' perceptions. This problem has to do with the validity of interpretations of group level phenomena by simply assessing individual perceptions. This remains a thorny methodological issue and is a limitation of the Team Development Survey that was not addressed adequately by the authors and needs to be taken into account in future assessments.

SUMMARY. In conclusion, although there are concerns about the methodological issues of assessing higher order phenomena such as team performance by using individual team members' perceptions and the partial assessment of criterion-related validity, the Team Development Survey is rigorously developed and shows psychometrically sound measurement of team performance that has few parallels or competitors. For example, I refer to the Teamness Index, which was reviewed in *The Eleventh Mental Measurements Yearbook* (11:417) as a comparison and that particular scale has no psychometric validation whatsoever. The TDS is a conceptually developed scale that measures all the major dimensions of team performance and effectiveness quite adequately. The Team Development Survey can be recommended for group organizational interventions and assessment notwithstanding the methodological issues discussed earlier.

REVIEWER'S REFERENCES

James, L. R., & Jones, A. P. (1974). Organizational climate: A review of theory and research. *Psychological Bulletin, 81,* 1096–1112.

Dunnette, M. D. (Ed.). (1976). *Handbook of industrial and organizational psychology.* Chicago: Rand McNally.

Parker, G. M. (1990). *Team players and team work: The new competitive business strategy.* San Francisco: Jossey-Bass.

Katzenbach, J. R., & Smith, D. K. (1993). *The wisdom of teams: Creating the high-performance organization.* Boston: Harvard Business School.

Review of the Campbell-Hallam Team Development Survey by MARY A. LEWIS, Director, Human Resources, Chlor-Alkali and Derivatives, PPG Industries, Inc., Pittsburgh, PA:

The Campbell-Hallam Team Development Survey (TDS) consists of two forms: a 72-item Member Survey for team members (with the option of adding up to 15 supplemental questions) and a 22-item Observer Survey for customers, managers, consultants, or others who work with the team. Minimum team member size is three, and the number of observers can range from 4 to 10. The administrator's guide is well organized and easy to follow, and the survey questionnaires are also well prepared and intuitively easy to complete.

Scores are provided on 18 scales organized around four categories and an overall score based on all items. Each scale is based on from three to six items, and the scale score is reported as a T score, standardized with a mean of 50 and a standard deviation of 10 (note: the Satisfaction scale was designed with a mean of 51). Five items are considered team performance items. The norms were developed from a sample of 1,881 individuals representing 194 teams covering a wide variety of levels and functions. Reliability was estimated for both internal consistency (median Cronbach's alpha = .69) and test-retest (median correlation .80 over a 27-day span).

Two types of reports are provided: a team report, to be used by the facilitator, and a member report. Each member report includes the team profile and team item responses as well as the individual member's personal responses. A narrative summary is also provided, which includes suggested strengths, areas for improvement, and suggested actions for improvement. The team report is similar, without the individual information, and also includes suggested steps for discussing the results. A team facilitator's guide provides detailed and more elaborate recommendations on a process to review and use the results.

The TDS was developed based on an extensive review of theory and research, as well as the practical experience of the authors. This review, which is well documented in the manual provided, led to the development of the Team Success Model. This model, on which the survey is based, proposes that teams build resources, find ways to use them, attend to process that will help them improve, and then measure success based on team performance and team member satisfaction. A 166-item version of the survey was developed and, after several iterations of data collection and refinement, reduced to the 72-item member survey.

The data were then rescored using all samples to develop the norms referred to earlier. During the item development and refinement process, an observer booklet was created to get an outside perspective on the team. Observer items were written for each of the 18 scales and five performance items in the Member Booklet.

The TDS manual provides a great deal of data on scale intercorrelations (they are moderate to high) and item intercorrelations by scale (they, too, are moderate to high). Although the scales are conceptually independent, they do not appear to be statistically independent. The validity evidence includes a cursory discussion of face validity and an interesting philosophical treatise on construct validity that raises the issue of the relevance of the concept of "true score" for perception of a team function. Statistical support for construct validity is nonetheless provided through member/observer scale/item correlations. Concurrent validity was calculated using the average of the five performance items for team members, for team leaders, and for observers as criterion measures. These three criteria were correlated with the 18 scale scores and the overall score. Median correlations were .37 for average leaders performance items, .5 for average observer, and .6 for average team member. These correlations are moderate to high, and are slightly higher than the intercorrelations of the scales.

It is conceivable that the 18 scales of the TDS are actually some much smaller number of empirical scales, and that the reporting process could be simplified into much fewer dimensions. However, the primary purpose of this tool is to develop teams. The conceptual scales this instrument represents are easily understood by team members, observers, leaders, and facilitators. The instrument is designed to be used with little external support, other than scoring of results, by organization members who have had little technical training. For that reason, the use of these scales makes a great deal of sense. Scale independence is not necessarily an accurate representation of the real world, and in fact is an artifact imposed by statistical models. In this case, scale understanding seems to be a legitimate test construction goal.

Scale scores were examined by a number of demographic characteristics, including gender, age, and race, by dividing teams up into categorical groupings such as all male, all female, and mixed teams to describe the composition of the sample.

In addition, scale scores were correlated with such variables as proportion of females on the team, or average leader age. In general, these demographic variables appeared to have little relationship to scale scores, although leader age seemed to be positively related to scale score ($r = .21$) and number of meetings per week was negatively related to scale score ($r = -.16$). It would appear that the scales work equally well across a wide range of teams, both in terms of demographics and job function.

The manual also provides supplemental material on content, importance, and action items for each of the scales. This material, coupled with the facilitator's guide, should provide enough support to allow effective team development sessions.

SUMMARY. The TDS is a well designed, easy-to-administer tool that can provide feedback to drive a team building/team development process. The materials and scales are easily understood, rest on sound theory, were developed using appropriate techniques, and should provide a solid basis for team building. The administrator's guide is self-explanatory, the facilitators' guide is well thought out, and the manual provided enough background information to thoroughly understand the scales and their meaning. I would recommend the TDS as a team building tool, but would strongly recommend that the facilitator selected be someone from outside the team, with presentation and facilitator training.

[61]

Canadian Achievement Survey Tests for Adults.

Purpose: "Designed to measure achievement in reading, language, and mathematics ... subject areas commonly found in adult basic education curricula."

Population: Adults.

Publication Date: 1994

Acronym: CAST.

Scores, 6: Reading (Vocabulary, Comprehension), Language (Language Mechanics, Language Expression), Mathematics (Mathematics Computation, Mathematics Concepts and Applications).

Administration: Group.

Levels, 3: Completed up to Grade 6, completed Grades 7 to 9, completed Grades 10 and above.

Price Data, 1997: $63 per 25 test booklets (specify level); $32 per 25 hand-scorable answer sheets; $58 per 50 machine scorable answer sheets; $44 per manual (53 pages); $21 per review kit including brochure, 1 copy each of Levels 1, 2, and 3 test booklets, hand-scorable answer sheet, machine-scorable answer sheet, and directions for administering.

Time: (90) minutes.

Author: Canadian Test Centre.

Publisher: Canadian Test Centre, Educational Assessment Services [Canada].

Review of the Canadian Achievement Survey Tests for Adults by JOHN O. ANDERSON, Professor, Faculty of Education, University of Victoria, Victoria, British Columbia, Canada:

The Canadian Achievement Survey Tests for Adults (CAST) is a battery of multiple-choice tests of reading, language, and mathematics developed for three levels of respondent. It has been adapted from the Comprehensive Tests of Basic Skills (T5:665). The tests are intended to provide information to better inform placement and admission decisions about adult learners for basic education programs.

The CAST consists of six subtests of 15 to 18 items each: Vocabulary, Comprehension, Language Mechanics, Language Expression, Mathematics Computation, and Mathematics Concepts and Applications. Each of the three levels of the test is contained within a single booklet consisting of four-option multiple-choice items. The battery should take about 90 minutes to complete. The user has the choice of machine-scorable answer sheets or a U-Score answer sheet that provides an easy-to-use scoring key incorporated into the sheet itself. A test manual is provided that outlines the development, structure, and scoring of the CAST. The test manual also provides detailed instructions for administering the tests.

The levels of the test correspond to grade levels in Canadian schools and the tests have been normed in 1992 with a sample of over 16,000 Canadian students from grades 5 to 12 with the unexplained exception of grade 9 students. To facilitate meaningful results it is suggested that the appropriate level of the test be given to the respondent. To assist with this a *locator test* is available, and the test manual suggests that some consideration be given to the nature of the program for which the test is being used in order to use an appropriate level.

The test results are to be converted into grade-relevant percentiles, stanines, and scale scores. Through the use of the percentiles, stanines, or scale scores, the user can locate a respondent within a relevant grade level based upon the norms provided. Although the test manual does provide a brief introduction to grade-equivalent scores, the publishers have wisely decided against the use of grade-equivalent scores with the CAST.

The reliability of the CAST was estimated by comparing CAST scores with scores on the Canadian Achievement Tests, 2nd Edition (CAT/2) for students at different grade levels who took both tests. The correlation between the CAST and the related CAT/2 test was used as the index of reliability. These values hovered at about the .90 value suggesting that the two sets of scores were quite similar. The standard errors of measurement are also provided in the test manual with a welcome caution about the use of test scores as estimates of respondent ability. The *SEM*s ranged from 1.5 to 1.9 on the subtests, which would mean that they constitute about 10% of the score range (maximum subtest scores are 15 to 18). This would further translate into the fact that the 95% confidence interval would encompass about 40% of the score range for each subtest. So it is indeed important for the user to treat scores as estimates of respondent ability rather than as firm point values.

The norms provided with the CAST are of two types. The grade-relevant norms were derived from samples of 1,800 to 3,600 students from Grades 5 to 12 and are provided for each of the six subtests at each of the three levels of the CAST. The user can easily convert the raw score to stanines or percentiles for the grades most relevant to that level of the test. The program-relevant norms are developed for Level 3 of the CAST and appear to be based on samples of convenience drawn from programs largely in Ontario and British Columbia with samples ranging in size for 85 to 624. The test manual points out that these may provide helpful information in score interpretation, but caution must be taken in using these norms for any decisions about respondents. To assist the user in score interpretation, some examples of score transformations and interpretations would be most helpful.

SUMMARY. The CAST presents itself as a convenient means to provide information relevant to student placement in adult education programs—a difficult and complex task. The test is convenient and does provide information on student abilities in the kinds of tasks for which multiple-choice testing is suited in the areas of language and computation. The selection and placement of individuals in the wide range of adult education programs will require some program-specific analysis to evaluate the quality of decisions made and the effectiveness of information such as that provided by instruments such as the CAST.

Review of the Canadian Achievement Survey Tests for Adults by MARK H. DANIEL, Associate Director of Development, American Guidance Service, Circle Pines, MN:

The Canadian Achievement Survey Tests for Adults (CAST) is a paper-and-pencil, multiple-choice test battery designed to assess the reading, language, and mathematics skills of adults in basic education programs. Its primary purposes are to assist in placement into instructional programs and to measure growth in skills following instruction.

Each of the three levels of the CAST consists of six tests, two each in Reading (Vocabulary and Comprehension), Language (Mechanics and Expression), and Mathematics (Computation and Concepts/Applications). With one minor exception, norms are provided only for tests and not for composites. Thus, the publisher intends the instrument to be interpreted at the level of the individual tests. Indeed, promotional literature suggests that users may administer the tests selectively to suit the purpose of evaluation.

The three levels are designed for individuals who have completed different amounts of schooling: Level 1 for up to Grade 6, Level 2 for Grades 7–9, and Level 3 for Grade 10 or higher. More precise assignment of levels to examinees may be achieved with the Locator Test, which consists of 20 Vocabulary and 20 Mathematics items. There are two levels of the Locator Test, one for examinees with 6 years of schooling or less, and the other for those with 7 or more years.

The three levels of the CAST are identical in the number of items per test, in the overall and test directions, and in the number of answer choices per item. The tests are administered under strict time limits, which are the same across levels. A common answer sheet, in either scannable or self-score format, serves all three levels (all of which have the same scoring key). For these reasons, and because there are no dictated items, all three levels of the CAST may easily be administered simultaneously to a single group.

CONTENT AND PRESENTATION. The CAST item content appears to be well suited to Canadian adults. The subject matter is relevant to adult interests and activities, and the spellings, measurement units, and postal addresses are Canadian. The items appear to have been carefully edited, and the test booklets and answer sheets are well designed and attractive, with ample white space.

Vocabulary (18 items). This test uses synonym, antonym, and sentence completion items.

Reading Comprehension (15 items). Each level includes three reading selections, which are interesting and appropriate for adults. Many of the questions rely on inference.

Language Mechanics (15 items). This test focuses on capitalization and punctuation. Items ask the examinee to add necessary punctuation, or select the sentence or sentence fragment that has correct capitalization and punctuation. Several questions on each level refer to a business letter.

Language Expression (18 items). This test concerns language usage and sentence and paragraph structure. Items ask the examinee to identify the correctly written word, phrase, or sentence; combine two sentences; or select the sentence that fits a particular location in a paragraph or develops a topic sentence.

Mathematics Computation (15 items). This test consists of calculation problems covering arithmetic, fractions, decimals, percents, signed numbers, and algebraic expressions. Each five-choice item includes the option "none of these," which forces the examinee to work out each answer precisely.

Mathematics Concepts and Applications (15 items). This test contains word problems dealing with measurement, algebra, numeration, and data interpretation.

LOCATOR TESTS. Each of the two Locator Tests consists of 20 synonym items and 20 mathematics calculation items. The content of the Level 1 Locator Test is noticeably easier than the content of Level 1 of the CAST, which is surprising because the purpose of this Locator Test is to select between Levels 1 and 2 of the CAST. An examinee must score at least 90% correct (36 out of 40) on the Level 1 Locator Test to be assigned Level 2 of the CAST. Thus, the Level 1 Locator Test is inefficient for its purpose. It appears from a content examination that examinees who score near the middle of the raw score range on the Level 1 Locator Test will find Level 1 of the CAST quite difficult. Level 2 of the Locator Test is better suited to its function, with the cutting score for choosing between CAST Levels 2 and 3 occurring near a raw score of 20.

DEVELOPMENT. A "Test Manual Working Draft," the only available documentation, provides minimal information about the development and psychometric properties of the CAST. The CAST is made up of items taken from the Canadian Achievement Tests, Second Edition (CAT/2; T5:384), which itself is adapted from the Comprehensive Test of Basic Skills, Fourth Edition (T5:665). Items were selected according to their appropriateness for adults; cosmetic changes were made to some items to make them suitable for adults. There is no discussion in the manual of the rationale behind the CAST item blueprint, other than that items were chosen for their relevance to adult basic education curricula and to the demands of today's society.

RELIABILITY AND VALIDITY. All information about the psychometric properties of the CAST is derived from CAT/2 standardization data for students in Grades 5–8 and 10–12. No information on the reliability and validity of scores from the CAST for adults is reported, despite the availability of data for 2,289 community-college and technical-college students who took Level 3 and for whom program-specific norms are presented in the manual.

For school-age examinees, reliabilities are not provided in the manual but they may be computed from the raw-score standard deviations and standard errors of measurement reported for each grade level. (According to personal communication from the publisher, these standard errors are based on internal-consistency reliabilities.) The reliabilities thus computed are similar across tests and grade levels. Median test reliabilities are: Vocabulary, .77; Reading Comprehension, .71; Language Mechanics, .67; Language Expression, .75; Mathematics Computation, .77; and Mathematics Concepts and Applications, .72.

For several reasons, it is difficult to predict from these data what the test score reliabilities will be for adult students. The program-specific norm tables for Level 3 show raw-score standard deviations for the Reading and Language tests that are similar to or smaller than those for the reliability samples for Grades 10–12, suggesting that, for these tests, score reliabilities for adult students are lower than the values reported above. For the Mathematics tests, the program-specific samples have somewhat higher standard deviations than the high-school samples, which would imply higher score reliabilities.

However, looking at just one level of the CAST (in this case, Level 3) is an incomplete way of evaluating the reliability of the scores from the instrument, which is a multilevel system. Presumably, different individuals in a group being assessed are routed to different CAST levels. The group routed to a particular level is a restricted-range subsample of the original group. What a user should want to know is the reliability of the overall CAST system for the entire group. One would expect this overall reliability to be higher than the reliability of a single level. However, from the information given it is not possible to estimate that overall reliability.

Correlations between scores from the CAST and the CAT/2, based on the large samples (4,300 to 8,800 students per level) used in the equating study, are offered as measures of alternate-form reliability. The correlations between corresponding tests are high (median = .91), but inasmuch as the CAST is made up of CAT/2 items there is item overlap between the variables being correlated. These appear to be correlations between two different scorings of a single administration of CAT/2. As such, they have little bearing on reliability.

Reliability is important for achieving one of the CAST's state goals, to provide measurement of growth in skills following instruction. Assuming a score reliability of .75, the standard error of the difference between two scores on the test is approximately .7 of a standard deviation. The modest reliabilities and relatively small number of items on each test weaken their suitability for assessing change.

No validity data of any kind are presented for the CAST. Users must rely on their judgment of the face validity of the items.

NORMS. There are two sets of norms. One set is for elementary and secondary school students in the 1992 CAT/2 norming study, based on an equating of CAST and CAT/2 scores. These norms are of questionable relevance for evaluating adults. The way in which they are presented further limits their usefulness. Each CAST level has norms for a different range of grades, and the ranges do not overlap (Level 1, Grades 4–6; Level 2, 7–9; and Level 3, 10–12). Thus, different examinees assigned to different CAST levels cannot be scored on the same grade norms.

Actually, a mechanism does exist by which raw scores from all CAST levels could be placed on a single score scale, thereby providing access to a wider range of norm groups. This is the system of "scale scores" printed in the grade-norm tables for each test. However, these scale scores are not used in scoring the CAST (with one minor exception). Instead, each level is treated as an independent instrument with its own limited set of norms. A resourceful user could utilize the scale scores, but this is not explained in the manual.

The other set of norms, called "program-specific" norms, are for seven samples (averaging about 325 cases each) of first-year students in various technical, engineering, trade, health-sciences, and business programs in Canadian colleges. These norms are limited to CAST Level 3. There is little difference among the norms for the seven groups on the Reading and Language tests, although on the Mathematics tests the engineering and technical students score higher than the other groups.

One final type of normative data is provided: grade equivalents for a literacy composite (the average scale score on the Reading and Language tests) and a numeracy composite (the average on the Mathematics tests). Grade equivalents extend from Grade 6 to Grade 12. This is the only use of the scale scores in the CAST.

As noted earlier, CAST Level 1 appears to be considerably more difficult than Level 1 of the Locator Test, and will likely be challenging for low-functioning adults. It is appropriate in difficulty for the average child in Grade 5 or 6. Thus, it may be excessively difficult for some of the intended examinees (i.e., "Adults entering or enroled [sic] in basic education programs, requiring beginning literacy," manual, p. 1).

SUMMARY. The strengths of the CAST are its content, which appears to be interesting to and appropriate for adults, its attractive presentation, and its brevity and ease of administration. The quality of the technical and normative information is not, however, at a similarly high level. It appears little effort has been made to provide the user with information or scoring procedures appropriate to a multilevel instrument that incorporates routing. The available reliabilities (which may underestimate the instrument's true reliability) are modest, and do not encourage use of the instrument for one of its stated purposes, measuring growth following instruction. Normative data likewise suffer from failure to treat the instrument as a multilevel system. The absence of any reliability or validity

information for adults is a serious lack. Fortunately, most of these problems could be corrected through appropriate data collection and analysis, which it is hoped will be included when the final version of the manual (as opposed to the working draft) is published.

[62]
Career Decision-Making Self-Efficacy Scale.

Purpose: "Measures an individual's degree of belief that he/she can successfully complete tasks necessary to making career decisions."

Population: College students.

Publication Date: 1983–1994.

Acronym: CDMSE.

Scores, 6: Self-Appraisal, Occupational Information, Goal Selection, Planning, Problem Solving, Total.

Administration: Group.

Price Data: Available from publisher.

Time: Administration time not reported.

Comments: A 25-item short form is also available.

Authors: Nancy E. Betz and Karen M. Taylor.

Publisher: Nancy E. Betz (the author).

Cross References: See T5:403 (1 reference).

Review of the Career Decision-Making Self-Efficacy Scale by JAMES K. BENISH, School Psychologist, Helena Public Schools, Adjunct Professor of Special Education, Carroll College, Helena, MT:

The Career Decision-Making Self-Efficacy Scale (CDMSE) is a tool for measuring "an individual's degree of belief that he/she can successfully complete tasks necessary to making career decisions" (manual, p. 8). The scale was developed for group administration to college students, and has as its foundation Bandura's sources of information regarding the concept of self-efficacy expectations. Previous studies conducted by the authors apply the theories of self-efficacy to vocational psychology and counseling through the application of "Crites' (1978) model of career maturity and assessed in the Career Maturity Inventory" (manual, p. 8). There has been much research in the area of career decision making, and this scale is based on that research.

The CDMSE was developed to provide information regarding "Self-Appraisal, Occupational Information, Goal Selection, Planning, and Problems-Solving" (manual, p. 10). The 50-item scale is intended to be administered in a group setting utilizing generic answer sheets provided by the user. A short version (25-item scale) is also available and retains the same five-factor structure as the complete CDMSE. User qualifications necessitate knowledge of career development and the theories from which this test was based. The CDMSE is a research tool that can be used for career counseling within a classroom setting. Although graduate level training is not specified, it would appear that familiarity with psychometric principles should be adhered to in administering either form. No time limit is given for administration of either form; however, completion time would depend on number of subjects and whether answers are scored electronically or manually. The individual subscales each contain 10 items that, according to the authors, have a "perceived difficulty of career decision-making tasks" (manual, Table 1). Test subjects must respond to each 10-point scale ranging from "Complete Confidence [9] to No Confidence [0]" (manual, p. 9), with each response based on the subject's preconceived ability to accomplish each task.

STANDARDIZATION AND NORMS. The CDMSE was initially administered to 346 midwest college students attending either a private liberal arts college or a large public university. This 1983 validation of the test was used to establish scoring and administration criteria. Of the 346, there were 128 males and 218 females, and data gathered were used to support reliability and validity of the scores including factor analysis. Since then, there have been numerous studies reported in an extensive reference section of the manual. An accompanying journal article underscores the authors' (and others) continuing research of the CDMSE (Betz, & Luzzo, 1996). Clear, concise tables were listed in the manual for item analysis, mean and standard deviation of scores, and gender comparisons for the combined subject group. However, statistical analysis for other normative data, including reliability and validity evidence, was contained within the text of the manual rather than being arranged in a more readable table form.

RELIABILITY. Internal consistency reliability was estimated with coefficient alpha on the five subscales of the CDMSE. These values for Self-Appraisal, Occupational Information, Goal Selection, Planning, and Problem-Solving were .88, .89, .87, .89, and .86 respectively. Total reliability for scores from the 50-item test was .97, and the accompanying journal article reported the 25-item

alpha value of .94. These very respectable reliability findings were replicated in more recent follow-up studies provided by the authors and others involved in comparing the CDMSE with other questionnaires. Another unpublished study "reported a coefficient alpha of .93 and test-retest reliability of .83 over a one and one-half month interval" (manual, p. 10).

VALIDITY. A rather expansive narrative within the administration manual highlights various studies and conclusions regarding the authors' discussions of the evidence of content, concurrent, and construct validity of the CDMSE, and how it compares with other tests and research tools. The authors also presented evidence for predictive and discriminant validity based on a plethora of research found throughout the narrative portion of the test manual. Although the test findings support most validity factors, there remains evidence of the need for further study and interpretation of data gathered from the above mentioned research. The CDMSE scores were found to have statistically significant nonzero correlation with scores from Holland, Daiger, and Powers' (1980) My Vocational Situation, with values ranging from .28 to .40. Another interesting finding involving construct validity came from a 1990 study that "reported that the CDMSE significantly differentiated three groups of students categorized on the basis of college major status: Declared Majors (M = 335), Tentative Major Choice (M = 3.8) and Undecided (M = 283)" (manual, p. 15). Finally, although the predictive validity for the CDMSE appears strong, much of the research presented within the manual contains disjointed references of questionable importance for the practitioner.

SUMMARY. The usefulness of the application of the CDMSE for use in vocational psychology and career counseling is strong, especially for students who lack the self-efficacy and career decision making needed for setting goals or achieving success in college. Providing students with the information obtained from their responses might facilitate decision-making skills and reduce frustration with future career planning. As a guidance tool for college age students, the CDMSE is a practical tool that should be given strong consideration. As a research instrument, the CDMSE has proved useful as a forum for ongoing follow-up and scrutiny. It would appear that it has become a standard with which to compare other instruments. Also, it would appear that it has been used to develop new hypotheses for research studies. It appears to be continually evolving as a test instrument to study, and based on the presentation on validity evidence in the manual, for example, this may not be useful for the practitioner searching for a validity table, and finding only a lengthy narrative. Perhaps publishing the CDMSE into a finalized, bound copy would further its practicality and application for those choosing to use it as an assessment tool.

REVIEWER'S REFERENCE
Betz, N. E., & Luzzo, D. A. (1996). Career assessment and the Career Decision-Making Self-Efficacy Scale. *Journal of Career Assessment, 4,* 413–428.

Review of the Career Decision-Making Self-Efficacy Scale by RICHARD W. JOHNSON, Adjunct Professor of Counseling Psychology and Associate Director Emeritus of Counseling & Consultation Services, University Health Services, University of Wisconsin—Madison, Madison, WI:

According to Albert Bandura's theory of self-efficacy, a person's belief in his or her ability to perform a particular behavior significantly affects that person's choices, performance, and persistence. Karen Taylor and Nancy Betz developed the Career Decision-Making Self-Efficacy Scale (CDMSE) as a means of assessing the relevance of this theory to career choice and development.

SCALE COMPOSITION. The CDMSE consists of 50 items that represent critical skills involved in career planning. The authors prepared 10 items to measure each of five career-planning competencies (accurate self-appraisal, gathering occupational information, goal selection, making plans for the future, and problem solving) identified by John Crites (1978) in his model of career maturity. For each item, respondents indicate on a 10-point scale their degree of self-confidence in performing the task mentioned in that item.

NORMATIVE DATA. The CDMSE manual provides means and standard deviations for the Total score, 5 subscales, and 50 items for 346 college students who participated in validation studies. The test authors found little or no significant differences in the mean test scores for men and women or for students enrolled in different types of colleges. Most of the students (79%) in the normative sample were first-year students.

The CDMSE has been designed to be used with college students; however, it can be readily adapted for use with other populations. Relatively little information regarding the influence of cultural background on test scores is available. One study cited in the manual reported that African-American students scored higher than did students from other racial or ethnic groups. Somewhat inconsistent results have been reported in regard to the influence of age, sex, and academic achievement on CDMSE scores.

The average student marked "much confidence" (between 6 and 7 on a scale that runs from 0 to 9) for most of the items. For this reason, the CDMSE may not discriminate as well among students as it would if it had a higher ceiling.

RELIABILITY. Alpha coefficients of consistency are relatively high for all of the subscales (alphas ranged from .86 to .89 for the normative sample described above). The alphas coefficient for the Total score was .97, which indicates that the item content is highly consistent across all 50 items. A test-retest reliability of .83 has been reported for the Total score over a 6-week period.

VALIDITY. Factor analyses do not support the use of the five categories obtained from Crites' theory. The authors suggest that the CDMSE be viewed as "a generalized career self-efficacy measure covering a multifaceted domain of career decision-making behaviors" (p. 11). Despite the results of the factor analyses, the authors recommend retaining the five subscales as a "useful framework" to orient clients to the process of career counseling and career education.

Scores on the CDMSE are highly correlated with scores on other measures of self-confidence, such as self-esteem and occupational self-efficacy scales; however, they also tap unique aspects of self-confidence associated with career planning. In several multiple regression studies, the CDMSE explained more of the variance in career decidedness than all other variables, including measures of self-esteem, occupational self-efficacy, career salience, locus of control, anxiety, verbal ability, and math ability.

As expected, a number of research studies have found high correlation coefficients between scores on the CDMSE and measures of career indecision such as the Career Decision Scale, My Vocational Situation, Career Maturity Inventory, and Fear of Commitment Scale (Betz & Luzzo, 1996). CDMSE scores also have differentiated among students with declared majors, tentative majors, and no majors in the expected manner. All of these studies support the convergent validity of the CDMSE.

To serve as a relatively pure measure of self-confidence in career planning, scores on the CDMSE scores should be independent of ability and social desirability measures. Research studies show low correlations between CDMSE scores and career decision-making skills (as opposed to attitudes), SAT scores, or ACT scores. These data support the discriminant validity of the instrument. No studies of the relationship between CDMSE scores and scores on a measure of social desirability have been reported.

Most of the validity studies conducted with the CDMSE have been based on the relationship between scores on the CDMSE and other measures obtained at the same time or within a short time interval. Longitudinal research studies are needed to determine if CDMSE scores can effectively predict behavioral criteria such as career decidedness, engagement in career planning tasks, and career persistence over longer time periods.

RECENT DEVELOPMENTS. The authors have recently prepared a short, 25-item form of the inventory consisting of the best five items from each subscale (Betz, Klein, & Taylor, 1996). Research conducted thus far with the short form indicates that it may produce higher validity coefficients than the full-scale form. The alpha reliability coefficient for the total scale remains high (alpha = .94). In addition, the authors have recently proposed that the 10-point response continuum be reduced to 5 points to further simplify the form (N. E. Betz, personal communication, March 15, 1998).

SUMMARY AND CONCLUSIONS. The CDMSE has been shown to provide reliable and valid measures of self-confidence in making career decisions in a number of different situations. As such, it can serve a valuable purpose in both research and counseling. In research, it can be used to study factors associated with the causes and consequences of self-confidence in career decision making. In counseling, it can be used to assess the client's need for treatment on this issue and his or her responsiveness to different interventions designed to improve self-confidence in career decision making. Because of its brevity, the short form can be particularly valuable in situations where the instrument is administered more

than once. Additional research on the instrument itself is needed in regard to the relationship between the long and short forms, its use in different cultures or with different populations, and its validity in predicting behavioral criteria.

REVIEWER'S REFERENCES

Crites, J. O. (1978). Career Maturity Inventory. Monterey, CA: CTB/McGraw-Hill.

Betz, N. E., Klein, K. L., & Taylor, K. M. (1996). Evaluation of a short form of the Career Decision-Making Self-Efficacy Scale. *Journal of Career Assessment, 4,* 47–57.

Betz, N. E., & Luzzo, D. A. (1996). Career assessment and the Career Decision-Making Self-Efficacy Scale. *Journal of Career Assessment, 4,* 413–428.

[63]

Career Factors Inventory.

Purpose: Designed to provide an understanding of career decision-making readiness.
Population: Ages 13 and over.
Publication Date: 1997.
Acronym: CFI.
Scores, 4: Need for Career Information, Need for Self-Knowledge, Career Choice Anxiety, Generalized Indecisiveness.
Administration: Group.
Price Data, 1999: $4.95 per client kit including self-scorable item booklet and answer sheet and interpretation; $31 per kit including self-scorable item booklet and answer sheet, interpretation, and Applications and Technical Guide (37 pages); $16.50 per 10 self-scorable booklets; $2.20 per single self-scorable booklet; $30 per Applications and Technical Guide.
Time: (5–10) minutes.
Comments: Inventory is untimed; also part of the careerhub.org website.
Authors: Judy M. Chartrand, Steven B. Robbins, and Weston H. Morrill.
Publisher: Consulting Psychologists Press, Inc.

Review of the Career Factors Inventory by AYRES D'COSTA, Associate Professor of Education, The Ohio State University, Columbus, OH:

The Career Factors Inventory (CFI) is "designed to help people determine whether they are ready to engage in the career decision-making process" (Applications and Technical Guide, p. 1). It consists of 21 items requiring Likert-type response, using five rating levels ranging from Strongly Disagree (1) to Strongly Agree (5). The CFI can be conveniently administered by a counselor to clients, on an individual or group basis in about 5 to 10 minutes, and provides scores on four scales (Need for Career Information, Need for Knowledge, Career Choice Anxiety, and Generalized Indecisiveness). Another good feature is that the Inventory is self-scorable and provides assistance for plotting an Individual Profile based on these four scores, and for interpreting this Profile.

The Applications and Technical Guide claims that the CFI "has been used successfully in a variety of educational, business, and counseling settings" (p. 15). Materials available to this reviewer were this Guide and the Self-Scorable Booklet and Interpretation.

TECHNICAL AND PSYCHOMETRIC ISSUES. Career choice is a critical challenge in vocational counseling, and the CFI, which claims to address career indecision, therefore has the potential to be an important counseling tool. The CFI postulates two causes for such indecision: a lack of information about oneself or about careers, and poor decision-making approaches due to anxiety or general indecisiveness. The CFI does not address counseling challenges related to diagnosing or following up bad career choices.

Given its simplicity and obvious patency, the CFI is a remarkable tool with respect to its construct definition efforts. The Guide indicates that 31 items were initially written to represent five constructs associated with career decision making, based on a review of literature. Principal components factor analyses, including confirmatory factor analysis, were utilized to decide on the current four constructs. The individual item error variances reported are quite high, indicating a serious problem for this item style. The test-retest (2-week and 3-month administration intervals) and internal consistency reliability indexes range in the 60s and 80s, the higher values occurring for the only trait measure among the four scales, General Indecisiveness. These reliability indexes are modest.

The goodness of fit results for the four constructs, as well as the other discriminant/convergent validity studies, appeared reasonably convincing to this reviewer. The validity of the four scales, based on correlations with similar scales from other instruments, appear to be supportive of the authors' claims, although there are some glaring exceptions. Several of the correlations are low (below .30), and a couple appear to be in a direction opposite to that ordinarily expected. One table that is noteworthy is the change in CFI scores following counseling intervention. In other words, assuming the intervention was indeed effective, CFI was able to document it, although one wishes statistical tests of significance were also available.

Gender differences were noted only for "General Indecisiveness," with females reporting greater indecisiveness. No ethnic group differences were noted. Again, no statistical tests were conducted.

SCORING AND INTERPRETATION ISSUES. The administration instructions recommend that, before taking the CFI, students be helped to understand its purpose and the four scales it measures. Although this clarifies its intent, it also makes this self-report instrument extremely easy to fake. The scoring is simplistic, and no latent trait attempts have been made to justify the addition of the item ratings within a scale.

The norms used in interpreting CFI scores are based on convenience samples of college students in general psychology courses at two universities, presumably associated with the authors. No justification is provided, other than "career decision making was deemed salient for these individuals" (p. 7). To judge other more diverse clients, such as high school students and special adult groups, using the distribution of scores obtained by this select college group, appears obviously inappropriate. No attempts are apparent in the Guide to pool data for better norms given the wide variety of clients claimed to have been successfully tested using the CFI.

The interpretation of scores identifies three regions using two arbitrary statistical cutoffs, "Mean" and the "Mean plus one Standard Deviation," and assumes a normal distribution of scores. No justification, theoretical or empirical, is provided for these assumptions or interpretations.

The Guide also recommends plotting the four scale scores and joining these points to obtain a polygon-like profile. This approach can lead to overinterpretation. There is no rationale for the sequence of the four scales, other than they belong together in pairs to two major constructs, Lack of Information and Difficulty in Decision-making. Nevertheless, this reviewer was impressed by the very practical Interpretation Model and the clinical counseling approach presented in chapter 4 of the Guide. The case studies presented with the relevant CFI profiles should be very helpful to counselors.

OVERALL UTILITY AND EVALUATION. Despite its overarching and therefore inappropriate title, the CFI must be recognized as a quick and simple tool designed to do a limited job, namely determine readiness for career decision-making in terms of four factors assumed to be the key problems. It should not be expected to do any more than that. The term "career factors inventory" used in the title is misleading because it is too broad. The CFI is not a typical career decision-making tool in that clients are not enabled to make good career decisions. Nor is it an inventory of all factors related to careers or the choice thereof. It merely addresses readiness to make decisions, and that, too, in a very simplistic way.

Another major problem in the CFI is an inherent weakness in the wording of several of the items, which, in the mind of this reviewer, poses a serious validity concern. The phrase, "Before choosing or entering a particular career area, I *need to ...*" (italics added), is intended by the authors to reflect a compelling feeling, which is then scored as a deficit or need. Students who agree are deemed to indicate a deficit, therefore, a lack of readiness for career decision making. Unfortunately, this choice of phrasing can also be understood as asking a student to reflect a belief about what is appropriate to do in the particular circumstance. It is quite reasonable to Agree to the special "need" as an appropriate or wise step you believe you should first take. For example, it is wise to need to talk to, or recognize the importance of talking to engineers before choosing engineering as a career. Therefore, scoring this response as a deficit could add to the item error variance and also adversely impact the validity (interpretation) of the CFI scores. The high item error variance and low validity coefficients reported in the Guide might be reflections of this problem.

SUMMARY. Assuming that the confusing phrase mentioned above will be clarified in the CFI administration process, this reviewer believes that the CFI is a limited but reasonable counseling tool. A change in title would also be in order to more accurately reflect what this Inventory is designed to do. With these limitations recognized and corrected, this reviewer applauds the authors' efforts to meet the psychometric standards appropriate to this potentially useful counseling instrument.

[64]

Career IQ Test.

Purpose: "Developed to assist individual in self exploration, vocational exploration, and career development."

Population: Ages 13–adults.

Publication Date: 1997.

Scores, 18: Aptitude (Verbal, Numerical, Spatial, Perceptual, Manual Dexterity, General Ability); Interest (Artistic, Scientific, Nature, Protective, Mechanical, Industrial, Business Detail, Selling, Accommodating, Humanitarian, Leading-Influencing, Physical Performing).

Administration: Group.

Price Data, 1997: $49 per complete kit including manual (42 pages) and CD-ROM with user's guide; $27 per manual.

Time: Administration time not reported.

Comments: Computer administered; Windows 3.1 or higher or Windows 95, MS-DOS Version 5.0 or later, or Macintosh System 7.0 or higher required.

Author: Virtual Knowledge.

Publisher: Virtual Knowledge.

Review of the Career IQ Test by WAYNE CAMARA, Executive Director of Research & Development, The College Board, New York, NY:

The Career IQ and Interest Test is a multimedia-based self-assessment designed to assess individuals' career interests and aptitudes and provide a match to over 400 job classifications. It includes an aptitude and interest test, results of which are then compared with results from self-assessments of one's interests and abilities and provides a match with about 400 occupations.

This product is primarily a software and entertainment product rather than a serious career assessment. There is no information in published materials concerning the validity, reliability, or normative basis for the product, and despite repeated inquiries to the distributor and publisher, no information was provided. "The results of this program should be used to motivate self-exploration, vocational exploration and career development" (manual, p. 7) among individuals from the ages of 13 through adult. The software appears to be an effective motivational product for individuals who may be willing to self-explore careers and jobs. The product takes advantage of audio, photography, and colorful graphics in the introduction and provides a useful menu for getting through the program. Overall, it is an attractive package, with little to no substance beyond that available free from the Department of Labor's occupational database.

The test taker first completes the introduction where he or she is presented with some basic information on the assessment and career exploration in general, followed by self-assessments. One is asked to rate their aptitude in six areas and their interests in 12 vocational areas: Artistic, Scientific,

Nature, Protective, Mechanical, Industrial, Business Detail, Selling, Accommodating, Humanitarian, Leading-Influencing, and Physical Performing. Ratings are completed using a 5-point scale from 1-very low to 5-very high. Results from the self-assessment are plotted for the test taker after completion. Anchors are provided for each of the scale-points (e.g., rank 5: 90–99 percentile); however, because they are only provided in the directions, users are likely to forget the descriptors when checking their self-ratings. After completing the ratings, test takers are presented with a profile of aptitude self-ratings and interest self-ratings. The profile simply reports back the ratings the test taker just generated and provides no additional information.

Following the self-assessments, test takers then complete an Aptitude test, which is composed of five-subtests. Each subtest provides one or more screens of instructions, followed by an example. Two of the subtests are highly speeded and questions move from easy to difficult as testing continues. Each test has a timer in the top of the screen and the manual notes "some of the tests are designed so that many individuals will not complete all of the items in the time allowed" (p. 6). The five subtests include:

1. Vocabulary Aptitude requires the test taker to select two words from the four provided that are either synonyms or antonyms (the test does not tell you which you are looking for and these vary by item). This includes 20 items and must be completed in 4.5 minutes.

2. Numerical Aptitude contains 15 items with a 6-minute time limit. It is composed of basic computational problems in a multiple-choice format with five choices.

3. Spatial Aptitude requires the individual to determine which of four three-dimensional figures can be constructed for a two-dimensional stimulus object. The subtest relies heavily on visual perception and discrimination and contains 10 items to be completed in a 4-minute time limit.

4. Perceptual Aptitude also relies on visual perception, but of text or numbers. The test taker must determine if two sets of words (e.g., names, titles, addresses) or numbers are the same or different. With 100 items and a 2.5-minute time limit, this is the most heavily speeded measure.

5. Manual Dexterity is similar to the coding subtest found on popular intelligence tests, requiring test takers to type a numeric value that corresponds to a symbol. A coding grid is provided, but speed and facility with computer keyboards affect a test taker's score in this area and it does not appear to measure manual dexterity in the same way paper-based versions do because of the keyboard effect.

Separate scores are computed for each of these five aptitude tests as well as a general ability score obtained by summing the raw scores from the Verbal and Numerical Aptitude subtests. Scores are reported based on norms yet no description of the normative group (size, demographic background, date) is provided or available from the publisher. Scores range from 1 (very low-bottom 10%) to 5 (very high-top 10%). Brief two to three sentence descriptions of each aptitude are provided on screen or in the manual with no examples to aid in interpretation. However, the descriptions are of the construct (e.g., numeric aptitude) and no indication of the score meaning (what a "4" means) is provided to aid in interpretation of scores.

The Interest Test contains 132 items scored on a 3-point scale. Test takers read a job title and indicate if they "like," "dislike," or are "neutral" toward each job. Items correspond to one of the 12 interest scales and scores ranging from 1 (very low–bottom 10%) to 5 (very high–top 10%) are reported for each scale. Again, the same brief descriptive paragraph is generated to explain a score of 1 or 5 on each scale, with no interpretative information helping the individual interpret their score. For example, in completing the interest test my score on the Selling scale was only a 2 out of 5, yet the analyses did not inform me of what a "2" indicated, but read "High scores on this scale indicate an interest in providing information on a product and persuading others of its value and desirability. Jobs that satisfy this interest involve selling products or services in stores, offices, or customer's homes." This is exactly the same text printed in the manual (p. 10) and provides no distinction between Scores 1–5. Again, this test does not provide useful interpretations to users that can inform them what a particular score means.

The final step in the program is to generate a career search mapping just over 400 jobs to the aptitude and interest profiles associated with data from the 1996–1997 *Occupational Outlook Handbook* published by the U.S. Department of Labor. The manual notes that individuals may obtain an empirical estimate of their interests and abilities, matched to the interests and abilities in the Handbook. However, there is no information on the validity, reliability, or normative base used to arrive at the Aptitude and Interest scores, and without such information, these claims appear overly exaggerated.

Once the career search is completed, the user may print out the results, which indicate jobs with a high, moderate, and low match. The career search tends to generate a large number of potential occupations (well over 40 that have a high match, and over 80 with a moderate match), which vary in a number of conditions in three trials of the software with students. The resulting number of jobs may simply overwhelm many users who are looking for broader descriptions of the types of occupations (rather than specific jobs), which are most associated with their aptitudes and interests. Finally, the user can obtain a substantial amount of information on occupations because the program contains the content of the 1996–1997 *Occupational Outlook Handbook* published by the U.S. Department of Labor. For each occupation, the user can review: (a) the nature of work; (b) working conditions; (c) employment; (d) training and other qualifications, and advancement; (e) job outlook; (f) earnings; (g) related occupations; and (h) sources of additional information. This detailed information may be the most useful component of the program, yet this information is taken directly from the Handbook.

The Career IQ and Interest Test has no supporting documentation to review concerning the validity or reliability of the scores that are generated. Despite several calls to the distributor, publisher, and other persons associated with the program no evidence was ever forwarded to this reviewer or even cited by the publisher. One must assume that the data from the U.S. Department of Labor are used to match profiles of aptitudes and interests to the various occupations because these data are already contained in the handbook (U.S. Department of Labor, 1997). However, the scores generated from this program must be greatly suspect, given the lack of documentation, evidence of validation, and the actual items used on several of the subtests.

SUMMARY. The Career IQ and Interest Test does not meet even minimal standards for a test as set forth in professional guidelines (AERA, APA, & NCME, 1985). It appears to be more of an entertainment program than to have any scientific basis for its scoring and associated career

search. The manual and materials address installation of the software, troubleshooting, and basically reprint the job database and text from the Handbook (U.S. Department of Labor, 1997). The manual does not address any technical aspects of the test itself and is inadequate in nearly all respects when judged by professional standards. Without evidence to support the scores or results from the career search, the Career IQ and Interest Test should not be used to initiate career exploration or guidance activities. Individuals interested in initial career exploration may benefit by choosing among a variety of paper-and-pencil-based interest inventories such as the Self Directed Search, which are much less expensive than this software program and have developed manuals and supporting documentation to address issues of validity, reliability, and appropriate use.

REVIEWER'S REFERENCES
American Educational Research Association, American Psychological Association, & National Council on Measurement in Education. (1985). *Standards for educational and psychological testing*. Washington, DC: American Psychological Association.
U.S. Department of Labor. (1997). *Occupational outlook handbook*. Washington, DC: Government Printing Office.

Review of the Career IQ Test by DONALD THOMPSON, Dean and Professor of Counseling and Psychology, Troy State University Montgomery, Montgomery, AL:

The Career IQ and Interest Test (CIQIT) is a computer-based aptitude test, interest inventory and report generator. The tests are administered and scored by computer, and the computer generates a diagnostic career report based on the interests and aptitude measures. The publisher's description indicates that the CIQIT "provides individuals with a unique solution through the matching of their IQ and interests with specific occupations." The obvious equating of "IQ" with aptitudes could be troublesome to those who are involved with psychometrics. The CIQIT is designed for use by persons from age 13 through adult, and the average time for administration appears to be between one hour and one and one-half hours. The most appropriate statement that can be made about the CIQIT is that it *is not* a test. It should be considered a career planning tool only. Therefore, this review will focus on its value in this context.

The test package is delivered on one CDROM disk and is designed for use on computers running Windows 3.11, Windows 95, and with some work, it will run with Windows 98. MSDOS and MAC (System 7) versions are also available but were not used for this review. The package must be installed on a computer hard-disk drive and requires about 8 megabytes of disk space, but the original CDROM must also be in the computer during each administration.

Because the CIQIT is, in fact, a computer-based system, some discussion of the technical merits of the software is necessary. The system requirements are stated on the package, and one must have a system that meets the minimum hardware requirements or the program will not install or run properly. In fact, there appear to be some computer system issues and problems that are not addressed in the minimum hardware requirements. This reviewer attempted to install the program on five different computers. On one, a 486 laptop that appeared to meet all the minimum hardware specifications, the program installed but would not run. The problem seemed to be the lack of an adequate sound card (there is no mention of this in minimum hardware requirements). In several attempts to install the program on high-end desktops running Windows 98, an installation error occurred each time. Only after all Windows start-up programs were disabled did the program finally install. The same problem occurred on a computer running Windows 95, and the same solution was found. Unfortunately, no caveats were contained in the documentation about this type of problem. The publisher does have a web site at www.virtent.com, which provides some limited assistance in this regard. However, their technical assistance response time is excellent, and when a request for assistance was emailed to the site, a helpful response was emailed back within one day. Other than the above-mentioned problems with installation, the program ran well thereafter. There is one minor operational problem with the program. Many of the instruction screens include both forward and back buttons even after a user has reached the last screen (and thus, one cannot move forward). This could prove confusing to some test takers.

Although the program is intended primarily as a personal career planning tool and seems to be targeted for purchase by individuals rather than schools or testing centers, the package contains a test management system that allows the purchaser to test and track the results of multiple users. The purchaser of the software is authorized to use the software on one machine for unlimited administrations of the tests and associated report preparation.

The key features of the Career IQ Test include an aptitude test that assesses six aptitude areas: General Ability, Manual Dexterity, Verbal, Numerical, Perceptual, and Spatial. Each section is timed, and the total time allotment for the Aptitude portion is about 17 minutes. The Interest test has 132 items and measures 12 interest factors directly correlated to data in the Dictionary of Occupational Titles (DOT) Guide for Occupational Exploration from the U.S. Employment Service. Also, the CIQIT includes a Self-Appraisal Test that inventories an individual's self-assessed abilities; likes and dislikes related to work; a Career Match Wizard that matches test results and/or self-appraisals with occupations contained in the U.S. Department of Labor *Occupational Outlook Handbook;* and a Career Search Database that provides information for hundreds of occupations. The database includes detailed job descriptions, earnings, training requirements, and an employment outlook to the year 2005. Finally, the program prints the complete test results, with career matches and job descriptions. The program will generate a report from either responses entered to the self-appraisal, or for the scores achieved on the Aptitude test and Interest inventory. The on-line help feature is adequate, and the graphics used throughout the program are of good photographic quality.

There is a 39-page user's manual (23 pages are devoted to tables of occupational/aptitude relationships). Much of the same material is provided on-line during the testing process. However, no reliability or validity data are provided for either the aptitude or interest test. No information is provided concerning the source of items for either test or how the tests were developed, and no normative data are provided. The user's manual has no value as a source of technical information.

The user's manual includes the following statement regarding the use and value of the CIQIT: "The results of this program should be used to motivate self-exploration, vocational exploration and career development" (p. 7). Clearly, the CIQIT should not be considered as a psychometric tool for the accurate assessment of aptitudes and interests, but rather as a career planning tool. Viewed in this regard, one must ask, does it accomplish its intended purpose?

SUMMARY. Even though the empirical psychometric data regarding the CIQIT are not available, in general, it is this reviewer's conclusion that the CIQIT is a reasonably good computer-based test administration and management system that could prove useful as a career exploration tool. There are several positive features of the CIQIT. Once the initial purchase is made, there is no additional cost for each use. After some initial installation problems, there were no technical problems with the software during multiple uses. Several of the test subjects for this review indicated that they enjoyed the test process and felt that the results were consistent with their self-assessments of aptitudes, interests, and career goals. The only major complaint from subjects was the short time limits for the aptitude measures. The program seems to take maximum advantage of the capabilities of the computer for test administration and report generation. Both graphics and sound quality are excellent. If one assumes that the aptitude and interest assessments are providing an accurate portrayal of a client, the computer-generated report could be an effective tool for career guidance and counseling.

However, as a psychometric device, there are many limitations to the CIQIT. There is no empirical evidence to suggest that the aptitude and interest test results provide an accurate assessment of a client, and therefore results may be of questionable value in providing data to assist clients in making specific career decisions. If the program is used in conjunction with a good career counselor, the CIQIT may have some positive value as a career planning tool.

[65]

Career Occupational Preference System—Professional Level Interest Inventory.

Purpose: Designed to measure career interest for those wanting to focus on the professional level careers.
Population: College and adult professionals, college-bound senior high school students.
Publication Dates: 1982–1989.
Acronym: COPS-P.
Scores: Scores in the 16 COPSystem Career Clusters: Service-Social, Service-Instructional, Science-Physical, Science-Medical/Life, Technology-Civil, Technology-Electrical, Technology-Mechanical, Outdoor-Agribusiness, Outdoor-Nature, Business-Management, Business-Finance, Computation, Communication-Written, Communication-Oral, Arts-Design, Arts-Performing.

Administration: Group.
Price Data, 1998: $13 per 25 self-scoring forms [$46.75 per 100, $220.50 per 500]; $12.50 per 25 Self-Interpretation Profiles and Guide [$44.50 per 100, $206.75 per 500]; $13.50 per 25 machine-scoring forms [$47.50 per 100, $223.50 per 500]; $1.60 each scoring by publisher; $22.25 per hand-scoring keys; $5 per technical manual ('89, 37 pages); $2.75 per examiner's manual ('89, 15 pages); $22.75 per set of COPS-P Visuals; $9 per specimen set.
Time: (15–20) minutes.
Authors: Lisa Knapp-Lee, Lila F. Knapp, Robert R. Knapp.
Publisher: EdITS/Educational and Industrial Testing Service.
Cross References: See T5:416 (1 reference).
[Editor's Note: The following reviews are based on materials received prior to January 2000. The publisher advises that a revision was done in 2000.]

Review of the Career Occupational Preference System—Professional Level Interest Inventory by MARK A. ALBANESE, Professor, Preventive Medicine and Director, Medical Education Research and Development, University of Wisconsin—Madison, Madison, WI:

The Career Occupational Preference System—Professional Level Interest Inventory (COPS-P) truly is a system. It is composed of a set of instruments and referral materials designed to aid college and adult professionals and college-bound high school students in not only identifying career options consistent with their interests and aptitudes, but also to provide in-depth material about each of various career possibilities. Based upon the degree to which the individual likes/dislikes 192 job activity descriptions, it first creates a profile of 16 career clusters based upon the degree to which each is consistent with the individual's interests. The second step identifies specific jobs within each cluster that are most consistent with the individual's interests. Each occupational cluster is also keyed to related college majors to enable examinees to select courses of training that will prepare them for entry into occupations in the cluster. If aptitude is a factor in making a career decision, the authors have an aptitude test available to help users determine the relative feasibility of different career options. Documents providing detailed career information and labor statistics compiled by the United States government are part of the referral materials to help users gain as deep an understanding as possible about what various jobs entail in terms of work type, salary expectations, traveling required, etc. (*Occupational Outlook Handbook* and the *Dictionary of Occupational Titles, Fourth Edition Revised*). Although machine scoring is available, the authors encourage self-scoring to enable users to gain a deeper understanding of what their scores mean. Overall, it is a relatively short, carefully crafted, well thought out system of career counseling materials.

The development of the system is described as "following the pattern of postulated theory, tested by exploratory factor analytic research and, finally, confirmatory factor analysis" (manual, p. 12). Median reliability estimates based upon internal consistency (alpha—6,343 college students) and test-retest correlations over a one-week time lapse (154 entering college students) were .89 and .94, respectively. Studies examining the long-term stability of job interests indicate that from 40–45% of the students who take the inventory will have the same area of greatest interest from one year to the next and virtually all will maintain one of their top three areas of greatest interest over that period.

The authors argue that the validity of the inventory is based upon items being written as clearly as possible to represent activities performed in the occupations incorporated within each cluster and that self-scoring further enhances the "face" validity. Exploratory factor analysis and confirmatory factor analysis results are reported in a separate technical manual. Correlations between conceptually similar scales of the COPS-P and then COPS Interest Inventory ranged from .70 to .93 with a median correlation of .84. Correlations between the COPS-P and the Strong Campbell Interest Inventory and the Vocational Preference Inventory are reported in the technical manual. The most recent norms were obtained in 1988 based upon a sample of 3,616 that was stratified according to populations in five regions of the country. Separate norms are reported for males and females acknowledging the fact that there is a gender by career interaction in career interests that needs to be adjusted to meet the Title IX and Federal and State Legislation requirements to minimize sex bias.

CRITIQUE. The best thing about the COPS-P is that it is a full service career interest inventory. It is based upon a reasonably well-accepted theory of career selection and has been created by exploratory and confirmatory factor analysis. With companion tests to assess aptitude and professional

attitudes and values, as well as references detailing what various jobs are like, it gives the user a complete set of materials to assist in career selection. As one might expect from the use of factor analysis in its development, the scale scores have demonstrated very good internal consistency reliability estimates (median = .89). The test-retest reliability estimates are particularly impressive (mean = .94). Another strength of the instrument is its use of tasks that are very concretely tied to various jobs to assess the examinee's likes and dislikes. Further, using an open format as opposed to forced choice makes the results easier to interpret. Finally, providing separate norms for males and females is important for an instrument that measures career interests in light of known gender differences.

Even though this is a well-designed and useful instrument, there are some issues that are of concern. First, the most recent norming data are from 1988. Given the warp speed with which the web-economy has expanded, whole new classes of positions have been created in recent years. Although the general classifications of jobs probably continue to be valid, the differentiation within the computation cluster has expanded greatly.

A second issue pertains to ethnicity differences that might affect likes and dislikes for various job activities. Although ethnicity may not differentially affect responses, the potential for problems in this regard is as great as it is for gender. Data regarding the instrument's sensitivity (or insensitivity) to ethnicity should be reported.

Although the data on the validity are reasonable from an internal structure and concurrent validity stand point, there are no data that suggest that individuals who are in a given occupation or who are training to enter a given occupation have scores on the inventory that would lead to them being counseled to enter that occupation. Information of this type would be very helpful in establishing the validity of scores from the instrument.

A final issue pertains to several of the items addressing health careers. All items on the COPS-P are framed in terms of actions that individuals in a job do on a regular, or at least a common basis. Examples of items include: Write critical reviews for a newspaper, act in a movie or play, and work in a mental hospital diagnosing problems. Note that although the first two are actual behaviors (write, act), the third (work) is a generic term reflecting any number of activities or that one's behaviors in the setting will be paid for. The action is actually diagnosing problems. If it were reworded to be: diagnose psychological problems affecting patients in a mental hospital, it would seem more appropriate and informative.

A second health-related issue pertains to how some of the questions are presented. For instance, one item is: Remove teeth and perform oral surgery. Although the intent may be to find out if the respondent might be interested in becoming a dentist or oral surgeon, it could just as easily reflect propensity to become chief interrogator in a medieval torture chamber. If someone responds that they really like to do these things, you would not be able to determine if they are a born dentist or psychopath. This is not an isolated item, another reads: Cut open a chest cavity to implant a device to maintain life. In the health sciences, students learn that in order to help people, doctors sometimes have to do brutal things to them. Admissions committees to the health sciences look foremost for applicants who are compassionate and want to help people. During the course of their health sciences education, students learn that in order to help, they must sometimes do harm. I cannot conceive of a situation where an applicant who said they were interested in becoming a physician because they like to cut open chests or remove tumors would seriously be considered for admission. The implication of this problem is that the health professions cluster may not be as valid as are other clusters.

SUMMARY. The COPS-P is a very carefully developed and validated career interest inventory that provides a full complement of materials and support references for helping individuals decide upon a career path. It is brief (taking only about 15–20 minutes to complete the inventory and another 10–20 minutes to self-score) and inexpensive (less than $1 per person if ordered in bulk). It has demonstrated strong psychometric properties in terms of internal consistency and test-retest reliabilities and convergent and discriminant validity (correlates higher with scales measuring similar traits and lower with scales measuring different traits.) Separate norms are provided for males and females. An area in need of attention is that the norms are over 12 years old and should be updated with new data and careers should be updated to include those dealing with the internet and world wide web. Data from indi-

viduals who are presently in a job or who are training to enter a job that suggest that they would be counseled to enter that job would bolster the validity of the instrument. Data reflecting ethnicity differences would help determine if the instrument should have separate norms for individuals with different ethnic backgrounds. Finally, some of the health sciences questions are framed in ways that would not be viewed positively in the professions were individuals to profess liking the activities portrayed (removing teeth, cutting open chests), detracting from the validity of the results from that component of the inventory.

Review of the Career Occupational Preference System—Professional Level Interest Inventory by JEFFREY A. JENKINS, Assistant Professor, Roger Williams University, Bristol, RI:

The Career Occupational Preference System—Professional Level Interest Inventory (COPS-P) is the form of the well-established COPS Interest Inventory directed toward professional, college-trained individuals. The COPS-P is intended to be used as a brief measure of an individual's preferences about job activities required by professional occupations such as those in the medical, technology, business, and artistic fields. It may be used beneficially with college students, adults returning to the work force, or for those who contemplate a career change.

The COPS-P divides professional occupations into eight broad areas: Science, Technology, Outdoor, Business, Computation, Communication, Arts, and Service. These areas are further divided into 16 subclusters that form the instrument subscales used in interpretation of a respondent's occupational interests and preferences. The broad categories and the subscales are derived from factor analytic studies of the underlying dimensions of occupational choice and are as follows: Science (Medical-Life, Physical); Technology (Civil, Electrical, Mechanical); Outdoor (Agribusiness, Nature); Business (Management, Finance Computation); Communication (Written, Oral); Arts (Design, Performing); and Service (Social-Health, Instructional).

After creation of a COPS-P profile of the 16 subscales, a respondent can engage in career planning by reference to the Self-Interpretation Profile and Guide that lists specific occupations within each of the subscales, the *Occupational*

Outlook Handbook and *Dictionary of Occupational Titles* references for those occupations, as well as a list of skills and abilities needed for each job. An understanding of an individual's occupational preferences in terms of these clusters and subclusters can be used in the career counseling session to narrow the individual's choices and focus on a limited number of occupations consistent with the person's interests and aptitudes.

Items in the COPS-P consist of statements relating to specific job activities: for example, "Remove teeth and perform oral surgery," "Prosecute criminals in court," "Outline an advertising campaign for a new product." Respondents indicate their degree of interest or disinterest in each job activity on a 4-point Likert scale (*like very much, like moderately, dislike moderately, dislike very much*). The 192 job activity items are presented in a short, self-administered booklet with an included response sheet for machine scoring. The inventory can also be hand-scored. The instructions are brief and easily understood. Scores on the COPS-P are produced for each of the 16 subscales within the eight broad categories of occupations, from which a profile is created.

The technical characteristics of the COPS-P are very good for this type of inventory. Internal consistency reliability based on a sample of 6,343 college students yielded coefficient alpha estimates for the subscales from .81 to .94, with a median of .89. Test-retest reliability (administration interval = 1 week) for a sample of 154 college students yielded estimates from .85 to .99, with a median of .99. The publisher has taken a convergent approach to demonstrating validity of the COPS-P. As noted earlier, the technical manual reports factor analytic studies that have provided evidence of the existence of the 16 subscales and, thus, construct validity. Evidence of concurrent validity is reported through additional research on the relationship between COPS-P and COPS Interest Inventory, the Strong Campbell Interest Inventory, and the Vocational Preference Inventory. Some evidence of predictive validity also is reported in a study of the relationship between COPS-P scores and students' declared college majors. Norms for the COPS-P were originally based on data collected in 1983 from a national sample of over 3,500 college students in both 2-year and 4-year institutions. The normative information was updated in 1988.

SUMMARY. As one of many career interest measures available, the COPS-P makes a contribution to interest assessment and can be used beneficially for self-interpretation of interests and by career counselors. Despite its solid technical characteristics and usefulness, a minor criticism might be made that the overall appearance of the instrument and interpretive materials should be updated. Both the color of the ink used, the printing, and the formatting of the test booklet and interpretive guide give the impression that the instrument is dated. Particularly as the technological and service industries continue to change at a rapid pace, such an appearance may, in the user's mind, contradict the clear benefits that one may continue to derive from the instrument.

[66]
Career Thoughts Inventory.

Purpose: Constructed to assess "dysfunctional thinking in career problem solving and decision making."
Population: Adults, college students, and high school students.
Publication Dates: 1994–1996.
Acronym: CTI.
Scores, 4: Decision Making Confusion, Commitment Anxiety, External Conflict, Total.
Administration: Group.
Price Data, 2001: $146 per introductory kit including manual ('96, 99 pages), 25 test booklets, and 10 workbooks ('96, 39 pages); $45 per 25 test booklets; $75 per 10 workbooks; $33 per manual.
Time: (7–15) minutes.
Authors: James P. Samson, Jr., Gary W. Peterson, Janet G. Lenz, Robert C. Reardon, and Denise E. Saunders.
Publisher: Psychological Assessment Resources, Inc.

Review of the Career Thoughts Inventory by JANET H. FONTAINE, Associate Professor of Counseling, Indiana University of Pennsylvania, Indiana, PA:

The Career Thoughts Inventory (CTI) is one of a relatively new breed of career assessment devices that seeks to provide the career client and helping professional with innovative self-knowledge in the area of cognitive dysfunction as it relates to career decision making. Its three construct scales identify specific areas of thought dysfunction: Decision Making Confusion/DMC (14 items that assess a person's inability to initiate or sustain the decision process), Commitment Anxiety/CA (10 items measuring the degree to which anxiety-producing thoughts may be contributing to indecision), and External Conflict/ EC (5 items assessing the client's ability to balance self-perceptions with the input from significant others). The CTI provides a Total score, a global indicator of dysfunctional career thinking.

The CTI is a theoretically based instrument, generating subscale content from the cognitive information processing (CIP) model (Peterson, Sampson, & Reardon, 1991; Peterson, Sampson, Reardon, & Lenz, 1996). Its 48 statements require test takers to select one of four responses ranging from strongly agree to strongly disagree. All statements are expressed negatively (no counterbalancing) to avoid complications in the use of the accompanying workbook, *Improving Your Career Thoughts: A Workbook for the Career Thoughts Inventory* (Sampson, Peterson, Lenz, Reardon, & Saunders, 1996). The workbook provides exercises to assist in identifying and altering a client's dysfunctional career thinking. It is this "package" of diagnostic and treatment products that make the CTI uniquely appealing to career service providers.

The Inventory itself is self-administering and combines the test booklet with answer and scoring sheet (carbonless paper), as well as profile form. Directions for scoring are somewhat confusing, however, and if client-scored as indicated appropriate in the manual, scores should be rechecked by a professional. The instrument seems fairly robust as the authors indicate that results are invalid only if 10% (5 items) or more were omitted.

Scores are reported as *T* scores and percentiles. The profile form is easy to use and shaded in gradients of 10 *T*-score points from white to grayblue to emphasize higher scores.

The authors indicate the CTI can be used for high school and college students seeking a college major or choosing an occupation as well as adults considering an occupational change or reentering the labor market. It can serve as a screening measure to identify individuals likely to experience career choice problems, as a needs assessment to identify the specific nature of the dysfunctional thinking, and as a learning resource (in conjunction with the workbook), assisting clients to identify and challenge their specific dysfunctional thoughts. The authors suggest, however, that professional counselors assist in this latter phase.

Although professionals and professionals in training (under supervision) who possess general knowledge of helping skills, assessment, and career development concepts are legitimate users, some background in cognitive-behavior therapy and familiarity with the Inventory manual are necessary. The manual goes into great depth (10 pages) explaining its theoretical underpinnings in Cognitive Information Processing (CIP) and cognitive therapy research. Without a substantial investment of time, the practitioner not already familiar with cognitive therapy and CIP concepts and terminology (e.g., self-talk, metacognitions, self-monitoring, the CAVSE cycle, executive processing domain, etc.) will find great difficulty in digesting this theoretical information in sufficient detail to ensure effective use of the CTI and its workbook.

The CTI authors caution throughout the manual that cultural values may impact some scores and consistently suggest the establishment of local norms to ensure cultural perspectives are not pathologized as dysfunctional thoughts (e.g., amount of impact of significant others on career choice in an Asian population would not necessarily indicate dysfunctional thinking).

TECHNICAL CHARACTERISTICS. The Career Thoughts Inventory utilized well-established test construction procedures in its development and the product is a psychometrically sound instrument. A representative normative sample was provided for the three populations it is designed to serve: high school students (n = 396), college students (n = 595), and adults (n = 571). Although norms were stratified by geographic area (south, midwest, north eastern, and western regions), ethnicity, and gender (a higher proportion of women in each sample is explained by the fact that more women seek counseling services), no mention was made of how these subjects were specifically selected.

RELIABILITY. Internal consistency and testretest reliabilities were examined for all four CTI scales using 1,562 adults, college and high school students, and clients seeking career services. Results were very promising. For all groups, alpha coefficients were determined for CTI Total score (alpha = .93–.97), DMC (alpha = .90–.94), CA (alpha = .79–.91), EC (alpha = .74–.81).

Test-retest coefficients over a 4-week period were provided for only college and high school students (n = 121). Higher reliability was obtained for the college student sample (n = 86, Total Score) than the high school sample (n = 69, Total

Score). Although these coefficients are marginally acceptable, the authors claim that the overall Total Score reliability for the high school sample was attenuated due to the External Conflict subscale's limited number of items (5). Because the high school sample's EC coefficient was .52, this would seem a reasonable explanation if it were not for the fact that the college student sample had no corresponding depressed EC coefficient.

VALIDITY. The Career Thoughts Inventory has high face validity as all items seem logically affiliated with thinking about the general career selection process. Construct validity was evaluated through principal components analyses that identified three interpretable factors (Decision Making Confusion [DMC], Commitment Anxiety [CA], and External Conflict [EC]). What is curious about this factor analysis, however, is that only 29 of the total 48 Inventory items were included in the three factor scales identified. The remaining 19 (close to 40% of total test items) appear to contribute only to the Total Inventory Score and may have been retained more for content validity purposes. The authors provide no rationale for the inclusion of these apparently "independent" items in the final version of the CTI.

Content validity is tied to CPI theory components and briefly explained in the manual. Because the test authors are also the developers of the CIP theory, expert content analysis would seem to be adequate. An appendix provides the reader a detailed list of which CTI questions cover each of the eight CPI components, with no redundancy.

The CTI's ability to discriminate between groups of college students seeking career services (n = 199) and those not seeking services (n = 149) documented concurrent criterion-related validity. Using MANOVA techniques, significant differences were found on all subtests between these two groups as well as on 26 of the 48 items.

SUMMARY. The Career Thoughts Inventory is a well-constructed instrument for its slated purpose (i.e., to identify specific dysfunctional thinking patterns associated with career decision making). Although other instruments may address some of the same components as those measured by the CTI, its unique contribution is its cognitive dysfunction perspective. Its brief administration time and accompanying treatment workbook make it an appealing addition to available career tools. Although the reading levels for the CTI and

workbook are Grade 6.4 and 7.7, respectively, it is possible a number of career clients may not have the reading skills necessary to utilize either.

Practitioners may have difficulty envisioning how the CTI can be consistently integrated into their practice other than on a case-by-case basis and evidence of the workbook's ability to correct dysfunctional career thinking is still missing. A last caveat is that scoring done by clients should be rechecked until scoring directions are rewritten. Local norms are encouraged to ensure cultural bias is minimized.

The CTI has a unique place in the armamentaria of career service providers. It is a well-constructed instrument that has utility for its stated purposes.

REVIEWER'S REFERENCES
Peterson, G. W., Sampson, J. P., Jr., & Reardon, R. C. (1991). *Career development and services: A cognitive approach.* Pacific Grove, CA: Brooks/Cole Publishing Company.
Peterson, G. W., Sampson, J. P., Jr., Reardon, R. C., & Lenz, J. G. (1996). A cognitive information processing approach to career problem solving and decision making. In D. Brown, L. Brooks, & Associates (Eds.), *Career choice and development* (pp. 423–475). San Francisco: Jossey-Bass Publishers.
Sampson, J. P., Jr., Peterson, G. W., Lenz, J. G., Reardon, R. C., & Saunders, D. E. (1996). *Improving your career thoughts: A workbook for the Career Thoughts Inventory.* Odessa, FL: Psychological Assessment Resources, Inc.
Gilbert, H. B. (1997, January). *Career Thoughts Inventory: A review and critique.* Paper presented at the Annual Meeting of the Southwest Educational Research Association, Austin, TX.

[67]
Caregiver-Teacher Report Form.

Purpose: Designed "to assess behavioral/emotional problems and identify syndromes of problems that tend to occur together."

Population: Ages 2–5.

Publication Date: 1997.

Acronym: C-TRF.

Scores, 10: Anxious/Obsessive, Depressed/Withdrawn, Fears, Somatic Problems, Immature, Attention Problems, Aggressive Behavior, Internalizing, Externalizing, Total.

Administration: Group.

Price Data, 1997: $10 per 25 test booklets; $10 per 25 profiles for hand scoring; $10 per guide (67 pages); $7 per templates for hand scoring; $135 per computer scoring program.

Time: Administration time not reported.

Comments: Ratings by daycare providers and preschool teachers.

Author: Thomas M. Achenbach.

Publisher: Child Behavior Checklist.

Review of the Caregiver-Teacher Report Form by KAREN T. CAREY, Professor of Psychology, California State University, Fresno, CA:

The Caregiver-Teacher Report Form (C-TRF) is designed to be completed by daycare providers and preschool teachers who respond to 99 problem area items and several open-ended items. Items are grouped into three categories labeled Internalizing, Neither Internalizing or Externalizing, and Externalizing. These are further broken down into syndromes. The Internalizing grouping is composed of Anxious/Obsessive, Depressed/Withdrawn, and Fears syndromes; the Neither Internalizing or Externalizing grouping is composed of Somatic Problems and Immature syndromes, and the Externalizing grouping is composed of Aggressive Behavior and Attention Problems syndromes. A total scale score is also obtained. The manual provides specific information related to the procedures used for constructing the scale.

Each item is scored 0 for *not true*, 1 for *somewhat or sometimes true*, and 2 for *very true or often true*. Item number 100 provides space for the caregiver/teacher to write in any additional problems the child has that were not addressed by other items of the scale. Three additional open-ended items can be completed that include whether the child has any illness or disability, what concerns the caregiver most about the child, and what the child does best. A profile consisting of each of the seven syndromes can be generated using the protocol and plotting results using *T*-scores or percentiles.

The norm group consisted of 1,076 children between the ages of 2 and 5 with 536 boys and 539 girls from 12 states and Holland. Demographic characteristics include socioeconomic status (upper, middle, and lower), ethnicity (NonLatino White, African-American, Latino, Mixed or Other), region of U.S.A. (Northeast, North Central, South, West), and respondent (Caregiver and Teacher). Children from upper socioeconomic status, described as NonLatino White, and residing in the Northeast region appear to be overrepresented and caregiver respondents (78) seem to overrepresented as compared to teachers (23) in the sample.

T-scores are obtained from each syndrome and are assigned on the basis of percentiles. Different numbers of items compose each of the syndromes. Normalized *T*-scores were assigned to raw scores on the basis of the percentile represented by raw scores in the norm sample. The *T*-scores were also truncated to low scores so that a child who obtained 0 on two scales did not appear to have more problems in one area than in another. A *T*-score of 50 was assigned to all raw scores that fell at midpoint percentiles up to the 50th percentile. At the high end of the scale *T*-scores were assigned from 71 to 100 in increments because most children obtained scores below the maximum number possible on each syndrome scale. Normal, borderline, and clinical ranges are identified for all scale scores.

In the manual the author states that further reliability and validity studies are needed as this is the first edition of this instrument. However, the initial studies appear to provide adequate technical data. Test-retest reliability of .84 was obtained over intervals averaging 8.7 days. Mean interrater reliability of .66 was obtained. Correlations of the C-TRF with the Child Behavior Checklists/2-3 and 4/18 scales ranged from .14 to .64.

Content validity evidence was based on examination of the items by professionals in the field, parents' feedback, and by findings that respondents' ratings significantly discriminated between referred and nonreferred children. Criterion-related validity was examined based on the ability of each item to discriminate between children who had been referred for behavioral/emotional problems and children from the norm group. Results indicated that the referred sample did differ significantly from the norm sample on most items and scales.

SUMMARY. The C-TRF appears to be a useful instrument to identify behavioral and emotional problems in young children and technical evidence is adequate. Although further studies are needed to confirm technical adequacy, it appears that this instrument will gain the same widespread use as the Child Behavior Checklist (T5:451).

Review of the Caregiver-Teacher Report Form by MICHAEL FURLONG, Professor, and RENEE PAVELSKI, Doctoral Candidate, Counseling, Clinical, School Psychology Program, University of California, Santa Barbara, Graduate School of Education, Santa Barbara, CA:

The Caregiver-Teacher Report Form (C-TRF/2–5), a general measure of child behavioral and emotional problems, is designed to be completed by daycare providers and preschool teachers who have known the child in a school or daycare setting. The C-TRF/2–5, appropriate for 2- to 5-year-olds attending prekindergarten programs or day care, is part of a family of assessment tools including: (a) the Child Behavior Checklist (CBCL/2–3), (b) the CBCL/4–18, (c) the Teacher's Report Form (TRF/

5–18), (d) the Youth Self-Report (YSR), (e) the Young Adult Self-Report (YASR), (f) the Young Adult Behavior Checklist (YABCL), (g) the Direct Observation Form (DOF), and (h) the Semistructured Clinical Interview for Children (SCIC). The C-TRF can be thought of as a downward extension of the TRF and as a teacher version of the CBCL. The validity of these tools has been documented in empirical research. Therefore, Achenbach advises that they be used as an integrative unit where appropriate for the age of the individual.

The format of the C-TRF/2–5 is similar to that of the CBCL/2–3. Both contain 99 questions and open-ended items used for describing illnesses, disabilities, concerns the respondent has most about the child, and the best things about the child. Specifically, 82 questions have counterparts on the CBCL/2–3, 56 questions have counterparts on the CBCL/4–18, and 65 questions have counterparts on the TRF.

ADMINISTRATION. The instructions for the C-TRF/2–5 state that staff members who have the most experience with the child over the longest period of time (for a minimum of 2 months) are the best respondents. Responses should be based on the child's behavior within the past 2 months. The same 2-month period used in the Teacher Rating Form (ages 6–17) was selected as sufficient for children's behavior to stabilize in new settings and for respondents to become well acquainted with the children (C-TRF/2–5 manual, p. 49).

The administration of the C-TRF requires no special training and can be completed by assistant and trainee providers and teachers, as well as by more experienced personnel. As different staff members see the child in unique settings, it is best to have as many personnel as possible complete separate C-TRFs on the child based on their individual views. To clarify the role of the respondent, the C-TRF asks about their training and the experience of the child in their care. The type and size of the facility are described, as well as how many hours per week the child attends. If a child has a disability or is in a special class, respondents should base their answers on expectations for typical peers of the child's age. If the respondents lack the information to answer certain questions, one should write in "No chance to observe" or mark 0 to indicate "Not True (as far as you know)."

RESPONSE SCALE. The checklist uses a three-option response scale (from 0 to 2) for each problem item: 0 = *not true (as far as you know) of the child;* 1 = *somewhat or sometimes true;* and 2 = *very true or often true.* It is important to think about these responses in context as each item is weighed equally in subscale scores. The three-option scale, although convenient and economical, assumes that these responses are equally meaningful for all items. It is important for clinicians to get a sense of the caregivers' understanding of these categories in terms of their implied frequency and tolerance/intolerance of specific behaviors.

CONTENT AND SCORING. The scoring profile of the C-TRF/2–5 includes: (a) seven syndrome scales (Anxious/Obsessive, Depressed/Withdrawn, Fears, Somatic Problems, Immature Behavior, Attention Problems, and Aggressive Behavior); (b) a composite Internalizing problem scale score; (c) a composite Externalizing problem scale score; and (d) a Total Problem scale score. Raw scores and their corresponding *T*-scores for each subscale may be hand tallied and graphed on a profile using templates, or computer-scoring programs can be purchased that will score the profiles based on key entered or machine-read forms.

A number of the items, such as #27 ("Doesn't seem to feel guilty after misbehaving") and #90 ("Unhappy, sad or depressed") involve subjective judgements. The manual emphasizes the importance of obtaining multiple informants to minimize the subjectivity and identify agreements and disagreements between their judgments. Question #100 asks the informant to write in any problems the child has that were not listed above. Proper use requires a thorough review of all item responses prior to any hand or computer scoring.

NORMS. Normative data for the C-TRF/2–5 were drawn from a sample of 1,075 children (536 boys and 539 girls) from a variety of settings at 15 sites in 12 states and Holland. The National Institute of Child Health and Development (NICHD) Study of early Child Care provided data for 753 of these children. This sample is composed of approximately 71% Caucasian, 18% African American, 5% Latino, and 5% mixed or other, and a high representation from upper class SES (47%). The settings included daycare centers, Headstart programs, and preschools. One of the confusing matters of creating a preschool caretaker/teacher report form is that not all preschool youth attend a formal program. Thus, defining what the "norm" sample should be in problematic.

The C-TRF/2–5 should not be misunderstood to be an assessment of all preschool children. Eventually it will be necessary to establish norms that describe meaningful subgroupings of children in formal and informal preschool caretaker settings. Another matter is that no data were given in the manual regarding the education level, age, or gender of respondents. This is problematic in outlining norms as this data could confound the interpretation of the results. Greater description of caregiver and teacher demographics would aid in gaining a fuller understanding of these norms. In the future, information about the number of child ratings provided by each caregiver should be provided.

The fact that the C-TRF, like all the other Achenbach scales, focuses exclusively on pathology means that the distribution of subscale scores is highly skewed. Thus, it was necessary to rescale the scores using what is referred to as a "normalized T-score." Of what use are these normalized T-scores for the researcher and the clinician wishing to interpret a child's behavior emotional profile? This is very unclear. The normalized T-score are supposed to provide a more "bell-shaped curve" to the distribution of scores. The user of the C-TRF should recognize that the subscale normalized T-scores are not normally distributed over a full range of behaviors. Because the C-TRF focuses exclusively on problematic behaviors it is only tapping the upper range of the behavioral/emotional continuum. In addition, some of the subscales do a better job of this than others, particularly Depression/Withdrawn, Immaturity, Attention Problems, and Aggressive Behavior. These subscales have a sufficient number of items and these behaviors occur frequently enough among preschool children to obtain a smooth spread of scores across a wider distribution. This means that higher and lower scores on these subscales, in particular, may have clinical meaning. In summary, at the syndrome subscale level, given the various distribution problems, it would be best to use percentile ranking to interpret profiles and to explain them to parents and other consumers.

RELIABILITY. Agreement between different daycare and preschool staff members rating the same child was indicated by a mean r = .66. The test/retest reliability of C-TRF scale scores was supported by a mean r = .84 over intervals averaging 8.7 days (ranging from .64 to .91). These results should be read with caution, as the sample size was small. However, the cross-informant reliability index for somatic problems was inadequate (.33). This result is surprising, as the questions tend to be less subjective. Curiously, the majority of the test-retest data were derived from ratings provided by Dutch teachers. Given that the C-TRF was developed in English this hardly seems adequate to examine its score stability. The Achenbach series has a long tradition of being translated into other languages, but given that this manual describes its original development and validation, one would have hoped that its psychometric properties would have been firmly established with the English version prior to extending its use to another language and culture. Despite the need for collecting additional reliability data for various sociocultural groups in whichever country the C-TRF is used, the data that are presented show that scores decreased some over about an 8-day interval. The changes were small, but this downward trend is consistent with other research showing that other Achenbach scales produce lower scores on readministration. This is undesirable when used as an outcome measure in program evaluations. This pattern should be kept in mind by clinicians and researchers when evaluating program effectiveness.

VALIDITY. Several kinds of support are presented for validity of scores from the C-TRF. Feedback was received from professionals, parents, teachers, and caregivers. Most of the items and scales scored from the C-TRF ratings discriminated significantly between the referred and normative samples of children. Age, ethnic, and SES differences had little effect on the C-TRF scores. Because the C-TRF/2-5 draws upon the extensive tradition of the Achenbach scales, it has a solid foundation in empirical research about children's mental health.

When considering the validity of scores from the scale, users should recognize that the C-TRF/2-5 has greater power to detect and evaluate externalizing problems. In regression analyses, the syndrome and composite scores were significant predictors of referral status (few differences were found for socioeconomic status, age, or Non-Latino White versus other ethnicities). However, the strongest predictors of referral status were Attention Problems, Aggressive Behavior, and the Externalizing composite. This also may reflect the fact that caregivers identify children in need by observing troubling behaviors as opposed to emotional/internal problems. Preschool children may also be more likely to exhibit their internal turmoil through their behavior. Additional discriminant analyses showed that only the Externalizing composite was a significant predictor of referral status for both boys and girls.

SUMMARY. The C-TRF/2-5 is an interesting component of a complex, evolving, and continually improving assessment package that has become a collection of landmark instruments. Over 1,700 studies have utilized one or more of these instruments and the assessment package has gained international recognition. As a result, the measurements are endorsed and validated by a diverse group of researchers and have been translated into 50 different languages. As a research tool, the C-TRF/2-5 is well established, easy to use, and affordable. Although the long-term utility of the C-TRF/2-5 awaits empirical validation and clinical research, current users of the Achenbach battery of instruments will certainly want to add this instrument to their assessment libraries.

[68]
Carey Temperament Scales.

Purpose: Designed to assess "temperamental characteristics in infants and children."
Population: Ages 0-1 to 12-0.
Publication Dates: 1996–1998.
Acronym: CTS.
Scores, 9: Activity, Rhythmicity, Approach, Adaptability, Intensity, Mood, Persistence, Distractibility, Threshold.
Administration: Individual.
Price Data: Available from publisher.
Time: [15–20] minutes.
Comments: IBM or Macintosh computer scoring software available.
Authors: William B. Carey, Sean C. McDevitt, Barbara Medoff-Cooper, William Fullard, and Robin L. Hegvik.
Publisher: Behavioral-Developmental Initiatives.

Review of the Carey Temperament Scales by AIMÉE LANGLOIS, Professor, Department of Child Development, Humboldt State University, Arcata, CA:

SYNOPSIS. The Carey Temperament Scales (CTS) are designed to assess the temperamental traits of children from 1 month to 12 years of age for either clinical or research purposes. The CTS can be used clinically to specify the nature of issues

that pertain to children's behavior and parenting, and to help caregivers learn about the individuality of a particular child. However, the authors caution that data obtained from administering the CTS for this purpose should be used with other sources of assessment and information.

The CTS comprises five questionnaires that assess the same nine temperament traits (Activity, Rhythmicity, Approach-Withdrawal, Adaptability, Intensity, Mood, Persistence, Distractibility, and Sensitivity) at each of the following age levels: 1 to 4 months, 4 to 11 months, 1 and 2 years, 3 to 7 years, and 8 to 12 years. Each scale contains between 86 and 110 items that describe various behaviors typical of children at the identified ages. The individual who fills out a questionnaire about a child is identified as "rater" and should be familiar with the child; he or she rates each item on a scale of 1 to 6 that reflects whether the behavior occurs from *almost never* to *almost always*. The "user" or professional who will interpret the scores enters the ratings by hand on a "Scoring Sheet" appropriate to the child's age group and then computes a "Category Score" for each temperament characteristic on the basis of the data entered. The category scores thus obtained are then transferred to an age-appropriate "Profile Sheet" on which means and standard deviations for each trait are provided. The child's profile can then be compared to norms for his or her age group and interpreted. An electronic version of the scoring sheet allows the examiner to enter questionnaire item scores directly into a computer; a "Caregiver Report" and a "Professional Report" are then generated from the data provided. In addition, the computer program can create separate "Profile" and "Quickscore" reports.

Instructions are given for administering the questionnaires to the "rater," entering and scoring the responses, and using the computer program. These instructions are detailed in the test manual and user's guide that accompany the CTS. The manual also has sections on test development and standardization, as well as on reliability and validity. A reference list, an appendix, and a section on limitations of questionnaire data complete the manual.

CRITIQUE. The author provides a good rationale for the design of the CTS and its use; however, the limitation of the scales, highlighted by the authors themselves, and the potential for human error in arriving at category scores limit the usefulness of this instrument. These issues are discussed below on the basis of criteria delineated by Rudner (1994), McCauley (1988), and McCauley and Swisher (1984).

DEFINITION OF THE STANDARDIZATION SAMPLE. The manual provides evidence that the CTS was standardized on 200–500 children from 1 month to 12 years of age, the population for which it is intended. However, the authors refer the reader to earlier studies about the CTB development and its standardization. As a result, unless one accesses these studies (some of which were conducted more than 30 years ago), information about the "normalcy" of the children in the standardization sample is unknown. The authors acknowledge that the subjects in the standardization sample were a homogeneous group of white middle-class children and that the norms may not apply to "specialized settings" or "special subgroups." They suggest that additional research is needed to document if ethnic and/or socioeconomic differences exist and that restandardization may be needed with other groups. In light of the increasing diversity of the U.S. population, the use of the CTS is thus limited to a narrow section of society. Without complete and up-to-date information about additional samples, determining whether and how a particular child's temperament compares to that of his or her peers is uncertain.

RELIABILITY. The manual provides evidence that reliability testing was conducted to determine the stability of test scores over time. Test-retest reliability (administration interval of 20–75 days) scores range from .64 to .94 and increase from infancy to the oldest age group, possibly reflecting the variability of infants from 1 month to 3 years of age. The CTS would therefore be more valuable for use with children between 3 and 12 years of age.

The low test-retest reliability of some scales is compounded by the absence of information on interexaminer reliability. Transferring the responses from the questionnaire to the scoring sheet requires minute attention to detail and undivided attention; depending on the scale used, the examiner must fill out between 86 and 110 "bubbles," each representing the rating of an item on the questionnaire. Given that 16 "bubbles" represent each item that reflects the rating scale, and given that the items on the scoring sheet are not in the order in which they appear on the questionnaire, the possibility for error appears high. In addition, the computation of a category score for each temperament trait on the scoring sheet requires several mathematical computations that must be done in a specific order. Again, this requires minute attention not only to detail but also to sequence, further adding to possible examiner error and negatively affecting interexaminer reliability. The computer version of the CTS is likely to minimize examiner error associated with scoring but without data it remains a matter of conjecture and weakens the usefulness of the test.

VALIDITY. The CTS is based on well-known temperament theory and as such has high construct validity. In addition, the authors provide ample evidence that they used quantitative methods to study and control item validity. The resultant questionnaires therefore have content validity and the behaviors described compare favorably with those identified in the literature as specific to different age groups of children. The authors deplore the fact that they could not attempt external measures of external validity because of a "lack of a standardized observational scheme against which to compare the questionnaire" (technical manual, p. 14). However, they refer the reader to additional literature to highlight the relationship "between temperament and external events" (p. 15), and the "validity and appropriate use of temperament data in practice" (p. 15).

TEST ADMINISTRATION. The administration process is described quite specifically in terms of what the "user" is to do before giving the questionnaire to the "rater" and after receiving the questionnaire. Specific instructions help determine which of the five scales to select and identify the individual who can provide accurate ratings about a child. Other instructions pertain to briefing the "rater," transferring responses to the scoring sheet, computing category scores, transferring them to the profile sheet, and using the computerized version of the CTS. All instructions are provided in a conversational style and are thus easy to follow. However, the number of steps one has to follow to derive the category scores might require several readings of the relevant paragraphs. Fortunately, these instructions are provided both in the user's guide and on the scoring sheet.

QUALIFICATIONS OF RATER. The user's guide specifies that the individual completing the questionnaire should be someone who has "sufficient experience with the child over a 4 to 6 week period to provide accurate ratings" (manual, p. 5). However, the authors caution that because completion of any of the scales requires an early high school reading level, "users" might consider administering the CTS verbally to "raters" whose reading skills are below par. Issues such as whether parents and caregivers would be willing to admit to reading difficulties and how much time it takes to administer the CTS verbally are not addressed. In addition, unless raters are familiar with questionnaires and rating scales, the process may be daunting even if their reading skills are adequate. Almost every page is filled with about 35 sentences each describing a specific behavior; next to each sentence is a series of six numbered "bubbles" that reflect the rating scale; after reading each sentence raters must select which number reflects the rating that they assign the child for that item, and then fill out the corresponding bubble. Fatigue and frustration are likely to play a role in this process; furthermore individuals with mild learning disabilities such as attention deficits or visual figure-ground discrimination problems would be overwhelmed by the layout of the questionnaire. However, the authors do not address these issues, which may partially explain the low reliability (.70) between caregivers. The authors also recognize the possibility that raters may distort their responses. On the basis of the above factors, errors accumulated during rating would then impact test scores and interpretation, and thus compromise the usefulness of the scales.

QUALIFICATIONS OF USERS. The authors specify that only licensed or certified professionals should use the CTS. For clinical purposes they identify qualified users as individuals who "provide care for children and their parents" (user's guide, p. 4) and students under supervision of such. To remove any doubt as to who can be considered as qualified, a long list of professionals is provided. For research purposes the authors recommend that faculty and supervised graduate students be from accredited institutions. To ensure that high professional standards are maintained for test use the authors invite the reader who does not meet the above requirements to return the test for a full refund. This type of attention to user qualifications is likely to ensure a somewhat rigorous use of the scales. However, unless licensed users are familiar with tempera-

ment theory and the work supporting it, the CTS becomes a dangerous instrument leading to possible misinterpretation and worse misdiagnosis. This last issue is not addressed in the manual.

SUMMARY. In spite of its high construct and content validity, and attention to the qualifications of professionals using it, the CTS has limited usefulness. The absence of norms for diverse groups narrows its use to the white middle class; the lack of interexaminer reliability data fails to address the numerous potential sources of errors for both raters and examiners. These factors undermine the CTS's usefulness as a means of assessing temperamental characteristics. However, on the basis of their high content validity, professionals can use the items on the questionnaires as guidelines to interview parents or caregivers when gathering information about a child. Professionals well versed in temperament theory are likely to find these items useful; yet, depending on their knowledge and expertise, they may find a more expedient way to assess temperament. Conversely, qualified professionals who are only vaguely familiar with temperament issues could misuse the test. Determining a child's temperament is a valuable undertaking on many fronts. However, unless the current CTS is revised to include diverse groups and address the numerous sources of errors discussed above, its value is limited as a clinical tool.

REVIEWER'S REFERENCES

McCauley, R. J., & Swisher, L. (1984). Psychometric review of language and articulation tests for preschool children. *Journal of Speech and Hearing Disorders, 49,* 34–42.

McCauley, R. J. (1988, Spring). Measurement as a dangerous activity. *HEARSAY,* 6–9.

Rudner, L. M. (1994, April). *Questions to ask when evaluating tests.* ERIC/AE Digest (Report No. TM024537). Washington, DC: ERIC Clearinghouse on Measurements and Evaluation. (ERIC Document and Reproduction Services No. ED385607)

Review of the Carey Temperament Scales by E. JEAN NEWMAN, Assistant Professor, University of South Alabama, Mobile, AL:

The Carey Temperament Scales represent three decades of research and development. There are five separate scales: The Early Infancy Temperament Questionnaire (EITQ; ages 1–4 months), the Revised Infant Temperament Questionnaire (RITQ; ages 4–11 months), the Toddler Temperament Scale (TTS; ages 1 and 2 years), the Behavioral Style Questionnaire (BSQ; ages 3–7 years), and the Middle Childhood Temperament Questionnaire (MCTQ; ages 8–12 years). The scales are designed for parents to complete, and contain 76 (EITQ) to 110 (BSQ) items on a 1–6 scale (1 = *almost never*, 6 = *almost always*) format.

The scales are intended to explain possible reasons for children's behaviors and reaction patterns, and the impact of these behaviors on the caregivers. Responses are tabulated to give the nine cluster scores. Overall, diagnostic scores are used to indicate cluster scores of "easy, intermediate low, slow to warm up, intermediate high, and difficulty" (manual, p. 4).

The use of caregiver ratings (and sometimes teacher ratings) provides information from those who spend the most time with the child, and therefore can observe behaviors and patterns. The author concedes that such methods have been criticized because of subjective bias. However, the authors refer to evidence of high correlations between rater responses and corroboration with documentable data such as medical records, professional observations and assessments, and developmental level assessment. There are also documented reliability estimates between caregivers, with an average of .70. When there are discrepancies between caregiver ratings, or between repeated ratings over time, the authors suggest more in-depth interviewing for clarification.

Although each scale was developed and validated separately over the past 30 years, the basic sequence and process have remained consistent: The scale is developed, followed by pretest and standardization.

Items in each scale were developed based on behavioral cluster indicators from an original New York Longitudinal Study (Thomas, Chess, Birch, Hertzig, & Korn). Items were rewritten after submission to faculty and graduate students familiar with research. Items were randomly placed on the instruments. Pretesting for each scale included 50–75 children for each scale. Items with correlation scores below .30 were rewritten or eliminated, and the process was repeated. For standardization, a pool of 200–500 children per scale was used, with even age representation throughout the range of each scale. Age and gender analyses were performed, and again items were removed or rewritten.

Sample demographics reveal that most subjects were Euro-American, middle socioeconomic level, and living in the eastern portion of the United States. This may be the source of barriers to generalization. Because the most practical use of the results would be to assist parents in understanding their own interaction patterns with their children, and because environment plays such a crucial role in such assessment, members of other cultures and races, and particularly those of low socioeconomic status, may not find results and recommendations accurate or useful. Several caveats are offered by the authors in relation to the scales. First, the RITQ was standardized on 4–8-month-olds. No norming data are available for 10- and 11-month-olds and for children 7 years, 4 months to 8 years. Second, the variable labeled "distractibility" is measured differently in the EITQ and RITQ, as compared to the other scales, to assess the original Thomas et al. (1963) factor labeled "soothability," whereas the higher-aged scales define distractibility in the context of distraction from tasks. Likewise, the variable labeled "rhythmicity" in infancy could be rather "tightly" defined and assessed in physical patterns such as eating and sleeping; however, in older children this variable became more appropriately "predictability." Therefore, the former refers more to the biological/physical realm, and the latter to the social realm.

Reliability of scores from each scale was assessed by using test-retest and internal consistency methods. As might be expected, the test-retest ranges (administration interval = 20–25 days) were lowest for infants (EITQ = .64–.79; RITQ = .66–.81). Likewise, estimates of internal consistency reliability were lower for these two groups (.43–.76 and .49–.71, respectively). However, careful analysis of summaries from the original samples as compared to analogous scales such as the Bayley Scales of Infant Development (BSID and BSID-II; Bayley, 1969; 1993), show that these results are within acceptable ranges.

Similarly, the validity of the scales increases with age. Most infant scales are found to be low in predictive validity (Cohen & Swerdlik, 1999). However, as pointed out in the authors' own text (Carey & McDevitt, 1995) related to validity assessment, the Carey Scales reflect, as do most other infant scales that rely on caregiver ratings, "at least moderate levels of validity" (manual, p. 14).

In the user's guide and test manual for the Carey Temperament Scales, careful attention is given to reporting and interpretation of the results. The authors point out that assessment is a dynamic interaction of child, caregiver, and setting. Therefore, certain attributes of the caregiver must be taken into account before deciding what type and degree of information is given to caregivers directly (variables include caregiver's knowledge of temperament literature, clinician assessment of the environment, and assessment of child behavior). Therefore, the experience and expertise of the test administrator are crucial to this process, as well as their ability to probe in individual interview. The manual provides careful consideration of all these variables. For example, the list of potentially qualified test users includes only trained and qualified professionals. In addition, careful instructions are provided for preparation, administration, scoring, writing, and interpreting the professional report. Samples of computer-generated scores and reports are included, and helplines are given for assistance in training, report-writing, and report printing. Extensive attention has been given to a computer version of these scales. Technical reports are available for the scales, a website is available, and data analysis is swift and comprehensive via the computer software for scoring.

SUMMARY. As the authors state, assessment of temperament is not as concrete in psychometric terms as some other assessment constructs. Whenever one attempts to explain the "why" of behavior, the reliability and validity of assessment instruments will always be accompanied by caveats and limitations. However, given the constraints inherent in such an undertaking, the Carey Scales represent an attempt that relies on sound theory, research, methodology and psychometric analysis. The only limiting factor is the generalizability to race and SES backgrounds not included in sampling demographics. Therefore, the scales would be most appropriate for middle SES, Euro-Americans in the United States.

REVIEWER'S REFERENCES

Thomas, A., Chess, S., Birch, H. G., Hertzig, M. E., & Korn, S. (1963). *Behavioral individuality in early childhood.* New York: New York University Press.

Bayley, N. (1969). Bayley Scales of Infant Development: Birth to two years. New York: The Psychological Corporation.

Bayley, N. (1993). *Bayley Scales of Infant Development (2nd ed.) manual.* San Antonio: The Psychological Corporation.

Carey, W. B., & McDevitt, S. C. (1995). *Coping with children's temperament: A guide for professionals.* New York: Basic Books.

Cohen, R. J., & Swerdlik, M. E. (1999). *Psychological testing and assessment: An introduction to tests and measurements.* (4th ed.). Mountain View, CA: Mayfield Publishing Company.

[69]
Carroll Depression Scales.

Purpose: Designed as a measure of depression; providing diagnostic as well as level of severity information.
Population: 18 years and over.
Publication Date: 1998.

Scores, 5: Major Depression, Dysthymic Disorder, Melancholic and Atypical Features, HDRS, Total.
Administration: Group.
Price Data, 2001: $93 per complete kit including 25 CDS-R QuikScore™ forms and technical manual (96 pages); $35 per CDS-R 25 QuikScore™ forms (English or French-Canadian); $28 per 25 Brief QuikScore™ forms (English or French-Canadian); $45 per technical manual; $57 per specimen set including 3 CDS-R QuikScore™ forms, 3 Brief CDS-R QuikScore™ forms, and technical manual.
Comments: Self-report; interpretation by qualified professionals only.
Foreign Language Editions: French-Canadian QuikScore™ forms available.
Author: Bernard Carroll.
Publisher: Multi-Health Systems, Inc.
 a) CARROLL DEPRESSION SCALES.
Acronym: CDS-R.
Time: (20) minutes.
Comments: A 52-item self-report measure.
 b) CARROLL DEPRESSION SCALE—REVISED.
Acronym: CDS-R.
Time: (10) minutes.
Comments: A 52-item self-report measure; includes diagnostic index in addition to severity score provided by CDS.
 c) BRIEF CARROLL DEPRESSION INVENTORY.
Acronym: Brief CDS-R.
Time: (2) minutes.
Comments: A 12-item self-report rapid screening measure of depressive symptoms.

Review of the Carroll Depression Scales by SUSAN M. SWEARER, Assistant Professor of School Psychology, University of Nebraska—Lincoln, Lincoln, NE:

The Carroll Depression Scales are self-report measures of depressive symptoms in older adolescents (above age 17) and adults. There is no upper age limit for the Scales. Three scales make up the Carroll Depression Scales: the Carroll Depression Scale (CDS), the Carroll Depression Scale—Revised (CDS-R), and the Brief Carroll Depression Scale (Brief CDS). The CDS was first released in 1981, and the revised version was designed to reflect all the symptoms of depressive disorders in DSM-IV (American Psychiatric Association, 1994). The Brief CDS, developed from the original CDS, was designed as a screening instrument of depressive symptoms. There is also in development a computer-administered CDS-R and Brief CDS.

The Carroll Depression Scales were originally developed in order to match the item content of the Hamilton Depression Rating Scales (HDRS; T5:2216). Additionally, the CDS-R was designed for the assessment of key subtypes of depression; other self-report measures do not assess for subtypes. The manual notes that the CDS-R is a particularly efficient instrument in identifying depression among the elderly and the seriously depressed because the "yes-no" response format of the CDS-R lessens the cognitive burden required in completing self-report measures. As stated in the manual, other self-report measures of depression can be problematic for these populations as they have more complicated responses patterns (i.e., the Beck Depression Inventory [BDI; 37] and the Center for Epidermiologic Studies of Depression Scale [CES-D]).

The original 52 CDS items are included in the CDS-R that was developed in 1996. The CDS-R is a 61-item measure that includes statements that assess all the depression-related symptoms in the DSM-IV. The CDS-R yields four Diagnostic Support Indices that summarize the symptom pattern for corresponding DSM-IV depressive disorder diagnoses. The four indices reflecting DSM-IV criteria use all 61 statements on the CDS-R and yield diagnostic algorithms for symptoms of Major Depression, Dysthymic Disorder, and the modifiers "with melancholic features" and "with atypical features." The total CDS score (52 items from the original CDS) reflects the severity of the patient's depression.

The Brief CDS is composed of 12 of the original 52 CDS statements. The total score on the Brief CDS correlates highly (.92) with the CDS-R total score. When the main objective is to determine the severity of an individual's depressive symptoms, the full CDS-R and the brief CDS will yield similar results. However, when a detailed profile of depressive symptoms or extensive clinical information is needed, the CDS-R is recommended.

Administration and scoring of the CDS-R is relatively simple. The CDS-R takes approximately 10 minutes to complete and the Brief CDS takes a few minutes to complete. The Carroll scales can be completed by older adolescents and adults with a sixth grade reading level. Raw scores, T-scores, and percentiles can be obtained. A patient's responses can be compared to two sets of norms: a control group and a depressed group. However, there are no age norms reported in the manual. There are six scores that can be derived

from the CDS-R. They are: (a) a total score that reflects the severity of the patient's depression, (b) a Diagnostic Support Index for Major Depression, (c) a Diagnostic Support Index for atypical features of Major Depression, (d) a Diagnostic Support Index for melancholic features of Major Depression, (e) a Diagnostic Support Index for Dysthymic Disorder, and (f) scores from the 17 HDRS items.

The severity score on the CDS-R ranges from 0 to 52 and from 0 to 12 on the Brief CDS. A CDS-R score of 10 and a Brief CDS score of 3 differentiates mildly depressed patients from nondepressed patients. Cutoffs were established by 417 community control subjects who completed the Brief CDS and 248 community control subjects who completed the CDS.

Six phases of development of the CDS are described in the manual. Field trials of the CDS were conducted at the University of Michigan, Ann Arbor in the 1970s. Additionally, the CDS has been adopted for use at Duke University Medical Center. Thus, the aggregate data from these two settings have been combined to yield a sample of 959 depressed patients and 248 nondepressed subjects. These groups are used in a variety of the reliability and validity studies.

Validity data are reported in the manual. Face validity, convergent validity, and discriminant validity evidence are all reported. The primary indication of face validity is the correlation of .80 between the CDS and the HRDS. Convergent validity is demonstrated by correlations of the CDS with the Montgomery-Asberg Depression Rating Scale (MADRS) of .71, with the Clinical Global Rating of Depression (CGRD) of .63, with the Beck Depression Inventory (BDI) of .86, with the Center for Epidemiological Studies of Depression Scale (CES-D) of .67, and with the Visual Analog Scale (VAS) of -.71. The CDS displays good discriminant validity in its ability to differentiate between depressed and anxious patients. The correlation between the CDS and State-Trait Anxiety Inventory is .26.

Reliability estimates are also provided in the manual. Split-half reliability between even and odd items on the CDS is .87. Cronbach's coefficient alpha for the CDS is .95. Test-retest reliability estimates were conducted on 16 patients who completed the CDS with between 5 hours to 4 weeks of time between administrations. The

Pearson correlation coefficient was .96. However, in order to be considered in the analysis, the CDS scores had to have a HDRS score that did not vary by more than two points (meaning the 17 HDRS items could not vary by more than two points between administrations). The manual justifies this decision by stating that the CDS is a state measure rather than a trait measure. However, given this parameter, it appears that the test-retest reliability is an inflated estimate.

A major weakness of the CDS is that the comparison groups of 248 normal control respondents (for the CDS-R) and the 417 normal control respondents (for the Brief CDS) are never described. Additionally, *T*-scores and percentiles are derived based on a "pooled cohort" (manual, p. 32) of 959 inpatients and outpatients from two different settings (University of Michigan and Duke University). Methodologically, this is problematic. The CDS-R was constructed during 1996 and reliability and validity information on the revised version are not reported in the manual.

One of the most confusing aspects of the manual is the fact that the data for validity and reliability come from different samples and from aggregate samples. The demographic characteristics of the samples are not adequately described. In fact, only the study sample for the screening abilities of the CDS are described. One hundred percent of the patients and controls were Caucasian. Thus, the utility of the CDS for diverse populations is questionable. The manual states that the CDS has been translated in many languages (Spanish, French, German, Japanese, Chinese, Greek, and American Sign Language). This potentially makes the CDS a useful instrument for individuals from various cultural backgrounds. However, cultural norms are not provided, thus the utility of the CDS for different cultural groups is unknown.

Forty-three research studies from 1979 to 1996 using the CDS are reported in an appendix of the manual. The results of these studies support the efficacy of the CDS as a self-report measure for depressive symptoms.

SUMMARY. It appears the CDS is a useful self-report measure for assessing depressive symptoms in severely depressed individuals and/or in the elderly. Given the importance of multi-modal and multi-informant assessment in depression, the manual acknowledges that the Carroll scales should not be used as the only source of clinical information

(manual, p. 13). Thus, in combination with other sources of data, the Carroll scales appear to be an effective screening tool for assessing depression in the severely depressed and in the elderly.

REVIEWER'S REFERENCE
American Psychiatric Association. (1994). *Diagnostic and statistical manual of mental disorders* (4th ed.). Washington, DC: Author.

[70]
Change Abilitator.
Purpose: Designed to identify six types of concerns people experience when change is introduced into their organization.
Population: Teams.
Publication Date: 1995.
Scores, 6: Information, Personal, Operational, Impact, Collaboration, Transforming.
Administration: Group.
Price Data, 1998: $7.95 per questionnaire; $34.95 per Leader's Guide (149 pages).
Time: (15) minutes.
Comments: Revision of the Stages of Concern Questionnaire.
Author: LHE, INC.
Publisher: Human Resource Development Press.

Review of the Change Abilitator by CYNTHIA A. LARSON-DAUGHERTY, Adjunct Professor, Psychology Department, Towson University, Towson, MD, and Director of Training & Development, Federal Reserve Bank, Baltimore, MD:

SUMMARY. The Change Abilitator Questionnaire and support materials (Leader's Guide) are useful resources for identifying and addressing six typical employee concerns regarding organization change. Overall, the instrument is clearly focused, well-designed, and easy to use. The purpose and results are clear and easy to follow. There are relatively few criticisms of the instrument, and from a practitioner's perspective, should not necessarily dissuade an organization from using it and potentially benefiting from the data it can generate.

TEST COVERAGE AND USAGE. Practitioners should not allow the brevity and lack of depth in the Change Abilitator's initial introduction to dissuade them from using the instrument. What the instrument is capable of generating, and how those data can be effectively used to help employees address concerns about organizational change is further explained in Section 2, "Why Use the Change Abilitator."

The instrument focuses on six typical stages of concern during organization change. Development and design of the instrument appears to have been methodical and deliberate. The instrument aids in generating employee concern, offers anonymity, provides baseline and progressive follow-up data collection, and the ability to create individual, work group, department, and organization profiles.

TEST VALIDATION AND NORMING. There are no data reported for the Change Abilitator. All of the technical information reported is from the previous version, Stages of Concern.

TEST ADMINISTRATION. Test-taker instructions are clear and the instrument is relatively easy to complete. No reference is made in the instructions regarding time limitations, use of reference materials, etc. Scoring and simple interpretation of results are presented in a clear and user-friendly format. Use of a pencil is referenced for the first transferring of results to the scoring profile form. Future edits/revisions or reproduction of the test should note the use of a pencil, time limitations, and reference materials specified in the introduction.

Administration instructions are clear and easy to follow. The Leader's Guide provides several useful options for instrument application (individual, group, department, and organization). The Guide serves as an excellent resource for facilitating lesson plans around the instrument's results.

TEST REPORTING. Test result reporting methods are laid out in a methodical, step-by-step user-friendly format. Result category labels, descriptions, and illustrations are clear and helpful for developing and understanding participant profiles.

TEST AND ITEM BIAS. During the instrument developmental phase, measures were taken to reduce item bias. As noted previously, certain items were recognized as weak or inconsistent and were removed from the final version.

The language of the instrument is easy to follow and terms are readily defined. An individual outside the field of Human Resource Development could easily work their way through the material, complete the test, develop a profile, and interpret the results on a basic level. As a result, the instrument is very appealing.

SUMMARY. Overall, aside from the minor notation cited in the evaluation, the purpose, design, and content delivery of the instrument make it a good test for identifying and addressing the six typical employee organization change concerns.

Review of the Change Abilitator by RICH-ARD J. McCOWAN, Professor Emeritus, State University College at Buffalo and Director, Research and Education, Center for Development of Human Services, Buffalo, NY, and SHEILA C. McCOWAN, Doctoral Candidate in Counseling Psychology, State University of New York at Buffalo, Buffalo, NY:

Organizations are often confronted with situations that require change, such as declining performance, social issues, marketing changes, and legislative mandates. It is difficult to manage change because staff are forced to move from comfortable, familiar settings into an ill-defined future where old rules and procedures can no longer be used. Change forces people to replace routines used successfully in the past with new, untested procedures.

The Change Abilitator is a revised version of the Stages of Concern (SoC) Questionnaire that was developed to identify concerns about change among preservice and in-service teachers. The manual notes that in developing the SoC the author created a pilot instrument of 195 items that was sent to a sample of teachers and college faculty stratified by "years of experience with an innovation" (manual, p. 137). Item correlation and factor analyses were conducted using the 359 returned questionnaires. The hypothesized scales corresponded to the seven factors that explained over 60% of the common variance.

Based on these results, the author selected 35 items representing each factor from the 195-item questionnaire and created the SoC, which was subsequently revised to become the Change Abilitator. This questionnaire was designed to help managers identify employee concerns before changes were implemented. Items use an 8-point scale ranging from *irrelevant* through *very true*. Each item examines an aspect of change in an organization such as "I am concerned about conflict between my interests and my responsibilities" and "I would like to help other employees in their use of the change."

The Change Abilitator identifies six types (or stages) of concern that people experience when change is introduced into an organization including: Information (What does the change involve?); Personal (How will the change affect me?); Operational (How will the change be implemented?); Impact (How will change affect people in the organization?); Collaboration (How can I help implement the change?); Transforming (Can change be accomplished in a different way?). The instrument includes a self-scoring two-part carbonless form. The top sheet contains circles that correspond to normative scores where respondents shade in total scores for each stage. The second page is a profile sheet containing a grid that is used to develop a profile of an individual's or group's concerns about the change. The test is easy to complete, and scoring instructions are very clear. The questionnaire includes descriptions of each stage of concern and describes why the information is important for people and the organization. It includes a guide for developing a personal action plan and a brief description of the research base of the stages of concern. Individual profiles can be averaged to provide an organizational profile.

The Change Abilitator manual contains lesson plans and materials for a workshop based on questionnaire results, including masters for overhead transparencies. These materials provide a complete package for conducting a workshop for organizational staff involved in change and innovation.

SUMMARY. As a training activity, the Change Abilitator is well designed and attractive. However, the factor analysis conducted to develop the instrument was questionable, primarily in the limited, selected, and nonrandom sample of 359 returned questionnaires from a group that only included teachers and college faculty. The manual did not provide the response rate for the sample survey. When factors are standardized and sample variability is reduced, factor weights and intercorrelations are also reduced. In addition, factor analysis requires large samples. The most popular recommendation is the "rule of 10" suggesting at lest 10 cases for each item in the instrument, whereas other methodologists suggest an item-to-variables ratio no lower than 5. Finally, because the sample used for the factor analysis was restricted to teachers and college professors, the construct validity of the instrument is consequently limited to comparable samples until other populations are included in the validation process.

[71]
Child Development Review.

Purpose: A brief screening inventory "designed to help identify children with developmental, behavioral, or health problems."
Population: 18 months to age 5.
Publication Date: 1994.
Acronym: CDR.
Scores, 5: Development (Social, Self-Help, Gross Motor, Fine Motor, Language), Possible Problems, Child Description, Parents' Questions/Concerns, Parents' Functioning.
Administration: Individual.
Price Data, 1998: $10 per 25 parent questionnaire/child development charts; $10 per manual (22 pages).
Time: Administration time not reported.
Comments: Parent-completed questionnaire; scores reflect parents' report of child's present functioning-development.
Author: Harold Ireton.
Publisher: Behavior Science Systems, Inc.

Review of the Child Development Review by TERRY OVERTON, President, Learning and Behavioral Therapies, Inc., Farmville, VA:

DESCRIPTION AND PURPOSE. The Child Development Review manual includes information about the Child Development Review System. This system is composed of the Child Development Review, the Child Development Chart—First Five Years, the Infant Development Inventory, and the Child Development Chart—First 21 Months. This system was designed to serve as a format for reviewing a child's development with the child's parents and to screen for children who may be having developmental problems. The five areas of development assessed are Social, Self-Help, Gross Motor, Fine Motor, and Language. The Child Development Review consists of six open-ended questions for parents concerning the child's strengths, weaknesses, and concerns. A 26-item checklist, containing developmental and behavioral items completes this questionnaire. The parent, the examiner, or both, complete the Child Development Chart—First Five Years, which lists developmental milestones in the five areas. The chart assists with structuring observations or in asking parents for additional information. The final piece of the system is the problems list questions. This is composed of 25 possible problems experienced by children ages birth through 5 years. The Infant Development Inventory and the Child Development Chart are similar instruments to the Child Development Review. These two instruments, for earlier ages, provide a more detailed month-by-month guide of development within the first 21 months of life. The author states that possible developmental problem areas may be further assessed by using a clinical interview format. The author provides examples of using the instrument to structure clinical interview questions.

ADMINISTRATION AND SCORING. The Child Development Review system is administered as an informal criterion-referenced assessment instrument. The parent is given the appropriate interview form for the child's age. This paper-pencil format is easy to administer. The examiner reviews the parents' responses and asks probes about specific problem areas. The examiner and the parent complete the appropriate developmental chart. Instructions for scoring the developmental chart are provided in the manual. The Child Development Chart is scored to determine children whose development is advanced, which is indicated by behavior that is 30% above the level expected for his or her age, around the age expected (behavior is within 30% of the actual age), questionable behavior (behavior that is immature or 30% below the level expected for age), and developmentally delayed (more than 50% below the level expected for age). Suggestions are provided for the examiner to use the results to discuss areas of concern with the parents.

TECHNICAL INFORMATION. The Child Development Review Parent Questionnaire was researched in conjunction with the Preschool Development Questionnaire and the Child Development Review. The manual includes research on all three of these instruments. The sample sizes included in the research ranged from 46 to 2,225 in the four studies. The author reports conclusions from these studies on age and sex differences, common problem areas according to parents, most common problem items, more common problems of early childhood/special education children, and problem items predictive of poor kindergarten performance. The manual does not include specific information on instrument design, item selection, standardization efforts, criterion-related validity data, or detailed descriptive information regarding the samples. The percentages of parents endorsing specific items as problems for their children are included on a table based on a sample of 411 parents. A normative table for ages of 12 months through 5 years is provided for the 30% below and 30% above behaviors for the Child Development Chart—First Five Years. Information about the sample for this table is not included in the table. Several references are provided that list the studies of the various instruments of the system.

EVALUATION. The Child Development Review System's most appealing attribute is its ease of use for parents, attractiveness, and face validity. The instrument seems to be in line with expected developmental milestones; however, the author fails to explain specific details and provide important research explaining the development of the instrument. This information is imperative for potential consumers in various professions in early childhood. The manual does not include sufficient information about validity and reliability. The construct validity would be greatly enhanced by research on developmental progress using longitudinal research. The manual's format and presentation of specific information is confusing and seems to have little continuity from page to page. The system includes several pieces and each part of the system should receive its own section in the manual rather than requiring the consumer to attempt to sort out research or instructions on one piece from another. Because of the ease of administration and minimum time and effort required for scoring, research on the various pieces of this system in a variety of settings, with both average and clinical samples, would be easily conducted. The individual components of the instrument are affordable.

In summary, this system seems to have great appeal because of its ease of use and understanding by parents, short administration and scoring time, and attractiveness. In order for this instrument to have greater appeal for test consumers, the author should include additional research information and redesign the test manual.

Review of the Child Development Review by GARY J. STAINBACK, *Senior Psychologist I, Developmental Evaluation Clinic, East Carolina University School of Medicine, Department of Pediatrics, Greenville, NC:*

The Child Development Review (CDR) is a 99-item parent report form that spans the developmental ages from birth to 5 years of age. Areas of Social Development, Self-Help, Gross Motor, Fine-Motor, and Language are addressed. In addition to the 99 developmental items, there are 25 items of possible problems addressing the child's health, growth, habits, vision and hearing, language, motor, and behavioral problems. Developmental behaviors are included within an age interval whereby 75% of normally developing children have developed the behavior by that age.

Parents are directed to examine the chart and check those items that describe what their child is doing regularly, or moderately well. Items are marked with a "B" if their child is only just beginning to do them or does them only sometimes. Items not marked mean the child is not yet doing that developmental task. Parents are further instructed to stop marking in a column representing an area of development (e.g., Social, Self-Help) when three NOs (blanks) in a row have been encountered. For infants under the age of 18 months, it is recommended by the author that a more detailed chart of infant development be used: the Infant Development Inventory (IDI, Ireton, 1994), a copy of which is provided in the Appendix of the CDR.

The CDR is intended to help professionals review the development of young children with the child's parents. It is intended to be a screening instrument for children who may have a developmental problem. It is also intended to be a means for parents to use when talking about their child's development with a professional or child specialist. The CDR has reportedly been used in preschool settings for screening of development, pediatric practices as part of Well Child exams, and as a parent education tool. Items are based on child development research that has included the Minnesota Child Development Inventory (Ireton & Thwing, 1972), Infant Development Inventory (Ireton, 1994), Early Child Development Inventory (Ireton, 1988), and Preschool Development Inventory (Ireton, 1988). Reportedly, this research has included normally developing children, children at risk, and those with developmental disabilities.

Perhaps the most useful purpose of the CDR would be as part of a developmental interview, where direct yes/no questions are avoided. The suggested starting point for a child is one age level below the child's actual age. The suggested stopping point is when all items within a given age interval are answered "NO" or when three items in a row are answered "NO," or when it "makes sense to stop."

Scale interpretation requires using both the problems items and the developmental items. The author points out that 60% of parents of 3- and 4-year-olds check one or more of the problem items, and gives guidance related to the likelihood of various items accounted for by parents. Scoring the developmental items is accomplished by drawing a line on the chart representing the child's actual age, then two more horizontal lines representing a Below Age Line and Above Age Line. The Below Age Line is drawn at 70% of the

child's actual age, and the Above Age Line at 130%. For each area of development, the child's level of development is rated either: *A = Advanced, AA = Around Age, ?D = Questionable Development,* or *DD = Delayed Development.* Advanced is for behavior over 30% above age level, AA for behavior with 30% of the actual age, ?D for behavior that is 30% younger, and DD for behavior that is 50% or more delayed. A chart is provided in the manual starting at 12 months and ascending in 1-month increments up to 5 years, and provides the 30% age levels above and below the given age.

CDR research is addressed through the earlier instruments from which its items have been drawn. These instruments include the Preschool Development Inventory and the Child Development Inventory. Research on the CDR has also been done in a statewide Early Childhood program that screened 3-year-olds, and in a pediatric well-child care program. Each piece of research spoke to the CDR's usefulness for addressing issues pertaining to the child's development and allowing for further discussion, referral for further evaluation, or the provisions for early childhood education services.

No information is provided regarding norms or standardization, nor for reliability or validity of the instrument. The author has been very active in the development of child development inventories, and comparison of the CDR with a separate measure, different from one of his own, would certainly help to provide evidence with regard to validity. Multi-observer ratings may also help to estimate reliability.

In summary, the CDR is a brief parent report measure of the developmental functioning of young children between birth and 5 years of age. It has been used in medical well-child assessments and in settings to help determine eligibility of preschool children for early intervention. It is also useful as a tool to gather parent observations pertaining to their child's development, and direct attention to their developmental concerns. Unfortunately, the CDR does not provide norms or standardization data, nor are issues of reliability or validity addressed. Reported in the manual are some testimonials of the utility of the instrument. More useful, however, would be data relating to criterion-related validity. The CDR appears to be useful as an aid in the medical-parent interview pertaining to the developmental status of the child, but should not be used alone in this process. It should also be used cautiously as a measure of a child's development and for determining eligibility of Early Intervention services.

REVIEWER'S REFERENCES

Ireton, H. R., & Thwing, E. (1972). *Manual for the Minnesota Child Development Inventory.* Minneapolis: Behavior Science Systems.

Ireton, H. (1988). *Early Child Development Inventory manual.* Minneapolis: Behavior Science Systems.

Ireton, H. (1988). *Preschool Development Inventory manual.* Minneapolis: Behavior Science Systems.

Ireton, H. (1992). *Manual for the Child Development Inventory.* Minneapolis: Behavior Science Systems.

Ireton, H. (1994). The Infant Development Inventory. Minneapolis: Behavior Science Systems.

[72]
Child Sexual Behavior Inventory.

Purpose: Designed as a "measure of sexual behavior in children"; used in the identification of sexual abuse.
Population: Ages 2–12.
Publication Dates: 1986–1997.
Acronym: CSBI.
Scores, 3: Developmentally Related Sexual Behaviors, Sexual Abuse Specific Items, Total.
Administration: Individual.
Price Data, 2001: $120 per introductory kit including manual ('97, 61 pages) and 50 test booklets; $40 per manual; $45 per 25 test booklets.
Time: Administration time not reported.
Comments: Completed by a child's primary caregiver.
Author: William N. Friedrich.
Publisher: Psychological Assessment Resources, Inc.
Cross References: See T5:457 (1 reference).

Review of the Child Sexual Behavior Inventory by FRANK M. BERNT, Associate Professor, Health Services Department, St. Joseph's University, Philadelphia, PA:

The Child Sexual Behavior Inventory (CSBI) is a 38-item parental report instrument that assesses the occurrence of a wide range of sexual behaviors in children ages 2 through 12. Mothers or primary female caregivers indicate the frequency with which they have observed a variety of sexual behaviors on a 4-point rating scale (0 equals *never*, 3 equals *at least once a week*). Its primary use is to evaluate children who have been (or who are suspected of having been) sexually abused; it has also been used to monitor changes in sexual behavior as a result of receiving therapy (Berliner & Saunder, 1996; Hall-Marley & Damon, 1993).

Its original version (Friedrich et al., 1992) represented a departure from the Child Behavior Checklist (T5:451; Achenbach & Edelbrock, 1983); by focusing specifically upon child sexual behaviors, it avoided many of the limitations of a broad-scale assessment of symptoms that had yielded a less consistent pattern of relationships to a history of sexual abuse. The result was an instrument that yielded higher levels of both specificity and sensitivity and a higher overall accuracy in classifying abused versus nonabused cases (highest sensitivity levels were for males ages 2–6; lowest, for females ages 7–12).

The CSBI taps nine different domains of sexual behavior, including boundary problems, exhibitionism, gender role behavior, self-stimulation, sexual anxiety, sexual interest, sexual intrusiveness, sexual knowledge and voyeuristic behavior. In its original version, it yielded five subscale scores. The current version yields a Total score and two subscale scores: a Developmentally Related Sexual Behavior (DRSB) score, which reflects level of age- and gender-appropriate behavior; and a Sexual Abuse Specific Items (SASI) score, which is directly aimed at identifying a history of sexual abuse. Items for the DRSB scale were identified as those endorsed by at least 20% of the norming sample; accordingly, this scale represents an emphasis upon certain sexual behaviors as being normal. Given the dearth of data on "what is normal sexual behavior" (professional manual, p. 1) for children, this feature seems to represent a positive contribution in its own right.

The CSBI is administered in paper-and-pencil format. Its author suggests that it might also be administered via interview, but notes that the CSBI was normed with individuals completing the written version. It takes less than 10 minutes to complete. Scoring is done by hand and can be done in less than 5 minutes. Items are written at a fifth-grade reading level. Potential users should note that item content is necessarily explicit, given the subject matter being assessed. Although administration of the CSBI requires no formal training, the interpretation of CSBI scores requires graduate training in a psychology- or psychiatry-related field as well as coursework in the interpretation of psychological tests; in addition, given the complexity of the problem of child sexual abuse and the dire consequences of faulty conclusions, any user should also be well-versed in the field of child sexual abuse. The author provides useful direction regarding the interpretation of CSBI results in the manual, by listing key questions to consider in addition to CSBI results and by including eight detailed clinical case studies to illustrate issues in interpretation.

One of the apparent improvements represented by the current version is its more comprehensive norming sample. Although the norm sample is larger than for the earlier version, the description of sample selection and screening criteria, as well as of which portions of which samples are used in various studies, is not always clear or consistent. In addition, the norm sample is drawn exclusively from nonclinical groups in Minnesota and in Los Angeles county. Given the weight given to cultural contexts in which sexual behavior occurs (Lamb, 1994), a norm sample that represents a wider range of geographic areas seems called for. One definite advantage of the current version is its providing norms for three separate age groups (2–5, 6–9, and 10–12 years) as well as for each gender.

Although norms are generated using only responses from mothers or primary female caregivers, its potential use with other care providers (fathers, teachers, day care providers, etc.) is addressed in the manual—particularly, the advantage of having information about the child's sexual behavior from more than one observer and in a variety of settings. Studies of interrater reliability have found high to moderate correlations between mother (or female primary caretakers) and father ratings ($r = .83$); between mothers and psychiatric primary nurses ($r = .43$); and between mothers and teachers ($r = .40$). Results were preliminary at best, given very small sample sizes.

Internal consistency estimates for the CSBI Total scale (alpha coefficient) were .72 for the normative sample and .92 for the sexually abused sample. Test-retest reliability over 2 weeks was .91; over 4 weeks, .85. The CSBI (in its earlier or later versions) has been found to be correlated with the Children's Attributions and Perceptions Scale (Mannarino, Cohen, & Berman, 1994); to the Children's Behavior Checklist Internalizing and Externalizing Scores (Cosentino, Meyer-Bahlburg, Alpert, Weinberg, & Gaines, 1995: Friedrich, Grambsch, Broughton, Kuiper, & Beilka, 1991); and to the Sexual Abuse Sensitive measure (SAS: White, Halpin, Strom, & Santilli, 1988). The CSBI's discriminant validity has been explored in several studies. The CSBI Total raw score has been found to discriminate between sexually abused and nonabused preschoolers; between sexually abused school-age children and

children treated for emotional/psychiatric problems with no such history; between sexually aggressive (with no history of sexual abuse) and nonaggressive sexually abuse children; and between sexually aggressive and physically aggressive and nonaggressive children (professional manual, p. 40).

SUMMARY. The CSBI's author is careful to note that, although the SASI's ability to classify children minimizes the occurrence of false positives, it is nonetheless necessary to use the CSBI as "only *one* component of a more comprehensive evaluation" (emphasis in original; professional manual, p. 42). This point needs repeated underscoring. The CSBI's promised utility as a means of identifying children who have been sexually abused rests primarily upon its discriminative power. Discriminant analyses have yielded overall classification levels ranging from 68% to 83% for the CSBI Total score and from 71% to 87% for the SASI. Such numbers would be impressive in many clinical contexts; however, the catastrophic consequences of either a false positive or a false negative in making decisions about whether child sexual abuse has occurred should make the user cautious. The CSBI is arguably the best scale of its kind, and it certainly provides useful supplemental information not available through other commonly used data sources (projective tests, child interviews, physical examinations) and avoids the shortcomings associated with child interviews and subjective clinical judgment (Kuehnle, 1998).

However, the challenge that it faces is proportionate to the complexity of the problem it addresses. "Child sexual abuse does not result in the development of a syndrome of specific symptoms but rather, it is a life event or series of events that will produce a broad range of behaviors in child victims" (Kuehnle, 1998, p. 7). The breadth of that range is further complicated by the particular cultural context in which sexual behaviors of all sorts occur (Lamb, 1994). Accordingly, one area in need of further development is the norming of samples drawn from sites other than Minnesota and California. On the other hand, if used cautiously, it provides a valuable device for indicating the need for further assessment (Dammeyer, 1998).

REVIEWER'S REFERENCES

Achenbach, T., & Edelbrock, C. S. (1983). *Manual for the Child Behavior Checklist and Revised Child Behavior Profile.* Burlington: University of Vermont, Department of Psychiatry.

White, S., Halpin, B. M., Strom, G. A., & Santilli, G. (1988). Behavioral comparisons of young sexually abused, neglected, and nonreferred children. *Journal of Clinical Child Psychology, 17,* 53–61.

Friedrich, W. N., Grambsch, P., Broughton, D., Kuiper, J., & Beilke, R. L. (1991). Normative sexual behavior in children. *Pediatrics, 88,* 456–464.

Friedrich, W. N., Grambsch, P., Damon, L., Hewitt, S. K., Koverola, C., Lang, R. A., Wolfe, V., & Broughton, D. (1992). Child Sexual Behavior Inventory: Normative and clinical comparisons. *Psychological Assessment, 4,* 303–311.

Hall-Marley, S. E., & Damon, L. (1993). Impact of structured group therapy on young victims of sexual abuse. *Journal of Child and Adolescent Group Therapy, 3,* 41–48.

Lamb, M. E. (1994). The investigation of child sexual abuse: An interdisciplinary consensus statement. *Child Abuse and Neglect, 18,* 1021–1028.

Mannarino, A. P., Cohen, J. A., & Berman, S. R. (1994). The Children's Attributions and Perceptions Scale: A new measure of sexual abuse-related factors. *Journal of Clinical Child Psychology, 23,* 204–211.

Cosentino, C. E., Meyer-Bahlburg, H. F. L., Alpert, J. L., Weinberg, S. L., & Gaines, R. (1995). Sexual behavior problems and psychopathology symptoms in sexually abused girls. *Journal of the American Academy of Child and Adolescent Psychiatry, 32,* 940–947.

Berliner, L., & Saunder, B. (1996). Treating fear and anxiety in sexually abused children: Results of a controlled, 2-year follow-up study. *Child Maltreatment, 1,* 294–311.

Dammeyer, M. D. (1998). The assessment of child sexual abuse allegations: Using research to guide clinical decision making. *Behavioral Sciences and the Law, 16,* 21–34.

Kuehnle, K. (1998). Child sexual abuse evaluations: The scientist-practitioner model. *Behavioral Sciences and the Law, 16,* 5–20.

Review of the Child Sexual Behavior Inventory by THOMAS McKNIGHT, Psychologist, Private Practice, Spokane, WA:

The Child Sexual Behavior Inventory (CSBI) is intended to evaluate "children who have been sexually abused or who are suspected of having been sexually abused" (professional manual, p. 1). This 38-item questionnaire looks at a number of sexual behaviors in various areas, including boundary problems, exhibitionism, gender-related behavior, self-stimulation, sexual anxiety, sexual interest, sexual intrusiveness on another person, sexual knowledge, and voyeuristic behavior. Behavioral information is provided by the mother or "primary female care giver" (professional manual, p. 8).

The inventory can be administered individually or in groups. Directions for administration and scoring are generally clear, items are rather specific, and instructions provided the respondent(s) are detailed enough to eliminate the impact of these issues on reliability and validity. In addition to the total score (CSBI Total), raw scores are summed for two additional scales: Developmentally Related Sexual Behaviors (DRSB) and Sexual Abuse Specific Items (SASI), which are scored separately for girls and boys in three different age groups (2–5, 6–9, 10–12 years). The raw scores are then converted into *T* scores and a score above 65 is considered "clinically significant" (professional manual, p. 13). Any *T* score between 60 and 64 suggests difficulty and possibly significant behavior problems, and 59 and below are considered "nonsignificant." The basis for these conclusions is not clarified in the manual.

The instrument was standardized using 1,114 children in three "nonclinical samples" (two from Minnesota and one from California). Children with a substantiated or suspected history of sexual abuse were excluded. A sexual abuse sample included 512 children from more diverse geographical regions. The means and standard deviations of the CSBI and DRSB, and SASI raw scores are provided for the normative sample and the sexually abused sample, separated by gender and age group. Typically, the standard deviation is greater than the mean score, which is somewhat problematic but actually often seen in checklists.

Reliability analysis of the CSBI Total scale found rather modest internal consistency with an alpha coefficient of .72. However, internal consistency for the sexual abuse sample was more impressive with an alpha coefficient of .92. Test-retest reliability, with a 2-week interval, was .91 and interrater reliability (mother and father ratings) was .83 for the CSBI Total raw score. However, when ratings by primary care nurses were compared to rating by the mothers or foster mothers of 19 psychiatric inpatient children, the coefficient dropped to .43.

The manual notes that when the nonclinical group was contrasted with the sexual abuse group, the latter had higher CSBI Total raw scores across each of the six age-gender groups. Classification accuracy (nonclinical vs. sexual abuse) varied but was reported to be greater than 68% in all cases and as high as 82.8% in two of the six groups. Correct classification, using the SASI score, ranged from 71.4% to 86.8%. However, the manual does not provide information about actual hit rates of the four possible categories: true positive, false positive, true negative, false negative, and this is a serious limitation. Additionally, it is unclear whether a *T* score of 65 or another score was used as the "cutoff."

SUMMARY. In the future, the Child Sexual Behavior Inventory may be a valuable component of a comprehensive evaluation of children who are suspected victims of sexual abuse. Currently, it must be considered a research instrument and as the author points out, utility "depends on continuing research" to understand the relationship between sexual abuse and "different aspects of sexual behavior in children" (professional manual, p. 42). Continued research with a larger sample of children with greater geographic representation is needed. Specific information about accuracy in classification is also needed; providing the percent of children correctly classified is of limited value without the actual breakdown of this information and the actual cutoff scores necessary for optimal classification.

Although a number of case studies are reported in the manual, statistical information needs to be expanded significantly and more detail about the research referenced in the manual will be of value. The inclusion of the DSRB scale (Developmentally Related Sexual Behaviors) in this inventory makes it clear certain sexual behaviors are age appropriate and not symptoms. Expanded information in this area will be useful.

There are a number of cautions in the Child Sexual Behavior Inventory manual. The author notes it is important to clarify information provided by the parent who responds to the inventory in order to assure accuracy of responding to a specific item. He also notes it is "essential" this instrument be used in combination with clinical measures and procedures "to best understand children and assure their safety" (professional manual, p. 42). However, there is great concern someone will use this inventory, in spite of the author's caution, to support an otherwise unfounded allegation of sexual abuse.

[73]
Childhood Trauma Questionnaire.

Purpose: Designed as a self-report inventory for "screening for histories of abuse and neglect."
Population: Ages 12 and up.
Publication Dates: 1997–1998.
Acronym: CTQ.
Scores, 5: Emotional Abuse, Physical Abuse, Sexual Abuse, Emotional and Physical Neglect and Minimization/Denial of Abuse.
Administration: Individual.
Price Data, 2000: $84.50 per complete kit including 25 READYSCORE answer documents and manual ('98, 76 pages); $34 per 25 READYSCORE answer documents; $62 per manual.
Time: (5) minutes.
Comments: A 28-item, self-report inventory.
Authors: David P. Bernstein and Laura Fink.
Publisher: The Psychological Corporation.
Cross References: See T5:460 (2 references).

Review of the Childhood Trauma Questionnaire by MICHAEL FURLONG, Professor, and RENEE PAVELSKI, Doctoral Candidate, Counseling, Clinical, School Psychology Program, University of California, Santa Barbara, Graduate School of Education, Santa Barbara, CA:

The Childhood Trauma Questionnaire (CTQ) is a 28-item retrospective, self-report measure of childhood (and adolescent for adult respondents) abuse and neglect experiences and is offered for use with individuals ages 12 and older. Its stated uses are (a) for rapid abuse-history taking for treatment planning, (b) to encourage disclosure of childhood abuse as part of clinical assessments, and (c) for use in epidemiological and correctional studies involving childhood abuse. Ironically, although the word "trauma" is used in the title, this instrument is not a measure of the impact that abuse or neglect has on a person. Furthermore, it does not assess factors associated with abuse-related trauma such as the use of force and the relationship of the victim to the perpetrator in sexual abuse.

The CTQ contains five subscales, three assessing abuse (Emotional, Physical, and Sexual) and two assessing neglect (Emotional and Physical). Each subscale has five items and there is a three-item Minimization/Denial subscale to check for extreme response bias, specifically attempts by respondents to minimize their childhood abuse experiences. A 5-point frequency of occurrence scale is utilized: (1) *never true*, (2) *rarely true*, (3) *sometimes true*, (4) *often true*, and (5) *very often true*. Each subscale score ranges from 5 (no history of abuse or neglect) to 25 (very extreme history of abuse and neglect).

CONTENT AND SCORING. The CTQ initially had 70 items derived from a review of the maltreatment literature and a review of other trauma scales. The items were written in behavioral terms so as to avoid using stigmatizing words such as "abuse." Most of the items are presented in the past tense and ask the respondent to indicate how often a behavior occurred during childhood (or adolescence) (e.g., "I was punished with a belt, a board, a cord, or some other object"). Curiously, however, three key items specifically ask if the respondent believes he or she was "emotionally abused," "sexually abuse," or "physically abused." These three items stand out as being different than the other CTQ items.

The Emotional Neglect subscale is unique because all five of its items describe positive childhood experiences (e.g., #28. "My family was a source of strength and support"). The authors argue that the absence or infrequent expression of positive affect and support constitutes emotional neglect. This is likely to be a matter of debate for some users of this scale. A psychometric analogy would be to have a set of items all stating positive mood states (e.g., "I was happy as a child") to be reverse scored and then purported to measure depression. Nonetheless, this subscale is a nice strength-based measure, which, only because of its reverse scoring, is forced into a pathology model. Similarly, Physical Neglect may not assess outright lack of physical care. Responses to items about not having enough to eat, wearing dirty clothes, and being taken to the doctor are influenced by a person's experiences with poverty in childhood, not necessarily neglect.

NORMS. Norms were derived from six samples, only three of which had more than 300 respondents: (a) 378 mostly Black, male inpatient substance abusers; (b) 398 adolescent psychiatric inpatients; and (c) 1,225 all female, mostly White HMO members (although in the manual, one table gives 1,187 as the number of HMO members). These three subsamples comprise 2,001 of the 2,201 individuals in the CTQ norm group. The former two subsamples are from New York psychiatric facilities and the latter sample was derived from the Pacific Northwest. Despite using nonrepresentative samples, the authors offer "norms" for each of these subsamples. The adult substance user norms present percentile ranks derived from just 58 female respondents. Percentile ranks are also provided for adolescent psychiatric patients and are derived from just 171 males and 227 females. As pointed out by the authors, the distributions of scores, even in these high-risk samples, were quite skewed—most individuals reported little to no abuse or neglect. The mean raw score associated with the 50th percentile for both the male and female adolescents was 7, just 2 points higher than the lowest score possible.

The CTQ norms were also used to create the severity classification categories of (1) *None or Minimal,* (2) *Low to Moderate,* (3) *Moderate to Severe,* and (4) *Severe to Extreme.* For three of the subscales (Physical Abuse, Sexual Abuse, and Physical Neglect) scores of 13 or higher fall in the Severe to Extreme classification. Practically, this means that if an individual answers three of five subscale items as "rarely true" and two items as "sometimes true," they would have a raw score of 13. How these classifications apply to regional groups in the U.S. is completely unknown. These categories should be used with extreme caution.

RELIABILITY. Internal consistency coefficients are offered for all of the subsamples with generally favorable patterns reported. Focusing on the three largest subsamples, the Sexual Abuse (alphas of .93 to .95) and Emotional Neglect (alphas of .88 to .92) are the most reliable subscales. Emotional Abuse (alphas of .84 to .89) and Physical Abuse (alphas of .81 to .86) have acceptable reliabilities. The internal consistency of Physical Neglect (alphas of .63 to .78) is marginal. Test-retest reliabilities were derived from a small sample of 40 methadone-maintained outpatients who completed the scales twice over an average 3.6-month period. All stability coefficients were near .80, suggesting good consistency of responses over time.

VALIDITY. The CTQ's validity was examined first by conducting an exploratory factor analysis of the 70-item version using data from the adult substance abusers and the adolescent psychiatric inpatients. The results of this analysis are presented in previous publications, but no results are presented in the manual, which is an oversight. The exploratory factor analyses produced four factors with the adult sample and five factors with the adolescent sample. The authors used these findings to reduce the length of the scale to its current 25 items (plus 3 bias response items). The manual presents the results of confirmatory factor analyses in greater detail. These analyses tested the goodness of fit of the five-factor CTQ subscale model for the adult substance abusers, the adolescent psychiatric inpatients, and a subsample of the HMO members. The results showed structural invariance across the three samples suggesting that they measured the same constructs across groups.

SUMMARY. The CTQ authors are to be commended for constructing an instrument that attempts to measure all major categories of abuse and neglect, which is not an easy task. The CTQ is a well-packaged instrument that has potential value when included in an outpatient or inpatient clinical assessment with adults. Its regular use provides an efficient way to ensure that all clients are given the opportunity to disclose abusive childhood experiences and likewise will encourage the therapist to explore the influence of abusive experiences as part of the client's case history. It is only in this context that it is likely to uncover previously repressed memories of childhood trauma-producing events. Its more common and appropriate use would be as part of epidemiological studies, with consenting adults. Such studies would help establish abuse and neglect base rates in the general population and better establish the impacts of abuse and neglect across clinical and nonclinical populations.

Despite potential beneficial uses of the CTQ with individuals who have experienced abuse, the manual devotes limited attention to the issue of how to debrief individuals who disclose abuse in their CTQ responses. This may not be a critical issue in clinical settings that serve known victims of abuse; however, administering the CTQ as a screening tool with adolescents in schools or as part of the evaluation of demonstration mental health projects raises significant ethical issues. It will be necessary to consider how informed consent will be handled when disclosures about abuse or neglect would require clinicians or researchers, as mandated reporters, to inform local child protective agencies of any suspected abuse.

Review of the Childhood Trauma Questionnaire by JONATHAN SANDOVAL, Professor of Education, Division of Education, University of California, Davis, Davis, CA:

To begin, it is important to note that the name, Childhood Trauma Questionnaire (CTQ), is misleading for this short questionnaire. The central constructs underlying the questionnaire are emotional, physical, and sexual abuse. Other traumatic events that may occur during childhood, such as the death of a parent or a major illness, are not assessed. Nevertheless, as a screening tool to identify individuals with a childhood history of abuse and neglect, this device may have utility.

The format of the questionnaire is straightforward and easy to use. The examinee responds to 28 simple questions on a 5-point Likert scale ranging from *Never True* to *Very Often True*. The hand-scoring features of the answer sheet lend themselves to accurate scoring with few clerical errors. Comparison group norms are available for male and female adult substance abusers, male and female adolescent psychiatric inpatients, and female middle-class HMO members from the northwestern United States. Because of unknown bias operating in the selection of these groups, the norms should be used with extreme caution. Undoubtedly, there are differences in the culture-based conceptualization of abuse, so that further research on this scale will have to be undertaken with clearly defined culturally homogeneous groups.

The manual accompanying the CTQ is complete in describing the development of the questionnaire, in setting forth guidelines for administration and scoring, and in reporting the psychometric characteristics of the test. Inquiring into issues surrounding childhood abuse raises a number of questions of sensitivity, intrusiveness and, in the case of adolescents, legal obligations. These facets of test use have been addressed nicely in the chapter on general testing guidelines.

The content of the CTQ items seems to derive logically from the underlying construct. The three items correlating highest with their respective scales are "I believe that I was physically abused," "Someone molested me," and "I believe that I was emotionally abused." Other items have been phrased to avoid potentially pejorative terms. Because the items are stated so directly, it would seem that the questionnaire would duplicate a number of common intake interview forms. The virtue of the CTQ is that the item wordings here have been scrupulously tested and are now standardized.

The items are written at a sixth grade reading level and the manual is clear that reading level and intellectual functioning should be assessed before administering the scale. Although the manual suggests the CTQ may be given to individuals as young as age 12, it is probably best used with older adolescents and adults. Directions in the manual anticipate a number of contingencies in administration.

The psychometric qualities of the test are acceptable, although continued validation of the test is certainly warranted. The internal consistency reliability estimate for the four scales are good across seven samples used in the test development (typically between .80 and .93), although the Physical Neglect Scale alpha coefficients are only moderate (median .66). The test-retest reliability estimate (administration interval 3–4-month average) clustered around .80 for the scales in a group of 40 methadone-maintained outpatients. It would be useful to have stability estimates for a more typical population.

Construct validity was examined through somewhat incompletely described exploratory and confirmatory factor analysis. There is evidence for the existence of the five factors used in the scale, although the physical and emotional abuse factors seem highly correlated. We are not told how well other models might fit. For example, the emotional neglect factor, which is made up of items framed as positive statements, is highly correlated with the emotional abuse factor. The authors do acknowledge that these factors are, and should be, correlated.

Additional evidence for construct validity is presented in the mean scores of various groups (e.g., college undergraduates, adult substance abusers, female fibromyalgia patients). The more "normal" populations have lower scores, as expected. It would have been more helpful had some of the groups been further broken down into those who had been abused and those who had not. Demonstrating a significant difference between those with a history of abuse and those without would have been more persuasive. It is curious this information was not reported.

The manual does indicate good correlations between scores on the CTQ and ratings derived from semistructured interviews administered by clinicians and ratings by therapists. The correspondence of the CTQ scores with ratings of Sexual Abuse and Physical Abuse seem particularly noteworthy (typically correlations from .50 to .75).

The CTQ authors evidently view abuse or neglect to be on a continuum ranging from minimal to extreme. They offer score levels or cut scores to indicate each of four categories (none or minimal, low to moderate, moderate to severe, and severe to extreme). These scores were derived by determining the point at which the maximum number of individuals were correctly classified as abused and the maximum number of individuals were also correctly classified as having experienced little abuse. These points were calculated for adolescent psychiatric inpatients and for female HMO members but the latter are recommended and tabled in the manual. The user should be aware that these categories were derived from the self-reports of middle-class females. Use with other populations should proceed only after further research is completed.

Included on the CTQ is a three-item Minimization/Denial Scale. This scale functions somewhat as a social desirability scale and is designed to detect the underreporting of maltreatment. Scores from this short scale do correlate with like measures of social desirability and it is probably a useful adjunct to interpretation. The scale does not have a protection against faking abuse, and it would be easy to dissemble on this test.

SUMMARY. This test does fill a gap in screening for abuse and neglect. As a new test, more research will have to be done to document its utility for a variety of groups. It obviously should not be used alone to make clinical decisions, but should help to identify individuals for further interviewing and treatment around issues of abuse.

[74]
Children's Depression Rating Scale, Revised.

Purpose: Constructed as a "screening instrument, diagnostic tool, and severity measure of depression in children."
Population: Ages 6–12.
Publication Date: 1996.
Acronym: CDRS—R.
Scores: Total score only.
Administration: Group.
Price Data, 1999: $62.50 per complete kit including manual (91 pages), and 25 administration booklets; $18.50 per 25 administration booklets; $48 per manual.
Time: (15—20) minutes.
Comments: Ratings by health care professionals.
Authors: Elva O. Poznanski and Hartmut B. Mokros.
Publisher: Western Psychological Services.
Cross References: See T5:473 (8 references).

Review of the Children's Depression Rating Scale, Revised by E. THOMAS DOWD, Professor of Psychology, Kent State University, Kent, OH:

The Children's Depression Rating Scale, Revised (CDRS-R) is a clinician-rated scale for assessing childhood depression that is modeled after the Hamilton Rating Scale for Depression, an adult measure. It was designed to be used with children between the ages of 6 and 12. It is an interview-based instrument by which a sensitive clinician elicits information that is used to assess depression in 17 symptom areas. It takes about 20–30 minutes to complete. In addition, the same interview-based scale can be used to obtain information about the child's level of depression from parents and other significant others such as teachers. Thus, it is possible to obtain a comprehensive assessment of the level of childhood depression, a phenomenon that the authors say has been and is considerably underreported. The authors state that this instrument should be used as a preliminary finding to support a follow-up with more exhaustive assessment of childhood depression.

The CDRS-R comes with a manual and an administration booklet. The manual includes an introduction and subsequent chapters on administration and scoring, interpretation and case examples, an excellent review of the literature on depressive disorders in childhood, development and standardization of the instrument, and psychometric properties. There are also two appendices, an interview guide and sample responses for child interviews, and a corresponding guide for parents (and by implication other significant figures in the child's life).

One administration booklet is required for each administration. It consists of a 5- or 7-point rating scale for each of the 17 domains, along with descriptors of each rating and space for comments by the interviewer. The front page contains a "depression thermometer" which includes a total raw score (the Summary Score) as well as a conversion to *t*-scores and percentiles. The *t*-scores are then given an interpretation. There is also a comparison of symptom ratings from all sources (i.e., child, parent, other, as well as a combination Best Descriptor of Child). Apparently, the interpretation is based on previously collected normative data although that is not entirely clear.

The instrument, according to the manual, is administered according to a semistructured interview. This means that, although the interview follows a standard format in conducting the assessment interview, the authors also encourage flexibility in jumping ahead and exploring topics that arise spontaneously even though they may be out off place sequentially. This should be done, according to the manual, to avoid reinforcing any existing sense of alienation and isolation on the part of the child and combine rigor with empathy. Indeed, the consistent demonstration of sensitivity to children in collecting the data is one of the strengths of this instrument and its approach. The appendices provide suggested topics and prompts and sample responses. There are also four case examples to provide guidance in conducting these interviews and scoring the results although, given the flexible approach required, more than four might have been helpful. The flexibility of approach is also demonstrated in the overall Best Description of the Child, which is not simply a rigid and standardized combination of the three separate assessments (child, parent, other). Rather, depending on the circumstances, the child's data may be given precedence or the parent's or teacher's data might. With such a flexible approach, I wondered if extensive training might be necessary to fully utilize the CDRS-R (actually, I still do). However, interrater reliability estimates for the original unrevised instrument between interviewers familiar with the instrument and those unfa-

miliar with it resulted in similar scores, although there is no definition of "familiarity." Interrater reliability was .74 for interviewers familiar with it and .75 for those unfamiliar with it. Item-total correlations for interviewers familiar with the CDRS had a median of .62 whereas item-total correlations for interviewers unfamiliar with it had a median of .61. Nevertheless, my assessment of the instrument is that training would be required before it could be used well. The very flexibility that allows for empathy and sensitivity may also reduce the standardization and reliability unless the interviewer has had supervised practice.

The original instrument was first published in 1979. Its interrater reliability estimates at that time were good, ranging between .92 and .96. Internal consistency reliability estimates, conducted by correlating each item with a Global Rating of Depression and the Summary Score, resulted in a median correlation of .70. I should note that these reliabilities appear to be based on child assessments only, not parents or others. The CDRS was later revised by adding two symptom areas (Excessive Guilt and Depressed Feelings), renaming some of the symptom areas, and revising the rating anchors. Interrater reliability for the revised scale was estimated as .92 and test-retest (2-week interval) reliability was estimated as .80. Internal consistency reliability (estimated using coefficient alpha) was reported as .85. Validity was demonstrated by a correlation of .87 between the CDRS-R Summary Score and an independently assigned Global Rating of Depression, by a correlation of .48 between the CDRS-R and a modified version of the Hamilton Rating Scale for Depression, and by the ability of the CDRS-R to predict psychiatrically referred children diagnosed with depressive disorders. Scores on the CDRS-R were also found to be associated with independent assessments of suicidal ideation and behavior as well as other depressive symptoms.

SUMMARY. This appears to be a well-designed and researched instrument with years of development, reliability, and validity studies behind it. Its strengths include the semistructured interview-based approach, which is helpful in assessing children who may be more reticent than adults in describing and admitting symptoms. In addition, the authors quite appropriately describe the use of this instrument as a first step in a more comprehensive assessment. Strengths also include the provision for multiple sources of data from parents and others and the flexible combination of these data into a Best Description of the Child.

This very flexibility, however, can lead to loss of both reliability and validity if a standardized format is not followed to some extent. Therefore, I would suggest, perhaps more than the authors do, supervised training and experience in using the CDRS-R. The manual is dense and packed with considerable information, leading to some difficulties in understanding clearly what the authors are saying. This is especially noticeable in Chapter 5, Development and Standardization, and Chapter 6, Psychometric Properties, where reliability and validity data are presented in confusing ways. It would be helpful, for example, to have all the reliability information in one place followed by the validity information. As it is reliability information is provided in both chapters and validity information in Chapter 6 only, leading me to wonder if no validity studies were conducted on the original instrument at all. Some of the terms (e.g., Global Rating of Depression) are not well-defined so that the reader must search throughout the manual to determine what they mean. The interrater reliabilities especially are presented in confusing ways and it was not easy to determine what was being compared to what.

In summary, this appears to be a good instrument for an initial assessment of childhood depression. It should be used by a trained rater, however, and cannot be administered as easily as paper-and-pencil measures.

Review of the Children's Depression Rating Scale, Revised by DONALD LEE STOVALL, Associate Professor of Counseling & School Psychology, University of Wisconsin—River Falls, River Falls, WI:

The Children's Depression Rating Scale, Revised (CDRS-R) is designed to help psychologists and mental health clinicians assess the level of depression in children from ages 6 through 12. The authors assert the instrument has been used as a screening instrument, diagnostic tool, or as a measure of severity of a child's depression. In clinical settings, the instrument can be used to confirm or document a diagnosis of depression. In nonclinical settings, such as a school psychologist's or physician's office, the CDRS-R can be used to screen for depression in children. A clinical psy-

chologist, clinical social worker, or psychiatrist could refer children in nonclinical settings who obtain an elevated rating on the CDRS-R for a more extensive assessment. As stated by the authors, the CDRS-R is a "first step" in a clinical assessment of a child referred for evaluation. In addition to its use as a diagnostic tool in clinical settings, or as a screening tool in school settings, the CDRS-R also has applications as a research tool involving studies of depression in children. It can be used as a pre- or posttest measure regarding the effectiveness of interventions applied to children.

The CDRS-R assesses 17 symptoms of depression, including those found in the *Diagnostic and Statistical Manual of Mental Disorders* (DSM-IV; American Psychiatric Association, 1994). The symptoms assessed by the instrument include social withdrawal, sleep disturbance, excessive fatigue, and suicidal ideation, among others. The CDRS-R is completed as a semistructured interview with the child, or with the child's parent. The examiner evaluates the child on 14 symptoms, and three other ratings of the child are based upon observations of the child's nonverbal behavior during the interview.

Each symptom covered by the CDRS-R is presented on a continuum and rated on a scale from 1 to 5, or 1 to 7. The lowest score (1) is reserved for "no difficulties." The highest score (5 on 5-point scale, 6/7 on 7-point scale) is reserved for "severe clinically significant difficulties." The scale for Suicidal ideation, for example, begins with a rating of 1 indicating that the child has an understanding of the word suicide, but he or she does not apply that term to himself or herself. The scale for Suicidal Ideation ends with a rating of 7 if the child had made a suicide attempt within the last month, or is considered actively suicidal. Although the rating scale for each item may range from 1 to 5 or 1 to 7, not each scale point has an associated descriptor. The authors present "anchor points," which give the rater specific standards to score. The examiner may use points in between the "anchor points" if he or she is uncertain of the degree to which to rate a child's symptom.

In the manual for the CDRS-R, the authors provide a useful interview guide for conducting an interview with the child, or in conducting the interview with the parent of the child. These guides are contained in the Appendix and they include sample responses and information about how those sample responses would be rated. The protocol is structured to allow results from an interview with the child to be compared with those of the parent, or other person familiar with the child. Additionally, if multiple ratings have been obtained, the clinician can combine information from multiple ratings to develop a summary of the "Best Description of the Child."

The child's raw score on the CDRS-R is converted to a *T*-score. Interpretation is based upon the *T*-score range that contains the child's score. If a child obtains a *T*-score in the 65–74 range, the interpretation is that a depressive disorder "is likely to be confirmed" by a comprehensive diagnostic evaluation. A *T*-score range of 75–84 indicates that a depressive disorder diagnosis is "very likely" to be confirmed. A *T*-score of 85 or higher indicates that a depressive disorder diagnosis is "almost certain" to be confirmed. At a *T*-score level of 85 or higher, the recommendation is made to intervene and evaluate the needs of the child immediately. It is clear from the manual and from the descriptive statements associated with the *T*-scores that no diagnosis of depression or dysthymic disorder should ever be made based solely on the results of the CDRS-R. The CDRS-R would be one element in a comprehensive assessment of a child, particularly in cases where there are concerns about depression.

The CDRS-R offers a comprehensive set of descriptions of behaviors associated with a clinical diagnosis of depression. The authors present detailed definitions of symptoms of depression that increase the likelihood that users of the measure understand the items, and how symptoms should be rated. The use of "anchor points" provides a good foundation for those rating a child. Both the specificity of the definitions of the symptoms provided by the authors in the manual and the use of the "anchor points" are important elements with regards to the reliability of scores from the instrument, and the usefulness of the instrument as a research tool.

STANDARDIZATION. The CDRS-R norms were developed from a clinical and school sample. The standardization sample, however, is not nationally representative. The sample used is also not culturally diverse. These issues do present some cautions about the use of the instrument. The clinical sample, which involved 78 children, was drawn from children who were involved with the Youth Affective Disorders Clinic at the University of Illinois Medical Center, and the Rush-Presbyterian-St. Luke's Medical Center. These centers were located in Chicago, Illinois. The children in the clinical sample initially met the DSM-III criteria for a depressive disorder, and were followed at 6-week, 6-month, and one-year intervals. The authors reported that 77% of the clinical sample met the criteria for a Depressive Disorder Diagnosis and that 23% met the criteria for some other psychiatric diagnosis. The school sample involved a one-time assessment of 223 children from a magnet school in the Chicago public school system. These children were randomly selected for participation in the study. In addition to the children who were interviewed, 109 parent interviews were also conducted.

The authors do not provide a breakdown of the clinical sample based upon age. This information is provided for the school sample. The authors did not report an attempt to match the sample to a specific census based upon several commonly used demographic or racial factors. They report that both the clinical sample and the school sample fell into the categories of white, black, or mostly Hispanic. Children from Asian or Native-American heritage did not appear to be represented in the sample. Examiners who might work with a significant number of children whose heritage is Asian or Native American would need to be cautious about using the instrument. Certainly, use with more diverse populations is an area of research with the CDRS-R. The age range of the CDRS-R spans children from age 6 through age 12. This also creates some caution about the standardization. Given the size of the clinical sample, and lack of a specific breakdown based upon age, certain age ranges may have small numbers of children who were involved in the standardization. Again, further research with specific age groups is suggested.

The authors reported various forms of reliability data. Based upon 25 interviews of children within the clinical sample, conducted by pairs of child psychiatrists, a product moment correlation of .92 was reported. Test-retest reliability estimate, based upon a 2-week post intake assessment, was reported at .80. Based upon these assessments of reliability, the CDRS-R appears to produce reliable scores. Reliability when assessing depression can be influenced by many factors, as depression can be a variable state. Some fluctuation in assessments of depression in children can be expected.

The authors reported various forms of validity data. Convergent validity evidence involved the comparison of the CDRS-R with other measures of depression. The authors report a comparison of the CDRS-R results with a Global Rating of Depression score. The Global Rating of Depression score represented clinical judgement assigned by clinicians regarding the severity of depression. The results of the CDRS-R were compared to this score, and a correlation of .87 was found. The summary score from the CDRS-R was also compared to the summary score from the Hamilton Rating Scale for Depression. This comparison yielded a correlation of .46, with $p<.01$. The authors also provide information in the manual indicating that the results from the CDRS-R were able to discriminate children diagnosed with depression from those with some other diagnosis or from children without a diagnosis.

SUMMARY. The CDRS-R is presented as a tool to assist in the diagnosis of depression in children ages 6–12. In nonclinical settings, it can be used as a tool to help professionals screen children for depression. In clinical settings, it can be used as a component in an overall assessment of a child's needs. It can be used as a baseline measure for depression, with the ability to compare data from multiple perspectives. The authors present a detailed manual that provides clear definitions of symptoms associated with depression, and samples of how items might be scored. The use of anchor points provides structure to ratings given by examiners. Information is included in the manual regarding the development and standardization of the instrument. The usefulness of the CDRS-R as a screening device for depression, or as a research tool, is supported. The weakness of the CDRS-R relates to a lack of a national standardization, and failure to include Asian or Native-American children in the clinical or norm sample.

REVIEWER'S REFERENCE

American Psychiatric Association. (1994). *Diagnostic and statistical manual of mental disorders* (4ᵗʰ ed.). Washington, DC: Author.

[75]
Children's Memory Scale.

Purpose: "Designed to evaluate learning and memory functioning" in children and adolescents.
Population: Ages 5–16.
Publication Dates: 1997–1998.
Acronym: CMS.

Scores, 34: 14 Core Battery Subtest Scores: Dot Locations (Learning, Total Score, Long Delay); Stories (Immediate, Delayed, Delayed Recognition); Faces (Immediate, Delayed); Word Pairs (Learning, Total Score, Long Delay, Delayed Recognition); Numbers (Total Score); Sequences (Total Score); 6 supplemental scores: Dot Locations (Short Delay), Stories (Immediate Thematic, Delayed Thematic), Word Pairs (Immediate), Numbers (Forward, Backward); 6 Supplemental scores from 3 Supplemental Subtests: Word Lists (Learning, Delayed, Delayed Recognition), Picture Locations (Total Score), Family Pictures (Immediate, Delayed); 8 Indexes: Visual Immediate, Visual Delayed, Verbal Immediate, Verbal Delayed, General Memory, Attention/Concentration, Learning, Delayed Recognition.
Administration: Individual.
Levels, 2: 5–8, 9–16.
Price Data, 1999: $345.80 per complete kit including manual ('97, 288 pages), 25 record forms for both age levels, 2 stimulus booklets, response grid, 8 chips in a pouch, and 5 family picture cards; $33.50 per record forms (specify level); $84 per manual ('97, 288 pages); $83 per computer Scoring Assistant (available for Windows or Macintosh).
Time: (20–50) minutes.
Author: Morris J. Cohen.
Publisher: The Psychological Corporation.

Review of the Children's Memory Scale by SCOTT A. NAPOLITANO, Adjunct Assistant Professor, Department of Educational Psychology, University of Nebraska-Lincoln, Lincoln, NE, and Pediatric Neuropsychologist, Lincoln Pediatric Group, Lincoln, NE:

The Children's Memory Scale (CMS) is an individually administered instrument developed to evaluate learning and memory in individuals ranging in age from 5 to 16. The complete CMS consists of nine subtests that assess functioning in three domains: (a) auditory/verbal, (b) visual/nonverbal, and (c) attention/concentration. Each domain includes two core subtests and one supplemental subtest. Each subtest in the auditory/verbal domain and the visual/nonverbal domain contains both an immediate memory component and a delayed memory component, with a delay of approximately 30 minutes between the two components. Different combinations of subtests are combined to yield eight index scores: Verbal Immediate, Verbal Delayed, Delayed Recognition, Learning, Visual Immediate, Visual Delayed, Attention/Concentration, and General Memory.

The CMS manual is well written and the test instructions are clearly explained and easy to understand. Comprehensive and easy-to-follow test instructions are also printed directly in the stimulus booklets, facilitating ease of administration. The core battery may be administered in approximately 30–35 minutes of actual test time, and the supplementary battery adds an additional 10–15 minutes of testing time. Each subtest in the auditory/verbal as well as the visual/nonverbal domains also includes a delay task that requires a 30-minute delay from the completion of the immediate memory tasks. The CMS has an optional scoring assistant that greatly simplifies scoring and includes many different report options from a simple summary of index scores to a complete report including background information, score comparisons, and graphs. One drawback to the current version of the scoring assistant is that case reports may not be saved for later review or printing.

The standardization sample for the CMS was stratified by age, sex, race/ethnicity, geographic region, and parent educational level. Census data (U.S. Bureau of the Census, 1995) was utilized for stratification of race/ethnicity, geographic region, and parent education level. The entire sample consisted of 1,000 children equally divided into 10 age groups: 5, 6, 7, 8, 9, 10, 11, 12, 13–14, and 15–16. The sample consisted of 500 males and 500 females, with 50 males and 50 females included in each age group. In terms of race/ethnicity, categories included were: White, African American, Hispanic, Native American, Eskimo, Aleut, Asian American, Pacific Islander, and Other. In terms of geographic region, the following regions were specified: Northeast, North Central, South, and West. In terms of parent education, the following five categories were included: 8th grade or less, 9th through 12th grade, high school graduate or equivalent, 1 to 3 years of college or technical school, and 4 or more years of college. Overall, the sample closely matched the Census data; however, some case weighting was used to adjust the race/ethnicity and parent education level proportions to those in the Census data.

A unique feature of the CMS is that a subgroup of examinees, referred to as the "linking sample," was also administered either the Wechsler Intelligence Scale for Children—Third Edition (WISC-III) or the Wechsler Preschool and Primary Scale of Intelligence—Revised (WPPSI-R). The linking sample consisted of 300 children, 273 of whom were administered the WISC-III and 27 of whom were administered the WPPSI-R. This feature allows for exploration of relationships and discrepancies between memory and IQ.

Internal consistency was assessed for the majority of subtests using split-half reliabilities corrected by the Spearman-Brown formula. For six subtests, reliability coefficients were estimated using generalizability coefficients due to uniqueness of these subtests, item presentation formats, and inter-item dependency. Reliability coefficients are reported for all age groups across all subtests. Average reliability coefficients for the index scores ranged from .76 to .91. Again averaged across age groups, coefficients for the core battery of subtests ranged from .71 to .91, with an average value of .78. Likewise, average coefficients for the supplementary subtests ranged from .54 to .86, with an overall average value of .72.

Test-retest reliability coefficients were more variable. The mean test-retest interval was 59.6 days. Across all ages, test-retest reliability coefficients ranged from .26 to .88, with a mean value of .71. When these values were corrected for the variability of CMS scores on the first testing, the reliabilities ranged from .29 to .89, with a mean value of .71. Given the low test-retest reliabilities, stability of test scores was further examined by examining the consistency with which a subject was classified into one of the following categories: impaired, borderline to low average, and average to above average. For the index scores, decision consistency coefficients range from .61 to .93 with a mean value of .78. A practice effect of up to one standard deviation for most scores was revealed, and the CMS manual warns that retesting an examinee within 6 to 8 weeks may result in large practice effects. Interrater reliability was assessed for a subsample of 112 subjects randomly chosen from the standardization sample. Using intraclass correlations, coefficients were obtained that range from .88 to 1.00, with a mean value of .99.

The CMS manual presents information regarding the content, construct, and criterion-related validity of the instrument. Evidence of content validity consists of a description of the test construction procedures. Evidence of construct validity includes subtest and index intercorrelations and results from confirmatory factor analysis. Results from the factor analysis appear to support a three-factor model consisting of Auditory/Verbal memory, Visual/Nonverbal Memory, and Attention/Concentration. To address criterion-related validity, the manual presents data from a series of studies comparing performance on the CMS to performance on measures of general cognitive ability, achievement and academic performance, executive functioning, language skills, and other measures of memory. Additionally, data concerning the CMS performance of children with neurological and neurodevelopmental disorders are also presented. Overall, adequate evidence for the validity of the CMS is presented, thus providing initial support for the use of the instrument. Given the newness of the instrument, further research regarding the validity of the CMS is needed.

SUMMARY. The CMS is an individually administered instrument that was developed to assess memory and learning in children ranging in age from 5 to 16. The CMS is well-designed and standardized, comprehensive, and very user friendly. Furthermore the tasks are engaging and child friendly. The psychometric properties of the CMS are generally quite acceptable, yet users should note that there tends to be a decrease in reliability coefficients for the individual subtests as compared to the index scores, and that the low test-retest reliabilities indicate that the CMS should not be given twice within a 6- to 8-week time frame. There is good evidence for the construct validity of the CMS as well as initial support for the convergent/divergent and discriminant validity of the test. Given these factors, the CMS is not only a welcomed addition to currently available memory assessment tools for children, it is poised to become the instrument of choice for assessing memory and learning in children.

Review of the Children's Memory Scale by MARGOT B. STEIN, Clinical Assistant Professor of Psychiatry, UNC School of Medicine, Director of Training, Center for the Study of Development and Learning, University of North Carolina at Chapel Hill, Chapel Hill, NC:

The Children's Memory Scale (CMS) "was developed to provide school psychologists, child neuropsychologists, and clinical psychologists with a standardized instrument that evaluates the important processes involved in learning and memory" (manual, p. 1). It was designed to help professionals not only to evaluate memory functions of children with neurodevelopmental disabilities such as attention deficit/hyperactivity disorder, speech/language impairment, and learning disabilities, or

various neurological disorders such as epilepsy, traumatic brain injury, and brain tumors, but also to formulate treatment recommendations for them.

The battery consists of nine subtests that assess functioning in each of three domains: (a) auditory/verbal learning and memory (verbal), (b) visual/nonverbal learning and memory (visual), and (c) attention/concentration. Each domain is assessed through two core subtests and one supplemental subtest. Core subtests include: Stories, Word Pairs, Dot Locations, Faces, Numbers, and Sequences. Supplemental subtests consist of Word Lists, Family Pictures, and Picture Locations. The core subtest battery can be administered in about 30–35 minutes, according to the manual; the supplemental battery takes an additional 10–15 minutes to administer. There is approximately a 30-minute delay between the immediate memory and the delayed memory portion of each subtest. For each subtest, normative scores are provided for evaluating specific abilities. The index scores associated with each domain reflect various aspects of learning and memory functioning such as short-term memory, delayed memory, learning, and attention/concentration. The General Memory Index represents global memory functioning.

The CMS is intended to be consistent with current theoretical models of memory and learning and with research findings from the neuropsychological assessment of patients with disorders of memory and learning. It also is intended to account for the developmental changes that are expected to occur between ages 5 through 16 and to evaluate the relationship between memory and intelligence. Finally, it is intended to be able to evaluate questions regarding a child's learning style and ability to remember as well as to be "child friendly" (e.g., interesting and motivating) within the constraints of a typical standardized testing situation. As such, the CMS has both clinical and research applications.

In terms of administration and materials, the complete CMS kit includes the administration and scoring manual, test materials, and scoring protocols. There are two different protocols for children of ages 5 to 8 and children of ages 9 to 16. The administration and scoring procedures are clear and easy to follow, but a period of practice contributes significantly to efficiency in both areas. A carrying case is provided and is necessary to carry the test materials conveniently. These materials are well designed, colorful, and sensitive to current issues of gender and culture, holding the interest of the examinees.

The CMS manual contains a great deal of detail about the representativeness of the normal sample. The CMS was normed and standardized based on a sample of 1,000 "normal" children in 10 age groups ranging from age 5 to age 16. These age groups were 5, 6, 7, 8, 9, 10, 11, 12, 13–14, and 15–16, and each age group consisted of 100 children. The sample included 500 females and 500 males from both private and public school settings, with an equal number of both sexes in each of the 10 age groups. In terms of race/ethnicity, the proportion of Whites, African-Americans, Hispanics, and other race/ethnic groups was based on the race/ethnic group proportions of U.S. children ages 5 through 16, based on the 1995 Census. In terms of geographical distribution, children were chosen for the standardized sample in accordance with the proportion of children living in each of four regions of the United States (e.g., Northeast, North Central, South, and West). Specific exclusion criteria for the normal sample included reading below grade level, having repeated a grade, a previous diagnosis of a neurological disorder, referral or receipt of any type of special education or Chapter I remedial services, or previous injury placing one at risk for memory impairment. In addition, in order to assess the clinical sensitivity/utility of CMS data, the CMS was administered to various clinical groups with different neurodevelopmental and neurological disabilities and to a normal control group matched for age, race, sex, and parent education level.

The administration manual also contains an impressive amount of detail on the psychometric properties of the CMS. Reliability coefficients (split-half corrected using Spearman-Brown) are provided for each of the nine subtests for each age, and range from .70 to .94. Scores generally remain relatively stable as children grow older, with the exception of the Long Delay task for Word Pairs and the Verbal Delayed Index score. Indeed, reliability coefficients of the Index scores are greater than the individual subtests making up the index. Test-retest stability coefficients (59.6 mean interval) for CMS Index scores are generally adequate for each of three age bands (5–8, 9–12, 13–16), with the notable exception of Visual Immediate and Visual Delayed Indexes. Information also is included concerning the standard error of measurement for each subtest and index score for each age group.

The manual also includes correlations between scores on the CMS and other standardized measures of general cognitive ability, such as the Wechsler Intelligence Scale for Children—Third Edition (WISC-III), Wechsler Preschool and Primary Scale of Intelligence—Revised (WPPSI-R), Differential Abilities Scale (DAS), and the Otis-Lennon School Ability Test, Sixth Edition (OLSAT-6). These data suggest that the CMS General Memory Index shows a consistent, moderate, positive correlation with general, verbal, and nonverbal intellectual abilities regardless of the instrument used to measure IQ. The Attention/Concentration Index correlates highly with other measures of complex attention, and moderately with most measures of cognitive ability. Correlations of the CMS with measures of academic achievement such as the Wechsler Individual Achievement Test (WIAT), again show a moderate, positive relationship between most CMS measure and measures of academic achievement. The strongest relationship was displayed between the Attention/Concentration Index and total academic achievement. In addition, the manual also presents correlations between the CMS and measures of executive functioning such as the Wisconsin Card Sorting Test (1993) and the Children's Category Test (1993), with measures of language functioning such as the Clinical Evaluation of Language Fundamentals—Third Edition (1995), and with other measures of memory functioning such as the Wechsler Memory Scale—Third Edition (1997), the Wide Range Assessment of Memory and Learning (1990), and the California Verbal Learning Test—Children's Version (1994).

The CMS joins two other well-established memory scales: the Wechsler Memory Scale—Third Edition (WMS-III; 416); and the Wide Range Assessment of Memory and Learning (WRAML; T5:2880). Though the WMS-III is primarily used with adults, like the WRAML, it has norms for adolescents age 16–17. Correlations between the WRAML and CMS indexes are low to high, with the highest correlation between indexes measuring the same subdomain. The WRAML does not have an attention index, although there is a high correlation between the CMS Attention/Concentration Index and three out of four WRAML indexes, which suggests that attention plays an important role in children's performance on that test as well.

To assess the clinical utility of the CMS, data were collected on small clinical groups with various neurological and neurodevelopmental disabilities including children with Temporal Lobe Epilepsy and Traumatic Brain Injury, and children with brain tumors, learning disabilities, Attention Deficit/Hyperactivity Disorder, and specific language impairment. Clinical sensitivity of the CMS in detecting mild to moderate memory problems in children with neurodevelopmental disabilities was noted. However, the CMS should have greater sensitivity to learning and memory dysfunction in children with neurological disorders.

SUMMARY. The CMS represents a very valuable contribution to the assessment of children's memory and learning. It is conceptually well grounded in current research, elegantly laid out, and relatively easy to administer and score. To be sure, it has some limitations. In the reviewer's experience, the CMS takes 15 to 30 minutes longer to administer than does the WRAML. Delayed recall procedures on both tests occur no more than 30 minutes after the initial presentation, limiting the assessment of long-term memory accordingly. In addition, it should be noted that a CMS administration with elementary-age children with psychiatric and/or more severe neuropsychological problems can take considerably longer than the estimated administration time. This may compromise the proper administration of delayed tasks. The CMS also makes no attempt to formally evaluate procedural memory. However, its strengths are notable in terms of its conceptual integration of Baddeley and Hitch's "working memory" models (1986, 1994) and other research on the neuroanatomy of memory, its comprehensive approach to memory assessment, and its potential for increasing our understanding and remediation of children's learning problems.

REVIEWER'S REFERENCES

Baddeley, A. (1986). *Working memory.* Oxford, England: Clarendon Press.
Baddeley, A. D., & Hitch, G. J. (1994). Development in the concept of working memory. *Neuropsychology, 8,* 485–493.

[76]

Clinical Evaluation of Language Fundamentals, Third Edition—Observational Rating Scales.

Purpose: Designed to measure "a student's classroom communication and language learning difficulties."

Population: Ages 6–21.
Publication Date: 1996.
Acronym: CELF-3ORS.
Scores: 4 sections: Listening, Speaking, Reading, Writing.
Administration: Individual or group.
Forms, 4: Parent, Teacher, Student, Summary.
Price Data, 1999: $52.50 per complete kit including rating scales, summary forms, and guide (86 pages); $12.50 per Teacher rating forms; $12.50 per Parent rating forms; $16 per summary forms; $21 per guide.
Time: Administration time not reported.
Comments: Ratings by parents, teachers, and students.
Authors: Eleanor Semel, Elisabeth H. Wiig, and Wayne A. Secord.
Publisher: The Psychological Corporation.
Cross References: See T5:541 (1 reference).

Review of the Clinical Evaluation of Language Fundamentals, Third Edition—Observational Rating Scales by ROBERT R. HACCOUN, Professor and Chair, I-O Psychology, Université de Montréal, Montreal, Quebec, Canada:

The Clinical Evaluation of Language Fundamentals, Third Edition—Observational Rating Scales (CELF-3) is designed to help speech-language pathologists and school based teams of professionals target language problem zones for students—aged 6 to 21 years—referred to them. It is intended also to provide a convenient set of tools for assessing progress (or lack thereof) following remedial treatment. It is not designed to identify the causes of the problems nor does it provide, by itself, help in defining specific treatments. The overall goal is to improve classroom performance.

The CELF-3 consists of three color-coded sets of observation scales and a summary sheet. The rating scales are filled in by people who are familiar with the student's language skills. Forms are provided to gather ratings from teachers, parents, and the student (self-ratings) although the administrator is invited to supplement these sources if he or she feels the need to do so.

The three groups of raters are asked identically worded questions. Each form contains 40 ratings scales that focus on four zones of language: Listening (9 items), Speaking (19 items), Reading (6 items), and Writing (6 items). Examples of the rating scales are "has trouble paying attention" (Listening); "has trouble answering questions people ask of him or her" (Speaking); "has trouble sounding out words when he or she is reading"

(Reading); "has trouble writing what he or she is thinking" (Writing). For each scale, the observation is gathered on a 4-point frequency scale (*never, sometimes, often, always*). Raters who are unable to answer a question may indicate this by penning DK (don't know) next to an item for the Listening and Speaking sections. However, a specific rating point labeled N/A "not applicable" is printed for the Reading and Writing sections. The scales are formatted such that higher scores reflect greater levels of potential problem.

After completing the form, the raters are to return to it and circle the specific items that concern them the most. Finally, at the end of the form, space is provided for the respondents to list, in an open-ended format, any other concerns they have about the child's listening, speaking, reading, and writing skills. The information provided on these forms is then reproduced onto the summary sheet.

The manual makes a number of specific recommendations covering the administration procedures. It is presumed that teachers and most parents would be able to fill in the form themselves with little input from professionals and suggests that the rating scales may be answered on the phone. The manual warns that self-ratings completed by children should be administered using a face-to-face procedure because children may need help, especially if they have language difficulties. In all cases, however, the person in charge of the evaluation may chose to paraphrase and/or give examples to help the raters answer questions they consider troublesome.

Following the administration, the summary form is used to organize the data and as a guide for the follow-up interview required to complete the assessment; but once again, the administrator may "adapt" the form at will. Although data may be gathered from the various sources outlined, the teacher data are considered the most important and it is this person who is to be interviewed. The manual suggests that teacher-generated information should be given the greatest weight in defining the problem and the remedial strategies to be recommended. However, the parent and student data may be contrasted to that produced by teachers. Although the manual briefly touches upon cases of convergence between the ratings, it remains strangely silent with regard to disagreements. This is troubling considering the (relatively low) intersource agreement levels that are reported (see the technical section below). The interview protocol recommended is a "patterned interview" where teachers are prompted to provide concrete behavioral examples of the problem areas. Presumably, disagreements between sources would be discussed during the interview but nothing is said of this in the documentation.

Technical Information.

DEVELOPMENT OF THE SCALE. The scale items were generated following interviews conducted with teachers, parents, and students (aged 5–17 years). This process generated a Research Edition that was administered to about 5,000 people. Of these, 1,208 CELF-3 were completed by students, their teacher, and their parent(s). Additionally, data are provided for ratings conducted with 117 "language disordered" students.

RELIABILITY: CORRELATION BETWEEN SOURCES. As these are observation scales the level of correlation between sources (students, parents, and teachers) is very important. Although the correlations between the sources on each of the items are generally significant, they are not, as a rule, very high (ranging in the .20 range for non-language-disordered cases to the .30 range for language-disordered ones). The correlation between the sources for the aggregated parameters (Listening, Speaking, etc.) is somewhat higher (in the .30–.40 range), which is expected as aggregated scores will be more reliable than individual ratings. Parents and teachers show moderate levels of agreement but the lowest agreement levels are between teachers and students. Finally, parents agree with their children more than teachers do.

More modest levels of intersource convergence is often noted in these "360 degree" types of evaluations where information is gathered from a multiplicity of sources. After all, reality is often a function of the observer. Yet one is left with a troubling question: Who is right? The test developers lean towards the view that the teachers are because they are the most informed and the most responsible for academic performance of children. However, some tangible empirical evidence demonstrating their point would be welcomed.

VALIDITY. The evidence of criterion-related validity of the CELF-3 Observation Scales was obtained by correlating the results obtained by the two samples (1,208 with no language disorders and 117 with language disorders) with the results obtained on the CELF-3 (a test that purports to diagnose possible language disorders). This latter measure produces "receptive" and "expressive" language scores. The concurrent correlation between these ratings provided on the four parameters of the CELF-Observation Scales and the two dimensions of the CELF-3 are in the right direction and significant, ranging from .32 to .43 for teacher sources. The concurrent validity coefficients for the parent and the student ratings are significant though lower. Although the coefficients obtained on the sample with language disorder are slightly higher (ranging from .31 to .46) all validity coefficients reported should be considered moderate at best.

Worrisome, however, is the pattern of undifferentiated correlation between the scales. The expressive language score should reflect verbal production (expressing information), whereas the receptive language scores should reflect verbal acquisition (gaining information). One would then expect that the Listening and Reading scores on the CELF-3 Observation Scales correlate more strongly with the "receptive" scores than with the "expressive" scores obtained on the CELF-3. Similarly, Speaking and Writing on the CELF-3 Observation Scales should correlate more strongly with the "expressive" and less with the "receptive" scores. Although the manual does not report statistical tests of these values, visual inspection of the reported data does not reveal this expected pattern of correlation. This evidence casts some doubts as to the overall validity of the CELF-3 Observation Scales, the CELF-3, or both.

Finally, the CELF-3 Observation Scales are intended to help in zeroing in on specific language difficulties to better target possible interventions. Such an ambition requires that the dimensions (Listening, Speaking, Reading, and Writing) be reasonably independent. Unfortunately, the manual does not report this information. Moreover, the dimension scores are useful in targeting the potential problem zone (Listening or Reading, for example). Each of these scores is constructed by aggregating the individual ratings assigned to that dimension. At the very least, therefore, one would expect that scales assigned to a particular dimension should correlate more strongly with that dimension than scales assigned to any other dimension. Such statistical analyses are not reported but they should be.

ITEM BIAS. No data are reported on possible ethnic, race, or gender biases. Given the weight given to teacher ratings it is far from evident that such problems of bias do not exist in this measure.

OVERALL EVALUATION. The CELF-3 Observational Rating Scales appear to be relatively easy to use and on surface seem to tap the key elements of language skills with children. Moreover, the scales appear to allow for much latitude in the administration and interpretation of the results, which allows for its use in a wide set of circumstances. However, flexibility is a double-edged sword in that the increased practicality of the instrument may be attained at the risk of creating potential variations in the conclusions that may be reached for the same children across administrators and situations. The fact that no attempt appears to have been made to assess the same children on several occasions or across the same children with different teachers does not serve to alleviate concern about this potential problem.

The reliability of the observation system is insufficiently demonstrated. Part of the problem may stem from the response scale chosen. Generic descriptors such as the ones used ("sometimes," etc.) are subject to idiosyncratic interpretations that may cause all manner of disagreements between people. As for the validity of the scale, that too is lacking. The evidence is really limited to a simple concurrent design (which tends to produce overestimates of validity because of method variance problems). In spite of this "built-in" advantage, the coefficients obtained are modest (though significant).

Further, it is not at all clear why parents and students are involved in the process, beyond obtaining their participation and cooperation with the diagnosis-intervention process. The data they produce are not, in the final analysis, given much weight.

Finally, indicating that a child has problems with any area described by the Observation Scales may or may not indicate that the problem is at the language level. For example, noting that a child always has trouble "paying attention" may be explained by a listening "problem" or, alternatively, by a myriad of other issues including behavioral, attitudinal, motivational, attention, neurological, or cognitive ones. To be fair, the authors do recognize this issue and suitable warning is provided to potential users. Therefore, it is crucial that the results obtained using the form be conceived as a starting point for problem diagnosis to be supplemented by additional assessment procedures. Considerable interviewing skills and clinical acumen are required to make a successful use of this measurement tool.

Review of the Clinical Evaluation of Language Fundamentals, Third Edition—Observational Rating Scales by DAVID P. HURFORD, Director of the Center for the Assessment and Remediation of Reading Difficulties and Professor of Psychology and Counseling, Pittsburg State University, Pittsburg, KS:

The Clinical Evaluation of Language Fundamentals, Third Edition (CELF-3) Observational Rating Scales (ORS) is to be used to identify specific communication and language difficulties in children aged 6 to 21 years who are experiencing listening, speaking, reading, and/or writing deficits. The ORS is completed by the student, his or her teacher(s), and his or her parent(s).

The responsibility of diagnosing children who are experiencing academic difficulties and to build appropriate interventions for them is much more of a collaborative effort today than has been the case in the past. As such, it is critical that team members have a common language to discuss the child's needs as well as behavioral examples provided from ecologically valid situations to guide the diagnosis and intervention process. The ORS was created to meet this need.

The ORS comprises the Teacher, Parent, and Student Rating Forms, and the Summary Form. Each of the three rating forms is color coded and has the same 40 statements that depict difficulties in listening, speaking, reading, and/or writing that a child suspected of having communication and/or language deficits might be experiencing. The Summary Form is used by the test administrator to summarize the information obtained with the rating forms and to recommend appropriate interventions based on information gained from the rating forms and through further interviews with the student's teacher and parent(s).

The ORS is completed by the teacher, parent, and student by circling *Never, Sometimes, Often,* or *Always* for each of the 40 statements. For example, the first item refers to attention (The student has trouble paying attention/My child has trouble paying attention/I have trouble paying attention, depending on who is making the rat-

ing). There are 9 items with regard to Listening, 19 for Speaking, and 6 each for Reading and Writing. If the rater cannot make a judgment he or she is instructed to write DK (don't know) next to the statement. There is also a note to raters for 6- and 7-year-old students that NA (not applicable) can also be written next to a statement for the Reading and Writing sections because it is quite likely that these students have not engaged much in these activities. When the rater has completed each of the 40 items, he or she is then instructed to circle the item numbers that concern him or her the most. It is recommended that assistance be given to student raters, particularly students who are younger or who have poor reading ability, language difficulties, or reduced cognitive functioning. Given that the student has been suspected of having language difficulties, and hence is the reason for completing the form, a great many student raters will need assistance. This, however, is not detrimental to the ORS because information can be gathered from the student as a result of the interaction between the student and the test administrator that will be useful for diagnosis and planning. Finally, each rater is asked to produce any other problems that he or she has with regard to the student and to rate them (*Never, Sometimes, Often,* or *Always*).

The focus of the Summary Form is to identify accurately the problem areas and to provide information to guide and plan appropriate interventions based on the data gathered from the ORS. Because the primary concern of the interventions is to improve the student's classroom functioning, the teacher is seen as the most accurate judge, and his or her concerns are given priority. It is suggested that the classroom teacher be included in the team that will be planning the interventions. The Summary Form has space for the test administrator to list the problems that were of concern to the teacher along with their frequency of occurrence (*Sometimes, Often,* or *Always*). Once these have been entered the next step involves interviewing the teacher to further define the problem areas with specific behaviors and examples. During the interview the teacher is asked to provide at least two examples of the identified problem areas for each section. The teacher is also asked to rank the top five problems in terms of level of concern and necessity for intervention. During the process of the interview other problems may surface that were not originally identified with the Teacher Rating Form. The last step in completing the Summary Form is to summarize the 5 top-ranked concerns with comments, to provide conclusions and recommendations for intervention, and to provide three goals for intervention. The goals should address the parents' concerns. If they do not, it is suggested that the parents be contacted to provide them with information as to why their concerns were not incorporated or to discuss with the teacher how the parents' concerns could be addressed.

The ORS was developed by interviewing 240 students aged 5 through 17 who had language or communication disorders, at least one of each of their teachers, and at least one of their parents or guardians. The statements comprising the ORS were selected from a pool of concerns that were generated by the students, parents/guardians, and teachers during the interviews. The most frequently occurring statements relevant to language and communication difficulties were edited, collapsed when there was redundancy, and then included on the ORS.

A total of 1,208 students participated in the standardization of the research edition of the ORS; all of the students who were part of the standardization sample were also involved with standardization of the CELF-3. This latter addition was used to evaluate reliability and validity and assigned numbers to the "Happens" column's responses of *Never* (1), *Sometimes* (2), *Often* (3), and *Always* (4). In addition, a new column was created for the research edition in which the rater indicated how "concerned" he or she was with each statement: *Not at All* (1), *A Little* (2), and *A Lot* (3). Of approximately 5,000 returned ORS research forms, 1,208 were complete sets composed of returned forms from a student, one of his or her parents, and one from one of his or her teachers. In addition to the 1,208 complete sets, 117 complete sets were returned from language-disordered students. A positive correlation between "Happens" and "Concerned" would indicate that the more often an individual indicated a particular problem behavior occurred the more concerned the respondent became with that behavior. The correlation coefficients for each of the statements were all significant (at $p < .001$) and ranged between .71 and .95 within each of the parent, teacher, and student groups. Agreement between

the various groups on the "Happens" variable were mostly significant, and were much smaller (range: .00 to .50). For the non-language-disordered students, all of the correlation coefficients between each group were significant by section (Listening, Speaking, Reading, and Writing) and were generally consistent across the various groups (parents-teachers, parents-students, teachers-students). For the language-disordered students, only the correlation coefficients for the parents and teachers group by section were significant. The manual does not include mean "Happens" for each group, which would be quite interesting in determining the nature of the low correlations for the language-disordered students.

Validity issues were examined with content, criterion-related, and construct validity. Content validity evidence included interviews with children who were diagnosed as language disordered and who were receiving services for that diagnosis, one of their parents, and one of their teachers to determine a pool of items that reflected their listening, speaking, reading, and writing difficulties. The most frequently occurring items from that pool were edited to reduce redundancy and to insure that the items were related to language and communication. Criterion-related validity was assessed using the Receptive, Expressive, and Total Language Scores from the CELF-3 (T5:540). These scores were inversely related to the four sections of the ORS, which was expected. The lower the CELF-3 score the poorer the performance. The more frequently a behavior occurred, the higher the ratings (on the ORS). In other words, as performance declines (on the ORS), the frequency ratings should increase. Generally, the correlation coefficients were modest ranging from .00 to -.46. The correlation coefficients from the teachers' ratings were the highest, whereas the correlation coefficients from the students' ratings were the lowest. Criterion-related validity was also assessed by assigning students to groups based on their CELF-3 total scores. For the students without language disorders, the groups were composed of those individuals who scored 1 standard deviation (*sd*) or more above the mean on the CELF-3, individuals who scored between the mean and 1 *sd* above the mean, individuals who scored between the mean and 1 *sd* below the mean, and individuals who scored 1 *sd* or more below the mean. For the group that scored 1 *sd* or more above the CELF-3 mean, nearly all of the ORS ratings were *Never* and *Sometimes*. As group membership represented decreasing performance, the frequency of *Never* and *Sometimes* ratings decreased and the frequency of *Often* and *Always* ratings increased. The same procedure was used with the students who had language disorders except that there was no group of students who scores greater than 1 *sd* above the CELF-3 mean, with similar results. Finally, construct validity was assessed by comparing the student, teacher, and parent ratings on the ORS of students with and without language disorders on each of the statements. It was proposed that construct validity of the ORS would be established if the ratings were significantly different between the groups of children with and without language disorders, a defensible argument (except that validity is never "established"). There were significant differences in ratings between the students with and without language disorders for the parents and teachers for all but four statements for the teachers and all but four statements for the parents. Two of the statements in which there were no differences in ratings were the same for the parents and teachers. The same was not true for the student ratings. There were only differences for 12 of 40 statements for the students. Unfortunately, the authors do not explain the statistical procedure that was performed on these data, most likely, *t*-tests were employed.

In summary, the Clinical Evaluation of Language Fundamentals, Third Edition (CELF-3) Observational Rating Scales seems to be a very useful instrument to assist in the identification of language and communication difficulties and to assist in the planning of interventions. It provides a forum for professionals to discuss relevant problem behaviors that have been identified by students, parents, and teachers. Most importantly, the same statements comprise each of the Student, Parent, and Teacher forms so that a common language and metric is being used to gather the information. It should be clear that this instrument does not provide standardized test results. Its main purpose is to help accumulate information that will be relevant, appropriate, and useful for the planning of interventions for students who have language or communication disorders.

[77]

Clinical Observations of Motor and Postural Skills.

Purpose: Designed to assist occupational therapists in performing assessments of children with suspected developmental and coordination disorders.

Population: Ages 5–9.
Publication Date: 1994.
Acronym: COMPS.
Scores: 6 items: Slow Movements, Finger-Nose Touching, Rapid Forearm Rotation, Prone Extension Posture, Asymmetrical Tonic Neck Reflex, Supine Flexion Posture.
Administration: Individual.
Price Data: Not available.
Time: (15–20) minutes.
Comments: Ratings by therapist.
Authors: Brenda N. Wilson, Nancy Pollock, Bonnie J. Kaplan, and Mary Law.
Publisher: The Psychological Corporation.
[Note: The publisher advised in December 1998 that this test is now out of print.]

Review of the Clinical Observations of Motor and Postural Skills by GLEN P. AYLWARD, Professor of Pediatrics, Psychiatry and Behavioral and Social Sciences, Southern Illinois University School of Medicine, Springfield, IL:

The Clinical Observations of Motor and Postural Skills (COMPS) is a screening tool designed to identify subtle, developmental motor coordination problems or "dyspraxias" (manual, p. 2) in children. The test is reported to take 15 to 20 minutes to administer, and is recommended as a general screening tool in situations such as kindergarten motor screening. The COMPS is geared for use by occupational therapists and is not recommended to be given to children with significant motor or cognitive impairments. The COMPS is a descriptive, versus evaluative, tool and basically is a revision and elaboration of clinical observation protocols from Ayres (1976) and others. Therefore, no diagnosis, per se, is derived. The authors of the COMPS have essentially standardized administration and made scoring procedures more objective than was the case with previous clinical observations. Because most of the indicators are "mature" by age 7 to 8 years, the COMPS is applicable for children in the 5- to 9-year age range. The test can be given to older children, and in such applications a positive finding would be of clinical utility (indicating dysfunction); however, a negative finding would not be as clinically meaningful.

The COMPS consists of six indicators. These are: (a) Slow Movements measuring the child's ability to move the upper extremities slowly and symmetrically. This indicator is considered to measure cerebellar function over a 6-second time span, with symmetry, quality of performance, and speed each being scored on a 3-point scale. (b) Rapid Forearm Rotation assessing the number of forearm rotations accurately completed within 10-seconds. Diadochokinesis (cerebellar-vestibular integrity), assessed in this manner, matures at age 7–8 years. (c) Finger-Nose Touching requires the child to touch the nose and then the finger of the other hand that is extended as far as possible from the face. The task is performed both with eyes open and closed. This maneuver is thought to reflect cerebellar coordination and also matures by age 7 years. (d) Prone Extension Posture measures the child's ability to assume and maintain an arched-back position against gravity with arms and legs extended in a sort of "superman" or "supergirl" flying posture. It involves vestibular-proprioceptive function. (e) Asymmetrical Tonic Neck Reflex (ATNR) measures the presence of the asymmetrical tonic neck reflex in the quadruped position. This item requires the attachment of a plastic measuring tool to the child's arms in order to measure elbow flexion. (f) Supine Flexion Posture assesses the child's ability to assume and maintain a flexed posture in the supine position, with the child bringing knees to the chest and crunching up in a "ball." Duration and measurement of six flexion components is involved.

COMPS materials include a manual, four-page scoring forms, two plastic measuring devices with velcro fasteners (with lines to facilitate measuring elbow angles), and a carrying case. A stopwatch, mat, and two chairs are necessary, and this reviewer suggests use of a calculator as well. The authors recommend that the sequence of item presentation remain as outlined, this being underscored for the last three items in particular because of the facilitation effects of stretch and flexor activities.

The authors emphasize that one of the strengths of the COMPS lies in its objective scoring. However, the scoring is somewhat complex and time-consuming for a screening test. Scores are summed and then compared to one of three weighted score tables that are based on age (5 years 0 months to 5 years 11 months, 6 years 0 months to 7 years 11 months, and 8 years 0 months to 9 years 11 months). Converted scores range from -2.16 to 7.92, depending on task and age of the child. The six weighted scores are then totaled, an "adjustment" is subtracted (7.61, 8.54, or 9.80, depending on age), and a weighted total score is derived. A weighted total score less than

zero is considered indicative of problems in postural and motor skills, and scores greater than zero are indicative of normal functioning. Interpretation of a score of exactly zero is not specified.

The normative sample consisted of 123 children, 67 who displayed developmental coordination disorders (DCD), and 56 children with no known motor problems. Diagnostic criteria warranting the diagnosis of DCD, ages of the children, gender, and other demographic information are not contained in the manual. Instead, the prospective test user is referred to an article by Wilson, Pollock, Kaplan, Law, and Farris (1992) for more detailed information on test development. It would seem that this information should be provided in the manual, as a substantial number of test users might not necessarily attempt to seek out the reference. Moreover, the high base rate of purported coordination/motor problems would affect statistical descriptors such as sensitivity.

Test-retest reliability over a 2-week time span in the total sample ($r - 48$) was estimated to be .93; it was .87 in the DCD group ($n = 20$) and .76 in the non-DCD group ($n = 28$). Interrater reliability was measured using four individuals: two with experience in pediatrics, one with no experience in pediatrics, and one occupational therapy student. Sample sizes used for comparisons ranged from 30 to 72, and reported intraclass correlation coefficients ranged from .57 to .90. The highest correlations were found between the two "pediatrics experienced" examiners. In general, test-retest reliability needs to be more rigorously examined.

Internal consistency reliability, using Cronbach's alpha coefficient, was estimated to be .77 for the total test. Correlations between the individual items and total test score ranged from .33 (ATNR) to .53 (finger-nose touching).

Construct validity was measured via use of MANOVAs, with age as a covariate (MANCOVA). DCD and non-DCD children ($n = 64$) were compared on total COMPS scores (not weighted total scores) and were found to differ significantly. Additional comparisons, not covarying for age, revealed significant between-group differences as well ($ns = 22, 22$, and 20, for each of the three age groups). Discriminant analyses (DCD and non-DCD group membership as grouping variable) produced a reported 73% correct classification rate. Weights derived from this procedure were employed in the aforementioned three age-specific weighted score conversion tables in the manual, which are used in the computation of the final weighted total score. The previously mentioned adjustment score is an intercept that is subtracted to denote the cutoff score of zero, which is the same for all ages.

The authors also report sensitivity and specificity values for a sample of 64 children (ages not specified). Reported sensitivity ranged from 82% to 100%; specificity from 63% to 90%. However, given the vagueness of the reference diagnosis, the high base rate of "dysfunction," and the lack of specific numbers in the comparisons, these terms may not be appropriate. Co-positivity and co-negativity may be more applicable.

Concurrent validity involving score comparisons between the COMPS weighted total score and the Test of Visual Motor Integration, Standing Balance-Eyes Open and Closed tests, the Motor Accuracy Test—Revised, and the Bruininks-Oseretsky Test of Motor Proficiency produced correlations ranging from .18 to .48 (*n*s ranging from 27 to 64). Correlations between the six COMPS subtest scores and these concurrent measures ranged from .07 to .65. The authors also describe at length a comparison between eight children with motor and sensory integration problems who also had been given the COMPS and the Sensory Integration and Praxis Tests (SIPT; Ayres, 1989). Given the small sample size, this discussion is of limited utility and is rather speculative.

SUMMARY. In summary, the main strength of the COMPS is found in the emphasis on refinement of administration and scoring of clinical observations of motor coordination items, frequently used to assess neurologic "soft signs." Administration directions are well presented and clear. Moreover, in addition to occupational therapists, the test can be useful for other professionals such as early developmental neuropsychologists (Aylward, 1997). That being said, drawbacks include a small sample size (with inadequate description in the manual), a high base rate for motor problems in the original sample, a relatively lengthy administration time and labor-intensive scoring (if the test is to be used as a screen), and the need for additional research as to the "diagnostic utility" of the COMPS.

REVIEWER'S REFERENCES

Ayres, A. J. (1976). *Interpreting the Southern California sensory integration tests.* Los Angeles: Western Psychological Services.
Ayres, A. J. (1989). *Sensory integration and praxis tests.* Los Angeles: Western Psychological Services.
Wilson, B., Pollack, N., Kaplan, B. J., Law, M., & Faris, P. (1992). Reliability and construct validity of the Clinical Observations of Motor and Postural Skills. *The American Journal of Occupational Therapy, 9,* 775–783.
Aylward, G. P. (1997). *Infant and early childhood neuropsychology.* New York: Plenum.

Review of the Clinical Observations of Motor and Postural Skills by WILLIAM R. MERZ, SR., Professor-School Psychology Training Program, California State University, Sacramento, CA:

The Clinical Observation of Motor and Postural Skills (COMPS) is designed to assist occupational therapists in performing valid and reliable assessments of suspected developmental coordination disorders in children ages 5 to 9. It is a revision of and elaboration on clinical observations used by pediatric occupational therapists. Standardizing tasks and developing objective scoring criteria were the primary goals for developing the COMPS. The COMPS is a screening tool rather than an evaluative instrument for assessing change over time. Although screening for the presence or absence of motor problems that have a postural component is the instrument's primary function, it also accurately identifies from 73% to 95% of children in the norm group with motor problems that have a postural component. The COMPS is made up of six tasks: Slow Movements: the ability to move slowly and symmetrically—a reflection of cerebellar function; Rapid Forearm Rotation: the number of forearm rotations accurately completed within 10 seconds—a test of cerebellar-vestibular integrity; Finger-Nose Touching: the ability to touch index finger to nose and then touch finger to the extended index finger of the other hand—a measure of cerebellar coordination; Prone Extension Posture: the ability to assume and maintain an arched back position against gravity—a task related to vestibular-proprioceptive processing dysfunction; Asymmetrical Tonic Neck Reflex: the degree of inhibition of the Asymmetrical Tonic Neck Reflex—a measure of postural stability; and Supine Flexion Posture: the ability to assume and maintain a flexed posture in the supine position over time—a task associated with somato-dyspraxia.

It takes 15 to 20 minutes to administer the COMPS as a general screening device for motor problems in children 5 to 9 years old. The authors warn against using it with children younger than 5 years. They urge cautious use with children older than 9 years when a child has motor difficulties but, then, only as an indication that the child has motor difficulties. They also recommend against using it with children who have known neurological or neuromotor problems or with children who manifest general intellectual delays. As a screening tool it gives a global picture of a child's functional performance. The authors do not presently recommend it as a measure of change over time. Occupational therapists and physical therapists with some experience in assessing children can use this set of observations. Although students and therapists without pediatric experience can use the COMPS, the authors suggest that examiners have at least 1 to 2 years of experience in testing children.

This set of observations uses a 3- or 4-point scale based on qualitative descriptions of behaviors to derive scores; the values are presumed to be on an equal interval scale. The order of administration proceeds from easier, briefer tasks and progresses to more complex tasks. Raw scores are converted weighted scores for each of three age groups (5-0 to 5-11, 6-0 to 7-11, and 8-0 to 9-11). These weighted scores are summed across tasks and an adjustment number is subtracted to yield a weighted total score. Scores less than zero indicate problems in Postural and Motor Skills; scores greater than zero indicate normal function. The authors suggest in the section of the manual on interpretation that the assessor examine each of the subtest results to look for tasks that may be more difficult for the child. They also state that performance may be used to aid in treatment planning with children who already have identified problems. They maintain that the six tasks tap different areas of neuromotor function but caution that they are not totally discrete. Therefore, they suggest that the COMPS be interpreted primarily as a cluster of skills in light of presenting functional problems.

The test was developed, standardized, and normed in Canada on a small sample of children in the Province of Alberta. Although the authors do not report the actual sample size of the norm group, the numbers in the reliability and validity studies range from 20 to 119; that number gives an idea of how small the norm group may be. The authors report estimates of test-retest (within a 2-week period) reliabilities of .76 for their nondisabled sample, .87 for their disabled sample, and .93 for the entire sample. Interrater reliabilities are wider ranging and a good deal lower for the disabled

group: .57 to .76; they are .81 to .90 in the nondisabled group. Internal consistency reliabilities computed as correlations between item and total test score range from .33 to .53 and from .46 to .54 when computed as Cronbach's alpha with the item score deleted. These coefficients urge caution in generalizing behavior based on these observations to typical behaviors.

Construct evidence of validity is presented by analyzing scores of 64 children with MANOVA and Discriminant Function Analysis. Using age as a covariate, mean differences on total test scores between the disabled and nondisabled were statistically significant. Means between the disabled and nondisabled children for the different age groups without covariation were statistically significant for all age groups. Discriminant functions were statistically significant for each of the six tasks and indicated that the scores detect dysfunction correctly 73% of the time across age groups. The authors report concurrent evidence of validity by correlating COMPS nonweighted scores with measures collected during the same period. Correlations for nonweighted item scores with the other tasks range from .07 to .65; correlations for weighted total scores with the other measures range from .18 to .48. One can infer content evidence of validity from the authors' drawing tasks reported in the current literature on motor skills and tasks commonly used by pediatric therapists.

SUMMARY. The COMPS is a test with a narrow purpose designed for professionally trained pediatric occupational and physical therapists to use for screening 5- to 9-year-olds for motor problems. Trials with small samples demonstrate that the COMPS discriminates fairly well between children who have motor problems and those who do not. The evidence about reliability and validity needs further exploration because, at first glance, the magnitudes of correlations do not seem impressive. Examples are the magnitude of the reliability coefficients among tasks taken by the disabled group and item correlations with criterion measures used to present evidence of validity. Because the disabled group is smaller, has a more restricted range of scores, and more than likely has less variability than the nondisabled group, the magnitudes of correlation coefficients are attenuated. With item-total score correlations, restriction in range would attenuate correlation magnitudes. Discussion of these issues would better describe how the instrument functions in achieving its screening purpose.

There is great need for instruments that assess motor skills in the 5- to 9-year-old population. Psychologists use fairly gross measures; more specialized measures used by people trained specifically in the motor function of children would help identify children who need accommodation. It would help delineate the nature and specifics of that accommodation. In that regard, the COMPS has much to recommend. It does, however, need more work with larger sample sizes taken from a more geographically diverse population. Working with the COMPS in American public schools would provide valuable information on an extremely diverse population of children. Assessment of motor skills in the United States would benefit from standardized, norm-referenced instruments that identify children with need and evaluate progress with training. Instruments that allow assessment of progress during training would be very helpful, as well. Standardized, norm-referenced assessment tools for children age 10 or older would be extremely helpful.

The COMPS must be used cautiously by trained professionals who recognize that generalization is restricted by the norm group and standardization sample. It is a valuable step in the right direction.

[78]
The Clock Test.

Purpose: "Developed as a screening tool for the assessment of dementia in the elderly."
Population: Ages 65 and older.
Publication Date: 1995.
Scores, 3: Clock Reading, Clock Drawing, Clock Setting.
Administration: Individual.
Price Data, 1999: $160 per test kit including 25 QuikScore™ forms, 25 profile sheets, administration test, and manual (85 pages); $60 per 25 QuikScore™ forms; $10 per 25 profile sheets; $60 per administration tent; $40 per manual.
Time: [15–30] minutes.
Authors: H. Tuokko, T. Hadjistavropoulos, J. A. Miller, A. Horton, and B. L. Beattie.
Publisher: Multi-Health Systems, Inc.

Review of The Clock Test by HOWARD A. LLOYD, Neuropsychologist, Hawaii State Hospital, Kaneohe, HI:

The Clock Test was designed as a screening tool for assessment of cognitive impairment in the elderly. The authors have attempted to standardize the administration and scoring of traditional clock drawing tasks while adding components to measure clock setting and clock reading abilities. The manual provides a thorough and detailed explanation of the uses of the Clock Drawing Test, as well as a historical review of similar techniques. This serves to educate the user of this test about the conceptual foundations upon which The Clock Test is based. To their credit, the authors clearly state the limitations of this measure and caution against the use of The Clock Test as the sole diagnostic measure of cognitive impairment. User qualifications are also clearly delineated in the manual.

The Clock Test comprises three separate tasks. Clock Drawing requires subjects to place numbers on a predrawn clock face and set the hands of the clock to a specified time (10 after 11). Clock Setting requires the subject to set the hands on five predrawn clocks with the number omitted, to five different times (1 o'clock, 10 after 11, 3 o'clock, 9:15, and 7:30). Clock reading requires subjects to read the time set on five predrawn clocks (numbers omitted) with the hands set at the same times used in the clock setting task. Scoring of the Clock Drawing and Clock Setting conditions is facilitated by a standard scoring form on which the stimuli are printed. Carbon paper is used to transfer the subject's drawings onto this form. The one flaw to this system is that the carbon paper must be placed properly for the form to work as it was designed. There is no instruction in the manual about this and the forms received by this reviewer for review required that the carbon paper be reversed in order to work. This is a minor flaw but one that may result in some initial administration errors due to failure to have the subject's drawings transferred to the scoring form. Otherwise, the scoring form serves its purpose of facilitating ease of scoring this test in a standardized manner. The manual provides detailed scoring instructions and examples.

The Clock Test was normed on a sample of 1,753 normal elderly subjects ranging in age from 65 to 100. A clinical sample of 269 subjects over the age of 65 who had been diagnosed with dementia was also included. An additional sample of 64 community dwelling older adults aged 50 and above was used for cross-validation purposes. This normative sample appears appropriate to the purpose of this test and is of sufficient size to allow for reasonable standardization. The psychometric properties of The Clock Test are well within acceptable ranges.

Interrater reliability for the scoring procedures ranged from .90 to .99, which is quite high. This high interrater reliability is particularly important given the nature of The Clock Test as a screening tool for cognitive impairment. Test-retest reliability (time interval specified as "within days") was assessed for the Clock Drawing Test using a subsample of the clinical group. Retesting resulted in a test-retest reliability coefficient of .70. This is actually rather low, particularly for such a short retest interval. Although the test-retest reliability of such a measure may be less important than interrater reliability, it is also unfortunate that the authors did not conduct a similar examination of the stability of scores on The Clock Test for a subsample of their normal group. This would have been a more appropriate measure of the test-retest reliability of The Clock Test.

The validity of The Clock Test was investigated using multiple approaches including measures of sensitivity and specificity, and convergent and discriminant validity. The authors clearly put considerable effort into analyzing the validity of scores from The Clock Test. Detailed information is provided in the manual that strongly supports the validity of scores from this test. Sensitivity indices ranged from 80% to 93% and specificity indices ranged from 82% to 94%. The Clock Test correlates well with a variety of traditional neuropsychological measures. The authors have done a good job establishing strong evidence of the validity of scores from The Clock Test using a variety of appropriate approaches to validity estimation.

SUMMARY. In summary, The Clock Test has been well designed and has strong normative and psychometric properties. One minor design flaw was noted in an otherwise admirable attempt to facilitate standard scoring of The Clock Test. This measure is likely to be useful to generalist psychologists as well as specialists in neuropsychology. The authors should be commended for standardizing a frequently used, but heretofore often qualitatively interpreted, screening task.

Review of The Clock Test by ANTHONY M. PAOLO, Coordinator of Assessment and Evaluation, University of Kansas Medical Center, Kansas City, KS:

The Clock Test was designed as a brief screening test for dementia in the elderly. It measures visuo-spatial construction, visual perception, and abstract conceptualization. The test consists of three subtests: Clock Drawing, Clock Setting, and Clock Reading. The interrelation for normal persons among the three subtests ranges from -.26 for Clock Drawing and Reading to .38 for Clock Reading and Setting. These relatively small relationships are to be expected because the tasks are different, but all of them tap some component of cognitive functioning. The correlations increase in magnitude for persons with dementia ranging from -.51 to .71. The higher correlations likely reflect increased variability of performance in persons with brain dysfunction.

To obtain a total score, the user counts different types of errors that the patient makes. There are seven error types and at least three subcategories under each error type. Interrater reliability for raters scoring the clock test was very good and ranged from .73–1.00 for Clock Drawing, .95 to .98 for Clock Setting, and .99 for Clock Reading. Test-retest stability over a 4-day period for 32 persons with suspected dementia was .70 for Clock Drawing. Although the magnitude of this coefficient is adequate, the 4-day test-retest interval is not one typically used in clinical settings. The stability of the Clock Setting and Clock Reading subtests is not provided. In addition, standard errors should be provided to allow users to be able to compute when changes in Clock Drawing scores reflect real change, rather than measurement error.

The Clock Test demonstrates adequate convergent and divergent validity evidenced by moderate correlations of -.27 to .77 with other measures of cognitive abilities (i.e., selected subtests from the Wechsler Adult Intelligence Scale—Revised, verbal fluency, and Buschke Cued Recall) and lower correlations (.05 to -.19) with measures of mood (i.e., selected subtests from the Multifocal Assessment Scale). Additional evidence of validity comes from The Clock Test's ability to distinguish normal elderly persons from those with suspected dementia. In general, the sensitivity and specificity estimates are good and range from 80% to 94%. The manual notes that distinguishing between normal and demented elderly is better for the young-old group (i.e., ages 65 to 70) rather than the older groups (i.e., persons older than 70 years). This suggests that The Clock Test may be best suited as a screening tool for the young-old rather than the old-old.

Age-dependent cutoff scores are provided for a large (N = 1,753) healthy elderly sample. This sample was 58% female and ranged in age from 65 to 100 years (Median = 75 years). The median education level was 11 years. No information is provided concerning how representative this sample is of elderly persons. If the sample is not representative, but merely a sample of convenience, then the results presented in the manual may not generalize well to other elderly persons. The manual does refer users to an article published in the *Canadian Medical Association Journal* that may provide users with a more detailed description of the standardization sample. It is this reviewer's opinion that test authors and publishers should provide all relevant information in the test manual. Finally, the normative information provided is only for total scores. No information on the prevalence of the different error types among normal or demented elderly is provided. This is unfortunate because the presence of certain clock errors (i.e., stimulus boundness) have a long clinical heritage. Providing hard numbers to such a clinical heritage would be extremely helpful for clinicians.

The use of clock drawing as a screening device for cognitive impairment has a long history. This version of The Clock Test provides a large norm sample and good standardized administration and scoring procedures. The reported reliability and validity values for scores from The Clock Test are adequate for a screening device. Providing sensitivity and specificity information is essential for a screening device and the authors are commended for presenting this data. The lack of a clinically relevant retest interval and standard errors makes any change in scores on retesting difficult to interpret. Knowing how representative the standardization sample is would also be helpful. Overall, The Clock Test is a good choice for persons needing a well-standardized version of a screening device that has a long and rich history in neurology and neuropsychology.

[79]
Closed Head Injury Screener.

Purpose: "Designed to help medical doctors and psychologists assess whether patient symptoms are suggestive of closed-head injuries."
Population: English-speaking adults.

Publication Date: 1994.
Acronym: CHIS.
Scores: 3 ratings: Medical Facts, Presenting Complaints, Response Validity.
Administration: Individual.
Price Data, 1998: $25 per sampler set including manual (20 pages), questionnaire/answer sheet, and scoring directions; $100 per permission set including sampler set plus permission to reproduce up to 200 copies of the instrument.
Time: Approximately 30 minutes.
Comments: To be used as a supplement to a full face-to-face patient interview; partial paper and pencil/ partial oral interview; results interpreted by administrator; not to be used with patients with cognitive deficits that are explainable by a previous diagnosis.
Author: Michael Ivan Friedman.
Publisher: Mind Garden, Inc.

Review of the Closed Head Injury Screener by THOMAS J. CULLEN, JR., *Clinical Psychologist, Cullen Psychological Services, P.C., Fairless Hills, PA:*

The author makes a clear statement regarding the appropriate uses of the Closed Head Injury Screener. He notes that clinicians are often faced with situations where they must make decisions regarding the necessity of referring patients for neuropsychological evaluation. He also notes that in many cases symptoms may be biased as a function of situations involving legal actions. Therefore, the test is designed to aid the clinician in screening for the consequences of a closed-head injury while at the same time helping the clinician to be alert to the possibility of bias in a patient's responding.

He cites the case that the conceptual status of post-concussion syndrome as a diagnostic entity has been controversial and has changed over the years. He presents a definition of the syndrome as encompassing a variety of emotional symptoms and motivational and cognitive deficits that make their appearance shortly after the patient has been involved in a concussive event of some sort. He goes on to note that the cognitive deficits typically involve the areas of attention, memory, and reasoning. The motivational deficits are noted to include sleep disruption and poor general vitality as well as disinterest in appetitive, recreational, and social behavior. The emotional symptoms include both dysphoria and irritability. He states that the most commonly encountered concussive event is the motor vehicle accident with additional significant contributions from both assault and sports.

He goes on to present studies by a number of authors showing the effects of concussive events including those involving no contact with the head and only very brief unconsciousness. The studies found disruptive effects in skill and a characteristic distribution of microscopic lesions. From these studies, it has been concluded that concussions are acceleration-deceleration injuries. As such, the author notes that there is a high incidence of events that may produce such acceleration-deceleration injuries. Indeed, today's clinician may be faced with any number of situations where neuropsychological examination appears appropriate. It is noted that neurobehavioral consequences of closed-head injuries, especially in milder forms, are often quite subtle and are often ascribed to an emotional response to physical trauma. At the same time, the clinician must be aware of the possibility of biased responding by individuals simply seeking compensations for damages. The Closed Head Injury Screener therefore provides a structure for an interview that elicits symptoms of post-concussion syndrome and provides guidelines for the interpretations of the obtained results. It also enables the clinician to be aware of biased responding before proceeding with a lengthy testing process.

The author notes that for the most part the Screener is administered in a question-and-answer format over a period of about one-half hour. (There is also a Questionnaire Format that is intended as an adjunct to the full interview and that may allow a considerable saving of time in the case of patients who are capable of responding "to" and responding "in" written form.) There are four sections to the full interview instrument. The first elicits medical facts associated with the events of the trauma. The second prompts the report of any neurobehavioral symptoms that appear to be consequentially related to the initial trauma. The last two sections provide an indication of the validity of the patient's responses to the interview.

The manual is clear and presents the administration procedures in a straightforward manner. The instrument reporting procedures are also elucidated. It is noted that certain evidence documenting compromised cortical functions, the existence of a concussive event, and a certain score on the Learning and Recall sections must be present before suggesting there is evidence of a closed-head injury. Nevertheless, the author makes it clear that because the instrument is a screener, it cannot provide the basis for a diagnosis of a closed-head injury. Its stated purpose is to assist the clinician in judging whether a full neuropsychological evaluation is appropriate in a particular case. It is important to note that no reliability data are presented. And no predictive validity data are presented. The content validity is such that the Screener closely mimics the areas of impairment noted in the stated definition of post-concussion syndrome. The instrument is not biased with regard to any demographic characteristics except for English-language proficiency.

SUMMARY. Overall, the Closed Head Injury Screener provides a useful tool in the battery of tests available to psychologists working with possible closed-head injury patients. It taps a number of areas typically measured by a variety of other tests. In this sense it provides a relatively quick measure of possible neuropsychological impairment. It also provides an important measure of a patient's motivational integrity. However, it should be noted that it does not measure every possible area and misses some of the major cognitive functional areas tapped by other specialized tests. A variety of functional areas have been identified as being important in a neuropsychological screening instrument. These areas include lateral dominance; motor functioning; auditory, tactile, and visual sensation; spatial-perceptual organization; language skills; general information; and memory processes. The Closed Head Injury screener does not measure lateral dominance, motor functioning, tactile sensation, spatial-perceptual organization, language skills, general information, or specific memory processes beyond self-reported global memory difficulties. It does, however, detail the elements of post-concussion syndrome quite well.

Review of the Closed Head Injury Screener by SCOTT A. NAPOLITANO, Adjunct Assistant Professor, Department of Educational Psychology, University of Nebraska–Lincoln, Lincoln, NE, and Pediatric Neuropsychologist, Lincoln Pediatric Group, Lincoln, NE:

The Closed Head Injury Screener (CHIS) is a semi-structured interview designed "to assess whether or not the presentation of a given case suggests a closed-head injury" (manual, p. 18), and "to assist the clinician in judging whether or not a full neuro-psychological evaluation is appropriate in any particular case" (manual, p. 17). The CHIS consists of four sections: (a) Medical Facts, (b) Presenting Complaints, (c) Learning, and (d) Recall. The Medical Facts section of the interview elicits information from the patient regarding the medical facts of the injury such as loss of consciousness, confusion, and post-traumatic amnesia. The Presenting Complaints section of the interview elicits information from the patient regarding neurobehavioral changes following an injury such as changes in memory, attention, and sensory abilities. The Learning and Recall sections are included as a validity index of the patient's truthfulness in responding. The patient is first presented with a list of 20 words and instructed to learn them and be able to remember them. Then the patient is shown a list of 20 word pairs. In each pair there is one familiar word and one new word, and the patient must indicate which word is the familiar word. In addition to the four sections described above, the CHIS includes an optional Questionnaire Format, which can serve as an adjunct to the complete interview. When the Questionnaire Format is utilized, the patient first completes the questionnaire, which is in yes/no format and which parallels the full interview, and then the examiner reviews the questionnaire with the patient eliciting further detail.

The CHIS manual is quite brief and is lacking much information that seems necessary to use the instrument in clinical practice or to make a decision as to whether or not to proceed with further neuropsychological testing, which is one of the stated purposes of the test. To begin with, no information regarding for what ages the CHIS is appropriate has been provided. It seems as though many of the questions would be difficult for children to answer. The author does state that the Questionnaire Format is not appropriate for children, but does not provide specific ages or reading levels at which it becomes appropriate. No objective rating, scoring, or decision-making system is explained, with the exception of the validity index, on which the author states that at least 16 correct recognitions should be achieved to be sure of the patient's motivational integrity. Furthermore, even though this criterion is provided, no specific empirical rationale for using 16 as a cutoff is provided. Again, related to the age issue, it is unclear whether the author is advocating the use of this cutoff for all ages (i.e., is 16 the cutoff for both a 5-year-old and a 35-year old?). As far as the other scales are concerned, the manual is

very vague regarding making decisions about whether a closed-head injury is present or not. For example, for the Presenting Complaints section the manual states "as the number of complaints increases, so does the probability of a positive screening decision" (p. 18). However, no specific numbers or cutoffs are described to aid in the decision-making process.

No information regarding the CHIS's psychometric properties is presented in the CHIS manual. Additionally, no research studies are presented to support the CHIS's usefulness for the purposes for which it was designed. Specifically, no examination of interrater reliability, test-retest reliability, construct validity, or the criterion-related validity of the CHIS is presented. Although the CHIS would appear to be somewhat useful in obtaining a thorough clinical history, the absence of this information makes it unacceptable for its intended purpose of making significant decisions regarding whether or not to identify as having a closed-head injury, or whether or not to complete a neuropsychological assessment following a head injury.

SUMMARY. Given the serious limitations of the CHIS described above including the lack of sufficient decision criteria and the complete absence of research investigating reliability and validity, it is not possible to recommend this instrument for clinical use. The author has the obligation to provide sufficient information regarding the basic psychometric properties of an instrument, including whether it measures what it is supposed to measure.

[80]
Closed High School Placement Test.

Purpose: Designed as a measure of cognitive and basic skills to assist in placement decisions for entering freshmen.

Population: Eighth grade students.

Publication Dates: 1985–1991.

Acronym: HSPT.

Scores, 8: Cognitive Skills (Verbal, Quantitative, Total), Basic Skills (Reading, Mathematics, Language, Total), Composite.

Administration: Group.

Price Data, 1997: Available only through Lease/Score program including school rental of test materials and scoring service; $4.85 per student, minimum scoring service charge of $42.35 required.

Time: (140) minutes plus (15–25) minutes per optional test.

Comments: Optional tests include science, mechanical aptitude, and Catholic religion.

Author: Scholastic Testing Service, Inc.
Publisher: Scholastic Testing Service, Inc.
Cross References: See T5:547 (1 reference) and T3:2324 (1 reference); for reviews by Leonard S. Cahen and Irvin J. Lehmann, see 8:26 (1 reference); see also 7:21 (2 references); for reviews by Marion F. Shaycoft and James R. Hayden of an earlier series, see 6:6; for reviews by William C. Cottle and Robert A. Jones of the 1955 "open" test, see 5:15.

Review of the Closed High School Placement Test by GEORGE ENGELHARD, JR., Professor of Educational Studies, Emory University, Atlanta, GA:

The purpose of the High School Placement Test (HSPT) is to aid with the task of selection and/or placement of students entering high school. The HSPT is recommended to assist with admission decisions, placement in high school classes, remediation efforts with incoming high school students, and scholarship awards. The target population is eighth grade students who plan to attend high school. The HSPT provides scores related to Basic Skills (Reading, Mathematics, Language, Total Basic Skills), Cognitive Skills (Verbal, Quantitative, and Total Cognitive Skills), Battery Composite, and optional tests (Science, Mechanical Aptitude, Catholic religion). New forms of the HSPT are created annually.

SCORES, NORMS, AND EQUATING. Local percentile ranks, national percentile ranks, standard scores, and stanine scores are provided for all subtests. Grade equivalent scores are available for the Basic Skills Tests, and an ability scale (Cognitive Skills Quotient with a mean of 100 and standard deviation of 15) is provided based on the Total Cognitive Skills Test. The manuals provide clear and detailed instructions for test administration. The score reports are described fully in the manuals along with appropriate cautions for interpreting the scores on the HSPT.

Potential users of the HSPT should be cautioned that all of the norm-referenced scores (national percentile ranks, stanine scores, and grade equivalents) are derived from user-based norms, and not a nationally representative sample of eighth grade students in the United States. In several places, the authors incorrectly refer to these user-based norms as a "national representative sample of eighth-graders" (e.g., Technical Supplement for Form QQ, p. 2). It is unclear how many students are included in the user-based norms (5,000 students are mentioned in one section of the manual and 50,000 in another

section). No data are provided regarding the number of students in the total user sample, and no information is available regarding the demographic characteristics of the user-based norms. Without minimal information regarding the demographic composition of the subgroups that define user-based norms, such as proportion of males/females, race/ethnicity, urban/suburban/rural, geographic region, school size, and socioeconomic levels, it is virtually impossible for potential users to evaluate the adequacy of the norms.

As pointed out earlier, new forms of the HSPT are created every year. The Rasch Measurement Model (RMM) is used to equate these annual forms. The number of common items and the content representation of the items used to link annual forms are not described. In addition to using common-item equating based on the RMM, equipercentile equating based on randomly equivalent groups (up to 1,000 students) is also used to link annual forms. No information is provided on how potential discrepancies between these two equating methods are handled in the equating process.

RELIABILITY. In support of the reliability of scores on the HSPT, the manual provides estimates of KR20 and KR21. Overall, the reliability estimates are quite good for this type of instrument. The lowest reliability coefficient is .83 for the language subtest of the Basic Skills Test, and the highest is .97 for the Composite Test. No evidence of the stability of the scores over time, such as test-retest reliability coefficients, is provided. No equivalent forms reliability coefficients are reported; because a new form of the HSPT is created annually, evidence regarding the stability and equivalence of scores across forms should be provided. The authors should be complimented for providing standard errors of measurement for the raw score and derived score scales. The high internal consistency estimates of reliability (KR20 and KR21) are large enough to warrant the use of HSPT scores for individual student decisions regarding admission and placement.

ITEM SELECTION. The selection of items for the HSPT was based on a consideration of traditional indices of item quality, such as item difficulty and item discrimination, and also on the goodness-of-fit statistics associated with the Rasch Measurement Model (one-parameter, Item Response Theory model). Unfortunately, the authors do not take full advantage of the strengths of the Rasch Measurement Model (RMM). For example, the authors should consider reporting variable maps using the item calibrations to illustrate the variables being measured by the HSPT. It should be stressed that the invariance properties associated with the RMM, item-invariant measurement of examinees and sample-invariant calibration of items, are not inherent properties of the RMM (Engelhard, 1994; Hambleton & Jones, 1993). The invariance properties are essentially hypotheses that must be examined for each test. The fit statistics that provide evidence regarding invariance, and other Rasch-related statistics (e.g., reliability of item separation) are not reported in the manuals. This information is required in addition to the traditional psychometric data (e.g., KR20 and KR21) in order to fully evaluate the psychometric quality of the HSPT.

VALIDITY. In support of the content-related validity of the HSPT, the authors provide a short description of the objectives and number of items included in each area. According to the authors, the content of the Basic Skills Test (Reading, Mathematics, and Language) is reviewed each year to ensure current curricular emphasis. No details are provided regarding how this process is conducted. Several key questions are left unanswered, such as: (a) How was the content validity study conducted? (b) What changes have occurred in the content of the tests over time? And (c) What was the composition of the expert panel used to examine content validity? Potential users have minimal information to make a decision regarding the appropriateness of content included on the HSPT for their intended uses. No detail is provided regarding changes over time in the content of the Cognitive Skills Test.

Because the major purpose of the HSPT is to make selection and placement decisions, information regarding predictive validity is essential. Extensive evidence regarding the predictive validity of the HSPT is provided. Correlations with a variety of tests, such as the PSAT, SAT, and ACT are reported. The correlations between scores on the HSPT with other high school performance measures are quite high. Correlations between scores on the HSPT and 11th grade GPA are also quite high (.33 to .73 for HSPT Total Basic Skills, and .32 to .69 for HSPT Battery). Information regarding predictive validity is not provided in the annual technical supplements that are provided to most users. Given the critical nature of this information for the potential user of the HSPT, a short summary of the predictive validity evidence should be included in these yearly technical supplements.

The intercorrelations of the subtest and total scores on the HSPT are also reported. These correlations are quite high and range from .64 to .98. These are typical of what would be expected for these types of tests.

There is no evidence that the content of the HSPT was reviewed for item or test bias. No information is provided regarding any analyses of differential item functioning across subgroups of examinees. Analyses of the predictive validity of the HSPT across subgroups are also not described in the technical manual. Given the importance of the selection and placement decisions that may be made on the basis of the HSPT, it is critically important that detailed information concerning potential item and test bias be provided in the manual.

SUMMARY. The HSPT appears to reflect sound professional test development, administration, and scoring strategies; however, the technical documentation is somewhat weak and lacks sufficient detail needed to evaluate the HSPT. More information should be included in the annual technical supplements in support of the psychometric quality of the HSPT, and in support of its usefulness as a placement test. The lack of a detailed description of the norms makes it difficult to evaluate the usefulness of the HSPT for its recommended purposes. The authors should consider making greater use of the strengths of the Rasch Measurement Model in support of the psychometric quality of the HSPT. As pointed out above, potential users need to be careful that the user-based norms are not misinterpreted to be national norms.

REVIEWER'S REFERENCES
Hambleton, R. K., & Jones, R. W. (1993). Comparisons of classical test theory and item response theory and their applications to test development. *Educational Measurement: Issues and Practice, 12*(3), 38–47.
Engelhard, G., Jr. (1994). Historical views of the concept of invariance in measurement theory. In M. Wilson (Ed.), *Objective measurement: Theory into practice* (vol. 2) (pp. 73–99). Norwood, NJ: Ablex.

Review of the Closed High School Placement Test by ERNEST KIMMEL, Executive Director, Office of Public Leadership, Educational Testing Service, Princeton, NJ:

Opening the packet of materials submitted for review created the sensation that one had opened a file that had been resting in the back of a filing cabinet for many years. Both the physical appearance of the materials and the conceptual and psychometric models underlying the test reflect the state-of-the-art of past decades. Descriptive, technical, and interpretive information is scattered among a number of publications. Because the dates of these publications span more than two decades, it is difficult to know whether and which data pertain to the current versions of the test and resulting scores.

USE. Although the title of the instrument suggests that the intended use of the test is for placing incoming high school students into appropriate programs and courses, the 1997 report on validity cites selection for admission, remediation, and scholarship selection as other primary uses of the battery. The battery is administered to eighth graders under closed (i.e., secure) procedures by high schools or school systems. Although no information is provided about the types of schools and systems using the HSPT, the publishers report that 97% of the respondents to a 1996 survey of users represented private schools. Of the responding schools, 61% have a selective admissions policy and 38% used the results of the HSPT to determine scholarship awards.

DESCRIPTION. The HSPT measures broad Cognitive Skills and a set of Basic Skills. The Cognitive Skills test provides a Verbal (60 items), Quantitative (52 items), and Total score; the Basic Skills test has a Reading (62 items), Mathematics (64 items), Language (60 items), and Total score. These are combined in a Battery Composite Score. In addition to a raw score, local percentile ranks, national percentile ranks, standard scores, and stanine scores are provided for all subtests. For the Basic Skills scores, Grade-Equivalents are provided. The Total Cognitive Skills score is transformed to a Cognitive Skills Quotient on a scale with a mean of 100 and a standard deviation of 15. A new battery of tests is developed annually and can be used only under secure conditions.

In addition to the above tests, users can choose an optional test and have its results reported along with the scores of the HSPT battery. Optional tests are available in Religion, Mechanical Aptitude, and Science.

CONTENT. We are told that "The Basic Skills content is reviewed each year to ensure that the test reflects current curricular emphasis." Further, "each form reflects changes in curricular emphases that occur from year to year" (HSPT Technical Supplement for Form QQ [1990], p.

9). "A thorough analysis of curricular trends is made, using textbooks and related materials plus statistical evidence from the previous year's STS-HSPT" (The High School Placement Test Technical Report [1976], p. 8). Unfortunately, no information is provided as to how the publisher chooses textbooks or other information about current curricula or from whom such information was solicited. Nor are we told who makes judgements about the changes needed in the battery or who sets the test specifications that allocate the weight given to different topics. Because of this absence of information, it is impossible to judge the extent to which the test does reflect the eighth-grade curriculum for some undefined group of schools.

The Cognitive Skills content is defined in terms of "generally accepted item-types associated with both the Verbal and Quantitative Cognitive Skills." The user is implicitly asked to "trust" the publisher because no rationale or research evidence is presented to justify the item types that are used or the relative weights assigned to each. It would also be very helpful to know what experts were involved in making these decisions.

New test items are "experimentally tested in schools with students comparable to those who will ultimately use the new form" (technical report, p. 8). Such tryouts and subsequent item analyses are apparently inadequate to eliminate all inadequate items because a number of items in the form submitted for review had multiple correct answers or very dated content. A thorough review by a panel of qualified teachers would seem like a worthwhile investment—by eliminating faulty items and adding a degree of credibility. Several of the item formats seem unnecessarily artificial, posing tasks in ways that occur neither in school nor in subsequent life (e.g., when is one given four decontextualized words and asked to choose which one does not belong? Or four unrelated sentences and asked to choose the one with "errors in capitalization, punctuation, or usage"?).

MEASUREMENT PROPERTIES. As indicated above, no information is provided that would enable the user to make judgments about the curricular or construct facets of validity. A 1997 publication, *STS Validity Studies: Relating Performance on the STS High School Placement Test* presents data from 33 schools in 10 states. Some of the data relate the HSPT scores to criteria collected later (i.e., predictive); other data were collected concurrently with the HSPT data. Although these data are described as showing the relationship of the HSPT "to subsequent high school performance," most of the data presented use other tests as the criterion. Only one table in the report uses school performance (i.e., Grade 11 GPA) as the criterion. The median correlations between the HSPT—Battery Average and Grade 11 GPA are around .55, with a range from .32–.69. It would be useful to know the characteristics of the schools reporting the extremes of this range. The reported correlations are similar to the relationship one finds between many tests of general academic ability and performance several years later. The correlations reported between the HSPT and a variety of other tests suggests a substantial degree of overlap in the skills measured by the several tests. Although called a "placement" test, no evidence is provided to support the use of either the total or the subscores in making decisions about differential educational treatment (i.e., placement into classes that use different approaches or move at different paces).

The reliabilities (KR_{21} and KR_{20}) reported for the Cognitive Skills Total, the Basic Skills Total, and the Composite for Form QQ are in the .92–.97 range—a level appropriate for making admission and scholarship decisions about individual students. The reliability estimates provided for the subtests of this form range from .81 to .90—suggesting that they are appropriate for making reversible decisions such as placement into particular classes. The estimates of the standard error of measurement show a similar pattern. It would be very helpful if the publisher also reported the standard error of differences to aid users in judging whether the difference between the scores of two students reflects a "true" difference or is likely to be an artifact of the errors of measurement.

The survey of users shows that a substantial majority use subtest scores as part of the criteria for placement, especially into English and Mathematics. Yet there is substantial intercorrelation among the subtests and the total scores (e.g., the Mathematics and Quantitative scores correlate .80 with each other and .87–.88 with the composite score). As an earlier reviewer (8:26) indicated, one needs to question whether any differences among subscores reflects actual differences in student achievement or only measurement noise. The Technical Supplement is cautious in indicating

that the coefficients among the part scores "allow some degree of independent use in placement and/or counseling" (Technical Supplement, p. 6). The Interpretive Manual also cautions that "Individual subtest scores should be carefully evaluated when placing students in specific courses" (Interpretive Manual, p. 6). It would be very helpful if more information were provided about the ability of the subtests to discriminate among real differences in achievement.

RESULTS. As indicated above, student performance on the HSPT is reported on several scales. Most prominent is the national norm scale and the associated stanine scale. Each year this scale is cross-validated using "data accumulated for that year's battery" (HSPT Technical Report [1976], p. 2). Elsewhere we are told that the norms are developed using "a random sample of students ... drawn from the national eighth-grade population who are taking the test and definitely intending to attend a secondary school" (HSPT Technical Supplement for Form QQ [1990], p. 3). Still elsewhere, we are told that the "percentile norms ... use as a base only those grade 8 students who plan to attend an academic high school" (HSPT STS Validity Studies [1997], p. 15). These norms would be more accurately categorized as "program" norms because the label "national" implies that they are representative of all eighth graders in the U.S., or at least those planning to attend high school. No information is provided about the schools that are included in the database from which the stratified random sample of students is drawn nor is there any information that would permit one to judge whether these norms can be interpreted in any way beyond the context of the limited number of schools that choose to use the HSPT.

In 1980, the HSPT introduced a normalized standard score scale for all subtest and total scores. With a mean of 500 and a standard deviation of 100, the standard score scale is described as invariant from year to year. Each new form is equated to the 1980 scale through a Rasch latent trait model. The publishers particularly stress the use of the standard score scale as a fixed frame of reference for making group comparisons across years. They also suggest using the standard score scale, rather than a normative scale, in situations where a cutoff score is used—again as a better way of maintaining consistency in decision making. It would seem appropriate for the publisher to give greater emphasis to the standard score scale in all applications and to rely less on percentile ranks as the primary score.

SUMMARY. There is little to distinguish the HSPT from other measures of skills and abilities related to subsequent learning. Because of the lack of information, one cannot judge the extent to which the Basic Skills battery reflects any particular eighth grade curriculum. No evidence or rationale is provided for the choice of item types used in the Cognitive Skills measure. The sample test indicates that a more thorough review could eliminate a number of hard-to-defend items. Even though there appears to be a reasonably strong relationship between the HSPT and subsequent grade average in high school, no evidence is provided to support its eponymous purpose of placement.

[81]
Cognistat (The Neurobehavioral Cognitive Status Examination).

Purpose: Designed to assess intellectual functioning.
Population: Adults.
Publication Dates: 1983–1995.
Acronym: Cognistat.
Scores, 11: Level of Consciousness, Orientation, Attention, Language (Comprehension, Repetition, Naming), Constructional Ability, Memory, Calculations, Reasoning (Similarities, Judgment).
Administration: Individual.
Price Data: Available from publisher.
Time: Administration time not reported.
Authors: R. J. Kiernan, J. Mueller, and J. W. Langston.
Publisher: Northern California Neurobehavioral Group, Inc.

Review of the Cognistat (The Neurobehavioral Cognitive Status Examination) by CHARLES J. LONG, Professor of Psychology, and FAITH GUNNING-DIXON, Research Assistant, Psychology Department, The University of Memphis, Memphis, TN:

The Cognistat was designed to assess cognitive functioning in the following areas of abilities: Memory, Language, Construction, Calculations, and Reasoning. In addition, Level of Consciousneess, Orientation, and Attention are assessed during the examination. The test was designed as a brief assessment tool to screen for cognitive dysfunction. The target population is

not specified in the manual, but normative data are provided for adults only (20 to 66 years). A primary goal of this instrument is to provide finer discriminations among the aforementioned areas of abilities than is provided by other brief cognitive screening instruments. The authors clearly state that the Cognistat was not meant to replace traditional neuropsychological tests, but to detect areas of weakness, which could then be more thoroughly assessed using additional measures.

The instrument consists of five major ability areas (Language, Constructional Ability, Calculations, Reasoning, and Memory) as well as sections assessing Level of Consciousness, Attention, and Orientation. The average length of administration is approximately 5 minutes for normally functioning individuals, whereas administration takes 10 to 20 minutes when assessing cognitively impaired patients (Kiernan, Mueller, Langston, & Van Dyke, 1987). With the exception of the Memory and orientation sections, each ability area contains a screening item that is administered to each individual. If the examinee passes the screening item for any particular section, then he or she receives full credit for that specific portion of the test. However, if the screening item is failed then the metric items are administered. The metric items are administered by level of difficulty, beginning at the easiest level. For each section, the screening item is designed to be the most difficult item, although Oehlert et al. (1997) suggest that the more conservative approach of administering all the items yields a lower false negative rate. This screen and metric approach does allow for quick administration of the instrument when testing individuals with normal cognitive functioning while allowing for a more in-depth assessment of individuals who exhibit difficulty on screening items.

The testing stimulus material and the testing manual are both very functional. Complete directions for the administration and scoring of the Cognistat instrument are located in the manual. After administering the entire scale, the examiner adds up the total points earned within each section and plots the raw scores on the graph located on the front cover of the test protocol. The graphical display of scores on the front cover of the test booklet provides the examiner information about level of the examinee's performance (average, mild impairment, moderate impairment, and severe impairment). Overall, the directions for administration and scoring are clear and easy to follow. However, the results would be more meaningful if raw scores were converted to age-normed standard scores for each section. In addition a global index of cognitive functioning would serve to supplement the information provided by the scores obtained for each area.

Normative data for the Cognistat were collected on 60 subjects ranging in age from 20 to 66. Participants were nonprofessional members of the staff at medical centers. Although subjects were apparently screened for a history positive for medical and other neurological problems, little detail is provide regarding the specific exclusion criteria. Additional normative data were collected for a geriatric group composed of 59 individuals with a mean age of 77, as well as a group of 30 neurological patients (mean age of 54) who had documented brain lesions from a variety of etiologies (i.e., CVA, neoplasm, etc.). The failure to provide more details regarding the neurological sample and the relatively small *N* limits the utility of the normative data. Providing normative data in the manual for different types of neurological groups (i.e., DAT) would be useful for the clinician. These data should include information regarding the frequency with which different types of individuals perform at each level. Finally, normative data have been collected for a sample of 866 psychiatric inpatients (Logue, Tupler, D'Amico, & Schmitt, 1993) but this study is not referenced in the Cognistat manual.

The authors fail to provide information about the selection of items for the instrument. Although superficially the items do appear to assess the constructs they are supposed to measure, neither statistical analyses nor theoretical rationale are provided for test construction. Due to both the screen and metric design of the test and the goal of the test to provide discriminations amongst different areas of abilities, data regarding the construct validity of the scores from this instrument are particularly imperative for interpretation of performance. Results of factor analysis have yielded only very limited support for the construct validity of the different areas of ability (i.e., reasoning) (Logue, Tupler, D'Amico, & Schmitt, 1993). The authors fail to provide adequate information about both concurrent and predictive validity. The test was found to have far fewer false negatives in populations of neurosurgery patients; however, the study was not designed to consider false positives

(Schwamm, Van Dyke, Kiernan, Merrin, & Mueller, 1987). Research conducted with CVA patients does suggest that the Cognistat may be more sensitive to cognitive dysfunction than both the Mini Mental State Exam and the Albert's Test and that it is a better predictor of functional outcome in such patients (Mysiw, Beegan, & Gatens, 1989).

Additionally, the authors of the Cognistat apparently do not assess the reliability of scores from the instrument. They state that the standard measurements of test-retest reliability are not appropriate for this scale due to the relative lack of variability in performance in the normal population which may lead to misleading reliability coefficients. The authors also state that split-half reliability is statistically inappropriate due to the limited number of items on the scale. Although the aforementioned concerns may be valid, reliability should still be assessed. One viable option is to assess test-retest reliability in both the normal population and in neurological populations, and qualify the results of the reliability studies with cautions about interpretation. Another approach that would enhance the utility of this instrument is to develop an alternative form of the test. This option would serve both to provide an opportunity to assess alternate form reliability, as well as to attenuate practice effects when the instrument is used to track the course of a disorder.

SUMMARY. The test is well designed for ease and brevity of administration. Also it appears to be a relatively sensitive screening test for cognitive dysfunction. The instrument's stated purpose of providing a measure that allows for finer distinctions among areas of cognitive dysfunction is an important contribution. This is accomplished by evaluating cognitive functions individually rather than as a single global score. It is further aided by the use of a mental status profile. However, the authors' failure to provide information about the statistical properties of this scale, particularly studies of both construct and concurrent validity as well as reliability, is a severe limitation. Clearly, what is needed is a comparison of screening tests such as the Cognistat with established measures of cognitive function in both older controls and patients of different etiologies. In conclusion, the Cognistat appears to have the potential to improve upon already existent brief cognitive screening instruments that provide just a global index of cognitive functioning, but the authors' failure to provide the user sufficient information about the statistical properties of this scale significantly limits its utility.

REVIEWER'S REFERENCES

Kiernan, R. J., Mueller, J., Langston, W., & Van Dyke, C. (1987). The Neurobehavioral Cognitive Status Examination: A brief but differentiated approach to cognitive assessment. *Annals of Internal Medicine, 107,* 481–485.

Schwamm, L. H., Van Dyke, C., Kiernan, R. J., Merrin, E. L., & Mueller, J. (1987). The Neurobehavioral Cognitive Status Examination: Comparison with the Cognitive Capacity Screening Examination and the Mini-Mental State Examination in a neurosurgical population. *Annals of Internal Medicine, 107,* 486–491.

Mysiw, W. J., Beegan, J. G., & Gatens, P. F. (1989). Prospective cognitive assessment of stroke patients before inpatient rehabilitation: The relationship of the Neurobehavioral Cognitive Status Examination to functional improvement. *American Journal of Physical Medicine Rehabilitation, 68,* 168–171.

Logue, P. E., Tupler, L. A., D'Amico, C., & Schmitt, F. A. (1993). The Neurobehavioral Cognitive Status Examination: Psychometric properties in use with psychiatric inpatients. *Journal of Clinical Psychology, 49,* 80–89.

Oehlert, M. E., Haas, S. D., Freeman, M. R., Williams, M. D., Ryan, J. J., & Sumerall, S. W. (1997). The Neurobehavioral Cognitive Status Examination: Accuracy of the "screen-metric" approach in a clinical sample. *Journal of Clinical Psychology, 53,* 733–737.

Review of the Cognistat (The Neurobehavioral Cognitive Status Examination) by STEVEN R. SHAW, Lead School Psychologist, Department of Developmental Pediatrics, The Children's Hospital, Greenville, SC:

DESCRIPTION. Cognistat is a hybrid of structured neurological status interview and standardized screening battery for neuropsychological dysfunction. The result is a useful and brief instrument for use when there is need for a detailed neurological status interview. The purpose of the Cognistat is to determine if a person's cognitive functioning is in the average range, mildly impaired, moderately impaired, or severely impaired level for each of five areas.

Five areas of cognitive functioning are assessed: Language, Constructions, Memory, Calculations, and Reasoning. Reasoning is made up of subtests called Similarities and Judgment. The other areas consist of a single subtest. Levels of Consciousness, Orientation, and Attention are assessed independently of the five areas of cognitive functioning.

Materials consist of a well-organized protocol for each administration. A stimulus booklet and a set of red, white, and red and white tiles for the construction subtest are also included. The manual provides detailed instructions for administration and scoring. All materials required for administration could easily be carried on a clipboard.

ADMINISTRATION AND SCORING. The Cognistat uses a screen and metric approach to administration. For each subtest, the client is administered a single item (i.e., the screen). If the screen item is passed, then the patient is considered to be in the average range for that task and that subtest is terminated. The authors state that

about 20% of normal individuals fail the screen. This seems like a reasonable figure, but there is no supporting evidence presented. If the screen item is failed, then the client is administered four to eight additional items (i.e., metric items). These items assist in determining the degree of impairment in each cognitive area.

Although no typical administration time is supplied in the manual, six trial administrations by the reviewer with adolescents in a developmental pediatrics setting yielded administration times ranging from 5 to 35 minutes. If all screen items are passed, then the Cognistat is an extremely concise test. However, when metric items are to be administered, the Cognistat becomes more than a brief screen.

Scoring is clear and objective for most subtests. The exceptions are the subtests of the Reasoning Area, which requires some interpretation. The Similarities subtest is analogous to Similarities subtest on Wechsler Intelligence scales. The Judgment subtest is analogous to the Comprehension subtest on Wechsler Intelligence scales. Rules for differentiating 0-, 1-, or 2-point responses are not completely clear—noting that answers must be "appropriate and reasonably well explained." Some examples of 0-, 1-, and 2-point responses are given. Examples of appropriate queries are also provided. Overall, scoring criteria are clear.

There are no standard scores, percentile ranks, or similar metrics used. Raw scores are transferred to a chart on the front of the protocol. Results are presented as Average, Mild Impairment, Moderate Impairment, or Severe Impairment for each subtest and the five areas. Nor is the rationale for associating raw scores with a given impairment level entirely clear. No index of global or overall impairment is presented.

TECHNICAL INFORMATION. The normative group consisted of 60 subjects who were volunteers from the nonprofessional staff at medical centers. Thirty were in the 20–30-year-old group and 30 were in the 40–66-year-old group. There were minimal differences between groups on the Cognistat. There was little variance among individuals for these nonimpaired groups. Data were also presented for 59 geriatric patients and 30 neurosurgical patients. The geriatric patients had no history of medical issues, psychiatric concerns, or medications known to affect cognitive functioning. The neurosurgical patient sample had some form of brain lesion (e.g., tumor, stroke). Means and standard deviations for all normative samples were reported.

No reliability data were presented. The authors note that common reliability criteria are inappropriate for the screening and metric format. Split-half reliability coefficients would invariably be quite low because there are few items on the test. The authors also note that measures applied to pathological patients are notoriously unstable. All of these concerns are legitimate. However, data on stability for the different populations and interexaminer reliability would have been useful.

Validity data are sparse. The neurosurgical and geriatric populations scored lower than the other normative groups. However, no other validity studies were presented. The manual provides a list of journal articles, book chapters, presentations, and posters relating to the use of the Cognistat. However, a detailed review of validity studies was not presented. The manual also provides a listing of 30 ongoing projects using the Cognistat. Five case studies were presented to illustrate interpretation of cognitive profiles. Minimal validity data are provided in the manual.

Interpretation of the Cognistat can be challenging. Two pages in the manual are devoted to detailed explanations of the cautions in interpreting the Cognistat. Some of the cautions include insensitivity to issues concerning premorbid intelligence, insensitivity to some frontal lobe lesions, and absence of reading, writing, and spelling items. Sensory deficits, impaired levels of consciousness, attention deficits, language disturbances, learning disabilities, and low general mental ability are all cited as confounding variables when interpreting the Cognistat. As with all assessment instruments, interpretation of the Cognistat requires integration with other medical and psychological data, family history, motivation, and a host of other factors.

SUMMARY. As a structured neurological status interview, the Cognistat is a detailed and well-considered improvement over the 10-second interview commonly administered in emergency rooms and crisis care environments. As a screening instrument, the Cognistat may provide useful qualitative information, but fails to meet minimal psychometric standards for decision making. Because of these shortcomings, the person administering and interpreting the Cognistat must have extensive expertise in the issues in administration and interpretation of qualitative neurological status examinations.

[82]
Cognitive Symptom Checklists.

Purpose: "Developed to assist in the identification and treatment of problems in five basic cognitive areas."
Population: Ages 16 and older.
Publication Date: 1993.
Acronym: CSC.
Scores: 5 checklists: Attention/Concentration, Memory, Visual Processes, Language, Executive Functions.
Administration: Group.
Price Data: Price data available from publisher for complete kit including manual (26 pages), and 10 each of Attention/Concentration, Memory, Visual Processes, Language, and Executive Functions checklists.
Time: (10) minutes per checklist.
Comments: Checklists can be used separately or in any combination.
Authors: Christine O'Hara, Minnie Harrell, Eileen Bellingrath, and Katherine Lisicia.
Publisher: Psychological Assessment Resources, Inc.

Review of the Cognitive Symptom Checklists by THOMAS J. CULLEN, JR., Clinical Psychologist, Cullen Psychological Services, P.C., Fairless Hills, PA:

The Cognitive Symptom Checklists (CSC) are actually a set of five checklists that were designed to elicit information about difficulties in daily living that a client may be experiencing as a result of impaired cognitive functioning. The authors state that the CSC may be used with individuals 16 years of age and older who have neurological disorders or developmental disorders. The appropriate settings for the use of the test, according to the authors, includes residential settings, outpatient facilities, school settings, and clinician's offices. The instrument was reportedly developed for use within a treatment model that focuses on identifying cognitive problems, teaching strategies, and generalizing strategies and skills to real-life situations. The authors further state that the CSC was developed as "a clinical tool to assist clients in determining missing links and to target real-life, functional areas in treatment" (clinician's guide, p. 21).

The administration of the CSC is accomplished in four phases. These are the Checklist Selection, Administration, Inquiry, and Interpretation. The authors note that the Administration may be carried out by individuals with no formal training in psychology so long as that individual is familiar with self-report instruments and that individual has access to a supervising clinician for consultation. The Selection, Inquiry, and Interpretation phases must be carried out by a clinician familiar with brain/behavior relationships and with therapeutic approaches to rehabilitation of cognition. The authors also state that the instrument may be self-administered. It is also stated that the five checklists may be used either individually or in various combinations depending on the needs of the client or the clinician. As examples, the authors cite the difference in needs of a client with diffuse brain injury as compared to the needs of a client with a learning disability.

The five checklists correspond to "five core cognitive areas in which clients often experience problems" (p. 1). The five areas, as well as the individual items, were apparently chosen by the authors as "representing critical problems observed in their clinical work and reported by survivors of brain injury and other neurological disorders" (p. 21). They note that the CSC was "developed to provide information that is typically not obtained through the use of traditional standardized tests" (p. 21). Indeed, this last statement seems to be eminently clear. Although formal neuropsychological evaluation often yields invaluable information, the day-to-day or real-life consequences of neurological dysfunction often go unspoken. It is in this area that the CSC excels. It provides a vehicle for conveying the much needed objective descriptions of some of the problems encountered by the client with neurological dysfunction. By reporting on specific identified behaviors, the clinician is able to tie the abstract conceptualizations presented in a neuropsychological evaluation to the more concrete and real problems experienced by the individual client.

Despite the need for behavioral checklists in the area of neuropsychological dysfunction, it should be noted that the psychometric value of the instrument is questioned. In line with this, the authors appropriately cite several clinical caveats for use of the CSC. They point out that, "As with all self-report instruments, the CSC may not accurately reflect all of a client's symptoms" (p. 7). It is also noted that there may be an under- or overreporting of information by the client due to a number of factors. It is noted that the CSC is a clinical tool and not a standardized test. This is of utmost importance and must be firmly stressed. It is appropriately

stated that the checklists were not designed for formal scoring beyond an examination of specific items and clusters of symptoms. The CSC is designed to supplement and complement other clinical tools.

SUMMARY. The sample population is not clearly identified or defined. The authors state that "validation of sections occurred through consensus of four clinicians, representing psychology, speech, and counseling disciplines, who independently identified, grouped, and categorized items" (p. 21). Nevertheless, despite face validity for certain clinical populations, there are no data presented to quantify the validity or reliability of scores from the instrument. Therefore, although the authors suggest that the instrument might be used to measure treatment progress or to establish a baseline for cognitive problem areas, it must be used with much caution in this respect. There are no quantified reliability measures making the instrument of questionable utility as a psychometric instrument.

Review of the Cognitive Symptom Checklists by MICHAEL LEE RUSSELL, Commander, 47th Combat Support Hospital, Fort Lewis, WA:

The Cognitive Symptom Checklists (CSC) is a useful set of structured inventories that can assist in the identification of neurological problem areas. The CSC will allow the clinician to refine which symptoms of cognitive difficulty may require more formal neuropsychological testing. The format of these questionnaires is actually five separate four-page booklets, each of which is color coded and targeted to a different cognitive function. They can be given in any combination, depending on the patient's presenting problem, and average approximately 70 questions per inventory. These checklists, when combined with a brief screening instrument such as the COGNISTAT (Northern California Neurobehavioral Group, 1995) can make a fairly comprehensive 50-minute neuro-screening interview.

The questions asked in the inventory are fairly standard neurological and neuropsychological screening questions used by most clinicians. The great advantage of this instrument is that its standardized format would insure that important areas are not omitted in an interview, and to allow administration by a technician for later review by the clinician. The manual suggests self-administration as another option, but I would only recommend this for a very high functioning neurological population: The questions asked are sometimes complex, and there are a large number of them (389 plus 7 redundant demographic questions if all 5 questionnaires are given). It asks the individual to rate difficulties in several subtests of cognitive function, then to go back and circle those areas of most concern. The manual suggests that a clinician remain present until the questionnaires are completed to provide structure and answer questions, which is certainly prudent.

The fundamental flaw of the questionnaire approach in assessing cognitive dysfunction is that it presupposes accurate self-appraisal: The individual must be cognitively intact enough to realize their own limitations in order to accurately report them. In essence, they must manifest intact executive ability for the data collected to be meaningful. Even though this is often the case in stroke and attention-deficit disorders, it is unlikely for most cases of cortical dementia. As the manual cautions, it is clearly a problem in the Executive and Memory questionnaires, and these should not be seen as a substitute for an objective memory test or a set of objective mental problems, which may be of more value in observing dysfunction in these areas.

The manual is well written, and addresses well the theoretical basis and limitations of the questionnaires. The administration instructions are clear and well written, including a procedure for inquiry. There are no formal scoring criteria.

SUMMARY. The development and validation of the CSC was as a "clinical tool," rather than a psychological test: The items were selected by clinical judgment of the authors, sampling items they felt to be critical in assessing a patient's cognitive ability, and guided by their own Rehabilitation Model. They refined the tool with the input of other clinicians and patients, although no formal reliability or validity data are reported. As their clinical judgment of what constitutes important questions to ask closely aligns with my own, it appears as a fairly useful clinical tool, as long as it is used in conjunction with formal testing and objective assessment methods.

REVIEWER'S REFERENCE

The Northern California Neurobehavioral Group. (1995). *Manual for COGNISTAT (The Neurobehavioral Cognitive Status Examination).* Fairfax, CA: Author.

[83]

CogScreen Aeromedical Edition.

Purpose: "Designed to rapidly assess deficits or changes in" various cognitive abilities associated with flying.

Population: Aviators ages 25–73 with 12 or more years of education.
Publication Date: 1995.
Acronym: CogScreen—AE.
Scores, 65: 19 Speed Measures (Math Speed, Visual Sequence Comparison Speed, Matching-to-Sample Speed, Manikin Speed, Divided Attention Sequence Comparison Speed, Divided Attention Indicator Alone Speed, Divided Attention Indicator Dual Speed, Auditory Sequence Comparison Speed, Pathfinder Number Speed, Pathfinder Letter Speed, Pathfinder Combined Speed, Shifting Attention Arrow Direction Speed, Shifting Attention Arrow Color Speed, Shifting Attention Instruction Speed, Shifting Attention Discovery Speed, Dual Task Previous Number Alone Speed, Dual Task Previous Number Dual Speed, Dual Task Tracking Alone Error, Dual Task Tracking Dual Error), 19 Accuracy Measures (Backward Digit Span Accuracy, Math Accuracy, Visual Sequence Comparison Accuracy, Symbol Digit Coding Accuracy, Symbol Digit Coding Immediate Recall Accuracy, Symbol Digit Coding Delayed Recall Accuracy, Matching-to-Sample Accuracy, Manikin Accuracy, Divided Attention Sequence Comparison Accuracy, Auditory Sequence Comparison Accuracy, Pathfinder Number Accuracy, Pathfinder Letter Accuracy, Pathfinder Combined Accuracy, Shifting Attention Arrow Direction Accuracy, Shifting Attention Arrow Color Accuracy, Shifting Attention Instruction Accuracy, Shifting Attention Discovery Accuracy, Dual Task Previous Number Alone Accuracy, Dual Task Previous Number Dual Accuracy), 16 Thruput Measures (Math Thruput, Visual Sequence Comparison Thruput, Symbol Digit Coding Thruput, Matching-to-Sample Thruput, Manikin Thruput, Divided Attention Sequence Comparison Thruput, Auditory Sequence Comparison Thruput, Pathfinder Number Thruput, Pathfinder Letter Thruput, Pathfinder Combined Thruput, Shifting Attention Arrow Direction Thruput, Shifting Attention Arrow Color Thruput, Shifting Attention Instruction Thruput, Shifting Attention Discovery Thruput, Dual Task Previous Number Alone Thruput, Dual Task Previous Number Dual Thruput), 11 Process Measures (Divided Attention Indicator Alone Premature Responses, Divided Attention Indicator Dual Premature Responses, Pathfinder Number Coordination, Pathfinder Letter Coordination, Pathfinder Combined Coordination, Shifting Attention Discovery Rule Shifts Completed, Shifting Attention Discovery Failures to Maintain Set, Shifting Attention Discovery Nonconceptual Responses, Shifting Attention Discovery Perseverative Errors, Dual Task Tracking Alone Boundary Hits, Dual Task Tracking Dual Boundary Hits).
Administration: Individual.
Price Data, 1996: $849 per software kit including manual (148 pages), quick start guide, internal light pen

package, and Testkey with 10 administrations (specify 3.5-inch or 5.25-inch disk); $69 per manual; $29.50 per administration with Testkey unlock; $75 per extra Testkey (with no administration); $375 per internal light pen package.

Time: (45–60) minutes.

Comments: Requires IBM or compatible 640K, EGA or VGA graphics card, color monitor, and light pen.

Author: Gary G. Kay.

Publisher: CogScreen LLC.

Review of the CogScreen Aeromedical Edition by ROBERT W. ELLIOTT, Director, Aviation Psychology Center, Los Angeles, CA:

DESCRIPTION. The CogScreen Aeromedical Edition (CS-AE) is an integrated, computer-self-administered neuropsychological/cognitive-screening battery and software scoring system designed to assess attention, immediate and short-term memory, visual-perceptual functions, sequencing functions, logical problem solving, math calculation skills, reaction time, simultaneous information processing abilities, and executive functioning skills. The CS-AE "was initially designed to meet the Federal Aviation Administration's (FAA) need for an instrument that could detect subtle changes in cognitive functioning: 'changes which left unnoticed may result in poor pilot judgment or slow reaction time in critical operational situations and use in the medical recertification evaluation of pilots with known or suspected neurological and/or psychiatric conditions'" (manual, p. 1). The CS-AE requires that the subject input responses by touching a light pen onto a cathode ray tube monitor on 10 of the 11 subtests. There are 12 alternate forms to CS-AE that may be used for repeated test administrations for the same individual. The approximately one-hour examination is self-administered and automatically scored. The individual's performance can be compared against a specific age group or against the entire sample of commercial aviators. After scoring of the individual's performance, a 10-page report of test score performances can be generated.

The 11 subtests include Backward Digit Span (recall of visually presented digits in reverse order), Math (multiple-choice math word problems), Visual Sequence Comparison (comparison of two simultaneously presented series of letters and numbers), Symbol Digit Coding (substitution of digits for symbols with immediate delayed recall of symbol-digit pairs), Matching To Sample (recognition of a checkerboard pattern), Manikin (identification of the hand in which a rotated human figure is holding a flag), Divided Attention (monitoring of the vertical movements of a bar within a circle, presented alone and in combination with the Visual Sequence Comparison test), Auditory Sequence Comparison (comparison of tone patterns), Pathfinder (sequencing numbers and letters and alternating a set of numbers and letters), Shifting Attention (identifying a rule for a visual task and then applying the rule until feedback indicates the rule has changed), and Dual Task (a visual-motor tracking test combined with a continuous memory task involving recall of a previously presented number). These 11 subtests are not tests of aviation knowledge or flying skills but are designed to assess the underlying perceptual, cognitive, and information-processing abilities associated with flying.

The CS-AE has also been used in a number of research applications involving use of antihyperintensive drugs, alcohol effects on cognitive performance, age, sleep apnea, HIV effects, military preflight training, head injury, and other medical and performance issues. A number of these studies are reported in peer-reviewed and government publications but are not compiled in any systematic journal or collection.

MATERIALS. The CS-AE package includes a single IBM 3.25-inch diskette, light pen package, and Testkey with 10 administrations. Minimal system requirements include an IBM-compatible computer (80286 processor or higher), EGA or VGA graphics card, color monitor, 20-megabyte hard disk drive, and a standard 101-keyboard. Currently, the CS-AE is accessed through the DOS system and has been updated to operate on Pentium-II and III systems. The CS-AE is not available for a Windows environment but development of this capability is currently in process.

PROGRAM USE. The CS-AE version currently in use was originally refined and marketed by Psychological Assessment Resources, Inc. (PAR) and includes their easy-to-use opening screens for general demographic information including age, education, aviation history, medical history and reason for referral, computer experience, alertness, and mood. The client is instructed on use of the light pen and then begins administration of the first of the 11 subtests.

Instructions emphasize that both speed and accuracy are assessed. In addition, there are scores that will be generated that record the number of correct responses per minute (thruput), and a number of qualitative and process-oriented performance characteristics. Speed on the CS-AE is assessed to the hundredth of a second.

Reliable administration of the CS-AE requires an eighth-grade reading level, normal vision, and adequate hearing. Administration of the CS-AE can be accomplished with trained personnel with a background in the fundamentals of test administration. A full interpretation of CS-AE results requires professional training in neuropsychology and familiarity with the CS-AE subtests.

The CS-AE is designed to be largely self-administered, but the test administrator needs to be available if the client experiences difficulty with administration. A unique feature of the CS-AE is the inclusion of a practice session before each task is actually scored. The practice session requires a predetermined level of proficiency before the subtest is administered. If the respondent fails two consecutive attempts to complete the practice session, the test will not proceed without the intervention of the administrator. The administrator has the choice then or repeating the instructions, running the exercise, or skipping the exercise.

At the conclusion of the one-hour test administration, a screen indicates that the test has ended. An important feature of the CS-AE is that not all tests need to be entered to derive standardized scores other than the summary logistic regression estimated probability of brain dysfunction score (LRPV). Generation of the LRPV requires that all tests be administered.

OUTPUT. The CS-AE report can be immediately scored and printed out, viewed on the screen, or exported to a data file. At the conclusion of the administration there is an opportunity for insertion of comments that may have affected test administration. The 10-page report is divided into the previously inserted demographic information and medical notes, and interpretative considerations. The report produces accuracy, reaction time, thruput, and/or process scores for each of the 11 subtests. There are 65 separate raw scores produced. The option of generating scores that compare the respondent's performance against commercial pilots of all ages or the age group that corresponds to the respondent's age is available.

The report presents the respondent's raw scores in order of subtest presentation, a base rate analysis showing the number of scores falling at or below the 15th and 5th percentiles, frequency (percentile) of occurrence of this level of performance compared to the standardization population, and a predicted value for brain dysfunction score based on the respondent's performance (LRPV). The author warns that an LRPV score greater than .60 for pilots under the age of 45 is highly suggestive of impairment. For older pilots, a score greater than .60 is "less abnormal" (manual, p. 87). The remaining pages present bar graphs displaying the respondent's performance relative to a previously selected comparison group in raw score, percentile, and *T*-score format. This information is provided in separate graphs for Speed, Accuracy, Thruput, and Process. Interpretation of the data is aided with a chapter in the manual.

The output report is well-organized in its graphic representations of percentile ranks and *T*-scores and each of the domains (Speed, Accuracy, Thruput, and Process). Because all of the respondent's performances are reported as standardized scores, comparison can be made directly either within or across the four domains.

The CS-AE was designed initially as a screening test and is not a substitution for a comprehensive neuropsychological evaluation. As the author points out, the CS-AE minimally assesses language, memory, and perceptual-motor integration skills. There are several different methods for interpreting the respondent's performance. These methods include single versus dual test performance, base rate approach, logistic regression approach, profile interpretation, or performance on individual subtests. A unique feature of the CS-AE is the use of the LRPV, which was based on the performance of a young sample of mildly brain-damaged and functionally intact individuals. LRPV scores above .60 suggest impairment and a need for a thorough neuropsychological evaluation. The author warns that "under no circumstances should the LRPV score be used as the primary performance assessment technique" (manual, p. 88).

STANDARDIZATION. The development of the CS-AE is based on coordinated norming because the tests in the computerized battery were simultaneously normed on the same standardization samples. The use of *T*-scores provides the option for scale norming that allows each performance to be compared to an equivalent standard scale on any other test in the battery. In addition, the individual's performance across multiple administrations can be profiled across multiple evaluations.

The standardization sample for the CS-AE included 584 commercial airline pilots, aged 25 to 67 years, with 12 or more years of education, in the United States, and 225 pilots in Russia. The U.S. sample excluded pilots who had a history of neuropsycholpgically significant neurologic or psychiatric conditions, substance abuse, and those taking psychoactive medications. In the development of the standardization sample, the CS-AE was rigorous in eliminating many of the confounds compromising the development of most psychometric tests.

The early development of the CS-AE, healthy pilots were compared with age- and IQ-matched nonpilot normals and mildly brain damaged patients on conventional neuropsychological measures and computerized performance tests of aviation-related abilities. The CS-AE correctly classified 32 out of 40 patients with brain dysfunction and incorrectly classified only 3 healthy pilots. The conventional neuropsychological measures correctly classified 20 of the 40 patients and incorrectly classified 2 pilots.

RELIABILITY AND VALIDITY. After initial administration of the CS-AE to the standardization pilot group, 199 returned for readministration at 6- and 12-month intervals. Comparison of Thruput and Speed measures at the three test periods generated test-retest reliability coefficients for the Thruput and Speed measure ranging from .63 to .91. The average test-retest reliability level was approximately .80.

Several forms of validity were examined, including content, construct, factorial, and criterion. Content validity was considered by assessing the opinions of a group of pilots on the relevance of each CS-AE subtest to cognitive tasks essential for skilled aviation performance. Rating of each subtest varied from 48% to 84%. To assess construct validity, correlations were computed between CS-AE domains and subtest scores and the Trail Making Test, Tactual Performance Test, California Verbal Learning Test, Category Test, Paced Auditory Serial Addition Test, Rey Complex Figure Test, Seashore Rhythm Test, Speech Sounds Perception Test, Wisconsin Card Sorting Test, and Wechsler Adult Intelligence Scale—Revised (WAIS-R). CS-AE performance was minimally correlated with general intelligence. Factor analytic studies revealed a nine-factor solution that accounted for 67.1% of the variance. Criterion validity studies focused on determining the sensitivity and specificity of CS-AE in the detection of mild brain dysfunction when compared with conventional neuropsychological screening measures. A discriminate functional analysis on CS-AE correctly classified 87.5% of patients and 90.5% of the pilots. The conventional neuropsychological screening battery correctly classified 32 of 41 pilots, 33 of 40 patients, and 27 of 42 nonpilot normals, for an overall accuracy rate of 80.25%. these results indicate a sensitivity (true positive) rate with CS-AE of 73% and a specificity (true negative) of 90%.

Aviation performance studies indicate that CS-AE is predictive of specific elements of flight performance. In a joint Russian-American, FAA-funded research project, flight performance data were collected on 75 Russian Aeroflot pilots from flight data recorders over a 3-year-period. An index of flight violations was used as a measure of skilled aviation performance. The index was found to be significantly correlated ($r = -.23$ through $-.51$, $p < .01$) with nine CS-AE measures. Research by Taylor, O'Hara, Mumenthaler, and Yesavage (2000) found that general cognitive speed and working memory efficiency on the CS-AE could explain 33% of the variance in overall flight performance in a Frasca-141 flight simulator with a group of 100 civilian pilots between 50–69 years of age.

CONCLUSIONS. The CS-AE is a screening instrument designed to detect subtle changes in cognitive functioning in pilots. Although this measure is highly correlated with traditional neuropsychological measures, there is minimal assessment of memory and visual perceptual processes, and no assessment of language, which are all cognitive processes integral to brain functioning. There is no question that use of the CS-AE is a time saver because traditional neuropsychological tests are both labor intensive and time-consuming for both patients and the examiner. Many neuropsychological tests are not sensitive to subtle decrements in performance, are dramatically impacted by repeated administrations, and must be administered in an individual setting. The CS-AE can be group administered, is designed to detect subtle changes in selected areas of cognitive functioning, and has 12 parallel forms available for repeat administrations. Additionally, the scoring process assures that there is a direct conversion of the respondent's raw score performances to standard scores, and all scores are standardized and referenced to the same *T*-scaling.

The printout report is well-designed and displays a summary of the scores in both graphic and numerical formats. For scoring, the examiner may choose comparison populations and/or intraindividual comparison across multiple administrations.

Cognitive measures not assessed in most neuropsychological tests include simultaneous information processing and divided attention. Both are assessed with the CS-AE. Even though CS-AE scoring profiles provide normative performance information, interpretation of the performance is left up to the examiner, who should have received specialized training in neuropsychology. This process of interpretation is aided by a well-designed and comprehensive professional manual. Missing from the manual are published norms for nonpilot populations, norms corrected for intelligence and education or a correction factor for these confounds, norms or correction factors for gender (females), and an LRPV value that can be corrected for age. Additionally, the nonavailability of the specific scores responsible for the LRPV value make it difficult for the end user to identify specific reasons for a weak performance when base rate scores may be within the normal range.

The CS-AE's format is the future of neuropsychological testing and scoring procedures. The advantage of computer-based assessment systems is that they can provide a sensitive and accurate timing system, capability for administration of simultaneous information processing tasks, and a reduction of variability and error that may be introduced by examiner characteristics.

Many of the tasks in the CS-AE are performed at ceiling levels on the accuracy measures, resulting in minimal variance of accuracy scores and unstable inferential statistical results. Thus, interpretation of accuracy scores is difficult with high-functioning individuals and may limit interpretation of performance of intact high-functioning individual.

SUMMARY. The CS-AE is one of the most rigorously normed and user-friendly cognitive screening batteries available for administration and scoring of cognitive functions. Design and layout of the test, the scoring profiles, and the manual are user-friendly but need to be updated. The manual needs to reflect new ownership, and the CS-AE needs to provide a Windows operating environment capability. As an alternative to the CS-AE, users may want to consider MicroCog (T5:1665), published by The Psychological Corporation (1993). MicroCog assesses a broad range of cognitive functions but was developed without the rigorous controls on selection of the standardization sample population used in the development of the CS-AE. There are other computer-administered neurocognitive batteries that have been developed, such as the Multidimensional Aptitude Battery (MAB; Jackson, Barton, & Blokker, 1991; T5:1731), and Automated Neuropsychological Assessment Metrics (ANAM; Reeves et al., 1992), but these batteries tend to be limited to military application and/or research on drug effects.

REVIEWER'S REFERENCES

Jackson, D. N., Barton, C. F., & Blokker, H. C. (1992). *User's Manual for the Multidimensional Aptitude Battery (MAB) Software Program.* London, Ontario, Canada: Sigma Assessment Systems.

Reeves, D. L., Winter, K., LaCour, S., Ransford, K., Kay, G., Elsmre, T., & Hegge, F. kW. (1992) *Automated neuropsychological assessment metrics documentation: Vo. I Test administration guide.* Washington, DC: Office of Military Performance Assessment Technology: Walter Reed Army Institute of Research.

Powell, D. H., Kaplan, E. F., Whitla, D., Weintraub, S., Catlin, R., & Funkenstein, H. H. (1993). *MicroCog: Assessment of Cognitive Functioning.* San Antonio, TX: The Psychological Corporation.

Taylor, J. L., O'Hara, R., Mumenthaler, M. S., & Yesavage, J. A. (2000). *Relationship of CogScreen-AE to flight simulator performance and pilot age. Aviation, Space, and Environmental Medicine, 71*(4), 373–380.

Review of the CogScreen Aeromedical Edition by HILDA WING, Personnel Psychologist, Federal Aviation Administration, Washington, DC:

The CogScreen Aeromedical Edition is a computer-administered battery of 13 cognitive and perceptual/psychomotor tests, with scores from each representing either the test or its components. The Speed and Accuracy scores are self-explanatory; the Thruput scores are rates of correct responses per unit time; the Process measures are a heterogeneous mix of premature errors, perseverative errors, and coordination. The battery takes about a half-hour to administer.

The battery was designed to evaluate a pilot's fitness for duty by an assessment of cognitive functioning. The research background for the test is based in the neuropsychiatric branch of science rather more than from the educational, psychological, or psychometric areas. The normative database includes 584 experienced commercial pilots, representing large, medium, and small U.S. airlines, who range in age from less than 35 to more than 54. This sample is overwhelmingly male with above-average educational levels. No racial or ethnic statistics were presented; my assumption is that this sample is mostly white. Many of this sample returned for a second ($n = 317$) and third ($n = 199$) administration, 6 and 12 months after the initial administration. The manual includes data from additional studies of, for example, Russian pilots, normals, nonpilot controls, and individuals with diagnosed brain dysfunction. Data from the last named group suggest that an additional use of CogScreen-AE could be as a screen for possible neurological problems.

The system itself is DOS-based and requires at least an IBM-type PC with a 286 chip or higher with printer, a hard drive, a floppy disk drive, etc. The test equipment provided by the publisher includes the software, a light pen, and a Testkey, a security device that permits only a set number (here, 5) of test administrations. By following the explicit and careful directions in the manual, I was able to set up my home computer to administer CogScreen-AE, and the battery was straightforward to administer and to take. The system is fairly user-friendly, considering that it is DOS-based. I can only say that 1995, the date of publication, seems like light-years ago in terms of computer software accessibility and ease of use.

Chapter 9 of the test manual, "Reliability and Validity," includes 34 8.5 x 11-inch, two-column pages, and incorporates 36 tables and two figures. Overall, I found the data presentation to be user-unfriendly. The text material accompanying the various statistics, typically one or more pages removed from the table itself, was strictly at a descriptive level without any overarching framework into which to put these findings. Perhaps this would not be a problem for someone with extensive neuropsychiatric experience. My experience is in psychometrics, so I will limit my comments to that arena.

Most of the analyses are performed separately for the four large classes of measure types: Speed, Accuracy, Thruput, and Process. Test-retest reliabilities were calculated for the Speed and Thruput measures only, because their score frequencies met probability distributions and practice effects assumptions more adequately than the Accuracy and Process measures. The average level of test-retest reliability obtained was about .80, surprisingly high for such short tests. The mean scores for the Accuracy and Process measures were fairly stable from the initial to the 6-month to the 12-month intervals, suggesting stability of these measures to the test author. I am not as confident. Perhaps only those pilots who were more stable in the first place were also those more likely to come back a second and a third time for retesting. The subsequent discussions on validity, although discussing results by the class of measures, include both class types where reliability statistics were available (Speed, Thruput) and where they were not (Accuracy, Process).

Evidence for three perspectives of the battery's validity is presented. The content of the tests has a research base of aviation cognitive task analysis. An Aviation Design Review Committee consisting of eminent individuals with different specialties of aviation expertise supported test selection and development. A sample of pilots taking an earlier version of the battery and a sizable number from the normative sample provided judgments of aviation-relevance. I agree with the author's judgment that the tests in CogScreen-AE are relevant and appropriate for use by aircraft pilots.

For construct validity, the author identified 120 pilots from the normative base who also were administered a number of paper-and-pencil neuropsychological tests as well as the Wechsler Adult Intelligence Scale—Revised (WAIS-R). Most of the data displayed suggest significant but moderate correlations with such instruments. The author discusses the limits of generalizability of the results because of the methods differences between these two groups of tests: one set is computer-administered and the other is in paper-and-pencil form. The author does not discuss two other limitations, that of imperfect reliability, especially for the Speed and Process measures, and that of restricted range. It should be expected, when the validation sample has a mean WAIS-R IQ of over one standard deviation above the stated adult mean, to obtain scores showing lower correlations of the CogScreen-AE tests with the WAIS-R and other clinical tests. To the extent that the battery is used with actual pilot examinees, correction for range restriction is less appropriate because a plausible estimate of the mean IQ for the population of aircraft pilots would be one standard deviation above the mean IQ for the general population. To the extent that the battery is used as a neuropsychiatric screen for nonpilots, as discussed in the subsequent section on criterion validity, range restriction is an important consideration. The final discussion of the construct validity section covers factor analyses of data from the U.S. and Russian combined pilot sample. The results of five factor analyses are presented. The first used 26 "selected" CogScreen-AE measures to yield a nine-factor solution that appears to me to reflect the 11 different tests. The next two factor analyses are of the Speed measures, for the total sample and for the U.S. pilots alone. The final two analyses are of the Thruput measures, again for the total sample and then for the U.S. sample. Both classes of measures have adequate and large estimates of reliability. Although the verbal descriptions of the results are fine as far as they go, I wondered what further inferences might be drawn using more recent statistical approaches such as structural equation modeling. These could support higher-level and more meaningful conceptual inferences of human cognitive processing.

The final section, on criterion validity, discusses five clinical studies comparing pilots, from both the U.S. and Russia, with or without performance referrals, with nonpilot controls and with patients having diagnosed mild brain dysfunction. The evidence, based on small samples, does not contradict the inference that battery results can distinguish normal people, including pilots without performance referrals, from those with mild brain disorders. Again, more sophisticated analyses might support broader inferences.

The manual concludes with a thoughtful and cautious discussion of appropriate and limited interpretations of CogScreen-AE test results. Included as appendices are tabled base rates for the numbers of scores at or below the 15th and the 5th percentile for the total U.S. pilot sample, and for the different age groups within this sample. Norms are provided by class of measure (Speed, Thruput, etc.). This concerns me because the comparability of a Speed score from, for example, Math with one from Divided Attention is not clear. Discussion of any possible difference score concerns me more because there is insufficient documentation of the psychometric frailties inherent in difference scores.

SUMMARY. The CogScreen-AE is a sophisticated computerized battery of cognitive tests that can be used as a screen for aircraft pilots referred for medical examination based on performance. The battery appears to have some potential as a screen for neuropsychiatric dysfunction as well, but more research is needed. The Professional Manual, or test manual, provides a great deal of data that are not well presented and that do not support many inferences about neurological functioning in particular and cognitive processing in general. Developing a user-friendly description based on sophisticated data analysis procedures could support a better-understood instrument as well as greater empirically based support of cognitive information processing theories.

[84]
Communication Activities of Daily Living, Second Edition.

Purpose: "To assess the functional communication skills of adults with neurogenic communication disorders."
Population: Aphasic adults.
Publication Dates: 1980–1999.
Acronym: CADL-2.
Scores: Total score only.
Administration: Individual.
Price Data, 1999: $177 per complete kit.
Time: (25–35) minutes.
Comments: Previous edition entitled Communicative Abilities in Daily Living.
Authors: Audrey Holland, Carol Frattali, and David Fromm.
Publisher: PRO-ED.
Cross References: For a review by Rita Sloan Berndt of an earlier edition, see 10:69 (2 references).

Review of the Communication Activities of Daily Living Scale, Second Edition by CAROLYN MITCHELL PERSON, Associate Professor of Urban and Ethnic Communication Disorders, Southern University, Baton Rouge, LA:

TEST COVERAGE AND USE. The intended use of the Communication Activities of Daily Living, Second Edition (CADL-2) is to measure the functional communication abilities in adults who have brain damage. The original CADL was intended to be used as a test of functional communication for adults with aphasia. According to the authors, the CADL-2 is based on sociolinguistic theory and a holistic framework of functional communication that supports assessment using contextualized methods. The CADL-2 evaluates behavior in terms of reading, writing, or using numbers; social interactions; divergent communication; contextual communication; nonverbal communication; sequential relationships; and humor/metaphor/absurdity. The original CADL included role playing in addition to the behavioral categories just described. Role-playing is excluded in the CADL-2. The authors state that the CADL-2 measures rudimentary aspects of functional communication and that it does not measure the extent of the restrictions on participation in a full social life nor does it pretend to address the scope of the complex enterprise of conversation. Users of the CADL-2 are cautioned about the test's utility in long-term care settings and that scores resulting from tests, rating scales, or other forms of measurement should not be used alone for diagnostic purposes.

TEST VALIDATION AND NORMING. The CADL-2 was standardized on a sample of 175 individuals with neurogenically based communication disorders who were between 20 and 96 years of age ($M = 67$, $SD = 17$). The authors state that the subjects are drawn from 17 states (Alabama, Arizona, California, Georgia, Idaho, Indiana, Louisiana, Michigan, New Hampshire, New Jersey, New York, Ohio, Oklahoma, Pennsylvania, and Texas); however, only 15 are reported. Each demographic characteristic was compared to the percentages reported in the *Statistical Abstract of the United States* (U.S. Bureau of the Census, 1997). The sample was found to be nationally representative. The sample size appears adequate and sufficiently representative to establish the percentiles and stanines representing overall communicative abilities, to substantiate validity statements, and to support conclusions regarding the use of the CADL-2 for the intended purpose.

RELIABILITY. Reliability estimates are reported for three types of errors: content sampling, time sampling, and scorer differences. Appropriate statistical methods are reported. A coefficient alpha was computed to estimate the degree of homogeneity among the items within the CADL-2 (content sampling). The standard error of measurement (SEM) was used to estimate a confidence interval surrounding particular test scores. The test-retest technique was calculated to measure how constant the test performance of the 175 subjects was over a median time of 2 months 20 days (time sampling). A relational index of agreement was computed to test errors due to examiner

variability, clerical mistakes, and failure of the examiner to use the standard score table correctly (scorer differences). The magnitudes of the coefficients addressing the three sources of test error reported are: content sampling .93, time sampling .85, and scorer differences .99. Prior to the calculation of the coefficients, the authors stated that coefficients approximating or exceeding .80 in magnitude would be considered as minimally reliable and that those approximating or exceeding .90 would be considered most desirable. The magnitudes of the coefficients suggest that the CADL-2 possesses little test error. The subjects were drawn from more than one state; however, the test-retest study was conducted with the subjects with chronic aphasia from the state of Arizona.

VALIDITY. Three types of validity were examined: content, criterion-related, and construct validity. Content validity refers to the extent to which the test questions represent the knowledge, behaviors, and skills in the specified domain of interest. Criterion-related validity addresses the question of whether or not the test predicts performance. Construct validity refers to whether or not the underlying traits of a test can be identified and if these traits reflect the theoretical model on which the test is based.

There is a clear statement of the behaviors represented by the test in that the examiners, who all had experience in adult neurological disorders, agreed that the CADL-2 categories and items covered the scope of functional communication of adults with neurological disorders. Examiners, who were certified and licensed speech-language pathologists, validate the scope and appropriateness of the CADL-2 categories, items, and stimulus pictures. Judgments were elicited from the examiners by questionnaires. Additionally, the authors conducted an item-discrimination analysis. Questionnaire and item-discrimination results provided evidence of content validity.

Empirical evidence in support of criterion-related validity must include a comparison of performance on the test against performance on outside criteria. The Western Aphasia Battery (Kertesz, 1982), a standardized inventory of aphasic impairment, was used as the measure to evaluate validity. The rationale for choosing this measure appears to be that because the CADL-2 measures communication abilities of daily living of individuals with aphasia, then it should correlate with other measures of communication in individuals with aphasia such as the Western Aphasia Battery. The Western Aphasia Battery (WAB) yields an aphasia quotient score whereas the CADL-2 yields a stanine score. Pearson product-moment correlation coefficients were calculated and indicated a moderately high relation between the CADL-2 stanine score and the WAB aphasia quotient score.

Evidence in support of construct validity can take many forms. One approach is to demonstrate that the test behaves as one would expect a measure of the construct to behave. The conceptual framework for each tested construct should be clear and well founded. The basis for concluding that the construct is related to the purposes of the test should be stated. Whether or not the framework provides a basis for testable hypotheses concerning the construct should be discussed. The degree to which these hypotheses are supported by empirical data should also be addressed. Three constructs were established by the CADL-2 authors: (a) It should differentiate between groups of individuals who have communication limitations resulting from neurological damage and groups of individuals with no damage (group differentiation); (b) it should correlate with clinicians' overall ratings of communication based on patients' performance on traditional language and cognitive tests (item validity); and (c) it should correlate with the examiners' ratings of the patients' communication disorders (relationship to other measures). The constructs were supported by the data. The results of the *t*-test calculated to study group differentiation data indicated that the differences were statistically significant. The coefficients calculated to study item validity exceeded the coefficient value for acceptability. The CADL-2 was also found to be significantly related to other measures.

TEST ADMINISTRATION. CADL-2 examiners should be licensed (where applicable) and certified speech-language pathologists with experience in assessment and treatment of individuals with neurogenic communication disorders. The authors provide detailed and clear instructions for test administration, scoring, and interpreting results.

TEST AND ITEM BIAS. The CADL-2 does not appear to be biased or offensive with regard to race, sex, ethnic origin, geographic region, or other factors. All subjects spoke English as their primary language. Review of the stimulus pictures that are photographs indicates that the authors attempted to racially balance the photographs. Other pictures are common objects or depict common everyday situations. Even though the CADL-2 appears bias-free, there is no indication that the items were statistically analyzed for possible bias, that the test was specifically analyzed for differential validity across ethnolinguistically diverse groups, or that the test was analyzed to determine the English language proficiency required of test takers.

SUMMARY. The CADL-2 was developed to assess the functional communication skills of adults with neurogenic disorders. It meets the key test evaluation standards discussed above. As part of the assessment protocol for individuals with aphasia, the CADL-2 can yield valuable information that contributes to objective assessment of and decision making about an individual.

REVIEWER'S REFERENCES

Kertesz, A. (1982). Western Aphasia Battery. San Antonio: Psychological Corporation.
U.S. Bureau of the Census. (1997). *Statistical abstract of the United States: The national data book.* Washington, DC: U.S. Department of Commerce.

Review of the Communication Activities of Daily Living Scale, Second Edition by KATHARINE SNYDER, Assistant Professor of Psychology, Shepherd College, Shepherdstown, WV:

The purpose of the Communication Activities of Daily Living Scale, Second Edition (CADL-2) is to assess functional communication abilities of aphasic individuals on adaptive daily tasks. Because detailed administration and observation are required, the test is designed for certified or licensed professionals in speech-language pathology. Like traditional neuropsychological assessments (e.g., the Luria-Nebraska; T5:1524), a 3-point scoring system with room for qualitative assessment (e.g., G for gestural cues) is an asset. Normative findings with the original CADL were extended to include a wider clinical population of individuals with traumatic brain injury, mental retardation, and Alzheimer's disease (Aten, Caligiuri, & Holland, 1982; Fromm & Holland, 1989). Successful Spanish and Japanese versions of the CADL were also developed and standardized (Honda, Mitachi, & Watamori, 1999; Martin, Manning, Munoz, & Montero, 1990).

One of the most significant changes in the updated CADL-2 is the elimination of the environmental sounds and role-playing components as well as narrowing down the definitional categories. With the elimination of the controversial role playing and environmental sounds components of the CADL-2, more color photographs, items of everyday scenarios, universal signs, and common reference materials were added (e.g., maps & schedules). This adds to the internal consistency of the CADL-2 as well as reduces the potential for poor performance resulting from attentional problems rather than language comprehension issues.

Normative data for the CADL-2 was gathered by 19 licensed clinicians from 175 (ages 26–96) patients with neurological damage to either hemisphere resulting primarily from strokes. All of the patients were previously judged as having a communication disorder. Total scores on the CADL-2 are converted into stanines and percentiles, which are derived from the distribution of the normative sample.

In addressing the difficult content validity question of what typical/functional communication activities are, questions for each of the following categories were developed: Reading, Writing, or Using Numbers (e.g., signs and making change); Social Interactions (e.g., pragmatic use of gestures); Divergent Communications (e.g., which clock is the best time for eating lunch); Contextual Communication (e.g., what to wear on a rainy day); Nonverbal Communication (e.g., facial expression of emotion); Sequential Relationships (e.g., the behavioral steps in making a phone call); and Humor/Metaphor/Absurdity. The Social Interactions Category of the CADL-2 is a combination of the Social Conventions and Speech Acts Categories of the original CADL. Similarly, the Nonverbal Communications Category on the CADL-2 is a combination of the Nonverbal/Symbolic and Deixis Categories of the original CADL. Given the global nature of these categories, the content validity for each category in isolation is questionable. However, CADL-2 scoring does not separate these categories and the categories are used for definitional purposes only. Hence, the reduction in the number of categories in the CADL-2 is an excellent feature.

Reliability, criterion-related validity, and construct validity assessments with the CADL-2 are impressive. Interitem correlations, test-retest coefficients, and interrater reliability coefficients were impressive, suggesting that the CADL-2 is a reliable measure of functional communication patterns. The ability of the CADL-2 to predict results on other well-known aphasia measures, such as the Western Aphasia Battery, is also impressive ($r = .66$), supporting the criterion-related validity of the CADL-2. Because individuals without communication disorders would score at or above the 96th percentile, the CADL-2 also has a high degree of construct validity in separating individuals with or without aphasia. However, caution should be used in saying that construct validity extends to the differentiation of brain-damaged and non-brain-damaged individuals, as psychological, medical, intellectual, and attentional factors may also be involved in CADL-2 performance.

SUMMARY. The CADL-2 is a very useful measure of functional communication, especially when used as an additional measure of expressive/receptive speech and aphasia by well-trained individuals. Qualitative changes in the updated CADL-2 have enhanced reliability/validity and the progress towards standardizing the test into other languages is impressive. When administered in conjunction with a history evaluation, a mental status examination, and a psychological or neuropsychological evaluation, the CADL-2 is a very useful measure for speech/language therapists.

REVIEWER'S REFERENCES

Aten, J. L., Caligiuri, M. P., & Holland, A. L. (1982). Efficacy of functional communication therapy for chronic aphasia patients. *Journal of Speech and Hearing Disorders, 47*(1), 93–96.

Fromm, D., & Holland, A. L. (1989). Functional communication in Alzheimer's disease. *Journal of Speech and Hearing Disorder, 54*(4), 535–540.

Martin, P., Manning, L., Munoz, P., & Montero, I. (1990). Communicative abilities in daily living: Spanish standardization. *Evaluacion Psicologica, 6*(3), 369–384.

Honda, R., Mitachi, M., & Watamori, T. S. (1999). Production of discourse in high-functioning individuals with aphasia—with reference to performance on the Japanese CADL. *Aphasiology, 13*(6), 475–493.

[85]

Communication Profile: A Functional Skills Survey.

Purpose: Designed to assess the importance of 26 everyday communication skills to elderly clients from diverse educational, cultural, and socioeconomic backgrounds.

Population: Elderly adults.

Publication Date: 1994.

Scores: Item scores only.

Administration: Individual.

Price Data: Not available.

Time: Administration time not reported.

Comments: Orally administered; survey used for elderly clients with health problems that have impaired or potentially could impair the ability to communicate; administrator scored.

Author: Joan C. Payne.
Publisher: The Psychological Corporation.
[Note: The publisher advised in March 1999 that this test is now out of print.]

Review of the Communication Profile: A Functional Skills Survey by ELAINE CLARK, Professor of Educational Psychology, University of Utah, Salt Lake City, UT:

The Communication Profile: A Functional Skills Survey assesses the importance of a broad range of communication skills in the daily lives of older adults (e.g., verbal expression and comprehension, reading comprehension, writing, and math). It is intended to be used in treatment planning for elderly people who are experiencing functional communication problems. The 26 items in the survey were chosen for their "broad applicability to the lives of older adults, regardless of their heterogeneity in education, living circumstances, financial resources, gender, ethnic background, or job experiences" (manual, p. 1). According to the author, there are similar measures of communication problems (e.g., Sarno's Functional Communication Profile and Lomas' Communication Effectiveness Index); however, the Communication Profile is unique in its assessment of what examinees perceive to be important communication skills. For example, the Profile asks adults to rate how important it is for them to be able to read an appointment card, talk on the phone with family and friends, or write checks to pay bills. It does not, however, assess a person's competence to perform these tasks. The title may be somewhat misleading to potential users who do not read carefully that this is a survey, not a functional skills analysis. The Profile is intended to be used alone or in conjunction with other measures; however, from this reviewer's perspective, there would be little advantage to give only the Communication Profile. For one, there would be no way to verify if a communication problem exists. Secondly, it would be ineffective, not to mention inefficient, to target only perceived problems for rehabilitation.

ADMINISTRATION AND SCORING. According to the manual, the Communication Profile is to be administered by a clinician. It is not entirely clear, however, to whom the term clinician refers. One might assume that this refers to someone who has experience with an aging population, or those for whom the instrument was intended. The fact the author felt compelled to include in the manual suggestions to insure examinees can see the materials and hear the questions (e.g., wearing their glasses and hearing aids), however, suggests that more novice examiners are expected to administer the survey. There are no indications that any training is needed to administer the scale, or that there are any requirements other than the ability to read the 26 items in a face-to-face situation. Administration instructions are clearly written and, for the most part, the scoring is self-explanatory.

All survey items are answered using either a 1-to-5 or 1-to-3 Likert-type rating scale. Although the 1-to-5 scale is the standard format, a shorter 3-point rating scale can be used by those who are unable to use a 5-point scale. It is unclear who should use the shorter rating system, as no suggestions were made in the manual. If examiners elect to use the short form rating scale, however, they need to be cautious in scoring the items. The examiner's scoring form only has the 5-point ratings, and the numbers assigned to the 3-point rating system (i.e., 1 = *not important at all*, 2 = *somewhat important*, and 3 = *important*) are not the same as the 5-point system (1 = *not important at all*, 2 = *not too important*, 3 = *somewhat important*, 4 = *important*, and 5 = *very important*). This may make it somewhat confusing to examiners and could lead to scoring errors. For example, if an examinee taking the test uses the 3-point scale and responds to an item with a rating of 2, the examiner is apt to record the answer as "not too important," whereas the correct answer would be "somewhat important." This is a rather minor problem, and is certainly not insurmountable; however, some mention of this in the manual (or an additional scoring sheet with the 3-point scale) may be helpful. The author did include two separate rating scale sheets for examinees to refer to while rating the survey questions. One is to be used for the 5-point scale, and the other for the 3-point scale. The two rating sheets are reproducible and have large block letters to assist those with reduced vision.

A Personal Profile form is also included and is to be used in conjunction with the 26-item survey. The form asks demographic questions but is extremely limited (e.g., asks questions about the examinee's age, gender, ethnic background, level of education, type of job and employment status, annual income, and living situation). It is surprising that the form does not ask questions about the examinee's health history, especially given the author's statement on page 2 of the manual that the Communication Profile is intended to be used with aging adults whose health has compromised their ability to communicate. Because it is assumed that this includes adults with stroke histories and dementing illnesses, some place on the form needs to be provided to obtain this information. Targeting high-risk aging adults (e.g., adults at risk for aphasic disorders secondary to cerebral vascular accidents) may extend the usefulness of the Communication Profile. As the Personal Profile form stands, there is no place to write any additional comments that may be relevant to assessment and treatment of communication problems.

SCALE DEVELOPMENT, RELIABILITY, AND VALIDITY. Survey items were developed by a work group that consisted of the author and three individuals who had experience with the "normal elderly" and elderly individuals in rehabilitation settings (e.g., a gerontologist, geriatric social worker, and speech and language pathologist). The work group who constructed the items also had experience with elderly people from culturally diverse backgrounds. In addition to these individuals, four speech and language pathologists were asked to evaluate a preliminary survey to determine if the items met the following criteria: independence of each item, appropriateness for the elderly, appropriateness for elderly from culturally diverse backgrounds, and items representing functional communication. The interjudge agreement among the four evaluators was .97.

Following pilot testing and reviews, the final 26-item Communication Profile was administered to 257 elderly adults (100 males and 157 females; 143 African-American and 114 Caucasian) for field testing. The sample was "selected" (it is not clear how) from 300 elderly adults in churches, nursing homes, and senior centers in the midwest and northeastern region of the United States. Staff at the various sites apparently referred potential subjects for testing if they felt they met criteria (i.e., no history of neurological damage, significant unaided hearing problems, or dementia). The subjects were between the ages of 65 and 94 (139 were 65 to 74, and 118 were between the ages of 75 and 94), and lived in community or institutional settings. The number of individuals with annual incomes over or below $30,000 was approxi-

mately equal; however, there was an overrepresentation of individuals with post-high school education and white collar jobs.

Results of the field testing showed that there were no significant group differences for gender, ethnicity, or education. There were, however, significant differences for community-living status (i.e., living alone or with others), living arrangements (community or nursing home), personal income, and type of job. Summary profile information across the eight demographic variables is provided to assist users in understanding what skills the field-test group found particularly important; that is, what they consistently rated as skills having high priority for them. For example, subjects living in the community who have a high school education or less rated "telling the doctor what bothers you" as being a more important skill than did the other groups. Individuals 75 or older and living in nursing homes rated being able to read prescription labels as being highly important, and more so than the other groups.

Internal consistency reliability data are provided. The Cronbach alpha for the 26-item survey was .82. The number of subjects used to calculate the alpha for the 26-item survey was 257. The Guttman split-half technique and the Spearman-Brown formula were also calculated for the reliability of the 26-item survey (the Guttman produced a coefficient of .74 and the Spearman-Brown, a reliability coefficient of .77). No test-retest reliability data were provided, which is unfortunate given the potential for variable responding by elderly adults who have dementing illnesses and other neurologic problems compromising their communication. The only analyses reported in the manual for adults with disabilities were those pertaining to 100 aging adults with mental retardation, and 100 aging adults with hearing impairments. The reported data, however, were limited to Cronbach alpha coefficients.

TEST SCORE INTERPRETATION. The survey is intended to provide a "profile" of skills viewed as important for therapy. There is no total score to be derived, and according to the author, "there are no right or wrong answers ... no basal or ceiling scores" (manual, p. 2). The author suggests that examiners look for items that receive a score of 4 (important) or 5 (very important) when planning for treatment. Obviously, this system has to be adapted for examinees who use the 3-point scale (e.g., targeting items that are given a rating of 3, a score that represents an "important" skill).

Although the author states that examiners can use the fieled-test profile data provided in the manual to compare examinees' responses to those of nonneurologically impaired adults with similar demographic features, it is unclear how useful this information would be. The fact that nonneurologically impaired adults 65 to 75 years of age, living in the community, and having an annual income of less than $30,000, rate being able to ask the date as more important than other groups provides little information on which to base an intervention program. In addition, given the way information is presented, it is not even practical to look up this type of data. It also seems impractical to compare an examinee's skill rating with their own demographic data (i.e., data provided on the Personal Profile). Although the author suggests using the Profile data in this manner, interpretive suggestions such as these do not appear helpful, and are difficult to understand.

CONCLUSIONS. The Communication Profile represents a good attempt at providing information about communication skills that older adults view as important in their daily life. Although the Profile does not lend itself to the direct assessment of skill deficits, and provides little in the way of treatment information (i.e., other than information about examinees' perceptions of skill importance), the Communication Profile can be used to help target skills that may need further evaluation and intervention. Fortunately, the survey is easy to use and takes very little time to administer and score. Potential users, however, need to be aware of the limited information that is derived from the Profile, and the limited population with which the instrument was field tested. No older adults with neurologic impairments such as strokes and dementias were included in the field tests. In fact, the only groups tested besides normals (i.e., nonneurologically impaired older adults) were aging adults with mental retardation and hearing impairments. As a result, it is difficult to determine who would actually benefit from being given the Profile. Although the 26 items appear appropriate for demented adults and those with strokes, these data are missing. It is hoped that data supporting the usefulness of the instrument will be forthcoming, in particular, the relationship between the survey data and intervention strategies.

Review of the Communication Profile: A Functional Skills Survey by D. ASHLEY COHEN, Clinical Neuropsychologist, CogniMetrix, San Jose, CA:

Statements at the beginning of the Communication Profile (CP) manual are ones with which almost everyone in the gerontology field would agree: that intact functional language skills aid elders in being able to remain independent and maintain well-being, and that the "systematic study" of these everyday communication skills in older adults has been lacking. Sadly, this instrument will do little to help professionals restore functional communication skills to those who have lost a portion of them, and nothing to help maintain the skills in unimpaired elders.

Despite its title, the CP does not survey or measure in any way the *actual* functional communication skills of examinees. What is rated is the perceived importance of various communication skills to the person being interviewed. Perhaps of most concern is that only a skewed sample of very healthy subjects with little or no communication problems was used in standardization, even though the test is recommended for use with older adults with various speech and language handicaps, along with other cognitive and physical impairments.

NORMATIVE SAMPLE AND INSTRUMENT DEVELOPMENT. Items were generated by a committee of four persons, and informally validated by four others. We are told that "the theoretical framework for the CP was developed from a nontraditional paradigm of a broad range of variables that should be considered for aging clients" (manual, p. 7). However, the theories discussed—relating to racial and sexual differences—bear little relation to the instrument presented.

Diversity and ethnicity are heavily discussed, but the author concludes that Black and White older adults did not differ significantly in their responses. Although she also quotes others that aging is "a gendered process," most of her results show no differences based on gender. Further, because one of the author's stated aims is to develop more ethnically and culturally relevant instruments, it is unfortunate that no older Hispanics or Asians were included.

The final normative sample of 257 was 61% female, 56% Black and 44% White. Demographic data were tabulated in the manual, although only in raw numbers, leaving the reader to calculate percentages. This table would have been more meaningful if the sample data were compared with figures from U.S. citizens age 65 and over. For example, her data reveal that 52% of the sample had some college education up to post-graduate degrees, which is far from representative of the current cohort of older adults.

The normative sample was drawn from the northeastern U.S. and some midwestern sites. This limitation is regrettable as a recent study (Klein, 1998) found that the counties in the U.S. with the highest percentage of seniors are located in Florida, California, Arizona, and Nevada.

Subjects were obtained from senior centers, churches, and nursing homes; potential subjects were suggested by ministers or staff members. Thus, no independent-living subjects were included if they were not affiliated with a social organization of some type. As has often been observed (Birren, Sloane, & Cohen, 1992; Butler, Lewis, & Sunderland, 1991) elders who are not involved in activities such as church or senior centers can be very different from older adults who do belong to these organizations: Some are more isolated, ill or depressed, whereas others are much more independent.

Only very healthy elders were selected for inclusion; even subjects with hearing loss were excluded. Particularly when studying older persons, restricting one's sample to the healthy restricts the range acutely (by as much as 80%), and decreases the variance unacceptably, as well as making generalization to the entire elderly population a questionable proposition (LaRue & Markee, 1995).

The manual concedes that "there is a certain amount of selection bias in how subjects were identified and included in the study" (p. 24). The manual then reassures us: "However, it was felt that the size of the sample would eliminate much of the bias in subject selection" (p. 24). In the opinion of this reviewer, 257 individuals is not that large a sample for development of a new instrument. Second, and most important, it is impossible to make up for a restriction of range in a population sample simply by adding more subjects who are essentially the same; heterogeneity cannot be produced in a homogenous sample, no matter how many similar cases are included.

USES FOR THIS INSTRUMENT. The manual identified the primary purpose of this instrument as being determination of the importance of various practical language skills to older adults who have a language impairment. Other uses suggested were assisting therapists in selecting training goals important to the patient, measuring changes in the patient's priorities following a change in situation, and employing the instrument as a component of a thorough language assessment. Finally, it is said the Communication Profile can provide comparative premorbid and postmorbid data.

Regarding the last suggested use, the author seems to be suggesting using the rankings of her healthy normative sample to gauge the likely past importance of certain language skills to a current patient, prior to the onset of his or her brain disorder, and then compare that hypothesized ranking to the patient's present ranking. No means is conceivable to validate this use based on the test development data described in the manual.

The manual lists four groups with whom the test can be used effectively: (a) diffuse neurological disorders, (b) hearing impairments, (c) mental retardation, and (d) aphasia (mild to moderate) from cerebrovascular accidents and traumatic brain injuries.

Although older mentally retarded adults and older persons with hearing impairments were "field tested" in the development of this instrument, none of the findings from these two groups is presented in the manual, nor are data presented for those with neurological disorders or aphasia. It is troubling that the author suggests using the CP with demented, CVA, and TBI patients, who often have extensive and multifaceted cognitive difficulties, when they have not been examined during test development. For example, persons with language impairments may not understand the test items, or may not be able to rate them accurately.

POSITIVE FEATURES. As the test developer noted, there is a need for instruments targeted to elders, and she has attempted to address this need both in her normative sampling and in the format of her measure. For example, two levels of response complexity are available for more intact or more impaired persons. It is also welcome that individuals can respond by speaking their answers, gesturing, or writing, in an attempt to accommodate those with various physical handicaps.

Administration instructions are clear. The manual discusses common problems that may arise during testing, and suggests strategies for overcoming them. Purchasers are urged to reproduce pages of the manual for their own use. There are

"Additional Activities" and situational role playing items suggested for therapy, which may expand the possible use of the instrument.

MINOR PROBLEMS. There is an excessive amount of repetition in the manual. This did not produce an overly long document, however, as the entire text runs to 24 pages, with large type and very generous margins. Unusual or incorrect usage of neuropsychological terms is annoyingly frequent. For example, on page 5 she writes "partial or complete blindness in one eye (hemiopsia) [sic]" and on page 2 she lists "Diffuse neurological disorders (e.g., Alzheimer's and progressive neuropathies)." There are minor inaccuracies in other areas as well (e.g., in Table I, instead of 257 subjects described elsewhere, a total of 272 subjects were reported for Income Data).

In the author's Conclusions section, many of the explanations advanced for the findings appear post hoc. For example, it was found that persons who lived with others put more importance on communication skills than those who lived alone. The author reasons that one would need better ability to communicate when living with someone else, but it could as easily be argued that those who live alone have no one else on whom to depend, and must therefore have reliable functional communication skills.

SUMMARY. Did this need to be a "test" at all? With improved statistical analysis, this work may have made an interesting journal article, and could have been the beginning of a useful instrument, particularly if it had included measurement of actual skills, along with patient ratings of their priorities.

Despite its attention to the needs of older adults, and to the priorities of patients in rehabilitation, the CP's deficiencies—a demographically limited and skewed normative sample, standardization on only very healthy older persons, and faulty and inadequate statistical analysis—seriously limit the usefulness of this measure.

REVIEWER'S REFERENCES

Butler, R. N., Lewis, M., & Sunderland, T. (1991). *Aging and mental health* (4th ed.). New York: Macmillan.
Birren, J. E., Sloane, R. B., & Cohen, G. D. (Eds.). (1992). *Handbook of mental health and aging.* San Diego: Academic Press.
LaRue, A., & Markee, T. (1995). Clinical assessment research with older adults. *Psychological Assessment, 7*(3), 376–386.
Klein, H. E. (1998). Retirement migration in America. *Psychotherapy Finances—Special Report; Statistics and Demographics, 24*(1), 6.

[86]
Communication Skills Profile.

Purpose: "Designed to help people who want to gain a thorough knowledge of the processes of communica-

tion and to improve their effectiveness as communicators."
Population: Individuals or teams within organizations.
Publication Date: 1997.
Scores: 6 scales: Slowing My Thought Processes, Making Myself Understood, Testing My Conclusions, Listening Constructively, Getting to the Essence, Exploring Disagreement.
Administration: Group.
Price Data, 1997: $12.95 per test booklet.
Time: Administration time not reported.
Author: Elena Tosca.
Publisher: Jossey-Bass Pfeiffer.

Review of the Communication Skills Profile by ROBERT BROWN, Carl A. Happold Distinguished Professor of Educational Psychology Emeritus, University of Nebraska-Lincoln, and Senior Associate, Aspen Professional Development Associates, Lincoln, NE:

The Communication Skills Profile (CSP) is a self-report instrument that includes eight questions for each of the six subscales, three of which focus on expressing one's own opinions (Slowing Thought Processes, Making Myself Understood, and Testing My Conclusions) and three on Listening and Understanding (Listening Constructively, Getting to the Essence, and Exploring Disagreement). Respondents use a 6-point Likert-like scale (6 = *Nearly always true*, 1 = *Never true*) to respond. After completing the scales, respondents are asked to predict their average score for each of the subscales before calculating their actual average scores.

Next, respondents plot their scores within a circle that has lines representing the six scales radiating from the center with gradations from "1" near the center to "6" near the circumference. The dots representing the scores are then connected to form a polygon. Sample polygons represent profiles with generally low scores, mixed high and low scores, and generally high scores. The author suggests that a "gap analysis" be made between the individual's score and the ideal score of "6." At this juncture, the respondent reads a page-length set of bromides for each of the six scales, which suggest how to improve his or her communication skills. Finally, the respondent is asked to develop an action plan for improvement and obtain feedback from others.

The manual includes no psychometric data regarding norms, reliability, or validity so it is not possible to comment on these characteristics of the instrument from a data-based perspective. The CSP appears to be a tool that would be more useful in a workshop setting than as an instrument to analyze an individual's communication skills for any diagnostic or prescriptive purposes. Nevertheless, the author asserts that the CSP "was designed to help people who want to gain a thorough knowledge of the processes of communication and to improve their effectiveness as communicators" (manual, p. 1); as such, the psychometric properties of the CSP should be available to potential users.

Choosing among alternative instruments will depend on the specific purposes of the users. Even if the user desires only to stimulate discussion within a group, the CSP might not be the best alternative. Many of the questions are abstract and, though understandable, may not provide individuals with enough concrete feedback to enable them to understand, much less improve, their communication skills. And how valid are self-perceptions of one's communication skills? The discrepancies between what an individual thinks he or she has communicated and what the listener understands are too frequent in everyday life for much credibility to be given to a self-report skill profile.

Assessment of communication skills lends itself naturally to a performance-based approach to measurement. Having individuals make presentations or observing individuals in communications settings is just one alternative. Televised vignettes or role-playing situations could be used to provide respondents with a context in which they could comment on the portrayals or even be asked to suggest how they would handle the situation. The creative possibilities are numerous and they could be tailor-made for the specific communication setting.

SUMMARY. Examination of the CSP may provide potential users with useful ideas if they are thinking about a workshop-like situation. Even then, without major adaptations to the specific context, the CSP would not likely be of much benefit. If the user wants a true assessment of communications skills, consideration must be given to a performance-based assessment procedure. I cannot recommend the CSP.

Review of the Communication Skills Profile by THOMAS P. HOGAN, *Professor of Psychology, University of Scranton, Scranton, PA:*
PURPOSE AND TARGET POPULATION. The Communication Skills Profile (CSP) is a 48-item, self-report questionnaire regarding one's own communication practices. According to the CSP booklet, it is "designed to help people who want to gain a thorough knowledge of the processes of communication and to improve their effectiveness as communicators" (manual, p. 1). Communication, of course, is a very broad topic, encompassing reading, writing, public speaking, the broadcast media, etc. The CSP booklet does not explicitly differentiate among these subdivisions of the field. However, discussion in the booklet makes it clear that the CSP focuses on interpersonal communication of the one-on-one or one-on-small group variety, especially in the oral mode.

The CSP booklet indicates that the questionnaire may be completed individually or in groups. Beyond that, the booklet does not identify a target audience or administration procedures. One infers from the discussions in the CSP booklet that the target audience is adults working in organizational settings. There are no time limits or suggested timing arrangements. It appears that an adult of normal intelligence and motivation could complete the questionnaire in about 15 minutes.

MATERIALS, ITEMS, SCORES. The CSP consists of a 48-page booklet that provides a description of the rationale for the questionnaire, the questionnaire items themselves, pages for profiling scores, and suggestions for follow-up activities. Each person completing the questionnaire gets one of these booklets.

The CSP's 48 items are divided into the following six sections, with 8 items per section: Slowing My Thought Processes, Making Myself Understood, Testing My Conclusions, Listening Constructively, Getting to the Essence, and Exploring Disagreement. The booklet indicates that the first three of these sections comprise Area 1: The Ability to Express One's Own Opinion, and the last three sections comprise Area 2: The Ability to Listen and Understand Others. However, neither the text nor the score profiles suggest obtaining total scores from the section scores for these two broader areas.

Each of the 48 items calls for a self-report on a 6-point Likert-type scale ranging from 6: *nearly always true* to 1: *never true*. Each item is a one-sentence statement, such as "I try to find the cause of a disagreement in order to understand its origins." Numerical responses to the items are summed within each section, then averaged (divided by 8), and profiled. Two types of profiles are provided in the CSP booklet. The first is a bar chart showing the six scores. The second is a Holland-type hexagon with the six scales radiating from the center. Unfortunately, this arrangement easily gives the impression that high points on certain scales form polar opposites. This was probably not intended and the CSP text does not suggest it. Nevertheless, the visual appearance of the axes in the polygon invites such an interpretation.

TECHNICAL CHARACTERISTICS. The CSP has no norms, no reliability data, and no validity data. In fact, none of these terms nor concepts related to them are mentioned in the CSP booklet. The author and publisher are, apparently, oblivious to these concepts or simply consider them irrelevant for the CSP.

In the absence of any normative data, one could conceivably view the average scores on the six scales and their accompanying bar charts or polygon projections as amenable to criterion-referenced interpretation. In fact, that is what the CSP booklet does, without calling it criterion-referenced interpretation. However, there does not seem to be any basis for such interpretation of the scores. No rationale is provided for claiming that the statements in each of the six areas are somehow representative of their respective domains. A low score in one area may be a function of the peculiar wording of a few items in that area rather than a real deficiency in the area. The CSP booklet contains no discussion of how the eight items in each area were constructed or why they are thought to be representative of the area.

The CSP booklet contains no reliability data or any discussion of the concept of stability of scores. One infers that the author just assumes that responses to the items are perfectly reliable. The CSP booklet contains no data on the validity of the measures. At the most elementary level, even lacking any data, one would expect presentation of a rationale for having 6 scales rather than 1, or 10, or 30. No such rationale is provided.

SUMMARY. The CSP should not be considered a test or psychometric measure in any ordinary sense of those terms. It has no standardized administrative procedure, no rationale for interpreting scores (either norm-referenced or criterion-referenced), no systematic method of development, no reliability data, and no validity data. The CSP may be useful for purposes of generating discussion in professional development seminars. However, it is not useful for measurement purposes. If one needs a measure of interpersonal communication skills or knowledge of such skills, one needs to look elsewhere.

[87]
Community College Student Experiences Questionnaire, Second Edition.

Purpose: Designed to assess community college students' "quality of effort" toward maximizing college opportunities and achieving their goals.
Population: Community college students.
Publication Dates: 1990–1995.
Acronym: CCSEQ-2.
Scores: 9 scales: Quality of Effort (Course Activities, Library Activities, Faculty-Student Acquaintances, Art, Music and Theater, Writing Activities, Science Activities, Vocational Skills), Satisfaction.
Administration: Group.
Price Data, 1997: $.75 per copy of questionnaire; $1.50 per copy for processing; $11 per test manual ('95, 95 pages); $70 per diskette containing results and summary computer report.
Time: (20–30) minutes.
Comments: For use with students fluent in English.
Authors: Penny W. Lehman, Corinna A. Ethington, and Tissy B. Polizzi.
Publisher: Center for the Study of Higher Education, The University of Memphis.
Cross References: For reviews by Charles Houston and by Rosemary E. Sutton and Hinsdale Bernard of the original edition, see 12:87.

Review of the Community College Student Experiences Questionnaire, Second Edition by CANDICE HAAS HOLLINGSEAD, Assistant Professor, Department of Special Education, Minnesota State University, Mankato, MN:

TEST COVERAGE AND USE. The Community College Student Experiences Questionnaire, Second Edition (CCSEQ-2) was published in 1995. CCSEQ-1, the original questionnaire, was published in 1990. The purpose of the measure is not clearly specified. However, the instrument states "quality of" student "effort" is the main concept examined and focuses on four elements of that effort: student description and motivation for attendance, how and to what extent the student uses institution resources, student impressions of the institution, and student self-evaluation of progress to goals. "Quality of Effort is defined as the amount, scope, and quality of effort students put into taking advantage of the opportunities offered to them by the college" (manual, p. 10). The instrument states it is designed to "fit" student diversity found in community colleges. The instrument is designed for community college students who are fluent in English and is therefore not suitable for students with limited English proficiency. Another limitation is its lack of suitability for students who are enrolled in programs that are not academic or vocational.

The instrument content covers six sections: Background, Work, and Family (age, gender, ethnicity, native language, time spent on job, effects of job responsibilities on college work, effects of family responsibilities on college work), College Program (term units, overall units, class meetings, grades, hours spent in studying, attendance motivation), College Courses, College Activities (83 items in 12 topical areas), Estimate of Gains (student self-evaluation on 23 educational goals), and College Environment.

Two score types can be determined from section scores: "Quality of Effort" and "Satisfaction." Quality of Effort scales can be calculated from the first eight topical areas (61 items) of College Activities. Each of the eight topical area scores vary in the number of items available. For example, the topical area of "faculty" has 8 items with possible scores ranging from 8 to 32 whereas the topical area of "course activities" has 10 items with possible scores ranging from 10 to 40. Quality of Effort scales permits colleges to derive total student score means by topical areas. These data can then be used to determine student activities by program, gender, ethnicity, and enrollment status resulting in improved college services.

The Satisfaction scale is drawn from five of the seven College Environment items. The score represents the College Environment from a student's point of view. The range of possible scores is 5 (low) to 25 (high).

RELIABILITY AND VALIDITY. Comparative data are provided from 56 community colleges, institutions, and students. The samples are not representative nationally and are not meant to be interpreted as norms. Three comparative data samples are All Students (n = 17,993), Transfer Students (n = 9,026), and Vocational Students (n = 3,161). Comparative information is provided in table format (manual, pp. 23–53). All tables depict response frequencies to items as percentages.

The eight Quality of Effort scores drawn from the College Activities section are the only items included in the manual's description of psychometric properties. Interitem Pearson correlations were calculated within each of the eight topical areas in College Activities scales. Correlations were all positive but primarily below .50. Cronbach's alpha was used to measure internal consistency. These coefficients ranged from .82 to .94. Factor analysis for each scale was performed using a one-factor solution; loadings ranged from .49 to .91. The relationship between College Activities and estimate of Gains was examined between the two sections for patterns of correlations. Correlations ranged from .02 to .55. The following combinations yielded the highest correlations: Science Activities with Mathematics, Science, and Technology (.55) and Art, Music, and Theater with Arts (.55).

APPLICATION. The manual provides guidelines for the planning and implementation of a college's student population completion of a study using this instrument. The resulting frequencies and crosstabs can provide the college useful information about the experiences they provide to diverse students. Colleges can use this information to improve their services to students and for public relations.

SUMMARY. The Community College Student Experiences Questionnaire, Second Edition provides community colleges with information regarding the services they provide to a variety of students, which in turn can impact the policy decisions the college makes. The CCSEQ-2's strength lies in the information it can provide a college if the participant sample size is high. The instrument does have limitations. The one of greatest concern is that all data are from student self-report, influencing the potential participant response rate and the accuracy of the data received. Another concern is the limited amount of reliability and validity support of instrument scores.

Review of the Community College Student Experiences Questionnaire, Second Edition by JAMES P. VAN HANEGHAN, Associate Professor, Department of Behavioral Studies and Educational Technology, University of South Alabama, Mobile, AL:

The Community College Student Experiences Questionnaire, Second Edition (CCSEQ), is a survey instrument designed to examine the degree of involvement of students in the academic and other activities at community colleges. The second edition of the instrument is not substantively different from the original version. The only change in the manual involves a larger sample of community colleges serving to double the sample size of the original group reported in the first edition. There were two prior reviews of this instrument, and many of the issues raised by the earlier reviewers are still valid (see 12:87).

As in the first edition, the purpose of the CCSEQ is to collect student demographic information, information about student involvement in academic and nonacademic activities, students' use of services at the college (counseling, study skills, etc.), estimated gains the students perceive they have made in various domains, and their opinions about the college environment. It takes about 30 minutes to administer, and the questionnaire is computer scored. Hence, it is easy to use.

The CCSEQ yields a variety of scores, but the central construct the instrument focuses on is the notion of "quality of effort." This construct encompasses how engaged students are in classes and activities and how engaged students are in using the facilities and programs offered by the college. Nine different scores are generated from questions in various areas. The areas include: Course Activities, Library Activities, Faculty Contact, Student Acquaintances, Fine Arts, Writing, Science, and Vocational.

The suggested uses of the CCSEQ include: college self-studies, evaluations, and other institutional uses that might help colleges improve the quality of their service to their students. The appendices in the manual provide suggestions for how to administer and use the CCSEQ for various purposes. However, this information is sparse and could be better presented. For example, there is some information about using different sampling units (individuals versus classes), but the authors really never identify the use of classes as an instance of cluster sampling. They imply that perhaps some kind of multistage sampling might be done, but there is not enough detail to provide much help. There are only two pages on how to organize and report results. Although the variety of potential uses may make it difficult to specify exactly how someone might write up the results, more than a few pages in an appendix are warranted on interpretation.

There are comparative data to help anchor the results based on a national sample of 56 community colleges. However, although the sample is national, it is not necessarily representative. Further, although the scores are broken down into students who are transferring to 4-year schools versus those who are in vocational/technical programs, there are other dimensions along which scores need be broken down in order to use the information fruitfully. For instance, the scores are not broken down by the number of credit hours, the size of the school, demographics of schools, and so on. Further, there is the introduction of overall satisfaction variable in this data without any explanation of where the score comes from in the CCSEQ. The only place that shows how that score was derived was in an appendix that contained some computer code for running statistical analyses, and this information apparently excludes one variable in the summation that leads to the score, because the compute statement leaves out one variable that was supposed to be recoded to construct the score.

In spite of the large sample, the authors provide inadequate psychometric analysis of their questionnaire in the manual. The authors present two types of evidence for the "quality of effort" construct. There are factor analyses based on several thousand cases that suggest that the items in the various domains do cluster together, and there is evidence that the scores on the quality of effort scales correlate moderately with self-reported gains in various academic and nonacademic areas. There are no objective criterion measures reported in the manual. The authors need to include evidence that the scores are predictive of measures other than those found within the questionnaire itself. Further, limited reliability evidence is presented. The authors present internal consistency reliability estimates that are reasonable, but do not present any test-retest reliability. This would especially be important in any attempt to follow students longitudinally.

Given the diverse missions of community colleges, it is unclear whether the "Quality of Effort" construct will be suitable for some colleges. For example, community colleges are engaging in more distance learning via the internet. If the trend toward distance education continues, the CCSEQ will need to be altered to consider what involvement means to students taking distance education courses. For example, students taking a course via the internet may never visit the facilities of the college, yet may be highly engaged in learning. Also, many community colleges serve culturally and linguistically diverse populations. The CCSEQ is designed for fluent English speakers, and does not deal with some of the issues specific to culturally diverse groups.

SUMMARY. Overall, the CCSEQ is an interesting instrument that may provide community college administrators with useful information about how involved their students are with their institution. However, more psychometric work is needed to validate the construct, the manual needs to be expanded to provide more detailed and useful information about how to use the CCSEQ, and there are some concerns about the currency of the present form of the CCSEQ in that it does not take into account trends toward distance education in community colleges and increasingly diverse student populations.

[88]

Competency-Based Performance Improvement: Organizational Assessment Package.

Purpose: Used to assess an organization's performance improvement program(s) and to improve planning for future programs.

Population: Business managers.

Publication Date: 1995.

Scores, 7: 6 categories (Strategic Goals and Business Objectives, Needs Analysis/Assessment/Planning, Competency Modeling, Curriculum Planning, Learning Intervention Design and Development, Evaluation), Total.

Administration: Group.

Price Data, 1996: $59.95 per Administrator's Handbook (61 pages), and 10 data collection instruments; $34.95 per Administrator's Handbook; $2.95 per data collection instrument (volume discounts available).

Time: Administration time not reported.

Author: David D. Dubois.

Publisher: Human Resource Development Press.

Review of the Competency-Based Performance Improvement: Organizational Assessment Package by STEPHEN F. DAVIS, Professor of Psychology, Emporia State University, Emporia, KS:

This instrument is based on the contention that "Organization managers and human resource professionals are discovering that they cannot rely on employees to bring to the workplace the competencies they need to perform their jobs with

complete success" (administrator's handbook, p. 1). This situation led to the development of an assessment device to facilitate the creation and implementation of a high-impact, competency-based program. Unfortunately, it is not clear whether the Competency-Based Performance Improvement Organizational Assessment Package achieves this goal.

This assessment device is an extension of the Strategic Systems Model originally created by the author, David Dubois, in 1993. This somewhat simplistic model begins with a simultaneous consideration of goals/objectives/business plans and a front end needs analysis/planning/assessment. Subsequent stages include (in order) competency model development, curriculum planning, learning intervention design and development, and evaluation. Unfortunately, little concrete information concerning the adequacy of this model is provided.

The assessment instrument consists of 30 items (five items per each of the six dimensions deemed important for evaluating performance improvement programs). All items are answered "yes," "no," or "not sure." The presence of a line requesting the number of "yes" responses at the end of each dimension is noteworthy; these prompts might create strong demand characteristics and potentially inflate the number of "yes" responses per dimension. Likewise, the complete lack of any sort of technical data (e.g., normative, validity, and reliability measures) concerning the development of this instrument is distressing.

The lack of technical data is compensated by the thoroughness, almost to a fault, of the steps to be followed in preparation and survey administration. Even the most obvious and trivial points are elucidated. For example, potential users are cautioned that "as the number of respondents increases, so will the amount of manual effort that must be applied to the hand-scoring, analysis, and data interpretation process" (p. 8). The details of "Organizing and Planning the Data Collection Activities" also are compulsively delineated. In short, the author has a unique ability to state (and restate) the obvious and make trivial aspects appear more important than they really are. Despite the lengthy descriptions and copious examples, the assessment form and associated summary and analysis sheets are easy to complete.

The potential for introducing answer bias reappears in the section on "Data Handling and

Analysis Methods" (p. 16). Whereas some of the suggestions for contacting and encouraging specific individuals who have not responded may seem somewhat intimidating or overbearing, several of the procedures for "Data *Editing*" [emphasis added] are capricious at best. For example, potential users are told that "When a choice is not marked, the assumption will be made that the intended response to the item was either *No* or *Not Sure*" (p. 17) and that "When two or more response choices are marked (e.g., *Yes* and also *Not Sure*), the assumption will be made that the intended choice was not *Yes*" (p. 17). The logic that prompts these decisions is not readily apparent and certainly does not appear methodologically sound.

As noted, data-analytic procedures are handled at a rudimentary level. All requisite calculations can be accomplished with a simple hand calculator (or scratch pad and pencil). If the test user is able to add and divide, no difficulty will be experienced. Although the reader is told that "Other analyses of the data are possible by application of methods from mathematical statistics" (p. 17), these other analyses are never discussed. The goal of the data "analysis" (summarization is a more appropriate term) is to produce one of four profiles: (a) total organization performance improvement plan adequacy ratings as shown by individual employee groups, (b) total organization performance improvement plan adequacy ratings as shown by all employees, (c) adequacy ratings for each of the six program components using data from employee groups, and (d) adequacy ratings for each of the six program components using data from all employees. Sample worksheets and profile sheets, as well as *detailed* instructions for using them, are provided.

Interpretation of the data and program implementation revolve around an examination of "key organization players' perception of the status of the performance improvement in its entirety" (p. 21) and "the organization players' perceptions of the status of the subsystem elements" (p. 21). These objectives are best accomplished through the use of an "analysis table," which lists the perceptions (adequate, somewhat adequate, or inadequate) of the total program and the six subsystem elements for all employees and key groups, such as officers, executives, managers, etc. The different patterns of adequacy-inadequacy for these respective groups are compared and appropriate

actions contemplated. Two problems complicate this otherwise straightforward approach. First, the translation of numerical data into the three adequacy categories is simply a given; no supportive data are presented to tell the user why, for example, a score of 24 is "adequate" whereas a score of 23 is "somewhat adequate." Second, the illustrative example contains such authoritative phrases as "a major observation," "clearly differ," "data also indicate," and "this implies" without providing supportive statistics or explanations.

These apparent problems and issues notwithstanding, the Competency-Based Performance Improvement: Organizational Assessment Package has some redeeming features. It is easy to administer and score. It has the potential to stimulate relevant discussions that might lead to performance improvement. These aspects might suggest its appropriateness for certain situations.

Review of the Competency-Based Performance Improvement: Organizational Assessment Package by JERRY M. LOWE, *Associate Professor of Educational Leadership, Sam Houston State University, Huntsville, TX:*

The Competency-Based Performance Improvement: Organizational Assessment Package was developed to help organizations establish competency-based employee performance improvement programs. Focusing upon selected criteria from the Strategic Systems Model for Creating High-Impact and Competency-Based Performance Improvement Programs (SSM; Dubois, 1993), this diagnostic checklist is designed to provide organizations with the following program assessment information: (a) availability of learning opportunities for employee job performance improvement, and (b) an analysis of employee competencies that contribute to better job performance. Components of the SSM assessment package focus upon common organizational goals and objectives. The SSM addresses six broad domains the author considers important to organizational performance improvement: (a) Strategic Goals and Business Objectives; (b) Needs Analysis, Assessment, and Planning; (c) Competency Modeling; (d) Curriculum Planning; (e) Learning Intervention Design and Development; and (f) Evaluation. The 30-item SSM may be administered to groups or individual employees and other key personnel, as it is designed to accommodate a universal variety of organizational applications. Participants respond to one of three choices for each item: YES, NO, or NOT SURE.

ADMINISTRATION AND INTERPRETATION. The SSM checklist includes the following materials: (a) a manual that provides clear, step-by-step instructions for administration and scoring; (b) two survey plan worksheets that provide structure for conducting the survey; (c) four data analysis worksheets that assist in organizing, analyzing, and interpreting the data; and (d) four profile sheets that allow the survey data to be displayed numerically or graphically. There are no indications in the package regarding who may administer the instrument or under what conditions the survey should be conducted. Meaningful suggestions for administration of the surveys are included in the SSM package and include procedures for preparation, distribution, and management of the survey packets. Major shortcomings appear in this section of the administration information in that the author advocates data editing as a means of dealing with unclear response or nonresponse to items on the survey. Appropriate descriptive statistics may be used in interpretation of the data; however, the author advocates the development of four analysis profiles in order to enhance the timely completion and availability of the results. Utilizing specific worksheets provided in the SSM packet, the researcher may assemble the collected data to determine the following profiles: (a) total organization performance improvement program adequacy ratings based upon data from individual employee groups, (b) total organization performance improvement program adequacy rating based upon data from individual employees, (c) a profile of adequacy ratings for any or all of the six program components using data from any or all of the employee groups, and (d) a composite adequacy rating for any or all of the six components of the SSM.

NORMATIVE INFORMATION, RELIABILITY, AND VALIDITY. According to the author, the SSM was not normed, and procedures to establish reliability and validity were not conducted because the instrument was internally specific to the organization using it.

SUMMARY. The SSM appears to be a well-constructed instrument. The information included in the package is clear and well organized and serves to enhance the ease of administration and analysis. However, with the absence of reliability and validity information, the instrument may not be useful for making predictions about organizational effectiveness.

REVIEWER'S REFERENCE

Dubois, D. D. (1993). *Competency-based performance improvement: A strategy for organizational change.* Amherst, MA: Human Resource Development.

[89]
The Competent Speaker Speech Evaluation Form.

Purpose: Designed to measure public speaking competency.
Population: Post-secondary students.
Publication Date: 1993.
Scores, 9: Chooses and Narrows a Topic Appropriately for the Audience and Occasion, Communicates the Thesis/Specific Purpose in a Manner Appropriate for Audience and Occasion, Uses an Organizational Pattern Appropriate to Topic/Audience/Occasion and Purpose, Provides Appropriate Supporting Material Based on the Audience and Occasion, Uses Language That is Appropriate to the Audience/Occasion and Purpose, Uses Vocal Variety in Rate/Pitch and Intensity to Heighten and Maintain Interest, Uses Pronunciation/Grammar and Articulation Appropriate to the Designated Audience, Uses Physical Behaviors that Support the Verbal Message, Total.
Administration: Individual.
Price Data: Available from publisher.
Time: Administration time not reported.
Author: Speech Communication Association.
Publisher: National Communication Association.

Review of The Competent Speaker Speech Evaluation Form by SANDRA M. KETROW, Professor of Communication Studies, University of Rhode Island, Kingston, RI:

The National Communication Association (NCA [formerly Speech Communication Association]) began to publish formal methods to assess oral communication in the 1970s. Given the long history of focus on what constitutes the elements of effective public communication, the Competent Speaker Speech Evaluation Form (CSSE) produced by Morreale and colleagues under the auspices of NCA might be viewed as the culmination or distillation of many years of effort. At its time of publication (1993), this CSSE form was quite good. When compared to multiple other instruments available in various texts, instructor manuals, and student handbooks, this form stands out as exemplar. The editors of the CSSE report an extensive process to locate or derive, and then winnow, the criteria categories. They also provide an intensive testing process and results for technical quality. The claim made that this instrument may be used to assess public speaking competence at the target level of a college sophomore (14th grade) is accurate, and may be understated. The CSSE form may be used as stipulated to "evaluate informative and persuasive speeches in class" (p. 3) and it has potential as a feedback "tool for instructing and advising students" (p. 3). Given its implied large-scale testing in 10 or more higher-education institutions, the other two uses (for placement evaluation or to generate assessment data for institutional accountability) are valid. The authors also wish users to accept that microscopic-level items are adequate to infer macroscopic-level outcomes or perceptions, such as "dynamism," or "credibility." That performative skills reflect internal or cognitive processing, or knowledge, or cultural competence, is left to the form user to take on faith.

Unlike some communication competence or trait measures that have been used in validity studies with thousands of subjects, the editors evaluated the CSSE instrument using 12 evaluators. The report of "traditional analysis" states that from an initial pool of 40, videotaped speeches from 12 students were used to examine the reliability and validity of the form and its criteria.

Generally high interrater reliability coefficients (Ebel's and Cronbach's) are reported, although there is variation of magnitude of approximately .18 in these values. The instability of scores might contribute to these differences in magnitudes of the reliability estimates, as might the relative vagueness and subjectivity of the standards for each criterion. For example, what is "uses supporting material that is inappropriate in quality and variety"? (p. 12). The editors explain this standard as they do some others with "That is, supporting material is only vaguely related to the thesis of the speech, and variety is either too great or too little to do anything but detract from the effectiveness of the speech" (p. 12). With experience (and some training), an evaluator can make this kind of judgment based on the criteria furnished to the students prior to the speaking event. However, this level of abstraction leaves questions. The acceptable reliability coefficients generated by diverse groups of student evaluators, both for ethnicity and gender, are indicators that the form

is fairly free of certain biases. These data imply that the CSSE form may be used with minimal training for effective evaluation. However, an excellent training process is outlined for evaluators, and this reviewer recommends following their procedure.

The editors report convergent validity evidence with the Personal Report of Communication Apprehension (PRCA) (McCroskey, 1977). As scores from the PRCA are highly reliable, and show excellent convergent and divergent validity with scores from a number of other communication and psychology measures, the Competent Speaker Evaluation Form lines up well for construct validity. This is further emphasized by its convergent validity evidence with the Communication Competency Assessment Instrument (CCAI) (Rubin, 1982), although the CCAI is intended to measure broader communication competency.

The editors do not provide any data reflecting the levels of the convergent or divergent validity evidence, nor do they address establishing intrarater reliability. In reporting the results of a Rasch analysis for independent elements, it is troubling that the fit appears weak for "appropriate language" and "articulation." Nor do they examine validity or reliability for using the instrument to evaluate graduating high school seniors (or first-year college students). The editors of the CSSE report in their bibliography a scant few studies that provided limited predictive or external validity evidence (until 1985). It would be useful to examine more recent indicators, including the standards given by Berko, Morreale, Cooper, and Perry (1998) and Rubin and Hampton (1998) that relate to the national Goals 2000 for K–12, and for competencies required in our current work world.

SUMMARY. It is difficult to find fault with content and construct validity evidence given the ancestors of this instrument. However, some process of identifying a large number of microscopic skills as well as macroscopic ones, within both the content and delivery areas, and then refining them via a component analysis (or even more intriguing and useful, sequential equation, such as LISREL, modeling) would help instructors and evaluators be more relaxed with the selected items and their respective categories. History mitigates against content and construct validity for the CSSE Form, because the editors apparently begin by assuming that the use of certain items and categories repeatedly across centuries is adequate support for their utility. Research reported by Ketrow (1999) establishes clearly that nonverbal cues may account for anywhere from 60% or more of the meaning of a particular message. Thus, whether "vocal variety" and "articulation" should be separate, or "physical behavior" more finely distributed, remains to be seen. Items such as "adjustment to audience," especially as diversity increases in the United States, may become more and more important. Much printed competition exists for the Competent Speaker Evaluation Form, but none of these competitors documents reliability or validity evidence in such a comprehensive manner. Until some other challenger appears or this form is updated to more recent standards, this would appear to be the instrument of choice for those needing to evaluate college student (or equivalent) public speaking.

REVIEWER'S REFERENCES

McCroskey, J. C. (1977). Oral communication apprehension: A summary of recent theory and research. *Human Communication Research, 4*, 78–96.

Rubin, R. B. (1982). Communication Competency Assessment Instrument. Annandale, VA: Speech Communication Association.

McCroskey, J. C. (1997). *An introduction to rhetorical communication.* Boston, MA: Allyn and Bacon.

Berko, R. M., Morreale, S. P., Cooper, P. J., & Perry, C. D. (1998). Communication standards and competencies for kindergarten through grade 12: The role of the National Communication Association. *Communication Education, 47*, 174–182.

Rubin, D. L., & Hampton, S. (1998). National performance standards for oral communication K–12: New standards and speaking/listening/viewing. *Communication Education, 47*, 183–193.

Ketrow, S. M. (1999). Nonverbal aspects of group communication. In L. Frey (Ed.), *Handbook of group communication theory and research* (pp. 251–287). Thousand Oaks, CA: Sage.

Review of The Competent Speaker Speech Evaluation Form by JULIA Y. PORTER, Assistant Professor of Counselor Education, Mississippi State University, Meridian, MS:

Based upon an extensive review of recent communication research, The Competent Speaker Speech Evaluation Form is a criterion-based instrument designed to measure eight competencies that are divided into two categories: (a) Preparation and (b) Delivery. Developers' intended uses of the instrument include: "(a) evaluating informative and persuasive speeches in class; (b) testing-in or testing-out (placement) purposes; (c) as a tool for instructing and advising students about the preparation and presentation of public speeches; and (d) generating assessment data for accountability-related objectives of academic institutions" (manual, pp. 3–4). Only the first purpose, "evaluating informative and persuasive speeches in class," has been researched and documented at this time.

Instrument scoring is based on specific performance standards and criteria outlined in the test manual. Scores result in three levels of performance: (a) unsatisfactory, (2) satisfactory, and (3) excellent. Evaluators using this instrument can assign any numerical weighting system to these levels. These levels of performance categories are very broad and would require evaluator interpretation if the traditional five-letter (A, B, C, D, F) grading system is applied to the evaluation results. Another area of concern is that the quality of the instrument results are dependent on the expertise of the rater. A training video with 12 speeches was developed to train raters in the assessment of speakers. Interrater reliability results for speech communication professionals (N = 12; 8 females, 4 males; 11 Anglo, 1 Hispanic) gave an Ebel's coefficient of .92, graduate teaching assistants generated a Cronbach's alpha of .76 (N = 10; demographic data not available); and community college speech instructors generated a Cronbach coefficient of .84 (N = 3; demographic data not available). Although reliability coefficients were more than adequate, the small sample size makes the results questionable. Even if the reliability results are accepted, only speech professionals were included in the sample. Other evaluators interested in using The Competent Speaker Speech Evaluation Form may need extensive training before being able to adequately use the rating system. Content validity was examined through the use of competency items identified by an 11-member team who conducted the literature review. Convergent validity was studied by comparing scores from The Competent Speaker instrument with scores from the Communication Competency Assessment Instrument and the Personal Report of Communication Apprehension. Two studies that were conducted to investigate cultural bias found no significant differences in scores by ethnic group (White, Black, Hispanic, or Asian) or by gender. In the first study, N = 40 and in the second study N = 260. Again, the small sample sizes of these studies would not allow the data reported to be generalized to other populations.

SUMMARY. The Competent Speaker Speech Evaluation Form is the first standardized and psychometrically tested speech evaluation form. Due to the subjectivity of the evaluation form, rater training is extremely important. Results should be viewed with caution because of possible rater error and should be used in conjunction with other assessment measures.

Comprehensive Assessment of School Environments Information Management System.

Purpose: Designed to facilitate and encourage the use of data-based planning for school improvement projects.

Population: Secondary schools.

Publication Dates: 1991–1995.

Acronym: CASE-IMS.

Scores, 9: Principal Questionnaire, Teacher Report Form, Student Report Form, Teacher Satisfaction Survey, Student Satisfaction Survey, Parent Satisfaction Survey (optional), School Climate Survey for Teachers, School Climate Survey for Students, School Climate Survey for Parents (optional).

Administration: Group.

Price Data, 1995: $175 per MS/DOS 3.5-inch or 5.25-inch software and user's manual; $49 per Version 1.2 add-on disk and manual ('96, 87 pages); $195 per Version 1.5 scoring package update with scanner interface; $395 per Version 1.5 enhancement and scoring package update; $395 per Macintosh version; $6 per 35 surveys (specify School Climate, Student Satisfaction, Teacher Satisfaction or Parent Satisfaction); $5 per 35 answer sheets (specify NCS or Scantron); $5 per examiner's manual; $15 per technical manual; $5 per Climate/Satisfaction sampler kit including examiner's manual and one of each form; $135 per Mainframe scoring package; $95 per MS/DOS or Apple II/e scoring package; $1.50 per 35 Principal Questionnaire and Report Forms (specify NCS or Scantron); $7 per 35 Teacher or Student Report Forms (specify NCS or Scantron); $5 per computer demo disk.

Time: Administration time not reported.

Comments: Computer administered; available in MS/DOS (3.5-inch or 5.25-inch disks) or Macintosh (3.5-inch disk) format.

Author: National Association of Secondary School Principals Task Force on Effective School Environments.

Publisher: National Association of Secondary School Principals.

Review of the Comprehensive Assessment of School Environments Information Management System by JOSEPH R. MANDUCHI, Clinical Associate, Susquehanna Institute, Harrisburg, PA:

The Comprehensive Assessment of School Environments Information Management System (CASE-IMS) is a system for integrating and managing information about a school and its general climate. The system consists of several surveys that are administered to the school principal, teachers, students, and parents. After completion of the surveys, the data may be input into any IBM-compatible computer either by hand or by use of an electronic scanner.

The CASE-IMS was developed by the National Association of Secondary School Principals (NASSP) Task Force on Effective School Environments. The program package states that the CASE-IMS "is a total school profiling and planning software package that extends and incorporates data from NASSP's School Climate and Satisfaction Instrumentation" (manual, p. 1-5). There are seven instruments used in this version of the CASE-IMS. They are a (a) Principal Questionnaire, (b) Teacher Report Form, (c) Student Report Form, (d) Teacher Satisfaction Survey, (e) Student Satisfaction Survey, (f) Parent Satisfaction Survey, and a (g) School Climate Survey. These seven instruments comprise the data set by which school-based data are derived.

One criticism of the CASE-IMS is that there is not a well-defined method for the collection of the data. There are no instructions that provide for randomization of sampling and there is considerable latitude regarding how data may be collected. For example, under the instructions for Survey 3, the Student Report Form, it is recommended that it be administered to the entire student body or a "representative sample" (manual, p. 1-6). Without clear guidelines on the selection of a sample, any single principal or CASE-IMS review committee could develop sampling techniques that could easily lead to erroneous conclusions regarding the perceptions of the school. Although this is certainly a school responsibility, it would serve the test publishers well if firm guidelines for sampling were provided. Instructions on sampling procedures would be a plus.

The data are compiled into indicator variables that "provide systematic measurement of important input and mediating variables as outlined in the CASE model" (manual, p. 1-8). The indicator variables are further condensed into CASE Summary variables that are used for "prediction, forecasting, and planning" (manual, p. 1-9). Once aggregated, the data are designed to assist in the identification of successes and problems in the current performance of a school and to assist in the planning of school improvement projects.

To analyze the data, a number of easily understood reports are developed. The first is a series of graphs that compare the school's score on a variety of scales to national norms. Box graphs are provided for student, teacher, and parent climate and satisfaction. The norms are developed from what the manual describes as a "large normative study" (p. 1-9).

The manual does not describe this normative study in detail. The normative data base is included in the software and serves as the basis for developing predictive relationships called path equations. *T*-scores are provided to provide more precise interpretation of the data. The *T*-score tables are likewise easy to navigate and to understand.

Additional reports include a listing of the various indicators and annotation as to whether the studied school performed well below average to well above average in comparison to other schools in the national norm group. These reports are easy to scan and can serve as a jump-off point for further school climate planning projects.

The manual provides "Six Steps for Diagnosis and Planning Improvement" (pp. 6-1–6-12). The manual is instructional and again, easy to follow. The six steps lead to a "what if" analysis. In this last step, outcomes variables can be studied in relation to predictor indicators. The CASE-IM program using "path equations" can predict changes in outcome variables based on changes in predictor variables. The steps to perform the "what if" analysis are, once again, easy and do not require advanced computer literacy.

The software also provides suggested interventions that have been known to yield changes in the predictor indicators. These "suggested interventions" can serve as the basis for school improvement projects. The manual is clear to point out that the "suggested interventions" are not validated as proven strategies but widely accepted activities used by others to bring about change.

In reviewing the material, the CASE-IMS software and a demonstration data disc are provided. The software is installed easily and the manual is extremely user friendly. This reviewer encountered no problems in moving about the program, understanding commands, and obtaining reports. The ease of operations of this package is a definite advantage.

SUMMARY. The CASE-IMS is a comprehensive instrument for the study of school climate with input from a wide variety of sources. The pitfalls of the measure seem to demand that any use of the CASE-IMS be used in committee format with opportunity for oversight of methods, interpretation, and future planning.

Review of the Comprehensive Assessment of School Environments Information Management System by DANIEL L. YAZAK, Assistant Professor of Counseling and Human Services, Montana State University-Billings, Billings, MT:

Developed as a microcomputer program by the National Association of Secondary School Principals, the Comprehensive Assessment of School Environments (CASE) Information Management System facilitates assessment and future planning in schools. CASE operates on IBM/compatible microcomputers that use MS-DOS 4.0 or later versions, a printer, hard disk, and floppy-disk drive. Memory and processor speed requirements are not reported.

An extensive, detailed CASE users' manual is included with the CASE program. Although the level of detail is thorough and complete, familiarity with both data input and survey involvement should be considered a requisite before using CASE. The interrelated nature of several variables used in the CASE program make it necessary to insure both accuracy and understanding of inputs before meaningful conclusions can be drawn from CASE program results.

Construct variables for the CASE program evolved from a Task Force on Effective School Climate established by the National Association of Secondary School Principals (NASSP), which began its work in 1982. A review of the literature by the Task Force revealed inadequate methods and techniques for describing a general model depicting school and related environments. A complete discussion of the CASE model can be found in Keefe, Kelley, and Miller (1985). Diagrams of the model in the users' manual describe major headings of Societal, School District and Community, and School or Classroom Environments. These portions of the model are presented as important variables interacting to affect the entire School Environment.

Segments of the model are presented as additional subsets. For example, Societal Environments are divided into Societal Ideologies (Individual Ability, Schooling, Work, and Social Mobility). Next, Structures of Dominance are separated into Wealth and Social Class, Status and Occupational Hierarchy, and Caste (race, gender, etc.).

Finally, School or Classroom Environment variables include Inputs (Goals and Objectives, Organizational Characteristics, and Characteristics of Groups and Individuals), and Mediating Variables (School Climate and Student Outcomes—both satisfaction and productivity).

In order to facilitate the collection and use of variables outlined in the CASE model, the Task Force developed seven instruments for each of the following stakeholders identified during its research: principal, teacher (report and satisfaction perspectives), student (report and satisfaction perspectives), parent satisfaction, and school climate. The users' manual contains a brief description of each instrument along with references to other CASE manuals for more detailed information. Information concerning reliability and validity of scores from the instruments is not presented.

Four variable types evolve from the CASE model. First, output variables present a school's productivity in terms of student attitude and achievement on standardized tests. Second, input variables measure resources and efforts required to obtain that performance. Third, mediating variables are measures of attitudinal characteristics that may magnify or diminish the input effects on outputs. And finally, context indictors are obtained from demographic data. Emphasis is placed on the information gathered on the Principal Questionnaire and is subject to the bias of that individual and numerous sampling errors.

A large, normative study conducted by NASSP provided national norms (means and standard deviations) for indicator variables in addition to predictive relationships. Predictive relationships can be used to estimate output variables given changes in input and/or mediating variables. Size, composition, and sampling methods are not provided for the normative study. Type of predictive relationships and correlational statistics are not presented.

CASE also provides a means for comparisons of the four variables to national-school means and school T-scores. National norm T-scores have a mean of 50 and standard deviation of 10. These scores can then be used to review an individual school's standing vis-a-vis a national population and whether a statistically significant difference exists between national and local scores.

In addition to providing an extensive statistical description of inputs and variables to the CASE system, an analysis of possible interventions is included. Using both programmed logic and alternative variable analyses, a target variable is selected for possible change, inputs and/or moderator variables are previewed, and probable estimated effects can be calculated for review. Interpretation of the estimated effects should be made with caution given the nature of the NASSP norming study and programmed regression tendencies on subsequent proposed interventions.

SUMMARY. Utilizing conceptual variables such as Societal, School District and Community, and School or Classroom Environments, an assessment of a school's productivity can be made. The CASE model provides a way of comparing local to national school means and T-scores. This computer application was developed by the National Association of Secondary School Principals.

REVIEWER'S REFERENCE
Keefe, J. W., Kelley, E. A., & Miller, S. K. (1985). School climate: Clear definition and a model for a larger setting. *NASSP Bulletin, 69,* 70–77.

[91]
Comprehensive Identification Process [Revised].

Purpose: "Designed to identify children who may have problems that could interfere with their success in school."

Population: Ages 2–6.5.

Publication Dates: 1975–1997.

Acronym: CIP.

Administration: Individual.

Price Data, 1997: $249.95 per complete kit including Symbol booklet, Screening booklet, Parent Interview form, Observation of Behavior form, Speech and Expressive Language Record form, Child Record Folder, Interviewer's manual ('97, 40 pages), Administrator's Manual ('97, 54 pages) and manipulatives in carrying case.

Foreign Language Edition: Earlier edition available in Spanish.

Time: (25–35) minutes.

Comments: CIP screening team should include at least one member who has a background in early childhood education of the disabled and is skilled in screening and evaluation; alternatives to the standard screening, such as in-home screening or bilingual screening available.

Authors: R. Reid Zehrbach (test), and Joan Good Erickson (Speech and Expressive Language Record Form).

Publisher: Scholastic Testing Service, Inc.

a) CHILD: RECORD FOLDER.

Scores, 5: Hearing, Vision, Perceptual Motor, Cognitive-Verbal, Gross Motor.

Comment: Materials for hearing and vision screening must be obtained locally.
b) SPEECH AND EXPRESSIVE LANGUAGE RECORD FORM.
Scores, 6: Articulation/Phonology, Voice, Fluency, Expressive Language, Associated Factors, Total.
Author: Joan Good Erickson.
c) OBSERVATION OF BEHAVIOR FORM.
Scores, 7: Hearing, Vision, Physical/Motor Speech and Expressive Language, Social Behavior (Responses, Interaction), Affective Behavior.
d) PARENT INTERVIEW FORM.
Scores, 7: Pregnancy/Birth/Hospitalization, Walking/Toilet Training, Hearing, Vision, Speech and Expressive Language, Medical, Social Affect.
Comment: History and ratings by parent.
Cross References: See T4:616 (1 reference); for reviews by Robert P. Anderson and Phyllis L. Newcomer of an earlier version, see 8:425 (1 reference).

Review of the Comprehensive Identification Process [Revised] by J. JEFFREY GRILL, Professor and Chair, Special Education Department, Athens State University, Athens, AL:

The Comprehensive Identification Process (CIP) [Revised] is a screening instrument, developed in the 1970s, for use with children between the ages of 2 and 6 1/2 years. The CIP's stated purpose is to "identify every child in a community who is eligible for a special preschool program or who needs some kind of medical attention or therapy to function at full potential when he or she enters school" (Interviewer's Manual, p. 1).

All needed manuals and record forms, as well as most, but not all manipulable items are included in the kit. Several items must be provided by users of the CIP—paper of two sizes (i.e., 8 1/2 x 11 inches, 6 x 6 inches), pieces of cellophane tissue for wrapping a small toy, a sturdy box or chair of about 18 inches in height, access to a functioning doorknob (or a jar with a lid of about doorknob size), and a roll of masking tape. On site, various tables, chairs, and screens or dividers are needed as well as refreshments.

The CIP screening is conducted by a team, consisting of a leader, a parent interviewer, three to five child interviewers, speech and expressive language interviewers, and a hearing and vision team. At least one of the members should have a background in early childhood education of the disabled. The team leader makes local arrangements for the site of the screening, is available

during screenings to answer questions, and serves as the greeter for those arriving with children to be screened. The parent interviewer assists the parent with completion of the Parent Interview Form. Child interviewers conduct the screenings of individual children and record and score children's responses to the various tasks at the perceptual-motor, cognitive-verbal, and gross motor stations. These interviewers also note the child's behavioral and social-emotional development. Speech and expressive language interviewers should be speech-language pathologists, and these individuals collect and analyze elicited language samples, including recognizing voice and fluency disorders, and discriminating between dialect variations and language disorders. Likewise, the hearing and vision team should include professionals, but may consist of properly trained paraprofessionals. The Administrator's Manual (p. 21) indicates that, with a staff of seven to nine, about 60 children could be screened in 3 hours (80 children in 4 hours).

Screening consists of a brief series of tasks that the child interviewer presents to the child. These tasks are scored Pass or Fail. Overall results, based on the child's cumulative performance in each of the areas assessed results in a rating of Pass, or Review, or Evaluate. Children rated Pass have satisfactorily completed the screening, and evidence no notable problems. Those rated Evaluate are deemed to need a full, professionally conducted evaluation because their "behaviors reveal a high probability of need for special assistance" (Administrator's Manual, p. 8). Those rated Review generally have not performed well in one area, and may need to be evaluated or rescreened in that area. The team determines ratings.

Both the Administrator's and Interviewer's Manuals offer detailed, generally well-written, directives for all aspects of screening, but some information is ambiguous. For example, it is not clear if one child interviewer conducts all screening of one child, moving with the child from station to station, or if a different interviewer is present at each station. Also, the Administrator's Manual (p. 17) directs that "Each child should be administered the tasks that correspond to his or her age in months. If at all possible, it is important to screen the child at one age level *above* his or her actual age." For a child having difficulty, it might be more appropriate to screen at one age level below his or her actual age.

Tasks used in the screening seem appropriate and are consistent with the types of tasks typically used in preschool assessment instruments. However, notable in its absence is any assessment of the self-help behaviors commonly found in such instruments. The author states this area was omitted because "it is believed that children who are delayed in the self-help area will also manifest important delays in one or more of the areas that are screened by CIP" (Administrator's Manual, p. 6).

Little is offered to suggest that this "revised" edition provides anything new since its initial development in the 1970s. The rationale for the CIP focuses on research from the 1970s and citations are virtually all from the 1950s through 1970s. More important, empirical support for all significant aspects of the instrument is practically nonexistent. Specifically, no data are offered to support the specific item selection and assignment of items to particular age levels. No evidence is offered for the validity of the items or the instrument or the ratings. One might reasonably expect that a preschool screening instrument might provide at least some evidence of both concurrent and predictive criterion-related validity, but none is offered. No evidence is offered for the reliability of the instrument. With a screening instrument that employs several individuals, interrater reliability is of particular concern, yet no mention is made of any type of reliability. No norms are provided, although some detail is offered on numbers of children used in the initial development of the instrument. However, almost no demographic data on this initial group are offered. And, apparently no attempt has been made to select a new sample of children for the revision.

SUMMARY. The CIP [Revised] offers nothing new; avoids addressing current regulations affecting special education services; omits an important aspect of screening (self-help) that other, more recently developed or revised screening instruments provide; and offers no norms, no evidence of validity or reliability of any kind, and no empirical support for its use. Clearly, other instruments, such as Developmental Indicators for the Assessment of Learning (DIAL; 116) in its more recent revisions, are superior for screening preschool children at risk of needing special educational programs.

Comprehensive Personality Profile.

Purpose: "To identify individuals with personality traits that are compatible with both occupational and organizational demands."
Population: Adults.
Publication Date: 1985–1998.
Acronym: CPP.
Scores, 17: Primary Scales (Emotional Intensity, Intuition, Recognition Motivation, Sensitivity, Assertiveness, Trust, Exaggeration), Secondary Traits (Ego Drive, Interpersonal Warmth, Stability, Empathy, Objectivity, Independence, Aggressiveness, Decisiveness, Tolerance, Efficiency).
Administration: Group or individual.
Price Data, 2000: $125 per 5 kits including manual ('99, 105 pages), 5 questionnaires(quantity discounts available), and PC compatible scoring software or fax scoring.
Time: (15–25) minutes.
Comments: Also available in French and Spanish; title on questionnaire is CPP Compatibility Questionnaire.
Authors: Wonderlic, Inc. and Larry L. Craft (questionnaire).
Publisher: Wonderlic, Inc.
Cross References: See T4:617 (1 reference).

Review of the Comprehensive Personality Profile by SANFORD J. COHN, Professor, Division of Curriculum and Instruction, Arizona State University, Tempe, AZ:

The Comprehensive Personality Profile (CPP) is a personality profiling system designed to assess the degree of compatibility of individuals for specific jobs. It was derived through the use of factor analytic techniques. The authors recommend four uses for the CPP: employee selection, improvement of management effectiveness, employee development, and communication and team building. Although the title suggests a very broad application, the instrument is, in fact, intended for use in selecting and enhancing employees who have a lot of contact with customers, that is, employees in sales and service industries.

The CPP consists of four components: the CPP Questionnaire, the CPP Program Software, the Scoring Diskette, and the CPP Reports. The CPP Questionnaire consists of 88 true/false items that focus on the examinee's description of themselves, their feelings, and their preferences. This questionnaire can be administered manually, using the paper-and-pencil version, or via computer, using the CPP software, which guides the administrator through each step of the assessment process. Administration usually takes less than 30 minutes. Candidates must complete every item and mark a True or False response for both the Ideal and Real columns for each statement. Ideal CPP scores describe what the candidate feels is important for success in a given position, whereas Real CPP scores describe the candidate's personal characteristics. Five separate printout reports are available, each describing the examinee's personality from a different perspective: selection criteria, supervisory considerations, sales managers, sales training, and personal development (self-report).

Detailed directions are provided in the test manual for the installation and use of the program software. This reviewer examined the paper-and-pencil version of the questionnaire, which requires the administrator to transcribe examinees' responses into a computer-monitor screen for that purpose, included as part of the software package.

CPP results are broken down into 7 Primary and 10 Secondary personality traits, which the authors define as "consistent patterns of thoughts, feelings, or actions that individualize people" and are said to account "for much of the regularity and consistency in an individual's behavior both on and off the job" (user's manual, p. 31). The 7 Primary traits and their descriptions are provided in the manual.

Emotional Intensity (E)—assesses physical, mental, and social intensity levels (high scoring individuals are excitable and restless, whereas low scoring individuals are persistent and even-paced).

Intuition (I)—measures the degree to which a person relies upon experience and feelings to make decisions to solve a problem (high scorers tend to dislike detailed analysis of complex subject matter, whereas low scorers tend to use an analytical approach to problem solving).

Recognition Motivation (R)—assesses the need for status, prestige, or acknowledgement (high scorers are dependent on consistent feedback from others, whereas low scorers seek activities that provide private recognition and self-respect).

Sensitivity (S)—describes the degree to which an individual expressively demonstrates warmth and caring (high scorers are actively involved in helping and nurturing others, whereas low scorers are controlled and private).

Assertiveness (A)—measures the ability to influence the action of others (high scorers confi-

dently assert themselves, whereas low scorers have difficulty saying "no" when confronted).

Trust (T)—measures the individual's perception of the outside world (high scorers are open and trustworthy, whereas low scorers are skeptical).

Exaggeration (X)—assesses the degree to which the examinee is exaggerating strengths or downplaying weaknesses in order to appear more favorable to the job interviewer; it also serves to provide evidence of validity of the questionnaire (high scorers are intentionally or unintentionally presenting a more favorable image regarding conformity, self-control, or moral values, whereas low scorers are being more forthright and critical of their personal qualities).

The CPP also provides scales of 10 Secondary Traits, which, unlike the 7 Primary Traits, were created on the basis of experience, observations, and peer literature review, as opposed to a factor analytical process. The 10 Secondary Traits involve interacting combinations of the 7 Primary Traits: Ego Drive, Interpersonal Warmth, Stability, Empathy, Objectivity, Independence, Aggressiveness, Decisiveness, Tolerance, and Efficiency. In addition to these traits, the CPP applies additional combinations of Primary Traits to predict specific management, sales, and administrative performance.

The CPP reports interpret the Primary scale scores in terms of three interaction profiles, each reflecting the combination of two scale scores. For example, Temperament represents the interaction of the Emotional Intensity and Intuition scales. A median split appears to be the basis of deciding where on each scale an individual falls, which in turn determines which quadrant (Temperament Style: Intense, Active, Passive, or Easy-Going) is most descriptive of the examinee. In addition to the Temperament Style, the CPP yields an Ego Style and a Social Style. It must be noted that there is a distinct problem inherent in the use of the median split to categorize individuals. The median typically is the point in a normal distribution that contains the greatest number of scores. Given that imperfect reliability of any instrument results in errors of categorization, the median is often the place at which this error can influence the most possible scores.

The CPP uses a quadrant system to categorize each examinee's overall results into four personality types: Driver, Motivator, Thinker, and

Supporter. For each of these Personality Types, the CPP report provides a description, strengths, weaknesses, and career directions.

The CPP questionnaire asks examinees to respond to the items in the ideal case and the real case. The Ideal CPP scores do not describe the examinee's personality traits, but rather they describe what the candidate thinks is important for success in a given position. These scores provide administrators with potentially useful insight into the candidate's perception about the job for which he or she is applying. These perceptions in turn can be compared with the examinee's Real CPP scores. An Ideal/Real Match Percentage can be calculated by dividing the number of CPP items to which the candidate responded the same for both the Ideal and Real by the number responded to differently. This percentage is useful in describing the overall degree to which the candidate's impression of the job matches the candidate's personal characteristics. The higher the percentage, the greater the degree to which the candidate's personality is compatible with the demands of the job.

The CPP also provides an Accuracy Index to address the validity of an individual's results. This Index is affected by several CPP components including specific faking items, item contradiction, high exaggeration, and high Ideal/Real Match Percentages. The lower the Accuracy Index (on a scale from 0 to 10), the less valid the CPP results. The higher the Index, the more straightforward and frank the candidate was in completing the CPP questionnaire.

DEVELOPMENT. Over 400 personality and motivational assessment statements were examined to generate the 88-item CPP questionnaire. These statements addressed core, underlying, fundamental personality traits. Every effort was made by the development team to meet the rigid requirements of the American Psychological Association *Standards for Educational and Psychological Testing* (AERA, APA, & NCME, 1999). By 1998, more than 40,000 employees, job applicants, and students had been profiled using the CPP.

Four main considerations drove the development of the CPP questionnaire. The questionnaire had to be reliable and valid, job related, practical to administer, and fair.

The norm reference group consisted of 1,350 employees, job applicants, and business technology students. This group was equally distributed by gender and included 12% nonwhite occupational representatives.

RELIABILITY AND VALIDITY. CPP profiles needed to be reliable, that is, they needed to be relatively uninfluenced by transitory factors, such as fatigue, anger, or depression. CPP profiles also needed to be valid, that is, they had to be subjected to intense scrutiny to determine that they in fact measure the constructs they are purported to measure, and support intended interpretations and use.

The average estimate of internal reliability (Cronbach's alpha) was .78, ranging from .73 to .85. These statistics were based on 30,826 administrations. The average estimate of test-retest reliability over a 6-week interval was .77, ranging from .65 to .85. The test-retest statistics were based on a sample of 67 university students and 61 personnel consultants.

The reliability of this measure is also enhanced by the safeguards built in to signal attempts by examinees to distort their responses and bias scales in their favor.

Validity studies have centered on correlations with other personality measures, such as the 16PF and the Myers-Briggs Type Indicator (MBTI), as well as with specific scales from the Millon Clinical Multiaxial Inventory. In these studies, the constructs underlying the CPP have been supported in both convergent and divergent directions.

Criterion-related validity has been examined in numerous research studies. The test publishers, moreover, continue to collect validity data from organizations that employ the CPP and that agree to provide data for such studies (over 40,000 administrations as of 1998). Criteria against which performance on the CPP has been evaluated include sales productivity, work quality, and other aspects of job performance. An extensive set of appendices to the manual provide detailed discussion of a number of validity studies.

JOB-RELATED. Criterion-related validity evidence also addressed the degree to which the CPP was job-related in a study conducted in 1995. Five hundred and twenty organizations provided over 42,000 questionnaire results. The organizations' job titles were then linked to the Department of Labor's Dictionary of Occupational Titles (DOT). As a result of this study, the User's Manual introduced the Job Description Questionnaire (JDQ). The JDQ allows a hiring manager to evaluate the worker requirements of virtually any position. It aids in identifying job-related knowledge, skills, and abilities, and defining the target score ranges on the CPP that indicate a match between the job and the job candidate.

PRACTICAL TO ADMINISTER. The CPP requires the examinee to answer 88 true/false items in two contexts (Ideal and Real). It can be administered to groups via paper and pencil and to individual's via computer. Administration requires about 30 minutes. The interpretive structure of the CPP results in no experience being required to use the questionnaire and to interpret the profile results.

FAIRNESS. The examination of the fairness of the CPP included considerations of examinees' comfort and the likelihood that they would provide honest, thoughtful responses. To ensure these conditions, items selected for the questionnaire were noninvasive. Statistical analyses were conducted to determine the impact the CPP might have on protected groups, such as the rates at which members of protected groups were hired. Results indicated unfair impact if members of protected groups were hired at a rate less than 4/5 the majority hiring rate. Adverse impact studies also examined gender effects. Adverse impact was found only when a high number of scales (>5) were employed in selection cutoff procedures. Sex, age, race, and education were factors addressed by adverse impact studies.

SUMMARY. The CPP does indeed appear to be a useful test to aid in a number of human resources applications with the sales and service industries. It has been developed by a test-development group of long standing and excellent repute. It meets the excellent criteria against which it was evaluated. Reliability and validity evidence is presented through compelling results from numerous studies. The degree to which it is job-related is clearly established by means of its linkage to the Dictionary of Occupational Titles in a massive study that incorporated data from over 40,000 administrations by 520 companies. Little more could be done to make the CPP easier or more practical to administer and to interpret. The measure has been examined to determine potential adverse impact on members of protected groups. Factors studied include sex, age, race, and education.

REVIEWER'S REFERENCE

American Educational Research Association, American Psychological Association, & National Council on Measurement in Education. (1999). *Standards for educational and psychological testing.* Washington, DC: American Educational Research Association.

Review of the Comprehensive Personality Profile by IRA STUART KATZ, Clinical Psychologist, California Department of Corrections, Salinas Valley State Prison, Soledad, CA, and Licensed Clinical Psychologist, Private Practice, Salinas, CA:

A good man or woman is hard to find and keep, especially in Corporate America today. More than ever employers are seeking to attract and retain the best people to maintain a competitive edge and survive in the 21st century. The search for an easy-to-use, cost-effective, and meaningful instrument that is a win-win for prospective and current employees may have ended. Welcome the Comprehensive Personality Profile (CPP) to the plethora of organizational selection, retention, and team building instruments.

Can one instrument be all things to all people? Can one instrument help employers with attracting and retaining the best of the best sales personnel and help nurture team building and organizational integrity, too? That is a tall order for any instrument. How does the Comprehensive Personality Profile measure up? Let us find out.

The Comprehensive Personality Profile (CPP) is an 88-question instrument that is based on a factor-analytically derived personality system designed to assess adult personality in terms of job compatibility. It was developed by Larry L. Craft, Ph.D. Dr. Craft developed the instrument based on his experience as a human resource professional in the insurance industry. Using factor analysis based on over 40,000 candidates from a wide variety of positions, he identified traits of drive and motivation that he felt were critical to success in sales occupations. There immediately is some question about the generalizability of these data to other jobs and positions. That will be further discussed later in this review.

Dr. Craft isolated 7 personality traits that he felt were important to understanding an individual's behavior on and off the job. He also identified 10 secondary traits.

The CPP measures 7 Primary and 10 Secondary personality traits (factors). Dr. Craft believes that the Primary traits (Emotional Intensity, Intuition, Recognition Motivation, Sensitivity, Assertiveness, Trust, Exaggeration) and the Secondary traits (Ego Drive, Interpersonal Warmth, Stability, Empathy, Objectivity, Independence, Aggressiveness, Decisiveness, Tolerance, Efficiency) are unique and critical, yet often overlooked. The components of the CPP are most user-friendly.

The CPP is composed of the CPP Questionnaire, CPP Program Software, Scoring Diskette, and CPP Reports. Of significance here are the reports that describe the candidates' personalities in terms of selection criteria, supervisory considerations, sales performance, sales training, and personal development. To get to those points the data collected from the input document are broken out into four distinct personality types. It is important to note how the CPP defines personality in terms of understanding and interpreting CPP scores. For the CPP, personality traits are consistent patterns of thoughts, feelings, or actions that individualize people. These patterns are described in the CPP in terms of primary, Secondary, and Interaction traits. These traits are supposed to account for much of the regularity and consistency in an individual's behavior both on or off the job. The Interaction Profiles that are generated yield three interaction traits: (a) *Temperament*—which is seen as intense-active-passive or easy-going, (b) *Ego Style*—which is seen as proud-agreeable-aloof-genuine, or (c) *Social Style*—which is seen as Dominant-Sociable-Cautious-Compliant. Finally, the CPP uses a quadrant system to categorize each candidate's overall CPP results into four personality types: Driver, Motivator, Thinker, and Supporter. Each of these traits is further interpreted and evaluated on the basis of strengths, weaknesses, and career directions. This is a worthy and helpful placement tool. The last feature of psychometric note is the Ideal/Real Match Percentage.

The Ideal/Real Match Percentage is a calculation of dividing the number of CPP items to which the candidate responded the same for both the Ideal and Real by the number responded to differently (i.e., Ideal = T, Real = T vs. Ideal = T, Real = F). Specifically, Item 1 on the CPP asks the respondent to answer True (T) or False (F) to both IDEAL and REAL for this question: "1. I believe I would enjoy the independence, excitement, and risk that is associated with owning my own business." This is a good question to determine a candidate's potential for a career in sales. Consistency and/or inconsistency in response to the query should be helpful and/or an overall job placement assessment guide.

The strength of the CPP is in its limits. No one personality trait measure can be all things to all people. The CPP is not the Myers-Briggs Type Indicator (Briggs & Myers, 1998; 251), the Revised NEO Personality Inventory (Costa & McCrae, 1992; T5:2218), or the Millon Index of Personality Styles (Millon, 1994; T5:1688). It does share some common psychometric genealogy with all of them, but it is in some ways far more practical, yet limited.

The Comprehensive Personality Profile User's Manual does a good job of orienting the user to the mechanics of the instrument and the philosophical system on which it is based. It has a ways to go to convince this reviewer of the technical properties of the instrument based on what is read and available in the manual. Although there is reference to a normative data base of 500 positions in over 500 organizations, and the utilization of the *Dictionary of Occupational Titles* (DOT), there is still too much an element of mystery in the psychometric basis for the scores. Are we talking about sales positions per se, or are we seeking to have the instrument be used with other kinds of work? I am not convinced this instrument can easily be generalizable. At least that is not clear from this otherwise excellent manual that is written mostly in layman's terms. This is a plus because that will truly make it practical to administrators. Finally, the CPP is eminently fair. The items used are noninvasive, well thought out, clearly written, and should generate honest and thoughtful responses. The statistical analysis conducted regarding protected groups is also reassuring.

Overall, this reviewer believes that the CPP is fair and sensitive to the needs and concerns of both organizations and individuals. There are a number of uses for the CPP that also bear some reflection and analysis. The CPP shows real potential to be used to promote organizational communication and team building. Specifically, having the data generated from the CPP, corporate trainers and organizational development specialists would be able to utilize the various profile clusters to ensure that team formation and team conflict can be addressed in a defined and discreet manner as opposed to helter-skelter gut-shots. Blending the strengths and building out of trait diversity offers much potential. Team building utilizing the data generated by primary traits can be more focused and productive. The development and validation of the Job Description Questionnaire is a valuable adjunct to the CPP for the organizational decision maker, enabling a far more precise match between job-related competencies and individual test results. The Target Selection Report that is part of the CPP package displays ideal and acceptable selection ranges for each of the seven Primary traits of the CPP. This is another strength in this package.

Finally, in the Appendix of the manual, correlations with the Myers-Briggs Type Indicator and the Millon Clinical Multiaxial Inventory were presented. Statistical complementarity was somewhat limited and discouraging. Most compelling in the Appendix were the CPP Case Studies. These studies provide further support of the CPP in selection of sales and other personnel.

Once again, the overall data were strongest for selecting sale personnel. Yet there was some value in the study of Telecommunications/Dispatchers where a stepwise regression analysis was performed to determine criterion variance accounted for by CPP scores. A multiple r of .31 (p<.01) was obtained, resulting from strong criterion relationships for three of the seven CPP scales: Trust, Intuition, and Sensitivity. The results provided evidence that Trust, Intuition, and Sensitivity did predict job performance and turnover for public safety Telecommunication/Dispatchers. In fairness, the CPP is a fairly new instrument. Perhaps other studies will show more utilization and generalizability to nonsales type jobs. The early results are encouraging.

SUMMARY. The comprehensive Personality Profile is not all things to all people. It has both strengths and limitations. As a fairly user-friendly instrument for attracting, motivating, and retaining top-flight sales personnel, the CPP has much to offer. It can be hoped that further revisions of the instrument and the manual will reflect on some of its current limitations addressed above and make it even more a valuable standout in this overcrowded field. The CPP is a welcome and needed addition.

REVIEWER'S REFERENCES

Costa, P. T., Jr., & McCrae, R. R. (1992). The Revised NEO Personality Inventory. Odessa, FL: Psychological Assessment Resources, Inc.
Millon, T. (1994). Millon Index of Personality Styles. San Antonio, TX: The Psychological Corporation.
Briggs, K. C., & Myers, I. B. (1998). The Myers-Briggs Type Indicator, Form M. Palo Alto, CA: Consulting Psychologists Press, Inc.

[93]
Comprehensive Receptive and Expressive Vocabulary Test—Adult.

Purpose: To assess receptive and expressive oral vocabulary.
Population: Ages 18-0 to 89-11.
Publication Dates: 1994–1997.
Acronym: CREVT-A.
Scores, 3: Receptive Vocabulary, Expressive Vocabulary, Total.
Administration: Individual.
Price Data, 1999: $174 per complete kit.
Time: (20–30) minutes.
Comments: Youth version (CREVT; T5:655) available; two equivalent forms included in testing kit.
Authors: Gerald Wallace and Donald D. Hammill.
Publisher: PRO-ED.

Review of the Comprehensive Receptive and Expressive Vocabulary Test—Adult by MARGARET E. MALONE, Language Testing Specialist, Peace Corps, Washington, DC:

The Comprehensive Receptive and Expressive Vocabulary Test—Adult (CREVT-A) is designed for several purposes: to identify adults whose vocabulary development lags below their peers; to identify differences between expressive and receptive vocabulary skills; to measure progress in vocabulary development for program use; and for application to vocabulary use in research studies. According to the test booklet, this test can be used with adults between the ages of 18 and 89 who can understand the directions and speak English. This information points to the test's greatest downfall: the lack of information for applicability with non-native speakers of English. The test developers state that the test should not be used with the deaf or with people who speak no English, but make no reference to level of English language proficiency necessary to take this test.

The test has two forms, A and B. Each form includes a picture book with color photographs, an examiner's manual, and a preprinted record form for the examiner to complete. The picture book is used to conduct the test, and all answers are recorded by the examiner on the record form. Each form has two subtests, one for receptive vocabulary, or the examinee's ability to identify the picture that goes with the word spoken by the examiner, and one for expressive vocabulary. The directions are clear and easy to follow.

The test was normed on a sample of 778 adults from seven states and the District of Columbia. The sample was intended to be stratified to include appropriate samples of age, gender, race (African-American/White/Other), and ethnicity (African American, Hispanic, Asian, Native American, and Other). In addition, the population was stratified by urban/rural populations and included representation from the Northeast, North Central, South, and West. The population was intended to form a representative sample of the 1990 U.S. Census. The sample did not include representation from the Northwest, Midwest, or Southwest areas of the country.

The norming involved both reliability and validity studies. Reliability was investigated in several ways, including scorer reliability, alternate form reliability, and test/retest reliability. The interrater reliability estimate was .99 for both subtests. However, this coefficient is not based on the norming sample, but instead on a study conducted on 24 tests from the sample, each rated by two different members of the research team. Although this reliability estimate is indeed high, it applied only to a small part of the norming sample.

Test/retest reliability was also measured on a small subsample of the norming population. Over a 2-week period, 24 examinees took one form of the CREVT-A twice. Test/retest coefficients ranged from .84–.87. Again, this is a high correlation, but the sample size (12) for each form of the test was quite small. Overall, although the reported reliability coefficients are high, the sample on which reliability was tested was very small to be considered for generalizability.

After estimating the reliability coefficients of the test, the test was investigated for content and construct validity. Content validity was considered by examining test format and test items. Test format was construed as being appropriate because it was similar to formats of other vocabulary tests. In addition, the format of receptive vocabulary (identifying the picture that corresponds to a word) was considered a valid way of showing vocabulary understanding. Similarly, the expressive vocabulary subtest was considered valid because it allows examinees to speak at length to describe a vocabulary word.

To examine the test's construct validity, the test developers compared the scores on the subtests of the CREVT to each other, as well as compared scores of tests of intellectual abilities to the CREVT. The subtests do not correlate very highly; the correlations ranged from .56–.66. Additional investigations of construct ability were somewhat problematic. One study examined the performance of 26 examinees on the CREVT-A. These 26 examinees were selected because they had been classified as having low mental ability according to their performance on the Comprehensive Test of Nonverbal Intelligence. The study found that these 26 examinees had relatively lower scores on the CREVT-A than other examinees. Scores of 496 examinees on the CREVT-A were also compared to scores of the same examinees on the CTONI (Comprehensive Test of Nonverbal Intelligence). The correlations between these tests were quite low—.30–.53. The examiner's manual, however, states that the coefficients are highly significant, which is not really accurate.

In addition to investigating the content and construct validity of the test, the developers also investigated the test for gender and racial bias. The results indicated little or no gender or racial bias on the test.

SUMMARY. The test has many good features: the test booklet including vivid photographs, high scorer reliability, an excellent norm group stratification, low racial and gender bias, ease of administration, and clear directions. The test booklet is well laid-out and colorful. Its only drawback is that some of the photographs show rather outdated equipment. The scorer reliability and test reliability estimates are also high, although the method used to elicit this reliability included only a very small subsample (24) of test takers. This number is not large enough nor sufficiently well stratified to make broad generalizations.

Additional weaknesses of the test include the initial stratification and the validation studies. This test was normed on 798 speakers of English. However, the test developers do not differentiate among those examinees with different levels of English language proficiency. The test is clearly inappropriate, as stated in the test booklet, for those who do not speak English as a first language. However, no guidance is given on its appropriateness for use with non-native speakers of English, who constitute a part of the adult population in the United States. In addition, though the test was examined for bias on a white/nonwhite basis, it did not look into any bias among subgroups or ethnic groups.

The validation study is also troublesome. The content validity study was acceptable; it examined the test content in a thorough manner and cross-referenced scoring with the *Word Frequency Guide Book*. Though this book is quite out-of-date (1971), it nonetheless provided a reasonable methodology. The construct validation study was not as well constructed. First, the correlation between subtests was considered "high" when it actually ranged from .29–.73. Second, the study of group differences was troublesome. The 26 adults were preclassified as having low mental ability, but the examiner's manual does not specify how this classification was made. Finally, the comparison of scores between the CREVT-A and the CTONI was questionable. The correlations were quite low, and actually suggest that the two tests measure different abilities.

In sum, though the test has many strong characteristics, its construct validity is weak. In addition, the lack of direction in test applicability for nonnative speakers of English makes it unusable for many groups.

Review of the Comprehensive Receptive and Expressive Vocabulary Test—Adult by WAYNE H. SLATER, Associate Professor, Department of Curriculum and Instruction, University of Maryland, College Park, MD:

The Comprehensive Receptive and Expressive Vocabulary Test—Adult (CREVT-A), available in two equivalent forms, measures both receptive and expressive oral vocabulary. It is appropriate for use with individuals between the ages of 18-0 and 89-11. According to the examiner's manual, the CREVT-A has four major uses: (a) to identify individuals who are significantly below their peers in oral vocabulary proficiency, (b) to determine any discrepancy between receptive and expressive oral vocabulary skills, (c) to map progress in oral vocabulary development as a consequence of special intervention programs, and (d) to measure oral vocabulary in research studies. Individuals taking this test must be able to understand the directions of the subtests, must be able to formulate the necessary responses, and must be able to speak English. The CREVT-A should not be administered to people who are deaf or who speak no English.

According to the authors, the CREVT-A has four distinctive features: (a) Both receptive and expressive vocabulary are measured; (b) the scores for the receptive and expressive vocabulary subtests are based on the same normative sample; (c) the words assembled for both the receptive and expressive vocabulary subtests map onto the same 10 categories (animals, transportation, occupa-

tions, clothing, foods, personal grooming, tools, household appliances, recreation, and clerical materials) that the authors argue represent knowledge areas familiar to most people; and (d) the use of color photographs on the receptive vocabulary test is in contrast to the black-and-white drawings used in other vocabulary tests.

The CREVT-A consists of two subtests. The format of Subtest I, Receptive Vocabulary, is a variation of the familiar point-to-the-picture-of-the-word-I-say procedure. The examiner says a series of stimulus words, one at a time, and after each word the examinee selects from six pictures the one that best represents the stimulus word. This subtest is made up of 10 plates, each of which has six pictures. All of the pictures on a plate relate to one of the 10 categories mentioned earlier (e.g., animals, transportation, occupations, clothing). The format of Subtest II, Expressive Vocabulary, is based on the premise, if you want to determine if a person knows the meaning of a word, ask that person to define the word. According to the authors, this procedure reduces guessing to a minimum and permits the assessment of the depth of one's lexical knowledge. Because this approach requires the subject to describe the stimulus word in some detail, the authors argue it is ideal for an expressive vocabulary test. At a minimum the subject's response may be a one-word synonym, but more often it is an elaboration that includes characteristics, functions, and discriminating elements that relate to the stimulus words. The words on Subtest II are mapped onto the same 10 categories that are measured on Subtest I, Receptive Vocabulary (e.g., animals, transportation, occupations, clothing). No time limits are imposed on this test. The time required to give both subtests varies from 20 to 30 minutes. The Receptive Vocabulary and Expressive Vocabulary subtests rarely take more than 10 to 15 minutes each to administer.

The appropriate use of ceilings is an essential part of administering the CREVT-A. For the Receptive Vocabulary subtest, every subject begins with Item 1 and proceeds until he or she misses two items in a row (the ceiling). Scoring is fairly straightforward. The subject receives 1 point for every item passed before reaching the ceiling. Any items mistakenly given above the ceiling are scored as 0, no pass. On the Expressive Vocabulary subtest, testing also begins with the first item. The ceiling is three items missed in a row. Because the examiner may assume that any items above the ceiling would have been answered incorrectly, all items above the ceiling are automatically scored as incorrect. If for some reason items are given above the ceiling, any items that are passed are scored as incorrect.

The CREVT-A provides four types of scores: raw scores, standard scores for the subtests and composite, and percentiles. The raw scores is the total number of points that the subject earns for the items of a subtest. The standard scores provide the clearest indication of a subject's CREVT-A performance. Based on a normal distribution with a mean of 100 and a standard deviation of 15, standard scores for the subtests are converted from raw scores using the appropriate tables included in the examiner's manual. Standard scores for the composite are found by pooling the standard scores of the subtests and converting that value using the appropriate tables included in the examiner's manual. Standard scores allow the examiner to make comparisons between the CREVT-A subtests. Finally, percentiles, or percentile ranks can be obtained by converting standard scores for the subtests and composite using the appropriate tables in the examiner's manual.

The authors provide a fairly straightforward examiner's manual for the CREVT-A. It includes the following sections: Rationale and Overview, Information to Consider Before Testing, Administration and Scoring Procedures, Interpreting the CREVT-A's Results, Normative Procedures, Test Reliability, Validity of Test Results, Controlling for Bias, References, and Normative Tables. The Rationale and Overview needs to be updated and reworked significantly by including important insights from recent research, especially the work of Richard C. Anderson, Isabel L. Beck, Michael F. Graves, and William E. Nagy. In the section on Normative Procedures, the authors do not provide us with sufficient information on the precise selection criteria used to choose standardization sites and the 778 subjects tested (Anastasi & Urbina, 1997). At the same time, the authors build a case for the representativeness of their normative sample with regard to residence, race, ethnicity, geographic area, and family income by comparing their sample's percentages with those reported in the *Statistical Abstract of the United States* (U.S. Bureau of the Census, 1990).

SUMMARY. To conclude, this reviewer cautiously recommends the use of the Comprehensive Receptive and Expressive Vocabulary Test—Adult (CREVT-A) as an initial assessment of oral vocabulary for the following purposes (a) identification, (b) noting discrepancies between receptive and expressive oral vocabulary, (c) documentation of progress, and (d) research. The results of the CREVT-A may be useful in documenting a person's level of performance in oral vocabulary. If a person is found to be deficient in oral vocabulary on the CREVT-A, the examiner will need to refer him or her for more in-depth diagnostic procedures. The results of the CREVT-A may also be useful in determining any differences between a person's receptive and expressive oral vocabulary. If the problem identified is a general vocabulary deficit or if a deficiency exists in only the receptive or expressive modality, the CREVT-A may contribute important information to the diagnostic effort. The examiner will need to administer additional informal and formal assessments before any definitive conclusions can be drawn about an individual's oral vocabulary status. The third potential use is to provide clinicians, teachers, and administrators with a means of documenting a person's progress in remedial or other instructional programs. Again, the CREVT-A should be used with other informal and formal assessments for this purpose. Finally, the CREVT-A may serve as a valuable research tool, when used in concert with other informal and formal assessments, for investigators examining oral vocabulary development.

REVIEWER'S REFERENCE

Anastasi, A., & Urbina, S. (1997). *Psychological testing* (7th ed.). Upper Saddle River, NJ: Prentice Hall.

[94]

Computer-Based Test of English as a Foreign Language and Test of Written English.

Purpose: "To evaluate the English proficiency of people whose native language is not English."
Population: University and college applicants.
Publication Dates: 1964–1999.
Acronym: TOEFL, TWE.
Scores, 5: Listening, Structure, Reading, Writing, Test of Written English Score.
Administration: Group.
Price Data, 1999: (The following prices apply to quantities of 1–9 items; quantity discounts available on larger orders): $15 each for TOEFL Sampler CD ROM; $47 each for Test Preparation Kit, 2nd Edition; $16 each for Volume 1 paper-based Practice Tests; $24 each for Volume 2 paper-based Practice Tests; $14 each

for Volume 2 computer-based Practice Tests; $32 each for Volume 2 computer-based Practice Tests; $8 each for TOEFL Sample Test, 6th Ed.; $100 fee for taking Computer-Based TOEFL test.
Time: (155–205) minutes for TOEFL; 30 (35) minutes for TWE.
Comments: Tests administered at centers designated by the publisher; computer-based testing available throughout the year by appointment at centers in the U.S. and most countries; candidates may take the test not more than once a month; TOEFL may be administered separately but TWE given only in conjunction with TOEFL test at specific annually determined combined administrations; as of July 1998, the TOEFL program has gone to a computer-based delivery; the paper-based TOEFL/TWE is currently offered in limited areas (primarily in Asia); the paper-based TOEFL/TWE will be phased out (target date: 2000).
Authors: Jointly sponsored by College Entrance Examination Board, Graduate Records Examination Board, and Educational Testing Service.
Publisher: Educational Testing Service.
Cross References: See T5:666 (15 references) and T4:2757 (12 references); for reviews by Brenda H. Loyd and Kikumi K. Tatsuoka of an earlier edition of the TOEFL, see 9:1257 (1 reference); see also T3:2441 (9 references), 8:110 (15 references), and T2:238 (4 references); for reviews by Clinton I. Chase and George Domino of earlier forms, see 7:266 (10 references).

Review of the Computer-Based Test of English as a Foreign Language and the Test of Written English by R. J. DE AYALA, Associate Professor of Educational Psychology, University of Nebraska— Lincoln, Lincoln, NE:

The Computer-Based Test of English as a Foreign Language (TOEFL) and the Test of Written English (TWE) are examinations designed to measure an examinee's proficiency in English and his or her ability to write in English, respectively. In both cases these tests were designed to measure these proficiencies for individuals whose native language is not English and for students at the 11th grade level or above. Documentation provided described the development of the paper-based TOEFL questions and its various sections, Listening Comprehension, Structure and Written Expression, and Reading Comprehension. This development includes the use of language specialists for question writing, ETS test development specialists, review of all item specifications, questions, and final test forms for cultural and racial bias as well as content appropriateness. All test questions are pretested on representative groups of international groups of nonnative English-speaking students. Subsequent to the administration of each new form, statistical analyses are conducted in order to monitor the level of difficulty of the test, the reliability of the scores on the entire test and of each section, intercorrelations among sections, and time allotment. ETS documentation references a number of studies addressing content, criterion-related, and construct validity of the paper-based TOEFL.

As part of the TOEFL 2000 project, the TOEFL's administration was made computer-based (CBT) in July 1998. Although some of the questions on the CBT are similar to those found on the paper-based test, others utilize the multimedia capabilities in order to more closely reflect "real world" situations. For instance, photos and graphics are used to create context, as well as to complement and support the content of the listening stimuli. In addition, whereas the paper-based TOEFL consisted of multiple-choice questions, the CBT TOEFL utilizes multiple-choice questions, constructed-response items, and a Writing section that measures an examinee's ability to generate standard written English. The CBT TOEFL consists of four sections: Listening, Structure, Reading, and Writing. Purported advantages of CBT include year-round testing (although individuals may only take the CBT TOEFL once per month), individual scheduling, and faster score reporting (e.g., examinees have the option of viewing unofficial test "scores" upon the CBT's completion). Administration of the CBT TOEFL is at Sylvan Technology Centers, at computer test centers at certain universities and colleges, at ETS offices in the United States, and via mobile test centers.

The CBT TOEFL includes computer-adaptive testing (CAT) components and a nonadaptive (so-called linear) test. In a CAT the test is "tailored" or adapted to the examinee's ability thereby allowing for fewer questions than with traditional paper-based tests. In contrast, linear tests administer the same set of questions to all examinees without regard for their abilities. The Listening Comprehension and Structure sections of the CBT TOEFL are adaptive; the Reading section is linear. The Writing (essay) section consists of one essay prompt and may be answered by an examinee typing his or her response on the computer or by handwriting the essay. It should be noted that because the Reading section is a linear test, examinees may skip or change answers to questions, whereas for the adaptive sections once the examinees confirm their answer to a question the may not go back and change the answer. In addition, in the CAT sections examinees are not allowed to skip questions. Another implication of the use of a CAT in the Listening Comprehension and Structure sections is that more credit is given for correctly answering a difficult question than for correctly answering an easy question. Therefore, the scores on these sections will be a function of the correctness of the answers to the section's questions as well as the number of questions answered. For the Reading section the examinee receives one raw score point for each correctly answered question regardless of its difficulty. All examinees receive a test of the same length, question types, content distribution, and time. Total administrative testing time is approximately 4.0 to 4.5 hours and includes a mandatory Tutorial (most examinees take about 40 minutes to complete, but allotted time is unlimited) and a 10-minute break, a Listening Comprehension portion (30–50 questions, 40–60 minutes), a Structure portion (20–25 questions, 15–20 minutes), a Reading portion (44–60 questions, 70–90 minutes), and the Writing section (1 prompt, 30 minutes). Therefore, the total number of questions on the CBT TOEFL ranges from 95 to 136 questions, whereas for the paper-based version there were at least 140 questions. For all CBT administrations examinees will listen to directions and questions over headphones; individuals will be able to adjust their audio volume. Deaf examinees (with appropriate documentation) are not administered the Listening section and are allowed interpreters for spoken directions (Rebecca Bacon, personal communication, May 17, 2000).

The Listening section is designed to assess an examinee's ability to understand spoken English and Contains multiple-choice questions, questions with two answers, matching/ordering of text or objects questions, and graphical selection items. For example, examinees are presented with one or more relevant photos/graphics (e.g., a professor delivering a lecture in front of a blackboard) and listen on headphones to the lecture or dialog (what the examinee hears also appears on the screen). Following the passage, the examinee is visually and aurally presented questions to answer. The Structure section is designed to measure an examinee's ability to recognize appropriately written English. Questions in this section ask the user to either select the correct answer to complete an incomplete sentence or to identify words or phrases that represent unacceptable English. The Writing section measures an examinee's ability to generate and organize ideas, and then to compose a response in English to an assigned topic. The essays are scored by two independent certified readers trained in the Online Scoring Network. Certified readers log onto the network, are calibrated, and view the examinees' written responses. All essays are rated on a 0 to 6 scale. (The scoring rubric is available at the TOEFL website, www.toefl.org.) The average of the ratings is the examinee's score on the essay. If the two raters assigned to rate the essay are more than one point apart on their ratings, then a third rater is utilized. For scoring purposes the examinee's score from the Structure section is combined with the Writing section to obtain a single Structure/Writing scaled score equally weighted by the two section scores. The Reading section requires the examinee to read and understand four to five passages of approximately 250–350 words and to answer 10 to 14 multiple-choice questions concerning each passage.

The computerized TOEFL is reported on a scale that is different than that used for the paper-based version. The use of a different scale for the CBT TOEFL, although inconvenient, is justified by the use of questions that are not directly comparable to those in the paper-based version (e.g., CBT questions that utilize the multimedia capability of the computer). The use of a different scale reinforces the differences between the CBT TOEFL and its paper version. In contrast to the paper-based TOEFL Total Score scale (i.e., 310 to 677 [prior to 1998 the scale was 200 to 677]; section scale scores from 31 to 68, but for the Reading Comprehension section the range was 31 to 67), the computerized version Total Score has a range from 0 to 300; 0 to 30 for each of the three sections. Because the scores on the computerized TOEFL are not considered equivalent to those on the paper-based version, the score standards that were established by institutions using the paper version of the test should not be applied to computerized TOEFL scores without consideration of these scale differences. In short, new score standards will need to be established. To facilitate the interpretation of the CBT TOEFL scores and the transition from paper-based to CBT, ETS compared the scores of 6,556 examinees who took both the paper and computer-based TOEFL tests between November 1997 and March 1998. The results of this study are available as a series of Concordance Tables. These tables relate the section and total scores for the paper version to those of the computerized-based score. Moreover, the concordance of score ranges for the paper and computerized scores are provided. These ranges are particularly useful because, as indicated by the nonperfect reliability estimates of the test, test scores are not perfect measures of ability. As such, it is possible to conceptualize that the examinee's actual ability falls within a range of observed scores (the breadth of the range being a function of the standard error of measurement). Therefore, the concordance ranges take into account the error of measurement and allow for the handling of situations where one computer-based score corresponds to more than one paper-based score. Once the CBT TOEFL becomes operational in a given country the traditional paper based version will no longer be offered. Therefore, the use of these tables is an interim solution for the transition from paper-based to CBT. When the transition to CBT TOEFL is completed it should no longer be necessary to refer to these tables.

In order to address individuals who are unfamiliar with CBT and/or computers, the TOEFL program distributes a TOEFL Sampler CD. (The Sampler is a shorter package than the PowerPrep package that is also available for the TOEFL.) The TOEFL Sampler CD is an instructional CD-ROM that includes animated instructions on basic computer skills needed for taking the test (e.g., how to use a mouse, scrolling), practice questions and review, listening and reading practice, and practice writing topics. In addition, because the Sampler is in English it offers the nonnative speaker an additional (forced) practice opportunity. A feature lacking from the Sampler that would be useful would be a timer that the user could enable (if desired) and that would allow the user to mimic the timing of the CBT TOEFL. The Sampler CD also does not have adaptive components. System requirements are either a Macintosh or Intel/Compatible chip microcomputer (for the Macintosh a 68040 processor or higher and for the Intel/Compatible chip platform a 486 processor or higher with Windows 3.1 or higher). Both platforms require a CD-ROM drive, 8 megabytes of

RAM, a mouse, sound capability (e.g., a sound card), a Latin-alphabet keyboard, and a monitor capable of displaying 640X480 (documentation indicates that the monitor should be color, but this reviewer executed the program on both color and gray-scale monitors and the program's display was legible on the gray-scale monitor). The Sampler CD-ROM may be purchased (as mentioned above), downloaded from the TOEFL web site for U.S. $8, www.toefl.org/cbprpmat.html#Sampler (the downloadable version does not contain all of the Listening review features found on the CD-ROM), or the examinee may, via the Internet, view noninteractive PDF files containing sample questions and writing topics. Examples of essays at each of the six scale points are available for examinees to download and review at www.toefl.org/cbprpmat.html#topics.

In contrast to the TOEFL Sampler CD, the PowerPrep package contains two timed CBTs using actual TOEFL questions (Todd Acker, personal communication, May 18, 2000) and is apparently designed to simulate the Intel/Compatible chip platform and has the same hardware requirements as the Sampler CD with the additional requirement of 26 megabytes of hard-disk storage. For examinees without access to a computer, ETS has produced a paper document, *Preparing Students for the Computer-Based TOEFL Test*, that allows examinees to at least obtain an idea of what the CBT TOEFL will be like. However, it is difficult to believe that on the basis of this paper document and the CBT's Tutorial at the time of examination, an examinee without any previous computer experience will be as prepared and feel as comfortable as someone who has access to a computer. Regardless, a study conducted by ETS found that after administering a specially designed tutorial and adjusting for English language proficiency (as measured by the paper-based TOEFL), there was no evidence of adverse effects on performance on the computer-based TOEFL (Kirsch, Jamieson, Taylor, & Eignor, 1998; Taylor, Jamieson, Eignor & Kirsch, 1998).

ETS presents estimated reliabilities and standard errors of measurement for section and total scaled scores based on data from computer-based test simulations. These reliability estimates were .87 for Listening, .81 for Structure/Writing, .88 for Reading, and .94 for the Total scaled scores; the reliability estimation method was not specified

(ETS, 1998). For completeness, the paper-based TOEFL scores have reliability estimates (alphas) of .90 (Listening), .86 (Structure and Written Expression), .89 (Reading), and .95 for the total scaled scores (ETS, 1997). The standard errors of measurement for the paper-based TOEFL were 2.0 for Listening, 2.7 for Structure/Writing, 2.4 for Reading, and 13.9 for total scaled score, whereas for the CBT the corresponding standard errors were 1.6, 2.1, 1.6, and 10.4. ETS (1998) found that the intercorrelations between the paper-based and CBT TOEFL Listening, Structure/Writing, Reading, and Total scores were .82, .75, .82, and .89, respectively. Assuming that the CBT reliability estimates are coefficient alphas and that the simulation data are comparable to the empirical data used for the paper-based reliability estimates, then the two TOEFL formats yield comparably equivalent and high reliability estimates. No information was provided concerning interrater agreement for the Writing section on the CBT TOEFL. Because of the similarity in scoring of the Writing section and the Test of Written English (TWE), the interrater reliabilities from the TWE may give an indication of the quality of the scores from the Writing section. For the TWE the interrater Pearson correlations were between .77 and .81, whereas the coefficient alphas for the final scores based upon two readers per essay ranged from .87 to .89.

Information concerning validity for the CBT TOEFL was not available. According to ETS (1998), "validity evidence developed over many years for the paper-based test, in the absence of contrary evidence, is a good source of information about the computer-based version" (p. 36). This is an interesting perspective to espouse given the use of question formats specifically designed for the computer and the necessity of creating a new reporting scale for the CBT TOEFL. Validity evidence for the CBT TOEFL will need to be accumulated. In this regard, ETS provides a brochure, *Guidelines for TOEFL Institutional Validity Studies*, in order to aid institutional testing centers or Admissions Departments in performing local validity studies. These guidelines, written before the introduction of the CBT TOEFL, are concerned with content and criterion-related validity and contain suggestions for criteria selection, selection of predictors, and determining standards. This reviewer was not able to find any documentation indicating which item response theory (IRT)

model is being used for the CAT sections. Given that ability estimation for the CAT sections is dependent on the difficulty of the items and that the item pool is categorized by item content and difficulty, it would appear that a one-parameter model is being used.

The TWE was designed to assess writing proficiency and was the basis for the Writing section of the TOEFL. It was initially developed to complement the paper-based TOEFL's Structure and Written expression section; the TOEFL and TWE had to be taken on the same day. The TWE presents the examinee with a topic and gives him or her 30 minutes to plan, organize, and write an essay on the topic. The TWE differs from the Written section of the CBT TOEFL in that (a) the examinee's essay was scored on a 1- to 6-point holistic scale plus ratings of INR and OFF (INR [nonresponse] and OFF [did not write on assigned topic] are similar to the Writing sections' rating of 0), (b) the TWE score was separate from the TOEFL score, (c) reading and scoring of the essays were performed at a central location, and (d) responses were handwritten. The TWE essays were scored by two independent certified readers with a third rater used if the two raters initially assigned to rate the essay were more than one point apart on their ratings. According to the TOEFL 1999 Products and Services Catalog, the TWE was to be discontinued June 2000.

SUMMARY. This reviewer was unable to take or review the actual CBT TOEFL, nor did he have access to the PowerPrep package. Because the PowerPrep presents CBTs it would seem that this package may be more beneficial for the potential examinee to use in preparation for the CBT TOEFL. Insufficient information was available to determine how ETS's computer-based testing simulation was conducted in order to obtain reliability estimates. It should be noted that although in the context of IRT, the concept of reliability is not as paramount as it is in Classical Test Theory, it is possible to obtain reliability-like information for CAT using empirical data (Thissen, 2000). In addition, the validity of the CBT TOEFL could not be directly addressed. Presumably information in both of these areas will be forthcoming as the CBT TOEFL becomes more pervasive.

REVIEWER'S REFERENCES

ETS. (1997). *TOEFL test and score manual*. Princeton, NJ: Educational Testing Service.

ETS. (1998). *TOEFL Computer-Based TOEFL score user guide*. Princeton, NJ: Educational Testing Service.

Kirsch, I., Jamieson, J., Taylor, C., & Eignor, D. (1998). *Computer familiarity among TOEFL examinees*. (TOEFL Research Report No. 59, Research Report 98-6). Princeton, NJ: Educational Testing Service.

Taylor C., Jamieson, J., Eignor, D., & Kirsch, I. (1998). *The relationship between computer familiarity and performance on Computer-Based TOEFL test tasks*. (TOEFL Research Report No. 61, Research Report 98-8). Princeton, NJ: Educational Testing Service.

Thissen, D. (2000). Reliability and measurement precision. In H. Wainer, N. J. Dorans, D. Eignor, R. Flaugher, B. F. Green, R. J. Mislevy, L. Steinberg, & D. Thissen (Eds.), *Computerized adaptive testing: A primer* (2nd ed.) (pp. 159–184). Mahwah, NJ: Lawrence Erlbaum Associates.

Review of the Computer-Based Test of English as a Foreign Language and Test of Written English by ALAN SOLOMON, Research Associate, School District of Philadelphia, Philadelphia, PA:

The Test of English as a Foreign Language (TOEFL) is designed to assess the English proficiency of college and university applicants whose primary language is not English. The computer-based test is made up of four sections, Listening, Structure, Reading, and Writing. Examinees may take the test throughout the year by appointment. Testing time varies from 3 1/2 to 4 hours. A paper-based version of TOEFL was scheduled to be phased out by December 2000.

The Reading section follows a linear testing model. Here, examinees respond to questions that span the difficulty range. Each examinee responds to a unique set of items. However, each set is similar in terms of content and statistical features.

The Listening and Structure sections follow a computer-adaptive testing model. Examinees start their test with a moderately difficult item and receive subsequent items based on their responses. The publisher believes that the program estimates each examinee's ability in the section and selects items designed to refine that estimate.

Examinees work through TOEFL at their own pace and the time required to complete the test varies from one individual to another. However, each section has a time limit. The number of questions in each section may vary because the test publisher may add some for research purposes. Nevertheless, all examinees' scores are based on the same number of questions. The test publisher notes the number of questions in each section and the respective time limit on-screen.

The testing procedure begins with a mandated tutorial. Here, examinees learn the unique procedures necessary to take a computer-based test. Individual tutorials precede the Listening, Structure, and Reading sections because the response style varies for each one. The Writing test includes a tutorial for examinees who prefer to keyboard their essays rather than write them.

The Listening section includes from 30 to 50 items and requires 40 to 60 minutes to complete. It is designed to measure an individual's ability to comprehend North American English through its conversational features. The Structure section is made up of from 20 to 25 items and calls for 15 to 20 minutes of testing time. This section concerns the individual's ability to deal with standard written English through a formal approach.

For the test itself, students listen to passages through headphones and record their responses on the computer screen. In the computer-adaptive portion, examinees may not review their responses. They may do so in the linear position.

The TOEFL includes a student test preparation manual and an information bulletin. Both products are attractive, well-written, and should serve to facilitate student understanding of the TOEFL and promote their performance on the examination itself.

The publisher claims that reliability estimates for the TOEFL are within acceptable limits. These estimates vary from section to section: .81 for the Structure/Writing composite to .88 for Reading. However, the Total Score reliability is .94.

Sample size also varied by native language. Eight groups, Arabic, Chinese, Indonesian, Japanese, Korean, Russian, Spanish, and Thai had over 1,000 representatives in the sample. This finding may point to a bias linked to native language.

Brenda Loyd (1985) reviewed an earlier version of the TOEFL in the *Ninth Mental Measurements Yearbook*. She noted that TOEFL and subsequent GPAs do not have a strong relationship. Recent studies have continued this finding. Thus, the TOEFL may be assessing an individual's ability to get along in English rather than his or her ability to cope with the English used in our higher education programs.

With these shortcomings in mind, the TOEFL provides a sound means of assessing English ability among nonnative speakers. The publisher has listed a number of studies designed to assess the test's effectiveness and a list of useful tables that will assist the psychometrician in evaluating and analyzing the measure. Both the Loyd and Tatsuoka reviews (1985) are supportive. This reviewer takes the same position and acknowledges the continuing efforts of the publisher to improve this test along various dimensions.

REVIEWER'S REFERENCES

Lloyd, B. H. (1985). [Review of the Test of English as a Foreign Language]. In J. V. Mitchell, Jr. (Ed.), *The ninth mental measurements yearbook* (pp. 1568–1569). Lincoln, NE: Buros Institute of Mental Measurements.

Tatsuoka, K. K. (1985). [Review of the Test of English as a Foreign Language]. In J. V. Mitchell, Jr. (Ed.), *The ninth mental measurements yearbook* (pp. 1569–1570). Lincoln, NE: Buros Institute of Mental Measurements.

[95]
Computerized Assessment of Response Bias: Revised Edition.

Purpose: "To quantitatively assess a given patient's attitude (response bias) in taking neuropsychological or neurocognitive tests."

Population: Severely impaired neurologic patients, mild traumatic brain injury patients, non-neurologic simulators.

Publication Dates: 1992–1995.

Acronym: CARB.

Scores, 24: 4 actions (Block 1, 2, 3, Total) each with 6 scores: Total Correct, Number of Correct Responses Obtained with Left Hand, Number of Correct Responses Obtained with Right Hand, Reaction Time Average, Reaction Time Average for Correct Responses, Reaction Time Average for Incorrect Responses.

Administration: Individual

Forms, 4: Standard or Quick form, each with or without item-specific feedback.

Price Data, 1995: $175 for disk and comprehensive manual (63 pages).

Foreign Language Edition: Spanish language version available.

Time: (22–40) minutes.

Comments: Typically, this is a test of motivation, not ability or impairment; instructions for installing and operating CARB (DOS based) software are included in the manual.

Authors: Robert L. Conder, Jr., Lyle M. Allen, III, David R. Cox, and Carol M. King.

Publisher: CogniSyst, Inc.

Review of the Computerized Assessment of Response Bias: Revised Edition by M. ALLAN COOPERSTEIN, Clinical Psychologist & Forensic Examiner, Independent Practice, Willow Grove, PA:

Disguised as a tool for the assessment of a cognitive ability (visual digit recognition), the Computerized Assessment of Response Bias (CARB) is a criterion-referenced test constructed specifically to quantitatively measure test-taking attitude or response bias. This sensitizes a clinician to the possible effects of biased responding upon test data in (primarily) neuropsychological patients, although it may be applied to other populations.

Response bias refers to systematic error in the data produced due to intentional or unintentional erroneous recall or reporting. Caution is mandated when inferring the reliability of litigants because response biases may affect self-reports in a misleading fashion. For example, Lees-Haley, Williams, and English (1996) found that plaintiffs reported preinjury functioning greater than that of controls. After factor analyzing Minnesota Multiphasic Personality Inventory-1 (MMPI-1) validity scale items, Cloak, Kirklen, Strozier, and Reed (1997) stated that response bias scales are needed with more distinct definitions and greater internal consistency.

The CARB may complement neuropsychological, forensic, or disability evaluations by providing an independent and reliable method of assessing underperformance using a forced-choice visual digit recognition task that is easily passed by patients with severe brain injury and normal individuals. It measures reaction time, response patterns, and left-right performance differences, providing statistical analyses and an interpretive report.

TEST DEVELOPMENT AND RATIONALE. The authors assert that assessing response bias is an essential component of neuropsycholgical evaluation. They extend this to apply to any cognitive evaluation used to establish compensable damages or mitigation of criminal responsibility. Based upon motive, if a patient tends to perform worse than their actual ability level of neurologic impairment, the assessment will be misrepresented and clinical decision making will be adulterated. Tendencies to perform worse than one's actual ability should be identified and quantified. Consequently, response bias was chosen as having a neutral value as a construct and taking into consideration voluntary and involuntary processes and conscious and unconscious processes.

The authors further claim that clinical experience demonstrates that allowing the subject to function alone may increase symptom exaggeration, that patients may find it easier to exaggerate or feign symptoms while performing standardized measures in contrast to interpersonal interactions.

They submit that the best method for administration and scoring of a response bias test is a computer-human interface for reliable and autonomous administration to computer-naive subjects, the program providing immediate statistical feedback to the examiner for use in the ongoing evaluation. Thus the CARB was developed.

The CARB has been implemented with large varieties of patient groups, including severely impaired, nonlitigating neurologic patients who served as research controls. Other groups sought compensation, mild traumatic brain injury (TBI) patients, and non-neurologic simulators. In using the CARB, a clinician must decide if the patient has the minimal abilities to provide a valid performance using a computer. Patients with motor perseveration can take the CARB; special handling for the keyboard repeat function that informs the subject about held keys can be installed.

TEST FORM AND ADMINISTRATION. Documentation includes a manual on technical information, test characteristics and procedures used in test development, and a user's guide including information on test administration, scoring, normative data, and interpretation of results.

Instructions and practice are followed by exposure of a 5-digit number for 5 seconds (3 in the brief version). The patient then sees a request to count backwards from 20 to 1. Time periods for distraction range from 5 to 15 seconds in one version, 3 to 9 seconds in Quick CARB, and have been reduced further in CARB '97 (Allen, Conder, Green, & Cox, 1997) following investigations.

After the distraction, two choices are exposed on either side of the screen. The patient taps the left or right shift key, indicating the side where the target stimulus is seen.

Auditory and/or visual feedback may be implemented. The next target automatically appears after a brief delay. Following completion of each block, a message text congratulates him or her on successful performance and states that the next block of trials will be even more difficult. With completion, the computer tells the patient that the test is finished.

SCORING AND INTERPRETATION. CARB results are scored immediately and available on-screen, printed, or sent to a text file. The data compare the patient's performance to control populations of patients with severe traumatic brain injury (STBI). Z scores and probability values are provided for the three blocks of items, as well as the total number of items administered. Normative comparisons are made with the performance of other groups of subjects. To compare performance to various reference groups, "t" statistics and associated "p" values are provided.

The report presents the total correct and possible correct number, the percentage of right- and left-sided key presses, right and left visual half field differences, and individual item and average response times for selection of choice stimuli. These variables could be used as interim and outcome measures for recovery of cognitive functions.

NORMATIVE INFORMATION. Basing their approach on binomial probability theory, a patient's performance may be compared against chance performance to yield an exact probability value for the number of errors committed. In instances of gross response bias, this precludes the need for a control group. Patients attempting to bias their performance in a negative direction may show results significantly worse than those obtained by chance. These statistics are reported for individuals using z scores and probability values. Differences at or less than the .05 level are generally considered significant.

The CARB was normed first in a comparison study in which the performances of a brain-injured (BI) control group ($N = 8$) was compared with two simulated malingering or Fake Bad (FB) groups (both $N = 8$). All BI patients and simulators were able to independently operate the software. Significant differences were found between the three groups for total number correct and other measured parameters. Post hoc comparisons found that performance of the BI patients was superior to and significantly different from the "subtle" FB group and both groups were significantly better than the "gross" FB group. Probability values for pretenders using subtle FB strategy were not significantly different from chance errors; overall performance was significantly below that of the BI subjects. The combination of p values and group comparisons with the patient sample allowed detection of simulated subtle malingering not available from earlier studies.

A number of later studies have replicated and extended these findings in independent investigations, confirming that poor overall CARB performance is related to symptom exaggeration or incomplete effort, and CARB performance is not related to ability, age, sex, educational level, or the individual's IQ.

SOFTWARE. Cogshell is the proprietary DOS environment within which the battery of tests is housed. The CARB, however, is not yet capable of operating within a Windows environment and one must reboot and run it in DOS mode to administer it. An earlier test version ran smoothly and wrote to the disk, but at completion "crashed" and needed to be restarted to browse or print results. This has been remedied in later versions. The CARB will eventually be converted to a Windows platform, which should streamline its use and improve graphics.

DISCUSSION. The CARB may be applied to work and clinical experience in pain, chronic fatigue, and psychiatric assessment, aiding clinicians in assessing the impact of secondary gain, incomplete effort, feigning, symptom exaggeration, faking, and malingering, appearing robust in its capacity to assess at least one aspect of response bias.

The CARB supplements clinical decision making, and, as a single test, should not be used as a sole criterion to assess response bias. It may be combined, for example, with a structured interview approach, such as the Structured Interview of Reported Symptoms (SIRS) by Rogers, Bagby, and Dickens (1992), which systematically assessed deliberate distortions in the self-report of symptoms.

In addition, CARB authors suggest that results could be integrated with other data, such as EMT and/or police reports, emergency room and hospital reports, coma scores, Total Trauma Scores, and results of neurologic or neurophysiology examination. Psychometrics, however, can only detect biased responding. The ultimate determination of malingering must be based on overall clinical evaluation (Frederick, Sarfaty, Johnston, & Powel, 1994). However, the CARB does demonstrate respectable correlations with the Word Memory Test (WMT; 424), another measure of symptom exaggeration.

Other factors remain to be considered in researching response bias, such as attention deficits and psychomotor retardation. Brebion, Smith, and Widlocher (1997) deal with the controversy over the performance of depressed individuals on recognition memory tasks, attempting to assess whether there is impaired discrimination and conservative or liberal response bias according to signal detection theory. Individuals with depression demonstrated lower discrimination than controls although the index of response bias was not different between groups. Among individuals with depression, the general severity of depression was related to discrimination, whereas psychomotor retardation level was related to response bias.

Further research is assured by the authors. It is hoped that, in following through, a double-blind approach may be initiated with a variety of populations, including neuropsychological, emotional, litigants, nonlitigants, etc.

REVIEWER'S REFERENCES

Rogers, R., Bagby, R. M., & Dickens, S. E. (1992). *Structured Interview of Reported Symptoms: Professional manual.* Odessa, FL: Psychological Assessment Resources, Inc.

Frederick, R. I., Sarfaty, S. D., Johnston, J. D., & Powel, J. (1994). Validation of a detector of response bias on a forced-choice test of nonverbal ability. *Neuropsychology, 8,* 118–125.

Lees-Haley, P. R., Williams, C. W., & English, L. T. (1996). Response bias in self-reported history of plaintiffs compared with nonlitigating patients. *Psychological Reports, 79*(3, Pt. 1), 811–818.

Allen, L. A., III, Conder, R. L., Green, P., & Cox, D. R. (1997). CARB '97: Computerized assessment of response bias. Durham, NC: CogniSyst, Inc.

Brébion, G., Smith, M. J., & Widlocher, D. (1997). Discrimination and response bias in memory: Effects of depression severity and psychomotor retardation. *Psychiatry Research, 70,* 95–103.

Cloak, N. L., Kirklen, L. E., Strozier, A. L., & Reed, J. R. (1997). Factor analysis of Minnesota Multiphasic Personality Inventory-1 (MMPI-1) validity scale items. *Measurement & Evaluation in Counseling & Development, 30*(1), 40–49.

Review of the Computerized Assessment of Response Bias: Revised Edition by EDWARD E. GOTTS, Chief Psychologist, Madison State Hospital, Madison, IN:

Response bias refers here to those kinds of testing results that suggest, imply, or indicate a respondent may have exerted less than a "best effort" while completing a test. The Computerized Assessment of Response Bias: Revised Edition (CARB) (updated March 1999) thus was designed to address such issues as malingering, deception, and poorly motivated performance. These issues have been conceptualized and studied using varied response validity checks, with different methods being employed as a function of the particular types of psychological tests in question (Rogers, 1997). Specifically the CARB was developed as a means of addressing these issues during the administration of neuropsychological tests.

The CARB presents the examinee with a forced-choice task that calls for recognition, after a brief delay (8–9 seconds) interval, of a string of visually presented digits. This relatively easy task is made to appear more difficult by means of expectancies created through the directions given the examinee, by placing a distraction task between the stimulus presentation and recognition testing; and by varying the delay intervals used between presentation and testing. It is, hence, expected that motivated examinees will perform with relatively high accuracy of recognition, whereas poorly motivated, disinterested, or malingering examinees will deliver a less satisfactory performance. Differing degrees of "not remembering" can, accordingly, be used to infer subtle versus more obvious forms of poor motivation. The CARB's authors acknowledge that their method follows the lead of earlier work (Hiscock & Hiscock, 1989). Other developments in use of forced-choice recognition to evaluate malingering are reviewed by Pankratz and Binder (1997).

The literature verifies the wisdom of considering and evaluating the possible presence of response bias when performing assessments of persons who may be influenced by secondary gain issues (Rogers, 1997). This provides sufficient reason to seek instruments that increase the likelihood of detecting suboptimal test performance. The question to be weighed here is how well the CARB improves detection. First, however, the test's reliability will be considered. In one sample of 307 compensation cases, correlations among the three blocks of 37 items each ranged from .80 to .90. Retest after one week with a small sample ($n = 25$) yielded a stability coefficient of .92. High reliability in terms of internal consistency as expressed by the Cronbach alpha coefficients is not to be expected, because in another study of 1,752 cases it was found that persons who did not pass the CARB (i.e., those lacking adequate motivation) had interblock variability that was three to four times as great as that demonstrated by persons whose CARB scores exceeded the cutoff of 89% correct. Therefore, the presence of some variability in scores across blocks is not unexpected; rather it validly reflects the inconsistency that marks the performance of persons evidencing response bias. Traditional item analysis indicators of reliability are not reported in the manual for CARB '97.

The validity of the CARB is evaluated in terms of its ability to identify persons who have poor performance motivation and who, hence, are likely to do less than their best on other neuropsychological or intellectual measures. The CARB predictably spots these poorly motivated examinees. For example, scores disproportionately often fall well below established cutoffs for compensation-motivated examinees whose physical and lab findings fail to corroborate their claimed injuries. Contrastingly, well-documented cases of individuals with severe traumatic brain injury (STBI) and other neurological injury (i.e., tumor, burst aneurysm, post-CVA/stroke) who are not compensation motivated perform as well as normals. In one study, litigating patients' average CARB scores were only 47.9% correct, whereas nonlitigating patients averaged 82.9% correct. This finding attests directly to the validity and, at the same time, indicates that the CARB measures motivation to perform well rather than ability.

The CARB's validity has also been evaluated relative to a number of other response bias measures used in neuropsychology: CogniSyst's Word Memory Test (WMT), the Minnesota Multiphasic Personality Inventory (MMPI/MMPI-2), the California Verbal Learning Test (CVLT) (Millis, Putnam, Adams, & Ricker, 1995), the Recognition Memory Test (Warrington, 1984), and the 21-Item Test (Iverson, Franzen, & McCracken, 1991). Clearly the MMPI/MMPI-2 is the least satisfactory instrument of this group for classifying motivated and undermotivated examinees. The CARB consistently exhibits the best overall accuracy for identifying motivated examinees (positives) and the lowest misidentification of positives (i.e., false positives). Further, it offers the best overall correct identification of poorly motivated patients (negatives) and the smallest misidentification rate for negatives (i.e., false negatives). All of the foregoing instruments, however, classify more examinees as false negatives than is desirable. The CARB's authors conclude that this is perhaps the unavoidable consequence of the high response inconsistency found repeatedly among symptom exaggerators. Based on the foregoing findings and the need to reduce false negatives further, the CARB's authors recommend the conjoint use of at least two tests of response bias. For this purpose they suggest using their WMT and the CARB together.

The preceding recommendation is easily implemented because the validity portions of the WMT can be accessed along with the CARB from CogniSyst's application umbrella, CogShell, along with a review of demographics and memory complaints. The instruments in the CogShell group further can be called up as a battery that is predesignated by the examiner. Up to 10 batteries can be programmed and stored to meet varied patient needs.

The CARB applications have been extended by CogniSyst's research to include other patient groupings besides the STBI and other neurological categories. They have now shown, for example, that the CARB also identifies motivated and undermotivated examinees with complaints of chronic pain and chronic fatigue syndrome. They further have found that patient CARB scores are relatively unaffected by patient age (at least up to age 60), level of intelligence (from borderline through bright average), and clinical depression—in the same way that symptom exaggeration and actual memory problems are not confounded with each other by the CARB.

SUMMARY. The CARB improves the accuracy with which examinees can be identified as motivated versus undermotivated. Gross malingering can also be spotted by application of binomial probabilities. The incidence of suboptimal examinee performance during testing is in the range of 30% and calls for more than examiner clinical acumen to be detected. CogniSyst's considerable program of research has led to the setting of functional cutting scores relative to well-defined patient groupings. The CARB by itself is superior in accuracy of classification to a number of other instruments to which it has been compared. Nevertheless, examiners should use at least two differing measures of response bias in order to optimize identification/classification. Coaching of examinees by unscrupulous representatives prior to testing can invalidate the CARB and other response bias tests. Use of multiple tests may counteract this practice. The current CARB '97 manual (1999) is much improved over its predecessors, yet still requires clarification and further documentation in certain places. Technical support from CogniSyst will, in this reviewer's experience, generally make amends for these and other shortcomings.

REVIEWER'S REFERENCES

Warrington, E. K. (1984). *Recognition Memory Test: Manual.* Berkshire, UK: NFER-Nelson.

Hiscock, M., & Hiscock, C. K. (1989). Refining the forced-choice method for the detection of malingering. *Journal of Clinical and Experimental Neuropsychology, 11,* 967–974.

Iverson, G. L., Franzen, M. D., & McCracken, L. M. (1991). Evaluation of an objective assessment technique for the detection of malingered memory deficits. *Law and Human Behavior, 15,* 667–676.

Millis, S. R., Putnam, S. H., Adams, K. M., & Ricker, J. H. (1995). The California Verbal Learning Test in the detection of incomplete effort in neuropsychological evaluation. *Psychological Assessment, 7,* 463–471.

Pankratz, L., & Binder, L. M. (1997). Malingering on intellectual and neuropsychological measures. In R. Rogers (Ed.), *Clinical assessment of malingering and deception* (2nd ed., pp. 223–236). New York: Guilford.

Rogers, R. (1997). *Clinical assessment of malingering and deception* (2nd ed.). New York: Guilford.

[96]
Conflict Style Inventory.

Purpose: Designed to assess an individual's approach to conflict resolution.
Population: Adults.
Publication Dates: 1990–1995.
Acronym: CSI.
Scores, 15: Total Score, Individual [one-on-one] Conflict Situations, Group/Team Conflict Situations on 5 styles: (Avoiding, Smoothing, Bargaining, Forcing, Problem Solving).
Administration: Group.
Price Data, 1995: $24.95 per trainer's guide ('94, 47 pages); $6.50 per inventory; $4.95 per Managing Conflict Constructively Participant Handout.
Time: (20) minutes.
Comments: Self-scored.
Authors: Marshall Sashkin.
Publisher: Human Resource Development Press.

Review of the Conflict Style Inventory by TRENTON R. FERRO, Associate Professor of Adult and Community Education, Indiana University of Pennsylvania, Indiana, PA:

The Conflict Style Inventory (CSI), developed by Marshall Sashkin of George Washington University, is a packet of three booklets: The *Conflict Style Inventory* (rev. ed.) includes the inventory itself, together with scoring and interpretation guidelines; *Managing Conflict Constructively* (MCC) provides background information on the nature of conflict and how to deal with conflict; and the *Conflict Style Inventory Trainer Guide* (rev. ed.) describes the model on which the inventory is based (the model is also discussed in MCC), offers a brief section on technical considerations, provides guidelines and materials for using the inventory in a training and development seminar, and analyzes the 10 cases used in the CSI.

The CSI, developed to help respondents learn more about how they and others deal with conflict at work, consists of 10 mini-cases about work-related conflict situations. Each case is followed by five alternative actions that the respondent, if he or she were in that situation, might take. The respondent distributes a total of 10 points among the five alternatives to indicate which actions he or she would prefer; the respondent can assign all 10 points to one alternative or can divide the points among more than one alternative action. The points assigned to these 10 cases are then transferred to a scoring table made up of 10 columns, 2 each for each of the five primary strategies for dealing with conflict: Avoiding, Smoothing, Bargaining, Forcing, and Problem Solving. Total scores for each of these five strategies are then plotted on a chart to indicate how the respondent's scores compare (very high, high, average, low, very low) with typical scores obtained from various groups. The two subtotals within each primary strategy measure the extent to which the respondent uses each of the conflict styles in situations involving just one other person and in situations involving a group or team.

Although "the CSI continues to undergo psychometric development to determine how well the scales cohere and validation studies to measure the extent to which the scores actually tap behaviors representative of the styles they define" (Trainer Guide, p. 7), the normative data are quite limited. Data are provided for five samples, with a total *N* of 118: 36 clerical personnel, 21 personnel specialists, 4 top executives of a national cosmetics firm, 8 top executives of a national retail chain, and 49 professional employees of a major university library (including managers). No information is provided about how these samples were drawn; they have the appearance of being convenience samples. Consequently, the validity and generalizability of scores from the inventory have not yet been clearly established. Even though total means and standard deviations for the combined samples are provided, there is no indication that correlations have been calculated to explore the differences between and among the sample groups. The combined totals tend to obscure what appear to be differences in strategies preferred by the various samples. The author does promise that "three types of research are underway to study further the psychometric properties of the CSI" (Trainer Guide, p. 7): factor analysis of the 50 individual scores produced by respondents, a split-half reliability test of respondents' scores on the 10 cases, and comparing the individual and group conflict style scores (the subtotals for each of the five primary strategies).

Sashkin states that "this is not a 'test' and there are no 'right' or 'wrong' answers" (CSI, p. 1), yet he makes clear that "only problem solving has consistent positive outcomes" (CSI, p. 16). Although "the other three styles can be appropriate at times," yet "problem solving and bargaining are the most generally useful approaches to conflict" (MCC, p. 8). MCC also concludes with sections describing how to move from Fighting, Smoothing, Avoiding, and Bargaining to Problem Solving. Further, the author notes that some respondents, "particularly those who have been exposed to the conflict style concepts prior to completing the CSI, report that they are able to figure out the 'right' answers" (Trainer Guide, p. 7). This observation is confirmed by the data: Respondents consistently applied over 50% of their points to problem-solving actions (sample means are 50.03, 52.62, 66.75, 67.62, and 54.26; combined mean is 54.01). Do these data accurately reflect reality?

SUMMARY. The three booklets are well and clearly written and are based on sound theoretical bases. The user must be careful, however, not to overextend the potential applications of the CSI. It is most helpful as a descriptive measure that provides insight for self-development and can be used effectively individually and in small groups; it should not be used in a prescriptive manner nor as the basis for making decisions about the value, worth, or ability of individuals. Neither the theory nor the psychometric evidence support such an application.

Review of the Conflict Style Inventory by SCOTT T. MEIER, Associate Professor and Director of Training, Department of Counseling and Educational Psychology, SUNY Buffalo, Buffalo, NY:

Sashkin designed the Conflict Style Inventory (CSI) to help respondents learn more about their particular styles for dealing with interpersonal conflict. The CSI presents individuals with 10 brief vignettes and asks them to assign 10 points to one of five possible actions that deal with the described conflict. Scores are summed across the vignettes on five dimensions that correspond to the response choices: Avoiding, Smoothing, Bargaining, Forcing, and Problem-Solving. For each dimension test-takers also receive scores on their preferences for handling conflict in one-on-one situations and group situations.

The major distinction of the CSI is its 10 vignettes. Instead of simply asking respondents to respond to typical self-report statements, the CSI presents a realistic situation and asks the respondent to make judgments about their potential actions. For example, one case describes a supervisor, to whom you report, who has seriously mismanaged a project. The result is that the project is behind schedule, additional problems have arisen, and the company is losing money. Among your choices are to document your supervisor as the cause of the problems, keep a low profile, try to get transferred to another unit, or meet with your supervisor to discuss the problems. Sashkin notes that as many as 90% of respondents report they would use the problem-solving approach, an indication of the transparency of the correct answers on the CSI.

The CSI test booklet includes instructions for scoring as well as a description of the conflict resolution styles. Also available are a CSI Trainer's Guide and another booklet entitled "Managing Conflict Constructively." The nontechnical nature of these materials indicates that their most appropriate use is in workshops designed to intervene and improve users' styles for handling conflict. The accompanying booklets do provide basic theory and anecdotal information about conflicts—Sashkin describes the instrument as based on more than 30 years of research on conflict—but they are geared more towards the intended users of the materials than an academic audience.

Although the manual describes the CSI as undergoing continuing psychometric development, no reliability or validity information is currently provided for the CSI. Similarly, a search of PsycINFO found no published references for the CSI. The manual includes very elementary normative data for a sample of 118 individuals in five occupations with sample size ranges from 4 (executives) to 48 (professional university library employees). The reported means and standard deviations differ considerably for these occupational groups. For example, the mean Avoiding Score for 36 clerical personnel equaled 10.92 (*SD* = 9.42), whereas the mean score for the 49 library employees was 5.76 (*SD* = 6.38). These diverse scores raise doubts about the generalizability of the norms for both the described groups and other occupations.

SUMMARY. Given the lack of psychometric data, use of the CSI should be considered experimental. Whether the more realistic presentation of conflict stimuli via its innovative vignettes will translate into improved validity remains to be seen. Individual currently seeking scales with available reliability and validity information might consider the Teamwork-KSA Test (Stevens & Campion, 1994), which includes scales for conflict resolution and collaborative problem solving.

REVIEWER'S REFERENCE

Stevens, M. J., & Campion, M. A. (1994). *Teamwork-KSA test examiner's manual*. Rosemont, IL: NCS.

[97]
Conners' Continuous Performance Test.
Purpose: A computerized assessment tool used to assess attention problems and to measure treatment effectiveness.
Population: Ages 6 to adult.

Publication Dates: 1992–1996.
Acronym: CPT.
Scores, 13: Hits, Omissions, Commissions, Hit Response Time, Hit Response Time Standard Error, Variability of Standard Errors, Attentiveness, Risk Taking, Hit Response Time Block Change, Hit Standard Error Block Change, Hit Response Time Inter-Stimulus Interval Change, Hit Standard Error Inter-Stimulus Interval Change, Overall Index.
Administration: Individual.
Forms, 3: Standard, X, AX.
Price Data, 1999: $495 per computer program (IBM 3.5-inch disk); $35 per Preview Version (IBM 3.5-inch disk).
Time: (14) minutes.
Comments: Self-completed performance measure; computer administered; requires IBM or compatible with DOS 3.3 or better and at least 512K of RAM.
Author: C. Keith Conners.
Publisher: Multi-Health Systems, Inc.
Cross References: See T5:679 (2 references).

Review of the Conners' Continuous Performance Test by JAMES YSSELDYKE, Birkmaier Professor of Educational Leadership, University of Minnesota, Minneapolis, MN:

The materials for the Conners' Continuous Performance Test (CPT) consist of a computer disk and a user's manual. I read and reread the manual, and found that it would be confusing for all but those who are well versed in assessment of reaction time, vigilance, and arousal. I thought the user's manual assumed that the reader/user had a significant knowledge base and background experience in assessment of attention and hyperactivity disorders. I found it disorganized and difficult to follow.

The CPT is a vigilance or attention test for use in research or clinical settings. The test is administered and scored by computer, and is presented in a game-like format. The person being assessed pushes buttons when a specific letter or set of letters appears on the screen. The author contends that the CPT is useful in measuring attention and learning disorders in children and the effects of drug treatment in hyperactive children. In describing the theoretical background for the test the author talks in six paragraphs about vigilance, vigilance decrements, theories of low arousal in hyperactivity, event rates, floor effects, anticipatory and preparatory sets, criterion strictness, and reaction speed. The discussion is very brief and difficult to understand. Major terms and concepts are not defined. Those who already know the constructs and how they are measured may be able to follow the discussion.

There are two ways in which the Conners' CPT may be used: a standard mode and one customized by the clinician or researcher to gather specific kinds of data. The standard mode takes about 14 minutes to administer. The norm group for the standard mode is inadequately described as composed of "670 carefully studied patients with a variety of attentional problems and comorbid conditions, and 520 normal, unselected community children, adolescents, and adults" (p. 6). Of the 670 clinical cases, 186 were excluded from the norm group to be used in cross validation (130), because subjects were on medication (10), or because they were "outliers" (46). So, the clinical comparison group is composed of 484 cases. When the computer prints out test results, they are in the form of T scores and percentile calculations are based on comparisons to individuals of the same age and gender group, but the ages and genders of the comparison group are not reported in the manual.

The CPT computer program automatically prints reports for subjects after they have completed the test. The manual includes 19 pages of information on how to interpret the reports generated and examples of case studies.

Data on the technical adequacy of this measure are presented, but are difficult to follow. There are no data on the reliability of scores from the CPT. Data relative to validity consist of inadequately described studies of the extent to which the measure can discriminate between clinical types, the correlation of the measure with other continuous performance measures, and descriptions of the rates at which individuals make various types of errors on the test. There are additional pages of graphs showing the decline of reaction time over age, standard error of reaction time over age, omission and commission errors as a function of age, and changes in duration of reaction time for males, females, and clinical types.

SUMMARY. Clinicians and researchers who are well versed in the measurement of continuous performance and reaction time may find this a useful device in their work. Others are likely to find the test and the manual confusing and of limited use.

[98]
Conners' Rating Scales—Revised.

Purpose: Constructed to assess psychopathology and problem behaviors.

Population: Ages 3–17; self-report scales can be completed by 12- to 17-year-olds.

Publication Dates: 1989–1997.

Acronym: CRS-R.

Administration: Group.

Price Data, 1999: $425 per complete kit including manual ('97, 226 pages), 25 feedback forms for each of the CPRS-R:L, CPRS-R:S, CTRS-R:L, CTRS-R:S, CASS:L, CASS:S, CADS-Parent, CADS-Teacher, CADS-Self-Report, 25 Global Index-Teacher Forms, 25 Global Index-Parent Forms, 15 CRS-R Treatment Progress Color Plot, and 100 Teacher Information Forms; $26 per 25 Quick Score forms (specify test and version); $22 per feedback forms (specify test and version); $46 per technical manual; $40 per user's manual; $45 per Windows preview version including 3 administrations/interpretive reports, and user's manual; $10 per computer interpretive report; $4 per computer profile report.

Comments: Ratings by parents and teachers and adolescent self-report.

Author: C. Keith Conners.

Publisher: Multi-Health Systems, Inc.

a) CONNERS' PARENT RATING SCALE—REVISED.

Acronym: CPRS.

Scores, 13: Oppositional, Cognitive Problems/Inattention, Hyperactivity, Anxious-Shy, Perfectionism, Social Problems, Psychosomatic, ADHD Index, Conners' Global Index: Restless-Impulsive and Emotional Lability, DSM-IV Inattentive, DSM-IV Hyperactive-Impulsive, DSM-IV Total.

Forms, 2: Long, Short.

Time: (15–20) minutes.

b) CONNERS' TEACHER RATING SCALE—REVISED.

Acronym: CTRS.

Scores: Same as *a* above.

Forms, 2: Long, Short.

Time: (15) minutes.

c) CONNERS-WELLS' ADOLESCENT SELF-REPORT SCALE.

Acronym: CASS.

Scores, 10: Conduct Problems, Cognitive Problems/Inattention, Hyperactivity, ADHD Index, Family Problems, Anger Control Problems, Emotional Problems, DSM-IV Inattentive, DSM-IV Hyperactive-Impulsive, DSM-IV Total.

Forms, 2: Long, Short.

Time: (15–20) minutes.

d) CONNERS' GLOBAL INDEX.

Acronym: CGI.

Scores, 3: Emotional Lability, Restless-Impulsive, Total.
Forms, 2: Parent, Teacher.
Time: (5) minutes.
e) CONNERS' ADHD/DSM-IV™ SCALES.
Acronym: CADS.
Scores, 4: Conners' ADHD Index, DSM-IV: Inattentive, DSM-IV: Hyperactive/Impulsive, DSM-IV Total.
Forms, 3: Parent, Teacher, Adolescent.
Time: (5–10) minutes.
Cross References: See T5:681 (99 references) and T4:636 (50 references); for reviews by Brian K. Martens and Judy Oehler-Stinnett of the original edition, see 11:87 (83 references).

Review of the Conners' Rating Scales—Revised by ALLEN K. HESS, Distinguished Research Professor and Department Head, Department of Psychology, Auburn University at Montgomery, Montgomery, AL:

"Conners (1990–1991) has produced a family of rating scales that are [sic] useful for identifying hyperactivity and other behavioral problems in children" (Gregory, 1996, p. 327). The fruits of his three decades of work are provided in the Technical Manual for the Conners' Rating Scales (CRS), containing a wealth of information in its 208 pages. The CRS began as a brief set of phrases forming a checklist given free to clinicians to use with parents and teachers. It has grown to include both long- and short-form parent scales and teacher scales by which to rate boys and girls from ages 3 to 17, and a set of self-report adolescent scales for youth from 12 to 17 years of age.

The set of parent and teacher rating scales includes subscales putatively tapping Oppositionalism, Cognitive Problems, Hyperactivity, Anxiety-Shyness, Perfectionism, Social Problems, Psychosomatic Concerns (parent scales only), Global Hyperactivity (including emotional lability and restless-impulsive components), Attention-Deficit/Hyperactivity Disorder (ADHD), and DSM-IV Symptoms (including inattentive and hyperactive-impulsive components). The adolescent scales include subscales for Family Problems and Anger Control problems subscales in addition to the Conduct Problems, Cognitive Problems and DSM-IV Symptoms subscales, and a Hyperactivity ADHD index. The parent-teacher, parent-child, and teacher-child contrasts can yield fascinating information (e.g., if the child and teacher see problems that the parents do not perceive).

PSYCHOMETRIC CHARACTERISTICS. The Conners rating scales are face valid. Teachers respond to items such as "fidgets with hands or feet or squirms in seat," "disturbs other children," and "talks excessively"; parents respond to items such as "easily frustrated in efforts," "argues with adults," and "messy or disorganized at home or school." Children answer questions such as "I feel like crying," "I break rules," and "I am behind in my studies."

RELIABILITY. Standard errors of measurement are presented for observed and predicted scores. They show that the scales provide stable scores to assess both the individual at a given time and the changes that might occur in an individual over time. The items seem to cohere to their assigned scale as seen by the impressive internal reliability coefficients. However, no interjudge reliability estimates are presented. This is a serious omission in observer-based measures. Six- to 8-week test-retest reliability coefficients are as low as .47 for the CTRS-R:L Cognitive-Problems and DSM-IV-Hyperactive-Impulsive scales, and the CPRS-R:L Anxious-Shy scale. However, the other test-retest coefficients average in the .70s with the CTRS-R:L scales averaging .82. In contrast to the norms that have an 11,000 total subject base, the test-retest reliability coefficients for the teacher, parent, and adolescent scales are based on samples of but 50 subjects each.

NORMS. A Canadian- and United States-based sample provides norms in 3-year age groupings for the parent and teacher's forms (from 3–5, 6–8, 9–11, 12–14, and 15–17 years) and for the adolescent self-report form (from 12–14 and 15–17 years). Norms for the parent scales tend to overrepresent white and underrepresent black parents; norms for the teacher scales are racially proportional; the norms for the adolescent scales overrepresent blacks. Native-American norms were collected and reveal elevations on most scales when compared with the norms of other ethnic groups. The problem of whether to use one set of norms for all children, based on the fact that the test subjects will be measured by a societal standard, or whether to use norms as specific to the tested person as possible is a question that is larger than the Conners' Scales or this review can address adequately, but the CRS does provide enough information for the user to sculpt a test report for either perspective.

EMPIRICAL VALIDITY. The CRS have been used in a variety of studies over the years but surprisingly the manual does not refer to any of the studies. There is a serious need for the manual to examine concurrent and predictive validity. With the exception of a study using the Children's Depression Inventory, the research reviewed in the manual is exclusively concerned with the relationships between various forms of the CRS, and these relationships are modest.

The manual cites one study concerning "discriminant validity." Conners idiosyncratically defines discriminant validity as the "instrument's ability to distinguish between relevant subject groups" (manual, p. 133). In fact, discriminant validity is defined by psychometricians as the degree to which measures do not correlate with variables from which they should differ. The manual does not cite any discriminant validity studies that show, for example, elevated hyperactivity scales and nonelevated obsessive-compulsive or anxiety-shyness scales with a hyperactive sample. Conversely, a measure with discriminant validity would show elevations on anxiety-shyness scales but not on hyperactivity scales in a group of anxious children. Such studies would provide discriminant validity [previous *MMY* reviews cite such evidence (Martens, 1992; Oehler-Stinnett, 1992), but this manual is strangely silent on this issue. These two reviews in the *Eleventh MMY* are excellent, are still pertinent in their observations about the CRS, and are essential resources for the reader interested in using the CRS or one of its competitors].

Conners' definition of discriminant validity actually is closer to what is usually termed "classification efficiency," or the degree to which a measure correctly classifies people. Classification efficiency is often determined by linear discriminant function analysis, which may account for the definitional problem. The manual reports a study showing the subscales differ when assessing a "nonclinical," ADHD, and emotional disturbance group. However, the degree to which true positive and true negative (hits) and false positive and false negative (misses) decisions occur is not reported so we do not know how efficient the CPRS-R:L is in helping with classification decisions.

The differences between the groups portrayed on the scales are interesting, statistically significant, and consistent. But because the prevalence of hyperactivity is some 3% in the general population and the study included 91 "nonclinical," 91 ADHD, and 55 emotional problem children, there is no way to determine the utility of the CRS in detecting ADHD from the "nonclinical" and emotional problems group. That is, when the samples are roughly a third ADHD there are statistical differences but will the CRS be useful in detecting ADHD when applied to populations where the prevalence rate is closer to 3%? The *F*s were statistically significant but tell us nothing about classification efficiency nor the magnitude of effect or clinical significance of the differences. Sensitivity, the degree to which a measure detects disordered people in a population, and specificity, the degree to which a measure distinguishes between disorders, are yet to be determined for the CRS.

The manual shows male and female matrices to have similar factor solutions. Studies presented in the manual, and published in peer-reviewed journals only after the publication of the manual, appear to support three factor solutions featuring the Oppositionalism, Cognitive Problems, and Hyperactivity scales. Recall that the CRS posit six or more scales in the various forms. But surprisingly, a study supporting the six scales/factors model is not cited. Trites, Blouin, and Laprade (1982) report a six-factor solution for the CPRS-39, with the Hyperactivity factor accounting for 36% of the variance. There is little question that the CRS is tapping something important, that there is strong evidence for a three-factor structure, that the six scales model received only partial support, and that the factorial validity studies are consistent in showing the CRS to be useful in assessing ADHD at the least. But there is an equal certainty that more research by the author and by independent researchers needs to be published in peer-reviewed journals, and that the manual needs to include peer-reviewed validity research.

CONCLUSIONS. The 30-year anniversary is a time for Conners to celebrate the prominence of the CRS in clinical and research activities, particularly those addressing questions of hyperactivity. However, there is a greater urgency to address the paucity of peer-reviewed externally published validity research and the need to determine the classification accuracy of the CRS than there is a need to celebrate. Anyone engaging in educational or child clinical assessment or in research concerning child clinical syndromes generally and hyperactivity specifically, needs to consider using the CRS, weighing the limitations cited above against the flaws and benefits extant in other measures.

REVIEWER'S REFERENCES

Trites, R. L., Blouin, A. G. A., & Laprade, K. (1982). Factor analysis of the Conners' Teacher Rating Scale based on a large normative sample. *Journal of Consulting and Clinical Psychology, 50*, 615–623.

Martens, B. K. (1992). [Review of Conners' Rating Scales.] *The eleventh mental measurements yearbook* (pp. 233–234). Lincoln, NE: Buros Institute of Mental Measurements.

Oehler-Stinnett, J. (1992). [Review of Conners' Rating Scales.] *The eleventh mental measurements yearbook* (pp. 234–241). Lincoln, NE: Buros Institute of Mental Measurements.

Gregory, R. J. (1996). *Psychological testing: History, principles, and applications (2nd ed.).* Boston: Allyn and Bacon.

Review of the Conners' Rating Scales—Revised by HOWARD M. KNOFF, Professor of School Psychology, University of South Florida, Tampa, FL:

Published for the first time in 1989, the Conners' Rating Scales—Revised (CRS-R) has been revised and restandardized with three primary goals in mind: (a) to align the CRS-R with, especially, the Attention-Deficit/Hyperactivity Disorder (ADHD) criteria of the *Diagnostic and Statistical Manual of Mental Disorders* (4th Edition; DSM-IV; APA, 1994); (b) to update the norms using a large, representative normative sample; and (c) to add an adolescent self-report scale such that the CRS-R can now elicit multiple response sets from parents, teachers, and adolescents from ages 12 through 17 (to complement the parent and teacher analyses available from ages 3 to 11). With this restandardization and its main focus on the assessment of ADHD, the CRS-R reinforces its distinction as one of the best instruments in this area relative to development, psychometric integrity, and functional utility. As such, except for the three DSM-IV Symptom subscales on the Adolescent Self-Report Scales (Long and Short), the CRS-R can be used for screening, comprehensive assessment, treatment monitoring, and research.

The CRS-R actually comprises five clusters of scales: the Parent Rating Scales (Long and Short versions), the Teacher Rating Scales (Long and Short versions), the Adolescent Self-Report Scales (Long and Short versions), the Parent and Teacher Global Indexes, and the Parent, Teacher, and Adolescent versions of the ADHD/DSM-IV Scales. Usually given under the direction of a school psychologist or other psychologist, all of these scales can be used for children and youth aged 3 to 17, except the Adolescent Scales, which are used between the ages 12 and 17. Completed within the context of the child or adolescent's behavior during the last month, the Parent and Teacher scales have "reading ease" scores, using the Flesch Reading Ease Formula, at the 9th and 10th grade reading equivalents, and the Adolescent scales score at the 6th grade reading equivalent.

Overall, the CRS-R has short- and long-form versions for parents, teachers, and adolescents (via self-report), respectively. As organized by the items on its protocols, the Long version of the Parent Rating Scale (80 items) consists of seven "clinical" subscales (Oppositional, Cognitive Problems, Hyperactivity, Anxious-Shy, Perfectionism, Social Problems, Psychosomatic), the Global Indexes (Restless-Impulsive, Emotional Lability), the ADHD Index, and the DSM-IV subscale (with its Inattentive and Hyperactive-Impulsive factors). The Parent Rating Scale-Short Form (27 items) consists of three shortened clinical subscales (Oppositional, Cognitive Problems, Hyperactivity—which happen to be the three scales accounting for the most variance on the Long Form), and a shortened ADHD Index. Although there are separate protocols that allow the clinician to combine the Parent Rating Scale—Short Form (with its 27 items) with the Parent Global Index (10 items) and the Parent ADHD/DSM-IV Scales (26 items), it would appear easier and more clinically sound to give a parent *one* 80-item Parent Rating Scale—Long Form rather than *three separate* shorter form protocols totaling 63 items. Even though the Short Form scales have good psychometric properties, the integrated Long Form scale has more items (increasing its clinical reliability) and more explained variance.

Except for the Psychosomatic subscale, the Long Form of the Teacher Rating Scale (59 items) has the same subscales as the Parent Scale—Long Form along with a substantial, but not complete, overlap of individual items. The same is true for the Short Form of the Teacher Scale (28 items), which again consists of the three shortened Oppositional, Cognitive Problems, Hyperactivity subscales, and the shortened ADHD Index. The Long Form of the Adolescent Self-Report Scale (87 items) consists of six clinical subscales (Family, Emotional, Conduct, Cognitive, and Anger Control Problems, respectively, and Hyperactivity), the ADHD Index, and the DSM-IV subscales. The Adolescent Short Form (27 items) consists of the Conduct Problem, Cognitive Problem, Hyperactive-Impulsive, and ADHD Index subscales. Because some of the adapted items overlap across the Adolescent Scale and the Parent and Teacher scales, care needs to be taken when attempting to interpret results across these scales and their similar sounding subscales. This is especially true given the expected low or nonsignificant correlations between the Adolescent and the Parent and Teacher scales, respectively, that are reported in the manual.

DEVELOPMENT, PSYCHOMETRIC PROPERTIES, AND EVALUATION OF THE CRS-R. Relative to the development of the CRS-R, it appears that all of the scales, except for the DSM-IV Symptoms Subscales, were factor analytically derived (the manual reports that the DSM-IV subscales were rationally created). These factors were derived from a pilot study that involved 10 sites from eight states, and responses from (a) the parents of 2,200 students, (b) the teachers of 1,702 students, and (c) 1,749 self-reporting adolescents. Additional information about the pilot samples and the item loadings on the various factor analyses are needed (see evaluation below). The manual also needs to report the empirical research underlying the items chosen for the scales, and which items (of the 131 teacher, 193 parent, and 102 self-report items) were not retained in the scales' final versions. In addition, the author needs to clarify a statement in the manual (p. 86) that suggests the preliminary pool of items was selected to cover seven preselected content areas (i.e., conduct, activity, attention, learning, and social problems, respectively, and emotionality, and perfectionism). Although this a priori organization is not problematic per se, it *is* important to demonstrate that they have an empirical basis relative to ADHD. This preselection takes on additional importance when the final clinical scales, and their factor structures, are considered. Clearly, the close resemblance of the final scales with their original conceptualizations demonstrates the integrity of the item selection process, as well as the construct validity of the CRS-R.

Based on the factor analytic results of the pilot study, the final CRS-R norms were derived from over 8,000 cases from over 45 states and 10 provinces across the U.S. and Canada. The Long Form of the Parent Scale was based on 2,482 cases. The Short Form sample (involving 2,426 cases) overlapped substantially with the Long Form sample with the protocols simply being rescored to generate separate norms. Limited demographic and stratification data were provided (see below). The median annual household income for partici-

pating parents was between $40,001 and $50,000. As this appears to be above the median income for the country as a whole, the possibility exists that the norms may not be representative of "typical" children and adolescents in the U.S. either due to differences in parent perceptions and ratings or to the actual behavior of those in more upper-income homes. Ultimately, this is an empirical question that is offset by some of the convergent and discriminant validity data reported in the manual.

The Teacher and Adolescent Self-Report scales similarly used large samples in their norming processes (approximately 2,000 children and adolescents for the Teacher Scale and 3,400 adolescents for the Self-Report Scale). Their respective Short Form samples also largely overlapped with the Long Form samples through the rescoring of the reorganized protocols. Although the size of the normative samples used is impressive, discrepancies were noted relative to the racial distribution of rated children and adolescents. Specifically, the percentage of Caucasian students rated was approximately 83% for the Parent Scale, 78%–81% for the Teacher Scale, and 62% for the Adolescent Scale (the percentage ranges reflect differences between the Long and Short Forms of a scale). For African-American students rated, the percentages were 4%–5% for the Parent Scale, 7%–10% for the Teacher Scale, and 30% for the Adolescent Scale. The percentage of Hispanic students rated ranges from 3% to 6% of the sample across the three scales, and between 1% to 2% of the samples involved Asian, Native American, or other-racial-background students, respectively.

Although the impact of these discrepancies is unknown, the CRS-R manual did note a number of significant ethnic differences among certain scales across the Long and Short Forms of all three (Parent, Teacher, and Self-Report) CRS-R scales. In the end, clinicians will need to be careful when making comparisons and conclusions for profiles across the Parent, Teacher, and Self-Report scales of the CRS-R, both because of the demographic differences across the normative samples and the fact that correlations between these respondents are typically low.

From a psychometric perspective, the CRS-R manual reports the reliability and validity data expected for this type of tool. Relative to the reliability, internal consistency, reliability estimates appear acceptable, ranging from .72 to .95. Six- to

8-week test-retest reliabilities are similarly acceptable, ranging from .47 to .92. Relative to the validity, factorial validity was reported for the Long and Short Forms, respectively, of the Parent, Teacher, and Self-Report Scales looking at both the intercorrelations between the subscales and the factorial structures for males and females. Once again, based on the data provided in the manual, both the intercorrelations among the subtests for the Long and Short Forms of the three scales and the confirmatory factor analyses reported for the Short Forms of the scales appear acceptable.

Finally, the manual addresses construct validity by reporting the CRS-R's convergent validity (primarily through interrespondent correlations) and its discriminant validity (primarily through investigating three different clinical or nonclinical groups of adolescents). As expected, there was considerable variability in the intersubscale correlations between the parent and teacher ratings; low or nonsignificant correlations between parent and adolescent self-report ratings and teacher and adolescent self-report ratings also were reported. Although the samples and data collection methods used were not well-described, the discriminant validity findings across an ADHD, "emotional problem," and randomly selected CRS-R normative group did reveal significant differences in most of the predicted directions across all of the subscales for the Parent, Teacher, and Self-Report Scales, respectively.

CRITICAL OMISSIONS. Even though the CRS-R is well organized and is very detailed throughout, there are a number of omissions that made specific aspects of the CRS-R difficult to evaluate. Some of the notable omissions include the lack of information regarding: (a) how the sites and participants in the pilot and norming processes were chosen (e.g., randomly, by convenience, or in a different manner); (b) how reflective the 10 pilot sites were of the demographics of the country and (later) of the norming sample; (c) the specific item correlations from the pilot study's factor analytic results that largely determined which items were included in the final CRS-R; (d) demographic stratification of the parent participants *and the students who were rated* in the norming process across the country (especially by gender, age, race, and SES), and how these demographics compared with the U.S. Census; (e) the teachers and adolescents who participated in the norming

and their descriptive characteristics (e.g., the teachers' degrees, years of experience, gender with race, etc.; the adolescents' age and gender with race, their grade-point averages, etc.); (f) where and how the Canadian participants were fit into the norming process and statistical analyses; (g) how many mothers versus fathers participated in the Parent norming process, and the statistical analyses to demonstrate that the CRS-R's profiles can be used with either parent respondent; (h) the statistical rationale for separating the norms into the five (3–5, 6–8, 9–11, 12–14, 15–17 year) age group clusters, and the factor analytic/construct validity of the CRS-R across these age clusters; (i) the normative and discriminant validity support for the recommendation that children or youth scoring at the 65T level be evaluated further; and (j) how the CRS-R accommodated for the racial differences found and reported in the manual.

In the face of the large standardization sample and the reliability and validity data reported, these omissions are important but they do not undermine the overall strength of the CRS-R. Nonetheless, these issues should be addressed in future revisions of the manual. If done, this would only make the general use of the CRS-R unquestioned.

SUMMARY. Given its revision, restandardization, psychometric integrity, and functional utility, the Conners' Rating Scales—Revised maintains its place as one of the best instruments available relative to assessing ADHD and its concomitant behaviors for children and adolescents aged 3 to 17. The CRS-R now appears to be well aligned with the ADHD criteria of the DSM-IV, it has updated its norms using a large sample of children and adolescents drawn from across the country and Canada, and it has added an adolescent self-report scale (for ages 12 through 17) such that multirespondent data can be collected from parents, teachers, and adolescents.

The CRS-R is now composed of five clusters of scales: the Parent Rating Scales (Long and Short versions), the Teacher Rating Scales (Long and Short versions), the Adolescent Self-Report Scales (Long and Short versions), the Parent and Teacher Global Indexes, and the Parent, Teacher, and Adolescent versions of the ADHD/DSM-IV Scales. Each scale comes with a separate protocol and profile form that provides easy-to-understand directions and scoring approaches that minimize errors. Although the manual needs some added description, especially relative to the samples used to pilot and norm the CRS-R and the factor analyses used to demonstrate the scale's construct validity across the age and gender groups used, it provides an exceptional amount of information that is clear and well organized, and that includes interpretive guidelines and a series of prototypical case studies.

Overall, except for the three DSM-IV Symptom subscales on the Adolescent Self-Report Scales (Long and Short), the CRS-R can continue to be used for its intended screening, comprehensive assessment, treatment monitoring, and research purposes. Although additional research is needed to replicate and validate the work reported in the manual, it is clear that the CRS-R is a well-crafted and important tool in the assessment of ADHD children and adolescents.

[99]
Contextual Memory Test.

Purpose: Designed to assess awareness of memory capacity, strategy use, and recall in adults with memory dysfunction.
Population: Adults.
Publication Date: 1993.
Acronym: CMT.
Scores, 12: Recall Score (Immediate Recall, Delayed Recall, Total Recall), Cued Recall, Recognition, Awareness Score (Prediction, Estimation of Performance Following Recall, Response to General Questioning [Prior to Recall, Following Recall]), Strategy Use (Effect of Context, Order of Recall, Total Strategy Score).
Administration: Individual.
Price Data, 1999: $89 per complete kit including manual (138 pages), 2 test cards, 14 cut-apart sheets of 80 picture cards, 25 score sheets (12 pages), and carrying case; $32 per 25 score sheets.
Time: Administration time not reported.
Author: Joan P. Toglia.
Publisher: Therapy Skill Builders—A Division of The Psychological Corporation.

Review of the Contextual Memory Test by KAREN MACKLER, School Psychologist, Lawrence Public Schools, Lawrence, NY:

The Contextual Memory Test (CMT) examines different aspects of an individual's knowledge of their memory limitations, following such events as head trauma, CVAs, dementia, brain tumor, etc. It also assists in determining how responsive a patient is to using cues to enhance recall. The author states that "this information is directly related to choosing and designing a compensatory or remedial treatment program" (p. 1). It is understood that the instrument is not diagnostic in nature, and the information should be used to supplement more conventional measures of memory and cognition.

The CMT has two equivalent versions. Each consists of a picture card containing 20 drawings of items relating to either a Restaurant or a Morning scene. The test is given in two parts. Part I (noncontext) requires recall without being told the theme. Part II is given only if the patient scores below criterion on Part I, and the theme is told to the patient. If recall does not improve significantly after being given the schema, a task involving cued recall and recognition can be used. These additional tasks were not included in the original research. In addition to the recall tasks, the patient is asked to respond to questions regarding estimation of memory capacity, awareness of actual performance, and strategies used to recall.

The basic test takes approximately 5–10 minutes to administer, with a 15–20-minute time interval before the delayed recall task is given. If the patient demonstrates difficulty, the time is increased to include cued recall and recognition tasks.

The manual is written in a straightforward manner. Directions for administration become clearer upon familiarity with the protocol. Strengths and limitations of the measure are stated explicitly in the manual. Although administration is easy, scoring and interpretation are more difficult. Twelve scores are obtained. Raw scores are compared to norms to determine norm-referenced scores.

A weakness of this measure is its norms. The measure was standardized on 375 adults, ages 17 to 86, from the New York City area. Eighty-three percent of the sample was Caucasian, indicating inadequate ethnic diversity. In addition, 50% of the group held a college degree. Demographic variables such as educational level and age significantly influenced recall scores. The text offers many disclaimers as to the use of the scores. Perhaps more important than comparing scores to normed scores is to examine the pattern of scores relative to one's own performance. Many suggestions for remediation of specific weaknesses are included within the manual. These strategies are helpful and sensible. Several case studies are presented to illustrate different profiles.

The Morning and Restaurant versions of the measure are considered appropriate alternative forms if used with their corresponding standard score conversion tables. The tables are different to account for differences found in difficulty level between the two versions.

A sample population of 112 individuals with brain injury aged 17–88 was tested to assess reliability and validity. This group was similar in sex to the control group, but differed in education (lower), race (more diverse), and mean age (higher). In addition, these individuals covered a wide range of diagnoses. As such, it cannot be said with certainty that the scores obtained are representative for a specific patient experiencing memory impairment. Clinically it has been noted that some patients benefit from the context version of the test, whereas others do not.

Recall scores were analyzed for reliability using parallel form, test-retest, and Rasch analysis. Parallel form reliability compared the Morning and Restaurant versions of the test. These estimates ranged from .73 to .81, with higher reliability estimates for the context versions. A quasi-test-retest reliability estimate was obtained by correlating immediate recall scores with delayed recall scores. Full test administration procedures were not followed for the delayed score, voiding the potential for a true test-retest reliability score. These estimates ranged from .74 to .87 for the control group and .85 to .94 for the subjects with brain injury.

Rasch analysis generates item separation scores and person separation scores. For the full sample (control and patients with brain injury), person separation reliabilities ranged from .75 to .77 with immediate and delayed recall scores taken separately. When the recall scores were combined, reliability improved to .89 to .90. Overall reliability estimates indicate that the measure stands up over time.

Prediction scores were found to be highly reliable, with a correlation score of .90. Strategy scores correlated at .75 between the two versions of the test.

Concurrent validity was assessed by correlating recall scores on this measure with those obtained on the Rivermead Behavioral Memory Test. Results of these correlations were in the upper .70s to mid .80s.

Discriminant function analysis was used to assess the ability of the CMT to discriminate between nondisabled individuals and those with brain injury. An overall hit rate of .873 was obtained with immediate and delayed recall scores. Adding in the total strategy score resulted in a high rate of .911. The addition of the discrepancy score did not improve the hit rate (.907).

Overall, the Contextual Memory Test (CMT) is an easily administered measure that appears to have potential usefulness in the assessment of an individual's knowledge of and use of specific memory strategies. It is questionable how useful the normed scores are. Rather, the instrument provides a structured method for obtaining information regarding current strategies used and gives some useful suggestions for translating test performance into remediation and treatment goals.

Review of the Contextual Memory Test by ALAN J. RAPHAEL, President, International Assessment Systems, Inc., Miami, FL:

Published in 1993 by Therapy Skills Builders, a Division of The Psychological Corporation, the Contextual Memory Test (CMT) is a 40-item measure designed to assess awareness of memory capacity, strategy use, and recall in adults with bonafide memory dysfunction.

According to the test developer, the CMT is not diagnostic in purpose and is intended solely to provide information that can supplement traditional measures of memory and cognition. This distinction is contradictory and confusing, as it is labeled as a test, yet denies the essential diagnostic qualities of a test.

Although the test has a large normative sample of 375, the sample is biased with only about 25% of the subjects possessing a high school education or less. There is also an overemphasis on younger people, yet no material is provided on the interaction between age and education, which is likely to occur in skewed normative samples. The overemphasis on younger subjects is also problematic given that memory dysfunctions are more relevant to middle-aged and older populations. There is information on age and education correlates; however, norms provided present only gross correlations for age and none at all for education despite a higher correlation of education with test indices. Raw scores are transformed into "standard" scores; however, the mean and standard deviation of these scores is not provided (although standard error of the mean scores are presented).

There are clear directions for labeling scores normal or abnormal, but the reasoning behind such distinctions is unclear.

The normative data are questionable as well. The CMT has been standardized on subjects without obvious memory dysfunction who are 18 years old and older and has purportedly demonstrated evidence of reliable and valid interpretations for adults who have organic memory dysfunction. According to the author, the test is unique in that it examines different aspects of individuals' self-awareness of their memory limitations.

Testing based on one brain-injured group is presented, but the demographic characteristics of this and the normal groups are quite different. The brain-injured group consists primarily of people with CVAs, tumors, and dementia, and is much older and less educated than the normal group. The author makes no attempt to look at diagnostic differences between the brain-injured group and a matched group of control clients, although general comparisons are made on some score distributions without correcting for demographic information.

The test generates many measures that have unclear scoring. There are no factor analytic or other procedures to indicate how the different scores relate to one another.

Like many self-report measures, this instrument has no method of controlling for test-taking attitude or external influences like work avoidance, depression, malingering, deception, or random responding. This is particularly significant for memory measures that are often involved in rehabilitation matters or personal injury litigation where secondary gain matters like financial compensation abound.

Reliability data on the measure are generally good, with parallel form reliability estimated along with correlations with the Rivermead Behavioral Memory Test. Reliabilities generally fell in the .70+ range, consistent with other reliable tests of memory function. The authors also report what they call "quasi test-retest reliability" (p. 1) by correlating immediate and delayed memory.

Overall, from an empirical viewpoint, this test has value as a measure of memory function. However, the measure as it currently stands possesses significant limitations as a clinical instrument and should be limited to use as a research instrument until further research clarifies its value,

validity, and reliability for use in diverse populations. It should not be used to determine memory function or memory impairment in individuals whose status potentially or definitely supports a claim seeking compensation for injuries or illnesses related to memory impairment.

[100]
Continuous Visual Memory Test [Revised].

Purpose: Constructed to assess recognition memory, perception, and discrimination.
Population: Ages 7–80+.
Publication Dates: 1983–1997.
Acronym: CVMT.
Scores, 6: Acquisition (Hits, False Alarms, d-Prime, Total), Delayed Recognition, Visual Discrimination.
Administration: Individual.
Price Data, 2001: $139 per complete kit including manual ('88, 22 pages), norms manual ('97, 51 pages), stimulus cards, and 50 scoring forms; $29 per manual; $19 per norms manual; $64 per stimulus cards' $36 per 50 scoring forms.
Time: (45–50) minutes.
Authors: Donald E. Trahan and Glenn J. Larrabee.
Publisher: Psychological Assessment Resources, Inc.
Cross References: See T5:687 (4 references); for reviews by Nancy B. Bologna and Stephen F. Davis of an earlier edition, see 12:93; see also T4:642 (4 references).

Review of the Continuous Visual Memory Test by MICHAEL B. BROWN, Associate Professor of Psychology, East Carolina University, Greenville, NC:

The Continuous Visual Memory Test (CVMT) is a visual recognition memory test, designed to measure three aspects of visual memory. The Acquisition Task measures recognition memory by having the person differentiate previously learned stimuli from newly presented stimuli. A Delayed Recognition Task is presented after a 30-minute delay, and the examinee is required to identify stimuli previously presented from a set of similar stimuli. The Visual Discrimination Task assesses the ability of the examinee to accurately discriminate stimuli and thus help to differentiate between problems with visual discrimination and visual memory deficits. Administration time, including the 30-minute delay for the Delayed Recognition Task, is about 45–50 minutes. The test was designed to measure memory functions in persons with neurological impairments, and appropriate examinees must be able to understand the requirements of the tasks, have adequate visual acuity, and be capable of providing an appropriate response to the task. In addition, persons with severe psychiatric disorders usually have impaired scores on the CVMT and, therefore, the CVMT should not be administered until symptoms have subsided. The authors note that the test should be used with caution for children under 8 or persons over 80.

MATERIALS. The test materials consist of 137 bound stimulus cards and a four-page scoring form. Eleven stimulus cards are used as sample stimulus items, 112 cards are test items for the Acquisition Task, and 7 cards are used for the Visual Discrimination Task. There are also 7 cards that contain the items for the Delayed-Recognition Task. The four-page scoring form includes sections for recording demographic data about the examinee and has a scoring summary on the front page. The inside page has space to record the examinee's responses to the three tasks, and includes a useful visual representation of the Delayed Recognition and Visual Discrimination Tasks. The spacing and design are adequate. The second inside page and the last page are devoted to providing scoring formulas, cutoff scores, and a table of values to be used in scoring calculations. These items are probably of some utility for the examiner in the use of the test, although the examiner might just as easily refer to the manual, resulting in a savings of two pages of the scoring form and, presumably, a lower cost per use.

MANUAL. The CVMT manual comes in two parts. A 1988 manual contains information on the test, how it was constructed, administration and scoring, and norms for persons ages 18–70+. An additional manual, published in 1997, contains normative data for children and adolescents and older adults (ages 50 and above). The manuals are brief (the 1988 manual is 19 pages and the 1997 manual is 47 pages). Both are attractively printed and relatively easy to read. There is a very brief introduction to memory assessment and visual memory that consists mainly of information published prior to 1988. The 1997 manual provides some additional information about the technical characteristics of the test.

Administration and scoring are described, including sample directions for the three tasks. Scoring is fairly simple, as the examiner is required to note the examinee's responses by coding "0" next to any item the examinee identifies as previously shown or whether the response was correct or incorrect. Four variables are scored for the Acquisition Task. Hits are the correct recognition of a recurring item, and False Alarms are scored when the examinee identifies a new stimulus as a reoccurring one. The Total score is the number of Hits plus the number of correct identifications of new items. Finally, the concept of d-Prime is borrowed from signal detection theory, and this value is used as an overall measure of memory sensitivity.

TECHNICAL CHARACTERISTICS. The 1988 standardization group for the CVMT included 310 adults ranging from 18–91 years of age. The norm group was divided into four age ranges (18–29, 30–49, 50–69, and 70+), with groups ranging from 30 participants in the 70+ range to 139 in the 30–49-year age range. All participants were screened for neurological and psychiatric impairment and were considered healthy. The average level of education for each group included some college. No data were provided as to where or how the sample was chosen or how representative the sample was for racial or geographical variables. The 1997 Supplemental Norms include two studies using children, one with 138 American children in Grades 1 through 5 and 640 Canadian children from 9 to 15 years of age. Children in the American sample were elementary school students in one small Midwestern town. Children in the Canadian sample were selected from six elementary and middle schools in a large western Canadian city. Eighty-eight adults over age 50 from the 1988 norms were combined with 77 others from two additional studies to form a revised older adult norm group. The average level of education includes some college, and the residence of these adults included Texas, Florida, Montana, and Los Angeles, California. No data are supplied on ethnicity or socioeconomic variables.

Split-half reliability was calculated for 25 patients with severe closed head injury and 25 matched normal subjects (none of whom were included in the standardization sample). Reliability coefficients for recurring items were .80 and .98 for normal and neurological patients respectively, and .98 and .90 for nonrecurring items. Test-retest reliability (administration interval = 7 days) was examined in a sample of 12 normal adults, with correlations of .85 for the total score, .80 for d-Prime scores, and .76 for the Delayed Recognition Task over 7 days. Validity was demonstrated using test performance by persons with unilateral hemisphere lesions, finding that there was a difference in performance on the CVMT by persons with right versus left hemisphere cerebrovascular lesions. Other studies found that CVMT performance was impaired for persons with a variety of neurological disorders. Construct validity was assessed through factor studies demonstrating that CVMT delayed recognition performance is independent of verbal learning and that older participants did more poorly on the CVMT than did younger participants.

OVERALL EVALUATION. The use and interpretation of the CVMT is seriously compromised by the inadequate technical data gathered on the test. The standardization groups present obvious problems. The number of persons included in the samples is much too limited. Adults with very minimal education are not represented well in the norm group. The American children's group is much more homogenous than the Canadian children's group. We do not have information on how representative all of the samples are for racial or socioeconomic variables. The reliability data are provided by a small group, the ages of which are not revealed. The evidence for validity is somewhat better, but leaves a great deal to be desired in establishing a level of comfort with the test's validity. There are no studies that attempt to differentiate normal from neurologically impaired adults based on the use of the test. That the test cannot differentiate between neurologically and seriously psychiatrically impaired individuals removes one of the potential uses of this test for the practicing clinician.

Review of the Continuous Visual Memory Test by ALICE J. CORKILL, Associate Professor and Co-Director, Cognitive Interference Laboratory, University of Nevada, Las Vegas, NV:

The Continuous Visual Memory Test (CVMT) is designed to assess an individual's ability to recognize complex ambiguous figures that do not easily lend themselves to verbal labeling. It is appropriate for use with people age 7 through and beyond age 80. In particular, the three tests on the CVMT are designed to measure either learning or retention. Learning refers to the initial acquisition of new information. Retention refers to the storage of learned information beyond the normal limits of short-term memory. As

the authors state, on many tests, learning and retention are indistinguishable. The CVMT allegedly allows differentiation between learning and retention and, therefore, may allow a more specific understanding of memory impairment.

The authors provide a thorough description of the theoretical foundation for the test. Although the test has not changed since it was first published (1983), it is unfortunate that with the publication of additional normative data (1997) the authors did not update the "Memory Assessment" portion of the 1988 Professional Manual. Marked advances in the neurosciences between 1988 and 1997 have shed light on many links between the brain and cognitive functioning, among those localization of cognitive skills. The Professional Manual would have been well served by an update.

The CVMT consists of three tasks: an Acquisition Task, a Delayed Recognition Task, and a Visual Discrimination Task. During the Acquisition Task, which is designed to measure learning, subjects view 112 cards that contain geometric figures based on 70 different complex ambiguous designs. Seven of the 70 designs are recurring and appear seven times during the administration of this portion of the test. Each of the 7 recurring designs was created to portray one of the following categories: solid random 7-point polygons, hollow random 10-point polygons, solid random 12-point polygons, irregular nonsense figures, complex line drawings, checkerboard patterns, and randomized patterns of 14 stick segments. Furthermore, of the 70 different designs, 42 are distraction designs for each of the 7 recurring designs (6 distraction designs for each recurring design). The distraction designs are perceptually similar to the recurring designs. The 112 items are arranged in 16-item blocks for scoring purposes. In the first block of 16 all 7 recurring designs appear. In each subsequent block of 16 (7 blocks of 16 = 112 cards), an examinee will see the 7 recurring designs, 7 distraction designs (one of each of the recurring design categories), and 2 nonrecurring designs that are unrelated to the recurring design categories.

Examinees are instructed to identify whether they have previously seen a design by orally labeling each design as "old" or "new." Therefore, for the first block of 16 designs, the examinee should indicate that all 16 designs are "new." During subsequent blocks, however, the examinee should indicate that 7 of each block of 16 are "old" without labeling a distractor design as "old." The examinee, of course, does not know that the cards are arranged in blocks of 16. To the examinee, the cards simply appear as a sequence of 112 different designs.

Design cards are displayed at a rate of one card every 2 seconds. If examinees take longer than 2 seconds to provide a response, the examiner is to cover the figure with one hand, ask for a response, and then remind the examinee of the 2-second time limit. Examinees are encouraged to label the design as "old" or "new" as quickly as possible. Responses are recorded on a preprinted scoring form that indicates whether the design is new or old. Examiners are instructed to record the time the acquisition task was completed so that an appropriate delay interval can be allocated.

Thirty minutes after the completion of the Acquisition Task, examinees are administered the Delayed Recognition Task. Examinees are not informed that there will be a Delayed Recognition Task. Examinees may complete other tests during the delay interval as long as they do not contain visual stimuli similar to those used in the CVMT.

During the Delayed Recognition Task, which is designed to measure retention, examinees examine stimulus cards that contain a display of seven complex ambiguous figures, one of which is identical to a recurring figure from the acquisition phase of the test, the other six of which are identical to the six distractor figures that appeared only once during the Acquisition Task. Examinees are instructed to select the figure that appeared seven times during the Acquisition Task. Examinee responses are recorded on a preprinted scoring form that indicates the location of the recurring figure. Examinees are given up to 15 seconds to study the card before they are urged to provide a response.

Immediately following the Delayed Recognition Task, examinees complete the final portion of the CVMT, the Visual Discrimination Task. During the Visual Discrimination Task, examinees are shown a complex ambiguous figure on one card and are asked to identify which of seven designs on a second card is identical. Examinees are given up to 15 seconds to study the cards before they are urged to provide a response. Examinee responses are recorded on a preprinted scoring form that indicates the location of the identical figure.

The Acquisition Task results in 4 scores: Hits, False Alarms, d-Prime, and Total score. A Hit is the correct identification of a recurring design. A False Alarm is identification of a non-recurring design as a recurring design. Total score is the number of Hits plus the number of correct recognitions of new items. A simple formula is provided for calculating total score: Total score = (number of Hits) + 54 - (number of False Alarms). The d-Prime score represents an overall measure of memory sensitivity. It is predicated on signal detection theory and, therefore, is an indicator of "signal strength." Exactly what the d-Prime score means is not explained well. The d-Prime score is calculated with the following equation: d-Prime = z[Pr(Hits)] - z[Pr(False Alarms)]. The z values may be obtained from either the Appendix of the Professional Manual or the scoring form.

The Delayed Recognition Task responses are scored as either correct or incorrect. The scores for the Delayed Recognition Task range from 0–7. The Visual Discrimination Task responses are also scored as either correct or incorrect. The scores for the Visual Discrimination Task range from 0–7.

In the Professional Manual (1988), based on a sample of 310 adults ranging in age from 18–70+, norms are provided for 5 of the 6 scores: Hits, False Alarms, d-Prime, Total Score, and Delayed Recognition Task score. In the *Supplemental Normative Data for Children and Older Adults* (1997), based on three samples, three sets of norms are provided for 4 of the 6 scores: Hits, False Alarms, Total score, and Delayed Recognition Task score. Norms for d-Prime are not included due to problems associated with instances when numbers of Hits or False Alarms fall at or near the extremes of the distribution. Under such circumstances, Total scores and d-Prime scores may be dramatically different. The authors suggest that Total score is, as a result, the best score to use to indicate overall test performance. The three norm samples are based on (a) American children (n = 138) from age 7–11 (smallest n = 25, largest n = 30); (b) Canadian children (n = 640) from age 9–15 (smallest n = 11, largest n = 88 for the 65–79 group). In the American children and older adults norms, as well as the norms from the 1988 manual, percentiles are presented for age groups regardless of sex. In the Canadian children norms, however, norms for boys and girls are separate and different norm tables are provided based on IQ (greater than 110 and less than or equal to 110). In some instances, the number of examinees in a norm group is extremely low (e.g., n = 11) and, as a result, the reported percentiles should be considered unstable. It should also be noted that no norms are reported for ages 16 or 17. In addition, no normative information is reported for the Visual Discrimination portion of the CVMT.

Corrected split-half (odd—even) reliability estimates for the Acquisition Task and the Delayed Recognition Task for both neurologically impaired (n = 25) and matched normal controls (n = 25) range from .80 to .98. Test-retest reliability (administration interval = 7 days) for total recall (Acquisition Task), d-Prime (Acquisition Task), and the Delayed Recognition Task (n = 12) were .85, .80, and .76 respectively. In both instances, sample sizes are extremely low; as a result, the reliability estimates should be considered unstable. No reliability values were reported for the Visual Discrimination portion of the CVMT.

Estimates of construct validity are based primarily on two studies, one with 92 neurologically normal adults in the 18–61 age range and one with an unknown number of patients known to suffer from a neurological impairment (e.g., severe closed head injury, Alzheimer's type dementia, amnestic syndrome) associated with a high rate of memory deficits. In the study with neurologically normal adults, d-Prime was associated with general cognitive variables and Delayed Recognition Task scores were associated with an independent dimension of visual memory functioning. The study with the neurologically impaired sample showed that these subjects performed poorly on at least two CVMT scores (which scores are not reported in the Professional Manual). Two further studies are reported. These studies indicate that the CVMT shows neither significant differences between males and females on test scores nor between individuals with different levels of education. None of the studies report on the Visual Discrimination portion of the CVMT. It is unfortunate that with the publication of additional normative data (1997) the authors did not update the "Reliability" or "Validity" portions of the 1988 Professional Manual. No new reliability or validity information appears in the 1997 Supplement although at least two citations in the references indicate studies of construct validity since the 1988 professional Manual. In addition, no validity or reliability estimates are based on how children perform on the test.

SUMMARY. The Continuous Visual Memory Test is an instrument that is likely more appropriate for research uses than for assessing neurological impairment. A nice feature of the test is the separate tests for learning and retention. Although the test has not changed since it was first published (1983), it is unfortunate that with the publication of additional normative data (1997) the authors did not update the reliability and validity information or the memory assessment portion of the test manual. In its current form, the reliability and validity evidence for scores from the CVMT is questionable due to small sample sizes, no data for the visual discrimination test, and incomplete reports in the test manual.

[101]

The Conversational Skills Rating Scale: An Instructional Assessment of Interpersonal Competence.

Purpose: "To assess the skills domain of conversational competence."
Population: Secondary and post-secondary students.
Publication Date: 1995.
Acronym: CSRS.
Scores, 5: Altercentricism, Composure, Expressiveness, Interaction Management, Total.
Administration: Group.
Forms, 7: Rating of Partner Form, Rating of Self Form, Instructor Rating of Student Form, Self Frequency Version, Partner Frequency Version, Self Trait Rating Form, Other Trait Rating Form.
Price Data: Available from publisher.
Time: (5–15) minutes.
Author: Brian H. Spitzberg.
Publisher: National Communication Association.

Review of The Conversational Skills Rating Scale: An Instructional Assessment of Interpersonal Competence by SANDRA M. KETROW, Professor of Communication Studies, University of Rhode Island, Kingston, RI:

The Conversational Skills Rating Scale (CSRS) "was developed to provide a psychometrically sound instrument for assessing self or other interpersonal skills in the context of conversation" (manual, p. 1). It can be used to evaluate specific *or* general conversations in a "variety of populations." In addition, it can be used to generate "data for institutional accountability."

The author posits that because competence is context driven, the traditional expectations for reliability and validity coefficients approaching unity are less applicable. However, internal consistency "is usually in the high .80s to low .90s" (manual, p. 10). Validity measures of .33 for instructor vis-a-vis observer-ratings of molar skill, or lower for others (with higher levels hovering in .30–.45 range) are troubling. Further explication of the reliability evidence is warranted, given these other data.

The issue of applicability for general conversations is one of the problems Spitzberg (the test author) notes regarding competence—that it can be "episodic/contextual" or "dispositional/pancontextual" (manual, p. 4), and he further notes that competence skills can be particular to an individual or "relationship-specific." Also, social knowledge of the other, one's cognitive schema, as well as cultural standards for competence, may drive perceptions. So, although a person might be unskilled in an artificial, staged exchange, it is possible for him or her to be skilled in ongoing, developed relational episodes that occur longitudinally (or the converse). His 1991 study tested trait measures, including communication involvement, apprehension, attentiveness, and self-monitoring. The results indicated that competence is indeed context-specific. Other data Spitzberg cites demonstrate a trend of support for external and predictive validity. However, his measure fails to account for the mediating influence of other affect besides motivation. For example, some people are nervous about first encounters, and likely would be scored as less competent if the CSRS is used as a one-shot measure.

A collateral difficulty with Spitzberg's CSRS is the derivation of items and factor structures. In one case, a two-factor solution (Expressiveness and Interaction Management for instructors, and Expressiveness and Composure for partners and peers) is identified. As other research shows, this model is not stable, although Spitzberg cites a co-authored 1990 study in which he posits that a four- *and* a five-factor solution are supported. Spitzberg states that "the CSRS is best viewed as a factorially complex instrument" (manual, p. 9). This is one explanation for the failure to isolate stable factors across studies (including his own). Several studies cited had sample sizes large enough to support appropriate cross validation on split sample, but none of this seems to have been conducted or reported, nor were Wilks's lambda scores for significance.

Some suspicion is raised about content validity evidence. That is, are the 25 molecular and the 5 molar items either necessary or sufficient to establish interpersonal communication competence? The identification (or nomenclature) of vocalics versus the factors Expressiveness, Altercentrism, Composure, and Interaction Management seems to confuse behavior (vocalics) with interpretation of behavior. Several molecular items related to effective (vs. competent) use of nonverbal cues require judgments about negatives, whereas almost all the other items are neutrally or positively stated (e.g., "speaking disfluency" versus speaking fluency, or "unmotivated movements" versus body or body extremity movements). Spitzberg neglects or sidesteps any focus on knowledge or affect (which differs from motivation) except indirectly. These cognitive and affective dimensions underpin the performative. Other studies identify competencies required for molar assessment. Trenholm and Jensen (2000) present a model that includes an internal, or processual, dimension, composed of goal, role, self, perceptual, and message knowledge/repertoire/selection components. The second dimension of their model is external, or performative, consisting of appropriately and effectively used behaviors, such as listening or disclosure skills. This latter dimension is the area about which communication competence specialists most disagree. The primary difficulty in terms of construct validity is that "the constructs may not be conceptually tied to competence, either in general, or as operationalized by the CSRS" (manual, p. 10). If one only wishes to check light conversational competence, the CSRS may be appropriate. However, a claim that the CSRS measures a more generalized interpersonal communication competence goes far past the construct/content validity evidence provided for this instrument.

The CSRS appears to be culturally bound. One example of these limits lies in Spitzberg's claim that its use as a "get-acquainted conversation" is highly relevant to college students (indeed, probably to everyone)" (manual, p. 6). In some cultures, an elaborate process is employed for meeting others, particularly for young males and females. A second example is related to Expressiveness, which is not valued panculturally as stated in the CSRS ("facial expressiveness [neither blank nor exaggerated]"). Spitzberg does cite two studies that support cross-cultural generalization. However, other researchers (G. M. Chen, personal communication, January 23, 2001) have identified other atomistic and global areas. Chen argues that one problem with such measures as the CSRS is that they are presented as "one-size-fits-all," but that they cannot achieve that goal. Another issue is the focus on behavior as representing competence. Communication competence researchers argue, instead, that communication includes knowledge, motivation (affect), and skill.

A third problem area is sensitivity and awareness. Intercultural communication competence scholars use these terms to mean partly knowledge, but also perspective-taking, empathy, and generally "tuning in" to the other person. Spitzberg would argue that this is Altercentrism, which is partly accurate, but the behavioral items that comprise this factor include "asking questions," "nodding of head in response to partner statements," etc. Nonverbal communication scholars have pointed out that women and African Americans nod more as back-channel cues, and that this behavior means "I am listening." In contrast, males tend to use this cue to mean "I agree." At best, these behavioral measures tap listening indirectly. Thus, one large dilemma is that of cross- (and co-) cultural bypassing.

A final issue with intercultural and interpersonal communication competence researchers is the composition of the construct "competence." Chen (Chen & Starosta, 2000) and others have argued that effectiveness is only one component of competence. At least the CSRS asks for a perception rating of effectiveness and appropriateness. Spitzberg has the actor and the partner (or instructor or peer) rate for both. If the actor does not believe that she or he has achieved a conscious goal of making a new friend but the partner perceives that the actor is a good conversationalist and that the actor has achieved the exercise goal of engaging in a brief interaction, the ratings will be inconsistent and correlations will be low. Even trained observers' ratings show less than satisfactory reliability coefficients, and no interrater or intrarater reliabilities are reported. As it stands, then, the CSRS shows limitations with content, predictive, and external validity.

SUMMARY. If one is searching for an instrument to measure surface-level interpersonal *conversation* competence as demonstrated in some behaviors, particularly in a classroom or training setting, this instrument is an appropriate choice. An alternative choice might be the Iowa Commu-

nication Record (ICR) (Duck, Rutt, Hurst, & Strejc, 1991; Leatham & Duck, 1990). The ICR is much stronger with respect to measuring real interpersonal communication competence, although in some respects more subjective and relationship-bound. The larger and underlying dimensions of communication, social, and other knowledge, motivation (affect), and awareness remain unresolved in these instruments. Locating a single measure for interpersonal and intercultural communication competence is as yet unattainable.

REVIEWER'S REFERENCES

Leatham, G., & Duck, S. (1990). Conversations with friends and the dynamics of social support. In S. W. Duck & R. C. Silver (Eds.), *Personal relationships and social support* (pp. 23–27). London: Sage Publications.

Duck, S., Rutt, D. J., Hurst, M. H., & Strejc, H. (1991). Some evident truths about conversations in everyday relationships: All communications are not equal. *Human Communication Research, 18*, 228–267.

Spitzberg, B. (1991). An examination of trait measures of interpersonal competence. *Communication Reports, 4*, 22–29.

Chen, G. M., & Starosta, W. J. (2000). The development and validation of the intercultural communication sensitivity scale. *Human Communication, 3*, 1-15.

Trenholm, S., & Jensen, A. (2000). *Interpersonal communication* (4th ed.). Belmont, CA: Wadsworth.

Review of The Conversational Skills Rating Scale: An Instructional Assessment of Interpersonal Competence by JULIA Y. PORTER, Assistant Professor of Counselor Education, Mississippi State University, Meridian, MS:

The Conversational Skills Rating Scale (CSRS) examines 25 behavioral items that make up four skill clusters that are a part of interpersonal competence. According to Spitzberg (the test author), it is the evaluation of a behavior's appropriateness and effectiveness that determine its competence in any given context. This instrument can be used as an episodic measure to assess a specific conversational encounter or as a dispositional measure to assess a general cross-situational tendency. The CSRS has been used "(a) to assess students in class and provide diagnostic feedback on their conversational behavior; (b) to provide students feedback in ecologically representative settings; (c) to examine improvement from one point in time (i.e., assessing a particular conversational encounter) to another point in time (i.e., assessing a general cross-situational tendency); and (d) as a research instrument" (manual, p. 6).

There are seven CSRS rating scale forms: one for an instructor to rate a student, three forms for self-ratings, two forms for rating a conversational partner, and one form for an outside observer. The opportunity to triangulate instrument results strengths the accuracy of the ratings. Instructions found at the top of each rating form are clear and easy to follow. The 25 behavioral items to be evaluated on each of the rating forms are specific and easily identifiable. The CSRS manual contains a description of each of the 25 behavioral items and a definition of what each of the numerical ratings (1, 2, 3, 4, 5) under that item mean. Each item is ranked on a 5-point competence continuum scale with 1 = *inadequate* (meaning there is extensive room for improvement), 2 = *Fair*, 3 = *Adequate*, 4 = *Good*, and 5 = *Excellent* (meaning no room for improvement).

The most common use of the CSRS is by an instructor rating students who are interacting in a get-acquainted conversation or other stimulus conversation. The internal reliability coefficient was reported as consistently greater than .85. Interrater reliability was .75. Information about the norm group was not given. Face validity is demonstrated by a low level of abstraction in measuring competence. However, a limitation is that there may be other skills that reflect competence that have not yet been identified. Research is continuing on the CSRS to determine whether there are additional skill domains not represented in the current version.

SUMMARY. The Conversational Skills Rating Scale can be used to help students and individuals identify strengths and weaknesses in their conversational skills. The CSRS is easy to administer and interpret. It can be used in a variety of settings such as speech classes, counseling sessions, and employment interviews.

[102]
Coolidge Axis II Inventory.

Purpose: Designed as a measure of personality disorders.
Population: Ages 15 and older.
Publication Date: 1993.
Acronym: CATI.
Scores, 45: 13 Personality Disorder Scales (Antisocial, Avoidant, Borderline, Dependent, Histrionic, Narcissistic, Obsessive Compulsive, Paranoid, Passive Aggressive, Schizotypal, Schizoid, Sadistic, Self-Defeating); 4 Validity Scales (Random Responding, Tendency to Look Good or Bad, Tendency to Deny Blatant Pathology, Answer Choice Frequency); 7 Axis I Scales (Anxiety, Depression, Post-traumatic Stress Disorder, Schizophrenia, Psychotic Thinking, Social Phobia, Withdrawal); 4 Neuropsychological Dysfunction Scale and Subscales (Neuropsychological Dysfunction, Memory and Concentration, Language Dysfunction, Somatic); 4 Executive Functions Scale and Subscales (Executive Functions, Poor Planning, Decision-Making Problems, Task Incompletion); 3 Hostility Scales (Anger, Dangerousness, Impulsiveness); 4 other clinical scales (Indecisiveness, Emotional Lability, Apathy, Adjustment); Normal Clinical Scale (Introversion-Extraversion); 5 Non-normative scales (Drug and Alcohol, Sexuality, Depersonalization, Frustration Tolerance, Eccentricity).
Administration: Group.
Forms, 2: Self-report, Significant Other.
Price Data, 1996: $10 per evaluation kit including demo disk, manual on disk, 2 test booklets, and limited-use scoring software; $199 per complete kit including computer scoring software (unlimited use), manual ('93, 41 pages), and 25 test booklets; $349 per multi-user kit (same as complete kit, for use by 2 or more clinicians at the same address); $20 per 25 test booklets; $7.50 per manual.
Time: (30–45) minutes.
Comments: Computer scoring program requires DOS version 3.1 or higher and at least 640K RAM.
Author: Frederick L. Coolidge.
Publisher: The CATI Corporation.
Cross References: See T5:690 (3 references).

Review of the Coolidge Axis II Inventory by KEVIN L. MORELAND, Psychologist, Private Practice, Ft. Walton Beach, FL:

The Coolidge Axis II Inventory (CATI) was originally developed in the early 1980s to measure the personality disorders defined in the *DSM-III* (American Psychiatric Association, 1980; see Grana, Coolidge, & Merwin, 1989). The inventory was expanded to 200 items during the late 1980s, partly to help measure the two experimental personality disorders added to the *DSM-III-R* (1987), a number of Axis I scales, and three validity scales (Coolidge & Merwin, 1992). The current test booklet has 225 items, but the last 25 are not scored.

The inventory is advertised as *DSM-IV* (American Psychiatric Association, 1994) compatible, though no information is provided on alterations made to effect this change. That may not be as big a problem as it sounds for the Axis II scales. In the *DSM-IV*, Antisocial Personality (ASP) criteria were changed by deleting two items, combining two items, and simplifying the relationship between ASP and Conduct Disorder. One item was added to the Borderline (BDL) criteria. The Passive-Aggressive diagnosis was relegated to an appendix and two *DSM-III-R* experimental disorders, Sadistic and Self-Defeating, were dropped. This review will consider only those personality disorders listed in the *DSM-IV*.

ITEM AND SCALE DEVELOPMENT. The items were developed rationally. They are answered on a 4-point scale from *Strongly False* to *Strongly True*. Most of the scales include roughly half as many items keyed in the false direction as in the true direction to offset symptom claiming. The number of items per scale ranges from 16 for Avoidant Personality (AVD) to 45 for ASP. Considering two or more Axis II items keyed in the same direction, item overlap among scales ranges from 25% between AVD and the other scales to 64% between ASP and the other scales (cf. Coolidge & Merwin, 1992). It would be helpful to have a table of the empirical intercorrelations among the scales to evaluate its effects.

RELIABILITY. Thirty-nine college students took the CATI twice, one week apart. The mean stability coefficient was .90, with a range from .78 for the Obsessive-Compulsive (OCD) scale to .97 for the Schizoid (SZD) scale. Unfortunately, the individual values were not reported.

The coefficient alpha reliability estimates for all the scales were calculated on the 609 "purportedly normal" individuals who were predominantly young, Caucasian, single, and well educated. These reliabilities ranged from .68 for the OCD scale to .87 for the Dependent (DEP) scale with a median of .79.

STRUCTURAL VALIDITY. A principal factor analysis was conducted with varimax rotation on data from the 609 participants previously described. The three factors extracted accounted for about 65% of the common variance but did not conform to the rational classification used in the *DSM* or factors developed using other instruments. This may have been due to the presence of the three scales dropped from the *DSM-IV*. However, the three factors did match Horney's theory that people move toward others (Histrionic loading = .91), away from others (AVD = .89), or against others (ASP = .89).

CONTENT VALIDITY. In addition, Coolidge and Merwin (1992) asked mainly depressed clients of 11 "licensed clinicians" to complete the CATI and the Millon Clinical Multiaxial Inventory-II (MCMI-II; Millon, 1987), and the clinicians rated their clients on a personality disorder checklist. Using a criterion of 1 *SD* above the mean on the CATI as evidence of a disorder, the CATI and clinician diagnoses agreed 12 out of 24 times, using a Base Rate Score of 75 as a criterion, agreement was 14/24 with the MCMI-II.

The CATI was related to the original version of the NEO Personality Inventory (Costa & McCrae, 1985) for 223 college students (Coolidge, Becker, DiRito, Durham, Kinlaw, & Philbrick, 1994). Zero-order correlations were largely in line with theoretical expectations. Significant correlations between the CATI and NEO neuroticism scale were positive, except for SZD (-.41); the correlations with NEO Extraversion were negative except for Histrionic (HST; .46); the correlations with Agreeableness were negative, and, finally, the correlations with Conscientiousness were all negative.

Fifty-two married participants, mostly white, in their mid 30s, and with at least some college took the CATI and were rated on the Axis II constructs by their spouse and a friend. Participant/spouse correlations ranged from .27 (PAR, n.s.) to .63 (HIS) with a median of .57, and participant/friend correlations ranged from .22 (BDL, NAR, n.s.) to .61 (OCD) with a median of .40 (HIS). This is similar to correlations found in such studies with other instruments.

NORMS. The norm sample described in the 1993 test manual included 937 individuals. Most were female (62%), young (mean age = 29), Caucasian (89%), single (57%), and had at least some college (70%).

SUMMARY. Even though the CATI has been under thoughtful development for nearly 20 years, it has generated only a handful of studies published in the peer-reviewed literature. Moreover, Dr. Coolidge and his colleagues have published all these, most employing college students and other "purported normals" as participants.

Given these factors I cannot recommend the CATI for clinical use absent local trials. Even though scoring is unlimited, given the competition, the $200 (as of early 1999) price of the scoring software may be preventing practitioners and researchers from trying the CATI. Dr. Coolidge and his publisher may wish to rethink their marketing strategy.

REVIEWER'S REFERENCES

American Psychiatric Association. (1980). *Diagnostic and statistical manual of mental disorders* (3rd ed.). Washington, DC: Author.

Costa, P. T., Jr., & McCrae, R. R. (1985). *The NEO Personality Inventory manual*. Odessa, FL: Psychological Assessment Resources.

American Psychiatric Association. (1987). *Diagnostic and statistical manual of mental disorders* (3rd ed. Rev.). Washington, DC: Author.

Millon, T. (1987). *Millon Clinical Multiaxial Inventory-II: Manual for the MCMI-II*. Minneapolis: National Computer Systems.

Grana, A. S., Coolidge, F. L., & Merwin, M. M. (1989). Personality profiles of the morbidly obese. *Journal of Clinical Psychology, 45,* 762–765.

Coolidge, F. L., & Merwin, M. M. (1992). Reliability and validity of the Coolidge Axis II Inventory: A new inventory for the assessment of personality disorders. *Journal of Personality Assessment, 59,* 223–238.

American Psychiatric Association. (1994). *Diagnostic and statistical manual of mental disorders* (4ᵗʰ ed.). Washington, DC: Author.

Coolidge, F. L., Becker, L. A., DiRito, D. C., Durham, R. L., Kinlaw, M. M., & Philbrick, P. B. (1994). On the relationship of the five-factor personality model to personality disorders: Four reservations. *Psychological Reports, 75*, 11–21.

Review of the Coolidge Axis II Inventory by PAUL RETZLAFF, *Professor, Psychology Department, University of Northern Colorado, Greeley, CO:*

The Coolidge Axis II Inventory (CATI) is an odd mix of scales. Although the title implies personality disorder scales, the test also includes a number of Axis I scales, a few neuropsychological scales, some hostility scales, and, finally, a group of "other" scales.

Generally, the manual is dated both in terms of the discipline and the current version of the test. Much has changed since *DSM-III-R* and the MCMI-II. Further, the manual is at best barely adequate.

The test is primarily made up of *DSM-III-R* personality disorder criteria rewritten into psychological test item format. These items are endorsed by patients on a 1 to 4 *Strongly False* to *Strongly True* metric. The manual talks about a 200-item version of the test but the current test is 225 items. It is not readily apparent where the other 25 items came from.

The scales include 13 personality disorder scales (Antisocial, Avoidant, Borderline, Dependent, Histrionic, Narcissistic, Obsessive-Compulsive, Paranoid, Passive-Aggressive, Schizotypal, Schizoid, Sadistic, and Self-Defeating). There are 7 Axis I scales including Anxiety, Depression, Post-traumatic Stress Disorder, Psychotic Thinking, Social Phobia, and Withdrawal. There are 4 neuropsychological function scales, one an overall Neuropsychological Dysfunction scale and three subscales (Memory and Concentration, Language Dysfunction, and Somatic). There are 3 Hostility scales including Anger, Dangerousness, and Impulsiveness. There are 4 "Other Clinical Scales" including Indecisiveness (Executive Functions), Emotional Lability, Apathy, and Adjustment. There is 1 "Normal Clinical Scale," which is Introversion-Extraversion. Finally, there are 5 "Non-normative" scales including Drug and Alcohol, Sexuality, Depersonalization, Frustration Tolerance, and Eccentricity. This amounts to over 30 scales.

The biggest problem with the test is that it started out being a test of personality disorders and then became a test that included many domains. Those additional scales were built using the original personality disorder items. Judging from the item keying, the neuropsychology scales have new items but it is not apparent from the manual that many of the other scales were developed using new items.

The reliability estimates presented in the manual are only for the personality disorder scales and used "normal" subjects. Cronbach alphas are needed for all the scales. In addition, a large sample of patients is far more appropriate to the intent of the test.

Validity for scores from the personality disorder scales is unimpressive. A study with a total of 24 patients including only three males is presented as criterion validity evidence. No scale-specific validity evidence is presented due to the large number of scales per subject. The author has arbitrarily chosen a cutscore of 1 standard deviation above the normative sample's mean as indicative of a personality disorder. Obviously, a data-based decision would have been better. Construct validity evidence for scores from the Axis I scales correlated against MCMI-II and MMPI type scales are all generally in the .60s. An intercorrelation matrix of the CATI scales would have been nice to determine scale specificity.

The validity of scores from the neuropsychological scales hinges on a study of only 17 clinical subjects. Further, it appears that the subscales were developed through a factor analysis of the items using the normal subjects' data. Here, a development procedure that used actual patients would have been stronger. There appears to be no reliability or validity data for the Hostility scales, the "Other Clinical" scale, the "Normal Clinical" scale, or the "Non-normative" scales.

SUMMARY. In sum, the CATI provides an odd mixture of scales. Scores from some are probably reliable and some probably valid. The manual is inadequate and the number of actual clinical subjects is inadequate. Given that the competition is the MCMI-III (236), there is little reason to use the CATI.

[103]
Cooper Assessment for Stuttering Syndromes.

Purpose: Identifies and quantifies affective, behavioral, and cognitive components of stuttering syndromes.
Publication Date: 1995.
Price Data: Not available.

Time: [60] minutes.

Comments: Each CASS package includes both DOS and Windows® version; system requirements: DOS-1.5 MB hard disk space, Windows® (3.1 or higher)—1 MB hard disk space.

Authors: Eugene B. Cooper and Crystal S. Cooper.

Publisher: The Psychological Corporation.

a) CHILDREN'S VERSION.

Population: Ages 3–13 years.

Acronym: CASS-C.

Scores: 4 parts: Chronicity Prediction Checklist, Parent Assessment of Fluency Digest, Teacher Assessment of Fluency Digest, Child Fluency Assessment Digest.

b) ADOLESCENT AND ADULT VERSION.

Population: Adolescents and adults age 13 and over.

Scores: 5 parts: Speech Situation Avoidance Reactions, Frequency Disfluencies, Client's Assessment of the Fluency Problem, Clinician's Assessment of the Fluency Problem, Chronicity of the Fluency Problem.

[Editor's Note: The publisher advised in February 2001 that this test is now out of print.]

Review of the Cooper Assessment for Stuttering Syndromes by DAVID P. HURFORD, Director of the Center for the Assessment and Remediation of Reading Difficulties and Professor of Psychology and Counseling, Pittsburg State University, Pittsburg, KS:

The Cooper Assessment for Stuttering syndromes (CASS) is composed of two protocols, the Cooper Assessment for Stuttering syndromes: Children's Version (CASS-C), and the Cooper Assessment for Stuttering Syndromes: Adolescent and Adult Version (CASS-A). With regard to assessing stuttering behavior and its related cognitive and affective components, it is prudent to examine children and adolescents/adults separately. Approximately 75% of children who stutter will not stutter after the onset of puberty. Those who do, and who have not been assisted by treatment, are quite likely to stutter for the rest of their lives. One of the facets of the CASS-C is to determine the likelihood of sustained disfluency in oral language. The CASS-A and the CASS-C are both computer programs designed to assist the speech-language pathologist (SLP) in organizing important information regarding the behavioral, cognitive, and affective components of stuttering. The CASS-A/C is a self-contained protocol on a 3.5-inch diskette. No manual or supporting material accompanies the diskettes.

The CASS-C and CASS-A are not assessment instruments. They are fundamentally organizational protocols. The results of the CASS provide a summary of the data that were entered by the speech-language pathologist and derives a mean fluency disorder rating.

The CASS-C included the Chronicity Prediction Checklist, the Parent Fluency Assessment Digest, the Teacher Fluency Assessment Digest, and the Child Fluency Assessment Digest. From these, a report is derived that provides a useful compilation of the likelihood of continued stuttering difficulty, the parent's and teacher's judgment of the severity of the child's disfluency as well as observational information concerning the child's stuttering behavior, and his or her cognitive and affective response to stuttering. Last, there is an evaluation of the child's disfluency rate.

The CASS-A includes the Situation Avoidance Reactions, the Feelings and Attitudes Regarding Fluency, the Disfluency Frequency, Type and Duration, the Disfluency Concomitant Behaviors, the Client Perceptions of Severity, the Clinician Perceptions of Severity, and the Assessing Chronicity protocols. These components help to determine the severity of the individual's stuttering behavior, its etiology and development, as well as determining the nature of the cognitive and affective reactions to stuttering and the situations in which it occurs.

The strengths of the CASS-A/C are that the protocols include theoretically relevant items regarding not only the stuttering behavior, but also the secondary issues of the cognitive and affective responses to stuttering. Therapies have traditionally emphasized remediating the disfluencies rather than considering the individual's emotional and cognitive responses to stuttering. These can be quite disabling as well. Including the individual's cognitive and emotional responses to stuttering helps to provide a more complete understanding of the effect of stuttering on the client. Many of these concerns have grown out of failure of therapeutic interventions. In such cases, the client leaves the therapy with the stuttering intact and no support for the ancillary difficulties associated with disfluent speech. Cooper indicates that these individuals have chronic perseverative stuttering syndrome. Therapies should address the secondary issues related to stuttering for these individuals and should help them to develop compensatory mechanisms or other techniques for adjustment. Conversely, there are treatment programs that boast 93% initial success and 75% sustained success in which clients retain fluent speech for 1 to 4 years post-treatment (e.g., Hollins Communication Research Institute in Roanoke, Virginia).

The disadvantages of using the CASS-A/C for purposes other than organizing and summarizing are numerous. No psychometric properties were evaluated or reported for either version of the CASS. Not only will the results of the CASS be idiosyncratic to the professional doing the evaluation, there is no guidance to determine how to differentiate between a mild, moderate, severe, or a very severe problem, which the SLP must determine when administering the CASS. The mean fluency disorder score is based entirely on the values produced by the SLP, the client, and the parents/teachers. No studies of reliability or validity were conducted and no norming sample existed to determine the nature of the derived scores.

The CASS-A/C is relatively simple to use; however, the entire test is computer based with no supporting material. In fact, there is no manual. As a result, many potential users will find this device seriously lacking. Some time and effort is required to explore and to become familiar with the various aspects of the program.

SUMMARY. The CASS-A/C should only be used as an organizational vehicle. The items are appropriate for fully comprehending the nature of the individual's stuttering difficulty. However, the SLP will need to determine the meaning of the summary information. There are no norms associated with either version of the CASS. There is not evidence that individuals with appropriate fluency would respond any differently to many of the items on the CASS as compared to individuals with disfluency. It should be emphasized that no studies of reliability or validity were reported. As a result, there is no evidence that scores from the CASS-A/C are reliable or valid. Using the CASS-A or CASS-C for any purpose other than organizing clinical interview information is certainly not appropriate or warranted and definitely is not advised.

Review of the Cooper Assessment for Stuttering Syndromes by JANET NORRIS, Professor of Communication Disorders, Louisiana State University, Baton Rouge, LA:

The Cooper Assessment for Stuttering Syndromes is a computerized program designed to assist a practitioner in conducting an evaluation of stuttering. By following the directions in the program, a fluency protocol can be completed, with the resulting data automatically tabulated and computed for means and percentage of occurrence. The data then are organized into a report complete with an analysis of the results, including judgments of severity and prognosis. The results can be printed as a report complete with a personal heading or letterhead, or stored for later reference.

Two nearly identical versions of the program are available, one for children and one for adolescents and adults. Both versions begin by entering identifying information about the individual to be assessed, including name, address, and date of birth. This is followed by six tasks designed to examine common phenomena associated with stuttering. These include assessments of speech situation avoidance reactions, feelings and attitudes regarding stuttering, the percentage of disfluencies produced during differing speech tasks, types and duration of disfluencies exhibited, extraneous and distracting behaviors produced while speaking, and a perception of the individual's disorder as judged separately by the individual and the examiner. Additional comments also can be added to the report.

The protocol requires approximately one hour to complete and requires no materials except a reading passage that can be printed from the program. Most of the protocol is completed by asking the individual to respond to questions, making choices along a 5-point scale with descriptors such as "never," "frequently," or "always." Responses are entered directly into the computer using a keyboard positioned so that the examiner can observe and talk to the individual without having to shift out of typing position.

The questions presented are those traditionally asked in a fluency evaluation and are fairly comprehensive. For example, the speech situation avoidance subtest is composed of 50 questions, ranging from very general queries (i.e., How often do you avoid speaking situations?) to specific (How often do you avoid eating in restaurants?). Most common avoidance situations are addressed, including giving directions, giving one's name on the phone, talking to inattentive people, or talking in the classroom or during job interviews. The children's version includes the questions designed to address adult situations and vice versa, for which a "not appropriate" entry can be submitted. This is the longest task on the protocol and it is likely that children will begin to show distractibility or disinterest before the final item is reached. However, there is no restriction preventing conduction of the interview across more than one session and this may be an option for children and some adults.

Feelings and attitudes are similarly addressed, but with 25 questions responded to with "agree," "undecided," or "disagree." These questions are designed to evaluate self-perception (Fluency problems are my own fault) and attitudes (Stutterers should not be called on in class). The protocol calls for the individual's initial reaction, rather than a thoughtful analysis of the statement.

The third section of the protocol assesses actual speech production using recitation, spontaneous conversation, and reading. Recitation includes repeating the nursery rhyme "Mary had a little lamb," and the pledge of allegiance, as well as repeating six sentences. As the individual speaks, the examiner clicks the mouse for each disfluency detected. The program assumes that the examiner is a professional with knowledge of stuttering, because disfluencies are not defined nor are examples given. A percentage of the number of disfluently produced words from the total number of words is calculated by the program. Reading includes oral reading of a 100-word passage and 12 sentences that the individual must complete (e.g., 5 + 5 = _____).

Finally, a short sample (2–3 minutes) of conversation is obtained and analyzed subjectively by the examiner for a judgment of the percent of occurrence of disfluencies, while each disfluency heard is recorded by clicking the mouse. The tasks are most appropriate for older children and adults, especially the reading passage that appears to be at an upper elementary level. It is surprising that a passage with a lower readability level was not selected for the children's version.

The fourth section is a checklist of extraneous or secondary behaviors that commonly accompany disfluent speech. These include facial movements such as wrinkling the forehead or losing eye contact, body movements such as arm twitches or head jerks, and abnormal breathing patterns such as shallow breaths or rapid inhalations. Any behaviors observed during the assessment or known to be characteristic of the individual are to be indicated.

The fifth section is an assessment of the types and duration of dysfluencies. Type is defined by such characteristics as insertion of sounds, words, or phrases, episodes of silent prolongation or vocalized prolongation, or sound, word, or phrase substitutions while speaking. Vocal quality, such as unusual pitch, intensity, rate, or prosody also is indicated. Duration of the average disfluent moment is measured along a scale ranging from fleeting to greater than 4 seconds, with specification of the longest duration produced during the evaluation.

The final section measures the individual's and the examiner's perception of the disfluency. The individual provides perceptions of the frequency of their own disfluency, as well as how often they consider stuttering to be a problem, and how great a problem it is in daily life. The examiner answers similar questions as well as judgments of the individual's perception of the problem compared to the actual problem as measured by the protocol. The examination ends with a checklist of 10 yes/no questions regarding common developmental and behavioral characteristics of stuttering. This includes whether the problem began in early childhood, if periods of normal fluency and control are experienced, and if the problem has persisted 10 years or more.

The results of the assessment, including tables displaying the results of the different subsections complete with totals, means, and percentages are available nearly simultaneously with the final click of the mouse. The program also provides a syndrome indication, such as "remediable stutter syndrome" and a severity rating, such as "mild" or "severe."

The Cooper protocol is based on traditional methods of assessing the observable products of stuttering, treated as a series of separate "stutter events," as well as affective, behavioral, environmental, and cognitive components of the syndrome. No manual is provided that describes the theoretical frame for the components of the protocol nor explains how items were selected. However, Cooper and Cooper's (1985) integrated view of stuttering as a complex disorder influenced by multiple factors is well established in the literature. The questions and measures are based on decades of research that have explored the areas assessed in this protocol. It would be useful to have reliability data, such as test-retest performance for a variety of individuals exhibiting a range of stuttering severity, to assess the accuracy of this computerized method for gathering data. For example, the mouse clicks that are produced as the person speaks could be distracting or could add tension resulting in greater disfluencies, especially during the first administration when the procedure is unfamiliar. Validity data are also lacking. A determination of whether the severity rating and syndrome indication resulting from the protocol are consistent with actual severity and prognosis would be an important measure of construct validity.

SUMMARY. The Cooper Assessment for Stuttering Syndromes provides an assessment of a variety of factors related to stuttering, but each is treated as a separate component. The structure of this instrument thus limits the true interaction among the factors that cause and maintain stuttering. The Cooper can be used to provide a descriptive assessment of some of the products of stuttering, and it does this very efficiently. But this is only a beginning point for assessing and treating stuttering. To conduct an adequate assessment of the syndrome, the examiner must look beyond the surface to view the complex and dynamic interactions that occur among these and many other factors. This would include an analysis of the factors that limit or increase disruptions in fluency during conversations that differ on factors that limit or increase disruptions in fluency during conversations that differ on factors such as topic of discussion and speaking partners, and consideration of the dynamics between multiple factors simultaneously impacting speech (Smith & Kelly, 1997).

REVIEWER'S REFERENCES

Cooper, E. B., & Cooper, C. S. (1985). Cooper Personalized Fluency Control Therapy—Revised. Allen, TX: DLM Teaching Resources.
Smith, A., & Kelly, E. (1997). Stuttering: A dynamic, multifactorial model. In R. F. Curlee & G. M. Siegel (Eds.), *Nature and treatment of stuttering: New directions* (2nd ed.). Boston: Allyn & Bacon.

[104]
Coping Inventory for Stressful Situations.

Purpose: Scale for measuring multidimensional aspects of coping with stress.
Population: Adults, adolescents.
Publication Date: 1990.
Acronym: CISS.
Scores, 5: Task, Emotion, Avoidance, Distraction, Social Diversion.
Administration: Individual or group.
Forms, 2: Adult, Adolescent.

Price Data, 1999: $40 per complete kit including manual (78 pages) and 25 QuikScore™ forms (specify Adult or Adolescent Version); $22 per 25 Adult or Adolescent QuikScore™ forms; $25 per manual; $160 per IBM MS DOS 50-use 3.5-inch disk for administration and scoring.
Foreign Language Editions: French, German, Spanish editions available.
Time: (10) minutes.
Comments: Paper-and-pencil or computer administered.
Authors: Norman S. Endler and James D. A. Parker.
Publisher: Multi-Health Systems, Inc.
Cross References: See T5:696 (2 references).
[Editor's Note: The publisher advised in September 1999 that a Second Edition (1999) is now available for this test addressing several concerns raised by reviews of the 1990 edition. The Second Edition will be reviewed in the *15th MMY*.]

Review of the Coping Inventory for Stressful Situations by E. THOMAS DOWD, Professor of Psychology, Kent State University, Kent, OH:

The Coping Inventory for Stressful Situations (CISS) is a 48-item self-report, paper-and-pencil measure of coping along three dimensions consisting of 16 items each: Task-oriented, Emotion-oriented, and Avoidance-oriented coping. The latter scale in turn consists of two subscales, Distraction (8 items) and Social Diversion (5 items). The instrument is based theoretically on an interactional model of anxiety, stress, and coping, in which person variables (e.g., trait anxiety, vulnerability, cognitive style) interact with situation variables (e.g., life events, hassles, crises) to produce perception of threat, leading in turn to increases in state anxiety and subsequent physical and psychological reactions to this state anxiety. The model is presented as an integration of an intraindividual approach to coping (in which an individual's coping is compared across different types of situations) and an interindividual approach to coping (in which coping scores of the same individual are assessed over different occasions representing a stable score). These different approaches have differing implications for reliability estimates; one would expect it to be lower for the intraindividual approach than for the interindividual approach. Functionally, the CISS appears to be more interindividual, however; indeed, the manual states that it was developed to assess preferred coping *styles* or strategies *typically* used. Work on the instrument began in 1986 and it was formerly called the Multidimensional Coping

Inventory (MCI). There is both an adult and an adolescent version, the latter constructed by re-wording six items in the adult version in more simple words.

The package comes with a manual and a combination answer sheet and scoring grid, which enable the user to plot individual scores against normative data. The manual consists of seven chapters, including a general description of the instrument, computer administration and scoring instructions, interpretation and use, instrument development, description of normative samples, and reliability and validity evidence. There are several case studies indicating how the instrument might be used in clinical situations.

The inventory was created by developing a pool of 120 items representing (in the view of a number of psychologists and graduate students) diverse coping behaviors. This pool was reduced to 70 items by removing redundant and biased items (not stated is how this was done or what "biased" means). The 70 item scale was administered to 559 undergraduates and a factor analysis conducted, resulting in 19 factors. Based on the scree test criteria, the first three factors were rotated. Subsequently, items that did not load about .40 were discarded with a few exceptions. The resulting rotated factors were labeled "task-oriented coping," "emotion-oriented coping," and "avoidance-oriented coping." A later factor analysis identified two subfactors of the Avoidance scale. From the description, however, it is not clear how only three factors were ultimately identified. Were the three factors identified in advance or arrived at strictly empirically?

The authors present both coefficient alpha and test-retest reliability estimates. The former, by each factor and by gender, ranged from .92–.73, with the majority in the .90s and .80s. Test-retest reliabilities ranged from .73–.51. These reliabilities, although decent, are not high, especially the test-retest, indicating perhaps that coping style is not an especially stable construct. Item-remainder correlations (those between each item and the rest of the items) for each factor ranged from .12 to .71. Many of these correlations are quite low and I am surprised that some of the lower correlating items were not eliminated earlier in the test development.

Validity was investigated by factor analyses on subsequent samples, resulting in the same three factors, and by relatively low intercorrelations of the CISS factor scales. These results, the authors say, speak to the multidimensionality of the scale and presumably to validity. Construct validity was demonstrated by theoretically expected correlations between the factor scales of the CISS and the Ways of Coping Scale (WOC), the Basic Personality Inventory (BPI), the Beck Depression Inventory (BDI), the Endler Multidimensional Anxiety Scales (EMAS), the Eysenck Personality Inventory (EPI), and selected scales of the MMPI-2. Although the theoretical logic behind some of the many correlations was apparent, the logic behind others was not. In general, Emotion-focussed coping was related to various measures of psychological distress and Task-focussed coping either was not related to psychological distress or was negatively related. Avoidance-focussed coping was generally not related to psychological distress.

Emotion-focussed coping in this instrument appears to be an unmitigated problem with no redeeming features at all and associated with a wide variety of psychological problems. Aside from the situational differences in coping styles (one might use Task-focussed coping in one situation and Emotion-focussed in another), the stress literature does not present Emotion-focussed coping in such a universally negative light. Even the case examples present it this way; those individuals in distress are high on Emotion-focussed coping and low or moderate on Task-focussed and Avoidance-focussed coping. Indeed, I was left wondering how this instrument would have differential utility over instruments measuring general psychological distress.

SUMMARY. This is a reasonably well-designed instrument for which specific utility is not always clear. What, other than providing another look at general distress, is to be done with the results? Perhaps one implication is its use as an initial assessment instrument prior to training individual to use more Task-focussed and fewer Emotion-focussed coping strategies that are undefined by this instrument. In addition, I would suggest the authors revise the instrument to eliminate some of the very low item-remainder correlations. I suspect they might be reducing the reliability. Finally, I would like to know exactly how the specific factors and subfactors were identified.

Review of the Coping Inventory for Stressful Situations by STEPHANIE STEIN, Professor of Psychology, Central Washington University, Ellensburg, WA:

The Coping Inventory for Stressful Situations (CISS) is a revision of the former Multidimensional Coping Inventory. The CISS is a brief self-report measure of coping styles used by an individual in a "difficult, stressful, or upsetting situation" (manual, p. 5). Each item on the inventory is a single descriptive phrase that is rated by the respondent on a Likert-type scale from 1 *(not at all)* to 5 *(very much)*. The 48 items combine to provide *T*-scores in five types of coping styles: Task, Emotion, Avoidance, Avoidance-Distraction, and Avoidance-Social Diversion. The adolescent version of the inventory is apparently identical to the adult version except that some of the vocabulary is simplified. The inventory is quick and easy to administer and score.

The manual that accompanies the inventory is well organized and complete. It provides thorough guidelines on administration and scoring of the CISS. However, the chapter on interpretation of the inventory is a bit vague. The authors describe two methods of profile analysis: eyeballing and pattern analysis. It is surprising to see eyeballing listed as a recommended method of interpretation, especially without additional guidelines, because untrained individuals using that technique tend to underestimate or overestimate differences between the scales or differences over time. In contrast to the informal eyeballing method, the authors also recommend pattern analysis using "*statistically based decision rules regarding confidence intervals*" (manual, p. 14). However, they do not explain how to do this, nor do they provide confidence intervals or the standard error of measurement on the different scales. They do include several case studies, which are accompanied by score profiles. Unfortunately, the authors provide only very general interpretations of the case studies for the most part, indicating whether a scale score was high or low but not giving much information about the implications of these scores. Another minor problem with the case studies is that the interpretation of the scores is inconsistent. For example, the guidelines indicate that a *T*-score of 32 or 33 is "much below average" but in some of the case studies a score of 33 is described as "low" and in one case study a score of 32 is considered "somewhat below average." It is questionable whether the average test user would know how to interpret a CISS profile meaningfully after reading this chapter.

A detailed description is given of the development of the CISS including a theoretically based rationale for the inventory and factor analysis of the five scales. Several normative samples are described for the English version of the CISS: 537 adults, 1,242 college undergraduates, 302 psychiatric inpatients, 313 young adolescents between the ages of 13 and 15 years, and 504 older adolescents between the ages of 16 to 18 years. Other than gender, the manual does not provide any further information about the normative populations. Therefore, the test user has no way of knowing whether the normative sample is similar to the test user's subjects in terms of SES, race/ethnicity, geographic region, or any other relevant demographic characteristic. The authors only say that the adult and college samples were English-speaking North Americans, which is likely to mean Canadians because that is where the authors lived.

Reliability data on the CISS are adequate. The authors present internal consistency reliability coefficients ranging from a low of .69 for female psychiatric patients on the Distraction scale to a high of .92 for male early adolescents on the Task scale. Most of the Cronbach alpha coefficients are between .80 and .90. Test-retest reliability information (based on a 6-week interval) is also provided for a small subgroup of college undergraduates. The test-retest correlations range from .68 to .72 on the Task and Emotion scales and are slightly lower for the Avoidance scale and two subscales, ranging from .51 to .60.

In support of the validity of the CISS, the authors present factor analyses data that provide evidence for the multidimensionality of the inventory. In addition, nonsignificant or low intercorrelations were found between the Task, Emotion, and Avoidance scales. The intercorrelations were somewhat higher between the Avoidance scale and the two Avoidance subscales, which is not surprising because they share some of the same items in each scale. Finally, the authors present evidence for the construct validity of scores from their instrument by correlating scores with other instruments such as the Marlowe-Crowne Social Desirability Scales (low or nonsignificant correlations) and the Ways of Coping Questionnaire (moderate correlations). They also correlate the different CISS scales with various measures of psychopathology such as the Basic Personality Inventory, the MMPI-2, the

Beck Depression Inventory, the Psychosomatic Symptom Checklist, and others. The authors found that the Emotion scale was highly correlated with a number of measures of "psychological distress, psychopathology, and somatization. Task-oriented coping and avoidance-oriented coping, on the other hand, appear to be unrelated to these negative variables" (manual, p. 63). Actually, the Task scale is negatively correlated with some of the measures of psychopathology, which is consistent with the authors' theory. However, the general lack of correlation between the Avoidance scale and the two subscales of Distraction and Social Diversion with almost anything else leads one to question the inclusion of these scales.

SUMMARY. The CISS appears to be a technically adequate measure of coping styles. More information could and should be provided, though, on the characteristics of the norming samples so that test users can judge the appropriateness of the measure for their subjects. The biggest weakness of this instrument is that the implications of the scores are unclear, especially on the Avoidance scale and subscales. It leaves the test user responding "So what?" after the instrument is administered and scored. Additional guidelines from the authors on interpretation and use of the instrument would be helpful. Despite these problems, the CISS is probably the best measure of its kind because other measures of coping styles have even more problems related to reliability and factor structure.

[105]
Coping Responses Inventory—Adult and Youth.

Purpose: Constructed as "a measure of ... types of coping responses to stressful life circumstances."
Population: Ages 12–18, 18 and older.
Publication Date: 1993.
Acronym: CRI.
Scores: 8 scales: Logical Analysis, Positive Reappraisal, Seeking Guidance and Support, Problem Solving, Cognitive Avoidance, Acceptance or Resignation, Seeking Alternative Rewards, Emotional Discharge.
Administration: Group.
Levels, 2: Adult and Youth.
Forms, 2: Ideal, Actual.
Price Data, 2001: $109 per complete kit including manual (44 pages), 10 reusable item booklets (actual form and 50 answer sheets (specify adult or child); $17 per 10 reusable item booklets (specify adult or child and ideal or actual); $35 per 25 answer sheets (specify adult or child); $30 per manual (specify adult or child).

Time: (10–15) minutes.
Comments: Computer scoring system available from publisher.
Author: Rudolf H. Moos.
Publisher: Psychological Assessment Resources, Inc.
Cross References: See T5:699 (5 references).

Review of the Coping Responses Inventory— Adult and Youth by ASHRAF KAGEE, Postdoctoral Fellow, University of Pennsylvania, Philadelphia, PA:

The Coping Responses Inventory (CRI) is a 48-item Likert-type instrument that assesses eight different types of coping responses to stressful life events. The instrument uses the approach-avoidance framework and measures both cognitive and behavioral strategies of coping. Approach coping focuses on the problem at hand and reflects the individual's cognitive and behavioral efforts to resolve problems. Avoidance coping on the other hand tends to focus to a greater extent on emotions and reflects attempts to avoid thinking about the problem and its implications. The versatility of the test is reflected not only in the availability of both its adult and youth versions, but also in its utility with healthy individuals, psychiatric and substance abuse patients, and medical patients (e.g., cancer, chronic pain, AIDS, heart, stroke, diabetic, burn, and arthritis patients). Moreover, the test may be administered either as a self-report inventory or as a structured interview. The appeal of the CRI lies in its ease of use. It may be hand-scored in a few minutes by means of a scoring template attached to the answer sheet. A profile area is provided that permits transformation from raw scores to T scores. Also available from the publisher is a computerized scoring system designed to generate an Interpretive Report that is useful in assisting clinicians to understand CRI results and present them to their clients.

The CRI manuals are easy to read and understand, and provide informative case examples of profiles of subjects coping with various life experiences. The development of the test is adequately described. The normative group in the adult version was sufficiently large ($N = 1,800$). However, given the average age of 61 years it appears that these norms are more relevant to older rather than younger individuals.

The reliability coefficients of the CRI Adult subscales range from .58 to .74 and are presented separately for men and women, indicating moderate to high internal consistency for the test. The reliability coefficients for the CRI-Child subscales are similar, ranging from .55 to .79. Intercorrelations between the scales show the scales to be moderately positively correlated, and test-retest reliability (1-year interval) averaged around .45 for all the subscales. The professional manual also presents general findings of studies that support the validity of the instrument. Lacking in these reports, however, are actual validity indices reflecting the robustness of the measure in comparison with other instruments. Moreover, adequate descriptions of the research methods and selection procedures used to select the samples were not provided in these reports. The authors of the scale appear to have invested considerable effort in the test development process, from identifying coping domains, constructing items and expanding on the item pool, conducting field trials, and making final revisions based on the results of these. The apparent absence of factor analytic studies, however, detracts from the empirical rigor of the test development process. Despite these limitations in reporting, many studies presented in the manual focus on the coping strategies of problem drinkers and patients with medical problems, which are population groups for whom healthy and adaptive coping is of great importance.

Among the implicit claims of developers of most coping measures is the supposed universality of their application. This claim has been contested by assertions that situation-specific mechanisms are more appropriately examined given the unique set of stressors and challenges that arise in various contexts (e.g., Coyne & Smith, 1991). Despite its supposed universality, and in the absence of psychometrically sound instruments that focus on situation-specific coping (e.g., coping with positive HIV test results or chronic pain), the CRI represents a stable general measure that permits an approximation into the ways in which individuals cope with adverse circumstances.

REVIEWER'S REFERENCE

Coyne, J. C., & Smith, D. A. (1991). Couples coping with a myocardial infarction: A contextual perspective on wives' distress. *Journal of Personality & Social Psychology, 61,* 404–412.

Review of the Coping Responses Inventory— Adult and Youth by EVERETT V. SMITH, JR., Assistant Professor of Educational Psychology, University of Illinois, Chicago, IL:

This review of the Coping Responses Inventory (CRI) examines the Adult (CRI-A) and Youth (CRI-Y) Actual forms together and, where relevant, separately. Comments are also provided for the CRI-A Ideal form answer sheet.

The CRI is intended to measure eight different types of coping responses: Logical Analysis, Positive Reappraisal, Seeking Guidance and Support, Problem Solving, Cognitive Avoidance, Acceptance or Resignation, Seeking Alternative Rewards, and Emotional Discharge. The first four scales measure approach coping, the second set of four scales measure avoidance coping. Within each set of four scales, the first two scales represent cognitive coping strategies, the last two scales represent behavioral coping strategies. Each scale consists of 6 items. Respondents first describe a recent stressful event and then use a 4-point scale to rate their dependence on each of 48 coping items. The CRI also contains 10 items used to indicate how the respondent evaluates the stressful event. Responses to these 10 items provide additional diagnostic information and aid in the interpretation of coping profiles.

The CRI-A may be used with subjects 18 years of age and older from the following populations: healthy adults, adult psychiatric patients, adult substance abuse patients, and adult medical patients. The CRI-Y is intended to be used with subjects between the ages of 12 and 18 years from the following populations: healthy youth; youth with emotional, psychological, or behavioral problems; and youth with medical disorders. The format of the CRI permits its use as a self-report (approximately 15 minutes to complete) or as a structured interview (15 to 30 minutes to complete) assessment. The directions for administration are clear and easy to follow.

An answer sheet allows participants to provide demographic information and responses to the 10 evaluative and 48 coping items. A bottom sheet provides a simple and straightforward mechanism for obtaining the eight scale scores. If 1 or 2 items on a given scale have missing data, a correction factor is applied to reflect the full range of potential values. The reverse side of the answer sheet contains a profile form that allows a direct conversion of the raw scale scores to T-scores, ($M = 50$, $SD = 10$). This visual representation of a respondent's coping profile may help facilitate interpretation, which should be conducted by a qualified psychologist or counselor. The profile form also contains marked regions of T-scores and associated interpretative descriptors. The criteria for determining the cutscores for these regions and why the same cutscores apply across all eight scales are not detailed in the manual and users should be cautious in placing too much weight into these apparently judgmental categories. The manuals for the CRI-A and CRI-Y contain several clearly written case examples to demonstrate potential applications and interpretations. Applications may include case description (e.g., reliance on approach versus avoidance coping and cognitive versus behavioral strategies), treatment planning, and program evaluation.

The CRI-A has been developed over the course of three decades. The development of the CRI-Y is more recent, with the first version appearing in the 1980s. A review of the conceptual framework, the content analyses of how people deal with a wide variety of stressful situations, the interviews conducted, the judgmental evidence of item meaningfulness, and the empirical evidence (item-total correlations, response distributions, and scale intercorrelations) is provided in the manual. The CRI-Y was also reviewed by a reading expert to ensure a sixth-grade reading level.

The normative sample of the CRI-A contained over 1,900 participants from two field trials. The sample consisted of alcoholic, depressed, and arthritic patients and healthy controls. The majority (over 1,800) of the participants came from the second field trial. The mean age of participants in the second trial was 61 years (no *SD* provided) and 90% were Caucasian. These participants averaged 14.2 years of schooling and had a median income of $22,500 per year. Sixty-nine percent were currently married. The representativeness of this sample compared with the target population may be lacking. As noted in the manual, the CRI-A was designed for subjects age 18 and older, yet the mean age of participants from the second field trial was 61. However, without knowing the variability about the mean age, the representativeness of the normative sample is difficult to gauge. Based on the pooled sample (normative sample) from the two field trials, the author reports women to have higher coping scores on all eight scales compared to men. The manual only provides means and standard deviations for the eight scales for men and women. Noticeably lacking are normative data for each of the sampled populations and different ethnic groups. It could

be of great clinical value to have norms for each of these patient and ethnic group populations. The manual also details the correlations among the coping scales, the relationship of various sociodemographic characteristics with the coping responses, and the comparability of the scales on the current version with earlier versions of the CRI-A. Internal consistency estimates range from .61 to .74 for males and .58 to .71 for females. Such estimates should be kept in mind when making decisions at the individual level. Twelve-month stability coefficients were estimated based on data from over 90% of the participants in the second field trial. Averaged across the eight scales, stability estimates were .45 and .43 for men and women, respectively.

The normative sample for the CRI-Y contained 400 youths (179 boys and 221 girls) from the two field trials. The sample consisted of healthy youth, youth with depression and conduct disorders, and youth with rheumatic disease. The majority, 315 of the 400 participants, came from the first field trial. The mean ages of participants in this trial were 15.2 and 15.3 years (no *SD* provided) for boys and girls, respectively. Approximately 70% of the 315 participants were Caucasian. The fathers and mothers of these participants averaged 15.0 and 14.2 years of schooling, respectively. Based on the data from both field trials (the normative sample), the author reports girls to have higher coping scores on all eight scales compared to boys. As with the CRI-A, the CRI-Y manual only provides means and standard deviations for the eight scales for boys and girls. Normative data for each of the sampled populations and different ethnic groups could have clinical value. The manual provides partial correlations among the coping scales separately for boys and girls, controlling for the type, severity, and evaluation of the stressor. The relationship of various sociodemographic characteristics with the coping responses are also presented. Internal consistency estimates range from .55 to .72 for boys and .59 to .79 for girls. Again, when making decisions concerning individuals, these estimates should be kept in mind. Twelve-to 15-month stability coefficients were estimated based on data from 254 of the 315 participants in the first field trial. Averaged across the eight scales, stability estimates were .29 and .34 for boys and girls, respectively.

Evidence for validity follows the traditional paradigm of content, concurrent, predictive, and construct validity. Content validity was mentioned earlier in this review for both the CRI-A and CRI-Y forms. Evidence for concurrent, predictive, and construct validity comes from several studies. These studies focused on group differences, determinants of coping responses, and how responses are associated with various functioning outcomes. The populations sampled include problem drinkers, alcoholic and depressed patients, matched controls, and various medical patients for the studies involving the CRI-A; healthy youth and youth with depression, conduct disorders, and rheumatic disease were sampled for studies using the CRI-Y. In general, specific scales were able to discriminate between clinical groups and healthy controls. The studies also provide evidence in support of a model specifying that characteristics of a life crisis or transition, the evaluation of the stressor, and aspects of the personal and environmental systems are associated with the selection of specific coping responses. Findings relating coping responses with functioning outcomes demonstrated that approach coping is associated with resolution of stressors. Despite the impressive collection of studies reviewed in support of evidence for validity, the theory behind the interpretations is lacking. An elaboration of the theory underlying the findings would help potential users evaluate the evidence for validity and provide a theoretical foundation for interpretation.

An Ideal version, which may be used to assess what the respondent believes to be the best way to cope with the stressful event, is also available. Deviations from the actual coping style and the perceived best method of coping may be used to identify areas for intervention. The response format for the CRI-A Ideal (and presumably the CRI-Y Ideal) version is identical to the CRI-A Actual version. This may be problematic as the response format does not appear to be compatible with the question being asked. The introductory stem for the Ideal version states "The best way for you to deal with this problem is to:"; the response options consist of "No, Not at all," "Yes, Once or twice," "Yes, Sometimes," and "Yes, Fairly often." This apparent lack of compatibility may confuse or frustrate respondents. Future refinement of the CRI-A Ideal version should employ an alternative response format and investigate other procedures for comparing the Actual and Ideal responses. A computer program is available to score and facili-

tate interpretation of the coping profiles for both the CRI-A and CRI-Y. There is also a CRI-A form to assess work-related coping.

In conclusion, the CRI-A and CRI-Y have made significant contributions to the clinical and research work with respect to coping. The well-written manual provides numerous examples, detailed information about scale development and potential applications, and a comprehensive review of studies utilizing these inventories. This information will be a valuable asset to potential users.

[106]
Correctional Institutions Environment Scale, Second Edition.

Purpose: Designed to measure the "social climate of juvenile and adult correctional programs."

Population: Residents and staff of correctional facilities.

Publication Dates: 1974–1987.

Acronym: CIES.

Scores, 9: Involvement, Support, Expressiveness, Autonomy, Practical Orientation, Personal Problem Orientation, Order and Organization, Clarity, Staff Control.

Administration: Group.

Forms, 4: Real (R), Ideal (I), Expectations (E), Short (S).

Price Data, 1997: $25 per sampler set including manual ('87, 64 pages), test booklet (R, E, I, S) and scoring key; $90 per permission set.

Foreign Language Editions: Versions adapted for use in French Quebec, Slovenia, Sweden, Spain, and the United Kingdom.

Time: Administration time not reported.

Comments: Part of the Social Climate Scales (T5:2445).

Author: Rudolf H. Moos.

Publisher: Mind Garden, Inc.

Cross References: See T4:660 (3 references) and T3:612 (1 reference); for a review by Kenneth A. Carlson of an earlier version, see 8:531 (16 references). For a review of the Social Climate Scales, see 8:681.

Review of the Correctional Institutions Environment Scale, Second Edition by KEVIN J. McCARTHY, Assistant Clinical Professor of Psychiatry, Louisiana State University Health Sciences Center, Department of Psychiatry, New Orleans, LA:

The Correctional Institutions Environment Scale (CIES) is a social climate assessment inventory incorporating the dimensions of Relationship, Personal Growth, and System Maintenance, which differentiate among correctional programs by their orientation. Each dimension incorporates related subscales: Relationship includes Involvement, Support, and Expressiveness; Personal Growth includes Autonomy, Practical Orientation, and Personal Problem Orientation; System Maintenance includes Order and Organization, Clarity, and Staff Control. The scale reflects diversity in correctional social climates through an evaluation of the nine primary environmental factors that also support the identification and classification of adult and juvenile institutional custody facilities through a typology of correctional programs.

The scale is available in multiple formats representing a variety of research applications including the standard form (R), which incorporates a total of 90 items for use in measuring the viewpoint of institutional staff or residents regarding correctional programs. Form R is the primary scale on which substantial normative data have been developed. Forms S, I, and E are adaptations of Form R. The CIES manual contains the means and standard deviations for distinct juvenile, adult male, and adult female Form R normative samples: The short form (S) comprises 36 items drawn from the standard form (R). Form S is not intended for use in determining individual differences; rather, it is an instrument for quick assessment of correctional climates (R. H. Moos, personal correspondence, October 7, 1999).

The Ideal Form (I) with 90 reworded items, reflects differing value orientations, goals, and programmatic preferences among institutional staff and residents: Form E measures personal program expectations by incorporating 90 reworded items from Form R. No psychometric data were provided for Form E. Forms I and E are directly parallel to Form R with identical scoring keys. Supporting documentation states that the CIES has been adapted in a variety of languages and cross-cultural applications. Although the scale has also been adapted for a variety of uses in juvenile facilities and community correctional centers, there has been limited CIES-based research on the implementation of program changes in adult prisons.

Administration instructions are clear and scoring procedures are simplified through the use of a template. Each response is scored either true or false. Columns of responses are arranged to represent the subscales. Results are tabulated as raw scores that are subsequently converted into standard scores through the use of conversion tables. Appendices are provided for plotting unit level profiles for staff and residents in juvenile, adult male, and adult female units. Appendices also include tables for conversion of individual mean scores to standard scores in juvenile and adult male facilities. No adult female individual mean raw score to standard score conversion tables are provided in the manual (R. H. Moos, personal correspondence, October 7, 1999).

Internal consistency reliability estimates for Form R subscales ranged from .54 for residents and institutional staff to .75 for residents and .83 for staff members. Item-subscale correlations ranged from .38 for residents and .42 for staff to .50 for residents and .56 for facility staff. The documentation only provided subscale intercorrelations for the male juvenile sample of residents ($N = 713$) and staff ($N = 651$). These intercorrelations among the nine Form R subscales ranged from -.47 to .53 for residents and from -.50 to .57 for institutional staff. According to the manual (p. 21), estimates of the "overall CIES profile" stability across time were provided for a 1-week interval, 1-month interval, and 2-year interval, positing extended stable properties. Although the manual comments (p. 19) on internal consistencies and subscale intercorrelations for the adult sample, normative data were not provided.

Test-retest reliability ranged from .65 to .80 for the nine Form R subscales. These statistics were provided for 31 residents completing the "scale twice with a one-week interval between testings" (manual, p. 21). Further study is recommended to evaluate test-retest reliability over extended time intervals and across diverse samples of juvenile and adult residents and institutional staff. Normative data for Form S included means and standard deviations for residents and staff in juvenile, adult male, and adult female facilities; Form I norms included "combined results from juvenile and adult units" (manual, p. 16), which were presented for residents and facility staff.

Form A, a 194-item inventory, was developed and administered to a limited sample of correctional staff and residents. Subsequently, a 120-item Form B was derived from Form A and administered in diverse correctional institutions located in the United States and the United Kingdom. Form R was developed from the assimilated data "consistent with ... psychometric adequacy and subscale meaningfulness" (manual, p. 19).

The development of the CIES was rooted in the conceptualization of the correctional environment as a dynamic process incorporating four distinct determinates: (a) physical features; (b) organizational structure and policies; (c) suprapersonal factors; and (d) social climate (manual, p. 36).

Instrument validity was supported through the inclusion of approximately 20 research studies that focused upon evaluating the impact of essential aspects of the correctional environment including: physical features, size and staffing, correctional climates; morale, personality, and adaptive behaviors; disciplinary infractions; rates of absconding; parole performance; correctional environments and residents outcomes; and matching programs to residents. Content validity of the CIES is supported by a series of true or false statements about the correctional environment that are grounded in the meaningfulness of individual subscale domains.

The construct validity of this instrument is well developed in terms of potential assessment of juvenile and community treatment centers. The scales' predictive validity would yield best results when applied to juvenile and community-based populations. It is likely that the CIES will have limited usefulness as an assessment instrument in high security adult prisons. The predictive validity of this instrument in adult facilities is likely to be adversely affected by the highly polarized nature of these institutions.

SUMMARY. With a population of 5.9 million offenders (Bureau of Justice Statistics, 1999), the CIES is a useful instrument in the evaluation of correctional social climates. It provides researchers and practitioners with a comprehensive methodology to assess, identify, and strengthen programmatic approaches to behavior change through the evaluation of correctional environments. The practical usefulness of this instrument would be enhanced through the development of a dimension incorporating the evaluation of institutional, economic, and personal barriers to social access and the inclusion of familial influences as a potential stabilizing factor during incarceration, post-prison adjustment, and parole (Hairston, 1988; Knox & Greer, 1989). The Correctional Institutions Environment Scale is a well-constructed instrument for measuring the social climate of custodial facilities. Its properties lend themselves to research and clinical applications when used with normative populations.

REVIEWER'S REFERENCES
Hairston, C. F. (1988). *Family ties during imprisonment: Do they influence future criminal activity?* Federal Probation, 52(1), 48–52.
Knox, G. W., & Greer, B. (1989). *Family counseling and corrections: Research findings.* From the Annual Meeting of the American Correctional Association. Denver, CO: ACA.
Bureau of Justice Statistics. (1999). *U.S. correctional population reaches 5.9 million offenders.* Bureau of Justice Statistics Website. [Retrieved September 1999 from the World Wide Web: www.ojp.usdoj.gov/bjs.pub/press/ppus98.pr]

Review of the Correctional Institutions Environment Scale, Second Edition by M. DAVID MILLER, Professor, University of Florida, Gainesville, FL:

The Correctional Institutions Environment Scale, Second Edition (CIES) is one of 10 Social Climate Scales that is designed to measure the social climate of juvenile and adult correctional programs. The author suggests that the CIES can be used for clinical, evaluation, and research applications. The CIES measures three underlying domains: Relationship Dimensions, Personal Growth Dimensions, and System Maintenance Dimensions. Each of the dimensions consists of three subscales. The Relationship Dimensions are measured by Involvement, Support, and Expressiveness; the Personal Growth Dimensions are measured by Autonomy, Practical Orientation, and Personal Problem Orientation; and the System Maintenance Dimensions are measured by Order and Organization, Clarity, and Staff Control. Therefore, the CIES consists of nine subscales. The nine subscales appear on four forms of the assessment. The Real Form measures residents' and staff members' views of their correctional program. The Ideal Form measures preferences for a correctional program. The Expectations Form measures expectations about a correctional program that either a resident or staff member is about to enter. Finally, the Short Form is a shortened version of the Real Form.

Fairly extensive data have been collected and are reported on the Real Form and the Ideal Form. The Short Form has reasonably high intraclass correlations with the Real Form suggesting a similarity in the two forms. The Expectation Form is new and has no reported psychometric data limiting its utility until studies have been conducted. Data for the Real and Ideal Forms include norms, reliability estimates, and validity studies.

The norm data are based on reasonable sample sizes for juvenile, adult male, and adult female programs. Norms are reported separately for residents and staff members on both the Real Form, the Ideal Form, and the Short Form. In addition, norms are reported for individuals and units (note: the number of units is small for some of the norms), making interpretation within specific contexts simpler (e.g., adult female staff members for each subscale). Although the means and standard deviations look reasonable, the sampling of units is never fully described and is probably not randomly selected. Furthermore, the characteristics of the sample units, residents, and staff members are not fully detailed.

The test development process provides a rigorous development procedure that includes item statistics based on building reliable (e.g., high item to subscale correlations) and valid assessments (e.g., low correlations with the Crowne-Marlowe Social Desirability Scale). The net effect of this care in test construction is a reasonable level of reliability. Internal consistency coefficients are reported for the Real Form and range from a little low to moderately high for residents (range = .54 to .75, median = .68) and staff (range = .54 to .83, median = .69) for juvenile samples. In addition, test-retest reliabilities at one week are higher (range = .65 to .80, median = .77) and are reported to remain quite stable over relatively long periods. The author also reports that similar results were obtained for adult male samples (no mention is made of adult female samples). Overall, reliability evidence suggests that the subcategory scores can be reliably estimated for residents and staff on the Real Form for juveniles and adult males. Only limited data are provided for the other forms of the assessment, raising questions about their reliability as well as the Real Form reliabilities for adult females.

Validity evidence on the Real Form of the CIES is fairly extensive. The evidence includes correlations of the subcategories (moderate to low), higher order factor analyses, variation across correctional programs, relationship to age and length of stay (negligible), and correlations with social desirability scales (negligible). In addition, a sample profile is shown and interpreted. The role of the CIES in the evaluation of program changes and development is discussed along with extensive citations on uses of the CIES for program evaluation and comparison, and other research studies.

SUMMARY. The bulk of the validity evidence suggests that the Real and Ideal Forms can be used effectively to measure social climate in different correctional settings. Moreover, evidence suggests that the CIES will provide a valuable profile that can be used to guide program changes and development.

[107]
Cross-Cultural Adaptability Inventory.

Purpose: "Designed to provide information to an individual about his or her potential for cross-cultural effectiveness."

Population: Trainers and professionals who work with culturally diverse and cross-culturally oriented populations.

Publication Dates: 1987–1995.

Acronym: CCAI.

Scores: 4 scales: Emotional Resilience, Flexibility/Openness, Perceptual Acuity, Personal Autonomy.

Administration: Group.

Price Data, 1995: $44 per preview package including manual ('95, 88 pages), 3 Action Planning Guides, and 3 self-scoring individual surveys; $15 per multi-rater set including one individual survey, 3 feedback forms, 3 feedback form scoring sheets and directions for use; $5 per self-scoring individual survey including survey, scoring sheet, and profile and interpretive worksheet; $25 per manual; $10 per facilitator's guide; $4 per participant's workbook; $3 per Action Planning Guide.

Time: [15–30] minutes.

Comments: Observer-rating survey is optional.

Authors: Colleen Kelley and Judith Meyers.

Publisher: NCS (Minnetonka).

Review of the Cross-Cultural Adaptability Inventory by LYNN L. BROWN, Assistant Professor, Northern Arizona University, Phoenix, AZ:

The Cross-Cultural Adaptability Inventory (CCAI) is a self-report instrument of 50 Likert-scored items measuring four categories of cross-cultural effectiveness. The test is designed to be used as a self-assessment tool for individuals moving to a new culture or for those facing re-entry issues upon return to their country of origin. The test manual states that it can also be used as a source of information for counseling individuals facing acculturation stress or life transitions.

The reviewer was provided with optional materials: an Observer Form to be used to provide 360 degree feedback, a Cultural Passport to Anywhere training exercise with facilitator's guide, and an Action Planning Guide suggesting further group-related activities for post-scoring awareness. It was suggested that the CCAI be used as part of a larger training experience that could also include these materials.

INVENTORY DEVELOPMENT. An original checklist of items judged to be important to cross-cultural readiness was given to participants who had cross-cultural knowledge and who had also lived abroad. The top 16 items were then divided into five categories and 10 test items were written for each category. After three revisions based on pilot testing, one dimension, positive regard for others, was eliminated. In 1992, after further statistical analysis, the present version of the inventory was published. The CCAI has a Flesch-Kincaid reading grade level of 8.2.

ITEM FACTOR ANALYSIS. The test items were subject to factor analysis with varimax rotation yielding factor loadings ranging from .04 to .65 for Emotional Resilience (ER), .32 to .62 for Flexibility/Openness (FO), .32 to .62 for Perceptual Acuity (PAC), and .35 to .66 for Personal Autonomy (PA). Of the 50 items, 18 measure ER, 15 items measure FO, 10 items relate to PAC, and 7 assess PA. Response options range from "Definitely True" to "Definitely Not True" for each item. Nine of the items are reverse scored: 3 in the ER scale and 6 in FO scale. No items in the PAC or PA scales are reverse scored.

SCORING. Upon completion of the test, participants self-score their answers by breaking the test apart and allocating indicated point values for each item to the four scale categories. Point totals are then transferred to a stanine-equivalent circle grid that graphically shows high and low scores. The test authors stress that differences between score categories, rather than percentage rank, is the purpose of this scoring profile.

NORMING. Norming was done on 653 individuals. The sample seems skewed in that more than half (63%) were male, most (69%) were younger than 30, and a majority had some college experience. Although this is a test designed to measure cross-cultural effectiveness, no ethnic/racial demographics were provided for the 80% of the sample who were U.S. citizens, and the balance were only identified through a list of countries with no breakdown of specific group numbers. The current 1995 test manual provides no additional normative data to further generalize the data to a larger population.

VALIDITY. Although the manual says the test should not be used for screening purposes, the obvious direction of item responses may introduce social desirability contamination into validity considerations. For example, in the normative sample, 31 of the 50 items have a median score of 5 or greater (out of a possible 6). This skew has the effect of translating small differences in raw scores into major swings in stanine rank.

As complex personality traits are being assessed, small item sets can also bias results. This reviewer is concerned, for example, about the construct validity of a complex scale such as personal autonomy being measured with only seven items. Finally, no concurrent or predictive validity data are provided.

RELIABILITY. The inventory appears to have adequate internal consistency with Cronbach's alpha coefficients ranging from .68 for PA to .82 for ER.

SUMMARY. The experience base of the test authors is international organizational development, plus the pilot testing phase through the International Society for Intercultural Education Training and Research (SIETAR) are obvious strengths of the instrument. Ancillary materials included with the inventory, although somewhat basic in nature, point in the right direction of multimodal training effectiveness. The optional ratings by outside observers, if used, would also increase the usefulness of the scale measures. The inventory, however, could be strengthened by addition in the manual of more current research indicating some predictive validity of the constructs measured. Additionally, linking definitions to more fundamental theory in acculturation stress and adaptation to change would deepen the rationale for the factor scales.

Review of the Cross-Cultural Adaptability Inventory by WENDY NAUMANN, Assistant Professor, Department of Psychology, University of Memphis, Memphis, TN:

The Cross-Cultural Adaptability Inventory (CCAI) is a self-evaluation tool that is part of a training program intended to provide examinees information regarding their potential for cross-cultural effectiveness. The manual is brief but provides clear information on the scoring and uses of the CCAI. Commentaries are provided for each item in order to assist trainers and examinees with the interpretation of their scores on each of the subscales. Although normative data exist on the CCAI, the authors clearly state that the self-awareness purpose of the instrument is best met by using raw scores instead of standardized scores. Percentiles and stanine scores are available, but the test authors recommend plotting raw scores on a self-assessment profile. Individuals who have some college education and have traveled abroad are overrepresented in the normative sample, and the manual lacks descriptive information regarding the sample such as the geographical location of the examinees.

The original version of the CCAI was developed using a two-step process. First, an exhaustive literature search was conducted in order to identify characteristics of cross-cultural effectiveness. A composite list of 58 items was created based on the literature review and discussions with individuals who had specialization in the area. Secondly, this composite list was sent to 25 experts selected based on their cross-cultural knowledge and sophistication and their experiences abroad. These experts rated each of the items on importance, and the highest rated items were compared to the literature. Through the use of statistical analyses and four judges, the items were grouped into the four scales comprising the CCAI. Use of these procedures provided adequate content validity for the scales as a self-assessment tool. In addition to content validity, construct validity was assessed using exploratory factor analysis and item-to-scale correlations. These statistical procedures were conducted using data from the normative sample. This sample of 653 examinees overrepresented males, individuals below the age of 30, and individuals with at least some college experience. No information was provided regarding the techniques used to obtain the sample. Findings from the exploratory factor analysis and the item-to-scale correlations supported the scale structure of the instrument.

Overall, the reliability estimates of the CCAI are adequate for use of the instrument as a training tool. The Personal Autonomy subscale has the weakest overall psychometric properties with the largest percentage of items double loaded on more than one factor, the weakest correlation with the overall total score ($r = .55$), and the lowest Cronbach alpha (.68). The remaining subscale scores and total score have adequate internal consistencies ranging from .78 for Perceptual Acuity to .90 for the Total score. Correlations between the four subscales range from .27 to .59. Almost all of the 49 items are negatively skewed; however, this dynamic could be due to the large percentage of people in the normative sample who have traveled

abroad (70%). In spite of the skewness, the items and subscales do have an adequate degree of variability. The authors warn against the use of the CCAI for diagnostic purposes, and the psychometric properties of the instrument do not warrant such a use.

Other forms of validity evidence were also assessed. The authors address this issue of face validity and provide a reasonable argument for a high degree of face validity; however, no evidence is given for this assertion. No predictive validity information is included in the manual for this reason. One study assessing the discriminant validity is discussed; however, the sample used for this study was very limited in external validity. The authors describe the results of this study as "promising," but readers should be cautioned against placing too much emphasis on the findings.

SUMMARY. Overall, the psychometric properties of the CCAI are adequate for its use as a training tool. Although more validity information could be provided, the development of the scale and the existing reliability and validity evidence are satisfactory. The authors are also very clear in the manual regarding the appropriate uses of the instrument and warn against inappropriate uses.

[108]
Curriculum Frameworks Assessment System.

Purpose: "A series of tests based on the major educational outcomes stated in the four California Frameworks ... [which] ... provides teachers and administrators with one measure of whether students are attaining the educational goals recommended by the state framework committees."

Population: Students in grades 1–12 from the California public school districts.

Publication Dates: 1990–1992.

Scores, 4: History—Social Science, English—Language Arts, Mathematics, Science.

Administration: Group.

Parts: 2 formats: The Curriculum Frameworks Assessment System, The Curriculum Frameworks Assessment Supplement.

Levels, 10: 1–8, 9/10, 11/12.

Price Data, 1994: $28.65 per review materials including test booklet for each level with accompanying examiner's manual, and sample copies of the CompuScan answer sheets used at Levels 4–8 and 9–12 (both system and supplement); SYSTEM: $83.65 per 35 test books and 1 examiner's manual (Level 1: 1990, 61 pages; Level 2: 1990, 57 pages; Level 3: 1990, 53 pages); $52.50 per 35 hand-scorable test books, and 1 manual, Levels 1–3; $60.55 per 35 reusable test books (Levels

4–12) and 1 examiner's manual (Levels 4–8, 1990, 66 pages); SUPPLEMENT: $63 per 35 machine-scorable test books and 1 manual (Level 1, 1990, 54 pages; Level 2, 1990, 49 pages; Level 3, 1990, 45 pages); $42 per 35 reusable test books and manual (Levels 4–12); $45 per 50 answer booklets (grades 4–8, 9–12); $537.50 per 1,250 answer sheets, grades 4–8 continuous form (10P); $537.50 per 1,250 answer sheets, grades 9–12 continuous form (12P or 10P); $29 per student diagnostic profile sheet, grades 1–12; $5.65 per item classification tables (Levels 1–12); $8.35 per norms book and technical report (grades 1–12); price data for scoring service available from publisher.

Time: (5–75) minutes per test.

Comments: "The Curriculum Frameworks Assessment System consists of 6 tests which measure the [four] frameworks educational outcomes. The items ... provide statewide normative ... and framework outcome information"; "The Curriculum Frameworks Assessment Supplement consists of 3 tests. When [it] ... is administered in conjunction with the CTBS/4 Complete Battery, Form A, schools can receive the entire CTBS/4 information and the Curriculum Frameworks Assessment information"; item classification tables available for Levels 1–12.

Authors: CTB Macmillan/McGraw-Hill.

Publisher: CTB/McGraw-Hill.

Review of the Curriculum Frameworks Assessment System by GERALD S. HANNA, Professor of Education, Kansas State University, Manhattan, KS:

DEVELOPMENT AND DESCRIPTION. The Curriculum Frameworks Assessment (CFA) is aligned with educational outcomes for English—Language Arts, History—Social Sciences, Science, and Mathematics promulgated in various K–12 Curriculum Frameworks and Model Curriculum documents published by the California State Department of Education between 1984 and 1988.

First, items were identified in the Comprehensive Tests of Basic Skills, Fourth Edition (CTBS/4) Complete Battery, Form A, that matched the content and skills for each framework. Then, additional items were developed to better assess each curriculum framework. These latter items comprise the CFA Supplement, which can be administered along with Form A of the Complete Battery of CTBS/4 to secure national norms for the latter while assessing all parts of the Curriculum Frameworks that lend themselves to multiple-choice items.

Alternatively, one can use the CFA System in which the Supplement is packaged with the relevant parts of the CTBS/4, Form A. When so administered, percentile ranks and other derived scores are based on California reference groups, not national norms. This review focuses on the CFA System.

ASSESSMENT OF INTEGRATED CURRICULUM. In pursuit of assessing an integrated curriculum, the CFA departs from tradition both in relationship between subtests and subscores and in its item types.

TESTS AND SCORES. An interesting and creative feature of the CFA concerns its breaking out of the paradigm of a one-to-one correspondence between tests and scores. For example, at Grade 5 subtests are: Test 1—Reading, Test 2—Language, Test 3—Integrated Curriculum: Part 1, Test 3—Integrated Curriculum: Part 2, Test 4—Mathematics, Test 5—Mathematics Technology, and Test 6—Science. The English-Language score is computed from the sum of all the items in Tests 1 and 2 as well as some of the items in both parts of Test 3. The History-Social Science score is based on some of the items in both parts of Test 3. (Note the absence of a separate test for this score.) In general, the Mathematics score is the sum of all the items in Tests 4 and 5 (although sometimes items from Test 6 are included in determining the mathematics score). The Science score is based on all the items in Test 6. (In some grades, the Science score also draws from Test 3.)

This approach seems promising. Indeed, it would be nice to see it carried further in order to (a) exploit connections between science and social science at *all* grades and (b) capitalize upon relationships of mathematics to science and social science.

ITEM TYPES. Although the Integrated Curriculum tests employ some relatively conventional free-standing multiple-choice items, other items and the stimuli upon which they are based depart from convention in two ways. First, the interpretive exercises based on reading passages and graphic displays are designed not only to assess acquisition of information from the stimuli but also to assess student knowledge and experience. The answers to some items lie within the examinee rather than within the stimuli. Similarly, some items depend on examinees' abilities to combine their prior knowledge and experience with information provided by the stimuli.

This line of thinking would seem to have the capability of producing items that better simulate reality. In using everyday-life data sources (e.g., maps, recipes, or tabular material), we do indeed bring what we know to the situation, and some such sources require such requisite knowledge. Thus, the CFA posture may produce items with greater authenticity than conventional interpretive exercises. On the other hand, abandoning of the expectation of *dependence* of correct answers to items upon their stimuli may weaken the item type in assessment of transfer of learning. The latter may be a price that should not be paid without very careful consideration.

Second, some of the items in the integrated Curriculum test are unconventional in that they require examinees to integrate information from two or more sources, such as a map and a reading passage. This kind of interpretive exercise seem wonderfully suited for assessing higher-level mental processes, including transfer of learning, in relatively authentic ways.

DIRECTIONS AND TIME LIMITS. The directions read to students should be faulted for not addressing the issue of guessing when in doubt. In view of the use of number-correct scoring, students should have been informed that it is to their advantage to respond to every item. Validity is likely to be weakened by failure to remove this source of individual differences, which is not relevant to what the tests are intended to measure.

To make matters worse, instructions to examiners concerning guessing are confusing and contradictory. Examiners are instructed on the one hand to "encourage students to attempt all items" (examiner's manual, p. 17). On the other hand, they are later told to "advise students to skip any items they really do not know and go on to the next one" (examiner's manual, p. 17). Differences among examiners can be expected to produce a worrisome lack of uniformity in this respect.

Directions regarding the time limits are also problematic. Examiners are told to "observe the time estimates for each test sitting ...; however, allow ample time for most students to complete the section being administered. It may be necessary to end a sitting before *every* student has finished, especially if only one or two students are experiencing some difficulty" (examiner's manual, p. 15). The vagueness of these directions can be expected to produce rather unstandardized time limits; yet this problem would be expected to impact the scores of only those students who are in the slowest quarter or so of their respective classes.

VALIDITY AND RELIABILITY. Prospective users must judge the content-related validity evidence of the CFA for their own local use. The detailed item classification tables will be helpful in this regard. The CFA's tight articulation with the California curriculum will probably be a strength in some settings and a limitation in others.

The only kind of reliability data supplied is KR20, which unfortunately, is described as a lower-bound estimate of test reliability. Because KR20 is eroded not only by imperfect internal consistency but also by content heterogeneity, it could be described (for unspeeded tests) as a lower-bound estimate of *internal consistency* reliability. However, another major source of error variance in objective group tests is consistency over time, and KR20 does not reflect this. Hence, it would be more realistic to consider KR20 to *over*estimate the reliability that would be secured from the preferred kind of study— alternate forms administered a week or two apart by different examiners. The triple fault, then, is that (a) only internal consistency data are reported, (b) users are not warned that variations of examinee performance over time and across examiners are not reflected in the reliability estimates, and (c) the internal consistency estimates are described as lower-bound estimates of test reliability.

The KR20s for the four frameworks for each grade level appear to be acceptable, ranging across grades between .77 to .95 and having a median value of .90.

INTERPRETABILITY. Interpretation of a test can be referenced to a well-described reference group of other examinees or to a tightly described content domain. CFA materials suggest both kinds of interpretation.

NORM REFERENCING. Stratified cluster sampling was used to obtain California reference groups averaging about 2,000 public school pupils per grade. The most important stratification variable—socioeconomic status—appears to have been only roughly categorized into only two strata that were determined solely by the fraction of students in districts who received Chapter 1 funding. Stratification for the seemingly less important variables—region of the state and urbanicity—appear to have been more refined.

CURRICULUM REFERENCING. For each of the four frameworks per grade level, curriculum-referenced scores (e.g., raw and percent scores) are provided for each of the 3 to 10 outcomes. Three serious issues come to mind. First, how can a raw or percent score be meaningful for assessments that sample very large, open-ended domains such as higher-order thinking, economic literacy, or physical science? Obviously, they cannot. Thus, the curriculum-referenced scores cannot yield meaningful interpretations.

Second, how redundant are the separate outcome measures? In order to use subscores prudently, one needs to know that they enjoy some reasonable degree of mutual independence. Unfortunately, the manuals fail to report the correlations among the outcome measures. Hence, the curriculum-referenced scores cannot be used with confidence.

Third, are the outcomes measures reliable enough to justify their use with individual pupils? The Technical Reports fail to provide reliability coefficients for outcome measures, yet do report standard errors of measurement. However, the accuracy of these reported standard errors of measurement is questionable. Elsewhere these (but not other) standard errors of measurement are defined in a nonstandard manner that resembles a standard error of the mean; yet the figures reported in Table 7 seem too large to be that. Other inconsistent and confusing evidence is also reported, such as an Individual Performance Reports graphic display showing standard error bands that are much larger than the values reported in accompanying tables yet are puzzling in that they are all the same length in spite of a 100% variation in the number of items per outcome exhibited.

So are the outcome measures reliable enough to justify their use? Because the manuals are less than helpful in answering this question, one might best fall back on general knowledge. It seems unlikely that measures typically based on five to seven items will provide reliable scores.

Any one of these three issues would render the curriculum-referenced interpretation scores of the short outcome measures to be ill advised.

SUMMARY. The Curriculum Frameworks Assessment uses some promising item types and innovative relationships between scores and tests to assess student achievement of California curriculum. Test directions have some serious flaws. Internal consistency of the four major scores seems adequate. Curriculum-referenced interpretation of student performance on individual outcome measures suffers from three fatal flaws; I strongly urge users not to use these scores. Norm-referenced interpretation of student performance on major scores is referenced to California students who were not as fully described as they might have been. The norm-referenced uses of the CFA seem to be a reasonable choice for users who wish to focus assessment upon the California curriculum by use of California reference-group data.

[109]
Das-Naglieri Cognitive Assessment System.

Purpose: "Developed to evaluate cognitive processes of children … using the PASS theory of intelligence."
Population: Ages 5 to 17-11.
Publication Date: 1997.
Acronym: CAS.
Levels, 2: Ages 5–7, ages 8–17.
Price Data, 1999: $595 per complete kit with carrying case; $520 per complete kit without case; $48 per Administration and Scoring Manual (305 pages); $48 per Interpretive Handbook; $27 per 25 Record Forms (ages 5–17); $16.50 per 25 Response Books (specify ages 5–7 or ages 8–17); $16.50 per 25 Figure Memory Response Books (ages 5–17); $24 per 30 Multi-Pack of Forms; $64 per Assessment of Cognitive Processes: The PASS Theory of Intelligence (256 pages).
Comments: PASS theory reconceptualizes intelligence as cognitive processes.
Authors: Jack A. Naglieri and J. P. Das.
Publisher: Riverside Publishing.
  a) STANDARD BATTERY.
  Scores: 4 scales with 13 subtests: Planning (Matching Numbers, Planned Codes, Planned Connections), Simultaneous (Nonverbal Matrices, Verbal-Spatial Relations, Figure Memory), Attention (Expressive Attention, Number Detection, Receptive Attention), Successive (Word Series, Sentence Repetition, Speech Rate, Sentence Questions).
  Time: [60] minutes.
  b) BASIC BATTERY.
  Scores: 4 scales with 8 subtests: Planning (Matching Numbers, Planned Codes), Simultaneous (Nonverbal Matrices, Verbal-Spatial Relations), Attention (Expressive Attention, Number Detection), Successive (Word Series, Sentence Repetition).
  Time: [40] minutes.
Cross References: See T5:763 (5 references).

Review of the Das-Naglieri Cognitive Assessment System by JOYCE MEIKAMP, Associate Professor of Special Education, Marshall University Graduate College, South Charleston, WV:

NATURE AND USES. The Das-Naglieri Cognitive Assessment System (CAS) is a clinical instrument for assessing intelligence based on a battery of cognitive tasks. The CAS reflects the authors' more than 20 years of research and development. Utilizing an innovative, nontraditional approach for assessing individual differences in intelligence, both theory and applied psychology are incorporated in this instrument. Based upon Luria's PASS theory, intelligence is reconceptualized as consisting of four cognitive processes. These mental activities include planning, attention, simultaneous, and successive (PASS) processing. The CAS is designed for identifying relative cognitive processing strengths and weaknesses, predicting achievement or classification, determining eligibility, and designing treatment, instructional, or remedial programs.

Operationalizing the PASS theory, the CAS has two forms: a Standard Battery and a Basic Battery. Both forms consist of Planning, Attention, Simultaneous, and Successive Scales. For the Standard Battery, each of the four PASS scales consists of three subtests, whereas the Basic Battery PASS scales utilize two subtests each. Within each PASS scale scores are combined to yield a standard score with a mean of 100 and *SD* of 15. A Full Scale standard score, derived from the sum of the subtest scaled scores, is generated for either the Standard or Basic Batteries.

Each PASS scale subtest was developed to operationalize a particular process for task completion. These subtests incorporate a variety of tasks, representing diversity in content, modality, and complexity. Uniquely, the CAS employs Planning and Attention scales, two constructs not typically incorporated in traditional measures of intelligence. For example, the Planning scale subtests present relatively easy paper-and-pencil tasks requiring the individual to make decisions about solving novel tasks. Not only must a plan of action be created, but also applied, verified, and modified as needed.

Emphasizing cognitive processing strategies, the examiner records not only time and accuracy, but also the strategies the subject both appears to be and reports to be utilizing. Although this feature is unique and holds much promise for understanding an individual's cognitive processing, identification of relative strengths and weaknesses, and designing treatment and instructional programs, caution is in order for exceptional populations. For example, questioning individuals who may be ei-

ther mentally retarded or learning disabled is problematic because these populations frequently have great difficulty verbalizing strategies utilized to solve problems. Thus, there may be great uncertainty as to whether or not they are even utilizing problem-solving strategies. Moreover, given the examiner accuracy, timing, and observed and reported strategies requirements, and the nature of the demands placed on the examiner, potential for error exists for the Planning subtests.

Attention is felt by the authors to be central to cognitive processing. The Attention Scale requires the child to focus on a task, selectively attend to a specific stimulus, and suppress irrelevant stimuli. A variety of creative tasks with familiar stimuli are in each of the subtests.

Conversely, the Simultaneous scale subtests include a predominance of information coding tasks requiring perception of parts into wholes or a single gestalt. Interrelating parts into a perceptual whole, the subtests require the individual to acquire, store, and retrieve information. According to the CAS authors, simultaneous processing involves both nonverbal spatial as well as verbal-grammatical activities.

The Successive Processing subtests tasks require the processing of information in a linear and sequential manner. For each of the subtests the individual deals with verbally presented information in a specific chain-like order and for which the order drives the meaning. According to the CAS authors, each element is only related to those that precede it, and these stimuli are not interrelated. Unlike the other CAS scales, the Successive scale subtests stimuli are only presented auditorily to the individual and then the individual is asked to respond verbally. Given the diversity of modalities and modes of presentation utilized in the other Pass scales, one has to wonder why the authors uncharacteristically opted to rely so heavily on verbal task demands for this particular scale.

DEVELOPMENT AND STANDARDIZATION. The CAS was standardized on a national sample of 2,200 children (aged 5-0 to 17-11) randomly stratified for age, gender, race, Hispanic origin, geographic region, parental educational attainment, and community setting. Approximately 13% of the sample was drawn from children who were receiving special education services. All scores are expressed as normalized standard scores and as percentile ranks. Although conversions of CAS subtest raw scores to age equivalents are also available, the authors caution about doing so.

RELIABILITY AND VALIDITY. Split-half reliability coefficients ranging from .70 to .96 were reported for Simultaneous and Successive subtests (except Speech Rate). Test-retest reliability coefficients (median delay = 21 days) for the Planning and Attention subtests as well as Speech Rate ranged from .64 to .92. The formula for the reliability of linear combinations was utilized to compute reliability coefficients for the Standard and Basic Battery PASS scales and Full Scale standard scores. Standard Battery PASS scale reliability coefficients were from .84 to .95, and for the Basic Battery they ranged from .81 to .93. Standard Full Scale coefficients were from .95 to .97 and Basic Full Scale coefficients ranged from .85 to .90.

In addition to content validity built into the tests through item and subtest analyses via task analyses and examination, analyses conducted on the standardization sample contributed to evidence of construct validity. Data were provided from factor analyses of subtests, age differences, and internal consistency of subtests and scales, as well as CAS Basic and Standard Batteries. However, factor analyses of subtests indicated some support for a 4-factor PASS solution as well as for a 3-factor solution. Thus, Planning and Attention as separate factors may be debatable.

Criterion-related validity against the Woodcock-Johnson—Revised Tests of Achievement was investigated with a sample of 1,600, with resulting correlations appearing to be promising. Several other investigations, with small groups of exceptional children, also reported promising correlations.

INTERPRETIVE HAZARDS. An important goal of the CAS is to reconceptualize human cognitive processing in order to gain a broader understanding of both interindividual and intraindividual differences. Ultimately this information is to be used to make informed decisions about diagnosis, eligibility, and intervention. However, comparing the PASS scales and subtest scores for intraindividual differences and discrepancies may open the way for misinterpretation. Such ipsative interpretation is highly controversial given these procedures violate the assumptions of typical statistics (Kerlinger, 1973).

Regarding intervention, the authors acknowledge the validity of assessment-intervention linkages is ongoing and an emerging area of research. Although a summary of such research is provided, few intervention studies with exceptional populations are cited. Thus, caution should be exercised in prescribing PASS-based remedial instruction for exceptional students.

SUMMARY. The CAS is an innovative instrument and its development meets high standards of technical adequacy. Despite interpretation cautions with exceptional populations, this instrument creatively bridges the gap between theory and applied psychology.

REVIEWER'S REFERENCE

Kerlinger, F. N. (1973). *Foundations of behavioral research* (2nd ed.). New York: Holt, Rinehart, & Winston.

Review of the Das-Naglieri Cognitive Assessment System by DONALD THOMPSON, Dean and Professor of Counseling and Psychology, Troy State University Montgomery, Montgomery, AL:

The Das-Naglieri Cognitive Assessment System (CAS) is a test of general ability that consists of a battery of subtests designed to assess cognitive processing based on the authors' PASS theory of intellect "which reconceptualizes intelligence as cognitive processes" (Interpretive Handbook, p. 2). The user's manual indicates that the CAS was developed:

> To integrate theoretical and applied areas of psychological knowledge using a theory of cognitive processing and tests designed to measure those processes. More specifically, the CAS was developed to evaluate Planning, Attention, Simultaneous, and Successive (PASS) cognitive processes of individuals between the ages of 5 and 17 years. (p. 1)

The complete CAS kit includes the Administration and Scoring Manual, Interpretive Handbook, and 25 each of the Record Form, Response Book, and Figure Memory Response Books. The test has two forms: The Standard Battery is composed of 13 subtests (only 12 are used in any administration, however), and the Basic Battery is composed for 8 subtests. Although both the Standard and Basic Batteries include Planning, Attention, Simultaneous, and Successive (PASS) scales, in the Basic Battery the scales are composed of two subtests each, whereas on the Standard Battery, the scales have three subtests each. All subtests yield standard scores, and the standard score scale for each subtests has a mean of 10 and standard deviation of 3. The Full Scale score on the test is determined by combining the subtests scaled scores. The Full Scale score is a standard score scale that has a mean of 100 and a standard deviation of 15.

The CAS is an individually administered test that requires 40 minutes for the Basic Battery and 60 minutes for the Standard Battery. The reported reliability data for the Full Scale and PASS subscales indicate the test has high internal consistency and test-retest reliability. The Full Scale reliability coefficients range from .95 to .97 (Spearman corrected split-half estimate), and the average reliabilities for the Standard Battery PASS scales are reported as .88 (Planning), .88 (Attention), .93 (Simultaneous), and .93 (Successive). The Interpretive Handbook also reports data on content, construct, and criterion-related validity. These data provide generally strong support for the construct, and the criterion-related validity studies suggest that the CAS is highly correlated to other well-established measures of ability and achievement such as the Woodcock-Johnson Psycho-Educational Battery—Revised (WJ-R; T5:2901) and the Wechsler Preschool and Primary Scale of Intelligence—Revised (WPPSI-R; T5:2864).

CAS norms are based on a sample of 2,200 children ranging in age from 5 years to 17 years, 11 months. The standardization sample was distributed geographically to be representative of the United States for gender, age, racial and ethnic origin, and socioeconomic factors. The data reported in the Interpretive Handbook suggest that this was a very well-done standardization. The representativeness of the norm data should insure that the individual scores can be accurately interpreted for all individuals for whom the test is intended.

Although the primary purpose of the CAS is to assess cognitive processing (or general intellectual functioning/ability level), the authors suggest that PASS scores can be especially useful in the identification of attention-deficit/hyperactivity disorders, traumatic brain injury, learning disabilities, mental retardation, and giftedness.

The CAS has many strong features that make it a desirable test. It is not difficult to learn to administer the test, and the directions for administration and scoring are clear and straightforward. Also, when compared to other individually administered general ability tests, such as the Stanford-Binet (T5:2485) or the Wechsler scales (T5:2864; T5: 2862), it take less time to administer. As noted earlier, the CAS definition of cognitive functioning (intelligence) is based on the four components of planning, attention, simultaneous, and successive processing. This is a different view of intelligence, but it also makes sense if you follow the reasoning. Test administrators who used the CAS for this review liked the idea of four specific assessment areas rather than just Verbal or Quantitative scores provided by the Wechsler Scales. It is easy to explain the test scores to parents and teachers because the full scale and subtests scaled scores have means and standard deviations that are the same as the Wechsler Scales. This also makes it easy to interpret and compare to other test scores. In fact, the Record Form contains a very handy chart for making a direct calculation of ability/achievement discrepancy scores using the WJ-R Achievement Test results. The interpretive handbook is very helpful in making judgments regarding the meaning of test scores and making interpretations for individual test takers; however, the lack of an index made it difficult to find specific material quickly. Having the option of the Basic or Standard Battery adds flexibility and still provides the full scale score and all four cognitive processing scores.

The CAS is a relatively new entry into the field of ability testing. The amount of empirical research supporting the PASS construct is limited, and most of this comes from the authors. Although the test materials were generally judged to be of high quality, the administrators who used the CAS for this review were unimpressed with the scoring templates that are used as overlays on the subject's Response Book answer sheets. The overlays are made of translucent paper, as opposed to a more durable plastic material. The templates are likely to tear, fall apart, or be disfigured in long-term use. Several test subjects expressed dislike for the Sentence Repetition and Sentence Questions subtests. They complained that both the subtests were particularly difficult because the sentences were so silly. The Figure Memory subtest is similar to the Bock Design subtest on Wechsler Scales, but it is both more difficult to administer, and appears to be more difficult for subjects to perform. The ratio conversion scores are rather confusing. The method of scoring is clear, but the meaning of the scores is rather hazy. Although the complete test battery kit costs less than either the Wechsler or Binet Scales, the cost of consumables per administration (about $2.20) does raise the long range cost.

SUMMARY. Overall, the CAS was judged by this reviewer to be a strong entry into the ability testing field for children and adolescents. It would seem particularly useful for testing special populations as noted earlier. The PASS concept makes logical sense, but more empirical research is needed. The test materials are of generally high quality, and ease of use is a strong feature. Generally, I found the CAS to be a better measure than the current version of the Stanford-Binet, but in terms of ease of use and score interpretation, I prefer the Wechsler Scales.

[110]
Davidson Trauma Scale.

Purpose: Developed to assess post traumatic stress disorder (PTSD) symptoms and aid in treatment.
Population: Adults who have been exposed to a serious trauma.
Publication Date: 1996.
Acronym: DTS.
Scores, 4: Intrusion, Avoidance/Numbing, Hyperarousal, Total.
Administration: Individual or group.
Price Data, 1997: $45 per complete kit including manual (42 pages), and 25 QuikScore™ forms; $22 per 25 QuikScore™ forms; $27 per manual.
Foreign Language Edition: French-Canadian QuikScore™ forms available.
Time: (10) minutes.
Author: Jonathan Davidson.
Publisher: Multi-Health Systems, Inc.

Review of the Davidson Trauma Scale by JANET F. CARLSON, Professor of Counseling and Psychological Services, Associate Dean School of Education, Oswego State University, Oswego, NY:

The Davidson Trauma Scale (DTS) is a recently published, paper-and-pencil, self-report inventory that assesses frequency and severity of posttraumatic stress disorder (PTSD) symptoms in adults. The DTS was developed by Jonathan Davidson, Director of the Anxiety and Traumatic Stress Program at Duke University Medical Center. The items of the scale consist of 17 symptoms that mirror closely the diagnostic criteria of PTSD, contained in the fourth edition of the *Diagnostic and Statistical Manual of Mental Disorders* (DSM-IV; American Psychiatric Association, 1994). Using the past week as a frame of reference and a 0 to 4 rating scale, test takers are asked to rate each

item for the frequency of its occurrence and the subjective distress accompanying the symptom. The items comprise three symptom clusters associated with the major dimensions of PTSD symptomatology—intrusion into everyday life, acts or experiences that avoid or numb feelings connected with the trauma, and hyperarousal.

APPLICATIONS. The test author recommends the DTS for use in providing feedback to patients undergoing treatment for PTSD and to assess treatment response. Further, it may be used as a screening instrument or for research purposes. Appropriately, the test author advises potential users that the DTS is best regarded as an adjunct or supplement to clinical assessment, rather than as a replacement for same. It is not intended as a diagnostic instrument.

The intended uses of the DTS include the assessment of PTSD symptoms experienced by adults who have been exposed to serious traumata. In this context, trauma is a clinically significant term denoting an event that is "outside of everyday experience and [is] markedly distressing to the great majority" (manual, p. 2). The test author notes that such an event must have "involved actual or threatened death or serious injury, or threat to the physical integrity of self or others, and induced a response of intense fear, helplessness, or horror" (p. 1). Such events include but are not limited to criminal or sexual assault, combat, natural disaster, torture, and bereavement.

ADMINISTRATION, SCORING, AND INTERPRETATION. The DTS may be administered individually or in group format. It also is possible to modify procedures slightly to permit oral administration if, for instance, the test taker were visually impaired. Instructions to the test taker are simple, and the test author indicates that completion of the scale requires only an eighth-grade reading level. General guidelines for test administration are provided in the test manual, including suggestions for prompting respondents if necessary. Total administration time is no more than 10 minutes; scoring takes even less time than administration.

Test takers respond by writing numbers corresponding to their ratings of frequency and severity of the 17 symptoms in boxes on the record form. A carbonized sheet transfers responses to the underlying score sheet, consisting of a set of boxes that are meaningfully grouped to yield a

Total Frequency score, Total Severity score, and Total DTS score. In addition, separate cluster scores for Intrusion, Avoidance/Numbing, and Hyperarousal are readily obtained by simple addition.

Interpretation stems from tabled data that present relative frequencies of various Total DTS scores for persons with and without PTSD. The table appears in the manual and is reproduced as part of the DTS QuikScore form. Interpretation is based primarily on the total score, which may range from 0 to 136. The test author suggests that the tabled data provide a measure of diagnostic probability, and offers the score of 20 as "a useful flag that PTSD is a likely probability" (manual, p. 15). However, elsewhere in the manual (p. 23) a cut point of 40 is identified as "perhaps the most clinically accurate." As noted above, cluster scores are obtainable, but data-derived interpretive procedures are not specified in the test manual for scores other than the Total DTS score. The test author suggests that subscale scores, frequency, and severity ratings be examined to assist in treatment planning or assessment of treatment response.

TECHNICAL ASPECTS. The section of the test manual that covers psychometric characteristics presents information from four studies to generate reliability estimates and provide evidence of scale validation. All studies used clinical samples, ranging in size from 53 to 110. The study used to examine test-retest reliability consisted of 102 individuals, who completed the DTS two times, with a one-week interval, and an assessment by a third party that their clinical picture had remained constant. The resulting coefficient was .86. Split-half reliability estimates are reported as .95 and .97 for frequency and severity, respectively, but it is not clear from the manual how these coefficients were determined. Alpha reliability coefficients were based on combined data from these studies (n = 241). The test author describes the coefficients as "high" and indicates that the values exceeded .90 for the total scale and for the frequency and severity scale scores. A separate study of 50 women who survived childhood sexual abuse produced alpha reliability estimates of .93 for the total scale, and .85, .83, and .87 for Intrusion, Avoidance/ Numbing, and Hyperarousal cluster scores, respectively. Item-total correlations ranged from .60 to .89, with most falling in the .80s.

Validation evidence for the DTS is provided in the test manual with attention to classification accuracy, convergent validity, divergent validity, group differences, and treatment change. All of these are best viewed as construct validation efforts. The test author discusses classification accuracy in terms of the interdependence of sensitivity and specificity and provides examples of how each factor is clinically relevant, as well as how each is affected by the selection of different cut points. Convergent validity was assessed by comparing the DTS with the Clinician-Administered PTSD Scale (n = 102), the Impact of Events Scale (n = 180), and the Symptom Checklist-90-R (n = 123). Correlation coefficients of Total DTS scores with the corresponding total score for each of these instruments were .78, .64, and .57, respectively. A related study compared the frequency and severity scales of the DTS with the total score from the Trauma Symptom Checklist 40, with resulting coefficients of .31 and .24, respectively. In addressing divergent validity, the Total DTS score was compared with an extraversion measure from the Eysenck Personality Inventory, using 78 subjects. Appropriately, the scores were unrelated (r = .04). The test author reports significant findings concerning the scale's ability to discriminate PTSD from non-PTSD patients, and to distinguish patients who respond to treatment from those who do not. Changes in symptoms and overall clinical condition, as assessed by the treating physicians, paralleled changes in DTS scores.

A factor analysis using a clinical sample (n = 133) was conducted. Some of the findings are presented briefly in the test manual. The test author notes that in this analysis a single very strong factor emerged, with a second much weaker factor present. Other studies found three factors. The number of factors extracted may be due, in part, to the characteristics of the samples used, and the method of extraction employed.

CRITIQUE. Not surprisingly, the information presented in the test manual is favorable and supportive of the DTS as far as its use with the intended population. Still, potential users must be prepared to ferret out some information beyond that presented in the test manual that may affect their choice of instruments. In particular, test users should bear in mind that the DTS is not intended to be a diagnostic instrument, and should not be used as such. Thus, in clinical applications, it is best regarded as a screening instrument for PTSD or as an indicator of the frequency and extent of related symptoms.

The test manual is uneven in its presentation of information. In the discussion of studies bearing on the psychometric properties, for example, sample sizes or procedures employed are only sometimes specified. Other times, rather descriptive labels are used, making it difficult for a potential user to assess relevant features of the scale. Particularly problematic are the guidelines pertaining to interpretation, which appear driven almost exclusively by clinical judgment. Therefore, use of the DTS by persons who lack considerable clinical experience with trauma victims is not recommended. Use of the scale by persons with substantial experience will not add greatly to such persons' understanding of the patient or population with whom they work. However, as a means of documenting symptoms numerically, or assessing treatment response, experienced clinicians may find the DTS somewhat useful.

There are no filler items on the DTS, as all items contribute to the total score. Items clearly are aimed at assessing aspects of PTSD. The response options for each item are presented in order of increasing severity or frequency. The items themselves are grouped by clusters. Although these characteristics make administration, scoring, and interpretation straightforward and probably add to the intrinsic appeal of the instrument, they also make faking extremely easy, because what is being assessed and which responses will garner the greatest clinical "weight" are obvious. In cases where test takers might be motivated to deceive (e.g., competency to stand trial, custody hearings, involuntary commitment procedures, social desirability), the test user is advised to use additional or less transparent means of assessment. Test users are left to their own devices as far as the detection of malingering.

SUMMARY. The DTS is a relatively new instrument, intended to be used and integrated with other available information, in order to document and understand PTSD symptomatology among clinical populations. Likely, it will find applications in related arenas, including research, screening, and assessment of therapeutic outcomes. Working in its favor are the facts that it is a simple measure that is easily and rapidly administered and scored, may be modifiable for use with individuals with disabilities, encompasses the major symptoms of PTSD, and is reasonably priced. Evidence concerning its usefulness is most likely to accumulate from its use in clinical settings and data generated from these applications. In the test manual, the test author expresses interest in receiving such information.

REVIEWER'S REFERENCE
American Psychiatric Association. (1994). *Diagnostic and statistical manual of mental disorders* (4th ed.). Washington, DC: Author.

Review of the Davidson Trauma Scale by WILLIAM E. MARTIN, JR., *Professor of Educational Psychology, Northern Arizona University, Flagstaff, AZ:*

The Davidson Trauma Scale (DTS) was designed for use with adults who have experienced a serious trauma as operationalized by the 1994 *Diagnostic and Statistical Manual of Mental Disorders* (DSM-IV; American Psychiatric Association, 1994). The scale is intended to cover *all* types of trauma including accident, combat, sexual assault, criminal assault, natural disaster, torture, burns, loss of property, near death experiences, and bereavement.

The DTS consists of 17 questions organized into three subscales and three total scales that directly reflect the 17 symptoms of Criteria B, C, and D of the DSM-IV for Posttraumatic Stress Disorder (PTSD). The three subscales are Intrusion (5 questions/symptoms), Avoidance/Numbing (7 questions/symptoms), and Hyperarousal (5 questions/symptoms). Additionally, the three total scales are Total Frequency (17 questions/symptoms), Total Severity (17 questions/symptoms), and DTS Total (17 questions/symptoms).

ADMINISTRATION, SCORING, AND INTERPRETATION. A user of the DTS is asked first to provide an open-ended response that identifies the trauma that is most disturbing him or her. Then, the user responds in two ways to 17 questions reflecting trauma symptoms. First, the respondent is asked to identify the frequency of symptoms for the last week on each questions using a 5-point rating scale (0 = *Not At All*, 1 = *Once Only*, 2 = *2–3 Times*, 3 = *4–6 Times*, and 4 = *Every Day*). Second, the respondent identifies the severity of each symptom using a 5-point scale ranging from 0 = *Not At All Distressing* to 4 = *Extremely Distressing*. The DTS is presented on a carbonized 3-page form that is used for both administering and scoring the instrument. The test-taking process takes less than 10 minutes according to the DTS manual.

Completion of the DTS culminates in three subscale scores (Intrusion, Avoidance/Numbing,

Hyperarousal), a Total Frequency score, a Total Severity score, and a DTS Total score. The three subscale scores and the DTS Total score are obtained by combining the frequency and severity ratings for all those questions that are associated with the three subscales and the total scale.

The DTS manual provides guidelines for interpreting the DTS results that focus on examining the DTS Total score, subscale scores, and the frequency and severity of symptoms scores. A table containing ratios of expected number of individuals with PTSD to individuals without PTSD is provided to assist the examiner in interpreting the DTS Total scores. Accordingly, higher ratios indicate higher probability of having PTSD. Unfortunately, there is a lack of information on how the ratios furnished in the table were obtained. Likewise, it is unclear which scores to use given the information provided in the table. The manual presents interpretations for six case studies representing differing traumas and clinical contexts.

DEVELOPMENT OF THE SCALES. The DTS was constructed to reflect directly the DSM-IV Criteria B, C, and D for Posttraumatic Stress Disorder.

RELIABILITY AND VALIDITY. Estimates of reliability and validity for scores from the DTS were derived primarily from four clinical research studies. The clinical groups in the four studies were female rape victims ($n = 78$), hurricane victims ($n = 53$), male combat veterans ($n = 110$), and individuals in multicenter clinical trials ($n = 102$). The ethnocultural profile of the first three clinical groups was reported as African American (24%), Hispanic (6%), and Caucasian (70%).

A one-week test-retest reliability estimate of $r = .86$ ($n = 21$) was reported. A split-half reliability estimate was $r = .95$ but the sample used was not specified. Coefficient alphas were over .90 for the Frequency, Severity, and DTS Total scales using the first three clinical groups combined. Item-total correlations ($n = 241$) ranged from .60 to .88 for the frequency items and .76–.89 for the severity items.

Classification accuracy values were reported as indicators of validity. For example, a positive predictive value of .92, a negative predictive value of -.79, and a diagnostic accuracy of .83 were given for a Total DTS score of 40. It is unclear, however, how these values were derived. Scores from the DTS were correlated with three other related measures to demonstrate evidence of convergent validity. The measures and associated correlation coefficients of the total scores were: (a) PTSD Scale ($r = .78$, $n = 102$), (b) Impact of Events Scale ($r = .64$, $n = 180$), and (c) Symptom Checklist-90-R ($r = .57$, $n = 123$). Additionally, a divergent validity measure is reported at $r = .04$ ($n = 78$). Further evidence of construct validity was reported based upon studies demonstrating group differences, treatment change, and severity differences. Finally, a small sample size ($n = 131$) principal components analysis was briefly discussed indicating a lack of clarity as to the factor structure of the DTS.

SUMMARY. The DTS provides a clinician with standardized self-report information from a respondent, reflecting perceived symptomatology directly related to the DSM-IV criteria for Posttraumatic Stress Disorder. This information used in conjunction with other data sources, including clinical assessment, would be useful in screening and for supplementing diagnoses to develop intervention plans. However, the DTS should not be used singly for diagnosis of PTSD. Although there is evidence supporting the psychometric properties of the DTS, considerably more data are needed. For example, there is a need for additional studies with larger sample sizes representing more trauma types in varying contexts. Furthermore, it would be valuable to initiate an intentional research agenda to study more fully the effects of sex, ethnocultural background, and socioeconomic status on DTS scores.

The case studies presented in the manual were useful in demonstrating how the DTS can be interpreted in a variety of clinical contexts. However, the table of ratios of expected numbers of individuals with PTSD to individuals without PTSD needs further explanation relative to both its origin and its use in interpreting DTS scores. Moreover, the authors might consider developing specific norm-referenced scores to supplement the interpretation process. Not only would standard scores be useful for interpretation but they could generate valuable data for the next DSM revision.

Although there are empirical strengths to the DSM process used to develop the criteria for PTSD that constitute the DTS, there also are restrictions to using the results. The data gathered in the DSM process focus on providing evidence to support optimal clinical diagnostic decision making, not to discover the traits and factors that comprise the psychological construct of posttraumatic stress. As such, the DTS is most suited for clinicians who want to connect their diagnoses and interventions directly to the DSM process.

REVIEWER'S REFERENCE

American Psychiatric Association. (1994). *Diagnostic and statistical manual of mental disorders* (4th ed.). Washington, DC: Author.

[111]
Degrees of Reading Power [Revised].

Publication Dates: 1979–1995.
Acronym: DRP.
Scores: Total score only.
Administration: Group.
Price Data, 1998: $40 per Primary/Standard DRP Examination set including 1 copy each of test forms, practice exercises, and manuals); $35 per Advanced DRP examination set; $130 per classroom set of Primary DRP; $126 per classroom set of Standard DRP; $123 per classroom set of Advanced DRP (classroom sets include all manuals and testing materials for 30 students).
Time: (45–50) minutes.
Comments: Practice tests may be used to select appropriate test form for student; also provides readability analysis of instructional material in print; machine or hand-scored; group profiles available.
Author: Touchstone Applied Science Associates (TASA), Inc.
Publisher: Touchstone Applied Science Associates (TASA), Inc.

a) PRIMARY.
Purpose: Constructed to measure "how well students are able to construct meaning from prose material."
Population: Grades 1–3.
Forms, 2: G, H.
Levels, 3: 0, 9, 8.
Price Data: $90 per 30 machine-scorable test booklets (select form); $11.50 per 30 practice booklets.

b) STANDARD.
Purpose: Same as *a* above.
Population: Grades 3–12 and over.
Forms, 2: G, H.
Levels, 5: 8, 7, 6, 4, 2.
Price Data: $68 per 30 test booklets (select level and form); $12.50 per 30 practice booklets (select level S1 or S2); $16 per 30 NCS answer sheets.

c) ADVANCED.
Purpose: Constructed to measure "how well students are able to reason with text."
Population: Grades 6–12 and over.
Forms, 2: T, U.
Levels, 2: 2, 4.

Price Data: $75 per 30 test booklets (select level and form); $14.50 per 30 practice booklets; $16 per 30 NCS answer sheets.
Cross References: See T5:773 (5 references); for reviews by Darrell N. Caulley, Elaine Furniss, and Michael McNamara and by Lawrence Cross of an earlier edition, see 12:101 (9 references); see also T4:726 (14 references); for reviews of an earlier edition by Roger Bruning and Gerald S. Hanna, see 9:305 (1 reference).

Review of the Degrees of Reading Power [Revised] by FELICE J. GREEN, Professor of Education, University of North Alabama, Florence, AL:

Although the revised Degrees of Reading Power (DRP) has three tests available—Primary, Standard, and Advanced—this review is restricted to the Primary and Standard tests.

The Primary and Standard DRP tests are designed to assess students' comprehension of the surface meaning of textual material that increases in difficulty. Consisting of nonfiction paragraphs and/or passages, the tests are in a modified cloze format (deleted words in the passages with four or five words to choose from to fill each missing word) with no time limit.

Although the DRP tests are criterion referenced, yielding a measure of the comprehension ability of students at the independent, instructional, and frustration levels, the tests can be normed. Using conversion tables provided, percentile ranks, stanines, and Normal Curve Equivalents can be obtained.

For instructional purposes—choosing appropriate material for students, individualizing instruction, grouping (should one choose to do so), monitoring students' progress, etc.—the criterion-referenced DRP scores are most useful. A DRP score can be obtained for each student at the independent level (ability to read with 90% comprehension), instructional (75% comprehension) and frustration (50% comprehension) levels). The DRP score for each of these levels indicates the difficulty of the material a student can read at each level.

To facilitate teachers in selecting appropriate materials for their students, five volumes of DRP Readability Reports are available. Information concerning the readability, or difficulty, of approximately 4,000 classic, popular fiction, and popular nonfiction books is provided in *Readability of Literature and Popular Titles*, Volumes 1, 2, and 3. DRP difficulty values of books are listed in each volume. DRP values for thousands of widely used textbooks in reading and the content areas are listed in *Readability of Textbooks*, 9th Edition. *Readability of Textbooks in Series*, 9th Edition can be used to compare series to each other and to determine whether instructional materials are properly sequenced according to difficulty across the grades. To determine the readability values of reading materials that are not included in the Readability Reports, a microcomputer software program, MicRA -> DRP is available.

The Primary DRP is recommended for Grades 1–3 and the Standard DRP is recommended for Grades 3–12+, but there were no students in Grade 1 included in the norming sample. The number in the sample, approximately 30,500, was adequate for Grades 2–12, but one should question the omission of first grade students from the sample.

All of the students in the sample were in New York State, which is supported by the National Assessment of Educational Progress (NAEP) results. In 1992 the NAEP found that New York State was the only state where the average reading proficiency was identical to the nation. Schools were used with a large and diverse enough population to emulate characteristics of the national population, such as different school sizes and school district socioeconomic status. Both public and private schools were used with a population of students from several ethnicities.

The internal consistency reliability coefficient of the tests for Grades 4–12 range from .93 to .97, and the standard errors of measurement range from 2.2 to 3.8 (raw scores). The reliability estimate for Grade 2 is .91 and is .92 for Grade 3. The standard errors of measurement are 2.8 and 2.7, respectively. The reliability estimates of the tests are, therefore, high, and the standard errors are small, as they should be.

The publisher of the DRP, Touchstone Applied Science Associates, Inc. (TASA), offers a multitude of services for schools that use the DRP. In addition to the Readability Reports already mentioned, TASA publishes *The English Profiles Handbook*, which can be used to report teachers' observations of student proficiency and progress. As with other test publishers, scoring is available, but TASA offers more ways of reporting results than most test publishers. TASA not only provides The Individual Performance Chart that re-

ports test results to parents, the publisher will also write a narrative letter to parents printed on school letterhead to explain test results.

Two Class Rosters are available that report scores to schools, one of which includes normative information and the other includes item response patterns. TASA also will provide a Class Profile and Class Summary Report that show the distribution of student performance and measures of central tendency (e.g., mean, median). In addition, TASA will create graphic reports that can be very useful.

There is an excellent glossary in back of the DRP Handbook. The definitions of important terms are very clear and easy to understand.

SUMMARY. In conclusion, the DRP is an excellent test. The fact that it has no time limit means that students who read slowly are not penalized, and only comprehension abilities are assessed. The cloze procedure has been proven to be a good method for assessing comprehension of reading material, and all of the services and publications available for reporting and using test results make the DRP one of the most useful tests available.

REVIEWER'S REFERENCES

Touchstone Applied Science Associates. (1988). *Readability of literature and popular titles* (vol.1). Brewster, NY: Author.
Touchstone Applied Science Associates. (1991). *Readability of literature and popular titles* (vol.2). Brewster, NY: Author.
Touchstone Applied Science Associates. (1993). *Readability of Textbooks* (9th ed.). Brewster, NY: Author.
Touchstone Applied Science Associates. (1994). *Readability of textbooks in series* (9th ed.). Brewster, NY: Author.
Touchstone Applied Science Associates. (1995). *Readability of literature and popular titles* (vol.3). Brewster, NY: Author.

Review of the Degrees of Reading Power by HOWARD MARGOLIS, *Professor of Educational and Community Programs, Queens College of the City University of New York, Flushing, NY:*

The Primary and Standard Degrees of Reading Power (DRP) Tests are part of a larger program designed to measure a student's ability to comprehend the surface meaning of text and match this ability to materials that the DRP Program determines is at the student's instructional or independent reading levels. The link between the student's DRP test score and reading materials is a common DRP scale, used to report student performance on the DRP and to assess the readability of text. The publisher (Touchstone, TASA) claims that "Because the DRP Score scale is identical to the DRP readability scale, test scores can be interpreted directly in terms of the difficulty of materials students are able to read .... A student who earns a DRP Score of 50 should be able to read textual material that has a DRP difficulty of 50" (Touchstone, 1995, p. 43). However, the information available casts considerable doubt on the ability of the DRP Program to achieve this goal with the accuracy needed to make placement decisions about readers, especially those with reading or related problems.

TEST DESCRIPTION AND USES. According to the publisher, the DRP tests are designed to assess students' understanding of the surface meaning of text in Grades 1 through 12, adult basic education and GED programs, and college situations. The tests should not be administered until students have mastered decoding skills. Students must choose from a list of common words the one word omitted from a nonfiction passage. Each passage has several deletions. Correct answers require the student to understand the surface meaning of the passage rather than just the individual sentence. This is because each option makes semantic and syntactical sense in the single sentence, but the correct option alone makes sense in the context of the passage. The DRP is untimed, which may help slow and anxious readers. Of particular importance is the single, unvarying format of the test's items. This allows comparisons over time, with different DRP forms.

The DRP's authors have responded admirably to many of the criticisms of standardized tests and the modified cloze or maze procedure. By requiring students to understand the essence of a passage the DRP addresses the need for cloze tests to assess comprehension beyond the sentence level (Parker, Hasbrouck, & Tindal, 1992). The consistent nature of its items, along with their high face validity, support using the DRP to assess surface meaning over time. For reasons presented below, this support is limited to group comparisons, initial student surveying, or use in a more comprehensive assessment and placement process.

DRP materials assert that students do not require subject matter knowledge of a passage to choose correct answers. This appears accurate if limited to technical or specialized knowledge. However, test users should not read too much into this as vocabulary and subject matter knowledge are inextricably intertwined. Consider two nonsecured sample items. The first requires knowing that "group" refers to "pattern." The second requires knowing that a "boat" is a "vessel" and that both relate to "river traffic." Thus, for some

students, inadequate background knowledge and vocabulary may cause low scores.

The publisher's admonition not to administer the easiest DRP until students have mastered decoding skills is well advised. Its applicability, however, is ambiguous. Many average 2nd grade readers have not fully mastered decoding, word analysis, or word recognition. Research is needed to determine the threshold reading proficiency required to obtain valid DRP scores. In line with this, Estes and Estes (1989) concluded that "The DRP measures the reading skills associated with fluent reading ... mastered by the intermediate grade student. It does not measure the skills of readers prior to fluency" (p. 8).

RELIABILITY AND CONCURRENT VALIDITY. The DRP has adequate reliability for surveying groups of students. Alternate form test-retest reliability coefficients for two research versions given in Grades 4 and 6 between 1 and 2 weeks apart, ranged from .86 to .91 (Touchstone, 1995). A test-retest comparison of Operational and Pilot forms yielded coefficients of .80 to .89, for Grades 4, 6, and 8 (Touchstone, 1996).

Kuder-Richardson (K-R 20) internal-consistency reliability coefficients of .90 to .94 (Forms E & F, Grades 2 to 8) (Touchstone, 1995) and .92 to .96 (Form G, Grades 2 to 9) (Touchstone, 1996) support the publisher's contention that the DRP is a "single-objective test" that measures a specific reading construct.

Older DRP versions correlate fairly high with the reading portions of the California Achievement Test (CAT; .77 to .86, Grades 3 through 9) (Weiner & Kippel, 1984) and the Iowa Tests of Basic Skills (ITBS; .73 to .86, Grades 5 through 7) (Hildebrand & Hoover, 1987). Koslin, Zeno, Koslin, Wainer, and Ivens (1987) present similar findings. Touchstone (1995) reports DRP gains after 5 months of instruction, suggesting sensitivity to growth. Together, these studies support the validity of the DRP as a standardized group-administered survey of reading achievement.

In addition to using DRP scores to select independent and instructional level reading materials for individual students, Touchstone recommends that it be used to gauge school accountability and student progress toward specific reading goals (1995). As a quick, group-administered standardized test that correlates well with the CAT and ITBS, it should effectively meet accountability needs by estimating the reading achievement of student groups. However, its validity for assessing progress toward specific reading goals is quite limited, as DRP tests "are single-objective tests measuring how well students understand the surface meaning of what they read" (Touchstone, 1995, p. 1). Given the limited, invariant nature of the DRP items and its multiple-choice format, interpretation of progress should be limited to the type of cloze task measured and other short-paragraph, short-answer type tests with which it correlates highly. Generalization should not be made to areas it ignores (e.g., fluency, matching strategy to purpose, synthesizing large amounts of materials) without collecting ample data in these areas.

The DRP's reliability, and thus its validity for assessing poor readers and inconsistently motivated students, is suspect. First, the test and its student labels, narrative reports, class rosters, and parent reports offer only single DRP scores designating a student's independent, instructional, and frustration levels, without providing a standard error of measurement or guidance for interpreting scores within a confidence interval (e.g., 68%, 95%). The inference is that each score is a valid, accurate indicator of reading achievement rather than a number that represents a sample of behavior, subject to error. DRP materials do state that the standard error averages around 2.5 DRP units, is small in the center of the distribution, and "fairly large" at the extremes (Touchstone, 1996, p. 4). However, without more specific error information, pre-post score comparisons and the confidence that one can place in single scores is highly problematic, especially for poor readers. Second, the DRP is a group test. Often, this makes it impossible to accurately ascertain the reasons for a student's poor score. Typically, one has no way of knowing if the student fully understood the task, sustained concentration, or jumped from passage to passage in a disorganized, impulsive, and anxious manner. Consequently, most reading textbooks recommend that group test scores be considered hypotheses, to be validated through diagnostic teaching and observation. It is one reason why federal special education regulations (e.g., Individuals with Disabilities Act Amendments of 1997) mandate that important educational decisions not rely on group test scores or single sources of information.

THE DRP SCORE-READABILITY MATCH. The DRP Handbook correctly states that validity "actually refers to the appropriateness of the inferences that can be drawn from test scores .... A test may have many different kinds of validity" (Touchstone, 1995, p. 58). The evidence suggests that the DRP has ample validity for surveying the reading achievement of groups of students. Contrary to the publisher's literature (e.g., "Is this text of appropriate difficulty for the intended students? If DRP test scores are available for the students, *precise answers* to this question can be obtained"; Touchstone, 1999, p. 8, emphasis added), using DRP to match students with reading materials lacks justification. The publisher's interpretation lacks a firm research foundation, ignores the limitations of readability formulas, disregards factors that make text difficult for individual students, and neglects basic assessment principles.

Historically, DRP scores have inaccurately matched students to reading materials (Bieger, 1989; Bormuth, 1985; Carver, 1985, 1990). Carver (1985) concluded that "it is likely that users of the DRP test will be creating the mismatch problem that the test purports to solve" (p. 36). Estes, Richards, and Wetmore-Rogers (1989) found that DRP scores correlated only moderately with informal reading inventory instructional levels, raising concerns about DRP levels. To have confidence adequate to use DRP scores to select reading materials will require research demonstrating that students of various backgrounds and abilities successfully comprehend and are productive and comfortable with materials at their DRP levels.

The DRP Handbook (Touchstone, 1995) contains excellent information on readability. It notes that text difficulty, for individual students, is often a function of the student's background, interest, and motivation. Unfortunately, the test format and the Handbook's score interpretations neglect much of this information as well as the critical readability factors of text length, text structure, quality of writing, and instructional situation. This last factor assesses what student must do with reading materials. Different assignments, with the same material, can make dramatically different demands on students; one assignment may be at their independent level, whereas another may be at their instructional or frustration level. Thus, readability refers to personal interactions with text that are mediated by task requirements. Although no test can account for all readability factors, the interpretations given by the DRP

Handbook (Touchstone, 1995) and DRP reports need to provide a more comprehensive, interactive perspective. Otherwise, mismatches between readers and materials will likely occur.

Frequently DRP materials (e.g., Touchstone, 1995) violate basic assessment principles by interpreting DRP scores as absolutes, rather than as samples of behavior that assist in decision making, contain error, and are affected by the student's instructional environment (Witt, Elliott, Daly, Gresham, & Kramer, 1998). By showing how to use and interpret DRP scores in conjunction with basic assessment principles (e.g., continuous monitoring of progress) and other factors that influence text difficulty for individual students, the publisher could improve the DRP's validity for matching reading materials to student needs.

THE DRP SCORE AS CRITERION-REFERENCED. The DRP is offered as a criterion- and a norm-referenced measure. The publisher considers the DRP criterion-referenced because it identifies the most difficult school and real world materials (e.g., newspapers, job-related items) a student can read with a specific level of comprehension (Touchstone, 1995).

Criterion-referenced interpretations of DRP scores are problematic. First, it is uncertain that DRP scores accurately identify the materials students can read with predicted levels of comprehension. As Bormuth (1985) noted, "the formula used with the Degrees of Reading Power test ... overestimates the difficulty of the simple materials ... while underestimating the difficulty of the advanced materials" (p. 46). Second, the DRP does not directly assess student performance on typical classroom or real world materials. Typically, such materials are more complex, lengthy, variable, and demanding than DRP items, making accurate prediction uncertain. Third, the publisher does not present sufficient research to demonstrate that DRP scores accurately predict performance on typical classroom and real world reading tasks. This limits criterion-referenced interpretations to the narrow, multiple-choice DRP task, which differ dramatically from classroom and real world reading tasks, which typically require the application of information. Consistent with this, King, Rasool, and Judge (1994) found that Standard Form DRP scores do not accurately predict the academic performance of students in college courses with heavy reading loads.

SUMMARY. The Primary and Standard DRP are a series of well-conceived tests with adequate validity for surveying students' understanding of the surface meaning of text. Sufficient research has yet to demonstrate that the tests accurately match students to reading materials of varied difficulty or that they accurately predict students' performance with typical classroom and real world reading materials. Revising the DRP's reporting and interpretative materials to treat its scores as limited samples of behavior to consider in concert with other factors critical to reading placement would improve the validity and usefulness of DRP interpretations.

REVIEWER'S REFERENCES
Weiner, M., & Kippel, G. (1984). The Relationship of the California Achievement Test to the Degrees of Reading Power test. *Educational and Psychological Measurement, 44*(2), 497–500.
Bormuth, J. R. (1985). A Response to "Is the Degrees of Reading Power Test Valid or Invalid?" *Journal of Reading, 29*(1), 42–47.
Carver, R. P. (1985). Is the Degrees of Reading Power test valid or invalid? *Journal of Reading, 29*(1), 34–41.
Hildebrand, M., & Hoover, H. D. (1987). A comparative study of the reliability and validity of the Degrees of Reading Power and the Iowa Tests of Basic Skills. *Educational and Psychological Measurement, 47,* 1091–1098.
Koslin, B. L., Zeno, S., Koslin, S., Wainer, H., & Ivens, S. H. (1987). *The DRP: An effectiveness measure in reading.* NY: The College Board.
Bieger, E. M. (1989). The Degrees of Reading Power—A testing and teaching tool? *Reading Improvement, 26*(3), 203–207.
Estes, T. H., & Estes, J. J. (1989, Spring). Degree of Reading Power as Virginia's passport to literacy. *Reading in Virginia,* pp. 6–13.
Estes, T. H., Richards, H. C., Wetmore-Rogers, E. (1989, November/December). *Construct validity of the Degrees of Reading Power test.* Paper presented at the 39th Annual Meeting of the National Reading Conference, Austin, TX. (ERIC Document Reproduction No. ED-316-841)
Carver, R. P. (1990). Rescaling the degrees of reading power test to provide valid scores for selecting materials at the instructional level. *Journal of Reading Behavior, 22*(1), 1–18.
Parker, R., Hasbrouch, J. E., & Tindal, G. (1992). The maze as a classroom-based reading measure: Construction methods, reliability, and validity. *Journal of Special Education, 26*(2), 195–218.
King, B. W., Rasool, J. A., & Judge, J. J. (1994). The relationship between college performance and basic skills assessment using SAT scores, the Nelson Denny Reading Test and Degrees of Reading Power. *Research and Teaching in Developmental Education, 11*(1), 5–13.
Touchstone Applied Science Associates, Inc. (1995). *DRP handbook: G&H test forms.* Brewster, NY: Author.
Touchstone Applied Science Associates, Inc. (1996, December). *Reliability and standard errors of measurement for Degrees of Reading Power (DRP) tests.* Brewster, NY: Author.
Witt, J. C., Elliott, S. N., Daly, E. D., III, Gresham, F. M., & Kramer, J. J. (1998). *Assessment of at-risk and special needs children* (2nd ed.). Boston, MA: McGraw-Hill.
Touchstone Applied Science Associates, Inc. (1999). *DRP Program: The readability standard.* Brewster, NY: The author.

[112]
Derogatis Affects Balance Scale [Revised].

Purpose: Designed as a multidimensional mood and affects inventory to "measure the affects profile of community, medical, and psychiatric respondents."

Population: Adults.

Publication Dates: 1975–1996.

Acronym: DABS.

Scores, 13: Joy, Contentment, Vigor, Affection, Anxiety, Depression, Guilt, Hostility, Positive Score Total, Negative Score Total, Affects Balance Index, Affects Expressiveness Index, Positive Affects Ratio.

Administration: Individual.

Forms, 2: DABS, DABS-SF (Short Form).

Price Data, 1999: $50 per 50 tests; $25 per 50 profiles; $29.50 per manual ('96, 58 pages).

Time: (5) minutes (DABS); (2–3) minutes (Short Form).

Comments: Self-report inventory, for clinical or research uses; formerly published as the Affects Balance Scale (ABS).

Author: Leonard R. Derogatis.

Publisher: Clinical Psychometric Research, Inc.

Cross References: See T5:791 (16 references), T4:132 (6 references), and 9:61 (6 references).

Review of the Derogatis Affects Balance Scale [Revised] by MARK. J. ATKINSON, Associate Professor of Psychiatry and Applied Psychology, University of Calgary, Calgary, Alberta, Canada:

The Derogatis Affects Balance Scale (DABS) operationalizes the well-researched constructs of negative and positive affectivity, affective balance, and affective intensity. The self-report instrument has been developed primarily for use with clinically ill populations (i.e., depression, anxiety, sexual dysfunction, cancer, and asthma), although a norming table is included for use with nonpatient populations. The instrument is not suited for use with mentally or physically impaired persons who might provide a distorted or exaggerated report. It is written at a Grade 8 level and takes under 5 minutes to complete.

The DABS measures affectivity via eight primary emotional dimensions and affects balance via five derived "higher order" scores. The full version of the DABS consists of 40 affective terms or items (e.g., Cheerful, Miserable, Relaxed, etc.), each of which is rated according to frequency of occurrence, from *Never* (0) to *Always* (4). Respondents' ratings are summed across five conceptually related emotional terms to provide scale scores on four, "lower order" positive emotional dimensions (i.e., Joy, Contentment, Vigor, and Affection) as well as four lower order negative dimensions (i.e., Anxiety, Depression, Guilt, and Hostility). Item scores are also used to produce several higher order variables: Total Positive and Negative Affect (PTOT & NTOT), Affective Balance (AB Index), Affective Expressiveness (AE Index), and, a more recently defined, Positive Affects Ratio (PAR).

RELIABILITY. Estimates of internal consistency (Cronbach's alpha) for both lower order and higher order scales are reported using response data from a sample of 355 psychiatric inpatients. For this sample, these estimates range from moderate to high, .84–.92, for the positive affect scales, and .79–.85 for the negative affect scales. Internal consistency estimates reported for the derived global measures range from .86–.94. Although a norming table is provided for nonclinical populations, the reliability of the DABS scales for such populations is not reported in the manual. It is possible that reliability estimates using clinical samples are not representative of those that might be found using nonclinical samples, because on might expect greater positive-negative affective variation in a non-distressed sample.

Test-retest coefficients of 1 week, 1 month, and 2 months are reported from several small studies using patients with breast cancer, and two samples of seniors. It is unclear why such small samples were used or how the retest time intervals were chosen. Nevertheless, among breast cancer patients, the adequate test-retest reliability estimates for both the lower and higher order scales are reported (range: .78–.84). For the geriatric samples, only test-retest reliability estimates for higher order scales are provided. It is unclear why lower order reliability estimates were omitted for these samples. With the exception of low Affects Expressions Index (AEI) test-retest reliability reported for the Alzheimer's sample (.40), the remaining test-retest coefficients for the higher order scales were moderate to high, .62–.87.

Alternate form reliability coefficients between the full DABS and the DABS-Short Form are presented on the global scales. There are insufficient items on the DABS-SF to reliably measure lower order dimensions. The alternate form reliabilities were high and ranged between .94 and .97 for a group of community respondents.

CONSTRUCT VALIDITY. A factor analysis, using data from a psychiatric inpatient population, identified six of the eight theoretical lower order dimensions of the DABS. The existence of Vigor, Affection, Anxiety, and Hostility were shown to be distinct. The remaining two positive affect dimensions, Joy-Contentment, were not identified as distinct factors, nor were two negative affect dimensions, Depression-Guilt. Various explanations are possible, one is an item ordering effect resulting from cognitive priming of item responses. Importantly, these findings do not present a serious deterrent to use the higher order scales, but should serve as a caveat to those conducting research with a focus on these nonindependent dimensions. The DABS items effectively tap the discrete higher order constructs of positive and negative dimensions of affective experience. A two-factor analytic solution cleanly revealed the predicted negative and positive dimensions (NTOT & PTOT).

CRITERION-RELATED VALIDITY (CONCURRENT & PREDICTIVE). Both lower and higher order DABS measures have been shown to identify changes in affective experiences over the course of various medical and psychotherapeutic treatments for cancer, sexual dysfunction, clinical anxiety, and depression. The DABS has also been used successfully to examine life stress, coping, and psychosocial function among caregivers to Alzheimer's patients and a medical student sample. The results of several oncology studies suggest that the DABS can discriminate between longer and shorter survival rates in two samples of cancer patients. However, given the controversy around this topic and the small sample sizes, these findings should be interpreted tentatively. In another study, lower order affects, in combination with the "fighting spirit" scale of the Mental Adjustment to Cancer Scale (MAC), correctly predicted patient compliance with chemotherapy regimens in 86% of the study participants.

Affective subtype patterns, identified using dichotomized PTOT and NTOT scores, have been used to characterize a normal student sample, a sexual dysfunction sample, and a sample of psychiatric inpatients. The proportions of each sample classified by the four affective subtypes were distributed as clinically expected for each sample. Evidence for convergent validation with other measures of psychological distress and psychological symptoms is sparse, and although the manual mentions convergence of higher order DABS scores with the Global Severity index of the SCL-90-R no actual coefficients are reported. Nevertheless, higher order scales have been shown to exhibit differences between personality types that are consistent with what is known about affective disposition.

SUMMARY. A founding principle of the DABS is the meaningful contribution of affects balance to the manifestation to psychopathology, stress, and health. A convincing body of validation research is provided to support the clinical utility and validity of this supposition, primarily with samples of patients with clinical depression or various forms of sexual dysfunction. Much of the psychometric development work contained in the DABS manual has been previously published (Derogatis & Rutigliano, 1996).

REVIEWER'S REFERENCE

Derogatis, L. R., & Rutigliano, P. J. (1996). The Derogatis Affects Balance Scale DABS. In B. Spilker (Ed.), *Quality of life and pharmacoeconomics in clinical trials* (2nd ed.) (pp. 107–118). Philadelphia: Lippincott-Raven.

Review of the Derogatis Affects Balance Scale [Revised] by CARLEN HENINGTON, Associate Professor of Educational Psychology, Mississippi State University, Starkville, MS:

PURPOSE AND RATIONALE. The Derogatis Affects Balance Scale (DABS) is a 40-item multidimensional mood and affects inventory designed to measure current level of affect and the balance between positive and negative affect, in either state or trait form. The typical time reference, "the past 7 days including today" (manual, p. 9), is a measure of state characteristics and makes this instrument appropriate for research and treatment effectiveness purposes.

The original measure, developed and normed in 1975, was known as the Affects Balance Scale (ABS). In 1994, a short form (20 items) was developed and normed, combined with the previous version, and renamed the DABS. Within the DABS, two domains of affect are presented: Negative Affect (NA)—general psychological distress including anxiety, anger, and depression and Positive Affect (PA)—feelings of high energy, enthusiasm, and capacity for pleasurable engagement. Within each domain four dimensions can be measured as determined through the principal components analysis. PA contains the following dimensions: (a) Joy (emotional feeling state of happiness), (b) Contentment (cognitive component of self-satisfaction, positive emotional status), (c) Vigor (enabling energy sources to fuel productivity), and (d) Affection (capacity to engage in positive emotional correspondence with others). NA contains: (a) Anxiety (fear-based, future-oriented affect with a strong cognitive component), (b) Depression (characterized by sadness, apathy, dejection, dysphoria), (c) Guilt (perception or belief of failure to assume significant responsibilities), and (d) Hostility (anger-based emotion arising from conflict and discord).

TEST CONTENT AND MATERIALS. The DABS is a self-report rating scale that requires an eighth grade reading level. Using a Likert-type rating scale, the respondent indicates the degree (0 = *Never* to 4 = *Always*) that a single word is descriptive of themselves. Each of the eight primary affect dimensions are measured with five single-word descriptors for a total of 40 descriptors. The author does not indicate how descriptors were selected for inclusion.

The manual provides psychometric information, theoretical basis for the instrument, and a list of studies to support the usefulness and validity of the instrument. The manual also provides a series of vignette profiles combined from several clinical diagnoses to illustrate key components of the instrument and aid in interpretation. These profiles are also used to support validity studies indicating usefulness of specific global scores.

ADMINISTRATION AND SCORING. Administration time is brief (5 minutes) with similarly brief scoring requirements. The respondent reads a descriptor and circles the corresponding number indicating the degree to which it is descriptive of their feelings. Descriptors are presented in a mixed order with equal spacing between dimension descriptors (i.e., a descriptor from a specific dimension followed by a descriptor from each of the other dimensions).

Scoring is straightforward and involves adding the scores for each of the five responses in the eight primary dimensions. A raw score for each dimension is calculated by totaling the corresponding rating for all five descriptors in each column corresponding to one of the eight dimensions. The corresponding sums of the four dimensions within each of the positive and negative affects are then totaled to determine the Positive Affective raw total score (PTOT) and Negative Affective raw total score (NTOT). The instrument also yields three additional global scores: (a) Affects Balance Index (ABI), the principal DABS measure of affects balance and well-being representing the relative standing on both affective states, is calculated by determining the difference between the PTOT and the NTOT and then divided by 20 [i.e., ABI = PTOT-NTOT)/20]; (b) Affects Expressiveness Index (AEI), an indication of the respondent's overall affect intensity, is calculated by summing the score of all 40 item responses; and (c) Positive Affects Ratio (PAR), useful in tracking response to intervention, is calculated by determining the ratio of positive affectivity to total affectivity (i.e., PAR = PTOT/AEI).

Raw scores for the eight dimensions and five global domains are converted to *T* scores using one of three norming groups (i.e., community norms, *n* = 480; inpatient depression norms, *n* = 339; asthmatic medical outpatient norms, *n* = 100). Norms are available for the short form using a community population. The author provides limited demographic data (i.e., gender, race, religion) for each of the norm groups.

RELIABILITY. Acceptable reliability has been determined through internal consistency and test-retest for the dimension and global scores. Using a large sample of psychiatric inpatients (*n* = 355), the internal consistency ranged from .79 to .92 on the dimension scores and from .86 to .94 on the global scores. The one-week test-retest reliability for a small sample of cancer patients (*n* = 16) yielded coefficients ranging from .78 to .84 on the eight dimensions. Two other test-retest studies examining reliability of the global domains were also reported using small samples of normal volunteers over age 60 years (*n* = 21, across 2 months) and patients with dementia (*n* = 13, across 1 month). Coefficients ranged from .70 to .87 for the normal group and .40 to .71 for the dementia group.

VALIDITY. Validity was illustrated with a variety of studies examining the DABS scores of cancer patients and their spouses, caregivers of chronically ill patients, patients with anxiety, etc. and report acceptable validity based on correlational data, predictive discrimination, and response to treatment over time. In many of these studies, the author provided summaries of relationships rather than quantitative data to support validity statements.

SUMMARY. The DABS is a measure of affectivity suitable for research or tracking treatment effectiveness. Depending upon the referent time, it can be a measure of state or trait affective levels and can be administered across several weeks or months. It has acceptable reliability and appears to have acceptable validity with a variety of respondents. The lack of information about the development of the descriptors is of slight concern, as is the period of time since norms were collected. Additionally, there is no evidence to support the use of the DABS as a diagnostic measure.

[113]
Detroit Tests of Learning Aptitude, Fourth Edition.

Purpose: Designed to measure both general intelligence and discrete ability areas.

Population: Ages 6-0 to 17-11.

Publication Dates: 1935–1998.

Acronym: DTLA-4.

Scores: 10 subtest scores: Word Opposites, Design Sequences, Sentence Imitation, Reversed Letters, Story Construction, Design Reproduction, Basic Information, Symbolic Relations, Word Sequences, Story Sequences; and 16 composite scores: General Mental Ability Composite, Optimal Composite, Domain Composites (Verbal, Nonverbal, Attention-Enhanced, Attention-Reduced, Motor-Enhanced, Motor-Reduced, Total), Theoretical Composites (Fluid Intelligence, Crystallized Intelligence, Associative Level, Cognitive Level, Simultaneous Processing, Successive Processing, Verbal Scale, Performance Scale, Total).

Administration: Individual.

Price Data, 2001: $329 per complete kit including examiner's manual ('98, 247 pages), Picture Books 1 and 2, 25 Profile/Summary forms, 25 Examiner Record Booklets, 25 response forms, Story Sequence Chips, and Design Sequence Cubes; $69 per examiner's manual; $89 per Picture Book 1 (for Design Sequences, Design Reproduction and Symbolic Relations); $29 per Picture Book 2 (for Story Sequences and Story Construction); $24 per 25 Profile/Summary forms; $44 per 25 Examiner Record Booklets; $24 per 25 response forms; $20 per Story Sequence Chips; $49 per Design Sequence Cubes; $109 per software scoring and report system (Windows).

Time: (40–120) minutes.

Author: Donald D. Hammill.

Publisher: PRO-ED.

Cross References: See T5:798 (27 references); for reviews by William A. Mehrens and Michael Poteat of an earlier edition, see 12:107 (4 references); see also T4:752 (7 references); for reviews by Arthur B. Silverstein and Joan Silverstein of an earlier edition, see 10:85 (15 references); see also 9:320 (11 references), and T3:691 (20 references); for a review by Arthur B. Silverstein of an earlier edition, see 8:213 (14 references); see also T2:493 (3 references), and 7:406 (10 references); for a review by F. L. Wells, see 3:275 (1 reference); for reviews by Anne Anastasi and Henry Feinburg and an excerpted review by D. A. Worcester (with S. M. Corey), see 1:1058.

Review of the Detroit Tests of Learning Aptitude, Fourth Edition by JEFFREY K. SMITH, Professor of Educational Psychology, Rutgers, the State University of New Jersey, New Brunswick, NJ:

The Detroit Tests of Learning Aptitude, Fourth Edition (DTLA-4) is the most recent edition of the DTLA, first published in 1935. The DTLA-4 is designed to measure the cognitive abilities commonly understood to be intelligence or aptitude. The use of the phrase "Fourth Edition" is somewhat problematic here, as the DTLA-4 is fundamentally the same test as the DTLA-3. As noted in the technical manual, "the items of the DTLA-3 and the DTLA-4 are identical" (p. 104). The DTLA-4 is primarily a response to criticisms and shortcomings of the DTLA-4, particularly with regard to the technical support for the use of the test. The improvements of the DTLA-4 over the previous edition concern the additional research that is provided concerning the norming, reliability, and validity information in support of the interpretation of the test scores. The only differences of substance in the test itself from the previous edition are the elimination of the Pictures Fragments subtest, and the use of color illustrations as opposed to black and white.

The DTLA-4 consists of 10 subtests: Word Opposites, Design Sequences, Sentence Imitation, Reversed Letters, Story Construction, Design Reproduction, Basic Information, Symbolic Relations, Word Sequences, and Story Sequences. These subtests can be combined into any of 16 composite scores including a General Mental Ability Composite (consisting of the sum of the standard scores of all subtests), a Verbal Composite, a Nonverbal Composite, an Attention-Enhanced Composite, an Attention-Reduced Composite, a Motor-Enhanced Composite, a Motor-Reduced Composite, a set of eight composites based on various theories of intelligence, and an Optimal Composite consisting of the four highest subtest scores for any individual. The number of subtests in these composites ranges from 4 to 10.

The testing time necessary to administer the DTLA-4 ranges from 50 to 120 minutes, somewhat long, but not unreasonable given that one usually does not administer a measure such as this unless the results are to be put to an important use. The examiner's manual states that examiners should have some formal training in assessment, but does not specify any certification necessary to be an examiner; potential examiners are referred to policies of school boards, state regulations, or professional associations to see what competencies or certifications are required to be an examiner.

The DTLA-4 appears to be a well-designed and executed measure of the cognitive abilities of children, aged 6–17. The fact that the DTLA has remained in publication since 1935 argues for its popularity among practitioners in the field. The additional technical studies that have been conducted in support of the measure are welcome and represent a distinct improvement over the previous edition. In particular, it was good to see the inclusion of test-retest measures indicating the stability of the tests over time, and the reporting of reliabilities for subgroups of test-takers. The reliabilities of the scales are adequate for their intended purposes and the measure correlates well with other well-established measures of cognitive ability such as the Wechsler Intelligence Scale for Children—III (T5:2862) and the Kaufman Assessment Battery for Children (T5:1379).

There are still technical and conceptual problems with the DTLA-4 that need to be noted. Perhaps the most distressing of these difficulties concerns the 16 composite scores that can be constructed out of different combinations of the 10 initial subtests. The problem here is that the author is claiming more than he really has. To begin, 2 of the composites are identical to 2 others, reducing the unique number of composites to 14. Next, several of the composites are only one subtest different from other composites. For example, to develop the Motoric Domain of composites (consisting of the Motor-Enhanced Composite and the Motor-Reduced Composite), one simply needs to make a modest adjustment from the Linguistic Domain (taking the Symbolic Relations subtest out of the Nonverbal Composite and moving it to the Verbal Composite). One would imagine that some of these composites would correlate with one another so highly as to make their distinctions trivial; composite intercorrelations are not provided.

The final problem with regard to the composites is the Optimal Composite. This consists of the highest four subtest scores for any examinee. Thus, the Optimal Composite will consist of different subtests for different examinees. The idea here is to show the examinee at his or her best. It is referred to as an estimate of the person's potential in terms of likelihood of doing well under optimal circumstances. The Optimal Composite appears to be an attempt to formalize a desire to look for an individual's strengths, a laudable posture. There are two problems with this approach.

First, the Optimal Composite is almost certain to exacerbate measurement error. That is, for any given individual, the four best subtest scores are likely to contain more positive measurement error than the remaining six scores. This will lead to an inflated estimate. Second, the forming of the four highest scores into an "Optimal Composite" suggests that this score has some level of formal standing in the assessment. If it does, can it be used for purposes of discrepancy analysis for identification of learning disabilities? It seems clear that it should not be used for such purposes. Although the examiner's manual does not give any indication that it *can* be used for identification of learning disabilities, it also does not warn against such usage.

Another area of concern has to do with the analysis of items for technical quality and for lack of bias. The section on Conventional Item Analysis indicates that several of the subtests have a number of items that fall below typically accepted levels of quality. The examiner's manual glosses over this shortcoming by saying that, "On the average, the test items satisfy the requirements previously described and present evidence of content validity" (p. 135). The following section looks at Differential Item Functioning Analysis. The manual cites Camilli and Shepard (1994) in calling for test developers to conduct studies looking for item bias. This is commendable, but then the manual presents an item bias study using Jensen's (1980) approach, which Camilli and Shepard expressly recommend against using because of its likelihood for missing real occurrences of bias. Much more powerful techniques are available.

SUMMARY. From the perspective of technical support for the interpretation of the test scores, the DTLA-4 is an improvement over the DTLA-3, and addresses a number of the criticisms in the earlier version. There is still work to be done from a technical perspective. Additionally, it is recommended that the 16 Domain Composites be reduced to 3, eliminating all but the General, the Verbal, and the Nonverbal. The Optimal Composite has technical and theoretical weaknesses, and may encourage inappropriate usage. The rest of the composites are either too similar to one another to be useful, or are simply indications that the DTLA-4 subtests can be combined to look like other theoretical approaches to measuring intelligence. This distracts the user from the primary purpose of the instrument.

REVIEWER'S REFERENCES

Jensen, A. R. (1980). *Bias in mental testing.* New York: Free Press.
Camilli, G., & Shepard, L. A. (1994). *Methods for identifying biased test items.* Thousand Oaks, CA: Sage Publications, Inc.

Review of the Detroit Tests of Learning Aptitude, Fourth Edition by ROSS E. TRAUB, Professor, Department of Curriculum, Teaching and Learning, The Ontario Institute for Studies in Education, the University of Toronto, Toronto, Ontario, Canada:

According to the manual, these 10 tests can be used to (a) inventory relative strengths and weaknesses in the intellectual abilities they assess, (b) identify mental deficiency, (c) predict future success in academic endeavours, and (d) support the conduct of research into intellectual functioning (pp. 24 & 25). Unfortunately, the manual is inaccurate and deficient in ways that leave me wondering whether these purposes can be well-served by the Detroit Tests of Learning Aptitude. The following comments, which simplify my concerns, are organized under the headings Administration and Scoring, Test Scores and Score Interpretations, Norms, Reliability, Content Validity, Construct Validity, and Bias.

ADMINISTRATION AND SCORING. The directions for administering the Detroit Tests are reasonably clear and comprehensive, but psychometrists new to them will find it difficult to score the Design Reproduction test. Despite the inclusion of practice responses in the manual, the scoring guide for Design Reproduction includes no models for "2" on the score scale; the only assistance offered is this: "If an examinee's drawing lies between the qualities exhibited by the drawings in Columns 3 [1 point] and 5 [3 points], then a score of 2 points is achieved" (manual, p. 56).

TEST SCORES AND SCORE INTERPRETATIONS. Raw scores on the tests are converted to standard scores, which range from 0 to 20 (mean 10, standard deviation 3). These scores are then aggregated, over all or various combinations of the tests, with the resulting sums converted into scores resembling deviation IQs (mean 100, standard deviation 15). Test users are encouraged to compare an examinee's performances across the 10 tests by looking for significant differences between pairs of standard scores. A table of critical differences is provided for help in this. Another table of critical values is provided for testing differences in the IQ-like scores for any of the seven complementary pairs of composites (e.g., Verbal vs. Nonverbal) listed in the manual. Alternatively, a user can refer to tabled values of "clinically useful" differences, which are considerably larger than those needed for statistical significance. Users are properly cautioned to be aware of state laws regarding the use and interpretation of intelligence test scores, and to be cognizant of the effect on performance of such factors as unreliability.

NORMS. This version of the Detroit Tests was normed on a sample of 1,350 persons from 37 of the United States. (No reason is given for the exclusion of some states.) This sample combined two cohorts, separated in time by 7 years. (No information is provided on cohort differences, if any.) The representativeness of the norms sample was evaluated with regard to geographic area, gender, race, urban/rural split, family income, parental education, and disability status vis-a-vis the U.S. population of school-age children. The sample is shown to compare quite closely to the population on all these characteristics, save perhaps that of income. Standard scores and percentile ranks are provided for each test in half-year age ranges. IQ-like scores and corresponding percentile ranks are provided for composite scores on all 10 tests, and on combinations of 6, 5, and 4 tests. A table for converting raw scores to age equivalents is also provided for individual tests. (Appropriately, the author urges caution in the use of age-equivalent scores.)

RELIABILITY. Coefficients of internal consistency and test-retest reliability are reported, together with an assessment of interrater agreement. At first glance, these appear to be satisfactory for both individual tests (e.g., alpha coefficients of .86 on average over age levels and tests, test-retest coefficients [administration interval of 1 week] of .84 on average) and composite scales (even larger coefficients). (Surprisingly and questionably, the test-retest coefficients listed for grades 7–12 are identical to those listed for the total sample!) Unfortunately, this reliability evidence was collected piecemeal, not in a coordinated generalizability study that would provide estimates of the error variances attributable to items, occasions, and raters, and their interactions. As none of the coefficients reported in the manual are affected by all of these sources of error, it seems likely that reliability is overestimated to a degree that will remain unknown until a suitable G-study has been conducted.

CONTENT VALIDITY. The Detroit Tests include tasks commonly associated with individually administered tests of intelligence. The description provided in the manual for each test informs us of its source, and indicates whether a test is identical to or different from one included in previous editions of the Detroit Tests, how it compares to tests found in other individually administered instruments (e.g., the Wechsler scales), why it has been included, and what mental factors are thought needed to perform the test well. Some of the latter claims seem incoherent. For example, the Reversed Letters Test is said to be "definitely a measure of spatial memory and visual-motor integration ability" (manual, p. 17), but also a measure of "attention, visual sequencing, and memory, as well as fine motor ability" (manual, p. 83). The latter of these two descriptions seems more apt.

CONSTRUCT VALIDITY. The Detroit Tests, so it is claimed, can be combined to form 16 different composite scores. Further, we read that:

> All of the composite scores estimate general mental ability (or "overall aptitude," "scholastic aptitude," or "global intelligence," whichever term the reader prefers). However, they all do so in a somewhat different manner. Some scores emphasize important psychological variables such as attention, language, and manual dexterity; some relate to current theoretical constructs; others stress additional psychological perspectives. Because of this, the examiner can interpret the battery's scores from a variety of orientations. (manual, p. 19)

For this claim to be true, either the tests must be independent of one another, or each must tap specific, yet reliably measured, factors not measured by other tests in the set.

Evidence regarding common and specific factors can be derived from a table of intercorrelation coefficients among the tests (manual, p. 147). These coefficients were computed from the standard scores on the 10 tests of all 1,350 members of the norms sample. The manual also includes a report of the results of "principal components exploratory factor analyses" (p. 152) of this intercorrelation matrix, with selected results from the analyses reported in Table 9.12 (p. 152). My eye was caught by the eigenvalues reported for an unrotated, two-factor model—4.07 and 4.10 respectively. These eigenvalues imply two common factors accounting for more than 80% of the total variance of the 10 tests, an impossible result for a correlation matrix with no off-diagonal coefficient greater than

.74 and with 12 of the 45 distinct coefficients less than .30. (As well, we cannot possibly know what is meant by a "principal components factor analysis." See McDonald, 1985, for a description of the differences between principal components analysis and factor analysis.)

I conducted an exploratory factor analysis of this matrix of intercorrelations using the unweighted least squares method available in SPSS (1997). The first two eigenvalues of the correlation matrix were 4.34 and 1.05, in line with expectation. The scree plot of all 10 eigenvalues suggested only one important factor. (Although the second eigenvalue is larger than 1 and so exceeds Kaiser's 1960 criterion for inclusion in the model, the scree plot provides no justification for a second factor if the third and subsequent factors are deemed inconsequential.) Study of the residuals reveals, as must be the case, that a two-factor model fits the data somewhat better than a one-factor model does, but it is far from clear that the two factor model yields interpretable results.

Table 9.12 of the manual contains the pattern matrix from a Promax (oblique) rotation of the two-factor model that was fit in the author's analysis. The corresponding Promax rotation from my analysis looks quite different. In particular, Factor I of Table 9.12 of the manual is defined exclusively by Word Sequences, Sentence Imitation, Word Opposites, Story Construction, and Basic Information, with pattern coefficients of .82, .87, .80, .51, and .66, respectively; in my analysis, the most similar factor had coefficients for these variables of .85, .95, .36, .22, and .22, respectively. The coefficients for the latter three variables were higher for the other factor in my analysis (.46, .29, and .57). Although the author's analysis would appear to support Wechsler-like verbal and performance composites for the Detroit Tests, my analysis brings this interpretation into question.

In a further effort to support the various composites suggested for the tests, the author presents the results of several confirmatory factor analyses. These results are LISREL (Jöreskog & Sörbom, 1998) statistics from attempts to fit the models implied by the seven complementary combinations of two composite scores suggested for the Detroit Tests. I fit two of the models—those implied by Cattell and Horn's theory of fluid and crystallized intelligence, and Wechsler's concept of verbal and performance aptitude. Table 9.13

records chi-square misfit statistics for these models of 167 and 157, respectively, whereas my analyses produced corresponding chi-square values of 614 and 588. For whatever reason, the results presented in the manual appear to misrepresent the degree of model misfit, at least as measured by the chi-square statistic.

What can be concluded from this? Subject to the limitation that the factor results are based on only one sample, albeit the important norms sample, we can hazard that the common factor variance among the Detroit Tests is modeled reasonably well by a single factor. For the recommended composites to possess the interpretations ascribed to them, the specific components of the 10 tests must account for a substantial amount of test variance, and elicit the unique mental qualities said to be assessed by each composite. In support of this scenario is my finding that the minimum proportion of unique variance (specific plus error) attributable to a test under the one-factor model is .40; the maximum proportion is .88. If the reliability coefficients are .85 or more, then a substantial proportion of the variance of each test is specific to the instrument, and might well support the large number of differential composite score interpretations claimed for the tests. Further evidence favoring the idea of a number of distinct score composites would be a table of correlation coefficients among scores on the various composites, provided the coefficients were reasonably small. Unfortunately, the manual does not include such a table.

BIAS. The topic is dealt with in a section on differential item functioning in the chapter on validity, and again in a separate chapter entitled "Controlling for Test Bias." The Detroit Tests are said to be unbiased because (a) the normative sample represents all population subgroups of interest, (b) the tests yield equal reliability and validity coefficients for the population subgroups that were considered, and (c) the items comprising the tests are free from differential item functioning. Regarding this argument, I would make the following points: (a) That a norms sample is representative means only that the norms are unbiased for the population, not that the test is free from bias against one or another subpopulation as a measure of a construct. (b) Equality of reliability and validity coefficients across groups is reassuring, but this equality can be realized even for tests biased against one or another subpopulation. (c)

The author claims to have used the Delta Score approach (Jensen, 1980) to assess differential item functioning, but simply correlating item delta statistics from two groups—this is what appears to have been done—is not what Jensen recommended. Even if Jensen's method had been applied correctly, however, we could not accept the results as indicative of DIF (Camilli & Shepard, 1994, ch. 2). Perhaps the Detroit Tests are unbiased, but the manual contains no compelling psychometric evidence to support the claim.

CONCLUDING REMARKS. The Detroit Tests assess abilities thought related to success in school and other spheres of intellectual functioning. They may do so very well, but to convince prospective users, the author needs to improve the information contained in the manual regarding the psychometric quality of the instruments.

REVIEWER'S REFERENCES
Kaiser, H. F. (1960). The application of electronic computers to factor analysis. *Educational and Psychological Measurement, 20*, 141–151.
Jensen, A. R. (1980). *Bias in mental testing.* New York: The Free Press.
McDonald, R. P. (1985). *Factor analysis and related methods.* Hillsdale, NJ: Lawrence Erlbaum Associates.
Camilli, G., & Shepard, L. A. (1994). *Methods for identifying biased test items.* Thousand Oaks, CA: Sage Publications.
SPSS. (1997). SPSS for Windows (Release 8.0.0). Chicago: SPSS, Inc.
Jöreskog, K. G., & Sörbom, D. (1998). *LISREL 8.20.* Chicago: Scientific Software International.

[114]
Developing the High-Performance Workplace.

Purpose: "Created to give organizational members a tool for assessing employee opinions about the status of high-performance workplace characteristics in their work environments."

Population: Organizational employees.

Publication Date: 1996.

Scores, 18: Importance Ratings (Training and Continuous Learning, Information Sharing, Employee Participation, Organization Structure, Worker-Management Partnerships, Compensation Linked to Performance and Skills, Employment Security, Supportive Work Environment, Overall HPW Rating), Quality Ratings (Training and Continuous Learning, Information Sharing, Employee Participation, Organization Structure, Worker-Management Partnerships, Compensation Linked to Performance and Skills, Employment Security, Supportive Work Environment, Overall HPW Rating).

Administration: Group.

Price Data, 1996: $64.95 per complete kit including administrator's handbook (77 pages), and 10 collection instruments; $2.95 per collection instrument; $39.95 per administrator's handbook.

Time: Administration time not reported.
Authors: David D. Dubois and William J. Rothwell.
Publisher: Human Resource Development Press.

Review of the Developing the High-Performance Workplace by M. DAVID MILLER, Professor, University of Florida, Gainesville, FL:

Developing the High-Performance Workplace is an instrument and research process that is intended to help organizations examine the status, or implementation, of high-performance workplace (HPW) practices. The results of the assessment would then be used to evaluate organizations and guide them in implementing changes that would lead to better jobs and increased productivity.

The instrument consists of 55 Likert items that reflect employees' opinions about the implementation of HPW practices. The items were based on themes that were identified by the U.S. Department of Labor's Office of American Workplace (OAW) as the most common elements of a high-performance workplace. The OAW identified four broad categories: (a) skills and information; (b) participation, organization, and partnership; (c) compensation, security, and the work environment; and (d) putting it all together. The categories were further divided into eight subcategories that served as the scales for the instrument. The eight subcategories were Training and Continuous Learning (5 items), Information Sharing (6 items), Employee Participation (10 items), Organization Structure (4 items), Worker-Management Partnerships (9 items), Compensation Linked to Performance and Skills (7 items), Employment Security (3 items), and Supportive Work Environment (11 items). The instruments also provide separate ratings for importance and quality of each of the HPW practices.

The Administrator's Handbook describes in a clear manner a seven-step process for evaluating HPW practices within an organization that includes a HPW Task Group that sets initial objectives, surveys employees, and analyzes and interprets results. In addition, the Handbook includes multiple examples of how to score, report, and interpret survey results. This process provides some assurance of clear and valid use of the survey. That is, it is through the local determination of objectives and their alignment with the survey that content validity occurs. The authors suggest that organizations "determine the precise objectives of your HPW research project within the context of the organization" (administrator's handbook, p. 23).

On the other hand, the locally implemented process and the linking of the items with the HPW practices as identified by the Office of the American Workplace are the only attempt at validation of the survey and the research process. No data are provided on prior validation or reliability studies to convince the user of the psychometric quality of the survey or the survey process. For example, no systematic content review is reported; no correlations with other instruments are provided; and no reliability estimates are reported for the subcategories (e.g., no internal consistencies). In addition, score interpretation relies heavily on the interpretation of the value labels (e.g., very important, important) and the clarity with which a mean score falls close to one of the values. No norms are provided and there are no clear standards for interpreting the mean levels of the scores.

SUMMARY. In short, the survey outlines a reasonable process for examining the work environment. However, the psychometric quality of the survey is unknown, at best. To the extent that it prompts discussion and implementation of HPW practices within an organization, the instrument is worthwhile and it does follow the suggested subcategories from the OAW report; but organizations should be cautious in relying on data that have not been shown to be valid or reliable. Any use of the instrument to make important decisions about organizations should require local examination of validity and reliability issues prior to using the instrument.

Review of the Developing the High-Performance Workplace by DENIZ S. ONES, Hellervik Professor of Industrial-Organizational Psychology, Department of Psychology, University of Minnesota, Minneapolis, MN:

What employer does not want a high performance workplace? But, how does one go about developing such a workplace? The answer to the latter question goes to the heart of our economy, the welfare of the organizations, and the welfare of the employees in them. A good place to start identifying the characteristics of the organization at hand is through the use of organizational diagnostic tools. Developing the High-Performance Workplace (HPW) is an organizational survey instrument designed to assess employee perceptions of the importance and existence of a variety of organizational characteristics and practices. The use of the survey would most likely inform organizational change and development efforts.

DESCRIPTION OF THE SURVEY. This instrument assesses the importance and actual usage of a variety of workplace innovations that may be valuable in improving work performance and the way that workers are treated. It is designed to help organizational leaders and change agents understand existing organizational cultures, the way business is conducted in their organizations, and employee perceptions. The test measures employee values and organizational practices around various workplace characteristics that have been identified as those existing in high performance workplaces.

There are 55 characteristics of high-performance workplaces rated on two dimensions: (a) the perceived importance of that characteristic for the achievement of high performance in the organization under consideration and (b) the existence of such conditions in the organization. That is, each rater is asked to respond to two questions for each high performance workplace characteristic. Parenthetically, the authors use the word *quality* when instructing respondents to rate the existence of conditions in their organization. In my opinion, *quality* is the wrong word. The meaning of what is being rated would be clearer if the instructions to the respondents were to rate current conditions in the organization.

Each question is rated on a 6-point Likert scale ranging from *important* to *unimportant* for the importance question and, ranging from *excellent* to *poor* for the existence question. "Not applicable/do not know" is also a response option. The importance ratings are to be used for discussion and to answer the question of what is valued and what is not valued in the particular organization or work unit. The quality ratings are used to suggest action: What needs to be done so that organization can become a high-performance workplace?

The manual indicates that the HPW practices were taken from a 29-page document titled "Road to High-Performance Workplaces: A Guide to Better Jobs and Better Business Results" published by U.S. Department of Labor's (DOL) Office of the American Workplace (U.S. Department of Labor, 1994). All the items (criteria) are therefore in the public domain. The materials supporting the instrument do not tell us for what

purpose these 55 criteria were originally developed and how they were originally intended to be used in organizational data collection efforts. Reading through the 55 items, it is apparent that there is much management faddish language used, and there are many conceptual redundancies that make me suspect that this list of high-performance workplace characteristics might be the outcome of some brain-storming session, rather than a careful psychometrically oriented development effort.

Across the 55 items, four general sets of characteristics about the workplace are assessed: (a) "Skills and Information": Items that include characteristics about training and development; (b) "Participation, Organization and Partnership": Items that revolve around communications between the employees and the organization, organizational structure, and conflict; (c) "Compensation, Security and Work Environment": Items that tap into pay practices, security concerns, and working conditions; and (d) "Putting it all together": Items that are intended to measure the linkages between HPW and other firm level practices and strategies.

The authors of the survey divide the 55 items into eight thematic areas, item clusters that are at a more homogenous level than the four general sets of characteristics identified above. The eight item clusters are Training and Continuous Learning (5 items), Information Sharing (6 items), Employee Participation (10 items), Organization Structure (4 items), Worker-Management Partnerships (8 items), Compensation Linked to Performance and Skills (7 items), Employment Security (3 items), and Supportive Work Environment (11 items). Eight cluster ratings and an overall rating are generated for interpretation of the results of data collection efforts.

MEASUREMENT AND PSYCHOMETRIC PROPERTIES. No psychometric information (including reliability, construct validity, etc.) about this instrument is reported. At the very least, the instrument developers and publishers should be conducting and reporting internal consistency reliability analyses as well as factor structure analyses supporting the eight item clusters used. Further, it would be very helpful to present empirical data supporting the usefulness of the instrument in organizational development efforts. How does one judge whether or not the instrument is supported in its use in organizations if no empirical research is conducted or reported on it? To ensure that I was not overlooking any research that may have been conducted using the Developing HPW instrument, I conducted a literature search of the PsychINFO database but could not find any studies using or reporting on the instrument. There were no references to this instrument in the competitively refereed psychological or human resource management literature. This indicates that it has not been used in any applied research. Similarly, a call to the senior author of the instrument turned up no research studies or results. It was indicated that the test publishers expect the purchasing organizations to conduct their own analyses. Apparently, one reason for not being able to report any psychometric information about the instrument is that organizations oftentimes customize the survey to their needs, adding or deleting items. However, all this flexibility is purchased at the price of using data collection instruments with unknown psychometric properties.

ADMINISTRATION AND USE. The information from the survey is intended to assess employee opinions about their own values and present existence of a whole host of high performance workplace characteristics. Intended users for the instrument are both for-profit and non-profit organizations.

The instrument is expected to help with "planning and executing a successful transition to a high performance workplace" (administrator's handbook, p. 1). The instrument developers suggest that it may also be used as an organizational diagnostic tool in assessing how change efforts may be working. The usability of the instrument might be enhanced due to its flexibility and customization according to the requests of organizations.

MANUALS AND SUPPORTING DOCUMENTS. The only document available on the instrument is a 77-page administrator's manual. Personal communication with the senior author of the test indicated that there are no other internal technical reports and the authors or the publisher do not keep track of data collected with the instrument. This is despite the fact test authors specifically call on instrument users to share their results with the test developers (administrator's handbook, p. 2).

The administrator's manual contains very detailed and useful information for collecting, analyzing, and interpreting data from the HPW survey. The manual is divided into four main sections: (a) Introduction to the Organization Assessment Process and Its Administration, (b) Planning and Conducting data Collection Activities, (c) Data Handling and Analysis Methods, and (d) Interpreting the Data and Program Implementation. It provides mostly sound and sensible advice about data collection and organizational development efforts in general (e.g., the need to have top management support for the change or organization development effort to be successful). There is also good advice on how to administer and make use of the survey. Practical issues are addressed: who to survey, how many respondents, how to handle sensitive information, etc. Even the most inexperienced human resources manager should be able to use this instrument with ease.

The list of references and additional readings offered at the end of the manual are also useful. Some of the academic literature on human resource management interventions to create high performance workplaces were listed in this list of references. The interested user is made aware of where to go for more information.

SUMMARY. The data collection instrument may be a good first shot at measuring some areas of organizational culture, values, and efforts and the importance of various organizational characteristics. However, the fact that there is currently no psychometric information about this tool is a major drawback for organizations that may be interested in using it in the assessment phase of their organizational development methods. There needs to be much more empirical work from publishers and authors. Users should make an attempt to make sure that psychometric properties of the survey are not compromised in real world applications and usage. That is, organizations using the instrument should collect data on the psychometric properties of the version of the instrument they are using to ensure that professional standards are met. Also, one needs empirical data from multiple organizations to verify some of the currently unsupported claims (e.g., "HPW practices have utterly transformed some organizations, helping them achieve quantum leaps in performance improvement," administrator's handbook, p. 3).

Despite the shortcomings described above, there are a number of things to commend about this instrument. It is flexible and adaptable to organizational needs. The administrator's manual is written very clearly and takes the administrator step-by-step through the entire data collection, interpretation, and recommended action generation phases of organizational change. The advice about organizational development efforts is reliable, if not plain sensible. Future editions of the instrument need to bolster these desirable characteristics of the "Developing High-Performance Workplace" survey with empirical data from organizations.

REVIEWER'S REFERENCE
U.S. Department of Labor. (1994). *Road to high-performance workplaces: A guide to better jobs and better business results.* Washington, DC: U.S. Government Printing Office, Superintendent of Documents.

[115]
Developmental Assessment of Young Children.

Purpose: Designed to measure "developmental abilities."
Population: Birth to age 5-11.
Publication Date: 1998.
Acronym: DAYC.
Scores: General Development Quotient.
Administration: Individual.
Price Data, 1999: $164 per complete kit including examiner's manual (67 pages), 25 each of Adaptive, Cognitive, Communication, Physical, and Social-Emotional scoring forms, and 25 profile/summary forms; $24 per 25 scoring forms (specify domain); $14 per 25 profile/summary forms; $37 per manual.
Time: (10–20) minutes per subtest.
Comments: Rating by examiner; subtests may be used alone or in any combination.
Authors: Judith K. Voress and Taddy Maddox.
Publisher: PRO-ED.

a) COGNITIVE SUBTEST.
Purpose: Designed to measure "skills and abilities that are conceptual in nature."
Scores: Total score only.
b) COMMUNICATION SUBTEST.
Purpose: Constructed to assess "the exchange of ideas, information, and feelings."
Scores: Total score only.
c) SOCIAL-EMOTIONAL SUBTEST.
Purpose: Designed to measure "social awareness, social relationships, and social competence."
Scores: Total score only.
d) PHYSICAL DEVELOPMENT SUBTEST.
Purpose: Designed to measure "motor development."
Scores: Total score only.
e) ADAPTIVE BEHAVIOR SUBTEST.
Purpose: Designed to assess "independent functioning."
Scores: Total score only.

Review of the Developmental Assessment of Young Children by BILLY T. OGLETREE, Associate Professor, Communication Disorders Program, Western Carolina University, Cullowhee, NC:

The Developmental Assessment of Young Children (DAYC) is a five-subtest battery that measures different but interrelated developmental abilities. It is designed for children between the ages of birth and 5 years, 11 months. The DAYC has four major uses: (a) the identification of children with developmental delays; (b) the determination of specific strengths and weaknesses in young children; (c) the documentation of children's progress; and (d) the measurement of young children's developmental abilities for research purposes. Components of the DAYC include an examiner's manual, scoring forms, and scoring summary sheets.

The DAYC's five subtests are intended to measure the developmental areas mandated by IDEA (i.e., Cognitive, Communicative, Social-Emotional, Physical, and Adaptive Abilities). The Cognitive subtest consists of 78 items that measure concept-development. Areas assessed include attention, memory, purposive planning, decision making, and discrimination. The Communication subtest includes 78 items spanning receptive/expressive language and verbal/nonverbal abilities. The Social-Emotional development subtest consists of 58 items that measure social awareness, relationships, and social competence. The Physical Development subtest consists of 87 items measuring motor development. Finally, the Adaptive Behavior subtest consists of 62 items that measure independent functioning in self-help.

The DAYC can be administered in 1 hour and 40 minutes (each subtest requires approximately 20 minutes). Testing may occur over more than one assessment period but should be completed as soon as possible. Examiners administering the DAYC should be knowledgeable with respect to test statistics, administration of standardized measures, test scoring, and score interpretation.

Administration of the DAYC is fairly simple. Entry points for each subtest are provided according to age. Subtests are completed through either observation, interview, or direct assessment. Items passed receive 1 point and items failed receive 0 points. Subtest ceilings are established when 3 of 5 items are failed. Basals are established by three consecutive passes. If necessary, examiners may administer items below the entry point to determine subtest basals.

DAYC data are recorded on the subtest scoring forms and the profile/examiner summary sheet. Subtest scoring forms contain all items for the subtest and sections for identifying information, score recording, summary scores from other related test instruments, information specific to the test administration conditions, and score interpretation/recommendation.

The DAYC yields five types of scores including subtest raw scores, subtest age equivalents, subtest standard scores, a quotient standard score, and percentiles. Raw scores are described as the total number of points earned for each subtest. Raw scores for the DAYC can be converted into the derived scores mentioned above using DAYC appendices. The examiner's manual cautions against the use of DAYC age equivalent scores, but includes them due to their widespread use by agencies and school systems. Finally, the DAYC provides guidelines for comparing subtest scores for statistical significance and comparing the DAYC quotient to other developmental tests.

The DAYC was normed on a sample of 1,269 children residing in 27 states. The normative sample was comparable to the general population of the United States in terms of geographic region, gender, race, rural or urban residence, ethnicity, family income, educational attainment of parents, and disability status.

The psychometric properties of the DAYC are discussed at length in the examiner's manual. Three types of reliability are reviewed. First, data are reported specific to content sampling error. Internal consistency reliability coefficients are provided for each subtest using groupings (in 6-month intervals) of the normative sample. All coefficients round to or exceed .90. Coefficients for the composite are equal to or greater than .95. These values suggest that test items for subtests are related to each other. Time sampling reliability is reported using the test-retest method with two groups of children ($r = 31$; $n = 18$). One group included children with known disabilities. The time period between assessment for each study was 15 days. Test-retest coefficients for the subtests were all greater than .90. The final reliability type reported related to interscorer differences. Two individuals independently scored 39 DAYC protocols randomly selected from the normative sample. Coefficients for all subtests were .99.

The DAYC examiner's manual discusses three types of validity including content-description, criterion-prediction, and construct-identification. The manual notes that three demonstrations of content validity are offered for DAYC subtests. First, a detailed rationale for each subtest is presented. Second, the results of conventional item analysis are included. Finally, items are shown not to give advantages to one group over another. To assess criterion-prediction validity, the DAYC was compared to the Revised Gesell and Amatruda Developmental and Neurologic Examination and the Battelle Developmental Inventory Screening Test. Correlations are described as "very high" (manual, p. 39). Finally, the DAYC reports data specific to construct-identification validity. This type of validity indicates the degree to which underlying traits of a test can be identified and reflect the theoretical model upon which the test is based. The examiner's manual for the DAYC states the five basic constructs of the instrument and reports statistical data supporting each construct.

SUMMARY. In conclusion, the DAYC is a comprehensive tool for infants and young children. It assesses the primary developmental domains and provides useful data with respect to developmental status. These data would appear appropriate for both identifying disability and monitoring progress. A possible weakness of the DAYC could be time required to administer the entire battery. In sum, most examiners find it difficult to complete instruments requiring well over an hour to administer. Of course, the examiner's manual suggests that administration of the DAYC can span several test periods.

Finally, although it is not recommended in the examiner's manual, this reviewer would consider the DAYC an excellent tool for use in dynamic assessment. Olswang and Bain (1996) note that dynamic assessment attempts to determine if systematic modifications of contextual cues may improve children's performance. Although this type of assessment may violate standardized administration guidelines, it can clearly assist with identifying the child's potential as well as their current status. Using the principles of dynamic assessment, the DAYC would appear to be an ideal tool for the provision of information useful in treatment planning.

REVIEWER'S REFERENCE

Olswang, L. B., & Bain, B. A. (1996). Assessment information for predicting upcoming change in language production. *Journal of Speech and Hearing Research, 39,* 414–423.

Review of the Developmental Assessment of Young Children by T. STEUART WATSON, Professor of Counselor Education/Educational Psychology, Mississippi State University, Starkville, MS:

The Developmental Assessment of Young Children (DAYC) is one of many instruments available to assess the developmental status of children from birth to 6 years of age. It measures the five areas of developmental functioning mandated by IDEA using one of three assessment methods: observation, parent interview, and testing the child. The stated uses of the DAYC are for identifying children with developmental delays, diagnosing strengths and weaknesses in developmental areas, and documenting change as a result of programmatic intervention.

MATERIALS. The kit contains an examiner's manual, profile examiner summary sheets, and subtest scoring forms for each of the five developmental domains. The examiner's manual begins with a concise rationale, description, and recommended use of the instrument as well as a brief review of the legislative history that has impacted the use of early childhood assessment instruments. The authors do a nice job of acquainting the reader with some of the difficulties in designing psychometrically sound instruments for use with this population. Overall, the manual is well organized, easily understandable, and well written.

The profile examiner summary sheet is simply a means of condensing information (Identifying Information, Record of DAYC Scores, Summary of Other Test Results, Profile of Standard Scores, Referral Information, and Interpretation/Recommendations) onto a single source. The subtest scoring forms are easily understood and should pose no problems for examiners with very little testing experience. It is probably inappropriate, however, to have an Interpretation/Recommendation section on the front of each of the scoring forms due to the potential abuse by some examiners of attempting to make recommendations based on the results of each individual subtest.

The most notable omission is the lack of materials that are sometimes necessary for completion of the items if the subtest is being completed via testing the child. For example, Item 40 on the

Cognitive subtest requires blocks and Item 49 requires that the examiner provide the child with pictures or objects from at least two categories. The lack of appropriate materials in the test kit is the greatest drawback to using the DAYC and would be especially problematic for inexperienced examiners. Lack of these materials may also impact child performance either positively or negatively, depending upon the type of materials chosen by the examiner and also brings into question the probability of providing a standardize administration (a crucial component of a standardized test).

ADMINISTRATION AND SCORING. Administration is simple and straightforward with the easiest modes being observation and testing the child. As the authors describe the conditions necessary to make an interview a valid means of obtaining information, it is apparent that persons with minimal experience and training may have difficulty with hesitant parents, which could impact the results of the assessment.

Entry points and basal and ceiling rules are well described in text and with a table using five examples. Scoring is easy as items are either passed (1) or not passed (0). Raw scores are derived by summing the points on each page and carrying them over to the last page for a final computation. The raw scores for each of the subtests are then entered on the profile/examiner summary sheet and converted to percentiles, age equivalents, and standard scores via tables in the back of the manual. The standard scores from the five subtests are summed and converted to a General Development Quotient that, unfortunately, will probably be interpreted by most who use the test as the equivalent of an IQ score.

Chapter 4 of the manual provides guidelines for interpreting the results of the DAYC. In the section on subtest age equivalents, the authors correctly note their concerns regarding age equivalent scores and the American Psychological Association's (1992) position against using them. The go on to state that because many agencies require these scores, they "reluctantly" provide them. The bind the authors are in is certainly understandable. To sell the test, it has to be useful to consumers. For many test users, age equivalents make the test more usable. On the other hand, test authors have not only an ethical obligation but a professional obligation as well to stop providing these scores, which in turn may change the practice of using age equivalents. Perhaps the least appropriate, but probably most used, method of interpretation is discrepancy analysis—that is, computing the significance of the difference scores among the DAYC subtests and with scores from other tests. Whether or not a score is clinically or statistically significant from another score has very little relevance for diagnostic decisions or programming recommendations. In addition, there are no data reported for the reliability of difference scores, which are absolutely necessary if one is interpreting score differences. To the authors' credit, on page 23 of the manual they state, "To make accurate diagnoses and clinical decisions, examiners should require information exceeding that which is available from tests."

Although it may not be a problem given the population for whom the test is intended, it seems as though there may be an inadequate floor and ceiling at some of the age ranges. For example, beginning at age 16 months, one cannot obtain a standard score of less than 50 on the Cognitive subtest nor a standard score greater than 115 at 66–71 months of age.

STANDARDIZATION. The normative sample is more than adequate as it included 1,269 children from 27 geographically diverse states and British Columbia, Canada. The sample was chosen based on age, geographic location, gender, race, urban or rural residence, ethnicity, family income, education level of parents, and disability status (learning disabilities, speech-language delays, and mental retardation). The percentage of children in the sample closely matched the 1996 U.S. Census data on each of the variables. The sample also includes an "at-risk" category that appears to be taken from those identified as having no disability but having either an established, biological, or environmental risk.

RELIABILITY. Internal consistency, test-retest, and interscorer reliability were computed for the DAYC. Estimates of internal consistency, using coefficient alphas, indicated high reliability (.90 or higher) across all eight 6-month age intervals. The lowest coefficients were found in the 6–11-month age group, but were still above .90. Coefficient alphas were also computed based on ethnic status, gender, and disability status subgroups. Again, the reliability estimates were quite high with none lower than .98 for any of the subgroups across the five domains and composite

score. The corresponding standard errors of measurement at each of the age intervals were acceptable, with most ranging from 1.50 to 3.00. The largest *SEM*s were found at the 6–11-month age interval (range 1.50 on the Composite to 4.74 on Adaptive Behavior). Test-retest reliability (administration interval = 15 days) was based on two studies of 31 and 18 children from a single day care facility in a southern and a northern state, respectively. Although the correlation coefficients ranged from .94 to .99, two studies with extremely limited samples preclude definitive statements about test-retest reliability. To demonstrate interscorer reliability, two staff persons from the publisher's research department scored 39 protocols. The correlation between the standard scores was .99. Despite this rather robust coefficient, interscorer reliability would have been much more impressive had the authors used field-based examiners to simultaneously score protocols. It seems to be a bit of "fishing from the swimming pool" to use highly skilled and expert staff to illustrate that the test has minimal error due to differences between scorers.

VALIDITY. Content validity of the DAYC was quantitatively established by computing item discrimination coefficients at each of eight age intervals and correlating Delta scores of different subgroups for each of the subtests. Item discrimination coefficients for the normative sample ranged from .41 to .94, indicating adequate item discrimination. The correlations between Delta scores for five subgroup iterations (gender, ethnicity, disability status) ranged from .94 to .99, indicating that the relative item difficulty for each of the subgroups was extremely similar (i.e., virtually no systematic item bias). Criterion-related validity is based on two studies; the first involving 26 children residing in one of three states and the second comprising 18 children. Scores from the DAYC subtests were correlated with composite scores from the Battelle Developmental Inventory Screening Test (Study 1) and the Revised Gesell and Amatruda Developmental and Neurologic Examination (Study 2). All coefficients were significant at the .01 level with the Battelle (range from .47 to .61) and at the .05 level with the Gesell (range from .41 to .53). Given that there are only two studies with extremely small sample sizes, it would be premature to make definitive conclusions regarding the criterion-related validity of the DAYC. Construct validity was demonstrated by examining the mean scores across 12 age intervals, correlating age and subtest scores, examining mean scores of different subgroups, correlating subtests with one another, and conducting a factor analysis. As expected, there was a strong correlation between age and subtest scores (from .90 to .94) and a corresponding increase in mean scores with advancing age. Again, as expected, subjects who were nondisabled had higher mean scores than subjects at risk who, in turn, had higher mean scores than subjects with disabilities. It is important to mention, however, that the standard deviations for subjects in the disabled subgroup ranged from 21.58 (Cognitive) to 60.37 (Physical Development), which actually exceeded the mean score of the Physical Development subtest! Intercorrelations between the subtests were computed for the entire sample and for seven subgroups. Median coefficients ranged from .83 (Hispanic Americans) to .94 (females). Results of the exploratory factor analysis for the normative sample indicated a single factor underlying test performance. A principal components factor analysis for seven subgroups indicated one factor for each of the subgroups. Thus, it appears that for all subjects *within* the normative sample, the DAYC is measuring a single construct, namely developmental skills.

SUMMARY. The DAYC joins a long list of instruments designed to measure the developmental status of young children. All of the material in the test kit is well organized, easy to understand, and relatively simple to use. The primary limitation of this test is that there are no supplementary materials available to assist in administering the items, which could seriously affect test performance and jeopardize standardized administration. Although scores are supported with excellent reliability data, the validity of scores from the test has not been firmly established. Considering the purposes for which the test was designed, it appears to be appropriate for use as a means of identifying children either with developmental delays or children at risk for developing developmental delays. It may be appropriate for determining relative strengths and weaknesses in developmental areas, but the value of engaging in such a practice is highly questionable, especially given the lack of data on the reliability of difference scores. It is not appropriate for evaluating change as a result of programmatic intervention primarily because there are no data presented to show that the test is sensitive to treatment effects. Despite these weaknesses, the DAYC covers a broader age range than many other instruments, has more recent and representative norms, has excellent reliability and some validity data reported, and assesses a wide range of developmental skills. In weighing the advantages and disadvantages of the test, the DAYC is recommended by this reviewer as one part of the overall screening process for children birth to 6 years but should not be the sole factor in making either diagnostic or placement decisions. Examiners should also secure all possibly needed supplementary materials prior to testing to facilitate ease of administration.

REVIEWER'S REFERENCE

American Psychological Association. (1992). *Ethical principles of psychologists* (rev. ed.). Washington, DC: Author.

[116]

Developmental Indicators for the Assessment of Learning, Third Edition.

Purpose: Designed as "an individually administered developmental screening test designed to identify young children in need of further diagnostic assessment."
Population: Ages 3-0 to 6-11.
Publication Dates: 1983–1998.
Acronym: DIAL-3.
Scores, 7: Motor, Concepts, Language, DIAL-3 Total, Self-Help Development, Social Development, Speed DIAL.
Administration: Individual.
Subtests, 5: Motor, Concepts, Language, Self-Help Development, Social Development.
Price Data, 1999: $349.95 per complete kit including manual ('98, 136 pages), 50 record forms (English), 1 record form (Spanish), 50 cutting cards, 50 parent questionnaires (English), manipulatives, dials, operator's handbooks in English and Spanish for motor, concepts and language areas, Speed DIAL, and training packet; $349.95 per complete kit in Spanish; $49.95 per DIAL-3 administration forms (specify English or Spanish) including 50 record forms, 50 cutting cards, and 50 parent questionnaires; $34.95 per 50 cutting cards and 50 record forms (specify English or Spanish); $21.95 per 50 parent/child activity forms (specify English or Spanish); $69.95 per training video; $149.95 per computer program (specify Windows or Macintosh).
Foreign Language Editions: Spanish edition available.
Time: (20–30) minutes; Speed DIAL: (15–20) minutes.
Comments: In contrast to DIAL-R, the DIAL-3 has two formats: the full version and the short version (called the Speed DIAL).

Authors: Carol Mardell-Czudnowski and Dorothea S. Goldenberg.
Publisher: American Guidance Service, Inc.
Cross References: See T5:809 (2 references); for reviews by Darrell L. Sabers and Scott Spreat of an earlier edition, see 12:110 (1 reference); see also T4:762 (6 references); for reviews by David W. Barnett and G. Michael Poteat of an earlier version, see 10:89 (6 references); see also 9:326 (1 reference) and T3:696 (2 references); for reviews by J. Jeffrey Grill and James J. McCarthy of an earlier edition, see 8:428 (3 references).

Review of the Developmental Indicators for the Assessment of Learning, Third Edition by GREGORY J. CIZEK, Associate Professor of Educational Measurement and Evaluation, University of North Carolina, Chapel Hill, NC:

The Developmental Indicators for the Assessment of Learning, Third Edition (DIAL-3) is the most recent version of a developmental screening measure for young children that was first introduced in 1975 as the DIAL and, as a result of revisions in 1983 and 1990 became known as the DIAL-R. Past revisions resulted in improved materials and technical characteristics; the DIAL-3 represents a continuation of this trajectory.

PURPOSE. The DIAL-3 was designed to be one component of a larger program to identify potential difficulties for, primarily, children at school-entering age. The authors of the DIAL-3 differentiate between several related concepts—ability, development, intelligence, school readiness—and state that the test is correctly used only as a preliminary screen for developmental delays in children from, roughly, ages 3 to 7. This age range represents a one-year older expansion of the range covered by the DIAL-R.

Five developmental areas are assessed by the full version of the DIAL-3. These include the three basic areas assessed in the previous version of the test (Motor Skills, Concepts, and Language) and two new areas (Self-Help and Social Development) so that developmental coverage of the DIAL-3 corresponds to the five areas mandated for assessment by the Individuals with Disabilities Education Act (IDEA, 1997). A short form of the DIAL-3 is also available, called the Speed DIAL. The short form assesses only the three basic areas, and can be administered in half the time required to administer the long form (15 vs. 30 minutes). All materials and norms tables are also available for a Spanish version of the DIAL-3. The remainder of this review concerns the long form, with only occasional references to the DIAL-3 or Spanish version when a distinction is necessary.

MATERIALS. The materials that comprise the DIAL-3 exhibit attention to detail at every step of the assessment process. For example, videotape instructional materials are available for training screening program personnel, self-tests are included for assessing the competence of those who will be administering the screening; questions are suggested for conducting an evaluation of the screening program. Complete information is presented in the DIAL-3 manual for planning and implementing a large scale screening, on topics such as locating children to be served, designing floor plans for the screening area, handling "overly helpful parents," and discussing results following the screening.

Administrator instructions, record forms, and screening materials are well organized and easy to use. Also included are masters that can be photocopied to prepare child name tags, parent report forms, and handouts for parents describing developmentally appropriate activities for their children. Materials necessary for administering the DIAL-3 are packaged in bold-colored tote bags that are color-coordinated for the Motor, Concepts, and Language areas. These materials include items such as: bean bags, scissors, blocks, and other manipulatives used by the children, and large cardstock wheels that are rotated to reveal picture prompts (one at a time). It is from these wheels or "dials" that the assessment derives its name.

ADMINISTRATION. Although it is an individual screening, the DIAL-3 is administered in a setting in which three children at a time are observed in a specially designed screening area staffed by several members of an administration team. It is recommended that the team consists of a coordinator who leads the team and is a professionally trained in special education, early childhood education, psychology, or other related area. Three operators staff each of three stations in the screening area, which is set up "to simulate a relaxed, early childhood setting in which many gamelike activities are occurring simultaneously" (manual, p. 3). It is also recommended that a suitable number of volunteers are on hand to assist in maintaining an efficient flow of activities, especially if a large number of children are being screened, or if the other screening-related activities (such as hearing and vision screening) are conducted concurrently.

Administration of the DIAL-3 requires children to move through the three stations and, at each station, to respond to questions or perform tasks related to one of the areas assessed. For example, at the Motor station, a child is asked to perform movements such as jumping, skipping, cutting with scissors, and building block towers. At the Concepts station, tasks include naming body parts, colors and counting, and sorting shapes. The Language station asks a student to pronounce words, and to respond to oral questions about his or her name, birthdate, and letter sounds, among other things. In these three areas, the tasks that make up the DIAL-3 are similar to those assessed in its predecessor the DIAL-R, although the majority of the tasks have been revised, several were dropped in the current version, and at least two are completely new. According to the manual for the DIAL-3, these changes were precipitated both by new insights into developmentally sensitive tasks and Item Response Theory (Rasch) analyses that helped identify misfitting items.

While the child is progressing from station to station, observations are also being recorded by the operators for behaviors that may indicate the need for further assessment in social, affective, or speech/language areas. At the same time, the child's parent completes a Parent Questionnaire designed to elicit the parent's perceptions of possible medical, self-help, or social issues; these questions form the remaining two areas assessed by the DIAL-3, namely, Self-Help Development and Social Development.

SCORING. Scoring for the Motor, Language, and Concepts areas is accomplished by first converting the raw scores assigned to a child's responses into scaled scores. This process is easily performed by referring to conversions printed directly on the forms where the child's task performance is recorded. No scaled score conversions are required for the Self-Help and Social areas, although these raw scores must be obtained using scoring overlays. All scores are then recorded on the front of the DIAL-3 record form. Scores in all five areas can be obtained; a score called the DIAL-3 Total is also available, which is a composite formed from the Motor, Language, and Concepts scores.

Overall results from the assessment are reported as a dichotomy: A child's performance is identified as *Potential delay* or *OK*. These two classifications differ from previous versions of the DIAL, which also included a *Potential advanced* category. The authors strongly advise that children who are identified as *Potential delay* should not have important educational decisions made based on this classification, but should be referred to a competent professional for confirmation or further investigation of the child's developmental status.

NORMS. Data for national norms for English-speaking children were obtained from 1995–1997. The data collection resulted in a nationally representative sample of 1,560 children, stratified by gender, race/ethnicity, geographical region, and parental education (a proxy for socioeconomic status). A separate sample of 605 Spanish-speaking children was obtained for norming the Spanish version, although this sample was not as carefully constructed to match population characteristics, and Spanish-speaking children from the U.S. as well as Puerto Rico and Panama were included. Characteristics of both samples are presented in the DIAL-3 manual, which includes well-presented tables showing the joint frequencies of key variables used for stratification.

Overall, although precise information about how these samples were selected for inclusion in the norming study is not presented in the manual, the validity of the norms for English-speaking children appears to be much more defensible than for Spanish-speaking children. Along these same lines, the manual reports that separate norms for Spanish-speaking children were not actually constructed, but a correspondence between the performance of English- and Spanish-speaking children was established through equating. Although there is a reasonable rationale for this choice, the actual equating procedures may have introduced an additional cause for cautious use of the DIAL-3 with Spanish-speaking children. For example, the procedure simply defined items as being "common" if their Rasch calibrated difficulties were not "very different," with that criterion met by items with differences in calibrated difficulties of "about one logit or more" (manual, p. 77). This operational definition seems not only ill-specified, but also extremely liberal when compared to the differences in performance that would exclude items from consideration as common items in other contexts.

VALIDITY. Development of the DIAL-3 followed procedures that would generally promote valid interpretations. The authors of the DIAL-3 manual recognize the importance of clarity regarding appropriate interpretations of scores. For example, the manual cautions users that the DIAL-3 is *not* a readiness, diagnostic, or intelligence test and that screening should not be viewed as a one-shot test upon which critical decisions should automatically be based. Instead, the assessment is intended as "the first step in a process of identification of young children in need of special services" (manual, p. 6).

Development procedures for the DIAL-3 included grounding in the literature of child development, task tryouts and refinements, and bias reviews. Extensive content validity evidence is presented in the manual for each of the 20 tasks in the Motor, Concepts, and Language areas; however, comparatively skimpy content validity evidence is presented for the Self-Help and Social areas.

Much data related to convergent and discriminant validity evidence is also provided; most of the evidence supports the intended use of the DIAL-3. For example, intercorrelations between the five areas assessed by the DIAL-3 are generally low (as would be desired), ranging from .23 for the Social and Motor areas, to .65 for Concepts and Language. The attention given to correlations between the DIAL-3 and its predecessor (i.e., the DIAL-R) is not very helpful. More helpful are the correlations reported between the DIAL-3 and numerous other tests that assess related constructs, although these seem lower than would be desirable, perhaps due in part to the time interval between administrations of the tests. Correlations are reported between performance on the DIAL-3 and Early Screening Profiles (ESP; Harrison et al., 1990). The correlation between the ESP Cognitive/Language Profile and the DIAL-3 Total was a modest .61; the Concepts subtests of the two measures correlated only .48. Similarly, the correlation between the DIAL-3 Total and the ESP Basic School Skills composite was .56; the correlation between the DIAL-3 and the Battelle Developmental Inventory Screening Test (Newborg, Stack, Winek, Guidubaldi, & Swinicki, 1984) Total was .55; and the correlation between the DIAL-3 Total and the Brigance Preschool Screen (Brigance, 1985) Total score was .53. On the other hand, the correlation between General Conceptual Ability composite scores on the Different Ability Scales (Elliott, 1990) and the DIAL-3 Total scores was .79.

Although the pattern of correlations provides some evidence that the DIAL-3 does measure the intended construct, a different question is whether scores on the DIAL-3 can be confidently used for making refer/do not refer classifications or decisions. This issue is strikingly illustrated in the decision cutoff tables provided in the manual. Users of the DIAL-3 are advised to "choose one of five cutoffs that best fit [sic] the screening needs of their community" (p. 52). The five cutoff choices will identify approximately 16%, 10%, 7%, 5%, and 2% of children screened if the community is representative of the norming sample. These cutoffs appear to be arbitrary, as does the choice of cutoff, except for the advice that the use of too liberal a cutoff could identify more children as "at risk" than could practically be referred for further assessment. From a technical perspective, what is missing in the validity data presented for the DIAL-3 is predictive evidence bearing on the relationships between the suggested cutoffs and subsequent indicators of child functioning in school and other settings.

From a more practical standpoint, the DIAL-3 manual does not provide guidance regarding how a screening coordinator would go about choosing an operational cutoff in the first place. Although the manual suggests that the cutoff be "adjusted" if too many or too few children are identified as at-risk, any adjustment would be too late for those already identified, and the problems associated with recontacting parents already informed of their child's (potentially incorrect) classification are not discussed.

RELIABILITY. Evidence that the DIAL-3 produces dependable scores is also available, and the authors should be commended for including a helpful discussion of the nature of errors in decision making and the relative costs of over- and underidentification. Alpha coefficients for the total test and subareas are greatest in the preschool age range for which the assessment will most likely be used (i.e., around age 5) and lower as the age of the child approaches the extremes of 3 and 7 years. For 5-year-olds, internal consistency estimates are .90 for the DIAL-3 Total and range from .71 to .85 for the subareas (Motor and Social Development, respectively). Stability was estimated by giving the DIAL-3 to 158 students with a median interval of 28 days; test-retest coefficients were in the .80s for the Total test, and predictably lower for the subareas, though never lower than .69 (Motor, younger students).

Although the manual notes that "the single score from the DIAL-3 Total is likely to be less useful than the separate area scores" (p. 10), this advice should clearly be tempered by recognition of the comparatively weaker dependability of the area scores. Naturally, accurate information about specific areas of developmental need would be desirable from an intervention perspective, and scores in some subareas of the DIAL-3 have acceptable dependability. However, other areas (notably, Motor Development) are not sufficiently reliable for decision making. And, although standard errors at relevant age ranges are provided, two concerns are immediately apparent. First, although reported for age intervals, standard errors at the critical classification cutoff points are not reported. Second, although the 95% confidence bands are typically only as large as 6–8 points in the range in which the DIAL-3 would most commonly be used for school screenings, the standard errors are unacceptably large in other age ranges, especially very young children.

SUMMARY. The DIAL-3 is easy to use, score, and interpret. There is sufficient evidence for users to have confidence in the dependability of scores on the DIAL-3, although additional information should be developed regarding reliability at critical decision points. Validity evidence is—like the colorful totes in which the DIAL-3 is provided—a mixed bag, however. A great deal of content validity evidence supports the inclusion of many of the tasks that appear on the assessment, but predictive validity evidence is missing. The lack of evidence supporting the cutoff points is a more critical omission. The norms developed for English-speaking children appear to be reasonably representative of the national population; however, the equating procedures used to create norms for Spanish-speaking children are suspect.

Overall, the new version of the DIAL represents an improvement over the previous version and, compared to some of the alternatives that exist for accomplishing its purpose, the DIAL-3 provides a defensible way to help educators identify children at risk for school failure resulting from developmental delays. The DIAL-3 also incorporates much that makes it a successful revision of its predecessor, the DIAL-R. In fact, in a review of that version, a reviewer commented that

he had "never showed the DIAL-R to anyone who didn't like it" (Sabers, 1995, p. 285). The same conclusion applies to the DIAL-3. This instrument will appeal to those who seek a quick method of screening young children who may need additional assessment for developmental delays in five key areas.

REVIEWER'S REFERENCES
Newborg, J., Stock, J. R., Winek, L., Guidubaldi, J., & Svinicki, J. (1984). Battelle Developmental Inventory. Chicago: Riverside.
Brigance, A. H. (1985). Brigance Preschool Screen. Northern Billerica, MA: Curriculum Associates.
Elliott, C. D. (1990). *Differential Ability Scales: Administration and scoring manual.* San Antonio, TX: Psychological Corporation.
Harrison, P. L., Kaufman, A. S., Kaufman, N. L., Bruininks, R. H., Rynders, J., Ilmer, S., Sparrow, S. S., & Cichetti, D. V. (1990). AGS Early Screening Profiles. Circle Pines, MN: American Guidance Service.
Sabers, D. L. (1995) [Review of the Developmental Indicators for the Assessment of Learning, Revised/AGS Edition.] In J. C. Conoley & J. C. Impara (Eds.), *The twelfth mental measurements yearbook* (pp. 283-285). Lincoln, NE: Buros Institute of Mental Measurements.
Individuals with Disabilities Education Act [IDEA]. P.L. 105-17, 111 Stat 37-157 (1997).

Review of the Developmental Indicators for the Assessment of Learning, Third Edition by DOREEN WARD FAIRBANK, Associate Professor of Psychology, Meredith College, Raleigh, NC:

The Developmental indicators for the Assessment of Learning, Third Edition (DIAL-3) was developed and written by Carol Mardell-Czudnowski and Dorothea S. Goldenberg. The DIAL-3 is an individually administered developmental screening test used to identify young children in need of further diagnostic assessment. This instrument directly assesses motoric, conceptual, and language behaviors. The DIAL-3 Parent Questionnaire, completed by a parent or caregiver during the screening, provides normed scores for the child's self-help and social skills as well as information on personal/medical information, and overall development. In order to further assess the psychosocial area the testers also complete a rating scale during the screening.

This is the third revision since the original DIAL was developed in the 1970s. This revision includes modifications, additions, and deletions in test items based on current research to appropriately screen the five developmental areas (Motor, Concepts, Language, Self-Help, and Social Skills) mandated in the Individuals with Disabilities Education Act (IDEA; 1997). Other revisions include updated norms, a change in the testing age from 2-0 through 5-11 years in the DIAL-R to 3-0 through 6-11 years for the DIAL-3, and an additional shortened, separate format, the Speed DIAL. The DIAL-3 takes approximately 30 minutes to complete, whereas the Speed DIAL only requires about 15 minutes. The Speed DIAL was designed to provide a shortened format that may be used for quicker screening (e.g., a child who enters a program after the initial screening was completed).

The DIAL-3 also was revised to be available in both English and Spanish. The Spanish edition was normed on a separate national sample of young Spanish-speaking children. The items are similar but tailored to match the requirements of each language and culture.

The DIAL-3 items are empirically based, developmentally sequenced, and assess the developmental skills that are considered the foundation for academic learning. The test areas and related academic areas are as follows: The Motor area relates to learning arithmetic, and items in the Language area are related to learning to read.

The DIAL-3 kit comes in an attractive large cloth storage bag that houses three additional cloth storage bags each containing a separate section of the test. Each bag contains the Operator's Handbook, a movable dial-testing format to expose a single stimulus at a time, the necessary manipulatives, and answer sheets for that section. The Parent Questionnaires, training packets, record forms, the test manual, and the Speed DIAL Operator's Handbook and record forms are all contained within the larger blue bag.

The DIAL-3's administration is usually completed in an arena setting to test large numbers of children in a short span of time and requires one professional coordinator and three professional or paraprofessional operators (testers) and optional volunteers. The DIAL-3 kit contains an extensive training program for the staff to complete prior to testing. The training materials include a training overview, training materials packet, written tests, and a training video (optional). The training comes in both English and Spanish and should take about 4 hours to complete. The manual provides the details concerning the conditions, facilities, and procedures for the screening. The children move from section to section while the coordinator instructs the parents to complete the Parent Questionnaire. The manual recommends entry levels and possible exit points for each child by age. After each item is completed the operator circles the appropriate raw score according to the task-scoring criteria given for each item in the manual. The scaled score for that item is then determined by reading up the column on the answer sheet to the large bold number printed at the top of the column (0, 1, 2, 3, or 4). When the testing is completed in each section, a Scale Score Total is determined. The operator should score the series of the nine behaviors in the behavioral observation section during this time. The Total Score and each area Scale Score Total or Speed DIAL Total Score should then be compared on the appropriate cutoff tables in the manual. If the performance is below the average range of scores this may indicate a potential learning delay, whereas a performance within the average range of scores indicates age-appropriate skill development. The manual suggests score interpretations, possible follow-up assessment procedures, and methods to conduct conferences with parents on the results.

A national normative sample of 1,560 children aged 3-0 through 6-11 was completed from 1995–1997. The standardization sample was selected to match U.S. Census data from the March 1994 Current Population Survey. The sample was stratified within each age group by the following criteria: gender, race/ethnicity, geographic region, and parents' education level. The sample was taken from 36 states and Washington, DC. Children with disabilities were included in the sample, but their data were not separated out and only their services were recorded. Spanish-speaking children from sites in Puerto Rico and Panama also were recruited. The sample appears to be improved from the last revision.

The internal consistency reliability estimates across age groups varied among the areas (from .45 to .90) with the Motor area being consistently the lowest (median reliability was .66; the other areas ranged from .77 to .87). The median reliability for the DIAL-3 Total score was .87 but Speed DIAL was only .80. Test-retest reliability (administration intervals ranged from 12 to 65 days) was calculated using two groups and was found to be .88 for the DIAL-3 and .84 for Speed DIAL for Group 1 ($N = 80$, aged 3-6 to 4-5) and to be .84 for the DIAL-3 and .82 for Speed DIAL Group 2 ($N = 78$, aged 4-6 to 5-10).

The earlier versions of the DIAL document the content validity. The DIAL-3 utilized the Rasch Item Analysis to identify any items that were not consistent with others in the test. The item content of the DIAL-3 was also reviewed by a number of expert reviewers. Together with the results from the Item Analysis, items were deleted or modified for this revision. Construct validity was examined for each area as well as the Total Scores. Correlations with the Battelle Developmental Inventory Screening test were .55 for the DIAL-3 Total Score and .63 for the Speed DIAL. The individual areas correlated with a range from .26 in Self-Help to .67 in Language. The DIAL-3 Language area and the Peabody Picture Vocabulary Test showed corrected correlations of .69 for the younger age group and .57 for the older age group. The Social Skills Rating System's parent Social Skills rating had a strong correlation with both the DIAL-3 Self-Help area (.66) and with the Social Development score (.72).

SUMMARY. The DIAL-3 appears to be a stronger and better standardized screening instrument than the earlier editions. The authors have addressed concerns and incorporated changes suggested by earlier reviewers. The DIAL-3 is a useful tool in developmental screening programs, but should be used only as a screening instrument with caution taken in overinterpreting the results.

[117]
Developmental Tasks for Kindergarten Readiness—II.

Purpose: Designed to provide "objective data about the school-readiness of pre-kindergarten children so that effective educational programming can be planned for them."

Population: Pre-kindergarten children.

Publication Dates: 1978–1994.

Acronym: DTKR-II.

Scores, 19: Composite Score (Social Interaction, Name Printing, Body Concepts—Awareness, Body Concepts—Use, Auditory Sequencing, Auditory Association, Visual Discrimination, Visual Memory, Visual Motor, Color Naming, Relational Concepts, Number Counting, Number Use, Number Naming, Alphabet Knowledge), Acquired Knowledge, Verbal-Conceptual, Visual Skills.

Administration: Individual.

Price Data, 1999: $98 per kit including manual ('94, 97 pages), materials book (cards), and 25 test booklets; $39 per 25 test booklets; $23 per materials book; $39 per test manual.

Time: (20–40) minutes.

Comments: Administered by school personnel for diagnostic-remedial purposes.

Authors: Walter J. Lesiak and Judi Lucas Lesiak.

Publisher: PRO-ED.

Cross References: See T4:766 (1 reference); for reviews by Carol A. Gray and Sue White of an earlier edition, see 9:328.

Review of the Developmental Tasks for Kindergarten Readiness—II by JOSEPH O. PREWITT DIAZ, School Psychologist, Chester Upland School District, Chester, PA:

This test is a revision of the Developmental Tasks for Kindergarten Readiness (DTKR; Lesniak, 1978). The test can be used for screening and diagnostic-remedial purposes of children ages 4 years, 6 months to 6 years, 2 months. The major changes include: (a) standardization, (b) the use of standard scores rather than the letter grading system used by the DTKR, and (c) inclusion in the manual of a chapter presenting intervention strategies. The test is designed to address several developmental tasks related to early childhood learning. Fifteen subtests were developed to cover areas of oral language, visual motor skill, cognitive knowledge, and social development.

Lesniak and Lesniak (the authors of the 1994 revision) report that the test was constructed after an examination of curriculum guides, review of the literature, and consultation with 50 school districts to determine specific instructional objectives for Kindergarten. There is no discussion on the linguistic and cultural applicability of the items. A consideration about the world-view of children who are recent arrivals to the united States and the skills that these children bring to school, makes the use of this test in some geographical areas of the country difficult to recommend.

The test kit is composed of an examiner's manual, a spiral-bound materials book, and individual test booklets. In addition, the examiner will need a pencil, an eraser, 10 plastic chips, pennies, or blocks, and one 8 1/2-inch x 11-inch sheet of blank paper.

School psychologists, teachers, other school personnel, or trained paraprofessionals can administer the test. The manual suggests that "parents have frequently administered the test with proper training; however, they should not assess their own children" (manual, p. 5). The attitude of the developers of the test about who can administer the test is of concern. The training of test administrators takes about 2 hours. The content of this training is not clearly articulated and thus presents a problem relating to validity of the results. The administration time ranges between 20 and 30 minutes. The examination time should be consistent with the child's skill level.

The instructions for administration and scoring of the items are clearly articulated and easy to follow. The test is designed in such a way that activities are clustered in ways that follow the same method of responding. The examiner's manual includes examples for scoring that assist the examiner in making scoring determination in the subtests of Visual Memory and Visual Motor Skills. An improvement of this test from its predecessor is that it includes a chapter on intervention strategies. There are suggestions made for each of the subtests as well as a list of publishers. The discussion on the chapter of interventions allows the diagnostician to recommend specific strategies to the classroom teacher. There is no discussion of examiners' translation of instructions and how this may affect the results of the test.

A great deal of effort is placed on presenting the technical data for this instrument. The demographic characteristics of the sample present some problems in terms of the use of this instrument in areas of the country with large numbers of limited-English and non-English speakers. The majority of the sample is from the north central part of the country. There is no discussion of the number of rural versus urban school districts that participated in the standardization process. There is no documentation pertaining to any children who may be handicapped or have been diagnosed with a physical developmental disorder. There is no discussion as to prior preschool experience for children in the sample.

The size of the standardization sample for the test was 2,521. The sample was equally distributed between males and females. The age range was from 4 years, 6 months to 6 years, 2 months. The average school age for Kindergarten children is 5 years, 5 months. There is no discussion of the qualification of the examiner and their effect on the test results. About 11.2% of the sample is composed of children 5 years, 10 months up to 6 years, 2 months. Children generally enter first grade at age 6. There is no explanation for the inclusion of children past Kindergarten age, especially troubling because the test developer indicates that this test is a screening test for Kindergarten.

The small sample size representing Hispanics and Asians is a major problem in development and standardization of this test. There is no documentation about the country of origin of the Hispanics and Asians. There is no discussion of cultural applicability of the items. There is no discussion about the time in the U.S. for the sample categorized as Hispanic or Asian. These deficiencies raise some concerns about the use of this test in urban areas with large numbers of culturally and linguistically diverse children.

The psychometric evidence for scores from the test is presented and discussed. The test-retest reliability estimates range from a low of .82 for the Social Interaction subtest to a high of .97 for the Number Naming subtest (the test-retest intervals ranged from 2 weeks to 1 month). A predictive validity study was conducted between the DTKR and the California Achievement Test. These validity data are from the original test and not representative of the current revised version of the test.

Results of a factor analysis are presented in the manual. Three factors were identified in a varimax rotation: Acquired Knowledge, Verbal/Conceptual, and Visual Skills. Acquired Knowledge included Number Naming, Number Use, and Number Counting, Color Naming, Alphabet Knowledge, and Name Printing. For the Verbal/Conceptual factor, Body Concepts, Auditory Association and Relational Concepts were included. In the third factor, Visual Skills, subtests included are Visual Motor, Memory, and Discrimination.

SUMMARY. The test has some areas of strengths including the use of a standard scores system similar to other tests currently used in the school setting. Secondly, the theory base for the test is clearly articulated and the process of test construction appears scientifically sound. Third, a chapter presenting intervention strategies is included. The interventions are organized to address each subtest.

The greatest problem is that the normative sample is not representative of the national distribution of school-age population. Test interpretations do not account for issues of validity for culturally and linguistically diverse populations. The use of this test in a large school district with a diverse population should be done with caution. A deeper look at the changing demographic face of the country and the applicability of items is important for the educational world. The chapter on strategies is heavily grounded in the literature and offers a limited amount of practical suggestions. It recommends sources of materials that might not be readily available to the teacher.

REVIEWER'S REFERENCE

Lesniak, W., Jr. (1978). Developmental Tasks for Kindergarten Readiness: An Assessment of Abilities and Skills in Preschool Children to Determine Kindergarten Readiness. Brandon, VT: Clinical Psychology Publishing.

Review of the Developmental Tasks for Kindergarten Readiness—II by THERESA GRAHAM, Assistant Professor of Educational Psychology, University of Nebraska—Lincoln, Lincoln, NE:

OVERVIEW. The Developmental Tasks for Kindergarten Readiness—II (DTKR-II) is an assessment tool for "school districts who wish to institute a kindergarten assessment program that advocates a diagnostic-prescriptive model" (manual, p. 2). The test consists of 15 subtests covering the areas of oral language development, visual motor development, cognitive development, and social development. The subtests include Social Interaction, Name Printing, Body Concepts—Awareness, Body Concepts—Use, Auditory Sequencing, Auditory Association, Visual Discrimination, Visual Memory, Visual Motor, Color Naming, Relational Concepts, Number Knowledge (counting, use, naming), and Alphabet Knowledge.

INSTRUMENT RATIONALE. The DTKR-II is designed to assess basic skill level to determine strengths and weaknesses of children just prior to or in the first few weeks of kindergarten. The DTKR-II is not intended to measure kindergarten readiness, but rather to examine kindergarten curriculum to meet the needs of children. In addition, the authors state that the subtests were derived based on relevant literature and match instructional objectives for kindergarten. Unfortunately, little literature regarding kindergarten curriculum is cited. Moreover, there are a number of kindergarten objectives mentioned that are not assessed in the DTKR-II (e.g., knowledge of shapes), and some of the objectives are minimally assessed (e.g., social development). Finally, it is difficult to understand why the authors would not expect schools and personnel to use the DTKR-II as a readiness measure because "kindergarten readiness" is in the title.

ADMINISTRATION AND SCORING. The information regarding test administration and scoring is relatively straightforward. However, there are a few weaknesses in this area. First, the authors state that parents may be in the testing room with the child if the child is hesitant about the testing. Unfortunately there is no place to indicate this on the test booklet. This should be noted because performance on subtests (e.g., Social Interaction) might be affected. Second, the examiner is given flexibility to change the order of subtests, but again, there is no place in the test booklet to note this accommodation.

Scoring is also problematic and may penalize groups of children. For example, on the body part subtest, the examiner is instructed that he or she may use the first three body part items as a pretest if the child is hesitant to begin the task but that the child is not able to receive credit for knowledge of those items. This direction seems to penalize children who may be shy. Scoring is also problematic on the visual motor task. No examples are provided of circles that would receive a "zero" score.

RECORDING AND INTERPRETING SCORES. Problems may arise in interpreting scores due to items that are confounding or problems with the test protocol. For example, knowledge of right and left is confounded with body knowledge ("point to your right hand"). If a child makes an error, it is not clear whether that is related to body part knowledge or right-left knowledge. In other cases, the protocol may lead to improper interpretations. For example, in Auditory Sequencing, the children do not necessarily receive each item (if they succeed on the first trial they then proceed to the next "level" skipping the other trials on a given level). This protocol makes item analysis difficult.

Overall, the method to record the scores for the DTKR-II is much better than the letter grading system used in the prior version. The present system uses scaled scores with a mean of 10 (*s.d.* = 3; maximum = 16) for the subtests and factor scores and a mean of 100 (*s.d.* = 15; maximum = 130) for the composite score. To compute the scaled scores, the examiner computes the raw scores and then converts the raw score using the norm table in the manual. The composite score is computed by adding up all of the raw scores and then converting the total raw score with the norm table. The validity of the composite score is questionable. Because the raw scores on the subtests are not comparable, it is unclear how a composite score based on the sum of the subtests is valid. This would be especially true for a child whose scores are extremely variable.

The qualitative interpretations may also be questionable. Although an item analysis can give a sense of the skills the child possesses, the authors do not cite evidence to support their claim that the items to be analyzed are truly indicative of any measurable construct. Secondly, appropriate qualitative interpretation requires knowledge of kindergarten curriculum. If parents are considered appropriate examiners, it may be important that they have training to understand what "reversals, rotations, and/or inversions" mean and what are the consequences of such results.

TECHNICAL DATA. The authors give information regarding the standardization sample of the DTKR-II. Unfortunately, they fail to indicate when the sample was recruited, when they took the test, or any information regarding the examiners. In addition, the information regarding the reliability is somewhat vague. Although they report an interrater reliability rate of 90%, they do not provide any information regarding the ages of the children whose protocols they selected to assess interrater reliability. It may be that older children who may be more proficient in certain areas are easier to score than younger children, yielding a superficially high interrater reliability. Also, they did not report reliability for the Social Interaction subtest, a test with a higher degree of subjective evaluation.

Although a study found a .90 test-retest reliability coefficient (with a 2-week interval), specific information regarding the subsample used is lacking. No indication of when the study was done or the exact percentage of ages of children was provided. In addition, it would be interesting to see if the same alphas could be found for the different age groups. Is there similar internal consistency across the different age groups?

Predictive validity was assessed by comparing scores on the DTKR-II with prereading and math California Achievement Test (CAT) scores. These are the same data that were obtained for the DTKR. Again, information regarding the sample is lacking. Therefore, validity is difficult to assess. Finally, more information regarding the step-wise regression analysis would have been helpful. For example, why would Number Knowledge (in terms of counting and naming) predict prereading scores but not math scores on the CAT?

SUMMARY. The DTKR-II is intended to be diagnostic and prescriptive. However, the title will suggest to users that it will provide something else. In addition, the reliability and validity data are weak. Given that this is a norm-referenced test, the usefulness of this measure is called into question.

[118]
Developmental Teaching Objectives and Rating Form—Revised.

Purpose: Designed "for assessing social and emotional development of children and youth."
Population: Ages 0–16 years.
Publication Dates: 1992–1998.
Acronym: DTORF-R.
Scores, 5: Behavior, Communication, Socialization, Academics/Cognition, Total.
Administration: Individual.
Price Data, 1997: $52 per kit including 4 subscale booklets, user's manual ('97, 63 pages), technical report ('97, 29 pages), and rating forms; $16 per additional packet of 4 subscale booklets; $36 per set of 4 software disks (specify PC or Mac).
Time: Administration time not reported.
Comments: Rating form filled out by people familiar with the child, following observations; older students (and also their parents) participate in their own team ratings.
Authors: Mary M. Wood; The Developmental Therapy Institute, Inc.
Publisher: Developmental Therapy Institute, Inc.

Review of the Developmental Teaching Objectives and Rating Form—Revised by SHARON H. deFUR, Assistant Professor, School of Education, College of William and Mary, Williamsburg, VA:

The Developmental Teaching Objectives and Rating Form—Revised (DTORF-R) is a 171-item rating scale designed for collaborative use by educational professionals and parents to assess a child or youth's social and emotional development in the domains of Behavior (acting), Communication (saying), Socialization (caring), and Academics/Cognition (thinking). Use of this rating scale theoretically provides a profile of sequential skills for these four domains across a developmental age span from infancy to adolescence. The primary target groups are children and youth who are experiencing challenges in appropriate social and emotional behaviors. According to the information provided, there are six intended uses for this rating scale: (a) To assist in the identification of students in need of referral to special education; (b) to assist in making decisions regarding special education placement and instructional grouping; (c) to assist in identifying instructional objectives; (d) to plan curricular activities that foster social emotional competency; (e) to document student progress in these areas; and (f) to evaluate the effectiveness of programs using this model.

The DTORF-R represents a revision of the DTORF (1979), both of which evolved from a research and development field project aimed at improving the social and behavioral skills of children and youth with emotional and behavioral disabilities. The test publishers do not articulate exact numbers or demographics of the subjects who were used in test development and revision. They state that the instrument has been used with "several thousand children and youth with emotional, social, and behavioral handicaps from 18 months to 16 years of age, enrolled in special education throughout the United States" (technical report, p. 1). Furthermore, they report that some students without disabilities as well as students in other countries have been included in instrument usage. In addition, the instrument has been translated into several other languages. In one limited study, no statistical differences are reported when comparing geocultural or economic groupings. From the information provided, one can only presume that this instrument has been primarily used with students with emotional and behavioral disabilities (predominantly boys). The authors suggest that cultural bias is reduced due to the fact that this instrument is completed within the cultural context of the student. This may only hold true if the rater(s) share the same cultural and economic values as those of the student's culture.

Although additional demographic information concerning the use of this instrument and its applicability would be helpful in evaluating the documented value, this may not be the critical determinant regarding the rating scale's utility for the practitioner. Current special education requirements ask for education professionals and families to collect information regarding functional behavior and to develop behavior intervention plans. As such, the DTORF-R offers a tool to analyze behavior and identify skills in need of improvement. Furthermore, the individuals with Disabilities Act of 1997 stresses the importance of assessment information that yields instructional implications, which is one of the stated purposes of this instrument. The fact that the instrument has relatively worthwhile content and construct validity may reduce the practitioner's concern regarding limited historical demographic information.

The 171 items for the DTORF-R were constructed based on an extensive review of developmental theory, social learning theory, and research that has been widely accepted and validated. Panels of experts from the field of special education, teacher training, and developmental psychology have reviewed items and made comparisons to other developmental scales and report favorable comparisons. The DTORF-R has been field tested for practical relevance and revised to insure that subscale items represent an appropriate developmental sequence. These approaches add credibility to the validity of the content of the DTORF-R. Moreover, the evidence for construct validity of the DTORF-R does not appear debatable, at least at face value. The test publishers present two grids, one of scope and sequence, and one of developmental content, that represent a synthesis of the theory and research of 160 authors and form the basis for items within the DTORF-R. Extensive research resulted in a calibration of item sequences defining distinct levels of difficulty between each item and provides a strong sequence of infancy to adolescence developmental milestones in the four domains.

The test publishers claim high degrees of interrater reliability (.95 and .98). Further reading reveals that this report is based on two raters who had been trained using a standard rater training program; additional studies of interrater reliability would make this claim more credible. Internal consistency reliability has been supported through empirical research. It is important to note that the technical report states "The DTORF-R can be used with confidence as a reliable instrument as intended *trained raters*…" (p. 5).

The DTORF-R is a nonrestricted test, although it is recommended for use by educational professionals. Parents are also included as potential users. Although this instrument is nonrestricted, all of the validity analyses and reliability measures were collected using raters who had been trained in the use of the instrument. To the credit of the test publishers, the User's Manual includes a practice section with review questions, rating error analysis, profile interpretation, and case studies to use for practice in rating observed behaviors. Video tapes and audioslide presentations are available for self-training. However, there is no clear measure of when a novice user would become proficient based on such self-study. Furthermore, all the effectiveness research that was reported used raters who were evaluated as being highly proficient in their use of the instrument and most of these raters had participated in a 6-week inservice program.

Test administration requires student observation and completion of each item of the rating scale. The publishers claim an easier format for using the subscale booklets, but I found them awkward although the user's manual addresses the scoring process, the number of errors that constitute a ceiling (although that term is not used), and the number of items that constitute mastery of one stage, close study of the manual is needed to understand what would be expected regarding administration, scoring, and interpretation. The publishers have developed numerous profile options and forms including item-by-item forms, progress rating forms, proportional scores comparing the four domains, and percentage comparison forms. Developmental age scores can be calculated as well as T scores for standardized comparisons. I would caution against placing much value on the use of the percentage comparisons as the number of subscale items are not equal between scales, plus the numbers of items within domains or stages are too small to yield valid representation of gains or losses. The publishers have created a progress reporting form that would be useful for special educators in reporting progress to parents as required by the IDEA of 1997.

The test publishers recommend that a team of people (parents and professionals) collaborate to arrive at a consensus decision regarding each rating for the child/youth, although this consensus method is not required. This approach offers challenges and opportunities to the evaluation team. The most prominent challenge would be the skill development needed to enhance reliability and the reality that raters need to understand the developmental constructs and content of the subscale items. On the other hand, this would offer an opportunity for parents to be actively involved and contribute to the evaluation process, another intention of IDEA 1997. It could provide a shared understanding among these team members and create a more cohesive team approach to instruction in the curriculum areas of behavior, communication, socialization, and academics/cognition.

SUMMARY. As a criterion-referenced developmental behavior rating scale, the DTORF-R has potential to assist special educators as described in the intended uses of the instrument and in meeting some of the new requirements of IDEA 1997. Its deceptive rating scale simplicity should not mask the complex skills required to accomplish these tasks effectively, and users should take the role of preparation and training seriously prior to adopting this instrument as central to special education decision making.

[119]
Developmental Test of Visual-Motor Integration, 4th Edition, Revised.

Purpose: "Designed to assess the extent to which individuals can integrate their visual and motor abilities."
Population: Ages 3-0 to 17-11.
Publication Dates: 1967—1997.
Acronym: VMI.
Scores, 3: VMI, Visual, Motor.
Administration: Group.
Price Data: Available from publisher.
Time: Administration time not reported.
Authors: Keith E. Beery (test and manual) and Norman A. Buktenica (test).
Publisher: Modern Curriculum Press.
Cross References: See T5:815 (52 references); for reviews by Darrell L. Sabers and James E. Ysseldyke of the Third Revision, see 12:111 (25 references); see also T4:768 (42 references), 9:329 (15 references), and T3:701 (57 references); for reviews by Donald A. Leton and James A. Rice of an earlier edition, see 8:870 (24 references); see also T2:1875 (6 references); for a review by Brad S. Chissom of an earlier edition, see 7:867 (5 references).

Review of the Developmental Test of Visual-Motor Integration, 4ᵗʰ Edition, Revised by JAN VISSER, Assistant Professor of Kinesiology, Pennsylvania State University, State College, PA:

DESCRIPTION. According to the test manual "the Beery-Buktenica Developmental Test of Visual-Motor Integration (VMI) is a developmental sequence of geometric forms to be copied with paper and pencil. The purposes of the VMI are to help identify, through early screening, children who may need special assistance, to obtain needed services, to test the effectiveness of educational and other interventions, and to advance research" (manual, p. 5). Two versions of the test are available: an 18-item version for ages 3 to 7, and a 27-item version for use with preschool children through adults. The latter differs from the former only in that it contains an additional set of 9 more difficult items.

Two supplemental tests have been added to the 1997 edition of the VMI. These subtests, the VMI Visual Perception and the VMI Motor Coordination, use the same stimulus forms as the VMI and are used as follow ups to determine if a child experiences problems in the visual or motor domain, rather than in perceptual-motor integration. The Visual subtest measures the ability to recognize the geometric forms, whereas the Motor subtest measures the ability to trace the forms. In the Motor subtest, starting dots and double-lined paths are used as visual guides for the required motor performance to reduce visual perceptual demands. Despite the introduction of these subtests, the authors advise to use the existing clinical "Testing the Limits procedure" to meaningfully assess visual, motor, and other factors that may affect VMI performance.

Compared to the 1989 edition, two major changes have taken place. One is the use of a new, well-defined norm sample. This is a clear improvement as the norm samples in previous editions were very poorly described, making any comparison with normative data methodologically unsound. A second change is that the authors decided to revitalize the one-point-per-item scoring, which was used in all editions prior to 1989. In the 1989 edition a system of weighted scoring was used, with scores ranging from 1 to 4. Further changes include updated reports of important advances in the use of the VMI in recent years and the availability of standard scores at 2- and 4-month intervals for ages 3 to adults.

TEST COVERAGE AND USE. Basically, the VMI measures the coordination of visual perception and finger-hand movements. The actual purpose of the VMI goes far beyond the simple measurement of visual-motor integration, however. As stated in the manual, the identification of visual-motor difficulties indicates children who are at risk and in need of services of various kinds. These services include, but are not necessarily limited to, visual-motor intervention. The purpose of the test is grounded on perceptual-motor theories that state that higher levels of thinking and behavior require the ability to integrate sensory inputs and motor action. These ideas are supported by the correlations that have been found between form-copying and some forms of school and other successes, and it is believed that remediation of visual motor difficulties can improve academic achievement. There is a serious lack of scientific evidence supporting this notion, however. Although the authors acknowledge that

the supposed relationship between a remediation of visual-motor difficulties and later success in academic performance has not been proven and that automatic transfer does not usually occur, this belief is still one of the key elements underlying the purposes of the VMI.

NORMS. The norms of the 1996 version are based on a well-defined sample of 2,614 children from 3 through 17 years of age, representative of the 1990 U.S. Census. All reliability and validity measures presented are based on this sample. The norms should not be used to evaluate the scores of adults aged 18 and older.

RELIABILITY. A coefficient alpha of .82 and an odd-even split-half correlation of .88 indicate a sufficient level of internal consistency for the VMI.

Interrater reliabilities of .94 for the VMI, .98 for the Visual subtest, and .95 for the Motor subtest are given. These levels are surprisingly high, as an inspection of the examples of scored responses on VMI items suggests that decisions regarding the application of the scoring criteria are not at all straightforward. Neither the scorers' background and education level, nor their level of experience with the test is provided, which makes it somewhat difficult to interpret the interrater reliabilities. However, the authors explicitly state that experience is a major factor in the level of interrater reliability. Reliability studies based on previous norm samples indicate that interrater reliabilities over .90 are acquired after as little as 3 hours of preparation.

VALIDITY.

Construct validity. The main constructs that are thought to be related to test performance are: development, nonverbal intelligence, and academic achievement. Clear correlations with age have been found (R = .83, .75, and .74, for the VMI, the VMI Visual, and the VMI Motor, respectively), indicating that test performance is a function of development. Correlations with nonverbal intelligence (performance IQ, as measured with the Wechsler Intelligence Scale for Children—Revised [WISC-R] are .66, .58, and .55, respectively. Surprisingly, correlations with the verbal component of the WISC-R are also relatively high (.48, .43, and .41). Correlations with the Comprehensive Test of Basic Skills (CTBS) are .63, .29, and .40, indicating some relationship with academic performance.

Concurrent validity. A different way to look at construct validity is to compare the test with other instruments that measure similar constructs. Moderately high correlations have been found with the copying subtest of the Developmental Test of Visual Perception (DTVP-2) ($R = .75$) and the drawing subtest of the Wide Range Assessment of Visual Motor Abilities (WRAVMA) ($R = .52$).

Content validity. The item construction and selection procedures are clearly described. The items were selected after a review of the literature. As a second step, some items were discarded, and others were modified on the basis of studies on children's performance. It is unclear who made these decisions. Item analysis has indicated that the items differentiate between individuals.

Predictive validity. In combination with other measures, the test predicts achievement in school, such as reading ability. The manual does not state what the contribution of the VMI is in this prediction, however. Considering the alleged usefulness of the VMI as a predictive instrument, more information should be available on this point.

TEST ADMINISTRATION AND REPORTING. The manual clearly describes the requirements for test administration and interpretation. The user can choose from a vast number of ways to report the results. Apart from raw score, it is possible to use standard scores, scaled scores, stanines, percentiles, or age and grade equivalents. Also, a student's strengths and weaknesses can be presented in a profile.

TEST AND ITEM BIAS. Statistically significant differences have been found between different cultures and different socioeconomic groups. However, these differences were very small and accounted for only 1%–3% of the variance in the sample. No differences based on either gender or residence have been found.

SUMMARY. The VMI is a well-documented test of visual-motor integration, providing norms for children from ages 3 through 17. The test has good psychometric properties, with sufficient levels of reliability and validity. It is a valuable screening instrument for the measurement of problems in visual-motor integration. However, using the VMI with the intention to prevent or remediate academic failure is highly questionable.

Review of the Developmental Test of Visual-Motor Integration, 4th Edition, Revised by MAR-TIN J. WIESE, Licensed Psychologist/Certified School Psychologist, Lincoln Public Schools, Lincoln, NE:

The Developmental Test of Visual-Motor Integration (VMI), 4th Edition, Revised is the latest version of the VMI originally published in 1967. The VMI is a culture-free, developmental sequence of 24 geometric forms to be copied with paper and pencil and used to assess visual perception and motor coordination abilities (visual-motor integration). The manual defines visual-motor integration as "the degree to which visual perception and finger-hand movements are well coordinated" (manual, p. 19).

In addition to the 24 geometric designs to be copied, the VMI fourth edition now includes two supplemental tests, Visual perception and Motor Coordination. In the Visual Perception test, the child is required to select and point to one geometric form that is an exact match to a stimulus design. Pointing reduces the motor requirements of the task and focuses on the visual perception qualities of the task. In contrast, the Motor Coordination test requires the child to trace the stimulus forms with a pencil and provides information about the child's motor performance while reducing the visual perceptual demands of the task. It is not necessary to administer all three tests but if the examiner chooses to administer all three, it is important to follow the specified sequence: VMI, then the Visual Perception test, and finally the Motor Coordination test.

Scoring of the current edition of the VMI is somewhat simpler than with the third edition as each figure is scored pass or fail (one point or zero points). The fourth edition also adds an opportunity for children to imitate the first three designs if they are unable to successfully copy them from the model presented. The manual provides clear scoring criteria and numerous examples of correct scoring of each design. Both the Visual Perception and Motor Coordination tests are easily scored and examples of correct scoring are also provided. Tables are provided to convert the subject's raw scores to a standard score, scaled score, and percentile rank.

The demographic characteristics of the normative sample are clearly presented and include breakdowns by gender, ethnicity, geographic area, and age. A substantial effort was made to match the normative sample with U.S. Census information. The manual presents evidence for acceptable reliability (internal consistency, interscorer reliability, and test-retest reliability) of the VMI and the two supplemental tests. Evidence of the validity of scores is also presented and there exists strong support for adequate content validity, concurrent validity, construct validity, and predictive validity. A short section on teaching children how to improve visual-motor (handwriting) skills is also included.

SUMMARY. Compared to the Bender-Gestalt Test (T5:301), the VMI has the distinct advantage of a standardized administration procedure and a clearly described normative sample. The VMI also presents evidence of reliability whereas the Bender-Gestalt (Hutt, 1969, 1977, 1985) does not. In summary, the VMI is a well-constructed, technically adequate measure of a child's visual-motor skills.

REVIEWER'S REFERENCES

Hutt, M. L. (1969). The Hutt adaptation of the Bender-Gestalt Test (2nd ed.). New York: Grune and Stratton.
Hutt, M. L. (1977). The Hutt adaptation of the Bender-Gestalt Test (3rd ed.). New York: Grune and Stratton.
Hutt, M. L. (1985). The Hutt adaptation of the Bender-Gestalt Test: Rapid screening and intensive diagnosis (4th ed.). Orlando, FL: Grune and Stratton.

[120]
Devereux Scales of Mental Disorders.

Purpose: Constructed for "evaluating behaviors associated with psychopathology."
Population: Ages 5–12, 13–18.
Publication Dates: 1993–1996.
Acronym: DSMD.
Scores, 10: Conduct, Attention/Delinquency, Anxiety, Depression, Autism, Acute Problems, Internalizing Composite, Externalizing Composite, Critical Pathology Composite, Total.
Administration: Group or individual.
Forms, 2: Child Form, Adolescent Form.
Price Data, 1999: $170.50 per complete kit including manual ('94, 300 pages), and 25 ReadyScore™ answer documents for each Child Form and Adolescent Form; $52.50 per ReadyScore™ answer documents (specify form); $65.50 per manual; $205 per DSMD Scoring Assistant including user's guide ('96, 77 pages), 2 disks, 5 child's record forms, and 5 adolescent record forms.
Time: (15) minutes.
Comments: Revision of Devereux Child Behavior Rating Scale (T3:703) and Devereux Adolescent Behavior Rating Scale (T3:702); ratings by parents, teachers, or other professionals; Scoring Assistant available to provide narrative interpretive reports and other information.
Authors: Jack A. Naglieri, Paul A. LeBuffe, and Steven I. Pfeiffer.
Publisher: The Psychological Corporation.
Cross References: See T5:818 (1 reference).

Review of the Devereux Scales of Mental Disorders by COLIN COOPER, Senior Lecturer, School of Psychology, The Queen's University, Belfast, United Kingdom:

These scales are successors to the Devereux Child Behavior Rating Scale and the Devereux Adolescent Behavior Rating Scale, and are designed to assess psychopathological and behavioral problems in children and adolescents. There are two versions of the scales, one designed for use with children aged 5–12, and the other with adolescents aged 13–18. Each version consists of approximately 110 items describing problem behaviors, about 65% of which are common to both versions. Assessments are made by asking an individual who is familiar with the individual to rate how often each behavior has occurred during the previous month. Such ratings are made using a 5-point scale ranging from *never* to *very frequently*. The items in the children's version of the questionnaire are scored to produce measures of conduct problems, attentional problems, anxiety, depression, autism, and acute (psychotic) problems. The adolescent version produces scores on conduct-disorder, delinquency, anxiety, depression, autism, and acute problems. The conduct and attention/delinquency scales may also be combined to produce a composite score known as externalizing; combining the anxiety and depression yields an internalizing score, and combining the autism and acute-problem scales produces a critical pathology composite. A total pathology score may also be derived by summing standardized scores on the six primary scales.

The items in both of the questionnaires were derived from the earlier Devereux scales and by identifying behaviors associated with developmental psychopathology according to the DSM-III-R and DSM-IV criteria and other sources, including literature reviews and interviews with caregivers. Indeed, two substantial tables detail the precise diagnostic significance of each item according to DSM-III and DSM-IV. Thus, it certainly seems as though the items are relevant to psychopathology, providing evidence of the scales' content validity. Substantial tables of norms are derived from over 3,000 cases, carefully sampled so as to comprise a representative sample of the normal U.S. child and adolescent population. The test manual contains tables allowing test users to transform raw scores into *T*-scores and percentiles for the primary scales, and to transform the summed *T*-scores from the appropriate primary scales into *T*-scores and percentiles for the four derived scales.

Items were assigned to scales on the basis of exploratory factor analysis, but much detail is missing (including information about the size and composition of the sample). The scoring scheme for the Devereux Scales of Mental Disorders (DSMD) exactly reflects the salient loadings reported in the test manual and so it seems probable that the analysis reported in the test manual was the one that was used to assign items to scales. Thus, the test manual does not show whether the factor structure is replicable. One published study (Gimpel & Nagle, 1996) suggests that it is not—a conclusion that has implications for the discriminant validity of the scales. VARIMAX rotation was used, which is curious given that an attempt was then made to perform higher order confirmatory factor analyses on the scale scores, a procedure that only makes sense if the primary scales are intercorrelated.

The confirmatory factor analyses analyzed the covariances between the primary scale scores. Unfortunately, reports of these analyses lack vital detail, including any mention of exactly which models are being tested, the parameter estimates (factor loadings) that emerged, and the composition of the sample. Thus, it is impossible to comment on the quality of the composite scales. The only results that are presented from the confirmatory factor analysis are goodness-of-fit indices. Given what is now known about the relationship between the size of fit indices and sample size (Hu & Bentler, 1995) the authors may be a little optimistic when describing the fit of their models.

The internal-consistency reliability estimates of the scales are very high (over .9 for most of the six primary scales for each version of the questionnaire), but these may be artificially elevated for three reasons. First, no mention is made of the sample used to calculate the reliabilities. If it comprises the normative group plus the seriously behaviorally disturbed children whose scores are reported elsewhere in the manual, the within-group variation would be much larger than within the normal population, which would inflate coefficient alpha. Second, it is possible that age may act as a covariate. For example, all the young children may show low levels of the behaviors that form a particular scale, whereas many of the older children may show much higher levels (e.g., of swearing or running away from home). This will also elevate the apparent reliability of the scale. It is most surprising to find that the pathological implications of the various behaviors are assumed to be the same at all ages, for age is never considered when norming the scores. Finally, some of the items are highly similar in content. If a rater indicates that a child often has temper tantrums then this surely determines how the rater must respond to other items in the scale, such as "suddenly changes mood" or "becomes angry when frustrated." The items are not logically independent of each other, and this too will inflate coefficient alpha (Cooper, 1998).

There are two other potential problems with the rating format that have not been explored in the test manual. It is quite possible that the raters will use the scales consistently, but in different ways. When an assessor is asked to rate how often a child "has difficulty separating fact from fantasy," for example, should they do this with reference to other children of the same age? Or by comparing them with *all* children aged between 5–12? And if the assessor works with behaviorally disturbed children, should the comparison be made with reference to the other behaviorally disturbed children, or children in the general population? This may not affect the reliability of the scores, but could well influence their validity. A second problem concerns the attributional processes of the raters. A rater may believe, through their experiences of working with a child, that this individual is depressed, autistic, conduct-disordered, etc., and so may consciously or unconsciously distort their responses to the checklist items so as to over- or underestimate the prevalence of certain behaviors. It is noteworthy that the interrater reliabilities for the various scales (.44–.66) are very much lower than the internal consistency reliabilities. This seems to suggest that the raters are using the scales in different (but consistent) ways. There may be value in refining the instructions given to raters, making it clear what is meant by terms such as "rarely within the last four weeks," perhaps by using age-related guidelines and specifying the comparison group.

The validity studies clearly show that children and adolescents with various diagnoses of behavioral problems show extreme scores (often two or more standard deviations above the population mean) on the various scales of the Devereux checklist. The scales have diagnostic potential in that they can effectively discriminate between samples of normal and hospitalized children and adolescents, the accuracy of predictions typically being between 70% and 90%. The discriminant validity of the scales is less clear. Although those diagnosed as depressed, autistic, etc. do indeed have elevated scores on the appropriate DSMD scales, their scores on all the *other* scales are also elevated. Curiously, the manual does not appear to show the correlations between the primary scales.

SUMMARY. The items in the Devereux scales have obviously been carefully constructed, and the normative data have been painstakingly gathered. However, questions must arise about the need for age-related norms within each scale, and improved specification of how raters should use terms such as "rarely" when performing assessments, perhaps introducing age-related measures of frequency. The test is clearly able to discriminate between normal children and those with behavioral problems, but there are important unresolved issues concerning the factorial and discriminant validity of the scales.

REVIEWER'S REFERENCES

Hu, L., & Bentler, P. M. (1995). Evaluating model fit. In R. H. Hoyle (Ed.), *Structural equation modeling: Concepts, issues, and applications* (pp. 76–99). Thousand Oaks, CA: Sage Publications.

Gimpel, G. A., & Nagle, R. J. (1996). Factorial validity of the Devereux Behavior Rating Scale—School Form. *Journal of Psychoeducational Assessment, 14*, 334–348.

Cooper, C. (1998). Why many personality scales may be trivial. In J. Bermudez (Ed.), *Personality psychology in Europe* (pp. 33–39). Tilberg, Netherlands: Tilberg University Press.

Review of the Devereux Scales of Mental Disorders by CHARLES A. PETERSON, Staff Clinical Psychologist, Department of Veteran's Affairs, Minneapolis Medical Center, and Associate Clinical Professor of Psychology, University of Minnesota, Minneapolis, MN:

The Buros Institute "test[s] ... the tests" (Plake, n.d., p. 2), proudly encouraging, criticizing, and helping tests improve. Almost everybody—even the heaven-sent gaze of Oscar K. Buros himself—will be happier with the revised Devereux Scales of Mental Disorders (hereafter, DSMD). This is a decidedly improved version, collapsing the earlier Devereux Child Behavior Rating Scale (Spivack & Spotts, 1966; see T3:703) and the Devereux Adolescent Behavior Rating Scale (Spivack, Spotts, & Haimes, 1967; T3:702; see also *MMY* 13:96 for a review of the spin-off Devereux Behavior Rating Scale—School Version). This ambitious revision features one manual and two sets of items—one set for children 5–12 and the other for adolescents 13–18 with a 65% item overlap—incarnate on two "ready score" carbon-paper-backed answer sheets, the bottom sheet's grid facilitating scoring. Test language was updated, modernized, and purged of unacceptable content (e.g., no sexist language). Items, response format (from 7-point to 5-point scale), scoring, and interpretation were simplified. The items were further modified to heighten content validity and congruence with the categories in the *Diagnostic and Statistical Manual* (DSM-V; American Psychiatric Association, 1994). Finally, new reliability and validity data are presented to support the tests' use. The DSMD also benefits from an improved standardization sample, intended to be closely representative of the U.S. population.

Professionals using this scale will benefit from the consistent, objective approach to behaviors associated with psychopathology in children and adolescents within the ages of 5–18. The subject (i.e., the child or adolescent) does NOT take this test. His or her behavior is rated. On one side of the testing table, the authors first address the qualifications of "examiners," who are defined as the person who administers, scores, and interprets the results. Examiners should be familiar with developmental psychopathology, mental disorders, and, somewhat vaguely, "the use of normative data" (manual, p. 4). The latter is necessary but not sufficient and should include formal training in test construction and psychometrics. A "rehabilitation counselor" may not use the test in a manner as sophisticated and responsible as a clinical psychologist. The authors next address the qualifications of "raters," described as anyone with "sufficient exposure to the child or adolescent over the past four weeks" (manual, p. 5). Raters are mostly a bimodal group, typically parents or teachers, but could include counselors at a group home, vocational counselors, foster parents, and more. Raters must have a minimum sixth grade reading ability. Here sits an important question: Will an undertrained counselor at a group home rate behavior in a manner (acceptably) equivalent to a clinical psychologist on a residential treatment unit? Or, will ego-involved parents, enmeshed in family psychopathology, provide "accurate" ratings, or merely provide "their view" from within the undifferentiated ego mass (Bowen, 1976) of the family? The answer is "no" but the test does feature different norms for teachers and parents (cf. Fiske, 1971, for a careful discussion of how the relationship between observer and subject influences the ratings; in brief, different relationship to the subject equals different ratings). The data on different raters is a good example of the DSMD's fine attention to psychometric detail; the manual literally bulges with normative data. Internal reliability (alpha) is good, all hovering around .90, or higher. Test-retest reliability over a 24-hour period is also quite good, with most scores in the .80s or .90s. It is possible that the preceding values are artificially inflated by the very short time lapse between ratings. Interrater reliability is less favorable, with most correlation coefficients reported in the mid .40s or .50s; these scores were obtained comparing teachers and teachers' aides, perhaps likely to share similar perspectives. A more crucial test of interrater reliability—upon which we wait—would pair psychologists (who might suffer from procrustean overinterpretation) or teachers with parents across contexts (or how about comparing one parent's view with that of the other parent?). Males and females might also differ in their rating of different behaviors (e.g., aggression; cf. Rogers, 1995, for a discussion of various influences on raters and ratings).

Validity is also assessed on many levels. Content validity is good: The items show a strong congruence with DSM-IV criteria for the behavior under examination. Construct validity evidence is good, but it might be even better if the nomological net surrounding these variables were more carefully woven and articulated (Cronbach & Meehl, 1955). Principal components and confirmatory factor analyses lend support for the six component and the three composite scales (a cynic might argue that this factor solution is almost inevitable; cf. Eysenck, 1953; Peterson, 1965). Criterion-related validity evidence is persuasive (e.g., conduct disorders and attention-deficit-hyperactivity disorders are associated with the Externalizing composite scale; depressive and anxiety diagnoses are associated with the Internalizing composite scale and so on). Further, the DSMD was able to correctly classify roughly 77% of the children and adolescents according to intervention-setting (e.g., outpatient vs. residential, reflecting presumed level of severity).

Raw scores are transformed into T-scores; percentiles are accompanied by confidence intervals. The test produces factorially derived scales; factor retention was based both on size of the eigenvalue (presumably the "scree," too; cf. Cattell, 1966) and psychological/conceptual meaningfulness. The test output includes Conduct and Delinquent scores and a composite Externalizing score; Anxiety and Depression scores; Autism and Acute Problems scores and a composite Critical Pathology score, and finally, a Total Score. The differential elevations on different scales contribute to diagnosis and treatment planning. Caution is warranted here: No data are provided on the degree of relationship (correlation) among the different scales, making interpretation of individual scales a risky venture.

This test sits poised on the edge of the millennium, packing its own computer program, known as the "DSMD Scoring Assistant." This requires a PC with a processor rated at 386 or higher, 4MB of RAM, 1.4MB disk drive, 5MB of free space on the hard drive, Microsoft Windows version 3.1 or later, Microsoft MS-DOS operating system 5.1 or later. After this program is installed, one can enter and score profile sheets, print out reports of varying levels and purposes (e.g., single point or comparison assessments), and create databases. Although good help is hard to find, the manual accompanying the two disks is very readable and the computer program is reasonably user friendly; just in case, tech support is also available for the computer program. A narrative output summarizes the scale scores. Qualitative descriptions (e.g., "Very Elevated") may also be appended to the scores/scales. Similar to the Koss-Butcher (1973) MMPI critical items (although it is not clear whether in this instance the items were related to external criteria), a list of "problem items" is provided in the automated narrative for the psychometrically more risky analysis of individual items within trouble areas (e.g., "Self-Injury" or "Illegal Behavior"). The "Scoring Assistant" also provides a "DSM-IV Cluster Inquiry," which shows which keyed items indicate the possibility that the criteria for a DSM-IV diagnosis may have been met.

SUMMARY. The Devereux Scale of Mental Disorders was designed to identify psychopathology in children and adolescents from ages 5–18. This latest edition/revision is built upon careful psychometric work. The manual is replete with data upon which to base the interpretive work.

However, it must be noted that this revision is young and imperfect; problems persist. Some critics will object to the test's exclusive focus on problems, rather than healthy behaviors; however, the test is devoted to spelunking psychopathology and should not be criticized for what it did not intend. Problems with insufficient cross-context (home and school) interrater (teacher vs. parent vs. psychologist and more) reliability threaten the test's use. Further, inadequate data on the relationship among the various scales makes interpretation of differential scale elevations risky at the present time.

Recalling Freud's (1937) comments on the near impossibility for parents to be totally satisfied with their children, this test is imperfect, but still, an offspring of which both authors and publishers can be proud. To their credit, the test publishers give clarion call for psychometrically responsible use, reminding "examiners" to use the test in a manner consistent with the test's limits and the *Standards for Educational and Psychological Testing* (American Educational Research Association, American Psychological Association, & National Council on Measurement in Education, 1999), which inspire and shape our psychometric habits. Despite a few problems clamoring for attention in the next revision, this test mostly meets those lofty ideals.

REVIEWER'S REFERENCES

Freud, S. (1937/1964). Analysis terminable and interminable. In J. Strachey (Ed. & Trans.), *The standard edition of the complete psychological works of Sigmund Freud* (vol. 23, pp. 211–253). London: Hogarth (originally published 1937).

Eysenck, H. J. (1953). *The structure of human personality.* London: Methuen.

Cronbach, L. J., & Meehl, P. E. (1955). Construct validity in psychological tests. *Psychological Bulletin, 52,* 281–302.

Peterson, D. R. (1965). The scope and generality of verbally defined personality factors. *Psychological Review, 72,* 48–59.

Cattell, R. B. (1966). The scree test for the number of factors. *Multivariate Behavioral Research, 1,* 245–276.

Spivack, G., & Spotts, J. (1966). Devereux Child Behavior Rating Scale. Devon, PA: Devereux Foundation Press.

Spivack, G., Spotts, M. J., & Haimes, P. E. (1967). Devereux Adolescent Behavior Rating Scale. Devon, PA: Devereux Foundation Press.

Fiske, D. W. (1971). *Measuring the concepts of personality.* Chicago: Aldine.

Koss, M. P., & Butcher, J. N. (1973). A comparison of psychiatric patients' self-report with other sources of clinical information. *Journal of Research in Personality, 7,* 225–236.

Bowen, M. (1976). Theory in the practice of psychotherapy. In P. J. Guerin (Ed.), *Family therapy: Theory and practice* (pp. 42–90). New York: Halstead Press.

American Psychiatric Association. (1994). *Diagnostic and statistical manual of mental disorders* (4th ed.). Washington, DC: American Psychiatric Association.

Rogers, R. (1995). *Diagnostic and structured interviewing.* Odessa, FL: Psychological Assessment Resources.

American Educational Research Association, American Psychological Association, & National Council on Measurement in Education. (1999). *Standards for educational and psychological testing.* Washington, DC: American Educational Research search.

Plake, B. S. (n.d.) *Oscar and Luella Buros Center for Testing.* Unpublished manuscript.

[121]
The Differential Diagnostic Technique.

Purpose: "A projective drawing test" designed to "provide an indication of an individual's ego functioning and organization."

Publication Date: 1995.

Acronym: DDT.

Scores, 30: 6 scores (Personality Rigidity, Intellectual Control, Energy Output, Impulsiveness, Dissociation Summary) in 5 areas (Total-Area, H-Area, P-Area, H-P Area, Memory).

Administration: Group.

Forms, 2: Adult, Children's

Price Data, 1998: $35 per test (specify Adult or Children's form); $20 per scoring stencils; $10 per scoring charts; $50 per manual ('95, 135 pages).

Time: Untimed.

Authors: Otto Weininger and D. Barry Cook.

Publisher: Otto Weininger (the author).

a) DDT—ADULT FORM.

Population: Age 12 and over.

b) DDT—CHILDREN'S FORM.

Population: Ages 6–12 years.

Review of The Differential Diagnostic Technique by SANDRA A. LOEW, Assistant Professor, Counselor Education, University of North Alabama, Florence, AL:

The Differential Diagnostic Technique is a visual-motor projective test designed to assess ego functioning and organization. The test-taker copies 12 figures from stimulus cards that are shown individually then, after having drawn all of the figures, the cards are removed and the individual redraws them based on memory. There are four straight-line figures, four curved-line figures and four figures made up of straight and curved lines. Each group of figures comprises an area, with the straight-line figures in the area termed "hostility" (H), the curved-line figures termed "passivity" (P), and mixed figures termed "interpersonal" (HP) area. There are 26 qualities that are manifestations of ego control, loss of ego control, or emotional energy that is available to the compromise between ego control and loss of ego control. Those factors fit into the five categories of Personality Rigidity (PR), Intellectual Control (IC), Impulsiveness (IMP), Dissociation (DIS), and Energy Output (EO). The categories of Personality Rigidity and Intellectual Control symbolize the area of ego control, and Impulsiveness and Dissociation are indicative of loss of ego control, whereas Energy Output is related to the emotional energy available to the individual. To obtain a control score (C), the PR and IC scores are added together, and the sum of IMP and DIS provides a loss of control score (LC). Subtracting the LC in each area from the C in each area provides a Control Index (CI). To determine the Differential Index of Control (DI), which is an indication of the core pattern of personality defenses, the CI of P is algebraically subtracted from the CI of H. The Total Index of Control (TI) or the CI for the Total area is an indication of the efficiency functioning of the test-taker.

The totals are recorded in a histogram that provides a picture or "psychogram" in each of the areas. The categories (PR, IC, IMP, DIS, EO) are on the vertical axis and the areas (hostility, passivity, interpersonal, total, and memory) are on the horizontal axis. This provides the scorer with a graphic description of the five categories in each of the five areas.

The administration instructions for the instrument are very clear and easy to follow. There is no time limit to the testing and it can be administered in a group or individually. Several sheets of blank paper, sharpened pencils with no erasers and a smooth writing surface, in addition to the stimulus cards, are the required testing materials. Although the scoring instructions are more difficult to understand, there are examples of figures in each section to explain the concepts being evaluated. For instance, in evaluating the arrangement of the figures on the paper, there are a number of examples that show possible arrangements such as methodical, logical, etc. The scoring section of the manual is arranged beginning with the factors that do not require stencils followed by the factors requiring stencils. "Harmony" is a factor that is scored based on the scoring of other factors that follow in the manual. It seems to have been placed out of logical sequence and the scorer must refer back to that section after scoring other factors. The scoring is complicated but becomes easier with each subsequent administration of the test.

The manual provides no statement indicating the population for which this measure was designed, nor is there a clear statement of recommended use. Therefore, it is difficult to know when The Differential Diagnostic Technique is an appropriate measure and what would constitute inappropriate applications. One may deduce from the name of this instrument that this might be a useful measure for a clinical population; however, there is limited information to determine age range or any other factors that might impact the outcome of the assessment. Clinicians and researchers should not have to make presumptions about the appropriateness of instruments that they might purchase.

Weininger (1989) reported that this assessment was used to compare mothers of children with autism with mothers with normal children, to assess learning disabled children, and to assess mothers in infant stimulation groups. He also found personality organization as measured by The Differential Diagnostic Technique a "useful index" for "predicting frequency and duration of containment" (p. 64) for adolescents in residential treatment.

Weininger, Erdman, and Ammons (1993) found this to be useful in treatment planning for young offenders, suggesting that the information garnered from this assessment would indicate the ability of the offender to engage in a therapeutic relationship, and the youth's need for a structured environment. Additional information is available in unpublished manuscripts; nevertheless, this information is not in the manual and not helpful to someone trying to determine if this would be a useful investment.

Having no information on the population on which this instrument was normed makes it impossible to know if this is a useful instrument for any particular setting or population. The manual provides no information concerning validity or reliability so the user has no way of knowing if this instrument assesses what it purports to assess, and if it does so consistently.

In summary, The Differential Diagnostic Technique is a visual-motor projective test that may be useful in treatment planning for adolescents in residential treatment. However, the manual does not provide any information on norming, validity, and reliability so a professional cannot use this instrument responsibly or make ethical decisions concerning this instrument without this information. Therefore, there is no justification for purchasing The Differential Diagnostic Technique at this time.

REVIEWER'S REFERENCES

Weininger, O. (1989). The Differential Diagnostic Technique: A visual-motor projective test: Further research. *Psychological Reports, 65*, 64–66.
Weininger, O., Erdman, J. E., & Ammons, W. J. (1993). Further research on personality organization using The Differential Diagnostic Technique. *Psychological Reports, 73*, 1247–1250.

[122]
Digit Vigilance Test.

Purpose: Designed to measure vigilance during rapid visual tracking and accurate selection of target stimuli.
Population: Ages 17–80.
Publication Date: 1995.
Acronym: DVT.

Scores, 2: Total Time, Total Errors.
Administration: Individual.
Forms, 2: 6s, 9s.
Price Data, 1996: $45 per introductory kit including Professional User's Guide (12 pages), 25 test booklets, and set of 4 scoring templates; $13 per Professional User's Guide; $21 per 25 test booklets; $21 per set of 4 scoring keys.
Time: (10) minutes.
Author: Ronald F. Lewis.
Publisher: Psychological Assessment Resources, Inc.

Review of the Digit Vigilance Test by RAYMOND S. DEAN, Director, and SCOTT KRISTIAN HILL, Co-Director, Neuropsychology Laboratory, Ball State University, Muncie, IN:

The Digit Vigilance Test (DVT) is part of the Repeatable Cognitive Perceptual Motor (RCPM) Battery (Lewis & Rennick, 1979). The RCPM was developed to measure subtle changes in neuropsychological status and purports to be robust to practice and repeated administrations. According to the Professional User's Guide that accompanies the instrument, the DVT was designed to assess psychomotor speed, visual-motor tracking, and visual attention while minimizing the influence of attentional components such as selectivity and processing capacity. Specifically, subjects are asked to scan two pages of numbers and cross out every 6 (9s are used for the alternate form). Scores are calculated for Total Time, errors of commission, omission, and Total Errors. Lewis (the author of the test and of the Professional User's Guide) does not provide recommended age limits for the DVT. Rather, the reader may infer the intended age range from references to normative data published elsewhere. These references contain norms on two adult samples: ages 20 to 80 (Heaton, Grant, & Matthews, 1991) and 17 to 79 years (Lewis, Kelland, & Kupke, 1990).

The materials are simple and straightforward. The test manual/guide is brief and provides details regarding materials, qualifications for examiners, administration, and scoring. Examiners with limited experience should have little difficulty learning the administration and scoring of the measure. However, norms for the DVT are provided in two separate publications (Heaton, Grant, & Matthews, 1991; Lewis, Kelland, & Kupke, 1990). Derivation of scaled scores and *T*-scores can prove rather inconvenient for consumers who do not have these publications in their libraries. Raw scores are converted to scaled scores, which are then converted to *T*-scores.

Although the DVT is purported to be sensitive to frontal lobe function, Lewis cautions against such interpretations until such a relationship has been empirically validated. On the other hand, Lewis asserts that the DVT is better suited to detect change in neuropsychological status associated with clinical or psychopharmacological interventions. The standardization sample included 280 individuals aged 20 to 80 years; however, the user's guide is unclear regarding the age range of this sample. Participants denied a history of neurologic, psychiatric, or other disorders that might affect performance. When poor performance is thought to be a pathognomonic indicator of CNS dysfunction the use of normal nonimpaired participants for standardization is not uncommon in neuropsychology. However, examination of the normative data revealed that nearly 14% of the standardization sample performed in the impaired range. This may result in false positives as only 5% to 8% of the general population would be expected to exhibit neuropsychological impairment. Norms for the scaled scores utilize the entire sample whereas more precise conversions for *T*-scores are based on age and education. Again, the conversion tables and normative information are found outside the Professional User's Guide. The 10 age and 6 education ranges result in a total of 60 groups with an average of less than 5 individuals in each group, which questions the reliability of scoring.

The DVT is accompanied by a Professional User's Guide rather than a manual. This document is very brief and lacks appropriate detail for evaluation and utilization of the measure without additional references. However, the guide cites a number of studies that shed some light on the psychometric properties of the measure. A review of the pertinent literature demonstrated the DVT to be psychometrically sound. Kelland and Lewis (1996) provided test-retest reliability estimates of the Total Time score to be high for a one-week interval (on both forms and Page 1 times) and moderate for the Total Errors score and Page 1 errors. Kelland and Lewis also reported practice effects between two trials given in the same session but not with a third session one week later. The three trials over two sessions were used to determine both the reliability and practice effects. However, it is unclear the length of the delay between the first two trials and which scores were used for the reliability analysis. The inclusion of these in the guide would be most helpful to the user.

In support of the predictive validity of the measure Lewis stated in the user's guide that the DVT significantly discriminated between differing stages of HIV infections and placebo/diazepam conditions. However, no information was provided regarding the other variables included, the relative contribution of the DVT to the discriminant, or the accuracy of group prediction. Additional support for the validity of the DVT, presented in the guide, comes from the observation of mean differences between normal controls and hypoxemic patients using Total Time (Prigatano, Parsons, Wright, Levin, & Hawryluk, 1983). Prigatano et al. showed the Total Errors score to be less useful in discriminating and is unrelated to speed. Consequently, Lewis cautions against using it for diagnostic or research purposes and recommends qualitative interpretation of errors only when an unusual number of omission or commission errors are demonstrated.

Construct validity of the DVT was supported through factor analysis of the RCPM (Lewis et al., 1990) and is presented in the Professional User's Guide. The Total Time score loaded highest on a factor reflecting speed of information processing. Concurrent validity was estimated by zero-order correlations with other measures seen as sensitive to psychomotor speed (Trails B of the Halstead-Reitan Battery and Digit Symbol of the Wechsler Adult Intelligence Scale [WAIS]). However, DVT Total Time was not significantly correlated with a measure of sustained attention and discriminant reaction time (Kelland & Lewis, 1996). Thus, as purported the DVT appears to be more sensitive to psychomotor speed or speed of information processing than attentional components or reaction time.

SUMMARY. The DVT was designed to be a measure of psychomotor speed, visual attention, and visual-motor tracking. However, recent research supports the Total Time score as a measure of psychomotor speed component. The standardization sample appears appropriate for scaled scores but the ratio of subjects to groups and the relatively high proportion of the standardization sample that performed in the impaired range leads one to question the utility of the age- and education-corrected *T*-scores. Nevertheless, research indi-

cated scores from the DVT to be reliable and it has demonstrated adequate validity despite methodological flaws in several of the validation studies. Although the DVT may be useful in monitoring the effects of clinical and/or pharmacological treatment, it is our impression that this measure is more of a clinical instrument than a standardized measure. Moreover, the manual or in this case the Professional User's Guide is extremely brief and lacking numerous details regarding psychometrics, validity research, and normative information necessary for interpretation of the measure. Regardless, one important question remains unanswered, why is the DVT being published individually rather than as part of the RCPM?

REVIEWERS' REFERENCES

Lewis, R. F., & Rennick, P. M. (1979). *Manual for the Repeatable Cognitive-Perceptual-Motor Battery.* Grosse Pointe Park, MI: Axon Publishing.

Prigatano, G. P., Parsons, O., Wright, E., Levin, D. C., Hawryluk, G. (1983). Neuropsychological test performance in mildly hypoxemic patients with chronic obstructive pulmonary disease. *Journal of Consulting and Clinical Psychology, 51,* 108–116.

Lewis, R. F., Kelland, D. Z., & Kupke, T. (1990). A normative study of the Repeatable Cognitive-Perceptual-Motor Battery. *Archives of Clinical Neuropsychology, 5,* 187

Heaton, R. K., Grant, I., & Matthews, C. G. (1991). *Comprehensive norms for an expanded Halstead-Reitan Battery: Demographic corrections, research findings, and clinical applications.* Odessa, FL: Psychological Assessment Resources.

Kelland, D. Z., & Lewis, R. F. (1996). The Digit Vigilance Test: Reliability, validity, and sensitivity to diazepam. *Archives of Clinical Neuropsychology, 11*(4), 339–344.

Review of the Digit Vigilance Test by DANIEL C. MILLER, Associate Professor of Psychology, Texas Woman's University, Denton, TX:

PURPOSE. "The Digit Vigilance Test (DVT) is a paper-and-pencil task designed to measure vigilance during rapid tracking and accurate election of target stimuli. The task appears to isolate alertness and vigilance and to place minimal demands on the selectivity and capacity components of attention" (user's guide, p. 3). The author suggests that the DVT test is often administered as part of a Repeatable Cognitive Perceptual Motor Battery (RCPM; Lewis & Rennick, 1979) but it is being marketed as a stand-alone instrument. The DVT requires no special training to be administered and can be completed in approximately 10 minutes. The examinee is presented with a sheet filled with 59 rows of 35 single digits and asked to cross out each occurrence of a target number (e.g., 6) as quickly as possible. Completion time and (omissions + commissions) errors across two sheet of numbers serve as the scores for the test.

The Professional User's Guide that accompanies the test is inadequate. The author reports that the DVT was standardized on two adult samples: (a) ages 20–80 years (Heaton, Grant, & Matthews, 1991) and (b) ages 17–79 years (Lewis, Kelland, & Kupke, 1990). A serious limitation of the DVT is that the test cannot be scored using the author's administration manual. To determine standard score conversions for adults ages 20–80, the test user must purchase a separate publication, the Heaton et al. (1991) norms, from the same publisher. For the 17–19-year-olds, means and standard deviations for the Total Time and Errors of omission are included in the administration manual, however; there is no conversion table for standard scores for this age group. Another major concern is related to the fact that only the mean and standard deviation for the errors of omission are reported in the DVT administration manual for the 17–19-year-old norm group, which is not the correct information required to score the test. Standard scores are to be reported for the total time and the total number of omission errors plus the total number of commission errors, not just the total number of omission errors.

The author reports that the DVT was developed as a component of the RCPM battery. Even though the DVT is being marketed as a stand-alone test the samples used for test validation and norming are not described in the DVT manual. To determine the adequacy of the standardization and norming sample, the user would have to purchase an additional publication, the RCPM manual (Lewis & Rennick, 1979) from a different publisher. The DVT test author provides no justification or empirical support for using the test as a stand-alone instrument rather than a part of the larger RCPM test battery as it was originally standardized.

The reliability of the DVT was addressed in the administration manual. In one unpublished study, test-retest reliability coefficients, within a one-week interval (n = 40), were .91 for Total Time, .80 for Page 1 Time, .66 for Total Errors, and .61 for Page 1 Errors. Alternative forms reliability (n = 20) coefficients were .90 for Total Time and .93 for Page 1 Time. These results included no specifics on the demographic characteristics of the subjects; thus generalizability of these reliability estimates is difficult. At best, the DVT Total Time may be a stable measure over a brief period of time, but the stability of the error score is suspect. The author reported that the DVT has practice effects from the first to second

trial, but that the effect diminished thereafter. Researchers and clinicians using the DVT as a pre-post test should be cautious in interpreting performance changes without controlling for these reported practice effects.

Several validity studies were reported in the administration manual. Two studies were reported to investigate the construct validity of the DVT that demonstrated the adverse effect of a single clinical dose of diazepam on the DVT time score. Principal component analysis with a sample of 202 normal volunteers yielded a two-factor solution and accounted for 65% of the total test variance. The first factor was thought to represent speed of information processing and the second was thought to represent simpler motor function. Several predictive validity studies were also reported. Differences in Total Test Time were found in several clinical groups including mildly hypoxemic. COPD patients, multiple sclerosis patients, insulin-dependent diabetes mellitus patients, and patients with early stages of HIV infection.

SUMMARY. The DVT in its present stand-alone form appears to be inadequate. In a major oversight, the Professional User's Guide does not provide norm tables to score the test. Users of the test would have to purchase one or two more manuals in order to find the appropriate norms based on the age of the subject. Preliminary evidence is provided for the reliability and validity of scores from the test, however; clinicians and researchers using the DVT for test-retest changes must be concerned about the reported practice effects. The DVT has the potential to be a valuable measure of vigilance but all of the test validation and standardization data along with expanded psychometric properties need to be reported in a single administration manual.

REVIEWER'S REFERENCES

Lewis, R. F., & Rennick, P. M. (1979). *Manual for the Repeatable Cognitive Perceptual Motor Battery*. Grosse Point Park, MI: Axon Publishing.

Lewis, R. F., Kelland, D. Z., & Kupke, T. (1990). A normative study of the Repeatable Cognitive-Perceptual-Motor Battery. *Archives of Clinical Neuropsychology, 5*, 201.

Heaton, R. K., Grant, I., & Matthews, C. G. (1991). *Comprehensive norms for the expanded Halstead-Reitan Battery: Demographic corrections, research findings, and clinical applications*. Odessa, FL: Psychological Assessment Resources, Inc.

[123]
Dimensions of Excellence Scales [1991 Edition].

Purpose: Designed to identify, describe and validate successful programs and practices of a school district, as well as to forecast future needs.

Population: Schools or districts.
Publication Dates: 1988–1990.
Acronym: DOES.
Administration: Group.
Price Data;, 1998: $2 per school staff survey; $1.25 per parent survey; $1.25 per student survey; $23.95 per manual ('90, 71 pages).
Comments: Ratings by students, parents, and school staff.
Authors: Russel A. Dusewicz and Francine S. Beyer.
Publisher: Research for Better Schools, Inc.

a) STUDENT SCALE.
Scores: 4 dimensions: School Climate, Teacher Behavior, Monitoring and Assessment, Student Discipline and Behavior.
Time: (30) minutes.

b) PARENT SCALE.
Scores, 8: Same as *a* above plus Leadership, Curriculum, Staff Development, Parent Involvement.
Time: (20–30) minutes.

c) SCHOOL STAFF SCALE.
Scores, 8: Same as *b* above.
Time: (45) minutes.

Cross References: For reviews by Janet F. Carlson and William P. Erchul of an earlier edition, see 11:112.

Review of the Dimensions of Excellence Scales [1991 Edition] by ANDREW A. McCONNEY, Associate Research Professor, Teaching Research Division, Western Oregon University, Monmouth, OR:

The Dimensions of Excellence Scales (DOES) consist of three survey instruments (i.e., School Staff, Parent, and Student) that assess perceptions on eight dimensions suggested as important for K–12 school effectiveness. The eight dimensions are School Climate, Leadership, Teacher Behavior, Curriculum, Monitoring and Assessment, Student Discipline and Behavior, Staff Development, and Parent Involvement. The DOES was developed "to assist local education agencies in gathering reliable information about their schools' performance in their effort to diagnose problems, identify strengths, and improve school operations" (manual, p. 1).

Both Research for Better Schools (RBS) and Harford County Public Schools (MD) staff wrote the initial pool of DOES items. All survey items are 5-point Likert-type with the anchors *almost always* to *almost never*. The School Staff scale consists of 200 items, and the other two scales (Parents and Students) were developed on the basis of this item pool. The Parent scale has 71 items and the Student scale 44 items covering four of the eight dimensions thought most appropriate to students. A total of 26 schools participated in the field test of the DOES in 1985 and 1986.

Three groups of issues impact the quality and potential usefulness of the DOES. These concerns are unchanged from those noted in two previous reviews of the DOES that appear in the 11th edition of the *Mental Measurements Yearbook* (Carlson, 1992; Erchul, 1992). Perhaps this is because the initial development and field testing of the DOES was conducted under the auspices of RBS during the time that agency received federal support from the U.S. Department of Education's Office of Educational Research and Improvement (OERI) as the mid-Atlantic regional educational laboratory. RBS no longer serves as a regional lab although it currently operates the Mid-Atlantic Eisenhower Consortium for Mathematics and Science Education.

VALIDITY. Most critically, the validity of the DOES, although seemingly promising, is as yet undetermined. The DOES authors report that Harford County school staff in conjunction with RBS staff constructed the initial item pool and that the eight dimensions and component items are grounded in school effectiveness research. The authors further note that content validity is the most important type of validity for the scales. The problem is that no reference list or bibliography is provided to let readers or users know what research underlies the scales. Therefore, it is not possible from the supporting information provided to know whether the content of the survey items is aligned with the content of a reasonably comprehensive or reputable body of research on school effectiveness. On the face of it, the items in the three scales do appear reasonable and could be assumed related to school effectiveness. It would, however, strengthen the authors' case for the validity of the scales if they were to provide a bibliography of the research to which they refer, and perhaps specific references that relate to or support each indicator, or at least each dimension of school effectiveness.

Related to this issue, the DOES was developed and field tested in the late 1980s, and without subsequent revision could not have taken consideration of a more recent and growing body of research that addresses school reform and improvement (e.g., Hargreaves, 1997). For example, the substantial literature on recent standards-based school reform is not reflected in the scales, and school leaders may find the DOES somewhat dated with respect to the focus of their current efforts in school improvement.

RELIABILITY. The reliability of the scales remains in question. Only measures of internal consistency (Cronbach's alpha) are reported, and only for one of the three scales (School Staff). Although the alphas reported are high, this indicates only that the items that comprise each of the eight dimensions are consistent with each other, that is, measure the same construct in the view of school staff. The authors should also report reliability estimates for the other two scales (Parents and Students), as it is less than acceptable to assume that estimates of internal consistency would be similarly high for the two considerably shorter scales. Further, estimates of scale stability (test-retest) would be helpful in gauging the consistency of the DOES, particularly if related to other assessments of school change or effectiveness. Stability estimates, particularly in relationship to other measures of school effectiveness, would also bolster the authors' implied case for the criterion-related validity of the DOES. At present, we have no way of knowing whether the instruments accurately diagnose areas of needed school improvement, or whether they accurately gauge school change or program success.

Similarly, the characteristics of the norm group of schools that field tested the DOES in 6 and 1985 are not reported. School demographics and some description of what the DOES revealed in terms of school effectiveness, along with subsequent changes in the schools, would help potential users determine the applicability of the scales for their own situations, as well as potentially strengthen the case for the validity of the DOES.

OPPORTUNITY TO OBSERVE. Many authorities on the construction of survey instruments have noted that scale developers should take great care in providing items that respondents will have had the opportunity to directly observe or experience (e.g., Thorndike, Cunningham, Thorndike, & Hagen, 1991). Alternatively, if respondents' opportunities to observe are in question, the scales should provide the option for respondents to answer "cannot say" or "not observed." As noted previously by Carlson (1992) the omission of such an option is "troubling" (p. 284). This is particularly so for items in the Parent scale

such as "school leaders perform staff evaluations on a regular basis" or "teachers give positive feedback to every student," and items in the Student scale such as "the superintendent visits my school and is interested in what we do in school" or "the teachers are fair in grading all students."

SUMMARY. The DOES is a potentially useful set of survey instruments for diagnosing needs as well as gauging school improvement efforts from the perspective of school staff, parents, and students. However, the reliability and validity of scores from the DOES remain in question, and the scales may now be somewhat dated as they will not have taken into account a large body of recent research on school reform and improvement.

REVIEWER'S REFERENCES

Thorndike, R. M., Cunningham, G. K., Thorndike, R. L., & Hagen, E. P. (1991). *Measurement and evaluation in psychology and education* (5th ed.). New York: Macmillan.

Carlson, J. F. (1992). [Review of the Dimensions of Excellence Scales.] In J. J. Kramer & J. C. Conoley (Eds.), *The eleventh mental measurements yearbook* (p. 284). Lincoln, NE: Buros Institute of Mental Measurements.

Erchul, W. P. (1992). [Review of the Dimensions of Excellence Scales.] In J. J. Kramer & J. C. Conoley (Eds.), *The eleventh mental measurements yearbook* (p. 285). Lincoln, NE: Buros Institute of Mental Measurements.

Hargreaves, A. (Ed.) (1997). *ASCD yearbook: Rethinking educational change with heart and mind.* Alexandria, VA: Association for Supervision and Curriculum Development.

[124]
The Diversity Management Survey.

Purpose: To determine how the structural components of an organization's inner workings contribute to the effective management of diversity in the workplace.

Population: Business managers and workers.

Publication Date: 1995.

Acronym: DMS.

Scores, 8: Strategies, Structures, Systems, Style, Skills, Staffing, Shared Values, Total.

Administration: Group.

Price Data, 1995: $3.95 or less per survey (volume discounts available) including Consulting Guide to Administration and Implementation (31 pages).

Time: (20) minutes.

Comments: Self-administered, self-scored.

Author: Cresencio Torres.

Publisher: Human Resource Development Press.

[Editor's Note: The publisher advised in October 1998 that this test is now out of print.]

Review of The Diversity Management Survey by RICHARD HARDING, Director of Research, Kanexa Corporation, Lincoln, NE:

The Diversity Management Survey (DMS) has, as a purpose, "to help determine how the structural components of an organization's inner workings contribute to the effective management of diversity in the workplace" (manual, p. 1).

The Survey is intended to be administered to managers and employees in an organization. The information collected is to be utilized by people within an organization whose responsibilities include managing diversity in the workplace (e.g., human resource personnel, consultants, managers, and people who do training within the organization).

The Survey is composed of 21 statements that are spread equally across seven variables. The seven variables are referred to as the Opportunity Model based on the McKinsey 7-S framework. The seven variables are Strategies, Structures, Systems, Style, Skills, Staffing, and Shared Values. Each statement is keyed to one of these seven variables, yielding three statements per variable. The administration of the DMS can be done on an individual or group basis, and respondents have 20 minutes to complete the DMS. Additionally, there are two open ended questions that people are asked to answer. The 21 statements are rated on a 5-point scale, from *Strongly Disagree* to *Strongly Agree*.

The validity of scores from the DMS was studied through a content validity effort, utilizing the judgment of managers, workers, and organizational development specialists. These individuals were administered the DMS and then asked to answer questions about the DMS. These questions ranged from how well the DMS addressed diversity issues, how easy the DMS was to read and understand, and whether the DMS can be used effectively to assess diversity management issues.

There were five questions used in evaluating the DMS, and the only validity evidence listed is the mean scores for those five questions for the "yes" responses. Five organizational development specialists were asked to evaluate the definitions of each of the seven variables and whether the statements within each of the categories accurately described the variable being measured. One other attempt to investigate validity was referenced in the brief manual. This involved 150 managers and employees in both government and private business. How many organizations were represented was not given, nor were any other demographic data made available on this sample. The group was given the DMS and then asked to respond to the five evaluation questions: Their mean scores to the

five questions ranged from .71 to .86 (Yes responses). No data were presented on the actual DMS items.

Many questions remain about the validity of scores from the DMS. For example, how were the questions derived? Were there any empirical methods for assigning statements to one of the seven variables? Were other statements tested, etc., and were there any other empirically derived measures collected at the item or variable level?

There are many concerns about the statements and what they are actually measuring. Specifically, there are several statements included that would be very difficult for any employee to know, including the term "all employees" (Survey, p. 7), thus casting shadows on the interpretation of the statement. Others are double-barreled statements where it seemed as if they would have provided cleaner information had they been split into two statements. The wording on some of the statements was very difficult to understand, much less provide a valid response. The above raises questions about the viability of the statements, the variables, and the interpretation and usefulness of the collected data.

A section on scoring the DMS is included, with three score ranges being suggested. A low score indicates the variable may be "creating a barrier" (manual, p. 19) to the diversity efforts of an organization; a moderate score maintains the status quo; and a high score supports the management of diversity in the organization. How these score ranges were derived was not included in the manual. Based upon the scores received by each of the items within the Survey, one can then go to the intervention options section in the manual and select an activity or an intervention that can be used in an effort to raise a low score. Some of the interventions seemed very straightforward and could help the organization to reach its diversity goals, but some seemed to be of limited value and extremely difficult to implement.

SUMMARY. Caution should be applied in the use of the DMS. Reliability and validity information is virtually nonexistent. The statements are of dubious quality, difficult to understand, and double-barreled. Much more information is needed about the use of this Survey in organizations. Basic issues, such as reliability and validity, should be addressed. In addition, more study should be given to the usefulness of the Survey in meeting diversity goals and/or increasing the diversity within an organization through using this Survey. Another basic question to be answered is, how practical and relevant are the 21 interventions suggested? Given all these unknowns, this reviewer would have a difficult time recommending the DMS for use.

Review of The Diversity Management Survey by GEORGE C. THORNTON III, Professor of Psychology, Colorado State University, Fort Collins, CO:

The Diversity Management Survey (DMS) is currently (October 1998) out of print and the publisher has no plans to reprint the survey. In addition, virtually no information about the test was found beyond a brief and inadequate manual, even after correspondence with the author and publisher and after extensive computer and manual searches for relevant documents. Nevertheless, some readers may have used the survey or may be contemplating designing a comparable instrument. Thus, this review will describe the content of the DMS, the limitations of the current questionnaire and manual, and suggestions for improvement.

The DMS was designed to determine how several features of an organization might contribute to the effective management of diversity at work. It consists of three statements for each of seven organizational variables listed above alleged to contribute to organizational effectiveness. No evidence is provided to support the contention that these factors are important, or that the specific statements under each factor are theoretically or empirically related to organizational effectiveness, member satisfaction, or any other index of effectiveness in managing diversity.

Examples of statements for selected scales include: "My organization's vision of the future includes valuing cultural differences in the workplace" (Strategies); "My organization makes sure that women and minorities are placed in visible positions, e.g., line management, planning groups, or special task forces" (Systems); "In my organization, men and women feel that valuing diversity is an important part of the organizational culture" (Shared Values). All are quite reasonable statements to be sure, but there is no evidence to demonstrate that the items in the scales are related to each other (e.g., coefficient alpha), or that the scales are independent of each other or related to any organizational outcome.

Respondents evaluate the organization on a 5-point scale from *Strongly Disagree* to *Strongly Agree*. A scoring sheet is provided in each survey booklet to add up scores for the three items in a scale and then to total all seven subscores. Subscores ranging from 3–6 are considered Low (this factor is a barrier), 7–9 is Moderate (this pattern maintains the status quo), and 10–15 is High (indicating support for the management of diversity). These designations appear completely arbitrary. The manual includes no norms to show if groupings are appropriate or to provide information to interpret the meaning of scale scores.

The guide to administration and interpretation of the survey provides no data to support its reliability or validity. The guide provides only very brief descriptions of the origin of the instrument, difficulties organizations may face in managing diversity, and something called the McKinsey model of opportunity, which displays the seven areas covered by the survey. No references to any other sources are provided.

One short section titled "validity" describes a survey of managers who agreed with such questions as "Does the DMS address diversity issues in your organization?" and "Is the DMS easy to read and understand?" Another survey of five unspecified organizational development specialists agreed with the definitions and the appropriateness of the statements for each variable. Such endorsements are nice but hardly the level of evidence of validity contemplated by any professional standards for supporting the validity of any test.

SUMMARY. The dearth of evidence does not comply with even minimal standards expected of test authors or publishers. Before anyone could endorse the use of the DMS, one would insist on more data to support any inferences from scores on the questionnaire for any practical use in an organizational setting.

Future survey developers may learn from the fledgling efforts displayed in this survey. The content could be matched more clearly to variables found to be relevant to successful diversity management efforts established in theory or empirical research studies. The issues facing organizations in the management of diversity involving different groups of special populations, such as women, Hispanics, workers from different countries, and older workers could be incorporated into the survey. Basic normative data should be collected and reported from different groups of individuals for the perceptions of organizations' diversity management efforts. It is certainly reasonable to expect differences in points of view from managers versus staff members, men versus women, minorities versus majority group members. Such differences could be displayed in norm tables to foster better interpretation of scores. Basic psychometric evidence of reliability (e.g., indices of homogeneity and stability) and validity (e.g., evidence that ratings of these structural variables are accurate measures of organizational reality) should be reported.

Unfortunately, the DMS provides no such data and we are left with the frustrating situation of not knowing anything about the quality of this instrument. We can only hope that someone might use this primitive instrument as a stimulant to develop and evaluate some method for assessing the quality of diversity management efforts in organizations.

[125]
Domestic Violence Inventory.

Purpose: "Designed specifically for risk and needs assessment of people who have committed physical, emotional and verbal abuse."
Population: Ages 12–18, adults.
Publication Dates: 1991–1995.
Acronym: DVI.
Scores: 6 scales: Truthfulness, Violence, Alcohol, Drugs, Control, Stress Coping Ability.
Administration: Group.
Forms, 2: Adult, Juvenile.
Price Data: Available from publisher.
Time: (30) minutes.
Comments: Available in English and Spanish; both computer version and paper-pencil format are scored on IBM-PC compatibles.
Author: Risk & Needs Assessment, Inc.
Publisher: Risk & Needs Assessment, Inc.

Review of the Domestic Violence Inventory by CAROL COLLINS, Family Counseling and Research Center, Caldwell, ID:

The Domestic Violence Inventory (DVI) is a 155-question self-report instrument designed to measure the risk of committing domestic violence and to assess treatment needs. The publisher suggests the inventory would be helpful in evaluating violence prone offenders, alcohol or drug abusers, and the emotionally disturbed. The six separate scales produce truth-corrected scores in which the amount of error variance associated with untruthfulness is identified and automatically applied to each scale score.

ADMINISTRATION AND SCORING. Respondents are presented a survey with 155 questions designed to assess level of risk of committing domestic violence. The test can be administered either individually or in groups. All answers are given as "True" or "False." Answers are marked on a separate sheet with the pencil-and-paper version, and on the computer with the computerized version.

If the pencil-and-paper version is used, the answers must be entered into the computer to generate scores. Once they are entered, scores are interpreted and available within 5 minutes. A thorough orientation and training manual gives instructions to the interviewer.

Space is available on the form to enter subjective observations of the evaluator and to enter the evaluator's recommendations for treatment. The publisher cautions that results should be considered in conjunction with any significant observations by the evaluator. They acknowledge that treatment recommendations made as a result of DVI testing can have life and death implications.

Percentile scores are given on each of the six measures. Each scale score is classified in terms of the range of risk it represents. Risk rank is identified as "Low Risk," "Medium Risk," "Problem Risk," and "Severe Problem Risk."

NORMING INFORMATION. Detailed norming information and research history are provided with the test, which has been standardized on the domestic violence offender population. Several summaries of specific studies are included with the test package.

Based on research identifying significant gender differences on two of the scales, gender-specific norms have been established for the Truthfulness Scale and the Violence Scale. Publishers are careful to note that gender differences may vary depending on the geographical area.

One of the strong features of the test is the ongoing research program that allows annual updates to the norming information database. Each filled test diskette must be returned to the publisher before another can be purchased. This provides continual input to be added to their database and contributes to the ongoing improvement of the test.

RELIABILITY. In summary of scientific findings, the publisher states that "reliability refers to consistency of results regardless of who uses the instrument. DVI results are objective, verifiable and reproducible" (p. 13). Statistical data provided support the internal consistency of the DVI. In one study Cronbach alpha coefficients for the six scales ranged from .83 to .92.

VALIDITY. Extensive research is cited summarizing validity studies of the DVI. In validity studies, each of the six scales is treated separately. For example, the Stress Coping measure was compared with scores from the Taylor Manifest Scale and with the Cornell Index. The correlations were significant in the predicted direction.

Concurrent validity was examined by comparing scores from four DVI scales with scores on comparable scales on the Minnesota Multiphasic Personality Inventory (MMPI). Scales correlated were Truthfulness, Alcohol, Drugs, and Stress Coping.

SUMMARY. The Domestic Violence Inventory (DVI) can be useful to evaluators attempting to determine the level of risk of offenders. It should be considered a tool to aid the evaluator, who must consider test results in conjunction with his or her subjective observations and professional judgment. A possible danger is that an evaluator who has many respondents to assess may use the test in an assembly-line fashion, taking the test scores at face value, without adding his or her own experiential wisdom and without considering significant information provided by the respondent. The test publisher cautions evaluators to consider the grave consequences of their recommendations.

With these cautions in mind, the DVI is a convenient, easy-to-take test that provides immediate scoring results. This reviewer believes the DVI is a satisfactory and useful instrument for the purpose for which it is designed.

Review of the Domestic Violence Inventory by DAVID M. KAPLAN, Professor and Director of the Graduate Program in Counseling, Alfred University, Alfred, NY, and MOLLY L. VANDUSER, Alfred University, Alfred, NY:

The Domestic Violence Inventory (DVI) is a 155-question self-report instrument designed to assess both the risk and needs of perpetrators of physical, emotional, and verbal abuse. There are two versions: a juvenile form designed for ages 12–18, and an adult form designed for those over 18. Both versions are available in English and Spanish. The instrument can be completed by most individuals in 35–40 minutes and requires a sixth grade reading level.

The DVI can be administered individually or in groups, and the client can use paper and pencil or computer. Scoring and interpretation are computer generated on-site within 4 minutes. DVI software must be run on an IBM-PC compatible computer with a minimum of 640K memory. The instrument comes with a computer disc, a "Computer Operating Guide," an "Orientation and Training Manual," an "Inventory of Scientific Findings," and a "Community Corrections, Georgia Summary Report."

The DVI contains seven scales: Truthfulness, a lie scale; Violence, a measure of anger, hostility and lethality; Alcohol, a measure of frequency and magnitude of ethanol-related problems; Drugs, a measure of substance abuse and related problems; Control, a measure of attempts to control oneself and others; Stress Coping Ability, a measure of effectiveness in coping with stress, tension and pressure; and Treatment Needs, a needs assessment. Separate gender norms are utilized for Alcohol, Drugs, and Violence Scales.

The DVI was developed by pooling items from experienced doctoral level psychologists at treatment agencies, shelters, and batterers programs. Final items were then selected by "statistically relating" items to known domestic violence offender groups (the specific method for "statistically relating" these items is not presented). Final items were then normed on 1,478 domestic violence offenders in Georgia. Demographics of this population are detailed in the "Community Corrections, Georgia Summary Report."

Psychometric information is contained in the "Inventory of Scientific Findings." Reliability data focus on internal consistency. The Cronbach alpha ranges for each scale are solid: Truthfulness .85–.87; Violence .81–.90; Alcohol .89–.94; Drugs .88–.92; Control .83–.88; and Stress Coping Ability .90–.93. No test-retest reliability information is provided. In addition to supporting internal consistency reliability, the Cronbach alpha correlations described above provide evidence for the construct validity of the DVI.

The "Inventory of Scientific Findings" also describes a number of studies that focus on concurrent validity. Perhaps the most important statement along these lines is that "the DVI does differentiate between 'normals' and domestic violence offenders" (p. 8). However, no specifics are provided to support this declaration.

Concurrent validity studies are reported that correlate the DVI with related instruments. Correlations of DVI scales with related MMPI scales range from .31–.78. Correlations between DVI scales and related SAQ-Adult Probation scales range from .34–.76. Correlations of professional staff ratings, following a screening interview, with DVI scales, were substantially lower, ranging from .03–.54.

A shortcoming of the DVI is the lack of document organization. There is no traditional manual with discrete sections on inventory development, normative information, reliability data, and validity data. Instead, information is spread out among the "Orientation and Training Manual," "Computer Operating Guide," "Inventory of Scientific Findings," and "Community Corrections, Georgia Summary Report."

The "Computer Operating Guide" is fairly straightforward but requires a rather high degree of computer literacy. Testers unfamiliar with computer applications may become anxious when trying to read and implement the instructions contained within this document.

The "Orientation and Training Manual" contains much useful information. However, as stated above, this information would better serve the tester if it were organized along the lines of a traditional inventory manual.

The "Community Corrections, Georgia Summary Report" seems to report data on the norm group upon which the DVI was developed. However, this is inferred, and the document never makes this statement directly.

Finally, the "Inventory of Scientific Findings" provides important psychometric data. However, for some unknown reason, the data are presented chronologically, rather than grouped under the headings of "Reliability" and "Validity" and their subcategories, as is traditional. The chronological listings of studies makes it difficult to evaluate the overall worth of the instrument.

SUMMARY. The DVI appears to be a promising instrument that focuses on not only evaluating, but also assisting, perpetrators of domestic violence. Data are provided that support the reliability and validity of the instrument (although additional data focusing on test-retest reliability, content validity, and predictive validity would be useful). The major shortcoming of the DVI is the lack of organization of accompanying materials.

Dos Amigos Verbal Language Scales.

Purpose: Designed to assess the level of both English and Spanish language development in children.
Population: Ages 5-0 to 13-5.
Publication Dates: 1973–1996.
Scores, 3: English, Spanish, Dominant Language.
Administration: Individual.
Price Data, 1999: $35 per complete test kit including manual ('96, 17 pages), and 25 test forms; $15 per 25 test forms.
Time: (20) minutes.
Comments: No reading by examinees; examiner must read and speak Spanish and English; the manual for this 1996 edition suggests this is a "criterion-referenced test" with scoring based on previous normative material used in earlier test editions.
Author: Donald E. Critchlow.
Publisher: Academic Therapy Publications.

Review of the Dos Amigos Verbal Language Scales by ROBERT B. FRARY, Professor Emeritus, Virginia Polytechnic Institute and State University, Blacksburg, VA:

Dos Amigos is described in its accompanying manual as "a quick, easily-administered screening tool" (p. 6). It was developed for use with children whose first language is Spanish and is administered individually. Stimuli and responses are oral. Two lists of 85 words each, one in English and the other in Spanish, comprise the scales, both of which are administered to a subject. The examiner reads the words, and the subject responds with antonyms. For some stimuli, two or three responses are keyed as correct, but most allow only a single correct response. If the subject makes a correct response that does not match the key, the examiner asks for another answer. The score is the number of responses that match the key. A scoring/reporting sheet provides the examiner with the stimuli and correct responses.

This publication is a reissue of an earlier version listed in *Tests in Print III* (Mitchell, 1983). However, a search of several archives reveals no reviews or research reports concerning its use. The manual has been updated for use with the reissued test. It has been expanded to include a discussion of children's language acquisition. Norming data from the original version have not been updated.

The manual provides no justification for the narrow cognitive requirements of the test (i.e., simple provision of antonyms, claiming, however, that the test "was intended to utilize children's antonym understanding as a practical and effective means to sample English and Spanish language development and conceptualization," p. 9). There is no discussion of the fact that vocabulary level must be a strong determiner of performance on the scales quite apart from "language development and conceptualization" (p. 9). The manual also states that selection of words in the two scales was based on "two years of observing oral language activities in kindergarten through sixth grade classrooms" (p. 11). Advice from a panel of consultants in Mexican-American culture eventually led to the two 85 word lists, each of which contains mostly equivalent stimulus-response pairs (e.g., recordar-olvidar and remember-forget). The lists are in ascending order of difficulty as determined by "preliminary testing responses" (manual, p. 12). The source or number of these responses is not specified.

The scales were field-tested on 1,224 elementary students in Laredo, Texas. They were of Mexican-American ancestry and had learned Spanish first. The manual provides means and standard deviations for the number of correct responses in English and Spanish separately for eight age strata covering ages 5 years, 0 months through 13 years, 5 months. The strata contain 90 to 172 subjects. Also provided is a table of "smoothed" means and standard deviations, which eliminates irregularities peculiar to an age group. One standard deviation below the smoothed age group means was (apparently arbitrarily) selected as a "cutoff score" for each age group. The manual refers to the smoothed means and cutoff scores as "criterion referenced" score points (p. 6). Nevertheless, they are a direct reflection of the 25-year-old norms, and no criteria are established on which to base them.

The manual makes various recommendations for students who score below the means and/or below the cutoff scores on the English and Spanish scales or both. No justification is offered for the recommendations, but they are relatively benign (e.g., evaluate further to determine whether the problem lies with language skills or cognitive ability). Scores on the scales are also purported to identify the dominant language of the subject according to whether the Spanish or English score is higher, with no consideration of measurement error in the case of scores that are relatively close. Indeed, the internal consistency reliability estimates needed to produce the standard errors of measurement for the two scales were apparently not computed, though the data required for this process would have been available from the field test described above.

DISCUSSION. This publication is essentially a re-presentation of a 25-year-old test with no updating of its norms. Moreover, even 25 years ago, the narrow focus of Dos Amigos on local Mexican-American culture and students limited its potential validity in other settings. Over the 25-year period, there have apparently been no studies to evaluate its validity or reliability empirically.

With respect to content validity, one might well question a number of the stimulus-response pairs. For example, "slender" is the *only* keyed response for the stimulus "corpulent," whereas in Spanish the more commonplace "delgado" is the keyed response for "corpulento." Surely a meaningful proportion of subjects must be able to respond with "thin" but not "slender." The keyed responses for "ignorant/ignorante" are "intelligent/intelegente," which is simply incorrect in English and correct only colloquially if at all in Spanish. A bright subject might respond to "ignorant/ignorante" with "informed/culto," which would be counted wrong in both scales.

The field test means for the various age strata seem very low. For example, the means for the highest stratum (12 years, 6 months through 13 years, 5 months) are 34 and 33 (out of 85) for Spanish and English respectively. This result may be due to the requirement that testing be discontinued after five consecutive incorrect responses (manual, p. 16). Quite possibly subjects for whom testing is curtailed would respond correctly to a number of additional stimuli if given the opportunity. Users of Dos Amigos might well experiment with a more liberal mode of administration.

SUMMARY. All things considered, Dos Amigos offers nothing more than the convenience of two preprinted lists of words that can be used to identify students with clearly deficient or advanced Spanish/English vocabularies. This information might be useful in the absence of any prior knowledge about a student but would probably be superfluous otherwise. Users should avoid any serious dependence on the 25-year-old norms and associated norm-referenced (not criterion-referenced) score cut points.

REVIEWER'S REFERENCE

Mitchell, J. V., Jr. (Ed.). (1983). *Tests in print III*. Lincoln, NE: Buros Institute of Mental Measurements.

Review of the Dos Amigos Verbal Language Scales by MARIA DEL R. MEDINA-DIAZ, Associate Professor, Department of Graduate Studies, University of Puerto Rico, Rio Piedras, PR:

Dos Amigos Verbal Language Scales consist of two sets of 85 words in Spanish and English, where the examinee has to answer with the opposite word. These scales were designed to determine the dominant language (English or Spanish) of the elementary school children. Scale words were randomly selected from a pool of the most commonly used words of kindergartners through sixth-graders. The item selection was accomplished after a 2-year period of observing oral language activities in the classrooms. The words were paired with the opposites identified at each grade level, field tested, and reviewed by a consultant panel. There is no information with regard to the classroom's geographic regions and its demographic composition, or to the persons in charge of selecting the words. Other Spanish-speaking groups, different from Mexican-Americans, may have other equivalent words and appropriate responses. For instance, they may use "negro" instead of "moreno," "viejo" for "rancio," "superficial" for "encimado," and "perder" instead of "derrotar." In addition, the Spanish scale shows a gender language preference because many of the words (about 34%) are presented in terms of male orientation (for example, using "delgado" instead of "delgada").

Both Spanish and English scales are administered individually and orally to the examinee. The author indicates that each scale can be given and scored in about 10 minutes. However, there is no information about the administration time supporting this. Particularly, when the scales are given to younger examinees, the administration time will be longer. There are no indications for the administration pace of the stimulus words and the waiting time for the answer. There is a suggestion for an informal pre-screening prompt in order to determine if the examinee understands what an opposite word is. A problem may be dealing with an examinee who does not know the opposite of the exemplary word or does not understand the prompt. In this case, should the scale be administered? There is no provision regarding the administration order of the scales. The user may start with the Spanish scale because it is the first one in the scoring sheet. Another important issue is the language used at the beginning and during the administration of the scales. There are no directions in Spanish to the examinees. This is a serious omission for an instrument that purports to help bilingual children.

The directions indicate that it is not required to present every stimulus word listed to the examinee. However, there is no suggestion of other procedures to follow when administering the scales. Another drawback in this regard is the lack of clarity in how the stimulus word will be said to the examinee: Should it always be framed in a question format (e.g., Which is the opposite of ____?) or can each word be spoken singly? Also, directions are provided for giving feedback to the examinees but it is not clear if this practice should be done for every correct answer. Neither has it been indicated how many times the examinee can attempt to give an answer. Apparently the administration will continue until the examinee misses five consecutive words. Because both scales are to be administered, a transition procedure should be included.

According to the author, the scales can be "administered by any person who has reading and speaking knowledge of Spanish and English. The examiner should also have a thorough understanding of Dos Amigos Scales" (manual, p. 15). These qualifications are important as well as the pronunciation and verbal fluency of the examiner in Spanish and English.

The author claims that the scales will help to identify the English and Spanish language development levels of the children. However, this instrument does not provide language proficiency levels. Instead, an overall measure of a student's ability to identify antonyms is provided. It is stated in the introduction section of the manual that there is a link between the language development level and the cognitive skills of encoding, integration, and decoding. However, there is no clear connection between identifying antonyms and dominance in a particular language. Some construct validity issues are missing in the information about the background and rationale for the scales such as the difference between knowing the opposite of a given word and being capable of using it, and the relationship between identifying antonyms and conceptualization as cognitive skills for developing word meaning. More theoretical background and recent studies are needed for determining children's language development or domain of a language using only the scales' results.

This instrument is an expanded version of a norm-referenced form published 24 years ago. The 1996 edition is purported to be criterion-referenced; norm-referenced data were not available. The scales will be reissued as a norm-referenced tool in the next edition. However, some normative data were collected and used for establishing the scoring criteria. The norm sample used for this purpose was local and convenient, thus not representative of the Spanish-population groups in the United States. A total sample of 1,167 elementary students of Mexican-American ancestry was used to compute the mean and standard deviation in the field test. Thirty bilingual students were selected by their teachers to participate in the clinical pilot study. Using this sample, criterion-validity studies were performed. No statistical data are shown related to these results. The author argues "strong evidence" and "positive relationship" between the Dos Amigos Verbal Language Scales and the criterion measures but the magnitude of the correlations are not reported. An informal procedure for documenting the scales' validity is also reported such as a conversation with the special reading teacher of the pilot study students.

No reliability and item analysis information is available in the test manual. The author indicates that the items are ordered by difficulty levels but item difficulty indexes are missing. Some of the items are not in the same order in the two versions of the test and there is no report on the effect of the item order in the difficulty levels.

The scoring sheet includes both lists of 85 words in Spanish and English with their antonyms. A few directions for scoring and interpretations are provided. Some directions regarding the use of the scoring sheet are missing (for instance, how to complete the information on the first page). The student oral answer is compared with the opposite word provided in the scoring-sheet. A "+" is recorded if the answer is correct and a "0" if it is incorrect.

Cutoff scores for each language scale by age group were derived from the raw data of the field testing group, and set at one standard deviation below the smoothed mean. The rationale for choosing this point is not presented. The passing scores for the Spanish scales ranged from 3 to 20 and for the English scale from 0 to 24. For the English scale the cutoff scores are lower for the examinees between 5 through 8.5 years of age, and higher

after 9.6 years of age. A student's score is compared with both cutoff scores. The higher score indicates examinee dominant language. The score interpretations should be done with the results of both scales. A couple of exemplary interpretations are provided but some combinations of results and interpretations are missing (e.g., passing score in English and no passing score in Spanish, and passing scores in both scales). Some suggestions for instructional assistance and further evaluation (if needed) are also given. The case of a cutoff score of zero in the English scale for the younger examinees (5.0 to 6.5 years old) needs some explanation.

SUMMARY. Dos Amigos Verbal Language Scales could be used to identify kindergartners' through sixth-graders' knowledge of opposite words in both English and Spanish. It is a long test and can be shortened in the administration protocol but exactly how this is done is not clear. There are serious conceptual, cognitive, and cultural drawbacks that weaken the intention of determining the dominant language of the examinee. The scarce evidence of validity and reliability as well as the flaws in the administration procedures can result in misleading interpretation of the results. Despite the above limitations, this instrument may serve as a screening tool for additional, more comprehensive evaluation of the child's dominant language. Using these scales as the only tool for this purpose is not recommended because of insufficient technical information and the lack of research support.

[127]
Driver Risk Inventory—II.

Purpose: "Designed for DUI/DWI offender screening."

Population: Convicted DUI and DWI offenders.

Publication Dates: 1986–1997.

Acronym: DRI-II.

Scores, 6: Truthfulness, Alcohol, Driver Risk, Drug, Stress Coping, Dependency.

Price Data: Available from publisher.

Time: (30–35) minutes.

Comments: Self-administered, computer-scored test.

Author: Behavior Data Systems, Ltd.

Publisher: Behavior Data Systems, Ltd.

Cross References: For a review by Frank Gresham of an earlier version, see 12:125.

Review of the Driver Risk Inventory—II by TONY CELLUCCI, Associate Professor and Director of the Psychology Training Clinic, Idaho State University, Pocatello, ID:

The Driver Risk Inventory—II (DRI-II) is the revision of a computer-scored DUI/DWI assessment instrument first developed in the 1980s. It is self-administered (sixth grade reading level) and consists of 140 items divided into the following response formats: 84 true/false, 34 Likert, and 22 multiple-choice items. Five measurement and one classification scale are derived. Self-report items are combined with arrest records to indicate risk level—low (0–39th percentile), medium (40th–69th percentile), problem (70th–89th percentile), and severe (90th–100th percentile). The computer printout generates a disclaimer that "no diagnosis or decision should be based solely upon DRI-II results."

In evaluating the DRI-II, one is presented with an incongruity. The publisher had forwarded a large number of testimonials from state programs and organizations including the National Highway Traffic Safety Administration (NHTSA). Yet there is no published scientific literature on the DRI, which relates to the proprietary nature of the instrument. The publisher provided an orientation and training manual, an inventory of statistical findings, and a 1997 validation study from Florida involving 1,114 DUI offenders. It was necessary to talk to professional staff to clarify these materials.

The items on the measurement scales were initially constructed from a rational definition of each scale and then revised statistically. The Driver Risk scale was changed minimally and the Stress-Coping ability scale is identical to previous test versions. There is no item overlap between scales although one item can contribute to the School or the Drug scale depending upon how it is answered (Don Davignon, personal communication, May 13, 1999). Although these scales are said to measure tendency as well as problems, most items appear face valid. No test-retest information is available but alpha coefficients for the scales are good. These coefficients and validity information are provided for each scale below.

The Truthfulness scale (21 items, alpha = .87) is said to measure truthfulness in completing the inventory versus a guarded or minimizing style. It has been shown to be highly correlated (.67) with the Minnesota Multiphasic Personality Inventory-2 (MMPI-2) L-scale. Scores on this scale are used to correct the other DRI-II measurement scales based on shared variance.

The Alcohol scale (23 items, alpha = .93) is reported to be statistically related to the number of alcohol arrests although no specific correlation is reported. It is moderately correlated with other alcohol abuse instruments such as the MAST (.38), Mortimer-Filkins (.45), and the MAC-R (.29). The Drug scale (22 items, alpha = .87) is an independent measure of illicit drug abuse. It is reportedly associated with drug-related arrests and correlated (.62) with the DAST.

The Driver Risk scale (25 items, alpha = .83) measures driving risk (e.g., irresponsible or aggressive) independent of substance involvement. It is said to be associated with the number of traffic violations and accidents and has been previously correlated (.40) with a measure of aggressivity.

The Stress-Coping ability scale (30 items, alpha = .92) is a measure of the capacity to handle stress. Past research has shown that it is correlated with the Taylor Manifest Anxiety Scale (-.70), Cornell Neuroticism Index (-.75), and Ego Strength on the 16PF (.69) as well as more moderately with a number of MMPI scales.

The Substance Dependence/Abuse scale (30 items, alpha = .81) is a new addition and provides a classification (i.e., abuse or dependence) based on items keyed to the seven dependence and four abuse criteria in the DSM-IV. It is possible for first time offenders not to receive a diagnosis (Don Davignon, personal correspondence, May 13, 1999). This self-report scale was correlated with a DSM-IV criterion test (.94) and is associated with the Alcohol scale (.63), which is viewed as more of a severity measure.

The scale scores of the DRI-II are corrected for truthfulness and converted to percentiles. There are minimum percentile scores for several scales based on arrest history. For example, number of alcohol arrests with blood alcohol concentration (BAC) at time of arrest establish a minimum for the Alcohol scale. These individual minimums are used to correct for underreporting and did not contaminate the criterion coefficients reported above (Don Davignon, personal communication, May 13, 1999). Even when using BAC to correct for tolerance, only 11.7% of the Florida sample met dependence criteria. The DRI-II was constructed so as to identify a predicted percentage of DUI offenders as having low (39%), medium (30%), problem (20%), and severe (11%) risk, and the scores adhere closely to these expected percentages.

A major limitation of the DRI-II is that the standardization group is inadequately described.

The publisher's materials state that the test has been developed on over 350,000 offenders in 39 states and Canada. However, there are actually separate databases maintained for different states in which given legal definitions of DUI differ. Test scores from a DUI evaluator in a state without a database will be compared to a standard database comparable in size to that in the Florida study (Don Davignon, personal communication, May 13, 1999). Inspection of the statistical findings provided revealed that tested groups were similar demographically. For example, most groups were 80% male, 70%–75% Caucasian, with an average age in the 30s, and a high school education level. Between 20%–40% were multiple DUI offenders. Gender differences have been found on the Truthfulness, Alcohol, and Driver Risk scales, and gender influences the scoring of these scales.

The psychosocial assessment of DUI offenders has all too often been considered a less than professional activity not requiring a clinician. Research suggests that all such assessments should draw on multiple sources of information including official records (Chang & Lapham, 1996). Interestingly, because the base rate for recidivism is relatively low, test instruments may inform clinician decisions (Leshowitz & Meyers, 1996). Including an assessment of driver risk and traffic offenses is supported in the literature (Donovan, Umlauf, & Salzberg, 1990) as is considering client truthfulness or self-report validity in conjunction with alcohol measures (Lapham et al., 1995). However, there is still a need for prospective validation.

SUMMARY. No single test is definitive in the evaluation of substance abuse and DUI risk. However, this instrument is a reasonable choice for assessing DUI offenders. Certainly the ease for adopting the DRI-II would be enhanced if the publisher would develop an appropriate technical manual including a clear description of the standard database and more complete validity data. Several statements in the informal materials were disturbingly inaccurate or sensational (e.g., truth-corrected scores reveal what the client is trying to hide). This test appears better than the promotional materials designed to sell it.

REVIEWER'S REFERENCES

Donovan, D. M., Umlauf, R. L., & Salzberg, P. M. (1990). Bad drivers: Identification of a target group for alcohol-related prevention and early intervention. *Journal of Studies on Alcohol, 51,* 136–141.

Lapham, S. C., Skipper, B. J., Owen, J. P., Kleyboecker, T., Teaf, D., Thompson, B., & Simpson, G. (1995). Alcohol abuse screening instruments: Normative test data collected from a first DWI offender screening program. *Journal of Studies on Alcohol, 56,* 51–59.

Chang, I., & Lapham, S. C. (1996). Validity of self-reported criminal offenses and traffic violations in screening of driving-while intoxicated offenders. *Alcohol & Alcoholism, 31,* 583–590.

Leshowitz, B., & Meyers, J. M. (1996). Application of decision theory to DUI assessment. *Alcoholism: Clinical and Experimental Research, 20,* 1148–1152.

Review of the Driver Risk Inventory—II by KEVIN J. McCARTHY, Assistant Clinical Professor of Psychiatry, Louisiana State University, Health Sciences Center, New Orleans, LA:

The Driver Risk Inventory—II (DRI-II) is a computerized screening instrument for use among individuals who have been convicted of drinking or drug-related offenses. The instrument was developed to assist courts, probation officers, and treatment personnel in the evaluation of individuals arrested for impaired or intoxicated driving. It affords third party interests an opportunity to evaluate these individuals in terms of drinking or drug taking behaviors and their future recidivism risk level. The data developed through this instrument may also be used to identify those convicted individuals suitable for placement in treatment options. The DRI-II may be used to direct participation in mandated alcohol and drug educational processes.

The instrument consists of 140 questions that are computer administered or it may be completed with the assistance of computer audio. Testing is easily administered, requiring approximately 30 minutes to complete, score, and report individual results. A paper edition is available, which requires scanning and computer scoring. The instrument is available in both an English and Spanish format. The DRI-II requires that the participant read and comprehend at a sixth grade level. The manual describes the DRI-II as "the highest rated automated assessment or test" in a study sponsored by the National Highway Safety Administration. Accompanying literature suggests that the DRI-I was the instrument evaluated in the NHSA study (DRI: An Inventory of Scientific Findings, p. 28).

Although the literature submitted was extensive, the format precluded quick access to supporting reliability and validity data. Because the literature contained information on two tests (DRI-I and DRI-II) it was occasionally contradictory and distracting, often obscuring the distinction between the two instruments. The publisher's research methodology uses an annual database study as their primary research mechanism, noting that the "annual database analysis is new, and in many respects innovative. Since we have and continue to do annual databases analysis we have adapted a reporting strategy in line with the annual database studies" (Don Davignon, personal communication, July 27, 2000).

Information was often presented in a promotional framework. The publisher's nontraditional reporting approach limits the instrument's usefulness regarding easily accessed reliability and validity data. The manual needs to be updated, integrated, and supported by consistent data analysis that facilitate meaningful comparisons. The manual notes that "the DRI-II has been researched and normed on the DUI/DWI offender population" (training manual, p. 5) though it lacks substantive demographic data regarding participants in the normative sample.

According to accompanying literature (DRI: An Inventory of Scientific Findings, p. 7), "Different scoring procedures have been established for male and female clients. Age, ethnicity and educational factors continue to be studied and reviewed." The publisher also conducts an annual state-by-state analysis. Results of an analysis of data from the State of Florida were submitted for review. Those data were based upon administration of the "DRI-Short Form" and "DRI-Standard Tests" rather than the instrument under review. Additionally, the supporting documentation included a substantial intermixing of data from DRI-I and DRI-II studies. Accompanying literature discussed testing instruments not under review.

The Driver Risk Inventory-II utilizes multiple evaluative approaches for assessing and reporting data, including a Substance Dependency/Abuse Scale that was developed as a classification category, having been correlated ($r = .964$) with rewritten DSM-IV criterion items. The DRI-II uses five core measures including a Truthfulness validity scale, identifying underreporting of problems or "truth-corrected scores reveal(ing) what the offender is trying to hide" (Scientific Findings, p. 23) and individual scales for assessing Alcohol and Drug use. The Driver Risk Scale identifies aggressively irresponsible drivers—independent of substance abuse." The Stress Coping Scale measures the individual's ability to cope with stress "which can affect a person's driving ability."

Although documentation noted that validity of the DRI-II was ascertained though correlational studies with other criterion instruments (A validation Study of the DRI-II in a large sample of DUI offenders, pp.3–4) both the Driver Risk Scale and the Stress Coping Abilities Scale "were not included in this study because of time constraints involved in testing." The publisher noted that these scales "were not the focus of this study" (p. 4) and suggested that there had been little change. They also noted that "each of these scales had been studied extensively" (p. 4) in previous research of this instrument's predecessor, the DRI-I. These components represent a meaningful component of the reported DRI-II profile and appear to be integral to the goal of assessing the risk associated with individual drivers and their substance-abusing behaviors.

DRI-II profile scores are reported as percentiles with rankings of low, medium, problem, and maximum risk levels. The reporting scheme identifies low risk as 0–39th percentile, medium risk as 40–69th percentile, problem risk as 70–89th percentile, and maximum risk as 90–100 percentile. Results of an ANOVA comparing mean score differences between Abuse, Dependence, and No Classification groups was reported as "very significantly different (all p's <.0001)" (validity study, p. 13). The inventory also incorporates a psychometric technique identified as "truth-corrected scores" that provides computational modifications of the Alcohol, Drug, Driver Risk, and Stress Coping Scales.

Reliability data included Cronbach's alpha ($N = 1,014$) for measuring internal consistency of inventory scales ranging from .81 (Substance Abuse/Dependency Scale) to .93 (Alcohol Scale). Validity data included correlational studies with correlations that ranged from $r = .291$ for comparisons between the Alcohol measurement scale and the Mac-Andrews Alcoholism Scale to $r = .618$, for comparisons between the Drug measurement scale and the Drug/Abuse Screening Test. Coefficient alphas were also obtained for criterion test scales including the MMPI-2 "L" Scale = .72; Mac-Andrews Scale = .56; Drug Abuse Screening Test = .85, and DSM-IV items = .81.

SUMMARY. The six empirically based scales are the essential elements of this instrument, yet their value is seriously undermined by a lack of normative DRI-II data provided in a uniform and useable manner. The publisher recommends that this instrument be used in conjunction with an interview conducted by experienced staff. It should also be supplemented with court-related records to ensure maximum screening effectiveness. It is suggested that the instrument should not be used for diagnostic purposes without clinical judgment. Its usefulness is restricted to courts and mandated referral programs because the publisher specifically recommends that the DRI-II report *not be given to the DUI offender.*

The instrument appears to have no linkage to treatment interventions or measures of progress among clients active in recovery or educational programs. Ethical issues regarding the right to privacy, data storage and management as well as the need to secure permission for future disclosure are largely unacknowledged. Efforts to ensure client confidentiality apparently depend upon the deletion of participant names, prior to returning the used diskettes for inclusion in the publisher's database. The publisher notes that "test users establish their own pre-test disclosure policies" (Don Davignon, personal communication, July 28, 2000).

The publisher maintains an expanding database that is analyzed annually, providing a basis for ongoing instrument restandardization. Nevertheless, the transfer and potential use of driving records, family income records (reporting varies by state), arrest records, and diagnostic classifications may require full disclosure notification to participants, in light of the sensitive nature of this information. In a narrowly proscribed group of informed individuals, this instrument is likely to be useful in identifying those at-risk individuals who may incur future DUI/DWI arrests.

[128]
Drug-Taking Confidence Questionnaire.

Purpose: "As an assessment tool, the DTCQ identifies a client's coping self-efficacy in relation to 50 drinking or drug-taking situations."
Population: Clients of addiction treatment.
Publication Date: 1997.
Acronym: DTCQ.
Scores: Situation profiles in two areas: Personal States, Situations Involving Other People; 8 subscales: Unpleasant Emotions, Physical Discomfort, Pleasant Emotions, Testing Personal Control, Urges and Temptations to Use, Conflict with Others, Social Pressure to Use, Pleasant Times with Others.
Administration: Group.
Price Data, 1998: C$34.95 per user's guide; C$14.95 per 30 questionnaires (specify alcohol or drug); C$39.95 per sample pack including user's guide and 40 questionnaires (10 alcohol and 30 drug); C$75 per 50 uses of computer-administration software (DOS format).

Time: (15) minutes.
Comments: User's guide written in both English (160 pages) and French (69 pages); "French versions of DTCQ have not been scientifically validated."
Authors: Helen M. Annis, Sherrilyn M. Sklar, and Nigel E. Turner.
Publisher: Centre for Addiction and Mental Health [Canada].

Review of the Drug-Taking Confidence Questionnaire by MICHAEL H. CAMPBELL, Director of Residential Life, New College of University of South Florida at Sarasota, Sarasota, FL:

TEST COVERAGE AND USE. The Drug-Taking Confidence Questionnaire (DTCQ) is a 50-item self-report instrument designed to measure self-efficacy regarding substance abuse in a wide variety of psychological states and social situations. The authors state that the DTCQ is an appropriate tool for the initial assessment of clients entering treatment for alcohol or drug addiction; however, the instrument can be re-administered during the course of treatment to monitor progress or to suggest a honing of treatment focus to particular problem areas. Additionally, the DTCQ can be used as a treatment outcome indicator for either research or clinical purposes.

Once clear advantage of the instrument is flexibility with regard to specific substances. Test materials include two forms. The first measures alcohol-related self-efficacy in each of 50 situations; the second allows clients to specify specific substances. Clients may identify up to three substances (including alcohol).

TEST CONSTRUCTION. The manual does not provide a detailed description of item selection procedures, but the authors do state that the DTCQ is based on Bandura's (1977) theory of self-efficacy applied to eight categories of drinking or drug-taking situations proposed by Marlatt (e.g., 1978, 1979). Self-efficacy is operationalized in terms of the client's anticipatory confidence that he or she "would be able to resist the urge to drink heavily" in each of 50 situations representative of Marlatt's eight categories. The test employs a Likert-style response format ranging in 20-point increments from 0% (*not at all confident*) to 100% (*very confident*). The DTCQ items produce subscale scores measuring self-efficacy in situations involving Personal States (Unpleasant Emotions, Physical Discomfort, Pleasant Emotions, Testing Personal Control, and Urges/Temptations to Use) or

Situations Involving Other People (Conflict with Others, Social Pressure to Use, and Pleasant Times with Others). Most subscales are composed of 5 items; the scales measuring unpleasant emotions and conflict with others each contain 10 items. Items are face-valid, and test takers could easily fake good or bad.

The authors report on a series of confirmatory factor-analytic studies used to verify the appropriateness of Marlatt's eight-factor model in comparison to several alternatives. Although all models leave a significant amount of covariance unexplained, the eight-factor solution provides the best fit to the data. The manual also details results of a second-order factor analysis suggesting a three-factor structure (negative situations, positive situations, and temptation situations). Overall, the factor-analytic data provide only limited support for the construct validity of an eight-factor subscale structure.

ADMINISTRATION AND SCORING. Ease of use is a major strength of the DTCQ. The manual provides simple, clear instructions, and the instructions to clients are clear and concise. The instrument is available in paper-and-pencil and computerized formats, each of which requires about 15 minutes to complete per substance. The authors report data documenting the equivalence of written and computerized versions of the test.

The result of scoring is a confidence score on each scale for each substance assessed. Test users should be careful not to confuse the terms confidence score and confidence intervals. The DTCQ does not yield confidence intervals. Rather, the confidence score reflects the strength of the test taker's confidence in his or her ability to "drink heavily" or "use drugs" in each category of situation.

NORMS. The total sample size for normative data was 713, subdivided into 344 alcohol clients, 253 cocaine clients, and 116 other drug clients. The participants were recruited from clients seeking treatment at a facility in Toronto. Characteristics of the sample suggest some caution regarding the range of populations with which the test may be used appropriately. First, many clients were self-selected in that they were in treatment for addictions; those not self-selected were mandated court referrals, which constituted 16.6% of the total sample. Second, samples for each of the three substance groups were predominately male (ranging from 73.9% to 77.9% of each group). Third, over 40% of the total sample were unemployed. Finally, the majority of clients had received prior treatment. The characteristics of the sample suggest that norms are based on a sample with relatively debilitating, chronic patterns of abuse. Therefore, clinicians should use caution when using the DTCQ for clients with less severe or long-standing substance abuse problems (e.g., in a college counseling center setting). The lack of demographic data regarding the sample is a serious limitation of this instrument. The manual does not list the ethnic or racial composition of the sample and no such data are used in any analysis.

RELIABILITY. The internal consistency of the DTCQ appears good. Cronbach's alpha coefficients for each subscale ranged from .79 to .95 in separate analyses of the alcohol, cocaine, and other drug samples. The authors do not report test-retest or alternate form reliability data.

VALIDITY. The authors first focus on validating the DTCQ as a measure of self-efficacy by correlating subscales with consumption variables (e.g., quantity and frequency of use), social context of use (social pressure and percentage of time spent drinking alone), and use-related criteria (e.g., years of drug use and motivation to quit). Second, they correlate subscales with several psychometric instruments. Correlations were generally in the predicted directions, but the strengths of relationship do not provide compelling evidence of validity. A more serious issue, however, is the authors' choice of types of validity evidence to evaluate. The studies reported in the manual do provide evidence of convergent and discriminant construct validity using several self-reported historical behaviors as well as a broad array of criterion instruments (e.g., the Depression Subscale of the SCL-90-R, the Stages of Change Readiness and Treatment Eagerness Scale, and the Beck Depression Inventory). However, no attention is given to the predictive validity of scores from the instrument in terms of treatment prognosis or outcome, with the exception of a reference to previously published data regarding the positive impact of self-efficacy on treatment outcome.

SUMMARY. The available data suggest that the DTCQ shows promise as a convenient, cost-effective tool for assessment of clients in treatment for substance abuse, particularly in programs with a cognitive-behavioral emphasis. However, the initial sampling procedures are vulnerable to several serious criticisms, and further research is needed to provide stronger documentation of validity. In particular, research demonstrating the predictive validity of scores from the DTCQ would increase its viability as a clinical tool.

REVIEWER'S REFERENCES

Bandura, A. (1977). Self-efficacy: Toward a unifying theory of behavioral change. *Psychological Review, 84,* 191–215.

Marlatt, G. A. (1978). Craving for alcohol, loss of control, and relapse: A cognitive-behavioral analysis. In P. E. Nathan, G. A. Marlatt, & T. Loberg (Eds.), *Alcoholism: New directions in behavioral research* (pp. 271–314). New York: Plenum Press.

Marlatt, G. A. (1979). Alcohol use and problem drinking: A cognitive-behavioral analysis. In P. C. Kendall & S. D. Hollon (Eds.), *Cognitive-behavioral interventions: Theory, research, and procedures* (pp. 319–355). New York: Academic Press.

Review of the Drug-Taking Confidence Questionnaire by GLENN B. GELMAN, Executive Director, Northern Illinois Counseling Associates, P.C., Arlington Heights, IL, and Adjunct Professor of Psychology, Roosevelt University, Schaumburg, IL:

The Drug-Taking Confidence Questionnaire (DTCQ) is a 50-item self-report questionnaire designed to assess anticipatory coping self-efficacy across a range of addictive behaviors. Clients are asked to "imagine" themselves in each of 50 relapse crisis situations and to rate their level of confidence to resist the urge to drink heavily or use a specific drug in that situation. Clients indicate their confidence on a six-level scoring scale. For example, if the client believes he or she is 80% confident that he or she could resist the urge to drink, if, for example, feeling happy, the client would answer "80." According to the User's Guide, the DTCQ can be used with different treatment approaches and in various clinical settings, including individual and group counseling programs. Moreover, it can be administered and re-administered during treatment to chart self-confidence and identify relapse risks, at the end of treatment to determine progress, and as a post-treatment outcome measure.

Like its companion instrument, the Inventory of Drug-Taking Situations (IDTS; 186), the DTCQ employs two questionnaires: one specific to alcohol use, and the other specific to the use of other drugs. Similarly, the DTCQ is administered separately for each substance the client reports having used, so that information can be obtained about the use of specific drugs or (10) drug classes.

In fact, the DTCQ provides an intriguing complement to the IDTS. For example, the IDTS evaluates risk on the basis of past behavior. The DTCQ, on the other hand, evaluates risk on the basis of (imagined) future behavior. Taken together, the assessment of relapse risk can be formidable. The 50 risk situations sample a relevant cross-section of real-life experiences. Then, the client's responses are profiled, based on Alan Marlatt's well-regarded eight-category classification system. The categories are clinically useful because they portend practical steps that can be taken to enhance risk-prevention competencies, across specific drugs used and specific situations.

The questionnaires are easy to administer, answer, score, and interpret. Each inventory can be completed in about 15 minutes. Although a required reading level is not specified, item contents are worded clearly and simply. (Note that this reviewer examined the English version only; therefore, these comments are not meant to apply to the French version.)

The idea to ask clients to anticipate their substance use behavior in specific situations derives from Bandura's well-known theory of self-efficacy. The authors note that high self-efficacy has been associated with positive treatment outcomes. What one imagines about his or her likely conduct presumably correlates with—or even predicts—what one might actually do in a given risk situation. By understanding the client's own perceptions about coping self-efficacy, treatment interventions and prevention strategies can be better focused. To this reviewer, the reliance on self-estimations of risk behavior appears most useful for clients who have demonstrated positive motivation and/or are well into the recovery process.

One strength of the DTCQ is that it encourages the client to participate in his or her own treatment planning. A "sober" test-taking approach will no doubt reveal vital information about one's relapse-risk propensities. However, because the content of the DTCQ is obvious, it readily invites "faking-good" or "faking-bad" response patterns. To be sure, this is a common problem when assessing any clinical population, let alone one predisposed to minimization and denial. The authors do attempt to address this issue by suggesting that even low elevation profiles can be clinically useful. Still, the "power" of the DTCQ would be significantly increased by adding validity indicators with which to analyze a client's response tendencies.

The User's Guide devotes a significant discussion of correlating DTCQ scores with those of other assessment instruments (e.g., Beck Depression Inventory, Drinking-Related Locus of Control Scale). For example, clients who score high on depression were found to have reported lower levels of confidence in their ability to resist the urge to drink heavily. Other variables addressed include sex and age differences, differences between primary drugs, and the effects of drug consumption on DTCQ scores. More research is indicated to analyze the effects of other psychological, psychosocial, and sociodemographic variables. For example, one might consider the effects of an antisocial personality disorder, or indigence, on self-ratings of coping self-efficacy.

One subtle problem with the DTCQ is its use of the word "abuse." For example, each questionnaire asks the client the following question, "Is this your MAIN substance of abuse? [*sic*]" The use of this phrasing implies, a priori, that the client agrees that his or her pattern of use can be labeled as such. For an instrument with as much utility as the DTCQ, this represents a needless limitation.

The DTCQ may be completed using hand-scoring or computerized formats. This reviewer examined only the hand-scoring materials; however, it should be noted that the computerized version requires an IBM-compatible computer and a DOS format. For this instrument to gain wider user acceptance, requisite upgrades are clearly indicated. This seems especially the case because in the (otherwise thorough) User's Guide, instructions for the would-be hand-scorer are limited. Scoring the DTCQ is a simple matter, once one deciphers the methodology. Although scoring instructions are stated on the hand-scoring form, the steps should be better articulated in the user's Guide. Another pitfall is that the names of the eight categories, and their respective computation formulas, are printed right on the hand-scoring form that is completed by the client. Although this design allows for expedient scoring, it seems unduly distracting and can potentially bias the client's answers.

The Client Confidence Profile is visually appealing. Results, represented by a bar-graph, are immediately interpretable. From a clinical perspective, reviewing the data with the client could well serve to highlight relapse risk patterns, and generate situation-specific relapse prevention strategies. In this regard, the DTCQ shines.

SUMMARY. The DTCQ is based on a promising model of coping self-efficacy. Several of the problems appear to diminish its range of applica-

bility. The DTCQ is at its best for clients who have demonstrated that they are motivated and/or well into their recovery program. Its value is augmented when used in conjunction with the closely aligned IDTS. Even with its present limitations, the DTCQ offers a useful clinical tool in identifying situations that may place an individual at risk.

[129]
Dysarthria Examination Battery.

Purpose: Designed to "assess motor speech disorders."
Population: Children and adults.
Publication Date: 1993.
Scores, 5: Respiration, Phonation, Resonation, Articulation, Prosody.
Administration: Individual.
Price Data, 1999: $68 per complete kit including test booklet, 3 stimulus cards, 20 scoring forms, and manual (47 pages); $18 per 20 scoring forms.
Time: (60) minutes.
Author: Sakina S. Drummond.
Publisher: Communication Skill Builders—A Division of The Psychological Corporation.

Review of the Dysarthria Examination Battery by STEVEN B. LEDER, Professor, Department of Surgery, Section of Otolaryngology, Yale University School of Medicine, New Haven, CT:

The Dysarthria Examination Battery (DEB) is a comprehensive clinical tool that encompasses all aspects of speech production (i.e., Respiration, Phonation, Resonation, Articulation, and Prosody). These general areas are assessed by 23 specific tasks that provide the clinician with an in-depth evaluation of speech production. Severity of dysarthria is determined by what percentage of these tasks are abnormal. Thus, all tasks are weighted equally in determining dysarthria severity.

The DEB examination manual is comprehensive and easy to use, with both explicit instructions and rationales for each task as well as detailed interpretation of results. Normative data are provided by task in an easy-to-read table, with clear parameters for determination of normal/abnormal performance for each task. Summary tables provide a concise reference to facilitate scoring and rating dysarthria severity.

The response form lists each task separately and with adequate space to record data. A separate column is provided to record abnormal responses for easy identification of problem areas and summing of responses. However, no summary box was provided in which to record the overall dysarthria severity score.

Due to the thoroughness of the DEB, estimated administration time is 1 hour. In today's budget-conscious health care environment, evaluation time is limited and patients often have multiple speech and language problems, making a 1-hour dysarthria assessment difficult to justify. In addition, proper administration of the DEB requires computerized voice analysis equipment that is not readily available to most clinicians and, if available, is not easily transported into facilities where patients are evaluated at bedside.

It was claimed that the DEB can also be used in the assessment of dysphagia and dysphonia. Even though the task analysis as it is presented necessitates overlap into these areas, the DEB does not present sufficient data to be used to evaluate either dysphagia or dysphonia in a reliable or comprehensive manner.

Although the DEB is comprehensive in that it considers all five aspects of speech production and their component tasks, the manner in which the overall severity of dysarthria is determined suggests that the instrument should be used with caution. The simplicity of the normal/abnormal forced-choice system and the fact that all tasks are treated equally may lead to an overall severity rating that does not correspond to a perceptual dysarthria severity rating. That is, certain general areas and specific tasks are more important than others. For example, articulation is generally more important than respiration, and speech intelligibility in words and sentences is generally more important than velar movement and s/z ratio in the overall picture of dysarthria severity.

Review of the Dysarthria Examination Battery by MALCOLM R. McNEIL, Professor and Chair, Department of Communication Science and Disorders, University of Pittsburgh, Pittsburgh, PA:

The Dysarthria Examination Battery (DEB) requires three stimulus cards, a stopwatch, an audiotape recorder with microphone, a dry spirometer, a flashlight, a disposable tongue depressor, a laryngeal mirror, a bite block, and acoustic analysis hardware/software (e.g., VisiPitch/PM, Pitch Analyzer/Sona Graph, Computer Speech Laboratory, etc.).

The DEB consists of a number of tasks designed to assess each of the speech processes:

five Respiration, six Phonation, three Resonation, six Articulation, and three Prosody. Each of these tasks yields data that are both quantifiable (save for the Resonance tasks) and perceptually rated using a 1–5 point category rating scale. Ratings are made for respiration; vocal quality of vowels and speech; labial, mandibular, and lingual movements and resistance; stress and intonation as well as for palatal and pharyngeal reflexes and lingual, velar and labial tactile sensation. These 23 independent and 36 dependent measures were selected from an original list of 47 dependent measures derived from the literature on the nature and assessment of motor speech disorders.

Drummond, the DEB author, defined dysarthria as "a speech disorder resulting from neuromuscular problems involving more than one level of the vocal tract" (manual, p. 1). Although this is a unique and theoretically and clinically untenable definition, its invocation does not necessarily obviate the DEB for some of the purposes for which it was designed. Consistent with the majority of assessment tools for dysarthria, nonspeech as well as speech behaviors are elicited and judged/measured. However, no theoretical rationale is provided for their inclusion.

There are several stated purposes for administering the DEB. These include (a) detection of dysarthria; (b) differential diagnosis of dysarthria from disorders resembling it; (c) determining treatment candidacy directed toward speech production versus augmentative communication; (d) determining severity of dysarthria by speech process involved, which is judged as either "minimally" or "maximally" impaired; and (e) determining the specific speech process to be targeted in treatment. It is also stated that the DEB can be used in the assessment of dysphagia and dysphonia (of assumed nonneurogenic origin). The DEB makes no attempt to differentially diagnose by "type" of dysarthria (e.g., using the Darley, Aronson, & Brown [1969a;b] classification system) and does not attempt differentiation by disease process or anatomic (neural or structural) region involved. Explicit criteria for satisfying any of the stated purposes are not provided.

VALIDITY. The content validity of the DEB is reasonably consistent with other dysarthria examination batteries such as the Oral Speech Mechanism Screening Examination—Revised (St. Louis & Ruscello, 1987), the Frenchay Dysarthria

Assessment (Enderby, 1994), and the Dworkin-Culatta Oral Mechanism Examination (Dworkin & Cullata, 1980) in terms of the behavioral elicitation procedures and in the types of judgments/measurements used for their quantification/description. The number of behaviors elicited for each task are relatively few (in an attempt to keep the test time to a minimum) and threatens the reliability of the test, given the large variability in some individuals and in some types of dysarthria. A brief description of each task arranged by speech process follows.

Respiration is assessed while the patient is at rest and is judged for rate (cycles per second) and type (abdominal, thoracic, clavicular oppositional, mixed). Criteria for judging adequacy for both variables are given. Words per exhalation are counted during serial speech (counting) and during the reading of the "grandfather" passage (with conversational speech used as a substitute if the patient is unable to read). Cutoff scores for the serial speech and read productions are provided. Using spirometry, vital capacity is assessed. Both maximum phonation time (during vowel prolongation) and the S/Z ratio are measured as an index of air flow regulation, glottic efficiency, respiratory musculature control, lung tissue pressures, and the ability to overcome respiratory gravitational forces. Cutoff scores for both measures are provided.

Phonation is assessed, and pathology judged from performance on six tasks. Habitual pitch and loudness are assessed during a single sustained vowel (/i/ or /a/) and during the production of the patient's single repetition of a single word ("one"). Acoustic instrumentation is used to derive the frequency ("pitch") and intensity ("loudness") values. The assumption is that these data collected on these productions represent the patient's "habitual" vocal fundamental frequency and intensity, an assumption that is often unjustified depending on the nature and severity of the dysarthria. Frequency range is assessed instrumentally via ascending and descending productions of /a:/ (alternatively through a "pitch glide" procedure) and intensity range is assessed instrumentally via ascending and descending repetitions of "one-one-one-one," etc. Optimal frequency and intensity are also assessed instrumentally. Optimal frequency is defined as the frequency in the production of /a:/. Optimal intensity is defined as the intensity in the production of serial "one" productions. Both optimal frequency and intensity are identified as

the point on the visual waveform at which the patient's performance is "smoothest." Vocal quality is assessed through sustained vowel productions and through connected speech elicited from passage reading. Quality is rated perceptually on a 5-point category scale with scores of 2–5 representing pathological quality. The scale encompasses the physiological parameters of vocal fold abduction/adduction, timing, onset, maintenance, and superimposed noise. Criteria for rating the most severely deviant quality is the presence of three or more behaviors from among breathiness, hoarseness, pitch breaks, loudness breaks, hard/breathy glottal attack, monotonous pitch, monotonous loudness, vocal decay, or tremulous quality. No explicit criteria are given for determining the "smoothest" portion of the waveform for either frequency or intensity and no rationale or concurrent validation data are given for the criteria of three or more signs for assigning the most severe quality.

Resonation is assessed, and pathology judged from performance on three tasks. Velar movements are rated for those that are (a) consistent, smooth, symmetrical; (b) asymetrical but with maintained movement; (c) deterioration across trials; (d) minimal movement; and (e) no movement as elicited from five repetitions of "ah." Specific criteria for symmetry, smoothness, and actual movement are not provided and ultimately rely on the skill, bias, and knowledge of the examiner. Fogging of the nasal mirror is used to determine nasal emission using alternate productions for "may" and "pay." The degree of hypo/hypernasality is assessed perceptually using a 5-point category scale from the auditory recording of connected speech and from the previous task.

Articulation is assessed in six domains (speech intelligibility, labial movements, mandibular movement, and lingual movements for speech and nonspeech and during active resistance). Intelligibility scores are derived from words (10) and sentences (12) that are assumed to "adequately provide an index of the patient's functional communications" (manual, p. 12). Stimuli are read or repeated and intelligibility is determined from orthographic transcriptions of recorded productions by the examiner. These procedures for eliciting and judging intelligibility leave multiple sources of bias in the transcriptions and ultimately in the intelligibility score.

Labial movements are assessed for range and rate of movement for both speech and nonspeech (pursing/spreading/smiling and repetitive /pa/) behaviors. The range of mandibular movement is assessed for opening and closing, and both behaviors are judged on 5-point category scales. Likewise, lingual movements are assessed for speech and nonspeech and also judged on different 5-point category scales. Muscle tone is also assessed with a single lingual protrusion with resistance against a tongue depressor. Explicit criteria for assigning any of five categories for each of the structures or movements rely on the skill, bias, and knowledge of the examiner.

Prosody is assessed via reading rate on the "grandfather" passage (or alternately from contextual speaking rate) and from the acoustic and perceptual judgment of stress and intonation. Speech rate can be calculated rather objectively, and criteria are provided for judging normalcy/deviance. Although intensity, fundamental frequency, and duration of voicing can be measured acoustically with high validity and reliability, their relationships to the perceptual measures of the same behaviors are often substantively discordant. Although the 5-point category scale for judging stress and intonation is often difficult to objectify and hence difficult to measure reliably even by highly trained judges, the preliminary reliability data provided for this measure appear adequate for the DEB.

Other, supplementary, measures of oral motor performance include palatal and pharyngeal gag reflex and oral sensitivity to tactile stimulation. As with most clinical neurologic examinations, the delivery of stimulation and judgment of responses rely on the skills, biases, and experience of the examiner and are therefore susceptible to unreliability.

Construct validity is poorly addressed. Where it is inferred, it is minimally explained and in those rare instances where there is an explanation (e.g., the definition of dysarthria), it is difficult to reconcile with known phenomenology and mechanisms of the family of dysarthrias. A substantive limitation of the DEB is the lack of rationale or data for the ordinality or intervality of each of the 5-point category scales. Without such evidence, it is difficult to determine with confidence that an assigned rating represents an improvement or decrement in performance, either within or between individuals with dysarthria.

Concurrent and predictive validities were not addressed in the DEB.

RELIABILITY. Interjudge reliability was estimated using six graduate students who had completed two semesters of coursework in voice and (presumably) the dysarthrias. Three were trained in the administration and scoring (amount and nature unspecified) of the DEB and three were not. Ten of the 15 measures that require perceptual ratings were videotaped from 18 heterogeneous (with respect to etiology) subjects with dysarthria. No explanation was given for the omission of the other measures other than that the nonspeech and lingual resistance judgments were excluded because they could not be observed clearly from videotape replay. Nine of the 10 measures demonstrated significant correlation coefficients that were all high and ranged from .73 to .98 on the first ratings and .36 (nonsignificant, $p > .05$) to .96 on the second rating. Inexperienced (untrained) DEB scorers had significantly poorer interjudge reliability for 2 of the 10 measures (vocal speech quality and nasality) compared to the experienced raters.

Intrajudge reliability was examined by having the same six judges who were used in the interjudge analysis repeat the judgments from videotape, one week later. Correlation coefficients for the second experienced judge were low and nonsignificant for 1 of the 10 measures (nasality), as was 1 measure for Judge 3 (vocal speech quality). The significant correlation coefficients were generally high and ranged from .63 to .98 for these judges. The inexperienced judges' reliability was somewhat poorer with two nonsignificant correlation coefficients (vocal speech quality and lingual elevation/depression) for Judge 1, two for Judge 2 (vocal speech quality and nasality), and one for Judge 3 (nasality). The significant correlation coefficients were generally high and ranged from .47 to .92.

Test-retest reliability was not addressed in the DEB.

ADMINISTRATION. The speech and nonspeech tasks are relatively simple to administer by the clinician and perform by the patient. The patient instructions are generally relatively free from ambiguity and administration procedures are reasonably well specified and likely to provide the context for replicable test performance. However, the number of trials or tokens elicited for many measures is small and provides a threat to the accurate (valid) measurement of the frequently variable performance of many of the dysarthrias.

STRENGTHS. The DEB is unique in its integration of acoustic and physiologic with the auditory/visual perceptual measures in the examination of the speech production system in dysarthria. It is unusual in its lack of reliance on maximum performance tasks. Most tasks and judgments are framed around the dynamic range of "typical" speech production. This characteristic may provide a more socially valid measure of dysarthria than most other examinations.

Reference data for each of the measures (perceptual as well as acoustic and physiologic) are provided with suggested cutoff scores for the diagnosis of "abnormal/deviant" performance. This is rare in dysarthria assessments and provides a useful guide to the clinician or researcher. This provision also leaves the battery open to criticism for a lack of validation of these cutoff scores.

Although the data must be considered preliminary in terms of number of judges evaluated and the number of tasks measured, interjudge and intrajudge reliabilities are encouraging. This is especially true for the notoriously low reliability of many of the measures that use 5-point category scales such as those used in this battery.

WEAKNESSES. Although cutoff scores are provided for 23 of the 47 dependent measures, there is no concurrent validation of them for any of the purposes for which the test was developed. Neither sensitivity nor specificity data are provided for any of the tasks or for the test as a whole. Without test-retest reliability evidence, the DEB cannot be recommended for any of the purposes for which it was designed.

Reliability evidence was not reported for one third of the perceptual measures or for any of the acoustic or physiologic measures that play a critical role in the ultimate validity and utility of scores from the DEB. Although instrumental measures are generally considered to be more reliable than perceptual measures, this reliability is dependent on the behavioral sample from which the measurements are taken. With the relatively small number of tokens/trials for each of the tasks, it is possible/likely that these measures would be unstable or perhaps provide an invalid representation of a specific person's behavior on that task/measure. Reliability evidence for these measures is essential to examine before the DEB can be recommended for any of the purposes for which it was constructed.

The 5-point category scales on which each of the perceptual measures was based were apparently assembled to provide ordinal and interval-level data. No demonstration of this scaling was presented and hence the reliability data may be suspect.

SUMMARY. Overall utility and comparison to other dysarthria assessments: Although most tests for dysarthria use tasks very similar to those of the DEB, few others provide cutoff data for determining abnormal performance. In this way, the DEB provides an advantage over most of the other protocols. The DEB's omission of test-retest reliability and established sensitivity and specificity data place it in close approximation with most other published tests of dysarthria. Without these data the DEB cannot be recommended for any of the purposes for which it was designed. However, the systematic guide of tasks through the speech processes offered by the DEB is an important improvement over an unstructured, haphazard, and nonreplicable assessment often used by clinicians in the assessment of dysarthria.

REVIEWER'S REFERENCES

Darley, F. L., Aronson, A. E., & Brown J. R. (1969a). Clusters of deviant speech dimensions in the dysarthrias. *Journal of Speech & Hearing Research, 12,* 462–496.
Darley, F. L., Aronson, A. E., & Brown, J. R. (1969b). Differential diagnostic patterns of dysarthria. *Journal of Speech and Hearing Research, 12,* 246–269.
Dworkin, J. P., & Culatta, R. A. (1980). Dworkin-Culatta Oral Mechanism Examination. Nicholasville, KY: Edgewood Press, Inc.
St. Louis, K., & Ruscello, D. (1987). The Oral Mechanism Screening Examination. Baltimore: University Park Press.
Enderby, P. M. (1994). Frenchay Dysarthria Assessment. Austin, TX: PRO-ED, Inc.

[130]
Dyslexia Screening Instrument.

Purpose: Designed to identify students with dyslexia.
Population: Grades 1–12, ages 6–21.
Publication Date: 1994.
Scores, 4: Passed, Failed, Inconclusive, Cannot Be Scored.
Administration: Individual.
Price Data, 1999: $74.50 per complete kit including teacher rating scale, manual (40 pages), and scoring program software; $13 per 50 rating forms.
Time: (15–20) minutes.
Comments: Rating form is completed by student's teacher; computer scored, DOS 3.0 or higher.
Authors: Kathryn B. Coon, Mary Jo Polk, and Melissa McCoy Waguespack.
Publisher: The Psychological Corporation.

Review of the Dyslexia Screening Instrument by JANET E. SPECTOR, Assistant Professor of Education and Human Development, University of Maine, Orono, ME:

The Dyslexia Screening Instrument (DSI) assesses the degree to which a student displays characteristics associated with Dyslexia. According to the authors, the DSI is useful for screening students in grades 1–12 to identify those at risk for dyslexia. The authors also recommend the DSI as part of a multidisciplinary evaluation to document a student's disability as required by either Section 504 of the Rehabilitation Act of 1973 or the Individuals with Disabilities Education Act (IDEA).

The measure comprises 33 statements, each of which describes a problem (e.g., inadequate spelling for grade level; low self-esteem). A rater, typically the target student's teacher, indicates on a 5-point Likert-type scale the degree to which the student demonstrates each behavior. Administration is easily accomplished, even for novice evaluators. Scoring is slightly less straightforward. Because items are weighted to reflect their contribution in discriminating between students with and without dyslexia, the measure must be scored using software that comes with the scale. The program is available only for PC users, a notable limitation for teachers in schools with Apple or Macintosh computers. For PC users, the computer software is easy to use. According to the authors, rating and scoring takes no more than 15 to 20 minutes per student.

The DSI yields a classification rather than a norm-referenced score such as a standard score of percentile rank: *Passed* (i.e., the student's score is most similar to students in the norm group who did not have dyslexia); *Failed* (i.e., the student's score is most similar to students in the norm group who were identified as dyslexic); *Inconclusive* (i.e., the score is not similar to either of the above groups); and *Cannot Be Scored* (i.e., more than three items were omitted by the rater). For students who fail the screening, the manual recommends completion of additional assessments in accordance with state and district policies for identifying students with special education needs. Follow-up is also recommended for students with an inconclusive rating and for students who pass the screening if they were referred due to academic problems.

The test manual contains brief but well-organized sections on reliability, validity, and standardization procedures. Test reliability was estimated using two approaches, internal consistency and interrater reliability. Although it would be desirable to study interrater reliability in a larger sample and to investigate test-retest reliability, the measure shows sufficient reliability for a screening device (i.e., all coefficients exceeded .85).

The DSI may appeal to school personnel who are searching for a quick way to identify students at risk for dyslexia. Unfortunately, it has several serious shortcomings. First, the authors fail to provide a definition of dyslexia, a construct for which meaning varies widely across researchers, practitioners, and policy makers (e.g., Lyon, 1995). Without a definition, it is impossible to judge construct or content validity. The only definition the authors provide is for learning disabilities, and this serves merely to document that dyslexia is widely regarded as a form of learning disability. The manual includes a brief discussion of content validity that focuses on item selection. Items were generated based on a review of the literature and then validated by teachers and other professionals with prior experience with dyslexia. The final set of items was selected for their ability to distinguish between dyslexic and nondyslexic students in the standardization sample. The authors acknowledge that the behaviors on the scale also describe students with learning disabilities and attentional or behavioral difficulties, but they do not believe that this undermines the use of the measure for differential diagnosis. Their argument would be more compelling if they were able to relate the behaviors to a definition of dyslexia and, better still, to a theory of dyslexia. In addition, the authors do not indicate to prospective users which items contribute most to student scores. If this information were provided, it might be possible to evaluate retrospectively the match between items and current definitions and theories of dyslexia.

A second weakness of the DSI is the nonrepresentativeness of its norms, a problem that compromises its potential as a screening device. The scale was developed in a single metropolitan school district with a sample of 386 students ranging in age from 5 to 21 years old. In comparison to the U.S. population, DSI race and socioeconomic breakdowns reflect overrepresentation of Africa-American students (36.8% of the sample) and students from lower socioeconomic levels (47.7% of the sample qualified for free or reduced-price lunch). Users in geographic regions or districts with noncomparable demographics should definitely not use the DSI. Similarly, prospective users cannot assume comparability between the

DSI's dyslexic/nondyslexic students and the dyslexic/nondyslexic population in their district. Unfortunately, no achievement or cognitive data are provided to enable a comparison.

Finally, although the authors present some promising statistics to support validity, key questions remain unaddressed. Two studies are described that demonstrate potential for differential diagnosis. One study indicated the effectiveness of the instrument in not identifying high-performing students (n = 74) as dyslexic (100% accuracy). Another study investigated the DSI's ability to distinguish between ADD and dyslexia. Among students with ADD (n = 51), the percentage of students (63%) who received passing (i.e., nondyslexic) scores was consistent with results of previous research on the percentage of students with ADD who do not have reading and spelling problems (i.e., 50%).

With respect to predictive validity, the DSI was about 73% accurate in identifying which second graders (n = 34) who had been referred for a dyslexia program would be found to be dyslexic based on more lengthy diagnostic procedures and teacher judgment. Among nine middle and high school students, DSI results and district diagnostic procedures were congruent in all but one case. In a more comprehensive study, the test was used to screen for dyslexia in a population of 762 elementary, middle, and high school students who had never been referred for testing. The demographics of the sample resembled that of the standardization sample (i.e., overrepresentation of African-Americans and students from a lower socioeconomic group). The DSI identified 20% of the students (n = 152) as Failing (i.e., dyslexic) or Inconclusive. Unfortunately, the rate of hits and false positives cannot be established because outcomes for failing and inconclusive scores are not separated. However, among these students, only 24% (n = 36) were later diagnosed as dyslexic, suggesting a potentially high rate of false positives. False negatives cannot be estimated because no follow-up testing was done for students who passed the screening.

Is the DSI an efficient and effective screening measure? Clearly, additional data are needed to address this question. In particular, it would be helpful to compare the DSI's hit rate to that of other measures. Many school districts use group-administered achievement tests to identify students with problems such as dyslexia. If the DSI is not a better predictor of dyslexia than achievement data, it will be superfluous in districts with group-administered testing programs.

Overall, the DSI is an easily administered rating scale that may be attractive to school personnel who need to identify students who are at risk for dyslexia. However, given the absence of a guiding definition of dyslexia, the nonrepresentativeness of the standardization sample, and the indeterminacy of validity studies, the measure falls short of its promise. Until the authors address these issues, the test is not recommended as a screening measure.

REVIEWER'S REFERENCE

Lyon, G. R. (1995). Toward a definition of dyslexia. *Annals of Dyslexia, 45*, 3–31.

Review of the Dyslexia Screening Instrument by BETSY WATERMAN, Associate Professor, Counseling and Psychological Services Department, State University of New York at Oswego, Oswego, NY:

The Dyslexia Screening Instrument is a recently developed (1994) measure for which the purpose is to help identify children or adolescents who demonstrate those characteristics often associated with dyslexia (i.e., reading, spelling, writing, or language-processing difficulties). It is also suggested that the results of this test may help to provide information required for documentation of eligibility for services under Section 504 of the Rehabilitation Act of 1973 and the Individuals with Disabilities Education Act (IDEA).

The Dyslexia Screening Instrument is a 5-point rating scale that is completed by a teacher who is acquainted with the targeted student's reading, English, or language abilities. The scale consists of 33 declarative phrases (e.g., "easily distracted") to which a teacher may respond with one of five possible numbers: 1-never exhibits; 2-seldom exhibits; 3-sometimes exhibits; 4-often exhibits; and, 5-always exhibits. Scoring is completed using an IBM-format computer program that accompanies the test. Concrete instructions for installing and using the computerized program are included in the manual. There are four possible outcomes or "scores" that may be assigned to the targeted student based on the teacher's responses—Passed (behavioral characteristics not consistent with dyslexia), Failed (behavioral characteristics consistent with dyslexia), Inconclusive (behavioral characteristics that are inconsistent with either group), and Cannot Be Scored (the result of more than three questions unanswered).

In developing this instrument, an initial pool of 70 research-based statements was reviewed by teachers, and later, by other professionals (i.e., psychologists, college teachers, and reading specialists) with 43 statements retained.

A total of 386 students, 172 from elementary grades and 214 from secondary grades, from a large, city school district, made up the development sample. Of these students, 103 were in the dyslexia program. In an effort to determine the "best weighted combination of statement scores" (manual, p. 17), the 43 items were subjected to discriminant analysis. Those items that had low discriminant weights, were highly correlated with each other, or were frequently omitted during testing were ultimately eliminated from the statement pool. The 33 items that remained comprise the current test. The authors also used the posterior probability of group membership, with the probability set at 95% in order to be classified as a member of a given group.

Internal consistency for items on the Dyslexia Screening Instrument was reported at .99 for the elementary students and .98 for the secondary students. Interrater reliability was completed with 27 elementary and 29 secondary at-risk students who had received multiple teacher ratings. A correlation of .86 was reported for elementary students and .91 for secondary students. The authors reported 100% and 97% agreement on classification for elementary and secondary students respectively.

Content, construct, and predictive validity studies were also conducted. The test authors report that the Dyslexia Screening Instrument is based on current research and reviewed by experts in the field. The authors report that discriminant analysis predicted placement with 98.2% at the elementary level and 98.6% at the secondary level and 100% accuracy with high achieving students at both elementary and secondary levels. In a study completed with children classified with Attention Deficit Disorder (ADD), the test authors found that 63% of ADD children were classified as nondyslexic, 25% were classified as dyslexic, and 12% as "Inconclusive," consistent with other research findings on ADD/dyslexia overlap. Predictive validity was investigated in two studies using students who had been referred for dyslexia screen-

ing. These students were rated by teachers using the Dyslexia Screening Instrument and also evaluated in the school district's typical manner (i.e., cognitive assessment, discrepancies in achievement performances). The authors report that 73% to 100% of students who "Failed" the Dyslexia Screening Instrument were classified as dyslexic and over 73% of those who "Passed" the Dyslexia Screening Instrument were not classified as dyslexic. A final screening study was completed on 474 elementary, 189 middle school, and 99 high school students who had never been referred for testing. White (322), African-American (416), and other (24) racial groups were represented. Students who "Failed" or were classified as "Inconclusive" were further assessed for cognitive and achievement abilities. Of those, 54% of elementary students, 70% of middle school students, and 100% of high school students were ultimately diagnosed as dyslexic.

SUMMARY. The Dyslexia Screening Instrument appears to be a quick measure that is useful in identifying students who have behavioral characteristics that are consistent with other students diagnosed with dyslexia and that shows reasonable evidence for score validity and reliability. Statements on the rating scale appear consistent with current literature in the field and are written in generally concrete, observable, "non-child-blaming" terms. From a psychometric standpoint, the instrument appears adequate although samples are small and from one geographic area. The greatest concern related to the current measure is the absence of any discussion related to the definition of dyslexia. Because this term is not universally used in state definitions of disabilities and it is used in many different ways by both lay people and professionals, the lack of a clear definition may result in confusion as this test is applied and interpreted. Finally, although the computer scoring program is generally easy to use, the instructions need to be updated to include the latest versions of Windows currently in use (i.e., Windows 3.X, and Window 95 and 98). Also, the program generates a report so brief that it offers little specific useful information.

Overall, this screening instrument appears appropriate for the purpose for which it is intended and may offer preliminary information that would be helpful in further assessment and in the development of interventions.

[131]
Dysphagia Evaluation Protocol.

Purpose: Developed to "assist in evaluating swallowing functioning in adult patients."

Population: Adult patients.

Publication Date: 1997.

Acronym: DEP.

Scores: 14 ratings: History and Observations (Feeding History, Nutritional Status, Respiratory Status), Clinical Evaluation of Swallowing (Observations, Oral Control, Primitive and Abnormal Reflexes, Pharyngeal Control), Feeding Trial (Appetite/Willingness to Participate, Ability to Swallow Without Food Bolus, Oral State, Pharyngeal Stage), Impressions (Summary, Functional Level, Recommendations/Plan).

Administration: Individual.

Price Data: Not available.

Time: Administration time not reported.

Authors: Wendy Avery-Smith, Abbey Brod Rosen, and Donna M. Dellarosa.

Publisher: Therapy Skill Builders—A Division of The Psychological Corporation.

[Editor's Note: The publisher advised in February 2001 that this test is now out of print.]

Review of the Dysphagia Evaluation Protocol by MAYNARD D. FILTER, Professor of Speech-Language Pathology, James Madison University, Harrisonburg, VA:

The Dysphagia Evaluation Protocol (DEP) was developed for the purpose of assisting the trained professional "in evaluating swallowing function in adult patients, based on behavioral observation without the use of technical equipment" (manual, p. 3). The DEP consists of a protocol for the bedside evaluation of adults with suspected dysphagia. The authors have indicated that no published protocols for the evaluation of adults with dysphasia have been tested for reliability. The DEP record form is a four-page check sheet that includes limited space for comments.

A noninstrumental evaluation of feeding and swallowing is considered a routine, necessary procedure that will provide the examiner with important diagnostic or descriptive information. The concise, check-sheet format of the DEP allows the examiner to organize data in an orderly systematic manner. The major areas important for swallowing and feeding are included in the DEP. Comments on specific items of the DEP follow: Under General Status, a judgment must be made (after the feeding trial) about the patient's ability to recognize the swallowing problem. A judgment of "No insight" assumes that the patient is "unaware of or actively denies the problem" (manual, p. 8). In order to make a judgment, the examiner must know if the patient really has a problem; administration of the DEP cannot determine whether the patient really has a swallowing problem. Under the category of Oral Control, judgments must be made about muscle tone during palpation; how reliable are these judgments even when the examiner is familiar with these procedures? Under Vocal Quality, the terms "low, harsh, hoarse" are not defined. Also, the authors state that hypo- [*sic*] and hypernasality may signify weakness of the uvula; there are many reasons for hypernasality and hyponasality but weakness of the uvula is not among them.

Under Volitional Cough, a deep cough is not defined. Under the Oral Stage, a judgment of "normal bolus containment in oral cavity" (manual, p. 18) is made if there is no drooling, leakage from lips, or spillover into the pharynx; the spillover cannot be observed without instrumentation. Judgments of "bolus formation" are judgments of "bolus clearing," not "bolus formation." Judgments of bolus propulsion cannot be made during swallows because the mouth should be closed as soon as a bolus is presented. Silent aspiration is listed as one of the criteria for deferring or discontinuing the feeding trial; the signs and symptoms of silent aspiration are not explained.

Interrater reliability data were not gathered from independent administrations of the DEP; one examiner administered the DEP and the other examiner observed. The research study results found that 58 of 96 or 60% of individuals showing difficulty on some aspect of the DEP also showed evidence of aspiration, penetration, or pooling during the modified barium swallow study (MBS), even though MBS procedures and methods of rating/judging were not specified. Because the DEP evaluation resulted in 40% false positives for symptoms of pharyngeal stage dysphagia, DEP results should not be used to determine if an MBA study should be recommended. No correlation of DEP data with MBS data was reported. Also, on Charts 3.1 and 3.2 in the manual, the number of subjects under DEP and MBS is not clear.

A noninstrumental dysphagia evaluation should assist in the identification of those patients who do not need further (expensive) testing, and should help predict those patients who might present aspiration, penetration, or pooling. The authors found that no individual items or groups of items showed definitive predictive ability; however, 13 items from the DEP appeared to be "most closely linked to impairment or difficulty on at least one area of the MBS" (manual, p. 35). In the summary of the research study the authors indicate that clinicians may use the DEP results in identifying [*sic*] specific variables or elements of swallowing function that are problematic. The problematic variables listed in the research study are broad (nonspecific) areas such as oral control, pharyngeal control, bolus formulation, and bolus propulsion, the latter two of which cannot be evaluated without instrumentation.

The seven purposes of the DEP follow with comments related to each purpose. The DEP (accurately documents the status of clients; the DEP provides an organization that allows the examiner to document the status of the client; (b) encourages the use of uniform terminology among staff; terminology such as: harsh voice quality, deep cough, bolus formation, and bolus propulsion should be defined and clarified; (c) assists in identifying an individual's type of dysphagia; results of the DEP could rule out oral dysphagia; therefore, the ability to identify type of dysphagia is limited; (d) is useful as a consistent measure when comparing the performance of different clients at different stages of disease and treatment; if all examiners used the DEP, results from different administrations of the DEP could be compared; (e) is useful to classify and standardize treatment for specific types of dysphagia; DEP data are not related to classifying or standardizing treatment; (f) is helpful to determine which clients are appropriate for videofleuroscopy or other imaging procedures; DEP data do not predict which patients should receive further tests and which should not; (g) is useful as a reevaluation measure to assess the effectiveness of therapeutic techniques; when test and retest materials are identical, reliability increases.

Most authorities in dysphagia agree that a (noninstrumental) clinical evaluation provides important data that will be useful for differential diagnosis. Dysphagia clinical evaluation outlines and forms are available in the literature; Goodrich and Walker (1997) have developed a two-page form as has Miller (1997). Swigert (1996) has developed a two-page form for the acute care setting and a two-page form for the skilled nursing facility setting. Swigert includes complete directions and cover sheets that allow the examiner to rate swallowing performance on the ASHA Functional Communication Measure/Swallowing. The most complete noninstrumental clinical evaluation protocol for dysphagia is the Clinical Evaluation of Dysphagia (CED) developed at the Rehabilitation Institute of Chicago (RIC) by Cherney, Pannell, and Cantieri (1994); it includes a very complete seven-page outline. During trial feeding, 14 areas may be assessed for six different types of bolus presentations; however, no reliability or validity data on scores from the RIC-CED are available.

SUMMARY. The DEP covers the major areas related to feeding and swallowing; the protocol is concise and organized. Reliability and validity data suggest that the DEP will provide dependable data when administered by an experienced examiner. The DEP does provide important diagnostic information and gives the examiner a "standardized" outline format. Integrating information from standardized protocols is included among the purposes of the clinical examination listed in the guidelines "Clinical Indicators for Instrumental Assessment of Dysphagia" drafted by ASHA Special Interest Division 13 (1998); the DEP could serve as an acceptable standardized protocol.

REVIEWER'S REFERENCES

Cherney, L. R., Pannell, J. J., & Cantieri, C. A. (1994). *Clinical evaluation of dysphagia in adults.* In L. R. Cherney (Ed.), Clinical management of dysphagia in adults and children (2nd ed.) (pp. 49–69). Gaithersburg, MD: Aspen Publishers, Inc.
Swigert, N. B. (1996). *The source for dysphagia.* East Moline, IL: LinguiSystems, Inc.
Goodrich, S. J., & Walker, A. I. (1997). Clinical swallow evaluation. In R. Leonard & K. Kendall (Eds.), *Dysphagia assessment and treatment planning. A team approach* (pp. 59–72). San Diego: Singular Publishing Group, Inc.
Miller, R. M. (1997). Clinical examination for dysphagia. In M. E. Groher (Ed.), Dysphagia diagnosis and management (3rd ed.) (pp. 143–162). Boston: Butterworth-Heinemann.
ASHA Special Interest Division 13. (1998). *Guidelines—Clinical indicators for instrumental assessment of dysphagia.* Rockville, MD: American Speech-Language-Hearing Association.

[132]
Early Childhood Attention Deficit Disorders Evaluation Scale.

Purpose: Designed to document behaviors and measure the characteristics of ADHD in school and home environments.

Population: Ages 24–84 months.

Publication Date: 1995.

Acronym: ECADDES.

Scores, 3: Inattentive, Hyperactive-Impulsive, Total Percentile Rank.

Administration: Individual.

Forms, 3: Home, School, ECADDES/DSM-IV.

Price Data, 1999: $142 per complete kit including 50 School Version rating forms, 50 Home Version rating forms, 50 ECADDES/DSM-IV forms, School Version technical manual (42 pages), Home Version technical manual (42 pages), ECADDES Intervention manual (147 pages), and Parent's Guide (134 pages); $31 per 50 rating forms (specify School Version or Home Version); $31 per 50 Home Version Spanish rating forms; $20 per 50 ECADDES/DSM-IV forms; $12.50 per technical manual (specify School Version or Home Version); $22 per ECADDES Intervention manual; $13 per Parent's Guide; $35 per computerized Quick Score program (IBM); $149 per computerized Intervention manual (IBM); $149 per computerized Parent's Guide (IBM).

Time: (15–20) minutes.

Comments: Ratings by persons familiar with the child's behavior patterns in home or school settings.

Authors: Stephen B. McCarney and Nancy W. Johnson (Intervention Manual and Parent's Guide).

Publisher: Hawthorne Educational Services, Inc.

Review of the Early Childhood Attention Deficit Disorders Evaluation Scale by LIBBY G. COHEN, Professor of Special Education, University of Southern Maine, Gorham, ME:

The overall purpose of the Early Childhood Attention Deficit Disorders Evaluation Scale (ECADDES) is to assist in the identification of children ages 2.0 through 6.0 years who have Attention-Deficit/Hyperactivity Disorder (ADHD). The ECADDES consists of Home and School Versions. The American Psychiatric Association *Diagnostic and Statistical Manual of Mental Disorders, Fourth Edition* (DSM-IV; 1994) has defined ADHD and has established five criteria for determining ADHD. The Home and School Versions are observational scales designed to be used together and document the prevalence of the characteristics of ADHD.

The DSM-IV definition of ADHD requires that the existence of ADHD be documented in at least two settings. Thus, the Home and School Versions should both be used when documenting the characteristics of ADHD. The manuals correctly caution that the scales only confirm characteristics of ADHD and that the information obtained from the scales should be used to make referrals for further assessment or as part of a comprehensive evaluation.

Both the Home and School Versions are composed of two subscales, Inattentive and Hyperactive-Impulsive, that are similar in format. The Home Version contains 50 items and the School Version contains 56 items. The items were developed based on the five criteria of ADHD specified in DSM-IV.

Both versions are administered in a similar fashion. A rater, usually a parent or a teacher who is familiar with the child, completes the rating form. Each item is rated from 0 (*does not engage in the behavior*) to 4 (*one to several times per hour*). If the rater has not observed the child engaging in a behavior, the behavior is rated 0. It takes between 15 and 20 minutes to complete the form.

Few details about the standardization samples for both versions of this test are provided. The Home Version was standardized on 1,896 children, ages 2 through 6 years, from 28 states. The School Version was standardized on 2,887 children, ages 2 through 6 years, from 30 states. The subjects were identified by school districts, randomly selected by a commercially available mailing list. When comparisons of the subjects' characteristics are made with the Statistical Abstract of the United States (1992) numerous discrepancies can be found. For the Home Version, there is an overrepresentation of children whose parents hold white collar jobs, severe underrepresentation of children residing in the West, overrepresentation of children who are categorized as white, underrepresentation of children categorized as African-American, and an overrepresentation of males. For the School Version, there is an underrepresentation of parents who hold white collar jobs, an overrepresentation of parents who hold blue collar jobs, a severe underrepresentation of children living in the West, overrepresentation of children who are categorized as white, underrepresentation of children categorized as African-American, and an overrepresentation of males. Although both versions are intended to be used together, there is no evidence that they were co-normed.

Test-retest reliability for the School Version was examined using a sample of 65 children. The test-retest interval was 30 days. All coefficients were in the mid to high .90s. Test-retest reliability for the Home Version was estimated using a sample of 67 children. The test-retest interval was 30 days. All coefficients were in the mid to high .80s. Interrater reliability was investigated for both versions. Depending on the version, sets of parents or educators rated 97 children. For the Home Version, coefficients ranged from .70 to .72. The coefficients for the School Version ranged from .64 to .67. Internal consistency was measured for both versions using Cronbach's alpha. The coefficients were in the high .90s for both versions.

The manual attempts to demonstrate that the ECADDES has content validity. This type of validity is not appropriate for an instrument of this sort because a theoretical construct, attention-deficit/hyperactivity, is being measured. The manual for each version states that content validity was established by diagnosticians and educators who matched DSM-IV criteria with scale items. In fact, this is not content validity; it is face validity, which should not be confused with content validity.

Evidence of criterion-related validity was documented in several ways. The ratings of 71 randomly selected children from the normative sample were similar to the ratings of children who were diagnosed as having ADHD. This is not surprising because the children in both the standardization sample and the clinical group were already identified as having ADHD.

Evidence of criterion-validity was also considered by administering the ECADDES with the Conners' Rating Scale and the Attention Deficit/Hyperactivity Test to 68 children. The resulting coefficients demonstrated that each of the instruments evaluates somewhat similar, but not identical characteristics.

Although the test purports to measure a theoretical construct, ADHD, minimal evidence is provided about that construct, how to evaluate it, and the diagnostic utility of the results.

SUMMARY. The ECADDES is based on the DSM-IV criteria for attention-deficit/hyperactivity disorder. Although intuitively appealing, this instrument should be used very cautiously. Glaring weaknesses include lack of an appropriate standardization sample and inadequate evidence of validity. When developing an instrument that proposes to assess a theoretical construct, such as attention-deficit/hyperactivity disorder, evidence of construct validity is essential. Unfortunately, evidence of construct validity is very weak.

REVIEWER'S REFERENCE

American Psychiatric Association. (1994). *Diagnostic and statistical manual of mental disorders* (4th ed.). Washington, DC: Author.

Review of the Early Childhood Attention Deficit Disorders Evaluation Scale by HAROLD R. KELLER, Professor and Chair, Department of Educational Psychology, University of Nebraska—Lincoln, Lincoln, NE:

The Early Childhood Attention Deficit Disorders Evaluation Scale (ECADDES) includes a 50-item Home Version and a 56-item School Version. Ratings are provided by sets of caregivers and teachers. Norms are established for males and females ages 2 through 6, yielding standard scores for inattentive and hyperactive-impulsive behaviors, with separate norms for the Home and School Versions.

The technical manuals for Home and School Versions are accompanied by *The Parent's Guide to Early Childhood Attention Deficit Disorders* and *The Early Childhood Attention Deficit Disorders Intervention Manual*. The ECADDES was targeted specifically to the criteria for ADHD within DSM-IV. The authors state that ECADDES may be used for multiple purposes: (a) to screen for characteristics of ADHD; (b) to provide a measure of ADHD behavior for any children referred by the school or parents; (c) to provide information that may contribute to the diagnostic process for ADHD; (d) to develop program goals and objectives; and (e) to identify intervention activities for ADHD in the educational/home environment.

Multiple raters who are familiar with the child and who have primary observational opportunities in the setting are encouraged. Frequency of behaviors observed in each setting are rated on a 5-point scale, from 0 (*does not engage in the behavior* or not observed) to 4 (*one to several times per hour*). The frequency designations certainly represent an improvement over prior scales where ratings range from *not at all* to *very much* (Conners, 1989) and from *not a problem* to *severe problem* (Gilliam, 1995). Ratings are summed for raw scores, then converted to subscale standard scores (mean of 10 and standard deviation of 3), a sum of subscale standard scores, standard errors of measurement, and percentile score. It should be noted that the example in the School Version manual for computing subscale standard scores is incorrect, based upon information from the wrong columns.

Items were based upon characteristics of ADHD from DSM-IV and were developed from recommendations of unspecified diagnosticians and educators/other professionals. A total of 56 professionals supplied a list of indicators of ADHD, then suggested refinements of initial item pools. The scales were then field tested with children in 10 school districts in Missouri, with teachers and parents of children from all grades (K–12). The grade range for the field testing is problematic because the scale ranges from ages 2 to 6. Item analyses were conducted and resulted in the final item sets for the two versions.

Normative data for the School Version were gathered from 2,887 children from 52 school systems in 30 states. The Home Version included normative data from 1,896 children in 28 states. There is no description of the school settings, particularly at the preschool level where considerable variability in context, and educational and social goals might be expected. In comparison to national proportions, both samples were underrepresented by ethnic minority groups. The North Central region and children from rural residences were overrepresented in both samples, whereas the West region and urban/suburban settings were underrepresented. The School and Home Versions were not co-normed and that might have been useful for decision-making purposes. The numbers of 6-year-old children in each sample (111 and 276 for the School and Home Versions, respectively) were quite small, particularly because there are separate standardization groups by age and gender. Although DSM-IV criteria indicate that symptoms must be present prior to age 7, most ADHD diagnoses are made with school-age children (Barkley, 1998; DuPaul & Stoner, 1994).

Test-retest reliabilities, based upon random samples of children from the normative samples rated at a 30-day interval, were in the .90s for the School Version and in the .80s for the Home Version across all scores and age by gender groups. These reliability estimates are consistent with prior literature (Achenbach & Edelbrock, 1978). Interrater reliabilities were in the .70s and .60s, for the School and Home Versions, respectively. Internal consistencies for both versions were .96 to .98 for the total scale.

Generally principal components analyses support the identification of two subscales, relating to inattention and hyperactive-impulsive factors. Diagnostic validity on each version was determined by comparing the ratings of randomly selected sets of children with corresponding groups of children identified as ADHD in the same school systems. On both versions, group differences were significant in the expected direction. Correlations with other home and school measures (Conners, 1989; Gilliam, 1995) were signifi-

cant, supporting criterion-related validity. However, the order of magnitude of the correlations was not always in the anticipated direction. For example, the Conners Hyperactivity subscale correlated higher with the ECADDES Inattention subscale than with the Hyperactive-Impulsivity subscale. Similarly, Gilliam's Impulsivity subscale correlated higher with the ECADDES Inattention subscale than with the Hyperactive-Impulsivity subscale.

The most important concerns about these scales relate to the authors' proposed uses for the scales. With regard to screening, measuring, and providing information that might contribute to the diagnostic process for ADHD, the authors explicitly state that ratings from parents and teachers are not the sole determinants of diagnosis of ADHD. They provide a good list of what is included in a comprehensive assessment for ADHD. Placing a bold-faced statement that ratings are not sole determinants of diagnosis on both rating forms would lend this important point greater prominence. Reliance upon only ratings occurs too frequently in practice, and every effort should be made to prevent misuse and misunderstanding of such measures. The manuals provide no guidance for how to use these scales in the assessment and diagnostic process. The authors appropriately recommend the administration of both the School and Home Versions, with multiple respondents for each version. However, they provide no guidance for how to deal with inconsistent ratings within or across settings (Costenbader & Keller, 1990).

The intervention and parent guide manuals are designed to address the development of program goals and objectives, and identification of interventions in both settings. The authors also state that the scales can be used to monitor progress toward intervention goals. No data are presented on scale sensitivity to intervention and behavior change with multiple administrations. Intervention programs for children with ADHD are more effective when there is collaboration between home and school settings. There is no guidance in either manual concerning the importance of collaboration, how to collaborate, the focuses of collaboration, and the importance of jointly monitoring intervention effectiveness.

In each manual for each behavior presented, a set of goals, objectives, and interventions are listed, implying there is a one-to-one correspondence. No evidence is presented to support a direct relationship between the rated behaviors and the goals, objectives, and interventions. Many of the strategies appear reasonable; some are commonsense approaches, but there is no evidence presented to support their application based upon the ratings. There is some research that supports some of the strategies, but others lack research support. Some of the interventions represent important ways to interact with children, but they appear unrelated to the behaviors and no supportive data are presented.

There is no guidance in the selection of behaviors to be changed. For each behavior, multiple goals, objectives, and interventions are listed. The manuals may be useful for the generation of ideas to be evaluated systematically on an individual basis. The authors state that some interventions apply to most children and should be considered first in order to provide a more general approach to ADHD. Other interventions are purported to be more specific and should be individually selected for children. There are no guidelines as to which interventions are general and which are specific, and no guidelines for the selection of strategies to address problem behaviors. The problem seems to be compounded in the parent manual, where the authors claim that the strategies are so straightforward there is no need for a therapist or professional to explain to parents how to implement any of the strategies. The difficulty in this suggestion is illustrated in the authors' brief definition of a behavioral contract. There is extensive literature on behavioral contracts, but no empirically based guidance is provided with respect to how to implement a behavioral contract. The manuals also provide no guidance with respect to how to evaluate progress in behavioral change or how long to try strategies before modifying them. There is no discussion of the fact that behavior often gets worse or escalates before it gets better when new behavior change strategies are implemented.

SUMMARY. The School and Home Versions of the ECADDES appear to be psychometrically sound for the purposes of screening, measuring, and providing useful information as part of the diagnosis of ADHD. The emphasis that such ratings provide only partial information is not stated strongly or prominently enough. The problem is compounded by the inclusion of parent and school intervention guides that present goals,

objectives, and interventions directly tied to each rated behavior. No evidence is presented to support the use of the scales for the development of goals and objectives, or the identification of interventions in the home and school settings. No guidance is provided on home-school collaboration, selection of behaviors to be changed, or selection of goals, objectives, or interventions. No evidence is presented to support the claim that the scales can be used to monitor intervention success.

REVIEWER'S REFERENCES

Achenbach, T. M., & Edelbrock, C. S. (1978). The classification of child psychopathology: A review and analysis of empirical efforts. *Psychological Bulletin, 85,* 1275–1301.
Conners, C. K. (1989). *Conners' Rating Scales manual.* North Tonawanda, NY: Multi-Health Systems, Inc.
Costenbader, V. K., & Keller, H. R. (1990). Behavioral ratings of emotionally handicapped, learning disabled, and nonreferred children: Scale and source consistency. *Journal of Psychoeducational Assessment, 8,* 485–496.
DuPaul, G. J., & Stoner, G. (1994). *ADHD in the schools: Assessment and intervention strategies.* New York: Guilford.
Gilliam, J. E. (1995). Attention-Deficit/Hyperactivity Disorder Test. Austin, TX: PRO-ED.
Barkley, R. A. (1998). *Attention-deficit hyperactivity disorder: A handbook for diagnosis and treatment* (2nd ed.). New York: Guilford.

[133]
Early Childhood Environment Rating Scale—Revised Edition.

Purpose: Designed to measure the quality of the environments in early childhood programs.
Population: Early childhood programs or classrooms (excluding infant and toddler programs).
Publication Dates: 1980–1998.
Acronym: ECERS-R.
Scores, 8: Space and Furnishings, Personal Care Routines, Language-Reasoning, Activities, Interaction, Program Structure, Parents and Staff, Total.
Administration: Group.
Price Data: Available from publisher.
Foreign Language Editions: Translations of the original ECERS in Italian, Swedish, German, Portuguese, Spanish, and Icelandic.
Time: (140) minutes.
Comments: Can be completed by an outside observer or as a self-assessment by program staff.
Authors: Thelma Harms, Richard M. Clifford, and Debbie Cryer.
Publisher: Teachers College Press.
Cross References: See T5:875 (11 references) and T4:833 (7 references); for reviews by Richard Elardo and Cathy Fultz Telzrow of the original version, see 9:365.

Review of the Early Childhood Environment Rating Scale—Revised Edition by KATHLEEN D. PAGET, Director of Research and Evaluation, The Center for Child and Family Studies, College of Social Work, University of South Carolina, Columbia, SC:

Quality programming for preschool-aged children is one of the most important challenges facing professionals committed to the well-being of young children and their families. In the 20 years since the Early Childhood Environment Rating Scale (ECERS) was published, the field of early childhood education has witnessed significant progress, both in the quality of programs for young children and in the measurement of program quality. As the authors of the ECERS state on the first page of the manual, a process of self-examination has taken place in the field of early childhood education and has resulted in a broadening of what program quality is—to emphasize cultural diversity, family concerns, and individual children's needs. To keep pace with these defining features, the authors of the ECERS have conducted an extensive revision process of their measurement tool to emphasize the inclusion of children with disabilities and greater sensitivity to cultural diversity. Guided by input from researchers and practitioners who had used the ECERS in a variety of ways, the revised product was field tested in 45 classrooms in 35 different centers and emerged as a sound and versatile tool for research, for all phases of program planning and development, and for formative and summative evaluation.

The manual that accompanies the ECERS-R describes the revision process, the changes made to the original measure, the evidence of technical quality of the scores from the revised measure, instructions for proper use, the specific subscales and items, a sample score sheet and profile, and a score sheet from which multiple copies can be made. On the first page of the manual, the authors describe the revision as a "long and exacting process" comprising three focus groups with practitioners, feedback sessions with researchers, and distribution of a questionnaire to users of the ECERS in the United States, Canada, and Europe. This process left the original scale's definition of the environment intact: "those spatial, programmatic, and interpersonal features that directly affect the children and adults in an early childhood setting" (manual, p. 1).

The subscales of the revised measure are very comprehensive and are named Space and Furnishings; Personal Care Routines; Language-Reasoning; Activities; Interaction; Program Structure; and Parents and Staff. The 43 items comprising these subscales are scored on a scale of 1 to 7, with detailed, graduated criteria and examples enhancing ease of use. In the category of Personal Care Routines, for example, a score of 5.1 is achieved if "Each child is greeted individually (Ex. Staff say 'hello' and use child's name; use child's primary language spoken at home to say 'hello')" (manual, p. 17). A score of 5.3 is given if "Parents are greeted warmly by staff" (manual, p. 17). A score of 7.1 is attained if "When they arrive, children are helped to become involved in activities, if needed" (manual, p. 17); and a score of 7.3 is given if "Staff use greeting and departure as information sharing time with parents" (manual, p. 17). The care given to the details of scoring combines with the authors' expertise in early childhood development to provide the user a sense of confidence that all relevant features of quality programming are being examined. Because of the comprehensiveness of the scale, the authors suggest at least 2 hours for completion and *recommend* that users anticipate needing more than 2 hours.

The face validity of the measure is supplemented by empirical support for its psychometric soundness through internal consistency and interrater reliability (weighted Kappa) data for individual items and for subscales. With the exception of one item, all Kappas are .50 and higher. The manual does not provide data on the stability of scores, and the authors do not provide a rationale as to why test-retest studies have not been conducted. In addition, the manual does not provide specific validity information; instead, the authors cite studies supporting the predictive validity of the ECERS (Peisner-Feinberg & Burchinal, 1997; Whitebook, Howes, & Phillips, 1990) and state that the revised version would "be expected to maintain that form of validity" (manual, p. 2). Similarly, with respect to construct validity, the authors cite earlier studies (Rossbach, Clifford, & Harms, 1991; Whitebook et al., 1990), that have yielded two factors within the ECERS (teaching aspect of environments; provision of opportunities), and appropriately state the need for further research to determine whether the ECERS-R has the same empirical dimensions. Certainly, a measurement tool that contributes so significantly to the quality of programs for young children deserves more sustained empirical support and more widespread dissemination through refereed publications.

The section of the manual entitled "Instructions for Using the ECERS-R" is clearly written and includes clarification on scoring issues, definitions of terms, extensive "notes for clarification," and sample questions to pose to teachers to assist in arriving at accurate scores. The section effectively illustrates that conducting an accurate observation of a preschool environment is a process that requires a high level of sophistication. Although the first paragraph informs the reader that a video training package is available from Teachers College Press and recommends a training sequence led by an experienced ECERS-R trainer, this important information could be overlooked by a reader of the manual. Thus, the documentation accompanying the scale would be strengthened if a videotape and accompanying training manual were included with each manual that is distributed. Because of the subjectivity inherent in conducting classroom observations, the training materials certainly warrant more visibility.

SUMMARY. In conclusion, practitioners, parents, program evaluators, and researchers will find the ECERS-R to be an excellent tool and an improved product over its innovative and popular predecessor. The ECERS-R sets a standard for the monitoring of program quality and, in so doing, makes an effective statement regarding the importance of early childhood environments and their influence on young children's development.

REVIEWER'S REFERENCES

Whitebook, M., Howes, C., & Phillips, D. (1990). *Who cares? Child care teachers and the quality of care in America. Final report of the National Child Care Staffing Study.* Oakland, CA: Child Care Employee Project.

Rossbach, H. G., Clifford, R. M., & Harms, T. (1991, April). *Dimensions of learning environments: Cross-national validation of the Early Childhood Environment Rating Scale.* Paper presented at the annual meeting of the American Educational Research Association, Chicago.

Peisner-Feinberg, E. S., & Burchinal, M. R. (1997). Relations between preschool children's child care experiences and concurrent development: The cost, quality, and outcomes study. *Merrill-Palmer Quarterly, 43,* 451–477.

Review of the Early Childhood Environment Rating Scale—Revised Edition by GENE SCHWARTING, Assistant Professor, Department of Education/Special Education, Fontbonne College, St. Louis, MO:

This 1998 revision of the original Early Childhood Environment Rating Scale (ECERS), published in 1980, is designed as a standardized tool to be used for the assessment of facilities serving young children (ages 2 1/2 through 5 years) such as day care centers, preschools, and prekindergartens. It is presented as appropriate for program evaluation, monitoring, improvement, or research and might be administered by an outside evaluator or program staff. It is recommended that completion involve an observation of at least 2 hours duration, followed by a 20-minute discussion with staff regarding indicators not observed.

The ECERS was revised based upon analyzing its relationship to other standards for early childhood environments, input of past users of the instrument, and reviewing the results of studies using the ECERS. Goals expressed by the authors include updating content, modifications in format and scoring instructions, and adding indicator scores to improve specificity. Field testing followed by further changes resulted in the ECERS-R.

The 43 items on the ECERS-R are divided into groups of 4 to 10 items among the following seven subscales: Space and Furnishings, Personal Care Routines, Language-Reasoning, Activities, Interaction, Program Structure, and Parents and Staff. Each item is scored on a 7-point scale, with 1 = *inadequate* and 7 = *excellent*, using descriptors provided to assist in the determination of the value to be assigned. Consumers must note that a score of 1 is obtained if any item under the first descriptor is positive; higher scores are based upon all items under the first descriptor being negative with indicators under higher descriptors scored positive. Scores of 3, 5, or 7 require that all indicators for that value be scored "yes"; scores of 2, 4, or 6 require that at least half of the indicators for the next higher value are scored "yes." For the seven subscale areas, averages are to be calculated. There are no norms tables to use for making judgment, nor is there a total or overall score to obtain. Rather, the results of the scale are used to compare strengths and needs within a facility; or, one assumes, to compare different environments.

Reliability information provided indicates that the percentage of agreement across all indicators is 86%, whereas at the item level, raters agreed within a score of 1 point 71% of the time. Weighted Kappa interrater scores for each item vary from .28 through .90, with only one item (Language for Reasoning) being below .5. Interrater correlations for the subscales range from .71 through .88, with a total scale internal consistency reliability estimate of .92.

Information regarding the validity of the ECERS-R is not provided; rather, it is noted that the original version was found to have adequate predictive validity and therefore the revision should maintain that level. Face and content validity certainly appear adequate, as the items address the major criteria by which one would evaluate an early childhood center. The scores assigned to the descriptors for the items, however, appear to be related to individual philosophy and values.

Provision for special populations is made throughout items rather than as a separate section, encouraging inclusion of children with disabilities as opposed to separation. Scoring is made somewhat complex by the system utilized, but through practice will become familiar. Using means rather than medians for subscales may result in extreme scores influencing the value for an area.

SUMMARY. The availability of norms, as well as some type of overall score, would extend the usefulness of the instrument. Nevertheless, the ECERS-R is an improvement over the original and continues to be one of the few available in the field that could be effectively used to evaluate an early childhood facility. The authors' recommendation that further research be conducted with the instrument is appropriate, but should not stand in the way of the use of the instrument for the designated purposes.

[134]
Early Childhood Inventory—4.

Purpose: Constructed to assess the "behavioral, affective, and cognitive symptoms of childhood psychiatric disorders."
Population: Ages 3–6.
Publication Dates: 1996–1997.
Acronym: ECI-4.
Scores, 25: AD/HD Inattentive, AD/HD Hyperactive-Impulsive, AD/HD Combined, Oppositional Defiant Disorder, Conduct Disorder, Peer Conflict Scale, Separation Anxiety Disorder, Specific Phobia, Obsessions, Compulsions, Motor Tics, Vocal Tics, Generalized Anxiety Disorder, Selective Mutism, Major Depressive Disorder, Dysthymic Disorder, Adjustment Disorder, Social Phobia, Sleep Problems, Elimination Problems, Posttraumatic Stress Disorder, Feeding Problems, Reactive Attachment Disorder, Autistic Disorder, Asperger's Disorder.
Administration: Group.
Forms, 2: Parent Checklist, Teacher Checklist.
Price Data, 1997: $102 per deluxe kit including screening manual ('96, 72 pages), norms manual ('97, 190 pages), 25 parent checklists, 25 teacher checklists, 50 parent score sheets, and 50 teacher score sheets; $32 per 25 parent checklists and score sheets; $23 per 25 teacher checklists and score sheets; $22 per screening manual; $22 per norms manual.
Time: (10–15) minutes.
Comments: Instrument is designed to correspond to the DSM-IV classification system.

Authors: Kenneth D. Gadow and Joyce Sprafkin.
Publisher: Checkmate Plus, Ltd.

Review of the Early Childhood Inventory—4 by ROBERT C. REINEHR, Professor of Psychology, Southwestern University, Georgetown, TX:

The Early Childhood Inventories (ECI) are paper-and-pencil checklists completed by parents and teachers. The items in the *ECI* are based on the diagnostic criteria specified in the American Psychiatric Association's *Diagnostic and Statistical Manual of Mental Disorders* (DSM-IV) and are closely modeled on the Child Symptom Inventory (CSI) and the Adolescent Symptom Inventory (ASI), DSM-based instruments published previously by the same authors.

The purpose of the ECI is to facilitate the gathering of information in clinical settings from parents and teachers and to systematize the exchange of information between the school and the clinician regarding children who have been referred for clinical evaluation. Use of the checklists offers an alternative to structured psychiatric interviews, and assists in the provision of the DSM categorical label typically required by insurance reimbursement forms.

The ECI are scored in two different ways: the Screening cutoff score method and the Symptom Severity score method. The Screening cutoff method is intended to indicate whether the total number of symptoms rated for a given DSM disorder is sufficient to be of clinical concern. The primary focus of the ECI manual is the Screening cutoff score; no information is provided pertaining to the use of the Symptom Severity score.

The ECI manual presents no normative data and no reliability or validity information pertaining to either the parent or teacher checklist. Although several dimensional rating scales are mentioned in the manual as possible standards for the validation of ECI scores, no data are presented with respect to the relationship between ECI scores and any other dimensional measure. Neither are there any comparisons with structured interviews or clinical diagnoses. [Editor's Note: A separate norms manual, published in 1997, includes extensive reliability and validity information.]

Some comparisons are reported between previous versions of the ECI and the present version, and some comparisons between ECI scores of children who had been referred for psychiatric screening and those of children who were enrolled in a community day-care program. Some of the latter children were receiving special education services. Analyses and results vary between diagnostic groups, but in general, children who have been referred for psychiatric evaluation score more highly on the ECI than do the other comparison groups.

SUMMARY. The authors point out that some questions about the psychometric properties of the ECI cannot be answered satisfactorily because they are linked to the reliability and validity of the diagnostic categories on which the ECI are based. The ECI thus reflects the conceptual limitations inherent in the DSM classification system.

The shortcomings of the diagnostic system do not, however, relieve the authors of the ECI of the obligation to provide reliability and validity information to users, and the ECI manual provides no data of this kind. As a result, the ECI have essentially no psychometric value. [Editor's Note: This information is available in the 1997 norms manual.] Their value as a clinical technique is of course a matter of practitioner opinion.

[135]
Early Screening Inventory—Revised.

Purpose: Designed to identify children at risk for possible school failure.
Population: Ages 3–6.
Publication Dates: 1976–1997.
Acronym: ESI-R.
Scores, 3: Visual-Motor/Adaptive, Language and Cognition, Gross Motor.
Administration: Individual.
Levels, 2: Preschool (3 to 4 1/2 years old), Kindergarten (4 1/2 to 6 years old).
Price Data, 1997: $96 per complete kit including examiner's manual ('97, 195 pages), 30 score sheets, 30 parent questionnaires, screening materials, tote; $75 per package including trainer's manual ('97, 91 pages), introductory and training videos; $44.50 per examiner's manual $19.50 per trainer's manual; $19.50 per 30 score sheets; $29.50 per introductory video (25 minutes); $39.50 per training video (60 minutes); $17.50 per package of screening materials.
Foreign Language Edition: All screening materials available in Spanish.
Time: (15–20) minutes.
Comments: Originally introduced as the Eliot-Pearson Screening Inventory.
Authors: Samuel J. Meisels, Dorothea B. Marsden, Martha Stone Wiske, and Laura W. Henderson.
Publisher: Rebus Inc.
Cross References: See T5:889 (1 reference); for reviews by Denise M. Dezolt and Kevin Menefee of an earlier edition, see 11:122 (1 reference).

Review of the Early Screening Inventory—Revised by ERNEST KIMMEL, Executive Director, Office of Public Leadership, Educational Testing Service, Princeton, NJ:

This is the latest revision of a screening inventory that was first introduced in 1975 as the Eliot-Pearson Screening Inventory. It is a brief assessment procedure "intended to identify children who may need further evaluation in order to determine if they have a condition that may place them at risk for school failure" (examiner's manual, p. 2). The current early Screening Inventory—Revised (ESI-R) is available in two versions: The ESI-P (Preschool) that is standardized on children ages 3 to 4.5 years and the ESI-K (Kindergarten) for children ages 4.5 to 6 years. The authors are to be commended for making clear the purpose of the instrument and for stressing that "The ESI-R should be used only to identify the *possibility* of a learning or handicapping condition that might affect a child's overall potential for success in school" (examiner's manual, p. 2). They point out that any child who falls into the "Refer" category on the ESI-R needs to be further evaluated using a variety of other assessments and supplementary information.

The ESI-R is built on a well-articulated model of child development in the areas of Visual-Motor/Adaptive, Language and Cognition, and Gross Motor with the item types clearly linked to these developmental areas. All screening recommendations, however, are to be based on the total score across these three areas.

There are very clear directions for administering and scoring each task or item and a training kit, including two videos, is provided to help new testers develop the skills necessary to accurately and consistently administer and score the inventory and to analyze the results so as to provide further insights into the child's development in comparison with others of the same age.

The standardization of the ESI-R is well documented and the authors are careful to note some aspects where the normative information may not be representative. It is unfortunate that the data reported for their norming sample do not break out the Hispanic students from the catch-all "Other" category. In July 1994, during the period when the authors were collecting their norming data, the U.S. Census Bureau estimated that 14.2% of the 3- to 6-year-olds in the U.S. were Hispanic, only slightly smaller than the proportion (15.1%) of African-Americans in that age cohort. This rapidly growing segment of the population should be separately reported so that users can judge the representativeness of the norming sample.

The procedure by which the cut scores were determined is clearly explained and particular attention is given to the ability to use the inventory to discriminate between those students who are at-risk and those who are developing as expected. The evidence for both versions shows that the recommended cut scores on the ESI-R are very effective at identifying those who are at risk while excluding from further evaluation most of the children who are not at risk. There is a very low probability that a child who, in fact, needs further screening will not be identified in the "Refer" category. This is achieved at the cost of overreferring a number of students who are not at-risk. However, in the real world situation, it is preferable to have such false positives rather than to run the risk of missing children who need help.

There is evidence of high interrater reliability in the scoring of the ESI-R. The correlations between two trained scorers of the same performance are all in the .97–.99 range. The test-retest correlations (using different testers/scorers for the two occasions; time interval of 7–10 days) range from .68 to .98. The standard errors of measurement are all very small. The ESI-R has been validated against the General Cognitive Index (GCI) of the McCarthy Scales of Children's Abilities administered several months later. For both the ESI-K and the ESI-P, the correlation between the ESI score and the GCI is .73. It would be helpful if the authors would provide validity data using additional criteria, such as performance in kindergarten or in the primary grades. This was done for an earlier edition of the Inventory and one can only hope that the authors are accumulating such performance data for the students in the 1992–1994 sample. Because the authors have regularly published research regarding the Early Screening Inventory, potential users can examine the evidence for themselves.

The ESI-R was normed on English-speaking children. A version for Spanish-speaking children is available but was not included in this review. In view of the striking growth in the number of children in U.S. schools who come from homes where English is not the dominant language, it is important that the authors study how the ESI-R can be used with such children. It would provide an important service to the children and their teachers if the ESI could distinguish between delayed development and not yet being fluent in English.

SUMMARY. Overall, the ESI-R appears to be carefully developed and standardized and the authors have paid considerable attention to providing the tools for training testers/scorers to be accurate and consistent. Schools, agencies, and others working with young children should find this a useful tool for its intended purpose of identifying children who should receive a more thorough, multifaceted evaluation of their developmental needs.

Review of the Early Screening Inventory— Revised by KATHLEEN D. PAGET, Director of Research and Evaluation, The Center for Child and Family Studies, College of Social Work, University of South Carolina, Columbia, SC:

In the introductory video to the Early Screening Inventory—Revised (ESI-R), the lead author, Samuel Meisels, greets the viewer and states that he and his colleagues have been "refining, revising, and researching" the Early Screening Inventory (ESI) for 20 years. It is this reviewer's conclusion that this 20-year process has resulted in a developmental screening instrument that sets the gold standard for others who wish to develop screening instruments for use with young children.

Like its popular and well-respected predecessor, the ESI-R (pronounced "easy-r") is a brief developmental screening instrument that is individually administered to children and is designed "to identify children who may need special education services in order to perform successfully in school" (examiner's manual, p. 2). Among the improvements made during the revision process are an expansion in age range to include 3-year-olds, the addition of a parent questionnaire, an expansion of the normative sample to include 6,000 children, improvements in training materials, the development of a Spanish-language version, and an increased number of empirical studies of psychometric soundness. Comprising two versions, the preschool version (the ESI-P, for children between the ages of 3 and 4-1/2 years) and the Kindergarten version (the ESI-K, for children between the ages of 4-1/2 and 6 years), the revision reflects the differences in development between these two age groups and, in doing so, sensitively highlights the rapid growth and development of very young children.

The materials included in the ESI-R are noteworthy in a number of ways. The objects and toys used for administration are few in number, are nicely packaged, and are durable. The inclusion of a "tote bag" instead of a briefcase for carrying the materials is a child- and parent-friendly feature that reflects the sensitivity of the co-authors to the possibility of anxiety among some young children and their parents. Two videotapes are included and provide excellent information. The "Introductory Video: A Demonstration of Administrative Procedures" provides an overview of what developmental screening is, what it is not, and issues related to the presence of parents during screening. Most of this introductory video consists of the demonstration of one administration of the ESI-R, followed by an interpretation of the results. A training video provides the trainee an opportunity to view a co-author administering the ESI-R to four children between the ages of 3 and 6 years. With use of a trainer's manual during and after the video, the trainee learns how the examiner scores and interprets the four children's performances and what the "examiner's notes" indicate about each child's behavior and approach to the screening experience. For these four children, it is very clear to the trainee how the examiner arrives at one of the three possible recommendations: to refer for diagnostic assessment, to rescreen, or to give the child "OK" status. In addition, the training manual includes suggestions for new examiners, a sample letter to a family, a roster of children screened, information about the features of successful screening experiences, and details of organizing training sessions for others in using the ESI-R. It is important to note that, although a section of the manual is entitled "Suggestions for Discussing Screening Results with Parents," the section is only one-third of a page long and could be improved with case examples. In general, however, the training materials communicate the essentials of the ESI-R in a very clear way while also providing an excellent overview of the salient issues in developmental screening.

The examiner's manual supplements the administration, scoring, and interpretive information provided in the trainer's manual and provides an impressive amount of information related to the standardization, reliability, and validity of both the ESI-P and ESI-K. Results of item analyses and studies of interrater and test-retest reliability, standard error, predictive validity, and the sensitivity and specificity of cutoff scores provide strong evidence of psychometric soundness of the ESI-R. It is important to note that the psychometric information provided in the examiner's manual does not pertain to the Parent Questionnaire. On two pages of the manual, the authors provide an overview of the Parent Questionnaire and note that the Questionnaire should only be used as supplementary information rather than for making explicit screening decisions. This is an important caveat for users of the ESI-R until earlier research into the relationship between the Questionnaire and ESI screening decisions (e.g., Henderson & Meisels, 1994) is replicated.

Even though the addition of the Parent Questionnaire is an asset of the ESI-R, its inclusion also raises a number of important issues related to parent involvement in the screening process. Because of the importance of parental input and family systems issues pertaining to very young children's development, much information remains to be published and disseminated about the Parent Questionnaire. These efforts should include a videotaped demonstration of a parent interview, how the questionnaire is scored, and how results are interpreted, especially when compared with results from the child's performance on the ESI-R. This reviewer looks forward to the continued work of the co-authors in researching the validity of the Parent Questionnaire, incorporating it fully into the accompanying training materials, and continuing to emphasize the appropriate involvement of parents in the developmental screening process.

SUMMARY. It is clear that 20 years of "refining, revising, and researching" have resulted in an excellent instrument for developmental screening. At the same time that the clarity and comprehensiveness of the ESI-R make the process of instrument development look "easy," the number of years devoted by the authors to this process provide an essential backdrop for anyone who uses this measure or is interested in developing other measures for screening young children. The field of early childhood assessment would benefit from such a level of sustained commitment from others interested in the screening and well-being of very young children and their parents.

REVIEWER'S REFERENCE

Henderson, L. W., & Meisels, S. J. (1994). Parental involvement in the developmental screening of their young children: A multiple-source perspective. *Journal of Early Intervention, 18,* 141–154.

[136]
Early Screening Project.

Purpose: "Allows for the cost-effective screening of problem behaviors to aid in the early remediation of behavior disorders."
Population: Ages 3–6.
Publication Date: 1995.
Acronym: ESP.
Scores, 4: Critical Events Index, Aggressive Behavior Scale [Externalizers], Social Interaction Scale [Internalizers], Combined Frequency Index Adaptive Behavior, Combined Frequency Index Maladaptive Behavior.
Administration: Individual or group.
Price Data, 1995: $95 per complete kit including manual (103 pages), instrument packet, social observation training video, and a stopwatch.
Time: [60] minutes total/group.
Authors: Hill M. Walker, Herbert H. Severson, and Edward G. Feil.
Publisher: Sopris West.

Review of the Early Screening Project by J. JEFFREY GRILL, Professor and Chair, Special Education Department, Athens State University, Athens, AL:

The Early Screening Project (ESP) is a deceptively simple, multistage screening procedure for identifying "at-risk" children of ages 3 to 5 years. Specifically, the ESP is a downward extension of the earlier Systematic Screening for Behavior Disorders (SSBD; T5:2607), developed previously by two of this instrument's authors. The ESP kit contains a manual, a stopwatch, an extensive set of protocols, and a 15-minute video for training users in the observation procedures required at Stage Three of the procedure.

The ESP provides a procedure to screen preschool children at risk for a variety of potential school problems. The ESP "allows for proactive screening and evaluation … [and] … screens/identifies both acting-out and withdrawn behavior patterns" (manual, p. 1). Federal legislation has long mandated that states engage in "child find" activities—that is, states must actively seek out youngsters with disabilities who need special edu-

cation services. Further, the authors of the ESP cite numerous sources to support the need for early identification of such children. Nonetheless, early identification remains a difficult undertaking. Clearly, the ESP is intended to fill a significant need.

The manual clearly describes the screening procedures, and suggests that Stage One and Two procedures (i.e., ranking all children in a class along two dimensions, and then rating the top three in each group using two additional scales) could be completed for an entire preschool in a group administration. Stage One focuses on identifying children in a teacher's class for either externalizing (e.g., disruptive, acting out behavior) or internalizing (e.g., social isolation, phobias, withdrawal) behavior problems. In Stage One, teachers first must read and understand the authors' clear definitions and explicit examples of externalizing and internalizing behavior problems, and then rank order the children in their classes according to the degree to which each child matches the externalizing and internalizing profiles. Next, teachers must identify the top five children in each group. The authors emphasize that five children must be identified as externalizers and as internalizers, and that the groups must be mutually exclusive. The three highest ranking children in each group automatically pass on to Stage Two screening.

The purpose of Stage Two is to gather information to make normative comparisons on measures included in the ESP: the Critical Events Index, and either the Aggressive Behavior Scale (for Externalizers) or the Social Interaction Scale (for Internalizers), and the Combines Frequency Indices for Adaptive and Maladaptive Behavior. The Critical Events Index lists 16 behaviors, ranging from "Exhibits painful shyness," to "Sets fires," to "Vomits after eating" (p. 16). Teachers check each behavior that has occurred for that child during the school year, even if the teacher has not directly observed the behavior. For Externalizers, teachers rate each child on the Aggressive Behavior Scale, a list of nine items, among them, "Has tantrums" and "uses obscene language" (p. 18). Teachers use a 5-point scale to rate the frequency (*never* to *frequently*) with which each behavior occurs for the child. Similarly, teachers rate the Internalizers on the Social Interaction Scale, a list of eight items, among them, "Shares laughter with classmates," "Freely takes a leadership role" (p. 20). Teachers use a 7-point scale to rate the frequency of occurrence (*Not Descriptive or True* to *Very Descriptive or True*) for each behavior. Finally, in this stage, teachers complete two indices, one for adaptive behavior (eight items) and one for maladaptive behavior (nine items), and rate each of the six identified children on a 5-point frequency of occurrence scale (*Never* to *Frequently*).

Scoring the scales is straightforward. The Critical Events Index score is simply the sum of items checked on the scale (0 to 16). For each of the remaining scales used in Stage Two, the score is the sum of the numbers circled on each. Separate Normative Comparison charts are provided for boys and for girls, and each chart indicates critical scores for three levels of risk (at-risk, high risk, extreme risk) for each of the scales and indices used in Stage Two.

Stage Three of the process is optional, but recommended for any child who may be referred to a child study team. This stage involves administration of a Parent Questionnaire, and a direct Social Behavior Observation of the child during free play. Thorough directions and a training videotape are provided to ensure accurate coding of observed behaviors. Additionally, the manual offers extensive information on uses of ESP results, including suggested interventions for specific types of behaviors.

The manual also offers specific procedures for group administration, and several appendices that provide case studies, an observation quiz, sample form letters, description of technical adequacy, practice scores for the training videotape, scaled scores, and First Steps, a home-school intervention program.

The normative sample for the ESP included 2,853 children between the ages of 3 and 6 years, clearly an adequate sample. However, geographic representation is weighted heavily to the Southeastern United States, with more than one third of the sample (1,073) from Kentucky and Louisiana. Northeastern states are represented by only 25 subjects from New Hampshire. Girls comprise 46% of the sample, boys, 54%. There is a slight overrepresentation of children eligible for special education services (22%). Although racial groups are adequately represented, low-income (58%) and rural (63%) children seem to be overrepresented.

The authors report two kinds of reliability: interrater, and test-retest. Interrater reliability for Stage One was based on cross-tabulations of teacher/assistant teacher pairs of ratings, and used the Kappa

coefficient. These ranged from .42 to .70. Stage Two teachers' and assistant teachers' scaled scores for children were correlated using the Pearson r, and these coefficients ranged from .48 to .79. Generally, interrater reliability seems adequate for screening purposes. Interrater reliability for observation was calculated using a sample of 20% of the 541 observations. These coefficients were derived by dividing the smaller observation score by the larger score and resulted in coefficients of .87 and .88 in two studies.

Test-retest reliability, spanning a 6-month period, involved cross-tabulation of teacher and assistant teacher ratings. Results yielded coefficients of .59 for Externalizers and .25 for Internalizers. Fall and Spring ratings for Critical Events, Adaptive, and Maladaptive scales yielded correlation coefficients ranging from .75 to .91. These results seem adequate for screening although 6 months may be too long an interval especially with preschoolers.

The authors report that the ESP clearly discriminates between groups of Externalizers and normal children across all measures; such discrimination is less clear between groups of Internalizers and normal children.

The discussion of validity focuses on content, concurrent, and discriminative validity. For content validity the authors used a panel of experts to judge the instrument, and relied on previous research and feedback from teachers. Concurrent validity was studied using correlation with the Behar and the Conners rating scales. These studies yielded coefficients ranging from .19 to .95. Unfortunately, the authors provide no further information on sample size or on the specific correlational procedure used. Using discriminant function analysis, the authors examined the ESP's percentages of true positive and true negatives. Results yielded percentages ranging from 62 to 100, and 94 to 100 respectively, clearly adequate for screening.

SUMMARY. Overall the ESP provides a much needed, relatively simple procedure for screening preschoolers who may be at-risk for school difficulties. The manual is very clearly written, and offers much valuable information, beyond merely the instructions for administration. Relative ease and speed of use in group settings make the ESP a valuable screening instrument, despite its few flaws (i.e., disproportionate representation of some groups, and less than adequate reporting of what seems to be adequate levels of reliability and validity).

Review of the Early Screening Project by HOWARD M. KNOFF, Professor of School Psychology, University of South Florida, Tampa, FL:

The Early Screening Project (ESP) is a preschool screening tool (for ages 3 to 5 years) that helps to determine whether children with apparent externalizing or internalizing behavior problems need more in-depth assessment and intervention in their classrooms. Organized in a three-stage, multiple-gating screening process, the ESP is a downward extension of the Systematic Screening for Behavior Disorders instrument (Walker & Severeson, 1990; T5:2607), and it can be used as part of the Child Find requirement of the federal, special education Individuals with Disabilities Education Act (IDEA).

Normed on over 2,800 children, aged 3 to 6 years old, the ESP has classroom teachers (a) rank order the five most externalizing students and, separately, the five most internalizing students in their classrooms based on some fairly general behavioral descriptions of these two domains (Stage 1); and (b) complete (Stage 2) the Critical Events Index, Aggressive Behavior Scale (for externalizing students), Social Interaction Scale (for Internalizing students), and Combined Frequency Indices (Adaptive and Maladaptive Behavior) on the top three externalizing and internalizing students, respectively, from the Stage 1 list. In the optional Stage 3, students who have been identified as "At Risk" (one standard deviation above the scale means of the normative sample), "At High Risk" (two standard deviations above the means), or "At Extreme Risk" (three standard deviations above) are observed in the classroom for at least two 10-minute periods of time using the Social Behavior Observation form, and parents complete the Parent Questionnaire to determine if the same classroom problem behaviors are occurring at home.

Expanding on the multiple-gating stage process, the ESP manual recommends that teachers evaluate their students twice per year (October/November and February/March) first using the rank ordering procedures of Stage 1. Given the screening nature of this process, the descriptions of the inappropriate externalizing and internalizing behavior to which teachers are asked to compare their students, respectively, are broad and general (almost too general), and teachers are strongly encouraged to identify five problematic students in each of these two areas with no overlapping students. Although subsequent assessments at Stages 2 and 3 do appear to decrease the potential for "false positive" errors, the manual needs to more fully describe the empirical research underlying the descriptions provided, and how they accurately and consistently apply to male and female preschoolers from ages 3 to 5 and from all of the diverse geographic, socioeconomic, racial, and other backgrounds evident across the United States. Although this issue is seemingly addressed through the normative and psychometric data provided in the manual, there are some problems with these data (see below).

At Stage 2, teachers complete three of four scales for six of the students identified in Stage 1. The Critical Events Index lists 16 (one open-ended) specific behavior problems that teachers might observe in the classroom. Three of the behaviors (setting fires, being sexually abused or touched in private areas, and nightmares or sleeping problems) and a fourth (showing evidence of physical abuse) are likely to occur outside of the classroom. Teachers are encouraged to rate these four events if they have reliable and accurate information about them. The Aggressive Behavior Scale (for students identified with externalizing problems) consists of nine items rated on a 5-point frequency scale. The Social Interaction scale (for students identified with internalizing problems) consists of eight items rated on a 7-point frequency scale. And, the Combined Frequency Indices consist of eight Adaptive and nine Maladaptive behaviors also rated on 5-point frequency scales.

According to the manual, items for the Stage 2 scales were selected from the empirical research, from (undefined or described) teacher and expert feedback, and through adaptations of the SSBD (for the Critical Events Index and Aggressive Behavior Scale) and the Social Interaction Rating Scale (Hops, Walker, & Greenwood, 1988; for the Social Interaction Scale). No information on the development of the Combined Frequency Indices was evident. Overall, the information provided on the development of these scales (e.g., the rational and/or empirical decision-making rules relative to item inclusion or exclusion), the ability of individual items to discriminate at-risk versus "typical" children, and their factor structure and construct validity across student age, gender, socioeconomic strata, and race needs to be strengthened.

Relative to normative data, the Stage 2 scales were given to 1,401 preschool and kindergarten children, aged 3 to 6, in typical and specialized programs in eight states between 1991 and 1994. Given the ESP's gating process, 137 three-year-old, 721 four-year-old, and 448 five-year-old children participated in the Stage 2 norming process. Critically, the manual does not report the demographic (gender, socioeconomic, race) stratification or characteristics of these three groups, nor are any statistical analyses apparent to determine the need for separate norm tables across these variables. In addition, the geographic distribution of the normative sample is weak relative to children from the Southeast and Atlantic Seaboard (none are represented), the Northeast (only 25 children from New Hampshire are represented), and the Northern parts of the country (Utah, Nebraska, and Kentucky were the northernmost states represented between Oregon and New Hampshire).

Relative to the psychometric integrity of the Stage 2 scales, the manual reported ESP data for interrater reliability, test-retest reliability (for the Critical Events and Adaptive/Maladaptive Scales), consistency across measures, content validity, concurrent validity, discriminative validity, and treatment utility. Construct and convergent validity data were noticeably missing, and the discriminative validity study reportedly used *teacher recommendations* of students for Behavior Disorders (BD) eligibility status, rather than clinically identified BD students, for the discriminant function analyses performed. Although the psychometric data reported for these areas appear quite acceptable, additional and specific descriptions as to the samples used (including the numbers of students participating and where they were from), the demographic variables analyzed, and all of the statistics and results generated are needed. Indeed, other than norm tables for the Stage 2 scales, no other statistical tables fully outlining the psychometric data for these tools were provided. Clearly, this information is needed in order to be able to comprehensively evaluate the ESP for its field and clinical use across the country.

Stage 3 assessments are completed on children identified at Stage 2 with "At Risk" or more extreme behavior. Although the Stage 3 assessments are identified as optional in the ESP manual, behavior rating information from a referred child's parents and behavioral observations in the setting where concerns have been identified (here, in the classroom) are critical to a multi-setting, multi-instrument, multi-respondent evaluation. Even from a screening perspective, these assessments should be required in order to minimize incorrectly screened children. Regardless, the ESP's Stage 3 Parent Questionnaire consists of 12 items divided into three areas (Playing with other children, Getting along with caregivers, and Playing with materials and self-care). The Social Behavior Observation process involves free play or unstructured activity observations of identified children to determine the percentage of time that they spend in prosocial, antisocial, and nonsocial behavior. Although cross-referenced to specific items in the Stage 2 scales, the Parent Questionnaire has the same strengths and, especially, weaknesses as the other scales described above. And, although the ESP comes with a training tape that describes its behavior observation process and definitions for the specific categories used, the Social Behavior Observation process provides only a minimal level of descriptive data, and virtually no functional assessment data. It is unsettling to imagine what teachers will do with the information supplied by the observations completed (normative data are provided, but again, from an undescribed sample of students). Psychologists, significantly, will probably defer to a more comprehensive and sensitive observation system and approach.

There are a number of initial concerns inherent in the ESP (or any early screening or identification process). These include the potential (a) to misinterpret behavior that falls within the broad range of *typical* behavior for a preschooler as inappropriate or "disordered," (b) to believe that students identified by a screening tool *de facto* have a need for interventions, (c) to prematurely categorize or label children with these behaviors as special needs or special education students, and (d) to assume that screening or other assessment tools automatically link with *specific* interventions. Significantly, all of these concerns are addressed directly by the authors of the ESP, and they did respond successfully about ways to minimize their potential negative outcomes for children. However, these concerns remain given that the manual never really prescribed who should oversee the administration and interpretation of the ESP.

Although school psychologists and other related service specialists were referenced relative to this role, the manual should have more strongly required their direct supervision given the psychometric and behavioral assessment and intervention decisions required by the ESP, and the potential legal use (e.g., through IDEA) of its outcomes. This is especially true given that the primary outcome of the ESP is the classification of children into "Not at Risk," "At Risk," "At High Risk," or "At Extreme Risk" categories, and that additional psychological and behavioral assessments, functional analyses linking these assessments to effective interventions, and the monitoring of intervention progress are required. Even with preschoolers, these latter tasks are best done by psychologists or those with advanced test interpretation and behavioral intervention skills.

SUMMARY. With supervision and follow-up evaluations by psychologists or others similarly trained, the Early Screening Project (ESP) will likely be a useful tool to help teachers identify preschool children who are having externalizing or internalizing difficulties in the classroom. Although additional normative and psychometric data are needed for greater comfort and clinical use, the data available appear to support the ESP's ability to accurately screen for children "at-risk" for and demonstrating more severe internalizing and externalizing behavior problems. The ESP manual is straightforward and well-organized, and teachers and parents should be able to understand its process, completing and scoring its various scales with relative ease. Overall, the "first generation" of this instrument has created a good foundation for a (hopefully) revised and updated version that extends its empirical and research base.

REVIEWER'S REFERENCES

Hops, H., Walker, H. M., & Greenwood, C. R. (1988). *Social Interaction Rating Scale.* Longmont, CO: Sopris West.
Walker, H. M., & Severson, H. H. (1990). *Systematic Screening for Behavior Disorders (SSBD). User's guide and administration manual.* Longmont, CO: Sopris West.

[137]
Employee Aptitude Survey, Second Edition.

Purpose: Designed to predict future job performance.
Population: Ages 16 to adult.
Publication Dates: 1952–1995.
Acronym: EAS.
Administration: Group.
Price Data: Price data available from publisher for test materials including Technical Manual ('94, 91 pages), Examiner's Manual ('94, 66 pages), and Supplemental Norms Report ('95, 92 pages).
Time: (5–10) minutes.

Comments: Tests available separately.
Authors: G. Grimsley (a–h), F. L. Ruch (a–g, i, j), N. D. Warren (a–g), and J. S. Ford (a, c, e–g).
Publisher: Psychological Services, Inc.

a) TEST 1, VERBAL COMPREHENSION.
Publication Dates: 1956–1984.
Scores: Total score only.

b) TEST 2, NUMERICAL ABILITY.
Publication Dates: 1952–1963.
Scores: Total score only.

c) TEST 3, VISUAL PURSUIT.
Publication Date: 1956.
Scores: Total score only.

d) TEST 4, VISUAL SPEED AND ACCURACY.
Publication Dates: 1952–1980.
Scores: Total score only.

e) TEST 5, SPACE VISUALIZATION.
Publication Dates: 1952–1980.
Scores: Total score only.

f) TEST 6, NUMERICAL REASONING.
Publication Dates: 1957–1985.
Scores: Total score only.

g) TEST 7, VERBAL REASONING.
Publication Dates: 1952–1963.
Scores: Total score only.

h) TEST 8, WORD FLUENCY.
Publication Dates: 1953–1963.
Scores: Total score only.

i) TEST 9, MANUAL SPEED AND ACCURACY.
Publication Dates: 1953–1963.
Scores: Total score only.

j) TEST 10, SYMBOLIC REASONING.
Publication Dates: 1957–1985.
Scores: Total score only.

Cross References: See T5:937 (4 references), T4:894 (1 reference), T3:799 (4 references), and T2:1071 (14 references); for reviews by Paul F. Ross and Erwin K. Taylor, and an excerpted review by John O. Crites of an earlier edition, see 6:769 (4 references); for reviews by Dorothy C. Adkins and S. Rains Wallace of an earlier edition, see 5:607.

Review of the Employee Aptitude Survey, Second Edition by BRIAN ENGDAHL, Counseling Psychologist, U.S. Department of Veterans Affairs Medical Center, and Clinical Associate Professor, Department of Psychology, University of Minnesota, Minneapolis, MN:

The Employee Aptitude Survey (EAS) was reviewed by three authors in *The Sixth Mental Measurements Yearbook.* Since those reviews, a new edition of the Examiner's Manual was published in 1994, and a Technical Manual (1994) and Supplemental Norms Report (1995) have also been published, although the test battery itself has not been revised. The Examiner's Manual remains a model of clarity and should meet the needs of anyone who administers the tests. The Technical Manual and Norms Report repeat most of the information presented in earlier publications, but the authors have gone well beyond that, responding to previous reviewers' concerns by gathering and presenting more validity data. This provides us with an expanded basis for evaluating and using the EAS.

The EAS has two primary purposes: employee selection and vocational guidance. A concept guiding the development of the EAS was "maximum validity per minute of testing time" (technical manual, p. 3). Largely derived from earlier tests of abilities and skills, it is a battery of 10 short tests that may be given singly or in any combination. There are alternate forms for 9 of the tests. The authors emphasize that the test is easily administered, easily (hand) scored, and easily interpreted. I agree with the first two claims, but have problems with the third. They claim that advanced training is not required to interpret the EAS test scores, but recommend that the user be familiar with general testing concepts and descriptive statistics. The lack of detailed validity studies and the lack of validated cutpoints for criteria of interest place a considerable burden on the user of the EAS, especially when employee selection is the goal. One wishing to make the fullest use of the EAS should have a background in Industrial/Organizational psychology and selection, and preferably be prepared to conduct local studies to gather evidence of validity and utility of EAS scores.

The overall lack of detail on the validation samples diminishes the EAS's value in selection situations where local validation studies cannot be readily conducted, that is, those situations where reliance would have to be placed on well-detailed validation studies. Few EAS validity studies have been published in peer-reviewed journals. A meta-analysis of prediction studies contained in the Technical Manual suggests that the EAS has substantial predictive validity across a variety of occupational and educational settings. Some detail about the meta-analysis samples is presented, although it is less than a scholarly review would demand. The authors state that they have shared all the technical information that they have available to them, and that much of it was provided by EAS test users. It is not clear which data were contributed by EAS users and which were developed by the authors themselves.

There are very few helpful facts associated with the norms other than an occupational title and sample size. Out of 80 occupational (nonstudent) groups, only 27 go beyond this. Even in these 27, the information is so sketchy as to be of limited usefulness. For example, the year of data collection is given for only 11 samples. These range from 1976–1983. The average age is noted for only 3 of the samples. More importantly, few if any subgroup differences are discernable from the Norms Report as a whole. Information is lacking about the gender, race, and geographic makeup of the samples. The only basis for speculation about gender differences in EAS test scores is provided by the set of male and female college student norms. Needless to say, evidence for differential validity across groups is not included.

The reader is presented with 86 pages of norm tables in the Supplemental Norms report, plus those contained in the Examiner's Manual. Tables that appear in both volumes at times represent the same sample, and at other times appear to represent different samples. The lack of accompanying sample detail makes selecting the appropriate norm group difficult if not impossible. Only tables in the Examiner's Manual incorporate battery norms (for groups where they have been developed).

Nowhere is the user warned that the norm tables do not constitute validity data, as the groups were not selected on some criterion of success. At best, I have found the norm tables useful as rough guides in career counseling. Individuals may be interested in their standing relative to one or more of the groups on tests that appear important to successful job performance. Only the validity coefficients in the Technical Manual and its meta-analysis have been empirically validated for such predictions. These coefficients are fewer in number, and grouped into eight broad occupational categories. They, too, provide a basis only for rough speculation about training or occupational success, because the EAS system lacks cutpoints for individual predictions.

The section on reliability is limited to a summary of studies in which alternate forms were administered within a single testing session to a number of groups. Although the resulting coefficients are impressive, they are probably overestimates of reliability, as the tests are highly speeded.

No internal consistency data are presented, although ICRs would likely be high, given the above, the results of factor analyses presented in the Technical Manual, and the homogeneity of test content. No test-retest (stability) data are presented (with one exception on the Manual Speed Accuracy Test).

A brief and apparently hypothetical illustration of the EAS's potential to increase selection validity (and therefore achieve cost savings) is provided in a section titled "Utility." To a neophyte, the potential cost savings suggested in this rosy example may appear almost too good to be true. The authors would do well to note that anyone considering developing a selection program using ability tests should be cognizant of the complexities and pitfalls inherent in test utility analysis, or seek appropriate consultation. No cross validation results are presented.

Scrutiny of the Supplemental Norms Report revealed what past reviewers have noted: ceiling problems across several tests (i.e., Verbal Comprehension) in upper level occupational groups (actuary, scientist/mathematician, etc.). As previous reviewers have noted, this suggests that the EAS may not be suitable for jobs and educational programs requiring top ability levels. A few minor concerns also surfaced in my review: The manuals are bound in such a way that the pages easily detach, soon leaving me with a looseleaf collection of pages. Administration instructions suggest (without citing supporting data) that administering the EAS to individuals or groups makes no difference, except that group administration saves examiners' time.

SUMMARY. Although a number of concerns and criticisms have been raised, in my opinion, the EAS compares very favorably with other multifactor ability batteries I have used over the years in vocational and educational counseling, including the USES General Aptitude Test Battery (GATB; T5:2797), the Differential Aptitude Tests (DAT; T5:838), and the Armed Services Vocational Aptitude Battery (ASVAB; T5:180). Despite the shortcomings in validity data noted above, I remain impressed with this battery and the usefulness of the tests in career counseling. The EAS has a solid heritage, and a long record of usefulness in industrial selection and vocational prediction situations.

Review of the Employee Aptitude Survey, Second Edition by PAUL M. MUCHINSKY, Joseph M.

Bryan Distinguished Professor of Business, The University of North Carolina at Greensboro, Greensboro, NC:

The Employee Aptitude Survey (EAS) consists of 10 ability tests: (a) Verbal Comprehension, (b) Numerical Ability, (c) Visual Pursuit, (d) Visual Speed and Accuracy, (e) Space Visualization, (f) Numerical Reasoning, (g) Verbal Reasoning, (h) Word Fluency, (i) Manual Speed and Accuracy, and (j) Symbolic Reasoning. In constructing the EAS the guiding concept was maximum validity per minute of testing time. Originally published in the 1950s, the hallmark of these tests is their very brief administration time. Nine of the tests have a 5-minute time limit, and one test (Numerical Ability) has a 10-minute time limit. Thus, in theory, a 10-factor set of human abilities could be assessed in less than 1 hour.

The 10 tests can either be hand scored or machine scored. I am also aware that the publisher will soon be offering a computerized version of the test. Three different manuals are available for the user: Technical Manual, Examiner's Manual, and a Supplemental Norms Report. These manuals are among the most comprehensive that I have seen provided by a publisher. The Technical and Examiner's Manuals are both over 60 pages in length, whereas the Norms Report is almost 100 pages. These manuals provide extensive information on reliability, validity, practice effects, creating test batteries for various occupational groups, meta-analytic research findings on the test's ability to forecast job-related criteria, directions for scoring, instructions for administration, and references. The norms are presented by DOT job code and job title, are very detailed, and are easy to read. Many test publishers could take a lesson on how to construct manuals from those designed for the EAS.

The fundamental issue to be addressed in using these tests is the degree to which the user accepts the premise that a meaningful inference about a job candidate can be drawn from a 5-minute sample of (test) behavior. The EAS was constructed on the basis of incremental validity per minute of testing time. The 5-minute testing time limit was established by the publisher to achieve an acceptable level of validity. The validation evidence presented in the manual supports this conclusion. The underlying premise is that assessment can be a time-consuming and costly process. Therefore, reducing test time but not sacrificing validity meets a desirable organizational objective. My opinion of that premise is a qualified "maybe," and the qualifications depend on the job level. If the job level in question is on the lower end of the distribution of job complexity (and particularly if there are many candidates to assess), I would strongly endorse the logic of this test. However, if the job is at the upper end of the distribution of job complexity (and thus value to the organization), in no way would I ever recommend any 5-minute test be used as a basis to make a major personnel selection decision. The norm tables include jobs as bank teller, clerk, sales representative, and computer programmer. For such jobs I would readily endorse the EAS. The norm tables also include jobs as top manager, middle manager, scientist/mathematician, and engineer. For such jobs I would want to assess many factors including intelligence, and I would want more than a 5-minute assessment of verbal comprehension or numerical reasoning. I would rather use the Watson-Glaser Critical Thinking Appraisal (1980; T5:2856) for such important jobs. I would gladly accept greater testing time (as 30–45 minutes) as a trade-off for having greater confidence and organizational acceptability in the results of the assessment. Consider the following scenario. You are responsible for selecting a "top manager" for a company. You assess the candidate with a battery of 5-minute tests, recommend hire, the candidate is hired on the basis of your recommendation, and is subsequently dismissed after a brief period of time on the job for poor performance. The disappointed company president then asks you on what basis you made a recommendation to hire that individual. Your reply is the results of a series of 5-minute tests. You might then justifiably find yourself in line with the former top manager at the unemployment office.

Five-minute assessments of abilities ignore the social validity of the tests. The empirical validity of these "quickie" tests as reported in the manuals does not address the more sensitive issue of the acceptability of the assessment to the organization. I strongly believe the organizational acceptability of a 5-minute assessment is heavily influenced by the job level in question. As Messick (1995) stated, consideration of construct validity also includes the issues of appropriateness and acceptability. No meta-analytic analysis of empirical validity coefficients addresses such considerations.

I have used the EAS on many occasions over the course of my career. My experiences have all been positive. I am particularly impressed with the Space Visualization test, which I found to be very useful in the selection of packers and shippers. I know of no other test that assesses spatial ability in this way.

SUMMARY. In short, I think highly of the EAS for making efficient assessments of selected abilities that have organizational relevance. The manuals provided by the publisher are first-rate. However, I recommend temperance be exercised in using the EAS to select personnel for upper level jobs where issues other than empirical validity will be of salience to the hiring organization.

REVIEWER'S REFERENCES
Watson, G., & Glaser, E. M. (1980). Watson-Glaser Critical Thinking Appraisal. San Antonio: The Psychological Corporation.
Messick, S. (1995). Validity of psychological assessment: Validation of inferences from persons' responses and performances as scientific inquiry into score meaning. *American Psychologist, 50,* 741–749.

[138]
Employee Assistance Program Inventory.

Purpose: "Designed as an intake or screening tool for professionals in Employee Assistance Programs (EAPs)."
Population: Working adults seeking counseling.
Publication Date: 1994.
Acronym: EAPI.
Scores: 10 scales: Anxiety, Depression, Self-Esteem Problems, Marital Problems, Family Problems, External Stressors, Interpersonal Conflict, Work Adjustment, Problem Minimization, Effects of Substance Abuse.
Administration: Group or individual.
Price Data, 2000: $89 per introductory kit including manual (44 pages), 25 reusable item booklets, and 25 answer sheet/profiles; $32 per 25 item booklets; $32 per 25 answer sheet/profiles; $29 per manual.
Time: (20) minutes.
Authors: William D. Anton and James R. Reed.
Publisher: Psychological Assessment Resources, Inc.

Review of the Employee Assistance Program Inventory by MICHAEL G. KAVAN, Associate Dean for Student Affairs and Associate Professor of Family Practice, Creighton University School of Medicine, Omaha, NE:

The Employee Assistance Program Inventory (EAPI) is a 120-item self-report intake or screening tool for use in employee assistance programs (EAPs). It is meant to "rapidly identify common psychological problems of employed adults and may be used to guide appropriate referrals or short-term interventions" (professional manual, p. 1). The authors suggest that the EAPI may also be used to evaluate the efficacy of interventions used with an employee. The U.S. Public Health Service National Institute for Occupational Safety and health (NIOSH) stated that surveillance measures such as this are considered a "cornerstone" for protecting the mental health of workers (Sauter, 1992).

ADMINISTRATION AND SCORING. The EAPI may be administered to individuals or groups ages 18 and older. The authors report that a third grade reading level is necessary to complete the EAPI. Although the authors suggest that no training is required to administer and score the EAPI, they recommend that those interpreting the EAPI must have graduate training in clinical, counseling, or educational psychology, or in social work or a related field of study. For administration, respondents are required to possess both the reusable EAPI Item Booklet, which contains the directions for administration and the items, and a separate answer/scoring sheet with profile. Before starting the inventory, the test administrator is to read aloud specific instructions for taking the inventory. Respondents are instructed to complete basic demographic information and then to select the answer that "best represents your opinion about the accuracy of the statement" by circling "F" for false or not at all true, "S" for slightly true, "M" for mainly true, and "V" for very true. Administration time is estimated to be 20 minutes with an additional 5 minutes necessary for scoring and profiling. Scoring of the EAPI entails ripping off the perforated strip on the top of the answer sheet, which exposes the scoring sheet, and then calculating raw scores by summing each domain column. These are then plotted onto a profile located on the back of the scoring sheet. Although this process may appear simple, those scoring the EAPI must be careful when transferring scores from the scoring sheet to the profile as the ordering of scores varies between the two sheets.

The EAPI assesses problems in 10 domain areas including Anxiety, Depression, Self-Esteem Problems, Marital Problems, Family Problems, External Stressors, Interpersonal Conflict, Work Adjustment, Problem Minimization, and Effects of Substance Abuse. In addition, the profile sheet includes a critical item section meant to assess suicidal ideation. Raw scores may be easily compared to T-scores on the profile sheet or to percentile scores in Appendix B of the manual. T-scores equal to or greater than 70 are considered significant, whereas scores within the 60 to 69 range suggest "difficulty" in a particular domain area. The interpretation of the Substance Abuse scale is handled differently due to an extremely positively skewed distribution for the standardization sample. Here, a raw score of 16 is considered significant because it is predicted to identify approximately 78% of persons experiencing substance problems. In using this recommended cutoff score, 14% of persons would be wrongly identified as having a substance abuse problem. The risks involved with the overidentification of problems such as this include potentially harmful labeling as well as unnecessary additional testing and/or treatment. Thus, EAPs must be extremely careful about interpreting and following up on significant Substance Abuse scale scores.

Information on the interpretation of EAPI scores is limited to T-score conversion tables and tables comparing employee scores with percentile scores for the standardization sample. The manual does provide limited descriptive information on each domain scale and seven brief case illustrations; however, no other interpretive information is provided by the authors. The authors do suggest that "interpretive hypotheses should be confirmed by other, more detailed methods of evaluation such as consultation interviews, personal histories, mental status exams, and assessments of personality or psychopathology" (manual, p. 8).

RELIABILITY. Limited reliability data are provided within the manual. Internal consistency reliability coefficients (Cronbach, 1951), calculated on 215 employed adults, range from .73 to .92 with a mean of .86. The manual includes no references to test-retest reliability information; this is unfortunate, especially because the authors suggest that the EAPI may be readministered to evaluate intervention efficacy.

VALIDITY. In regard to content validity, the EAPI was developed by sending a survey form to 200 randomly selected EAP professionals requesting information on their assessment needs; however, only 38% returned the survey. Of the 50 possible assessment areas listed on the survey, the authors selected 9 frequently endorsed assessment areas and then added a problem minimization scale meant to assess the respondent's receptivity to treatment. Following a literature review, 344 items were developed representing the various content areas. An item analysis and an internal consistency study were used for refinement and/or elimination of items resulting in the current scale. Seven convergent and discriminant validity studies were then conducted at 44 EAP sites throughout the United States and Canada. Results from these validation studies indicated that scores on the Substance Abuse scale correlated .79 with those from the Michigan Alcoholism Screening Test and .67 with scores from the Drug Abuse Screening Test. The Self-Esteem Problems scale correlated between -.45 and -.56 with the Tennessee Self-Concept Scales. The Anxiety scale correlated .76 with the State-Trait Anxiety Inventory (STAI) State Anxiety scale and .82 with the STAI Trait Anxiety Scale. The Depression scale correlated .85 with the Beck Depression Inventory. The Marital Problems scale correlated between -.47 and -.79 with scales from the Dyadic Adjustment Scales, whereas the Family Problems scale correlated between -.48 and -.54 with subscales of the Family Adaptability and Cohesion Evaluation Scales II. The Work Adjustment scale correlated between .46 and .81 with scores from the Occupational Stress Inventory. The External Stressors scale correlated .49 with the Holmes-Rahe Social Readjustment Rating Scale. The Interpersonal Conflict scale correlated -.34 with the NEO Personality Inventory—Revised (NEO PI-R) Warmth facet scale and -.38 with its Compliance facet scale, whereas the correlation was .59 with the Angry Hostility facet scale. Finally, the Problem Minimization scale correlated -.44 with the NEO PI-R Vulnerability Scale and .54 with the Personality Assessment Inventory Treatment Rejection subscale. An additional simulation study was completed and demonstrated that for the most part the Problem Minimization scale was responsive to the intentional under- or overreporting of problems.

NORMS. Normative data are provided on 1,266 employed adults ages 18 through 76 years from Colorado, Florida, Mississippi, Ohio, Tennessee, and Texas. The composition of the sample is said to mirror the projected U.S. civilian labor force in the year 2000; however, there is a slight overrepresentation of African-American women in the standardization sample. The sample included persons from a variety of occupational fields; however, no data are provided within the manual as to how this relates to national statistics.

SUMMARY. The EAPI is a fairly comprehensive self-report screening measure or intake tool used to identify common employee problems. It is relatively easy and quick to administer. Internal consistency reliability evidence is good; however, support for the validity of scores from the individual EAPI scales is variable. Whereas the authors' validation studies demonstrated fairly strong correlations between the Substance Abuse, Anxiety, Depression, Marital Problems, and Work Adjustment scales and related external measures, to date, only mild to moderate correlations have been shown between the Self-Esteem Problems, Family Problems, External Stressors, Interpersonal Conflict, and Problem Minimization scales and measures of related constructs. Additional studies, therefore, are encouraged to assess the validity of scores from the domain scales with other measures and groups. In particular, it would be beneficial to relate EAPI domain scale scores with functional measures such as productivity, absenteeism, turnover, and so forth. Until completed, users of the EAPI are cautioned against making major EAP decisions based solely on this inventory. Also, although measures such as the EAPI have the potential to play an important role in tertiary prevention efforts of EAPs, emphasis should continue to be placed on primary prevention, or work site health promotion efforts (DeJoy & Wilson, 1995).

REVIEWER'S REFERENCES

Cronbach, L. J. (1951). Coefficient alpha and the internal structure of tests. *Psychometrika, 16,* 297–334.

Sauter, S. L. (1992). Introduction to the NIOSH proposed national strategy. In G. P. Keita & S. L. Sauter (Eds.), *Work and well-being: An agenda for the 1990s* (pp. 11–16). Washington, DC: American Psychological Association.

DeJoy, D. M., & Wilson, M. G. (Eds.). (1995). *Critical issues in worksite health promotion.* Needham, MA: Allyn and Bacon.

Review of the Employee Assistance Program Inventory by DAVID J. PITTENGER, Associate Professor of Psychology, The University of Tennessee at Chattanooga, Chattanooga, TN:

The stated purpose of the Employee Assistance Program Inventory (EAPI) is to provide therapists and counselors with a simple-to-administer intake instrument that screens for a host of common psychological problems. The designers of the EAPI created the instrument specifically for use with employee assistance programs. There is no reason, however, to expect that the instrument could not be used in any mental health setting that offers counseling services to the general nonchronic population. The authors of the EAPI make clear that the instrument is not a diagnostic tool. Rather, the EAPI is an indicator of potential psychological problems that may require additional testing and evaluation.

The test consists of a reusable questionnaire containing 120 descriptive statements (e.g., I take pride in my work) that are answered on a 4-point scale ranging from "False, not at all true" to "Very true." Clients respond using a carbonless paper answer sheet that contains the scoring template. The statements are clearly and objectively written leaving little room for ambiguity about what the instrument measures. Administration of the EAPI does not require any formal training and may be administered individually or to groups.

The EAPI consists of 10 scales consisting of 12 statements each. The first 9 scales are indicators of Anxiety, Depression, Substance Abuse, Self-Esteem, Marital Problems (defined as problems with one's spouse or partner), Family Problems (defined as intrafamily discord), External Stressors (defined as significant personal health, legal, or financial problems), Interpersonal Conflict with Coworkers, and Work Adjustment (defined as a measure of satisfaction with current employment). The 10th scale, Problem Minimization, is a validity scale designed to determine if the client underestimates or denies personal problems, or wishes to avoid a psychological intervention. Three of the items in the Depression scale are said to be critical indicators of suicide.

Scoring consists of adding the responses to the 12 items for each scale. The manual contains tables that allow the user to convert the raw score to a T score with a mean of 50 and a standard deviation of 10. This transformation is based on a normative sample conducted by the test designers. Scales in which the client answers fewer than 10 statements are not considered valid. According to the manual, the entire test results are invalid if the client fails to answer 24 or more items.

For the majority of the scales, the authors recommend that scores one standard deviation above the mean indicate potential problems that warrant further investigation. The exceptions to this rule are the Substance Abuse and Problem Minimization scales. For the Substance Abuse scale, the authors recommend that a raw score of 16 be used to indicate a potential problem. For the Problem Minimization scale, the authors suggest that scores two standard deviations above the mean represent obvious attempts to conceal one's problems.

Although the EAPI appears to have much to offer as a screening tool, it leaves much to be desired regarding its psychometric properties. A careful review of the supporting evidence offered for the validity of the EAPI indicates that the evidence is incomplete and does not ensure that the instrument can make the distinctions it claims to make.

The only reliability data consist of internal consistency coefficients for each of the 10 scales. Although coefficient alpha is a useful index, it by no means informs us of the temporal stability of an instrument. Test-retest reliability data, even for a short interest interval, would allow more informed interpretations of the results.

The evidence used to support the existence of nine clinical scales is also sparse. For example, the authors of the EAPI made no attempt to subject the results of their normative data to confirmatory factor analysis. Similarly absent is any information concerning the intercorrelations among the scales. Although the internal consistency coefficients for the individual scales are high ($M = .86$) there is no indication that these coefficients would change if one or more of the scales were combined.

Although the authors report the results of eight convergent and discriminant validity studies, the data represent mostly concurrent validity analysis. The authors of the EAPI did not employ traditional multitrait multimethod procedures to ascertain the convergent and discriminant validity of the subscales. Furthermore, for each validation study, the participants were employees seeking treatment through their EAP as opposed to employees in general. In other words, these samples were not truly representative of the general population for whom the test was constructed. Similarly, there was no attempt to determine whether groups representing different employment classification (e.g., management vs. laborer) produce different response profiles.

Of the nine clinical scales, the Substance Abuse (SA) scale appears to demonstrate the greatest level of concurrent validity. Specifically, there are strong correlations between SA scores and self-report substance abuse screening inventories. In addition, these alternative measures of substance abuse do not correlate with the other scales in the EAPI. The Marital Problem and Family Problem scales also demonstrate fair concurrent validity with similar psychometric measures.

The results for the other scales are not as clear. For example, there are only moderate correlations between the Anxiety and Depression scales and popular alternative measures of state-trait anxiety and depression. Furthermore, the Self-Esteem, Family Problem, and External Stressor scales also correlate strongly with the concurrent measures of anxiety and depression. These data again raise questions concerning the independence of the individual scales.

SUMMARY. The EAPI appears to be a noble attempt to offer a compact and ready screening instrument for general mental health problems. At present, however, the EAPI should be considered a prototype in need of much additional research to confirm the utility of the instrument.

[139]
Employment Values Inventory.

Purpose: "A measure of personal values associated with work and the working environment."
Population: Adults.
Publication Dates: 1988–1992.
Scores, 14: Work Ethic, Social Outgoingness, Risk-Taking, Stability, Responsibility, Need For Achievement, Task Orientation, Leadership, Training and Development, Innovation, Intellectual Demands, Status, Structure, Inclusion.
Administration: Individual or group.
Price Data: Available from publisher.
Time: (30–40) minutes.
Comments: Computer administration and scoring available.
Author: Selby MillSmith Limited.
Publisher: Selby MillSmith Limited [England].

Review of the Employment Values Inventory by JULIE A. ALLISON, Associate Professor of Psychology, Pittsburg State University, Pittsburg, KS:

The Employment Values Inventory (EVI) is a 168-item self-report scale designed to measure values underlying behavior at work. The EVI was designed primarily for adults who are already familiar with their work behavior, ideally due to previous/current work experience. The EVI is available in both pencil-and-paper format or a computerized version, which also offers immediate scoring and score interpretations. Respondents of the EVI are asked to indicate on a 4-point Likert scale their reactions (from 0 = *negative* to 3 = *very positive*) to each of the 168 brief statements regarding their values and/or behavior at work. The scale is simple to complete, taking approximately

40 minutes for paper-and-pencil or 30 minutes for computer. Scoring reports are available in one of three ways. A score chart provides raw scores and STEN scores for each of the 14 scales along with bar chart summaries for each. Full narratives give scale-by-scale ratings of each of the scores, along with a personalized paragraph about each scale. The standard narrative provides individual STEN scores compared with particular norms (general, clerical, graduate) and a standard paragraph describing each scale.

THEORETICAL RATIONALE. The developers of the EVI define values as attitudes and preferences that are followed consistently. Their theoretical premise holds that values affect us in three ways. First, values affect us as an individual working at work. For example, what jobs we prefer, in what context, will be impacted by what values we hold more strongly. Values also affect us as an individual working as part of a group. Individual differences prevail in society and at work. Consequently, what values the individuals of a group hold, in comparison with the values of the group as a whole, are important. Finally, the values of an individual in the context of the organizational values are important and have strong implications for both job satisfaction and work productivity. The EVI was designed to provide insight into how an individual's values might impact his/her work in each of these contexts.

FOURTEEN WORK-RELATED VALUES. Given this theoretical premise, the EVI was designed to measure 14 values, each categorized into one of six broader value classifications. Job values includes Work Ethic, Task Orientation, and Need to Achieve. People values includes Social Outgoingness, and Inclusion or the desire to include others in teamwork settings. Management values include Leadership and Responsibility. Professional values include Innovation, Intellectual Demands, and Risk-Taking. Organizational values include the appreciation of Stability, Structure, and Status; and finally, Personal values deals with one's striving to acquire more Training and Development.

VALIDITY AND RELIABILITY. Although the scale and scale items make intrinsic sense, little support for the theoretical rationale is provided. Furthermore, and more troublesome, is the paucity of data offered to support either the validity or the reliability of the scale. No descriptions are offered on test item development or test item inclusion. No empirical evidence is provided to support the inclusion of 14 separate scales within the total scale, nor is there any discussion of the relationships between the scales. Validity research has been limited to assessing the relationship between scores on the EVI and three independent scales including the Myers-Briggs Type Indicator, FIRO-B, and the Jackson Personality Inventory. Results indicate support for validity: Correlations between EVI scales and subscales on each of the three independent scales are significant in the expected directions, but moderate in value. It should be noted, however, that even this research is limited in nature, with Ns ranging from 105–138.

Similar problems exist with the reliability data. Although coefficient alphas are reported and are in the acceptable ranges (from .72 for Work Ethic to .88 for Inclusion), there is no information provided on either the participants or the methodology used to obtain such results.

As stated earlier, normative data are available, and descriptive interpretations are available in light of this data. Normative data are also based, however, on a limited total sample of $N = 459$ (demographics not reported), and should be heeded with caution.

Because of the potential uses and consequent insights of the EVI, it is the hope of this reviewer that validity and reliability research be continued, with larger samples and more careful reporting strategies. Research assessing the predictive validity of the scale for persons at work is also needed.

USES OF THE EVI. The authors of the EVI manual report that uses of the scale include but are not limited to two purposes. First, they can be used for defining training and development needs of the employee. A second purpose of the EVI may include identifying areas of career counseling and development.

SUMMARY. Because of the lack of data supporting the validity of this scale, particularly predictive validity, the purposes of the EVI should be limited to informational/educational. The EVI could potentially be quite useful in the areas of career counseling and planning. Results of the EVI may also be helpful for employees at work so long as there are no employee evaluation criteria attached. To use the EVI as any kind of evaluation criterion or to attempt to develop intervention strategies based on the results of this scale, however, seems premature and imprudent.

Review of the Employment Values Inventory by NAMBURY S. RAJU, Distinguished Professor, Institute of Psychology, Illinois Institute of Technology, Chicago, IL:

The Employment Values Inventory (EVI) consists of 168 items, with four options (0 = Negative, 1 = Neutral, 2 = Positive, and 3 = Very Positive) per item. It yields 14 different value scores: Work Ethic, Social Outgoingness, Risk-Taking, Stability, Responsibility, Need to Achieve, Task Orientation, Leadership, Development, Innovation, Intellectual Demands, Status, Structure, and Inclusion. Scores on each of the 14 values are reported on a standard, 10-point scale, STEN 1–STEN 10. The EVI is primarily designed for measuring values in adults. It is intended for use with individuals in a counseling situation or with a group of individuals in an industrial setting. The inventory is expected to take about 10–15 minutes and has a machine-scorable answer sheet.

RELIABILITY. Alpha estimates of reliability are reported for the 14 scales, which range from a low of .72 for Work Ethic to a high of .88 for Inclusion. Six of the reliability estimates are in the .80s, and the rest in the .70s. It appears that the sample for reliability analysis consisted of 459 subjects from the U.K. Because the number of items contributing to each scale is not reported in the manual and user guide, it is difficult to evaluate the magnitude of these reliability estimates. Because the EVI consists of 168 items, it may be assumed that each of the 14 scales contains 12 distinct items. For scales with 12 Likert-type items, the reported alpha estimates of reliability appear reasonable, although a bit on the low side. There is almost no description given in the guide of the sample used for the reliability analysis, except to refer to it as the General Population (U.K.). There is also no mention of test-retest and parallel form reliability estimates in the guide.

VALIDITY. As evidence of construct validity, the guide provides the correlations between the 14 EVI scales and the Myers-Briggs Type Indicator, FIRO-B, and Jackson Personality Inventory. Even though the EVI is not a personality inventory, some degree of relationship between the EVI scales and personality traits would be expected and hence the reason for reporting these correlations. Most of the correlations are in the .20 to .30 range. The sample sizes were 138, 138, and 106 for the Myers-Briggs Type indicator,

FIRO-B, and Jackson Personality Inventory, respectively. There is no description of the samples in the guide; it is not even clear if the same sample was used for the Myers-Briggs Type indicator and FIRO-B measures. Without an adequate description of the samples used, it is difficult to evaluate the relevance and generalizability of the reported correlations to other populations. No data were presented in support of either criterion-related or content validity. Evidence of criterion-related validity would have been very relevant because the EVI is designed for use in the industry.

NORMS. Normative data were reported for three different populations: General Population (U.K.), Clinical Population (U.K.), and Graduate Population (U.K.). The sample size for the General Population norms was 459, and no sample size information was provided in the guide for the other two populations. In addition, no demographic information about the three samples is reported in the guide.

The reported normative data are not typical of what one would expect to find in a section on norms. The number of raw scores corresponding to each of the STEN points is displayed in the norms tables, separately by scale. Also shown in these tables are the raw score mean and standard deviation by EVI scale. There is no description in the guide on how to use the data contained in the norms tables. There are no percentile scores as such.

SUMMARY. The guide contains detailed descriptions of the 14 values in the EVI, and it also describes how the inventory may be used with individuals, groups of individuals, and in organizations. The guide provides limited information about the reliability of the EVI scales, but none about criterion-related validity. This latter validity information is especially relevant because the EVI is intended for use in organizations. The description of samples used for various psychometric analyses is almost nonexistent. Also, there is no information on item development or item tryout. In summary, it is difficult to assess the psychometric quality of the EVI scales because of the lack of relevant statistical information.

[140]
Endicott Work Productivity Scale.

Purpose: "Designed to describe types of behavior and subjective feelings that are highly likely to reduce productivity and efficiency in work activities."
Population: Adults.

Publication Dates: 1994–1997.
Acronym: EWPS.
Scores: Total score only.
Administration: Individual.
Manual: No manual.
Price Data, 1997: $.50 per questionnaire.
Time: [3–5] minutes.
Author: Jean Endicott.
Publisher: Department of Research Assessment and Training, Columbia University.

Review of the Endicott Work Productivity Scale by ANDREW A. COX, Professor of Counseling and Psychology, Troy State University, Phenix City, AL:

The Endicott Work Productivity Scale is a self-report questionnaire that assesses behaviors, feelings, or attitudes that may reduce work productivity and efficiency. The purpose of the test is to assess the degree that psychological or medical conditions may affect the test respondent's work functioning. Individuals endorse test items using the time perspective of one week prior to completing the test.

The 25 test items are completed by circling a 5-point Likert scale as follows: 0 = *Never;* 1 = *Rarely;* 2 = *Sometimes;* 3 = *Often;* and 4 = *Almost Always.* Items are direct in nature, assessing behaviors, feelings, or attitudes that are detrimental to work productivity. Item directness is a desirable quality for instruments assessing short-term behavioral or attitudinal change (Berger & Patchner, 1988).

A manual is not available for the instrument. All scoring, interpretative, and descriptive information for the measure is provided in Endicott and Nee (1997). Test scoring is accomplished by summing numerical ratings for each test item in order to obtain a total score. A maximum total score of 100 is possible. The total score is compared to mean total scores for a group of depressed patients receiving treatment in a outpatient facility and community nonpatient sample reported in Endicott and Nee (1997). Other than comparison of the obtained total score to the described mean scores, other interpretation data for the obtained score are not provided.

Normative data consist of results from 77 outpatients diagnosed with major depressive disorder and 66 individuals residing within the community who were not diagnosed with psychopathology. Fifty percent of the depressed patients were female with a mean age of 41. The nondepressed community sample was 70% female. The age for the community sample was not reported. Other than these two samples, additional normative data for the test are not indicated.

Reliability and validity information are reported for the test in Endicott and Nee (1997). Test-retest and internal consistency reliability data are reported for the instrument. Reliability data are reported only with the clinical sample of depressed outpatients and nondepressed community samples used in establishing the test's norms. A test-retest reliability coefficient (interval = 10 days to 2 weeks) of .92 was obtained for the group of depressed outpatients who were administered the Endicott Work Productivity Scale. An internal consistency index of .93 was attained for both the clinical and community normative samples. Preliminary evidence of the reliability of the scores from the instrument is presented.

Concurrent validity was assessed using the Hamilton Rating Scale for Depression, the Symptom Checklist 90 (SCL-90), Clinical Global Impressions Severity of Illness and Global Improvement Scale (National Institute of Mental Health, 1985), and Self-Report Scale to Diagnose Major Depressive Disorder (Zimmerman, Coryell, Corenthal, & Wilson, 1986). Moderate correlations with these measures are indicated. The author concludes that the test scores possess acceptable validity as a measure of severity of illness. Validity data are reported only for the normative sample described in developing the test instrument. Validation data for other medical or psychiatric diagnostic patient groups are not described for the measure.

This test should be considered a research instrument in preliminary form at present. Additional study is necessary to establish the instrument's psychometric properties using additional clinical populations other than those diagnosed with depression. Additional clinical and nonclinical samples are also required to establish a representative normative sample for interpretation as well as to further substantiate the technical characteristics of the test. Reliability results for this measure appear to be promising. Additional assessment of the measure's validity is necessary. Further information is needed relative to the clinical utility and interpretation of the total score. The establishment of a cutting score or range of critical score values for interpretation would be helpful. A manual should be developed to aid the test user in administration, interpretation, and use of the test.

SUMMARY. The instrument is brief and direct. A minimal amount of critical clinical time is required for test completion. Though not reported in descriptive material, the test items could be comprehended by most adults in a clinical setting. Undoubtedly, the instrument could be administered orally to individuals who manifest reading deficits. Preliminary reliability and validity data are presented for the instrument. The test would be useful within a battery of test measures to assess outcomes of clinical interventions. With further research, to include additional clinical and nonclinical normative groups, this measure could serve a useful note in delineating the impact of medical and psychological factors on work behaviors.

REVIEWER'S REFERENCES

National Institute of Mental Health. (1985). Special feature: Rating scales and assessment instruments for use in pediatric psychopharmacology research. *Psychopharmacology Bulletin, 21,* 839–843.

Zimmerman, M., Coryell, W., Corenthal, C., & Wilson, S. (1986). A self-report scale to diagnose major depressive disorder. *Archives of General Psychiatry, 43,* 1076–1081.

Berger, R. M., & Patchner, M. A. (1988). *Implementing the research plan: A guide for the helping professions.* Newbury Park, CA: Sage.

Endicott, J., & Nee, J. (1997). Endicott work productivity scale (EWPS): A new measure to assess treatment effects. *Psychopharmacology Bulletin, 33,* 13–16.

Review of the Endicott Work Productivity Scale by WILLIAM C. TIRRE, Senior Research Psychologist, Air Force Research Laboratory, Brooks Air Force Base, TX:

TEST COVERAGE AND USE. The Endicott Work Productivity Scale (EWPS) was designed to assess the extent to which a person's work productivity and efficiency is adversely affected by a medical condition, for example, depressive disorder. The test developer intended the EWPS be used as a research tool in assessing the effectiveness of treatments on mental disorders. The goal was to have a measure that was sensitive enough to discriminate among levels of work productivity within a sample of persons who were depressed (or otherwise impaired) but still working. This intended use appears to be appropriate. The test developer did not indicate test uses that would be inappropriate. For example, we do not know how the test developer would feel about the EWPS being used by clinicians to assess an individual client's progress toward recovery from depression.

APPROPRIATENESS OF SAMPLES FOR TEST VALIDATION AND NORMING. Only the most preliminary of test validation studies on the EWPS has been reported so far. Endicott and Nee (1997) administered the EWPS to a sample of 42 outpatients being treated for a major depressive disorder but still working, and to a sample of 66 community members who were not being treated for any mental disorder. Fifty percent of the outpatient sample was male and 30% of the community sample was male. Four of the 66 community participants met the criteria for a major depressive disorder by an independent criterion. No norms were reported, just mean scores for the clinical sample at intake ($N = 35$) and endpoint ($N = 42$), and mean scores for the community sample ($N = 66$). The samples were appropriate in composition for preliminary test validation but inadequate in size.

RELIABILITY. Two types of reliability estimates were reported. Internal consistency was estimated with the alpha method (Kuder & Richardson, 1937) for both the clinical sample (alpha = .92) and the community sample (alpha = .93). These estimates suggest that the EWPS is internally consistent (the items measure one trait) for both clinical and community samples. Test-retest reliability was estimated as the intraclass correlation between test scores collected 10 to 14 days apart on a sample of 16 outpatients whose condition "had not changed greatly in severity of illness" (Endicott & Nee, 1997, p. 14). The intraclass correlation was .92. It is not clear why the intraclass correlation was used, when a simple Pearson correlation would be appropriate. The sample size is woefully inadequate for reliability estimation, and the sample composition was not representative of the population to which an investigator might want to generalize. It would have been better to estimate test-retest reliability on an unrestricted sample of outpatients and on an unrestricted sample of community members who were not outpatients at the clinic.

VALIDITY. Three types of construct validity evidence were reported. Nomological validity (Messick, 1981) (called concurrent validity by Endicott and Nee, 1997) was assessed by examining the correlations of the EWPS with measures of severity of illness, including the Hamilton Rating Scale for Depression (Hamilton, 1960), the Clinical Global Impressions Severity of Illness and Global Improvement Scale (National Institute of Mental Health, 1985), and the Symptom Checklist 90 (Derogatis, Lipman, & Covi, 1973). For both the clinical and community samples these measures appeared to be moderately correlated in the expected direction, but significance levels were not reported. When I applied the usual two-tailed test of significance, I found that the Hamilton Rating Scale for Depression was not significantly correlated with the EWPS at intake ($r = .27$, $N = 35$) but was significantly correlated at the endpoint ($r = .61$, $N = 42$). Endicott and Nee also report that the EWPS correlates significantly with change scores on the Hamilton scale ($r = .29$, $N = 35$), which is a true statement only if a one-tailed test is appropriate. Unfortunately, insufficient data were reported to interpret this finding. I am assuming that a simple difference score was used (e.g., Hamilton Depression score at intake minus score at endpoint—an improvement score). If this is true, then one possibility is a nonlinear relationship such that only the mildly depressed outpatients really show any improvement. The nondepressed would be likely to stay that way, and the profoundly depressed would be unlikely to improve. Another possibility is that the nondepressed would stay that way, and the depressed outpatients would tend to improve. A scatterplot should be reported and the goodness of fit of a nonlinear function should be tested. Also offered as evidence for the validity of the EWPS to identify depressed individuals were t-tests comparing the mean EWPS scores of the depressed outpatients at intake and at endpoint with the mean EWPS scores of the community sample. The outpatient sample had a significantly higher mean score than the community sample at intake but not after a placebo treatment (which was not described in the article).

The validity evidence offered is at least a step in the right direction, but much more needs to be accomplished to document the construct validity of the EWPS. I would recommend a study in which the EWPS is administered to a sample of persons seeking outpatient treatment for mental disorders and to a community sample not seeking treatment. In addition to the EWPS, I would administer comprehensive tests of personality that measure both the normal and clinical traits. This strategy would help locate work productivity in the space defined by the major personality traits. I would also administer tests of traits that might provide alternative explanations of work productivity variance. Broadbent's Cognitive Failures Questionnaires (Broadbent, Cooper, FitzGerald, & Parkes, 1982) and various job satisfaction scales come to mind.

TEST ADMINISTRATION. The EWPS is basically a self-administered rating scale that should be usable by a wide variety of persons. The reading level is relatively simple, but the test developers caution that persons who are severely ill or are poor readers might need to have the test items read to them.

TEST REPORTING. Because the test was designed as an evaluation or research tool, the test developers have not provided any special report or interpretive guides for use by clinicians.

TEST AND ITEM BIAS. There are insufficient data on the EWPS to conduct analyses of test and item bias.

SUMMARY. The EWPS is a research instrument that merits attention by investigators interested in assessing the effects of clinical treatments on work productivity. Only the most preliminary level of psychometric data is available on this instrument. Reliability and validity studies need to be accomplished with larger samples that better represent the clinical and general populations to which researchers might want to generalize. The construct of work productivity needs to be understood in terms of basic personality traits and alternative interpretations of the trait need to be explored.

REVIEWER'S REFERENCES

Kuder, G. F., & Richardson, M. W. (1937). The theory of the estimation of test reliability. *Psychometrika, 2*, 151–160.

Hamilton, M. (1960). A rating scale for depression. *Journal of Neurology, Neurosurgery, and Psychiatry, 23*, 56–62.

Derogatis, L. R., Lipman, R. S., & Covi, L. (1973). SCL-90: An outpatient psychiatric rating scale: Preliminary report. *Psychopharmacology Bulletin, 9*, 13–28.

Messick, S. (1981). Constructs and their vicissitudes in educational and psychological measurement. *Psychological Bulletin, 80*, 575–588.

Broadbent, D. E., Cooper, P. F., FitzGerald, P., & Parkes, K. R. (1982). The Cognitive Failures Questionnaire (CFQ) and its correlates. *British Journal of Clinical Psychology, 21*, 1–16.

National Institute of Mental Health. (1985). Special feature: Ratings scales and assessment instruments for use in pediatric psychopharmacology research. *Psychopharmacology Bulletin, 21*, 839–843.

Endicott, J., & Nee, J. (1997). Endicott work productivity scale (EWPS): A new measure to assess treatment effects. *Psychopharmacology Bulletin, 33*, 13–16.

[141]
EQ Questionnaire.

Purpose: "To measure entrepreneurial and executive effectiveness to be used as a personal and organizational development tool."

Population: Adults.

Publication Date: 1993–1998.

Acronym: EQ Questionnaire.

Scores, 12: Adaptability, Managerial Traits (Risk Tolerance, Time Management, Creativity, Strategic Thinking, Planning, Goal-Orientation), Personality Traits (Extroversion, Intuition, Thinking, Perceiving), EQ Index.

Administration: Group.

Price Data, 1998: $75 per 5 questionnaires including user's manual ('95, 32 pages) and scoring software; volume discounts available.

Time: [25–35] minutes.

Comments: Test booklet title is EQ Questionnaire; manual title is Entrepreneurial Quotient; administered with paper and pencil and scored using PC or administered and scored using PC (requires IBM or compatible computer).

Authors: Wonderlic, Inc. and Edward J. Fasiska.

Publisher: Wonderlic, Inc.

Review of the EQ Questionnaire by JAMES T. AUSTIN, Research Specialist, Ohio State University, Columbus, OH:

The Entrepreneurial Quotient (EQ) instrument is published by Wonderlic, Inc. The instrument proper consists of an introduction and directions, two information sections, and 100 binary response items (preferences) that were developed to assess the entrepreneurial profile of applicants or incumbents. The user's manual (1995) describes the system, its computer scoring, interpretation of the EQ summary scales (Adaptability, Managerial Traits, Personality Traits), and the overall EQ Index, model development, and validation. An EQ guide (16 pages) is printed by the scoring program. The underlying model was developed by Fasiska (1992), who also authored *The EQ Factor* (Fasiska, 1994). My review proceeds sequentially through the manual and instrument, then provides conclusions.

USER'S MANUAL. A 1-page introduction establishes history, context, and a dictionary definition of the entrepreneur as an "individual who assumes business risk for the sake of profit" (p. 2). Subsequently, one operational definition used is an individual who starts and operates a business for a period of 5 years. Immediately following, the scoring program for Microsoft Windows Operating System (Ver 3.1) is described. The presentation includes system requirements, text conventions, installation to a PC hard drive, running the program, scoring an EQ Questionnaire, editing examinee information, security, reports, exiting the program, and maintaining databases. Demographics and instrument responses are entered by hand.

One positive feature of the scoring program is that response information may not be altered, although there is no way to protect against reentering a person's responses. I have minor criticisms and one major one. It is not clear whether the program operates under more current versions of the operating system (e.g., Windows 95/98/NT). The exact purpose of the EQ guide is also not clear whether score reporting, interpretation, or a combination. For usability, it would be helpful to have illustrations of various screens (i.e., screen shots) of the scoring/database program in the user's manual. Most serious problems, however, were the minimal literature review and the lack of a solid conceptual framework to support a network of relationships among constructs that determine managerial and personality types and the construct itself, and those that affect constructs that are a function of managerial and personality types. Such a model should be laid out at the outset to provide a source of hypotheses for testing and content specifications for developing an item pool.

In the next section of the manual, a scoring foundation is proposed. It is called the gravitational theory and asserts that those who have persisted and succeeded as entrepreneurs are (a) comfortable yet challenged and (b) capable of assessment to identify the characteristics required for entrepreneurial success.

The next section, *Interpreting EQ Results,* provides more report format description than guidance on interpretation. The components of Adaptability, Managerial Traits and Typing, and Personality Scales and Typing are described. Managerial traits are six in number, and typing (i.e., categorizing) is based on a model, apparently derived by Fasiska, that sequences goal achievement into four steps: idea generation, strategy development, planning, and implementation. Sixteen types or categories result from four sets of binary preferences. It seems that little use was made of existing theory on management competencies or goal striving in the domains of organizational behavior or human resource management. This lack of use indicates little attempt to relate a new instrument to theories and instruments that are currently available. Personality typing, a complement to the managerial typing, is based on the theory of Carl Jung, and mention is made of validation against the Myers-Briggs Type Indicator. A standard 16-category system is proposed. It would be useful to clarify the relationship(s) among the personality and managerial traits and types, perhaps with an illustration.

Model development, apparently completed by Fasiska (1992), is described as an iterative process, using interviews and decision-making analyses with a relatively small sample of 55 entrepreneurs and executives and 50 persons who were not self-employed. In an initial phase, only personality types were used. Specifically, they were validated against the Myers-Briggs Type Indicator (96 of 105 individuals exactly matched types). These results indicated that the typical entrepreneur exhibited an ENTP profile (Introversion-*Extroversion,* *Intuition*-Sensing, *Thinking*-Feeling, and *Perceiving*-Judging). The manual states that the results of this phase were not completely satisfactory. Therefore, a second phase of model development involved adding the management functions and readministering the instrument to a sample comprising 155 managers, 220 self-employed individuals, and 235 employed individuals from the general public. It is claimed on page 19 that "statistically analyzed results were used to refine the model to its present form which incorporates 11 variables." It would be helpful to provide these analyses and results. Finally, it is stated that two further interactions using all 11 variables were implemented with "several thousand" individuals in those three subgroups. No data from these groups are provided, however. This area of the manual is lacking because there is insufficient detail pertaining to statistical results to support evaluation by a reader.

Wonderlic gathered validity data for the instrument after model development. Most of this unpublished research used reasonably large samples and known groups method (which compares self-reported entrepreneurs with other groups, here executives and the general public). In the first phase, "ideal" profiles were developed using 320 executives, 690 entrepreneurs, and 1,075 general population individuals. Means on the 11 variables were compared among the groups, and dimensional weights were derived in proportion to each variable's sensitivity in differentiating the three groups. None of the details of these analyses are provided, and thus it is impossible to evaluate the appropriateness of the weighting. Even if proprietary information, the general weighting techniques should have been described. In the next paragraph (p. 20), a statement is made that the "original EQ model was developed and refined" using responses from 2,085 persons, and that "This original validation was conducted using 1260 data profiles." Along this general line, it was difficult to track all of the phases, samples, and subgroups. For example, the totals for the subgroups (180 executives, 420 entrepreneurs, and 680 employed individuals) do not add up to 1,260 but to 1,280. A chart describing them and the methods of sample selection (convenience, random, or other) would be extremely helpful. Tables on page 21 illustrate mean differences and significance tests on the three groups for the EnQ and ExQ. I have several concerns about this presentation. First, each of the tables would benefit from better labeling. Are the bold values in Tables 2a and 3a means and the values below in parentheses standard deviations? Second, it would be useful to see attention to effect size and statistical power. Finally, I believe that analysis of variance might be more useful than separate t-tests in this situation.

The manual discusses two subsequent studies. In Phase II, a small sample of 52 was divided into two subgroups, 31 successful entrepreneurs and 21 successful executives, based on peer judgments that are not described in detail. The same sorts of tables were used to report the results, and the first two critiques from Phase I still apply. It occurs to this reviewer that a personality variable—autonomy or need for independence—might also be useful in a network of variables surrounding the entrepreneurial construct given that the individuals work for themselves. Next, *Further EQ Model Development* describes validation enhancements performed using a mailed survey addressed to individuals who had responded to the EQ Questionnaire. The survey is not described in detail, the response rate was 23%, and no comparisons of responders/nonresponders were presented. Survey responses were used to categorize individuals into four categories (two entrepreneurial and two executive) and an undetermined group.

Summary statistics on 10 EQ traits and four summary scales are presented for a sample of 1,523 individuals (whose selection or recruitment was not described). This sample is described by gender and ethnic breakdown, with most of the sample reporting male, Caucasian status. The ethnic part of this table is headed gender. In Tables 10 and 11, the EQ components are compared across the gender and ethnic subgroups. With the exception of Planning, which has a 14-point difference favoring females, most of the gender means are equal or within 1 point. Greater differences are observed among ethnic groups, with the ranges across groups (i.e., within a column defined by an EQ scale or dimension) falling between 3 and 11 points. It is good to see these breakdowns, but

tests of significance and effect sizes would be more helpful in determining disparate impact.

THE INSTRUMENT. The 100 items are binary choices between two preferences. There appears to be a possibility of social desirability due to transparency in some items, and the publisher to date has provided no studies of this biasing factor.

CONCLUSIONS. It is encouraging to see an instrument that addresses entrepreneurial and executive functions, especially given the changes that are occurring in the business sectors of the industrialized nations (e.g., global markets, web-based commerce). Some evaluative evidence has been provided by the developer and the publisher. The current instrument and documentation, however, leave something to be desired. The flaws, however, can be corrected. Minor flaws in the manual included the lack of usability of some portions, typographical errors, and omissions of relevant data or explanations. More serious flaws, although not fatal, involve the failure to provide a conceptual rationale and model to organize the entrepreneurial and executive dimensions and a failure to provide richer validation evidence. With respect to additional construct validity evidence, it would be useful to see retest reliability estimates, clarification of internal consistency estimates, and social desirability correlations. Additional evidence is needed in the form of relationships of the EQ with multiple criteria assessed from multiple perspectives (cf. Murphy, Trailer, & Hill, 1996). Further evidence could be provided through a training intervention approach to entrepreneurship, with the EQ used pre- and posttraining to assess participant gain in the skills assessed. Additional evidence could be obtained by relating the EQ instrument to typologies of entrepreneurship, such as the one validated by Miner (1997). Miner's types are personal achievers, real managers, expert idea generators, and empathetic supersalespeople. Finally, it seems feasible to study the EQ Questionnaire in the context of entrepreneurship education. Low, Venkataraman, and Srivatsan (1994), for example, proposed a simulation game for teaching and research purposes that would easily blend with the EQ Questionnaire.

SUMMARY. This instrument has potential if cosmetic and substantive changes are made in the instrument, the user's manual, and in the evidence provided by the publisher. This evidence should be provided before the instrument can be recommended wholeheartedly for personnel selection. Research with the instrument is appropriate given that any decisions based on score interpretation have much less consequence for individuals.

REVIEWER'S REFERENCES

Fasiska, E. J. (1992). Managerial type determination and its role in the development of an Executive/Entrepreneurial Quotient (EQ) instrument. *International Journal of Value-Based Management, 5,* 17.

Fasiska, E. J. (1994). *The EQ factor.* North Versailles, PA: LaserLight Publishing.

Low, M., Venkataraman, S., & Srivatsan, V. (1994). Developing an entrepreneurship game for teaching and research. *Simulation and Gaming, 25,* 383–401.

Murphy, G. B., Trailer, J. W., & Hill, R. C. (1996). Measuring performance in entrepreneurship research. *Journal of Business Research, 36,* 15–23.

Miner, J. B. (1997). *A psychological typology of successful entrepreneurs.* Westport, CT: Quorum Books.

Review of the EQ Questionnaire by PAUL M. MUCHINSKY, Joseph M. Bryan Distinguished Professor of Business, The University of North Carolina at Greensboro, Greensboro, NC:

The EQ (Entrepreneurial Quotient) Questionnaire ostensibly assesses a job candidate's suitability for entrepreneurial and executive functions. The instrument consists of 100 questions requiring the candidate to indicate which of two answers is the more self-descriptive. One such question is as follows: "If your company was sponsoring a golf outing and you loved to play golf and had your choice of golfing with your favorite foursome, or an invited group that you didn't know but had a reputation of being good golfers, which group would you choose to golf with? (a) your favorite foursome; (b) The invited group" (instrument disk).

The instrument yields several scores that reflect various aspects of the candidate's suitability, which include managerial style and psychological type preferences. Four bipolar managerial style dimensions are presented: Creative vs. Traditional; Strategic vs. Functional; Planning vs. Reacting; and Goal-oriented vs. Activity-oriented. With two levels to each dimension, 16 possible types can be manifested. According to the publisher, a "managerial profile may be considered as the operational or applied counterpart of a personality profile which represents the predisposed innate nature of an individual's thinking and proposed behavior patterns" (manual, p. 12). The EQ Questionnaire also presents assessments of personality based on the Jungian model of psychological type. The resulting types are identical to those found in the Myers-Briggs Type Indicator: Extroversion vs. Intraversion; Intuition vs. Sensing; Thinking vs. Feeling; and Perceiving vs. Judging. The confluence of all the assessed dimensions

is to produce a single overall score called the "EQ" (Entrepreneurial Quotient), which is to be used to make personnel decisions. The underlying premise is that successful entrepreneurs exhibit certain managerial and personality types, and this instrument will be useful in identifying such people.

My overall opinion of this instrument is mixed, as many issues influence my judgment. The quality of the validational evidence is uneven. No mention is made in the test manual regarding how the 100 questions were derived either through empirical methods (as factor analysis) or rational selection. No item statistics are presented, so we have no basis to understand the inclusion of the question on golf, for example, or what it measures. The method of contrasted groups (self-reported entrepreneurs, executives, and "others") was used to provide validational evidence for the meaning of the EQ index. The overall sample size used to make validity assessments was larger than found in similar research (in excess of 2,000). However, little is said of the "other" or "general population" group that served as the contrasted sample. In practice this instrument would be used to make differentiations among candidates with basically similar vocational interests and aspirations through the self-selection process. Thus the real value of this instrument would be to make more fine-grained differentiations among applicants who are more alike than different, and thus the predictive accuracy of the instrument is overestimated. However, such a criticism applies to many contrasted-group validation designs.

I was impressed with the publisher's statement that there is a contingent relationship between the ideal profile for a candidate and differing kinds of entrepreneurial work activity. It is recommended that certain managerial types may be blended more effectively than others to produce successful and satisfying outcomes. However, this sensitivity to matching certain types of people to certain types of environments is lost in the usage of the overall EQ index. To quote from the user's manual, "In terms of EQ results, the EQ Index is the 'bottom line' in that it represents the candidate's overall entrepreneurial potential as measured by the EQ Questionnaire" (p. 16). The EQ Index itself is based upon some questionable psychometric assumptions. The average score on each subdimension of the instrument, as based on the entrepreneurs who served as the norm group, is considered as the "ideal profile." According to the manual, "when individuals have skills and traits that differ from the ideal, they are less likely to attempt and/or succeed in starting a new business" (p. 24). The EQ Index is derived in part from the difference of the candidate's scores on the subscales and the ideal profile. Thus, a candidate's scores that are greater than the "ideal" are statistically regarded as equivalent to scores that are less than the "ideal." This statistical algorithm is at odds with the theoretical premise that higher scores indicate a stronger tendency to consistently think or behave in the desired manner.

I was pleased with the publisher's attempt to provide a theoretical linkage between managerial type and personality type. The validational evidence on this association was most positive. I also commend the publisher for articulating a conceptual basis for successful entrepreneurial activity. As best I can infer, the critical underlying psychological construct behind successful entrepreneurs is achievement striving. At a fundamental level perhaps that is what this instrument does—identifies candidates with higher achievement motivation. However, I found the operational issues associated with generating the EQ Index (the "bottom line") to be confusing at best and internally contradictory at worst. I doubt if the non-technically trained user of this instrument will be sufficiently knowledgeable to realize that there are questionable links and assumptions between the model upon which the instrument is based and the derivation of the single EQ Index score that will be used to make personnel decisions. I found some disturbing disconnects between a sound theoretical model and the ultimate "bottom line" score.

The manual describes more norm-group validational evidence and procedures that found in many test manuals. However, more information should have been presented on the EQ Index, such as the properties of the score distribution, deciles, stanines, or any similar type of reference information to better understand this all-important score. Six pages of the manual are devoted to giving detailed instructions on how to set up the EQ scoring program for Windows.

SUMMARY. In conclusion, given the great amount of current social interest in entrepreneurial activity, I commend the publisher for attempting to create an instrument deemed useful in facilitating such activity. However, on several occasions I had considerable difficulty understanding "how they got there from here" in the derivation of the EQ index and its associated interpretation.

[142]
Evaluation of Basic Skills.

Purpose: Designed to provide a concept-based measurement of reading, writing, and mathematics.
Population: Ages 3 to 18.
Publication Dates: 1995–1996.
Scores, 3: Reading, Writing, Mathematics.
Administration: Individual.
Price Data, 1998: $49.95 per complete start-up kit including administration manual ('95, 27 pages), 50 test forms, and 25 pre-test/post-test word tests; $15.95 per administration manual; $17.95 per 2-tape audio cassette set "Administering the Test"; $95 per application fee as test administrator; $25 per 50 test forms; $20 per 50 pre-test/post-test word tests.
Time: (10) minutes for Mathematics section; untimed for Reading and Writing sections.
Author: Lee Havis.
Publisher: Trust Tutoring.

Review of the Evaluation of Basic Skills by
ELEANOR E. SANFORD, Director of Technical Research, MetaMetrics, Inc., Durham, NC:

The Evaluation of Basic Skills test was "designed to provide a simple, effective, and reliable means of evaluating 'basic skills' of children aged 3–18" (manual, p. 1) in the areas of writing, reading, and mathematics. In addition, the test was designed to identify learning difficulties and to prescribe appropriate instructional approaches for each examinee. Subtests include each significant skill ability in the various areas, from basic to advanced, with completion of all skills defining the reasonable expected level of adult functioning in a literate, technological world (i.e., roughly comparable to a high school diploma in the United States). The Mathematics and Writing subtests are designed to be individually administered, but can be group administered if the examinees are about the same age; the Reading subtest must be individually administered. Only the Mathematics subtest is timed (10 minutes).

DEVELOPMENT. The development of each subtest was based on the author's experiences working with young children. General test specifications are provided, but there is no theoretical framework for the test. The Writing subtest measures spelling ("the act of writing, not the process"), the Reading subtest measures an examinee's sight vocabulary, and the Mathematics subtest measures mathematics concepts. The items for each subtest are arranged in sequence from most basic to most advanced, although very little research and no empirical data are provided to validate the sequencing. Based on an examination of the Mathematics items, it appears that the items are ordered by topic rather than difficulty or instructional sequence (addition of decimals comes after division of fractions with unlike denominators). In addition, because of presentation mode (horizontal versus vertical), some of the items do not assess the concept specified (place value).

TEST ADMINISTRATION. Because the items on each subtest are sequenced, different starting points for different ages are provided. When not starting with the first item, it is assumed that the student would answer all of the prior items correctly. The test administrator is directed to stop the test when the examinee misses five items in a row. This may be hard to do on the Writing and Mathematics subtests because the administrator will need to be scoring the examinee's responses as the test is being administered.

NORMS. The norming population for the test consisted of 147 examinees ages 8 to 18 in grades 2 through 4, grade 6, and high school. Only students at three schools in Maryland were tested and there was no mention as to the representativeness of the sample in relation to the intended population. If one assumes that the examinees in each sample are equally distributed in terms of age, then the samples at each age (ages 7 through 18) range from 8 for ages 12 and 13 to 21 for age 8. No examinees aged 3 to 6 or 14 were tested. The raw data were smoothed to develop the raw score to age scale conversion; in addition, scores for ages below 6 were extrapolated. The norming data were obtained from nonstandard administrations of the test (for the Writing and Mathematics subtests, all items were administered in a group setting; and the Mathematics subtest was untimed).

RELIABILITY. No information is provided concerning the consistency or stability of the scores or the scoring process.

VALIDITY. The results of the test are to be interpreted in relation to what is typical performance on each of the subtests for the age. Although the scores for each age go up similar to growth curves from other assessments, the sample sizes are so small that caution must be exercised when interpreting the results from the assessment.

Even though the test was designed to match the skills associated with a high school diploma, no studies were described that compared scores on the assessment and completion of high school.

SUMMARY. General test specifications are provided, but no content or construct validity information is provided. This assessment may be useful as a quick screening instrument when first working with an examinee, but it should not be used to determine an examinee's strengths and weaknesses in a content area, analyze learning difficulties, or develop instructional plans.

Although age-equivalent scores may be intuitively appealing, they are fraught with misunderstanding. When an examinee receives an age-equivalent score higher than his or her age, it is often misinterpreted that the examinee is performing at the higher level and is ready for even higher-level material. The appropriate interpretation is that the student performed better than an older examinee on the same material and is ready for more challenging material than his or her age (not more challenging than the age-equivalent score).

Review of the Evaluation of Basic Skills by LORAINE J. SPENCINER, *Professor of Special Education, University of Maine at Farmington, Farmington, ME:*

The Evaluation of Basic Skills assesses writing, reading, and mathematics for children and youth, ages 3–18. According to the administration manual, this test is designed to "help organize a successful instructional approach to improve learning and diagnose specific academic needs of the individual student" (manual, p. 1). The instrument comes with an administration manual, test protocols, pretest/post-test phonetic word tests, and two tapes (4 hours) of instruction on administration. The test is administered individually to students, although the manual states that the writing and math sections may be administered to groups of children if the age level is about the same.

According to the manual, there is no required order in administering the three subject areas. The Writing section contains a total of "50 basic writing problems." These "problems" are spelling words, ranging from common phonetic words to words with irregular spellings. The test does not contain any sentence, paragraph, or essay writing. Similarly, the Reading section contains a total of "50 problems" consisting of reading words from a word list. No information is provided in terms of analyzing word reading skills. The Mathematics section consists of 57 computation questions, ranging from counting items in a set to trigonometry and beginning calculus. No word problems are included.

Scoring involves calculating a raw score for each test section then looking up the "age level performance score" (manual, p. 9) in a conversion table in the manual. The "age level performance scores" are based on a sample group of children who were given the test in 1995. This sample consisted of one second grade class of 24 children (ages 7–8); one third grade class of 28 children (ages 8–10); one fourth grade class of 26 children; one sixth grade class of 23 children (ages 11–13); and 46 students ages 15–18. All the children were enrolled in one of two schools in Maryland. No additional information about the sample is provided. The manual furnishes no information concerning the technical characteristics of the test including test development, reliability, or validity of scores from the instrument.

SUMMARY. The Evaluation of Basic Skills is not adequate for assessing reading, writing, and mathematics. The test items do not begin to reflect the skills that students are expected to demonstrate as described in national standards of education reform. Furthermore, the "age level performance scores" are based on a very limited sample of children ages 7–18. Information about the characteristics of the sample is lacking. No information is provided about scores for children 3–6 years of age, although the test manual states that the instrument is appropriate for children ages 3–18. This test is not recommended for any purpose.

An additional aspect of this instrument is of concern. Accompanying the test kit is a brochure describing how one can "earn money with your own testing service" (brochure, p. 2) by becoming a certified test administrator. The process of becoming "certified" involves obtaining two character references, attaching verification of one's educational background, purchasing a "start-up kit" for $49.95, and submitting a $95 application fee. Applicants are required to administer one test and submit it to the publisher for "review and approval."

The brochure describes the "valuable service to students, teachers, and parents"; yet the publisher encourages and supports a process that will result in unqualified test examiners. The publisher does not mention a minimum level of education for individuals administering the test; in fact, "high school degree or equivalent" is mentioned as an option. Second, the examiner needs to submit only one practice protocol to receive "approval." To become proficient in administering, scoring, and interpreting a new assessment instrument, examiners must have an appropriate educational background and multiple opportunities to use the assessment before becoming "proficient." Test publishers must share the responsibility for encouraging and specifying high standards for individuals preparing to use their instruments.

[143]
Expressive Vocabulary Test.

Purpose: Designed to assess expressive vocabulary and word retrieval.

Population: Ages 2.5–90 years.

Publication Date: 1997.

Acronym: EVT.

Scores: Total score only.

Administration: Individual.

Price Data, 2001: $139.95 per complete kit including test easel, 25 record forms, and manual (176 pages); $26.95 per 25 record forms; $149.95 per AGS Computer ASSIST™ for the EVT (IBM or Macintosh).

Time: (15) minutes.

Comments: Conormed with the Peabody Picture Vocabulary Test—III; comparison between EVT and PPVT-III standard scores yields an evaluation of word retrieval; ; scoring ASSIST™ provides extended norms below 40 and includes vocabulary-building exercises.

Author: Kathleen T. Williams.

Publisher: American Guidance Service, Inc.

Review of the Expressive Vocabulary Test by FREDERICK BESSAI, Professor of Education, University of Regina, Regina, Saskatchewan, Canada:

The Expressive Vocabulary Test (EVT) is a useful addition to the general area of clinical tests of language development and language functioning. It has been conormed with the third edition of the Peabody Picture Vocabulary Test (PPVT-III; 280). Basically, it measures expressive vocabulary and thus complements the receptive vocabulary measures of the Peabody Test. When the scores of an individual are compared on both these tests, a measure of word retrieval can be derived and interpreted. The EVT consists of 190 items, excluding practice items; the first 38 are labeling items and the rest are synonym items in which the examiner presents a picture and a word and the examinee responds with a synonym.

Generally, the test materials are attractive and well laid out. The stimulus pictures are clear, uncluttered, and colorful. The record forms and the manual are well organized and easy to use. The acceptable and incorrect responses are clearly differentiated and color coded on the record form. Prompting procedures are clearly indicated and basic and ceiling rules are well explained. The norms are primarily standard scores with conversion tables for percentile ranks, normal curve equivalents, and stanines. Brief explanatory statements are given in the manual concerning the interpretation of each of these scores. The information on interpretation of score differences on the EVT and PPVT-III, however, is quite brief and more suggestions about the possible meanings of statistically significant differences between expressive and receptive vocabulary performance should be given. No doubt future research will help to clarify this clinically important issue.

VALIDITY. The development of the test followed good psychometric practices. Suitable item development and selection along with pilot studies and classical and Rasch item analysis lend some assurance of content and construct validity. The two main constructs, namely vocabulary knowledge and word retrieval, are defined and clearly distinguished. Clear evidence of age differentiation is given and median correlations of .79 and .77 with the PPVT-III Forms-III A and III B, respectively, give evidence of both discriminant and convergent validity. Corrections of the correlations for restriction of range are noted. The evidence for the clinical validity of the test with special needs groups such as individuals with speech and language impairment is encouraging. Clinical cases selected for study were matched with individuals from the norming sample on age, gender, race, and SES. A speech-impaired group showed no significant differences on their mean EVT score when compared to a matched control group but a language-impaired group as well as a mentally retarded group had significantly lower scores.

The mean EVT score differences of over 50 points between a learning disabled group and matched controls is dramatic. This suggests that the EVT might well be a very useful instrument for use in elementary school settings and particularly useful in diagnosing reading difficulties and learning disabilities of various kinds.

The norming of the test is exemplary. The same standardization sample as that used with the PPVT-III was employed. It consisted of 2,725 examinees tested at 240 sites in the United States. The characteristics of the sample based on gender, race, SES, and geographic region closely match those of a 1994 national survey conducted for the Bureau of Labor Statistics. Examiners were carefully trained and were required to do practice cases before collecting the norming data. What remains is that the test now needs to be normed in other English-speaking countries.

RELIABILITY. Evidence of reliability of the EVT is abundant. Corrected split-half coefficients ranging from .83 to .97 are reported. This was done across 25 age ranges in the standardization sample. The Rasch ability estimate was used to estimate the examinee's ability on each half of the test. Test-retest reliability estimates (mean interval of 42 days) are somewhat lower as could be expected. Coefficients of .77 to .90 are reported. These were derived from a total sample of 226 randomly selected subjects in four age categories. The standard error of measurement computed from split-half reliabilities is acceptable for individual use in most age ranges. A median SEM of 4.6 across the 25 age categories is quite adequate for a confident interpretation of the obtained scores.

SUMMARY. Generally, the EVT should be a useful clinical instrument for assessing expressive vocabulary and, when used with the PPVT-III, for the assessment of word retrieval. It can be recommended for use in educational settings where normal language development as well as language abnormalities and learning disabilities need to be assessed. It can also be recommended for adults but in a more limited way because different clinical groups (such as individuals who are aphasic or those with hearing or visual impairment) cannot be assessed with the existing norms. The test can be strongly recommended for research use by cognitive psychologists and others interested in language development and language functioning.

Review of the Expressive Vocabulary Test by OREST EUGENE WASYLIW, *Director of Adult Clinical Psychology, Isaac Ray Center, Rush-Presbyterian—St. Luke's Medical Center, Chicago, IL:*

The Expressive Vocabulary Test (EVT) is an untimed, individually administered test of expressive vocabulary and word retrieval that was conormed with the Peabody Picture Vocabulary Test, Third Edition (PPVT-III, Dunn & Dunn,

1997; 280). There are no alternate forms. The test consists of four examples and 190 items divided into age-group sets. The test kit includes a stimulus folder that converts into an easel, an examiner's manual for administration and scoring, and record sheets. The first 38 items require labeling, and the rest require synonyms. Most stimuli are large, colored-drawing pictures, but sometimes the examiner is required to point to something, such as part of the body. Occasionally, several different questions are asked for the same visual stimuli (e.g., what is this? What color?). The EVT is designed to be given by technicians. Teaching items are provided that help facilitate understanding of the purpose of this test.

The manual reports average administration times for separate age groups from youngest examinees (age 2 1/2) to oldest (age 90+). These times range from 9.0 to 25.1 with a mean of 15 minutes. The record form conveniently has basal and ceiling criteria repeated on each page, and examples of correct and incorrect responses. The manual has larger correct/incorrect response lists, and provides rationales for scoring. Correct answers must correspond to the picture and also match stimulus words in form and tense. The manual mentions considerations for testing special populations. Articulation errors are not counted, so that younger children are not penalized for improper pronunciation. Raw scores can be converted to standard scores, normal curve equivalents, test-age equivalents, and confidence intervals.

TEST AND ITEM DEVELOPMENT. Stimulus words were selected from eight different vocabulary or word-frequency lists, and synonyms were added to extend the effective age range of this test. Two pilot studies of participants aged 3 to 21 years were conducted. Classical and Rasch item analyses were completed. A bias-review panel was used to identify any offensive or apparently biased stimuli. A national tryout of 908 participants spanning age 2 to 21 years from all major regions and ethnic groupings with the U.S. was conducted at 73 sites.

RELIABILITY. Reliability statistics are reported for 25 age ranges from 2 to 90+ years, with a total of 2,725 participants tested at 240 sites nationwide. Alpha coefficients range from .90 to .98, and odd/even split-half, corrected reliability coefficients range from .83 to .97. Test-retest reliabilities were computed for intervals of 8 to

203 days between tests. The corrected test-retest reliability coefficient for the 2- to 5-year age groups ($N = 67$) was .77, whereas reliabilities for older groups ranged from .84 to .90. Although the greatest change (or growth) in language abilities is expected at the youngest age levels, possible reasons for the rather low reliability for the youngest group are not discussed in the manual.

VALIDITY. The reference manual includes very detailed information concerning geographic representation, educational level, ethnic breakdown, socioeconomic status, gender, and special group representation of the standardization group. Content validity was addressed by selecting test words on the basis of frequency and common usage in Standard American English. Construct validity is argued on the basis of frequency and common usage in Standard American English. Construct validity is argued on this same basis, plus data showing a developmental progression in scores. Tryout data show an inverse relationship between item frequency and difficulty. The manual argues that the validity of EVT scores is supported by its intercorrelations with the PPVT-III (a test of receptive vocabulary) that range from .61 to .88 depending on age. However, just how these data support the validity of EVT scores as a measure of word retrieval is not explained.

Internal validity data are provided through assessments of item homogeneity, item growth curves, and age differentiation. As expected, average scores increase appropriately with age, and the steepest part of the growth curve occurs at the earliest ages.

Concurrent validation studies found that EVT scores are more highly correlated with Verbal than Performance IQ on the Wechsler Intelligence Scale for Children—Third Edition (WISC-III; Wechsler, 1991), and with the Oral Expression Scale than the Listening Comprehension Scale of the Oral and Written Language Scales (OWLS; Carrow-Woolfolk, 1995). However, contrary to expectations, EVT scores were not more highly correlated with crystallized than fluid intelligence on the Kaufman Adolescent and Adult Intelligence Test (KAIT; Kaufman & Kaufman, 1993).

Studies of special groups showed no differences on EVT scores between speech-impaired participants (defined by articulation problems only) and controls. Learning-disabled (for reading), language-impaired, language-delayed, and mentally retarded groups all showed lower EVT scores than did controls, with the lowest scores being for the MR and LD groups. All groups showed better PPVT-III than EVT scores except for the gifted group, whose scores were equivalent on both tests.

INTERPRETATION. The manual lists possible areas of application, and a computer-scoring program, called ASSIST™, is also available that allows for graphing of repeated testing results and suggests vocabulary-building exercises. Tables are provided with significance and prevalence rates for differences between EVT and PPVT-III standard scores. However, a better discussion of the implications of difference scores between these two tests would be appreciated, particularly for the unusual circumstance in which a person shows better oral production than receptive vocabulary.

SUMMARY. The chief advantage of the EVT appears to be its ease of use and conorming with the newest version of the highly popular, well-regarded, and very well-researched receptive vocabulary test, the PPVT-III. The EVT is designed to be easily administered and to be given by technicians and people with a variety of backgrounds. It appears successful in this regard. Instructions, stimuli, and scoring procedures are very clear. The EVT does appear very easy to learn and administer, and easy for examinees to understand. The training items are also a welcomed aspect of this instrument.

In regard to limitations, scoring rules take some learning and not all the case examples are intuitive. Test-retest reliabilities appear rather low for the youngest age ranges, which may limit the effectiveness of this test for preschoolers. The EVT can be uncomfortably long to administer to older examinees and to special populations such as language-impaired clients. Instructions for early items are extremely clear. However, there should be a more prominent warning when a blank card is presented and the examiner is required to point to something else, such as a body part. Ambiguities in scoring still occur despite attempts in the manual to delineate the rationale for scoring. Initial validation shows positive correlations of this test with measures of verbal intelligence and expressive speech, but did not find expected correlations with subtests of several widely used developmental speech and language tests.

The EVT is a cued-recall test, in which synonyms are double-cued, with both a word and a picture. This may reduce the sensitivity of this test for people with word-finding problems. The reason for this multimodal cuing is never explained. Giving the EVT together with the conormed PPVT-III may be helpful, as the authors recommend. However, if word-finding problems are suspected, the evaluator may also wish to complement the EVT with single-cued and free recall format tests, such as the Oral Vocabulary subtest of the Woodcock-Johnson Psycho-Educational Battery—Revised (WJ-R; Woodcock & Johnson, 1987; T5:2901). In general, the EVT appears to be a useful and user-friendly test, but it is best administered in a battery of tests and may have limited utility for preschoolers and for older clients.

REVIEWER'S REFERENCES

Woodcock, R. W., & Johnson, W. B. (1987). Woodcock Johnson Psychoeducational Battery—Revised. Itasca, IL: Riverside Publishing.
Wechsler, D. (1991). Wechsler Intelligence Scale for Children—Third edition. San Antonio, TX: Harcourt Brace Educational Measurement.
Kaufman, A. S., & Kaufman, N. L. (1993). Kaufman Adolescent and Adult Intelligence Test. Circle Pines, MN: American Guidance Service, Inc.
Carrow-Woolfolk, E. (1995). Oral and Written Language Scales: Listening Comprehension and Oral Expression. Circle Pines, MN: American Guidance Service, Inc.
Dunn, L. M., & Dunn, L. M. (1997). Peabody Picture Vocabulary Test, Third Edition. Circle Pines, MN: American Guidance Service, Inc.

[144]

Family Assessment Form: A Practice-Based Approach to Assessing Family Functioning.

Purpose: Constructed to "standardize the assessment of family functioning and service planning for families receiving home-based services."

Population: Families receiving home-based services.

Publication Date: 1997.

Acronym: FAF.

Scores: 6 scales: Parent-Child Interactions, Living Conditions, Caregiver Interactions, Supports for Parents, Financial Conditions, Developmental Stimulation.

Administration: Group.

Price Data, 1997: $18.95 per test booklet/manual (79 pages).

Time: (60–90) minutes.

Comments: Ratings by child welfare practitioners.

Author: Children's Bureau of Southern California.

Publisher: Child Welfare League of America, Inc.

Cross References: See T5:1007 (1 reference).

Review of the Family Assessment Form: A Practice-Based Approach to Assessing Family Functioning by CINDY CARLSON, Professor of Educational Psychology, University of Texas at Austin, Austin, TX:

The Family Assessment Form (FAF) is a practice-based instrument designed to help child welfare practitioners standardize the assessment of family functioning and service planning for families receiving home-based services. Thus, its primary purpose is to facilitate clinical practice. It is secondarily useful in research and primarily in program evaluation. The FAF package includes a Face Sheet, a Behavioral Concerns/Observation Checklist, a Service Plan, a Closing Summary form, and a rating scale of six areas of family functioning. The FAF family functioning rating scale is considered to be a standardized measure for which psychometric properties have been evaluated, whereas the other forms may be modified by users to fit their needs. In the remainder of this review, FAF will be used to refer only to the standardized family functioning rating scale.

The FAF rates six domains of family functioning on a 9-point scale. Five levels of ratings are clearly defined on the rating form facilitating interrater reliability. Within each level ratings may reflect either a whole number or a midway point between two numbers, (e.g., 2 or 2.5). Interrater reliability, based on double coding of tape-recorded research interviews yielding 970 comparisons, found exact correspondence to be 50%, +/- a half step in rating 73.5%, and +/- a full step 89.2%.

In terms of validity, rating domains were developed by practitioners to reflect central areas of concern to child welfare practice with families; thus, the measure can be considered to have good face content validity. Construct validity was examined using a factor analysis of the FAF research interview based on 240 cases. Six interpretable factors were derived with factor loadings above .4 and with no item loading higher on another factor than where placed. Subscales derived from the factor analysis yielded inter-item reliability (Cronbach's alpha) estimates ranging from .71 to .92. Comparisons of the research interview analyses with the worker ratings of family functioning yielded similar alpha coefficients. No additional validity studies are reported.

Use of the FAF is enhanced by the availability of a comprehensive manual and rater-training by the measure's development staff. The manual clearly specifies the nature and purpose of the instrument, development and psychometric validation, training essentials, directions for completion and scoring, and differential use of the measure for clinical practice and program evaluation. Research on the measure appears to be ongoing, and it is hoped will provide additional indications of psychometric quality to support use of the instrument.

SUMMARY. The FAF is a well-developed rating scale of family functioning designed explicitly for the purposes of assessing the needs and monitoring change in child welfare families who receive home-based services. The measure has been thoughtfully developed and psychometric validation data are promising. Continuing research will establish this measure as a valuable clinical and research tool.

Review of the Family Assessment Form: A Practice-Based Approach to Assessing Family Functioning by MARY LOU KELLEY, Professor of Psychology, Louisiana State University, Baton Rouge, LA:

The Family Assessment Form (FAF) is intended to help standardize the assessment of family functioning and service delivery by child welfare workers. Information for completing the instrument is obtained from a variety of sources including parent interview, records and report by others, and observation. The measure is unique in that it focuses on identifying the strengths and weaknesses of each family member rather than a single individual. The instrument is intended for use by practitioners and the authors state that the measure may be modified to meet the needs of a particular agency.

The FAF consists of five separate sections: a demographic face sheet; family functioning; caregiver history and characteristics; child behavior problem and temperament; and service plan. The section on family functioning evaluates the family's physical environment, financial status, social support, parent-child interactions including discipline and parental bonding with the child, developmental stimulation of the child, and interactions between caregivers. Each section contains several items and each item is rated on a 9-point scale with the anchors ranging from an unusual strength to severe family dysfunction/child should be removed. Operational definitions of functioning at each of five anchors are provided for each item.

The section on the caregiver(s) history and characteristics is used to rate the parents' abuse history, current psychological adjustment such as substance use, emotional stability, and self-esteem. Separate ratings are obtained on each caretaker and using the same format noted above.

The section evaluating behavior problems is completed by checking whether each child exhibits a variety of externalizing and internalizing behavior problems. Each behavior problem has an operational definition written next to it. The final section provides space for listing target family problems, treatment goals, and method of achieving each goal as well as a section on goal achievement.

The FAF was developed and revised to meet practitioners' needs for standardized information on clients and not for placing the client in a category by summing responses. However, ratings can be used to assess goal achievement. The authors provide a description of procedures for training case workers to complete the FAF that is logical and practical. The directions for completing the FAF are described clearly and specifically.

Research on the FAF is limited and normative data on the items have not been obtained. The authors do provide some initial interrater and inter-item reliability estimates as well as construct validity data based on factor analyses. However, other forms of validity data, such as predictive and discriminant, are not provided. Furthermore, the reliability and validity data were obtained through client interview and not through typical administration procedures. This lack of psychometric data significantly limits the utility of the FAF. Little is known about whether all important areas are assessed or whether additional areas of functioning are important to family functioning. Likewise, whether some areas of functioning may provide little important data to the issue of service planning is not known. Furthermore, it may be that certain items should be weighed more heavily than others in the information-gathering process. Finally, the operational definitions of behaviors and functioning at each of the anchors should be very useful for examining rater reliability.

SUMMARY. In spite of the shortcomings of the FAF, the instrument appears to have good face validity and considerable support in the form of agency adoptions. It is likely the instrument provides more standardized data on families that could be useful to many welfare agencies. Importantly, the FAF can be reproduced for use within an agency for the intended purposes. Thus, agencies on restricted budgets in need of a more consistent data base on their individual clients may find the FAF appealing. Moreover, the instrument design would lend itself to validity research (e.g., predicting client outcomes).

Family Assessment Measure Version III.

Purpose: "Provides quantitative indices of family strengths and weaknesses."

Population: Families.

Publication Dates: 1993–1995.

Acronym: FAM-III.

Scores, 26: General scale (Task Accomplishment, Role Performance, Communication, Affective Expression, Involvement, Control, Values and Norms, Social Desirability, Defensiveness, Total), Dyadic Relationships (Task Accomplishment, Role Performance, Communication, Affective Expression, Involvement, Control, Values and Norms, Total), Self-Rating (Task Accomplishment, Role Performance, Communication, Affective Expression, Involvement, Control, Values and Norms, Total).

Administration: Individual.

Price Data, 1999: $125 per starter kit including manual ('95, 90 pages), 25 General Scale QuikScore™ forms, 25 Dyadic Relationship Scale QuikScore™ forms, 25 Self-Rating Scale QuikScore™ forms, and 15 MHS ColorPlot Profile of Family Perceptions; $25 per 25 General Scale QuikScore™ forms (English, Spanish, or French-Canadian); $25 per 25 Dyadic Relationship Scale QuikScore™ forms (English, Spanish, or French-Canadian); $25 per 25 Self-Rating Scale QuikScore™ forms (English, Spanish, or French-Canadian); $22 per 15 Progress Color Plot Profiles; $22 per 15 MHS ColorPlot Profile of Family Perceptions; $40 per manual; $45 per specimen set including 5 General Scale QuikScore™ forms, 10 Dyadic Relationship Scale QuikScore™ forms, 1 MHS ColorPlot Profile of Family Perceptions, and 1 Progress ColorPlot.

Foreign Language Editions: Spanish and French-Canadian QuikScore™ forms available.

Time: (30–40) minutes.

Authors: Harvey A. Skinner, Paul D. Steinhauer, and Jack Santa-Barbara.

Publisher: Multi-Health Systems, Inc.

Cross References: See T5:1008 (3 references).

Review of the Family Assessment Measure Version III by KENNETH J. MANGES, Director, Kenneth J. Manges & Associates, Inc., Cincinnati, OH:

The Family Assessment Measure Version III (FAM-III) is a novel, significantly researched (247 "normal" adults and 65 "normal" adolescents) instrument with a well-organized and comprehensive manual. Software support and internet access are two additional points to consider for using this assessment tool.

The instrument consists of the manual and three easily scorable carbon sheets for the three scales listed as: General, Self-Rating, and Dyadic

Relationship. The General scale consists of 50 forced-choice questions (*strongly agree, agree, disagree,* and *strongly disagree*). The scale can be used as a baseline or used at some point after therapy has been initiated to measure change. The Self-Rating and Dyadic scales each have 42 similarly scored forced-choice questions. There are guidelines for interpretation of the scores along with four case studies. Scores are based on a mean of 50 and a standard deviation of 10. Each forced-choice response is converted by the protocol into a numeric value, which can be easily calculated and transformed onto a FAM-III Color-Coded Profile of Family Perceptions. Each family member can be compared to each other and their scores plotted on the profile.

Each scale has an entry for the following headings: Task Accomplishment, Role Performance, Communication, Affective Expression, Involvement, Control, Values, and Norms. On the General scale there is a separate cumulative score for Overall Rating as well as two additional scores for Social Desirability and Defensiveness. The color-coded form allows a visual comparison as well as a quick interpretation based on the color range within which the score falls.

The manual suggests a low refusal rate for participants (2%) with a somewhat higher (unspecified) refusal rate for different clinical populations. To this writer, familiar with adolescents and institutionalized children, the refusal rate is potentially significantly higher.

The test authors advocate introducing the questionnaire as part of the intake assessment and not as an introductory first experience with the therapist/evaluator. Suggested time for the questionnaire is 30 to 40 minutes depending on whether all three FAM scales are administered and the number of people (dyads) within the family.

The multiple forms necessitated by the stepfamily member can be daunting, as each member will require multiple forms for pairing with other family members. For example, within a stepfamily of two children with involved grandparents you can have six dyads for each child (for a total of 12 forms for the two children) and an additional 6 forms for each adult you evaluate. Although not an insurmountable obstacle, the numerous forms and subsequent interpretation time pose a challenge to the clinician attempting to manage their billable time.

Time management is an issue. The manual's authors indicate that the time to administer and easily score the instrument is minimal. But they go on to state "interpretation of the FAM should be based upon individual's item responses, the total FAM score, the factor scores and their elevations, and an integration of the test data with information from additional sources which might include clinical interviews and direct observation of family members" (manual, p. 3).

A first-hand experience taught this writer not to accept assumptions that the test is anything less than time-consuming (count on 2 hours for scoring and interpretation for a four-member non-stepfamily household with a non-existent-grandparent household). The administrator can also anticipate clients raising questions about some of the scale questions. In addition, it is imperative for the therapist/evaluator considering use of this instrument to specify the time frame for which the questions are to be answered (one month, one year, etc.). In stepfamilies and foster care or institutionally housed children you can also anticipate skewed scores as a natural by-product inherent in the nontraditional family relationship.

Step-by-step guidelines within the manual are helpful as are warnings about misinterpretation of elevations. An example of such a warning is the statement, "*Social Desirability* and *Defensiveness Scales* below 40 do *not* guarantee the validity of the clinical scales, as there may be other distortions that are not being measured (i.e., projection)" (manual, p. 23).

The FAM-III has some limitations that are addressed in the manual and some that are not. Those not prominently mentioned in the manual are the more difficult instances frequently encountered when evaluations are used with managed care referrals or where custody decisions are being evaluated and stepfamily loyalties-problems are at issue.

Managed care is a reality for the clinician. The administration and interpretation are time-consuming. The authors are not at fault. The instrument provides a valuable objective measure that can be used in the therapy process or in a forensic evaluation as a point of focus and evaluation discussion. However, the time consumed with the administration and interpretation are questionable billable hours for the therapist.

When custody decisions are being considered there is an ever-present threat to an evaluation that gives the appearance of objectivity. This test is a self-report and not objective. It does not account for manipulation on the part of the test taker. Alienation of parental rights, a child's or parent's loyalty, and disturbed or inconsistent responding are not addressed.

The clinician has the opportunity to use the distortion as a means of discussion for constructive change. The forensic evaluator has the opportunity to question the validity of the measure when they have inconsistencies between test and observed behavior.

SUMMARY. The FAM-III is a valuable addition to the field of family evaluation tests. The authors have conducted thorough research on the instrument. They offer the clinician and forensic evaluator a means to compare baseline and intervention strategies. The use of standardized questions and a statistical yardstick for comparison are helpful to the evaluator considering the instrument. The comprehensive manual with case examples is insightful. Computer access, which will shorten scoring and interpretation, and internet access are helpful adjuncts for the user. Limitations include the need for multiple forms with involved families and time-consuming interpretation.

Review of the Family Assessment Measure Version III by STEPHEN A. SPILLANE, Learning and Training Specialist, Centerville, MA:

The Family Assessment Measure Version III (FAM-III) is a self-report instrument that the authors assert may be used as a diagnostic tool, to measure therapy outcomes, or for basic research on family strengths, weaknesses, and processes. It is designed to provide an assessment of family functioning that integrates individual members and collective characteristics in the past and the present. Potential users should be familiar with the *Standards for Psychological and Educational Testing* (AERA, APA, & NCME, 1985).

Construct validity evidence is presented through a clear and sound description of the Process Model of Family Function. The concepts examined include Task Accomplishment, Role Performance, Communication, Affective Expression, Involvement, Control, and Values and Norms. Three scales are derived for General, Dyadic Relationships, and Self-Rating.

Evidence for content validity was provided by successive pilot tests of items to establish ad-

equate levels of internal consistency reliability estimates. Principal component analyses suggest parsimony. Reported coefficient alpha reliabilities for overall General, Dyadic Relationships, and Self-Rating scales ranged from .86 to .95 for adult and children samples. Predictive validity was examined by a multiple discriminant analysis that yielded four discriminators significant at the .001 level—two of which accounted for 84% of the between group dispersion. No analysis of multicollinearity was reported. Median coefficients for test-retest reliability for subscales ranged from .57 to .66 with a test-retest average delay of 12 days.

Several studies of special populations are reported including: alcoholic or depressed father; "Problem Families"; school phobia; emotionally disturbed children; Cystic Fibrosis; "Distressed Relationships"; pain and headaches; anorexia; bulimia; anxiety disorders; adopted children with special needs; and manic-depressive parents. Discriminant validity studies examining group differences are "inconsistent" according to the author.

The FAM-III manual and materials provide clear instructions for administration and outline appropriate procedures to produce and interpret test results. The author recognizes that the variety of forms to be used requires the user to invest adequate time and practice in administration. Computerized scoring is available.

In summary, the FAM-III is a useful addition to diagnostic and research tools in family assessment. It is recommended particularly for probing characteristics and processes of families that include members with disabilities. However, as the author points out, it should be used as an adjunct rather than a substitute for clinical observations in diagnostic and therapeutic applications.

REVIEWER'S REFERENCE

American Educational Research Association, American Psychological Association, & National Council on Measurement in Education. (1985). *Standards for educational and psychological testing.* Washington, DC: American Psychological Association, Inc.

[146]
Family Environment Scale [Third Edition Manual].

Purpose: Designed to assess family members' perceptions of their social environment.
Population: Ages 11–adult.
Publication Dates: 1974–1994.
Acronym: FES.
Scores, 11: Cohesion, Expressiveness, Conflict, Independence, Achievement, Intellectual-Cultural, Ac-

tive-Recreational, Moral-Religious, Organization, Control, Incongruence.

Administration: Group.

Forms, 4: Real (Form R), Ideal (Form I), Expectations (Form E), Children's Version.

Price Data, 1999: $52.75 per preview kit including Form R item booklet, self-scorable answer sheet, interpretive report form, and third edition manual ('94, 96 pages); $27.75 per 25 Form R reusable item booklets; $41.50 per 25 Form I or Form E reusable item booklets; $13.75 per 25 nonprepaid answer sheets for use with item booklets; $8.50 per 25 profiles; $29.50 per 25 interpretive report forms; $13.20 per scoring key; $34.70 per 25 self-scorable answer sheets for use with item booklets; $48.40 per third edition manual; $27.75 per Social Climate Scales user's guide, revised.

Time: (15–20) minutes.

Comments: One component of the Social Climate Scales (T5:2445).

Authors: Rudolf H. Moos and Bernice S. Moos.

Publisher: Consulting Psychologists Press, Inc.

Cross References: See T5:1010 (138 references); for reviews by Julie A. Allison and Brenda H. Loyd of an earlier edition, see 12:151 (76 references); see also T4:961 (136 references); for reviews by Nancy A. Busch-Rossnagel and Nadine M. Lambert of an earlier edition, see 9:408 (18 references); see also T3:872 (14 references); for a review by Philip H. Dreyer, see 8:557 (4 references). For a review of the Social Climate Series, see 8:681.

Review of the Family Environment Scale [Third Edition Manual] by JAY A. MANCINI, Professor of Human Development, Virginia Polytechnic Institute & State University, Blacksburg, VA:

The Family Environment Scale (FES) is part of the family of the Social Climate Scales. Although the scale manual is in its third edition, the scale itself appears unchanged from its earlier versions (earlier manuals published in 1974 and 1986). This third edition of the FES manual does contain additional normative information, as well as more in-depth discussions of research applications. The manual also includes a substantial bibliography of articles, book chapters, and reports published up through 1994. The FES itself contains 90 items that are responded to by "true" or "false" answers. There are four forms of the FES: Real, Ideal, Expectations, and a children's version. The children's version is not reviewed here. There are 10 subscales, each of which contains 9 items: Cohesion, Expressiveness, Conflict, Independence, Achievement Orientation, Intellectual-Cultural Orientation, Active-Recreational Orientation,

Moral-Religious Emphasis, Organization, and Control. The manual includes definitions of these subscales. For example, Cohesion is defined as "the degree of commitment, help, and support family members provide for one another" (manual, p. 1). Items are in statement form for example, "Family members really help and support one another," "We tell each other about our personal problems," and "Being on time is very important in our family." The test developers have also constructed two summary indices, one called the Family Relationships Index and the other the Family Social Integration Index; each index contains 27 items drawn from the 10 subscales. The test manual does not clearly indicate the item content of any of the subscales or indices, though it is evident that some items are likely to be part of a particular subscale. A careful studying of the scoring sheet does lead to seeing which items are attached to each subscale.

THEORETICAL CONTEXT. One merit of the FES is the theoretical context that has informed it and that it in turn informs. In the section on research applications and validity the test manual presents and discusses a conceptual framework that is grounded in stress and coping theory. This framework includes the family environment concept (components of relationship, growth, and maintenance), a set of determinants (adult and child individual characteristics and well-being, and extrafamilial context factors such as ongoing stressors and resources) and a set of outcomes (adult and child coping and well-being, and extrafamilial context factors).

CLINICAL AND RESEARCH APPLICATIONS. This third edition of the scale manual provides an array of excellent descriptions of how the FES has been used and the range of its applications. For example, there is a section on clinical applications that focuses on depressed patients' families, alcoholic patients' families, and on an adolescent in an emotionally disengaged and disorganized family. The typology of family environments developed for clinicians includes personal growth-oriented families (these families include those that are in independent-, achievement-, and moral-religious-oriented groupings), relationship-oriented families (these families include those that are in support- and conflict-oriented groupings), and system-maintenance-oriented families (those families that are disorganized). The section in the manual that discusses research applications demonstrates the broad-based use of the FES. For example, the FES has been used in research on youth with conduct disorders, substance abuse problems, and learning disabilities; in research on families with child illnesses that include asthma, diabetes, and juvenile arthritis; in research on families with a history of physical or sexual abuse; and in research on families whose members have phobias, personality disorders, depression, and schizophrenia. Many other applications are described in the manual.

TECHNICAL PROPERTIES (RELIABILITY AND VALIDITY) OF THE SCALE. The manual contains in-depth descriptions of how the scale was developed, and indicates that the developers followed accepted standards. The rationale underlying construction of the FES is explained as an introduction to discussing reliability and validity. Information on internal consistency and on test-retest reliability is provided. Across the subscales internal consistency (alpha) ranged from .61 to .78. Corrected average item-subscale correlations ranged from .27 to .44. Test-retest reliability at 2 months ranged from .68 to .86 across the subscales, and at 4 months ranged from .54 to .86. The sample on which the internal consistency and item-subscale correlations was based was quite large ($n = 1,067$) whereas the test-retest information was based on sample sizes that were quite small ($n = 47$ for 2 months and $n = 35$ for 4 months). Data are also provided that compare normal ($n = 1,432$) and distressed ($n = 788$) families on the FES subscales. These data suggest that the FES does discriminate on dimensions such as Cohesion, Expressiveness, Independence, Intellectual and Recreational Orientation, and on Conflict. The test developers also report on two longitudinal research projects in which subscale stabilities were examined. Overall stability decreased over time, especially at 10 years from the beginning of the study. Of the subscales, Moral-Religious Orientation and Organization showed the greatest stability.

Various studies have addressed construct and discriminant validity of the FES. The manual describes in detail those FES constructs that have been shown to correlate with other constructs and measures to which it should and should not relate. All things considered, the FES demonstrates sufficient evidence of acceptable validity. This is not surprising given the care with which the FES has been grounded in theory and the initial care taken in item construction. In their own work the test developers report that their Moral-Religious subscale was highly related to religious participation, and that their Conflict subscale was appropriately associated with how much family members report actual disagreements. This information is supplemented with information that gives means and standard deviations for a range of special groups, including distressed adults and adolescents, families of different sizes, one-parent families, African-American and Latino adults, and African-American adolescents.

SUMMARY. The Family Environment Scale has been used in clinical and research work for over 25 years. Given its widespread use, the FES has certainly been accepted by researchers for application in a number of family settings. In comparison with other measures that are employed to address aspects of family living, the FES has been the subject of much scrutiny. Based on how the scale was developed and how it has been examined and used over time, it is recommended for situations in which researchers desire an omnibus assessment of the quality of family life. It is unclear whether a systematic evaluation of the FES has occurred in recent years, that is, an evaluation for which the goal is to consider possible revisions. At the very least the language used in the items should be critiqued (as has been pointed out in earlier *MMY* reviews, items appear to have a middle-class bias), and consideration should be given to the context in which families live in the 21st Century and the increasingly varying forms that families take. As with any test or measure, there must be a valid match with the research question, the theory underlying the research, and those persons who are the focus of the study. Otherwise validity and reliability are compromised.

Review of the Family Environment Scale [Third Edition Manual] by MICHAEL J. SPORAKOWSKI, Professor Emeritus of Human Development, Virginia Polytechnic Institute and State University, Blacksburg, VA:

The Family Environment Scale (FES) has had two fairly recent reviews in *The Twelfth Mental Measurements Yearbook* (12:151) that quite thoroughly detail many of the essential materials regarding the instrument. This commentary looks at the third edition FES manual and summarizes its offerings with a perspective focused on the instrument's utility in researching and clinically working with couples, families, and similar relationships.

The most recent edition of the FES manual (1994) offers considerably updated and expanded sections on research references, new normative data, and expanded information on how the instrument may be used in clinical work, program evaluation, and consulting. The scale itself is used in viewing relationships, personal growth, and systems maintenance that reflect linkages between the family and its larger social context. The FES is a 90-item, self-report, True-False format instrument that taps those dimensions.

The scale comes in three forms: The Real Form (R)—measuring perceptions of the respondent's current family environment; The Ideal Form (I)—measuring people's preferences about ideal family environments; and, The Expectations Form (E)—measuring expectations about family settings (expectations about what a family would be like). A Children's Version, a 30-item Pictorial version, is available for use with children ages 5 to 11 years.

Subscales of the FES are seen as representing: Relationship Dimensions—Cohesion, Expressiveness, and Conflict; Personal Growth Dimensions—Independence, Achievement Orientation, Intellectual-Cultural Orientation, Active-Recreational Orientation, and Moral-Religious Emphasis; and System Maintenance Dimensions—Organization and Control. A well-presented 11-page chapter on "Development, normative samples and psychometric characteristics" shows data about methodological and statistical considerations regarding the continuing developmental process of this scale. Detailed descriptions of the psychometrics behind these subscales are presented in some depth, as is evidence of reliability and validity. This chapter and the appendix materials provide a great deal of useful data about group comparisons on the scales (e.g., Distressed vs. Normal Adolescents), as well as data related to some of the diverse samples used in the scale's ongoing development (e.g., means and standard deviations for African-American and Latino Adults, and African-American Adolescents). Scoring and profiling of the results of the administration can be done by the administrator or may be sent to the publisher for a narrative report.

Research articles and chapters related to the FES number over 550 items in the "references section" representing a great variety of journals, books, and other resources. This should be most helpful to the wide variety of potential users of this instrument. Research applications are summarized in 41 pages of referenced narrative discussions in the manual. This reviewer was most positively impressed with this very helpful, categorical section which included sections such as: Families with a physically ill child; Families with a history of physical or sexual abuse; Families of substance abuse patients; A conceptual framework; Determinants of family climate; Coping with transitions and crises; Family environment and child development; and, Family environment and adult adaptation.

From my viewpoint as family researcher and clinician, the most useful section of this new manual is the section entitled "Applications for clinicians, consultants, and program evaluators." It discusses the timing and utilization of family assessment, integrating family assessment as part of educational programming and therapeutic interventions, promoting family growth, and utilization in the training of professionals, especially those dealing with families and other close relationships. Integral to this section is the combined use of FES profiles and case studies in discussing the whys, whens, and hows of employing this device in practice.

SUMMARY. My overall impression of the FES is that it is a theoretically grounded, solidly developed instrument useful in the assessment and description of family and other close relationships. It offers the possibility of within-family assessment using its various self-report formats, thus offering glimpses of both the internal and external family climate influences bearing upon family functioning. It may be a very useful, complementary device in assisting practitioners who do individual work as well, by helping to provide a larger context for behavior.

[147]
Feelings, Attitudes, and Behaviors Scale for Children.

Purpose: "Designed to assess a range of emotional and behavioral problems."
Population: Ages 6–13.
Publication Dates: 1996.
Acronym: FAB-C.
Scores, 7: Conduct Problems, Self Image, Worry, Negative Peer Relationships, Antisocial, Lie, Problem Index.
Administration: Group.

Price Data, 1999: $55 per complete kit including manual (59 pages), and 25 QuikScore™ forms; $27 per 25 QuikScore™ forms; $30 per manual; $32.95 per specimen set including manual and 3 QuikScore™ forms.

Time: (10) minutes.

Comments: Self-report.

Author: Joseph H. Beitchman.

Publisher: Multi-Health Systems, Inc.

Review of the Feelings, Attitudes, and Behaviors Scale for Children by PATTI L. HARRISON, Professor of School Psychology and Assistant Dean of the Graduate School, The University of Alabama, Tuscaloosa, AL:

The Feelings, Attitudes, and Behaviors Scale for Children (FAB-C) for children ages 6–13 years is reported by the author to be a screening instrument designed to assess a range of emotional and behavior problems of children. Children respond to the 48 items on a score form or computer administration program by selecting a "yes" or "no" response for each item. A reading level for the items is not given in the manual, and the author indicates that items may be read to children who are younger or have poor reading skills.

The items are combined to assess six dimensions: Conduct Problems (11 items), Self-Image (7 items), Worry (7 items), Negative Peer Relations (5 items), Antisocial (6 items), and Lie (8 items). A Problem Index is formed by first totaling raw scores for the Conduct Problems and Lie Scales with 4 supplemental items not assigned to a dimension and, then, subtracting the Worry dimension raw score from this total. It should be noted that, unlike many other self-report measures, the Lie Scale is interpreted by the author as a measure of defensive response style and immaturity, in addition to an assessment of the examinee's validity in responding to items.

CONCEPTUAL FOUNDATION. A major concern about the FAB-C is the author's failure to provide a conceptual or theoretical framework to form a foundation for its use in practical settings or to guide development of items, support interpretation of the scores, or plan validity studies. In the first sections of the manual, the author offers very limited discussion of the possible use of the FAB-C and only notes that it may be used as a routine screening device in a number of settings that serve children. The lack of framework for the use of the instrument results in no standards by which to judge the evidence for validity or the appropriateness of the interpretation guidelines.

The lack of a conceptual or theoretical framework is very apparent in the development of the items and content of the scale. The author originally hypothesized 10 clinical dimensions, but, as a result of the factor analyses and pilot studies, 6 dimensions are assessed on the final instrument, representing only 3 of the original 10 dimensions. The content of some items in the final dimensions does not seem consistent with standard conceptual definitions. For example, as noted earlier, the Lie Scale is interpreted as an index of defensive responding or immaturity and includes items such as "I like everyone I know" and "I always tell the truth." Items measuring more internalizing problems, such as "It's hard for me to keep my mind on anything" and "My parents expect too much of me," are found on the Conduct Problems scale, along with externalizing problems, such as "I often get into trouble." The Antisocial scale appears to consist primarily of items related to permissive, impulsive behavior, such as "It's OK to show off," "It's OK for kids to bite their fingernails," and "It's OK to get angry."

TECHNICAL DATA. Development of the FAB-C began with several pilot studies designed to identify items that should be modified or deleted and to investigate the factor structure of the items. Unfortunately, the manual provides very little information about the initial studies, and the reader is referred to other publications by the author. Following the pilot studies, the instrument was normed with a sample of 1,988 children selected to represent the population of Ontario, Canada. No demographic information is provided for the normative sample, except for the age and gender of the children, and the author indicates that it was impossible to collect data about cultural background and socioeconomic status. The lack of demographic information is a significant limitation of the sample.

Internal consistency reliability coefficients and, for factor scores only, test-retest (10-day and 28-day intervals) reliability coefficients are provided for all scales except the Problem Index. In general, the low to moderate values of the coefficients ($a = .50–.79$; $r = .46–.81$) suggest that scores should be interpreted very cautiously.

The results of several validity studies are reported in the manual. Confirmatory factor analyses appear to support the scales of the FAB-C, and moderate intercorrelations between the scales suggest that they may be measuring fairly distinct constructs. In a discriminant function analysis of scores for a group of children attending a psychiatric hospital and a group of children with no problems, the Lie, Conduct Problems, Worry, and supplemental items resulted in the greatest discrimination. These scales were combined to form the Problem Index, and the Problem index correctly classified about 71% of the children in the two groups. As a result of these findings, the author concludes that the Problem Index scale may be used as a screening assessment to identify children who may be assessed with a more comprehensive clinical assessment.

Correlations between FAB-C scores and several criteria (i.e., parents' scores on the Child Behavior Checklist, teacher's scores on the Conners' Teacher Rating Scale, clinicians' ratings of symptoms and positive health items) were primarily in the .20s and .30s. Correlations between the FAB-C and the Children's Depression Inventory were in the low to moderate range, but significant, for the Conduct Problems, Self-Image, Worry, and Peer Relations scales and nonsignificant for the Antisocial and Lie scales and Problem Index.

SCORING AND INTERPRETATION. Normative scores are reported separately for boys and girls in 2-year age intervals. However, steep growth curves for some scales, as shown in graphs of mean scores by 1-year age intervals and statistically significant differences for mean scores of age groups, suggest that the author should have provided norms in intervals of 1 year or less. Scores for the seven scales are linear T scores, with higher T scores associated with more problems. As is common with scales that measure children's problems, the score distributions are skewed and, for two scales, the range of T scores is constricted. For example, the maximum T score for some scales is 63 or 64. A computer scoring program is available.

The author defines a "clinically elevated test score" (manual, p. 13) as one that is above 65, especially if one is in a "high base rate group" such as a group of children in a clinical setting. Further, the author recommends using a much higher criterion score (e.g., 70 or 75) if a child is in a "low base rate group," such as a group of children without identified behavioral problems. Unfortunately, the author does not provide a rationale for these criterion scores or explain the need to use different criterion scores for different groups.

Throughout the manual, the author recommends integrating results from the FAB-C with other test scores and other observations. The author is commended for emphasizing that the FAB-C should never be the only source of information. However, guidelines for interpretation are very brief and do not directly address the use of the FAB-C as a screening instrument. The author does not provide directions for using the FAB-C to plan more comprehensive assessment, a common use of a screening instrument. Several case studies are included in the chapter on interpretation, but provide only brief summaries of the FAB-C scores and do not support how the FAB-C added relevant or additional information to the assessment of the children.

SUMMARY. Although the FAB-C record form is well designed and the manual is clearly written and includes some important technical data, the FAB-C is not recommended for use. The author provides little information about the use and interpretation of the instrument and its conceptual framework, and, after reading the manual, major questions are "What does the instrument measure?" and "Why should it be used?" The validity of using a self-report rating scale with children as young as 6 years is questionable; many social-emotional rating systems do not include children's self-reports until they are 8–10 years of age or older.

The technical data suggest some important limitations of the instrument. The instrument was normed only with children who live in Ontario, and the lack of information about important demographic variables results in concerns about using the instrument with Ontario children. Internal consistency and test-retest reliability coefficients for scales are low to moderate and suggest that examiners should use these scales with great caution. The reliability of the Problem Index is unknown, but, as a result of validity data, the author recommends the use of the problem Index as a screening measure. Other validity data provide some support for the structure of the FAB-C, but limited support for the relationship between the FAB-C and scores on important criterion measures. Unfortunately, test-retest reliability data and some validity data are reported for factor scores, instead of the final scale scores of the instrument.

Several other assessments of behavioral and emotional problems are recommended for professionals. Both the Behavior Assessment System for

Children (40; Reynolds & Kamphaus, 1992) and the Child Behavior Checklist (T5:451; Achenbach, 1991a, 1991b, 1991c) are comprehensive systems that include children's self-reports, as well as parent and teacher reports. These assessment systems have a strong conceptual and research foundation and a wealth of technical data to support their use.

REVIEWER'S REFERENCES

Achenbach, T. M. (1991a). *Manual for the Child Behavior Checklist/4–8 and 1991 Profile.* Burlington, VT: University of Vermont Department of Psychiatry.
Achenbach, T. M. (1991b). *Manual for the Teacher's Report Form and 1991 Profile.* Burlington, VT: University of Vermont Department of Psychiatry.
Achenbach, T. M. (1991c). *Manual for the Youth Self-Report and 1991 Profile.* Burlington, VT: University of Vermont Department of Psychiatry.
Reynolds, C. R., & Kamphaus, R. W. (1992). *Manual for the Behavior Assessment System for Children.* Circle Pines, MN: American Guidance Service.

Review of the Feelings, Attitudes, and Behaviors Scale for Children by MARY LOU KELLEY, Professor of Psychology, Louisiana State University, Baton Rouge, LA:

The Feelings, Attitudes, and Behaviors Scale for Children (FAB-C) is a self-report questionnaire for assessing a range of behavior and emotional problems in children aged 6–13. The FAB-C consists of 48 short statements answered yes or no. The FAB-C can be used as a screening measure in a variety of settings such as schools and outpatient clinics. The FAB-C contains six clinical scales: Conduct Problems, Self-Image, Worry, Negative Peer Relations, and Anti-Social Attitudes as well as a Lie Scale and Total Problem Index score. The questionnaire can be either computer or handscored using a carbon, quick-scoring system. The FAB-C takes approximately 15 minutes to complete and 10 minutes to hand score.

The manual accompanying the FAB-C is well written and provides a clear description of test administration and scoring procedures. The author provides adequate caution against the overreliance of the FAB-C in assessment and cautions against the use of the instrument without adequate knowledge of the principles and limitations of psychological testing. The author provides very clear guidelines for interpreting test profiles and discusses varying nuances in interpreting test data. The manual also describes several case vignettes and the obtained FAB-C profiles, which are likely to be very helpful to those relatively less familiar with test interpretation. The reliability and validity data are clearly described and presented.

The FAB-C was developed on the basis of the author's clinical experience and previous research. The author began with an initial pool of 200 items that appeared to tap into 10 hypothesized clinical dimensions. Through a series of studies, a 55-item scale with eight clinically distinct factors was produced. The final version of the scale eliminated the "sensitive-emotional" and the "positive-family relations" factors due to poor internal reliability with a new sample. However, the items from the "positive-family relations" factor were retained on the final form of the FAB-C as the items discriminated normal from clinical samples.

The FAB-C was normed on a large, heterogeneous sample of Canadian children aged 6–13. Norms are provided based on gender and age at 2-year intervals. The author provides data on age and gender differences across the varying factors of the FAB-C. The author reports adequate inter-item correlations for the FAB-C factors. However, internal consistency and test-retest reliability estimates were moderate at best. With regard to validity evidence, the FAB-C correctly classified 63% of the clinical sample and 74% of the normal sample yielding an overall classification rate of 71%. The Lie subscale and the conduct problems subscale made the greatest contribution to the discrimination of the normal and clinical groups. Relatively low, but generally significant, correlations were obtained between FAB-C factor scores and scale scores from parent and teacher measures as well as symptom ratings by psychiatrists.

SUMMARY. The FAB-C has many positive features including ease in administration and scoring and carefully derived factor structure tapping important dimensions of children's behavior and emotional problems. The measure likely will be useful as a screening measure and many of the items appear to tap important diagnostic information for follow-up in a comprehensive assessment. Although carefully constructed and normed, the reliability and the validity of scores from the FAB-C are only moderately supportive of the instrument. Although this may largely be due to the small number of items on each factor as well as the inherent unreliability of children's self-report, users should avoid overreliance and overemphasis on the results of the questionnaire as the assessment process.

[148]

The Filipino Work Values Scale.

Purpose: "Constructed to measure work values."

Population: Filipino employees and students.

Publication Dates: 1987–1988.
Acronym: FWVS.
Scores, 10: Environmental, Familial, Intellectual-Achievement Oriented, Interpersonal, Managerial, Material, Occupational, Organizational, Religious, Variety.
Administration: Group.
Forms, 2: Employee, Student.
Price Data, 1997: P2,000 per employee edition complete kit including manual ('87, 39 pages), 25 scale booklets, 25 answer sheets, and manual scoring keys; P2,500 per student edition complete kit including manual, 25 scale booklets, 25 answer sheets, and manual scoring keys; P40 per scale booklet; P4 per answer sheet; P500 per manual; P400 per manual scoring keys; computerized scoring keys available.
Foreign Language Editions: English, Cebuano, Filipino, Thai, and Pangasinense.
Time: (15–20) minutes.
Author: Vicentita M. Cervera.
Publisher: Vicentita M. Cervera [Philippines].

Review of The Filipino Work Values Scale by GARY J. DEAN, Associate Professor, Adult and Community Education, Indiana University of Pennsylvania, Indiana, PA:

INTRODUCTION. The Filipino Work Values Scale (FWVS) is an 80-item, self-report inventory that produces 10 scores: Environmental, Familial, Intellectual-Achievement Oriented, Interpersonal, Managerial, Material, Occupational, Organizational, Religious, and Variety. There are two versions, one for employees and one for students. Respondents rate each of the 80 items on a scale of 1 to 5 with 1 = *very unimportant*, 2 = *unimportant*, 3 = *neutral*, 4 = *important*, and 5 = *very important*. The instrument has been published in English, Cebuano, Filipino, and Pangasinense. Only the English version was reviewed.

The purpose of the FWVS is to measure a person's work values. Values are defined as "the stance that the self takes to the total environment as expressed through its behavior, ideas, body and feelings and imagination" (manual, p. 3). The specific values measured are the 10 identified above, plus a total score, which "were derived from a review of foreign and local literature and from a survey of the work values of Metro Manila workers" (manual, p. 3).

DEVELOPMENT. There were several phases to the development of the FWVS. The first phase involved item development by the author based on a review of the literature and Filipino culture and personality. A first draft of the instrument developed in this phase contained a total of 130 items.

The second phase of development consisted of a review of these items by experts from a variety of disciplines. This review resulted in decreasing the total number of items to 108. Further review reduced the total number of items to 100.

The resulting second draft of the instrument was then field tested with 249 employees in 39 companies in Metro Manila. This study allowed for the reduction in the total number of items to 80 for the final draft of the instrument. This systematic and thorough approach to test development is to be commended.

VALIDITY AND RELIABILITY. Validity was investigated through studies on both the second and final drafts of the instrument. The final draft was tested with 1,067 respondents. Item analysis, interitem correlations, and intersubscale correlations were computed for both drafts of the instrument. The author asserts that construct validity was studied by correlating the items of each subscale with one another and with the total subscale score. Cervera (the author) reports that the mean interitem correlations for each subscale ranged from a low of .26 (for the Occupational subscale) to .40 (Religious subscale). Further, he asserts that the "t-values of all items but one were significant at the .001 level. This means that each item discriminates the low from the high scores" (manual, p. 8).

In addition, the intersubscale correlations were computed. In this regard the correlations ranged from a low of .23 (Religious correlated with Intellectual-Achievement Orientation) to a high of .78 (Occupational correlated with Intellectual-Achievement Orientation).

Cervera claims that the subscales "are contributory to the measurement of work values which the FWVS aims to do, yet are distinct from one another, which means that they measure different aspects of work values" (manual, p. 9). Here one could observe that the number of correlations in the .6 to .7 range indicates that the distinctions among the subscales are somewhat less than desirable and that the value of having 10 subscales could be questioned. This reviewer is not in a position to question whether the 10 subscales adequately represent Filipino work values. Rather, it has been taken on the assumption that Cervera is accurate in his assessment of the work values to be assessed. The high intersubscale correlations, however, give rise to the question of how independent the measurement of these concepts is in the FWVS.

Reliability was investigated through computing the coefficient alpha for each subscale and the instrument as a whole, for both the second and final drafts of the instrument. The coefficient alpha correlations ranged from a low of .616 to a high of .857 for each of the subscales and was .905 for the total instrument on the final draft. In addition, F-ratios were computed for each subscale to determine the variance "between people" and "between measures (items)." All F-ratios were significant at the .01 level. This careful analysis leaves little question as to the reliability evidence for scores from the FWVS.

ADMINISTRATION AND SCORING. The FWVS is self-administered and takes approximately 15 to 20 minutes to complete. There is a separate answer sheet for both the employee and student versions. Hand scoring is achieved by laying 10 scoring guides one at a time over the answer sheet. Each scoring guide is for a different subscale of the instrument. For each subscale, the total number of times each response (1 = *very unimportant*, 2 = *unimportant*, 3 = *neutral*, 4 = *important*, and 5 = *very important*) is given are counted and then multiplied by that value to obtain a "weighted response." The weighted responses for each subscale are then added to obtain a raw score for that subscale for the respondent. This process is somewhat cumbersome but can be managed if there are not too many inventories to score. Directions for scoring the FWVS using Lotus 1-2-3 were included in the materials sent but this reviewer did not have access to the program to try it.

INTERPRETATION. Interpretation of the results of the inventory are obtained by comparing an individual's raw score for each subscale to an appropriate occupational group. Norms have been developed for the following occupational groups: (a) administrative, executive, and managerial workers; (b) clerical and related workers; (c) production and related workers and transport equipment operators; (d) professional technical related workers; (e) sales workers; and (f) service workers. Appendices provide specific job titles included in each of these occupational groups to assist in matching an individual with an appropriate norming table. Each table contains the percentile rank for the raw

scores for each of the 10 subscales as well as the mean score and standard deviation for each subscale. No special norms are provided for the student version; presumably they are to be interpreted by comparing raw scores to the norms provided for employees. Based on the extensive normative data provided, an individual's score for any subscale can be compared with an appropriate norm group.

SUMMARY. The purpose of the FWVS is to assess the work values of Filipinos in 10 subscales. The instrument appears to have been carefully researched and developed. The validity and reliability data are very complete. With the exception of the high interscale reliability coefficients, which indicate that the subscales may not be as independent of one another as is desirable, the instrument appears to be well thought out and developed. Administration is easy and should not present problems. Scoring, however, is somewhat cumbersome. Interpretation is facilitated by extensive norms developed with six different occupational groups. Overall, the FWVS appears to be a carefully developed and highly usable instrument. It should aid in career counseling and in helping individuals select occupations. Future work on the instrument should focus on decreasing the interrelationships among the subscales.

Review of The Filipino Work Values Scale by **WILLIAM I. SAUSER, JR.,** *Associate Dean and Professor, College of Business, Auburn University, Auburn, AL:*

The Filipino Work Values Scale (FWVS) is a carefully constructed and researched self-administered, self-paced scale of work values distinctive to the Filipino population. The scale is a product of the author's doctoral dissertation and is an effort to provide to Filipino researchers, counselors, and human resources professionals "a tool peculiar to our own culture and to our culture's needs" (manual, p. 2). It produces scores for 10 work values relevant to the culture of the Philippines, plus an overall "total" score.

The respondent is asked to rate agreement with each of 80 items on a 5-point scale ranging from *Very Important* to *Very Unimportant*. The wording of the 80 items in the two versions (Employee, Student) is virtually identical; the difference between the versions has to do with focus within the test-taking directions on current employment versus intended employment. Scoring and interpretive procedures for the two versions are identical. The items themselves are designed for a literate test-taker and include language and phraseology appropriate to the Filipino population. Most of the items are straightforward in nature, but some are grammatically cumbersome and would be confusing to some test-takers, for example: "Working with superiors who train you to integrate and coordinate organizational resources (men, material, money, time and space, for example) toward the accomplishment of objectives" (Item 19).

The test manual is impressive in its thoroughness and detail. The conceptual framework for the FWVS is explained, the highly sophisticated scale development process is described, administrative and scoring procedures are presented, validity and reliability data are provided, and norms for six different occupational groups are tabulated. These norms were calculated from 1,738 Filipino employees working in a wide variety of settings and job types. Each of the six occupational norming groups is described in detail. Sample sizes for the six groups range from 116 (Sales) to 718 (Professional/Technical).

The overall coefficient alpha reliability of the 80-item scale is .90; subscale reliabilities range from .61 (Variety) to .86 (Intellectual-Achievement Oriented). Though conceptually distinct and created in a manner to enhance content validity, there is evidence that the 10 subscales are in practice interrelated. Subscale intercorrelations range from .23 to .78. Item analysis indicates that each item discriminates low from high scorers. All in all, the FWVS thus appears psychometrically sound for its intended purpose. A list of studies conducted subsequent to the publication of the manual (supplied by the publisher) indicates that the FWVS is receiving continued attention by researchers in the Philippines and elsewhere.

This reviewer encountered difficulty with the paper template hand-scoring materials provided by the test publisher. The templates were poorly cut and did not always fit properly over the answer sheets, resulting in cumbersome and possibly inaccurate scoring. In one case (Environmental), a subscale item was omitted altogether from the template, thus resulting in an inaccurate score. Clearly this detail needs attention if the FWVS is to be commercially viable. Fortunately, the answer sheets are machine scorable, and this option appears preferable for mass application.

One highly desirable feature of the FWVS is its availability in four languages spoken in the Philippines. Considerable care was taken during the translation process to assure parallel content and interpretation no matter which version is used. For example, to create the Cebuano version from the English, directions and items were translated by a professional translator, then "retranslated" by a panel of experts. Discrepancies in interpretation were addressed, resulting in a very smooth translation. This version was then field-tested and further revised as needed.

SUMMARY. The Filipino Work Values Scale is well conceived and prepared, appears psychometrically sound, and—once the manual scoring templates are improved—should be relatively easy to administer, score, and interpret. As the author claims, it helps meet the need for a work values scale relevant for use in the Philippines and appears useful as a tool for research and application in "understanding the behavior of a Filipino at work" (manual, p. 2).

[149]
Firestone Assessment of Self-Destructive Thoughts.

Purpose: Constructed "for the clinical assessment of a patient's suicidal potential."
Population: Ages 16–80.
Publication Date: 1996.
Acronym: FAST.
Scores: No scores.
Administration: Group.
Price Data, 1998: $120.50 per complete kit including manual (176 pages) and 25 ReadyScore® response booklets; $51.50 per 25 response booklets, $73.50 per manual.
Time: (20) minutes.
Comments: Includes 11 levels of progressively self-destructive thoughts on a continuum ranging from Social Isolation, Eating Disorders, Substance Abuse, Self-Mutilation, and Suicide.
Authors: Robert W. Firestone and Lisa A. Firestone.
Publisher: The Psychological Corporation.

Review of the Firestone Assessment of Self-Destructive Thoughts by WILLIAM E. MARTIN, JR., Professor of Educational Psychology, Northern Arizona University, Flagstaff, AZ:

The Firestone Assessment of Self-Destructive Thoughts (FAST) is designed to measure the "Continuum of Negative Thought Patterns" as they relate to a client's level of self-destructive potential or suicidality. The authors recommend the FAST to be used for screening, diagnosis, treatment progress, treatment outcome, research, and therapy. The FAST is theoretically grounded in what the authors refer to as the "concept of the voice," which refers to negative thoughts and attitudes that are said to be at the core of maladaptive behavior.

The FAST consists of 84 items that provide self-report information from a respondent on how frequently he or she is experiencing various negative thoughts directed toward himself or herself. Four "composites" and 11 linked "continuum levels" comprise the FAST. One composite is named Self-Defeating and has five continuum levels (Self-Depreciation, Self-Denial, Cynical Attitudes, Isolation, and Self-Contempt). Addictions is another composite with addictions listed as its continuum level. A third composite is Self-Annihilating with four continuum levels (Hopelessness, Giving Up, Self-Harm, Suicide Plans, and Suicide Injunctions). The last composite is Suicide Intent and no continuum levels are identified.

ADMINISTRATION, SCORING, AND INTERPRETATION. The FAST instrument is a seven-page perforated, self-carbon form used for responding to items, scoring responses, and graphing the results. T scores are derived for the 11 continuum levels, four composites, and for the total score. Percentiles and 90% confidence interval bands also are available for use. The T scores are plotted on the T-Score profile graph, which has shaded partitions that indicate if the T scores fall within a *nonclinical range, equivocal range,* or clinical ranges that include *elevated* and *extremely elevated.*

The normative sample for the FAST was a clinical sample of outpatient clients undergoing psychotherapy. A T score of 50 on any scale represents the average performance of an individual who was in outpatient treatment with no suicide ideation from the normative sample. The nonclinical range is a T score between 20 and 41 whereas the equivocal range is 42–48. The two clinical ranges are elevated (42–59) and extremely elevated (60+). Any score that falls above the equivocal range is treated with concern and anyone scoring in the extremely elevated range on levels 7–11, the Self-Annihilating Composite, the Suicide Intent Composite, or the Total score should be immediately assessed for suicide potential.

DEVELOPMENT OF THE SCALES. The items for the FAST were derived from actual statements of 21 clinical outpatients who were receiving "voice therapy" in groups. Nine of the outpatients had a previous history of serious suicide attempts and the others exhibited less severe self-defeating behaviors including self-denial, isolation, substance abuse, and eating disorders. The list of items was further refined from a study conducted to select those factors that significantly discriminated between suicide attempters and nonattempters. Then items were retained or deleted based upon their psychometric relationship to hypothesized constructs, resulting in the current 84-item version of the FAST.

RELIABILITY AND VALIDITY. Cronbach's alpha reliability coefficients ranging from .76 to .91 (Mdn = .84) are reported for the 11 level scores. Standard errors of measurement and 90% confidence intervals also are provided. However, sample sizes and descriptions are not provided for these measures. Test-retest reliability coefficients (1–266 days) ranged from .63–.94 (M = .82) using a sample (N = 131) of nonclinical, psychotherapy outpatients, and psychiatric inpatients.

Content validity of the FAST was investigated using a Guttman Scalogram Analysis resulting in a coefficient of reproducibility of .91 and a coefficient of scalability of .66. FAST Total Scores were correlated with the Suicide Ideation subscale of the Suicide Probability Scale (r = .72) as indicators of convergent validity. An exploratory factor analysis was conducted using 579 outpatients resulting in a 3-factor solution (Self-Annihilating, Self-Defeating, and Addictions), which provided support for construct validity. Evidence for criterion-related validity was demonstrated from studies showing how FAST scores were able to discriminate inpatient and outpatient ideators from nonideators and to identify individuals who made prior suicide attempts.

SUMMARY. The authors have put forth empirical evidence that supports the psychometric properties of the FAST. However, continuing studies are needed, especially related to the effectiveness of the FAST in diagnosing and predicting chemical addictive behavior. Furthermore, the construct validity of scores from the FAST needs further consideration. First, the items for the FAST were generated from a small (N = 21) somewhat restricted focus group of persons receiving "voice therapy." Second, the FAST is closely anchored to a theoretical orientation known as "concept of the voice" in which additional studies are needed to validate.

Overall, the FAST is a measure worth considering for professionals working with individuals who have exhibited self-destructive potential or suicidality. However, I encourage professionals to study the theoretical orientation underlying the FAST and determine if it is congruent with their own expectations for clinical outcomes prior to extensive use of the instrument.

Review of the Firestone Assessment of Self-Destructive Thoughts by ROBERT C. REINEHR, Professor of Psychology, Southwestern University, Georgetown, TX:

The Firestone Assessment of Self-Destructive Thoughts (FAST) is a self-report questionnaire intended to provide clinicians with a tool for the assessment of a patient's suicide potential. Respondents are asked to endorse how frequently they are experiencing various negative thoughts directed toward themselves. The items were derived from the actual statements of clinical outpatients who were members of therapy groups in which the techniques of Voice Therapy were used.

Voice Therapy is a technique developed by the senior test author as a means of giving language to the negative thought processes that influence self-limiting, self-destructive behaviors and lifestyles. The FAST includes items intended to assess each of 11 levels of a Continuum of Negative Thought Patterns. Items were assigned to levels based on the judgments of advanced graduate students and psychologists with training in Voice Therapy.

In the standardization process, the FAST was administered to a sample of 478 clients who were currently receiving outpatient psychotherapy and who did not have any current (within the last month) suicide ideation, suicide threats, or suicide attempts. Standard scores were calculated for the Total Score, for four composite scores derived by factor analysis and other statistical procedures, and for each of the 11 levels of negative thought patterns.

Estimates of internal consistency are based on a single sample, the size of which is not reported in the manual. They range from .76 to .97, with the majority falling between .81 and .88. Test-retest reliability estimates are reported for three samples with intervals from 28–266 days in one study and 1–31 days in another: psychiatric inpatients (n = 28), psychotherapy outpatients (n = 68), and nonclinical college students (n = 35). Reliabilities for the various levels of the negative-thought continuum range from .63 to .94, with the higher coefficients generally being found among the nonclinical respondents. Test-retest reliability estimates for the various composite scores and for the total score are somewhat higher, ranging from .79 to .94.

As an indication of construct validity, FAST scores were compared to scores on the Beck Depression Inventory (BDI), the Beck Suicide Inventory (BSI), and the Suicide Probability Scale (SPS). The FAST Total score had its highest correlations with the BDI (.73), the BSI (.72), and the Suicide Ideations subscale of the SPS (.76). The composite scores and the various level scores had lower correlations with the subscales of the Beck instruments or the SPS.

The FAST was administered to groups of inpatients and outpatients with various diagnoses including Adjustment Disorder, Anxiety Disorder, Bipolar Disorder, Depression, Personality Disorder, Schizophrenia, and Substance Abuse, and to a nonclinical sample of 172 college students. Each of the clinical groups was further subdivided into suicide Ideators and Nonideators. Ideators had higher average FAST Total scores than did Nonideators and clinical groups had higher average FAST Total scores than did the nonclinical group. Information is provided in the manual with respect to the relationships between the various FAST subscales and the diagnostic groups and subgroups.

SUMMARY. In general, it would appear that the FAST is similar in many ways to other depression and suicide inventories. Total Scores tend to be higher for respondents in diagnostic groups than for nonclinical respondents, and within diagnostic groups, Suicide Ideators score more highly than do Nonideators.

Within the limits of these findings, the FAST may be useful to clinicians as an indication of how a given respondent's answers compare to those of various diagnostic groups. It might also be possible to use the scale as a clinical tool for the evaluation of change during therapy, although use as a psychometric instrument is not justified on the basis of the evidence presented in the manual.

[150]
First Words and First Sentences Tests.

Purpose: Designed to discriminate between moderate and severe language delay in very young children.
Population: Ages 18–36 months.

Publication Dates: 1997–1999.
Scores, 3: First Words Comprehension Screen, First Sentences Test, First Words Test.
Administration: Individual.
Forms, 2: A, B.
Price Data, 1998: £40 per Comprehension Screen picture book; £7.50 per 20 Comprehension Screen record forms; £49.99 per First Words Test Picture Books A & B; £9.99 per 20 First Words record forms; £39.99 per First Sentences Test Picture Books A & B; £9.99 per 20 First Sentences record forms; £19.99 per 10 "Helping Your Child" parent booklets; £9.99 per 20 parent checklists; £20.99 per manual ('97, 52 pages); £129.99 per starter pack including First Words and First Sentences Picture Books A & B, manual, one copy of "Helping Your Child," parent checklists and record sheets for assessing 20 children; £22.50 per sample pack including manual, one copy of "Helping Your Child," parent checklist and all record forms.
Time: Administration time not reported.
Authors: Bill Gillham, James Boyle, and Nicola Smith.
Publisher: Hodder & Stoughton Educational [England].

Review of the First Words and First Sentences Tests by SUSAN J. MALLER, Associate Professor of Educational Psychology, Purdue University, West Lafayette, IN:

The First Words and First Sentences Tests (FWFS) was constructed to identify potential language delay in children ages 15–36 months. The manual presents a somewhat sketchy theoretical rationale for the FWFS by citing several published articles concerning language development, delay, and assessment, without describing the findings in any detail. In addition, other language delay screening instruments are briefly described and criticized in an appendix. The FWFS actually consists of several tests that may be administered depending on the age and needs of the individual child. These tests include the First Words (FW) test (for children ages 20–36 months), the Parent Checklist (PC to be used without other FWFS tests for children ages 18–19 months, and with the First Words test for children 20–34 months), the First Sentences (FS) test (for children ages 28–36 months), and the Comprehension Screen (CS, for children who score at or below the 5th percentile on the FW test or the PC). The FW test includes two parallel forms that are composed of pictures of familiar objects that the child is required to name. The PC includes two forms, each composed of

several age-appropriate words. The FS test includes two parallel forms each consisting of 12 pictures of children engaging in activities that the child is required to describe. The parallel forms are provided for children with poor cooperation or performance on initial testing. Th CS Forms A and B include picture books that assess receptive vocabulary. The test kit also includes the Parent Booklet, which includes tips for encouraging language development, and the Next Action Record Forms, which provide criteria for "re-assessment, parental surveillance or specialist referral" (manual, p. 11).

The manual states that no specific training is needed to administer the FWFS, and the test is designed to be used by a variety of professionals (e.g., physicians, psychologists, teachers, speech therapists). The FW, FS, and CS tests are individually administered and untimed. Although the manual states that the administration of such types of assessment should require less than 10 minutes per test, the time required to administer the FWFS is not stated in the manual. It appears that the time required may vary depending on the age and attention span of the child being tested. There are no basal or ceiling rules. All children are administered all items.

Items on the FW test and PC are awarded a "check mark" or two points for words the child can say, an "X" or zero for words the child cannot say, and a "?" for words the parent is not sure if the child can say. The items scored as "?" are then awarded one point for near-miss. Item scores are summed to obtain raw scores, that are then converted to aged-based (by month) percentiles. The norms table provides scores only at the 50th percentile and below.

For each picture on the FS test, the longest response is recorded. Each age level (by month) by each sentence length (one to seven words or more) is noted as at the 50th percentile, below the 10th percentile, below the 5th percentile, or a "severe delay." For example, a 34-month-old child producing four-word sentences is below the 10th percentile and above the 5th percentile, whereas a 34-month-old child producing six-word sentences is at the 50th percentile. The table does not provide percentile ranks at each percentile; rather, only the rough grouping descriptors are provided. Therefore, a 34-month-old child producing a five-word sentence is somewhere between the 50th and 10th percentile.

Items scored as correct on the CS are summed to obtain a raw score. For children 22–30 months, these raw scores are labeled as "Below 5th percentile," "5th percentile," "10th percentile," and "15th percentile and above" (manual, p. 45).

The standardization sample for the FW test and PC included 485 children from the United Kingdom (U.K.), ages 18–36 months. Although the manual describes the sampling procedure, it does not provide sufficient detail concerning the representativeness of the sample. However, the little information provided concerning "social class" indicates that the sample is not representative of the U.K. population. The authors themselves state they encountered difficulty achieving sampling quotas. Even less information is provided concerning the standardization samples for the FS, which included 387 children ages 22–36 months, and the CS, which included 141 children ages 22–30 months, scoring at or below the 5th percentile on the FW test or PC. Furthermore, for the CS it is unclear (a) how the norms were created or (b) who was included in the representative peer group on which the percentiles are based. In addition, because there is an 8-month age range at a critical period of language development, age-based norms might have been more appropriate. Not only should there be concern among examiners in the U.S. concerning the small and unrepresentative standardization sample, but the normative data appear to be unrepresentative of children in the U.K.

No information is provided concerning the distributional properties of the scores on any of the FWFS tests. Thus, (a) interpretation of percentile ranks may be somewhat misleading if scores are highly skewed, and (b) subsequent correlational evidence of reliability and validity may be affected by nonnormality. Finally, the authors note that language delay in boys tends to be less persistent than delay in girls. Therefore, it seems logical that the authors should have provided separate norms and predictive validity evidence for boys and girls.

Parallel forms reliability coefficients were reported for the FW test ($N = 34$), PC ($N = 34$), and the FS test ($N = 23$), as .97., .93, and .81, respectively. Although the manual states that "some" administrations of the parallel form occurred 2 weeks subsequent to the first administration, thus providing for a more stringent test of reliability, it does not state the number of delayed administrations. Split-half reliability, using an odd-even split were reported ($N = 49$) for the FW test Form A (.97), FW test Form B (.97), PC Form A (.99), and PC Form B (.95). Because split-half

reliability coefficients may be influenced by the way the test was divided, coefficient alpha would have been a better estimate for internal consistency reliability.

Standard errors of measurement (*SEMs*) were based on the parallel forms reliability coefficients for the FW test, PC, and FS tests. Separate *SEMs* were not reported by age, probably because of the fact that reliability coefficients were not reported for the small samples at each age. Regardless, the standard errors of measurement were fairly large, especially for the FS test, which might be explained by the restricted scoring range. For example, a 32-month-old child might produce a two-word sentence, placing the child "Below the 5th percentile" (manual, p. 37). However, considering the one *SEM* (1.53), the child's score may fall between the "Severe Delay" and somewhere above the "Below the 10th percentile" level (remember that percentiles are grouped and thus, four- and five-word sentences are somewhere between the 10th and 50th percentiles). Considering two *SEMs*, the child's language skills may be severely delayed or as high as the 50th percentile. Thus, the examiner is left knowing as much about the child's language as before testing. Reliability evidence and *SEMs* are not reported for the CS.

The validity evidence is very limited. No evidence of content validity was provided. Justification is needed concerning the content included in the test materials (e.g., pictures of specific objects). Many of the picture contents are potentially gender, culturally, and geographically biased. For example, boys may not be as likely as girls to respond to the FW "hair" item, which is a picture of the profile of a girl with very long hair combed forward and covering most of her face. The picture of a brush appears to be more of a cleaning tool than a hairbrush. Scores on several items may be affected by exposure rather than language skills. For example, the picture of the "potty" may be unfamiliar to many children. The manual does not state whether a tryout version of the test was evaluated prior to standardization. Furthermore, neither the results of an item analysis nor an item level factor analysis were reported.

The statistically significant correlations between age and raw scores for all tests ($ps<.01$) were used as an indication of construct validity, although the specific correlation coefficients were not reported. Intercorrelations between the FW test, PC, and FS test were used as evidence of concurrent validity. The correlations were moderate to high and cannot be considered to be sufficient evidence of concurrent validity. Because the correlations were obtained on tests from the same battery of tests, correlations might have been affected by method bias. Correlations of the various FWFS tests with other published instruments would have served as more acceptable evidence of concurrent validity. The only evidence of predictive validity was the correlation of the FW test at 22 months with "mean length utterance (MLU) in morphemes" (manual, p. 38) at 30 months on the FS test. A correlation of .71 was reported for an extremely small sample of 15 children who are not described at all in terms of demographic characteristics. This evidence is inadequate, because (a) the sample was too small for correlational statistics and (b) the relationship again might have been a result of method bias. Predictive validity evidence of some external and meaningful criterion would have been more appropriate. The criterion should be selected based on whatever the FWFS tests claim to predict (e.g., future academic readiness or performance). Without this information, the examiner is left to wonder not only what the scores on the FWFS tests measure, but also what can be expected of children who obtain various scores on the FWFS. Finally, "clinical validation" evidence was provided by reporting scores on the PC, FW, and FS tests of 14 children diagnosed with language delay by speech and language therapists. All children scored below the 5th percentile, leading the authors to claim that the test resulted in 100% sensitivity. However, the particular sample of children was not compared to a control group of children without language delays. Validity evidence was not adequately provided for the CS.

SUMMARY. In conclusion, the results obtained for a child on the FWFS need to be interpreted cautiously because (a) the norms do not appear to be representative, (b) the scoring system is limited, (c) reliability evidence is insufficient, and (d) validity evidence is inadequate. For these reasons, the FWFS is not recommended and may lead to unwarranted concern regarding a child's language skills.

Review of the First Words and First Sentences Tests by DOROTHY M. SINGLETON, Associate Professor of Education, Winston-Salem State University, Winston-Salem, NC:

The First Words and First Sentences Tests, incorporating the First Words Comprehension Screen, are for children in an age group ranging from 18–36 months where language delay is suspected. The tests were published in 1997. The tests are designed to discriminate between moderate and severe delay in a child's language. The First Words Test has a natural communicative focus (picture-books) that is based on activities in which adults and children can engage normally. The First Sentences Test assesses language level, not by average performance, but by the utterance of sounds from the child. There are relationships between sounds and symbols, which would give children the maximum engaged-experiences, as possible.

The First Words and First Sentences Tests are for use by a wide range of professionals, including health visitors, speech therapists, general practitioners, pediatricians, psychologists, specialist teachers, and others who are involved in working with children who have delayed language. The authors have stated in the manual the empirical and theoretical basis for the tests. The empirical and theoretical bases have been identified as follows: (a) "because in both normal and delayed development receptive language is ahead of expressive language up to age 36 months; it follows that receptive delay, except in very rare and unusual cases, will always be signaled by expressive delay"; (b) "'flexible object naming' is a particularly powerful indicator of future language status under the age of 30 months"; and (c) "severity of delay in expressive language (conventionally the bottom 2.5% of the age level) is a strong indicator of future language difficulties" (manual, p. 5).

The First Words Test consists of Forms A and B. The test contains large color photographs of objects that research shows children talk about in their first hundred words. There are two developmentally parallel books of 28 pictures. There are also two Parent Checklists (A and B), a check of cross-validity.

The Parent Checklists are used for parents to indicate the level of their child's language, from prespeech comprehension to word combinations. These are cross-checked with the findings on the First Sentences Test.

There is a checklist of 43 words, including the nouns in the First Words Test. Additionally, other kinds of high frequency words are included.

Parents are asked to check words using certain symbols to note whether or not the child answered correctly.

For the First Sentences Test, Forms A and B, the responses are based on the frequency of one- to seven-word (or more) utterances. The First Words Comprehension Screen is a separate test for use with children who score at or below the 5th percentile on the expressive First Words Test and the Parent Checklist.

The administration of the tests is explicitly explained for the users. The directions are clear and can be easily read. Case studies have been outlined in the manual based on developmental history, observation, and evaluation at different age levels. The test is well written and user friendly.

There were 485 children who participated in the standardization sample. The First Words Test and associated Parent Checklist were administered to children in the 18–36-months age range. Parallel forms of the First Words Test and the Parent Checklist of different content provided a stringent measure of test-retest reliability. Split-half reliability coefficients were calculated for the First Words Test and the Parent Checklist, correlating the odd and even test item scores. Comparing scores across the age-range for developmental trend (developmental validity), correlating scores from First Words and First Sentences with those obtained from the parent checklist (concurrent validity), correlating scores at 20 and 22 months with those at 28 and 30 months (predictive validity), and obtaining test scores from children independently assessed as having clinically significant language problems will be used to assess the validity of scores from the tests.

The test scores are highly reliable and have good cross validation. One must be cognizant of the fact that language learning is based on modeling, imitation, practice, and selected reinforcement. These are strategies to be used to assess language acquisition.

Practitioners must be aware of different phases of language acquisition, based on age appropriateness and differences in culture, to determine if there is a possibility of language delay. These phases should include (a) general readiness, (b) reciprocal actions, (c) communicative signals, (d) early comprehension, and (e) early production. The interaction of children within their own environment and with others plays an important role in their acquisition of language.

SUMMARY. Scores from the First Words and First Sentences Tests are reliable but there are other tests that would be beneficial for assessment of language of 18–36-month-old children. The authors have identified several tests in their manual.

[151]

Fisher-Landau Early Childhood Screening [Experimental Version].

Purpose: "Designed to assess a young student's abilities and range of language, perceptual-motor, and readiness skills."
Population: Grades K–1.
Publication Date: 1995.
Acronym: FLECS.
Scores: 10 scales: Personal/General Information/Sequencing, Word Copying, Bender Visual Motor, Roswell-Chall Blending Test, Letter Naming, Sounds, Sentence Memory, Gates Word Matching, Picture Naming, Whole Word Learning.
Administration: Individual.
Price Data, 1997: $25.15 per specimen set including examiner's manual, 1 stimulus booklet, 1 examiner's test booklet, and 1 student's test booklet; $24 per 12 each examiner's test booklet/student test booklet; $14 per stimulus booklet; $9.15 per examiner's manual.
Time: (40) minutes.
Comments: Examiner's test booklet also includes optional teacher checklist designed to "provide a fuller picture of the child's language/learning and social/emotional development as seen in the context of the classroom."
Authors: Francee R. Sugar and Amy Stone Belkin.
Publisher: Educators Publishing Service, Inc.

Review of the Fisher-Landau Early Childhood Screening [Experimental Version] by LISA BISCHOFF, Associate Professor, School of Education, Indiana State University, Terre Haute, IN:

The Fisher-Landau Early Childhood Screening (FLECS) is an individually administered screening instrument designed to assess skills of children beginning in kindergarten or first grade. The authors state that the FLECS is intended to be a descriptive tool for classroom teachers to document current student performance, to design IEPs, and to modify curriculum; it is not intended to be a diagnostic or predictive test. The FLECS may also be used as a "postscreening" instrument to assess progress in late spring and to provide recommendations for the following year or to evaluate the child's readiness to begin learning to read.

The FLECS is appropriate for administration to all children entering kindergarten or first grade except those with "mental or physical" disabilities. The examiner's manual states that the test should be administered by "specialized school personnel … [such as] learning specialist, teacher, co-teacher, school psychologist, and speech and language pathologist" (p. 5). The examiner should be familiar to the child. Administration time is approximately 40 minutes. The FLECS should be completed in one session. The FLECS is composed of 10 subtests across areas including perceptual/motor skills, prereading/language skills, and behavioral observations. Skills assessed across the subtests are relevant to instruction at the kindergarten or beginning first grade level. A brief description of each task is provided in the examiner's manual.

Standardized instructions, a list of materials, and scoring criteria for each task are provided in the examiner's test booklet. Instructions for administration and scoring provide adequate detail for the examiner. Space for recording of behavioral observations is provided at the bottom of each page of the examiner's test booklet. The examiner's test booklet also includes an optional Teacher Checklist in which areas of strength and needs of the child over time may be recorded.

The current edition of the FLECS is described by the authors as "experimental." The FLECS is based in part on work by Jansky and deHirsch (1972) who developed the Jansky Predictive Index, a compilation of five subtests (Letter Naming, Gates Word Matching, Bender Motor Gestalt, and Binet Sentence Memory) designed to predict reading failure by second grade. The development of the FLECS involved modification of several of the subtests included in the Jansky Predictive Index as well as development of an additional four subtests. References regarding scoring and interpretation of the Bender are included in the examiner's manual. Information regarding development of other subtests is not included. Information regarding scoring are provided in the scoring manual, which is an appendix to the examiner's manual.

Information regarding standardization, reliability, and validity of individual subtests and of the screening battery as a whole is not provided. Subtests are scored on the administration/answer form of the examiner's test booklet and are transferred to the "Summary of Findings" also in the examiner's test booklet.

Results of the FLECS may be recorded for either qualitative or quantitative interpretation. Qualitative, or "clinical" interpretation is based on descriptive narrative of the child's performance on the items presented. The Summary of Findings sheet provides a column for recording such information. Quantitative interpretation involves recording a child's score in one of three columns including "concern," "possible concern," or "strength." Quantitative interpretation is based on "Minimum Achievement Scores (MAS)," which may be created by the examiner from a local sample. MASs are based on the frequency distribution of raw scores on particular subtests. Procedures for obtaining such MASs are provided in the examiner's manual. Alternatively, examiners may use MAS data derived from a New York City school that are included in the examiner's test booklet. Examples of results from several children included in the sample are provided to help teachers judge the appropriateness of the New York data for application in their own classrooms.

SUMMARY. The FLECS is described as "experimental" by the authors and is not intended for use as a predictive tool. Rather, it is designed to be used by teachers to assist in instructional planning. Little information is provided in terms of development, standardization, or psychometric properties of individual subtests or of the screening battery as a whole. The authors state in the examiner's manual that they hope to gather further data to be used to provide a revised version of the FLECS. Examiners are invited to share data with the authors and are provided a name and address to contact. The FLECS appears to provide information relevant to teachers of children entering kindergarten or first grade. The screening instrument is easy to use and information and the forms included provide for summarizing data across subtests for individual children and across children in a classroom. Although information regarding development, standardization, and psychometric properties of the instrument are not provided in this version of the FLECS, this instrument may be useful for teachers in instructional planning and progress monitoring.

REVIEWER'S REFERENCE

Jansky, J., & deHirsch, K. (1972). *Preventing reading failure: Prediction, diagnosis, intervention.* New York: Harper & Row.

[152]
Friedman Well-Being Scale.

Purpose: "Designed to assess the level of well-being of an individual."

Population: Adults.

Publication Dates: 1992–1994.

Acronym: FWBS.

Scores, 6: Composite/Total, Sociability, Self-Esteem, Joviality, Emotional Stability, Happiness.

Administration: Group.

Price Data, 1998: $25 per sampler set including manual ('92, 62 pages), questionnaire, and scoring materials; $100 per permission set including sampler set plus permission to reproduce up to 200 copies of the questionnaire.

Time: (2–3) minutes.

Comments: Scale for rating perception of others or for self-rating; self-administered, administrator scored.

Author: Phillip H. Friedman.

Publisher: Mind Garden, Inc.

Review of Friedman Well-Being Scale by JOHN W. FLEENOR, Director of Knowledge Management, Center for Creative Leadership, Greensboro, NC:

The Friedman Well-Being Scale (FWBS) consists of a series of 20 bipolar adjectives (e.g., angry-calm) designed to measure an adult's level of well-being. Respondents rate themselves (or another person) on each adjective pair using a 10-point semantic differential-type scale. According to the manual, the FWBS is easy to administer, score, and interpret. It can be scored for an overall measure of well-being, the Friedman Well-Being Composite (FWBC), as well as for five subscales: Emotional Stability (10 items); Self-esteem/Self-confidence (3 items); Joviality (3 items); Sociability (3 items); and Happiness (1 item). The results can be interpreted in terms of two models of well-being developed by Friedman (1989). According to the manual, the instrument is appropriate for use in counseling, psychotherapy, and other similar interventions (e.g., self-help groups, personal growth programs, etc.).

MANUAL. A 62-page manual, which describes both the administrative procedures and the technical documentation of the FWBS, was developed by the author in 1994. Much of the manual consists of tables that report the results of various psychometric studies conducted with the instrument.

ADMINISTRATION AND SCORING. According to the manual, it typically takes 2 or 3 minutes to complete the FWBS. Most test-takers should have no difficulty following the directions, which instruct respondents to circle a number from 1 to 10 on the answer sheet indicating the extent to which each set of adjectives describes them.

The test administrator scores the instrument using the scoring key included on the answer sheet. For an instrument that is otherwise fairly uncomplicated, the scoring of the FWBS is rather complex. First, the composite score is calculated by summing the responses on all 20 bipolar adjectives and dividing by 2. Then, the subscale scores are calculated by summing the scores for the items on that subscale, dividing by the number of items, then multiplying by 10. It is unclear why the responses to the items on each scale are not simply summed to calculate the scale scores. Apparently, the more complex scoring scheme was developed in order to create a 100-point scale (0–100) for each of the subscales.

Raw scores on the FWBS can be converted to standard scores using the conversion table in the manual. Although not explicitly stated, the standard scores appear to have a mean of 50 and a standard deviation of 10. The table for converting raw scores to standard scores is based on a small sample ($n = 69$) of normal adults.

NORMS. Norms are available for each bipolar adjective, the composite score, and the subscale scores. Normative data are presented for samples of normal adults ($n = 69$), college students ($n = 105$), and psychotherapy patients in high stress ($n = 51$) conditions.

RELIABILITY. Alpha coefficients are presented for the composite scores and the subscale scores of several samples of test-takers. The internal consistency reliability estimates of the composite scores range from .92 to .98, and the reliability estimates of the subscale scores range from .72 to .96. The Happiness subscale contains only one item, so it is not possible to calculate the alpha reliability of this subscale.

Split-half reliabilities, estimated with the college student sample, range from .69 to .96 for the bipolar adjectives. Test-retest reliabilities of the composite scores (with intervals from 3 to 13 weeks) range from .73 for the student sample to .85 for the patient sample.

VALIDITY. The manual reports correlations between the FWBS and over 100 clinical, personality, attitudinal, stress, relational, marital, and interpersonal scales and subscales. In fact, the number of reported validity coefficients is so great that it may be somewhat overwhelming to the average test user.

As evidence of external validity, the manual reports a study of 52 married couples in which each couple rated both themselves and their partner of the FWBS. A correlation of .61 was found between the self-report scores and the partner ratings.

As evidence of construct validity, the FWBS was correlated with a wide variety of scales as discussed previously. Among the most interesting results are the correlations with measures of the five-factor ("big five") model of personality (Costa & McCrae, 1992; Goldberg, 1992). With the sample of psychotherapy patients, the FWBS composite score was found to correlate .61 with Extraversion, .42 with Conscientiousness, .41 with Agreeableness, .13 with Openness, and -.81 with Neuroticism.

It also is informative to examine the intercorrelations among the FWBS composite score and the subscale scores. Correlations with the composite score range from .91 for Emotional Stability to .71 for Self-esteem/Self-confidence. Correlations between Emotional Stability and the other subscale scores range from .69 for Happiness to .49 for Social. In general, the intercorrelations among the FWBS scales appear to be higher than desirable for an instrument of this type. Judging from these correlations and the relationships with Neuroticism from the five factor model, the FWBS appears, to a large extent, to be measuring emotional stability, rather than any overall construct of well-being.

SUMMARY. Although the Friedman Well-Being Scale is fairly new, an impressive number of reliability and validity studies have been conducted with the instrument. However, the norms are based on sample sizes that are too small to be representative of potential test-takers, and, therefore, should be used with caution. These same small samples were used to develop the tables for converting raw scores to standard scores. Standardized scores, therefore, also should be used with caution.

Although the reliability evidence for the instrument appears to be adequate, the evidence of validity is less convincing. Although a large number of validity coefficients are presented, on closer inspection, some of the results do not appear to be fully supportive of the instrument as a measure of well-being. The FWBS is highly correlated with measures of emotional stability—so much so that it appears to be measuring this construct rather than overall well-being, as purported.

REVIEWER'S REFERENCES
Friedman, P. H. (1989). *Creating well-being: The healing path to love, peace, self-esteem, and happiness.* Saratoga, CA: R&E Publishers.
Costa, P., & McCrae, R. (1992). *NEO-PIR professional manual.* Odessa, FL: Psychological Assessment Resources.
Goldberg, L. (1992). The development of markers for the big five factor structure. *Psychological Assessment, 4,* 26–42.

[153]
General Ability Measure for Adults.

Purpose: "Designed to evaluate intellectual ability using abstract designs."
Population: Ages 18–96.
Publication Date: 1997.
Acronym: GAMA.
Scores, 5: Matching, Analogies, Sequences, Construction, GAMA IQ Score.
Administration: Individual and/or group.
Price Data: Available from publisher.
Time: (25) minutes.
Comments: May be self-administered.
Authors: Jack A. Naglieri and Achilles N. Bardos.
Publisher: NCS (Minnetonka).

Review of the General Ability Measure for Adults by ROBERT FITZPATRICK, Consulting Psychologist, Cranberry Township, PA:

The authors designed the General Ability Measure for Adults (GAMA) to measure general cognitive ability, or intelligence, in an efficient manner. It is nonverbal except for the instructions and requires no motor skill beyond filling in an answer sheet. It is normed for adults only. Readily administered to groups of examinees, it can even be self-administered. A Spanish language version is available.

For the most part, the GAMA appears to have been developed with care and with technical sophistication. Particular attention was paid to avoiding differential item functioning and other manifestations of bias. Whether justified or not, claims of bias against those who are culturally or otherwise out of the mainstream continue to plague tests of cognitive ability. Hence, any effort to achieve both the appearance and the reality of fairness is to be welcomed.

All items call for reasoning or problem solving based on abstract figures in two or more colors. Each of four subtests is intended to measure the same construct of general intelligence. Yet, the manual suggests comparing subtest scores for a given examinee. "Although variation among subtest scores is not considered to reflect different abilities (because the GAMA is a general ability test), varying scores could reflect performance differences related to the demands and structure of the individual subtests" (manual, p. 25). Suggested interpretations of subtest variations seem sensible enough, but are unsupported by evidence. It would be helpful to have data on the relationships of the subtests to a variety of spatial tests. Lacking such data, users are advised to be cautious in interpreting subtest scores.

The GAMA has 66 items, with a time limit of 25 minutes. The manual does not indicate what proportion of examinees can be expected to answer all the items, but it seems likely from inspection that such an event would be rare. The informed use of guessing, skipping item types the examinee finds especially difficult, and other coachable strategies might well be effective with the GAMA. Hence, the GAMA might be contraindicated for users potentially vulnerable to outside coaching.

Subtest scaled scores are based on norms from a United States standardization sample of more than 2,000, stratified by geographic region, age, gender, education, and race or ethnic group. Raw scores are converted to scaled scores and then to a deviation IQ score, based on norms for 11 age groups, ranging from 18–19 to 80+. (Sample sizes in the age groups range from 91 to 310.) Users should be aware that, with this type of scoring, the expected decrement of cognitive ability with age is taken into account, so that scores should be interpreted only in relation to those of others of similar age.

The test booklet and the manual are handsomely printed, partly in "colors that have been shown to be the least problematic for those with color-impaired vision" (p. 2). The test instructions are written at about a third-grade level of difficulty. The manual is generally well written, although the description of the self-scored answer sheet is hard to follow.

The results of internal consistency (average split-half correlations across the 11 age groups ranged from a low of .65 to a high of .81 for the subtests and equaled .90 for total GAMA IQ score; test-retest correlation was .67 for GAMA IQ score) and test-retest reliability studies are generally favorable though less so at the higher age levels. However, the test-retest (2–6-week interval) results are based on a single study with sample size of only 86, and should not be relied upon greatly.

The manual reports fairly high correlations of GAMA scores with those of other tests of cognitive ability, albeit more so for relatively nonverbal tests than for tests with high verbal content. Also reported are four studies using the GAMA to study special populations. In one of these studies, the GAMA was administered, with apparent success, to deaf adults using American Sign Language. The publisher has indicated that further studies are under way.

SUMMARY. A final verdict on the GAMA awaits those further studies and experience in application. Nevertheless, the evidence reported in the manual, along with the careful procedures in test development, support the authors' contention that the GAMA IQ score is an effective measure of cognitive ability for U.S. residents. It is not necessarily limited to special populations, but rather might be useful in a variety of situations where the user needs a short test that seems as fair to a variety of examinees as current test technology permits.

Review of the General Ability Measure for Adults by BERT A. GOLDMAN, Professor of Education, Curriculum and Instruction, School of Education, University of North Carolina at Greensboro, Greensboro, NC:

Naglieri and Bardos indicate that their "GAMA test evaluates an individual's overall general ability with items that require the application of reasoning and logic to solve problems that exclusively use abstract designs and shapes" (manual, p. 1). The test, consisting of four sample items followed by 66 items to be answered in 25 minutes, was normed on 2,360 people who ranged in age from 18 to 96.

The GAMA includes four subtests containing nonverbal items: Matching, Analogies, Sequences, and Construction. By using one of 11 age group conversion tables, the raw score earned on each subtest is converted to a scaled score with a mean of 10 and a standard deviation of 3. These four converted scores are summed and the total is converted to a GAMA IQ score that has a mean of 100 and a standard deviation of 15.

In addition to the test book and test manual, there are two kinds of answer sheets: a self-scoring answer sheet and a computer scannable one along with software scoring and reporting. All materials are attractively printed and the directions for administering, scoring, and interpreting scores are clearly presented and easily followed.

Detailed information concerning the GAMA standardization sample is presented and includes numbers and percentages of the various age groups, education levels, gender, geographic regions, and race or ethnic groups comprising the sample. The percentages of these groups are similar to the percentages obtained from the U.S. Department of Commerce, thus supporting the GAMA authors' claim that the test "was standardized using a carefully designed stratified random sampling plan" (manual, p. 31).

Reliability was estimated by the split-half method with the Spearman-Brown correction for each of the 11 age groups and for the total standardization sample. The average of these corrected reliabilities for two of the four subtests was low (i.e., .65 and .66). The other two were higher at .79 and .81. However, a linear composite of these reliabilities produced a coefficient of .90, which suggests a reliable total GAMA score.

Estimates of test-retest reliability within an interval of 2 to 6 weeks were determined from a sample of 86 people comprising both sexes, several ethnic or racial backgrounds, and varying education levels. The test means for each of the four subtests and for the total score are similar to those of the retest, suggesting that the scores remain stable over time. However, the test-retest reliability coefficient for each subtest and for the total score are low, ranging from .38 to .74, suggesting that over time the scores are not very stable.

The idea of providing a 25-minute nonverbal test of intellectual ability has merit. However, the authors provide little specific explanation for their selection of the four types of items comprising the GAMA. They indicate that "the GAMA test evaluates an individual's overall general ability; that it is designed to evaluate intellectual ability using abstract designs" (manual, p. 1). Although four types of items employing abstract designs are contained in the test format, this reviewer has difficulty accepting the notion that so limited an array of item types can adequately measure "overall general ability." The Full Scale WAIS-R, in this reviewer's opinion, may be considered more a test of an individual's overall general ability than the GAMA. A sample of 194 people provided a correlation of only .75 between the Full Scale WAIS-R and the GAMA. When the GAMA was compared to the Performance (nonverbal) half of the WAIS-R, a correlation of only .74 was produced.

Although these correlations are statistically significant at $p < .001$, they do not reveal, to a very high degree, that the GAMA measures "overall general ability."

Evidence is presented suggesting that the GAMA may be used with a variety of special populations including adults with learning disabilities, deaf adults, elderly nursing home residents, adults with traumatic brain injury, and adults with mental retardation. Again, to say that the GAMA is measuring the "overall general ability" of these groups may be misleading.

In summary, the GAMA appears to measure the ability to apply reasoning and logic to solve problems involving abstract designs and shapes. This reflects an aspect of intelligence rather than being a measure of overall general ability. The standardization sample was carefully selected to represent the U.S. population for ages 18 to 96. Internal consistency data for the total test are excellent, but test-retest reliability data suggest poor to fair stability of scores over time. Validity evidence for use of test scores as measures of overall general ability has not been shown. However, one might cautiously use the GAMA as a relatively quick screening device for measuring a limited aspect of intelligence.

[154]
General Processing Inventory.

Purpose: Designed to identify learning disabilities.
Population: Ages 5–75 years.
Publication Dates: 1986–1996.
Acronym: GPI.
Scores, 7: Graphomotor, Short Term Memory Retrieval, Long Term Memory Retrieval, Visual (Dyslexia), Auditory, Speech (Dysphasia), Total.
Subtests, 2: General Elementary Inventory of Language Skills (GEILS), General Elementary Inventory of Mathematics and Numeration (GEIMAN).
Administration: Individual.
Levels, 4: One (5 years old), Two (Above 6 years), Three (Above 8 years), Four (Above 10 years).
Price Data, 1999: $350 per test kit; $400 for training required to administer test.
Time: (60–180) minutes.
Comments: Training required; psychologists and other licensed test administrators will learn to tabulate errors and may send their results to publisher for report writing. There is a fee for report writing dependent on volume.
Author: Ruth M. Geiman.
Publisher: Ruth M. Geiman, Ph.D.

Review of the General Processing Inventory by SHERRY K. BAIN, Associate Professor, Department of Educational Psychology, University of Tennessee, Knoxville, TN:

RATIONALE AND STANDARDIZATION. The author states that the General Processing Inventory (GPI) is designed to provide "an accurate description of the behaviors underlying learning disabilities" (manual, p. 1), as well as to provide remediation and compensation guidelines for children with learning disabilities (LD). Specifically, the GPI purports to measure the presence of "subtle processing symptoms" via visual, auditory, oral, or written means as well as long and short-term memory deficits (p. 12).

Martin (the test author) states that norms are available for children and adults from 5 to 75 years of age. However, normative tables are not supplied in the test manual, and the samples described in test development do not actually include subjects above high school age. Curiously, the absence of normative tables does not preclude Martin from referring to the General Elementary Inventory of Mathematics and Numeration (GEIMAN) as a norm-referenced test. She refers to the General Elementary Inventory of Language Skills (GEILS) as the "criterion referenced companion" to the GEIMAN (p. 20). For all practical purposes, both the GEIMAN and GEILS subscales fit the criterion-referenced mold better than the norm-referenced mold.

In developing the GPI, Martin states she used nonparametric statistics, analyzing each item of the GEIMAN subscale based upon its probability of being passed or failed by students without learning disabilities. Her justification for abandoning parametric statistics is extensive; however, her reasoning is unclear to this reviewer. For example, she tries to demonstrate by explanation that the normal distribution does not apply in the case of characteristics of LD by hypothetically dividing the population of students into two samples, those without LD who make few or no decoding or memory errors and those with LD who make many errors. Martin presents two graphs, unlabeled on the ordinate and abscissa, to demonstrate her logic. Ignoring the indecipherable graphs, it is not difficult to recognize that a middle portion of students (those who make moderate levels of errors but do not perform badly enough to be labeled as LD) was left out of Martin's hypothetical sample, omitting a fairly large midsection of an erstwhile normal distribution of error rates. There is, apparently, no continuum for error-making behavior in Martin's book.

The actual sample used to develop the GPI consisted of four groups of students, totaling approximately 233 subjects across grade levels. Children were excluded from analyses if their school records showed academic problems or problems related to the characteristics of LD. All samples were drawn from the same geographic area (Ohio). Age, grade, racial/ethnic, or socioeconomic breakdowns of the samples were not provided in the manual.

RELIABILITY AND VALIDITY. Martin elects not to employ several traditional reliability and validity measures (e.g., split-half reliability, concurrent validity) based upon reasons too detailed to summarize here. Basically, because her product is criterion referenced instead of norm referenced, she argues that she only needs to consider the types of reliability and validity appropriate to criterion-referenced testing.

Martin does discuss item discrimination, for which she applied the Nolte Binomial Item Analysis, which sets a probability of zero errors for each item. She used this formula to choose items for the GEIMAN subscale, based upon her samples of children without LD. By this method, Martin produced a subscale of items that should be performed without errors by children with no apparent signs of learning problems.

Evidence of test-retest reliability (interval not reported) is supplied, based upon a sample of 11 students. The resulting correlation coefficient (.47), presumably across the entire test, led Martin to conclude there was lack of reliability; however, by deleting the Fact subtest from the GEIMAN subscale she obtained a reliability coefficient of .87. Because her data had limited variance, based upon a relatively error-free sample, one should expect the reliability coefficient to be low. It is difficult, however, to understand how Martin obtained such a huge difference by eliminating one subtest. Additional subscale and subtest data are not presented in the manual.

Evidence of construct validity is offered by Martin's listing of symptoms of processing disorder she had found in the literature, which guided item development. For content validity, she cites the inclusion of symbols, letters, digits, punctuation marks, etc., which represented the entire pool of items for each symptom, presumably listed under construct validity. Martin did, in fact, seek to include every item that she could determine would not be missed by a child without LD, causing a potentially long administration. She does designate age levels for specific administration, bypassing harder parts of the test for younger children.

Evidence for what Martin terms as criterion validity was presented in the form of results from two pilot studies of children diagnosed with brain damage or LD who were able to sit through the entire test administration without fatigue. Error patterns and overall results were apparently not an issue in these pilot studies. Her second body of evidence for criterion validity was the administration of the test in the four studies that constituted her purported normative sample, children without evident signs of LD. No data are presented comparing the performance of the two pilot studies with the performance of the norm sample, which might have actually supported criterion validity.

Evidence for concurrent validity and treatment validity is not offered by the test author. Recommendations, purportedly linked to testing results, are of a generic nature (e.g., "Write using a word processor," manual, p. 83). Although these are, without a doubt, helpful recommendations, they do not follow specifically or exclusively from results of the GPI.

ADMINISTRATION AND SCORING. Martin recommends that persons administering the GPI be licensed, certified examiners (no elaboration offered) and be trained for this particular test. Administration mimics that of several standardized intelligence tests (e.g., the Wechsler Intelligence Scale for Children, Third Edition [WISC-III]) with multiple subtests and several boxes of materials (letters, graduated rods, etc.). The child being tested is expected to use a mechanical pencil, supplied by the examiner, that is given to the child at the end of testing.

Administration and scoring instructions are extensive but, in some cases, unclear. Expected levels of performance based upon age and overall error rates are used in determining results. Scoring is complicated, involving coding each error by processing types, not explicitly defined in the instructions, tabulating the processing errors using another set of possibly obscure terms defined in a glossary (e.g., dyscopia), and finally determining appropriate recommendations under each general processing areas.

SUMMARY AND RECOMMENDATIONS. The GPI is, for all practical purposes, a criterion-referenced test, and not a norm-referenced test, for identifying children with the symptoms or behaviors associated with learning disability. Considered as a criterion-referenced test, the author has provided some reliability and validity evidence, although more is needed. If the GPI were to be used in making diagnostic decisions, traditional normative information should be gathered and construct, concurrent, and discriminant validity should be established. Until that time, potential users are strongly advised to consider alternative tests. Processing difficulties (e.g., auditory, visual, short-term memory) can be investigated using traditional ability tests, for instance, the WISC-III (12:412), or the Kaufman Assessment Battery for Children (K-ABC; T4:1343) (Wechsler, 1991; Kaufman & Kaufman, 1983; respectively), with normative information included. Academically related error patterns can be established through shorter, simpler tests (e.g., Gray Oral Reading Tests—Diagnostic by Bryant & Wiederhold, 1991, 12:166; KeyMath Revised by Connolly, 1988, T4:1355). Furthermore, until Martin is able to provide additional studies to establish that error patterns measured by the GPI remain constant within individuals, information from the GPI may be far less helpful for classroom recommendations than simpler and quicker curriculum-based assessment.

REVIEWER'S REFERENCES
Kaufman, A. S., & Kaufman, N. L. (1983). K-ABC: Kaufman Assessment Battery for Children. Circle Pines, MN: American Guidance Service.
Connolly, A. J. (1988). KeyMath Revised: A Diagnostic Inventory of Essential Mathematics. Circle Pines, MN: American Guidance Service.
Bryant, B. R., & Wiederholt, J. L. (1991). Gray Oral Reading Tests—Diagnostic. Austin, TX: PRO-ED, Inc.
Wechsler, D. (1991). Wechsler Intelligence Scale for Children, Third Edition. San Antonio: The Psychological Corporation.

Review of the General Processing Inventory by STEPHEN A. SPILLANE, *Learning Specialist/ Educational Consultant, Centerville, MA:*

According to the author, The General Processing Inventory (GPI) was created to address four areas of concern regarding learning disabilities and tests: They are not designed to measure learning disabilities; are either too global or too specific to measure learning; have not been standardized; and yield little remedial guidance. To respond to these concerns, the author claims to have spent 15 years compiling items to assess learning and recommendations based on that assessment.

The "boundaries of ... education, psychology, neurology, audiology, opthamology, medicine, and many others" (p. 2) were the source of the measures. The author states that two pilot studies, four norm samples, and 350 case histories were used to develop items that were combined to create two components of the GPI: the General Elementary Inventory of Mathematics and Numeration (GEIMAN) and the General Elementary Inventory of Language Skills (GEILS). The individual items consist of letters, digits, operation symbols, punctuation marks, and facts.

The author used idiosyncratic methods to gather the reliability and validity evidence for the GPI. She asserts that construct validity was established by "using the symptoms of subtle processing disorders recorded in the literature" (p. 25). Further, she posits that content validity was established because the items used were selected from those processing disorders. She argues that criterion validity was established by a series of pilot studies using small samples of students with and without brain damage and learning disabilities. Finally, the author reports a Pearson correlation coefficient of .47 for test-retest reliability (no interval reported).

The author asserts that parametric statistics were inappropriate to use for validation because of the absence of a normal distribution curve.

According to the author, the Nolte Binomial Item Analysis establishes a critical valued based on a 270.0% error probability with the standard error of measurement "set to the right of zero to accommodate for the unknown factors involved in the research" (p. 11). Items were included in the GPI if they did not have an error rate above the chance level.

The GPI materials consist of two test books, a manual, score sheets, tabulation sheets, chips, letters of the alphabet, four boxes of graduated rods, four letter cards, two word cards, and a coin card. Test administrators may tabulate results or send them to Dr. Geiman for report writing.

In summary, the GPI is a whole-hearted but ineffective attempt to add to the diagnostic tools available for the assessment of learning disabilities. Its development fails to meet procedures and criteria consistent with the *Standards for Educational and Psychological Testing* (APA, AERA, & NCME, 1985). It is not based on any identifiable

model of which I am aware in education, psychology, neurology, audiology, opthamology, or medicine. Unfortunately, the four areas of concern regarding learning disabilities and tests that were the impetus for the creation of the GPI were not addressed. The GPI, as designed, will not measure learning disabilities; is both too global and too specific to measure learning; has not been standardized; and consequently yields no valid nor reliable scores to use in remedial guidance. There are significantly better tools currently available in the learning disabilities tool box that provide reliable and valid diagnostic information such as the Wide Range Assessment of Memory and Learning (T4:2957) or the Woodcock-Johnson Psycho-Educational Battery—Revised (12:415).

REVIEWER'S REFERENCE

American Educational Research Association, American Psychological Association, & National Council on Measurement in Education. (1985). *Standards for educational and psychological testing.* Washington, DC: American Psychological Association, Inc.

[155]
Gibson Spiral Maze, Second Edition.

Purpose: Measures "the speed, accuracy, and general style of people's muscular reactions in response to carefully controlled stimuli."
Population: Children and adults.
Publication Dates: 1961–1965.
Scores, 2: Time score, Error score.
Administration: Individual.
Price Data, 1999: £10 per test 20 copies; manual and specimen set are now out of print.
Time: (2) minutes.
Comments: Forms part of the Clifton Assessment Procedures for the Elderly (T5:537).
Author: H. B. Gibson.
Publisher: Hodder and Stoughton Educational [England].
Cross References: See T4:1037 (3 references), T3:955 (1 reference), T2:1191 (3 references), 7:82 (3 references), and P:90 (2 references).

Review of the Gibson Spiral Maze, Second Edition by WILLIAM K. WILKINSON, Consulting Psychologist, Boleybeg, Barna, Co. Galway, Ireland:

The Gibson Spiral Maze (GSM) purports to measure psychomotor skill. It was first published in England in 1965 and the technical manual was updated in 1977. Why the instrument is under review 21 years later is a mystery. The potential user is immediately warned that the technical references are now outdated.

The GSM consists of a single Spiral figure made of continuously flowing concentric circles. Because the figure is not square and does not contain blind alleys, it is not a traditional maze, like the Mazes subtest of the Wechsler Intelligence Scale for Children, Third Edition (WISC-III). In fact, it may be more accurate to refer to it as the Gibson Spiral Figure, because reference to "Maze" may mislead potential users.

The Figure consists of small circles placed at different spacings within each spiral. The object is to trace an exit from the middle of the figure without touching the small circles or the path lines. The two scores available are Time (T) and Errors (E)—the latter score the sum total of the number of times the individual touched the inner circles or path walls.

Atypical in this test are the directions to test administrators to focus the test-taker on the time element. Specifically, at 15-second intervals the administrator is to sharply and authoritatively comment, "go as quickly as you can!" and to further stress speed by reiterating these comments at 15-second intervals. The author notes that the usefulness of the test depends on the administrator's skill in creating time-stress. I did not find a compelling rationale for emphasizing speed. One would think that the use of a stopwatch and the nature of the task would insure that examinees will work as quickly as they can. A serious difficulty with this procedure, as the author notes, is the creation of test administrator error (e.g., variations in voice tone, language, rapport with test-taker, etc.).

A positive feature of the GSM is that it is quick to administer and easy to score. The scores have demonstrated interrater reliability ($r = .98$). The manual provides limited test-retest reliability. It seems that in children ages 8 to 10, T decreases but E does not.

The author has developed a peculiar position with respect to norms. Because the test depends on the administrator's skill in stressing speed, the author urges GSM users to develop local norms. In addition, test scores will depend entirely on an individual sample's T and E score distribution. Therefore, the author suggests that GSM users obtain a sample's raw score distributions to form a scatterplot, with T and E regressed on each other. It is unclear how a test user interprets an individual's score before a sample distribution is obtained. Further, it is doubtful that test users will

believe it part of their responsibility to collect a GSM database and perform somewhat sophisticated statistical analyses on this data (unless they use the GSM purely for research purposes).

Based on regression analyses, the author developed four interpretive quadrants, "quick and accurate," "slow and accurate," "quick and careless," and "slow and careless." A person's score will fall into one of these four divisions after the local database is collected and analyzed.

At this point, the use of the GSM moves beyond its initial scope—as a measure of psychomotor speed. Using the four quadrants as a guide, it becomes a measure of "maladjustment," "neurotic styles," and purportedly discriminates between various clinical samples. For example, "naughty" boys are more likely to be quick and careless whereas "good" boys are more likely to be "quick and accurate." The lure for potential users is to consider the "styles" as indicative of personality disturbance. If anything, these are cognitive styles, because the test is purportedly a cognitive one. That is, psychomotor speed is a cognitive, neuropsychological variable first and foremost. If a test user wants to measure "personality" aberrations there are a number of "personality" tests specifically for this purpose.

An essential question is, "how well does the GSM measure psychomotor speed?" Although the GSM appears face valid as a measure of psychomotor speed, there is little construct validation evidence for this claim. There is a weak, albeit statistically significant, correlation of .33 with its precursor, the Porteus Mazes (Q-score). Unfortunately, greater effort is made to prove the usefulness of the GSM in distinguishing maladjusted children from their adjusted peers.

It is odd that the GSM was not correlated with other tests purporting to measure psychomotor speed. For example, the Coding and Symbol Search subtests of the Wechsler Intelligence Scale for Children—III (WISC-III; T5:2862) would seem parallel measures of paper-and-pencil speed. Oddly, the author compares the GSM to the WISC-III Block Design subtest, although it seems more similar to Coding and Symbol Search. Again, part of the problem is that the technical manual is outdated, so it is unknown how well the GSM correlates with more recently developed measures of psychomotor speed. For example, it would be interesting to see the correlation of the GSM on a reaction time measure, such as the processing Speed Index of the Continuous Performance Test (97). Convergent/Divergent validity studies such as these would seem a useful, indeed, essential, line of inquiry.

SUMMARY. Overall, the GSM may have a place in research, particularly neuropsychological research. However, the test is too limited and out of date to be considered a viable clinical instrument. If one wants to measure psychomotor speed the new Processing Speed Index of the WISC-III appears far more valid than the GSM. Again, one should not use this instrument as a measure of "personality" style or "deviation."

Review of the Gibson Spiral Maze, Second Edition by JAMES YSSELDYKE, Birkmaier Professor of Educational Leadership, University of Minnesota, Minneapolis, MN:

The Gibson Spiral Maze (GSM) test is a psychomotor test designed to measure the speed, accuracy, and style of people's muscular reactions in response to carefully designed stimuli. The authors claim that the test can be used in assessment of intelligence and "special skills," and in personality research. The conceptual/theoretical basis for the test is extremely dated, and there have been major developments in the assessment of psychomotor skills since the publication of the Gibson in 1965.

The GSM is a one-prompt test. Individuals are asked to trace a path through a spiral design printed on a large card. Small circles are in the spiral, and these are defined as "obstacles," which the examinee is to avoid. The test takes less than 2 minutes to administer. The administrator is instructed to tell the examinee in firm, sharp, repeated commands to go as quickly as he or she can. These injunctions to hurry are to be repeated every 15 seconds, and not more frequently. Thus, the test is described as a "time-stress" test.

The test is scored for time and number of errors. Errors are counted each time the subject touches an obstacle (1-point error), penetrates an obstacle or line (2-point error), or touches a line (1-point error if less than one inch, 2-point error if it touches for more than one inch). There are two ways to interpret the scores obtained. Users are told to construct their own norms by creating a graph in which time is plotted along the abscissa and errors plotted along the ordinate. Regression lines of Time on Error and Error on Time are plotted. The examiner uses the self-generated chart to assign one of four ratings to the subject: quick and careless, slow and careless, quick and accurate, and slow and accurate. An alternate way of reporting performance is to use norms printed in the test manual. These norms are based on data from 392 boys in primary schools. Other than knowing that the norms are for boys, the norm group is not described. The author also reports quartile and median scores for the following referent groups: office girls, factory girls, "approved school girls," secondary schoolboys, junior boys in a "remand" home, boys in a senior approved school, maladjusted schoolboys, and depressive patients (median age 55) before and after treatment (manual, p. 9).

Data on interscorer reliability are reported for secondary studies. Reliability estimates exceed .90. Data on test-retest reliability are also from secondary studies using samples, which are not described. Test-retest (over a period of one year) reliability estimates are consistently below .80. Data on validity are dated, limited, and highly questionable. For example, the author reports criterion group data on "good boys, average boys, and naughty boys" (manual, p. 11).

SUMMARY. In my opinion there is no specific reason why examiners would want to know how individuals perform on this test. If one did know, it is uncertain how the data would, could, or should be used. Very many superior devices are readily available for use in assessing psychomotor skills.

[156]
Gifted Evaluation Scale, Second Edition.

Purpose: Designed to help identify gifted students.
Population: Ages 4.5–19.
Publication Dates: 1987–1998.
Acronym: GES-2.
Scores, 8: 6 subscales (Intellectual Ability, Creativity, Specific Academic Aptitude, Leadership Ability, Performing and Visual Arts, Motivation [optional]), Quotient Score, Percentile Score.
Administration: Individual.
Price Data, 1998: $63.50 per complete kit including technical manual ('98, 60 pages), 50 rating forms, and Gifted Intervention Manual ('90, 107 pages); $10 per 50 motivation scoring forms; $12.50 per technical manual; $31 per 50 rating forms; $20 per Gifted Intervention Manual.
Time: (15–20) minutes.
Comments: Ratings by "anyone familiar with the student's behavior patterns and specific skills ... (e.g., teacher, counselor, etc.)."

Authors: Diana Henage (The Gifted Intervention Manual), Stephen B. McCarney and Paul D. Anderson (technical manual and subscale percentile tables).
Publisher: Hawthorne Educational Services, Inc.
Cross References: See T5:1089 (2 references); for reviews by Carolyn M. Callahan and Ross E. Traub of an earlier edition, see 12:162 (1 reference).

Review of the Gifted Evaluation Scale, Second Edition by DOUGLAS K. SMITH, Director of Programs in School Psychology, University at Albany— State University of New York, Albany, NY:

The Gifted Evaluation Scale, Second Edition (GES-2) was developed on the basis of a synthesis or integration of federal and state definitions of giftedness. These definitions emphasize that gifted students demonstrate well-developed abilities in one or more of the following areas: intellectual, aptitude, creativity, academic skills, leadership ability, and performing and visual arts. "The purpose of the GES-2 is to provide the primary observer of the student, the teacher, the opportunity to contribute an equal share of information which can be considered along with formal testing in decision-making for appropriate educational services" (technical manual, p. 7). Thus, the GES-2 is one facet in a comprehensive assessment process.

The authors of the GES-2 indicate that the instrument is appropriate for a number of functions ranging from screening students for gifted characteristics to developing program goals and objectives to specifying specific instructional strategies to data collection in research studies. To accomplish the instructional programming function of the GES-2, the Gifted Intervention Manual (Henage, 1990) was developed.

The GES-2 covers the age range of 5 years through 18 years and consists of 48 items that were developed on the basis of recommendations from educators of the gifted and educational diagnosticians. A rating scale is utilized for each item with scores ranging from (does not demonstrate the behavior or skill) to 5 (demonstrates the behavior or skill at all times [consistently]). The items are organized into five subscales: Intellectual, Creativity, Specific Academic Aptitude, Leadership Ability, and Performing and Visual Arts. An optional subscale, Motivation, is available for use by those requiring a measure of this characteristics.

Subscale raw scores are converted to standard scores (range of 1 to 20 with a mean of 10 and standard deviation of 3). The standard scores

for the five subscales are added together to produce the sum of subscale standard scores. This total is then converted to a quotient score (range of 50 to 150 with a mean of 100 and standard deviation of 15) and a percentile rank.

The 48 items on the GES-2 were developed on the basis of feedback from 37 educational diagnosticians and educational personnel in 1985. These consultants were initially asked to list the indicators of giftedness in students. From this item pool, 53 items were developed by combining items and eliminating items that were not feasible. This list was evaluated and modified by 31 of the original 37 consultants resulting in a list of 49 items. On the basis of face validity the items were assigned to the five subscales. Field testing was accomplished by randomly selecting 109 teachers from 10 districts in Missouri and asking them to complete the scale for four randomly selected students in their classes. On the basis of theses results, one item was eliminated resulting in a final scale consisting of 48 items.

Standardization occurred from August 1997 through April 1998 using a sample of 1,439 students from 14 states and 20 school systems, representing the four major geographical areas of the United States. Additional details regarding standardization procedures are not provided. Comparisons of the standardization sample with national census data show that the sample was predominantly white (89.3% vs. 73.1% in the U.S.) and urban/suburban (83.9% vs. 75.2% in the U.S.). The standardization sample, as compared to national census data, was overrepresented in the midwest and south and underrepresented in the northeast and west. Although data on the educational level of mothers and fathers show some variability with national census data, the discrepancies mostly occur at the 1–3 years of college and Associate's Degree level. The match between the two sets of data at the education extremes (less than high school and college degree) is closer.

Analysis of the standardization data by age and gender showed significant differences and led to the creation of 15 standardization groups. Thus, the norms tables are not organized based on age exclusively but rather on the basis of age and gender such as: Females, 5 years; Females, 6 years; Males, 5 years; Males, 6 years; etc.

Test-retest reliability data for 125 students randomly selected from the standardization sample and rerated after 30 days produced reliability coefficients ranging from .86 to .93, indicating substantial test-retest reliability. An important aspect of reliability for rating scales in interrater reliability. This was examined using 304 students rated by two educators "with equal knowledge of the students" (technical manual, p. 17). Pearson Product Moment correlations ranged from .69 to .91 for all age levels with Total Test reliability of .91. Thus, substantial interrater reliability is indicated. Finally, internal consistency reliability using coefficient alpha exceeded .91 for all subscales.

Validity of scores from the GES-2 was examined in several ways. Content validity is based on the item development procedures previously described. Correlations with the Gifted and Talented Evaluation Scale for a sample of 105 students on subscales measuring similar constructs ranged from .74 to .86 and were statistically significant. Factor analytic data for the GES-2 were also supportive of the instrument. Thus, the GES-2 appears to be a valid screening instrument for use in identifying students who are gifted and talented.

The GES-2 is easy to administer and score. The cover sheet of the School Version Rating Form provides very specific guidelines for rating the student. Elaborations of these guidelines are included in the technical manual. In addition, a thorough explanation of the rating scale descriptors are provided in the technical manual. Specific scoring procedures are provided in the technical manual as well as interpretive suggestions.

SUMMARY. The GES-2 is a screening instrument designed to be used as part of the assessment process in identifying students who are potentially gifted and talented. A rating scale format is used to identify behaviors in five areas that are based on current federal and state definitions of giftedness. The reliability data for the GES-2 are quite strong and the validity data, although limited, are supportive of the validity of scores from the instrument. Administration of the instrument is easily accomplished as is the scoring. The major weakness of the GES-2 is the standardization. The number of students involved is somewhat limited. Likewise, the norms are based on students in only 14 states and 20 school systems. Because the standardization sample was not stratified on major demographic variables (e.g., race/ethnicity, socioeconomic status, geographic region), the match with current census data is not

particularly close. Thus, users of the GES-2 should use the results cautiously and only for screening purposes as part of a multidimensional assessment process to identify students who may be gifted and talented.

Review of the Gifted Evaluation Scale, Second Edition by JOHN W. YOUNG, Associate Professor of Educational Statistics and Measurement, Rutgers University, New Brunswick, NJ:

The Gifted Evaluation Scale, Second Edition (GES-2) is a 48-item rating scale designed to assist in identifying students between the ages of 5 and 18 who may qualify for gifted education. All items use the same 5-point behavioral rating scale. Based on Seely's (1993) model for the assessment of gifted children, the GES-2 School Version Rating Form (the only form currently available) is intended to be completed by one or more of a student's educators with primary observational opportunities. This individual would typically be one of the student's teachers but could include aides or counselors. Multiple ratings by different teachers are acceptable if done independently but ratings done by a student's parent(s) are generally discouraged.

The most important aspect of the GES-2 is that it can provide a measure of giftedness that is relevant and meaningful to educational assessment. The usefulness of the GES-2 is based on the instrument's development using, at present, the most commonly accepted definitions of giftedness. The GES-2 was designed to identify and measure gifted students according to five characteristics: Intellectual, Creativity, Specific Academic Aptitude, Leadership Ability, and Performing and Visual Arts. GES-2 subscale scores, based on mutually exclusive sets of items, correspond to each of these characteristics. There is a sixth optional scale for Motivation that is based on 14 items from across the other five subscales. The Gifted Intervention Manual (Henage, 1990) is designed to be used in conjunction with the GES-2 for the purposes of developing program goals and objectives and identifying appropriate instructional activities.

STANDARDIZATION. The GES-2 was standardized in 1998 with a norming sample of 1,439 students from 20 school systems in 14 states. The norming sample included students from ages 5 to 18 but is not nationally representative of school-age children. The sample has too high a proportion of students from urban areas and from the southern United States and too low a proportion of racial/ethnic minority students. The sample is reflective of the national student body with respect to student's sex but not of parents' education.

VALIDITY. Evidence to support the construct validity of the GES-2 is based primarily on factor analysis results using the norming sample. The results in the test manual do not support a model of five distinct characteristics to giftedness. The empirical evidence supports the notion of a single construct because a dominant first factor accounts for nearly 65% of the variance in the item scores. This is the same criticism made of the original Gifted Evaluation Scale published in 1987 (Callahan, 1995; Traub, 1995). Although a four-factor solution was chosen, no justification is given as to why this is more meaningful than the one-factor solution. The four-factor solution is quite muddled with many items from different subscales often loading on two or more factors. Furthermore, reported correlations among the subscales are quite high with all of the intercorrelations of Intellectual, Creativity, and Specific Academic Aptitude above .90, and the correlations of Leadership Ability with these three subscores at .80 or higher.

One set of results from a concurrent validity study with 105 students is presented in the test manual. Students were rated using both the GES-2 and the Gifted and Talented Evaluation Scale (GATES) (Gilliam, Carpenter, & Christensen, 1996). Subscale scores from both instruments measuring the same construct had high correlations ranging from .74 to .86. However, correlations of scores from the two instruments that purported to assess different constructs were sometimes as high or higher. These results appear to support a unidimensional model of giftedness.

RELIABILITY. Test-retest reliability coefficients for a sample of 125 students rated twice 30 days apart are presented. For the six subscales, the reliability coefficients ranged from .86 to .93. In addition, interrater reliability values were computed using two raters for a sample of 304 students. These reliability coefficients for the six subscales ranged from .69 to .91. For both sets of reliability coefficients, the values appear to be adequate. Internal consistency reliability was calculated for each of the six subscales for the total

norming sample and for both sexes and five racial/ethnic groups (although two of the groups had 11 or fewer students). Most of the coefficient alpha values are quite high, typically between .94 and .96.

SUMMARY. Administration and scoring of the GES-2 is simple and straightforward and all of the items are understandable. The concept of using rating scale information based on teacher observations as a supplement to standardized tests for identifying gifted students is highly appealing. However, the GES-2 suffers from the same flaws as in the earlier edition. A norming sample that is more nationally representative would provide a more accurate basis for comparison. The use of five distinct subscales (plus an additional one for Motivation) on the GES-2 is not supported by the available empirical evidence. Given the extremely high correlations among at least three of the scales, there appears to be, at best, a single dominant construct of intellectual/academic aptitude with two secondary constructs of leadership and artistic abilities.

Although the GES-2 represents an improvement over the earlier edition, its use cannot be recommended until there is evidence to support the choice of its theoretical model or a more parsimonious model is adopted as the basis for this instrument's development.

REVIEWER'S REFERENCES

Henage, D. (1990). *The gifted intervention manual.* Columbia, MO: Hawthorne.

Seely, K. (1993). Giftedness in early childhood. In J. VanTassel-Baska (Ed.), *Excellence in educating gifted and talented learners* (pp. 67–81). Denver: Love Publishing Co.

Callahan, C. M. (1995). [Review of the Gifted Evaluation Scale]. In J. C. Conoley & J. C. Impara (Eds.), *The twelfth mental measurements yearbook* (pp. 415–416). Lincoln, NE: Buros Institute of Mental Measurements.

Traub, R. (1995). [Review of the Gifted Evaluation Scale]. In J. C. Conoley & J. C. Impara (Eds.), *The twelfth mental measurements yearbook* (pp. 416–418). Lincoln, NE: Buros Institute of Mental Measurements.

Gilliam, J. E., Carpenter, B. O., & Christensen, J. R. (1996). Gifted and talented evaluation scales. Austin, TX: PRO-Ed.

[157]

Graded Word Spelling Test, Second Edition.

Purpose: Designed to measure spelling achievement.
Population: Ages 6-0 to adults.
Publication Dates: 1977–1998.
Scores: Total words correct.
Administration: Group.
Price Data, 1999: £7.99 per test booklet/manual.
Time: (20–30) minutes.
Author: P. E. Vernon.
Publisher: Hodder & Stoughton Educational [England].
Cross References: See T5:1105 (1 reference); for a review by Carol E. Westby of an earlier edition, see 12:165 (3 references); see also T4:1056 (2 references).

Review of the Graded Word Spelling Test, Second Edition by DEBORAH L. BANDALOS, Associate Professor, Department of Educational Psychology, University of Nebraska—Lincoln, Lincoln, NE:

The Graded Word Spelling Test was originally published in Great Britain in 1977. The second edition, published in 1998, is essentially the same test with very minor revisions. The test is designed to be used with students aged 6 to 18 and consists of 80 words arranged in order of difficulty. Each word is read in the context of a sentence in order to avoid any confusion about the word that is to be spelled. The sentences to be used are specified in the manual and must be read as written in the manual to standardize administration procedures. Students are required to print each word on their test paper. Between 20 and 48 words are administered, depending on the age of the student. Younger children are given fewer words whereas older children are given relatively more.

An original pool of words was chosen from the Macmillan Spelling Series to include a wide range of difficulty levels. More difficult words were sampled randomly from a dictionary. The resulting 228 words were administered to a sample of 2,137 English students. Words that were found to be ambiguous, difficult to pronounce, or too abstruse were dropped, resulting in the current 80-word version of the test. The only differences between the first and second editions are seven minor changes in the sentences that accompany the words: All of the words are the same as in the first edition.

The manual accompanying the second edition states that the test yields "measures of attainment which are referenced to national norms and which can be used to assess and compare progress in spelling" (p. 3). Although this test would be useful for English or Canadian classroom teachers who want a quick assessment of the spelling abilities of their students, it is difficult to ascertain its utility for obtaining norm-referenced scores. The norms provided were based on convenience samples from England and Canada obtained in 1975. No new norm group was obtained for the second edition. The norm group consists of 3,313 English and 1,909 Canadian students. The English students were all from Northamptonshire whereas the Canadian sample was drawn from urban and rural areas in five unspecified provinces. No gender, ethnic, or other information is available about the sample. Thus the sample, although adequate in terms of size, is of questionable representativeness. This fact is acknowledged by the test's author, who nevertheless includes tables of age norms and "spelling quotients" derived from the percentile ranks of the norm group. The term "spelling quotient" is somewhat misleading as these scores are actually not quotients or ratios but are standardized scores with a mean of 100 and a standard deviation of 15.

Because of the unknown representativeness of the group on which they are based, the age norms and spelling quotients are of limited value for inferring how students' spelling abilities compare with others. They could, however, be useful for assessing the progress of individuals or groups of students across time.

The author reports split-half reliability coefficients over .9 for tests of 25 words at ages 9–10 and for tests of 40 words at ages 12–13. Although no further information is given regarding the groups of students from whom these coefficients were obtained, these levels of reliability are quite respectable and probably reflect, to some degree, the consistency obtained through using standardized procedures for administering the items. Careful instructions for administering the test are given in the manual and the importance of following these instructions is emphasized.

SUMMARY. No information on validity is reported, and there does not appear to have been any assessment of possible item bias. If the test were to be used to infer students' relative standings or levels of achievement in spelling, these omissions would be of serious concern. In particular, the possible inclusion of words that may not be familiar to all students is a serious concern.

[158]
Group Reading Test, Fourth Edition.

Purpose: Designed to measure "the reading of single words and of simple sentences."
Population: Ages 6:4 to 8:11 and less able children 8:0 to 11:11.
Publication Dates: 1968–1999.
Acronym: GRT.
Scores: Total score only.
Administration: Group.
Forms, 2: A, B.
Price Data, 1999: £5.99 per 20 Form A or Form B; £8.99 per manual ('99, 27 pages); £4.99 per template A or B; £9.99 per specimen set.
Time: (20) minutes.

Author: Dennis Young.
Publisher: Hodder & Stoughton Educational [England].
Cross References: For reviews by William R. Merz, Sr., and Diane J. Sawyer of an earlier edition, see 12:171 (1 reference); see also T4:1102 (4 references); for reviews by Patrick Groff and Douglas A. Pidgeon of the Second Edition, see 9:458 (1 reference); for a review by Ralph D. Dutch of the original edition, see 8:729.

Review of the Group Reading Test, Fourth Edition by GRETCHEN OWENS, Associate Professor of Child Study, St. Joseph's College, Patchogue, NY:

The Group Reading Test (GRT), developed for use in the British schools, is now in its fourth edition. Though the manual does not specify what changes have been made, the publisher's representative reports that it was updated mainly to reflect National Curriculum issues impacting English schools, and two items have been amended (e.g., "wireless" as a synonym for radio). The norms developed for the third edition have been retained in the fourth.

This brief measure is designed for administration by a general education classroom teacher to all his or her students during a single session. The author describes it as "suitable for children in the last term of Year 2, in Year 3 (especially the first term), and with older below-average juniors" (manual, p. 1), which translates in the U.S. to the end of first and the beginning of second grade, as well as older children who are reading at a first- or second-grade level.

For the first activity, Pictures, the child must look at each of 15 line drawings and circle the associated label from among a selection of three to five words. The 30 items in the Sentences section are all short (stems of two to six words followed by six options) so that the entire item appears on the same line. This makes for a compressed format that may be perceptually difficult for some children.

Detailed directions for group administration are provided, and hand scoring is relatively straightforward. (However, the instruction to put the template over the answer sheet and mark a "cross" on the item number of any error is awkward, as the template must be picked up each time to make the mark.) Raw scores are converted to standard scores, percentiles, and reading ages. Surprisingly, there is no table of grade equivalents, which teachers might use to help them arrive at tentative reading place-ments or to select trade books at the appropriate level. The two norms tables are broken down by grade level, each of which then provides quotients based on the child's age. The first table is for "Years 2 and 3," the second for "Year 4 and older juniors" (manual, pp. 10–11). It is unclear why first- and second-graders are lumped into the same comparison group, as their amount of exposure to reading differs. Both tables are inexplicably truncated, but the second one more so, with no way to look up raw scores under 11 or over 42, and no quotients below 70 or over 88 listed for those in the oldest group.

Standardization was done using 4 years' worth of score distributions from 2,585 children attending the same sample of schools used to norm the author's other tests. Though information about correspondence with census data may appear in the manuals of these other tests, the GRT manual contains nothing whatever about the students' race or ethnicity, socioeconomic level, residence (urban, rural), geographic region, or the numbers of students at each grade/age level. The user who tries to interpret scores from the GRT is comparing his or her students' results to those of an unspecified group of school children attending "junior and infant schools" (manual, p. 19) in an unknown part of England.

Minimal evidence is presented for content validity. The author asserts that the content was "determined by empirical investigation of what children of 7 to 9 years can do" (p. 23), but gives no further information regarding this investigation, the rationale for why he selected the specific test items he did, nor any indication of the extent to which they match up with standard reading curricula at this level. A total of 45 items covering 2 years of reading instruction is clearly insufficient to achieve high levels of content validity. In addition, the GRT presents a strong cultural component that may affect its validity for American users. Many of the vocabulary items are less familiar to North American children than to those who live in the U.K. For example, an American child who sees a picture of a faucet is likely to have difficulty associating it with the word "tap," and most primary-level children in America will not automatically know that "chips" are what one has with one's fish.

Concurrent and predictive validity evidence are acceptable, but no information on construct validity appears. The author acknowledges that the correlation of .73 with group intelligence test scores suggests that general verbal abilities may account for much of the association between the GRT and the other reading tests. Although he constructed the sentence items "to minimise demands on vocabulary, general knowledge, and intelligence" (manual, p. 17), nearly half the items in the Sentences portion require the child to provide a synonym. Because many of the test items and the response options are ones to which the average second-grader has not yet been exposed (e.g., "Cunning means—cat-fish cavalry cereal champion crafty cave"), poor scores on the test are just as likely to reflect lack of exposure as any difficulty with decoding skills or processing of content.

Reliability data are presented in the form of the standard error of measurement (rather than the more commonly reported reliability coefficients). Granting this substitution, the magnitude of the *SEM* and the reported levels of reliability for alternate forms and test-retest data are generally acceptable. Data on internal consistency are absent.

SUMMARY. The author suggests that the GRT can be used for screening, program evaluation, and progress evaluation, but not for diagnosis or instructional planning. However, with the increasing amount of ongoing, large-scale standardized testing being mandated in American schools, there seems to be little need in most classrooms for teachers to add yet another screening test. Further, classroom teachers in the primary grades today have better assessment methods, such as miscue analysis and reading records, that should be a regular part of their classroom routine and, as such, will provide an ecologically valid measure of reading skill in a context that does not heighten children's anxiety. Based on their ongoing classroom assessments, by the end of first grade teachers are aware of which students are experiencing difficulty, and for these students time is better spent on an individualized diagnostic test that will provide information regarding the specific skills to target for instruction. Given the psychometric and cultural limitations of the GRT that are cited above and the advantages of available alternative assessment methods, its use cannot be recommended at this time.

Review of the Group Reading Test, Fourth Edition by JOHN W. YOUNG, Associate Professor of Educational Statistics and Measurement, Rutgers University, New Brunswick, NJ:

The Group Reading Test, Fourth Edition (GRT-4) is a 45-item group-administered test designed to measure early and intermediate literacy skills based on the reading of single words and simple sentences. Primarily intended for use in the United Kingdom, the GRT-4 is best suited for children between the ages of 6 and 9 although it can be used with below-average readers up to age 12. The GRT-4 has two forms with scoring templates, A and B, each with 15 picture identification items (with a time limit of 4 minutes) and 30 sentence completion items (with a time limit of 9 minutes). An accompanying teacher's manual of 26 pages is available. In this manual, no information was provided regarding the development of the GRT-4 in relation to any current reading or literacy theories or models. The GRT-4 is described as a "comprehension test overlapping with the simpler items in passage comprehension tests" (manual, p. 4).

STANDARDIZATION. The norms for the GRT-4 were constructed to be compatible with the author's other tests for primary children (see Young, 1989, 1992, 1996, 1998a, 1998b). The norming sample was drawn from a nationally representative group of primary schools although it is unclear whether the national norms are for England only or for all of the countries of the United Kingdom. The norming sample consisted of 2,585 students (1,272 boys and 1,313 girls); no information as given on the age distribution in the sample. Raw scores are converted to standard scores (mean of 100, standard deviation of 15) for each 2-month age interval.

VALIDITY. The evidentiary basis for the validity of the GRT-4 is quite weak. Two types of information are presented regarding the validity: (a) a persuasive argument on the content validity of the GRT-4, and (b) empirical studies on the criterion-related validity of the GRT-4. With respect to content validity, the teacher's manual elaborates on this point with the following: "graded word reading-type tests are valid because they test what progress has been made in the basic skills of decoding" (manual, p. 21). In addition, "a valid reading test depends on what the children are being asked to do, and whether this is appropriate to the stage of development" (manual, p. 21). No reference to a particular literacy theory, model, or philosophy is given by the author. Furthermore, there do not appear to have been any attempts made to examine content validity through the use of expert judgments by content matter specialists.

With respect to criterion-related validity, a concurrent validity study was conducted using a sample of 80 students who were tested using the GRT-4, four other reading tests, and the Non-Reading Intelligence Tests (Young, 1989). In addition, teacher ratings of the students were obtained. Correlations between scores on the GRT-4 and those from other reading tests are moderate to high but no conclusions can be drawn from a single small study with minimal information on the students or on the nature of the other tests. Predictive validity results are given for two samples of students (*N*s of 130 and 230) tested using the GRT-4 and another reading test 3 years later. Again, moderate to high correlations were reported but note that correlations of a similar magnitude might have been found if the latter test was a measure of general intelligence or of academic aptitude.

RELIABILITY. Information on the parallel forms reliability of the GRT-4 is based on a sample of 100 children given both forms with a reported reliability coefficient of .945. Test-retest reliability is given in terms of differences between test and retest scores. For a sample of 886 students, the mean difference was 2.37 raw score points and 77% of students had scores no more than 3 points apart. However, note that the retest occurred immediately after the initial test so that a carryover effect, especially for older children, was likely to be a confounding factor.

SUMMARY. For several reasons, the GRT-4 cannot be recommended for use as a measure of reading ability for students in U.S. schools. The lack of a solid theoretical foundation in terms of the test's development is the principle weakness. The author does not make clear how literacy is defined and how the test items attempt to measure it. Some of the items require knowledge of objects or ideas that are incidental to measuring literacy, which degrades the test's construct validity. In addition, given that the GRT-4 is intended for use in English schools and was normed on English school children, these differences are sufficient to be of concern in adapting the test for use with American school children. A reference to fish and chips in one of the items will not be familiar to all students. Finally, the validity evidence in support of the GRT-4 is quite limited. No information regarding item development, pilot testing, or the

use of curriculum experts is available in the teacher's manual, which yields the impression that the GRT-4 has not been subjected to rigorous and effective scrutiny.

REVIEWER'S REFERENCES

Young, D. (1989). Non-Reading Intelligence Tests, Levels 1–3. London: Hodder & Stoughton.
Young, D. (1992). Cloze Reading Tests (2nd ed.). London: Hodder & Stoughton.
Young, D. (1996). Group Mathematics Test (3rd ed.). London, Hodder & Stoughton.
Young, D. (1998a). Parallel Spelling Tests (2nd ed.). London: Hodder & Stoughton.
Young, D. (1998b). SPAR Spelling & Reading Tests (3rd ed.). London: Hodder & Stoughton.

[159]
Hammill Multiability Achievement Test.

Purpose: Designed as a "measure of school achievement."
Population: Ages 7-0 to 17-11.
Publication Date: 1998.
Acronym: HAMAT.
Scores, 5: Reading, Writing, Arithmetic, Facts, General Achievement Quotient.
Administration: Individual.
Forms, 2: A, B.
Price Data, 1999: $184 per complete kit including manual (116 pages), 25 each Form A and Form B response booklets, and 25 each Form A and Form B record forms.
Time: (30–60) minutes.
Authors: Donald D. Hammill, Wayne P. Hresko, Jerome J. Ammer, Mary E. Cronin, and Sally S. Quinby.
Publisher: PRO-ED.

Review of the Hammill Multiability Achievement Test by JEFFREY A. JENKINS, Assistant Professor, Roger Williams University, Bristol, RI:

The Hammill Multiability Achievement Test (HAMAT) is a revised version of PRO-ED's Quick-Score Achievement Test. As an individually administered measure of student achievement, the HAMAT claims five specific uses: (a) identifying students who are significantly above or below their peers in academic achievement; (b) determining student strengths and weaknesses among basic academic abilities; (c) performing periodic reevaluations of achievement; (d) conducting research on student achievement; and (e) screening students. It seeks to measure student achievement in those areas comprising the curriculum in schools while avoiding test bias in an easy-to-administer-and-score format. The HAMAT achieves these goals and its utility in each of the above areas is warranted.

The HAMAT was designed to serve as a quick measure of student achievement in four areas: Reading (comprehension and word knowledge), Writing (spelling, punctuation, capitalization), Arithmetic (calculation), and Facts. The latter area involves factual questions relating to science, social studies, health, and language arts. Two forms, A and B, may be used. The HAMAT is intended for use with students from ages 7-0 to 17-11. It is not designed to be used diagnostically to create individualized instructional plans.

Item formats on the HAMAT vary for each of the four areas measured, which comprise subscales for the test. For Reading, a student is given a series of 17 short paragraphs, ordered by difficulty. Within each paragraph, the student must make word choices to correctly complete each of the three sentences. For example, "The boy has a bat. He holds it with his [dogs head hands dish]. He likes to hit [shoes birds shows balls] with the bat. He is [honey happy fish fly] when he plays." For Writing, the test administrator dictates 27 sentences that a student must write on lines provided in the test booklet (e.g., "She can row the boat"; "Ben, tell me about electricity"). The Arithmetic items range from single-digit addition and subtraction to fractions and decimals (e.g., "8 - ___ = 6; "5% of 32.15 = ___"). Finally, the Facts subtest consists of 22 factual questions (e.g., "Name the four seasons;" "What is the longest river on earth?"). Items from each subscale are well drafted and range appropriately in difficulty across the ages for which the HAMAT is designed. The items are clearly presented in a well-organized Response Booklet in which students can record their answers.

Administration of the test is untimed, but the publisher estimates 30 minutes to one hour of testing time. Given the uses of the HAMAT discussed above, it is designed to be individually administered. The Profile/Examiner Record Form organizes the administration instructions for each subscale, allows scoring of each item, and provides a simple method for calculating and recording subscale and total scores in terms of raw scores, grade equivalents, percentiles, and standard scores.

Along with the Profile/Examiner Record Form, the examiner's manual allows the test user to properly interpret HAMAT results, including a helpful explanation of the use of discrepancy analysis to examine differences between HAMAT subscales or between the HAMAT and various tests of intelligence. The manual also gives useful normative information based on a sample of 1,672 students from five states in representative geographic regions of the U.S. The norms are up-to-date, having been collected in 1996 and 1997. In general, the examiner's manual is an excellent resource for the test user, with chapters relating to administration, scoring, interpretation, norms, and technical characteristics of the HAMAT. Reliability of the HAMAT was estimated using internal consistency, parallel forms, and test-retest methods. Coefficient alpha ranged from .87 to .93 for both forms of the subscales, and yielded .96 and .95 on the composite score for Forms A and B, respectively. For the parallel forms and test6-retest estimates (with a 2-week interval) reliability was found to exceed .80 with many subscale estimates for various ages exceeding .90. Based on the estimates presented, reliability of scores from the HAMAT is outstanding given the relatively small number of items, compared to the generally high reliability of most lengthy achievement batteries.

The HAMAT's validity was examined in terms its content validity, criterion-related validity, and construct validity, as is appropriate for a test of achievement. To demonstrate content validity, the publisher offered a clear rationale for the item formats and subject matter covered by each subscale, compared the areas covered by the HAMAT to other achievement tests, and performed quantitative item analyses (item discrimination, difficulty, bias). The extensive discussion of these methods along with the evidence presented in the examiner's manual supports the content validity of the HAMAT in the areas it is designed to measure.

Likewise, criterion-related construct validity of the HAMAT is supported by fairly strong evidence for a newly constructed instrument. The correlation between composite scores on the HAMAT and the subscales of the Comprehensive Scales of Student Abilities ranged from .49 to .71, and the HAMAT's correlation with the Metropolitan Achievement Tests (7th Ed.) resulted in estimates from .69 to .80. Such validity coefficients are clearly adequate for a measure of this type. With respect to construct validation, the publisher adopted a multifaceted approach by examining various types of evidence. Of these, perhaps most significant is the factor analysis performed on the four subscales that resulted in the finding of a single general factor, overall achievement. Such a result is expected of an achievement measure.

SUMMARY. The HAMAT was developed using best test design and can be used for the individual assessment of achievement with confidence. It compares favorably with the widely used Woodcock-Johnson Psycho-Educational Battery—Revised (T5:2901), and offers ease of administration and scoring. The wealth of information that may be obtained from the HAMAT justifies its recommended uses in the individual assessment of student achievement.

Review of the Hammill Multiability Achievement Test by ELEANOR E. SANFORD, Director of Technical Research, MetaMetrics, Inc., Durham, NC:

The Hammill Multiability Achievement Test (HAMAT) is an individually administered achievement test designed to assess basic skills in reading, writing, and mathematics; general factual knowledge; and general achievement. The test is designed for use with students aged 7-0 (years-months) to 17-11. The test is not timed and is easy to administer and score. Results are provided in terms of scale scores, percentiles, age-equivalents, and grade-equivalents.

DEVELOPMENT. Each of the subtests—Reading, Writing, Arithmetic, and Facts—was developed according to a theoretical framework. Numerous basal series, study guides, textbooks, and assessment program specifications were consulted to determine the basic skills in each of the areas. The items on each form of the test are sequenced according to the grade level of the content. The factual knowledge items are based on basic facts taught in school.

The HAMAT was developed using a sample of 1,672 students in Grades 1 through 12 that was representative of the United States school-age population. Although the sample as a whole is representative, it is small when providing normative information (percentiles) for ages 7-0 to 17-11 (approximately 140 students per grade). The data were calculated at 6-month intervals and then converted to normalized standard scores at each interval. The resulting data across age levels were smoothed somewhat to maintain monotonically increasing growth curves. Because of the small sample size, scores could only be calculated at 6-month intervals and the remaining scores were derived through interpolation.

There are two forms of the HAMAT, A and B, but no item-level information is provided to show that the forms are equivalent in content or difficulty. Although for the overall sample, the Reading, Writing, and Arithmetic subtests give roughly the same median percentage of correct items (Reading, A = .78 and B = .82; Writing, A = .57 and B = .58; and Arithmetic, A = .58 and B = .61), the median difficulties for Factual Knowledge for the whole sample are markedly different (A = .64 and B = .53). At various ages the median correlations between the two forms are different (especially Factual Knowledge at most age levels). In addition, the median percent difficulties by age levels are not monotonically increasing (Reading). Because these median percent difficulties are only computed on items with variance, information needs to be provided to show that the abilities assessed do increase monotonically.

RELIABILITY. Reliability was calculated using coefficient alpha and test-retest indices. Coefficient alpha estimates are typically in the upper 80s and 90s; some of the coefficients at the elementary level (especially Factual Knowledge) are in the low 80s and 70s. Test-retest reliability estimates range from the mid-70s to the mid-90s over a 2-week interval. Standard errors of measurement (*SEM*) are only provided for the mean score.

The reliability of the scoring process was examined by having a sample of completed protocols for 32 high school students (15–17 years old) evaluated by two raters. Although the correlations between the ratings are high (mid- to upper-90s), no protocols from elementary-level students were examined. Scoring elementary-level protocols may be more problematic than scoring high-school-level protocols.

VALIDITY. The HAMAT scores correlate consistently with scores from other measures (both at the total score level and the subscore level) such as the Metropolitan Achievement Tests (MAT7) and the Comprehensive Scales of Student Abilities (CSSA). When the HAMAT subtests are correlated with age, the correlations are good for ages 7-0 to 12-11 (Reading, $r = .10–.15$; Arithmetic, $r = .14–.18$; and Factual Knowledge, $r = .19–.20$).

The HAMAT manual states that the General Achievement Quotient "is the best indicator of a student's over all mastery of school-taught subject matter. It is also the best single predictor of future school achievement, including school grades, vocational education success, graduation, and so forth" (p. 21). No information is provided to support the use of the HAMAT.

SUMMARY. The HAMAT is a well-developed test for assessing the level of basic skills in students ages 7-0 to 12-11 "to identify children and youths who are significantly below or above their peers in academic achievement" (manual, p. 5). The authors are very clear to state that the HAMAT "should not be used as the basis for planning instructional interventions for individual students" (manual, p. 5). As an informal assessment to provide global indications of strengths and weaknesses among the basic skill areas it is very good—it does what it was designed to do.

Validity and reliability information provided supports the uses of the test, especially to help determine strengths and weaknesses among basic academic achievement abilities. The authors have provided extensive discussions on discrepancy analyses, bias in testing, and the interpretation of scores, including cautions and examples of misinterpretations (such as can happen with grade equivalents).

[160]
Hammill Multiability Intelligence Test.

Purpose: Designed to "identify those children and adolescents who, as a result of their mental abilities, are likely to experience success or failure in school."
Population: Ages 6-0 to 17-0.
Publication Date: 1998.
Acronym: HAMIT.
Scores: 8 subtest scores: Word Opposites, Design Sequences, Sentence Imitation, Design Reproduction, Basic Information, Symbolic Relations, Word Sequences, Story Sequences; and 3 composite scores: General Intelligence Quotient, Verbal Intelligence Quotient, Nonverbal Intelligence Quotient.
Administration: Individual.
Price Data, 1999: $284 per complete kit including examiner's manual (213 pages), 2 picture books, 25 profile/examiner record forms, 25 response sheets, story sequence tiles, and design sequence cubes; $69 per examiner's manual; $89 per Picture Book 1; $29 per Picture Book 2; $44 per 25 profile/examiner record forms; $14 per 25 response sheets; $20 per set of story sequence tiles; $29 per design sequence cubes.
Time: (30–90) minutes.
Comments: Designed as a special use version of the Detroit Tests of Learning Aptitude (113); eight subtests of the HAMIT are identical to eight subtests of the DTLA-4.
Authors: Donald D. Hammill, Brian R. Bryant, and Nils A. Pearson.
Publisher: PRO-ED.

Cross References: For information and reviews of the Detroit Tests of Learning Aptitude, Fourth Edition, see 113.
[Editor's Note: The publisher advised in September 2000 that this test is now out of print.]

Review of the Hammill Multiability Intelligence Test by WILLIAM STEVE LANG, Associate Professor of Educational Measurement and Research, Department of Educational Measurement and Research, University of South Florida, St. Petersburg, FL:

The Hammill Multiability Intelligence Test (HAMIT) is a short form of the widely used and well-known Detroit Tests of Learning Aptitude—Fourth Edition (DTLA-4; 113). As such, this review does not repeat the comments and discussions of previous reviews of various version of the DTLA except to reiterate the most important criticisms. The HAMIT reports to give a "sound estimate of general intelligence" (manual, p. xiii) for diagnostic purposes, intellectual reevaluation, or research. It would be used with school-age (ages 6 to 17) persons. The test returns these composites from the eight subtests: a General Intelligence Composite, a Verbal Intelligence Composite, and a Nonverbal Intelligence Composite. Most users of the HAMIT, like the DTLA, should be examiners with experience and education in intelligence testing.

The HAMIT is simply a subset of 8 of the 10 subtests of the DTLA-4. All of the manual statistics are based on the same items. In fact, the HAMIT manual states, "the normative, reliability, ability, and validity data for the eight subtests are also identical ... because the HAMIT and the DTLA-3, as well as the DTLA-4, are composed of the same items" (manual, p. 15). Essentially, this is not so much a new instrument, but a repackaging of a shortened form of the DTLA.

Overall reliability of scores from the HAMIT seems good with regard to test-retest, internal consistency, and interscorer differences. The manual is confusing though, as it sometimes clearly states the sample size and demographics of the study, but at other times leaves the reader with little or no information. One has to refer to a previous chapter's description of the normative sample for Table 8.1, read the text to realize that Table 8.4 refers to a different sample with little description of subjects, and again refer to a third study for Table 8.5 where practically no description of subjects is given.

One criticism of previous versions of the DTLA is the length of administration time (up to 2.5 hours). The manual estimates the HAMIT would usually take 50 minutes to 1.5 hours. Another criticism of earlier versions of the DTLA (in previous *Mental Measurements Yearbooks*) has been a lack of construct validity. It seems that shortening the tests by removing two subtests as a whole may address one problem (lengthy administration times), but surely would weaken whatever theoretical reason one had for inclusion of those subtests originally. Even though the HAMIT makes the same historical arguments for the existence of certain subtests as the DTLA, it makes a much weaker argument for the specific form or choice of certain items as representative of those subtests. The HAMIT includes an argument that shortened versions of a test are sometimes appropriate, but fails to discuss effectively the reasons the specific eight subtests of the DTLA were chosen for inclusion and the two specific subtests removed were unnecessary.

The HAMIT gives essentially the same arguments for item inclusion and absence of bias as previously provided in the DTLA. These methods are based on classical techniques to determine item difficulty and differential item functioning. The HAMIT references Camilli and Shepard (1994) with regard to the need for detection of item bias, but then appears to use a classical method of detecting bias that the same publication recommends should be no longer used (Delta plot). In short, the HAMIT would benefit from an item response theory method of item analysis with regard to both the item difficulties and elimination of bias. This would greatly improve the defense of the choice of items, ordering the difficulty of the items, and arguments for lack of bias.

Finally, the HAMIT provides a number of criterion-related coefficients using the original DTLA, and a number of current, widely used measures of achievement and ability. Most of the subtest relationships with the DTLA were positive and ranged from .31 to .79. Full scale intelligence relationships ranged from .70 to .92. Even though this may mean that the HAMIT is an alternative, there is no obvious reason that the HAMIT has any benefit over the Wechsler Intelligence Scale for Children, Third Edition (T5:2862), the Kaufman Assessment Battery for Children (T5:1379), or the Test of Nonverbal

Intelligence, Second Edition (393). In fact, with the dated item analysis techniques used by the HAMIT, one of the other instruments in common use would provide more confidence.

SUMMARY. In conclusion, those needing an intelligence measure for placement or diagnosis would be advised to use the Wechsler Intelligence Scale for Children, Third Edition (T5:2862) unless one has previous reason or experience that the DTLA-4 is appropriate. In that case, there is no benefit of the HAMIT over the DTLA-4.

REVIEWER'S REFERENCE

Camilli, G., & Shepard, L. A. (1994). *Methods for identifying biased test items.* Thousand Oaks, CA: Sage Publications, Inc.

Review of the Hammill Multiability Intelligence Test by DAVID L. WODRICH, Director of Psychological Assessment Services, Phoenix Children's Hospital, Phoenix, AZ, and MARK E. SWERDLIK, Professor of Psychology, Illinois State University, Normal, IL:

The Hammill Multiability Intelligence Test (HAMIT) derives from the Detroit Tests of Learning Aptitude (DTLA; 113). The DTLA has undergone three revisions and improvements, culminating in the DTLA-4 (1998). The HAMIT comprises eight subtests "borrowed intact" from the DTLA-4. To support use of the HAMIT, its manual contains validity data on the DTLA-3 and DTLA-4 as the items for these tests are the same as those for the HAMITs. Although the HAMIT is identified as an abbreviation of the DTLA-4, no rationale for selecting these eight DTLA subtests, nor for eliminating only two others, is provided.

GENERAL DESCRIPTION. The HAMIT's eight individually administered subtests are suitable for children ages 6 to 17 years. They produce a verbal intelligence quotient, derived from Word Opposites, Sentence Imitation, Basic Information, and Word Sequences subtests, a nonverbal intelligence quotient, derived from Design Sequences, Design Reproduction, Symbolic Relations, and Story Sequences subtests, as well as an aggregate general intelligence quotient. IQ scores have a mean of 100 and standard deviation of 15; scale scores have means of 10 and standard deviations of 3. Percentiles and age equivalents are also reported. The HAMIT is designed to measure general intelligence in relation to issues of giftedness and mental retardation, learning disabilities (viz., ability-achievement discrepancy), routine special education reevaluations, and as a research variable.

TEST MATERIALS AND MANUAL. Material consists of spiral-bound picture books, sheets for drawing designs, cubes for sequencing, and small chips for denoting number sequences. Visual stimuli seem clear, although sometimes rather small. The materials are quite compact, portable, and appear durable and well constructed.

The test manual is organized and written well with chapters devoted to normative information, reliability, validity, controlling bias, and test interpretation. Also addressed are important issues such as theoretical models of intelligence and assessment of children from minority groups. Some of the material seems beyond the grasp of those without extensive measurement background and in-depth training in mental testing (the manual enumerates psychologists, diagnosticians, special educators, speech-language pathologists, and "others who are interested in examining the psychological constitution of examinees" [manual, p. 15] as test users). Also, the manual, although quite correctly championing the use of a regression approach for determining ability/achievement discrepancies, may inadvertently encourage use of other approaches because it lacks the necessary regression-based tables unless the HAMIT and the Hammill Multiability Achievement Test (HAMAT; 159; a related achievement test) are used. Tables are available for comparing the HAMIT with other achievement tests using a simple difference method, but test users would have to perform calculations using a formula to apply a regression approach to these other achievement measures.

STANDARDIZATION. The HAMIT used a large (1,350) standardization sample that matched census figures on geographic region, gender, race, urban vs. rural residency, ethnicity, family income, and parents' educational attainment. Additional commendable steps, such as matching the sample for ethnicity at each age, were also taken. Unfortunately, the HAMIT's sample is a mixture of cases collected in 1989–1990 and 1996–1997.

RELIABILITY. The manual cites adequate or better internal and test-retest reliability coefficients for composite (viz., IQ) scores, such as test-retest (administration interval = 1 week) values of .96, .91, and .96 for Verbal, Nonverbal, and General (composite) IQs. Test-retest values for two of the nonverbal subtests, Design Sequences and Story Sequences, of .71 and .76, respectively, raise

questions about the interpretability of these individual scales. The authors should be credited for reporting supplemental information such as interscorer reliability data (which are also apparently quite adequate).

VALIDITY. The authors carefully detail the need for content-descriptive, criterion-predictive, and construct validity and provide evidence of each. Nonetheless, some arguments for validity seem hollow. For example, noting that other ability tests (each of which is enumerated) include vocabulary subtests, the authors justify inclusion of the HAMIT's Word Opposites subtest because it, too, measures vocabulary. Inspection of the Word Opposites items, however, suggests that verbal relations and conceptual ability would also be tapped by this "vocabulary test."

Regarding criterion validity, the HAMIT seems to perform about as well as other general ability measures. Correlations with other ability (IQ) tests and with achievement tests, both concurrently and prospectively administered, are provided. Coefficients of validity are generally adequate with occasional disappointing values, such as a HAMIT nonverbal IQ/WISC-III performance IQ correlation (apparently concurrently administered) of only .54. Favorably, the manual contains intercorrelations of the HAMIT with a stunning array of ability (seven) and achievement (six) measures.

Factor analysis data concern the verbal/nonverbal dichotomy only, for which there is some support. Although arguing for a link between contemporary theories and intelligence measures, the manual delivers little here. The authors provide a figure with each HAMIT subtest placed (dichotomously) according each of several ability models (e.g., fluid/crystallized according to Cattell & Horn; simultaneous/successive according to Das). Unfortunately, how these categorical assignments were made and the empirical justification for their placement is unclear.

Despite laudatory attempts to tackle the issue of bias head-on (e.g., use of inclusive normative sampling, examining reliability and validity data for target groups), the HAMIT manual appears to overstate the capability to minimize group bias. For example, the HAMIT manual provides evidence of diminished black/white group differences (general IQ 102 versus 99) but not for European-American and Hispanic-American groups (general IQ 102 versus 95), yet it makes broad proclamations of lack of bias, in part, because all ethnic groups and genders are "within the normal range" (manual, p. 123). Pronouncements about unbiased assessment and expectations for minimal group differences seem particularly misplaced given the HAMIT's traditional composition and its own manual's confirmation of a heritage of measuring *g* that extends from Spearman, through Wechsler, to the HAMIT.

CONCLUSIONS. Regardless of its many appealing features, the HAMIT's role in contemporary assessment of intellectual ability is decidedly unclear. The test appears to be too long for a screening instrument. If one were seeking a traditional IQ measure, then there is little reason to select the HAMIT over the entrenched WISC-III (T5:2862). If one were seeking a cutting-edge instrument attuned to conceptual advances in mental abilities and compatible with recent research, then tests such as the Woodcock-Johnson Psycho-Educational Battery (T5:2901), Cognitive Assessment System (109), or Kaufman Intelligence Test for Adolescents and Adults would be preferable.

[161]
The Hand Test [Revised].

Purpose: Designed as "a diagnostic technique that uses pictures of hands as the projective medium."
Population: Ages 5 and older.
Publication Dates: 1959–1991.
Scores, 41: 24 quantitative scores: Interpersonal (Affection, Dependence, Communication, Exhibition, Direction, Aggression, Total), Environmental (Acquisition, Active, Passive, Total), Maladjustive (Tension, Crippled, Fear, Total), Withdrawal (Description, Bizarre, Failure, Total), Experience Ratio, Acting Out Ratio, Pathological, Average Initial Response Time, High Minus Low Score, plus 17 qualitative scores: Ambivalent, Automatic Phrase, Cylindrical, Denial, Emotion, Gross, Hiding, Immature, Inanimate, Movement, Oral, Perplexity, Sensual, Sexual, Original, Repetition.
Administration: Individual.
Price Data, 1999: $130 per complete kit including manual ('83, 94 pages), manual supplement: Interpreting Child and Adolescent Responses ('91, 41 pages), 25 scoring booklets, and 1 set of picture cards; $16.50 per 25 scoring booklets; $29.50 per set of picture cards; $48 per manual; $44.50 per manual supplement: Interpreting Child and Adolescent Responses.
Time: (10) minutes.
Author: Edwin E. Wagner.
Publisher: Western Psychological Services.

Cross References: See T5:1169 (6 references) and T4:1121 (17 references); for a review by Marcia B. Shaffer of an earlier edition, see 10:134 (5 references); see also 9:464 (16 references), T3:1053 (21 references), 8:575 (29 references), T2:1470 (15 references), and P:438 (12 references); for a review by Goldine C. Gleser and an excerpted review by Irving R. Stone of an earlier edition, see 6:216 (6 references).

Review of The Hand Test [Revised] by COLIN COOPER, Senior Lecturer, School of Psychology, The Queen's University, Belfast, United Kingdom:

The Hand Test is a projective technique in which participants are shown line drawings of single hands, and are invited to describe what each is doing. There are nine small cards in the series, together with a blank card that encourages the participant to describe the activity of an imaginary hand. Both left and right hands are included in the series. The test is quick to administer and score. Because it is enjoyable to take and requires only verbal responses, it can be given to both adults and children. There are two manuals, one of which describes how the test may be used to assess adult personality and behavior; the other focuses on the responses of children and adolescents. These manuals also contain norms and reliability and validity data.

This test is interesting because "the instrument mirrors the prototypical actions which are close to the surface and hence apt to be expressed behaviorally" (manual, p. vi). Indeed, the test seems free of the mysticism that sometimes surrounds projective techniques. The guiding assumption seems to be that if (for example) a person often shows affection to others, enjoys relaxing, or has strong negative emotions, then such tendencies will be reflected in their interpretation of The Hand Test cards. Two types of scores are derived from the participants' responses. First, quantitative measures are scored by assigning each person's response(s) to each card into 1 of 15 categories. These 15 categories fall into four groups: Interpersonal, Environmental, Maladjustive, and Withdrawal Activities. It seems that the categories were grouped on theoretical, rather than empirical, grounds. Thus, it is difficult to be certain that there are indeed four groups of categories (factors) underlying the responses. Second, addition to these content-based measures, 17 other variables (such as the time taken to respond to a card, the use of clichés, movement, sexual and original responses) may be coded. These seem to echo some aspects of the Rorschach scoring procedure, but, according to the author, "quantitative scores are concerned with methods of relating to the interpersonal or impersonal environment whereas the qualitative scores focus more on personal tendencies and the motivation behind these action tendencies" (manual, p. 24). This review follows the manual, and places most stress on the quantitative responses.

As with the Rorschach, participants are free to rotate the cards before responding. For example, an open palm with the fingers together but the thumb apart might make one think of a traffic policeman's "stop" command in one orientation, yet an invitation to shake hands when rotated. It seems odd that participants are allowed to choose to which of these very different images they wish to respond, and there seems to be no compelling rationale for allowing them to do so. When respondents' responses can be categorized in several different ways (e.g., "breaking down a door with a karate chop" could be scored as either "aggressive" [part of the Interpersonal group] or "active" [Environmental group]) the scorer is directed to "choose the category that seems to most appropriately express the psychological intent of the response" (manual, p. 11).

Norms are provided based on 100 individuals, half being midwestern university students and the remainder "individuals who had appeared at a clinic seeking vocational or other non-psychiatric counselling" (manual, p. 17). It is not obvious that this sample is representative of any population. It is also modest in size. The table of norms shows only the mean, standard deviation, and the 7th, 50th, 84th, and 94th centiles for each category and group, rather than full centile scores. The scores are heavily skewed to the right, with 8 of the 15 categories having a median (as well as a minimum) score of zero, and narrow ranges.

Interrater reliability estimates appear impressive. However, the only study that reports kappa coefficients is an unpublished conference paper. Corrected split-half reliability of the four groups of scores are encouragingly high (although based on a very diverse clinical sample). The test-retest reliability is impressive over short time periods, falling to a more modest level (.37 to .60) for periods of 1–10 years. However, samples that are small and/or unusual in composition yield much of the data. There is also an impressive range of validity information, much of it relating scores to

aggression. Unfortunately (a) studies sometimes use unconventional levels to assume statistical significance (e.g., .1 instead of .05); (b) none ensure that the family-wise alpha is maintained at .05; (c) it is not always clear why particular studies (such as those reporting that Hand Test scores discriminate between "good" versus "poor" workers with learning difficulties or "paid and unpaid volunteers") should be regarded as important evidence for the validity of the technique; and (d) multivariate techniques are occasionally performed on very small samples.

Chapter 4 of the manual presents Hand Test data from 11 diagnostic groups (alcoholic, schizophrenic, learning-disabled, etc.) and presents tables of norms from each of these groups, together with suggestions for using the test diagnostically. However, no statistical tests are performed to determine whether the patterns of response from any of the clinical groups differ in any way from those of the normative group. This may be because of the partially ipsatized nature of the test. Because each response is assigned to one scoring category, an individual could not show extreme scores on all categories. Thus, all the categories (and groups) will tend to be negatively correlated, which creates difficulties when relating test scores to other variables. The problem is not as bad for the Hand Test as for some other measures (as each person can produce more than one response to a card), but it will affect interpretation and analysis of scores on the test.

SUMMARY. The Hand Test is a conceptually simple tool that may be useful in identifying individuals who behave aggressively. Its strengths are its speed and ease of administration and scoring, and its apparent high reliability. Less impressive are its theoretical rationale, the small and atypical normative group, the lack of statistical tests to support the claim that clinical groups differ in their responses to the test, and the statistical problems posed by its partly ipsatized nature. Some aspects of the test (such as allowing respondents to rotate cards or make several responses) could perhaps have been incorporated better into the scoring system. The test merits more nonclinical research.

Review of The Hand Test [Revised] by SUSANA URBINA, Professor of Psychology, University of North Florida, Jacksonville, FL:

The Hand Test is deceptively simple at first glance. The test materials consist of a packet of 10 small picture cards, 9 of which depict line drawings of a human hand in different positions and 1 of which is blank. A four-page scoring booklet is available from the publisher, but not essential. Administration is easy. Examinees are shown the stimulus cards, one at a time, and asked to tell "what it looks like the hands might be doing" (Wagner, 1983, p. 6). Test-takers are free to give as many or as few responses as they wish to each card. Each response is scored for only one of the quantitative categories, whereas more than one qualitative scoring category may be used for a single response, if necessary. The scoring process is also simple and clearly described in the manual, which lists high percentages of interscorer agreement and kappa coefficients for most categories, with the exception of those with very low response frequencies. The total amount of time needed to give and score the test is short and its cost is relatively low once the initial investment in the manual and the cards is made.

As anyone familiar with such seemingly straightforward projective devices knows, the complications arise when one considers the intended uses and possible applications of the test. Initially, The Hand Test was designed to reveal attitudes and action tendencies that are close to the surface and likely to be translated into behaviors. Its original validation work was concerned with the prediction of acting-out behavior. Some of the scores from The Hand Test have differentiated samples of aggressive and nonaggressive subjects to a significant extent, across more than one study. A typical example is a recent investigation by Clemence, Hilsenroth, Sivec, and Rasch (1999) which appears to support the use of the Aggression and Acting Out scores in identifying aggressive tendencies in children. Since its initial development, however, claims about the purported usefulness of the test have escalated. For instance, even though readers are cautioned that The Hand Test was designed for use with other instruments—and that it is subject to possible environmental influences and sensitive to the examinee's present state—the manual also states that the test *may* be used alone as a short screening device (Wagner, 1982, p. 4). Elsewhere, the manual suggests that The Hand Test is a useful adjunct for general personality appraisal, for differential psychiatric diagnosis, and even for determining the presence of "organicity."

On the surface, The Hand Test appears to be solidly backed by an extensive literature of over 200

references that have accumulated in the four decades since the test was developed. In addition, Wagner, Rasch, and Marsico (1991) have published a manual supplement with norms and interpretive guidelines for children and adolescents, and Young and Wagner (1999) have edited a case book for various applications of The Hand Test in research and clinical practice. Furthermore, several major reviews of The Hand Test (Bodden, 1984; Shaffer, 1989; Sivec & Hilsenroth, 1994) have been quite favorable.

What then is the problem with an instrument that has proved so intriguing and appealing to so many investigators and practitioners? To put it simply, the problem is that the data supporting its clinical use are unconvincing. Although to casual observers the abundant research literature on The Hand Test may lend the technique an air of scientific respectability, upon closer inspection it turns out that a large portion of that literature is based on methodologically weak studies and contains information that is inconsistent, contradictory, and/or trivial. Thus, instead of lending support to the purported uses of the test, the net effect of its empirical literature is to obfuscate the issue.

The principal weaknesses of the data presented in The Hand Test manual and supplement concern two somewhat related areas, namely (a) the stability of its large array of scores and (b) the possibility of interpreting them normatively. With regard to the first problem, it should be noted that, to the extent that scores fluctuate arbitrarily, prediction is unreliable. Thus, the stability of scores is crucial to their potential use in any kind of prediction. In The Hand Test manual and supplement, a total of four test-retest reliability studies are presented. The resulting 75 test-retest reliability coefficients range in magnitude from .12 to .91, with a median of .62. Wide variations in the intervals between test and retest across the four studies complicate the interpretation of these figures. Nevertheless, the numbers obtained suggest that most of The Hand Test scores derived from a single administration are too unstable to interpret with any degree of confidence. For example, in the study with the shortest interval between administrations (14 days) the test-retest reliability coefficients for the two scores that are potentially most useful, namely, Aggression and Acting Out, were only .51 and .55, respectively.

With regard to the normative interpretation of Hand Test scores, and the consequent inferences that may be made based on these scores, there are two major problems. The first is the inadequacy of the norms presented in both manuals, in light of the requirements set by the *Standards for Educational and Psychological Testing* (American Educational Research Association, American Psychological Association, & National Council on Measurement in Education, 1999). Samples are poorly described and apparently selected on the basis of convenience. All of the norms presented in the new manual supplement (Wagner et al., 1991) are based on 389 students drawn exclusively from the Akron, Ohio public school system. Moreover, an inspection of the normative information tables shows that there are far too many scoring categories for which the frequencies are too low and for which the overlap across clinical samples is too great. The second major problem with regard to normative interpretation of The Hand Test scores is that of interindividual differences in response productivity. The total number of responses per examinee can fluctuate, with consequent differences in the frequencies of other scoring categories. Because most of The Hand Test scores are simple frequencies and because response productivity itself has been linked to other psychologically significant variables such as intelligence and age, it is easy to see how the interpretation of scores can be affected by productivity. This problem is not unique to The Hand Test and has been discussed at length in reference to the Rorschach (e.g., Anastasi & Urbina, 1997, pp. 415–416).

SUMMARY EVALUATION. For what purposes, if any, can The Hand Test be recommended? In spite of its ease and brevity, use of The Hand Test in neuropsychological or psychiatric diagnosis seems hard to justify. On the other hand, as long as its limitations are kept firmly in mind, the technique could prove useful for idiographic exploration of personality within a therapeutic setting, when more comprehensive projective methods (such as the Rorschach [323] or the Thematic Apperception Test [T5:2749]), are unavailable or inappropriate. The Hand Test could also be used as one possible indicator of proneness to violence, as long as other techniques are also used (e.g., Borum, 1996). In the latter context, The Hand Test should probably be administered on two different occasions and used only if the two sets of pertinent scores prove to be stable across both occasions.

REVIEWER'S REFERENCES

Wagner, E. E. (1983). *The Hand Test, Revised 1983: Manual.* Los Angeles: Western Psychological Services.

Bodden, J. L. (1984) [Review of The Hand Test.] In D. J. Keyser & R. C. Sweetland (Eds.) *Test critiques: Volume I* (pp. 315–321). Kansas City, MO: Test Corporation of America.

Shaffer, M. B. (1989). [Review of The Hand Test, Revised 1983.] In. J. C. Conoley & J. J. Kramer (Eds.), *The tenth mental measurements yearbook* (pp. 342–343). Lincoln, NE: The Buros Institute of Mental Measurements.

Wagner, E. E., Rasch, M., & Marsico, D. S. (1991). *Hand Test manual supplement: Interpreting child and adolescent responses.* Los Angeles: Western Psychological Services.

Sivec, H. J., & Hilsenroth, M. J. (1994). The use of The Hand Test with children and adolescents: A review. *School Psychology Review, 23,* 526–545.

Borum, R. (1996). Improving the clinical practice of violence risk assessment: Technology, guidelines, and training. *American Psychologist, 51,* 945–956.

Anastasi, A., & Urbina, S. (1997). *Psychological testing* (7th ed.). Upper Saddle River, NJ: Prentice Hall.

American Educational Research Association, American Psychological Association, & National Council on Measurement in Education. (1999). *Standards for educational and psychological testing.* Washington, DC: American Educational Research Association.

Clemence, A. J., Hilsenroth, M. J., Sivec, H. J., & Rasch, M. A. (1999). Hand test AGG and AOS variables: Relation with teacher rating of aggressiveness. *Journal of Personality Assessment, 73,* 334–344.

Young, G. R., & Wagner, E. E. (Eds.). (1999). *The Hand Test: Advances in application and research.* Melbourne, FL: Krieger.

[162]
Hare Psychopathy Checklist: Screening Version.

Purpose: To screen for psychopathy in forensic and nonforensic settings.

Population: Adults age 18 and over.

Publication Date: 1995.

Acronym: PCL:SV.

Scores, 3: Part 1, Part 2, Total.

Administration: Individual.

Price Data, 2001: $120 per kit including 25 interview guides, 25 QuikScore™ forms, and manual (82 pages); $90 per 25 interview guides/QuikScore™ forms; $45 per 25 interview guides; $45 per 25 QuikScore™ forms; $40 per manual; $30 per optional rating criteria clipboard; $42 per specimen set including manual, 3 interview guides, and 3 QuikScore™ forms.

Time: (30–60) minutes; case history review and scoring require further (20–30) minutes.

Comments: Shortened version of Hare Psychopathy Checklist—Revised (T5:1174).

Authors: S. D. Hart, D. N. Cox, and R. D. Hare.

Publisher: Multi-Health Systems, Inc.

Review of the Hare Psychopathy Checklist: Screening Version by RONALD J. GANELLEN, Director, Neuropsychology Service, Michael Reese Hospital and Medical Center, and Associate Professor, Northwestern Medical School, Chicago, IL:

The Hare Psychopathy Checklist: Screening Version (PCL:SV) was developed to screen for the presence of psychopathy in forensic, psychiatric, and non-clinical settings. The conceptual basis for the PCL:SV is the same as that used to construct the original and revised versions of the Psychopathy Checklist (Hare, 1980, 1991), which are recognized as psychometrically sophisticated, clinically useful, state-of-the-art instruments that have impressive concurrent and predictive validity (Salekin, Rogers, & Sewell, 1996).

The authors of the PCL:SV summarize their view of the nature of psychopathy and the difference between psychopathy and criminality, or antisocial behavior, in a well-written, informative overview contained in the manual. Briefly, they point out that the criteria for a diagnosis of an antisocial personality disorder, as defined in the DSM-IV, differs from the clinical conceptualization of psychopathy, originally formulated by Cleckley (1976) and operationalized by Hare (1985), in that the DSM-IV diagnosis focuses on overt delinquent and criminal behavior ignoring or minimizing interpersonal and affective features such as grandiosity, lack of empathy for others, difficulties forming long-lasting interpersonal attachments, shallow emotional reactions, and lack of remorse for one's actions.

The rational for developing the PCL:SV is that the version of the test in current use, the Hare Psychopathy Checklist—Revised (PCL-R), is time-consuming to administer, often requiring 3 hours to complete. The authors reasoned that a shorter test format, the PCL:SV, could be used to rule out psychopathy in some individuals while signaling a likelihood of psychopathy in others who could then be evaluated more carefully using the PCL-R. They argue that considerable professional time and effort could be saved if the PCL:SV was found both to be time efficient to administer and score, and to have acceptable psychometric properties.

The PCL:SV manual describes in considerable detail the impressive efforts made to develop and validate the PCL:SV so that it would conceptually parallel the PCL-R and assess the two factors that, according to Hare, define psychopathy, a factor involving an egocentric approach to interpersonal relationships marked by callous, manipulative exploitation of others, and another involving impulsive, irresponsible, and antisocial behavior. PCL:SV items measuring these characteristics were taken directly from a larger set of items on the PCL-R. Although the authors explain that the high internal consistency of the PCL-R indicated there was considerable redundancy among the set of items loading on PCL-R Factors 1 and 2, they do not explain why certain PCL-R items were selected to be used on

the PCL:SV and why others were rejected. It is not clear from the manual whether these decisions were made on conceptual or empirical grounds.

PCL:SV items are rated after the examiner completes a semi-structured interview and reviews available historical information obtained from charts and/or collateral informants. The importance of obtaining collateral information is appropriately stressed given the possibility that some individuals who are evaluated in a forensic context might be motivated to present a distorted, biased picture of their history. During a clinical interview, the rater attempts to obtain information about an individual's academic achievement, behavior in school, employment history, patterns of interpersonal relationships, and involvement with the legal system. The interview and collateral information is then used by the rater to decide how closely the individual matches a prototype for a specific category (e.g., deceitful, impulsive, grandiose). The manual contains clearly articulated guidelines to be used by raters to determine whether an individual matches the prototype for each category. Although these decisions are acknowledged to be subjective to a certain extent, the interrater reliability data presented in the manual indicate that trained raters using these criteria achieve respectable levels of agreement. For instance, the weighted mean interrater reliability averaged across seven validation studies conducted in different geographic regions and with diverse samples (e.g., prisoners, psychiatric inpatients, and college undergraduates) was .84 for the PCL:SV Total Score, .77 for PCL:SV Factor 1, and .82 for PCL:SV Factor 2.

The manual describes the data obtained from the PCL:SV validation studies that show impressive concurrent validity in terms of the relationships with the PCL-R, ratings of DSM-III-R criteria for antisocial personality disorder, self-report measures of psychopathy (e.g., the Millon Clinical Multiaxial Inventory [MCMI], and a semistructured interview designed to diagnose personality disorders, the Personality Disorder Examination. The pattern of convergent and discriminant validity reported for prison, psychiatric, and nonclinical samples supports the conceptualization of the PCL:SV as a measure of psychopathy. Furthermore, the results of confirmatory factor analysis show that, consistent with Hare's theoretical formulation, two factors better describe the dimensions of psychopathy measured by the PCL:SV than a unidimensional model.

One potential limitation of the validation studies is the small percentage of minorities included in the samples. For instance, the forensic/nonpsychiatric samples were predominantly white. Although data presented in the manual show no relationship between race and PCL:SV Total scores, further research is needed to show that the PCL:SV is not biased against minorities when used in applied settings.

The authors report that PCL:SV Total scores of 12 or below show minimal likelihood of psychopathy, as defined by scores on the PCL-R; PCL:SV scores of 18 or above are usually only obtained by PCL-R-defined psychopaths; and scores of 13–17 are considered ambiguous, but deserve further attention (manual, p. 15). However, the manual contains minimal information about how these cutoff scores were determined or about their clinical efficacy. This is unfortunate as the ultimate test of the PCL:SV is the extent to which PCL:SV ratings provide accurate, useful information to determine whether or not an individual requires further, more detailed evaluation concerning psychopathy. Given this limitation, one should be cautious about reaching firm conclusions about the presence or absence of psychopathy, particularly in nonforensic populations and particularly for scores in the "ambiguous" range, until further research more firmly establishes accurate cutting scores. This is a critical issue that deserves greater attention in future research, especially because the premise justifying the PCL:SV is that it is cost-effective.

The authors report that both PCL-R and PCL:SV ratings were obtained in five of the validation samples. Because the items on the PCL:SV are a subset of items from the PCL-R, one would expect the two versions of the test to have high levels of agreement. The authors report significant correlations between the two versions of the PCL, but do not report the degree to which classifications of psychopathy based on the two versions of the test agree (e.g., kappa coefficients).

SUMMARY. Overall, the PCL:SV is a promising screening measure of psychopathy based on a strong theoretical and an impressive empirical foundation. The data contained in the well-written manual demonstrate that the PCL:SV provides scores that permit reliable and valid screening decisions about the construct of psychopathy. Although additional data are needed to establish firm cutpoints to rule in and rule out psychopathy, the developers of the PCL:SV are well on the way toward achieving their goal of providing a technically sound, clinically useful screening measure of psychopathy.

REVIEWER'S REFERENCES

Cleckley, H. M. (1976). *The mask of sanity: An attempt to clarify some issues about the so-called psychopathic personality.* St. Louis: Mosby.

Hare, R. D. (1980). A research scale for the assessment of psychopathy in criminal populations. *Personality and Individual Differences, 1,* 111–119.

Hare, R. D. (1985). Comparison of procedures for the assessment of psychopathy. *Journal of Consulting and Clinical Psychology, 53,* 7–16.

Hare, R. D. (1991). *Manual for the Hare Psychopathy Checklist—Revised.* Toronto: Multi-Health Systems.

Salekin, R. T., Rogers, R., & Sewell, K. W. (1996). A review and meta-analysis of the Psychopathy Checklist and Psychopathy Checklist-Revised: Predictive validity of dangerousness. *Clinical Psychology: Science and Practice, 3,* 203–215.

Review of the Hare Psychopathy Checklist: Screening Version by NATHANIEL J. PALLONE, University Distinguished Professor (Psychology), Center of Alcohol Studies, Rutgers University, Piscataway, NJ, and JAMES J. HENNESSY, Professor, Graduate School of Education, Fordham University, New York, NY:

During the decade since its publication for general (rather than research) use, the Hare Psychopathy Checklist—Revised (PCL-R) has positioned itself as the instrument of choice, the connoisseur's gauge. Yet, as Hart, Cox, and Hare (authors of the Hare Psychopathy Checklist: Screening Version [PCL:SV]) recognize the parent PCL-R instrument "is rather time-consuming and expensive to administer," requiring "about two and a half to three hours of clinician time per patient" (manual, p. 2) and (in consequence of its standardization sample) limited in applicability to "forensic" subjects. Hence, they have produced a "screening version" that is presented as "a relatively quick and inexpensive way … to screen for psychopathy in forensic settings and to assess and diagnose psychopathy outside forensic settings" (manual, p. 1). In contrast to the parent instrument, the authors of the Hare Psychopathy Checklist: Screening Version (Hare PCLS:SV) estimate that administration and scoring of the screening version should consume only about half as much time per examinee (90 vs. 180 minutes). Nonetheless, although they assert that the instrument adduces "virtually no false negative errors," its authors acknowledge that the SV "overpredicts psychopathy" (i.e., yields false positive errors) so that confirmatory examination using the PCL-R should be undertaken to avoid falsely labeling high scorers. Thus, putative time savings in the processes either of diagnostic labeling in the clinical setting or "sorting" (e.g., for security and safety purposes) in the correctional setting cannot readily be calculated in advance.

The quasi-actuarial, but largely clinical, process that results in a single score per examinee begins with a "semi-structured interview," utilizing the Hare PCL: Screening Version Interview and Information Schedule, Part I, a protocol structured not unlike the NMH-endorsed Diagnostic Interview Schedule. The PCL:SV version consists of 65 questions organized around eight themes (school adjustment, work history, health problems, goals, family history, sexual relationships, and impulsive and antisocial behavior in childhood and adulthood). Some questions are relatively factual, requiring only accurate recall on the part of the respondent (e.g., "Where did you grow up?"), but others require substantial filtration and processing by respondent and clinician alike (e.g., "Have you ever been deeply in love?"). Part II, labeled a "collateral information schedule," requires that the clinician consult "charts and collateral information" to verify demographic data, educational and employment history, and, importantly in the correctional setting, history of arrests and convictions. With these sources of data, the clinician "scores" the examinee on a 3-point scale (from zero for "no" to 2 for "yes") on each of 12 dimensions of personality or behavior familiar in the conceptual and research literature as the generally accepted hallmarks of psychopathy: superficiality, grandiosity, deceitfulness, lack of remorse, lack of empathy, failure to accept responsibility, impassivity, poor behavioral control, lack of goals, irresponsibility, and antisocial behavior in adolescence and adulthood. Item scores are then summed to provide a total score, with a ceiling of 36. Norms for total score are provided for four major groupings of subjects—forensic, but nonpsychiatric; forensic-psychiatric; nonforensic but psychiatric; nonforensic and nonpsychiatric (a group composed of undergraduate students at two Canadian universities), respectively. According to the authors, "For diagnostic purposes, a cutoff score of =/+ 18 is recommended ... those scoring 12 or lower ... can be considered non-psychopathic. Those scoring 13 through 17 may be psychopathic and should be further evaluated with the PCL-R. Scores of 18 or higher offer a strong indication of

psychopathy and warrant further evaluation with the full PCL-R" (manual, p. 22).

The litany of characteristics assessed by the PCL:SV omits several key dimensions tapped by the PCL-R (e.g., manipulativeness, parasitic lifestyle, promiscuity, criminal versatility) of particular interest in the forensic setting but not altogether insignificant in the clinical setting either. Of course, the clinician is not limited to the PCL:SV interview schedule as his or her sole source of data but instead is encouraged to "collect historio-demographic data and to sample the individual's interpersonal style" through standard, free-ranging clinical probing. One suspects that even an experienced clinician will be reasonably hard-pressed to move through 65 questions, engage in amplificatory clinical probing, consult "charts and collateral information" for verification or disconfirmation, and assign scores on 12 scales within a time span of 90 minutes.

Internal consistency for total PCL:SV score calculated through Cronbach's coefficient alpha is reported at levels ranging from .69 (for undergraduates in Ontario) to a high of .91 (for undergraduates in British Columbia), with a weighted mean of .84, a level the authors regard as "acceptable for a clinical scale." Inter-item correlations demonstrate moderate item independence, ranging from .42 (for British Columbia undergraduates) to .17 (among both Ontario undergraduates and forensic inpatients), with a weighted mean of .32. Although no formal studies have yet been completed to assess the test-retest reliability of scores from the PCL:SV, the authors estimate that value to be .90, as derived from the test-retest reliability coefficient of the parent PCL-R, a process not altogether favored by the psychometric purist. However, interrater reliability for the total PCL:SV scores is reported through a series of intraclass coefficients, ranging from .67 (for forensic psychiatric inpatients) to .92 (for a "comparison" group composed of both traditionally aged and "adult" undergraduates), with a median of .82. It is a matter both of curiosity and concern that the median intraclass coefficient for undergraduates at two institutions in whom there is (virtually by design) little reason to expect a noticeable incidence of psychopathy, is higher at .90, than the median of .75 for four groups of forensic subjects (in- and outpatients and inmates in Federal and provincial correctional institutions, respectively), in whom there are many reasons to suspect a relatively high incidence of psychopathy. Such data may suggest that the instrument is more efficient at "ruling out" than at confirming psychopathy.

Concurrent validity is reported between PCL:SV total score and PCL-R total score at levels ranging from .55 for psychiatric inpatients to .84 for psychiatric outpatients, with a median of .81 (and, in this instance, with virtually no variation between coefficients for undergraduate comparison subjects, at .81, and forensic subjects, at a median of .80); enumeration of symptoms of antisocial personality disorder identified in DSM-IV, at levels ranging from .52 to .85; scores on the "Antisocial" scale of the Millon Clinical Multiaxial Inventory, Version II (MCMI-II), at .68; and scores on the "Socialization" scale of the California Psychological Inventory, at -.47. Coefficients of convergence are also reported with a variety of other data (e.g., scores on the Beck Depression Inventory and on each scale of the MCMI-II, assessment of alcohol and drug abuse history; and self-ratings by subjects).

According to its manual, users of the PCL:SV should hold a doctorate (specified as a Ph.D., Ed.D., or M.D.); be licensed or certified by a "state or provincial body that regulates the assessment and diagnosis of mental disorder" (p. 17); "have expertise ... in psychopathology and psychometric assessment" (p. 17); and "be familiar with the clinical and empirical literature pertaining to psychopathy, specifically with the research described in the manual for the Hare Psychopathy Checklist—Revised" (p. 17). That is a hefty set of constraints indeed for an instrument labeled unequivocally by the generators as a screening device only, especially when the instrument, according to its authors, "overpredicts psychopathy" because it is more efficient at "ruling out" than at "ruling in."

A cautionary note should be sounded concerning use of the PCL:SV in correctional settings in the United States. The standardization sample for the instrument contained a total of 586 participants, of whom 269 (46%) were either inmates or probationers (and some of whom also "had a diagnosis of serious mental disorder," typically psychosis). Of these 269 correctional subjects, 76% were Caucasian, likely reflecting the fact that fully 82% of them were either incarcerated or on probation in Canada; indeed, although U.S. subjects comprised only 18% ($N = 49$) of the correctional group, non-Caucasian U.S. subjects accounted for 65% of all non-Caucasians in the sample. In contrast to the aggregate correctional subjects on whom norms for use of the PCL:SV in forensic settings have been derived, U.S. Bureau of Justice Statistics data reveal that (in 1996) Caucasians accounted for only 40% of the inmates in the nations' prisons, so that Caucasians are overrepresented in the standardization sample at a ratio of very nearly 2:1 in relation to their representation in the prisons of the United States (and non-Caucasians are proportionally underrepresented). Rampant litigiousness among the denizens of U.S. prisons and jails would doubtless magnify such disparity in seeking judicial redress of any sort of decision grounded in inappropriate norms. To rectify that situation, an augmented set of norms segregated by race appears to be required.

SUMMARY. The PCL:SV is a quasi-actuarial, quasi-clinical, instrument that improves upon its parent instrument, the PCL-R, only in respect of paring a clinician's time from approximately 180 to 90 minutes for "administration" via interview schedule and interpretive scoring. Yet, to be considered a definitive indicator, a PCL:SV score must be validated by subsequent administration of the PCL-R, so that a total of 270 minutes of clinician time may be consumed in the progression from screen to definition. Especially in the forensic setting, where as Stevens (1993) observed, diagnosing psychopathy often resembles "searching for hay in a haystack," the utility of a screening device that produces only a tentative marker (or "soft sign") is not immediately self-evident. Surely researchers in both forensic and clinical settings, and very likely clinicians in forensic settings as well, will continue to regard the parent measure as the instrument of choice when an unequivocal index of psychopathy is required. In clinical use in forensic settings in the U.S., limitations in applicability issuing from the racial composition of the standardization sample need to be recognized and rectified.

REVIEWER'S REFERENCE

Stevens, G. F. (1993). Applying the diagnosis antisocial personality to imprisoned offenders: Looking for hay in a haystack. *Journal of Offender Rehabilitation, 19*(1/2), 1–26.

[163]
Hausa Speaking Test.

Purpose: To evaluate the level of oral proficiency in Hausa attained by non-native speakers.
Population: Adults.

Publication Date: 1989.
Acronym: HaST.
Scores: Total score only.
Administration: Individual or group.
Price Data: Available from publisher.
Time: (40) minutes.
Comments: Examinee responses recorded on test tape scored by publisher.
Author: Staff of the Division of Foreign Language Education.
Publisher: Center for Applied Linguistics.

Review of the Hausa Speaking Test by MAR-GARET E. MALONE, Language Specialist, Peace Corps, Washington, DC:

The Hausa Speaking Test (HaST) couples a new direction in oral proficiency testing—reliance on audio technology for oral proficiency testing—with a real need for oral proficiency testing in the less commonly taught languages. The combination of these two factors is the Hausa Speaking Test, a tape mediated test of oral proficiency. This test, commonly known as a Simulated Oral Proficiency Interview or SOPI, relies on a prerecorded test tape and test booklet to elicit speech from the test taker, rather than with a live interviewer. The examinee's resulting test tape can be rated by a trained rater at a later time. The HaST is one of 10 simulated oral proficiency interviews (SOPI) developed by the Center for Applied Linguistics (these are also available in Arabic, Mandarin Chinese, Hebrew, Indonesian, French, German, Japanese, Portuguese, and Spanish and will soon be available in English as a Second Language). Because the HaST was among the earliest of the tests of this type developed, it does not benefit from the improvements made in later SOPIs based on research performed in the earlier tests.

The HaST tests oral proficiency of native speakers of English studying Hausa as a second language. The specificity of audience—native speakers of English—is important, because all test directions and explanations of the items occur in English. The test manual states specifically that the examinee must be American or English-speaking to take this test.

The test has a number of potential uses, from assessment for students who wish to study abroad to assessment for professional purposes. Because the test developers conducted neither specific-use validation studies nor standard-setting studies to determine appropriate scores for differ-ent uses of the test, no information is supplied about either topic. Therefore, any group wishing to use the test should conduct their own validation study prior to use, particularly for high-stakes purposes.

The test does not take long to administer (40 minutes). The test can be administered both to a large group in a language laboratory or to an individual by using two tape recorders (one to play the test tape and one to record the responses). All test directions and items are read over the test tape and are written clearly in the test booklet. The test has five parts and an undisclosed number of items. The first part, the personal conversation, is the only part that includes any spoken language in Hausa. In this item, the examinee is asked to respond to 13 short, personal questions in Hausa, which are spoken on tape by a native speaker of Hausa. In the next part, the examinee uses a drawn map to give directions in Hausa. The next three items require the examinee to explain a sequence of four or five pictures on a page. The purpose of these three items is to elicit past and present narration, as well as to give instructions. The manual does not show any of the pictures; therefore, the clarity and quality of the illustrations is unknown.

The next part, Topical Discourse, has six items. Examinees speak about different topic areas. Finally, in the last part, the examinee is asked to imagine that she or he is in a real-life situation and to speak accordingly. The test is sent for rating to an HaST-trained rater and is scored according to the ACTFL Guidelines (1986).

The test and its development process have a number of positive and negative characteristics. On the negative side, the sample size of pilot study participants was small, the construct validity evidence of the test is unclear, and the specific applications of the test, based on the pilot population, are not validated. On the positive side, the test has high interrater and parallel form reliability as well as ease of administration and scoring.

The first issue relates to size and background of the pilot study. The size of the pilot study is small—only 13 participants. The backgrounds of the participants in the pilot study are not described in detail, except to say the backgrounds are "widely diverse." The lack of information on the pilot study is unfortunate because potential users cannot know if a person with his or her background has ever used the test. In addition, the test was not validated for any particular purpose, which leaves the responsibility for validity of test use with the potential user.

Though this study is small, it is important to note that the sample of nonnative speakers of Hausa in the United States is also rather small. Therefore, this possible source of error reflects reality: There are not many nonnative speakers of Hausa in the United States.

A second issue relates to the validity of the OPI, the test on which the SOPI is based, and the ACTFL Guidelines (1986), the scale used to score the HaST. A debate continues on the construct validity of the OPI, and the HaST, because it was modeled on the OPI, may also suffer from lack of construct validity. Similarly, the ACTFL Guidelines have been challenged by many (e.g., Lantolf & Frawley, 1985). Relying on the ACTFL Guidelines to rate any test automatically causes validity questions.

On the positive side, the test has good parallel form reliability, very high interrater reliability, content evidence validity, and ease of administration. There are two parallel forms of the HaST, A and B. Each participant took both forms of the test. Parallel form reliability when rated by the same rater ranged from .80–.82, and parallel form reliability when rated by different raters ranged from .76–.91. Interrater reliability, however, was higher, ranging from .88–.93. Only two raters scored the tests, and both had OPI and ACTFL training.

The content validity for scores from the test is also quite high. Unlike the OPI, the SOPI gives all directions for all items in English. Therefore, there is no confusion between the listening domain and the speaking domain because the only skill tested is speaking in Hausa.

Finally, the HaST administration is simple. The test booklet supplies detailed, step-by-step directions. The test is quite sensitive to less commonly taught languages because it can be administered virtually anywhere by any language lab technician or other personnel and can be rated at a later time in a different location.

SUMMARY. Many of the issues raised by the HaST are difficulties of testing any less commonly taught language. The test was developed because there are so few available OPI testers in Hausa. Because it is a less commonly taught language, there were few examinees available to take the pilot test. Overall, the test is a practical one, appropriate to nonnative speakers of Hausa who speak English as a primary language.

REVIEWER'S REFERENCES
Lantolf, J., & Frawley, W. (1985). Oral Proficiency Testing: A critical analysis. *Modern Language Journal, 69,* 337–345.
American Council on the Teaching of Foreign Languages. (1986). *ACTFL proficiency guidelines.* Hastings-on-Hudson, NY: Author.

[164]
Hay Aptitude Test Battery [Revised].

Purpose: "Helps select applicants with the ability to work quickly and accurately with numerical and alphabetical detail."

Population: Applicants for clerical and plant positions.

Publication Dates: 1947–1999.

Scores, 3: Number Perception, Name Finding, Number Series Completion.

Administration: Group or individual.

Price Data, 2001: $385 per test battery including all 4 tests, user's manual ('99, 32 pages), and scoring key; $55 per 25 Warm-Up Tests; $85 per 25 tests (specify Number Perception Test, Name Finding Test, or Number Series Completion Test); quantity discounts available.

Foreign Language Editions: French and Spanish versions available.

Time: 4 minutes per test; 1 minute per Warm-Up Test.

Author: Edward N. Hay.

Publisher: Wonderlic, Inc.

Cross References: For reviews by Sue M. Legg and M. David Miller of an earlier edition, see 12:179; for a review by Robert P. Vecchio of an earlier edition, see 9:470; see also T2:2132 (2 references) and 5:849 (2 references); for reviews by Reign H. Bittner and Edward E. Cureton, see 4:725 (8 references).

Review of the Hay Aptitude Test Battery [Revised] by MARK A. ALBANESE, Professor, Preventive Medicine and Director, Medical Education Research and Development, University of Wisconsin—Madison, Madison, WI:

The Hay Aptitude Test Battery is a very focused assessment used for screening applicants for positions that emphasize information-processing speed and accuracy, such as clerical and editorial-type positions. It purports to assess short-term memory and accuracy with numerical and alphabetical detail and numerical comprehension and logical thinking. It is composed of three tests, each assessing a different type of task: Number Perception (matching of 3–6-digit numbers—7623—7613 same, different?), Name Finding (converting a name from a common form to a reference-type form, i.e., changing from first, middle initial, last, to last, first initial, middle initial—Mark A. Albanese to Albanese, M. A.), and Number Series Completion (2 4 6 8 10 12 __ __). A one-minute warm-up test is administered before the three operational tests in order to reduce test-taker anxiety. The test takes relatively little time to administer (total testing time = 13 minutes, including the warm-up test, but not including directions and filling out identifying information).

The test is speeded, with penalties for incorrect answers being applied with varying severity. The Number Perceptions test is scored by subtracting from the number of items attempted (as defined by the last question answered) two times the number of items incorrect or omitted. Because the tests are basically pure speed tests, where it is assumed that examinees would get all items attempted correct if they had enough time, the scoring is equivalent to Right minus 2* (Wrong/omitted). Correcting for chance success would only be Right minus Wrong, thus the penalty involves both a doubling of the weight and including omits as wrong answers. This severe penalty is administered because "Carelessness in matching numbers is particularly common, and costly, to your organization" (user's manual, p. 7). The Name Finding Test also contains a penalty for incorrect and omitted items. It contains what are essentially four-option, multiple-choice questions. A name is presented as first name, middle initial (MI), and last name (LN) and the examinee's task is to check the match from among four options presented as LN, first initial, MI. Scoring involves recording the number of items attempted and the number incorrect/omitted. A net score is computed equivalent to Right minus Wrong/omitted. To simply correct for chance success, the net score would be computed as R—1/3 W. Thus, again, omitted items are considered equivalent to wrong answers and the penalty applied is three times more severe than would be applied to simply correct for chance success. The Number Sequence test contains items presenting six numbers in sequence followed by two blanks for the examinee to supply the next two numbers in the sequence. Both numbers must be correct, otherwise the item is considered wrong. A net score is again created by R-W/Omitted. Because supply-type items do not provide a finite probability of answering correctly by random guess-

ing, the severity of this correction cannot be precisely specified, but it is probably even more severe than that applied to the other tests.

The Hay Aptitude Test Battery was originally published in 1951. This revision provides normative data from 1992 studies as well as those from an earlier 1972 study for comparative purposes and combined norms. Generally, the results of the norming studies conducted in 1992 were similar to those conducted in 1972. The primary exception is that the Number Perceptions test showed a mean score increase of 10 points from the 1972 to 1992 norms, which amounts to a statistically significant ($p<.0001$) effect size of .37. This becomes relevant in that the 1972 and 1992 data are merged for reporting some of the norms. Although it could be argued that, for the other tests, merging the 1972 data with the 1992 data will provide more stable normative data, the results for the Number Perceptions test are likely to be distorted by combining the data. This is accentuated when in subsequent sections of the user's manual, norms are provided for individual occupations that only report the 1992 data. It would seem better practice to refrain from merging data from the two different norming dates for a test like this.

A further complicating matter is that no information is provided on how the norming samples were obtained nor the testing conditions, including the motivation for the members of the norming sample to perform their best on the tests. The authors encourage users to develop their own norms based upon the experience they have in using the test. Given the vagaries of the norming data, this seems like a very reasonable recommendation. Users should be cautious in interpreting the norms from the merged data. All norms provided in the manual, including the distributions of scores for workers from various occupations and the threshold scores suggested for selecting workers in various occupations should be considered tentative at best. Data on test score reliability report values of: Number Perceptions = .85 (test-retest administration interval not provided), Name Finding = .94 (split-half), Number Series Completion = .94 (split-half), but the data come from a document almost 50 years old (Aptitude Test Service; 1953). Even though split-half and test-retest score reliabilities are appropriate estimates of reliability given the speeded nature of the tests, the age of the studies is a problem. At the very least, split-half reliabilities of scores from the 1992 norming study should be reported.

The manual argues for the content validity of the tests on grounds that the tasks on the tests are "direct work samples of tasks found in the daily operations of a wide variety of jobs" (user's manual, p. 26). The criterion-related validity of the tests is supported by abstracts of 11 validation studies. These 11 validation studies involved from 21–110 workers and correlated Hay Aptitude Test performance with work outcomes. The types of workers in the studies included emergency telephone operators, police and fire dispatchers, clerical, data entry, bookkeepers, accounting clerks, and loan officers. Using employer performance ratings, work produced, and salary as operational definitions of work outcome, the ranges in correlations with the various Hay Tests were: Name Finding: .26–.60, Number Series Completion: .22–.56, and Number Perception: .40–.64. One of the studies determined that use of the Hay Tests in selection of clerical workers would result in "a gain in productivity of $2,149.25 per year per worker" (user's manual, p. 27). The criterion-related validity data indicate reasonably strong relationships with work outcomes and the potential for employers to see productivity gains by using the Hay Tests in worker hiring decisions appears to be established.

The validity data and conclusions must be tempered by two concerns: (a) Tables 1 and 2 suggest disparate impact by gender and ethnicity and (b) computers have changed how people do many of the types of jobs for which the Hay tests were created. Women scored higher than men on all three tests by a statistically significant margin: Number Perception Test (Effect size = .44), Name Finding Test (Effect Size = .52), Number Series Completion (Effect Size = .12). As for ethnicity, White (W) examinees scored higher than both African-American (AA) and Hispanic (H) examinees by statistically significant margins: Name Perception Test (Effect size—W vs. AA = .52, W vs. H = .69), Name Finding Test (Effect size—W vs. AA = .82, W vs. H = 1.08), and Number Series Completion Test (ES—W vs. AA = .91, W vs. H = 1.09). Interpreting these results is complicated due to the differing proportions of males in the different ethnic groups (W = 20% male, AA = 40% male, H = 63% male). It cannot be determined from the tables if these differences in performance are due to the overrepresentation of males (who do

more poorly than females on the tests) in the AA and H groups or the difference between genders being the result of the maldistribution of gender in the various ethnic groups. Providing tables with a breakdown by gender and ethnicity would help clarify this issue for users, but it does not address what to do about the fact that the Hay Aptitude Test Battery results in disparate impact for gender, ethnicity, or both. Any user will have to demonstrate that the tasks contained on the tests are directly tied to job performance in order to address the potential legal issues associated with disparate impact.

Spell checking programs, computer programs that perform automatic checks of data using double entry procedures, as well as other applications of computer technology have changed how many people work, especially those in the types of positions for which the Hay Tests were developed. Thus, the content validity of scores from the tests may be declining. Any potential user of the Hay Aptitude Test Battery will need to ensure that there is a match to the activities of the jobs for which they want to use the tests for selection purposes. The criterion-related validity data, although impressive, are based upon undated and unreferenced studies. If these data are as old as the reliability data, they badly need updating.

Another change in the environment that is important for this test is the Americans with Disabilities Act (ADA), which has been used to demand testing accommodations, such as increased time on tests, for students with learning disabilities. No mention of testing accommodations is made in the user manual. Because the Hay Tests are intrinsically speeded, some guidance on how to respond to examinees requesting accommodations for learning disabilities will need to be addressed at some point. If there have been instances where users of the Hay Tests have declined to permit testing accommodations and have successfully defended legal challenges, this would be important information to include in the user's manual.

CRITIQUE. The Hay Aptitude Test Battery has been in use for almost 50 years. The test is a very straightforward assessment of skills that would have been critical for individuals working in clerical, editorial, data-entry, and low-level accounting type positions at the time the test was developed and may still relate well to performance in the jobs even though computers have changed the ways in which such jobs are done. Data are provided that

531

support the criterion-related validity of the tests in terms of worker productivity. The amount of time needed to administer the tests is remarkably short considering the validity correlations reached as large as .64. Given the importance of the work done by people in clerical, editorial data-entry, and low-level accounting type positions, tests that predict work performance as well as does the Hay Aptitude Test Battery are an important part of the employee hiring process. The Hay Tests have a long history of use to support their value for this purpose.

Although the Hay Aptitude Test Battery has many positive characteristics, there are issues that need to be addressed, particularly those that pertain to changes that have occurred in the work place in the last 25 years. One unusual feature is that the test has only one form. This may be problematic because there are no data that indicate whether repeatedly taking the test improves performance to any degree. Given the brevity of the test and that, as the user's manual states, it is expected that all examinees should be able to answer all the questions given enough time, it would seem that data on the effect of repeatedly taking the tests would help employers gain a better grasp of how to interpret scores from applicants who may have gone through the application process many times in hopes of gaining employment. The nature of the tasks contained in the tests would lend themselves easily to creating new forms.

Another issue that needs to be addressed is modifications to the directions to examinees regarding how omitted items will be treated in scoring. The fact that points are subtracted for omitted items is unusual and examinees are likely to change their behavior if they are aware of this feature. Oddly, this feature is most likely to negatively affect examinees who have more education, especially those who have taken college entrance examinations such as the Scholastic Aptitude Test (SAT; T5:592) because the SAT applies a correction that is set at chance levels. Item omitting behavior appropriate for a test correcting at chance levels may not be appropriate for one that corrects at levels beyond chance.

There are several things that need to be added to the user's manual. First, if the test batteries have been changed in the last 50 years, it would be helpful to describe what those changes have been (the most recent copyright is 1997; something probably changed at that time to allow the copyright to be updated). At present, the only changes that can be detected are updated normative data in 1972 and 1992. Descriptions of how the norming samples were obtained need to be added to the manual to help the users understand how valid they are for their purposes. It would also help immensely to place dates and citations on the validity studies so users can evaluate to what extent the results may apply to their own organization. The reliability data need to be updated from the most recent norming period (with each norming, at least split-half reliability estimates should updated). Further, the references in the user's manual need to be updated, the most recent reference cited is 1985.

Perhaps the most important issue the user's manual needs to address concerns how test users should respond to requests for accommodation, particularly increased time, under ADA and how to respond to disparate impact by gender and ethnicity. Because both of these issues have great potential to result in litigation, they should be carefully addressed.

SUMMARY. The Hay Aptitude Test Battery appears to be a very useful instrument for what it was intended to do, screen applicants for clerical, data-entry, editing, and low-level accounting positions. The test produces scores with reasonably high split-half and test-retest reliabilities (.85–.94), relatively moderate intercorrelations (.49–.64), and impressive predictive validity estimates. However, the lack of multiple forms, severe penalties applied for incorrect and omitted items, incomplete descriptions of validity and norming studies, documented disparate impact by gender and ethnicity, and failure to address mechanisms for responding to accommodations mandated by ADA combine to offer major challenges to prospective test users.

Review of the Hay Aptitude Test Battery by MICHAEL KANE, Professor, Department of Kinesiology, University of Wisconsin, Madison, WI:

The Hay Aptitude Test Battery includes three tests—Number Perception, Name Finding, and Number Series Completion—each taking 4 minutes, plus a 1-minute warm-up test. In the Number Perception Test, the examinee must decide, for each of 200 pairs of numbers, whether the two numbers are identical or different. For the Name Finding Test, the examinee must match each of 32 names on the front of the answer sheet to the same name in a list of 128 names on the back of the page. For both of these tests, each item involves a simple matching task, but both tests are highly speeded.

The Number Series Completion Test contains 30 numerical sequences, with six numbers each, and the examinee must supply the next two numbers in the sequence. The tasks in this test seem more demanding than those in the other two tests, but they are still not very difficult. Nevertheless, doing 30 of these series in 4 minutes would present a challenge to most people.

The tests are short. The instructions, the response formats, and the scoring procedures are all efficient and clear. Each test provides a sample of performance on a specific kind of task: matching names exactly, checking one number against another, and completing simple numerical series.

PROPOSED INTERPRETATION. The user's manual suggests at least two levels of interpretation. On one level the tests are interpreted as samples of tasks found in certain jobs. On another level, some interpretations seem to be stated in terms of constructs. The Number Perception Test is said to assess "short-term memory and accuracy with numerical detail" (manual, p. 2). The Number Series Completion Test is said to assess "numerical comprehension and logical thinking" (manual, p. 2). The manual slides back and forth between different levels of interpretation.

According to the manual, the Hay Battery is designed to help identify applicants for employment who can work quickly and accurately with numerical and alphabetic data. The manual suggests that the cutscore for making hiring decisions can be based on local experience or can be derived from a table of median scores for various job categories. No rationale is provided for using the 50th percentile as a cutscore.

VALIDITY. The user's manual claims that the content validity of the Hay Battery "is easily established" because the tests are "direct work samples of tasks found in the daily operations of a wide variety of jobs," and that "these tasks are critical … to such jobs as bookkeeping, accounting, data entry" (p. 26). It is certainly reasonable to assert that many jobs call for speed and accuracy in handling data, but the manual provides no evidence that the specific tasks included in the Hay tests are critical to any job. The claim that the tasks in these tests are direct work samples is

simply taken for granted. Tasks like those in the Number Perception Test could arise in proofreading data, and the tasks in the Name Finding test would come up in checking files. However, the extent to which these specific tasks play a major role in any job is certainly questionable (especially in this age of computers).

Face validity, or the appearance of job relatedness, gets a lot of attention in the discussion of validity. The section on content validity ends with the extraordinary claim that, "face valid tests … are, by nature, content valid as well" (manual, p. 26). The larger question of the importance of any of these tasks in various jobs (i.e., the central question in developing a content-based validity argument) is not considered in the manual.

The tasks in the Number Series Completion Test (finding the next two numbers in a series) are not a routine part of any job. Rather, this kind of task is found mainly in tests of inductive reasoning. The manual says that the purpose of this test is to "identify applicants who understand numeric relationships and have the ability to perceive patterns using logic and reasoning skills" (p. 11), and relates the ability being measured to "general cognitive ability, or intelligence" (p. 11). The manual provides no evidence to support its claims for these construct interpretations.

The section on validity studies includes a number of studies of the relationships between Hay test scores and measures of performance in various jobs. The sample sizes tend to be quite small (most under 50 and almost all under 100). The criteria are generally not described in any detail, and references to more complete documentation are not provided. These studies seem to have been conducted by organizations using the Hay Battery, and it is not clear how representative these results are. The criterion-related validity evidence is quite weak.

The user's manual reports a test-retest reliability of .85 for the Number Perception Test (interval not reported) and reports split-halves reliabilities of .94 for both Name Finding and Number Series Completion. Given that all three of the tests are highly speeded, a split-halves coefficient is inappropriate. A test-retest or parallel-forms reliability should be reported. Furthermore, all of these coefficients are derived from "early studies" (1953) that are not described or adequately referenced in the manual. This lack of basic data on reliability is inexcusable in a test first published 50 years ago.

The manual reports user norms collected between 1972 and 1992 for the three tests. Each of these data sets contains about 7,000 individuals, but the extent to which they are representative of any current population is unclear. The manual also reports data from a 1992 study relating Hay scores to various demographic variables. The average scores for whites are considerably higher than those for various minority groups. Given the weakness of the available validity evidence, the potential for adverse impact should be a cause for concern.

SUMMARY. The Hay tests would be relatively quick and easy to administer and could be of use in evaluating speed and accuracy on the three types of tasks included in the battery. However, an employer who considers using them for making hiring decisions should certainly compare the job requirements to the content of the tests before adopting them. The user should conduct a local validity study, and if possible, should evaluate the test-retest reliability of the tests. The manual does not provide adequate evidence of reliability and validity.

[165]
Herrmann Brain Dominance Instrument [Revised].

Purpose: Designed to measure "a person's preference both for right-brained or left-brained thinking and for conceptual or experiential thinking."
Population: Adults.
Publication Dates: 1981–1995.
Acronym: HBDI.
Scores, 12: Left Mode Dominance, Right Mode Dominance, Quadrant (Upper Left, Lower Left, Upper Right, Lower Right), Adjective Pairs (subset of 4 Quadrant Scores), Cerebral Mode Dominance, Limbic Mode Dominance.
Administration: Group.
Manual: No manual.
Price Data, 1998: $52 per scored survey form including interpretation package.
Time: (15–20) minutes.
Comments: Self-administered; must be scored by publisher or certified practitioner.
Author: Ned Herrmann.
Publisher: Herrmann International.
Cross References: See T5:1197 (1 reference); for a review by Rik Carl D'Amato of an earlier edition, see 11:159 (7 references).

Review of the Herrmann Brain Dominance Instrument [Revised] by F. FELICIA FERRARA, Assistant Professor, College of Behavioral Sciences, The University of Sarasota, Sarasota, FL:

In general, the Herrmann Brain Dominance Instrument (HBDI) and accompanying supportive materials offer a technique for assessing one's dominant mode of performance based on brain dominance structures of a physiological nature. Several different documents were submitted for review, rendering materials cumbersome and somewhat excessive to read through. Even though substantial research was conducted on the instrument, the non-sequential organization of materials make it difficult to follow.

The 456-page, landscape-typefaced (11-inch x 8.5-inch) book accompanying the test material is awkward and cumbersome to handle. Format and chapter sequences and content often vacillate between first person dialogue describing various facets of brain dominance theory and vague reference to technical properties of the instrument. Furthermore, documentation of past research and theorists is scarce if existent at all. Similarly, one chapter discusses the evolution of HBDI concepts, including numerous experiments referenced (i.e., biofeedback, Berkeley Brain Tests); references are supplied at the end of the book. Consequently, exact references are difficult to track if access to cited sources are desired for follow-up reading.

PURPOSE. The purpose of the HBDI is cited as a personal preference survey intended to help individuals understand their personal manner of interacting with others and responding to events within their environment. However, the purpose is not easily tracked or delineated in the text provided except for vague references within the chapters. It is not clear if the accompanying text was intended to be a technical manual or simply a narrative account of the concept of brain dominance. Perhaps, reading materials would be best organized within clearly delegated focus with one book for discussion materials and a second shorter version of a technical manual that adheres solely to survey artifacts.

ADMINISTRATION. Separate handouts describe test administration with vague reference to standardization techniques (if any), time of administration, and beginning instructions for participants. Ample attention and emphasis cover the confidentiality of individualized protocols including allowance of private feedback time for individual protocols. Accommodations are recommended for half-day to 5-day workshops for group feedback. A 2–4-hour feedback time is suggested for individual participants.

SCORING. Scoring format is not clearly stated in a separate section other than one small section of the protocol, which provides a mail-in address, thus indicating that the author retains sole licensure for scoring the instrument. Although classification scores result in a two-factor bi-polar range of functioning with a third single polar right- or left-hand dominance factor, actual procedures for arriving at the classification scores are not clearly stated. Although the actual survey form is attractive, easy to read, and clearly written, response format changes from a 5-point Likert scale for Work Elements subsection, to a rank-order format for the Key Descriptors and Hobbies subsection, and a forced-choice format for the Adjective Pairs subsection. Another section on Introversion-Extroversion provides participants with a nine-section continuum with no demarcating definition of each of the nine sections. Thus, participants' perception of introvert versus extrovert may vary significantly, particularly without a definition of the concepts on the protocol. A final section, entitled simply Twenty Questions, might best be renamed, as current title appears superfluous. Demographic information is requested on the final page; however, again the participant is asked to rate him/herself on concepts such as rational, organized, interpersonal, and imaginative, yet operational definitions are not provided, thus leaving interpretation to wide variation across participants.

PARTICIPANTS. Sample group demographics are not provided, although on a profile of responses based on occupational classifications samples range as low as 49 females and 82 males for Art Directors to over 2,600 for clerical groups. Yet, given small sample sizes in most cases, the author does state that HBDI profiles are generalizable to other groups. Also, even though early sample groups were drawn during the early 1980s, no reference is made to societal or cultural trends over time and how changes might influence participants' manner of responding based on evolved societal expectations or environmental influences. Method of sample selection was not noted within profile projection materials either, which might have provided the potential test user with a greater ability to decide if the instrument is appropriate for specific groups.

TECHNICAL REPORTS. Reliability and validity are mentioned in various materials provided for review and at times are inappropriately introduced within sections that were said to be devoted to theory or applied use of the instrument. Perhaps, it would be best if the author would confine technical aspects of the instrument in one delegated section of a technical manual so that readers can easily access that information.

Reliability indexes are provided, rendering adequate reliability indexes for test-retest reliability across 78 repeated measures in a large database, but no reference is made to the remaining participants in the database. Because the indexes provided are offered as evidence of HBDI score stability, supportive documentation of demographic information of the 78 participants as well as additional information on the remaining large data base would be helpful. Also, interval periods between test-retest measures should be reported.

Validity is discussed in numerous sections of the main body of the book but only internal validity indexes are provided, generated through factor analysis of data results. Factor loadings in some cases are marginal, barely reaching the acceptable .30 or higher index normally used in interpreting adequate factor loading. External validity of the HBDI is not clearly demonstrated within materials provided. Predictive validity and generalizability of findings across varying groups should be examined cautiously as supportive empirical data are remiss. More detailed descriptions of sample groups and repeated reliability and validity procedures would be helpful. For example, use of Campbell and Fisk's (1959) procedure for multitrait, multimethod validation techniques could be helpful in studying validity properties for the HBDI.

SUMMARY. Even though empirical results to date appear encouraging, continued and more extensive studies for reliability and validity may enhance the plausibility of technical qualities of the HBDI; additional studies and detailed reports of methods and procedures used may greatly enhance the use of this survey. As a method of understanding personal manner of interactions, the HBDI may be helpful, but is also cumbersome to interpret—requiring lengthy time for interpretation of results. In the current format, data are difficult to find and survey materials need to be summarized in a more organized fashion. Perhaps, separating technical materials in a more organized manner in a separate manual with sections clearly delineated in acceptable format with the *Standards for Educational and Psychological Testing* (AERA,

APA, & NCME, 1999) would appropriately display the quality and significance of the HBDI in accordance with expressed intended use of the survey.

REVIEWER'S REFERENCES

Campell, D., & Fiske, D. (1959). Convergent and discriminant validation by the multitrait-multimethod matrix. *Psychological Bulletin, 56,* 81–105.

American Educational Research Association, American Psychological Association, & National Council on Measurement in Education. (1999). *Standards for educational and psychological testing.* Washington, DC: American Educational Research Association.

Review of the Herrmann Brain Dominance Instrument [Revised] by GABRIELE van LINGEN, Professor of Educational Studies, Leadership and Counseling, Murray State University, Murray, KY):

The Hermann Brain Dominance Instrument (HBDI) is in its 18th revision since its original development in the 1970s (Herrmann, 1994). It received a previous review that continues to be relevant (D'Amato, 1992). Applications and format do not appear to have been changed since that review, but the author provides additional research studies in support of the validity and relevance of the instrument.

The HBDI is described as a unique, scientific, broadly applicable tool for assessing thinking styles. The author claims that it is founded in brain physiology, at least metaphorically. It measures a person's preference for thinking in one or several of the four quadrants of the brain: cerebral left or the A quadrant, limbic left or the B quadrant, limbic right or the C quadrant, or cerebral right or the D quadrant. These preferences are related not only to thinking styles, but also to certain preferences in problem solving, decision making, and communicating, as well as to occupational satisfaction. The profile descriptions lead one to conclude that these preferences may reflect more than thinking styles, perhaps representing a broad typology. The Myers-Briggs Type Indicator (Myers & McCaulley, 1985) has figured strongly in both the development of and additional research on the HBDI (Herrmann, 1994; Power & Lundsten, 1997).

Among the applications and uses claimed for the HBDI are a better understanding of self, others, and occupational groups; enhanced communication and interpersonal relationships at work and at home; enhanced productivity and creativity at work; enhanced learning and teaching; and the capability of relating individual profiles to those of college majors, occupational groups, work groups, and families. These myriad purposes present problems for the validation of the instrument.

The HBDI is a 120-item self-report questionnaire. The items are presented in a variety of formats in 11 sections. The response requirements for each vary dramatically. Section 1 contains four items related to Biographical Information; Section 2 has two forced-choice items related to Handedness; a one-item forced priority ranking of three School Subjects makes up Section 3; 16 Work Elements are rated on a 5-point scale in Section 4; Section 5 involves the selection and prioritization of 8 of 25 Key Self-descriptors; Section 6 similarly results in the selection and prioritization of 6 of 22 Hobbies, including an open option; a one-item rating of Energy Level and a two-item rating of Motion Sickness make up Sections 7 and 8, respectively; Section 9 is a forced-choice selection between 24 Adjective pairs; Section 10 is based on a one-item self-rating of Introversion/Extroversion using a 9-point scale; and Section 11 consists of self-ratings on 20 questions using a 5-point scale. The form requests additional information related to birth order, occupations, and other self-descriptive information for confidential research purposes. It also provides a glossary of terms. The form must be returned to Herrmann International for scoring.

The resulting report contains a colorful Profile Overlay, a Data Summary Report, Profile Explanation, and Foursights Application Plan and Poster. The Profile Overlay consists of a pie chart divided into the four brain quadrants, each color-coded, that locates the individual's results as a quadrant profile score on a scale ranging from 0 in the center to 130 at the periphery. The author states that this score can extend over 150, however. The relevant items on which a score is based and the method of scaling are not specified. A table of Preference Codes for each quadrant, scaled from 1 = *Strong Preference* through 2 = *Intermediate Preference* to 3 = *Low Preference*, the results for Adjective Pairs analyzed according to quadrant, and the Profile Scores are also provided. Although the 1 to 3 ratings are each related to a range of profile scores, it is not clear how these ranges were determined.

The Data Summary Report provides general descriptions of each section of the assessment form. The Profile Explanation also explains each profile quadrant and modes (combined mental processes of two adjoining quadrants) in general terms, relates them to occupations, and provides descriptions of 35 profiles—9 single dominant, 17 double dominant, 8 triple dominant, and 1 quadruple dominant. The Foursights Poster provides a graphic organizer allowing the individual to apply these concepts and the individual results to the work environment and plans for future improvement. Thus, much of the specific interpretation and application of the HBDI is the responsibility of the report's recipient.

Before a test can be recommended for general use, objective information on reliability and validity must be available, providing direct checks on how accurately and well it actually measures its claims (Anastasi & Urbina, 1997). Bunderson (in Herrmann, 1994) presents information related to reliability and validity of scores from the HBDI, based on six studies. Most of these have not been published. Many of the conclusions are based on an unpublished doctoral dissertation conducted by Kevin Ho in 1988 with 7,989 subjects (in Herrmann, 1994).

With regard to reliability evidence, only test-retest reliability is addressed. Based on a subsample of 78 cases in Kevin Ho's study, the reported test-retest stability coefficients appear to be adequately high for the hemispheric (both left/right and cerebral/limbic) and quadrant scores, ranging from .86 (Quadrant A) to .97 (Quadrant D). The reliability for the Intro/Extroversion item was moderate at .73. The interval between assessments was not given and may have varied among subjects.

There are several problems with the six studies provided as evidence for internal construct validity. They are all based on factor analyses conducted in the development of the HBDI; therefore it would appear that at least five of them contain different items from the several versions of the questionnaire. Moreover, they include a variety of other tests in addition to the HBDI items, a procedure that confounds the results specific to this particular instrument. The presentation of the results also does not lead to clarity of interpretation. It seems evident that empirical validation for the various constructs or scores of the assessment is not available, other than for right/left hemispheric differences.

As evidence for external construct validation, Bunderson describes a study by Schkade on EEG differences in accountants and artists (*N* = 24). Again, only a global left/right difference is clearly established. Additional dissertation research that has used the HBDI also appears to be mainly consistent with regard to very general right/left distinctions. Moreover, the results of these studies appear to be inconsistently related to the profiles of various occupations that form a large part of the interpretation of the HBDI.

Herrmann maintains that there is a certain validity to the HBDI because it is a self-administered instrument and "we know more about ourselves than anyone else does" (p. 67, 1994). In fact, he claims that information about ourselves provided by others is significantly inaccurate by comparison. Not only does this orientation ignore the fact that many valid personality measures based on self-reports are related to observers' ratings (e.g., Gough, 1965; Hogan, Hogan, & Roberts, 1996), but it creates a major problem for the external validity of this instrument.

SUMMARY. The HBDI, although reportedly receiving a uniformly positive response from participants of Herrmann's management training workshops, cannot make claims for meeting test standards that would recommend it to the public domain. Appropriate reliability and validity studies are not available. The instrument's format itself would appear to present problems for establishing the former, whereas the variety of claimed purposes and constructs would present difficulties for demonstrating the latter. Despite decades of research, there is only minimal credible evidence that the HBDI results in scores that are temporally stable and that the scores relate to meaningful nontest behavior. Other instruments, with established psychometric properties, are better suited for the individual applications that the HBDI claims. For instance, the Myers-Briggs Type indicator (251) is a better instrument for assessing more general personality type or style. For career or occupational decision-making, the Hogan Personality Inventory (Hogan & Hogan, 1995; T5:1212) or the System of Interactive Guidance Information (SIGI-Plus; Katz, 1993), updated for adults, are better suited. Cognitive style is perhaps best assessed by the more established perceptual tasks such as the Embedded Figures Tests (Witkin, Oltman, Raskin & Karp, 1971; T5:926) or by exploring more complex processes, such as Sternberg's thinking styles (1994).

REVIEWER'S REFERENCES

Gough, H. G. (1965). Conceptual analysis of psychological test scores and other diagnostic variables. *Journal of Abnormal Psychology, 70,* 294–320.

Witkin, H. A., Oltman, P. K., Raskin, E., & Karp, S. A. (1971). *A manual for the Embedded Figures Tests.* Palo Alto, CA: Consulting Psychologists Press.

Myers, I. B., & McCaulley, M. H. (1985). *Manual: A guide to the development and use of the Myers-Briggs Type Indicator.* Palo Alto, CA: Consulting Psychologists Press.

D'Amato, R. C. (1992). [Review of the Herrmann Brain Dominance Instrument.] In J. J. Kramer & J. C. Conoley (Eds.), *The eleventh mental measurements yearbook* (pp. 377–378). Lincoln, NE: Buros Institute of Mental Measurements.

Katz, M. R. (1993). Computer-assisted career decision making: The guide in the machine. Hillsdale, NJ: Erlbaum.

Herrmann, N. (1994). *The creative brain* (2nd ed.). Lake Lure, NC: The Ned Herrmann Group.

Sternberg, R. J. (1994). Thinking styles: Theory and assessment at the interface between personality and intelligence. In R. J. Sternberg & P. Ruzgis (Eds.), *Intelligence and Personality*. New York: Cambridge University Press.

Hogan, R., Hogan, J., & Roberts, B. W. (1996). Personality measurement and employment decisions. *American Psychologist, 51*(5), 469–477.

Anastasi, A., & Urbina, S. (1997). *Psychological testing* (7th ed.). Upper Saddle River, NJ: Prentice-Hall, Inc.

Power, S. J., & Lundsten, L. L. (1997). Studies that compare type theory and left-brain/right-brain theory. *Journal of Psychological Type, 43*, 22–28.

[166]
High School Placement Test—Open Edition.

Purpose: Designed as a measure of cognitive and basic skills to assist in placement decisions for entering freshmen.

Population: Eighth grade students.

Publication Dates: 1982–1995.

Acronym: HSPT.

Scores, 5: Verbal Skills, Quantitative Skills, Reading, Mathematics, Language.

Administration: Group.

Restricted Distribution: Available for school purchase only.

Price Data, 1997: $98.09 per starter set including manual ('95, 15 pages), and 35 test booklets; $34.88 per 35 optional test booklets (specify subject); $5 per large-print test booklet; $28.34 per 50 answer sheets; $22.94 per scoring kit including manual for hand scoring and interpreting results, 1 answer key, and 2 class record sheets; $5.83 per manual; $6.33 per manual for handscoring and interpreting results; $7.96 per technical supplement; $.42 per pressure sensitive label; $.31 per student score folder; $18 per audio-cassette; $8.18 per 20 practice tests; $19.48 per specimen set.

Time: (135) minutes plus (15–25) minutes per optional test.

Comments: Optional tests available including science, mechanical aptitude, and Catholic religion.

Author: Scholastic Testing Service, Inc.

Publisher: Scholastic Testing Service, Inc.

Review of the High School Placement Test— Open Edition by JOHN O. ANDERSON, Professor, Faculty of Education, University of Victoria, Victoria, British Columbia, Canada:

The High School Placement Test (HSPT) has been published since 1955 and is intended to assist high schools in the selection and placement of freshmen students (Grade 9) by providing standardized estimates of verbal and quantitative abilities, and achievement in reading, language, and mathematics. In addition, there are three optional tests available in Science, Mechanical Aptitude, and Religion. The following comment will focus exclusively on the five-component HSPT consisting of the Quantitative, Verbal, Reading, Language, and Mathematics subtests.

Two versions of the HSPT are available: the open edition, which is the same test available one year to the next; and the closed edition, which allows for a high degree of test security by restricting item exposure. A new closed version is developed annually and normed on a U.S. national sample of 5,000 Grade 8 students. This development of multiple forms of the test creates a need for equating test scores across the different versions of the HSPT. The Scholastic Testing Service uses both equipercentile equating and one-parameter IRT approaches for equating. The 1980 administration of the test is the form to which all other versions have been equated. The equating procedures are briefly described in the technical manual but further information would have to be made in order to understand fully the procedures and evaluate the extent to which each version of the test does indeed generate equivalent results.

The test consists of 298 multiple-choice items and requires approximately 3 hours to administer. Students respond to the test on a single-page answer sheet. The test publishers, Scholastic Testing Service, provide a scoring service for the closed edition of the HSPT that generates standard scores, national and local percentiles, and grade equivalent scores for the five components of the HSPT, the composite score for the two cognitive abilities tests (called the Cognitive Skills Quotient), the composite score for the three academic skills tests (the Basic Skills Score), and the composite score for the whole battery of 298 items. In addition to student results, school and system level reports can be ordered as well as item analysis reports. The Open Edition of the test must be scored by school personnel to produce standard scores and national percentiles.

The HSPT is accompanied with an administration manual, an interpretive manual, a technical supplement, and a report on validity studies. The administration manual provides a concise overview of the tests, clearly lays out the directions for test administration, and includes a script of directions to be read to students. The interpretive manual provides a description and explanation of the scores generated by the tests and a discussion of how these scores may be interpreted and used. The technical manual provides information on the internal reliabilities of the tests and standard errors of measurement that further assist the user in the interpretation and use of the test results.

The construct or content validity of scores from the HSPT is not well addressed in any of the materials that accompany the test. The items comprising the HSPT are not clearly described in terms of the skills and abilities that are being measured. There is a listing of item types within each section of the HSPT and a note claiming great care was taken in the development of items, but no clear descriptions of the underlying framework or development procedures are provided. The composite verbal and quantitative ability estimate is reported as a Cognitive Skills Quotient (CSQ). The CSQ is described as analogous to an intelligence quotient (and reported on the same scale with a mean of 100) but it is claimed to be better because the underlying abilities are more closely related to academic performance and therefore more predictive of high school performance—a claim that is not substantiated in the documentation provided with the test. The Reading, Language, and Mathematics sections of the test are not described in terms of item development or in terms of linkage to curricular or theoretic frameworks and models of reading, writing, and mathematics. However, predictive validity has been extensively studies by the Scholastic Testing Service and is reported in a separate publication. The studies have correlated the scores generated by the HSPT (for Grade 8 students) with scores of the same students on various indicators of subsequent high school performance including the Scholastic Aptitude Test (SAT), American College Testing Program (ACT), Metropolitan Achievement Test, California Achievement Test, and Grade 11 grade-point averages. The correlations of the composite HSPT scores to the standardized tests (SAT, ACT, MAT, and CAT) are positive with the average correlation approximately .75. The correlations to Grade 11 grade-point average were lower (approximately .55) as would be expected given the variability in the composition and calculations of student grades. These results lend credence to the predictiveness of the HSPT in relation to high school performance 2 to 4 years after the administration of the test.

The use of grade equivalent scores is discussed in the interpretive manual and appropriate cautions about their use are given. However, and as noted in the manual, the use of grade equivalent scores is fraught with potential serious problems. Nonetheless, these scores are provided as part of the HSPT. Serious consideration should be given to discontinuing their presence in the HSPT.

SUMMARY. The HSPT is a test designed to predict performance in high school and the predictive validity studies support its use for this purpose. The HSPT provides a traditional standardized measure (multiple-choice item format) of basic academic skills of Grade 8 students and as such can find utility in making placement decisions for incoming high school students. If schools are in a position in which the student records from elementary school do not provide an adequate basis for making selection and placement decisions, the HSPT can provide useful, standardized information. In deciding on whether to use the HSPT, a school should carefully estimate the costs of using such a test and the following should be factored into the calculations: the purchase price for the test materials and the scoring service; the costs of administrative time of acquisition, distribution, student organization, and test interpretation; and the value of the 3 hours of student time required to write the test. In using the test a school should conduct its own validity studies in order to monitor the effectiveness of the HSPT in enhancing the accuracy of selection placement decisions for incoming students.

Review of the High School Placement Test— Open Edition by GENEVA D. HAERTEL, Senior Educational Researcher, SRI International, Menlo Park, CA:

The High School Placement Test (HSPT), published by the Scholastic Testing Service (STS), was the first test battery designed to assist high schools in making selection or placement decisions by objectively measuring the basic and cognitive skills of entering students from different elementary, middle, and junior high schools. Because the battery is designed to select high school applicants, test security has been a priority, and a new edition of the battery is developed each year. Only one form of the battery is available annually. In addition to the HSPT's use for student selection and placement, it is also used to guide remediation of incoming students in basic skill areas, and as part of a process to award scholarships.

The test battery assesses students' basic skills in reading, mathematics, and language, and their verbal and quantitative cognitive skills. In addition, optional tests are available to measure students' mechanical aptitude, knowledge of science, and the Catholic religion. The edition of the HSPT reviewed comprised 298 multiple-choice items, each of which had three or four distractors. One hundred and eighty six of these items were used to measure the three basic skill areas: Reading (comprehension, 40 items; vocabulary, 22 items); Mathematics (concepts, 24 items; problem-solving, 40 items); and language (capitalization, punctuation, and usage, 31 items; spelling, 10 items; miscellaneous, 19 items). One hundred and twelve items were used to measure cognitive skills; Verbal (60 items) and Quantitative (52 items). The same multiple-choice format is used in the optional tests in Science (1991 version) and the Catholic religion (1990 version). Each of the science and religion tests is composed of 40 multiple-choice items with four distractors. The mechanical aptitude test was not made available for this review. Students use mark-sense answer sheets to record their responses.

The HSPT provides normative scores for each calculated subscale, total, and composite score. Among the scores provided are national percentile ranks, local percentile ranks, grade equivalents, and standard scores. A cognitive skills quotient (CSQ) is provided and interpreted as a replacement for the traditional IQ score. It takes into account the student's age at the time of testing on the Verbal and Quantitative skill subscales. Optional test scores are presented as raw scores and national percentile ranks.

Although the other types of scores used to report performance on the HSPT are commonly employed in measures of academic performance, the use and interpretation of the CSQ is more unusual and open to challenge. In the HSPT Interpretive Manual, the CSQ is described as a predictive index of a student's future academic and learning potential and is to be interpreted as a traditional IQ score. Thus, a CSQ of 100–109 "represents academic potential that is found in the second quarter of the school population—50th to 75th percentiles" (Interpretive Manual, 1985, p. 4). Despite the test publisher's claims that the CSQ should be treated as a measure of academic potential, they provide no technical information supporting the validity of the CSQ, nor do they explain why a measure of academic potential rather than attainment should be employed as part of the selection process. Many legal challenges have been directed at the use of IQ tests in placing students in instructional programs and schools during the past two decades. If a district or school is committed to use a measure of IQ or learning potential in placement decisions, it would be wise to select an IQ measure that is supported by an abundance of high-quality reliability and validity data.

The 1995 Manual of Directions for the HSPT describes the battery, its subscales, and scores. It provides thorough instructions on time requirements, assessment materials needed, and use of the answer sheet. Scripts are provided for opening and closing the test period and for administering each of the subscales. The HSPT is a power test and is designed to estimate maximum performance of students in knowledge and skills. Time limits were established based on data showing that between 80% and 85% of students were able to attempt all items. The directions in the manual are clear and comprehensive and, if followed, increase the likelihood of a standardized administration.

The STS provides substantial interpretive and statistical information on the HSPT. The Interpretive Manual and the small brochure entitled "Your Scores on the STS High School Placement Test" provide excellent, user-friendly information on what the various scores mean. The psychometric data are presented in the *High School Placement Test: Technical Supplement,* which describes validity, reliability, item characteristics, norming procedures, standard errors of measurement, and subscale difficulty levels and discriminatory power.

The STS employs a two-step norming procedure to generate annual national norms for the HSPT. A norming sample of up to 1,000 students, composed of eighth graders who definitely intend to enroll in a secondary school, is selected and each student is randomly assigned to one of two groups—one group takes the new form of the HSPT and the second group takes the prior year's form. Using these randomly equivalent groups, the STS links the new and prior items and uses the Rasch model (Item Response Theory, one-parameter model) to equate the two versions of the test. The second step of developing the norms involves cross-validating the preceding year's norms.

Descriptive statistics are presented for each HSPT subscale. These statistics include average raw score, standard deviation, functional range of the subscale (i.e., the difference in the raw-score points between the 99th and 1st percentile rank), and the percent of items available for differentiating among the top 5% of students (i.e., difference between the maximum subscale score and the 95th percentile, expressed as a percentage of the full range of scores).

Statistics describing the subscales' difficulty levels reveal that the average percent correct (i.e., the mean score expressed as a proportion of the total number of items) ranges from 48% to 58%. The discriminatory power of the subscales is adequate for the HSPT's purposes: The functional ranges of the full subscales extend from 56% to 74%, whereas the functional range of the subscales between the 95th and 100th percentile extends from 14% to 23% (an average of about 19% of the items on each subscale are available to discriminate student performance at the highest levels). Because this battery is used to identify students at the top 5% to 10% of the national eighth-grade population, the subscales' ability to discriminate among scores at higher levels is essential. The HSPT subscales have an appropriate level of difficulty and discriminatory power given their purpose.

The Technical Supplement also provides item statistics that were used to develop the subscales. For each item, the mean difficulty index and the item discrimination index are presented. Most of the item discrimination indices on the HSPT range between .20 and .55. The item discrimination index presented for each item, in combination with the item's mean difficulty index, are at acceptable levels for such a selection test.

KR_{20} and KR_{21} reliability coefficients were presented for each of the cognitive and basic skills subscales and for the composite scores. The KR_{21} coefficients range from .85 to .97. The magnitude of these coefficients indicates that there is a high degree of item uniformity within each subscale. The use of the KR_{20} is sufficient as an estimate of the internal consistency of the HSPT's subscales; the addition of the KR_{21} adds little additional information. The Technical Supplement does not report test-retest reliabilities. The calculation of test-retest reliabilities would determine the amount of variance associated with the testing occasion, which is critical information when evaluating a selection test. Although the Technical Supplement reports reliabilities, there is little interpretation of them.

Three sets of standard errors of measurement (*SEM*) are reported. These include *SEM*s for (a) raw scores, (b) standard scores, and (c) the cognitive skills quotient and grade equivalents. As with the reliability data, the *SEM*s are interpreted. There is no discussion concerning the use of *SEM*s to construct confidence intervals that would identify the range of scores within which a student's true score is likely to fall with a specified probability.

Do the various HSPT subscales measure truly different knowledge and abilities? Intercorrelations among the basic skills and cognitive subscales range in magnitude from .64 to .83. Seven of the intercorrelations are below .75, and three are between .76 and .83. The magnitudes of these intercorrelations are moderate, which indicates that the scales are sufficiently independent to support their differential use in placement and counseling decisions.

High-quality validity data are essential for high-stakes tests. The HSPT presents content validity data in its Technical Supplement. Tables are presented that specify the number of items from each of the three basic-skill HSPT subscales that measure common eighth-grade curriculum objectives. The source of the eighth-grade curriculum objectives is not identified. In this age of educational reform and standards-based curriculum, there can be dramatic variations in the curriculum content emphasized in different schools, districts, and states. Currently, users of the test can examine these tables and see what overlap exists between the items on the HSPT, the curricula objectives specified in the tables, and the curriculum that is delivered in their school or district. It would be helpful if tables were provided that demonstrate the alignment of HSPT items with traditional and reform-based curricula objectives.

Determining the content validity of the cognitive subscales is very complex, given that the cognitive items measure skills that are not typically part of a curriculum. STS addresses the content validity of the cognitive subscales by indicating the number of HSPT items on the subscales that match the types of items traditionally used to measure cognitive skills (e.g., analogies, syllogisms, numeric sequencing). Advances in cognitive psychology have resulted in the development of numerous theories of cognition and not all of them contain the same skills. The rationale and theoretical basis for the selection of types of skills and items should be included.

Although the HSPT does assess a variety of valuable curriculum content and skills, its content validity can be challenged. For example, 27 computation items occur in the problem-solving section of the Mathematics basic skills subscale, as compared to 13 application items. Some mathematics educators would dispute such a reliance on computation items in a subscale labeled as "problem-solving." The number and types of items contained in the subscales should represent the depth of knowledge needed for students to perform successfully in high school. The STS should provide a rationale explaining the distribution of the items in the various subscales.

Statistical information on the HSPT's validity is reported in *STS Validity Studies: Relating Performance on the STS High School Placement Test.* This technical bulletin reports results of studies conducted from Spring 1992 through Spring 1996. Published in 1997, this document relates performance on the HSPT to subsequent high school performance using various criterion measures administered to students at different grade levels. The validity coefficients reported span from 1 to 4 years (studies correlate incoming freshmen's performance on the HSPT with their subsequent performance on various criterion measures at the 9th, 10th, 11th, or 12th grade levels) and represent results from over 90 separate predictive validity studies conducted in 33 schools in 10 different states. The following criterion measures were used in the studies: Preliminary Scholastic Aptitude Test; Scholastic Aptitude Test; American College Testing Program; National Educational Development Test; PLAN; Metropolitan Achievement Test; California Achievement Test; Stanford Achievement Battery; and grade point average in 11th grade.

For each annual edition of the test, criterion results are available 1 to 4 years after the battery was administered. Thus, results of predictive validity studies are reported by STS every 4 to 5 years. The magnitudes of the validity coefficients between the subscales of the HSPT and subscales of the various criterion measures reported in the 1997 technical bulletin ranged from $r = .44$ to .94, but concentrated around $r = .65$ to .75. The magnitude of correlations between the composite scores of the criterion measures and the HSPT battery total were greater. They ranged from $r = .32$ to .92, but centered $r = .80$. These very substantial validity coefficients provide ample evidence that the HSPT can be used for the purposes of selecting, placing, remediating, and awarding scholarships.

SUMMARY. The HSPT is a useful measure to assist high schools in making high-stakes decisions that affect the educational opportunities provided to individual students. Substantial statistical information is available on the test battery, but the absence of interpretive commentary on some of the test battery's technical qualities (i.e., reliability, standard errors of measurement, and item characteristics) reduces the test consumer's ability to judge the battery's appropriateness for their setting.

The market for test batteries such as the HSPT will grow in the next few years because of the public's strong interest in school choice. Schools and districts will be looking for psychometrically sound instruments to select and place students in schools with limited enrollments. The HSPT can be used for such high-stakes decisions, but additional technical and interpretive information should be provided about the CSQ to ensure that the consequences of using this particular score are defensible.

[167]
High/Scope Child Observation Record for Ages 2 1/2–6.

Purpose: Designed to assess children's development, learning, and interests.
Population: Ages 2 1/2–6 years.
Publication Date: 1992.
Acronym: COR.
Scores, 6: Initiative, Social Relations, Creative Representation, Music and Movement, Language and Literacy, Logic and Mathematics.
Administration: Group.
Price Data: Available from publisher.
Time: Administration time not reported.
Comments: Ratings by teachers.
Author: High/Scope Educational Research Foundation.
Publisher: High/Scope Educational Research Foundation.

Review of the High/Scope Child Observation Record for Ages 2 1/2–6 by GLEN P. AYLWARD, Professor of Pediatrics, Psychiatry and Behavioral and Social Sciences, Southern Illinois University School of Medicine, Springfield, IL:

The High/Scope Child Observation Record (COR) is an observational instrument designed to allow staff members of early childhood educational programs, preschools, and similar child-care facilities to record behaviors in children ages 2 years, 6 months to 6 years. Observations are made in normal program activities and are grouped into six developmental categories: (a) Initiative (expressing choices, solving problems, engaging in complex play, cooperating in program routines); (b) Social Relations (relating to adults, relating to other children, making friends with other children, engaging in problem solving, understanding and expressing feelings); (c) Creative Representation (making and building, drawing and painting, pretending), (d) Music and Movement (exhibiting body coordination, exhibiting manual coordination, imitating movements to a steady beat, following music and movement directions); (e) Language and Literacy (understanding speech, speaking, showing interest in reading activities, demonstrating knowledge about books, beginning reading, beginning writing), and (f) Logic and Mathematics (sorting, using the words *not, some, all,* arranging materials in graduated order, using comparison words, comparing numbers of objects, counting objects, describing spatial relations, describing sequence and time). The COR therefore contains a total of 30 items, each scored on a 5-point scale. Essentially, the observer chooses a statement that best represents the presumed highest level of behavior characteristic of the child under observation. For example, in the Initiative category, the *solving problems* subscale includes options ranging from "child does not yet identify problems" (score of 1) to "child tries alternative methods to solve a problem and is highly involved and persistent" (score of 5). Most items are initiated by the child, versus being elicited by the examiner.

The complete High/Scope COR kit includes a 52-page manual, assessment booklets (each can be used three times for the same child), anecdotal notecards, parent report forms, and a COR poster. The instrument can be used to evaluate individual children or groups, curricula (or parts of a curriculum), or specific characteristics of particular groups being served such as bilingual children or those with special needs. The COR can be used to provide feedback to parents, staff, administrators, program evaluators, or researchers.

The COR is the result of previous efforts to assess outcomes of the High/Scope Preschool Curriculum. Originally, items had three to seven scoring options, but in the present version, all have five possible scores; several items were added and others deleted from the original version to produce the current 30-item version. The end result is an instrument that could be applied to a variety of curricula.

A total of 64 teams, each consisting of a Head Start teacher and an assistant teacher collected data on 484 children who were attending preschool programs in southeastern Michigan. Of these, 51% were African American, 26% were white, 14% middle Eastern, 7% Hispanic, 2% Asian, and 1% Native American. A major drawback is that the specific ages of the children were not stated. Teams underwent 3 days of initial training and were supported and monitored throughout data collection. The authors emphasize the need for periodic refresher sessions to enhance reliability in routine COR usage.

Alpha coefficients for teachers ranged from .80 to .93; for assistants, values ranged from .72 to .91 (based on a sample of 50 teachers, 50 assistants, and 484 children). Pearson correlations between teacher and assistant scores ranged from .61 to .72.

"Factor loadings" for subscales and the six developmental categories, based on the responses of 51 teachers and 484 children, are reported to range from .57 to .82, with most being above .75. Correlations between the six factors (developmental scales) were .69 to .84 ($M = .75$), based on a sample of 484 children and 50 teachers. The authors report relationships between teacher-rated COR items from Fall to Spring, with ratings increasing by .9 points over this period, from 2.6 to 3.4; correlations between ratings ranged from .29 to .60. The samples were not described in detail, and they appeared to be of a mixed nature (i.e., cross-sectional and longitudinal, with ns of 484 and 415, respectively).

Validity evidence included correlations between COR ratings and the McCarthy Scales of Children's Abilities (MSC) ($n = 98$); these ranged from .27 to .66. The COR language and Literacy scale had the highest correlations with the MSCA (.53–.66), whereas Music and Movement had the lowest (.27–.46). In regard to demographic variables, correlations between COR ratings and age were .51–.61 ($n = 385$), gender .00–.07 ($n = 376$), and socioeconomic variables .14–.28 (parent schooling and employment). The socioeconomic variables are not well described and their influence may have been underestimated, due to the homogeneity (i.e., generally low SES) of the sample.

The COR Assessment Booklet contains a summary page where the examiner transfers subscale scores from preceding pages and produces an average score for each of the six developmental categories. Unfortunately, there are no directions as to what to do with these scores, or how best to interpret them. This issue underscores the problem of not specifying ages of the sample children. It would enhance interpretation if mean scores and standard deviations for each age were presented. Along these lines, item statistics (Table 1 in the manual) are rendered meaningless because the user has no idea as to the ages of the children involved. As it now stands, it is assumed that each subscale scoring option represents an increment in the child's developmental level, although it was not indicated how this assumed developmental sequence was validated.

The intent of the COR is in line with the new models or "visions" of developmental assessment of infants and young children, namely moving away from norm-referenced testing to criterion-referenced, curriculum-based, or performance assessments (particularly the latter). Given that the movement espouses assessment that involves multiple sources of information and multiple components, avoidance of unfamiliar surroundings, use of a familiar assessor, and decreased reliance on formal tests and tools, the COR has potential. However, the authors have indicated that individuals not familiar with a child would have a difficult time completing the COR, requiring at least three contacts before completing the instrument reliably. Moreover, time taken to complete the instrument is not specified. These factors may make the instrument rather time-consuming. Conversely, the COR does tap the child's level and pattern of organizing experience and functional capacities, with integration of cognitive, social, and emotional abilities. Moreover, it bridges the gap between assessment and intervention and allows for cultural and ethnic differences, particularly with the use of the option of additional descriptors. Unfortunately, it may do so at the cost of psychometric rigor.

Review of the High/Scope Child Observation Record for Ages 2 1/2–6 by MARY MATHAI CHITTOORAN, UC Foundation Assistant Profes-

sor of School Psychology, The University of Tennessee at Chattanooga, Chattanooga, TN:

The High/Scope Child Observation Record (COR) is described by the authors as a developmentally appropriate assessment instrument for use in early childhood settings. It is designed to allow teachers to assess young children's developmental progress by gathering semistructured observations of their behaviors over a period of several months. The COR offers a nonintrusive alternative to "artificial and limited testing situations" (manual, p. 3) and allows teachers to observe children as they engage in daily instructional activities. Observations may be made on six subscales: Initiative, which assesses the ability to begin and follow through on tasks; Social Relations, which assesses social interactions with peers and adults; Creative Representation, which measures the ability to represent objects and experiences through symbolic means such as imagination, language, and art; Music and Movement, which assesses musical abilities as well as fine and gross motor skills; Language and Literacy, which evaluates listening, speaking, reading, and writing; and finally, Logic and Mathematics, which assesses logical thinking and mathematical reasoning.

The COR has 30 items grouped under the major subscales. Each item includes five descriptive statements that represent a range of functioning, from very poor (rated 1) to very superior (rated 5). The rater selects the statement that best describes the functioning level of the child and adds relevant notes about the child's behaviors. Although behaviors are preferably self-initiated, the COR does allow observers to structure situations or ask questions to prompt a desired behavior. Ratings are transferred to the Summary of Scores sheet. Subscale scores, which represent the average rating for all items on a subscale during a single observation period, may be computed.

The COR was developed and validated over a 2-year period beginning in 1989. Sixty-four teaching teams and nine home-based teachers representing eight Head Start programs in Southeastern Michigan were recruited, trained, and paid for their involvement. Teaching teams were responsible for approximately 2,500 children a year who were ethnically representative of Head Start programs across the nation.

Teachers' COR ratings showed an average increase of .9 between fall and spring ratings for the 1990–1991 school year. Pearson product-moment correlations between the two sets of teacher ratings ranged from .29 to .60 and factor loadings of items completed for the six COR categories ranged from .57 to .82, with only four items loading below .70. Factor correlations between scales ranged from .69 to .84. With regard to reliability, the manual reports intraobserver alpha coefficients ranging from .80 to .93 for teachers and .72 to .91 for assistant teachers. Interobserver Pearson product-moment correlations for ratings completed by 50 teaching teams ($n = 484$) were found to range between .61 and .72.

Concurrent validity evidence was collected from a sample of 98 children who were evaluated with both the COR and the McCarthy Scales of Children's Abilities. The manual reports correlations ranging from a high of .66 between the COR's Language and Literacy subscale and the McCarthy's Perceptual-Performance scale and a low of .27 between the COR's Music and Movement subscale and the McCarthy's Verbal subscale. The manual also reports correlations ranging from a low of .37 to a high of .53 on four pairs of similar scales. COR ratings showed moderate correlations with children's age and low to negligible correlations with variables such as child's gender and parental schooling and employment. A related study demonstrated the feasibility of training teaching staff to use the COR; 10 research assistants were provided with 3 days of training and practice and achieved a 92.8% agreement rate.

CRITIQUE. The High/Scope Child Observation Record provides a systematic way of gathering information about young children that obviates the difficulties associated with traditional methods of assessment. COR materials are attractive and aid in ease of administration. Anecdotal notecards allow teachers to document children's behaviors over the course of several months and the Assessment Booklet, which can be used three times, provides a convenient summary of developmental progress. The items and their associated descriptors are particularly helpful. For example, on the item, "Child distinguishes between *some* and *all* and uses these terms in categorizing" the descriptor is, "When watering plants, Diana says, 'these are all plants; some of them are cactus plants.'" The Parent Report, also available in Spanish, affords teachers an easy way to communicate assessment information to parents. Behavioral indicators in each domain simplify the development of short-term instructional objectives and may be particularly useful for teachers of children with special needs.

One rather obvious omission in the manual is a clear discussion of how to interpret and use COR subscale scores. Such information would be invaluable for teachers who want to use assessment results for instructional planning. Factor correlations are rather high, indicating not only that children's behavior remains consistent across domains of functioning and that observers tend to rate individuals consistently, as the authors suggest, but that the six subscales may be related to one another, at least in this preschool population. A child's functioning in one domain may not be independent of his or her functioning in another domain.

The COR's technical features are its weakest area. The authors offer very little information about the actual development of the COR, stating only that it was developed in several versions over the course of a decade. With the exception of ethnic composition, there is little information provided about the validation sample or about the teaching teams who participated in the study. Such information would appear to be critically important. The issue of content validity is only tangentially addressed. Although the COR is based on the High/Scope Preschool Curriculum, there is no indication that efforts were made to judge the degree of agreement between the two, or between the COR and other preschool curricula. A panel of experts might have been profitably used to address content validity and to comment on item content and format. The manual does not provide evidence of construct validity although the COR purports to measure several important constructs in early childhood development. Concurrent validity correlations with scores on the McCarthy are low. The McCarthy differs from the COR in intent and format, so correlations could hardly be expected to be high. More information on criterion-related validity would be useful; for example, do documented delays at this stage necessarily mean that children will experience deficits later? Does superior performance on the COR suggest fewer problems in the elementary years? Given the purpose of Head Start and preschool programs like it, the answers to such questions may very well be important.

Internal consistency reliability estimates appear to be adequate; however, interobserver reliability is not as impressive. There are too few items, both on the total scale and on the subscales; for example, both the Initiative and the Music and Movement subscales only have four items. The feasibility study was conducted using research assistants, not regular teachers or teaching assistants, and as such, offers limited generalizability.

Technical issues must be addressed before the COR can be recommended without reservation. However, given its limitations, the COR may still be profitably used as part of a comprehensive assessment battery if results are interpreted with caution.

[168]
Hogan Development Survey.

Purpose: "Designed to assess eleven common dysfunctional dispositions."
Population: Ages 16 and older.
Publication Dates: 1995–1997.
Acronym: HDS.
Scores: 11 scales: Excitable, Skeptical, Cautious, Reserved, Leisurely, Bold, Mischievous, Colorful, Imaginative, Diligent, Dutiful.
Administration: Group.
Price Data, 1998: $2 per test booklet; $12.50 per 25 answer sheets; $45 per manual ('97, 74 pages); $30 per interpretive profile; $15 per graph or data file profile.
Time: (20) minutes.
Authors: Robert Hogan and Joyce Hogan (manual).
Publisher: Hogan Assessment Systems, Inc.

Review of the Hogan Development Survey by GLEN FOX, Clinical Psychologist, Occupational Psychology Services, Sevenoaks, Kent, England:

The Hogan Development Survey (HDS) is a self-administered personality questionnaire that focuses on personality disorders occupying the psychological space halfway between psychopathology and normal personality. The rationale for its use is the paucity of instruments mapping dysfunctional interpersonal behavior outside the clinical area, and the need to identify disorders that inhibit optimum functioning in the workplace or the home.

The HDS contains 11 scales and 168 items to which a respondent indicates "agree" or "disagree." There is no item overlap among the scales. The scales are Excitable, Skeptical, Cautious, Reserved, Leisurely, Bold, Mischievous, Colorful, Imaginative, Diligent, and Dutiful. Each of the scales maps onto one of the DSM-IV personality disorders, but in diluted form. Thus HDS "Skeptical" maps onto DSM-IV "Paranoia," HDS "Mischievous" onto DSM "Antisocial," HDS "Diligent" onto DSM "Obsessive-Compulsive," and so on. Like the California Psychological Inventory (CPI), based on the Minnesota Multiphasic Personality Inventory (MMPI), the instrument has its roots in the clinical field, but unlike the CPI's empirically based item content, or the factor analytic structure of the Sixteen Personality Factor Questionnaire (16PF) or the Personality Research Form (PRF), construction appears to be wholly deductive and depends on the views and expertise of the authors.

The HDS can be administered to individuals or small groups using either paper and pencil or computer software. The software can then be used to score the responses and generate a computer narrative report. An optical scanner can also be used to score paper responses, or alternatively a bureau fax/mail-in scoring service is available.

INTENDED USERS. The test is intended for use in coaching and development, and as a selection tool for high level appointments and for posts where personality disorders would be particularly dangerous, such as police officers or airline pilots.

STANDARDIZATION. The standardization sample consisted of over 2,000 adults, including employed adults, job applicants, prisoners, and graduate students. The proportions of these groups are not given, so it is not possible to tell how representative the sample is of the workplace population, although it is clear that women were substantially underrepresented. The ages in the samples ranged from 21 to 65, with a mean age of 38.5. The sample was made up of 1,532 men and 322 women; 150 identified themselves as black and 15% were college educated.

There is no indication given in the manual as to which questions relate to which scales. No item analyses are presented, although the authors do say that items were "screened" (they do not indicate how this was done) to avoid clinical themes, religious beliefs, or sexual preferences. No scoring keys are provided, so users have to rely on computer software or return the instrument for scoring and interpretation.

However, norms can be computed from means and standard deviations, which are given in the technical data. Each of the 11 scales appears to be more or less normally distributed, with the exception of the Diligence scale, which is somewhat skewed to the right.

RELIABILITY. The internal consistency indices for the scales range from .50 to .78. Cronbach's alpha is calculated on a sample of 2,071. All but 4 of these 11 reliability coefficients are below the minimum level of .70. Test-retest values show that the test's stability across time (3-month interval) is somewhat better, with coefficients ranging from .58 to .87, but these were calculated on a very small sample of 60 students.

Somewhat oddly, the authors assert that the standard error of measurement is consistent across the scales and averages .06, but it is clear that they have confused the standard error of the mean with standard error of measurement. The standard error of measurement actually varies between 1.02 and 1.48, which is a little over half a standard deviation for most scales. This is to be expected, given the relatively poor reliability of the instrument, but it must cast some doubt on the accuracy of reported results.

VALIDITY. Construct validity evidence is supplied in the form of correlations between scores on the HDS and those from other instruments, including two inventories devised by the same authors: the Motives, Values, Preferences Inventory (MVPI) and the Hogan Personality Inventory (HPI); the MMPI, on which the instrument is conceptually based; and, rather puzzlingly, the Watson Glaser Critical Thinking Appraisal and the Industrial Reading Test. There are some high correlations between the MMPI and HDS for appropriate scales. The Diligent scale, however, does not seem to correlate well with any of the other measures, even with the MMPI Compulsive scale ($r = .14$) on which it is based.

Further concurrent validation evidence is offered in the form of correlations between observers' descriptive ratings of individuals, and the HDS. These are not particularly strong, ranging from .13 to .3, with 65% of the correlations at or below .2.

FAIRNESS. Mean differences are given for each scale by gender ($N_M = 1,532$; $N_F = 322$), race ($N_{white} = 622$; $N_{black} = 150$) and age (907 under 40; 801 over 40). No t-test results are given, but in all cases the mean differences are substantially less than the standard error of measurement, indicating that the test is unlikely to show adverse impact, although the disproportion of males to females and the lack of information about the representative nature of each gender sample may make this a premature conclusion.

GUIDANCE RELATING TO USE. The manual indicates that the instrument can be used in the workplace as a selection and development instrument. The scores are given in three percentile bands: Average (0% to 40%), Elevated (41% to 89%), and High (90% to 100%). If these percentile ranges are derived from a group of adults from the normal population, it seems a little unusual to treat the bottom 40% of the group as average, and to presume that the majority of the standardization sample therefore had elevated scores. Again, it would be useful to know the true composition of the group. The banding also seems crude and a little risky, given the size of the standard error of the test. For example, a person with an Elevated rating might have been given a score of 60 (which given the standard error, might really represent a true score of 40, which falls in the average band) or they might have been given a score of 70 (which might really represent a true score of 90 [high]).

Scale by scale descriptions are given, with alternative comments for each of the three percentile bands. There are very sharp distinctions in the comments made for the various percentile bandings: "Average scorers may be described as quiet, modest and unassuming ... elevated scorers may be seen by others as unfocused and distractible ... High scorers are often described as self-promoting and not listening well" (manual, p. 34). In view of the size of the standard error, and the broad brush approach to the three bands, it seems speculative to imply such strong differences between them.

There are also some examples of integrated interpretation with whole profiles using attendant descriptions (e.g., "Litigious Profile" [high on Leisurely, Skeptical, Diligent, and Imaginative] and "Corporate Stalker Profile" [high on Reserved, Colorful, Imaginative, and Mischievous, and average on Dutiful, Leisurely and Diligent]). In view of the very strong statements made in these interpretations, (e.g., "This person should be suspicious, resentful, easily upset, and should have odd or unusual theories about others' intentions, as well as being fussy, picky, critical and judgmental" (p. 43), better validational data would have been more reassuring.

SUMMARY. The inventory appears conceptually to fill a need for a measure of personality disorders in the "normal" working population. However, there are a number of caveats. The standardization sample was largely non-college-educated, which may cast some doubt on the applicability of the instrument to higher educated clients. More information is needed on this norm group, which should be fully representative of the normal working population. The reliability of several of the scales is not particularly high, and the standard error is too large for the percentile bandings to be reliable, or for some of the comments made in the sample interpretations to be safely used in many applications. It might have been wiser for the authors to have described the "Elevated" band in more borderline terms, and to have made sharp distinctions only between the "Average" and "High" bands, in view of the ease with which a person scoring Elevated might (because of error) have a true Average score. The validational data relating to performance is also disappointing, both in quantity and quality. The measure may be of use in a developmental context, but more evidence is needed before the HDS can safely be offered as a selection tool.

Review of the Hogan Development Survey by E. SCOTT HUEBNER, *Professor of Psychology, University of South Carolina, Columbia, SC:*
The Hogan Development Survey (HDS) is a 168-item self-report scale designed to measure 11 dysfunctional dispositions in the work environment that would "be used primarily for professional development and coaching rather than personnel selection" (manual, p. 7). The 11 dispositions were derived from the personality disorder and managerial derailment literatures. High scores on the various dimensions were expected to be related to interpersonal difficulties in general and occupational difficulties in particular. The authors theorized that the HDS dimensions reflect core themes of the various personality disorders, which "occupy a psychological space halfway between the domain mapped by measures of normal personality … and measures of abnormal personality" (manual, p. 3). Scale names and items were crafted so as to deliberately avoid medical or psychiatric content.

The 80-page manual describes aspects of administration, scoring, interpretation, and technical properties. Administration procedures are outlined clearly. Three computerized scoring options are available, including mail-in/fax scoring. Manual scoring, however, is not possible. Although it is not entirely clear, it appears that test scores are limited to percentile ranks.

The HDS manual provides limited information regarding the standardization sample. Although the sample was large, its representativeness is questionable. Inadequate information is provided regarding a number of crucial sample variables, such as the number of participants per age group, the geographic location of the participants, and socioeconomic status levels of the participants. The ratio of males to females is about 5:1.

Although the authors state that the HDS involved six cycles of item development, no specific item analysis data are presented. Psychometric information concerning test bias (including item level bias) is also not presented.

Reliability evidence is mixed. Three-month test-retest coefficients appear acceptable; however, the research sample was limited to 60 graduate students. Alpha coefficients ranged from .50 to .78, with seven falling below .70, suggesting considerable caution with respect to the use of the scales in making decisions about individual clients.

Validity evidence supports the HDS for the most part, although much of the evidence is limited to research with other scales developed by the same authors. HDS intercorrelations support the separability of the dimensions. Factor analytic investigations of the scales also conform to expectations. For example, a principal components analysis of the HDS scales yielded support for three higher order dimensions that can be interpreted as reflecting Horney's three interpersonal styles of "moving against people," "moving toward people," and "moving away from people." Curiously, although the authors underscore the usefulness of this potential taxonomy of dysfunctional interaction dimensions, they fail to develop and investigate the reliability and validity of any such higher order scale scores for the HDS.

Convergent and discriminant validity correlations between the HDS and the Minnesota Multiphasic Personality Inventory (MMPI) Standard Scales and Personality Disorder Scales are encouraging as are correlations between the HDS and the Hogan Personality Inventory (Hogan & Hogan, 1995) and the Motives, Values, and Preferences Inventory (Hogan & Hogan, 1996). Modest, but meaningful correlations between HDS scores and managerial behavior ratings from an unspecified mix of subordinates, peers, and supervisors are also demonstrated.

Although the validity evidence appears promising, additional research is needed. For example, cross-sectional and longitudinal studies that investigate the ability of the HDS scores to discriminate important occupational outcomes (e.g., successful vs. derailed managers) are clearly needed as evidence of the utility of the HDS. For another example, studies of the correspondence between self- and other- (e.g., spouse, co-worker) ratings would be desirable.

The manual provides some useful interpretive guidelines. Important information is omitted, however. For example, although the authors encourage users to interpret a given scale score only in relation to other scale scores, no relevant guidelines for comparing scores (e.g., standard error of the difference) are included in the manual. Furthermore, limitations of percentile ranks are not mentioned.

SUMMARY. Overall, I believe that the HDS is an intriguing, innovative instrument that may eventually make a major contribution to the leadership and career development assessment areas. The authors provide a compelling argument for the need for a non-pathology-based instrument that captures the array of misguided interpersonal strategies that may "derail" employees from effective occupational functioning. Further development of the HDS, however, is required before it can be used confidently with individuals. At a minimum, future development should include: (a) a more detailed manual, (b) enhanced scale reliability, and (c) additional validation research. Until then, the HDS offers most promise as a research tool.

REVIEWER'S REFERENCES
Hogan, R., & Hogan, J. (1995). *Hogan Personality Inventory manual*. Tulsa, OK: Hogan Assessment Systems.
Hogan, J., & Hogan, R. (1996). *Motives, Values, Preferences Inventory manual*. Tulsa, OK: Hogan Assessment Systems.

[169]
Holden Psychological Screening Inventory.

Purpose: "To provide a very brief measure of psychiatric symptomatology, social symptomatology, and depression."
Population: Ages 14 and older.
Publication Date: 1996.
Acronym: HPSI.
Scores, 4: Psychiatric Symptomatology, Social Symptomatology, Depression, Total.
Administration: Individual or group.
Price Data, 1999: $48 per complete kit including manual (50 pages) and 25 QuikScore™ forms; $25 per 25 QuikScore™ forms (English or French-Canadian); $30 per manual; $33 per specimen set including manual and 3 QuikScore™ forms.
Comments: Windows™ version computer administration and scoring available on CD or 3.5-inch disk.
Foreign Language Editions: French-Canadian QuikScore™ forms available.
Time: [5–7] minutes.
Author: Ronald R. Holden.
Publisher: Multi-Health Systems, Inc.
Cross References: See T5:1213 (1 reference).

Review of the Holden Psychological Screening Inventory by STEPHEN N. AXFORD, Psychologist, Pueblo School District No. Sixty, Pueblo, CO, and University of Phoenix, Colorado Springs, CO:

The Holden psychological Screening Inventory (HPSI) is a self-report, paper-and-pencil format, individual- or group-administered clinical screening instrument, normed for use with adolescent and adult ("people over 14 years old," manual, p. 3) nonclinical, psychiatric, and forensic populations. As noted by the publisher, the HPSI can be used efficiently and quickly for determining potential need for more comprehensive assessment. The author states that although the HPSI "is not intended to offer a complete psychological assessment," it is designed to serve as a "component" of comprehensive diagnostic evaluation, to include "extensive interviewing, examining, and testing" (manual, p. 3). As stated by the author:

> The HPSI was developed to fulfill a need for a short, reliable, and valid questionnaire that focuses generally on the broad domain of psychopathology and, in particular, on the underlying dimensions associated with the MMPI. (manual, p. 3)

The HPSI purportedly can also be utilized for program evaluation and as a method for monitoring treatment efficacy. Truly a brief measure, the HPSI consists of 36 five-point Likert-type scale items and requires 5 to 7 minutes to complete. The author states that individuals with reading difficulties, psychiatric problems, or whose first language is not English may require "slightly" more administration time. The HPSI may not be appropriate for psychotic and certain physically disabled subjects, according to the author.

Comprising three scales, the HPSI is based on a three-factor model involving specific components of psychopathology: Psychiatric Symptomatology (aspects of hypochondriasis, persecutory ideas, anxiety, thinking disorders, and deviation), Social Symptomatology (aspects of interpersonal problems, alienation, persecutory ideas, impulse expression, and deviation), and Depression (aspects of depression, social introversion, and self-depreciation). The factors were identified through multivariate latent analysis of the Minnesota Multiphasic Personality Inventory (MMPI), Differential Personality Inventory, and Basic Personality Inventory.

A well-organized manual provides in-depth discussions on the HPSI's item development and psychometric properties. A detailed schematic illustration outlines steps in HPSI scale construction, including factor analysis, item selection, validation, and norming. The final version of the HPSI was normed on several samples: A general adult sample ranging in age from 18 years to above 70 years (main normative group, $N = 564$), high school students ($N = 139$), university students ($N = 326$), adult psychiatric patients ($N = 64$), and adult male psychiatric offenders ($N = 277$). The main normative group comprised respondents randomly selected from a community-based Canadian consumer mailing list. Although the norming samples represent a good start, the HPSI would benefit from additional norming employing larger sample sizes and broader demographic representation. As a point of reference for comparison, the Personality Assessment Screener (PAS; Morey, 1997)—a 22-item clinical screening instrument having similar purposes as the HPSI but derived from the Personality Assessment Inventory (PAI; T5:1959) instead of the MMPI (T5:1697)—is normed on a sample of 2,631 individuals in community and clinical settings, utilizing 1995 U.S. Census-based quotas.

As noted by the author, a major demographic concern regarding the norming samples is limited representation of racial/ethnic minorities. The HPSI adult normative sample yielded the following race/ethnicity composition percentages: White = 85.1, Asian = 7.5, African Canadian = 1.1, Hispanic = .7, First Nations = .4, and other = 5.3. As the author correctly points out, this places severe restrictions on generalizing normative results to non-Caucasian populations. Until additional norming is conducted with larger sample sizes, the HPSI should not be used with non-Caucasian subjects. In a section of the manual entitled "Directions for Future Research," the author acknowledges the HPSI was normed on pri-

marily English-speaking North American (Canadian) Caucasian samples and that studies sampling other populations are needed. As noted by the author, this would address the issues of: (a) whether separate norms may be needed for different ethnic/racial groups, and (b) "establishment of psychometric properties for the HPSI in non-white populations" (manual, p. 37).

As the HPSI may well receive attention in the United States, given the size of the U.S. market and the appeal of the HPSI as an efficient and economical screening instrument, it would be encouraging to see additional norming and validation research targeting Black, Hispanic, Native American, and Asian American populations. Indeed, as the HPSI manual identifies both U.S. and Canadian customer service centers, there seems to be intention to market in both nations.

Regarding internal consistency reliability, six studies are cited by the author, with median coefficient alpha values across samples (N ranging from 61 to 564) of .73 for Social Symptomatology, .74 for Psychiatric Symptomatology, .84 for Depression, and .83 for Total Psychopathology. As noted by the author, higher coefficient alpha values were observed for the clinical samples, as would be expected "where more measurement variance would be anticipated" (manual, p. 31). Regarding test-retest reliability, a single study is cited by the author, involving 108 undergraduates, with a 4-week retesting interval, yielding the following coefficients: Psychiatric Symptomatology = .83, Social Symptomatology = .84, Depression = .86, and Total Psychopathology = .88. Particularly for a screening instrument, these are adequate correlation coefficients, indicating internal consistency and stability. However, additional research in this area sampling a greater diversity of populations is needed.

A detailed section addressing validation is provided in the manual. HPSI scale validity coefficients ranging from .28 to .75 for two studies involving self-report and observer ratings for undergraduate and clinical populations are reported. Generally, coefficients were observed to be higher for the clinical population. Coefficients reported for the student population, involving roommate observations, are somewhat low, although in the direction predicted.

In an effort to address criterion validity, the author compares mean HPSI scores for clinical versus nonclinical populations, further differentiated by gender. For each gender, means differ significantly (.01 level) for all HPSI scales. In that the HPSI successfully differentiates clinical from nonclinical populations, this lends credence to the HPSI's criterion validity. It thus appears that the HPSI meets its main criterion as a clinical screening instrument.

Regarding convergent validity, the author reports correlations between the HPSI and theoretically connected self-report scales, specifically: the MMPI-2, Basic Personality Inventory (BPI), Carlson Psychological Survey (CPS), and Jackson Personality Inventory (JPI). In general, the coefficients are of sufficient magnitude and in the directions predicted, supporting the validity of the HPSI as this relates to measuring constructs it purports to measure.

The author also reports research investigating the HPSI's utility in detecting clinical change, thus addressing the claim that the instrument may appropriately be used in monitoring treatment and program effectiveness. In general, the research supports that the HPSI is a sensitive measure for detecting clinical change. Review of the HPSI answer sheet reveals clinically relevant and carefully constructed items, generally written in the present tense. From a face validity perspective, the HPSI presents as a useful instrument for monitoring intervention efficacy.

The HPSI manual's sections on test administration, scoring, interpretation, and use are concise and clear, with examples of scoring and sample case studies. Although the scoring materials are user friendly, requiring no templates or additional tables other than provided in the protocol, two options for computer administration and scoring are available utilizing IBM-compatible hardware and software: on-line administration (on-screen presentation of items) and a personal computer data entry and scoring program (QuikScore). Both options yield a computer-generated interpretive report. Network accessibility is available. HPSI computer services are retailed on a per use basis (i.e., the programs include an invisible counter).

The HPSI yields a composite *T*-score (Total psychopathology and *T*-scores for the three factors (Psychiatric Symptomatology Scale, Social Symptomatology Scale, and Depression Scale). Representing the only validity index for the HPSI, the Total Psychopathology raw score is used as a measure of excessive impression management (i.e.,

"faking good/faking bad"). The HPSI manual provides a table of cutoff scores for determining invalidity. According to the author, the HPSI validity index was empirically derived utilizing the fact that heavily biased responding results in substantially correlated scales; in contrast, a sincere pattern of responding should result in relatively independent scales. The author notes that "norms for general adult and general psychiatric patient populations" (p. 11) were also considered in the development of cutoff scores. To the author's credit, the test user is cautioned to utilize social ecological factors when interpreting validity index data. A high validity index score may accurately be indicative of severe maladjustment.

The author is to be commended for including a section in the HPSI manual on "Directions for Future Research" (p. 37) addressing limitations of the instrument and empirical issues requiring further investigation. Specifically, the HPSI is in need of additional norming utilizing larger and demographically representative samples, and specific HPSI scales require further investigation (e.g., how does the HPSI validity index compare to validity indicators for other measures? Does the Social Symptomatology Scale predict workplace adjustment?).

In summary, although considerable theoretically well-grounded work has been invested in item development/selection, the HPSI appears to be in its formative stages of development with regard to norming and research aiding interpretation of test results. The author has established a good foundation for future investigation of what appears to be a promising clinical screening instrument. The major limitation of the instrument, as the author acknowledges, is a limited norming sample. At the present time, the HPSI should be restricted to use with Caucasian subjects. Users of the HPSI should find the materials (manual, protocol, scoring forms) to be of professional quality and very convenient. The HPSI meets its primary goal as an efficient method for clinical screening. The prospect of the HPSI generating research that could potentially result in health services benefits related to efficient triage and treatment/program efficacy evaluation is encouraging.

REVIEWER'S REFERENCE

Morey, L. C. (1997). *Personality Assessment Screener professional manual.* Odessa, FL: Psychological Assessment Resources.

Review of the Holden Psychological Screening Inventory by JANET F. CARLSON, Professor of

Counseling and Psychological Services, Associate Dean School of Education, Oswego State University, Oswego, NY:

The Holden Psychological Screening Inventory (HPSI) is a recently published, brief, paper-and-pencil, self-report inventory that assesses three major dimensions of psychopathology in persons over the age of 14. The HPSI was developed with an eye toward psychometric soundness and practicality. The test author notes that the inventory is predicated on the scale structure of traditional but much lengthier personality inventories. The inventory consists of 36 five-point Likert-type items, with 12 items representing each of the major dimensions tapped—psychiatric symptoms, social symptoms, and depression. A total score is also obtained. Test takers are asked to rate some items according to the frequency with which the statements listed apply (e.g., "I behave recklessly"), and other items on the basis of the extent to which respondents agree or disagree with the statements posed (e.g., "Trying something new is scary").

APPLICATIONS. The test author recommends the HPSI for use with clinical and nonclinical populations, as a component of comprehensive assessment. The inventory may be used to assess treatment response, to screen for psychopathology or to identify areas where further testing is warranted, and for research purposes. Appropriately, the test author advises potential users that the HPSI is best regarded as an adjunct or supplement to clinical assessment, rather than as a replacement for same. It is not intended as a diagnostic instrument.

ADMINISTRATION, SCORING, AND INTERPRETATION. The HPSI may be administered individually or in group format. It may be possible to modify procedures slightly to permit oral administration if, for instance, the test taker were visually impaired. However, the test author warns that the inventory may not be appropriate for use with individuals with disabilities, generally. Its appropriateness would need to be considered in light of the nature of the disability. Instructions to the test taker are easy to understand and follow. General guidelines for test administration are provided in the test manual. Typically, administration time is between 5 and 7 minutes; scoring takes about the same amount of time as administration.

Test takers respond by circling letters corresponding to their ratings of frequency (Items 1–19) or agreement (Items 20–36) for each of the 36 statements on the record form. A carbonized sheet transfers responses to the underlying score sheet, consisting of a grid with differential shading that expedites scoring. Responses are associated with numerical ratings, shown on the score sheet that is beneath the carbonized sheet. To score the inventory, one simply transposes the numbers to one of three appropriately shaded columns, each of which corresponds to a scale. The values within each column are then summed to produce scale scores for Psychiatric Symptomatology, Social Symptomatology, and Depression. Raw scores for each scale may range from 0 to 48. Scale scores are summed to yield a Total Psychopathology score. The total raw score may range from 0 to 144. Raw scores are converted to T-scores by plotting the scores on a profile form, which is part of the QuikScore response sheet.

Interpretation begins with an assessment of profile validity, which is largely a function of the Total psychopathology score. In general, extreme scores (greater than 80 or less than 20) on the total scale are indicative of an invalid profile that typically is associated with dishonest responding. Less extreme scores (greater than 70 or less than 30) are suggestive of the possibility that the profile is not valid. The validity index is intended to detect faking or attempts to present oneself in an overly positive or overly negative way. Cutoff scores that assist in the assessment of deception were derived empirically. The test author is careful to note that working hypotheses other than faking—such as severe disturbance—should be considered, even when scores are extreme.

Narrative interpretive guidelines associated with T-score ranges are presented in the test manual, and are used to interpret the three scale scores once the profile has been deemed valid. As well, percentiles associated with raw score values are presented by sex, for each scale and the total score. The test author suggests that individual responses may be queried, in an effort to identify isolated areas of difficulty that may benefit from intervention. Further, the test author suggests that HPSI findings be integrated with other available assessment information. Computer software is available from the publisher. The HPSI Computer Program runs on IBM-compatible personal computers with Microsoft Windows installed, and is launched from PsychManger. The program scores and interprets the HPSI, as well as several other instruments developed by the same publisher.

TECHNICAL ASPECTS. Several types of samples were used to establish norms. The main normative group consisted of a community-based sample of 304 women and 259 men from Canada, sampled during 1994. Although demographic descriptions are provided in the test manual, comparison figures (e.g., from the U.S. Bureau of the Census) are not given, so it is not easy to establish the degree to which the sample mirrors any specific population. Still, with less than 15% of the normative group being nonwhite, it is apparent that the normative group overrepresents whites and underrepresents nonwhites, for North American populations. The test author acknowledges that "the current adult HPSI norms cannot be recommended for nonwhites" (manual, p. 30). It also appears that individuals whose marital status is separated or divorced were underrepresented, whereas individuals with at least a college education were overrepresented.

Additional data in the form of means and standard deviations for several groups with special characteristics are provided in tables in the test manual. For example, the manual contains normative data for high school students, university students, psychiatric patients, and psychiatric offenders. The test author specifies that the data for high school students should be used in place of the data on the profile forms when the respondent is between the ages of 14 and 17. Similar instructions are not provided for the other samples for whom normative data are provided.

The section of the test manual that covers psychometric characteristics presents information about reliability estimates and provides evidence of scale validation. Internal consistency reliability estimates were examined using eight studies, ranging in size from 61 to 564 respondents, and varying in composition from students, to male, females, offenders, and adults. Overall, the coefficients are high, generally running in the mid-.60s to .90 range. Test-retest reliability was examined in a single study, using a 4-week interval and 108 undergraduate students. The reliability coefficients for Psychiatric Symptomatology, Social Symptomatology, Depression, and Total Psychopathology were .83, .84, .86, and .88, respectively.

Validation evidence for the HPSI is provided in the test manual, including consideration of criterion validity, classification accuracy, convergent validity, and treatment change. Two sets of validity coefficients were determined using a nonclinical sample of 150 students and a clinical sample of 64 adult psychiatric patients. In both studies, respondents completed the HPSI, as did a second party who was well acquainted with the respondent but unaware of the HPSI results. Validity coefficients were at least in the moderate range, varying from .28 to .75.

Classification accuracy was assessed using an experimental faking study. The HPSI correctly classified 67% of respondents using the more conservative T-score cutoff of <30, and 77% when the less conservative T-score of <20 was used as the cutoff score. Further, mean scores for the three scales and the total score differed at the .01 level of probability, between clinical and nonclinical samples, indicating that individuals with and without psychiatric disorders can be discriminated on the basis of their HPSI profiles.

Convergent validity was assessed using a sample of 84 patients, and comparing HPSI Psychiatric Symptomatology scale scores with related MMPI-2 (Butcher, Dahlstrom, Graham, Tellegen, & Kaemmer, 1989) scales and Jackson's Basic Personality Inventory (Jackson, 1976). Resulting correlation coefficients averaged .56 and .58, respectively. Similar comparisons using the Social Symptomatology scale scores produced average coefficients of .37 and .51, respectively, and the Depression scale score yielded average coefficients of .57 and .60, respectively. Findings reported by other researchers, and presented in the HPSI test manual as well, were largely consistent with these results.

Two small scale studies are reported in the test manual in support of the HPSI's ability to detect clinical changes. Both studies were conducted using a pretest/posttest paradigm. In general, changes in scale scores and total score were in the predicted directions. The test author also presents the results of five factor analyses, employing anywhere from 64 to 564 participants, and confirmatory principal components analyses. On balance, the HPSI's factor structure supports the scoring key.

CRITIQUE. In favor of the HPSI is the fact that it is a straightforward measure that is easily and rapidly administered, and easily and rapidly scored and interpreted. Its theoretical base was borrowed from tried and true measures with lengthy histories of development and related research. For a rather recently published instrument, the HPSI has been well-researched, can be scored and interpreted via computer software, and is reasonably priced compared to other screening or research tools that require individual administration. Data accumulated to date concerning its psychometric properties are encouraging, in that they support the inventory's reliability and validity. The presence of a validity index, in the form of the Total Psychopathology score, is unusual but welcome in a brief instrument such as this one.

Test users should be mindful of the fact that the HPSI is not intended to be a diagnostic instrument, and should not be used as such. Thus, in clinical applications, it is best regarded as a screening instrument that assesses three traditional dimensions of psychopathology. As suggested earlier, it may function as an indicator of clinical change in paradigms examining treatment response or outcome, in clinical or empirical applications.

As noted by the test author, use of the HPSI with nonwhite individuals is not recommended, given the relative lack of nonwhite participants in the main normative group. Other questions about the representativeness of the normative group are present as well, as suggested earlier. In addition, the interpretation of scores for youth between the ages of 14 and 17 is considerably more complex, given that the manual instructs the test user to use the norms in the manual rather than those contained—and presented conveniently in graph form—on the QuikScore form. Procedures for using the data in the manual to interpret scores for adolescents are vague, leaving the test user somewhat to his or her own devices. A table of T-score conversions for this age group could be included in the test manual, which would spare this confusion.

SUMMARY. The HPSI is a relatively new instrument, although it has been in development for several years. The number of studies that support its psychometric soundness is larger than for most tests first published in 1996. It is intended to be used and integrated with other available information, as part of a more comprehensive psychological assessment aimed at illuminating major dimensions of psychopathology. Likely, the HPSI will find additional applications in related arenas, including research and assessment of therapeutic outcomes. It is a simple measure that is easily understood and rapidly administered, scored, and interpreted, and may be modifiable for use with some individuals with disabilities. Group administration is possible, and computer software for scoring is available. Additional evidence concerning the HPSI's usefulness is likely to accumulate from its use in clinical settings and data generated from these applications.

REVIEWER'S REFERENCES

Jackson, D. N. (1976). *Basic Personality Inventory*. Port Huron, MI: Sigma Assessment Systems.
Butcher, J. N., Dahlstrom, W. G., Graham, J. R., Tellegen, A., & Kaemmer, B. (1989). *Minnesota Multiphasic Personality Inventory-2: Manual for administration and scoring*. Minneapolis: University of Minnesota Press.

[170]
Human Figure Drawing Test.

Purpose: "Designed to provide an objective approach ..." to human figure drawings.
Population: Clients in psychotherapy.
Publication Date: 1993.
Acronym: HFDT.
Scores, 4: Impairment, Distortion, Simplification, Organic Factors Index.
Administration: Individual.
Price Data, 1999: $69.50 per complete kit including handbook (189 pages), 25 drawing forms, and 25 AUTOSCORE™ forms; $10.50 per 25 drawing forms; $27.50 per 25 AUTOSCORE™ forms; $49.50 per handbook.
Time: (5–20) minutes.
Authors: Jerry Mitchell, Richard Trent, and Roland McArthur.
Publisher: Western Psychological Services.
Cross References: See T5:1226 (4 references).

Review of the Human Figure Drawing Test by CHARLES A. PETERSON, Staff Clinical Psychologist, Department of Veterans Affairs, Minneapolis Medical Center, and Associate Clinical Professor of Psychology, University of Minnesota, Minneapolis, MN:

Projective drawings have long been part of the psychodiagnostician's repertoire. Surveys too numerous to mention document the procedure's robust popularity, one that has been relatively stable (never left the top 10) throughout clinical psychology's lifetime.

For better or for worse (yes, it seem like we are wedded to these procedures), human figure drawings rest on several assumptions: (a) Frank's (1939) classic statement of the projective hypothesis argues that the psychological structure of the individual will express itself as it organizes unstructured material (cf., Peterson & Johanson,

1993; Peterson & Schilling, 1983 on the classification issue). (b) The choice of the human person/body for graphomotor expression is a deft one because the ego is "first and foremost a body-ego" (Freud, 1923, p. 27). (c) The procedure achieves its projective/unstructured status with a simple instruction, one that asks the test subject to "draw a person," assiduously avoiding cues or rules that might guide or structure the production. (d) Finally, when the test subject draws a human form, the subject's personality structure and dynamics will be revealed to the psychologist for diagnostic scrutiny.

It may be that the unstructured nature of the task is useful for the test subject, as it facilitates the expression of personal material for the divination process. But, it is equally fair to note that the unstructured nature of the task is not good for the psychometrically minded psychologist.

The Human Figure Drawing Test (HFDT) is one more attempt to organize and systematize the interpretation of the unstructured projective procedure. The authors insist that their procedures will add some quantitative data to enhance—not replace—the more typical free-form qualitative analysis. This version of the Draw-A-Person provides a "Drawing Form" upon which demographic information is collated, and upon which the test subject draws a person. The clinician is encouraged to note unique reactions and differential interests as the subject does so. Using criteria illustrated in the manual, the same-sex drawing is scored according to 74 criteria, such as "elaborate belt or waist emphasis" or "chicken feet" (talons or multiple lines) on a convenient form, which has been cleverly backed with carbon paper, transferring scores to the "Interpretation Guide." In an amazing feat of prestidigitation, the scores yield written interpretations next to the score checked. For example, "waist emphasis" equals "concern over sexual control," and "chicken feet" equals "regression or retardation," and "disheveled hair" equals "sexually impulsive behavior" or "thought disorder." Certain scores are noted for "simplification" and other scores are tallied on a "distortion" index and later arithmetically manipulated to produce an "Organic Factors Index." References are provided for the interpretation of such factors as "thin, wasted or ribbonlike arms."

The test data are interpreted on multiple levels, several of which produce indices related to cognitive impairment: (a) The Impairment Scale provides information on whether or not the individual shows some cognitive impairment. The authors caution "the clinician must remember that this test is designed to detect only general variations in the level of cognitive functioning" (manual, p. 71). Translate: this test is not that accurate. Use a Wechsler and consult a neuropsychologist. Later on, Table 3 presents "features *believed* to represent organic impairment" (manual, p. 159; emphasis added). In other words, they present no data to indicate that such factors *are* related to organic impairment. It is also puzzling to be told that the same 74 indicators that were used to divine functional psychopathology are now the same factors believed to represent organic impairment. Further, the algorithm underlying these 74 factors uncritically assigns a weight of 1 to each indictor, many, no doubt, of differential predictive validity. (b) The test procedure also yields "Distortion" and "Simplification" scores, used in a very fuzzy manner to rarify the nature or severity of the subject's cognitive deficit as measured by the "Impairment Scale." (c) An "Organic Factors" score is obtained by subtracting the Simplification from the Distortion score. A range of scores indicates, at the antipodes of the scale, either an "organic condition" or "mental retardation" whereas scores in the middle neither confirm nor exclude the presence of either condition. (d) Finally, anchored by the above "quantitative" interpretations, the test results are now sifted for qualitative interpretation of such factors as "bare feet on a clothed figure" (equals "aggression" for the curious reader).

After 16 case examples, the reader arrives at a chapter on "development and psychometric properties" (manual, p. 159). Seven hundred subjects from a state hospital composed the clinical sample, and the nonclinical group was made of 100 hospital staffers not screened for psychopathology. Differences in age, race, education, and intelligence were noted among clinical and nonclinical samples, but the differences were not subjected to tests of significance. Each drawing was scored by three psychologists, and a two out of three agreement was required to score the presence of a particular sign such as "nostrils showing." Interrater reliability scores are not provided for individual items. Further, the manual is quite confusing on who is agreeing with whom, with both inexperienced raters and more experienced raters (psychologists) producing Cohen's kappas of .77, .42, .57, and

.23, none-too-impressive numbers for the major Impairment index. The various features of the drawings are tabulated in frequencies for each diagnostic group. It is not clear how these diagnoses were obtained. The manual offers some data to suggest that Impairment Scores are related more to diagnosis than IQ (not stating how the latter was obtained). Items on the Distortion and Simplification scales were factor analyzed and revised to discard low-weighted items and to enhance Cronbach's alpha. The two scales correlate .56 with one another, indicating considerable overlap. No test-retest data are provided. Each of the scales (i.e., Distortion, Simplification, total Impairment scale, and the Organic Factors Index) were able in discriminant analyses to differentiate among nonclinical, psychiatric, and organic/mentally retarded groups at a rate exceeding chance classification. Sensitivity and specificity data should have been provided here.

SUMMARY. Human figure drawings—for all their problems—continue to be used by a majority of clinical psychologists. The authors of *this version* of the draw-a-person may be commended for their effort to structure the interpretation of this unstructured technique. In general, there is more support for the composite indices than for individual items, here repeating Swenson's (1957) findings and cautions to focus on broad, robust factors such as adjustment—maladjustment. Whether it is worth going through all this to conclude a *patient* is maladjusted is open to serious doubt. In the end we may recall, but question, Freud's words (a February 28, 1934 letter to projective theorist Saul Rosenzweig): This type of research will convince no one, but "can do no harm" (quoted in Shakow & Rapaport, 1964). However, fuzzy research can do harm. If one makes the precarious decision to use figure drawings, then it could be argued that one should use a version that imposes structure on the diagnostician's divinations. Partisans on both sides of the aisle will no doubt continue to project their sketch of the utility of human figure drawings. Still, and staying within the metaphor, fancy raiment on a stick figure does not really improve the stick figure.

REVIEWER'S REFERENCES

Freud, S. (1923/1961). The ego and the id. In J. Strachey (Ed. & Trans), *The standard edition of the complete psychological works of Sigmund Freud* (vol. 19, 3–66). London: Hogarth (originally published 1923).
Frank, L. K. (1939). Projective methods for the study of personality. *Journal of Psychology, 8*, 389–413.
Swenson, C. H., Jr. (1957). Empirical evaluations of human figure drawings. *Psychological Bulletin, 54*, 431–466.
Shakow, D., & Rapaport, D. (1964). The influence of Freud on American Psychology. *Psychological Issues*, Monograph 13 (whole issue).
Peterson, C. A., & Schilling, K. M. (1983). Card pull in projective testing. *Journal of Personality Assessment, 47*, 265–275.
Peterson, C. A., & Johanson, T. J. (1993). A taxonomy of psychological tests. *British Journal of Projective Psychology, 38*, 63–70.

Review of the Human Figure Drawing Test by WILLIAM K. WILKINSON, *Consulting Psychologist, Boleybeg, Barna, County Galway, Ireland:*

It is increasingly common to see the application of quantitative methods to projective test development. A good example is John Exner's design of an objective scoring system for the Rorschach Ink Blot Test (323). In this regard, the authors of the Human Figure Drawing Test (HFDT) are to be commended for subjecting a traditional projective technique to the same scientific standards to which nonprojective measures aspire.

Briefly, the HFDT requires an individual to complete two human figure drawings (the second figure requested being of opposite gender to the first). Only the first drawing is scored, with the second drawing qualitatively analyzed. The figures are completed on an HFDT Drawing Form, which consists of a demographic cover page and opens to the blank pages used for the drawings. The authors suggest that the HFDT can be used with individuals 15 years or older, although this seems a rather arbitrary age limit.

The HFDT includes an Autoscore Form. One side of this form consists of a Profile Sheet with three major scores identified—Impairment, Distortion, and Simplification—along with a *T*-Score Scale for indexing the scores obtained. In addition, there is an organic Factors Index, which is a ratio of the Distortion and Simplification Scales. The back of the Profile Sheet contains the HFDT Scoring Sheet consisting of all 74 items and their individual interpretation. When scoring is completed, a carbon sheet inside the perforated Autoscore form automatically transfers item marks to their respective clinical scales (e.g., Distortion or Simplification). The Autoscore form is a handy feature because it greatly reduces HFDT scoring and interpretation time, especially when compared with other projective techniques.

The other essential item is the HFDT manual, which is referred to as an "Illustrated Handbook." For scoring purposes, the HFDT Handbook provides the 74 scoring items, each with definition and illustrated examples. An example is Item 15 which is "Thin, Wasted, or Ribbonlike Arms. This item is scored if the figure's arms are drawn without definition, or if they are thin and degenerate or look like tape or ribbon" (manual, p. 19). Under this item are two illustrations depicting when the item is present. In addition, the HFDT authors should be praised for devoting 80 pages of the Handbook to 12 case studies, each complete with drawings and completed Autoscore Forms. This is invaluable because the case studies can serve as a self-training module for new users. I recommend that prospective HFDT users independently score case study protocols until they reach 90% agreement with the authors across three consecutive drawings. This is necessary because scoring an item like Item 15 above may be somewhat subjective. The manual includes a section on interrater reliability, which for two "relatively inexperienced" scorers was 92% and 90% in agreement with the test authors' item scores (across a large sample of drawings). However, this should not lessen the need for new users to establish a level of scoring mastery.

The HFDT is correctly identified as a projective-type measure. As such, it can be included as part of a projective battery (e.g., Rorschach, TAT, Sentence Completion, etc.) for psychologists testing projective hypotheses. If used in this way, the HFDT qualitative scoring method (e.g., Item 31 "light lines" = anxiety, uncertainty, passivity) may be more relevant than the quantitatively derived scales. It should be noted that individual item interpretations are cross referenced in the Handbook with the author(s) first suggesting a particular interpretation. For example, the interpretation associated with Item 31 includes references to Jolles (1971), Buck (1969), Hammer (1968), Machover (1949), and Urban (1963). This cross-referenced system is another positive feature of the Handbook.

A second use of the HFDT is its inclusion as part of a diagnostic battery for psychiatric populations. It is in clinical diagnosis that the technical merits of the HFDT are advanced. For example, at a rudimentary level, the authors note that the underlying assumption of the HFDT is that drawings of nonclinical populations reliably differ from psychiatric groups. Indeed, the General Impairment Score, which is the sum total of the 74 items noted in a drawing, is substantially higher for psychiatric compared to nonpsychiatric groups.

A word of caution is that the standardization sample is restricted to psychiatric patients at the hospital where the HFDT was developed. Likewise, the nonclinic group consists entirely of hospital staff at the same hospital. It is most likely that the limited nature of the sample relates to the author's selection of a relatively low T-score cutoff of 56 in discriminating between "no/mild impairment" and "moderate/psychiatric impairment." One would expect this cutoff point to be closer to $T = 60$ because most measures of psychopathology use T values in excess of 60 to distinguish "psychiatric" from "nonpsychiatric" populations. That the HFDT cut-score is below 60 leads me to suspect positive skew in the raw score distribution, a problem likely due to the limited nature of the standardization sample. Although the authors do provide several histograms, they omit graphic display of General Impairment (GI) scores. The tabled percentages of GI scores do suggest positive skew, because they do not match the percentages predicted by a normal T-distribution (e.g., 77% of nonclinic sample below $T \leq 55$ is greater than the 69% predicted by a normal T-distribution; 0% of nonclinic sample $> T$ of 70 is less than the 2% above this value predicted by a normal T-distribution). Although the severity of skew is difficult to determine, the danger is the increased likelihood of false positives given the limited nature of the standardization sample.

I would be more confident if the nonclinical sample was significantly broadened in order to produce a more varied raw score distribution. This distribution should be put in histogram form so the test user can ascertain its "normality." Ideally, the cut-scores will increase such that "no impairment" equates to T-scores under 60, Mild Impairment defines a T-score between 60–65, the Moderate Index moves to 66–75, and the Severe category applies to T-scores above 76.

I also caution HFDT users to look critically at the descriptive categories applied to various T-score ranges. For example, "unimpaired overall cognitive functioning or only mild impairment" is noted for T-scores below 56. "Mild impairment" and "unimpaired" are very different interpretations, yet co-exist to define the least psychiatrically impaired individuals.

SUMMARY. Overall, the HFDT authors embarked on the arduous task of scientifically validating a projective measure. I view the HFDT as a step forward for projective drawings. Appropriate cautions are required with respect to the standardization sample and the delimiting influence of this sample on the interpretive value of the derived scores. It is hoped that these cautions will lessen as the HFDT continues to be validated.

[171]
IDEA Oral Language Proficiency Test.

Purpose: To "assist in the initial identification designation and redesignation of a student as being NES, LES, or FES (Non-Limited-Fluent English Speaking)."

Population: Preschool–grade 12.

Publication Dates: 1983–1998.

Acronym: IPT.

Scores, 4: Vocabulary, Comprehension, Syntax, Verbal Expression.

Administration: Individual.

Price Data: Available from publisher.

Foreign Language Edition: English and Spanish versions available for each level.

Publisher: Ballard & Tighe, Inc.

a) PRE-IPT.

Population: Ages 3–5.

Publication Date: 1988

Time: (8–13) minutes.

Authors: Constance O. Williams, Wanda S. Ballard, and Phyllis L. Tighe.

b) IPT-I.

Population: Grades K–6.

Publication Date: 1991.

Time: (14–19) minutes.

Authors: Wanda S. Ballard, Phyllis L. Tighe, and Enrique F. Dalton.

c) IPT-II.

Population: Grades 7–12.

Publication Date: 1998.

Time: (15–20) minutes.

Authors: Enrique F. Dalton and Beverly A. Amori.

Cross References: See T5:1234 (5 references).

Review of the IDEA Oral Language Proficiency Test by EMILIA C. LOPEZ, Assistant Professor, Queens College, City University of New York, Flushing, NY:

The IDEA Oral Language Proficiency Test (IPT) measures students' oral language proficiency skills in the areas of Vocabulary, Comprehension, Syntax, and Verbal Expression in Spanish and English. The tests include items that assess basic interpersonal as well as academic proficiency skills (Cummins, 1984). The authors developed the tests using sound procedures that included identifying a panel of experts to list the skills and competencies necessary for oral proficiency in Spanish and English and reviewing research studies in language proficiency.

The norming samples used in the Pre-IPT and the IPT-II in Spanish and English are relatively small (i.e., the English Pre-IPT was normed with 248 children whereas the Spanish version was normed with 312 children; the English version of the IPT-II was normed with 459 subjects and the Spanish version was normed with a total of 571 subjects). The IPT-I (Forms C & D) in English and the IPT-I in Spanish have larger norming samples (i.e., 1,054 and 948 subjects, respectively). The IPT-II English and the Pre-IPT Spanish and English versions were normed in California and Texas. The English and Spanish versions of the IPT-I and the Spanish version of the IPT-II in Spanish were normed in seven to eight different states that have large numbers of culturally and linguistically diverse children. Most of the subjects in the Spanish versions of the IPT tests were born in Mexico and the United States and very few subjects were included with backgrounds from Central America, South America, and the Caribbean. An approximately equal distribution of females and males was included in the norming samples.

Subjects in the norming samples of all the IDEA tests demonstrated a range of language proficiency levels. For example, in the Spanish version of the IPT-I subjects were chosen who ranged from non, limited, to fluent Spanish speakers. This breakdown in language proficiency is advantageous because it is representative of a wide range of Spanish speakers. However, unequal sample distributions were noted in all the IPT tests for English and Spanish language proficiency skill levels.

The manuals for the IDEA tests provide little information on the students' backgrounds. For example, the Spanish versions of the IPT-I and II as well as the English version of the IPT-I (Forms C & D) provide data on the students' primary languages and country of origin but manuals for the other IPT tests reviewed did not provide that information. Data on years in the United States and the ethnic backgrounds of the students are not available for any of the IPT tests. Control was not provided for parent education, socioeconomic background, or history of language development. The subjects' levels of language proficiency were determined solely through teacher and/or district opinion. The test manuals often showed missing data for the students' language proficiency levels in English and Spanish. When language proficiency data were included, the authors did not specify what measures or procedures were used by the districts to classify the students' levels of language proficiency. Information was also not available about the educational programs of the students and the background of the teachers who were rating the students' language skills (e.g., How many students were in bilingual programs vs. in monolingual English programs? Were native language skills ratings provided by teachers who instructed the students in Spanish and English?).

For most items, the authors provide estimates of interitem, split half, test-retest (1–2 weeks), and interrater reliability. Reliability estimates are also provided between forms for the IPT-I English Forms A and B. The test-retest reliability estimates for all the IDEA tests range from .43 (IPT-II English [A & B] manual, p. 60) to .93 (IPT-I English-Form C manual, p. 59). The combined test-retest and interrater reliability estimates for Form A of the English IPT-II is .43 and is the lowest and most questionable reliability estimate.

The most extensive data presented in the manuals referred to criterion and construct validity. Consumers of the IDEA tests are encouraged to read each manual carefully as the types of validity data presented vary from test to test. Among the validity data provided are correlations between test results and (a) teachers' predictions of the test performance; (b) teachers' opinions of students' oral language proficiency skills; (c) districts' ratings of students' language proficiency; (d) age; (e) teachers' opinions of academic ability; (f) grade; (g) time in country; (h) Comprehensive Test of Basic Skills scores in reading, language, and math; and (i) proficiency in reading, language, writing, and math. The validity studies tended to show significant relations between variables. However, the IPT-II English demonstrated low validity coefficients between the test results and several variables (e.g., age and grade). The Spanish and English versions of the IPT-I also yielded low correlations between the age of the students and the IPT scores. A significant number of students included in the IPT-II Spanish validation sample scored in the two highest levels of the test, putting into question the validity of results from this measure for students functioning in lower levels of the test.

SUMMARY. In general, some of the strengths of the IDEA include their availability in two languages and, for some of the English measures, their availability in two forms (e.g., the IPT-I in English includes versions C & D). The IDEA tests are also easy to administer in terms of time (i.e., test times vary from 8 to 20 minutes depending on the version of the test and the students' level of language proficiency) and procedures (Cook, 1995; Stansfield, 1991).

The tests' limitations far outweigh the strengths cited above. One limitation is that the authors failed to conduct validity studies that investigated how the test content relates to achievement. Thus, caution should be used when using the IPT tests to assess immigrant children with little or no previous educational experiences because many of the items assess academic related experiences that may not be familiar to students with such backgrounds.

The second limitation is that the IDEA tests focus on measuring discrete aspects of language proficiency (e.g., syntax, morphology, lexicon, and phonology) with less emphasis on pragmatic and functional aspects of language (Oller, 1979). The authors emphasize that responses must be grammatically and syntactically correct for many items, implying that functional language skills, a strength for many limited-English-proficiency children, are downplayed (Jitendra & Rohens-Diaz, 1996).

A third limitation is that the norming procedures used (i.e., small sample sizes and field testing in a few states) limits their validity for a wide range of children throughout the United States. Overall, further research is needed to provide more validity evidence for the IDEA tests especially in terms of predictive and construct validity (e.g., correlation with other language proficiency measures).

The tests' fourth limitation is due to the authors' failure to provide scoring procedures that would allow examiners to take into consideration regional differences in vocabulary. This criticism is particularly relevant for Spanish-speaking children living in the United States who come from a variety of Hispanic countries and demonstrate regional differences in vocabulary and colloquialisms. Although the authors acknowledge that such differences exist, they advise examiners that only those responses printed on the Spanish protocols are acceptable and that diverse but correct responses should be scored as incorrect.

Finally, in their reviews of the IPT-I in English, Cook (1995) and Stansfield (1991) comment that the test manual is poorly organized and lacks details as to how data were obtained. This criticism applies to all the manuals for the IDEA tests as the authors fail to describe how, for example, data on teacher opinion, teacher prediction, and district designation of language proficiency were obtained. In addition, the manuals did not clearly specify the process used by the panel of experts to choose the test items. Manuals for recent revisions of the Spanish versions of the IPT-I and IPT-II as well as the English IPT-I (Forms C & D) provide only a brief description of revision procedures.

REVIEWER'S REFERENCES

Oller, J. W., Jr. (1979). *Language tests at school: A pragmatic approach.* London, England: Longman Group.

Cummins, J. (1984). *Bilingualism and special education: Issues in assessment and pedagogy.* San Diego, CA: College-Hill.

Stansfield, C. W. (1991). [Review of IDEA Oral Language Proficiency Test]. In J. Keyser & R. C. Sweetland (Eds.), *Test critiques: Volume VIII* (pp. 264–269). Austin, TX: PRO-ED, Inc.

Cook, A. A. (1995, January). *A review of the IDEA Oral Language Proficiency Test, Text Forms C & D, English.* Paper presented at the Southwest Educational Research Association, Dallas, TX.

Jitendra, A. K., & Rohena-Diaz, E. (1996). Language assessment of students who are linguistically diverse: Why a discrete approach is not the answer. *School Psychology Review, 25,* 40–56.

Review of the IDEA Oral Language Proficiency Test by SALVADOR HECTOR OCHOA, Associate Professor, Department of Educational Psychology, Texas A&M University, College Station, TX:

The purpose of the IDEA Oral Language Proficiency Test (IPT) is to (a) assess a student's proficiency in English and/or Spanish and (b) determine a child's dominant language if both the English and Spanish version are used in conjunction with one another. There are 12 different IDEA tests: (a) PRE-IPT in English and Spanish for preschoolers, (b) IPT-I in English (Forms A, B, C, and D) and in Spanish (First and Second Editions) for kindergarten and elementary school-aged children, and (c) IPT-II in English (Forms A and B) and Spanish (First and Second Editions) for secondary school-aged students. It should be noted that although 12 of the IDEA Oral Language Proficiency Tests are being reviewed, 2 of these measures (IPT-I Oral English, Forms A & B) are now obsolete. All 12 measures, however are being included because they have not been previously reviewed in a *Mental Measurements Yearbook.*

PRE-IPT. The PRE-IPT in English and Spanish measures the following aspects of oral language proficiency: Vocabulary, Comprehension, Grammar/Syntax and Verbal Expression. A panel of experts in early childhood selected the test content and wrote items for both English and Spanish forms. Each form has 42 items. Sufficient information is provided in the manual and protocol about test administration and scoring.

ENGLISH FORM. There are several limitations to the standardization sample of the English Form of the PRE-IPT. The sample consisted of only 248 preschoolers. This is an insufficient number. Moreover, the sample size of preschoolers at particular age periods is insufficient. The manual reports that only 15 children between the ages of 3 years to 3 years 6 months and from 5 years 7 months to age 6 were included in the sample. Only preschoolers from California ($n = 171$) and Texas ($n = 77$) were included in the sample. The manual provides no information concerning the socioeconomic status of the sample. The sample is not representative of the United States Census.

The manual provides information on internal consistency and test-retest reliability. With respect to internal consistency, the manual reports that this form had a split-half reliability coefficient of .88 and a Cronbach's alpha of .96. The one-week test-retest reliability coefficient was .79. Given the lack of reliability usually displayed with preschool children, the reliability estimates are very good.

The test authors provide supportive data concerning the validity of the PRE-IPT. Content validity evidence is demonstrated via a test blueprint indicating how each item fits into the four major aspects of language proficiency assessed by this form. There are sufficient items for all four domains. Concurrent criterion-related validity evidence was provided by correlating teacher prediction of the PRE-IPT level by actual PRE-IPT level results. The contingency coefficient of .62 is acceptable. Construct validity evidence was provided by correlating PRE-IPT with (a) age and (b) "teacher opinion of academic ability." The contingency coefficient for the former was .34 and was .43 for the latter. Both of these coefficients are acceptable.

SPANISH FORM. As in the English form, there are major limitations about the standardization sample. The sample size of 312 is insufficient and the sample has too few preschoolers at particular age periods. The manual reports that only 8 children between the ages of 3 years to 3 years 5 months and 14 preschoolers from 3 years 6 months to 3 years 11 months were included in the sample. Only preschoolers from California (*n* = 264) and Texas (*n* = 48) were included in the sample. The manual provides no information concerning the socioeconomic status of the sample. The sample is not representative of the Spanish-speaking preschool population in the United States.

Internal consistency reliability is estimated by a Spearman-Brown adjusted split-half reliability coefficient of .84 and a Cronbach's alpha of .93. One-week test-retest reliability estimate was .82. The test-retest reliability estimate was also used as an indication of interrater reliability. All of the reliability coefficients are clearly acceptable.

The manual provides information concerning the different types of validity. Content validity is demonstrated via a test blueprint indicating how each item corresponds to one or more of the four aspects of language proficiency. Concurrent criterion-related validity evidence was provided by correlating teachers' prediction of PRE-IPT test results with actual PRE-IPT test results. There is, however, a discrepancy between what is reported in the text of the manual on page 15 (i.e., Pearson's correlation = .646) and the information reported in Table M (i.e., Pearson's correlation = .617) concerning this validity coefficient. Construct validity evidence was provided by correlating PRE-IPT results with (a) age (contingency coefficient of .53), (b) "socio-maturational age classification" (contingency coefficient of .52), and (c) "teacher opinion of academic ability" (contingency coefficient of .33).

IPT-I. The IPT-I in English and Spanish measures the following six components of oral language proficiency: syntax, morphology, phonology, lexicon, comprehension, and oral expression. All English forms and the first edition of the Spanish form have 83 items. The second edition of the Spanish form has 85 items. The test manual and protocol provide clear directions about test administration and scoring for both language forms.

ENGLISH FORMS A & B (1979). The standardization sample of the English Form A and B of the IPT-I has major shortcomings. The manual provides information regarding the gender, age, and grade level of the standardization sample. The manual reports that 59 seventh graders and 45 eighth graders were included in the standardization sample. The cover of the test manual, however, clearly states that the IPT-I is for grades K–6. The authors do not provide an explanation why

these 104 students are included in the sample. It appears that the sample of 2,061 is exclusively from California. The manual reports that 388 of the students were from rural districts, 953 pupils were from urban districts, and 720 from suburban districts. The authors fail to provide data indicating if this breakdown by type of district is representative of California. The manual provides no information concerning the ethnicity and socioeconomic status of the sample. The sample is not representative of the United State Census.

The manual reports several reliability estimates of the scores for English Forms A and B. With respect to internal consistency, the test authors report a Cronbach's alpha and corrected split-half coefficient of .99 for both Form A and B. One-week test-retest reliability coefficients for both Form A and B were .94. The alternate form reliability for Form A and B was .82. These reliability coefficients are good.

The test authors provide information about the three major types of validity. The test developers provide a test blueprint indicating how the six domains of oral language proficiency are assessed by items for both Form A and B. There are sufficient number of items for each domain. Concurrent criterion-related validity was demonstrated by correlating (a) "teacher's prediction of student oral language proficiency" with IPT-I test results (p. 19), (b) California's "state approved" oral language proficiency tests results with IPT-I test results (p. 21), and (c) "teacher's designation" of level of proficiency (i.e., non-English speaker, limited-English speaker, fluent-English speaker) with IPT-I designation level (p. 24). The validity coefficients of the concurrent criterion-related validity studies in the order listed above for Form A were (a) .79, (b) .75, and (c) .71. The validity coefficients of the concurrent criterion-related validity studies in the order mentioned above for Form B were (a) .66, (b) .59, and (c) .63. Construct validity evidence was provided by correlating IPT- score with age and grade level. The validity coefficient for the former was .59 and was .66 for the latter. All of the coefficients reported for concurrent criterion-related validity and construct validity are acceptable.

ENGLISH FORMS C & D (1990). The English Forms C and D were developed to improve Forms A and B. The publishers felt that creating new forms would provide educators in the field a wider selection of forms. "The authors decided to base the new Form C on the original Form A and the new Form D on the original Form B" (p. 2). Forms C and D measure the same six components of oral language proficiency as Forms A and B. "Approximately 20% of the test items in the original test were either revised, rewritten, rearranged or deleted in order to construct the new forms" (p. 2). Forms C and D are improvements over Forms A and B in that (a) all pictures in the test booklet are in color and (b) there is only one picture stimulus on each page.

The standardization sample for Forms C and D consisted of 551 and 503 elementary school-aged children, respectively. The test manual provides information on the following characteristics of the sample: age, gender, grade level, ethnicity, state, school district designation of the degree of English proficiency, and "teacher opinion of academic ability" (p. 11). Approximately 75% of the sample is from two states—California (53%) and Texas (22%). There is an insufficient number of students included at certain age periods. There are only 38 twelve-year-old students in the sample for both Form C and D. In the initial printing of the 1991 technical manual, the test authors report the ethnicity breakdown of the sample by language groups: i.e., Spanish, English, Korean, etc. Language group does not necessarily equate to ethnic status. It is possible that an English-speaking student is of Hispanic or Asian descent. It should be noted that the test publishers have corrected this typographical error in subsequent printing of the technical manual and have changed the label for Tables F and G from "ethnicity" to "primary language." The manual provides no information concerning the socioeconomic status of the sample. Although the standardization sample used for Forms C and D is an improvement over the one employed in English Forms A and B, it is not representative of the United States Census.

Reliability estimates reported for Forms C and D are acceptable in terms of their magnitude. With respect to internal consistency, the corrected split-half coefficients were .85 and .87 for Form C and D, respectively. Both forms had adequate Cronbach's alpha coefficient with .98 for Form C and .99 for Form D. The alternate form reliability coefficients were the following: Forms A and C = .88; Forms A and D = .87; Forms B and C = .95; Forms B and D = .76; and Forms C and D = .91. Interrater reliability

and one-week test-retest reliability coefficients were .93 for Form C and .87 for Form D.

With respect to validity, the test developers provide a test blueprint indicating how the six domains of oral language proficiency are assessed by items for both Form C and D. There are a sufficient number of items for each domain. Concurrent criterion-related validity was demonstrated by correlating IPT-I test results or designation level with (a) teacher's prediction of student oral language proficiency, (b) teacher opinion of academic ability, (c) district's designation of level of proficiency (i.e., non-English speaker, limited-English speaker, fluent-English speaker), and (d) teacher opinion of level of proficiency designation. The validity contingency coefficients of the concurrent criterion-related validity studies in the order listed above for Form C were (a) .68, (b) .36, (c) .59, and (d) .63. The validity contingency coefficients of the concurrent criterion-related validity studies in the order mentioned above for Form D were (a) .61, (b) .37, (c) .59, and (d) .61. Construct validity evidence was provided by correlating IPT tests results with (a) age (contingency coefficient of .37 for Form C and .40 for Form D) and (b) grade level (contingency coefficient of .40 for Form C and .47 for Form D).

SPANISH FORM—FIRST EDITION (1990). The standardization sample of the Spanish form has several limitations. The sample consisted of only 654 students. This is not a sufficient number to adequately assess ages 5 to approximately 12 or 13 and grades K to 6. The sample was only from Texas (27%) and California (73%). The manual does not provide information about the country of origin of the Spanish speakers. This information is important given that there are many different dialects of Spanish in the United States (e.g., Mexican, Cuban, Puerto Rican, etc.). Moreover, the manual does not provide information on the socioeconomic status of the sample. The sample is not representative of the Spanish-speaking elementary school-age population in the United States.

With respect to reliability, the manual only provides information on internal consistency. The corrected split-half reliability was .955. The Spanish form had a Cronbach's alpha of .99. These two reliability coefficients are very high. The test manual fails to provide information on test-retest reliability.

The manual provided information on only two types of validity. With respect to content validity, the test authors provide a test blueprint that demonstrates how the six domains of oral language proficiency are assessed by the 83 items. There are a sufficient number of items for each domain. Concurrent criterion-related validity was established by correlating actual IPT test results with (a) teacher's prediction of student oral proficiency and (b) district classification of oral language proficiency (p. 17). The validity coefficients for the former was .70 and was .67 for the latter. The manual also provides information to support the concurrent criterion validity of the IPT-I Spanish form with kindergartners. The manual fails to include any information on construct validity.

SPANISH FORM—SECOND EDITION (1996). The standardization sample consisted of 948 students from eight states. The test authors provide the following data on the standardization sample: age, gender, grade level, ethnicity, primary language, country of origin, district designation of the degree of English and Spanish proficiency, teacher opinion of the degree of English and Spanish proficiency, and teacher opinion of ability in several academic areas. One positive factor noted among the descriptive information is the presence of data pertaining to the samples' country of origin. Approximately 41% of the sample were born in the United States with the remaining 58% born outside the United States from 12 Latin American countries. The largest group of students (47%) in the standardization sample were born in Mexico. Inclusion of both native- and foreign-born limited-English-proficient students in the standardization sample is positive. Although the sample is not representative of the Spanish-speaking elementary school-aged population in the United States, the test authors have made a commendable attempt to include children who evidence a heterogeneity of Spanish dialects. Achieving this task is quite difficult. The sample included in the second edition is a vast improvement from the first edition. The manual, however, does not provide information pertaining to the socioeconomic status of the sample.

With respect to reliability, the technical manual provides evidence of internal consistency reliability by reporting a Cronbach's alpha of .99. The manual reports a test-retest reliability estimate across 2 weeks of .72.

The test manual provides information about the three major types of validity. As with the first Spanish edition, the test authors provide a test blueprint illustrating how each of the 85 items corresponds to the six domains of oral language proficiency assessed by the test. There are sufficient numbers of items for each domain. Concurrent criterion-related validity was addressed by correlating "teachers' prediction of student's oral proficiency" (p. 25) with actual IPT test results. The obtained validity coefficient of .72 is very good. Moreover, construct validity was examined by correlating IPT score levels with (a) age, (b) grade level, (c) "teacher opinion of academic ability," (d) "teacher opinion of Spanish reading ability," and (e) "teacher opinion of Spanish writing ability." The Pearson's correlation coefficients in the order listed above were: (a) .49, (b) .52, (c) .28, (d) .49, and (e) .46. The test authors report that all five coefficients are statistically significant at the .001 level. The authors do note that the coefficient of .28 for teacher opinion of academic ability is "relatively weak," but "is to be expected."

IPT-II. The IPT-II in English (Forms A and B) and Spanish assess the same six components of oral language proficiency that are measured by the IPT-I. Items were developed by the test authors and reviewed by language specialists. English forms A and B each have 91 items, and the first edition of the Spanish form has 81 items. The second edition of the Spanish form has 85 items. As in the PRE-IPT and IPT-I, the test manual and protocol provide clear directions about test administration and scoring for both language forms.

ENGLISH FORMS A & B (1983). The manual provides little information about the standardization sample. The only information included in the manual was that 459 students were from five school districts in California and that 306 of the students were English speakers and 153 were labeled "NES/LES/FES" [non-English speakers/limited-English speakers/fluent English speakers] population. The authors explain why two different language groups of students were included in the sample in the validity section of the manual by stating: "Acknowledging the fact that the English-Only sample population would provide sufficient data for establishing NES/LES designations and wishing to verify the FES designation with the population for which the test is intended, additional studies were conducted using native speakers of other languages" (p. 32). This reviewer was unable to ascertain if these 459 students were used to norm the instruments or for field testing. The manual fails to provide critical information about the sample with respect to gender, age, grade level, or socioeconomic status. The obtained sample is not representative of the United States Census.

With respect to reliability, information is reported for only certain language groups (i.e., English-Only vs. "NES/LES/FES" population). The authors report that "[a]n inter-item reliability study was conducted using an English-only student population .... Over 93% of the English-Only population scored on levels F and M [mastery], thereby providing insufficient variance on individual items to be utilized for this study" (p. 56). The interitem reliability estimate for the "NES/LES/FES" population was .99 for both Form A and B. Test-retest reliability, interrater reliability, and alternate form reliability were examined only with the English-only population. One-week test-retest and interrater reliability on 30 English-only-speaking students was .43 for Form A and .73 for Form B. Alternate form reliability was examined with 56 English-only students. The obtained contingency coefficient was .63 with a significance level of .0013.

Validity was examined with both English-only students and with "NES/LES/FES" students. With respect to content validity, the test authors provide a test blueprint showing how each item loaded with respect to the six components of oral language proficiency. There are sufficient items for each of the six components. The authors provide an appendix stating how each of the 91 items fits into the Basic Interpersonal Communication Skills (BICS) and Cognitive Academic Language Proficiency (CALP) language constructs. Concurrent criterion-related validity evidence was provided with the English-only students by correlating actual IPT-II test results with "teacher prediction of IPT II student levels" (p. 24). The resulting contingency coefficient was .36 for Form A and .40 for Form B. The authors state that "[t]he data presented for the criterion validity on the English-only population is not statistically significant" (p. 25). Concurrent criterion-related validity was examined with the "NES/LES/FES" population by correlating actual IPT-II tests results with (a) "teacher prediction of oral language proficiency" (p. 48), (b) "district designation" (p. 50), and (c) "teacher designation" (p. 52). The Pearson's correlation coefficients of the concur-

rent criterion-related validity studies in the order listed above for Form A were (a) .66, (b) .56, and (c) .69. The test authors report that these three coefficients were statistically significant at the .001 level. The Pearson's correlation coefficients of the concurrent criterion-related validity studies in the order mentioned above for Form B were (a) .43, (b) .35, and (c) .59. The test authors report that these three coefficients were statistically significant at the .001 level. With respect to construct validity, the authors conclude: "there does not exist a strong statistically significant correlation between age and IPT II Results for English for English-Only students at the secondary level. There is a slight correlation between grade and IPT II Results on Form B that is statistically significant ... [A]ll data was negatively skewed with a narrow range of scores. These data serve to validate the hypothesis that native speakers of English would score at the highest levels of IPT II" (p. 31). For the "NES/LES/FES" student population, construct validity was examined by correlating IPT-II test results with (a) age (Pearson's correlation of .14 for Form A and .53 for Form B), (b) grade level (Pearson's correlation of .12 for Form A and .01 for Form B), and (c) "time in country" (p. 43) (Pearson's correlation of .61 for Form A and .64 for Form B).

SPANISH FORM—FIRST EDITION (1987). The standardization sample of the IPT-II Spanish form has major limitations. First, the sample size of 481 is insufficient. The sample is only from California (89%) and Texas (11%). The manual does not include a separate section to describe the norming sample. The reader must assume that the sample of 481 described in the construct validity section of the technical manual (pp. 24–25) is the same 481 students mentioned in the standardization sample. If this, in fact, is the case, there is an insufficient number of seventh grade students ($n =$ 43) included in the sample. There is no information regarding ethnicity and socioeconomic status. The sample is not representative of the Spanish-speaking population of the United States.

With respect to reliability, the manual reports that the scores of the Spanish form have internal consistency as indicated by a Cronbach's alpha of .99. Test-retest reliability across a one-week period and interrater reliability studies, which were conducted on a sample size of 63, resulted in a Pearson's correlation of .62, which was significant at the .001 level.

The three major types of validity were addressed in the technical manual. With respect to content validity, the test authors provide a test blueprint showing how each item loaded with respect to the six components of oral language proficiency. There are sufficient items for each of the six components. Concurrent criterion-related validity was examined by correlating IPT-II test results with "teacher prediction of student's oral language proficiency" (p. 21). The Pearson's correlation coefficient for this analysis was .67. Construct validity was addressed by correlating IPT test results with (a) age (Pearson's correlation = .20), (b) grade (Pearson's correlation = .13), (c) "teacher opinion of academic ability" (p. 29) (Pearson's correlation = .25), and (d) "teacher opinion of Spanish language ability (p. 32) (Pearson's correlation = .70).

SPANISH FORM—SECOND EDITION (1996). Similar to the first edition of the Spanish form, the standardization sample of the IPT-II Spanish second edition has some limitation. First, the sample size of 571 is insufficient. There are insufficient numbers of students at each age level. Second, the sample is from only eight states (Arizona, California, Florida, Idaho, Illinois, New Mexico, New York, and Texas). Approximately 59% ($n = 335$) of the sample is from California and less than 1% is from Texas. The manual, however, does include information on ethnicity and country of origin. This was not done with the first Spanish edition. Similar to the second edition Spanish form of the IPT-I, the authors have made commendable effort to include both native-born (58%) and foreign-born limited-English children from the 13 Latin American countries in the standardization sample. The standardization sample, however, is not representative of the Spanish-speaking school-aged population in the United States.

The manual provides information on two types of reliability. Evidence of internal consistency reliability of this form was provided by a Cronbach's alpha of .99. A 2-week test-retest reliability estimate with a sample of 116 students resulted in a Pearson's correlation of .73.

The manual provides information on content, criterion-related, and construct validity. Similar to all IPT measures, the test authors provide a test blueprint displaying how each of the 85 items correspond to the six domains of oral language proficiency examined by this test. There are suffi-

cient numbers of items for each domain. The authors provide an appendix stating how each of the 85 items fits into the Basic Interpersonal Communication Skills (BICS) and Cognitive Academic Language Proficiency (CALP) language constructs. Evidence of criterion-related validity was demonstrated by correlating "teacher prediction of students' oral language proficiency" with IPT results. The obtained validity coefficient was .73. Construct validity was examined by correlating IPT score levels with (a) age, (b) grade level, (c) "teacher opinion of academic ability," (d) teacher opinion of Spanish reading ability, and (e) teacher opinion of Spanish writing ability. The Pearson's correlations in the order listed above were: (a) .14, (b) .13, (c) .11, (d) .50, and (e) .50. The authors interpreted the first two coefficients as "positive, statistically significant yet relatively weak correlation" (p. 28). Moreover, they state that this could be due to the lack of not having a "wide range of scores" (p. 28) with a secondary-age student population.

SUMMARY. The IDEA Oral Language Proficiency Test ($n = 12$) is better than most language proficiency tests currently on the market with respect to reliability and validity. The IPT-I and II cover a broad perspective of language by assessing six components of oral language proficiency. The primary limitation of all IDEA test is the standardization sample. The standardization sample for all the English forms is not representative of the United States student population. Similarly, the standardization sample for all the Spanish forms is not reflective of the Spanish-speaking student population of the United States. It should be noted, however, that the IPT-I and II Spanish Forms, second editions have included both native and foreign-born limited-English-proficient (LEP) students. This is a positive practice because many LEP students in the United States are foreign born. The authors should have conducted concurrent validity studies with other oral language proficiency measures on the market. Although the test authors state how each of the items fits into the BICS and CALP language constructs for some of the IDEA test measures, they fail to provide the test examiner with an exact score that indicates the student's performance with respect to CALP. Although the three-level language designation (non/limited/fluent speaker) provided by the IDEA measures is helpful, specific information on student's CALP would provide educators and/or test examiners with critical information.

[172]

IDEA Student Ratings of Instruction.

Purpose: Designed to provide student ratings of college instructors.

Population: College faculty.

Publication Dates: 1975–1998.

Scores: 5-part report compiled from ratings data: Overall Measures of Teaching Effectiveness, Student Ratings of Progress in Specific Objectives, Teaching Methods/Style, Course Description/Context, Statistical Detail.

Administration: Group.

Price Data: Available from publisher.

Time: (10–20) minutes.

Authors: Donald P. Hoyt, William H. Pallett, Amy B. Gross, Richard E. Owens, William E. Cashin (technical reports), Glenn R. Sixbury (technical reports, numbers 7–10), Yih-Fen Chen (technical report number 11).

Publisher: IDEA Center.

Cross References: See T4:1195 (1 reference); for a review by John C. Ory of an earlier edition, see 9:493 (2 references).

Review of the IDEA Student Ratings of Instruction by RAOUL A. ARREOLA, Professor and Director of Educational Evaluation and Development, The University of Tennessee Health Science Center, Memphis, TN:

PURPOSE OF THE SYSTEM. The IDEA Student Ratings of Instruction System is designed to gather student input concerning the effectiveness of instruction. The IDEA student rating forms come in both a "long" and "short" version, each of which focuses on student learning rather than instructor teaching behaviors. Using the instructor's own teaching goals, the student rating data are analyzed using a national database. The goal is to provide diagnostic information designed to assist the faculty in improving their teaching effectiveness.

FORMAT. The IDEA system requires instructors to describe their course objectives prior to administering the rating form. The instructor is asked to rate the importance, on a 3-point scale (essential, important, or minor importance), of each of 12 IDEA objectives. The importance the instructor assigns to each objective is taken into account in tabulating results. The optically scanned long rating form is divided into six parts: The Instructor, Progress on, The Course, Self-Rating, Extra Questions, and Comments. The short form is divided into three parts: Progress on, Self-Rating, and Extra Questions. The items in the

short form are identical to the corresponding parts of the long form. The short form is appropriate for summative but not formative evaluation.

The Instructor section consists of 20 items dealing with five dimensions of instruction: student-faculty contact, involving students, establishing expectations, clarity of communication, and assessment/feedback. Items are scored on a 5-point scale ranging from *hardly ever* to *almost always*. The Progress on section deals with the students' evaluation of their progress on 12 course objectives, including gaining factual knowledge, acquiring "team" skills, developing creative capacities, and clarifying/developing personal values. Students are asked to compare the progress made on each objective with the progress made in other courses. Each item is scored on a 5-point scale ranging from *low* (lowest 10% of courses taken) to *high* (highest 10% of courses taken). The Course section deals with three course characteristics: amount of reading, amount of work in other assignments, and difficulty of subject matter. Ratings are compared to other courses on a 5-point scale ranging from *much less than most* courses to *much more than most*. The Self-Rating section includes a self-rating of student attitudes and behaviors in the course. Each item is scored on a 5-point scale from *definitely false* to *definitely true*. Included in this section are five "experimental questions" that the IDEA Center is studying for possible inclusion in future revisions of the form. The Extra Questions section is for optional instructor-designed multiple-choice questions. Finally, the form provides a space for students to make open-ended comments.

RESULTS. The IDEA report consists of seven parts plus identifying information (faculty and course name, number of students enrolled, percent providing ratings). The first two parts summarize evaluation results for overall measures (Part I) and for specific objectives (Part II). Both "unadjusted" and "adjusted" averages are compared with results in a very large national database. "Adjusted" results take into account factors that influence ratings but are beyond the control of the instructor (class size, "course-related" student motivation, academic habits/effort, etc.) The overall evaluation measures, presented both numerically and graphically, include progress on instructor-chosen objectives, improved student attitude, overall excellence of the teacher, and overall excellence of the course.

Part II provides similar information for the specific objectives selected as "Important" or "Essential" by the instructor. Part III (Methods) summarizes responses to the 20 items dealing with teaching procedures found on Section I of the standard form (but not included on the short form). Averages are reported graphically for each item and for scales designed to measure five instructional dimensions. Items are labeled as "Strengths," "Weaknesses," or "In-Between," depending on how their averages differ from classes of similar size and student motivation level. A second section of Part III is intended to facilitate improvement efforts by identifying "strengths" and "weaknesses" that research by the Center has shown to be most relevant to specific teaching objectives. Part IV summarizes student descriptions of course characteristics, and also provides a course description supplied by the instructor (including principal instructional methods, intended audience, special circumstances, and the amount of emphasis given to such matters as writing, computer applications, and quantitative skills). Section V provides statistical detail—frequencies, averages, and standard deviations for all items (including optional instructor-designed items).

DEVELOPMENT AND VALIDATION. The development and initial validation of the IDEA system is described by Hoyt (1973) and Hoyt and Cashin (1977). Items on instructor objectives were originally formed from earlier taxonomic classifications, and factor analyses. The 1998 revision employed the advice of users in eliminating three items and adding five that reflect contemporary emphases in higher education on team skills, values, lifelong learning, and critical thinking. The 20 teaching method items (10 of which are new) were written to reflect Chickering and Gamson's seven principles and were selected on the basis of their unique contribution to the prediction of outcomes (Chickering & Gamson, 1987). Items on course management and student characteristics were included primarily to adjust outcome measures by taking into account factors that were beyond the control of the instructor. The reliability estimates of the five scales of teaching methods ranged from .76 to .91, averaging .86 for classes of 15–34 students. For individual items, reliabilities in similar classes ranged from .62 to .92, averaging .84. A principal indicator of validity was the finding that student ratings of progress on objectives were positively related to instructor ratings of importance of objectives. Also, relationships between teaching methods and progress on objectives were consistent with theoretical expectations. Multiple regression analyses showed that each of the 20 teaching methods made an independent contribution to the prediction of at least one progress rating, and that the relevance of specific instructor behaviors varied with class size. Factors that were used to adjust outcome measures included class size, student desire to take the course regardless of who taught it, the portion of "difficulty" ratings and of "effort" ratings that could not be attributed to the instructor, and a measure of "other student motivation." More recent technical reports (e.g., Cashin & Perrin, 1978; Sixbury & Cashin, 1995a, 1995b; Hoyt, Chen, Pallett, & Gross, 1998) provide additional data on reliability and validity as well as a description of the computational procedures and comparative data bases used in producing reports for the latest version of IDEA.

SUMMARY. The IDEA Student Rating system is a commercially provided service with forms designed to solicit information from students concerning primarily their reactions to the instructor's style and course design. These reactions are weighted by the instructor's own priorities and goals and the resulting analyses provide diagnostic information that may be used to improve teaching effectiveness. Forms must be ordered from the IDEA Center and returned to them for processing. Institutions receive three copies of the IDEA computer report that includes interpretation aids incorporated into the report. For an additional fee, participating institutions may receive "Group Summary Reports" (which combine results for all classes or for selected subgroups) and "Faculty Summary Reports" (which summarize all reports for a given faculty member over a specified period of time).

The IDEA Student Rating system is one of the oldest, most researched, technically sound tools for use in a comprehensive faculty evaluation and faculty development program. It stands as one of the three major commercially available student rating systems along with the Student Instructor Report II (SIRS II; Centra, 1972a, 1972b, 1976, 1998) from Educational Testing Service, and the Aleamoni Course/Instructor Evaluation Questionnaire (CIEQ; Aleamoni, 1978; Aleamoni & Spencer, 1973; Areola, 2000; Gilmore, 1973) from Comprehensive Data Evaluation Services.

REVIEWER'S REFERENCES

Centra, J. A. (1972a). *The student instructional report: Its development and uses.* (SIR Report No. 1). Princeton, NJ: Educational Testing Service.

Centra, J. A. (1972b). *Two studies on the utility of student ratings for instructional improvement. I. The effectiveness of student feedback in modifying college instruction. II. Self-ratings of college teachers: A comparison with student ratings.* (SIR Report No. 2). Princeton, NJ: Educational Testing Service.

Aleamoni, L. M., & Spencer, R. E. (1973). The Illinois course evaluation questionnaire: A description of its development and a report of some of its results. *Educational and Psychological Measurement, 33*, 669–684.

Gillmore, G. M. (1973). *Estimates of reliability coefficients for items and sub scales of the Illinois course evaluation questionnaire.* (Research Report No. 341). Urbana, IL: University of Illinois, Office of Instructional Resources, Measurement and Research Division.

Hoyt, D. P. (1973). Measurement of instructional effectiveness. *Research in Higher Education, 1*, 367–378.

Centra, J. A. (1976). *Two studies on the validity of the student instructional report: I. Student ratings of instruction and their relationship to student learning. II. The relationship between student, teacher, and course characteristics and student ratings of teacher effectiveness.* (SIR Report No. 4). Princeton, NJ: Educational Testing Service.

Hoyt, D. P., & Cashin, W. E. (1977). *Development of the IDEA system* (IDEA Technical Report No. 1). Manhattan, KS: Kansas State University, Center for Faculty Evaluation and Development.

Aleamoni, L. M. (1978). Development and factorial validation of the Arizona course/instructor evaluation questionnaire. *Educational and Psychological Measurement, 38*, 1063–1067.

Cashin, W. E., & Perrin, B. M. (1978). *Description of IDEA System Data Base* (IDEA Technical Report No. 4). Manhattan, KS: Kansas State University, Center for Faculty Evaluation and Development.

Chickering, A. W., & Gamson, Z. F. (1987). Seven principles for good practice in undergraduate education. *AAHE Bulletin, 39*, 3–7.

Sixbury, G. R., & Cashin, W. E. (1995a). *Description of database for the IDEA diagnostic form* (IDEA Technical Report No. 9). Manhattan, KS: Kansas State University, Center for Faculty Evaluation and Development.

Sixbury, G. R., & Cashin, W. E. (1995b). *Comparative data by academic field* (IDEA Technical Report No. 10). Manhattan, KS: Kansas State University, Center for Faculty Evaluation and Development.

Centra, J. A. (1998). *The development of the student instructional report II.* Princeton, NJ: Educational Testing Service.

Hoyt, D. P., Chen, Y., Pallett, W. H., & Gross, A. B. (1998). *Revising the IDEA system for obtaining student ratings of instructors and courses* (IDEA Technical Report No. 11). Manhattan, KS: Kansas State University, the IDEA Center.

Arreola, R. A. (2000). *Developing a Comprehensive Faculty Evaluation System.* Bolton, MA: Anker Publishing, Inc.

Review of the IDEA Student Ratings of Instruction by JENNIFER J. FAGER, Assistant Professor of Teaching, Learning, and Leadership, Western Michigan University, Kalamazoo, MI:

The Instructional Development Effectiveness Assessment (IDEA) System is an evaluation program designed to provide student ratings of classroom instruction and instructors. As described in the IDEA Technical Report No. 11, the original IDEA system was developed in 1969. Subsequent to the initial publication the IDEA was revised in 1975 and remained as such until the revision reviewed here. The authors identified the needs for revisions due to the many changes in higher education including technological advances, instructional approaches, settings, educational purposes, and teaching/learning conceptualizations. The new items represent six new objectives and 15 new methods and were pilot tested by 10 institutions. Despite the updates, the authors did not alter the original conception which, according to the authors, distinguishes the IDEA from other student evaluation programs. The original included

(a) focusing on student learning as the chief indicator of teaching effectiveness, (b) taking into account factors that affect student ratings but that are not under the instructor's control, and (c) focusing on guiding instructional improvement efforts.

The three premises are incorporated into the three forms that make up the IDEA system. The Faculty Information Form provides instructors with an opportunity to identify variables that affect student ratings (e.g., type of student, enrollment, primary instructional approach, course requirements, context) as well as general objectives of the course (e.g., gaining factual knowledge, developing skill in expressing oneself orally or in writing). The Long Form includes 47 items in categories for students to provide information regarding their instructor's skills, their own progress in learning, general feedback on the course, a self-rating focusing on their own motivation for taking the course, and general questions asking the students to rate the course in relation to other courses. The form also allows for 19 questions to be provided by individual instructors as well as a place for written comments. This form is quite thorough and addresses contemporary issues such as the use of technology, teamwork, and the links made between course content and "real life." The Short Form includes a subset of the 47 items from the Long Form and focuses primarily on the course and student progress toward course objectives. This form provides instructors with an opportunity to include 10 questions related to specific course goals/outcomes. Further, the Short Form asks for comments on how the instructor might improve the course or his/her teaching procedures and provides space on the back for students to respond. The instructions accompanying each of the forms are lengthy but clear and easy to follow. They all include words of caution and include a sample report to add clarity to interpretation of final results.

Individual faculty select either the Long or Short Form for a course and complete the Faculty Information Form. This form accounts for extraneous influences that affect teacher and course ratings. A number of regression analyses were performed during the piloting of the revised forms and in the initial development of the IDEA system. These analyses recognize both "biases" under instructor control and those beyond the instructor's control. The factors beyond the instructor's control are the ones the IDEA system "aspires to take into account" (manual, p. 39). In the original IDEA system two factors were identified as accounting for invalid ratings. The first was class size and the second was student motivation. Thus the results of individual course evaluations are compared to similar classes. "Similar" was defined by the authors as in the same size range and/or same student motivation group. "Class size" is defined as small (under 15), medium (15–34), large (35–99), and very large (over 99). "Student motivation group" was defined by the average response to the question, "I had a strong desire to take this course" using a 5-point Likert scale.

The process used to develop the IDEA system in its newest form is well grounded in research and development. This process is well documented in the accompanying technical report that includes many tables that are easily interpreted by those with a background in basic statistics and measurement.

There is no argument regarding the quality of the IDEA system; however, there may be a difference of opinion over its use versus course evaluation forms designed for individual departments, colleges, and/or universities or forms emphasizing instructional quality through methods other than student achievement. Some course and instructor evaluations allow faculty to select items from a database whereas other offer a fixed set of questions. The IDEA does allow for a college, department, or individual faculty member to add up to 19 questions relevant to particular programs or professional development issues. This is a strength of the IDEA system.

An additional issue involving the IDEA system is that of the reporting of results. Results are reported as comparisons between an individual instructor and all faculty who have used IDEA (across all schools using the system) or all faculty who have taught courses of similar size containing students with similar levels of motivation. Some potential users may prefer a more specific norm group such as that of their own department or college or professional focus. An additional down side to the comparison groups is cited in the technical report. A "large" class contains 35–99 students. Instructional strategies vary greatly between a class of 35 where the primary method of approach may be a seminar or a class of 99 where the primary method is lecture or discussion.

SUMMARY. IDEA is a well-documented system, easy to administer, and appropriate to use in higher education. The reporting of results is well designed for faculty and administrators and provides a clear set of useful information. It is recommended that, before adoption in a course or a department or college, individual attention be given to preference for evaluating instruction based on student achievement and for comparisons to national norms.

[173]
Incentives Management Index.

Purpose: Designed to make explicit sales managers' "assumptions, theories, and practices in the realm of sales motivation."
Population: Sales managers.
Publication Dates: 1972–1995.
Acronym: IMI.
Scores, 5: Basic Creative Comfort, Safety and Order, Belonging and Affiliation, Ego-Status, Actualization and Self-Expression.
Administration: Group.
Price Data, 1995: $8.95 per test booklet/manual ('95, 24 pages).
Time: Administration time not reported.
Comments: Self-administered; self-scored.
Authors: Jay Hall and Norman J. Seim.
Publisher: Teleometrics International, Inc.

Review of the Incentives Management Index by LESLIE H. KRIEGER, *Senior Consulting Psychologist, NCC Assessment Technologies, Jacksonville, FL:*

[Editor's Note: This review is similar, and much of it is identical, to the review of the Sales Motivation Survey (330) by the same reviewer. This similarity in reviews is due to the similarity of the tests.]

The Incentives Management Index (IMI) is a brief self-assessment that enables sales managers to examine their approaches to the motivation of their sales people and then compare those approaches to the expressed motivations of both a normative sales person sample and the actual sales people they oversee. The authors believe that many of "the mysteries of sales motivation" (test book/manual, p. 2) which consultants often are brought in to solve can be dealt with more effectively by allowing the sales manager the opportunity to systematically explore thoughts about sales approaches and incentives. The Index was designed in recognition of the fact that sales people who do not experience "need satisfaction" on the job often have lowered productivity and higher turnover. Both the individual sales person and the selling organization benefit when there is need congruency. When used in conjunction with the publisher's Sales Motivation Survey (330) for individual sales people, these complementary assessments set the stage for dialogue about individual sales career development and performance management strategy as well as appraisal of the adequacy of the sales manager's own approaches to meeting the needs of an effective sales team.

The needs assessed in the Incentives Management Index are those outlined in Maslow's Need Hierarchy Model onto which the authors overlay Herzberg's Hygiene-Motivator Theory. This theoretical amalgam results in two fundamental motivational types: Motivation Seekers who are motivated by the demands of the task and who have tolerance for poor environmental factors, and Maintenance Seekers who are motivated more by the nature of their environment. The questionnaire yields scores on each of the five Maslow need levels and an overall assessment of Motivation Seeker versus Maintenance Seeker style.

People unfamiliar with the theories of Maslow and Herzberg will find brief but quite insightful synopses of these models on the eight pages of the questionnaire booklet between the items themselves and the scoring grid. The authors provide concise definitions of each Maslow need level, linking these definitions to examples of actual sales motivation and behavior. They state their underlying rationale for focusing on these models is to enable sales managers to become aware of their own views on the operation of need systems and how these views might support or conflict with the needs of sales people on their team.

The assessment itself consists of 60 items, each of which contains the stem of a proposition about managing sales people and two possible alternative conclusions or reactions to that proposition. The somewhat unusual format carries the following instructions:

> For each survey item, you have five points to distribute between two alternative reactions to the situation described. If A is completely characteristic and B is completely uncharacteristic, give 5 points to A and 0 points to B. If A is considerably characteristic and B is somewhat characteristic, give 4 points to A and 1 point to B. If A is only slightly more characteristic than B, give 3 points to A and 2 points to B. Each of the three combinations also may be reversed. (test booklet/manual, p. 1)

Responses are written directly into boxes coded for one of the five themes. The scoring consists of counting the number of points in the boxes for each of the themes and transposing those totals onto a large banded profile sheet. The resulting profile reflects the sales manager's personal theory about what motivates sales people.

The real issue addressed here is the extent to which the sales manager's approach corresponds to the expressed needs experienced by sales people themselves. Normative bands on the profile sheet allow comparison of the manager's response to results derived from 409 sales people who are not further identified. No percentiles, standard scores, or other bases for score comparison are provided. Presumably, the sales manager also could collect results from the Sales motivation Surveys completed by sales people on their own team, summarizing these data on the profile sheet as the basis for more relevant comparison.

Although marketing materials from the publisher, Teleometrics, quote a research psychologist, "Reliability and validity studies on Teleometrics' materials were conducted within the stringent guidelines established by the American Psychological Association," repeated inquiries to the publisher confirmed that no such information was available for the Incentives Management Index. No test manual exists and there is no technical or psychometric documentation of any kind to support the design or use of the instrument.

SUMMARY. The complete absence of supporting psychometric data makes it impossible to recommend this attractively packaged assessment for anything other than a thought provoker or conversation starter on sales motivation issues. There appears to be no basis for its use in making decisions about one's own sales management style or the appropriateness of that style for enhancing the career opportunities or performance management strategies of a sales force.

Review of the Incentives Management Index by PATRICIA H. WHEELER, President and Principal Researcher, EREAPA Associates, Livermore, CA:

The Incentives Management Index (IMI) is designed as a self-assessment device for sales managers to help them understand the assumptions and practices that characterize the sales manager's attempts to motivate others. The title of the instrument implies a broader scope of management than sales managers and could be misleading to potential customers.

The instrument and interpretative materials are packaged in a single attractive booklet. The instrument, comprising the first half of the booklet, consists of 60 statements, each presenting a situation. For each statement, two potential responses or reactions are listed. The individual is to assign a total of 5 points to these two options, based on how he or she is likely to respond or react (i.e., what he/she would do) rather than what an ideal sales manager should do. The individual can assign all 5 points to one of the two options or divide them between the two, as long as they add up to 5 for each statement. Across all 60 statements, the total points assigned should equal 300 points.

The results are shown as a profile of need factors, based on Maslow's Need Hierarchy Model. The five need factors are: Basic-Creature Comfort, Safety and Order, Belonging and Affiliation, Ego-Status, and Actualization and Self-Expression. There is also some discussion of Herzberg's Hygiene-Motivation Theory and how it is linked to Maslow's theory.

Each of the five categories of need factors is assigned a letter code, and this code appears on the instrument next to the box where the individual enters a number ranging from 0 to 5. If the individual has looked through the second half of the booklet, it is extremely simple to respond in a certain manner to arrive at a desired profile. A more complex scoring strategy should be employed to minimize such a possibility.

The statements presented reflect the world of sales of the early 1970s when the instrument was originally developed. No mention is made of the more current term of "marketing." No items address the use of technology, the role of travel, the feasibility of telecommuting and working from home or car, or of the sale of services (only products). The statements need to fit the current structure of the marketing profession.

No data are provided for validity or reliability. Even the development of the statements and a review of them by sales managers and business leaders is not discussed, a minimum for content validation. How the options used for scoring were linked to the five need factors is not clear.

A profile summary is provided on which the average score of 409 sales persons is plotted and a shaded area that is 20 points wide (10 above and

10 below) is shown that "represents the 'average range' around those data points" (test booklet/manual, p. 15). It is unclear how they computed the so-called "average range," or even who was in this sample of 409 sales persons and when the data were collected. In addition, no comparable data are provided for sales managers.

This instrument has an accompanying one for sales staff, the Sales Motivation Survey (SMS), which was not covered by this review. It is also a self-scored device and, as pointed out in the IMI booklet, its results should be kept confidential. Yet the IMI booklet suggests profiling the IMI results for the sales manager's need factors against the profile for the sales person. It then says if there is a difference of 10 points between the two, in either direction, "it is significantly discrepant and worthy of consideration" (p. 22). If the difference is as high as 20 points, there is "a significant difference and [the difference in need levels] should become a focal point for consideration, discussion, and critique" (p. 22). The basis for these interpretations seems arbitrary. In addition, the fact that an employee and his or her manager have different need structures does not necessarily mean there is a problem that warrants attention. They have different job responsibilities, and satisfactory performance in a given position may require a different needs structure from that of another position (i.e., a sales manager and a sales person should not necessarily have the same need factor structure).

SUMMARY. The IMI is a self-assessment device for sales managers designed to help them gain a better insight about their own need structure. Although attractively packaged, the content is dated, it lacks technical quality, and it has inherent weaknesses in format that can easily allow an individual to give an inaccurate profile.

[174]
Independent Living Scales.

Purpose: Designed to assess adults' competence in instrumental activities of daily living.
Population: Adults with cognitive impairments.
Publication Date: 1996.
Acronym: ILS.
Scores, 6: Memory/Orientation, Managing Money, Managing Home and Transportation, Health and Safety, Social Adjustment, Total.
Administration: Individual.
Price Data, 1999: $209.50 per complete kit including manual (119 pages), 25 record forms, stimulus

booklet, and a pouch containing a facsimile of a driver's license, credit card, and key; $31 per 25 record forms.
Time: (45) minutes.
Comments: Four screening items are used to determine whether the examinee has a vision, speech, or hearing impairment; the stimulus booklet is designed for adults who can hear and those with a hearing impairment.
Author: Patricia Anderten Loeb.
Publisher: The Psychological Corporation.

Review of the Independent Living Scales by LIBBY G. COHEN, Professor of Special Education, University of Southern Maine, Gorham, ME:

The Independent Living Scales (ILS) is an individually administered test that ostensibly assesses selected independent living skills of adults. However, the specific purpose of the instrument is unclear because several different descriptions are used throughout the manual to indicate what the test assesses. These include: "instrumental activities of daily living" (manual, p. 1), "functional competence" (manual, p. 68), living arrangements, competency in managing personal property and affairs, guardianship decisions, needs for support services, adaptations, or instruction.

The ILS kit includes a manual, stimulus book, record forms, and a plastic case containing a key, a poor imitation of a credit card, and a driver's license. The examiner must provide the remaining materials needed for administration including a stopwatch, money (both coins and bills), a telephone book, and a telephone. The test consists of seven screening items and five subscales: Memory/Orientation (8 items), Managing Money (17 items), Managing Home and Transportation (15 items), Health and Safety (20 items), and Social Adjustment (10 items).

The subscales can be administered in any order. Several items are ambiguous or poorly worded. One example of a poorly worded item on the Managing Home and Transportation subscale is "What are two routine tasks that you do at home, but less often than every day?" One item asks the respondent to read the time on an analog clock rather than a digital clock. The stimulus book is used throughout the test administration.

Items are scored 2, 1, or 0. Although the manual provides suggested guidelines for scoring items, a great deal of interpretation is left to individual test administrators.

The development and administration of the ILS does not take into consideration the diversity of the U.S. population. The test assumes that respondents are able to read, write, hear, and speak English. There is no consideration for testing accommodations for adults who may have physical disabilities and many potential respondents of this test may have physical disabilities. The test scores of respondents who have one or more sensory disabilities may be penalized because of the way the items are administered and scored.

Several samples were used in the development of the ILS. A clinical sample composed of 248 adults, ages 17 years and older, had diverse clinical diagnoses including mental retardation, traumatic brain injury, psychiatric problems, or dementia. A nonclinical sample consisting of 590 adults, ages 65 years and older, was divided into three groups according to living status: Independent, Semi-independent, and Dependent. The ILS standard scores are only based on the Independent group. There is a great deal of disparity when the characteristics of the Independent group are compared to the U.S. population, ages 65 and older, according to the 1993 Census with regard to educational level, race/ethnicity, and geographical region.

Raw scores are converted to standard scores (standard T scores with a mean of 50 and a standard deviation of 10) for the subscales and both factors. The Full Scale is a sum of the five standard subscale scores (deviation IQ scores with a mean of 100 and a standard deviation of 15). All of the standard scores were derived from nonnormalized distributions because the distribution of the underlying raw scores was based on the minimal requirements for competence.

Reliability was determined only for the nonclinical sample and was not based on a sample of adults for whom this test is intended. Internal consistency reliability was based on the 590 respondents from the nonclinical sample. Coefficients for the subscales ranged from .72 (Social Adjustment) to .87 (Managing Money). As expected when the items were arranged into the two factors, the internal consistency reliability increased (Problem Solving .86, Performance/Information .92). Full Scale internal consistency was .88. Test-retest reliability (7–24-day interval) was based on 80 adults from the nonclinical sample. The coefficients for the subscales, factors, and Full Scale ranged from .81 (Social Adjustment) to .92 (Managing Money). Interrater reliabilities were all in the high .90s.

According to the manual, content validity was examined through the use of a Q sort. The test items were sorted into the subscales by areas of competence. For example, items relating to managing the home, transportation, mobility, communication, and use of the telephone were placed in the Managing Home and Transportation subscale. Although the ILS contains five subscales, the only two factors that were identified are problem solving and performance/information. Five of the 8 items on the Memory/Orientation subscale and 6 of the 10 items on the Social Adjustment subscale did not align with either of these factors.

The purpose of the cut scores is to aid in predicting the functional competence of the respondents to live independently. Criterion-referenced cut scores, according to living status, were developed for the subscale, factor, and Full Scale scores. Percentages of adults in the nonclinical Dependent and nonclinical Independent groups were classified as having dependent, semi-independent, or independent living status. There are several problems with the development of these cut scores. First, the samples from which the cut scores were derived are small and not representative of older adults according to the U.S. Census. Secondly, no studies are reported in the manual that confirm that these scores do, in fact, accurately predict functional competence. Finally, there is some support in the manual that demonstrates that, upon retesting, decision making is very inconsistent and unstable.

Several studies were conducted that investigated concurrent validity of the ILS. The Wechsler Adult Intelligence Scale—Revised (WAIS-R) was administered to 90 adults from the nonclinical sample. The results of this study demonstrated that the ILS and the WAIS-R assess different constructs. The MicroCog and the ILS were administered to 47 adults in the nonclinical sample. The MicroCog is a computer-administered and scored test of neurocognitive functioning. The results showed that the MicroCog and the ILS test similar constructs. The Activities of Daily Living Domain (ADL) and the ILS were administered to 90 adults from the nonclinical sample. The results demonstrated that the ADL and the ILS assess somewhat similar constructs.

The ILS was administered to small samples of individuals who were diagnosed with some type of cognitive impairments such as mental retarda-tion, traumatic brain injury, dementia, or psychiatric disturbance. These studies showed that the ILS is not a precise instrument and that the results are open to interpretation.

SUMMARY. The ILS is an instrument that should be used cautiously. Because of the emphasis on respondents being able to read, write, hear, and speak English, this instrument may not be useful with all individuals for whom it was intended. The standardization sample is not representative of the U.S. population. Although reliability is satisfactory, validity is inadequate. Caution should be exercised when interpreting the results of this instrument.

Review of the Independent Living Scales by JACK A. CUMMINGS, *Professor and Chair, Department of Counseling and Educational Psychology, Indiana University, Bloomington, IN:*

The Independent Living Scales (ILS) was designed to assess "adults' competence in instrumental activities of daily living" (manual, p. 1). The purpose of the ILS is to evaluate an individual's skills associated with various levels of independent living. In contrast to current measures, the ILS requires the individual to demonstrate various adaptive skills. The ILS does not rely on third party informants or self-report. Loeb's (the test author's) intent was to create a "direct, more objective assessment of functioning in daily life" (manual, p. 1).

STANDARDIZATION. A sample of 590 individuals, ages 65 and above, served as the standardization sample. The sample was stratified into five age groups at intervals of 5 years starting at age 65. Within the sample, individuals were in one of three living arrangements: Independent (*n* = 400), Semi-independent (*n* = 100), and Dependent (*n* = 90). Those classified as Independent typically lived in a private home and were capable of all self-care skills. Semi-independent individuals often lived in a retirement home and needed some assistance with a limited number of daily living activities. Those in the Dependent category needed full-time supervision and help with most daily living skills. Adults in the three categories of living arrangement were evenly distributed across the age levels. Men and women were proportionally represented.

In the section of the manual on standardization, Loeb reports that two samples were collected. She refers to the group of 590 adults as the "nonclinical" sample. The clinical sample was not actually a standardization sample, but rather separate validation samples including individuals with mental retardation, dementia, traumatic brain injury, and chronic psychiatric disturbances. No norms are provided for individuals representing the aforementioned groups. Despite the age stratification in the nonclinical sample, the norms are collapsed for all individuals. This means that regardless of the adult's age, there is a single norm table that is used to generate subscale and factor scores. As developmental cognitive and psychomotor changes have been documented with adults in the age range from 65 to 85+, there should have been some discussion in the manual of the relationship between age and performance on the ILS. Beyond the issue of age, the decision to aggregate the scores of individuals across independent, semi-independent, and dependent living situations also merits discussion by the author. As the standardization sample is composed, approximately two thirds are living independently, one sixth semi-independently, and one sixth dependently. What is the rationale for allocating those proportions in the sample? An alternative approach to the use of a single table would have been to have separate norms for those in the three levels of living with each category stratified by age. This would be similar to the use of separate norm tables with the AAMR Adaptive Behavior Scale—School, Second Edition (Lambert, Nihira, & Leland, 1993; T5:2).

RELIABILITY. Coefficient alphas were calculated to estimate the internal consistency of the Full Scale score, two factor scores, and five subscale scores. The coefficients for the Full Scale and factor scores exceeded .85. Scores from the subscales of Managing Money, Managing Home and Transportation, and Health and Safety were reported to have coefficients in the mid-80s. The reliability of scores from the Social Adjustment and Memory/Orientation subscales was slightly lower at .72 and .77, respectively. Loeb notes in the manual that the lower internal consistency estimates of the latter two subscales are a function of relatively fewer items as compared to the other subscales. Overall, the coefficient alphas provide support for the author's contention that scores from the ILS have adequate internal consistency.

Stability was assessed by readministering the scale to 80 nonclinical adults. The average interval between testings was 2 weeks (range 7 to 24 days). The coefficients were impressive: .91 for the Full

Scale, .90 and above for both factor scores, and .81 to .92 for the subscales. These coefficients indicate adequate stability.

Loeb also reports decision consistency based on the test-retest data. The question was whether an individual's classification as high, moderate, or low functioning would be comparable across testing sessions. For those initially scoring in the high classification, 92.6% scored high in the second administration. Likewise, there was consistency for those initially classified as functioning in the low range: 81.3% were in the same classification after the second testing. However, the stability of the classification for those labeled moderate was considerably less consistent. Only 47.6% were classified as moderate on the second testing. More than half of those in the moderate category on the first testing scored in the high range on the second administration. This is likely a function of a practice effect or, as Loeb suggests, partially explained by elderly individuals feeling more comfortable with the testing format on the second sitting.

VALIDITY. The description of the initial item development is vague. An unspecified number of "professionals knowledgeable about competency issues … [and] older adults" identified items and subscales that were important in regard to competent functioning (manual, p. 60). Once the items were developed, four experts in the psychology of aging sorted items into categories. The content validity phase of scale development could have been improved by having experts judge how effectively the various items represent a given domain, as well as judging the adequacy of the item format. Despite this caveat, the present reviewer does not see gaps in item coverage or problems with format.

Criterion-related validity was established with concurrent validity studies where scores from the ILS was correlated with scores from the Wechsler Adult Intelligence Scale—Revised (Wechsler, 1981), MicroCog (Powell, Kaplan, Whitla, Weintraub, & Funkenstein, 1993), and an unpublished activities of daily living self-report measure. Although the resultant coefficients were in the moderate range, none of the concurrent measures would have been expected to serve as an ideal anchor for the ILS. Another form of criterion-related validity was demonstrated by considering the performance of individuals in the three different living circumstances.

CONCLUSIONS AND SUMMARY. The value of the ILS lies in the selection of items; it provides a useful guide for a practitioner to reflect on the various roles associated with independent living. The ILS provides a format to observe an individual's response to common situations wherein adults have to perform actions to maintain an independent life style. This allows the examiner to gain another perspective on the individual's abilities, a perspective that can supplement data form third party informants. It is not a scale that should be interpreted rigidly. For instance, an individual may be performing at the top of the distribution in the areas of Memory/Orientation, Managing Money, Health and Safety, and Social Adjustment. A high Full Scale may place the individual in the independent category, but there could be a mobility issue that would require assistance. Loeb points to another issue: An individual may score poorly in a given area because a spouse or someone else takes responsibility for the function. As with other assessments, scores from the ILS must be interpreted in light of background information, observations, interviews, and other data.

REVIEWER'S REFERENCES

Wechsler, D. (1981). Wechsler Adult Intelligence Scale—Revised. San Antonio, TX: Psychological Corporation.
Lambert, N., Nihira, K., & Leland, H. (1993). AAMR Adaptive Behavior Scale—School, Second Edition. Austin, TX: PRO-ED.
Powell, D. H., Kaplan, E. F., Whitla, D., Weintraub, S., & Funkenstein, H. H. (1993). MicroCog: Assessment of Cognitive Functioning. San Antonio, TX: Psychological Corporation.

[175]

The Infanib.

Purpose: Designed to provide a systematic scorable method to assess the neurological status of infants, especially infants who are premature or have special conditions.
Population: Infants from birth to 18 months corrected gestational age.
Publication Date: 1994.
Scores, 20: Hands Open, Hands Closed, Scarf Sign, Heel-To-Ear, Popliteal Angle, Leg Abduction, Dorsiflexion of the Foot, The Foot Grasp, Tonic Labyrinthine Supine, Asymmetric Tonic Neck Reflex, Pull-To-Sitting, Body Denotative, Body Rotative, All-Fours, Tonic Labyrinthine Prone, Sitting, Sideways Parachute, Backwards Parachute, Standing-Positive Support Reaction, Forward Parachute.
Administration: Individual.
Price Data, 1999: $79 per complete kit including 50 screening forms and manual (131 pages); $23 per 50 screening forms.
Time: Untimed.

Comments: "Criterion-referenced" test with ratings determined by therapist.
Author: Patricia H. Ellison.
Publisher: The Psychological Corporation.

Review of The Infanib by JILL ANN JENKINS, Psychologist on Sabbatical, Barcelona, Spain:

The Infanib (Infant Neurological International Battery) is a 20-item neuromotor development test that was intended to assess infants with special needs, including those born prematurely, treated in neonatal units, those with developing sicknesses, and those who have generally slow development.

The test represents a selection of items found in the Milani-Comparetti and Gidoni (MCG) method (Milani-Comparetti & Gidoni, 1967a, b), the French Angles method (André-Thomas, Chesni, & Dargassies, 1960), the Primitive Reflex Profile (Capute, Accardo, Vining, Rubenstein, & Harryman, 1978), and items from the test developer's research with the National Collaborative Perinatal Project. The examination yields a score placing the infant's motor development into one of three ranges: "abnormal," "transient" (transient abnormalities), and "normal." Infants in the "abnormal" range are then subcategorized as falling into one of four categories: spastic tetraparesis/dyskinesia, spastic hemiparesis, spastic diplegia, and hypotonia. When scoring, the items are additionally divided into five factors including: Spasticity, Head and Trunk, Vestibular Function, Legs, and French Angles.

All of the 20 test items require physical manipulation of the infant. The examiner, therefore, needs to have experience in recognizing normal and abnormal tone and posture at different developmental ages. The test author seems to have envisioned the test to be used by the physical therapists, occupational therapists, nurses, and pediatric neurologists to which she so often refers.

The Infanib provides the examiner with pictorial examples of all of the test items being used on a child with abnormalities and without. It also provides four case studies (two with transient abnormalities, one with a marked abnormality, and one normal child). Although these are very helpful in understanding the test, it would have been more useful if the manual was accompanied by a videotape so that one could see the physical manipulations in action rather than frozen in a frame.

The manual itself is a useful and informative tool regarding the etiology, diagnosis, and prognosis of infants with neuromotor delay. In addition, it includes helpful information on giving test results to caretakers. However, it falls short of good professional standards with regard to providing references for general comments in numerous places (i.e., stating that "black infants ... often have neuromotor precocity but ... delay in the acquisition of language," p. 52), and authors referred to (i.e., discussing the "Bayley" without giving the full name of the test, date, or author of the test, manual, p. 100). In addition, one must constantly glance between chapters to find statistical and methodological aspects of the Infanib.

The scoring sheet itself for the Infanib also has its weaknesses. The examiner must constantly flip from front to back of its one-sheet format for scoring and interpretation. In addition, although one can assume that the five different boxes in which infant's scores are placed must be related to the five factors, they are not indicated as such.

STANDARDIZATION. Except for the very general statement that, "a large sample of infants who were initially treated in the neonatal care unit" (manual, p. 97) were used for the construction of the test, further description of this sample was not given. The excluded information about sample characteristics, including age range and mean age, sample size, demographics, and presenting issues in these subjects, has grave implications for the external validity of the test. The author does not, in fact, even provide the age range for which the test was designed to be used. The reader is left only to assume from the scoring sheet that it was included for infants ages birth to 18 months gestational age.

The examiners used for the test construction were all physical therapists, again threatening the external validity of the Infanib. As the author herself reasonably states earlier in the manual (p. 5), frequently there are disagreements on the interpretation of a measure depending on the field of the examiner. It probably would have been more beneficial to have a representative sample of different professionals who might have given assistance in the test construction.

Mean scores and standard deviations for the five factors and total score at ages 6 months and 12 months were calculated by Stavrakas, Kemmer-Gacura, Engelke, and Chenier (1991) for normal, transiently abnormal, and abnormal subjects, with an impressive sample of $n = 243$ infants. However, if the infant that one is testing does not fall at the 6- or 12-month level the examiner will not be able to statistically analyze the results for the five factors and total score.

VALIDITY. Predictive validity of each of the five factors and total score (with children evaluated at 6 and 12 months only) is discussed in the research by Stavrakas et al. (1991). The results indicated that the spasticity and head and trunk factors at 6 months were predictive of cerebral palsy at 12 months (86.8% and 87.1%, respectively). However, the predictive validity of the other factors and total score was not further discussed.

The author does discuss predictive validity related to her earlier research using the MCG method, for which there are overlapping test items with the Infanib (Ellison & Foster, 1992). Although showing acceptable correlations, these results must be interpreted cautiously as the MCG is simply NOT the Infanib.

To evaluate concurrent validity, the examiners in the original study of the Infanib were asked to first rate the infants as normal to abnormal on a 5-point scale before using the Infanib. The factor and overall scores of the Infanib were then correlated with these initial scores. If the author had provided the results it may have been quite enlightening. Because she did not, we are left to wonder about the concurrent validity evidence.

Content validity was not discussed by the author, and construct validity is discussed in vague terms (where the author devotes a section to discussing the importance of construct validity and then, quizzically, does not provide any information regarding the Infanib).

RELIABILITY. The manual provides better information on the reliability of the Infanib, boasting an interrater reliability of $r = .97$, and a 6–15 months test-retest reliability of $r = .95$ (Castro, deSanchez, & Landinez, 1985). Castro et al.'s study had an impressive $n = 65$ infants tested on two occasions by two testers, for a total of 234 assessments.

With regard to internal consistency reliability, the Infanib also shows quite acceptable results, with an alpha coefficient of .88 for infants 7 months of age or less, .93 for infants 8 months or more, and an overall score of .91. However, one must view these results cautiously as they were developed with a version of the Infanib that was later revised.

SUMMARY. The Infanib is a neuromotor developmental evaluation for infants ages birth to 18 months gestational age, which clearly needs further standardization and research regarding its validity. It does show evidence of high interrater and test-retest reliability estimates.

The Infanib manual itself has some quite serious flaws in omitting highly relevant data, not citing references, and poor organization of information. It is however, a very useful review of the current knowledge regarding etiology, diagnosis, and prognosis of neuromotor problems in children. The scoring sheet itself lacks clarity and is physically clumsy to use.

Despite the author's previous descriptions of the Infanib as a "neurological" test of infancy (Ellison, 1986, 1992) professionals should note that the Infanib only evaluates the *neuromotor* development of infants. It does not, therefore, look at other neurodevelopmental issues that one would find in the revised edition of the Bayley Scales of Infant Development (BSID-II) (Bayley, 1993; T5:270), or the Cattell Infant Intelligence Scale (Cattell, 1960; T5:433) including auditory response, visual responses, and primitive cognitive functioning.

REVIEWER'S REFERENCES

André-Thomas, C. Y., & Dargassies, S. A. (1960). *The neurological examination of the infant.* London: National Spastics Society.

Cattell, P. (1960). Cattell Infant Intelligence Scale. New York: Psychological Corporation.

Milani-Comparetti, A., & Gidoni, E. A. (1967a). Pattern analysis of motor development and its disorders. *Developmental Medicine and Child Neurology, 9,* 625–630.

Milani-Comparetti, A., & Gidoni, E. A. (1967b). Routine development examination in normal and retarded children. *Developmental Medicine and Child Neurology, 9,* 631–638.

Capute, A. J., Accardo, P. J., Vining, E. P. G., Rubenstein, J. E., & Harryman, S. (1978). *Primitive Reflex Profile.* Baltimore: University Park.

Castro, A. V., deSanchez, I. E., & Landinez, N. S. (1985). *Reliability of the infant neurological international battery (Infanib) for the assessment of neurological integrity in infancy to high risk Colombian infants.* Unpublished thesis, Instituto Materno, Infantil of Bogota, Bogota, Columbia.

Ellison, P. H. (1986). Scoring sheet for the Infant Neurological International Battery. *Physical Therapy, 66,* 548–550.

Stavrakas, P. A., Kemmer-Gacura, G. E., Engelke, S. C., & Chenier, T. C. (1991). Predictive validity of the infant neurological battery (Infanib). *Developmental medicine and Child Neurology Supplement.*

Ellison, P. (1992). Infant Neurological International Battery has high predictive validity, and test author is a pediatric neurologist. *American Journal of Occupational Therapy, 46*(9), 855.

Ellison, P. H., & Foster, M. (1992). Developmental pathways through childhood for children treated in the neonatal intensive care unit (NICU). *Acta Paediatrica Scandinavica Supplement, 380,* 28–35.

Bayley, N. (1993). Bayley Scales of Infant Development (2ⁿᵈ ed.). San Antonio: Psychological Corporation.

Review of The Infanib by JOHN J. VACCA, Certified School Psychologist, Assistant Professor of Special Education, Advisor, Graduate Program in Early Intervention, Loyola College, Baltimore, MD:

TEST COVERAGE AND USE. The purpose of the Infanib is to provide a systematic scorable method to assess the neurological status of infants (birth to 18 months corrected gestational age), especially those who are premature or have special conditions. Usage of the Infanib is designed for therapists, physicians, and nurses. The current revised issue of the Infanib stems in large part from Dr. Ellison's clinical experience in pediatric neurology. The primary focus of the Infanib is on the evaluation of neuromotor functioning in the young infant. Data collected from such an evaluation are believed to provide professionals with an overall indicator of both the developmental outcome and the neurological integrity of the infant's central nervous system.

Dr. Ellison concentrated her efforts in the development of the Infanib by including key aspects of documented approaches in the infant neurological examination. Included are the American pediatric neurology method, focusing on primitive reflexes, tapping of reflexes, and cranial nerves and the French method of neurological examination, incorporating the use of the French Angles (scarf sign, heel-to-ear, popliteal angle, and leg abduction). There are 20 items on the revised Infanib. These include: Hands Open, Hands Closed, Scarf Sign, Heel-to-Ear, Popliteal Angle, Leg Abduction, Dorsiflexion of the Foot, The Foot Grasp, Tonic Labyrinthine Supine, Asymmetric Tonic Neck Reflex, Pull-to-Sitting, Body Denotative, Body Rotative, All-Fours, Tonic Labyrinthine Prone, Sitting, Sideways Parachute, Backwards Parachute, Standing-Positive Support Reaction, and Forward Parachute. One of the many attributes of the Infanib includes the introductory chapters of the manual that address the instrument in general, an historical overview of the development of infant neuromotor assessment techniques, the manner in which the Infanib was developed through Dr. Ellison's clinical experience in pediatrics, suggestions for professionals to assist in the development of diagnoses, and a discussion on the need for a collaborative relationship among parents, caregivers, and professionals. Generally, Dr. Ellison's work with the Infanib is intended to guide professionals in their interpretation of neurological abnormalities in infancy and to provide a systematic and reliable set of procedures and a scoring rubric to "provide good guidelines for discussions with parents and recommendations for diagnostic testing and treatment" (manual, p. 6).

APPROPRIATE SAMPLES FOR TEST VALIDATION AND NORMING. In terms of the development of the Infanib, Ellison discussed several steps that were carried out. First, the items for the Infanib came from five sources: French Angles; Milani-Comparetti and Gidoni methods; research from Capute, Palmer, Shapiro, Wachtel, Ross, and Accardo; and research from the National Collaborative Perinatal Project. Second, Ellison mentioned that the list of items was "pruned" on the basis of experience and previous studies. The original list of items, however, was not identified. Additionally, Ellison stated that the items were scored, but she did not specify the scoring rubric.

Another step involved in the development of the Infanib was the "competent, compulsive examiners were requested to examine a large sample of infants who were initially treated in the neonatal intensive care unit" (manual, p. 97). In the manual, the way that the samples were to be drawn is not specified and the demographics of the infants who were evaluated are not identified. Ellison indicated that the examiners, however, needed to have certain qualities: "perseverance, patience, and willingness to fill in every data point for every child" (p. 98). Further, she stated that she was uninterested in the disciplines of the examiners (e.g., medicine, nursing, etc.), but she was more interested "that the project [was] done well" (p. 98). Although it is important that the project was conducted appropriately, such loose criteria regarding professional disciplines is a drawback of the instrument. In light of the nature of the population of infants addressed by the Infanib, and due to the fact that many professionals from different disciplines are involved in the care of infants (especially those from neonatal Intensive Care Units), the disciplines of persons participating in the pseudo-piloting of the Infanib could have been more specifically identified. Such consideration would have helped to provide more of an in-depth analysis of interrater reliability among all professionals involved in the care of infants considered high risk, rather than a discussion on interrater reliability among those professionals who ended up participating in the piloting of the Infanib. Therefore, in reviewing the values for interrater reliability (.97), it is questionable whether these results represented reliability among physicians only, for example, or if they represented reliability among physicians, nurses, physical therapists, and occupational therapists.

In terms of analysis, Ellison mentioned that the following methods were used: descriptive statistics, correlation matrices, and factor analyses. Upon completion of the analyses, Ellison identified that the four highest loading items for each of the five factors were selected. This resulted in the present 20-item scale.

RELIABILITY. Another asset of the Infanib is the way in which issues of reliability and validity are addressed in a separate section. Such openness helps professionals make informed decisions about which tests they will use in a given evaluation.

INTERNAL CONSISTENCY. Upon completion of development and piloting of the Infanib estimates for internal consistency were obtained for the five factors (Spasticity, Head and Trunk, Vestibular Function, Legs, and French Angles) and for the total scores for two different ages (above and below 8 months). The alpha coefficients were high (.88 for infants 7 months of age or less, .93 for infants 8 months or more, and .91 for all subjects).

INTERRATER RELIABILITY. According to the information presented in the manual, a study was conducted using the Infanib with 65 infants and seven evaluators (Castro, deSanches, & Landinez, 1985). Each infant was evaluated twice, independently by two examiners on two separate occasions. A total of 234 assessments were conducted, and estimates for interrater reliability using the Infanib were high ($r = .97$). Although these results are significant for this particular study, descriptions of the participants and examiners were not provided. Additionally, it is unclear whether the examiners had prior experience with the Infanib, which would have contributed to the high degree of concordance. In all, even though these results are impressive, more studies would need to be completed with varying types of neonatal difficulties and professionals to thoroughly examine interrater reliability of the Infanib.

TEST-RETEST RELIABILITY. Ellison reports that in the study cited previously for issues of interrater reliability, test-retest reliability was also high ($r = .95$). The demographics and the time interval between administrations of the study were not identified or discussed. Therefore, caution should be used when interpreting the results. Investigations that are more recent than 1985 are needed with the Infanib to prove that use of the scale will provide reliable results and assist professionals in making competent diagnostic decisions for the infants referred for evaluation.

PREDICTIVE VALIDITY. In terms of predictive validity, Ellison makes reference to a study that was conducted with 243 infants using the Infanib to evaluate the children at 6 and 12 months of age (Stavrakas, Kemmer-Gacura, Engelke, & Chenier, 1991). According to the information provided by Ellison, "the spasticity and head trunk subscales (factors) at 6 months were highly predictive of cerebral palsy at 12 months—86.8% and 87.1% respectively with discriminant function analyses" (p. 108). Ellison continues, however, stating that at present there are no data for predictive validity of the Infanib from infancy to older ages. Ellison made reference to two other assessment methods (Milani-Comparetti & Gidoni) and stated that values for predictive validity of these methods ranged from .42 to .64. She identified that similar results could be probable with the Infanib, but that additional investigations with the Infanib are needed to document this. In the initial chapters of the Infanib, Ellison makes an impressive case for the use of the neuromotor examination to predict future developmental difficulties, yet the data she presents do not involve the Infanib. Although the Infanib appears to represent an amalgamation of former neuromotor approaches, more data need to be provided in order to establish the overall utility of the scale with the infant population. Provision of additional data would help professionals to better anticipate the sequelae of early neurological-related difficulties in infancy.

CONCURRENT VALIDITY. Ellison mentions that a procedure was conducted during the initial stages of development of the Infanib to investigate concurrent validity, yet no values were reported.

CONSTRUCT VALIDITY. In terms of construct validity, Ellison does not provide values for the Infanib. She mentions, however, that "neonatal conditions should be better considered [in order] to provide better construct validity for neurologic abnormality on the scoring sheet" (manual, p. 109).

TEST ADMINISTRATION. The Infanib provides the professional with clear instructions on how to elicit each motor posture and how to record responses. It is not clear, however, how each response is scored and tabulated to render factor scores and a total score. The professional is provided with real life photographs of infants performing each motor movement. Additionally, pictures of infants at various age-month intervals are provided (0–3, 4–6, 7–9, 10–12 months respectively). Further, each set of pictures portrays both normal and abnormal postures. Along with the pictures for each item, Ellison includes a brief narrative, in which the relationship between early neuromotor abnormalities seen at the time of assessment with the Infanib and later development is discussed. The professional is not provided with adequate guidance, however, in how to interpret his or her own findings. Ellison appears to present conclusions based on her experience. Although the discussion of the relationship between early signs of neuromotor abnormality and later development is helpful, values for predictive validity are not fully established with the Infanib.

SUMMARY. Professionals should use caution when interpreting their own findings with the Infanib. Further, findings from the Infanib should be used in conjunction with results from other developmental measures in order to allow professionals to make appropriate diagnostic and prescriptive decisions for infants.

REVIEWER'S REFERENCES

Castro, A. V., deSanchez, I. E., & Landinez, N. S. (1985). *Reliability of the infant neurological international battery (Infanib) for the assessment of neurological integrity in infancy to high risk Colombian infants.* Unpublished thesis, Instituto Materno, Infantil of Bogota, Bogota, Columbia.
Stavrakas, P. A., Kemmer-Gacura, G. E., Engelke, S. C., & Chenier, T. C. (1991). Predictive validity of the infant neurological battery (Infanib). *Developmental Medicine and Child Neurology Supplement.*

[176]
Infant Development Inventory.

Purpose: Designed "for screening the development of infants in the first eighteen months."
Population: Birth to 18 months.
Publication Dates: 1980–1995.
Acronym: IDI.
Scores, 5: Social, Self-Help, Gross Motor, Fine Motor, Language.
Administration: Individual.
Manual: Brief Instructions only.
Price Data, 1995: $10 per 25 parent questionnaires.
Time: Administration time not reported.
Comments: New version of the Minnesota Infant Development Inventory (T4:1642); observations by mother.
Author: Harold Ireton.
Publisher: Behavior Science Systems.
Cross References: See T5:1259 (2 references); for information on the earlier edition, see T4:1642 (1 reference); for a review by Bonnie W. Camp of the earlier edition, see 9:714.

Review of the Infant Development Inventory by ALAN S. KAUFMAN, Clinical Professor of Psychology, Yale University School of Medicine, and

NADEEN L. KAUFMAN, Lecturer, Clinical Faculty, Yale University School of Medicine, New Haven, CT:

The Infant Development Inventory (IDI), for ages 1–18 months, is a revision of the Minnesota Infant Development Inventory (MIDI; Ireton & Thwing, 1980), which, in turn, evolved from Ireton's prior work with the Minnesota Child Development Inventory (MCDI; Ireton & Thwing, 1974). The IDI is intended to offer "a convenient way of obtaining and summarizing the mother's observations of her baby's development" (Ireton, 1995). The author sees the IDI as a time-saving device: "The professional may save time assessing the infant's development by reviewing the mother's IDI report before examining the baby, and then confirming a few age-relevant items by observation or testing" (IDI instructions, p. 1).

Mothers are shown a Child Development Chart that lists five columns of behaviors (Social, Self-Help, Gross Motor, Fine Motor, Language), which are sequenced developmentally from birth to 21 months. The Chart is constructed as a grid such that each column is composed of 17 boxes, the first 15 depicting one-month intervals (i.e., Birth–1 mo., 1–2 mos., and so forth, to 1–15 mos.), and the last two boxes denoting 3-month intervals (15–18 mos. and 18–21 mos.). Age-appropriate behaviors are printed in the pertinent box within each column. Mothers are supposed to check off the "behaviors that describe the things that your baby is doing regularly or pretty well" and to "mark with a B those things that your baby is only just beginning to do or only does sometimes." Mothers are to go down each column until they come to three "NOs" in a row; then they go on to the next column. There are a total of 89 behaviors listed, ranging from 13 in the Self-Help column to 22 in the Language column. Most boxes include a single behavior, although some boxes are empty (four in Self-Help) and several list two behaviors (six in Language and three in Gross Motor). In addition to filling out the Chart, mothers are asked to write, within two small boxes, a description of their baby and a response to "How are you doing as a parent?"

To use and interpret the IDI Chart, test users are provided with an 8.5 x 11-inch pink card. The front of the card tells about the uses of the IDI and instructs professionals, in three brief paragraphs, to integrate the parent's report with their professional observations and knowledge. The back of the card instructs test users how to graph the results of the mother's responses to the Chart, and provides a table for determining which age levels of behavior correspond to Delayed development (30% below the infant's chronological age) or Advanced development (30% above the infant's chronological age). When computing the infant's age, the days of prematurity are subtracted before the age is rounded down to the nearest half-month (below age 12 months) or month (age 12 months and above). Half-months can be gleaned from the Chart because each box is subdivided; some behaviors are printed in the top half of the box and others are printed in the bottom half. Advanced and Delayed development are determined for each of the five areas separately. When evaluating the infant's developmental level, test users are told to consider only the checked behaviors; those behaviors marked with a "B" are treated as secondary information.

The lack of a manual makes it difficult to evaluate the IDI. The author provided only the pink card, the copy of the Chart, a one-page Appendix that devoted the left column to the IDI, and an article that related the Bayley Scales of Infant Development (Bayley, 1969) Mental Scale to the earlier version of the IDI, the 1980 MIDI (Creighton & Sauve, 1988). The Appendix indicates that the IDI items were drawn from prior research with the MCDI and that "Developmental age norms have been established for these items." There is no mention of how these age norms were established or whether any attempt was made to obtain standardization data or otherwise update what are most likely outdated norms. No reliability or validity data are reported for the IDI.

The Creighton and Sauve (1988) investigation suggests that the MIDI shows promise as a predictor of Bayley Mental age performance for 86 high risk 7–10-month-olds (mean = 8 months). However, the Bayley's 30-year-old norms are long outdated—the most well-respected test of infant development has been replaced by a second edition (Bayley, 1993)—and the MIDI has been supplanted by the IDI. Ireton does not indicate how closely the IDI resembles its predecessor, whether items were moved from one age level to another based on new data, or what steps were undertaken to modify the MIDI. The fact that the IDI Chart lists some age levels with two items and others with none indicates that the IDI represents at least a slight modification of the MIDI. In her review of the MIDI in the *Ninth Mental Measurements Yearbook* (*MMY*), Camp (1985) noted, "There is one item for each month of age in each of five areas" (p. 995). Also, the "stop" rule was changed from 5 to 3 "NOs," and the directions to the mother are more precise in the IDI than for its predecessor; for the MIDI, mothers were asked "to read each statement and decide if it describes 'what your baby is doing'" (Camp, 1985, p. 995). Furthermore, the age range of birth to 18 months differs for the IDI from the birth-to-15-months range indicated for the MIDI in the *9th MMY*.

However, the major criticisms made by Camp (1985) of the MIDI still apply to the IDI: (a) the standardization of the MCDI did not include infants below age 6 months, so the criterion for placement of items below that level is unclear; (b) no validity or reliability data were provided either for Ireton's instrument or for the MCDI within the age range of the MIDI; (c) it is not possible to know exactly how parents will interpret the wording of the behavioral statements; (d) there is no justification for the 30% criterion for determining Delayed or Advanced development; and (e) it is unclear how to interpret Delayed development in a single area of behavior—what it denotes and what to do about it.

The wording of the IDI items is a concern because some of the behavioral statements are vague. For example, a 2-month Gross Motor item on the IDI is "Holds head steady when held sitting." On the Bayley Scales of Infant Development—Second Edition (Bayley-II; Bayley, 1993), holding one's head steady for 3 seconds is achieved at the age of one month whereas holding one's head steady for 15 seconds is 2-month behavior. Another illustration of wording that might confuse mothers is the distinction between the Fine Motor items "Marks with pencil or crayon" (listed on the Chart between 14 and 15 months) and "Scribbles with pencil or crayon" (between 15 and 18 months).

Of greater concern is the placement of items on the IDI Chart by Ireton in view of the questionable data base for making such decisions. An appropriate criterion for evaluating the "correctness" of the IDI developmental ages is the Bayley-II, for which norms are both representative and recent. A comparison of similar items on the IDI and Bayley-II reveals some notable differences. For example, "Kicks a ball forward" is an IDI Gross Motor item listed as occurring at about 18 to 19 months; on the Bayley-II, the item, "Swings leg to kick ball" has a developmental age of 26 months. "Imitates sounds that you make" is an IDI Language item listed as occurring at about 9 months; on the Bayley-II, "Imitates vocalization" has a developmental age of only 5 months. "Transfers objects from one hand to the other" is an IDI Fine Motor item listed as occurring at about 6 to 6.5 months; on the Bayley-II, the item, "Transfers object from hand to hand" is a 5-month item. Although a number of IDI items are placed correctly, based on the Bayley-II criterion, the discrepancies are numerous and occasionally extreme. The validity of the developmental ages yielded by the IDI in each of the five areas is, therefore, open to challenge. Whereas the burden of validating a test ordinarily falls on the author, this burden was not dealt with in any way by Ireton.

SUMMARY. The IDI is intended to provide a measure of an infant's development, Advanced and Delayed, in five areas of behavior, as observed by the mother. It lacks data-based support for its placement of behaviors at specific developmental levels, reliability or stability of the infant's obtained age levels, and validity of the mother's classifications of her infant as Advanced, Delayed, or "normal." The wording of some behaviors is imprecise and the developmental levels assigned to some behaviors differ substantially from the empirically derived levels reported for the Bayley-II (Bayley, 1993). Professionals who are seeking an instrument for obtaining an infant's developmental level based on the mother's (or, more appropriately, the primary caregiver's) observations are not advised to use the IDI. A much better choice is the Kent Infant Development (KID) Scale (3rd ed.) (Reuter & Wozniak, 1996; 192) for ages 1–15 months. The KID Scale is administered to the infant's primary caregiver. It includes a much wider array of behaviors than the IDI, and these behaviors were selected as a result of considerable test research and development efforts. Psychometric properties were addressed by the KID Scale authors, and its applications cross-culturally have been documented by empirical research.

REVIEWERS' REFERENCES

Bayley, N. (1969). *Bayley Scales of Infant Development manual.* San Antonio, TX: The Psychological Corporation.

Ireton, H., & Thwing, E. (1974). *Minnesota Child Development Inventory.* Minneapolis, MN: Behavior Science Systems.

Ireton, H., & Thwing, E. (1980). *Minnesota Infant Development Inventory.* Minneapolis, MN: Behavior Science Systems.

Camp, B. W. (1985) [Review of Minnesota Infant Development Inventory.] In J. V. Mitchell, Jr. (Ed.), *The ninth mental measurements yearbook* (pp. 995–996). Lincoln, NE: Buros Institute of Mental Measurements.

Creighton, D. E., & Sauve, R. S. (1988). The Minnesota Infant Development Inventory in the developmental screening of high-risk infants at eight months. *Canadian Journal of Behavioral Science, 20,* 424–433.

Bayley, N. (1993). *Bayley Scales of infant Development: Manual (2nd ed.).* San Antonio, TX: The Psychological Corporation.

Reuter, J. M., & Wozniak, J. R. (1996). *Kent Infant Development (KID) Scale (3rd ed.): User's guide & technical manual.* Kent, OH: Kent Developmental Metrics.

Review of the Infant Development Inventory by JOHN J. VACCA, Certified School Psychologist, Assistant Professor of Special Education, Advisor, Graduate Program in Early Intervention, Loyola College, Baltimore, MD:

TEST COVERAGE AND USE. The purpose of the Infant Development Inventory (IDI; adapted version of the Minnesota Infant Development Inventory, 1980) is to provide a means for professionals and mothers to screen the developmental status of infants in the first 18 months of life. Though a manual for the scale is not provided, a page of instructions for administration and interpretation is included for the professional, and a limited set of instructions is included for the mother. The format of the IDI is intended to assist mothers in summarizing their own observations of their infants' development. The author makes reference to the infant's mother only without indicating that another caregiver could complete the scale. In light of the changing makeup of today's family, the fact that the author only makes reference to the "mother" is a drawback of the scale. The child would be better assessed if the IDI could be completed by any caregiver directly familiar with the child, including the parents (if available) to allow multiple perspectives on the child's functioning capabilities. In combination, multiple perspectives are not only a legal requirement for early childhood assessment, but also help to provide a link between the results gained from formal and informal evaluation techniques.

Eighty-nine pass/fail items on the IDI are categorized according to the areas of Social, Self-Help, Gross Motor, Fine Motor, and Language. Additionally, a limited amount of space is provided for the mother to address the following open-ended questions: "Please describe your baby; What questions or concerns do you have about your baby's health: Development? Behavior? Other?; How are you doing as a parent?" Through review of these observations and answers to such questions, professionals are presumed to be able to determine whether the infant is developing in a normal pattern or has delays. Further, the author states that "the professional may save time assessing the infant's development by reviewing the mother's IDI report before examining the baby, and then confirming a few age-relevant items by observation or testing" (instructions, p. 1). Although the inclusion of parent/caregiver report is crucial in the appropriate evaluation of an infant or young child, this information should not be used to gauge time needed for an evaluation or to determine the amount of items from a normative measure to be administered to the child. Instead, the professional should comply with principles of best practice for assessment by employing a complete battery of evaluative measures with the child, and by using the data from observations to assist in the interpretation of the normative data. For instance, many infants may not respond to items the way the test author expected them to respond for a variety of reasons, including novelty of the testing situation (room, materials, clinician), motivation, sleep/awake cycles, illness, or fatigue. In these situations, observations about the child received from someone who sees the child on a daily basis may assist the professional to determine the representativeness of the child's responses on the items on the normative measure.

TEST ADMINISTRATION. With respect to procedures for test administration, the author does not provide suggestions for the professional regarding how and when to introduce the IDI to the infant's mother. Based on a review of the IDI material, it appears that the mother is given the IDI to complete first. This assumes that she is able to read and comprehend the statements. The author mentions that the IDI can be used as a guide in a parent interview when it is suspected that the mother is unable to complete the scale independently. Although this can be beneficial to the mother, such use of different forms of administration of the IDI can greatly affect the reliability of the results. For example, when the IDI is used in the context of a parent interview, verbal exchange occurs between the professional and the mother. This may facilitate a higher level of clarification regarding test items than that of a mother who completes the IDI independently and may make her own judgments on an item's meaning. Therefore, it would be critical for a professional using the IDI to always verify with the mother who completes the scale independently that she completely understands both the content of the items and the criteria for responding to the items.

According to the brief set of instructions provided for the mother, the first thing she is required to do is to answer the series of open-ended questions about her baby. Second, she is instructed to proceed to the back of the sheet and review the items that "tell us what [her] child is doing in each area of development." The mother places a check beside those things her baby is "doing regularly or pretty well," and a "B for those things that [the baby] is only just beginning to do or only does sometimes."

In terms of scoring, the directions for the professional are brief. They enable the professional to determine whether the child is considered by the mother to be functioning in a normal manner or to have delays. A score that falls 30% below the child's chronological age is used as the benchmark for determining developmental delay.

APPROPRIATE SAMPLES FOR TEST VALIDATION AND NORMING. No information relating to test validation and norming issues is included on the IDI instruction sheet. The instruction sheet simply indicates that the scale addresses development from birth to 21 months. The author states that the items on the IDI were drawn from earlier research with the Minnesota Child Development Inventory (1980), and that the developmental age norms have been established. Documentation supporting these statements is not included in the current IDI material. Therefore, it is not clear whether or with what population the IDI was field tested. It is also unclear how the items on the IDI were developed and subsequently selected. All of this information should be provided to allow the professional to determine if the scale would be appropriate for use with a given child and family.

RELIABILITY. In terms of reliability, the author did not include information on the revised IDI forms. An area that needs to be discussed in particular is internal consistency. Due to the fact that no information was available to address item selection, the degree to which the items are consistent with one another cannot be determined.

PREDICTIVE VALIDITY. In a study completed by Creighton and Sauve (1988), the Minnesota Infant Development Inventory (MIDI) was compared with the Bayley Scales of Infant Development (BSID) in the screening of capabilities of high-risk infants, 8 months of age ($n = 86$). Based on correlation results, the authors reported that the scores from the MIDI and BSID were significantly consistent ($p<.001$). Creighton and Sauve prefaced their discussion of results, however, by identifying that "the study sample was an abnormal sample ... and hence showed a higher frequency of developmental problems on the BSID than one would anticipate in an unselected population of infants" (p. 430). Therefore, because the children in the sample had a significant postnatal history for developmental problems, the similarities in the responses received for both the MIDI and BSID need to be treated cautiously. In looking at the results, the correlations for both raw scores and index scores ranged from .46 to .58. Although these reflect a moderate degree of relationship (although statistically significant), the authors indicated that the data "[did] not indicate whether the MIDI has predictive utility for later infancy and childhood development" (p. 431).

SUMMARY. A major strength of the IDI is that it was designed with the intent of capturing the opinions of mothers concerning their babies in a formal manner. Too often, the input of caregivers is heard but not formally appreciated in a given evaluation. The IDI provides a vehicle for parent input to be considered in tandem with other normative measures. It is this type of input that is vital to the appropriate assessment of an infant or young child. In some cases, parent input helps in the translation of scaled scores. Even though the intent of the IDI is to incorporate parent report into the eligibility equation, professionals are cautioned to ascertain fully whether the mother understands the items and completion requirements of the IDI. Parent report is often the vehicle by which children are referred for screening. It should not be, however, the only vehicle by which children are identified for services. If the concepts of sensitivity and specificity are to be upheld, parent report should be augmented by norm-referenced screening tools such as the Developmental Indicators for the Assessment of Learning—Revised (DIAL-R; 116), AGS Early Screening Profiles (T5:124), Screening Profile for the Battelle Developmental Inventory (T5:266), or the Early Screening Inventory (135). Throughout this review, issues regarding the utility of the IDI have been identified. Due to the fact that issues of sampling, item selection, validity, and reliability with the IDI have not been reconciled, professionals are urged to treat results from administration cautiously.

REVIEWER'S REFERENCE

Creighton, D. E., & Sauve, R. S. (1988). The Minnesota Infant Development Inventory in the developmental screening of high-risk infants at eight months. *Canadian Journal of Behavioral Science, 20,* 424–433.

[177]
Infant Developmental Screening Scale.

Purpose: Designed as a clinical instrument to be used to assess the current developmental status of the newborn.

Population: Newborns.

Publication Date: 1995.

Acronym: IDSS.

Scores, 24: Habituation, Attention/Interaction (Visual Orientation, Auditory Orientation, Alertness, Irritability), Motor Responses (General Tone, Movements, Activity Level, Symmetry), Physiological System (Respiratory/Circulation, Other Stress Signals), Abnormal Posture or Movements, Reflexes (Root, Suck, Hand Grasp, Toe Grasp, Babinski, Ankle Clonus, Positive Support, Walk, Placing, Crawl, Asymmetric Tonic Neck Reflex, Moro).

Administration: Individual.

Price Data: Not available.

Time: (10–20) minutes.

Author: W. June Proctor.

Publisher: The Psychological Corporation.

[Editor's Note: The publisher advised in March 1999 that this test is now out of print.]

Review of the Infant Developmental Screening Scale by JEFFREY A. ATLAS, Associate Clinical Professor (Psychiatry), Bronx Children's Psychiatric Center, Albert Einstein College of Medicine, Bronx, NY:

The Infant Development Screening Scale (IDSS) is described by the publisher as a "clinical instrument to be used to assess the current developmental status of the newborn" (manual, p. 1). In the 26-page manual, the IDSS is noted to be a "clinical tool in the experimental phase of construction" (p. 24), one for which the author invites feedback from users for further refinement of the scale. Although this invitation is a valuable one to the infant health community in the research and practical development of the field, it is important to consider the differences between a clinical instrument and an experimental scale carefully in determining the usefulness of the IDSS in particular applied settings.

The IDSS comprises scales for Habituation, Attention/Interaction, Motor Responses, Physiological Systems, Abnormal Movements, and Reflexes. The scales vary in construction from Reflex check-offs (e.g., Babinski absent or exaggerated) to observations combining physiological impressions and counts of stress signals, to multidimensional assessments combining stimulation of responses and general observation (Attention/Interaction). The ordinal scaling of these measures appears sensible, and their presumed treatment as equal-interval scales for purposes of later correlational analysis and predictive validity is not in serious contrast to psychometric principles. However, the variations in anchor points and summary stores (e.g., ranging from 1–3 for Habituation to 4 to 20 for Attention/Interaction and Motor Responses) is contrary to our expectations of more congruent scaling with such measures as the Brazelton Neonatal Assessment Scale (T4:321) from which the IDSS draws heavily. The Brazelton, in addition, contains some more refined individual measures, such as Defensive movements (to cloth on face), which this reviewer has found valuable in testing infants for viability of neurobehavioral integration. The more global assessments of the IDSS and its fledgling research status bring up the question of the need for an additional scale at this juncture.

One advantage of the IDSS is that, in part, due to its relative simplicity, extensive training is not required in contrast to the Brazelton. As such, it may find a current niche as a screening device in settings used to suggest the need for further evaluation or early intervention. It may also furnish a set of individual findings that may be psychoeducational for parents, sensitizing them to their baby's needs and possible problems. The manual presents some impressive follow-through studies showing significant predictive value of IDSS scores and infants' Bayley developmental quotient scores at 4-, 9-, and 15-month intervals. A number of qualifiers to these good results should be noted: the small (*n* = 106) and demographically restricted nature of the sample (the sample comprising a preponderance of inhabitants from Guam, and 1% ethnic Caucasions); interrater agreement estimates relying on global "percentage" of agreement versus proximity of agreement (e.g., such as used in alpha ratings); and a high number of false positives (50 of 81 children predicted by the IDSS to be at risk had normal Bayley scores).

In summary, the IDSS is to be recommended as a "work in progress" screening device for infants at risk (premature, exposed in-utero to toxic substances), which does not require an intense training regimen and which may provide useful information to parents in concert with pediatric health workers. Infant health professionals, researchers, and students desiring a more tested clinical instrument might do well to consider the revised Brazelton book as an established, and to this point preferred, alternative.

Review of the Infant Developmental Screening Scale by CYNTHIA A. ROHRBECK, Associate Professor of Psychology, The George Washington University, Washington, DC:

The Infant Developmental Screening Scale, or IDSS, was developed to provide an assessment of potential developmental delays in newborns from 38–42 weeks gestational age and to teach parents more about their babies' behavior. The IDSS manual also provides recommendations for using the IDSS to assess premature infants. IDSS items were developed from, and are similar to, items from other neonatal scales such as the Neonatal Behavioral Assessment Scale (Brazelton, 1984; T4:321).

In contrast to some of these other measures, the IDSS was designed to be administered and scored quickly and easily. According to the manual, it takes about 10–20 minutes to administer and 5–10 minutes to score. This aspect appears to be the only rationale for developing a new infant screener; other evidence for the IDSS' strengths compared to other infant screeners is not provided.

The IDSS includes 12 behavioral items (covering Habituation, Attention/Interaction, Motor Responses, Physiological System, and Abnormal Posture or Movements). Items are scored from "1" (the best score) to "5" (the least desirable) except for Habituation items, which are scored on a 1–3 scale. Summary scores for each behavioral area are recorded on a profile sheet, divided into "Normal," "Questionable," and "High Risk." Twelve reflex items are scored as "absent," "present/weak," "present/normal," or "exaggerated." A summary score is recorded on the profile sheet. The test comes with a bright toy and a rattle that are used as manipulatives.

It should be noted (and it is stated several times in the manual) that the IDSS should *not* be used as an isolated measure to predict future infant development or to make intervention decisions. In addition, results may vary depending on the infant's state when the test is administered. It is also suggested that the IDSS could be used as an intervention tool (e.g., demonstrating techniques of arousal and soothing to new parents) although there is no evidence of the measure's reliability or validity when used for that purpose.

In fact, there is limited reliability evidence for the IDSS in general. Interrater reliability estimates (ranging from .83 to .96) are based on percent agreement of only four examiners' scoring of eight infants. Internal consistency and test-retest reliability and norms are not available. Furthermore, it should be noted that this sample was from one hospital in Guam; further evidence of the measure's generalizability is needed.

The manual also provides only preliminary validity evidence for the IDSS. Content validity is suggested by basing the items on items from other neonatal scales. One sample of 106 at-risk (i.e., low birth weight, low Apgar score) infants at the University of Guam was used to provide preliminary evidence of construct validity. In this sample, the mean gestational age was 35, the sample was roughly equal boys and girls, and the predominant ethnic groups were Chamorro and Filipino. At follow-up visits, 4 months (n = 83), 9 months (n = 65), and 15 months (n = 60), the Bayley Scales were administered. At each follow-up, IDSS scores were significantly related to Bayley scores and predicted more of the variance in Bayley mental and psychomotor scores than other important variables such as birth weight, mother's education, or severity of neonatal complications (number of days hospitalized after birth). This study provides preliminary evidence for using the IDSS to identify infants eligible for intervention services.

SUMMARY. Future research is needed to provide additional evidence of test score validity. Studies need to sample from different populations to provide support for generalizability. As noted by the test developer, scores on newborn tests have not shown strong relationships with later development. Future research is needed to see whether or not the IDSS will predict future behavior better than other infant measures.

REVIEWER'S REFERENCE

Brazelton, T. B. (1984). Neonatal Behavioral Assessment Scale (2nd ed.). *Clinics in Developmental Medicine, No. 88.* Philadelphia: Lippincott.

[178]

Infant/Toddler Symptom Checklist.

Purpose: Designed as a screening instrument for infants and toddlers with regulatory and sensory-integrative disorders.

Population: 7–30 months.

Publication Date: 1995.

Scores, 9: Self-Regulation, Attention, Sleep, Eating or Feeding, Dressing/Bathing or Touch, Movement, Listening and Language, Looking and Sight, Attachment/Emotional Functioning.

Administration: Individual.

Levels, 6: 7–9 months, 10–12 months, 13–18 months, 19–24 months, 25–30 months, General Screening Version (when age specific administration is inconvenient).

Price Data, 1999: $54 per Infant/Toddler Symptom Checklist including manual (58 pages) in a vinyl storage portfolio; $32 per additional score sheets available in 6 sets of five sheets in 25-page pads.

Time: (10) minutes.

Comments: "Criterion-referenced"; checklist completed by parents or caregiver.

Authors: Georgia A. DeGangi, Susan Poisson, Ruth Z. Sickel, and Andrea Santman Wiener.

Publisher: Therapy Skill Builders—A Division of The Psychological Corporation.

Review of the Infant/Toddler Symptom Checklist by DEBORAH ERICKSON, Director of Clinical Psychology, University of Sydney, Sydney, Australia:

The Infant/Toddler Symptom Checklist was designed as a screening method for parents and professionals to use in determining when 7–30-month-old infants and toddlers exhibit regulatory disorders that lead to behavioral difficulties. The authors indicate that the checklist could be used to identify problems such as sensory-integration disorders, attentional deficits, and emotional or behavioral problems, in conjunction with a comprehensive evaluation. Identification is conducted by assessing 18–31 descriptors (depending on the age range) sporadically distributed in the domains of self-regulation; attention; sleep; eating or feeding; dressing, bathing, and touch; movement; listening and language; looking and sight; and attachment and emotional functioning. Although the intent is commendable, the test development process does not support the lofty aspirations.

There are five age range assessment checklists (7–9 months, 10–12 months, 13–18 months, 19–24 months, and 25–30 months) with a variety of descriptors at each age range that are not necessarily consistent with the other checklists. Scoring is in three categories: *never or sometimes, most times,* or *in the past.* The authors argue that the choice of descriptors was based upon an item analysis and that only specific questions that indicated the potential for self-regulatory problems at

each age level were used for that particular checklist.

For example, in the 7–9-month checklist, eight of the nine domains were assessed through 22 descriptors. In the Listening, Language, and Sound domain section, one descriptor, "Is distracted by sounds not normally noticed by average person" (p. 1) was used. In the 10–12-month checklist, eight of the nine domains were assessed through 18 descriptors and the Listening, Language, and Sound section was assessed by the same descriptor as already mentioned. In the 13- to 18-month checklist, 31 descriptors were used to assess eight of the nine domains with Listening, Language, and Sound being assessed this time by "Startles or is distressed by loud sounds such as vacuum, doorbell, or barking dog" (p. 2). In the 19–24-month checklist, nine of nine domains were assessed through 23 descriptors with Listening, Language, and Sound now assessed by a descriptor that was similar to, but not exactly worded as, the descriptor seen in the 7–9-month and 13–18-month checklists. The descriptor "Is distracted by sounds the average person doesn't notice" (p. 1) was included with two additional descriptors in this domain: "Doesn't respond to verbal cues (hearing not a problem)" and "Repeats or echoes previously heard words, phrases or sentences." In the 25- to 30-month checklist, this reviewer counted 17 descriptors in the formal checklist, although the number is counted as 18 in the interpretation section of the manual. There is no Listening, Language, and Sound section and only seven of nine domains are assessed at this age level.

To reiterate, each age checklist has a variety of a different number of descriptors assessing some of the domains and not necessarily all of the domains. In addition, the wording of similar descriptors is not exact. This apparent inconsistency raises questions of how the item analysis was used to discriminate which descriptors should be assessing which domains. No clear explanation, other than the sketchy section on item analysis, is given as to how and why certain descriptors were used for certain ages and why certain domains were assessed and others were not at different age levels.

To add to this difficulty in test construction, the standardization sample was only based upon 154 normal infants and 67 infants with regulatory disorders and only items with medium to large discrimination indexes differentiating between these normal and regulatory-disordered infants were used and reported at each age level. There is no clear discussion on why a descriptor such as "hates face and hair washed" was significant and used as a checklist descriptor for assessing dressing, bathing, and touch at age 7–9 months, NOT used at 10–12 months, used again at 13–18 months, NOT used at 19–24 months, and used again at 25–30 months. If there was some chronological consistency, then an argument could be made about different developmental milestones being assessed in these checklists. However, no such argument is purported and this looks to the reviewer much like random error due to a small sample size.

The administration and scoring section of the manual is clear and the scoring is easy. The interpretation section raises many questions in terms of how the cutoff scores for the different age ranges were actually determined. Reference was made to the validity section for further explanation. However, the validity section did not meet the criteria for descriptions of evidencing validity in test manuals recommended in the *Standards for Educational and Psychological Testing* (AERA, APA, & NCME, 1985) guidelines. The process described to validate scores from the test is not extensive nor convincing. For example, the section to evidence concurrent validity used the lack of correlations to other tests as evidence that the checklist assessed different functions from those of other early childhood measures. Even though this may be true, and would be a positive addition to the market of infant and toddler assessment tools, much more independent validation, with broader samples through numerous studies is necessary before drawing conclusions about what this assessment tool does or does not assess. There was no section in the manual to examine the reliability of scores from this assessment.

SUMMARY. In conclusion, the psychometric properties of the Infant/Toddler Symptom Checklist make it suspect in terms of what it actually assesses. The introduction section of the manual explaining the need for such an assessment and the original intent of the test development process is clear and well conceived. With further research, these checklists could be refined and validated more thoroughly. Enhancing the psychometric properties of these checklists would make this assessment process a viable option in screening for regulatory disorders that contribute

to future behavioral and emotional problems. There is no doubt that early diagnosis and intervention would be a proactive method to reduce the risk of these children developing dysfunctional behavior patterns later in life. However, until further work and research studies are completed on this checklist system, this reviewer does not recommend it for use as a screening tool for parents and professionals.

REVIEWER'S REFERENCE

American Educational Research Association, American Psychological Association, & National Council on Measurement in Education. (1985). *Standards for educational psychological testing.* Washington, DC: American Psychological Association, Inc.

Review of the Infant/Toddler Symptom Checklist by RUTH E. TOMES, Associate Professor, Early Childhood Education, Northeastern State University—Tulsa, Tulsa, OK:

The Infant/Toddler Symptom Checklist (I/TSC) measures behaviors exhibited by 7- to 30-month-old children said to be symptomatic of early regulatory disorders and associated with later learning and sensory-integrative disorders. The I/TSC was designed to serve two clinical functions. As a screening tool, the checklist helps identify those infants who should be referred for further diagnostic testing. It may also be used as a diagnostic tool in conjunction with traditional developmental tests and other clinical measures.

The construct of regulatory disorders is relatively new in the field of infant mental health (Mercer, 1998). Described by Greenspan (1993) and operationally defined in *Diagnostic Classification Task Force, Zero to Three* (1994), regulatory disorders are characterized by "difficulties in regulating behavior and physiological, sensory, attentional, motor or affective processes, and in organizing a calm, alert or affectively positive state" (manual, p. 31). The authors of the I/TSC devote 10 pages of the manual to discussion of the theoretical background of the disorder and related domains. Based on this theory, they developed nine domain specifications: (a) Self-Regulation, (b) Attention, (c) Sleep, (d) Feeding, (e) Dressing, Bathing, and Touch, (f) Movement, (g) Listening, Language, and Sound, (h) Looking and Sight, and (i) Attachment/Emotional Functioning. Test items were systematically generated from the domain specifications.

There are five age-related versions and one general screening version of the checklist. As a result of validity studies (discussed below), the total number of items and items within each domain varies among these versions. The 7–9-month checklist has 22 items; 10–12-month, 18 items; 13–18 month, 31 items, 19–24-month, 23 items; 25–30-month, 18 items; and the general version 21 items.

The I/TSC is designed to obtain parents' report of their infant's behaviors. The instrument is easy to administer and takes about 10 minutes to complete. The manual contains a reproducible cover sheet that describes the purpose of the checklist to the parent, gives instructions on how to rate the infant's behaviors, and asks for some background information. The two-page checklist is then completed either by the parent or via clinician interview in cases of illiteracy or cultural differences. Most items are rated as "never or sometimes" (0 points), "most times" (2 points), or "past," indicating the behavior was a problem in the past (1 point). An exception is one item regarding time spent calming the child. For this item, 0 points are assigned to 15–30 minutes, 1 point to 1–2 hours, and 2 points to 3 hours/plus per day. Points are tallied for the entire checklist. The total raw score is compared to a cutoff protocol for interpretation. Infants whose scores fall at or above the cutoff for their age group are considered at risk and further diagnosis is recommended. The scoring procedures are straightforward and should pose no difficulties for the examiner.

To be useful a measure must show evidence of score reliability. A serious flaw in the I/TSC is that no reliability data are provided. The test is marketed as a criterion-referenced measure, but it is better described as a criterion-related measure because it claims to discriminate between infants who are at risk for regulatory disorders and those who are not. Because the cutting score determines decisions that affect individual infants, classification errors may occur due to unreliability of the test measurement.

The authors do provide three kinds of data to give evidence of validity. A construct validity study demonstrated differences between two groups of infants (normal and regulatory-disordered) at each age range by item and for the total checklist. Based on these analyses, 14 of the original 57 items were eliminated. Items retained in each age version were those with medium to large discrimination indices. These data are clearly presented along with procedures used to locate optimal cutoff scores. A second study examined the utility of

the checklist for screening infants in pediatric practice. The false-delayed error rate (3% to 13%) and the false-normal rate (0% to 14%) were consistent with the construct validation study and are within acceptable ranges. Intercorrelations among the I/TSC, the Bayley Scales of Infant Development, Mental Scales, and other clinical measures were examined for evidence of concurrent validity. The manual states that the correlations were low and none were significant for the regulatory disordered sample. No numerical data are provided, however, relevant to the claim that the I/TSC provides information distinct from the other measures.

The samples of infants upon which the cutoff scores and validity studies are based were all drawn from the Washington, DC area and all but 6% were white and middle-class. The test authors recognize that these samples are not representative of the general population. The total norming sample consisted of 154 normal and 67 regulatory-disordered infants. When divided into the five age-range categories, some of the samples were too small (as few as eight in the 10–12-month disordered group) to provide effective item analysis.

SUMMARY. The Infant/Toddler Symptom Checklist is a commendable attempt to meet the need for a tool for screening regulatory-disordered infants. Given that the constructs assessed by the checklist have not been shown to be reliably assessed, data presented on validity are suspect. Further research needs to be done to document evidence of score reliability. Cross-validation studies with more samples of infants are needed before clinicians can use the checklist with confidence.

REVIEWER'S REFERENCES
Greenspan, S. I. (1993). Regulatory disorders. In C. H. Zeanah, Jr. (Ed.), *Handbook of infant mental health* (pp. 280–290). New York: Guilford Press.
Diagnostic Classification Task Force, Zero to Three. (1994). *Diagnostic classification: 0–3.* Arlington, VA: National Center for Clinical Infant Programs.
Mercer, J. (1998). *Infant development: A multidisciplinary introduction.* Pacific Grove, CA; Brooks/Cole.

[179]
INSIGHT Inventory [Revised].

Purpose: Designed to determine how an individual differs from other individuals in his or her style of influencing others, relating to others, responding to people, making decisions and taking action, and structuring time and handling details.

Population: Adults age 21 and over, students age 16–21.

Publication Dates: 1988–1993.

Scores: 4 traits: Getting Your Way (Direct, Indirect), Responding to People (Reserved, Outgoing), Pacing

Activity (Urgent, Steady), Dealing with Details (Unstructured, Precise).

Administration: Group.

Forms, 6: A (Adult Team-Building), B (Adult Communications), F (Adult Feedback/Others), I (Adult Job Interviewing), C (Student Communications), D (Student Feedback/Others).

Price Data, 1998: $6.50 per Forms B and I; $12 per Forms A and F; $3 per Forms C and D; $250 per Training Kit for adult version including video, training guide, technical manual, and transparency masters; $150 per Teaching Kit for student version including video, teaching guide, technical manual, and transparency masters; quantity discounts available for all materials.

Time: (15–20) minutes.

Comments: Users get two profiles, one reflecting how they see themselves in their work (school) environment and the other reflecting how they see themselves in their personal (at home) environment; "has field theory base which takes into account that participants may change their behavior from one environment (field) to another"; utilizes self-perception; supporting feedback sets provide perceptions of how five others see the user; 1993 revision based on a second collection of norms and a factor analysis of the items.

Author: Patrick Handley.

Publisher: Insight Institute, Inc.

Cross References: For a review by Susana Urbina, see 13:149.

Review of the INSIGHT Inventory [Revised] by SANFORD J. COHN, Professor, Division of Curriculum and Instruction, Arizona State University, Tempe, AZ:

One would do well to consider the INSIGHT Inventory, the instrument, in its context as the centerpiece in a well-developed curriculum for helping examinees interpret their results and engage in activities to enhance their understanding about how they relate to other people in different contexts. A primary purpose of the measure, then, is to provide a shared experience of self-reflections upon which a subsequent structured interaction (or interview) can be based.

The publishers provide two versions of the measure and its training kit: an adult version designed to facilitate understanding about oneself and how one operates both in a personal context and in a work context, and how the context influences or in part determines our behavior and our internal assessment of ourselves; and a version for late adolescents and young adults (ages 16–21) designed to be applied to personal and school (as opposed to work) contexts. A single 68-page

manual, copyright 1989, is included with each version. Each kit includes the test, the manual, score interpretation booklets, and detailed training books (including a video) to facilitate implementation of the respective attendant curriculum (adult or youth).

An additional component, the Style Feedback Set (SFS), offers the extra dimension of *how others see you* to the examinee. The SFS offers five other individuals the opportunity to use the same list of adjectives in an attempt to describe the examinee and provide feedback to him or her.

DEVELOPMENT. This self-report personality inventory consists of two identical lists of 32 adjectives (ordered differently) yielding two style profiles: one describing the examinee at work or at school and the other at home in his or her personal world. The normative groups for both versions of the inventory are described as normal adults and youths, inasmuch as the measure is designed for use with normal populations.

The manual provides brief overviews of the theoretical foundations underlying the conception and the empirical tools employed in the creation of the INSIGHT Inventory. The theoretical traditions include Field Theory, Trait Theory, and Factor Analysis. The use of adjectives as test items is also supported.

The 32 adjectives comprising the instrument were winnowed from a list that incorporated Allport and Odbert's (1936) original descriptive list of adjectives with adjectives more common to today's society and frequently used by both professional and lay people to describe differences between people. Factor analysis, using a sample of 1,540 adults, yielded eight scales that accounted for four theoretical factors. This same factor structure was supported in subsequent analyses based on new samples of 589 adults and 1,021 students in high school and college. Scales for the four theoretical factors were developed based on the factor loadings, with eight separate items loading on each of the four scales. The four theoretical factor scales are named: Getting Your Way, Responding to People, Pacing Activity, and Dealing with Details.

RELIABILITY.

Internal Consistency. The internal consistency of each of the four scales comprising the INSIGHT Inventory [Revised] (II-R) was determined through the computation of a coefficient alpha, which ranged from .71 to .85 with a mean of .77. These values are considered quite acceptable for personality measures.

Test-Retest. Test-retest reliability was based initially on a sample of 90 college students, with 6 weeks between administrations. The coefficients range from .54 to .82 with a mean of .73. A second study of test-retest reliability was conducted in the spring of 1998 (and added as a 1998 update to the manual). A sample of 38 graduate students enrolled in an introductory course on career development at the University of Kansas took the test twice with administrations 2 weeks apart. Test-retest reliability coefficients for this later study range from .64 to .91 with a mean of .77 for the four Work Style Scales and from .76 to .90 with a mean of .82 for the Personal Style Scales.

The II-R does not have alternate forms, so Alternate-Form reliability was not addressed.

VALIDITY. Empirical validation of the II-R has consisted of the comparison of its four scales with appropriately convergent or divergent scales from three other measures of similar personality characteristics: Myers-Briggs Type Indicator (MBTI), Sixteen Personality Factors (16PF), and Self-Directed Search (SDS). Detailed explanations for the patterns of Pearson correlation coefficient tables with respective convergent and divergent II-R scales are provided in the manual. The author argues that consistent support is shown for the constructs measured by the II-R.

Even though no claim is made that these few studies establish construct validity for the II-R, the overall impression one gets of the state of validity study reported in the manual is that it is very thin. The authors list nine excellent strategies for further studies of reliability and validity for the II-R. It is this reviewer's wish that some of these studies had been completed and added to the manual update for the current revised version of the test. It has been over a decade since the measure was created. Surely, this time span would allow for some of the follow-up studies to have been done and their progress reported.

SUMMARY. In its role as a stimulator of self-reflection in the context of training adults or students to understand themselves and others better in their personal and professional settings, the II-R makes sense. It yields a profile report that can serve as a springboard for a structured interview, counseling session, or class.

The technical manual is replete with descriptions of the theoretical justifications underlying the creation and application of the II-R. The empirical data supporting its reliability and validity are encouraging, but quite thin, especially with regard to validity. This reviewer encourages the author to continue full speed ahead with further studies designed to examine the validity of the II-R and its attendant training curriculum.

REVIEWER'S REFERENCE

Allport, G. W., & Odbert, H. S. (1936). *Trait-names: A psycholexical study.* Princeton, NJ: Psychological Review Company.

Review of the INSIGHT Inventory [Revised] by ELIZABETH L. JONES, Associate Professor of Psychology, Western Kentucky University, Bowling Green, KY:

The INSIGHT Inventory is a self-report inventory that assesses styles of interaction with others and styles for accomplishing tasks in order to enhance self-knowledge and understanding. The inventory is a part of a complete training package designed for improving self-knowledge in order to enhance communication, interpersonal, leadership, and team building skills. The inventory is designed for use with students (16–21 years) and adults with separate forms and ancillary materials provided for the student and adult levels. This inventory yields ratings in four main areas including two styles of interpersonal interaction (Getting Your Way and Responding to People) and two preferred styles of accomplishing tasks (Pacing Activity and Dealing with Details). Individuals respond on a carbonless form to adjectives on a 4-point scale in both "Work/School" context and a "Home" context. Profiles are then plotted for the four traits in the two contexts of work or school and home. The training program includes a video, overhead transparency masters, teaching guide, skill-building exercises, and a technical manual. The student program is cited as helpful for improving communication skills and relationships with others along with building self-esteem, valuing diversity, and developing leadership. The adult form is described as beneficial for communication, leadership, and career development.

As a comprehensive review of the development and technical properties of the INSIGHT Inventory is available (Urbina, 1998), the present review will provide only a brief review of this information and focus more on the application aspects of the training program not emphasized in the previous review. As an educational/training instrument, the INSIGHT Inventory is not held to as high a technical standard as required for diagnostic instruments. As an educational tool, the inventory evidences marginal to adequate reliability. Coefficient alpha reliability coefficients ranged from .71 to .85 with test-retest stability over 6 weeks from .54 to .82 across the four scales and the work/school and home contexts. Additional test-retest information was provided in a 1998 technical manual update indicating 2-week test-retest reliabilities of .64 to .91 for the work context and .76 to .90 for the home/personal context (n = 38). Evidence of construct validity was obtained through factor analysis during test development. Convergent and discriminant validity for the four trait scales were demonstrated through comparison with other well-known self-report inventories (Myers-Briggs Type Indicator, Sixteen Personality Factor Questionnaire, and Self-Directed Search). Validity data support the four scales of the inventory reasonably but not definitively. There is some overlap between the four INSIGHT Inventory scales and they do not always correspond strongly with the expected scales on the criterion measures.

Although the INSIGHT Inventory evidences reasonable technical properties to substantiate that the inventory measures the traits it purports to measure with reasonable reliability, it does not report any evidence to support the inventory's intended use with the training materials. The training package is based on the premise that knowledge of personal styles or traits revealed from use of the self-report inventory and subsequent training will benefit a person's knowledge and understanding of themselves and others. Knowledge gained from use of the INSIGHT Inventory for adults and the ancillary training materials is purported to benefit individuals in the general areas of communication, leadership, and career development. The student version is described as beneficial for improving communication skills and relationships with others; other applications include building self-esteem, valuing diversity, and developing leadership. It is a major shortcoming that there is no evidence that the self-report measure along with the training package does change or benefit individuals in the ways described. Without this evidence, consumers should be warned that although the package has some face validity, there is no evidence of the validity of the training package.

The ancillary materials in the training package include training/teaching guides, overhead transparency masters, skills-building exercises, and a training video for both the adult and student version. The training guides are well developed and cross reference the video, overheads, and skill-building exercises and provide suggestions for discussion activities. The overhead transparency masters for the most part are well developed; however, a few are too cluttered and the print is too small to be highly effective. The Skill Building Exercises booklet for participants provides a range of exercises to apply knowledge of the INSIGHT Inventory results. Exercises range from predicting behavior based on profiles to describing profiles based on examples of behavior and applying the understanding of the profiles to their own examples. The videos are designed to be used with the inventory and the training worksheets and provide step-by-step illustrations of how to mark responses, score, pilot profiles, and interpret results. Brief vignettes are also included to illustrate each of the four traits in both interpersonal and work/school contexts. Uses of the profiles are provided in the areas of responding to stress, "flexing" or adapting your style to communicate more effectively, team building (adult only), and conflict resolution (adult only). The videos are of good production quality and evidence good consistency with the printed training materials. The student materials are appropriate for the age range stipulated (16–21 years). The materials are not appropriate for use with students with mental retardation or other significant cognitive impairments. It appears that at least a 10th grade reading level is necessary for use of these materials; however, the reading level of the materials was not reported. Reading level should also be considered when using this with adult populations.

SUMMARY. As indicated previously, the use of this self-report inventory for the proposed uses (building self-esteem, building communication, and leadership skills, for example) has not been empirically supported. However, the INSIGHT Inventory in isolation evidences reasonable reliability and construct validity. The INSIGHT Inventory appears to be a reasonable measure of the traits for the purpose of self-descriptions and self-knowledge. It is not a measure that is designed for, or that has the technical adequacy of, a diagnostic measure. When the inventory is considered within the context of a training package or system, there is no evidence to validate the use of the training package. The system cannot be used with confidence until such evidence becomes available.

REVIEWER'S REFERENCE

Urbina, S. (1998). [Review of the INSIGHT Inventory.] In J. C. Impara & B. S. Plake (Eds.), *The thirteenth mental measurements yearbook* (pp. 509–510). Lincoln, NE: The Buros Institute of Mental Measurements.

[180]
Integrated Visual and Auditory Continuous Performance Test.

Purpose: Designed to assess visual and auditory response control, attention, and hyperactivity, providing data to help the clinician diagnose and differentiate between the four subtypes of Attention-Deficit/Hyperactivity Disorder outlined in the DSM-IV.

Population: Age 5 to adult.

Publication Dates: 1993–1999.

Acronym: IVA.

Scores, 28: Attention Quotient Auditory, Attention Quotient Full-Scale, Attention Quotient Visual, Balance, Comprehension Auditory, Comprehension Visual, Consistency Auditory, Consistency Visual, Fine Motor Regulation, Focus Auditory, Focus Visual, Persistence Auditory, Persistence Visual, Readiness Auditory, Readiness Visual, Response Control Quotient Auditory, Response Control Quotient Full-Scale, Response Control Quotient Visual, Sensory/Motor Auditory, Sensory/Motor Visual, Speed Auditory, Speed Visual, Stamina Auditory, Stamina Visual, Vigilance Auditory, Vigilance Visual.

Administration: Individual.

Price Data, 1999: Three options: Option 1: $295 per Starter Kit including software, Administration & Interpretation manual ('99, 116 pages), and 10 tests (licensed for use at 1 computer; 3.5-inch IBM disks); $99 per 10 additional tests; $249 per 30 additional tests; or Option 2: $598 per Registration Kit including software, Administration & Interpretation manual, and 10 tests (licensed for use at 1 computer; 3.5-inch IBM disks); $89 per 25 additional tests; or Option 3: $1,495 per unlimited use version including software, Administration & Interpretation manual, and unlimited tests (licensed for use at 1 computer; 3.5-inch IBM disks); $495 per unlimited use version for schools.

Time: 13 minutes.

Comments: Computer administered; requires MS/DOS or Windows compatible computer.

Authors: Joseph A. Sandford and Ann Turner.

Publisher: BrainTrain.

Review of the Integrated Visual and Auditory Continuous Performance Test by HARRISON KANE, Assistant Professor, Department of Special Education, University of Nevada—Las Vegas, Las Vegas, NV, and SUSAN C. WHISTON, Professor, Department of Educational Psychology, University of Nevada—Las Vegas, Las Vegas, NV:

The Integrated Visual and Auditory Continuous Performance Test (IVA) is a standardized, individually administered instrument that assesses inattention and impulsivity in a counterbalanced design across visual and auditory modalities. The IVA is expressly designed to measure response control and attention in reference to Attention Deficit Hyperactivity Disorder (ADHD). Other exceptionalities are addressed only in light of diagnosing and considering ADHD, either in terms of differential diagnosis or comorbidity. Specifically, the IVA is intended to help the clinician diagnose and differentiate between subtypes of ADHD (i.e., Predominant Inattentive Type and Predominantly Hyperactive-Impulsive Type).

Computer administered, the IVA requires the examinee to click a mouse button when he or she hears or sees the number "1" (target stimulus) and to refrain from responding when the number "2" (distractor stimulus) is presented. The test measures momentary lapses in visual and auditory attention and records errors of commission (i.e., impulsivity) and omission (i.e., inattention). For each trial, reaction time is recorded in milliseconds. A total of 500 trials are presented each lasting about 1.5 seconds. A brief initial practice period ensures that the examinee understands the task and minimizes practice effects. Including "Warm Up" and "Cool Down" trials, the entire test lasts about 20 minutes and fulfills the authors' intent of being "mildly boring and demanding of sustained attention" (manual, p. 1). Installing and administering the IVA is straightforward. The program is IBM compatible and requires a DOS environment. The authors advise the use of headphones and an ergonomic mouse. As with other continuous performance tests (CPTs), response sets form the basis for scores. Therefore, any interruption during the main test period terminates the entire testing session.

Norms are offered for ages 5 to 90 years of age. Sandford and Turner (the test authors) present only a minimal description of the normative sample, stating that "normative data were collected from individuals not known to have past neurological disorders ... and not known to have learning and or attentional problems or demonstrating hyperactivity" (manual, p. 97). Hence, the norming sample was not randomly selected. Rather, it is a homogenous group, which the authors contend makes the IVA more sensitive to discrepant scores in cognitive processing. The normative group is composed of 781 individuals across 10 age levels, stratified by gender. Past research with CPTs substantiates developmental and gender differences in performance (e.g., Barkley, 1995); therefore, stratification by age and gender seems appropriate. Norms are adequate for ages 5 to 44 years, with an average of 89 individuals in each of the age levels. For the two oldest age groups, however, the sample is rather scant. The 45- to 54- and 55- to 90-year-old levels are composed of 34 and 33 individuals in each group, respectively. Therefore, clinical comparisons with the norming sample are tenuous for older examinees. No mention is made of the geographic, racial, or ethnic composition of the norm group. Dates of standardization are not reported. The last update to the normative group is assumed to be 1995, as noted in a validity study included in the examiner's manual. Also, the standardization is further compromised by a noticeable absence of clinical samples. With the ease and accessibility of the Internet, the authors may want to consider an "on-line" version of the IVA, which could facilitate expanding the normative sample.

Based on 500 trials, the IVA produces computer-generated reports. Results are reported in standard scores with a mean of 100 and standard deviation of 15, which is comparable to many standardized IQ and achievement tests. This feature introduces a welcomed degree of familiarity when interpreting the varied quotients. In total, the IVA generates six global scales and 22 raw scale scores that are conceptually grouped into response, attention, attribute, and validity scales. Scales operationalize components of various theories of ADHD, with particular reference to the work of Barkley (e.g., Barkley, 1993). Furthermore, quotients and scales are tied to diagnostic criteria from the DSM-IV. Each scale subsumes a number of subscales. For example, the Vigilance, Focus, and Speed subscales contribute to the Full Scale Attention Quotient. In addition, two rating scales may be used to complement the computer-generated results of the IVA. The examiner completes one behavior-rating scale during administration of the IVA, and a self-report rating scale can be completed by the examinee at the end of testing. The examiner's manual is thorough in offering interpretive guidelines for the various scales

and quotients, but offers no supportive evidence or documentation that the suggested guidelines have any clinical or ecological validity.

Reliability data reported in the manual are somewhat meager. The authors report a small study with 70 individuals, ages 5 to 70 years. The sample was composed of individuals without identified problems of attention. Test-retest correlations (administration interval = 1 to 4 weeks) for the composite quotients ranged from .37 to .75. Generally, these findings suggest a moderate degree of stability for the IVA quotients and scales. However, the small sample size precludes any meaningful insight into developmental trends with regard to the stability of the IVA constructs.

Obviously, the clinical importance of the IVA is its accuracy in the diagnosis of ADHD. The authors present a small discriminative validity study that examined the IVA's accuracy relative to diagnoses made by psychologists and physicians. Two groups were formed. A group of 26 children diagnosed with ADHD was matched to a comparison group of 31 children with no history of ADHD or neurological impairment. Using only data obtained from the IVA, researchers correctly classified 24 children (92%) in the ADHD group. Children in the non-ADHD group were identified with 90% accuracy. The concurrent validity of the IVA with other CPTs (e.g., Gordon and TOVA) and rating scales was high, insofar as all measures were able to identify a high proportion of children with ADHD. The IVA had the lowest rate of false negatives among the varied measures used in the study, less than 10%. In light of this small study, the IVA has adequate sensitivity (92% correctly identified as ADHD) and specificity (90% correctly identified as non-ADHD) to be considered a viable diagnostic measure. However, the authors do not provide some expected validation evidence of the IVA. Specifically, there is no validity study using the IVA to distinguish between non-ADHD subjects and subtypes of ADHD (i.e., Predominantly Inattentive Type and Predominantly Hyperactive-Impulsive Type).

SUMMARY. By providing measures of visual and auditory attention in a single administration, the IVA has a clear advantage over several CPTs. In addition, administration and scoring are computerized, removing the element of human error. By providing a number of scales and quotients, the IVA attempts to measure the multidi-

mensionality of attention. Results are easily interpretable. However, there are some noteworthy
limitations. The standardization sample is small in
comparison to other CPTs such as the TOVA.
Adults are not adequately represented in the standardization, and it is difficult to ascertain the
ethnic makeup of the normative sample. Reliability data are insufficient to assess accurately the
stability of the IVA constructs across the age levels
in the normative sample. Results from the reported validity studies are impressive, but indicate
only a good start. There is no single diagnostic test
of ADHD in children, and any comprehensive
assessment of ADHD should involve multiple
methods from different sources. Continuous performance tests are among the most frequently
used laboratory-based measures in the identification and assessment of attentional deficits (Barkley,
1991). As part of a comprehensive assessment of
ADHD, the IVA is most appropriately used when
it complements information gained from interviews, rating scales, and observations. We recommend that the IVA not be used in isolation,
especially in light of its noted limitations. Further
study is clearly needed to examine the reliability
and validity of the IVA.

REVIEWER'S REFERENCES

Barkley, R. A. (1991). The ecological validity of laboratory and analogue
assessment methods of ADHD symptoms. *Journal of Abnormal Child Psychology, 19,*
149–178.
Barkley, R. A. (1993). A new theory of ADHD. *The ADHD Report 1*(5), 1–4.
Barkley, R. A. (1995). Sex differences in ADHD. *The ADHD Report, 3*(1), 1–4.

*Review of the Integrated Visual and Auditory
Continuous Performance Test by MARTIN J. WIESE,
Licensed Psychologist/Certified School Psychologist,
Lincoln Public Schools, Lincoln, NE:*

The Integrated Visual and Auditory Continuous Performance Test (IVA) is a computer-
administered test of visual and auditory attention.
The IVA is designed to measure inattention, impulsivity, and hyperactivity and therefore assist the
clinician in diagnosing Attention Deficit Hyperactivity Disorder (ADHD). The test lasts approximately 13 minutes during which 500 trials or
items are presented to the subject either on the
computer's screen or through the computer's speakers. Each trial last 1.5 seconds. The subject is
required to respond (by clicking the computer's
"mouse button") when a "1" is presented either
visually or auditorily. Conversely, the subject is
asked to inhibit responding (by not clicking the
"mouse button") when a "2" is presented either

visually or auditorily. A warm-up period and short
practice test are presented before the main test to
help the clinician determine whether the subject
understands the task requirements. A cool-down
period is also presented after the main test. The
IVA is intentionally boring, requires sustained
attention, and demands the subject to shift cognitive sets (visual and auditory) while taking the test.

The IVA provides six global composite scores
and 22 other scale scores divided into four groups:
Response Control, Attention, Attribute, and Validity. A global composite score summarizes the
subject's overall performance in terms of Response
Control (Prudence, Consistency, and Stamina)
and Attention (Vigilance, Focus, and Speed). After administration of the IVA a three-page report is
available for review and printing. The report presents
the test results in tables and graphs with limited
interpretation. If the clinician completes an optional
rating scale, the report includes a short narrative of
the examiner's observations and the subject's subjective experiences on an additional page.

Although the manual provides adequate details on the installation, startup, and administration of the IVA, information about sampling procedures, norm group development, reliability, and
validity are minimal or completely absent. According to the manual, "normative data were collected from individuals not known to have past
neurological disorders, not on medication (except
birth control and nasal spray), not currently active in
psychotherapy or counseling, and not known to have
learning and/or attentional problems or demonstrate
hyperactivity" (p. VIII-1). Remarkably, much of the
information about the norm group is found in promotional material included with the test manual.
The normative database file is also contained in a
computer file that can be accessed by the examiner
but it also contains very limited information.

The IVA was normed on 781 individuals
divided by gender and broken down into the
following age groups: ages 5–6 ($n = 61$), 7–8 ($n = 143$), 9–10 ($n = 116$) 14–17 ($n = 72$), 18–24 ($n = 64$), 25–34 ($n = 81$), 35–44 ($n = 74$), 45–54 ($n = 34$), and 55–91 ($n = 33$). It appears from careful
reading of the manual that additional normative
information (i.e., race, education, and geographic
area) was collected during standardization but this
information is not apparent in the database. It is
not directly stated in the manual but it appears
that the subjects' test scores are obtained through

the use of age- and gender-specific normative information but no reason is given for breaking down scores by either age or gender. Regardless, the lack of adequate normative information makes it extremely difficult to make adequate and appropriate interpretations based on the subject's test performance.

Besides an inadequate description of the norm sample, the IVA manual is also seriously lacking in other areas including convincing evidence of reliability and validity. One research article is presented discussing IVA's test-retest reliability (with a 1–4 week interval). The authors report that "overall changes in quotient scores were very small" and the "changes which occur in IVA scores over time can reliably be interpreted to reflect possible medication, treatment or environmental effects" (manual, p. VII-6). However, the correlation coefficients (Pearson r) among the six global composite scores range from .37 to .75, which appears to indicate inadequate reliability to make diagnostic decisions that affect children's lives.

The manual also contains one study on the IVA's predictive validity. Performance on the IVA was compared to the results of two other continuous performance tests (Gordon's CPT and the Test of Variables of Attention [T.O.V.A.]) and two behavior rating scales (Conners' Parent Rating Scale—39 and the Children's Attention Scale). The validity of scores from the IVA was evaluated by comparing the accuracy of the IVA CPT to diagnoses made by an independent physician or psychologist. Based on this single study, the authors report that "research supports the conclusion that clinicians now have a new, accurate cognitive test which can provide important objective data for inclusion in the multi-method assessment of ADHD." This reviewer takes issue with this statement on the grounds that insufficient data support the use of CPTs in identifying ADHD at all. Clinicians are required to make broad generalizations from performance on a computerized test of attention to actual behavior in the natural environment, particularly a classroom setting. Recent clinical practice guidelines issued by the American Academy of Pediatrics (AAP, 2000) indicate that an adequate diagnosis can be made only with appropriate history gathering, interviews with caregivers and teachers, and careful behavioral observations. Current data do not adequately support the use of continuous performance tests in the diagnosis of ADHD.

SUMMARY. Although the IVA is generally "user-friendly" in terms of administration, it fails to meet the *Standards for Educational and Psychological Testing* (AERA, APA, & NCME, 1985). In its present form the IVA lacks sufficient research and rationale for its use as a measure of inattention, impulsivity, and hyperactivity. Adequate descriptions of the IVA's development, normative data, and psychometric properties are severely lacking. More disturbing is the potential for its misuse and misinterpretation of the test results. Clinicians should avoid the temptation to diagnose ADHD or other behavioral disorders on the basis of this computer-administered test. Much additional research is needed to support the use of any continuous performance test in the diagnosis and treatment of the Attention Deficit Hyperactivity Disorder.

REVIEWER'S REFERENCES

American Educational Research Association, American Psychological Association, & National Council on Measurement in Education. (1985). *Standards for educational and psychological testing.* Washington, DC: American Psychological Association, Inc.
American Academy of Pediatrics. (2000). Clinical practice guideline: Diagnosis and evaluation of the child with attention-deficit/hyperactivity disorder. *Pediatrics, 105*(5), 1158–1170.

[181]
Integrated Writing Test.

Purpose: "Designed to evaluate major components of good writing in students' writing samples."
Population: Grades 2–12.
Publication Date: 1993.
Acronym: IWT.
Scores, 7: Productivity, Clarity, Vocabulary, Spelling, Punctuation, Legibility, Total Test Language Quotient.
Administration: Group.
Levels, 5: Grades 2/3, Grade 4, Grades 5/6, Grades 7 to 9, Grades 10 to 12.
Price Data, 1997: $132.95 per kit including manual (66 pages) and 35 booklets for each grade level; $22.95 per package of 35 booklets; $22.95 per manual.
Time: 15(20) minutes.
Comments: Academic extension of the Developmental Test of Visual-Motor Integration (119); also based upon the National Assessment of Educational Progress Writing Test.
Authors: Keith E. Beery with assistance from the Integrated Teaching Team.
Publisher: Golden Educational Center.

Review of the Integrated Writing Test by C. DALE CARPENTER, Professor of Special Education, Western Carolina University, Cullowhee, NC:

DESCRIPTION. The Integrated Writing Test (IWT) is a short, simple assessment tool designed to evaluate "good writing" by having students write for 15 minutes to a teacher-chosen prompt. Percentile ranks and standard scores are calculated for six subtests and the total test. Productivity is the number of words written. This is a standard method of assessing writing fluency. However, students are not allowed time to reflect on the topic nor are they allowed any other prewriting time to engage in brainstorming, webbing, outlining, discussing, or other activities that might lead to good writing and that are often suggested by written expression experts.

Clarity is a content score that refers to clarity of presentation. Students are told that they should write as if they were reporters for a newspaper. How well they address the following reportorial questions is evaluated: Who? When? Where? What? How? Why? Each of these questions receives a score of 0 for "Unclear" to 3 for "Detailed." This is the most subjective subtest and is at least partially dependent on the teacher-selected topic. Some topics such as "Discovery of America" might be more amenable to this kind of writing than others such as "Photosynthesis." Examiners are told to decide on a topic that will elicit the required questions and is interrelated with a topic being taught in a content area.

Vocabulary is scored by counting the number of words with seven or more letters and comparing this to the total number of words written yielding a ratio of long words to total words written. This is a standard, objective, and reliable method of scoring vocabulary. Spelling is also a ratio, counting number of words misspelled to total number of words. Unlike Vocabulary, which only counts the same long word once, misspelled words are counted whenever they occur even if they are consistently misspelled.

Punctuation is another ratio measure calculated the same way as Spelling except that punctuation errors are counted. Scorers are instructed to circle all punctuation errors including omissions. Examiners are directed to sections of dictionaries for punctuation rules. Although this subtest appears to be objective, all sources do not agree on punctuation rules, particularly on comma use, and examiners must have a basic knowledge to know where to question punctuation.

Legibility is a measure of number of words to total words with adequate legibility. A word with poor legibility includes such things as poor spacing, letter distortions, or any word that makes the reader pause to decipher.

The Total Test score is a composite of three or more subtests and is available as a quotient or percentile.

The Integrated Writing Test is based on the National Assessment of Educational Progress (NAEP) in Writing and is compared throughout the manual to the NAEP. Unlike the NAEP, the IWT allows examiners to score the entire writing sample or to score only five lines of the writing sample for all but the Clarity subtest. This approach reduces the time required to score each test and is reported in the manual to correlate at very high levels with full sample scoring.

A separate response form is required for each student to use and is also used to record. Five versions of the response form are available based on the grade level of the student and differ only in the line space provided. Besides a writing instrument, a watch, and the record form, the test requires no other materials to administer the test. A manual is required to score as well as is, presumably, a standard guide to punctuation rules.

NORM SAMPLE. The IWT was normed on approximately 1,000 students at 11 age levels with appropriate proportions of ethnic groups and balanced for gender. No information is provided about the inclusion of students with disabilities.

RELIABILITY. Because of the subjective nature of some of the scoring, interrater reliability is critical. On a sample of 20 protocols of fifth grade students, two scorers achieved interscorer reliabilities above .90 for all subtests except Legibility (.85) using the sample and full scoring methods. Internal consistency coefficients averaged .73 (Vocabulary) to .99 (Productivity). Test-retest reliability was estimated using two fourth grade classes writing within 2-days of each other. Coefficients using the sample method of scoring ranged from .23 (Punctuation) to .81 (Productivity) and using the full scoring method ranged from .49 (Punctuation) to .84 (Spelling).

VALIDITY. The authors present content validity information by stating reasons for each of the subtests and the method of scoring chosen. The topic selection for the writing sample is the most controversial aspect of the IWT and in this case, the manual states narratively, without presenting data, that no significant difference was found between action-oriented topics but significant differences were obtained between action-oriented topics and passive topics. Criterion-related validity is shown by comparing selected subtests of the IWT with the developmental curves of the NAEP Writing and comparing total test scores for the IWT with the Test of Written Language-2 and the California Test of Basic Skills. Construct validity evidence is presented in four ways. IWT subtest intercorrelations show low to moderate coefficients indicating that subtests do not assess the same thing. Developmental curves affirm that the constructs measured are indeed developmental. Third, the manual presents scores for 22 students identified as learning disabled showing their average scaled scores in an attempt to indicate group differentiation. Yet, the scores presented are not significantly different from nondisabled students in the standardization sample. Finally, the manual presents data from a study of two fourth grade classes using the test and showing gains after approximately 7 months of instruction.

SUMMARY. The Integrated Writing Test is promising and deserves to be used by researchers and practitioners. It offers a quick and authentic way to measure important aspects of writing. The manual provides reasonably clear directions for administering and scoring. However, the option of two scoring methods, a sample method and a full scoring method, may appear confusing to some users. The choice of a topic to which students are to write is the most problematic feature of the instrument. Although the authors address how to choose a topic, the information about variations in scores based on topic is not adequate.

Technical data regarding standardization sample, reliability, and validity are not overwhelming, but are adequate to merit further use of the instrument. Reliability and validity studies use small samples and focus on the intermediate grades rather than including the entire age range of the norm sample. Therefore, the IWT appears better suited to these grades than to second grade students and secondary aged students. The instrument would benefit, as would most, from more study. Nonetheless, the IWT currently offers an acceptable alternative to other popular writing tests.

Review of the Integrated Writing Test by RICHARD M. WOLF, Professor of Psychology and Education, Teachers College, Columbia University, New York, NY:

The Integrated Writing Test (IWT) is a test of reportorial writing ability intended for use by classroom teachers in grades 2–12. Students are given 15 minutes to write a passage on an assigned topic, pretending that he or she is a reporter "who is writing the story for a newspaper" (test booklet, p. 1). The test booklet, outside of a cover sheet for recording name and other information, consists simply of three pages of ruled lines on which to write the story. Unfortunately, teachers are furnished virtually no guidance about a topic on which students are to write. The manual simply says, "Decide upon [a] topic which will elicit the *Who?, When?, Where?, What?, How?, and Why?* questions of reportorial writing. The topic should also interrelate with a topic currently being taught in another subject such as Language, Science, or Social Studies" (manual, p. 5). Unfortunately, no examples of topics are furnished.

Scores are obtained on the following six dimensions: Productivity (the number of words in a five-line sample—usually lines 10 through 14 of the story), Vocabulary (the number of words of seven letters or more in a five-line sample), Spelling (number of misspelled words in a five-line sample), Punctuation (the number of punctuation errors in a five-line sample), Legibility (the number of words judged "poor legibility" in a five-line sample), and Clarity (a rating of 1 to 6 for judged clarity of the entire story). Except for Clarity, the scoring can be done on either the full story or a five-line sample from the story. Norms are provided for each of the dimensions. Scaled scores and percentile ranks are provided for each of the six dimensions whereas scaled scores, percentile ranks, "quotients," *T* scores, and NCEs (normal curve equivalents) are provided for total scores. The norms are based on samples ranging from 78 to 110 students at each grade level, drawn from different sections of the United States. The use of "quotients" is highly questionable for two reasons. First, they are not quotients at all, but rather standard scores with a mean of 100 and a standard deviation of 15. Second, they resemble Wechsler Intelligence Scale scores and thus may lead some users to regard them as immutable. This seems dangerous.

Validity evidence on the IWT inheres primarily in the selection of the dimensions on which the stories are scored. It appears to parallel the scoring dimensions of the National Assessment of Educational Progress (NAEP), Grill and Kerwin's

(1989) Written Language Assessment (WLA; T4:3005), and Hammill and Larsen's (1988) Test of Written Language (TOWL-2; T4:2804). However, the authors acknowledge that some of the scores may be less important than others, namely Clarity, Spelling, and Punctuation. Evidence of construct validity is furnished by showing that the developmental curves for many of the scores parallel those of other tests of writing proficiency. Raw score correlations with grade levels range from .36 for Punctuation and Legibility to .67 for Productivity. Correlations between IWT scores and other measures are fairly high (i.e., .6 to .7), although the samples sizes on which they are based are often quite small.

The author presents the results of a number of investigations undertaken to establish the reliabilities of the various scales. Although the results show generally high reliability estimates with values in the .7 to .9 range, these studies suffer from two defects. First, the sample sizes are generally quite small (as low as 10 students in an analysis). Second, analyses were conducted combining age/grade groups. This inflates the variability considerably and results in high correlations. It would have been better to conduct analyses separately at each age/grade level.

One issue of particular interest to test users, particularly teachers, is the amount of time required to score the IWT. The author provides two procedures. The first involves scoring the full story and the second requires only a scoring of five lines of the story (lines 10–14 are recommended). To determine whether the five-line scoring was sufficient, the author and a graduate student in English each scored 20 protocols from an average fifth grade class on both the five-line sample as well as the full scoring. As expected, the correlations for the full scoring were higher (.87 to .97) than for the five-line sample scoring (.85 to .97). The median correlation for the full story scoring was .965 whereas the median correlation for the sample scoring was .925. It appears that the five-line sample scoring is adequate although if there is a question about an individual's performance, full story scoring should probably be done.

In summary, the IWT appears to be a carefully developed measure of reportorial writing ability for students in grades 2–12. It yields scores on six dimensions. If these dimensions are ones that a teacher feels are important, then its use should be given consideration. If other types of writing are to be assessed (e.g., narrative writing), a user will need to look elsewhere or devise a different measure. Validity and reliability information are based on relatively small samples and may be somewhat inflated by combining results across age/grade levels. Unfortunately, users are given little guidance with regard to the selection of topics on which students should write.

REVIEWER'S REFERENCES
Hammill, D. D., & Larsen, S. C. (1988). Test of Written Language (TOWL-2). Austin, TX: PRO-ED.
Grill, J. J., & Kirwin, M. M. (1989). *Written Language Assessment Manual*. Novato, CA: Academic Therapy Publications.

[182]
Intermediate Booklet Category Test.

Purpose: Designed as a "test of higher order cognitive functions" to assess brain damage.
Population: Ages 9–14.
Publication Dates: 1985–1987.
Acronym: IBCT.
Scores: Total Error Score.
Administration: Individual.
Price Data: Price data available from publisher for complete kit including IBCT in 2 volumes, manual ('87, 19 pages), and 50 scoring forms.
Time: (30–60) minutes.
Author: Paul B. Byrd.
Publisher: Psychological Assessment Resources, Inc.

Review of the Intermediate Booklet Category Test by JAMES K. BENISH, School Psychologist, Helena Public Schools, Adjunct Professor of Special Education, Carroll College, Helena, MT:

The Intermediate Booklet Category Test (IBCT) is intended as an intermediate booklet version of the 1979 Booklet Category Test (BCT). As a "test of higher order cognitive functions" (manual, p. 7) to assess brain damage, the IBCT is an attempt to offer a more practical assessment tool to evaluate children than the Category Test (CT), which relies on antiquated, cumbersome laboratory equipment. Because the CT is an indicator of the Halstead-Reitan Battery (T5:1164), the author hopes to offer the IBCT as a similar, but more convenient alternative. The author notes that "research conducted on the Intermediate Booklet Category Test to this date is introductory and should be considered as a starting point" (manual, p. 3).

The Intermediate Booklet Category Test is designed for children 9 through 14 years of age. The Booklet Category Test version developed in

1979 is intended for adults. With more clinical attention drawn toward children and adolescents with learning problems, a need for more thorough neurological evaluations has increased. Hence, a new computerized version of the Category Test along with the Intermediate version has already been published and newly revised making the 1987 Intermediate Booklet Category Test a low technology-based evaluation tool.

Administration and scoring criteria were clearly and concisely written in the IBCT manual. Although the author did not discuss training needed to administer and interpret this test, it should be assumed that advanced graduate training in neuropsychological assessment would be essential. The examiner must be completely familiar with test items to prevent disruption of the flow in administering the IBCT. Based on review of the test content and administration requirements, it appears total testing time is about 30 to 60 minutes depending on age and temperament of the child. The IBCT is composed of six subtests contained within two test booklets. Clear, concise, highlighted instructions are presented within the administration manual for each subtest. The scoring form allows the examiner to mark a subject's response and give immediate feedback. Correct responses are shaded on the form, and allow for ease in scoring. Total error scores are calculated from computing each subtest error. The author notes that a total error score greater than 50 suggests "impaired performance on the CT" (manual, p. 13), and is therefore also an accepted clinical standard for the IBCT.

STANDARDIZATION AND NORMS. A 1986 study involved 24 learning disabled and 24 regular education children between ages 9 and 14 years. A year later, the IBCT and the CT were administered to "30 children receiving special education services for behavior disorders (BD) and 30 children in regular education (RE) classes" (manual, p. 15). No further studies were reported by the author since 1987, the most recent copyright. Page 13 of the IBCT manual contains Table 1, the "Classification of Category Test Error Scores." These classifications include "Normal to Above Average," "Slightly Below Normal," "Questionable Impairment," and "Significant Impairment." Selz and Reitan (1979) were the source for this table.

VALIDITY AND RELIABILITY. In Chapter V of the manual, the author reported on the two studies conducted that document very respectable evidence for concurrent validity between the IBCT and the CT. An overall "positive correlation of .894" was shown (manual, p. 14). Internal consistency of the IBCT is listed as .912 for the 1986 study, and .92 for the 1987 study, both using split-half analysis. Table 3 displays the correlation coefficients between the IBCT and the CT for the author's 1986 study. These correlation scores listed by group and age range are all respectable, and range from .797 to .965 for ages 9 through 14, and .794 and .864 for regular education and learning disabled groups respectively. Correlation coefficients were even higher for the 1987 study, with the behavior disorder group at .907, and the regular education group at .935.

SUMMARY. As mentioned above, another version of the Category Test was developed for desktop or notebook computer use. Entitled the Category Test Computer Program 6.0, this version of the Category Test allows the user to administer the Halstead Category Test including Russell's Revised Short Form, the Intermediate version (for ages 9 to 14), and a new Adaptive Category Test. Professionals trained in neurological assessment who would rather utilize a more technically advanced computerized version might consider the Category Test Computer Program 6.0. It would appear that another option exists that transcends the CT's problems with mobility and ease of administration. However, the IBCT still has a place among neuropsychological assessments, and as the author cautions, should not be used to "make clinical judgments based solely on a subject's performance on the IBCT" (manual, p. 13). When used in conjunction with other relevant tests, the IBCT should help to provide indicators of possible neurological dysfunction. Statistically, the IBCT is strong when administered and interpreted within the context in which it was developed.

REVIEWER'S REFERENCE

Selz, M., & Reitan, R. M. (1979). Rules for neuropsychological diagnosis: Classification of brain function in older children. *Journal of Consulting and Clinical Psychology, 47,* 258–264.

Review of The Intermediate Booklet Category Test by VINCENT J. SAMAR, Associate Professor, Department of Applied Language and Cognition Research, National Technical Institute for the Deaf, Rochester Institute of Technology, Rochester, NY:

The Intermediate Booklet Category Test (IBCT) is a test of complex concept formation and abstract reasoning intended to detect brain damage in older children. It is closely based on the Halstead Category Test (CT), the most sensitive indicator of brain damage in the Halstead-Reitan Neuropsychological Battery (T5:1164). However, unlike the original CT, which used a complicated projection box apparatus bound to a laboratory or clinical setting, the IBCT, like its cousin the Booklet Category Test—Adult (BCT-Adult), uses printed designs presented in a portable booklet format.

TEST FORMAT AND DESCRIPTION. The IBCT consists of a test manual, two booklets of stimulus items, and 50 manually scorable response forms. The IBCT contains 168 stimulus items (numerical and literal symbols and nonverbal designs) divided into six subtests. The items are white drawings on a black background, one item to a page. The item pages are bound in a two-volume ring-binder set, making the test very portable. The scoring form is a four-page bifold. The first page permits the examiner to enter a child's identifying information, subtest scores, and a brief observation for each subtest. The remaining three pages permit the examiner to record the child's response to each item by checking one of four response boxes. For each item, the correct response box is shaded to facilitate scoring and the provision of examiner feedback. For the examiner's quick reference, a replica of the stimulus item appears above the four response boxes for each item.

Each item of the IBCT is designed to remind the child of a number between 1 and 4. The child's task in responding to each item in a specific subtest is to find a principle or concept common to all the items within that subtest that determines the correct response number. For each item, the child indicates that number by pointing to one of the Arabic numerals 1, 2, 3, or 4 arrayed in a row on a cardboard response strip placed before the child.

The manual states, somewhat misleadingly, that the IBCT has retained the same 168 designs used in the CT. In fact, the CT and BCT-Adult contain 208 designs in seven subtests. The six-subtest IBCT has dropped a section.

Subtest I of the IBCT is composed of 8 items. Each item is one of the first four Roman numerals (I, II, III, IV). The child must point to the Arabic numeral on the response strip that corresponds to an item's Roman numeral. Subtest II is composed of 20 items. Each item contains from one to four simple objects, all of the same type. The possible item types are squares, circles, vertical lines, human stick figures, or letter strings. The child must point to the Arabic numeral on the response strip that corresponds to the number of separate objects on the page. Subtest III is composed of 40 items. Each item contains four simple geometric objects in a horizontal row (squares, triangles, and irregular pentagons) that share one or more features (fill, shape, or size). Within each item, one object fails to share a feature common to the other three. The child must point to the Arabic numeral on the response strip that corresponds to the position of that object in the row (numbered implicitly from left to right). Subtests IV and V are each composed of 40 items representing a variety of geometric and letter figures. The figures are drawn in a combination of different proportions of solid and dotted lines. The child must point to the Arabic numeral on the response strip that corresponds to the proportion of the figure that is drawn in solid lines (i.e., 1/4, 2/4, 3/4, or 4/4 of the figure may be drawn in solid lines). Subtest VI contains a sampling of 20 items from previous subtests. Therefore, there is no single principle across the Subtest VI items that determines the correct response for any item. Instead, the child must remember the correct principle for each item from its previous presentation.

The stimulus items are large and bold; they are easy for children to see, even for children who might have some degree of vision impairment. The four-page response form that the examiner must use, however, is visually crowded. Subtests begin and end wherever they happen to fall on the page with headings that are not sufficiently prominent to quickly guide the examiner's eye to the beginning of a specific subtest section. In this respect, the IBCT has not caught up with the latest version of the BCT-Adult, which employs response forms that represent each subtest on a new page.

TEST COVERAGE AND USE. The IBCT is intended to be an alternative form of administration of the CT for use with children ages 9–14 years. It was designed to extend the ages covered by the booklet form of the CT downward from the minimum age at which the BCT-Adult may be used (15 years and up).

The manual does not directly address the scope of applications of the IBCT. However, as an alternative form of the CT, it is clearly intended for use in discriminating neurologically intact from brain-damaged children in the 9–14-year-old age range. In addition, the manual presents data from two studies (Byrd & Warner, 1986; Byrd & Ingram, 1987, cited in Byrd, 1987) that suggest that the IBCT discriminates between regular education children and learning disabled (LD) children, and between regular education children and children with behavioral disorders (BD), respectively, in a manner comparable to the CT. However, the manual does not explicitly recommend the use of the IBCT to identify LD or BD children.

The manual is careful to point out that the same criteria and cautions that apply to the CT also apply to the IBCT. In particular, the manual stresses that the IBCT "should be interpreted only within the context of a pattern of test scores in making an interpretation regarding the presence of deficits attributable to brain dysfunction" (p. 13).

APPROPRIATENESS OF SAMPLES FOR TEST VALIDATION AND NORMING. Because of the extensive development and validation efforts of Halstead, Reitan, and others since 1935, the Halstead-Reitan Neuropsychological Battery is widely regarded by neuropsychologists as one of the most sensitive tools for detecting cognitive deficits among individuals with suspected neurological damage (Fischer, 1987). The CT alone is nearly as good a predictor of brain damage as the entire Halstead-Reitan Battery (Wheeler, Burke, & Reitan, 1963). The authors of the IBCT and the BCT-Adult intended to produce a precise alternative format to the original CT so that the normative data from the original test could be applied to the results of the booklet versions (DeFilippis & McCampbell, 1991). The IBCT's close modeling of the stimuli and instruction set of the CT should cause the IBCT to inherit the substantial validity and reliability characteristics of the CT, and presumably to enjoy the same factorial preeminence as the CT does when it is used as a substitute for the CT in the Halstead-Reitan Neuropsychological Battery. In principle, this situation should greatly reduce the required size and scope of new validation samples for the IBCT compared with a totally novel assessment instrument.

Nevertheless, the only normative data reported by the manual for the IBCT itself were published in 1986 and 1987. They are based on samples of only 24 regular education children and 24 LD children in one study (Byrd & Warner, 1986), and 30 regular education and 30 BD chil-

dren in a separate study (Byrd & Ingram, 1987). Because these samples were broken down further among six age groups (9–14 years), they are seriously inadequate to confidently ensure that the psychometric performance of the IBCT matches that of the CT.

This would remain a somewhat speculative concern if there were not new evidence to suggest that the booklet forms of the CT may produce scores in some individuals that are seriously deviant from the score produced by the original, better validated CT. DeFilippis, Jarvis, and Hamlin (1996) recently noted that despite the intended similarity in the instruction sets for the original CT and BCT-Adult, the latter test omits certain crucial instructional items. Those items refer to the requirement for the examiner to use extensive prompts to urge individuals to describe the test items verbally or to study the test items carefully and reflect on why they might be making errors. Without this prompting, some individuals who have more difficulty with the test produce much higher error scores than they should. DeFilippis et al. provided two case studies that indicate that interpreting such scores by reference to the normative data for the CT (Reitan, 1959, 1979) or through widely used interpretive systems (e.g., Jarvis & Barth, 1994) will either produce excessive false positive identifications of brain impairment or cause the severity of impairment to be overestimated in some individuals.

The IBCT suffers from the same omission of crucial instructions as the BCT-Adult, and so it should also suffer from reduced validity relative to the CT. The use of extremely low sample sizes and of a highly restricted range of presumed neurological impairments in the two validation studies reported in the manual for the IBCT make it difficult to estimate the extent of validity violations such as that reported by DeFilippis et al. (1996) for the 9–14-year-old age range covered by the IBCT. Clearly, then, the IBCT suffers from seriously inadequate population sampling for validation and norming, despite its derivative relationship to the CT.

RELIABILITY. The manual reports overall split-half internal consistency reliabilities from the two validation studies of .912 and .920. No data are presented for children with and without suspected brain damage at different ages. The lack of reliability estimates for different groups of normal and neurologically impaired children raises significant concern over the suitability of the IBCT for making decisions about individual children.

CONTENT AND CONSTRUCT VALIDITY. The content validity of the IBCT is comparable to that of the CT because its items are patterned directly after the items of the CT, which is generally regarded as having appropriate content validity. The construct validity of the IBCT may suffer from contamination by additional psychological factors (attentional set, risk taking behavior, etc.) stemming from the use of the altered instruction set recommended in the manual, as indicated by the work of DeFilippis et al. (1996) discussed above. Reverting to the original instruction set, which uses extensive prompts to circumvent the psychological idiosyncrasies of test-taking behavior in certain children and to drive children toward their best performance should obviate this construct contamination. Nevertheless, it remains necessary to demonstrate empirically that the IBCT, even with revised instructions, has adequate construct validity evidence.

TEST ADMINISTRATION. The manual provides test instructions that are intended to be read verbatim to the individual. They are clear, as far as they go. However, the manual should be revised to include a caveat to the examiner to heed the need for extensive prompts and to provide examples of appropriate prompting without giving away the principle. For example, Reitan (1979) suggests telling individuals to observe the items carefully, to describe the figure before answering, to state their reasons for selecting a specific response, to try to notice how the items change, and so on.

The manual says nothing about the optimal conditions of administration (lighting, pace of administration, positioning of the child, etc.). One concern not addressed in the manual is the need for the examiner to take care to shield the response form from the child. The correct answer is indicated on the response form for each item by a shaded box, and the item is reproduced in miniature on the form. Because the examiner must be close to the child in order to flip the item pages in the booklet while simultaneously recording the child's responses, there is a danger that a clever child could surreptitiously observe the correct responses and achieve a false negative score without ever identifying the relevant principle.

The IBCT requires 30–60 minutes of testing time. I verified the lower limit of the administration time by administering the IBCT to my daughter and one of her friends, both neurologically normal, academically advanced 12-year-olds, who required between 25–30 minutes to complete the test.

TEST AND ITEM BIAS. Arnold, Montgomery, Castaneda, and Longoria (1994) have provided direct evidence that the CT is affected by the level of acculturation of Hispanic groups in the U.S. This suggests that the use of the IBCT with culturally diverse groups and nonnative speakers of English is problematic, especially for children in the 9–14-year-old age range. Subtest I, for example, depends upon certain specific knowledge of the system of Roman numerals. This knowledge may or may not be within the purview of some of the youngest children for whom the test is intended or of members of certain cultural groups.

Additionally, the level of English vocabulary and idiom and the complexity of sentence grammar in the instructions (e.g., the use of passive voice and the use of embedded structures) is too high to ensure clear comprehension by some children in the 9–14-year-old age range, by many children who are nonnative users of English, by many children who are language learning disabled, or by many children who are deaf or hard-of-hearing. This concern is compounded by the failure of the instructions to explicitly require the examiner to prompt the individual with clarifying and focusing remarks during the test administration.

No doubt, the instructions of the IBCT will need to be simplified and refined to ensure cultural and communicative fairness. However, in doing so, it will be necessary to revisit the general validation process for each target population. Extreme caution must be exercised when using the IBCT as currently administered or with unvalidated modifications to assess brain damage in children from different cultural, ethnic, or language groups.

The manual states that Subtest VI "repeats items from the first five subtests and requires that the subject remember the correct principle from the previous subtests" (p. 9). However, no items are actually repeated from Subtest I. More importantly, 2 of the 20 items in Subtest VI (Items 8 and 20) are not correctly presented in the materials reviewed by this reviewer. They are the same as Item 5 in Subtest V and Item 14 in Subtest IV, respectively, but are rotated 180 degrees in the plane of the page. For these items, then, it appears that a mental operation of rotation is required to recognize the items as having been previously presented, although the rotation does not alter the correct response. [Editor's Note: PAR representatives state that this problem was due to a printing error in this one test booklet and not a universal problem with the test.]

SUMMARY. The IBCT is designed to closely parallel the contents of the CT and, therefore, to largely rely for its validation and norms on previous validation and norming studies of the CT. However, the IBCT has also been simplified by dropping 40 items. Importantly, the IBCT instructions deviate from the instructions of the CT in a way that has been shown to compromise the construct validity scores from the booklet versions of the CT, and the validation sample of the IBCT is seriously inadequate. Minimally, users of the IBCT should augment the administration procedures recommended in the manual's instructions with the use of extensive prompting as suggested by Reitan (1979). Moreover, the user should bear in mind that scores from the IBCT have not been adequately validated on the child population and should therefore not be used alone to evaluate brain damage in any population of children, even with the appropriately modified administration procedures.

REVIEWER'S REFERENCES

Wheeler, L., Burke, C. H., & Reitan, R. M. (1963). An application of discriminant functions to the problems of predicting brain damage using behavioral variables. *Perceptual and Motor Skills Monograph Supplement 3-V16, 16,* 417–440.

Reitan, R. M. (1979). *Manual for administration of neuropsychological test batteries for adults and children.* (Mimeographed manual). Indianapolis: Author.

Byrd, P., & Warner, P. (1986). Development of a booklet version of the Halstead Category Test for children ages nine through fourteen years: Preliminary validation with normal and learning disabled subjects. *Journal of Clinical Neuropsychology, 8,* 80–82.

Byrd, P. (1987). *The Intermediate Booklet Category Test manual.* Odessa, FL: Psychological Assessment Resources, Inc.

Fischer, W. E. (1987). [Review of the Halstead Category Test.] In D. Keyser & R. Sweetland (Eds.), *Test critiques* (vol. VI; pp. 208–215). Austin, TX: PRO-ED.

DeFilippis, N. A., & McCampbell, E. (1991). *Manual for the Booklet Category Test.* Odessa, FL: Psychological Assessment Resources, Inc.

Arnold, B. R., Montgomery, G. T., Castaneda, I., & Longoria, R. (1994). Acculturation and performance of Hispanics on selected Halstead-Reitan neuropsychological tests. *Assessment, 1,* 239–248.

Jarvis, P. E., & Barth, J. T. (1994). *Halstead-Reitan Neuropsychological Battery: A guide to interpretation and clinical applications.* Odessa, FL: Psychological Assessment Resources, Inc.

DeFilippis, N. A., Jarvis, P. E., & Hamlin, D. H. (1996). The Category Test and the Booklet Category Test: Equivalent tests but different instructions? *Bulletin of the National Academy of Neuropsychology, 1,* 13–15.

[183]

Internalizing Symptoms Scale for Children.

Purpose: Developed to provide a screening and assessment self-report tool for research and clinical evaluation of internalizing symptoms associated with depression, anxiety, somatic problems, social withdrawal, and various types of affect in children.

Population: Ages 8–13.
Publication Date: 1998.
Acronym: ISSC.
Scores, 3: Negative Affect/General Distress, Positive Affect, Total.
Administration: Group or individual.
Levels, 3: Normal, At-Risk, High Risk.
Price Data, 1999: $74 per complete kit.
Time: (20) minutes.
Authors: Kenneth W. Merrell and Amy S. Walters.
Publisher: PRO-ED.
Cross References: See T5:1288 (2 references).

Review of the Internalizing Symptoms Scale for Children by ROBERT CHRISTOPHER, President, International Mental Health Network, Ltd., Poway, CA:

The Internalizing Symptoms Scale for Children (ISSC) is a relatively new (1998) pencil-and-paper instrument with 48 items scored on a 4-point response scale and is intended to be administered to children in Grades 3 through 6, or ages 8 through 13. The ISSC was developed as a norm-referenced scale that utilizes a self-report format and is primarily intended to assess a spectrum of internalizing domain symptomatology ranging from emotional and cognitive to physiological symptoms.

The conceptual framework for the ISSC is based on the development of new approaches in classification and conceptualization of childhood psychopathology during the mid-1960s. The foundation of the new taxonomies was based on statistical analyses of child psychopathology categorized into two major dimensions: the internalizing domain (or overcontrolled and inner-directed behavior) and externalizing domain (or the undercontrolled and outer-directed behavior). The major categories of the internalizing domain include depression, anxiety, social withdrawal, and somatic problems. The externalizing domain includes primarily a range of behavioral disorders such as conduct disorder, antisocial and aggressive behaviors, and attention-deficit/hyperactivity disorder. Internalizing disturbances, such as depression, seem to be related to a child's difficulties in multiple areas of competence, from maladaptive social problem-solving styles, conflict-negotiation and affect regulation deficits, to peer rejection. Children with comorbid internalizing and externalizing spectrum of symptoms seem to generally suffer from the greatest social dysfunctionality (Rudolph, Hammer, & Burge, 1994).

The intent of the ISSC is primarily to focus on a general assessment of an area of a symptomatological spectrum, and not to provide specific clinical diagnostic impressions and formulations about specific child disorders. However, the intensity and directionality of the two ISSC factor scores may provide sufficient guidelines for formulation of diagnostic impressions. Thus, the ISSC may be appropriate in the following domains of clinical applications: (a) assessment and identification of children at risk for development of internalizing disorders; (b) assessment for and classification of eligibility for educational and mental health services; (c) development of behavioral, social, and emotional therapeutic interventions for children with diagnosed internalizing disorders; and, (d) research of child emotional spectrum symptomatology.

SELECTION OF ITEMS. Items for the ISSC were selected from available literature on depression, anxiety, somatic complaints, and social withdrawal. Initial selection of the items was based on 192 descriptors resulting in a selection of 76 items. Refinement of item characteristics, peer-review, and elimination of low item-total-correlations led to the current version of the ISSC with 48 items. The average item-total correlations of the current item set is .40, with the majority of items exceeding .25. It is therefore reasonable to assume that the existing item set adequately represents the domain of the chosen symptomatology intended to be measured in the target population consisting of elementary-age children. The average alpha coefficient for the ISSC total score is reported at .91, and the within-the-factor coefficients are .91 for Factor 1, and .85 for Factor 2.

ADMINISTRATION, SCORING, AND INTERPRETATION. Administration of the ISSC is uncomplicated; it does not require special technical qualifications, and it can be administered by a variety of persons, from psychologists, social workers, teachers, and counselors to paraprofessionals and clerical staff. The ISSC can be administered to children either individually or in group settings. Each child would be provided with the response sheet, and the testing can proceed with basic instructions. The response sheet contains the 48 items along with the boxes for each of four possible responses: *Never, Hardly ever, Sometimes,* and *Often.*

From the total set, 36 items describe negative affect and the presence of symptoms represen-

tative of internalizing disorders, and 12 additional items, reverse scored, identify positive characteristics incompatible with high levels of emotional distress. Because the second factor of the ISSC is scored reversely, indicating an absence of positive symptomatology, higher values for both sets of items are associated with higher levels of distress. The items are not designed to be the polar opposites of each other. Their dichotomous character is intended to represent the notion that internalizing and externalizing domains are not singular, unrelated, and mutually exclusive entities, but components of a single continuum of a constellation of children's emotional disturbances.

The examiner should remain available during the testing in an unobtrusive capacity. Only an English version of the ISSC is available. Administration of the test through an interpreter to children whose primary language is not English has not been tested for validity and is not recommended. Total administration time is estimated to be between 8 and 15 minutes.

Scoring and interpretation of the results should be done by professionals with training and experience in psychometrics or measurement. The raw scores are recorded by the examiner and converted to percentiles, standard deviation equivalents, and standard scores for both factors. The normative tables are included in the ISSC manual.

To form a profile, standard scores and the ISSC total score for each factor are recorded on an ISSC summary sheet, and plotted on a graphical display. The first graph shows the relationship between the two ISSC factors: Negative Affect/ General Distress and Positive Affect. The second graph shows the child's total score, which represents the overall level of internalizing symptoms. The graphs provide visual representations suitable for clarification and interpretation of test results.

A four-stage interpretation strategy of ISSC scores is recommended by the authors. The first stage involves matching of the obtained scores to the national standardization sample using percentile ranks, standard deviation equivalents, and standard scores as indicators of score placement. The second stage "involves identification of a general range of common scores in which a particular ISSC Total or factor score fits" (examiner's manual, p. 20). These general ranges are "Normal Level," "At-Risk Level," and "High-Risk Level."

The third stage involves making additional normative comparisons, such as gender x grade comparisons. Finally, the fourth stage of interpretation consists of qualitative examination of individual item responses when scores are at the At-Risk and High-Risk levels.

VALIDITY OF THE ISSC. The ISSC factor structure was examined by applying both exploratory and confirmatory factor analyses, which gave sufficient statistical support for the two-factor structure. The factors were identified as: the Negative Affect/General Distress Factor, consisting of 35 items, and highlighting negative affect symptomatology, and the Positive Affect Factor, consisting of 13 polar and 4 cross-loading items. The second factor indicates an increasing absence, rather than presence, of positive affect. Although the correlation between two factors (.41) gives sufficient statistical support for the two-factor structure of the ISSC, the total scale score is the best index of clinical findings and applications of this instrument.

ISSC convergent construct validity evidence was gathered by studying its relationship with five other self-report instruments also intended for assessment of various aspects of children's internalizing symptomatology. The significant correlations were found to exist with the Youth Self-Report (YSR; Achenbach, 1991), The Children's Depression Inventory (CDI; Kovacs, 1992), Revised Children's Manifest Anxiety Scale (RCMAS; Reynolds & Richmond, 1985), Reynolds Child Depression Scale (RCDS; Reynolds, 1992), and the State-Trait Anxiety Inventory for Children (STAIC; Spielberger, 1973).

The ISSC manual cites several studies that were conducted in order to measure both the criterion-related validity of the ISSC as a measure of internalizing symptomatology, and its sensitivity to theoretically based group differences. Results supported the scale's reliability in detecting gender differences, differences between externally identified internalizing and noninternalizing children, between emotionally disturbed and regular education students, and between gifted and nongifted students.

SUMMARY. The primary purpose of the ISSC is identification of general areas of children's emotional distress. Support for the psychometric quality of the ISSC does exist, indicating that it could be a valuable instrument in both research

and clinical assessment of internalizing symptoms in children between 8 and 12 years of age.

The ISSC's hit rate is estimated to be at about 75%. To offset the possibility of assessment failure through false positive and false negative results, and for the purpose of achieving an accurate baseline diagnostic formulation in clinical applications, the ISSC should be used in conjunction with other instruments that have more comprehensive and refined diagnostic systems of identification and classification of child psychopathology. Development of comprehensive computerized interpretive reporting would be beneficial for this instrument.

The usefulness of the ISSC may be in the fact that it can be utilized in a variety of applications requiring general assessment of children, and by a range of professionals, from clinicians to educators. The ISSC is an instrument that is relatively short in length and is easy to administer.

The statistical fit of the ISSC item set is also within an acceptable range. The two-factor structure of the ISSC is statistically supported, with the main interpretative emphasis on the first factor (Negative Affect). Various studies indicated the ISSC has good correlations with other standardized measures, and that it manifested a satisfactory degree of both convergent and discriminant construct validity.

The ISSC was standardized on a population of 2,149 children in Grades 3 through 6, from several states, representing each of the four U.S. regions. The racial/ethnic composition of the ISSC norm group is not consistent with the general U.S. population. The normative sample included a large percentage of children with learning disabilities. The ISSC's applicability in a variety of clinical and nonclinical settings, relative simplicity of the item content, and ease of administration are considered strengths of the instrument. Shortcomings of the ISSC include lack of standardization with children within the borderline intellectual functioning, and those who do not have an adequate command of the English language. Use of language interpreters is not recommended for administration of the ISSC.

Finally, in view of findings reporting temporal validity of internalizing symptomatology (Fischer, Rolf, Hasazi, & Cummings, 1984), the issue of recommended test-retest intervals and sequence should be addressed more thoroughly in the ISSC manual.

REVIEWER'S REFERENCES

Spielberger, C. D. (1973). *State-Trait Anxiety Inventory for Children.* Palo Alto, CA: Consulting Psychologists Press.

Fischer, M., Rolf, J. E., Hasazi, J. E., & Cummings, L. (1984). Follow-up of a preschool epidemiological sample: Cross-age continuities and predictions of later adjustment with internalizing and externalizing dimensions of behavior. *Child Development, 55,* 137–150.

Reynolds, C. R., & Richmond, B. O. (1985). *Revised Children's Manifest Anxiety Scale manual.* Los Angeles: Western Psychological Services.

Achenbach, T. M. (1991). *Manual for the Youth Self-Report and 1991 Profile.* Burlington, VT: University Associates in Psychiatry.

Kovacs, M. (1992). The Children's Depression Inventory. North Tonawanda, NY: Multi-Health Systems, Inc.

Reynolds, W. M. (1992). Reynolds Child Depression Scale. Odessa, FL: Psychological Assessment Resources.

Rudolph, K. D., Hammen, C., & Burge, D. (1994). Interpersonal functioning and depressive symptoms in childhood: Addressing the issues of specificity and comorbidity. *Journal of Abnormal Child Psychology, 22,* 355–371.

Review of the Internalizing Symptom Scale for Children by SUZANNE G. MARTIN, Director of Needs Assessment, Charter Fairmount Behavioral Health System, Philadelphia, PA:

TEST COVERAGE AND USE. The Internalizing Symptoms Scale for Children (ISSC) is designed for children in elementary school (Grades 3 through 6) to assess a child's perceptions of internalizing symptoms related to depression, and anxiety, somatic problems, and social withdrawal. It can be used in either the school or clinical setting and is also recommended as a research tool. It can be used as part of a comprehensive test battery or as a screening tool to identify high-risk children.

SAMPLES FOR TEST VALIDATION. The standardization group is representative of the national racial/clinic composition and includes a mix of suburban, rural, and urban settings as well as relatively equal numbers of boys and girls (51.6% and 48.4%, respectively). Participants were public school students across the United States. Socioeconomic status, race, and special education participation could only be estimated due to study constraints.

RELIABILITY. Extensive reliability testing of both test-retest, standard error of measurement, and internal consistency was conducted with results suggesting reliability levels at least similar and possibly superior to similar children's self-report tests. The standard error of measurement is modest, which indicates that the range of error that surrounds ISSC scores is small.

PREDICTIVE VALIDITY. No predictive validity data are reported. To date, one study (McClun, 1997) has examined the criterion-related validity of the ISSC. In this study, the total scores of the ISSC with internalizing broadband *T*-scores and internalizing status from the Child Behavior Checklist (CBCL) (Achenbach, 1991)

used two different methods. For each method, the correlation coefficient was within the acceptable minimum range.

CONTENT VALIDITY. Test questions are drawn directly from an expert panel of child mental health clinicians judging 76 preselected items (reduced from an initial pool of 192 potential symptom descriptors). The average item-total correlation for the ISSC test is .40, well above the cutoff of .25 recommended by some statisticians. However, 3 items were retained despite their low correlation (<.25) due to their perceived clinical importance.

CONSTRUCT VALIDITY. A variety of research studies support the convergent construct validity of the ISSC with five different children's self-report instruments that assess various aspects of internalizing symptoms. Correlational comaparisons have been obtained using the ISSC and other widely available and researched child self-report tests. These comparisons support the convergent construct validity of the ISSC as a broad measure of internalizing symptoms. Four studies, which assess the senssitivity of the ISSC to theoretically based group differences, provide additional support for the construct validity of the ISSC.

TEST ADMINISTRATION. The test can be read by the patient or read to the patient by the examiner (with equally valid field test results). It takes approximately 10 minutes to complete. Test administration and scoring instructions are provided. User qualifications are specified including the recommendation that examiners possess training in psychometrics and developmental psychology. Scores are reported in percentile ranks, standard deviation equivalents, and standard scores.

TEST REPORTING. Scoring is very clear and comparative information is provided. The authors suggest a four-level interpretive strategy of qualitative and quantitative information. No information is provided on reporting test results to parents or debriefing children about the test.

TEST AND ITEM BIAS. The theoretical foundation of the ISSC is based on empirical evidence that internalizing symptomatology in children is represented by four basic domains—depression, anxiety, somatic complaints, and social withdrawal. The expert panel used in the development of the test was asked to assure that items selected adequately captured internalizing symptoms and were free of cultural and gender bias. The authors report that research to date supports the use of the ISSC with an English-speaking clientele.

SUMMARY. The ISSC appears to be a useful screening tool for use in educational settings. It is doubtful that in a clinical population the ISSC would add any meaningful data that would not be available through a clinical interview. Nor would the ISSC add measurably to a standard personality battery. As is true of most self-report measures, the ISSC only captures information that the child is willing to share about his or her experiences. Although it is recommended that test examiners have a knowledge of psychometrics, this statement should be clarified and use of the test restricted to individuals competent to report and interpret psychometric data in a meaningful way.

REVIEWER'S REFERENCES

Achenbach, T. M. (1991). *Manual for the Child Behavior Checklist and 1991 Profile.* Burlington, VT: University Associates in Psychiatry.
McClun, L. A. (1997). *An investigation of criterion-related validity and clinical sensitivity of the Internalizing Symptoms Scale for Children.* Unpublished doctoral dissertation, Utah State University, Logan.

[184]
Interpersonal Adjective Scales.

Purpose: "A self-report instrument designed to measure two important dimensions of interpersonal transactions: Dominance and Nurturance."
Population: Ages 18 and up.
Publication Date: 1995.
Acronym: IAS.
Scores, 10: Assured-Dominant, Arrogant-Calculating, Cold-hearted, Aloof-Introverted, Unassured-Submissive, Unassuming-Ingenious, Warm-Agreeable, Gregarious-Extraverted, Dominance, Nurturance.
Administration: Individual or group.
Price Data: Price information available from publisher for introductory kit including manual (143 pages), 25 test booklets, 25 scoring booklets, and 25 glossaries.
Time: (15–20) minutes.
Comments: Separate norms are available for college students and adults; glossary is included to be used by subjects during testing.
Author: Jerry S. Wiggins.
Publisher: Psychological Assessment Resources, Inc.
Cross References: See T5:1288 (2 references).

Review of the Interpersonal Adjective Scales by STEVEN J. LINDNER, Executive Director, Industrial/Organizational Psychologist, The WorkPlace Group, Inc., Morristown, NJ:

The Interpersonal Adjective Scales (IAS) describe the behaviors individuals are likely to manifest when interacting with others. Individuals use an 8-point Likert scale to rate the extent to which 64 adjectives accurately describe them as a person. Based on these ratings, a profile of an individual's interpersonal behaviors is generated. Profiles show individuals' standings on eight different interpersonal scales arranged on a circle having two primary axes: Dominance and Nurturance. The shape of an individual's profile defines his or her general interpersonal style or type, the intensity with which behaviors associated with that type are likely to be manifested, and the likelihood of behaviors associated with each of the remaining interpersonal scales.

The IAS is appropriately used to assess the interpersonal styles of college students and adults. Normative data are provided for both college and adult men and women with separate norms available for each group. Separate norms for both college and adult men and women allow individuals' interpersonal profiles to be interpreted with respect to the most meaningful referent group.

The IAS requires a 10th grade reading level when administered with its accompanying glossary, which defines the 64 adjectives that appear in it. Because of its high reading level, the IAS may not be appropriate for individuals whose primary language is not English. However, the IAS has been translated into Chinese, Dutch, German, Spanish, and Swedish (manual, p. 59). Although no formal training is required for administering and scoring the IAS, professional training in psychology is required for interpreting the IAS. Only general information regarding interpersonal types and the behaviors associated with types are provided in the test's manual. A detailed interpretation of an individual's profile requires professional understanding of interpersonal behaviors, personality, psychopathology, clinical assessment, and for work place applications, "knowledge of laws governing the use of tests for that purpose, along with psychometric concepts such as job relevance" (manual, pp. 7–8).

In clinical settings, IAS profiles should not serve as the only diagnostic measure of psychopathology. Interpretation of an individual's IAS profile should be supported by information obtained from additional assessment instruments, such as personality measures, and family, social, and work histories.

In other settings, such as research or the workplace, the purpose and use of IAS scores may justify its appropriateness as a stand-alone test.

Each of the eight scales of the IAS has strong internal consistency, providing a reliability index that suggests items making up each of these scales are cohesive in measuring the underlying characteristics they have been assigned to measure. Although the scores from the IAS have strong reliability with respect to internal consistency, the test manual provides no information regarding the consistency with which individuals assess themselves over multiple occasions (test-retest reliability) or the extent to which ratings of individuals by independent others agree (interrater reliability).

With respect to validity, the structural arrangement of the IAS interpersonal scales along the dimensions of dominance and nurturance has substantial theoretical and conceptual support. This theoretical and conceptual evidence comes from research conducted by others examining concepts and constructs related to the IAS. In limited cases, the test manual refers directly to studies using the IAS.

Studies directly using the IAS have shown that peer ratings of dominance and nurturance correlate with corresponding facets of the NEO Personality Inventory (Costa & McCrae, 1992). In addition, IAS scales have been found to correspond with self-reported behaviors (Buss & Craik, 1983; Buss, 1984; Buss, Gomes, Higgins, & Lauterbach, 1987) and observed nonverbal behaviors (Gifford & O'Connor, 1987). Convergence between two different measures of similar characteristics suggests that the IAS is measuring the underlying interpersonal constructs it purports to measure. Correspondence between IAS ratings and behaviors also supports the notion that inferences made from individuals' standings on the IAS are descriptive of their actual behaviors.

SUMMARY. The IAS is a useful measure for assessing the interpersonal styles of adults and college students along two important dimensions of interpersonal behavior: dominance and nurturance. Those using the IAS to make clinical assessments need to supplement IAS results with information from other instruments and sources. Those using the IAS for making workplace-related decisions (e.g., employee selection) need to establish the job relatedness of the IAS for the jobs in question. The strong theoretical and conceptual foundation of the IAS, along with its substantial empirical evidence supporting the appropriateness of its structure, makes it a good instrument for describing the behaviors individuals are likely to manifest when interacting with others.

REVIEWER'S REFERENCES

Buss, D. M., & Craik, K. H. (1983). The act frequency approach to personality. *Psychological Review, 90*, 105–126.

Buss, D. M. (1984). Toward a psychology of person-environment (PE) correlation: The role of spouse selection. *Journal of Personality and Social Psychology, 47*, 361–377.

Buss, D. M., Gomes, M., Higgins, D. S., & Lauterbach, K. (1987). Tactics of manipulation. *Journal of Personality and Social Psychology, 52*, 1219–1229.

Gifford, R., & O'Connor, B. (1987). The interpersonal circumplex as a behavioral map. *Journal of Personality and Social Psychology, 52*, 1019–1026.

Costa, P. T., & McCrae, R. R. (1992, June). *Comparability of alternative measures of the five factor model.* Paper presented at the annual meeting of the American Psychological Society, San Diego, CA.

Review of the Interpersonal Adjective Scales by GERALD R. SCHNECK, *Professor of Rehabilitation Counseling, Mankato State University, Mankato, MN:*

The Interpersonal Adjective Scales (IAS) is a "self-report instrument that is designed to measure two important dimensions of interpersonal transactions: Dominance (DOM) and Nurturance (LOV)" (manual, p. 1). The IAS test booklet contains 64 items that consist of adjectives, which are descriptive of interpersonal interactions. The test respondent rates each of the items on an 8-point Likert scale, according to how accurately each adjective describes them as an individual. The accuracy of self-description is rated on the Likert scale, which ranges from 1 (Extremely Inaccurate) to 8 (Extremely Accurate). Scores on the instrument are "ordered around an interpersonal circumplex with Dominance and Nurturance as the primary axes" (manual, p. 1). The IAS also measure the respondents' interpersonal type and the intensity of type.

The majority of the content of the professional manual for the IAS centers its focus on the psychological and clinical assessment of individuals. It also includes a relatively thorough explanation of the development of the instrument, procedures for administration and scoring, normative group descriptions, and scoring tables, as well as developmental and psychometric properties of the instrument.

The author indicates that the IAS is appropriate for use with college students and adults, with separate norms being provided for each. A reading level analysis of the IAS test items and the IAS glossary sheet adjective definitions indicated that a 10th-grade reading ability is necessary to complete the test. It is recommended the test user use care in the administration of the IAS to persons whose native or first language is not English, and who do not have the physical and emotional capabilities for meeting "the normal demands of testing with self-report instrument" (manual, p. 7). Additional care is emphasized if the user will be testing persons with "psychological disorder(s), or who display confusion, psychomotor retardation, distractibility, or extreme emotional distress" (manual, p. 7).

Administration and scoring of the IAS "can be performed by individuals with no formal training in psychology or related fields." However, "(T)raining in the administration and scoring of the IAS should be provided by a qualified psychologist. In a psychiatric setting, for example, an appropriately trained ward staff member can administer the IAS" (manual, p. 7). The test manual does emphasize that "interpretation of the IAS requires professional training in clinical or counseling psychology," and that "interpretation should not be attempted without a firm understanding of theories of personality and psychopathology and a knowledge of the appropriate uses and limitations of self-report inventories" (manual, p. 7). Other professional qualifications may be essential, beyond these basic requirements, depending on the setting and the purpose(s) for which the IAS is utilized. In administering the IAS, the professional manual, a four-page IAS test booklet, a one-page glossary (printed definitions are included on both sides of the page), and a four-page scoring booklet are used. The respondent uses the glossary sheet whenever they are unsure of the meaning of one of the descriptive word items.

The manual states that most respondents will complete the instrument in approximately 10–15 minutes. The test administrator should encourage the respondent to complete all unanswered items, prior to completing scoring of the instrument. The scoring booklet is then used to complete the lengthy and involved manner of scoring the completed instrument. Raw octant scores, average raw octant scores, and T-scores are determined for each of eight personality type categories. T-score values for each of the personality type categories are then combined in order to calculate the Dominance (DOM) and Nurturance (LOV) scores. Angular location, vector length, and vector length T-score are then calculated prior to being plotted on the circumplex, which provides a graphic profile on the instrument for the respondent. A relatively extensive discussion and several case studies are offered and are meant to aid the qualified test user in interpreting the resulting respondent profile that is represented on the circumplex.

Normative samples for the IAS were drawn from several sources, including: (a) participants in the Baltimore Longitudinal Study of Aging (McCrae & Costa, 1989) (N = 344); (b) a volunteer sample that was recruited through churches and civic organizations (N = 377); (c) a sample of volunteer undergraduate college students from the University of British Columbia (Wiggins & Broughton, 1991) (N = 2,988); and (d) an employment sample of applicants for fire fighter positions in a large southwestern city (N = 362). Descriptive information regarding the composition of each normative group was provided and differences among sample groups were analyzed and resulting data were presented.

A very thorough discussion of the theoretical basis for inclusion of self-descriptive adjectives within the instrument, study of items to include and exclude for the final scales, reliability, structural and convergent validity, varying applications to which the instrument might be applied, and the evolution of the IAS circumplex as a behavioral map were presented within the manual. Internal consistency reliability of IAS scales was estimated using Cronbach's alpha; results for the IAS scales ranged from .755 to .865 for the Adult sample and from .733 to .865 for the College student sample. Factor analysis was performed as part of the structural validity analysis of the circumplex model. Correlational analysis of the IAS scales was performed as part of the convergent validity analysis of the instrument. A relatively extensive presentation of data and discussion of its implications was presented for both the structural and convergent validity analyses of the IAS.

The IAS appears to be a well-developed assessment tool based upon a substantial amount of theoretical foundation and research evidence. The professional manual and instrumentation provide a well-organized and thoughtfully written presentation of the information that would be most useful to a professional who wishes to identify and utilize an instrument such as this, within mental health or other therapeutic settings. The IAS presents itself as an important supportive tool within a therapeutic milieu and as a welcome adjunct to other measures of psychopathology or psychological type. In the hands of a well-qualified professional, significant information can be drawn from respondent results on this instrument, to aid in the exploration of those dimensions and issues that have brought the individual to seek out therapeutic assistance.

REVIEWER'S REFERENCES

McCrae, R. R., & Costa, P. T., Jr. (1989). The structure of interpersonal traits: Wiggins' circumplex and the five-factor model. *Journal of Personality and Social Psychology, 56*, 586–595.

Wiggins, J. S., & Broughton, R. (1991). A geometric taxonomy of personality scales. *European Journal of Personality, 5*, 343–365.

[185]
Interpersonal Trust Surveys.

Purpose: Designed to measure an individual's "propensity to trust and to build trust with other people."
Population: Adults.
Publication Dates: 1996–1997.
Acronym: ITS; ITS-O; OTS.
Forms, 3: Interpersonal Trust Survey, Interpersonal Trust Survey—Observer, Organizational Trust Survey.
Scores, 6: Shares Information, Reduces Control, Allows for Mutual Influences, Clarifies Expectations, Meets Others' Expectations, Total.
Administration: Group.
Price Data, 1998: $59.95 per kit including Interpersonal Trust Survey—Observer, Interpersonal Trust Survey, Organizational Trust Survey, scoring software, and facilitator's guide ('96, 172 pages); $5.95 per Interpersonal Trust Survey; $3.95 per Interpersonal Trust Survey-Observer; $3.95 per Organizational Trust Survey.
Time: Administration time not reported.
Comments: Scored for "My Behavior" and "Others' Behavior"; can be used as part of an educational workshop in interpersonal trust or as a tool for counseling; based on the "behavioral model of interpersonal trust"; scoring software available (must be run with Microsoft Excel).
Author: Guy L. DeFuria.
Publisher: Jossey-Bass Pfeiffer.

Review of the Interpersonal Trust Surveys by MARK E. SIBICKY, Associate Professor of Psychology, Marietta College, Marietta, OH:

The Interpersonal Trust Surveys kit contains three surveys that are intended to teach people about their trust-enhancing behaviors. The primary survey is the Interpersonal Trust Survey (ITS). The ITS is a 60-item self-report inventory in which respondents rate items (e.g., "I try to meet my responsibilities") on a 1 (*strongly disagree*) to a 9 (*strongly agree*) Likert scale. The items comprise 10 subscales, 5 of which measure the tendency to engage in trust-enhancing behaviors, and 5 that measure the respondent's expectations that others will use the trust-enhancing behaviors. Scoring the ITS involves computing subscale scores

and then using a scoring matrix to match scores against the average score from a normative database.

Also included in the kit is the Interpersonal Trust Survey—Observer (ITS-O). The ITS-O is similar to the ITS and is designed to accompany it. The ITS-O requires an observer to rate the target person's behavior on the five trust-enhancing behaviors, as well as rate their expectations of the target's behaviors. The purpose is to provide feedback to the target about other people's expectations and to stimulate discussion about interpersonal trust.

The third survey is Organizational Trust Survey (OTS), which is a 50-item Likert-type survey that measures perceptions of interpersonal trust at an organizational level. For example, the OTS can be used between supervisors and workers, upper management and workers, or at the level of the entire organization. Included in the survey kit is a facilitator's guide that contains easy administration and scoring instructions. Also included is material for lectures and guidelines for conducting a workshop on the Interpersonal Trust Surveys.

INTENDED USE AND THEORETICAL BACKGROUND. The stated purpose of the surveys is educational, the goal being to teach respondents how their trust-related behavior is perceived by others and to help respondents establish more trusting relationships. Possible users of the surveys are listed in the guide as being human resource trainers, organizational consultants, counseling psychologists, and researchers. A list of possible applications for the surveys includes business and government organizations, schools, health care settings, family counseling, cultural diversity training, and research.

All three surveys are based on the author's Behavioral Model of Interpersonal Trust (DeFuria, 1996) that proposes that a person's propensity to trust others derives from two sources. The first is a person's tendency to engage in the five types of trust-enhancing behaviors. These behaviors are: sharing relevant information with others, reducing controls, allowing for mutual influence, clarifying mutual expectations, and meeting expectations. The second is a person's expectation that others will use these trust behaviors.

In terms of background information, the facilitator's guide contains numerous research references that demonstrate the importance of interpersonal trust. Unfortunately, the author never explains how this research can be integrated into his Behavioral Model of Interpersonal Trust. Little explanation is given as to why specific constructs of trust were selected over others, or how items were developed to measure these constructs.

Interpersonal trust is an important, yet complex, social and psychological phenomenon. Unfortunately, the facilitator's guide presents a hodgepodge of research and a model of trust that seems both oversimplified and oversold. Furthermore, some readers of the guide may get the false impression that there is more empirical support for the Behavioral Model of Interpersonal Trust than there is. Currently, the only research directly relating to the model or to any of the surveys, is the author's own unpublished doctoral dissertation (i.e., DeFuria, 1996).

Another weakness appears in the section of the guide reporting on the author's own research. Although this section suffers from a lack of clarity, it appears that several important hypotheses were not supported by the results, including some that would have lent support to the construct validity of the surveys.

The facilitator's guide also states that the ITS can be used to teach people of different races and cultures how to increase their trust of each other. Yet no studies in this area have been done. Furthermore, there is no mention of a growing body of research indicating that differences exist between cultures, not only in the tendency to trust others but also in the way cultures define trust (e.g., Yamagishi & Yamagishi, 1994). With so little research having been done, many of the claims made in the facilitator's guide about the application of the surveys is speculative, with no evidence to support them.

PSYCHOMETRIC PROPERTIES. The author reports that a small group of subjects performed content analysis on potential ITS items. This content analysis does not appear to have been in a quantifiable form, as no content validity ratio measures are provided. The normative database of the ITS was established on a relatively small number of subjects ($N = 360$). The author provides little information about these subjects, other than their job titles, thus making it difficult to estimate how the survey will generalize to other populations. The internal reliability (alpha coefficient) for the ITS is reported to be .981 and test-retest reliability estimates were not performed.

No information on the psychometric properties of the ITS-O is provided. According to the facilitator's guide, none is needed because the ITS-O is used to provide ITS users with additional feedback.

The OTS was also standardized on a small sample of apparently homogenous employees ($N = 264$). Again, little information about the representativeness of subjects is provided. Coefficient alphas for the different organizational levels of the OTS are reported as .975, .981, and .989 and again no test-retest estimates are provided.

Both the ITS and OTS show evidence of internal consistency, in other words, significant correlations between average subscale scores and average total test scores. Although internal consistency is certainly a desirable quality, it should not have to bear the weight of test psychometric evidence alone. Other evidence for test validity (e.g., concurrent validity, discriminate validity, confirmatory factor analysis) as well as estimates of test-retest reliability need to be established for the surveys.

SUMMARY. The facilitator's guide states that the Interpersonal Trust Surveys can be used for educational purposes to help people enhance their interpersonal trust behaviors. However, the current validation evidence and theoretical foundation for the surveys are insufficient to justify the stated applications and claims made in the facilitator's guide. The Interpersonal Trust Surveys cannot be recommended, even for the purposes of self-education until a more cogent attempt is made to assess their psychometric properties. The potential for misuse and misinterpretation of survey results is too great.

REVIEWER'S REFERENCES

Yamagishi, T., & Yamagishi, M. (1994). Trust and commitment in the United States and Japan. *Motivation and Emotion, 18,* 129–166.

DeFuria, G. L. (1996). *A behavioral model of interpersonal trust.* Unpublished doctoral dissertation, St. John's University, Springfield, LA.

[186]
Inventory of Drug-Taking Situations.

Purpose: "Designed primarily as an assessment instrument, the IDTS generates an individualized profile detailing situations in which a client has used alcohol and/or other drugs over the past year."

Population: Drug or alcohol users.

Publication Date: 1997.

Acronym: IDTS.

Scores: Situation profiles in three areas: Negative Situations, Positive Situations, Temptation Situations; 8 subscales: Unpleasant Emotions, Physical Discomfort, Pleasant Emotions, Testing Personal Control, Urges/Temptations to Use, Conflict with Others, Social Pressure to Use, Pleasant Times with Others.

Administration: Group.

Price Data, 1998: C$34.95 per user's guide; C$14.95 per 30 questionnaires (specify alcohol or drug); C$39.95 per sample pack including user's guide, and 40 questionnaires (10 alcohol and 30 drug); C$75 per 50 uses of computer-administration software (DOS format).

Time: (15) minutes per each drug class.

Comments: User's guide written in both English (150 pages) and French (72 pages); French version of IDTS have not been scientifically validated; "The IDTS is administered separately for each of the client's major substances of abuse, not once for the client's overall use of drugs."

Authors: Helen M. Annis, Nigel E. Turner, and Sherrilyn M. Sklar.

Publisher: Centre for Addiction and Mental Health [Canada].

Review of the Inventory of Drug-Taking Situations by TONY CELLUCCI, Associate Professor and Director of Psychology Training Clinic, Department of Psychology, Idaho State University, Pocatello, ID:

This 50-item self-report inventory is designed to provide a profile of high-risk situations in which substance abusers have engaged in the last year. For each item, respondents indicate the frequency of their use on a 4-point scale (i.e., *never, rarely, frequently,* and *almost always*). There are separate forms for alcohol versus other drugs although the items are identical. The patient fills out the inventory for each major substance of abuse separately as situational triggers are said to vary by substance. The computerized format allows the clinician to specify alternative time frames. There are eight scales with problem index scores (percents) suggesting severity of drug use in that category of situation. Interpretation is based on an individual's situational profile. The primary use of this instrument would be in treatment planning as well as related substance abuse research.

The Inventory of Drug-Taking Situations (IDTS) was based on research conducted at the Addiction Research Foundation. It builds on past studies of the Inventory of Drinking Situations (IDS; 13:155), which it presumably replaces. The conceptual background to these tools was the early work of Marlatt and Gordon (1985) in deriving a taxonomy of relapse situations. The manual is silent on how IDTS items were selected, although Turner, Annis, and Sklar (1997) stated that the items were derived from previous research on the IDS and the antecedents of drug use reported by patients presenting for treatment. Examination of the IDS-42 items and the items on the newer IDTS indicate considerable revision. It would be necessary to know how items were selected, rewritten, and evaluated to address the issue of content validity.

As with the IDS, five scales reflect personal states (Unpleasant Emotions, Physical Discomfort, Pleasant Emotions, Testing Personal Control, and Urges/Temptations to Use) and three address interpersonal context (Conflict with Others, Social Pressure, and Pleasant Times). There are 10 items for Unpleasant Emotions and Conflict with Others; the remaining scales are limited to 5 items each. Variable scale lengths are reflected in the alpha coefficients for these scales (.92 to .70 for the total sample). Descriptive statistics are provided indicating evidence for a moderate amount of skewness. One limitation is the lack of test-retest data. Two hundred and thirty-one patients did take the IDTS via both computer and paper with a mean interval of 14 days. The scale correlations ranged from .66 to .78. Reading level is not indicated; however, examiners are instructed to assist patients who have trouble reading.

IDTS data are provided for a sample of 669 patients (ages 22 to 70) who presented for substance abuse services. Mean age was 35.3 years with an average of 11.9 years of education. There were 338 subjects presenting for alcohol problems, 226 for cocaine, and 135 related to various other drugs. Only 24% of the sample were female. Normative information is provided, but the user is discouraged from using T scores in lieu of directly interpreting problem index scores. The normative data are presented separately for alcohol versus cocaine patients and include sex and age breakdowns for those scales on which significant demographic differences were found.

The interpretation of the IDTS is more descriptive than normative. The manual provides a reliability estimate (.95) and validity coefficients for a total score; however, one is not calculated nor are any norms for the IDTS total score presented. There is an interesting discussion of the reasons for differentiated versus undifferentiated profiles (e.g., precontemplation stage, awareness of triggers), suggesting it would be informative to know what percentage of profiles might be considered undifferentiated (i.e., little variability between scale scores).

Psychometric research on the IDTS has centered on the factor structure of this and related instruments. A series of confirmatory factor analyses have supported a first-order model consistent with Marlatt's classification. All items significantly loaded on their designated factors with the model accounting for 85% of the covariance. Moreover, previous research suggested a smaller number of second-order factors for which several models were subsequently tested. Turner et al. (1997) reported the best fit was a three-factor solution involving (a) negative situations (unpleasant emotions, physical discomfort, and conflict with others), (b) positive situations (pleasant emotions and pleasant times), and (c) temptations (urges/temptations, testing personal control, and social pressure). Results suggested a consistent factor structure between alcohol and drug samples. Other researchers (Carrigan, Samoluk, & Stewart, 1998; Samoluk, Stewart, Conrod, Pihl, & Dongier, 1998), however, found that on the alcohol-focused IDS-42 the Social Pressure scale contributed more to the positive situations factor than temptations. Samoluk et al. (1998) attribute this discrepancy to respondents on the IDTS rating antecedents to the use of other drugs as well as alcohol, but further research is necessary to clarify if the factor structure differs between ratings of various drugs or the two instruments. A small comparability study between the IDTS alcohol and the IDS-42 is reported in the manual involving 121 alcohol patients; intercorrelations ranged from .76 to .92, but specific scale data were not reported. On the IDTS, the cocaine sample reported heaviest use on the Urges/Temptation items whereas alcohol patients' heaviest use involved situations related to Unpleasant Emotions.

Validity data for the IDTS are based on correlating the scales and a total score with various measures of self-reported consumption, dependence, and social-emotional context. For example, the number of standard drinks consumed on drinking days correlated with IDTS scales (.18 with Social Pressure to .31 with Physical Discomfort). The strongest pattern of correlations between severity of substance abuse and the IDTS involved the Negative Situation scales. There are also moderate negative correlations between using drugs alone and scores on the scales Social Pressure and Pleasant Times with Others. The alcohol dependency scale correlated .41 with the IDTS total score within the alcohol sample, and the DAST correlated .43 with the IDTS total score within

the cocaine sample. Moreover, SCL-90-R depression and somatization scores correlated as expected with Unpleasant Emotions and Physical Discomfort but not with the Pleasant Emotions scale. As with the earlier IDS, however, no evidence is available relating IDTS scores prospectively to relapse situations.

SUMMARY. The IDTS builds on previous research and provides a structured instrument for assessing both the antecedents to using alcohol as well as other drugs. Beyond the earlier development of the IDS, there is little information related regarding content validity. The internal consistency coefficients of the scales are acceptable. Because the authors recommend the interpretation of problem index scores, the benefits of standardized scores are forsaken. Seemingly, a total scale T score would have some value as a measure of substance abuse severity. The psychometric value of using the IDTS rests on its well-studied factor structure. Interestingly, current research is unclear regarding the placement of the social items that may differ for alcohol versus other drugs of abuse. The authors hope that this instrument will allow more systematic investigation and comparison of the situational factors involved in alcohol and other drug abuse. To this end, there is a need for more information on the stability of IDTS scales and especially for data on their predictive validity.

REVIEWER'S REFERENCES

Marlatt, G. A., & Gordon, J. R. (1985). *Relapse prevention: Maintenance strategies in the treatment of addictive behavior.* New York: Guilford Press.

Turner, N. E., Annis, H. M., & Sklar, S. M. (1997). Measurement of antecedents to drug and alcohol use: Psychometric properties of the Inventory of Drug-Taking Situations (IDTS). *Behaviour Research and Therapy, 35,* 465–483.

Carrigan, G., Samoluk, S. B., & Stewart, S. H. (1998). Examination of the short form of the Inventory of Drinking situations (IDS-42) in a young adult university sample. *Behaviour Research and Therapy, 36,* 789–807.

Samoluk, S. B., Stewart, S. H., Conrod, P. J., Pihl, R. O., & Dongier, M. (1998, November). *Psychometric evaluation of the short form of the Inventory of Drinking Situations (IDS-42) among women substance abusers.* Paper presented at the 32nd annual convention of the Association for the Advancement of Behavior Therapy, Washington, DC.

Review of the Inventory of Drug-Taking Situations by GLENN B. GELMAN, Executive Director, Northern Illinois Counseling Associates, P.C., Arlington Heights, IL, and Adjunct Professor of Psychology, Roosevelt University, Schaumburg, IL:

The Inventory of Drug-Taking Situations (IDTS) is a 50-item self-report questionnaire that aspires to profile situations in which a client has used alcohol and/or other drugs over the 12 past months. By rating the frequency of use in various risk situations, a client's "most problematic triggers to alcohol and/or drug use" (user's guide, p. 7) can be assessed. To accomplish this task, a typical 4-point scale is employed (ranging from 1 = *never* to 4 = *almost always*). According to the user's guide, the IDTS can help therapists and clients (a) recognize situations associated with heavy drinking or drug use; (b) anticipate situations in which risk of use may increase; (c) develop individualized treatment and/or aftercare plans; and, (d) develop strategies to cope with high-risk situations.

An interesting feature of the IDTS is that it is actually two questionnaires: one specific to alcohol use, and the other specific to the use of other drugs. Moreover, the IDTS is to be administered separately for each substance the client reports having used, to identify antecedents specific to each drug or drug class used. The 10 drug classes that can be assessed will be familiar to anyone who works with a substance-abusing client population.

The 50 risk situations are, of course, not exhaustive, but they do sample a relevant cross-section of real-life experiences. The client's responses, then, are profiled, based on Alan Marlatt's (Marlatt, 1978, 1979a, 1979b; Marlott & Gordon, 1980, 1985) well-regarded eight-category classification system. The categories are clinically useful because they allow practical inferences to be made about the client's drug-using patterns.

The questionnaires are easy to administer, answer, score, and interpret. Each inventory can be completed in about 15 minutes. Item contents are neither wordy nor written in hard-to-understand double negatives. In fact, its matter-of-fact language gives the IDTS a decided appeal. (Note that this reviewer examined the English version only; therefore these comments are not meant to apply to the French version.) Given its affordable purchase price, its ease of use, and the practical information obtained, this inventory should enjoy wide-spread utilization.

The IDTS can be administered in an individual or group format. It can be used repeatedly, for example, at the intake interview, during the course of treatment to track progress, during an aftercare phase, and to conduct follow-up reviews. Here, concerns such as instrumentation and practice effects are mitigated by the obvious, self-evident purpose for which the IDTS is used in the first place.

However, this strength belies an inherent weakness, namely, the ease with which one may "fake-good" or "fake-bad." To be sure, this is a common problem when assessing any clinical population, let alone one predisposed to minimization and denial. The authors do attempt to address this issue by suggesting that even low elevation profiles can be clinically useful. Still, the "power" of the IDTS would be significantly augmented by adding validity indicators with which to analyze a client's response tendencies.

One subtle problem with the IDTS is its use of the word "abuse." For example, each questionnaire asks the client the following question, "Is this your MAIN substance of abuse? [*sic*]" The use of this phrasing is presumptuous and implies, a priori, that the client agrees that his or her pattern of use can be labeled as such. One imagines attempting to administer the IDTS in a forensic case, or to an employer-referred individual. The client will likely decline to comply with this inventory at the outset, lest he or she admit to the presence of a problem before the assessment is even completed.

The IDTS may be completed using hand-scoring or computerized formats. This reviewer examined only the hand-scoring materials; however, it should be noted that the computerized version requires an IBM-compatible computer and a DOS format. For this instrument to gain wider user acceptance, requisite upgrades are clearly indicated. This seems especially the case because in the (otherwise thorough) user's guide, instructions for the would-be hand-scorer appear to have been omitted. Scoring the IDTS is actually quite simple, once one deciphers the methodology, but the steps should be articulated. Another pitfall is that the names of the eight categories, and their respective computation formulas, are printed right on the hand-scoring form that is completed by the client. Although this design allows for quick scoring, it seems unduly distracting and can potentially bias the client's answers.

Transferring the Problem Index Scores to the Client Profile is a simple matter. Results, represented by a bar-graph, are immediately interpretable. From a clinical perspective, reviewing the bar graph with the client could well serve to enlighten, clarify, and anticipate risky situations, and engender a collaborative spirit of recovery.

SUMMARY. The IDTS does do what it aims to do. Its elegance lies in its simplicity. It is easy to understand, and easy to administer, answer, score, and interpret. Several of the problems identified by this reviewer seem readily resolvable.

Even with its present limitations, the IDTS offers a useful clinical and research tool for identifying situations that may place an individual at risk.

REVIEWER'S REFERENCES

Marlatt, G. A. (1978). Craving for alcohol, loss of control and relapse: A cognitive-behavioral analysis. In P. E. Nathan, G. A. Marlatt, & T. Loberg (Eds.), *Alcoholism: New directions in behavioral research and treatment* (pp. 271–314). New York: Plenum.

Marlatt, G. A. (1979a). Alcohol use and problem drinking: A cognitive-behavioral analysis. In P. C. Kendall & S. D. Hollon (Eds.), *Cognitive-behavioral interventions: Theory, research and procedures* (pp. 319–355). New York: Academic Press.

Marlatt, G. A. (1979b). A cognitive-behavioral model of the relapse process. In N. A. Krasnegor (Ed.), *Behavioral analysis and treatment of substance abuse.* (National Institute on Drug Abuse Research Monograph, 25. Pp. 191–200). Rockville, MD.

Marlatt, G. A., & Gordon, J. R. (1980). Determinants of relapse: Implications for the maintenance of behavior change. In P. O. Davidson & S. M. Davidson (Eds.), *Behavioral medicine: Changing health lifestyles* (pp. 410–452). New York: Brunner-Mazel.

Marlatt, G. A., & Gordon, J. R. (1985). *Relapse prevention: Maintenance strategies in the treatment of addictive behaviors.* New York: Guilford.

[187]
Jackson Vocational Interest Survey [1995 Revision].

Purpose: Designed "to measure career interest with psychometric precision and to provide comprehensive information for educational and career planning."
Population: High school and above.
Publication Dates: 1977–1997.
Acronym: JVIS.
Scores, 50: 34 Basic Interest Scales (Creative Arts, Performing Arts, Mathematics, Physical Science, Engineering, Life Science, Social Science, Adventure, Nature-Agriculture, Skilled Trades, Personal Service, Family Activity, Medical Service, Dominant Leadership, Job Security, Stamina, Accountability, Teaching, Social Service, Elementary Education, Finance, Business, Office Work, Sales, Supervision, Human Relations Management, Law, Professional Advising, Author-Journalism, Academic Achievement, Technical Writing, Independence, Planfulness, Interpersonal, Confidence); 10 General Occupational Themes (Expressive, Logical, Inquiring, Practical, Assertive, Socialized, Helping, Conventional, Enterprising, Communicative); 3 Administrative Indices (Unscorable Responses, Response Consistency Index, Infrequency Index); Academic Satisfaction; Similarity to College Students; Similarity to Occupational Classifications.
Administration: Group.
Price Data, 1999: $67 per examination kit including one each manual ('77, 107 pages), JVIS Applications Handbook ('93, 92 pages), JVIS Occupations Guide ('95, 82 pages), hand-scorable answer sheet, profile sheet, and machine-scorable answer sheet for extended report; $18 per test manual; $32.95 per JVIS Applications Handbook; $20.95 per JVIS Occupations Guide; $28–$32 (depending on volume) per 25 test booklets; $9–$11 (depending on volume) per 25 hand-scorable answer sheets; $9–$11 (depending on volume) per 25 profile sheets; $73–$83 (depending on volume) per 10 machine-scorable answer sheets for extended reports; $42–$48 (depending on volume) per 10 machine-scorable answer sheets for basic reports; $99 per software package including disks, software manual for Windows, test manual, and 10 coupons for computer reports.
Foreign Language Editions: Available in French (booklets and extended reports) and Spanish (booklets only).
Time: (45–60) minutes.
Authors: Douglas N. Jackson and Marc Verhoeve (applications handbook).
Publisher: Sigma Assessment Systems, Inc., Research Psychologists Press Division.
Cross References: See T5:1334 (5 references) and T4:1297 (1 reference); for reviews by Douglas T. Brown and John W. Shepard of an earlier edition, see 10:158 (1 reference); for reviews by Charles Davidshofer and Ruth G. Thomas, see 9:542; see T3:1204 (1 reference).

Review of the Jackson Vocational Interest Survey [1995 Revision] by MICHAEL J. ROSZKOWSKI, Director, Institutional Research, La Salle University, Philadelphia, PA:

The Jackson Vocational Interest Survey (JVIS) is presented as an interest inventory intended to help high school students, college students, and adults make educational and vocational decisions, including ones involving midlife career transitions. The instrument consists of 289 pairs of statements in a forced-choice response format that requires the respondent to indicate a preference for one member of each pair. The items form 34 Basic Interest scales consisting of 17 items per scale. Twenty-seven of the Basic Interest scales measure interest in work roles and the remaining seven Basic Interest scales assess interest in work styles. Roles are more closely associated with an occupation or class of occupations (e.g., the Engineering scale) whereas styles involve preference for working in an environment that allows for the type of behavior in the title of the scale to be expressed (e.g., Independence scale). The 34 Basic Interest scales can be further summarized into 10 more global scales called General Occupational Themes, which are similar to Holland's typology of 6 work themes. Jackson believes that 10 rather than 6 themes emerge in factor analyses of the JVIS due to the larger number of interest scales and the greater independence between scales.

The JVIS can be either hand scored or machine scored. For hand scoring one uses the

JVIS answer sheet, which is arranged in a 289-item matrix with 17 pairs across and 17 pairs down. The JVIS can be hand scored easily by counting the number of A responses selected in each row of the first 17 scales and the number of B responses selected in the columns of the last 17 scales. Hand scoring results in a profile of only the Basic Interest scales. The computer-scored report is much more extensive. In addition to the Basic Interest scales, it includes scores on the General Occupation Themes, an Academic Satisfaction score, and measures of response quality. The nature of these scores is discussed in a narrative portion of the report.

The original norms for the JVIS were based on high school and college students drawn from three sources: 16 U.S. and Canadian colleges (n = 1,473), 12th grade students admitted to Pennsylvania State University (n = 1,907), and students from 28 high schools in Ontario, Canada (n = 4,430). These three groups were given equal weight in the development of a single set of norms. A subset of 1,000 subjects (500 males and 500 females) was identified that matched the larger sample with respect to the mean scores and related standard deviations. The stated purpose of this smaller sample is further normative work.

The manual, with a copyright date of 1997, does not reflect the recent modifications that have been made to the JVIS. A form titled "Your Guide to the New JVIS Report" indicates that the JVIS has been restandardized on a group of 2,500 high-school students and young adults, using data collected in 1994/1995. The Extended Report for the JVIS now presents the results in terms of percentile scores rather than standard scores. For the Basic Interest scales, percentiles relative to males, females, and a combined male-female group are reported, but only the percentiles relative to the combined norm group are plotted on a bar graph. On the General Occupational Themes, male percentiles and female percentiles are available, with sex-appropriate percentiles also being presented on a bar graph. Also reported is an Academic Satisfaction percentile score, previously called the Academic Orientation score, that indicates how strongly the respondent's interests match those of students who are satisfied in an academic environment.

The quality of an individual's responses can be assessed by means of two administrative indices: Response Consistency and the Infrequency Index. The Response Consistency Index (formerly called the Reliability Index) checks whether the answers are consistent when the questionnaire is split into two halves. It, too, is now reported as a percentile. Previously, it was reported as a correlation coefficient. The Infrequency Index examines responses to the 45 least popular items on the JVIS. In most instances, a high score on the infrequency index simply indicates unusual interests, but in combination with a Low Response consistency score, it could be indicative of careless-responding. If the administrative indices are out of normal range, a diagnostic message appears on the report.

The reliability of the JVIS is discussed in terms of internal consistency and temporal stability, examining the (a) individual Basic Scales, (b) General Occupational Themes, and (c) profiles (configuration of scores). The Internal consistency analysis of the individual Basic Interest Scales, based on a sample of high school students (n = 1,573), resulted in coefficients theta that ranged from .70 to .91, with a median of .82. (Theta was used instead of Cronbach's alpha because the latter may underestimate the reliability of scales with heterogeneous items.) The internal consistency reliability of profiles of Basic Interest was determined on a sample of high school students (n = 1,706) using a method that considers the person-reliability of each individual in the sample. Because this procedure was developed by Jackson and may not be familiar, a brief description is provided. For each person, the item scores on each of the Basic scales were ranked from 1 to 17. Next, the items with odd-numbered ranks from the 34 Basic scales were summed together into a score (X) and the items with the even-numbered ranks were totaled into another score (Y). A correlation was then computed between these two sum scores (i.e., the odd-ranked items with the even-ranked items) and corrected using the Spearman-Brown formula. The frequency distribution of the reliability coefficients, as depicted in the manual, is symmetrical in shape but with a distinct negative skew. The average person reliability is about .80.

Temporal stability evidence comes from three samples. The one-week test-retest of the individual Basic Interest scales in a sample of university students (n = 172) ranged from .73 to .91, with a median of .84; the profile had a median reliability of .88. In another sample of university students (n = 54), the Basic Interest scales showed a median one-week test-retest reliability of .87 (range: 59 to .96) and the profile had a mean stability coefficient of .94. In this same sample, the stability of the 10 General Occupational Themes ranged from .82 to .92 with a median of .89, and the stability of the profile based on the General Occupational Themes had a mean reliability of .94. Long-term profile stability of the Basic Interest scales was investigated in a sample of 102 medical applicants who first took the JVIS as part of the application process and then 6 months later as medical students; the correlation between the profiles based on Basic Interest scales was .84.

The reported reliability data are impressive, but the available data were not exploited fully for estimates of reliability. The internal consistency measures of reliability could have been computed on all samples. This would be valuable information given that the internal consistency evidence is derived from high school students, whereas the test-retest data are based on college students.

The JVIS was developed with a concern for construct validity. Evidence presented to support the validity of the JVIS consists of a demonstration of (a) the meaningfulness of the scales to the layperson, (b) low redundancy between scales, (c) convergent and discriminant validity of individual scales as well as profiles, and (d) substantive and meaningful differences in scale scores among different occupations. A more detailed review of this evidence follows.

A number of studies are reported demonstrating the construct validity of the JVIS. Three studies considered the meaningfulness of the JVIS to subjects who did not possess formal training in the study of occupations. In the first study, high school students (n = 359) expressed their global ratings of interest, on a 7-point scale, for each of the dimensions covered in the Basic Interest scales, which were identified only by name and a simple description. These single-item ratings were correlated with the subjects' actual scores on the Basic Interest scales. The resultant correlations were moderate in magnitude with a median of .38 for females and .33 for males; but in most instances, the global self-rating had its highest correlation with the targeted JVIS scale. The second study demonstrated that people could estimate the pattern of interests typical of a particular job simply by having the name of the occupation or a brief description of it. Undergraduates (n = 100) rated six occupations regarding the level of interest

members of these occupations would have on the 34 Basic Interest scales. Not only was there considerable congruence in the judges' inferences, but the inferences correlated with the actual interests shown by members of the five occupations who were administered the JVIS. In the third study, undergraduate students obtained a median validity coefficient of .56 when judging the Basic Interest scores of jobs representing each of the 32 job clusters in the Dictionary of Occupational Titles. Jackson feels that these results suggest that the Basic Interest scales are meaningful to people, even if they are not trained in psychology.

The nature of the interrelationship between the scales of the JVIS is the focus of a number of studies discussed in the manual. The 34 Basic Interest scales are shown to be fairly independent of each other, having average interscale correlations of only .28 among males and .24 among females. However, the first 17 Basic Interest scales form one cluster and the second 17 Basic Interest scales form another cluster because the first half of the JVIS consists of science-related scales whereas the second half contains business-related scales. There is a slight negative correlation between the two sets that is due to the forced-choice format. The Basic Interest scales can be reduced to no less than 10 orthogonal factors (i.e., the General Occupational Themes). The Basic Interest scales are also different from scholastic aptitude. Correlations between the JVIS scales and the Scholastic Aptitude Test in a sample of 2,154 students starting Penn State University were generally extremely small, with certain understandable exceptions. As would be expected, SAT Quantitative scores were correlated with the Mathematics (.37), Engineering (.28), and Physical Science (.24) scales. Likewise, it is logical that the Verbal portion of the SAT correlated with the Author-Journalism scale (.21) and Technical Writing scale (.20). A stepwise discriminant analysis using SAT scores and the JVIS to predict the area of study selected by college freshmen found that 23 variables entered the prediction equation for males and 20 variables entered for females, suggesting that the Basic Interest scales of the JVIS were contributing unique information. This study may also be seen as evidence for criterion-related validity.

A multitrait-multimethod analysis of the construct validity of the JVIS was conducted in an experiment on volunteering for experiments. Willingness to participate in the 51 hypothetical experiments and scores on 29 JVIS scales were factor analyzed, with 29 factors being extracted. The experiments and the JVIS scales defined the same interest factors. For example, Factor 3 was defined by willingness to participate in an experiment on Mental Arithmetic, an experiment on Coaching Effects on Mathematics, and the JVIS Mathematics Basic scale.

The most impressive study discussed in the manual involved subjects (Penn State freshmen) administered both the JVIS and the Strong Vocational Interest Blank (SVIB). The correlation matrix between the two instruments was used to estimate JVIS profiles for the 278 occupations originally defined in terms of their SVIB scores. The JVIS profile of these occupations conformed with expectations about which interest would be high and low for the occupations. For instance, accountants have the highest scores on Office Work, Finance, Business, and Planfulness. JVIS scores of members of certain occupations actually tested with this instrument (i.e., chemists, guidance counselors, teachers, ministers and real estate agents) support the results obtained using the SVIB to predict JVIS occupational profiles.

The forced-choice format of the JVIS has been highlighted as one of its strong points by its author. According to Jackson, the items in each dyad were equated for popularity and unlike Likert response formats, the forced-choice format in the JVIS is not subject to the response bias that accounts for as much as a third of the variance in scales using a like-dislike format. But Juni and Koenig (1982) contend that the forced-choice format of the JVIS leads to a number of artifacts, and may be troublesome to some respondents. To begin with, these investigators contend that the format invites a response bias, so that a person will consistently pick either the A or B option. Furthermore, it is claimed that the A options in each pair reflect scientific or intellectual pursuits whereas the B options are affective in nature. Certain combinations are more probable so that it is more likely to have an "adventurous mathematician" than a "mathematics teacher." The format may be irritating to some people because the choice in some pairs is between unrelated activities. Undeniably, the forced-choice format is more economical because it reduces by half the number of statements to be rated. The possible response bias

does not seem to occur very often, given the data presented by Jackson, and the Administrative indices will allow one to determine if it does happen.

SUMMARY. The JVIS was developed using multivariate statistical procedures. Jackson considers the following as the JVIS's unique features: (a) substantive definitions of the dimensions, (b) internal consistency of the dimensions, (c) low redundancy between dimensions, and (d) minimum response bias. Evidence presented in the manual supports these claims. The decision to report scores in the revised computer-generated report in terms of percentiles rather than standard scores was probably made because such scores are easier for the lay person to understand, at least on a superficial level. However, percentile scores have severe limitations if one wishes to conduct research, because they should not be averaged. The JVIS is not a brief instrument so its completion requires a serious commitment to the task. That, along with its focus on professional jobs, makes the instrument most appropriate for the serious student considering college studies. The manual is outdated given the revisions in the norms and report format.

REVIEWER'S REFERENCE
Juni, S., & Koenig, E. J. (1982). Contingency validity as a requirement in forced-choice item construction: A critique of the Jackson Vocational Interest Survey. *Measurement & Evaluation in Guidance, 14*, 202–207.

Review of the Jackson Vocational Interest Survey by EUGENE P. SHEEHAN, Professor of Psychology, University of Northern Colorado, Greeley, CO:

The Jackson Vocational interest Survey (JVIS) provides a measure of vocational interest for use in career counseling and decision making. The instrument consists of 289 pairs of statements describing specific occupational activities, such as "servicing customers' appliances." Respondents select the statement that best reflects their interests. A forced-choice format discourages neutral responding. The 289 item-pairs factor into 34 scales, each comprising 17 items. The scales are conceptualized into two kinds: 28 work role and 7 work style scales. Work role scales are associated with either a specific occupation or class of occupations, such as Social Science, Skilled Trades, Elementary Education, Law, and Human Relations Management. Work style scales indicate a preference for different kinds of work-related behaviors. Independence, for example, refers to a preference for autonomy in the workplace. A high score on Interpersonal Confidence indicates a disposition to work in environments containing the opportunity to work self-assuredly with others. Thus, the JVIS is comprehensive in breadth. Additionally, in contrast to other vocational guidance instruments, the JVIS is designed to encourage exploration of broad career interest areas, rather than specific occupations.

The JVIS was designed for use with several populations and with several purposes. The most common populations are college and high school students. The manual also suggests the JVIS can be used for research into vocational interests and work classification. Although the vocabulary is at the seventh grade level, several of the items seem more complex or abstract than a seventh grade level.

The JVIS can be scored either by hand or by computer. Although hand scoring is relatively easy to accomplish, the computer-scores version is much more useful as it provides an extended report containing much individualized information, including a profile and analysis of scores on the basic interest scales, scores on the general occupational themes, similarity to college students and occupational classifications, and where to go next in career exploration. The computer-scored version also provides an individual index of reliability for the respondent completing the instrument. Users can also obtain a JVIS Applications Handbook. The user's guide contains further information on career development, the JVIS (scales, themes, clusters), and various career profiles for use in career guidance.

The manual contains a comprehensive amount of psychometric information on the JVIS. Indeed, the manual is not for the psychometrically unsophisticated. It provides a detailed description of the test construction procedures, which conform to the highest standards of test development. This description includes information on item selection procedures, preliminary factor analysis, and item analyses. Not only does the manual describe the procedures used, it also provides the rationale for these procedures and, occasionally, the advantages of the approach employed over alternative approaches. For example, there is a discussion of the advantages of the use of basic scales over empirical item keying. The JVIS was developed using the national/empirical approach. This approach involved the identification of vocational interest areas and then composing items to assess these dimensions.

The psychometric properties of the JVIS are thoroughly researched. The manual, for example, contains information on four different types of reliability. In general, the psychometric properties of the JVIS are impressive. Internal consistency coefficients of the scales are high (median .82), as are estimates of test-retest reliability (one-week interval) (median .84). Studies also demonstrate the reliability of JVIS profiles to be more than adequate. Unfortunately, a few of these reliability studies used small numbers of subjects. Reliabilities based on larger numbers would be useful. Although the strategies used to norm the JVIS are appropriate, the size of the normative sample should be larger and more geographically dispersed.

Validity studies on the JVIS demonstrate that, for the limited number of occupational groups tested, appropriate clusters of JVIS scales are highly ranked. For example, a group of elementary teachers had their high scores on the Teaching, Elementary Education, and Social Science scales. Thus, different but appropriate scales were highly ranked by different occupational groups. Additionally, the individual items, scales, occupational clusters, and occupational themes all demonstrate good face validity as indicators of the ability of the JVIS to measure an individual's career interests. However, more extensive and systematic data on predictive and concurrent validity are necessary.

SUMMARY. The JVIS is an interesting instrument designed to assess the vocational interests and work preferences of adolescents and college students. The instrument has an impressive developmental background and solid psychometric support, although more extensive information on predictive and concurrent validity is needed. Certainly, the JVIS is a very functional tool for use in vocational guidance. This is especially the case given the large amount of useful information produced in the computerized printout's extended report. This report will provide those users of the JVIS in the career guidance field with much individual data for use in discussions with their clients. Overall, the JVIS compares well with its competitors.

[188]
The Jesness Inventory.
Purpose: Designed to measure "several relevant personality dimensions."
Population: Ages 8 and older.
Publication Dates: 1962–1996.
Acronym: JI.
Scores, 22: Conventional Scales (Social Maladjustment, Value Orientation, Immaturity, Autism, Alien-

ation, Manifest Aggression, Withdrawal-Depression, Social Anxiety, Repression, Denial, Asocial Index), Validity Scales (Lie, Random Response), Subtype Classification (Undersocialized—Active, Undersocialized—Passive, Immature Conformist/Conformist, Cultural Conformist/Group-Oriented, Manipulator/Pragmatist, Neurotic—Acting-out/Autonomy-Oriented, Neurotic—Anxious/Introspective, Situational/Inhibited, Cultural Identifier/Adaptive).

Administration: Individual or group.

Price Data, 1999: $70 per complete kit including manual, 10 test booklets, and 25 QuikScore™ forms; $13 per 10 reusable test booklets (specify English, Spanish or French-Canadian); $27 per 25 QuikScore™ forms (specify English or Spanish); $40 per manual; $42 per specimen set including manual, 1 test booklet, and 3 QuikScore™ forms; $75 per set of scoring templates and computer program for Windows.

Foreign Language Edition: Spanish and French-Canadian forms available.

Time: Administration time not reported.

Comments: Self-report; "Originally developed for use in the assessment and classification of male delinquent youths."

Author: Carl F. Jesness.

Publisher: Multi-Health Systems, Inc.

Cross References: See T5:1341 (3 references) and T3:1209 (9 references); for a review by Dorcas Susan Butt of an earlier edition, see 8:595 (14 references); see also T2:1249 (5 references); for a review by Sheldon A. Weintraub of the Youth Edition of the earlier edition, see 7:94 (10 references); see also P:133 (3 references).

Review of The Jesness Inventory by ROBERT M. GUION, Distinguished University Professor Emeritus, Bowling Green State University, Bowling Green, OH:

This 155-item inventory was initially developed for the assessment of "youth at risk," whether delinquents or those with psychological or behavioral problems; it is also suggested for adults. It was developed in recognition of the extensive individual differences among a less-than-homogeneous group known as delinquent. For respondents with at least a fourth grade reading level, it provides both a taxonomy of personality variables and a classification scheme, offering scores on 11 personality scales and 9 classification scales. It is an aid, not a substitute, for judgment; although administering and scoring the inventory is rather simple, interpretation of the scores requires advanced education and relevant experience. The emphasis in this review is on the basic personality scales.

The personality scales stem from an initial 250-item pool. Three of them (Social Maladjustment, Value Orientation, and Immaturity) were developed by item analyses comparing a priori groups. Seven scales resulted from cluster analysis. The 11th scale (Asocial Index) is a weighted composite of the other scales based on discriminant function analysis, distinguishing between offenders and nonoffenders. According to the manual, no item appears on more than one scale unless scored in opposite directions, but that assertion needs qualifying: An item scored for one of the seven cluster analytic scales is not scored in the same direction on any of the other six cluster scales. Several items are scored for a cluster scale and for two of the first three scales. Overlapping items produces some redundancy. For example, the 65-item Social Maladjustment scale and the 26-item Alienation scale have 14 items in common, and the correlation between them is .66. Correction for attenuation using the reported alpha coefficients raises the correlation estimate to .81—not quite totally redundant. Using the less friendly test-retest reliabilities, however, gives a corrected coefficient of .99. The median intercorrelation was lower, .38, but alpha coefficients were lower than one would wish (especially for the Immaturity scale, where alpha = .43) with several in the .60s. Coefficients reported for retesting after a year were lower still, although the likelihood that attitudes of delinquents would fluctuate suggested that moderate retest reliabilities simply reflect scale sensitivity. All things considered, several scales appear to be redundant, some do not. It seems likely that all useful variance could be expressed in not more than three factors—one very large factor, a secondary one combining Immaturity and Repression, and perhaps a third one defined mainly by the Social Anxiety scale. Is this a serious problem? Perhaps not. The manual emphasizes frequently that the inventory is to be an aid in assessment, not the sole basis. Such a caveat suggests that scores on individual scales are not considered definitive but can guide the search for other relevant information about individual respondents. For such screening, the reliabilities are probably adequate for most of the 11 scales, and there may be enough unique meaning in the scores to be useful in practice. The scales should not, however, be considered a scientifically useful taxonomy of personality variables.

The normative data samples, totaling more than 3,000 cases, included both male and female delinquents and nondelinquents. Ages ranged from 8 to 19, although there were no female delinquents under age 12. Scores of nondelinquents were converted to "T-scores" for the various age and sex groupings in the nondelinquent samples, and these are the reported norms. (The manual does not say whether these are normalized T-scores or linear transformations.) Data from these samples were collected in 1961 and 1962. Have there been enough social changes in the more than three decades since then to change the norms? Many modal attitudes have changed, including attitudes toward many kinds of behavior. Are girls under 12 still less likely than boys to be committed as delinquent? Is behavior once considered a form of delinquency now considered ordinary? Does it now require more serious social transgressions to be classed as delinquent? Do item responses mean now the same things they meant nearly 40 years ago? It seems to me that renorming is needed, and to whatever extent the reliability estimates come from these same data, they should be brought up to date as well.

Validity evidence, primarily construct validity, includes more recent studies. Many of these studies involve correlations with other measures. I would have liked to have seen more argument presented about why certain correlations are deemed to support the interpretations intended for scores from the various scales—not because of doubts but because the nature of the author's arguments would help clarify the sometimes murky nature of the intended constructs. It is nice to have sections of a test manual giving information in support of construct validity, but they are not very meaningful if the nature of the construct has not been well defined. For some of these scales, the nature of constructs is discernible but not wholly clear. For example, "Value Orientation" is (or "reflects") a "tendency to share attitudes characteristic of individuals of low socioeconomic status" (manual, p. 5). A statement of why a negative correlation with the CPI Tolerance scale, or a positive correlation with the MMPI Pt scale, supports such an inference would clarify the construct as the author has intended it. Other validity information seems more pragmatic. Data are presented showing that scores can distinguish delinquents from nondelinquents or first time from repeat offenders. However, prediction of delinquency is not very successful (because of low base rates, according to the manual).

SUMMARY. The Jesness Inventory was developed with a lot of thought and care. I do not doubt its usefulness in the practical setting of screening young people (or even adults) who may have violated laws—when such screening is done by well-trained people with access to supplementary information. I am concerned, however, about its age. Like far too many other personality measures, there is a tendency to assume that an instrument developed in one zeitgeist will retain all of its desirable characteristics as the zeitgeist changes—and maybe even discard any undesirable characteristics over time. Such assumptions need to be challenged, and developers of the instruments need to maintain a chronological history of various kinds of item statistics and evidences of scale validities. In the case of the Jesness Inventory, item revisions in 1972 were to make the inventory useful for adults and females. Further revision of one key scale (Social Maladjustment) was done in 1986. The reader is not told what effect these changes had on norms, reliabilities, or validities. Ten years after the most recent item changes the current manual was published—but it reflects little new information in its list of references. There may have been little or no psychometric reason to revise anything said about the inventory since 1972, but I see no sign that such an assumption has been investigated. This concern, of course, applies equally well to nearly all personality measures developed during the flurry of test development of the 1950s and 1960s.

Review of the Jesness Inventory by SUSANA URBINA, Professor of Psychology, University of North Florida, Jacksonville, FL:

BACKGROUND INFORMATION. The Jesness Inventory (JI) was developed, in the early 1960s, as part of a long-term project aimed at evaluating the effectiveness of a treatment program for young male delinquents. Its author, Carl F. Jesness, wanted a multidimensional instrument that could be used with subjects as young as 8 years of age and that would be helpful in predicting delinquency and assessing change. At the time the JI was developed, there were no other self-report inventories specifically designed for adolescents, let alone deviant adolescents. Thus, the JI was rightly seen by an earlier reviewer as "a useful addition to measurement in the study and treatment of young offenders" (Butt, 1978, p. 876).

Since its introduction, the JI has undergone minor revisions that purportedly make it appropriate for use with adults and with females, and there has been some refinement of two of its scales, but it has otherwise remained essentially unchanged. The inventory is being reviewed now because its manual has been revised to consolidate information spread over several publications and to incorporate more recent research. Therefore, this review will simply describe the basic components of the JI and outline its strengths and weaknesses from a contemporary perspective. Prospective users are urged to consult earlier *Mental Measurements Yearbooks* and Mooney's comprehensive review (1984) for additional details on the JI.

It is worth noting that since the 1960s, several instruments that could be used for the same population and purposes for which the JI was intended have been published. Among these are: the Basic Personality Inventory (BPI; T5:256), the Millon Adolescent Clinical Inventory (MACI; T5:1685), the Minnesota Multiphasic Personality Inventory—Adolescent (MMPI-A; T5: 1698), and the Personality Inventory for Youth (PIY; T5:1963), all of which attempt to assess maladaptive tendencies in adolescents. An instrument for adult male offenders, the Carlson Psychological Survey (CPS; T5: 427), has also been published. Thus, test users in the field can now choose the most suitable instrument(s) for their purposes from among several.

GENERAL DESCRIPTION. The JI comprises 155 true/false items that require approximately 30 minutes to complete and at least a fourth-grade reading level. Scoring can be done directly from the Quikscore™ answer form or by computer. The inventory can also be administered by computer and a computer-generated narrative report is available as well.

Normative samples for the JI consisted of 970 delinquent and 1,075 nondelinquent males between the ages of 8 and 18 as well as 450 delinquent females, aged 12 to 19, and 811 nondelinquent females between the ages of 8 and 18. Data were collected in California in 1961 and 1962. The nondelinquent samples, mostly lower class, came from 10 public schools and, according to Jesness, contained at least some delinquents.

Two distinct sets of results can be gathered from the JI. One set consists of 11 "conventional" personality scales and the other of nine "I-level" scales used to classify respondents. The personality scales aim to differentiate delinquents from nondelinquents and to describe respondents. *T*-score norm comparisons on these scales are based on the nondelinquent samples, separated by sex and age level. Three of the personality scales—Social Maladjustment (SM), Value Orientation (VO), and Immaturity (Imm)—have items that were selected based on whether they differentiated, respectively, (a) delinquents from nondelinquents, (b) youths from different social class groups, and (c) youths from different age groups. Seven other personality scales, developed through cluster analyses, assess maladaptive traits, such as Alienation, Manifest Aggression, and Withdrawal-Depression. The remaining personality scale score, an "Asocial Index" (AI) derived through discriminant function analysis, combines information from eight of the other personality scales and is regarded as the best JI measure of one's generalized tendency to transgress social rules.

Comprising the second set of JI results are nine "I-level" scales that classify respondents into types such as "Unsocialized Aggressive" or "Immature Conformist." Although the "I" in "I-level" is never spelled out in the manual, it apparently refers to interpersonal maturity level as postulated in M.Q. Warren's theory (cited in the manual, pp. 33-35), which was the basis for the JI typology. The I-level scales were constructed from the responses of 206 delinquents classified as "ideal" representatives of their types. Norms for each scale were then derived from a different sample of 2,000 delinquent males. The rules for classifying test takers into types were empirically determined based on combinations of scores on the nine scales. The goal of these scales is to help in differential treatment planning for those already identified as delinquents.

An evaluation of response sets that might invalidate results is particularly relevant for the population targeted by the JI. Yet, the inventory provides only two validity scales—of five items each—designed to assess random responding and tendency to "fake good." These scales, described as "experimental," are offered only with the JI scoring software and need empirical validation. Pinsoneault (1998), however, has recently developed two promising response inconsistency scales to detect random and acquiescent response sets on the JI.

EVALUATION OF STRENGTHS AND WEAKNESSES. It is easy to understand why, according to Pinkerman, Haynes, and Keiser (as cited by Pinsoneault, 1998), the JI is the second most widely used personality inventory in juvenile court clinics in the U.S. The inventory grew out of the author's extensive experience with delinquent youths and of his knowledge of the theoretical and empirical literature in the field. The JI has gathered a solid research base spanning thee decades and several countries (75 PsycINFO entries from 1967 to 1998). Its brevity, low reading level requirement, and normative base of (male) delinquents as young as 8 years make it uniquely suitable for juvenile forensic settings. In addition, validity data on the Asocial Index show that the JI can certainly contribute to identifying or predicting delinquency in young males. The remaining scales and subtype classification system provide a good source of hypotheses for individual assessment and research. Descriptions of typical attitudes, behavior, background variables, and treatment recommendations provided in the manual for each JI type should prove helpful to counselors and of heuristic value.

In spite of its potential usefulness, there are several areas in which the JI could be improved. First, and most important, is the issue of its applicability to groups other than adolescent male delinquents, which is questionable in light of the way the JI was developed. Adult norms are altogether lacking and norms for delinquent females are only available for ages 12 to 19. In addition, the JI norms now date back almost 40 years. Another matter, important in view of the goals of the inventory, is the generally low stability (ranging from coefficients of .40 to .79) of the personality scales over an 8-month interval, and the relatively low rate of subtype classification agreement (52%) over the same period. Furthermore, the manual has a number of errors that could easily be corrected. Among the more significant of these are the sketchy fashion in which validity data are provided, the allusion to an important table (4.2) that is not presented (manual, p. 27), and discrepancies between the text and the tables.

SUMMARY. The JI may prove clinically useful in the assessment of young delinquent males, especially if used in conjunction with other tools. For young female delinquents, clinical use is not as well supported and for adult offenders, it is not supported at all. Updating and extension of the JI norms, as well as further investigation of its stability and of its validity for females and adults, would be highly desirable.

REVIEWER'S REFERENCES

Butt, D. S. (1978). [Review of the Jesness Inventory.] In O. K. Buros (Ed.), *The eighth mental measurements yearbook* (pp. 876–878). Highland Park, NJ: The Gryphon Press.

Mooney, K. C. (1984). [Review of the Jesness Inventory.] In D. J. Keyser & R. C. Sweetland (Eds.), *Test critiques* (vol. I, pp. 380–392). Kansas City: Test Corporation of America.

Pinsoneault, T. B. (1998). A Variable Response Inconsistency scale and a True Response Inconsistency scale for the Jesness Inventory. *Psychological Assessment, 10,* 21–32.

[189]
Joliet 3-Minute Preschool Speech and Language Screen.

Purpose: "Differentiates individuals with intact skills from those with suspected problems in phonology, semantics, and grammar."
Population: 2.5–4.5 years.
Publication Date: 1992.
Scores: 3 areas: Grammar, Semantics, Phonology.
Administration: Individual.
Price Data, 1999: $66 per complete kit including 12 vocabulary plates on card stock, 2 reproducible scoring sheets, recordkeeping manual, and manual (57 pages); each kit includes Apple II series 5.25-inch recordkeeping disk and 3-ring binder with tabbed dividers.
Time: (3) minutes.
Author: Mary C. Kinzler.
Publisher: Communication Skill Builders—A Division of The Psychological Corporation.

Review of the Joliet 3-Minute Preschool Speech and Language Screen by CARLOS INCHAURRALDE, Professor of Linguistics and Psychologist, University of Zaragoza, Zaragoza, Spain:

The Joliet 3-Minute Preschool Speech and Language Screen (J3-M PSLS) provides a tool for differentiating the individuals who have intact skills in the 2.6- to 4.5-year age range from those with suspected problems in Phonology, Grammar, and Semantics. This test should be useful for professionals who work with small children especially educators, in enabling them to detect language problems. There are two separate individual forms: the Individual Development Screen for ages 2.6–2.11, and the individual primary Screen for ages 3.0–4.5. Both are administered in a similar way, with differences in the contents and the suggested cutoffs. There are sections for checking Vocabulary, Grammar, and Phonology, with precise scoring instructions. Voice and fluency are also scored, although in a more subjective manner, during the administration of the grammar section. The documentation of the test is good, with a manual section, reproducible forms, information about standardization, references and readings, and a vocabulary key and plates for the vocabulary exercises. There is also a diskette with a recordkeeping computer program that can be used in Apple II series or compatible computers.

TEST DEVELOPMENT. The J3-M PSLS was standardized using a population of 421 children grouped in 6-month intervals from 2 years 6 months to 4 years 5 months. This resulted in four age groups with a more or less similar number of subjects. Three major ethnic backgrounds (Black, White, and Hispanic-other) and three socioeconomic classes were represented in the analysis. Cutoff scores were calculated both in the Developmental and the Primary versions for Vocabulary, Grammar, and Phonology, following the formula Mean + Standard Deviation + Standard Error of Measurement.

RELIABILITY. Two types of estimates of reliability are reported: Test-Retest and Interscorer. The test-retest method should estimate the stability of measurement over time. A sample of 43 persons was used and the time interval between tests was 2 weeks. The test sections were presented in reverse order. Within sections only the presentation of the plates in the vocabulary section was reversed. All reliability coefficients yielded a value of more than .85 (and most were greater than .95). For score interpretation it is important to take into account the standard error of measurement (reported for each of the four age intervals and the three sections) at cutoff points, because dichotomous decisions may place subjects into separate categories, with important implications for diagnosis.

Grammar and Phonology were also scored by a second speech-language pathologist for a sample of 15 subjects. There was a percent agreement with the first scorer of 93%. This is a high value, but it was measured on a very small sample.

CONTENT VALIDITY. There was a concern to examine content validity in the final version of the test. The Vocabulary section underwent some changes in the development stage. Eight vocabulary plates were discarded because they did not achieve adequate mean difficulty levels. Items with discrimination values greater than .30 were considered acceptable, and most items had a value of more than .50.

The Grammar section shows the mean length of utterances according to age calculated in the development stage. Inclusion of sentences in this section was also determined by difficulty and discrimination values estimated with the sample. Content validity analyses in the Phonology section are also reported to have been included by means of item analysis, and by resorting to research findings in phonology about the difficulty of certain items (*th, z, v, dz*) before age 4 (Kenny & Prather, 1984; Irwin et al., 1994; McDonald, 1976).

CONSTRUCT VALIDITY. The correlation among the different sections are fairly low. The test designer accepts a critical value of at least .20 for significance at the .05 level for $N = 100$, and three values fall below that figure ($r = .17$ for Phonology/Vocabulary at age 2.6–2.11, $r = .04$ for Phonology/Vocabulary at age 3.0–3.5, $r = .16$ for Phonology/Grammar at age 3.6–3.11). However, it is argued that the three components should be assumed to be distinct entities that are interrelated, in a conception consistent with Bloom and Lahey's (1978) model.

The calculation of chi square values shows a relationship of socioeconomic level to grammar and vocabulary, whereas no significant relationship can be found for phonology. This is congruent with language performance prediction of economic status variables shown by the work of Bernstein (1970) and Lassman, Fisch, Vetter, and LaBenz (1980).

CRITERION VALIDITY. The Vocabulary section has high correlation values ($r = .719$, $r = .703$, $r = .824$, $r = .736$) with the Peabody Picture Vocabulary Test—Revised. The Grammar section also exceeds the critical value ($r = .20$ for significance for $p<.05$) for correlation with the Carrow Elicited Language Inventory ($r = .84$, $r = .90$, $r = .86$).

In addition, scores on the Phonology section also show high correlation with the Coarticulation Assessment in Meaningful Language with respect to the results concerning the phonemes *t, k, f, sh, ch, s, l, r*. The group correlation shows a value of .89. This section also shows significant Spearman rank-difference correlation coefficients (at $p<.05$) with respect to the Production Percentages from the Coarticulation Assessment in Meaningful Language.

The test therefore shows evidence of validity when contrasted with accepted criteria.

SUMMARY. This screen performs well in testing both form (Phonology and Grammar) and content (Grammar), as claimed in the manual's introduction. The use of the language (Pragmatics) is not screened at all. If we are interested in linguistic skills in communication, we would need to resort to another tool. The instrument meets technical standards in terms of reliability, content validity, and criterion validity, which makes it a trustworthy test. There are some areas that are not screened in an exhaustive way (e.g., phonology), but there is some justification for this on the grounds of available theory. The screen can be administered very quickly and the forms are easy to fill in, with very clear instructions. This makes the instrument very valuable for screening large groups of children and identifying those individuals with potential language problems. It is to be recommended but with the proviso that it is used within its own restricted domain of application.

REVIEWER'S REFERENCES

Bernstein, D. (1970). A sociolinguistic approach to socialization. With some reference to educability. In F. Williams (Ed.), *Language and poverty* (pp. 25–61). Chicago: Markham.

Irwin, J. V., Huskey, R., Knight, N., & Oltman, S. (1974). A longitudinal study of the spontaneous remission of articulatory defects on 1,685 school children in grades one, two and three. *Acta Symbolica, 5,* 1–17.

McDonald, E. T. (1976). Screening Deep Test of Articulation. Pittsburgh: Stanwix House.

Bloom, L., & Lahey, M. (1978). *Language development and language disorders.* New York: John Wiley and Sons.

Lassman, F., Fisch, R., Vetter, D., & LaBenz, E. (1980). *Early correlates of speech, language, and hearing.* Littleton, MA: PSG Publications.

Kenny, K. W., & Prather, E. M. (1984). Coarticulation Assessment in Meaningful Language. Tucson, AZ: Communication Skill Builders.

[190]
Juvenile Automated Substance Abuse Evaluation.

Purpose: Intended to "measure adolescent alcohol and drug use/abuse … attitudes and life-stress issues."
Population: Adolescents.
Publication Dates: 1989–1997.
Acronym: JASAE.
Scores, 6: Test Taking Attitude, Life Circumstance Evaluation, Drinking Evaluation Category, Alcohol Addiction Evaluation, Drug Use Evaluation, Summary.
Administration: Individual or group.
Price Data, 1998: $4.50 per evaluation.
Manual: No manual; Reference Guide available.
Time: (20) minutes.
Comments: Self-administered; computer-scored, IBM compatible with either DOS or Windows required; provides DSM–IV classification for alcohol and drug use and ASAM patient placement criteria for treatment recommendations; available in English and Spanish.
Author: ADE Incorporated.
Publisher: ADE Incorporated.

Review of the Juvenile Automated Substance Abuse Evaluation by MARK POPE, Associate Professor, Division of Counseling, University of Missouri—St. Louis, St. Louis, MO:

The Juvenile Automated Substance Abuse Evaluation (JASAE) is a 107-item self-report inventory first published in 1988 and designed as an adolescent alcohol and drug use/abuse evaluation. The JASAE also examines respondent attitudes and life stress issues to determine if problems exist and the degree, and then recommends appropriate interventions based on the results of the entire assessment. The version reviewed here was version 3.25, published in October 1997.

The JASAE "kit" consists of a question booklet, a scoring and report generation 3 1/2-inch diskette, a one-page descriptive flyer, various descriptive flyers for other ADE supplemental products, and various unpublished research manuscripts on a variety of ADE inventories.

The question booklet is a seven-page document printed in black ink on regular 20-pound white paper with a staple in the upper left corner. Along with this booklet came a one-page frontispiece that declared that this was a "master copy of the program survey" and invited the user to "(p)lease make additional copies of the survey as you need them" and that "(n)ew masters will be provided upon request." This is followed by a copyright warning to only use these "in conjunction with ADE, Inc.'s copyright assessment programs." There is a copyright line on the first page of the question booklet.

There is no technical manual; there is a "technical report," which reports on a large validation study of the instrument. A well-written technical manual that incorporates much of the included data but focuses on information important to administration and scoring is critical to the instrument's commercial publication and use.

The 107 items in the question booklet begin on page 2. In the first 10 items are seven demographic questions (age, race, sex, current educational status, years of school completed, current living status, current employment status), interspersed with three 9-point Likert-type items (feelings about educational status, living status, and employment status) anchored by *very worst* (lowest) to *very best* (highest). The next 97 items have a variety of formats with the primary format a question followed by a "Y/N" response format (yes/no). Again, interspersed throughout these final 97 items are items that require the respondent to fill in the blank (frequency of beer consumption), Likert-type items (ability to handle stress), and items that require the respondent to choose from a list (number of the items you have tried or used at least once). The variety of formats interspersed with each other is more likely to keep the attention of these adolescents and not allow them to get into patterned-responding (all Ys or all Ns). Responses are entered directly in the question booklet either by circling Y or N or by entering a specified number or letter. The response blank is printed in a column down the right side of each page of the question booklet with the item number reprinted next to the blank. Administration time is estimated to be 20 minutes.

The "kit" is contained in a textured pocket-folder with an embossed logo for ADE. The scoring and report generation diskette is included in a clear-plastic pocket on the interior of the folder. The responses are entered by a nonrespondent into a computer software program directly from the question booklet, estimated to take 3–5 minutes on the average. A narrative report is then generated.

The narrative report is a three-page report and begins with the reprinted demographic information. The main narrative report begins with the disclaimer that "(t)he following report should be viewed as a series of hypotheses which may require further investigation. Individuals interpreting this evaluation should be knowledgeable in substance abuse problems and possess screening and assessment skills" (pp. 9–11). The report is divided into three major sections.

The first section is a narrative report of the five major subscales of the report (Test Taking Attitude, Life Circumstance Evaluation, Drinking Evaluation Category, Alcohol Addiction Evaluation, and Drug Use Evaluation). Unfortunately for the user of the report, there is no consistency in type of reported score. Each of the subscales reports a nonstandard score followed by a one- or two-sentence interpretation of the score.

The second section reports recommended interventions and includes a suggested DSM-IV diagnosis for the respondent. The third section identifies specific item responses that are important and prints them into three categories (possible areas of concern, drug use symptoms, and low or unusual life circumstance ratings).

The remainder of the materials in the kit are either descriptive marketing pieces or studies. They are inadequate as either for the professional who is attempting to evaluate the effectiveness and ease of use of the JASAE. Let me repeat my earlier statement: This lack of professional use information is consistent for the JASAE. There is no technical manual; there is a "technical report" that reports on a large validation study of the instrument. A well-written technical manual, which incorporates much of the included data but focuses on information important to administration and scoring, is critical to the instrument's commercial publication and use.

The validation studies regarding the JASAE included in the review materials were all authored by Childers and Allred from East Carolina University. It is important to have a strong research base for assessment instruments; however, it is also important to have some variety in researchers to ensure replicability of results. No data are included in any of the JASAE studies that document the development of the inventory.

The reliability information for the instrument is based on one research study reporting test-retest reliability data on the subscales (.80 to .85) for a 14-day period. Test-retest data are especially important for longer term trait/personality measurement; however, for state/behavioral measurement the use of test-retest study data as a measure of reliability is not as useful. The JASAE is a state/behavioral measure, where we expect and hope for changes, especially in a positive direction with a population such as adolescents. A better way to measure reliability for state/behavioral assessment is through measures of within-scale, inter-item reliability.

Validity data are reported in several different studies included in the review materials, but these studies compare subscales on the JASAE to subscales on personality instruments such as the Minnesota Multiphasic Personality Inventory and the California Psychological Inventory. Again, the JASAE subscales are state/behavioral measures and comparing them to trait/personality measures does not provide evidence of construct validity. It would be a different story if the authors were discussing concurrent criterion-related validity. Unfortunately for the test user, the authors do not specify the type of validity for which they are presenting evidence. They leave it to the reader to determine and this is not the best way of presenting validity data.

The authors of the JASAE are to be commended for publishing the results of their findings of research conducted on this instrument at an American Psychological Association regional conference. This shows a commitment to the continued upgrading of the inventory and willingness to allow evaluation by other professionals.

SUMMARY. Overall, the JASAE may do an adequate job as an alcohol and drug abuse assessment; however, the lack of a professional technical manual, the confusion of validity evidence, the wrong type of reliability evidence along with the lack of any other type of reliability evidence, the lack of specific instructions and information for professional users, and the lack of researcher variety and replication are critical problems. Many of the problems of the JASAE could be corrected in a strong, well-written technical manual.

Review of the Juvenile Automated Substance Abuse Evaluation by JODY L. SWARTZ-KULSTAD, Assistant Professor of Counselor Education, University of Wisconsin—Superior, Superior, WI:

The Juvenile Automated Substance Abuse Evaluation (JASAE) is a 107-item computer-assisted, self-report measure of attitudes and behaviors associated with substance use/abuse. The JASAE also provides information on test taker attitude and life circumstances. Although the JASAE was originally developed for use with individuals in clinical and judicial settings, some support has been provided for group (e.g., school) settings. The primary goal of the JASAE is to facilitate assessment of substance use/abuse and, based upon the totality of assessment findings, provide enough information about aspects of the respondent's life to determine the appropriate level of intervention. ADE notes the assessment is used to refer the individual directly to education, treatment, or further evaluation and/or to provide a basis or reinforcer for a personal interview.

TEST INFORMATION. The JASAE is appropriate for adolescents ages 12–18, and is also available in Spanish. The JASAE is an "offspring" of an adult measure, the Substance Abuse Life Circumstances Evaluation (377), with item modifications made to increase the JASAE's appropriateness for adolescents. Reading level is rated at 5th grade; the questionnaire has a built-in process for detecting reading/comprehension problems and when identified, they are noted in the interpretive report. Test materials include paper administration forms that are manually entered or optically scanned into a computer scoring and interpretation program.

No manual is provided. Even though no qualifications are required for administration, individuals providing interpretation of the evaluation should be professionals who are knowledgeable about substance use/abuse problems and possess training in assessment. The JASAE takes approximately 20 minutes to complete and 3–5 minutes to enter scores and obtain an interpretation report. Of note, the measure is intended to be used in conjunction with its computer program; thus, manual scoring is not available. Additionally, the measure should not be used in isolation; the interpretation report specifically states "the following report should be viewed as a series of hypotheses that may require further investigation" (p. 9).

SUBSCALE INFORMATION. JASAE items are organized into five scales: Summary, Test Taking Attitudes (TTA), Life Circumstances Evaluation (LCE), Drinking Evaluation (DE), and Drug Use Evaluation (DUE). Scoring on each scale is based on analysis of the overall pattern of responses. The summary, TTA, and LCE scales provide continuous data that are converted to categories for interpretation purposes; the DE and DUE scales are categorical. The Summary scale assesses overall risk/need for intervention. The TTA scale provides test validity information and is essential for interpretation of the assessment. The LCE scale is a measure of life stresses (there are differences in categories between the individual and group administered). The DE and DUE scales measure extent of alcohol use and substance use other than alcohol, respectively. Although the interpretation report provides information on a sixth area, Alcohol Addiction Evaluation, no information regarding this area was available.

INTERPRETIVE REPORT. Test users are cautioned against drawing conclusions based on the JASAE alone. The interpretive report provides a good resource for information on each of the scales as well as a reporting of possible areas of concern, drug use symptoms, and low or unusual life circumstance ratings (to be used in conjunction with interpretation of the LCE scale). In addition, information on areas that need further clarification, DSM IV classification, recommended interventions, and possible referral needs for the individual are reported.

RELIABILITY. Based on results from a sample of college students (n = 73; Allred, Childers, & Ellis, 1992), the JASAE shows good test-retest reliability (14-day interval) for the three continuous scales (.80 to .85). Categorical agreement for the Drinking Evaluation and Drug Use Evaluation remained fairly stable, with 65.71% and 75.71% (respectively) categorical agreement across time. The available reliability data were obtained from a sample that technically falls outside the age range of the measure. This calls into question the utility of this data.

VALIDITY. According to ADE, the JASAE has been used in over 75,000 individual assessments in courts, schools, and mental health settings since 1988 and has over a 90% agreement rate (n = 466) with professional assessment interview results (ADE, 1997). For validation of use with groups, a study (Allred, Childers, & Ellis; 1991, 1992) was undertaken with 1,061 adolescents in grades 6–12. The sample was representative of the area (Northeast) from which the sample was obtained (representation by Euro-American and African-American students only). Results provide some support for convergent validity. For the total group sample, questions assessing self-report of use were significantly related to all scales of the JASAE. In addition, several subsamples (ranging in size from 108 to 230) were administered additional measures to provide evidence of the JASAE's convergent validity. The JASAE scales were low to moderately correlated with scores on the Beck Depression Inventory, the Zung Self-Rating Depression Scale, the Piers-Harris Self-Concept Scale, and Attitudes Toward School Questionnaire. Levinson's IPC measure of locus of control showed no relationship with the JASAE, despite hypothesized relationships.

Though the JASAE does appear to have some evidence of convergent validity, further investigation is warranted. As the primary purpose is to evaluate substance use/abuse, some evidence of convergent validity with substance use/abuse measures would be valuable. In the current validation study, assessments that measure aspects related to substance use/abuse were included, but none expressly provide information on assessment of substance use/abuse behavior. These may measure ancillary aspects or influences on the development, maintenance, and outcome of substance use, but they are not substance use.

ADDITIONAL INFORMATION. Users of the JASAE are provided with three additional programs: a Client Tracking program, an Incorporated Outcome Program, and a Data Analysis Program.

SUMMARY. The JASAE provides a potentially valuable tool to assist in the identification and intervention of substance use and abuse in the adolescent population. The JASAE's strengths lie in its translation of assessment results into viable intervention recommendations. An additional strength is the ancillary software available through the ADE, a particularly useful addition in this era of increased accountability.

Although the JASAE does show strong potential as both an individually administered and group-administered measure, several areas must be addressed. Scant information about the development of the instrument, the norm sample, how cutoff scores for category assignments were derived, and the measure's psychometric properties should serve as a caution for users. The lack of a manual severely hampers potential users' understanding of the test attributes and utility. For users unfamiliar with administration and scoring of the JASAE, lack of a manual can lead to some confusion, particularly related to understanding the intricacies of the measure itself. Related to validity, the questionnaires used to provide convergent validity miss the mark, to some degree. The JASAE does assess more than substance use/abuse, but because the primary purpose is to assess substance use/abuse, evidence of convergent validity with a substance-related measure is warranted. Moreover, the available information on the validity of the measure is limited solely to convergent validity; event though this is useful, gathering information on construct validity and predictive validity is an important next step.

REVIEWER'S REFERENCES

Allred, L. J., Childers, J. S., & Ellis, B. (1991). *Use of the Juvenile Automated Substance Abuse Evaluation (JASAE) with a public school sample.* Unpublished Technical Report. Clarkston, MI: ADE, Incorporated.

Allred, L. J., Childers, J. S., & Ellis, B. (1992). *Validation of the SALCE and JASAE as indicators of substance abuse in 12–21 year olds.* Symposium conducted at the 38th annual meeting of the Southeastern Psychological Association, Knoxville, TN.

ADE, Incorporated. (1997). *Juvenile Automated Substance Abuse Evaluation reference guide.* Unpublished report. Clarkston, MI: ADE, Incorporated.

[191]

Kaufman Test of Educational Achievement [1998 Normative Update].

Purpose: "Provides an analysis of a child's educational strengths and weaknesses in reading, mathematics, and spelling, to identify possible skill areas (e.g., reading comprehension, mathematics computation) needing remediation or enrichment."

Population: Grades 1 through 12, ages 6–22.
Publication Dates: 1985–1998.
Acronym: K-TEA.
Administration: Individual.
Price Data, 1999: $279.95 per special edition complete kit including brief form and comprehensive form, wipeable test plates, 2 test easels, 2 manuals, 50 record booklets, 2 sample reports to parents, and carry bag; $234.95 per regular edition complete kit including all of special edition kit except wipeable test plates.
Authors: Alan S. Kaufman and Nadeen L. Kaufman.
Publisher: American Guidance Service, Inc.

a) BRIEF FORM.
Purpose: "Screening of student on global achievement skills to determine the need for follow-up testing and evaluation."
Scores, 4: Reading, Mathematics, Spelling, Battery Composite.
Price Data: $109.95 per special edition Brief Form kit including 77 test plates in easel, 25 record booklets, sample reports to parents, wipeable test plates, carry bag, and manual ('98, 288 pages); $94.95 per regular edition Brief Form kit including all materials in special edition except wipeable test plates; $26.95 per 25 record booklets; $19.95 per 25 reports to parents; $31.95 per manual.
Time: (30) minutes.

b) COMPREHENSIVE FORM.
Purpose: "Provides an analysis of a child's educational strengths and weaknesses in reading, mathematics, and spelling, to identify possible skill areas (e.g., reading comprehension, mathematics computation) needing remediation or enrichment."
Scores, 8: Reading Decoding, Reading Comprehension, Reading Composite, Mathematics Applications, Mathematics Computation, Mathematics Composite, Spelling, Battery Composite.
Price Data: $184.95 per special edition Comprehensive Form kit including 133 test plates in easel, 25 record booklets (including error analyses), sample report to parents, wipeable test plates, carry bag, and manual ('98, 591 pages); $159.95 per regular edition Comprehensive Form kit including all materials in special edition except wipeable test plates; $34.95 per 25 record booklets; $21.95 per 25 reports to parents (available in Spanish); $52.95 per manual; $149.95 per software package (IBM or Macintosh); $189 per software package to run DOS/Windows on Macintosh.
Time: (60–75) minutes.
Cross References: See T5:1386 (26 references) and T4:1348 (5 references); for reviews by Elizabeth J. Doll and Jerome M. Sattler of an earlier edition, see 10:161.

Review of the Kaufman Test of Educational Achievement [1998 Normative Update] by JOHN POGGIO, Professor of Psychology and Research in Education, School of Education, University of Kansas, Lawrence, KS:

The Kaufman Test of Educational Achievement (K-TEA) is prepared as an individually administered measure of school achievement for children and adolescents in Grades 1 through 12. It offers age-based norms (6 years 0 months to 18 years 11 months) as well as grade-based norms by way of two separate and nonequivalent forms: a Comprehensive Form that yields scores in Reading Decoding (60 total items measuring letter identification, and pronunciation of phonetic and nonphonetic words), Reading Comprehension (50 total items measuring literal and inferential comprehension), Mathematics Applications (60 total items measured using word problems of basic arithmetic functions of increasing complexity), Mathematics Computation (60 total items measuring a range of increasingly difficult number operations), and Spelling (50 total items measured using a word list of increasing difficulty); and, a Brief Form that assesses in the areas of Reading (52 items total spanning decoding and comprehension-type questions), Mathematics (52 items total appraising basic computation, concepts, and word problems), and Spelling (40 items total using a graded word list).

The Brief and Comprehensive forms do not share items, and the forms were not prepared to assure their equivalence (e.g., sampling items to forms drawn from a common item pool). Though the manual suggests the two versions are alternate forms and may be used as such, there is a lack of content-related validation information to support such an assurance. Additionally, each form provides for a Battery Composite score that is created by summing the form's subtest scores. This procedure is suspect and the validity of the index compromised as there are different numbers of items on each subtest (in the extreme, varying by as much as 30% in the Brief Form, and 20% in the Comprehensive Form) and thus an individual's total score is unevenly weighted based on the number of items answered correctly (e.g., two students with scores of 50 could have very different achievement profiles). Were a battery composite score desired by the user, the more appropriate procedure would be to average the individual's standard scores derived for each subtest. Of course, existing K-TEA Battery score norms would be of no use were such a procedure followed by the user.

The content of the Comprehensive and Brief K-TEA have not been changed in any way since their introduction in 1985. Manuals are not updated to introduce new validation or bias studies. The present versions of the Brief and Comprehensive Forms offer only an updating of their respective norms. In this regard it appears that sampling to update the norms was completed based on samples of volunteers. Although overall data on the norm samples suggest a match to the 1994 U.S. population statistics on factors such as gender, race/ethnic composition, and parental education, geographic representation is not in evidence in the 1995–1996 norms (e.g., no students from Texas are represented in the norming sample or inland California, etc., and there is no documentation of the representation based on urban, suburban, and rural environments). No information is provided about the norming sample regarding representation of primary language of the student or language spoken in the home. Comparison of the original 1985 norms to the norms created based on 1995–1996 renorming does suggest significant changes in the score distributions. As such, it is difficult to justify that the standardization chapters from the original manuals were left intact and in place rather than being replaced, or at least updated, in the preparation of the new manuals. The new norming data are presented in an Appendix.

The documentation in the K-TEA manuals is sparse regarding the content and focus of the K-TEA assessments. Comprehensive test blueprints or tested skill specifications are not offered, thus the user must review individual items at the desired grade levels to acquire a sense of the constructs to be measured and the specific skills to be assessed. For assessments that assert measurement of school achievement, this lack of detail is an issue. A review of the currently offered K-TEA does suggest limitations with regard to mathematics and reading comprehension. In mathematics, today's schools tend to be oriented toward curricular expectations and instructional practices defined by the recent National Council of Teachers of Mathematics (NCTM) curricular standards. The K-TEA mathematics sections do not appear to conform to NCTM's curricular guidance. Also, reading instruction in the schools has moved toward

teaching and assessing reading comprehension based on authentic, rich, and lengthy texts on assorted modalities/text-types (e.g., narration, explaining, technical, etc.). The K-TEA remains very much composed of isolated, very short pieces (often fewer than 50 words). There does not appear to be good alignment for the K-TEA as measures of school achievement and the curricular or instructional experiences students are likely encountering in their reading and mathematics instruction.

An issue for the K-TEA is the adequacy of the studies that are available to suggest freedom from bias, offensiveness, and insensitivity for historically impacted groups (race, linguistic, gender, cultural, and disabled populations). As noted, there has been no recent work to support the psychometric properties of the K-TEA, thus only work of the past is available to address this area. The efforts of the past used a methodology (the Angoff delta analysis approach) for detection of item bias that has been found wanting and rarely in use. Also there is no discussion of the use of logical or rational reviews of test items by impacted group members. Present day testing standards make clear the need for tests to be evaluated by appropriate empirical methods to minimize bias. On this standard the K-TEA is notably deficient in so far as no investigations have been reported using newer, more appropriate empirical or logical review methods.

SUMMARY. For users desiring an appraisal of student achievement in mathematics and reading it is difficult to imagine a context where the K-TEA can be recommended over more current assessment tools, even group administered achievement instruments. Costs associated with an individually administered assessment, needed qualifications of and training for examiners, and reliance on basic knowledge test items coupled with almost multiple-choice like instructions for scoring make selection of the K-TEA a difficult option. Even though reliability estimates for the various scores scales are high, present documentation fails to report standard error of measurement at specific score points or score ranges; rather, the K-TEA continues to offer only total scale standard errors, again not supporting benefits associated with individualized administrations.

Review of the Kaufman Test of Educational Achievement [1998 Normative Update] by WILLIAM D. SCHAFER, Associate Professor of Measure-

ment, Statistics, and Evaluation, University of Maryland, College Park, MD and State Director of Student Assessment, Maryland State Department of Education, Baltimore, MD:

PURPOSE AND DESCRIPTION. The Kaufman Test of Educational Achievement is intended for use in decision making about individuals as well as for program evaluation. It consists of two forms, a Brief Form to be used for screening and a Comprehensive Form to allow exploration of individual students' strengths and weaknesses. Both forms are designed for students from Grades 1 through 12 and are administered individually using at different times an easel book and a paper-and-pencil format.

DEVELOPMENT. Each subtest began with a working definition for which items were developed, administered to tryout samples, analyzed, and evaluated for assignment to either form. Data from a later "standardization" were used to further refine the scales, dropping items that showed poor fit to the Rasch model or were not needed for acceptable reliability.

The original scales were renormed during 1995 and 1996 as part of a larger study in which the Peabody Individual Achievement Test—Revised (279), the KeyMath-Revised (194) and the Woodcock Reading Mastery Tests—Revised (423) along with these two batteries, were administered to nationally representative samples. Each member of the sample received one full battery along with one or more other subtests. Other samples received only those subtests that measured a common domain. The latter were used for linking purposes in a Rasch analysis that placed all items in the domain on the same ability scale. This interesting approach to norming provides rich opportunities for comparisons among the batteries, but there is no discussion of that being done in the manual. It also creates a potential for differences in the ways domains with perhaps nonidentical definitions can impact the common scaling. There is no discussion of that problem, nor, apparently, were the fits of the items from the different batteries compared with one another as part of the analysis.

There were five domains identified in the study: Reading Decoding, Reading Comprehension, Mathematics Computation, Mathematics Applications, and Spelling. All five areas are represented on the Comprehensive Form, but only the last three were administered from the Brief Form. In order to renorm the Reading subtest of the Brief Form, the equivalence relationship that was developed originally was used again.

SCORE INTERPRETATION. Numerous tables by age (and grade) allow easy conversion of raw scores on each subtest to standard scores with a mean of 100 and a standard deviation of 15. Another table allows conversions to other common reporting systems: percentile ranks, stanines, and normal curve equivalents. Confidence band widths are given for different ages (and grades), but are not associated with subtest score points. Other tables give the differences between standard scores that would be required for statistical significance between scores on different subtests and composites. Several other tables are also given and the manual discusses how the new norms compare with the earlier ones.

RELIABILITY. Unfortunately, reliability coefficients were not reestimated for the new sample. Earlier estimates suggest the subtests of the Comprehensive Form have homogeneity indices that range upwards from the high .80s with composite homogeneity indices in the .90s. The Brief Form's homogeneity indices were lower. More importantly, the standard errors on all of the Comprehensive Form subtests are less than 6, and on all of the Brief Form subtests are less than 8, on the standard score scale, which has a standard deviation of 15. The information the test provides can thus decrease the range of uncertainty by half or more.

VALIDITY. The validities of the subtests were examined through expert judgment. In each case, a definition of the domain to be sampled was developed and items were generated consistent with that definition. Correlations among subtests presented separately by age (and grade) show patterns that seem consistent with those from similar batteries.

As with any achievement battery, a potential user should be careful in deciding whether the subtests are valid in the local situation. Consistency with the domain that the student has been studying is an important consideration. Differences in curriculum imply that scores from any one test will not have equivalent validity across educational settings.

The manual lists several uses of the battery. These range from individual interpretation, to selection decisions, to program evaluation, to basic and applied research. Each of these settings has evidence needs that are idiosyncratic. Consequential evidence of validity should be sought for each of these intended uses of the test.

SUMMARY. The development and psychometric characteristics of the Kaufman Test of Educational Achievement place the battery among the best available. However, the need for an individually administered achievement test, particularly at older ages (and grades) is not clear. The manual indicates that it may be useful when a group test is inappropriate because the student has difficulty scoring well in the group setting or when clinical insight is desired. But the manual is not very helpful in providing guidance about how to interpret scores in those cases, nor was the renorming study designed to allow one to refer the scores earned to any group-administered test, because all the other tests that were in the study are also individually administered.

[192]
Kent Inventory of Developmental Skills [1996 Standardization].

Purpose: Designed to assess the developmental status and progress of healthy infants, infants at risk, and young children with developmental disabilities.

Population: Infants up to 15 months of age and young children whose developmental age is less than 15 months.

Publication Dates: 1978–1999.

Acronym: KIDS.

Scores, 12: Developmental Ages and Standard Scores for: Cognitive, Motor, Language, Self-Help, Social Domains, Full Scale.

Administration: Individual.

Price Data: Price information available from publisher for complete kit including 25 profile sheets, 25 answer sheets, reusable administration and scoring booklet, 5 scoring templates, set of developmental timetables, manual, and 2-use disk for on-site computer scoring and interpretation.

Time: (45) minutes.

Comments: Relies on caregiver report; also yields individualized developmental timetables; includes hand-scoring materials and an expanded computer report, including a list of developmentally appropriate activities selected to match each child's specific competencies; earlier editions entitled The Kent Infant Development Scale.

Authors: Jeanette Reuter with Lewis Katoff and Jeffrey Wozniak (3rd edition of the test manual and user's guide) and James Whiteman (computer-scoring disk).

Publisher: Western Psychological Services.

Cross References: See T5:1391 (2 references); for reviews by Candice Feiring and Edward S. Shapiro of an earlier edition, see 10:163 (2 references); for a review by Candice Feiring of an earlier version, see 9:567; see also T3:1246 (1 reference).

[Editor's Note: The publisher advised in September 1999 that this test has been changed but that the following reviews, based on materials for The Kent Infant Development Scale, Third Edition [1990 Standardization], are still appropriate for the new edition. Major changes are ones of packaging and usage. Hand scoring is now available as well as an expanded computer report.]

Review of The Kent Infant Development Scale, Third Edition [1990 Standardization] by DIANE J. SAWYER, Murfree Professor of Dyslexic Studies, Middle Tennessee State University, Murfreesboro, TN:

DESCRIPTION. The Kent Infant Development Scale, Third Edition, consists of 252 items sampling five domains of development: Cognitive, Motor, Language, Self-Help, and Social. These items are ordered in a hierarchical progression that the authors indicate are consistent with the developmental progression observed in normal children. The scale was designed to be used by any caretaker with at least a 4th grade level of reading ability. However, the authors indicate that the scale items may be read to caretakers who do not have reading skills consistent with the demands of the test. For each item, the caretaker indicates the child's current status—yes, the child can perform the task; yes, the child used to perform the task but outgrew it; no, the child cannot do this task yet. On the accompanying answer sheet, the caretaker fills in the #1 if the child can do the task, the #2 if the child has outgrown the task, or the #3 if the child cannot yet do the task.

Raw scores in each domain are calculated by counting the numbers of ones and twos that have been circled. Templates are provided to distinguish the items that fall into each domain. Raw scores are then converted into a Developmental Age, in months, using a profile sheet provided by the authors. The developmental age for each domain and for the full scale may be obtained. Finally, the developmental status may be determined by consulting the Delay Chart provided by the authors. This chart permits a comparison of the child's chronological age with the full scale developmental age obtained. Determination of status—no delay, at risk, or developmentally delayed—is based upon standard deviations from the mean of the norming sample. A classification of developmentally delayed would be associated with the difference between the developmental age and the chronological age of more than two full standard deviations. A computer scoring procedure is also available. Conversion of raw scores to standard scores (mean of 100, *S.D.* of 15) is possible for children ages 2–14 months using conversion tables provided. The authors state that the full scale standard score provides the best guide for determining developmental status (manual, p. 9).

To interpret developmental status, in each of the domains, into a plan for intervention, developmental timetables are provided. In these timetables, a given item number is associated with the age norm at which that item is expected to be accomplished. It is suggested that intervention begin at the point at which the caretaker identifies three consecutive items in the domain as #3 (child cannot do it yet). Intervention is interpreted as special attention from the caregivers. Professional consultation is suggested to assist the caregiver in interpreting the scale results, in planning intervention, or in determining if referral to early intervention programs or particular specialists should be made. A clinical case study is provided to assist test users in interpreting test results to determine the developmental status and to assess strengths and weaknesses.

DEVELOPMENT OF THE SCALE. The Kent Infant Development Scale has evolved through three separate normative studies. Profiles obtained on more than 1,500 children have contributed to item selection, and the development of all normative data provided. These children were described as normal, healthy babies and young children representing at least two different socioeconomic groups.

RELIABILITY. Reliability is reported with respect to internal consistency, test/retest reliability, and interjudge reliability. Internal consistency is high; Cronbach alpha coefficients of .93 to .99 are reported for the five domains and the Full Scale. Test/retest reliability coefficients (administration interval ranges from 2 weeks to 2 months) from four different studies are reported. Generally, these are high and consistent, ranging from .91 to .99 for the domain and full scale scores. One study, however, involving 331 children, yielded much lower coefficients. In this instance, coefficients ranged from .77 to .86. This particular study was part of the Hungarian language form of the scale. Interrater reliability is reported for six

studies. These studies include those associated with the development of the scales in other languages. Overall, the reliability coefficients ranged from .68 to .99. In all studies, mothers' and fathers' ratings were compared. However, a number of nonparental caregivers were also included in some of the computations. The two lowest coefficients attained across all studies involved samples of severely or profoundly mentally retarded children and children with diagnosed brain damage. Within both samples, the lowest coefficients were obtained for the Language domain.

VALIDITY. Validity of the scales was examined with respect to construct validity, concurrent validity, and predictive validity. With respect to construct validity, the authors note correlation coefficients of .88 to .93 for scores obtained on the scale with the ages represented in the samples of healthy infants.

Concurrent validity has been examined through a comparison of the scale with the Bayley Scales of Infant Development. Degrees of agreement in the assessment of "delayed or not delayed" across the two measures, over five studies, are reported to be between .44 and .91. Decision agreement based upon the Full Scale score only, ranged from .59 to .97.

The authors report three studies that explored the predictive validity of the scales. Two studies examined child behavior on the scales over periods of 4 months, 6 months, and 7 months. One study shows a high degree of predictive validity (.90 to .97) for a sample of 71 children tested at a 6-month interval. Much lower predictive values were obtained in another study which examined prediction over a 4-month span (a sample of 256 children) and a 7-month span (a sample of 96 children). Values of .70 to .77 were obtained for a 4-month interval and values of .41 to .54 were obtained for a 7-month interval. In a third study, the ability of the scales to predict outcome measures on the Bayley Scales and the Stanford-Binet was examined. This latter study yielded the lowest prediction values (.46 at 1 year of age), .33 at 2 years of age, and .20 at 3 years of age based upon an assessment at age 6 months).

SUMMARY. The Kent Infant Development Scale, Third Edition, is a relatively brief and easy-to-use instrument. It addresses development in five critical domains and is perhaps best suited as a screen for the possible identification of children with developmental delays. Reported test/retest reliability is reasonably strong but interrater reliability is relatively weaker. This may be due, of course, to the familiarity of the rater with the child's behavior on a day-to-day basis. Among mother/father pairs of raters, it is likely that one parent will have many more clock hours of contact with the child each day than may be possible for the other parent. The range of interrater reliability coefficients reported appears to underscore the importance of ratings obtained from the primary caregiver.

Estimates of concurrent validity vary greatly (.44 for the Self-Help to .91 for the Social and Motor domains) when compared to the Bayley Scales of Infant Development. When compared to the Vineland Adaptive Behavior Scales, the validity index ranges from .85 for the Self-Help scale to .97 for the Full Scale. These data, however, were derived from a sample of only 25 children. Again, the estimates of concurrent validity raises the question of rater familiarity with the child as well as the question of objectivity of the rater in the use of any of the scales for the evaluation of development.

The power of the Kent Scales to predict performance on these scales or other scales at a future time is extremely variable. Prediction to a second administration of the scales at 4 months was .77, at 6 months was .97, and at 7 months was .54 based upon the Full-Scale score, across three studies. Such wide variability may simply underscore individual variability in development among individuals previously diagnosed as developmentally delayed or disabled. The ability of the Kent Scales to predict performance on the Bayley Scales 6 months and 18 months later is quite low (.46 and .33 respectively).

The data presented by the authors suggests that the primary utility of the Kent Scales may be to identify developmental status at the time of assessment, but not to predict future behavior among individuals with developmental handicaps. As a screen, the Kent Scales may be facilitative in identifying areas of slower than expected development and in assisting with decisions regarding referral for further assessment or for supportive stimulation.

Review of The Kent Infant Development Scale, Third Edition [1990 Standardization] by GARY J. STAINBACK, Senior Psychologist I, Developmental Evaluation Clinic, East Carolina University School of Medicine, Department of Pediatrics, Greenville, NC:

The Kent Infant Development Scale, Third Edition (KID Scale) is a 252-item parent assessment of their child's development up to the age of 15 months. It precedes two earlier editions and normative studies from 1978, 1982, and 1990. The KID Scale is reported to be appropriate for the assessment of normally developing, at risk, and developmentally delayed children, even those whose level of developmental functioning falls below a 15-month level. The Full Scale score is recommended for determining the developmental status of an infant; however scales are also provided for Cognitive, Motor, Language, Self-Help, and Social domains. Developmental Age (DA) and Standard Scores are provided for the Full Scale score total, as well as for each domain scale. Several foreign language versions are available as well as a computer-scoring program, which offers a slightly greater analysis than would traditionally be available through hand scoring and analysis.

Parents or primary caregivers are asked to rate each of the 252 items, either 1 (Yes, can do it), 2 (Yes, used to do it but outgrew it), or 3 (No, cannot do it yet). The standardization sample of the third edition of the KID Scale consisted of 706 infants between .3 and 15.8 months of age, who by parent report were full term and without any significant medical complications or serious illnesses. An equivalent number of male and female infants were involved in the standardization. Developmental Ages were smoothed so Full Scale raw scores offer a DA in tenths of a month, ranging from .1 to 15.5. Standard scores have a mean of 100 and standard deviation of 15. In addition to standard scores and developmental ages, the manual offers item age norms and a Consistency Scale. Item age norms reflect the approximate age an item may be observed in the development of a child. The Consistency Scale can be used as a validity check on the scoring responses of the caregiver. In the KID Scale are 53 pairs of items that describe similar behaviors. If responses for essentially the same behavior are inconsistent, the caregiver may have responded carelessly and the resulting scores may not be valid. The Consistency Scale is equal to the number of item pairs that were found to be answered in an inconsistent manner. It is only available, however, when the KID Scale is scored by computer.

The KID Scale manual presents an impressive array of psychometric data, illustrating its sound evidence of reliability and validity. Internal consistency measures, test-retest, interjudge reliability, and generalizability indices are provided for reliability measures. Concurrent, predictive, and construct validity measures are also available and very acceptable. Normative studies have also been undertaken in the Netherlands (1990), Spain (1996), Hungary (1996), Germany (1992), the Czech Republic (1996), and South Vietnam (1989). The overall order of behavioral acquisition across all cultures was found to be very similar, with rank order correlations of .80 and above. However, some cultural variations were noted; therefore, cultural factors would need to be accounted for in assessing the developmental timetables for some cases.

Perhaps one of the more impressive features of the KID Scale came from research comparing scores from the KID Scale with those from the Bayley Scales of Infant Development (BSID), the Motor Scale and Mental Scale. Strong validity measures were obtained even for a clinical sample of developmentally disabled children, as well as with children at risk.

Scoring of the KID Scale may be accomplished through the use of templates or the computer-scoring program, that may be loaded on a personal computer or by mailing the results to the publisher. The computer program requires an IBM or compatible computer running Microsoft's Disk Operating System (MS-DOS) and having at least 350K of RAM and a floppy disk drive. From the computer program three report formats are available: short report (only scores and DAs, no narrative text), professional report (scores, DAs, list of items and their responses, and no narrative text), or the full report, which has all of the above plus a narrative text that explains the domains and scores. It is anticipated that about 6 to 12 minutes would be involved in keying in the client information and responses to the 252 items, and about 4 to 10 minutes to print the report. Template scoring is accomplished by counting the number of 1s and 2s on the answer sheet (without the template). Templates are used for determining the score for each domain. Tables are provided for converting Full Scale and Domain Raw Scores to DAs and Standard Scores. A graphic display is then plotted on the Profile Sheet, where approximate Domain and Full Scale Raw Scores can be read along the right and left hand margins. From this profile, strengths and areas of weakness may be identified.

If more than five items were left unanswered by the caregiver, the scale should be considered invalid. An invalid scale should also be considered if the Consistency Scale Score is greater than 4. Care should also be undertaken for computing the correct age of the child, as well as adjusting for chronological age when necessary, in order to obtain valid estimates of the child's developmental status. A Delay Chart is provided and provides a developmental status for the child's chronological age to the nearest .5 of a month, and a rating for the amount of delay. Delays are rated as No Delay, At Risk, or Developmentally Delayed, depending on the difference between the obtained score and the chronological age or corrected gestational age. Essentially, ratings of Developmentally Delayed represent standard scores <71 whereas At Risk represents standard scores between 70 and <86.

Analysis of results may also involve an analysis of the developmental timetables, where emergent behaviors may be identified. This may be particularly useful for programming purposes in Early Intervention programs, as well as an aid for programming for the clinically delayed. Emergent behaviors can then be identified for each domain area and activities provided to help the child in acquiring these behaviors within the next month (assuming a normal course of development).

SUMMARY. In review, the KID Scale follows a sound evolution of the scale from the doctoral dissertation of L. Katoff. Earlier editions were psychometrically sound (see ninth and tenth editions of the Buros *Mental Measurements Yearbooks* for reviews), and the current edition remains so. A computer-scoring program is also available, which makes possible an added level of analysis to the results, namely the Consistency Scale, which can serve as a validity check for scoring purposes. The KID Scale is recommended in the developmental assessment of children up to 15 months, or of those developmentally delayed and whose level of functioning falls within this range. It may even prove more useful in the developmental assessment of culturally different children, especially those whose family cultures follow very close to those of their heritage.

[193]
Kent Visual Perception Test.

Purpose: "Constructed for evaluating the visual perceptual skills of children."

Population: Ages 5–11.
Publication Date: 1995.
Acronym: KVPT.
Administration: Individual.
Price Data, 1996: $154 per complete kit including manual (122 pages), 20 Copy Tests, Memory Test, Discrimination Test, and 20 Scoring and Error Analysis Booklets; $59 per 20 Copy Tests; $12 per Memory Test; $16 per Discrimination Test; $39 per 20 Scoring and Error Analysis Booklets; $34 per manual.
Time: [20–30] minutes.
Author: Lawrence E. Melamed.
Publisher: PRO-ED, Inc.

a) KENT VISUAL PERCEPTION TEST—DISCRIMINATION.
Purpose: Designed to assess visual discrimination skills.
Acronym: KVPT-D.
Scores, 2: Error Analysis, Total.

b) KENT VISUAL PERCEPTION TEST—COPY.
Purpose: Designed to assess visual reproduction skills.
Acronym: KVPT-C.
Levels, 3: C1, C2, C3.
Scores, 4: C1, C2, C3, Total.

c) KENT VISUAL PERCEPTION TEST—MEMORY.
Purpose: Designed to assess immediate memory.
Acronym: KVPT-M.
Scores, 2: Error Analysis, Total.

[Editor's Note: The publisher advised in February 1999 that this test is now out of print.]

Review of the Kent Visual Perceptual Test by ANNIE W. WARD, Emeritus Professor, University of South Florida, Daytona Beach, FL:

The Kent Visual Perceptual Test (KVPT) is actually three tests, one of which has three levels: KVPT-C—Copy, C-1, C-2, and C-3; KVPT-D—Discrimination; and KVPT-M—Immediate Memory. These tests were developed to evaluate the visual perceptual skills of children from ages 5 to 11. All three instruments use the same shapes, but the task is different for each. For C, the task is to copy the stimulus form. For D the task is to select the shape that matches the stimulus, and for M the task is to match the shape from memory after the stimulus is removed.

The first chapter of the manual provides a brief discussion of the rationale for the development of the KVPT tests; however, it is not until chapter 8 that the taxonomy is presented and the procedures for development are discussed. The chapters in between provide administration and scoring directions.

There is little information about "Adverse Impact and Fairness" and no evidence to indicate whether these tests yield different results for children of different ethnic groups.

VALIDITY. In developing the KVPT, the author tried to follow procedures recommended in the literature. In order to define the construct, the author started with a review of the literature, from which he developed a taxonomy of "perceptual processing functions" (manual, p. 75). Much of this work was based on the work of Zusne (1970), along with that of Gibson (1969) and Massaro and Sanocki (1993).

The taxonomy is presented in Table 8-1. It covers four levels: Sensory Encoding, Perceptual Integration, Memorial Classification and Retrieval, and Cognitive Abstraction. For each level the "processing function" is identified, along with examples of associated "response functions."

DEVELOPMENT OF ITEMS. From the literature cited above, and the work of Gibson (1969) and Laughery (1971), the following features were selected: lines, curves, angle and point of intersection, open versus closed, symmetry, and "cyclic permutation" in which a feature is repeated (as in "M").

Over 200 stimulus items were created at three levels: Level 1: Single lines or curves, Level II: Two elements, and Level III: Two elements, plus organization elements as symmetry. The items were tried out first as *copy* items. The items were selected that demonstrated the clearest linear age-related improvement, except for a few items for which the success rate was less than 50% at age 12. The latter items were included in order to preclude a ceiling effect. The final version of the KVPT-C had 42 items, scattered across the three levels of complexity.

The KVPT-D was developed using the same 42 items, presented in a multiple-choice format. The KVPT-M was also created from the same 42 multiple-choice items, but the students are required to select the matching shape from memory, after a 5-second exposure.

STATISTICAL ANALYSIS. The items were administered to a sample of children ages 5–11. There were 741 children in the sample, with approximately 100 children at each age level, almost equally divided between boys and girls. Means and standard deviations were computed for each age/gender group.

In addition, a principal components factor analysis was conducted. Two factors were identified which accounted for 75% of the variance. The factors were identified as (a) Perceptual Integration and (b) Memorial Classification and Retrieval, which are the two middle levels of the taxonomy. No mention is made of the other two levels. However, earlier in chapter 8 there is a statement that the decision was made to focus on the two middle levels because, first, these are the processes most typically investigated by current visual perceptual tests and, second, there are already many good tests that address the fourth level, Cognitive Abstraction.

No correlations with scores on other instruments or with other criteria are reported, although it is mentioned that the KVPT scores are correlated with subsequent achievement scores.

RELIABILITY. Cronbach's alpha was computed as a measure of internal reliability. No values are reported; instead, there is a table that reports the level of significance. A small scale test-retest using 30 children 10 years of age yielded a reliability coefficient of .83 for the C Total score and .4 to .5 for the D and M tests. Actual correlations are not reported.

ADMINISTRATION AND SCORING. The tests are designed to be administered individually. The manual contains complete instructions for administering and scoring. There is a separate chapter for each of the three tests, with many samples of the scoring procedures.

Scoring is fairly simple, except for the analysis of errors, which is the most important part of the information to be derived from these tests. The author says the errors are carefully described so that scoring requires very few judgment calls. Unfortunately, these materials are not well organized and are difficult to follow, even though several samples are provided.

NORMS. Norms are reported in the appendices. Most of these are for children from 5 to 11 years of age, but there are norms for 18- to 22-year-olds and for older adults. The adult norms are described as "norms of convenience" and are based on very small sample sizes.

The norms for children are not very representative, either. They are based on the same 741-case sample of children on which the items were developed. They are described as overwhelmingly lower middle to middle class, from school districts in smaller cities and rural areas of northeastern Ohio.

In addition to the norms, chapter 7 presents information about "clinical interpretation with the KVPT" (manual, p. 59). Unfortunately, this discussion talks about "high scores" and "poor scores," and "average" and "moderately impaired," without defining what these are.

SUMMARY. The Kent Visual Perceptual Test has a good theoretical background and apparently well-developed items, but it needs more technical data.

First, there is a need for better norms. There is no way to know how well the available information fits other groups, especially minority or other language groups from large cities. Second, studies should be made and reported of the relationship between the various pieces of this test with some other instruments for which more information is available, in order that users may have more confidence that they know just what is being measured.

Also, better studies that demonstrate the relationship of scores on this test to evidence of other traits such as reading and mathematics achievement are badly needed. Even if one can demonstrate that the tests measure what was intended, the user needs more information to answer the question, "So what?"

Finally, the manual needs to be completely reorganized to make it easier to follow and easier to find important information. All information about the procedures for developing the tests, including the collection of technical information about validity and reliability, should be in one place. At the present time it is necessary to turn back and forth through several chapters to find it.

REVIEWER'S REFERENCES

Gibson, E. J. (1969). *Principles of perceptual learning and development*. New York: Appleton-Century-Crofts.
Zusne, L. (1970). *Visual perception of form*. New York: Academic Press.
Laughery, K. R. (1971). Computer simulation of short-term memory: A component decay model. In G. T. Bower & J. T. Spence (Eds.), *The psychology of learning and motivation: Advances in research and theory* (Vol. VI). New York: Academic Press.
Melamed, L. E., & Rugle, L. (1989). Neuropsychological correlates of school achievement in young children: Longitudinal findings with a construct valid perceptual processing instrument. *Journal of Clinical and Experimental Neuropsychology*, 11, 745–762.
Massaro, D. W., & Sanocki, T. (1993). Visual processing in reading. In D. M. Willows, R. S. Kruk, & E. Corcos (Eds.), *Visual processes in reading and reading disabilities* (pp. 139–161). Hillsdale, NJ: Erlbaum.

[194]

KeyMath Revised: A Diagnostic Inventory of Essential Mathematics [1998 Normative Update].

Purpose: Designed to assess understanding and applications of mathematics concepts and skills.
Population: Grades K–9, ages 6–22.
Publication Dates: 1971–1998.

Acronym: KeyMath-R.

Scores, 17: Basic Concepts (Numeration, Rational Numbers, Geometry, Total), Operations (Addition, Subtraction, Multiplication, Division, Mental Computation, Total), Applications (Measurement, Time and Money, Estimation, Interpreting Data, Problem Solving, Total), Total.

Administration: Individual.

Forms, 2: A, B.

Price Data, 1999: $389.95 per complete kit including Form A and B test easels, 25 each Form A and B test records, sample report to parents, and manual ('98, 255 pages); $209.95 per single form (A or B) kit including test easels, 25 test records, sample reports to parents, and manual; $39.95 per 25 test records (select A or B); $19.95 per 25 reports to parents; $44.95 per manual; $199.95 per complete ASSIST™ reporting software (Macintosh, DOS, or Windows).

Time: (35–50) minutes.

Comments: Revision of KeyMath Diagnostic Arithmetic Test; computerized reporting software available.

Author: Austin J. Connolly.

Publisher: American Guidance Service, Inc.

Cross References: See T5:1392 (15 references) and T4:1355 (5 references); for reviews by Michael D. Beck and Carmen J. Finley, see 11:191 (26 references); see also T3:1250 (12 references); for an excerpted review by Alex Bannatyne, see 8:305 (10 references).

Review of the KeyMath Revised: A Diagnostic Inventory of Essential Mathematics [1998 Normative Update] by G. GAGE KINGSBURY, Director of Research, Northwest Evaluation Association, Portland, OR:

KeyMath Revised with the 1998 Normative Update (KeyMath-R) is an individually administered inventory designed to identify a student's status in mathematics. KeyMath-R has norms for use with students from kindergarten to adult. KeyMath-R is designed to be administered to one student at a time. The person administering the test uses a small easel to present questions to the student, gives vocal directions, and records the student's responses on a scoring sheet. The expected time of administration is 35 to 50 minutes, although it is an untimed instrument with the exception of the Mental Computation strand.

KeyMath-R has two forms, each of which contains 258 items. A particular student will actually be administered far fewer than 258 questions, because basal and ceiling levels control the items that are administered within each strand. Subscores are available in primary areas of Basic Concepts, Operations, and Applications. In addition, scores are calculated for several strands within each primary area. Basic Concepts includes strands of Numeration, Rational Numbers, and Geometry. Operations includes strands of Addition, Subtraction, Multiplication, Division, and Mental Computation. Applications includes strands of Measurement, Time and Money, Estimation, Interpreting Data, and Problem Solving. Within each strand, up to four domain scores dealing with detailed aspects of the strand are computed for the test taker.

A student is administered KeyMath-R with one strand following another. In each strand, items are ordered from least difficult to most difficult. For the first strand (Numeration) a student starts at the item specified for the student's grade. As a student takes KeyMath-R, the test proctor scores each item administered and enters this information on a scoring form. The score for the Numeration strand is used to establish the item at which the student begins in each of the subsequent strands. In each strand, the student's test stops when three consecutive items are answered incorrectly.

Once a student completes the test, the test proctor may create some reports by hand, or enter the results into software designed to compute the subscores and produce several different types of reports. These reports include scaled scores, percentile ranks, grade equivalent scores, and other similar scores for the three major content areas. Reports also include scaled scores, score ranges, and percentile ranks for each strand. Domain indicators are also reported, detailing whether a student is "weak," "average," or "strong" in each domain. The scales scores are calculated using item response theory (the Rasch model, in particular). Finally, information about possible instructional needs for the student is reported in a narrative description of the student's performance, and in an analysis of the items missed by the student. The reporting software is available for DOS, Windows, and Mac-OS.

RELIABILITY AND VALIDITY. Split-half reliability and alternate-forms reliability coefficients are presented for the total test, the three primary areas of content, and each strand. For the total test, alternate-forms reliabilities range from .88 to .92, whereas adjusted split-half reliabilities range from .90 to .99. For the three primary areas of content, reliabilities are lower, with alternate-forms reliabilities ranging from .79 to .85, and split-half reliabilities ranging from .65 to .97. For the individual strands, the reliabilities are quite variable with alternate-forms reliabilities ranging from .53 to .80, and split-half reliabilities ranging from .07 to .94. Sample sizes for any particular reliability coefficient were modest, but information from the split-half study and the alternate-forms study were quite consistent.

In addition to these traditional measures of reliability, estimates of reliability based on item response theory are presented, as is an examination of expected error of measurement. The results of these studies confirm those from the traditional reliability studies. Total test score consistency was extremely high, consistency from the primary content areas was quite reasonable, and consistency for the strands was quite variable, but always positive.

One thing that should be noted about the reliability results is that they are probably influenced slightly by the scoring procedure used in KeyMath-R. Any item not seen during administration is given an imputed value. All items easier than the easiest item seen in a strand are assumed to be correct, whereas all items harder than the most difficult item seen are assumed to be incorrect. This is a reasonable procedure for administration, but it probably inflates the reliability coefficients slightly from what they would be if students responded to all items.

A very reasonable discussion of KeyMath-R content validity is included in the support materials. From this discussion, it is clear that KeyMath-R was developed in a thoughtful manner, with the assistance of many individuals with a substantial background in mathematics education. It is also clear that the domain structure and test blueprint used within KeyMath-R were designed to sample a wide variety of important mathematics concepts, while maintaining a needed specificity in the domains sampled.

Construct validity is addressed by three studies that investigated the relationships between scores from KeyMath-R and scores from the original KeyMath, CTBS math scores, and ITBS math scores. Total test correlations with the earlier version of KeyMath range from .86 to .93. Total test correlations with the Comprehensive Test of Basic Skills (CTBS) and Iowa Test of Basic Skills (ITBS) total mathematics scores were .66 and .76, respectively. The correlation with the earlier version of KeyMath is almost as high as allowed by the reliability of the tests. For the other two tests, the correlation with KeyMath-R is lower, and might suggest that there are some differences in the aspects of mathematics being measured. The sample sizes used in these comparisons are modest, but probably adequate to suggest that the various instruments are measuring similar constructs.

NORMING SAMPLE. This version of KeyMath-R differs from the 1988 version only in that it has a new norming sample. The actual questions and scoring have not changed. The norming sample, however, has improved substantially. Students from 40 states and the District of Columbia participated in the renorming of the test. Between 200 and 300 students were included in each grade from kindergarten to 12th grade. Representation of ethnic groups, geographical groups, and parental education in the total norming sample were quite similar to the national distribution of these characteristics in the most recent census.

STRENGTHS AND WEAKNESSES. A special education teacher might benefit from having an instrument like KeyMath-R available. It could be used to identify a student's primary strengths and weaknesses when the student enters the class. Its somewhat adaptive nature might also give KeyMath-R some advantages over a wide-range district-wide mathematics assessment for students in the lower portion of the achievement distribution within a grade. Finally, if a teacher is experienced in the use of KeyMath-R, it might help to pinpoint particular instructional needs for a student.

Given these uses though, KeyMath-R is still showing its age. The content of the test probably has more emphasis on computation than most school districts have had for the past 10 years. This is probably not appropriate if the test is to be used with the general student population. In addition, the use of calculators is quite common during assessments in some school districts. This practice will make KeyMath-R somewhat less useful in those districts.

Beyond content issues, KeyMath-R could benefit greatly from computer-based administration, or at least computer-based scoring. As it stands, individuals administering the test have to report by hand, or enter raw scores into the reporting program, to created computer-delivered reports. This adds to the possibility of error at several points in scoring and reporting. The computer-based reports are very well done, but the program for data entry lacks many features of current data-entry programs.

SUMMARY. In general, KeyMath-R seems to be a test that could be used in special settings to add information to a teacher's knowledge of a student's strengths and weaknesses in mathematics. It is a well-documented instrument with information about reliability, validity, and common performance in a national sample. On the other hand, KeyMath-R is somewhat dated in content, and somewhat more difficult to use than it might be with computer delivery or computer-based scoring. Finally, because KeyMath-R is designed to be used for students of many ages, it tends to lack content specificity that might make it more useful with students in any particular grade. It is likely that a broad range test written for a particular grade will be more useful to teachers in that grade than KeyMath-R will be.

Review of the KeyMath Revised: A Diagnostic Inventory of Essential Mathematics [1998 Normative Update] by JAMES A. WOLLACK, Assistant Scientist, Department of Testing & Evaluation, University of Wisconsin—Madison, Madison, WI:

For the past 30 years, the KeyMath assessment has been an invaluable tool for teachers and school districts for assessing the mathematical competencies of their students in kindergarten through ninth grade. KeyMath is an individually administered test that, in 35–50 minutes, provides detailed information about a student's mathematical understanding and skill in 3 broad areas (Basic Concepts, Operations, and Applications), 13 general subareas (Numeration, Rational Numbers, Geometry, Addition, Subtraction, Multiplication, Division, Mental Computation, Measurement, Time and Money, Estimation, Interpreting Data, and Problem Solving), and 43 very specific content domains, as well as an overall measure of mathematical achievement.

The original KeyMath, developed in 1971, was revised in 1988 (KeyMath-R) to reflect a variety of curricular changes that had taken place since the instrument was developed. In 1998, an updated set of norms tables were published for the KeyMath-R (KeyMath-R/NU). In all other aspects, the KeyMath-R/NU remains unchanged from the KeyMath-R. Beck (1992), Larson and Williams (1994), and Finley (1992) provide very good critiques of the KeyMath-R.

A detailed description of the normative update (NU) is included in the test manual. This renorming was part of a coordinated norming program involving four other individually administered achievement tests: The Kaufman Test of Educational Achievement (K-TEA; both the comprehensive and brief forms), the Peabody Individual Achievement Test—Revised (PIAT-R), and the Woodcock Reading Mastery Tests—Revised (WRMT-R). As part of this program, each participating student received one full test battery, along with at least one subtest from some of the other test batteries. The administration of the additional subtests accomplishes two goals. First, it allows items from different tests to be placed onto a common scale and, second, it ensures that the norms within each domain are based on adequate sample sizes. Because the WRMT-R does not include any mathematics items, students' responses to those items were not used in renorming the KeyMath-R. The sample used to update the norms on the KeyMath-R/NU was impressive. A total of 3,429 people (3,184 K–12 students and 245 young adults aged 18–22) participated in this cooperative, five-test norming effort, although only 2,802 completed the Operations Area and 2,809 people completed the Basic Concepts and Applications Areas of the KeyMath-R/NU. The updated sample contains approximately 1,000 more people than the 1988 norming. A total of 650 people received the entire KeyMath-R/NU battery, with the rest of the sample receiving at least one KeyMath-R/NU subtest. Sample sizes were similar for each grade, with approximately an even number of males and females at each grade level. Within each grade, the sample was carefully stratified to ensure that it was representative of the U.S. population with respect to sex, parental education (a proxy for socioeconomic status), race/ethnicity, geographic region, and educational placement (i.e., students in gifted and special education programs).

The norms were developed based on the ability distribution derived from application of the Rasch model for each domain at each grade or age level. Those distributions were smoothed and transformed into the metrics of interest (e.g., percentiles, grade or age equivalents, etc.). This process is explained in the manual, but unless the test user has considerable knowledge of statistical and measurement techniques, including Rasch scaling, it will be very difficult to follow. Finally, very detailed and well-organized tables are provided, separately by grade (fall and spring) and age, where appropriate, for total score, area scores, and subtest scores for computing (a) the standard or scaled scores; (b) percentile ranks, stanines, and normal curve equivalents; (c) age and grade equivalents; (d) minimum differences between area scores to achieve statistical significance; and (e) average domain scores, by ceiling item.

SUMMARY. Overall, the KeyMath-R/NU remains one of the very best test batteries for assessing a student's knowledge and understanding of basic mathematics and providing useful diagnostic information to the teachers. The availability of an updated set of well-designed norms tables should only encourage more people to seriously consider using the KeyMath-R/NU assessment.

REVIEWER'S REFERENCES

Beck, M. D. (1992). [Review of the KeyMath Revised: A Diagnostic Inventory of Essential Mathematics.] In J. J. Kramer & J. C. Conoley (Eds.), *The eleventh mental measurements yearbook* (pp. 437–438). Lincoln, NE: Buros Institute of Mental Measurements.

Finley, C. J. (1992). [Review of the KeyMath Revised: A Diagnostic Inventory of Essential Mathematics.] In J. J. Kramer & J. C. Conoley (Eds.), *The eleventh mental measurements yearbook* (pp. 438–439). Lincoln, NE: Buros Institute of Mental Measurements.

Larson, J. A., & Williams, J. D. (1994). KeyMath Revised: A Diagnostic Inventory of Essential Mathematics. In D. J. Keyser & R. C. Sweetland (Eds.), *Test critiques, Vol. X* (pp. 350–354). Austin, TX: PRO-ED, Inc.

[195]
KEYS: Assessing the Climate for Creativity.

Purpose: Designed to measure how "employees perceive stimulants and barriers to creativity."
Population: Employees.
Publication Date: 1995.
Scores, 10: 8 environment scales (6 environmental stimulants to creativity: Organizational Encouragement of Creativity, Supervisory Encouragement of Creativity, Work Group Supports, Freedom, Sufficient Resources, Challenging Work; 2 obstacles to creativity: Organizational Impediments, Workload Pressure); 2 outcome scales (Creativity, Productivity).
Administration: Group.
Price Data, 1998: $20 per survey booklet (5–50 booklets); quantity discounts available.
Time: (15–20) minutes.
Comments: Costs of survey booklets includes scoring, standard feedback results, one KEYS User's Guide (205 pages), and one KEYS: Interpreting the Results.
Authors: Teresa M. Amabile, Robert M. Burnside, and Stanley S. Gryskiewicz.
Publisher: Center for Creative Leadership.
Cross References: See T5:1393 (1 reference).

Review of the KEYS: Assessing the Climate for Creativity by CAROLYN M. CALLAHAN, Professor of Educational Leadership, Foundations, and Policy, Curry School of Education, University of Virginia, Charlottesville, VA:

KEYS is based on a sound theoretical and empirical framework regarding creative productivity in organizations. The items on the 81-item, objectively scored instrument are logically derived from interviews with informants working in a wide variety of organizations geared toward productive innovation. The authors carefully define creativity as "production of novel and useful ideas and things" (user's guide, p. 1) and innovations as "successful implementation of creative ideas by an organization" (user's guide, p. 1). Further, the authors take great care to point out that the instrument measures perceptions of the environment and not actual factors in the environment, or the creative productivity of individuals or organizations. While pointing out that there is an assumption that individuals working in an environment are likely to have perceptions corresponding to "objective" observations, they also argue that it is perceived environment that influences an individual's response to that environment. Further, they specify that the realm of assessment covered by KEYS is limited to the extent to which the work environment stimulates or inhibits creativity and warn users against other uses of the assessment tool such as a general assessment of the work environment or individual worker's creativity or adjustment to an organization.

The instrument is designed to reflect group perceptions of an environment. Response analysis and reporting is limited to results produced by a minimum of three individuals in an organization or a subgroup of the organization. Specific individual feedback may be provided to individuals so they may compare their scores to the group scores.

The reliability estimates on the subscale (internal consistency and test-retest for individual scores) range from moderate to high (.66 to .94), and given the specification of a minimum of three respondents for analysis, support confidence in consistent results on the subscales for either research or organizational analysis.

The authors have provided adequate factor analytic support justifying the assignment of items to the specific subscales. While acknowledging the loading of some items on more than one scale, the ways in which the data are to be used does not make the given assignments problematic. Evidence of convergent validity is derived from correlations with the Work Environment Scale (Insel & Moos, 1974). These correlations are moderate (except in areas of workload pressure and freedom) as would be expected. Nonsignificant correlations with a measure of personality variables associated with creativity and with a measure of cognitive style (-.27 to .14) support discriminant validity of the instrument (Amabile, Hill, Hennessey, & Tighe, 1994; Kirton, 1976).

The most important validity evidence is provided by a three-phase study of the ability of the scales to discriminate between perceptions of environments that are associated with productivity rated high and low on the dimension of creative innovation. Under the most stringent conditions in the study, five of the scales (Challenging Work, Organizational Encouragement, Work Group Supports, Supervisory Encouragement, and Organizational Impediments) discriminated significantly. Freedom and Workload Pressure and Sufficient Resources did not discriminate.

Purchase of the KEYS instrument is limited to individuals approved by the Center for Creative Leadership (CCL). The purchaser is required to have background in psychology, assessment, and/ or organizational development or may be trained by CCL. The user must agree to conditions for maintaining confidentiality of individual results. These specifications are tied to acknowledgement that the reliability and validity of scores from the instrument are dependent on specific assumptions about administration, the sampling of respondents from the organization or subgroup in the organization, and the confidentiality of the process. Because names are included on the form and sensitive work environment questions (especially some relating to supervisory support) are included, an outside interpreter and confidentiality is critical to obtaining meaningful results.

Scoring and reporting of results in relation to the norm group is carried out by CCL. The results may be reported for varying groups or subgroups within an organization (at extra charge in some cases). All subscale and individual item scores are reported in comparison to the full norm group composed of organizations that have used the instrument rather than a purposive sampling of organizations. These organizations represent a broad sample of organizations (but not necessarily assessed or grouped according to their creative innovation or creative productivity). The reports provided include graphic information presented in conjunction with classification of group scores as

Very High, High, Mid-range, Low, and Very Low on each subscale based on 10-point differences on *T*-score scales. There is no discussion of whether the scores from the norm group formed a normal distribution or were normalized. Differences of 10 points are suggested to be "meaningful" differences. However, neither the classification nor the interpretation of meaningful differences is supported by empirical evidence. To make it possible to judge the appropriate interpretation of score differences, data on the frequency distribution should be provided in the manual. Further, individual item reliabilities are not presented.

Careful and detailed directions are provided for sampling, establishing and maintaining trust, and interpretation of results. The format of the instrument is appealing and would likely have great face validity to the respondent.

SUMMARY. Overall, the authors and publisher provide clear and carefully documented evidence of reliability and validity for the intended purposes of KEYS. Users who follow the standards for administration and interpretation of results, who understand the limitations of the statement as outlined by the authors, and who interpret the norms cautiously are likely to have information useful in generating discussions around actions for improving the environments for creative innovation.

REVIEWER'S REFERENCES
Insel, P. M., & Moos, R. H. (1974). Work Environment Scale. Palo Alto, CA: Consulting Psychologists Press.
Kirton, M. (1976). Adaptors and innovators: A description and measures. *Journal of Applied Psychology, 61,* 622–629.
Amabile, T. M., Hill, K. G., Hennessey, B. A., & Tighe, E. (1994) The Work Preference Inventory: Assessing intrinsic and extrinsic motivational orientations. *Journal of Personality and Social Psychology, 66,* 950–967.

[196]
Kindergarten Language Screening Test, Second Edition.

Purpose: Designed to help identify children "who need further diagnostic testing to determine whether or not they have language deficits that will accelerate academic failure."

Population: Ages 4-0 through 6-11.

Publication Dates: 1978–1998.

Acronym: KLST-2.

Scores: Total score only.

Administration: Individual.

Price Data, 1999: $94 per complete kit including manual ('98, 30 pages), 50 profile/examiner record forms, picture book, and 3 picture cards; $29 per manual; $39 per 50 profile/examiner record forms; $29 per picture book; $5 per 3 picture cards.

Time: (5) minutes.

Authors: Sharon V. Gauthier and Charles L. Madison.

Publisher: PRO-ED.

Cross References: See T4:1359 (2 references).

Review of the Kindergarten Language Screening Test, Second Edition by TIMOTHY R. KONOLD, Assistant Professor of Education, University of Virginia, Charlottesville, VA:

According to the authors, the Kindergarten Language Screening Test, Second Edition (KLST-2) was designed to serve as a screening tool to aid in the identification of early language problems that may suggest the need for a more comprehensive evaluation for children. The test comprises 18 items, 17 of which combine to form a single score. Seven of these items remained unchanged from the original KLST. By contrast, 1 item was revised from its original form and 9 items represent new initiatives. The authors provide theoretical and/or empirical rationale to support children's ability to respond to each of the 17 items. However, users might benefit more from a better understanding of how each of these items relates to language. This lack of explicit link between items and the dimensions of language they were designed to address may result in interpretive difficulties for examiners who lack a good understanding of early language research. For example, the manual indicates that "should a child show poor performance on the KLST-2 in areas related to vocabulary, his or her ability could be further evaluated" (p. 7). However, the manual does not explicitly identify those items designed to measure vocabulary. A related concern is that the authors contend that the KLST-2 items were designed to measure both receptive and expressive language. However, no empirical (e.g., factor analysis) or theoretical evidence is provided to support this statement.

The technical characteristics reported in the manual are well explained and can easily be understood by users with minimal training in measurement or assessment. Evidence of reliability for KLST-2 scores is provided by way of internal consistency, test-retest, and scorer differences. The internal consistency estimates are favorably high across the three age groups that were investigated. Test-retest reliability was investigated in four samples of unreported size. These estimates suggest that children's scores on the KLST-2 are relatively stable across a 1- to 3-week interval. Scorer difference reliability was investigated by correlating the scores obtained from two independent PRO-ED staff members on 30 randomly selected protocols. The reported correlation of .99 suggests that scoring instructions are sufficiently comprehensive and should result in few calculation errors.

The KLST-2 manual also reports several studies intended to support the instrument's content, criterion-related, and construct validity. Content validity was addressed by providing a rationale for the test items and through classical item discrimination analyses. Concerns regarding the connection between the items and language development were previously addressed in the first paragraph. The median point biserial coefficients reported for each of the three age groups provide preliminary evidence that the items are able to discriminate, to some degree, between high and low scoring children. Criterion-related validity was investigated with correlations between the KLST-2 and three existing measures of early language ability. These results suggest that the KLST-2 similarly measures aspects of early language ability found in previously published assessments, most notably with he Preschool Language Scale—3 (Zimmerman, Steiner, & Pond, 1992). No evidence of discriminant validity was provided.

The most promising study conducted on the KLST-2's construct validity involved estimates of the measure's sensitivity and specificity with respect to distinguishing between known groups of children with and without language impairments. Results indicate that the KLST-2 was able to accurately identify children with known language impairments (sensitivity = .90), but was less successful identifying children without language impairments (specificity = .61). It is likely that examiners may incorrectly identify even more children as having language impairments when none actually exist, due to the discrepancy between the KLST-2 cutoff used in this study and that advocated for use by examiners. Namely, the KLST-2 cutoff score used in the aforementioned study was based on a prevalence rate of 16% (i.e., only 16% of the children would obtain lower scores). By contrast, the cutoff score advocated for use in the KLST-2 manual for generating language impairment hypotheses, and considering children for further assessment, is based on a prevalence rate of 23%. Given the more important goal of this screening measure, of identifying children with possible language impairments, this study suggests that the KLST-2 may be well suited for this purpose.

The standardization sample was well stratified in accordance with U.S. Census data on the variables of geographic region, gender, and two race categories (i.e., "white" and "black"). However, the relatively small sample sizes for each of the six age-based normative groups may result in percentile rank score misinterpretations. Raw score to percentile rank look-up tables are provided for each of the six age groups. However, only 9 of the possible 99 percentile rank values are listed in the table. As a result, examiners basing their interpretations on percentile ranks may tend to over- or understate the relative position of the examinee. For example, a raw score of 24, for a 4-year-old child, corresponds to a percentile rank of 51, and a raw score of 23 corresponds to a percentile rank of 32. This example illustrates that 19% of the sample would be expected to fall between these two percentile rank scores, despite the fact that a raw score between 23 and 24 cannot be obtained.

SUMMARY. The KLST-2 appears to be a useful tool for the identification of children with possible language impairments. The authors provide convincing evidence to support the reliability of the measure and offer some validity studies to support its various uses. The KLST-2 would benefit, however, from more empirical research on its factor structure to support the receptive and expressive components of language it was designed to assess. This research would also provide users with a better understanding of what each of the items was designed to assess and thereby provide for a more focused follow-up evaluation when indicated.

REVIEWER'S REFERENCE

Zimmerman, L. L., Steiner, V. G., & Pond, R. E. (1992). Preschool Language Scale-3. San Antonio, TX: Psychological Corporation.

Review of the Kindergarten Language Screening Test, Second Edition by LESLIE EASTMAN LUKIN, Assessment Specialist, Lincoln Public Schools/ ESU 18, Lincoln, NE:

The Kindergarten Language Screening Test, Second Edition (KLST-2) is a language screening test that was designed to identify children with potential language impairments. The instrument is intended for use with children between the ages of 4 years, 0 months and 6 years, 11 months. Because the KLST-2 was designed as a screening device, the authors strongly suggest that identified children receive additional diagnostic assessment. The KLST-2 consists of 18 items, 17 of which contribute to a total score that can be converted to a percentile rank and/or stanine. The first 17 items (tasks) are designed to measure verbal abilities that are considered normal for children between 4 and 7 years of age. The tasks include activities that reflect both receptive and expressive language competencies. The last item requires the test administrator to make a number of subjective judgments (good or poor) about the child's overall performance in the areas of intelligibility, attention to task, willingness to communicate, gestural communication, response rate, fluency, and voice. The authors suggest that in the majority of cases, the test administration time should be 5 minutes or less.

ADMINISTRATION AND SCORING. In general, the directions for administration and scoring are complete and clear. The only major concern with regard to scoring the KLST-2 items has to do with the scoring of Items 11 through 14. There are potential student responses that are not covered in the scoring criteria. This ambiguity may result in differences in scoring from one test administrator to another. Also, the scoring for Item 17 appears to be rather cumbersome in comparison to other items on the KLST-2.

NORMS. Norms expressed in terms of percentile ranks and stanines are available for six age groups, with each group representing a 6-month age span. A moderately sized norming sample (N = 519) was drawn from 16 states, representing various regions within the United States. The sample is described in the examiner's manual in terms of geographic region, gender, race, and age. The authors suggest that the percentages in the sample match the percentages reported in the U.S. Census for 1990. Although the reported percentages for the sample are fairly closely matched to the reported percentages for the U.S. Census, it is puzzling how the authors derived the value of 14% that is associated with the geographic area described as "West" given the list of states that is included in the examiner's manual. In addition, the Midwest is slightly underrepresented in the sample (17% versus 24% reported in the U.S. Census) and the South is slightly overrepresented (49% versus 36% reported in the U.S. Census).

RELIABILITY. Internal consistency estimates of reliability (Cronbach's alpha) were reported for three major age groups as well as the overall group. The estimates of reliability were in the acceptable range from .81 (5 years, 0 months through 5 years, 11 months) to .90 (4 years, 0 months through 4 years, 11 months). The authors also provided estimates of reliability that resulted from four separate test-retest studies. The time intervals between testing in the four studies ranged from 1 to 3 weeks. Sample sizes were not reported. The estimates of reliability were, once again, in the acceptable range, from .83 to .98. Finally, the authors provided information about the rate of agreement between raters. The authors reported a correlation of .99 that resulted from scores generated by two individuals who "independently scored a set of 30 completed protocols randomly selected from the normative sample" (manual, p. 12). This extremely high rate of agreement is likely to be artificially inflated by the fact that the scorers were "scoring" protocols that were already completed. A better test of rater agreement would have resulted if a second rater had observed test administration and independently completed and scored a protocol.

VALIDITY. The authors provided information about validation studies under three general headings: content validity, criterion-related validity, and construct validity. Under the heading of content validity, information is provided about how the construct (verbal competence) being measured by the KLST-2 is defined by the authors. In addition, information is provided about how items were identified for inclusion in the instrument and how these items compare to items that are included in other widely used instruments. In general, adequate justifications are provided for the majority of the items included in the KLST-2. The one exception is the inclusion of the picture arrangement item. This item does not appear to be directly related to either expressive or receptive language. Typically picture arrangement tasks are more strongly associated with performance scores as opposed to verbal scores on individually administered tests of intelligence such as the Wechsler Intelligence Scale for Children—Third Edition (WISC-III; T5:2862). Finally, empirical data from a traditional classical true-score approach to item analysis are presented in the form of item discrimination indices, specifically point biserial correlations. The authors stated that all the item point biserials met or exceeded the self-imposed criteria of .30.

Under the heading of criterion-related validity, the results of three studies focusing on criterion-related evidence are provided. Scores from the KLST-2 were correlated with scores from

three other measures of language: the Preschool Language Scale-3, the Test of Language Development—Primary, 3rd Edition, and the Clinical Evaluation of Language Fundamentals—Preschool. The sample sizes for all three studies were relatively small, ranging from 25 to 33. In addition, two of the three studies focused on children at the upper age range for the KLST-2, 6 years of age. Despite these limitations, all three studies resulted in moderate to high positive correlations between the KLST-2 and the other measures of language.

Finally, in the section entitled construct validity, the authors reported the results of two studies, one focused on group differentiation and the other on sensitivity. Group differentiation, according to the authors, results when children with language impairments score lower on an instrument designed to screen children for language than do children with "normally developing language" (manual, p. 18). Sensitivity focuses on the number of correct identifications of language impairment that result from the use of KLST-2 scores. A sample of 33 children, 14 of whom had been previously identified as having language impairments, were included in a study that yielded data that supported both group differentiation and sensitivity hypotheses.

SUMMARY. The KLST-2 appears to be a relatively well-constructed screening test for language impairments for use with kindergarten students. The authors provided clear information about the intended use of the instrument, the intended audience, the necessary qualifications for potential test users, how to administer and score items, and appropriate cautions concerning the use of KLST-2 scores. The authors also provided, throughout the manual, clear definitions of a number of relevant measurement terms such as item discrimination, reliability, and validity. In general, information about the norming sample and the evidence of reliability and validity were clearly presented and represented adequate levels of technical quality. The inclusion of a slightly larger norming sample, more representative of all regions of the United States, would be helpful. Also, the omission of sample sizes for the test-retest studies and the relatively small sample sizes for the validation studies (ranges from 25 to 33) is somewhat problematic. Despite some minor limitations, the KLST-2 appears to have promise as a language screening device that requires little training and time to administer and score.

The Kirkpatrick Management and Supervisory Skills Series.

Purpose: Designed to assess "Key management skills and practices."
Publication Date: 1995.
Scores: Total score only.
Administration: Group.
Price Data: Available from publisher.
Time: (20) minutes per inventory.
Author: Donald L. Kirkpatrick.
Publisher: Donald L. Kirkpatrick (the author).

a) COMMUNICATION INVENTORY.
Purpose: Constructed to "improve knowledge, attitudes, and skills" related to communication.
Population: Supervisors and all levels of managers.
Acronym: CI.

b) HUMAN RELATIONS INVENTORY.
Purpose: Constructed to assess "the relationships that exist between supervisor and subordinate."
Population: Same as *a* above.
Acronym: HRI.

c) MANAGING CHANGE INVENTORY.
Purpose: Designed to "cover principles, facts, and attitudes that are basic to managing change effectively."
Population: All levels of managers.
Acronym: MCI.

d) MANAGEMENT ROLES INVENTORY.
Purpose: Designed to measure "philosophy, principles, and approaches related to the effective performance of managers."
Population: Same as *c* above.
Acronym: MRI.

e) COACHING AND PERFORMANCE APPRAISAL INVENTORY.
Purpose: Constructed to assess "concepts, principles, and techniques that are important ingredients" of on-the-job coaching.
Population: Same as *c* above.
Acronym: CPAI.

f) TIME MANAGEMENT INVENTORY.
Purpose: Constructed to measure "Key factors in better time utilization and delegation."
Population: Same as *c* above.
Acronym: TMI.

g) LEADERSHIP, MOTIVATION, AND DECISION-MAKING INVENTORY.
Purpose: Constructed to "make managers more conscious of their need to be leaders."
Population: Same as *c* above.
Acronym: LMDMI.

Review of the Kirkpatrick Management and Supervisory Skills Series by L. CAROLYN PEARSON, Professor of Education, and LEE DROEGEMUELLER, Professor of Education, University of West Florida, Pensacola, FL:

The Kirkpatrick Management and Supervisory Skills Series consists of seven different inventories that measure Communication Skills (CI); Human Relations (HRI); Managing Change (MCI); Management Roles (MRI); Coaching and Performance Appraisal (CPAI); Time Management (TMI); and Leadership, Motivation, and Decision-Making (LMDMI). All of the inventories are usually used to determine training needs; stimulate discussion, especially in a conference setting; evaluate training programs; provide coaching information; and for four of the tests (HRI, MRI, MCI, LMDMI) to aid in the selection of managers.

The CI is designed to measure principles, facts, and techniques of communication. It is further subdivided into definitions of communication, philosophy and principles, oral and written communication skills, and listening skills. The HRI is designed to examine relationships between the supervisor and subordinate. It is further subdivided into the supervisor's role in management, understanding and motivating employees, developing positive employee attitudes, problem-solving techniques, and principles of learning and training. The MCI is designed to cover principles, facts, and attitudes that are basic to managing change effectively. It is further subdivided into the manager's role in change, why people resist/resent or accept/welcome change, and principles for managing change. The CPAI is designed to cover the concepts, principles, and techniques that are important for on-the-job coaching and performance appraisal and has two subscales, respectively. The TMI is designed to cover key factors in better time utilization and delegation and has no subscales. The LMDMI was developed to cover leadership, motivation, and decision-making and the items are grouped accordingly in an attempt to make managers more conscious of their need to be leaders.

The MRI can be used as a stand alone in that it is really a battery of inventories. The other inventories deal with a specific topic whereas this inventory contains subscales that cover eight different topics with 10 items each. The MRI measures leadership styles, selecting and training, communication, motivating, managing change, delegation, decision making, and managing time. The instrument is designed to cover the philosophy, principles, and approaches related to the effective performance of managers.

Lengths range from 45 items (CPAI) to 80 items (CI, HRI, MRI) and take from 15 to 20 minutes to complete. The items require the respondent to indicate whether they agree or disagree with the statements. A separate answer sheet that is self-scored and is not to be handed in is provided as part of the test booklet. Correct responses are recorded in a box underlying carbon paper and scoring is done by subtracting the incorrect responses from the total. The directions for taking the test are clear and the user is told to keep track of the incorrect responses so that they may be evaluated after the inventory is taken; however, the author does not give directions on what to do with items for which there is no response. The tests are arranged in such a way as to make hand scoring easy. Each inventory, in a separate answer booklet or in the back of the manual, has reasons for how each item is scored. The reasons are the author's opinions. The MCI contains a few appli cation items, and for 10 of the items there is more than one possible correct response. The LMDMI has 4 items that are not scored because the answers are given in percentages that are based on the opinion of the respondent.

Norming was scantily done on office and plant supervisors, middle and top management, personnel and training managers, human resource managers, and secretaries and social workers from more than 100 companies representing industry, government, business, and education from the United States and Canada. Each test was normed with different groups making interpretations across tests difficult. The only information provided was item means, standard deviations, and an analysis of which items were most frequently missed by the group; therefore, the inventories could hardly be considered to have adequate normative data on which to base score interpretations because there is no information presented concerning gender and ethnicity performance differences.

The author provides no rationale or theoretical framework for the statements that are used for each of the areas. There is no logical analysis presented on how the items were developed, pretested, or selected from the research on management/supervision. It is up to the user to determine if evidence for content validity exists for a particular job setting. As for predictive validity, the au-

thor warns that for managerial selection the inventories should be validated using job performance as the criterion. Consequently, in terms of empirical research, no reliability or validity data are reported; therefore, it is assumed that the inventories are probably only suitable for discussion purposes. The author also cautions the test user about using the instruments for screening purposes. There has been no research undertaken to determine if the items are free of bias.

SUMMARY. In conclusion, the Kirkpatrick Management and Supervisory Skills Series is in need of documentation of the research base from which it was derived. The items have good face validity; however, there is no indication of how they were derived from the research on management/supervision. Empirical evidence to support score reliability, validity, and biases has yet to be provided. We cannot recommend the series because there are no studies to support it as a measure of management skills.

[198]
Kirton Adaption-Innovation Inventory [1998 Edition].

Purpose: A measure of a person's preference for, or style of, creativity, problem solving, and decision making.
Population: British and U.S. adults and teenagers over age 14.
Publication Dates: 1976–1998.
Acronym: KAI.
Scores, 4: Sufficiency v. Proliferation of Originality, Efficiency, Rule/Group Conformity, Total.
Administration: Individual or group.
Price Data: Available from publisher.
Time: (5–10) minutes.
Comments: Translations available for Italian, Slovak, French, and Dutch adults and teenagers.
Author: Michael Kirton.
Publisher: Occupational Research Centre [England].
Cross References: See T5:1404 (15 references) and T4:1364 (9 references); for reviews by Gregory J. Boyle and Gerald E. DeMauro of an earlier edition, see 11:193 (8 references).

Review of the Kirton Adaption-Innovation Inventory [1998 Edition] by LYNN L. BROWN, Assistant Professor, Northern Arizona University, Phoenix, AZ:

The Kirton Adaption-Innovation Inventory (KAI) is an administrator-scored instrument of 32 Likert-scaled items measuring one broad construct, an innovation-adaption continuum. Items are not all scored in the same direction in order to avoid response set, and this variation is randomly distributed. The KAI is designed for adults literate in the language used, although recent norming studies have also established that the instrument can be used reliably with adolescents age 17 or above. The instrument is not a timed measure, but the inventory will take approximately 5–10 minutes to complete.

The 1998 edition is a further expansion of the original 1977 version. The inventory items remain the same; however, the manual has been expanded to include more recent research relating to use of the instrument together with revised statistical tables regarding construction methodology. In addition to the test manual and instrument, the reviewer was also provided a copy of a supplemental list of reference cites not included in the manual, as well as a copy of *Adaptors and Innovators* (Rev. Ed.) by Michael Kirton (1994) which further expands upon the underlying theoretical basis for the instrument.

THEORETICAL BASIS FOR INSTRUMENT. The test creator Michael Kirton asserts that creativity is not correlated with intelligence, but rather is present in all problem-solving behavior. He suggests a continuum of an individual's need for structure, with innovators needing less and adaptors needing more. Both individuals, however, can be creative: The adaptor is creative in working within existing structure to problem solve, whereas the innovator often goes beyond to find a solution. Finally, this continuum is described as a style or preferred method of behavior that remains relatively constant over time. The individual may use coping behavior from the opposite pole of this continuum, but the continued need to do so over a period of time results in stress and ultimate lack of productive work.

ITEM DEVELOPMENT. A list of statements consistent with the adaption-innovative typology was introduced to a group of 20 managers who augmented the list with additional suggestions. A second group of managers was asked to do a card sort to categorize a single individual's behavior, and then to expand the card sort to include both positive and negative attributes of such a person. With both groups of managers, a consistent division into "adaptors" and "innovators" was made. Pilot samples were then carried

out, items with high or low (≥80%; ≤20%) endorsements eliminated, and items failing to correlate ≥ .20 also dropped from the pool. This revised list was then tested on a general population sample (N = 355), further items were dropped or revised, and yet another sample population was tested.

FACTOR TRAITS. Although all items in the instrument are related to the common continuum of adaptive-innovative behavior, factor analysis using orthogonal rotation indicated that three subgroups could be formed: Sufficiency-Proliferation of Originality (SO) with 13 items, Style of Efficiency or Thoroughness (E), with 7 items, and Preference for operating within Rules, Policies, Mores, and Consensus (R), 12 items. Internal reliability estimates for each factor trait were: the SO subscale, .83; the E subscale, .76; and the R subscale, .83.

NORMING. The first norming population was drawn from local British populations representing women volunteers, business people, students, and hospital employees, with additional stratified subjects added to balance the group by age, sex, education, and occupational status (N = 532). No information on ethnicity was given. A replication sample of 276 subjects was used 7 months after the first group was tested, again balanced by the four demographic variables. Analysis of scores for both groups showed an almost perfect distribution curve. Although these first groups were drawn from one country, the instrument has subsequently been translated into numerous European languages, and has been used in United States, Australian, African, and Asian locations as well, with similar results.

RELIABILITY. Internal reliability, using the Kuder-Richardson 20 was .88 for the original sample. Calculations on the replication sample collected one year later also yielded a K-R 20 of .88. Numerous subsequent studies on various target populations in countries such as the United States, Australia, Canada, and France have yielded Cronbach alphas ranging from .79 to .91.

VALIDITY. The KAI has good face validity, being easy to take and score, with strong respondent cooperation. The manual asserts that concurrent validity is demonstrated by the fact that scores have produced a normal distribution curve for a human mental attribute over several populations in numerous languages. Discriminant validity is demonstrated by the failure of the KAI to correlate with instruments measuring human intelligence such as the Otis (High Form A) and Cattell (Factor B).

SUMMARY. Although the instrument is well designed and adequately normed, the accompanying manual could be more clearly organized for better understanding by the general test administrator. With the advent of the Internet, access to testing materials is certainly easier, but still an impediment to those not living in Britain. In addition, use of the test is limited to Certified Administrators only (i.e., those who have undergone a week of intensive training at limited locations in the U.S. or Britain). Nevertheless, the true originality of this instrument's underlying premise, plus its popularity in the arenas of business, education, and science will continue to give it prominence in the venue of human behavior measurement.

Review of the Kirton Adaption-Innovation Inventory [1998 Edition] by RIC BROWN, Associate Vice President for Research, Graduate and Extended Programs, California State University, Sacramento, Sacramento, CA:

The Kirton Adaption-Innovation Inventory (KAI) is reported to measure an adult's individual preferred style with respect to bringing about change. It is not a measure of intellectual capacity and does not suggest that being adaptive versus being innovative is more or less appropriate—just different. Thus, the KAI attempts to quantify the manner a person prefers to solve a problem, not the person's ability at problem solving.

The theory behind the KAI is that problem-solving style is on a bipolar continuum. At one end is the adaptor, a person who looks for structure and definition (e.g., creates by doing things better). The high adaptor, in response to problems, is seen as methodical, reliable, and precise, thereby producing sound and safe ideas. The opposite style, the innovator, is not as tolerant with regard to existing patterns or rules, but prefers change that does things differently. The high innovator is one who thinks tangentially and produces many ideas, some of which may be seen as "blue sky."

The manual accompanying the KAI provides an extensive theoretical background in support of the KAI's constructs. In addition to a total score, the KAI has three subscales. The SO (Sufficiency-Proliferation of Originality) person is described as the creative loner. An E (Adaptive

Efficiency) seeks improvement of the current structure. The R operates within rules and consensus. The KAI manual lists over 300 citations in support of the scale.

Extensive data are reported with respect to the construction of the scale including original item construction and item analysis with fairly large sample sizes. The validation samples were carefully constructed to include a wide range of occupations, age, gender, and education level. As well, data are reported with respect to controlling for social desirability. Most of the scale development was completed on samples from England. Some data are presented with respect to other language translations (Italian, French, Dutch, Czech). The general manual does not report any studies of cross-cultural validation (Brown, 2000), but refers to a language manual supplement.

Although the KAI is not a timed measure, it is suggested that approximately 10 minutes is necessary to complete the form. Either individual or group administration is suggested. The prompt asks the respondent to describe how easy or difficult it is for them to be "A person who" followed by 33 descriptors (e.g., A person who ...is thorough). For each of the items, the respondent is asked to mark a continuum from *very hard,* to *hard,* to *easy,* to *very easy* on a 17-point scale. A scoring guide is provided and the 17-point scale for each item is reduced to a 1 to 5 score; 1 for *very easy,* 5 for *very hard.* Several items are reversed to attempt to avoid response set. Scoring is to be done by a trained scorer and not self-scored by the respondent. Once the instrument is scored, the manual indicates that those scores are on a continuum that is normally distributed. Lower scores indicate an adaptor (e.g., the lowest scorers are very high adaptors). As the scores increase, individuals move into the mild adaptor to mild innovator range. Extremely high scorers are said to be very high innovators.

Extensive data are presented with respect to reliability of scores among the samples and subsamples with coefficients appropriately high at .8 and above. As well, extensive validity information is presented both in terms of content validity, factor analysis, and correlation of the KAI with other related personality traits.

Interestingly and importantly, the KAI manual offers a section on the ethical use of the instrument that includes a reminder for proper scoring, adequate feedback, and cautious interpretation. In addition, even though data are presented for nonadults, appropriate caveats are noted.

SUMMARY. As a measure of cognitive functioning, the KAI has been developed with an extensive theoretical underpinning. It would seem appropriate as a research tool to study style with respect to change. The manual implies an occupational focus, but there is no presentation of what such an applied use the scale might have. For example, even though norms are shown for various groups (bankers, managers, teachers, etc.), use in any applied setting involving these groups is not demonstrated.

REVIEWER'S REFERENCE

Brown, R. (2000). Measuring the construct of locus of control in an international setting. *Phi Beta Delta International Review, X*, 165–173.

[199]
The Kohlman Evaluation of Living Skills.

Purpose: "An occupational therapy evaluation that is designed to determine a person's ability to function in basic living skills."
Population: Occupational therapy clients with living skill deficits.
Publication Dates: 1981–1992.
Acronym: KELS.
Scores: 5 areas: Self-care, Safety and Health, Money Management, Transportation and Telephone, Work and Leisure.
Administration: Individual.
Price Data, 1998: $35 per administration booklet.
Time: (30–45) minutes.
Comments: Evaluation combines interview questions and tasks; can be used with the elderly, with persons who have cognitively disabling conditions, in court for the determination of commitment, and in discharge planning at acute-care hospitals.
Author: Linda Kohlman Thomson.
Publisher: The American Occupational Therapy Association, Inc.

Review of The Kohlman Evaluation of Living Skills by GABRIELE van LINGEN, Professor of Educational Studies, Leadership and Counseling, Murray State University, Murray, KY:

The Kohlman Evaluation of Living Skills (KELS) was developed for occupational therapists to assess an individual's basic living skills. It focuses on five main areas of basic living skills, grouped into Self-care, Safety and Health, Money Management, Transportation and Telephone, and Work and Leisure. It contains a total of 17 items, varying from two items to six items per area. The content is considerably more limited than normative measures of living skills (e.g., The Assessment of Living Skills and Resources; Williams et al., 1991), measures of impact of illness on daily functioning (e.g., The Sickness Impact Profile; Bergner, Bobbitt, Carter, & Gilson, 1981), and measures of adaptive behavior (e.g., AAMD Adaptive Behavior Scale; Nihira, Foster, Shellhaas, & Leland, 1974), which assess related capabilities. Overall, the KELS does not provide a comprehensive assessment; however, it may be useful as a quick screening instrument that by means of observation, interview, and limited demonstration assists occupational therapists in making a global determination about an individual's ability to perform limited aspects of the five content areas.

The KELS was originally developed for use in a short-term inpatient psychiatric unit. However, the manual states that it can also be an excellent tool for use with the elderly in making determinations of independent living, that it can be used in court for the determination of commitment and disability, and that it is appropriate for cognitively disabling conditions such as organic brain syndrome or Alzheimer's disease. These claims must be considered overly ambitious because of the limited content of the KELS. In particular, the absence of assessing physical abilities and housekeeping skills would make such use inappropriate.

The KELS defines "independent" as that "level of competency required to perform the basic living skills in a manner that maintains the safety and health of the individual without the direct assistance of other people" (manual, p. 39). The instrument's scoring categories are therefore "Independent" or "Needs Assistance." In addition, in case of special situations, the terms "Not Applicable" and "See Note" can be used. Criteria for the determination of "independence" vary and are specified for each item within each area. For the area of Self-care, a minimum standard for (a) appearance and (b) frequency of reported self-care activities is provided. For the area of Safety and Health, the client must (a) identify the dangerous elements in three pictures and the lack of danger in another; (b) identify and partially demonstrate actions to be taken for three instances of health-related problems; (c) identify or find, using a telephone book, the number to be called in an emergency; and (d) identify or find, using a telephone book, the name and location of a doctor and dentist. To be considered independent in the area of Money Management, the client must (a) recognize or correct the amount of change to be returned for the purchase of two small items, (b) report having or developing a source of income through employment, (c) report an appropriate monthly food budget, (d) appropriately budget for 3 of 10 monthly expense categories, (e) correctly complete and record a Checking Account Form or a Savings Account Form, and (f) correctly identify the amount due, due date, and a payment method for a bill. For the area of Transportation and Telephone, independence is established when a client (a) can report using a method of transportation without assistance, other than walking, within the past month; (b) can report a method of finding a bus to reach a destination; and (c) can demonstrate using directory assistance, locating a company's telephone number, and dialing for and repeating a recorded message. A client is assessed to be functioning independently in the area of Work and Leisure if (a) she or he plans to find an appropriate job by a realistic method and (b) is engaged in a minimum of three leisure activities within the past month, of which one must involve other people.

On the basis of these criteria, a final score can be computed, with "Independent," "Not Applicable," and "See Note" counted as 0 and each instance of "Needs Assistance" counted as 1, except for the two items for Work and Leisure which are one-half point each. The manual states that a score of 6 or more indicates that the client needs assistance to live in the community; scores in the range of 5 to 5.5 indicate borderline skills for independent living. It is suggested that both the total score and individual items rated "Needs Assistance" are used to develop recommendations for the client. The manual mentions and provides the Community Support Scale (Morrow, 1985) as a tool for quantifying the availability within the community of the assistance needed for a client to function independently.

Although the scoring criteria are well described and appear to be easily applied, the manual provides no information for the basis of item selection. They appear to have face validity for an urban setting, but no evidence is provided that would support their unique selection for an instrument of this nature. No mention is made of a validation sample, other than that the KELS was originally used with short-term psychiatric patients. Overall, the manual provides little if any research related to the instrument's development.

Six research studies related to reliability and validity are reported in the manual. However, none of these have been published. All of the studies used relatively small samples (50 or less). Three of the studies provided no details related to the number of subjects or research design, resulting in problems for interpretation. The three additional studies, one related to concurrent validity and two to predictive validity, were reported to have major design flaws.

For reliability, only interrater agreement percentages are reported. These are described as being in the acceptable to high range, with figures ranging from 74% to 100% provided across three studies. However, the limitations of these studies must be considered in accepting these results.

Concurrent validity coefficients ranging from .78 to .89 were reported for the KELS and the Global Assessment Scale and a -.84 was reported for the KELS and the Bay Area Functional Performance Evaluation (BaFPE). Both studies used psychiatric patients as subjects. A study of 20 people living independently and 20 people living in a halfway house found that the KELS score was lower, signifying greater independence for subjects in the former group. Ninety percent ($n = 18$) scored less than 5. However, the results of this and a study by Morrow (1985) on predictive validity suggest that a cutoff score of 5.5 for independent living may actually be an underestimate, with a considerable number of people with this score reportedly living independently. Again, the lack of adequate research procedures must be considered. The author is careful to point out that the KELS needs further research to document reliability and validity.

Two recent studies point out some additional weaknesses of the KELS. Rockwood, Joyce, and Stolee (1997) compared the effectiveness of various outcome measures, including the KELS, with Goal Attainment Scaling (GAS) for measuring the health status of 44 patients undergoing cognitive rehabilitation. They found that the KELS as well as the Rappaport Disability Rating Scale, the Milwaukee Evaluation of Daily Living, the Klein-Bell elimination scale and mobility scale, the Instrumental Activities of Daily Living Scale, and the Spitzer Quality of Life Index were all relatively insensitive to change using a relative efficiency statistic and effect size statistic. In a study of 24 homeless women, Davis and Kutter (1998) found that the KELS identified deficits in independent living skills, especially in the area of money management. This area has the greatest number of items, and therefore may most frequently provide the basis for identifying needs for assistance in independent functioning.

To administer the KELS, the examiner needs to obtain additional equipment and materials. These are specified in the manual and easily obtained. They include a local telephone book, deck of cards, bar of soap, dollar bills and various coins, checking account and savings account forms, and a current utility bill. A telephone should also be available. The actual administration and scoring can be easily accomplished, following the directives of the manual.

SUMMARY. The KELS is a brief screening instrument for independent functioning in the community with clearly described administration and scoring criteria. The scoring sheet is simple and easy to use. Materials can be obtained easily and are directly related to the tasks. Because of its ease of use and clear criteria for scoring, interrater reliability may reach acceptable levels. However, the evidence for the KELS scores' validity for determining an individual's levels of independence and for making recommendations for appropriate living situations needs to be determined. Although the KELS may possess some face validity, its brevity and limited content may function to restrict its utility. Moreover, the concentration of items on Money Management may actually have the effect of overidentifying individuals who need assistance in functioning in the community. Some areas necessary for independent functioning are not covered. The KELS is perhaps used most effectively as a screening instrument for specific independent living skills that should be supplemented by additional assessment utilizing observations or actual demonstrations of living skills that tap a wider scope of functioning.

REVIEWER'S REFERENCES

Nihira, K., Foster, R., Shellhaas, M., & Leland, H. (1974). AAMD Adaptive Behavior Scale (rev. ed.). Washington, DC: American Association of Mental Deficiency.

Bergner, M., Bobbitt, R. A., Carter, W. B., & Gilson, B. S. (1981). The Sickness Impact Profile: Development and final revision of a health status measure. *Medical Care, 19,* 787–788.

Morrow, M. (1985). *A predictive validity study of the Kohlman Evaluation of Living Skills.* Unpublished master's thesis, University of Washington, Seattle.

William, J. H., Drinka, T. J. K., Greenberg, J. R., Farrell-Holtan, J., Euhardy, R., & Schram, M. (1991). Development and testing of the Assessment of Living Skills and Resources (ALSAR) in elderly community-dwelling veterans. *The Gerontologist, 31,* 84–91.

Rockwood, K., Joyce, B., & Stolee, P. (1997). Use of goal attainment scaling in measuring clinically important change in cognitive rehabilitation patients. *Journal of Clinical Epidemiology, 50,* 581–588.

Davis, J., & Kutter, C. J. (1998). Independent living skills and posttraumatic stress disorder in women who are homeless: Implications for future practice. *American Journal of Occupational Therapy, 52*(1), 39–44.

[200]
Kolbe Conative Index.

Purpose: Designed to focus on the "predisposition of a subject to respond to specific behavioral settings with certain patterns of behavior."

Publication Dates: 1987–1997.

Administration: Group or individual.

Price Data: Available from publisher.

Comments: A series of instruments designed to enhance personnel selection and increase self-awareness about instructive talent and potential.

Author: Kathy Kolbe.

Publisher: Kolbe Corp.

a) KOLBE A™ INDEX.

Purpose: Designed to measure conative style.

Population: Adults.

Acronym: KCI-A.

Scores, 4: Fact Finder, Follow Thru, Quick Start, Implementor.

Time: (25) minutes.

b) KOLBE B™ INDEX.

Purpose: Designed to "identify the characteristics perceived as necessary to succeed in a given job."

Population: Job applicants.

Acronym: KCI-B.

Time: (15–20) minutes.

c) KOLBE C™ INDEX.

Purpose: Designed to "identify the characteristics necessary to function successfully in a specific job."

Population: Supervisors.

Acronym: KCI-C.

d) KOLBE R™ INDEX.

Purpose: Designed to identify "how you (the respondent) wish another person would take action."

Population: Adults.

Acronym: KCI-R.

e) KOLBE Y™ INDEX.

Purpose: Designed to assist the respondent in identifying his/her "talent for certain types of activities."

Population: Youth (5th grade reading level).

Acronym: KCI-Y.

f) KOLBE Z™ INDEX.

Purpose: Designed to give subjects the opportunity to identify the characteristics perceived as necessary to being a successful student.

Population: Students.

Acronym: KCI-Z.

Cross References: For reviews by Collie Wyatt Conoley and Frank Gresham of an earlier edition, see 12:208.

Review of the Kolbe Conative Index by RAOUL A. ARREOLA, Professor and Director of Educational Evaluation and Development, The University of Tennessee Health Science Center, Memphis, TN:

INTRODUCTION AND PURPOSE. The purpose of the Kolbe Conative Index (KCI) is to provide a measure of the underlying instincts that predispose an individual to respond to specific environmental settings with certain patterns of behavior (conation). Its primary use is as a tool in the selection and hiring process within a corporate or business setting although it also has applications in school settings.

The KCI is predicated on a psychological model that posits four major intellectual instincts: (a) the *probing* instinct that creates a need to investigate in depth; (b) the *patterning* instinct that causes the individual to seek a sense of order; (c) the *innovating* instinct that is the basis for the need to experiment; and (d) the *demonstrating* instinct that converts ideas into tangible form. In addition, individuals are seen as operating in one of three "zones" in the expression of these instincts: (a) the *prevention* zone that leads to the behavior of resistance; (b) the *response* zone that leads to the behavior of accommodation; and (c) the *initiation* zone that leads to an insistent "lets-get-on-with-it" behavior. The interactions between the four instincts and the three zones of expression define four Action Modes: (a) the *Fact Finder* mode that results from the instinct to probe; (b) the *Follow Thru* [*sic*] mode that results from the instinct to pattern; (c) the *Quick Start* mode that results from the instinct to innovate; and (d) the *Implementor* mode that results from the instinct to demonstrate. The KCI provides an indication of an individual's preferred Action Mode in resisting, accommodating, or facilitating various actions in a specific setting. This information may be used to determine the degree to which an individual's preferred Action Mode might facilitate or impede success in a specified work or school setting.

FORMAT. The Kolbe Conative Index (KCI) consists of a series of six paper-and-pencil instruments designed for either individual or group administration. Four instruments (Forms A, B, C, and R) are intended primarily for adults; two (Forms Y and Z) are intended for use with young people and students.

FORM A. This is the basic form of the KCI and generates results indicating the individual's normal preference for behaving in either the Fact Finder, Follow Thru, Quick Start, or Implementer Action Mode. The results from Form A provide an indication of the individual's customary preference patterns in responding to life situations.

FORM B. This form is used to determine the individual's perceptions about what performance or behavior characteristics are necessary to succeed in a job specified on the form. The form is flexible in that any job of interest may be specified. When contrasted with the results of Form A, an indication of the degree of "match" between an individual's "natural" Action Mode and their perceived requirements of the job may be seen.

FORM C. This form is intended for use primarily by a supervisor of a specific job and asks the respondent to indicate what type of actions they would reward or value in this position. Its intent is to identify the perceived performance characteristics of someone who would be successful in the job. Again, when compared with the results of Form A from an applicant for the position, the utility of this form in the selection and hiring process is obvious.

FORM R. This form is used to measure an individual's pattern of preferences in interacting with another individual in a relationship. Again, when used in conjunction with Form A, this tool may be used as part of the process of either (a) selecting members of a team who are most likely to succeed in accomplishing a given task, or (b) matching a supervisor with an employee for a specific job.

FORM Y. This form is intended for use by children who can read at least at the fifth grade level. It is essentially a child's version of Form A.

FORM Z. This form is intended for use by students, presumably above the fifth grade reading level, and is essentially a student version of Form B. That is, the specific "job situation" identified is the school/classroom setting with its attendant assignments, tests, projects, and teacher/student interactions. Once again, when used in conjunction with Form A, an indication of the degree of "match" between the student and the school setting may be obtained.

Each of the above forms uses a series of 36 forced-choice items that ask the individual to indicate which choice is "most" like the individual and which is the "least." Responses to each item are recorded on a separate optically scannable answer sheet that must be sent to a centralized processing office for scoring.

In addition to the core 36 items, each form contains a final section that includes between 6 and 16 items to which the individual is to respond by using a "Strongly Agree" to "Strongly Disagree" scale. Unlike the items that are well-constructed and use an appropriate response scale, the final section of each form contains a fundamental error in design. Forms A, B, C, Y, and Z have items in this section that require a "Strongly Agree" to "Strongly Disagree" response. However, what is provided is a 10-point scale where "Strongly Disagree" may be responded to as either a "3" or a "4," "Undecided" as either a "5" or a "6," "Agree" as either a "7" or an "8," and "Strongly Agree" as either a "9" or a 10." This violates the basic psychometric principle that each point on scales used this way must be clearly defined. In this section of each KCI form every agreement position on the scale may be responded to on one of two numerical choices. This produces a potential for decreased reliability in the form's results. In addition, the scale is flawed in that the middle position used is "Undecided" rather than "Neither Agree nor Disagree," which is the true middle position between Strongly Disagree and Strongly Agree. Finally, the individual is asked to record their responses on a separate answer sheet that contains only the positions "1" through "10" rather than abbreviations of the "Strongly Agree—Strongly Disagree" scale points.

On Form R, the problem in the last section is even more serious. The individual is asked to indicate degree of agreement or disagreement with 10 statements but the response scale provided uses "Excellent," "Good," "Acceptable," "Problematic," and "Unacceptable" response labels—again spread over 10 numbered response positions, 2 per response term. This scale not only fails to match the items, it is flawed in that it mixes the standard "Excellent—Poor" and "Highly Acceptable—Highly Unacceptable" scales as well as some undefined "problematic" scale. The revision of the last section in each form to use a simple SA = Strongly Agree, A = Agree, D = Disagree, SD = Strongly Disagree scale would undoubtedly enhance the reliability of the resultant data.

RESULTS. The personalized computer-generated report for Form A, which includes colored graphs, provides the individual with an indication of their tendencies to use each Action Mode. Based on a diagnostic analysis of the pattern of Action Mode tendencies, the report also includes recommendations on which instincts to trust, how to use time and energy productively, possible career paths, how to avoid stress, and how to communicate effectively. Using the same general rubric, the remaining forms provide indications of an expression of these Action Modes in specific situations—either work or school related.

DEVELOPMENT AND VALIDATION. Based on the three-faculty concept of the mind, which postulates cognitive, affective, and conative functions, the KCI involves the measurement of an individual's preferred pattern of translating will, desire, or motivation into effort and action (conation). Derived particularly from the work of John Dewey and Carl Jung, and originally developed in working with gifted children, the KCI's primary emphasis is in the selection of potentially successful individuals for specific jobs, although two forms of the KCI are also available for use in identifying elements contributing to student success in school.

The information provided by Kolbe relative to the reliability and validity of scores from the KCI was relatively weak with much of it in the form of case studies. The case studies sometimes included data from "other" unidentified non-KCI instruments, possessed infrequent standardization of administration procedures, and had reliability and validity reports that provided no overall summary of the reliability of scores from the instruments. However, the test-retest (with an 8- to 16-month interval) reliability of the Action Mode scales, as determined in preliminary studies, were Fact Finder (.69), Follow Thru (.71), Quick Start (.85), and Implementor (.77). Subsequent case studies indicated that the reliabilities of these scales range from .50 to .87.

The KCI reliability and validity data tend to indicate that the instruments is relatively unbiased in terms of race, national origin, gender, age, or disability. That is, the KCI does not select any group less than 80% as frequently as the most frequently selected group and thus is in compliance with the EEOC guidelines.

Overall, the KCI results appear to be sufficiently consistent in documented application to suggest that it provides a reasonably useful set of tools for aiding in the selection of potentially successful employees or students expected to perform in specific behavioral or work situations.

SUMMARY. The Kolbe Conative Index (KCI) consists of a series of instruments that provide a measure of underlying instincts that predispose an individual to respond in ways that may facilitate or impede success in either a specific work or school setting. The instruments may be administered in either an individual or group setting, with responses being recorded on separate optically scannable answer sheets. The answer sheets must be returned to the Kolbe Corporation in Phoenix, Arizona, for processing and a report is produced for each person.

Although founded on firm psychological principles and models, some sections of the KCI forms contain fundamental errors in scale construction. The results of the KCI are produced as a report that is personalized, colorful, and informative, but that unfortunately has the appearance of an astrologer's computerized "reading." The report includes not only a summary of primary Action Mode preferences relative to an identified work or school situation, but also suggests strategies for behaving in that situation so as to maximize the probability for success.

The KCI appears to be a useful set of tools for use as part of a larger, more complete selection and hiring procedure within a corporate setting. The KCI is marketed precisely for this purpose as the Kolbe RightFit procedure. Likewise, the KCI forms intended for use with children and students, when used as part of a larger and more complete assessment, may provide useful information in selecting and placing students in specific school settings where they may be more likely to succeed.

Review of the Kolbe Conative Index by CHOCKALINGAM VISWESVARAN, *Associate Professor, Florida International University, Miami, FL:*

The mind is construed as being shaped by cognition, affect (or personality), and conation, with plenty of measures available in the literature for assessing cognition and affect. Thus, to facilitate measurement of this tripartite conceptualization of the mind, the Kolbe Conative Index (KCI) was developed. Kolbe postulates four basic instincts (to probe, pattern, innovate, and demonstrate) that result in four characteristic modes of operation (Fact Finder, Follow Thru,

Quick Start, and Implementor). The KCI is designed to assess an individual's strength in each of the four action modes using a scale of 1–10. Typically, the four numbers sum to 20, which is consistent with Kolbe's view that everyone has the same conative energy but that we only differ in how we get things done.

Three zones (prevent, respond, initiate) are identified for each of the four scales. Scores of 1–3 lie in the prevent, 4–7 in respond, and 8–10 in the initiate zone. A person whose Fact Finder scores fall in the prevent zone will resist engaging in Fact Finder activities whereas if the score lies in the initiate zone a person will characteristically respond to a task by collecting all necessary specific facts. A person whose Fact Finder scores fall in the respond (or accommodate) zone will be able to tolerate fact finding activities but will not choose to engage in such detail-oriented activity, and similarly, for the other three action modes. A Follow Thru insistent will like to make detailed plans and follow through on any activity to completion. A Quick Start insistent is entrepreneurial, and an Implementor insistent likes to model and work with concrete objects. Persons in initiate, respond, and prevent zones for a particular mode are those who will function, are willing to function, and who won't function, respectively, in that mode. The KCI can be used either as an ipsative (detailing the relative strengths of an individual in each of the four modes) or as a norm-referenced (comparing your strengths with successful performers) measure.

Kolbe started with a 200-item index reflecting a taxonomy of unlearned behaviors that quantified the use of various paths to problem solving by 3rd to 12th grade students in Arizona. The pattern of behaviors did not distinguish between gifted, normal, and learning-disabled students, but Kolbe was able to predict whether a student could succeed in a given activity based on their characteristic action modes. Parallels were found on observation of adults and, based on reliability analyses, Kolbe settle on a 36-item instrument.

The manual states that interrater reliability is not an issue because the KCI is mechanically scored. Internal consistency estimates are not provided because minor changes have been made on the current version of the KCI and split-half studies are in progress. Based on responses from 70 individuals employed in either a Big 6 accounting firm or a marketing management firm who took the KCI between 8 and 15 months, test-retest correlations of .69, .71, .85, and .77 were reported for Fact Finder, Follow Thru, Quick Start, and Implementor action modes, respectively. Only 5.7% of the respondents changed scores by more than 2 units in any mode, and no significant differences were found in the means across the two administrations. In another study, similar results were found.

Contrast group design was used to assess criterion-related validity. The typical study analyzes the distribution of the four action modes in successful performers in a job, and develops cut scores for predicting future success. Studies are reported for legal ($n = 93$), engineering ($n = 124$), construction ($n = 100$), healthcare ($n = 222$), and manufacturing sales ($n = 164$) jobs. In a study involving 201 teams (Computer division of Eastman chemicals, and sales teams from Hersheys), the correlation between team validity assessments with the criteria of goal attainment and profitability were .79 and .92, respectively.

Correlations with the Myers-Briggs Type Indicator (MBTI) ranged from -.45 to .45 in one study ($n = 268$) and some correlations were in fact higher (.59 between Follow Thru insistence and Judging dimension of MBTI) in another study ($n = 44$). No correlations are reported with measures of intelligence or with standard measures of personality (e.g., the Big Five measures of personality). The six intercorrelations between scores on the four action modes ($n = 268$) were .32, -.53, -.39, -.77, -.03, and -.29. Given that these were observed correlations uncorrected for unreliability, the independence of the four action modes is suspect.

Extensive data ($n = 4,030$) are provided to show that there are no group differences between men and women in any of the four scores. Similarly, no group differences were found between racial groups. Individuals older than 40 years of age scored comparably to younger respondents. A separate analysis (also indicating no group differences) is reported for a particular organization ($n = 152$). No group differences were found between American and non-American respondents either. Analyses, based on 24,416 Kolbe scores from 51 professions each grouped into 10 levels, indicated that the four-fifths rule was satisfied for race, gender, and age groups. However, although extensive data were presented to show (a) no group differences, and (b) no adverse impact, no study

was reported examining predictive bias (systematic over- or underprediction of the criterion). The manual claims face validity based on responses given by test takers who mostly concurred with the interpretations presented to them.

SUMMARY. The central thesis of the KCI is that everyone is capable of being successful if they are true to their characteristic mode of operation. Stress and failure occur only when we are asked to work against our grain. Although I would like to believe in this optimistic view, my readings on individual differences render such a view of humanity untenable. Perhaps the KCI can be used to identify individual strengths, and facilitate better communication among people, teams, and organizations.

[201]
Language Sampling, Analysis, and Training—Third Edition.

Purpose: "Designed to analyze the syntax and morphology of children who are producing a significant number of utterances containing at least three morphemes."

Population: Children with language delay.

Publication Dates: 1974–1999.

Acronym: LSAT-3.

Scores, 39: Word Morpheme (Sentences Total, Words Total, Morphemes Total, Words/Sentences Means, Morphemes/Sentence Means, Word-Morpheme Index), Noun Phrase Constituents (Pronouns, Prepositions, Possessive Marker, Demonstratives, Articles, Plurals, Locatives, Conjunctions), Verb Phrase Constituents (Modals, Particles, Copula, Present Progressive Tense, Present Tense-3rd Singular, Past Tense, Irregular), Simple Sentence Constructions (Noun Phrase, Verb Phrase, Verb Phrase + Noun Phrase, Noun Phrase + Verb Phrase + [Noun Phrase], Noun Phrase + Copula + N/Adj, Unclassifiable Constructions), Complex Sentences (Coordination, Subordination-Infinitives, Adverbials, Indirect Questions, Verb + [that] + Sentence, Relatives, Direct Quotations, Complex in More Than One Way, Unclassifiable, Percentage Complex), Questions, Negatives.

Administration: Individual.

Price Data, 2001: $89 per complete kit including manual (1999, 163 pages), analysis forms, and transcription sheets; $34 per manual; $34 per analysis forms; $24 per transcription sheets.

Time: Administration time varies.

Comments: Visual and verbal stimuli for eliciting language sample determined by examiner; tape recording recommended for recording responses; a detailed tutorial with self-checking exercises covering all steps in the procedure, multicultural issues, setting targets, training, measuring and reporting change are new inclusions in the third edition handbook.

Authors: Dorothy Tyack and Gail Portnuff Venable.

Publisher: PRO-ED.

Cross References: For a review by Margaret C. Byrne of an earlier edition, see 9:590.

Review of the Language Sampling, Analysis, and Training—Third Edition by SHEILA PRATT, Assistant Professor of Communication Science & Disorders, University of Pittsburgh, Pittsburgh, PA:

The Language Sampling, Analysis, and Training—Third Edition (LSAT-3) is a protocol for assessing the grammatical structures (syntax and morphology) of children's spoken English. It was developed primarily for use by speech-language pathologists (SLPs) to evaluate the developmental level and error characteristics of language produced by children with language impairment. However, the authors have proposed extending its use to text analysis. The ultimate purpose for using the LSAT-3 is to determine appropriate levels and foci of language therapy and training for individual children.

The LSAT-3 uses a traditional approach to analyzing sentence-level grammar, and largely is based on transformational grammar, thus providing some theoretical justification and precedence. Moreover, by using a traditional approach the LSAT-3 includes categories and terms that are familiar to SLPs, linguists, and many special educators. The protocol is thorough and allows for the assessment of complex sentences, which increases its suitability for text analysis and the assessment of language produced by sophisticated speakers. An additional strength of the LSAT-3 is that its instructional and training sections are extensive, making the LSAT-3 very useful for student clinicians and SLPs who have limited background in recording, transcribing, and analyzing language samples of children. The training section is well organized and provides abundant feedback although it lacks a criterion for an acceptable level of training.

A major weakness of the LSAT-3 is that only limited information about its development is provided and no documentation of its psychometric properties is included in the manual. The authors provide no reliability or validity data although the complex-sentence analysis section of the protocol had been applied reliably by Tyack and Gottsleben (1986) with normal developing children. Moreover, similar spontaneous language

sample analysis protocols have been shown to be reliable with children with language impairment although intertranscriber and temporal reliability have been found to be dependent on the metric (e.g., mean length of utterance in morphemes, number of different words) and the sample-size used (Cole, Mills, & Dale, 1989; Gavin & Giles, 1996). The validity of numerous language sample measures also has been established in that they have been shown to be sensitive to developmental change and language disorder (see Gavin & Giles, 1996).

The practicalities of using the LSAT-3 is an additional concern in that it is cumbersome and time-intensive, preventing many SLPs from using it routinely. The authors argue against employing computer-based systems such as *Systematic Analysis of Language Transcripts* (Miller & Chapman, 1984) or the programs within the freeware program *Computerized Profiling* (Long, Fey, & Channell, 2000) because they believe that these programs excessively distance clinicians from language transcripts. However, computer analysis programs can reduce analysis time and error as well as increase analysis flexibility and complexity.

SUMMARY. The LSAT-3 is a traditional paper-and-pencil language sample analysis protocol. It includes extensive instructional and training materials although no criterion for acceptable training is provided. The psychometric properties of the LSAT-3 have not been adequately tested although analysis protocols that use a similar framework have been shown to be reliable and valid. A practical limitation of the LSAT-3 is that the analysis procedures have not been computerized.

REVIEWER'S REFERENCES

Miller, J., & Chapman, R. (1984). *SALT: Systematic analysis of language transcripts (manual).* Madison, WI: Language Analysis Laboratory, Wisconsin Center on Mental Retardation and Human Development, University of Wisconsin.

Tyack, D. L., & Gottsleben, R. H. (1986). Acquisition of complex sentences. *Language, Speech, and Hearing Services in Schools, 17,* 160–174.

Cole, K. N., Mills, P. E., & Dale, P. S. (1989). Examination of test-retest and split-half reliability for measures derived from language samples of young handicapped children. *Language, Speech, and Hearing Services in Schools, 20,* 258–268.

Gavin, W. J., & Giles, J. (1996). Sample size effects on temporal reliability of language sample measures of preschool children. *Journal of Speech and Hearing Research, 30,* 1258–1262.

Channell, R. W., & Johnson, B. W. (1999). Automated grammatical tagging of child language samples. *Journal of Speech, Language, and Hearing Research, 42,* 727–734.

Long, S. H., Fey, M. E., & Channell, R. W. (2000). Computerized Profiling (Version 9.2.7) [Computer software]. Cleveland, OH: Case Western Reserve University. Retrieved August 7, 2000 from the World Wide Web: www.cwru.edu/artsci/soci/cp.htm

[202]
Leader Behavior Questionnaire, Revised.

Purpose: Constructed as a measure of "organizational leadership."

Population: Managers and employees.
Publication Dates: 1988–1996.
Acronym: LBQ.
Scores: Visionary Leadership Behavior Scales (Clear Leadership, Communicative Leadership, Consistent Leadership, Caring Leadership, Creative Leadership) Visionary Leadership Characteristics Scales (Confident Leadership, Empowered Leadership, Visionary Leadership), Visionary Culture Building Scales (Organizational Leadership, Cultural Leadership).
Administration: Group.
Forms, 2: Self, Other.
Price Data, 1996: $7.95 per self questionnaire; $2.95 per other questionnaire; $24.95 per trainer's guide ('96, 63 pages).
Time: (10–20) minutes.
Author: Marshall Sashkin.
Publisher: Human Resource Development Press.

Review of the Leader Behavior Questionnaire, Revised by JANET BARNES-FARRELL, Associate Professor of Psychology, University of Connecticut, Storrs, CT:

The Leader Behavior Questionnaire, Revised, published in 1995, is a revision to the third edition of the Leader Behavior Questionnaire (LBQ). The LBQ was developed by Marshall Sashkin as a tool for measuring "Visionary Leadership" (also known as transformational leadership). According to descriptive information provided by the publisher, it is primarily designed as a diagnostic tool that can be used as part of training and development efforts for executives and supervisors or managers who aspire to take on executive-level roles in organizations. It has been used in a variety of settings, including manufacturing organizations, telecommunications organizations, nonprofit organizations, and public school administration.

The LBQ should not be confused with another popular measure of leader behavior, the Leader Behavior Description Questionnaire (LBDQ; T5:1437). The two instruments focus on different aspects of leader behavior. In contrast to the LBDQ and similar instruments that primarily measure leader behaviors associated with task-oriented and relationship-oriented aspects of *transactional* leadership, the LBQ focuses specifically on behaviors and behavior patterns that characterize *transformational* (visionary) leadership. The content of the LBQ is closely linked to theory on the nature of transformational leadership, particularly the work of Bennis (Bennis & Nanus, 1985), House (1988), Jaques (1986), Parsons (1960), and

Schein (1985), as well as the author's own theory of visionary leadership (Sashkin, 1988). Although the LBQ claims to be a comprehensive assessment instrument, it must be understood that the author uses the term comprehensive with respect to measurement of transformational (visionary) leadership only. In particular, the LBQ-Revised purports to measure three features of visionary leadership: Visional Leadership Behavior, Visionary Leadership Characteristics, and Visionary Culture Building. Earlier versions of the LBQ included items that measured aspects of transactional leadership (i.e., task- and relationship-oriented leadership behaviors); the current edition of the LBQ explicitly avoids those domains.

CHARACTERISTICS OF INSTRUMENT. The LBQ-Revised (1995) is available in two versions: LBQ-Self and LBQ-Other. The LBQ-Self is intended for self-assessment; the LBQ-Other is intended for coworkers, subordinates, or supervisors who are familiar with the behavior of the individual who is being assessed. Each form contains instructions, the scale, and a separate form for recording responses. The LBQ-Self also includes information for scoring and interpretation of scores. In addition, a trainer's manual provides background information about the development of the instrument; normative data for subscales, cluster scales, and total scores on the LBQ; summaries of validation work conducted with the instrument; and extensive information about how to use the LBQ in a training and development context.

Each instrument (-Self and -Other) is described as a measure of the extent to which an individual displays the behaviors characteristic of a "Visionary Leader." The LBQ-Self consists of 50 statements. Individuals completing the form are asked to consider each statement and indicate the extent to which that statement is true of their own behavior, using a 5-point scale that includes the following response choices: Completely True, Mostly True, Somewhat True, A Little True, Not At All True. The LBQ-Self is completed by individuals who are in positions of leadership or individuals who would like feedback about their potential to take on leadership roles. They are encouraged to complete the LBQ-Self, to ask some of their associates to complete the LBQ-Other, and to compare their self-assessments with the assessments of leadership potential provided by their associates.

The LBQ-Other (revised edition) consists of the same 50 statements, reworded to reflect descriptions of another individual's behavior. Individuals who complete the LBQ-Other are asked to indicate the extent to which they believe each statement is true of an associate's behavior, based on their own experiences and interactions with that person. The same 5-point scale described above is used to record responses. The LBQ-Other is completed anonymously by several individuals who are familiar with the behavior of the individual being assessed; the author recommends that it always be completed by a minimum of three associates, in order to protect the anonymity of responses. The trainer's manual also suggests that the trainer score and average responses on the LBQ-Other before providing this information to the individual who is being assessed.

SCORING AND INTERPRETATION. Scoring the LBQ-Revised is relatively straightforward. A carbonless copy scoring form and directions provided with the LBQ make this a very manageable task for those who complete the LBQ-Self. As noted above, the LBQ-Other should be scored and summarized by a trainer. It should *not* be scored by the individual who is being assessed.

The 50 items comprising the LBQ form 10 subscales. Each is represented by 5 items that are summed to form a scale score. Scores on the first 5 subscales—Clear Leadership, Communicative Leadership, Consistent Leadership, Caring Leadership, and Creative Leadership—are summed to provide a cluster score for Visionary Leadership Behavior. Scores on the next three subscales—Confident Leadership, Empowered Leadership, and Visionary Leadership—are summed to provide a cluster score for Visionary Leadership Characteristics. Scores on the final two subscales—Organizational Leadership and Cultural Leadership—are summed to provide a cluster score for Visionary Culture Building. An unweighted sum of scores on all 10 subscales provides a Visionary Leadership Total Score. Grids that graphically convert scores to percentile ranks (based on combined normative information for all occupations in the norm groups available to the author) are included to assist individuals in interpreting their Visionary Behavior, Characteristics, and Culture Building scores. In addition, examples and interpretations of different kinds of LBQ profiles are provided.

PSYCHOMETRIC CONSIDERATIONS. The author provides several kinds of evidence regarding the reliability and validity scores from the LBQ. At the time the trainer's manual was prepared, much of this evidence was based on unpublished doctoral dissertations and works still in progress. Test-retest reliability estimates, which would appear to be relevant to the uses for which the LBQ is designed, were not yet available. Internal consistency estimates for the 10 subscales are weak to moderate. They ranged from .52 to .75 in a study that included scales in the Behavior cluster. A later study reported internal consistency estimates for the Characteristics and Culture Building subscales ranging from .31 to .88. Comparisons of responses provided to the LBQ-Self and the LBQ-Other suggest that there is generally high similarity between the pattern and level of responses provided by self-assessments and other-assessments on the 50 items comprising the LBQ.

Validity evidence provided by the author includes descriptions of the results of several factor-analytic studies, relationships between LBQ scores and other measures of transformational leadership, and concurrent validity studies that examined the relationship between LBQ total scores and several measures of organizational effectiveness. This evidence generally supports the following conclusions: (a) There is evidence of convergent validity, supported by significant appropriate relationships between scores on LBQ subscales and similar scales on other measures of transformational leadership; (b) factor-analytic studies suggest that the items in the LBQ form interpretable subscales, but they are often different from the scale structure that the author planned; and (c) total scores on the LBQ are significantly related to indicators of effective organizational culture, organizational productivity, and quality of work life, although the magnitude of these relationships is not clear.

Normative data provided with the trainer's guide include means and standard deviations on all LBQ subscales, cluster scores, and total scores for 13 samples who completed the LBQ-Self and the LBQ-Other (sample sizes ranged from 18 to 200) and an additional 16 samples who completed an earlier version of the 5 Visionary Behavior subscales.

SUMMARY. The LBQ-Revised is a relatively brief instrument for the measurement of three aspects of visionary leadership. Its strengths are that the items comprising the measure are well-grounded in theory on transformational leadership, it is practical to use and easy to score, and the author provides valuable guidance for interpreting scores on the three aspects of visionary leadership measured by the LBQ and using that information for leader development. Its primary weakness at this point is relatively weak evidence that individual subscales provide independent, internally consistent information about the behavioral categories they were intended to represent. As such, it may be misleading to interpret and use scores on individual subscales. In addition, more detailed information about the characteristics and outcomes of criterion-related validity studies conducted with this measure are needed to make the argument that the visionary leader behaviors advocated by the author are demonstrably related to the kinds of organizational outcomes that leaders and organizations hope to achieve.

REVIEWER'S REFERENCES

Parsons, T. (1960). *Structure and process in modern societies.* Glencoe, IL: Free Press.

Bennis, W. G., & Nanus, B. (1985). *Leaders: The strategies for taking charge.* New York: Harper & Row.

Schein, E. H. (1985). *Organizational culture and leadership.* San Francisco: Jossey-Bass.

Jaques, E. (1986). The development of intellectual capability: A discussion of stratified systems theory. *Journal of Applied Behavioral Science, 22,* 361–383.

House, R. J. (1988). Leadership research: Some forgotten, ignored, or overlooked findings. In J. G. Hunt, B. R. Baliga, H. P. Dachler, & C. A. Schrishein (Eds.), *Emerging leadership vistas* (pp. 245–260). Lexington, MA: Lexington Books.

Sashkin, M. (1988). The visionary leader: A new theory of organizational leadership. In J. A. Conger & R. N. Kanungo (Eds.), *Charismatic leadership: The elusive factor in organizational effectiveness* (pp. 122–160). San Francisco: Jossey-Bass.

Review of the Leader Behavior Questionnaire, Revised by HILDA WING, Personnel Psychologist, Federal Aviation Administration, Washington, DC:

The Leader Behavior Questionnaire, Revised (LBQ) is a 50-item instrument for individuals in organizations to use for self-assessment and development for management. Each item is a statement that "describes a certain leadership behavior, characteristic, or effect that a leader might have on the organization" (questionnaire booklet, p. 1). The Likert-scale response format provides the respondent with a 5-point verbal scale (Completely True, Mostly True, Somewhat True, A Little True, Not At All True) to indicate how true the statement is, of either the Self, or some Other asked to evaluate the respondent. There are 10 scale scores of 5 items each: five scales for Visionary Leadership Behavior, three scales for Visionary Leadership Characteristics, and two scales for Visionary Culture Building. For each scale, 3 of the items are scored positively and 2 negatively. There

is a separate answer sheet for the Self and for each of several Others; the answer sheet is two-part no-carbon-required with the Response Form in front and the Scoring Form underneath. Scoring procedures are straightforward and easy for the respondent (Self) and the trainer to follow.

This instrument has the desirable characteristic of being based on a well-explicated, complex, and plausible theory of visionary leadership. Both the Trainer Guide and the Self Guide include substantive information about this theory that should be useful. The Self Guide includes interpretive information for the respondent. The Trainer Guide includes a more detailed description of the theory, statistical data, and outlines of training sessions using the LBQ for individuals' self-discovery. In the minimal and not well-presented statistical presentation lies the source of my frustration with this instrument.

There has been a great deal of informative research supporting this questionnaire but few data pertain to its intended use, training. And there certainly is minimal evidence for using the LBQ for any type of personnel decision. I will organize most of my comments according to the format of the Trainer Guide, which I consider as a test manual. Although the document may succeed as a training guide, it leaves a lot to be desired as a repository of necessary and sufficient information about the LBQ as an instrument.

Section I, Background and Introduction, and Section II, Elements of Visionary Leadership Theory, are comprehensive but could be organized more systematically for a crisp coverage of where the theory came from and how the scales and areas (Behavior, Characteristics, Culture Building) follow from this research. Some of the research referenced was not included in the References list, which in itself cites many reports that are not readily available to a reader. The Guide mentions "over 100 doctoral dissertations" (p. 3) but gives little further detail. Although these two sections are well written and are most plausible, the documentation was, to me, obscure.

Section III, Technical Information is of limited usefulness. Reliability and validity data are buried in text rather than organized into tables and graphs. The Reliability subsection describes how the 10 scales were developed and revised. Current discussions of this concept stress the many facets of reliability and how various indexes illustrate these facets. Reliabilities across occasions, across raters, and across items, as per generalizability theory, provide different insights about the instrument. Most of the discussion here, however, focuses on the difficulties of collecting and interpreting data. Two sets of Cronbach alphas for the scales are presented, one from a sample of unknown size and description, the other from a sample of 31 otherwise unknown respondents. A description of Self-Other reliability references some research in progress but includes no statistics, although there is mention that Self scores are typically slightly lower than Other scores. Again, no data are available, although one validation study is mentioned in which the scores of 50 retail store managers for whom the Self-Other comparisons showed "high consistency" were positively related to indicators of profit and shrinkage.

The research discussed for Construct Validity and Factor Analytic Studies has the potential for providing strong empirical support for the instrument and the theory, but the only numbers mentioned referred to the numbers of LBQ-Self reports and of LBQ-Other reports. One study of church leader effectiveness was described in more verbal detail but was not cited in the References list. Where are the tables of factor loadings, of correlations for discriminant and convergent validity with other instruments such as general ability, Locus of Control? Where are the figures of orthogonal and oblique factors? My frustration with these components is based on my assumption that the necessary and sufficient data were available to the writer(s) who composed this guide but are not made available to the test user.

The next component of Section III, Other Validity Research, starts off with the misstatement that "the relationship between LBQ scores and leadership effectiveness" (p. 15) reflects concurrent validation, when this is actually criterion-related validation. Again, brief textual summaries, with only general description of the occupations or settings of the respondents, are presented, accompanied by no data. Not only is this inadequate evidence, it is irrelevant for the stated purpose of the LBQ, self-assessment and development. That "leaders' LBQ scores are clearly and significantly associated with a variety of measures of organizational effectiveness" (p. 15) can imply that this instrument is worth more attention, but it does not support its use in training.

The final component of Technical Information is found under Appendix A, LBQ Norms. These 29 sets of data, providing sample sizes, means, and standard deviations of samples varying in size and composition, for Self or Other and frequently both, for however many scales were available at the (unstated) dates of data collection, are not very useful as they are given. The information would be more helpful if the samples were grouped into larger clusters based on occupational setting, educational level, and so forth. Also, the scoring interpretations provided elsewhere in the Trainer Guide, and the Self guide, are stated to be based on percentile norms, yet no percentiles are given here. Because the means and score ranges suggest that the score distributions are positively skewed, using the standard deviations with the assumption of a normal distribution to estimate equivalent percentile regions of the same, or other area scales, is problematic at best. How the percentiles were developed, and based on which samples, is a mystery.

The concluding Section IV, The LBQ Booklet—Organization, Scales and Items, presents extensive discussion of the LBQ items and how they are supposed to work, as well as suggestions for using the instrument "in management training and development" (p. 28). The instrument certainly appears face-valid, an important consideration for its intended use. Two outlines for a trainer to follow, for half or a full day, appear to be useful.

SUMMARY. The LBQ appears to be a useful instrument for individual development of leadership, using a sophisticated and up-to-date model. It should be easy to administer and to understand. I give it an unqualified recommendation for research use. For any other use, however, the information available in the Trainer Guide provides insufficient documentation.

[203]
Leadership Practices Inventory—Delta.

Purpose: Designed to identify practices and behaviors associated with effective leadership and to measure empirically personal and organizational progress in leadership development.

Population: Managers and employees.

Publication Dates: 1988–1992.

Acronym: LPI-Delta.

Scores, 5: Challenging the Process, Inspiring A Shared Vision, Enabling Others to Act, Modeling the Way, Encouraging the Heart.

Administration: Group.

Forms, 2: Self, Observer.

Price Data, 1998: $49.95 per kit including facilitator's guide, self and observer instruments, and scoring software.

Time: Administration time not reported.

Comments: Designed as a component of a leadership training workshop based on the authors' model of leadership qualities; can be used as a pre-/posttest; interpretive information based on both self and observer forms.

Authors: James M. Kouzes and Barry Z. Posner.

Publisher: Jossey-Bass Pfeiffer.

Cross References: For reviews by Frederick T. L. Leong and Mary A. Lewis of the LPI (non-delta version), see 12:213; see also T4:1411 (2 references). [Editor's Note: The publisher advised in November 2000 that this test is now out of print.]

Review of the Leadership Practices Inventory—Delta by MARK E. SIBICKY, Associate Professor of Psychology, Marietta College, Marietta, OH:

The Leadership Practices Inventory—Delta (LPI-Delta) is a slightly altered version of Kouzes and Posner's popular Leadership Practices Inventory (LPI; T5:1448). Like the LPI, the LPI-Delta is derived from Kouzes and Posner's (1987) model that views effective leadership as a set of behaviors that can be learned and practiced. The five key sets of behavior are: (a) Challenging the Process, (b) Inspiring a Shared Vision, (c) Enabling Others to Act, (d) Modeling the Way, and (e) Encouraging the Heart. Kouzes and Posner maintain that anyone who can increase the frequency of these behaviors will increase their leadership effectiveness.

The LPI was developed to provide users with a baseline evaluation of the frequency of their effective leadership. The test was not intended to assess the degree of change in leadership behavior. However, users of the LPI asked for more developmental feedback about changes in their leadership behavior. To meet this need, Kouzes and Posner modified the LPI into the LPI-Delta. The authors suggest that a user first complete the LPI and then, after a few months, complete the LPI-Delta. Scores from the LPI-Delta should then be used to assess ones' progress in developing more effective leadership behaviors.

Like the LPI, the LPI-Delta consists of two 30-item test forms. One form of the test is completed by a user about their leadership behavior (Self-form), and the other is given to a subordinate to provide ratings of the user's leadership behavior (Observer form). Both test forms contain the same descriptive behavioral statements (e.g., "treats others with dignity and respect") for each of the five key practices. Respondents rate changes in the frequency of the described behavior on a 5-point Likert scale, ranging from 1 (somewhat decreased) to 5 (substantially increased). Following each item, respondents are also asked to indicate how appropriate they feel the level of the behavior is by rating it either: (a) ok, (b) should do somewhat more frequently, or (c) should do much more frequently.

The LPI-Delta test package also includes a user test manual and a workshop-trainer's manual that contain background and developmental information on both the LPI and LPI-Delta. The trainer's manual also describes procedures for conducting a 4- to 6-hour-long training workshop based on the LPI-Delta. Overall, the test forms and manuals are clear and well organized, and the test appears easy to administer and score.

Regarding the psychometric properties of the LPI-Delta, the trainer's manual contains an appendix with some descriptive statistics and a table listing the authors' findings on test reliability. Internal reliability coefficients for the five key leadership behaviors are reported as ranging from .68 to .80 for the Self-form and .76 to .88 for the Observer form of the LPI-Delta. Unfortunately, the majority of information provided in the manual on reliability and validity, including references to studies, only applies to the LPI and not the LPI-Delta. Apparently, the authors believe that the changes made to the LPI-Delta are so minimal that both tests possess equivalent psychometric properties. This may or may not be the case. Unfortunately, because there are so few empirical data provided in the LPI-Delta manual, nor apparently any published studies, it makes it impossible to evaluate the authors' claims about the test.

The LPI-Delta does appear to be an easy-to-use test and one would guess that it is destined to become as popular as its twin sibling the LPI. Yet, potential users should be aware of some relevant criticisms of Kouzes and Posner's model of leadership, which serves as the basis of the LPI-Delta.

For example, Chemers (1997) proposes that Kouzes and Posner's model is overly simplistic, with a romanticized and narrowly focused view of leadership. He points out that Kouzes and Posner used nonsystematic interviewing techniques and self-report questionnaires on a select sample of successful leaders and followers. Although these data may have uses, this also may represent an overly romanticized image of "heroic leaders." In a sense, the model may only represent subjects' implicit theories of leadership and their post-hoc explanations for organizational change. Like many popular theories of leadership, Kouzes and Posner's model fails to consider situational variables, and this may be "oversimplified and oversold" (Chemers, 1997, p. 84). These criticisms are relevant to the LPI-Delta in two areas.

First, the section of the LPI-Delta test manual pertaining to score interpretation and feedback does contain a series of vague, self-reflective questions that are similar to questions found in many popular self-help books. For example, "What do you need to do to become more effective at inspiring a Shared Vision?" Also, "How do you feel about your progress?" No specific theoretical explanation is provided concerning what a score means, or how a user can change their behavior in a specific situation.

Also relevant is the question of what LPI-Delta is really measuring. Is it measuring changes in behavior that will truly allow anyone, anywhere, to become a more effective leader as the authors suggest, or is it simply measuring peoples' prototypical image of what a leader should look like? Unfortunately, the current research evidence on both the LPI and LPI-Delta leaves these questions unanswered. As other reviewers have noted (see reviews of the LPI, 12:313), there is a strong need for more validation research on these tests. In particular, studies addressing predictive validity need to be conducted and these studies need to go beyond concurrent validity with other self-report measures of leadership.

SUMMARY. In conclusion, the LPI-Delta may be a useful tool for personal self-reflection, or for simply discussing changes in ones' image as a leader. However, users should interpret their scores with caution. Until more research is conducted on the psychometric properties of the LPI-Delta, especially more extensive validation studies, its worth as a measure of leadership effectiveness cannot be judged.

REVIEWER'S REFERENCES

Kouzes, J. M., & Posner, B. Z. (1987). *The leadership challenge: How to get extraordinary things done in organizations.* San Francisco: Jossey-Bass.
Chemers, M. M. (1997). *An integrative theory of leadership.* Mahwah, NJ: Lawrence Erlbaum Associates.

[204]
Leadership Practices Inventory—Individual Contributor [Second Edition].

Purpose: "Designed to assist a nonmanagerial leader in assessing the extent to which he or she engages in certain leadership behaviors."
Population: Nonmanagerial leaders.
Publication Dates: 1990–1997.
Acronym: LPI-IC.
Scores, 5: Challenging, Inspiring, Enabling, Modeling, Encouraging.
Administration: Group.
Forms, 2: Self, Observer.
Price Data, 1999: $49.95 per kit including workbook, Self and Other forms, and scoring software; $12.95 per Self form plus workbook; $3.95 per Other form.
Time: Administration time not reported.
Comments: Nonmanagerial version of the Leadership Practices Inventory (T5:1448); a 30-item Self or Observer rating; hand or computer scored (computer scoring recommended); computer scoring software available.
Authors: James M. Kouzes and Barry Z. Posner.
Publisher: Jossey-Bass/Pfeiffer.
Cross References: For reviews by Frederick T. L. Leong and Mary A. Lewis of an earlier edition of the Leadership Practices Inventory, see 12:213; see also T4:1411 (2 references).

Review of the Leadership Practices Inventory— Individual Contributor [Second Edition] by JOHN M. ENGER, Professor of Education, Barry University, Miami Shores, FL:

The Leadership Practices Inventory (LPI) is a widely marketed tool for facilitating workshops primarily for formative evaluation of a supervisor's performance. Interpretations are based on the responses to questionnaires completed by the supervisor (Self) and various others (Observers) who have had the opportunity to see this individual in the leadership role (facilitator's guide, p. 40). Normative data supplied in the package are also used to interpret these responses. The LPI was developed in the mid-1980s by James Kouzes and Barry Posner, members of the California-based Tom Peters group. Recently, a change in the response scale from a 5-point to a 10-point Likert scale modified the instruments. The rationale for the change was to produce more sensitive instruments.

The LPI consists of two 30-item questionnaires. A supervisor for whom the evaluation is being conducted completes one and those familiar with the performance of the supervisor complete copies of a second questionnaire. Those who constitute the "observers" group may be supervisees, managers, peers, and customers (identified by the authors as constituents, managers, peers, and others). Responses from the completed questionnaires are entered into a computer program provided with the LPI package. The resulting printouts form the basis of a daylong workshop to review various aspects of the supervisor's performance. Printouts reflect the perceptions of the various groups, contrasts of these perceptions, and comparisons to the LPI normative information.

Since being introduced onto the market, the LPI has been used in numerous studies. Although this review addresses the Leadership Practices Inventory for Individuals, Kouzes and Posner also market editions for managers, teams, and student leaders (see Posner & Brodsky, 1992).

As reported by the authors, the LPI was carefully planned and extensively developed during the mid-1980s (Posner & Kouzes, 1988). Based on numerous interviews and item tryouts, the LPI represents well-thought-out instrumentation for administration and interpretation. Reliability and validity evidence is presented and represents high levels by any standards. Subsequent analysis based on a large sample produced a factor structure consistent with the original 5-factor scale (Posner & Kouzes, 1993). This set of five factors was identified as behavior or distinct practices leaders engage in and named by the authors as (a) challenging the process, (b) inspiring a shared vision, (c) enabling others to act, (d) modeling the way, and (e) encouraging the heart. For a thorough review and discussion of the technical aspects of the development and validation of the original LPI, see the review by Leong (1995) in *The Twelfth Mental Measurements Yearbook*. More recent study (Fields & Herold, 1997) produced statistics and reliability estimates on the five scales consistent with those reported by the authors. Also, a confirmatory factor analysis reproduced the five-factor model reported by Posner and Kouzes (1993).

The older normative data were developed with the 5-point response scale (1 = *Rarely or Never do what is described in the statement*, 2 = *Once in a while do what is described in the statement*, 3 = *Sometimes do what is described in the statement*, 4 = *Fairly often do what is described in the statement*, 5 = *Very Frequently, if not Always, do what is described in the statement*). To create more sensitive interpretations of these perceptions, the authors changed to a 10-point response scale (1 = *Almost Never*, 2 = *Rarely*, 3 = *Seldom*, 4 = *Once in a While*, 5 = *Occasionally*, 6 = *Sometimes*, 7 = *Fairly Often*, 8 = *Usually*, 9 = *Very Frequently*, 10 = *Almost Always*). No data are presented or analyses performed to establish the case that this scale, in fact, is more sensitive.

SUMMARY. Overall, Kouzes and Posner have developed a very usable and popular Leadership Practices Inventory that has stood the test of time and continues to hold a prominent place in the market of instruments used primarily for formative evaluation of leaders at various levels of an organization.

REVIEWER'S REFERENCES

Posner, B. Z., & Kouzes, J. M. (1988). Development and validation of the Leadership Practices Inventory. *Educational and Psychological Measurement, 48*, 483–496.

Posner, B. Z., & Brodsky, B. (1992). A leadership development instrument for college students. *Journal of College Student Development, 33*, 231–237.

Posner, B. Z., & Kouzes, J. M. (1993). Psychometric properties of the Leadership Practices Inventory—updated. *Educational and Psychological Measurement, 53*, 191–199.

Leong, F. T. L. (1995). [Review of the Leadership Practices Inventory]. In J. C. Conoley & J. C. Impara (Eds.), *The twelfth mental measurements yearbook* (pp. 555–557). Lincoln, NE: Buros Institute of Mental Measurements.

Fields, D. L., & Herold, D. M. (1997). Using the Leadership Practices Inventory to measure transformational and transactional leadership. *Educational and Psychological Measurement, 57*, 569–579.

Review of the Leadership Practices Inventory—Individual Contributor [Second Edition] by L. CAROLYN PEARSON, Professor of Education, University of West Florida, Pensacola, FL:

The Leadership Practices Inventory—Individual Contributor (LPI-IC) is designed for non-managerial leaders and measures five leadership practices including: Challenging the Process, Inspiring a Shared Vision, Enabling Others to Act, Modeling the Way, and Encouraging the Heart. Each of the five areas is further subdivided into two components that the authors describe as the 10 commitments of leadership. Developed from the original LPI (T5:1448), the individual contributor form also comes in two versions, Self and Observer, that are to be used by nonmanagerial leaders with direct observation when using the Observer form. Both versions, like the original, also consist of 30 items with 6 items per subscale that can be self-scored; however, the items have been updated based on the authors' latest research. The original 5-point Likert scale has been expanded to a 10-point scale to encourage more specific responses, to eliminate the prior neutral position, to eliminate the need for a separate instrument to assess change (customers indicated the LPI-Delta [203] was difficult to use), and to be more sensitive in detecting progress over time. PC scoring software is also available. The directions for taking the instrument are clear and a separate perforated answer sheet allows for easy transfer of scores. Although not indicated, it is estimated that time for administration is about 15 minutes.

Included with the LPI-IC is a facilitator's guide that provides comprehensive information on workshop training and instrument usage and is intended to support either a half-day or full-day session. In the section of the guide on preparing to conduct training, a concise overview of the model on which the instrument is based, including updates, is provided. In the section on conducting training, in addition to clear administration directions for both forms, the authors also provide a detailed section on providing feedback from a hypothetical leader's scores, how to analyze that feedback, and how to make an action plan to address any deficiencies. The appendices also include masters for overhead transparencies and psychometric properties of the instrument. As a supplement, a participant's workbook is also included that closely follows, yet does not duplicate, the facilitator's guide.

As stated in prior reviews, the original LPI was developed and refined with data gathered from more than 1,200 managers. The analysis involved a multi-year study in which managers responded to a survey in which behavioral statements were content analyzed and sorted into various category labels. From these cases the five leadership practice categories were identified and items were written accordingly. After refinement, the LPI was administered to over 2,100 managers and their subordinates. The data were factor analyzed to examine construct validity, and reliability indices were obtained, resulting in the final version of the instrument. An additional 2,876 managers and subordinates yielded final reliability and validity estimates for the LPI with internal reliability estimates ranging from .70 to .85 for the original Self-version and .81 to .92 for the original Other-version, with test-retest reliability estimates ranging from .93 to .95. Various validation efforts have resulted in the 30 items loading on the appropriate dimension and have remained stable. Gender and cross-cultural studies over the years have revealed few biases with the LPI, and there is now a Spanish-language version. Additional re-

search by the authors also provided strong evidence of discriminant and predictive validity using a Leadership Effectiveness Scale, and significant relationships were found between the LPI and job satisfaction, organizational commitment, and productivity.

In more recent research involving the LPI and LPI-IC, the instruments have been examined in various settings including the development of a modified version for use with college students and a Spanish-language version. Identifying and analyzing practices utilized in achieving their "personal best" with coaches and superintendents are additional examples of how the LPI and LPI-IC have been used. Other populations include school-based and centralized-management administrators and teachers; presidents and vice-presidents of four-year colleges and universities; hospital administrators; protestant congregations; recreation sport, leisure, and lifestyle leaders; community leaders; and nursing staff. All of the studies yielded further validation evidence of the LPI and LPI IC and demonstrated their utility.

SUMMARY. In conclusion, over the years there has been much empirical research to provide evidence of the reliability and validity of scores from the LPI and LPI-IC. Grounded in a solid conceptual framework, research continues to demonstrate not only that the LPI has good psychometric properties, but also that it demonstrates utility in various settings. The LPI-IC, its instructions, and the facilitator's guide are well written and easy to use. The materials provided in the facilitator's guide are excellent for providing workshop training. I highly recommend the LPI-IC as a useful tool for use with managers and in meeting training needs.

[205]

Learning and Memory Battery.

Purpose: Used for assessing both specificity and sensitivity to diverse memory problems.
Population: Ages 20 to 80.
Publication Date: 1995.
Acronym: LAMB.
Scores: 7 subtests: Paragraph Learning, Word List, Word Pairs, Digit Span, Supraspan Digit, Simple Figure, Complex Figure.
Administration: Individual.
Price Data, 1999: $295 per complete kit including 25 recording forms, 25 profile/summary sheets, 100 Simple and Complex Figure drawing forms, administration tents, standard score conversion booklet, and

manual (171 pages); $55 per manual; $65 per 25 recording forms; $12 per Standard Score Conversion Booklet; $10 per 100 Simple and Complex Figure Drawing Forms; $180 per administration tents (set of 2); $295 per LAMB Score Windows™ CD or 3.5-inch disk (unlimited use); price information available from publisher for Administration Windows™ 3.5-inch (per usage).

Time: (45–60) minutes.

Authors: James P. Schmidt and Tom N. Tombaugh.

Publisher: Multi-Health Systems, Inc.

Review of the Learning and Memory Battery by CHARLES J. LONG, Professor of Psychology, and MICHELE L. RIES, Research Assistant, Psychology Department, The University of Memphis, Memphis, TN:

The Learning and Memory Battery (LAMB) was designed to serve as a relatively comprehensive measure of learning and memory abilities. This instrument was developed to overcome the limited scope, weak theoretical foundations, and psychometric deficits found in many of the other memory tests that are presently available. The selection of memory constructs assessed by the LAMB was based on research literature on those memory types that have been found to be anatomically and functionally distinct as well as clinically useful. The content of several of the subtests was largely derived from already established memory tests, and therefore should be familiar to clinicians and researchers who evaluate memory functions. Subtests of this battery were selected to assess various types of memory (e.g., verbal vs. nonverbal) and various phases of memory (e.g., short-term vs. long-term). Repeated presentation of materials within each subtest provides information on the rate and pattern of learning over multiple exposures. Immediate free recall, cued recall, recognition, and delayed recall measures are utilized to distinguish among problems in consolidation, storage, retrieval, etc.

The instrument consists of seven subtests. Three subtests are verbal (Paragraph Learning, Word List, and Word Pairs); two are numerical (Digit Span and Supraspan Digit); and two are visual (Simple and Complex Figure). The test is relatively easy to administer and score, but this process is rather time intensive. About 60 to 90 minutes should be allotted for the full administration; about 30 to 60 minutes should be allotted for scoring. Meaningful information can be derived by administering individual subtests (without com-

pleting the full battery of tests) because each subtest is independent in content and has its own normative data. The test materials include two administration tents, Simple and Complex Figure drawing sheets, recording forms, trial-by-trial summary sheets, and profile sheets. A computerized scoring program called LAMB Score is also available for purchase. Directions for the administration and scoring of the LAMB are available in the manual and on the side of the administration tents viewed by the examiner. Overall, the materials are user-friendly and instructions are clear and easy for the examiner and test taker to understand.

Raw scores are obtained for each trial within each subtest by tallying the correct answers obtained during that trial. Cumulative percentile scores for each trial can be found in the manual. Total raw scores for each subtest are obtained by summing raw scores of the learning trials. The raw scores for trial 1, total, and retention are entered onto the summary table on the front page of the recording form. Standard scores are available in the Standard Scores Conversions Tables booklet (these scores are broken down by age groups); the standard error of measurement for total learning scores is reported in the manual. Because the authors stress the independence of the memory functions evaluated by this instrument, and thus the independence of the subtest scores, no composite memory score is calculated.

The normative sample for this instrument included 480 individuals age 20 to 79 who had no history of neurological disease or depression. The gender, education level, and intelligence of the normative group paralleled that of the normal population. The effect of age on memory test performance was controlled for by establishing separate norms for 10-year age groups from ages 20 to 60 and 5-year age groups from ages 60 to 80. Seventy individuals were included in each of the first four groups; 50 individuals were included in each of the last four groups.

The authors of this instrument employed coefficient alpha and split-half reliability measures as indices of internal consistency. Subtest reliabilities obtained by calculating coefficient alphas range from .62 to .95. Lower reliabilities found for verbal tests were explained in several ways (e.g., recency and primacy effects in list memorization act to mitigate against the equal chance of items to be answered in a certain direction). Subtest reliabilities obtained by computing split-half reliability coefficients ranged from .76 to .96. Simple Figure was the only subtest that displayed low reliability estimates for both measures of internal consistency (.74 and .76 respectively). The authors state that this low reliability level reflects the ease of this task that leads to a rapid ceiling effect in most test takers. Interrater reliability was evaluated for the scoring of the Simple and Complex Figure subtests. High interrater reliability (.99) was demonstrated for both subtests. Test-retest reliability was evaluated using a sample of 20 neuropsychologically impaired individuals (the specific impairments were not described). The mean time lapse between administrations of the LAMB was 15.4 months (range 4 to 46 months). The authors report reliability coefficients ranging from -.03 to .86 (median = .73). The use of a neuropsychologically impaired sample in assessing test-retest reliability makes it difficult to interpret these coefficients (especially because the specific impairments of those within the sample are not described). Individuals in this clinical population may exhibit variability in performance due to progression of their neurological condition. It is thus difficult to ascertain how much fluctuation in test scores is due to instability of the test itself and how much reflects an actual change in performance of the individuals due to progression of neurological impairment. The effort to determine the test-retest reliability of any memory test encounters problems because practice effects and long-term retention of material render two administrations of the test nonindependent. The only logical way to attempt to overcome this difficulty would be to administer the battery to a sample of normal individuals with a lengthy time lapse between the administrations.

The LAMB is presented as a comprehensive measure of memory, yet it obviously does not tap every empirically validated form of memory. In the test manual, the authors provide a thorough overview of the domains of memory assessed by the LAMB and a rationale for this choice of targeted memory domains. To assess concurrent validity of the LAMB, the verbal and visual subtests were compared to other established tests of verbal and visual memory (e.g., Wechsler Memory Scale—Revised [WMS-R], Benton Visual Retention Test, Rey Auditory Verbal Learning Test). The LAMB subtests correlated significantly with these memory tests, yet these correlations were only of moderate size (ranging from .17 to .59). The authors attributed the moderate correlation sizes to low reliability of the established memory measures. The LAMB demonstrated sufficient ability to discriminate between individuals with neurological deficits (i.e., individuals with traumatic brain injury, epilepsy, and Alzheimer's disease) and normal individuals. Sensitivity and specificity of the LAMB for detection of neurological deficits was not reported.

The LAMB serves as a useful instrument for the assessment of memory. It is comparable to the WMS-R in its psychometric properties. The use of multiple learning trials on all subtests and the availability of trial-by-trial performance norms for the evaluation of learning curves are unique features of the LAMB. Other unique features include a comprehensive manual outlining the theoretical rationale for the subtests, comprehensive age-based norms, individual subtest scoring, an easy-to-interpret profile of subtest performance, and a number of representative clinical cases. In conclusion, although the clinical information obtained through the use of the LAMB may be redundant with that which is assessed by other memory tests, it does serve as another source of valid and reliable information about a number of clinically relevant memory types.

REVIEWER'S REFERENCE
Tombaugh, T. N., & Schmidt, J. P. (1992). The Learning and Memory Battery (LAMB): Development and standardization. *Psychological Assessment, 4,* 193–206.

Review of the Learning and Memory Battery by WILFRED G. VAN GORP, Professor of Psychology in Psychiatry, Director, Neuropsychology, New York Hospital—Cornell Medical Center Mental Health System, New York, NY:

The test authors assert that the Learning and Memory Battery (LAMB) was developed based upon an information-processing framework in response to significant failings of prior memory measures. The authors note that historically, memory tests have been limited because multiple aspects of memory processes have not been adequately assessed.

In response to this perceived need, the authors developed a new memory battery that assesses a range of processes including delayed recall of paragraph information as well as recognition of this information. The battery also assesses learning, as well as free and cued recall, of a word list in addition to word pairs, emphasizing the "difficult" word pairs. Nonverbal memory is assessed through recall of simple and complex figures. Primary memory is assessed by both digit span and supraspan learning tasks. The authors have collected normative data from a final sample of 480 subjects, recruited largely from Ottawa, Canada (potential subjects were excluded who scored greater than 12 on the Geriatric Depression Scale or less than 25 on the Mini-Mental State Examination).

From a psychometric perspective, the scores from the LAMB appear to be adequately reliable. Internal consistency estimates (Cronbach's alpha) for the various subtests of the LAMB range from .62 for Digit Span backwards to .95 for the Complex Figure subtest (Table 7–9, p. 87, manual). Subsequent factor analytic studies reported in the manual have demonstrated three factors underlying the LAMB: a verbal factor, a visual factor, as well as a general intelligence factor (Table 7–14, p. 91, manual). The authors further provide useful data on the validity of scores from the battery by comparing performance on the seven subtests for four different clinical populations.

The authors are to be commended for working hard to develop an improved aggregate memory battery relative to what existed when they began their work. Ten years ago, when the LAMB was first developed, there was a critical need to improve upon existing memory measures in neuropsychology; the original Wechsler Memory Scale, which was in widespread use, did not include measures of delayed recall. Additionally, there was an emphasis in the original Wechsler Memory Scale upon an aggregate "memory quotient," which implied that memory was a unitary phenomenon and largely ignored its component parts. The LAMB was developed in order to improve upon these and other limitations of existing instruments.

Things have changed greatly in the past 10 years, and the authors' publication of the LAMB may be just a bit too late to make it a widely used and popular memory test. Around the time of the development of the LAMB, others noted the same need for improved memory measures, and this resulted in such developments as the Wechsler Memory Scale—Revised (WMS-R: T4:2940), which included index scores of attention and concentration, verbal memory, nonverbal memory, general memory, and delayed memory. There is now a third edition of the Wechsler Memory Scale (Wechsler Memory Scale—III, WMS-III; 416), which contains further improvements upon the WMS-R with a number of new subscales and indices. Perhaps the greatest strength of the WMS-III is that the norms are based upon a large and nationwide sample of demographically heterogeneous adults.

This strength of the WMS-III also represents the greatest limitation of the LAMB. The normative data for the LAMB are based upon a Canadian sample, largely from one location, of 480 subjects that appears to be a "sample of convenience" in that individuals were recruited by word of mouth, from shopping malls, personal contacts, etc. Information on the ethnicity of the sample is not given, though in the absence of information to the contrary, it is assumed to be a relatively homogeneous sample. It is not clear the degree to which the norms from the LAMB may be appropriately applied to other North American or English-speaking groups, or to individuals of various ethnicities. This factor alone is sufficient for the WMS-III to be considered a superior tool to the LAMB in order to assess a range of memory functions for most adults in North America.

The test stimuli for the LAMB are quite appropriate and are a strength of the battery. The stimuli are presented in booklet format in very large print and are shown to the patient or subject. They are easily read (particularly important for older adults who may have vision difficulties) and appear to be easily administered. The manual is very readable and contains complete information on administration, scoring, and interpretation.

In sum, the greatest limitation of the LAMB is that it has now been replaced by a new generation of memory measures that contain even more sophisticated methods of assessment of memory processes, generate a broader range of test scores, and contain a more appropriate, demographically heterogeneous standardization sample than is true for the LAMB. As such, despite admirable efforts, it may be that some of the same criticisms that have been leveled at older measures of memory by the authors of the LAMB may now be leveled, unfortunately, at this test.

[206]
Learning Disabilities Diagnostic Inventory.

Purpose: Designed to identify specific learning disabilities and to help diagnose dysphasia, dyslexia, dys-

graphia, dyscalculia, and disorders in executive function.
Population: Ages 8-0 to 17-11.
Publication Date: 1998.
Acronym: LDDI.
Scores, 6: Listening, Speaking, Reading, Writing, Mathematics, Reasoning.
Administration: Individual.
Price Data, 2001: $109 per complete kit including examiner's manual (106 pages) and 50 rating summary booklets; $42 per examiner's manual; $69 per 50 rating summary booklets.
Time: (10–20) minutes.
Authors: Donald D. Hammill and Brian R. Bryant.
Publisher: PRO-ED.

Review of the Learning Disabilities Diagnostic Inventory by TERRY B. GUTKIN, Professor of Educational Psychology, University of Nebraska—Lincoln, Lincoln, NE:

Given the on-going confusion and difficulties associated with diagnosing learning disabilities in children and youth, the appearance of a new assessment device that takes a novel approach to this complex professional problem is welcome indeed. It is refreshing to consider the work of test authors who are beginning to think "out of the box" in relationship to this set of professional problems. Despite having broken some new ground, however, the Learning Disabilities Diagnostic Inventory (LDDI) is far from being free of its own unique set of problems.

PURPOSES, BASIC CONCEPTUALIZATION, AND GENERAL UTILITY. The LDDI is intended, first and foremost, as a tool for diagnosing children and youth with learning disabilities in one or more of six specific areas (i.e., Listening, Speaking, Reading, Writing, Mathematics, and Reasoning). Rather than relying on traditional discrepancy methodologies, comparing levels of intellectual and academic attainment, it is a 90-item behavior checklist completed by professionals who have worked very closely with referred individuals and had sufficient opportunity to observe their performance in areas of suspected disabilities. Each of these behavior descriptions is purported to have been identified in the research literature as an overt manifestation of learning disabilities. The basic premise of the LDDI is that persons demonstrating high numbers of these behaviors have a high probability of being learning disabled.

Despite some encouraging technical data (discussed below), the utility of the LDDI in daily practice seems quite limited. In particular, this instrument appears to be an "add on" rather than a replacement for traditional diagnostic methods. The authors note it should never be used in isolation from other test data (presumably traditional intelligence and norm-referenced achievement measures) and that it "should be considered in conjunction with the results of aptitude-achievement discrepancy formulas, especially in states where the formulas are required" (p. 51) by law. Even as an "add on," however, it could be of significant pragmatic value if the instrument reduced the number of false positives or false negatives identified by more traditional procedures. Given that the authors present no such argument, it is assumed there is no supportive evidence in this regard. Making matters worse, the authors also note explicitly that the LDDI "*should not* be used as a basis for planning individual instructional programs" (examiner's manual, p. 14). As such, there is no evidence that the LDDI either saves time, increases diagnostic accuracy, or enhances treatment information in comparison to more traditional assessment procedures. Thus, it is hard to discern why practitioners would want to employ this test on a regular (or even irregular) basis.

Secondarily, the LDDI is designed to advance research pertaining to learning disabilities. Although no specific directions are delineated in this regard, it would appear that the different approach to learning disability diagnosis (i.e., behavior checklist versus aptitude-achievement discrepancies) does open up a range of potentially fruitful lines of empirical investigation. For example, it creates new opportunities for multimethod research in this area. A particularly interesting group to study would be those students who meet the traditional criteria for LD but do not qualify for this diagnosis with the LDDI (and vice versa).

Psychometric Qualities.
NORMATIVE SAMPLE. The norm sample consists of 522 educational professionals (90% special education teachers) who rated the behaviors of 2,152 students who were previously identified as learning disabled. The raters were drawn from 43 states and the District of Columbia. The sample seems to be a reasonable demographic match with educators who work with LD students, although it is probably overweighted with both females (87%) and Euro-Americans (91%). Given that no national statistics are available in

this area, it is not possible to discern the quality of this sample with any precision. Regarding the students, the authors did a nice job of matching 1995 U.S. Census data in relationship to gender, race, ethnicity, placement location, geographic region, and family income. This sample includes 151–286 students for each age group between 8–18. It is noteworthy that the normative statistics developed for each of the six scales of the LDDI (i.e., Listening, Speaking, Reading, Writing, Mathematics, and Reasoning) were drawn only from children in the sample identified as having learning problems in those specific area(s) rather than from the sample as a whole.

RELIABILITY. The reliability data reported for the LDDI are generally quite solid, although a number of critical issues remain unaddressed. Coefficient alphas for the Listening, Speaking, Reading, Writing, Mathematics, and Reasoning scales are all quite good, with averages across the age range of .92–.95 and none falling below .84 when subdivided by demographic characteristics. Test-retest reliabilities varied from .84–.90; however, these were over only a one-week period. Given the hypothesized physiological basis for learning disabilities presented by the authors, a more stringent examination of score differences over time should have been employed. Additionally, because the interpretation of the LDDI depends on profile analysis of its six scale scores (evaluating if scores are above, equal to, or below a stanine of 6), the stability of student profiles should have been assessed. Even though the manual indicates that the average scores on each individual scale correlated highly across the one-week test-retest period, there is no information regarding how many children might have been diagnosed differently due to changes in their individual test profiles. Finally, strong interrater agreement rates were reported (.82–.93 across the six scales). However, these data are also somewhat tainted. First, there were only two pairs of two raters employed for these assessments. Second, there is no indication of base rates and whether agreement levels exceeded chance. If the two pairs of raters suspected that all or most of the students they rated were LD, there would likely have been very high rates of agreement due to chance alone.

VALIDITY. As acknowledged by the authors, the LDDI test manual provides only a "starter set" (examiner's manual, p. 49) of validity data. In terms of content validity, the authors provide a list of research articles that are purported to support the empirical basis for each and every item on the instrument, along with a number of item analyses showing that LDDI items are free from racial and gender bias. For criterion-related validity, data show a moderate relationship between LDDI scale scores and teachers' identification of academic problem areas for 115 LD students. Finally, a variety of data are presented regarding construct validity. Even though generally positive, this latter set of data is less than compelling. Due to space limitations, commentary will be limited to only the two most central analyses.

First, how well does the LDDI differentiate among LD and non-LD students? Although only 4% of "normal" students had LDDI "profiles indicative of LD" (examiner's manual, p. 72), this analysis seems less critical than whether the LDDI can discriminate among LD and non-LD students who are struggling academically. Along these lines, it is significant that only 70% and 16% of MR and emotionally disturbed participants, respectively, had LDDI profiles that were not indicative of LD. Also, only 69% of LD students were categorized with the LDDI as "likely" (as opposed to "possibly" and "unlikely") to have learning disabilities. Unfortunately, the most important analysis along these lines was not even reported in the test manual. That is, how many low-achieving but nonhandicapped students are identified as LD by the LDDI? It is hoped that future researchers will assess this critical diagnostic question.

Second, utilizing Varimax and Promax factor analytic procedures, only one and three factors, respectively, were found rather than the six that should have emerged if the six LDDI scales had high construct validity. The authors attempt to "explain away" the singular orthogonal factor by arguing that "because all the scales measure some type of learning disability, they should load on a single factor" (examiner's manual, p. 73). Unfortunately, this logic flies in the face of arguments made repeatedly throughout the manual that the profile of differences among the six LDDI scores, rather than the total LDDI score, is critical to the diagnosis of LD with this instrument. Additionally, finding only three oblique factors undercuts the construct validity of the six LDDI scales, despite the authors' arguments to the contrary that these results were "anticipated" (examiner's manual, p. 74).

One other comment on the validity section of the test manual is that there are too many instances of explicitly or implicitly overstepping the data reported. Exemplifying this problem is the statement that LDDI scale discrepancies are "as diagnostically interesting, if not more so, than the aptitude-achievement discrepancy" (examiner's manual, p. 51) traditionally used to diagnose LD. If true, this would be a critical argument supporting the use of the LDDI in clinical practice. Unfortunately, no rationale or data are provided regarding this point.

SUMMARY. The LDDI represents a new and potentially important approach to diagnosing learning disabilities in children and youth. It has a strong normative sample, and a variety of supportive reliability and validity data. The principal shortcomings of this instrument are twofold. First, its clinical utility is unclear. Specifically, no data were presented demonstrating how the LDDI is either superior to or complements more traditional diagnostic practices. Second, additional investigation (e.g., how well does the LDDI differentiate among nonhandicapped low achievers and LD students) is necessary before either researchers or practitioners can be secure regarding its technical qualities.

Review of the Learning Disabilities Diagnostic Inventory by JOHN MacDONALD, School Psychologist, North Kitsap School District, Poulsbo, WA:

The authors intend the Learning Disabilities Diagnostic Inventory (LDDI) to assist in the evaluation of intrinsic processing disorders underlying Specific Learning Disabilities (SLD). The LDDI consists of six rating scales, with 15 items each in Listening, Speaking, Reading, Writing, Mathematics, and Reasoning.

The authors state that examiners interpreting LDDI ratings should be school psychologists, educational diagnosticians, SLD specialists, or speech-language pathologists. Examiners are to select the most competent and experienced person to rate the student on the LDDI. Raters should be general or special educators or speech-language pathologists.

Each item states a problem behavior, and is rated from "Frequently" (1) to "Rarely" (9) "exhibits the behavior." Ratings are summed, yielding total scores ranging from 15 to 135 for each scale. Sums are converted to stanine scores. Stanines 1 to 5 indicate that a disability is "Likely," 6 indicates "Possible," and 7 to 9 "Unlikely."

Norms are based on 522 teachers rating 2,152 subjects "officially diagnosed" as SLD and placed in special education programs in Grades 3 through 12. They were recruited from a commercial mailing list of 15,000 teachers working in the field of learning disabilities. Most were special education teachers with Master's degrees and more than 5 years of experience.

There were 151 to 286 students in each one-year age group. They were representative of the SLD population in terms of gender, race/ethnicity, placement location, and family income. There were only 12 Asian and 14 Native American students in the entire sample.

Scores from the LDDI appear reliable. Internal consistency estimates averaged above .90 for each scale. One-week test-retest reliability coefficients varied from .84 to .90. Interexaminer reliability coefficients based on two examiners independently rating 40 protocols, were above .95 for each scale, and the examiners agreed on 97% of the protocols as indicating presence or absence of a disability. Interrater agreement was .82 to .93, assessed by comparing ratings of teachers and co-teachers of 24 students.

For content validity evidence, the authors describe scale development. Based on a literature review, 157 items were written describing behaviors indicative of "neurologically based LD" (examiner's manual, p. 36). Thirty-six experts rated these for relevance to the SLD definition in federal law: They judged 61% of items as evident of SLD, 32% "somewhat" evident, and 7% as "minimally" evident of SLD. No evidence is provided about expert belief that the items measured intrinsic processing deficits.

Criterion-related validity evidence comes from a study of 115 subjects with SLD who were not part of the norming study. Between 57% (Speaking) and 70% (Reading) were identified by the LDDI as "Likely" having a disability in the same areas their teachers said were weak. This is poor evidence: The LDDI would miss 43% of students with severe deficits in Speaking. Further, 61% of a population is expected to have stanine scores under 6 (have LDDI scores of "Likely" disabled), and the base rate for reading disability in a population of SLD students is about 70%. Allowing teachers to note more than one area as a "weakness" increased the likelihood of agreement on at least one scale.

Construct validity evidence seems to be the LDDI's greatest weakness. First, is the LDDI developmentally valid? The authors cite the low correlation between age and LDDI scores (.20) as evidence for construct validity. They argue there should be no developmental progression in scores because SLD students have widely varying skills at all ages. However, in the normal population, skills improve with age. Shouldn't developmental progression in the normal population be appropriate evidence for the construct validity of the LDDI? No such evidence is presented.

Is the LDDI factorially valid? The authors state confirmatory factor analysis suggests a six-factor solution underlying LDDI scores. However, this analysis involved treating each scale as a separate structural equation model, and really confirms only that each scale was measuring primarily one factor. In an analysis of all LDDI scales together, a principal component factor analysis did yield a single factor solution, accounting for 53% of the variance. Factor loadings on the single factor were above .70 on all scales but Mathematics (.64). A "Promax" rotation yielded a three-factor solution, but these were moderately correlated: .49 for Factors 1 and 2, .50 for Factors 2 and 3, and .41 for Factors 1 and 3 (Elizabeth Allen, personal communication, December 9, 1998). Thus, all six LDDI scales appear to be measuring one construct.

Does the LDDI have adequate convergent validity? It has moderate relationships with the Woodcock-Johnson—Revised Tests of Achievement, with rs around .70 for corresponding subtests. Even noncorresponding subtests correlated highly. LDDI Reading correlated .69 with Woodcock-Johnson—Revised (WJ-R) Broad mathematics, and the median correlation of all LDDI scales and WJ-R subtests is .61.

Does the LDDI have adequate discriminant validity? The authors report a study with 260 normal subjects, 47 with Mental Retardation, and 32 with Severe Emotional Disturbance, along with students from the norming study with SLD. Normal students obtained an average stanine of 8 to 9, students with MR 1 to 4, students with SED 6 to 7, 7 for SLD students with weaknesses in areas other than the scale in question, and 5 for SLD students with weaknesses in the same area as the scale. Considering that 5 is at the extreme high end of the "Likely" Disability category, this also makes the discriminant validity of the LDDI questionable. It is likely that a large proportion of SLD students will be missed. This, combined with the uniformly low scores of the subjects with MR, begs the question of what the LDDI measures beyond intellectual ability.

SUMMARY. The LDDI's construct validity and utility are questionable. If used to screen students likely to have SLD, it would miss as many as 43%. The authors appear to take a reductionistic approach to assessing cognitive process (e.g., the underlying cognitive process in reading is reading behavior). This reviewer doubts that this instrument adds to a comprehensive SLD evaluation, nor can it substitute for any part of such an evaluation.

[207]
Learning Disability Evaluation Scale (Renormed).

Purpose: "Developed to aid in diagnosis, placement, and planning for learning disabled children and adolescents."
Population: Grades K–12.
Publication Dates: 1983–1996.
Acronym: LDES.
Scores, 8: Listening, Thinking, Speaking, Reading, Writing, Spelling, Mathematical Calculations, Total.
Administration: Individual.
Price Data, 1999: $133.50 per complete kit including 50 Pre-Referral Learning Problem Checklist forms, 50 Pre-Referral Intervention Strategies Documentation forms, 50 LDES rating forms, LDES technical manual ('96, 71 pages), Learning Disability Intervention manual ('95, 223 pages), and Parents' Guide to Learning Disabilities ('91, 200 pages); $26 per 50 Pre-Referral Learning Problem Checklist forms; $26 per 50 Pre-Referral Intervention Strategies Documentation forms; $31 per 50 LDES rating forms; $12.50 per technical manual; $22 per Learning Disability Intervention manual; $16 per Parents' Guide to Learning Disabilities; $20 per computerized Quick Score (specify IBM or Macintosh); $149 per computerized manual (specify IBM or Macintosh).
Time: (15–20) minutes.
Comments: Ratings by teacher; the 1996 edition is renormed but content is not revised.
Authors: Stephen B. McCarney (test and manual) and Angela Marie Bauer (manual).
Publisher: Hawthorne Educational Services, Inc.
Cross References: For reviews by Glen P. Aylward and Scott W. Brown, see 12:214 (1 reference).

Review of the Learning Disability Evaluation Scale (Renormed) by PATRICIA B. KEITH, Assistant Professor, Psychology Department, University of South Carolina, Columbia, SC:

The Learning Disability Evaluation Scale (LDES) has been renormed (McCarney, 1996). The original instrument developed by McCarney and Bauer (1988) was previously reviewed (Aylward, 1995; Brown, 1995). It was thought to have well-defined norms, the validity and reliability estimates were found to be within acceptable ranges, the directions for administration of the instrument were declared to be clear, and the scoring system was believed to be appropriate (Brown, 1995). Although, the LDES was thought to be basically psychometrically sound, many good suggestions were made by previous reviewers that appear not to have not been incorporated into the new LDES. This reviewer thinks that the instrument may not be as acceptable as other reviewers have thought. A cost-benefit analysis should be done before an examiner purchases the instrument.

The utility of the complete package (LDES, Parent's Guide to Learning Disabilities, and Learning Disability Intervention Manual) is best suited for use with elementary and high school children who are experiencing academic problems. The constructs measured by the test are: Listening, Thinking, Speaking, Reading, Writing, Spelling, and Mathematical Calculations. Although the instrument was designed to provide information for referral, assessment, and later treatment of children with learning disabilities, Aylward (1995) cautions test users to view results as "indicative" and not "definitive"—or to put it another way—the results may or may not indicate that the child has a learning disability and the support manuals may or may not indicate what could be done for that child in the classroom.

McCarney, one of the original developers of the LDES, is responsible for the renorming of the LDES. McCarney is to be congratulated for knowing that well-trained examiners are not interested in using evaluation scales with norms over 15 years old (the original LDES was developed and normed in 1984). The development and technical characteristics of the recently renormed LDES are documented in the manual.

The development of LDES items is important. Yet, items on the LDES appear not to have been reviewed to determine if they still adequately reflected current research findings regarding characteristics of children with learning problems or learning disabilities. Teachers may find items difficult to answer unless they work in a traditional classroom setting and are responsible for the reading, math, spelling, and writing components of the child's education program. Furthermore, the items do not consider differences in children's temperaments, cultural or ethnic backgrounds, or general adolescent development (a period of development often characterized by inconsistency in listening, thinking, and speaking practices).

The "quantifiers" or teachers are asked to use a rating system (1 = *rarely or never*; 2 = *inconsistently*, and 3 = *all or most of the time*) that appear to be improperly sequenced. For example, a student who *never* does something should not get a score the same as a student who *rarely* does something. Similarly, a student who does something *most of the time* should not get the same score as a student who does something *all* of the time. Additionally, the item analysis section (specifically the "analysis of the response pattern of the item," p. 13) may lead examiners to question the quality of some items and their ability to discriminate accurately the variable that is being measured.

It has been almost three decades since PL94-142 was put into law. The way professionals conceptualize the assessment of students experiencing learning problems in schools has somewhat changed. Yet, the new LDES manual does not appear to recognized important policy shifts in federal and state mandates (e.g., IDEA and 504), paradigm changes in service delivery patterns for children with learning problems (e.g., inclusion practices, noncategorical placements), and the implications these changes have for serving children experiencing academic problems. The author may want to revise the manual to provide support and a rationale for the instrument that is not couched in 1970s terminology and draws for recent empirical research on characteristics of students experiencing learning problems.

Perhaps the LDES renorming analyses were not done using a 1970 version of SPSS, yet, the reference section of the manual only refers to this very dated software statistical package (Nie, Bent, & Hull, 1970). Test users should be troubled by the use of dated statistical software packages. During the last decade many theoretical and statistical advances have been made in the measurement field. Therefore, the author may want to incorporate more modern measurement techniques in establishing the technical characteristics of the LDES (e.g., IRT, SEM, hierarchical factor analysis).

Professionals, trainers, and examiners in the field no longer use the Wechsler Intelligence Scale for Children—Revised (WISC-R), the Peabody Individual Achievement Test (PIAT), and the Woodcock Reading Mastery Test. These instruments have been revised long ago, so there is no justification for using old tests with old norms to establish the criterion-related validity when renorming the LDES. Additionally, small sample sizes (less than 100) were used during the validation investigations. With 6,160 students serving as the normative sample (1995), one would expect a much larger sample size to be used in these analyses.

SUMMARY. The newly normed LDES may be able to provide some information to educators regarding students' learning and related behavior problems. However, it may be prudent for examiners to refrain from making normative statements about results obtained from this scale. Much work still needs to be done to establish norms from a nationally representative sample of children before the LDES scale can be effectively used with students experiencing learning and related behavioral problems in schools and to justify the cost of the scale. Therefore, this instrument is recommended for use in research settings and not for use in schools today.

REVIEWER'S REFERENCES

Nie, N., Bent, D., & Hull, H. (1970). *Statistical package for the Social Sciences.* New York: McGraw-Hill.
Aylward, G. P. (1995). [Review of the Learning Disability Evaluation Scale.] In J. C. Conoley & J. C. Impara (Eds.), *The twelfth mental measurements yearbook* (pp. 557–559). Lincoln, NE: Buros Institute of Mental Measurements.
Brown, S. W. (1995). [Review of the Learning Disability Evaluation Scale.] In J. C. Conoley & J. C. Impara (Eds.), *The twelfth mental measurements yearbook* (pp. 559–560). Lincoln, NE: Buros Institute of Mental Measurements.

Review of the Learning Disability Evaluation Scale (Renormed) by LORAINE J. SPENCINER, Professor of Special Education, University of Maine at Farmington, Farmington, ME:

The Learning Disability Evaluation Scale (LDES) (Renormed) was designed to provide a norm-referenced tool to aid in screening, diagnosis, placement, and planning for children and adolescents with learning disabilities. The instrument addresses areas of difficulty in Listening, Thinking, Speaking, Reading, Writing, Spelling, and Mathematical Calculations. Although the test manual does not state the age range of children for whom this instrument may be used, the norms include students ages 5 years, 5 months through 18 years.

The LDES-Renormed consists of three forms, an examiner's manual, and two booklets. The forms include: the Pre-referral Learning Problem Checklist, The Learning Disability Evaluation Scale (School Version), and the Intervention Strategies Documentation Form. The booklets for teachers and parents, The Learning Disability Intervention Manual—Revised, and The Parent's Guide to Learning Disabilities, are included to assist with program planning and intervention.

The Pre-referral Learning Problem Checklist form consists of 88 items that can be checked if the teacher has observed the student demonstrate the behavior during the past month.

The Learning Disability Evaluation Scale (School Version) form consists of the same 88 items in the Checklist rated as (1) *rarely or never*, (2) *inconsistently*, or (3) *all or most of the time*. The manual includes descriptors of each of these quantifiers. The items are clustered in seven subscales reflecting concerns in Listening, Thinking, Speaking, Reading, Writing, Spelling, and Mathematical Calculations. The form is completed by the student's teacher and takes approximately 20 minutes. Raw scores may be converted to standard scores, percentiles, or a global index of learning difficulties. The global index, or learning quotient, has a mean of 100 and a standard deviation of 15.

The Intervention Strategies Documentation Form provides a convenient way to organize student history, learning or behavior concerns, and the interventions implemented.

The Learning Disability Evaluation Scale (Renormed) is the test manual. Detailed information about the development of the test and the technical characteristics is included. Separate sections describe administration, scoring, and interpretation.

The Learning Disability Intervention Manual—Revised, an ancillary booklet, consists of goals, objectives, and intervention suggestions that relate to each of the seven subscales of learning or behavior difficulties. This manual provides helpful suggestions and starting points in planning intervention strategies that would be of interest to both special education and regular classroom teachers.

The Parent's Guide to Learning Disabilities, an ancillary booklet, provides suggestions of intervention strategies for family members. The organization does not follow the seven subscales above but rather lists interventions in the following areas: (a) memory, organization, and following directions; (b) general academics; (c) reading; (d) written/expressive language and speech; (e) math; (f) handwriting; and (g) self-control.

During March—May 1995, 6,160 students from 26 states participated in the renorming of this instrument. The demographic characteristics of this sample approximated those of the 1994 Statistical Abstract of the U.S. in terms of gender, residence, race, and occupational status of parents. The norming sample did not provide adequate approximation of geographic representation: The Northeast was underrepresented and the North Central area was overrepresented.

The technical characteristics of this test are generally adequate, based on several small studies reported in the manual. Additional studies should be completed. A test-retest reliability study was completed by 87 teachers 30 days after the initial testing. Scores of younger children (ages 5–7) were more reliable ($r = .90$–$.93$) than those of adolescents ($r = .80$–$.81$). Interrater reliability ranged from $.96$–$.98$ across age levels. Internal consistency was adequate ($>.80$).

The manual presents evidence of both content and criterion-related validity. The criterion-related validity study (71 students) found high correlations between the subscales of the LDES-Renormed and Wechsler Intelligence Scale for Children—Revised, the Peabody Individual Achievement Test, and the Woodcock Reading Mastery Tests. In order to assure examiners that criterion-related validity is sufficiently strong, new instruments should be compared with instruments currently in use. Unfortunately, the author chose to use the earlier, rather than the revised versions of these instruments in this study.

In an additional validity study, 92 students were randomly selected from the normative sample and compared with a corresponding group of 92 students who were identified as having learning disabilities. Raw score mean differences between the two groups were statistically significant ($p<.001$) for all subscales and the Learning Quotient. Although this study suggests that the instrument has diagnostic validity for identifying a student with a learning disability, additional studies are warranted.

SUMMARY. The LDES-Renormed is a well-constructed instrument to assist in the diagnosis and planning for children and adolescents with learning disabilities. Initial studies provide evidence that scores from this instrument have adequate validity and reliability, although additional studies are needed to support these findings. The examiner's manual states that the instrument may be used for screening purposes; however, no information is included regarding screening procedures. A small but essential task is to edit the examiner's manual to reflect "people-first" language.

[208]
Learning Organization Practices Profile.

Purpose: Designed "to facilitate a diagnostic process by which an organization can measure its capacity as a learning organization."
Population: Organizations.
Publication Date: 1994.
Acronym: LOPP.
Scores, 12: Vision and Strategy, Executive Practices, Managerial Practices, Climate, Organizational and Job Structure, Information Flow, Individual and Team Practices, Work Processes, Performance Goals and Feedback, Training and Education, Rewards and Recognition, Individual and Team Development.
Administration: Group.
Price Data, 1997: $24.95 per set including manual (43 pages) and 1 profile booklet; $7.95 per profile; quantity pricing available.
Time: Administration time not reported.
Author: Michael J. O'Brien.
Publisher: Jossey-Bass/Pfeiffer.

Review of the Learning Organization Practices Profile by NEIL P. LEWIS, Management Psychologist, Marietta, GA:

The Learning Organization Practices Profile (LOPP) is a self-administered paper-and-pencil inventory for use with the employees of an organization. It consists of 60 items (each a 6-point Likert scale) that query people on their perceptions of multiple traditional aspects of organizational functioning. Each of the 12 aspects is addressed by five items. Employees fill out the instrument—either on their own or in a group setting—then self-score. The author recommends interpreting the scores and giving feedback in a group setting with the employees.

The LOPP is not a psychological test in the traditional use of the term. It measures no traits, characteristics, knowledge, skills, or abilities of the test taker nor does the test manual present any standardization, reliability, or validity data. Rather, the LOPP is a normless attitude survey purporting to measure one particular aspect of organizational functioning—"Organizational Learning"—which the author defines as a continuous and enhanced capacity to learn, adapt, and change that is woven into the fabric of an organization's character. Overall, the LOPP does comprehensively measure the extent to which this somewhat esoteric construct is present or absent in an organization.

The accompanying 38-page LOPP Guide to Administration and Implementation provides a comprehensive, well-organized primer including useful templates for how to approach an organizational study and how to address a range of problems commonly encountered in organizations. The chapter "Using the Parts to Create a Greater Whole" presents a workable, though somewhat academic and idealistic, description of some key dimensions of how organizations work to achieve their objectives. The chapter "What Now? Acting on Results" offers a very useful blueprint for how to initiate an organizational change program.

Although the author states that scores do not imply good or bad—just the extent to which the organization is strong versus where it can grow and improve—clearly he is operating from the implicit assumption that being a Learning Organization is good, and not being a Learning Organization is bad. Even though such a position has an intuitive appeal, he does not offer any data that support the position that Learning Organizations are more effective or successful over time by whatever criteria are appropriate (i.e., goal-attainment, sales, profitability, growth, stockholder/owner value, etc.), rather than just being more hospitable places to work.

In addition, the concept of the Learning Organization is not so widely accepted in the mainstream business community that most organizations' CEOs would readily undertake an assessment of the dimension and implement organizational changes to increase it. At present, the concept is embraced more by academics, organizational development practitioners, and consultants than by line operating managers. Accordingly, the LOPP would have a limited application as to the kinds of organizations where it would be accepted and therefore useful. Nontraditional, loosely structured, dynamic, start up/early stage, or matrix organizations would be more appropriate. Traditional, mature, bureaucratic, or conventionally organized and managed organizations would likely have little interest in it.

There are some specific criticisms of the instrument itself. All the items are worded so that the "agree" responses identify the presence of strongly socially desirable (and somewhat idealistic) attributes in the character and functioning of the organization. By not balancing the wording with negatively phrased items requiring "disagree" responses to endorse desirable qualities, there is a much increased likelihood of the respondent adopting a response set.

In addition, the overall reading level of the questions appears to be on the high side. The items are more abstract and more conceptual than those customarily dealt with by most rank-and-file workers. Thus, the instrument is better suited for use with brighter, more literate people who would generally be found in technical, professional, or managerial work groups. Furthermore, use of the term "executive" is unfortunate as it is rarely used day-to-day by most people in contemporary business organizations. Although the author does make a distinction between middle management and top management (the more common terms), the differences need to be made more explicit and better defined.

Finally, the inexperienced practitioner is cautioned not to use the LOPP alone as a basis to make significant changes in an organization. Before any such effort is undertaken, it is critical to conduct a comprehensive organizational review sequentially assessing first the adequacy of the organization's strategy, then its structure, then its processes (the dimensions that the LOPP primarily measures), and finally its people, to identify where the real problems lie and determine what changes, if any, are required.

SUMMARY. The LOPP is a normless 60-item attitude survey (rather than a psychological test) that purports to measure the extent to which the employees of an organization perceive it to be a "Learning Organization" (i.e., able to learn and adapt). Although it suffers from a few structural problems, the instrument comprehensively assesses the extent to which an organization fits the rather academic and theoretical "Learning Organization" model. The accompanying Guide to Administration and Implementation is a well-done primer for how to approach one narrow component of a comprehensive organization assessment and then initiate a program of organizational intervention and development based on this dimension only.

Review of the Learning Organization Practices Profile by MICHAEL J. ZICKAR, Assistant Professor of Industrial-Organizational Psychology, Bowling Green State University, Bowling Green, OH:

The Learning Organization Practices Profile (LOPP) is designed to assess the quality of organizational processes and practices that foster individual learning and growth. There are 12 dimensions of organizational practices relevant to learning practices that are measured with the LOPP; these dimensions range from "Vision and Strategy" to "Individual and Team Development." Potential uses of the scale mentioned in the administration guide include stimulating dialogue related to organizational learning and evaluating a change resulting from organizational programs designed to enhance learning. In short, the LOPP is designed to provide a rough organizational overview.

Each of the 12 dimensions is measured with five items. Each item presents a description of an organizational practice or characteristic that relates to the organization's emphasis on learning. For example, one item states "managers admit their own mistakes." The response scale for each item is 6-point scale that ranges from *strongly disagree* to *strongly agree*. The respondent is given the option of using the entire organization or their business unit or department as the unit of analysis. The items are written with clear language and are easily completed. Average administration times are not given but I would estimate that most people could complete the LOPP in 30 minutes or less. Straightforward instructions for handscoring the instrument are presented at the end of the test booklet. Employees could be allowed to complete the instrument at their leisure because all relevant instructions are included in the test booklet. Overall, the testing booklet is attractive and functional.

Unfortunately, it was difficult to evaluate the psychometric properties of the LOPP because the test developers appear to have devoted minimal attention to examining the reliability and validity of scores from this instrument. The only relevant information presented in the administration guide is a brief description of the rational approach used to develop the LOPP. An unspecified number of organizational development experts were used to classify items into relevant dimensions and also to eliminate items. It is unclear whether the 12 LOPP dimensions were identified before the item review or were an outcome of that process. An ongoing reliability study is mentioned in the administration guide but none of the results of this study are presented. I cannot evaluate the psychometric adequacy of the LOPP without such a study.

Two other pieces of information needed to recommend the LOPP are also missing from the administration guide. The LOPP appears to have no evidence for construct or predictive validity. The administration guide also lacks norms that would be important for judging the meaningfulness of scores.

SUMMARY. The LOPP appears to be a useful tool for stimulating dialogue related to how an organization can improve its individual members' capacities to learn. The dimensions measured by the LOPP seem to span the possible range of organizational dimensions quite well; hence, the process of having team members complete the instrument and then meeting to discuss individual results would provide a useful springboard for discussion of a variety of issues. The administration guide provides information on how to structure these feedback meetings. However, until further psychometric research (both reliability and validity) is conducted, I cannot recommend using the LOPP as a basis for organizational decisions such as allocation of training resources or evaluation of training programs. The process of completing the LOPP may be useful for some employees but the resulting scores are difficult to interpret without further information.

[209]
Learning Styles Inventory [Educational Activities, Inc.].

Purpose: Designed to assess an individual's learning style of receiving and expressing information.
Population: Intermediate and secondary level students.
Publication Date: 1993.
Acronym: LSI.
Scores, 9: Visual Language, Visual Numeric, Auditory Language, Auditory Numeric, Tactile Concrete, Social Individual, Social Group, Oral Expressiveness, Written Expressiveness.
Administration: Group.
Price Data, 1994: $98 per 2 diskettes, 2 backups, management, and documentation; $395 per kit for class, school, or district batch processing using IBM PC or models 25, 30, etc. with an NCS 3000 or SCANTRON 1400 scanner.
Time: Administration time not reported.
Comments: Pencil and paper or computer (Apple/MS-DOS/Windows/Mac) administered.
Authors: Jerry F. Brown and Richard M. Cooper.
Publisher: Educational Activities, Inc.

Review of the Learning Styles Inventory [Educational Activities, Inc.] by ROBERT BROWN, Carl A. Happold Distinguished Professor of Educational Psychology Emeritus, University of Nebraska—Lincoln, and Senior Associate, Aspen Professional Development Associates, Lincoln, NE:

The Learning Styles Inventory (LSI) is a 45-item, self-report survey of student learning style preferences divided into three categories: Cognitive Style (Visual Language, Visual Numeric, Auditory Language, Auditory Numeric, and Tactile Concrete), Social Style (Individual, Group), and Expressiveness Style (Oral and Written). Respondents read descriptive statements (e.g., "I would rather tell a story than write it") and use a 4-point, Likert-like response format to indicate whether the statement is *Most Like Me* (score = 4) or *Least Like Me* (score = 1). Intermediate response categories of "3" and "2" have no verbal descriptors. The inventory is intended for use with intermediate and secondary students. The manual authors suggest that teachers might also want to complete the survey to determine their own preferences.

The LSI can be completed in a paper-and-pencil format or on a computer; disks are provided for Macintosh, Apple, or MS-DOS versions of the inventory.

The manual provides a brief explanation regarding learning styles with the expectation that the inventory will assist teachers in diagnosing individual student learning styles. The authors cite no literature supporting their views of learning styles and the few references provided all pre-date 1980. A computer analysis, using the disk provided makes it possible for teachers to compare individual students to the rest of the class and the teacher's preference style to those of individual students and the entire class.

For each of the nine subscales, the manual describes how a respondent scoring high on the scale would prefer to learn and provides suggested teaching techniques best employed for high scoring students. Teachers are encouraged to shape their teaching strategies to meet the learning styles of the students. Nearly twice as many pages of the manual are devoted to how to use the program disks to record data and print out graphical formats than are devoted to the purpose and usages of the inventory.

No normative data are provided. Presumably, a respondent's highest scale score would indicate that this is his or her preferred learning style. Yet, it is possible for a respondent to score high or low on all the scales. Presumably such students would have no preferred distinctive learning style.

Critical psychometric information, such as reliability and validity data, are absent. Supplementary information (copies of a report) provided independently of the manual report reliability data derived during the early developmental stages of the LSI. Reported odd-even, split-half reliabilities range from .25 (Visual Numerical) to .95 (Expressive Oral and Auditory Numerical). Only four scales had reported reliabilities above .75 (Auditory Numerical, $r = .95$, Expressive Oral, $r = .95$, Expressive Written, $r = .81$, and Group Learner, $r = .93$). These findings suggest great caution in making educational prescriptions for individual students based on the LSI scores.

What is the most troublesome is the lack of even the most rudimentary discussion of validity issues of which there are many. The concept of learning styles seems on first examination to be self-explanatory and valid and as such has a level of acceptance among perhaps many educators. After all don't some of us prefer to listen to a lecture rather than to read a book on the same topic; and vice versa? Unfortunately, there is almost a cult-like behavior among believers who use a variety of instruments (e.g., Myers-Briggs Type Indicator; 251) to provide "insights" to test-takers regarding their learning styles (and often personality profiles) with suggestions on how the learners should be matched with appropriate instructors. This is not the place for a full discussion of these issues but educators planning to use a learning style inventory, particularly for prescriptive purposes with individual students, owe it to their students to be thoroughly informed regarding the pros and cons of such uses.

Validity issues regarding the LSI include: (a) The formulation of the constructs for the scales. What is their theoretical derivation? How interrelated are the scales? What constructs would a factor analysis yield? (b) The differences between "preferences" and actual learning style behaviors. The LSI assesses respondent preferences. No data are provided that support a relationship between what teaching strategies a student says he or she prefers (e.g., lecture vs. discussion) and whether or not the student would make the same choice when provided with an actual opportunity to choose among several learning formats. (c) The impact of different learning style matches and mismatches on student achievement. Do students scoring high on the auditory scales perform better when the same material is provided auditorially versus in written form? These are just examples of validity issues needing attention.

Other questions must also be addressed. Is it possible, for example, that learning style preference might vary depending on the content of the material? What about the context of the learning situation? How would student motivation affect learning style preferences?

Even if learning styles are critical influences of student achievement, a question remains as to the ultimate educational value of matching student learning styles to instructional teaching strategies. What is the relative value of matching learning and teaching styles compared to teaching students how to cope with mismatches? Finally, what are the risks of teachers and/or students attaching descriptive labels to themselves?

Other learning style preference inventories exist that give more attention to issues of reliability and validity. (See reviews in *The Eleventh MMY* [1991] and subsequent editions.) This reviewer, however, is not aware of any instrument with sufficient theoretical or psychometric support to warrant use for making prescriptive statements for individual students. The Learning Process Questionnaire (T5:1466) attempts to assess how students approach learning, their motives and strategies, and is a better instrument for its purposes, but it cannot be recommended for use with individual students or without considerable awareness by the user of the relevant research and theoretical literature.

SUMMARY. Being attentive to and responding to the needs, interests, and abilities of individual students seems like a worthwhile goal for teachers, whatever context within which they teach. Providing more individualized instruction remains an ideal goal. However, doing so is much more complex than administering a learning style inventory and matching teaching strategies to student learning styles. The LSI needs extensive analysis before any consideration should be given for using it for other than research purposes. It should not be used by teachers who are not knowledgeable about its weaknesses and its potential for harm.

Review of the Learning Styles Inventory [Educational Activities, Inc.] by ROBERT J.

DRUMMOND, Professor, Division of Educational Services and Research, University of North Florida, Jacksonville, FL:

The Learning Styles Inventory (LSI) is designed to measure the preferred method of receiving and expressing information of intermediate and secondary students. The purpose of the LSI is to aid teachers in diagnosis and for identifying appropriate instructional strategies.

COMPOSITION. The inventory consists of 45 statements using a 4-point scale, *least like me* to *most like me.* Three categories are assessed: Cognitive Style, Social Style, and Expressive Style. The Cognitive Style measures five dimensions of the student's preference in acquiring information: Auditory Language, Visual Language, Auditory Numerical, Visual Numerical, and Tactile Concrete. Social style has two subscales, Individual Learning and Group Learning, as does the Expressive Style Scale with oral Expressive and Written Expressive.

ADMINISTRATION AND SCORING. There are two versions of the LSI, a pencil/paper version and a computer-assisted version. The teacher can enter the responses on the students' answer sheets and get the results for the class. The authors suggest that teachers may wish to take the test and compare their profile with the students in their classes. The teacher can print individual student data and a class composite, and compare the students' results to the class results. The software is available for both Apple and IBM computers. The software produces these graphs for the teacher.

The technical supplement states that the LSI at its present state of development is in its infancy and that validity studies should be considered. Item reliability studies have been conducted. Cronbach alphas or scale reliability coefficients are reported. The LSI manual does provide a few examples of how the teacher could use the results.

No factor analytical studies were reported to support the three dimensions and nine scales. The authors do not provide any information on how and why the range of scores was chosen. A score of 32 to 40 in a given area is considered to represent a major learning style. Prescriptive information provided on one of the frames is to help the teacher plan effective strategies to use with students.

SUMMARY. The LSI has appeal because of its computer-assisted feature that provides immediate feedback to the teacher. Although the test appears to have face validity, more thorough construct validation evidence is needed. In addition, more thorough reliability studies would be in order such as test-retest comparisons in addition to Cronbach's alphas for internal consistency. There is no normative information such as grade or gender. Are there grade differences or gender differences on any of the scales? The citations and reference sources are dated. No review of literature is reported to support the structure of the test. Although the LSI has potential, much more work is needed for it to become a widely accepted and used inventory.

[210]
Leatherman Leadership Questionnaire: 360 Degree Leadership Profile.

Purpose: "To provide specific feedback to individuals, groups, and organizations about their leadership behaviors."
Population: Leaders, managers, supervisors, team leaders, potential leaders, supervisors, and executives.
Publication Dates: 1987–1996.
Acronym: LLQ-360.
Scores, 28: Assigning Work, Career Counseling, Coaching Employees, One-on-One Oral Communication, Managing Change, Handling Employee Complaints, Dealing with Employee Conflicts, Counseling on Attendance, Performance and Work Habits, Helping an Employee Make Decisions, Delegating, Taking Disciplinary Action, Handling Emotional Situations, Setting Goals and Objectives and Planning with Employees, Handling Employee Grievances, Conducting Employee Meetings, Giving Positive Feedback, Negotiating, Conducting Performance Appraisals, Establishing Performance Standards, Persuading/Influencing Employees, Making Presentations to Employees, Problem Solving with Employees, Conducting Selection Interviews, Team Building, Conducting Termination Interviews, Helping an Employee Manage Time, One-on-One Training, Total.
Administration: Group.
Price Data, 1998: $1,500 per Basic LLQ-360 Degree administrator's kit including administrator's manual ('96, 207 pages), overhead transparencies (43), rater's booklets, 10 answer sheets for participants, 50 answer sheets for "others," scoring service for 10 participants which includes group summary reports in hardcopy and overhead transparencies, development manual ('92, 365 pages), and self-development action planner; $75 per additional answer sheets and scoring service with development manual; $55 per additional answer sheets and scoring service without development manual; $5 per additional answer sheet for "Others";

$10 per additional rater's booklet ('96, 24 pages); $10 per self-development action planners ('96, 16 pages); $29.95 per additional self-development manual; $750 per additional administrator's kit (no scoring service).
Time: (30) minutes.
Comments: Machine-scored by publisher; related to but separate from the Leatherman Leadership Questionnaire (T5:1479).
Author: Richard W. Leatherman.
Publisher: International Training Consultants, Inc.

Review of the Leatherman Leadership Questionnaire: 360 Degree Leadership Profile by CLAUDIA J. MORNER, Professor and University Librarian, University of New Hampshire, Durham, NH:

The Leatherman Leadership Questionnaire: 360 Degree Leadership Profile (LLQ-360) is a thoroughly developed instrument with an extensive package of materials available to support the test administrator and the person taking the questionnaire. Based on the Leatherman Leadership Questionnaire (LLQ; T5:1479), it is designed to provide 360 degree evaluation of a manager or supervisor's leadership behaviors in 27 categories. What this means is that the instrument may be taken not only by the person wanting to rate or understand his or her leadership behaviors, but is also designed to be administered to the person's subordinates, peers, customers, and boss so that the manager can determine how his or her behaviors are perceived by a wide range of people at work. This is what gives the 360 degree perspective of the person being evaluated. Unlike the LLQ, which is a measurement of a person's knowledge of leadership, the LLQ-360 rates how associates perceive a person and how the manager self-rates. In addition to rating the person on each of the 27 categories of leadership, each item gives the rater the opportunity to note the confidence in the accuracy of each rating and the rater's view of the importance of each task for the job done by the person being evaluated. The test developer when computing the individual's scores considers these factors of confidence and importance.

The developers of the LLQ-360 have left nothing to chance when it comes to preparing the administrator with all necessary information and advice. Their packet, contained in a carrying case, includes two large three-ring binders and some handbooks and guides. Information for people who would administer the questionnaire is extensive and helpful with no details omitted. Included, for example, is a checklist of supplies and equipment needed, and a discussion of standards of administration. Detailed scripts and overhead transparencies are supplied. These help to ensure that the questionnaire is administered appropriately. Also included are instructions on using an overhead projector, appropriate setting, time necessary to administer the instrument, reading level information, and guidance on how to help people understand the results.

Questionnaires are returned to the developers for scoring and the results are returned for the group and individuals, listing all the information on one sheet. For each of the 27 tasks, the scores (in percentages) are given for the person's rating, the boss's rating, the person's importance rating, the boss's importance and then the others in the 360 degree rating: subordinates, peers, and customers. The number of people in each of these last three categories are also given. Also on the rating sheet is the average of others' scores and an average of everyone including the subject and all others who rated him or her. Bar graphs are used to show the person's strengths and weaknesses over the 27 items and there is a category that compares this person's average score with norms based on all others who have completed this questionnaire. Also given are the person's LLQ score, if appropriate, and the group average score of the work group being evaluated and the group norm compared with all other groups who have completed the LLQ-360. The size of the database of these norms is given at more than 20,000. What is often missing in other questionnaires of this type is follow-through. What do you do with the results? Here the developers have extensive advice for group/small group discussion of the results. For additional follow-up on an individual basis, the developers include a 346-page paperback, the *LLQ Development Manual*. It gives detailed information on each of the 27 categories of leadership, with helpful advice for a person who has taken the questionnaire and would like to improve in specific areas.

The developers are thorough in their description of how the LLQ, on which the LLQ-360 was based, was developed. They discuss in detail who should use it and how it should be used and how content validity was examined. The developers describe the work of the panel of eight industry leaders, the 21 studies used to develop the

content and the 223 participants from seven organizations such as city fire department, state agency, retail sales company, hospital, and an electric utility company. Members of these diverse groups rated the items similarly in nearly all of the tasks. All of this analysis has been previously reported in the reviews of the LLQ by Rain (1995) and Rudner (1995) in the *Twelfth Mental Measurements Yearbook*. Although the developers give advice on ways to gather local evidence of validity, particularly measuring the LLQ-360 results against a knowledge-based instrument such as the LLQ, they do not provide in their voluminous information any data on the reliability of scores based on their large databank. Because the LLQ-360 developers do all the scoring for their customers, they should have sufficient data to make a case for reliability. Much space is given to show the thorough work done on content validity, but nothing is given about how the questionnaire might be free from measurement error or about other measures of reliability.

SUMMARY. This appears to be a promising instrument for employers to use for leadership developmental assessment, career counseling, and for understanding the leadership strengths or weaknesses in an organization. Further work on examining the reliability of scores from the instrument, or presenting these data, is recommended in future editions of the LLQ: 360 Degree Leadership Profile. The developers offer the instrument freely for academic research projects, so it is expected that more research will be conducted on this important leadership instrument.

REVIEWER'S REFERENCES
Rain, J. S. (1995). [Review of the Leatherman Leadership Questionnaire [Revised].] In J. C. Conoley & J. C. Impara (Eds.), *The twelfth mental measurements yearbook* (pp. 571–572). Lincoln, NE: Buros Institute of Mental Measurements.
Rudner, L. M. (1995). [Review of the Leatherman Leadership Questionnaire [Revised].] In J. C. Conoley & J. C. Impara (Eds.), *The twelfth mental measurements yearbook* (pp. 572–574). Lincoln, NE: Buros Institute of Mental Measurements.

Review of the Leatherman Leadership Questionnaire: 360 Degree Leadership Profile by WILLIAM VERDI, Manager Employment Testing and Validation, Long Island Railroad, Middle Village, NY:

The Leatherman Leadership Questionnaire: 360 Degree Leadership Profile (LLQ-360) defines leadership as "those interactive behaviors that occur between a team leader, supervisor, manager, or executive and his or her subordinates, boss, peers, and 'customers' (internal or external)" (technical manual, p. 1). It does not evaluate a candidate's ability to budget, administrate, or communicate effectively in a written format, or to motivate individuals. The LLQ-360 evaluates 27 different facets of leadership (number of items for each dimension are in parentheses): Assigning Work (8); Career Counseling (10); Coaching Employees (10); One-on-One Oral Communication (10); Managing Change (10); Handling Employee Complaints (9); Dealing with Employee Conflicts (9); Counseling on Attendance, Performance and Work Habits (10); Helping an Employee Make Decisions (8); Delegating (10); Taking Disciplinary Action (10); Handling Emotional Situations (10); Setting Goals and Objectives and Planning with Employees (9), Handling Employee Grievances (10); Conducting Employee Meetings (10); Giving Positive Feedback (8); Negotiating (10); Conducting Performance Appraisals (10); Establishing Performance Standards (8); Persuading/Influencing Employees (6); Making Presentations to Employees (10); Problem Solving with Employees (10); Conducting Selection Interviews (10); Team Building (10); Conducting Termination Interviews (10); Helping an Employee Manage Time (8); and One-on-One Training (10).

Raters and the individual being rated are asked to make three separate ratings for each item: using the item presented, (a) "rate the quality of the person's performance"; (b) the rater's "confidence or accuracy" of the rating made; and (c) how important the task is to the overall job. Scores for each of the 27 leadership dimensions and an overall score are available. Raters can be anyone who is familiar with both the candidate's job and his or her specific job performance. This means multiple raters from various levels (above, below, and on the same level as the ratee) can be obtained. The Rater's Guide indicates that it should only take about 30 minutes to complete; but to obtain accurate ratings, this reviewer feels more time will be required (up to one hour).

Normative data either in the form of specific organizational norms (other respondents within the same company who completed the LLQ-360 if enough have done so) or general norms based upon all who have completed the LLQ-360 are available. Reports are provided for the individual, group (department level or function), and company-wide level. Overhead transparencies and feedback presentations are also available for the various levels. Users of the LLQ are provided with a *How to Complete the LLQ* (Rater's Guide) and a manual on how to interpret the feedback scores (Action Planner). Both documents are written for the novice user, so no special training or education are required. Familiarity with leadership theory or 360 degree feedback instruments would be a plus. For the uninformed, customer service is available. This reviewer cannot evaluate the level nor the accuracy of such support. The publishers pledge to provide customers with complete support including site visitation.

The LLQ-360 should *not be used* for preemployment or prepromotion screening. There is a lack of research showing the ability of the LLQ to predict successful job performance, tenure, or promotability. Given the lack of validation research presented (research showing that LLQ-360 scores are somehow related to performance in a leadership position) any use of the LLQ-360 for promotion or hiring would require the development of local normative data. Given that success in most leadership positions is part situational (the environment) and part dispositional (the person) one would be ill advised to assume a candidate's success as a leader could be determined by looking at their ability level alone.

The LLQ-360 can be used to identify a candidate's developmental strengths and weaknesses, to identify training areas to address, to perform pre/post managerial training evaluations, or to give an individual the opportunity to receive feedback from peers/colleagues, subordinates, and supervisors. Users of the LLQ-360 will obtain a wealth of technical information pertaining to administrative and interpretative issues. They will also receive a thorough report delineating multiple areas for development.

SUMMARY. The LLQ-360, given its depth of coverage and ease of use, is best suited for use within a leadership development or training program. Trainers can get rapid assessments of several dimensions from multiple rating sources. The lack of research evidence for the LLQ-360's ability to successfully identify candidates with leadership skills is not reason enough to dismiss its use. Future research and practical experience with the LLQ-360 will demonstrate its usefulness. This reviewer cannot make such an evaluation at this time. Trainers and personnel who want to use the LLQ-360 should first ensure that the dimensions covered by the LLQ-360 are applicable and then decide how important the applicable dimensions are to successful performance.

In conclusion, the advantages of the LLQ-360 are ease of use and administration, detailed feedback reports, and a wide coverage of the several dimensions of leadership. The drawbacks of the LLQ-360 are: scant research or practical evidence demonstrating the LLQ-360's ability to differentiate ratees on leadership ability or the LLQ-360's success in past use, limited theoretical foundation for its development, and no information on how the instrument was constructed. Given these limitations, substantive employment and development decisions should not be made using the LLQ-360 as the sole source or method of evaluation. I cannot evaluate the LLQ-360's technical properties (how well it differentiates high from low leadership candidates) or how well it was developed because that information was not available at the time of this review.

[211]
Leiter International Performance Scale—Revised.

Purpose: Constructed as a "nonverbal cognitive assessment."

Population: Ages 2.0–20.11, adults.

Publication Dates: 1936–1998.

Acronym: Leiter-R.

Scores, 31: Visualization and Reasoning (Figure Ground, Design Analogies, Form Completion, Matching, Sequential Order, Repeated Patterns, Picture Context, Classification, Paper Folding, Figure Rotation), VR Composite (Fluid Reasoning, Brief IQ, Fundamental Visualization, Spatial Visualization, Full IQ), Attention and Memory Associated Pairs, Immediate Recognition, Forward Memory, Attention Sustained, Reverse Memory, Visual Coding, Spatial Memory, Delayed Pairs, Delayed Recognition, Attention Divided), AM Composite (Memory Screen, Associative Memory, Memory Span, Attention, Memory Process, Recognition Memory).

Administration: Individual.

Price Data, 2000: $850 per complete kit (in cloth carrying case) including manual ('97, 378 pages), 3 easel books, VR response cards, AM response cards, manipulatives, 20 each VR and AM record forms, Attention Sustained booklets A, B, and C, and the Growth Profile Booklet and the rating scales; $25 per 20 record forms (specify battery); $15 per 20 Attention Sustained booklets (specify form); $10 per 20 rating scale record forms (specify form); $25 per 20 Growth Profile booklets, $75 per manual.

Time: (90) minutes.

Comments: May calculate growth scores (criterion-referenced scores) to assess improvement in cognitive skills; computer scoring software available requiring Windows 3.1, Windows 95 or Windows 98 operating systems.

Authors: Gale H. Roid and Lucy J. Miller.

Publisher: Stoelting Co.

Cross References: See T5:1485 (64 references), T4:1446 (33 references), T3:1319 (16 references), and T2:505 (18 references); for a review of the original version by Emmy E. Werner, see 6:526 (10 references); see also 5:408 (17 references); for a review by Gwen F. Arnold and an excerpted review by Laurance F. Shaffer, see 4:349 (25 references).

Review of the Leiter International Performance Scale—Revised by GARY L. MARCO, Consultant, Chapin, SC:

The Leiter International Performance Scale has recently been updated and standardized on over 2,000 children and adolescents. Its primary purpose continues to be assessing in a nonverbal way the cognitive development of special populations of individuals aged 2 years up to 21 years for whom the usual tests of cognitive abilities are inappropriate. Examples of these populations include those who are deaf, mentally handicapped, speech and language impaired, learning disabled, brain injured, and ESL populations. It is also intended for use in evaluating speech and language disorders, including attention deficit disorders. The revision, based on modern psychometric and cognitive theory, is substantial; most of the subtests and materials used for the test have been revised and new subtests have been added. The revision and its supporting documentation are impressive, and in this reviewer's judgment makes the instrument an outstanding example of nonverbal cognitive assessment. Because of the instrument's complexity, this review does not cover some aspects (e.g., cut-scores) of instrument development.

TEST DESCRIPTION. The Leiter International Performance Scale—Revised (Leiter-R) consists of 20 subtests in four domains. The first 10 subtests form the Visualization and Reasoning (VR) Battery; the second 10, the Attention and Memory (AM) Battery. The AM Battery was added to this edition to make the scale more useful for individuals with learning disabilities. The VR and AM batteries take about 40 minutes each to administer and may be administered separately, depending on the needs of the individual to be assessed. Optional rating scales (Examiner, Parent, Self, and Teacher) may be used to collect additional, observational information about an individual. Brief versions of the VR Battery ("IQ screener") and AM Battery ("Memory Process screener") are available to make tentative decisions about intellectual development or to distinguish individuals with attention deficit disorders from those with learning disabilities.

Carroll's (1993) work and Gustafsson's (1984) hierarchical model of cognitive abilities guided the revision. This development is impressive in that it represents a major rework of the item content of the battery. Although the primary domains (Reasoning, Visualization, Attention, Memory, and Memory Span) are represented at each of the age levels tested by the battery, the subdomains change somewhat and increase in complexity with age.

TEST KIT. The test kit consists of an impressive set of materials that are geared towards making the test materials lighter and easier to use than those in the previous version. Foremost among these materials are the three plastic easel books that provide the 20 subtest items and directions for administration and scoring. The three item types represented on the Leiter-R are those that require the examinee to (a) place response cards in the easel tray, (b) arrange manipulative response shapes, and (c) point to stimulus material. Besides the easel booklets, the kit includes three Attention Sustained booklets for ages 2–3, 4–5, and 6–21 and a packet containing scoring keys, laminated grids, and picture plates for three of the AM subtests.

Other testing materials for the examinee include response cards and manipulative response shapes. Materials for the examiner include record forms for the VR and AM batteries and record forms for growth scores and rating scales. Also included in the kit are the rating scales for examiner (provided at the end of the record forms), teacher, parent, and self. A timer and a colored marker complete the kit.

TEST ADMINISTRATION. The Leiter-R is administered individually using response easels and stimulus cards. Test materials consist of three easels of stimulus material, picture cards, physical objects (manipulatives), and printed material. The examinee is asked to place the cards and manipulatives into slots on a frame. Not all subtests are appropriate for each age level. The Examiners Manual lists the recommended subtests for a given age level and the order of administration (p. 20).

The directions for administering and scoring the subtest tasks are conveniently given on the back side of the easel sheet on which the task is presented. They are also shown in the Examiners Manual. The directions are clear but may still pose some difficulty in administration until the examiner is well acquainted with the subtests. The method of communicating directions to the examinees is through pantomime. The examiner is, however, permitted considerable freedom in pantomiming the instructions—this could possibly lead to individual differences that depend on examiner variation. The directions provided in the Examiners Manual and the easel charts are very thorough and thus, except for the pantomiming requirement, go a long way toward providing the necessary standardization.

Examiners are well advised to practice giving the battery before actually using it in an operational setting. In this reviewer's opinion, to ensure smooth standardized administrations, supplemental practice and instruction in giving the instrument are necessary. Special training in administering the battery is available through the test publisher as well as college and university courses.

SCORING. The scoring directions for each subtest are provided in the Examiners Manual and on the back of the appropriate easel card. The directions are very clear, and forms are provided for recording the test results.

The test publisher also makes available a Computer Scoring Software System and User's Guide that prepares a score report for an examinee once scores are entered into templates. The system works with Windows 95 and Windows 98 operating systems. Chapters in the User's Manual tell how to install the system, how to use the basic system, how to input data, how to prepare reports, and how to interpret scores (selected portions from the Leiter-R Examiners Manual). Although the scoring software and guide are very clear, the printed reports generated are very ordinary in appearance. In this modern era of personal computers, scoring software is a welcome addition to the testing battery.

SCALED SCORES. The normative scales for the VR Battery are based on a nationally representative sample of 1,719 individuals; those for the AM Battery, on 763 individuals. Subtest scores are expressed on a normative scale with a mean of 10 and a standard deviation of 3 for each age group (55 age brackets, ranging from 2 years,

0 months to 20 years, 11 months). For general intellectual ability a deviation IQ (mean of 100 and standard deviation of 15) is used based on the subtest scaled scores. Growth increments are expressed on a scale developed using the Rasch item response theory model (see Embretson, 1996; Hambleton, Swaminathan, & Rogers, 1991; Wright & Stone, 1979). Extensive documentation of the scaling and tables for converting raw scores to scaled scores is provided in the Examiners Manual.

SCORE USE. The Examiners Manual appropriately recommends that the test results not be used apart from nontest information (e.g., academic and family background). It also suggests caution in using the battery with individuals from cultures that may not be familiar with testing.

The Examiners Manual suggests that score interpretation proceed from general IQ scores, to composite scores on two or more subtests, to specific subtest scores, and finally to detailed, diagnostic level information. In addition, it shows how to use growth scores, based on item response theory, and provides for measuring growth between two testings. Interpretive information provided with growth scores includes item difficulty values that are on the same scale as the test scores and growth norms. In the chapter on score interpretation, the Examiners Manual provides a number of useful examples of various types of score uses, including clinical interpretation, and describes what the subtests measure. This chapter should be very helpful to score users.

TRYOUT AND STANDARDIZATION ADMINISTRATIONS. Tryout testing occurred in 1994, and standardization testing in 1995. The total sample for the pilot administration consisted of 550 children and adults, including 225 children without disabilities. For the separate age groups, the sample sizes for these analyses were small, numbering no more than 50 at each of five age brackets for the pilot testing.

Two samples were used for the standardization administration, one for the VR Battery and one for the AM Battery. The VR sample consisted of 1,719 typical children and the AM sample, 763 typical children—a subset of the VR sample—administered both batteries on two occasions. The AM sample provide at least 42 examinees for each of 18 age brackets. Such sample sizes within age brackets may seem small compared to those in norming samples for nationally normed individu-

ally administered intelligence tests, but compare favorably with those used for other memory and neuropsychological instruments such as the Wechsler Memory Scale (416). In addition, the standardization edition was administered to 701 atypical children with such disabilities as severe speech or language impairment, severe hearing impairment, and significant cognitive delay, and with ESL, LD, and ADD/ADHD groups.

Representation in terms of geographic region, community size, socioeconomic status, gender, race, and ethnicity for both the tryout and standardization administrations was slightly non-representative in some cases, but certainly adequate for purposes of the item analyses, scaling, and other statistical analyses that were carried out. Hispanic and Afro-American subjects were oversampled for item tryouts so that nearly equal sample sizes of white, Hispanic, and Afro-American subjects were achieved.

ITEM AND SUBTEST SELECTION. Twenty-three subtests and 704 items were included in the tryout edition of the test. Based on the item analyses, 20 subtests and 691 items were included in the standardization edition, and 20 subtests and 549 items were chosen for the final edition. For both the tryout and standardization administrations, items were selected by examining a number of variables (e.g., item difficulties, item-total correlations, Rasch fit statistics, internal consistency of items within subtests, correlations with criterion variables, differential item function indices, and ratings by examiners). The extensiveness of the item selection for the Leiter-R is impressive and led to an appropriately refined final edition.

NORMS. Norms for different population segments are not provided in the Examiners Manual. However, the scores themselves are normative in that they have set means and standard deviations (e.g., 10 and 3 for subtests) and as such may be referred to the normal curve to obtain percentile ranks. The Examiners Manual does provide mean scores for 11 special criterion groups (severe speech or language impairment, severe hearing impairment, etc.), and percentile ranks and Normal Curve Equivalents for the rating composite standardized scores. Additional normative data by gender and racial/ethnic group would help with score interpretation.

RELIABILITY INFORMATION AND SCORE DIFFERENCES. Consistent with modern psychometric developments, classical and item response theory approaches to reliability were used. Reliability information reported in the Examiners Manual consisted of internal consistency reliabilities (alpha coefficients), test-retest reliabilities, standard errors of measurement, and test information curves. The average coefficients (alphas) across the various age brackets range from .75 to .90 for the VR subtests. The average coefficients (alphas and retest reliabilities—for times subtests) range from .69 to .87 for the AM subtests. Reliability coefficients and standard errors of measurement are also reported for the AM Battery Special Diagnostic Scales and for rating subscales for the examiner, parent, teacher, and self-rating scales. In addition, reliabilities of IQ and composite scores are reported for three age brackets. Moreover, test-retest reliability coefficients are reported based on samples of 163 children and adolescents for the VR Battery and 45 children for the AM Battery. (The time between occasions is not reported in the Examiners Manual but was presumably only a few days.) The sizes of the test-retest reliability coefficients vary considerably because of the small sample sizes but still are reasonably similar to the alpha coefficients. Several of the subtests and composite scores showed practice effects. Also, scores on the AM Battery subtests and composite scores were less stable than scores on the VR Battery.

Decision consistency reliability is reported for the Brief IQ Screener and the Full Scale IQ for identifying children with cognitive delay (those below the cutoff scores). In addition, test information curves are reported for these scales. This kind of reliability information is more relevant than coefficient alphas and retest reliabilities for such decisions.

These reliability analyses, although based on small sample sizes, are clearly presented and comprehensive. The test publisher's use of modern psychometric theory for developing reliability information is to be commended. The reliability information reported in the manual should provide users with what they need to evaluate score consistency.

A caveat here is that the reliability analyses and some of the analyses to be reported under validity were apparently derived from test scores generated by dropping items from tests given in the 1995 standardization administration. Others were apparently based on the actual tests given at the tryout and standardization administrations. Reliability and validity results would best be based on scores from a real administration of the final edition of the Leiter-R and not from administrations of the tryout and standardization editions. Presumably studies reporting reliabilities and validities based on giving the final edition of the Leiter-R will be forthcoming in the research literature.

VALIDITY. The validity perspective taken with respect to the Leiter-R is one that stresses the importance of multiple validities for the various interpretations of test scores. This view is consistent with current testing standards. Obviously, studying validity is an ongoing process; thus, one can only expect the publisher's documentation to provide evidence for the most important validity considerations.

CONTENT VALIDITY. Content validity evidence for the test comes from ratings provided by 60 examiners involved in the tryout phase and 114 examiners involved in the standardization phase of data collection. Carroll's (1993) delineation of cognitive factors was used to categorize both the original Leiter items and the items that were added later. Only those subtests that received high ratings were retained in the final version of the test. Content validity evidence also comes from the careful procedures used to select the items for the subtests (see the section on item and subtest selection).

CRITERION-RELATED VALIDITY. Criterion-related validity evidence consisted of percentages of correctly classified examinees, correlations among the Leiter-R scores and scores on other intellectual ability tests, and differences between typical and atypical examinees. The Examiners manual provided information on classification accuracy in identifying cognitive delay or giftedness and attention deficit disorders or learning disabilities. The classification results are very promising, but the Examiners Manual wisely cautions score users not to use the Leiter-R scores in isolation for clinical diagnosis. The classification accuracy is especially good for identifying cognitive delay.

Criterion-related information was also represented in the form of correlations with other instruments that measure similar abilities. Included in the manual are correlations of the Brief IQ, Full IQ, and certain other scores on the Leiter-R with scores on the original Leiter, the Wechsler Intelligence Scale for Children (WISC-III), selected subtests on the Stanford-Binet Intelligence Scale—Fourth Edition, the Wide Range Assessment of

Learning and Memory, and the Test of memory and Learning. These data also suffer from small sample sizes (ranging from 18 to slightly over 100). Correlations with the original Leiter were quite high (.85 to .93). The other correlations tended to be lower but still high enough to suggest that similar abilities are being measured.

Other criterion-related validity information consisted of correlations with group-administered achievement tests (from the California Achievement Test, Comprehensive Test of Basic Skills, and Stanford Achievement Test batteries). All of these correlations were in the low to moderate range.

CONSTRUCT VALIDITY. A number of analyses relevant to construct validity were completed on the tryout and standardization editions of the Leiter-R. Mean scores on the Growth Scale (based on four Brief IQ subtests) increased monotonically with age, starting to level off at about 10 years of age and plateauing at about 15 years of age. In addition, factor analytic studies (both exploratory and confirmatory) provided evidence for the multidimensionality of the Leiter-R and for the existence of reasoning, visualization, attention, and memory factors (Bos, 1995, and Bos, Gridley, and Roid, 1996). One confirmatory analysis supported four- or five-factor hierarchical models for the Leiter-R for three different age brackets. Moreover, the ideal patterns of common variance greater than specific variance and specific variance greater than error variance were generally supported, although four of the subtests had very low specific variances. A cross-battery analysis demonstrated the convergence of nonverbal factors on the WISC-III and the Leiter-R.

A final piece of construct validity evidence relates to fairness across ethnic groups. Studies of bias at the subtest level yielded few significant differences between Caucasian and Hispanic samples and between Navajo and normative samples (see, for example, Flemmer & Roid, 1996). Clearly, however, more fairness studies are needed.

For a test that is new the validity evidence presented in the Examiners Manual is reasonably comprehensive and supports the factorial nature of the Leiter-R. Other validity evidence will accumulate as researchers undertake special studies and present their results. This reviewer encourages the test publisher to study particularly the validity of the test for discriminating among different types of special groups.

SUMMARY. The Leiter-R is a carefully developed battery that is based on a well-specific cognitive model. Excellent test materials, along with a comprehensive Examiners Manual that also serves as a technical manual, go a long way toward making the Leiter-R a solid measurement instrument. Although more study is needed, the evidence so far suggests that the Leiter-R is an effective instrument for identifying and evaluating those with speech and language disorders and for estimating the cognitive ability of such individuals.

REVIEWER'S REFERENCES

Wright, B. D., & Stone, M. H. (1979). *Best test design.* Chicago: MESA Press.
Gustafsson, J. E. (1984). A unifying model for the structure of intellectual abilities. *Intelligence, 8,* 179–203.
Hambleton, R. K., Swaminathan, H., & Rogers, H. J. (1991). *Fundamentals of item response theory.* Newbury Park, CA: Sage.
Carroll, J. B. (1993). *Human cognitive abilities: A survey of factor-analytic studies.* New York: Cambridge University Press.
Bos, J. (1995). *Factor structure of the field edition of the Leiter International Performance Scale—Revised.* Unpublished doctoral dissertation, George Fox University, Newberg, OR.
Bos, J., Gridley, B. E., & Roid, G. H. (1996, August). *Factor structure of nonverbal cognitive abilities: Construct validity of Leiter-R.* Paper presented at the annual meeting of the American Psychological Association, Toronto, Canada.
Embretson, S. E. (1996). The new rules of measurement. *Psychological Assessment, 8,* 341–349.
Flemmer, D., & Roid, G. H. (1996, August). *Nonverbal cognitive performance of Hispanic and speech-impaired adolescents.* Paper presented at the annual meeting of the American Psychological Association, Toronto, Canada.

Review of the Leiter International Performance Scale—Revised by TERRY A. STINNETT, Associate Professor, School Psychology Programs, Oklahoma State University, Stillwater, OK:

The Leiter International Performance Scale—Revised (Leiter-R) represents a significant modernization and upgrade of an historic icon. The instrument measures nonverbal intellectual ability, memory, and attention and is appropriate for use with children and youth aged 2 years through 20 years, 11 months. It may be particularly useful for children with communication disorders, cognitive delays, English as a second language, hearing impairments, motor impairments, traumatic brain injury, and attention and/or learning difficulties.

The Leiter-R contains 20 subtests that comprise two batteries, Visualization and Reasoning (VR) and Attention and Memory (AM). They have separate record forms. There are four optional rating scales including separate forms for the Examiner, Parent, Self, and Teacher. The subtests given for the VR and AM batteries vary for different age groups and not all subtests are administered at a given age. There is a recommended order of administration for the four distinct age groupings of 2–3, 4–5, 6–10, and 11–20 years. The items to be presented to a child are based on specific age-based starting points and all subtests begin with teaching trials. Items are presented through pointing, gesture, facial expression, and pantomime. There are three types of response formats; the child might place response cards in a particular order, or arrange manipulative shapes, or point to the correct response on the easel. There are standard rules for restarting if the start-point items are too difficult for the child and standard discontinue rules based on cumulative rather than consecutive errors. All subtest demands, materials, teaching items, and scoring guides are printed on the back of easel pages before the first item of each subtest. The record forms also include start points, stop rules, time limits, and some cues for item content to facilitate administration.

There are 10 VR subtests: Figure Ground (FG), Design Analogies (DA), Form Completion (FC), Matching (M), Sequential Order (SO), Repeated Patterns (RP), Picture Context (PC), Classification (C), Paper Folding (PF), and Figure Rotation (FR). There are 10 AM subtests: Associated Pairs (AP), Immediate Recognition (IR), Forward Memory (FM), Attention Sustained (AS), Reverse Memory (RM), Visual Coding (VC), Spatial Memory (SM), Delayed Pairs (DP), Delayed Recognition (DR), and Attention Divided (AD).

LEITER-R RATING SCALES. The optional rating scales are to assess social-emotional functioning and all four yield composite scores for Cognitive/Social and Emotions/Regulation. The Examiner Rating Scale includes the subscales of Attention, Organization/Impulse Control, Activity Level, Sociability, Energy and Feelings, Mood and Regulation, Anxiety, and Sensory Reactivity. The Parent Rating Scale subscales include Attention, Activity Level, Impulsivity, Social Abilities, Adaptation, Moods and Confidence, Energy and Feelings, and Sensitivity and Regulation. The Self Rating Scale (used only for children aged 9–20 years) has four subscales: Organization/Responsibility, Activity Level and Mood, Feelings and Reactions, and Self Esteem. The Teacher Rating Scale subscales are Attention, Organization/Impulsivity, Activity Level, Social Abilities, Mood and Regulation, Temperament, Reactivity, and Adaptation. The Examiner and Teacher Scales both have excellent internal consistency reliability (Cronbach's alphas) across the ages (mid .80s to

upper .90s). The Parent Scale generally has very good internal consistency (alphas generally in the mid .80s). The estimates for the Self Rating Scale were lower (range from .69 to .83). The temporal stability of the Examiner Rating Scale was also examined, but the length of the interval between ratings was not specified. The test-retest stability was best at the 2–5-year level with all estimates falling in the upper .80s and .90s. Estimates were lower at the other two age groups. The Cognitive/Social composite reliabilities were acceptable across the three age groups (2–5 years = .90; 6–10 = .87; and 11–20 = .80). The Emotions/Regulation composite followed a similar pattern but was not very stable at the 11–20-year age group (2–5, .94; 6–10, .87; and 11–20, .76).

A series of factor analyses of the rating scales suggested two fairly distinct factors, Cognitive/Social (CS) and Emotions/Regulation (ER). Although the scales appear structurally sound, the authors indicate additional validity work is needed. The Leiter-R manual is not too specific about how to use the rating scale information. It suggests the rating scale data can be combined with the battery data to develop hypotheses. The authors did report studies that used cutoff scores for the Examiner C/S composite to examine classification accuracy in samples of children with ADHD, but the results were not promising. I would recommend that systems like the Behavior Assessment System for Children (Reynolds & Kamphaus, 1992; 49) or the Child Behavior Checklist (Achenbach, 1991; T5:451) be used for assessment of behavioral and emotional adjustment until further support for the Leiter-R scales is accumulated.

LEITER-R SCORES. Raw scores for each of the VR and AM subtests can be converted to age-based scaled scores ($M = 10$, $SD = 3$) that range from 1 to 19. Percentile rank scores for the subtests are not available in the manual but can be derived through the Leiter-R computer scoring software (described later in this review). [Editor's Note: The publisher advises the percentile ranks for the subtests may be found in Appendix K.] Combinations of VR battery subtests scaled scores yield estimates of nonverbal general ability ($M = 100$, $SD = 15$). There is a Full Scale IQ for ages 2–5 and 6–20 and a Brief IQ Screener for all ages. The authors state the IQ score reflects nonverbal "g." The VR battery subtests can also provide composite scores for Fluid Reasoning, Fundamental Visualization, and Spatial Visualization, but the test's authors recommend calculating only those composites that are needed to answer questions specific to the child being assessed. There are six AM composite scores that reflect aspects of attention or memory: Memory Screener (for ages 2–20), Associative Memory (6–20), Memory Span (6–20), Attention (6–20), Memory Process (6–20), and Recognition Memory (4–10).

The IQ and composite score norms are collapsed into a single table for all ages rather than being separated by age groups. Percentile rank scores for the IQ derivatives and VR and AM composite scores are available. The standard errors of measurement for all Leiter-R scores are also presented in the manual. Confidence intervals at the .95, .90, and .68 levels can also be calculated and the values needed to construct the intervals are presented in the manual for three age groups (2–5, 6–10, and 11–20). Examiners should note that the confidence intervals are based on obtained score rather than the predicted true score method that is most appropriate for describing the examinee's current functioning on a given test at that point in time they were tested (Glutting, McDermott, & Stanley, 1987). The Leiter-R also provides Growth Scores for all subtests, composites, and IQs for interpreting a child's performance in a criterion-referenced fashion. Because the child's overall ability and task performance ability are placed on the same continuum, these scores can be considered in conjunction to allow for estimation of the difficulty that items may have for the child, which can then be used to target skills at the appropriate level for intervention.

LEITER-R COMPUTER SCORING SOFTWARE. The manual recommends a hierarchical interpretive model to describe the child's cognitive strengths and weaknesses. For the convenience of their users, a computer scoring software system and user guide (Roid & Madsen, 1998) can be purchased separately. Those familiar with the score-difference method will recognize the Leiter-R interpretive model as similar (e.g., see Kaufman, 1979, 1994; Wechsler, 1991; Sattler, 1992). There is disagreement in the literature among experts about the value of subtest-level interpretation (Glutting, McDermott, Watkins, Kush, & Konold, 1997; Kaufman, 1994; Sattler, 1992). However, the authors do stress that not all levels of the interpretive model must be used. They also em-

phasize that the statistical significance of score differences as well as the frequency of differences in the normative population (base rate) should be evaluated. To be maximally clinically useful, a score difference needs to be statistically significant and rare in the normal population.

Raw score data are entered by the examiner and automatically converted to scaled scores and IQs. There are six data entry forms: Identification, VR Battery, AM Battery, AM Diagnostic Scales, Examiner and Parent (EP) Rating Scales, and Teacher and Student (TS) Rating Scales. Two report versions can be printed: a five-page summary of tables of the results and a nine-page report containing tables and profiles. The system does not provide interpretive narratives and does not generate hypotheses for the user, which should prohibit those without sufficient background with the test's theory and concepts from using the program to write reports. As would be expected, the system allows its summaries to be saved to a file so that a user can access and edit them with other software such as a word processing program. Most would likely use this feature to reduce the standard output before cutting, copying, and pasting Leiter-R results into a more individualized, comprehensive interpretive psychological or psycho-educational assessment report. The program calculates 90% confidence intervals for all score points and there is no way to specify otherwise. The authors include a brief section in the guide related to ethics and computer-assisted interpretation.

DEVELOPMENT AND CONTENT VALIDITY. The Leiter-R was developed with careful attention to theoretical and psychometric excellence. A literature review and input from subject matter experts and Leiter users were used to compile a variety of items into 23 subtests that reflected the content that logically would be expected for a nonverbal IQ test. Examiners at both the tryout and standardization phase provided content and procedural ratings for each subtest. Only subtests that received high ratings were retained without revision. Items were also categorized according to Carroll's (1993) groupings of cognitive factors. This was an impressive effort to make the Leiter-R a solid theoretically based test. A comparison of the proposed structure of the test to the theory shows that it was designed to reflect nonverbal components of a multifactor, hierarchical "g" model like the three-stratum theory of cognitive abilities (see Carroll, 1993; Carroll, 1997; Gustafson, 1984). Item-level analyses included calculation of item difficulties for five age groups, estimation of item-total correlations, assessment of item stability (test-retest), differential item functioning between gender and ethnic subgroups, qualitative analysis of items by examiners and examinees, and item-response theory scaling.

CONSTRUCT VALIDITY. After the item analyses, subtest-level analyses were completed. Exploratory and confirmatory factor analyses generated a series of models to describe the Leiter-R's internal structure (Bos, 1995; Bos, Gridley, & Roid, 1996 as cited in the 1997 Leiter-R Examiners Manual.). In sum, the Leiter-R tryout edition fit the underlying theoretical model fairly well with adolescents showing more differentiated cognitive abilities than younger children did and an invariant, unidimensional, and robust "g" factor composed of the FG, FC, RP, and SO subtests was demonstrated at all ages. The Leiter-R final edition was also subjected to a series of exploratory and confirmatory factor analyses. The exploratory analyses (principal axes) employed four age groups (2–3, 4–5, 6–10, and 11–20 years) to reflect the different starting ages of the subtests. Reasoning, visualization, attention, and memory factors emerged across all age groups although there was some variation in the way the subtests loaded across the ages. Confirmation models were again examined following the exploratory analyses and justified four factors at ages 4–5 and five-factor models at ages 6–10 and 11–20 as the best fitting. All are hierarchical models with "g" at the highest level, with subordinate second-level broad abilities, followed by even more specific and narrow third level abilities. For the 4–5-year age group Fluid Reasoning, Broad Visualization, Attention, and Recognition Memory were confirmed; at ages 6–10 Nonverbal Reasoning, Visuospatial Reasoning, Attention, Recognition Memory, and Associative Memory Span were confirmed; and at ages 11–20 Nonverbal Reasoning, Visuospatial Reasoning, Attention, Associative Memory, and Span Working Memory were confirmed.

At the 2–5-year-old age group most of the individual subtests were fair estimates of "g" with C, FC, M, and AS (loadings ranged from .60 to .66) providing the strongest measures of the construct. The best measures of "g" at the 6–10-year

group were only fair: FG, FC, DR, SO (.55 to .65), DA and DP (both at .53), and IR (.49). For the 11–20-year group SO (.70) and PF (.70) were strongly associated with "g" whereas DA, FC, RP, FR, AP, VC, and SM were good measures of "g" (.54 to .62).

STANDARDIZATION. The test has a superb standardization sample that is nationally representative. A stratified random sampling design was used based on the population survey of the 1993 U.S. Census. The VR Battery was standardized on 1,719 children and the AM Battery on a subset ($N = 763$) of that group. There is an impressive match between the sample demographics and the census data on gender, ethnicity (including Caucasian, African-American, Hispanic, Asian, and Native American), parental education level, and geographic region. The sample is specified into 18 age groupings; for the VR Battery there are approximately 100 children in each half-year grouping for ages 2–5 and about 100 children and youth in each of the remaining 10 age groups. For the AM Battery sample there are a minimum of 42 children at each of 18 age levels. The standardization sample is presented in cross-tabulated form for a variety of variables and users can evaluate the relevance of the sample for their uses in great detail.

LEITER-R RELIABILITY. Stability over time was estimated for Leiter-R VR subtests and composite scores for three age groups (2–5, 6–10, 11–20) but there is no indication of the length of the interval between testing. The AM battery data are also presented but were derived from a single 6–17-year-old group. The VR subtests were more reliable at the 11–20-year age group than at the other age groups with most test-retest coefficients falling in the .80s. The estimates for these subtests at the younger ages were lower. The reliabilities for the composite scores and IQs for the VR battery were acceptable (upper .80s or .90s) except for Fluid Reasoning at the 2–5- and 6–10-year levels (both were .83). The AM battery subtests generally were too low to be considered stable over time. They ranged from .55 to .85 with a median estimate of .62. The AM composite score reliabilities were somewhat better ranging from .61 to .85. However, only the Attention composite (.85) was sufficiently stable to be used for diagnostic purposes. None of the other test-retest estimates broke .80.

Internal consistency reliabilities are reported for the VR battery subtests, the AM battery subtests, and the special diagnostic scales of the AM battery. Most of the estimates are Cronbach's alpha coefficients, except for the timed AS and AD tests, which are test-retest estimates. For the VR battery the average alpha reliabilities ranged from .75 to .90 with a median alpha value of .82. For the AM battery the average reliabilities ranged from .67 to .87 with a median alpha value of .83. The alphas for the AM special diagnostic scales ranged from .74 to .87.

SUBTEST SPECIFICITY ESTIMATES. Common, specific, and error variance associated with the Leiter-R subtests are presented in the manual and were derived using the communalities from the principal axes analyses of the three age groupings and the reliability estimates just presented. For the most part, the Leiter-R subtests follow the Common > Unique > Error variance pattern. To their credit the authors caution users about subtests at different ages, which have excess error variance.

ADDITIONAL VALIDITY STUDIES. Classification accuracy statistics are reported for the Leiter-R for a variety of groups (e.g., children with mental retardation, children who are gifted, children with learning disabilities including verbal and nonverbal subgroups, and children with ADHD including hyperactive and inattentive without hyperactivity subgroups). Using a cutoff IQ score of 70 resulted in good specificity and sensitivity with low rates of false positives and false negatives for the children with mental retardation. The Leiter-R was not very effective in reclassifying students who had previously been identified as gifted. The Leiter-R fared even worse for classifying children with attention problems and children with learning disabilities. Various cutpoints were examined using the Memory Process Composite (MPC), the Examiner rating scale Cognitive/Social Composite, and the two combined for classification of these groups. The best classification compromise was a combination of the MPC cutoff score of 90 and C/S composite score of 85, which produced moderate sensitivity (.50 to .60) and an acceptable false positive rate (5.4 to 6.3). Classification of the LD groups was also problematic with a similar pattern of low sensitivity (.40 to .67) using the MPC and unacceptable false positive rates (.20 to .24).

A variety of criterion groups were also contrasted by comparison of group means. For "typical" children the median IQ was 101, whereas children with mental retardation had a median IQ of 58, and children who had been identified as gifted-talented had a median IQ of 115. The hearing-impaired and English-as-Second Language groups were only approximately a third of a standard deviation below the normative sample mean. Also the Growth Scale scores show an increase across age, which suggests the scores are age-sensitive and performing as expected.

The Leiter-R Brief and Full IQs are also correlated with the WISC-III Full Scale and Performance IQs (.85 to .86). The Leiter-R AM Memory Process Composite was related to the WISC-III Freedom from Distractibility Index (.78) and the AM Attention composite was related to the WISC-III Processing Speed Index (.83). These data indicate the Leiter-R has convergent validity with established independent measures of intelligence but is also capable of providing some additional description of a child's intellectual abilities that would not be evident with the Wechsler.

The Leiter-R IQs are also moderately related to certain subtests of the Stanford-Binet Intelligence Scale—Fourth Edition (SB-IV, Thorndike, Hagen, & Sattler, 1986), and to subtests of the Wide Range Assessment of Learning and Memory (WRAML, Adams & Sheslow, 1990), and to subtests of the Test of Memory and Learning (TOMAL, Reynolds & Bigler, 1994). Taken as a whole these data support that the Leiter-R has overlapping variance between independent measures of reasoning, visualization, and memory.

The Leiter-R IQs are also related to tests of academic achievement including the Wechsler Individual Achievement Test (WIAT; Psychological Corporation, 1992) Reading and Math (.69 to .83), the Woodcock-Johnson Psycho-Educational Battery—Revised (WJ-R; Woodcock & Johnson, 1989) Broad Reading and Mathematics (.79 to .82), and the Wide Range Achievement Test—3 (WRAT-3; Wilkinson, 1993) Word Recognition and Arithmetic subtests (.62 to .73). The Leiter-R IQs are also related to several group-administered achievement tests (e.g., California Achievement Test [CAT], Comprehensive Test of Basic Skills [CTBS], and Stanford Achievement Test [SAT]). The SAT Math and Reading and the CAT Math were moderately related to the Leiter-R scores (.48 to .70). The Leiter-R was not highly related to the CAT Reading, CTBS Math, and CTBS Reading scores (.24 to .31).

SUMMARY. The Leiter-R is recommended as an excellent contemporary test of nonverbal intellectual ability. This is a theoretically derived instrument and careful attention has been paid to all aspects of its development and psychometric qualities. Does the Leiter-R have some problems? Yes, but the test's strong points far outweigh its negatives and to their credit, the test authors have presented the test's strengths and weaknesses in an honest and straightforward manner. They have left no stone unturned. It will be exciting to observe the further validation of the Leiter-R by independent researchers in the years to come. No doubt this revision has ensured the Leiter-R will continue to be used by modern psychologists rather than becoming a historical artifact.

REVIEWER'S REFERENCES

Kaufman, A. S. (1979). *Intelligent testing with the WISC-R.* New York: John Wiley & Sons, Inc.

Gustafsson, J. E. (1984). A unifying model for the structure of intellectual abilities. *Intelligence, 8,* 179–203.

Thorndike, R. L., Hagen, E. P., & Sattler, J. M. *Assessment of children* (3rd Ed. Rev. and updated). San Diego: The author.

Glutting, J. J., McDermott, P. A., & Stanley, J. C. (1987). Resolving differences among methods of establishing confidence limits for test scores. *Educational and Psychological Measurement, 45,* 607–614.

Woodcock, R. W., & Johnson, M. B. (1989). Woodcock-Johnson Psycho-Educational Battery—Revised. Itasca, IL: Riverside.

Adams, W., & Sheslow, D. (1990). Wide Range Assessment of Memory and Learning (WRAML). Wilmington, DE: Wide Range, Inc.

Achenbach, T. M. (1991). *Manual for the Child Behavior Checklist/4–18 and 1991 Profile.* Burlington: University of Vermont, Department of Psychiatry.

Wechsler, D. (1991). *Manual for the Wechsler Intelligence Scale for Children* (3rd Ed.). San Antonio: The Psychological Corporation.

Psychological Corporation. (1992). Wechsler Individual Achievement Test. San Antonio, TX: The author.

Reynolds, C. R., & Kamphaus, R. W. (1992). Behavior Assessment System for Children. Circle Pines, MN: American Guidance Service.

Sattler, J. M. (1992). *Assessment of children* (3rd Ed. Rev. and updated). San Diego: The author.

Carroll, J. B. (1993). *Human cognitive abilities: A survey of factor-analytic studies.* New York: Cambridge University Press.

Wilkinson, G. S. (1993). Wide Range Achievement Test-3. Wilmington, DE: Jastak Associates/Wide Range, Inc.

Kaufman, A. S. (1994). *Intelligent testing with the WISC-III.* New York: John Wiley & Sons, Inc.

Reynolds, C. R., & Bigler, E. D. (1994). Test of Memory and Learning (TOMAL). Austin, TX: PRO-ED.

Carroll, J. B. (1997). The three-stratum theory of cognitive abilities. In D. P. Flanagan, J. L. Genshaft, & P. L. Harrison (Eds.), *Contemporary intellectual assessment: Theories, tests, and issues* (pp. 122–130). New York: The Guilford Press.

Glutting, J. J., McDermott, P. A., Watkins, M. M., Kush, J. C., & Konold, T. R. (1997). The base rate problem and its consequences for interpreting children's ability profiles. *School Psychology Review, 26,* 176–188.

Roid, G. H., & Madsen, D. H. (1998). *Leiter-R computer scoring software system user's guide.* Wood Dale, IL: Stoelting Company.

[212]
The Level of Service Inventory—Revised.

Purpose: Constructed as "a quantitative survey of attributes of offenders and their situations relevant to level of supervision and treatment decisions."

Population: Ages 16 and older.

Publication Date: 1995.

Acronym: LSI-R.

Scores: Total score only.

Administration: Individual.

Price Data, 2001: $130 per complete kit including manual (53 pages), 25 interview guides, 25 QuikScore™ forms, and 25 ColorPlot profiles; $60 per 25 interview guides; $35 per 25 QuikScore™ forms; $18 per 25 ColorPlot profiles; $45 per manual; $55 per specimen set including manual, 3 interview guides, 3 QuikScore™ forms, and 3 ColorPlot profiles.

Time: (30–45) minutes.

Foreign Language Editions: Spanish guides and forms available; information for French-Canadian version available from publisher.

Comments: Ratings by probation officers, parole officers, and/or correctional workers to provide a comprehensive risk/needs assessment important to offender treatment planning; Windows™ computerized version available on CD or 3.5-inch disk.

Authors: D. A. Andrews and James L. Bonta.

Publisher: Multi-Health Systems, Inc.

Review of The Level of Service Inventory—Revised by SOLOMON M. FULERO, Chair, Department of Psychology, Sinclair College, Dayton, OH:

According to the authors, the Level of Service Inventory—Revised (LSI-R) was designed "to assist in the implementation of the least restrictive and least onerous interpretation of a criminal sanction and to identify dynamic areas of risk/need that may be addressed by programming in order to reduce risk" (manual, p. viii). The authors indicate that the content of the LSI-R is drawn from the recidivism literature, and that the LSI-R has been widely used in the risk assessment area. The scale takes a social learning approach to criminal behavior.

The LSI-R is a quantitative survey of attributes of offenders and their situations, emphasizing what has been found in prior research to be relevant to level of service decisions. It is composed of 54 items, each answered with either a Yes or No, or a 0–3 rating. The items cover subcomponents including Criminal History, Education/Employment, Financial, Family/Marital, Accommodation, Leisure/Recreation, Companions, Alcohol/Drug Problems, Emotional/Personal, and Attitudes/Orientation. It is noted that many of these are what are referred to as "dynamic" risk factors (as opposed to "static" or unchanging ones such as gender), and as such they can function as treatment targets that could reduce the risk of recidivism if addressed. Indeed, the authors note that psychometric and factor analytic research on the scale suggests that the total score measures an underlying dimension of "propensity for rule violations" (manual, pp. 38–39). Data on the LSI-R are collected on a Profile Form that yields a Total Score and scores on each of the 10 subcomponents. Computer scoring and interpretation are available, either on-line or on disk. So-called "cut-off scores" are given for decisions that include probation (minimum, medium, maximum), halfway house placement (highly appropriate, appropriate with close supervision, or not appropriate unless with intensive supervision and treatment), and institutional classification (e.g., minimum, medium, maximum).

The authors describe research with probationers in which scores on the LSI-R predicted, at above-chance levels, officer judgments of appropriate levels of supervision at intake, officer judgments of appropriate levels of supervision while in progress, office judgments of the success of supervision, actual amount of supervision activity, early versus regular terminations, early closures versus active supervision, evidence of in-program recidivism, multiple reconvictions, incarceration, and officially undetected self-reported criminal activity. They also describe research with incarcerated offenders that predicted success in correctional halfway houses, institutional misconduct, parole outcome, and recidivism one year post-release (manual, p. 3).

The psychometric properties of the LSI-R are reasonably impressive, with interrater and test-retest reliability scores in the .80–.99 range, depending on the length of time between assessments. Internal consistency alpha coefficients are in the .70–.90 range, though the subcomponent alphas are lower, ranging from .06–.86. Measures of face and construct validity are also discussed, with reasonable outcomes.

There are at least two important (perhaps critical) limitations of the scale that impact on its usefulness and generalizability. First, the male and female normative groups were both from Ontario. Notably absent from the manual is any discussion (or listing in the references) of research that has extended the findings into the United States, though the manual indicates that the instrument has been adopted for use by the State of Colorado. Also, the "cutoff scores" given in the manual are those that have been "recommended in Ontario"

(manual, p. 16). The manual says that "individual jurisdictions are encouraged to develop their own guidelines" (p. 16). However, to do so would involve research studies of the thorough sort that the authors have done in Ontario, and there is a real danger that such studies will be neglected in favor of rote or blind use of the numbers given in the test manual.

SUMMARY. The LSI-R offers an intriguing empirical approach to risk assessment in the area of correctional decisions. However, it is clear that much work remains to be done before the authors can hope for general applicability of the scale. Jurisdictions that intend to consider use of the LSI-R should be prepared to conduct their own independent follow-up research before actual implementation, in order to establish cutoff scores that work in their settings.

Review of the Level of Service Inventory—Revised by ROMEO VITELLI, Staff Psychologist, Milbrook Correctional Centre, Milbrook, Ontario, Canada:

The Level of Service Inventory—Revised (LSI-R) is the newest version of the criminal risk/need assessment instrument originally developed by Donald Andrews and James Bonta and is based on their social learning theory of criminal conduct (Andrews & Bonta, 1994). It was originally titled the Level of Supervision Inventory; hence, the name was changed to its current form as a reflection of the increasing use of the inventory in noncustodial settings. The test is described as "a checklist sampling a number and variety of risk factors that are supported by research, professional opinion, and a broad social learning perspective on criminal conduct" (manual, p. viii). Potential uses for the LSI-R include classifying offenders, allocating treatment and security resources, monitoring offender risk, making halfway house placement decisions, deciding appropriate security level classification, making probation supervision decisions, and assessing likelihood of recidivism.

The 54 items of the LSI-R are scored using either a "YES/NO" or "0–3" rating format based on item content. The risk factors sampled by the LSI-R include: Criminal History, Education/Employment History, Financial Status, Family/Marital Status, Accommodation, Leisure/Recreation, Companions, Alcohol/Drug Problem, and Criminal Attitudes/Orientation. The accompanying Interview Guide provides a protocol for gathering the information needed to administer and score the inventory. Specific cautions are raised by the authors recommending that all information obtained in interviews be verified using collateral sources of information (i.e., available records or interviewing others familiar with the client's history).

NORMS AND INTERPRETATION. Information relating to the development and interpretation of the LSI-R is provided in chapter 3 of the manual. The LSI-R was developed using a male sample (n = 956) and a female sample (n = 1,414) obtained from detention and correctional centres in the province of Ontario. Raw scores obtained on the LSI-R are converted to percentiles based on comparison with the appropriate normative group.

Interpretation of the LSI-R scores involves comparison of the total LSI-R score with normative data, examination of specific risk factors, and assigning clients to High, Medium, Moderate, Low/Moderate, or Low risk/needs categories based on recommended cutoff scores. Due to the need for further research on female offender classification, no cutoff scores are available for female clients. As a further aid to interpretation, a series of case studies are provided to demonstrate LSI-R profiles for high, medium, and low-risk clients.

RELIABILITY AND VALIDITY. Information on the psychometric properties of the LSI-R is provided in chapter 5 of the manual. This includes a summary of reliability and validity studies of the LSI-R and its previous versions dating back over the last 15 years. Due to the dynamic nature of most of the LSI-R items that are thus subject to change over time, research has consistently shown that test-retest reliability varies based on time interval between tests. One representative study showed that test-retest reliability ranged from .92 for no test-retest interval to .84 following a 6-month test-retest interval (Andrews & Robinson, 1984). Interrater reliability for the LSI-R has been shown to be quite good (.99–.94 range) with obtained differences between raters being five points or less with few disagreements as to assignment of risk/need category. Internal consistency for the LSI-items has been determined using alpha coefficients and intercorrelations between the various subcomponents of the inventory. Coefficient alpha values are usually in the .7 to .8 range; correlations between the individual subcomponents and the corrected LSI-R total score

tend to fall in the .45 range. It is suggested by the authors that the good internal consistency shown by the findings indicates that the 52 LSI-R items measure a common "propensity for rule violations" dimension.

Chapter 5 of the manual outlines numerous validity studies of the LSI-R that have focused on comparisons between the LSI-R and various measures of outcome success. These methods include multiple reconvictions (r = .40, p<.001), postprogram recidivism (r = .37, p<.001), selection for parole (r = .53, p<.001), violation of parole (r = .35, p<.05), reincarceration after parole (r = .47, p<.01), institutional misconducts (r = .36, p<.001), halfway-house success (r = .39, p<.01), and new charges (r = .51, p<.001). The manual also outlines research comparing the LSI-R with other criminal risk scales (i.e., the Salient Factor Score, the Megargee MMPI-based system [Megargee & Bohn, 1979], and the Statistical Information of Recidivism), which have shown that the LSI-R was the best predictor of program outcome and recidivism. Extensive cross-validation studies have shown good generalization across a diversity of client populations including male and female juvenile offenders, male and female adult offenders, halfway house candidates, child welfare cases, and mentally disordered offenders.

Overall, the LSI-R has been shown to have strong evidence of reliability and validity and is the most well-developed offender classification instrument used in Canada and the United States.

SUMMARY. The LSI-R is a well-designed and useful measure of offender risk that appears to be highly sensitive to the static and dynamic predictors of criminal conduct identified by empirical research (Andrews & Bonta, 1994). A potential area for further validity research may be to investigate the role of psychopathy in criminal risk through the comparison of the LSI-R to established measures of psychopathy such as the Psychopathy Checklist-R (Hare, 1991; T5:1174). Concern may also be raised about the sensitivity of the LSI-R to sex offender recidivism, which is predicted by a different set of factors than those factors used to predict general and nonsexual violent recidivism. As such, objective criminal risk scales have been found to be quite poor in predicting sexual recidivism (Hanson & Bussiere, 1996). Despite these potential drawbacks, the LSI-R appears to be a valuable tool for the detection of "propensity of rule violations" in offenders.

REVIEWER'S REFERENCES

Megargee, E. I., & Bohn, M. J., Jr. (1979). *Classifying criminal offenders: A new system based on the MMPI.* Beverly Hills, CA: Sage.

Andrews, D. A., & Robinson, D. (1984). *The Level of Supervision Inventory: Second Report. A report to Research Services.* Toronto: Ontario Ministry of Correctional Services.

Hare, R. D. (1991). The Hare Psychopathy Checklist—Revised. Toronto, Ontario: Multi-Health Systems, Inc.

Andrews, D. A., & Bonta, J. (1994). *The psychology of criminal conduct.* Cincinnati: Anderson Publishing Co.

Hanson, R. K., & Bussiere, M. T. (1997). Predictors of sexual offender recidivism: A meta-analysis (User Report No. 1996–04). Ottawa: Department of the Solicitor General of Canada.

[213]

Listen Up: Skills Assessment.

Purpose: Designed to measure listening comprehension, interpretation, and ability to follow directions.

Population: Grades 7–12 and adults.

Publication Dates: 1985–1995.

Scores, 6: Evaluating Message Content, Understanding Meaning in Conversations, Understanding and Remembering Lectures, Evaluating Emotional Meanings in Messages, Following Instructions and Directions, Total.

Administration: Group.

Price Data, 1998: $295 per one-day program including facilitator's guide ('95, 48 pages), two 40-minute videos (Forms A and B), and 25 answer sheets (Forms A and B); $195 per half-day program including facilitator's guide ('95, 32 pages), one 20-minute video, and 25 answer sheets; $24.95 per 25 answer sheets (Forms A or B).

Time: [40–80] minutes.

Authors: Kittie W. Watson and Larry L. Barker.

Publisher: Jossey-Bass/Pfeiffer.

Review of Listen Up: Skills Assessment by CLEBORNE D. MADDUX, Professor of Educational Psychology and Information Technology in Education, University of Nevada, Reno, NV, and RHODA CUMMINGS, Professor of Educational Psychology and Human Growth and Development, University of Nevada, Reno, NV:

Listen Up: Skills Assessment is a standardized, multiple-choice test of listening skills. The manual states that the purpose of the test is "to meet the needs of corporate and academic listening-training programs" (p. 2).

The test includes two equivalent forms, each yielding raw scores for five, 10-item subtests: (a) Evaluating Message Content, (b) Understanding Meaning in Conversations, (c) Understanding and Remembering Lectures, (d) Evaluating Emotional Meanings in Messages, and (e) Following Instructions and Directions.

Examinees watch and listen to brief, videotaped simulations of conversations between individuals speaking English with a variety of accents or dialects (Southern U.S., British, etc.). After each enactment, the screen displays, and a narrator reads, a question and four possible answers. The examinee chooses one answer and marks it on an NCR answer sheet. The last page of the answer sheet is the instructor's record sheet, which includes a key to correct answers and blank fields for calculating and listing subtest and total scores.

Unfortunately, the videotaped simulations are amateurish, and many of the actors are somewhat bizarre in appearance and dress. This tends to be amusing and could distract the examinee from the message itself. This is a serious problem because many of the simulations are quite brief and cannot be repeated. Another problem is that the questions appear only briefly on the screen and disappear too rapidly to permit rereading. Then too, many of the choices are ambiguous, making it difficult to determine why a given choice is scored as correct. Another problem is that the instructions preceding each simulation often use advanced vocabulary, which could cause examinees to make errors unrelated to their listening ability.

Scores available are subtest and total raw scores. For either form of the test, each item is assigned two points, producing five possible subtest scores of 20, and a total possible raw score of 100. The manual includes a table with national mean scores for both forms for either of two comparison groups: (a) undergraduate college students, and (b) managers, supervisors, and professionals. Another table makes it possible to derive percentiles for the total score based on either national comparison group.

The major shortcoming of the test is the lack of adequate standardization and psychometric information. The authors refer to piloting an earlier version of the test with "several thousand subjects representing a number of states and geographical regions in the United States and including executives, professionals, government employees, and undergraduate/graduate college students from a variety of universities and curricula" (p. 14). The manual goes on to state that these pilot tests were then subjected to factor analyses, item analyses, reliability tests, and descriptive analyses. However, the adequacy of these procedures cannot be judged because no further details are furnished.

The manual states that test-retest reliability coefficients were also calculated for the earlier, non-video version of the test, and found to be significant. However, the coefficients themselves are not listed and there are no details given. A few references are given to reliability studies conducted during the 1980s and early 1990s with the earlier version of the test. However, no details of these studies are provided. No reliability data were reported for the current version of the test. Validity data are also totally missing, although the manual provides some references to validity studies that were conducted with the earlier version of the test.

SUMMARY. Listen Up: Skills Assessment is an attempt to provide a standardized, alternate form test to assess listening skills of college students or business professionals for use in corporate and academic listening-training programs. The test is administered by playing a videotape of actors simulating conversations in various English accents and dialects. At the conclusion of each simulation, a narrator reads questions and multiple-choice answers that are displayed briefly on the screen. Examinees record answers on an NCR answer sheet. Examiners score the responses and record five subtest raw scores and a total score. These scores can be compared to national means and percentiles of either students or business professionals.

The videotaped simulations are of poor technical and artistic quality and may be distracting to examinees. Psychometric and standardization data are missing or incomplete, and reliability and validity studies appear to have been conducted with an earlier version of the test. The test should be improved by providing better quality videotapes and more detailed descriptions of how and why items were selected, as well as more extensive and up-to-date investigations of reliability and validity. Until these problems are solved, the test will be of limited, experimental value.

Review of Listen Up: Skills Assessment by SANDRA J. WANNER, Professor of Education and Director of Special Education, University of Mary Hardin-Baylor, Belton, TX:

Listen Up: Skills Assessment is both a training tool and a standard testing instrument. The current test (1995) is designed to meet the needs of corporate and academic training programs and is appropriate for students in grades 7 through 12 and adults.

Listen Up is designed as a group assessment although it can be used for an individual assessment. It comes in two forms (A and B) and is made up of five parts designed to evaluate types of listening comprehension ability rather than content knowledge. Part 1 measures an individual's skills in interpreting message content. Part 2 tests an individual's understanding of meaning in his or her conversations. Part 3 tests an individual's ability to remember lecture information. Part 4 measures an individual's skill in interpreting emotional meaning. This part involves listening to how something is said as well as to what is said. Part 5 measures an individual's ability to follow directions.

Parts 1, 2, and 4 are designed to measure the listening skills that participants use in brief listening situations and Parts 3 and 5 are designed to measure the listening skills used in longer listening situations.

In test reporting, Listen Up provides five separate scores—one for each part as well as an overall score. Overall scores range from 0 to 100 with each decile (10% range) given a rating (Excellent, Very Good, Good, Average, Below Average, Poor, and Very Poor). To aid in interpreting test results a Listening-Skill Area Score Sheet is provided where respondents can compare their individual scores to National Average scores.

Average scores for respondents and scores are provided for each decile within the total distribution of scores. The authors admit, "that test scores may be affected by a variety of external factors." And suggest that the "primary emphasis in interpreting individual scores should be on building positive-listening behaviors" (facilitator's guide, p. 9).

The manual is easy to read and comprehend. Administration instructions for Listen Up (10 steps) are easy to follow even by those without test-administration experience. The 1995 video version presents all test questions and possible responses orally and visually. The only written materials for participants are self-scoring answer sheets (NCR paper). The suggested administration time is 35 minutes.

The normative data, percentiles, and average scores provided are for the Adult Version (1991) of Listen Up and need to be updated for this 1995 version. No data are provided on the 7th through 12th grade norm group. Student references in the manual refer to 20,000 plus undergraduate college students in the age range of 18 to 27 years enrolled in speech classes.

The adult norm group (7,500 plus) includes managers, supervisors, and professionals in business, government, education, and industry in the age range of 26 to 64 years representing a wide range of corporations and organizations. No mention was made of blue-collar workers or persons who had not attended college. "In evaluating a test's norms users should consider not only whether the norms are generally representative, but also the age of the norms" (Salvia & Ysseldyke, 2001, p. 118).

In the "Message to the Facilitators" on page 10 of the manual, the authors indicate they want to provide test users with current normative data. They request copies of participants' test scores along with their occupation, age, subtest scores, total test scores, gender, and geographic location. They intend to use the data to provide updated norms for the user. This indicates the normative data are in process.

When Listen Up is used for listening awareness or training purposes, the authors suggest that participants can score their own tests. In addition, facilitators are encouraged to allow 30 minutes for participants to process Listen Up by encouraging thoughtful responses to 10 questions that are provided.

The appendix in the test manual provides a list of activities divided into Parts 1 through 5 matching the areas tested. These activities come from Listen Up: Learning Activities (not provided in facilitator's guide) and are to help "participants target areas for improvement and begin the process of becoming better listeners" (facilitator's manual, p. 55).

Reliability evidence is weak. Only alternate form reliability was determined for the alternate Forms A and B because Listen Up is designed to be used for test-retest purposes. The Pearson Product—Moment Correlation was used and the manual indicates, "significant positive correlations were found between forms A and B and the abbreviated version of Form A" (facilitator's guide, p. 14). No specific coefficients were listed.

Validity was examined by correlating Listen Up to the Receiver Apprehension Test (Wheeless, 1975). Fitch-Hauser and Villaume (1991) report that Listen Up is sensitive to inferential and literal-listening strategies.

An item analysis was conducted on results from earlier versions of Listen Up. Selected items were designed to discriminate among effective and ineffective test performances. Items identified as too difficult or too easy were deleted from the final version of both test forms. Developers attempted to include diverse vocal dialects, ages, and genders. The same individuals appear in both forms of the assessment videos and thus provide a one-to-one correspondence between videos. Directions were both voiced and provided in visual form to benefit all respondents.

An extensive reference list is provided for those desiring to pursue research in the area of listening comprehension assessment. A reference list for "Sources for Listening Instruction" is also provided.

SUMMARY. Listen Up: Skills Assessment is easy to give, quick to score, and provides instant feedback to respondents to help determine their skill in listening comprehension. Though lacking strong evidence of reliability and validity, Listen Up can be used as a screening instrument to see if participants need further testing or could be helped with listening comprehension learning activities.

The need for communication skills is evident in workforce development, educational institutions, and in families. Listen Up can indicate weak areas in the listening comprehension of youth and adults so remediation can begin immediately. Listening plays an ever-growing role in effective communication and the ability to listen effectively is a key to management, teaching, and parenting success.

REVIEWER'S REFERENCES

Wheeless, L. (1975). An investigation of receiver apprehension and social context dimensions of communication apprehension. *Speech Teacher, 24,* 261–268.
Fitch-Hauser, M., & Villaume, W. (1991, March). *Listening to problematic texts: inferences in response to textual disturbance.* Paper presented at the International Listening Association Conference, Jacksonville, FL.
Salvia, J., & Ysseldyke, J. E. (2001). *Assessment* (8th ed.). New York: Houghton Mifflin Company.

[214]
Listening Styles Profile.

Purpose: "Designed to identify habitual listening responses and to encourage participants to think about how preference traits might be expressed in actual settings."

Population: Adults.

Publication Date: 1995.

Scores, 4: People Oriented, Action Oriented, Content Oriented, Time Oriented.

Administration: Group.

Price Data, 1998: $19.95 per trainer's package including facilitator's guide (24 pages), profile, and answer sheet: $69.95 per complete kit; quantity discounts available.

Time: (5–10) minutes.

Comments: Can be used to evaluate self or another person.

Authors: Kittee W. Watson and Larry L. Barker.
Publisher: Jossey-Bass Pfeiffer.

Review of the Listening Styles Profile by
MILDRED MURRAY-WARD, Professor of Edu-
cation, School of Education, California Lutheran Uni-
versity, Thousand Oaks, CA:

The Listening Styles Profile is an instrument apparently designed primarily for business professionals. The instrument is described by the authors as a tool designed to identify habitual listening responses and to encourage participants to think about listening traits exhibited in actual settings. The authors also claim that the instrument may be used to help individuals learn to adapt their listening styles to the speakers' needs, time constraints, and settings.

The inventory consists of an answer sheet, facilitator's (examiner's) manual, and a detailed information sheet for inventory results analysis of self or others. In the earlier section of the manual or guide the authors propose a four-category system of listener styles: People-Oriented, Action-Oriented, Content-Oriented, and Time-Oriented together in an acronym (PACT). Information on the characteristics of listeners who fall into or cross multiple areas of these categories are described in great detail.

The manual is written in an informal, friendly style. This is both refreshing and a great limitation of the instrument. It is refreshing because the information is clearly presented. It appears to be written for a person with minimal assessment training. However, the guide also fails to present many important pieces of information. The absence of this information makes the use of the inventory for its proposed purposes highly questionable.

First, development of the instrument is poorly described. The authors stated that the inventory stemmed from research and the authors' experience with listener characteristics. Although a reference list is provided, the nature and extent of the research and author experience are never discussed. The authors began with a pool of 30 items, later reduced to 24. The origins and evolution of the items and item data are not provided. No information on the composition or size of the norm sample is offered. Furthermore, normative data and procedures are missing.

Second, no research base for a listening styles construct is provided. The authors state that the items from the instrument were derived from

the research literature and personal experience. A reference list related to listening appears at the end of the guide, but no citations are offered to support the instrument's origins. Furthermore, the nature of the authors' experiences are not described. Ironically, literature is offered on the fact that people may change or train their styles.

Third, much validity evidence is missing. Even though the authors did factor analyze the items, the lack of information on the construct and the origin of the items makes the analysis less useful. Furthermore, the analysis procedures are quite sketchy. The authors indicated that "some" items did not fit the four-factor solution, but did not offer their actual number. In addition, the writers state that two other versions of the instrument were created and also factor analyzed. The result was the current inventory, but the reader is left with no information on the origins of these items, impact of the additional items, or the specific changes made to the items on the original instrument. Furthermore, no factor analysis procedures or loadings are provided for any of these analyses.

As was stated earlier, the authors claim that the inventory identifies styles and helps an individual change or adapt styles. However, no predictive or concurrent validity studies have been done to support the descriptions of people with these styles. Claims based only on the research of others on gender listening differences and multiple listening preferences are made for the inventory. The most curious claim is the one in which a certain scoring pattern indicates listening avoidance. Certainly, no evidence is presented that this inventory is effective in determining any of these response patterns.

Fourth, reliability information is not provided. The use of the instrument for rating self and others makes such information essential. The problem is made more complex by author instructions to the facilitator (examiner) to set the context for the listening responses because context impacts these responses. How does the context change responses? In what ways?

Fifth, the actual administration procedures, although detailed, are not standardized, making interpretation even more questionable. The directions on the instrument may be read to the examinees, but the instructions are quite vague. The respondent is not even told if the response should be for him- or herself or others. The facilitator also sets the context or settings for the listening acts. No information is offered to help the facilitator make this determination. Finally, the analysis procedures for self or others are described in detail. However, as was noted earlier, these procedures have not been validated in any manner.

Finally, interpretation of the results is quite complex, but appears to be unsupported by data. Scoring and interpretation involve a four-quadrant box drawing and instructions to the respondent for scoring on a 5-point scale for each item. The respondent is to place the scores on the correct section of the drawing. Inferences from the results include major listening preference, possible multiple preferences, and listening avoidance. However, limited empirical evidence for these inferences is available to the respondent or the facilitator.

SUMMARY. Because of the major limitations noted in this review, this reviewer suggests that this inventory be used with extreme caution. The lack of developmental, normative, validity, and reliability evidence make the meaning of the scores impossible to interpret. Overinterpretation of the results is a major problem with this inventory. Complex inferences from the instrument are not supported by empirical evidence. Certainly, if the inventory is used in business settings, employment, promotion, or even training decisions based on the results of this instrument are highly questionable, at best. If the reader is interested in assessing listening, many other factors such as the listener's education level, experience, listening training, social context, and physical limitations should be considered before using the results of this instrument.

Review of the Listening Styles Profile by SANDRA WARD, Associate Professor of Education, The College of William and Mary, Williamsburg, VA:

The Listening Styles Profile is based on the premise that people find it easier to listen to certain speakers and certain kinds of information. Consequently, they habitually rely on comfortable patterns of listening behavior, rather than adapt to a unique situation. The Listening Styles Profile is designed to identify habitual listening responses and encourage participants to think about how preferences might affect communication with others. The authors profess that by using the Listening Styles Profile, participants can learn to adapt their preferred behaviors to match the speaker's style and situation. The authors designate and describe four types of listening styles, including people-oriented, content-oriented, action-oriented, and time-oriented. There are no references in support of these styles.

The initial items for the Listening Styles Profile were generated from the literature and the authors' professional experience. A pool of listening experts screened the items. However, the credentials of these experts are not described, nor is it explained what they were attending to in the screening process. The first instruments were administered to pilot groups for analysis of contextual understanding and ease of administration. No description of these groups is provided. Item analysis resulted in 24 items that were submitted to a factor analysis. Although the authors report that the results supported the four categories of listening styles listed above, there is no description of the type of factor analysis used. Furthermore, the authors do not provide any results so the reader lacks any information on the factor loadings or the percentage of variance accounted for by each factor. The validity data for this instrument are insufficient, and its reliability is not documented. Although the authors provide summaries of studies on gender differences, multiple preferences, and listening avoidance, they do not reveal the data analysis or specific results. Consequently, the reader only receives the authors' interpretations. The manual provides more advice than technical information.

The administration of the instrument is easy and does not require training. The participants rate themselves or others on 20 items using a Likert scale that ranges from 1 (never) to 5 (always). In order to score the profile, participants count the number of 4 and 5 responses in each of the four categories, and the highest total indicates their strongest listening preference. Because normative data are not available, it is impossible to evaluate the meaning of these scores. Additionally, there are no data to support the differential diagnosis of listening styles.

SUMMARY. The Listening Styles profile represents an instrument that does not meet the *Standards for Educational and Psychological Testing* (AERA, APA, & NCME, 1985). No norms are available. The validity data are insufficient and the reliability data are absent. The measure is comparable to surveys one finds in popular magazines. Although the topic may be interesting, there are no data to support the scores or their interpretation. Extreme caution is warranted in the use of this instrument to detect listening profiles. Furthermore, there is no convincing evidence that knowledge of listening styles will encourage changes in habitual listening responses.

REVIEWER'S REFERENCE

American Educational Research Association, American Psychological Association, & National Council on Measurement in Education. (1985). *Standards for educational and psychological testing.* Washington, DC: American Psychological Association, Inc.

[215]
Lore Leadership Assessment.

Purpose: Designed to "measure behaviors, skills, and impacts desirable in a leader."
Population: Adults working in organizations.
Publication Date: 1998.
Scores, 6: Overall Leadership Effectiveness, Moral Leadership, Intellectual Leadership, Courage, Collaboration, Visionary/Inspirational.
Administration: Group.
Forms, 2: Self-Assessment, Assessment of Other.
Manual: No manual.
Price Data, 1998: $99 per set including questionnaires and answer sheets.
Time: [30] minutes.
Comments: Test forms are mailed to publisher for scoring and interpretation.
Author: Terry R. Bacon and International LearningWorks.
Publisher: International LearningWorks®.

Review of the Lore Leadership Assessment by CONNIE KUBO DELLA-PIANA, *Director of Evaluation, Model Institutions for Excellence and the Partnership for Excellence in Teacher Education, The University of Texas at El Paso, El Paso, TX:*

According to the test developer, the Lore Leadership Assessment is a tool that measure behaviors, traits, skills/competencies, and impacts desirable in a leader. The Lore Leadership Assessment instruments are designed to measure both strengths and weaknesses in leadership effectiveness of the leader, who is to be assessed based on self-perception, the perception of others, and a comparison to norms. The design, analysis, and interpretation of the Self-Assessment and the Assessment By Others instruments are based upon the five-dimensional Lore Leadership Model. The five dimensions of the model are Moral Leadership, Intellectual Leadership, Courageous Leadership, Collaborative Leadership, and Visionary/Inspirational Leadership. The test developer states

that the comprehensive multidimensional model and the assessment of leadership effectiveness, which is based on the model, are a result of "years of research and experience in the practice of leadership" (Test booklets, Self Assessment & Assessment By Others). One assessment packet consists of 1 Self-Assessment Questionnaire and 15 Assessment by Others Questionnaires. (Survey Control Sheet, answer sheets, respondent envelopes, and business reply envelopes are also provided.) No manual or references are provided with the packet or the Feedback Report, but the test developer provided the reviewer with an example of the Feedback Report that is sent to the person who is being assessed for leadership effectiveness. In the rest of the review, this person is referred to as the "target person."

The target person and the respondents (selected others) are required to answer a set of items using a 7-point Likert-scale (*strongly agree* to *strongly disagree*) and an open-ended "narrative question" on recommendations for improvement. The Self-Assessment contains 79 items. Each item presents a statement about a person's leadership effectiveness and is followed by an elaboration or descriptive definition. The Assessment By Others contains a set of items that parallels the 79 items on the Self-Assessment form. In addition, there are 35 items on "leadership impact" of the target person on the respondents, four items on the level of "situational trust and confidence" the respondents have in the target person, and the open-ended narrative question that asks respondents for recommendations for improvement. Once the items are completed and the questionnaires are mailed to the test developer the items are analyzed and a feedback report is generated for the target person.

The feedback report contains a summary of results, narrative recommendations, the person's dimensions of leadership, others' level of trust in the target person's leadership, and detailed results by type of respondent who completed the Assessment By Others form. The Feedback Report provides instructions on how to interpret the information in the report and presents the person's self-scores, the average score from others' ratings on each item, a norm score for each item, a difference score for each item (difference between the score of the target person and the norm), and the target person's Leadership Quotient (Lore Leadership Assessment Report). According to the test developer, the norm scores reflect the average ratings of professionals from around the world in business, industry, and government whose scores are in [the organization's] extensive assessment database. Norm scores are presented as benchmarks and are reference points for the radar graph of the target person's score for each dimension in comparison to the norm score for each dimension to facilitate the interpretation of results in terms of strengths and weaknesses (Lore Leadership Assessment Feedback Report). The Leadership Quotient has a mean of 100. To help with the interpretation of the difference score, the test developer claims that a difference score on an item that is greater than .5 is significant, that is, the difference between the self-assessed score (response to the item) is significantly different from the norm score for that item.

The Detailed Results section of the Feedback Report lists each item or leadership skill or behavior by dimension. Items are classified, grouped, and presented under each of the dimensions along with the results of the analysis of responses to the item. Scores for each item from each group of respondents are also presented in graphic form (bar graphs). In the Narrative Recommendations section of the Introduction to the report, the test developer cautions the recipient of the report that he or she must determine for himself or herself whether the recommendations are appropriate, accurate, and indicative of the directions that should be taken to increase effectiveness as a leader. The test developer notes that the recommendations for improvement are based on a small amount of information from a limited number of people. The test developer provides an 800 telephone number and a P.O. Box number for further questions about the results.

Completion of either the Self-Assessment or the Assessment By Others questionnaire requires about 30 minutes. Another 30 minutes is needed to organize the administration of the instruments. The target person is required to select respondents, although criteria for selection are not provided. Categories of selected respondents appear in the Assessment By Others Test Booklet. No instructions are provided on how to enlist respondents, to inform them of the voluntary nature of participation, and to follow-up on initial requests for participation and the completion of the form. The target person must list the names of the selected respondents on the Survey Control Sheet, write the names of these persons on each of the business reply envelopes, and write the target person's name and the name of his or her organization on top of each answer sheet. In addition, the target person must address each respondent envelope, insert the required documents into it, and distribute this envelope to each selected respondent. The target person is also required to design an instruction sheet for the respondents. Brief instructions appear at the end of the Lore Leadership Assessment answer sheet. Although a FAX number appears in the instructions, specific instructions not to FAX answer sheets are given on the instruction sheet for the target person.

Although claiming that the test has been extensively administered in government, business, and industry, the test developer does not provide any evidence of the reliability of the test or the validity of the interpretation and use of the results or a full description of the individuals used to establish the norm scores. An analysis of the classification of items by leadership dimensions suggests that the items are reasonable descriptions or definitions of the five leadership dimensions. No evidence is provided to inform the test user of types of methods used to validate the claim that the items form five dimensions or factors.

SUMMARY. Although a comparison of self-perception, others' perception of leadership effectiveness, and norms are designed for no facilitated debriefing or counseling, more support for the interpretation of results and understanding of the recommendations is needed, in the view of this reviewer. The Lore Leadership Assessment is a component of a complete leadership training and development program. The results could be better understood when examined within the context of the complete program and with the help of trained facilitators and/or counselors. Based on promotional literature, the highest impact of the results from the assessment tools is gained through "one-on-one counseling sessions with experienced program faculty" (Lore International Institute Promotional Literature).

[216]
Malingering Probability Scale.

Purpose: Designed to "assess whether an individual is attempting to produce false evidence of psychological distress."
Population: Ages 17 and over.
Publication Date: 1998.
Acronym: MPS.

Scores, 6: Depression and Anxiety, Dissociative Disorders, Post-Traumatic Stress, Schizophrenia, Inconsistency, Malingering.
Administration: Individual.
Price Data, 2001: $129.50 per kit for mail-in computer scoring including reusable administration card, 5 prepaid mail-in answer sheets, and manual; $360 per kit for on-site computer scoring including reusable administration card, 20-use disk, 100 PC answer sheets, and manual; $4.95 per reusable administration card; $49.50 per manual; $18.50 per mail-in answer sheet; $310 per 20-use disk (PC with Microsoft Windows); $15 per 100 PC answer sheets; $16 per FAX Service Scoring charge.
Time: (20) minutes.
Comments: May be administered by paper and pencil or personal computer; computer scored (only) and interpreted locally or by publisher FAX or mail-in service.
Authors: Leigh Silverton and Chris Gruber (manual).
Publisher: Western Psychological Services.

Review of the Malingering Probability Scale by SOLOMON M. FULERO, Chair, Department of Psychology, Sinclair College, Dayton, OH:

For anyone who does forensic work, the issue of malingering—the voluntary production of psychological symptoms for purposes of secondary gain—is an overarching one. The Malingering Probability Scale (MPS) is one of a series of instruments that have been designed over the years to attempt to discriminate those with genuine problems from those who are feigning or exaggerating.

The stated purpose of the MPS is to assess "whether an individual is attempting to produce false evidence of psychological distress" (manual, p. 1). The test assesses malingering in two ways: the evaluation of a person's inconsistency of response to test questions (the INC scale) and the tendency to endorse items that describe spurious yet seemingly authentic symptoms of psychological distress (the MAL scale). These symptoms concentrate in four areas: Depression/Anxiety, Dissociative Disorders, Post-Traumatic Stress Disorder, and Schizophrenia. In addition, the MPS features four clinical scales covering these same four areas (the DEP, DIS, PTS, and SCH scales, respectively).

The test is a 139-item objective inventory, answered in true-false fashion. If 14 or more items are left blank, the test cannot be scored. It is designed for use with persons 17 years of age or older. Reading level was measured at third to fourth grade. Test users will immediately note one

drawback of the MPS, at least for some: All administrations must be computer-scored by means of mail-in or fax service, though a computer disk is available as well (this last option also allows on-line administration). The primary rationale for this, according to the authors, is that the use of computer scoring "effectively blocks dishonest individuals from obtaining information that would help them to 'figure out' the MPS" (manual, p. 1), though the authors also acknowledge that scoring in this way also protects the "proprietary value of the MPS to its copyright holders" (manual, p. 2).

The data presented in the manual show reasonably good levels of reliability, using measures of internal consistency, test-retest reliability, and temporal stability, and using samples of nonreferred individuals from the general population (college students), individuals from populations in whom malingering tendencies are often assessed (prison and forensically referred samples), and individuals referred for clinical but nonforensic evaluation. The authors note that this compares favorably with the one-week test-retest correlations for the Minnesota Multiphasic Personality Inventory (MMPI) Content Scales, which were in the .70–.90 range.

Another set of studies sets forth the validation data. These studies used techniques of dissimulation (for college students and prison inmates) and guided dissimulation in which the subjects were given the DSM criteria for the disorders. Scores were also obtained from samples of inpatients and referred forensic and clinical outpatient clients. A notable weakness in this regard is a failure to present data that link scores on the MPS to obtained scores on other malingering measures (e.g., the MMPI-2, T5:1697; the Structured Interview of Reported Symptoms; etc.).

Interpretation of the MPS begins with an analysis of the INC scale. With a high INC score, the remainder of the scale is likely uninterpretable. High INC scores may be produced by a failure to understand the test items by a person who, for example, is dyslexic or for whom English is not the first language. Alternatively, a response pattern such as all True or all False responses, as well as mechanically alternating responses, will also produce high INC scores. If the elevation is less than a T-score of 70, however, the remainder of the test is interpretable.

The authors' discussion (manual, pp. 6–10) of the meaning of a score on the MAL scale is important reading for all clinicians. Clearly, a conclusion that a person is malingering is a probability statement. More importantly, the probability score relates directly to the base rate of the underlying construct. The authors present graphs of the distribution of "honest" and "dishonest" MAL scores under different base rate assumptions. For example, if a person obtains an MAL *T*-score of 73, where the base rate of malingering is assumed to be 50%, 20%, or 10%, the concluded probability of malingering is either 72%, 38%, or 22%. A very convenient feature of the interpretive report is that it sets forth these different probabilities of malingering under what they term "strong" (50%), "moderate" (20%), or "weak" (10%) base rate assumptions. This will be helpful in explaining the meaning of scores on the MPS to persons (i.e., courts, lawyers, juries) who are unfamiliar with psychological scoring jargon and thus more prone to misinterpretation.

There is one other interesting and ironic issue: How do you tell if people are faking on a test of malingering? The authors argue that malingering on the MPS is highly unlikely, because such a person would "need a sufficient understanding of relevant scientific literature" and would have to "make 139 such multifaceted distinctions in the course of an MPS administration ... and do so in a relatively short time" (manual, p. 1). Although these are reasonable arguments, additional data on the ability of reasonably well-versed persons to fool the test (e.g., psychology graduate students, etc.) would be helpful.

SUMMARY. All in all, the Malingering Probability Scale is a welcome addition to a field that is, at this point, relatively underaddressed by forensically relevant scales. The MPS needs additional validation work, however, particularly in its correlational relationship to other malingering measures such as the SIRS. Nonetheless, its careful presentation of the issue of base rate is a major strength, and clinicians who make forensic judgments in areas other than malingering (e.g., risk assessment probabilities for recidivism in sexual predator cases) would do well to consider including the sort of information presented in the interpretive report on this test.

Review of the Malingering Probability Scale by RADHIKA KRISHNAMURTHY, Associate Professor, School of Psychology, Florida Institute of Technology, Melbourne, FL:

The Malingering Probability Scale (MPS) is a 139-item true-false measure developed for the specific purpose of detecting psychological symptom exaggeration. With this narrow focus, the scale's application appears largely limited to clients in civil or criminal proceedings who would benefit from appearing severely distressed. The scale is said to secondarily assess for actual psychological disorder although in this application it is, at best, a crude screening measure of questionable value.

The process of developing and standardizing the MPS appears to comply with current standards of test development and is reasonably well described in the test manual. The standardization sample of 1,016 adults, ages 17+, selected from four regions of the U.S. and tested between 1995 and 1996, certainly meets expectations in terms of being large, contemporary, and nationally representative. However, although the sample matches the 1994 U.S. Census data adequately in terms of ethnic distribution, the actual *number* of ethnic minority participants is quite small (e.g., Asian = 15, Native American = 24, Hispanic = 56). Consequently, despite the authors' report of the test's fairness for minority groups based on their statistical evaluation of moderating factors, caution is needed in interpreting MPS results for ethnic minority persons.

The test manual provides minimal information on the structure and composition of the scales, purportedly to prevent the target populations from obtaining facts that could enable response manipulation. Unfortunately, such concealment also precludes qualified users from scrutinizing the test for its psychometric adequacy. For example, the manual reports that the Inconsistency (INC) scale consists of 20 item pairs that are correlated, similar in meaning, and that should be answered in the same direction. However, neither the item composition of the scales nor the raw score to *T*-score conversion data are furnished in the manual. The other major scale, Malingering (MAL), is reported to contain a "large number of statements" (manual, p. 6) that simulate symptoms of psychological distress but there is no disclosure in the manual of the number of items. The test examiner will have to take the authors' word on the appropriateness of assignment of items to scales and of the distinctions between genuine distress items of the test and pseudo-symptom items of the MAL. Nonetheless, the

MPS appears to have been carefully validated by the test authors. In particular, validation procedures for INC and MAL are well designed and implemented in ways consistent with procedures used in recent research studies on malingering. The validation of the clinical scales is more cursory. Test-test reliability (one-week interval) and temporal stability results of the MPS warrant replication as they were based on small samples of 33 and 31 participants, respectively.

The MPS is easy to administer and makes minimal demands on time and reading level. However, test examiners will find the scoring procedures mysterious as the scale can only be scored by the publisher, Western Psychological Services, again for the expressed purpose of maintaining test security. Such lack of information, combined with the cost of mail-in or on-line scoring and time delays involved in mail-in procedures, are likely to limit the usage of this measure, which already has limited applicability. Of the scoring options available, on-line scoring appears the most cost-effective but only for settings where malingering would be frequently assessed.

Test interpretation begins with, and is focused on, evaluation of INC and MAL scores to identify problematic response styles. The MAL scale is the sole indicator of malingering. The fact that only one of six scales on this malingering test actually assesses malingering may cause the test to be viewed with some skepticism. Further, one might consider this a simplified approach to evaluating malingering, given the more complex alternatives presented in tests such as the Personality Assessment Inventory (Morey, 1991; T5:1959) where a malingering index is derived from a set of multiple configural features, or the Minnesota Multiphasic Personality Invengory-2 (Butcher, Dahlstrom, Graham, Tellegen, & Kaemmer, 1989; T5:1697) where configural patterns and indices form the bases of malingering judgments. On the other hand, the developers of the MPS have given thoughtful consideration to base rate issues and limitations of cutting scores, which they have addressed by furnishing probability scores for MAL. Specifically, the interpretive report indicates the probability of malingering using a 20% base rate assumption and also offers alternative probabilities for 50% and 10% base rates. This approach to score interpretation is conceptually sophisticated but is practically limited by the fact that the probability data are based on a sample of fewer than 200 psychology students and consequently have questionable generalizability.

Interpretation of the four clinical scales—Depression and Anxiety (DEP), Dissociative Disorders (DIS), Post-Traumatic Stress Disorder (PTS), and Schizophrenia (SCH)—is guided by the use of two cutting scores, $T = 60$ and $T = 65$, representing different levels of confidence. The test authors have extended appropriate cautions around the interpretation of these scales, particularly with regards to negative results. However, the very inclusion of these scales into the MPS confounds the purpose of this measure and is arguably a mistake. Specifically, it is not clear whether clinical scale items were selected for their effectiveness in obscuring the pseudo-symptom items or to reflect clinical disorders in their own right, and it is highly unlikely that they can address both purposes effectively.

The MPS interpretive report provides all the necessary information concerning malingering detection including T-score values and the probability scores mentioned earlier. The report also furnishes item response data which, in the absence of knowledge of scale membership of items, have no apparent purpose.

SUMMARY. The MPS is a unique malingering scale that is unidimensional and less comprehensive compared to indices of malingering on several personality inventories. Determining whether the simplicity of this measure is an asset or liability requires clinical trials in the intended settings. The use of the MPS for identifying the presence of true distress is not supportable in light of limits to the types of distress measured and limited validation of the relevant scales, and it certainly cannot be construed as a face valid distress measure. One of the greatest limitations of the MPS is that protection of the test materials and procedures have been overemphasized at the cost of furnishing needed information for determining the adequacy of this scale. The MPS will likely be used only in a limited number of settings for its intended limited purpose, but usage even at that level may partly depend on making scoring procedures more user-friendly.

REVIEWER'S REFERENCES

Butcher, J. N., Dahlstrom, W. G., Graham, J. R., Tellegen, A., & Kaemmer, B. (1989). *MMPI-2: Manual for administration and scoring*. Minneapolis: University of Minnesota Press.
Morey, L. C. (1991). *The Personality Assessment Inventory professional manual*. Odessa, FL: Psychological Assessment Resources.

Management & Leadership Systems.

Purpose: Designed to assess management and leadership skills and team effectiveness.
Population: Management personnel.
Publication Dates: 1992–1996.
Acronym: MLS
Administration: Group.
Price Data, 1996: $295 per facilitator's kit including manual ('96, 207 pages), Guide to Management & Leadership, Project Management Workbook, 6 Management Leadership Profiles, 6 Team Effectiveness Profiles, and transparency masters; $35 per Guide to Management & Leadership; $40 per Project Management Workbook; $95 per scoring software including software disks (specify 3.5-inch or 5.25-inch), Code Lock, Operating manual.
Foreign Language Editions: Available in English, Spanish, and French.
Time: Administration time not reported.
Comments: Microcomputer software requirements are DOS version 3.0 or newer, 1 MB RAM, 1 MB free in hard drive; the option to have ASI generate the MLP and TEP is available, thus eliminating purchase of the scoring software.
Author: Curtiss S. Peck.
Publisher: Assessment Systems International, Inc.

a) MANAGEMENT & LEADERSHIP PROFILE.
Purpose: Designed to measure "both present behavior and desired behavior based on the needs and expectations of the people who are evaluating the manager."
Acronym: MLS.
Scores, 15: Clarity of Purpose (Goals, Communication), Planning and problem Avoidance (Planning, Involvement, Decision Making), Task Accomplishment (Competence, Motivation, Work Facilitation), Providing Feedback (Feedback), Exercising Control (Managing Performance, Accountability, Delegation), Individual & Team Relationships (Relationships, Linking, Teamwork).

b) TEAM EFFECTIVENESS PROFILE.
Purpose: "Provides a way of measuring and giving feedback to teams on how they manage their processes and projects."
Acronym: TEP.
Scores, 15: Clarity of Purpose (Goals, Communication), Planning and Problem Avoidance (Planning, Involvement, Innovation/Risk, Decision Making), Task Accomplishment (Values, Competence, Motivation, Quality/Continuous Improvement), Providing Feedback (Feedback), Exercising Control (Control, Delegation), Individual & Team Relationships (Linking, Teamwork).

Review of the Management & Leadership Systems by STEPHEN F. DAVIS, Professor of Psychology, Emporia State University, Emporia, KS:

The core of the Management & Leadership Systems (MLS) consists of the Management & Leadership Profile (MLP) and the Team Effectiveness Profile (TEP). (Other components not available for review include the *Guide to Management & Leadership, Project Management Workbook, High-Performing Teams Workbook,* and scoring software.) The MLS User's Manual indicates that the goals of the MLS are to "develop and/or strengthen the management and leadership skills of people who will be instrumental in inspiring commitment to the positive changes needed for companies to be competitive and successful" (p. 1) and to evaluate and provide guidance and evaluation to teams within an organization. It is felt that "teams can be incredibly successful when they have guidance and regularly evaluate and discuss their work processes, rather than just focusing on their outputs" (p. 1).

According to Curtiss S. Peck, the developer of these materials, a two-fold impetus prompted the development of the MLS: A large number of managers have never read any material on management and leadership skills, whereas other managers have received academic training that does not transfer to the work environment. These two situations pointed to the need to provide assistance for managers and leaders in business. In turn, Peck developed the Work Flow Process Model, which is well-suited for facilitating collaborative relationships and "empowering people at all levels to do the right things at the right times" (p. 11). All components of this theoretical model revolve around customers and mission. "Satisfying the needs of the customers and the mission of the organization, function, and/or team" (p. 12) interfaces with the next layer of the model: the six phases that guide action. In order these phases are Clarity of Purpose, Planning and Problem Avoidance, Task Accomplishment, Feedback, Exercising Control, and Individual and Team Relationships. The final (outermost) layer of the model involves the process of continuous improvement and utilizes such steps as Plan/Replan, Activity, Performance Measurement, and Analysis. Because the MLP and TEP are driven by the Work Flow Process Model, it is important to understand the model. The User's Manual clearly describes the basic model and how it supports these two instruments. (The User's Manual is a definite plus for the MLS package. In addition to providing information on the theoretical background of the system, this extensive manual presents detailed, yet readable, chapters on the MLP and TEP, feedback, project administration, and statistical analysis.)

The 15 dimensions or categories measured by the MLP are embedded within the six phases that guide action. For example, Managing Performance, Accountability, and Delegation are the dimensions measured within the Exercising Control phase. The MLP consists of 119 questions that are answered on a Likert-type scale ranging from 1 (*never*) to 5 (*always*). The respondent provides two answers for each question. One answer indicates the current frequency of occurrence (*Is*), whereas the second answer indicates how often the described behavior *Should* occur.

The TEP also evaluates 15 dimensions or categories that are embedded within the six phases that guide action. For example, Values, Competence, Motivation, and Quality/Continuous Improvement are the dimensions measured within the Task Accomplishment phase. The TEP consists of 87 questions that are answered on the same scale and in the same manner as are the questions on the MLP. The questions that comprise the MLP and TEP are easily understood; moreover, the physical layout of each answer sheet facilitates responding.

Although provisions and instructions are included for the involvement of both an internal coordinator and an external consultant, the responsibilities of these two positions are sufficiently similar that the project can be handled by one of these individuals. In any event, the designated individual will be in charge of coordinating the entire test administration program, arranging for the scoring of the profiles, providing feedback once the scored profiles are returned, and conducting reassessment to ascertain program effectiveness.

Once the MLP and TEP profiles are completed, the user can opt to have them scored by Assessment Systems International, Inc. (ASI) or the forms can be scored in house using software purchased from ASI. Although the latter alternative is appealing, there appear to be several potential drawbacks. First, because the ASI software is now quite dated (e.g., it was designed for 3.0 DOS and is available on 3.5-inch and 5.25-inch disks), some users may not choose this option because of system limitations. Second, an individual must undergo ASI certification training in order to be able to use the software. Third, in-house scoring appears to be reasonably expensive. Finally, the fact that the employment of an external consultant (likely an ASI employee) is highly recommended makes processing of profiles by ASI easier and more appealing.

The scored materials for the MLP and TEP are presented in graphical form that depicts both the "Is" and "Should" scores for the major categories and on a question-by-question basis. For the MLP these Is and Should scores are depicted for specific individuals, as well as the individual's boss and staff.

Likewise, the TEP depicts the value of the differential between "Is" and "Should" for the 15 major categories and for each individual question. These responses are presented for the team leader, the team members, and customers.

This approach to scoring makes it easy to determine strengths (small or no gaps between "Is" and "Should") and improvement areas (large gaps between "Is" and "Should") as perceived by the various constituencies. Plotting the "Is" and "Should" differential also lends itself quite well to evaluating the effects of change via a subsequent reassessment(s).

SUMMARY. The ease of coordination, administration, and interpretation suggest that the MLP and TEP have the potential to be effective instruments in an organization's evaluation of its effectiveness. The option to readminister these scales in order to determine the effectiveness of a program or modification that has been implemented is an appealing bonus. Strong support services from ASI also are desirable aspects of the overall evaluation program. However, before deciding to use the MLP or TEP, the costs involved should be considered; they may be substantial. However, the benefits to be derived may clearly outweigh the costs.

Review of the Management & Leadership Systems by WILLIAM J. WALDRON, Administrator, Employee Testing & Assessment, TECO Energy, Inc., Tampa, FL:

INTRODUCTION. The Management & Leadership Systems (MLS) is a package of multirater feedback instruments and support materials designed to assess management and leadership skills (the *Management & Leadership Profile; MLP*) and team effectiveness (the *Team Effectiveness Profile; TEP*). A detailed manual/facilitators' guide accompanies the instruments, and optional workbooks and other associated developmental materials are available. Scoring of the instruments and report generation are typically performed by the publisher, but DOS/Windows software is available for on-site scoring as well. The publisher conducts training workshops for organizations that want to conduct the entire feedback process in-house.

Both the MLP and TEP instruments are based upon the publisher's own theory of effectiveness, referred to as either the "Work Flow Process" or "Management Task Cycle" model in various parts of the manual/guide. This model describes management and team effectiveness in terms of 15 dimensions grouped into six broad areas. The MLP contains 119 behavioral statements, each of which is rated on two 5-point frequency scales: How often *does* this occur, and how often *should* this occur. The TEP contains 90 statements, each of which is rated using the same two scales.

Both instruments are designed to be used by multiple raters: For a manager using the MLP, ratings would typically be performed by self, boss, direct reports, and peers; for the TEP, the team rates itself, as does the team leader and perhaps customers. The reports graphically present the "is" and "should" dimension ratings by each source, as well as normative percentiles on the "is" scales. A summary of top-rated strengths and development areas is provided, as is a detailed section containing individual item results.

CRITIQUE. The quality of the guide/manual accompanying the instruments is variable. The quality of the sections describing administration procedures is very high, with attention paid to the proper use and potential misuses of the instruments. Many other sections, however, are written in rather rambling and unclear prose; the manual is much longer than it needs to be to convey the information it contains. Even given its length (143 pages plus appendices), there is a clear lack of information describing the development of the theory/model underlying the instruments.

The feedback reports provided by the publisher are nicely done, presenting the results in a clear fashion. The reports would be further improved by expanding the introductory section about the reports' contents and how to use them; in particular, information about the source of the normative data (percentiles) presented in the reports is needed but missing.

SUMMARY. Multirater or "360-degree" feedback is currently extremely popular in organizations today. As an organizational development intervention, the effectiveness of these programs is a function of many factors, among them (a) the quality of the instrument (including the fit between the dimensions measured and the organization's particular needs), (b) the clarity and ease-of-use of reports and supporting materials, and (c) the skills of the external and/or internal staff implementing them. I cannot evaluate the Management & Leadership Systems on the third factor; on the first two, perhaps all that can be said is that these instruments should be among those reviewed by organizations desiring to implement a multirater feedback program. Others are of course available, many with a more fully described theoretical foundation and better quality statistical data available (Clark & Clark, 1990). The publisher would do well to rewrite key sections of the manual to improve their clarity and incorporate more and better information about the statistical characteristics of the instruments.

REVIEWER'S REFERENCE

Clark, K. E., & Clark, M. B. (Eds.). (1990). *Measures of leadership*. West Orange, NJ: Leadership Library of America.

[218]
MAPP: Motivational Appraisal of Personal Potential.

Purpose: Intended to measure "an individual's potential and motivation for given areas of work."
Population: Employees at all levels.
Publication Date: 1995.
Acronym: MAPP.
Scores, 13: Interest in Job Content, Temperament for the Job, Aptitude for the Job, Orientation to People, Affinity for Objects and Things, Approach to Data and Information, Reasoning and Thinking Style, Mathematical Capability, Language Levels, Personal Style, Personal Traits, Interpersonal and Social Tendencies, Learning Style.
Administration: Group.
Price Data, 1997: $350 per job profile (direct or composite); $10 per database input; $200 per personal appraisal; $150 per executive appraisal; $40 per job match summary; $80 per job match analysis; $120 per work team; $30 per people to job match; $30 per job to people match; $950 per corporate training; $1,800 per consultant training.
Time: (20–25) minutes.
Comments: Available as paper-and-pencil or computerized version.

Authors: International Assessment Network.
Publisher: International Assessment Network.

Review of the MAPP: Motivational Appraisal of Personal Potential by MARTHA E. HENNEN, Consultant, The Pittman McLenagan Group, L.C., Bethesda, MD:

The Motivational Appraisal of Personal Potential (MAPP) measures individual potential in terms of occupational and vocational interests. The instrument consists of 71 triadic items; the examinee is instructed to mark which of three areas he or she most prefers and which he or she least prefers.

SCORING PROCESS. The system may be administered either on computer or in paper-and-pencil form. Scoring must be completed by computer using the "Preference Record Software" in order to translate item responses to percentile ranks. The MAPP generates five analyses for each respondent: Narrative Interpretation, Worker Trait Code Analysis, Vocational Analysis, Personal Analysis, and Educational Analysis. Each provides information about specific aspects of the respondent's motivations. Nowhere in the materials reviewed or presented is there a description of the scoring process for translating individual responses.

The Narrative Interpretation provides detailed verbal descriptions of the individual's: Interest in the Job Contents; Temperament for the Job; Data: Priority and Preference of Mind Activity; People: Relationships, Roles, Interactions; Things: Engineering, Operating, Sensory/Perceptual; Aptitude: Mental, Perceptual, Sensory/Perceptual; Reasoning: Mental Processes Required by the Job; Mathematics: Math Functions Required by the Job; and Language: Literary and Communicative Requirements. Each description summarizes the analysis of the respondent's motivations towards each area based upon responses to the MAPP items.

The Worker Trait Code System takes a detailed look at the individual's motivations for specific vocations. The author drew upon the job coding inherent in the Dictionary of Occupational Titles (DOT) to create worker trait codes. The coordination of job coding and worker coding allows for matching of job content to personal motivations. A summary table is created for each of the areas listed in the Narrative Interpretation, showing level of motivation toward the characteristics involved. In addition, graphs present those levels of motivation visually.

The Vocational Analysis compares the respondent's motivations with the normative population of respondents in 19 occupational categories defined by the Department of Labor. From this analysis, the MAPP system also generates a list of the "Top Ten Vocational Areas" for a specific individual.

The scale's Personal Analysis describes levels of motivation toward 23 traits. This set of traits is the basis for all the other analyses and is referred to as the "Core." The traits are based loosely upon the general interests of the Kuder Profile Records (technical reference manual, 1995). Percentiles are calculated for each trait representing the strength of the respondent's motivations as compared to the normative population. Percentiles are presented in rank order. Each trait is also converted onto a 1–5 point scale (1 = *Dedicated Motivation*, 2 = *Strong Motivation*, 3 = *Moderate Motivation*, 4 = *Disinterest*, and 5 = *Avoidance*) to help identify the most and least motivating traits.

A second aspect of the Personal Analysis addresses 40 Psychological Factors. Although included in all appraisals, these factors are "especially suitable and valuable for counselors, case workers, psychologists, and psychiatrists" (technical reference manual, p. 24). Dorothy Neils assisted with much of this section's development, creating this list of factors through her research on the work of Henry Murray and her experiences in evaluating women felons prior to sentencing in criminal court cases. Her experience with a criminal population may show limited applicability to the general audience targeted by the MAPP. Research to determine the applicability of these factors to a normal population is not described. Caution may be needed in interpreting these results.

The final section of the Personal Analysis, the Personal Orientation, is designed to stand alone and summarizes the individual's motivations. This analysis presents several factors of motivation including: Leadership factors, Interpersonal factors, Social factors, Performance, Mechanical Orientation, Mechanical Repair, Mechanical Maintenance.

The Educational Analysis was included in the MAPP based upon the work of and in conjunction with Dr. David Barbee. This section of the measure attempts to quantify the respondent's "motivational characteristics and learning styles" (technical reference manual, p. 35). The Educational Analysis assesses: Mental Orientation, Perceptual Orientation, Learning Environments and Perceptions Regarding Input Media, Coping with Learning Environments, Coping with Classroom Environments, and Skills for Testing Procedures. The purpose of information is to assist in the design of skills acquisition programs.

JOB ANALYSIS. In addition to providing individual analysis, the MAPP may be used by employers to analyze the underlying motivations for specific jobs. The MAPP system suggests three methods for collecting job analysis information: (a) Averaging the worker trait codes of at least six persons highly competent in the job; (b) rating the job with provided Job Analysis forms and factors for Worker Trait importance; and (c) converting standard job analysis functions to Worker Trait ratings and codes and averaging the codes for all functions into a total job code. There are no guidelines provided for who should be involved in the second or third job analysis procedures. Job analysis procedures based upon the MAPP follow the same model as the Worker Trait codes to facilitate comparison or matching of individuals to jobs. Factors are rated on a 5-point scale of importance. Job Matching occurs by ranking the motivations within each factor and comparing the resulting rank orders for jobs and respondents.

NORMS. The technical reference points out that the personal analysis comparisons and percentile ranks are made based upon the population database (technical reference manual, p. 13). Elsewhere, the technical reference mentions "historic files of over 11,000 persons" (p. 32). Nowhere does the technical reference provide a description of the make-up of the normative sample.

VALIDITY AND RELIABILITY. The technical reference includes a presentation on the author's interpretation of validity. The author, Kenneth Neils, suggests that the greatest argument for the instrument's "validity" is that the "Validation on all appraisals since 1955 exceeds 99%" (p. 7). More than 99% of the assessed individuals, when asked whether the information sounds familiar or rings true, agreed with the assessment results. Neils also suggests that a construct validity approach should be taken for the MAPP. However, there are no supporting data in the technical reference to indicate that the measure does in fact support construct validity evidence, beyond the agreement statistic above. There

is no discussion in the technical reference about reliability of scores.

Available on the International Assessment Network's website is information about a research study conducted by an independent consultant with 32 respondents (Gilbert, 1997a). All research participants were employed full time; the sample was 62.5% male; their median age was 49; each took the MAPP two times. The time interval between MAPP administrations was approximately 9 months. Such a small sample size clearly limits the generalizability of the research results. However, the reliability evidence was fairly strong. Test-retest reliability was assessed in three ways: correlations between worker trait codes across time (median r_{xx} = .90), correlations of job ratings across time (median r_{xx} = .95), and correlations between specific item responses across time r_{xx} = .71). The study included a range of occupations. Follow-up studies focusing on specific occupations are mentioned but not described.

To assess construct validity, the research participants simultaneously responded to the Strong Vocational Interest Inventory (Gilbert, 1997b). Prior to the study, three managers matched the Strong occupational interests and the MAPP occupations. Correlations with the Strong Inventory for scores on five dissimilar occupational profiles were low (.14 to .41), suggesting some discriminant validity. Scores on 75 occupation profiles of more similar content ranged from .50 to .92 with a median correlation of .67, suggesting convergent validity. The limits of the research study strongly suggest the need for further evaluation.

SUMMARY: AREAS OF STRENGTH. To its credit, this instrument is easy to administer and provides a great deal of information to the respondent. In recent years, the idea of finding a match between individual characteristics and organizational and position characteristics (e.g., person—job fit) has become more widespread. The MAPP provides pertinent information on that issue.

SUMMARY: AREAS OF CONCERN. However, from the information provided and the technical reference, it would appear that this instrument is trying to accomplish a great many loosely related goals. The appraisal results are highly detailed and difficult for the naive user to wade through. In addition, the research supporting this instrument is weak at best. The Kuder Occupational Interest Survey (reviewed by Herr, 1989, and Tenopyr, 1989), upon which some of this instrument is itself based, seems simpler to interpret and has a long research history supporting its development and interpretation.

REVIEWER'S REFERENCES

Herr, E. L. (1989). [Review of the Kuder Occupational Interest Survey, Revised (Form DD)]. In J. C. Conoley & J. J. Kramer (Eds.), *The tenth mental measurements yearbook* (pp. 425–427). Lincoln, NE: Buros Institute of Mental Measurements.

Tenopyr, M. L. (1989). [Review of the Kuder Occupational Interest Survey, Revised (Form DD)]. In J. C. Conoley & J. J. Kramer (Eds.), *The tenth mental measurements yearbook* (pp. 427–429). Lincoln, NE: Buros Institute of Mental Measurements.

Gilbert, L. (1997a). *Test-retest reliability study of MAPP.* Unpublished report prepared for the International Assessment Network, Inc.

Gilbert, L. (1997b). *Construct validity study.* Unpublished report prepared for the International Assessment Network, Inc.

Review of the MAPP: Motivational Appraisal of Personal Potential by ABBOT PACKARD, Instructor, Educational Psychology and Foundations, University of Northern Iowa, Cedar Falls, IA:

The MAPP (Motivational Appraisal of Personal Potential) is a personnel appraisal system composed of a 71-question inventory. There are two versions, computer and paper, which can be taken in approximately 20–25 minutes. Automated scoring and analysis are available immediately via modem or may be faxed or mailed. There are three major areas of concentration: Job Profiling, Job Matching, and Team Work Capabilities. The MAPP is to be used by company personnel officers and consulting agents and agencies to assist in placing and/or promoting individuals to a position. The function suggested is to match skills and potential skills of personnel to the functional requirements of a job.

No data are supplied to suggest that a psychometric evaluation was done on questions. The match of skills and employees can be done by comparing results of the prospective employee with existing knowledge of a database of persons in similar positions created over a period of 40 years.

Only individuals who are trained and authorized in the use and evaluation of the MAPP system can administer this test. Information was not available to determine these procedures and their standardization.

Results are available in numerous forms including a narrative report described in the brochure as 27 pages in length. This report explains how the individual's traits compare to the given job. In addition a spider graph represents the traits of successful individuals in this position compared to the interviewee. This type of graph presents a very visual comparison between individuals within

a job or it can be used to compare individuals to the skills required of the position.

SUMMARY. The use of the MAPP system appears to be limited to business and industry. The material offered for review left the reviewer limited information to perform a thorough assessment. The only information given by the publisher was knowledge of a database of similar positions built over 40 years to compare potential employees. Effectiveness of the MAPP requires the user to become familiar with the descriptions with the database in order to make valid judgements on whether the MAPP system would be effective in aiding their hiring practices.

[219]
Marital Satisfaction Inventory—Revised.

Purpose: Designed to "identify, separately for each partner in a relationship, the nature and extent of distress along several key dimensions of their relationship."

Population: Couples who are married or living together.

Publication Dates: 1979–1998.

Acronym: MSI-R.

Scores, 13: Conventionalization, Global Distress, Affective Communication, Problem-Solving Communication, Aggression, Time Together, Disagreement About Finances, Sexual Dissatisfaction, Role Orientation, Family History of Distress, Dissatisfaction with Children, Conflict over Child Rearing, Inconsistency.

Administration: Group.

Price Data, 1999: $118 per complete kit including 20 AutoScore™ answer forms, 2 test report prepaid mail-in answer booklets for computer scoring and interpretation, 2-use disk and 2 PC answer sheets for on-site computer scoring and interpretation, and manual ('97, 126 pages); $26.50 per 20 AutoScore™ answer forms; $48 per manual; $12.50 per 6 Spanish research administration booklets; $17 per mail-in answer booklet; $199.50 per 20-use disk (PC with Microsoft Windows); $15 per 100 PC answer sheets; $9.50 per FAX Service Scoring charge.

Foreign Language Edition: Spanish research edition administration booklet available but without separate norms.

Time: (25) minutes.

Comments: 150-item self-report inventory; hand or computer scoring available; computer-generated interpretation available.

Author: Douglas K. Snyder.

Publisher: Western Psychological Services.

Cross References: See T5:1582 (15 references) and T4:1538 (7 references); for reviews by David N.

Dixon and E. M. Waring of an earlier edition, see 9:652 (2 references).

Review of the Marital Satisfaction Inventory—Revised by FRANK BERNT, Associate Professor of Health Services, St. Joseph's University, Philadelphia, PA:

Both the Marital Satisfaction Inventory—Revised (MSI-R) and its predecessor, the MSI (1981), seem to have been designed primarily for use by therapists, counselors, and others working with couples considering or beginning conjoint therapy. Although its original version was designed for couples who have been married or living together for "at least six months" (manual, p. 6), the author suggests that the revised version can be used effectively with a wide range of couples, including same-gender couples and couples during courtship or engagement. The MSI-R serves several functions in the clinical context: diagnosis and goal-setting; rapport-building and facilitation of communication; and measuring therapy progress and outcome.

Revision of the original MSI focused upon four principal improvements: (a) reducing the number of items from 280 to 150; (b) restandardizing the instrument using a larger, more representative norming sample; (c) rewording several items to permit appropriate use of the scale with nontraditional couples; and (d) the addition of two new scales (Inconsistency and Aggression).

The 150 true-false items provide subscores for 13 subscales, with higher scores indicating greater distress or dissatisfaction. The Inconsistency scale represents a second validity measure, which was added to identify individuals who may be random or careless in their responding, confused about test content or directions, or deliberately noncompliant. Its addition seems warranted, given research indicating that response set issues are a common problem among the instrument's target population (Fowers & Applegate, 1995).

Retention of items in the revised instrument was based not simply upon their contribution to subscales' internal consistencies but also upon their reflecting a wide range of endorsement rates and item content. As a result, internal consistency estimates are somewhat lower than for the original MSI, dropping from a mean alpha of .88 to a mean alpha of .82 (range .70–.93). Test-retest reliability coefficients on 12 of the subscales for a 6-week period for the same 12 subscales dropped from a mean of .89 to a mean of .79 (range of .74–.88). The revised scales on the MSI-R measure virtually the same constructs as those in the original version of the instrument: Correlations between the original scales and their MSI-R counterparts range from .94 to .97.

The new, larger standardization sample consists of 1,020 couples (2,040 individuals). Data were collected from 53 different sites in 22 states representing all major geographic regions in the U.S. The author provides a detailed and convincing description of how the resulting sample reflects the general population with respect to gender, age, educational level, geographic region, ethnicity, and occupation. Significant differences with respect to gender were consistent with previous research; accordingly, separate norms for males and females are provided. A thoughtful analysis of the effects of age, educational level, and ethnicity upon norms revealed moderator effects for several of the scales. The author provides a reasonable argument for why such effects do not warrant separate norms for these groups.

The convergent validity of the original MSI was well established, with moderate to high correlations between the Global Distress subscale and other well-established measures of "relational accord" (ranging .66–.90). In addition, other subscales were found to be correlated with intuitively similar scales on the Minnesota Multiphasic Personality Inventory (MMPI) as well as with behavioral measures, observer ratings, and treatment outcomes. Both the MSI and MSI-R effectively discriminate between clinical and nonclinical groups and have been used to measure differences in pre- versus posttreatment comparisons (Snyder & Wills, 1989).

A principal components factor analysis of the 12 content scales (excluding inconsistency) yielded three components that accounted for 64% of the total variance. The general factor accounting for most of the common variance includes subscales related to affective and communicative aspects of the relationship; the remaining specific factors reflected child-related concerns as well as attitudes about parental and marital roles.

An "actuarial approach" described by Snyder, Lachar, Freiman, and Hoover (1991) is used to generate an empirical basis for interpreting individual test scores. The technique involves identifying relationships between MSI-R subtest scores and various external criteria, then constructing contingent-frequency tables and identifying ranges of scores that correspond to above-chance likelihoods that the external criterion will present (to a moderate or extensive degree).

The MSI-R can be self-administered in either a computer or a paper-and-pencil format. Instructions and items are written to be readable at a sixth-grade level. The paper-and-pencil version can be easily completed in 25 minutes. Scoring can be done manually (using an auto-score answer form) or by computer. The computerized version provides a computer-generated test report that includes an interpretation of test results. Scannable response forms are also available; these can be sent to Western Psychological Services for scoring. Both methods of scoring yield normalized T-scores (normed separately for males and females); T-scores are graphically presented on the MSI-R Profile Form, which locates both responding partners' scores relative to their respective norm groups identifies areas in which potential or actual problems exist (except for the Role Orientation scale).

The test manual provides an extensive discussion of how to interpret the scales, including detailed descriptions of scales as well as their clinical implications. This discussion is following by a careful outline of a seven-step procedure for analyzing results, followed by eight separate case studies illustrating how the procedure is applied.

SUMMARY. Reviewers of the original MSI agreed that, though it had some limitations, it was arguably the best of its kind available and that the author was committed to and capable of its further development. Time has revealed their judgment to be quite accurate. The manual is clear, well organized, and thorough in its descriptions of all aspects of the MSI-R, and its development of a system for interpreting scores rests upon an empirically based actuarial method.

The MSI-R seems especially well suited for clinical settings. The question arises whether it is equally suited for use by researchers. A brief review of the literature suggests that the Marital Adjustment Scale (Locke & Wallace, 1959) and the Dyadic Adjustment Scale (Spanier, 1976; T5:863) are still the most frequently used of all such scales, but that the MSI's use has increased over time in research settings. Perhaps its original length made it less appealing for researchers seeking a unidimensional measure of marital satisfac-

tion; this obstacle has been ameliorated by reducing its length. Equally likely is that these two scales are brief and easily available as part of the public domain. Both are acceptable as global, unidimensional measures of marital satisfaction (Fowers, 1990). The MSI-R, though more expensive, offers a number of advantages: It is thoroughly described; it is normed on a more representative sample; its recent revision of items makes it less dated; and perhaps most importantly, the inclusion of 11 different subscales measuring different aspects of relationships makes it a much more powerful instrument. With recent improvements, the MSI-R's appeal may well result in wider use by researchers interested in measuring a wide range of relationship qualities for couples.

REVIEWER'S REFERENCES
Locke, H. J., & Wallace, K. M. (1959). Short marital adjustment and prediction tests: Their reliability and validity. *Journal of Marriage and the Family, 21,* 251–255.
Spanier, G. B. (1976). Measuring dyadic adjustment: New scales for assessing the quality of marriage and similar dyads. *Journal of Marriage and the Family, 38,* 15–28.
Snyder, D. K., & Wills, R. M. (1989). Behavioral versus insight-oriented marital therapy: Effects on individual and interspousal functioning. *Journal of Consulting and Clinical Psychology, 57,* 39–46.
Fowers, B. J. (1990). An interactional approach to standardized marital assessment: A literature review. *Family Relations, 39,* 368–377.
Snyder, D. K., Lachar, D., Freiman, K. E., & Hoover, D. W. (1991). Toward the actuarial assessment of couples' relationships. In J. P. Vincent (Ed.), *Advances in family intervention, assessment, and theory* (vol. 5; pp. 89–122). London: Kingsley Publishers.
Fowers, B. J., & Applegate, B. (1995). Do marital conventionalization scales measure a social desirability response bias? A confirmatory factor analysis. *Journal of Marriage and the Family, 57,* 237–241.

Review of the Marital Satisfaction Inventory— Revised by MARY LOU BRYANT FRANK, Professor and Department Head of Psychology, North Georgia College & State University, Dahlonega, GA:

One of the most used and cited couple and marital inventories for the past 15 years has been the Marital Satisfaction Inventory. In a field with multiple, varied measures, it remains a respected standard and one of the better, less expensive instruments. The purpose of the inventory is "identifying the nature and extent of relationship distress with couples considering or beginning conjoint therapy" (manual, p. 1). Through assessing the couple on 13 scales, the therapist can gather information important to initial assessment, assess efficacy of therapy, diagnose a couple's strengths and weaknesses, and assess the home environment for emotionally or behaviorally troubled children or adolescents. It can also be used as a post-assessment tool.

First published in 1981, the new version of the Marital Satisfaction Inventory—Revised (MSI-

R) is the first complete revision. The MSI-R (1997) was based on a larger, more representative standardization sample (1,020 couples), a reduction in the number of inventory items, the addition of a scale to assess aggression in the relationship, and the addition of a scale to assess random responding. The current version has been used in cross-cultural comparisons (Negy & Snyder, 1997; Hahlweg & Klann, 1997), has been used across various age groups, has incorporated individuals across the country (as well as the world), has been used with individuals from various levels of education, and has been updated with more inclusive terminology (e.g., using terms such as "partner" and "relationship" rather than "spouse" or "marriage"). The addition of a scale to measure aggression extends its usefulness to abusive relationships and abusive family environments. The MSI-R offers mail-in, fax, self, and microcomputer scoring that can include an extensive test report. The revisions would seem to keep the MSI-R in the forefront of relationship assessment.

The MSI-R has included some additional modifications to increase its usefulness and improve its validation and normative base. Utilizing data collected since its initial release as well as rescaled data from the original instrument, it represents studies of couples from a variety of groups (e.g., clinical and nonclinical, pre- and posttreatment, divorced, partner abuse, financial counseling, sexual dysfunction, adult psychiatric, and child/adolescent psychiatric). Comparison scales and profiles are provided in the manual.

Reliability information reflects numerous studies and careful attention to maintain the integrity of the previous instrument. The MSI-R has from 9 to 19 items for each question with the internal consistency ranging from .70 to .93, with a mean coefficient of .82. This compares to 15 to 43 items for each scale on the MSI-R with internal consistencies ranging from .80 to .97 and a mean of .88. Test-retest reliabilities are also comparable to those of the previous instrument. One hundred and five couples took the MSI-R at the beginning and the end of a 6-week period. The test-retest coefficients ranged from .74 to .88, with a mean coefficient of .79. Previous scores on the MSI had correlations ranging from .84 to .94, with a mean rating of .89. Fewer items (150 on the MSI-R and 280 on the MSI) with resultantly less administration time (reportedly down from 30 to 25 minutes) would seem to account for the slight change in reliability coefficients.

Validity information is likewise comparable with the previous instrument; however, the MSI-R has benefited from additional data and comparisons. The correlations between the original and revised scales range from .94 to .98, with a median of 95.5. The newer norms with the broader standardization sample used normalized (rather than linear) T-scores. The 13 scales were found to be highly interrelated, with three primary components emerging from a factor analysis. The first and primary factor measured affect and communication in the relationship, the second factor reflected child-related concerns, and the third factor reflected the couple's attitudes toward marital and parental roles. Multiple studies illustrated that the MSI-R adequately distinguishes (discriminant validity) between group differences (e.g., clinical and nonclinical, pre- and posttreatment, divorced, partner abuse, financial counseling, sexual dysfunction, adult psychiatric, and child/adolescent psychiatric). Correlational studies addressed convergent validity by showing that the scales relate to the key aspects of couple relatedness, and that they are able to distinguish between those who will most likely benefit from relationship counseling. Studies also looked at the meaning of the scaled scores utilizing actuarial validity that forms the basis of the current interpretation system.

The content and scales vary only slightly from the MSI to the MSI-R. Given the previous reviews (Dixon, 1985; Waring, 1985), the 11 primary scales do not differ substantively and will not be repeated herein. However, the two additional scales include the Inconsistency (INC) scale and the Aggression (AGG) scale. The INC scale represents another validity index to reflect response consistency and random responding. Items have either highly similar content (most likely these items would elicit the same response) or highly opposite content (in which case the responses would be different). The AGG scale measures verbal/nonphysical and physical aggressiveness. The potential for a partner to begin utilizing intimidation and then become physically aggressive is supported by the literature and, as such, a scale measuring these tendencies has clinical and research value.

The manual for the MSI-R is comprehensive and user friendly (although an index would have improved its utility). It not only provides excellent information on psychometrics and statistical information, but it also provides a detailed systematic interpretation with multiple case studies. The previous concerns with this instrument appear to be addressed in this revision.

Society has changed substantively since 1981. Although in the standardization of the MSI-R Inventory, the terminology was updated, the entire focus needed to be reviewed and updated. Standardization should have included nonmarried heterosexual as well as gay and lesbian couples. The inventory's utility would seem to be broader than just as a marital inventory and has proven itself in multiple studies to be effective with a wide variety of individuals. This would increase its scope and utility. Many of the other questions regarding this instrument have been adequately addressed; bringing the instrument current within the culture would seem to be an important next step.

SUMMARY. Substantive changes have continued to be made for the MSI-R to make it a more valid and reliable, usable, and efficient instrument for measuring couple distress. Although modifications are recommended for continued development and sensitivity to all couples in this society, it will remain one of the key instruments in the field of couples and relationship counseling. I believe it will continue to be useful as a research and a clinical tool.

REVIEWER'S REFERENCES

Dixon, D. N. (1985). [Review of the Marital Satisfaction Inventory]. In J. V. Mitchell, Jr. (Ed.), *The ninth mental measurements yearbook* (pp. 894–895). Lincoln, NE: Buros Institute of Mental Measurements.

Waring, E. M. (1985). [Review of the Marital Satisfaction Inventory]. In J. V. Mitchell, Jr. (Ed.), *The ninth mental measurements yearbook* (pp. 895–896). Lincoln, NE: Buros Institute of Mental Measurements.

Hahlweg, K., & Klann, N. (1997). The effectiveness of marital counseling in Germany: A *contribution* to health services research. *Journal of Family Psychology, 11*, 410–421.

Negy, C., & Snyder, D. (1997). Ethnicity and acculturation: Assessing Mexican American couples' relationships using the Marital Satisfaction Inventory—Revised. *Psychological Assessment, 9*, 414–421.

[220]
Maryland Addictions Questionnaire.

Purpose: Intended to survey "issues relevant to the severity of patients' alcohol and drug abuse history."
Population: Ages 17 and older.
Publication Date: 1997.
Acronym: MAQ.
Scores, 15: Validity (Response Inconsistency, Defensiveness), Summary (Emotional Distress, Resistance to Treatment, Admission of Problems), Substance Abuse (Alcoholism Severity, Drug Abuse Severity, Craving, Substance Abuse Control, Resentment), Treatment (Motivation for Treatment, Social Anxiety, Antisocial Behaviors, Cognitive Symptoms, Affective Disturbance).

Administration: Group.
Price Data, 1999: $99.50 per complete kit including manual (102 pages), 20 AutoScore™ answer sheets, 2 prepaid mail-in answer sheets for computer scoring and interpretation, and 2-use disk and 2 PC answer sheets for on-site computer scoring and interpretation; $28.50 per 20 AutoScore™ answer sheets; $13.50 per mail-in answer sheet; $15 per 100 microcomputer answer sheets; $45 per manual; $235 per microcomputer disk good for 25 uses (3.5-inch, Microsoft Windows required); $10.50 per FAX Scoring Service.
Time: (15–20) minutes.
Comments: Author suggests should be administered as an intake measure for individuals entering addiction treatment programs.
Author: William E. O'Donnell, Clinton B. DeSoto, and Janet L. DeSoto.
Publisher: Western Psychological Services, Inc.

Review of the Maryland Addictions Questionnaire by CARL ISENHART, Coordinator, Addictive Disorders Section, VA Medical Center, Minneapolis, MN:

The Maryland Addictions Questionnaire (MAQ) is a 111-item self-report questionnaire that assesses substance abuse history, attitudes, and beliefs of individuals seeking substance abuse treatment. The instrument consists of five Substance Abuse scales (Alcoholism Severity, Drug Abuse Severity, Craving, Control, and Resentment), five Treatment scales (Motivation, Social Anxiety, Antisocial Behaviors, Cognitive Symptoms, and Affective Disturbance), three Summary scores (Emotional Distress, Resistance to Treatment, and Admission of Problems), and two Validity scales (Inconsistency and Defensiveness). It was designed for ages 17 and older, requires a fifth grade reading level, and can be completed in 15–20 minutes. There is a 30-item version (MAQ-30) that takes 5–10 minutes and yields scores that are equivalent to the three Summary scores and five Substance Abuse and Treatment-related scores. The 30-item version and a computerized version will not be reviewed here.

STANDARDIZATION AND ITEM DEVELOPMENT. The authors developed "face valid" items that were compatible with the conceptual domains deemed to be a priority. The domains were based on current substance abuse typologies, paradigms, and treatment criteria. Also, 22 addiction counselors were interviewed for input regarding important treatment issues. The Summary scales were generated from factor analysis of the MAQ scales.

The MAQ was normed on a group of 983 people (758 males and 225 females) from the following types of programs: outpatient (67%), residential services for individuals convicted of alcohol-related driving offenses (24%), and half-way house programs (9%). Those individuals self-identified their addiction status as: 30% alcohol and drugs, 19% drugs only, 27% alcohol only, and 24% not addicted. The average age was 32.5 years ($SD = 9$) and the average level of education was 11.8 ($SD = 2$).

The authors examined differential MAQ scoring across subgroups who differed on gender, ethnicity, age, and education. Overall, their analysis suggested some clinically significant differences between men and women and between different age groups. However, although "effect size" estimates were provided, except for age, there was no presentation of statistical significance of the MAQ scale differences between the subgroups. Significant differences should be identified first then the effect size of that difference evaluated to determine clinical relevance. Also, with the age comparison, there was no control for multiple comparisons.

ADMINISTRATION, SCORING, AND INTERPRETATION. The MAQ manual provided very good instructions and examples for scoring the instrument. The examinee responds to a 5-point scale from 0 (not at all) to 4 (extremely) to indicate the extent the experience applies to him or her, and the response is transferred to a scoring sheet used by the examiner to tally the raw scores for each scale. The raw scores are transferred to a profile sheet where the scores are converted to T-scores and percentiles and plotted on a profile sheet.

The manual provided information to facilitate interpretation; this included an assessment of profile validity by reviewing the Defensiveness and Inconsistency scales, suggestions for interpreting the Substance Abuse and Treatment scales, and eight case examples. One concern, however, has to do with the three Summary scales (Emotional Distress [EMO], Resistance to Treatment [RES], and Admission of Problems [ADM]). The manual described "profiles" of different combinations of Summary score scales (e.g., EMO/RES/ADM, or EMO/ADM/RES, etc.). The manual stated that there should be at least five T-score points between the highest and lowest Summary score. This seems too liberal to this reviewer in that there should

be a minimal distance between all three Summary scales; for example, one standard error of measurement *SEM*. The authors could calculate *SEM*s to develop confidence intervals for determining "well-defined" summary score profiles.

RELIABILITY. The authors supported the instrument's reliability with internal consistency and test-retest reliability estimates. The coefficient alphas for the total standardization sample ranged from .72 (Resentment) to .93 (Alcoholism Severity, Craving, and Affective Disturbance). Test-retest reliabilities were reported for two different patient samples: the residential DWI facility (average test-retest interval was 1.34 weeks) and the outpatient substance abuse treatment program (average test-retest interval was 28 days). The correlations for the first sample ranged from .50 (Inconsistency) to .93 (Alcohol and Drug Severity), and all but a total of four scales had correlations >.80. The correlations for the second sample ranged from .50 (Inconsistency) to .92 (Admission of Problems), and all but a total of three scales had correlations >.80.

VALIDITY. The authors presented an extensive discussion to support the instrument's validity. The instrument's internal structure was supported with a factor analytic study that demonstrated that the individual items generally loaded on the theoretical scale. Convergent validity was assessed by correlating the MAQ scores with instruments that assess alcohol use, alcohol and drug-related problems, expectations, denial, cognitive performance and symptoms, psychopathology and social instability, and substance abuse severity indexes. Also, the MAQ scales were correlated with Brief Symptom Inventory scales and with counselor ratings of patients. Generally, the expected relationships were found and the authors discussed any exceptions. However, the sheer number of correlations made interpretation difficult. An alternative strategy would involve regressing the MAQ scores onto the convergent measures. This would identify the MAQ scales that significantly correlate most with the convergent measure and provide clearer support for validity.

Discriminant validity was demonstrated by comparing the MAQ scores of individuals with differences, types, and severity of substance abuse: substance abusers and nonclinical volunteers, different numbers of DWI and treatment episodes, inpatients and outpatients, and patients in public and private programs. Also, MAW scores for the four standardization subgroups were analyzed. Overall, predicted differences were obtained between the comparison groups; however, in some of the comparisons the tests of significance were not reported and, where they were, frequently no corrections were made for multiple comparisons.

SUMMARY. The MAQ provides an assessment of substance-related domains that are not readily available from other instruments, and it assesses areas that may not be directly related to substance abuse but that are still important to consider in treatment planning. The manual is well organized and functional. The standardization sample is well described, the reliability data are reasonable, and, notwithstanding some concerns about some statistical procedures, there is evidence for the validity of the scores. However, procedures need to be established to determine "well-defined" summary score profiles. The instrument may be too biased towards more "traditional" concepts of substance abuse. For example, admission of being an "alcoholic" is scored on the "Motivation" subscale but "hating" to attend AA meetings is scored on the "Resistance" subscale. Clearly, people have changed their substance abuse patterns without admitting they are an alcoholic and without attending AA. Also, there may be many reasons why a person does not like to attend AA (e.g., psychiatric disorders). Given these concerns, however, this instrument warrants continued clinical use and being subjected to additional psychometric research.

Review of the Maryland Addictions Questionnaire by JOHN A. MILLS, Professor, Counseling and Student Development, Indiana University of Pennsylvania, Indiana, PA:

The Maryland Addictions Questionnaire (MAQ) is a 111-item inventory designed to assist in the assessment of the needs of individuals entering drug abuse evaluation or treatment programs. The full MAQ may be administered, or a short form may be used if the examinee has completed at least the first 30 items. The standard form of the instrument yields 11 scales, including 5 scales pertaining to substance abuse treatment and 5 scales pertaining to broader treatment-related issues. The MAQ is designed for a specific population, and appears to be an efficient instrument that may be administered repeatedly. A

technician may administer the MAQ, but the manual is clear that interpretation should only be conducted by a professional with training in psychological assessment and addiction treatment.

The MAQ uses self-report to address key elements of an evaluation for drug abuse treatment, including Alcoholism Severity, Drug Abuse Severity, Craving, Substance Abuse Control, and Resentment. The treatment-related issues include Motivation for Treatment, Social Anxiety, Antisocial Behaviors, Cognitive Symptoms, and Affective Disturbance. In addition to the specific content areas, there are two validity indices, addressing Inconsistency of Responses and Defensiveness. Three Summary scores are developed, which are described as Emotional Distress, Resistance to Treatment, and Admission of Problems.

The first part of the two-part manual for the MAQ includes extensive information regarding administration and scoring of the instrument. The second part provides technical information regarding item selection and scale development, and provides clear descriptions of standard score interpretation and the nature of the reference group through which standardization was developed. The development of the instrument is clear and complete, with a good quality rationale for scale development and extensive data in support of the psychometric properties of the instrument.

On the basis of the rational and empirical strength of the instrument, the authors described a procedure for systematic interpretation of the well-organized output of results. This strategy includes use of the validity scales and the clinical scales, and is made stronger through the use of groupings of clinical scales and use of item content. The instrument does not provide a diagnosis, and the technical materials make it clear that the results represent the subjective point of view of the respondent. This means that additional methods of assessment and verification of assessment data are essential companions to any MAQ findings.

The MAQ may be given on a computer or using a pencil-and-paper format. It is important that the respondent use the proper form for the type of scoring to be conducted. Users of the MAQ must be mindful of the warning to use the instrument with persons over 17 years old, who are willing to be responsive to the instrument, and who can read at least at the fifth grade reading level.

In addition to the evidence for reliability and construct validity, the MAQ appears to have good utility for treatment planning and exhibits good face validity. The instrument reflects a design that is readily accessible to the persons taking the instrument and the professionals who will use it. With the clear organization of the multifaceted instrument, there is a clear method for extracting and applying the most relevant information. The instructions give clear guidelines for use and explicit cautions about possible ways that the instrument might be misused.

SUMMARY. The MAQ appears to be a highly useful instrument with strong psychometric properties. It is an empirically supported and well-described instrument, which can make an important contribution to clinical decisions at the time of a respondent's admission or reassessment to drug and alcohol treatment. The validation information allows the user to make a well-founded interpretation in the context of relevant norm groups. Because of the clarity and distinctness of the 11 scales, an individual's results are readily useful for treatment planning and re-evaluation.

[221]
Matching Person and Technology.

Purpose: Designed for "selecting and evaluating technologies used in rehabilitation, education, the workplace and other settings."
Population: Clients, students, or employees.
Publication Dates: 1991–1994.
Acronym: MPT.
Administration: Group.
Forms, 2: Consumer, Professional.
Price Data: Available from publisher.
Time: (15) minutes per test.
Author: Marcia J. Scherer.
Publisher: The Institute for Matching Person & Technology, Inc.
  a) SURVEY OF TECHNOLOGY USE.
  Purpose: Constructed to measure "the consumer's present experiences and feelings toward technological devices."
  Acronym: SOTU.
  Scores: 4 categories: Experience with Current Technologies, Perspectives on Technologies, Typical Activities, Personal/Social Characteristics.
  b) ASSISTIVE TECHNOLOGY DEVICE PREDISPOSITION ASSESSMENT.
  Purpose: Designed to "help individuals select appropriate assistive technologies."
  Acronym: ATD PA.

Scores: 5 categories: Disability, Environment, Temperament, Device, Degree of Match.
  c) EDUCATIONAL TECHNOLOGY PREDISPOSITION ASSESSMENT.
  Purpose: Designed "for teachers who are helping students use technology to reach educational goals."
  Acronym: ET PA.
  Scores: 4 categories: Educational Goal, The Student, Educational Technology, Educational Environment.
  d) WORKPLACE TECHNOLOGY PREDISPOSITION ASSESSMENT.
  Purpose: "Designed to assist employers in identifying factors that might inhibit the acceptance or use of a new technology in the workplace."
  Acronym: WT PA.
  Scores: 4 categories: The Technology, The Employee Being Trained to Use the Technology, The Workplace Environment, Match Between Person and Technology.
  e) HEALTH CARE TECHNOLOGY PREDISPOSITION ASSESSMENT.
  Purpose: "Developed to assist health care professionals in identifying factors that might inhibit the acceptance or appropriate use of health care technologies."
  Acronym: HCT PA.
  Scores: 5 categories: Health Problem, Consequences of HCT Use, Characteristics of the Health Care Technology, Personal Issues, Attitudes of Others.

Review of Matching Person and Technology by PATRICIA A. BACHELOR, *Professor of Psychology, California State University at Long Beach, Long Beach, CA:*

Matching Person and Technology (MPT) is designed to be a series of assessment instruments to facilitate the selection and evaluation of technologies used in education, rehabilitation, and workplace settings. The five assessment instruments are the Survey of Technology Use (SOTU), the Assistive Technology Device Predisposition Assessment (ATD PA), the Educational Technology Predisposition Assessment (ET PA), the Workplace Technology Predisposition Assessment (WT PA), and the Health Care Technology Predisposition Assessment (HCT PA). The SOTU elicits present experiences and feelings about technological devices. Issues of self-esteem and well-being surrounding the use of technology are assessed using a 3-point semantic differential. The ATD PA is used by rehabilitation specialists to aid individuals in selecting assistive technologies. The checklist taps satisfaction with current progress and prioritizes aspects of recovery. The user's view about an assistive device or devices is captured on a 5-point or 7-point scale. The ET PA uses a checklist to identify educational goals/targets as well as student, teacher, and psychosocial environmental characteristics. The WT PA is designed to identify factors that may inhibit the use or acceptance of technology in the workplace. Employers can thereby plan training to assist employees in skill enhancement. The HCT PA was designed to assist health care professionals to identify factors that may facilitate or inhibit the acceptance of appropriate use of health care devices. Except for the HCT PA, each instrument has a version designed for the provider of technologies (therapist, rehabilitator, teacher, trainer, etc.) and a version designed for the user of technology (client, student, employee, etc.).

The MPT assessment process enables the individual to enter into a collaborative decision-making environment designed to assist technology users and providers in making choices based upon the needs of the user, the environment, and the personality of the user. Users' expectations and preferences, personal and social factors, economic and situational characteristics, as well as the training requirements will add to the blend of qualities and traits needed for an effective/successful pairing of person and technology. The successful pairing of each user to the appropriate technological device should save the frustration and economic losses of a mismatch.

No specific scoring system is used. However, the patterns of positive and negative responses are expected to reveal to the users and providers sufficient insight to select a technological device with the best chance of success.

The targeted population includes individuals with physical or sensory disabilities. No specific age limits are recommended; however, the ability to read is required.

RELIABILITY. The interrater agreement of the SOTU was reported to be 80% or higher on more than two-thirds of the items. Eighty-six to 91% was the consistency reported across ET PA raters. Overall, the agreement is higher among technology items than on user psychosocial characteristics. These findings provide a preliminary step in the process of demonstrating the consis-

tency of the MPT scales. In order to conform with the *Standards for Educational and Psychological Testing* (AERA, APA, & NCME, 1985), estimates of internal consistency need to be assessed prior to an enthusiastic acceptance of the psychometric merit of the MPT scales. Without evidence of internal consistency, the dependability of assessments made with the instrument is dubious. Consequently, the application and use of the MPT scales should be restricted to research applications.

VALIDITY. Content validity was suggested by using items reflective of a person's actual experiences with technology. Discussions with professionals and ongoing literature reviews were offered as evidence for content validity of the scales. A few contrasted group studies were used to support claims of criterion-related validity. The SOTU and ET PA were used in a study designed to identify the characteristics of 120 students from eight schools in Maine who would be successful in a distance learning course in American Sign Language. Results indicated that selected items from the SOTU and ET PA were modest predictors of grades and satisfaction/proficiency with course technologies. The ET PA was used in a study with 59 middle-school students to assess successful performance in multimedia instruction. Results based on descriptive outcome measures were suggestive of a relationship between the ET PA and performance. These predominantly descriptive studies are not compelling evidence of the predictive and/or criterion-related validity of scores from the MPT. Further research studies are needed to show convincing support for claims of predictive and/or criterion-related validity of all of the MPT scales. The careful appraisal of such validity will enable users to use and interpret the scales with confidence about the accuracy of the test results. The dissemination of evidence based upon validity studies is warranted prior to use of the MPT scales beyond research settings.

NORMATIVE GROUPS. Limited information was provided on the standardization sample or normative groups. The purpose of the MPT does not readily lend itself to such comparisons. This is primarily a personalized assessment strategy.

SUMMARY. The MPT system is an innovative approach to the difficult issue of pairing persons with sensory or physical disabilities with assistive technology. The needs, abilities, environment, personality, and social characteristics of the individual are used to facilitate a match. These aspects blend to create technology matches that one hopes will avoid frustration and mismatches leading to nonuse and economic losses. These types of assessments are particularly important now that technology is available in many forms for disabled and sensory impaired persons. Support for the psychometric qualities of the MPT subscales has been, to date, preliminary and basically descriptive. Appropriate evaluations of the internal consistency and criterion-related validity are expected to be conducted prior to an enthusiastic endorsement of the psychometric merit of the scales of the MPT.

REVIEWER'S REFERENCE

American Educational Research Association, American Psychological Association, & National Council on Measurement in Education. (1985). *Standards for educational and psychological testing*. Washington, DC: American Psychological Association, Inc.

Review of Matching Person and Technology by LAURA L. B. BARNES, Associate Professor of Educational Research and Evaluation, School of Education Studies, and CARRIE L. WINTEROWD, Assistant Professor of Counseling Psychology, College of Education, Oklahoma State University, Tulsa, OK:

Matching Person and Technology (MPT) is a collection of five individual assessments designed for use by technology providers (educators, rehabilitation professionals, health care professionals, or employers) to help identify obstacles to the successful use of technology for each individual consumer. These assessments help professionals consider whether or not a technology is a good match for individual consumers given personal and environmental factors. The individual assessments target somewhat different populations of technology users and providers. Except for the Assistive Technology Device Predisposition Assessment (ATD PA), there appear to be no restrictions placed on the types of technology under consideration. For example, the Educational Technology Predisposition Assessment (ET PA) may be appropriate for studying the outcomes of distance learning with general undergraduate students, or it may be used to evaluate the feasibility of using special computer enhancements for a student with a physical disability.

The MPT is described as being grounded in a theoretical model in which the degree of successful technology use depends on characteristics of the technology user in interaction with characteristics of the technology and the environment in which the technology is being used. Thus, each of the MPT assessments contains items developed to measure each of these three areas. Each of the assessment instruments (except for the Health Care Technology Predisposition Assessment; HCT PA) is a pair of instruments—one to be completed by the technology user and a similar one for use by the technology provider to help the user and provider work together to make choices about technologies and training strategies.

There are no norms reported for any of the MPT assessments. Scores on the individual instruments are to be interpreted subjectively and used to supplement clinical judgement. For some of the instruments, discrepancies between the technology user's self-report ratings and the technology provider's ratings of the same or similar items can provide useful insight into differing perspectives on the barriers that influence technology use. The amount of interpretive guidance given in the manual varies across the instruments, from a great deal for the ADT PA to very little for the WT PA.

In general, there is very little psychometric information contained in the brief (48-page) manual. The shortage of information on the reliability and validity of MPT scores pertains to all five of the instruments. Neither does the manual describe how the instruments were developed, though test development is often cited in the manual as the basis for validity. For example, the author claims content validity for the Survey of Technology Use (SOTU) because "the SOTU was created from the experiences of people who used or did not use a technology provided to them" (manual, p. 10) but provides no supportive information about the instrument's development. Likewise, the manual provides no information to support the statement that the Assistive Technology Device Predisposition Assessment (ATD PA) was developed from research that examined differences between users and nonusers of assistive technology. Purchasers of the MPT assessments are promised reliability and validity updates as they become available.

Following are brief reviews of each of the instruments in the MPT collection.

SURVEY OF TECHNOLOGY USE (SOTU). The Survey of Technology Use is a two-part survey. The first part purports to measure attitudes toward technology experiences; the second part seeks to measure aspects of general affect, mood, and typical activities. The SOTU could help professionals evaluate the effectiveness of technology interventions, particularly with consumers who are initially reluctant to use technology, and to identify those who may be at risk of abandoning technology.

With respect to reliability, interrater agreement of 80% on most of the SOTU items was reported for a group of undergraduate students (no sample size given) who were shown a videotape of a "student considering using a computer" (manual, p. 9). A semester-long test-retest study involving self-ratings by the same students was reported, according to the author, to show reasonable stability although no coefficients or other statistics were presented. No validity evidence is presented in the manual. One study not included in the manual (Keefe, Scherer, & McKee, 1996) showed SOTU items and ET PA items were predictive of course grades and teacher ratings in two distance learning courses in which American Sign Language was taught. The same study reported a fairly strong correlation (.64) between nonspecified items from the SOTU and ET PA with the Tennessee Self-Concept scale.

EDUCATIONAL TECHNOLOGY PREDISPOSITION ASSESSMENT (ET PA). The Educational Technology Predisposition Assessment was developed to identify characteristics of (a) the educational goals, (b) the technology, (c) the learner, and (d) the learning environment that would influence the successful use of the technology. Both the teacher and student forms provide a checklist of learner characteristics (e.g., impatience, physical dexterity, preference for group or individual work, likes computers). Questions about the technology and the educational environment must be responded to separately for each different type of technology being considered.

Scoring of the ET PA can be extremely complex and requires a great deal of time, effort, and subjective judgment on the part of the teacher/professional. For each of the 32 learner characteristic items on both the teacher and student forms, the teacher must decide whether that characteristic will facilitate or discourage the use of the particular technology under consideration. Once each item has been marked as an incentive or disincentive, the teacher must then assign to each item a strength rating from 1 (strong disincentive) to 5 (strong incentive). Items not selected as representing this particular learner's characteristics must be scored in reverse (e.g., a score of 1 would

be assigned to a strong incentive item that was not selected). A similar process is required on the Educational Environment section of the student form. The whole scoring process for this assessment instrument is so cumbersome and time-consuming that it seems improbable it would facilitate decision making more than once. On the other hand, the ET PA might be a reasonably useful tool if only a single technology were used repeatedly so that the strength ratings could be pre-assigned. Further, it may be informative to have the students themselves evaluate whether or not their own responses (regarding personal and learning characteristics and educational environment issues) would facilitate or hinder their use of educational technology.

In a study published subsequent to the publication of the MPT, Albaugh and Fayne (1996) reported an average interrater agreement of 87% for nine incentive items and 91% for nine disincentive items when CD-ROM technology was the target. Some evidence for validity comes from studies reported in the manual and two other studies (Albaugh & Fayne, 1996; Keefe, Scherer, & McKee, 1996) that showed some items from the ET PA were useful in predicting student satisfaction and grade outcomes for courses delivered electronically (computer conferencing, HyperCard, satellite video, CD-ROM).

The ET PA has some very practical applications for educators who work with students needing educational technology services. The Educational Goal section of the Student Form may be useful in promoting successful use of educational technology devices by helping educators better understand student perceptions of the goal and their levels of motivation in achieving such a goal. The manual also provides examples of educational goals and a useful discussion on matching educational goals with instructional strategies.

ASSISTIVE TECHNOLOGY DEVICE PREDISPOSITION ASSESSMENT (ATD PA). The Assistive Technology Device Predisposition Assessment is designed to promote collaboration between professionals and consumers in selecting assistive devices. The consumer form primarily assesses the influences of disability, environment, consumer personality, and device characteristics on ATD use. The professional form helps assess consumer and environmental characteristics that may affect ATD use and evaluate device requirements compared to consumer resources. The ATD PA has scoring requirements similar to the ET PA. Once again, scoring of either form is a daunting task (there are 6 pages of scoring instructions) and represents a major drawback to use.

Predictive validity of the instrument would appear to be critical; however, the only information given in the manual is that the ATD PA was more sensitive than another instrument in distinguishing between users and nonusers of listening devices in two groups of hearing-impaired adults. The only reference to reliability for the ATD PA was a report of "good inter-rater reliability, particularly for items regarding the AT and disability" (manual, p. 23) among a group of psychology students and four groups of rehabilitation professionals.

Although the author does not specify when the ATD PA should be administered, it is assumed that it could be administered prior to discharge from a rehabilitation hospital by a rehabilitation professional who has a good working relationship with the client. In addition, the ATD PA could be administered in an outpatient vocational rehabilitation setting after the rehabilitation counselor has developed a good working relationship with the client. The ATD PA would not be appropriate to administer until the professional has a good understanding of the client's attitudes, feelings, personality style, and level of environmental support.

In general, the forms hold a great deal of promise for rehabilitation professionals and their clients. The professional form may help rehabilitation professionals organize their conceptualizations about the client-technology match.

WORKPLACE TECHNOLOGY PREDISPOSITION ASSESSMENT (WT PA). The Workplace Technology Predisposition Assessment is designed to supply employers with "individual information on your employees' perspectives of new technologies" (manual, p. 37) to facilitate decisions about training, orientations, "even to the point of accommodating differing learning styles" (p. 37). The employer and employee forms ask for ratings to be given to aspects of the technology (e.g., length of time for training), the person using the technology (e.g., previous success with new technology), and the workplace (e.g., is mastery of technology rewarded?). The items appear highly relevant to issues that influence the successful implementation of a new technology in the work-

place. Both forms provide space for respondents to identify any discrepancies between the employee's and employer's perceptions of work technology use by the employee or any potential negative influences on such use. In addition, space is provided to document necessary accommodations, interventions, and/or training plans to increase workplace technology use. The WT PA has the potential to be very useful in helping employers or workplace consultants identify employees' concerns about technology implementation and could be an important planning tool. For example, it may provide information that would be useful in establishing an implementation and training schedule in a company that is adopting a complex new database system, or it may help employers and employees work together to comply with the Americans with Disabilities Act by adding or modifying technology. Unfortunately, no reliability nor validity data were available in the manual or made available for this review.

HEALTH CARE TECHNOLOGIES PREDISPOSITION ASSESSMENT (HCT PA). The Health Care Technologies Predisposition Assessment is a checklist to be completed by the healthcare provider. The HCT PA contains 43 items that address characteristics of the health problem, consequences of health care technology use, characteristics of the health care technology, personal issues, and attitudes of others. The categories represented in the instrument are said to be "areas of influence that impact most on a patient's use or non-use of a technology" (manual, p. 40). The HCT PA has no scoring criteria and may be used as an interview guide and "visual aid to help you organize your impressions about your patient" (p. 41). Again, no reliability nor validity data were presented. It would be important to know how the items were developed and the degree to which responses to these items do, in fact, point to barriers to successful technology use.

The advantage of the HCT PA is its short, checklist format for screening potential barriers to health care technology use. However, the fact that there is no scoring system may make it difficult to scan the items quickly for meaning or to identify major themes. A factor analysis of this instrument may help to identify specific constructs related to health care technology use.

GENERAL COMMENTS ON THE MPT. The only way in which the organization of the

MPT suggests its use as a "battery" is through two worksheets and flowchart. One worksheet is used to record the technology user's specific limitations, goals, and desired interventions in 11 potential areas. Examples are provided of technologies and environmental accommodations for each of these areas to help professionals develop goals and/or interventions with the consumer. The other worksheet helps professionals identify: (a) the person's limitation(s); (b) technologies that the person is currently using (includes months used, percent of daily use, and level of satisfaction with technology); (c) technologies used previously (includes months used, percent of daily use, satisfaction with technology, and reasons for not using this technology now); and (d) technologies needed for that person. These two worksheets provide professionals with a well-organized format to document client/consumer information pertinent to technology use. Depending on the type of interventions planned, the technology provider is directed by the flowchart to one or more of the MPT assessment instruments. Unfortunately, the manual's interpretive guides for scores are strictly "within instrument." There are no discussions aimed at examining profiles across tests for consistency or discrepancies. Further, several of the instruments measure the same basic characteristics—for example, both the AT PA and the ET PA measure family support, self-concept, coping skills, etc., which must be evaluated as an incentive or disincentive to using each specific technology being considered. If multiple assessments are to be used, the instrument should be organized to minimize redundancy. In the current format, several of the assessments are far too long for reasonable use in combination.

Although these assessment instruments were developed to supplement professional opinions, one major limitation of these assessments is the lack of specific scoring keys to interpret item responses or subscale scores. For the SOTU, the ATD PA, and the ET PA, professionals simply look at subscale scores or tallies and determine which subscale has the lowest score or tally. The lowest subscale score is then identified as an "area of concern" to discuss further with the consumer. For the HCT PA and the WT PA, professionals have to extrapolate major themes on their own by exploring individual item responses. It is unclear how this current scoring system provides meaning to the items, except to identify areas for further assessment.

SUMMARY. Our general impression of the MPT is that the author has tried to do too much with it and has succeeded in doing only some of it well. If the MPT is thought of as a conventional test, it fails in many respects—many of the instruments are too long, the scoring is cumbersome and time-consuming, there is no formal mechanism for interpreting the scores so laboriously obtained, and data are sorely lacking on the reliability and validity of the scores. Very little information is presented on the validity of the instruments for counseling and rehabilitation—almost nothing, in fact. Though some information is provided to support their use as outcomes measures, it is still inadequate. This is unfortunate because there appears to be a great need for outcome measures, particularly in the area of assistive technology. However, if the process of completing and scoring the MPT can be viewed as part of a helping process—as a vehicle for fostering collaborative decision making and goal setting, and for promoting self-understanding, then these shortcomings become less serious. This would suggest that the consumer/client become more involved in the scoring process of these instruments than the manual suggests—for example, by deciding to what extent personal and environmental characteristics are incentives or disincentives to technology use. If the MPT is to be used as a guide to organizing therapeutic approaches to technology decision making, or as a learning activity, it may be highly effective. However, we cannot recommend that scores derived from the MPT be used for ranking, sorting, classifying, categorizing, describing, predicting, or for any other purpose that assumes the scores have meaning. There is simply too little evidence to support such traditional use. The strength of the MPT is the theoretical model upon which it is based and its wide applicability.

REVIEWERS' REFERENCES

Albaugh, P. R., & Fayne, H. (1996). The ETPA for predicting technology success with learning disabled students: Lessons from a multimedia study. *Technology and Disability, 5,* 313–318.

Keefe, B., Scherer, M. J., & McKee, B. G. (1996). Mainepoint: Outcomes of teaching American sign language via distance learning. *Technology and Disability, 5,* 319–326.

[222]

Mathematics Competency Test.

Purpose: Constructed to assess "mathematics achievement."

Population: Ages 11 to adult.

Publication Dates: 1995–1996.

Scores: Total score only.

Administration: Group.
Price Data: Available from publisher.
Time: (40) minutes.
Authors: P. E. Vernon, K. M. Miller, and J. F. Izard.
Publisher: Australian Council for Educational Research [Australia] and Hodder & Stoughton Educational [England].

Review of the Mathematics Competency Test by JOSEPH C. CIECHALSKI, Professor of Counselor and Adult Education, East Carolina University, Greenville, NC:

The Mathematics Competency Test (MCT) is the descendant of the Graded Arithmetic Test (GAT) published in 1949 and later revised in 1971 and 1976. Published in 1995–96, the MCT retained 18 items from the 1976 GAT and added 28 new items for a total of 46 items.

All of the items are open-ended and were constructed to assess math skills in four areas. These areas include: Using and Applying Mathematics (12 items), Number and Algebra (20 items), Shape and Space (8 items), and Handling Data (6 items). Items are arranged in order of difficulty. The MCT may be used in schools, colleges, and employment settings.

ADMINISTRATION AND SCORING. The administration section in the manual is divided into three parts: preparation, instructions for administration, and using the test with poor readers. This section of the manual was well written and informative.

Scoring the test is easy. The authors point out that, unlike scoring multiple-choice items, more skill is needed to score open-ended questions. Scorers of the MCT must be able to recognize alternate correct answers. Therefore, the scoring key contains acceptable alternate answers as well as information on responses that are not acceptable. The scoring key, included in the manual, was designed to correspond with the responses made by the examinee in the test booklet. Directions for scoring the test also included suggestions for avoiding errors in determining the total score and the scores for each of the subscales.

Scores are reported in raw score, percentiles, stanines, percentile ranges, and MCT scaled scores using the conversion Table (Table 2). Error scores are also reported in Table 2. In addition, percentile ranks by age group are provided in Table 3.

NORMS. The norming group was developed by sampling students and employment applicants from the United Kingdom ($n = 575$) and Australia ($n = 264$). It was noted by the authors that, because of the voluntary nature of the sample, the norms may not be a representative sample. The norming data for both sample groups were combined because a statistical analysis indicated that the level of difficulty for individual items was consistent between the two groups. Unfortunately, the difficulty indices for individual items were not included in the manual. Table 4 also includes the means, standard deviations, internal consistencies estimates, and standard errors of measurement of the norming group ($n = 839$) for the full test and subscales.

RELIABILITY. Evidence for reliability was reported by calculating the internal consistency estimates for the total test and the four subscales. The reliability coefficients ranged from .65 for the Handling Data subscale to a high of .94 for the total test. However, the manual does not describe which internal consistency method was used in calculating these coefficients. Standard errors were reported for the MCT and ranged from .95 for Handling Data to 2.55 for the total test.

No evidence of test-retest reliability is reported in the manual. Although the scoring key contains alternative correct answers that may be supplied by the examinee, scorers still must be able to recognize other correct responses. Therefore, evidence of scorer reliability is needed.

VALIDITY. Evidence of content validity was reported in the table of specifications (Table 1). This table contains information on the four content areas, the specific items included in each area, and the total number of items in each area.

Concurrent validity coefficient was reported as .80 by correlating the MCT with the ACER Test of Employment Entry Mathematics (TEEM). The tests were administered so that half of the group took the TEEM first and the other half took it second.

Test validation by means of interscale correlations was reported. The four subscales were correlated with each other and with the total test. Coefficients among the subscales ranged from .66 to .82 and from .84 to .96 between each subscale and the total test.

INTERPRETATION. A profile is provided on the back page of the test booklet to aid in the interpretation of test scores. Using the profile, information about an individual's total score and subscale scores can be easily obtained. The directions for interpreting the results are clearly written and the examples are straightforward.

The total score can be interpreted easily by completing the graph on the right side of the profile. When completed, this graph provides a shaded region representing a banded score based on the standard error of measurement for the total test. Using this banded score, one may compare the results of several individuals or the results of an individual who was retested. When the graphs are aligned, one can readily determine whether the shaded regions overlap or not. If they overlap, then one may assume that the level of mathematics skills is likely the same. Likewise, if they do not overlap, then the level of mathematics skills is most likely not the same. In addition, spaces are provided at the bottom of the profile for recording stanine, percentile rank, and percentile range scores for the total test.

To interpret the results of the four subscales, graphs representing each subscale are included on the profile. These graphs contain a list of the item numbers for each subscale arranged in order of difficulty. To complete these graphs, one needs to find the items missed on the test and mark them on the corresponding graph. Using these results, one may determine which mathematics skills need additional work.

SUMMARY. The MCT is designed to assess mathematics skills. Directions for administering, scoring, and interpreting the test are clearly presented in the manual and illustrated with easy-to-follow examples. The profiles provide useful information that can be used to determine math achievement as well as areas needing improvement. Although evidence of validity and reliability are reported, evidence of test-retest and scorer reliability are not. The MCT is a power test; however, no information is provided in the manual on the difficulty index of individual items. These concerns need to be considered before selecting this instrument.

Review of the Mathematics Competency Test by G. MICHAEL POTEAT, Associate Professor of Psychology, East Carolina University, Greenville, NC:

The Mathematics Competency Test (MCT) is a brief (46-item), group-administered, timed (30 minutes) instrument designed to measure the math skills of individuals from 11 years of age to adulthood. The test is designed as a measure that will allow: (a) the identification of individuals with ability or weakness in mathematical skills, (b) the identification of group strengths and weaknesses, (c) information to use in instructional planning, and (d) the development of a profile of individual math skills. The questions on the MCT are intended to measure four areas of mathematical skill: (a) Using and Applying Mathematics (12 items), (b) Number and Algebra Skills (20 items), (c) the Use of Shape and Space (8 items), and (d) the Ability to Handle Data (6 items). The MCT is recommended by the test developers for use in employment, school, and college settings.

An 8-page test booklet consists of a cover page, 6 pages of items, and a profile sheet. Simple instructions for administering the test are included in the 31-page user's manual. The 46 items are hand scored and a scoring key is included. A number of the items require responses that would not be amenable to the use of a multiple-choice format and the development of machine scoring would not appear to be practical. The MCT was developed and published in the United Kingdom and Australia, and several of the items would need modification to be used in the U.S. (e.g., the substitution of dollars for pounds). Inspection of the content of the items suggests the MCT covers material no more difficult than what would be taught in a typical high school general mathematics course in the U.S. Examples of two of the more difficult items are to compute the square of a decimal fraction and determine the hypotenuse of a right triangle—which requires computing the square root of a perfect square.

The profile sheet is used to plot raw scores for the total score and the four subscales. The number correct on each subscale corresponds to different heights on the profile bars because of the variation in the number of items between the subscales. The total test raw score can be converted to percentile ranks, stanines, and MCT scaled scores (which range from -5.2 to 4.97). Percentile ranks are also provided for the total score by 6-month intervals starting at 11 years, 6 months to 15 years, 11 months. MCT scaled scores are provided for the four subscales, but Shape and Space and Handling Data consist of so few items that the interpretation of the subscales is problematic.

Technically the MCT can be characterized as underdeveloped. Norms are based on samples of

575 subjects from the United Kingdom and 264 subjects from Australia. The reference group is otherwise not described and is not claimed to be representative. The manual addresses this weakness by making an argument for the use of the MCT as a measure of skill (i.e., as a criterion-referenced test). A measure of internal consistency reliability is provided for the total test (.94) and for each of the subscales. Handling Data, which consists of only six items, has a reported internal consistency value of .65 and a standard error of measurement of .95. The other three subscales have internal consistency coefficients of .78 (Using and Applying Mathematics), .89 (Number and Algebra), and .73 (Shape and Space). Content validity is addressed by stating that the items on the MCT are similar to items in other mathematics tests. Criterion-related validity is addressed by reporting a correlation of .80 between a short form of the ACER Test of Employment Entry Mathematics and the MCT. The administration of the two instruments was counterbalanced, but the number of subjects involved was not specified.

The MCT contains some interesting items and can be administered quickly by individuals with little training in testing. The scoring of responses and converting of raw score to percentile ranks should present no problem to anyone who has even minimal training in statistics or testing. However, the use of the MCT cannot be recommended. The norms are totally inadequate and the evidence for both content and criterion-related validity is extremely limited. The internal consistency reliability estimates for the total test and "number and algebra" subscale are adequate, but the other three subscales should only be interpreted with extreme caution. The use of the MCT scaled score is confusing, and the basis for its calculation is not clear. If the number of items on the MCT was increased and adequate norms developed, it might potentially provide useful information especially in the employment applications. In its present form it is inadequately developed and there are a number of other measures of mathematical ability that provide more reliable information. As a measure of mathematical competence, the MCT does provide some criterion-related information, but similar and more complete data could be obtained by developing a mathematics test based on any of a number of standard curricula.

[223]
Mathematics Self-Efficacy Scale.

Purpose: Intended to measure beliefs regarding ability to perform various math-related tasks and behaviors.
Population: College freshmen.
Publication Date: 1993.
Acronym: MSES.
Scores, 3: Mathematics Task Self-Efficacy, Math-Related School Subjects Self-Efficacy, Total Mathematics Self-Efficacy Score.
Administration: Group.
Forms, 2: A, B.
Price Data, 1998: $25 per sampler set including manual (22 pages); $100 per one-year permission to reproduce up to 200 administrations of the test.
Time: (15) minutes.
Authors: Nancy E. Betz and Gail Hackett.
Publisher: Mind Garden, Inc.
Cross References: See T5:1602 (1 reference).

Review of the Mathematics Self-Efficacy Scale by JOSEPH C. CIECHALSKI, Professor of Counselor and Adult Education, East Carolina University, Greenville, NC:

The Mathematics Self-Efficacy Scale (MSES) is designed to assess one's beliefs that he or she is capable of performing math-related tasks and behaviors. Although the manual indicates otherwise, there is only one form of the test. The MSES contains 34 items divided into two parts: Everyday Math Tasks (18 items) and Math-Related Courses (16 items).

In Part 1, examinees rate each item based on how much confidence they have in themselves to solve everyday math problems. Part 2 contains a list of 16 math-related courses that require examinees to rate the amount of confidence they have in completing the courses with a grade of "A" or "B."

Development of the MSES is extensive. The original instrument contained 75 items divided into three parts: math problems (18 items), math tasks (30 items), and a list of math-related college courses (27 items). An analysis of these items resulted in the development of the 1983 version. This version contained 52 items divided into three parts: Math Tasks (18 items), Math Problems (18 items), and Math-Related Courses (16 items). According to the manual, the 1993 version of the MSES retained only the Math Tasks and Math Problems subscales. However, in reviewing the test booklet, the two subscales that were actually retained were the Math Tasks and Math Courses.

ADMINISTRATION. The directions for administering the MSES are clearly written. A practice example is provided in Part 1 to ensure that the examinees understand how they are to respond to each item on the test. The test is not timed but should take no more than 15 minutes to administer. According to the manual, the MSES is designed to be used with an answer sheet; however, no answer sheet was included in the package. In reviewing the example in the test booklet, it appears that examinees are expected to respond to each item by circling their response in the test booklet.

Examinees rate each item based on a 10-point scale ranging from 0 to 9: *No Confidence at All* (0); *Very Little Confidence* (1–3); *Some Confidence* (4–5); *Much Confidence* (6–7); and *Complete Confidence* (8–9). Some examinees may have a problem in using this 10-point scale. For example, examinees who believe that they have "very little confidence" with a given math task may have difficulty deciding whether to rate their response a 1, 2, or 3. A 5-point scale may be sufficient.

SCORING. Scoring the MSES is easy. The MSES yields three subscale scores ranging from 0 to 162 (Math Tasks); 0 to 144 (College Courses); and 0 to 306 (Total score). Directions for obtaining average scores for each part and a total average score are described in detail. The total average score may be converted to percentiles using the conversion table (Table 2). According to the manual, the most useful score is the total average score.

NORMS. Table 1 includes the norming data developed from a 1983 sample population of undergraduates from the Ohio State University (*n* = 262). Norming data developed from a 1989 sample population of undergraduates from the University of Utah (*n* = 148) are also included in Table 1. No norming data are reported for the 1993 version of the MSES.

RELIABILITY. The authors report internal consistency reliability coefficients of .96 for the Total scale, and .92, .96, and .92 for the Math Tasks, Problems (no longer a part of the MSES), and Courses subscales respectively. In addition, coefficient alpha (.92) and test-retest reliability (2-week interval) (.94) are reported. However, all of the reliability estimates reported are for the 1983 version. No reliability coefficients are reported for the 1993 version.

VALIDITY. Evidence of content, concurrent, and construct validity coefficients are re-ported in the studies cited, but all are based on the 1983 version of the MSES. No validity coefficients are reported for the 1993 version.

INTERPRETATION. To interpret an individual's score, a table (Table 2) of percentile equivalents is used. Using this table, one can convert a person's total average score into percentile equivalents based on gender. The authors are careful to point out that these scores should not be overinterpreted due to significant gender differences regarding math self-efficacy. Again, the information contained in this table is based on the 1983 norming group. therefore, users of the 1993 version need to be extremely cautious when interpreting the results.

SUMMARY. It is evident that extensive research and effort went into the development of the MSES. Like the 1983 version, the 1993 MSES is theory based and easy to administer and score. Unfortunately, what is troublesome for this reviewer is that there are problems with some of the information contained in the manual. Almost all of the information contained in it refers to the 1983 version. For example, the manual indicates that there are two forms of the MSES (FORMS A & B) but only one form is available. The norms included in the manual are old and need to be revised for the 1993 version of the MSES. Validity and reliability coefficients are reported in the manual but are all based on the 1983 version. In addition, some information contained in the manual needs to be rewritten or corrected. Until these problems and concerns are corrected in the manual, the 1993 version of the MSES cannot be recommended for use.

Review of the Mathematics Self-Efficacy Scale by EVERETT V. SMITH JR., Assistant Professor of Educational Psychology, University of Illinois, Chicago, IL:

The Mathematics Self-Efficacy Scale (MSES) is intended to measure a person's beliefs in their ability to accomplish math tasks and related behaviors. The MSES consists of 34 self-report items answered on a 0 to 9 confidence scale with labels of *No Confidence at all* (0 on the response scale), *Very Little Confidence* (1, 2, or 3), *Some Confidence* (4 or 5), *Much Confidence* (6 or 7), and *Complete Confidence* (8 or 9). Modification of this 10-point response scale may be desirable as the current scale does not evenly distribute the rating points among the anchors. For example, there are 3 rating points to choose from for *Very Little Confidence*, 1 point for *No Confidence at all*, and 2 points for *Complete Confidence*. This distribution loads the response scale in favor of *Very Little Confidence*. In addition, if one can have more than one level of *Complete Confidence*, why not more than one level of *No Confidence at all*?

The first 18 items of the MSES are intended to measure Mathematics Task Self-Efficacy. Instructions ask participants to respond to the question "Please indicate how much confidence you have that you could *successfully* [emphasis added] accomplish each of these tasks by circling the number according to the following 10-point confidence scale." Examples of math tasks include "Determining the amount of sales tax on a clothing purchase" and "Calculating recipe quantities for a dinner for 3 when the original recipe is for 12 people." The remaining 16 items are intended to measure Math-Related School Subjects Self-Efficacy. Instructions ask participants to "Please rate the following college courses according to how much *confidence* [emphasis added] you have that you could complete the course with a *final grade* [emphasis added] of 'A' or 'B.' Circle your answer according to the 10-point scale below." Examples of math-related school subjects include Economics, Calculus, Accounting, and Biochemistry.

The MSES is easily administered to individuals or groups of participants. Completion time is estimated to take no longer than 15 minutes. Scoring for each dimension (Math Tasks and Math-Related School Subjects) follows the traditional summated rating scale technique in which the responses to the items corresponding to each dimension are summed and then divided by the number of items representing each dimension. The authors also suggest calculating an average score by summing the responses to all 34 items and dividing by 34. The justification provided in the manual for creating an average total score is that "The most useful score is the Total Mathematics Self-Efficacy Scale score ... because it includes both types of item content" (manual, p. 11). Implicit in the creation of this average total score is the notion that both scales measure the same construct. However, no empirical evidence (a simple correlation would suffice) is provided to justify combining the two scales to form a single

scale. In addition, no evidence is provided to support the statement that the average total score is the most useful of the three scores. Until such evidence is accumulated, it is recommended that the two scale scores be used as two indicators of mathematics self-efficacy. With respect to missing data, the authors suggest that if less than four responses are omitted, then simply sum the responses to the items that were completed and divide by the number of items completed to arrive at a scale score. If four or more responses are omitted, the authors claim the scores can no longer be considered valid.

Evidence for the reliability of the scores consists of estimates of internal consistency and test-retest coefficients. Across studies the internal consistency estimates were all above .90 for the original three scales (discussed below) and the total scale. A modified version of the Math-Related School Subjects scale had a 2-week test-retest coefficient of .94. A Japanese version had test-retest coefficients (4-week interval) of .68, .72, and .75 for the Math Tasks, Math Problems, and Math-Related School Subjects scales, respectively. A significant omission is information regarding the standard error of measurement, which would be essential for interpreting individual scores.

Validity evidence is reported in the traditional content, concurrent, and construct validity paradigm. The content of the original MSES was based on a review of existing measures of mathematics anxiety and confidence. From this review three domains were identified: solving math problems, math behaviors in everyday life, and college math-related courses. Seventy-five items were generated for these three domains by adapting items from existing measures, using examples of math tasks generated by students, and using courses perceived by college students as requiring a math background and knowledge. Using data from 115 undergraduates, the authors used traditional item discrimination and internal consistency indices as well as item difficulty ratings provided by the students and an examination of item content to reduce the total item pool to 52. The manual elaborates only on the Math Tasks and Math-Related School Subjects scales. The Math Problems scale was dropped from this version for "ease of administration and simplicity of instructions" (manual, p. 9). Evidence for concurrent validity is supported using correlations with other measures of attitude toward mathematics. Specifically, the MSES Total score was found to be correlated with math anxiety ($r = .56$; because this correlation is positive, it is assumed that higher scores on the math anxiety measure indicate lower levels of anxiety as self-efficacy and anxiety are hypothesized to be inversely related), confidence in doing math ($r = .66$), perceived usefulness of math ($r = .47$), and effectance motivation in math ($r = .46$) (Betz & Hackett, 1983). Studies have also found that math self-efficacy contributes to the selection of science-based college majors, perceived math- and nonmath-related career options, and to the prediction of mathematics performance. Construct validity evidence is supported using the "known" groups technique. The authors hypothesized that because math has traditionally been a male domain, females would report lower levels of math self-efficacy. These hypothesized relationships have been demonstrated in a number of studies (Betz & Hackett, 1983; Lapan, Boggs, & Morrill, 1989) for all three of the original scales as well as the total scale score. It is noted that these differences may exist as the result of females having fewer mathematics courses.

Normative data were obtained on samples of undergraduates (predominantly freshman) from two research universities. A series of studies conducted comparing males and females at each university on the Math Tasks, Math-Related School Subjects, and average Total scores indicated statistically significant differences on all three scores, with males demonstrating higher levels of self-efficacy. Score interpretation is facilitated by a table of approximate percentile equivalents based on the average Total scores. These percentiles are provided for each gender and are derived from an averaging of the average total scores and standard deviations from the two samples. With the samples being drawn from two large research universities and the intended population being college freshman, the representativeness of the normative sample may not be adequate. Potential users of the MSES may wish to develop local norms.

The manual recommends that the MSES be used to help investigate problems associated with low math self-efficacy and the related math avoidance and approach behaviors with respect to the pursuit of careers in science and engineering by women and minorities. The manual also suggests that the MSES may be used to help identify students in need of an "efficacy" intervention with treatment focusing on the four influences on self-efficacy (i.e., performance accomplishments, vicarious learning, verbal persuasion, and emotional arousal).

The manual itself contains several typographical errors and oversights, making for difficult and frustrating reading. For example, the cover of the manual, the Table of Contents, the test booklet, and the scoring guide indicate that two forms of the MSES exist. However, this reviewer found no evidence of a second version. Other minor typographical errors or oversights include incorrect page numbering in the Table of Contents, incorrectly stating the number of items per scale at various points in the manual, stating that the Math Problems scale was retained for this version when in fact the Math-Related School Subjects scale was retained, an incorrect spelling of an author's name, the failure to create separate headings for the evidence of concurrent and construct validity (the manual lists the evidence of content, concurrent, and construct validity all under the heading of Content Validity), and the unusual practice of citing Table 2 prior to citing Table 1. For those wishing to pursue the topic of mathematics self-efficacy further, the list of references may also prove problematic. More than 10 citations in the manual had no corresponding entry in the Reference section.

In conclusion, the MSES has made an important contribution toward the measurement of mathematics self-efficacy. It is a simple and short assessment that may be used for research, assessment, and intervention purposes. It is recommended that future versions of the MSES include a more representative norming sample, additional psychometric studies investigating the dimensionality of the responses, and attention to the other recommendations mentioned in this review.

REVIEWER'S REFERENCES
Betz, N. E., & Hackett, G. (1983). The relationship of mathematics self-efficacy expectations to the selection of science-based college majors. *Journal of Vocational Behavior, 23,* 329–345.
Lapan, R. T., Boggs, K. R., & Morrill, W. H. (1989). Self-efficacy as a mediator of Investigative and Realistic General Occupational Themes on the Strong Interest Inventory. *Journal of Counseling Psychology, 36,* 176–182.

[224]
Mather-Woodcock Group Writing Tests.
Purpose: "Designed for early identification of problems/weaknesses, measurement of growth in writing skills, instructional planning, and curriculum evaluation."

Population: Grades 2.0–16.9.
Publication Date: 1997.
Acronym: GWT.
Scores: 3 clusters (Total Writing, Basic Writing Skills, Expressive Writing Ability), and 4 subtests (Dictation Spelling, Writing Samples, Editing, Writing Fluency).
Administration: Group.
Price Data, 2001: $185 per package including 25 student booklets, administration directions, scoring key, 25 writing evaluation scales, GWT manual ('97, 96 pages), and scoring disk (specify Basic, Intermediate or Advanced package, and specify Windows or Macintosh); $72 per 25 writing booklets (specify Basic, Intermediate or Advanced).
Time: (60) minutes or less.
Authors: Nancy Mather and Richard W. Woodcock.
Publisher: Riverside Publishing.

Review of the Mather-Woodcock Group Writing Tests by BRUCE THOMPSON, Professor and Distinguished Research Scholar, Department of Educational Psychology, Texas A&M University, and Adjunct Professor of Community Medicine, Baylor College of Medicine, College Station, TX:

The Mather-Woodcock Group Writing Tests (GWT) are an adaptation of the individually administered Woodcock-Johnson Psycho-Educational Battery—Revised (WJ-R; T5:2901) writing tests. However, although items from both measures are similar in format, all GWT items are new. The manual asserts that the GWT provides "both norm-referenced and criterion-referenced information about several facets of writing skill, including basic writing skills and expressive writing" (p. 5). The tests can be administered in about one hour. The GWT measures six aspects of writing skills: punctuation, capitalization, spelling, usage, writing fluency, and quality of written expression.

The GWT is intended to facilitate the early diagnosis of writing problems, measurement of writing skill growth, design of instructional programs, and program evaluation. Three forms are available: Basic (Grades 2 to 3), Intermediate (Grades 4 to 7), and Advanced (Grades 8 to 16). However, the measure may be administered to adults as well, by selecting the form and levels best matching estimated educational achievement.

Within each of the three forms from one to three different levels of the tests are available, depending upon the test area and form. For example, for the Basic form (Grades 2 to 3) there are three different test levels available for measuring Dictation Spelling. However, for the Advanced form (Grades 8 to 16) there is only one test level available for Writing Samples.

The GWT provides a total writing score representing an overall measure of writing proficiency that is a combined measure of all four subtests. A basic writing skill score is also provided that evaluates spelling and editing skills. And an expressive writing skills score is provided as a measure of ability to produce sentences.

Scores of various types are provided. Examples of the more conventional scores that are available include raw, age equivalent, grade equivalent, standard scores, and percentile ranks. An "instructional zone" score is also available, which might indicate, for example, that a student in the eighth month of the fifth grade has writing skills comparable to those of the average student in the third grade and can perform writing tasks below the Grade 2.3 level quite easily but would find tasks above the Grade 3.8 level quite difficult. Obviously this "instructional zone" score would be quite useful in designing instructional activities.

During the test development process, the GWT items were statistically linked to the difficulty scale underlying the WJ-R item pool. This was done by having participants complete the new GWT items and 15 to 20 linking items from the WJ-R item pool and then using one-parameter Rasch modeling procedures. Some have questioned the appropriateness of the Rasch model (cf. Fan, 1998) as opposed to more classical measurement procedures. Nevertheless, this strategy made group GWT results more directly comparable with those likely to be provided by individually administered WJ-R assessments.

The normative sample included 3,345 participants aged 6 to 18 years, and 2,135 participants aged 19 to 90 years. More than 100 diverse communities from various regions of the United States were represented in the sample. A comparison of the sample with a U.S. Census profile suggests a close SES match with education, household income, and employment and occupational status.

STATISTICAL CHARACTERISTICS. Score reliabilities were evaluated using split-half coefficients corrected by the Spearman-Brown formula. Most of these reliabilities were in the high .80s or the .90s.

However, for some reason coefficients were only provided for a subset of age groups from the normative sample. Additionally, it is unclear why for these analyses the sample sizes within age groups fluctuated for different skill scores. For example, the sample size for the dictation spelling coefficient for 20- to 29-year-olds was 713, but for the same age group the sample size for the coefficient for the total writing scores was 334.

Several sets of validity studies are presented in the manual. The concurrent validity studies involved 72, 51, and 29 participants, and 4, 4, or 1 other test batteries, respectively. Another study was characterized as a "construct validity" report and involved merely presenting intercorrelations among scores on the GWT scales.

The correlations reported in this "construct validity" study were all quite large. For example, for 10-year-olds the correlations ranged from .58 to .97. Such large correlations raise the question of whether discrete scores, as opposed to a single generic score, are appropriate.

SUMMARY. The GWT is useful for a wide range of age and ability levels. The measure has been carefully normed. The reliabilities of GWT scores tend to be high. However, additional validity studies are certainly necessary if users are to be confident in the integrity of GWT scores. In the final analysis, scores that are reliable but not valid are of little if any utility. However, additional validity studies are likely forthcoming.

REVIEWER'S REFERENCE

Fan, X. (1998). Item Response Theory and classical test theory: An empirical comparison of their item/person statistics. *Educational and Psychological Measurement, 58*, 357–381.

[225]

The MbM Questionnaire: Managing by Motivation, Third Edition.

Purpose: Designed for "helping managers understand their own needs" … and "to identify the needs of their employees."
Population: Managers and supervisors.
Publication Dates: 1986–1996.
Acronym: The MbM Questionnaire.
Scores: 4 scales: Safety/Security, Social/Belonging, Self-Esteem, Self-Actualization.
Administration: Group.
Price Data: Available from publisher.
Time: (10) minutes.
Author: Marshall Sashkin.
Publisher: Human Resource Development Press.

Review of The MbM Questionnaire: Managing by Motivation, Third Edition by JOHN W. FLEENOR, Director of Knowledge Management, Center for Creative Leadership, Greensboro, NC:

Based on Maslow's (1943) classic theory of motivation, the MbM Questionnaire: Managing by Motivation (MbM) is designed to increase the effectiveness of managers by improving their motivational skills. The MbM provides scores on four scales representing Maslow's hierarchy of needs—Security, Social, Self-Esteem, and Self-Actualization. Security includes safety and survival needs, Social includes the need for belonging, Self-Esteem includes the need for interpersonal relationships, and Self-Actualization includes the need for self-development. The instrument is intended to help managers understand their own motivations, as well as their employees' motivations, related to job performance. According to the author, the MbM encourages managers to focus on the intrinsic motivators of their employees, rather than on external motivators that are less relevant.

The first edition of the MbM was developed for training purposes in 1985; the second edition was published in 1990. The third edition of the MbM which includes revised scoring and interpretive material, was published in 1996. A form was included in the third edition on which respondents can plot and visually compare their scale scores. Additionally, the discussion of the underlying theories of motivation was expanded in the third edition.

The MbM is a 20-item questionnaire that can be completed and self-scored in 10–15 minutes. Directions for scoring and brief interpretive materials are included in the test booklet. On the instrument, respondents indicate the extent to which they agree or disagree with each item (e.g., "Chasing after dreams is a waste of time"). According to the author, the MbM is primarily a tool for increasing self-understanding; therefore, there are no right or wrong answers.

MANUAL. A 24-page trainer's guide includes a summary of theories of motivation, suggestions for workshop design, norms, technical information, and references.

ADMINISTRATION AND SCORING. The instrument is self-scored. Directions instruct test-takers on how to convert their responses to numerical scores. One score is calculated for each of the four needs (Security, Social, Self-Esteem, and Self-Actualization). There are five items on each scale; possible scores range from 5 to 25.

NORMS. Norms are available for the scores on each need. Normative data are presented for five samples: Managers ($n = 46$), team leaders ($n = 30$), retail store managers ($n = 54$), MBA students ($n = 13$), and sales clerks ($n = 188$).

RELIABILITY. According to the manual, interitem correlations were calculated using a large dataset during the second revision of the MbM. Items that did not correlate highly with others on the same scales were revised. Although scale reliabilities are alluded to in the manual, no reliability data are reported for the instrument.

VALIDITY. The manual indicates that construct validity of the scale scores was investigated using factor analyses. Eight factors were identified which were combined to form the four dimensions of Maslow's (1943) model; however, no further description of the factor structure is presented. The manual states that the result of this analysis "does not mean that The MbM Questionnaire accurately measures an individual's motivational state or that the questionnaire accurately predicts individuals' behaviors" (p. 5). The primary purpose of the instrument, therefore, is to acquaint managers with the basic concepts of work motivation, rather than attempting to measure the levels of motivation present in the respondents.

SUMMARY. The MbM is a fairly engaging presentation of Maslow's (1943) hierarchy which can be used to provide managers with a hands-on technique for understanding work motivation. It shows some promise as a training tool to increase managers' self-insights in areas related to motivation. The author clearly states that the MbM has not been validated as a measure of work motivation, and he presents no reliability or validity data for the instrument. Additionally, the norms for the MbM are based on small samples and are probably not representative of the population of test-takers. The norms, therefore, should be used with caution. In summary, the instrument was not developed, nor is it recommended, for use as a measure of individual differences in levels of motivation.

REVIEWER'S REFERENCE

Maslow, A. (1943). A theory of human motivation. *Psychological Review, 50,* 370–396.

Review of The MbM Questionnaire: Managing by Motivation, Third Edition by ROBERT K. GABLE, Professor of Educational Psychology, and Associate Director, Bureau of Educational Research and Service, University of Connecticut, Storrs, CT:

The Managing by Motivation (MbM) self-report questionnaire is based on Maslow's Need Hierarchy and Herzberg's Motivator-Hygiene theories. The 20-item questionnaire purports to assess four dimensions, each with five items. An atypical 5-point Likert scale is employed and contains four gradations of agree and one disagree option (*Agree Completely, Agree Mostly, Agree Partly, Agree Slightly, Do Not Agree*). Although the four "agree" labels appear to represent a continuum, no empirical evidence or discussion is offered to support the use of the rating format. It may be that previous pilots of traditionally balanced "disagree-agree" formats resulted in extremely skewed distributions favoring the "agree" option. Item response theory assessment of the accuracy of these multi-step response options is necessary before this format can be supported.

ADMINISTRATION. The author's suggestion that The MbM Questionnaire can be group administered in 10 minutes is appropriate.

VALIDITY. Although not labeled as such, the content validity of The MbM Questionnaire is well supported through discussions of the Maslow and Herzberg theories. In addition to brief literature reviews, the Trainer Guide provides a content analysis/rationale for each item-dimension assignment. Unfortunately, the Technical Considerations section contains no empirical evidence of construct validity. The statement "The technical development of this instrument has demonstrated ... the validity of the constructs, the basic ideas of the dimensions (as shown by the factor analyses)" (p. 5) does not meet the *Standards for Educational and Psychological Testing* (APA, AERA, NCME, 1985). Readers need access to exploratory or confirmatory factor analytic studies that support this statement. The author's statement that "The purpose of this instrument is to teach people, especially managers, some basic concepts of human work motivation" (p. 5) does not preclude the inclusion of empirical support for the constructs underlying meaningful score interpretations.

Five of the 20 items are negative statements (e.g., "Job security is not especially important to me"). Given the confirmatory factor analysis (Pilotte & Gable, 1990) and item response theory (Wright & Masters, 1982) research on the use of positive/negative item stems, the inclusion of some "reversed scored" items is an empirically unsupported approach to instrument development. It could be that the positive and negative items access different aspects of the targeted affective constructs.

RELIABILITY. The earlier reference to technical development demonstrating "a degree of scale reliability (as shown by intercorrelations)" (p. 5) is not adequate. Item analysis and scale level alpha internal consistency and possibly stability reliabilities are necessary before users can be confident that The MbM Questionnaire provides accurate assessments. Following the statement regarding reliability and validity (p. 5) the author states: "This does not mean that the MbM accurately measures an individual's motivational state or that the questionnaire accurately predicts individual's behaviors" (p. 5). Again, we note that stating that "the purpose of the instrument is to teach people ... basic concepts of human work motivation" (p. 5) does not excuse the author from following the *Standards* by providing users with empirical evidence of reliability and validity to allow accurate and meaningful score interpretations.

SCORING AND SCORE INTERPRETATION. The MbM Questionnaire booklet contains an easily used scoring grid to facilitate hand scoring. The scores can then be plotted on a chart for comparison with some small norm groups (e.g., MBA students, $N = 46$; retail store managers, $N = 54$; female retail sales personnel—national cosmetics firm, $N = 188$). The Trainer's Guide presents scale-level means and standard deviations for five such groups. The Guide also contains a form for respondents to indicate expected and actual scores. A well-done interpretive guide section is also included based on Maslow's and Herzberg's theories.

SUMMARY. The MbM Questionnaire is clearly designed to introduce basic concepts of motivation during leadership training seminars. Although the questionnaire is based on well-documented theories of motivation, the materials available lack any empirical evidence of construct validity and reliability. Without the empirical information required by the *Standards for Educational and Psychological Testing* (AERA, APA, & NCME, 1985), it is unclear if the data obtained provide valid interpretations. Unfortunately, several users will ignore the lack of validity and reliability data and assume their score interpretations are meaningful and accurate, but the jury is still out.

REVIEWER'S REFERENCES

Wright, B. D., & Masters, G. N. (1982). *Rating scale analysis.* Chicago: Mesa Press.

American Educational Research Association, American Psychological Association, & National Council on Measurement in Education. (1985). *Standards for educational and psychological testing.* Washington, DC: American Psychological Association, Inc.

Pilotte, W. J., & Gable, R. K. (1990). The impact of positive and negative item stems on the validity of a computer anxiety scale. *Educational and Psychological Measurement, 50,* 603–610.

[226]
McDowell Vision Screening Kit.

Purpose: "Designed for screening children's vision problems."
Population: Birth to age 21.
Publication Date: 1994.
Scores, 15: Distance Vision, Near Point Vision, Ocular Alignment/Motility (Cover/Uncover, Light Reflex), Color Perception, Ocular Function (Pupils, Scanning, Shifts Attention, Blink, Tracking, Convergence, Conjugate Gaze, Visual Fields, Distant/Near Accommodation, Nystagmus).
Administration: Individual.
Price Data, 1999: $115 per kit including all test materials, 100 recording forms, and manual (40 pages); $19.50 per 100 recording forms; $38 per manual.
Time: (10–20) minutes.
Comments: Recording form for use in screening young children or disabled students; administrator scored.
Authors: P. Marlene McDowell and Richard L. McDowell.
Publisher: Western Psychological Services.

Review of the McDowell Vision Screening Kit by CYNTHIA A. ROHRBECK, Associate Professor of Psychology, The George Washington University, Washington, DC:

The McDowell Vision Screening Kit is designed to screen for vision problems in children with behavioral or mental problems who cannot complete more conventional screeners. It assesses for visual acuity (distance vision), near point acuity (near vision), eye alignment and motility, color vision, and "ocular function" (e.g., tracking, blink reflex, etc.). The manual notes that children who might easily be distracted or become disengaged with traditional vision tests will, in most cases, be able to complete the McDowell Vision Screening. This screener takes 10–20 minutes to complete and has a simple "pass/fail" scoring system. It should be noted (and the manual stresses this point) that the McDowell Vision Screening Kit should only be used to identify vision problems that require further evaluation by eye care specialists; it should not be used to make diagnostic decisions.

The manual provides detailed descriptions of how the testing situation should be set up, which should help examiners to follow a standardized procedure. Suggestions are given for helping young and/or disabled children cope with the assessment. The kit includes the necessary manipulatives for all screening procedures, such as penlights, plastic animals, bright colored blocks, etc. These items would probably be familiar and appealing to most children. Several case studies provide guidelines for use of the tests and interpretation of test results.

With regard to content validity, the McDowell does not attempt to screen for all possible visual problems, but does include several common visual problems that can often be identified in a brief screening procedure. In brief, distance vision is screened by observation of the child's ability to track stimuli (red "pom-pom" balls in Snellen equivalent sizes). Near vision is screened by observation of the child's ability to position his or her finger on black dots (standard Snellen equivalents) on white cards 15 inches away. Ocular alignment and motility are screened by covering and uncovering each eye while the child is focusing on an interesting toy placed at various distances. Pupillary light reflex is assessed by shining a small penlight in the eye and observing the position of the light reflection in the pupil. To assess color perception, the child is asked to match blocks of the same color. Although, according to the manual, standardized tests do not exist for assessment of "ocular function," the McDowell includes procedures to check for additional abilities, such as pupil accommodation, scanning ability, shifts of attention, blink reflex, tracking, etc.

The McDowell Vision Screening Kit's test-retest reliability and concurrent validity evidence was gathered with a sample of 181 developmentally disabled preschoolers from Albuquerque's public school districts. A subsample ($n = 34$) completed the screening twice, after a one-week delay. Test-retest reliability coefficients ranged from .89 to 1.00. For the entire sample, the correlation between scores from the McDowell's distance vision screening with standard distance vision screening (either HOTV or Goodlite Symbol 10-foot chart) was .90. The McDowell's near point screening procedure correlated .93 with standard near point vision screening (the HOTV or Goodlite symbol near point cards). It should be noted that less than 2% of participants failed to complete this McDowell screening procedure, and that 10% were unable to complete the standard near point screening test. Standard tests of ocular

alignment (Random Dot E or the Titmus fly test, the Cover-Uncover test, and the Pupillary Light Reflex test) showed a perfect correlation with the McDowell alignment screener. In addition, all subjects were able to complete that screening procedure, whereas 11% failed to complete the standard test. There was also a perfect correlation between results on the McDowell test for color vision and the standard test (Ishihara color vision plates). Many subjects (44%) were unable to complete the standard test in this case, whereas only 6% failed to complete the McDowell color vision procedure.

It should be noted that in this subsample, 17% of children were found to have some type of vision deficit. Half of those subjects were already under the care of an eye care specialist, the remaining half were referred ($n = 16$). Eye care specialists' reports were returned for 10 of those subjects, which generally confirmed the referral vision problems; intervention was needed in 5 of the 10 cases. Although promising, further evidence is needed to support McDowell's predictive validity.

SUMMARY. The McDowell Vision Screening Kit was designed to provide an easy-to-administer and easy-to-complete vision screener for young or disabled children. It has preliminary evidence of test-retest reliability and concurrent validity with other visual screeners. In addition, more children appear able to complete the McDowell screening tests compared to standard vision screening tests. Further research is needed to provide support for the McDowell Vision Screening Kit's predictive validity. Finally, nationally representative norms are not available for this measure and further research is needed to support its generalizability.

[227]
The McGill Pain Questionnaire.

Purpose: Designed to locate and specify the qualities of pain and to measure all dimensions of pain meaningful to patients.
Population: People in pain.
Publication Date: 1975.
Acronym: MPQ.
Scores, 4: Sensory, Affective, Evaluative, Miscellaneous.
Administration: Individual.
Manual: No manual.
Price Data, 1998: $.10 per copy and/or per use.
Time: (5–10) minutes.
Comments: Instructions for the pain questionnaire may be obtained from the publisher.

Author: Ronald Melzack.
Publisher: International Association for the Study of Pain.
Cross References: See T5:1615 (1 reference).

Review of The McGill Pain Questionnaire by GREGORY J. BOYLE, Professor of Psychology, Bond University, Gold Coast, Queensland, and Visiting Professor, Department of Psychiatry, University of Queensland, Royal Brisbane Hospital, Hesston, Australia:

The McGill Pain Questionnaire or MPQ (see Melzack, 1985; Melzack & Katz, 1992) is a multidimensional 84-item self-report questionnaire intended for the psychometric assessment of pain syndromes. The MPQ (now a quarter century in existence) is the most frequently used and most highly cited pain assessment instrument worldwide. Indicative of its enormous popularity is the fact that it has been translated into numerous different/diverse languages. The MPQ instrument contains 20 separate subcategories of verbal (single-word) pain descriptors. These subcategories are assigned to Sensory, Affective, and Evaluative domains respectively, with a further grouping of four miscellaneous subcategories. Word descriptors of pain are ranked according to intensity within each subcategory. A Present Pain Index (PPI) measures overall pain intensity (based on six descriptors only). Testing time ranges initially from 15–20 minutes, down to only 5–10 minutes on retest. A short-form (MPQ-SF) consists of only 15 (11 Sensory, 4 Affective) descriptor subcategories (Melzack, 1987), and includes the PPI and Visual Analogue Scale (VAS) measures of pain intensity.

Nevertheless, and despite its international popularity, scoring systems for the MPQ remain psychometrically complicated, raising ongoing doubts about the reliability of subcategory scores (Bernt, 1991). Subcategories include widely differing numbers of pain descriptors (ranging from two to six descriptor words each), thereby accounting for greatly discrepant proportions of variance, and preventing direct comparison between subcategory scores. In addition, the number of subcategories allocated to each domain differs widely—Sensory (10), Affective (5), and Evaluative (1). Consequently, in comparison with the Sensory domain, the proportion of variance accounted for by the Affective domain is only 50%, whereas for the Evaluative domain a mere 10% of variance is measured. Recourse to sophisticated

scoring systems (e.g., Deschamps, Band, & Coldman, 1988) has not overcome these problematic psychometric complexities (Jensen, Karoly, O'Riordan, Bland, & Burns, 1989) brought about by the structural composition and design of the MPQ instrument itself.

In regard to concurrent validity, MPQ and VAS correlations can sometimes be inconsistent, suggesting that MPQ psychometric properties may vary for different subgroups of pain patients (Bernt, 1991). Irrespective of concurrent validity though, the discriminative and predictive validity of the MPQ instrument remains less than optimal. Some MPQ word descriptors (e.g., *lancinating* and *rasping* are not easily understood by the average pain patient, and others are ambiguous in that they describe multiple qualities of pain (e.g., *flashing* pertains to brightness as well as frequency) yet are confined to single subcategories in the MPQ (Fernandez & Towery, 1996). Consequently, MPQ descriptor words selected by pain patients are seldom clearly suggestive of particular pain syndromes. In a similar vein, Wilkie, Savedra, Holemer, Tesler, and Paul (1990) reported that most pain patients designate only a minority of MPQ descriptor words. On logical grounds alone, Hase (1992) has suggested an extensive reclassification of many of the MPQ descriptors among subcategories, which seems compelling. Likewise, Clark, Fletcher, Janal, and Carroll (1995), on the basis of a hierarchical clustering analysis, have proposed an extensive reclassification of MPQ descriptors.

In addition, the construct validity of the MPQ has been drawn into question. For example, Jerome, Holroyd, Theofanous, Pingel, Lake, and Saper (1988) concluded that reliance on only the tripartite (Sensory, Affective, and Evaluative) domains may lead to loss of diagnostic information due to restriction of variance associated with possible underfactoring. On the other hand, using a confirmatory factor analytic approach, Turk, Rudy, and Salovey (1985) reported that the tripartite structure of the MPQ was in doubt, due to excessive overlap among the factors. Evidently, the MPQ factor structure still remains somewhat uncertain, as many exploratory factor analytic studies involving the instrument have been flawed by insufficient sample sizes, and reliance on less than optimal and/or inappropriate methodology (see Fernandez & Turk, 1992; Holroyd et al., 1992).

In regard to reliability, a study by Graham, Bond, Gerkovish, and Cook (1980) showed that the consistency of choice of pain descriptor subcategories ranged from 66% to 80% over four administrations of the MPQ in cancer outpatients. Although there is clearly some consistency in choice of verbal descriptors, immediate test-retest correlations (dependability coefficients— because the MPQ is a state measure) are not reported, and consequently the reliability of subcategories remains unknown. Also, there is no indication of item homogeneity of subcategories, leaving doubts about internal consistency versus item redundancy (cf. Boyle, 1987, 1991). Motivational distortion (e.g., inconsistent responding, faking good, faking bad, and other response sets) is not addressed, making determination of invalid profiles especially difficult. Absence of a comprehensive, up-to-date test manual is a severe limitation that could very easily be rectified, as empirical research findings involving the MPQ, which have accumulated over the last three decades, are now considerable.

SUMMARY. Clearly, the MPQ instrument does appear to make a unique contribution to pain assessment, using the language of pain to describe perceived pain intensity as well as different perceived qualities of pain (Melzack, 1985; Melzack & Katz, 1992). Although the MPQ instrument includes relatively current terminology, and avoids colloquial or slang expressions, it is nevertheless apparent that some of its descriptor words warrant exclusion, that others need to be recategorized, and that some of the subcategories need to be relabelled (Fernandez & Towery, 1996). It is now evident from the empirical research findings that considerable refinement of the MPQ psychometric structure and properties is urgently needed, as originally called for by the test author. Particular emphasis might be paid to issues of discriminative and predictive validity. In view of its great popularity within both the medical and psychological professions worldwide, it is to be hoped that revisions to the structure of the MPQ instrument will soon be forthcoming.

REVIEWER'S REFERENCES

Graham, C., Bond, S. S., Gerkovish, M. M., & Cook, M. R. (1980). Use of the McGill Pain Questionnaire in the assessment of cancer pain: Replicability and consistency. *Pain, 8,* 377–387.

Melzack, R. (1985). Discriminative capacity of the McGill Pain Questionnaire. *Pain, 23,* 201–203.

Turk, D. C., Rudy, T. E., & Salovey, P. (1985). The McGill Pain Questionnaire reconsidered: Confirming the factor structure and examining appropriate uses. *Pain, 21,* 385–397.

Boyle, G. J. (1987). Review of the (1985) "Standards for educational and psychological testing: AERA, APA, & NCME." *Australian Journal of Psychology, 39,* 235–237.

Melzack, R. (1987). The short-form McGill Pain Questionnaire. *Pain, 30,* 191–197.

Deschamps, M., Band, P. R., & Coldman, A. J. (1988). Assessment of adult cancer pain: Assessment of current methods. *Pain, 32,* 133–139.

Jerome, A., Holroyd, K. A., Theofanous, A. G., Pingel, J. D., Lake, A. E., & Saper, J. R. (1988). Cluster headache pain vs. other vascular headache pain: Differences revealed with two approaches to the McGill Pain Questionnaire. *Pain, 34,* 35–42.

Jensen, M. P., Karoly, P., O'Riordan, E. F., Bland, F., Jr., & Burns, R. S. (1989). The subjective experience of acute pain: An assessment of the utility of 10 indices. *Clinical Journal of Pain, 5,* 153–159.

Wilkie, D. J., Savedra, M. C., Holemer, W. L., Tesler, M. D., & Paul, S. M. (1990). Use of the McGill Pain Questionnaire to measure pain: A meta-analysis. *Nursing Research, 39,* 36–41.

Bernt, F. M. (1991). Review of the McGill Pain Questionnaire. *Test Critiques, 8,* 402–412.

Boyle, G. J. (1991). Does item homogeneity indicate internal consistency or item redundancy in psychometric scales? *Personality and Individual Differences, 12,* 291–294.

Fernandez, E., & Turk, D. C. (1992). Sensory and affective components of pain: Separation and synthesis. *Psychological Bulletin, 112,* 205–217.

Hase, H. D. (1991). McGill Pain Questionnaire: Revised format. In L. VandeCreek, S. Knapp, and T. L. Jackson (Eds.), *Innovations in clinical practice: A source book* (vol. 11; pp. 285–291). Sarasota, FL: Professional Resource Press.

Holroyd, K. A., Holm, J. E., Keefe, F. J., Turner, J. A., Bradley, L. A., Murphy, W. D., Johnson, P., Anderson, K., Hinkle, A. L., & O'Malley, W. B. (1992). A multi-center evaluation of the McGill Pain Questionnaire: Results from more than 1700 chronic pain patients. *Pain, 48,* 301–311.

Melzack, R., & Katz, J. (1992). The McGill Pain Questionnaire: Appraisal and current status. In D. G. Turk & R. Melzack (Eds.), *Handbook of pain assessment* (pp. 152–168). New York: Guilford.

Clark, W. C., Fletcher, J. D., Janal, M. N., & Carroll, J. D. (1995). Hierarchical clustering of pain and emotion descriptors: Toward a revision of the McGill Pain Questionnaire. In B. Bromm & J. Desmedt (Eds.), *Pain and the brain: From nociception to cortical activity* (pp. 319–330). New York: Raven.

Fernandez, E., & Towery, S. (1996). A parsimonious set of verbal descriptors of pain sensation derived from the McGill Pain Questionnaire. *Pain, 66,* 31–37.

Review of The McGill Pain Questionnaire by EPHREM FERNANDEZ, *Associate Professor of Clinical Psychology, Southern Methodist University, Dallas, TX:*

At its birth, the McGill Pain Questionnaire (Melzack, 1975) became the first systematic attempt to organize the (English) vocabulary of pain into an instrument for measurement and diagnosis of pain. Now in its 25th anniversary, the McGill Pain Questionnaire (MPQ) has become the most widely cited instrument in pain research (approximately 1,000 citations in MEDLINE). It is possibly the most widely used pain assessment questionnaire, having also been translated into 15 languages ranging from Japanese to Portuguese.

The core of the MPQ is a list of 78 single-word descriptors of pain distributed across the Sensory, Affective, and Evaluative domains, plus another six words for present pain intensity. Within the Sensory domain are 10 subcategories capturing various sensory qualities of pain: dullness, brightness, coldness, hotness, traction, constrictive pressure, incisive pressure, punctuate pressure, spatial, and temporal. Within the Affective domain are four subcategories related to emotion: tension, autonomic, fear, and punishment, and within the single Evaluative category are words describing the intensity of pain. These are supplemented by four miscellaneous subcategories of words. Each word has a place in one of the above subcategories and an intensity value and intensity rank relative to other words in that subcategory. For example, the word "burning" is in the hotness subcategory and has an intensity value of 2.95 on an interval scale of 1–5, and a rank of 2 because it is the second least intense of four words in the hotness group. On the other hand, the word "terrifying" is in the fear subcategory and has an intensity value of 3.95 on the 5-point scale and a rank of 3 because it is the highest in implied intensity among three words in that subgroup. By simply summing the intensity values or ranks of words selected in the appropriate categories, a quantitative index can be obtained of a person's pain sensation, pain-related affect, and pain as a whole. One caveat is that rank values are confounded by the unequal numbers of words in each subcategory. Therefore, different scoring methods have been adopted including the use of a visual analogue scale rating of each descriptor (Charter & Nehemkis, 1993), a ratio of the rank score to the maximum rank score of that subcategory (Deschamps, Band, & Coldman, 1988), and weighting of the ranks by a correction factor (Melzack, Katz, & Jeans, 1985). Subcategory scores are then summed to yield category scores for Sensory, Affective, and Evaluative dimensions of pain.

The tripartite structure of the MPQ received support from the first generation of factor analytic studies in this area although evidence for a distinct Evaluative factor was usually weak. This factor was often confounded with the Affective factor (e.g., Bailey & Davidson, 1976; Burckhardt, 1984), and understandably so, because many of the words in the MPQ evaluative category (such as "annoying" and "troublesome") do describe affect.

It was not until Turk, Rudy, and Salovey (1985) that the construct validity of the MPQ was first seriously questioned. Using confirmatory factor analysis, they discovered higher cross-construct correlations than within-construct correlations in the MPQ. This multicollinearity led to questions about the distinctiveness of the Sensory, Affective, and Evaluative factors of the instrument. Could they all be measuring one and the same thing? Melzack (1985) issued a reminder that high intercorrelations also exist between many

other attributes such as color and texture, yet we do not cease to distinguish between such constructs.

The issue of the tripartite structure of the MPQ has been more effectively addressed in a statistically rigorous study of almost 2,000 chronic pain sufferers from six pain treatment programs (Holroyd et al., 1992). Although a three-factor model fit better than a one-factor model, hierarchical factor analysis revealed that two-thirds of the variance explained by even the best-fitting factor structure was shared variance common to the three first-order factors. This has remained one of the strongest challenges to the theoretical factor structure of the MPQ.

Embedded in the problem of category distinctiveness are questions about the very membership of verbal descriptors within subcategories. Torgerson, BenDebba, and Mason (1988) have used multidimensional scaling to show that many of these descriptors can fit into multiple subcategories. Hase (1992) has come up with a rationally driven regrouping of the existing MPQ words and relabelling of some of the subcategories. Clark, Fletcher, Janal, and Carroll (1995) have empirically generated an expanded list of pain descriptors organized along new dimensions based on hierarchical clustering.

The solution is not to dismantle or dispose of the MPQ. This instrument has provided fundamental clues to pain assessment, and its potential can be maximized by careful refinements. Along such lines, Fernandez and colleagues (Fernandez & Towery, 1996; Towery & Fernandez, 1996; Fernandez & Boyle, 1996) have derived a subset of MPQ words that satisfy a strict decision rule for membership in subcategories. Specifically, the criteria of absolute frequency, relative frequency, and unimodality of assignment to subcategories were applied to identify and exclude MPQ words that are underused, incomprehensible, or ambiguous, while preserving the more efficient descriptors of pain. Subcategory labels were also subject to refinement. Some of the Affective subcategories like tension and fear had too much overlap in meaning to allow unequivocal classification of descriptors. These can be substituted with the labels of fear, sadness, and anger, which are relatively discrete and appropriate for distinguishing the common affective correlates of pain. In the Sensory domain, the temporal and spatial labels seem misplaced as subcategories at the same level as dullness, hotness, etc. Rather, temporal and spatial are superordinate classes for characterizing any pain sensation described in the subcategories. Thus, it makes sense to speak of an aching pain that is also episodic and located in the back. For this reason, temporal and spatial should be regarded as dimensions or axes beyond the sensory qualities of pain, as in the taxonomy proposed by the International Association for the Study of Pain (Merskey, 1986).

With the above refinements, the emergent system of pain descriptors and subcategories is smaller than that of the original MPQ but essentially similar in structure. Moreover, intensity values of the descriptors need no amendments because they correlate very highly with those originally reported by Melzack and Torgerson (1971). Thus, a more parsimonious version of the MPQ is now possible, although it still awaits clinical validation.

In pain assessment, the clinical utility of an instrument is manifested by its capacity to discriminate varying levels of pain as well as its capacity to differentiate various types of pain. With regard to the first of these, the MPQ shares concurrent validity with visual analogue scale ratings of pain (Walsh & Leber, 1983) and is quite sensitive to changes in pain following medication and recovery (Van Buren & Kleinknecht, 1979). However, the second goal of diagnostic validity has only been partially fulfilled. There is some indication of different patterns of word choice between acute and chronic pain (e.g., Tearnan & Dar, 1986) and between functional versus organic pain (Leavitt & Garron, 1980), but the evidence is mixed as far as specificity between words and pain syndromes like back pain, headache, arthritic pain, and so on. Most of the reported differences in pain descriptor choice in relation to pain syndrome are blurred and post hoc in nature, thus making it difficult to actually diagnose patients on the basis of the MPQ. It is quite likely though, that the aforementioned refinements of the MPQ will improve the diagnostic validity of this instrument.

The issue of predictive validity also warrants further investigation. Published research is still lacking on whether the MPQ can predict the risk of disability, the course of pain if untreated, and who will respond best to specific types of treatments. Such screening and pretreatment decisions are presently addressed by a handful of other instruments designed to assess an array of psychosocial factors relevant to pain.

SUMMARY. The language of pain is indispensable in understanding the pain patient, and the McGill Pain Questionnaire was the first to organize the vast pain lexicon into a format for pain assessment. Twenty five years after its first appearance, the instrument remains widely used in research and practice. It is sensitive to pain intensity but its diagnostic validity is somewhat limited by the lack of specificity between pain descriptors and particular pain syndromes. This has stimulated efforts to refine the instrument using new statistical approaches. This notion of refinement was indeed part of the vision expressed by Melzack (1975) in his publication of the MPQ.

REVIEWER'S REFERENCES

Melzack, R., & Torgerson, W. S. (1971). On the language of pain. *Anesthesiology, 34,* 50–59.

Melzack, R. (1975). The McGill Pain Questionnaire: Major properties and scoring methods. *Pain, 1,* 277–299.

Bailey, C. A., & Davidson, P. O. (1976). The language of pain: Intensity. *Pain, 2,* 319–324.

Van Buren, J., & Kleinknecht, R. A. (1979). An evaluation of the McGill Pain Questionnaire for use in dental pain assessment. *Pain, 6,* 23–33.

Leavitt, F., & Garron, D. C. (1980). Validity of a back pain classification scale for detecting psychological disturbance as measured by the MMPI. *Journal of Clinical Psychology, 36,* 186–189.

Charter, R. A., & Nehemkis, A. M. (1983). The language of pain intensity and complexity: New methods of scoring the McGill Pain Questionnaire. *Perceptual and Motor Skills, 56,* 519–537.

Walsh, T. D., & Leber, B. (1983). Measurement of chronic pain: Visual analog scales and McGill Melzack pain questionnaire compared. In J. J. Bonica, U. Lindblom, & A. Iggon (Eds.), *Proceedings of the Third World Congress on Pain: Advances in pain research and therapy* (vol.5; pp. 897–899). New York: Raven Press.

Burckhardt, C. S. (1984). The use of the McGill Pain Questionnaire in assessing arthritis pain. *Pain, 19,* 305–314.

Melzack, R. (1985). Discriminative capacity of the McGill Pain Questionnaire. *Pain, 23,* 201–203.

Melzack, R., Katz, J., & Jeans, M. E. (1985). The role of compensation in chronic pain: Analysis using a new method of scoring the McGill Pain Questionnaire. *Pain, 23,* 101–112.

Turk, D. C., Rudy, T. E., & Salovey, P. (1985). The McGill Pain Questionnaire reconsidered: Confirming the factor structure and examining appropriate uses. *Pain, 21,* 385–397.

Merskey, H. (1986). Classification of chronic pain: Descriptions of chronic pain syndromes and definitions of pain terms. *Pain, Suppl. 3,* S21–S225.

Tearnan, B. H., & Dar, R. (1986). Physician ratings of pain descriptors: Potential diagnostic utility. *Pain, 26,* 45–51.

Deschamps, M., Band, P. R., & Coldman, A. J. (1988). Assessment of adult cancer pain: Shortcomings of current methods. *Pain, 32,* 133–139.

Torgerson, W. S., BenDebba, M., & Mason, K. J. (1988). Varieties of pain. In R. Dubner, G. F. Gebhart, & M. R. Bond (Eds.), *Proceedings of the Vth World Congress on Pain* (pp. 368–374). Amsterdam: Elsevier Science.

Hase, H. D. (1992). McGill Pain Questionnaire: Revised format. In L. VandeCreek, S. Knapp, & T. L. Jackson (Eds.), *Innovations in clinical practice: A source book, Vol. 11* (pp. 285–291). Sarasota, FL: Professional Resource Press.

Holroyd, K. A., Holm, J. E., Keefe, F. J., Turner, J. A., Bradley, L. A., Murphy, W. D., Johnson, P., Anderson, K., Hinkle, A. L., & O'Malley, W. B. (1992). A multi-center evaluation of the McGill Pain Questionnaire: Results from more than 1700 chronic pain patients. *Pain, 48,* 301–311.

Clark, W. C., Fletcher, J. D., Janal, M. N., & Carroll, J. D. (1995). Hierarchical clustering of pain and emotion descriptors: Toward a revision of the McGill Pain Questionnaire. In B. Bromm & J. Desmedt (Eds.), *Pain and the brain: From nociception to cortical activity* (pp. 319–330). New York: Raven Press.

Fernandez, E., & Boyle, G. J. (1996). *Affective and evaluative descriptors in the MPQ: Room for revision.* Sixteenth Annual Meeting of the American Pain Society, New Orleans.

Fernandez, E., & Towery, S. (1996). A parsimonious set of verbal descriptors of pain sensation derived from the McGill Pain Questionnaire. *Pain, 66,* 31–37.

Towery, S., & Fernandez, E. (1996). Reclassification and rescaling of McGill Pain Questionnaire verbal descriptors of pain sensation: A replication. *Clinical Journal of Pain, 12,* 270–276.

[228]
Measure of Questioning Skills.

Purpose: Designed "to measure the quantity and quality of questions."

Population: Grades 3–10.

Publication Dates: 1986–1993.

Scores, 4: Gathering Information, Organizing Information, Extending Information, Composite.

Administration: Group.

Forms, 2: A, B.

Price Data, 1997: $40.27 per complete kit including manual ('93, 61 pages), 20 activity booklets, 20 tally sheets, 20 result forms, 20 individual profile charts, and 1 class record sheet (specify form); $27.20 per 20 activity booklets, 20 tally sheets, and 1 class record sheet (specify form); $15.57 per manual; $18.80 per specimen set.

Time: (20) minutes.

Authors: Ralph Himsl and Garnet Miller.

Publisher: Scholastic Testing Service, Inc.

Review of the Measure of Questioning Skills by DARRELL L. SABERS, Professor of Educational Psychology, University of Arizona, Tucson, AZ:

The Measure of Questioning Skills (MQS) should be considered a work in progress rather than a standardized instrument. The User's Guidebook presents a rationale for having an instrument that measures the number and quality of students' questions, but does not provide data to support the MQS as that measure.

Each form of the test includes four pictures. The student is instructed to spend 4 minutes on each picture, writing "as many different questions as you can about each picture" (user's guidebook, p. 15). Each produced question is categorized into one of the three stages of managing information (Gathering Information, Organizing Information, and Extending Information). The frequency in each category and the sum across the three categories are recorded as the scores for the student.

The instructions for administration do not appear to be fair to the student who desires to maximize performance on the task. The instructions include "try to think of questions that no one else will think of," which is misleading to the student when the score reflects only the number of questions generated. The current scoring system for individuals does not reward originality; either the directions for administration or for scoring must be modified to be fair to the students.

It also seems unrealistic to expect the scorer to examine each question to determine classification into the correct stage if that classification will not be used in assessment of the individuals. It would be expected that students in instructional programs emphasizing questioning would have a major advantage in taking the MQS, yet the use of norms produced by counting questions might not reflect the better quality of the questions asked by these students.

The extensive discussion on the content validity of the test model leads one to expect a measure of the quality of the questions asked by students. Yet this expectation is not met with the current scoring system. The goal of developing student proficiency in asking better questions that guided the formation of the classification system was not used in the preparation of a student reporting system.

Strengths of the MQS include two forms, clear instructions for administration and scoring, and a Handbook of Tips and Strategies for Teachers (not reviewed). Weaknesses are the dearth of data and the nature of the convenience sample (numbers per grade varying from 52 third grade students to 11 sixth graders to 33 tenth graders)—and the norms are not accompanied by information on the selection of students in the sample. Data are available for performance on individual parts (pictures) of the test as well as the total; however, these data are suspect because the student is allowed four additional minutes to spend on any of the four parts, and this allowance destroys the basis for comparability across individual parts. If the MQS were used as an instructional tool rather than as a test, these potential individual variations would not be a problem.

All students in the sample took both forms, but there is no indication which students took which form first. There are no data reported on the test-retest correlations or the expected change in performance due to experience taking the test. There are no reliability data reported; data are limited to means, standard deviations, and number of students by sex for each grade. No data address predictive or construct validity. There is no support for an appropriate way to report scores to or for individual students—only a suggestion that the "teacher can determine whether a student is above or below the average for a particular grade level" (user's guidebook, p. 18).

SUMMARY. The MQS might have appeal to teachers looking for an instructional supplement to increase their students' abilities to ask good questions. The classification system will be useful for this purpose, but the scoring system will not be. At this stage of development the MQS should be considered an experimental version of a measurement instrument. Further development of the scoring system is encouraged.

[229]
Memory and Behavior Problems Checklist and The Burden Interview.

Publication Dates: 1983–1990.
Administration: Individual.
Price Data, 1998: $5.25 per manual including the instruments.
Authors: Steven H. Zarit and Judy M. Zarit.
Publisher: Gerontology Center, The Pennsylvania State University.
a) MEMORY AND BEHAVIOR PROBLEMS CHECKLIST.
Purpose: Designed to "determine how frequently a dementia patient engages in problematic behaviors and which problems are especially upsetting for family members."
Population: Dementia patients and their families.
Acronym: MBPC.
Scores, 3: Frequency of Problems, Severity of Functional Behavior Problems, Mean Distress.
Comments: Administered by an interviewer to family members of a dementia patient.
b) THE BURDEN INTERVIEW.
Purpose: "Designed to assess the stresses experienced by family caregivers of elderly and disabled persons."
Population: Caregivers of elderly and disabled persons.
Scores, 2: Personal Strain, Role Strain.
Comments: Administered by an interviewer or self-administered.
Cross References: See T5:1643 (2 references).

Review of the Memory and Behavior Problems Checklist and The Burden Interview by SALLY KUHLENSCHMIDT, Associate Professor of Psychology, Western Kentucky University:

The best part of the Memory and Behavior Problems Checklist (MBPC) and The Burden Interview are two reprints (Zarit, 1992, 1994) provided with the instruments. These articles provide thoughtful measurement recommendations that ought to be reified in these instruments. Instead, these two assessment tools suffer from lack of attention to detail, starting with the manual.

No justification is provided for including The Burden Interview and the MBPC in the same manual. The manual fails to explicitly relate the two assessment tools to prior literature, does not explain why and how the MBPC was revised, reports no theoretical issues, does not provide current reliability and validity information for the MBPC, and muddies administration.

MBPC. The MBPC was revised 9 years ago but neither current data nor clear information on the nature of the revision are provided. Item changes seem to have been the main alteration, deletion of some items, and addition of a few addressing affective problems and lower rates of behavior. Some current problems with items include grammatical errors (spelling, shifting person from "you" to "I") and inconsistently dealing with extremes of talking and eating behavior (asking if either extreme occurs in one question but asking about the extremes separately for the other behavior). The MBPC respondent is asked to indicate the extent to which each identified behavior problem has "bothered or upset" the caregiver. Given varied interpretations of "bothered" and "upset," this core question should be rephrased. More explicit anchors (as opposed to the current "very much" or "extremely") would be useful in assessing the need to intervene. My impression is that the authors followed no clear theory of disruptive behavior or caregiver stress to guide the selection of items or development of this instrument.

Administration as explained in the manual is confusing. Procedures are more effectively explained on the test protocol. No validation or normative sample is identified for the MBPC. Without norms, the user is left to rely on clinical impressions in interpreting the results. Reliability and validity information on the original MBPC appeared promising but has apparently not been further developed, based on the manual. The authors suggest multiple potential scores (total, cross-products, etc.), without exploring the strengths, weaknesses, or interpretation. Currently, the MBPC contributes only a structured approach to collecting information that could as easily be gathered from an interview.

THE BURDEN INTERVIEW. The Burden Interview also suffers from poor editing. The target population is reported to be those caring for another person but all of the questions refer to a "relative," requiring a rewrite to use it with nurses and others who are professional caregivers. Again, several of the 22 items are poorly written (e.g., "Do you feel that your relative seems to expect you to take care of him/her, as if you were the only one he/she could depend on?"). One item assumes illness, as opposed to some other problem, is the cause for caregiving. To reduce the floor and ceiling effects often encountered in this area I recommend restructuring The Burden Interview to use behavioral referents, "I ..." sentences, anchor points of "strongly agree" to "disagree," and a 7-point scale. The current scale strongly conveys the assumption that the caregiver is, indeed, experiencing stress. Such a mental set is likely to influence responses. Zarit (1992, 1994) mentions that coping, social support, and family factors, among others, are significant aspects of dealing with caregiving. These dimensions are not adequately measured in this scale. Positive aspects of caregiving that might reduce feelings of burden are ignored. Despite these conceptual weaknesses, the reliability evidence of the instrument seems adequate (alphas from .88 to .91). Some work has been done on validity (total Burden score with a global rating of burden $r = .71$; total Burden score with total Brief Symptom Inventory score $r = .41$). Confirmatory factor analysis revealed two subscales (Personal Strain alpha = .80; Role Strain alpha = .81).

SUMMARY. The Memory and Behavior Problems Checklist is a research instrument. The psychometric information is simply not adequate for clinical work. If used in a clinical setting it should be considered a structured interview and scores should be interpreted very cautiously, if at all. The Burden Interview is in slightly better psychometric shape but the clinician will need to supplement the questions to assess some significant areas affecting caregiver stress. Both devices and the manual would benefit from more thorough editing. Most seriously, the procedures do not appear to have benefited from the knowledge and experiences of the creators. In the research articles accompanying the devices several major concerns with assessment in the area are raised (e.g., the impact of family, the role of caregiver/receiver demographic characteristics, the heterogeneity of caregivers). The instruments do not address these concerns. There is no explicit collection of important demographic information, for example. A clinician with some expertise in the area could create a structured interview that was at least as effective in determining ongoing problems and caregiver stress. A researcher would likely want to refine these scales before using them. The topic is worthy of a thorough, comprehensive, and well-constructed assessment tool that addresses the latest research findings. The articles accompanying the MBPC and The Burden Interview provide excellent guidance in such a pursuit.

REVIEWER'S REFERENCES
Zarit, S. (1992). Measures in family caregiving research. In B. Bauer (Ed.), *Conceptual and methodological issues in family caregiving research. Invitational conference on family caregiving research* (pp. 1–19). Toronto: University of Toronto.
Zarit, S. H. (1994). Methodological considerations in caregiver intervention and outcome research. In E. Light, G. Niederehe, & B. Lebowitz (Eds.), *Stress effects on family caregivers of Alzheimer's patients* (pp. 351–369). New York: Springer.

Review of the Memory and Behavior Problems Checklist and The Burden Interview by RICHARD A. WANTZ, Associate Professor of Human Services, College of Education and Human Services, and Associate Clinical Professor of Psychiatry, School of Medicine, Wright State University, Dayton, OH, and BENJAMIN D. BARKER, Research and Clinical Associate, Wright State University, Dayton, OH:

CHECKLIST COVERAGE AND USE. The purpose of this checklist is to "determine how frequently a dementia patient engages in problematic behaviors and which problems are especially upsetting for family members" (p. 2). This checklist may be administered by a mental health professional during the interview process to the patient and their family. The checklist is in two parts. The first outlines type and frequency of behavior problems. The second part, entitled The Burden Interview, determines the amount of burden these behaviors have on the patient's family. The checklist is only intended for those suffering from dementia and the family members caring for the patient. If the patient and family are not interacting then this assessment should not be used. The focus of the assessment is less on the patient but on reaction of the family.

APPROPRIATE SAMPLES FOR VALIDATION. The checklist under review is the 1990R version of the checklist. Psychometric properties appear to refer to the 1982 form of the checklist. Limitations of the information in the manual include: (a) The manual does not provide information on the development of the checklist, pilot testing, validation, or norming; (b) sample size is not reported; and (c) item difficulty levels are not provided.

RELIABILITY. No reliability evidence is provided in the manual for the 1990R version of the checklist. According to the author, the 1982 version has a Guttman split-half reliability of .65. The distress ratings have a split-half reliability estimate of .66. Test-retest correlation is .80 for the frequency measure and .56 for the distress measure (administration interval not provided).

VALIDITY. No validity evidence is provided in the manual for the 1990R version of the checklist. The author claims that the previous checklist measures four factors: Depression, Disruptive Behaviors, Memory Impairment, and Retardation or low rates of behavior. The manual reports moderate predictive validity evidence between the checklist and the Mental Status Questionnaire, Face-Hand Test, Folstein Mini-mental State Examination, and Brief Symptom Inventory.

PREDICTIVE VALIDITY. The manual indicates that validity has been estimated by correlating the frequency measure with global estimates of severity of cognitive impairment. The checklist does not predict future performance. It records problem behavior and the reaction of those problems with family members. It may be used to show behavior patterns over time.

CONTENT VALIDITY. The manual does not cite any judgments made by experts regarding content validity. For The Burden Interview, evidence is presented for two factors: Personal Strain and Role Strain. However, 4 out of the 22 questions were unassigned (Items 7, 10, 15, and 22).

CHECKLIST ADMINISTRATION. Instructions are clear but not logical. In the scoring of the checklist, a Likert Scale ranging from 0 to 4 is used. However, a 9 is also included under "Frequency" to convey "Don't know/not applicable." Confusion arises when the instructions state to sum all the scores to find the total.

CHECKLIST REPORTING. Concerns about scoring include: (a) Results are explained in terms of the summation of total points accumulated for "Frequency" and "Reaction"; (b) results do not indicate if a score is low, high, or in the normal range; and (c) normative data are not available for comparison.

CHECKLIST AND ITEM BIAS. Neither the items nor the checklist were analyzed by the author for bias. The checklist is not translated into any additional languages.

SUMMARY. The checklist is undeveloped and should be considered experimental. The clinician should consider using the Scales of Adult Independence, Language and Recall (SAILR; 336) or another measure until this checklist has accumulated sufficient validity evidence to document adequate score reliability.

[230]
Metropolitan Performance Assessment: Integrated Performance Tasks.

Purpose: Designed to show progression in the "acquisition of concepts, strategies, and skills needed to perform language/literacy and quantitative/mathematics tasks" usually taught through kindergarten.

Population: Ages 4-4 to 6-3; ages 5-5 to 7-0.

Publication Date: 1995.

Acronym: MPA.

Scores, 3: Holistic, Analytic (Language/Literacy, Quantitative/Mathematics).

Administration: Group.

Levels, 2: 1, 2.

Price Data, 1999: $33.75 per examination kit including task booklet, set of manipulative sheets, directions for administering, scoring guide, and teacher observation form (Level 1 or Level 2); $40.75 per task package including 25 booklets, 25 sets of manipulative sheets, directions for administering, and teacher observation form (Level 1 or Level 2); $22 per scoring guide (Level 1 or Level 2); $5.25 per directions for administering (Level 1 or Level 2); $41 per preliteracy inventory including 25 record forms, Homer the Goose Storybook, and directions for administering; $19.75 per developmental inventory; $10.75 per portfolio assessment guidelines with information for interpreting preliteracy and developmental inventories; $14 per literacy environment inventory; $54 per Handbook of Early Childhood Activities.

Time: Untimed.

Comments: Handbook of Early Childhood Activities covers many areas assessed in the MPA, but may also be used independently of the program.

Author: Joanne R. Nurss.

Publisher: The Psychological Corporation.

Review of the Metropolitan Performance Assessment: Integrated Performance Tasks by THEODORE COLADARCI, Professor of Education, University of Maine, Orono, ME:

The Metropolitan Integrated Performance Tasks (MIPT) are designed to engage students in a series of activities that "show how each child is progressing in acquiring the concepts, strategies, and skills needed to perform language/literacy and quantitative tasks typically introduced in PreKindergarten and Kindergarten" (scoring guide, p. 5). Unlike conventional tests, these performance tasks are intended to "mirror active, hands-on instruction." For example, a component of one task asks students to match a numeral with the correct number of objects. This is accomplished by having students (a) cut out 15 large dots from a sheet of paper; (b) examine a page in the test booklet that presents a row of numerals, each with an empty box above it; and (c) paste the correct number of dots in each box. A component of another task involves the sequencing of story events: Students cut out pictures of events from a story that had been read to them moments before, and then they paste the pictures in the test booklet in proper chronology. The teacher plays a facilitative role, in that he or she "should motivate, guide, and encourage children to produce their best work."

There are two levels of the MIPT; each level offers two tasks, and each task comprises six activities. Level 1 tasks correspond to objectives usually taught in prekindergarten and early kindergarten; Level 2 tasks reflect those objectives taught toward the end of kindergarten or the beginning of first grade. All tasks are "thematic." For example, activities for the Level 1 task *Birthday Surprise* are situated in a story of a girl who is selecting a birthday gift for her grandfather.

The Metropolitan Integrated Performance Tasks are designed to assess two general sets of objectives: "Language/Literacy" (e.g., follow oral directions, copy print, classify objects, predict a story ending, sequence story events, tell a story from pictures, comprehend a story, identify beginning consonants and consonant blends, understand positional words) and "Quantitative/Mathematics" (e.g., count, understand numerical sequence, demonstrate number/numeral correspondence, understand ordinal numbers, measure objects in a picture, understand relational concepts, compute, understand fractions, complete number sentences, write and solve a story problem, extend patterns).

Performance task activities can be spread over several days, or even weeks. Further the MIPT can be administered to any size group, from one child to the entire class. A few activities have "cooperative" components.

ADMINISTRATION. Extensive directions are provided for administering the performance tasks: Teachers are told what materials are needed for each task, how to introduce the task theme, and how to conduct the task's six activities. My sense is that many teachers will find the adminis-tration of the MIPT to be, at best, logistically daunting. First, each activity has multiple steps and instructions; with a classroom of young children, complications and confusion easily arise. Second, teachers are instructed to "circulate" among students to query each child about his or her work and, if necessary, to write clarifying information in the test booklet regarding a student's response. Third, an accompanying observation form requires teachers to note each student's behavior during the activities (e.g., works without being distracted, tries a variety of solutions, takes turns).

SCORING. Each of the four tasks yields a single "Holistic" score, as well as an "Analytic" score for Language/Literacy and for Quantitative/Mathematics. All scores fall on a 3-point scale. The Holistic score "represents the scorer's overall impression of a child's performance" (scoring guide, p. 7) across the task's six activities. That is, does the student demonstrate "the strategies, concepts, and processes" relevant to the task's activities? Holistic scores take on values of 3 (*all or almost all*), 2 (*some*), or 1 (*few or none*). In contrast, Analytic scores reflect the student's mastery of area-specific objectives. On a Level 1 task, for example, a Quantitative/Mathematics Analytic score of 3 is reserved for students who (a) demonstrate understanding of number/numeral correspondence, (b) sequence numbers and sets correctly, (c) graph toys correctly, and (d) record the total numbers of graphed toys accurately. This score signifies that "performance in this area is successful." An Analytic score of 2 reflects "a combination of strengths and weaknesses" in the area, and a score of 1 corresponds to "largely unsuccessful" performance. Data from the observation component are not considered in determining these scores.

For each task, a scoring guide provides detailed rubrics for both Holistic and Analytic scoring, along with "hints" and "tips." Sample responses, illustrating various levels of proficiency, are provided for each task. Holistic and Analytic scores accompany each sample response, along with explanatory annotations. Finally, teachers can score a practice exercise and compare their scores to those of experienced raters. The MIPT author, Joanne Nurss, is to be commended for assembling this rather impressive Scoring Guide. Nevertheless, I suspect that many teachers will question whether several 3-point scores are worth the tedium of administering the MIPT.

RELIABILITY. Interrater agreement was examined with raters trained at The Psychological Corporation. Exact agreement in Holistic scoring was obtained for 82% to 90% of these raters, depending on the task; the figures for Analytic scoring were 81% to 86%. Agreement was always within 1 point on these 3-point scales. A subsequent analysis was conducted using novice raters (classroom teachers). No further information is provided about this analysis, other than that "agreement [between these teachers and] the trained scorers was *nearly* as high as that between trained scorers" (emphasis added). I take this to mean that some of the exact agreement percentages may have dropped below 80%, which is rather low when there are only 3 score points. These reliability data suggest that the MIPT scoring rubrics and explanatory annotations should more clearly differentiate adjacent performance levels.

VALIDITY. The validity argument for the MIPT is thin. In regard to content validity, we are told only that the objectives and content of this instrument were informed by an "extensive review of the literature" concerning developmentally appropriate curricula, emerging literacy, and the like. Although Nurss acknowledges that the content of the MIPT should be of demonstrable relevance to "the processes and strategies important for success in beginning reading, writing, numeracy, and problem solving" (scoring guide), this relevance is not demonstrated to the prospective user. As for construct validity, Nurss implies that the face validity of the MIPT is sufficient evidence, "because the tasks and the behaviors they measure are exactly the same." This betrays an unusual definition of construct validity and, in any case, does nothing to assure prospective users that MIPT scores permit meaningful inferences about the knowledge and skills measured by this instrument. For example, a Level 1 activity asks students to match uppercase and lower case letters by connecting a series of labeled dots (*A* to *a*, *B* to *b*, etc.), which ultimately forms the outline of a familiar object. Does this problem reveal a student's knowledge of uppercase and lowercase letters or, rather, the ability to complete a picture? In some instances, the mere configuration of dots makes a correct response seemingly unavoidable, even for students who do not know their Ps and Qs.

The author's fondness for face validity notwithstanding, correlations between MIPT performance and Metropolitan Readiness Tests (MRT;

231) scores are available—although, surprisingly, one must order the MRT norms book to see them. The Level 1 MIPT holistic score and the Level 1 MRT Total Test Composite are moderately correlated ($r = .51$, $n = 76$), as are the Level 2 tests ($r = .54$, $n = 49$); correlations between MIPT analytic scores and MRT subscale scores are generally smaller ($rs = .29$ to $.53$). These validity coefficients are somewhat modest, although the restricted scale of MIPT scores doubtless is at play.

No evidence of predictive validity is provided because, curiously, "predictive validity is not relevant" (scoring guide) to the MIPT. Although the MIPT was not designed for making formal predictions about subsequent performance, one nonetheless would expect that MIPT scores are related to academic progress. Evidence of this should be furnished.

Nurss embraces the important notion of consequential validity, which she defines as "the extent to which an assessment leads to improvement of instruction and learning in the classroom" (scoring guide). Surprisingly, no evidence is provided in this regard, nor is there even any discussion of how the MIPT can be used to inform instruction. In short, the instructional value and utility of this instrument remains undemonstrated.

CONCLUSION. Reliability and validity evidence for the MIPT is generally weak. Further, although it is true that many of the performance tasks have the feel of authentic activities, this authenticity, perhaps ironically, calls into question the need for such an instrument. Because most early education teachers routinely engage students in such activities, there is little reason to believe that the MIPT will yield information about students that their teachers do not already know. To be sure, some teachers may not be accustomed to deriving general ratings from naturally occurring instructional activities. But rather than purchase off-the-shelf assessments that duplicate instructional practice, a school district would be better advised to invest in staff development (e.g., constructing and using scoring rubrics) so that teachers can extract reliable and valid information from the classroom activities in which they routinely engage their students.

Review of the Metropolitan Performance Assessment: Integrated Performance Tasks by DELWYN L. HARNISCH, Professor of Curriculum and In-

struction, University of Nebraska–Lincoln, Lincoln, NE:

The purpose of the Metropolitan Performance Assessment (MPA) Integrated Performance Tasks is to assess children's developing levels of Language/Literacy and Quantitative/Mathematics concepts with classroom activities. The Integrated Performance Tasks vary from measuring individual performances to measuring both the individual and group performance. The Tasks were designed to mirror everyday active, hands-on instruction.

There are two levels to the Integrated Performance Tasks. Level 1 tasks are for Prekindergarten or beginning Kindergarten children and Level 2 tasks are for Kindergarten or beginning Grade 1 children. The author designed this test to match with primary instructional methods. The tasks have instructional and assessment value. Level 1 tasks engage the children in play-like interactions to maximize student performance and Level 2 tasks are designed to measure the performances of children actively involved in learning more complex language/literacy and mathematics.

There are six activities for each of the two separate booklets for Level 1 (*One, Two, Buckle My Shoe* and *Houses*) and for Level 2 (*Birthday Surprise* and *Pizza*).

The Scoring Guides were designed to guide the teachers on how to score the Integrated Performance Tasks holistically and analytically. The Holistic score is to reflect the child's performance on the set of six activities as a whole in terms of the level of integration of Language and Literacy with Quantitative concepts, strategies, and processes. The Analytic score is to reflect a separate proficiency score for both the Language/Literacy and Quantitative/Mathematics areas.

Teachers not familiar with using rubrics may feel uncomfortable giving a score for the students' work. There is no right answer. The scoring is left entirely up to the teacher's discretion, which makes some teachers and administrators uncomfortable. Teachers must also consider the student's performance as a whole. There are no scores on individual activities. To help the teachers with the scoring, the publisher provides a scoring guide with sample scores and practice booklets.

A Teacher Observation Form is included for the teacher to record observations of the child's active and interactive behaviors while completing the Integrated Performance Tasks. In the Scoring Guide is a Parent-Teacher Conference Report that allows the teacher to provide feedback regarding strengths and areas with which the child needs help for Language/Literacy and for Quantitative/Mathematics activities.

PERFORMANCE TASKS. For Level 1, the Language/Literacy set of activities focuses on having children demonstrate their ability to recognize and understand rhyming words, match uppercase and lowercase letters, copy print, draw a picture about a rhyme and write or tell about the pictures, and understand positional words. In the second booklet the children are asked to demonstrate their ability to apply the basic concepts of same and different, classify pictures of houses, draw a picture of their own house and write or tell about the picture, and match colors and shapes. The Quantitative/Mathematics activities focus on having the children demonstrate their understanding and ability to match the correct number of objects with a numeral, put numbers and sets of objects in numerical sequence, and color in squares on a graph to show numbers of like objects. The second booklet of activities engages the children in demonstrating their understanding of and ability to apply the concept of ordinal numbers, compare the height and width of objects, apply the concepts of more and fewer, measure objects in pictures, show number/numeral correspondence, and identify objects that are tallest and shortest.

For Level 2 the performance activities associated with Language/Literacy ask the children to demonstrate their ability to draw and write an ending to a story, sequence story events, tell a story from a sequence of pictures, arrange sets of pictures to show the structure of stories, write a title for a story, and match pictures that begin with the same consonant sounds or consonant blends. The second booklet on Pizza asks the children to demonstrate their ability to draw a picture of their favorite kind of pizza and provide a title and labels for the drawing; write a story about the favorite kind of pizza; sequence the steps of a task to show what is done first, second, etc.; draw, title, and label an imaginary pizza and write a price for and a description of the imaginary pizza that he or she drew. The performance activities associated with Level 2 Quantitative/Mathematics ask the children to demonstrate their understanding of and ability to apply one-to-one correspondence, write whole numbers and fractions, count forward and backward, complete number sentences, subtract, extend patterns, and count money. The second booklet asks the children to demonstrate their understanding of and ability to sequence numbers up to 50, count forward and backward, add and subtract, count by fives and tens, complete number problems, write a story problem and solve it, and extend picture patterns.

TEST ADMINISTRATION. Associated with each of the tasks are separate booklets containing the general and specific directions for administration. No time limits are set for the performance tasks. The guidelines suggest that teachers use their judgment in determining an appropriate amount of time, spread over several days, for children to work on activities. Children are encouraged to do their best work and to understand that they need not be on the same step of an activity as their classmate. Tasks may be administered individually, to a small group, or to an entire class. Teachers are encouraged to have a performance environment that is similar to the normal teaching/learning activities conducted in the classroom. The teacher's role is to be that of a "coach." Teachers are encouraged to motivate, guide, and encourage children to produce their best work. The guidebook notes that teachers should document the amount and type of assistance that is shared with each student to assist in determining the proficiency level of the child in language and literacy and in mathematics concepts and skills. Children taking the tasks are encouraged to have ample opportunity to cut, draw, paste, write, and solve problems without being disturbed by others. The manual does not include a discussion of how this type of support from the examiner or differences in administration from standard directions between examiners may affect individual student performance and affect the reliability and validity of the resultant scores. Several times it appears on the tasks that the teacher is to write a translation of the child's work to facilitate scoring at a later time.

SCORING PROCEDURES. The tasks are scored holistically and analytically using a 3-point scale. None of the activities are rated separately but instead they are rated as a whole set for each booklet of six activities. The analytic rubric is based on a score on the Language/Literacy or Quantitative/Mathematics scale. At Level 2, five of the six activities measure only one of the two Analytical areas with four Language/Literacy areas

represented. For Level 2, each of the six activities measure only one of the Analytical areas with one booklet having four activities in Language/Literacy whereas the other has three activities in Language/Literacy.

The Scoring Guide provides a list of instructional objective measures by each task along with scoring tips. The scoring tips identify areas where children received credit for their performances. The Guide provides six scored student booklets with Holistic and Analytic scores ranging from 1 to 3 along with annotations or justifications for the scores given to the student performances. The Guide also provides two booklets for the teacher to practice using the scoring rubrics.

TEST VALIDITY. No description of the sample data is provided for the performance tasks. For Level 1, approximately 350 students from Prekindergarten and Kindergarten participated in the study. Score distributions on the Holistic and Analytic areas were given with mean score changes on the Holistic scale from 1.78 to 2.35 and from 1.53 to 2.47 for students from the Prekindergarten and Kindergarten levels. These changes reflect a difference between 1 and 1.5 standard deviation on their respective scales across the one-year levels. Percentage agreement between trained raters on Holistic scale scores were higher (85% and 87%) compared to analytical scores (82% and 81%). Correlations among the three scores (Holistic and Analytical areas—Literacy and Quantitative) were highest between the Holistic and Quantitative (values ranged from .71 to .84) area. Correlations between Literacy and Quantitative scores ranged from .42 to .59 for Prekindergarten and Kindergarten scores.

For Level 2, approximately 350 students from Kindergarten and Grade 1 participated in the study. Score distributions on the Holistic and Analytic areas were given with mean score changes on the Holistic scale from 1.68 to 2.31 and from 1.71 to 2.13 for students from the Prekindergarten and Kindergarten levels. These changes reflect a difference between 2/3 and 1 standard deviation on their respective scales across the one-year levels. Percentage agreement between trained raters on Holistic scale scores were higher (90% and 82%) compared to Analytical scores (86% and 83%). Correlations among the three scores (Holistic and Analytical areas—Literacy and Quantitative) were highest between the Holistic and Literacy (values ranged from .67 to .76) areas. Correlations between Literacy and Quantitative scores ranged from .33 to .46 for Kindergarten and Grade 1 scores.

No comparisons are made with student performance on the MPA tasks and their performance on multiple-choice tests. It is difficult to determine the level of student performance from the collaboration and support from the classroom teacher. Another area of validity concern has to do with the conceptual clarity of the tasks with the Analytical areas. It is not clear from the Scoring Guide the extent to which logical analysis of task content and expected performance were undertaken. The author in making her revisions for her next edition would do well to address the linkage between the performance tasks and the teaching and learning process. Clear statements of purpose and uses of assessment should be provided. In addition, the author may understand the scoring criteria for the booklets but having it understood by the teachers and students on each of the performance tasks remains a challenge. In short, the development of the Performance Tasks reflects the changes in early childhood education and the Postmodern World that emphasizes embeddedness, particularity, and irregularity as accepted educational reform concepts (Elkind, 1994).

On several of the activities the demands on the teacher/test administrator are heavy for making interpretations of student work. The MPA uses, at most, a quasi-structured administration process that is heavily dependent on the teacher for an objective and unbiased assessment of the child—even prior to interpretation. That is, without a standardized posttest inquiry, the potential that a teacher could self-select specific question components for elaboration, based on the student, and bias both the responses and the interpretation of the instrument is likely. Furthermore, many of the assumptions inherent in the suggested administration directions are untested or, at least, the author cites no research to validate her recommended procedures.

OTHER CONCERNS. A number of critical issues have already been addressed; however, some additional critique is warranted and described below.

Special attention needs to be given to clarifying the concepts and terminology in the MPA. Greater attention is needed to have an improved understanding of the student thinking process that is represented when doing the particular activities associates with the theme-based assessment. No mention is made of the selection of the tasks and/or activities for each. No research is provided that represents how the tasks are connected with instructional practice and how they contribute to improved learning. No data are given that reflect the extent to which the student's knowledge is generalizable and transferable to new situations from the specific performance tasks found in these two booklets.

SUGGESTIONS. The test could be improved if the objectives covered by each activity were listed. This listing could help teachers identify the specific areas in which students need help. For the teachers who want to integrate more activities such as the ones included in the assessment, the publisher does provide a handbook of early childhood activities. Research by Shepard et al. (1996) on the effects of introducing classroom performance assessments on learning show no immediate improvements in overall student learning, but some positive changes were shown in mathematics.

SUMMARY. In closing, the authentic nature of the MPA performance tasks is quite appealing. However, the realism of performance assessments comes at the cost of limitations in the generalizability of the results. Educators need to realize the restrictions that directly or indirectly limit generalizability, such as limitations on student time leading to reductions in the number of tasks possible, rater quality, and task quality. With the MPA, educators need to remember also that assessments requiring considerable student time may result in student scores that are not dependable if each score is based on few tasks and if the student-task variance is large (Harnisch, 1994).

REVIEWER'S REFERENCES

Elkind, D. (1994). Early childhood education and the postmodern world. *Principal, 73*(5), 6–7.
Harnisch, D. L. (1994). Performance assessments in review: New directions for assessing student understanding. *International Journal of Educational Research, 21*(3), 341–350.
Shepard, L. A., Flexer, R. J., Hiebert, E. H., Marion, S. F., Mayfield, V., & Weston, T. J. (1996). Effects of introducing classroom performance assessments on student learning. *Educational Measurement: Issues and Practice, 15*, 7–18.

[231]
Metropolitan Readiness Tests®, Sixth Edition.

Purpose: Designed to assess basic and advanced skills important in beginning reading and mathematics.
Population: Prekindergarten through grade 1.
Publication Dates: 1933–1995.

Acronym: MRT®6.

Administration: Individual (Level 1) or Group (Level 2).

Price Data, 1999: $16 per 25 parent-teacher conference reports (specify level); $16 per story comprehension big book.

Time: (85) minutes per level; (10) minutes for the practice items for each level.

Authors: Joanne R. Nurss and Mary E. McGauvran.

Publisher: The Psychological Corporation.

a) LEVEL 1.

Population: Prekindergarten and beginning kindergarten.

Administration: Individual

Scores: 5 tests: Beginning Reading Skill Area (Visual Discrimination, Beginning Consonants, Sound-Letter Correspondence), Story Comprehension, Quantitative Concepts and Reasoning, plus Prereading Composite.

Price Data: $101 per complete kit including stimulus manual, story comprehension big book, manual ('95, 43 pages), 25 parent-teacher conference reports, and 25 student record forms; $26.75 per 25 student record forms; $25.25 per manual; $47 per stimulus manual; $24.50 per exam kit including Level I flyer, story comprehension big book flyer, manual, student record form, and parent-teacher conference report.

b) LEVEL 2.

Population: Middle and end of kindergarten and beginning of grade 1.

Administration: Group.

Scores: 5 tests: Beginning Reading Skill Area (Beginning Consonants, Sound-Letter Correspondence, Aural Cloze with Letter), Story Comprehension, Quantitative Concepts and Reasoning, plus Prereading Composite.

Price Data: $135.25 per starter kit including 25 test booklets, directions for administering, story comprehension big book, 25 practice booklets, class record and analysis chart, norms book, answer keys, parent-teacher conference reports, 25 Birthday Surprise Task booklets, 25 Birthday Surprise manipulative sheets, Birthday Surprise directions for administering, scoring guide, and teacher observation form; $67.50 per 25 test booklets also including directions for administration, 25 practice booklets, and class record and analysis chart; $24.50 per answer keys; $33.75 per manual; $25.25 per norms book ('95, 72 pages); $14 per exam kit including test booklet, directions for administering, practice booklet, class record and analysis chart, and parent-teacher conference report.

Cross References: See T5:1659 (14 references) and T4:1619 (35 references); for a review by Michael M. Ravitch of an earlier edition, see 9:700 (11 references); see also T3:1479 (73 references), 8:802 (111 references), and T2:1716 (55 references); for reviews by Robert Dykstra and Harry Singer of an earlier edition, see 7:757 (124 references); for a review by Eric F. Gardner and an excerpted review by Fay Griffith, see 4:570 (3 references); for a review by Irving H. Anderson, see 3:518 (5 references); for a review by W. J. Osburn, see 2:1552 (10 references).

Review of the Metropolitan Readiness Tests, Sixth Edition by R. W. KAMPHAUS, Professor, Department of Educational Psychology, The University of Georgia, Athens, GA:

The sixth edition of the Metropolitan Readiness Tests (MRT6) represents the latest version of the core instruments of the Metropolitan Early Childhood Assessment Program. Given the extent of the entire assessment system, this review focuses exclusively on the MRT6 consisting of Levels 1 and 2. Level 1 is individually administered and designed to assess the "emergent literacy and mathematics strategies" (Interpreting Manual, p. 5) in prekindergarten and beginning kindergarten. Level 2, which is group administered, assesses "strategies and processes in beginning reading and mathematics" (Interpreting Manual, p. 5).

The MRT-5 was previously reviewed for *The Twelfth Mental Measurements Yearbook.* Both reviewers noted some strengths; however, numerous deficiencies were identified as well, especially an absence of adequate validation studies. Specifically, the review by Mabry (1995) cited numerous inadequacies and concluded:

> Although developers of the MRT have exercised the conventional strategies in constructing their test and offered the usual caveats to users, these are insufficient. The test is outdated, passé in terms of learning theory, technically inadequate, confusing to targeted audiences, and likely detrimental to children and schools. (p. 612)

In addition, Stoner (1995) cited a lack of validity evidence for some of the major uses of the scale. One of his summary paragraphs stated:

> The Metropolitan Readiness Tests (MRT), Fifth Edition materials are well written and user friendly. However, the purported usefulness of the tests for making educational decisions about curricula and instruction are unsubstantiated. In the absence of further research and data, current use of the MRT should be limited to screening decisions to determine which children in a classroom might

benefit from further assessment or from on-going monitoring of their skill development. (p. 614)

Based on these thorough reviews of the MRT5 it is reasonable to expect the developers of the MRT6 to respond to the majority of these prior concerns. In addition, the MRT6, although published in 1995, should be held to the same set of standards as all tests currently in use, specifically, the latest version of the *Standards for Educational and Psychological Testing* (AERA, APA, & NCME, 1999; hereafter referred to as the *Test Standards*). Therefore, the purpose of this review is twofold. The degree to which the MRT6 has accumulated adequate validity evidence to support its intended uses will be assessed. Second, the extent to which the MRT6 meets the *Test Standards* for modern usage will be evaluated.

The MRT6, like its most recent predecessor, has limited evidence of validity. A mere two pages of validity evidence is reported. Two of the three investigations reported in the Norms Book are predictive validity studies where Level 2 of the MRT6 is used as a predictor of Metropolitan Achievement Tests and Stanford Achievement Test scores. Level 2 scores correlated moderately with Metropolitan scores (coefficients in the .50s) and better with the Stanford (coefficients in the .60s and .70s). The last study reported is a table of intercorrelations for the Level 2 subtests accompanied by the following explanation: "Further evidence of the validity of the MRT can be derived from the intercorrelations among the subtests and Skill Areas of the MRT." (p. 48).

In other words, the test developers present no validity evidence for Level 1 and virtually none for Level 2. The prior reviewers of the MRT were correct, validity evidence was lacking then and it is lacking now. Even if held to the lower standards of the previous edition of the *Test Standards*, the validation of the MRT6 is unacceptable for supporting its routine use for the screening of academic achievement in prekindergarten and kindergarten.

The Manual for Interpreting provides some indication of the type of validity evidence that should be gathered to support use of the MRT6. The Manual for Interpreting suggests, for example, that "The content-referenced results provided by the MRT6 Performance Ratings can be helpful in the instructional process" (p. 31). This statement suggests that validity evidence should

be presented in support of at least the content selection methods and the performance ratings assigned.

Toward that end the content selection methods are described as follows: "An extensive review of the literature was conducted prior to the tests' development to provide evidence that the results are assessing those skills that are important to early learning" (p. 48). The results of this analysis are provided in the Manual for Interpreting where the performance objectives and associated items are listed. These stated objectives, however, are not listed on any of the content-referenced interpretive charts provided. The interpretive charts and record forms include only subtest ratings of performance and norm-referenced scores by subtests, thereby deemphasizing analyses by instructional objective. If, in fact, the content is usefully organized by instructional objective it would seem reasonable to in some way assist the user in applying this information to instructional design.

Another notable problem in this regard is that although a statement was made that an extensive review of the literature was conducted, there are no references to this literature given. Thus, interested test users are unable to make an informed decision about the applicability of the test content to their classroom and instructional programs. Furthermore, no evidence is given regarding the qualifications of the individuals who selected the content based on this review. A list of curriculum consultants is not provided, nor is a comparison between the objectives and subtests selected and popular curricula articulated. In other words, MRT6 users are unable to make an intelligent decision regarding whether or not the test content is relevant for their use without engaging in considerable effort to independently articulate the relationship between the MRT6 content and the research literature, typical curricula, and their curriculum. This lack of information regarding content selection is likely inconsistent with Test Standards 1.6 and 1.7, which state the need for a well-articulated content blueprint and a description of expert judgments utilized.

A related content interpretation problem is the system of Performance Ratings for the individual subtests. These ratings are "content-referenced indicators of the child's performance on the skills measured by the tests" (p. 17). Essentially, a child is assigned a plus sign, check mark, or minus sign for each test based on "author's judgments of the degree of proficiency demonstrated by specific raw-score ranges on each test" (p. 17). By logical extension, validity evidence should be provided in support of the author's decisions. Such evidence is not provided.

Additional validity shortcomings could be identified by making direct comparisons between the manuals and the *Test Standards*. This analysis would be exhaustive given that so little evidence is provided in the manuals. One could conclude that Level 1 is essentially unvalidated and that Level 2 possesses only limited evidence for the predictive validity of its norm-referenced scores. One additional validity problem, however, must be mentioned.

A glaring discrepancy exists between the MRT6 and the *Test Standards* in the former's lack of attention to issues of fairness. Topics such as proper populations for application of the MRT6, preparation for testing for children from diverse backgrounds, statistical analyses of bias, appropriateness of test content for children from diverse backgrounds, and interpretation of results for non-English or limited-English speakers are given no or little attention. This shortcoming makes the MRT6 inadequate by modern standards, given that an entire chapter of the *Test Standards* is now devoted to issues of fairness. The Manual for Interpreting does suggest that a child's educational background and language be taken into account when assigning meaning to the results. Nevertheless, the manual does not explain how this information should be used to effect proper interpretation.

SUMMARY. There are at least two valuations that may be assigned to the MRT6. Either it is a good test that is simply poorly documented, or it is unusable due to poor design at every phase of development. The answer to this question is unknown based upon reading the manuals. As such it is probably most reasonable to assume that it is unusable unless locally validated. Unfortunately, many school districts do not have the personnel or other resources required to build the necessary validity foundation or to provide guidelines for responding to issues of fairness.

One could argue that the authors were simply trying to write manuals that were easily understood by teachers causing the authors to avoid technical language or complex measurement concepts. This point of view is easily countered by the fact that many of the points made in the manual are simply not adequately developed, thereby precluding the nontechnical reader from making adequate use of the scale. Simple language could have been used to give the user adequate information to make informed judgments regarding selection and use of the MRT6.

REVIEWER'S REFERENCES
Mabry, L. (1995). [Review of the Metropolitan Readiness Tests, Fifth Edition.] In J. C. Conoley & J. C. Impara (Eds.), *The twelfth mental measurements yearbook* p. 611–612). Lincoln, NE: Buros Institute of Mental Measurements.
Stoner, G. (1995). [Review of the Metropolitan Readiness Tests, Fifth Edition.] In J. C. Conoley & J. C. Impara (Eds.), *The twelfth mental measurements yearbook* p. 612–614). Lincoln, NE: Buros Institute of Mental Measurements.
American Educational Research Association, American Psychological Association, & National Council on Measurement in Education. (1999). *Standards for educational and psychological testing.* Washington, DC: American Educational Research Association.

Review of the Metropolitan Readiness Tests, Sixth Edition by CHRISTINE NOVAK, Clinical Assistant Professor, Division of Psychological and Quantitative Foundations, The University of Iowa, Iowa City, IA:

The Metropolitan Readiness Tests, Sixth Edition (MRT6) is a component of the Metropolitan Early Childhood Assessment program, geared toward identifying skill strengths and weaknesses in prereading and prematics to assist with curricular planning. Two primary groups are targeted as users: classroom teachers and administrators.

Instructions for administering Level 1 (individual) and Level 2 (group) are straightforward. Clear examples show how to summarize the information obtained and how to use this information to guide instructional decisions for individuals or groups of children. Useful features included the Class Record and Analysis Charts and the Parent-Teacher Conference Report. The Class Record allows the user to see at a glance which children require additional instruction in which areas. The Conference Report provides a simple description of the child's performance along with explanations of each of the areas tested and a sample of activities that parents can use at home to help develop these skills. One change that would make the test easier to use would be to put all of the Level 1 information in one manual and all of the Level 2 information in another manual. As it is now, there are four manuals (Level 1 Manual, Level 2 Directions for Administration, Norms Book, and Manual for Interpretation).

The types of scores available include percentile ranks, stanines, normal curve equivalents, scaled scores, and standard scores (Level 1 only). Emphasis is placed on using stanines and percentiles for interpretation. Little information is provided for guiding the use of NCEs or scaled scores; in fact, the mean and standard deviation for the scaled scores is not reported. It is explained that scaled scores might be of more interest to researchers and those wanting to determine growth in skills over time.

Additional interpretive information includes the Content-Referenced Performance Rating and the Stanine Classification. The Performance Rating is used in reporting results to parents and determining groups for instructional purposes. There are three ratings: one indicating proficiency, one indicating acquisition, and one indicating needed instruction. Ratings are based on raw scores and justified purely on the basis of the authors' judgment. As reported in the Manual for Interpreting, Performance Ratings may not always coincide with Stanine Classifications, which assign Above Average, Average, or Below Average labels according to normative standards. A good example of how different the resulting pictures of students might be can be drawn from the sample class data provided in the Norms Book (pp. 22–24). Raw scores of 8 and 9 on the Story Comprehension subtest yield percentiles and stanines of 1; however, the Performance Rating of one is considered to be in the acquisition stage, whereas the second is considered to need instruction in this skill area.

A further difficulty in using the Performance Ratings for determining instructional groups is that the scores represent different skills achieved within an area. Looking at the item content for each skill area, it is apparent that some subskills are represented by only one item; furthermore, some items measure more than one subskill. For example, Level 1 Quantitative Concepts and Reasoning includes 20 items measuring 10 different objectives. Part-whole relationships, linear estimations, classification, and linear measurement are each represented by only one item. In contrast, associating numerals with numbers of objects and counting objects are both represented by five identical items. If the teacher looks only at the number of items missed, valuable information is lost relative to whether the child's need is in a variety of areas or one specific area.

It is also important when interpreting scores to take into consideration measurement error. The Manual for Interpreting addresses this issue briefly, stating that "As a general rule, the *SEM* for the

MRT6 is about one stanine" (p. 24). The Norms Book reports standard errors of measurement based on internal consistency estimates for skill areas and composites ranging from 1–4 raw score points (with larger *SEM*s associated with the composite scores). Using this information, a prekindergarten child obtaining a raw score of 18 on Story Comprehension could be said to perform anywhere from the 60th to 98th percentile (or from Stanine 6–9); the same score for a midyear kindergartner results in an even larger confidence interval from the 34th to 95th percentile, or Stanine 4–8.

Internal consistency estimates are reported for both levels across grades and time of testing except for Level 1 at the fall of first grade. Total Test Composites are within the acceptable range for making important decisions about individual students (.90 or above) except for Level 1 midyear prekindergarten, midyear kindergarten, and spring kindergarten. The Level 2 Prereading Composites also have strong internal consistency (most estimates in the .90s); however, Level 1 Prereading Composites are more suitable for screening because most of the estimates are in the .80s.

Likewise, Quantitative Concepts and Reasoning can be used for screening purposes at Level 1 spring prekindergarten or Level 2 midyear and spring kindergarten; the remaining estimates are below .80 and insufficient for decision-making about individual students. Story Comprehension overall has weak consistency (range .53 to .77).

The usefulness of the Story Comprehension scores is questionable, not only in terms of internal consistency, but also in relation to what is being measured. In the validity data reported, Story Comprehension (Level 2) was shown to correlate more highly with Quantitative Concepts and Reasoning than with the other reading measures contained in the MRT6. It also correlated more highly with Total Math than Total Reading on the Stanford Early School Achievement Test (9th Edition) (SESAT9). Despite this oddity, the limited validity studies showed the MRT6 (Level 2) to provide adequate prediction for kindergartners of subsequent achievement as measured by the Metropolitan Achievement Test 7 and the SESAT9. Additionally, concurrent validity studies supported the MRT6 in relation to similar achievement scales.

The normative sample for the MRT6 is generally representative of the 1990 U.S. Census.

Although the sample appears to be sufficiently large, there is no breakdown of numbers by grade. No information is reported relative to possible test bias.

SUMMARY. In conclusion, the MRT6 provides information that could be useful in determining early academic or "readiness" skills in reading and math. However, users are cautioned against overinterpretation for individual students particularly in relation to profile analysis of strengths and weaknesses.

[232]
Michigan Alcoholism Screening Test.

Purpose: Designed as a screening test for assessing alcohol abuse.
Population: Adults.
Publication Dates: 1971–1980.
Acronym: MAST.
Scores: Total score only.
Administration: Group or individual.
Manual: No manual available.
Price Data, 1996: $40 per copy, which includes scoring key and permission to duplicate the test.
Foreign Language Edition: Spanish and Japanese versions available.
Time: (10) minutes.
Comments: Can be self-administered.
Author: Melvin L. Selzer.
Publisher: Melvin L. Selzer.
Cross References: See T5:1661 (85 references).

Review of the Michigan Alcoholism Screening Test by JANE CLOSE CONOLEY, Dean, College of Education, Texas A&M University, College Station, TX, and JEFF REESE, Psychology Intern, Texas Tech University, Lubbock, TX:

INTRODUCTION. The Michigan Alcoholism Screening Test (MAST) is a 25-item questionnaire developed by Selzer in 1971 to provide a convenient and efficient measure of lifetime alcoholism and alcohol-related problems. The MAST is intended for screening purposes and not as a stand-alone diagnostic tool for alcoholism (Connors & Tarbox, 1985). All of the items require a "yes" or "no" response and are face valid in nature. The items, except one, are differentially weighted and are summed to provide a total score. The majority of items have a weight of 2 (e.g., "Do friends or relatives think you are a normal drinker?") if answered in the alcoholic direction. The rest of the items have a weight of 1 (e.g., "Have you gotten into physical fights when drinking?") or 5 ("Have you ever attended a meeting of Alcoholics

Anonymous?"). Scores range from 0 to 53 with higher scores indicative of a problem with alcohol. Items address drinking behavior, consequences for drinking, and attempts to receive help for drinking problems.

Although details on the development of the items for the MAST are incomplete, the instrument was apparently devised by drawing items from other alcohol survey studies and by items written by Selzer himself (Connors & Tarbox, 1985). The weighting system was determined by optimizing the ability of each item to discriminate between alcoholics and nonalcoholics based on data from a control group and a hospitalized alcoholic group. Interestingly, Selzer (1971) used the MAST to exclude individuals in the control group who had high MAST scores reasoning that some of these individuals were likely to have alcohol difficulties. This is an example of criterion contamination (Gray, 1996).

The MAST has been revised several times, including the use of more inclusive language and changing the wording of some items, and/or omitting Item 7, which is not scored in the original version. However, as evidenced by the research literature, the original MAST is still the most popular version and the minor changes seem to have had little influence in its subsequent use.

ADMINISTRATION, SCORING, AND INTERPRETATION. The MAST can be administered either orally or in written form. Although originally designed to be administered orally by both professional and nonprofessional personnel, Selzer, Vinokur, and van Rooijen (1975) found high reliability and validity indices with a sample using a paper-and-pencil format. Computerized versions also exist.

Different suggestions have been made for scoring the MAST, but the approach outlined by Selzer in his original report (1971) is the most commonly used. A score of 3 or less is nonalcoholic, a score of 4 is possible alcoholism, and a score of 5 is alcoholic. In a later study, however, Selzer et al. (1975) recommended the cutoff scores be elevated to increase specificity. He suggested a score of 4 or less to be nonalcoholic, a score of 5–6 to be possible alcoholism, and 7 or more to be alcoholic. Further, Hedlund and Vieweg (1984) noted that Selzer's (1971) recommendations for future use, assigning 2 points for each arrest of driving under the influence or other drunken behavior (Items 23 and 24) and giving 5 points for a positive response to a history of delirium tremens (Item 18), are not explicitly denoted in many studies.

The face validity of the MAST is cause for some concern. Although Selzer (1971) asserted that faking good was not a threat to accurate interpretation, some more recent work has illustrated that although nonalcoholics do not substantially change their scores when told to lie, alcoholics can successfully depress their scores when given instructions to "look good" (Lapham et al., 1995).

USE AND POPULARITY. The MAST is arguably the most researched and frequently used instrument for detecting alcoholism (Connors & Tarbox, 1985; Parsons, Wallbrown, & Myers, 1994). The MAST has been administered in a variety of settings and to a variety of respondents, including persons convicted of drunken driving, psychiatric patients, general medical patients, and college students, among others. Further, the MAST has often been used as a criterion for establishing validity in other alcohol screening instruments.

Evidence for the popularity of the MAST can be seen in its world-wide use, having been translated into several languages including Tamil and Japanese, and the many modified versions that have been adapted from the original MAST. Some of the more common adaptations are shortened versions, including the 10-item Brief MAST (bMAST; Pokorny, Miller, & Kaplan, 1972), the 13-item Short MAST (SMAST; Selzer et al., 1975), and the 9-item Malmo modification of the bMAST (Mm-MAST; Kristenson & Trell, 1982). Modified versions also exist for subpopulations, including a 24-item version for the elderly (MAST-G; Blow et al., 1992), a 35-item Self-Administered Alcoholism Screening Test (SAAST; Swenson & Morse, 1975) for general medical populations and for assessing an individual's mother's (M-SMAST) and father's (F-SMAST) alcohol abuse, both of which are variants of the SMAST (Crews & Sher, 1992). Despite all of these adaptations, the original MAST (Selzer, 1971) remains the most popular version. It is a cheap and easy instrument that attracts attention from researchers worldwide (e.g., Tulevski, 1989).

PSYCHOMETRIC PROPERTIES. Although the development of the MAST is somewhat flawed by criterion contamination, the psychometric properties of the instrument are impressive. Internal consistencies average about .84 across a number of studies. The standard error of measurement is usually about 3.42. Point biserial correlations range from .13 to .72. The MAST correlates well with other measures of alcoholism, counselor ratings of alcoholism, and with DSM-IV diagnoses for substance abuse.

The validity of the MAST is best viewed by examining its: (a) predictive positive values, that is, ratio of true positive results to all positive results; (b) predictive negative values, that is, ratio of true negative results to all negative results; (c) sensitivity, that is, proportion of persons with alcohol problems who score positive on the MAST; and (d) specificity, that is, proportion of persons with no alcohol problems who score negative on the MAST (Storgaard, Nielsen, & Gluud, 1994).

Positive predictive values of the MAST range between .24 and .96. Predictive negative values range between .78 and 1.0. The Storgaard et al. (1994) review also found that sensitivity of the MAST is high ranging from a high of 1 to a low of .36 depending on the criterion and the population under study. Specificity of the MAST is not as strong. Although some studies show specificities in the .90s, more modest values between .30 and .80 are common.

The MAST is not equally valid, apparently, for every group. Women, whatever their alcohol status, tend to score lower than men score. Older respondents score lower than younger ones (Blankfield & Maritz, 1990). Individuals with serious mental disorders are not identified well by the MAST despite the high comorbidity of alcoholism and mental illness (McHugo, Paskus, & Drake, 1993). Although the MAST is generally found to be more sensitive than the CAGE (Magruder-Habib, Stevens, & Alling, 1993), the CAGE may be more sensitive with elderly patients (Jones, Lindsey, Yount, Soltys, & Farani-Enayat, 1993). The MAST is not useful in identifying levels or intensity of substance abuse (Maisto, Connors, & Allen, 1995).

A debate in the MAST literature has revolved around its factor structure. Recent analyses suggest a strong general factor of alcoholism in addition to several other specific factors (Parsons et al., 1994). Whether treatment implications can be drawn from such an interpretation remains unclear.

SUMMARY. Among the various alcohol screening devices available (e.g., the CAGE, Self-

Administered Alcoholism Screening Test) the MAST is the most frequently given and researched. Its high sensitivity and lower specificity are appropriate for its role as a screening device. Overidentification is preferable to underidentification.

Problems with its use are related to definitional problems with alcoholism and the likelihood that responders in the general population can easily fake good. As part of a multimodal diagnostic approach, however, the MAST offers practitioners an avenue for further exploration.

REVIEWERS' REFERENCES

Selzer, M. L. (1971). The Michigan Alcoholism Screening Test: The quest for a new diagnostic instrument. *American Journal of Psychiatry, 127,* 1653–1658.

Pokorny, A. D., Miller, B. A., & Kaplan, H. B. (1972). The brief MAST: A shortened version of the Michigan Alcoholism Screening Test. *American Journal of Psychiatry, 129,* 342–345.

Selzer, M. L., Vinokur, A., & van Rooijen, L. (1975). A self-administered Short Michigan Alcoholism Screening Test (SMAST). *Journal of Studies on Alcohol, 36,* 117–126.

Swenson, W. M., & Morse, R. M. (1975). The use of a self-administered alcoholism screen test (SAAST) in a medical center. *Mayo Clinic Proceedings, 50,* 204–208.

Kristenson, H., & Trell, E. (1982). Indicators of alcohol consumption: Comparisons between a questionnaire (Mm-MAST), interviews and Serum Glutamyl Transferase (GGT) in a health survey of middle-aged males. *British Journal of Addiction, 77,* 297–304.

Hedlund, J. L., & Vieweg, B. W. (1984). The Michigan Alcoholism Screening Test (MAST): A comprehensive review. *Journal of Operational Psychiatry, 15,* 55–64.

Connors, G. J., & Tarbox, A. R. (1985). Michigan Alcoholism Screening Test. In D. J. Keyser & R. C. Sweetland (Eds.), *Test critiques: Volume 3* (pp. 439–446). Kansas City, MO: Westport.

Tuvelski, I. G. (1989). Michigan Alcoholism Screening Test (MAST)—its possibilities and shortcomings as a screening device in a pre-selected non-clinical population. *Drug and Alcohol Dependence, 24,* 255–260.

Blankfield, A., & Maritz, J. S. (1990). Female alcoholics: III. Some clinical associations of the Michigan Alcoholism Screening Test and diagnostic implications. *Acta Psychiatrica Scandinavica, 81,* 483–487.

Blow, F. C., Brower, K. J., Schulenberg, J. E., Demo-Dananberg, L. M., Young, J. P., & Beresford, T. P. (1992). The Michigan Alcoholism Screening Test—Geriatric Version (MAST-G): A new elderly specific screening instrument. *Alcoholism, Clinical, & Experimental Research, 16,* 372.

Crews, T. M., & Sher, K. J. (1992). Using adapted short MASTs for assessing parental alcoholism: Reliability and validity. *Alcoholism, Clinical, & Experimental Research, 16,* 576–584.

Jones, T. V., Lindsey, B. A., Yount, P., Soltys, R., & Farani-Enayat, B. (1993). Alcoholism screening questionnaires: Are they valid in elderly medical outpatients? *Journal of General Internal Medicine, 8,* 674–678.

Magruder-Habib, K., Stevens, H. A., & Alling, W. C. (1993). Relative performance of the MAST, VAST, and CAGE versus DSM-III-R criteria for alcohol dependence. *Journal of Clinical Epidemiology, 46,* 435–441.

McHugo, G. J., Paskus, T. S., & Drake, R. E. (1993). Detection of alcoholism in schizophrenia using the MAST. *Alcoholism: Clinical and Experimental Research, 17,* 187–191.

Parsons, K. J., Wallbrown, F. H., & Myers, R. W. (1994). Michigan Alcoholism Screening Test: Evidence supporting general as well as specific factors. *Educational and Psychological Measurement, 54,* 530–536.

Storgaard, H., Nielsen, S. D., & Gluud, C. (1994). The validity of the Michigan Alcoholism Screening Test (MAST). *Alcohol & Alcoholism, 29,* 493–502.

Lapham, S. C., Skipper, B. J., Owen, J. P., Kleyboecker, K., Teaf, D., Thompson, B., & Simpson, G. (1995). Alcohol abuse screening instruments: Normative test data collected from a first DWI offender screening program. *Journal of Studies on Alcohol, 56,* 51–59.

Maisto, S. A., Connors, G. J., & Allen, J. P. (1995). Contrasting self-report screens for alcohol problems: A review. *Alcoholism: Clinical and Experimental Research, 19,* 1510–1516.

Gray, B. T. (1996), *A review of selected substance abuse screening instruments.* Paper presented at the annual meeting of the Texas Psychological Association, Dallas, Texas.

Review of the Michigan Alcoholism Screening Test by JANICE W. MURDOCH, Professor of Psychology, Clemson University, Clemson, SC:

The Michigan Alcoholism Screening Test (MAST) is a 24-item inventory designed as an initial detection device for alcoholism. The MAST is simple to administer and to score and can be completed in less than 15 minutes. The MAST has been used in a wide variety of populations and contexts, including both clinical and research applications (see Hedlund & Vieweg, 1984, for a review). A MAST score of 4 is considered suggestive of alcoholism and 5 is considered to indicate alcoholism.

RELIABILITY. The MAST has been found to have good internal consistency and test-retest reliability (Hedlund & Vieweg, 1984; Skinner & Sheu, 1982). Hedlund and Vieweg report six studies of the MAST's internal consistency, with estimates ranging from .83 to .95, indicating that total scores are quite reliable. Test-retest estimates range from .97 for a one-day interval (Zung, 1982) to .84 for an average 4.8-month interval (Skinner & Sheu, 1982).

Individual items show greater variability in reliability. Test-retest coefficients for MAST items range from .86 (for "Have you ever been arrested for drunk driving or driving after drinking?") to .29 (for "Do you feel you are a normal drinker?") (Skinner & Sheu, 1982). Item-total score correlations have been found to range from .30 (for "Have you gotten into fights when drinking?") to .79 (for "Have you ever attended a meeting of AA?") (Zung & Charalampous, 1975). Some items on the MAST tend to be endorsed infrequently (such as "Have you ever been told you have liver trouble? Cirrhosis?"), reducing their contribution to discriminating between alcoholics and nonalcoholics.

VALIDITY. The items on the MAST are directly related to drinking behavior and to negative consequences associated with drinking, making it highly face valid. The high face validity of the measure suggests that it is possible for alcoholics to deliberately avoid detection by giving the obviously "non-alcoholic" response. Although this is clearly a possibility, the low cutoff score for the MAST is intended to minimize false negatives. An alcoholic who minimizes negative consequences of drinking may still reach the cutoff score. Ehrlich and Selzer (1967) found that 92% of a group of known alcoholics who were instructed to lie on the measure were correctly classified. Consistent with the item content of the MAST, factor analytic studies (Skinner, 1979; Zung, 1980) have found that most of the total score variance is explained by a single factor indicating general alcohol-related impairment.

The MAST has been found to correlate with other measures of alcohol use, including the General Alcoholism Factor of the Alcohol Use Inventory ($r = .83$; Skinner, 1979) and the MacAndrew Alcoholism Scale ($r = .31$ to $.46$; Friedrich & Loftsgard, 1978a, b). These findings indicate reasonable concurrent validity for scores for the MAST.

Given the concern about the high face validity of the MAST, its correlation with social desirability measures is also of interest. Correlations of $-.11$ to $-.18$ have been found between the MAST and the Crowne-Marlowe Social Desirability Scale Deny-Bad subscale (Selzer, Vinokur, & van Rooijen, 1975); however, a correlation of $-.32$ was found with the Personality Research Form Desirability Scale (Skinner, 1979).

Hedlund and Vieweg (1984) reviewed the validity of scores from the MAST for classifying individuals. They found that the ability of scores from the MAST to correctly identify alcoholics ranged from 79% to 100%, and their ability to identify nonalcoholics ranged from 36% to 95%. The MAST tends to produce a high rate of false positives and overall only a moderate rate of accurate classification in general psychiatric populations. As with any cutoff score, the lower the base rate of alcoholism in the population to be screened, the more false positives will be produced by the MAST. Given the low cutoff score and the high point values assigned to some individual items, it is important to remember that the MAST is intended to be used as a screening device and scores should not be overinterpreted.

SUMMARY. The MAST is a well-known and frequently used screening device for alcoholism. It assesses alcohol-related behaviors and negative consequences associated with drinking. It is quickly and easily administered and scored. There is a large fund of research on the psychometric properties of the instrument. It has been found that scores have good reliability and adequate validity for use as a screening device. In some populations, including the general psychiatric population, the MAST produces a high number of false positive classifications.

REVIEWER'S REFERENCES

Ehrlich, N. J., & Selzer, M. L. (1967). A screening program to detect alcoholism in traffic offenders. In M. L. Selzer, P. W. Gikas, & D. F. Huelke (Eds.), *The prevention of highway injury* (pp. 44–40). Ann Arbor: University of Michigan Highway Safety Research Institute.

Selzer, M. L., Vinokur, A., & van Rooijen, L. (1975). A self-administered short Michigan Alcoholism Screening Test (SMAST). *Journal of Studies on Alcohol, 36*, 117–126.

Zung, B. J., & Charalampous, K. D. (1975). Item analysis of the Michigan Alcoholism Screening Test. *Journal of Studies on Alcohol, 36*, 127–132.

Friedrich, W. N., & Loftsgard, S. O. (1978a). Comparison of two alcoholism scales with alcoholics and their wives. *Journal of Clinical Psychology, 34*, 784–786.

Friedrich, W. N., & Loftsgard, S. O. (1978b). A comparison of the MacAndrew Alcoholism scale and the Michigan Alcoholism Screening Test in a sample of problem drinkers. *Journal of Studies on Alcohol, 39*, 1940–1944.

Skinner, H. A. (1979). A multivariate evaluation of the MAST. *Journal of Studies on Alcohol, 40*, 831–844.

Zung, B. J. (1980). Factor structure of the Michigan Alcoholism Screening Test (MAST) in a psychiatric outpatient population. *Journal of Clinical Psychology, 36*, 1024–1030.

Skinner, H. A., & Sheu, W-J. (1982). Reliability of alcohol use indices: The lifetime drinking history and the MAST. *Journal of Studies on Alcohol, 43*, 1157–1170.

Zung, B. J. (1982). Evaluation of the Michigan Alcoholism Screening Test (MAST) in assessing lifetime and recent problems. *Journal of Clinical Psychology, 38*, 425–439.

Hedlund, J. L., & Vieweg, B. W. (1984). The Michigan Alcoholism Screening Test (MAST): A comprehensive review. *Journal of Operational Psychiatry, 15*, 55–64.

[233]
Michigan English Language Assessment Battery.

Purpose: Designed "to evaluate the advanced level English language proficiency of adult non-native speakers of English."

Population: Adult non-native speakers of English.

Publication Dates: 1985–1998.

Acronym: MELAB.

Scores, 5: Writing, Listening, GCVR [includes Grammar, Cloze Reading, Vocabulary Synonym, Vocabulary Completion, Reading] Final Score, Speaking Test (optional).

Administration: Group or individual.

Forms: Multiple equivalent forms.

Price Data, 1998: $35 per registration for Standard Individual MELAB; $25 per examiner's fee; $15 per Oral Interview; additional price information available from publisher.

Time: (135–150) minutes for complete battery; (30) minutes for Writing; (30) minutes for Listening; (75) minutes for Grammar/Cloze/Vocabulary/Reading; (15) minutes for optional oral interview.

Comments: "Used primarily to draw inferences about a test-taker's ability to study in an institution where English is the medium of instruction" or for test takers who require evidence of English language ability for professional purposes; candidates register to take exam through the publisher, which authorizes every examination (at a group test center or by certified examiner), marks all papers, and issues official score report directly to institutions selected by examinee.

Author: The English Language Institute Testing and Certification Division.

Publisher: English Language Institute, The University of Michigan.

Review of the Michigan English Language Assessment Battery by AYRES D'COSTA, Associate Professor of Education, The Ohio State University, Columbus, OH:

The history of development of the Michigan English Language Assessment Battery (MELAB) dates back to the English Language Institute founded in 1941 at the University of Michigan by Professor Robert Lado. Lado introduced objective listening and speaking assessment approaches, thus moving away from the British tradition that focused on "dictation, reading aloud, written essays, translations and commentaries on specific English language assignments" (technical manual, p. 66).

The MELAB's validity appears to be founded on Lado's descriptive analysis of English language proficiency for nonnative speakers. He stressed the importance of English as it is spoken by native speakers, rather than on written English or what was said about the language. In this sense, this pragmatic definition is reminiscent of Alfred Binet's approach to defining intelligence by the set of skills included in his I.Q. test. Also, just as Binet was measuring "readiness for schooling," Lado proposed to measure the readiness of non-English-speaking students for academic study in the U.S. by emphasizing listening and understanding skills.

The MELAB is the outcome of several decades of revisions of the original Lado tests. It is perhaps fair to say that the MELAB influenced the development of the Test of English as a Foreign language (TOEFL; 94) by Educational Testing Service (ETS) in 1963, but it has since been eclipsed by this faster developing and more popular rival. The TOEFL is now much more widely used and has recently been adapted to the computer-based mode of administration. Nonetheless, Lado's pioneering work is remarkable not only because he introduced objective assessment approaches into language testing, but also because of his recognition that "language proficiency is only one factor in predicting academic success; and other factors, such as type of course work attempted, prior academic background, and motivation, are also significant" (technical manual, p. 67).

At the present time, the MELAB has four parts. The first part assesses impromptu written composition on an assigned topic; the second is a listening test delivered via a tape-recording; and the third assesses grammar, reading comprehension, and vocabulary. The fourth part is optional and assesses speaking ability. It might be useful to mention that the TOEFL also has similar components: Listening, Language Structure, Reading Comprehension, and Writing.

It thus appears that the MELAB adheres to a fairly well-accepted competency model or test specifications matrix. This model presumes that international students who wish to attend a U.S. institution of higher learning must demonstrate sufficient proficiency in the following parts of the test battery; Part 1—Composition: The examinee must write a short essay on an assigned topic in which a position is taken and defended. It is expected that personal experience will be utilized to describe or explain a problem and offer possible solutions. Part 2—Listening: This tests how well an examinee understands spoken English. It includes audio-recorded conversational statements or mini-lectures followed by short questions in multiple-choice format. Part 3—Grammar, Cloze, Vocabulary, Reading: The purpose here is to assess both simple grammatical usage and comprehension of written English. The Cloze technique requires the candidate to find an appropriate word to fill in a blank in a passage or sentence, thus assessing language understanding in the context of a topic or theme that is presented. Part 4—(Optional) Speaking test: The examiner rates the candidate for fluency, intelligibility, grammar, vocabulary, understanding, and functional use of language.

Scoring and Reporting is done at the University of Michigan using somewhat traditional methods. For instance, the compositions (Part 1) are rated by a small pool of raters "who assess compositions daily," and provide a numeric level of the writing quality along with a letter code to indicate features that are especially good or bad given the writing level. Although, efforts are said to be made to ensure interrater reliability, one wonders how the pool of qualified raters is kept trained, motivated, and quality-controlled. Parts 2 and 3 are in multiple-choice mode, but the manual (p. 11) indicates that they are still "hand-scored with a scoring stencil," instead of using some of the more convenient computer-scoring methods that are now used by most reputable testing companies. New forms are created to ensure similar content, and the percentile method of equating is used to compare forms. The manual states (p. 10) that "the specific conversion scale for each Form varies from one Form to another." Obviously, item-response-theory-based approaches are not used.

The interpretation of MELAB scores, including the Final Total Score, is based on a scaled score system, which uses a percentile-based approach. The scaled scores are related to a 5-step interpretive rating, but there was no indication as to how this was validated other than on a general normative basis. This was particularly troublesome to this reviewer, given the strong argument to criterion-reference such tests.

The manual does include several useful normative tables broken down by reason for testing, gender, age, and native language. This effort demonstrates sensitivity of the authors to these variables; however, it seems insufficient to leave the reader with these tables and little guidance as to how to use them for differential interpretation or use of test scores.

The reliability indexes for the three parts are carefully presented in terms of internal consistency measures, alternate forms and test-retest reliability, and interrater and intrarater reliability as appropriate. The reported indexes seem respectable, ranging from .82 for Part 2 test-retest to .95 for the internal consistency index for Part 3.

The section presenting the validity evidence (administration interval not reported) for scores from the test is perhaps the best feature of the MELAB. Aside from its historical theoretical underpinnings, good efforts are made to describe the content of each component in reasonable depth. This ensures content stability and clarity as new forms are developed and users try to interpret the scores of the test battery. Several construct analyses were conducted to demonstrate the single-factor structure of each part of the test battery, when examined separately. However, a two-factor solution appears to suffice for the entire battery, with Parts 1 and 3 as the written language component and Part 2 as the aural component. Additionally, the manual reports a Pearson correlation coefficient with the TOEFL as .704 ($N = 72$), and "a moderately strong relationship" with independent teacher assessment of English proficiency.

SUMMARY. Thus the MELAB, although in serious need of modernization, appears to be a reasonably well-developed test battery for assessing the English language proficiency of international applicants to U.S. institutions.

Review of the Michigan English Language Assessment Battery by ALAN GARFINKEL, Professor of Spanish and Education, Department of Foreign Languages and Literature, Purdue University, West Lafayette, IN:

The Michigan English Language Assessment Battery (MELAB) has a history of over 50

years of development and use "by adult non-native speakers of English who will need to use English for academic purposes at the college and university levels" (Information Bulletin, p. 2). The test "is also administered to professionals who will need to use English in their work" (p. 2). The MELAB is administered to groups in testing centers around the world. It is meticulously described in the MELAB technical manual, which has caused the test to earn its wide range of acceptance among graduate schools. Administration of the test requires between 2 1/2 and 3 1/2 hours including check-in at the registration site.

The MELAB has three parts. Part 1 generates a composition score; Part 2 tests listening comprehension; and Part 3 gives a rating based on grammar, CLOZE, vocabulary, and reading items. An optional speaking test is available and the instructions for its use indicate that test producers have a strong familiarity with the literature of oral proficiency testing.

General and specific reliability coefficients are provided, as appropriate, for the composition, listening, and grammar (including CLOZE, vocabulary, and reading) segments of the test. These are based on very large samples, and KR 21 estimates of internal consistency reliability on one of the four forms range from .87 to .95. Also impressive are interrater reliability estimates for the composition section (.90) which, though based on smaller samples, are strengthened by a well-constructed chart of qualitative descriptions that have been given numerical values.

The MELAB technical manual makes a strong case for validity in terms of content and construct validity. These arguments are supported with scores of those claiming English as their native language, the pattern of which suggests that the MELAB is indeed a test of English language proficiency. Further support is provided by the fact that there is a moderately high and statistically significant correlation between MELAB scores and estimates made by teachers in one small sample.

Test administration and reporting are, as noted above, done on a secure basis and the final MELAB score is reported in a useful fashion. Those using the test are cautioned by the authors of the manual not to use a single, rigid, cutoff point because of error of measurement.

There is no mention of cultural bias in the manual. This seems appropriate for a test designed to measure linguistic proficiency in the language of a mainstream culture in which people of various linguistic and cultural backgrounds are expected to function.

Mary C. Spaan's *A Student's Guide to the MELAB* (1992) is published by the University of Michigan Press (ISBN 0-472-08146-2) to assist prospective test takers with self-assessments, self-study guides, practice tests, and scoring keys. The English Language Institute provides a 16-page bulletin describing the test for prospective test takers free of charge. It may be downloaded (as of June 1999) from www.lsa.umich.edu/eli/pdfdocs/pdfdocs.htm on the world wide web. [Editor's Note: In June 2000, we were able to retrieve the 87-page MELAB Technical Manual and the 21-page 1999–2000 MELAB Information Bulletin and Registration Forms from this web site.]

SUMMARY. In conclusion, this reviewer believes that the Michigan Language Assessment Battery is a psychometrically sound instrument that is fully deserving of the confidence placed in it by its acceptance by academic and professional groups across the country.

REVIEWER'S REFERENCE

Spaan, M. C. (1992). A student's guide to the MELAB (Michigan English Language Assessment Battery). Ann Arbor, MI: University of Michigan Press.

[234]
The MIDAS: Multiple Intelligence Developmental Assessment Scales.

Purpose: "Designed to provide an objective measure of the multiple intelligences."
Population: Age 14 to adult.
Publication Dates: 1994–1996.
Acronym: MIDAS.
Scores: 10 scales with 27 subscales: Musical (Appreciation, Instrument, Vocal, Composer), Kinesthetic (Athletic, Dexterity), Logical-Mathematical (School Math, Science, Logic Games, Everyday Math, Everyday Problem-Solving), Spatial (Spatial Awareness, Art Design, Working with Objects), Linguistic (Expressive, Rhetorical, Written/Reading), Interpersonal (Persuasion, Sensitivity, Working with People), Intrapersonal (Personal Knowledge, Calculations, Spatial Problem-Solving, Effectiveness), Leadership (Communication, Management, Social), General Logic, Innovative.
Administration: Group.
Price Data, 1996: $25 (plus shipping and handling) per manual ('96, 128 pages).
Time: (30) minutes.
Comments: May be group administered via self-completion or individually as a structured interview;

based on Howard Gardner's theory of Multiple Intelligences.
Author: C. Branton Shearer.
Publisher: Multiple Intelligences Research and Consulting, Inc.

Review of the MIDAS: Multiple Intelligence Developmental Assessment Scales by ABBOT PACKARD, Instructor, Educational Psychology and Foundations, University of Northern Iowa, Cedar Falls, IA:

This test is intended as a screening instrument to determine the characteristics of an individual's multiple-intelligence disposition. The Multiple Intelligence Developmental Assessment Scales (MIDAS) are proposed to provide an objective measure of the multiple intelligences as reported by the person or by a knowledgeable informant. The test was created to provide information about the individual's intellectual development and/or to aid curriculum design and enhance the counseling process. The MIDAS is based on Howard Gardner's theory of multiple intelligence providing information in four broad categories. First, it gives an estimate of the person's intellectual abilities in each of the seven constructs (Linguistic, Logical-Mathematical, Spatial, Musical, Kinesthetic, Interpersonal, and Intrapersonal). Second, it give 25 types of skills that are associated with each type of intelligence (e.g., navigator and advertising for Spatial). Third, three additional scales assess the person's inclination for Innovation, General Logic, and Leadership. Fourth, qualitative information is provided to deepen information gained through the measure's questions.

This test is intended for use with individuals from 14 years of age through adulthood. It can be a self-completion test or it can be administered via a structured interview. Individuals who are unable to read at a sixth grade level should have the test administered via a structured interview. Other individuals who should have the test administered by structured interview are those who are either unable or unwilling to cooperate in responding in an honest manner. Respondents with a very limited education or conceptual ability should answer the questions with the aid of a knowledgeable friend or family member. The publisher suggests that the users of the MIDAS instrument should have "an understanding of basic assessment principles and the limitations of psychometric interpretation" (manual, p. 11). Anyone interpreting results of the test should be trained in the use of this instrument with a minimum of a master's degree in psychology, education, or a related field to insure proper use and interpretation.

Psychometric properties were assessed against standards used to evaluate objective tests. An exploratory study using 349 participants addressed the question of whether the MIDAS was able to determine the seven distinct scales or constructs as described by Gardner's theory of multiple intelligences. The results indicated that seven hypothetical constructs could be determined. Discriminant and convergent validity were investigated yielding evidence that the MIDAS had the ability to discriminate each construct. The information provided the reviewer stated "while these results are not perfect they provide evidence that the questionnaire obtain a 'reasonable estimate' of a person's multiple intelligence profile" (manual, p. 67). Four studies were conducted over a 6-year period using more than 700 individuals. Construct validity was examined using 349 participants to determine if the MIDAS was able to assess specific intellectual abilities (constructs) suggested by H. Gardner. During this stage it was determined that the questionnaire was able to distinguish the hypothetical constructs. Concurrent validity was examined using 56 participants to determine that the MIDAS's subscales and appropriate cognitive tests showed correlational values ranging from .35 to .65 (most values above .48). Predictive validity evidence was gathered using 224 university students. These college students' self-reports were compared with "expert ratings" provided by their instructors; an 86% agreement was found for one category.

Four studies examined the internal consistency of the items in each scale. The mean alpha coefficients for the seven scales ranges from .76 for Kinesthetic to .87 for three other scales giving a grand mean of .85 for all seven scales. Temporal stability examination was conducted using two studies to determine if respondents changed their rating during the retest of the questionnaire. Twenty subjects in phase one completed the retest with a week delay yielding an 89% agreement. A later study using 32 participants with an 8–10-week delay indicated an average .81 agreement. An interrater reliability study was conducted to estimate the reliability of an informant's responses as well as to obtain information regarding construct validity. The rate of pairwise agreement for

individual items ranged from 75% to 85% using a total of 212 people. Cultural bias was investigated using 119 college students with the results suggesting that the MIDAS is not prone to cultural bias.

Complete instructions are given with forms for both self-assessment and assessment by a knowledgeable informant. The steps in administration are simple and direct, providing guidance for each step and condition. The test is scored by two methods: DOS-based computerized scoring program or a mail-in computerized scoring service. The results are reported with a multipage profile of the individual.

The profile includes several items to help with the interpretation of the MIDAS results: (a) an introduction to the assessment with its limitations and definitions of terms, (b) seven main scale scores, (c) 25 subscale scores, and (d) a listing of high and low key items (available in the extended report option). An interpretative packet is available for educational, career, and counseling uses. Included are the following items: (a) Cover letter introducing the nature of profile, (b) brief learning and skill summary describing areas of both strength and limitations, (c) brief descriptions of the main and subscales, (d) strategies for each intelligence, (e) college majors selection help, and (f) activities and occupations associated with the multiple intelligences. Also included are steps to understanding, interpretation, and action planning.

SUMMARY. Further studies are needed to support the value of the initial assessments. With more support, the strength of estimating a person's intellectual skills in H. Gardner's seven constructs would increase the test's desirability. This information could aid in developing a curriculum design or adding information to the counseling proceeding of an individual.

Review of the MIDAS: Multiple Intelligence Developmental Assessment Scales by MICHAEL S. TREVISAN, Assistant Professor, Department of Educational Leadership and Counseling Psychology, Washington State University, Pullman, WA:

Gardner (1993) has offered a multiple-intelligence model that includes the following dimensions: linguistic, logical-mathematical, spatial, kinesthetic, musical, interpersonal, and intrapersonal. These intelligences are flexible and dynamic and can be enhanced or improved through education and/or life experiences.

Ideas of multiple intelligences, particularly Gardner's model, resonate well with many educators. A school district in Washington state, for example, has instituted a curriculum designed specifically to foster Gardner's multiple intelligences at the elementary school years. Recently, a school district in the midwest posted a position announcement with the job responsibility of developing, implementing, and evaluating a curriculum focused on Gardner's multiple intelligences.

Given the movement in some school districts toward embracing Gardner's multiple-intelligence model, the development of the Multiple Intelligence Development Assessment Scales (MIDAS) seems a timely and welcome addition to the current curricular and instructional strategies designed to enhance Gardner's multiple intelligences. In fact, this reviewer is not aware of any other existing psychometric assessment designed to assess Gardner's multiple intelligences.

The MIDAS was developed in 1996 and is designed to be administered to individuals from age 14 to adulthood. The questionnaire consists of 106 five-point Likert scales with scale anchors specific to the content of the item. The reading level of the questionnaire is approximately sixth grade. Items ask the respondents about their (a) level of skill, (b) amount of participation, or (c) amount of enthusiasm, relative to the activities of personal preferences reflected in the item.

In addition to the aforementioned seven constructs from Gardner (1993), the items provide information on 25 subskills associated with each intelligence. Three "research scales" are also provided, which assess an individual's tendency for Innovation, General Logic, and Leadership.

The MIDAS can be individually or group administered and takes approximately 25–35 minutes. The MIDAS can also be administered with a structured interview, which takes approximately an hour. Clear, readable directions for administration are provided in the documentation accompanying the MIDAS, although there are some misspelled words in the administration manual that should be located and corrected in future documentation. The manual includes directions for both self-completion and when conducting administration with an interview.

Two options exist for scoring. One, a DOS scoring system, can be obtained from the publisher and used in-house. Two, a computerized scoring service, is available from the publisher. The second approach requires the use of a computer-scannable answer sheet. Directions for preparation of the scannable forms are included with the MIDAS documentation.

Two key sets of documents form the basis for score interpretation and consultation with the respondent. The first is referred to as the MIDAS Profile. The profile provides percent scores for the seven Gardner (1993) constructs, 25 subscales, and three research scales. A brief description of the assessment and limitations is also provided with the profile.

The Interpretative Packet is the second set of documents provided for consultation with clients. Included in the packet are a description of the scale and ways of interpreting the results, study strategies for each intelligence, strategies for selecting a college major, and activities and occupations associated with each intelligence.

Several reliability studies were conducted to estimate the consistency of scores obtained from the MIDAS. The first study estimated the extent to which the items within a scale go together or are internally consistent. Reliability estimates ranged from a low of .76 to a high of .87, providing evidence that items within a scale are measuring the same dimensions. Second, test-retest reliability estimates (based on a one-week interval) were computed to determine whether respondents change their ratings during a second administration of the questionnaire. Reliability estimates ranged from a low of .69 to a high of .86, suggesting that scores obtained from the MIDAS are relatively stable over time. Third, two studies were conducted to determine level of rater agreement, particularly when an informant conducts a structured interview with a test taker. However, the presentation of this section of the reliability studies is somewhat confusing. The author states, for example, that items not meeting agreement expectations were slated for removal or reconsidered but does not specifically state what actually happened to the items (although in a previous chapter the author specifically states that items were, in fact, eliminated). The author also defines anything below 65% agreement as unacceptable but no rationale was given for this arbitrary cutoff. Given the importance of accurately documenting test taker responses in a structured interview, this reviewer recommends rethinking the reliability evidence for rater agreement and its presentation. Assuming high agreement is desired, the author is encouraged to consider two central facets of high rater agreement when further refining the MIDAS: (a) clear criteria, and (b) training of raters (Herman, Aschbacher, & Winters, 1992).

Attempts to develop a scale that will produce valid scores is apparent in the documentation. Specifically, in the initial stages of development, items were written that were thought to tap into the various intelligences. After statistical analysis and expert review (including Howard Gardner as a reviewer) a finished set of items was retained that showed evidence for the seven scales inherent in Gardner's (1993) multiple intelligence theory. Further study showed moderate correlations with similar measures of intelligence, providing evidence of concurrent validity. In yet another validity study, a sample of college students' MIDAS scores showed some agreement with their college instructors' assessment of their multiple intelligences. Also, little evidence of cultural bias was shown in an investigation of its existence in the MIDAS.

These validity studies, however, appear to be unconnected. When the MIDAS is revised, the author is urged to develop a validity framework (Shepard, 1993) rather than an unconnected collection of validity studies. Given the high goal of assessing Gardner's (1993) multiple intelligences, this practice should markedly improve the assessment.

The MIDAS is a self-report measure. The author is clear about this limitation and offers guidelines for assessing whether an individual is capable of this type of reflection. Nevertheless, caution is warranted, particularly when using this measure for classification or diagnostic purposes in the context of a local program. Moreover, because this is a self-report measure of what one thinks their ability and cognitive styles might be rather than an actual measure of cognitive ability, in its current form the MIDAS is not equivalent to conventional intelligence and ability tests such as the Stanford-Binet or Wechsler Scales. Thus, even though the term "intelligence" appears in the title, this measure does not currently provide the kind of information needed for classification and diagnosis in the context of federal programs such as special education.

SUMMARY. Despite limitations previously mentioned, this measure appears to be a fine addition to the field. Some district officials made complementary statements about the MIDAS in the accompanying documentation and applaud its use. The author has made a professional attempt to build a quality psychometric assessment and further refinement will ensure its continued use in the future.

REVIEWER'S REFERENCES

Herman, J. L., Aschbacher, P. R., & Winters, L. (1992). *A practical guide to alternative assessment.* Alexandria, VA: Association for Supervision and Curriculum Development.
Gardner, H. (1993). *Frames of mind* (rev. ed.). New York, NY: Basic Books.
Shepard, L. A. (1993). Evaluating test validity. In L. Darling-Hammond (Ed.), *Review of research in education* (vol. 19, pp. 405–450). Washington, DC: American Educational Research Association.

[235]
Middle Grades Assessment Program.

Purpose: An assessment approach designed to collect the data essential to inform middle school improvement.

Population: Middle schools.

Publication Dates: 1981–1995.

Acronym: MGAP.

Scores: Interviews (Administrator, Teacher, Librarian/Media Specialist, Guidance Counselor, Support Staff, Student, Parent), Observations (Physical Facilities, General Environment, Library, Media Center, Classroom Instruction), Summarizing Sheets (Safety, Academic Effectiveness, Diverse Learning Opportunities, Self-Definition, Participation, Social Interaction, Physical Activity, Competence and Achievement, Structure and Limits).

Administration: Individual in part.

Price Data: Not available.

Time: Administration time not reported.

Comments: As a self-assessment, MGAP is conducted by and for a school; an assessment team approach is used.

Authors: Gayle Dorman; revised by Robin Pulver with Beth Leibson Hawkins and Kathy Hytten.

Publisher: Search Institute.

[Editor's Note: Publisher advised in December 1998 that this test is now out of print.]

Review of the Middle Grades Assessment Program by MICHAEL HARWELL, Professor, Research Methodology, Department of Educational Psychology, Minneapolis, MN:

The Middle Grades Assessment Program (MGAP) is an assessment tool designed to collect data needed for middle school change and improvement (e.g., to help assess whether particular kinds of curriculum changes in a school would have the desired outcomes or whether specific programs should be adopted or rejected). Essentially, it is an in-house assessment of school-related practices and attitudes. MGAP materials are used by an assessment team to interview and observe members of the school community with the goal of providing recommendations that would strengthen a school in prescribed ways. Information is usually obtained from one person at a time with no response time limit. As presented, the MGAP is a purely qualitative tool that is intended to serve as a vehicle for discussion and change, and is not concerned with traditional measurement notions of norms, reliability, and validity.

The manual states that there are five phases associated with using MGAP: (a) A decision to conduct an assessment is made, usually by a principal or school governance committee. This is followed by formation of an assessment team that includes the school principal, one or two team leaders selected by the principal, usually staff members, and other team members typically consisting of 6 to 12 staff members including teachers, two to eight parents and community members, and possibly a district administrator and one or two school board members. All members of the assessment team are volunteers. (b) Team members are trained to use and interpret MGAP materials, which consist of seven interview forms (Administrator Form, Teacher Form, Librarian/Media Specialist Form, Guidance Counselor Form, Support Staff Form, Student Form, Parent Form), four Observation Forms (Physical Facilities, General Environment, Library/Media Center, Classroom Instruction), and Summarizing Sheets that are used to help team members summarize information from their interviews. Teams consist of two interview administrators, librarians, and guidance counselors; each team member interviews several teachers, parents, and support staff members and observes school activities. (c) The assessment is conducted over 4–6 weeks. Various schedules for interviewing and observing are possible, for example, a few hours a day for 4–6 weeks or one day per week for 4–6 weeks. (d) Team members compile their findings individually and then spend 2 days summarizing their findings as a group in an attempt to reach a consensus on recommendations to strengthen the school. (e) Planning for school improvement is done over another 4–6-week period, presumably resulting in a written document.

Nine literature-based criteria described in the manual as important for assessing middle schools guide the process and underlie the interviewer and observation forms. These are Safety and Academic Effectiveness of the school, and seven developmental needs of young adolescents: Diverse Learning Opportunities, Self-Definition, Participation, Social Interaction, Physical Activity, Competence and Achievement, and Structure and Limits. The manual describes ideal characteristics associated with each criterion. For example, the manual lists 11 characteristics of an academically effective school, such as a curriculum that balances higher-level learning and basic skills mastery and school leadership that provides a strong focus on improving curriculum and instruction. Because no weighting scheme is described it is not clear whether the nine criteria are to be weighted equally, although this seems unlikely. The number of characteristics per criterion also varies within and across interviewing and observation forms. For example, in the Teacher Interview Form, 10 of the characteristics are associated with Academic Effectiveness, 8 with Competence and Achievement, and 3 with Social Interactions. For the Administrator Interview Form, 9 of the characteristics focus on Academic Effectiveness, 6 on Competence and Achievement, and 1 on Social Interactions.

CHOOSING TEAM MEMBERS AND RESPONDENTS. The user's manual indicates that members of the assessment team as well as respondents will consist of school administrators, teachers, librarian/media specialists, guidance counselors, support staff, students, and parents. The manual highlights the importance of characterizing the assessment as a collaborative enterprise among members of the school community who care about middle school students and about finding ways to improve the students' educational experiences. The manual emphasizes that the valid use of the interview and observation forms depends on (a) informing and involving the school community in the assessment, (b) the interviewing and observation skills of team members doing the assessment, (c) team members understanding that schools do not all look alike, (d) team members being able to look beyond observable behaviors to determine whether they are indicators of a desirable characteristic, (e) team members understanding that schools need to be observed over time to obtain an accurate picture of a school, and (f) team members who are committed to improving the school.

However, the manual is silent on two issues that shadow almost every page. One is the importance of selecting team members and respondents in a way that does not predispose or bias the results of the assessment. That most assessments are likely to be initiated and steered by the school principal raises one set of concerns; that most team members will be teachers working in the school being assessed raises another set of concerns. Although counter to the spirit of the MGAP, the possibility of biased results seems so strong that it needs to be attended to in the manual. For example, principals and teachers may have a vested interest in assessment results that reflect favorably on the school, and the innocent or deliberate selection of particular staff to the assessment team and other staff to serve as respondents could reflect that vested interest. Similarly, it is difficult to imagine how teachers in a school could be expected to respond honestly to questions such as "Do you like this school?" when the person who initiated the assessment was the principal of the school and the person asking the question is a member of the local school board! It is also easy to imagine cases in which those who volunteer to participate in the assessment, either as team members or as respondents, may not be representative of the school community. In fairness, the manual does mention the importance of obtaining a representative sample of the school community, but offers no advice on how to do so.

A second issue is that those schools that could realize the authors' portrait of an assessment as a collaborative enterprise in which all parties work toward a common goal are also likely to be those least in need of improvement, whereas schools in which the assessment results may prompt difficult decisions (e.g., staff reductions) are precisely the settings where collaboration may be most difficult and biased results most likely. For example, a well-funded school in a suburban district in which the MGAP is used to assess which extracurricular academic programs should be continued may involve a different set of dynamics as compared to an underfunded school in a large urban district in which the MGAP is used to assess ways to improve teachers' relationships with students from disadvantaged backgrounds.

These concerns are not a criticism of the MGAP per se, but raise the question of the kinds of middle schools where the MGAP may work best. If the authors believe the MGAP can work well in any setting they have a responsibility to explain why they believe this. Readers who are considering using the MGAP are well-advised to evaluate how credible the results of an assessment are likely to be for their school.

EASE OF USE. The user's manual is well-written and includes an extensive description, rationale, and bibliography for the nine criteria and for the suggestions for using the MGAP. Only after reading the user's manual, which at 136 pages of relatively small print is no mean feat, are the effort and the resources necessary to use the MGAP clear. The manual recommends that team leaders be trained by an external consultant before training other team members to interview respondents, observe aspects of a school, and to interpret their results. Team leaders use the Leader's Manual (136 pp.) to train team members over a 2-day period. How people with little or no interviewing or school-related experience (e.g., parents) can be adequately trained in 2 days is not discussed. Once trained, team members use interview forms to interview respondents. The interview forms contain well-structured questions that are marked yes or no, and follow-up questions. The interview forms incorporate the nine criteria described earlier.

However, an examination of questions on the forms again raises concerns about response bias. For example, questions in the Teacher Interview Form include "Do you believe all children can learn?" and "Do you like this school," whereas the Administrator Form includes the question "Are you available to teachers as a resource on classroom instruction?" Under what conditions would a teacher respond that they do not think all children could learn or that they do not like the school, or a principal admit they were not available to teachers? Similarly, the Student Form includes the question "Do you think that almost every student at this school has at least one adult staff member with whom he/she has a close and supportive relationship?" When would a student have this kind of information? It is important to note that many of the same questions are posed to those with different roles in the school community as an agreement check. For example, the question of whether an administrator is available as a resource to teachers is also posed to teachers. However, agreement across respondents (e.g., principals and teachers) may still reflect a response bias.

Assessment team members also complete observation forms for Physical Facilities, General Environment, Library/Media Center, and Classroom Instruction. All are marked yes or no based on the nine criteria listed earlier and present the same problems just described. The most serious problems involve the Classroom Instruction Form because it requires judgments on the part of team members for which even experienced classroom observers may have difficulty. For example, "Teacher makes smooth, quick, clear transitions from one activity to another" and "Teacher builds on students' comments and ideas" may be difficult behaviors to discern even for experienced classroom observers. Why the authors believe such behaviors can be adequately discerned by an observer who may have a total of two days of training and no school-related experience is not clear.

INTERPRETING THE RESULTS. After completing their interviews and observations, team members individually compile their findings. Summarizing sheets are available to assist team members in this task. Then the team meets as a group for 2 days to attempt to reach a consensus on the assessment results. Why the authors believe team members would be able to correctly interpret the results of their interviewing and observing is not discussed. Nor is it clear why a small group of school community members, some of whom have extensive school-related experience and others who may have little or none, would be expected to participate equally in the consensus-building process. The authors have a responsibility to offer credible advice on using this tool to team members with varying backgrounds and experiences.

CONCLUSION. As stated in the manual, the Middle Grades Assessment Program is best suited for middle schools in which members of the school community enthusiastically participate in an assessment with the common goal of improving the educational experiences of students. Such settings should minimize the possibility of biased results occurring as a function of the way that team members or respondents were selected. For middle school settings in which biased results are possible, users are advised to use the Middle Grades Assessment Program cautiously if at all. Given the concerns surrounding this tool, it seems reasonable to ask about the difference in information obtained from the Middle Grades Assessment Program, which may depend on minimally trained interviewers with little or substantial investments in a school, versus that obtained from an impartial and experienced external evaluator. The manual argues that external evaluators often fail to engage school personnel in meaningful ways, resulting in a set of recommendations that are not connected to actual practices within the school and, hence, that fail to motivate change. This may be, but the possibility of obtaining biased results using the Middle Grades Assessment Program with members of the school community seems at least as likely. Perhaps a reasonable compromise is for schools to consider contracting a highly trained, experienced, and impartial external evaluator to use the Middle Grades Assessment Program.

Review of the Middle Grades Assessment Program by STEPHEN H. IVENS, Vice President, Touchstone Applied Science Associates, Brewster, NY:

The Middle Grades Assessment Program (MGAP) is designed to provide middle school administrators, teachers, parents, and policymakers with tools to assess current practices and policies and compare them to similar characteristics of successful schools. The MGAP consists of seven interview forms and four observation forms. There are separate interview forms for Administrators, Teachers, Librarian/Media Specialists, Guidance Counselors, Support Staff, Students, and Parents. The four observational forms cover Physical Facilities, General Environment, Library/Media Center, and Classroom Instruction. MGAP instruments do not evaluate individual teacher performance nor do they assess student achievement levels.

The interview observation forms are designed to solicit information regarding perceptions of school safety, academic effectiveness, diversity of learning opportunities, development of student self-definition, student participation, social interaction, physical activity, competence and achievement, and structure and limits. For each of these areas, the MGAP User's Manual provides a series of statements reflecting an ideal school. Each item on the interview and observation forms is keyed to one of these nine criteria. Summary forms are used to collate the information and observations gathered across the separate forms.

There are five phases in conducting a MGAP assessment: (a) preparing to conduct an assessment of the educational policies, programs, and practices in a school; (b) training the assessment team members in the philosophy and use of the MGAP; (c) conducting interviews and observations; (d) sharing findings and reaching a consensus on recommendations to strengthen the school; and, (e) developing an action plan for school improvement. These five phases can be directed by the assessment team leader using the MGAP Leader's Guide and user's Manual. Alternatively, schools may retain an experienced MGAP trainer to lead one or more of the phases of the assessment by contacting the publisher.

The time to complete the MGAP will necessarily vary across schools. The publisher estimates that the assessment process can be completed over a 2- to 4-month period. Costs, too, will vary across schools. Each member of the assessment team needs copies of the MGAP User's Manual. In addition, there will be variable costs associated with released time or overtime for assessment team members, consultants, secretarial support, and supplies.

The primary focus of the Leader's Manual is on the training of the project assessment team. It is structured, detailed, and comprehensive. The User's Manual is focused primarily on the use of the interview and observational forms, and the collation of the information collected into a more useful summary format. Chapters 2 and 3 of this manual provide the reader with an excellent summary of the research literature on young adolescent learners and successful schools for them, respectively. A thoughtful feature in this manual is a well-annotated bibliography for further reading on a number of related topics.

SUMMARY. The instruments are conceptually sound; however, there is no evidence provided for the traditional concepts of reliability and validity. As noted in the Leader's Manual, the MGAP is not likely to be of much assistance in schools that are "out of control, i.e., schools where leadership is lacking, staff are unusually apathetic, students are out of control, and urgent concerns about physical safety exist" (p. 16). Conversely, the MGAP is likely to be most successful in situations where there is sufficient time to conduct the assessment and where the building and/or district administrators (a) exercise leadership for the assessment process, (b) are open to scrutiny from within, (c) are not afraid of shared decision- making with staff and parents, and (d) are willing to act on one or more of the team's recommendations.

[236]
Millon Clinical Multiaxial Inventory—III [Manual Second Edition].

Purpose: Designed to provide diagnostic and treatment information to clinicians in the areas of personality disorders and clinical syndromes.

Population: "Adults [18+] who are seeking [or in] mental health treatment and who have eighth-grade reading skills."

Publication Dates: 1976–1997.

Acronym: MCMI-III.

Scores, 28: Modifying Indices (Disclosure, Desirability, Debasement, Validity), Clinical Personality Patterns (Schizoid, Avoidant, Depressive, Dependent, Histrionic, Narcissistic, Antisocial, Aggressive (Sadistic), Compulsive, Passive-Aggressive (Negativistic), Self-Defeating), Severe Personality Pathology (Schizotypal, Borderline, Paranoid), Clinical Syndromes (Anxiety, Somatoform, Bipolar: Manic, Dysthymia, Alcohol Dependence, Drug Dependence, Post-Traumatic Stress Disorder), Severe Clinical Syndromes (Thought Disorder, Major Depression, Delusional Disorder).

Administration: Individual or group.

Price Data, 2001: $121.75 per preview package (specify mail-in or Microtest Q); $302 per handscoring starter kit including manual ('97, 216 pages), handscoring user's guide ('94, 9 pages), 10 test booklets, 50 answer sheets, 50 worksheets, 50 profile forms, and answer keys; $34 per prepaid interpretive mail-in answer sheet (specify English or Hispanic); $35.45 per prepaid corrections interpretive mail-in answer sheet (specify English or Hispanic); $17 per prepaid profile mail-in answer sheet (specify English of Hispanic); $18.50 per 25 Microtest Q answer sheets (specify English or Hispanic); $32 per interpretive Microtest Q report; $33.45 per corrections interpretive Microtest Q report; $15 per profile Microtest Q report; $27 per 10 handscoring test booklets; $45 per manual; $17.50 per Corrections Report User's Guide ('98, 56 pages); $65 per audiocassette (specify English of Hispanic).

Time: [25] minutes.

Comments: Designed to coordinate with DSM-IV categories of clinical syndromes and personality disorders; revision of the Millon Clinical Multiaxial Inventory—III (13:201); includes optional Corrections Report for use with correctional inmates.

Authors: Theodore Millon, Roger Davis, and Carrie Millon.

Publisher: NCS (Minnetonka).

Cross References: See T5:1687 (47 references); for reviews by Allen K. Hess and Paul Retzlaff of the third edition, see 13:201 (81 references); see T4:1635 (104 references); for reviews by Thomas M. Haladyna and Cecil K. Reynolds of the second edition, see 11:239 (74 references); for reviews by Allen K. Hess and

Thomas A. Widiger of the original edition, see 9:709 (1 reference); see also T3:1488 (3 references).

Review of the Millon Clinical Multiaxial Inventory—III [Manual Second Edition] by JAMES P. CHOCA, Director of Doctoral Studies, School of Psychology, Roosevelt University, Chicago, IL:

During a discussion at the convention of the American Psychological Association (APA), Raymond Fowler, APA Executive Director, lamented that the most commonly used psychological tests today are the same as those that were most popular 50 years ago (Fowler, 1999). It would appear that the field has not been able to duplicate, during the second half of the 20th century, the creativity of the first 50 years. The Stanford-Binet (T5:2485), the Rorschach (323), the Thematic Apperception Test (TAT; T5:2749), the Minnesota Multiphasic Personality Inventory (MMPI; T5:1697), the Wechsler batteries (414, T5:2862, T5:2864, 416, T5:2861), and the Halstead-Reitan Neuropsychological Test Battery (T5:1164) all originated during that time. Of course, there have been new editions, scoring systems, and refinements for many of the important tools of our trade. There has been an explosion of literature and several new journals dedicated exclusively to testing. There have even been a myriad of minor instruments added to our repertoire. These accomplishments, however, seem modest in comparison to the accomplishments of the first half of the century.

Perhaps the most notable exception to this trend has been the Millon Clinical Multiaxial Inventory (MCMI; Millon, 1977, 1982, 1994). In spite of its relatively brief history, this instrument has become a commonly used clinical tool (Piotrowski & Keller, 1989; Piotrowski & Lubin, 1990; Watkins, Campbell, Nieberding, & Hallmark, 1995). Three books have been entirely dedicated to the MCMI (Choca & Van Denburg, 1997; Craig, 1993a, 1993b), and the test has been repeatedly included in textbooks dealing with psychological assessment (e.g., Beutler & Berren, 1995; Craig, 1999a; Groth-Marnat, 1997; Koocher, Norcross, & Hill, 1998; Maruish, 1994; McCann & Dyer, 1996; Millon, 1997a; Newmark, 1996; Strack, 1999). More than 500 published studies have used the MCMI to collect data (Craig, 1999b); in fact, only two personality tests (the MMPI and the Rorschach) have been the subject of more published studies than the MCMI in the recent past (Butcher & Rouse, 1996; Ritzler, 1996). Numerous reviews and critiques are available (Dana & Cantrell, 1988; Greer, 1984; Haladyna, 1992; Hess, 1985; Lanyon, 1984; McCabe, 1984; Reynolds, 1992; Wetzler, 1990; Wetzler & Marlowe, 1992; Widiger, 1985). The test is being used in other countries and has been translated into several other languages (Jackson, Rudd, Gazis, & Edwards, 1991; Luteijn, 1990; Montag & Comrey, 1987; Mortensen & Simonsen, 1990; Simonsen & Mortensen, 1990).

The MCMI has many advantages over its main competitor, the MMPI-2. For one thing, the instrument was especially designed to measure personality traits; although an assessment of the personality make-up can also be obtained from the MMPI-2, this reviewer believes that the MCMI offers a clearer and more comprehensive evaluation of the personality dimensions. In spite of being much shorter, the MCMI is just as valid and reliable as the MMPI-2. The instrument was normed with psychiatric patients and uses a new weighted score, the Base Rate Score (BRS), that takes into account the prevalence of the specific disorder in the psychiatric population. Finally, Millon has been eager to adjust the inventory in order to incorporate theoretical developments, as well as changes in the classification system for mental disorders. In contrast, the basic clinical scales of the MMPI were not changed appreciably during the recent revision, and are still tied to a diagnostic system that is now archaic. Recent developments linking the theory into systems of treatment planning and psychotherapy (Choca & Van Denburg, 1997; Hyer, 1994; Retzlaff, 1995; Millon, 1999) make the test useful in situations where the interest is more therapeutic than diagnostic.

Compared with other instruments designed to measure personality traits (e.g., the NEO Personality Inventory, Costa & McCrae, 1985; T5:2218), the MCMI is a clinical inventory. It conceptualizes personality in the way clinicians think, using prototypes that have been part of the clinical literature for years. Because it also offers scales measuring clinical syndromes (Axis I of the DSM-IV), the diagnostician does not have to resort to a different instrument in order to assess those areas of functioning.

The MCMI is routinely used by itself as a screening instrument or as part of a test battery. When used as part of a battery, the referral question and history are typically considered in order to determine what other tests should be included. A typical battery to evaluate emotional problems may include more specialized self-report questionnaires (e.g., the Eating Disorders Inventory; T5:893) and projective tests such as the Rorschach and the TAT. The MCMI has also been used as part of a neuropsychological battery to evaluate brain dysfunction.

As is often the case, some of the disadvantages of the MCMI are the direct result of advantages listed above. The fact that it is based on Millon's theory has limited, in the past, the degree of compatibility equivalent scales have had with the DSM disorders (Widiger & Sanderson, 1987; Widiger, Williams, Spitzer, & Frances, 1985). The current version (MCMI-III) has three personality scales that do not have a DSM-IV equivalent. Moreover, the efforts to make the test more DSM compatible may be limiting its compatibility with Millon's theory (Widiger, 1999). In his eagerness to move the MCMI along, Millon has already produced three editions of this test. The end result is that, in spite of the wealth of literature available on the original MCMI and the MCMI-II, clinicians using the current version will not have access to much empirical data for a few years to come. Given the drastic changes that were made (95 of the 175 items of the MCMI-II were replaced to create the MCMI-III), one can not assume that anything that was true of an earlier version remains true with the current version.

The scoring used for the MCMI-III has been criticized for being unduly complex in ways that do not improve the performance of the test (Retzlaff, 1991; Retzlaff, Sheehand, & Lorr, 1990; Streiner, Goldberg, & Miller, 1993; Streiner & Miller, 1989). The test derives 24 scales from 175 items or the equivalent of about 7 items per scale. It accomplishes this feat by having items load on more than one scale, but that causes psychometric problems and leads to some scales that are excessively intercorrelated.

In pushing the psychological testing envelope, Millon accepted the notion of publishing operating characteristics, or the number of examinees that the test correctly diagnoses. This idea was originally proposed by Gibertini, Brandenburg, and Retzlaff (1986) for the MCMI, and the operating characteristics of the first two editions spoke well for those instruments. In contrast, the oper-

ating characteristics for the MCMI-III left something to be desired (Millon, 1994; Retzlaff, 1996). A second study was done by Roger Davis in an attempt to correct the problem, but the research design allowed clinicians who had seen the MCMI-III results to assign the diagnoses, obviously contaminating the data (study described in Millon, 1997b). It should be noted that having reasonable operating characteristics represents a very high standard for our current level of development. Even the most valid tests in our repertoire, such as the Wechsler Adult Intelligence Scale (WAIS-III; 415), would probably fare poorly if we were to demand that—in the absence of any other information—the test results lead to an accurate DSM-IV diagnosis.

SUMMARY. In closing, it should be noted that some of the most arduous critics of the MCMI have continued to use this instrument in preference of anything else. As implied above, this reviewer sees this test as one of the greatest contributions made to the field during his professional life.

REVIEWER'S REFERENCES

Millon, T. (1977). Millon Clinical Multiaxial Inventory. Minneapolis, MN: National Computer Systems.

Millon, T. (1982). Manual for the MCMI-II. Minneapolis, MN: National Computer Systems.

Greer, S. (1984). Testing the test: A review of the Millon Clinical Multiaxial Inventory. Journal of Counseling and Development, 63, 262–263.

Lanyon, R. I. (1984). Personality assessment. Annual Review of Psychology, 35, 667–701.

McCabe, S. (1984). [Review of the Millon Clinical Multiaxial Inventory.] In D. Keyser & R. Sweetland (Eds.), Test critiques (Vol. 1, pp. 455–465). Kansas City, MO: Test Corporation of America.

Costa, P. T., & McCrae, R. R. (1985). The NEO Personality Inventory manual, Form S and Form R. Odessa, FL: Psychological Assessment Resources.

Hess, A. K. (1985). [Review of the Millon Clinical Multiaxial Inventory.] In J. V. Mitchell, Jr. (Ed.), The ninth mental measurements yearbook (pp. 984–986). Lincoln, NE: Buros Institute of Mental Measurements.

Widiger, T. A. (1985). [Review of the Millon Clinical Multiaxial Inventory.] In J. V. Mitchell, Jr. (Ed.), The ninth mental measurements yearbook (pp. 986–988). Lincoln, NE: Buros Institute of Mental Measurements.

Widiger, T. A., Williams, J. B. W., Spitzer, R. L., & Frances, A. (1985). The MCMI as a measure of DSM-III. Journal of Personality Assessment, 49, 366–378.

Gibertini, M., Brandenburg, N. A., & Retzlaff, P. D. (1986). The operating characteristics of the Millon Clinical Multiaxial Inventory. Journal of Personality Assessment, 50, 554–567.

Montag, I., & Comrey, A. L. (1987). Millon MCMI scales factor analyzed and correlated with MMPI and CPS scales. Multivariate Behavioral Research, 22, 401–413.

Widiger, T. A., & Sanderson, C. (1987). The convergent and discriminant validity of the MCMI as a measure of the DSM-III personality disorders. Journal of Personality Assessment, 51, 228–242.

Dana, R., & Cantrell, J. (1988). An update on the Millon Clinical Multiaxial Inventory (MCMI). Journal of Clinical Psychology, 44, 760–763.

Piotrowski, C., & Keller, J. W. (1989). Psychological testing in outpatient mental health facilities: A national study. Professional Psychology, Research and Practice, 20, 423–425.

Streiner, D. L., & Miller, H. R. (1989). The MCMI-II: How much better than the MCMI? Journal of Personality Assessment, 53, 81–84.

Luteijn, F. (1990). The MCMI in the Netherlands: First findings. Journal of Personality Disorders, 4, 297–302.

Mortensen, E. L., & Simonsen, E. (1990). Psychometric properties of the Danish MCMI-I translation. Scandinavian Journal of Psychology, 31, 149–153.

Piotrowski, C., & Lubin, B. (1990). Assessment practices of health psychologists: Survey of APA Division 38 clinicians. Professional Psychology: Research and Practice, 21, 99–106.

Retzlaff, P. D., Sheehan, E. P., & Lorr, M. (1990). MCMI-II scoring: Weighted and unweighted algorithms. Journal of Personality Assessment, 55, 219–223.

Simonsen, E., & Mortensen, E. L. (1990). Difficulties in translation of personality scales. *Journal of Personality Disorders, 4,* 290–296.

Wetzler, S. (1990). The Millon Clinical Multiaxial Inventory (MCMI): A review. *Journal of Personality Assessment, 55,* 445–464.

Jackson, H. J., Rudd, R., Gazis, J., & Edwards, J. (1991). Using the MCMI-I to diagnose personality disorders in inpatients: Axis I/Axis II associations and sex differences. *Australian Psychologist, 26,* 37–41.

Retzlaff, P. D. (1991, August). *MCMI-II scoring challenges: Multi-weight items and site specific algorithms.* Paper presented at the 99th Annual Convention of the American Psychological Association, San Francisco, CA.

Haladyna, T. M. (1992). [Review of the Millon Clinical Multiaxial Inventory–II.] In J. J. Kramer & J. C. Conoley (Eds.), *The eleventh mental measurements yearbook* (pp. 532–533). Lincoln, NE: Buros Institute of Mental Measurements.

Reynolds, C. R. (1992). [Review of the Millon Clinical Multiaxial Inventory–II.] In J. J. Kramer & J. C. Conoley (Eds.), *The eleventh mental measurements yearbook* (pp. 533–535). Lincoln, NE: Buros Institute of Mental Measurements.

Wetzler, S., & Marlowe, D. (1992). What they don't tell you in the test manual: A response to Millon. *Journal of Counseling and Development, 70,* 427–428.

Craig, R. J. (Ed.). (1993a). *The Millon Clinical Multiaxial Inventory: A clinical research information synthesis.* Hillsdale, NJ: Lawrence Erlbaum.

Craig, R. J. (1993b). *Psychological assessment with the Millon Clinical Multiaxial Inventory (II): An interpretative guide.* Odessa, FL: Psychological Assessment Resources.

Streiner, D. L., Goldberg, J. O., & Miller, H. R. (1993). MCMI-II item weights: Their lack of effectiveness. *Journal of Personality Assessment, 60,* 471–476.

Hyer, L. (Ed.). (1994). *Trauma victim: Theoretical issues and practical suggestions.* Muncie, IN: Accelerated Development Incorporated.

Maruish, M. E. (Ed.). (1994). *The use of psychological testing for treatment planning and outcome.* Hillsdale, NJ: Erlbaum.

Millon, T. (1994). *Millon Clinical Multiaxial Inventory—III manual.* (1st ed.). Minneapolis, MN: National Computer Systems.

Beutler, L. E., & Berren, M. R. (Eds.). (1995). *Integrative assessment of adult personality.* New York: Guilford.

Retzlaff, P. D. (Ed.). (1995). *Tactical psychotherapy of the personality disorders: An MCMI-III based approach.* Boston: Allyn & Bacon.

Watkins, C. E., Jr., Campbell, V. L., Nieberding, R., & Hallmark, R. (1995). Contemporary practices of psychological assessment by clinical psychologists. *Professional Psychology: Research and Practice, 26,* 54–60.

Butcher, J. N., & Rouse, S. V. (1996). Personality: Individual differences and clinical assessment. *Annual Review of Psychology, 47,* 87–111.

McCann, J. T., & Dyer, F. J. (1996). *Forensic assessment with the Millon inventories.* New York: Guilford Press.

Newmark, C. S. (Ed.). (1996). *Major psychological assessment instruments* (Vol. II). Boston: Allyn & Bacon.

Retzlaff, P. (1996). MCMI-III diagnostic validity: Bad test or bad validity study? *Journal of Personality Assessment, 66,* 431–437.

Ritzler, B. (1996, Spring/Summer). Personality assessment and research: The state of the union. *SPA Exchange, 6,* 15.

Choca, J. P., & Van Denburg, E. (1997). *Interpretative guide to the Millon Clinical Multiaxial Inventory* (2nd ed.). Washington, DC: American Psychological Association.

Groth-Marnat, G. (1997). *Handbook of psychological assessment* (3rd ed.). New York: Wiley.

Millon, T. (1997a). *The Millon inventories: Clinical and personality assessment.* New York: Guilford.

Millon, T. (1997b). *Millon Clinical Multiaxial Inventory—III manual* (2nd ed.). Minneapolis, MN: National Computer Systems.

Koocher, G. P., Norcross, J. C., & Hill, S. S., III. (Eds.). (1998). *Psychologists' desk reference.* New York: Oxford University Press.

Craig, R. J. (1999a). *Interpreting personality tests: A clinical manual for the MMPI-2, MCMI-III, CPI-R, and 16PF.* New York: Wiley.

Craig, R. J. (1999b). Overview and current status of the Millon Clinical Multiaxial Inventory. *Journal of Personality Assessment, 72,* 390–406.

Fowler, R. D. (1999, August). Discussion. In S. Urbina (Chair), *Challenges and innovations in psychological testing and assessment.* Symposium conducted at the 107th annual convention of the American Psychological Association, Boston.

Millon, T. (1999). *Personality-guided therapy.* New York: Wiley.

Strack, S. N. (Ed.). (1999). *Essentials of Millon inventory assessments.* New York: Wiley.

Widiger, T. A. (1999). Millon's dimensional polarities. *Journal of Personality Assessment, 72,* 365–389.

Review of the Millon Clinical Multiaxial Inventory—III [Manual Second Edition] by THOMAS A. WIDIGER, Department of Psychology, University of Kentucky, Lexington, KY:

The Millon Clinical Multiaxial Inventory—III (MCMI-III) is a 175-item true-false self-report inventory for the assessment of psychopathology. Its major competing alternatives are the Minnesota Multiphasic Personality Inventory—II (MMPI-II; Butcher, Dahlstrom, Graham, Tellegen, & Kaemmer, 1989; T5:1697) and the Personality Assessment Inventory (PAI; Morey, 1991; T5:1959). Its principal advantages relative to these instruments are the inclusion of scales devoted to the diagnosis of the personality disorders included within the fourth edition of the American Psychiatric Association's (APA) *Diagnostic and Statistical Manual of Mental Disorders* (DSM-IV; APA, 1994). Personality disorders are placed on a separate axis in DSM-IV to encourage their diagnosis in clinical practice because they have been shown to have a substantial impact on the course and treatment of most other mental disorders (Widiger & Sanderson, 1995). The primary author of the MCMI-III has been a leading theorist in the diagnosis and classification of personality disorders and was instrumental in the development of the diagnostic criteria for both the avoidant and passive-aggressive personality disorders.

However, the extent to which the MCMI-III scales are in fact coordinated with the DSM-IV personality disorders has been controversial (Zimmerman, 1994). There has been a substantial amount of research on the convergence of various editions of the MCMI with other personality disorder instruments. A surprising omission from the MCMI-III test manual is any reference to this extensive research. The research summarized within the manual is confined to unpublished validation studies conducted by the test authors. Studies published in peer-reviewed journals by independent researchers have generally indicated good to excellent convergence with respect to the assessment of the avoidant, dependent, borderline, and passive-aggressive personality disorders, but inconsistent, problematic, and perhaps even poor convergence for the obsessive-compulsive, antisocial, histrionic, and narcissistic personality disorders (Widiger & Sanderson, 1995). In fact, many studies have reported significant negative convergent validity coefficients for the Obsessive-Compulsive scale. It is problematic enough to fail to obtain convergent validity but, apparently, persons who elevate on the MCMI-III Obsessive-Compulsive scale might even be less likely to have this personality disorder than persons who do not obtain an elevation.

Some of the weak convergence appears to be attributable to a different emphasis within the

MCMI-III scales on various components of, or theoretical model for, a respective personality disorder. For example, the MCMI-III scales for the assessment of the obsessive-compulsive, narcissistic, and histrionic personality disorders include a substantial proportion of items that assess adaptive rather than maladaptive functioning. The Histrionic scale includes items that assess adaptive gregariousness (e.g., #57: "I think I am a very sociable and outgoing person"; and #80: "It's easy for me to make many friends"), the Narcissistic scale includes items that assess normal, adaptive self-confidence (e.g., #40: "I guess I'm a fearful and inhibited person," keyed false; and #69: "I avoid most social situations because I expect people to criticize or reject me," keyed false), and the Obsessive-Compulsive scale includes items that assess normal, adaptive constraint (e.g., #22: "I'm a very erratic person, changing my mind and feelings all the time," keyed false; and #53: "Punishment never stopped me from doing what I wanted," keyed false). Persons with the respective personality disorder might endorse the item in the respective direction, but it is also evident that persons who do not have maladaptive personality traits would have to endorse these items in the same direction. Clinicians might consider readministering the MCMI-III after treatment has been completed. They may at times find that their psychotherapy has apparently created rather than cured their patient of narcissistic, histrionic, or obsessive-compulsive symptomatology, as scores on these scales have been shown to increase after treatment has been completed (Widiger & Saylor, 1998).

Potential limitations of items that assess adaptive rather than maladaptive functioning can be offset to some extent by confining their administration to persons known to have the respective symptomatology. The "normative data and transformation scores for the MCMI-III are based entirely on clinical samples and are applicable only to individuals who evidence problematic emotional and interpersonal symptoms or who are undergoing professional psychotherapy or a psychodiagnostic evaluation" (manual, 1997, p. 6). "An important feature that distinguishes the MCMI from other inventories is its use of actuarial base rate data rather than normalized standard score transformations" (manual, 1997, p. 5). Most other instruments determine cutoff points for scale interpretation on the basis of the extent of deviation from a population norm (e.g., Butcher et al., 1989; Morey, 1991). A limitation of such cutoff points is the false assumption that scale interpretation should be governed simply by statistical deviance. Cutoff scores that are coordinated with the actual base rate of a disorder will provide more accurate diagnoses.

However, the advantages of using base rate data to set a cutoff point are lost if the prevalence rate for the disorder varies significantly across different settings. This was demonstrated vividly by Retzlaff (1996). Retzlaff noted that the 1994 version of the MCMI-III test manual failed to report the probability of having a disorder given the obtainment of a cutoff point. Retzlaff therefore calculated this probability using the data provided within the test manual. The probability values ranged from a low of .00 (Sadistic) to a high of only .32 (Histrionic). Sensitivity rates (proportion of persons with a disorder who obtained a particular cutoff point) ranged from a low of .00 (Sadistic) to a high of only .40 (Dependent). These were remarkably poor results, yet they were based on the test authors' own validation data provided within the MCMI-III manual. For example, only 4% of the persons with an antisocial personality disorder included within the test authors' own validation sample would have been identified by the MCMI-III's cutoff points.

The second edition of the MCMI-III test manual was published the following year, along with new sensitivity and probability values that were now within acceptable ranges (e.g., the Obsessive-Compulsive scale had a sensitivity of .73 rather than .07). There was no indication of what correction was made to the validation data, to the scales, or to the cutoff points that provided this substantial improvement. However, perhaps the lesson learned from Retzlaff (1996) is that the diagnostic accuracy of the scales may vary substantially across different clinical settings. As indicated by the test authors, "local base rates and cutting lines must still be developed for special settings" (manual, p. 5). Millon et al. (authors of the 2nd edition test manual) suggest that "the MCMI can be used on a routine basis in outpatient clinics, community agencies, mental health centers, college counseling programs, general and mental hospitals, independent and group practice offices, and in court" (manual, p. 5). However, clinicians working within clinical settings in which substantial clinical symptomatology is not commonplace (e.g., college counseling or divorce mediation center) might find that the MCMI-III overestimates the extent and breadth of psychopathology.

Millon, Davis, and Millon (1998) provide a supplementary manual for applications of the MCMI-III within correctional (prison) settings. As indicated in this manual, the MCMI-III Interpretive Report provided by the National Computer Systems would most likely be inaccurate within a prison setting. "BR (base rate) modifications were made for those [personality disorder scales] where differences in prevalence were found between correctional inmates and psychiatric patients" (Millon et al., 1998, p. 5). Adjustments are made to the cutoff points for eight of the personality disorder scales when administered to male inmates, and to six scales when administered to female inmates. "The norms for the other MCMI-III scales remain the same ... because of their general applicability to diverse respondents" (Millon et al., 1998, p. 5). Surprisingly, no adjustments were made to the MCMI-III Antisocial Personality Disorder scale. The prevalence rate Millon et al. (1998) obtained for antisocial personality disorder symptomatology within their inmate setting was not substantially different from the base rate of antisocial symptomatology obtained by the MCMI-III in general psychiatric settings. In fact, Millon et al. (1998) indicated that if there is any difference, their research suggested that "male inmates are less likely than psychiatric patients to exhibit ... antisocial (Scale 6A; 14.4% versus 17.9%) ... characteristics" (p. 10). These findings are so discrepant from clinical expectations that some caution should perhaps still be exercised. Nevertheless, the effort of Millon et al. (1998) to develop separate MCMI-III norms for different clinical settings is an important advance in the scoring of this instrument.

Clinicians could make their own corrections to the cutoff points based on their own estimates of the prevalence rates within their local setting. Hand-scoring templates for the scoring of the MCMI-III are available at minimal cost. However, clinicians might find these templates to be somewhat cumbersome. There are 14 steps to complete, some of which closely resemble a complicated tax form. This complexity is due largely to the admirable efforts of the test authors to make adjustments to each scale for the many different variables that can impact a particular test score

(e.g., gender, setting, mood state, and response set). However, the test authors themselves estimate that it takes approximately 40–60 minutes to administer each hand-scoring template, which is appreciably longer than the 20–30 minutes it probably took for the respondent to complete the instrument. One might be better off using the 40–60 minutes to conduct a detailed interview of the patient.

SUMMARY. The MCMI-III is among the most popular self-report instruments for the assessment of personality disorders but given a number of important limitations it should be used with substantial caution and skepticism. Elevations on a particular scale should perhaps be interpreted as only suggestions for possible diagnoses that need to be verified with a systematic interview.

REVIEWER'S REFERENCES

Butcher, J. N., Dahlstrom, W. G., Graham, J. R., Tellegen, A., & Kaemmer, B. (1989). *Minnesota Multiphasic Personality Inventory (MMPI-2): Manual for administration and scoring.* Minneapolis: University of Minnesota Press.
Morey, L. C. (1991). *The Personality Assessment Inventory professional manual.* Odessa, FL: Psychological Assessment Resources.
American Psychiatric Association. (1994). *Diagnostic and statistical manual of mental disorders* (4th ed.). Washington, DC: American Psychiatric Association.
Zimmerman, M. (1994). Diagnosing personality disorders. A review of issues and research methods. *Archives of General Psychiatry, 51,* 225–245.
Widiger, T. A., & Sanderson, C. J. (1995). Assessing personality disorders. In J. N. Butcher (Ed.), *Clinical personality assessment: Practical approaches* (pp. 380–394). New York: Oxford University Press.
Retzlaff, P. (1996). MCMI-III diagnostic validity: Bad test or bad validity study. *Journal of Personality Assessment, 66,* 431–437.
Millon, T., Davis, R., & Millon, C. (1998). *Millon Clinical Multiaxial Inventory—III corrections report user's guide.* Minneapolis, MN: National Computer Systems, Inc.
Widiger, T. A., & Saylor, K. I. (1998). Personality assessment. In A. S. Bellack & M. Hersen (Eds.), *Comprehensive clinical psychology* (pp. 145–167). New York: Pergamon Press.

[237]
Minnesota Clerical Assessment Battery.

Purpose: "Designed to assess knowledge and skills required for a number of clerical jobs."
Population: Secretaries and other clerical workers.
Publication Dates: 1988–1995.
Acronym: MCAB.
Scores: 3 composite scores: Secretaries, Clerk-Typists, Generalists.
Administration: Group.
Price Data, 1995: $260 per complete system, limited-use license administration units; $1,495 per single machine, unlimited-use license; $5,995 per single building site license; additional license and volume discount information available from publisher.
Comments: Composite scores are derived from two or more subtests; requires MS-DOS or PC-DOS computer to administer.
Author: Assessment Systems Corporation.
Publisher: Assessment Systems Corporation.
　　a) TYPING/KEYBOARDING.
　　Scores, 3: Gross Speed, Accuracy, Net Speed.
　　Time: (2–4) minutes.

b) PROOFREADING.

Scores, 3: Initially Incorrect, Initially Correct, Total.

Time: (45) minutes.

c) FILING.

Scores, 3: Alphabetical, Numerical, Total.

Time: (50) minutes.

d) BUSINESS VOCABULARY.

Scores: Total score only.

Time: (25) minutes.

e) BUSINESS MATH.

Scores: Total score only.

Time: (60) minutes.

f) CLERICAL KNOWLEDGE.

Scores: Total score only.

Time: (25) minutes.

Review of the Minnesota Clerical Assessment Battery by ROBERT FITZPATRICK, Consulting Psychologist, Cranberry Township, PA:

The Minnesota Clerical Assessment Battery (MCAB), not to be confused with the Minnesota Clerical Test (T5:1693), is administered and scored by personal computer using a DOS operating system. The tests can be administered separately or in batteries. The using organization may use predesigned batteries or may specify its own.

The tests were developed by a content strategy; that is, a job analysis presumably dictated the choice and development of the tests. According to the user's manual, "a test is valid for the job if it consists of a sample of the types of things that a person could be expected to do on that job" (p. 5-1). Hence, it is said, there is no need for other evidence of validity. No criterion-related evidence, to show that test scores are related to clerical job performance, is presented. A weak claim for construct validity is based on data showing that test scores tended to be higher for norm group members who had relatively more reported experience with matters related to test content. The manual asserts that the user must "determine whether the tests are valid for a particular purpose and intended use" (p. 5-1). Most users, however, are limited in the resources they can devote to validation, and expect at least initial evidence and guidance from the publisher.

Even for the limited purpose of describing a content strategy, the manual is inadequate. The job analysis, insofar as it relates to the content of the tests, is described in quite general terms: Two previous job analysis studies (dated 1975 and 1981) and three secretarial handbooks were reviewed, and somehow the tests and their contents were derived. Further job analysis efforts were devoted to (a) establishing three norm groups representing different types of clerical workers and (b) aiding in the assignment of weights to test scores when tests are used in battery to produce an overall score. These efforts seem only marginally useful.

Except for the Typing/Keyboarding test, ample time is allowed, so that almost all examinees can finish each test. In some ways, this is a desirable feature because the psychometric characteristics of speeded tests are difficult to interpret. On the other hand, some clerical tasks call for quick *and* accurate work, so that pure accuracy is not necessarily what is wanted. Time to administer all six tests, judging from the experience of the norm groups, would average about 2 hours, and it could take as long as 4 hours.

The norm groups are limited in size and representativeness. The groups are made up of incumbent clerical workers, for most purposes divided into secretaries, typists, and "generalists" on the basis of time and importance of clerical activities in which the workers engage.

Reliabilities were estimated from internal consistency statistics for most of the tests. For the Typing/Keyboarding and Proofreading tests, the two parts were treated as alternate forms for the purpose of estimating reliability. The reliability numbers are high enough to be encouraging, but the lack of other reliability evidence is unfortunate. Test-retest correlations ought to have been obtained.

No information is provided about the intercorrelations of the tests, or of any of the tests with other measures. The tests appear to be similar to a number of other tests of clerical aptitude or ability. However, in the absence of data showing similarity in use, it would be risky to assume that scores from these tests are as valid for selecting successful clerks as others have been shown to be.

TYPING/KEYBOARDING. This is a straight copy test using two short passages that appear to be reasonably similar to material often encountered in a typical office. The text is shown in the top half of a split computer screen, and the examinee's production appears in the bottom half. The examinee is told that errors may be corrected only before the next word is completed. However, it is not clear whether it is good strategy for the examinee to correct errors. Scoring is automatic and complicated; it is doubtful that the scores are comparable to those that would be obtained in the usual typing test from separate printed copy.

PROOFREADING. This test is not a proofreading test in the traditional sense of detecting deviations from error-free copy. Rather, it presents 3 brief passages with a number of errors in spelling, grammar, capitalization, and punctuation. The examinee is to detect the errors and use the computer keyboard to correct them. Problems can arise if an examinee chooses to change the passage in ways not recognized by the program, or if an error is made in attempting a recognized correction.

FILING. This is a test of ability to place items in alphabetical or numerical order. Requiring up to an hour to administer, it seems inordinately long. Other similar tests can be completed in 10 minutes or so, with little if any loss in reliability.

BUSINESS VOCABULARY. The stem words for this test are said by the manual to have been "drawn from indices and glossaries of three secretarial handbooks" (p. 10-1), selecting words "that appeared both difficult and significant enough to include in a test" (p. 10-1). The sampling method is vaguely described and seems inadequate. Some of the keyed answers are difficult to justify, even after reference to a dictionary. (The tests are not accompanied by keys to correct responses, so that the user is apparently expected to trust the publisher to have keyed correctly.) It seems likely that this test is highly similar in function to a typical test of word knowledge or to a test of general cognitive ability.

BUSINESS MATH. This test deals with discounts and other percentage problems, fractions, and decimals. Items were partly based on the contents of three business math textbooks. Calculators are not allowed, but it is suggested that paper and pencil be made available. Surely, most clerks these days do not make calculations in this way.

CLERICAL KNOWLEDGE. The content of this test was based on the same three secretarial handbooks used for the Business Vocabulary Test, along with input from seven "business teachers from vocational-technical schools" (p. 12-1). Internal consistency reliability estimates for these items are relatively low (alpha = .80); it is not clear just what this test is measuring. It seems likely that it is substantially correlated with Business Vocabulary and general cognitive ability.

SUMMARY. These tests might be useful to an organization for which the content can be shown to be job-relevant and in which testing time is not an important consideration. For others, the doubtful job analysis and content relevance, the high testing time, the dearth of validity and other data, the limited reliability information, and the absence of justification for adding to the already bulging store of clerical tests make the MCAB a poor investment. An efficient alternative for most of the tests can be found, for example, in the Short Tests of Clerical Ability (T5:2408) or the Office Skills Tests (T5:1836), both of which come with ample validity and other evidence and which can be computer administered.

Review of the Minnesota Clerical Assessment Battery by BIKKAR S. RANDHAWA, Professor of Educational Psychology, University of Saskatchewan, Saskatoon, Canada:

The Minnesota Clerical Assessment Battery (MCAB), Edition 1.5, was published in 1995. It was intended for use in assessing the knowledge and skills of prospective employees for secretarial, clerical, and general clerical and secretarial positions, labeled here as "generalists." The previous version of this battery (Edition 1.0) was released in 1988 and reviewed by Stutzman and Veres III (1990). From the current manual it is not clear if any changes were made to the content of the tests in the battery, norms, results, and the manual itself.

The battery consists of six separate tests: Typing, Proofreading, Filing, Business Vocabulary, Business Math, and Clerical Knowledge. An interesting and a novel feature of this battery is that it is administered and scored on an IBM-compatible personal computer. As a result, it requires that the test administrator be reasonably computer literate and have the ability to cope with frustrations due to unexpected computer- or software-related glitches. The supplied diskettes do not allow making a backup copy of the MCAB Key Diskette to be used in case of a computer emergency. I can appreciate the need to control for the unauthorized use of the battery. However, the user's inability to have a working backup diskette handy in case of emergency is a serious problem. The planned testing cannot proceed unless a replacement is released by the publisher, which might take days. I personally ran into difficulties in accessing the tests for review. I either had to wait for days to get a replacement from the supplier after they had received the defective diskette back or receive a replacement from the Buros Institute personnel immediately after I informed them of my dilemma via e-mail. There ought to be another alternative for the developers to consider what is more convenient for the administrators of the battery in case something goes wrong with the original diskette.

The test development was preceded by an analysis of the jobs performed by clerical personnel in public service and the insurance industry. From this initial analysis the basic content of the six MCAB tests was determined. Also, a 25-task questionnaire, partitioned into seven content areas, was developed.

The job analysis questionnaire and the initial battery of six tests were administered to 414 employees from six organizations. The range of the number of examinees in the so-called "norming sample" from these organizations was 3 to 189. However, 46 of these examinees were excluded from the norming study because these respondents did not meet the criterion for inclusion, that is, spending at least half of their time doing tasks directly related to the tasks appropriate for the MCAB. These excluded examinees from the norming study were "combined with another sample of nonclerical individuals for use in refining the psychometric quality of the tests" (manual, p. 6-4). No further details of this group and how they were used for the above purpose are given in the manual. The remaining sample of 368 examinees were divided based on an iterative cluster analysis procedure into three subgroups, secretarial (187), clerk-typist (98), and general office clerk (83), for establishing separate norms. It is not evident how the cluster analysis categories represent actual reported job classifications of the individuals. Therefore, how one would relate to the norms results from MCAB for recruitment for a specific job is problematic.

The total sample consisted of 17 males and 346 females. The manual also reports the ethnic distribution of the total norming sample and concludes that "minority representation in the sample was slightly higher than that in the United States population at the time of the norming study" (manual, p. 6-4). Furthermore, norming samples clearly were convenience samples only and their representativeness or not to the U.S. population is incidental.

The Typing/Keyboarding Test was purportedly designed to measure the six tasks included in the job analysis questionnaire for this cluster. This is a direct typing test displayed on a split-monitor screen such that the stimulus text appears in the top window of the screen and the text that an examinee types appears in the bottom window. The examinee is given instructions on the computer screen on how to take the test and a practice passage is presented. Timing for typing the passage begins with the examinee's first keystroke. In terms of keystroke intensity and syllabic intensity as measures of difficulty, it is claimed that the first passage is typical of most general office correspondence and that the second passage is representative of professional or technical writing. Although three scores (gross speed, accuracy, and net) are obtained for each passage, standard error of measurement (*SEM*) is provided only for the gross speed for each passage and for the average gross speed.

The Proofreading Test consists of three passages, each about 100 words in length and contains 20 typographical errors, about two per line of text. It assesses, therefore, the examinee's ability to find and correct typographical errors on the computer screen. The developers admit that the proofreading passages are not authentic because it is rare to find a document in a business environment that would contain, on the average, two errors per line of text (manual, p. 8-1). The lack of authenticity is further exacerbated because there are 39 spelling errors in total, which would be rare to find given that most modern offices are equipped with the automated spelling checker. The exaggeration of errors was necessitated, it is argued, in order to make the test of reasonable length.

The primary score for the Proofreading Test is the net correctness, errors corrected minus the number of errors introduced, over the three passages. The minimum score may be less than zero. This results when an examinee introduces more errors than are corrected. The authors claim that several intermediate results are also provided for this test for diagnostic purposes (manual, p. 8-2). Interpretative guidance is provided for the use of these diagnostic scores through descriptive data in separate tables. However, norms are available by subgroup for the net correctness score. The internal consistency reported as alpha reliability coefficient, .92, for this score is reasonable.

The Filing Test is designed to assess the basic ability to file and retrieve items alphabetically and numerically. It is claimed to be a power test because 99% of the sample tested finished the test within the 25-minute limit imposed separately for the numerical and alphabetical portions of the test. Each portion of the test consists of two kinds of items. The first requires the examinee to indicate which of the nine labeled drawers will be selected for filing or retrieving a given document. The other requires the examinee to identify which in a list of nine has a pair of names or numbers out of sequence. The test consists of a total of 100 items, 50 alphabetical and 50 numerical.

Three raw scores and their corresponding standard scores are produced from the Filing Test, alphabetical, numerical, and total. For this test, norms are provided for the total group because the means for the three subgroups were not statistically different. However, the number of examinees used for establishing the norms for this test was considerably smaller (254) than the total eligible group of 353. There is no explanation for this discrepancy in the number of examinees. From the examination of the mean scores for the alphabetical (45), numerical (46), and total (91), it is obvious that this test was too easy and nondiscriminating. The test suffers from the ceiling effect and the placement of examinees into different skill levels with a difference between raw scores of one point for two successive levels in the top six levels of alphabetical and numerical components is not advisable. For these components, the authors report the alpha reliabilities of .90 and .91, respectively.

The Business Vocabulary Test, consisting of 60 items, assesses familiarity with words required for business communication. The items are four option multiple choice. The examinee is instructed to choose the word most similar to the stem word. There is no other text that accompanies each item. The stem words were chosen from indices and glossaries of three secretarial handbooks published between 1981 and 1984. As a result, some of the contemporary words in the business environment of computer applications are not represented in these items. Although a time limit of 25 minutes is set for this test, 99% of the examinees completed it within this time frame. A single raw score, representing the items answered correctly, is computed for this test. Norms for the total sample used are provided because it is claimed the subgroups were not significantly different on this test.

However, no statistical data for the subgroups are provided in the manual.

The mean and standard deviation of the total score was 46 and 9, respectively with an alpha reliability coefficient of .91. The test was again quite easy for the norming group because the average score was 77% correct and it is reported that "some examinees were able to answer all of the items correctly" (manual, p. 10-2). The minimum score on the test was 13, which is slightly below the chance score of 15. In spite of these problems, the reliability estimate was reasonable.

The Business Math Test consists of 25 four-option multiple-choice items. The items test examinees' problem-solving ability, presented as word problems involving decimals, percentages or proportions, and fractions. Examinees in the norming group were not allowed to use calculators. Thus, the manual recommends that future "examinees be allowed to use only paper and pencil. This will control for differential familiarity with calculators, result in more standardization across examinees, and match the conditions under which norming data were collected" (manual, pp. 11-2, 11-3). This is sound advice to the test users. The maximum time allowed for the test was 60 minutes and about 98% of the examinees in the norming sample completed all the test items.

Norms for the total group are provide because there were no significant differences in the means of the various subgroups.

The Clerical Knowledge Test initially administered to the norming group consisted of 110 items but reduced after administration to 60 items. A serious problem arises from changing the length and context of the items in the original in order to assemble the final version of the test without readministering it. Fatigue would be a critical factor in such a drastic reduction from 110 items to 60 items. Also, other psychological processes such as proactive and retroactive facilitation and inhibition are ignored in making these changes to the content of the test.

A single raw score was obtained and was linked to the corresponding *T*-score. It is stated that the means of the subgroups on this test were significantly different. Therefore, norms for each subgroup are provided.

Users are encouraged to create their weighting system for creating composite scores for assessing secretaries, clerk-typists, and generalists.

For the user-created weighting system for tests to be included, the MCAB provides skill-level norms in terms of *T*-scores. There is much emphasis put on the job analysis questionnaire originally used with the standardization of the MCAB. However, users are advised to assess the time spent on taks and the importance of those in a test to approximate the weights to be used. The composite score norms in the manual suffer from the lack of separation among the top six skill levels as has been the case with the individual tests in this battery. If group-specific composites are justified, I do not see the need to include the norms for the total group in the norming sample. A serious limitation in these composites is the absence of descriptive statistics necessary for interpreting the results.

Validity evidence for the tests rests on the job analysis and the content contained in the early 1980s handbooks for secretarial courses. Much has changed since in terms of technology and office practices. Content validity of the six tests in the battery in terms of tasks and their importance on the job is important but it is not the only requirement for tests that might be used for selection and promotion in various organizations. Other aspects of validity evidence are also necessary (see Messick, 1989; American Educational Research Association, American Psychological Association, & National Council on Measurement in Education, 1985). The only reliability evidence provided for the various tests in the MCAB is the internal consistency estimate. Can we interpret the test results properly if examinees are retested? How stable are the test scores? What are the actual and potential consequences of misplacements of examinees in skill levels? The impression given in the tables of norms is that the skill level of an examinee is the absolute placement without any regard to the measurement problems, notably the *SEM*. Suitable cautions in the interpretation of scores that suffer from drastic misclassifications are essential. Not much evidence of this is given in the manual. Also, users should be cautioned of the consequences of alterations to the content of tests in terms of the measured constructs. Altering the content of an instrument in a small way might seriously compromise the initial conception intended in the design and validation of the test. This battery encourages users to alter the content of the tests. How could they still use the norms provided for the tests? It is possible to simulate the

norms for composites based on different weightings by the users but it would not be possible to provide suitable interpretative aids if tests are altered.

The norming group was a convenience sample of experienced employees in related occupations. Unless research evidence is available that shows that new recruits perform as well as the norming group(s) on the tests in the MCAB, the use of this battery should be made with extreme caution. Also, extreme caution is necessary if tests are altered by the user organization. Regardless, local norms or criterion scores should be established before altered tests are used for selection purposes.

SUMMARY. The MCAB is an interesting computer-administered instrument for assessing clerical and secretarial skills. Prospective and current employees can be classified into skill categories. However, caution is recommended because separations between successive skill levels are not sufficiently large to permit such decisions with confidence.

REVIEWER'S REFERENCES

American Educational Research Association, American Psychological Association, & National Council on Measurement in Education. (1985). *Standards for educational and psychological testing*. Washington, DC: American Psychological Association, Inc.
Messick, S. (1989). Validity. In R. L. Linn (Ed.), *Educational measurement* (pp. 13–103). New York: Macmillan Publishing Company.
Stutzman, T. M., & Veres, J. G., III. (1990). Review of the Minnesota Clerical Assessment Battery. In J. Hogan & R. Hogan (Eds.), *Business and industry testing: Current practices and test reviews* (pp. 493–507). Austin, TX: PRO-ED.

[238]
Monitoring Basic Skills Progress—Second Edition.

Purpose: "Designed to monitor students' acquisition of basic skills in one of three academic areas" using curriculum-based measurements.

Publication Dates: 1990–1999.

Administration: Group, via individual personal computers.

Price Data, 2001: $329 per complete program including Basic Reading, Basic Math Computation, Basic Math Concepts and Applications, and Basic Spelling; $119 per Basic Reading—Second Edition; $229 per Math Complete kit; $119 per Basic Math Computation—Second Edition; $129 per Math Concepts and Applications; $19 per Basic Math Computation, Second Edition blackline masters; $39 per Math Concepts and Applications blackline masters.

Comments: "Derived from the curriculum-based measurement (CBM) model of student monitoring"; for use in general or special education classrooms; computer administered and scored (requires Macintosh 68020 or higher CPU with System 7.1 or later).

Authors: Lynn S. Fuchs, Carol L. Hamlett, and Douglas Fuchs.
Publisher: PRO-ED.
  a) BASIC READING.
  Purpose: Designed to "monitor student progress, identify students who require intervention, and improve instructional programs" in reading.
  Population: Grades 1–7.
  Scores: Total score only.
  Time: (2.5) minutes.
  b) BASIC MATH COMPUTATION.
  Purpose: Designed to "monitor student progress, identify students who require intervention, and improve instructional programs" in mathematics.
  Population: Grades 1–6.
  Scores: Total score only.
  Time: (2–6) minutes.
  c) BASIC SPELLING.
  Purpose: To monitor students' acquisition of basic skills in spelling.
  Time: (3) minutes.
  Comments: Orally administered.
Cross References: For a review by Joseph C. Witt and Kevin M. Jones of an earlier edition, see 12:241. [Editor's Note: Only the Math and Reading components have been revised since this instrument was reviewed in the *12th MMY*. The Spelling component will be revised at a later date and will be reviewed then.]

Review of Monitoring Basic Skills Progress—Second Edition by MARY J. McLELLAN, Associate Professor, Northern Arizona University, Flagstaff, AZ:

Monitoring Basic Skills Progress (MBSP) was revised in 1998 from the original 1990 version. The purpose of the second edition was to bring the software up to date from the Apple to the MAC platform. The MBSP is not available on the IBM platform with the justification that most educators work with MAC systems. This test, authored by some of the most well-known proponents of curriculum-based assessment, is designed to track students' progress in the areas of Basic Math and Basic Reading (Basic Spelling is also part of the instrument but the revision is not yet available for this area). Each of the areas has separate manuals and computer disks. Computer administration is the only option. The manuals provide directions regarding the installation and use of the program. In addition, there is a wealth of information about application options available for teachers.

The basic intent of the MBSP—Second Edition is the close monitoring of student progress in the two areas identified above. Students take short tests (on a weekly or bi-weekly basis) that are selected based on previous performance. Their results are placed on a graph, enabling the student and teacher to visually monitor their progress. In addition, the manual encourages and guides the teacher through the process of determining when alternative-teaching approaches may need to be introduced. The results of the alternative approaches can be tracked in terms of student's progress. The graphic presentation provides good representation of the results for students, teachers, and parents.

The Basic Math Computation section consists of 30 tests at each grade level with 25 problems in each test. These tests are printed in a spiral notebook that can be easily reproduced. The student completes the appropriate sheet and the student or the teacher transfers the answers to the computer program. The computer scores the responses and gives feedback via a test score. The computation tests are administered up to two times per week and are between 2 and 6 minutes in duration, depending on the grade level. The students are required to complete as many problems as they can in that short interval of time. The computer program plots the student's score and saves the information. As the student takes more tests the information is plotted so progress can be tracked. The authors provide information about how the application can be used for individual students, classrooms, or an entire school. There is a companion program of Basic Math Concepts and Applications that is sold separately by PRO-ED and was not reviewed here. The two math programs can be integrated on the computer for a comprehensive math assessment.

The Basic Reading portion of the MBSP is computer administered. The student sits in front of the computer and is exposed to a reading passage with blanks. The student uses the "mouse" to click a "blank" and three different words are provided as options with each click on the blank. When the student is satisfied with the response, he or she moves to the next blank. The material is exposed for 2 1/2 minutes and then the computer screen changes and the scores for the student are presented. There are 30 passages at seven grade levels. The difficulty of the reading passages are based on Fry's readability formula.

The spelling portion of the MBSP was not included in this review because it has not yet been published in the second edition.

The psychometric properties of the MBSP are satisfactory. The emphasis of the measure is on accurate tracking of progress for small groups or individuals rather than normative comparison to large samples. Hence, the reliability of the measure was calculated by assessing the stability of scores (at one-week interval) with alternate forms and over multiple administrations, although other measures of score reliability are also reported (e.g., internal consistency human vs. computer-scoring). Both measures of reliability were reported to be satisfactory, ranging from .73 to .99. Student ability to record responses independently was also found to be accurate. Expert opinion of content was used to assess validity and high agreement was noted. Adequate criterion validity was reported when student performance was compared to the Math Computations Test by Fuchs, Fuchs, Hamlett, and Stecher (1991) and the Comprehensive Reading Assessment Battery by Fuchs, Fuchs, and Maxwell (1988).

SUMMARY. The MBSP is a computer-assisted package that provides a systematic approach to curriculum-based assessment of Reading and Math skills. The package is quite comprehensive and offers a well-constructed set of assessment materials. In the tradition of CBM, students are assessed frequently so their progress can be monitored closely. Many short administrations are encouraged with the test offering multiple versions of assessments of similar skills. Adjustments to individual student curriculum are encouraged and outcomes can be tracked closely. Validity comparisons were made with tests constructed by the two primary authors. A comparison to other widely used achievement measures could have strengthened the authors' claims of strong criterion validity. The most significant change to the second edition is the adaptation from the Apple to MAC platform. This test provides the opportunity for carefully monitoring student progress and achieves its intended purpose.

Review of Monitoring Basic Skills Progress— Second Edition by JEFFREY K. SMITH, Professor of Educational Psychology, Rutgers, the State University of New Jersey, New Brunswick, NJ:

Monitoring Basic Skills Progress—Second Edition is a computer-based program of testing and analysis designed to allow teachers to monitor the progress of their students in the areas of Basic Reading, Basic Math Computation, and Basic Spelling. For this review, only the reading and mathematics portion of the program were available. (Additionally available is a Basic Math Concepts and Applications program, which is not part of this review.) The program consists of 30 tests for each grade level for Grades 1–6 in Mathematics and Grades 1–7 in Reading. The program also provides for computerized scoring and graphing of results for individual students and classes. It is designed primarily for use in a curriculum-based measurement approach that closely monitors student achievement on a regularly scheduled basis. It can be used both for students in a general educational program and for students with Individual Educational Programs (IEPs).

In the Reading program, the tests are based on the cloze technique of omitting every seventh word in a reading passage and providing the students with three options, one of which is the omitted word. There are 60 omitted words on each test. Tests are passages between 350 and 400 words long that have been located at various grade levels by using the Fry readability formula. Students have 2 1/2 minutes to complete the test and are asked not to guess. The test is administered on computer, which then scores and graphs the student's performance. Teachers are encouraged to test students once a week, or twice a week for students with IEPs. In the Mathematics program, there are also 30 tests at each grade level, with each test consisting of 25 items. The content of the Mathematics tests progresses over the grades reflecting the typical school curriculum. Subtest scores are also provided, such as "multiplying by one digit." Again, the program is computer administered, scored, and analyzed. Time for administration ranges from 2 minutes at Grade 1 to 6 minutes for Grade 6.

The Monitoring Basic Skills Progress program is intended to provide a close monitoring system that will allow for frequent re-evaluation of student progress by looking at how many items a student gets correct on each successive test. Growth is determined by graphing the number of items correct. This approach rests heavily on the assumption that the tests are of equal difficulty within a grade. In essence, the tests are intended to be 30 parallel forms in each grade level. Establishing this equivalence would require an arduous research program, particularly considering that the measures are intended for use by disabled as well as nondisabled students. Such a program of research is not provided. The authors do provide a sampling of the reliability and validity of the measures, and then basically rely on the similarity of the measures and the fact that they were all developed in the same fashion to infer that the measures not assessed would have the same measurement characteristics. The data that are provided, stability-based reliability coefficients and criterion-related validity coefficients, are adequate as far as they go, but they are only based on a small number of the tests, and use very small sample sizes. No data are provided on the fundamental equivalence of the measures, that is, do they have the same means, standard deviations, and reliabilities? Thus, if two somewhat difficult tests are administered in succession, a teacher may draw the conclusion that a student is not doing well under current instruction, when in fact what is happening is a measurement artifact.

The Reading program fundamentally defines reading as performance on the cloze procedure. Although this is a reasonable approach to measuring reading comprehension, it is a fairly limited view of reading. The program also encourages assessing oral reading rate, but even combined, these do not represent the broader, more language-arts approach to literacy that currently dominates the field. The problem here is that an assessment program that is primarily concerned with performance on the cloze procedure would lead to teaching that might overemphasize skills related to that procedure.

SUMMARY. Having looked at the shortcomings of the program, and they are not trivial, one needs to put those criticisms into the overall context of the program. The authors have worked on this program over a number of years, and published their findings in rigorous journals. Their program attempts to relate testing to instruction in a very serious fashion, and they have evidence that use of the curriculum-based measurement model leads to achievement with students who face substantial learning challenges. Although it is clear that from a purely measurement perspective there is much work left to be done on the program, from the perspective of attempting to realize a practical and powerful merging of testing with instruction, the program holds great promise. The use of frequent, brief formative tests, and the careful monitoring of student progress has proved to be an effective approach to working with student who have difficulty learning. Monitoring Basic Skills Progress provides the mechanism for implementing such a system. As additional evidence of the equivalence of the measures in the program becomes available, it could prove to be an exceptionally well-conceived and well-executed approach to using measurement in the service of instruction.

[239]
Motivation Assessment Scale.

Purpose: Designed to assess the motivation underlying problem behaviors so as to curb those behaviors.
Population: People with mental disabilities.
Publication Date: 1992.
Scores, 4: Sensory, Escape, Attention, Tangible.
Administration: Individual.
Price Data: Available from publisher.
Time: Administration time not reported.
Comments: A rating tool to be completed by someone in close contact with the target individual; can be completed by paper and pencil or as an interview.
Authors: V. Mark Durand and Daniel B. Crimmins.
Publisher: Monaco and Associates, Inc.
Cross References: See T5:1722 (2 references).

Review of the Motivation Assessment Scale by ROGER A. BOOTHROYD, Associate Professor, Department of Mental Health Law and Policy, Louis de la Parte Florida Mental Health Institute, University of South Florida, Tampa, FL:

DESCRIPTION. The Motivation Assessment Scale (MAS) is a 16-item rating scale designed to "find out why people's problem behaviors persist" (administration guide, p. 21). This individually administered measure was developed primarily for use with individuals with developmental disabilities to determine what motivates problem behaviors such as aggression and self-injurious behaviors. Each item is rated on a 7-point Likert-type scale from 0 (*never*) to 6 (*always*). The authors indicate that the items examine four categories of reinforcement or motivation: Attention (4 items), Tangible (4 items), Escape (4 items), and Sensory (4 items).

SCALE DEVELOPMENT. The administration guide does not provide very much detail about how the MAS was developed. The authors do indicate that the scale was developed over 4 years with input from individuals with different perspectives (e.g., teachers, parents, service providers) who had direct contact with persons with autism and other developmental disabilities. Additionally, they note that questions were added and deleted until raters could "adequately report how these individuals would behave in [various] situations" (p. 22).

ADMINISTRATION. Prior to completing the MAS, raters must provide a specific description of the individual's problem behavior to be assessed as well as a description of the setting in which the behavior is a problem. Although the MAS was designed to be completed by any number of raters (e.g., parents, teachers, caregivers, service providers), the authors indicate that it is critical that individuals "completing the MAS have experience in direct observation of and/or interaction with the individual over several weeks time" (administration guide, p. 31). Additionally, the authors indicate that raters must "be familiar with the intended meaning of each item" (administration guide, p. 22). To facilitate this, an explanation of the intent of each of the 16 items as well as comments from the authors on some items regarding how to score them in the event of special circumstances, is provided in the administration guide. The authors do not specify if the observation length should be for a fixed, minimum, or maximum period of time but do state that the MAS should never be completed for an entire day.

SCORING AND INTERPRETATION. The MAS is hand scored directly on the rating sheet. Individual item scores are transferred to a scoring grid. A total score is obtained for each of the four motivation categories by summing the individual's ratings from the four items in that category. Means scores are then obtained by dividing the total score of each category by 4, and finally the relative rankings (i.e., 1–4) for each are assigned based on the category means. The category with the highest mean score is considered the most likely motivation for the persistence of the problem behavior rated, the category with the second highest, the second most likely motivation, and so on. The authors state that when interpreting the MAS, users should rely most heavily on the relative rankings of the motivational categories and not on the individual's total category scores or mean category scores. In instances where two motivational categories receive high scores, the authors recommend reevaluating the individual in addition to making sure the behavior being assessed and the setting have been clearly defined. When there is a

tie for the highest score or when the mean scores between two categories are .50 or less, then both categories are considered as equally likely reasons for promoting the continuation of the problem behavior.

RELIABILITY. Interrater reliability was assessed by comparing the MAS ratings of teachers and assistant teachers of 50 students exhibiting self-injurious behavior. Pearson correlations between raters ranged between .80 and .95 (administration guide, p. 47). Thirty-day test-retest reliabilities ranged from .89 to .98. The administration guide does not provide individual test-retest or internal consistency reliability estimates for the four motivational categories or scales.

VALIDITY. The authors provide support for the validity of the four MAS scales, citing the results of a factor analytic study conducted by Bihm, Kienlen, Ness, and Poindexter (1991) in which they conclude that "the four factors were essentially equivalent to the subscales proposed by Durand and Crimmins (1988)" (p. 1237). Evidence of construct validity is demonstrated through two studies in which "teachers' ratings on the scale predicted how individuals would behave in analogue settings" (administration guide, p. 49) and that MAS scores and ABC charts (Antecedent-Behavior-Consequence charts) were better at identifying sensory function for behaviors in adults with profound mental retardation relative to analogue assessments.

COMMENTARY/REVIEW. Given the sparsity of the psychometric information in the administration guide and the fact that the copyright date of the guide was 1992, a quick literature review was conducted in PsychINFO, to determine if additional psychometric information was available on the MAS. Nine articles were found that focused specifically on the reliability and validity evidence for the MAS. A review of these articles suggests that the psychometric properties of the MAS are somewhat suspect, particularly when compared to those reported in the administration guide.

Concerns arise with respect to attempts to replicate the Pearson correlation interrater reliabilities reported in the administration guide as found by Durand and Crimmins (1988). Eight of these studies (Akande, 1994; Conroy, Fox, Bucklin, & Good, 1996; Duker & Sigafoos, 1998; Kearney, 1994; Newton & Sturmey, 1991; Sigafoos, Kerr, & Roberts, 1994; Spreat & Connelly, 1996;

Zarcone, Rodgers, Iwata, Rouke, & Dorsey, 1991) evaluated the interrater reliability of the MAS and found it to be dramatically lower than the reliability reported in the administration guide. Although the lower interrater reliability found in these studies could be partially attributed to differences in the culture of the children assessed, the range of problem behaviors and settings examined, the varied conditions under which the MAS was administered, and/or the backgrounds of the raters, the consistently low to moderate agreement found across raters raises serious concerns regarding the adequacy of reliability of the MAS's scores. If the MAS is to be used "to guide the design of treatments," as is recommended (administration guide, p. 49), then a greater level of interrater reliability is needed as these studies found it to be consistently below .80, the generally accepted standard (Kazdin, 1980).

These studies also indicate that agreement on the source or motive of reinforcement for the behavior was low. Zarcone, Rodgers, Iwata, Rouke, and Dorsey (1991) found only 29% of the raters agreed on the category of reinforcement maintaining their client's behavior. Sigafoos, Kerr, and Roberts (1994) found a slightly higher rate of agreement among raters (44%) and Duker and Sigafoos (1998) found still higher at 67%. Given that Durand and Crimmins (the authors of the MAS) indicate that treatment for a behavioral problem should be designed based on the category that ranks highest, one would desire a substantially higher level of agreement across raters regarding the motives for an individual's behavior.

Support for the factor structure and the scales' internal consistency was found in these articles. The one article that examined the MAS's factor structure (Singh et al., 1993) found it to be consistent with the study by Bihm, Kienlen, Ness, and Poindexter (1991) cited in the administration guide. With respect to the internal consistency of the MAS's scales, four articles (Akande, 1994; Duker & Sigafoos, 1998; Sigafoos, Kerr, & Roberts, 1994; Spreat & Connelly, 1996) report Cronbach alpha coefficients ranging from .67 to .74 for Sensory, .68 to .88 for Escape, .86 for Attention, and .67 to .91 for Tangible, also similar to those reported in the administration guide.

SUMMARY. Overall the MAS may have some utility in treatment planning in that it attempts systematically to identify and understand the reasons why an individual's problem behavior persists. Given the concerns with its interrater reliability, and thus its questionable validity, I strongly urge that the numerical ratings and rankings of the MAS not be relied on too heavily when developing treatment plans. I also strongly support and echo the authors' advice and caution that "assessment efforts should not involve the use of *just this device* [italics added]" (administration guide, p. 29).

REVIEWER'S REFERENCES

Kazdin, A. E. (1980). *Behavior modification in applied settings* (rev. ed). Homewood, IL: The Dorsy Press.

Durand, M. V., & Crimmins, D. B. (1988). Identifying the variables maintaining self-injurious behavior. *Journal of Autism and Developmental Disorders, 18,* 99–117.

Bihm, E. M., Kienlen, T. L., Ness, M. E., & Poindexter, A. R. (1991). Factor structure of the Motivation Assessment Scale for persons with mental retardation. *Psychological Reports, 68,* 1235–1238.

Newton, J. T., & Sturmey, P. (1991). The Motivation Assessment Scale: Inter-rater reliability and internal consistency in a British sample. *Journal of Mental Deficiency Research, 35,* 472–474.

Zarcone, J. R., Rodgers, T. A., Iwata, B. A., Rouke, D. A., & Dorsey, M. F. (1991). Reliability analysis of the Motivation Assessment Scale: A failure to replicate. *Research in Developmental Disabilities, 12,* 349–360.

Singh, N. N., Donatelli, L. S., Best, A., Williams, D. E., Barrera, F. J., Lenz, M. W., Landrum, T. J., Ellis, C. R., & Moe, T. L. (1993). Factor structure of the Motivation Assessment Scale. *Journal of Intellectual Disability Research, 37,* 65–74.

Akande, A. (1994). The motivation assessment profiles of low functioning children. *Early Child Development and Care, 101,* 101–107.

Kearney, C. A. (1994). Interrater reliability of the Motivation Assessment Scale: Another, closer look. *Journal of the Association for Persons with Severe Handicaps, 19,* 139–142.

Sigafoos, J., Kerr, M., & Roberts, D. (1994). Interrater reliability of the Motivation Assessment Scale: Failure to replicate with aggressive behavior. *Research in Developmental Disabilities, 15,* 333–342.

Conroy, M. A., Fox, J. J., Bucklin, A., & Good, W. (1996). An analysis of the reliability and stability of the Motivation Assessment Scale in assessing the challenging behaviors of persons with developmental disabilities. *Education and Training in Mental Retardation and Developmental Disabilities, 31,* 243–250.

Spreat, S., & Connelly, L. (1996). Reliability analysis of the Motivation Assessment Scale. *American Journal of Mental Retardation, 100,* 528–532.

Duker, P. C., & Sigafoos, J. (1998). The Motivation Assessment Scale: Reliability and construct validity across three topographies of behavior. *Research in Developmental Disabilities, 19,* 131–141.

Review of the Motivation Assessment Scale by JAMES P. VAN HANEGHAN, *Associate Professor, Department of Behavioral Studies and Educational Technology, University of South Alabama, Mobile, AL:*

The Motivation Assessment Scale (MAS) is a tool developed to help determine the functional basis for problem behaviors in individuals with developmental disabilities. The goal of the scale is to provide a quick and convenient assessment that can be used to help develop treatment plans. The scale is meant to be used as a starting point that can help quicken the intervention process by allowing the behavior analyst to develop some potential treatment plans based specifically on the function of behavior without having to do an extensive functional analysis of behavior. The authors point out that not only are functional analyses potentially time-consuming, but that they may actually increase the amount of aberrant behavior in the trial-and-error search for the factor or factors that maintain a behavior. Hence, the MAS has great potential in helping clinicians and teachers find ways to treat problem behavior.

The instrument is filled out by someone who is familiar with the individual (teacher, therapist, parent, etc.). It contains 16 items that make up four, four-item summated rating scales. The four scales rate the frequency with which aberrant behaviors (e.g., hand biting, punching, etc.) occur in conjunction with different types of reinforcing consequences. The different types of potential reinforcers for problem behaviors mentioned are: social attention, tangibles, escape, and sensory feedback. Each of the items involves a situation where the behavior may or may not occur. For example, one of the social attention items asks, "Does the behavior occur whenever you stop attending to the person?" Each item is rated on a 1 to 6 scale, with 1 indicating that the behavior never occurs in the situation described and 6 indicating that the behavior always occurs in the situation described. The items are nicely described in the manual by the authors, and they have done a good job in attempting to clear up any problems individuals might have in interpreting the items.

The scores on the four scales represent the mean ratings for each of the four reinforcement types. The user interprets the scores by ranking the different reinforcement type scores and then planning treatments based on the highest scoring motivation. Difficulties in interpretation occur when there is more than one high scoring area. The authors suggest reassessing whether the behavior being rated was defined too broadly (e.g., using a global label like tantrums versus specific behavior like pounding his fist on the table). If upon a second look, the behavior was not defined too broadly, they suggest that perhaps both types of reinforcers may be motivating the behavior. One issue not well addressed in score interpretation concerns the relative frequency ratings themselves. What if none of the motivations have a mean of 3 or greater (a score of 3 means that the reinforcer occurs half the time)? If none of the scales have means greater than 3, does taking the highest ranked scale still provide useful information? The authors suggest that when none of the potential motivations seem to be relevant, the Sensory Feedback score will be highest. However, they provide little guidance about what to do concerning the actual values of the ratings.

Along with suggestions for interpretation, the authors provide some guidelines for how to decide what to assess, who should do the assessment, and in what setting or settings the assessment will occur. These suggestions are helpful, but they involve judgments for which some assessors will do better than others. The authors suggest focusing on one specific behavior and assessing that behavior separately in different settings because the behavior might be maintained for different reasons in different settings. However, there are other possible scenarios (e.g., many different behaviors performed for the same underlying reason; multiple motivations for a single behavior in one setting) that could be addressed in more detail.

There are a variety of other issues to consider that may create difficulties in using the MAS productively: the level of functioning of the individual, the role and experience of the person rating the individual, the frequency of the behavior, and the co-occurrence of a behavior with others. Each of these factors may influence the reliability and validity of the motivational ratings. For example, an individual with severe developmental disabilities who has a small repertoire of behaviors may use the same aberrant behavior for a variety of different reasons.

These issues are reflected in psychometric analyses of the MAS. Although the authors report reasonable interrater agreement, internal consistency reliability, and a factor analysis confirming the item grouping into different categories, these findings have not been replicated easily by others (see Sturmey, 1994 for a review). Sturmey points out that some reliability and validity problems may be artifactual. For example, two different individuals may have different ratings of the same individual because their relationship with the individual is different (e.g., teacher versus teacher's aide), even though they may see that person at the same time each day. On the other hand, the nature of the scale may create some problems. For instance, Sturmey mentions that the number of items in each scale (four) may lower the internal consistency reliability of the scales. Sturmey suggests that some of the problems are related to the MAS not including items concerning the antecedent and setting events in the instrument. He points out that the failure to consider these events makes it difficult for users of the MAS to evaluate whether behaviors are a function of more complex contingencies. The authors do report several successful single-case studies that involve successful intervention based on recommendations from the

MAS. However, Sturmey reports that evidence for the criterion-related validity for scores from the MAS is mixed. For example, Sturmey reports evidence that in some cases where there were no clearly recommended strategies from MAS scores, other methods were more successful in identifying the relevant motivations.

SUMMARY. Overall, the MAS is an ambitious attempt to develop a very simple instrument to address the cause of serious behavioral problems. Although there is some merit to the MAS, the mixed results individuals have had in successfully using it suggest that more work needs to be done to make the scale more reliable and valid. Whether further revisions will make the instrument better remains to be seen. Sturmey's (1994) review of instruments like the MAS did not find any to be satisfactory in terms of reliability and validity. Hence, it may be that more labor intensive data collection efforts rather than questionnaires and interviews are needed to establish the causes of problematic behavior.

REVIEWER'S REFERENCE

Sturmey, P. (1994). Assessing the functions of aberrant behaviors: A review of psychometric instruments. *Journal of Autism and Developmental Disorders, 24,* 293–304.

[240]
Motives, Values, Preferences Inventory.

Purpose: Designed to assess "the fit between an individual and the organizational culture" and "a person's motives."
Population: Adults.
Publication Dates: 1987–1996.
Acronym: MVPI.
Scores, 10: Aesthetic, Affiliation, Altruistic, Commercial, Hedonistic, Power, Recognition, Scientific, Security, Tradition.
Administration: Group.
Price Data, 1998: $2 per test booklet; $12.50 per 25 answer sheets; $45 per manual ('96, 90 pages); $75 per software starter kit; $30 per interpretive profile; $15 per graph or data file.
Time: (20) minutes.
Authors: Joyce Hogan and Robert Hogan.
Publisher: Hogan Assessment Systems, Inc.

Review of the Motives, Values, Preferences Inventory by BRENT W. ROBERTS, Assistant Professor of Psychology, The University of Illinois, Champaign, IL:

The Motives, Values, Preferences Inventory (MVPI) was designed to achieve two goals. First, the MVPI is meant to be a comprehensive, direct assessment of a person's motives, values, and preferences. Although there are numerous short surveys of values (e.g., Rokeach, 1973; Super, 1973), and implicit motives (McClelland, 1980), the only comparable inventory of values, motives, and interests is the out-of-date Allport, Vernon, Lindzey Study of Values (1960). Thus, the MVPI attempts to fill an assessment void that has been overlooked by personality psychologists for several decades. The second goal of the MVPI is to be used to aid in determining the match between individuals and the culture of the organization in which they work. As opposed to many tests that are created on, and for, undergraduate psychology majors, the MVPI was created to serve the needs of industry.

The 200-item inventory consists of 10 primary scales: Aesthetic, Affiliation, Altruistic, Commercial, Hedonistic, Power, Recognition, Scientific, Security, and Tradition. The items were derived "rationally from hypotheses about the likes, dislikes, and aversions of the 'ideal' exemplar of each motive" (manual, p. 16). Each scale is composed of five themes: lifestyles, beliefs, occupational preferences, aversions, and preferred associates (kinds of persons desired as coworkers and friends). Items concerning sexual preferences, religious beliefs, illegal behavior, ethnic attitudes, and attitudes toward the disabled were avoided, which should allay concerns about invasions of privacy.

The validity of rationally developed scales depends almost exclusively on the test authors' understanding of the theory behind each construct to be developed. To their credit, the test authors performed an extensive review before developing the MVPI scales. The authors reviewed theories relevant to values, motives, and preferences by Spranger (1928), Strong (1943), Rokeach (1973), Super (1973), Holland (1997), and Rounds (1995). The 10 primary scales appear to be comprehensive capturing the dimensions that underlie Rokeach's list of values and compilation of values that make up the "universal taxonomy" of values (Schwartz & Bilsky, 1987).

Furthermore, the test authors do a remarkable job of synthesizing the diffuse and confused literature describing interests, preferences, motives, and values. They make two clarifying arguments. First, they argue appropriately that there is great overlap, both conceptually and empirically, among interests, preferences, motives, and values. Second, they argue that these constructs "can be placed in a hierarchy of abstraction with interests as the most concrete and values as the most abstract" (manual, p. 1). Rather than duplicating the efforts of tests designed to assess more narrow constructs such as occupational interests, the MVPI attempts to assess motives, interests, and values at a trans-situational level that can help to explain behavior across many different contexts such as workplaces, relationships, and leisure activities.

Construct validity was investigated by relating scores on the MVPI to those from major interest inventories, personality tests, intelligence tests, and observer descriptions from peers, supervisors, and subordinates. The evidence for convergent validity across numerous tests and self-report and observer methods was consistent with scale definitions. The only area of weakness appears to be that none of the scales tap the "Realistic" interest domain (Holland, 1997). The evidence for the discriminant validity of the MVPI was also quite strong. The intercorrelations among the MVPI scales averaged .18, which was rather low in comparison to most personality tests. Also, the relations between the MVPI and measures of cognitive ability were all below .30 and averaged .13, which indicates that the MVPI scales could be used in conjunction with intelligence tests in selection situations in order to capture unique variance in outcomes such as job performance. A principal components analysis of the MVPI scales produced four interpretable factors: Dominance (Recognition, Power, Hedonistic), Affiliation (Altruistic, Affiliation, Tradition), Security (Security, Commercial), and Aesthetic (Aesthetic, Scientific).

The 10 primary scales show sufficient evidence of reliability according to usual psychometric standards. Internal consistency estimates ranged from a low of .70 to a high of .84 with an average of .77. Three-month test-retest reliability estimates ranged from .64 to .88 with an average of .77. The test authors should be given credit for listing the average inter-item correlation for each scale, which provides an estimate of internal consistency that is unaffected by scale length. These estimates, which were quite consistent with averages for most reliable and valid personality scales, ranged from .11 to .22.

The MVPI manual provides norms based on an archival sample of 3,015 adults, most of whom were job applicants or employees. Sex, race, and age differences are also provided, although very few meaningful differences were found. The manual also provides scale-by-scale interpretive information and information on administering and scoring the test.

Three unique aspects of the MVPI deserve praise. First, the theoretical overview and the sophisticated discussion of the bandwidth relations among interests, values, motives, and preferences are highly informative and deserving of wider dissemination. The average psychologist would learn something by reading the MVPI manual. Second, the manual reads like a description of a "mature" test, such as the California Psychological Inventory (Gough, 1996). For example, in addition to the standard information on test development and scale interpretation, the manual provides profile interpretations of scale scores that link the test to the gold standard in interest assessment—the Holland typology (Holland, 1997). Third, the MVPI was developed and validated in applied settings for applied purposes. The authors obviously believe that their test has a job to do, and have designed it accordingly.

Two weaknesses should be addressed in future updates of the MVPI. First, more information could be provided about the norm sample so that test users could feel more confident in comparing values from specific samples to the norm sample. Furthermore, norms by industry and occupation would enhance the interpretation of scale scores greatly. Second, the evidence for convergent validity could be enhanced if the authors related the MVPI to more specific values assessment instruments such as Super's (1973) Work Values Inventory.

SUMMARY. The MVPI fills a void in the range of personality assessment tools. Not since the Allport, Vernon, Lindzey Study of Values (1960) have we had a straightforward, comprehensive assessment tool designed to assess motives, values, and interests. Furthermore, the MVPI is based on a rich understanding of the motives and values domain, the scales demonstrate relatively strong-evidence of reliability and validity, and the authors imbed the interpretation of their test in the context that they intend for its use—with employed adults. The MVPI should find numerous useful applications.

REVIEWER'S REFERENCES

Spranger, E. (1928). *Types of men: The psychology and ethics of personality*. Halle: Max Niemeyer Verlag.
Strong, E. K., Jr. (1943). *Vocational interests of men and women*. Stanford, CA: Stanford University Press.

Allport, G. W., Vernon, P. E., & Lindzey, G. (1960). *Study of values: Manual and test booklet* (3rd ed.). Boston: Houghton Mifflin.

Rokeach, M. (1973). *The nature of human values.* New York: Free Press.

Super, D. E. (1973). Work Values Inventory. In D. G. Zytowski (Ed.), *Contemporary approaches to interest measurement* (pp. 189–205). Minneapolis, MN: University of Minnesota Press.

McClelland, D. C. (1980). Motive dispositions: The merits of operant and respondent measures. In L. Wheeler (Ed.), *Review of personality and social psychology* (Vol. 1, pp. 10–41). Beverly Hills, CA: Sage.

Schwartz, S. H., & Bilsky, W. (1987). Toward a universal psychological structure of human values. *Journal of Personality and Social Psychology, 53,* 550–562.

Rounds, J. B. (1995). Vocational interests: Evaluating structural hypotheses. In D. Lubinski & R. V. Dawis (Eds.), *Assessing individual differences in human behavior: New concepts, methods, and findings* (pp. 177–232). Minneapolis, MN: University of Minnesota Press.

Gough, H. (1996). *California Psychological Inventory manual* (3rd ed.). Palo Alto, CA: Consulting Psychologists Press.

Holland, J. L. (1997). *Making vocational choices: A theory of vocational personalities and work environments.* Odessa, FL: Psychological Assessment Resources, Inc.

Review of the Motives, Values, Preferences Inventory by SHELDON ZEDECK, Chair and Professor of Psychology, Department of Psychology, University of California, Berkeley, CA:

The Motives, Values, Preferences Inventory (MVPI) is composed of 200 items that measure a respondent's fit to an organization's culture as well as provide an assessment of that respondent's motives, interests, and values. Responses to items are on a 3-point scale: Agree, Uncertain (no opinion), and Disagree. There is a paper-and-pencil version as well as computer on-line testing. Scoring is by optical scanning or by use of a mail-in or FAX scoring system.

The 10 scales measured by the MVPI (Aesthetic, Affiliation, Altruistic, Commercial, Hedonistic, Power, Recognition, Scientific, Security, and Tradition) were developed on a rational basis. Each scale contains 20 items about the likes and dislikes of the "exemplar" of each motive. Each scale is composed of five themes: (a) lifestyles, or the manner in which a person would like to live; (b) beliefs, focusing on ideal goals; (c) occupational preferences, or the work a person would like to do; (d) aversions, reflecting attitudes and behaviors that are disliked; and (e) preferred associates, focusing on the kind of persons desired as coworkers and friends. The items provide direct assessments of a person's motives and feelings about the subject as opposed to requiring inferences.

The manual accompanying the MVPI is quite comprehensive. There is an extensive discussion of the literature pertaining to the measurement of motives, values, and interests. Of special significance is the discussion on the differences between personality and interests. There is an excellent discussion of Holland's taxonomy for organizing individuals and occupations, a tax-onomy that focuses on personality types that result in a hexagonal configuration (realistic, investigative, artistic, social, enterprising, and conventional types). The psychometric properties a user should consider are well represented in the manual. The sample size on which the MVPI psychometric data are determined is 3,015, a reasonable-sized norming group for a relatively new instrument. The reliability estimates reported for both internal consistency (from .70 for Security to .84 for Aesthetic) and test-retest (average reliability of .77 in 3-week and 8-week interval studies) are good. One analysis that I have not frequently seen reported in test manuals, reading level, shows that the inventory requires a third grade level. The table with the descriptive statistics for each scale presents results for males and females, blacks and whites, and "under 40" and "40 and above." Unfortunately, sample sizes for these categories are not presented; thus, we cannot determine if there is an adequate sample of, for example, blacks that would provide confidence in making comparisons from a black respondent to the norm sample. Also, it is hoped that future manuals will include information on other ethnic groups as well as provide breakdowns on different job or occupational titles.

A reported principal components analysis shows that four components account for 67% of the variance in the intercorrelation matrix. These four components are not specifically labeled by the authors, but are compared to factors that have appeared in the personality and interest literature.

Validity information is provided for content, construct, and empirical strategies. The presentation on content validity focuses on the item content and the premise that the item directly measures motives, values, and interests. The construct validity evidence is based on the correlation between the MVPI and other tests of interests, normal personality, dysfunctional personality, and cognitive ability. There is a thorough discussion of the relationship between the MVPI and each of these types of tests. In summary of the construct strategy, the evidence presented is impressive given that hypothesized relationships are obtained, thereby suggesting that the MVPI is measuring a unique aspect of a respondent's motives, values, and interests.

The strategy for obtaining evidence of empirical validity is based on examining correlations between the MVPI and observer descriptions about real world performance. Accordingly, results are presented for six samples in two organizations where respondents completed the MVPI and anonymous observers described these respondents using special checklists. The results reveal expected patterns of correlations between the MVPI scales and the ratings of behaviors known to be associated with effective and ineffective organizational performance.

The section in the manual on interpretations and use is somewhat limited. A sample report presented in the Appendix shows how the respondent compares to the normative sample (graphic profile) as well as provides interpretive information for each of the 10 scales. There is no interpretation or information on the pattern of responses (i.e., there is no suggestion, for example, that those scoring high on Scales 1, 4, 7, and 9 are satisfied in a particular type [Holland's typology] of occupation or types of organizations). Given that the test is designed to help people choose occupations or careers and to evaluate the fit between a person's values and the climate of a particular organization, more information about occupations, careers, and one's organization needs to be incorporated into the feedback. One would hope this guidance can be incorporated into future manuals as more data are collected on the MVPI.

SUMMARY. Overall, the MVPI is a good instrument to measure motives, values, and interests of people seeking vocational information or desiring to assess their work styles and orientations.

[241]
Motor-Free Visual Perception Test— Revised.

Purpose: Designed as a test of visual perception that avoids any motor involvement.
Population: Ages 4–11, adults.
Publication Dates: 1972–1996.
Acronym: MVPT-R.
Scores, 2: Perceptual Quotient, Perceptual Age.
Administration: Individual.
Price Data, 2000: $85 per test kit including manual ('96, 40 pages), test plates, and 50 recording forms in vinyl folder; $27 per manual; $40 per test plates; $15 per 50 recording forms; $9 per pad of 50 remedial checklists (optional); $27 per specimen set including manual and sample form.
Time: (10) minutes.
Authors: Ronald P. Colarusso and Donald D. Hammill.
Publisher: Academic Therapy Publications, Inc.
Cross References: See T5:1725 (8 references) and T4:1677 (6 references); for a review by Carl L. Rosen

of an earlier edition and an excerpted review by Alan Krichev, see 8:883 (9 references).

Review of the Motor-Free Visual Perception Test—Revised by NANCY B. BOLOGNA, Clinical Assistant Professor of Psychiatry, Louisiana State University Medical Center, Program Director, Touro Senior Day Center, New Orleans, LA:

The Motor-Free Visual Perception Test—Revised (MVPT-R) is an updated edition of the Motor Free Visual Perception Test first introduced in 1972. The revised edition offers norms from a new standardization sample, and an expanded age range (4 through 11 years vs. the original 4 through 8 years). The original MVPT was developed to provide a general measure of visual perceptual processing ability that is uncontaminated by motor performance. Although the new edition offers norms for ages 4 through 11 years, the maturity of the human visual perceptual system by age 10 to 11 years suggests that the age 11 norms would be appropriate for adult use. In fact, a review of the raw score means for each age in the standardization sample reveals a negatively accelerating curve, reaching a plateau at about age 9 years, further supporting the use of age 11 norms as "adult." The MVPT-R has been used with both children and adults in a wide range of clinical populations, including mentally retarded children and adults, schizophrenics, cerebral palsied individuals, and brain-damaged adults. Because the test does not rely on graphemic responses, unlike many other visual perceptual measures, it may be particularly useful with populations who are motorically impaired.

The standardization sample consisted of 912 children residing in northern California and Georgia. The numbers of children in each age group ranged from a low of 100 (age 9) to a high of 135 (age 11). Fifty percent of the children in the total population were male and 50% female, with the gender ratio within each age nearly 50/50. The racial characteristics of the population were close to those reported by the U.S. Bureau of the Census, 1988. Sixty three percent of the sample population was white (compared to 70% of the U.S. population), 10% black, 16% Hispanic and 11% "other" (as compared to 15%, 11%, and 4%, respectively, from the census data). Children included in the standardization sample were described as "not identified as having motor, sensory or learning disabilities" (manual, p. 13), but no details were provided of any screening techniques used to eliminate such individuals. Although the test manual mentions studies in clinical populations, no norms are presented for comparison with similarly impaired individuals.

The selection of individual test items for the revised edition was determined by point biserial correlation of each potential item with the total score. Those yielding coefficients between .30 and .80 were considered acceptable for inclusion. Test-retest, split half, and Kuder-Richardson reliabilities were determined for the original Motor-Free Visual Perception Test within each age range (4 years through 8 years). All reliability coefficients were noted to fall between .71 and .84. Reliability measures were not calculated for the revised edition and are not available for the expanded age range. Similarly, the validity coefficients offered reflect studies with the original MVPT. In fairness, strong correlations between the original MVPT and the MVPT-R support the carryover of both reliability and validity measures from the original edition.

There are five aspects of visual perception that are sampled by the MVPT-R: spatial relationships, visual discrimination (of form, color, and position), figure-ground discrimination, visual closure, and visual memory. Although the test provides items in each of these areas, only a single composite score is generated, reflecting a general perceptual ability. The authors clearly warn against attempting to use item cluster scores as measures of subareas of visual perception, citing significant interrelatedness among these abilities. Even through skills, such as visual closure, may in theory exist separately from other aspects of visual perception, studies as far back as Thurstone (1944) have consistently reported strong intercorrelations among the various constructs that form visual perception.

The MVPT-R is an individually administered, multiple-choice test. Instructions are simple and straightforward. The 40 multiple-choice test items are presented in a spiral-bound book that includes on each page clear, easy-to-read instructions to the examiner. Test items seem engaging, and are well presented with little chance for confusion about instructions or other nonperceptual factors. Although the test is not timed, completion should take less than 10 minutes. Scoring the MVPT-R consists of simply summing the number of correct responses, then comparing that raw

score to the correct column in a normative table to derive a perceptual quotient and a perceptual age. A perceptual quotient of 85 or less (1 standard deviation below the mean) is considered indicative of visual perceptual inadequacy. Perceptual age is reported as a range (based on the mean and standard error of measurement), generally used as an easily interpreted value for lay persons.

SUMMARY. The MVPT-R is a quick, easily administered measure of general visual perceptual ability. Reliability and validity evidence have been presented for an earlier version of the instrument, which correlates well with the revised edition. The instrument will be useful within its limited scope. Independent research articles may provide suggestions for using this instrument in clinical populations; however, no norms currently exist for that purpose.

REVIEWER'S REFERENCE
Thurstone, L. L. (1944). *A factorial study of perception.* Chicago, IL: The University of Chicago Press.

Review of the Motor-Free Visual Perception Test—Revised by THERESA VOLPE-JOHNSTONE, Clinical and School Psychologist, Pleasanton, CA:

The Motor-Free Visual Perception Test—Revised (MVPT-R) is a revision of the original test developed by Ronald P. Colarusso and Donald D. Hammill in 1972. It is an untimed, individually administered test "designed for screening, diagnostic, and research purposes ... of overall visual perceptual processing ability in children and adults" (manual, p. 7). The items themselves do not require knowledge, skill, or ability outside the visual perceptual realm. The MVPT-R requires no graphomotor output. Therefore, visual perception can be isolated from populations with a visual motor or motor skill deficit. Primary changes to the original include updated norms, an expanded age range (through age 11 years), and the addition of four new test plates bringing the item total to 40. Administration directions are easy to follow and accompany each plate. Plates consist of a target stimulus with horizontally placed response choices. Subjects may respond by pointing or may use another gestural system. The one-page scoring sheet is simple, objective, and inexpensive, with correct responses in boldface type. Each category has an example for which the correct answer may be given with an explanation should the examinee incorrectly respond.

The original MVPT had norm data for children without any specific disability. The authors suggest that the revised test can be used for a variety of purposes with different populations but did not perform any analyses to confirm group differences. The MVPT-R seemed relatively pure for item bias. The use of Delta values yielded high correlations (.78 to .92) for all racial groups with no significant differences upon comparison.

Interpretation of test results is explained in the introduction section. The two scores that may be obtained are perceptual quotients and perceptual ages. This reviewer recommends perceptual quotients because perceptual ages may be misleading, particularly below age 5 or above age 10. The manual specifically indicates that no attempt should be made to generate subtests scores for the five separate visual perceptual skills or to identify specific strengths or weaknesses in the subareas. This suggestion is a good one because there are too few items in some groupings to make definitive statements. Further, the authors do not establish that these five areas are mutually exclusive (Compton, 1990), nor do they adequately define the areas.

In terms of test construction, the test is divided into five areas by category for ease of administration. These areas are visual discrimination, visual closure, visual memory, spatial relationships, and figure-ground. Based on the revised test item analysis distribution, it seemed that most of one's visual perceptual development is complete by about age 8-0, supported by item difficulty greater than .75 for approximately 70% of total items by this age. Unless there was compelling rationale for administering the first three categories past age 8, there was not enough variation in scores to be useful once the skill is fully developed. Barring neurological injury to visual processing or perceptual areas, the MVPT-R would permit stable estimates of performance above the test age range without re-administration of the test. The test is objectively scored and although coefficients for interrater reliability were not indicated, the scoring format would likely yield high correlations.

Reliability and validity were not established for scores from the revised MVPT. The data from the original sample were referenced because the authors concluded that the extremely high correlation between the original and the revised edition ($r = .85$) would allow it. Because the visual perceptual construct is dependent upon neurophysiological maturation, this would make sense. However, when considering using this test, one should keep in mind that the original studies used an N of 881 for ages 4 through 8 (racial composition not reported), with uneven distribution through the age range. Reliability and validity coefficients for age 4 was based on a small N and there are no data for groups over age 8 years. Interpretation for these age groups should be cautious. Current demographics have an $N = 912$ with over 100 at each age group between 4 and 11 years. Its racial composition is weighted slightly more heavily toward minorities. It seems, therefore, that using the MVPT-R as a screening tool would be appropriate up to age 8, but should be interpreted very cautiously for ages 4, 9, and above.

If accepting data from the MVPT regarding reliability and validity, the reliability coefficients would suggest that scores from the test do have a high degree of stability. This is presumed more from split-half and Kuder-Richardson reliability coefficients because test-retest data may have been confounded by time-sampling (standardization population was tested 20 days after pretesting). Mean coefficients were .86 (KR-20) and .88 (split half), yielding a split-half coefficient stronger than that for all other motor-free tests referenced in the manual.

Validity was reported to be discussed in three ways: content, construct, and criterion-related. Content validity was investigated by the degree that there is high correlation with other tests that purport to measure the same domain. Construct validity was reportedly demonstrated based on low discriminant validity coefficients and high convergent validity coefficients. A criticism is that these test coefficients were based on infrequently used tests, tests that have since been renormed and/or revised in some important way, or tests that were not highly reliable themselves. Internal consistency was considered using the point biserial correlation technique with Plates 1–36 evidencing statistical significance at least once for the age range 5 through 7 years. The MVPT-R did not give information showing that the test accurately distinguishes between people who are known to have different levels of the construct due to poor neurophysiological growth but did report age differentiation based on the original MVPT sample population. Criterion-related validity was not discussed but it seemed likely that performance on the MVPT-R would be used to estimate current status and not be used in a predictive way.

SUMMARY. Primary benefits of the MVPT-R include easy administration and scoring, clear and simple instructions in the manual, and total testing time of about 10 minutes. Additionally, no verbal responses are required, the test can be used for individuals with limited language ability, receptive language requirements are minimal, and it can easily be interpreted to other languages. Further, additional instructions are permitted on trial items, slow response time is not penalized, and the authors are planning a vertical position plate booklet for individuals with hemispatial visual neglect. Limitations include the reliability and validity data being based on the 1972 sample and no research cited to support the suggestion that the visual perceptual system was completely developed by age 10 years 11 months (except the high pass rate in the item analysis summary). There was no evidence that the four additional plates substantially discriminated at half-year intervals from year 9-0 through 11-6, which could then be extrapolated to adult populations based on item difficulty levels. Further, based on reviewer administration of 17-year-old females, new information was not attained because of the additional plates. Correlation data between the MVPT and other tests of visual perception did not describe the children in the comparison. Content validity was not adequately established and the resources referenced for instructional materials and ideas were from 1964–1971.

REVIEWER'S REFERENCE

Compton, C. (1990). "Motor-Free Visual Perception Test" in *A guide to 85 tests for special education.* Fearon, Janus, Quercas: Belmont, CA.

[242]
Motor-Free Visual Perception Test—Vertical.

Purpose: Designed to assess problems in visual perception in individuals with hemispatial visual neglect.
Population: People with brain injuries.
Publication Date: 1997.
Acronym: MVPT-V.
Scores: Total score only.
Administration: Individual
Price Data, 1999: $80 per complete test kit including manual (35 pages), test plates, and 50 recording forms; $16 per 50 recording forms; $38 per test plates; $23 per manual.
Time: (10) minutes.
Comments: Contents of test based on the Motor-Free Visual Perception Test (241).

Authors: Louisette Mercier, Rejean Hebert, Ronald Colarusso, and Donald Hammill.
Publisher: Academic Therapy Publications.

Review of the Motor-Free Visual Perception Test—Vertical by MATTHEW E. LAMBERT, Research Neuropsychologist, Neurology Research Education Center at St. Mary Hospital, Lubbock, TX:

The Motor-Free Visual Perception Test—Vertical format (MVPT-V) is a revision of the original Motor-Free Visual Perception Test (MVPT) developed by Colarusso and Hammill (1972). The MVPT-V is an outgrowth of a master's thesis conducted by Louisette Mercier at the University of Sherbrooke in Canada. The main revision involves reorienting that test stimuli from a horizontal to a vertical perspective and including a horizontal line under each target stimulus to make it more conspicuous, while retaining all of the original 36 items without any additions. Additionally, the page size is changed from 8.5 x 11 inches to 8.5 x 14 inches to allow enough space for a vertical presentation of the target and answer graphics, maintaining the distance between graphic figures. Apart from these changes, administration instructions and scoring remain the same as for the original MVPT. The 36 stimulus pages are spiral bound with instructions printed on opposite pages to aid administration. Responses are reported on a scoring sheet that facilitates tallying of raw score totals. The rationale for this adaptation is to allow a more accurate assessment of visual-perceptual functioning following cerebral impairment while controlling for potential interference from hemispatial visual neglect (HVN).

Psychometric properties of the MVPT-V are described in the 35-page manual, which discusses the theoretical underpinnings of the test and its revisions as well as administration, scoring, and interpretation information. Scoring is essentially the same as in the original test version and involves compiling raw scores or correct responses. Yet, throughout the manual references are made to "AB" and "AD" responses as having some differential meaning. At no point in the manual, however, is there a discussion of "AB" and "AD" responses or how they are differentially scored or interpreted.

Unfortunately, there is a dearth of interpretive information in the manual such that only the grossest descriptive statements can be made based on any scores. The manual states "adults *without* a history of head injury or HVN can be expected to show an *overall* raw score in the range of 28 to 36.

Adults *with* a history of head injury should first be tested for HVN. If HVN is present, the MVPT-V can be used to assess more accurately the nature of the visual-perceptual problems" (p. 23, original italics included). This raises the question of how this actually should occur and suggests more emphasis has been placed on how the original MVPT should be revised rather than its applicability to clinical or research practice.

The interpretive limitations noted are not surprising because it appears insufficient attention has been applied to understanding the psychometric characteristics of the new test. A basic assumption is made that the item characteristics of the MVPT-V are identical to the original MVPT. In fact, the Item Selection section of the MVPT-V manual is reprinted from the 1972 MVPT manual. This assumption is inappropriate in that the reorientation of the items fundamentally changes them and necessitates a formal assessment of their psychometric properties to determine if they are equivalent to the parallel items in the original test.

This assumption is also used as a basis for justifying the internal consistency of the MVPT-V. Again, the internal consistency information from the 1972 MVPT manual is reprinted in the current manual instead of estimating the internal consistency of the current instrument. MVPT data are further presented as evidence for the MVPT-V's test item homogeneity and comparability to other visual perception tests. The admonition can only be made again that the MVPT and MVPT-V are fundamentally different tests and independent evaluation of the psychometric properties of the MVPT-V must be undertaken in order to justify its stated purpose.

Although the more basic psychometric properties of the MVPT-V were not assessed, an attempt was made to establish test-retest reliability. Data were apparently obtained from the normative sample used in the MVPT-V validation study that included non-cerebrally impaired controls and cerebrally impaired persons with and without HVN. Subjects were readministered the MVPT-V at a 5- to 8-day interval. The manual presents Pearson correlation values for both the horizontal ($r = .95$) and vertical ($r = .93$) formats. Additionally, intraclass correlation coefficients were presented for the horizontal ($r = .94$) and vertical ($r = .92$) formats. These correlations are of sufficient magnitude for their purposes. Standard test development practices, however, require

separate samples be used for determining reliability and validity properties.

The "Validity" section of the test manual addresses issues of construct, concurrent, and diagnostic validity. For construct validity, reference is made to the consistency in scores for individuals (with or without head injury) who did not suffer HVN, between the horizontal and vertical formats and the inconsistency of scores between formats for individuals suffering HVN. Aside from the difficulty in understanding the basis for the scores used (e.g., AB responses), another assumption is made that the test adaptation actually controls for the HVN construct. Comparison to other measures of visual perception that could or could not be affected by HVN would be a more appropriate way to examine construct validity. As it is, adequate construct validity evidence is lacking. This criticism also applies to the statements about concurrent validity based on comparisons between scores of unimpaired controls and head-injured patients without HVN.

An interesting finding is noted when addressing the issue of diagnostic validity. Comparison is made between the MVPT-V and the Bell Test for determining HVN. Apparently, the "Bell Test diagnosed 100 percent of the subjects with clinically-evident age HVN, while 55 percent of those persons showed possible evidence of HVN using the MVPT-V" (manual, p. 20). Use of the MVPT-V as an HVN diagnostic tool would, therefore, seem inefficient as compared to the Bell Test.

Additional statements are made regarding diagnostic validity through a discussion of differential performance patterns for individuals in various age categories. Their utility, however, is questioned in relating to uncertainty about how visual-perception functions in normal individuals at different ages.

SUMMARY. Numerous questions are present regarding the MVPT-V's psychometric properties that are not satisfactorily answered based on the limited developmental data presented in the test manual. Its use as a clinical or research tool at this time is inappropriate. A great deal more research is needed to examine the reliability and validity of scores from this adaptation. Once this research is completed, and assuming the data support use of the adapted instrument, significantly greater attention needs to be given to making the manual instructive and facilitative to the test user. In its current form it is obfuscating and distracting.

[243]

Movement Assessment Battery for Children.

Purpose: Designed to assess motor skills and motor development difficulties.

Population: Ages 4–12 years.

Publication Dates: 1972–1992.

Acronym: Movement ABC.

Administration: Individual or group.

Price Data, 1999: $463.50 per complete kit including checklist, manual ('92, 250 pages), record forms, and all necessary manipulatives in an attaché case; $14 per 50 checklists; $40 per 25 record forms (specify level).

Authors: Sheila E. Henderson and David A. Sugden.

Publisher: The Psychological Corporation Limited [United Kingdom]; distributed by The Psychological Corporation.

a) MOVEMENT ABC.

Scores, 3: Manual Dexterity, Ball Skills, Static and Dynamic Balance.

Administration: Individual.

Levels, 4: Age Band 1 (Ages 4–6); Age Band 2 (Ages 7–8); Age Band 3 (Ages 9–10); Age Band 4 (Ages 11–12).

Time: (20–30) minutes.

Comments: Developed from the Test of Motor Impairment (9:1265).

b) MOVEMENT ABC CHECKLIST.

Scores, 5: Child Stationary/Environment Stable, Child Moving/Environment Stable, Child Stationary/Environment Changing, Child Moving/Environment Changing, Behavioral Problems Related to Motor Difficulties.

Administration: Individual or group.

Time: Administration time not reported.

Comments: Behavior checklist used by teachers, parents, and other professionals.

Cross References: See T5:1725 (8 references); for a review by Jerome D. Pauker of an earlier edition, see 8:881 (2 references); see also T2:1904 (4 references).

Review of the Movement Assessment Battery for Children by LARRY M. BOLEN, Professor and School Psychology Trainer, East Carolina University, Greenville, NC:

The Movement Assessment Battery for Children is the product of 20 years of research and provides a comprehensive and systematic assessment system for screening, identifying, planning intervention, and program evaluation for children with motor problems. The test battery is composed of three basic parts: The Movement ABC Test, designed by S. E. Henderson, D. H. Stott, and F. A. Moyes; The Movement ABC Checklist,

developed by D. A. Sugden and L. Sugden; and The Movement ABC Manual, which includes a thorough presentation of a Cognitive-Motor theoretical approach to intervention, compiled by Henderson and Sugden.

The Movement ABC Test is based in large part on the Test of Motor Impairment (TOMI; Stott, D. H., Moyes, F. A., & Henderson, S. E., 1972). Specifically, the Movement ABC Test follows from the 1984 revision of the TOMI by Henderson (Stott, D. H., Moyes, F. A., & Henderson, S. E., 1984). The 1972 TOMI had 45 items, 5 at each of nine age levels, reflecting the format of the Oseretsky Test of Motor Proficiency (Oseretsky, 1923, 1948). The Henderson revision of the TOMI (1984) involved substantial modifications. The 1984 TOMI was reorganized into three sections covering Manual Dexterity, Ball Skills, and Static and Dynamic Balance. Additionally, a decision was made to increase sensitivity at the lower end of the scale. Thus, test items were organized into four sets of eight, with each set corresponding to one of four age bands ranging from age 4 to 12.

The Movement ABC is the direct descendant of the TOMI and includes all features of the 1984 Henderson revision of the TOMI. Two additions, however, make the clinical usefulness of the Movement ABC superior to the TOMI: First, the authors utilize a strong underlying theoretical (Cognitive-Motor) framework in interpreting and developing practical interventions for children with motor problems. Second, the refinement of Stott's (1972) Checklist and inclusion as part of the current test battery extends the scope for classroom-based assessment and screening as well as for home-based assessment and screening.

Standardization and item representation remain basically unchanged from the Henderson revision of the 1984 TOMI. Modifications involved clarifying test instructions, providing pictorials to help standardize test item presentation, improving the scoring system (from a 3-point scale to a 6-point scale) to sensitize measurement for small improvements in motor performance, and expanding the record form. A major modification involved the addition of norms for children 4 years of age, recognizing the need for preschool assessment and screening.

The United States standardization of the Movement ABC included 1,234 children divided into four geographic samples: Northeast, North

Central, South, and West. Both urban and rural areas were represented with 24 testing centers across the U.S. The case quotas spanned four age bands from 4 through 12 years: Age Band 1: 4 to 6 years of age (n = 493); Age Band 2: 7 to 8 (n = 264); Age Band 3: 9 to 10 (n = 257); and Age Band 4: 11 and over (n = 220).

The South sample was underrepresented (U.S. population percentage 34.6, test sample 12.6%) and the West sample was overrepresented (U.S. 18.9%, test sample 34.6%). Ethnicity was very adequately represented across the four age bands proportionally to U.S. population percentages. Although standardization was also stratified based on parents' educational background, the test norms do not adequately represent the less educated parent. Children with motor problems with parents having 12 years or less of education are significantly underrepresented and the better educated parents are slightly overrepresented. The authors state that the effect on the norms is considered slight. Followup analysis of "socioeconomic status," represented as mother's education level, and Movement ABC test scores supports this notion. Analysis of a group of children aged 4 to 6 years and of children aged 7 to 12 found no significant relationship of Total impairment scores and mother's educational level.

Item reliability data were provided for samples of children for Age Bands 1, 2, and 3 over a 2-week period. Percentage agreement for each of the eight items comprising each age band ranged from 62% to 100%. The median agreement for Age Band 1 was 90%; Age Band 2 = 84%; and Age Band 3 = 80%. These percentage agreements are quite high considering they represent individual items rather than total score. The stability of the Total impairment scores were: 97% for Age Band 1, 91% for Age Band 2, and 73% for Age Band 3. Percentage agreement data for Age Band 4 was not reported and should be presumed as low.

Validity evidence was assessed in a number of ways. Concurrent validity was considered by comparing performance on the Movement ABC with the Bruininks-Oseretsky (n = 63). Construct validity was investigated by comparing assessment outcome with various experts (e.g., teachers, therapists, pediatricians, various clinics, etc., where children with known impairment received services). In all cases, the Movement ABC differentiated motor-impaired children from matched samples of normal functioning children. Moreover, the test was also able to discriminate subtle changes in motor movement following intervention efforts.

The Movement ABC Checklist, designed to be used by teachers, parents, and other professionals, provides a qualitative aspect to the standardized assessment. Originally developed in 1972 by Sugden, the content of the Checklist was modified as well as reorganized following a behavior-environment interactional model. This allows for examining children's motor behavior (passive/moving) in different settings as well as contrasting environmental demand differences (stable/changing). As with the Movement ABC Test, the Checklist is thoroughly explained and detailed in the manual.

Although user qualifications are discussed, the authors maintain no special training is required. Keeping in mind that only experienced professionals, including special service teachers, would be expected to use the test, it seems quite clear that the usefulness of the test will directly reflect the background and training of the professional using it. It is my opinion that not only training in standardized procedures is necessary but that adequate background knowledge with regard to motor development is essential for proper and effective utilization of this test.

The test equipment is first rate. The design and motor behavior measured have high face validity. The manual is clear and detailed. The manual is also a monograph outlining in considerable depth the theory, structure, and evolution of the Movement ABC (i.e., providing detailed background knowledge in motor movement). The authors utilize a persuasive Cognitive-Motor theoretical framework for understanding test performance (degree and kind of motor impairment) and effect on the learning process. For therapist and teachers, the manual presents chapters on intervention, linking assessment to behavior management, and the teaching of individual skills.

In sum, the Movement ABC appears to be an excellent instrument for the measurement of motor difficulties for young children. Caution is advised in the use of the test for Age Band 4 (ages 11–12) until data are provided showing reliability and validity of measurement at this level.

Review of the Movement Assessment Battery for Children by CAROL E. KESSLER, Assistant Professor of Education, Chestnut Hill College, Phila-

delphia, PA, and Adjunct Professor of Special Education, West Chester University, West Chester, PA:

This Battery, appropriate for children 4–12 years of age, originated from the works of Stott (who developed the Test of Motor Impairment [TOMI]) and Keogh (who produced the original Checklist). Thirty years of work have produced this new package. The main test (TOMI) was first published in 1972, revised by Henderson in 1984, and newly formatted as The Movement ABC in 1992 by Henderson and Sugden. This hybrid is a direct descendent of these previous editions, but additionally emphasizes practical application and intervention, creating fresh opportunities for classroom-based screening and assessment. Stott was concerned with investigating the relationship between possible perinatal trauma and later developmental disorders, specifically "clumsiness" in childhood; whereas Keogh, working with another strand of inquiry, was interested in alerting teachers to movement difficulties and their subsequent educational significance in children

The Movement Assessment Battery for Children (Movement ABC) incorporates both of these perspectives into an assessment battery that contains two component parts. The "performance Test" requires individual administration and entails a series of motor tasks that the child must complete in a standardized fashion. It contains 32 items organized in four age bands of eight tasks. The first age band is for ages 4–6; the next is for children 7–8 years; the third band is for 9–10 year-old-children; and finally, the last band is for youngsters between the ages of 11 and 12 years. The requirements are identical for each of the eight tasks within the four bands. The eight test items or tasks are grouped under three dimensions: Manual Dexterity (3), Ball Skills (2), and Static (1)/Dynamic Behavior (2). The total score is a composite of these eight estimates of movement competence and is translated in terms of age-related norms. Additionally, a section where qualitative observations are to be noted accompanies each task. Further, upon conclusion of the test administration, the examiner is to comment on the influences on performance and summarize the qualitative observations. This portion should take 20–40 minutes, thereby easily maintaining the interest of the child. The Total Impairment Score on the Test portion indicates the extent to which a child demonstrates movement difficulties when compared to her/his same-age peers. Any score below the 5th percentile indicates a definite motor delay requiring immediate intervention. Similarly, a score between the 5th and 15th percentile suggests borderline motoric functioning.

The Checklist, ideal for screening purposes, is the second component of the Battery. This section is to be completed by an adult who is very familiar with the child's everyday movement capabilities. The 48 items are divided into four sections, each of which entails evaluating and rating the child in progressively more complex situations (Child Stationary/Environment Stable, Child Moving/Environment Stable, Child Stationary/Environment Changing, Child Moving/Environment Changing). Section 5 of the Checklist provides a qualitative assessment regarding the child's feelings and attitudes that may affect movement functioning. The Checklist, according to the manual, will probably identify more children as having deficits than will the Movement ABC Test, but will most likely yield similar scores for youngsters who are competent. This combination of quantitative and qualitative information is a definite strength of this assessment device.

The format of this well-constructed test is easy to follow. The instrument is designed to measure a child's motoric competence, not the ability to remember or understand directions. Therefore, numerous demonstrations can be given; instructions can be simplified, modified, and/or repeated; and testing may be done over the course of more than one session. A 0 item score indicates success whereas the measure of motor impairments is tabulated using a 1–5 score range.

In general, the manual is comprehensible and each item description has a matching picture of a child performing the task, which is extremely helpful. The instructions and scoring criteria are very clear, as well. Thus, the Test is easy to administer and score and is appropriate for the age range tested. Also, the instrument does not seem to pose any risk of physical injury, would be equally relevant to various cultural backgrounds, and includes tasks that are equally familiar to both sexes. Further, all of the materials supplied (my kit was missing the pegboard with 16 green pegs as well as the plastic target disk) were of very high quality. In addition, all of the necessary items fit neatly into the attaché case provided. One limitation inherent in the test pertains to the specifications regarding the room requirements, which are: a space that is at least 18 by 12 feet, a floor that is uncarpeted, and a blank wall that is smooth (I suppose the school gymnasium would satisfactorily meet these stipulations). The manual indicates that the instructions have been clarified, the scoring system has been improved, and norms for 4-year-olds have been added in the 1992 Battery—very critical improvements when compared to the previous editions. Also, the addition of the Checklist and the explanation of the cognitive-motor approach to educational intervention (which appears in the manual) are very helpful.

The age norms for the Test, which are provided for children 4–12 years of age, are based on a representative sample of 1,234 youngsters. For the Test, the geographic spread included the Northeast, North Central, South, and West regions (the standardization of the Test was completed in the United States whereas the Checklist was based in the United Kingdom). Both rural and urban areas were represented. Further, in terms of gender, parental education, and ethnic origin, the sample seems to satisfactorily represent the general population of children in the U.S.

In preparing the impairment score scale and the test items for the newest edition, there was a deliberate focus on the low end of the distribution of motor proficiency. Because there was a statistically significant difference in variability among the 4–5-year-old band and the older children on the Total Impairment scores, two sets of total score norms were prepared.

When examining the reliability data for the Test, there seems to be stability over time when the items and Total Impairment scores are statistically analyzed. However, additional reliability data are necessary because the sample size was small. In investigating the construct validity for the Test, comparisons between groups of children known to have difficulties were made. In various studies, children with learning disabilities, as well as children with low birth weight and/or prematurity were compared with the standardization sample. These high-risk children consistently demonstrated motor difficulties (obtained elevated scores) in comparison to normal children. Additionally, the Movement ABC Test was examined in relationship to the Bruininks-Oseretsky Test. Although these tests are similar in some respects, they also differ radically. The ABC Test focuses primarily on the identification of impairment and the Bruininks Test is intended to indicate ability across the entire spectrum. A coefficient of -0.53 resulted (the true direction of the relationship is positive because the composite scores of these tests are scaled in the opposite direction). Because these two tests are only moderately comparable (a very high correlation should not be expected to occur), it is suggested that additional test comparisons be conducted to gain a more comprehensive validity examination of scores from the Test.

When examining the statistical adequacy of the Checklist, only children between the ages of 6–10 years were examined. The authors make a commitment to collect data in the future that include children who have just begun school and those who are entering puberty.

It can be hoped that with more extensive study these limitations regarding the technical characteristics of this instrument will be addressed adequately. In summation, I recommend this Battery for examiners who are interested in assessing a child's movement capabilities and in increasing their knowledge pertaining to the management and remediation of motor impairments.

[244]
Mullen Scales of Early Learning: AGS Edition.

Purpose: A comprehensive measure of cognitive functioning for infants and preschool children.
Population: Birth to 68 months.
Publication Dates: 1984–1995.
Scores, 6: Gross Motor Scale, Cognitive Scales (Visual Reception, Fine Motor, Receptive Language, Expressive Language), Early Learning Composite.
Administration: Individual.
Price Data, 1999: $599 per complete kit; $25.95 per 25 record forms; $149.95 per Mullen ASSIST (specify for IBM, Macintosh, or Windows).
Time: (15–60) minutes.
Comments: Previous editions entitled Infant Mullen Scales of Early Learning and Preschool Mullen Scales of Early Learning.
Author: Eileen M. Mullen.
Publisher: American Guidance Service, Inc.
Cross References: See T5:1728 (2 references); for a review by Verna Hart of the earlier edition, see 11:177.

Review of the Mullen Scales of Early Learning: AGS Edition by MARY MATHAI CHITTOORAN, UC Foundation Assistant Professor of School Psychol-

ogy, The University of Tennessee at Chattanooga, Chattanooga, TN:

The Mullen Scales of Early Learning: AGS Edition is a revised version of the original Mullen Scales of Early Learning (MSEL) and combines the Infant MSEL with the Preschool MSEL. It is an individually administered, standardized measure of cognitive functioning in infants and preschoolers from birth through 68 months. The Mullen is theory-based and consists of a Gross Motor Scale, which is administered to children from birth through 33 months, and four Cognitive Scales (Visual Reception, Fine Motor, Receptive Language, and Expressive Language), which can be used with children from birth through 68 months. Performance on individual scales is reported as T-scores ($X = 50$; $SD = 10$) and the optional Early Learning Composite ($X = 100$; $SD = 15$) is a derivation from the T-scores of the four Cognitive Scales, and serves as an overall estimate of cognitive functioning. Also available are percentile ranks and age equivalents. Because scales on the Mullen correspond with federal mandates for infant and preschool assessment, results of the test may be used for eligibility decisions, as well as for program planning and early intervention services.

The test kit includes a number of bright and attractive test materials. Although they are generally durable and safe for use with young children, there were some notable exceptions; cards for some items are flimsy and unlikely to stand up to continued use, the table leg arrived broken, and the formboard, which appears to be made of painted particle board, is poorly sanded and was covered with paint flakes. Examiners are also expected to supply supplemental materials such as paper and coins; however, the author does provide a comprehensive list of necessary materials. The Item Administration Book includes directions for administration and scoring and is nicely done; however, there are only a few items in each area, and in some cases only two at certain age levels. The Stimulus Booklet may have been more useful with an easel back. Further, its small size, and the fact that there are often many items crowded onto a page, may be problematic for young children. The single-sheet fold-out Record Form could have been better designed; the print is miniscule, giving it a rather "busy" appearance, and the flap that contains stimuli for items on the Receptive and Expressive Language Scales is oddly placed.

Training requirements are minimal and administration should be simple for those with early childhood experience. The examiner may choose to give all or some of the subscales without sacrificing accuracy and is allowed to vary the order of administration to maintain examinee interest. Although most items involve observing the child actually performing a task, there are some that may be scored by interviewing the parent, and others that allow the parent to assist in elicitation of a response. Scoring and interpretation are enhanced by the inclusion of clearly organized tables, case studies, and ASSIST software.

Seventy-one clinicians participated in the standardization of the Mullen over a period of 8 years. The normative sample included 1,849 children between the ages of 2 days and 69 months grouped into 16 age groups ranging from 2-month age intervals at the youngest age level to 5-month age intervals at the upper age level. Children in the normative sample were 51.3% male and 48.7% female and included Caucasian, African American, Hispanic, and Native American individuals in proportion to the U.S. Census of 1990. Females are underrepresented at some age levels (e.g., 5–6 months) and males are underrepresented at others (e.g., 27–32 months). Other stratification variables included socioeconomic status, geographic region, and community size. Results of the Mullen may be affected by the fact that the standardization sample did not include children with a primary language other than English or children with known exceptionalities; separate norms for children with special needs might have been useful. Also potentially problematic is the fact that the sample only included children whose parents gave permission for participation.

Item analyses using the Rasch one-parameter IRT model were conducted to determine the final item set for all five scales of the Mullen as well as to establish basal and ceiling rules. Developmental progression of raw scores and intercorrelations between scales are offered as evidence of construct validity and principal-factor loadings (ranging from .55 to .90) lend support for the Early Learning Composite as a measure of general cognitive ability.

Concurrent validity with the Bayley Scales of Infant Development was studied in a sample of 103 "normal" children ages 6 to 15 months. Moderately high correlations were obtained between the Bayley's Mental Development Index and both the Early Learning Composite (.70) and the four cognitive scales (.53 to .59). The Gross Motor Scale correlated with the Bayley's Psychomotor Development Index at .76. Divergent validity was illustrated by relatively low correlations with scales measuring unrelated abilities. High convergent and divergent validity were also established by examining correlations between measures of receptive and expressive abilities on the Mullen and the Preschool Language Assessment ($N = 65$; ages 15–59 months). The Mullen had high to moderate correlations with the Motor subtest of the Brigance, the Peabody Fine Motor Scale, and the Metropolitan Readiness Test. According to the author, the Mullen is able to discriminate between children with developmental delays and those without. Content validity is not directly mentioned; however, evidence of criterion-related and construct validity can also be used to establish content validity.

Modified split-half internal consistency coefficients for the scales had median values ranging from .75 to .83 and the composite had a median value of .91. Four coefficients were not used in the calculation of median values because of ceiling effects on the Visual Reception Scale and floor and ceiling effects on the Receptive Language Scale. The standard error of measurement had median values ranging from 4.1 to 5.0 for the Cognitive Scales and 4.5 for the Early Learning Composite. Test-retest reliability was measured for two age groups (1–24 months and 25–56 months) with a mean retest interval of 11 days. Among the younger age group, stability coefficients ranged from a low of .82 for the Fine Motor Scale ($N = 50$) to a high of .96 for the Gross Motor Scale ($N = 38$); among the older age group, coefficients ranged from a low of .71 for the Expressive Language Scale ($N = 47$) to a high of .79 for the Fine Motor Scale ($N = 47$). Interscorer reliability for four age groups of children between 1 and 44 months ($N = 81$) ranged from .91 to .99. Although validity and reliability evidence appears to be adequate, it must be mentioned that results reported are based on studies completed with previous versions of the Mullen and samples that are either rather small or that have inadequate representation of older children.

SUMMARY. The concerns noted with regard to standardization, reliability, and validity warrant a cautious interpretation of the test, particularly for older children or children with exceptionalities. Despite these deficiencies, the Mullen appears to be a satisfactory alternative to other measures of functioning for early childhood populations, particularly if it is used as part of a comprehensive assessment battery.

Review of the Mullen Scales of Early Learning: AGS Edition by CAROL E. KESSLER, Assistant Professor of Education, Chestnut Hill College, Philadelphia, PA, and Adjunct Professor of Special Education, West Chester University, West Chester, PA:

There is an increased need to assess young children, particularly those from birth to 68 months, because of the passage of P.L. 999-457. The Mullen Scales enables early childhood specialists to design developmentally appropriate individualized educational plans based on the child's profile of cognitive abilities and weaknesses, which underlies her/his learning style. These Scales assist the examiner in facilitating eligibility decisions regarding the need for special services but, as the author notes, should be used in conjunction with measures of social-emotional development and adaptive skills to provide a comprehensive assessment.

Dr. Eileen M. Mullen, a developmental psychologist, has extensive experience in diagnosing children with developmental disabilities. This interactive test model, which includes both intrasensory and intersensory components, views intelligence as "a network of interrelated but functionally distinct cognitive skills" (manual, p. 1). This assessment device consists of a Gross Motor Scale and four Cognitive Scales (Visual Reception, Fine Motor, Receptive Language, Expressive Language). Also, an Early Learning Composite score is included, which represents general intelligence.

In her theoretical framework, Mullen asserts that visual and auditory conceptual development has as its foundation gross motor learning. Each score provides a T score, percentile rank, descriptive category (which is very helpful for the practitioner), and an age equivalent. T scores are to be used for program eligibility. If a child receives a T score of 30 or less on any Scale (2 standard deviations or more below the mean), this would indicate a significant delay and would certainly warrant early intervention services. Further, T scores of 31–35 (1.5 standard deviations below the mean) are indicative of a child at risk for delay and should also be considered for special services.

The manual provides outstanding explanations regarding all the important features of the

Scales and includes examples of profile interpretations within case study reports. The test kit contains an ASSIST computer software program, which is available in Macintosh, DOS, and Windows versions. The program calculates derived scores and give interpretive information for the five Scales and the Early Learning Composite. Also, it includes activities for intervention for birth through 36 months. It is suggested that these intervention tasks be extended upward to include children 45+ months. Further, the manipulatives included are of high interest to young children and are of very sturdy quality. An exception would be the child's safety scissors. These should be of a higher quality if children are expected to cut accurately and comfortably for Item 24 of the Fine Motor Scale. Also, white chalk and/or a 10-foot colored tape should be included (specified in the manual to be supplied by the examiner). Inclusion of these items would make preparation a great deal easier for the examiner.

The Scales are presented in nontechnical terms and are easy to administer and score. Also, the directions have numerous diagrams to aid comprehension and are of very superior quality. The administration time, 15–60 minutes, is certainly within an acceptable range and thus allows the interest of the child to be maintained easily. All five scores can stand alone for scoring and administrative purposes. Separate scores are available for both receptive and expressive responses, which should be considered a definite strength of this test.

Standardization data are provided on 1,849 children ranging in age from 2 days to 69 months. More than 100 sites, in four geographic regions of the U.S. (Northeast, South, West, Central), were used. The standardization testing began in the Northeast region and continued over a period of 8 years. Stratified variables included sex, race/ethnicity, father's occupation, and urban/rural residence. The description of the sample indicates that it is a very close representation of the U.S. population. The examiner should be cognizant of the fact that only children with parental consent were included in the sample. An item analysis and normative scores (these recomputed norms are different from the ones provided in previous versions) are provided.

The psychometric properties appear technically adequate. Internal consistency was estimated using a split-half procedure. Very satisfactory median internal consistency values for the five Scales were obtained (.75 to .83). However, some ceiling effect is present for the Perceptive Language Scale and the Visual Perception Scale. Also, a floor effect is evident for the Receptive Language Scale, which reflects reduced score variance and concomitantly reduces reliability estimates. Negligible practice effects were demonstrated (test-retest reliability), which indicates a high degree of score stability over time. The interscorer reliability ranges from .91 to .99 and thus the Scales appear to be interpreted similarly by multiple examiners. Further, the construct and concurrent validity appears to be technically sound. The author uses developmental progression of scores, intercorrelations of the Scales, and principal-axis factor analysis in support of the construct validity of this assessment instrument. Also, concurrent validity was substantiated using the Bayley Scales of Infant Development, the Preschool Language Assessment, and the Peabody Fine Motor Scale with different age ranges. Again, correlations between the Mullen Measures and the Bayley Measures support convergent and divergent validity of the scores. The results, when compared to the PLA Measures, yield similarly good evidence. Finally, when investigating and comparing the fine motor scales, again the Mullen Scale shows substantial correlations supporting the concurrent validity of this instrument.

Some of the earlier psychometric concerns regarding the Infant Mullen Scales of Early Learning have been addressed adequately and thus the examiner can be more confident when using these Scales to assess learning patterns and capacities of children. In summary, I highly recommend this assessment tool when the examiner is interested in measuring a young child's cognitive abilities and gross motor base for learning.

[245]
The Multidimensional Addictions and Personality Profile.

Purpose: Designed as "an objective measure of substance abuse and personal adjustment problems."
Population: Adolescents and adults experiencing substance abuse and mental health disorders.
Publication Dates: 1988–1996.
Acronym: MAPP.
Scores, 15: Substance Abuse Subscales (Psychological Dependence, Abusive/Secretive/Irresponsible Use, Interference, Signs of Withdrawal, Total), Personal Adjustment Subscales (Frustration Problems, Interper-

sonal Problems, Self-Image Problems, Total), Defensiveness and Inconsistency Scores (Defensiveness, Inconsistency, Total); Minimizing Response Pattern Scales (Substance Abuse, Personal Adjustment, Total).

Administration: Group or individual.

Price Data, 1995: $65 per 50 answer booklets; $30 per manual ('96, 110 pages); $22 per French and Spanish translation package including written and audiotaped instructions and questions; $170 per Advanced Computer scoring package including 50 tests and a research module.

Foreign Language Edition: French and Spanish translation package available (including printed questions with audio tape).

Time: (20–25) minutes.

Comments: Previous edition entitled The COMPASS; IBM or compatible with 2 disk drives and at least 640K RAM, monitor, and printer required for computer scoring option.

Authors: John R. Craig and Phyllis Craig.

Publisher: Diagnostic Counseling Services, Inc.

Review of The Multidimensional Addictions and Personality Profile by CARL ISENHART, Coordinator, Addictive Disorders Section, VA Medical Center, Minneapolis, MN:

The Multidimensional Addictions and Personality Profile (MAPP; a revision of "The COMPASS") is a 98-item self-report questionnaire that assesses an individual's (adolescent or adult) substance abuse and personal adjustment. It can be administered in 20–25 minutes either individually or in a group. The manual states that "no minimum reading skill or educational level is required" (manual, p. 19) because an illiterate person could have the items read to him or her.

The Substance Abuse section consists of four, 14-item subscales and one total scale that assess Psychological Dependence; Abusive, Secretive, and Irresponsible Use; Interference; and Signs of Withdrawal. The Personal Adjustment scales consists of three, 14-item subscales (actually, seven, 2-item pairs with opposite content) and one total scale that assess Frustration, Interpersonal Problems, and Self-Image Problems. An Inconsistency and Defensiveness scale are derived from the Personal Adjustment items. The Inconsistency scale assesses the test-taker's response consistency and contains the 21, 2-item Personal Adjustment scale items. The Defensiveness scale assesses the person's willingness to admit to problems. The response options for all the items consist of five options: *always, usually, occasionally, seldom,* and *never.* Each

text term is associated with a number; for example, *always* = 4 and *never* = 0.

ADMINISTRATION AND SCORING. The MAPP items are administered orally or in writing, and the examinee's responses are transferred via a carbonless sheet to a scoring sheet that is used by the examiner to tally the raw scores. The scale scores are obtained by tallying the examinee's responses to each item then converting the raw scores to percentiles. The Defensiveness score is obtained by counting the number of *never* responses on the three Personal Adjustment subscales. The Inconsistency score is obtained by summing the absolute differences between the 21 pairs of items that make up the Personal Adjustment subscales. The manual provides guidelines (but no rationale) for when to question or reject protocols based on the Defensiveness and Inconsistency scales.

NORMS. There are major problems with the standardization description. The standardization sample consisted of "inpatients" and the "general population"; a table provides details of each sample's sex, race, and age. There is no description of the inpatient sample in terms of background or substance use dimensions, and there was no discussion of how these individuals were selected for inclusion. There was a large age difference between the inpatient and general population sample (31% of the inpatient and 71% of the general population was under 21, respectively), but there was no analysis of the statistical significance of that and other possible differences between the two groups. The authors do not provide the means and standard deviations of the standardization sample's scores from the MAPP. The only means and standard deviations that are provided are from a sample of 131 people used in the test-retest reliability sample. With this limited sample, the standard deviations show a high level of variation. There is no information about the distribution of the samples. There was no evaluation of any demographic differences on any of the MAPP scales.

SCALE DEVELOPMENT AND CONTENT. The substance abuse scale items "were selected primarily from rational-theoretical considerations rather than by factor-analytical or empirical techniques ... to meet the definition of substance abuse as set forth in this manual and in DSM-III-R" (manual, p. 9). These items were "provided to substance abuse evaluation specialists" (manual, p. 9) for further refinement. The Personal Adjustment scale items were "limited to those areas which dealt with the most commonly occurring problems of daily living" (manual, p. 9). There is no discussion of the refinement of items and justification for the types and number of items in each scale. For example, there was no empirical evaluation of whether the subscales assess truly unique and independent dimensions: The reported Substance Abuse subscale correlations ranged from .57 to .85. There was also no justification for needing 21 pairs of items for the Inconsistency scale; it is likely fewer items would serve the same purpose. Also, there is no empirical support that the Inconsistency scale item pairs do represent opposite content.

RELIABILITY. The quality of the reliability data is poor. Test-retest reliability was reported for 131 people with an interval of 7 days between administrations; no other intervals were reported. The correlations ranged from .50 to .91. Each scale's standard error of measurement (*SEM*) was reported; however, the large *SEMs* seem to actually call into question the test's reliability. For example, the *SEM* is approximately 11 for the Total Substance Abuse score. Given a score of 23 (which is at the 50th percentile), 68% of the time the true score will fall between a range of 12 and 34; this represents percentiles of 30 and 65, respectively. This is a large range and questions the repeatability and consistency of the scores. Of course, this problem is further exacerbated if two *SEMs* were to be used (which is typical). In addition, the authors reported "internal consistency measures" to support reliability. However, instead of examining the consistency of item responses within the subscales and total scales and calculating coefficient alphas, they correlated the subscales with the total scale. This does not represent item consistency but rather shared variance across the scales (which is different). Because they reported substance abuse subscales and the total score correlations between .83 to almost .86, this further questions the independence and uniqueness of these scales.

VALIDITY. The validity data presented in the manual are weak. *T*-test analysis showed that the MAPP scales significantly differentiated between "chemically dependent" patients and the general population and between a new sample of inpatients (again, there is no demographic or background information provided) and patients with a first and prior arrests and those with and without prior DUIs. However, *t*-tests do not control for making multiple comparisons and do not control for the high correlations between the subscales. These results do little to support the validity of the instrument. In addition, because of the high correlations between the substance abuse and distress scales, the differences that do occur between the inpatients and the general population may be attributable to the distress and not substance use per se. Demographic differences, which were not examined, could also explain the differences. There are no comparisons of the MAPP scores with external criteria, such as other measures of substance abuse, diagnostic criteria, or other indicators of substance-related problems.

SUMMARY. This reviewer cannot support the use of the MAPP. The evaluation of the MAPP vis a vis the standardization sample is inadequate, and there is limited support for the reliability and validity of the instrument.

Review of The Multidimensional Addictions and Personality Profile by KEITH F. WIDAMAN, Professor of Psychology, University of California at Davis, Davis, CA:

The Multidimensional Addictions and Personality profile (MAPP) is a measure of substance use problems and accompanying personal adjustment problems. Alcohol and drug use and abuse are pressing problems in the U.S. so reliable and valid measures of substance use problems are valuable tools in psychological evaluation in general and personnel selection in particular. Personal adjustment problems may precipitate substance use problems or may result from such problems. The MAPP takes no stand on the causal relations between substance use and personal adjustment problems, simply opting to assess the types of adjustment problems that appear to represent significant comorbidity with substance abuse.

DESCRIPTION. The MAPP is a 98-item scale that contains items answered on a frequency scale, ranging from 0 = *Never* to 4 = *Always*. The 98 items are divided into seven primary content scales, with 14 items per scale. Four content scales directly assess substance use problems. These four scales are labeled Psychological Dependence (PD), Abusive, Secretive, and Irresponsible Use (ASI), Interference (INT), and Signs of Withdrawal (SOW). These scale scores can be aggregated into an overall Total Substance Abuse Scales score, which is the simple sum of the PD, ASI, INT, and SOW scale scores. All substance use questions are positively worded (i.e., none are negatively worded), so acquiescence response bias might well be confounded in all four substance use problems scales.

The remaining three content scales measure Personal Adjustment problems accompanying substance use problems. These three scales are Frustration Problems (FP), Interpersonal Problems (IP), and Self-Image Problems (SIP). The aggregated Total Personal Adjustment Scales score is the simple sum of the FP, IP, and SIP scale scores. One-half of the items for each personal Adjustment problem scale are positively worded, and one-half are negatively worded, which would control for acquiescence response bias.

There are also two sets of style scales. The first set consists of two scales, Defensiveness (DEF) and Inconsistency (INC), which can be summed into a total score. The second set of style scales consists of "minimizing" response style scales. One may obtain a score for each subject on a Substance Abuse Minimizing Response Pattern Scale, a Personal Adjustment Minimizing Response Pattern Scale, and a Total Minimizing Response Pattern Scale, which is the sum of the previous two scale scores.

ADMINISTRATION. The MAPP may be administered in either group or individual formats. The instructions for the MAPP are simple and straightforward, with the respondent told to describe his or her behavior during the past 6 months when choosing a response on the 0 = *Never* to 4 = *Always* scale for each item. One confusing aspect of the MAPP is the fact that the 98 items are presented under the title of COMPASS Questionnaire. The COMPASS was an earlier name for the questionnaire now identified as the MAPP, and this inconsistency should be rectified.

SCORING. The scoring of the seven content scales is easily completed. As respondents answer each item, a carbon copy of item responses is transferred directly onto a scoring template, and item scores are easily summed into scale scores for the seven content scales.

With regard to style scales, the DEF scale score is obtained by counting the number of 0 (or *never*) responses across the Personal Adjustment problem scales of FP, IP, and SIP. The INC scale scores is the absolute difference between responses on pairs of items from the FP, IP, and SIP scales,

after appropriate reversing of the scores on negatively worded items. This rescoring of the items from the Personal Adjustment problems scales may be problematic, leading to contaminated correlations among scale scores due to item overlap. In addition, the DEF and INC scales are fairly crude attempts to identify defensiveness and inconsistency of responding. The final style scales, identified as "minimizing response pattern" scales, are poorly described, and the method for obtaining scale scores on these items is not included in the MAPP scoring template.

The standardization samples consisted of an inpatient sample of 424 persons and a general population sample of 1,668 persons. In the general population sample, 1,180 persons were under 21 years of age, 460 were 21 years and over, and 28 declined to state their age. These samples were used to generate two conversion tables, one for persons under 21 years of age and the second for those 21 years and older. The conversion tables provide only percentile scores, which have a uniform distribution. The knowledgeable user could use these conversion tables to transform scores into a T-score or IQ score metric, but this would require a nonlinear transformation of percentiles into another metric and is not provided in the manual. Also, raw scores on each of the seven content scales have a potential range from 0 to 56. The raw scores on these scales are likely to be positively skewed, so conversion to another metric using percentiles would be recommended when using these variables in statistical models.

RELIABILITY. Test-retest reliability estimates based on a sample of 131 respondents, are reported for all content scales and for the DEF and INC style scales, as well as the total scores derived from the several sections. The test-retest interval was 7 days. The test-retest reliability coefficients for the substance use problems scales were fairly high, ranging from .89 to .91. The reliability estimates for the interpersonal adjustment problems scales were lower, ranging from .78 to .87. Test-retest reliability estimates for the style scales of Defensiveness and Inconsistency were much lower, ranging between .50 and .67. No test-retest reliabilities were provided for the Minimizing response pattern scales.

The accompanying values for the standard error of measurement (*SEM*) for each scale are given for the raw score metric only. The *SEM* values appear reasonably small for most scales, but are difficult to interpret given the differing means and standard deviations for each scale.

VALIDITY. The authors reported correlations among Substance Abuse scales and among Personal Adjustment problem scales, referring to these as indices of internal consistency reliability. However, these are more correctly seen as indices of validity, particularly discriminant validity. That is, correlations among scales within a given domain should be sufficiently low to support a contention that empirically distinct constructs are assessed. Across the three samples of persons under 21 years, persons 21 years and over, and inpatients, the correlations among the substance abuse scales ranged between .57 and .85. Across these same three samples, the correlations among the Personal Adjustment scales ranged between .50 and .76. If corrected for attenuation (or unreliability), most of these correlations among scales would be over .80, with many above .90. These results suggest that there is little discriminant validity among the four Substance Abuse scales and little discriminant validity among the Personal Adjustment scales. No correlations were provided between Substance Abuse and Personal Adjustment scales, so the discriminant validity between these two domains is unknown. Also, no correlations among style scales were reported in the manual.

The only other type of validity evidence presented is a series of group mean comparisons between the inpatient sample with other contrast groups. The inpatient sample had a mean level of response placing them at or beyond the 99th percentile on most scales, representing a rather extreme contrast group. Not surprisingly, the inpatient sample had significantly different mean scores on all scales when compared to persons under 21 years of age, persons 21 years and older, persons with a first offense for drug use, persons with two or more arrests for drug use, and persons arrested for driving under the influence with or without prior arrests. No comparisons among the latter groups were reported.

No factor analytic results on the MAPP are reported, and no correlations with other similar instruments are reported. As a result, the dimensional structure of the MAPP has yet to be tested.

SUMMARY. The MAPP is an easy-to-administer, direct measure of substance abuse and the personal adjustment problems associated with substance use. Although levels of reliability are adequate, the MAPP has several deficiencies.

Among these deficiencies are the potential contamination of acquiescence response bias on the substance use scales and the lack of clear discriminant validity among many of the scales derived from the MAPP. Persons wanting a measure of alcohol use might consider the Alcohol Use Inventory (T5:136), by K. W. Wanberg, J. L. Horn, and F. M. Foster, which has a much wider array of reliability and validity information available. The MAPP appears to be a promising instrument, but additional reliability and validity data are needed to ensure confident interpretation of its scale scores.

[246]
Multidimensional Anxiety Scale for Children.

Purpose: "Designed to assess a variety of anxiety dimensions in children and adolescents."

Population: Ages 8–19.

Publication Date: 1997.

Administration: Group.

Price Data, 1999: $55 per MASC complete kit including manual (62 pages) and 25 QuikScore™ forms; $32 per MASC specimen set including manual, 3 MASC QuikScore™ forms, and 3 MASC-10 QuikScore™ forms; $30 per manual; $26 per 25 MASC QuikScore™ forms; $78 per MASC-10 complete kit including 25 MASC QuikScore™ forms and 25 MASC-10 QuikScore™ forms; $22 per 25 MASC-10 QuikScore™ forms.

Comments: Self-report.

Author: John March.

Publisher: Multi-Health Systems, Inc.

a) MULTIDIMENSIONAL ANXIETY SCALE FOR CHILDREN.

Acronym: MASC.

Scores, 13: Physical Symptoms (Tense Symptom Subscale, Somatic Symptoms Subscale, Total), Harm Avoidance (Perfectionism Subscale, Anxious Coping Subscale, Total), Social Anxiety (Humiliation Fears Subscale, Performance Fears Subscale, Total), Separation/Panic, Total Anxiety, Anxiety Disorders Index, Inconsistency Index.

Time: (15) minutes.

Comments: Self-report measure; can be orally administered to young children or poor readers; for use only by psychology professionals with training in assessment.

b) MASC-10: MULTIDIMENSIONAL ANXIETY SCALE FOR CHILDREN—10 ITEM.

Acronym: MASC-10.

Scores, 4: Physical Symptoms, Harm Avoidance, Social Anxiety, Separation/Panic.

Time: (2–5) minutes.

Comments: A shortened, 10-item version of the MASC tapping the four basic anxiety scales.

Review of the Multidimensional Anxiety Scale for Children by JOHN C. CARUSO, Assistant Professor of Psychology, University of Montana, Missoula, MT:

The Multidimensional Anxiety Scale for Children (MASC) is a very brief measure of self-reported anxiety symptoms and it has acceptable reliability and validity to be recommended for use in a wide variety of circumstances. The strengths of the MASC are the detailed hierarchical structure, which allows for potential differentiation between alternative manifestations of anxiety and good item selection and scale development, which allows for some degree of confidence in the use of the scales. The weaknesses of the MASC are a biased normative sample, which makes the use of the test with specific minority groups questionable, and unacceptably low reliability for some scales and subscales.

Administering and scoring the MASC (which takes approximately 15 minutes) results in a total of 13 scores. At the highest level of organization is the Total Anxiety Scale (the sum of the 39 items), which consists of four subscales: Physical Symptoms (further divided into Tense and Somatic subscales), Harm Avoidance (consisting of the Perfectionism and Anxious Coping subscales), Social Anxiety (consisting of the Humiliation Fears and Performance Fears subscales), and Separation/Panic (which has no subscales). In addition to these 11 scales, an Anxiety Disorders Index and a validity scale provide measures of symptoms related to DSM-IV diagnoses of anxiety disorders and response inconsistency respectively.

Although a large sample was used in norming the MASC, there was a serious omission. The Hispanic/Latino representation in the total sample (*N* = 2,698) was 19 (.7%), drastically different from current census figures. Based on this fact alone, use of the test with Hispanic children is questionable. Although the representation of Hispanics and Asians was inadequate, analyses presented in the manual showed no significant differences between the ethnic groups. Considering the small representation, however, further investigation in this area is warranted. Finally, although the fourth-grade reading level of the test was acceptably verified, no examination of the ability of nonnative English speakers to accurately complete the test was conducted.

The reliability estimates of most of the MASC scales are acceptable with some exceptions. Using a liberal internal consistency reliability criterion of .65, the following subtests did not produce reliable scores in the normative sample: the Harm Avoidance Scale and its Perfectionism and Anxious Coping Subscales, the Performance Fears Subscale of the Social Anxiety Scale, and the Anxiety Disorders Index. This indicates that these scales are not composed of homogenous items, which is not surprising in the case of the Anxiety Disorders Index because there are several accepted, diagnosable anxiety disorders. For the other scales, however, this indicates that a degree of caution should be used when interpreting scores. Test-retest coefficients (administration interval = 3 months) were higher but based on only 24 subjects.

The validity evidence for scores from the MASC was demonstrated both internally (via confirmatory factor analysis that supported the four-factor structure) and externally (via a series of discriminant analyses). The four main scores of the MASC successfully discriminated between a DSM-IV anxiety disorder sample (68 of 76 subjects correctly classified) and a random subset from the normative sample (64 of 76 subjects correctly classified). The Anxiety Disorders Index correctly discriminated between a separate sample of children with DSM-IV diagnosed anxiety disorders (30 of 36 subjects correctly classified) and a random subset from the normative sample (33 of 36 subjects correctly classified). These analyses provide the bulk of the validation information for scores from the MASC indicating that although initial results are promising, further validity studies are required. Paramount would be studies examining the discriminating capabilities of the four main scales with respect to children with different DSM-IV anxiety disorders as opposed to the heterogeneous groups used in the MASC manual.

The MASC-10 is a short version of the MASC and includes items from each of the four main subscales but provides only a single score to be used as a quick screening instrument. Unfortunately, the internal consistency estimates of the MASC-10 score for the normative sample were generally less than .70 (the exception being males in the 16- to 19-year-old age group), indicating that caution be used in interpreting these scores. Test-retest reliability coefficients (administration interval = 3 months) were again higher than internal consistency, but are again questionable due to the small sample size. Validity evidence for scores from the MASC-10 was only partially addressed in the MASC manual.

SUMMARY. The four main scales of the MASC as well as the Anxiety Disorders Index are useful in discriminating between children with diagnosable anxiety disorders and those without. The test, therefore, could provide a valuable piece of corroborating evidence or the impetus for a more thorough examination of a particular child. The validity and usefulness of the subscales of the four main scales are questionable especially in those cases in which reliability is low. The MASC-10 may be useful as a quick screening device, but other instruments have higher reliability and more adequately established validity.

Review of the Multidimensional Anxiety Scale for Children by ROBERT CHRISTOPHER, President, International Mental Health Network, Ltd., Poway, CA:

The Multidimensional Anxiety Scale for Children (MASC) is a self-report measure intended for assessment of anxiety symptoms in children and adolescents ranging in age from 8 to 19 years. It is a brief measure intended to be used as a component of an overall clinical evaluation as well as in research settings. Recommended uses for the MASC include routine screening in settings such as schools, outpatient clinics, residential treatment centers, child protective services, juvenile detention centers, and private practice offices. Potential users of the instrument identified by the author include psychologists, physicians, social workers, counselors, teachers, and pediatric nurses.

The MASC consists of 39 continuous items that are distributed across four basic scales: Physical Symptoms, Harm Avoidance, Social Anxiety, and Separation/Panic. The first three scales also contain the following subscales: Tense Symptoms and Somatic Symptoms, Perfectionism and Anxious Coping, and Humiliation Fears and Performance Fears.

The MASC also utilizes two major indexes: Anxiety Disorders and Inconsistency. The Anxiety Disorders Index identifies respondents who may require a more detailed clinical assessment, and the Inconsistency Index is used for identification of random or careless responding. To develop this index, eight item pairs were selected, and the index was computed by calculating the absolute value of the difference in the response to each item pair and summing up these eight differences. High scores on the Inconsistency Index are interpreted as the respondent's lack of motivation, lack of

comprehension of the items, careless responding, deliberate distortions in self-disclosure, poor insight, or lack of self-awareness. However, the manual cautions that relatively low scores on this index do not guarantee validity of results, and that a generally random response pattern may also produce a low Inconsistency Index score.

Creation of the Anxiety Disorders Index was based on identification and selection of items that had high discriminant validity between clinical and nonclinical groups. A total of 15 items was selected, and statistical validation of their predictive value was performed retaining only the 10 items with a standardized discriminant-function coefficient above .25. This index is used in identification of children and adolescents who are likely to be diagnosed with an anxiety disorder. However, this index is not recommended as a measure for detection of obsessive-compulsive disorder because subjects with this disorder were not included in the initial group of 40 youths (24 males and 16 females) selected for development of the Anxiety Disorders Index.

A fourth grade reading level is required, and the manual suggests utilization of assistance of clinicians or other trained interviewers when the scale is administered to children under the age of 10. The MASC uses a 4-point, Likert-type format and the respondents are asked to rate each item according to their own experience. The responses are rated as "0" for *Never true about me,* "1" for *rarely true about me,* "2" for *sometimes true about me,* and "3" for *often true about me.* All items are phrased in a positive direction, and the increasing scores on all scales and subscales indicate increasing levels of emotional problems.

Estimated administration time is about 15 minutes, and total estimated scoring time is less than 10 minutes. A separate form is also available that contains only 10 items (MASC-10) and is recommended for general assessment of anxiety symptoms. This abbreviated version of the MASC is intended for repeated testing and monitoring of treatment progress. It is recommended by the author for applications where a fast, routine assessment is required or for group administrations. Scoring of the MASC-10 requires approximately 5 minutes.

The normative sample for the development of the MASC consisted of 2,698 children and adolescents (1,261 males and 1,437 females). The racial distribution of the sample consisted of 53.3%

Caucasians, 39.2% African Americans, .7% Hispanic/Latin Americans, 1.4% Asian Americans, 2.4% Native Americans, and 3% classified as "other." No separate norms were developed for any of the racial groups. Separate norms are available for males and females in 4-year intervals for ages 8 through 19. Recommendations for interpretation of the MASC indicate that it should be based on individual item responses, *T*-scores for the various scales and subscales, and the Anxiety Disorders Index and the Inconsistency Index.

The MASC is not recommended as a single information source, and the scale results should be integrated with other more comprehensive and detailed clinical material in order to formulate baseline clinical impressions and diagnostic and treatment considerations.

Respondents completing the MASC record their responses on a QuikScore™ form, and the scoring key is located between the answer sheets for the MASC, and underneath the answer sheet for the MASC-10. The score key is formatted like a grid and all the scoring is done on it. The scales and subscales are identified horizontally across the top of the grid. Not including the Inconsistency Index, a total of 12 raw scores is generated for the MASC, and 1 raw score for the MASC-10. The raw scores are converted into standard *T*-scores (mean of 50 and a standard deviation of 10) on the MASC Profile forms. The Profile form is two-sided, with *T*-scores for males on one side, and for females on the other. The MASC-10 Profile form lists information for both male and female subjects on the same page. *T*-score information is available for three different age groups: 8- to 11-year-olds, 12- to 15-year-olds, and 16- to 19-year-olds.

Interpretation of the MASC includes assessing the validity of the results, evaluating profile patterns, analyzing scale and subscale scores, and examination of individual items. The manual recommends six steps in the interpretation of individual test results:

1. Determining validity of information about anxiety symptoms obtained with the MASC: This step includes examination of the Inconsistency Index and making a comparison with index scores of other respondents.

2. Determining the overall level of anxiety symptomatology: *T*-scores above 65 would represent clinically significant symptoms in a "high base rate" group such as the clinical subjects with iden-

tifiable emotional and behavioral disturbances; use of a higher criterion (a *T*-score of 70 to 75) may be recommended for the "low base rate" groups, or subjects without identifiable psychological and behavioral problems.

3. Determining if all scales are elevated or if there is a pattern suggesting a specific type of anxiety disorder: This step includes evaluation and identification of problem areas that may represent diagnostic groupings, versus those that do not appear to be clinically symptomatic.

4. Determining which item responses are elevated: This step is recommended as a possible aid in formulation of target questions during the clinical interview and selection of treatment approaches.

5. Integration of information from the MASC with other clinical data about the subject such as other psychometric instruments, parent/child interviews, teacher reports, and data from other clinical sources such as other mental health professionals. This step is intended to determine clinical significance of the MASC results.

6. Defining a need and recommendations for additional assessment and/or interventions: This step would be beneficial in the development of treatment plans, length of treatment, and collaboration with other components of the child's support system such as parents and educators.

The MASC exhibits a good internal consistency of items with the alpha coefficient averaging over .65 for both males and females. The test/retest reliability at 3-month intervals, with a sample of 24 white subjects, allowed good temporal stability of the MASC.

Confirmatory factor analysis of the MASC four-factor structure was done with two different groups of subjects: 2,698 nonclinical subjects and 390 clinical subjects. The multifactorial model showed good fit to data in both the clinical and nonclinical samples. Further support for this model was found in the statistically sound intercorrelation of MASC scales. Examination of the discriminant validity of MASC scales indicated sensitivity of 90%, the overall correct classification rate was 87%, and kappa at .74. These results indicated the MASC can successfully identify those subjects who have elevated levels of anxiety disorders and who may benefit from further, and more detailed, clinical assessment. The sensitivity of the MASC Anxiety Index was 83%, specificity 92%, the overall correct classification rate 88%, and kappa 0.75.

A test of convergent validity of the MASC with the Revised Children's Manifest Anxiety Scale yielded moderate to high correlations with the MASC Physical Symptoms Scale and the Social Anxiety Scale. Low to moderate correlations were found with the Harm Avoidance Scale and Separation/Panic Scale. Lower overall correlations were found with the Children's Depression Inventory-Short (CDI-S).

SUMMARY. The MASC may find applications in a variety of situations where global assessment of anxiety disturbances in children and adolescents is required. It is a brief instrument that can be used by a variety of professionals. The scale identifies general areas of anxiety disturbances, but does not provide sufficient support for formulation of baseline diagnostic impressions about specific diagnostic groupings. Its applications are perhaps most suitable in settings such as private physicians offices, school counseling, and pediatric nursing where repeated measurements or quick administration are needed. Further research and cross-validation of this instrument with other well-standardized measures for assessment of children and adolescents may reinforce its diagnostic value. To ensure diagnostic certainty, the MASC should only be used in conjunction with other clinical methods and instruments.

[247]
Multidimensional Health Profile.

Purpose: "Developed to provide a brief but comprehensive assessment of psychological characteristics relevant to mental and physical health."
Population: Ages 18 and over.
Publication Dates: 1992–1998.
Administration: Group or individual.
Forms, 2: Health Functioning, Psychosocial Functioning.
Price Data: Available from publisher.
Time: (15) minutes for either form.
Authors: Linda S. Ruehlman, Richard I. Lanyon, and Paul Karoly.
Publisher: Psychological Assessment Resources, Inc.
a) MULTIDIMENSIONAL HEALTH PROFILE—PSYCHOSOCIAL FUNCTIONING.
Acronym: MHP-P.
Scores, 17: Number of Stressful Events, Perceived Stress, Coping Skills, Total Social Support, Emotional Support, Informational Support, Tangible Support, Negative Social Exchange, Total Psychological Distress, Depressed Affect, Guilt, Motor Retardation, Anxious Affect, Somatic Com-

plaints, Cognitive Disturbance, Life Satisfaction, Global Stress.
Comments: 58-item self-report questionnaire to assess psychosocial functioning.
b) MULTIDIMENSIONAL HEALTH PROFILE—HEALTH FUNCTIONING.
Acronym: MHP-H.
Scores, 20: Self-Help, Professional Help, Help from Friends, Spiritual Help, Positive Health Habits, Negative Health Habits, Self-Efficacy, Health Vigilance, Health Values, Trust in Health Care Personnel, Trust in Health Care System, Hypochondriasis, Overall Health, Recent Health, Presence of a Chronic Illness, Impairment Due to a Chronic Illness, Office Visits, Overnight Hospital Treatment, Emergency Room Treatment, Over the Counter Medication.
Comments: 69-item self-report questionnaire to assess health functioning.

Review of the Multidimensional Health Profile by WENDY NAUMANN, *Assistant Professor, Department of Psychology, University of Memphis, Memphis, TN:*

The Multidimensional Health Profile (MHP) is intended as a screening instrument only, assessing psychological factors relevant to mental and physical health. This instrument is for adults only and is not recommended for adolescents under the age of 18 years. Although two record booklets of the MHP are provided (Mental Health Profile—Psychosocial Functioning, Mental Health Profile—Health Functioning), this division of the scales is intended for ease of administration and does not represent two different forms of the test. Administration of the test is easy and the instructions provided are clear.

Because previous tests have focused on only one or two dimensions of health-related characteristics, the MHP was designed to provide a comprehensive screening battery that would be feasible for physicians to use with patients in primary health care settings. With this purpose in mind, the authors used a two-step process to begin development for the scale. This process was rather comprehensive, and the documentation provided reflects a significant degree of thoughtfulness in creating the underlying framework for the instrument. The first step included conducting a comprehensive review of the current research and measurement tools assessing health-related antecedents, outcomes, and mediators. The areas identified included life stress, coping skills, social resources, mental health, response to illness, health habits (also includes Adult Health History and Health Care Utilization), and health beliefs and attitudes. These areas were then used to create a 70-item survey that was administered to about 416 physicians in order to determine perceived importance. Results of this second step indicate that all of the physicians completing a survey attached at least some degree of importance to all of the 70 items. These areas and the relevant research for each area are well described in the manual.

Further development of the MHP refined the scales through the use of statistical procedures. An outpatient sample in Phoenix, Arizona (n = 325) was used to identify items to be deleted by using a specific set of criteria and then conducting an exploratory factor analysis on scales with more than one item. The size of this sample is adequate given the analyses performed; however, the demographic makeup limits the external validity of the sample. Based on the results of the exploratory factor analyses, items with low factor loadings (<.40), low communalities (<.40), or double loadings were deleted and new items were added to the scales. A national development sample (n = 673) stratified by age and gender was created next in order to complete a confirmatory factor analysis on 10 of the scales. This second sample is much more substantial in size and has satisfactory representativeness. All scales either met the fit criterion (CFI>.90) or problematic items were deleted until the fit criterion was met. Results of the confirmatory factor analyses appear to validate the hypothesized conceptual structure of the MHP.

The norm group was representative of the adult population nationally especially with respect to gender and age groups. The national sample used for the norm group consisted of over 2,400 examinees with equal numbers of gender-by-age groupings. The administration for the norm group, however, is not consistent with the administration most widely used by test administrators. Examinees in the norm group completed their protocols via a phone interview, and yet the authors of the test assert that even if a protocol is read to an individual, the examinee should complete the protocol. The authors reviewed survey research assessing differences between the two administration techniques, and reported the most common finding being one of no difference. However, these differences were not assessed within the norm group or with any sample of examples using the MHP.

Using the norm group, overall psychometric properties were examined for the instrument. Because so many of the scales comprise only one item, test-retest reliability was used to determine the stability of the items over time. Using a subgroup of 122 and a test-retest period of 3 weeks, low to adequate reliability estimates were found for each of the scales. The mental health scales ask examinees to report symptoms within the last week instead of 3 weeks, thus these items were revalidated on a sample of undergraduate students using the 1-week time frame. The reliabilities for the scales using this sample were adequate at .71 or higher. However, the external validity of the sample is questionable and should be considered when evaluating the mental health scales. The reliability values for the remaining scales ranged from .44 to .89 with 18 of the 29 scales resulting in low reliabilities below .70. The response to illness scales were particularly low. Convergent and divergent validity coefficients were obtained for various scales using subsamples of approximately 125. Although the overall pattern of significance for these correlations was consistent with expectations regarding convergent and discriminant validity, the magnitude of the correlations assessing convergent validity was quite low. Very few of these correlations were above .60. No predictive validity evidence was reported, thus an estimate of false positives and false negatives found in the norm group was not provided. Although no scales assessing "faking good" or "faking bad" are provided, correlations between the MHP scales and social desirability scores are low indicating that responses are not susceptible to examinees faking good. Finally, T-score cutoffs for the scales are provided to guide determination of further assessment; however, no empirical support is provided for these cutoffs.

SUMMARY. Overall, the MHP has mixed psychometric properties. The development of each of the scales is adequate for its use as a screening instrument. However, even though the authors warn against using the MHP for diagnostic purposes, the low values for convergent validity and the lack of predictive validity evidence make it difficult to assess how well the MHP will function as a screening device. Physicians using this instrument should complement scores on the MHP with other patient information before making a decision to conduct further testing. Additional validity evidence is needed in order to determine the screening accuracy of the MHP.

Review of the Multidimensional Health Profile by TERRI L. WEAVER, Assistant Professor of Psychology, Saint Louis University, St. Louis, MO:

The Multidimensional Health Profile (MHP) is a relatively brief, yet comprehensive screening instrument that was designed for use with patients in primary care settings. There are two test booklets associated with the MHP: One booklet contains items tapping psychosocial areas of functioning and the other booklet contains items tapping health-related areas of functioning. A strength of the instrument is that it is one of the few instruments to bridge psychosocial risk factors, protective factors, and health attitudes and practices.

In developing the items for the MHP, authors conducted comprehensive searches of relevant literature, examining constructs that have been found to influence health functioning. It is helpful to have the two separate booklets, allowing health-care providers to elect to focus on one of the areas, if they so choose. Administration time may be somewhat underestimated (the manual estimates 30 minutes for administration of both packets but administration of a slightly longer version of the interview, by telephone, took 42 minutes, on average). The layout of the booklet is clear. Wording is generally straightforward, and is reported to be at the 4th grade reading level. Authors received responses from 46% (192/416) of physicians (both urban and a smaller sample of rural) who reported that both the psychosocial and more traditional health-related areas were equally relevant and important.

Standardization of the instrument was comprehensive and included a gender- and age-stratified sample of 2,411 participants. Participants were similar to the 1998 population demographic characteristics cited by the U.S. Bureau of the Census, making the sample representative of the population at large. Scales are interpreted using T scores with a score greater than 1 standard deviation above the mean (60–69) leading to suggested follow-up and a score 2 or more standard deviations above the mean (≥ 70) leading to strongly recommended follow-up. For purposes of consistency, all MHP T scores are scaled so that higher T scores indicate greater levels of presumed risk for problems in a given domain. Although this does provide consistency, for subscales with adaptive names (e.g., Positive Health Habits), it can be difficult to remember that "higher" scores indicate less adaptive functioning on the measure. Renaming the subscales to reflect the results that higher scores indicate more difficulty would have been more conceptually consistent. There are several subscales (e.g., Response to Illness subscales), in which T scores less than 40 also suggest a need for follow-up evaluation, specifically when these low rates of help-seeking or coping are paired with a serious or very serious illness.

Reliability or stability of scores from the instrument was initially assessed using a subsample of a national development sample ($N = 122$), who completed the MHP on a second occasion, approximately 3 weeks after the initial interview. The national development sample (different from the national standardization sample described above) consisted of a representative sample of adults stratified by age and gender ($N = 673$). Relatively lower reliabilities were found for two global mental health items and several of the psychological distress subscales. Authors posited that these attenuated reliability estimates may have resulted from the Time 2 assessment period, in which participants were asked to rate their responses over the past week, which did not overlap with the rating done during the initial test period. In an effort to examine this hypothesis, authors reconducted the reliability assessment with an undergraduate sample and created a 2-day, test-retest interval and found that reliability estimates were improved. Although they interpreted this increase in reliability as yielding support for their supposition that the nonoverlapping time frame may have attenuated reliability estimates, it may have been somewhat more accurate to acknowledge other competing hypotheses. That is, the time period itself was markedly shorter (2 days versus 3 weeks). Also, it would have been helpful for the authors to provide some data on why psychological measures may have been more sensitive to nonoverlapping time periods (more variable) compared with some of the other constructs. Convergent and discriminant validity were examined by administering a number of relevant measures in a series of five subgroups of the national development sample. In addition, 100 spouses rated their partner for stress, response to illness, health habits, health history, health care utilization, and health beliefs and attitudes. Overall, convergent and discriminant validity appeared to be well established and efforts were painstaking and commendable. Predictive validity was not evaluated.

Based on the relative T scores, the MHP offers recommendations should respondents score within the elevated ranges. Some of the recommended follow-ups appeared to be more specific and somewhat more helpful than others. For example, specific recommendations were suggested for respondents reporting few positive health habits (i.e., it was suggested that they be given "information concerning related behavioral health risks, the existence of formal and informal resources to assist the individual" [p. 19], etc.) whereas follow-up was simply suggested or strongly recommended (but not elaborated) for those reporting low self-efficacy.

Essentially, there may be a number of cases in which the feedback from the screening instrument would alert the health care provider that there was a deficiency in a particular area without providing information about where or how to proceed with follow-up care. Although having prescriptive recommendations may well be beyond the scope of such a screening instrument, it is more the inconsistency with which such specific recommendations were made (i.e., for some subscales but not for others) that made this more of an issue.

SUMMARY. Overall, the MHP appears to be a very valuable and unique screening tool that is likely to hold much promise for use within primary care settings and for health-related research.

[248]
Multifactor Leadership Questionnaire for Research.

Purpose: Designed to access the full range of leadership styles.
Population: Management personnel.
Publication Dates: 1985–1995.
Acronym: MLQ.
Scores, 12: Idealized Influence (Attributed to You), Idealized Influence (Behaviors You Display), Inspirational Motivational, Intellectual Stimulation, Individualized Consideration, Contingent Reward, Management-by-Exception (Active), Management-by-Exception (Passive), Laissez-Faire, Extra Effort, Effectiveness, Satisfaction.
Administration: Group.
Forms, 2: Leader, Rater.
Price Data, 1998: $25 per Sampler set including manual ('95, 41 pages), and one each of the components

used to administer, score, and interpret the MLQ; $100 per Permission set including the Sampler set along with an agreement to reproduce up to 200 copies of the instrument for personal and non-commercial use for one year.
Time: Administration time not reported.
Authors: Bernard M. Bass and Bruce J. Avolio.
Publisher: Mind Garden, Inc.
Cross References: See T5:1736 (5 references); for reviews by Frederick Bessai and Jean Powell Kirnan and Brooke Snyder of an earlier edition, see 12:247 (5 references); see also T4:1684 (5 references).

Review of the Multifactor Leadership Questionnaire for Research by DAVID J. PITTENGER, Associate Professor of Psychology, The University of Tennessee at Chattanooga, Chattanooga, TN:

The distinction between transformational and transactional leadership styles has been popular since Burns's (1978) exposition on leadership. Bass (1985) expanded upon this paradigm and has spent considerable time refining the Multifactor Leadership Questionnaire (MLQ) as a measure of these leadership styles. Since its introduction in 1985, the MLQ has been the subject of considerable empirical analysis and subsequent revision.

There are two versions of the MLQ, each consisting of 45 statements. The Leader version contains statements that describe the individual's leadership behavior (e.g., "I lead a group that is effective"). The Rater version contains similar statements (e.g., "Leads a group that is effective") that ask the respondent to evaluate an identified leader, typically a superior. Both forms use a 5-point Likert scale representing the relative frequency of each behavior. The forms are designed for machine scoring. The test user submits the completed forms to the publisher who, in turn, prepares a computer-generated commentary of the results. One can score the forms by hand, but the task is tedious and not facilitated by a simple-to-follow key.

According to the manual, the MLQ measures four broad characteristics of leadership behavior, each of which consist of several smaller facets. The first characteristic is transformational leadership, which refers to leaders who use charismatic and inspirational techniques to motivate others. The construct consists of four subscales. The first two subscales are refinements of the Charisma scale used in a previous version of the MLQ. The new scales are Idealized Influence (attributed to the leader), and Idealized Influence (exhibited by the leader's behavior). The remaining subscales measure the degree to which the leader provides inspirational motivation and intellectual stimulation for the subordinates.

The second characteristic is transactional leadership, which the authors describe as a leadership style that relies upon the exchange of tangible outcomes between the leader and follower. According to the authors, transactional and transformational leadership styles are not mutually exclusive processes. Three separate facets define transactional leadership: Contingent Reward, Active Management by Exceptions, and Passive Management by Exception.

The third leadership characteristic implies the absence of any leadership behavior. Appropriately, the authors call this leadership style Laissez-Faire. There is a single scale to measure this propensity.

The last set of scales determines the degree to which the leader is seen as being effective and creating satisfaction among followers. There are three subscales for this factor: Extra Effort, Effectiveness, and Satisfaction.

Given the ubiquitous and sometimes casual discussion of leadership in contemporary industrial and organizational settings, more information and detail than the manual provides is needed. Although the authors provide some limited information concerning the evidence of reliability and validity for scores from the instrument, the careful reader may be struck by the information that is missing. This omission is especially apparent given the lively and lucid accounts of leadership and the MLQ that Bass provided in other venues (e.g., Bass, 1985, 1997).

To begin, the manual contains no clear and definitive description of the purpose of the instrument. There is no attempt to describe the situations or contexts for which the test's use is appropriate or inappropriate. Similarly, there is no attempt to identify the parameters of reasonable inferences one may make from the test scores. Indeed, the MLQ appears to be available to any user regardless of training and expertise with psychological tests. These are critical issues to address, especially if an employer decides to use the MLQ in conjunction with retention and promotion reviews.

Equally absent is a clear explication of the nomological network that describes the theoretical interrelations among the scales of this instrument.

The reader will be hard pressed to understand the specific theoretical importance of the four major characteristics of leadership behavior. As an example, the authors describe how transformational leadership augments transactional leadership styles. Further, these styles are identified as being not mutually exclusive. The rationale for these distinctions is not clear as they are not examined in the manual. Given the exceptional range of behaviors and attitudes that the MLQ attempts to measure, a greater explication of the underlying theory is highly desirable.

The authors provide traditional descriptive statistics for the scales as well as an elaborate review of a confirmatory factor analysis. Although the data appear to support the distinctions created by the MLQ, there are several questions that have not been addressed.

First, transformational leadership is not the only leadership theory found in the current literature. A casual review of any textbook on the topic reveals many competing theoretical constructs. In addition, there are many alternative measures of leadership behavior. Furthermore, many of the MLQ dimensions appear to be personality factors described in the context of leadership. It is not clear whether behaviors associated with transformational leadership might reflect components of the Big-5 theory of personality such as extroversion, openness to experience, or conscientiousness. Given these observations, it is disappointing to find no comparison between the MLQ, alternative measures of leadership, or broad measures of personality.

Further, it is not clear whether the MLQ measures attributes unique to the person being evaluated or merely reflects the evaluator's schema for effective leadership. Meindl (1990) identified the "romance of leadership" phenomenon to describe an individual's implicit theories of leadership and leadership behavior. Because one may believe that leadership exists, and that certain types of leadership are preferable to others, one may be more likely to attribute the results of situational factors to the behavior of the individual. Therefore, the personal dynamics associated with transformational and transactional leadership styles may reflect a person's idealized expectations of a leader's behavior. Using the MLQ may, as a consequence, exaggerate the importance of a leader's behavior and remove attention from important interpersonal and situational factors.

In summary, Bass's theory of transformational and transactional leadership is popular and has spawned much empirical research. The available research does provide evidence that the instrument consistently measures constructs in keeping with Bass's theory. Whether these constructs afford a better understanding of leadership will require considerably more research. Similarly, whether the MLQ measures a unique collection of constructs or can be used to identify differences among individuals requires additional support.

REVIEWER'S REFERENCES

Burns, J. M. (1978). *Leadership*. New York: Harper & Row.

Bass, B. M. (1985). *Leadership and performance beyond expectations*. New York: Free Press.

Meindl, J. R. (1990). On leadership: An alternative to the conventional wisdom. In B. A. Staw (Ed.), *Research in organizational behavior* (vol. 12, pp. 159–203). New York: JAI Press.

Bass, B. M. (1997). Does the transactional-transformational leadership paradigm transcend organizational and national boundaries? *American Psychologist, 52*, 130–139.

[249]
Multilingual Aphasia Examination, Third Edition.

Purpose: Designed to evaluate the presence, severity, and qualitative aspects of aphasic disorder.

Population: Ages 6–69.

Publication Dates: 1978–1994.

Acronym: MAE.

Scores, 11: Visual Naming, Sentence Repetition, Controlled Word Association, Oral Spelling, Written Spelling, Block Spelling, MAE Token Test, Aural Comprehension of Words and Phrases, Reading Comprehension of Words and Phrases, Rating of Articulation, Rating of Praxic Features of Writing.

Administration: Individual.

Price Data, 1994: $170 per complete set including manual ('94, 56 pages), Visual Naming stimulus booklet, Reading Comprehension stimulus booklet, Block Spelling test letters, Token Test tokens and 100 record forms, and 100 each of Record Forms A, B, C, D, and E; $25 per manual; $16.10 per Visual Naming stimulus booklet; $21.50 per Reading Comprehension stimulus booklet; $14 per 100 record forms (specify Form A, B, C, D, or E).

Foreign Language Edition: Spanish edition available.

Time: Administration time not reported.

Authors: A. L. Benton, deS. Hamsher, and A. B. Sivan.

Publisher: AJA Associates.

Cross References: See T5:1740 (36 references).

Review of the Multilingual Aphasia Examination, Third Edition by NANCY B. BOLOGNA, Clinical Assistant Professor of Psychiatry, Louisiana State University Medical Center, and Program Director, Touro Senior Day Center, New Orleans, LA:

The Multilingual Aphasia Examination (MAE) is a test battery designed to evaluate the presence and severity of language disorders. Its name implies that it is available in different languages—and "multi" is generally reserved for more than two. The MAE Third Edition (1994) manual reports a Spanish version published in 1992, but makes no claim of other versions currently available or in preparation. No information regarding the determination of functional equivalence between the versions is provided in the Third Edition (English language) that was reviewed. Although this may seem unimportant to a novice tester, equivalence of item difficulty and vocabulary familiarity is a major concern in translated tests. Test users interested in the Spanish version are advised to contact the authors for additional information.

Aside from a rather misleading name, the MAE (3rd edition) has many advantages. The 11 tests that make up the MAE battery (Visual Naming, Sentence Repetition, Controlled Word Association, Oral Spelling, Written Spelling, Block Spelling, MAE Token Test, Aural Comprehension of Words and Phrases, Reading Comprehension of Words and Phrases, Rating of Articulation, and Rating of Praxic Features of Writing) provide ample sampling of the many aspects of receptive and expressive language. Many tests provide alternate forms to allow repeated testing without concern for carryover. Performance on each test and comparative performance on related tests allow fine distinctions in the evaluation of aphasic disorders. In addition, the MAE (3rd edition) provides several excellent sets of norms, a feature lacking in most popular aphasia batteries.

A sample of 360 persons, ranging in age from 16 to 69 years, all of whom spoke English as their primary language, was used to generate adults norms. Individuals were excluded from the normative sample if they demonstrated evidence or history of hemispheric brain disease, psychiatric illness, or mental retardation. Based on performance of the sample population, corrections for age, education, and gender (as well as factorial combinations of these characteristics) were established for each test as appropriate. In clinical use, these norms allow clear interpretation without concern for uncontrolled effects of age, education, and gender. A second normative sample included

229 children, all of normal intelligence, grouped by grade level rather than chronological age. The range covers from Kindergarten to Sixth grade.

Interpretation of performance on each test is further enhanced by comparison with the performance of a clinical reference group. The reference group consisted of nearly 50 frankly aphasic adult patients with no confounding pathology such as the presence of dementia or serious articulatory difficulties. The reference group included both fluent and nonfluent aphasics. In addition to this reference group, data are provided from an independent study of 60 nonaphasic subjects in the age range 70 to 89 years. Although the results of the study support the use of the younger normative standards, in that no significant deterioration of language was found in otherwise healthy elderly volunteers, mildly subnormal performance was noted in subjects aged 80 to 89 on both the Token Test and Sentence Repetition. Detailed study findings are presented to allow the performance of elderly test takers to be interpreted more clearly, assisting in the differentiation of "normal" age-related change from pathology.

Administering the MAE (3rd edition) is fairly straightforward and the spiral-bound stimulus books are sturdy. Standardized instructions are provided for the examiner, but are written only in the manual. The manual devotes one section to each test, including a description of the task, administration instructions, recording and scoring instructions, and interpretation. The result of this organization is that administration instructions are not easily visible and smooth administration requires frequent page turning to find the appropriate test instructions. Flip-chart-style stimulus books, with instructions printed facing the examiner, are easier to use. Responses are recorded on a collection of individual sheets rather than a booklet. Although this approach makes the use of individual tests in a stand-alone fashion more convenient, it is not desirable when the full battery is given. Each page requires full identifying and demographic information to be recorded.

Scoring the MAE (3rd edition) is facilitated by examples of acceptable and incorrect responses. Interpretation of results relies on easy-to-read charts that convert raw scores to percentiles with verbal classifications of performance ranging from severely defective to superior. As mentioned above, adjustments of raw scores control for effects of age, education, and gender, as appropriate. The manual includes information based on clinical reference groups to further interpret performance on each test.

SUMMARY. The MAE (3rd edition) manual provides no specific information on either reliability or validity. The notion of validity is certainly addressed indirectly by the normative and clinical reference group data. Reliability is addressed only briefly with largely unsupported statements regarding the equivalence of the alternate forms provided for some tests. In spite of this shortcoming, the MAE (3rd edition) represents a major improvement over older aphasia batteries that offer limited quantitative scoring and no normative standards.

Review of the Multilingual Aphasia Examination, Third Edition by MALCOLM R. McNEIL, Professor and Chair, Department of Communication Science and Disorders, University of Pittsburgh, and WILTRUD FASSBINDER, Doctoral Student, Department of Communication Science and Disorders, University of Pittsburgh, Pittsburgh, PA:

OVERVIEW. The Multilingual Aphasia Examination (MAE) consists of 11 subtests that assess spoken language production, verbal comprehension, reading comprehension, and writing. Three subtests target oral expression: Visual Naming, Sentence Repetition, and Controlled Word Association. Auditory and reading comprehension is assessed in the MAE Token Test, and in Aural Comprehension Words and Phrases. Oral, Written, and Block Spelling evaluate spelling ability. Rating scales for articulation and praxic features of writing are used to aid in separating motor-level impairments in speech and writing from aphasic impairments in language processing. For several subtests (Sentence Repetition, Controlled Oral Word Association, Token Test, and Oral, Written, and Block Spelling) two parallel forms are available.

ADMINISTRATION. In most cases instructions for administration are detailed and comprehensive, including time limits, instructions for repetitions, and discontinuation criteria.

STANDARDIZATION. Norms are provided for adult nonaphasic subjects stratified by education, age, and gender; for children (stratified by grade level); and for elderly adults. Normative data on aphasic subjects are available for all subtests except the spelling subtests.

SCORING. Scoring is based primarily on a pass/fail system, rendering the possibility of high reliability but also making the test insensitive to smaller changes within and between patients' performance. The examiner is encouraged to note qualitative aspects of the performance that are not captured by the scoring system. However, this procedure relies on the knowledge, biases, and clinical skills of the examiner and is frequently unreliable.

CONSTRUCT VALIDITY. Construct validity of the MAE is poorly addressed. The MAE was originally intended as a portion of a project designed to develop equivalent versions of a cross-linguistic aphasia test (Benton, 1969). Although this goal was never realized, a standardized version of the MAE is available in Spanish (Rey & Benton, 1992). The criteria for establishing an aphasia test that would yield comparability across languages were not discussed. Likewise, the linguistic characteristics of the MAE that justify its "multilingual" title are not discussed. The manual does not provide an explicit theoretical background that guided the development of the test, theoretical position on the nature of aphasia, or a rationale for the selection of the specific tasks, stimuli, or scoring procedures. Consistent with this weak theoretical development, the theoretical or clinical rationale for the differential diagnosis of fluency/nonfluency is unmotivated by the authors, in spite of the fact that this differential diagnosis is a primary goal of the test.

CONTENT VALIDITY. The MAE is a relatively brief test of aphasia compared to many other aphasia batteries as it includes fewer subtests with fewer stimulus items per subtest. Most of the tasks selected are also commonly used in other aphasia tests, and the general validity of the tasks has been established through its similarity to other aphasia batteries.

The Visual (confrontation) Naming subtest uses 10 pictures that require 30 naming responses. Without a stated rationale, correct responses are scored as 2, and incorrect responses are scored as zero points. Only phonologically correct target words, synonyms, or synonymous descriptions are scored as correct. Including phonological paraphasias as errors contradicts the stated purpose for the subtest, which is to: "assess the capacity to apply semantically correct verbal labels to visually perceived stimuli" (manual, p. 3). Furthermore, in order to determine phonological errors,

the test requires the examiner to distinguish between "articulation" errors and phonological paraphasias. This error dichotomy has been disputed on theoretical (Miller, 1995), as well as methodological grounds (Buckingham & Yule, 1987: McNeil, 1989). The authors acknowledge that some errors cannot be assigned reliably to either category, but assume that the distinction can be made in most cases. No validity or reliability data are reported that support this assumption (or for the other two production tests).

The sentence repetition subtest includes 14 items of increasing length (3–18 words) and assesses different grammatical constructions. Although other aphasia batteries that are guided by the "syndrome approach" have included repetition tests for the differential diagnosis of conduction aphasia (e.g., Boston Diagnostic Aphasia Examination [BDAE], Achen Aphasia Test [AAT]), and for assessing phonological and syntactic deficits (AAT), no explicit rationale is given for its inclusion in the MAE. The repetition subtest functions as a test of verbal short-term memory and is obliquely mentioned but not discussed in the test's interpretation.

The "Token Test" subtest is based on the principles outlined by DeRenzi and Vignolo (1962), requiring comprehension of nonredundant spoken imperative sentences. Based on a systematic increase in the complexity of commands through adjectival padding and syntactic form, patients point to and manipulate colored circles and squares. The MAE Token Test subtest consists of 22 items, and is the most sensitive test of the battery. Scoring is based on a 3-point scale (2, 1, 0 points), with 1 point awarded for correct responses with repetition.

Aural and Reading Comprehension subtests assess basic levels of comprehension, using pointing responses from an array of four pictures to 18 spoken or written test items, ranging from single words to short phrases. The items in both the listening and reading tests are intended to correspond in difficulty to allow a direct comparison between the two modalities. Differences in administration make the validity of this comparison unlikely. No evidence is given that the two lists are indeed equivalent.

Oral, Written, and Block Spelling evaluate spelling in three modalities: naming the letters in correct order, writing, and manipulating plastic letters from a choice of 11. Each task comprises 11 words that increase in difficulty and length (3–8 letters), which are presented in isolation and sentences. The three word lists are also intended as parallel forms for each task. However, graphemic and morphological structures of the words in the three lists are not completely equivalent. To determine differences between the three tasks that suggest a dissociation in performance, a table presents the percentages of differences in raw scores from the nonaphasic sample. These differences, however, cannot be directly applied to aphasic patients.

Articulation and Praxic Features Of Writing are scored on 9-point equal-appearing interval scales evaluating the degree of the "articulation" disorder and visuopraxic disorders of writing, respectively. They are intended to quantify the impression of the examiner on the degree to which errors in speaking and writing derive from these disorders rather than from aphasic errors, which influence scoring in the expressive subtests. Adjectives and sentence descriptors are given for the even numbers of the rating scale. The descriptions do not use the common terminology associated with descriptions of speech production deficits such as that provided for a score of 4 (e.g., "labored speech production; frequent slurring and/or misarticulation but speech is intelligible") and the descriptions are substantively different between speech and writing.

The articulation rating, together with informal observations on phrase length and prosody, is used in determining the patient's "fluency" classification. However, the judgment for both scales is based on the subjective impression of the examiner from both conversation and test performance. The authors claim that "interjudge agreement is satisfactory" (manual, p. 35).

The behaviors assessed through the Controlled Oral Word Association (COWA) subtest are frequently called "word fluency" or "verbal fluency." However, word association is unrelated to the fluency/nonfluency categorization of aphasia. In the COWA subtest, patients produce as many words as possible, with a given initial letter in one minute. Forms A and B use three letters that are matched in frequency.

As pointed out by the authors, word association can be impaired in patients who do not demonstrate aphasia. The underlying cognitive functions of word association are incompletely understood, but certainly include psycholinguistic

mechanisms involved in retrieval and maintenance of a selective set, verbal working memory, processing resource allocation, and other executive functions.

Performance on this test is usually considered to be particularly sensitive to lesions in the left frontal lobe. However, defective performance in word association can also result from focal damage in other areas as well as from multifocal and diffuse damage such as that caused by some degenerative diseases. Word association deficits in nonaphasic patients are not usually related to language production deficits in conversational speech or in writing. Deficits in the word fluency subtest of the MAE are not explicated either within the task or in the evaluation (scoring) procedures. This leaves the interpretation to the subjectivity of the examiner.

STANDARDIZATION AND NORMS. Normative data (presented in percentiles) for the nonaphasic group are based on a large sample of over 350 subjects. Based on this sample, score adjustments for age, education, and sex are available. Neither the standard error of measurement nor confidence intervals are provided, which makes the interpretation of results for a single case difficult. The manual does not provide information detailing when these norms were collected, or from where the sample was taken. Recently, Ruff, Light, and Parker (1996) provided norms for nonaphasic subjects on the COWA subtest, based on a similar sample of 360 subjects, described as "less rural-based." These normative values are generally higher than the ones reported in the MAE.

MAE normative data for the aphasic group are derived from a group of over 40 aphasic subjects, except for the three spelling tests. The sample appears to be too small to capture variability in performance of aphasic clients. Subjects with "an articulatory disturbance ... so severe that speech was not understandable" were excluded. This description is not completely clear. It could mean that severely dysarthric subjects were excluded, or that nonverbal aphasic individuals were excluded. This would limit the generalizability of the norms.

RELIABILITY. Many of the questions raised about this test could be addressed with adequate reliability data. The primary shortcoming of the MAE is that no appropriate reliability measures are reported. No standard error of measurement is provided for the aphasic, normal adult, or normal child samples. Inter- and intratest reliability have not been examined, save for the inadequate suggestions for the rating scales. Parallel forms of the test provide an excellent opportunity to estimate reliability; however, with the exception of that for the COWA, none were reported for aphasic subjects. Reliability scores for the nonaphasic group cannot be assumed to apply to persons with aphasia.

SUMMARY. The MAE is an aphasia battery designed to be a relatively brief test designed to detect the presence, severity, and qualitative aspects of aphasia. Its subtests provide assessment of all four modalities of aphasia: speaking, listening, reading, and writing. Particular strengths of this test are the normative data on nonaphasic individuals, the short administration time, and the availability of parallel forms for many of the subtests. However, additional background about the standardization procedure, aphasic norms based on larger sample, and measures of reliability need to be reported before this tool can be recommended for the purposes for which it was designed.

REVIEWERS' REFERENCES

DeRenzi, E., & Vignolo, L. A. (1962). The Token Test: A sensitive test to detect receptive disturbances in aphasics. *Brain, 85,* 665–678.

Benton, A. L. (1969). Development of a multilingual aphasia battery: Progress and problems. *Journal of the Neurological Sciences, 9,* 39–48.

Buckingham, H. W., & Yule, G. (1987). Phonemic false evaluation: Theoretical and clinical aspects. *Clinical Linguistics & Phonetics, 1,* 113–125.

McNeil, M. R. (1989). [Review of The Assessment of Aphasia and Related Disorders, Second Edition.] In J. C. Conoley & J. J. Kramer (Eds.), *The tenth mental measurements yearbook* (pp. 37–43). Lincoln, NE: Buros Institute of Mental Measurements.

Rey, G. J., & Benton, A. L. (1992). *Examen de Afasia Multilingue.* Iowa City: AJA Associates.

Miller, N. (1995). Pronunciation errors in acquired speech disorders: The errors of our ways. *European Journal of Disorders of Communication, 30,* 346–362.

Ruff, R. M., Light, R. H., & Parker, S. B. (1996). Benton controlled oral word association test: Reliability and updated norms. *Archives of Clinical Neuropsychology, 11,* 329–338.

[250]

Multiscore Depression Inventory for Children.

Purpose: Designed to assess depression and "features related to depression."

Population: Ages 8–17.

Publication Date: 1996.

Acronym: MDI-C.

Scores, 9: Anxiety, Self-Esteem, Sad Mood, Instrumental Helplessness, Social Introversion, Low Energy, Pessimism, Defiance, Total.

Administration: Group.

Price Data, 1999: $125 per complete kit including manual (54 pages), 25 AutoScore™ test forms, 25 profile forms, 2 prepaid mail-in answer sheets for computer scoring and interpretation, 2-use disk, and 2 PC answer sheets for on-site computer scoring and interpretation; $32.50 per 25 AutoScore™ test forms; $16.50 per mail-in answer sheet; $14.50 per 50 profile forms;

$45 per manual; $299 per MDI-C microcomputer disk including 25 uses (IBM or compatible and Microsoft Windows 3.1 or above; 3.5-inch); $15 per 100 microcomputer answer sheets; $12.50 per FAX service scoring.

Time: (10–20) minutes.

Authors: David J. Berndt and Charles F. Kaiser.

Publisher: Western Psychological Services.

Review of the Multiscore Depression Inventory for Children by JILL ANN JENKINS, Psychologist on Sabbatical, Barcelona, Spain:

The Multiscore Depression Inventory for Children (MDI-C) is a 79-item self-report depression inventory for children ages 8 to 17. Based on the adult Multiscore Depression Inventory (MDI) (Berndt, 1986; T4:1693), administration time is approximately 20 minutes and the test can be given on a group or individual basis.

The MDI-C was developed to investigate not only whether depression is present, but also what different features of depression are manifested in the children tested. It therefore boasts not only the ability to diagnose depression as do other self-report tools such as the Children's Depression Inventory (CDI) (Kovacs & Beck, 1977) and the Center for Epidemiologic Depression Studies—Depression Scale Modified for Children (CES-DC) (Weissman, Orvaschel, & Padian, 1980), but assists in specific treatment planning on an individual basis. The only other self-report depression inventory for children that also investigates characteristics of depression is the Children's Depression Scale (CDS) (Tisher & Lang, 1983). The CDS scales, however, are fewer and less specific than those found in the MDI-C.

The MDI for adults analyzes 12 constructs of depression. Two of the 10 constructs of the MDI were altered to conform to child-related issues for the MDI-C. The first, "Irritability" was transformed into "Defiance" to measure symptoms related to Oppositional Defiant Disorder and Conduct Disorder. Some of the items from "Cognitive Difficulty" (which relates to indecision, confusion, and bewilderment) were added to an "Anxiety" construct for children.

After an impressive sampling of 1,465 children ages 8 to 17 years from a geographically diverse sample in the USA, two of the initial scales were eliminated (Guilt and Learned Helplessness) due to inadequate reliability, as were two additional constructs that had been added (Somatic Problems and Suicidal Ideation). In the final version, the authors added a single question regarding suicidal ideation, which is to be analyzed separately from the remaining eight constructs (Anxiety, Self-Esteem, Social Introversion, Instrumental Helplessness, Sad Mood, Pessimism, Low Energy, and Defiance). The item questions themselves were written by children to ensure that the language was suited to children.

The sample of 1,465 children described above also provided the means and standard deviations for scoring. The sample was divided into three age groups: 8 through 10, 11 through 13, and 14 through 17.

The internal consistency reliability of the MDI-C total score and scales scores was evaluated for children in the age range of 11 to 13, with all of the alpha coefficients at or above .75. The other two age ranges, although showing very acceptable total score alphas (.92 for ages 8–10 years and .92 for ages 14–17), found six of the eight scales unable to meet alpha coefficients of .70. The upper and lower age groupings perhaps would have yielded better internal consistency scores if divided into more age ranges. It seems quite plausible, for example, in the upper age range grouping, that a girl of 14.0 years would have different developmental issues related to depression than a girl of 17.11 years.

Showing more optimistic findings, a cross validation sample of 254 junior high school and high school students found all of the scales, except for Pessimism, to be at or above alpha .70. Incidentally, Pessimism was also one of the scales that did not reach alpha of .70 with the normative sample as well.

Test-retest reliability was examined with a sample of 145 junior high and high school aged subjects ranging in age from 11 to 18. Subjects were tested 4 weeks after completing their initial MDI-C. Test-retest reliability estimates were quite high, with a Pearson correlation for the total score of .92, and a range of acceptable scale correlations from .77 to .86. Despite the homogeneity of the sample used (where all of the subjects were from the same demographic area), the results are quite impressive.

In a study of diverse, nonclinical children ages 9 to 17 (N = 163), criterion validity investigations found a correlation of .84 between the popularly used CDI (Kovacs, 1981) and the MDI-C total scores.

The correlation of the scales of the MDI-C and the CDI total score were lower (ranging from a correlation of .52 to .76), indicating that although the two scales are testing for the same overall concept of depression, the scales of the MDI-C are tapping different issues (as they were intended to do).

Seventy-one children (age range not provided) with various psychiatric diagnosis were also pooled to evaluate the predictive validity of the MDI-C. Predictive validity with clinician's ratings and the MDI-C of severity of depression was .61 (a substantial difference from that with the currently popular CDI, which was .44). Scores of the MDI-C were also highly predictive of the Piers-Harris Children's Self-Concept Scale (Piers & Harris, 1983) in a study of 147 children in the age range of 11 to 13.

When both the adult MDI and MDI-C were given to adolescents (n = 170) ranging from ages 13 to 18, moderate to high correlations were indicated between the scales, despite the fact that the scales of the MDI were altered to be more developmentally appropriate. The total score of the MDI and MDI-C had a very respectable correlation of .83.

The test was carefully constructed to ensure content validity. Items of the scale were included if a point biserial correlation of the item with its corresponding scale was higher than the item's correlation with any of the other seven scales. Initial and cross validation samples found highly significant total correlations of each item and their corresponding scales (p<.001).

Face validity was also fully analyzed and found to be satisfactory and the readability of the questionnaire acceptable. Construct validity via factor analyses on all of the MDI-C items was thoroughly evaluated with the normative sample (n = 1,114) and a cross-validation sample (N = 250). In both instances it was found to be acceptable.

SUMMARY. Scores from the MDI-C provide valid and reliable evidence of child depression. The inventory has been well researched. It offers the unique characteristic of looking at features of depression, in addition to indicating an overall score for depression, allowing the examiner to use it for not only diagnosis but also treatment planning. The well-established evidence of test-retest reliability may additionally be useful in screening and in research evaluating treatment effectiveness.

Research indicates that scale results are more valid for children in the age range of 11 to 13. The Pessimism scale should be viewed cautiously due to lower validity scores. If the clinician is looking for a tool that offers a wider age range for which to test, they may be better suited with the CDI, which has norms for children ages 6 to 17. In addition, there are other tests available which, unlike the MDI-C, allow for parent, teacher, and sibling evaluations of the child simultaneously to the child's self-report, such as the Children's Depression Scale (Tisher & Lang, 1983), the structured interview Kiddie SADS (Puig-Antich & Ryan, 1986), and the Bellvue Index of Depression (Petti, 1978). This may be critically important due to the current belief that agreement from more than one source is essential for appropriate assessment of childhood depression (Kaslow & Rehm, 1991).

REVIEWER'S REFERENCES

Kovacs, M., & Beck, A. T. (1977). An empirical-clinical approach toward a definition of childhood depression. In J. G. Schulterbrandt & A. Rasking (Eds.), *Depression in childhood: Diagnosis, treatment, and conceptual models* (pp. 1–25). New York: Raven Press.

Petti, T. A. (1978). Depression in hospitalized child psychiatry patients. *Journal of the American Academy of Child Psychiatry, 17,* 49–59.

Weissman, M. M., Orvaschel, H., & Padian, N. (1980). Children's symptom and social functioning self report scales: Comparison of mothers' and children's reports. *Journal of Nervous and Mental Disease, 168,* 736–740.

Kovacs, M. (1981). Rating scales to assess depression in school aged children. *Acta Paedopsychiatrica, 46,* 305–315.

Piers, E. V., & Harris, D. B. (1983). Piers-Harris Children's Self-Concept Scale (PHCSCS). Los Angeles, CA: Western Psychological Services.

Tisher, M., & Lang, M. (1983). The children's depression scale: Review and further developments. In D. P. Cantwell & G. A. Carlson (Eds.), *Affective disorders in childhood and adolescence: An update* (pp. 375–415). New York: Spectrum.

Berndt, D. J. (1986). *Multiscore Depression Inventory (MDI) manual.* Los Angeles, CA: Western Psychological Services.

Puig-Antich, J., & Ryan, N. (1986). *Schedule for affective disorder and schizophrenia for school-age children (6–18 years)—Kiddie SADS (K-SADS).* Unpublished manuscript. Pittsburgh: Western Psychiatric Institute and Clinic.

Kaslow, N. J., & Rehm, L. P. (1991). Childhood depression. In R. R. Kratochwill & R. J. Morris (Eds.), *The practice of child therapy* (2nd ed.) (pp. 43–75). New York: Pergamon.

Review of the Multiscore Depression Inventory for Children by MICHAEL G. KAVAN, Associate Dean for Student Affairs and Associate Professor of Family Practice, Creighton University School of Medicine, Omaha, NE:

The Multiscore Depression Inventory for Children (MDI-C) is a 79-item self-report measure designed to assess "depression and features related to depression" (manual, p. 1) in children between the ages of 8 and 17 years. It is meant to be used both as a screening instrument to "identify high risk children and as an aid in clinical assessment" (manual, p. 1). The MDI-C is adapted from the well-developed and respected adult Multiscore Depression Inventory (MDI; T4:1693). Like its predecessor, the MDI-C provides a total score for depression and subscale scores deemed useful in a broad range of clinical applications.

ADMINISTRATION AND SCORING. The MDI-C may be administered and scored by an "appropriately trained and supervised clerk" (p. 3) to individuals or to groups. For administration of the MDI-C, children are requested to complete the necessary background information on the answer form. They are then asked to read the printed instructions silently as the administrator reads them aloud. Children are to respond by circling "T" (true) or "F" (false) to each item by indicating how they "usually feel." The manual states that the items are readable at a mid first-grade reading level in one section, a second-grade reading level in another section, and a third-grade reading level in yet another section. Despite the authors' lack of clarity on this issue, experience with the MDI-C demonstrates that most MDI-C items are, in fact, clear and easy to understand. However, some younger children may have difficulty with the meaning of "suicide" and thus, the administrator may need to assist them in defining this word. Administration time is predicted to be 20 minutes, but most children should be able to complete the measure within 10 minutes.

The MDI-C may be scored by hand or microcomputer. Scoring may also be done by the test publisher through fax or mail services. For hand scoring, the administrator tears the perforated answer form in order to reveal the scoring page. A total score, which is meant to measure the severity of overall depression, and eight subscale scores (i.e., Anxiety, Self-Esteem, Sad Mood, Instrumental Helplessness, Social Introversion, Low Energy, Pessimism, and Defiance) are tabulated on this page and then transferred to a profile form for plotting. A suicide item is also included and contributes to the total score, but does not appear on any subscale. In addition, the scoring form includes an infrequency score column in order to measure response bias and/or malingering. Total scores can range from 0 to 79, whereas subscale scores can range from 8 to 13. The manual includes information on profile validity, total and subscale definitions, along with several case examples to assist in the interpretation of the MDI-C.

RELIABILITY. Within the manual, information is provided on both internal consistency and test-retest reliability. Coefficient alpha was figured for each MDI-C scale using the 1,465 children within the normative sample. Alpha coefficients for the entire group ranged from .70 (Low Energy) to .94 (Total score). Internal consistency holds up fairly well when examined within the three age ranges. One will, however, want to interpret some subscales within certain age groups with caution because alpha coefficients occasionally dip into the mid .60s. Internal consistencies were also calculated on a separate group of 254 junior high school and high school students (no other information was provided within the manual on this group) with alpha coefficients ranging from .66 (Pessimism) to .94 (Total). Four-week test-retest reliability was examined with 145 junior high and senior high school students (ages 11 to 18 years) from Charleston, South Carolina. Reliability coefficients ranged from .77 (Low Energy) to .92 (Total) indicating that the total score and subscale scores are fairly stable over time. No data, however, were provided on test-retest reliability for younger children. Therefore, caution should be urged when using the MDI-C for measuring treatment efficacy in younger children.

VALIDITY. The authors borrowed test construction techniques from the MDI in developing the MDI-C. Items were generated by the authors to match scales roughly equivalent to the MDI. These were then rewritten with the assistance of children so that a younger audience could more easily understand them. A survey by the authors found that most children viewed the items as age appropriate and a Q-sort demonstrated that children participating were able to sort successfully the majority of items into their respective subscale piles. Other evidence of content validity comes from the MDI-C coverage of the *Diagnostic and Statistical Manual of Mental Disorders—Fourth Edition* (DSM-IV) (APA, 1994) criteria for major depressive episode. With depression in children and adolescents being similar to that in adults, except for some age-specific symptoms, the MDI-C items cover fully or partially eight of nine DSM-IV symptom categories. The MDI-C does not, however, assess the temporal dimensions of the mood problem, nor does it address exclusion criteria as recommended by the DSM-IV. In terms of criterion-related validity, the MDI-C total score has been shown to correlate .84 with the Children's Depression Inventory in a sample of children and adolescents from the Midwest and Southeast. It correlated .83 with the MDI total scores (subscale

range from .12 to .82) in a sample of adolescents ages 13 to 18 years. The MDI-C total score was also found to correlate -.83 with the total score from the Piers-Harris Self-Concept Scale (subscale range from -.26 to -.83). The authors failed to assess any children within the normative sample with both the MDI-C and a clinical or structured interview, which is typically thought of as the "gold standard" for diagnostic purposes. They do cite item and scale development procedures along with convergent and discriminant validity for the MDI-C in support of construct validity. Their own factor-analytic studies found that "scales intercorrelated sufficiently to justify use of a single general dimension and were sufficiently different to justify a preliminary view of the scales as separate" (p. 31). Further analyses identified five factors consisting of demoralization, tension and stress, alienation, defiance, and an "uninterpretable" factor.

NORMS. The normative sample for the MDI-C consisted of 1,465 children between the ages of 8 and 17 years within grades 3 to 12 in Florida, Illinois, Michigan, Montana, Nebraska, North Carolina, South Carolina, and Washington. The authors note that a review of participating school demographics indicate that the relative proportion of Blacks and Native Americans to the general population is most likely high, whereas the number of Asians and Hispanics is low. No data, however, were specifically collected on the normative sample regarding this issue. Despite research suggesting that racial differences exist in the expression of depression in children (Politano, Nelson, Evans, Sorenson, & Zeman, 1986), no racial data are provided for the MDI-C within the manual.

SUMMARY. The MDI-C is a well-constructed self-report measure designed to assess depression and related features in children and adolescents. Administration and scoring of the MDI-C to children individually or in groups is quick and easy. Test-retest reliability and internal consistency reliability are solid for the total score and most subscale scores. Validity evidence appears strong in the limited studies that have been completed on the MDI-C to date. Interpretation will be made easier and more accurate as additional research data are generated on the MDI-C. Normative data for minority children and adolescents are sketchy at best, and thus, may limit the use of the MDI-C in these populations. In general, the MDI-C is a promising instrument for the assessment of depression in children and adolescents in both research and clinical settings. As additional validity data accumulates, the MDI-C is likely to develop into one of the best, if not the best, screening instrument available for this purpose. For diagnostic purposes, the MDI-C, as with any self-report measure, should only be used as part of a larger battery that includes a structured clinical interview (Fristad, Emery, & Beck, 1997).

REVIEWER'S REFERENCES

Politano, P. M., Nelson, W. M., Evans, H. E., Sorenson, S. B., & Zeman, D. J. (1986). Factor analytic evaluation of differences between Black and Caucasian emotionally disturbed children on the Children's Depression Inventory. *Journal of Psychopathology and Behavioral Assessment, 8,* 1–7.

American Psychiatric Association. (1994). *Diagnostic and statistical manual of mental disorders* (4th ed., rev.). Washington, DC: Author.

Fristad, M. A., Emery, B. L., & Beck, S. J. (1997). Use and abuse of the Children's Depression Inventory. *Journal of Consulting and Clinical Psychology, 65,* 699–702.

[251]
Myers-Briggs Type Indicator, Form M.

Purpose: Designed for "the identification of basic preferences on each of the four dichotomies specified or implicit in Jung's theory" and "the identification and description of the 16 personality types that result from interactions among the preferences."

Population: Ages 14 and older.

Publication Dates: 1943–1998.

Acronym: MBTI.

Scores, 4: Extraversion vs. Introversion, Sensing vs. Intuition, Thinking vs. Feeling, Judging vs. Perceiving.

Administration: Group.

Foreign Language Edition: Spanish (Form M Template scoring) edition available.

Price Data, 1999: $50 per 10 MBTI Form M self-scorable; $60 per manual ('98, 420 pages); $4.75 per Introduction to Type, Sixth Edition ('98, 43 pages); $7 per Introduction to Type in Organizations, Third Edition; $65 per 10 Form M prepaid profile combined item booklet/answer sheets; $100 per 10 Form M prepaid interpretive report combined item booklet/answer sheets; $120 per 10 Form M prepaid Interpretive Report for Organizations combined item booklet/answer sheets; $130 per 10 Form M prepaid Team Report answer sheets; $80 per 10 Form M prepaid Career Report combined item booklet/answer sheets; $62.50 per Form M item booklets; $15 per 25 nonprepaid answer sheets; $40 per 4 templates (for nonprepaid answer sheets).

Time: (15–25) minutes.

Comments: Scoring options: Self-scorable, template scoring, software on-site scoring, mail-in scoring; administration also available via software and internet; Spanish (Form M template scoring) edition available; based on personality theory of C. G. Jung; Forms F and G still available.

Authors: Katharine C. Briggs, Isabel Briggs Myers, Mary H. McCaulley (revised manual), Naomi L. Quenk (revised manual), and Allen L. Hammer (revised manual).

Publisher: Consulting Psychologists Press, Inc.

Cross References: See T5:1755 (78 references) and T4:1702 (45 references); for a review by Jerry S. Wiggins, see 10:206 (42 references); for a review by Anthony J. DeVito, see 9:739 (19 references); see also T3:1555 (42 references); for a review by Richard W. Coan, see 8:630 (115 references); see also T2:1294 (120 references) and P:177 (56 references); for reviews by Gerald A. Mendelson and Norman D. Sundberg and an excerpted review by Laurence Siegel, see 6:147 (10 references).

Review of the Myers–Briggs Type Indicator, Form M by JOHN W. FLEENOR, Director of Knowledge Management, Center for Creative Leadership, Greensboro, NC:

Based on Jung's (1923) theory of psychological types, the Myers-Briggs Type Indicator (MBTI) is designed to identify an individual's preferences on eight characteristics implicit in Jung's theory. The initial development on the MBTI began in 1942 when the mother-daughter team of Katharine Briggs and Isabel Myers started on their quest to operationalize Jung's theory. Over the years, the instrument has undergone extensive revisions, with the most recent version (Form M) being published in 1998. The MBTI provides scores on four dichotomous scales: Extraversion-Introversion (EI), Sensing-Intuition (SN), Thinking-Feeling (TF), and Judging-Perceiving (JP). The various combinations of these four scales result in 16 possible personality types, each represented by a four-letter code indicating the preference for each of the dichotomies (e.g., ESTJ).

According to its publisher, the MBTI is "the most widely used personality inventory in history" (manual, p. 9). Because of its popularity, however, there is a danger that the instrument may be used for purposes for which it was never intended. In the introduction to the manual, the authors address common misconceptions about the MBTI that may lead to its misuse. These include: (a) the instrument does not measure competencies—it identifies preferences; (b) the preferences identified by the MBTI are not personality traits, but represent a typology in which individuals with opposite preferences are qualitatively different; and (c) the interactions among these preferences are critical to understanding the instrument (i.e., the whole is greater than the sum of its parts).

THEORY. Jung (1923) posited that individual differences in personality can be explained by two basic human attitudes, extraversion and introversion. Extraverts draw their energy primarily from the outer world of other people and events. Introverts, on the other hand, draw their energy from their inner thoughts and experiences. Later, Jung added two additional dichotomies, which he called functions, to this theory: sensation and intuition, and thinking and feeling. Sensation (called sensing by Myers and Briggs) refers to perceptions that are observable by the five senses; intuition refers to the perception of possibilities and meaning by way of the unconscious. The thinking function refers to making decisions by using logic, whereas feeling refers to making decisions by considering one's personal values. The judging/perceiving orientation was not part of Jung's original theory, but was added by Myers and Briggs to identify one's orientation to the outer world. Judging is concerned with planning, organizing, making decisions, and coming to closure. Perceiving is concerned with being flexible and spontaneous, and with collecting additional information before making decisions.

On the surface, the theory behind the MBTI appears to be fairly simple. However, it is actually very complex, and casual users may have problems fully understanding its implications. According to Myers and Briggs, each four-letter type represents a complex set of relationships among the functions (S, N, T, and F), attitudes (E and I), and attitudes toward the outer world (J and P). These various interactions are known as type dynamics. For example, in addition to their preferred (dominant) function, individuals also have auxiliary, tertiary, and inferior (least preferred) functions. For Extraverts, their dominant function is extraverted (shown to others), whereas their auxiliary function is introverted. For introverts, the opposite is true—they show their auxiliary function to the outside world, and save their dominant function for their inner world.

MANUAL. The 420-page manual (1998) contains extensive information on the theory, development, psychometrics, and interpretation of the MBTI. It is one of the strengths of this instrument.

ADMINISTRATION AND SCORING. Form M of the MBTI contains 93 items written at the seventh-grade reading level. The respondents answer forced-choice items that are written to reflect the poles of the dichotomies. Form M has both computer and hand-scored versions. Instructions to the respondents are included on the cover of the question booklets. The hand-scored version uses unit weights for the items (i.e., each response is counted as one point). The points are summed for each scale, and an individual's preference on a scale is the pole of the dichotomy with the most points.

For the computer-scored version of the MBTI, an IRT (item response theory) scoring method is used. According to the authors, IRT scoring provides a more accurate indication of preference, especially around the cutoff points of the scales.

An IRT procedure was also used to select the item content for Form M. Through the use of DIF (differential item functioning) analyses, items that demonstrated significantly different responses by gender were eliminated form the item pool. This eliminated the need for different scoring procedures for males and females. The use of IRT in the development of Form M also makes it virtually impossible to score at the midpoint of a scale, thus eliminating ties on the scales. On previous forms, ties were broken by a decision-rule that arbitrarily assigned individuals to a preference (i.e., I, N, F, or P).

STANDARDIZATION SAMPLE. A representative national sample of U.S. adults over age 18 was used for the item analyses and item weighting ($N = 3,009$).

RELIABILITY. The authors report the usual estimates of reliability, including split-half, coefficient alpha, and test-retest reliabilities, which indicate acceptable levels of reliability for the scores. Most of these reliabilities, however, are based on the use of the continuous preference scores from the instrument. Such analyses are contrary to the theory underlying the MBTI—that the instrument is designed to sort individuals into types rather than to assign continuous scores to them. One reliability analysis is included that reports the percentage of agreement for the dichotomies for three test-retest samples. The percentage of participants reporting the identical four preferences after a 4-week interval range from 55% to 80%, with an average of 65%.

VALIDITY. The construct validity of the four-factor model of the MBTI was investigated using confirmatory factor analysis. The predicted four-factor model appeared to be the best fit for the data, compared to two competing models. In the manual, numerous validity studies are reported that correlated MBTI continuous scores with other instruments, such as the California Psychological Inventory (CPI). Again, the use of continuous scores is contrary to the theory underlying the instrument, so these results should be interpreted with caution.

CONCLUSION. With the publication of Form M, significant improvements are evident in the MBTI. Weaknesses in earlier scoring procedures have been reduced by the use of IRT techniques in the development of Form M. Additionally, previous gender differences in the scoring of some scales have been eliminated through the use of DIF analyses.

The MBTI appears to have some value as a tool for increasing self-insight, and for helping people to understand individual differences in personality type. For example, participants in management development programs and students undergoing career counseling may benefit from taking the instrument. The authors, however, continue to report studies that employ continuous scores as evidence of reliability and validity for the instrument, although they continue to stress that the instrument is not designed to measure personality traits on a continuous scale. The MBTI, therefore, cannot be recommended without reservation until additional analyses that are appropriate for categorical data are conducted and reported in the manual.

REVIEWER'S REFERENCE

Jung, C. (1923). *Psychological types; or, the psychology of individuation.* Princeton, NJ: Princeton University Press.

Review of the Myers-Briggs Type Indicator, Form M by PAUL M. MASTRANGELO, Associate Professor, Division of Applied Psychology & Quantitative Methods, University of Baltimore, Baltimore, MD:

The Myers-Briggs Type Indicator (MBTI) is a user-friendly personality assessment instrument—easy to administer, score, and interpret. The simplicity of the MBTI score (a four-letter "type" based on four dichotomous scale scores) especially contributes to its popularity among professionals who lack training in psychological assessment; however, this same feature contributes to the disdain among professionals who are trained in psychometrics. Many MBTI users are unaware of the instrument's theoretical assumptions and

subsequent limitations. For example, the MBTI is not designed to measure personality traits and therefore should *not* be used as a personnel screening device (p. 108 in the manual). Even though many scientific criticisms are addressed in the manual, the rejoinders are frequently misleading, perpetuating the gap between practitioners and scientists.

The manual is somewhat deceptive regarding score reliability (i.e., consistency), which asks how likely it is for one individual to receive the same score from different administrations of the MBTI. If one uses the four MBTI scales (scored continuously) as the unit of analysis, then responses show very high levels of internal consistency (mostly >.90) and acceptable levels of test-retest reliability (.83–.97 for a 4-week interval). However, the authors clearly state that the MBTI is meant to identify a person's whole type (e.g., ENTP). As a result the true test of reliability is the MBTI's ability to consistently indicate the same four preferences for any individual. Only one such study is reported in the manual for Form M (p. 163). After a mere 4 weeks, only 65% of the 424 respondents in the retest sample scored the same. Most of the remaining 35% showed consistency in three of the four scales, which is somewhat comforting, but less than adequate given the emphasis on holistic interpretation of the four preferences. Thus, the typical estimates of reliability are quite high, but they provide an inappropriate estimate for this scoring system; the *appropriate* reliability estimate shows consistent classification for only 65% of respondents, and that is less impressive.

Similar confusion exists when reviewing the MBTI's validity results, which address whether the MBTI scores measure the concepts they were designed to measure. Again, the answer depends on whether one violates the assumptions on which the MBTI is based. A traditional approach to estimating construct validity would be to correlate the MBTI scores with other measures of personality. Studies using this approach tend to use a continuous score for the four MBTI scales rather than the dichotomous score, violating the MBTI assumptions. Such studies suggest that the four MBTI scales correspond to four of the Big Five personality domains, excluding the Emotional Stability domain (also called Neuroticism). Because the Big Five model is the current framework for personality assessment, these demonstrations of convergent validity aid the interpretation of Jungian terminology.

However, demonstrations of validity for whole type scores (not continuous numeric scores) are ambiguous and wanting. The best test of the purported interaction among the four dichotomies was the calculation of the F-test for four-way interactions to predict various variables such as work preferences, job satisfaction, and values (p. 202). If a person's type is really more than just the sum of four dichotomies, then this four-way interaction term should predict many variables—certainly more than the four separate dichotomous scores. In fact, the four-way interaction term predicted only 3 of 73 dependent variables whereas the four main effects predicted 16 to 36 variables. To make matters worse, there is no listing of specific dependent variables or specific p-values that were significantly predicted in this analysis, which is very misleading as it preys on less sophisticated consumers of statistical results. The dearth of significant four-way interactions directly contradicts the fundamental assumption that the *combination* of the four preference scores is more important than the individual scores. Thus, the MBTI does show evidence of validity as four separate personality scales, but there is little evidence of a synergistic combination that creates the 16 types.

The authors should be commended for their efforts to apply Item Response Theory (IRT) to improve the reliability and validity of the four dichotomous scores in Form M, which replaces Form G as the standard form. IRT permits a psychometric examination of the reliability of each item at specific levels of the underlying trait being measured. Because the MBTI is used to indicate "how clearly a respondent prefers one of two opposite poles" (manual, p. 5), IRT was used to improve the accuracy of classifications when the respondent's preference was equivocal. The manual describes a study used to determine the cutting score for theta that separates each dichotomous preference score. Classifications based on IRT were compared to each participant's self-report of the type best suiting him or her. Each of the four preference scales showed over 90% agreement with self-reported best fit, and the combination of all four preferences agreed with self-reports 78% of the time. This study, however, suffered from rather obvious flaws. The sample size was a paltry 157, the self-reports were sometimes administered to

people who already knew their MBTI results, and the scoring procedures were never cross-validated—another example of misleading research in the manual.

SUMMARY. The MBTI should not be ignored by scientists or embraced by practitioners to the extent that it currently is. The MBTI is best used in situations where basic information regarding personality must be presented to lay individuals for self-understanding; it should not be used to make specific decisions about an individual (e.g., hiring). Adhering to four dichotomous scores restricts the MBTI's utility and demands more rigorous research than that found in the manual. Future research should address the consistency and interpretation of scores for those individuals who show a weak preference on a particular scale. Furthermore, this research needs to be presented in journals besides the *Journal of Psychological Type*, which is solely dedicated to the MBTI. The most widely used psychological measure should demand scientific scrutiny to improve service to the public.

[252]
Naglieri Nonverbal Ability Test.

Purpose: A "measure of nonverbal reasoning and problem solving independent of educational curricula and cultural or language background."

Population: Grades K–12.

Publication Dates: 1996–1997.

Acronym: NNAT.

Scores, 5: Pattern Completion (PC), Reasoning by Analogy (RA), Serial Reasoning (SR), Spatial Visualization (SV), Total (Nonverbal Ability Index—NAI).

Administration: Group.

Levels, 7: A (Kindergarten), B (Grade 1), C (Grade 2), D (Grades 3–4), E (Grades 5–6), F (Grades 7–9), G (Grades 10–12).

Price Data: Available from publisher.

Time: 30 (45) minutes.

Comments: An extension and revision of the Matrix Analogies Test (T5:1607); appropriate for non-English-speaking students, students with hearing, language, or motor impairment, and impaired color vision; a general measure of ability or identification of students with learning problems.

Author: Jack A. Naglieri.

Publisher: Harcourt Brace Educational Measurement.

Review of the Naglieri Nonverbal Ability Test by TERRY A. STINNETT, Associate Professor, School Psychology Programs, Oklahoma State University, Stillwater, OK:

The Naglieri Nonverbal Ability Test (NNAT), the latest expansion and revision of the Matrix Analogies Test (MAT; T5:1607), is based upon the MAT—Expanded Form (MAT-EF; Naglieri, 1985a) and the MAT—Short Form (MAT-SF; Naglieri, 1985b). The Naglieri Nonverbal Ability Test—Multilevel Form (NNAT-MF) is a group-administered, brief nonverbal measure of school ability for children from kindergarten through 12th grade. [Editor's Note: The publisher advises that the NNAT Individual Form is under development.] The instruments have been claimed to be predictive of academic achievement, to be appropriate for use with children of culturally and socioeconomically diverse backgrounds including those with limited English, and for identifying children with learning problems. The tests are narrow-scope; all items are matrix-solution type and use figural stimuli. Users who require individually administered, broad-scope, comprehensive, multi-construct nonverbal intellectual assessment should consider either the Leiter International Performance Scale—Revised (Leiter-R, Roid & Miller, 1997; 211) or the Universal Nonverbal Intelligence Test (UNIT, Bracken & McCallum, 1998; 404).

The NNAT-MF has seven separate levels: kindergarten, 1st, and 2nd grades each have their own, and grades 3 and 4, 5 and 6, 7–9, and 10–12 are grouped into those respective levels. There are 38 items for each level. Each level has a separate test booklet and the stimulus items for the level are in the booklet. There are machine-scorable answer forms and the students must fill in the circle (1–5) on the form that corresponds to their answers for the items. The catalogue suggests that users of the test have the option of purchasing the scoring service from Harcourt Brace Educational Measurement, or may conduct on-site local scoring using a reflected light scanner.

The items are grouped into the same four clusters as the scale's MAT predecessors: Pattern Completion (PC), Reasoning by Analogy (RA), Serial Reasoning (SR), and Spatial Visualization (SV). Naglieri, in the technical manual, contends that each cluster, to a certain extent, reflects general ability in a somewhat unique way and that the items are not biased for gender, race, or ethnicity. There are items that signify these four domains at every level except kindergarten, which does not contain Serial Reasoning or Spatial Visualization

items, and 1st grade, which does not contain Spatial Visualization items. Although information can be generated about a child's performance on each of the cluster areas, the test author recommends that the raw scores from these domains be combined to yield the Nonverbal Ability Index (NAI), described as a measure of general ability. It is probably wise to emphasize the NAI over the separate domains, as factor analysis of the MAT-EF yielded only three factors: PC, SR, and SV (see Naglieri & Insko, 1986) and many of the items were cross-loaded on them. Reasoning by Analogy and Serial Reasoning were particularly confounded (see McMorris, Rule, & Steinberg, 1989). Also, as was the case with the MAT, there are items on the NNAT that were not placed with a cluster, but do contribute to the overall NAI.

Raw scores can be transformed into scaled scores. NNAT scaled scores were developed with Item Response Theory methods and the NAI was developed specifically with the Rasch Model. The Rasch model relates the child's ability level to item difficulty level or the probability of answering an item correctly. Thus, because items are evaluated on a common scale or continuum of difficulty, the scores can be considered to reflect a universal ability scale across the age range of the test (i.e., the child's overall and task performance ability are placed on the same continuum). Careful attention was placed upon equating difficulty level among adjacent levels of the NNAT to ensure there was a continuous Rasch ability scale across all levels of the test. Correlations between each level and the next higher adjacent level were quite high (all fell at or between .80 to .82). A linear transformation of the ability scale was performed last so that the scores would be represented by positive numerals.

The NAI standard score has a mean of 100 and a standard deviation of 15, a common intelligence test standard score metric. The NAI can be converted to age or grade-based percentile ranks, and to age or grade-based stanine scores. Users might also choose to transform the NAI into a Normal Curve Equivalent. Cluster scores can be derived to describe the child's performance on the subareas that comprise the NAI. The technical manual mentions but does not describe them. Finally, the test yields Age-Equivalent scores.

The standardization samples (Fall and Spring) are very large and the NNAT was conjointly standardized with the Stanford Achievement Test Series, 9th edition (SAT-9; Harcourt Brace Educational Measurement, 1997) and the Aprenda, Segunda edición (Aprenda2; Harcourt Brace Educational Measurement, 1998). A stratified random sampling procedure was employed. The Fall norms are based on 22,600 children and the Spring norms included 67,000. Both samples covered the range of kindergarten–12th grade. The demographic characteristics (geographic region, socioeconomic status, urbanicity, ethnicity, and private school placement) mirrored the 1993–1994 National Center for Education Statistics (NCES) estimates fairly impressively. However, there was some overrepresentation of students from the Midwest region in the Spring Norms (30.2% vs. 23.8%) and a large degree of underrepresentation of urban students (5.6% vs. 26.8%) in the Fall sample compared to the NCES estimates. The norms also included children with disabilities and those with limited English proficiency.

No test-retest reliability estimates are presented for the NNAT-MF. Kuder-Richardson Formula 20 (KR-20) internal consistency reliability estimates based on raw scores for the total test by age and grade and by grade for the test cluster areas were calculated. Standard errors of measurement are also presented for raw scores. Probably of more interest to NNAT-MF users, however, are the standard errors of measurement for the NAI scaled scores. These were consistent across all levels and ranged from 5.6 to 5.8 points. The total score grade-based internal consistency coefficients are good and ranged from .83 to .93. The age-based KR-20s for total score are also good and ranged from .81 to .88. The estimates for the cluster areas were generally lower and much more variable than were the total score coefficients. In fact, the majority of the cluster area coefficients (68 of 86 or 79% of the coefficients) were unacceptable (.70 or lower). This could be in part due to various cluster areas having a relatively small number of items at certain test levels, or that the cluster areas are not factorially pure.

The NNAT-MF and MAT-SF total scores were correlated. It would be expected that the two would be strongly related as the NNAT is derived from the MAT. The two were related with rs ranging from .63 to .78 (median r = 75). Apparently the NNAT-MF and the MAT-SF, to a certain extent, measure the same cognitive ability. They should not be considered equivalent though.

The NNAT-MF showed good criterion-related validity with the Stanford Achievement Test—Form S (SAT). The NNAT-MF was moderately related to the SAT Total Reading, Mathematics, Language, Thinking Skills, and the Complete Battery scores (the majority of the correlation coefficients were in the .50s to .60s). The NNAT-MF was also related to the Aprenda2 Total Reading, Mathematics, Total Mathematics, Basic Battery, Language, and Thinking Skills. These correlations were lower and more variable. The correlations for the NNAT and the Aprenda2 scores were: Total Reading (.07 to .51, median r = .32), Mathematics (.39 to .56, median r = .51), Total Mathematics (.51 to .77, median r = .59), Basic Battery (.26 to .67, median r = .47), Language (.15 to .61, median r = .41), and Thinking Skills (.29 to .67, median r = .47).

The NNAT-MF score progression was also examined in terms of age differentiation to provide further evidence of validity. If the NNAT-MF items were related to academic functioning, then it would be expected that they would be progressively easier for older students than for younger ones (across levels). Also that pattern might be expected within levels (i.e., that items become progressively easier as students become older and have academic exposure over the course of the academic year). Examination of the mean p values and raw score means for the NNAT generally provided support for both expectations.

Finally biserial correlations were calculated for the NNAT for all levels to determine whether the test could separate high- from low-scoring students. The exact procedures used were not specified in the manual. However, this analysis can provide a measure of the item-criterion relationship that is independent of item difficulty (Anastasi, 1988, p. 219). The median correlations and ranges are presented. For the Fall sample the median r_{bis}s range from .50 to .73, whereas in the Spring sample they range from .51 to .60.

SUMMARY. In terms of the technical characteristics that are presented in the manual, the NNAT-MF appears adequate. Although the technical manual did present much of the psychometric data for the test in tables, the exact procedures used in the development and refinement of the NNAT-MF were not very detailed. Nevertheless, like its MAT parent, this is a satisfactory narrow-scope measure of nonverbal intellectual ability.

There are some key psychometric pieces missing, however. At a minimum, the test's temporal stability needs to be examined and further investigation of the test's underlying structure ought to be conducted. Also it would be hoped that the onsite scoring software would be available soon. Otherwise potential purchasers of the NNAT-MF may want to consider whether the cost-benefit ratio is acceptable for their uses, especially if there are plans to use the test repeatedly over a period of time. The test is well suited for assessment of students whose performance could be negatively impacted because of language differences or problems, hearing impairment, or cultural or socioeconomic background, etc. And if IQ were used as an admissions criterion, the test could also be effectively used to screen students for eligibility for gifted and/or talented programs. Another use for the NNAT-MF would be for research purposes when a measure of general ability is specified in the design.

Questions could be raised about other suggested applications of the instrument. The author suggests that the NNAT-MF could be used to identify students with low general ability and thus may indicate potential academic problems. Given the multilevel and group administration format of the test one could assume that it might be given to large numbers of students, perhaps an entire grade-level, school, or even district wide. Caution is warranted. Intellectual ability or "IQ" is an often-misunderstood construct by nonpsychologists as it is and the purchase of the NNAT-MF only requires a level "B" user qualification. Test users with a master's-level degree in Psychology or Education, or the equivalent in a related field with training in assessment are eligible to purchase level "B" materials. Gathering of intellectual ability data by nonpsychologists without specific a priori questions tailored to unambiguous referral concerns is bound to create problems in terms of interpretation and use. Why not identify with academic problems more directly and cheaply by record review, teacher and parent report, or by examining student performance on group achievement tests such as those that most districts already use? In closing, the NNAT-MF could be an acceptable instrument for users who need a quick, narrow-score estimate of nonverbal general intellectual ability. Test purchasers should decide for themselves whether the NNAT-MF is cost effective for their intended purposes.

REVIEWER'S REFERENCES

Naglieri, J. A. (1985a). Matrix Analogies Test—Expanded Form. San Antonio, TX: Psychological Corporation.
Naglieri, J. A. (1985b). Matrix Analogies Test—Short Form. San Antonio, TX: Psychological Corporation.
Naglieri, J. A., & Insko, W. R. (1986). Construct validity of the Matrix Analogies Test—Expanded Form. Journal of Psychoeducational Assessment, 4, 243–255.
Anastasi, A. (1988). Psychological testing (6th ed.). New York: Macmillan Publishing Co.
McMorris, R. F., Rule, D. L., & Steinberg, W. J. (1989). [Review of the Matrix Analogies Test]. In J. C. Conoley & J. J. Kramer (Eds.), The tenth mental measurements yearbook (pp. 479–481). Lincoln, NE: Buros Institute of Mental Measurements.
Harcourt Brace Educational Measurement. (1997). Stanford Achievement Test Series (9th ed.). San Antonio, TX: The author.
Roid, G. H., & Miller, L. J. (1997). Leiter International Performance Scale—Revised. Wood Dale, IL: Stoelting Co.
Bracken, B. A., & McCallum, R. S. (1998). Universal Nonverbal Intelligence Test. Itasca, IL: Riverside Publishing.
Harcourt Brace Educational Measurement. (1998). Aprenda: La prueba de logros en español (2nd ed.). San Antonio, TX: The author.

Review of the Naglieri Nonverbal Ability Test by MICHAEL S. TREVISAN, Assistant Professor, Department of Educational Leadership and Counseling Psychology, Washington State University, Pullman, WA:

OVERVIEW. Obtaining sound, rigorous school ability information for students with physical or learning disabilities, culturally diverse backgrounds, or languages other than English, can present significant challenges for school personnel. Moreover, conventional testing practices that require the student to read and respond to a test in English, relying heavily on verbal ability, are often inadequate for these difficult testing situations.

These unique realities in our schools may warrant innovative testing strategies in response. The development of the Naglieri Nonverbal Ability Test (NNAT) is one attempt at addressing these testing issues and is perhaps a welcome addition to the repertoire of educators and school support personnel. The NNAT is designed to provide an assessment of school ability and predict future academic performance by using items that contain only shapes and designs, requiring respondents to rely on *reasoning skills rather than verbal ability* to answer the items. In addition, NNAT items are thought to be "universal," allowing use with a "diverse population of students" (technical manual, p. 1). The NNAT is a revision of the expanded and short forms of the Matrix Analogies Test (T5:1607).

The NNAT is composed of seven levels that span Kindergarten through Grade 12 or ages 5 to 17. Each level consists of 38 five-choice items that form reasoning and ability clusters as follows: Pattern Completion, Reasoning by Analogy, Serial Reasoning, and Spatial Visualization. All items require respondents to "examine the relationships among the parts of the design (called a matrix) and determine which response is the correct one based on the information inherent in the item" (technical manual, p. 2).

SCORING AND ADMINISTRATION. Two forms of the NNAT are available: the Multilevel Form for group administration and the Individual Form. The NNAT can be completed in 35–45 minutes including preparing the machine-scorable answer sheets and conducting the practice exercises. Clear, easy-to-follow directions are available in the Directions for Administration document.

STANDARDIZATION. Fall and spring standardization of the NNAT took place in 1995 and 1996, respectively, with a combined sample size of nearly 90,000 students selected through a nationally stratified, random sampling scheme. Stratification was done by state with socioeconomic status, urbanicity, and ethnicity as stratification variables.

Derived scores are provided based on age or grade norms. The main derived score is referred to as the Nonverbal Ability Index (NAI). The NAI has a mean of 100 and a standard deviation of 15, similar to scaled scores from other ability measures. Percentiles, stanines, and normal curve equivalents are also available as well as cluster scores. However, all four clusters do not exist across the seven levels of the test.

RELIABILITY, VALIDITY, AND BIAS ELIMINATION. Reliability of data obtained from the NNAT was computed in the form of internal consistency estimates for both fall and spring at each level and computed separately for age and grade. Reliability data for cluster scores are also provided. Internal consistency estimates (KR-20) for total scores were quite good ranging from a low of .80 to a high of .93. Thus, by closely following the instructions, internally consistent scores can be obtained from administration of the NNAT. Reliability estimates (KR-21) for cluster scores were poor, with some reliability estimates in the mid-.20s, suggesting a lack of internal consistency in scores obtained at the cluster level.

Three types of validity data were evident in the technical manual. First, some content validity evidence was provided. Content validity evidence was examined by the author of the NNAT making a professional judgment to determine which items assess nonverbal ability and including only those items in the test. Second, criterion-related validity evidence was obtained by correlating scores from the NNAT with the Stanford Achievement Test, Ninth Edition (SAT9), a current standardized norm-referenced achievement test. The magnitude of correlations for various SAT9 subtest scores with scores from the NNAT range from the mid-.50s to the mid-.60s. Correlations were also obtained between NNAT scores and scores form the Aprenda2, a Spanish norm-referenced achievement test. These correlations were much lower, with a low of .07. Third, although limited construct validity data are available in the technical manual, a recent study shows moderate correlations between total and subtest scores from the Otis-Lennon School Ability Test (OLSAT) and scores from the NNAT (Naglieri, 1998). These correlations provide evidence that the NNAT is in part measuring a similar construct to that measured by the OLSAT, a well-accepted, conventional school ability test.

Bias was controlled for by using accepted industry procedures. In this case, scores on items were statistically contrasted between males and females, between Whites and African Americans, and Whites and Hispanics. Items showing statistically significant differences between these groups were eliminated.

CAUTIONS, CRITICISMS, AND RECOMMENDATIONS. The testing format used in the NNAT, geometric shapes and figures, dates back to the Army Beta tests used in World War I (Bruce Bracken, personal communication, September 2, 1998). Despite its history and length of use, no study or paper could be found that explicates fundamental issues of nonverbal ability testing. This reviewer also perused several common, recently published, or revised psychological testing textbooks and found little information on nonverbal ability testing.

Despite the lack of available information, nonverbal ability testing is an emerging testing technology that for some holds great promise (e.g., Anastasi & Urbina, 1997), particularly given the critical need to assess school ability for a rapidly growing diverse student population. In fact, at least three competing nonverbal ability tests have been published within the last 3 years and an entire symposium on the topic of nonverbal ability testing was conducted at the 1998 American Psychological Association annual convention (Bracken, 1998; Naglieri, 1998).

Until further work concerning nonverbal ability testing is more widely available, the following *cautions* and *criticisms* are offered. First, the NNAT may not be accepted by many states for placing students into special programs. A check with appropriate state officials on this matter is warranted. Second, the NNAT does not provide any connection or information about a student's verbal ability. Although this feature is by design, a student's ability to deal with verbally mediated information is fundamental to academic achievement. The Universal Nonverbal Intelligence Test (UNIT) offers an assessment of material conducive to internal verbal mediation such as labeling, organizing, and categorizing (Bracken, 1998) and thus may warrant consideration. Third, the validity evidence for the NNAT is insufficient. The evidence lacks integration and in some instances is of poor quality. The author's suggestion for potential users to conduct their own "content validity study" is inadequate. Further validity work is clearly needed. Also, in a review of the Matrix Analogies Test (MAT), McMorris, Rule, and Steinberg (1989) suggested an examination into the quality of the distractors. Because the NNAT is an extension of the MAT and no examination of distractors was apparent in the technical manual, this suggestion and criticism is extended to the NNAT.

SUMMARY. The author is commended for creativity in attempting to address a critical problem facing our schools today. Many features of the test and its development meet high psychometric standards. The additional validity evidence offered through correlations with the OLSAT suggests the author is working to address validity deficiencies. With additional work, the NNAT has the potential to become a critical tool for use in our schools. Educators or support personnel in search of an ability test for use with a diverse student population should give the NNAT serious consideration.

REVIEWER'S REFERENCES

McMorris, R. F., Rule, D. L., & Steinberg, W. J. (1989). [Review of the Matrix Analogies Test: Expanded Form]. In J. J. Kramer & J. C. Conoley (Eds.), *The tenth mental measurements yearbook* (pp. 479–481). Lincoln, NE: Buros Institute of Mental Measurements.

Anastasi, A., & Urbina, S. (1997). *Psychological testing* (7th ed.). New Jersey: Prentice Hall.

Bracken, B. (1998, August). Testing diverse populations with the Universal Nonverbal Intelligence Test. In J. A. Naglieri (Chair), *Testing diverse populations with new nonverbal intelligence tests.* Symposium conducted at the 106th annual meeting of the American Psychological Association, San Francisco.

Naglieri, J. A. (1998, August). Testing diverse populations with the Naglieri Ability Tests. In J. A. Naglieri (Chair), *Testing diverse populations with new nonverbal intelligence tests.* Symposium conducted at the 106th annual meeting of the American Psychological Association, San Francisco.

NEEDS Survey.

Purpose: Designed "to provide a concise but comprehensive profile of an individual's functioning" relative to the treatment of substance abuse.
Population: Adults.
Publication Date: 1994.
Acronym: NEEDS.
Scores, 10: Test Taking Attitude, Basic Problem Solving and Reading, Emotional Stability, Substance Abuse, Employment, Personal Relationship and Support System, Physical Health, Education, Criminal History, Overall "Needs."
Administration: Individual or group.
Manual: No manual; Reference Guide available.
Price Data, 1998: $6 per evaluation.
Time: (26) minutes.
Comments: Self-administered; computer-scored, IBM compatible with either DOS or Windows required; provides DSM-IV classification for alcohol and drug abuse and ASAM patient placement criteria for treatment recommendations; available in English or Spanish.
Author: ADE Incorporated.
Publisher: ADE Incorporated.

Review of the NEEDS Survey by ANITA M. HUBLEY, Assistant Professor of Educational and Consulting Psychology, and Special Education, The University of British Columbia, Vancouver, British Columbia, Canada:

The NEEDS Survey is a comprehensive measure of alcohol and drug use/abuse and related issues in adults. An extension of the Substance Abuse/Life Circumstance Evaluation (SALCE) Survey (377), the 130-item NEEDS Survey provides information that can be used to determine an initial level of intervention.

The NEEDS Survey is self-administered and computer scored. Ten areas are assessed:

1. Test Taking Attitude (TTA) describes the respondent's attitude toward the test using one of six categories. The majority of TTA items consist of a simple rephrasing of many of the Marlowe-Crowne Social Desirability Scale items, although the source of these items does not appear to be acknowledged.

2. Basic Problem-Solving Skills assesses the respondent's reading, comprehension, and problem-solving ability.

3. Emotional Stability Evaluation (ESE) assesses the respondent's history of emotional problems, reported life stresses, coping ability, and patterns of violent or aggressive behavior.

4. Substance Abuse Evaluation (SAE) evaluates the respondent's level of alcohol and drug use/abuse and any attempts made to address these problems. Two other subscales: Drinking Evaluation Category (DEC) and Drug Use Evaluation (DUE) are included.

5. Employment Assessment evaluates the respondent's current and previous 3 years of employment as well as financial difficulties.

6. Personal Relationship and Support System Assessment evaluates the stability of personal relationships and the degree to which family relationships are positive or negative.

7. Physical Health Assessment evaluates the degree to which the respondent feels hindered by physical health issues.

8. Educational Assessment evaluates years of formal education completed as well as the person's basic problem-solving skills and employment stability.

9. Criminal History Assessment reports the respondent's history of criminal activity.

10. Overall Needs provides a summary of the other subscales, a suggested level of supervision, and a referral recommendation.

Unfortunately, no information is provided regarding which items comprise each subscale, how the subscale categories were derived or validated, or how the suggested levels of supervision and intervention were determined. More information needs to be provided about the development and scoring of this measure. Lack of detail regarding scoring is particularly problematic when computerized scoring is used because the test user is further removed from this process (see Butcher, 1994, and Most, 1987).

The computerized data entry program for the NEEDS Survey provides plenty of instructions and is easy to use. The program requires that all data be entered twice. If the doubly entered responses to an item do not match, the person is then cued to correct the discrepancy. A difficulty with this approach is that the initial row of data is visible on the screen while the data are being entered the second time and so there is nothing to prevent the user from simply re-entering the data using the data on the screen rather than the raw data from the inventory. Not only should the computer instructions remind users of the extremely common likelihood of making errors (and the associated impact on scores and interpreta-

tion), but the initial line of data also should not be visible to the user when entering the data the second time.

Normative data are available for undergraduate students (Meyers, 1996; Thompson & Childers, 1995), adults (Childers, Cole et al., 1996), general correctional offenders (Childers, Meyers, & Wuensch, 1996), and domestic violence offenders (Childers, Meyers et al., 1996). The student norms consist of predominantly Caucasian samples; however, the norms for adults and offenders are based on both Caucasian and minority samples. These norms provide a good base. Further normative work needs to focus on large samples of (minority and nonminority) male and female inpatient and outpatient substance abusers, DWI offenders, and pregnant users/abusers.

No reliability evidence is provided for the NEEDS Survey. Information regarding the validity of inferences made from this measure is limited. Low to moderate positive correlations were found between the majority of Brief Symptom Inventory scales and both ESE and Overall Needs. Significant correlations were not found, however, with the substance use subscales (i.e., DEC, DUE, and SAE; Childers, Cole et al., 1996). Thompson and Childers (1995) presented summary profiles on the Brief Symptom Inventory for low and high scorers on DEC and DUE that suggested high scorers experience more symptomatology and distress than low scorers. Unfortunately, they did not indicate how many participants were in each of the low and high scorer groups, nor did they report the results of any statistical tests examining whether differences between these two groups were statistically significant. Low to moderate positive correlations were also found between the majority of SCL-90-R scales and each of ESE, Overall Needs, and SAE, indicating greater symptomatology among individuals with greater emotional instability, higher needs, and more substance (particularly alcohol) abuse (Meyers, 1996). Finally, Childers, Meyers et al. (1996) found that three individual NEEDS Survey items (i.e., number of dependent children, number of traffic tickets, and number of assault convictions) as well as scores on SAE and ESE were useful in discriminating between a general correctional population and domestic violence offenders.

A consistent pattern of gender differences has emerged for several NEEDS Survey subscales—

notably DEC and SAE (Childers, Cole et al., 1996; Meyers, 1996; Thompson & Childers, 1995). Some studies have shown gender differences on TTA (Meyers, 1996; Thompson & Childers, 1995) and ESE (Thompson & Childers, 1995).

An examination of correlations among the subscales of the NEEDS Survey raises the issue of whether all of the subscales are needed (Childers, Cole et al., 1996; Meyers, 1996; Thompson & Childers, 1995). High positive correlations are consistently found between SAE and DEC (r = .70 to .83), SAE and DUE (r =.76 to .82), Overall Needs and ESE (r = .72 to .73), and Overall Needs and SAE (r = .69 to .83). Although moderate correlations are expected because SAE incorporates DEC and DUE and all subscales are included in Overall Needs, the observed correlations seem overly high.

The role of TTA in the NEEDS Survey also needs further examination. Is TTA a validity (or bias) measure or is it a personality or situation-based characteristic? The meaning ascribed to TTA has important consequences for interpreting the low to moderate negative correlations found between TTA and each of ESE (r = -.55 to -.62), SAE (r = -.28 to -.38), DEC (r = -.19 to -.35), DUE (r = -.12 to -.27), and Overall Needs (r = -.36 to -.37) (Childers, Cole et al., 1996; Meyers, 1996; Thompson & Childers, 1995).

SUMMARY. The NEEDS Survey is a promising multidimensional measure of substance abuse and related demographic and psychosocial issues. Normative data are available for undergraduate students, adults, general correctional offenders, and domestic violence offenders. The presence of gender differences on some subscales suggests the need for separate norms by gender. At present, reliability evidence is lacking and validity evidence is somewhat limited, although it must be kept in mind that this is a relatively new measure. Two additional problems that need to be addressed include: (a) the lack of transparency in the scoring and interpretation of the subscales, and (b) the lack of published material in peer-reviewed and widely available outlets. There is no manual; all available material consists of conference presentations, unpublished reports, and a Master's thesis. Although promising, the NEEDS Survey does not have the psychometric evidence available to support its use over more established measures such as the Addiction Severity Index (McLellan, Lubrosky, Woody, & O'Brien, 1980).

REVIEWER'S REFERENCES

McLellan, A. T., Luborsky, L., Woody, G. E., & O'Brien, C. P. (1980). An improved diagnostic evaluation instrument for substance abuse patients: The Addiction Severity Index. *Journal of Nervous and Mental Diseases, 168*, 26–33.

Most, R. (1987). Levels of error in computerised psychological inventories. *Applied Psychology: An International Review, 36*, 375-383.

Butcher, J. N. (1994). Psychological assessment by computer: Potential gains and problems to avoid. *Psychiatric Annals, 24*, 20–24.

Thompson, M. A., & Childers, J. S. (1995, June). *College student norms and concurrent validity for the NEEDS (ADE)*. Presented at the 7th annual conference of the American Psychological Society, New York, NY.

Childers, J. S., Cole, L., Allred, L., Harker, B., Satterwhite, T., Wall, C., & Childers, A. S. (1996, June). *NEEDS (ADE, 1994) adult profiles, norms and concurrent validity*. Presented at the 8th annual conference of the American Psychological Society, San Francisco, CA.

Childers, J. S., Meyers, C., & Wuensch, K. (1996, March). *A domestic violence offender profile using the NEEDS Assessment Instrument (ADE, 1994)*. Presented to the Southeastern Psychological Association, Norfolk, VA.

Meyers, C. L. (1996). *College student norms and concurrent validity for the NEEDS Assessment Instrument*. Unpublished Master's thesis, East Carolina University.

Review of the NEEDS Survey by PAUL MASTRANGELO, Associate Professor, Division of Applied Psychology and Quantitative Methods, University of Baltimore, Baltimore, MD:

The NEEDS Survey is designed to assist probation officers, counselors, and law enforcement officials in evaluating recent offenders (individuals who have broken the law or terms of probation). Although the publisher touts the instrument as being widely used across the country, it is disappointing to see the promotion of a psychodiagnostic tool with (a) no user's manual, (b) no explanation for cutoff scores for diagnoses, and (c) no published research to support its accuracy.

The instrument consists of seven scales that measure risk areas, a cognitive ability scale that can be used to assess low-level mental functioning, and an "attitude" scale that seems like a measure of social desirability, but is reportedly an indicator of how well a person will respond to treatment. Scores are reported using continuous scores that correspond to five categories (no problem, beginning of problem, middle of problem, and severe problem). No percentile scores are provided, and there is no attempt to verify the meaning of the categories.

Evaluating the accuracy of the NEEDS scoring system is nearly impossible. There is very little information provided that supports the most basic psychometric properties, such as reliability and validity. Unlike most instruments, which provide the test user with a manual that includes relevant research findings, the NEEDS Survey comes with a couple of pages of research summaries that provide less information than a standard journal abstract. For this review, the publisher provided copies of recent conference presentations and student theses; however, I received no published research on the NEEDS Survey. In my own search of the PsychInfo and ERIC databases, I found no record of publication when searching for the NEEDS Survey or its predecessor, the SALCE. By relying solely on presentations and student theses to substantiate the instrument's validity and reliability, the publisher offers no research that has been critically reviewed for publication by peers.

The few studies that exist are too simplistic. For example, no study examines the instrument's susceptibility to faking. Much like the diagnostic measure from the 1920s, the Woodworth Personal Data Sheet, the NEEDS Survey is a list of questions that would likely be asked in a clinical interview. Most have a transparent purpose (e.g., Have you ever heard voices that others could not hear or seen things others could not see?). Lacking one-on-one contact with an interviewer, a client may be highly motivated to fake good (or bad) on the paper-and-pencil items. To be successful in this deceit, the test taker must avoid endorsing the items in the "attitude" scale (social desirability), but these items are easily identified. Given the dearth of research on this instrument, the degree to which faking can and does invalidate NEEDS Survey scores remains unknown. However, one of the unpublished studies noted that the SALCE summary score correlates positively with the MMPI-2's F scale ($r = .44$, $p<.01$) and negatively with L ($r = -.19$, $p<.01$) and K ($r = -.32$, $p<.01$). These findings suggest that the SALCE, which is the NEEDS Survey's predecessor, may be easily manipulated by the test taker. Alternatively, a more favorable interpretation can be made based on findings that alcoholics score higher on the F scale in comparison to non-alcoholics (cf. Hoffmann, Loper, & Kammeier, 1974), providing evidence of validity for the SALCE. Clearly, what little psychometric research exists leaves more questions than answers for the validity of the NEEDS Survey.

SUMMARY. In conclusion, the NEEDS Survey has "face validity," but appearances are not empirical evidence. Rather its transparent purpose may detract from the instrument's usefulness. Until more effort is paid to researching the psychometric properties and potential faking effects of the NEEDS Survey, users should be wary of results and seriously consider another instrument.

REVIEWER'S REFERENCE

Hoffmann, H., Loper, R. G., & Kammeier, M. L. (1974). Identifying future alcoholics with MMPI alcoholism scales. *Quarterly Journal of Studies on Alcohol, 35*, 490–498.

[254]

NEO-4.

Purpose: Designed as a four-factor version of the Revised NEO Personality Inventory (12:330).

Population: Ages 17 and older.

Publication Date: 1998.

Scores, 28: Extraversion (Warmth, Gregariousness, Assertiveness, Activity, Excitement-Seeking, Positive Emotions, Total); Openness to Experience (Fantasy, Aesthetics, Feelings, Actions, Ideas, Values, Total); Agreeableness (Trust, Straightforwardness, Altruism, Compliance, Modesty, Tender-Mindedness, Total); Conscientiousness (Competence, Order, Dutifulness, Achievement Striving, Self-Discipline, Deliberation, Total).

Administration: Group or individual.

Forms, 2: Form S (self-reports), Form R (observer ratings).

Price Data, 2001: $219 per comprehensive kit including NEO PI-R manual (101 pages), NEO-4 manual supplement (19 pages), 10 each Form S and Form R reusable item booklets, 25 hand-scorable answer sheets, 25 profile forms, 25 style graph booklets, 25 summary forms, and set of 8 overhead transparencies; $175 per introductory kit including all items in comprehensive kit except the NEO PI-R manual; $28 per 10 reusable item booklets (specify form); $28 per 25 hand-scorable answer sheets; $28 per 25 profile forms; $28 per 25 summary forms; $28 per 25 style graph booklets; $17 per NEO-4 manual supplement; $33 per NEO PI-R professional manual; $30 per set of 8 overhead transparencies.

Time: [25–35] minutes.

Comments: Questionnaire items, scoring keys, and scale norms are identical to those found in the Revised NEO Personality Inventory (NEO PI-R; T5:2218) for the four factors of Extraversion, Openness to Experience, Agreeableness, and Conscientiousness and users are encouraged to consult the professional manual for the NEO PI-R.

Authors: Paul T. Costa and Robert R. McCrae.

Publisher: Psychological Assessment Resources, Inc.

Review of the NEO-4 by THERESA M. BAHNS, Licensed Psychologist, Heartspring, Wichita, KS:

The NEO-4 is a personality inventory created through modification of the Revised NEO Personality Inventory (NEO-PI-R; T5:2218). The authors of the NEO-4 made one major change to the NEO-PI-R to create the new inventory. They removed all items on the Neuroticism scale, which relates to human differences on such traits as anxiety, depression, and vulnerability. The authors note the NEO-4 is intended for use in situations such as career counseling, career development, employee training, and personal growth, where positive traits are of primary interest. The resulting instrument is therefore shorter and, according to the authors, more appropriate for uses with such groups of individuals as those participating in workshops where results are more public.

The NEO-4 is composed entirely of NEO-PI-R items, therefore a brief overview of the NEO-PI-R is provided. The NEO-PI-R is based on the Five-Factor Model of personality. The factors have been named Neuroticism, Extraversion, Openness, Agreeableness, and Conscientiousness. The NEO-PI-R manual presents psychometric data providing support for the five-factor structure. A facet is defined as an individual trait. Intercorrelated traits, or facets, are clustered in domains or factors.

The NEO-PI-R has been used in an extensive number of studies and has been thoroughly critiqued (Botwin, 1995; Juni, 1995). The NEO-4, like the NEO-PI-R, has two versions, S (self-report) and R (other respondent). It consists of 192 items of the original 240 items in the NEO-PI-R. The items are assigned to one of 24 facets from the NEO-PI-R that were grouped on one of six styles. In addition, the authors also created a circle graph to demonstrate the organization of the four factors into six personality "styles": (a) Interests, (b) Interactions, (c) Activity, (d) Attitudes, (e) Learning, and (f) Character. This constitutes the second change between the NEO-PI-R and the NEO-4; however, it is more an elaboration than a change. These styles were described in the NEO-PI-R manual (p. 19) although not highlighted and named as "Styles."

The manual supplement contains a style graph for each of the six styles permitting the assessor to plot a respondent's scores on each graph. The reader is instructed to use the NEO-4 summary sheets to interpret the NEO-PI-R terms of personality styles (again, this would not address N factor information).

The authors note that the four domains assessed by the NEO-4 are very similar to the domains or preferences measured by the Myers Briggs Type Indicator (MBTI). The authors note that several differences between the MBTI and the NEO-4 support the NEO-4 as a superior instrument. These differences include: (a) traits presented as continuous rather than dichotomous

preferences, (b) six specific facets assessed within each domain, and (c) people characterized in terms of six different personality styles instead of a single psychological style or type (p. 10). The authors do not indicate how this was determined, by comparative analysis of items or by some other method.

Because the NEO-4 is simply a shortened version of the NEO-PI-R, most of the criticisms directed toward the NEO-PI-R are still appropriate. In particular, still present are issues involving the use of items: (a) that are negatively worded, (b) that combine two traits in one statement, and (c) that ask the respondent to report on others' perceptions of the respondent.

The review by Juni (1995) identifies several problems with items contained in the NEO-PI-R. Some items labeled as self-report are actually reports of others' perceptions of self; some items contain more than one issue. Other items use qualifiers that would permit many respondents to endorse the item. These criticisms are not addressed in this revision. The reading level was noted to be of concern in the original test and remains a concern with this particular form.

Indeed, it appears that none of the problems identified in the previous edition were addressed with this form with the exception of the criticism regarding use of the test to identify pathology. (Removing the N scale effectively eliminates that possibility.) The authors do not deny the existence of the Neuroticism factor. They simply do not measure it in this new inventory, creating a new measure that is more acceptable in public settings, the value of which is not clear. In the manual for the NEO-PI-R the user is cautioned against the omission of any scales, citing the probability that important relations with other criteria may be missed (p. 4). In other published works, the authors identify the Neuroticism scale as one of the fundamental dimensions of personality (Costa & McCrae, 1998).

The most surprising thing about the NEO-4 is that no new statistical analyses were conducted for the new form. The authors state that the psychometric data from the NEO-PI-R will suffice for the NEO-4. The manual for the NEO-4 is titled "supplement" and directs the reader to the NEO-PI-R manual for information on the rationale for the development of the test, standardization, norms, reliability, and validity. No new standardization data were collected on the new form. The original standardization data from the NEO-

PI-R were not even reanalyzed with the data from the Neuroticism scale eliminated. They do not address issues of how a shorter test, removal of items that are intrusive, and item order effect would affect a participant's performance. There is ample evidence that such factors as test length, item order, and item content influence responses.

The one previous validity study involved participants' evaluation of the accuracy of descriptions of themselves. One would only expect this kind of validity to go up, now that the N scale is removed and the clients can review their personality descriptions without facing their demons.

Because no new standardization work was conducted, the limitations of the earlier norm group have not been remedied. The sample is not particularly well related to the intended population. The norm group compared to the U.S. sample was well matched on age, gender, and race, but better educated. More importantly, the sample was a volunteer group rather than a random sample.

Although the NEO-PI-R is available in other languages (and critiqued for its failure to address response variations across cultures), the NEO-4 is available only in English. Considerable effort would have been required to gather normative ratings across cultures. Therefore, the English-only decision appears to be the wisest course at the present time.

The NEO-4 permits an analysis of six different styles. Limited data are presented to support the grouping of facets on styles (or the pairing of factors into different styles). Two styles have some research, specifically the pairing of Extroversion and Agreeableness and the pairing of Extroversion and Openness to Experience. The other styles are created from all other possible combinations of the four domains, apparently patterned after the procedure followed for the first two, and the meanings of each style created by rational method. Little explanation is provided for the assignment of meaning or interpretation of the facets or items. Additional research is needed to support the pairing of factors into different styles.

It is acceptable to score the test when a respondent omits as many as 32 items (16.7% of total information requested). Individual facet scales with more than 3 missing items are to be interpreted only "with caution." There are 8 items for each facet score so "more than 3" means 50% of the information is missing. This seems to be a very low criterion for interpreting anything beyond a failure to respond for some unexplained reason.

SUMMARY. Two previous criticisms have been addressed by reduction of materials: sensitivity issues inherent in the N scale and recommended use in foreign languages. It appears that the most meaningful work associated with developing a modified test was not completed, however, for the NEO-4.

A potential benefit of the NEO-4 is reduced risk when used in the public sector as an employee-training tool, or as a strategy to engage workers in group projects. Risk is reduced by not making available any negative information that may be derived from the N scale. The NEO-4 may be widely accepted for this specific purpose, but may be more acceptable than it is useful. The authors state that the N factor is largely unrelated to interests, so N scores contribute little to the vocational counseling use of the NEO.

It seems an uncomfortable compromise to eliminate a scale after completing extensive work to demonstrate that the scale, along with the remaining four, provides a comprehensive description of personality. If the Five Factor Model on which each progressive version of the BWI0OU has been developed is indeed an appropriate construct for personality, then four factors are not enough! It seems unlikely that persons seeking vocational guidance will receive adequate information to make best choices without discussion of emotional stability that is assessed only by the N factor. It may have been a better choice to eliminate the manual content correlating N scores to personality disorder indicators and to keep the interpretation for job-related personality-based responses.

This modification of the NEO-PI-R seems akin to NeoClassicism, which has nothing to do with reflecting the ideals of Greek architecture. Holding onto the name NEO has more to do with name recognition than meaning. It would be better named the PPI for Public Personality Inventory, a more palatable, protective personality inventory.

REVIEWER'S REFERENCES

Botwin, M. (1995). [Review of the Revised NEO Personality Inventory.] In J. C. Conoley & J. C. Impara (Eds.), *The twelfth mental measurements yearbook* (pp. 862–863). Lincoln, NE: Buros Institute of Mental Measurements.

Juni, S. (1995). [Review of the Revised NEO Personality Inventory.] In J. C. Conoley & J. C. Impara (Eds.), *The twelfth mental measurements yearbook* (pp. 863–868). Lincoln, NE: Buros Institute of Mental Measurements.

Costa, P. T., Jr., & McCrae R. R. (1998). The Revised NEO Personality Inventory (NEO-PI-R). In S. R. Briggs, J. M. Cheek, & E. M. Donahue (Eds.), *Handbook of adult personality inventories*. New York: Plenum.

Review of the NEO-4 by CARLEN HENINGTON, Associate Professor of Educational Psychology, Mississippi State University, Starkville, MS:

RATIONALE AND PURPOSE. The NEO-4 is the latest version of the NEO Personality Inventories based upon the five-factor model of personality (i.e., emotional, interpersonal, experiential, attitudinal, and motivational). See Botwin, 1995; Hess, 1992; Hogan, 1989; and Juni, 1995 for reviews of the NEO Personality Inventory. This 192-item version, completed in reference to self or another, measures personality traits in four domains (i.e., Extraversion, Openness to Experience, Agreeableness, and Conscientiousness), each composed of six facet scales. Items for the four domains are identical to those contained in the Revised NEO Personality Inventory (NEO PI-R; T5:2218). All items related to the Neuroticism domain have been eliminated. Incidentally, this makes the name "NEO-4" (taken from the first three domains assessed in the original NEO: Neuroticism, Extroversion, and Openness) inaccurate. The authors have also added six personality styles based on combinations of the four domains. These styles are intended to provide insight into an individual's personality and are: (a) Style of Interests (Openness/Extraversion), (b) Style of Activity (Extraversion/Conscientiousness), (c) Style of Attitudes (Openness/Agreeableness), (d) Style of Learning (Openness/Conscientiousness), (e) Style of Character (Agreeableness/Conscientiousness), and (f) Style of Interactions (Extraversion/Agreeableness).

ADMINISTRATION, SCORING, AND INTERPRETATION. Users of the NEO PI-R will find administration and scoring of the NEO-4 profile to be familiar. Because the substantive difference of the NEO-4 is the addition of the six styles, this section will focus only on scoring of this dimension. The NEO-4 includes six two-dimensional style graphs on which T scores of the two relevant domains can be plotted with the vertical axis corresponding to one domain and the horizontal axis corresponding to the other. The graph is divided into quadrants, with 50T as the intersection point of the axes. T scores, ranging from 20 to 80, for the two domains are plotted on the graph. The intersection of the two determines in which quadrant the individual's score for that personality style falls. Each quadrant comes with a short descriptor specific to the style. For example,

within Style of Learning (i.e., Openness and Conscientiousness domains) the quadrants are: high Openness/low Conscientiousness = Dreamers, high Openness/high Conscientiousness = Good Students, low Openness/high Conscientiousness = By-the-Bookers, and low Openness/low Conscientiousness = Reluctant Scholars. Each quadrant also contains a 2–3-sentence profile description.

The graph contains three areas delineated by concentric circles: an inner shaded area in which T scores in both areas fall between 45 and 55, a middle area with T scores between 35 and 65, and an outer area with T scores at the extremes (beyond 35 and 65). The shaded area is undifferentiated (i.e., individuals may be expected to exhibit characteristics of all four quadrants). The most accurate interpretations, according to the authors, can be made for those individuals whose intersecting scores fall close to a line drawn in the middle of a quadrant and within the two outer circles. Interpretation accuracy is also dependent upon the uniformity of the facet scores within each domain.

RELIABILITY AND VALIDITY. No reliability or validity data are presented by the authors in the Manual Supplement for the NEO-4. Reliability and validity reported for the NEO PI-R have been described as excellent, with reliability estimates ranging from .85 to .95 at the domain level and .56 to .90 at the facet level. Consensual agreement between multiple respondents, correlations with other personality inventories (e.g., MBTI, MMPI, CPI), and predictive validity have been presented for earlier versions. However, with the elimination of an entire section of the instrument, these psychometric properties can be expected to change. Little psychometric support is offered for this latest version of the NEO nor for the personality styles. Apparently intended as a validation study, the authors indicate that three groups of individuals (i.e., 28 graduate counseling students, 13 human resource development professionals, 18 graduate I/O students) positively evaluated the NEO-4, relative to other measures, for accuracy of results and clarity of instructions. However, no methodology was reported for this study. The accuracy ratings appear to have been subjective and the comparative data lack reference as to which measures were used. This lack of psychometric information specific to the NEO-4 and the new styles leads to the assumption that there is insufficient support for these personality styles and possibly for the modification of the NEO in general. Although the authors indicate that further research is warranted, this is in reference to modifications of the instruction for specific settings, rather than to this version of the NEO or the six personality styles. It would be appropriate to support the personality styles with a theoretical foundation and to conduct empirically based validity studies of profiles.

SUMMARY. In general, all versions of the NEO are best suited to research purposes and should not be used for diagnostic purposes. This version of the NEO was developed to be used when only four domains are of interest (e.g., during personal growth workshops and employee training seminars, in career development and career counseling). Three major differences between the NEO-4 and the Myers-Briggs Type Indicator (MBTI) are presented, the NEO-4: (a) regards personality traits as continuous dimensions rather than dichotomous preferences, (b) assesses six specific facets in each domain, and (c) characterizes six different personal styles rather than one psychological type. Reliability and validity studies specific to the NEO-4 are inadequate.

There are three important criticisms to be made about the NEO-4. First, the authors indicated in the NEO PI-R manual that users should not make modifications to tap specific domains. Although none of the reasons previously provided were compelling, this is exactly what they have done to their own instrument. Second, the NEO-4 joins an extensive list of instruments with an identical purpose, appears to be more difficult to score, and may not add to the plethora of typological instruments. The authors correctly state that the four global domains are similar to the MBTI preferences "when these are treated as continuous scales." In fact, one reviewer (Juni, 1995) stated that the NEO PI-R does not assess personality dynamics and that this instrument does not significantly differ from other similar instruments. Finally, the apparent strength presented by the authors of the NEO-4 is the addition of the six personality styles. No empirical studies are available to support these styles; the conceptual framework, and its attending theoretical basis, is absent. Rather, the styles are presented as constructs conceptualized from the authors' understanding of relevant research to that construct. Additionally, earlier reviewers argued that the theoretical base of

the NEO PI-R lacks conceptualization. Thus, a conceptually weak instrument has been further weakened by an additional interpretation component without a theoretic base.

REVIEWER'S REFERENCES

Hogan, R. (1989). [Review of the NEO Personality Inventory.] In J. C. Conoley & J. J. Kramer (Eds.), *The tenth mental measurements yearbook* (pp. 546–547). Lincoln, NE: Buros Institute of Mental Measurements.

Hess, A. K. (1992). [Review of the NEO Personality Inventory.] In J. J. Kramer & J. C. Conoley (Eds.), *The eleventh mental measurements yearbook* (pp. 603–605). Lincoln, NE: Buros Institute of Mental Measurements.

Botwin, M. D. (1995). [Review of the Revised NEO Personality Inventory.] In J. C. Conoley & J. C. Impara (Eds.), *The twelfth mental measurements yearbook* (pp. 862–863). Lincoln, NE: Buros Institute of Mental Measurements.

Juni, S. (1995). [Review of the Revised NEO Personality Inventory.] In J. C. Conoley & J. C. Impara (Eds.), *The twelfth mental measurements yearbook* (pp. 863–868). Lincoln, NE: Buros Institute of Mental Measurements.

[255]
Neonatal Behavioral Assessment Scale, 3rd Edition.

Purpose: Designed to evaluate an infant's behavioral and neurological status.

Population: Ages 3 days through 2 months.

Publication Dates: 1973–1995.

Acronym: NBAS.

Scores, 53: (Each item represents a score) in 3 domains: Behavioral (28 items), Supplementary (7 items), Reflex (18 items).

Administration: Individual.

Price Data, 1998: $33.95 per assessment.

Time: (20–30) minutes.

Comments: Previous version entitled Brazelton Neonatal Behavioral Assessment Scale-380; a 53-item rating scale of infant behavior and reflexes; not for use with infants recovering from illness or premature birth; to be administered by clinicians trained in neonatal behavior.

Authors: T. Berry Brazelton and J. Kevin Nugent.

Publisher: Cambridge University Press.

Cross References: See T5:1770 (17 references), T4:321 (9 references), 9:157 (9 references), and T3:311 (31 references); for a review by Anita Miller Sostek, and an excerpted review by Stephen Wolkind of an earlier edition, see 8:208 (15 references).

Review of the Neonatal Behavioral Assessment Scale, 3rd Edition by CAROL M. McGREGOR, Associate Professor of Education, School of Education and Human Development, Brenau University, Gainesville, GA:

The Neonatal Behavioral Assessment Scale (NBAS) was originally designed as a clinical and research tool to assess infant changes in state and behavior as the infant adapts to a new environment outside the uterus. A great deal of information has been gained on the status of newborns since the first edition of the NBAS was published in 1973, and the present version of the instrument has incorporated that knowledge to improve the items. Another important change of focus is the shift from use only as a clinical tool to including use with parents in making them aware of the developmental status of their newborn infants.

The NBAS evaluates a wide range of behaviors in newborns from birth to 2 months of age and takes about 25 minutes to administer. It contains 28 behavioral items scored on a 9-point scale and 18 reflex items scored on a 4-point scale.

The domains assessed include the autonomic, motor, state, and social-interactive systems. In the 1984 second edition of the NBAS, a set of Supplementary Items were added to evaluate the quality of responsiveness of at-risk infants and those seven items have been retained in the current edition.

The Scale is used to study the effects of maternal substance abuse, cross-cultural issues, caesarian deliveries, and other pre- and perinatal concerns. The NBAS requires training for effective and reliable results. Along with its worth as a research instrument, the NBAS would be useful for professionals dealing with at-risk infants, such as neonatoligists, pediatricians, nurses, psychologists, and early intervention specialists.

TEST NORMING. The normative base and standardization for the NBAS is limited or not available. Standardization is made difficult by the wide variance of factors surrounding the newborn, such as levels of obstetric intervention, medication, length of labor, specificity of gestational age, and other pre- and perinatal determiners of the newborn's condition. The authors believe that defining a normal population in a multicultural society is extremely difficult. This instrument, however, has been used over the years in many research projects and is considered a useful tool.

RELIABILITY AND VALIDITY. No statistics are presented in the test manual but numerous studies are cited that have examined test-retest reliability. Because rapid changes in the infant's behaviors are expected and serial administration of the instrument is recommended, test-retest reliability may not be appropriate for this type of assessment instrument. Change rather than stability is measured, and that degree of change will be based on innumerable variables. Although it is difficult to define reliability for the test itself, the authors strongly encourage training in which reliability

among raters is expected to be at a 90% level in order to be considered proficient with the instrument.

Again, no statistics are offered in the manual, but studies are cited that have evaluated the predictive validity of the NBAS as well as other measurements which, when combined with the NBAS, may be good predictors of later developmental outcomes. Various studies of data reduction techniques are quoted for the purpose of making the information gathered manageable and easier to interpret. Several studies have used factor analysis whereas others are of a nonparametric nature. Although content validity is not discussed, the experts used in each of the editions of the NBAS are well-qualified professionals with significant knowledge of newborn behavior. The fact that this instrument is in its third edition speaks to its usability and inferred validity for the purposes for which it was designed.

TEST ADMINISTRATION AND REPORTING. The administration and scoring criteria for each item of the NBAS is carefully described in detail. Many of the items have pictures depicting examples of state levels or handling preferences. There is a sequence of items recommended by the authors, and they fall into seven clusters: Habituation, Social-interactive, Motor System, State Organization, State Regulation, Autonomic System, Supplementary items, and Reflexes. Appendix 1 in the book is the NBAS Scoring Form, which is easy to use and to follow. When being used with parents, it is suggested that they be present for most of the test and then results shared with them following the evaluation. The book includes a section on clinical uses of the NBAS to assist professional groups with guidelines and applications in various settings, scoring procedures, and matters of interpretation.

SUMMARY. The NBAS is a tool for evaluating the quality of expected behaviors and states of the newborn and the infant's ability to adapt to extrauterine life. This edition has expanded its usage beyond a more clinical instrument to one that can be used by a variety of professionals experienced in the care of the neonate. The newborn's behaviors can be assessed for degree of normality and a functional behavioral profile can be produced both for clinical use and for sharing information with parents. Although there are few statistical data available in the book upon which to evaluate this test, several studies are cited that are accessible to the test user. This type of test does not lend itself to traditional statistical analysis due to the variability within subjects as well as environmental conditions. Training accounts for rater reliability and expert preparation provides evidence for content validity. The fact that there are no current, similar well-researched instruments available makes this a viable choice for the purposes for which it is intended.

Review of the Neonatal Behavioral Assessment Scale, 3rd Edition by HOI K. SUEN, Professor of Educational Psychology, Pennsylvania State University, University Park, PA:

This is the third edition of the Neonatal Behavioral Assessment Scale (NBAS), the first edition of which was published in 1973. The purpose of the NBAS is to assess the infant's adjustment to labor, delivery, and the new environment during the first 2 months of life. As with earlier editions, the guiding theory for the NBAS is the belief that the newborn infant is both competent and complexly organized.

Three types of items are included in the scale. These include 28 Behavioral items such as "response to decrement to rattle," and "hand-to-mouth"; 18 Reflex items such as "plantar grasp" and "rooting"; and 7 Supplemental items such as "general irritability" and "quality of alertness." The examiner rates the interaction on each of these items. For the Behavioral and Supplemental items, a 9-point rating scale is used. For the Reflex items, a 4-point scale is used. Explicit rubrics are provided for each of the items.

Items are administered in a predetermined order with some flexibility. The examiner is to administer each item interactively rather than in a static stimulus-response manner. The items are clustered into five "packages" and each package is administered in an established order. Through interaction with the infant, the examiner plays a major role in the assessment process, not just as an observer and scorer. The administration of the items is to progress from minimally intrusive tactile items, which do not require the handling of the baby, toward more stimulating massive vestibular items.

Examiners are required to undergo an extensive and systematic training regimen. The goal of the training is to maximize rating reliability and rater flexibility. Examiners are trained until a high degree of interscorer consistency is attained.

Trained examiners are certified to use the scale and only certified examiners are to use the scale.

The NBAS is primarily designed to be a research tool, although the authors suggest that it is also appropriate for individual clinical assessment. Extensive psychometric and validation analyses have been performed over the past two decades. The results have been somewhat mixed. First, there are only limited and incomplete standardization data, making it difficult to compare between infants or to interpret scores. The reliability studies have primarily relied on the classical test-retest approach. These studies have typically yielded low estimates of score reliability. Given the inherent rapid changes a typical infant undergoes during the first 2 months of life, these are unlikely to be accurate estimates of score reliability. Consequently, the reliability of the scores is essentially unknown. Scores on the scale were also found not to be a good predictor of developmental outcomes in some studies. This may be an indirect indicator of poor score reliability. The authors suggested that a change score derived from several administrations to the same infant during the first 2 months would have been a better indicator of infant adjustment, although no particular procedure was suggested for this purpose.

On the positive side, numerous other validation studies have been conducted that have tended to support the interpretation of the scores as measuring infant adjustment. These studies have tested many different hypotheses in an implicit nomological net. The preponderance of the evidence is in support of the interpretation of the scores as indicators of infant adjustment. These studies have included many studies in each of the following areas: Studies of at-risk infants, studies of relationship with obstetric medication and mode of delivery, studies of relationship with prenatal substance exposure, cross-cultural studies of neonatal behavior, and studies of predictive relationship with parent-child interaction and developmental outcome measures. The NBAS has even been used to study chimpanzee behaviors.

Because the primary goal of the NBAS is to be a research tool, the lack of reliability information is not detrimental. A high reliability would have enhanced the power of statistical analyses in research in general. However, because research typically involves group statistics rather than individual scores, the data used can be expected to have small standard errors of measurement. Given the preponderance of evidence in support of valid interpretation, one can conclude that the scale is an appropriate and meaningful tool for neonatal infant research.

It should be noted that the third edition of the scale was published in 1995. In this edition, some "minor modifications" have been made with the scoring rubric. It appears that all the validation studies have been done with early editions of the NBAS. No study specific to the third edition with the modified scoring was explicitly reported.

SUMMARY. The authors also cited many studies that have purported to demonstrate clinical utility. These studies have accumulated evidence that the use of the NBAS in clinical settings will help to improve maternal confidence and self-esteem, paternal attitudes toward and involvement in caregiving, parent-child interaction, and improved developmental outcome. It is difficult to separate these claims from the construct-related validation studies cited earlier. However, the authors suggested that the scale might serve as a diagnostic screen. This is an explicit claim of clinical utility. Unfortunately, although the authors reported numerous supports for the use of the scale as a research tool, they did not report any evidence that would support the scale as an effective and useful diagnostic or screening tool. Therefore, the NBAS may best be considered a valid tool for researchers. Until evidence of diagnostic and screening utility is demonstrated, it is best not used for individual infant diagnosis, screening for special treatment programs, or to guide intervention.

[256]

NEPSY: A Developmental Neuropsychological Assessment.

Purpose: "Designed to assess neuropsychological development.:
Population: Ages 3–12.
Publication Date: 1998.
Acronym: NEPSY.
Scores, 32: Attention/Executive (Tower, Auditory Attention and Response Set, Visual Attention, Statue, Design Fluency, Knock and Tap, Total), Language (Body Part Naming, Phonological Processing, Speeded Naming, Comprehension of Instructions, Repetition of Nonsense Words, Verbal Fluency, Oromotor Sequences, Total), Sensorimotor (Fingertip Tapping, Imitating Hand Positions, Visuomotor Precision, Manual Motor Sequences, Finger Discrimination, Total), Visuospatial (Design Copying, Arrows, Block Construction, Route Finding, Total), Memory and Learning (Memory for Faces, Memory for Names, Narrative Memory, Sentence Repetition, List Learning, Total).
Administration: Individual.
Forms, 2: Ages 3–4, Ages 5–12.
Price Data, 1999: $499 per complete kit including manual (464 pages), 10 record forms for both Ages 3–4 version and Ages 5–12 version, 10 response booklets for both Ages 3–4 version and Ages 5–12 version, scoring templates and manipulables packaged in a bright nylon bag; $21 per 25 Ages 3–4 response booklets; $26.50 per 25 Ages 5–12 response booklets; $23.50 per 25 Ages 3–4 record forms; $29 per 25 Ages 5–12 record forms; $79 per manual; $93.50 per stimulus booklet; $79 per tower (with 3 balls).
Time: (45–60) minutes for preschool-aged children; (65–120) minutes for school-aged children.
Comments: Also includes optional qualitative behavioral observations and supplemental scores.
Authors: Marit Korkman, Ursula Kirk, and Sally Kemp.
Publisher: The Psychological Corporation.

Review of the NEPSY: A Developmental Neuropsychological Assessment by SANDRA D. HAYNES, Assistant Professor, Department of Human Services, The Metropolitan State College of Denver, Denver, CO:

The shortened title, NEPSY, could easily leave one wondering about the purpose of this test instrument. Even knowledge of the acronym's origin, however, provides scanty information regarding the purpose of the test. NEPSY is an acronym taken from the word neuropsychology, with NE representing neuro and PSY representing psychology. After reviewing or using NEPSY, however, the aim of the test is unmistakable.

NEPSY, as the extended title suggests, was designed to assess neuropsychological development in children ages 3–12, with separate forms for children ages 3–4 and 5–12. The development of a measure specifically for children is a distinction among comprehensive neuropsychological tests that have historically been designed to assess neurological function in adults and then modified for use with children (e.g., the Halstead-Reitan Neuropsychological Test Battery, T5:1164).

The NEPSY was developed for four interrelated purposes. The first purpose is to detect subtle deficiencies that might interfere with a child's learning. Secondly, the NEPSY can be used to detect and clarify the degree to which brain damage or dysfunction affects the capacity to process information in a particular area of neuropsychological functioning or functional domain, such as language. In addition, the NEPSY can be used to determine how this impairment may impact or be impacted by the child's operating capacity in other functional domains. The third purpose is to provide for long-term follow-up of a patient to determine how functioning changes over time and with development. Finally, the NEPSY was designed "to create a reliable and valid instrument for the study of normal and atypical neuropsychological development in preschool and school-age children" (manual, p. 3). Two of these purposes are particularly noteworthy. First, the comparison between functional domains is in line with Luria's theory that emphasizes the interrelatedness of brain operations. This feature of the NEPSY allows the clinician to design more complete treatment plans with attention to all areas that may need remediation. Secondly, attention to continued research into normal and abnormal neuropsychological development is an important contribution of the NEPSY.

The NEPSY assesses the development of five neuropsychological domains: Attention/Executive Functions, Language, Sensorimotor Functions, Visuospatial Processing, and Memory and Learning. Thus the NEPSY focuses on assessment of impairment in the major categories of neuropsychological functioning. Further, functioning in each domain is measured using a graduated series of subtests with six in the Attention/Executive Functions domain, seven in the Language domain, five in the Sensorimotor Functions domain, four in the Visuospatial Processing domain, and five in the Memory and Learning domain for a total of 27 subtests. In addition to a score for each individual subtest, each domain yields a total score for an overall total of 32 scores. Supplemental scores for many subtests can also be calculated in the Attention/Executive Function, Language, Sensorimotor Function, and Memory and Learning domains. Such scores provide additional useful information regarding neuropsychological functioning such as time to completion, response set, immediate and delayed memory, and free versus cued recall. Subtest scores are based on sound neuropsychological theory (especially Luria). Raw scores are converted into scaled scores based on age or, as in the case of some of the Expanded Range subtests, into percentile ranks. The test manual provides information

for forming confidence intervals for each score and a place for listing this information is found on the profile sheet. Such flexibility in score representation and attention to reporting confidence intervals is a strength of this test.

Not all subtests are administered in all cases. Tests to be given depend on the child's age, referral question, needs of the child, time constraints, and setting. Subtests within each domain are divided into core subtests and expanded subtests. Core subtests represent a sample of performance from each domain and were chosen based on the psychometric qualities of the test as well as "clinical considerations." Expanded subtests provide additional information regarding functioning within each of the domains. The test authors recommend administering all core subtests for all individuals to obtain a good overview of function in all five domains. When only core subtests are used the assessment is referred to as a Core assessment. The authors identify three other types of assessment: Expanded, Selective, and Full. Expanded assessment involves the administration of all core subtests and administration of expanded subtests only within a domain in which there has been a previously identified problem. Selective assessment involves the administration of expanded subtests in different domains that may help to explain difficulties noted during administration of NEPSY core subtests. The authors recommend that expanded subtests be selected not only from domains in which the child demonstrated difficulty but also from domains that may be related to the apparent impairment. Thus, selection of expanded subtests should be based on theory and research findings. In this way, further information can be gathered regarding what deficiencies underlie the difficulties noted. Again, flexibility is a plus for this test as is use of multiple-domain assessment. Clinicians are able to measure relative strengths and weaknesses of each child within and across different functional domains. Knowledge of the interrelatedness of strengths and weaknesses can be used to develop the best treatment/education plan. Additionally, the profile approach can provide the clinician with invaluable information that can be easily communicated to others involved in the child's treatment. At first glance, the existence of 27 subtests appears time-consuming. In actuality the test requires only 45 minutes to 2 hours to administer, another strength of this test especially given that it is designed for children.

Although having a number of representative subtests is a strength, it is also the primary difficulty with NEPSY. One must be highly familiar with all subtests to do an efficient administration including knowing where to start within the subtest, when to return to the beginning, and when to stop subtest administration. Given 27 subtests, this can be quite a task. Practice is also necessary as appropriate use of props, hand positions, and written materials is required.

The NEPSY was originally developed and used in Finland (1980 & 1988). After proving successful in that country, the authors set to revising the instrument for use in the United States (1998). Revisions take into account the multicultural nature of the United States population; diversity in geographic, socioeconomic, urban, suburban, and rural living situations; and age at which children begin formal education. Normative data for the U.S. version of the NEPSY were developed using an adequate sample with regard to size and heterogeneity of subjects.

Perhaps the greatest strength of the NEPSY is the comprehensive evaluation of reliability and validity that produced consistently laudable results. Internal consistency was measured via split-half or test-retest reliability measures depending on the nature of the subtest. The average length of time between test administration for test-retest measures was 38 days. The results indicate that scores from most of the NEPSY subtests have moderate to high stability. Scores from tests requiring some degree of subjective scoring (e.g., design copying) were evaluated using interrater reliability and found to have a high degree of reliability.

Criterion-related validity was assessed in a number of published clinical studies using subtests from the 1988 Finnish version of the NEPSY. Most of the subtests in the current NEPSY had a high degree of correspondence to the Finnish version. Additionally more validity studies comparing various clinical groups to matched controls (on the current version) are provided in the NEPSY manual. Content validity was assessed via literature searches, and review by a panel of experts that included pediatric neuropsychologists and school psychologist from around the United States. Finally, construct validity was assessed by comparing the NEPSY to several other tests measuring similar content, including the Wechsler Intelligence Scale for Children, Third Edition and its subscales, the Wechsler Preschool and Primary Scale of Intelligence, Bayley Scales of Infant Development, Second Edition, the Wechsler Individual Achievement Test, the Benton Neuropsychological Tests, and several single neuropsychological tests. The results suggest that the NEPSY exhibits evidence for convergent and discriminant validity.

Perhaps a minor flaw but nonetheless a vexatious aspect of the NEPSY is the set-up of the manual and protocol forms. A great deal of complicated information is put into a paperback manual with no index, making access to information laborious and reading instructions during test administration unwieldy. Additionally, both the manual and protocol forms have poor figure-ground configuration. More attention paid to these details would make administration and scoring a much easier task.

SUMMARY. Overall, the NEPSY appears to be a strong developmental neuropsychological instrument based on sound theory and research that should prove a valuable assessment instrument in the field.

Review of the NEPSY: A Developmental Neuropsychological Assessment by DANIEL C. MILLER, Associate Professor of Psychology, Texas Woman's University, Denton, TX:

In the past, neuropsychological assessment with children has been principally restricted to downward extensions of tests initially designed for adults. The NEPSY has shattered that mold in an elegant fashion. The NEPSY is a comprehensive instrument designed to assess neuropsychological development in preschool and school age children. The authors point out that the NEPSY is unique as compared to other neuropsychological tests because: It is specifically designed for children ages 3–12, the subtests were standardized on a single sample of children, and the test was administered concurrently with other validity measures. The NEPSY was developed with four purposes in mind: (a) a psychometrically sound instrument sensitive to subtle neuropsychological deficits; (b) an instrument that helps evaluate "the effects of brain damage in young children"; (c) an instrument that could be used for "long-term follow-up"; and (d) an instrument for "the study of normal and atypical neuropsychological development in preschool and school-age children" (manual, pp. 2–3).

The NEPSY has a strong theoretical foundation in the Lurian perspective that is reflected in the assessment of a child's neuropsychological status across five functional domains, and in both quantitative and qualitative scoring. The five functional domains include: (a) Attention/Executive Functions, (b) Language, (c) Sensorimotor Functions, (d) Visuospatial Processing, and (e) Memory and Learning. The test consists of 27 subtests used in various combinations based upon the needs of the child and the assessment goals of the examiner. There is a suggested set of Core subtests for children ages 3–4 and 5–12, and a suggested set of Expanded subtests for the same age ranges. The administration times vary from 45–120 minutes based on the number of subtests administered and the age of the child.

The NEPSY comes with an administration, scoring, and interpretation manual, a stimulus booklet, and several manipulatives, all within a carrying case. The NEPSY manual is well organized with an easy-to-use guide indicating what materials are to be used with each subtest. The record forms are also easy to use and conceptually well designed, with discontinuation rules and time guidelines clearly printed. The NEPSY manual provides a variety of scores used in the quantification of a child's neuropsychological status, including standard scores, scaled scores, and percentile ranks. Most subtests also include supplemental scores that allow for intrasubtest pattern analysis of performance strengths and weaknesses. Finally, the qualitative behaviors observed during testing may be compared to the frequency of occurrence within the standardization sample.

From a neurocognitive interpretative perspective, the most useful features of the NEPSY are the different levels of scoring and interpretation, particularly the supplemental scores and qualitative analyses. It may be too easy for some users to report only the standard scores for the Core domains and perhaps the scaled scores of the subtests, without interpreting the pattern of the child's strengths and weaknesses and qualitative behaviors. Potential users of the NEPSY should seek out training specific to the test administration and interpretation, and have some graduate-level training in brain-behavior relationships.

Most NEPSY subtests are easy to administer and score; however, a few of the subtests such as Tower and Auditory Attention and Response Set require practice before actual administration. Currently, the NEPSY must be hand-scored; however, it is hoped that user demand will encourage

the publisher to release a computer-scoring program in the future. [Editor's Note: The publisher has advised in October 1999 that a computer-scoring program was recently released.] The NEPSY manual that accompanies the test kit is excellent, with chapters on the theoretical foundations and history, development and standardization, testing and scoring considerations, subtest administration, psychometric and statistical properties, and interpretation. The appendices of the manual include several useful forms including a Comprehensive Clinical History form, a Handedness Inventory, and an Orientation (a mini mental status exam) interview form. The Handedness Inventory and the Orientation Form have helpful norm tables that compare to the frequencies of the standardization sample.

The NEPSY standardization sample was derived from an adequate, stratified random group of children based on 1995 U.S. Census data. The Core Domain Scores exhibit moderately high internal consistency scores ranging from .69 to .91 and moderate stability coefficients ranging from .67 to .76 across the five domains for the average 5–12 age groups. The authors reported that there is a practice effect evident on the test-retest administrations of the NEPSY, particularly in subtests that measure memory or learning. Actually, there is a fairly strong practice effect across all domains, which increases with age, thus lowering the stability coefficients as age increases.

The NEPSY manual includes an excellent chapter on the validity evidence for the test. The content validity was reviewed twice for possible item biases and face validity by a panel of experts. The patterns of the correlations among the Domain subtests provide good support for the construct validity of the NEPSY, particularly within the Language Domain. Ample evidence for the convergent and divergent validity of the NEPSY's scores is provided in the manual based on correlational studies with the test compared to general measures of cognitive abilities, tests and indicators of achievement, and specific tests of neuropsychological functions. The Validity chapter of the manual also reports on several studies of the NEPSY used with several clinical groups including Attention-Deficit/Hyperactivity Disorder, ADHD with a Learning Disability, Reading Disabled, Language Disorders, Pervasive Developmental Disorders—Autistic Disorder, Fetal Alcohol Syndrome, Traumatic Brain Injury, and

Hearing Impaired. Norms for each clinical group along with matched control sample norms and areas of clinical significance are presented in the manual. Future research needs to better control for clinical group membership and examine potential within-group or subtype differences. For example, the clinical group composed of ADHD with a Learning Disability is too broad given the subtypes of ADHD and LD.

SUMMARY. The NEPSY is a welcome addition to the fields of child clinical neuropsychology and school psychology. The test is rooted in strong theory and prior years of clinical research and is relatively easy to administer and score. Interpretation of scores from the NEPSY will be the challenge to some users. It is recommended that potential users of the test seek out training in the test's administration and score interpretation. Given the good psychometric properties of the NEPSY, the test is ideally suited for research into the neurodevelopmental functioning of school-age children who may have a wide variety of acquired and congenital brain impairments. The clinical validity studies reported in the manual are a good first step in understanding the clinical utility of the test.

[257]
The Neuropsychological Impairment Scale.

Purpose: Designed to screen for "neuropsychological symptoms."
Population: Ages 18 and older.
Publication Date: 1994.
Acronym: NIS.
Scores, 14: Defensiveness, Affective Disturbance, Response Inconsistency, Subjective Distortion Index, Global Measure of Impairment, Total Items Circled, Symptom Intensity Measure, Critical Items, Cognitive Efficiency, Attention, Memory, Frustration Tolerance, Learning-Verbal, Academic Skills.
Administration: Group.
Forms, 3: Self-Report, Observer Report, Senior Interview.
Price Data, 2001: $129.50 per complete kit including 25 self-report AutoScore™ answer forms, 25 observer-report AutoScore™ answer forms, and manual (71 pages) with Senior Interview Supplement and Response Card; $34.50 per 25 self-report AutoScore™ answer forms; $31.50 per 25 observer-report AutoScore™ answer forms; $56 per manual; $85 per Senior Interview kit including 25 Senior Interview AutoScore™ answer forms, 1 manual with Senior Interview Supplement and Response Card, and 25 Mini Mental Status Exam record forms; $34.50 per 25 Se-

nior Interview AutoScore™ answer forms; $15 per 100 Mini Mental Status Exam record forms.
Time: (15–20) minutes.
Comments: Self-Report form and Observer-Report form both utilize the 14 scores listed above, Senior Interview provides Global Measure of Impairment and scores for Defensiveness, Affective Disturbance, and Inconsistency.
Authors: William E. O'Donnell, Clinton B. DeSoto, Janet L. DeSoto, and Don McQ. Reynolds.
Publisher: Western Psychological Services.
Cross References: See T5:1775 (3 references).

Review of The Neuropsychological Impairment Scale by ROBERT A. LEARK, Associate Professor, Psychology Department, Pacific Christian College, Fullerton, CA:

The Neuropsychological Impairment Scale (NIS) is a 95-item self-report paper-and-pencil rating scale. The authors cite that the NIS is a "screening instrument designed to serve as an 'early warning system,' which may be used to identify areas for inquiry, to focus treatment efforts, or to determine service efficacy as patients enter and progress through treatment" (manual, p. 1). The argument by the authors is that "individuals, for a variety of reasons, frequently do not report symptoms or histories that may be diagnostically important" (manual, p. 1). Thus, they sought to create a simple rating scale designed to help the clinician make certain key predictors of brain impairment are not overlooked.

The 95 items consist of 80 neuropsychological symptoms, 10 items measuring affective disturbance, and 5 items measuring test taking attitudes. Each item uses a 5-point scale (not at all, a little bit, moderately, quite a bit, and extremely). The assessment is completed in 15 to 20 minutes (a fifth grade reading level minimum is required). The authors note that the NIS can be used in "nonclinical and clinical" settings with the test used as an "intake measure." The two forms contain the same 95 items; however, only the self-report form has been standardized. The NIS Observer Report form is described as a "nonstandardized way to allow family members or other individuals familiar with the patient to describe how they perceive him or her in terms of neuropsychological symptoms or cognitive impairment" (manual, p. 1). The clinician is encouraged to compare the patient's self-report to the observer's report, even though this comparison is entirely subjective, lacking statistical reliability or validity.

DEVELOPMENT AND STANDARDIZA-
TION OF THE TEST. The impetus for the NIS
derived out of early research and subsequent development of the Cognitive Deficit Scale of the Symptom
Checklist 90—Revised (SCL-90-R; Derogatis, 1977)
by O'Donnell, DeSoto, and Reynolds (1984). This
research led to an initial version (and subsequent
versions) of the NIS, "designed specifically to screen
for symptoms relevant to the differential diagnosis of
neuropsychological impairment on a check list model"
(manual, p. 37).

For the current version of the NIS, the items
were developed primarily with cognitive impaired
patients all who were post acute and involved in
cognitive rehabilitation. From here, a nonclinical
standardization sample was obtained. The standardization sample is stratified by race, gender, and age
based upon the projections from the U.S. Bureau of
Census for 1995.

Mean education level for the sample is 13.5
years (comparable to the mean educational level of
12.7 for people over 25 years of age). The normalized T scores used to interpret the NIS are derived
from this 1,000-person sample. Items were analyzed for age, gender, and race effects. Racial
differences were not found to influence the NIS.
Age effects are noted and corrected by using age
groupings for the test. Gender was found to affect
only the TIC scale, with men endorsing fewer
items than females. A neuropsychiatric sample (N
= 534), was used for comparison purposes. Head-
injured patients comprise the largest sample (N =
134, all post acute), CVAs the second largest (N =
58), and Major Depression (N = 46) the third
largest clinical sample. All clinical patients met
criteria of a DSM-III-R or ICD-9-CM diagnosis.

RELIABILITY AND VALIDITY. Split-half,
internal consistency Cronbach alpha coefficients
and test-retest reliability estimates were the methods used to assess the score reliability. The split-
half approach used the first 40 and last 40 neuropsychological items for the neuropsychiatric sample.
Split-half coefficient of .87 between first and last
40 items is reported. The authors corrected for
attenuation, with a resulting coefficient of .93.

Cronbach alpha internal consistency coefficients for both nonclinical and neuropsychiatric
samples are reported. Nonclinical sample values
for each scale range from .66 (Defensiveness) to
.96 (Global Measure of Impairment), and from
.67 (Defensiveness) to .97 (GMI) for the clinical

sample. Median values for the scales are .79
(nonclinical) and .86 (clinical).

Test-retest reliability was examined by using
four different groups. Group 1 was 25 college-aged
subjects administered the NIS with an average 7-day
interval. Average correlation was .90, ranging from
.64 (DEF) to .98 (GMI). Group 2 included 25
neuropsychiatric outpatients with an average of about
14 days between testing. Average coefficient was .91,
ranging from .78 (DEF) to .94 (TIC and CRIT).
Group 3 used neurological patients administered at
three different times. Average time interval between
Test 1 and Test 2 was 5.44 weeks, and between Test
1 and Test 3 time was 14.36 weeks. Reliability
coefficients were not reported for this study, rather
the mean of the average standardized differences is
given. The data show that the scores decrease over
time. Given the coefficients for 2-week intervals
from Group 2, clearly 5-week and 14-week test-
retest intervals show considerable decrease in item
reporting. Group 4 consisted of 25 outpatient rehabilitation subjects tested about 1 year apart. Interestingly, compared to Group 3 data, the coefficients
show stable item reporting for this sample. Average
coefficient was .83, ranging from .72 (SIM) to .88
(COG and GMI).

The construct validity of the NIS examined
the scale correlations and factor structure of the test.
An interscale correlation table is presented for both
the nonclinical and clinical samples. The GMI scale
correlates the highest with most other scales for both
samples. The factor structure compared both the
nonclinical and clinical samples. There was no distinct item overlap between factors for either sample.
Each sample produced five-factor loading, although
with difference in order. Factor I, the general
factor, contained items from COG, ATT, MEM,
L-V, and ACD scales for both samples. Factor I
accounted for 23% and 29.1% (nonclinical and
clinical respectively) of the explained variance.
Each of the remaining four factors accounted for
no more than 4.4% of the explained variance.

Criterion validity was examined by looking at
both convergent measures, screening effectiveness
and discriminant analysis. Tests sensitive to cognitive
impairment (i.e., WAIS-R subtests and IQ scores,
Halstead-Reitan Battery [HRB] tests and Wechsler
Memory Scale) showed moderate correlation, suggesting that the NIS is sensitive to cognitive impairments. Screening effectiveness (hit rate, sensitivity,
and specificity) compared GMI scores of 70 or

greater to HRB Impairment Indexes of .5 or greater. A hit rate of .80 was achieved for this comparison. Using the same criteria, a sensitivity of .91 and a specificity of .76 was obtained. Discriminant analysis was explored by using 40 head-injured patients, 25 Affective Disorder patients, and 25 nonclinical volunteers. The classification matrix from the discriminant analysis yielded overall 90% correct classification.

SUMMARY. The NIS had reported solid reliability and validity data. As is typical for most WPS products, the manual reports all the data in readable and clearly understandable tables. The scoring of the NIS is relatively easy; the test forms convert to scoring pages. Items are clearly indicated and easy to sum, and a profile page is found within the test form. Thus, administering and scoring the NIS is very easy and self-directed. The manual provides assistance with interpretation. The NIS is probably best used by health clinicians (including psychologists) who have a background in the mental status examination.

Given that the NIS is a self-report screening instrument, this reviewer is somewhat puzzled as to why the instrument would be used. Most clinicians would give a thorough history and mental status examination to each patient, reducing (or replicating at best) the need for the NIS. However, if clinicians have little understanding of how cognitive impairments present themselves in the clinical population, then the use of the NIS makes sense.

REVIEWER'S REFERENCES

Derogatis, L. R. (1977). *SCL-90-R: Administration, scoring & procedures manual-II.* Towson, MD: Clinical Psychometric Research.
O'Donnell, W. E., DeSoto, C. B., & Reynolds, D. M. (1984). A cognitive deficit subscale of the SCL-90-R. *Journal of Clinical Psychology, 40,* 241–246.

[258]
Neuropsychology Behavior and Affect Profile.

Purpose: Designed to assess psychological changes in personality that accompany selective neurological disorders.

Population: Brain-impaired individuals ages 15 and over.

Publication Dates: 1989–1994.

Acronym: NBAP.

Scores, 5: Indifference, Inappropriateness, Pragnosia, Depression, Mania.

Administration: Individual.

Forms, 2: Form S, Form O.

Price Data, 1998: $25 per sampler set including manual ('94, 65 pages); $100 per one-year permission to reproduce up to 200 administrations of the test.

Time: Administration time not reported.

Comments: Form S is self-administered by patients judged capable of accurate self-report; Form O is filled out by significant other when Form S is deemed inappropriate.

Authors: Linda Nelson, Paul Satz, and Louis F. D'Elia.

Publisher: Mind Garden, Inc.

Review of the Neuropsychology Behavior and Affect Profile by SURENDRA P. SINGH, Professor and Clinical Neuropsychologist, College of Education, University of South Florida, Tampa, FL:

The test developers for the Neuropsychology Behavior and Affect Profile (NBAP) have partially succeeded in developing and gathering validity evidence on a test designed to assess neuropsychological behaviors and affects due to brain damage. The test design includes 106 test statement items ("sensitive to behavioral and affective change"), and five scales representing a construct ("commonly associated with neurological disorders," manual, p. 11). In accordance with the theoretical framework utilized by the test developers, the test items were designed to be answered twice by respondents: once as a descriptor of perceived premorbid status and again as an indication of perceived current functioning. According to the test manual, "The respondent circles the 'A' with a pencil if they mostly AGREE with the statement or the 'D' if they mostly DISAGREE" (manual, p. 9). The sum of "agree" responses for five scales and two subscales (Before and Now) yield raw scores that are converted into percentage or *T*-scores. There are two forms: Form S (a self-report measure) and Form O to be completed by an "individual closest to the patient" (manual, p. 6). The test is designed to assess current pattern of emotional response change (Now) associated with focal or lateralized brain dysfunction from premorbid (Before) condition.

Four studies (Nelson et al., 1989) were conducted to examine content validity, internal consistency, stability over time, and discriminant validity. According to these studies, results showed moderate levels of internal consistency across the five scales, with slightly higher coefficients (.68–.82) obtained for present (vs. premorbid) emotional status. High test-retest reliability was found (intraclass correlation coefficients ranged from .92 to .99). Study 4 examined discriminant validity; the instrument differentiated 61 demented subjects from 88 normal elderly controls on the basis of present behavioral affective style.

The item construction and content validation processes appear to meet the statistical validation requirement. However, making judgment regarding complex neuropsychological conditions such as depression, mania, denial, pragnosia, and unusual or bizarre behaviors based on self-rating or perceived rating is a difficult proposition. For example, neuropsychological overt behaviors in themselves such as asthenia and akinesia may appear as depression. In addition, we need to remind ourselves, given the complexity of neuropsychological behaviors affected by complex sets of variabilities, that the statistical significance with all its predictive value in and of itself is not a system of meaningful significance in predicting the neuropsychological effect.

The availability of two forms is an asset. Also, the test design that obtains current and premorbid self-rating or perceived rating by other is indeed unique. The use of the absolute dichotomous judgment response (Agree-Disagree) method in assessing the complex phenomenon is too limiting.

The test manual provides validation data for dementia, stroke, and closed-head-injury patients. NBAP validation data for dorsolateral frontal or orbitofrontal are not yet available. Cross-validation of the NBAP in stroke patients yields coefficients in the range of .70–.82 for "Now" scales and .66–.82 for "Before" scales. Cross-validation studies cited in the manual, except for closed-head injury, provide satisfactory statistics. The manual could use some updating. The missing figures on page 20 are critical and must be included. The test construct and rationale as evolved in the field of neuropsychology, although well documented and cited for the period ending 1994, are in need of updating.

The test developers identified observer variabilities (halo effects, leniency or severity bias, and central tendency/restriction of range) and claimed that rigorous efforts were made to control potential rater inaccuracies. However, these methods for controlling rater inaccuracies are not provided in the manual. It is advised that the test developers include such information in the manual, and consider the use of kappa statistics for ensuring the level of agreement among observers.

Directions for administration and scoring of the test are clear. However, professional requirements for administering and scoring the instru-ment are too liberal, requiring no "formal professional training in neuropsychology and related fields" (manual, p. 8). The test score interpretations are as good as the quality of the test scores. The qualities of test scores are affected by the individual administering the test. Even though the role of the individual administering NBAP is limited, this reviewer considers the test administrator's role as pivotal. Any attempt to marginalize the qualification of test administration is problematic.

The test developers are rightfully cautious regarding the interpretation of strict brain/behavior relationships including making the inferences regarding localized cerebral dysfunction based on the test results. The radiological procedures such as MRI and PET are better instruments to ascertain localized structural brain damage. However, following the structural brain damage diagnoses, the NBAP could be used as a screening device to assess evolving, static, and/or improving emotional response.

The recommendations that the scores are to be interpreted by professionals trained in neuropsychology, clinical psychology, neurology, or related fields, and that "a qualified professional should be available to monitor interpretation of scores in keeping with the Standards for Educational and Psychological Testing (American Psychological Association, 1985)" (manual, p. 8) are appreciated.

SUMMARY. The instrument design has excellent potential. It is advised that in the present form the test should be used as a screening device. The test needs more validation studies, and sound interrater reliability evidence. The test developers may consider the use of the Rasch Model to analyze item response data. The Rasch Model could simplify the task of constructing the parallel test and make the instrument more practical in practice as well as in research.

REVIEWER'S REFERENCE

Nelson, L., Satz, P., Mitrushina, M., Van Gorp, W., Cicchetti, D., Lewis, R., & Van Lancker, D. (1989). Development and validation of the Neuropsychology Behavior and Affect Profile. *Psychological Assessment, 1,* 266–272.

[259]
Noncognitive Variables and Questionnaire.

Purpose: To aid in admission decisions and advising regarding minority college student applicants.
Population: Minority college student applicants.
Publication Dates: 1978–1998.
Acronym: NCQ.

Scores, 8: Positive Self-Concept or Confidence, Realistic Self-Appraisal, Understands and Deals with Racism, Prefers Long-Range Goals to Short-Term or Immediate Needs, Availability of Strong Support Person, Successful Leadership Experience, Demonstrated Community Service, Knowledge Acquired in a Field.
Administration: Group.
Manual: No manual.
Price Data, 1998: $20 per packet including copies of research reports and/or journal article reprints, admission reference list, copy of NCQ questionnaire, and scoring key; $35 per subscription to Counseling Center Report Series for the academic year.
Time: [20] minutes.
Author: William E. Sedlacek.
Publisher: University of Maryland, University Counseling Center.

Review of the Noncognitive Variables and Questionnaire by GREGORY J. MARCHANT, Associate Professor, Educational Psychology, Ball State University, Muncie, IN:

A large number of factors contribute to the success of students at college. Although standardized college aptitude tests are accepted predictors of achievement, other variables obviously play a role in student success. Even the Educational Testing Service (1999), producers of the Scholastic Aptitude Test (SAT; T5:592), conducted research on "strivers," students who succeed beyond what their SAT scores might suggest. This research looked at background information of applicants to provide a "context" to be considered when evaluating a candidate's SAT scores. William Sedlacek explored noncognitive variables that contribute to college student success for two decades. The Noncognitive Questionnaire (NCQ) was the result of some of his early research, and he continued to explore college admissions, success, and retention along with the predictive ability of his instrument. His involvement with the NCQ and minority admissions decisions was evident in the 33 articles included in the packet of materials accompanying the instrument. Also included is a scoring key and profiles of high and low scorers.

The Noncognitive Questionnaire or Supplementary Admissions Questionnaire II is a two-page instrument designed to provide information regarding qualities that might impact success at college for applicants and students. Of the 29 items, 6 request demographic information; 2 require choosing a response concerning predicted lifetime level of education and potential reasons for dropping out of college; 3 ask for lists of goals, accomplishments, and high school and community involvement; and 18 are statements requiring a response on a Likert-type agreement scale (13 of which are reverse coded). Some of the wording in the items is unclear. Item 8 asks to list "goals that you have for yourself right now" and then suggests that responses like "to become president of a Fortune 500 company" should receive the highest rating, even though a respondent might consider the response outside of the "right now" time frame. Item 9 asks what the likely cause would be if the student were to leave the university without a degree, then the only response receiving the highest rating is "absolutely certain that I will obtain a degree" (all other responses including no response receive a score of a 2). The phrase in Item 16, "you get it in the neck," may also be confusing to some.

Tracey and Sedlacek (1984a) reported good construct validity of the scales and stated that the factor structure was "similar" for both racial groups (Blacks and Whites). However, the items in the factors (reported only for the Black sample) did not always match the items in the established scales, and 5 of the 23 items had loadings less than .30. Depending on how dissimilar the factor structure was, it may be inappropriate to use the scales across racial groups. It was curious that the following items were included on the NCQ Understands and Deals with Racism scale: (Item 18) I expect to have a harder time than most students UMCP [University of Maryland, College Park]; (Item 26) If course tutoring is made available on campus at no cost, I would attend regularly; (Item 27) I want a chance to prove myself academically. Face validity issues arise when interpretation of the scales based on their title and description may be inappropriate considering the nature of some of the items.

The predictive validity of scores from the instrument was tested by using multiple regression methods to predict college GPA and continued enrollment. However, in some studies the authors appear to use multiple regression equations including all of the individual items, selected items based on previous regressions, all of the scales, and selected scales based on stepwise regression. In one study (Tracey & Sedlacek, 1984b) 14 of the 23 individual items were identified as significant predictors; but it was not clear whether all of the individual items or just the significant items were then used to predict success. Scores from the instrument appeared to be a fair predictor of GPA (R = .29 to .48) and a good predictor of continued enrollment for the Black sample. However, because the multiple regression equation used individual items, which weights each item to maximize its predictive ability, it would be impossible to determine whether the scales or the total instrument as a whole would be significant predictors of achievement (without the unique item weightings). None of the studies reviewed used the total NCQ score as a predictor of GPA.

Another study (Tracey & Sedlacek, 1984a) looked at the NCQ scales prediction of GPA by comparing ridge regression to ordinary least squares regression (OLS), but failed to report the significance of the multiple regressions (OLS total sample N = 825, Whites R = .39, Black R = .03, Total R = .37). This study explored the cross validation of the instrument using the two methods. For both racial groups and the total the R rose considerably from the small sample (n = 30 to 50, R = .67 to .61) to the total sample indicated above. In discussing the poor cross validation and failure of ridge regression to correct it, the authors suggested that the problems could be due in part to the fact "the NCQ factors may not have the well developed psychometric properties typically associated with measures like SAT scores" (Tracey & Sedlacek, 1984a, p. 349).

A manual was not included with the instrument. Therefore, there were no directions for administration, there was no synthesis of studies identifying reliability nor validity, nor were there norms for the instrument. To his credit, Sedlacek has done extensive analysis of his instrument with some fairly positive results. For instance, test-retest reliability of .85 (however, only after 2 weeks) and interrater reliability on open-ended items r = .83 to 1.00 (however, the N was only 18); and a principal components factor analysis showed the NCQ variables to be relatively independent of one another (Tracey & Sedlacek, 1984). Sedlacek should be commended for his research efforts related to the use of noncognitive variables as predictors of college student success; however, the NCQ does not appear to have the psychometric properties to warrant its use in anything other than research. It would be inappropriate to use the instrument as a whole, its scales, or individual items as the basis for admission decisions without further research and development.

REVIEWER'S REFERENCES

Tracey, T. J., & Sedlacek, W. E. (1984a). Noncognitive variables in predicting academic success by race. *Measurement and Evaluation in Guidance, 16*(4), 171–178.
Tracey, T. J., & Sedlacek, W. E. (1984b). Using ridge regression with noncognitive variables by race in admissions. *College and University, 59*, 345–350.
Educational Testing Service. (1999, September). *ETS issues clarification on "strivers" research study.* Press release retrieved April 4, 2000 from the World Wide Web: http://www.ets.org/aboutets/news/newswire.html

Review of the Noncognitive Variables and Questionnaire by LISA F. SMITH, Assistant Professor, Psychology Department, Kean University, Union, NJ:

The Noncognitive Variables and Questionnaire (NCQ) is intended to support student selection and retention, in particular for minority students. The author maintains that traditional criteria and procedures for college admissions have been validated using Caucasian samples, and are therefore inappropriate for other groups. He further maintains that noncognitive variables are more predictive of academic success for minority students than is academic ability alone. The NCQ assesses eight noncognitive variables purported to be related to academic success for all groups, but particularly for minority students. These variables are (a) Positive Self-Concept or Confidence, (b) Realistic Self-Appraisal, (c) Understands and Deals with Racism, (d) Prefers Long-Range Goals to Short-Term or Immediate Needs, (e) Availability of Strong Support Person, (f) Successful Leadership Experience, (g) Demonstrated Community, and (h) Knowledge Acquired in a Field.

Although no test manual is supplied, the test materials provide a description for each of the noncognitive variables, profiles for high and low scorers for each noncognitive variable, a scoring key with a worksheet, and a summary of item numbers pertaining to each noncognitive variable.

TEST DESCRIPTION AND SCORING. The NCQ is made up of 29 items: 4 demographic items (social security number, sex, age, and race); 2 items requesting father's and mother's occupations; 2 items pertaining to educational expectations and retention expectations; 2 open-ended items asking the student to list three personal goals and 3 "things that you are proud of having done;" 18 Likert-type items on personal college expectations, support systems, and self-assessment; and a final item requesting a list of "offices held and/or groups belonged to in high school or your community."

The scoring key is straightforward and clearly written. Detailed instructions are given for scoring all non-Likert items. Directions (+ or -) are provided for scoring the Likert items.

NCQ NORMS. To assist in the interpretation and application of the scores obtained, high and low profiles are described for each of the noncognitive variables. No norming data on the development of these profiles are provided in the supporting documentation.

RELIABILITY. Adequate reliability data are provided in the supporting materials. A reliability study on all but the last noncognitive variable (knowledge acquired in a field) used a sample of 1,529 entering freshmen in 1979 ($n = 1,339$ Caucasian; $n = 190$ African American). Two-week test-retest correlations ($N = 18$) for the Likert-type items ranged from .70 to .94, with a median of .85. Interrater reliabilities for the open-ended items ranged from $r = .83$ (academic goals) to $r = 1.00$ (number of activities reported).

VALIDITY. Evidence of the validity of the NCQ is provided in a variety of studies conducted by the author and others. Factor analytic studies support the argument for the structure of the NCQ. A series of studies of the predictive validity of the NCQ have been conducted and published in journal articles. In this research, the NCQ has been related to college success for samples of white and black students. Results are generally supportive of the validity of the NCQ, sometimes strongly so. The NCQ typically adds power to regressions predicting grade-point average and graduation rate. However, there do not appear to be any cross-validation studies of the NCQ. Different factors turn out to be predictive of performance with different samples, making the use of the NCQ for admissions purposes somewhat problematical. Generally speaking, however, the efforts of the author to validate the measure are admirable.

Additional studies on various groups (e.g., international students, Asian American students, medical students, pharmaceutical students, student athletes) also yielded evidence of predictive validity.

SUMMARY. The NCQ appears to be a technically sound instrument for assisting in admission decisions and for predicting success in college, particularly for minority students. The questionnaire as written pertains specifically to the University of Maryland—College Park, but can be easily modified. Overall, when used in conjunction with other, more traditional criteria, the NCQ has the potential to enhance admissions practices in general, and assist in eliminating bias associated with admission decisions for minority students.

[260]
Occupational Stress Inventory—Revised Edition.

Purpose: Designed as a "measure of three dimensions of occupational adjustment: occupational stress, psychological strain, and coping resources."

Population: Age 18 years and over.

Publication Dates: 1981–1998.

Acronym: OSI-R.

Scores, 14: Occupational Roles Questionnaire (Role Overload, Role Insufficiency, Role Ambiguity, Role Boundary, Responsibility, Physical Environment); Personal Strain Questionnaire (Vocational Strain, Psychological Strain, Interpersonal Strain, Physical Strain); Personal Resources Questionnaire (Recreation, Self-Care, Social Support, Rational Cognitive Coping).

Administration: Individual or group.

Price Data: Available from publisher.

Time: (30) minutes.

Comments: Self-administered.

Author: Samuel H. Osipow.

Publisher: Psychological Assessment Resources, Inc.

Cross References: See T5:1825 (7 references) and T4:1870 (4 references); for reviews by Mary Ann Bunda and Larry Cochran of an earlier edition, see 11:269 (1 reference).

Review of the Occupational Stress Inventory— Revised Edition by PATRICIA K. FREITAG, Assistant Professor of Education Research, The George Washington University, Washington, DC:

The Occupational Stress Inventory—Revised Edition (OSI-R) is designed to measure Occupational Roles, Psychological Strain, and an employee's Personal Resources for coping with stress in the workplace. Each domain is divided into multiple subscales, consisting of 10 items each, that may provide additional diagnostic information. Occupational Roles includes: Role Overload (RO), Role Insufficiency (RI), Role Ambiguity (RA), Role Boundary (RB), Responsibility (R), and Physical Environment (PE); Psychological Strain has four component subscales: Vocational Strain (VS), Psychological Strain (PSY), Interpersonal Strain (IS), and Physical Strain (PHS); and Personal Resources includes subscales for Recreation (RE), Self-Care (SC), Social Support (SS), and Rational/Cognitive Coping (RC). The measure is specifically designed to assess individuals across a broad spectrum of work environments. The author suggests that this instrument could be used as a screening tool by employers to assess employees or "to identify the sources of stress and symptoms of strain prevalent in a given occupational unit or group" (manual, p. 2). There is some evidence that this instrument could provide data on outcomes from specific treatments or interventions. Programs aimed at reducing workplace stress or increasing the effective use of coping strategies for individuals or employee groups may benefit from using this instrument as a posttest measure. Similarly, specific interventions for individuals may be planned using the diagnostic information available in this inventory. However, some of the subscales may not be reliable enough to infer that changes in scores can be ascribed specifically to the intervention.

The instrument is designed for use with employed men and women, ages 18 and older. Data reported show no significant difference between males and females in subscale scores of each domain. The author cautions against interpreting total scores in any domain of the instrument, in favor of using the more detailed and accurate information provided by the subscale scores. In addition, it is recommended that the OSI-R be used in combination with other measures of occupational interests for a more comprehensive assessment of work-related stresses, strains, and resources.

In general, the items for the Organizational Roles domain are more complex than those of the Psychological Strain questionnaire in terms of length and the expression of feelings rather than specific behaviors. The questionnaires clearly group related items. This makes the forms easy to read and makes corresponding responses easily encoded on the scan sheets and transferred to the profile form provided. However, this format may also lead the respondent to indicate similar frequency ratings for related questions. This opens the possibility of some self-report bias and may have influenced factor loadings. In some cases items that seem to have similar function appear in several different scales. For example: "I'm good at my job," "I feel good about the work I do," and "My job fits my skills and interests" each appear in different sections of the questionnaire. Though these items may be used to provide an internal consistency check they also cause some overlap between scales. Future studies might look more specifically at the factor structure of the instrument overall and within the Organizational Roles domain.

The author asserts that: "This revision updates and provides normative data for both gender and occupation categories (i.e., executive, professional, technical, administrative support, public service/safety, and agricultural/production/laborer); it also modifies several existing items and generates new ones for each of the three OSI domains" (manual, p. 1). However, sample sizes used to establish norms vary widely and thus may not adequately represent the various occupation categories and levels. Specifically, marketing and agricultural occupations are underrepresented in the normative sample and may not be adequate norms for comparison. The scale score norms may not be as stable within some occupations at specific occupational levels.

Internal reliability estimates are high for each domain of the instrument and also generally good for the individual scales (range .70–.89) and are similar to those reported for the original Occupational Stress Inventory. Intercorrelations among the total questionnaire scores and the 14 scales align as expected with the underlying theory of the instrument. These correlations also suggest that each scale is important to the overall instrument construct. Factor analyses results also confirm the multiple dimensions of the stress, strain, and resource domains.

One weakness in this instrument is that each item depends on the respondent's own definition/perception of the workplace in responding. The questions are posed in the general form and thus each respondent must characterize their own role identity, think of context-specific sources of stress and strain, and rate the frequency of their own habits. Consequently, the use of this instrument for diagnosis, reflection, and supervision depends on shared meanings between the respondent and instrument scorer. The author cautions that this instrument "should not be used for the purposes of selection, retention, promotion, job performance evaluation, or compensation" (manual, p. 5).

The presentation of several specific cases of employee scores, analyses, and interpretations in the OSI-R Professional Manual illustrate how the author anticipates this instrument can be effectively used. These cases bring out the strength of the diagnostic information embedded in the relationships between the various scores and in a variety of work environments. The underlying theory provides considerable explanatory power and the characterizations of attributes of persons with high scores on each scale are provided. It would be helpful to the additional cases developed for the use of this instrument with work groups and/or specific occupations and occupation levels. The extensive references to studies and investigators who have worked with this instrument (and the previous OSI) attest to its functional utility in the workplace.

SUMMARY. The results from validity and reliability analyses of this revised version have improved specification of this instrument and established its general utility. Broader use of this instrument will make it possible to overcome these limitations. In the future it would be most helpful to provide more accurate norms for particular occupations and occupational levels by gender. Overall the instrument and scale scores show good correspondence with scores on other instruments that are valid measures of stress, strain, or resources in the employed adult population.

Review of the Occupational Stress Inventory—Revised Edition by ROBERT WALL, Professor of Reading, Special Education and Instructional Technology, Towson State University, Towson, MD:

The Occupational Stress Inventory—Revised Edition (OSI-R) is a refinement of the Occupational Stress Inventory that was copyrighted in 1981. There are 140 items distributed among 14 scales of 10 items each. These 14 scales address various aspects of occupational role stress, personal response to workplace stress, and the individual's coping resources.

In the revised version, approximately 20% of the items were changed (manual, p. 23). The internal consistency coefficients for the OSI-R were based on the 983 members of the norming sample. These coefficients ranged from .70 to .89. The two studies cited correlated responses of the OSI with the OSI-R based on data from 62 Air Force cadets and 45 Highway Patrol cadets. In general, the factor analysis data reported supports the current assignment of the items to the various scales.

The overwhelming majority of the more than 50 studies cited in the manual evaluating the instrument's psychometric properties are based on the original OSI, not the OSI-R. Anyone using the OSI-R will need to decide if the changes in the OSI-R require cautious application of studies based on the earlier version of the inventory. Many may decide to conduct their own validity and reliability studies.

In addition, prospective test users must determine if the OSI-R's norming sample and objec-tives are appropriate for their needs. The OSI-R norms were based on a sample of men and women, 73% with more than a high school degree. In the OSI-R norming sample, 75% were classified as belonging to the executive, public service/safety, professional, and administrative support occupa-tions. When compared to census data the execu-tive, administrative support, and public service/safety groups were overrepresented.

The author presents an extensive listing of the relationship between OSI scores and various criterion variables. Unfortunately for the reader, there is little information concerning sample sizes and statistical significance of the findings. Many of the correlations reported are too small to use in making individual predictions or decisions.

SUMMARY. The directions for the admin-istration of the test seem well thought out with appropriate examples and suggestions. The dis-cussion for how the inventory might be used and the case studies are useful. The author quite appropriately lists the needs for further valida-tion studies. This inventory could provide a good beginning point for discussing an individual's perceived stress and coping skills. However, given the concerns expressed about the reliability and validity information concerning this instrument, it should not be the only source of data.

[261]
Occupational Type Profile.

Purpose: Designed to measure individual's prefer-ences related to the manner in which they acquire information and make decisions based on that informa-tion.

Population: Adults.

Publication Date: 1991.

Scores, 5: Extraversion/Introversion, Sensing/Intu-ition, Thinking/Feeling, Judgement/Perception, Un-certainty.

Administration: Individual or group.

Price Data: Available from publisher.

Time: (20) minutes.

Comments: Computer administration and scoring available.

Author: Selby MillSmith Ltd.

Publisher: Selby MillSmith Ltd. [England].

Review of the Occupational Type Profile by STEVEN J. LINDNER, Industrial/Organizational Psychologist, The WorkPlace Group, Inc., Morristown, NJ:

The Occupational Type Profile assesses five characteristics of individual personality: Extraversion/Introversion, Sensing/Intuition, Thinking/Feeling, Judgement/Perception, and Uncertainty. Paper-and-pencil and computerized administration of the profile are available. Question booklets are reusable and answer sheets are scored by sending them directly to the publisher or by using Selby MillSmith's ASSESSOR system. Computerized administration requires the ASSESSOR system and training in its use.

The Occupational Type Profile contains 88 multiple-choice questions. Each of these questions was derived by applying Jung's theory of personality type to organizational behavior. Questions on the Profile refer to "practices and behaviors common to work" and are written so that it can "be appropriately administered to all types of personnel" (Manual & User Guide, p. 2).

Individuals' responses on the Occupational Type profile generate two reports: a score chart and a full narrative. The score chart shows raw and sten scores, and graphically illustrates individuals' standing on the five characteristics measured. Common to all Jungian scales, scores identify an individual's personality as one of 16 possible types. The full narrative report describes a person's "preferred decision making, thinking and managerial style" with respect to his or her personality type (Sample Reports, p. 1).

Those who use the Occupational Type Profile are cautioned about its established norms and reported reliability and validity. The normative data available in the Manual & User Guide and the ASSESSOR system are based on 67 individuals who ranged in age from 22 to 60 years old, held managerial jobs, and were from the United Kingdom. This normative sample poorly represents the general population. In addition to more extensive normative data, separate norms for, at least, gender and nationality are needed.

In order for the Occupational Type Profile to more accurately identify a person's standing on a personality characteristic and predict how those characteristics are likely to be manifested on the job, gender and culture specific norms are needed. Research has shown that (a) males and females have nonequivalent ranges of personality characteristics (McCrae & Costa, 1987) and (b) culture influences how personality characteristics are demonstrated in everyday life (Digman, 1990). There-

fore, describing and predicting the effects of individuals' personality characteristics on organizational decision making, thinking, and management is partly a function of their gender and culture.

With respect to scores from the Profile, two indices are presented: test-retest and internal consistency. The Profile's test-retest reliability was assessed using scores from eight people who took the test twice with an average interval of 2.5 weeks between the first and second testing. The Profile's internal consistency was assessed using the scores of 50 people. High levels of test-retest reliability ($r > .9$ for all scales except Uncertainty) and internal consistency ($r > .7$) were found.

The validity of four of the five characteristic scores assessed by the Occupational Type Profile was evaluated by correlating individual scores on these characteristics with their scores on the Myers-Briggs Type Indicator, a well-respected measure of the same characteristics. Correlations between like characteristics on these two measures were higher ($.72 > r < .50$) than the correlations between unlike characteristics ($.47 > r < .00$). This suggests that the Occupational Type Profile assessed the same characteristics as the Myers-Briggs Type Indicator. This pattern of correlations shows that scores from the profile have moderate and acceptable levels of validity for the characteristics Extraversion/Introversion, Sensing/Intuition, Thinking/Feeling, and Judgment/Perception (Gatewood & Feild, 1990).

Unique to instruments based on Jung's personality theory is the Occupational Type Profile's fifth characteristic, Uncertainty. Unlike the other four characteristics assessed by the Profile, no specific questions were written to assess Uncertainty. Uncertainty is determined by the "number of individual items for which a person has selected the middle response" (Manual & User Guide, p. 10). Interpreting the Uncertainty score is problematic because several possible interpretations could be applied. High scores on the Uncertainty scale could mean that an individual did not understand the question, does not know himself or herself well enough to answer, refused to accurately report his or her thinking or behavioral preference, or does not have a preferred behavioral or thinking style. When the true meaning of a scale cannot be determined it means that the scale lacks construct validity. The publishers of the

Profile are encouraged to further define the Uncertainty scale and show evidence of what it truly measures. In the interim, those who use the Profile are cautioned about using the Uncertainty scale to describe individuals' personalities or make predictions about their behaviors and thinking styles.

Overall, the number of individuals used to investigate the reliability and validity of scores from the Occupational Type Profile was inadequate. In addition, the extent to which the reported reliability and validity evidence could be due to chance is unknown because the statistical significance of reliability and validity coefficients was not reported. The lack of reliability and validity evidence also makes the narrative report, which the Profile generates, of questionable accuracy. The descriptions and predictions made of individuals in the narrative report assume that the Profile has accurately identified personality type. This assumption cannot be made given the validity data presented. In order to demonstrate that the Occupational Type Profile provides reliable and valid measures of individual personality, reliability and validity coefficients need to be replicated on larger samples, and statistical significance needs to be reported.

SUMMARY. The Occupational Type Profile is an alternative measure to the Myers-Briggs Type Indicator (251). Its desirable features are the relevance of its items to organizational behavior, the ease with which it can be administered, and the availability of computerized administration and scoring. However, without more convincing reliability and validity evidence and norms that better represent the general population's organizational behaviors, the Profile has limited usefulness and questionable accuracy. Those who choose to use the Occupational Type Profile will need to gather validity evidence and establish their own norms for the Profile in order to use it to accurately describe individuals' personality types and make predictions of how individuals' characteristics are likely to be manifested in the work place.

REVIEWER'S REFERENCES

McCrae, R. R., & Costa, P. T., Jr. (1987). Validation of the five-factor model of personality across instruments and observers. *Journal of Personality and Social Psychology, 52,* 81–90.

Digman, J. (1990). Personality structure: Emergence of the five-factor model. In M. R. Rosenzweig & L. W. Porter (Eds.), *Annual review of psychology* (vol. 41; pp. 417–440). Palo Alto, CA: Annual Reviews Inc.

Gatewood, R. D., & Feild, H. S. (1990). *Human resource selection* (2nd ed.). Orlando, FL: The Dryden Press.

[262]

Oetting Michaels Anchored Ratings for Therapists.

Purpose: Designed for use by supervisors to rate therapists in training.

Population: Graduate students and interns in counseling and clinical training.

Publication Date: 1989.

Acronym: OMART.

Scores: Developmental ratings on 34 dimensions of therapist effectiveness: Interviewing (Relationship with the Client, Dealing with Therapist Identification Issues, Personal Style, Exploration of Client Goals, Exploration of Issues, Exploration of Feelings, Time During the Interview, Responsiveness to Nonverbal Cues, Use of Language), Conceptualization of Therapy (Knowledge of Personality Theory, Applying Psychotherapy Theory, Knowledge of DSM III, Ability to Analyze Course of Therapy, Treatment Plans), Reaction to Supervision (Interaction During Supervision, Openness to Feedback, Confidence, Self Evaluation), Sensitivity to Client Issues (Dealing with Dependency, Dealing with Client/Therapist Sexual Feelings, Awareness of Environmental Influences, Sensitivity to Cultural Differences, Sensitivity to Sex-Role Stereotypes, Handling of Conflicts of Client/Therapist Values), Trainee Issues (Management of Personal Stress, Interference Because of Therapist's Adjustment Problems, Self-Direction of Professional Development), Other (Dealing with Ambiguity, Therapist's Attitudes to Authority, Writing Reports, General Test Interpretation, Intellective Assessment, Appropriate Handling of Sexual Material).

Administration: Individual.

Price Data: Available from publisher (license to reproduce provided for Ph.D.s or Ed.D.s).

Time: [20–30] minutes.

Comments: Completed by supervisor.

Authors: E. R. Oetting and Laurie Michaels.

Publisher: E. R. Oetting, Colorado State University.

Review of the Oetting Michaels Anchored Ratings for Therapists by JOHN S. GEISLER, Professor, College of Education, Western Michigan University, Kalamazoo, MI:

The Oetting Michaels Anchored Ratings for Therapists (OMART) is a series of 34 factors/scales developed for the purpose of providing supervisors with a framework to assess their supervisee's progress and development. The OMART is neither copyrighted nor dated. The 34 scales are grouped into six categories: (a) Interviewing (9 items), (b) Conceptualization of Therapy (5 items), (c) Reaction to Supervision (5 items),

(d) Sensitivity to Client Issues (6 items), (e) Trainee Issues (3 items), and (f) Other (including Dealing with Ambiguity, Writing Reports, Intellective Assessment, etc.) (6 items). No mention is made about the origin, justification, rationale, or development of the 34 scales. There is no evidence that they were developed as a result of either a survey of supervision literature or empirical research.

Supervisees' behaviors/performance are assessed by two methods: (a) behavioral descriptions and (b) a Likert-type scale (0 to 10). The two assessment methods are presented on opposing pages of a spiral-bound booklet. On the left page supervisors are to write out descriptions of typical behaviors (relating to one of the 34 scales) displayed by supervisees. The right hand page is a vertical Likert-type scale with accompanying statements that are to be used as guides for scoring. For example, under the Dealing with Ambiguity scale, the five guideline statements range from "Wants the 'right' answers from authority" to "Attacks very complex problems with pleasure. When unresolved, is comfortably able to let the problem 'ripen.'" Directions are provided for both methods. The introductory statement for scoring on the second page is somewhat interesting: "Rate your description of the scale." It might better read: "Rate your supervisee's performance on this factor (or scale)." It would be expected that within each of the 10 Likert-type scale sections there would be 10 descriptive statements. Such is not the case. The number of descriptive statements used as guidelines in scoring each scale range from five to seven across the 34 scales. And they are not equally spaced across the 11 points of the scales. In the example previously stated, the lowest rated descriptive phrase, "Wants the 'right' answers from authority" is physically placed near Point 3 on the scale and the phrase "Attacks very complex problems with pleasure. When unresolved, is comfortably able to let the problem 'ripen,'" is placed between Likert points 8 and 9. No phrases are lower or higher than these two, respectively.

The rationale for the development of the descriptive phrases is not provided nor is there any rationale for the placement of the phrases on the scale. Some of the descriptive phrases lack clarity, are dated, or are quaint. In the Writing for Reports scale the following descriptions of a supervisee's behavior receives a Likert score of 3+:

"Much of the material is 'Aunt Fanny'—accurate, but if your Aunt Fanny were in that setting the same things could be said about her." On the Knowledge of DSM III scale the following descriptive phrase would receive a score of about 2: "Never heard of the DSM II or III." Not only is the phrase dated, but a score of 2 (on a scale of 0 to 10) is most generous.

One scale deserves special mention: Dealing with Client/Therapist Sexual Feelings. This is the first of two scales dealing with sexual issues. Certainly these are issues that arise during the course of some therapy sessions and are a legitimate concern for therapist/supervisees and supervisors. However, these are two distinct and separate issues: (a) dealing with clients' sexual feelings and (b) dealing with the therapist's sexual feelings. They may have an impact, one upon the other, but the descriptive phrases used to judge the behaviors of the therapist have them lumped together (e.g., "Comfortable, direct and tactful in discussing client/therapist sexual feelings on both sides"). When scoring the therapist's performance on this scale a legitimate question arises, namely, is it the manner in which the supervisee/therapist deals with the client's sexual feelings, or is it the therapist's sexual feelings that are of concern, or both? No guidance is provided on this matter.

No reliability, validity, or field testing data were reported. There is no evidence that the instrument has been subjected to any form of factor analysis. There are no norm groups and there is no indication that reactions or feedback from practitioners was sought. No technical information of any type was provided. In their introductory remarks the authors suggest that they had hoped to have data available at a later date to assist in developing performance standards. No such data are available, yet it would appear that a significant amount of time has passed since the publication of the original instrument and that if such data were available they could have been provided.

SUMMARY. The OMART cannot be considered as an adequate, acceptable instrument for supervisee training. With no rationale provided for either scale development or scoring, with no technical data available to assess reliability and validity, with questionable placement and development of descriptive behavior/skill statements, the OMART must be considered an experimental instrument with extremely limited usefulness.

[263]
Ohio Functional Assessment Battery: Standardized Tests for Leisure and Living Skills.

Purpose: Designed to determine the functional level of a client's abilities in order to develop measurable treatment objectives.

Population: Adults experiencing slight to profound impairment in cognitive ability.

Publication Date: 1994.

Scores: 3 test options: the Functional Living Skills Assessment (FLSA), the Quick Functional Screening Test (QFST), and the Recreation and Leisure Profile (RLP).

Administration: Individual.

Price Data, 1999: $299 per complete battery including 25 recordkeeping forms, dominos, beads, and manual (83 pages); $49 per 25 recordkeeping forms.

Time: (15–65) minutes.

Comments: Ratings by therapist; test options utilize some or all of six activities: Recreation and Leisure Profile, Domino Patterns, Draw a Box, Beads, Sporting Goods Shopping Trip, and A Rainy Day.

Author: Roy H. Olsson, Jr.

Publisher: Therapy Skill Builders—A Division of The Psychological Corporation.

Review of the Ohio Functional Assessment Battery: Standardized Tests for Leisure and Living Skills by GARY L. CANIVEZ, Assistant Professor of Psychology, Eastern Illinois University, Charleston, IL:

The Ohio Functional Assessment Battery: Standardized Tests for Leisure and Living Skills (OFAB) was constructed as a "therapy tool designed to obtain the functional level of a client in order to develop measurable treatment objectives" (manual, p. 1). It was reportedly based on a leisurability model (Peterson & Gunn, 1984) that provides for interventions in (a) treatment, (b) leisure education, and (c) recreation. Cognitive and behavioral functioning is assessed based on the assumption that substantial limitations in these areas need to be remediated in order for an individual to participate in leisure activities or leisure education.

The activities and verbatim instructions seem adequate, although the activities seem to be quite complicated for clients in the severe range of cognitive impairment. As the verbatim instructions are printed in the same print style, size, and color, it seemed a bit difficult to read the instructions to the client in a smooth manner. Providing the instructions in a larger font and in a different color would be a helpful addition to future editions.

The Functional Living Skills Assessment (FLSA) is used with clients with cognitive impairments in the lower-moderate to severe range to assess three options, but upon closer inspection, it appears that there are actually two options as one activity, Recreation and Leisure Profile (RLP), is common to both the Quick Functional Screening Test (QFST) and the FLSA.

Information on the rationale for these tests was lacking. Also lacking was a description of the target population(s) including age, developmental, and disability considerations. Scoring examples and research studies reported in the manual suggest that it would be used with adults (and perhaps older adolescents) who were disabled in some manner. This, however, should be explicitly stated by the author so test users know exactly the populations with which this test could and should be used. A more elaborate description of the theoretical basis of this test and its development is also sorely needed.

Descriptions of parameter meanings are provided to assist in the interpretation of the results; however, there are no criteria presented to assist the user in determining whether a score or result is high, low, or otherwise. This is a limiting factor for criterion-referenced interpretations. Stating acceptable performance levels or levels of mastery and establishing external criteria for these levels would help in interpretation. There is also a lack of normative data to provide meaning to the obtained scores.

Technical data in the manual are presented in a somewhat awkward way by presenting validity data before reliability data. Reliability estimates were provided through the use of test-retest and interrater methods; however, there are no estimates of internal consistency for the functional parameters or other scores. Although the stability and interrater correlations are reported to be high, none of the reliability or validity studies are described in sufficient detail and include very small sample sizes of individuals from unknown geographic, ethnic, or socioeconomic status characteristics. It seems quite unlikely that these samples were demographically representative of the U.S. population. There are no descriptions of how the interrater reliability data were collected nor were there indications of the test-retest interval. This limits conclusions that might be made of the high correlations obtained in these studies.

Also lacking were factor analytic studies to determine the number of underlying traits or characteristics being assessed. The moderate to high intercorrelations among many parameters suggests that many of the cognitive parameters seem to be measuring a similar trait (general intelligence). With no indexes of parameter or subtest specificity, it is not possible to determine whether or not there is sufficient unique variability to interpret the separate parameters as meaningful above the likely general cognitive factor. Given the extremely small samples on which these correlations are based, it would not be possible to conduct such factor analyses.

On a more serious note, no validity studies have compared the OFAB cognitive parameters with other more psychometrically sound, objective instruments of cognitive or neuropsychological functioning such as the Wechsler scales (WISC-III [T5:2862], WAIS-R [9:1348], WAIS-III [415]), Stanford-Binet (SB:FE; T5:2485), or Halstead-Reitan (HRNPB; T5:1164). Such studies are necessary to validate the method used in the OFAB to assess these important characteristics.

SUMMARY. Although the OFAB is presented as a "therapy tool" (manual, p. 1) serious limitations discussed above suggest that this instrument should be used as a research instrument until further reliability and validity studies are conducted with better descriptions of the sample's cognitive, communication, and behavioral skills through a series of six activities requiring them to attend, retain information in short term memory, learn, retrieve information from long-term memory, problem solve, and perform motorically.

The OFAB reportedly provides three testing options and methods of investigation. Furthermore, if these are to be criterion-referenced tests, better guidelines need to be developed (and investigated) in order to guide interpretations. If these tests are to provide normative comparisons, then a nationally representative standardization sample for various disabilities is needed to provide appropriate comparisons that guide interpretations and provide meaning to the scores. The $299 cost of this instrument places it near the range of costs for intelligence, neuropsychological, and achievement tests that have much more reliability and validity research support and well-developed criteria and normative samples to guide interpretations. The OFAB may assist in helping understand an individual's limitations and leisure interests but it does not appear to be particularly cost effective.

REVIEWER'S REFERENCE
Peterson, C. A., & Gunn, S. L. (1984). *Therapeutic recreation program design: Principles and procedures* (2nd ed.). Englewood Cliffs, NJ: Prentice-Hall.

Review of the Ohio Functional Assessment Battery: Standardized Tests for Leisure and Living Skills by KATHARINE SNYDER, *Assistant Professor of Psychology, Shepherd College, Shepherdstown, WV:*

The Ohio Functional Assessment Battery (OFAB) was designed to assist occupational and recreational therapists in evaluating the adaptive skills of previously diagnosed cognitively impaired individuals. Those with severe impairments either take the Functional Living Skills Assessment (FLSA) or a shorter Quick Functional Screening Test. Individuals with mild impairments are given the Recreation and Leisure Profile (RLP), a structured interview/questionnaire assessing interests, resources, participation, motivation, and barriers to therapy.

Validity and reliability data for the FLSA are impressive. In support of criterion-related validity, the FLSA strongly predicts performance on the Comprehensive Occupational Therapy Evaluation Scale, with coefficients ranging from .87 to .98. Interrater and interitem reliability coefficients are also strong for all three components. Results are encouraging and support the utility of the OFAB in the design and assessment of recreation/occupational therapy programs.

Using six activities, the FLSA provides a standardized rating format for 19 critical parameters in designing and evaluating therapy programs. The six activities include placing chips in order of most to least preferred on top of activities on leisure charts, copying domino patterns, drawing/coloring a box, stringing beads (same size, color, and shape), shopping for sporting goods, and picking out activities for a rainy day. Before any activities, reality orientation is rated by asking individuals to verify their name, address, phone number, date, and time. The abilities to organize time/materials and to follow directions are also rated throughout the FLSA.

An excellent feature of the FLSA is in rating emotional/behavioral variables that could impact test performance. For instance, attention span and nonproductive behaviors are recorded during time spent off-task. Self-esteem ratings are based on personal presentation (e.g., neat appearance), general demeanor (e.g., smiling, frequency of self-deprecating remarks), and two additional questions. Perception of the test situation can influence the frequency of self-deprecating comments. A good feature of the FLSA is separating frustration tolerance, leisure motivation, cooperative behavior, and attention-seeking ratings from self-esteem. A needed clarification is that depression cannot be assessed by the FLSA and a psychological evaluation would be very helpful prior to administration of the FLSA.

Learning skills are a critical area to evaluate for the design and implementation of effective therapy programs. Learning skills are defined in the FLSA by the following factors: New learning, old learning, retention span, decision making, and problem solving. Retention span ratings are based on ability to verbally repeat directions immediately after being given, whereas ratings of new learning are based on the completion of novel activities (e.g., bead stringing). A suggestion for another rating of retention span and new learning is to have individuals repeat directions after a short period of time, with or without distractions. Old learning ratings are based on the level of recognition of the previously presented leisure cards. Another clarification is that pre- and postmorbid leisure skills cannot be evaluated in the FLSA. The addition of a detailed history evaluation could address this and would make the FLSA an even more useful measure to guide progress and development of therapy programs.

Standardized ratings of decision making and problem solving could occur for all six activities. Decision making is rated based on ability to choose appropriate activities on a rainy day, whereas problem solving is related to money management in the sporting goods shopping trip. A suggestion to further assess problem solving is to rate the ability of individuals to switch to a different size, shape, or color dimension on the bead-stringing task.

The FLSA is an excellent resource for evaluation of motor skills, an important skill in recreational and occupational activities. Fine motor skills and hand-eye coordination are rated during the bead-stringing activity. In fact, the drawing-a-box activity resembles the well-known neuropsychological draw-a-clock test and is a good method of observing hemispatial neglect or motor perseveration. A suggestion is to incorporate ratings for additional neuropsychological motor factors, such as motor slowing, awkwardness, and impersistence. A clarification is also needed in the literature, in that anosognosia is the unawareness or denial of an illness, which may or may not be comorbid with hemispatial neglect.

Verbal communication and nonverbal communication are also prerequisites for successful performance in therapeutic programs. Verbal communication is rated by whether or not individuals answer questions in a clear, direct, and logical way, whereas nonverbal communication is rated by how well the individual makes context-appropriate eye contact and gestures. These general ratings suit the purpose of the OFAB; however, additional testing is required to assess aphasia.

SUMMARY. The OFAB is a well-done measure of functional skills for the creation and evaluation of occupational and recreational therapy programs. Reliability and validity findings of all three components of the FLSA, Quick Screening Test, and RLP structured interview/questionnaire are impressive. As use of the OFAB expands, further normative research with different patient populations will be exciting. Overlap of factors is a possibility, yet this does not affect the ability of the OFAB to provide much needed information to occupational and recreational therapists for the creation and evaluation of programs. The OFAB is a very useful tool for therapists, especially when used in conjunction with other assessments. Training in the use of the measure is critical because the quality of assessment greatly depends on examiner skill.

[264]
Older Persons Counseling Needs Survey.

Purpose: To assess the needs of older persons and their desires for counseling.
Population: Ages 60 and over.
Publication Date: 1993.
Scores, 3: Needs, Desires, Total.
Administration: Group or individual.
Price Data, 1998: $25 per sampler set including manual (16 pages) and test booklet; $100 per one-year permission to reproduce up to 200 administrations of the test.
Time: (10–15) minutes.
Author: Jane E. Myers.
Publisher: Mind Garden, Inc.

Review of the Older Persons Counseling Needs Survey by DENNIS C. HARPER, Professor of Pediatrics and Rehabilitation, College of Medicine, University of Iowa, Iowa City, IA:

PURPOSE AND OVERVIEW. The Older Persons Counseling Needs Survey (OPCNS) was initially developed in 1978 for use with adults age 60 and older and focuses on assessing the needs of older persons and their stated desires for counseling. The author notes that the item development for the OPCNS was based upon a review of the literature in gerontology, psychology, and counseling involving older adult populations. Areas of specific concern identified by the author are in four categories: Personal concerns, social or interpersonal concerns, activity concerns, and environmental concerns. The review of these issues touches on a comprehensive list of issues such as death and dying, mental health needs, spirituality, physical and health concerns, relationship issues, actuality, group memberships, work, leisure time pursuits, independence issues, physical limitations in the environment, legal services, transportation, and housing. The authors have operationally defined counseling as an expressed desire to talk to someone about a series of needs endorsed on the OPCNS.

The OPCNS was initially field tested in 1978 with 850 older adults from Florida. The author notes groups of older persons evidencing high need states and/or high desires for counseling were identified as a primary target for counseling interventions in the use of this instrument. Such individuals included single or widowed, members of ethnic minority races, those who live in homes of relatives or friends, those who live in adult congregate living facilities or foster homes for adults, those who have low levels of education, and those with low incomes. Interestingly, the author indicates that in this survey high needs as stated by adults were related to living in either very rural or very urban areas. The OPCNS, Form S, may be used for research on the counseling needs of older persons according to the author. Furthermore the two subscales may be used to identify those older persons in need of counseling assistance as well as the specific concerns they might bring to a professional counselor.

ADMINISTRATION AND SCORING. The OPCNS can be administered individually or in groups and takes approximately 10 to 15 minutes for completion. It requires a fifth grade reading level according to the authors. The user may chose to administer the entire 56-item instrument or one of two 28-item subscales. The test booklet provided has the statements divided by Needs (identified as Items 1–28) and Desires (identified as Items 29–56) to facilitate ease of administration and scoring. Elders with physical disabilities particularly visual in nature may require oral administration resulting in a 30-minute test time for completion. Respondents are requested to endorse items that may be true "for your personally." A Likert scale with four response choices is presented: SA=Strongly Agree, A=Agree, D=Disagree, and SD=Strongly Disagree. Scoring is simple and values are assigned to each response ranging from strongly agree=4 to strongly disagree=1. Interpretation is based upon agreement or disagreement on the specific subscale (e.g., Needs subscale, Desires subscale). Higher scores are interpreted as indicative of greater Needs or Desires.

NORMATIVE INFORMATION. The OPCNS Form A was normed on a stratified random sample of 850 older persons in Florida in 1978 as indicated by the author. Means and standard deviations are reported for males and females and also presented for Caucasians and ethnic minorities. The author notes that Blake and Dickel (1980) obtained similar results on a sample of 500 older persons in Nebraska.

RELIABILITY AND VALIDITY. The subscale scores for Form S are derived by adding the numerical values for the first 28 items (Needs subscale) and the second 28 items (Desires subscale). Scores for the total instrument are derived by adding the scores for each of the 56 (Form S) items. Missing values are counted as zero. Full scale scores range as follows: Needs subscale 28–112, Desires subscale 28–112, and total score 56–224. A 2-week test-retest reliability with a sample of 32 older persons attending a senior center in 1978 was calculated for each of the items, the subscales, and the total score. Individual item correlations, all of which were significant at the .01 level, ranged from .39 to .81, with a median correlation of .56. The test-retest reliability coefficient for the Needs subscale was .68 and for the counseling Desires subscale .76. The intercorrelation between subscales for Form A was .86.

Content validity for OPCNS scores was examined through review (by experts in gerontology, assessment, and counseling) of item categories identified by the author in the manual and individual items. Opinions of these experts were that the categories represented an adequate sample of the possible needs of the older persons. No data are presented to clarify this statement. Concurrent validity was investigated using subgroups of the original sample of persons who completed the OPCNS. The author reports a series of instruments in which intercorrelations concurrently were completed on the Multiple Affect Adjective Checklist, the Death Concern Scale, the Survey of Personal Values, the Survey of Interpersonal Values, and the Life Satisfaction Index, Adams Modification. Correlations on these five instruments between the Needs and Counseling Desires subscales ranged from a high of .49 to a low of -.44. A majority of correlations reported concurrently between the OPCNS and these five instruments were nonsignificant. The authors also completed a principal axes factor analysis with an oblique rotation yielding six factors. All factors were noted to correlate highly with one another. Additional factor analyses led to the conclusion that the OPCNS is unidimensional in that it measures a global factor of needs for counseling, which is closely related to a global indication of desires for counseling.

SUMMARY. The OPCNS is an assessment focused on needs and desires for counseling in older adults. Its item content appears appropriate as stated. It is a straightforward survey with face validity. This is not a diagnostic instrument but a device to explore common concerns of older adults in a reasonably comprehensive fashion.

REVIEWER'S REFERENCE

Blake, R., & Dickel, T. (1980). Counseling needs of older Nebraskans. Unpublished paper. Omaha, NE: University of Nebraska at Omaha.

Review of the Older Persons Counseling Needs Survey by LAWRENCE J. RYAN, Core Faculty, The Graduate College of The Union Institute, Cincinnati, OH, and Vice President and Academic Dean, St. John's Seminary College, Camarillo, CA:

The Older Persons Counseling Needs Survey (OPCNS) is a self-report instrument that was constructed in 1978 for use with individuals over 60 years of age. The OPCNS appears to have its greatest potential utilization when employed as a research instrument. The single form questionnaire (Form S) includes nine demographic items that precede the 56 subscale items. For all of the subscale items an easy to follow Likert-type response format is utilized. The items that constitute the OPCNS were appropriately derived from

a literature review of concerns relative to the older population. The first 28 items of the OPCNS yield a subscale score that identifies the "need for counseling." The second 28 items (parallel to the first 28) yield a subscore that identifies the "desire for counseling." The only difference between the first 28 and the second 28 items is in the initial wording of each item. The first set of items identifies need areas, and the second set identifies the desire for assistance in the need areas. The instrument appears to be free of any racial, ethnic, or other bias.

The instruments was designed for individuals with a fifth grade education or better and can typically be completed in 10–15 minutes. If necessary, the instrument can be administered orally by an examiner as well. Appropriate administrative and scoring directions are clearly articulated. The OPCNS was normed on 850 older persons in Florida in 1978. In 1993 the authors revised the instrument to include an additional item tapping spirituality in each of the subscales. Surprisingly, subsequent to that revision no additional normative data were reported. The 1978 data include the report of 2-week test-retest reliabilities for a subsample of 32 subjects (median = .56). The instrument has excellent face validity. Concurrent validity of the OPCNS is reported through correlation data comparing the OPCNS with five other instruments. Significant correlation ratios are manifest between the Counseling Desires subscale and the Multiple Affect Adjective Checklist and for the Life Satisfaction Index-Z. No data relative to predictive validity are reported. Although the instrument claims to have two subscales, there is a question whether the two scales actually measure two different factors or a single factor. Factor analysis data regarding the OPCNS was unclear. The authors conclude that all factors identified are highly correlated with one another, and thus identify the OPCNS as a unidimensional instrument. The single factor identified is the global factor of "needs for counseling," which is closely related to a global indication of "desires for counseling."

SUMMARY. Similar in format to a number of other self-report instruments, the OPCNS has excellent potential for use, especially in gerontological research studies for the identification of specific factors that individual older persons or groups of older persons find bothersome in their lives. In clinical settings the OPCNS could be useful as a quick screening device for individuals or for large or small groups of older persons to assess the current level of satisfaction and adaptation to typical life stressful situations and the possible need for professional counseling service referral. The OPCNS is an uncomplicated and straightforward instrument with excellent face validity. It is a psychometrically sound and useful instrument for use in research studies that require data regarding the life problems faced by older persons.

[265]
Opinions About Deaf People Scale.

Purpose: To measure hearing adults' beliefs about the capabilities of deaf adults.
Population: Adults.
Publication Date: Undated.
Scores: Total score only.
Administration: Group.
Price Data, 1995: $11.50 per development and validation manual (127 pages); $1 per administration guide including reproducible copy of the scale; $5 per disk of both.
Time: Administration time not reported.
Authors: Paul James Berkay, J. Emmett Gardener, and Patricia L. Smith.
Publisher: National Clearinghouse of Rehabilitation Training Materials.

Review of Opinions About Deaf People Scale by JEFFERY P. BRADEN, Professor, School Psychology Program, Department of Educational Psychology, University of Wisconsin-Madison, Madison, WI:

TEST COVERAGE AND USE. The Opinions about Deaf People Scale (ODPS) is a 20-item, Likert-scale instrument intended to measure the opinions people hold regarding persons who are deaf. [Reviewer's Note: In keeping with the authors of the scale, and the customs of the Deaf community in North America, I will use "deaf people" instead of "people who are deaf" throughout the rest of this review.] The suggested uses of the instrument include measuring (and targeting for change) negative attitudes to improve relationships among deaf and hearing employees, and measuring how parental attitudes towards deaf people affects the performance of their deaf children in scholastic tasks.

SCALE DEVELOPMENT. The ODPS was developed in a three-step process: (a) specification of the domain to be sampled, (b) development and trial of a 35-item pilot version on a small (N = 35) group of undergraduate students; and (c) a second administration to a larger (N = 299) group of students. The authors (Berkay et al.) meticulously describe the decisions made in the domain specification, item generation, item selection, and final scale format and content stages of scale development (see also Berkay, Gardner, & Smith, 1995).

RELIABILITY. The reliability of scores from the ODPS was estimated via internal item consistency. Two versions of the ODPS are described in the manual: a preliminary version of 35 items, and a final version of 20 items. The reliability indices for the preliminary version were good to excellent (a = .90; split-half r = .86). The reliability estimates of the final 20-item version were good (alpha = .83; split-half r = .82). No stability (test-retest correlations) are reported, nor are parallel forms or other measures of reliability included in the manual.

VALIDITY. The validity of scores from the ODPS was investigated in two ways. First, Berkay et al. define the domain of attitudes towards deafness using a content/item mapping strategy. That is, they identified the types of attitudes (especially negative stereotypes) that individuals might have about deaf people in a number of domains (e.g., the intelligence of deaf people, their work skills, their academic abilities). They then explained how the ODPS sampled from these domains. This procedure culminated in appropriate item sampling of the identified domains, and reflected the relative weights that Berkay et al. assigned to these domains. Furthermore, items were constructed to be scored positively or negatively to balance response set tendencies across content domains.

The second method for validating scores from the ODPS was to correlate it with the Attitudes to Deafness (AD) Scale (Cowen, Rockway, Bobrove, & Stevenson, 1967). The AD scale also purports to measure attitudes about deafness. Berkay et al. do not explain why a second scale to measure attitudes about deafness is needed, although they refer to the dated content and norms of the AD scale. The correlation between the ODPS and the AD scale was high (r = .75), suggesting convergence between the two scales.

Unfortunately, Berkay et al. did not study the validity of the scores from the ODPS for either of its stated purposes. That is, Berkay et al. do not provide evidence regarding how the ODPS might identify negative attitudes in the workplace, evaluate the efficacy of programs intended to change attitudes, or how the ODPS might be used in research to link attitudes to other psychologically relevant constructs. Although Berkay et al. suggest the ODPS has treatment utility for changing attitudes among employees (that is, the instrument would point to treatments that would alter or improve the attitudes people may hold about deaf people), they do not provide evidence to support this use. Likewise, they do not demonstrate its use in measuring parental attitudes towards their deaf children, nor the link between those attitudes and the academic achievement of deaf children.

DISCUSSION. The ODPS appears to sample attitudes (hearing) people have toward deaf people. The items appear to have appropriate content validity, and the item/domain mapping employed in the development of the scale is exceptionally clear and rigorous. The instrument also demonstrates good internal consistency. A third virtue of this instrument is its cost—Berkay et al. clearly want to make this instrument available to people without regard to fiscal remuneration. It is inexpensive to order, and is available in the public domain (Berkay, Gardner, & Smith, 1994). I wish other test developers shared Berkay et al.'s scholarly values on this point.

The ODPS has some significant shortcomings. The definition of the domain sampled (that is, which domains one should sample in assessing people's attitudes toward deaf people) is arbitrary. I do not fault Berkay et al.'s choice of domains, but I do not have a clear sense that they chose the best domains to sample. The scoring of some items also appears arbitrary. For example, agreement with the pilot item "Deaf people do not have levels of achievement commensurate with hearing people" was indicative of a negative attitude. However, objective data show that deaf people have high rates of functional illiteracy, and the median reading level for deaf individuals who *graduate* from high school is approximately a fourth grade level. Although this pilot item does not appear on the final version of the ODPS, it illustrates the problem of defining the domain of attitudes towards deaf people, and of separating negative stereotyping from accurate appraisal.

A second shortcoming of this instrument is its insufficient validation. Berkay et al. wisely avoid recommending score classifications (e.g., cutoffs to identify positive, neutral, or negative attitudes) from their college sample data. However,

by failing to develop meaningful score standards, they undermine the use of the ODPS for its stated purpose. For example, how would employers know which ODPS scores reflect negative attitudes?

The other purpose of the ODPS (studying the relationship between parental attitudes and their deaf children's achievements) is unusually narrow. I suspect Berkay et al. intend the broader purpose of facilitating research on how opinions of deaf people influence behaviors and outcomes, but this purpose is not stated. Neither the narrow purpose, nor the broader application to research, is directly studied in the manual.

Given the current level of knowledge regarding the ODPS, its most appropriate use would be further research on the instrument itself. Item content suggests that it samples people's attitudes toward deaf adults, the reliability indexes suggest it does so with reasonable accuracy, and it has some construct validity support. There is no evidence in the manual to support the clinical/applied use of the ODPS, although the ODPS offers a promising (and inexpensive) platform for facilitating research.

REVIEWER'S REFERENCES
Cowen, E. L., Rockway, A. M., Bobrove, P. H., & Stevenson, J. (1967). Development and evaluation of an attitudes to deafness scale. *Journal of Personality and Social Psychology, 6*(2), 183–191.

Berkay, P. J., Gardner, J. E., & Smith, P. L. (1994, April). *Administration guide for the Opinion about Deaf People Scale: A Scale to Measure Hearing Adults' Beliefs about the Capabilities of Deaf Adults* (ERIC Document No. ED372122). Paper presented at the Annual Meeting of the American Educational Research Association, New Orleans, LA.

Berkay, P. J., Gardner, J. E., & Smith, P. L. (1995). The development of the Opinions about Deaf People Scale: A Scale to Measure Hearing Adults' Beliefs about the Capabilities of Deaf Adults. *Educational and Psychological Measurement, 55*(1), 105–114.

Review of the Opinions About Deaf People Scale by VINCENT J. SAMAR, Associate Professor, and ILA PARASNIS, Associate Professor, Department of Applied Language and Cognition Research, National Technical Institute for the Deaf, Rochester Institute of Technology, Rochester, NY:

The Opinions About Deaf People Scale (OADP) is a 20-item scale designed to measure the beliefs of hearing adults about the capabilities of deaf adults. The authors' intention in developing this scale was to provide a research tool and was motivated by the "belief that one of the first steps in changing negative attitudes toward deaf people is to measure and determine the attitudes that need to be changed" (Development and Validation manual, p. i). As a contemporary research instrument, however, the scale suffers from construct validity problems as detailed below.

TEST FORMAT AND DESCRIPTION. The OADP scale is supplied with an administration guide and a separate unpublished booklet that exhaustively documents the development and validation efforts for scores from the scale. The final version of the OADP scale contains 20 scale items, each of which requires respondents to indicate their agreement with the item using a 4-point Likert scale. The four anchors are: *strongly disagree, mildly disagree, mildly agree,* and *strongly agree.* The absence of a neutral point was based on the assumption that there is generally no neutral attitude toward deaf people (Development and Validation manual, p. 18) and was intended to prevent respondents from avoiding comment on what might be uncomfortable subjects.

The items on the OADP scale fall into six major categories of attitudes toward deaf people. These categories are intelligence, ability to deal with traffic, job skills, ability to live independently, communication skills, and academic skills. The nature of the categories is based on the perceptions of deaf and hearing professionals and previous literature on the nature of common misconceptions about deaf people. The numbers of items in each category are proportional to the frequency with which deaf and hearing informants and literature sources identified specific misconceptions about deaf people in each category. There are an equal number of negatively and positively phrased items.

TEST COVERAGE AND USE. The OADP scale is intended for use with hearing adults. The scale items are designed to measure beliefs about a specific subset of the deaf population. The subset includes young to middle-aged deaf adults only. The OADP scale was explicitly not intended to measure beliefs about deaf children and senior citizens. The authors believe that there are certain distinct misconceptions held by hearing people regarding these latter groups of deaf people and that attempting to include them in the same scale would produce too general an instrument. Given the authors' explicitly stated belief and their careful consideration of the scope of use of their scale during its development, it is unfortunate that they chose to title the instrument as if it applied to all deaf people, rather than indicating directly in the title that the targeted population was only young and middle-aged deaf adults. Because there is no mention of this restriction in the administration guide itself, there is a real danger that the scale might be indiscriminately used in research and other data gathering settings that apply to deaf children or senior citizens.

A second difficulty with the scope of the OADP scale is the operational definition that the authors assumed of a deaf individual. They define a deaf individual as follows:

> A deaf individual is someone who cannot hear and/or distinguish speech sounds even with amplification. Although the primary mode of communication for most deaf adults in the United States is American Sign Language, many of them take advantage of their residual (remaining) hearing and use speech and lip-reading skills to some extent. There are also deaf oralists who communicate through lip reading and speech and do not use sign language. Deaf individuals should be differentiated from hard-of-hearing individuals who can hear and distinguish speech sounds with amplification and primarily communicate through speech and lipreading. (Development and Validation manual, p. 1)

It is good that the authors recognize that individuals with significant hearing losses comprise diverse language and cultural groups. However, their audiometric definition of the target population for their instrument is both overly restrictive and itself suffers from a serious misconception about deaf people. The deaf community in the United States certainly does not define itself audiometrically, that is, according to whether or not its members "can hear and/or distinguish speech sounds even with amplification." Many members of the deaf community have some degree of residual hearing useful for perceiving speech sounds.

Nor is it reasonable to believe that the intended respondents for this scale, namely hearing individuals as a group, use such a restrictive audiometric criterion to determine whether or not a person is deaf. In fact, the most visible emblem to a hearing person of an individual's deafness is a hearing aid, most likely indicating to the hearing person that some deaf people have usable hearing. Even the authors' definition above suggests this conclusion when they point out that many deaf adults take advantage of their residual hearing.

Finally, the relevance of the ability to "hear and/or distinguish speech sounds" to the classification of individuals as members of the deaf versus hard-of-hearing community is a topic of ongoing debate. Although subgroup membership tends to correlate somewhat with audiometric characteristics, it is not a foregone conclusion that speech perception skill or the total lack of it is a necessary criterion for membership in either of these subgroups. In fact, the total absence of hearing and speech discrimination is even more restrictive than the standard audiometric definition of deaf and hard-of-hearing individuals. In any case, there are no instructions to hearing respondents in the OADP scale administration guide that would direct them to restrict their opinions to an audiometrically deaf as opposed to a hard-of-hearing population as restrictively defined by the authors. Therefore, it is doubtful that the authors' scale selectively targets deaf individuals who "cannot hear and/or distinguish speech sounds even with amplification." In reality, the scope of the OADP scale is more likely to be individuals who are perceived by hearing people to be members of the larger deaf community, including, potentially, at least some audiometrically hard-of-hearing individuals and not including, potentially, some audiometrically deaf individuals. This is a much more diverse group with much more varied communication characteristics than the authors envision their scale to address.

APPROPRIATENESS OF SAMPLES FOR TEST VALIDATION AND NORMING. An initial 35-item version of the OADP scale was piloted on a sample of 38 hearing students from an upper-level teacher education program population. Based on the results of the pilot administration, the final 20-item OADP scale was normed on a sample of 290 undergraduate students whom the authors regard as representative of a typical upper-level undergraduate student population. However, the sampling was not random over the university, but rather was restricted to students in a particular general education course entitled "Sociology of Family." This resulted in a high proportion of students from the college of arts and sciences (53%) and relatively low proportions of students from other colleges (e.g., only 7% of the sample were students from the College of Engineering). Therefore, not only are the norms for the OADP scale based on a highly educated population, they also tend to underrepresent populations from several significant academic and professional sectors.

This sampling bias in the normative data is potentially very important. The authors' intention

in developing this scale was to provide a research instrument to assess hearing people's attitudes toward deaf people as a prelude to designing effective methods to change the beliefs of hearing people toward deaf people. And, they explicitly state that they intend this instrument to be used in a variety of settings, including employment settings such as large corporations and with parent groups (Development and Validation manual, p. v). Presumably, future users of this instrument will be motivated to apply it in the settings that are most likely to engender negative attitudes toward deaf people. Undoubtedly, the attitudes of the target populations in these settings will be influenced by factors such as their level of education, the cultural history of their profession, their familiarity with deafness, and the social, communication, and functional demands of the setting. It seems unlikely that the population of students interested in the sociology of family can provide a suitable normative model for the sorts of real world employment settings where negative perspectives on deaf employees are likely to be harbored. Neither does it seem reasonable that this student population is an adequate model for the general population of hearing parents of deaf children, most of whom will be confronted rather suddenly with their child's deafness and its real implications for their child's education and development and for the social dynamics of their family. Therefore, extreme caution must be exercised in applying this scale to populations other than the unlikely one on which it was normed.

RELIABILITY. The documentation reports a coefficient alpha reliability estimate of .91 and a Guttman split-half reliability value of .92. These results suggest generally good internal consistency reliability for the instrument.

CONTENT AND CONSTRUCT VALIDITY. The content of the OADP scale is based on the perspective of a few deaf informants and previous researchers on the misconceptions that typify hearing people's attitudes toward deaf people. A reasonably good correlation ($r = 75$) with the widely used Attitudes to Deafness Scale (Cowen, Rockway, Bobrove, & Stevenson, 1967) suggests that the general construct assessed by the OADP scale is in line with the construct underlying that measure. However, the construct underlying the Attitudes to Deafness Scale was developed 30 years ago, when the general hearing society was not as informed about deafness and deaf people as it is today. Therefore, this correlation is not strong evidence for good construct validity for the OADP scale.

It is difficult to assess the actual construct validity of the OADP scale. Presumably, the intended construct for the OADP scale is the full spectrum of significant misconceptions about deaf people held by hearing people in today's society. However, it is questionable to what extent the OADP scale samples this domain fairly. The process of generating the prototype list of misconceptions for the OADP scale involved interviewing a group of "deaf professionals and deaf people" with a series of open-ended critical-incident questions. (Oddly, the OADP scale documentation refers to these informants as including hearing people working in the field of deafness.) This is a reasonable approach to identifying the universe of significant contemporary misconceptions that comprise the construct. However, there is no information given on the number of people interviewed, on their professional roles and experiences with deaf people, on their demographic characteristics, or on their cultural identities. Therefore, it is impossible to determine to what extent the sampling of misconceptions generated by this group is representative of the educated experiences of professionals working in deafness or of the deaf community itself.

The authors speculate, based on their literature review and informants' responses, that there are two subconstructs measured by the OADP items, namely attitudes toward the intelligence of deaf people and attitudes toward the skills of deaf people. Their factor analysis data intimate but do not clearly show differential factor loading patterns for the intelligence and skill items respectively. However, the scale only included two clear intelligence-related items, so it is difficult to assess the factor structure in this respect.

More importantly, it appears from the factor analyses on both the 35-item pilot version and the 20-item final version that the construct underlying hearing people's attitudes toward deaf people is intricate. These factor structures suggest that additional subconstructs determining hearing people's attitudes may include a dimension of perceived danger stemming from the inability to hear and a consequent concern for the safety of deaf people in specific situations, a dimension of concern regarding the existence of barriers to equal access in educational settings, a dimension of specific knowledge about the relationship between speech and intelligence, a dimension of knowledge about the nature of sign language, a dimension of general knowledge of deafness, and a dimension of conceptions about the roles and responsibilities of interpreters. If so, then further revisions of the OADP scale are in order to refine the item sampling of such constructs. In this sense, the construct validity of the OADP scale at this stage, even for the limited population on which it was normed, is incomplete in its sensitivity to the full range of attitude-relevant subconstructs that appear to influence the scale as it stands.

Furthermore, it is clear that the OADP scale falls short on at least two major dimensions of misconceptions held by hearing people, namely the communication and language abilities of deaf people and the cultural identities of deaf people. There is only one question related to sign language on the OADP scale, and that question only probes for the understanding that sign language is a fully developed human language like spoken languages. There are no items that would assess the respondent's understanding of the relationships among American Sign Language, signed English, and spoken English, the bilingual and bicultural status of deaf individuals in American society, the ability of deaf individuals to read and write and to communicate with hearing individuals in a variety of modes and a variety of settings, the existence of cross-cultural differences between deaf and hearing cultures, the existence of cultural diversity within the deaf population itself, and so on. Clearly, a research instrument intended to help change negative attitudes toward deaf people must expose the crucial underpinnings of those attitudes on the part of hearing people today. Historically, those underpinnings have proven to be misconceptions about language, thought, and culture. The OADP scale is inadequate in this respect. It does not assess attitudes regarding the major contemporary themes that educators and other professionals currently regard as central to the development, acceptance, and success of deaf people in society today.

Finally, it should be noted that attitudes toward deafness and deaf people held by hearing people (DeCaro, Dowaliby, & Maruggi, 1983; Parasnis, DeCaro, & Raman, 1996) and deaf people (Parasnis, Samar, & Mandke, 1996) vary from society to society. Hence, the construct represented by the OADP scale or its possible future revisions based on American respondents may not generalize to other countries.

TEST ADMINISTRATION. The administration of the OADP scale is relatively straightforward and should require about 5–10 minutes to complete. Care must be taken, however, in tallying the scores because both negative and positively stated items occur. This requires the user to reverse the numerical values assigned to half of the scale items. The authors have provided a scoring key to remind the user which items must be assigned which order of numerical values.

There is a troubling issue about the administration guide. The administration guide contains the following statement:

This scale measures hearing adults' beliefs about the capabilities of deaf adults. It should be apparent that there is a discrepancy between the scale's title and its actual measure. There was some concern that if the intent of the scale was explicitly stated, subjects might respond in a socially desirable manner. That is why the scale's title is somewhat ambiguous. If this scale is used to conduct research, subjects should be debriefed and informed of the scale's true purpose following the collection of data. (p. 1)

We find this statement mysterious and uninterpretable. The nature of the supposed discrepancy between the title and the stated purpose of the scale is, in fact, not apparent. This statement, therefore, is likely to confuse scale administrators and possibly to create a significant source of variation in their instructions to respondents if they try to compensate for whatever they imagine the discrepancy to be. The authors should revise their instructions to eliminate this claim or to include a specific and clear statement of its meaning and implications for administration.

SUMMARY. The OADP scale is a very limited instrument. It was validated on a population that is not representative of the populations to which the scale would most likely be applied and it does not sample the range of attitudes toward deafness that is needed in a useful research instrument today. The contemporary attitudes of hearing people toward deaf people are determined by greater subtleties of misconception than in previous times due to changes in people's world knowledge and their exposure to specific information and misinformation about deafness and deaf people.

The OADP scale fails to capture these subtleties. It might be useful, for example, for crude screening in organizational settings. However, it is inadequate for use in serious psychosocial or organizational research.

REVIEWERS' REFERENCES

Cowen, E. L., Bobrove, P. H., Rockway, A. M., & Stevenson, J. (1967). Development and evaluation of an attitudes to deafness scale. *Journal of Personality and Social Psychology, 6*(2), 183–191.

DeCaro, J. J., Dowaliby, F. J., & Maruggi, E. A. (1983). A cross-cultural examination of parents' and teachers' expectations for deaf youth regarding careers. *British Journal of Educational Psychology, 53,* 358–363.

Parasnis, I., DeCaro, J. J., & Raman, M. (1996). Attitudes of teachers and parents in India toward career choices for deaf and hearing people. *American Annals of the Deaf, 141,* 303–308.

Parasnis, I., Samar, V. J., & Mandke, K. (1996). Deaf adults' attitudes toward career choices for deaf and hearing people in India. *American Annals of the Deaf, 141,* 333–339.

[266]
Oral and Written Language Scales: Listening Comprehension and Oral Expression.

Purpose: Designed to assess "receptive and expressive … language."
Population: Ages 3–21.
Publication Date: 1995.
Acronym: OWLS.
Scores, 3: Listening Comprehension, Oral Expression, Oral Composite.
Administration: Individual.
Price Data, 1999: $169.95 per complete kit including manual (212 pages), Listening Comprehension Easel, Oral Expression Easel, and 25 record forms; $24.95 per 25 record forms; $149.95 per AGS computer ASSIST™ for OWLS LC/OE (IBM or Macintosh).
Time: (15–40) minutes.
Author: Elizabeth Carrow-Woolfolk.
Publisher: American Guidance Service, Inc.

Review of the Oral and Written Language Scales: Listening Comprehension and Oral Expression by STEVE GRAHAM, Professor of Special Education, University of Maryland, College Park, MD:

The Oral and Written Language Scales (OWLS) contains three subtests: Listening Comprehension, Oral Expression, and Written Expression. Although the three subtests were developed and normed as part of the same assessment, the Written Expression subtest was packaged as a separate test (267) and is not reviewed here. The decision to package the Written Expression subtest separately was unfortunate, as it complicates comparing students' performance in these three areas.

The Listening Comprehension and Oral Expression subtests of the OWLS are administered individually to children and young adults, aged 3 to 21. Listening Comprehension is measured by asking the examinee to select one of four pictures that best depicts a statement (e.g., "In which picture is she not walking to school") made by the examiner. Oral expression is assessed by asking the examinee to look at one or more line drawings and respond verbally to a statement made by the examiner (e.g., "Tell me what is happening here and how the mother feels"). Contrary to the author's claim, these tasks are not typical of those found in the classroom, and like other language tests of this nature, concerns about the ecological validity of the instrument need to be addressed in the test manual.

An interesting feature of the Oral Expression subtest is that the examiner can conduct a descriptive analysis of correct and incorrect responses. For all but 30 of the 96 items on this subtest, correct responses can be categorized as preferred or acceptable responses, providing additional information on how well the examinee understood the oral expression task. In contrast, incorrect responses can further be classified as a miscue involving grammar or a miscue involving semantic and/or pragmatic aspects of language. Although the manual provides item-by-item scoring rules for making these decisions, no data are provided on the reliability of these scores.

A notable strength of the OWLS is that both the Listening Comprehension and Oral Expression subtests were constructed on the basis of a strong theoretical foundation. Items were constructed to measure important aspects of listening and oral language performance. The author's description of this process is incomplete, however, as no table was provided to indicate what each item supposedly measured nor was the expert review process adequately described.

Both subtests are easy to administer, requiring only about 15 to 40 minutes depending upon the age of the child. The establishment of the basal and ceiling for the Oral Expression subtest involves some uncertainty, as the scoring information provided on the record form may not be adequate for correctly scoring all items. More complete scoring information is provided in the test manual. A solution to this problem is to provide the needed information in the same place that instructions for administering each item are provided.

The authors are to be commended for providing clear and easy-to-follow directions for scoring as well as determining normative scores. More attention, however, should have been directed to establishing the cautions that examiners need to exercise in interpreting these scores. This is especially the case for test-age equivalents that can be derived for each subtest and a composite score for the whole test.

According to the author, the OWLS provides a broad measure of an individual's competence in listening comprehension and oral expression. It is also claimed that the instrument can be used to help in the identification of students with learning disabilities, predict academic success, and monitor progress over time. The support that the author provided for each of these claims was uneven. For example, seven studies demonstrated that students with special needs scored lower on the OWLS than children included in the standardization sample that were matched on age, gender, race/ethnicity, and SES. This included children with learning disabilities in reading, learning disabilities in general academic skills, speech impairments, language delays, language impairments, hearing difficulties, and mental handicaps. The findings from these studies provide strong support for using the OWLS to help in the identification of students with learning disabilities as well as other disabilities involving language and cognitive difficulties.

In contrast, little evidence was available to support the claim that the instrument can be used to monitor progress over time. The only evidence relevant to this claim was the means and standard deviations for the raw scores of each subtest for the standardization sample. The standard deviations for each age level were typically larger than the mean difference between ages, and differences between one age level and the next were relatively small after children reached the age of 9. Notably absent in the test manual were data showing that scores for the OWLS are responsive to the effects of instruction.

The claim that the instrument can be used to predict academic success was only partially substantiated by the information provided by the author. In several studies conducted in conjunction with standardization of the OWLS, children's performance on the instrument was related to their current academic performance and, as noted earlier, students with severe academic difficulties (e.g., learning disabilities) did not perform as well on the test as matched students in the standardization sample. Nevertheless, there was no statistically significant difference in the test scores of students with less severe academic difficulties and a matched sample of students participating in the standardization process. Even more importantly, studies examining the validity of using scores from the OWLS to predict future academic performance were conspicuously absent in the test manual.

Finally, there was relatively strong support for the author's primary claim that the instrument provides a valid measure of general listening and speaking skills. First, scores on the OWLS were moderately to highly correlated with scores on other measures of language development. Second, measures of achievement and cognitive development were also moderately to highly correlated with OWLS scores. Previous research has established that school learning is dependent on language ability and that there is a substantial relationship between the development of cognitive and language skills. Third, mean scores of students in the standardization sample increased from one age to the next. As expected, differentiation was greatest for young children and least for older students and young adults. Fourth, as noted earlier, students with language difficulties, such as a hearing or language impairment, obtained lower scores on the test than matched students in the standardization sample.

With the exception of the Listening Comprehension scale, the reliability of scores from the instrument was adequate. Correlations for test-retest reliability and internal consistency for the Oral Expression scale and the composite score for both scales were almost always above .80. For the Listening Comprehension subtest, however, measures of reliability were below .80 for children aged 6 to 9, suggesting that this particular scales appears to be best suited as a screening device at these ages.

Finally, the OWLS was standardized on 1,795 examinees at 74 sites nationwide. The author is to be commended for the care taken in conducting the standardization, and the resulting sample was reasonably representative of the population of children in the United States in 1991.

In summary, the OWLS provides reliable and valid scores for determining the language competence of individual children. The only exception involves the Listening Comprehension measure, which appears to be best suited as a screening device for children 6 to 9 years of age.

Review of the Oral and Written Language Scales: Listening Comprehension and Oral Expression by KORESSA KUTSICK MALCOLM, School Psychologist, Augusta County School Board, Fishersville, VA:

The development of the Oral and Written Language Scales (OWLS) represents a positive advancement in the realm of language assessment. The OWLS was created to provide a quick and comprehensive evaluation of expressive and receptive language functions. The author indicated that her test can be used to determine "broad levels of language skills as well as specific performance in the areas of listening, speaking, and writing" (p. 1). The OWLS addresses these areas in a fashion that taps into everyday language functioning more so than do other language tests. Because the Listening Comprehension and Oral Expression Scales are packaged separated from the Written Expression Scale, they will be reviewed together. A review of the Written Expression Scale will be presented on its own in this *MMY* (267).

The Listening Comprehension Scale taps the understanding of spoken language. This scale requires examinees to select one of four pictures that depicts the verbal information presented by the examiner. Three levels of language skills are assessed by the Listening Comprehension Scale. These three levels include lexical, syntactic, and supralinguistic skills. Administration time takes 5 to 15 minutes, depending on the age of the examinee.

The Oral Expression scale was developed to measure the understanding and use of spoken language. Examinees must respond to questions, complete a sentence, or generate one or more sentences, based on a presented verbal and pictorial stimuli. This scale takes 10 to 25 minutes to administer.

The items on both the Listening Comprehension and Oral Expression Scales are presented in ascending developmental order. Basal and ceiling rules are clearly presented. The ceiling rule of stopping after failing five out of seven items on the Listening Comprehension Scale and six out of seven on the Oral Expression scale is always cumbersome for examiners. Rationales presented in the manual for this procedure, however, provide good reasoning for using this process to increase the reliability of the test while decreasing effects of fatigue on test performance.

The manual for the Listening Comprehension and Oral Expression Scales of the OWLS is very clear and informative. Administration and scoring procedures are presented in good detail. Administration of both scales is relatively easy. Scoring may present some challenge until examiners are familiar with necessary criteria. Many examples are provided that will help examiners work through the scoring of these scales.

Several positive administration and scoring procedures are present in the OWLS. Each scale provides ample items to help examinees understand presented directions. Teaching of these items is also possible when examinees do not grasp the direction. Another positive feature of this test is that the OWLS allows for an item analysis for examining the types of errors or patterns of language that the examinee tends to demonstrate. This analysis allows examiners to pinpoint specific functions of an examinee's language that need to be addressed in therapy.

Computer scoring and interpretation are available for both the Listening Comprehension and Oral Expression Scales. IBM and Windows versions of these programs are available. The usual normative scores as well as descriptive reports can be obtained from the use of the programs.

The most positive feature of the OWLS is its base in theoretical constructs related to the development of language processes. The manual highlights the essential theoretic positions utilized to formulate the purposes of the OWLS. A clear relationship was established between these positions and the applications and purposes of the OWLS scales.

Whereas previous tests of language development tend to focus only on the receptive or expressive components of language, and then only at the one-word level in many cases, the OWLS attempts to capture the pragmatic and supralinguistic (higher order thinking) structures of language. The test provides an opportunity to observe an examinee's ability to understand and produce connected language. Students with language processing difficulties often score well on more traditional measures of singular dimension language tests, yet have great difficulty using language to function in school or social settings. These students miss subtle nuances of language that cause communication difficulties in real life settings. The Listening Comprehension and Oral Expression Scales attempt to incorporate processes of language constructions not directly related to lexical or grammatical information. These scales attempt to tap the understanding of idioms, humor, exaggerations, and sarcasm used in conversational speech.

There are several positive test construction features of the Listening Comprehension and Oral Expression Scales of the OWLS. The author stated that items were written and reviewed by many experts in the fields of speech/language pathology, school psychology, and other related disciplines. Correct responses for the Oral Expression scale were not formulated a priori. Rather, responses from the standardization sample were reviewed to determine the language content and structures used by the examinees. Scoring criteria were then developed based on this sample of responses.

The standardization process of the Listening Comprehension and Oral Expression Scales was very appropriate. The sample size consisted of 1,795 subjects who ranged in age from 3 to 21 years. Subjects were grouped by 6-month age intervals for ages 3-0 to 4-11; 1-year intervals for ages 5-0 to 11-0; and then by ages 12–13, 14–15, 16–18, and 19–21. The total sample was representative of the U.S. population for gender, geographical region, race/ethnicity, and socioeconomic status as determined by maternal employment. Norms were established by age level. Mean scaled scores for both the Listening Comprehension and Oral Expression Scales were 100 with a standard deviation of 15. This makes comparisons with scores obtained on most of the major psychological and educational batteries easily done.

The OWLS Listening Comprehension and Oral Expression Scales can be administered to children and young adults ages 3 to 21 years. The upper age levels of this span are very positive features for this test. Many of the language tests only provide norms to the middle teen years. The band to age 21 allows examiners to assess language functions in older students and to trace the development of language competencies throughout their school careers.

The only apparent weakness of this test is its art work. Stimulus materials consist of black-and-white line drawings. Many of these drawings seem vague to the concepts to be tapped by the items. As the items increase in developmental difficulty, they become much more detailed and subtle in their differences. Students who do not attend well to visual detail, or who have short attention spans, may miss the cues and details presented in the materials that are used to prompt them for the appropriate language responses.

Statistical properties of the OWLS are good and reflect the trends in test development to provide this information before a test is marketed. Reliability studies conducted for the scales were not as extensive as the validity reports; however, they were adequate. Test-retest reliability for the short term (median of 8 weeks) by three different age groups was within the .58 to .85 range. One interrater reliability study evidenced good consistency in scoring with trained examiners for the Oral Expression Scale. Reliability coefficients ranged from .90 to .99.

Validity information presented in the manual was very impressive. Several studies were highlighted that compare results of the Listening Comprehension and Oral Expression Scales, by age levels, with commonly used measures of ability (Kaufman Assessment Battery for Children, Wechsler Intelligence Scales for Children—Third Edition, and the Kaufman Brief Intelligence Scale) other measures of language (Test for Auditory Comprehension of Language—Revised, Peabody Picture Vocabulary Test—Revised, and Clinical Evaluation of Language Fundamentals—Revised) and tests of academic achievement (Kaufman Test of Educational Achievement, Comprehensive Form, Peabody Individual Achievement Test—Revised, and Woodcock Reading Mastery Test—Revised). Correlations with other language tests were moderate to high, reflecting similarities between the tests. The use of the OWLS can be justified by the more extensive nature of the test and its age ranges. Correlations with IQ measures indicate strong positive relationships between the Listening Comprehension and Oral Expression Scales and various tests of verbal ability. Moderate correlations were obtained between these scales and the nonverbal sections of the IQ batteries. Moderate correlations were also obtained between the OWLS Scales and various measures of verbal achievement. Low correlations were obtained between these scales and measures of math achievement. The author offered these correlations as evidence of divergent validity, especially in areas where low correlations were obtained between the OWLS and various subtests of math achievement. Validity studies conducted with clinical populations (students with speech impairments, language

delays, and language impairments) indicated the more involved the speech or language difficulty, the lower the scores on the OWLS. This would indicate that the test is able to identify students with difficulties in the language functions.

SUMMARY. The OWLS Listening Comprehension and Oral Expression Scales may prove to be one of the more popular and widely used language tests. The scales can be administered by school psychologists, speech pathologists, educational diagnosticians, and other professionals who need to assess language functions in students. Examiners may find that the OWLS provides information on language functions that are not tapped by other language tests they are currently using.

[267]

Oral and Written Language Scales: Written Expression.

Purpose: Constructed as an "assessment of written language."
Population: Ages 5–21.
Publication Date: 1996.
Acronym: OWLS Written Expression.
Scores, 2: Written Expression, Language Composite (when used with OWL Listening Comprehension and Oral Expression Scales).
Administration: Individual or group.
Price Data, 1999: $84.95 per complete kit including manual (255 pages), response booklets, record forms, and administration card; $23.95 per 25 response booklets; $19.95 per 25 record forms; $62.95 per manual; $149.95 per AGS Computer ASSIST™ for OWLS Written Expression (IBM or Macintosh).
Time: (15–25) minutes.
Comments: May be used alone or in combination with OWLS Listening Comprehension and Oral Expression (266).
Author: Elizabeth Carrow-Woolfolk.
Publisher: American Guidance Service, Inc.

Review of the Oral and Written Language Scales: Written Expression by C. DALE CARPENTER, Professor of Special Education, Western Carolina University, Cullowhee, NC:

DESCRIPTION. The Oral and Written Language Scales: Written Expression (OWLS Written Expression) is intended to assess three aspects of written expression—Conventions, Linguistics, and Content. It may also be used as part of three scales comprising Oral and Written Language Scales, the other two being Listening Comprehension and Oral Expression (266). Although these three scales were conormed, they may be used individually and provide useful independent data.

OWLS Written Expression contains 39 items grouped in four overlapping sets for children ages 5 to 7, 8 to 11, 12 to 14, and youth 15 to 21. There are no basals and ceilings as all the items in a set are administered depending on the child's age. The following tasks are included: (a) Students write dictated sentences; (b) students write questions or notes, or interpret information from a table; (c) students complete stories; (d) students retell stories; (e) students use brief descriptive writing such as interpreting a quote or describing a cartoon character; (f) students use expository writing to convey information. All of the items are relatively short and, with rare exception, students receive a score of 1 or 0 for a point on an item. Some items are scored for only one point such as spelling whereas others are scored for as many as 7 or more points including such domains as meaningful content, details, and supporting ideas.

OWLS Written Expression is designed to be administered individually but may be administered to small groups. Administration requires a response booklet, record form, and a laminated Written Expression Scale administration card. All are well designed for clarity and ease of use. The manual may be used in lieu of the administration card and is necessary for scoring.

Scoring is complex and examiners must carefully read and understand the overall scoring scheme as well as follow instructions for each item. The manual provides clear, detailed instructions and examples of correct and incorrect answers for each item. Age- and grade-based standard scores are available as well as percentiles, normal curve equivalents (NCEs), stanines, and age and grade equivalents. OWLS comes with software for Macintosh and Windows formats to assist with finding and reporting derived scores. If the Listening Comprehension and Oral Expression scales are used, a Language Composite standard score is also available. In addition, the manual provides a reproducible Descriptive Analysis Worksheet for each of the four sets of items. This allows the examiner to conduct error analysis in each of the three major areas of Conventions, Linguistics, and Content.

NORM SAMPLE. OWLS Written Expression was administered individually to a national sample of 1,373 subjects. The norm sample appropriately reflects characteristics of the population in age, gender, race, region, and socioeconomic status (determined by mother's education level).

RELIABILITY. Split-half, test-retest, and interrater reliability coefficients are provided. For all but 19-to-21-year old subjects, split-half reliability coefficients are .84 or higher. Test-retest reliability was studied with a median 9-week interval between test administrations using a group of 54 students between the ages of 8 and 11 and a group of 30 students ages 16-0 to 18-11. Coefficients were .88 and .87. Because of the subjective nature of much of the scoring, interrater reliability is critical. Interrater reliability was estimated using 15 subjects in each of the four age classes of students and the mean interrater reliability coefficient was .95.

VALIDITY. The author presents information about content, construct, criterion-related, and clinical validity. Content validity rests on the author's construction of a model of language and adherence in item generation to that model. No other information is provided.

The evidence for construct validity is presented as intercorrelations among the three OWLS scales. By age, the mean correlation coefficients of the Written Expression scale is .57 with Listening Comprehension and .66 with Oral Expression. One would expect a stronger relationship between Written Expression and Oral Expression than between Written Expression and Listening Comprehension.

Scores on the OWLS Written Expression were correlated with scores on the following achievement instruments in separate studies: Kaufman Test of Educational Achievement (KTEA), Peabody individual Achievement Test—Revised (PIAT-R), and Woodcock Reading Mastery Test—Revised (WRMT-R). Most of the correlation coefficients exceed .80 for subtests of reading and spelling with OWLS Written Expression. Unfortunately, there are no criterion-related studies reported in the manual showing the relationship of scores on the OWLS Written Expression and other achievement measures of written expression such as the Test of Written Language-3 (TOWL-3; T5:2731).

Separate groups of students with language impairments, mental retardation, hearing impairments, and learning disabilities were studied with significant results upholding the clinical validity premise that these groups do score systematically lower than peer groups on the OWLS Written Expression.

SUMMARY. OWLS Written Expression provides educational diagnosticians and researchers with a reliable and valid measure of written expression for a wide range of ages of students. Using the Written Expression scale in conjunction with Listening Comprehension and Oral Expression is an advantage over some other instruments because a Language Composite is available. Although the instrument is relatively easy to administer, scoring takes more time initially, but instructions are relatively clear given the subjective components of the instrument. Accompanying software aids in scoring and reporting.

OWLS Written Expression is a good assessment instrument. In the area of written language the instrument uses many frequently used means of measuring achievement and some formats that are less common. Common formats include writing sentences from dictation, combining sentences, and finishing stories. Less common formats include creating a cartoon character and writing a note to your mother. OWLS Written Expression does not require the subject to produce an extended writing sample like some other instruments such as the TOWL-3. Except for the lack of this feature used by some other written expression instruments, OWLS Written Expression appears to adequately measure important aspects of writing achievement.

Review of the Oral and Written Language Scales: Written Expression by KORESSA KUTSICK MALCOLM, School Psychologist, Augusta County School Board, Fishersville, VA:

It has been difficult to find a test of written language that taps into a broad array of writing skills, that measures the mechanics of writing as well as the creative process of written expression, that can be administered quickly and easily, and that carries good psychometric properties. The Written Expression Scale of the Oral and Written Language Scales is a test that might address these assessment needs.

The Oral and Written Language Scales are composed of three separate scales: Listening Comprehension, Oral Expression, and Written Expression. The author advocates the administration of all three scales as part of a comprehensive assessment of language functioning; however, each scale may be administered independent of the other scales.

The Written Expression Scale of the OWLS was designed as a standardized test that measures an examinee's functional writing skills. Three major parts of the writing process are measured by this scale. These parts consist of: Conventions, measuring the applications of spelling, punctuation, and capitalization rules; Linguistics, measuring the use of language forms such as modifiers, phrases, verb forms, and complex sentences; and Content, measuring appropriate subject matter, coherence in writing, word choices, etc. Evaluation tasks of the Written Expression Scale require subjects to respond to a variety of open-ended writing tasks presented verbally by the examiner. Some tasks have accompanying pictures or printed materials. The writing tasks of this scale were designed to reflect typical writing assignments a student might encounter in a classroom setting. Writing activities include transcribing dictated sentences, writing notes or letters, retelling a story, completing a story, producing descriptive writing, and producing brief expository writing.

Administration of the Written Expression Scale takes 10 to 30 minutes depending on the age and skill levels of an examinee. Each examinee is presented a band of age-appropriate items. Items are arranged in ascending developmental order. This arrangement of items and levels allows for a good sampling of writing skills, while minimizing the effects of fatigue and frustration. Out-of-level testing is permitted to better assess the writing skills of lower functioning individuals or to tap into the upper limits of a bright student's writing skill range. The Written Expression Scale may be administered to examinees aged 5 to 21 years.

The Written Expression Scale may be given to individual or small groups of students. The ability to administer the scale to small groups of students may be of great value to special education teachers, school psychologists, and other professionals who must assess the writing skills of a large number of students each year. If group administration is used, examiners should limit the group size according to the age of the examinees. For example, three to five children would be the optimal group size for younger children as they might need more attention during the writing activities. As many as 10–15 students might comprise an assessment group of older students who are more independent in their writing habits.

Administration of the Written Expression Scale is straightforward. The manual is very clear in its presentation of the administration procedures of this test. The only materials needed for the administration process are a record booklet and an item card that contains the specific instructions for the test.

Scoring of the Written Expression Scale might prove to be somewhat of a challenge. Multiple scoring criteria are presented for each item. Practice will be necessary for examiners to master the specifics of the scoring rules. Scoring time can take as long as 17 minutes for the more advanced writing levels. The manual does provide good examples and explanations of scoring options for each item.

There are several positive features of the Written Expression Scale of the OWLS. Like the Listening Comprehension and Oral Expression Scales of this test, the Written Expression Scale is based on a strong theoretical foundation of language development and processes. All three scales were conormed, which allows for comparisons to be made between the different processes of language functioning. The range of obtainable standard scores for all three of the scales is another positive feature of the OWLS. Standard scores from 40 to 160 may be obtained. Few of the available writing tests on the market today provide this wide a range of standard scores. For example, on some assessments a score of 78 is the lowest standard score that can be obtained for some examinees. This level of score does not allow examiners to demonstrate point differences between ability and achievement that are often needed to document specific learning disabilities. With its lower range of standard scores, the Written Expression Scale of the OWLS may become the test of choice for many examiners charged with the task of defining significant weaknesses in a client's writing skills. A related positive feature of the Written Expression Scale of the OWLS is that it provides a Descriptive Analysis Sheet that allows examiners to chart items that examinees have passed or failed. Completion of the sheet provides a diagnostic view of particular writing strengths and weaknesses demonstrated by an examinee that can be translated into remedial activities.

No test is perfect and the Written Expression Scales does have a few weaknesses. The oral directions presented to examinees might be too complex. This may be especially true for those individuals who do have language processing difficulties. Even though readability estimates were

presented for the directions read to the examinee, lower functioning individuals may have trouble understanding what is being asked of them.

The Written Expression Scale of the OWLS was standardized on 1,373 subjects ages 5 to 21 years. The standardization sample was representative of U.S. Census data for gender, geographic region, socioeconomic status (by mother's education level), and race/ethnicity.

The statistical properties of the test are good. Strong positive correlations were reported in the various reliability studies presented in the manual. Internal split-half correlations ranged from .77 to .94. The standard error of measurement of 5.5 points also gave support to the reliability of the scale. Test-retest studies with intervals from 18 to 165 days yielded correlations of .88 for younger subjects and .87 for older subjects. Interrater reliability correlations ranged from .91 to .98 depending on the level of items reviewed.

The author of the Written Expression Scale also provided good information on the validity of this scale. Content and construct validity support was offered through the descriptions of the development process of the scale. Construct validity evidence using interscale correlations ranged from .30 to .75 when the three scales of the OWLS were compared to each other. The Written Expression Scale tended to correlate higher with the Oral Expression Scale than with the Listening Comprehension Scale. The explanation for this was that both the Written Expression and Oral Expression Scales tapped into forms of language expression, whereas the Listening Comprehension Scale measured receptive language functioning. Comparisons of scores obtained by subjects on other language-based tests with results of the Written Expression Scale yielded similar results. The Written Expression Scale tended to correlate more positively with tests of expressive language than it did with tests of receptive language.

Criterion-related validity was investigated by comparing scores from the Written Expression Scale with those obtained by subjects on various measures of achievement (the Peabody Individual Achievement Test—Revised, Kaufman Test of Educational Achievement, Woodcock-Reading Master Test—Revised). Strong positive correlations ranging from .63 —.88 were obtained. This is somewhat unusual for a test of written language, and may lend positive support for the inclusion of this scale in a battery of educational tests. Moderate to strong positive correlations (.41–.72) were also obtained between the Written Expression Scaled Score and scaled scores obtained on various measures of intellectual ability (such as the Wechsler Intelligence Scale for Children—Third Edition [WISC-III] and Kaufman Brief Intelligence Test). The Written Expression Scale tended to have stronger correlations with scales of verbal functioning than it did with scales of nonverbal abilities. Clinical studies conducted with the Written Expression Scale indicated that the test is able to discriminate between clients with language difficulties and those who do not demonstrate these problems.

With its assortment of writing tasks, ease of administration, and strong psychometric properties, the Written Expression Scale of the OWLS may become an instrument of choice when examiners must assess the written expression skills of school-aged individuals. The scale seems to meet many of the needs of a written language test, yet it is easy to administer and can be done so in a timely fashion.

[268]
Oral Speech Mechanism Screening Examination, Third Edition.

Purpose: "To provide the speech-language pathologist and other professionals with a method for assessing the adequacy of the oral mechanism for speech and related functions."
Population: Age 5 through adults.
Publication Dates: 1981–2000.
Acronym: OSMSE-3.
Scores: 9 areas: Lips, Tongue, Jaw, Teeth, Hard Palate, Soft Palate, Pharynx, Breathing, Diadochokinesis.
Administration: Individual.
Price Data: Available from publisher.
Time: (10–15) minutes.
Authors: Kenneth O. St. Louis and Dennis M. Ruscello.
Publisher: PRO-ED.
Cross References: See T5:1852 (6 references) and T4:1900 (4 references); for reviews by Charles Wm. Martin and Malcolm R. McNeil of an earlier edition, see 11:272.

Review of the Oral Speech Mechanism Screening Examination, Third Edition by ROGER L. TOWNE, Associate Professor and Head, Department of Communication Disorders, Northern Michigan University, Marquette, MI:

As noted by the authors, the Oral Speech Mechanism Screening Examination, Third Edition (OSMSE-3) "was designed to provide ... a screening examination that is reliable, relatively easy and quick to administer, and appropriate for children and adults in a variety of clinical settings" (examiner's manual, p. v). Although the test was developed to be utilized primarily by clinical speech-language pathologists, other professionals who have interest and knowledge or oral structure and function might also find it useful. The OSMSE-3 provides a highly structured format by which the individual components of the oral speech mechanism (i.e., lips, tongue, jaw, teeth, hard palate, soft palate, pharynx) can be assessed for structural and functional normalcy and deviance. Also included are guidelines for assessing breathing and speech diadochokinesis. It is estimated by the authors that administration of the OSMSE-3 by trained and experienced examiners will take 10 to 15 minutes.

Although the OSMSE-3 is indeed a short screening examination, the key to its successful use rests in the knowledge and observational skills of the examiner. To assist the examiner in this task the authors have prepared a very thorough examiner's manual in which each structure examined is described relative to its normal appearance and function, as well as typical deviations that might be encountered. A series of 12 black-and-white line drawings and 16 colored photographs now have been included for illustration and clarification of each structure. The newly shaded scoring form is organized to be user friendly, although its friendliness increases with familiarization and use. An audio training tape is also provided that instructs the examiner in the appropriate way in which to evaluate speech diadochokinesis and obtain reliable and consistent performance measures.

Few other tools for examining the oral speech mechanism have a scoring system and normative data as does the OSMSE-3. The examination scores 31 structure points and 24 function points from which noted deviations are subtracted. This results in a Total Score (55 minus number of deviations) that can then be compared to cutoff scores appropriate for the examinee's age. In addition, diadochokinetic performance can be compared to age-appropriate cutoff scores as well. Failure to stay below established cutoff scores for the three areas (i.e., structure, function, and diadochokinesis) results in failing the OSMSE-3.

Considering the fact that both structural development and neuromotor function are correlated with age, the ability to compare a person's performance with established age-related norms is a useful component. Additional data are also provided that allow some cursory comparison to individuals having phonological, stuttering, or head injury problems.

The OSMSE-3 is the third revision of the original OSMSE (1981) and the revised version of the OSMSE-R (1987). Normative data for the OSMSE and OSMSE-R were collected from 7 examiners testing 187 normal subjects in 12 age groups ranging in age from 5 to 77 years. Variability of standard deviations within and across age groups was quite small (1.1–3.1 for Total) leading the authors to conclude "scores are consistently high, uniform, and relatively invariant among normal subjects over the age of 5" (examiner's manual, p. 32). Test reliability, based on interjudge agreement, was examined using 8 examiners and 45 subjects and ranged between 89.4% and 100%. Interjudge agreement was examined using 9 different examines and 30 subjects and ranged between 81.7% and 98.3%. Because the content of the OSMSE-3 and its assessment procedures were not altered from the two previous versions of the test the normative and reliability data remain unchanged. Test validity was not formally assessed although the examiner's manual does present investigative data relative to construct and criterion-related validity that suggest that the OSMSE-3 has met some criteria relative to measuring what is intended.

SUMMARY. Although its content has remained unchanged from previous versions, the OSMSE-3 has been significantly improved in terms of its scoring form and examples provided in the examiner's manual. As a screening tool it accomplishes its purpose of providing a quick, yet thorough, cursory assessment of the oral mechanism's structure and function. It appears to be a reasonably sensitive instrument that would be capable of detecting mild and moderate deviations. The test's ability to score and compare scores to normative data relative to a client's age is a relatively unique and useful feature, especially when attempting to quantify baseline and changing conditions. As with other oral mechanism assessment tools, a thorough understanding of oral structure and function is necessary in order for an accurate and reliable assessment to be made. Despite the clear descriptions of normal and deviant characteristics that appear in the examiner's manual, this examination should only be given by qualified professionals such as clinical speech-language pathologists. If one is comfortable using the current OSMSE-R then there may not be an overwhelming benefit in purchasing this new revision. However, if one is looking for a relatively simple, yet comprehensive, oral mechanism screening instrument, then the OSMSE-3 should be given careful consideration.

[269]
Organizational Beliefs Questionnaire.

Purpose: "Intended to give concerned managers a deeper understanding of their own organization's culture."
Population: Organizations.
Publication Date: 1997.
Acronym: OBQ.
Scores, 10: Work Can Be As Much Fun As Play, Seek Constant Improvement, Accept Specific And Difficult Goals, Accept Responsibility For Your Actions, Care About One Another, Quality Is Crucially Important, Work Together To Get The Job Done, Have Concern For Measures Of Our Success, There Must Be Hands-On Management, A Strong Set Of Shared Values And Beliefs Guide Our Actions.
Administration: Group.
Price Data, 1997: $195 per basic assessment package; $49.95 per additional reports; $99.95 per 50 additional answer sheets.
Time: Administration time not reported.
Comments: Computerized interpretive information provided by publisher, including scale summaries and individual item analyses.
Author: Marshall Sashkin.
Publisher: Human Resource Development Press, Inc.

Review of the Organizational Beliefs Questionnaire by CYNTHIA A. LARSON-DAUGHERTY, Adjunct Professor, Psychology Department, Towson University, Towson, MD, and Director of Training & Development, Federal Reserve Bank, Baltimore, MD:

The revisions to the Organizational Beliefs Questionnaire (OBQ) and support materials (Administrator's Guide) are timely and relevant. The materials are incredibly detailed and helpful resources for managers in the pursuit of performance improvement via understanding organizational culture. Using scales, the instrument identifies 10 "dimensions of excellence cultures" (manual,

p. 3). The instrument is written for practitioners, but clearly presents the theoretical premise and research development that meets the rigor of academic standards. The instructions and explanation are rather lengthy, but provide the necessary depth to make the user comfortable and the results effective. The Executive Summary captures key themes and provides a useful introduction to the detailed report.

This instrument is not intended for those looking for a simple answer or quick fix. The detailed statistical summary with the qualitative items/statements may overwhelm the average practitioner, but those who are committed to understanding organizational culture through member values and beliefs in an effort to strategically enhance the long-term performance of their company will find that this is the instrument of choice. The criticisms of the OBQ are few and should not dissuade a manager or organization committed to cultural organizational diagnosis and performance improvement from using the instrument.

TEST COVERAGE AND USAGE. Organization managers considering the use and administration of the Organizational Beliefs Questionnaire (OBQ) will appreciate the level of detail provided by the author. The instrument's capability to generate data from all levels of the organization (employee, supervisor, and manager) assists managers, or more specifically organizational change agents, with the ability to gain a deeper and better understanding of their organization's culture.

The instrument asks participants their opinion regarding other organization members' viewpoints or beliefs. There are 10 values and belief scales that were derived based on their ability to support organizational excellence. Development and design of the instrument has been iterative based on research that has revealed changes in society and the workplace over the last two decades. The instrument, now in its third revision, has experienced both minor and major changes. The research methodology applied to review and revise the instrument appears to be timely and relevant. The instrument clearly aids in generating employee opinions about values and beliefs related to organizational culture. It provides participant anonymity and relatively detailed demographic data.

TEST VALIDATION AND NORMING. The instrument's sampling for validation and norming meets established standards. The author of the OBQ is relatively renowned in the field of organizational diagnosis and for instrumentation development, design, and testing. Traditional testing of samples was done and redone for each OBQ revision following the same rigorous methodology. Noted in the statistical summary of testing for norms and validity were the instrument's results when applied to organizations that Peters and Waterman (1988), authors of *In Search of Excellence,* and Collins and Porras (1994), researchers of organizations that have a history of long-term performance excellence, identified as excellent. The results of the most recent instrument, research based on a very large data set of over 1,400 respondents, indicates the instrument results show a relevant degree of scientific validity. The section on the development of the OBQ provides detailed information on norming, and validity evidence, and clearly identifies the reasons for instrument revisions and continued research.

RELIABILITY. Sufficient reliability measures were conducted to ensure internal reliability and qualification for meeting minimum standards for educational and psychological testing.

PREDICTIVE, CONTENT, AND CONSTRUCT VALIDITY. The author goes to great lengths to first explain types of validity, and then the relationship of different levels of validity to the instrument. The details about the revisions and the various levels, or strengths of content and construct validity, provide a user with enough confidence that scores from the instrument have high enough validity evidence to make the resulting data useful. The author clearly notes historical weaknesses and measures/changes initiated to correct them.

TEST ADMINISTRATION. The administrator/leader's preparatory guide is very helpful. The guide, similar to a "how-to" training manual, provides excellent content for planning the delivering of the instrument, administration, and follow-up. Participant instructions, an explanatory participant memo, and then brief instructions on the instrument, are clear and the instrument is easy to complete. The instrument is completed with a #2 pencil or dark blue or black ball-point pen. The OBQ is forwarded to HRD Press where scoring is processed and automated interpretations of results are generated. The results provide both an Executive Summary and item-by-item and cluster detail reports. If the administrator of the OBQ has questions or needs basic clarification on the results, the author provides an 800 phone number for questions.

Planning, administration instructions, and the follow-up guide are clear and easy to use. The manual serves as an excellent resource for facilitating planning for instrument implementation and conducting results discussions.

TEST REPORTING. Instrument results reporting methods are laid out in a methodical, step-by-step, user-friendly format. The Executive Summary captures key theme data and provides an excellent context for introducing results to participants. Result category headers and brief descriptions are clear and provide statistical data that point to key issue areas for further analysis.

TEST AND ITEM BIAS. A brief discussion about items within the instrument and revisions indicates that some questions were changed or modified to address their relationship to other questions and impact on the results. Most poignant and interesting, and important to note about this instrument, is that monitoring test and item bias are a continuing process. As an administrator of the instrument identifies and selects participants, it is critical that the sample and sample size represent the true mix of the organization's population. Clear instructions are presented on how to carefully oversee this critical process; and it clearly points out that there is administrator responsibility for reducing or eliminating test bias.

The language in the administrator's manual and on the instrument is clear. The author goes to great lengths to provide detail. This appears to be done in order to offer greater confidence in the instrument. An experienced manager familiar with instrument administration would have little problem using this instrument. A less experienced manager may need to spend more preparation time in order to ensure they administer the instrument accurately. In either case, the data this instrument generates are highly worthwhile for understanding organizational culture values and beliefs.

SUMMARY. Overall, aside from the quantity of data produced from the instrument (i.e., over 25 pages of data in sample results), review of the instrument suggests that it is a highly useful tool for managers to derive meaningful data about organization cultural values and beliefs. Ultimately, the data should help guide a manager through cultural issues that impede organizational performance and tap into those that support and promote performance excellence.

REVIEWER'S REFERENCES

Peters, T., & Waterman, R. (1988). *In search of excellance: Lessons from America's best run companies.* New York: Warner Books.

Collins, J. C., & Porras, J. I. (1994). *Built to last: Successful habits of visionary companies.* New York: HarperCollins.

Review of the Organizational Beliefs Questionnaire by MARY ROZNOWSKI, Associate Professor of Psychology, Ohio State University, Columbus, OH:

The Organizational Beliefs Questionnaire (OBQ) is a 50-item measure aimed at assessing perceptions of organizational climate. The developers of the OBQ have employed the frameworks of Hayes and Abernathy (1980) and Peters and Waterman (1982) to conceptualize and write items for the measure. To do this, organizations with long-term histories of excellent performance were examined and qualities of the climates within those organizations were used to derive content categories for the OBQ.

Culture, according to the OBQ, refers to patterns of shared beliefs. Thus, employees within an organizational setting must be queried as to their perceptions of values and beliefs within the organization. Some degree of correspondence among organizational members in perceptions is thus necessary for a valid measure of culture. Examples of values and beliefs that support organizational excellence are "work can be as much fun as play" and (employees in this organization) "seek constant improvement." There are 10 OBQ scales, each representing a separate dimension of excellent culture.

There are 50 items in the measure, and organizational members respond to these items on a 5-point scale from *strongly agree* to *strongly disagree.* Individuals respond to the items from the perspective of "people in this organization" rather than from the perspective of self, in order to minimize social desirability. Thus, individuals would respond that people in their organization believe that work can be as fun as play, for instance.

Considerable information for organizations is given in the technical manual. The OBQ was designed as a means of providing feedback to managers and considerable information of a tutorial nature is provided. Each scale is reviewed and discussed, as are each of the 50 items within the measure. It becomes clear that many of the items are less descriptive than they are evaluative and affectively oriented. This issue is not discussed by the author of the measure and may lead to excessive measurement error and socially desirable responding. Further, some of the items are a bit wordy and cumbersome, thereby potentially detracting from precise measurement as well.

To counter social desirability further, some items were written in the negative so that it would not be obvious to respondents which statement was positive and which negative. This could have been achieved by simply writing the items to be more descriptive and less affectively loaded.

"Norms" were obtained for a large number of organizations. These normative data are presented in a table that is unclear, however, and that does not really correspond to the text given in the technical manual. There is some concern regarding the method used to test variability to determine if there is more variability across than within organizations. In order to achieve this it is necessary to have an estimate of across-organizational variability. Who are members of the mixed sample? Many such questions are left unanswered. This grouping method makes less sense than combining individuals within groups (an across-groups term). Further, sample sizes for organizations are simply too small.

Data are needed on reliabilities, item analyses, and factor analyses. Inadequate reporting and few, if any, analyses are included here. There is very little validation information as well.

SUMMARY. It is true that assessing organizational culture is a very difficult task. The designers of the OBQ have made a reasonable first start, but much work could be done, and should be done, before a psychometrically sound, useful instrument results.

REVIEWER'S REFERENCES

Hayes, R. H., & Abernathy, W. J. (1980, July/August). Managing our way to economic decline. *Harvard Business Review,* 67–77.
Peters, T. J., & Waterman, R. H., Jr. (1982). *In search of excellence.* New York: Harper and Row.

[270]
Organizational Change-Readiness Scale.

Purpose: Constructed "to analyze the ability of an organization to manage change effectively and to plan improvement actions."
Population: Employees.
Publication Date: 1996.
Acronym: OCRS.
Scores: 5 scales: Structural Readiness, Technological Readiness, Climatic Readiness, Systemic Readiness, People Readiness.
Administration: Group.
Price Data, 1996: $6.50 per assessment inventory; $24.95 per facilitator's guide (24 pages).

Time: (20) minutes.
Comments: Redevelopment of Organizational Change-Readiness Survey.
Authors: John E. Jones and William L. Bearley.
Publisher: Human Resource Development Press.

Review of the Organizational Change-Readiness Scale by GARY J. DEAN, Associate Professor, Department of Adult and Community Education, Indiana University of Pennsylvania, Indiana, PA:

INTRODUCTION. The Organizational Change-Readiness Scale (OCRS) is a self-report measure through which members of an organization rate on a scale of 1 = *not at all,* 2 = *to a very little degree,* 3 = *to a little degree,* 4 = *to some degree,* 5 = *to a great degree,* and 6 = *to a very great degree,* 76 items regarding their organization's readiness for change. The items are grouped into five scales: Structural Readiness (21 items), Technological Readiness (6 items), Climatic Readiness (19 items), Systematic Readiness (13 items), and People Readiness (17 items). Each of these scales is measured in terms of both supports for change and barriers to change in a force-field analysis model. There are two booklets with the instrument: the inventory (which contains an interpretation guide) and a Facilitator's Guide.

DEVELOPMENT. The authors of the OCRS state that it is "a redevelopment of an instrument published earlier under the title *Organizational Change—Readiness Survey*" (facilitator's guide, p. 6), which was published in 1985 by Organization Design & Development. According to the authors, the model for the OCRS (the five scales of the instrument) is based on a thorough review of the literature on change readiness in organizations. The authors, stating that there is a scarcity of literature on the topic of change readiness in organizations, cite only two references, including what appears to be their primary source, an article by Pfeiffer and Jones (1978). Based on this review of literature and the previous Organizational Change-Readiness Survey, items were then developed for the OCRS to measure each of the five scales. The items were reviewed by "human resource development expert judges" (facilitator's guide, p. 6) and revised based on their comments. The resulting instrument was field tested prior to publishing the final version of the OCRS.

VALIDITY AND RELIABILITY. In the section of the Facilitator's Guide headed "Reliability and Validity," the authors discuss reliability but make no mention of specific attempts to establish validity beyond what is discussed in the section on the development of the OCRS. Because the authors provide only two references and no indication of the other literature they reviewed, it is difficult to determine the extent to which the five scales of the OCRS actually do reflect what the literature says.

Reliability was investigated using a small sample (n = 88), which was not further described. The following correlation coefficients were calculated for each scale using Cronbach's alpha: Structural Readiness = .79; Technological Readiness = .71; Climatic Readiness = .82; Systematic Readiness = .73; and People Readiness = .81. The authors correctly point out that the correlation coefficients for Technology and Systems are lower because of the limited number of items in these scales (6 and 13 respectively). In addition, the interscale correlations were calculated based on the same sample. These range from a low of .55 (Technology correlated with People) to a high of .80 (Comatic Correlated with People). The generally high interscale correlations indicate the interdependence of the scales, which the authors also acknowledge.

ADMINISTRATION AND SCORING. The inventory is contained in a booklet that includes an interpretation guide. The responses are recorded on NCR paper, the top page of which allows respondents to record their responses, and the bottom page of which allows for scoring. It took this reviewer less than 20 minutes to complete and score the inventory. The second page of the NCR answer sheet is divided so that the five scales appear as columns and are easily identifiable. Scoring is accomplished by recording the extreme positive and negative scores for each item. Items to which a respondent marked 1 (not at all) or 2 (to a very little degree) are recorded as an "X." Items to which a respondent marked 5 (to a great degree) or 6 (to a very great degree) are recorded as an "0." Items marked 3 (to a little degree) or 4 (to some degree) are not counted in computing the final scores for each scale. The effect of this system is that the scores are grouped into three categories: Scores of "1" and "2" are recorded as barriers (X), scores of "3" and "4" are disregarded, and scores of "5" and "6" are recorded as supports (0) for change readiness. These scores are recorded at the bottom of the second NCR page and again on an interpretation diagram.

INTERPRETATION. The total number of Xs for each scale indicates the extent to which

there are barriers to change readiness, and the total number of 0s indicates the extent to which change readiness is supported in the organization. These scores are marked on a diagram based on Kurt Levin's model of force-field analysis. Supports can then be weighed against barriers to help determine what needs to be done to facilitate change readiness in the organization. The authors provide descriptions and examples for each of the scales to aid in interpretation. The inventory booklet also provides a section entitled, "Action Planning for Improving Change-Readiness," which respondents can use to help them become more specific about how to build on the supports as well as reduce the impact of the barrier that have been identified by the OCRS. In addition, the Facilitator's Guide describes three ways to use the OCRS and the Inventory provides 13 strategies to facilitate change in an organization.

The layout of the NCR answer sheet and the inventory booklet make them easy to use and understand. The facilitator's guide is also easy to use and has good material to help facilitators employ the OCRS effectively in their organizations.

SUMMARY. The OCRS is a well-designed instrument, which can be used effectively for the purposes described by the authors: as a tool to promote discussion and understanding of change readiness in an organization. The lack of specifics provided by the authors regarding the development and validity evidence of the instrument does promote some concern. The authors state that the instrument was designed as "a professional tool, not a research instrument" (Facilitator's Guide, p. 6). The applied nature of the instrument, however, does not excuse the authors from supplying more detailed information on the literature reviewed, the derivation of the conceptual basis for the instrument, and procedures used to develop items and field test the instrument. In short, scores from the instrument can be considered valid only to the extent particular users believe the five scales and the items used to measure those scales accurately reflect change-readiness issues in their organization.

REVIEWER'S REFERENCE

Pfeiffer, J. W., & Jones, J. E. (1978). OD readiness. In J. W. Pfeiffer and J. E. Jones, (Eds.), *The 1978 annual handbook for group facilitators* (pp. 219–228). San Diego, CA: University Associates.

Review of the Organizational Change-Readiness Scale by EUGENE P. SHEEHAN, Professor of Psychology, University of Northern Colorado, Greeley, CO:

The Organizational Change-Readiness Scale (OCRS) is a 76-item attitude survey designed to assess employees' perceptions of an organization's ability and readiness to change. The OCRS was developed from a literature review in which the authors identified the dimensions deemed critical to organizational change-readiness. This resulted in the questions being groups into five readiness scales: Structural 921 items), People (17 items), Systemic (13 items), Climatic (19 items), and Technological (6 items). Respondents indicate on a 6-point scale the degree to which their organization has a particular change-related characteristics (e.g., To what degree does this organization "stay on the lookout for new technology?" [facilitator's guide, p. 2]).

The instrument is professionally presented in a booklet (inventory), which also contains scoring directions, an Organizational Change-Readiness Profile, Force-Field Analysis of Change-Readiness, description of major change strategies, and an Action Plan for Improving Change-Readiness. Directions for responding to and scoring the inventory are clear and easily followed. Scoring is completed on an answer sheet that is separate from the inventory booklet. Respondents identify and graph supports and barriers to the change process in the Force-Field Analysis of Change-Readiness. This graph provides an indication of the organization's current standing with respect to organizational change-readiness. it also provides the impetus for discussion about how an organization might best initiate change. The outline of major organizational change strategies and Action Plan for Improving Change-Readiness are designed to augment and provide direction to this discussion. An accompanying facilitator's guide describes how the instrument can be used in several settings: training module, team-building session, and one-on-one consultation. Thus, it would seem that the most common use of the OCRS is to stimulate spirited and practical discussion regarding an organization's readiness for change and how to position an organization so as to increase its adaptability.

In both the inventory booklet and the facilitator's guide, the authors liken the concept of change readiness to reading readiness and go on to assert that once a child is ready to read almost any method of reading instruction will work. I would disagree with this assertion. Extensive research shows that learning to read is not a unidimensional task. Reading requires numerous intellec-tual processes and may depend on a variety of instructional strategies (Pressley & McCormick, 1995). Organizational change is a similarly complex process and the effectiveness of change strategies will vary across organizations and depend on the context in which change is implemented.

The OCRS facilitator's guide provides little psychometric data. The authors maintain the instrument is ideographic, designed for use in separate and idiosyncratic organizations, and thus any norms would be misleading. I would argue that the development of norms for any psychometric instrument is both useful and necessary. The authors wrote items they believed assess the five change-readiness dimensions. Human resource development experts reviewed these items, which the authors then rewrote. They also report testing different forms of the instrument with training and consulting groups prior to the development of the final version. However, the facilitator's guide provides no information regarding the criteria used to select or reject items. Similarly, it does not provide any details of the groups used to test early versions of the instrument.

Reliability estimates (Cronbach's alpha) on the change-readiness dimensions and intercorrelations between the dimensions are the only psychometric data provided. The reliability estimates very between .71 and .82. These estimates are based on responses from 88 cases, a very small sample. It would be useful to have other types of reliability, especially both short- and long-term reliability.

The intercorrelations among the five dimensions range from .55 to .80, suggesting, according to the authors, the existence of a general factor underlying organizational change-readiness. it would be useful to have data from a factor analysis to support this contention. We do not know that the instrument has the factor structure proposed. indeed, the authors propose that those who use the OCRS with large populations conduct their own factor analysis.

No validity evidence is provided. Data on the following two validity questions should be provided: How does this instrument fare when taken by employees from organizations with known differences in organizational change-readiness? Additionally, what are the correlations between this instrument and other organizational change instruments? Answers to these questions would provide some evidence regarding whether the OCRS is measuring change-readiness.

SUMMARY. Overall, the OCRS is an interesting instrument designed to assess organizational change-readiness. The graphic representation of the results, combined with the other literature presented to OCRS users in the inventory and facilitator's guide, should provoke an interesting discussion about the concept of organizational change-readiness and specifically the state of the users' organization with respect to change-readiness. The psychometric data, however, are sparse and in need of further development. This lack of data is a clear weakness of the OCRS.

REVIEWER'S REFERENCE

Pressley, M., & McCormick, C. (1995). *Advanced educational psychology for educators, researchers, and policymakers.* New York: Harper Collins.

[271]
Otis-Lennon School Ability Test®, Seventh Edition.

Purpose: "Designed to measure abstract thinking and reasoning ability."
Population: Grades K–12.
Publication Dates: 1977–1996.
Acronym: OLSAT®.
Scores, 3: Verbal, Nonverbal, Total.
Administration: Group.
Levels, 7: A, B, C, D, E, F, G.
Forms, 3: 1, 2, 3.
Price Data, 1999: $22.50 per examination kit including one test booklet and directions for administering (Form 3, Levels AG); $83.50 per 25 Type 1 machine-scorable test booklets including 1 directions for administering (Form 3, Levels AD); $60.50 per 25 test booklets (specify reusable or hand scorable, and level); $25.25 per 25 Type 1 machine-scorable answer documents; $25.25 per 25 hand-scorable answer documents; $65.25 per technical manual; $12.75 per separate directions for administering; $42.25 per side-by-side keys for hand-scorable test booklets; $22 per stencil keys for hand-scorable answer documents; $22 per overlay keys for Type 1 machine-scorable answer documents; $5.25 per response keys (Form 3, specify level); $12.75 per 25 practice tests, including 1 directions for administering (Form 3, specify level); $6 per separate directions for administering practice tests; $65.25 per norms book; $5.75 per class records (Form 3, specify level).
Comments: Originally titled Otis-Lennon Mental Ability Test.
Authors: Arthur S. Otis and Roger T. Lennon.
Publisher: Harcourt Brace Educational Measurement—the educational testing division of The Psychological Corporation.
a) LEVEL A.
Population: Grade K.

Time: (70) minutes over 2 sessions.
Comments: Orally administered.
b) LEVEL B.
Population: Grade 1.
Time: Same as *a* above.
Comments: Orally administered.
c) LEVEL C.
Population: Grade 2.
Time: Same as *a* above.
Comments: Partially self-administered.
d) LEVEL D.
Population: Grade 3.
Time: (60) minutes.
Comments: Self-administered.
e) LEVEL E.
Population: Grades 4–5.
Time: Same as *d* above.
Comments: Self-administered.
f) LEVEL F.
Population: Grades 6–8.
Time: Same as *d* above.
Comments: Self-administered.
g) LEVEL G.
Population: Grades 9–12.
Time: Same as *d* above.
Comments: Self-administered.
Cross References: See T5:1866 (45 references) and T4:1913 (8 references); for reviews by Anne Anastasi and Mark E. Swerdlik, see 11:274 (48 references); for reviews by Calvin O. Dyer and Thomas Oakland, see 9:913 (7 references); see also T3:1754 (64 references); 8:198 (35 references), and T2:424 (10 references); for a review by John E. Milholland and excerpted reviews by Arden Grotelueschen and Arthur E. Smith, see 7:370 (6 references).

Review of the Otis-Lennon School Ability Test, Seventh Edition by LIZANNE DeSTEFANO, Professor of Educational Psychology, University of Illinois at Urbana-Champaign, Champaign, IL:

TEST BACKGROUND AND USES. The Seventh Edition of the Otis-Lennon School Ability Test (OLSAT-7) is the most recent in a series that began in 1918 with the Otis Group Intelligence Scale. The OLSAT is designed to measure abstract thinking and reasoning ability. The term "mental ability" has been changed from previous versions to "school ability" to reflect the purpose for which the current test is intended to serve: "To assess examinees' ability to cope with school learning tasks, to suggest their possible placement for school learning functions, and to evaluate their achievement in relation to the talents they bring to school learning situations" (Directions for Administration, p. 5). The use of "school ability" is also intended to discourage overgeneralization of the nature of the ability being measured (e.g., general intelligence). According to its publishers, the OLSAT is "based on the notion that to learn new things, students must be able to perceive accurately, to recognize and recall what has been perceived, to think logically, to understand relationships, to abstract from a set of particulars, and to apply generalizations to new and different contexts" (Directions for Administration, p. 5). Specific recommendations for appropriate uses and cautions against misuses of the OLSAT in educational settings, however, are not offered.

The Seventh Edition of the OLSAT contains items from the Fifth and Sixth Editions as well as new items. All items were reviewed and edited by editorial staff, measurement specialists, and psychologists for clarity, appropriateness of content, accuracy of correct answers, appropriateness of vocabulary, and absence of stereotyping or bias. Other than the changes made to item constituency, no discernible differences between the OLSAT Sixth and Seventh Editions were detected.

TEST STRUCTURE AND CONTENT. The OLSAT comprises seven levels (A through G) that are used for students in kindergarten to the 12th grade. Four separate levels are used for the early years (K through Grade 3) in order to provide a more precise measure of school ability during a developmental period recognized for steep gains in intellectual growth. One level, Level E, serves Grades 4 and 5; Level F serves Grades 6–8 and Level G Serves Grades 9–12. Levels A through G were normed using examinees whose age ranged from one year under and one year over designated school grades. Thus, out-of-level testing is possible within these limits.

Twenty-one different item types are organized into five clusters: Verbal Comprehension, Verbal Reasoning, Pictorial Reasoning, Figural Reasoning, and Quantitative Reasoning. Clusters I and II comprise the VERBAL component of the OLSAT and Clusters III-V form the NONVERBAL component. The classification of test items as verbal or nonverbal "hinges upon whether knowledge of language is requisite to answering the items" (Directions for Administering, p. 6). Verbal Comprehension includes Following Directions (Levels A–C), Antonyms (D–G), Sentence Completion (D–G), and Sentence Arrangement (D–G). Verbal Reasoning includes Aural Reasoning (A–C), Arithmetic Reasoning (A–G), Logical Selection (D–G), Word/Letter Matrix (D–G), Verbal Analogies (D–G), Verbal Classification (D–G), and Inference (E–G). Pictorial Reasoning includes Picture Classification (A–C), Picture Analogies (A–C), and Picture Series (K only). Figural Reasoning includes Figural Classification (A–D), Figural Analogies (A–G), Pattern Matrix (A–G), and Figural Series (A–G). Quantitative Reasoning is briefly samples (7 items) at Grade 3 (Level D), and used more extensively in Levels E through G. This cluster includes Number Series, Numeric Inference, and Number Matrix.

ITEM CHARACTERISTICS. All items on OLSAT tests use a multiple-choice format. Within each level, items are arranged according to certain criteria. For Levels A–C, items are arranged according to the kind of task performed by examinees (e.g., classifying or analogizing) and whether item stems are dictated by their teacher. This allows younger children, for whom test-taking may be an unfamiliar experience, to become more comfortable with these tasks. Within each of these three parts, items are spiraled by difficulty, with harder items "cushioned" by easier items so that children do not become discouraged once they have sensed that items are becoming increasingly more difficult to answer. At Levels E–G, items are arranged in a spiral omnibus format, wherein they are rotated throughout the test according to difficulty and item type. Level D (Grade 3) contains a section with figural and verbal items arranged according to increasing difficulty. In all other sections of Level D, items are arranged according to the spiral omnibus format of Levels E–G.

Equal numbers of verbal and nonverbal items are included in each level of the OLSAT. Levels A–C contain 30 items in both verbal and nonverbal components, whereas Level D contains 32 items and Levels E–G contain 36 items in each component.

CONSTRUCTION, DEVELOPMENT, AND STANDARDIZATION. OLSAT test development and norming efforts are extensive. The most recent national item tryout was conducted in 1994 with 10,000 students from schools across the country. School districts were selected according to a random sampling technique that resulted in samples of students that reflected the national school population in terms of SES, school district enrollment, and geographic region. Field-test items underwent a revision process that was intended to eliminate stereotypes and differential item functioning (DIF) with regard to gender and ethnic groups. Items that depicted differences in activities, emotions, occupations, or personality attributes with regard to gender, ethnic, or cultural group were identified by item editors, psychologists, and an advisor panel of minority educators and were subsequently removed from the OLSAT item pool. Following this review and elimination process, retained items were analyzed using the Mantel-Haenszel procedure to detect statistical differential item functioning (DIF) between gender and ethnic groups of students.

A stratified random sampling technique was invoked within each state to obtain standardization samples of examinees that were proportionate to total U.S. public and private school enrollment, and reflected percentages of students from different geographic, SES, and ethnic groups. The purpose of the standardization effort was to obtain normative and descriptive OLSAT data on students nationwide, to equate the levels of the Seventh Edition, to equate Sixth and Seventh Editions, and to document the statistical reliability and validity properties of scores from the test. Students participating in the OLSAT standardization samples were also administered the Ninth Edition of the Stanford Achievement Test Series (this is discussed in more detail in the section on Validity). Approximately 463,000 students participated in test standardization efforts in the Spring and Fall of 1995. The OLSAT Preliminary Technical Manual (PTM, released Spring, 1996) and Technical Manual (TM, 1997) provide information about standardization samples and statistical data relevant to test development including raw score means, standard deviations, and standard errors of measurement.

TEST SCORES. Total raw scores as well as those derived from Verbal and Nonverbal components of the OLSAT are converted to School Ability Indexes (SAIs), percentile ranks, stanines, and scaled scores SAIs (Mean = 100, Standard Deviation = 16). SAIs have been calculated for each 3-month age group (from 4 years, 6 months to 18 years, 2 months). SAIs have also been converted to stanines and percentile ranks—though not directly to scaled scores—within the same age groups. Although SAIs appear very similar to IQ scores, their exact meaning and significance are not clear. Scaled scores were developed by ad-

ministering two adjacent OLSAT levels to student samples from Grades 1–4, 5, and 9. This allowed the scaled score system of the OLSAT to provide a single, continuous, uniform scale that allows comparison of performance of students across all levels of the tests, irrespective of the age or grade of the examinee. Uses of the scaled scores include comparing scores from different levels of the test, measuring changes in performance over time, and testing out of level. The OLSAT norming manual, the compendium that contains score information, is well organized, easy to read, and allows for quick conversions back and forth between raw scores, SAIs, stanines, and percentile ranks. It is not clear, however, how each type of score should be interpreted nor what the relative advantages and limitations of each are. Examples of students' score reports with explanations to the user would have been welcomed.

RELIABILITY. Estimates of internal consistency (Kuder-Richardson 20) for Total, Verbal, and Nonverbal components of the OLSAT are presented in the PTM. Within each level, separate estimates were calculated for 3-month age groups. The youngest age group used was 5 years, 2 months (Level A). The oldest was 19 years, 11 months (Level G). For total scores, estimates of reliability ranged from .78 (Level D, age 11 years, 0–2 months) to .97 (Level F, age 10 years, 0–2 months and Level G, age 13 years, 3–5 and 6–9 months). Estimates of reliability for the Verbal component ranged from .68 (Level A, 5 years 0–2 months and Level B, 8 years, 3–5 months) to .96 (Level G, 13 years, 6–9 months). Finally, KR-20 coefficients for the Nonverbal component ranged from .63 (Level D, 11 years, 0–2 months) to .95 (Level F, 10 years, 0–2 months and Level G, 13 years, 3–5 months). Low numbers of examinees in some of the age groups and extreme out-of-level testing groups may have contributed to lower-bound estimates of reliability. Measures of the stability of OLSAT scores over time, however, are not available.

VALIDITY. Separate sections of the Technical Manual address content, criterion-related, construct validity of the OLSAT. Correlational data are presented as the primary evidence of test validity with regard to these three issues. First, correlations between Sixth and Seventh Editions of the OLSAT are shown in order to demonstrate the relationship between the content of these two versions. Total score correlations for the Sixth and

Seventh Editions range from .77 (Level F) to .87 (Level E). Ranges for Verbal and Nonverbal components range from .69 (Level A) to .83 (Level E) and .68 (Level F) to .83 (Level E), respectively. Correlations between the OLSAT and the Stanford Achievement Test (9th Edition) are presented to demonstrate the relationship between the OLSAT and academic achievement. Finally, the construct validity is evidenced by correlations between adjacent levels of the OLSAT. Correlations between Verbal components of Levels A and B, for example, would demonstrate the degree of consistency of the OLSAT in assessing the same skills across these levels. The level-to-level relationship is strongest for Total score, as would be expected for a scale comprising twice as many items as its two component scales. Correlations between Verbal components at adjacent levels range from .68 (Levels (C–D) to .82 (Levels B–C and E–F). Nonverbal component correlations range from .73 (Levels D–E) to .81 (Levels E–F). Correlations between Verbal and Nonverbal components at each testing level (and in each grade when one level is used to test multiple grade groups) are also presented. Correlations range from .67 (Level C) to .84 (Level E, Grade 5). The degree of these correlations indicates the extent to which each component (i.e., construct) contributes unique content to the test.

ADMINISTRATION, SCORING, AND REPORTING. Levels A–B are for use with Kindergartners and first graders, respectively. As such, these tests are dictated to examinees. Test items are organized into three sections and in a format that includes practice items. The first two sections are administered in one sitting; the third in a separate session, though it is not clear whether this should be scheduled on the same or a different day than the first two sections. Presumably, this decision is left to the discretion of the school/administrator. Level C (Grade 2) also has three sections, the last of which is dictated. Sections 1 and 2 are self-administered. Levels A–C each take approximately one hour to administer (37 minutes of actual testing time) and include examples of test items that students can try for practice. The "bubbles" that students use to indicate their responses are quite small, which may be a concern for youngsters who have underdeveloped fine motor skills. Levels D (two sections) and E–G (one section) are entirely self-administered in a one-

hour session (40 minutes of actual testing time). Practice items precede each section in Levels D–G.

Manuals for administering all levels of the OLSAT include an introductory section that provides information on the background, structure, and content of the test, and general and specific directions for test administration. General directions include information about the scheduling of the test, the materials needed, and the use of machine-scorable answer booklets. Specific directions include step-by-step instructions on the distribution of materials and procedures and scripted directions to students.

Directions for administration are for the most part clear, straightforward, and concise. There are, however, some ambiguous references to supplemental testing materials (e.g., an achievement test battery) and confusing instructions on how to complete/coordinate student identification information on both kinds of test forms. Nevertheless, no specific training in test administration is required, although the publishers recommend that proctors take the test prior to actual administration. Directions to students are also easy to follow. For Levels A–C, place markers are available to students. These and the scripted instructions that are read aloud by the proctor reduce the likelihood that students will become distracted or get lost during testing.

Test items for all levels use a multiple-choice format. Students mark their responses in the test booklets for Levels A–D. All levels can either be machine scored or scored by hand. Separate answer forms are provided for Levels E–G and include two options: a combination answer-folder, OLSAT machine-scorable answer document, or OLSAT hand-scorable answer document. Based on the materials provided for review, it is not clear what the relative advantages and disadvantages of any of these scoring options are.

Practice tests are available for all levels of the OLSAT. According to its publishers, the Practice Tests, which include items and procedures that resemble those on the actual test, "help students understand what to expect …, thus reducing anxiety." The practice tests also offer students, particularly the younger ones, an opportunity to practice the mechanics of coding their answers and personal information on separate documents. The publishers recommend that practice tests are administered one week prior to actual test administration.

OLSAT scores are reported at student and classroom levels. Raw scores, SAIs, scaled scores, stanines, and age and grade percentiles are included in both reports. Narratives that include brief descriptions of the skills tested by each item cluster as well as students' performance relative to same age and grade cohorts are presented in the student reports.

SUMMARY OF CONCERNS. Despite the thorough treatment given to OLSAT development and relative ease with which it can be administered to large groups of students, the following limitations are noted as deserving special attention.

1. Perhaps the most serious weakness of the Seventh Edition of the OLSAT is the validity evidence presented in the Technical Manual. Moderate to high correlations between current and previous versions of a test are not sufficient evidence of content validity. Furthermore, readers of the Technical Manual must take OLSAT publishers on faith when they allude to an ongoing external review process that assesses the relationship between the skills measured by each item and the stated purpose of the test. A more detailed description of this process would have been welcome. Second, evidence of the construct validity of the OLSAT is also weakly presented. Again, correlations—this time between total and component scores at adjacent levels and between Verbal and Nonverbal components within each level of the test—are insufficient. Results from confirmatory factor analyses that substantiate the differentiation of the verbal and nonverbal constructs of the OLSAT (and the degree to which each contributes to overall score variance) at all of its testing levels would also have been welcome. Third, correlations between the OLSAT and the Stanford Achievement Test scores represent an indirect measure of criterion-related validity in that a score on one measure can be used only to predict the score on another rather than the behavior of interest which, according to OLSAT publishers, is students' "ability to cope with school learning tasks." Direct evidence of this relationship as well as the implied relevance of the OLSAT to general success in school would improve the test's marketability among potential users. Another issue relevant to the validity of the OLSAT is whether total scores and those derived from its verbal and nonverbal components predict "school ability" equally well at all grade levels. That is, do OLSAT scores have greater relevance in the primary years

of schooling when curriculum, it could be argued, is less differentiated than in the middle and upper levels when instructional content is more specialized? Furthermore, the use of the OLSAT for high school students would be a curious choice for at least two reasons. First, many high school students are nearing completion of their formal schooling. If this is true, then, what is the practical value of the OLSAT? Second, if college is an option for high schoolers, then use of the OLSAT seems less likely given the array of well-established measures of first-year college (e.g., ACT, SAT).

2. Despite extensive summaries of descriptive, correlational, and normative data, the interpretation of OLSAT scores is an ambiguous endeavor and thus increased the risk of misuse. The publishers should be more clear about what the OLSAT can and cannot do, particularly in the reports returned to teachers and other audiences; recommendations for OLSAT use should be accompanied by acknowledgment of its limitations.

3. The history of the OLSAT can be traced back to a period of testing that was dominated by hierarchical theories of intelligence that devolve from a general, omnibus single intelligence factor *g* into more specialized, though correlated, factors. In light of recent advances in cognitive theory, the theoretical foundations of the OLSAT should be questioned.

4. Satisfactory internal consistency estimates are presented, but no data relating to the stability of OLSAT scores over time are currently available.

SUMMARY. If the test users acknowledge the limitations of the test noted above and accept it as one of a variety of instruments that could be used for screening purposes (i.e., to identify students who may need extra help), then the technical characteristics of the OLSAT qualify its use for this limited role.

Review of the Otis-Lennon School Ability Test, Seventh Edition by BERT A. GOLDMAN, Professor of Education, Curriculum and Instruction, University of North Carolina at Greensboro, Greensboro, NC:

The Otis-Lennon School Ability Test, Seventh Edition (OLSAT-7) is the latest version of a series of ability tests begun by Arthur Otis with his Otis Group Intelligence Scale in 1918 and further enhanced by the work of Roger Lennon with the introduction into the series of the Otis-Lennon

Mental Ability Test. This latest version employs "the same general conceptualization of the nature of ability" and "the same psychometric approaches" (Directions for Administration, p. 5) as its predecessors to measure thinking and reasoning abilities that are most relevant to school achievement. Given that the instrument is to be used in the school setting for the purposes of assessing school learning ability, suggesting school learning placement, and evaluating school achievement with respect to school learning potential, the label "school ability" is used rather than the label "mental ability." Also the term "school ability" is "intended to discourage overinterpretation of the nature of the ability being assessed" (Directions for Administration, p. 5).

Seven interrelated levels (A through G) of the test attempt to measure the ability range of students in Grades k through 12: Level A (Kindergarten), Level B (Grade 1), Level C (Grade 2), Level D (Grade 3), Level E (Grades 45), Level F (Grades 6–8), and Level G (Grades 9–12). Testing time per testing session takes from 27 minutes (Level C) to 50 minutes (each Level D–F) with Levels A, B, and C each requiring two testing sessions plus a 5-minute rest period within each session.

All levels contain both Verbal and Nonverbal items. The Verbal part consists of Verbal Comprehension, which includes four subtests: Following Directions, Antonyms, Sentence Completion, and Sentence Arrangement; and Verbal Reasoning, which includes seven subtests: Aural Reasoning, Arithmetic Reasoning, Logical Selection, Word/Letter Matrix, Verbal Analogies, Verbal Classification, and Inference. The Nonverbal part consists of Pictorial Reasoning, which includes three subtests: Picture Classification, Picture Analogies, and Picture Series; Figural Reasoning, which includes four subtests: Figural Classification, Figural Analogies, Pattern Matrix, and Figural Series; and Quantitative Reasoning, which includes three subtests: Number Series, Numeric Inference, and Number Matrix. Although all levels contain Verbal and Nonverbal items, no level contains all subtests. For example, only Levels A, B, and C contain the Following Directions subtest.

Each test level has a separate brief practice test designed to familiarize students with that level's types of items to be administered in a session prior to the regular test session or sessions. Clearly written and easily followed directions are given in manuals for each test level.

Two types of answer sheet are available: machine-scorable by the test publisher and hand-scorable. A Preliminary Technical Manual and booklet containing National Spring Norms are provided. Demographic characteristics of the standardization samples are presented in the Preliminary Technical Manual and closely resemble those given for the total U.S. school enrollment. The demographics include: Geographic Region, SES Status, Urbanicity, Ethnicity, and Nonpublic Schools. Handicapping conditions are also included, but without comparable U.S. School Enrollment data.

Reliability data are given in the form of K-R 20 coefficients for Verbal, Nonverbal, and Total scores for each grade and for each age in years and months. Most of the coefficients appear to be in the .80s and .90s with a few in the .70s and one low of .68 for Level A, Verbal, 5 years 0–2 months. Although these coefficients are mostly good to excellent, they represent internal consistency rather than test-retest stability.

Given the one purpose of the OLSAT-7 is to assess school learning ability, it seems reasonable to expect that there be validity data showing the relationship between OLSAT scores and grades in school. No such data are given in the Preliminary Technical Manual. Perhaps there will be a forthcoming technical manual containing this information. [Editor's Note: This information is provided on page 43 of the Technical Manual, which was provided in 1999 after this review was prepared.]

Data are presented containing correlations between the OLSAT-6 and OLSAT-7 for each grade levels (A–G) Total, Verbal, and Nonverbal scores. These correlations range from a low of .68 (Level F Nonverbal) to a high of .87 (Level E Total) with most in the upper .70s and mid to low .80s. Although all of these correlations appear to be statistically significant, if there are no major changes between the two test versions, one might expect the correlation to be much higher. This brings up the question of whether there are any major changes between OLSAT-6 and OLSAT-7. The Preliminary Technical Manual, Spring 1996, provides none.

Additional comparisons between the OLSAT-6 and OLSAT-7 are presented in the form of School Ability Index Scores (SAI) by age in years and months, which are one and two standard deviations above and below the mean.

Generally, most of the mean SAI scores for OLSAT-6 and OLSAT-7 differ by one, two, or three points revealing similarity between the two instruments.

There appears to be consistency between each successive level and its preceding level as evidenced by correlations between them ranging from a low .68 to a high of .88 with most in the mid to upper .70s and low to mid .80s. Further consistency within the test appears in the correlations between Verbal and Nonverbal means for each grade level K–12. These correlations range from .65 to .84 with most in the low .80s.

Mean item difficulty levels for Total, Verbal, and Nonverbal items are presented for each grade K–12. The difficulty levels range from .49 to .63 and appear to be satisfactory. Median item discrimination indexes are presented for Grades K–12 and also appear to be satisfactory ranging from .48 to .61.

The OLSAT-7 National Spring Norms booklet enables raw scores to be converted to percentile ranks, stanines, or scaled scores. However, no information is given concerning the mean and standard deviation of these scaled scores. Also the Norms booklet enables raw scores to be converted to School Ability Indexes (SAI), which in turn may be converted to percentile ranks and stanines. There is no explanation of what the SAIs represent. They resemble IQs, but because this test is not presented as an intelligence test this reviewer wonders what they are and why they are introduced.

SUMMARY. The OLSAT-7 is designed to measure school ability for grades K through 12 by means of Verbal and Nonverbal items. It is a group test for which general conceptualization and psychometric approaches are those of its predecessors dating back to 1918. The demographic characteristics of the standardization samples closely resemble those of the total U.S. school enrollment. Estimates of reliability in the form of K-R 20 coefficients are mostly good to excellent. However, these data represent internal consistency rather than test-retest stability. Given that one purpose of the OLSAT-7 is to assess school learning ability, it is troubling that no validity data showing the relationship between OLSAT scores and school grades are provided.

Although the correlations between the OLSAT-6 and OLSAT-7 appear to be statistically significant, if there are no major changes

between the two test versions (and we are not told whether there are), we should expect higher correlations between them. There appears to be consistency within the test as demonstrated by substantial correlations between successive levels and between Verbal and Nonverbal halves of the test. Item difficulty and item discrimination indexes appear to be satisfactory. Raw scores may be converted to School Ability Indexes, but there is no explanation of what these indexes are, although they resemble IQs. Until a more complete technical manual addressing the doubts raised by this review is prepared to replace the Preliminary Technical Manual, one should proceed with caution in using this instrument.

[272]
Pain Assessment Battery, Research Edition.

Purpose: Constructed as "a comprehensive assessment tool for evaluating and documenting the physical, experiential, behavioral, and psychological dimensions of chronic pain."

Population: Patients with chronic pain.

Publication Dates: 1993—1995.

Acronym: PAB-RE.

Scores: 7 tests: Pain History and Status Interview, Pain Imagery Interview, Pain Experience Scale, Pain Coping Interview—Research Edition, Stress Symptoms Checklist, Coping Style Profile, Interview Behavior Checklist.

Administration: Individual.

Price Data: Available from publisher.

Time: Administration time not reported.

Comments: Research instrument; computer-administered (DOS version only).

Authors: Bruce N. Eimer and Lyle M. Allen, III.

Publisher: CogniSyst, Inc.

Review of the Pain Assessment Battery, Research Edition by M. ALLAN COOPERSTEIN, Clinical Psychologist & Forensic Examiner: Independent Practice, Willow Grove, PA:

Chronic pain is a complex phenomenon involving a variety of dimensions that should be addressed in the assessment of pain patients. These dimensions include medical, physiological, psychological, and social factors (Cole, 1998). Secondary gains (e.g., increased attention, fiscal gain, and the avoidance of personal and vocational responsibilities) often obscure a clear view of a patient's pain. Hence the need for an accurate, economic assessment of chronic pain patients has pragmatic underpinnings in terms of diagnosis and treatment as well as the identification of possible symptom exaggeration and malingering.

This issue was recently studied by Gatchel, Polatin, and Kinney (1995). They examined whether a comprehensive assessment of psychosocial measures would be of use in identifying acute low back pain sufferers who would subsequently develop chronic pain disability. Results demonstrated the existence of a psychosocial disability variable (associated with injured workers likely to develop chronic problems) that was linked with the Hysteria scale of the Minnesota Multiphasic Personality Inventory (MMPI).

Similarly, the Pain Assessment Battery (PAB) aims towards comprehensively assessing the multidimensional characteristics of pain, offering a means of designing treatment, predicting success in treatment, and discriminating between genuine pain sufferers and those exaggerating or feigning symptoms.

My evaluation of the PAB has been an attempt to appraise a test battery still under development. Since receiving the first software, changes have occurred and the product has evolved. This review must be considered in that light and cannot address the ultimate form that the PAB will take, as a rereview at a later point will be necessary. In addition, because computer software is increasingly becoming a part of the clinician's toolbox (although not directly related to evaluation of the test instrument itself) I have relegated comments on software to a separate section.

PROPOSED USES OF THE TEST. Composed of seven components, the PAB purports to calculate 20 scales arranged under five dimensions. These include Physical and Temporal Dimensions of Pain, Pain Interference, Health-Related Behaviors, and Psychological Adjustment and Maladjustment. It also assesses Pain Coping, Nociception, Treatment Resistance and Alienation, and Global Pain Impairment. Extreme or critical responses are flagged. Components include a Pain History and Status Questionnaire, Pain Experience Scale, Stress Symptoms Checklist, and Coping Style Profile. These are said to offer a comprehensive view of the pain patient with indications for treatment and outcome studies.

TEST DEVELOPMENT. Bruce Eimer, the clinical author of the PAB, states that the test evolved from his need for a pain assessment instrument that could meet his clinical requirements, that would be easy to administer, have face validity for pain patients, be easily interpretable, and help clarify therapy goals outcomes. Basing his approach upon an earlier study (Eimer, 1988) that was influenced by Lazarus' (1981) multimodal psychotherapy, Eimer attempted to encompass physical and temporal dimensions of pain, behavioral factors, coping styles, affective and motivational factors, cognitive variables, interpersonal factors, and historical factors.

Drawing from a host of extant psychometric resources and attempting to compensate for their perceived deficits, he and Lyle Allen III, the co-author and publisher, developed an integrated, computerized assessment from which pain could be assessed, the generalizing effects of chronic pain could be identified, and through which a chronic pain patient's outcome to treatment could be predicted.

The authors' criteria for a clinically useful assessment of chronic pain and disability includes quantification, serial administrations to track treatment progress, a means to differentiate therapeutic approach and predict the likely success of interventions, immediate feedback, and face validity that is apparent to individuals suffering from pain to justify their discomfort in taking the test.

TEST FORM. The following is a description of the various formats and components of the PAB:

INTERVIEW FORMAT.

The Pain History and Status Interview (PHSI). This is a computer-administered, structured interview that identifies the primary pain source and secondary areas, a pain history and status, medical information, employment information and social environment.

The Pain Imagery Interview (PII). The Pain Imagery Interview elicits images of pain, negative cognitions and emotions, pain relief images, and positive cognitions useful in treatment planning. Development of the interview was partly influenced by Shapiro's (1995) multimodal model. Assessed are the present complaint, pain experience, pain onset, severity, imagery, and other aspects of the impact of pain in other areas of life.

INVENTORY FORMAT.

Pain Coping Inventory (PCI). The PCI is the nucleus of the PAB. It is a 92-item, comprehensive, patient self-report questionnaire aimed at an eighth grade reading level. It provides 18 scales measuring pain severity, interference, coping strategies, pain-related beliefs, self-efficacy perceptions, personality dysfunction secondary to chronic pain, psychological distress, psychological adjustment, quality of life issues, treatment resistance, patient alienation, and symptom magnification. The PCI may be administered as a paper-and-pencil questionnaire, then computer-scored, or administered and scored on computer. Computed scores and graphs are available as output.

The Stress Symptoms Checklist (SSCL). The Stress Symptoms Checklist is a 38-item self-report developed to assess anxiety-related and stress symptoms, including post-traumatic stress associated with chronic pain. Respondents rate the frequency that they have experienced each symptom over the prior 2 weeks on a 7-point verbal-numerical Likert scale.

The Pain Experience Scale (PES). The Pain Experience Scale identifies and focuses upon primary pain source areas, quantifies pain frequency and severity, and provides qualitative pain descriptors. Up to three pain sources may be identified and evaluated.

The Interview Behavior Checklist (IBCL). The Interview Behavior Checklist documents the clinician's observations of the patient's mental status and behavior during their interaction. This is provided as a large checklist from which the clinician may select descriptors that are compiled into a report upon completion.

The Coping Style Profile (CSP). The Coping Style Profile assesses the patient's basic modes of coping with chronic pain. Nine coping modality categories are addressed including behavior, affect, sensation, imagery, cognition, medication, social, diet, and exercise. Again a 7-point Likert scale is implemented. Although no normative data are provided, coping modalities are ranked using asterisks according to the value assigned from levels 5–7.

ADMINISTRATION, SCORING, AND INTERPRETATION. Patients complete the assessments on a computer or using paper and pencil. Scoring is accomplished by the program. Normative data for the PCI and SSCL are provided. Software also reports *T*-score values.

Administration of the PCI and SSCL took a total of approximately 20 minutes, dependent upon the reading level of the respondent, and was answered easily by an eighth grade volunteer. Interviewing and the completion of all PAB sections would take approximately 1 hour.

NORMATIVE INFORMATION. Normative data are available only for the Pain Coping Inventory and Stress Symptoms Checklist.

PAIN COPING INVENTORY. A normative sample of 444 chronic pain patients was used. These were individuals referred to outpatient behavioral chronic pain treatment programs for evaluation or treatment. The mean age was 40.8 years (*SD* = 12.12 years). Forty-three percent were male; 57% were female. Ninety-two percent reported primary pain complaints greater than 3 months in duration. The majority of patients experienced pain of 2–3 years in duration.

The most common pain was low back, headaches (all types), whole body, and neck and jaw related pain, respectively. The most frequent diagnoses were related to lumbar and cervical disc disease, chronic headaches, myofascitis, diffuse musculoskeletal pain, and fibromyalgia. Demographics pertaining to the percentages of patients involved in concurrent litigation or Worker's Compensation were not provided.

Stability and equivalence reliability was not assessed. Internal consistency alpha coefficients ranged from a low of .18 (perceived self-efficacy) to a high of .95 (global impairment index).

Construct validity was evaluated against the Multidimensional Pain Inventory (Kerns, Turk, & Rudy, 1985). Pearson correlations were calculated between scales and indices of the two instruments with a subsample of 80 patients taking both tests. Significantly positive correlations between the MPI and PCI Global Impairment Index were found for pain severity; the PCI Physical Severity Index correlating positively with the MPI Pain Severity Index. Two anticipated low correlations were found on indices on unique PCI Indices. In addition, a principal components factor analysis yielded a five-factor solution, accounting for 39% of the total variance.

Assessing biased response, the PCI was validated against the Computerized Assessment of Response Bias (CARB; see 95 for review) a forced-choice visual digit recognition task assessing subject effort and symptom exaggeration. A sample of 93 disability claimants were evaluated for pain disorder using the PCI in combination with the CARB. Significant differences were detected in which patients demonstrating exaggerated cognitive deficits on the CARB presented significantly lower scores on PCI coping measures while evidencing higher scores on PCI measures of pain-related impairment and dysfunction. This suggests that the combined use of the PCI and CARB may prove to be of use in discriminating exaggerating and malingering patients. However, this must be supported by further research involving larger samples in a variety of settings.

STRESS-SYMPTOMS CHECKLIST. The 38-item Stress Symptoms Checklist (SSCL) was subjected to a principal components factor analysis from which a two-factor simple structure solution was derived, accounting for 42.74% of the total variance. An internal consistency reliability estimate of both factors—Posttraumatic Anxiety Symptoms and Pain and Impairment—based upon coefficient alpha is excellent (PTAS - .93; PI - .91). Test-retest reliability was assessed with a sample of 20 nonpatients over a one-week period. A Pearson correlation of .67 was found for the total sum of ratings. Construct validity was also assessed with respectable correlations between the SSCL and the Anxiety Symptoms Questionnaire, the Cognitive Error Questionnaire, and the Irrational Belief Scale.

SOFTWARE. Cogshell is the proprietary DOS environment within which the battery of tests is housed and is capable of operating within Windows 95. Some problems were encountered in dealing with the software. The company provided updates as they became available.

Difficulties experienced included having to load the PII on drive C, although Cogshell and the remaining test battery were on another drive. There were failed attempts to select the option of a test battery, although tests could be administered individually with no difficulty. At the completion of certain tests, although they were written to disk, the program then "crashed" and had to be restarted in order to browse or print the results. Printing graphs was also problematic as the choice of printers is narrowly restricted at this time and graphics produced were rather inadequate.

I have learned that the PAB is to be converted into a Windows format. This should, it is hoped, reduce some of the difficulties encountered with the software.

DISCUSSION. The PAB is an ambitious undertaking which, as stated earlier, must be considered as still in development. A co-author (Allen) informed me that one of the goals is to gather data continuously from PAB users in an ongoing re-finement and development process. With larger sample sizes and further refinement the PAB (and its relationship to the CARB) should provide a rich source for further investigations into the complex phenomenology of pain.

Although content and construct validity are satisfactorily addressed and concurrent validity is examined via the MPI, data on predictive validity are lacking. There is also a question regarding a possible threat to external validity as all indications point to the standardization of the test using only pain populations and/or disability samples without sufficient reference to pain-free "normals" or those having pain who have not required or sought treatment.

Although the battery requires further refinement and standardization, the PAB/CARB combination appears to have immediate utility. The PCI and SSCL appear to be of greatest empirical value. The Coping Style Profile is also helpful in identifying patient propensities and pointing out areas of possible intervention that could be remedial. Although convenient, the Pain History & Status Inventory (PHSI) and Interview Behavior Checklist (IBCL) may be too limiting for clinicians with an established proficiency in this type of data gathering. The Pain Imagery Inventory could be considered an extension of the PHSI, as could the Pain Experience Scale, as its primary focus is to identify areas of pain and assign severity ratings and descriptors. This raises the question of whether increased parsimony, perhaps through item analysis, would result in a condensed form of the PAB while maintaining its essential goals.

I found the authors' overall model of pain to be somewhat unclear, appearing to be largely empirically derived and cognitive-behavioral in orientation. Although the PCI derives five factors and the SSCL derives two, the manual does not relate these clearly to each other although the Posttraumatic Anxiety Symptoms of the SSCL should impact the General Psychological Adjustment factor of the PCI and both are responses to pain and stress. Again, this may suggest a need to reconceptualize and/or redefine the overall structure of the PAB and better integrate its components.

SUMMARY. Computerized psychometrics first appeared in the early 1970s. Since that time, the diversity and level of sophistication was evolved exponentially. Clearly, computerized testing will play a more pervasive role in clinical and forensic practices. PAB is a vanguard approach to the area of pain detection and treatment, one of the most complex phenomena in human experience. We must respect the test developers' impressive initial efforts and their continuing data gathering endeavors and research-based refinements.

REVIEWER'S REFERENCES

Lazarus, A. A. (1981). *The practice of multimodal therapy: Systematic, comprehensive and effective psychotherapy.* New York: McGraw-Hill Book Company.

Kerns, R. D., Turk, D. C., & Rudy, T. E. (1985). The West Haven-Yale Multidimensional Pain Inventory (WHYMPI). *Pain, 23*(4), 345–356.

Eimer, B. N. (1988). The chronic pain patient: Multimodal assessment and psychotherapy. *International Journal of Medical Psychotherapy, 1,* 23–40.

Emerson, J., Pankratz, L., Joos, S., & Smith, S. (1994). Personality disorders in problematic medical patients. *Psychosomatics, 35*(5), 469–473.

Gatchel, R. J., Polatin, P. B., & Kinney, R. K. (1995). Predicting outcome of chronic back pain using clinical predictors of psychopathology: A prospective analysis. *Health Psychology, 14*(5), 415–420.

Shapiro, F. (1995). *Eye movement desensitization and reprocessing: Basic principles, protocols and procedures.* New York: Guilford Press.

Cole, J. (1998, Winter). To market, to market: Psychotherapy with chronic pain patients. *The Independent Practitioner, Bulletin of Independent Practice, Division 42, American Psychological Association, 18*(1), 29–30. Washington, DC: American Psychological Association.

Review of the Pain Assessment Battery, Research Edition by F. FELICIA FERRARA, Assistant Professor, College of Behavioral Sciences, The University of Sarasota, Sarasota, FL:

As reported in the research version manual of the Pain Assessment Battery (PAB), the instrument is intended to measure pain across five dimensions, with 18 subscales, and 92 items. Precise directions for test administration were not included in this manual. Examples of interpreting individual profiles are included, which greatly enhance the final interpretative means. A final scale entitled Coping Mechanisms is intended to allow the practitioner to match the client's expressed means of coping with pain and the prescribed treatment modality (i.e., if medication is taken to alleviate pain, then a medication-oriented treatment plan should be taken). Needless to say, this is an oversimplification of the treatment plan as extraneous issues need to be addressed. For example, the client may have a propensity to abuse the use of substances to alleviate the pain, which would call for alternate interpretations made from this scale.

Similarly, the concept of further subdividing the five dimensions of the PAB to an additional 18 subscales is cumbersome. Additionally, the empirical means used to establish subscale diagnostic cut scores was not clear. Attention may be given to Jaeger (1979) for reference in standard-setting models. Because no preliminary pilot study results or norming information were included in the research version, it is difficult to assess how the cut scores or diagnostic categories were derived

(Crocker & Algina, 1986). The intended sample groups to be used for research purposes were not addressed. For example, although the sample may be pain-injured individuals, what setting, types of injuries, or facilities will be sought out for sampling purposes?

Empirical analyses were not conducted to data; consequently, inferences to reliability or validity of this version of the instrument are not possible at this time. However, the conceptual and theoretical underpinnings of the PAB are well grounded and heavily documented in the research manual. Consequently, the instrument does lend itself to testable hypotheses testing at a future date.

Test administration is not addressed in this edition; for instance, will administrator training be required or is the instrument to be taken alone by the client, in a group format, or individually? It would appear that based on a 92-item instrument, extensive time for completion will be needed. If a client were in pain, would that require several visits or interrupted sessions to complete the instrument? Based on the length and complexity of the scoring of subscales, a scoring key format could be included to reduce scoring time (Thorndike, 1982).

Item bias was not observed in terms of age, race, or ethnic groups. However, items that were blatantly worded or seemingly intrusive to specific groups were found. For instance, one item asks, "Have you ever been sexually abused or molested as a child?" This item appears blatantly out of place, without a theoretical underpinning; a question that asks about a previous car accident, or broken arm or leg, might set a better precedence for assessing pain thresholds as perceived in trauma. In the History and Status Interview, Item 19, "Are you involved in Litigation related to your pain?" is a very blatant item, which may inhibit the client from honestly answering subsequent items. A more simplistic question might say, "Is there an attorney involved?" Several items appear to be redundant (i.e., Items 5 & 6, 3 & 7) (Crocker & Algina, 1986).

SUMMARY. Extensive research and theoretical work is included in the development research version of the PAB, thus indicative of a potentially psychometrically sound instrument. However, without substantial pilot test information, measures of internal consistency, or anticipated sample population data, it is premature to assess this instrument as an appropriate measure of pain and coping with pain, sufficient enough to develop treatment plans. Administration, scoring, readability level, time of completion, and item review all need to be conducted as related above (Gall, Borg, & Gall, 1996).

A computer version is available which may reduce administration time, and allow for computer scoring of the instrument. Clients may be offered either format, written or computer, depending on their existing computer skills.

REVIEWER'S REFERENCES

Jaeger, R. M. (1979). Measurement consequences of selected standard-setting models. In M. A. Bunda & J. R. Sanders (Eds.), *Practices and problems in competency-based education.* Washington, DC: National Council on Measurement in Education.
Thorndike, R. L. (1982). *Applied psychometrics.* Boston, Houghton Mifflin.
Crocker, L., & Algina, J. (1986). *Introduction to classical and modern test theory.* New York: Harcourt Brace Jovanovich.
Gall, M. D., Borg, W. R., & Gall, J. P. (1996). *Educational research: An introduction.* London: Longman Publishers.

[273]
Pain Patient Profile.

Purpose: Designed to identify patients who are experiencing emotional distress associated with primary complaints of pain and assess the severity of distress in comparison to community and pain patient population national sample.
Population: Pain patients aged 17–76.
Publication Dates: 1992–1995.
Acronym: P-3.
Scores, 4: Depression, Anxiety, Somatization, Validity Index.
Administration: Group.
Price Data, 2000: $62 per preview package including manual ('95, 89 pages), and answer sheets with test items for three assessments (specify Microtest or mail-in scoring); $82 per 50 hand-scorable answer sheets; $9.75 per MICROTEST Q interpretive report; $11.75 per mail-in interpretive report (also includes answer sheet with test items); $28 per manual.
Time: (10–15) minutes.
Authors: C. David Tollison and Jerry C. Langley.
Publisher: NCS (Minnetonka).

Review of the Pain Patient Profile by GREGORY J. BOYLE, Professor of Psychology, Bond University, Gold Coast, Queensland, and Visiting Professor, Department of Psychiatry, University of Queensland, Royal Brisbane Hospital, Hesston, Australia:

The Pain Patient Profile (P-3) is a 44-item multiple-choice paper-and-pencil inventory designed to measure the psychological aspects of pain in physically injured patients. The P-3 instrument purports to measure three psychological constructs (Depression, Anxiety, and Somatiza-tion—excessive somatic ideation), which are considered to contribute to pain perception (Tollison & Satterthwaite, 1991). A Validity Index assesses the random responding, inadequate reading skill, and symptom exaggeration. Unlike many standard psychological tests, the P-3 was designed specifically for pain patients, enabling comparison of a given patient's scores with those of the average pain patient. This has the advantage of providing a more realistic assessment within the pain patient population itself. Some practical administration limitations are briefly identified in the P-3 manual, although psychometric limitations as such are not addressed.

Although separate community and patient norms are provided in the manual, it is evident that sample sizes were too small ($N = 254$, and $N = 243$, respectively) to provide stable normative data within the 17–76-year range. Because elderly people are likely to be overrepresented among chronic pain patients, it might be beneficial to extend the norms for elderly patients in future versions of the instrument.

Short-term stability coefficients (mean retest interval of only 7 days, but ranging all the way from 1 to 16 days) were high: .99 (Depression), .98 (Anxiety), and .98 (Somatization). In view of this excessive variation in retest intervals, it is likely that the above reliability coefficients provide only a crude approximation to actual scale stabilities. Furthermore, no comparison of immediate retest (dependability) versus longer-term stability was provided in the manual, so that the reliability of the P-3 scales over differing time intervals remains uncertain. Cronbach alpha coefficients ranged from .70 to .91 ($M = .83$) for the separate scales across community and patient samples, suggesting some narrowness of measurement, and the possibility of some redundant items. Moderate item-homogeneity (not higher than .70) would seem preferable (cf. Boyle, 1991).

Concurrent/convergent validity correlations with related Minnesota Multiphasic Personality Inventory (MMPI) scales provided some evidence of validity of the separate P-3 scales, with correlations ranging from .13 to .82 ($M = .47$). However, as no factor analytic evidence (based on item-parcel intercorrelations) was reported in the manual, the construct validity of the three scales remains somewhat uncertain. A brief five-item validity scale serves as a crude validity index only. The issue of motivational distortion (inconsistent responding, faking good, faking bad, response sets, etc.) was not addressed adequately, leaving the determination of invalid profiles problematic.

Differing numbers of items across the P-3 scales is also problematic, causing slight discrepancies in measurement variance, thereby unnecessarily complicating comparison of a pain patient's raw scores across the three scales (cf. Boyle & Fernandez, 1995). Furthermore, the P-3 does not differentiate between state and trait measures, and no information is provided in the manual regarding item-response characteristics (cf. Boyle, 1987).

On the positive side, the P-3 includes current items, and avoids colloquial or slang expressions. Items considered potentially biased (on gender, ethnic, economic, religious, or other grounds) were excluded. Although the P-3 manual is relatively informative, further psychometric details are needed. Even so, two of the three psychological constructs measured in the P-3 (Depression and Anxiety) can also be quantified adequately in a wide range of existing psychological mood-state scales such as the Profile of Mood States (POMS; T5:2076), the Differential Emotions Scale (DES-IV), or the Eight State Questionnaire (8SQ; T5:915). Indeed, these latter instruments also have the advantage of providing measurement of a range of additional clinically important mood states, applicable to pain patients. Especially important is the role of Anger in chronic pain (Fernandez & Turk, 1995). In this respect, the P-3 is too restrictive in its assessment of the psychological concomitants of pain.

Moreover, additional research into the psychometric properties of the P-3 is recommended, especially its construct and factor analytic validity. Also, development of cross-cultural norms would greatly facilitate the valid use of the instrument outside the United States.

SUMMARY. Compared with other psychological instruments, the P-3 enables comparison of three emotional factors among pain patients using normative data derived from such patients. Although these psychological aspects of pain are important, it is evident nonetheless that the P-3 is somewhat restricted in its breadth of coverage of psychological variables. Aside from affective components of pain, cognitive and sensory components also need to be addressed (cf. Fernandez & Turk, 1992, 1993). Although the assumption that psychological assessment and intervention plays

an important role in the treatment of physically injured patients seems soundly based, the P-3 instrument needs further development and refinement before its routine use in hospital and clinical settings can be fully recommended.

REVIEWER'S REFERENCES

Boyle, G. J. (1987). Review of the (1985) "Standards for educational and psychological testing: AERA, APA and NCME." *Australian Journal of Psychology, 39*, 235–237.

Boyle, G. J. (1991). Does item homogeneity indicate internal consistency or item redundancy in psychometric scales? *Personality and Individual Differences, 12*, 291–294.

Tollison, C. D., & Satterthwaite, J. R. (1991). Chronic benign pain: Diagnosis and behavioral management. *Journal of Musculoskeletal Medicine, 8*, 55–66.

Fernandez, E., & Turk, D. C. (1992). Sensory and affective components of pain: Separation and synthesis. *Psychological Bulletin, 112*, 205–217.

Fernandez, E., & Turk, D. C. (1993). Anger in chronic pain patients: A neglected target of attention. *American Pain Society Bulletin, 3*, 5–7.

Boyle, G. J., & Fernandez, E. (1995). *Evaluation of the language of pain as indexed in the McGill Pain Questionnaire.* Paper presented at the 30th Annual Conference of the Australian Psychological Society, Perth, Australia.

Fernandez, E., & Turk, D. C. (1995). The scope and significance of anger in the experience of chronic pain. *Pain, 61*, 165–175.

Review of the Pain Patient Profile by RONALD J. GANELLEN, Director, Neuropsychology Service, Michael Reese Hospital and Medical Center, and Associate Professor, Northwestern Medical School, Chicago, IL:

The Pain Patient Profile (P-3) was developed to assess pain patients' emotional state and identify the presence of emotional variables that influence either patients' perception of pain or their cooperation with treatment interventions. The authors assert it is inappropriate to use existing psychological tests for these purposes as existing tests were developed to be administered to patients with a primary psychiatric disorder rather than a primary pain disorder, contain content that is inappropriate for pain patients, and do not have norms suitable to be used with pain patients. In addition, the authors claim that pain patients will be less threatened if evaluated with the P-3 than with commonly used psychological measures as the P-3 minimizes the possibility patients will think they are being asked to complete a self-report inventory about their emotional state because they are perceived as having a "mental" problem.

The P-3 was developed to be used by health care professionals with an advanced degree who are licensed to practice independently, such as physicians, chiropractors, psychologists, and physical therapists. The P-3 can be scored either by hand or by using an NCS computer program that also generates an interpretive report. The results of the P-3 are intended to show whether signs of depression, anxiety, or obsessive preoccupation with somatic concerns exist, and presents implications for treatment planning, including the need for consultation with a mental health professional.

The authors wrote all items for the P-3 and attempted to create scales to assess Depression, Anxiety, and Somatization, as well as whether the results should be considered valid. An initial pool of 49 items was developed and administered to a sample of 100 pain patients. Items were examined to determine whether the distribution was skewed and whether items correlated highly enough with the overall scale. One item was eliminated using these criteria. In a second study using 130 patients and 144 university students, the 48 items of the P-3 were found to be correlated with their parent scale at a level greater than .30. In a third study, using "more than 200 pain patients and more than 200 community subjects" the validity scales were revised and "some items were assigned to different scales to maximize content validity and reliability" (manual, p. 5).

The descriptions of these studies are sparse. For instance, it is not clear whether the samples in these three studies were independent or whether subjects from the first study were also used in the second and/or third studies. Furthermore, the authors do not detail the criteria they used to modify placement or items on different scales. The authors apparently did not conduct a factor analysis of the items to determine whether the P-3 yields four factors, as they intended. They do present statistics showing satisfactory item-scale correlations, excellent internal consistency, and high test-retest stability over a brief period of time (average 7-day interval).

Evidence concerning the validity of the P-3 is quite limited. The only validity data contained in the manual involves correlations between the P-3 Depression, Anxiety, and Somatization scales and related Minnesota Multiphasic Personality Inventory (MMPI) scales. No other information concerning validity is presented.

The paucity of adequate validity data should raise questions for potential users as to what scores on the P-3 mean. For instance, the P-3 contains five items "designed to detect random responding, reading comprehension problems, and magnification of symptoms" (p. 19). A score greater than 11 on the Validity Index is interpreted as raising concerns about symptom magnification. In addition, a clinical scale is considered invalid if more than one item on the scale is omitted. However, the authors present no data showing that these

criteria identify individuals who responded randomly; were unable to attend to, read, and understand the P-3 items; or exaggerated their problems. The absence of any data demonstrating that the P-3 validity scale operates as intended is a significant liability as psychological evaluations are often used to address questions as to whether pain patients, many of whom are involved in litigation, are reporting symptoms honestly.

It is also problematic that one validity scale is expected to measure three separate dimensions related to biased or distorted responding. Other commonly used psychological tests, such as the Minnesota Multiphasic Personality Inventory—2 (MMPI-2; T5:1697), Personality Assessment Inventory (PAI; T5:1959), and Millon Behavioral Health Inventory (MBHI; T5:1686) contain multiple validity indices designed to discriminate among different types of distorted responding. No evidence is provided showing that the one P-3 validity scale delivers everything it promises.

Raw scores for each P-3 scale are converted into linear T scores. The description of how the T scores were developed is quite confusing as raw scores for each scale can be converted either into a T score based on a sample of 243 pain patients or a T score based on a community sample of 254 individuals. Information about the demographic characteristics of these two samples is limited and incomplete. Users of the P-3 are encouraged to rely on comparison of a patient's score to the T scores for pain patients. This approach differs from that used in other widely used measures, such as the MMPI-2, which developed T-score distributions based on a nonclinical sample and, in clinical practice, interprets those scales that differ significantly from the range seen for normals. No compelling rationale for developing T scores for the P-3 based on the sample of pain patients rather than the pain-free community sample was provided.

Interpretation of the T scores for the P-3 scales is also confusing. Although the authors state that P-3 T scores have a mean of 50 and a standard deviation of 10, the authors recommend interpreting scores greater than half a standard deviation above the mean of 50 as being significantly elevated. The P-3 manual also defines the average and elevated ranges differently for different scales. For instance, for the P-3 Depression scale the average range is 47–54, whereas the average range for the P-3 Anxiety and Somatization scales is 46–

55. No rationale is provided for using these cutoffs as opposed to more commonly used cutoffs.

Although the authors contend that the P-3 will be less threatening to pain patients than existing psychological measures, an inspection of the items shows a great deal of similarity between the content of P-3 items and items on conceptually related measures. For instance, items on the P-3 Depression scale are quite similar to items on the Beck Depression Inventory (BDI, 37). P-3 items are generally face valid. For instance, the item "I sometimes think that everybody would be better off if I were dead" is obviously related to suicide potential and the item "I am almost always sad" is clearly related to dysphoric mood. There does not appear to be an appreciable difference in the content of P-3 items and items on other, brief, self-report measures of depression and anxiety. Given the obvious nature of the items on the P-3, it does not seem that patients asked to take the P-3 will be any more or less comfortable than if asked to complete related measures, such as the BDI. Thus, the P-3 offers no advantage in terms of minimizing the extent to which patients know their mental health is being evaluated, as the authors intended. Of course, one should also consider whether the discomfort the authors are attempting to avoid is a function of a test itself, or the way in which referrals for a psychological evaluation are handled.

SUMMARY. Overall, given the limited data concerning the validity of the P-3, I cannot recommend using it in clinical practice. Health care professionals attempting to address important questions concerning pain patients' emotional state and the extent to which psychological factors affect response to treatment are advised instead to rely on established measures.

[274]
Paper and Pencil Games.

Purpose: Constructed to measure "figural, quantitative and verbal skills closely related to scholastic achievement."
Population: Pupils in their second, third and fourth years in South African school system.
Publication Date: 1996.
Acronym: PPG.
Administration: Group.
Levels, 2: 2, 3.
Price Data, 1997: R5.13 per test booklet (specify level); R3.99 per Level 2 short version test booklet; R1.14 per practice test; R39.90 per manual (90 pages)

(English only); R28.50 per directions for administration (specify language).
Time: (150–180) minutes including 20-minute break.
Comments: Available in Afrikaans, Ndebele, Northern Sotho, Swati, Southern Sotho, Tsonga, Tswana, Venda, Xhosa, and Zulu.
Author: N. C. W. Claassen.
Publisher: Human Sciences Research Council [South Africa].
  a) LEVEL 2.
  Population: School years 2–3.
  Scores, 5: Classification, Verbal and Quantitative Reasoning, Figure Series, Comprehension, Pattern Completion.
  b) LEVEL 3.
  Population: School years 3–4.
  Scores, 5: Figure Series, Verbal and Quantitative Reasoning, Pattern Completion, Comprehension, Number Series.

Review of the Paper and Pencil Games by GARY L. MARCO, Consultant, Chapin, SC:

Paper and Pencil Games (PPG) is a group test designed to measure general scholastic reasoning in terms of figural, quantitative, and verbal skills. It is offered in the 11 official languages of South Africa. Level 2 is suitable for second and third graders; Level 3 for third and fourth graders. The test results are used to provide information helpful in identifying students who can benefit from standard instruction and to identify those students who have limited developed ability and who should be followed up with individual assessment. The tests are needed in the different languages because the schools offer instruction in the local language in the first three school years. The test information reviewed here is provided in the manual developed for the PPG.

Two general observations are relevant before proceeding with the review itself. First, the manual uses terminology such as Sub B, Standard 1, and Standard 2 that are undoubtedly familiar to Republic of South African users. But if the test publisher would like the PPG to be used outside the Republic of South Africa, the publisher is well advised to provide a description of these terms and how these levels might relate to levels of achievement in other countries. Second, the comparability of the test battery from one language group to another is assumed by the test publisher. Because of language differences, comparability should in fact be established via translations and back translations of items and empirical study. Here back translation occurred only for test directions.

TEST DESCRIPTION. PPG consists of 84 items at Level 2 and 100 items at Level 3. A short, 52-item version at Level 2 is also available. At Level 2 five item types are used: Classification, Figure Series, and Pattern Completion nonverbal items and Verbal and Quantitative Reasoning and Comprehension verbal items. At Level 3, five item types are also used. The item types are the same except that Number Series takes the place of Classification. An equal number of verbal and nonverbal items is used at each level. An optional test is available for administration to test takers who need practice with the materials prior to the actual testing.

TEST DEVELOPMENT. The theory underlying the PPG is that to learn at school students must be able to perceive accurately, recognize and recall what is perceived, understand relationships, think logically, infer from particulars, and apply generalizations. The item types making up the PPG appear to be appropriate for testing scholastic abilities, although empirical evidence is weak in this regard (see validity section).

In 1992 item pools were administered to 4,000 pupils. A year later revised and extended item pools were administered to about 3,700 students. At each pretesting items were selected on the basis of differential item functioning (DIF) indices (delta plot method) by gender, socioeconomic status, and language. Item types were also dropped as the result of the item and test analyses.

Presumably other factors (e.g., item difficulty and item-total correlations) besides DIF were taken into consideration in selecting items for the final item pool, but the manual makes no mention of such factors. Certainly, more than DIF should have been considered for item selection.

The final item pool, which contained approximately 50% more items than needed for the final battery, was administered in 1994 to approximately 10,000 students. A random sample of schools was drawn and the battery was administered to random samples of 20 Sub B and 20 Std 1 students in each school. Some additional testing was done on children of minority languages and Std 2 students. For purposes of norming, older students were eliminated from the sample. Some students took the battery 2 weeks later to estimate test-reliability.

Items were selected for the final battery on the basis of DIF information (in this case the Mantel-Haenszel statistic). The Comparison item type was dropped at this time because it correlated lowest with scholastic achievement. Because the final battery was intended to discriminate among lower performing students, easier items were selected for the final battery. In addition, difficulties were spread across the ability range so that a range of ability would be covered. Point biserial correlations with the item type score were also considered in selecting items for the final battery.

TEST ADMINISTRATION. The test takers are led through the test item by item. Depending on the item type, three to six practice items are administered before operational items are administered. No time limit is established, but groups on average take about 2 and a half to 3 hours (including a 20-minute break). This amount of testing time in one sitting—even with a 20-minute break—seems somewhat long for the students in the second through the fourth years in school. Test takers pencil in their answers right on the test booklet. The test directions in the manual are very clear as to how to proceed with the testing.

Because the test takers take the PPG one item at a time, there is a security concern that the test manual does not address. Presumably test takers could easily cheat on the test battery by getting answers from their neighbors. The manual does say something about protecting the security of the test materials, but does not address the cheating issue per se.

SCORES. Scoring is accomplished by hand by matching the test taker's answer with the keyed response. The following number-right scores are produced: item type raw scores, verbal and nonverbal raw scores (determined by adding the raw scores on the relevant item types), and a total raw score. Verbal, nonverbal, and total raw scores are referred to tables that show stanines for every half-year interval at a grade level. Although referring raw scores to stanines for these various levels provides appropriate norming information, a better practice in the opinion of this reviewer is to convert raw scores to a single scaled score, and then refer that score to the various norms tables. This type of scaling avoids the confusion of having multiple scaled scores.

SCORE INTERPRETATION. Test users are advised to interpret the nonverbal, verbal, and total scores. Test users are appropriately advised to use item type scores and scores on individual items with caution. Because raw scores are obviously affected by item difficulty, one cannot simply infer that because one raw score is better in percentage terms than another, a test taker should "work" on that area.

Test takers with stanine scores in the 3 to 7 range are considered to have the level of ability needed to benefit from standard instruction. Those with higher scores are considered capable of taking on instructional challenges and independent study, whereas those with lower scores are considered likely not to keep up with the standard instructional pace. Whether the inferences about ability to benefit from instruction for students scoring in these ranges are valid needs to be determined from studies of how well test takers do in school. This essential linkage to success in school is lacking.

TECHNICAL INFORMATION. Information regarding factor structure is presented in the form of correlations among item type raw scores for Levels 2 and 3, respectively. The correlations suggest moderate relationships—ranging from .37 to .63 for Level 2 and .34 to .73 for Level 3. The correlations among item types, including those not in the final battery, were factor analyzed by the principal factor method and the results rotated by the varimax procedure. This type of factor analysis, however, is inappropriate for two primary reasons: (a) It does not take account of unreliability and in fact assumes reliabilities of 1 for the measures, and (b) it results in uncorrelated factors (item type factors would not be expected to be independent). Hence, the factor analysis was not likely to yield meaningful results. More investigation is needed to confirm the verbal and nonverbal factors.

Reliability information for the verbal, nonverbal, and total scores is provided in the form of KR 20 (alpha) reliability coefficients, associated standard errors of measurement, and test-retest correlations. These data are provided for all students as well as for those who were environmentally disadvantaged. At level 2 all but three of the KR 20 coefficients are above .80, indicating a reasonable amount of homogeneity among the part scores. At Level 3 all of the coefficients exceed this value.

Standard errors are expressed in stanines, but how they were converted to this scale is not obvious and also not specified. The test-retest samples were smaller and the correlations slightly lower generally than the KR 20 reliabilities as might be expected. This result obtained particularly for the environmentally disadvantaged group. The lowest reliability regardless of method was for

the verbal subscore for this group, suggesting that the nonverbal score might indeed be a better measure of general scholastic ability than the verbal measure.

Criterion-related validity evidence is presented in the form of correlations with scholastic achievement (teacher evaluations and a mathematics achievement test) for both environmentally disadvantaged and nonenvironmentally disadvantaged groups. The correlations were lower for the former group, and in general were moderate in size (.20s to .40s) except for those with the achievement test, which were .30 or so points higher. Although these correlations suggest a moderate amount of predictive power, more validity evidence is needed. In particular the test publisher should try to determine whether stanine levels of 3 to 7 indicate standard instruction, whereas stanines above or below these levels justify enrichment or special instruction.

SUMMARY. The PPG battery is a verbal and nonverbal test battery that appears to cover important aspects of the verbal and nonverbal domains appropriate for scholastic achievement. The test is available in the 11 official languages recognized for instruction in the Republic of South Africa. The validity evidence does not clearly establish verbal and nonverbal factors; more study is needed. The empirical data do indicate that the test battery is probably useful for assessing the ability to benefit from normal instruction in schools, although the score levels suggested as cutoffs are not well established. Whether the battery has value for students in other countries would need to be determined through separate investigations.

[275]
Parallel Spelling Tests, Second Edition.

Purpose: Designed to help "chart children's progress in spelling."
Population: Ages 6 to 13 years.
Publication Dates: 1983–1998.
Scores: Total score only.
Administration: Group.
Price Data, 1999: £9.99 per test booklet/manual ('98, 40 pages).
Time: (20) minutes per test.
Comments: Teachers create tests from two banks of items: A (for ages 6 to 10) and B (for ages 9 to 13).
Author: Dennis Young.
Publisher: Hodder & Stoughton Educational [England].

Cross References: For reviews by Steven R. Shaw and Mark E. Swerdlik and by Claudia R. Wright, see 12:277.

Review of the Parallel Spelling Tests, Second Edition by THERESA G. SISKIND, Assessment Coordinator, South Carolina Education Oversight Committee, Columbia, SC:

The Parallel Spelling Tests are designed to measure spelling frameworks for the national curriculum in England and Wales, Scotland, and Northern Ireland. They are clearly not designed to measure spelling skills of students in the United States.

The theoretical basis for the tests is somewhat obscure. The author states that it is preferable and more valid to assess spelling in context but implies that it is more reliable to assess spelling with an objective test or one in which the examinee is required to write each word correctly as it is announced. The Parallel Spelling Tests are an example of this objective format.

The Parallel Spelling Tests include two banks of items. Bank A is composed of items designed to measure the spelling ability of children in Years 2–4 of British schools (ages 6:4–9:11) and Bank B is composed of items appropriate for children in Years 5–7 (ages 9:0–12:11). The banks contain sets of six item-pairs. Each item-pair includes two words to spell. The first word is dictated; a sentence is read with the word in context; the word is dictated again. The same procedure is followed for the second word. The examiner is advised to select one item-pair from each set of six until the maximum recommended number of item-pairs has been reached for each Year group. The banks include a total of 576 items with many possible combinations, providing numerous parallel forms—hence living up to their name.

Although the Parallel Spelling Tests are purported to be standardized, examiners are allowed to substitute their own sentences as long as the prescribed dictation procedure is followed. Additionally, examiners may select item-pairs utilizing any type of system as long as the item-pairs are not split. The rationale for maintaining the item pairs intact appears to rest on empirical item difficulty rather than on spelling construct. For example, the words are said to be ordered by spelling patterns, common letter strings, prefixes and suffixes, word families, etc. However, when reviewing the word pairs, it is immediately apparent that the word pairs rarely assess the same phonemic pattern.

Test administrations are advised to check student work to see that items are numbered correctly and that students do not write the sentences along with the spelling words. Some confusion could probably be alleviated if the test included oral directions to the children and simplified directions for selecting and numbering items.

Tests are scored by awarding a point for each correctly "spelt" (manual, p. 7) word. Raw scores may be converted to either a spelling age, which appears to be similar to an age equivalent, or to a quotient similar to an intelligence quotient. Standardization samples appear rather small to support such generalizations. The samples are described as representative, yet no data are given to justify this claim.

Test-retest reliabilities and stability estimates are all quite respectable ranging from the low to mid .90s. Non-identical samples of words were used to calculate these estimates. The effect of pronunciation on reliability is noted. Test-retest coefficients (administration interval not reported) using two different presenters for each of 11 samples were reported as .94 and .93, respectively, for the two banks. Interrater agreement in scoring may vary as a function of handwriting. Scorers are advised to ignore letter reversals, to ask examinees to read unclearly written letters, and to give credit where there is any doubt of correctness.

The utility of the test is questionable when one considers the discussion of test interpretation. Teachers are instructed to compare raw test scores with their own perceptions of children's spelling ability. If there is a discrepancy, they are advised to recheck the scoring of the test. "If the raw score proves to be correct, consider the possibility that the discrepancy may be due to the unreliability of testing" (manual, p. 32). Teachers are advised to retest with a parallel form. It is, presumably, when there is still a discrepancy that the following advice applies: "it is when the test result differs from the teacher's opinion that it may be most informative" (manual, p. 32).

Examples of norm-referenced interpretations of spelling ability using spelling age and progress in spelling using spelling quotient are given in the manual and provide some useful information. Educators are advised to view the spelling scores in concert with scores in reading and mathematics and oral intelligence with an "underlying assumption that it is valid to base our expectations on success in other fields" (manual, p. 32). Ultimately, however, teachers are advised to interpret all results based on their own knowledge of the child.

Error analysis—examining individual words and error patterns—can provide useful instructional information. This section of the manual provides a valuable discussion that could be expanded.

SUMMARY. The Parallel Spelling Tests provide what they claim in their name: numerous parallel forms of spelling tests for children in Years 2–7 of the British school system. They measure an important skill as defined by the national curriculum. The time spent in testing, scoring, and interpreting scores might better be spent in classroom testing using "a spelling book with words grouped by similarity of structure rather than to rely on spur-of-the-moment recall" (manual, p. 33), a similarly reliable method and one surely more instructionally valid in the measurement of spelling achievement for individual pupils.

Review of the Parallel Spelling Tests, Second Edition by LISA F. SMITH, Assistant Professor, Psychology Department, Kean University, Union, NJ:

The Parallel Spelling Tests, Second Edition (PST) are dictated spelling tests intended for students in England, Wales, Scotland, and Northern Ireland. The author states that the content and progression of the words used in the tests provide summative measures of the attainment of the goals put forth by the National Curriculum for English and the National Literacy Strategy Framework for Teaching. The author also states that the PST can provide a formative evaluation in that it can "reveal the types of words and spelling patterns that are causing difficulties at individual, class or whole-school levels" (manual, p. 4).

The manual is clearly written and provides basic and complete instructions on the rationale, construction, and uses of the PST. The author states that "the main purpose of the tests is normative" (manual, p. 36), yet goes into detail on how the results can be interpreted for and applied to individual children. No supportive data are supplied for these assertions.

Generalizability of the PST to students in the United States may be limited. The use of Standard British Language does not pose a problem in understanding the manual, and adjustments to the Standard British language spellings (e.g., theatre, flavour, programme, aeroplane) could be accomplished easily. However, the sentences themselves would need to be examined carefully and in several cases revised to correct unfamiliar words (e.g., pram), unfamiliar usage of words (e.g., He liked the house but not its *situation*), and take into consideration cultural sensitivity (e.g., In December, we decorate the Christmas tree).

TEST CONSTRUCTION, ADMINISTRATION, AND SCORING. The PST is arranged into two banks of items; Form A is intended for school years (in Great Britain) 2 to 4 (ages 6:4 to 9:11) and Form B is intended for years 5 to 7 (ages 9:0 to 12:11). The number of words to be used on a given test is determined by the year, ranging from 34 words for Year 2 to 50 words for Years 6 and 7. The test banks are divided into sections, each containing six pairs of items. A test is constructed by selecting one pair from each section until reaching the appropriate number of items. In this way, 12 tests can be constructed with no overlap of material.

The format for the administration of the test is: Announce the item number, dictate a word, read the word in a sentence, and then repeat the word. A time limit of 20 seconds per item is recommended for younger examinees. Time limits for older examinees are 15 seconds per item for easier items and 25 to 30 seconds per item for more difficult items. Two issues arise that may threaten the validity of the PST. First, although the author cautions against splitting the pairs, he states that the sentences themselves can be changed. Second, he suggests that children having great difficulty with the test should be redirected to another previously prepared activity.

Scoring involves a simple right or wrong decision, allowing for subjective knowledge of the child's handwriting or a comparison to other words on the test. Tables for raw scores and quotients are easily understood. The raw scores can be converted to spelling ages ranging from 6.7 to 15.0 years. The author states that the raw scores correspond to teachers' impressions of their students' abilities and can be useful for forming ability groups. No data are provided to support this assertion. The quotients are deviation scores with a mean of 100 and a standard deviation of 15 that give relative positions within the same month of age, ranging from age 6:4 to 12:11. The author states that quotients may be more appropriate for school records, in particular when a score for a younger child could be unfavorably compared to the scores of the older children in the same class.

PST NORMS. The norming sample came from 19 schools reported to be representative of national standards. The samples for Test A ($n =$ 1,981) and Test B ($n =$ 1,923) contained roughly equal numbers of boys and girls. Gender differences were reported in Years 2–6, with girls outperforming boys. Age norms and correlations compared favorably with the earlier edition of the Vernon Graded Word Spelling Test (1998; 157).

RELIABILITY. Test-retest reliabilities (administration interval not provided) on five samples of students ranging from 7-year-olds to 11-year-olds ranged from .925 to .956. Internal consistency coefficients are not obtainable, as items are combined differently for each administration. A study with a one-year delayed post-test showed a pre/post correlation of .918.

VALIDITY. Ninety percent of the 576 words in the PST were selected from *A Study of the Vocabulary of Young Children* (Burroughs, 1957); the remaining 10% were chosen from other sources. The author claims that the words selected from the Burroughs' study ensure that "the majority of the words in the banks are within the understanding of at least some 7-year-old children" (manual, p. 36), the remaining words extend the range to higher ability levels, and that the words demonstrate satisfactory discriminating power for English students. No data are presented to support these claims. The author provides correlations of the PST with a variety of other school measures developed by the author for samples ranging in age from 7 to 11 years. These correlations converge rather strongly with the PST, suggesting some level of method variance among the measures. There are no correlations with spelling ability measured from student essays or other work, nor are there correlations with teacher estimates.

SUMMARY. Overall, the PST seems a reasonably well-executed attempt to provide a measure of spelling ability for ages 6–13 in the United Kingdom. There could be more work done in establishing the validity of the measure, but the reliability appears to be quite good. A more established test, such as the spelling subtests of the Stanford Achievement Test (T5:2484), The Test of Written Language—Third Edition (T5:2731), or the National Achievement Tests would be more appropriate for use in the United States. For students in Great Britain, the PST may serve as a useful test of dictated spelling; caution should be exercised in the interpretation of results beyond that purpose.

REVIEWER'S REFERENCES

Burroughs, G. E. R. (1957). *A study of the vocabulary of young children.* Scotland: Oliver & Boyd.
Vernon, P. E. (1998). Graded Word Spelling Test (2nd ed.). London: Hodder & Stoughton.

[276]
Parenting Satisfaction Scale™.

Purpose: Designed to assess "parents' attitudes toward parenting."
Population: Adults with dependent children.
Publication Date: 1994.
Acronym: PSS.
Scores, 3: Satisfaction with Spouse/Ex-Spouse Parenting Performance, Satisfaction with the Parent-Child Relationship, Satisfaction with Parenting Performance.
Administration: Individual.
Price Data, 1999: $96.50 per comprehensive kit including manual (47 pages) and 25 ReadyScore® answer documents; $31 per 25 ReadyScore® answer documents; $70.50 per manual.
Time: (30) minutes.
Authors: John Guidubaldi and Helen K. Cleminshaw.
Publisher: The Psychological Corporation.
Cross References: See T5:1888 (1 reference).

Review of the Parenting Satisfaction Scale by IRA STUART KATZ, Clinical Psychologist, California Department of Corrections, Salinas Valley State Prison, Soledad, CA, and Licensed Clinical Psychologist, Private Practice, Salinas, CA:

OVERVIEW AND USES. The American family is under siege. Attacks on parents from the left and right are not uncommon. Biology thrusts individuals into social roles often unprepared, unschooled, and undifferentiated. The results of this lack of awareness, assessment, alignment, and attunement may lead to dysfunction and distress. Parenting role satisfaction appears to be related to behavioral outcomes. The Parenting Satisfaction Scale (PSS) is a refreshing step forward in closing the gap of awareness and promoting parenting skills and family healing.

The Parenting Satisfaction Scale (PSS) is a 45-item standardized assessment of parent's attitudes toward parenting with three discrete scales: Satisfaction with Spouse/Ex-Spouse Parenting

Performance, Satisfaction with the Parent-Child Relationship, and Satisfaction with Parenting Performance.

A unique feature of the PSS is the recognition that more and more families are blended and fragmented. Parenting role behavior is not limited by court decrees. As an empathetic communication tool in assessing various issues in custodial disputes, such as parental support, the PSS offers practical hope to both clients and clinicians. Equally compelling about the PSS is the potential of increasing empathy among family members by having the spouse or child complete the scale as though he or she was the responding parent.

The PSS is a very client-friendly instrument. It is easy to administer and score. Each scale contains 15 items. The PSS can be completed in 20 minutes. The reading level eases administration. The ReadyScore Answer Document instructs parents to respond to each item by circling the dot for their response that appears in front of the item. This is easy on the parent and makes the process of responding easier. Clients have shared with me their satisfaction with the ease of reading and scoring of the PSS. More impressive to them was the clear focus of the items covered. These were issues that often came up in family therapy. That client endorsement reinforces the PSS as a good adjunct clinical tool.

John Guidubaldi and Helen Cleminshaw, who authored the PSS, provide an excellent 43-page manual that, like the PSS, is very reader- and clinician-friendly. A brief review of what the manual covers is in order.

TEST MATERIALS. The PSS is a 4-page self-score instrument. The ReadyScore Answer Document is very easy to understand and use. Parents (and/or respondents) are asked to provide responses that describe how she or he feel about the spouse's (or ex-spouse's) parenting, how the parent feels about his or her relationship with the child(ren), and how the parent feels about her or his own parenting. The parent may choose to strongly agree, agree, disagree, or strongly disagree with each statement. The administration and scoring are refreshingly straightforward. The overall feel of the PSS is more clinical than psychometric. This is based on the fact that "parenting satisfaction" per se is not expected to follow a normal distribution in the entire population.

NORMS AND STANDARDIZATION. Standardization of the PSS involved three steps: a pilot phase including item generalization, and the establishment of reliability, face validity, investigations of construct (initial factor analyses) and criterion-related validity evidence, a standardization phase involving administering the PSS to a large nationwide sample, a second factor analysis, calculating reliability, and further analyses of criterion validity, and the final phase was a 2-year follow-up study. The purpose of the final phase was to reassess reliability and establish validity over time. There are sample inherent limits in the norm and standardization process. The pilot sample was composed of 130 parents (78 mothers and 52 fathers). Of the participants, 122 were married, and 8 were single parents.

Ninety-one percent of the sample was White. This does not appear to promote psychometric generalization. Norms in this pilot sample may not be truly representative of the current increasingly diverse American family millennial mosaic. There are alternative self-report inventories that may address this concern.

The Parent-Child Relationship Inventory (PCRI; 13:220) for example, authored by Anthony Gerard, was standardized with over 1,100 parents across the United States. An additional feature of the PCRI is that two validity scales alert the clinician to the possibility that a parent is responding inconsistently or portraying the parent-child relationship in an unrealistically positive light. The PCRI is also sensitive to the fact that "single dads" are becoming a more common factor in the parenting equation. The PSS could be strengthened in further revisions in these areas.

RELIABILITY. The PSS's internal consistency reliability indices, estimated using Cronbach's alpha, were very high with scores as follows: Satisfaction with Spouse/Ex-Spouse Parenting Performance, $r = .96$; Satisfaction with Parent-Child Relationship, $r = .86$; and Satisfaction with Parenting Performance, $r = .82$. A 2-year follow-up measuring internal reliability and test-retest reliability estimates indicated they were fair to good. Over a 2-year time period, satisfaction with the spouse's or ex-spouse's parenting style appears more stable than satisfaction with the parent-child relationship or than with one's own parenting style.

VALIDITY. Validity studies indicate good correlational factors of note. Specifically, correlations were shown between parenting satisfaction and children's social and academic performance, health ratings of family members, and between measures of family environment and the quality of the child's relationship with others. Worth noting here are two additional validity studies focusing on women, stress, and a Chinese Nationwide Child Adjustment Project. The women's project indicated parenting satisfaction highly correlates to satisfaction in spousal and employee roles as well as to life satisfaction in general. Stressors were shown to correlate negatively to parent satisfaction. The Chinese study resulted in expected correlations. The PSS was translated into Chinese and completed by 1,746 Chinese parents throughout the People's Republic of China. This is an exciting and needed step forward in bridging cultural and diversity gaps.

SUMMARY. The Parent Satisfaction Scale (PSS) is a clinically important tool that can help promote better understanding of the behavioral impact of various parenting roles. Its assessment of parent's attitudes toward parenting can be helpful to clients and clinicians. It can be strengthened by being more sensitive to various diversity issues including parental gender diversity. The PSS ease of reading and scoring are commendable and very client- and clinician-friendly. Future revisions should offer even more insights and clinical wisdom on the impact of parental roles attitude on behavior, communication, family relationships, therapy, and change. Drs. Guidubaldi and Cleminshaw have provided the gift of an excellent first step on a journey of needed clinical understanding for those focused on strengthening relationships and prosocial behaviors in families.

Review of the Parenting Satisfaction Scale by JANET V. SMITH, Associate Professor of Psychology and Counseling, Pittsburg State University, Pittsburg, KS:

The Parenting Satisfaction Scale (PSS) is a 45-item self-report questionnaire designed to measure attitudes toward parenting and satisfaction with the parenting role. It can be used to assess satisfaction with parenting in general, or satisfaction with parenting of a specific child. The scale generates a total satisfaction score as well as scores on three separate subscales. Subscale 1 (Satisfaction with Spouse/Ex-Spouse Parenting Performance) provides information about satisfaction with a partner's role in parenting. Subscale 2 (Satisfaction with the Parent-Child Relationship)

assesses level of satisfaction in the parent's relationship with their own child. Subscale 3 (Satisfaction with Parenting Performance) provides a measure of a parent's level of satisfaction with their own parenting role. The PSS was designed through a National Association of School Psychologists (NASP) project to predict child and family outcomes from levels of parenting satisfaction.

Test items were developed through relevant literature review as well as interviews with a nonclinical sample of adults to identify factors that were considered to be important to satisfaction and dissatisfaction with the parenting role. From this information, potential items were developed and these were reviewed by parents as well as experts in the field of child and family development. This process resulted in a pool of 211 items, which was then piloted on a sample of 130 parents to produce the final item selection for the test.

Test materials are very well designed, and the PSS is extremely simple and quick to both administer and score. The reading level of the test is upper elementary school. As the manual cautions, there is no check for social desirability, which could cause a problem given the high face validity of test items. The manual is comprehensive and easy to follow. Minimal qualifications are needed to administer and interpret the test. Although the manual suggests that the PSS may be completed in a parent's home, it would be desirable for the test to be taken in an office setting to ensure standardized administration conditions are met.

The normative sample appears adequate, other than fathers being significantly underrepresented in the sample. Of more concern is that the norms are already somewhat outdated, as the normative data were collected in 1981/1982. Tables are provided to obtain standard scores and percentile ranks. Standard scores are reported as nonnormalized *T* scores, which seems appropriate given that the distribution of raw scores on two of the subscales is somewhat skewed.

The test scores show adequate levels of reliability. Internal consistency was calculated using Cronbach's alpha and was found to be .96 for Satisfaction with Spouse/Ex-Spouse Parenting Performance scale, .86 for Satisfaction with Parent-Child Relationship scale, and .82 for Satisfaction with Parenting Performance scale. Test-retest reliability was investigated with 137 parents from the original normative sample, with a time interval of 2 years. Test-retest reliability coefficients were substantially lower than the internal consistency estimates: $r = .81$ for Satisfaction with Spouse/Ex-Spouse Parenting Performance, .59 for Satisfaction with Parent-Child Relationship, and .64 for Satisfaction with Parenting Performance. Although these coefficient values are rather low, this does not necessarily represent a problem with the test as it is quite reasonable to expect parenting satisfaction to change over time.

Factor analysis supports the existence of the three subscales on the PSS, although a small number of items do show rather low factor loadings. Alpha factor loadings for Factor 1 (Satisfaction with Spouse/Ex-Spouse Parenting Performance) vary from .61 to .84; for Factor 2 (Satisfaction with the Parent-Child Relationship) values range from .38 to .70; and for Factor 3 (Satisfaction with Parenting Performance) values range from .19 to .62.

Because no acceptable criterion for parenting satisfaction is available, evidence is provided for construct validity. In the pilot phase, the PSS was found to show significant correlations with other measures of satisfaction, although the scales used were measures of general life satisfaction and marital satisfaction rather than specific to the parenting role. The normative sample for the PSS was given a wide variety of instruments along with the PSS as part of the NASP project, and the three subscales of the PSS showed significant correlations with a large number of measures. Again, however, despite the vast amount of data collected, none of the measures were directly related to parenting satisfaction, but rather were predominantly in the areas of child's social competence, child's academic and intellectual achievement, family health, and family environment.

The authors describe several clinical applications of the test. For example, other family members may complete the PSS as though they were the responding parent, and this information could be used to increase communication and empathy. It should be noted, however, that these alternative applications may generate useful clinical hypotheses and qualitative impressions rather than psychometrically sound data, as no supporting data are provided in the manual.

SUMMARY. In summary, the test provides a much needed measure to assess levels of parenting satisfaction. The test provides a quick and easy measure of current levels of satisfaction, although

it is not necessarily predictive of future levels. Psychometric properties are adequate for research purposes as well as for generating clinical hypotheses or facilitating the clinical/counseling process with families. However, additional evidence of validity would be helpful, rather than reliance on measures that have at best an indirect association with parenting satisfaction. Overall, the test fills a valuable role, as there previously has been no accepted measure of parenting satisfaction available.

[277]
Parents' Evaluation of Developmental Status.
Purpose: Designed to help "identify children at risk for school problems and those with undetected developmental and behavioral disabilities"; "helps providers decide when to refer, reassure, advise, wait and see versus screen."
Population: Birth–8 years.
Publication Dates: 1997–1998.
Acronym: PEDS.
Scores, 3: Low Risk, Medium Risk, High Risk.
Administration: Individual.
Price Data, 1997: $30 per complete set including Brief Administration and Scoring Guide ('97, 8 pages), 50 PEDS Response Forms, and 50 Score/Interpretation Forms (same price for English and Spanish versions); $15 per 50 scoring or response forms; $3.50 per brief scoring guide; $69.95 per PEDS manual ('98, 157 pages); Bulk order discount available.
Foreign Language Edition: Spanish version available.
Time: (2–5) minutes.
Comments: Questionnaire for parents about children; can be administered as an interview or in paper and pencil form.
Author: Frances Page Glascoe.
Publisher: Ellsworth & Vandermeer Press, Ltd.

Review of the Parents' Evaluation of Developmental Status by LISA BISCHOFF, Associate Professor, School of Education, Indiana State University, Terre Haute, IN:

The Parents' Evaluation of Developmental Status (PEDS) is described by the author as a guidance system or triage process designed to assist early childhood and health care professionals in detecting and addressing developmental and behavioral difficulties in children from birth to age 8. Specifically, information obtained from administration of the PEDS may help determine the probability of a disability diagnosis for a specific child and to determine if the child should be referred for in-depth evaluation or further screening, or if parents should be provided with information and education, or if routine monitoring is sufficient to address a child's needs. The PEDS is not intended to take the place of in-depth evaluation where such evaluation is warranted.

The PEDS consists of 10 items that may be administered to parents in written questionnaire or interview format. Administration and scoring time is approximately 2 minutes. Areas assessed by the PEDS include global/cognitive, expressive language and articulation, receptive language, fine motor, gross motor, behavior, social-emotional, self-help, school, and other. One item is presented in each of the areas listed. Detailed administration, scoring, and interpretation guidelines are provided in the manual entitled "Collaborating with parents: Using Parents' Evaluations of Developmental Status in Screening, Surveillance and Promotion."

The PEDS was developed in response to a need for a brief, accurate screening instrument that could be used routinely and easily by health care providers to assist in determining the likelihood of developmental problems in children and the logical course of action for helping families deal with concerns. Development of the PEDS is based on research literature regarding the use of information provided by parents and on research literature regarding child development. The author reviews literature in the manual and provides a clear rationale for the use of parental concerns as indicators of developmental and behavioral problems. Furthermore, the author provides data and references for pilot studies conducted throughout the development of the PEDS.

The PEDS was standardized with 771 families in five states representing the South, South Central, North, Central, and West areas of the United States. Participants were recruited from a variety of sources including children attending public schools and daycare centers and nonenrolled siblings, private pediatric offices, and outpatient pediatrics clinics. Girls and boys were nearly equally represented in the sample and racial background closely resembled the 1996 U.S. Census data. Data regarding a number of family characteristics of the sample were provided in the manual. Information regarding variance in types of concerns expressed by parents with different child, parent, and family characteristics is provided in the manual.

Reliability data provided for the PEDS suggest that the scores from the instrument are highly reliable. Interrater reliability data suggest examiner agreement on the classification of parental concerns from 80% to 100% across categories with an average of 95%. Additional interrater reliability data suggest examiner agreement on elicited parental concerns from 80% to 100% with an average of 88%. Test-retest reliability data indicate stability over time with agreement of screenings administered 2 weeks apart of 80% to 100% with an average of 88%. Internal consistency data suggest that concerns included in the PEDS are independent and unique and overlap in a logical manner (e.g., fine and gross motor are correlated) yet demonstrate reasonable internal consistency (coefficient alpha = .81).

Information regarding concurrent validity, discriminant validity, and criterion-related validity are provided in the manual. Data were obtained through administration of a battery of tests to each of the 771 children in the standardization sample. The battery included measures of fine motor, gross motor, expressive language and articulation, receptive language, self-help, socialization, behavior, cognitive, and academic/preacademic skills. Description of procedures and tables summarizing data are provided in the manual. Concurrent validity data suggest moderate correlations between parental concerns in specific domains and scores on measures of similar content.

Discriminant validity is examined through a process in which children were classified by disability using criteria drawn from federal law and then regression analyses were used to identify concerns most closely related to specific disability categories. Results suggest that the PEDS does discriminate between types of problems based on expressed parental concerns. Finally, the PEDS demonstrates criterion-related validity in that the probability of a child having a disability based on expressed parental concern is 70% or greater across areas. Detailed information regarding specific concerns and child, parent, and family characteristics is presented in the manual.

SUMMARY. The PEDS is a screening instrument that has been carefully constructed and standardized. This brief, easily administered instrument can be incorporated into health care routines for children. Scores are based on expressed parental concerns and appear to provide reliable and valid indications of probable disabilities. The manual provides detailed information regarding administration, scoring, and interpretation and guides the examiner through the decision-making process following screening.

Review of the Parents' Evaluation of Developmental Status by MARK W. ROBERTS, Professor of Psychology, Idaho State University, Pocatello, ID:

Glascoe and her colleagues have constructed a 10-item prescreening instrument for health care providers (physicians, nurses) to assess systematically the risk of developmental disabilities in young children. On the Parents' Evaluation of Developmental Status, or PEDS, parents report any "concerns" they might have about their birth to 8-year-old child across major developmental domains: global/cognitive, expressive language and articulation, receptive language, fine motor, gross motor, behavior, social-emotional, self-help, school, and an open-ended "other" category. The PEDS format provides "No," "Yes," or "A Little" response options plus space for written comments. Parents can self-administer PEDS in 2 to 5 minutes or the health care provider can present items orally. Based on PEDS data, specific alternative decisions ("paths") are recommended: Refer for diagnostic testing, screen or refer for screening, provide brief counseling, or monitor progress with PEDS at the next office visit.

Most health care providers probably question parents about child development at some level. The PEDS, however, prompts the provider to do so systematically and repetitively, and provides empirical bases for alternative recommendations. The PEDS has the potential to reduce the number of undetected children (false negatives) with developmental disabilities, which is an important goal. There is no comparable instrument available. The test is inexpensive and quickly administered. Therefore, there is much to recommend the routine use of the PEDS by health care providers.

At present, however, the PEDS suffers from some important psychometric limitations. First, it is unclear how representative the standardization sample ($n = 771$) is of the population of young children contacting health care providers. Subjects included 514 nonpatients recruited from educational settings. Parents of nonpatients may have different "concerns" than a parent taking a child to a health care setting (Glascoe, Foster, & Wolraich, 1997). Second, although an impressive multisite method was employed, African-Americans and low-income families appear to be overrepresented. Third, the sample included a substantial number of younger siblings ($n = 225$) of youth recruited from educational settings, thereby rendering many informants nonindependent (because they reported concerns for two or more children). Finally, the informants were overwhelmingly mothers or stepmothers (89.2%), which virtually precludes the use of the PEDS with male informants.

The reliability of the PEDS has not been adequately examined. Providers use PEDS scores by summing the number of "significant" concerns (i.e., those items validated against disability criteria) and summing the number of "nonsignificant" concerns (i.e., those items not associated with disabilities). The number of significant items ranges from 4 to 7, depending on age group; conversely, the number of nonsignificant items ranges from 3 to 6. At a minimum the test-retest reliability and the standard errors of measurement of these two total scores should be reported. They are not. Instead, the manual reports agreement ratios obtained during pilot testing to demonstrate consistency across raters in assigning parent responses to the appropriate developmental domains for the two open-ended questions (Item 1: "Please list any concerns about your child's learning, development, and behavior"; Item 10: "Please list any other concerns"). Professional raters appear able to do this quite well; the average agreement ratio was 95%. Unfortunately, the only reported index of reliability that allowed nonspecific temporal effects to vary was a 2-week phone follow-up of 20% of the pilot sample. Comparison of the parent concerns reported on the two occasions indicated an average agreement ratio of 88%; however, that index is inflated by agreement over nonconcerns. The frequency distribution of "concerns" should be positively skewed with low item difficulty scores, hovering about the national disability base rate (16% to 18%). Therefore, in the analysis of test-retest parent consistency, the author should have limited agreements to the occurrence of concerns, thereby avoiding the spurious inflation inherent in agreements on nonoccurrence that accompanies low base rate phenomena.

The validity of PEDS data is summarized in Chapters X–XI of the manual. Several different criterion measures were used to screen or diagnose common developmental disabilities. An examination of the measures and the criteria used for disability classification revealed high quality measurements and standard classification rules. The only detectable problems were the lack of a reading comprehension measure for school age participants (the author relied on the Letter-Word Identification Scale from the Woodcock-Johnson) and a limited measure of social-emotional development, the Eyberg Child Behavior Inventory, which screens for externalizing disorders and omits internalizing disorders.

Three validation strategies were employed to evaluate the PEDS. First, many PEDS items correlated significantly with criterion measures. Second, some PEDS items were significantly associated with disability classifications across the age range and for specific age groups, yielding elevated prevalence data for youth with significant parental concerns. Third, PEDS sensitivity and specificity for identifying youth with disabilities appears consistently to exceed 70%. Therefore, substantial data do support the author's contention that PEDS data can be used as a prescreening device for developmental problems. At a minimum, those youngsters identified by significant concerns on the PEDS should be referred for a broad spectrum, validated screening test like the Battelle Developmental Inventory Screening Test (T5:266) or the Denver-II (T5:788). The screening does need to be comprehensive, however, because specific parental concerns raised on the PEDS do not correspond well with specific disabilities. For example, concerns about expressive or receptive language development do not enter into regression equations for predicting speech-language impairment.

The validity data are not without limitations. Most importantly, the prevalence data and sensitivity/specificity indices are probably overestimates. Validity data reported in the PEDS manual capitalize on sample specific covariance that might "shrink" dramatically when using the significant concerns identified in the current sample with a new sample of subjects. Until such cross-validation has been completed, test users are cautioned to view specific PEDS recommendations as tentative. For example, the PEDS delineates five alternative "paths" (i.e., decision-making branching systems). Alternative paths are based on prevalence, sensitivity, and specificity data cited in the manual. Unfortunately, all the sensitivity/specificity data are suspect because the items found to be "significant" were then used to quantify prevalence, sensitivity, and specificity levels in the same sample of subjects.

SUMMARY. Based on the data provided by the PEDS research team to date, I recommend that health-care providers routinely and repetitively administer the PEDS to prescreen children for developmental disabilities. The measure is inexpensive, quick, valid as a prescreen, and should reduce the rate of undetected children. When a youth's female parent has any concerns on those items that correlate with disabilities (the "significant" items), the provider can justifiably recommend a broad spectrum developmental screening by a competent developmental specialist. It is hoped that PEDS researchers will establish the test-retest reliability of the relevant total score (the sum of the significant items) and cross-validate the prevalence, specificity, and sensitivity of the PEDS on a new sample of representative children.

REVIEWER'S REFERENCE

Glascoe, F. P., Foster, E. M., & Wolraich, M. L. (1997). An economic analysis of developmental detection methods. *Pediatrics, 99,* 830–837.

[278]

PDI Employment Inventory and PDI Customer Service Inventory.

Purpose: Designed to identify job applicants most likely to display positive employee traits.
Population: Job applicants.
Publication Dates: 1985–1993.
Administration: Group.
Price Data: Available from publisher.
Time: (30) minutes.
Comments: Paper and pencil inventories of attitudes and self-descriptions; oral instructions; computer-scored.
Authors: George E. Paajanen, Timothy L. Hansen, and Richard A. McLellan.
Publisher: Personnel Decisions, Inc.

a) PDI EMPLOYMENT INVENTORY.
Purpose: Designed to identify job applicants who will be likely to be productive and to stay on the job at least 3 months.
Publication Dates: 1985–1993.
Acronym: PDI-EI.
Scores, 2: Performance, Tenure.
Foreign Language and Other Special Editions: Foreign and bilingual editions available include American Spanish/English, French-Canadian English, Mexican Spanish, British English, and Vietnamese/English.

b) PDI CUSTOMER SERVICE INVENTORY.
Purpose: Designed to identify job applicants most likely to exhibit helpful and positive behaviors in interacting with customers.

Publication Dates: 1991–1993.
Acronym: PDI-CSI.
Score: Customer Service Knowledge and Skills (Total).
Foreign Language Edition: Spanish-English edition available.

Review of the PDI Employment Inventory and PDI Customer Service Inventory by GORDON C. BRUNER II, Associate Professor, Marketing Department, Director, Office of Scale Research, Southern Illinois University, Carbondale, IL:

The PDI Employment Inventory (EI) was designed as a preemployment test to assist in the identification of applicants who are most likely to be productive and stay on the job for at least 3 months. The developers have positioned the instrument to be most appropriate for hourly workers who must be dependable but do not necessarily need high level skills. Likewise, the PDI Customer Service Inventory (CSI) was constructed in order to help identify applicants most likely to exhibit satisfactory behaviors related to interaction with customers of a business. The EI and the CSI can be administered separately or together, the latter being a 145-item form.

An impressive number of studies have been conducted to develop, purify, and gather validity evidence on the instruments. Evidence is provided to indicate that the tests meet the Federal Uniform Guidelines on Employee Selection Procedures as well as the Civil Rights Act of 1991.

The EI has four broad dimensions: Performance, Tenure, Infrequency, and Frankness, the last two being included as checks on careless and socially desirable responding, respectively. The authors described the items comprising the performance portion as representing 13 constructs but the instrument produces just one score to represent the set. Not surprisingly this leads to a low internal consistency (.74) as well as low one-month stability ($r = .62$). The reliability of the tenure portion of the EI was even lower (.64 [internal consistency], $r = .59$ [stability]). As for the CSI, it was developed to tap into some 16 personality dimensions that were thought to influence customer service behavior regardless of the work setting. The internal consistency estimate was .73 and the one-month stability value was .86. For both the EI and the CSI the authors argued that stability was the more important indicator of reliability. However, that position stands in opposition to what is now commonly accepted in psychometrics, that stability measures are confounded by various factors and should not be depended upon (e.g., Kelly & McGrath, 1988; Nunnally & Bernstein, 1994, p. 255). Further, if the score from an instrument is to be used for purposes such as hiring rather than just comparing groups then the internal consistency of the measure should be very high (i.e., greater than .90; Devellis, 1991, p. 86; Nunnally & Bernstein, 1994, p. 265).

Given this, it is this reviewer's position that due to the lack of unidimensionality and high reliability, the evidence of validity of scores from the instruments has not been established (e.g., Gerbing & Anderson, 1988). Only if we loosen that restriction are we impressed by the sheer quantity and variety of data presented in the manual in support of the validity of various uses in scores from the instrument.

Well over 100 correlation coefficients of the EI with other tests of personality and basic ability skills are presented in the manual as evidence of discriminant and convergent validity (pp. 31–35). Because the EI is multidimensional it is difficult to know how to interpret its correlation or lack thereof with the many other scales. On the positive side, it did have a moderate correlation with an employee reliability index; on the other hand, it had a much higher correlation with a test of reading comprehension. Obviously, it is premature for the authors to claim that the pattern of correlations shows a "sensible pattern" and is evidence of EI's validity (p. 31).

A variety of correlations are cited in support of the criterion validity of the EI and CSI. The figures are similar to what has been found in other recent studies of the effect of personality variables on customer service that indicate the portion of variance in service performance explained by personality ranges between 3% and 20% (e.g., Hurley, 1998). Although this suggests that some personality factors do appear to have a significant impact, especially in some settings, we must also be careful not to exaggerate personality's importance across work settings.

SUMMARY. In summary, the good news is that independent studies do appear to support the ability of the PDI (EI) to facilitate discrimination between employees based upon some sort of commitment factor (Collins & Schmidt, 1993; Woolley & Hakstian, 1992). The bad news is that the evidence of dimensionality, reliability, and validity of scores from the instruments are weak primarily because it is inappropriate for so many variables to be represented in the global scores composing PDI EI and CSI. Finally, managers should keep in mind that personality variables by themselves may not be the only or the best predictors of performance, and care must be taken not to overattribute causation to scores from any instruments that focus exclusively on such factors.

REVIEWER'S REFERENCES

Gerbing, D. W., & Anderson, J. C. (1988, May). An updated paradigm for scale development incorporating unidimensionality and its assessment. *Journal of Marketing Research, 25*, 186–192.

Kelly, J. R., & McGrath, J. E. (1988). *On time and method.* Beverly Hills, CA: Sage.

Devellis, R. F. (1991). *Scale development: Theory and applications.* Newbury Park, CA: Sage Publications, Inc.

Woolley, R. M., & Hakstian, A. R. (1992). An examination of the construct validity of personality-based and overt measures of integrity. *Educational and Psychological Measurement, 52*, 475–489.

Collins, J. M., & Schmidt, F. L. (1993). Personality, integrity, and white collar crime: A construct validity study. *Personnel Psychology, 46*, 295–311.

Nunnally, J. C., & Bernstein, I. H. (1994). *Psychometric theory* (3rd ed.). New York: McGraw-Hill.

Hurley, R. F. (1998). Customer service behavior in retail settings: A study of the effect of service provider personality. *Journal of the Academy of Marketing Science, 26*(Spring), 115–127.

Review of the PDI Employment Inventory and PDI Customer Service Inventory by ANNIE W. WARD, Emeritus Professor, University of South Florida, Daytona Beach, FL:

The PDI Employment Inventory (EI) and the PDI Customer Service Inventory (CSI) were developed by Personnel Decisions, Inc. to assist businesses and industries in making employment decisions. Both inventories deal with noncognitive aspects of employee behavior.

The inventories are quite short and they are available either in separate booklets or in a single booklet that combines both inventories. There are three types of items in both inventories: True-false; three-choice multiple-choice; and four-choice multiple-choice. The inventories are available in several language versions: American Spanish/English, British English, French-Canadian/English, Mexican Spanish, and Vietnamese/English. Three scores are reported on the combined inventories: Performance Score (EI), Tenure Score (EI), and Customer Service Score (CSI).

Although the test booklets themselves are not impressive, the manual is. It is well-written and contains much informative, useful information. Although it is directed primarily toward those who are responsible for hiring large groups of hourly employees, it also contains an impressive amount of technical information.

The manual starts with a brief discussion of personality tests in general and a longer discussion of counterproductive behavior and its relationship to satisfactory employee behavior. Then the authors describe the procedures used to develop the PDI inventories.

The authors are careful to recommend that users conduct their own studies and set their own cutoff scores based on local data. They also recommend that these inventories be used as only a part of hiring criteria, and that they be used in conjunction with other information. There is also a good discussion of "Adverse Impact and Fairness" and evidence to indicate that the PDI inventories are unbiased.

VALIDITY.

Development of the Employment Inventory (EI). In developing the EI, the authors followed procedures recommended in the literature. In order to define the construct, they started with a review of the literature, then they interviewed executives and managers of large companies and examined such materials as job descriptions, employee handbooks, training guides, and case files of counterproductive behavior.

From these materials they developed a set of 25 predictor constructs, mostly negative, separated into 10 major categories, which they used for item development. During the item development process they looked at a number of other instruments that seemed to be related to at least one of the constructs. A large number of items were written, but some of the constructs did not lend themselves to item writing, so the original 25 constructs were reduced to 13. Two of the original major headings were no longer there: "Excitement seeking" and "social influence." One subheading was apparently changed from "anomie" to "alienation." Careful study of the definition of the original constructs suggests that a different term for some of them might have been more informative. For example, the major heading "socialization," which has a positive connotation, is defined by the three headings of "delinquency," "fringe involvement," and "undeveloped values." Similarly, all of the subheadings under "Attitudes" are negative. It is clear that the items were directed at "nonproductiveness," which was the intent of the authors, but the terms used for some of them do not make this clear. The items were subjected to try-outs, concurrently with a sample of college students and with employees of a large retail chain.

Factor Analysis. Although the EI was not intended to be a factorially pure construct, a factor analysis was conducted with the data from the large department store. Of the 13 constructs that resulted from the original study and item writing, only five factors were identified and these factors accounted for only 15.7% of the total variance.

Predictive Studies. Scores on the EI were correlated with measures of job performance, with most of them being low positive (except when the hypothesized relationship is negative). Of the 167 relationships reported, 44% of the correlations were in the .20s and 27% were in the .30s. Eleven percent were higher than .40.

A comparison was also made of the percentage of satisfactory job performances of employees of one industry for those who "failed" and those who "passed" the EI, and for the situation with no use of the EI. There was a slight gain in the percentage of satisfactory employees with the use of the EI, ranging from 5–7% depending on where the cutting score was set.

Development of the Customer Service Inventory (CSI). The development of the CSI was based primarily on a study of the literature. Sixteen dimensions of personality that influence customer service were identified. Items were developed and administered to two groups of current employees and two groups of job applicants. Job analysis questionnaires were also administered to both job incumbents and supervisors. Four indicators of employee performance were developed and rank ordered. Only items that were related to job performance in more than one organization were selected for the final form of the inventory, which consists of 64 items.

Factor Analysis. Although the CSI was not intended to measure a factorially pure construct, a factor analysis was conducted. This analysis identified 10 factors that contributed 43.3% of the total variance of the inventory. The 5 largest factors contributed 28.2% of the total variance. It is easy to see the relationship between these factors and some of the original hypothesized constructs. However, a large percentage of the items did not load on any factor.

Predictive Studies. Scores on the CSI were correlated with four job ratings for eight employee groups. The correlations were mostly in the .20s.

A comparison was also made of the percentage of satisfactory job performances of employees of one industry for those who "failed" and those who "passed" the CSI, and for the situation with no use of the CSI. There was a slight gain in the percentage of satisfactory employees with the use of the EI, ranging from 3%–8%, depending on where the cutting score was set.

RELIABILITY. The internal reliability of the EI is reported as in the .60s and .70s, which the authors describe as acceptable, because the inventories were developed specifically to measure several different traits. The 4 week test-retest reliability estimate for the EI was only .60, which the authors attribute to the fact that it was obtained on a sample of university students, for which the scores have a restricted range.

For the CSI, the internal reliability was .73 and the one-month test-retest reliability was an impressive .86.

ADMINISTRATION AND SCORING. Both the EI and the SCI are essentially self-administering. There is a set of instructions to be read by the examiner while the examinee follows. A glossary of terms is provided in case the examinee needs help with a word.

There are 97 items on the EI, 64 on CSI, and 145 on the combined instrument. Although there are no time limits, most examinees finish in less than 30 minutes. Both inventories use a set of "infrequent response" items to identify examinees who are not responding validly.

Both inventories may be scored quickly with the use of a computer disk. The disk keeps a record of each examinee and summarizes the records.

SUMMARY. In contrast with many other noncognitive instruments, the PDI inventories have much to commend them. The authors followed recommended procedures for identifying the constructs and writing items. They also collected empirical information, which they used to validate and select the items included in the inventories. Also, although the reliability information and the construct validation information came from the "convenient sample" of university students, the predictive validity data came from employees and supervisors in businesses and industry, as it should.

There are some problems, however. Unfortunately, neither the reliability nor the validity information is good enough to warrant uncritical use of these inventories as the sole, or even the primary, source of information to be used in making hiring decisions. This is true of most instruments of this nature. Whether use of the PDI inventories as part of the employment process will improve the percentage of satisfactory job performances depends very much on the local situation.

As is usual with noncognitive inventories, the statistical evidence for validity is not impressive. Scores on the inventories were correlated with scores on other personality and ability instruments and, in general, the significant correlations were in the hypothesized direction. Correlations were also run between scores on the inventories and supervisors' ratings, and again the correlations were in the right direction, but low. And some limited studies of satisfactory job performance demonstrated slight gains with the use of the inventories.

In addition to the relatively low statistical evidence, there are some problems with the face validity of the inventories. Although the concept of face validity is not highly regarded, it is still important in some situations. Testing for employment would seem to be one of those. With the low correlations between inventory scores and job performance ratings, it would be reassuring to find that the items look as if they would educe important information. This does not appear to be so for many of the items.

Examination of the items raises some question about just what is being measured by some of them. Furthermore, some of them require a great deal more self-insight than many of the targeted examinees are apt to have. And some items and/or options are so obviously negative that *aware* examinees would not choose them. It may be that these specific items are those that are included as a part of the "Infrequency scale," but they do not seem to be so.

CONCLUSION. As the authors correctly point out, no single instrument should be used as the sole basis for making decisions about hiring. Also, the PDI inventories deal only with attitude and ethics. Of even more importance for many jobs is the matter of the knowledge and skills needed to handle the job, which would have to be evaluated from some other data. The authors of the PDI inventories feel that with hourly (by which they apparently mean "low-level") employees, the attitude and ethics questions may be of equal importance. In situations in which this is true, these inventories may be useful adjuncts to the hiring information.

The information could make an important contribution to those decisions in certain situations. First, the situation would be one in which there was the need to hire large numbers of hourly employees. Second, a job analysis should be made to determine that the traits needed by the employees are essentially the same as those addressed on one or both of these inventories. And, finally, the employer would need to conduct an ongoing validation study to investigate whether scores on the inventory are really a help in identifying potential employee problems.

[279]

Peabody Individual Achievement Test—Revised [1998 Normative Update].

Purpose: Designed to measure academic achievement.

Population: Grades K–12.

Publication Dates: 1970–1998.

Acronym: PIAT-R.

Scores, 9: General Information, Reading Recognition, Reading Comprehension, Total Reading, Mathematics, Spelling, Total Test, Written Expression, Written Language.

Administration: Individual.

Levels: 2 for Written Expression subtest (Level I: Grades K–1; Level II: Grades 2–12).

Price Data, 1999: $279.95 per complete kit including 50 combined test record and written response booklets, and manual ('98, 271 pages); $69.95 per 50 combined record/response booklets; $79.95 per manual; $15.95 per pronunciation guide cassette; $199.95 per software package (specify DOS 3.5-inch or 5.25-inch, Windows, or Macintosh).

Time: (60) minutes.

Comments: This test (PIAT-R [1998 Normative Update]) is the same as the PIAT-R (1989) but with new norms.

Author: Frederick C. Markwardt, Jr.

Publisher: American Guidance Service, Inc.

Cross References: See T5:1902 (103 references) and T4:1944 (33 references); for reviews by Kathryn M. Benes and Bruce G. Rogers of an earlier version, see 11:280 (125 references); see also 9:923 (39 references), T4:1944 (33 references), and T3:1769 (67 references); for excerpted reviews by Alex Bannatyne and Barton B. Proger of the original edition, see 8:24 (36 references); see also T2:26 (2 references); for a review by Howard B. Lyman of the original edition, see 7:17.

Review of the Peabody Individual Achievement Test—Revised [1998 Normative Update] by LAWRENCE H. CROSS, Professor of Educational Research and Evaluation, Virginia Polytechnic Institute, Blacksburg, VA:

The 1998 edition of the Peabody Individual Achievement Test—Revised/Normative Update

(PIAT-R/NU) is identical to the 1989 edition but with new norms. Data for the normative update were collected in 1995–1996, whereas data for previous norms were collected in 1986. The manual that accompanies the PIAT-R/NU is essentially unchanged from the 1989 edition except for the updated norms tables and a description of the norming process. The revised norms are also conveniently available on a computer program called ASSIST, which produces score reports and eliminates the need to look up normative scaled scores in the manual. This review focuses primarily on the new norms, with only limited attention given to the tests per se, or the psychometric properties of the test scores. Comprehensive reviews of the PIAT-R by Kathryn Benes (1992) and Bruce Rogers (1992) that appear in the *Eleventh Mental Measurements Yearbook* provide more detailed descriptions of the tests and summarize the reliability and validity evidence available at the time.

THE TESTS. The primary battery of the PIAT-R consists of six individually administered subtests which, in order of administration, are: General Information, Reading Recognition, Reading Comprehension, Mathematics, Spelling, and Written Expression. The latter subtest was introduced with the 1989 revision, but it is not included in the composite score for the battery, in part, due to the characteristically modest reliability and validity evidence associated with writing assessments. Except for the General Information and Written Expression subtests, the subtests consist mostly of multiple-choice questions, each with four choices. The items are well written, having survived extensive review and pilot testing. All six tests are contained in a four-volume Book of Plates, which incorporates an easel stand for ease of administering and scoring of the tests. The tests are designed for use with examinees in Grades K–12 and ages 5–19. Because examinees are administered only a small subset of items within the "critical range" of their achievement level, the manual suggests that one hour is sufficient time to administer the entire battery to a typical examinee.

NORMATIVE UPDATE PROCEDURES. The latest norming of the PIAT-R was conducted in conjunction with the norming of four other tests published by the American Guidance Service (AGS): The Kaufman Test of Educational Achievement (191), both the comprehensive and brief forms, the KeyMath—Revised (194), and

the Woodcock Reading Mastery Tests (423). A novel strategy was used to establish norms for all these tests using a common norming sample. The overall sample consisted of 3,184 students in Grades K–12 and 245 young adults ages 18–22 from 129 sites across 40 states in the continental U.S. Each of the five test batteries was administered to approximately one fifth of this sample, with 749 assigned to take the PIAT-R. In addition to their primary battery, small groups of individuals were administered one or more subtests from the other batteries in order to link the subtests across batteries. Subtests measuring similar content across the five batteries were grouped into five achievement domains. The five domains are Mathematics Computation, Mathematics Applications, Word Reading, Reading Comprehension, and Spelling. The Rasch scaling program BIGSTEPS was used with the linking samples to calibrate item difficulties across subtests measuring these five domains. For example, spelling items from the PIAT-R and both forms of the Kaufman Tests of Educational Achievement were placed on a common difficulty scale using data obtained from examinees who had taken two or more of these subtests. The linking samples, which were analyzed independently of the norming samples, ranged in size from 88 subjects for the Spelling domain to 312 for the Mathematics Application domain. Using the calibrated item difficulties, the program BIGSTEPS produced Rasch ability (achievement) estimates for all examinees in the norming sample who had taken any of the subtests defining each of the five domains. The norms for the PIAT-R were based on these Rasch ability estimates within each of the five achievement domains for each age and grade level. These ability estimates were then translated into raw scores in order to prepare the norms tables for the PIAT-R/NU.

The numbers of students for which domain ability estimates were obtained ranged from a low of 2,056 for the Spelling domain to a high of 2,809 for the Mathematics Applications domain. Because the General Information and Written Expression subtests are not measures of these domains, they were normed separately on sample sizes of 1,338 and 1,285, respectively. The demographic breakdown of the overall norming sample, and the samples represented for each of five achievement domains, compare favorably with percentages given for the total U.S. population in terms of sex, ethnicity, and parental educational levels, and less well for regions of the country wherein the Northeast and West are somewhat underrepresented relative to the North Central and South. The percentages of special education and gifted students represented in the overall norming sample closely mirrored population percentages for the U.S. Separate demographic profiles are not given for any of the PIAT-R subtests, including the General Information and Written Expression subtests for which independent norming samples were obtained.

THE ASSIST PROGRAM. This computer program will be a welcome addition to anyone who uses the PIAT-R on a regular basis. It is very simple to use and will greatly reduce the time needed to convert raw scores to derived scores and to generate various score reports. The program is available in DOS, Windows, and Mac versions. The program is accompanied with its own manual, which provides all the information necessary to use the program and interpret the score reports. The ASSIST manual also offers the same description of the norming study contained in the primary manual.

The first page of output contains a Score Summary that echoes the demographic information and the raw scores input for each subtest. For each raw score it provides the corresponding grade-equivalent, age equivalent, standard score, national percentile rank, and a normal curve equivalent score. The same set of scores is also provided for three composites: Total Test, Total Reading, and Written Language. The latter combines performance in Spelling and Written Expression if the writing assessment is given. Only developmental scales scores and grade-based stanines are reported for the Written Expression subtest. All scores are reported along with the upper and lower limits of either 68%, 90%, or 95% confidence intervals, depending on the option selected by the user. The first page also provides the aptitude-achievement discrepancy results.

In addition to the Score Summary described above, users can select one or more optional score reports. These include an age-equivalent profile, a standard-score profile, a subtest comparison, and an age-based narrative report. The default is for all reports to be generated.

COMMENTARY ON THE ASSIST PROGRAM. The ASSIST program, and its accompanying manual, should greatly facilitate reporting and interpreting PIAT-R test results. Not only is the program easy to install and use, but it has the potential to eliminate clerical errors associated with translating raw scores to norm-based scores. The reports are presented in a format that should pose few interpretative problems for school personnel or parents. The reporting of confidence intervals in all but the narrative report should help minimize undue concern over performance differences across subtests that may well be accounted for by measurement error.

SUMMARY. The PIAT-R is a well-developed battery of achievement tests designed to be individually administered to examinees across a wide range of age and grade-levels. As the manual appropriately notes, the PIAT-R is designed to provide a broad survey of educational achievement, and is not meant to yield formal diagnostic information.

In addition, the psychometric evidence needs to be updated. The 1989 manual provides an elegant summary of reliability and validity evidence from studies conducted in the 1970s and 1980s, but the new manual has not been updated in this regard. Assuming such evidence is forthcoming, I urge the publishers to acknowledge two artifacts unique to interpreting such evidence for individually administered wide-range achievement test. First, as noted by Rogers (1992) in his review, "The user needs to be aware that such high [reliability] coefficients are due, in part, to the procedure of counting all items below the basal score as correct and all items above the ceiling as incorrect" (p. 654). Second, the users should be made aware that reliability and validity coefficients computed using scores across a wide range of age or grade levels are inflated in comparison to coefficients based on age or grade specific groups. Failure to alert practitioners to these artifacts can lead to misleading psychometric inferences, especially when comparing wide-range individually administered achievement tests to group-administered tests that report grade or age specific coefficients.

REVIEWER'S REFERENCES

Benes, K. M. (1992). [Review of the Peabody Individual Achievement Test—Revised.] In J. J. Kramer & J. C. Conoley (Eds.), *The eleventh mental measurements yearbook* (pp. 649–652). Lincoln, NE: Buros Institute of Mental Measurements.

Rogers, B. G. (1992). [Review of the Peabody Individual Achievement Test—Revised.] In J. J. Kramer & J. C. Conoley (Eds.), *The eleventh mental measurements yearbook* (pp. 652–654). Lincoln, NE: Buros Institute of Mental Measurements.

Review of the Peabody Individual Achievement Test—Revised [1998 Normative Update] by JENNIFER J. FAGER, Assistant Professor, Teach-

ing, Learning, and Leadership, Western Michigan University, Kalamazoo, MI:

The Peabody Individual Achievement Test—Revised (PIAT-R) is an individually administered achievement battery that provides wide-range assessment in six content areas including General Information, Reading Recognition, Reading Comprehension, Mathematics, Spelling, and Written Expression. The PIAT-R provides norm-referenced measures for students from kindergarten through Grade 12 (ages 5-0 to 18-11). It is a revised test of the original developed in 1970. The following is a review of the normative update prepared by the author. The normative update is the essential and only difference between the current version of the PIAT-R and the original text published in 1989. (See reviews of the PIAT-R in 11:280 by Kathryn M. Benes and Bruce G. Rogers.) The test materials are unchanged with the exception of additional checkboxes for examiners to indicate whether original or updated norms were used when scoring a case.

The 1998 edition of the PIAT-R reflects the updated norms based on data collected in 1995–1996. Four achievement batteries were involved in the norming program and included the PIAT-R, the Kaufman Test of Educational Achievement (K-TEA), the KeyMath—Revised, and the Woodcock Reading Mastery Tests—Revised (WRMT-R). During the norming process no changes were made to the content of the batteries. The new norm tables were developed on a representative sample of 3,184 students in kindergarten through 12th grade in 129 sites in 40 states. The researchers used a stratified multistage sampling procedure to ensure selection of a nationally representative group at each grade. Sampling targets were based on the March 1994 U.S. Census Bureau data. An additional 245 subjects were tested representing an adult population aged 18–22. These subjects were from educational institutions including 2- and 4-year colleges and vocational training programs and some were paid for their participation.

School-based sampling was accomplished by site coordinators who distributed bilingual consent forms (Spanish and English) so that Spanish-speaking parents could complete the forms for English-speaking children. Parents were asked to provide information including birthdate, sex, race, grade, highest grade completed, and whether the child is proficient in English. Individuals not proficient in English are not included in the norm sample. Information was also collected from site coordinators on special education classifications, if any, applied to students in the norm sample. The sample selection process was completed by targeting 150 students in kindergarten and 125 students each at Grades 1 through 12 at both the fall and spring data collections. For ages 18–19 and 20–22 the target was 200 cases per group and time of year (fall or spring) was not considered in the sampling process.

The overall grade-norm sample was stratified for each grade from kindergarten through Grade 12. The author used census data to determine a representative sample for sex, socioeconomic status (as defined by parent[s] educational attainment), and race/ethnicity. Additional stratification variables included geographic region and gifted or special education students. The PIAT-R Normative Update clearly identifies these data in a series of well-constructed tables that are easy to read and interpret. The norm development process used by the author follows sound psychometric principles and thus meets statistical requirements.

It has been almost 10 years since norms were developed for the current PIAT-R. The author acknowledges changes that may have affected levels of academic achievement as represented in the updated norms. These changes include curriculum and educational practice, population demographics, and general cultural environment. Overall, average level performance has fallen in Grades 1 through 3 but has either remained the same or shown increases in the secondary level. In five of the subtests (Reading Recognition, Reading Comprehension, Total Reading, Mathematics, Spelling) students below average in Grades 1–12 have had a decline in performance since the original norms in 1989. Overall, the normative update identified a tendency for scores to be more variable than the original norms. This, as identified above in the five subtests, is due particularly to a decline in the level of performance of below-average students, at all grade levels except kindergarten.

SUMMARY. Overall, the normative update provides users with critical information when administering the PIAT-R. The sample is representative of the most current census data available at the time of the update. It is important to note that variability has increased in the time period between norming processes. Other issues to consider for administrators when using the new tables for interpretation include the requirement of English proficiency. With a sample representative of changing demographics (13% of the U.S. population self-identifies as Hispanic) it is important to caution administrators of the PIAT-R that the battery may not be appropriate for a portion of their populations.

[280]
Peabody Picture Vocabulary Test—III.

Purpose: Designed to measure receptive vocabulary attainment for standard English and can also be used as a screening test of verbal ability.
Population: Ages 2.5–90.
Publication Dates: 1959–1997.
Acronym: PPVT-III.
Scores: Total score only.
Administration: Individual.
Forms, 2: IIIA, IIIB.
Price Data, 2001: $239.95 per complete kit including all testing materials for Forms IIIA and IIIB, 2 norms booklets ('97, 48 pages), 2 examiner's manuals ('97, 78 pages), 25 performance records for Form IIIA, and 25 performance records for Form IIIB; $139.95 per PPVT-IIIA test kit; $139.95 per PPVT-IIIB test kit; $26.95 per 25 performance records; $149.95 per AGS Computer ASSIST™ for the PPVT-III (IBM or Macintosh); $35.95 per Technical References to the PPVT-III.
Time: (11–12) minutes.
Comments: Orally administered, norm-referenced test; only for use with standard-English-speaking individuals.
Authors: Lloyd M. Dunn, Leota M. Dunn, Kathleen T. Williams (technical supplement), and Jing-Jen Wang (technical supplement).
Publisher: American Guidance Service, Inc.
Cross References: See T5:1903 (585 references) and T4:1945 (426 references); for reviews by R. Steve McCallum and Elisabeth H. Wiig of an earlier edition, see 9:926 (117 references); see also T3:1771 (301 references), 8:222 (213 references), T2:516 (77 references), and 7:417 (201 references); for reviews by Howard B. Lyman and Ellen V. Piers, see 6:530 (21 references).

Review of the Peabody Picture Vocabulary Test—III by FREDERICK BESSAI, Professor of Education, University of Regina, Regina, Saskatchewan, Canada:

The Peabody Picture Vocabulary Test—III (PPVT—III) is a welcome revision of its two predecessors, the original PPVT 1959 edition and the 1981 PPVT-R. The overall test package is attractive and has a separate examiner's manual, a norms booklet and a carrying case that converts into an easel for convenient presentation of the picture plates. A software package, the PPVT—III ASSIST™, can be purchased separately and is very useful for the preparation of individual and group reports. It is available in both IBM (DOS and Windows) and Macintosh versions. The Technical References manual contains a clear and detailed presentation of the norming of the test as well as evidence of reliability and validity. In the Technical References and in the examiner's manual there is only a brief statement about what the test measures, namely receptive vocabulary and the comprehension of spoken English. Its potential uses as a vocabulary test or as a screening device in various clinical settings are clearly given. The authors warn that the test measures only the listening vocabulary which is a more restricted aspect of overall linguistic and cognitive functioning. Test scores should not be overinterpreted.

The instructions for administering and scoring the test are clear and easy to follow. The examiner's manual presents useful detail on different types of reliability coefficients and normative scores. Helpful explanations are given for users who may not be completely familiar with concepts such as a standard error of measurement or a normal curve equivalent.

The careful selection of items and their calibration for difficulty using both classical item statistics and the more sophisticated Rasch item analysis is evidence of content validity. The authors are also to be commended for submitting their items to a bias review panel to ensure that none of the items contain racial, ethnic, or gender biases. Construct validity is more difficult to establish. The authors do present evidence of age differentiation but they also admit that this is necessary but not sufficient evidence of the construct validity of scores from the PPVT—III. The criterion-related validity evidence is very good. Correlations with the Wechsler Intelligence Scale for Children, Third Edition (WISC-III) are .91 and .92 for Forms II A and II B respectively. Abundant evidence of lower correlations with nonverbal IQ measures is also given.

The reliability of the test has been thoroughly investigated. The internal consistency estimate is high. Alpha and split-half reliability coefficients are in the range of .86 to .98 for both

Forms A and B. Parallel forms reliabilities are also in the .88 to .96 range with the lower coefficients in the lowest and highest chronological age groups. The standard errors of measurement presented for the various chronological age groups are equally impressive. Some are as low as 3.0 and predictably the highest value was obtained with the youngest age group. A value of 5.2 is reported for the 2 year, 6 month age group. These reliability estimates are sufficiently high for the intended clinical use.

The selection of the standardization sample to match the demographic census data of a 1994 United States population survey make the norms truly national. The major variables taken into account were the four major geographic areas, ethnicity, educational level, and gender. The final standardization sample consisted of 2,725 examinees of whom 1,476 were tested with Form III A and 1,249 with Form III B. Clear and adequate evidence of a representative norming sample is evident in the Technical Reference manual. Users of the test are also cautioned that the standardization sample did not include individuals with evidence of impaired vision, hearing loss, or limited ability in English.

The difficulty level of the PPVT—III compared to its predecessor, the PPVT-R, is somewhat different. There is some evidence that the PPVT—III is slightly easier for persons in the 4- to 16-year chronological age range and slightly more difficult for the adult group. For researchers doing longitudinal or comparative studies, the technical manual provides a conversion table so that scores from the older edition can be converted to PPVT—III equivalents. This is a very useful feature.

SUMMARY. Generally, the PPVT—III can be recommended for use in educational and clinical settings to measure receptive vocabulary and to screen for English language ability and general language development. It has a wide range and can be used as readily with preschool children as it can with adolescents and adults. It does not require specialized training or highly technical knowledge to administer and score. The older editions of the test were widely used in research. The current edition should be very useful for researchers interested in language development, verbal intelligence, and related cognitive functions. What remains is to extend the norming process to include other English-speaking countries. This would make the test more applicable for potential users in these countries.

Review of the Peabody Picture Vocabulary Test—III by OREST EUGENE WASYLIW, Director of Adult Clinical Psychology, Isaac Ray Center, Rush-Presbyterian—St. Luke's Medical Center, Chicago, IL:

The Peabody Picture Vocabulary Test (Dunn, 1959) was originally designed as a brief intelligence test. This third edition is designed to measure receptive vocabulary in Standard English, provide a screening test of verbal ability, and serve as one element in a test battery of cognitive processes. There are two alternate forms (PPVT-IIIA & PPVT-IIIB) that can be purchased jointly or independently. The test folder converts into an easel for ease of administration. Stimuli consist of large, clear, black-and-white drawings, with four pictures per plate. Each form has 204 items that are now grouped into 17 sets of 12 items. For each set of items, the 3 easiest items are placed first, the 6 most difficult are randomly placed in the middle, and 3 relatively easy ones conclude each item set. This arrangement allows the examinee to end each set with some success. Norms are provided from age 2 1/2 to 90+, with age range intervals of 2 months up to age 19, 2 years up to age 25, 5 years up to age 41, and 10 years thereafter. The manual provides standard scores, age equivalents, percentile ranks, normal curve equivalents, and stanines.

ADMINISTRATION. The PPVT-III is designed to be administered by technicians. Administration rules and guidelines are very clearly and unambiguously spelled out. Examinees are shown four pictures and are read a word. The examinee must either point to the picture most closely depicting the correct word or state the number of the correct picture. Training items are provided. The examiner is allowed a variety of options in instructing the examinee, but commands are very simple. There are no time limits, but the examinee is encouraged to make a choice after 15 seconds. The examiner starts with the age-appropriate stimulus set unless the clinical circumstances dictate otherwise or the examinee does not achieve a basal level. Criteria for basal and ceiling levels are very clearly spelled out on the record form and in Part 2 of the PPVT-III manual.

ITEM DEVELOPMENT. Item selection began through the acquisition of 3,885 words (from the 1953 Webster's Collegiate Dictionary) that could be easily visually demonstrated. Other dictionaries and vocabulary sources were also consulted. A panel representing women and various minorities reviewed items to identify any offensive or apparently biased stimulus pictures or words. Various surveys of current PPVT-R (Dunn & Dunn, 1981) users were conducted, including focus groups at a convention, to review the artwork, administration, and scoring rules. A national tryout of the PPVT-III was conducted on 908 participants aged 2 1/2 to 21 years, at 73 sites. The tryout sample included representation from all major regions and ethnic groupings within the U.S. Items were calibrated for difficulty, and an item-bias analysis using the Rasch scaling model was conducted.

RELIABILITY. Data are reported for 25 standardization groups (25 age ranges from 2 to 90+ years), with a total 2,725 participants tested at 240 sites nationwide. Alternative-form reliability coefficients between Forms IIIA and IIIB range from .88 to .96 for standard scores and from .89 to .99 for raw scores. Alpha coefficients were based on all 204 items, and range from .92 to .98. Odd/even split-half, corrected reliability coefficients ranged from .86 to .97, with a median of .94 for both forms. Test-retest reliabilities for 8- to 203-day intervals between testing ranged from .91 to .94. Reliabilities for the PPVT-III are consistently higher than for the PPVT-R.

VALIDITY. The reference manual includes very detailed information concerning geographic representation, educational and socioeconomic level, ethnic breakdown, and gender of the standardization group. Groups of learning-disabled, speech-impaired, child and adult mentally retarded, hearing-impaired, gifted, and talented individuals were also represented in proportion to the general population.

Content validity is defined by all words being taken from major English dictionaries. For construct validity, studies showing close correlations between receptive vocabulary and overall intelligence on a variety of standardized tests are emphasized. Internal validity data are provided through assessments of item homogeneity, item growth curves, and age differentiation. As expected, average scores increase appropriately with age, and the steepest part of the growth curve occurs at the earlier ages. Interestingly, a positive growth curve was still seen up to age 60, which is consistent with recent normative data for verbal intelligence acquired for the Wechsler Adult Intelligence Scale—Third Edition (WAIS-III; Wechsler, 1997a, b).

Concurrent validation lies in findings that PPVT-III scores are more highly correlated with Verbal than with Performance IQ on the WISC-III (Wechsler, 1991), with crystallized than with fluid intelligence on the Kaufman Adolescent and Adult Intelligence Test (Kaufman & Kaufman 1993), and with vocabulary than with matrices on the Kaufman Brief Intelligence Test (Kaufman & Kaufman, 1990). Comparison data for several clinical groups are also described. As expected, there was only a slight reduction on the PPVT-III for speech-impaired subjects (defined by articulation problem only) compared to controls. Learning-disabled (for reading), language-impaired, language-delayed, and mentally retarded groups all showed substantially lower scores than did controls, with the lowest scores being for the MR and LD groups. As expected, a gifted group showed exceptionally high scores.

INTERPRETATION. Tables are provided for conversion of scores between the PPVT-R and PPVT-III. A computer-scoring program, called ASSIST™, is also available and provides brief explanations of terms and scores, allows for graphing of repeated testing, provides extended norms below a standard score of 40, and includes vocabulary-building exercises. The manual emphasizes that the PPVT-III is a screening device, such that test results should not be overgeneralized, and that its purpose is limited to measuring receptive vocabulary. The standardization sample did not include persons with visual problems or those who have limited English proficiency.

COMMENTS. The PPVT-III is one of the most user-friendly psychometric instruments of its kind I have yet seen. The PPVT-III is much easier to administer than the PPVT-R. Administration and scoring instructions are spelled out very clearly, simply, and logically, with clear, step-by-step instructions for raw score conversions and advice for selecting appropriate confidence intervals. The organization of test materials is better and establishing basal and ceiling levels is easier. The stimulus items and record forms are well organized.

A few of the visual stimulus cards appear on both Forms IIIA and IIIB, but with different prompts. This increases stimulus similarity between forms. The PPVT-III has improved reliability and updated norms. There are different instructions for different age levels. This avoids the prospect of talking down to clients. The record form includes a very convenient pronunciation key. Attempts to make the PPVT-III clinically balanced were supported in a recent study by Washington and Craig (1999) of African-American male and female children. They found no significant differences from the standard normal distribution. This was in contrast to their earlier findings suggesting that PPVT-R scores may be significantly lower for minority, at-risk kindergartners and preschoolers.

SUMMARY. The authors and publisher should be commended for a very well-written, well-organized, and conscientiously developed instrument that is easy to use and incredibly well documented. It should serve as a worthy successor to the highly popular PPVT-R, and would be a useful component of any testing armamentarium in educational, speech and language, or research settings.

REVIEWER'S REFERENCES

Dunn, L. M. (1959). Peabody Picture Vocabulary Test. Circle Pines, MN: American Guidance Service, Inc.

Dunn, L. M., & Dunn, L. M. (1981). Peabody Picture Vocabulary Test Revised. Circle Pines, MN: American Guidance Service, Inc.

Kaufman, A. S., & Kaufman, N. L. (1990). Kaufman Brief Intelligence Test. Circle Pines, MN: American Guidance Service, Inc.

Wechsler, D. (1991). Wechsler Intelligence Scale for Children—Third edition. San Antonio, TX: Harcourt Brace Educational Measurement.

Kaufman, A. S., & Kaufman, N. L. (1993). Kaufman Adolescent and Adult Intelligence Test. Circle Pines, MN: American Guidance Service, Inc.

Wechsler, D. (1997a). Wechsler Adult Intelligence Scale—Third edition. San Antonio, TX: Harcourt Brace Educational Measurement.

Wechsler, D. (1997b). WAIS-III WMS-III technical manual. San Antonio, TX: Harcourt Brace Educational Measurement.

Washington, J., & Craig, H. (1999). Performances of at-risk, African-American preschoolers on the Peabody Picture Vocabulary Test—III. Language, Speech, and Hearing Services in Schools, 30, 75–82.

[281]
Pediatric Evaluation of Disability Inventory.

Purpose: Designed as a "comprehensive clinical assessment instrument that samples key functional capabilities and performance."

Population: Ages 6 months to 7.5 years.

Publication Date: 1992.

Acronym: PEDI.

Scores, 9: Self-Care (Functional Skills, Caregiver Assistance, Modification Frequencies), Mobility (Functional Skills, Caregiver Assistance, Modification Frequencies), Social Function (Functional Skills, Caregiver Assistance, Modification Frequencies).

Administration: Individual.

Price Data: Available from publisher.

Time: (45–60) minutes.

Comments: Should be completed by the person or group of persons familiar with the child's typical performance in the domains surveyed; software program (IBM-compatible) available for data entry, scoring, and generation of individual summary score profiles.

Authors: Stephen M. Haley, Wendy J. Coster, Larry H. Ludlow, Jane T. Haltiwanger, and Peter J. Andrellos.

Publisher: Center for Rehabilitation Effectiveness, Boston University.

Review of the Pediatric Evaluation of Disability Inventory by BILLY T. OGLETREE, Associate Professor, Communication Disorders Program, Western Carolina University, Cullowhee, NC:

The Pediatric Evaluation of Disability Inventory (PEDI) is a comprehensive clinical assessment tool designed to sample functional capabilities and performance in children between 6 months and 7.5 years of age. Although intended for young children, the PEDI can be used with older children who function below 7.5 years developmentally. The authors of the PEDI state that it is most applicable for measuring functioning in children with physical or combined physical and cognitive deficits and would not likely be a preferred assessment tool for infants. Components of the PEDI include an administration manual, score forms, and an optional software (IBM compatible) for data entry and score analysis.

The PEDI can be administered within an hour. Recommended examiners include allied health professionals familiar with the child's typical performance (e.g., physical therapists, occupational therapists, nurses, speech-language pathologists, special educators, psychologists). Administration can occur by means of professional observation and judgment or by structured interview/parent report. Administration training guidelines are provided in the test manual.

The PEDI contains three distinct measurement sections. Part I measures functional skills and consists of a checklist of current capabilities. Part II measures caregiver assistance and requires judgments specific to the amount of aid provided during functional activities. Part III measure modifications needed to support functioning. These three sections are used to assess skills in Self-Care, Mobility, and Social Function domains. The PEDI consists of 197 functional skill items and 20 items that assess caregiver assistance and modifications. Items for the PEDI were taken and adapted from several sources including currently published tests and materials.

The Functional Skills Scale measures the child's current capability to perform specific skills. Items are scored as either 1 (the child demonstrates capability) or 0 (the child has yet to demonstrate capability). A score of 1 is awarded if the child is capable but chooses not to demonstrate behaviors. If items involve multiple components, the child must be capable of all aspects of the item to receive a score of 1. No items are to be left blank.

The Caregiver Assistance Scale measures the caregiver's contributions to the completion of basic functional activities. Items are scored on a 6-point rating scale ranging from independent (5) to total assistance (0). Scoring guidelines are available from the three broad assessment domains (Self-Care, Mobility, and Social Function). All items must be scored.

The Modifications Scale identifies functional activities for which modifications are required. Items are scored using N = no modifications, C = child-oriented modifications (e.g., use of child-size utensils), R = specialized rehabilitative equipment, and E = extensive modifications (e.g., suspension slings, feeders). Some items in the Social Function domain do not include the rating category of child-oriented modifications. Again, all items must be scored.

Raw summary scores for the Functional Skill Scales are calculated by adding scores for all items in each content domain. Raw scores for the Caregiver Assistance Scales are determined by summing ratings for each item. Raw scores for the Modifications Scale consist of frequency counts reflecting the number of times each modification category is used throughout the test. All raw scores are transferred to the composite score section of the score sheet. Raw scores are then converted into normative or scaled scores. The authors of the PEDI suggest the use of normative standard scores for children under 7.5 years and scaled scores for children above this age. Standard errors are provided for both standard and scaled scores and can be displayed in confidence intervals and illustrated graphically on the score form. The authors recommend that a confidence interval of two standard errors above and below the score be calculated. Finally, a Rasch model goodness-of-fit statistic can be calculated on the Functional Skills and Caregiver Assistance Scales with the optional software program. This score provides a validity check on the child's pattern of responses. The PEDI manual provides interpretive guidelines for all scores.

The PEDI was standardized on a sample of 412 children from the Northeastern United States. Children from Connecticut, Massachusetts, and New York were included. These states were selected due to the fact that they closely approximated the demographic characteristics of the United States in general. The sample was equally distributed with respect to age, gender, race, parent education level, and community size. The PEDI manual provides exhaustive item analysis data from the normative sample.

Three groups of children comprised clinical samples for validation purposes. The first group consisted of 46 children under the age of 6 who had experienced relatively minor injuries. Some of these children, however, had serious residual functional skills deficits. The second group consisted of 32 children between 1 and 9.8 years of age. These children had severe disabilities and were enrolled in a hospital-based day school program. The final group consisted of 24 children between 3.5 and 10.4 years who were also enrolled in a hospital-based day school program. These children functioned below the 7-year level. The PEDI manual provides normative standard and scaled scores for these groups.

The psychometric properties of the PEDI are discussed at length in the examiner's manual. Three types of reliability are reported. First, the manual reports internal consistency reliability coefficients for all six scales of the PEDI ranging from .95 to .99 indicating excellent internal consistency within these scales. Second, interinterviewer reliability estimates are reported for the normative and clinical samples on the caregiver assistance and modification scales. Interinterviewer reliability estimates were derived from independent scoring of the PEDI during interviews. Intraclass correlation coefficients ranged from .79 to .99 on the normative sample. The lowest agreement value was obtained on the Social Function domain of the Modifications scale. Intraclass correlation coefficients ranged from .84 to 1.0 on the clinical sample. A third type of reliability reported was examiners' agreements upon the functional status of individual children. This was addressed with a sample of 24 children with significant disabilities. Relatively high reliability was reported for all scales from two groups of respondents (intraclass correlation coefficients of .74 to .96). Again, the Social Function domain of the modifications scale yielded the lowest agreement value. This resulted in the removal of the child-oriented modifications rating category for some items.

The PEDI manual presents information specific to the instrument's construct, concurrent, discriminant, and evaluative validity. Construct validity is supported by data suggesting that changes in functional behaviors are age-related and that functional skills and caregiver assistance represent different dimensions of function (these are the two primary assumptions of the PEDI). Concurrent validity is reported from comparisons of the PEDI to the Battell Developmental Inventory Screening Test (BDIST). Both instruments were administered to matched groups of children with and without disabilities. Overall correlations between the two tests in the group with disabilities were reported to be moderate (r = .70 to .73). The lowest correlation reported was for the BDIST and the Caregiver Assistance score for children without disabilities (r = .62). The correlation between the Functional Skills scale and the BDIST for the children without disabilities was .81. Additional correlation data were reported from the PEDI, the BDIST, and the Wee-FIM (i.e., a children's version of the Functional Independence Measure—part of the Uniform Data Base for Medical Rehabilitation) on a sample of children with more severe disabilities. Correlations were reported to be high (r = .80 to .97). Discriminant validity is reported specific to the PEDI's ability to predict disability or nondisability status for children. In sum, the PEDI Modifications and Functional Skills scales were better predictors than the Battelle. Data are also reported from discriminant validity analysis between the PEDI's normative and clinical samples. Reported scores clearly discriminated between these groups. Finally, the PEDI's evaluative validity measures considered the instrument's ability to detect change in functional capability over time. Two samples of children with disabilities received two administrations of the PEDI over time. The PEDI was noted to be sensitive to change in children with mild to moderate traumatic injuries and severe disabilities.

SUMMARY. In conclusion, the PEDI is a comprehensive assessment instrument that samples functional capabilities and performance in children who are chronologically or developmentally young. It is well constructed and appears to be a good instrument to determine the presence of functional deficits in children and monitor their progress. Finally, the PEDI is truly unique in that it allows for the measurement of caregiver assistance and modifications. These data are invaluable as providers communicate with each other and assist with life transitions.

Review of the Pediatric Evaluation of Disability Inventory by GENE SCHWARTING, Assistant Professor, Department of Education/Special Education, Fontbonne College, St. Louis, MO:

The Pediatric Evaluation of Disability Inventory (PEDI) is a measure of the functional skills of children ages 6 months to 7.5 years in Self-Care, Mobility, and Social Development. It may be used to determine the existence and extent of developmental delays, to monitor progress of children in special education or rehabilitation programs, or for program evaluation. A Functional Skills scale consists of 197 items across these three domains to assess the actual capability of the child. An additional 20 items comprise the Caregiver Assistance and Modifications Scales that measure the amount of help and the extent of needed environmental adjustments and equipment required by the child. The PEDI was designed for professionals who work with a pediatric population with disabilities such as physical and occupational therapists, nurses and physicians, psychologists, speech/language pathologists, and special educators.

PEDI items were originally selected following a review of the literature, input from clinicians and practitioners, and similar instruments. Field testing was used to refine these items, with norming conducted in 1990–91 by trained pediatric nurse practitioners. The norm group included 412 nondisabled children from Massachusetts, Connecticut, and New York. An attempt was made to include a representative stratified quota sample, but African Americans and college-educated parents were overrepresented in the final group. The Rasch scaling model was applied to the Functional Skills and Caregiver Assistant scales, but not for the Modifications scale, during the development and scale construction of the PEDI.

The Functional Skills section may be completed by a parent or individuals well acquainted with the child, either through direct scoring or interview. The authors recommend that parent completion be followed with review by a professional to clarify any questionable scores, whereas professional assessment should be followed by discussion with the parent to verify the responses. For the Caregiver Assistance and Modifications sections, a structured interview format is recommended. There are no required examiner qualifications although it is suggested that the professional have a background in pediatrics and experience with children with disabilities. Total administration time is estimated at 45–60 minutes.

Functional Skills items are scored either 1 or 0, with no basal or ceiling as all items are to be scored. Examiners are encouraged not to confuse the capability to perform a task with preference or compliance issues. The Self-Care and Mobility areas are phrased as positives (the child can perform the task) whereas the Social Functions area involves negatives (the child does not have the skill). The Caregiver Assistance section is scored on a 6-point scale with 5 representing complete independence and 0 total dependence. The Modifications section scores are descriptive rather than numerical, with options being: none, child-oriented, rehabilitation equipment, or extensive modifications. Normative standard T-scale scores and scaled scores indicating performance on a 100-point continuum are available for 6-month age intervals. In addition to the norms tables presented in the manual, an optional software scoring program is available.

Content validity was assessed by a panel of experts from the fields of physical therapy, occupational therapy, medicine, education, and speech/language; clinical validation studies were conducted on three small hospital-based samples. Construct validity relies on the strong relationship of the PEDI with chronological age. Concurrent validity studies with the PEDI, the Battelle Developmental Inventory Screening Test, and the children's version of the Functional Independence Measure (Wee-FIM; Msall et al., 1994) found the PEDI to discriminate accurately between groups of children with and without disabilities.

Reliability measures include internal consistency, with coefficient alpha results varying from .95 through .99 for the Functional Skills and Caregiver Assistance Scales, and interinterviewer scoring reliability based on small samples showing correlations varying from .79 through 1.0 with most results in the high .9 range for all three scales.

The norm groups of the PEDI are not representative of the national population. The point scale for the Caregiver Assistance section may be misleading due to the need to distinguish between scores of 2 (frequent adjustments needed), 1 (very frequent adjustments needed), and 0 (almost constant adjustments needed). Items are descriptive, and appear to sample adequately the domains involved.

SUMMARY. Overall, the instrument is well-designed and compares favorably with others in the field. The three scales provide a dimension missing in other instruments, and should enhance the use of the PEDI for the population for whom it was designed.

REVIEWER'S REFERENCE

Msall, M., DiGaudio, K., Rogers, B. T., LaForest, S., Catangaro, N. L., Campbell, J., Willzenski, F., & Duffy, L. C. (1994). The Functional Independence Measure for Children (Wee-FIM): Conceptual bases and pilot use in children with developmental disabilities. *Clinical Pediatrics, 33*, 421–430.

[282]
Pediatric Examination of Educational Readiness at Middle Childhood [Revised].

Purpose: Constructed to "survey neurodevelopmental areas that may be associated with academic difficulties."
Population: Ages 9 to 14-11.
Publication Dates: 1984–1996.
Acronym: PEERAMID-2.
Scores: 6 major sections: Fine Motor/Graphomotor Functions, Attention Checkpoints, Language Functions, Gross Motor Functions, Memory Functions, Visual Processing Functions.
Administration: Individual.
Price Data, 1998: $72.90 (6+ sets) or $109.35 (1–5 sets) per complete kit including manual ('96, 80 pages), stimulus booklet, PEERAMID 2 kit, 12 record forms, and 12 response booklets; $47.75 (6+ sets) or $71.65 (1–5 sets) per 12 record forms and 12 response booklets; $12 (6+) or $18 (1–5) per stimulus booklet; $3 (6+ kits) or $4.50 (1–5 kits) per PEERAMID 2 kit (cup and ball); $10.25 (6+) or $15.40 (1–5) per manual; $13 (6+ sets) or $19.50 (1–5 sets) per specimen set (parent observation form, record form, and manual); $30 (6+) or $45 (1–5) per clinician's training videotape.
Time: (60) minutes.
Comments: Publisher suggests should only be used as a part of a multifaceted evaluation.
Author: Melvin D. Levine.
Publisher: Educators Publishing Service, Inc.
Cross References: See T5:1908 (1 reference); for reviews of the original edition by Cathy W. Hall and Jan N. Hughes, see 10:273.

Review of the Pediatric Examination of Educational Readiness at Middle Childhood [Revised] by JOSEPH C. KUSH, Associate Professor and Coordinator School Psychology Program, Duquesne University, Pittsburgh, PA:

The Pediatric Examination of Educational Readiness at Middle Childhood 2 (PEERAMID 2), is designed to provide standardized observation procedures—techniques that can be applied in health-care settings to help clinicians characterize children's functional health and its relationship to their neurodevelopmental and physical status. The PEERAMID 2 is designed for children ages 9 through 15 and is an upward extension of a family of instruments including the Pediatric Extended Examination at Three (PEET; T5:1909), the Pediatric Examination of Educational Readiness (PEER; T5:1907), and the Pediatric Early Elementary Examination (PEEX 2; 13:224). Unfortunately, however, very little has changed in the revised edition of the PEERAMID 2 and many of the limitations that characterized the early version of the scale remain.

Administration of the PEERAMID 2 requires approximately one hour and is designed to augment a more comprehensive physical, sensory, and neurological examination. The scale is designed to assess performance on 32 tasks in six specific areas: fine-motor function, language, gross-motor function, graphomotor function, memory, and visual functioning. Additionally, selective attention is rated at four intervals and two brief behavior inventories are completed at the end of the examination. The PEERAMID 2 Record Form contains information for administration and scoring the assessment and includes a clinical summary, a general health assessment, and a task analysis. An accompanying stimulus booklet contains stimuli for selected language, temporal-sequential organization, and visual processing tasks, and a separate PEERAMID 2 kit contains a cup and ball for the Eye-Hand Coordination task. Finally, a separate Observer's Guide allows users to record notes on the child's performance during the examination. Administration of the scale requires examiners to record pass/fail performance for each item and make specific observations of the child's performance. However, these assessments remain extremely subjective and will likely be based to a great degree on the pre-existing knowledge of normal child development held by the examiner. This possibility of inappropriate administration and interpretation is greatly increased given that no examiner qualifications are provided; given the differences in developmental training and clinical expertise, a beginning level examiner with an entry-level degree is very likely to score items differently than a more experienced examiner with an advanced degree.

The description of the revision process underlying the PEERAMID 2 is understated and vague. Phrases such as "Some tasks have been added based on evidence from recent research," and "Some sections of the PEERAMID 2 have been reduced in length," are unsubstantiated and unclear. Similarly, although the author indicates that the process of revision was "undertaken systematically" and references to factorial and concurrent validity studies are made, more descriptive and detailed information fails to be provided. Even an apparent attempt at establishing face validity falls short with statements such as "feedback was obtained from many clinicians all over North America" (manual, p. 2) and "several nationally-renowned experts were consultants on the content of the instruments" (manual, p. 2) coming as close to data as the author ever comes. Perhaps the statement, "Some of these changes, although regrettable, were felt to be in the interest of developing an outstanding and supportable instrument" (manual, p. 2) is the most telling. Why would making changes in terms or scales that were not reliable or valid be "regrettable"? Most test revisions highlight the improvement of the test following the incorporation of new items rather than take a seemingly apologetic tone of personal disappointment when empirical research identifies areas of needed improvement.

Although it is certainly inappropriate to use the PEERAMID 2 as a diagnostic instrument, extreme caution must also be used when considering the use of the scale as a screening instrument given that the PEERAMID 2 is neither a norm-referenced nor a criterion-referenced scale. The PEERAMID 2 examiner's manual continues to fail to provide absolutely any evidence that would allow intended users (pediatricians, family physicians, nurses, and health and other health-care professionals) to appraise the clinical utility of the scale before using it with young adolescents. No normative data are provided and basic psychometric information regarding the technical quality of the scale remains glaringly absent. A brief paragraph in the Introduction section of the examiner's manual indicates that "the process of revision was undertaken systematically, using … results of validity studies that examined the factor structure of the original PEERAMID and concurrent relationships with other measures" (manual, p. 2). The paragraph continues by stating, "Although published data on the neurodevelopmental tests are yet limited, relevant references are provided at the end of this manual" (manual, p. 2). Even though references are provided, only 6 of the references occur in peer-reviewed journals and only 4 appear to relate to the age ranges assessed by the PEERAMID 2.

Although the examiner's manual contains a section entitled Normative Data, there is no indication of where these data were collected. Only a single sentence, "The PEERAMID 2 is for children between the ages of 9 and 14-11" (manual, p. 3) provides even a vague reference to how many students or how or where (if at all) the normative database was derived. This factor is somewhat mysterious given that the earlier version of the scale indicated a normative database from "three public school systems in New England blue- and white-collar communities." Although even this description of a normative sample is less than stellar, and certainly not likely to be highly generalizable, it reflects an improvement over the PEERAMID 2. In the absence of any reported demographic variables such as gender, ethnic status, SES, or geographic region, potential users are simply unable to reach any meaningful interpretive conclusions about a child's performance on the scale. The examiner's manual appears to recognize this limitation ("It is important that the examiner be aware of the need for local norms. It is likely, for example, that severely economically deprived children may perform on the PEERAMID 2 in a manner that differs considerably from middle-class suburban children," (p. 3) but forces the individual user to do the work that should have been completed by the scale author and/or publisher.

Given the developmental nature of the scale, the lack of developmental norms is particularly striking. The scale attempts to provide these data by defining "normal" performance in a series of age-bands on the 32 groups of test items. Average performance is defined by scores falling between +/- one standard deviation from the means; however, neither corresponding means or standard deviations are provided, nor is the percentage of children who fall within the normal range. Similarly, no type of standardized scores including T-score, z-score, percentile ranks, or even age-equivalents are provided. As a result, users of the scale are unable to make empirically based interpretations regarding a child's normative performance. The examiner's manual does warn that the

PEERAMID 2 "is not intended for use in isolation" and does not "yield an overall score or even subtest scores" (p. 1), and later, "Success or failure on any particular item can have multiple possible causes" (p. 2); however, these cautions only serve to udnerscore the severe diagnostic and interpretive limitations imposed by the scale's omission of standardization procedures, normative data, and measures of central tendency.

The addition of even basic reliability data would allow potential users the ability to estimate the consistency of their assessment scores across time and examiners. In its present format, the PEERAMID 2 provides no indication of what changes in scale scores one should expect from administration to administration. Similarly, the examiner's manual provides no evidence that two examiners rating the same child should expect to derive comparable scores. This omission is particularly troublesome given the developmental nature of the scale. For example, an examiner who uses the PEERAMID 2 to assess a 9-year-old student and then reexamines the same student 2 or 3 years later would expect developmental progress on most, if not all, scales included in the instrument. This fluctuation in scores, although expected, will result in a lower test-retest reliability coefficient than will other scales where the construct being measured is expected to remain more constant. Developmental scales, therefore, are expected to have lower test-retest reliability coefficients than tests of intelligence, for example, because by definition developmental scores should increase over time whereas intelligence tests are typically more stable. In the absence of test-retest data or resulting standard errors of measurement, potential users of the PEERAMID 2 are unable to determine whether changes in a child's score over time reflect normal developmental progress, possible abnormal developmental etiology, or simply items that are being measured inconsistently across time by the examiner.

Equally troubling is the lack of empirical evidence relating PEERAMID 2 scores to other developmental instruments or tests of neurological or educational performance. Given a lack of established, or even preliminary validity studies, clinicians are severely restricted in the confidence they can derive from even basic diagnostic hypotheses. Without concurrent or predictive validity data it remains unclear how a PEERAMID 2 score fits into the more comprehensive neurological battery recommended in the examiner's manual.

SUMMARY. The PEERAMID 2 continues to lack even basic psychometric evidence for standardization, reliability, and validity. Examiner qualifications and training are unspecified, a factor that compounds measurement accuracy given that many of the items are highly subjectively scored. And even though many of these limitations were identified on the earlier version of the instrument, the author has unfortunately made little, if any, substantial improvements in the current revision. As a result, it remains unclear what clinical utility or unique contribution the PEERAMID 2 will add to already established neurodevelopmental batteries.

Review of the Pediatric Examination of Educational Readiness at Middle Childhood [Revised] by ROBERT G. MORWOOD, Professor of Education, Assistant Director Pasadena Campus, Point Loma Nazarene University, Pasadena, CA:

The Pediatric Examination of Educational Readiness at Middle Childhood 2 manual states the PEERAMID 2 is a neurodevelopmental examination for children between the ages of 9 and 15. It enables health care and other professionals to derive an empirical description of a child's development and functional neurological status. It is an advanced level of a series of neurodevelopmental examinations including the Pediatric Extended Examination at Three (PEET; ages 3 to 4; T5:1909), the Pediatric Examination of Educational Readiness (PEER; ages 4 to 6; T5:1907), and the Pediatric Early Examination 2 (PEEX 2; ages 6 to 9; 13:224). The stated purpose of the PEERAMID 2 is to survey neurodevelopment that may be associated with academic difficulties in this age group. This instrument is a developmental screening test that does not yield a definitive or total evaluation of function in any particular area. It does not generate an overall score, rather the end product is usually a narrative description of findings.

The test developers recommend that the neurodevelopmental test should never be used in isolation. The instrument is intended to be supplemental in nature and to be used in conjunction with additional testing and historical information collected and contributed by parents, clinicians, and school personnel.

The PEERAMID 2 assesses a child's performance on 32 tasks in six specific areas: fine-motor function, language, gross motor function, graphomotor function, visual processing, and memory (including items on visual and verbal recall, motor memory, short term memory, and the rate of retrieval). The author provides rating systems to evaluate work strategies, attention, behavior, and effort.

The revised PEERAMID 2 has added a section of phonology and increased the emphasis on memory. Also, selective attention is rated at four different times throughout the exam and two brief inventories are evaluated at the end of the testing.

The examiner's manual describes administration, interpretation, and scoring, and discusses each task's relevance to learning and behavior. The manual also includes samples of completed record forms, response booklets, and pertinent references.

The PEERAMID 2 examiner's manual alludes to the use of normative data in the development of test questions. They have included a normative key to the left of each task on the record form booklet; however, the manual is absent of normative data. In response to this the test developers specify "It is important that the examiner be aware of local norms" (p. 6). The manual also states "validation studies of the neurodevelopmental examinations are currently underway" (p. 6). This reviewer was unable to find or evaluate validation studies an/or normative data in the manual. The test developers recommend that "clinicians using the neurodevelopmental examination should have proper training as well as sufficient practice in their use. Ideally, they should attend courses on neurodevelopmental function and variation" (p. 6). It appears that a great deal of responsibility is placed on the clinician administering the examination to be familiar with the conceptual framework and knowledge base used to develop this instrument. This tends to allow for a great deal of variability depending upon the examiner's knowledge and experience in the field. The test manual gives adequate information on administration but once again the scoring requires subjective judgments on the part of the examiner. This, in addition to the absence of adequate normative data and evidence of reliability, allows for a wide range of test interpretation and overgeneralization by test users with appropriate training and knowledge of neuropsychology and learning disabilities.

SUMMARY. The PEERAMID 2 has potential as a research instrument in the area of middle childhood neurodevelopment and learning disabilities. However, much work is still necessary in normative data and reliability studies. Standardization of qualifications of test examiners must be clearly established. It should continue to be emphasized that this instrument only be used in conjunction with other standardized instruments and interpreted by appropriately trained clinicians.

[283]

PEEK—Perceptions, Expectations, Emotions, and Knowledge About College.
Purpose: "Designed to assess prospective student's expectations about what college will be like."
Population: Prospective college students.
Publication Date: 1995.
Acronym: PEEK.
Scores, 3: Academic Expectations, Personal Expectations, Social Expectations.
Administration: Group.
Price Data, 1996: $1.75 per publisher scored form; $1.25 per software scored form (volume discounts available); $10 per software scoring kit (one-time purchase).
Time: (15–25) minutes.
Comments: Self-report questionnaire; can be machine scored by publisher, locally via software, or by hand in classroom settings.
Authors: Claire E. Weinstein, David R. Palmer, and Gary R. Hanson.
Publisher: H & H Publishing Company, Inc.

Review of the PEEK—Perceptions, Expectations, Emotions, and Knowledge About College by DAVID GILLESPIE, Social Science Faculty, Detroit College of Business, Warren, MI:

The PEEK—Perceptions, Expectations, Emotions, and Knowledge About College was designed to assess student expectations regarding college. Three domains of expectations are considered: Academic, Personal, and Social. Students compare their expectations to those of other individuals from the same institution who have also completed the questionnaire. This within-institution comparison was designed to provide more relevant comparisons. The authors believe that students who have unrealistic expectations are at-risk to encounter academic difficulties. Intervention and retention efforts could be targeted to these individuals who report unrealistic expectations.

The PEEK is a single-page, paper-and-pencil questionnaire consisting of 30 items. This questionnaire can be administered individually or in a group setting. Expectations for each area are assessed by 10 questions. Test respondents use a 4-point rating scale for their responses. The alternatives on this scale range from *Not at all likely* to *Extremely likely*.

The tests was constructed by polling over 3,000 college faculty and students over 4 years regarding expectations about college. The resulting information was used to develop a database of 300 items regarding differences in the personal, social, and academic environments of different colleges and schools. Test items were then selected from this pool.

The authors believe that a formal background in psychological test administration is not needed in order to administer, score, and interpret the results of this test. However, faculty or university staff using this test should have a thorough understanding of the information in the test manual, use of test results, and standard test administration. Test instructions are clearly written on the front of the questionnaire.

Although the PEEK can be hand scored, computer scoring and interpretation is also available. If computer scoring is desired, completed tests can be sent to the publishing company for scoring or software can be purchased for on-site scoring. The PEEK scoring software can generate three types of reports: PEEK Distribution Report, Peek Individual Report, and Peek Summary Report. The PEEK Distribution Report provides descriptive data for each of the 10 questions in each category, across all subjects who completed the form. The Individual Report provides the student who completed the questionnaire a comparison of his or her responses to those of peers, and the PEEK Summary Report provides summative information for all the students who completed the form.

The PEEK Individual Report uses z-scores to describe student responses. The patterns of these responses are compared to those of other students and faculty at the host institution. Although most students will be unfamiliar with the direct interpretation of z-scores, the manual and computer-generated reports provide good explanations of test interpretations.

The PEEK has a number of strengths. It can be quickly administered and scored. There is strong theoretical support for the effect cognitions have on behavior. The results of the PEEK can be used to increase student awareness of their own expectations and in student advising. These results can also assist the institution in better serving its students. Once discrepant cognitions are identified, a range of intervention options can be instituted. The PEEK and its scoring software are very reasonably priced. The PEEK is also easily hand scored.

Although the PEEK has its strengths, it also has a number of limitations. The manual is unclear as to how the final 30 test questions were selected. A review of the manual suggests the test developers made the final decisions based on their preferences and experiences. The use of z-scores as compared to the more commonly employed scaled scores could contribute to difficulty in score interpretation. As stated in the manual, the use of z-scores may lead to some counter-intuitive interpretations in extreme circumstances. Although z-scores are designed to indicate relative agreement/disagreement between the expectations of a particular student in relation to those of a larger group of students, certain circumstances could complicate score interpretation. If the majority of students agree in their expectations with the institution, a low z-score may still indicate general agreement with institutional expectations. If a majority of students differ in their expectations from those of the institution, high z-scores may show little agreement with institutional expectations.

A related area of concern focuses on the comparison group used for score interpretation. The manual suggests that faculty, as well as students, complete the test. These respondents serve as the formal comparison group. However, this raises a number of issues. What relevance does a faculty member's perceptions have in relation to the expectations of the average undergraduate? It might be more effective to have upper-level students complete the PEEK based on their experiences. This information could serve as the comparison group for entry-level students. The authors of the PEEK also do not provide normative data to be used in test interpretation. This requires in-house comparisons. Although such comparisons can be useful, the issue of cohort effects can challenge the validity of test interpretation.

The scoring software also contains a default scoring system. This default scoring was created by the authors of the PEEK to reflect their experience with a number of institutions in the development of the instrument. The manual states that most institutions will find the default scoring is in close agreement with their own situations. How-

ever, there is no research cited to support this claim. The manual also states that the weights given to each of the 30 responses can be adjusted to reflect the expectations of the institution. However, an individual would need expertise in test construction and statistics before undertaking such a process. Additionally, when tests are hand scored, there is no procedure provided for aggregating the data across advisors for score comparisons and interpretation. There is no indication of how many students would be needed for a valid sample of the expectations of a general group of students. Perhaps most importantly, there are no psychometric data provided in the manual related to validity or reliability for score interpretation and use. This lack of information presents a formidable obstacle.

SUMMARY. The PEEK is a 30-item questionnaire used to assess entering college student's expectations related to college life in personal, academic, and social areas. It can easily be administered individually or in a group. Scoring can be facilitated by use of the computer-scoring package. Test results can be used by advisors or counselors to assist students in reformulating inaccurate expectations of college life. The weaknesses of the test include the lack of psychometric data, the use of z-scores to interpret test results, the lack of established comparison groups, and scanty information on test construction methods or institutional information related to its default scoring system.

Review of the PEEK—Perceptions, Expectations, Emotions, and Knowledge About College by DANIEL L. YAZAK, Assistant Professor and Chair, Department of Counseling and Human Services, Montana State University—Billings, Billings, MT:

Perceptions, Expectations, Emotions, and Knowledge (PEEK) About College is a 30-question self-report instrument designed to elicit responses that can be categorized according to Academic, Personal, and Social Expectations. Target users include prospective and current students, faculty, staff, and administrators in institutions of higher education. Results of the test can be used to provide an individual perspective or an individual score that can be compared with a peer group or another group using the PEEK. Uses of results include a basis for exploration of perceptions categorized into Academic, Personal, and Social experiences. The authors suggest that psychometric properties are established on a site-specific basis.

The PEEK was developed over a 7-year period. During that time, in excess of 3,000 individuals have contributed to the evolution of the 30-question item pool. No specific information is provided concerning psychometric properties of reliability and validity. National norms are not presented as PEEK is intended to provide information that can be compared on an institution-specific, time-limited basis. For example, perceptions, emotions, expectations, and knowledge data obtained from administering the PEEK can be used to identify differences within and between locally constituted groups. This idiosyncratic use of the test can be further developed by utilizing z-scores for additional comparisons. Software developed for the PC is available to provide percent responses of a local group, expanding comparison possibilities.

As no national norms have been developed for the PEEK, sources of error measure have not been reported. The self-report results are elicited from a Likert-type scale ranging from *not at all likely to be a part of my college experience* to *extremely likely to be a part of my college experience*. These results do not lend themselves to standard error of measure calculations. One test form is available for use. Due to the fact that local comparison situations are encouraged, interrater reliability calculations are not presented. Comparisons among groups by the test user is suggested; reliability estimates for different groups have not been made. Decisions concerning similarities and differences are possible using group data given the constraints of reliability evidence.

The PEEK relies on the self-report of individuals and/or groups at a specific location. Outside criteria have not been suggests to calculate correlations. As no distribution of scores for outside criteria has been presented, predictive accuracy is not appropriate in the case of the PEEK. The individual nature of self-report responses suggests use of the scores for comparison purposes without validity calculations.

Instructions for test administration are provided in the PEEK User's Manual. Group or individual administrations are appropriate for the test. Individuals familiar with standard test administration procedures will be able to administer the PEEK. Explanations for taking the test and potential uses of the PEEK are printed on one side of the test instrument. Test directions are made available in the PEEK User's Manual for use in group administration. An example question and response set is provided for test takers so that a uniform understanding among test takers is established. Likert-scale explanations are also provided so the test taker can consistently differentiate between the qualifying statements of the answer sequence.

Directions for test completion do not indicate a time limit. As the test seeks self-report information no reference materials or calculators are necessary. Standard testing requirements of a well-lit, well-ventilated room with minimal distractions are necessary. Test takers will require a writing surface and a number 2 pencil to complete the test.

A distribution report is available, which provides site score groups in three categories: Academic Expectations, Personal Expectations, and Social Expectations. Raw scores and percent responses are reported in addition to standard deviation, mean, median, and mode statistics for the category. Individual reports are available which convert raw scores to z-scores for the site and category. Summary reports provide a listing of individuals and z-scores by category. Interpretation of the individual z-score is provided in a narrative format along with a description of the category.

The PEEK is available in English written at a level appropriate for students who are able to read information concerning perceptions, expectations, emotions, and knowledge about academic, personal, and social experiences.

SUMMARY. Self-reported perspectives of Academic, Personal, and Social Expectations about College are elicited from a 30-question instrument. These reports provide individual and site-specific comparisons.

[284]
Performance Skills Leader.

Purpose: Designed to identify "leadership strengths and developmental needs."

Population: Employees in leadership positions.

Publication Date: 1996.

Acronym: PS Leader.

Scores, 24: Strategic Focus (Vision, Business Knowledge, Change Management), Business Focus (Quality Centered, Planning and Executing, Budgeting, Technology Management and Application), Work Force Focus (Coaching, Team Leadership, Creativity and Innovation, Commitment to Work Force Diversity, Human Resource Management), Interpersonal Focus (Interpersonal Skills, Oral Communication, Influencing, Writing, Conflict Resolution and Negotiation),

Personal Focus (Self-Development, Action Orientation, Results Focus, Flexibility, Problem Solving and Decision Making, Role Modeling, Time Management).
Administration: Group.
Price Data, 1996: $65 per assessment disk per leader; $800 per half-day seminar plus $65 per leader for assessment disk; $1,500 per full-day seminar plus $65 per leader for assessment disk (also includes Insight Inventory); $150 per group report; $49.95 per administrator's manual (110 pages).
Time: Administration time not reported.
Author: Human Technology, Inc.
Publisher: HRD Press.

Review of the Performance Skills Leaders by
TRENTON R. FERRO, Associate Professor of Adult and Community Education, Indiana University of Pennsylvania, Indiana, PA:
DESCRIPTION OF INSTRUMENT AND SUPPORTING MATERIALS. The Performance Skills Leader (PS Leader) assessment is based, according to the developers, on 24 competencies, divided into five key areas or foci (Strategic, Business, Workforce, Interpersonal, and Personal) that "describe both *what* successful leaders do ... and the characteristics that enable them to do it–*how* they do it" (Administrator's Guide, p. 1-1). The instrument consists of 82 items, which are statements of specific behaviors that describe each of the 24 competencies. These items, or behaviors, are intended to measure current proficiency levels of skills possessed by leaders at all levels and, by comparing current proficiency levels with required proficiency levels, to indicate leaders' job strengths (where current proficiency levels meet or exceed required proficiency levels) or development needs (where current proficiency levels are below required proficiency levels). These comparisons are achieved by rating each of the 82 items on a scale of 1 to 5, with 1 representing "No Proficiency" and 5 representing "Very High Proficiency."

The instruments are completed by the leaders themselves, by their supervisor, by three to nine persons reporting directly to them, and by three to nine of the leaders' peers. These instruments are stored on four discs (labeled Self, Supervisor, Direct Report, and Peer, respectively). When each respondent completes an assessment, that respondent must lock in the data she or he has entered. Such locking in ensures confidentiality and makes the data available for analysis and reporting; any data that are not locked in are not used.

After all respondents have completed their individual assessments, the disks are sent to the instrument's publisher for analysis. This analysis is contained in a report that is returned in a sealed envelope directly to the leader who is the subject of the assessment. Each leader's confidential report compares the leader's perception of job requirements with the supervisor's perception, ranks the 24 competencies by comparing those in which the leader is relatively stronger with those in which she or he may have greater development needs, identifies five behaviors in which the leader shows relatively more job strengths according to each perspective, identifies five behaviors in which the leader has relatively stronger development needs according to each perspective, presents the ratings for each task and activity on the assessment instrument from each of the four rater groups, and provides suggestions for improving skill levels in four areas of strength and eight areas of need.

The PS Leader is composed of three sets of materials. First is a package that includes four computer disks on which members of the four rater groups will provide their assessment of the leader; instructions for distributing, collecting, and returning the disks; and a tracking sheet to facilitate the data collection process. Second is a Participant Package that includes a list of the 82 leadership behaviors divided into the 24 leadership competency areas, a participant Interpretation Booklet, and sample reports. The Participant Interpretation Booklet, in turn, provides an overview of the PS Leader, information on understanding the feedback report, and suggestions and guidelines for undertaking a plan for ongoing professional development based on the results of the feedback report. Third, the Administrator's Guide gives an introduction to, and description of, the PS Leader, explains how to administer the instrument and, when received, distribute the feedback packets (reports) to participating leaders; provides a detailed lesson plan and supporting materials for conducting a PS Leader interpretation session (which can last from 2 1/2 hours to one day in length); a sample of a feedback report; and a copy of the instrument.

EVALUATION OF THE PS LEADER. The producers of this instrument claim that "the PS Leader assessment measures leadership skills based on a well-researched competency model .... The PS Leader competencies were determined based on an extensive research effort with more than 12,000 supervisors, managers, and executives in both public and private sector organizations" (Administrator's Guide, pp. 3–4; cf. p. 1-1 and Participant Interpretation Booklet, p. 2). However, these assertions are not supported by any evidence, documentation, citations, or references in either the Administrator's Guide or the Participant Package. Users are not provided any information regarding the source or derivation of the model, its 24 competencies, and the 82 items (i.e., the specific behaviors that describe these competencies) contained in the instrument. Further, there is no reference to, or citation of, any testing of the instrument to examine its psychometric properties. A thorough search of research databases has turned up neither independent analyses of the Performance Skills Leader nor any studies that have used this instrument for collecting data.

On the other hand, the instrument appears to possess face validity. Further, the assessment process and resulting report are completely confidential. When each rater completes the assessment, she or he locks in the data she or he has entered. No one else can access that data. All disks are submitted in mailers sealed by the leader/participant, and each feedback report is returned to the leader/participant in a sealed envelope. These procedures assure that the instrument is used strictly for its intended purpose—self-development and self-improvement of the leader using the assessment. To use the instrument otherwise (e.g., for diagnostic purposes or performance evaluation) would be a misuse.

The materials do require some editing. Particularly bothersome is the misspelling or truncation of the word "Very" as "Vry" on the instrument (although there is no apparent need to shorten the word); the rather persistent use of "their" to refer to a singular antecedent (e.g., "As *each* direct report completes *their* assessment"; italics added; Participant Instructions, p. 5); and a missing apostrophe for the possessive in the Supervisor's Assessment Disk (e.g., "Identify your direct reports [*sic*] current proficiency level").

SUMMARY. The Performance Skills Leader appears to be a useful tool for self-assessment. However, no evidence is presented to support the claims that it is based on a well-researched model and that the development of the competencies was based on extensive research. In light of this lack of evidence, prospective users will want to consider carefully the considerable financial investment needed to use this assessment instrument properly and fully.

Review of the Performance Skills Leader by GEORGE C. THORNTON III, *Professor of Psychology, Colorado State University, Fort Collins, CO:*

Performance Skills Leader (PS Leader) is one of numerous 360 degree feedback instruments for evaluating leader/manager's performance from multiple sources: The individual (self ratings), supervisor, peers, and subordinates. Sometimes other sources of evaluation can be used (e.g., customers or clients). PS Leader follows the pattern of most of these instruments and their ancillary programs by providing a set of materials for administering and interpreting the results. Unlike other leading multirater offerings, the material for PS Leader provides absolutely no data to support the claims that the instrument measures the intended skills.

The administrator's guide asserts that the questionnaire measures leadership skills based on a well-researched competency model. This model includes 24 competencies (e.g., Vision) arranged into the five general areas listed above (e.g., Strategic Focus). There is no further reference to source documents about the model listed, and the manual provides no information about how the model was developed or its theoretical bases. At a very minimum the publisher should describe how the test was developed and provide evidence of reliability (e.g., estimates of internal consistency of items within the scale, intercorrelations among the 24 competencies, and factor analysis to support the grouping of the competencies in the five general areas).

The manual also asserts that collecting feedback about these performance areas and providing feedback to leaders will lead to improvements in performance effectiveness. Again, no data are provided to support this assertion. At a very minimum, there should be some evidence of validity (e.g., in the form of correlations among the ratings from different sources, or the correlations of the ratings with some other source of leadership skill evaluations).

The questionnaire consists of 82 behavioral statements that are aggregated into the 24 competencies. Informants provide two ratings (on 5-point scales) for each behavior: One rating indicates the level of proficiency required on the job, and the second indicates the leader's current level of performance. Various combinations of these two ratings from the perspective of multiple raters are provided in the feedback reports: Job requirements consist of ratings from the self and supervisor; competency ratings come from all sources; strengths are identified when there is a small difference between job requirements and current levels of skills; developmental needs are identified when there is a large difference between job requirements and current levels of skills.

The reports also show profile graphs displaying self-ratings in comparison with supervisor and subordinate ratings. Additional parts of the report show lists of developmental needs identified by each rater source. Detailed reports show ratings from all sources on each of the 82 behaviors. No norms, which might allow interpretation of the meaning of scores, are provided in the manual.

The support materials include detailed guides for the administration of the questionnaires to the various informants. Responses are sent to HRD Press for scoring and report preparation. Both individual and group reports are available.

Extensive support material is provided for the conduct of interpretive feedback sessions with participants. The materials cover the description of the model, how to prepare leaders for feedback, the form and format of the feedback report, how to interpret the data, and examples of developmental actions that can be taken to address developmental needs. A booklet is also provided for the participants. No data are provided to support the contention that feedback provided in this manner has any positive impact on participants (e.g., do they accept it, do they intend to act upon it?). Of course, the ultimate questions are does developmental planning take place, do participants follow through with the developmental activities, and do their leadership skills improve as a result of the processes proposed here. Answers to those questions hinge on much more than the quality of the instrument per se, but the publisher has an obligation to make some effort to demonstrate positive outcomes from applying its package of assessment and development materials.

Professional standards admonish authors and publishers to provide evidence to support intended uses of test instruments. Data to support inferences to be made from test scores might be presented in manuals, tech reports, research publications, or case studies. Requests for information from this publisher and extensive search of the literature via manual and computer searches yielded only one source, and that was, at best, only tangentially related to the quality of the instrument.

SUMMARY. There is no evidence to support any of the recommended applications of PS Leader. Therefore, I cannot endorse this instrument, especially in light of the extensive research evidence supporting other multirater instruments (Van Velson & Leslie, 1991).

REVIEWER'S REFERENCE

Van Velson, E., & Leslie, J. B. (1991). *Feedback to managers.* Greensboro, NC: Center for Creative Leadership.

[285]
Personal Orientation Dimensions.

Purpose: Designed to "measure attitudes and values in terms of concepts of the actualizing person."
Population: High school, college, and adults.
Publication Dates: 1975–1977.
Acronym: POD.
Scores, 13: Orientation (Time Orientation, Core Centeredness), Polarities (Strength, Weakness, Anger, Love), Integration (Synergistic Integration, Potentiation), Awareness (Being, Trust in Humanity, Creative Living, Mission, Manipulation Awareness).
Administration: Group.
Price Data, 1998: $20.25 per 25 reusable test booklets; $13.75 per 50 answer sheets (machine-scoring) [$136.25 per 500]; $1.60 for EdITS scoring; $8 per specimen set; $4 per manual ('77, 14 pages).
Time: Administration time not reported.
Comments: A refinement and extension of concepts first measured by the Personal Orientation Inventory (T5:1939); self-administering.
Author: Everett L. Shostrom.
Publisher: EdITS/Educational and Industrial Testing Service.
Cross References: See T5:1938 (1 reference) and T4:1977 (1 reference).

Review of the Personal Orientation Dimensions by GLORIA MACCOW, School Psychologist, Guilford County Schools, Greensboro, NC:

The Personal Orientation Dimensions scales (POD) are a refined and extended version of the Personal Orientation Inventory (POI), which was published by Shostrom in 1963 and 1974. The POD is a comprehensive measure of values and behaviors seen to be of importance to actualizing and positive mental health as opposed to psychopathology. The instrument consists of 13 scales. There are 20 items on each scale making a total of

260 items in the Inventory. Each item is a two-choice, paired opposite statement of comparative value and behavior judgment. The author believes that double-statement items are useful in therapy situations. (The scales are described in detail in the manual.)

The POD was developed for use by counselors, therapists, and researchers as a comprehensive measure of concepts of humanistic psychology. It is used in colleges, business and industrial settings, clinics, and counseling agencies. The data can be used to plan intervention/treatment because of the instrument's focus on the client's mental health. The author describes the POD as self-administering. Examinees record their answers on a specially designed answer sheet that is returned to EdITS for processing. The POD should be interpreted by professionals trained in measurement, in POD interpretation, and in the concepts of Actualizing Therapy. A profile sheet is provided listing a T-score for each of the 13 scales. If most of the scale scores fall above the mean line, the individual is probably functioning effectively and is more highly actualizing than the average person.

Items for the POD were developed based on value judgments of therapists, counselors, and leaders in the field of human behavior. The POD was based on research with the POI and on theoretical conceptualizations of leaders in humanistic, existential, and Gestalt therapies. The items were administered to 402 college freshmen and their responses were submitted to nonotonicity analysis. This resulted in 13 factors, which represent a person's psychological being in terms of the concepts of Actualizing Therapy.

The technical properties of the POD are questionable. Although the POD has more items than the POI, the author appears to infer from the POI predictive and factorial validity of the POD. The factor structure was derived from the responses of a relatively small sample ($n = 402$) of college freshmen. Several studies are reported to demonstrate that the POD differentiates between actualizing ($n = 20$) and nonactualizing ($n = 21$) individuals, and between actualizing individuals and hospitalized psychiatric patients ($n = 91$). The actualizing group scored higher than the other two groups on all 13 scales.

The samples used to investigate reliability also were small. In one study, the instrument was administered to 40 participants and then re-administered one week later. Forty-six participants retook the test after a 3-month interval. The coefficients ranged from .53 to .79. Test-retest correlations are reported but these were based on the last research edition of the POD, which preceded this published version. It is not clear how the current version of the POD differs from the research edition.

SUMMARY. Several factors limit the utility of the POD. First, the instrument is useful for counselors and therapists who are skilled in actualizing therapy. Therapists who do not use this theoretical approach will require training in order to interpret the findings to their clients and to incorporate the data into treatment programs. Second, the tests must be mailed to the publisher for scoring. This is time-consuming and could prevent counselors from implementing treatment programs in a timely manner.

The instrument was published in the 1970s and does not conform to recent developments in test construction. For example, the manual does not describe the ethnicity and gender of standardization samples; the instrument cannot be scored without the assistance of the publisher. There are two concerns regarding the standardization samples. First, all of the studies used relative small samples. Second, the data were collected over 20 years ago and the responses of the participants may not be comparable to responses that would be obtained today.

Review of the Personal Orientation Dimensions by CLAUDIA R. WRIGHT, Professor, Educational Psychology, California State University, Long Beach, Long Beach, CA:

The Personal Orientation Dimensions (POD) was designed to provide an assessment of values and behavior judgments derived from actualization theories underlying humanistic, existential, and gestalt therapy. The inventory is intended for use in research and for applications in college, business, counseling, and clinical settings to assess a client's level of positive mental health. The POD is a 13-scale, self-administered inventory made up of 260 forced-choice item-pairs and closely related to the Personal Orientation inventory (POI; Shostrom, 1963; 1974) in both content and form. In the construction of the 13 POD scales, Shostrom (1977) retained 10 POI scales that had demonstrated both predictive and factorial-related validity. Based on practitioner feedback, research, and theory-based reconceptualizations of the actualizing person, some of the items from these retained scales were rewritten and new items added. The retained scales are Time Orientation (TO), Core Centeredness (CC), Strength (S), Weakness (W), Anger (A), Love (L), Synergistic Integration (SI), Potentiation (PO), Being (BE), and Trust in Humanity (TH). Three newly constructed scales are Creative Living (CL) and Mission (M), based on Maslow's (1971) later writings on self-actualizing, and Manipulation Awareness (MA) based upon Shostrom's (1967) conceptual framework.

SCORING AND INTERPRETATION. Each of the 260 item-pairs contains both a positive and a negative statement representing a value or behavior judgment related to an underlying conceptual continuum consistent with 1 of 13 actualizing dimensions. The respondent is instructed to select one statement from each pair that "most consistently applies" to him or her. The higher the score for each scale, the more positive the mental health of the respondent. To aid interpretation, a POD profile is generated for each examinee. The technical manual provides three profiles for comparison, which display patterns of mean scores across the 13 actualizing scales. These profiles are based upon responses from 20 nominated actualizing persons, 21 nominated nonactualizing persons, and 91 hospitalized psychiatric patients. In addition, for each of these groups and for a sample of 424 entering college freshmen, means and standard deviations for each scale are provided.

RELIABILITY. Insufficient evidence was provided to support the reliability of the POD scale scores. The only information about the reliability of scale scores was inferred from studies employing quasi-experimental, pretest-posttest designs to examine effects of various therapeutic or counselor training interventions. Correlation coefficients, ranging from .53 to .79 for the 13 scales, were obtained between pre- and postintervention test scores and represented as "lower-bound estimates" of reliability—the implicit assumption being that if no intervention had been present, the coefficients would have been higher. More appropriate reliability analyses would include internal-consistency estimates and/or stability coefficients that have not been confounded by the possible effects of an intervention.

VALIDITY. Several validation approaches were cited in the technical manual to support POD scale scores: (a) differentiation between selected criterion groups, (b) response bias, and (c) concurrent and construct validity studies. Differentiation between selected criterion groups (e.g., nominated groups of "actualizing" and "nonactualizing" or "clinical and "nonclinical" samples) provided validity evidence. Respondents classified as actualizing ($n = 20$) scored higher on all POD scales than those classified as nonactualizing ($n = 21$) (all $p < .05$); no statistically significant gender differences were found. POD scale means and standard deviations obtained from the sample of 424 freshmen were similar to those reported for the nominated nonactualizing group. Comparing data from the actualizing sample and from a clinical sample, 12 of the 13 POD scales were found to differentiate between the two groups at the .001 level; the Mission scale did not. In a study of 51 psychiatric inpatients classified as either paranoid or nonparanoid schizophrenic; only two POD scale scores, Time Orientation and Trust in Humanity, distinguished the two groups.

Response bias was examined by instructing respondents to "fake a good impression" leading to consistently lower POD scale scores indicating that POD items are resistant to manipulation. An inspection of item content suggests that "nonactualizing" value statements reflect tendencies toward societal conformity and pleasing others. Thus, respondents might have interpreted "faking a good impression" to mean "faking a socially desirable" response rather than an "actualizing" one.

Concurrent-related validity was examined by correlating POD scale scores with scores from other widely used personality measures such as the Eysenck Personality Questionnaire (EPQ; Eysenck & Eysenck, 1975), Myers-Briggs Type Indicator (MBTI; Myers & Briggs, 1943/1962), and Clinical Analysis Questionnaire (CAQ; Delhees & Cattell, 1970–1971). An examination of relationships between scores on the POD and the EPQ yielded, as hypothesized, negative validity coefficients between the POD scale scores and both EPQ scales of Neuroticism (-.55 to .29, mdn = -.34) and Psychoticism (-.48 to .18, mdn = -.25); and, moderate positive coefficients with the EPQ Extraversion scale (-.04 to .58; mdn = .38). Additional concurrent validity evidence was reported for 7 of 13 POD scales (namely, TO, CC, W, A, L, SI, and TH) in relationship to the MBTI Extraversion scale (.23 to .50, mdn = .31, all p < .05); 3 POD scales (A, L, and SI) were moderately correlated with the MBTI Sensing scale (r = .33, .37, and .36, respectively); 2 POD scales (L and TH) were correlated with the Thinking scale (r = .42 and .35, respectively); and, only the MA scale yielded a low but statistically significant correlation with the MBTI Judgment scale (r = -.30). Finally, low to moderate coefficients (-.51 to .46; mdn = 26.5) between the 28 CAQ and 13 POD scale scores were observed. However, out of a total of 74 validity coefficients reported, only 15 attained a magnitude of ± .40 or larger, suggesting minor overlap between the sets of scale scores. The strongest relationships were observed between the POD Anger scale and CAQ Outgoing (.46), Less Intelligent (-.48), Practical (.41), Uncontrolled (-.41), and High Psychasthenia (.45) scales.

Construct validity evidence was based on correlations among scores on the POD and the POI (Shostrom, 1963). As many POD items were similar to and/or modified from the POI, one might have expected greater overlap between the two measures than observed. Correlation coefficients between pairs of selected POD and POI scale scores that were purported to be conceptually similar to one another ranged from .50 to .70 (mdn = .68) suggesting moderate support for construct validity but that the POD scale scores might be tapping constructs not measured by the POI. In addition, two POD scales, Creative Living and Mission—derived from Maslow's later works, attained moderate coefficients with the POI scale Self-actualizing Value (SAV) (.41 and .44, respectively).

SUMMARY. Overall, the POD appears conceptually well grounded in theories and concepts of humanistic psychology as these apply to the actualizing person. Scores on the POD scales differentiate between groups of individuals classified as actualizing or nonactualizing as well as between respondents identified as actualizing or diagnosed with some psychiatric disorder. Concurrent validity findings suggest that selected POD scales demonstrate moderate overlap with the three EPQ scales (positively with Extraversion and negatively with Psychoticism and Neuroticism), the MBTI Extraversion scale, and with selected CAQ scales. Few instruments devoted to the assessment of actualizing behaviors, other than the POI (Shostrom, 1963), were found in a review of the

literature. Insufficient psychometric evidence has been offered to support the reliability of scale scores, to reinforce validity claims built on small sample sizes, to confirm that the POD scale scores are free from cultural biases, or to address cohort concerns.

REVIEWER'S REFERENCES

Myers, I. B., & Briggs, K. C. (1943/1962). The Myers-Briggs Type Indicator. Palo Alto, CA: Consulting Psychologists Press.
Shostrom, E. L. (1963). Personal Orientations Inventory. San Diego, CA: EdITS.
Shostrom, E. L. (1967). *Man, the manipulator: The inner journey from manipulations to actualization.* Nashville, TN: Abingdon Press.
Delhees, K. H., & Cattell, R. B. (1970–1971). Clinical Analysis Questionnaire. Champaign, IL: Institute for Personality and Ability Testing, Inc.
Maslow, A. (1971). *The further reaches of human nature.* New York: Viking.
Shostrom, E. L. (1974). *Manual for the Personal Orientation Inventory.* San Diego, CA: EdITS.
Eysenck, H. J., & Eysenck, S. B. G. (1975). The Eysenck Personality Questionnaire. San Diego, CA: EdITS.
Shostrom, E. L. (1977). *EdITS manual: Personal Orientation Dimensions.* San Diego, CA: EdITS.

[286]
Personal Stress Assessment Inventory.

Purpose: A self-assessment instrument designed to identify those who would most likely benefit from participation in stress-management training.
Population: Adults.
Publication Dates: 1981–1993.
Acronym: PSAI.
Scores, 6: Predisposition, Resilience, Sources of Stress, Overall Stress Factor, Health Symptoms, Personal Reactions.
Administration: Group.
Price Data, 1998: $7.50 per inventory (volume discounts available).
Time: (20–30) minutes.
Comments: Self-administered; self-scored.
Author: Herbert S. Kindler.
Publisher: The Center for Management Effectiveness.

Review of the Personal Stress Assessment Inventory by E. SCOTT HUEBNER, Professor of Psychology, University of South Carolina, Columbia, SC:

The Personal Stress Assessment Inventory (PSAI) was designed "to reflect which respondents would most likely benefit from participation in stress-management training" (Kindler & Schorr, 1991, p. 4). This self-report inventory includes six scales: Predisposition, Resilience, Sources of Stress, Health Symptoms, Overall Stress, and a social desirability scale.

Scoring and interpretation procedures are described in a one-page attachment to the test protocol. Cut-points for elevated scores are provided. However, no data are offered to support their accuracy.

Overall, limited information is available regarding the technical properties of the PSAI. Item analysis information is absent. The standardization sample was small and described inadequately. No descriptive statistics for the sample are indicated.

Reliability information is limited to estimates of internal consistency (i.e., coefficient alpha), presumably for the five subscales (even though a total stress factor scores is calculated and interpreted). The alphas ranged from .51 (Predisposition scale) to .91 (unspecified scale); however, the authors state "the Predisposition scale was revised following this study and brought up to an adequate level of reliability" (p. 6). Nevertheless, further information regarding the manner in which the Predisposition scale (which was designed to measure Type A behavioral tendencies) was modified and the resulting reliability coefficient is not specified.

Validity information is also lacking. The authors state that intercorrelations among the scales were assessed, but fail to provide the correlation coefficients. Similarly, the authors state that the PSAI is unrelated to social desirability responding, but provide no data. On a positive note, the PSAI Predisposition, Resilience, and Sources of Stress scales cumulatively predicted the PSAI Health Symptoms score, and the various PSAI scales (except Predisposition) discriminated a group of employees enrolled in a stress management program from a group of employees "under more typical employee pressures" (p. 7). Nevertheless, considerable additional information is needed to support the content, criterion (including predictive), and construct validity of scores from the PSAI before it can be used confidently in individual decision making. For one example, factor analytic studies are crucial to the determination of the construct validity of the scale. For another example, evidence of convergent validity with respect to other more established measures of the same constructs (e.g., other Type A measures, stressful events measures), including reports from other raters (e.g., spouses, coworkers), would be helpful. Furthermore, the PSAI should be scrutinized to rule out the possibility of any racial or gender bias.

In sum, the PSAI should be considered to be in the preliminary stage of development. It awaits considerable further research support before it can be used for any purpose, even research purposes.

REVIEWER'S REFERENCE

Kindler, H. S., & Schorr, D. (1991). Stress management training programmes: Motivating participation using a self-diagnostic inventory. *Employee Counseling Today, 3*(1), 4–8.

Review of the Personal Stress Assessment Inventory by NORMAN D. SUNDBERG, Professor Emeritus, Department of Psychology, University of Oregon, Eugene, OR:

Appropriately the cover of the Personal Stress Assessment Inventory (PSAI) is a calming picture of flowers by the seaside. Inside, the 10 pages give instructions followed by 10 to 33 items and scoring instructions. The following examples illustrate the flavor of the item content and method of answering: (a) For the Predisposition scale respondents must choose along a line of numbers from 1 to 10 between *I often got annoyed when I waited in line* and *I rarely got annoyed when I waited in line.* (b) For Resilience on the next page, respondents must choose from 1 to 4 (*Frequently, to Not in the Last 30 Days*) on such items as *I seek places where I can find serenity.* (c) For Stress Sources on two pages, they write 1 to 10 (low to major impact) on personal items such as *A person close to me died,* and separately on work items *I was criticized by my boss.* (d) On an additional two pages they rate other sets of Stress Source items for whether each condition is within one's power to change or not. (e) For Personal Reactions, they write T or F by items measuring social desirability, such as *I like to gossip at times.* (f) Health Symptom items call for circling 1 to 4 on frequency for Physical Symptoms such as "Diarrhea" and Psychological Symptoms such as "Frightening dreams." The last two pages cover scoring and interpretation.

The content of PSAI items incorporates a variety of the ideas in the stress literature, particularly drawing on work on Type A and life change ideas. However, the changing nature of the method of answering the items could be confusing and the scoring is rather complex. The description says that the time required is 20 to 30 minutes. However, it seems likely that it would take longer, especially for people not used to taking tests, perhaps more than a half hour to answer and 15 minutes to score. The inventory could be improved by reducing it to only one or two different ways of answering the items and a simpler scoring system.

The purpose of the PSAI is to identify those who would benefit from stress-management training (Kindler & Schorr, 1991). As presented by Kindler and Schorr, the PSAI is used in the first session of a three-session group program and is self-administered and scored. They emphasize confidentiality of results and the voluntary nature of the training. Unless the inventory is a regular part of a training program, the respondents not only would need to take and score the instrument by themselves but also to self-identify and be motivated to seek training or counseling. There are no studies of whether tested employees actually seek help outside the training sessions.

The last page of the inventory tells respondents how to interpret their scores. The author, Herbert Kindler, does not present a table of norms or indicate how he chose the critical scores such as the following: On Resilience "scores above 50 suggest more caring attention can be given to gaining better emotional, physical, mental and spiritual balance," and on the Overall Stress Factor scores above 55 or below 15 deserve special attention. The current form of the PSAI evidently is revised; the instrument was originally copyrighted in 1981.

A survey of psychology publications revealed no reports on the psychometric properties of the PSAI other than the Kindler and Schorr article (1991), although Kindler has some articles on stress management training. The Kindler and Schorr study may serve as a manual but it is not so labeled. It is a report of the use of the PSAI with a sample of 82 white-collar middle managers and professionals from a variety of organizations and another sample of 20 employees who reported to the company medical department because of stress-related symptoms. All scales except Predisposition (.51) showed adequate internal consistency (.79 to .91), but no test-retest reliability is given. A table of intercorrelations among scales is not shown, but the authors report that social desirability (the Personal Reactions scale) did not affect other scales in a significant way. Except for the Predisposition scale, scales were significantly correlated with health symptoms, indicating some evidence of concurrent validity. Also a comparison of the two samples showed significantly more perceived stress with those employees who had reported for medical services with stress-related symptoms on all scales except Predisposition. The Predisposition scale, which is derived from Type A theory about proneness to heart trouble, did not work well in several instances; the authors argue that Type A theory is flawed and that irritability and hostility are symptoms that are easy to cover up. A regression analysis on health symptoms showed that Resilience and non-work sources of stress were particularly important in accounting for variance separate from other stress indicators. There is, therefore, some evidence of concurrent and construct validity, but no report on predictive validity. In the article the authors conclude that low resilience is an excellent "predictor" of excessive stress symptoms. Their recommendation for balance in life is mentioned but not theoretically explicated.

Several *Mental Measurements Yearbooks* contain reviews of self-report instruments for working adults. The closest to the PSAI seem to be the Meta-Motivation Inventory (9:698) published in 1979, the Stress Resiliency Profile (13:301) published in 1992, and the Work Temperament Inventory (13:368) published in 1993. None of these have been used in research efforts comparing them with the PSAI, and their purposes are somewhat different. The first one is the closest, because it is intended to help managers and others in leadership positions evaluate their own development in management and personal growth. It provides feedback on thinking styles relative to management theories. It would be useful to have some research comparing these and other such stress-related instruments. The Kindler and Schorr article makes no reference to the instruments just mentioned. They report that the PSAI is widely used in North America and the United Kingdom and has been translated into Japanese.

SUMMARY. What might one conclude about the PSAI? This self-report inventory offers an array of material about stress and its sources. It seems that it would be helpful for alerting employed people to possible problems in their own thinking and their work and non-work environments. It may be useful as a teaching tool in stress management programs. However, research on the inventory is very limited, and the format of the inventory is rather complex for self-administration and scoring. The jury is out about whether the inventory would add anything to an employee assistance program beyond being a teaching tool alerting people to the nature of stress.

REVIEWER'S REFERENCE

Kindler, H. S., & Schorr, D. (1991). Stress-management training programmes: Motivating participation using a self-diagnostic inventory. *Employee Counseling Today, 3*(1), 4–8.

[287]
Personal Style Inventory.

Purpose: Designed "to assess Rational/Intuitive personal style preferences."

Population: Adults.

Publication Dates: 1991–1993.

Acronym: PSI.

Scores, 6: Planning, Analysis, Control, Vision, Insight, Sharing.

Administration: Group.

Price Data: Not available.

Time: Administration time not reported.

Comments: Designed to be part of a 1- or 2-day workshop.

Authors: William Taggart and Barbara Taggart-Hausladen.

Publisher: Psychological Assessment Resources, Inc.

Cross References: See T5:1953 (3 references).

[Editor's Note: The publisher advised in March 2001 that this test has been out-of-print since September 2000.]

Review of the Personal Style Inventory by STEVEN V. OWEN, Senior Biostatistician, Department of Preventive Medicine and Community Health, University of Texas Medical Branch, Galveston, TX:

The 1990s witnessed a dramatic growth of self-help materials and programs. The Personal Style Inventory (hereafter, PSI) is an outgrowth of that phenomenon. The PSI is not so much a measurement as an entire program for directing personal change. The main manual for the program is called the trainer's manual, and the PSI is typically run by a coordinator of a workshop in an organizational setting. The trainer's manual implies, though, that the program may also be organized by oneself, for oneself. The general goal of the PSI is to enhance organizational function through improvements in "personal flexibility." The focus is on interpersonal behaviors, although the PSI can presumably be aimed at nonsocial behaviors as well, such as reducing procrastination, improving study skills, or understanding others' motives. Strong claims are made about the potency and generalizability of the PSI program to alter many forms of behavior, in many settings, but a few anonymous quotations from previous PSI participants are the only evidence offered.

The PSI package consists of four booklets, only one of which—the Survey—is related to assessment. The remaining booklets comprise activities that are based on scores on the Survey.

Curiously, although the Survey development and psychometric evidence focus on six subscales, training interventions developed from the Survey data rely on individual items. Interventions are targeted at reducing the most frequent personal behaviors and building the least frequent behaviors, as though frequency of a behavior were a more important criterion than functionality. Subscale scores seem to be emphasized in organizing diverse training groups and offering insight about personal style.

The theoretical context for the PSI is claimed to be neuropsychological, but it includes a poorly integrated hodgepodge of Taoist philosophy, selected ideas from management literature, poorly connected ideas from brain physiology, and a collection of assumptions (e.g., "people know their true inner needs"). From the "theory," three personal preference modes were derived for a Rational Style (Analysis, Planning, and Control), and three paired and generally opposing modes for an Intuitive Style (Insight, Vision, and Sharing). Thus, for example, a person who prefers Analysis may well avoid Insight.

INSTRUMENT DEVELOPMENT. The measurement aspect of the PSI is limited to the brief, 30-item self-administered PSI Survey. The PSI authors began with an initial pool of 500 items collected from 10 unnamed surveys, and attempted to sort them into the six personal preference categories. No standard is reported for keeping or discarding items. The sorting exercise retained 87 items from the original item pool. In three subsequent rounds of content validation, four "expert judges" and a measurement specialist refined and expanded the item group to 90 items, 30 for each pair of preference modes.

For the final item winnowing, pilot data were gathered from 378 undergraduates, all of whom were majoring in business administration. The 90 items were given a 6-point response scale, with the poles assigned socially undesirable labels *Never* and *Always*. In between are ordinal labels: *Once in a while, Sometimes, Quite Often,* and *Frequently but not always.* Three common factor analyses, each with a varimax rotation, were run for the 30-item sets reflecting the three pairs of modes. Each analysis was constrained to a 2-factor solution. Items were retained for the final instrument if they had both large loadings on their expected factor, and large absolute discrepancies in loadings for the opposite factor. The aim was to finish with 5 items per mode, or 10 per pair of modes, for a total of 30 items. The tidiness of the factor results was likely an artifact of forcing an orthogonal solution, and avoiding a factoring of all 90 items together.

PSYCHOMETRIC EVIDENCE. Alpha reliability estimates for the six factor scales, based on the same pilot sample, ranged from .53 (Control) to .83 (Planning). The average reliability for the three Rational scales was .70; for the three Intuitive scales, .66.

The trainer's manual asserts that validity evidence was compiled through a multitrait/multimethod approach, but only a monomethod was used. The authors declare that their approach "is more rigorous than required by the multitrait-multimethod analyses" (trainer's manual, p. 79). The resulting multitrait correlation matrix, collected from the same pilot sample as the factor analysis, gives less support than claimed by the authors. Predictably, the Rational subscales showed positive intercorrelations, and negative correlations with their Intuitive counterparts. The authors interpret this as strong convergent and divergent evidence, but these correlations are partly a function of the way subscale items were selected based on the pattern of their factor loadings. Among PSI traits proposed to be inversely related, four of nine correlations are not significantly different from zero.

Examining PSI correlations with other measures (the Learning Style Inventory [LSI] and the Myers-Briggs Type Indicator [MBTI], which are both ipsative in format), coefficients as small as .20 between comparable traits are characterized as "relatively large." A series of correlations between PSI subscales and the Active Experimentation subscale from the LSI range from -.05 to +.05. The authors explain this in that "active experimentation ... is neither a Rational nor an Intuitive behavior" (trainer's manual, p. 77). In fairness, though, the multitrait matrix does have groups of correlations that give some support for discriminant and convergent validity. The results may have been even stronger had the authors chosen other measures that were not ipsative.

Norms were created from the same university sample used throughout the Survey development, and are thus limited in their generality. The single norms table (trainer's manual, p. 18) is merely a translation of raw subscale scores to percentile ranks, with no demographic breakdown. The table mistakenly shows quite a few percentile ranks of zero and 100. No other descriptive data—ranges, means, standard deviations—are given, so it is not possible to calculate standard errors of measurement or confidence intervals for the Survey subscores.

SUMMARY. The Survey portion of the Personal Style Inventory is a brief and superficial self-report measure that is claimed to reveal a typology of behavioral preferences. It joins other popular measures, such as the LSI and the MBTI (251), that are frequently used in school and corporate training programs. Unlike the LSI and MBTI, the PSI Survey does not suffer a forced-choice response format. However, like its companion tools, there is surprisingly little evidence that such measures are suitable for evaluation research aimed at personal training programs.

The PSI Survey has an uncertain and rambling theoretical basis, and it is especially scant on psychometric and normative data. It needs far more extensive analysis, examination, and supportive evidence. And to be taken seriously, it needs a full-fledged technical manual, not an appendix in a training manual. Given these limitations, it is hard to recommend it except as a rough experimental tool.

Review of the Personal Style Inventory by ALAN J. RAPHAEL, President, International Assessment Systems, Inc., Miami, FL:

Published in 1993 by Psychological Assessment Resources, Inc. (PAR), the Personal Style Inventory (PSI) is both a 30-item "survey" and a second 30-item "personal development program." It is based on work on managerial decision styles published by one of the authors in 1981. However, there has been almost no discernible effort to upgrade or improve the measure since its introduction in 1981.

The trainer's manual describes the PSI as a "self-administering, self-scoring, self-interpreting package to assess Rational/Intuitive personal style preferences" (p. iii). However, the manual essentially negates itself by stating "This Trainer's Manual provides information to help you use the PSI. However, you do not have to read the entire Trainer's Manual to start using the PSI .... Later, read any chapters that you believe will help you get more out of the PSI package" (p. iii). If the training manual, administration, scoring, and interpreting components are deleted or included based on the subjective inclination of the user, the measure does not appear to possess sufficient empirical psychometric properties to be of any objective value.

The PSI was developed by the authors using concepts from a Human Information Processing (HIP) metaphor that they report "is the theoretical foundation for the PSI Assessment package" (p. 4). The authors report "This approach uses the human nervous system as the basis for inferring broad categories of individual behavior" (p. 59). However, there were no references on HIP found in the reference section but there were references entitled "A source book in Chinese philosophy," "The Prophet," and the "Tao of Power."

The authors' definition of the PSI approach states "The PSI package focuses a participant's attention on enhancing his or her own inner resources through self-assessment" (p. 4). The authors believe that fundamental changes in behavior are possible when individuals determine what kinds of changes they wish to make. According to the authors, the PSI materials offer a powerful approach for helping an individual work toward greater personal flexibility. This, in turn, helps the organization deal effectively with situations where the underlying issues are problems of interpersonal dynamics. This work suffers from underdevelopment in all spheres, most importantly in the theoretical, statistical, and research domains. The authors would be well advised to rethink and redefine their theoretical foundation. From that foundation, they would be in a better position to objectively quantify the validity, reliability, and normative group data at sufficient levels to meet at least minimal psychometric standards.

This approach also purports to provide a behavioral change agent based simply on reading the manual for those who seek "determining for themselves what kinds of changes they wish to make" (trainer's manual, p. v). This statement disregards the accepted scientific basis for change as requiring professional therapeutic assistance.

There are very few psychometric data in the test manual. The first draft of the survey was given to a sample of 378 participants who were predominantly Hispanic (188) and Caucasian (135). Participants came from college courses and, in general, possessed strong management backgrounds. The application of these findings to other populations is questionable.

Items on each preliminary scale were paired successively with items on their opposite measure (for example, a comparison of analysis and insight items) using factor analysis to determine which items best loaded on each dimension with the least overlap with the opposite dimension. This determined which items were on each scale.

The authors also present normative data and correlation with the authors' own HIP scale, the Learning Style Inventory, and with the Myers-Briggs Type Indicator. All of these are similar self-report measures. In general, the correlations with these scales are in the predicted direction, but their magnitude is less than one expects from a theoretical model.

The authors also confuse "significance" with meaningfulness, because correlations as low as .09 are significant in a sample of this size. The authors also provide a measure of reliability for each scale (ranging from .53 to .83), but it is unclear whether this is test-retest or split-half reliability. Either way, these reliabilities are generally low and suggest instability in the specific scores. Of greatest concern is the absence of any data beyond this initial sample.

The authors attempt to justify their model with a physiological explanation that oversimplifies and misstates current knowledge about the brain. Although not essential to the model overall, it gives a misleading aura of scientific validity to the test that does not appear to be well supported.

SUMMARY. Those seeking a scientific, psychometrically and theoretically sound management process will be disappointed. This self-reporting process lacks a validity scale or any method for controlling for test-taking attitude or external influences such as self-serving behavior, secondary gain motivation, denial, rationalization, or random responding. This is particularly significant for use with all populations possessing a serious motive for such training or screening. This measure is extremely limited due to its reliance on the veracity, forthrightness, self-awareness, motivation, and comprehension of the user. The manual presents a limited list of research articles dealing with ancillary theoretical and statistical factors.

Overall, from an empirical viewpoint there is very little this process has to offer to the user.

Personality Assessment Screener.

Purpose: "Designed to identify individuals in need of further assessment for emotional problems, behavioral problems, or both."

Population: Ages 18 and older.

Publication Dates: 1991–1997.

Acronym: PAS.

Scores, 11: Negative Affect, Acting Out, Health Problems, Psychotic Features, Social Withdrawal, Hostile Control, Suicidal Thinking, Alienation, Alcohol Problem, Anger Control, Total.

Administration: Group.

Price Data, 2001: $70 per complete kit including manual ('97, 73 pages) and 25 response forms; $81 per 50 response forms; $32 per manual; $195 per PAI Software Portfolio with PAS module including IBM 3.5-inch disk for Windows, key disk with 25 uses, PAI-SP software manual, and 25 item/response sheets; $20 per software manual; $75 per IBM 3.5-inch key disk with 50 uses and 50 item/response sheets.

Time: (5) minutes.

Comments: Screening version of the Personality Assessment Inventory (T5:1959).

Author: Leslie C. Morey.

Publisher: Psychological Assessment Resources, Inc.

Review of the Personality Assessment Screener by MATTHEW BURNS, Assistant Professor of School Psychology, Central Michigan University, Mt. Pleasant, MI:

The Personality Assessment Screener (PAS) is a self-report objective measure for adults designed to provide a brief assessment of information applicable to various clinical difficulties and to focus further assessment efforts. The 22 items of the PAS are based on factor analyses of its parent scale, the Personality Assessment Inventory (PAI). Test developers emphasize the breadth and brevity of the PAS which results in a Total score and 10 Element scores.

PAS scores are reported in terms of a P score that represents the likelihood that the respondent would demonstrate a problematic profile on the PAI. A P of 48 on the Total score suggests a 48% chance that the respondent would demonstrate some clinical difficulty on the PAI, and is listed as the cutoff score for a moderate elevation. It is suggested that the Element scores not be interpreted unless the Total score is at least moderately elevated. Although the P score may be somewhat confusing at first, it seems to be quite consistent with the goal of a screening instrument.

ADMINISTRATION AND SCORING. The PAS can be administered in both group and individual settings. A reported reading ability of fourth grade is necessary to complete the items, but the manual recommends reading items and defining words for respondents who have difficulty with the items. Caution is recommended when the respondent's primary language is not English.

Each item consists of a statement that is rated as False, Slightly True, Mainly True, or Very True. The response form includes a self-carbon bottom page that is attached to the top page and converts the responses to a zero-to-three Likert format scale. A scoring grid is also provided that separates the item scores into the 10 clinical elements and computes the PAS Total score. Scoring is relatively straightforward and simple.

NORMS. The PAS is normed on the same three independent samples as the PAI: (a) 1,000 census-matched community dwellers, (b) 1,246 adult patients from various clinical settings, and (c) 1,051 psychology students from seven universities. Data are provided about the samples on several variables including age, gender, ethnicity, education, marital status, and occupation. The samples generally match the 1995 census data, and although females are underrepresented in the Clinical sample and males are underrepresented in the College-Student sample, both are probably typical ratios for those populations. However, the African-American population was somewhat underrepresented in the College-Student sample. The Clinical sample includes representation of various primary clinical diagnoses and matches the 1986 National Institute of Mental Health data.

Raw scores are converted to P scores by comparing them to one of the samples listed above, or to a combined Community Dwelling and Clinical sample consisting of 2,631 participants. Demographic data for the Combined sample match census data and provide an adequate norm group. The three additional norm groups may provide potential clinically useful data, but more information describing appropriate use of each norm group is needed.

RELIABILITY. Internal consistency estimates are provided for the element scores and the PAS total score using coefficient alpha and the Spearman-Brown formula. The authors suggest that due to the brevity and breadth of the scale, low internal consistency estimates are expected and desirable. Although it is acceptable for screening instruments to demonstrate lower reliability, coefficients of .70 (Murphy & Davidshofer, 2001) or .80 (Anastasi & Urbina, 1997) remain appropriate standards.

The internal consistency coefficients for the PAS score ranged from .751 for the community sample to .791 for the clinical sample. The only element score for the Community and College samples with an internal consistency coefficient that was above .70 was Social Withdrawal. However, data from the Clinical sample participants resulted in internal consistency coefficients that were above .70 for Negative Affect, Health Problems, Psychotic Features, and Social Withdrawal elements, and the Suicidal Thinking coefficient was above .80 among the Clinical sample. Nine of the 10 elements for the College sample and all 10 of the Community sample scores were below .70.

Low internal consistency coefficients are at least partially due to the small number of items for each element. The total scale includes 22 items for 10 elements. Although this number is sufficient for the total score, each element contains only 2 or 3 items. Therefore, the total score demonstrated adequate internal consistency for a screening instrument, but data provided from the element scores may lack sufficient internal consistency for even screening decisions.

Internal consistency coefficients were also provided for the PAS Total score as a function of demographic status. The reliability coefficients were provided for groups based on gender (male and female), age (<40 years and ≥40 years), race (white and nonwhite), and education (<14 years completed and ≥14 years completed). All of the coefficients for these groups were above .70 and suggested that these variables had little effect on the scale's internal consistency.

Test-retest reliability was assessed with 75 participants from the Community sample and 80 participants from the College sample using a 24- to 28-day retest interval. The stability coefficient for the PAS score equaled .886 for the Community sample, .853 for the College sample, and .863 for the combination of the two samples. Element coefficients ranged from .466 for the Alienation element with the College sample to .922 for the Community Sample's Alcohol Problems score. Six of the 10 test-retest coefficients for the combined sample were above .70. Data from participants

from the Community sample resulted in eight coefficients that were above .70 with only Alienation and Anger Control failing to meet that standard, and six of the 10 element scores for the College sample were below .70. Much like the internal consistency coefficients, the PAS demonstrated adequate test-retest reliability for the Total score, but only the Negative Affect, Acting Out, Social Withdrawal, and Alcohol Problems elements demonstrated adequate stability reliability coefficients for screening decisions.

VALIDITY. Extensive convergent validity data were provided by correlating the PAS Total and element scores with scores from several scales including the PAI, Minnesota Multiphasic Personality Inventory (MMPI), NEO-Five Factor Inventory (NEO-FFI), and others. The resulting coefficients were generally moderate to strong when comparing corresponding subscales. The PAS Total score correlated mostly in the moderate to strong range with PAI scales, and in the weak to moderate range with the MMPI, NEO-FFI, and other scales.

Score means for 13 groups of participants diagnosed with neurotic, psychotic, and behavior disorders were provided as further validity evidence. The mean PAS Total score was above the interpretative cutoff of 50 for each group, with most falling in the 70–80 range. Mean element scores were not as high as the Total score, but almost all were above 50. Although these data provide useful information, a comparative control group of normals would significantly add to their utility.

Test items for the PAS were selected based on factor analyses of the PAI, and their ability to predict clinically significant scores on the PAI. This approach to item selection seems consistent with the purpose of the PAS, and is also adequate demonstration of construct validity.

SUMMARY. The PAS appears to be a well-developed screening instrument based on an impressive parent scale. The manual is clearly written and contains an adequate description of norms, reliability, and validity data. The Total score seems to be reliable enough to use for screening decisions. However, some caution is necessary when interpreting element scores due to low reliability estimates of the subscales that contain only two or three items each. A screening instrument that was developed to predict clinically significant scores on more detailed assessments, rather than simply being a shortened version of a parent scale, is an interesting and welcome addition to the field of objective personality assessment.

REVIEWER'S REFERENCES

Anastasi, A., & Urbina, S. (1997). *Psychological testing* (7th ed.). Upper Saddle River, NJ: Prentice Hall.

Murphy, K. R., & Davidshofer, C. O. (2001). *Psychological testing: Principles and applications* (5th ed.). Upper Saddle River, NJ: Prentice Hall.

[289]
Personality Disorder Interview—IV: A Semistructured Interview for the Assessment of Personality Disorders.

Purpose: Constructed to "facilitate reliable and valid interview assessments of ... personality disorders."
Population: Ages 18 and older.
Publication Date: 1994–1995.
Acronym: PDI—IV.
Scores, 21: 12 Personality Disorder Scores (Antisocial, Avoidant, Borderline, Dependent, Histrionic, Narcissistic, Obsessive-Compulsive, Paranoid, Schizoid, Schizotypal, Depressive, Passive-Aggressive); 9 Thematic Content Area Scores (Attitudes Toward Self, Attitudes Toward Others, Security/Comfort with Others, Friendships and Relationships, Conflicts and Disagreements, Work and Leisure, Social Norms, Mood, Appearance and Perception).
Administration: Individual.
Price Data, 1996: $85 per complete kit including hardcover manual ('95, 277 pages), Personality Disorders Interview Booklet, Thematic Content Areas Interview Booklet, and 10 profile booklets; $11 per interview booklet (specify Personality Disorders or Thematic Content Areas); $19 per 10 profile booklets; $42 per hardcover manual.
Time: [120] minutes.
Comments: Corresponds with DSM—IV Personality Disorder diagnosis criteria.
Authors: Thomas A. Widiger, Steve Mangine, Elizabeth M. Corbitt, Cynthia G. Ellis and Glenn V. Thomas.
Publisher: Psychological Assessment Resources, Inc.

Review of the Personality Disorder Interview—IV: A Semistructured Interview for the Assessment of Personality Disorders by SAMUEL JUNI, Professor, Department of Applied Psychology, New York University, New York, NY:

The Personality Disorder Interview-IV (PDI-IV) is presented by its authors as a nonvalidated instrument intended to facilitate a more systematic assessment that may provide reliable and valid scores. The PDI does not include a validity scale, and it relies heavily on self-report, which is then evaluated unsystematically by each interviewer. Interviewers are free to implement revisions and are encouraged to ask additional questions. Requests for examples are to be considered for each question. The authors state: "An advantage of a semi-structured interview is that everyone who uses it will presumably be providing consistent, uniform assessments." I find this assertion inconsistent with the inherent unreliability of the procedure. To a psychometrician, the attempt to evaluate an instrument billed by its authors as lacking validity and having questionable reliability can be perplexing. As such, I have taken the approach of evaluating the PDI as a general outgrowth of DSM.

The instrument consists of a book, two questionnaires, and sheets for responses, scoring, and scaling. The book presents, for each criterion, an overview of history and rationale, the PDI-IV ratings, the interview questions, and a discussion of problems and issues. The interview consists of questions for each of the 93 diagnostic criteria of the 12 personality disorders. The inventory is apparently limited to adults over the age of 25. Two questionnaires are available, arranged in thematic and DSM order respectively. The advantages of the two interview formats are discussed. Notable is the caution against contextual distortions for interviewers who use the thematic content format. For an axis that is a relatively small part of DSM, the PDI is very large. One can only imagine the encyclopedic proportions of such a protocol were it to be developed for the entire DSM.

Despite the recommendation in DSM-IV to rank multiple diagnoses, no algorithm for such ranking is offered in the PDI-IV. The ratings differ from competing systems (e.g., the Personality Disorder Interview [PIQ] revisions of which were the predecessors of the PDI) by dispensing with the cumbersome 10-point scales in favor of just 3. However, being that DSM requires only a "hit" or "miss" for the items, the inclusion of a third supra-clinical rating for severity is excessive and ultimately complicates an already threateningly large protocol. Similarly, the PDI procedures that differentiate among PD items (both within and between criteria sets) exceed the requirements of DSM and unduly complicate the process.

The PDI is contrasted to alternate protocols, which measure some of the PDs with little room for professional judgement in item scoring, yielding more reliable but less valid results. Some of these, because they take self-reports at face value, result in overdiagnoses of PDs.

Each interview begins with a solicitation of major events, issues, and incidents experienced since late childhood. Overall, the PDI calls for open-ended clinical techniques to elicit information, by having the diagnostician ask for examples liberally. This feature is so important that it probably should have been featured in the actual interview booklets instead of being contained only in the book. Specifically, I would have spelled out two useful queries: "Tell me more" and the open-ended "How come?"

PDI questions are presented as initial inquiries. In addition, many items are assessed by indirect questions. Interviewers are discouraged from skipping an entire criterion even if its designation seems to be a foregone conclusion, but may skip items. Some "issues and problems" occasionally presented may not seem problematical to the seasoned diagnostician. Consider the "problem" of assessing flat affect. The authors of the PDI fail to include the elementary questions: "How often do you cry?" or "Do you laugh a lot?" stressing instead observational data, insisting that the evaluation of this criterion must be left to observation. The authors recognize validational problems with interviewing, such as mood distortions. Also discussed in this context are the more general "state vs. trait" issues, which complicate characterological diagnostics.

The PDI can be administered by lay interviewers, given appropriate training and supervision. Besides experience, this would require certain qualification of the "good interviewer" characteristics that are difficult to assess. The authors pay lip service to these problems, but do little to resolve them. The interview is estimated to last 2 hours. The authors suggest verifying data by interviewing an additional informant. The authors encourage the interviewer to verify data using a self-report inventory. They are reminiscent of limitations one may put at the end of the study as suggestive for further research, but are not appropriate in a document intended as a practical guide to diagnostics.

In the introduction to the interview, the respondent is informed that the assessment is related to the respondent's personality. Because personality is basically deduced from the responses to behavioral or affective questions, I fail to see the rationale of burdening (or biasing) the respondent with the information that the interview is personality oriented. I do not see the ethics of informed consent as invading such nuances of information-gathering intentions.

In the book, the authors demonstrate their detailed knowledge of DSM history, and the detailed evolution of this system. It is most interesting for artifactual historians of the politics of psychopathology or to those interested in the social evolution of nosology or the taxonomy of disorder. It is, moreover, a wide window into the world of clinical committee deliberations. Much of the book is irrelevant, given its detail, to the clinician or objective researcher. The book seems more of a vehicle for the authors to present historical aspects of the DSM, and this washes out the salience of its most relevant aspects. I would suggest a condensed manual separate from the book (similar to that for the Wechsler Adult Intelligence Scale, Third Edition; WAIS-III), although it is likely that the questionnaires as they exist now may well suffice and render a manual unnecessary.

The authors place heavy emphasis on the DSM criteria. The literal value of DSM is gleaned from vexing issues, where the authors grapple with the designation of disorders within Axis I versus Axis II, with the notion that differential diagnostic or treatment implications would follow. Such debates referenced throughout the book suggest that the categorization issues have taken precedence over the more conceptual issues that probably served as the basis for these opinions. At times, the debate seems to be functionally autonomous from the issues, as occurs (for example) when the options of multiple diagnoses are referenced almost as nosologically pure entities rather than clinically determined questions. Consider, for example, the statement, "Multiple PD diagnoses are inconsistent with the theory that personality disorders represent distinct clinical symptoms." It would appear that the authors are confusing the rules of clinical classification with theory.

Overall, well-worded questions and queries operationalize the DSM items. Pitfalls and distracters are well ironed out. To the professional, the questions appear quite intuitive and straightforward. To the inexperienced in diagnostics, some of the items will doubtless appear as arbitrary. It is not clear, however, toward which level of professional this work is oriented. It would appear that the detailed questions would be unnecessarily stifling for the experienced professional if they were to be taken as a set protocol. The inexperienced will likely be daunted by the seemingly excessive details and will probably find the protocol overwhelming. Experienced professionals will probably use the questionnaire minimally. I view it as a transitional tool for the new diagnostician as she or he establishes comfort with Axis II. Ultimately, such interviewers will either modify the questionnaire idiosyncratically, or dispense with it altogether. Thus, the tool is probably destined to become obsolete as users become more familiar with it.

Although primarily user friendly, the readability of the book is hampered by acronyms. Some of these Axis II abbreviations are not quite intuitive. Consider, for example, AVD for Avoidant, PND for Paranoid, DPS for Depressive, BDL for Borderline, OCP for Obsessive-Compulsive, and ANT for Anti-Social. It is inexcusable that these acronyms are not even defined until chapter 4, well after countless mentions in the previous chapters. Inexplicably, the acronyms are defined outright only in the Thematic Content Area Interview Booklet, but not in the PDI-IV Interview Booklet. In addition, some acronyms for Axis I diagnoses are defined once and then used liberally in the text, with little chance the reader will memorize them (e.g., GSP, etc.). The PDI-IV Interview Booklet, furthermore, begins with the ATS personality disorder, first featuring ATS-C, where the meaning of C is not explained, although one might judge contextually that it refers to conduct disorder. This is followed by criteria ATS-A1 through ATS-A7, where the appended A is never explained. This contrasts with the subsequent personality disorders where the criteria are simply sequenced in number (e.g., AVD-1 through AVD-7) with no letters appended at all.

The PDI uses occasional idioms in good taste (e.g., "stick to your guns" in OBC-8-g, "wallflower" in HST-1-b) but sounds rather pedantic at times. I would suggest more idioms to keep rapport with respondents maximal. For example, paranoid ideation can be elicited by asking patients whether they felt that others "had it in for them."

Some of the language in items seems to be oriented toward a relatively sophisticated level. Consider, for example, "moral code" (OBC-4-a), "defeatist" (DPS-6-c) which is used to substitute for the simpler term of "pessimistic" used in the actual DSM criterion, "luckless" (PAG-6-b), "sullen" (DPS-1-b), "delegating responsibility" (OBC-6-0b), and "promoted to their level of incompetence" (PAG-4-a).

One of the hazards of true-false item construction is the inclusion of conjunctives that render the intent of an item response ambiguous (Juni & Koenig, 1982) because it is not clear whether the respondent refers to all or some of the item elements. The presence of these conjunctives in the PDI is due to the fact that its authors simply mirrored multidimensional DSM criteria. Alas, what holds true for multifaceted criteria cannot simply be transformed into items. As examples, consider the question whether others find one's behaviors as peculiar, odd, *or* weird (SZT-7-a); whether the respondent feels uncomfortable *or* nervous (AVD-1-a). Conjunctives unnecessarily muddy the form of nontest PDI items as well. Even the very introductory question, where respondents are asked to describe major issues in their life, includes the options of referring to events since late childhood *or* adolescence. Why offer such options, which will only introduce nonuniformity into the responses? A problem related to the inclusion of conjunctives in items results from some question formats that reference a supposition and its qualification. In such a case, it is no clear to which of these the respondent is reacting. Consider, for example, the question whether one feels guilty about one's defiance (PAG-7-c). Does the response of "No" signify the lack of guilt or the lack of defiance?

One feature of the PDI is to have occasional items where the respondent is asked to become the diagnostician. Consider the question: "Do you think that some of much of this behavior represents a difficulty within your own personality?" (PAG-7-c). Other items ask the respondents whether others have considered them to have a personality problem. Consider the question, for example, "Has anyone ever accused you of being passive-aggressive?" (PAG-1-d). Are these unnamed others being used as ad hoc diagnosticians? Are these items meant to save the diagnostician time or energy, and are they reliable means of assessment? Similar item inadequacies are reflected in the question: "Do you have any unusual superstitions?" (SZT-2-a). Is it wise to leave the categorization of beliefs, and their normative frequency, to the respondent?

SUMMARY. This is a large work, approaching unwieldiness, with questionable utility. Its intent ranges from operationalizing Axis II to the elaboration of its history and related issues. These are accomplished only partially. The use of this tool as a research instrument is viable, but some item anomalies impact on its overall reliability.

REVIEWER'S REFERENCE

Juni, S., & Koenig, E. J. (1982). Contingency validity as a requirement in forced-choice item construction: A critique of the Jackson Vocational Interest Survey. *Measurement and Evaluation in Guidance, 14*, 202–207.

Review of the Personality Disorder Interview-IV: A Semistructured Interview for the Assessment of Personality Disorders by PAUL RETZLAFF, Professor, Psychology Department, University of Northern Colorado, Greeley, CO:

The Personality Disorder Interview-IV (PDI-IV) is an interview process that aids in the diagnosis of personality disorders. It provides extensive information on the criteria associated with 12 personality disorders. The "test" is primarily a book and associated worksheets. It is not conceptualized as a test in the formal sense and therein lie some problems.

The text provides detailed descriptions for each of the personality disorders including Antisocial, Avoidant, Borderline, Dependent, Histrionic, Narcissistic, Obsessive-Compulsive, Paranoid, Schizoid, Schizotypal, Depressive, and Passive-Aggressive. The descriptions cover the changes in the criteria from DSM-III-R to DSM-IV. Rationale for the changes are detailed. Then each of the DSM-IV criteria are presented, discussed, and examples are given. There are three worksheets. The first is a very extensive 66-page Interview Booklet that includes the DSM-IV criteria, a 3-point rating of the answer, and further questions to flesh out the effect on the patient's life. The second booklet covers the content from a thematic perspective and is 65 pages in length. The final worksheet is a summary sheet with the number of criteria met for each of the disorders. The cover of this sheet includes a profile system that attaches levels to various numbers of criteria met. Disorder levels are categorized as absent, traits, subthreshold, threshold, moderate, or extreme.

As available with the text and worksheets, the interview procedure is rich in history, clinical insight, and political agreement. As a test, however, the materials are well below that expected. As it stands, the questions may be viewed as items keyed to the 12 scales. These are well presented. There is, however, no evidence of norms nor evidence of reliability or validity for the current version.

Indeed, there is no evidence in the current text that the interview was ever given to a group of subjects.

Earlier versions of the interview are briefly mentioned in the first few pages of the first chapter. Here there is some evidence of psychometric quality of these earlier versions. Kappa statistics indicating agreement between judges are presented and for earlier versions are generally in the .30 to .80 ranges with medians in the .60 to .70 range. There is no mention of sample norms nor internal consistency reliabilities for the earlier questions.

The PDI-IV needs some data. There should be some evidence of the types of scores one would find for various samples of patients. Are the means for the scales higher for chronic alcohol abusers than for college students? What are the means and standard deviations for a mixed sample of inpatients and outpatients? Further, the data should be submitted to internal consistency analysis. What are the reliabilities of the scales? Do the ratings of the individual items tend to load well within scales? What are the item-total correlations for the questions? Do some items correlate higher with other scales than their own?

An intercorrelation of scales would be nice. Are the scales specific or do a number of scales correlate highly with one another? What is the factor structure to the 12 scales? With regard to judge variability, what are the Kappa statistics or simple correlations for the current version of the interview? Are all scales equally reliable with regard to interviewers? A study looking at judge agreement with several hundred subjects is necessary.

Finally, are the scale scores valid? Where is the evidence that the scores from the interview scales validly predict personality disorders? A study looking at patients of known diagnosis is needed. Failing that, a study of construct validity would be useful. A number of tests such as the Millon Clinical Multiaxial Inventory (MCMI; 236) are cited early in the work as a basis for some of the decisions. Where is the study correlating the interview with psychological tests such as the MCMI-III (236) or MMPI-II (T5:1697)? Along this same line, work is needed to validate the cut scores. There is no evidence that a score of 4 on Paranoid is at "threshold" or a score of 4 on Schizotypal is "subthreshold."

SUMMARY. A great deal of work has gone into the PDI-IV. It is clinically very rich. It does an excellent job of making the reader think about criteria and the questions necessary to map those criteria. As a textbook, it is excellent. As a test, however, it is very poorly documented. There are no norms, specific or broad-based. There is no evidence of reliability or validity. As such, users are cautioned.

[290]
Personnel Relations Survey [Revised].

Purpose: "Designed to assess the understanding and behavior of managers in their interpersonal relationships."
Population: Managers.
Publication Dates: 1967–1995.
Acronym: PRS.
Scores, 6: Relationships with Employees (Exposure, Feedback); Relationships with Colleagues (Exposure, Feedback); Relationships with Superiors (Exposure, Feedback).
Administration: Group.
Manual: No manual.
Price Data, 1997: $8.95 per test booklet.
Time: Administration time not reported.
Comments: Self-administered, self-scored; based on the Johari Window Model of interpersonal relationships.
Authors: Jay Hall and Martha S. Williams.
Publisher: Teleometrics International, Inc.

Review of the Personnel Relations Survey [Revised] by MATTHEW E. LAMBERT, Research Neuropsychologist, Neurology Research Education Center at St. Mary Hospital, Lubbock, TX:

The Personnel Relations Survey [Revised] (PRS) is a 1986 revision designed to update the Personnel Relations Survey originally developed by Jay Hall and Martha S. Williams in 1967. The PRS is a self-evaluation instrument designed to help managers understand how they contribute to and control informational processes between themselves and others. It is based on the Johari Window model of interpersonal relations developed during the latter 1960s and stemmed from work in group dynamics training. The goal of the instrument is to provide the manager with an understanding of his or her interpersonal communication style in relation to employees, colleagues, and supervisors. Interpersonal communication style is defined in terms of two informational sources, self and others; or the willingness to disclose information about self to others (Exposure) and the willingness to elicit information from others (Feedback). As a result of gaining awareness of

interpersonal style, the manager should then be able to make adjustments in behavior to improve interpersonal communication and organizational efficiency.

The PRS consists of the first six pages of a 15 page booklet that also includes scoring, interpretation, and psychometric data about the instrument. A discussion of the Johari Window model of interpersonal relations is also included and designed to assist the manager completing the PRS to understand how his or her individual profile may reflect positive and negative experiences with employees, colleagues, and supervisors. The PRS is divided into three 20-item sections each addressing relationships with employees, colleagues, and supervisors. Ten items in each section address interpersonal style related to Exposure, with 10 corresponding items addressing interpersonal style related to Feedback. The items are ordered so as to alternate between those associated with Exposure and Feedback. Raw Exposure and Feedback scores are tallied for each section then converted to percentiles and plotted on a Johari Window grid. Interpretation can then be undertaken by comparing the plotted profile to four interpersonal style types described in the manual, and what would be considered desirable in terms of exposure and feedback for a given interpersonal relationship. Comparison can also be made between individual scores for Exposure and feedback and those produced by managers in eight different organizational settings.

Reliability and validity data presented in the booklet are rather sparse, however. This may be due to the way in which the survey is packaged: as an instrument to be self-administered, self-scored, and self-interpreted. Yet, sufficient information should be provided to allow an adequate assessment of the instrument and its applicability to the situation or purpose for which it is selected. This includes a full description of the populations used for determining reliability and validity, which is not provided in the booklet. A footnote is included with the scoring instructions indicating normative data are based on scores of 12,809 managers who completed the PRS. It is stated that the PRS norms are updated periodically and the above number represents the current PRS sample being used.

As such, no information is provided as to how items were generated and then selected for inclusion in the final instrument. Reliability is described in terms of internal consistency with alpha coefficients of .78 and .80 for the Exposure and Feedback dimensions and a mean coefficient of equivalence for the revised version of .78. Test-retest reliability is not evaluated. A brief discussion of validity is included within the paragraph that also discusses reliability. According to that information, "the instrument discriminates among high, average, and low achieving managers, some thirteen organizational types and five Managerial Grid styles" (p. 6). Discrimination coefficients are not provided, however. Nor is there any discussion of how managerial achievement was determined or the organizational types and Managerial Grid styles to which reference is made. Construct and concurrent validities are stated to have been established through analyses with the Minnesota Multiphasic Personality Inventory (MMPI), the Comprehensive Personality Inventory (CPI), and Bass's Famous Sayings Test, with canonical correlations being .69, .87, and .79, respectively. Again, specific constructs used are not discussed so that understanding of the validity being ascribed to the PRS can be determined. Probably of greater concern, there does not appear to have been a direct test to determine if the PRS actually measures the constructs of Exposure and Feedback embodied in this particular adaptation of the Johari Window model of interpersonal relations. Numerous references to previous studies in which the PRS has been used are presented along with discussion of the major findings from each study.

SUMMARY. In conclusion, the PRS poses to have significant potential for understanding aspects of managers' interpersonal communication styles. An understanding of exposure and feedback styles may then enable managers to alter behavior so as to improve their communication and improve managerial effectiveness. Nevertheless, insufficient information is included in the booklet to fully examine its reliability and validity data such that reasonable decisions can be made when selecting the instrument for specific purposes. This could easily be addressed by including additional information in the booklet or providing a supplement that provides detailed reliability and validity data.

[291]
Photo Articulation Test, Third Edition.

Purpose: Constructed as a "systematic method for eliciting speech sounds from children and identifying errors in articulation."

Population: Ages 3–8.
Publication Dates: 1969–1997.
Acronym: PAT-3.
Scores: Total score only.
Administration: Individual.
Price Data, 1999: $144 per complete kit.
Time: (20) minutes.
Authors: Barbara A. Lippke, Stanley E. Dickey, John W. Selmar, and Anton L. Sodor.
Publisher: PRO-ED.
Cross References: See T5:1982 (15 references), T4:2017 (12 references), 9:957 (2 references), and T3:1814 (5 references); for a review of an earlier edition by Lawrence D. Shriberg, see 8:969 (1 reference); see also 7:962 (2 references).

Review of the Photo Articulation Test, Third Edition by DAVID P. HURFORD, Director of the Center for the Assessment and Remediation of Reading Difficulties and Professor of Psychology and Counseling, Pittsburg State University, Pittsburg, KS:

The Photo Articulation Test, Third Edition (PAT-3) is an articulation inventory that is used to elicit speech sounds from children aged 3 through 8 years so that errors in articulation can be identified. As is the case with any test of articulation, the administrator should have formal training in the assessment of articulation. Although the PAT-3 has no time limits, administration typically is completed in 10 to 15 minutes. The inventory is composed of 69 photographs, which the child is asked to name, and 6 items in which the child is either asked to repeat a word (e.g., say "measure," "beige," etc.) or to answer a particular question to elicit the particular speech sounds of interest. Last, the child is asked to tell a story about the last set of three stimulus pictures (Frames 70 to 72) to evaluate not only specific speech sounds, but to evaluate the child's speech and language characteristics (i.e., voice quality, language use, fluency, and intelligibility).

The PAT-3 was standardized with a norming group of 800 children from 24 states that included children with speech and language disabilities. The normative sample was very similar to the demographic characteristics of the United States population. The PAT-3 provides standard scores, percentiles, and age equivalents. Although age equivalents have been extensively criticized, the authors of the PAT-3 reluctantly provide them for administrative purposes of the agencies that use the inventory.

Reliability was evaluated by using internal consistency and interrater reliability indices. Internal consistency was assessed by computing coefficient alphas for each of the six age levels (3, 4, 5, 6, 7, and 8 years). Coefficient alphas ranged from .87 (for 7-year-olds) to .94 (for 5-year-olds) with a mean of .91 when age level was collapsed. Coefficient alpha estimates were also calculated for males, females, African Americans, Hispanics, and children with speech and language disorders by age level. These values were quite similar to those reported above with a range of .75 to .98 and a mean of approximately .92. These values indicate that scores from the PAT-3 produce a reliable measure of articulation for children between 3 and 8 years of age regardless of gender, minority group status, or speech and language status.

Interscorer reliability was evaluated by examining the results of two individuals who independently scored 20 completed PAT-3 protocols. Although this method assesses the likelihood of arriving at similar results when the protocols have been completed by a speech-language pathologist, it does not directly evaluate interrater reliability. To adequately evaluate this type of reliability requires that two individuals independently administer the PAT-3 to the same child, transcribe the utterances of the child, and then score the protocol. Although the authors report an average internal consistency reliability coefficient of .92 and an interscorer reliability of .96, a comprehensive analysis of reliability would have included interrater reliability.

Validity was examined by considering content validity, criterion-related validity, and construct validity. The PAT-3 assesses all of the consonants, vowels, and diphthongs used in the English language. The PAT-3 also includes nine blends. The stimulus items that form the inventory came from the first 4,000 words of the Thorndike and Lorge (1944) word list. Although there are more contemporary word lists available, the Thorndike and Lorge word list is adequate. Item discrimination was also used to examine content validity. There is an inherent difficulty in using item discrimination in a test such as the PAT-3 in which most individuals taking the test will respond incorrectly on very few of the items. In fact, most children taking the PAT-3 made fewer than 10% incorrect responses. As such, it seems that the test would not be capable of discriminating between individuals who have varying ability. It must be remembered that the purpose of the PAT-3 is to identify children who have not appropriately developed their speech and language skills. As a result, item discrimination is not as compelling as it might be for other types of tests. Although moderate, the item discrimination coefficients ranged from .29 (for 7-year-olds) to .39 (for 6-year-olds) and are sufficient for an articulation inventory. Delta scores were computed to evaluate item bias. The Delta scores for the dichotomous groups of gender (male/female), race (white/nonwhite), and ethnicity (Hispanic/non-Hispanic) were .97, .89, and .94. These values strongly indicate that the items are not biased.

Concurrent validity was evaluated by comparing the PAT-3 scores with those of the Test of Language Development—Primary, Third Edition (TOLD-P:3). Twenty children aged 47 to 70 months were given the PAT-3 and the Word Articulation subtest of the TOLD-P:3. The resulting correlation coefficient was .85 indicating that the PAT-3 scores were closely related to another test purporting to assess articulation.

Evidence for construct validity was provided by examining age and group differentiation. Articulation ability develops with age. Therefore, the PAT-3 scores, which reflect articulation errors, should be inversely related with age. For males the correlation coefficient was -.52 and for females was -.47. These values reflect what was theoretically expected, thus providing evidence of construct validity. Group differentiation refers to the PAT-3's ability to identify children with known articulation difficulties from those who do not have articulation difficulties. The mean standard score of the group of 335 children with articulation disorders evaluated in the standardization sample was 77. This value represents a group mean more than a standard deviation below the standardized group mean and supports the contention that the PAT-3 has construct validity.

The manual is concise and complete. The novice user of the PAT-3 will not find it difficult to comprehend the administration or scoring procedures. The PAT-3 is a very useful test to assess articulation difficulties. If the speech-language pathologist takes extensive notes, it would be possible to develop constructive remedial interventions for children whose speech and language skills have not properly developed. Conversely, the manual does not indicate uses other than as a test for articulation difficulties. No framework has been developed to guide speech-language pathologists to use the PAT-3 for remedial processes.

SUMMARY. The PAT-3 is an articulation inventory developed for children aged 3 to 8 years. The photographs used to elicit the speech sounds are engaging. It has acceptable psychometric properties, excluding interrater reliability, which was not addressed.

[292]
Police Selection Test.

Purpose: "Designed to measure abilities important for successful performance in training and on-the-job" as a police officer.
Population: Police officer applicants.
Publication Dates: 1989–1995.
Acronym: PST.
Scores: Total score only.
Administration: Group.
Price Data: Price information available from publisher for test material including Technical manual ('90, 17 pages), Administrator's Guide ('90, 8 pages), and Study Guide and sample questions ('90, 21 pages).
Time: (120) minutes.
Comments: Measures reading comprehension, quantitative problem solving, data interpretation, writing skills, and verbal problem solving.
Author: Psychological Services, Inc.
Publisher: Psychological Services, Inc.

Review of the Police Selection Test by JIM C. FORTUNE, Professor of Educational Research and Evaluation, Virginia Tech University, Blacksburg, VA:

PURPOSE. The Police Selection Test was designed to measure abilities important for successful performances in police training and on-the-job. The test is an entry-level test designed to select candidates for admission to the basic training program for police work.

DESCRIPTION. The test is a group-administered, multiple-choice test made up of 100 items organized in five sections. These sections include:

Section 1—reading comprehension—19 items measuring the ability to read, interpret, and apply information associated with police work.

Section 2—quantitative problem solving—20 items measuring the ability to work with number relationships, patterns, and organization principles.

Section 3—interpretation—23 items measuring the ability to read and use charts, tables, and maps and to follow written directions.

Section 4—writing skills—15 items measuring the ability to communicate with written language.

Section 5—verbal problem solving—23 items measuring the ability to use facts and make judgments from them.

RATIONALE. Criteria for any selection test for employment include: linkage of its content with the jobs for which the selection is being made and coverage of the relevant content, reliability, administrative ease, and production of results from which valid interpretations can be made. The linkage of content with the jobs for which the selection is being made is established through a quality job analysis. The coverage of the relevant content is assured through the table of specifications. Reliability must be adequate to make decisions on individuals and is shown through prestudy of the test performance. The manual for test administration gives evidence of administrative ease. The production of results from which valid interpretations can be made is evidenced through reported validity studies. These criteria form the basis for the review of the technical characteristics of this selection test.

TECHNICAL INFORMATION. The Technical Manual is concise, written with clarity, and easy to use. Perhaps its greatest fault is the omission of details needed to track the test development process.

The Technical Manual refers to but does not adequately describe the job analysis. The developers of the test report that three sources of information were used to determine job-relevant item types. It is assumed that determination of "item types" actually means test content. The sources were comprehensive job analysis, research literature, and police personnel. The job analysis was not described and a brief description of a meta-analysis is the information given on the literature search. Content selection appeared to be linked to training tests through current validity studies with training tests. Police personnel were asked to remember items that differentiated the most between superior and poor police performers. It appears that the linkage of content was made with the training for the job rather than with the job. It is unclear how the test developers assured the coverage of the relevant content. The Technical Manual does include a paragraph explaining that knowledge of the law, department rules and regulations, and police procedures must be obtained on the job and are not appropriate for entry-level testing. Knowledge of human psychology and behavior should be part of the test as well as trainee personality and philosophical traits.

In the Technical Manual reliability in the form of coefficient alpha was reported for what was described as the total test scores, but it was actually a pooled estimate of the reliabilities of the subtest scores. This coefficient was .94, which is judged to be adequate to make decisions on individuals. The subtest reliabilities were not reported. The manual for test administration is brief and straightforward, serving as evidence of administrative ease. The production of results from which valid interpretations can be made is evidenced through reported validity studies linking test performance to training outcomes. The validation study linking the test to outcomes provided a product moment correlation of .53 corrected up for attenuation to .65. Note that this validity index is for success in the training program and not on the job.

EVALUATION. The test contains similar content to other police selection tests, but it is very important to note that the content is directed toward selection for training and not for the job. The test does not appear comprehensive enough to serve as a total criterion for selection, but it appears to be quite useful as part of a selection battery.

Review of the Police Selection Test by DENIZ S. ONES, Hellervik Professor of Industrial-Organizational Psychology, Department of Psychology, University of Minnesota, Minneapolis, MN:

As early as 1917, industrial-organizational psychologists looked for, created, or used ability tests in police personnel selection (e.g., Terman et al., 1917). This is with good reason: Police are entrusted with public safety and hiring incompetent police officers endangers public safety. The Police Selection Test (PST) was designed to test some of the abilities important to successful law enforcement and therefore, presumably, was developed to enable police departments to select the highest ability job applicants for the job.

DESCRIPTION. The purpose of the PST is to measure the ability of entry-level job candidates for police officer jobs. That is, the test is designed to predict "successful performance in training and on the job" (technical manual, p. 1) for police officers. It is intended for use with law enforcement job applicants. This ability test has a total of 100 items and is composed of five subsections

with various numbers of items (see test development description below).

TEST DEVELOPMENT. Test development focused on abilities rather than job knowledge because it was important to be able to test job applicants at the entry level prior to acquiring specific job knowledge. It is expected that most of the job knowledge required to be a successful police officer would be acquired in training or later on the job. The domains to be tested by the PST were identified by drawing upon three sources: (a) job analytic information, (b) the research literature, and (c) job experts (police lieutenants). That is, development of the content of the PST was based on a detailed and comprehensive review of job analyses for police officer jobs coupled with a quantitative literature review on police selection using ability measures. In particular, test development heavily drew upon the findings of the Hirsch, Northrop, and Schmidt (1986) meta-analysis showing that across multiple studies and police departments, ability test showed sizable operational validities for predicting performance in training. In this meta-analysis, the operational validity of verbal ability tests for predicting training performance was .62. Police lieutenants were also involved in test development as job experts. They were asked to think of superior and unsuccessful police officers they knew and then to identify the characteristics that differentiated them. Characteristics that were consistently identified were included in the PST.

The subsections of the test are as follows: (a) reading comprehension, (b) quantitative problem solving (number series), (c) interpretation (ability to read charts, tables, maps, and instructions), (d) writing skills, and (e) verbal problem solving (verbal reasoning). Initially, 200 items were written and administered to 2,112 police officer job applicants (of the developmental sample providing demographic information on sex and race, the breakdown was as follows: 1,615 males, 487 females, 973 Whites, 876 Blacks, and 107 Hispanics). Items were written so that they did not contain any material that could be offensive to any ethnic group or sex. Two members of the test development team examined each item that was included on the experimental test.

Item analyses examined item difficulty, effectiveness of multiple-choice response option distracters, item-total and item-remainder correlations, and item bias. Items that were too difficult or too easy were eliminated. Poor distracters were identified by excluding those items with high distracter-total correlations. Also, distracters that were not being selected by many respondents were also identified as poor. Item-total correlations were examined to select those items yielding the highest item-total correlations. Item bias analyses used two different methods. First, items that were found to have differential probability of correct response for persons of the same ability level but different race were removed (Berk, 1982). Second, items that were disproportionately difficult for Hispanics and Blacks were removed (Angoff, 1982; Angoff & Ford, 1973).

The final measure includes 100 questions: 19 reading comprehension questions, 20 quantitative problem-solving questions, 23 interpretation questions, 15 writing skills questions, and 23 verbal problem-solving questions. All items are multiple choice. All but the verbal problem-solving questions use four response options (the last subscale uses three response options). Readability analyses of the test indicate that the mean reading ease index is at the 10th grade reading level.

RELIABILITY. The technical manual reports the reliability of the full test as .94 (reliability of the composite of five subsections included on the test). This reliability was computed on the developmental sample (n = 2,112).

CRITERION-RELATED VALIDITY. Given that for ability tests concurrent validities have been shown to approximate predictive validities (Barrett, Phillips, & Alexander, 1981), concurrent validity was investigated for the PST. For a sample of 105 police officers in training, overall scores on the PST were correlated with mean training test scores. In this validation study, the criterion was the mean of three job knowledge tests completed during training. Job relatedness of the criterion measures was established by expert judgments (by police officers). The observed correlation was .53. When this correlation was corrected for the downward biasing effects of unreliability in the criterion and direct range restriction, one obtains a more accurate estimate of the evaluation of the criterion-related validity of the test for performance in police training. This corrected correlation was .65. Thus, the PST is a valid predictor of acquiring the job knowledge necessary to be a good police officer. This level of criterion-related validity for training performance mirrors the previous litera-

ture on the validities of scores from ability tests for police work (Hirsch et al., 1986).

Another consideration relating to criterion-related validity is transportability of the validity. The technical manual makes a suggestion to ensure validity generalization to other law enforcement jobs: The test users should examine whether or not the job at hand is similar to the job for which the criterion-related validity was demonstrated. The cumulative literature from industrial psychology indicates that ability is the best predictor of job performance for entry level jobs and that validity generalizes across organizations, jobs, and situations (Schmidt, Ones, & Hunter, 1992). There is no reason to suspect that the validity of the PST will not be generalizable.

TEST FAIRNESS. The PST does reveal mean score differences between minorities and Whites (based on the information reported in the technical manual, I computed the mean Black-White difference to be .94 standard deviation units, favoring Whites). However, mean differences were also found on the criterion. The test publishers have examined the fairness of their test by computing subgroup validities for Blacks and Whites separately. Further, the regression lines for Blacks and Whites were compared. The results of these investigations revealed no differential validities for Blacks and Whites. Based on these data, the test was demonstrated to be fair to both Blacks and Whites in that training performance was not underestimated for Blacks.

NORMS. Mean and standard deviation information is available for the initial 2,112-participant developmental sample, as well as the 205-participant validation sample (broken out by racial group).

ADMINISTRATION AND USE. The subsections of the test are not separately timed but there is an overall 2-hour time limit to complete the 100 questions of the test. All the correct responses across all the sections of the test are summed to obtain an overall test score for each job applicant. The administrator's guide provides full text instructions to be read when administering the test. Scoring can be done by hand or by scanning machine. The scores on the PST can be used for ranking the job applicants, or a cutoff score can be established for hiring.

The ability items on the instrument are all job related, and therefore the test as a whole is likely to be perceived by applicants to be face valid. For example, the reading passage materials for the reading comprehension portion of the test were based on police introductory texts, police departmental notices, and manuals. This may enhance the usability of the measure for personnel selection. Further, because the test is not a measure of job knowledge and thus does not require any prior specialized training or knowledge, the test's usability for selecting entry level police work is enhanced.

MANUALS AND SUPPORTING DOCUMENTS. There are several manuals and supporting documents that accompany the PST. These are an informational brochure (7 pages), a study guide and sample questions (21 pages), an administrator's guide (8 pages), and a technical manual (17 pages). I found these materials to be extremely useful. Particularly the technical manual contained much of the psychometric information on the test.

SUMMARY. The PST is a good instrument. It is exemplary in making use of the past meta-analytic literature to guide test development. Further, the test's development and validation comply with the *Uniform Guidelines on Employee Selection Procedures* (U.S. Equal Employment Opportunity Commission, 1978) and the *Standards for Educational and Psychological Testing* of the American Psychological Association (AERA, APA, & NCME, 1985). The only psychometric data I found to be missing were on construct validity. Particularly, I would have liked to see some evidence of convergent and divergent validity. This should be reported in test manuals and can provide critically important information to potential users of the PST in designing *selection systems*. Also, both the test developers and users should continue to gather criterion-related validity for the criterion of job performance. These validity studies with the PST can contribute to future meta-analyses and can answer some important practical and scientific questions. Typically, ability tests have been shown to yield somewhat lower validities for job performance criteria than they do for training criteria (Hirsch et al., 1986). This has been attributed to both poor performance criteria (where raters have insufficient opportunity to observe) and the potential importance of noncognitive factors in police performance. To disentangle these two effects, it is essential that future validation studies with the PST attempt to develop good job performance criteria.

In 1917, Terman et al. wrote, "we know that 'general intelligence' can be measured with a fair degree of success, and we have reason to believe that this general intelligence, however we define it, is the most important single factor, apart from moral integrity, in determining fitness" (p. 18) for police positions. This statement still rings true over 80 years later. The PST appears to be a good measure of general cognitive ability and can be used as the cognitive ability component of police selection systems. As for "moral integrity," a class of tests referred to as integrity tests with fairly high demonstrated levels of criterion-related validity can be useful (Ones, Viswesvaran, & Schmidt, 1993).

REVIEWER'S REFERENCES

Terman, L. M., Otis, A. S., Dickson, V., Hubbard, J. K., Howard, L., Flanders, J. K., & Cassingham, C. C. (1917). A trial of mental and pedagogical tests in a civil service examination for policemen and firemen. *Journal of Applied Psychology, 1*(1), 17–29.

Angoff, W. H., & Ford, S. F. (1973). Item-race interaction on a test of scholastic aptitude. *Journal of Educational Measurement, 10*, 95–105.

U.S. Equal Employment Opportunity Commission, U.S. Civil Service Commission, U.S. Department of Labor, & U.S. Department of Justice. (1978). Uniform guidelines on employee selection procedures. *Federal Register, 43*, (166), 38295–38309.

Barrett, G. V., Phillips, J. S., & Alexander, R. A. (1981). Concurrent and predictive validity designs: A critical reanalysis. *Journal of Applied Psychology, 66*, 1–6.

Angoff, W. H. (1982). Use of difficulty and discrimination indices for detecting item bias. In R. A. Berk (Ed.), *Handbook of methods for detecting item bias* (pp. 96–116). Baltimore and London: The John Hopkins University Press.

Berk, R. A. (Ed.). (1982). *Handbook of methods for detecting item bias*. Baltimore, MD: The John Hopkins University Press.

American Educational Research Association, American Psychological Association, & National Council on Measurement in Education. (1985). *Standards for Educational and Psychological Testing*. Washington, DC: American Psychological Association, Inc.

Hirsch, H. R., Northrop, L. C., & Schmidt, F. L. (1986). Validity generalization results for law enforcement occupations. *Personnel Psychology, 39*, 399–420.

Schmidt, F. L., Ones, D. S., & Hunter, J. (1992). Personnel selection. *Annual Review of Psychology, 43*, 627–670.

Ones, D. S., Viswesvaran, C., & Schmidt, F. L. (1993). Comprehensive meta-analysis of integrity test validities: Findings and implications for personnel selection and theories of job performance. *Journal of Applied Psychology [Monograph], 78*, 679–703.

[293]
Portland Problem Behavior Checklist—Revised.

Purpose: "Developed to aid school and mental health personnel to identify problem behaviors, make classification or diagnostic decisions, and evaluate counseling, intervention, or behavior consultation procedures."

Population: Grades K–12.

Publication Dates: 1980–1992.

Acronym: PPBC-R.

Administration: Individual.

Price Data, 2001: $45 per complete kit; $20 per 25 male or female forms.

Time: Untimed.

Comments: Respondents are professionals working with children; scoring form also includes opportunity to report on "other" problems (those not specifically included as a subscale).

Author: Steven A. Waksman.
Publisher: Enrichment Press.
    a) FORM FOR FEMALES, GRADES K–6.
    Scores, 4: Conduct Problems, Peer Problems, Personal Problems, Total.
    b) FORM FOR FEMALES, GRADES 7–12.
    Scores, 5: Academic Problems, Personal Problems, Conduct Problems, Anxiety Problems, Total.
    c) FORM FOR MALES, GRADES K–6.
    Scores, 5: Conduct Problems, Academic Problems, Anxiety Problems, Peer Problems, Total.
    d) FORM FOR MALES, GRADES 7–12.
    Scores, 6: Academic Problems, Anxiety Problems, Peer Problems, Conduct Problems, Personal Problems, Total.
Cross References: For reviews by Terry A. Stinnett and John G. Svinicki of an earlier edition, see 10:287 (1 reference).

Review of the Portland Problem Behavior Checklist—Revised by THOMAS McKNIGHT, Psychologist, Private Practice, Spokane, WA:

The revised edition of the Portland Problem Behavior Checklist (PPBC-R), like its predecessor, is designed to help school personnel and mental health workers "identify problem behaviors, make classification or diagnostic decisions, and evaluate counseling, intervention, or behavioral consultation procedures" (manual, p. 1). This checklist rates 29 behaviors on a scale from 0–5 (*no problem* to *severe*) and provides a total score and a percentile rank for males, females, and the combined group, for students in Grades K–6 and Grades 7–12; mean scores, standard deviations, and standard errors of measurement are also available for different groupings. Identified problem areas for Grades K–6 boys include Conduct Problems, Academic Problems, Anxiety Problems, and Peer Problems. Identified problem areas for girls in these grades include only Conduct Problems, Peer Problems, and Personal Problems. For older students (Grades 7–12) identified problems for girls include Academic Problems, Personal Problems, Conduct Problems, and Anxiety Problems; added to the list for boys, in Grades 7–12, are Peer Problems.

Although designed for completion by a classroom teacher who has daily contact with the student, the checklist could be used with anyone (teacher, parent, school aid, counselor) who has ongoing contact with a student. Directions for administration and scoring are relatively clear but specific items seem rather general and there are no guidelines for "minor, moderate, severe" ratings.

From reading the manual, there is no sense this checklist was actually revised. Rather, it seems to have been renormed on 306 students from the "greater metropolitan" Portland, Oregon area, who were in Grades K–12, during the 1982–1983 school year. Information about numbers of male and female students in the sample and the number of students in the two grade groups (K–6 and 7–12) is presented in the manual but there is no information about ethnicity, family income, or level of intelligence. Thus, use of this checklist outside the greater Portland, Oregon area seems highly questionable and with normative information that is 17 years old, applicability even to this "greater metropolitan" area is questionable.

Split-half reliability estimate for all 306 subjects in the normative sample was high (alpha = .94). Test-retest reliability was based on one-month and one-week intervals. Correlations for the one-month interval varied from .61 for 6th grade students to .99 for 5th grade students. For the one-week interval, as expected, reliability coefficients are higher but information is not broken down by grade. The manual provides information about content and face validity for the checklist but construct validity studies produced rather weak correlation coefficients where scores on this checklist were compared to student scores on similar instruments. Concurrent validity is apparently based on a single study where the mean and standard deviation of the normative sample were compared to those for a group of 24 children "classified as emotionally disturbed" (manual, p. 8) and there was indication the PPBC-R did discriminate well between the two groups. No other concurrent validity studies were reported and there was no report of predictive validity.

SUMMARY. The author's notation that this checklist "appears to be an internally strong and very reliable instrument with excellent content and face validity" (manual, p. 8) seems reasonably supported by information reported in the manual. However, the conclusion it "also has good concurrent and construct validity" (manual, p. 8) is somewhat of an overstatement. The checklist is dated; normative information is some 17 years old and based on a very limited sample from a very small region. Normative information for this checklist is so limited that its utility is questionable, in almost any arena and adds little to the proliferation of behavior checklists. It cannot be recommended for general use by clinicians or school personnel where significant decisions about programs or students are made.

Review of the Portland Problem Behavior Checklist—Revised by ROBERT SPIES, Associate Director, Buros Institute of Mental Measurements, University of Nebraska—Lincoln, Lincoln, NE:

The Portland Problem Behavior Checklist— Revised (PPBC-R) is a 29-item, teacher-completed checklist of behavioral difficulties developed for students ranging from kindergarten through 12th grade. Each of the potential problems (e.g., overactive) is rated in a 6-point Likert-type format ranging from (0) *no problem* to (5) *severe*. Items are clustered into three to five factors depending on the student's sex and age, and two different hand-scored protocols exist that allow the checklist results to be easily computed into percentile only scores.

The PPBC-R has been reviewed previously and a variety of major and minor deficiencies with the instrument were specified (see 10:287). For additional detail on the substantive conceptual problems using the PPBC-R, the reader is referred to these reviews. However, because the publisher has updated the manual, the possibility existed that the checklist might have been subject to specific improvements. For this reason, this instrument was reexamined. Alas, hopes for systematic improvement in the PPBC-R were unrealized. The updated manual consists of only 12 pages and any changes made were cosmetic rather than substantive.

TEST DEVELOPMENT/STANDARDIZATION. Items were developed from a list of 275 problem behaviors listed by teachers in Portland, Oregon during the 1976–1977 school year. Teachers represented areas of expertise ranging from Head Start to high school. From this initial grouping of specific problems, the 29 most frequently mentioned behaviors were compiled. The initial sample population consisted of 217 randomly selected students in Portland, Oregon. During the 1982–1983 school year, data from another sample of 306 students were collected within the same geographic area for the revised version of this test. However, the data provided in the manual describing this process are limited and must be viewed as insufficient to generalize the results to different regional populations. In addition, the

stability of factor scores is especially questionable. Several scores (e.g., Peer Problems, Personal Problems, and Anxiety Problems) can be computed with as few as two or three checklist responses. The catchall category of "other problems" varies in item number (depending on sex and age) from 4 to 11. The PPBC-R (with only 29 initial items) is abbreviated by any standards as a useful instrument in the complex area of behavioral development. With the loss of these "other" items from its overall profile, the utility of the instrument becomes especially problematic.

RELIABILITY. The PPBC-R reports the results of a variety of split-half, test-retest, and interrater reliability studies that are within an acceptable range. Split-half reliability was .94 (n = 160) for males and .95 (n = 146) for females. Test-retest reliability for one-week intervals totaled .98 (n = 80) and one-month intervals were .81 (n = 239). Interrater reliability was reported at a modest .54 based upon the completion of the PPBC-R by a group of 35 participating teachers and a limited sample of their high school students (n = 37). No evidence of interrater reliability was cited for elementary school students who are the most likely subjects of a behavioral label. The most troublesome of all of these results is the absence of reliability data by their individual factors. Conclusions about the student difficulties should be substantiated by reference to both overall test reliability and to factor reliability. No tables are available in the manual to describe these crucial data.

VALIDITY. The manual reports a variety of statistical comparisons of the PPBC-R with other behavioral assessment instruments in an attempt to establish its construct validity. The AML Checklist, the Walker Problem Behavior Identification Checklist, the Piers-Harris Children's Self Concept Scale, and the Waksman Social Skills Rating Scale had modest overall correlations to the PPBC-R of .49 to .66. In addition, an analysis of a group of emotionally disturbed residential children contrasted to a normative sample suggested that the PPBC-R could discriminate between the two groupings of students. In light of the conceptual expansion of validity outlined by Messick (1989), however, these attempts to substantiate the PPBC-R as a valid instrument must be considered wholly insufficient.

SUMMARY. Previous reviewers of the PPBC-R have found numerous difficulties with this instrument that limit or preclude its use. These objections include insufficient numbers of test items and factors, inadequate manual documentation, limited scoring flexibility (percentile only), marginal evidence of some types of reliability and validity, and restricted potential for interpretation due to regional norms. Several other behavioral assessment instruments were suggested in place of the PPBC-R. From the time of the original publication of this checklist to the present time, instruments have become more sophisticated both as behavioral screeners (e.g., Systematic Screening for Behavior Disorders; Walker & Severson, 1992; T5:2607) and as multidimensional assessments (e.g., Behavior Assessment System for Children; Reynolds & Kamphaus, 1992; 40). In an environment that carries profound implications for students labeled emotionally or behaviorally disabled, the PPBC-R might best be regarded as an historical anachronism and relegated to the clinician's closet.

REVIEWER'S REFERENCES

Messick, S. (1989). Validity. In R. L. Linn (Ed.), *Educational measurement* (3rd ed., pp. 13–103). Washington, DC: American Council on Education and National Council for Measurement in Education.

Reynolds, C. R., & Kamphaus, R. W. (1992). *Behavior Assessment System for Children test and manual.* Circle Pines, MN: American Guidance System, Inc.

Walker, H. M., & Severson, H. H. (1992). *Systematic Screening for Behavior Disorders test and observer training manual.* Longmont, CO: Sopris West, Inc.

[294]
Posttraumatic Stress Diagnostic Scale.

Purpose: "Designed to aid in the diagnosis of posttraumatic stress disorder."
Population: Ages 17–65.
Publication Date: 1995.
Acronym: PDS.
Scores, 5: Symptom Severity Score, Number of Symptoms Endorsed, Symptom Severity Rating, Level of Impairment in Functioning, PTSD Diagnosis.
Administration: Group.
Price Data, 1997: $35 per hand scoring starter kit including manual (54 pages), 10 answer sheets, 10 scoring worksheets, and 1 scoring sheet; $117 per hand scoring reorder kit including 50 answer sheets, 50 scoring worksheets, and 1 scoring sheet; $17 per 25 MICROTEST Q answer sheets; $4.25 per MICROTEST Q profile report; $26 per manual; $35 per MICROTEST Q preview package including manual, answer sheets, and materials for 3 assessments.
Time: (10–15) minutes.
Author: Edna B. Foa.
Publisher: NCS (Minnetonka).
Cross References: See T5:2018 (1 reference).

Review of the Posttraumatic Stress Diagnostic Scale by STEPHEN N. AXFORD, Psychologist, Pueblo School District No. Sixty, Pueblo, CO, and University of Phoenix, Colorado Springs, CO:

With content aligned to DSM-IV criteria, the Posttraumatic Stress Diagnostic Scale (PDS) is a 49-item, paper-and-pencil or on-line, self-report clinical screening instrument designed to support assessment of the presence and severity of posttraumatic stress disorder (PTSD). As such, it is intended also to be used as a method for monitoring treatment progress. In fact, a computer-generated graphic Progress Report is available, utilizing NCS Assessments MICROTEST Q SYSTEM software, charting Symptom Severity and Number of Symptoms Endorsed. Although the PDS can be hand scored, a professional quality computer-generated interpretive report with tables, the Profile Report, is also available using the same software. The PDS requires approximately 10 to 15 minutes to administer and 5 minutes to score. Validated on clinical populations aged 18 to 65 years, the PDS is intended to be used with adults with at least eighth-grade reading level ability. As noted by the author, although clinical judgment may be used in deciding whether to administer the PDS to individuals falling outside the age range on which the PDS was normed, it should not be given to children because of the respective different DSM-IV criteria for diagnosing PTSD.

A well-written manual, cogently detailed, suitably addresses the conceptual and technical aspects of the PDS. As stated by the author and very evident in reviewing the test items, "the PDS was designed to correspond to DSM-IV diagnostic criteria for PTSD" (p. 3). Test items were revised following expert review. The PDS answer sheet, utilizing a combination of weighted or Likert-type, dichotomous-choice (i.e., "yes/no"), and multiple-selection formats, is well organized and professional appearing, offering ample face validity.

Subjects were recruited for the normative sample (N = 248) from: Veterans Administration hospitals, anxiety and PTSD treatment clinics, women's shelters, emergency/trauma centers, fire stations, ambulance corps, and residential rehabilitation centers. A prerequisite for inclusion in the study was that the trauma-inducing event had to occur at least one month prior to administration of the PDS.

The author provides a detailed summary of the demographic characteristics for the PDS normative sample, specifically by: age, race, marital status, religion, employment status, occupation, education, and income. The author also furnishes a tabulation of types of traumatic events reported by the normative sample. As noted by the author, the distribution of traumas represented in the PDS normative sample "should not be considered indicative of the likelihood of a particular type of trauma producing PTSD or of the general population of individuals with PTSD" (p. 5). The author further states that the frequency distribution observed "is in part a reflection of the sites at which the data were collected" (p. 5). Indeed, a review of the norming sample demographics supports this disclaimer. For example, under the category of religion, only 20.2% of the participants are listed as Protestant, whereas 30.8% are listed as Catholic. This is an understandable sampling limitation given that the PDS focuses on such a very specific area of differential diagnosis, with PTSD having relatively limited representation in the general population. Nevertheless, future studies involving the PDS, particularly as this relates to norming, should attempt larger and more representative samples.

Although norm-referenced scores are not reported, the test results for the PDS include six components: PTSD Diagnosis (i.e., "yes/no"), Symptom Severity Score (ranging from 0 to 51, based on summation of weighted responses for items corresponding to the 17 DSM-IV PTSD Criteria B, C, and D), Number of Symptoms Endorsed, symptom onset and duration specifiers (Acute, Chronic, With Delayed Onset), Symptom Severity Rating (Mild, Moderate, Moderate to Severe, Severe), and Level of Impairment of Functioning (No Impairment, Mild, Moderate, Severe). No validity index (e.g., measure of impression management) is provided. Future development and revision of the PDS should consider incorporation of such a component.

According to the author, "a diagnosis of PTSD is made if all six DSM-IV criteria ... are met" (p. 5), specifically: exposure to a traumatic event, reexperiencing symptoms, avoidance symptoms, arousal symptoms, symptom duration of one month or more, and distress or impairment in functioning. Cut-points for the Symptom Severity Ratings "are based on the author's clinical judgment and experience ... derived from a sample of 280 recent female assault victims and from a sample of 96 female assault victims with chronic

PTSD" (p. 10). Future validation of the Symptom Severity Rating index should involve independent review of the cut-points by a group of experts. In addition, to the author's credit, users of the PDS are encouraged to interpret Symptom Severity Ratings data with caution, due to lack of validation research and because only female subjects were employed in establishing the cut-points. Of course, this could potentially affect generalizability of results. The author states that "at present, these cutoffs should be used only to roughly estimate the relative symptom severity manifested by a given individual compared to other trauma victims" (p. 10). However, even this practice would be questionable with regard to male subjects until further validation research is conducted on the Symptom Severity Rating index.

The manual for the PDS provides detailed discussion of the inventory's psychometric properties. Included is a summary of means and standard deviations for the Symptom Severity Score and Number of Symptoms Endorsed indexes, for subjects meeting ($n = 128$) and not meeting ($n = 120$) Structured Clinical Interview for DSM-III-R (SCID) PTSD criteria. Mean scores for subjects meeting SCID criteria for PTSD are significantly higher ($p < .001$) than for subjects not meeting SCID criteria. The study also compares PDS and SCID percent diagnostic agreement, yielding 79.4% agreement between the two measures, with a kappa of .59. PDS sensitivity (ability to correctly identify PTSD subjects) is reported to be 82.0% for the study. Specificity for the study (ability to correctly identify subjects not having PTSD) is reported to be 76.7%. These findings lend support that scores from the PDS are valid for screening for PTSD.

Convergent validity for the PDS was investigated by correlating ($N = 230$) the Symptom Severity Score with scales measuring constructs (depression, intrusion, avoidance, anxiety) associated with PTSD. This approach was taken because of the dearth of scales, particularly screening instruments, specifically designed to identify PTSD. Correlations between the PDS and the scales measuring related constructs are as follows: Beck Depression Inventory = .79, State-Trait Anxiety Inventory (State index) = .73, State-Trait Anxiety Inventory (Trait index) = .74, Impact of Event Scale (Intrusion index) = .80, Impact of Event Scale (Avoidance index) = .66. Although these data support the convergent validity of scores from the PDS, future research employing comprehensive scales that can be used in the differential diagnosis of PTSD (e.g., Personality Assessment Inventory [Morey, 1991; 12:290]) would further address, perhaps more directly, the issue.

Both internal consistency and test-retest stability were examined in investigating the reliability of scores from the PDS. A Cronbach alpha of .92 is reported for the 17 items used to calculate the Symptom Severity Score, indicating that this index has high internal consistency. Representing 110 retests with an average interval between administration of 16.1 days, a kappa of .74 is reported, with 87.3% diagnostic agreement between administrations. These data support the internal consistency and stability of scores from the PDS.

SUMMARY. The PDS represents a substantial achievement in the initial development of a conceptually and psychometrically sound PTSD screening instrument based on DSM-IV criteria. Besides providing professional quality interpretive reports, the PDS offers the innovative advantage of a convenient method for charting treatment progress. However, as the author notes, additional validation research is needed for more precise interpretation of the Symptom Severity Rating index (one of six PDS test results components provided). Nevertheless, the PDS meets its main objective of validly and reliably differentiating PTSD from non-PTSD subjects. In addition, both in the manual and computer-generated diagnostic report, to the author's credit, appropriate interpretation and use of PDS results are adequately addressed. Although the PDS would benefit from additional validation research utilizing larger and perhaps demographically more representative samples, the PDS can appropriately be used as a clinical screening instrument for determining the presence of PTSD and charting changes in symptoms.

REVIEWER'S REFERENCE

Morey, L. C. (1991). Personality Assessment Inventory. Odessa, FL: Psychological Assessment Resources.

Review of the Posttraumatic Stress Diagnostic Scale by BETH DOLL, Associate Professor of Educational Psychology, University of Nebraska-Lincoln, Lincoln, NE:

The author describes the Posttraumatic Stress Diagnostic Scale (PDS) as a 49-item, self-report scale to assist clinicians and researchers in diagnosing and judging the severity of Posttraumatic Stress Disorder as it is defined in the DSM-IV

(*Diagnostic and Statistical Manual of Mental Disorders, Fourth Edition*; American Psychiatric Association, 1994). Despite this description, the PDS should be used principally as a research tool because evidence of its reliability and validity currently rests with a single, unreplicated study. As further evidence of the scale's technical adequacy emerges, the PDS could also prove to be a promising clinical tool.

The manual describes the use of the PDS in appropriately cautious terms. The author carefully advises that the scale not replace structured diagnostic interviews in making clinical decisions. The manual also notes that the scale should not be administered to persons under the age of 18, because the DSM-IV criteria are somewhat different for children and adolescents, and these differences are not represented in the PDS items. This latter caution may prove confusing to the scale's users because a prominent table in the manual maps the PDS against both adult and child criteria for the DSM-IV diagnosis of Posttraumatic Stress Disorder (PTSD). PDS items represent translations of the DSM-IV's technical language into common-use language suitable for adult clients: Items 1 through 21 serve to verify the respondent's experience of a traumatic event that involved actual or threatened death or injury to themselves or others and that left them feeling fearful and helpless (APA, 1994). Items 22 through 38 describe specific current symptoms of PTSD; respondents answer by indicating the presence and frequency of each symptom. Finally, Items 39 through 40 describe the duration of the symptoms and the degree to which these are interfering with the respondents' life.

Like all translations, the PDS language loses some of the richness of the original DSM-IV definition, and it is unclear how critical such omissions are. For example, the DSM-IV experience of "intense fear, helplessness or horror" (APA, 1994, p. 428) is translated into two items: "Did you feel helpless?" and "Did you feel terrified?" Is terror the same as intense fear? Are these the same as horror? The author reports that the item language was reviewed by other experts in the field in an attempt to evaluate the translations but stops short of describing how many experts reviewed the scale or the nature of their expertise. Consequently, the face validity of the scale's language is not entirely established.

Results of the PDS yield three judgments: (a) whether the six critical diagnostic criteria for PTSD have been met; (b) the Level of Impairment as judged by counting the number of life areas affected; and (c) the Symptom Severity Score created by summing severity ratings for the current symptoms list.

Although the manual refers to a "normative sample" underlying the PDS, the scale is not a norm-referenced measure. Instead, the PDS is criterion-referenced, with the objective of determining the degree to which PDS responses accurately reflect the "correct" DSM-IV diagnostic decision. Clinical labels are attached to the Level of Impairment and Symptom Severity Scores, but these labels do not appear to be derived from the performance of subjects in the scale's validity study.

Information assessing the reliability of the PDS and its adequacy as a criterion measure of the PTSD diagnosis is drawn wholly from a single 248-subject study reported in the manual. Unfortunately, the manual's description of the study omits critical information, whereas other details suggest that the study was not sufficiently representative to stand as a sole evidence of the technical adequacy of the scale. For example, subjects were drawn from agencies serving high-trauma populations in five East Coast states and two Midwestern cities. Figures presented in the PDS manual suggest that low- and upper-income subjects were somewhat overrepresented in the sample, and that Hispanic-American subjects and those of other minority groups were somewhat underrepresented. Subjects were included only if they had experienced a traumatic event meeting the DSM-IV criteria no less than one month before the study; consequently, the scale is most appropriately used to screen for PTSD among persons known to have experienced trauma.

Subjects were administered both the PDS and the Structured Clinical Interview for DSM-III-R (SCID; Williams et al., 1992), with the latter serving as the criterion measure against which the PDS was evaluated. The author never directly addresses the error introduced into the study by the SCID's origins in an earlier version of the DSM (the DSM-III-R; American Psychiatric Association, 1987). Moreover, the accuracy of such clinical interviews is highly dependent upon the skills of the interviewer, so it is a serious omission when the manual provides no information about the qualifications of the persons administering the SCID, the training those persons received, and interrater reliability of their diagnostic decisions.

These shortcomings aside, the results of the single validity study showed that diagnostic decisions made using the PDS agreed with those made using the SCID 79% of the time. Results suggest that the scale is both adequately sensitive (correctly identifying PTSD 82.0% of the time) and specific (correctly identifying non-PTSD 76.7% of the time). The robustness of these results would be more convincing if different examiners had administered the interview and the PDS, but the manual does not note whether this was the case.

Using the same study to assess scale reliability, the manual reports an impressive internal consistency alpha of .92 for the Symptom Severity Score. The more practical estimate of reliability is the percent agreement of diagnoses from two independent administrations of the PDS, separated by 10–22-day intervals. These diagnoses agreed 87.3% of the time, a relatively high degree of reliability. Again, these results would be most impressive if the two administrations were completed independently by different clinicians, but the manual fails to note whether this was the case.

SUMMARY. The PDS is a highly promising research tool developed to discriminate between those persons who, having experienced a significant traumatic event, do or do not meet the criteria for PTSD. Written to be parallel to the DSM-IV diagnostic criteria, a single validity study has shown the PDS to have high test-retest reliability across a 2-week interval and to show high agreement with a clinical interview designed around an earlier version of diagnostic criteria. The scale does not yet meet standards for general clinical use because it is based on a single, incompletely described and unreplicated validity study with a predominantly East Coast sample. The author acknowledges the scale's research status in recommending uses such as monitoring treatment outcomes or estimating prevalence of PTSD within specific populations.

REVIEWER'S REFERENCES

American Psychiatric Association. (1987). *Diagnostic and statistical manual of mental disorders* (3rd ed., rev.). Washington, DC: Author.
Williams, J. B. W., Gibbon, M., First, M. B., Spitzer, R. L., Davies, M., Borus, J., Howes, M. J., Kane, J., Pope, H. G., Rounsaville, B., & Wittchen, H. U. (1992). The structured clinical interview for DSM-III-R (SCID). *Archives of General Psychiatry, 49*, 630–636.
American Psychiatric Association. (1994). *Diagnostic and statistical manual of mental disorders* (4th ed.). Washington, DC: Author.

PREPARE/ENRICH.

Purpose: Designed as a series of tests for use in assessing couples' relationships.

Population: Couples.

Scores: 17 scores common to all four tests: Idealistic Distortion, Personality Issues, Communication, Conflict Resolution, Financial Management, Leisure Activities, Sexual Expectations, Role Relationship, Spiritual Beliefs, Couple Closeness, Couple Flexibility, Family Closeness, Family Flexibility, Self-Confidence, Assertiveness, Avoidance, Partner Dominance.

Administration: Group.

Price Data: Available from publisher.

Time: Administration time not reported.

Comments: Available as a compiled series of 4 tests with one manual.

Publisher: Life Innovations, Inc.

a) PREMARITAL PERSONAL AND RELATIONSHIP EVALUATION.

Purpose: Designed to help couples getting reading for marriage (who do not have children) assess their relationship.

Population: Couples planning to marry who do not have children.

Acronym: PREPARE.

Publication Dates: 1978–1998.

Scores, 20: 17 scores common to all 4 tests plus Marital Expectations, Children and Parenting, Family and Friends.

Authors: David H. Olson, David G. Fournier, and Joan M. Druckman.

b) PREMARITAL PERSONAL AND RELATIONSHIP EVALUATION—MARRIED WITH CHILDREN.

Purpose: Designed to help couples who are planning to marry (and who already have children) assess their relationship and identify important issues.

Population: Couples planning to marry who have children.

Publication Dates: 1981–1998.

Acronym: PREPARE-MC.

Scores, 20: Same as *a* above.

Authors: David H. Olson, David G. Fournier, and Joan M. Druckman.

c) ENRICHING RELATIONSHIP ISSUES, COMMUNICATION AND HAPPINESS.

Purpose: Designed to assess relationship strengths and areas for growth.

Population: Married couples or couples who have cohabited for 2 or more years.

Publication Dates: 1981–1998.

Acronym: ENRICH.

Scores, 19: 17 scores common to all 4 tests plus: Marital Satisfaction, Children and Parenting.

Authors: David H. Olson, David G. Fournier, and Joan M. Druckman.

d) MATURE AGE TRANSITION EVALUATION.

Purpose: Designed to help mature couples who are preparing for marriage assess their relationships.

Population: Couples over 50 planning marriage.

Publication Dates: 1995–1998.

Acronym: MATE.

Scores, 20: 17 scores common to all 4 tests plus: Life Transitions, Intergenerational Issues, Health Issues.

Authors: David H. Olson and Elinor Adams.

Cross References: See T5:2034 (7 references).

Review of the PREPARE/ENRICH by CORINE FITZPATRICK, Associate Professor of Counseling Psychology, Manhattan College, Riverdale, NY:

The PREPARE/ENRICH is a series of four tests developed to help counselors and clergy to work with premarital and married couples. The original PREPARE was developed in 1978 and has been revised three times (1982, 1986, 1996). It appears to have a dual purpose: assessment of conflict areas for couples and provision of a comprehensive skill-based program for couples based on the assessment. The assessment is designed to identify areas of conflict, relationship strength, and areas of growth with the relevant inventory. The skill-based program includes feedback using six couple exercises.

The PREPARE/ENRICH is composed of four couple inventories, each containing 165 items designed to identify and measure the couple relationship in 20 areas. There are 12 content areas, four personality scores, and four scales focusing on family-of-origin issues. A few scales are unique to some of the inventories. For example, PREPARE and PREPARE-MC have a marriage expectations area, ENRICH has a marriage satisfaction area, and MATE has a Life Transitions area. In addition, where the PREPARE and ENRICH have a Children and Parenting Area, that area is referred to as Integenerational Issues in MATE. Four personality scales have been added to enable better understanding of couple dynamics. Two additional scales assess information about the individual's family of origin and two scales look at the type of marriage. A Revised Individual Score (REV) is designed to give an accurate assessment of how each person perceives the relationship in each area. A separate Idealistic Distortion Scale serves as a correction score for idealism or the tendency to answer questions in a socially acceptable way. In addition, a Positive Couple Agreement score (PCA) indicates the level of positive agreement partners report in each of the content areas.

DEVELOPMENT OF THE SCALES. The current set of scales is an expansion of a previous act of scales that had been developed by the author in 1978 and had been revised in 1986 and 1996. The goal of this latest revision was to build on the strengths of the previous inventories, and to add a more comprehensive skill-based program for couples. The 20 categories were expanded and revised so there are now 165 items in each inventory as compared to 125. In this revision, 40% of the items are new, 30% were extensively revised, and 30% had minor revisions. The authors mention expansion of areas and the need to increase clarity and quality in explaining the reason for these changes. It would have been helpful to have a more detailed rationale as to why 70% of the inventory was changed. For example, how was the generation of new test items determined? The manual should have stated the criteria used.

The sampling procedure for this version is not described. The manual mentions that there is a "large national norm base" for the current version, but no further detail is given there or in the section on research studies about the particular sample used for this version. Detailed descriptions of normalizing populations must be clearly evident and described in detail in a manual.

RELIABILITY AND VALIDITY. Internal consistency and test-retest reliabilities are reported first, excluding the newly developed personality scales. Internal consistency reliabilities for the subscales range from .73 to .90, with average reliabilities for each of the tests ranging from .75 for the PREPARE and PREPARE-MC to .83 for the MATE. Test-retest reliability scores (administration interval not reported) are only reported for the PREPARE (.80) and ENRICH (.86). Both the internal consistency and the test-retest reliabilities have improved from those reported by Larson et al. (1995) for a previous version (e.g., internal consistency range from .64 to .85; test-retest $r = .73$). Clearly, unreliable items must have been dropped in this revision and the data suggest that the instrument has very good reliability. The reliability data for the Personality scales are less adequate. Only internal reliability (alpha) is reported with a range from .71 to .82.

Regarding validity, the authors cite research done on prior versions of the scale as the basis for concurrent, construct, and predictive validity. Those studies clearly indicate that scores from earlier versions of the instrument are valid. Considering that the current version has been substantially modified, as stated by the author, more evidence specific to this version is necessary. Citations of earlier studies, although supportive, do not replace the need to provide validity evidence for this version. The description of validity studies in the manual was vague. The inventory was given to a "panel of clinicians" who in general gave it high ratings. In addition, Larson et al. (1995) noted that PREPARE assesses most (85%) of the premarital factors defined in their research as good predictors. One must assume that the version of PREPARE mentioned in that study is not the current version. We have no information regarding whether a similar statistic is available for the current version. Clearly, the validity needs to be addressed more strongly psychometrically.

ADMINISTRATION, SCORING, AND INTERPRETATION. The inventory is given to the individual to self-administer using paper and pencil. Directions are easy and test length is appropriately short. Computer scoring is the only method available. There are many avenues of interpretation given the numerous subscales and composite subscales (e.g., personality scales). A strength of this instrument is its comprehensiveness for interpretation. In addition, the skill-based program is particularly innovative and its inclusion makes this instrument unique in its development of a skill-based program built around the findings of an assessment.

SUMMARY. This measure was developed within the framework of a strong body of research and prior measure development. The current version has been built on the basis of this research. There is a serious concern about the theoretical basis for recent item additions and more importantly about the validity. More research is needed on the validity and a more detailed description of the norming population is necessary in order to support this instrument as psychometrically sound. When those limitations are addressed, the comprehensiveness of this instrument and the inclusion of an additional set of exercises connected to it should enable this measure to develop as one of the most widely useful assessments in this area.

REVIEWER'S REFERENCE
Larson, J. H., Holman, T. B., Klein, D. M., Busby, D. M., Stahmann, R. F., & Peterson, D. (1995). A review of comprehensive questionnaires used in premarital education and counseling. *Family Relations, 44,* 245–252.

Review of the PREPARE/ENRICH by JAY A. MANCINI, *Professor of Human Development, Virginia Polytechnic Institute & State University, Blacksburg, VA:*

This array of couple relationship inventories, including PREPARE, PREPARE-MC, ENRICH, and MATE, have been developed by David H. Olson and colleagues over the past 25 years. These inventories are mainly designed to be used by counselors with couples who are considering marriage. The program in which these inventories are imbedded has two components. First, there is an assessment of the couple with the appropriate inventory. Second, there are feedback sessions with the counselor who uses a set of accompanying exercises that assist couples in processing information. PREPARE (Premarital Personal and Relationship Evaluation), PREPARE-MC (Premarital Personal and Relationship Evaluation—Marriage with Children), ENNRICH (Enriching Relationship Issues, Communication and Happiness), and MATE (Mature Age Transitional Evaluation) are discussed in great detail in the PREPARE/ENRICH manual, which also serves as a guideline for clinicians. These inventories are typically used within the context of counseling and have also been used in research studies. The manual on PREPARE/ENRICH is well written and comprehensive. It includes an overview of the inventories, administration procedures, an overview of the computer report generated by the test developers and returned to the counselor, guidelines for the counselor on organizing inventory results and giving feedback, a discussion of the personality assessments using the couple and family map, use of the inventories in group settings, a summary of the research studies on the inventories, a discussion of the items in the subscales, other resources for counselors and couples, a glossary of key terms, copies of all inventories and answer sheets, and training materials.

CONCEPTUAL GROUNDING. These inventories are based in the literature from the fields of family studies and of marital and family therapy. The test developers believe that relationship issues can be classified into four categories: personality, intrapersonal, interpersonal, and external issues. Conceptual areas in the PREPARE/ENRICH inventories that address these relationship issues are: Assertiveness, Self-Confidence, Avoidance, Partner Dominance, Idealistic Distortion, Personality Issues, Spiritual Beliefs, Leisure Activities, Marriage Expectations, Marriage Satisfaction, Communication, Conflict Resolution, Children and Parenting, Couple Closeness, Role Relationship, Sexual Relationship, Family-of-Origin, Family and Friends, and Financial Management. Definitions of these terms and their accompanying measures are included in the manual. For example, the measure of Idealistic Distortion "assesses the tendency of individuals to answer personal questions in a socially desirable manner" (manual, p. 15), the measure of Marriage Expectations "assesses an individual's expectation about love, commitment and conflicts in his/her relationship" (manual, p. 16), and the measure of Personality Assessment "assesses each individual's perception and satisfaction with the personality characteristics of their partner as expressed through their behavioral traits" (manual, p. 16). As each of these measures is described the test developers provide a narrative of the meaning of high scores, moderate scores, and low scores.

INVENTORY HISTORY, DEVELOPMENT, AND CHARACTERISTICS. The initial work on these inventories began in 1977. Over the years the inventories have been updated as the test developers evaluated them from both a conceptual and a research perspective. It appears that the most recent revisions occurred in 1996 and 1997 (except in the case of the MATE, first developed in 1995). It is to their credit that attention has been paid periodically to improving these measures. It should be mentioned that these inventories are not designed for the fainthearted test-taker. Each inventory contains 165 items. For most items the respondent is asked to indicate her or his level of agreement (strongly disagree, disagree, undecided, agree, and strongly agree) with a declarative statement.

Once completed the inventories are returned to Life Innovations, Inc. for scoring and interpretation. The counselor receives an elaborate report of 15 pages that provides an analysis of all inventory dimensions, as well as a Couple and Family Map analysis. The manual provides a great deal of guidance to the counselor for using the results with the clients.

RELIABILITY AND VALIDITY. In the manual, the test developers define various indicators of reliability and validity prior to presenting their results. Their analysis of internal consistency shows that alphas ranged from .73 to .90 across all subscales and across all four inventories. For PRE-PARE the average internal consistency was .75, for PREPARE-MC the average was .75, for ENRICH the average was .81, and for MATE the average internal consistency coefficient was .83. These reliabilities were computed on relatively large samples (sample size ranges from 456 to 1,742). They present test-retest reliability information (administration interval not specified) on PREPARE and on EN-RICH. These reliabilities ranged from .74 to .93, with average test-retest reliability of .80 for PRE-PARE and .86 for ENRICH. The analysis of subscale intercorrelations indicates associations between -.09 to .83; most were between .40 and .60. Although theoretically these scales should interrelate, in some instances the test developers should consider combining scales in the interest of parsimony. The four measures of personality (Assertiveness, Self-Confidence, Avoidance, and Dominance) also demonstrated good internal consistency, with alphas ranging from .71 to .82. These personality measures were correlated appropriately with subscales in PREPARE.

Content validity was originally examined by subjecting the inventory items to a panel of clinicians. The test developers report that these ratings supported the content of the subscales (however, empirical results are not presented in this manual). Concurrent validity was reported in a doctoral dissertation completed in the late 1970s. This study found the PREPARE subscales correlated as expected with other relationship measures, including marital satisfaction, conflict, self-esteem, communication, and cohesion. This same dissertation also provided support for the construct validity of PREPARE, finding that most subscales were unidimensional (these same findings were used to make additional changes in the measures). Apparently there are no more recent studies that have looked at concurrent and construct validity. The test developers also provide data on the predictive validity of PREPARE. They report that by using PREPARE scores they were able to predict with 80% to 85% accuracy couples that are likely to experience satisfaction with their marriage from those who are having problems. There is also a discussion of the validity of scores from EN-RICH. Research completed in the late 1980s

suggests that ENRICH shows good concurrent validity, in that it correlates highly with other measures of marital satisfaction, and that EN-RICH discriminates between stressed and nonstressed couples with over 90% accuracy. Studies on the validity of scores from PREPARE-MC and MATE apparently have not been conducted.

SUMMARY. The PREPARE/ENRICH Couple Inventories provide the counselor with a rich array of items that reflect the many dimensions of relationships. Olson and his colleagues have systematically addressed relationships through their inventory development over a number of years. Their own reports indicate that these measures are not only useful to counselors but are based on the research literature and provide good evidence of reliability and validity. The manual that is provided is thorough and easy to navigate, and most importantly it provides the user with a good sense of the clinical and research issues that the inventories address. What is not provided, however, are indications of how others outside of the test developer's team have used these inventories in either clinical or research work. The applicability of these inventories to diverse family groups and family contexts is also unclear, and is a direction that future research should take.

[296]
Preschool Skills Test.

Purpose: "Designed to assess the [developmental] skills of preschool-aged, early elementary or mentally handicapped children."
Population: Age 2 through Grade 2 level children.
Publication Dates: 1983–1993.
Scores: 7 developmental areas: Fine Motor, Personal/Social, Visual, Visual Identification, Number Concepts, Discrimination/Matching, Readiness/Academic.
Administration: Individual.
Price Data, 1998: $225 per complete kit; $35 per 50 answer sheets; $50 per 50 fine motor drawing sheets.
Time: [20–30] minutes.
Comments: Previous edition entitled Preschool Screening Test.
Author: Carol Lepera.
Publisher: Preschool Skills Test.
Cross References: For a review by Ruth Tomes of an earlier edition, see 12:303.

Review of the Preschool Skills Test by DOREEN WARD FAIRBANK, Associate Professor of Psychology, Meredith College, Raleigh, NC:

The Preschool Skills Test by Carol Lepera was originally developed in 1981 as the Preschool Screening Test. After several revisions, it was republished in 1991 as the Preschool Skills Test for children from age 2 through Grade 2 level. The test also can be applicable with all ages of children who are more severely mentally disabled because those children may function at this readiness to Grade 2 level. According to the author, "it was designed to yield a 'Readiness Age' to indicate a child's academic functioning level, as well as academic goals in a chronological developmental order" (technical manual, p. 3). The new revision includes additional statistical analyses on specific handicapped populations, an upgrading of the technical manual, and gives a "Readiness Age," a standard score, and a "Readiness Quotient."

The Preschool Skills Test contains 100 items divided by developmental skills and age/grade levels. The seven developmental skill areas are as follows: Fine Motor, Personal/Social, Visual Discrimination/Matching, Language Concepts, Number Concepts, Visual identification, and Readiness/Academic. The areas are then divided into the following age/grade levels: 24–30 months, 30–36 months, 36–48 months, 48–60 months, 60–72 months, Grade 1, and Grade 2. The spiral-bound test manual contains the questions for the 100 items and most of the test stimuli. Additional manipulative items are included with this test and they include: 10 blocks, 6 colored discs, 1 small bead, 1 box of crayons, and 1 pair of scissors. The test also includes the Fine Motor drawing sheets and the answer sheets.

The Preschool Skills test can easily be administered in 20–30 minutes. The manual does not state the level of qualifications for the administrator, but the test appears to be straightforward and the directions are very clear and concise, therefore suggesting that anyone with testing experience could administer this test. Testing should begin with Fine Motor followed by the Personal/Social area. Once these sections have been completed, the tester should start the rest of the test at the level where successes were still being achieved (basal) on the two previous sections and just before the level where failures (ceiling) had started. Scoring is completed as follows: a "+" for all possible answers in a section correct and the child passes all criteria indicated for that level; a "checkmark" indicating some items are passed but not all,

therefore implying an emerging skill; and a "0" for no answers were correct indicating that the child probably does not understand the task. A child's "Readiness Age" is defined by the author "as the age level between the basal and ceiling where at least three-fourths of the items are passed with a (+)" (technical manual, p. 5). Scoring is to be used to estimate a range of functioning, or a "Readiness Age." The author further states that "the test is designed to indicate areas of weakness, so educational goals may be written" (technical manual, p. 5). A summary box for the total raw score and standard score is included on the Preschool Skills Test answer sheet; however, there are no instructions in the manual for determining the raw score. There is a chart for converting the raw score to the standard scores at the end of the manual, but there is no available information in order to use the "Standard Scores" for comparison. The directions for determining the "Readiness Quotient" were found in the handicapped, referral population validity section of the technical manual and caution was given regarding its use in programming.

The Preschool Skills Test was originally standardized on 170 school-aged children selected from kindergarten, first, and second grade classes in an Indianapolis township and on 34 preschool-aged children from the same area. When this test was originally reviewed (Thomas, 1995), several problems were stated regarding this standardization. The primary problem was the small sample size, especially at the preschool level. Several of the statistical analyses were questioned because of the very small sample size. This was not corrected with this current revision and the original standardization is still given in the manual. However, the author did include a separate standardization by administering the test to 202 mentally disabled children, ages 34 months to 20 years, with 98% of the sample functioning with an IQ below 80 and 73% functioning below an IQ of 75. The author states that "the two standardization samples were not combined for analysis, since the mentally disabled sample was not selected randomly" (technical manual, p. 4). The disabled students were served through RISE Special Services. Preschool children in the standardization study were those referred by their parents to an agency to determine special education needs, similar to the original study, the sample size is very small for the preschool population (N = 21) and without a breakdown of ages.

The split-half reliability coefficient for the total sample with Spearman-Brown estimation was .98 for the original sample. A subtest-total test intercorrelation ranged from .79 to .96 for the original sample and .86 to .97 with the disabled sample. Test-retest reliability was not given for the original sample, but was determined to be .92 for the disabled sample ($N = 26$) (administration interval ranged from 7 months to 51 months with an average interval of 35.7 months).

Validity was examined by correlating the Preschool Skills Test with grades (grade-point average) obtained in school during the first grading period. The manual states that "the subtest scores correlated significantly at the .05 level in all areas for Kindergarten students and at the .01 level for students in Grade 1. Correlations were significant at the .05 level for students in Grade 2 in all areas except Fine Motor and Academic/Readiness (technical manual, p. 12). However, no validity data were given for the preschool age group. The validity scores for the disabled sample were based on an additional battery of tests including the Stanford-Binet Scale, Forms L-M, the Peabody Picture Vocabulary Test—Revised, and the Developmental Test of Visual-Motor Integration (Beery). Correlations were significant with all instruments and were highest when comparing the "Readiness Quotient" and the Stanford-Binet L-M IQ (.90).

Although item analyses were given to support the difficulty and progression of the test items, there was no evidence in the manual describing how the Preschool Skills Test was developed and why certain items were included. Also missing is a description for how the "Readiness Age" was developed.

SUMMARY. Overall, the Preschool Skills Test is an easy-to-administer test to determine certain strengths and weaknesses of children from the age of 2 to Grade 2. There are, however, several problems with the standardization of this test that need to be taken into account when attempting to use the results for purposes other than just determining the strengths and weaknesses of a child.

REVIEWER'S REFERENCE

Tomes, R. E. (1995). [Review of the Preschool Screening Test]. In J. C. Conoley & J. C. Impara (Eds.), *The twelfth mental measurements yearbook* (pp. 799–800). Lincoln, NE: Buros Institute of Mental Measurements.

Review of the Preschool Skills Test by MARK E. SWERDLIK, Professor of Psychology, Illinois State University, Normal, IL, and DAVID L. WODRICH, Director of Psychological Assessment Services, Phoenix Children's Hospital, Phoenix, AZ:

The Preschool Skills Test is designed to serve as a "quick yet accurate, screening instrument and to indicate a child's academic functioning level, as well as academic goals in a chronological developmental order" (technical manual, p. 3). Test materials, including manipulatives (e.g., colored discs, beads) are generally attractive to young children with brightly colored pictures of objects, animals, and cartoon figures. However, no minorities are pictured in any of the items portraying humans and some of the picture do not appear realistic (e.g., pictures of coins).

The 100 items are organized into seven developmental areas with some items appearing at more than one age level but with different scoring standards. The first two sections of the item booklet are organized by type of task (Fine Motor and Personal/Social) followed by items grouped by age/grade.

Test users should have little difficulty with administration. Some directions are incomplete (e.g., use of scratch paper for math). Examiners are instructed to begin by administering the Fine Motor subtest (essentially a visual-motor design-copying task) and then all items on the Personal/Social scale (tapping knowledge of personal information) with subsequent items administered beginning at the level at which successes are still being achieved but before failures begin occurring. No rationale is provided for this adaptive testing format. Some scoring examples are provided for the visual-motor tasks but scoring criteria for many items are ambiguous. Differential credit is allowed for most items. Most items permit a nonverbal response suggesting usefulness with children who are nonverbal or physically limited.

The norms are based on two separate standardization samples collected at three different times between 1983 and 1990. The first included 170 school-age children tested in 1986 and 34 preschool-age children tested in 1988, all combined and analyzed as one. The elementary-age participants were selected randomly from kindergarten through 2nd grade classes in one Indiana school district. The second standardization sample, collected between 1983 and 1990, consists of 202 "mentally handicapped children" ages 13 months to 20 years with 98% of the sample functioning below an IQ of 80 and 73% below an IQ of 75. A IQ range of below 80 for "mentally handicapped" is above the typical cutoff of 70. Significantly more males were included in this sample. The nonrandom sample of students with mental retardation was selected from a special education cooperative on the southern border of the Indianapolis metropolitan area. The preschool sample was selected from one preschool in the local area. General descriptions are provided related to the SES (e.g., majority are blue collar workers) and racial/ethnic composition of the areas from which the samples were drawn. It is not noted at all if the subjects are English-speaking. Qualifications of the examiners whose cases were included in the standardization samples were not described. This apparent "convenience sample" is quite restricted in size, geographical, and racial/ethnic representativeness and does not permit the test user to determine adequately how the sample compares to their potential subjects. The Preschool Skills Test yields standard scores (with a mean of 100 and a standard deviation of 15) for children in Grades K–2. A Readiness Quotient, representing a simple ratio of a child's Readiness Age divided by chronological age, can be computed for any age. The Readiness Age (defined as that level between the basal and ceiling where at least 3/4 of the items are passed) is recommended for use when discussing total scores for preschool-age children. The limitations of using age equivalents or the Readiness Quotient (similar to a ratio IQ score) were not addressed.

Internal consistency reliability (split-half with Spearman-Brown correction and coefficient alpha) for various age levels of the standardization sample consisting of preschool and elementary age students is satisfactory for a screening test (.98 for the total test and above .90 for all grades except Grade 2). Satisfactory (above .90) test/retest reliability evidence (administration interval ranged from 7 months to 51 months with an average interval of 35.7 months) is reported for a small (n = 26) sample of students who are mentally retarded. No other reliability data, based on separate studies apart from analysis of the standardization sample, are available. No interrater reliability is provided for subtests that require subjective judgment (e.g., fine motor).

No information is provided related to how or why the particular sample of skills/tasks were chosen. Construct validity evidence includes analyses of the K–2 norm sample indicating no differences in performance between males and females. Test performance in all areas (except Readiness/Academic) increases as age increases, although the test does not discriminate well above 84 months. Results of item difficulty levels (p-values), correlations of individual items with total and area scores, generally support the overall placement of items by difficulty levels. Similar support for the construct validity of the test for use with students who are mentally retarded is presented. For students in Grades K–2, criterion-related validity evidence of correlations of test scores with grades were all significant (median correlations for the different grades and total GPA above .44). However, the reliability of the criterion of teacher-assigned grades is suspect. Criterion-related validity evidence, for the group of subjects who are mentally retarded, includes high correlations with four criterion measures, two of which are no longer currently in use (Stanford-Binet Scale, Forms L-M [S-B L-M] and Peabody Picture Vocabulary Test—Revised [PPVT-R]). No validity evidence is presented for the preschool-age sample and all validity evidence is based on an inadequate and poorly defined norming sample.

No evidence is presented to assist the test user in determining if the test is equally useful for children from different racial/ethnic groups and items were not analyzed for possible bias or differential validity across groups. No factor analytic data are provided to support the grouping of the items into the various areas nor are adequate descriptions given for the various areas. Although the purpose of the test is to develop academic goals and for use as a screening test, no validity data are presented regarding using the Preschool Skills Test for these purposes.

SUMMARY. The Preschool Skills Test contains items that are generally attractive to young children. However, the norms are limited in size, geographical, racial/ethnic, and SES representativeness. Reliability and validity data are limited and based on norms that are highly suspect. The test has improved little since it was first published and is not recommended for use. Test users would be better served using screening tests such as the Battelle (T5:266) and criterion-referenced tests such as the Brigance series for developing academic goals.

Prison Inmate Inventory.
Purpose: "Designed for inmate risk assessment and needs identification."
Population: Prison inmates.
Publication Date: 1996.
Acronym: PII.
Scores: 10 scales: Truthfulness, Violence, Antisocial, Adjustment, Self-Esteem, Alcohol, Drugs, Judgment, Distress, Stress Coping Abilities.
Administration: Group.
Price Data: Available from publisher.
Time: (35) minutes.
Comments: Available in English and Spanish; both computer version and paper-pencil format are scored on IBM-PC compatibles.
Author: Risk & Needs Assessment, Inc.
Publisher: Risk & Needs Assessment, Inc.

Review of the Prison Inmate Inventory by R. J. DE AYALA, Associate Professor of Educational Psychology, University of Nebraska—Lincoln, Lincoln, NE:

The Prison Inmate Inventory (PII) is a 189-item self-report instrument for risk assessment and risk identification for prison inmates. The PII can be administered on a computer (IBM-PC) or in paper-based format. In either format the inventory utilizes software that produces a report that may be helpful in determining risk, establishing appropriate supervision levels, assessing inmate needs, and facilitating inmate awareness. To administer the PII on a computer, a staff member would execute the program and access the appropriate screens for providing preliminary inmate information (e.g., name, age, sex, etc.). After entering this preliminary information, the staff member would then allow the inmate to take the inventory. If administered in a paper-based format, the inmate would complete an answer sheet that would subsequently be entered by a staff member into the program. After data entry is complete the staff member may request a report that contains the inmate's percentile rank on each scale. All inmate responses are numeric and item formats consist of True/False and 4- or 5-point Likert scales. Inmates are required to answer all items. The PII requires that the inmate have, at a minimum, a sixth grade reading level and it is available in English and Spanish. Some questions make note of a time frame (6 months) within which the inmate should consider his or her behavior (e.g., in the last six months I …). Therefore, the PII cannot be administered more frequently than every 6 months. The instrument is intended to supplement, not replace, correctional employees' assessments.

The PII consists of 10 scales: Truthfulness (Validity), Violence, Antisocial, Self-Esteem, Alcohol, Drug, Distress, Judgment, Stress Coping Abilities, and Risk. The Risk scale is intended to measure the inmate's risk of continuing his or her "problem prone adjustment" (p. 2) and the Stress Coping Ability measure is concerned with mental health and related emotional/adjustment problems. The Drug and Alcohol scales are independent measures of inmate drug abuse/proneness or alcohol proneness, respectively. Judgment is designed to assess an inmate's capacity for both understanding and comprehension, whereas the Distress scale is concerned with measuring an inmate's distress. According to the PII developers, distress is a major reason why people seek help or counseling. The Distress scale is intended to assess both anxiety and depression. The Self-Esteem, Violence, and Antisocial scales are measures of an inmate's perception of his or her self-worth, tendency towards the use of violence, and "antisocial" behaviors, respectively. Antisocial behaviors are defined as lying, being uncaring, and/or being irresponsible. According to the PII description, the Truthfulness scale (also referred to as the "Validity" scale) is a measure designed to establish how truthful the inmate was while completing the inventory. A high Truthfulness scale score may be indicative that the other scales are invalid and is a feature the instrument's developers feel distinguishes the PII from other self-report measures. The developers contend that a problem with these latter self-report measures is that it is too easy for the inmate to fake responses. As a result the corresponding scores reflect only what the inmate wants the evaluator to know. With the PII the Truthfulness scale is used to "correct" the raw scores on the scales to produce "truth-corrected" (An Inventory of Scientific Findings, p. 3) scores. The developers of the PII state that these scores reflect what the inmate is trying to hide and, as such, are more accurate than simple raw scores.

As mentioned above, the staff member may request a report. This report contains the inmate's percentile rank (PR) on each scale. These percentile ranks are based on a prison population norm group. This information is also displayed as a bar chart with each bar representing a different scale.

The graphic also incorporates a classification of the inmate as Low Risk, Medium Risk, Problem Risk, and Maximum Risk on each scale. These percentile ranks and risk-related classifications indicate, relative to the norm group, how the inmate's score compares to other inmates' scores on a particular scale. To facilitate the staff member's understanding of the report, each scale is presented with the inmate's PR, risk assessment, and text that "interprets" the inmate's ranking on the scale. This reviewer did not have access to the actual software, but it does not appear that there is any artificial intelligence used to interpret the inmate's ranking. Instead, it appears that all inmates who receive the same Risk assessment classification on a particular scale will receive the same "interpretation" of his or her PR on that scale. However, this feature does relieve the staff member the burden of having to either remember or look up how to interpret each scale's possible rankings. In addition, certain items may be identified by the software as indicative of unusual or problematic responses of which the staff should be made aware.

Documentation did not identify which items were associated with which scale. Therefore, it was not possible to unequivocally evaluate the content validity of each scale. Although some items can be clearly associated with certain scales (e.g., an item concerned with drinking would be measuring on the Alcohol scale), others appeared not to be easy to associate with a particular scale.

The developers of the PII provided a review of scientific findings on the PII (An Inventory of Scientific Findings). This document contains an overview of studies conducted during the period of 1980 to 1995 on the PII or some of its scales using various populations (e.g., psychotherapy patients, job applicants, prison inmates). Although dates are given for the various studies, no references were provided for these studies. These studies may not have been published. In addition, although this document refers to the PII as a 219-item self-report test (p. 1) and as having 11 scales (p. 2), it describes only 10 scales and the PII answer sheet as well as the PII inventory itself have only 189 items. This document also specifies that the PII requires approximately 45 minutes to complete; however, this completion time is probably for the 219-item PII. The 189-item PII is described in a different document as requiring approximately 35 minutes to complete.

Risk assessment of the inmate (Low, Medium, Problem, and Maximum Risk) is done by comparing the inmate's PR to predefined cutpoints. Low Risk is defined as a PR within the range 0 to 39, Medium Risk as a PR within the range 40 to 69, Problem Risk requires a PR within the range 70 to 89, and the Maximum Risk classification is used for inmates with a PR above 90. For example, an inmate with a PR of 53 on the Distress Scale would be classified as a Medium Risk. The documentation does not elucidate what is meant by "risk." Moreover, it is not clear how these cutpoints were determined. The only information concerning the validity of these risk assessment classifications is found in the scientific findings review document and consists of "the close approximation of the obtained risk range percentages to predicted percentages" (p. 27) demonstrates the accuracy of the PII. However, by the definition of a percentile rank, the application of PR cutpoints would by necessity result in observed risk range percentages that would have close agreement with the "predicted" percentages. For the inmate population all reliability estimates (coefficient alpha) for the various scale scores were in the range of .70 to .95 and all were significantly different from zero. The developers of the PII state that a highly significant coefficient alpha for a scale reflects that the scale measures "one factor" (p. 16 and p. 21). However, large coefficient alpha does not necessarily indicate that an item set measures a single factor.

Because percentile ranks have meaning only within a distribution or across similar distributions it should be noted that of the three studies involving inmates that had complete demographic information, one study contained approximately 3% female inmates, in another study 2% were female, and 10% were female in a third study. Therefore, the standardization population is not very representative of female inmates and as a consequence it is unclear whether the cutpoints should be applied to female inmates. Furthermore, the standardization population across three different studies had a maximum of 1.2% Hispanic inmates, 1.0% Asian inmates, and 3% American Indians. The application of the PII to these ethnic groups may not be appropriate. The developers of the PII note that the PII is not appropriate for either sex offenders or inmates sentenced to execution. However, as the PII is introduced into additional prisons the Risk and Needs Assessment, Inc. will standardize the PII on the first group of inmates tested at the prison. Because the PII is standardized annually, inmates may produce identical or similar truth-corrected scores in two different years that when transformed to percentile ranks result in a different risk assessment classification. To facilitate this annual restandardization, users of the PII must return used diskettes to Risk and Needs Assessment, Inc. so that relevant data may be merged with the PII Expanding Database in order that the PII can be restandardized, an annual summary report generated for users of the PII, and for use in ongoing PII research. Purchasers of the PII inventory are allowed 25 or 50 test applications.

It appears that in at least one scale, the PR is a transformation of a composite score. For the Stress Coping scale a stress quotient (SQ) is calculated using the relationship $SQ = CS/S \times K$ (where CS is a coping skill score, S is a stress score, K is an undefined constant). (Presumably, CS and S are "truth-corrected" scores.) SQ is the Stress Coping score that is apparently transformed to the PR scale. There is no mention of the use of composite scores for the other scales.

The truth-corrected scores are, according to the PII developers, more accurate that the raw scores and reveal what the inmate is trying to hide. No empirical evidence is presented to support this contention. The specific procedure by which the raw scores are adjusted ("corrected") is not presented. The PII authors simply state that the correlation between the Truthfulness (Validity) scale and each other PII scale is used to identify error variance associated with untruthfulness and to add it back to the raw scores in order to produce the truth-corrected scores. It is not possible to discern from the PII's generated report how much correction is performed on a given inmate's profile. Greater information concerning how this adjustment to raw scores is performed as well as presenting the inmate's uncorrected profile (or at least the corrected and uncorrected percentile points for each scale) would be beneficial to staff members.

SUMMARY. The PII is intended to supplement correctional employees' assessments. The inventory's developers note that users should integrate the PII with other information to provide a more complete picture of the inmate. As such, the PII provides a means of profiling inmates that may be beneficial to correctional staff members.

Review of the Prison Inmate Inventory by JOHN A. MILLS, Professor, Counseling and Student Development, Indiana University of Pennsylvania, Indiana, PA:

The Prison Inmate Inventory (PII) is a 189-item inventory designed to assess the placement needs of prison inmates. In particular, the PII addresses risks associated with placement and classification changes and issues of level of supervision. The instrument is designed for a specific population, and particularly excludes death row inmates (who were not represented in the development samples) and incarcerated sex offenders. The PII authors reported that sex offenders should be administered the Sexual Adjustment Inventory, though it is not clear how the PII is inappropriate for their general conditions of incarceration.

The PII may be given on a computer or using a pencil-and-paper format. Both formats yield an automated report that is well organized and may be stripped of identifying information. This facility with the data is particularly useful for individuals wishing to build a database of such information. In some places, the documentation indicates that there are 219 items (reported in the "Inventory of Scientific Findings"), though the materials describe 189 items in other places. The materials actually reflect 189 items that contribute directly to the resulting scale scores, with supplemental information items for overall interpretive procedure. The usefulness of the PII is somewhat reduced because of the fact that the inventory is designed for use by persons functioning at least at the sixth grade reading level.

The three-part documentation includes an "Orientation and Training Manual," "An Inventory of Scientific Findings," and a "Computer Operating Guide." Among the three parts, there is redundancy in description of clinical scales and some difficulty in readability. The Orientation and Training Manual presents an overview of the instrument, including rationale for its use, basic scale information, and information about administration of the instrument. An Inventory of Scientific Findings redescribes the clinical scales, albeit in more detail. It also describes the potential benefits of use of the instrument, and describes the evidence for reliability and validity of the PII. The Computer Operating Guide has useful instructions for administration, scoring, and the creation of reports. The Computer Operating Guide is also accompanied by a Scoring and Quick Reference sheet that has useful information regarding basic procedures.

There is a lack of clear or complete information regarding the psychometric properties of the PII. The PII includes a single Truthfulness scale, which was normed on a sizable population. The authors indicate that the multifaceted scale provides a correction method. It does not, however, indicate how this is achieved using one scale. Nor does it present data to support specific problematic response tests. This makes it difficult to make sure interpretation of the exact nature of apparently untruthful responding.

The rationale for each clinical scale is well described and appears to address important elements of the domain. At the same time, the psychometric properties of the clinical scales are lacking. Although the scale descriptions and interpretive instructions are clear, it is difficult to substantiate interpretive conclusions on empirical grounds. There are extensive data demonstrating a relatively strong level of internal consistency and subscale discreteness for the clinical scales. There are also some data suggesting strong associations between several of the clinical scales and selected scales of the Minnesota Multiphasic Personality Inventory (MMPI), but this evidence is insufficient for a broad range of interpretive possibilities. No data was presented that appeared to associate scale scores with other external criteria. If the data exist in other sources, there were no references to direct the potential user of the PII. In spite of the seemingly hyperbolic claims of criterion validity, there is little support for the predictive, concurrent, or construct validity of the clinical measures.

SUMMARY. In spite of significant omissions in the demonstration of adequate validation of the PII, it could still be a useful instrument as a part of an overall assessment of the risk and placement dimensions for prison inmates. The normative information could be used to compare inmates to the normative sample on the clinical dimension, and professionals could develop local comparative norms using the data archiving capabilities of the computer software. Because of the good descriptive labels for behavioral, cognitive, and affective components of the scales, results of an individual's responding could be very useful for treatment planning and structuring of discussions with inmates seeking intervention.

[298]
Project Management Knowledge & Skills Assessment.

Purpose: Constructed to assess "Key areas of the Project Management Body of Knowledge."

Population: Project managers.
Publication Date: 1996.
Scores: 8 scales: Scope Management, Quality Management, Time Management, Cost Management, Risk Management, Human Resources Management, Contract/Procurement Management, Communications Management.
Administration: Group.
Manual: No manual.
Price Data, 1996: $11 per survey; $60 per composite report.
Time: Administration time not reported.
Comments: Can be used alone or in conjunction with Project Management Competency Assessment (T5:2097).
Author: Clark L. Wilson.
Publisher: Clark Wilson Group for the exclusive use of Educational Services Institute.

Review of the Project Management Knowledge & Skills Assessment by JERRY M. LOWE, Associate Professor of Educational Leadership, Sam Houston State University, Huntsville, TX:

The Project Management Knowledge and Skills Assessment instrument was developed to help organizations and individuals identify their strengths and weaknesses in the area of project management. By responding to 96 multiple-choice questions, participant knowledge and skill level are tested in relation to the following eight areas that compose the Project Management Institute's (PMI) project management body of knowledge: (a) Scope Management, (b) Quality Management, (c) Time Management, (d) Cost Management, (e) Risk Management, (f) Human Resources Management, (g) Procurement Management, and (h) Communication Management. There are 12 questions on the assessment for each of the eight areas. The 1996 revision of the Project Management Body of Knowledge includes a ninth area identified as Project Integration Management. This area is not included in the instrument being reviewed here because it does not yet appear on the PMI certification examination.

ADMINISTRATION, SCORING, AND INTERPRETATION. Materials found in the assessment package include an information sheet, a test booklet containing the 96 multiple-choice questions, and a scoring and resource guide. Also included is a summary matrix that is designed to indicate strengths and weaknesses in relation to the eight PMI knowledge-base areas. Using the answer key included within the packet, self-scorted by each individual participant. wers are matched on the matrix to the knowledge-base areas in order to provide an indication of program management strengths and weaknesses. Interpretation is very simple; the more correct answers that appear under each particular knowledge-base area, the greater the knowledge and skill on the participant appears to be. Organizations can use these data to help establish more meaningful training priorities for individuals as well as groups of employees.

NORMATIVE INFORMATION, RELIABILITY, AND VALIDITY. No normative information or reliability and validity information was included in the assessment information.

SUMMARY. The Project Management Knowledge and Skills Assessment Instrument appears to be well constructed with indicators that are specific to the knowledge-base established by PMI. Generalizability does not appear to be evident to any population other than persons involved in the area of project management. Information on the technical quality of the instrument should be included in the testing packet.

Review of the Project Management Knowledge & Skills Assessment by WILLIAM J. WALDRON, Administrator, Employee Testing & Assessment, TECO Energy, Inc., Tampa, FL:

This test, according to its publisher, was developed to help identify individual and organizational levels of knowledge and skill in project management; specifically, it is intended to measure the eight areas of the Project Management Institute's (PMI) Project Management Body of Knowledge (Project Management Institute, 1996). Although not stated explicitly, it would seem that one use of this test would be to assist individuals in preparing for the PMI certification examination covering this body of knowledge.

The test consists of 96 five-option multiple-choice items, 12 covering each of the eight knowledge and skill areas. The test is untimed; no instructions for administering the test are provided. The test is designed to be self-scored by the examinee, using an answer key provided as part of a four-page Scoring and Resource Guide provided; optionally, scoring by the publisher is available. This guide provides a matrix where the individual can plot their raw scores for each area, and suggests developmental resources (courses, books) for each area.

No manual for this test is available, so it is essentially impossible to address the quality of the instrument. The publisher would be well-advised to create such a manual, so that an informed test user could evaluate it for potential use. Information about the item development/content sampling strategy used is critical, as is basic reliability information for each area, because these eight scores are intended to be treated as a profile of strengths and developmental needs.

SUMMARY. The Project Management Knowledge and Skills Assessment could potentially serve a very useful purpose in assisting organizations to evaluate and develop their project management staff. However, a test manual with clear information about the test's development and psychometric characteristics must be provided so that potential users can realistically evaluate the suitability of the test for their purposes.

REVIEWER'S REFERENCE

Project Management Institute. (1996). *A guide to the project management body of knowledge.* Upper Darby, PA: Project Management Institute. (Available for order from PMI's web site: http://www.pmi.org/).

[299]

Prospector: Discovering the Ability to Learn and to Lead.

Purpose: "Designed to assess the ability to learn and openness to learning experiences."
Population: Managers and executives.
Publication Date: 1996.
Scores, 11: Seeks Opportunities to Learn, Has the Courage to Take Risks, Seeks Broad Business Knowledge, Adapts to Cultural Differences, Acts with Integrity, Is Committed to Making a Difference, Brings Out the Best in People, Is Insightful: Sees Things from New Angles, Seeks and Uses Feedback, Learns from Mistakes, Is Open to Criticism.
Administration: Group.
Price Data, 1998: $195 per 1–50 complete Prospector set including one self survey, 10 "other" surveys, one feedback report, one learning guide, and one user's guide (96 pages); quantity discounts available.
Time: Administration time not reported.
Authors: Morgan W. McCall, Gretchen M. Spreitzer, and Joan Jay Mahoney.
Publisher: Center for Creative Leadership.

Review of the Prospector: Discovering the Ability to Learn and to Lead by THEODORE L. HAYES, Research Analyst, U.S. Immigration and Naturalization Service, Washington, DC:

The Prospector's instructions state that it is a brief assessment of "your ability to learn, over the course of your career, the skills important to your effectiveness" (user's guide, p. I-1). The materials consist of a 57-item scannable form. When used as part of a multisource feedback (e.g., a "360-degree" rating) program, raters are asked for information about the target person's performance in his or her current role as well as an estimate of the target's likely future performance. Feedback materials consist of a graphical report showing scores on the Prospector's dimensions, brief instructions on score interpretation, and a self-development guide. The Prospector is one of a tripartite "suite" of measurements available from the Center for Creative Leadership, though it would seem that the Prospector could be used separately from its sisters.

OVERVIEW. The consulting utility of the Prospector far outweighs its psychometric properties. Further research may right this imbalance, but the current value of the instrument will be limited by the skill of the consultant using it.

VALIDITY. The authors are unclear in their construct description of the Prospector. In several places in their technical manual, they state that the prospector is an assessment of "ability to learn," yet at other points they state that it is meant to identify managers with higher potential for expatriate assignments. It would be reasonable to infer that the authors mean Prospector to reflect the ability to learn for the sake of expatriate success. However, "ability to learn" is a personality-oriented cognate of general mental ability, or g, but the authors do not clarify the extent to which this personality-oriented cognate diverges from g, nor the extent to which higher scores are indicative of management potential in general as opposed to success in expatriate assignments in particular.

The authors state that the item content was derived from an initial rational consideration of "19 learning-based attributes of leadership potential" (user's guide, p. II-1) followed by a self-report survey of 47 managers. The surviving items were grouped into 11 dimensions. The items reflect major aspects of the "Big Five" factor model of personality (e.g., emotional stability, extraversion), empathy, and a smattering of business acumen. About five items are explicitly worded to reflect potential expatriate success.

The authors report on a concurrent criterion-validity study in the technical manual. This study involved supervisor ratings of 838 direct reports working in multinational organizations.

The authors' description is not entirely clear, but it seems that 662 managers provided item-level evaluations of one direct report each, whereas apparently 88 managers provided evaluations of two direct reports each. The average dimension intercorrelation reported in the manual is .52. The true average dimension intercorrelation rises to .70 after correcting for measurement error in each dimension (using an overly generous reliability estimate of .75). The authors further divide the Prospector dimensions into two sets: "ability to learn from experience" consisting of four dimensions (Seeks Opportunities to Learn, Seeks and Uses Feedback, Learns From Mistakes, and Is Open to Criticism), and "end-state characteristics [competencies] of executive potential" composed of seven dimensions (Seeks Broad Business Knowledge, Adapts to Cultural Differences, Is Insightful: Sees Things from New Angles, Acts with Integrity, Brings Out the Best in People, Has the Courage to Take Risks, and Is Committed to Making a Difference). The average uncorrected dimension intercorrelation for the first set is .65 (corrected, .86), and for the second set it is .46 (corrected, .62). The distinction between the dimension sets seems reasonable, but the authors do not consistently pursue this distinction throughout their manual. However, the high intercorrelation within each dimension set and among all 11 dimensions raises empirical questions about the alleged multidimensionality of the Prospector.

Unfortunately, the authors asked their participating managers to provide job performance ratings and estimates of future potential along with Prospector ratings. No independent external criteria were assessed. The authors interpret the ensuing monomethod and highly multicolinear correlations as if they represented "evidence" for the validity of the Prospector. Rather, every correlational table presented in the Prospector manual shows that halo is indeed ubiquitous. Low Prospector scores seem to be symptoms, rather than independent predictors, of petulance, derailment, lack of mental agility, and low management potential. In sum, contrary to the authors' claims, no psychometric evidence is presented that the Prospector has multidimensional qualities, nor that it has correlational linkages to external criteria.

RELIABILITY. The authors state that they measured dimensional reliability using internal consistency estimates. This is appropriate for an instrument development study, yet because the Prospector's purpose is to identify areas for change and improvement, this internal consistency evidence does not address the more important issue of whether the dimensions are stable over time, or even whether they should be. The authors need to address growth and stability issues in order to provide individuals with guidance to know how much they should expect their scores to change and over what time period.

CONSULTING UTILITY. The value of the Prospector lies not in its psychometric properties, but in the heuristic, conceptual framework it provides the consultant who would interpret results as part of a feedback session. The Prospector's consulting-related validity comes from its well-thought-out feedback booklet, suggestions for self-monitoring, and its dimensions, which at least seem appropriate. The best use of the Prospector would be as part of a leadership retreat where the manager is able to receive dimensional feedback in a nonthreatening format. The consultant could then help the individual think through some self-development opportunities based on his or her strengths, as well as how to manage weaknesses. Presumably, the consultant should be trained in the use of the Prospector and its sister measurements in order to facilitate growth opportunities. The greatest growth might occur in situations where the individual's manager was included in the planning and feedback process. Although the degree of developmental intervention would be dictated by the available resources and budget, it would be inappropriate to expect most individuals to interpret and integrate Prospector feedback without consultation. Also, the consultant should be wary of managers who would seek to justify deleterious personnel decisions through low Prospector scores.

The authors believe that personal change is possible given one's talent and the right learning opportunities. Maybe this is true to a limited extent, and it is certainly more palatable than saying that interpersonal style is pretty well immutable by one's early 30s. However, the authors leave many critical questions unanswered. To be fair, these questions are endemic to the "360-degree rating" industry, but they are salient nevertheless. For example, how much can a person using Prospector really change? Which dimensions can be expected to change and which cannot? Would managers who give low ratings to

their direct reports be willing to consider change when making expatriate recommendations, or are low Prospector scores only the last signs of derailment? How does Prospector relate to cognitive ability measures? One may hope that the authors have been assembling data to address these and other issues.

SUMMARY. The Prospector may have some utility for organizing feedback to a client in a leadership feedback session, but its psychometric properties are still suspect.

Review of the Prospector: Discovering the Ability to Learn and to Lead by NEIL P. LEWIS, Management Psychologist, Marietta, GA:

Prospector: Discovering the Ability to Learn and to Lead is a paper-and-pencil questionnaire designed for use with the managers of an organization. It purports to measure one aspect of managerial behavior—learning ability and willingness to take advantage of growth experiences—that the authors believe are critical for managers in order to adapt to changing business environments, function effectively within various international cultures, and quickly embrace new technologies. They further believe that managers must be able to build on (learn from) experiences in order to meet the challenges of present and future leadership roles. They describe the Prospector as useful for individual assessment and development, as a tool to facilitate the design of training programs, as a tool to improve on-the-job development, and as a tool to support the development of learning organizations.

The Prospector uses the 360-degree assessment/feedback format. This class of instrument (also known as multirater assessment/feedback, mutisource assessment/feedback, full circle appraisal, and peer evaluation) typically consists of a participant rating himself or herself on a set of criteria. The participant's peers, superiors, and subordinates in the organization also rate him or her on the same dimensions. The participant receives a gap analysis identifying differences between how he or she see themselves and how those who work with them see these same attributes. The most effective use of 360-degree feedback is when its purpose is for management development rather than for administrative purposes such as salary administration or making promotion decisions. In fact, the Prospector is not suitable to use for such purposes.

As with most instruments published by the Center for Creative Leadership in Greensboro, NC, the Prospector shows scholarly development. The test manual describes a careful approach to item generation based on a review of the literature on executive development and on revisions including input from the International Consortium of Executive Development Research. It includes items sensitive to cross-cultural issues within an international environment. The final scale construction makes use of factor analysis. Four of the 11 scales are explicitly learning-oriented whereas the remainder include some dimensions described as end-state competencies, though the authors feel they contain learning implications as well.

The test manual describes acceptably high reliability and validity coefficients. However, company ratings of the norm group members were used as criterion-measures. The authors do not say whether or not the same managers who made or contributed to the company ratings were also people rating the participants using the Prospector. If they were, the validity coefficients may have been inflated somewhat due to lack of independence.

Overall, the Prospector is useful for its described purpose. If an organization wants to use a 360-degree feedback survey with a cross section of its managers primarily to measure to what extent they fit the learning organization model and to provide feedback to them to help them to become more that way, the Prospector is an appropriate instrument. However, employing a 360-degree approach takes a lot of time and commitment from the senior level people of an organization and thus is an expensive use of resources. Most of the other commercially available 360-degree feedback instruments assess a wider array of managerial behaviors than does the Prospector and some can be custom tailored to the particular needs or current issues that top management wants to address in the organization. Therefore, unless you are interested specifically in the learning organization dimension, one of the many broader, general purpose 360-degree instruments may be more cost effective.

Unlike many 360-degree instruments, the Prospector's test manual provides normative information including reliability and validity data. That it does may be an advantage but some take the position that such psychometric refinements are not needed given the usual purposes and applications of 360-degree instruments. The manual also provides a good framework for how to implement the 360-degree feedback process in an organization and gives guidelines for how to structure and approach the all-important feedback process with those who have been participants.

The authors clearly believe that if a manager is going to be successful and adapt to the changes that are already occurring and will occur in the future, he or she will need to strongly embrace principles of a learning organization. This position has an intuitive, commonsense appeal and most people would readily agree that adaptation to changing conditions is required to survive. Yet the overriding importance that is attributed to this dimension by the academics, organizational development practitioners, and consultants who work in this area has yet to be widely shared by line operating managers in the mainstream business community.

In minor criticism of the instrument itself, nearly all the items are worded so that the "agree" responses identify the presence of strongly socially desirable traits and behaviors. By not balancing the wording with negatively phrased items requiring "disagree" responses to endorse desirable qualities, there is an increased likelihood of the respondent adopting a response set.

SUMMARY. The Prospector is a well-designed, psychometrically sound, paper-and-pencil 360-degree assessment/feedback questionnaire designed for use with the managers of an organization. It purports to measure primarily one aspect of managerial behavior—learning ability and the willingness to take advantage of growth experiences—that the authors believe are critical for managers in order to adapt to changing business environments.

The typical application consists of a manager rating himself or herself on a set of criteria. That person's peers, superiors, and subordinates in the organization also rate the person on the same dimensions. The participant receives a gap analysis identifying differences between how they see themselves and how those who work with them see these same attributes.

The Prospector is properly used when its purpose is for manager feedback and development rather than for administrative purposes such as salary administration or making promotion decisions. But unless the user is primarily interested in measuring the learning organization dimensions of managerial behavior, one of the more comprehensive 360-degree instruments not tied to any one theoretical position may have broader application and give the organization more return for its 360-degree assessment expenditure.

[300]
Psychiatric Content Analysis and Diagnosis.

Purpose: "For measuring the magnitude of various psychological states and traits from the content analysis of verbal behavior."
Population: Children and adults.
Publication Dates: 1993—2000.
Acronym: PCAD.
Scores, 13: Anxiety Scale, Hostility Scales (Hostility Directed Outward, Hostility Directed Inward, Ambivalent Hostility), Social Alienation—Personal Disorganization Scale, Cognitive and Intellectual Impairment Scale, Depression Scale, Hope Scale, Health-Sickness Scale, Achievement Striving Scale, Human Relations Scale, Dependency Strivings Scale, Quality of Life Scale.
Administration: Group.
Price Data, 2001: $299.95 per software license including media and manual (2000, 83 pages).
Time: Administration time not reported.
Comment: Earlier version listed in previous Buros publications as Psychologic and Neuropsychiatric Assessment Manual.
Authors: Louis A. Gottschalk and Robert Bechtel.
Publisher: GB Software LLC.

Review of the Psychiatric Content Analysis and Diagnosis by WILLIAM M. REYNOLDS, Professor, Department of Psychology, Humboldt State University, Arcata, CA:

The Psychiatric Content Analysis and Diagnosis (PCAD) by Louis A. Gottschalk and Robert Bechtel is a computerized scoring procedure for the evaluation of speech samples using the Gottschalk-Gleser Content Analysis Method (Gottschalk & Gleser, 1969). There is a long and substantial history behind the current formulation of this measure, including the seminal publication by Gottschalk and Gleser (1969) providing the basic description of the method of content analysis of verbal behavior for the evaluation of psychological states. This procedure has been used in over 100 studies, including psychophysiological, pharmacological, neuropsychiatric, psychotherapy, and other research domains. The assessment focus of the PCAD is on the "content analysis approach to the measurement of psychological dimensions" (manual, p. 14).

Initial work on a computer-scoring procedure to emulate the detailed content analysis guidelines developed by Gottschalk and Gleser was reported by Gottschalk, Hausmann, and Brown in 1975, demonstrating that a program running on a PDP-10 computer (a small mainframe that allowed for "remote" terminals) could provide scores reasonably consistent with those of a trained clinician. Continued development and refinement of the computer program and the formulation of additional content scales and subscales resulted in the current version. The computer version, known as the PCAD is available on a compact disk (CD) or diskettes (3) designed for use with IBM compatible personal computers (PCs).

The PCAD scoring program evaluates 10 primary psychological scales along with associated subscales, including: Anxiety (with subscales of Death, Mutilation, Separation, Guilt, Shame, and Diffuse Anxiety), Hostility (with subscales of Hostility Directed Outward, Hostility Directed Inward, and Ambivalent Hostility), Social Alienation-Personal Disorganization, Cognitive and Intellectual Impairment, Depression (with subscales of Hopelessness, Self-Accusation, Psychomotor Retardation, Somatic Concerns, Death and Mutilation Depression, Separation Depression, and Hostility Outward), Hope, Human Relations, Achievement Strivings, Dependency Strivings, and Health-Sickness. The latter four scales are new additions to the PCAD from the 1993 version of the computer scoring program as previously described in the Psychologic and Neuropsychiatric Assessment Survey manual (Gottschalk & Bechtel, 1993). The PCAD manual provides a brief description of each of the content analysis scales, with descriptions varying in specificity and length. The scoring program also provides recommendations as to possible DSM-IV diagnoses for further evaluation.

Materials for this measure are few, consisting of just the manual and the computer program. Prior to the recent formulation of the PCAD, the computer program for analyzing verbal text and producing a report was not commercially available, although persons could send a diskette with the transcribed speech sample to the authors for scoring. To obtain scores using the PCAD, a speech sample (of approximately 5 minutes or more in duration) is used as the response sample. The sample of speech for analysis may be solicited using what is referred to as "Standard Procedure" that involves a relatively neutral (nondirective) set of instructions that require speaking for 5 minutes.

The authors suggest that this will provide a reliable sample of speech for purposes of computer analysis. In addition, the authors note that both clinical and research applications may need to use more directive instructions depending on the purpose of the assessment situation. For example, speech derived during psychotherapy, clinical interviews, respondent reports of attitudes or feelings, or even descriptions of dreams may be used. Once the speech sample is obtained, the next step is transcription and the creation of a computer text file for analysis.

The speech sample is transcribed onto a computer file and saved as an ASCII or text file, or as a WordPerfect 5.0, 5.1, or 6.x file. The PCAD manual provides suggestions for the transcription of audiotaped speech samples. The PCAD, similar to previous versions of this program, focuses on the clause as the coding unit of the sentence. The PCAD uses regular grammatical punctuation as conclusions of clauses or a user-inserted slash character in the transcript to mark the end of a clause. In this manner the user indicates different scorable ideas that may be in a compound or complex sentence. The specific scoring, that is the content analysis of speech used by the PCAD, is too complex to describe in this review; however, the research on this procedure has evolved for over 30 years with extensive research providing support for this methodology. Scoring is predicated on the Gottschalk-Gleser content analysis method initially developed in the 1960s (Gottschalk, 1982; Gottschalk & Gleser, 1969; Gottschalk, Winget, & Gleser, 1969) with computerized scoring developed in the 1970s (Gottschalk, Hausmann, & Brown, 1975), and refined in the 1980s (Gottschalk & Bechtel, 1982). The computer program scores the speech sample for the various scales and subscales and provides a report that includes the computer-generated scores for all scales, weighted scores that estimate human scorers, and other indices. The weighted human score is based on research showing that the computer-scoring algorithms, although showing a strong correlation with scoring done by the clinicians, underestimates the latter (Gottschalk & Bechtel, 1982).

The PCAD manual fails to meet most of the criteria and recommendations of the American Educational Research Association, American Psychological Association, and National Council on Measurement in Education (1999) for the documentation of psychometric characteristics. No information on reliability or validity is provided in the manual, although references to published and unpublished sources of information are provided. Users must glean through multiple publications going back several decades to find reliability and validity information on the various scales. The manual would be greatly improved by the inclusion of a chapter on reliability and validity of the scales, with information provided that summarizes the results of studies. Because several of the scales on the PCAD appear to be new, in that they do not appear on the previous version of the manual, reliability and validity data on these scales are needed.

Norms for the PCAD appear to be derived from the various development studies of individual scales, and although several hundred adults and children were used (Louis A. Gottschalk, personal communication, 2000), the normative sample size for each individual scale is more limited. In the PCAD manual, there is no description of the normative sample, although an appendix in the previous manual (Gottschalk & Bechtel, 1993) lists norms for scales separately for adult males and females and child males and females. The number of persons in each group is not provided, although some of this information can be ascertained from the published research. For example, the development of the Depression scale is reported by Gottschalk and Hoigaard-Martin (1986), wherein normative scores for the Depression scale and subscales are reported for samples of 29 male and 29 female adults and 16 male and 16 female children and adolescents drawn from Grades K through 12. The means and standard deviations of these samples in the 1986 publication are those for the Depression scale norms in the 1993 manual. Norms for other scales appear to be based on larger samples. As with reliability and validity, the manual would benefit from greater description of the normative sample.

SUMMARY. As a psychological test, the PCAD is a relatively unique assessment device. With over three decades of research evidence and a very wide range of clinical and research applications, the Gottschalk-Gleser Content Analysis Method has demonstrated its utility as an alternative methodology to projective and self-report objective assessment procedures. The PCAD provides for the computerized evaluation and interpretation of verbal behavior. Although relatively lacking in the manual are descriptions of reliability, validity, and the normative sample, much of this information has been reported in the research literature. With the creation of a PC version of this complex scoring and analysis procedure, there is even greater potential for the exploration and psychological evaluation of persons' verbal behavior. The PCAD should provide clinicians and researchers with a useful alternative assessment methodology.

REVIEWER'S REFERENCES

Gottschalk, L. A., & Gleser, G. C. (1969). *The measurement of psychological states through the content analysis of verbal behavior.* Berkeley: University of California Press.

Gottschalk, L. A., Winget, C. N., & Gleser, G. C. (1969). *Manual of instructions for using the Gottschalk–Gleser Content Analysis Scales: Anxiety, hostility, social alienation, personal disorganization.* Berkeley: University of California Press.

Gottschalk, L. A., Hausmann, C., & Brown, J. S. (1975). A computerized scoring system for use with content analysis scales. *Comprehensive Psychiatry, 16,* 77–90.

Gottschalk, L. A. (1982). Manual of uses and applications of the Gottschalk-Gleser verbal behavior scales. *Research Communications in Psychology, Psychiatry & Behavior, 7,* 273–327.

Gottschalk, L. A., & Bechtel, R. J. (1982). The measurement of anxiety through the computer analysis of verbal samples. *Comprehensive Psychiatry, 23,* 364–369.

Gottschalk, L. A., & Hoigaard-Martin, J. (1986). A depression scale applicable to verbal samples. *Psychiatry Research, 17,* 213–227.

Gottschalk, L. A., & Bechtel, R. J. (1993). *Psychologic and neuropsychiatric assessment survey: Computerized content analysis of natural language or verbal texts.* Palo Alto, CA: Mind Garden.

American Educational Research Association, American Psychological Association, & National Council on Measurement in Education. (1999). *Standards for educational and psychological testing.* Washington, DC: American Educational Research Association.

[301]
Psychosocial Pain Inventory [Revised].

Purpose: "Provides a standardized method of evaluating psychosocial factors important in maintaining and exacerbating chronic pain problems."
Population: Chronic pain patients.
Publication Dates: 1980–1985.
Acronym: PSPI.
Scores: Item scores only.
Administration: Individual.
Price Data: Price information available from publisher for complete kit including manual ('85, 38 pages) and 25 forms.
Time: Administration time not reported.
Authors: R. K. Heaton, R. A. W. Lehman, and C. J. Getto.
Publisher: Psychological Assessment Resources, Inc.
Cross References: See T4:2162 (1 reference).

Review of the Psychosocial Pain Inventory [Revised] by JULIE A. ALLISON, Associate Professor of Psychology, Pittsburg State University, Pittsburg, KS:

The Psychosocial Pain Inventory (PSPI) was developed to provide a standardized method of quantitatively evaluating psychosocial factors that

may play a role in chronic pain. A basic assumption underlying the PSPI argues that both the genesis and the maintenance of chronic pain may be determined by a complexity of factors, including organic pathology, psychopathological factors, and psychosocial factors. Traditionally, chronic pain absent of organic pathology has often been considered psychopathological in nature. Because psychopathology may (or may not) play a role, and the authors of the PSPI advocate obtaining Minnesota Multiphasic Personality Inventory (MMPI) results in juxtaposition with PSPI scores. In addition to a thorough physical/neurological evaluation, many psychosocial factors may contribute significantly to both the experience and the expressions of pain. These factors could be important to treatment programs for pain patients and may include, but are not limited to: (a) social reinforcement (both positive and negative) for behavioral expressions of pain; (b) financial compensation for pain; (c) emotional responses to environmental stress, which may be experienced as pain; (d) self-handicapping through pain; (e) using pain to obtain or validate the use of addictive drugs or alcohol; (f) social learning of pain behavior; (g) iatrogenic (induced inadvertently by physician or treatment) influences of present experiences with the health-care system; and (h) personality factors, which provide impetus for patient roles. The PSPI was designed specifically to measure these psychosocial categories.

The PSPI is an 8-page, 25-item structured interview for patients and their spouses. The interview begins with asking questions in an open-ended manner and any spontaneous responses are recorded following these responses, closed questions assessing frequencies for specific behaviors are given. Information from these latter questions are quantitatively coded. Even though a clear structure is provided by the PSPI, patients are encouraged to elaborate on problems not specifically covered in the interview, and clinicians are free to pursue issues that may seem important to a specific case. Upon completion of the structured interview, the patient is given a final total score based on the quantitative data obtained (instructions for scoring are clear and provided in the manual), which may range from 0 to 68. Higher scores indicate higher levels of psychosocial pain.

The content of PSPI items is quite extensive, and each is included with either a theoretical, clinical, or empirical rationale. They include duration of pain problem, disability income/litigation, life changes primary to pain problem, operations, time in hospital, number of primary physicians, relief obtained from previous treatments, pain-related stress, pain behavior at home, social reinforcement for pain behavior, pain-reducing behaviors, home/family-related responsibilities, work history, change in work status, plans if pain decreases, current medications, patient's past medical history, family history, history of physician usage, history of medication usage, alcohol abuse, pain contingent down time, and interview behavior.

RELIABILITY AND VALIDITY. Interrater reliability for the scoring of the PSPI was estimated as high ($r = .98$).

Data from validity studies on the PSPI do provide preliminary support for validity, but the research is not at a level that supports a general conclusion that scores from the measure are valid. All items on the scale have been found to correlate significantly with PSPI total scores. Significant correlations have been found between PSPI scores and several scores on the McGill Pain Questionnaire. And the authors report that research participants identified as improving 6 months post-treatment by their physician had originally scored significantly lower on the PSPI than those deemed to have not improved or even worsened. This support for the predictive validity of the PSPI is potentially weakened, however, by the confounding variable of treatment type, for which no results are reported. Furthermore, no additional studies replicating these results have been reported.

Normative data ($N = 169$) are provided from a sample of pain patients. These data may be helpful in identifying relative levels of psychosocial pain. The authors also suggest a cutoff level of 30 as a score that may predict poorer responses to treatments, particularly those that may put the patient at risk. However, the low N and the clinically derived cutoff level suggest that caution should be made in drawing any conclusions based on the PSPI score without corroborating information and/or data.

More research on the validity of scores from the PSPI is needed. Keeping this in mind, the PSPI does appear to be a potentially promising tool for identifying both the origins and the maintenance of pain and pain-related behaviors. In addition to identifying relative levels of both specific and general psychosocial pain, the PSPI may be used to aid in the identification of treatment for psychosocial components of pain, and to assist in the evaluation of treatment plans for pain patients. It is worth investigating.

Review of the Psychosocial Pain Inventory [Revised] by DENNIS C. HARPER, Professor of Pediatrics and Rehabilitation, College of Medicine, University of Iowa, Iowa City, IA:

PURPOSE. The Psychosocial Pain Inventory (PSPI) was designed to standardize the format of a clinical interview with adults who report chronic pain, and to provide a way to quantify data obtained in the interview. The authors described this process in the manual and in order to achieve these objectives they selected a structured interview format described by Fordyce (1976) as the basis for this interview. The authors describe a process without detail or verification of item development. Accordingly, the initial interview was subjected to pilot studies at the University of Colorado Pain Clinic. These deliberations reportedly resulted in a 31-item inventory; this inventory was employed in subsequent normative study validations. The information is vague as to its development.

NORMATIVE STUDY SAMPLE. The normative data on the PSPI were obtained from 169 consecutive chronic pain patients presenting at the University of Colorado Pain Clinic, date or type unspecified. Additional assessments were also completed on these patients, specifically the Minnesota Multiphasic Personality Inventory (MMPI) and the McGill Pain Questionnaire. The manual subsequently presents a series of MMPI profiles based on some group identification in relation to pain complaints. The authors present correlational data on the relationship between the Psychosocial Pain Inventory, general pain factors, the Minnesota Multiphasic Personality Inventory, and the McGill Pain Questionnaire. They conclude that the findings indicate that the Psychosocial Pain Inventory and the Minnesota Multiphasic Personality Inventory measure different variables in a population of patients with chronic pain. The authors also report correlational relationships between the McGill Pain Questionnaire and the Psychosocial Pain Inventory.

VALIDATION STUDIES. Two validation studies described in the manual attempt to identify relationships between specific responses on the Psychosocial Pain Inventory and specific patient indicators of pain and chronic disease. These authors indicate that the studies supported the conclusion that "it thus appeared that the total PSPI score could be used to predict outcome of treatment. Higher PSPI scores would predict increasing influence of psychosocial factors and poorer response to treatment plan" (p. 15). No other identifying information is provided.

GUIDELINES FOR ADMINISTRATION. The test authors have very specific guidelines for test administration and require that the questions be asked as written. Additional clinical suggestions for interviewing patients are offered as well. The manual then outlines the remaining 25 questions and the rationale and scoring for each. These are largely clinical interpretations.

SUMMARY. The Psychosocial Pain Inventory is a structured method of evaluating psychosocial factors common to chronic pain patients. The data presented by the authors in this manual are likely clinically useful; however, only limited, and insufficient, evidence of validity and reliability are presented. The PSPI seems useful as a structured interview based upon its face validity.

REVIEWER'S REFERENCE

Fordyce, W. R. (1976). *Behavioral methods for chronic pain and illness*. St. Louis: Mosby.

[302]

Psychotherapy Outcome Kit (Including Quality of Emotional Life Self-Report).

Purpose: Designed to assist mental health care providers in collecting treatment outcome data.
Publication Date: 1994.
Acronym: QELSR.
Scores: Total score only.
Administration: Individual.
Price Data, 1997: $25 per sampler set including QELSR, data sheet, clinical summary form, clinical summary end of treatment form, Psychotherapy Outcome Profile, and manual (52 pages, including sample forms) for child and adult versions; $100 per permission set including sampler set and permission to reproduce 200 copies of the test.
Time: No administration time reported.
Author: David P. Isenberg.
Publisher: Mind Garden, Inc.
  a) CHILD VERSION.
  Population: Age 15 and under.
  Comments: Child Version QELSR completed by parent/guardian.
  b) ADULT VERSION.
  Population: Age 16 and older.
  Comments: Adult Version QELSR completed by patient.

Review of the Psychotherapy Outcome Kit (Including Quality of Emotional Life Self-Report) by MATTHEW BURNS, Assistant Professor of School Psychology, Central Michigan University, Mt. Pleasant, MI:

The author of the Psychotherapy Outcome Kit (POK) cites several sources calling for an increase in concrete documentation of mental health care outcome data. To meet this need, and to provide a clinical summary that can be sent to primary care physicians, several data collection forms were compiled into the POK, the primary form of which is the Quality of Emotional Life Self-Report (QELSR).

A form of the QELSR is provided both for adults ages 16 and older and for children ages 15 and younger. The adult version is a 17-item self-report scale, and the child version contains 18 items to be completed by a parent or guardian. Resulting total scores reportedly range from 17 to 85 for the adult scale and 18 to 90 for the child version. It is recommended that the QELSR be completed before the 1st session, 10th session, termination session, and a 1-month follow-up session in order to establish progress. The test author suggests that a 5-point change in total score is evidence of improvement. However, the manual provides no other information regarding the interpretation of the total scores and the 5-point criteria were based on the author's use of the scale rather than sound research. Additional research examining the degree of change associated with positive treatment outcomes is necessary before the test can be used for its primary purpose.

Several data sheets are provided to compile and compare the QELSR total scores. The demographic portion of the data sheets includes the patient's name, age, gender, education, and ethnic background. Additional pages include primary diagnosis, prevalent diagnostic category, and a place to record four sets of item scores. Although these pages are concise enough to make the record-keeping process organized, they offer nothing innovative or particularly useful. Mind Garden, the POK publisher, will provide a database and outcome profiles from the data, but again little information is included to persuade a user that Mind Garden's services are preferable to utilizing any standard database software program.

Administration and scoring of the QELSR seems simple and straightforward. The manual also provides several samples of cover letters and explanation forms, which could be quite useful.

TEST CONSTRUCTION. The items of the QELSR are rated on a 5-point Likert scale. The length of the items ranges from short descriptions above each Likert Point such as *Very Unhappy with Relationships with Friends or No Friends,* to long descriptions of clinical conditions such as depression and anxiety with Likert anchors such as *Very Depressed* and *Never or Almost Never Depressed.* Each item attempts to be descriptive of a psychological dimension, but it seems somewhat unreasonable to assess constructs such as depression, anxiety, self-esteem, and feeling persecuted with only one item.

No norms are currently available for the QELSR because it is described as an ipsative scale, which suggests that the individual is the norm. The author should be commended for providing a scale for which the primary function is intraindividual comparison. However, given that the QELSR is a measure of treatment outcome, rather than a diagnostic tool, norms developed specifically to compare progress might be helpful. Furthermore, little information was provided about how the test was constructed or the scores established. The only information provided indicated that the QELSR was developed to demonstrate high face validity and that some items include descriptions of dimensions based on DSM-III-R and DSM-IV classifications. No other validity or reliability data were provided. In fact, the manual was largely void of psychometric data, description of test construction, guidelines for interpretation, administration time, and theoretical basis. It was mentioned that studies of psychometric properties are currently underway, but until those data are provided, use of the scale is not recommended.

SUMMARY. The Psychotherapy Outcome Kit is an attempt to meet an important need among mental health care providers. The manual provides useful examples of cover letters and explanation forms, but lacks data about the construction, psychometric properties, and interpretation of the QELSR, the kit's primary form. Therefore, use of the QELSR as a measure of treatment outcome is not recommended until additional research is conducted. Practitioners interested in measuring therapy outcomes could examine the detailed discussion provided by Maruish (1999). The use of a broad-band scale, such as the

QELSR, to measure treatment outcome seems somewhat ineffective given its predominate use of single-construct tools based on specific treatment goals.

REVIEWER'S REFERENCE
Maruish, M. E. (1999). *The use of psychological testing for treatment planning and outcome assessment* (2nd ed.). Mahwah, NJ: Lawrence Erlbaum Associates.

Review of the Psychotherapy Outcome Kit (Including Quality of Emotional Life Self-Report) by GEORGE DOMINO, Professor of Psychology, University of Arizona, Tucson, AZ:

The Psychotherapy Outcome Kit is made up of a 17-item rating scale called the Quality of Emotional Life Self-Report (QELSR) to be filled out by the patient, with an 18-item child's version to be filled out by the parent or guardian, and a set of office forms including cover letters, summary sheets, and diagnostic guidelines taken from the *Diagnostic and Statistical Manual of Mental Disorders, Fourth Edition* (American Psychiatric Association, 1994).

This kit is designed for psychotherapists who, within the framework of managed mental health care, must document clinical information when corresponding with primary care physicians and managed health organizations. As a set of office procedures, the kit represents a contribution and can be of use to the busy clinician who does not have the time or office skills to generate his or her own forms. They are forms, however, not tests, and thus are not in the purview of the *Mental Measurements Yearbook.* The QELSR is, however, a rating scale and can be legitimately analyzed from a psychometric perspective.

The QELSR items ask the respondents to indicate on a 5-point scale their self-evaluation on such dimensions as happiness, depression, anxiety, self-esteem, and alcohol or drug use. The items are clearly written, with dimensions like anxiety and compulsivity clearly defined, and each of the five response options (that differ from item to item) are clearly defined.

The kit is accompanied by a "manual" that describes the kit and the use of the various forms. There is, however, no psychometric information of any kind available. The manual contains the statement that "research is under way to carry out reliability, validity, and normative studies" (manual, p. 9), but although that statement was made in 1994 no such data were made available to this reviewer 4 years later. Thus, although the QELSR could potentially provide reliable and valid scores, its commercial publication is premature and contrary to the *Standards for Educational and Psychological Testing* (AERA, APA, & NCME, 1985).

At the very minimum, the author could have indicated how the items of the QELSR were generated and given some tentative data to support statements such as "a five point change" between initial and final QELSR reflects therapeutic improvement. Surely the form was administered to some clients before being presented to the world, and even some individual case profiles would have been better than no information.

SUMMARY. I would consider the QELSR a pilot rating scale with potential, but currently no psychometric support.

REVIEWER'S REFERENCES

American Educational Research Association, American Psychological Association, & National Council on Measurement in Education (Joint Committee). (1985). *Standards for Educational and Psychological Testing.* Washington, DC: APA.

American Psychiatric Association. (1994). *Diagnostic and statistical manual of mental disorders* (4th ed.). Washington, DC: American Psychiatric Association.

[303]
Quality of Life Enjoyment and Satisfaction Questionnaire.

Purpose: Designed to measure the "degree of enjoyment and satisfaction experienced by subjects in various areas of daily functioning."

Population: Adults with mental or medical disorders.

Publication Date: 1990.

Acronym: Q-LES-Q.

Forms, 2: Regular Form, Short Form.

Scores, 9: 6 scores (Physical Health, Subjective Feelings, Leisure Time Activities, Social Relationships, General Activities, Overall Life Enjoyment and Satisfaction); 3 optional scores (Work, Household Duties, School/Coursework).

Administration: Group.

Price Data, 1998: $1 per Regular Form; $1.50 per Summary Scale Scores.

Time: Regular Form: [5–15] minutes; Short Form: [3–5] minutes.

Comments: Self-report measure.

Author: Jean Endicott.

Publisher: Department of Research Assessment and Training, Columbia University.

Review of the Quality of Life Enjoyment and Satisfaction Questionnaire by JOHN C. CARUSO, Assistant Professor of Psychology, University of Montana, Missoula, MT:

The Quality of Life Enjoyment and Satisfaction Questionnaire (Q-LES-Q) is a brief (5–15 minutes) measure of self-reported life satisfaction generally and for a variety of facets. The five composite scores are for general life satisfaction, satisfaction with physical health, subjective satisfaction, satisfaction with leisure time activities, and satisfaction with social relationships. The general life satisfaction score is not the sum of other scores (in fact, no such composite is described), but based on a separate set of items. Three optional composite scores assess satisfaction with work, household duties, and school, for those individuals engaged in those activities. Additionally, single items assess satisfaction with medication (if any) and overall life satisfaction. Preliminary reliability and validity data are positive, but unfortunately there is no adequate normative sample, the scoring and interpretational system is inadequate, and the discriminant validity of the facets has yet to be demonstrated. These factors limit the utility of the Q-LES-Q.

The scoring system for the Q-LES-Q consists of summing the scores on the individual items (measured on 5-point Likert scales from *not at all or never* to *frequently or all the time*) making up a scale and determining the percentage of the total possible satisfaction points achieved. (For example, a person who marked a "3" for each of the 13 physical health items would have a percentage of [3X13]/[5X13] = 39/65 = 60%.) This percentage, and this percentage alone, is the basis for interpretation. It is unclear if this percentage is to be interpreted literally as the percentage of maximum satisfaction a person is experiencing, which would seem to be somewhat farfetched, or if not, why this percentage is computed at all. In any case, the raw scores and percentages are poor substitutes for descriptive statistics from relevant comparison groups. No norms or percentiles from any relevant sample have been reported. Thus, the Q-LES-Q is less useful for examining levels of satisfaction relative to one's peers than for examining changes in levels of satisfaction or intraindividual areas of greater or lesser satisfaction.

Information regarding item selection and development were incompletely described. Similarly, analysis of groups of items via exploratory or confirmatory factor analysis have not been reported. These are important omissions that must be addressed if this measure is to be recommended for general use.

Several studies (both from the test publishers and independent researchers) have reported internal consistency reliability estimates for the five main scales and each estimate has exceeded .85 indicating that the main scale scores are reliable. The preliminary validity evidence indicates that levels of satisfaction, as measured by the eight composite scores from the Q-LES-Q, are negatively correlated with the Clinical Global Impressions' Severity of Illness scale, and that changes in Q-LES-Q scores are negatively related to changes in scores on the Hamilton Rating Scale for Depression. Although these relationships indicate a degree of convergent validity for scores from the Q-LES-Q, discriminant validity has not been demonstrated.

SUMMARY. Before the Q-LES-Q can be recommended for general use, systematic psychometric analyses of items and composite scores must be conducted. Additionally, data from a large normative sample must be collected and a more sophisticated scoring system developed so that scores may be interpreted in terms of satisfaction relative to other individuals in appropriate reference groups. In spite of these limitations, the main scale scores have been shown to be highly reliable and have demonstrated convergent validity with other clinical measures.

Review of the Quality of Life Enjoyment and Satisfaction Questionnaire by MARY LOU BRYANT FRANK, Professor and Department Head of Psychology, North Georgia College & State University, Dahlonega, GA:

Measuring complex constructs is, by its very nature, a lengthy process. It generally involves not only defining the construct, but establishing the reliability of the measure, and validating its ability to measure the construct as well as assessing it in comparison to other concepts/measures. However, the criticisms leveled at instruments attempting to assess these more nebulous topics are often harsh due, in fact, to the central need to validate the credibility of the concept itself as well as the scores from the instrument being used. I believe that at least in part, the Quality of Life Enjoyment and Satisfaction Questionnaire (Q-LES-Q) suffers from a lack of diligence in statistically delving into this important construct as well as the inherent difficulty of the concept being measured. This is not to say that the instrument lacks utility, only that if it is going to gain wider acceptance, it will need to address the deficiencies in its current form.

The Quality of Life Enjoyment and Satisfaction Questionnaire (Q-LES-Q) is "designed to help assess the degree of enjoyment and satisfaction experienced during the past week." The self-report questionnaire has 93 items providing information on nine scales. The five scales used for all individuals are: Physical Health (13 items), Subjective Feelings (14 items), Leisure Time Activities (6 items), Social Relationships (11 items), and General Activities (15 items). The optional scales, used for those individuals for whom they apply, include Work (13 items), Household Duties (10 items), and School/Course Work (10 items). Two individual items are also scored as scales: Satisfaction With Medication (if the individual is on medication) and Overall Life Satisfaction and Contentment. The instrument uses a 5-point Likert-type scale format and the content appears to cover general items related to physical and emotional satisfaction. The Q-LES-Q seems to be an easy questionnaire to give and would probably take 15 minutes for the complete administration. It is a simple instrument, but lacking in documentation, background, and evidence of technical quality.

There is no manual for the Q-LES-Q. The questionnaire appears to be available only in a hand-scored version. Overall scoring instructions are minimal and no detailed interpretation recommendations are given. Although a simple instrument, the lack of directions, guidelines, and basic information for the Q-LES-Q cause the instrument to appear poorly conceived.

The reliability information on the Q-LES-Q are likewise sparse. Relatively small samples (n = 54 and 83) also negatively impact the generalizability of results. Test-retest reliability (time interval not indicated) was limited to depressed patients, although they were reported to be homogenous. The internal consistency reliability of the Q-LES-Q was seen as high; however, it is important to note the impact on generalizability of the limited sample size and composition.

Validity evidence shows a good start, but is not sufficient. The concurrent validity examination of the Q-LES-Q looked at the correlation of the scales with the severity of illness measured within the study. The scale appears to discriminate between depressives, and has relatively low shared variance. The Q-LES-Q seems to be sensitive to individual changes. The Q-LES-Q provides no validity indices and does not control for individuals responding in a socially desirable manner or who are more conscious in being deceptive. In medical settings, these might become important variables. Additional studies indicate that the Q-LES-Q has been used with a variety of individuals: dysthymics, women with PMS, alcoholics, severe mental illness, individuals needing stabilization/hospitalization, schizophrenics, adults 60 and over, and medical trials.

The lack of coherent information about the Q-LES-Q is compounded by the availability of alternative instruments that measure quality of life. The Health Related Quality of Life (Fitzpatrick, 1996; Andresen, Rothenberg, Pranzer, Katz, & McDermott, 1998), the Quality of Life Outcome Measure (Mohtadi, 1998), and the Quality of Life measure (Fallowfield, 1996) are a few of those that are available. A concerted effort is needed to evaluate all of these instruments and compare their utility in various settings. It would seem that medical usefulness of this concept would support a thorough evaluation of these varied measures.

SUMMARY. As an objective assessment, this questionnaire has many areas needing attention. Still, I would think if used thoughtfully as a tool to increase discussion about quality of life issues, it has utility. As a research tool, it would seem to need additional studies to sufficiently make the Q-LES-Q an easy-to-use, clear, and sound instrument.

REVIEWER'S REFERENCES

Fallowfield, L. (1996). Quality of quality of life data. *Lancet, 348,* 421–422.
Fitzpatrick, R. (1996). The international assessment of health-related quality of life: Theory, translation, measurement and analysis. *Journal of Medical Ethics, 22,* 248–249.
Andresen, E. M., Rothenberg, B. M., Panzer, R., Katz, P., & McDermott, M. P. (1998). Selecting a generic measure of health-related quality of life for use among older adults: A comparison of candidate instruments. *Evaluation and the Health Professions, 21,* 244–264.
Mohtadi, N. (1998). Development and validation of the quality of life outcome measure (questionnaire) for chronic anterior cruciate ligament deficiency. *American Journal of Sports Medicine, 26*(3), 350–359.

[304]
Quality of Life Inventory.

Purpose: Developed to provide a measure of a person's quality of life and their satisfaction with life.
Population: Ages 18 and over.
Publication Date: 1994.
Acronym: QOLI.
Scores: 17 scales: Health, Self-Esteem, Goals-and-Values, Money, Work, Play, Learning, Creativity, Helping, Love, Friends, Children, Relatives, Home, Neighborhood, Community, Overall Quality of Life.
Administration: Group or individual.
Price Data, 1999: $80 per starter kit for handscoring including manual (84 pages), 50 answer sheets, and 50 worksheets; $44 per preview package for computer scoring including manual, 10 answer sheets, materials needed for 10 assessments, and 10 profile reports; $63.50 per reorder kit for handscoring including 50 answer sheets and 50 worksheets; $17 per 25 computer answer sheets; $1.70 per profile report, $32.50 per manual.
Time: (5) minutes.
Comments: Useful for outcomes measurement as well as individual counseling.
Author: Michael B. Frisch.
Publisher: NCS (Minnetonka).

Review of the Quality of Life Inventory by LAURA L. B. BARNES, Associate Professor of Educational Research and Evaluation, School of Educational Studies, Oklahoma State University, Stillwater, OK:

The Quality of Life Inventory (QOLI) is theoretically grounded in a view of life satisfaction as a discrepancy between what a person has and what a person desires in valued areas of life. The model is linear and additive (i.e., overall satisfaction is the sum of satisfactions in particular areas of life deemed important). Satisfaction in highly valued areas is assumed to have greater influence on evaluations of overall life satisfaction than areas of equal satisfaction that are judged to be less important. The QOLI was developed as a measure of positive mental health to supplement measures of negative affect and psychiatric symptoms in both outcome assessment and treatment planning and to "focus the attention of health providers on a client's sources of fulfillment" (manual, p. 6). A chapter in the manual is devoted to general cognitively oriented treatment strategies for addressing the life areas assessed by the QOLI.

PRACTICAL EVALUATION. The QOLI can be administered via paper and pencil or online; scoring of the paper-pencil version can be accomplished by hand or by using available software. Only the hand-scoring version includes a form inviting respondents to identify problems that interfere with satisfaction in each of the 16 areas. The test materials are attractively packaged and easy to use. The meaning of the 16 areas is clearly defined for respondents. They are asked to rate both the importance of the area to their overall happiness and their level of satisfaction with that aspect of their life. The labels on the 6-point satisfaction scale may present a problem, however, because the scoring scheme assumes a higher level of satisfaction for a "somewhat satisfied" or a "a little satisfied" response than a "somewhat dissatisfied" or "a little dissatisfied" response. For some respondents, to be only a little satisfied may seem more negative than to be only a little dissatisfied. The scale values suggest the intended interpretation because positive numbers are assigned to satisfied responses and negative numbers to dissatisfied responses. Nevertheless, I found the scale labels to be somewhat counterintuitive and distracting. Labeling only the end-points of the scale or using some other scale format would solve this problem.

Hand scoring is easily accomplished with step-by-step instructions on the worksheet. Total scale raw scores are converted to T-scores and percentiles, and finally to an overall classification (very low, low, average, high) by consulting the manual. A respondent's score profile across the 16 areas may also be plotted.

Interpretation of both the total satisfaction score and the life area profile is facilitated by a generally well-written section on test interpretation. According to the manual the overall QOLI classification scheme is based on both normative data from the standardization sample and on clinical data and suggests that the 20th percentile appears to distinguish between clinical and nonclinical samples. It would be helpful to have more specific information validating the classification cutoffs. Also lacking is a discussion of measurement error and confidence bands in the section on interpretation.

STANDARDIZATION. The nonclinical standardization sample matched the 1992 U.S. Census fairly closely with respect to race, but its match on other relevant characteristics cannot be determined from the manual. The sample consisted of 798 out of 1,924 individuals samples from 12 states across the U.S. The sampling procedure was not described but appears to have been a convenience sample (e.g., some respondents were paid). The description of the sample in the manual is inadequate for making judgments about its appropriateness.

RELIABILITY AND VALIDITY. The QOLI reports stability (2-week interval) and internal consistency reliabilities in the .70s. The samples were quite small ($n = 55$) and not described. Validity of scores of the QOLI was presented through moderate to large correlations with two other life satisfaction scales and a small correlation with the Marlowe-Crowne Social Desirability Scale. Significant results from a study of 13 clinically depressed patients treated with bibliotherapy were presented as evidenced for sensitivity to clinical treatment. An array of correlational data from a previous version of the QOLI showed moderate positive correlations with other measures of subjective well-being and moderate negative correlations with measures of psychopathology.

SUMMARY. The QOLI appears to be theoretically grounded and well integrated into a cognitive therapeutic modality. The discrepancy model upon which the instrument is based is not disguised in the instrument design. This may be a drawback psychometrically in that a person's awareness of discrepancy between what they value and what they have may influence their subsequent responses. On the other hand, this awareness of discrepancy may facilitate therapy. The QOLI has acceptable, but not outstanding, evidence of score reliability. The standard error of measurement must be taken into consideration in score interpretation and in assessing pre-post change. Validity data from the manual are scant but potentially promising. More information on the standardization sample and procedures needs to be made available—normative comparisons are tenuous at best without a clearer description of the make-up of the comparison group. The test itself appears to be solid and may be used with appropriate caution for its stated purpose.

Review of the Quality of Life Inventory by RICHARD W. JOHNSON, Adjunct Professor of Counseling Psychology and Associate Director Emeritus of Counseling & Consultation Services, University Health Services, University of Wisconsin—Madison, Madison, WI:

The Quality of Life Inventory (QOLI) provides a broad measure of life satisfaction that complements measures of psychopathology used in clinical assessment. It evaluates one's quality of life in 16 different areas, such as Work, Love, and Health. Information of this nature is helpful in obtaining a fuller understanding of a client's issues and resources.

TEST DEVELOPMENT. The QOLI was developed by Michael Frisch based on a quality of life model that assumes four components underlie satisfaction with life in each of 16 areas. These four components (objective circumstances, attitudes toward one's circumstance, standards for evaluating one's situation, and relative importance attributed to an area of living) can be used both to explain an individual's scores and to suggest possible treatment approaches for improving scores.

The QOLI measures "weighted satisfaction" in each of the 16 life areas by the use of two questions for each area. Clients are asked first to rate their level of satisfaction (on a 6-point scale ranging from -3 to +3) for an area and then to indicate the relative importance (0, 1, or 2) that they place on that area. Satisfaction scores are multiplied by importance scores to obtain a total of 16 weighted satisfaction scores (ranging from -6 to +6), which are then added together to produce the QOLI Total score. The test questions, which are written at a 6th-grade reading level, are easy to understand and relevant to most therapy situations.

Most people can complete the QOLI in 5 or 6 minutes. Hand scoring of the instrument can be completed in 1 or 2 minutes. Because of its brevity, the inventory can be easily readministered to clients to help evaluate their progress in therapy.

Computer scoring is available as well as hand scoring. The hand-scoring version has the advantage of written comments supplied by the client that indicate the nature of problems or concerns in each of the 16 life areas. The computer version allows test scores from different administrations to be plotted in charts as a means of evaluating progress. All scores are reported as raw scores. Tables are provided for converting the Total score (but not the area scores) to T-scores or percentiles.

PSYCHOMETRIC CHARACTERISTICS. The QOLI has been standardized on a national sample that roughly matches the U.S. Census in regard to the distribution of racial and ethnic groups. The test results show no significant differences among the scores of Blacks, Whites, or Others; however, Hispanic respondents scored significantly higher (about one-third of a standard deviation) than both Blacks and Whites, indicating a higher quality of life for the Hispanic population. These results may be an artifact of the sampling process; additional research on this topic is needed. The author points out the value of collecting local norms for helping to determine treatment goals.

No significant sex or age differences were noted in the test scores. Test scores had low correlation ($r = .10$) with years of education. These data indicate that separate norms are not needed for different groups based on sex, age, or education.

The only test-retest reliability study reported in the manual for the current version of the QOLI yielded a relatively low correlation coefficient ($r = .73$ over a 2-week period). This result suggests a standard error of measurement of over one-half of a standard deviation unit. Two test-retest reliability studies reported in the appendix of the manual for an earlier version of the QOLI show higher correlations ($r = .91$ over 33 days and $r = .80$ over 18 days). This issue deserves further study.

Estimates of internal consistency for the Total score have been moderately high. Alpha coefficients have ranged from .77 to .89 for studies conducted with the original and revised version of the QOLI. These results indicate that the Total score is a relatively homogeneous measure of quality of life.

Validation studies show both convergent and discriminant validity. QOLI Total scores of subjects in the normative sample were significantly correlated with two other measures of quality of life, the Satisfaction with Life Scale and the Quality of Life Index. Total scores for these same subjects were relatively independent of scores on a measure of social desirability. Similar studies conducted with the original version of the QOLI (which closely resembles the current version) also support the validity of scores from the instrument.

Additional validation studies are needed. What are the relationships among the 16 areas of living scores? What factors account for most of the variance in the QOLI scores? Do low QOLI scores predict clinical depression, sensitivity to pain, immune system vulnerability, or other health or psychological problems as suggested by the author? Information on each of these topics would help to clarify further the validity of the QOLI.

INTERPRETATION OF SCORES. Total scores are interpreted in terms of four levels, ranging from very low (10th percentile and below) to high (above 80th percentile). Scores at or below the 20th percentile indicate areas of concern that should be explored further in counseling. The manual is unusually helpful in listing possible causes for low scores in each of the 16 categories and in suggesting possible treatment strategies. Case studies indicate that the QOLI scores of clients are highly sensitive to changes in one's situation.

CONCLUSIONS. The QOLI inventory possesses the following advantages: It is brief, comprehensive in its scope, easy to administer and score, and closely related to a quality of life model that can be helpful both in explaining scores and in suggesting possible treatments. It is a new instrument that still needs research on a number of issues, including separate scale norms, test-retest reliability, construct (factorial) validity, predictive validity, and cross-cultural applications. Research and clinical experience thus far indicates that the instrument can provide valuable information in conceptualizing a case, in suggesting treatment approaches, and in measuring outcomes of interventions. It is the best instrument of which I am aware for evaluating a client's quality of life.

[305]
Quality Potential Assessment.

Purpose: "Designed to provide information about an organization, such as data on its policies, practices, and logistics, and the degree to which the data contribute to encouraging staff to give their best to the organization."
Population: Adults.
Publication Date: 1992.
Acronym: QPA.
Scores: Actual and Desired ratings in 10 areas: Collaboration (Management Values, Support Structure, Managerial Credibility, Climate), Commitment (Impact, Relevance, Community), Creativity (Task Environment, Social Context, Problem Solving).
Administration: Group.
Price Data: Available from publisher.
Time: Administration time not reported.
Author: Jay Hall.
Publisher: Teleometrics International.

Review of the Quality Potential Assessment by THEODORE L. HAYES, *Research Analyst, U.S. Immigration and Naturalization Service, Washington, DC:*

The author states that the Quality Potential Assessment (QPA) is designed to "quantify what life is like in an organization" (manual, p. 2) by measuring the conditions of work that either facilitate or inhibit competent performance; the main focus is on inhibitors of performance. The basis for this measurement plan is "Competence Theory," which is described in a book by the company's founder and chairman, Jay Hall. Response materials allow for hand- or computer-scoring of the 40-item QPA questionnaire. Each questionnaire item is meant to be evaluated in terms of "As it is" and "As I would like it to be." Training manuals and feedback materials are designed to explain results

in terms of the Competence Theory model, which reflects the degrees of Collaboration, Commitment, and Creativity in the work place.

OVERVIEW. The goal is to assess the perceived gaps between organizational practice and some desired state on a set of items encompassing familiar organizational development (OD) dimensions such as task structure, management style, interpersonal relations, mission, and company climate. Better instruments than the QPA are available for this task.

VALIDITY AND RELIABILITY. The QPA measurement model is built around the three principles of Competence Theory: Balance among the Collaboration, Commitment, and Creativity dimensions; Polarity of these three dimensions; and Sequence of the three dimensions. The 40 OD-oriented items substantiate in turn the three dimensions. This order reflects the deductive nature of the instrument, and also the highly idiosyncratic constructs alleged to underlie its implementation. The authors refer to studies conducted in several organizations that support the validity of the QPA, but no data are presented to support this claim. A table is provided for conversion of raw scores to percentile scores based on a "normative sample" of over 1,000 respondents. The discussion of percentile scores is the most lucid section in the QPA materials.

Potential users not familiar with Competence Theory and who are looking for validity evidence will find this incredible elision in the accompanying marketing materials: "The easiest way for a trainer to establish the validity of a given approach [such as the QPA] is to ask the producer or publisher for proof that it works. And the proof is … in the facts about the theoretical and research bases for the particular program … When using [the QPA] the trainer must decide two things: whether the model itself is valid and if the instrument actually measures behavior according to the model. No publisher of reliable instruments should have any problem answering these questions to your satisfaction" (Feedback, pp. 6–7). Fair enough, yet the QPA materials do not offer any standard factual validity or reliability evidence about the QPA's research bases.

The QPA materials are remarkable for their pointless and grandiose verbosity. The effect is to lard the modest measurements resulting from the QPA—which are gap scores for 10 standard OD-related dimensions (task structure, etc.)—with Competence Theory parlance. Practically, the question response options require careful reading as they change from question to question. The reading level demands for this instrument are high, possibly putting it out of reach of many nonprofessional or nonmanagement jobs. Also, given the idiosyncratic and stilted language, transient response error is likely quite pronounced. This is exacerbated by the gap score response format ("As it is" vs. "As I would like it to be").

CONSULTING UTILITY. I am not familiar enough with Competence Theory to say whether the QPA is a good measure of it. However, a Competence Theory-based consultant would have slim pickings among other OD intervention measurements, so the QPA might serve this tiny group of consultants quite well. Any other consultant or trainer who is not wedded to Competency Theory would have much better options in almost any other measurement instrument. The interested party should consult Fleishman and Quaintance's (1984) fine review of human and organizational performance measurements, such as the well-researched Job Diagnostic Inventory (Hackman and Oldham, 1980) and its progeny. Algera (1998) has a more recent review from a European perspective.

SUMMARY. The author presents several compelling reasons why OD measurement and intervention are necessary. None of the arguments support the usage of the QPA in particular.

REVIEWER'S REFERENCES
Hackman, J. R., & Oldham, G. R. (1980). *Work redesign.* Reading, MA: Addison-Wesley.
Fleishman, E. A., & Quaintance, M. K. (1984). *Taxonomies of human performance: The description of human tasks.* Orlando, FL: Academic Press.
Algera, J. A. (1998). Task characteristics. In P. J. D. Drenth, H. Thierry, & C. J. de Wolff (Eds.), *Handbook of work and organizational psychology* (2ⁿᵈ ed.; vol. 3: Personnel Psychology; pp. 123–139). Hove, East Sussex, UK: Psychology Press.

Review of the Quality Potential Assessment by MICHAEL J. ZICKAR, *Assistant Professor of Industrial-Organizational Psychology, Bowling Green State University, Bowling Green, OH:*

The development of the Quality Potential Assessment (QPA) was based on a path model theory of "the structure of competence" (manual, p. 8), which states that positive collaboration leads to positive commitment and creativity, which both in turn lead to quality performance. Consequently, the QPA is designed to provide feedback on the three hypothesized antecedents of effective organizational performance.

There are 40 items on the QPA with three response options each. An example item is, "How much agreement with a decision must there be by people in your part of the organization before it will be implemented?" Each of the response options consists of several statements that describe potential organizational practices with respect to the item stem; the three options vary in terms of effectiveness. The order of response options varies throughout the questionnaire so that Response A does not always correspond to the best answer. Respondents are allowed to qualify responses so that Option A may be chosen as the most descriptive option yet Option B may be chosen as partially descriptive. Respondents are instructed to answer each item once to describe the organization "as it is" and a second time to describe the organization "as it should be." Large discrepancies between these two scores are supposed to indicate potential problem areas.

There are two options for scoring. A scannable answer sheet can be completed and computer-scored by Teleometrics International. A hand-scored version is also available, which is easily tabulated. The average completion time of the QPA is not given in the manual but I estimated it to be around 40 minutes.

The reliability evidence for the QPA consists of high internal consistency reliability coefficients (ranging from .91 to .94), computed from unspecified samples. There is no evidence to evaluate the stability of QPA scores across time. Because many of the questions deal with perceptions of organizational policies, it is unexpected that there would be much variation in scores over short time periods, barring change in management. It would be important, however, to demonstrate empirically this expected stability.

Validity evidence was gathered by assessing high- and low-performing groups within nine organizations that represented a variety of public and private industries. In each organization, a top-performing unit was compared to a poor-performing unit. An unspecified statistical test was conducted that showed a statistically significant difference between high- and low-performing groups across the nine organizations. The manual also reported that high-performing groups had less discrepancy between actual and desired scores than low-performing groups. Again, the statistical test was unspecified. I consider the criterion-related validity evidence to be preliminary. Future research should focus on predicting performance across the whole range of possible performance, not just the extreme ranges.

Norms were developed based on data from over 1,000 respondents from a wide variety of large and small organizations across several industries. Therefore, comparison to the average organization can be made; however, there are no breakdowns by industry or company size. Norms by company size may be important because it seems plausible that smaller-sized companies would have higher amounts of collaboration due to smaller numbers of layers between top management and the lowest-level of employee.

Overall, the documentation focuses on the theoretical model that underlies the QPA as well as a description of the generally deplorable state of management in the United States; documentation of the psychometric properties of the instrument is minimal. Important information, such as the correlations between the three major dimensions, is not presented. Additionally, construct validity could be supported by relating the test to other established measures of the same constructs. For example, the scale developers should relate their commitment dimension to the well-known commitment scale of Mowday, Steers, and Porter (1979).

SUMMARY. I think the QPA could be useful for identifying areas of an organization that might benefit from remedial training. However, decisions that require serious allocation of resources should be made with much other corroborating information. In the future, more emphasis should be made in documenting the psychometric properties of the QPA.

REVIEWER'S REFERENCE

Mowday, R. T., Steers, R. M., & Porter, L. W. (1979). The measurement of organizational commitment. *Journal of Vocational Behavior, 14*, 224–247.

[306]
Quick Neurological Screening Test, 2nd Revised Edition.

Purpose: "Designed to assess areas of neurological integration as they relate to learning."
Population: Ages 5–18.
Publication Dates: 1974–1998.
Acronym: QNST-II.
Scores, 15: Hand Skill, Figure Recognition and Production, Palm Form Recognition, Eye Tracking, Sound Patterns, Finger to Nose, Thumb and Finger Circle, Double Simultaneous Stimulation of Hand and Cheek, Rapidly Reversing Repetitive Hand Movements, Arm and Leg Extensions, Tandem Walk, Standing on One Leg, Skipping, Left-Right Discrimination, Behavioral Irregularities.
Administration: Individual.
Price Data, 1999: $80 per test kit including manual (93 pages), 25 scoring forms, 25 geometric form reproduction sheets, 25 remedial guideline forms, and cue cards; $27 per manual; $15 per 25 scoring forms; $10 per 25 geometric form reproduction sheets; $10 per 25 remedial guideline forms; $15 per directions for administration and scoring printed on 20 cue cards; $257 per specimen set (manual and sample forms).
Time: (20–30) minutes.
Comments: Screening for early identification of learning disabilities; 1998 edition provides extensive literature reviews, clarified directions for administration, and reformatted test protocol sheets.
Authors: Margaret C. Mutti, Harold M. Sterling, Nancy A. Martin, and Norma V. Spalding.
Publisher: Academic Therapy Publications.
Cross References: See T5:2141 (1 reference) and T4:2183 (3 references); for a review by Russell L. Adams of an earlier edition, see 9:1027.

Review of the Quick Neurological Screening Test, 2nd Revised Edition by EDWARD E. GOTTS, Chief Psychologist, Madison State Hospital, Madison, IN:

The original edition of this test came out 20 years ago and was reviewed 15 years ago by Adams (1985). Adams (1985) at that time identified with precision a number of empirical shortcomings that needed to be remedied by further study in order for the test to realize its promise. Unfortunately, the Quick Neurological Screening Test, 2nd Revised Edition (QNST-II) shows little evidence of progress in filling in those gaps. Adams' review (1985) should be consulted regarding his concerns that evidence of both reliability and validity were insufficient or flawed. He further found to be insupportable the claim that the test had applicability to adults as well as to children, and he judged that its claim to deal with *learning disability* was too general and was not validated in terms of specific varieties of learning disability. Perhaps few fundamental advances have been made in this revision due to the authors' considered belief, as stated in the Preface to the 1998 manual, that their original data remain solidly related to basic human neurological functioning, inasmuch as neural functions continue unchanged. It is, thus, needless to repeat in the present review those specific matters that Adams (1985) has previously covered. Instead, attention will be directed to additional issues that are germane to the evaluation of this revised edition.

Items within the 15 individual subtests are weighted either as *1* or *3*, with the "severe" score (3) designating greater deviation from expected performance. A rationale for weighting is presented briefly in the Administration and Scoring chapter and further explicated as "soft signs" only much later in the Test Development chapter. In any event, the assigned weights remain essentially unvalidated within the context of the QNST-II authors' creative processes of item selection and differentiation in terms of the seriousness of one developmental deviation versus another. The empirical validation efforts, rather, have been limited to the subtest item clusters, as discussed below.

Subtest validation efforts are mentioned as part of a "Pilot Study" that the authors conducted at some unspecified time (i.e., no date is given) with an age-partitioned sample: "under 9 years, age 9 years 1 month to 11 years 11 months, and 12 years and older" (manual, p. 72). Those in the three age groups are further divided into learning disabled (LD) and non-LD. They then present findings for most of the subtests, omitting comparison of "Left-Right Discrimination" and merging "Stand on One Leg" and "Skip" into a single subtest for comparison.

This Pilot Study, coincidentally, provides one line of evidence that seems counter to the authors' assigned item weights. Specifically, they have assigned weights of 3 to three of the five items (i.e., 60% heavily weighted) in the "Double Simultaneous Stimulation of Hand and Cheek" subtest. The composite scores for this subtest, however, failed to discriminate between the LD and non-LD children at any of the three age levels. On the other hand, "Figure Recognition and Production," which subtest assigns weights of 3 to only 2 of its 10 items (i.e., only 20% more heavily weighted) differentiated between LD and non-LD children at each of the three age levels and for the combined sample at highly significant levels. If a 60% seriously weighted cluster failed to discriminate groups, how does one account for a 20% seriously weighted cluster performing in a highly discriminating manner? This single, opportunistic comparison does not, of course, discredit the overall accuracy of the author-assigned weights,

but it certainly does raise questions about them that call for further study. Likewise, one may question assertions in the Educational Implications chapter about the relation between LD and the three QNST-II subtests that failed in the Pilot Study to differentiate LD and non-LD children.

In a related matter, the QNST-II authors categorize test performances for the 15 subtests combined as revealing a "moderate discrepancy" (MD) for total scores in the range 26–50 and a "severe discrepancy" (SD) for total scores exceeding 50 points. It is, nevertheless, hypothetically possible to obtain a total score of 62 points (i.e., severe) by missing 1-point items only (i.e., without ever being assigned a 3). If indeed 3-point items are the only ones signaling severe learning difficulties, it would seem odd empirically that one could exceed the "severe discrepancy" total-point score of 51 without having missed a single "severe" 3-point item. As it turns out, the manual neither presents nor cites a study through which normal range (NR<25) MD and SD cutoffs were established. Because means for total score are not presented in the Test Development chapter, it is not possible by inspection to learn if the specified ranges and cutoffs in any way correspond to some of their findings. Therefore, until further documentation is produced, 26–50 (MD) and greater than 51 (SD) points cannot be viewed as reliable guidelines for interpreting the significance of total scores obtained on QNST-II. Following a similar line of inquiry, the subtest scores shown on the recording Form as MD and SD cutoffs for each subtest must likewise be treated as untested hypotheses: No evidence appears in the manual for these cutoffs, nor are means reported for subtests that might permit preliminary, informal inferences to be made by inspection of existing data.

Significant variances were found among the (a) "Cue Cards" used in test administration, (b) manual's Administration and Scoring chapter, and (c) Recording Form. These can be illustrated briefly: Cue Cards omit directions for observing hand-eye-leg preference (Subtests 1, 4, and 12, respectively), whereas the manual specified these; there is an important wording difference for Subtest 9, Rapidly Reversing Repetitive Hand Movements; for 11, Tandem Walk, emphasis on observing S's performance with eyes open is omitted from the Cue Cards, and order of items on Recording Form departs from that in the manual; alternate use of letters on 3, Palm Form Recognition, is absent from Cue Cards; wording variation for 6, Finger to Nose; wording variation for 10, Arm and Leg Extension. Further, there are obvious typographical errors on Cue Card 9 (Subtest 5) and Card 13 (Subtest 6). Hence, before attempting to administer the QNST-II, the user is well advised to make personal annotations on the Cue Cards based on the preceding observations.

Not surprisingly, in view of the foregoing editorial lapses, the manual is marred by innumerable irregularities of style, the majority of which involve citation of references in text and in the references list. A few studies are cited in text and absent from the list of references; alphabetic order is disregarded at times in the references list; occasionally volume number or pages are missing; APA style is generally followed but with evidence of inconsistency throughout. A most glaring error of citation is the attribution to the American Psychological Association of DSM-IV, which should read American Psychiatric Association.

Despite the many obvious shortcomings just cited, the manual is readable and easy to follow. Extensive and valuable literature is explored relative to learning disabilities in the Educational Implications chapter. A parallel remark can be made for the Medical Implications chapter. Nevertheless, reviews of some of the literature in both of these chapters lack a critical quality. A Case Study and Sample Protocol appears following the balance of the text (pp. 75–82). This would have been more valuable to the reader if it had been accompanied by discussion and appraisal of findings by the authors.

SUMMARY. The status of QNST-II is similar to that of its first edition, as reviewed by Adams (1985): Its reliability is uncertain (i.e., no new reliability evidence); its validity remains to be established, despite the several studies that have employed one or another edition of the screening test. Classification of overall test performances as NR, MD, and SD, relative to cutting scores, is not supported by objective evidence. Similarly, classification of subtest performances is not warranted due to absence of relevant studies. Challenges are raised regarding current weights assigned to individual items in the subtests. Unevenness of quality of documentation is evident in variations of test administration directions between Cue Cards and the manual as well as in the many stylistic errors

noted. This continues to be a promising instrument for which promise awaits further realization.

REVIEWER'S REFERENCE

Adams, R. L. (1985). [Review of the Quick Neurological Screening Test]. In J. V. Mitchell, Jr. (Ed.), *The ninth mental measurements yearbook* (pp. 1256–1257). Lincoln, NE: Buros Institute of Mental Measurements.

[307]

RAND-36 Health Status Inventory.

Purpose: Designed to assess "general health status."
Population: Adults.
Publication Date: 1998.
Acronym: R-36 HSI.
Scores, 10: Physical Functioning, Role Limitations Due to Physical Health Problems, Pain, General Health Perceptions, Emotional Well-Being, Role Limitations Due to Emotional Problems, Social Functioning, Energy/Fatigue/Physical Health Composite, Mental Health Composite, Global Health Composite.
Administration: Group or individual.
Forms, 2: RAND-36, RAND-12 (a short form).
Price Data, 1999: $50 per complete kit including manual (126 pages), 25 question/answer sheets, and 25 hand-scoring worksheets; $7 per 25 question/answer sheets; $7 per 25 hand-scoring worksheets; $7 per 25 RAND-12 HSI question/answer sheets; $41 per manual.
Time: Administration time not reported.
Comments: Paper-and-pencil or computer administered; hand-scoring forms also available.
Author: Ron D. Hays.
Publisher: The Psychological Corporation.

Review of the RAND–36 Health Status Inventory by CORINE FITZPATRICK, Associate Professor of Counseling Psychology, Manhattan College, Riverdale, NY:

The RAND–36 Health Status Inventory (RAND–36 HSI), according to the foreword in the manual, asks probably the most commonly asked health status questions worldwide. It appears to have a dual purpose: benchmark assessment of general health status and the potential to evaluate change in that status. The benchmark assessment is designed to provide a measure of "general health status," including both physical functioning and mental well being. The change in health status purports to enable one to evaluate the clinical meaningfulness of change scores, thereby allowing more objective assessment of whether an individual has benefited from a particular intervention.

The RAND–36 HSI is composed of 36 questions that ask for responses of yes/no; yes, limited a lot; yes, limited a little; no, not limited at all, on 16 questions and for responses on variations of a Likert-type scale for the others. The yes/no questions seemed to be too restrictive; this is of concern because there are only 36 questions in the survey and all the other questions offer at least three choices. The restricted yes/no questions include three that address the relationship between emotional concerns and work and activities. These questions, in particular, should have a broader set of choices. Twenty-one questions generate four subscales (see scores above) that become the basis for the Physical Health Composite score. The remaining 14 questions generate four subscales that become the basis for the Mental Health Composite score. A Global Health Composite score is obtained from all eight subscales.

The RAND–36 HSI is used to generate individual reports that compare an individual's score to those of the standardized sample in two ways: An individual's health status may be compared to a representative sample of adults in the individual's age cohort and to a representative sample by gender.

DEVELOPMENT OF THE SCALES. The current inventory was derived from a long-form inventory that had been utilized by the author in previous research. Although the author cites work describing the long forms and indicating that items for the current survey were "selected to maximize their associations" with the long forms, it would have been helpful to know in some detail what was reduced. This is particularly important in determining whether a 36-item inventory has the breadth of a longer inventory.

Item Response Theory scoring the RAND–36 HSI was used in order to consider the relative item weights within each scale and item response weights within each item simultaneously. The manual provides a thorough theoretical rationale for the inclusion of this procedure. It should be noted that the items, which offered only two responses, did not show a significant difference between weighted scores and simple summed scores; this may be a methodology effect, but is may also suggest that these particular items should be reexamined with regard to breadth of responses.

The methodological decision to base the development of the three composite scales on principal axis factor analysis makes sense given the research, cited in the manual, indicating sufficient common variance. In addition, the oblique rotation is then the correct procedure and the results were reported ap-

propriately. The report of a goodness-of-fit test would enhance this discussion. In addition, although the factor loadings for the two subscales are reported, the factor loadings on the Global Health Composite should have been reported as well. It is noted in the foreword that the use of a Global Health Composite score is unique and, for that reason alone, the factor loadings and any other pertinent information should have been discussed.

The sampling procedure is impressive in allowing for two standardization samples, the age-based sample and an age-stratified sample. In addition, for the standardization across age groups, stratification was done by age, race/ethnicity, and educational level according to the U.S. population. As the authors point out, having both age-based norms and general norms allows for viewing one's health status from the perspective of what is characteristic at given points within the life cycle and from the perspective of changes across the life cycle. This is a particular strength.

RELIABILITY AND VALIDITY. With regard to internal consistency, estimates (alphas) indicate that all scales, ranging from .71 on the Social Functioning Scale to a high of .90 on the Physical Functioning Scale, reach levels of consistency considered necessary for group comparisons (.70). Only the Physical Functioning Scale meets the necessary level for individual comparisons (.90). Composite alphas for the Global Health and the Physical Health achieve the necessary level of reliability recommended for individual comparison. Within the Mental Health Composite, the 18–24-year age group and the greater-than-65-years group in the age-based sample do not reach the criterion. Thus, these composites can be used for individual clinical use, but the Mental Health Composite for these two groups should be interpreted cautiously. Test-retest reliability scores for six of the eight tests were greater than .70. The reliability of Role Limitations due to the Emotional Problems Scale (.59) and that of the Social Functioning Scale (.61) were below the necessary level. Composite score test-retest (median interval of 7 days) reliabilities all exceeded .80.

Regarding validity, the authors cite previous research on the items and scales. Some attempt should have been made to incorporate some of those findings in this manual. At the composite level, previous research work with earlier versions of the scale is mentioned as supporting validity;

this work should have been discussed in more detail. A particular strength in the reporting of validity evidence was the comparison of the Mental Health Composite Scale with the Beck Depression Inventory—Second Edition (BDI-II), the Beck Anxiety Inventory (BAI), and the Beck Hopelessness Scale (BHS). The Mental Health Composite score was most highly correlated with the BDI-II (-.57) and the BAI (-.54). These results suggest that the Mental Health Composite score is a good indicator of the psychological symptoms of depression and anxiety.

ADMINISTRATION, SCORING, AND INTERPRETATION. The inventory is given to the individual to self-administer using paper and pencil or computer. Directions are easy as is hand scoring of the form. Instructions for hand scoring were easy to follow, as were the appendices for conversion of raw scores to *t*-scores and cumulative percentages. The manual provides an excellent description of guidelines for interpretation, including a well-thought-out discussion of the sensitivity to and limitations of clinical interpretation of this scale.

SUMMARY. This measure was developed within the framework of a strong body of research and prior measure development. Although there are some concerns about reliability and validity, the authors address these limitations. Other measures, such as the Health and Daily Living Form (T5:1181) and the Lifestyle Assessment Questionnaire (13:186) are less targeted to assess both physical and mental functioning together. Thus, this measure will provide practitioners with valuable data for comparison on these clinically important questions.

Review of the RAND–36 Health Status Inventory by RICHARD I. FREDERICK, Staff Psychologist, U.S. Medical Center for Federal Prisoners, Springfield, MO:

The RAND–36 Health Status Inventory (RAND–36 HSI) is a 36-item measure of perceived health status. It was derived from the Health-Related Quality of Life Survey developed at the RAND Corporation for use in a Medical Outcomes Study and has the same item construction as the 36-item short-form version of the survey, known as the SF-36 Health Survey (352; see e.g., Ware & Sherbourne, 1992). The SF-36 depends on a simple summation of responses to derive total score and scale scores. The distinction of the RAND–36 HSI is that it incorporates a scaling methodology based on item response theory (IRT) and factor-based composite scores. The RAND–36 HSI is intended to allow clinicians to track perceived health status changes over time. For group measurement, the test is ostensibly intended to assist in the monitoring of population health, estimating the impact of different physical and mental conditions, estimating the impacts of clinical trials, and evaluating quality-assurance in hospital-based outpatient clinics.

The RAND–36 HSI may be administered by paper and pencil or by computer with software provided by the publisher. Respondents are asked to answer all 36 items about their health functioning for the preceding 4-week time period. Completion of the response sheet requires just a few minutes. For hand scoring, a worksheet is available from the publisher, or users can follow the directions for scoring given in the manual. Alternatively, item responses can be scored by computer software.

The following constructs are captured by the RAND–36 HSI: Physical Functioning, Role Limitations Due to Physical Health Problems, Pain, General Health Perceptions, Emotional Well-Being, Role Limitations Due to Emotional Problems, Social Functioning, and Energy/Fatigue. Obviously, given that only 36 items comprise the inventory, these scales are derived from a small number of items. Two scales represent only two items. Three composite scales are also derived: the Physical Health Composite, the Mental Health Composite, and the General Health Composite (which is, in reality, a composite of the Physical Health and Mental Health Composites).

Scoring for the RAND–36 HSI scales is based on a one-parameter IRT model. As explained by the author, in the IRT model, the expected score of a respondent on a particular item is a function of both the item difficulty and the ability (latent trait) of the respondent. The author's explanation of what constituted "item difficulty" or "ability" of the respondent for this Likert-response attitudinal inventory is inadequate. Given that the IRT recalibration of the SF-36 is apparently the only basis to adopt the SF-36, this limitation is critical. Apparently, the intent of the author was to make the RAND–36 HSI a more sensitive instrument in the clinical setting by conducting this recalibration. Although there is a comparison of the simple summation scoring provided by the SF-36 and the IRT-based scoring method of the RAND–36 HSI, this does not include predicting individual and group characteristics. There are no comparisons of the composite scales that were derived by different methods of factor analysis. Consequently, it is not at all clear why the revision was necessary or what the revision contributes beyond the SF-36. Finally, because the RAND–36 HSI does not appear to have any practical clinical utility, one wonders on what basis it is marketed.

The RAND–36 HSI was normed on a national standardization sample of 800 respondents representative of the U.S. population of adults aged 18–65+ years (based on the 1993 U.S. Census). The normative information obtained in the validation process is used to make interpretive statements by comparing respondent scores to their counterparts in age range. Reliability coefficients of individual scales (Cronbach's alpha) ranged from .71 to .90. Test-retest (median administration interval = 7 days) reliability coefficients were also moderate ranging from .59 to .89. Reliability coefficients (Cronbach's alpha) for the composite scales were substantially higher (.88 to .96). The same trend was evident in attempts to establish the validity of scores from the individual scales and the composite scores. Correlations with a variety of concurrently administered symptom checklists and health status scales were consistently moderate for the individual scales and somewhat higher for the composite scores. Correlations with a variety of concurrently administered symptom checklists and health status scales were consistently moderate for the individual scales and somewhat higher for the composite scores.

Interpretation of the RAND–36 HSI proves enigmatic. A copy of the scoring summary sheet presents the derived T score for each scale and composite as well as the cumulative percentage associated with that score. The interpretive report is nothing more than these percentages placed in declarative form for each scale. Despite convincing evidence throughout the manual that the individual scales lack sufficient reliability and meaning, they nevertheless represent the majority of the scoring summary sheet and interpretive report. Although the author cautions in the manual against basing interpretation on the individual scales, there is no caution on the scoring summary sheet or interpretive report.

SUMMARY. Use of the RAND–36 HSI for individual assessment of well-being does not appear warranted and will certainly frustrate examiners who try to determine what results actually mean. Use of the RAND–36 HSI for program review or clinical trials for groups does appear warranted, but the author has not sufficiently established why the SF-36 should not be used instead.

REVIEWER'S REFERENCE

Ware, J. E., Jr., & Sherbourne, C. D. (1992). The MOS 36-Item Short-Form Health Survey (SF-36): I. Conceptual framework and item selection. *Medical Care, 30,* 473–483.

[308]
Reading Comprehension Battery for Aphasia, Second Edition.

Purpose: "Designed to provide systematic evaluation of the nature and degree of reading impairment in adolescents and adults with aphasia."

Population: Pre-adolescent to geriatric aphasic people.

Publication Dates: 1979–1998.

Acronym: RCBA-2.

Scores, 19: Word–Visual, Word–Auditory, Word–Semantic, Functional Reading, Synonyms, Sentence–Picture, Paragraph–Picture, Paragraph–Factual, Paragraph–Inferential, Morpho–Syntax, Overall Score of Core Subtests, Letter Discrimination, Letter Naming, Letter Recognition, Lexical Decision, Semantic Categorization, Oral Reading: Words, Oral Reading: Sentences, Overall Score of Supplemental Subtests.

Administration: Individual.

Price Data, 1999: $149 per complete kit including examiner's manual ('98, 38 pages), picture book, supplementary picture book, and 25 profile/summary record forms; $19 per examiner's manual, $48 per picture book or supplementary picture book; $39 per 25 profile/summary record forms.

Time: (30) minutes.

Comments: Instrument is criterion-referenced.

Authors: Leonard L. LaPointe and Jennifer Horner.

Publisher: PRO-ED.

Cross References: See T5:2172 (1 reference), T4:2220 (5 references), and 9:1033 (1 reference).

Review of the Reading Comprehension Battery for Aphasia, Second Edition by CANDICE HAAS HOLLINGSEAD, Assistant Professor of Special Education, Minnesota State University, Mankato, MN:

TEST COVERAGE AND USE. The Reading Comprehension Battery for Aphasia, Second

Edition (RCBA-2) was originally (1979, First Edition) developed in response to practicing clinicians' (speech-language pathologists, neuropsychologists, neurolinguists) perceived need in evaluating the reading comprehension skills of individuals with brain damage, specifically aphasia regularities and peculiarities. The RCBA-2's purpose goes beyond the measurement of reading comprehension; it acts as a guide to therapy focus, rather than simply academic interest, in areas of identified impairment. Although limitations exist, the RCBA-2 is "designed to provide systematic evaluation of the nature and degree of reading impairment in adolescents and adults with aphasia" (manual, p. 1). The examiner's manual provides an overview schematic of reading modes and brief dyslexia variety descriptions.

Ten subtests constitute the RCBA-2 Core Battery. Each subtest, consisting of 10 items each, provides accuracy and completion time raw scores. The subtests are: I-Single Word Comprehension: Visual Confusions, II-Single Word Comprehension: Auditory Confusions, III-Single Word Comprehension: Semantic Confusions, IV-Functional Reading, V-Synonyms, VI-Sentence Comprehension: Picture, VII-Short Paragraph Comprehension: Picture, VIII-Paragraphs: Factual Comprehension, IX-Paragraphs: Inferential Comprehension, and X-Morpho-Syntactic Reading with Lexical Controls.

The Second Edition of the RCBA includes a separately bound and labeled Supplemental Picture Book (RCBA-S). The purpose of the RCBA-S is to "reveal reading prerequisite abilities such as letter recognition and letter naming" (manual, p. vi). Seven subtests constitute the RCBA-S. Each subtest, containing 5 to 40 items, provides accuracy and completion time raw scores. The subtests are: XI-Letter Discrimination (40 items), XII-Letter Naming (5 items), XIII-Letter Recognition (5 items), XIV-Lexical Decision (20 items), XV-Semantic Categorization (40 items), XVI-Oral Reading: Words (30 items), and XVII-Oral Reading: Sentences.

The RCBA-2 Core Battery and RCBA-S Supplemental Battery are similar in their presentation format. They both employ the use of an easel with test items on one side and examiner script/answers on the opposite side. The pages have appropriate white space, large bold-print, and pictures. The batteries differ in their response formats. The Core Battery involves silent reading comprehension (oral is allowed but not encour-

aged) and pointing recognition tasks. The Supplemental Battery involves oral reading comprehension, recall, recognition, and pointing tasks. There are warm-up items in the Supplementary Battery for the following skills: letter matching, letter naming, auditory-visual letter name recognition.

Usage of the results/scores are to be considered aids to clinical judgment. A limitation, as stipulated in the examiner's manual, is a statement concerning diagnosis. A diagnosis should only be made, by a professional, after multiple points of data have been gathered and analyzed. A strength of this assessment measure is the coverage of both silent and oral reading comprehension abilities in specific skill delineations. An error was found in the examiner's manual on page 17. The entire page is a duplicate of page 16 rather than an example of subtest recording for XIV and XV.

ADMINISTRATION, SCORING, AND INTERPRETATION. The RCBA-2 should be administered/interpreted by a professional who has received assessment training When the results are going to be used to diagnose, the examiner should consult the appropriate professional organization policies/procedures.

All subtests should be timed. No basals or ceilings exist. The RCBA-2 (both batteries) should take approximately one hour to administer. The amount of time used for each subtest is recorded on the Profile/Summary Record Form.

Each item tested is scored correct or incorrect on the Profile/Summary Record Form, which provides ample space to transcribe incorrect responses for error analysis. A summarization graph, for the Core Battery, is included on the record form in order to provide a visualization of subtest scores. A strength of the record form is space provided to document additional specific medical information. A concern of the record form is the space provided to document a percentile score. No information in the examiner's manual is provided by which to calculate a percentile score.

The RCBA-2 is a criterion-referenced measure yielding scores of accuracy and speed. These scores can be examined for quantity (number correct and time used) and quality (type of errors). Additionally, a strength of the measure is the opportunity to document specific skill performances over successive testings for the same individual longitudinally tracked. Changes can then be quantified and documented along with opportunity to target specific interventions in areas of greatest need. The examiner's manual provides a listing of intervention principles advocated for testing reading disorders accompanying aphasia.

RELIABILITY AND VALIDITY. The RCBA-2 construction was guided by literature on reading process and aphasia. Attention was given to adult interest and suitability, nondemeaning items. The examiner's manual provides detailed information outlining the incorporation of subtest controls. These are extensive. Examples are: movement from concrete to abstract, with increasing difficulty in word construction, and passage readability.

A study to determine stability reliability, internal consistency reliability, and criterion-referenced validity of the RCBA-2 was conducted by Van Demark, Lemmer, and Drake (1982). Test stability was high as indicated by reliability coefficient of $r = .94$ (df = 13, $p > 0.001$). Internal consistency reliability coefficient was .96, using KR-20 (administration interval not documented). This score demonstrates across individuals and within items high homogeneity. Criterion-referenced validity correlation coefficients were $r = .80$ ($p > .001$) using Gates Silent Reading Test and $r = .87$ ($p > 0.001$) using Porch Index of Communicative Ability, Van Demark et al. (1982) concluded the RCBA-2 was psychometrically sound.

Additional studies were conducted by Pasternack and LaPointe (1982), Nicholas, MacLennan, and Brookshire (1986), Jackson and Tompkins (1991), and Wertz et al. (1986). Each of these investigations underscored the reliability/validity findings of Van Demark et al. (1982).

SUMMARY. The Reading Comprehension Battery for Aphasia, Second Edition Core and Supplemental Batteries are criterion-referenced measures evaluating performance of "functional reading, reading prerequisite skills, and lexical decision making in individuals with aphasia" (manual, p. 30). The RCBA-2 purpose is a contribution of data to the clinician decisions in assessing disabilities in reading comprehension for adults impaired by cerebrovascular accident and adults/adolescents indicating traumatic brain injury. The batteries, which are easy to administer, provide quantitative/qualitative results supported by reliability/validity studies.

REVIEWER'S REFERENCES

Pasternack, K. F., & LaPointe, L. L. (1982). *Aphasic-nonaphasic performance on the Reading Comprehension Battery for Aphasia (RCBA)*. Presentation at the annual convention of the American Speech-Language Hearing Association, Toronto, Ontario, Canada.

Van Demark, A. A., Lemmer, E. C. J., & Drake, M. L. (1982). Measurement of reading comprehension in aphasia with the RCBA. *Journal of Speech and Hearing Disorders, 47*, 288–291.

Nicholas, L. E., MacLennan, D. L., & Brookshire, R. (1986). Validity of multiple-sentence reading comprehension tests for aphasic adults. *Journal of Speech and Hearing Disorders, 51*, 82–87.

Wertz, R. T., Weiss, D. G., Aten, J. L., Brookshire, R. H., Garcia-Buñuel, L., Holland, A. L., Kurtzke, J. F., LaPointe, L. L., Milianti, F. J., Brannegan, R., Greenbaum, H., Marshall, R. C., Vogel, D., Carter, J., Barnes, N. S., & Goodman, R. (1986). Comparison of clinic, home, and deferred language treatment for aphasia: A Veterans Administration cooperative study. *Archives of Neurology, 43*, 653–658.

Jackson, S. T., & Tompkins, C. A. (1991). Supplemental aphasia tests: Frequency of use and psychometric properties. *Clinical Aphasiology, 20*, 91–99.

Review of the Reading Comprehension Battery for Aphasia, Second Edition by ROBERT WALL, Professor of Reading, Special Education and Instructional Technology, Towson State University, Towson, MD:

The Reading Comprehension Battery for Aphasia, Second Edition (RCBA-2) is an update of the 1979 edition of the Reading Comprehension Battery for Aphasia. The revised edition includes 7 new supplemental subtests in addition to the original 10 subscales. According to the manual, the artwork and format of the original scales were updated. No other information is provided concerning what changes, if any, were made to the original items or subscales. "No studies have been conducted with the RCBA supplemental subtests" (manual, p. 29).

The difficulties in finding appropriate populations for developing tests such as the RCBA-2 are illustrated by the study cited in the manual as the study that used "by far" the most subjects and only involved 120 subjects. The studies cited in the manual as providing reliability and validity information ranged in size from 5–26 subjects. Although there is a paucity of studies related to the validity and reliability of scores of the RCBA, the manual's suggestions for administration, scoring and interpretation of test results seem appropriate and practical. This reviewer infers that the test authors have learned from their and others' clinical experience with the original RCBA. The directions for administration and scoring are clear and concise with practical suggestions.

As with many individual clinical tests, the directions allow considerable latitude to the test administrator. Given the small amount of information available concerning the relationship of the various scale scores with degree and type of aphasia, clinicians must create their own pool of information to guide them in choices of scales to use, interpreting scale scores, interpreting scale score patterns, and designing appropriate interventions. The individual using this test needs to be knowledgeable about the reading process as well as an expert in dealing with the various manifestations of aphasia.

This reviewer does take exception to one aspect of the answer sheet (Profile/Summary Record Form). If, as the manual asserts, the RCBA-2 is criterion-referenced rather than norm-referenced, it seems inappropriate to label percent correct as a percentile; however, Section III of the Profile/Summary Record Form does this. Percentile is a norm-based score and is defined as the percent scoring below a specific score.

Although the illustrative case study (including the sample completed profile/summary record form) is useful, some subscales were presented twice and other subscale results are missing.

The directions for the administration of the test seem well thought out with appropriate examples and suggestions. The answer sheet appears to be well designed for recording responses, timing subtests, and scoring, with a useful performance summary chart on the first page. The discussion of the RCBA-2's uses and case studies is useful.

SUMMARY. This inventory could provide a good beginning point for discussing an individual's reading comprehension skills. As indicated earlier, when using this battery test administrators must determine if the RCBA-2's 17 subtests provide information appropriate for their needs. The paucity of validity and reliability information is reason for caution concerning adoption of this battery without appropriate experience and other patient information. However, given the concerns expressed about the reliability and validity information provided for this instrument, it should not be the only source of data.

[309]
Reading Evaluation Adult Diagnosis, Fifth Edition.

Purpose: Designed for assessing existing reading competencies.
Population: Illiterate adult students.
Publication Dates: 1972–1999.
Acronym: READ.
Scores: 3 parts, 21 scores: Sight Words (List 1, List 2, List 3, List 4), Word Analysis Skills (Letter Sound Relationships, Letter Names [Upper-Case], Letter Names [Lower-Case], Reversals, CVC, CV[CC], Final Digraphs, Initial Digraphs, Final Blends, Initial Blends, Multi-Syllabic Words, Silent Letters, Soft C & G, Suffixes), Reading/Listening Inventory (Word Rec-

ognition, Reading Comprehension, Listening Comprehension).
Administration: Individual.
Price Data, 1999: $8 per test booklet/manual ('99, 51 pages); $2.50 per answer pad.
Time: Administration time not reported.
Authors: Original test by Ruth J. Colvin and Jane H. Root; 1999 revision by Kathleen A. Hinchman and Rebecca Schoultz.
Publisher: Literacy Volunteers of America, Inc.
Cross References: For reviews by Mary E. Huba and Diane J. Sawyer of an earlier edition, see 11:326 (1 reference).

Review of the Reading Evaluation Adult Diagnosis, Fifth Edition by HOWARD MARGOLIS, Professor of Educational and Community Programs, Queens College of the City University of New York, Flushing, NY:

The Reading Evaluation Adult Diagnosis, Fifth Edition (READ) is an individually administered informal reading inventory (IRI) developed by the Literacy Volunteers of America (LVA). It has three parts: Sight Words, Word Analysis Skills, and Reading/Listening Inventory.

Like most IRIs, READ tries to identify a student's instructional, independent, and frustration reading and listening levels for passages. It also assesses word recognition and word analysis skills. This information is essential for designing precisely focused instruction that is challenging, but not frustrating.

LVA developed READ for nonprofessional volunteer tutors to use with adults who are poor readers or nonreaders. Unfortunately, this edition of READ, like its predecessors, falls far short of the mark. Given the reliability and validity issues, discussed below, one cannot have adequate confidence that READ will routinely provide accurate information. This is of great concern, as instructional decisions derived from inaccurate information can impede progress and motivation.

RELIABILITY CONCERNS. READ fails to provide even the most rudimentary of reliability data, despite more than a decade of criticism to this effect (Fox & Fingeret, 1984; Huba, 1972). This makes it difficult to knowledgeably interpret READ findings or to have confidence in the instructional recommendations derived from them.

The reliability of the Sight Words part is probably compromised by having too few items and using criteria that may prematurely terminate testing. This part has four lists on Form A for initial assessment and four lists on Form B for reassessment. Each list has 10 commonly occurring words that students read aloud. Testing terminates after three errors on a list. Together, the small number of words per list and the termination criteria give situational error a considerable chance to influence the outcome. Maintaining the same 30% error rate with 20-word lists is likely to yield a more accurate estimate of word recognition abilities. The reliability of the 13 Word Analysis Skills subtests is probably also compromised by too few test items and criteria that may prematurely end testing.

The READ authors advise tutors to use Reading/Listening Inventory passages to assess progress. This recommendation is not justified as (a) the lack of alternate-form reliability data makes it impossible to assess passage equivalence, and (b) the absence of test-retest reliability data precludes knowing the frequency with which instructional levels change without commensurate changes in reading ability. Moreover, the Reading/Listening Inventory passages are extremely short and contain too few comprehension questions. One possible reason for this is the anxiety and embarrassment that many adults with reading problems experience in test situations. To meet the need for short passages, and to obtain an adequate sample of reading, the number of passages per level might be increased from four to eight so tutors can initially administer and cumulatively score several selections of equivalent difficulty over one or several sessions. This would likely increase the reliability of findings.

VALIDITY CONCERNS. Each READ part has serious problems that can significantly diminish the validity of its findings.

Sight Words Part: This test has the student read short lists of words aloud. READ correctly states that the "skill [measured by the Sight Word subtest] is thought to be necessary for fluent reading" (p. 40). However, examiner directions fail to specify the maximum response time allowed for a word to qualify as a sight word. According to Leslie and Caldwell (1995), students must pronounce a word within a second or so of exposure for it to be considered a sight word. Some tutors, however, might score a word a sight word if correctly pronounced after 8 seconds of effort; others might not. By ignoring this critical factor, READ supports both decisions, adding to validity concerns.

Word Analysis Skills Part: This test has 13 subtests, ranging from letter naming to pronouncing multisyllabic words. Many of the subtests have students read real words aloud. This is faulty if students already know some of these words. For example, on the Initial Blends subtest a student may correctly pronounce "cram" (not a word on the subtest) because it is a previously known word. The student may not know the sound made by "cr" or, if known, be able to rapidly apply it when decoding.

READ suggests that Word Analysis errors guide instruction. However, the scoring procedures could lead to faulty conclusions. According to READ directions, a word is marked wrong if the student correctly pronounces the targeted sound but mispronounces other parts of the word. This erroneously indicates that the specific sound-symbol relationship was unknown.

Several subtests lack mastery scores. Without specific criteria volunteer tutors may misinterpret findings.

Reading/Listening Inventory Part: This section has five sets of graded passages for students to read orally and listen to. There are four passages per level, ranging from first to fifth grade. Passage difficulty was determined by readability formula averages alone. This can produce a distorted picture of reading achievement as readability formulas often ignore factors responsible for passage difficulty.

Passages are excessively short. The average passage length for first grade is 47.75 words; for fifth grade it is 123.75 words. As a reference point, first and fifth grade passages on the Qualitative Reading Inventory II (Leslie & Caldwell, 1995), designed for elementary and secondary students with reading problems, average 162.50 and 290.50 words, respectively. Short passages may not produce representative samples of reading behavior.

During passage reading, the type of word recognition errors (word substitutions, insertions, omissions, self-corrections, and words supplied by the tutor) made by the student and their number are recorded. Reading is terminated after a specified number of errors. Across passages, the median is 4 errors for first grade and 8.5 errors for fifth grade. In many cases, the combination of short passages and low number of allowable errors will create an erroneous picture of a student's reading ability.

READ encourages tutors to plan instruction around the student's oral reading errors. The validity of an oral reading error analysis by nonprofessionals is problematic for several reasons. First, accurately recording oral reading requires a great deal of supervised practice, which volunteers may not get. Second, oral reading is quite variable; the kinds of errors made change with the type of materials read and the testing conditions. This limits the instructional generalizations that can be made from error analysis. READ ignores this limitation. Third, READ's oral reading selections are short and the test's ceiling is low, making it likely that students will often not produce a representative pattern of instructional level word analysis difficulties. Unfortunately, READ does not warn tutors to avoid error analysis at the frustration level. Errors at this level often differ from instructional level errors and are more numerous, creating a distorted picture of instructional needs. Finally, graduate reading majors find error analysis a difficult task that may take several semesters to master. Consequently interpretations of error patterns by nonprofessionals must be considered suspect.

To assess comprehension, the student is asked to retell each passage from memory immediately after reading or listening to it. Each passage lists five questions that can be asked to assess what was omitted in the retelling. Testing is terminated after two incorrect answers (although a tutor can continue testing if the tutor thinks the student has greater reading ability). Similar to other parts of READ, too few questions may provide an inaccurate picture of the student's reading abilities.

INFORMING INSTRUCTION. To obtain instructionally relevant information from an IRI requires an instrument that reliably assesses how well students read materials like those encountered in instruction. It also requires guidelines for skilled, flexible administration and interpretations supported by research. READ falls short in all these areas. For READ, the latter two concerns are especially important as it is designed for volunteers. Nonprofessionals may not know, for example, specific factors to consider in determining whether to continue testing beyond the student's statistical frustration level. They may not know that accurate but slow word-by-word reading can seriously impede comprehension and require instruction at very easy levels of word recognition. These concerns must be addressed before READ can be considered a valid instrument for informing instruction.

STRENGTHS. READ's Reading/Listening Inventory has several strengths that future editions

should maintain. Offering four selections per level gives it flexibility. Its passage topics (family, work, self, and community) are excellent for adults. The recommendation that students choose a passage to read may prove highly motivating to some students.

Unlike many tests, READ advises tutors to view its findings as tentative. This is sound advice.

CONCLUSION. READ is a poor choice for planning instruction. Reasons include a total lack of reliability and validity information, an inadequate number of Sight Words and Word Analysis Skills items, the possible influence of sight vocabulary on word analysis results, problematic test termination criteria, faulty word analysis scoring rules, failure to provide Word Analysis mastery criteria for all subtests, and extremely brief Reading/Listening Inventory passages. Future editions must address these criticisms for READ to effectively serve a very important and neglected need.

REVIEWER'S REFERENCES

Fox, B. J., & Fingeret, A. (1984). Test review: Reading Evaluation Adult Diagnosis (Revised). *Journal of Reading, 28,* 258–261.

Huba, M. E. (1992). [Review of the Reading Evaluation Adult Diagnosis (Revised)]. In J. J. Kramer & J. C. Conoley (Eds.), *The eleventh mental measurements yearbook* (pp. 750–751). Lincoln, NE: The Buros Institute of Mental Measurements.

Leslie, L., & Caldwell, J. (1995). Qualitative Reading Inventory, II. New York: HarperCollins College Publishers.

Review of the Reading Evaluation Adult Diagnosis, Fifth Edition by TIMOTHY SHANAHAN, Professor of Urban Education, University of Illinois at Chicago, Chicago, IL:

Reading Evaluation Adult Diagnosis (READ) is an informal reading inventory for adults. This is the only informal measure for making instructional decisions for this population. Standardized tests provide little information for helping instructors to target their lessons on student needs. That is where READ comes in. READ is an individually administered battery that is used to "systematically evaluate students' oral reading" (manual, p. 3) to help teachers figure out what instruction to provide. It is used to determine how well students can read the most common words in print, what strategies are known for recognizing words, and the level of material a student can read comfortably.

Adult literacy instructors could use reading inventories for children. That approach has several drawbacks, however, not the least of which is that adults would be asked to read texts that most would find childish. READ uses passages written for adults on topics such as the workplace, job searches, and adult students' experiences. Also, elementary inventories take an hour or more to administer, but given the short duration of instruction provided to most adult literacy students, the less time spent on assessment the better. READ is a kind of shortened informal inventory that can be administered quickly, perhaps in as little as 30 minutes. Informal reading inventories depend upon professional teacher knowledge. But volunteers deliver most adult literacy instruction, and READ was designed for the Literacy Volunteers of America (LVA) to be used by volunteers with little training. The brief directions for administration and interpretation are straightforward, with no technical information. READ is now in its fifth edition, and with its ties to LVA, is likely to be around for a long time.

READ includes a 48-page manual and a pad for recording and summarizing responses. The test manual has 9 pages of test directions (interspersed throughout), graded word lists for analyzing sight vocabulary, lists of letters and words for appraising word analysis skills, graded reading or listening passages, and 7 pages about how to use the results. The recording pad includes two copies each of the forms used for summarizing student's sight vocabulary and word analysis responses and for recording oral reading errors and comprehension responses for each passage, and a summary sheet. There is also a TUTOR manual—not a part of the test battery—that offers instructional recommendations referenced to the READ results.

The Sight Word vocabulary test includes two forms of four lists of 10 common words. Although grade levels are not provided, the lists are comparable to primer, first, second, and third grade levels. Students who can read the most common words, but who struggle with more advanced sight vocabulary, will not be distinguished by this test. These lists are short compared to other measures of sight vocabulary, and because of this the reliabilities of these are suspect, though no reliability data are included. However, given the purpose of determining a starting place for individual instruction, there is little cost for being wrong and this approach seems reasonable.

The Word Analysis section has only a single form, and consists of 13 lists that tap what students know about phonics. One list includes 19 consonants and the student is to tell the sound

usually associated with each letter. Another list presents all lower case letters and most upper case ones to determine knowledge of letter names. Other lists get at a student's ability to read words with simple spelling patterns or that include particular phonics elements like blends and digraphs or that have multiple syllables. There is even a list dealing with reversible words like *pot* or *saw*. These sections vary in length from as few as four items (Final Digraphs) to as many as 45 (Letter Names). Clearly, these subsections are not equally reliable, and teachers should use greater care in making sense of the shortest tests. Given that research has rejected reversals as a hallmark of reading disability, it is surprising that a section is devoted to this. Phonics tests, like this one, that rely upon word reading have a tendency to overestimate phonics skills, as students can read the words from memory. The authors have attempted to minimize this through the use of less frequently used words, but this is uneven and not necessarily effective. User beware. High scores on this part of the test may or may not indicate sound phonics skills.

The Reading/Listening Inventory includes passages at five levels of difficulty. There are four forms of each passage. Passages are short ranging in length from 40–100 words. Again, there are no grade level designations, though their readabilities range from first through fifth grade level. As with sight vocabulary, this test will only be useful with the lowest performing adult literacy students. Students are asked to read the passages orally while miscues are recorded, or to listen to the passage being read; after reading or listening their understanding of the passage is evaluated through retelling and questioning.

No traditional measures of readability, reliability, or validity are reported for this test. Readabilities are appropriate when checked against standard formulas; the passages and word lists seem to get increasingly difficult as are moves through the battery. It would be helpful to have data based on student performances that show this, and that support the equivalence of forms, but such data are not available. The problems with reliability have been noted, but these are acceptable given the fair tradeoff between reliability and efficiency. No validity information is provided. It would help to know if READ results are consistent with other measure or expert judgments. Even the basic construct validity of this measure is open to question. Some evidence with children shows that this type of reading level designation can place students in texts from which they learn best or read most comfortably. However, I know of no such evidence with adults. Reading levels might not have the same general value with adults.

SUMMARY. READ is well-designed, simple, informal reading assessment for use with adult literacy students who are functioning at low levels (up to about Grade 5). The manual provides appropriate suggestions for instructional decision making. No evidence is provided that shows that teachers make better decisions with this test or that the test results are consistent with other measures. READ appears to provide sound information for judging students' reading levels, but it is not clear how useful such judgments are for providing sound instruction as there have been no studies of the construct validity of instructional level with adults.

[310]
Receptive Oral Language Inventory.

Purpose: "Designed as a screening tool that examines a child's skills in listening comprehension, grammar, vocabulary, verbal analogies, and phonics" and to identify "students who would benefit from further diagnostic teaching or evaluation."
Population: Grade 1.
Publication Date: 1995.
Acronym: ROLI.
Scores, 11: Listening Comprehension, Grammar, Vocabulary, Verbal Analogies, Words in Sentences, Word Parts, Same/Different, Beginning Sounds, Ending Sounds, Position of Sound, Sound Analogies.
Administration: Group.
Price Data, 1999: $40 per test kit including manual (64 pages) and 10 test booklets; $17 per manual; $20 per 10 test booklets; $17 per specimen set including manual and sample forms.
Time: (30–45) minutes.
Author: Annabelle M. Markoff.
Publisher: Academic Therapy Publications.
[Editor's note: The publisher advised in January 2001 that this test is now out of print.]

Review of the Receptive Oral Language Inventory by CAROLYN MITCHELL-PERSON, Associate Professor of Communication Disorders, Southern University, Baton Rouge, LA:

The Receptive Oral Language Inventory (ROLI) was published in 1995. According to its author, the ROLI is intended only as a prereading

receptive language observation. It is not intended in and of itself as a definitive diagnostic instrument (manual, p. 7). The ROLI is not intended as a power evaluation instrument. Instead, it is designed as an "easy" observation that attempts to survey entry-level achievement in the receptive language area (manual, p. 15). The author does not define what is meant by entry-level achievement in the receptive language area.

The ROLI has two primary goals. It is designed to function as a screening observation and as a teacher-training instrument. As a screening observation, it is intended to evaluate semantics, syntax, morphology, and phonology necessary to develop reading readiness. The author reports that the ROLI is a prereading receptive language observation that identifies groups of students as well as individual students who would benefit from further diagnostic teaching or evaluation. The ROLI is a teacher training instrument and the author designed it as a reading curriculum development aid. Reading instructional activities based on the ROLI diagnostic levels are also provided. The development, administration, and interpretation of the ROLI are discussed within the context of diagnostic instruction based on ROLI diagnostic levels. The suggested diagnostic instructional activities are based on the author's assumption that children need an instructional program based on developmental oral language issues, thinking, and problem solving (manual, p. 6).

The ROLI is designed to be administered to first grade students before reading instruction begins as well as for the identification of students in the second and third grade without a strong receptive language base. The author claims, "the ROLI identified the 'at risk' populations in all three grade levels with very few exceptions" (manual, p. 28). Evidence supporting this claim is lacking.

The ROLI consists of five subtests: Subtest I, Listening Comprehension; Subtest II, Grammar; Subtest III, Vocabulary; Subtest IV, Analogies; and Subtest V, Word Discrimination. The test contains an answer booklet with 20 pages of black-and-white drawings with answer blocks that correspond to the subtests and a manual. The stimulus drawings are of common objects and events arranged in rows of four.

The ROLI is described as an observation of receptive oral language. This description and its title are somewhat misleading because none of the subtests require an oral response. Furthermore, the author states that nonverbal behaviors may cause poor ROLI performance. These behaviors are quality of attention, individual attention span, sustained motivation in a test-taking situation, the individual's speed of response matched to time allotted, and simultaneous processing ability demanding cognitive and motor modes in performance.

CONTENT VALIDITY. Content validation procedures involve the systematic examination of the test content to determine whether it covers a representative sample of the behavior domain to be measured. It is not clear whether the test development procedure followed a rational approach to ensure appropriate content. There is no evidence that the ROLI was validated by a panel of receptive language or reading experts in its development stages.

PREDICTIVE VALIDITY. No predictive validity data are offered or discussed for the ROLI. The author conducted a chi-square analysis to compare second and third grade students' performance on the ROLI with their performance on the Metropolitan Achievement Test. The author's rationale for conducting this analysis was based on the observation that students whose ROLI scores were in the lowest quartile were largely the same students who scored in the lowest quartile on the Iowa Tests of Basic Skills. The author does not discuss the analysis of scores that preceded the calculation of quartiles. The author does not give a clear rationale or discussion to support the use of a chi-square analysis. Perhaps the analysis was the author's attempt to demonstrate the relationship between the test needing to be validated (the ROLI) and subsequent performance on outside criteria (predictive validity). Any chi-square analysis can only indicate that the two phenomenon (test performances) might be related.

Even if the analysis was appropriate, the manner in which the results are reported is problematic. The author does not report how many of the 11 tests of the Iowa Tests of Basic Skills were administered, test conditions, examiner characteristics, etc. There is no reference citation in the text for the Iowa Tests of Basic Skills. Performance on the reading subtest of the Metropolitan Achievement Test was reported to be the basis for the chi-square analysis; however, the author cites the Language Instruction Test of the Metropolitan Achievement Test. The author repeatedly makes the point that the ROLI is an ideal test for children in the first grade; however, no data are reported for first graders. Vague conclusions are made based on the chi-square analysis.

CONSTRUCT VALIDITY. The construct validity of a test is the extent to which the test measures a theoretical construct or trait. There are three steps that are generally followed. First, several constructs thought to account for test performance are identified. Second, tentative assumptions are generated that are based on the identified constructs. Third, the tentative assumptions are verified by logical or empirical methods. It appears the author attempted to address construct validity by generating constructs on which to base the ROLI. The somewhat vague constructs appeared to be based on phonics, balance in instruction, perceptual deficit theories, developmental issues, early language interaction, static development, reading as a language process, analysis of the reading process, and language assessment.

The theoretical assumptions underlying the ROLI include: (a) Language skills can be improved in students; (b) classroom teachers can evaluate and instruct students whose skills are not at "readiness" levels with first grade teachers, the logical choice for this task; (c) readiness testing must provide information about the receptive aspect of oral language; and (d) more emphasis should be placed on language in natural communication activities based on personal relevance (manual, p. 21). The author did not discuss how the assumptions were generated based on the identified constructs.

There is no evidence that the basic constructs assumed to underlie the ROLI were related to testable questions and verified by logical or empirical methods.

ADMINISTRATION AND SCORING. Instructions for administration and scoring are stated but are not always clear. The lack of clarity may have introduced unidentified examiner or test bias. At the beginning of each subtest the examiner is told what to say and practice items are provided. Students are required to listen to material that is read to them by the examiner in each subtest. Using a multiple-choice format, students make choices from a series of black-and-white drawings and mark choices by making an "X" on the box in which drawings are located. The scoring key indicates that each correct answer receives one point.

The points of each subtest are summed resulting in a raw score for each subtest. On the cover sheet of the answer booklet instructions are given to circle each subtest's raw score. Areas are provided for recording both the subtest raw scores and the total score. The 25th percentile and raw scores said to fall below it have been calculated (no data are provided) and indicated on the answer booklet. Apparently, if a student's scores fall below the 25th percentile at any language level, the author claims that the student should be considered "at risk" and in need of further evaluation. As no supportive data are provided in the manual, this claim must be questioned. A specific section is not provided in the manual for scoring instructions. Brief mention is made in two unrelated sections of the manual (pp. 9, 49).

Instructions for ROLI administration are sometimes vague. For example, in Subtest I, Listening Comprehension, it is not clear how the students should correct their mistakes (manual, p. 31); however, clearer instructions are given for the same situation in Subtest II, Grammar (manual, p. 35). Subtest I is inconsistently labeled. It is referred to as Listening Comprehension and as Comprehension (manual, pp. 23 and 31, respectively).

Parts B, C, and F of Subtest V, Word Discrimination, are the most problematic in terms of instructions. In Part B, Number of Parts in Words (Syllables), examiners are not told how to say the syllables. Generally, authors of tests targeting syllable repetition instruct examiners to say syllables in a naturalistic manner preserving intonation, stress, and phonological characteristics. In Part B, examiners are instructed to say the word "another" as AN-OTH-ER (manual, p. 42). Speakers of Standard American English and some dialects say the word "another" with the phoneme /n/ as part of the second syllable. It is possible that variations in speech production may introduce bias as well as be perceptually confusing to some students.

In Part C, Same/Different, examiners are instructed to produce word pairs. Students are instructed to tell the examiner if the words are the same or different. Examiners are not told how to say the word pairs. Generally, authors of tests targeting word pair discrimination presented in same/different formats instruct examiners to say the pairs in a consistent manner. The pairs are usually said separated by a 2–3 second interval. The pairs are also said without falling intonation after the second word. Some students might per-

ceive word pairs said with falling intonation after the second word as one multisyllabic word.

Part F of Subtest V appears to have two conflicting labels as well as misleading instructions. According to instructions and the manner in which the words are written in the manual (p. 46), examiners will produce syllables. Students are instructed to listen for "sounds" and to indicate whether the "sounds" are heard in the beginning, middle, or end of the word. The directions given to students might imply that they are to listen for individual sounds and not groups of sounds. Examiners are not instructed to pause after each "sound," which might result in students being confused about what to listen for. For example, the examiner is directed to say "STARTED 'START'" (manual, p. 46) and is then to ask, "Where is the sound START in the word STARTED?" Other examples are FUL in BEAUTIFUL, VA in VACATION, and LEC in ELECTRIC (manual, p. 46). Part F is labeled as *Position of Sounds (Top Lines of Boxes)* in the manual (p. 45) and as *Number of Parts in Words* in the answer booklet (p. 20). No explanation is given for the part of the title in parenthesis *(Top Lines of Boxes)*. The task in Part F appears to be similar to the parts-of-words task as presented in Part B, Number of Parts in Words (Syllables). It appears that misleading instructions are given to students requiring them to listen for individual sounds and not syllables.

The stimulus black-and-white drawings in the answer booklet are generally adequate; however, some are ambiguous (pp. 1, 3, 10, & 12). Three pictures in Subtest I are problematic. First, the appropriate response to Item 1 requires the student to mark the picture of a dog "working" for someone. The picture is of a man "walking" a dog. Second, Item 11 requires the student to mark the picture of the animal that dogs help hunters find. The correct picture is of a wolf but it barely resembles a wolf. Third, Item 15 requires students to mark the picture that shows what dogs can see that people cannot see. The appropriate response is a dog's tail with marks intended to indicate motion ("). The dog's tail and the motion marks are barely noticeable. Item 10 of Subtest III requires students to mark the picture of a tire. The object in the picture cannot be clearly discriminated as a tire because it lacks depth. The picture of the bird being eaten by the cat in Subtest II (p. 7) could be offensive to some individuals.

RELIABILITY. The concept of reliability refers to the consistency of measurement. It is a key concept in measurement theory because it relates to the practical usefulness of all types and systems of measurement. The study of reliability of test scores centers on estimating the amount of error associated with the scores. For a test such as the ROLI, one might expect reports of interjudge, test-retest, and internal consistency types of reliability. Reliability data are not presented or discussed.

TEST DEVELOPMENT AND NORMING. Data for the process of selecting the sample, test stimuli, tasks, or scoring procedures are not provided. Grade level is the only subject demographic stated. The ROLI was administered to 74 undefined and undescribed children (50 second graders and 24 third graders). Even though the author states that the ROLI was developed to meet the need for a group-administered language test to be used by first grade classroom teachers (manual, p. 5), no data are available for first grade students. The procedures for selecting the first, second, and third grade students are not discussed.

The Code of Fair Testing Practices in Education (1988) specifies that test developers should identify and eliminate biased instruments. When there are no demographic characteristics given for subjects, one can assume that bias exists because there are no indicators that bias has been identified or eliminated (H. Albert, personal communication, April 29, 1999).

Examiner qualifications are implied. The author refers several times to first grade teachers being the logical choice for the task of assessing readiness levels with the ROLI. It appears that credentials held by a first grade teacher are basic examiner qualifications.

SUMMARY. There is no clear and sufficient theoretical framework in which to couch the ROLI's development or to interpret test results. The validity with which the ROLI's diagnostic levels can be used to identify, evaluate, and remediate receptive language weaknesses that might influence reading performance has not been adequately addressed. The concepts presented in the ROLI manual are not easy to follow. The relations between the concepts and the goals of the test are difficult to ascertain. This reviewer has concern about recommending the ROLI for the purposes for which it was designed.

REVIEWER'S REFERENCE

Joint Committee on Testing Practice. (1988). *Code of fair testing practices in education.* Washington, DC.

Review of the Receptive Oral Language Inventory by RUTH E. TOMES, Associate Professor, Early Childhood Education, Northeastern State University—Tulsa, Tulsa, OK:

The Receptive Oral Language Inventory (ROLI) is a group-administered assessment of receptive oral language skills purportedly related to a child's need for diagnostic instruction or further evaluation. The ROLI was designed for use at the end of kindergarten or beginning of first grade before formal reading instruction begins. It may also be used with the "at risk" second and third graders and with classes learning English as a second language.

The ROLI samples four components of language said to relate to reading: Phonology, Morphology, Syntax, and Semantics. The 111 ROLI items are divided into five subtests: Listening Comprehension (16 items), Grammar (20 items), Vocabulary (20 items), Verbal Analogy (20 items), and Word Discrimination (35 items). The latter is further subdivided into tests of Number of Words in Sentences, Number of Parts in Words (2 subtests), Same/Different, Beginning Sounds, and Sound Analogies. The manual provides a statement of rationale for each subtest with broad reference to theory, the author's experiences, and research findings. However, nowhere in the manual is any information provided on how items were selected or constructed.

The ROLI is administered using a consumable test booklet consisting of 20 pages of content, a page for comments, and a cover page for record of the child's scores. The items are presented in multiple-choice format. Each requires the child to choose a response from a series of pictures or numerals and mark an "X" on the selected response. If an error is made, the child may draw a line through the incorrect choice and mark another response.

Stimulus symbols are black-and-white line drawings of acceptable quality. However, they may confuse some kindergarten and early first grade students. There are too many on a page and some are too small. A switch in response format from horizontal to vertical presentation may further pose problems for some students.

The author states that the ROLI is designed to be administered by teachers to groups of students. Test administration instructions consist only of test directions. The teacher reads from the manual and instructs the students to mark in their test booklets. No information is provided regarding time requirements. Given the length of the test, it seems that several testing sessions would be needed. No detail is provided regarding the testing environment or preparation of the students. The administration of tests to young children in group settings is a questionable practice. Many factors could contribute to performance including group size, background noise, and confusion regarding the tasks. The manual does not address these issues. It does, however, state that characteristics of the children such as attention span, speed of performance matched to time allotted, and visual motor skills may influence test performance and that these behaviors should be considered when scoring the test. Not stated is how this information should be tracked or how it should be considered in scoring.

Scoring consists of simply counting the number of correct responses out of those possible for each subtest by comparing the child's choice to the answer key. These raw scores are recorded on the test booklet cover where a total score may also be recorded. The manual contains no explicit instructions for score interpretation. The subtest raw scores may be compared with a 25th percentile cutoff line. No information is provided about how this cutoff is determined. Scores below this cutoff presumably indicate a child's areas of deficient language skills and thus areas in need of diagnostic instruction. Several pages of suggestions for such instruction are included in the manual.

The ROLI does not have norms. No mention of test reliability is made in the manual. Concurrent validity was addressed by comparing performance of second and third graders on the ROLI and their Metropolitan Achievement Test (MAT) reading scores. Students who scored below the 5th stanine on the MAT scored in the bottom quartile on the ROLI. These data are of dubious value given questions about reliability, unknown sample sizes, and lack of information about subject characteristics except grade level. Of more importance, no validity studies are described for first graders who are the primary targets for the ROLI.

SUMMARY. The ROLI may have some value as an informal inventory of receptive language skills. However, the empirical basis linking the assessed skills and success in learning to read

is lacking. Additional problems and weaknesses are present throughout the test. No information pertaining to item selection, no evidence of validity, and totally inadequate evidence of reliability are serious technical flaws. Imprecise instructions for test administration and interpretation, problems of too many test items, and confusing format are other weaknesses. Finally, the group administration of tests to young children is fraught with problems not addressed in the manual.

[311]
Recovery Attitude and Treatment Evaluator.

Purpose: Intended for use after diagnosis of alcohol or other drug dependency to determine the "patient's level of resistance to treatment and other important information" to be considered in treatment planning.
Population: Adults.
Publication Dates: 1987–1996.
Acronym: RAATE–CE; RAATE–QI.
Scores: 5 dimensions: Resistance to Treatment, Resistance to Continuing Care, Acuity of Biomedical Problems, Acuity of Psychiatric/Psychological Problems, Social/Family Environmental Status.
Administration: Individual.
Forms, 3: Clinical Evaluation, Initial Questionnaire, Automated RAATE–QI.
Price Data: Available from publisher.
Time: (30–45) minutes for Clinical Evaluation; [20–30] minutes for Initial Questionnaire or Automated RAATE–QI.
Comments: Automated RAATE–QI requires minimum 386 IBM compatible with Windows 3.1 or later, 8 MB RAM, mouse, printer, and color monitor.
Authors: David Mee-Lee, Norman G. Hoffmann, and Maurice B. Smith (manual).
Publisher: New Standards, Inc.

Review of the Recovery Attitude and Treatment Evaluator by PHILIP ASH, Director, Ash, Blackstone and Cates, Blacksburg, VA:

The Recovery Attitude and Treatment Evaluator (RAATE) instruments were developed in response to what was perceived as a need for more consistent and objective measures to plan treatment and to place into appropriate levels of care patients suffering from substance dependence and addiction problems. Clinical work with such patients, surveys of policies and criteria for patient care in several treatment facilities, and review of published reviews and research led to the identification of five dimensions on which to establish a clinically relevant and useful severity profile for the individual patient.

These dimensions as finally formulated include:

Dimension A. Resistance to Treatment: degree of resistance to treatment (including denial of addiction problems);

Dimension B. Resistance to Continuing Care: commitment to on-going recovery and degree of resistance to continuing care;

Dimension C. Acuity of Biomedical Problems: withdrawal problems, to determine the acuity and intensity of any needed physical treatment;

Dimension D. Acuity of Psychiatric Problems: whether independent of or secondary to addiction; and

Dimension E. Social/Family Environmental Status: degree to which the psychosocial environment is supportive of or detrimental to recovery (user's guide, p. 1-1).

An initial attempt to develop a 5-point rating scale for each of these dimensions, and a corresponding set of placement criteria, failed to be sufficient. This led to the development of two instruments, The Clinical Evaluation (RAATE-CE) (Smith, Hoffman, & Nederhoed, 1992) and the Questionnaire I (RAATE-QI) (Smith et al., 1992). The Questionnaire I (RAATE-QI) is in a pencil-and-paper-administered format; it is also available in a computer-compatible form, Automated RAATE-QI.

The RAATE-CE includes 35 Likert-type four-choice (from "Definitely Yes" to "Definitely NO," where the MOST FAVORABLE response, indicating lack of illness or a favorable condition, is scored "1") items in a structured clinical interview. It may be administered by a trained clinician or counselor in 20–30 minutes. The questions are divided among the five dimensions listed above (A = 6, B = 5, C = 6, D = 8, E = 10). A Guidelines table is provided to reduce each dimension to a 5-point LOW (1)/HIGH (5) Severity Profile score, which is further encoded to a Level of Care evaluation.

The RAATE-QI is a 94-item true-false self-report questionnaire that is answered by the patient, taking about 30–45 minutes to complete. The questions are divided among the five dimensions listed above. In the pencil-and-paper version, the five dimensions are scored by use of plastic templates. The raw scores are transferred to the QI Severity Profile, and converted to QI Severity Profile Scaled Scores, yielding a RAATE-QI Severity Profile. Finally, for each RAATE-QI

dimension, the clinician circles the RAATE Severity Profile Scaled Scores under the appropriate ASAM (American Society of Addiction Medicine) Level of Care (Levels I–IV), where Level I is the most modest.

The RAATE manual presents a detailed introduction to the development and rationale of the RAATE, specific directions for administration and interpretation, and results of a reliability and validity study for the standardization sample ($N = 153$) drawn from recent enrollees of the Milwaukee County Mental Health Complex. Women comprised 43% of the sample, men 57%. The sample was largely composed of African-American drug abusers. The manual also includes an outline of desirable future studies and an extensive list of references.

RELIABILITIES. The RAATE-CE average interrater reliability estimates (across three clinicians) ranged from .59 to .77 ($N = 143$) and the internal consistency reliability values ranged from .65 to .87. The RAATE-QI internal consistency (KR-20) reliability ranged from .63 to .78, whereas test-retest reliabilities (over 24 hours) ranged from .73 to .87 (Allen & Megan, 1995, p. 476). Earlier, the manual (p. 5-5) reported test-retest (40 patients, 24 hours apart) reliability coefficients of .58 to .87 for the five dimensions. For the RAATE-CE, interrater reliabilities, by dimension, ranged from .58 to .70 (76 patients, 5 rater pairs) and from .51 to .87 (39 patients, one rater pair). Similar data were reported from the RAATE-CE by Smith et al. (1992, p. 361). The manual also contains extensive item analysis statistics.

As yet, very little evidence of criterion-related validity has been found by this reviewer, although a persuasive case may be made for the existence of content validity, as well as for arguing that the content and structure of the RAATE provides a basis for at least some components of construct validity. The manual itself suggests that "the intercorrelations of the five dimensions of the RAATE-CE demonstrated preliminary convergent and discriminant construct validity" (p. 5-4). Although the first two dimensions ("Resistance to treatment" and "Resistance to continuing care") were highly correlated, the other three dimensions appeared to be relatively independent, suggesting that the cited preliminary conclusion was justifiable.

SUMMARY. The RAATE-CE and RAATE-QI do seem to provide a way for trained clinicians to improve the accuracy and cost-effectiveness of treatment planning decisions for chemically dependent individuals. The instruments bring into focus issues in treatment decision-making that have not been extensively explored in available substance-abuse assessment devices. As the manual itself points out (pp. 6-1 to 6-3), extensive validity research is needed. Conduct of these studies should support the expectations set by the RAATE.

REVIEWER'S REFERENCES

Smith, M. B., Hoffmann, N. G., & Nederhoed, R. (1992). The development and reliability of the RAATE-CE. *Journal of Substance Abuse, 4,* 355–363.

Allen, P., & Megan, C. (Eds.). (1995). *Assessing alcohol problems: A guide for clinicians and researchers.* Washington, DC: National Institute on Alcohol Abuse and Alcoholism, NIAAA Treatment Handbook Series 4. Recovery Attitude and Treatment Evaluator (RAATE), pp. 474–477.

Review of the Recovery Attitude and Treatment Evaluator by TONY TONEATTO, Scientist, Clinical, Social and Research Department, Addiction Research Foundation, Toronto, Ontario, Canada:

The Recovery Attitude and Treatment Evaluator (RAATE) is the outcome of a program of clinical work conducted by David Mee-Lee (1988) who identified a small number of core variables critical to making clinical decisions about treatment placement, readiness for treatment, and treatment planning. Mee-Lee (1988) identified five key variables that form the basis of the five dimensions comprising the RAATE: (a) Resistance to Treatment (i.e., 6 items measuring awareness and acceptance of an addiction problem); (b) Resistance to Continuing Care, (i.e., 5 items measuring commitment to recovery); (c) Acuity of Biomedical Problems, (i.e., 6 items measuring health status); (d) Acuity of Psychiatric/Psychological Problems (i.e., 8 items assessing psychiatric status); and (e) Social/Family Environmental Status (i.e., 11 items assessing family support). There are presently two instruments that assess these dimensions, the 35-item RAATE-Clinical Evaluation (CE) to be administered in interview format, and the 94-item, true-false RAATE-Initial Questionnaire (QI), which is self-administered. The RAATE-CE items are rated on a 4-point scale. Both instruments require between 30 and 45 minutes to complete. The authors of the test manual state that neither instrument is designed to render psychiatric diagnoses nor to assess severity of addiction. Furthermore, the results of administering the two instruments are not intended to be compared directly because the content is not identical. Information describing the administration, scoring, interpretation, and psychometric properties of the two tests is provided in good detail in the 1992 test manual.

The interrater reliability of the RAATE-CE, based on 139 subjects, is suspect, due to the utilization of the Pearson product moment correlation coefficient, which "merely assesses the extent to which scores go together and not whether they are close to each other in absolute terms" (p. 58, Kazdin, 1982). Consequently, the coefficient may be quite high despite radically divergent scores by the raters. The appropriate statistic to assess interrater reliability would have been the intraclass correlation coefficient. It should be noted, however, that Smith, Hoffman, and Nederhoed (1992) reported a different reliability statistic (i.e., Fisher's r, p. 360) from the 1992 manual for these data. In any case, the correlations reported for the total scores averaged over the three interrater pairs ranged from .59 to .77, which can be judged to be fair to good. More recently, Najavits, Gastfriend, Nakayama et al. (1994) reported somewhat better interrater reliability coefficients, with a range of .66 to .92 for the five dimensions using a research version (RAATE-R) of the RAATE-CE in a sample of 116 cocaine-dependent outpatients. The internal consistency reliabilities reported in the 1992 test manual for each of the five dimensions are generally good (ranging between .79 and .86) with the exception of the dimension assessing availability of social support for which an unacceptable internal consistency estimate of .65 was reported. Najavits et al. (1997) reported internal consistency reliabilities for the five dimensions ranging from .45 to .71, which is generally considered poor.

Test-retest reliability on the RAATE-QI, based on two administrations of the test 8 to 10 hours apart (at least 24 hours may have been preferable), yielded generally excellent reliabilities, ranging between .73 to .87 with internal consistency (assessed with the KR-20 statistic) ranging between .63 and .77, which can be considered good. The relatively small number of items for most of the dimensions may have impacted on the estimates of reliability. A revised RAATE-QI, formed by deleting 17 items with low average item-scale correlations (< .25) and average test-retest correlations < .35, did not yield greatly improved internal consistency or test-retest reliabilities.

Construct validity for the two instruments was investigated by conducting interdimension correlations. The results show that for both instruments, Dimensions A and B, assessing Resistance to Treatment and Resistance to Continuing Care, tap into similar but not identical constructs ($r = .76$ and $r = .73$ between Dimensions A and B for RAATE-CE and RAATE-QI, respectively). Najavits et al. (1997) reported an r of $.42$ for RAATE-R between Dimensions A and B in cocaine abusers, considerably lower than would be desirable. The remaining three dimensions appear to be relatively independent constructs, with interdimension correlations ranging from $-.06$ to $.45$ for RAATE-CE and $-.30$ to $.47$ for RAATE-QI. Convergent-discriminant validity was further explored with the Multi-Trait Multi-Method approach, correlating the dimensions for both instruments. The result showed modest convergent validity, with coefficients ranging from $.28$ to $.54$, and good divergent validity with coefficients ranging from $-.17$ to $.25$. Najavits et al. (1997) found low correlations between the RAATE-R and the Circumstances, Motivation, Readiness, and Suitability Scales for Substance Abuse Treatment (CMRS; DeLeon, Melnick, Kressel et al., 1994) suggesting that the concurrent validity for scores from this instrument has yet to be established.

Further evidence for the construct validity of the measures (e.g., item-level factor analysis) and predictive validity have been planned but have yet to be reported. In addition, additional evidence for concurrent validity with other measures of readiness to change or psychiatric problems, for example, need to be conducted. There is some concern with the face validity of the RAATE-CE, particularly the Dimensions C and D measuring Acuity of Biomedical Problems and Acuity of Psychiatric/Psychological Problems. The questions comprising these dimensions require the patient to be able to assess what may often be very serious medical and psychiatric status, conditions best left to experts (i.e., physicians, psychiatrists). Many of the questions for Dimension D assess symptoms in a very superficial, general manner, and expect the patient to have insight into the relationship between symptoms and substance use, demanding interviewers be highly skilled in order to elicit valid responses. Thus, there is concern that considerable error can be introduced if the interview is administered by staff who are not highly skilled in medical or psychiatric diagnosis.

In summary, the RAATE-CE and RAATE-QI are intended to aid in the treatment planning and placement of treatment-seeking alcohol and drug abusers. However, the evidence for the reliability and validity for both instruments is, at present, too weak to conclude that this goal has been achieved. Representativeness of the sample and concerns about the size of the sample used in the psychometric analyses and the lack of extensive validity data (although the reliability data are generally good), indicate that further research is necessary before both instruments can achieve their goals.

REVIEWER'S REFERENCES

Kazdin, A. E. (1982). *Single-case research designs: Methods for clinical and applied settings.* New York: Oxford University Press.
Mee-Lee, D. (1988). An instrument for treatment progress and matching: The Recovery Attitude and Treatment Evaluator (RAATE). *Journal of Substance Abuse Treatment, 5,* 183–186.
Smith, M. B., Hoffmann, N. G., & Nederhoed, R. (1992). The development and reliability of the RAATE-CE. *Journal of Substance Abuse, 4,* 355–363.
DeLeon, G., Melnick, G., Kressel, D., & Jainchill, N. (1994). Circumstances, motivation, readiness, and suitability (The CMS Scales): Predicting retention in therapeutic community treatment. *American Journal of Drug and Alcohol Abuse, 20,* 495–515.
Najavits, L. M., Gastfriend, D. R., Nakayama, E. Y., Barber, J. P., Blaine, J., Frank, A., Muenz, L. R., & Thase, M. (1997). A measure of readiness for substance abuse treatment: Psychometric properties of the RAATE-R interview. *American Journal on Addictions, 6,* 74–82.

[312]
REHAB: Rehabilitation Evaluation Hall and Baker.

Purpose: "Designed to assess people with a major psychiatric handicap."

Population: Psychiatric patients who live in residential care.

Publication Dates: 1984–1994.

Acronym: REHAB.

Scores, 8: Deviant Behaviour, General Behaviour (Social Activity, Speech Disturbance, Self Care, Community Skills, Overall Rating), Speech Skills.

Administration: Individual.

Price Data, 1998: $405 (£215) per complete set including 50 assessment forms, 5 rater guides, 1 scoring key, 25 score sheets, 25 individual presentation sheets, 25 group presentation sheets, manual ('94, 136 pages), and carrying case; $33 (£17.50) per 25 assessment forms; $44 (£23) per 5 raters guides; $34 (£17.50) per scoring key; $19.50 (£10.50) per 25 score sheets; $27.50 (£14.50) per 25 individual presentation sheets; $46 (£26) per 25 group presentation sheets; $88 (£45.50) per manual; $105 (£60) per carrying case.

Time: (1 week).

Comments: A multipurpose behavior rating scale requiring observation of the target client over a period of one week; raters can include any direct care staff.

Authors: Roger Baker and John N. Hall.

Publisher: Vine Publishing Ltd. [England].

Cross References: See T5:2195 (2 references).

Review of the REHAB: Rehabilitation Evaluation Hall and Baker by JAMES P. CHOCA, Director of Doctoral Studies, School of Psychology, Roosevelt University, Chicago, IL:

The Rehabilitation Evaluation Hall and Baker (REHAB) is a rating scale for psychiatrically disabled individuals. The scale is split into two areas of functioning: Deviant Behaviour and General Behaviour. Results are grouped into five factor scores: Social Activity, Disturbed Speech, Speech Skills, Self Care, and Community Skills. The instrument was developed in the United Kingdom but has been translated into several languages including Dutch, Japanese, German, Spanish, French, Italian, and Hebrew (Baker & Hall, 1994). In addition to the user's manual, a rater's guide is available to train professionals on the use of the scale. The items seemed easily understood and the system was user friendly.

Originally designed to select patients with potential for moving from a psychiatric facility into the community, REHAB now has found a variety of other uses. Such uses have included the establishment of the patient's level of functioning, the assessment of change in the patient's behavior, treatment planning for individual patients, and planning or reorganization of psychiatric wards (Baker & Hall, 1994).

REHAB has the usual disadvantages of a rating scale. If used by only one professional, the scale can be used to organize the areas about which opinions are given. In such a case, however, the ratings would probably not be very revealing in that they would simply represent the opinion of that particular professional.

The instrument would be most helpful when several professionals will be using it to record their opinions on the same patient. In that case, the professionals would have to be trained so that the ratings will be done in a consistent manner. Such ratings by well-trained professionals would obviously be an ideal way of developing data about patients. Such a system is considered the "golden standard" by which all other methods of diagnosis are judged. However, the procedure becomes time-consuming and, as a result, expensive.

Finally, like any rating scale, there is a certain rigidity about the areas that can be rated and the way in which the rating is done (Mulhall, 1985). This is necessary in order to provide reliable ratings, but may occasionally lead to the disregard of important information.

SUMMARY. In conclusion, REHAB appears to be a good rating scale for evaluating the functioning of chronically disabled psychiatric patients. Having several trained professionals complete this instrument becomes an expensive proposition but one that would lead to useful and reliable data about the chronically disabled psychiatric population.

REVIEWER'S REFERENCES

Mulhall, D. J. (1985). Rehabilitation Evaluation, Hall and Baker—REHAB. *Behavioural Psychotherapy, 13*, 256–263.
Baker, R., & Hall, J. (1994). A review of the applications of the REHAB Assessment System. *Behavioural and Cognitive Psychotherapy, 22*, 211–231.

Review of the REHAB: Rehabilitation Evaluation Hall and Baker by PAMILLA MORALES, Senior Lecturer, Bolton Institute, Bolton, Lancashire, England:

The Rehabilitation Evaluation Hall and Baker (REHAB) is designed to assess people with major psychiatric disorders currently living in a restricted environmental/institutional setting. This instrument provides information on general daily behavior and is completed by staff over a one-week observation time period. The instrument can be applied in a variety of situations found within psychiatric rehabilitation and can be used in hospitals, day care centers, and institutions. The test can be administered to either individual patients or entire groups and contains forms for both types of assessment. The instrument provides information in six basic areas: Deviant Behaviour, General Behaviour/Social Activity, Speech Disturbance, Self Care, Community Skills, and an Overall Behaviour rating. There are 13 items generating Likert-style responses divided into two basic sections: Deviant Behaviour (7 items) and General Behaviour (16 items). The items were derived from research studies conducted in the 1970s into behavioral approaches to psychiatric rehabilitation, with particular emphasis on token economies with chronic psychiatric patients. Construction of the actual instrument took place in three phases. In the first phase, large numbers of psychiatric nurses, social workers, and relatives of patients were asked what they considered to be "important" behavior. The second phase was to incorporate studies with statistically related behavior and successful rehabilitation outcome. The last phase was to measure the frequency of behavior on wards. These three phases were integrated and the instrument was then pilot tested using 168 patients who were under 65 years of age and had been in a hospital over 2 years. Subsequently, the scale was revised and used in a wide variety of clinical situations utilizing 821 patients from six different sites in Great Britain. These data provide the current norming base.

Kendall correlation coefficients were calculated between every item and indicated an uneven pattern specifically in the first section, Deviant Behaviour, with only half of the intercorrelations being statistically significant. In addition, the factor analysis suggests that Deviant Behaviour is not a single factor but has four separate elements within the seven items. The second part, General Behaviour, appears to be a more cohesive scale with all of the correlation coefficients being significant. Factor analysis indicated that the first factor, accounting for 70% of the variance and labeled "Self Care," had item weights ranging from .7 to .9. The second factor, entitled "Social Activity," had item weights ranging from .45 to .8.

Interrater reliability correlation coefficients were calculated on eight different pairs of raters within the same institution on 47 patients. These coefficients ranged from .61 to .91. Three different concurrent correlational validity studies indicated that the pilot version of the REHAB showed good agreement with other independent measures of behavior in a residential setting, but poor agreement with measures based on patient interview.

Concurrent discriminative validity indicated that the instrument is able to discriminate satisfactorily between groups of patients at both the least and most handicapped ends of the distribution of scores.

Four separate studies, completely independent of each other, showed that the instrument is sensitive to change over time for the second part of the instrument only. The first part, Deviant Behavior, appears not to be a uniform behavioral dimension and was a less sensitive measure of change.

Test-retest reliability was conducted and was somewhat problematic as during the 5-year period between administrations there was a significant patient drop-out rate from an initial 37 patients to 17. Scores were reported for the General Behaviour section of the instrument and ranged from .80 to .90. It was reported that the scores for the Deviant Behaviour section of the instrument were more varied (.30–.80).

The manual is well written and detailed. It is divided into two parts; the first part contains information on how to organize the ratings, training of raters, scoring, and interpretation as well as an example of a completed group presentation sheet. The second part provides the background information, reliability, validity, and other technical information. The manual also contains a section on how to present findings as well as cutoff scores for individual patients who may be eligible for discharge into a less restrictive environmental setting. Included with the test is a separate booklet called the "raters guide," which is very useful with good explanations as well as definitions of specific behaviors, such as physical violence.

Scoring the test for the first seven items is fairly basic. The rater places a check in one of three boxes provided detailing the specific behavior using a scale indicating more than once a week, once a week, or no occurrence of the behavior. The remaining items are scored on a Likert-type scale. The rater places a mark through the line at the place that best describes the patient's behavior on a continuum from worst possible behavior to best possible behavior. A scoring key is then used that is a transparent template with 10 divisions. The scoring key is placed over the assessment form. The score for that item is the number given to that division on the scoring key. If the mark is on the exact dividing line, the manual suggests using the lower score.

SUMMARY. The REHAB is a very basic instrument and should not be used beyond rating and assessing the most rudimentary behaviors (i.e., incontinence, shouting/swearing, sexually offensive, and basic socializing within the restrictive environment). The cutoff points provided in the manual for discharge are a single-criterion approach and are not detailed enough for specific individual patient program planning or deciding what type of environment will be necessary following discharge. Positive aspects of this test are that it is easy to use, any member of the professional staff can utilize the instrument and rate patients, an entire ward can be assessed, and baselines can be established with programs and then implemented into practice.

[313]
Rehabilitation Compliance Scale.

Purpose: Intended to provide a measurement of compliance to a rehabilitation program in the severely injured musculoskeletal patient.

Population: Severely injured patients ages 17–85 years.

Publication Date: 1994.

Administration: Group.

Price Data, 1998: $25 per sampler set including manual, test, and scoring sheets; $100 per one-year permission to reproduce up to 200 administrations of the test.

Time: Administration time not reported.

Author: Neil W. Rheiner.

Publisher: Mind Garden, Inc.

    a) REHABILITATION COMPLIANCE SCALE.

    Acronym: RCS.

    Scores, 3: Appointment Compliance, Participation in Therapy, Progress in Therapy.

    Forms, 2: A, B.

    b) PATIENT EXPERIENCE QUESTIONNAIRE.

    Acronym: IEQ.

    Score: Total score only.

Review of the Rehabilitation Compliance Scale by MICHAEL P. GAMACHE, Clinical Assistant Professor of Psychology, Department of Neurology, University of South Florida, College of Medicine, Tampa, FL:

TEST COVERAGE AND USE. Musculoskeletal injuries are common and costly in terms of time loss from productive activities and the cost of rehabilitation. Despite advances in the ability to effect positive rehabilitation from these injuries, the cost effectiveness of rehabilitation efforts and the practical efficacy of such efforts is severely compromised by problems associated with noncompliance or failure to adhere to rehabilitation regimens. The Rehabilitation Compliance Scale (RSC) is a rating scale designed as a measure of compliance for the population of patients undergoing long-term rehabilitation from musculoskeletal injury in inpatient settings. The scale is completed by health care professionals (e.g., nurse, occupational therapist, physical therapist). It is most appropriate for use with severely injured, adult patients who are expected to remain hospitalized for at least a month or more and who do not suffer from injuries that would alter their cognitive status (i.e., head injury).

SIZE AND REPRESENTATIVENESS OF SAMPLE FOR VALIDATION AND NORMING. The test manual reports one validation study involving 50 patients undergoing long-term rehabilitation at a "Midwestern rehabilitation institution" (manual, p. 25). The patient sample was selected based on six criteria, including permission of attending physicians, willingness to participate, and the expectation that the severity of the patient's condition would require a minimum of 4 weeks of intensive inpatient rehabilitation. The author indicates that "40–50 percent" (p. 33) of the subjects selected were lost to the study because they did not remain available for the minimum 4-week observation period. It is not clear why they present a range of subject attrition rather than the specific percentage. There is no discussion of the percentage of patients excluded from the sample because of their unwillingness to participate in the study and how this may have affected the representativeness of the sample, particularly when the ultimate issue is compliance. The sample subjects were 60% male and 40% female and ranged in age from 17 to 85, with a mean age of 57 years. Despite characterizing the study sample as musculoskeletal injury patients, a review of the descriptive statistics regarding diagnosis, which were contained in a table in the manual, indicates that the primary diagnosis in more than one-third of the cases (38.0%) was neurological in nature and the modal diagnosis was cerebrovascular disease. In a discussion of subject selection problems the author states that subjects who were confused, aphasic, or who had head injury were excluded from the sample, which suggests that the criteria for determining the existence of confusion or other cognitive impairment were not particularly rigorous given the large number of neurological cases.

RELIABILITY. Reliability data for the RCS were derived from comparisons of the ratings of different disciplines (nurse vs. occupational therapist or physical therapist), different forms (Form A vs. Form B), and item analysis. The correlation between Form A and Form B was poor ($r = .167$), leading the author to conclude that Form B is measuring another construct than compliance and that further research is needed to determine the appropriate use of this form that they designed to be equivalent to Form A. The author also reports statistically significant differences between health care disciplines and their ratings of the same patients using the same form. They conclude that this finding is consistent with previous studies that have found differing perceptions of compliance between different disciplines. Despite acknowledging these differences, they offer a single mean score without differentiating between the professional disciplines of the raters. Internal consistency coefficients ranged from a low of .001 to a high of .916. Item correlation with total scores was only .167.

VALIDITY. The validity of the RCS was assessed by comparing RCS ratings with three external compliance measures: percentage of appointments kept, a rating of participation in therapy, and a rating by a multidisciplinary team of the patient's progress in therapy. The correlations were generally poor for the latter two. The only meaningful relationship was between the RCS and appointment keeping, which is the only one of the three criterion measures that is consistent with the usual definition of compliance. The correlation between Form A and the percentage of appointments kept was .737. Interestingly, in interpreting the study results, the author concludes that these criteria are "poor indicators of compliance" rather than concluding that the RCS is a poor predictor of compliance.

Content validity and item construction were based on the critical incident technique (Flanagan, 1954). The process entailed a survey of 330 health care professionals who provided representative descriptions of two examples of compliant behavior and two examples of noncompliant behavior each. A total of 2,201 critical incidents were generated for analysis and these were categorized and reduced to 28 types or categories of critical incidents for inclusion in a preliminary form of the rating scale, equally divided between examples of compliant and noncompliant behavior. They submitted this form to the original 330 health care professionals in order to obtain their opinion regarding the appropriateness of item content. Based on the feedback from these providers, the final form was revised to 24 items with a 5-point Likert rating for each item.

TEST ADMINISTRATION. The RCS is a 24-item Likert rating scale completed by a designated health care professional. For optimal analysis, the provider should have had direct contact with the patient to be rated for a minimum of at least 5 days before providing the rating. The patient should have been admitted to the rehabilitation program at least 2 weeks prior to rating, with at least 7 days of participation in a planned rehabilitation program, and an expected additional hospitalization of at least 4 weeks. The ratings are completed in pencil-and-paper format and a scoring key is included in the manual. The test would appear to take between 2 and 10 minutes to complete.

TEST REPORTING. There is no formal test reporting or interpretation offered. The author

suggests that the mean score of 44 be used "as the point of demarcation between measurement of compliance and noncompliance" (p. 46). However, he rightfully cautions against the use of this score as a cutoff score suggesting instead that the greater the patient's score above 40, the less likely they are to comply with rehabilitation. This, in turn, might suggest that patients obtaining high ratings would be desirable candidates for some type of intervention aimed at improving compliance and reducing resistance to rehabilitation efforts. Factor analysis suggests that the test measures four aspects of compliance: self-destructive behavior, self-directing behavior, information seeking, and contradictory behavior.

TEST BIAS. There is insufficient normative data to determine test bias. The clinical validation sample was 60% male and had a mean age of 57. No other demographic data are offered.

SUMMARY. The ability to effectively and reliably predict compliance with rehabilitation regimens could be very important in tailoring rehabilitation techniques and resources to individual patients. Some research has demonstrated effective techniques for improving compliance and the ability to identify patients in advance who are likely to benefit from compliance interventions would be useful. The RCS is a rating scale for use with professionals involved in the rehabilitation process. It is derived from observations made by these professionals of critical incidents representative of compliance and noncompliance. It does not, however, have sufficient reliability or validity evidence at this time for use in practical decisions regarding treatment and patient compliance. The experimental or informal use of this instrument is all that can be recommended at this time. Such use might facilitate further interaction and discussion across disciplines with respect to the likely compliance or need for other interventions to facilitate rehabilitation.

REVIEWER'S REFERENCE

Flanagan, J. C. (1954). The critical incident technique. *Psychological Bulletin, 51,* 327–358.

Review of the Rehabilitation Compliance Scale by ROBERT A. LEARK, Associate Professor, Psychology Department, Pacific Christian College, Fullerton, CA:

INTRODUCTION. The Rehabilitation Compliance Scale (RCS) consists of two 24-item rating scales (Forms A & B). Items are rated using the following scale: *unable to determine, very much like, somewhat like, unlike,* and *very much unlike.* The rater circles the appropriate response on the one-page (front/back) response form.

The RCS is designed to measure "compliance to a rehabilitation program in the severely injured musculoskeletal patient" (manual, p. 5). The basis for the test is found in the author's logical statement:

> If one accepts the assumption that compliance to an effective rehabilitation regimen is desirable if the patient is to return to a maximal functional state, it follows that compliance to a rehabilitation program will lead to improved rehabilitation outcomes. Compliance, therefore, may lead to reduction in the length of major treatment regimes, the time in which the health team is involved in carrying out specific therapeutic programs, and the amount of medical facilities utilized at any one time by the injured. A marked improvement in rehabilitation outcomes offers the potential for dramatically reducing expenditures in the care of the injured. (Manual, p. 7).

VALIDITY AND RELIABILITY. The author utilized a critical incident technique to obtain items reported by health care professionals as significant in the outcome of severely injured patient rehabilitation. Initially, analysis of 2,201 behavioral indicators produced 246 specific behaviors with equal frequency by raters. This draft of items was distributed to health care professionals. At the end of the analysis and recommendations, the two 24-item parallel forms were created. These forms were then tested on a 50-patient sample undergoing a 24-month rehabilitation program. Each form has a mean score possible of 44. Thus, 44 was selected as the cut score for indications of compliance, scores above are seen as less indicative of compliance, scores below as more compliant. The overall predictive validity of scores from the RCS is limited. For example, correlations to Participation in Therapy (.178) and Progress in Therapy (.121) for the RCS Form A are disappointing.

Reliability of scores from the RCS was determined by calculating Cronbach alpha coefficients. RCS alpha coefficients are .806 for Form A and .854 for Form B. Factor analysis yielded four distinct factors (self-destructive behavior, self-directing behavior, information-seeking behavior, and contradictory behavior) for both forms. Individual item correlation between the two forms is weak (r = .167 for total scores).

COMMENTS. The RCS, Forms A and B, presents a novel attempt to measure rehabilitation outcome behaviors. Unfortunately, they fall far short of the mark. The author of the scales recommends continued research with Form A.

Clearly, continued research is needed for the RCS. However, a blanket disregard for the test is not warranted. The rehabilitation field is in need of outcome measures that can identify behaviors predictive of successful treatment. Rather than totally disregarding this instrument, the reader is encouraged to take up the author's call for further research. The author has gone to great lengths to begin the process for a successful outcome mesure for a highly specific patient population.

[314]
The Renfrew Bus Story.

Purpose: Designed as a "test of narrative recall."
Population: Ages 3.6–7.0.
Publication Date: 1994.
Scores, 4: Information, Sentence Length, Complexity, Independence.
Administration: Individual.
Price Data, 1997: $45 per complete kit including manual (56 pages), 15 record forms, and story booklet; $5 per 15 record forms.
Time: Administration time not reported.
Comments: American adaptation of original British version.
Authors: Judy Cowley and Cheryl Glasgow.
Publisher: Centreville School.

Review of The Renfrew Bus Story by SHERRY K. BAIN, Associate Professor, Department of Educational Psychology, University of Tennessee, Knoxville, TN:

RATIONALE FOR TEST. The Renfrew Bus Story (RBS) is an American adaptation of a British screening test of narrative recall for young children (Renfrew, 1977). The test involves measuring a child's ability to retell a story presented orally and with pictures by the examiner.

Cowley and Glasgow, the RBS authors, offer extensive justification for the use of a narrative testing format and cite several references to support their positions. In general, they claim that the narrative format of testing is more sensitive to language problems than traditional language tests involving short answers or brief, one-word responses. The narrative format requires that the child integrate and organize several skills, including visual and audio input, listening comprehension, memory, sentence formation, and narrative schema understanding. In addition, the task of narrative recall simulates natural occurrences in daily interactions as well as typical classroom demands.

ADMINISTRATION AND SCORING. To administer the RBS, the examiner reads a script to the child while sequentially exposing 12 pictures in a booklet. The child is then audio taped retelling the story, with the examiner supplying a prompt and a story-starting line. The child uses the same sequenced pictures to retell the story, which is transcribed from the audio tape, and scored by the examiner.

Scoring is based upon quantitative categories including (a) Information, described as content memory; (b) Sentence Length; (c) Complexity, described as sentences containing subordinate or relative clauses or attempts at using these clauses; and (d) Independence, measured by the absence of prompts from the examiner. Raw scores for Information and Sentence Length can be transformed into standard scores (x = 100, sd = 15) and percentiles according to tabled norms for 6-month age blocks. A qualitative assessment can also be completed using guidelines from the manual, and a style sheet may be filled out, indicating a child's positive and negative behaviors observed during testing.

Recommendations for training to administer the RBS could not be found in the manual. The complexity of recording and scoring young children's narratives indicates the need for several practice sessions on the examiner's part. The test is quick to administer, taking 15 or 20 minutes at the most, but results can be slow to transcribe and score initially. Instructions seem clear and fairly explicit although there are bound to be occasional problems with scoring children's language usage. Several examples of scored record forms are provided in the manual. Dialect variations are acceptable.

STANDARDIZATION, RELIABILITY, AND VALIDITY. Normative information for the RBS is provided in the manual; however, some gaps in information are apparent. The normative group included 418 children enrolled in public, private, and parochial schools across several states in the mid-Atlantic area (states not specified), Florida, and Illinois. Children were excluded if they did not speak English as a first language, or were hearing-impaired, language-delayed, learning-disabled, or suspected of having similar problems by their teachers. In addition, children not responding to the examiner's prompts to retell the story were excluded from analyses. Children's ages were distributed fairly evenly across the range for which the test was designed. Demographic information for gender, urban versus rural setting, and racial/ethnic groups are displayed in the manual along with raw score means for each demographic breakdown. The authors state that these results were investigated for bias and that none was found. For racial/ethnic makeup, the normative sample consisted of approximately 89% Caucasian, 8% Black, and 3% Hispanic or Other. The authors stated that a range of socioeconomic levels was represented but did not elaborate on this.

Evidence of test-retest and interrater reliability is presented in the RBS manual. Test-retest reliability estimates, based on a small sample (n = 27), produced an average coefficient of .70 (for a 4-week interval) across three subtests: Information, Sentence Length, and Complexity (range across subtests = .58 to .79). Interrater reliability estimates across three raters ranged from .22 to .92 across the same three subtests, with Complexity averaging .38. Low to moderate test-retest and interrater reliability coefficients are a strong indication that the RBS should remain a screening test, as the authors suggest, and not a formal assessment instrument.

The authors present evidence for validity of the RBS based on increasing means across subtests as ages increase. Concurrent validity evidence is based upon comparison of the British and American versions of the test, producing correlation coefficients of .98 for both Information and Sentence Length subtests. Further information about the number of subjects and their nationality was not provided for concurrent validity results. It is assumed the RBS authors were the experimenters.

Previous studies using the earlier British version of the RBS are cited by the test authors as providing discriminant validity for children with language delays. However, if studies cited originated in the United Kingdom, this could seriously affect generalizability of results to U.S. samples because of differences in diagnostic standards.

CONCLUSION. The RBS testing package is small, well organized, and attractively designed. It consists of an Examiner's Manual with administration instructions and normative tables, a *Story Booklet*, and a set of record forms. Instructions are clear and easy to follow. Administration is quick and straightforward. Scoring may require more time than does administration. Evidence of test-retest reliability and interrater reliability are provided with appropriate cautions. Construct and concurrent validity have been investigated for the RBS although more information should be gathered.

Some limitations of the RBS merit reviewing here. First, the test has a limited, geographically proscribed normative sample and specific information about the socioeconomic status of children in the sample is not supplied. Potential users are cautioned regarding the match between local populations and children represented in the normative data. In areas such as the Southeastern states, where racial makeup and socioeconomic conditions differ drastically from the RBS's normative sample, minority children and children from economically deprived backgrounds may find themselves overidentified and placed on a list for formal assessment. Locally collected norms for this screening test would provide an advantage in some geographic areas.

Secondly, children with identified language or learning problems or with suspected problems were intentionally excluded from the normative sample altogether, which may translate into poorer standard scores than these children might have received if such a group had been included. The normative sample should be extended to include these children. In addition, the need for updated research regarding discriminant validity based upon a sample of American children is evident. Additional concurrent validity based upon other language screeners would also be a welcome addition.

A third concern involves caution in scoring and interpreting the Complexity subtest, which exhibits the weakest reliability data and appears to have an inadequate floor at lower age levels. The test authors do advise caution in using this subtest. On the other hand, the Complexity subtest might prove useful in screening for characteristics of giftedness, an issue not discussed in manual, but perhaps worth investigating.

SUMMARY. The RBS is recommended by its authors as a language-screening instrument, a research instrument, or a tool within a battery of language tests. In general, these recommendations seem appropriate. The test could provide an inexpensive addition to screening packages for children suspected of having language problems if limitations of the normative sample are considered.

REVIEWER'S REFERENCE

Renfrew, C. E. (1977). *The bus story*. Oxford, England: 2a North Place, Old Headington.

Review of The Renfrew Bus Story by ROBERT R. HACCOUN, Professor and Chair, I-O Psychology, Université de Montréal, Montreal, Quebec, Canada:

The Renfrew Bus Story is the U.S.-based version of a British scale developed by C. Renfrew. The test is presumed to assess in young children (aged 3-6—6-11) the "ability to give a coherent description of a continuous series of events" (p. 1). Such ability is said to be useful in the analysis of the state of a child's progress towards the development of higher language skills. These skills are presumably required for academic achievement.

Performance on this task depends on a complex set of skills including the coordination of auditory and visual cues, attention, comprehension, and memory. The development of the test is based on an analysis of the dimensions that, on theoretical ground, appear to underlie language development and academic achievement. The test is supposed to indicate a need for further testing and it is not intended as a stand-alone diagnostic instrument that would lead to specific remedial interventions.

Examiners must read a story to the child who is prompted to retell it in his or her own words. The story itself is very short, recounting the experiences of a bus that runs away from its driver. Twelve pictures describing the key elements of the story are also presented and the child peruses the pictures as he or she is read the story and as it is retold to the examiner. The entire protocol is tape recorded and a content analysis is conducted by the test administrator who scores the verbal production along four dimensions: Information (level of story detail reproduced), Sentence Length (mean number of words for the five longest sentences), Complexity (use of sentences that contain subordinate and-or relative clauses), and Independence (level of prompting required). In addition, the examiner notes, on specific templates, information that may form the basis of a qualitative assessment. Specifically, the examiner may score the child's production for sequencing problems, off-topic remarks, organizational weaknesses, word difficulties, self-correction, and syntax. The examiner is also required to ask some questions that prompt the child to draw some logical inferences.

Finally, the child's response style is also judged and recorded on a specific form.

The manual spends considerable time describing and exemplifying the scoring system. Appropriately, given the "open-ended" nature of the responses to be analyzed, scoring correctly is the essence of this measure. Very explicit directions and forms are provided to help the examiner in the scoring of a large number of possible verbal productions relevant to the information and the sentence length dimensions. Scoring for the Complexity and the Independence scores is explained with considerably less detail. Even though, based on the statistical information reported in the manual, these dimensions may prove more difficult to score reliably.

Test Properties.

TEST STABILITY. The stability of the test results was assessed using a test-retest procedure with a 4-week delay with a sample of children aged 4 years 6 months to 6 years 11 months. Very young children (3.5 to 4.5 years) are not included in the sample. Data came from 27 children who were administered the test and their results were scored twice (by nondescribed raters).

The values of the pre-post correlations were .79 for Information, .73 for Sentence Length, and .58 for Complexity. The level of reliability estimate for scores from the Independence dimension is not reported. Except for the Complexity score, which is low (and the nonexistent information on Independence), the remaining coefficients are reasonable. However, the reliability estimates are based on a rather small sample and no information is provided as to the composition of the sample in terms of race, gender, or other parameters of importance. Moreover, the manual does not describe the raters nor the extent of their familiarity and training with the test. Of special significance is that the manual offers no information to define the reliability of protocols for the different age groups, which is important because scores are especially sensitive to age. The omission of data for the youngest people for whom the test is intended is also a glaring omission that requires correction.

INTERRATER AGREEMENT. Because the test involves the scoring of "open ended" response, the issue of interrater reliability is crucial. Here again, the authors conclude that the obtained label of interrater reliability is adequate. It is not clear how the procedure was carried out exactly though

it appears that the mean rating obtained between the two authors was correlated with the results obtained by two (presumably independent) "special education teachers." These correlation coefficients, based on a sample of 25 children, ranged .70 to .90 for the Information scores; .79 and .81 for Sentence Length; and from .22 to .60 for the Complexity scores.

This methodology is suboptimal and interrater reliability level may be overestimated. First, any scoring variations between the authors would be washed out. Of course, it is possible that rather than the mean ratings obtained by the authors, each contributed an independent rating for some of the protocols. In this case, separate analyses for each author should have been reported. Second, the use of the correlation coefficient as opposed to the Kappa statistic as a basis for the estimation of agreement is not totally appropriate. Correlation coefficients are insensitive to any mean differences between raters, producing artificially high interrater agreement.

Despite the use of the problematic procedure, the reliability estimate of the Complexity scores is unacceptably low. Although the authors are prudent in advising test users to be especially diligent in scoring the test for complexity, it is doubtful that this prescription alone is sufficient. One can easily assume that the raters used in generating the results reported in the manual would have been very carefully monitored by the test authors. Therefore, the correlations obtained from their scores should be higher than those that would likely be found with raters in the field, where control over their training would most likely be less stringent. Consequently, and based on the reported data, it does not appear, at this point, that the Complexity scores are reliable enough to justify the use of this dimension to enable substantive decisions about children. The absence of technical information about the Independence score should trigger a great deal of caution in accepting the authors' claims about the usefulness of this dimension.

INDEPENDENCE OF THE DIMENSIONS. The manual does not report any information as to the intercorrelations between the dimensions. This is an important omission and a weakness that should be corrected. Until this is done, there is no basis for interpreting the dimensions separately.

VALIDITY. The validity of the use of scores from the scale requires further documentation. As a basis for validity the authors report a very high (r

= .98+) concurrent correlation with the British version of the scale. However, no methodology is reported in the manual. The validity claim is further bolstered by the observation that the scores obtained by subjects increase "smoothly" with age. Once again, however, no statistical tests or, for that matter, description of the methodology used to support these claims, is presented. Given the paucity of the supporting documentation, validity claims would need considerable bolstering before one can agree with the authors that the test produces valid scores for identifying potential language difficulties.

TEST OR ITEM BIAS. The bus driver-mechanic in the story is a woman, which is a nice touch. The authors claim that the test appears to show no gender or race bias and present a table showing means (without variance information) for different groups. No further statistical information is available. Perusal of the table, however, shows that Black children (and to a lesser degree Hispanic children) appear to obtain lower scores. Therefore, and given the available evidence, the claim of no test bias—especially with regard to Blacks and Hispanics (populations of special importance in the United States)—is not entirely convincing.

NORMS AND INTERPRETATION. Norms are reported based on a sample of 418 children enrolled in school in the Mid-Atlantic states, Florida, and Illinois. The protocols for the normative samples were scored by the authors of the test. Here caution is required: (a) The reference sample excluded children for whom English was a second language or who did not respond to any prompts to tell the story as well as children who were previously identified as suffering from hearing loss, language delay, learning disabilities, or who were the object of unspecified "concerns" by the teacher; (b) the resulting sample is composed of 10 times more Caucasian than visible minorities though the gender balance is better; (c) the size of the normative sample for the various age groups is unknown; (d) given the low total sample sizes, the normative information for Blacks and Hispanics broken down by age group may be excessively thin.

The results are expressed as raw scores and a table in the manual translates these into standard scores and percentiles. The tables for the Information and Sentence Length dimensions are quite detailed and provided for children at 6-month intervals (3 years 6 months to 6 years 11 months).

The norms tables are presented in a different format for the Complexity and the Independence scores leaving the impression that the two former scores are more important than the latter two. The reference chart for the Complexity dimension provides specific interpretations ("superior" to "concern") but the Independence chart only provides a global "average range" scores distribution. Separate norms are not given for gender, race, or other descriptions of the normative sample.

SUMMARY. The Renfrew Bus Story appears to be easy to administer and most young children might find it interesting. The scoring of the test, however, appears to be considerably more complex and difficult and errors are likely. Although some of the reliability information is encouraging (though perhaps overestimated) the validity information is, at this point, much too scanty. Unless that information is seriously updated and strengthened, the test user who still chooses to use the test should follow the authors' advice and supplement it with additional testing. The claim of nonbias with respect to minority groups is not convincing. Of special significance, the test should not be used with those for whom English is a second language, who suffer previously diagnosed learning disabilities, or who have various sensory impairments as the norms sample specifically excludes these children. Leaving aside the omissions and technical ambiguities, the interpretation of results may prove somewhat taxing in practice.

Only the Complexity dimension (low scores flag "caution") is associated with explicit interpretation labels. This dimension is the very one that shows the weakest psychometric qualities.

The percentile information on the other dimensions may indicate a child's relative performance, but in the absence of validity information, it becomes difficult for the test interpreter to prepare any sort of convincing conclusion. We simply do not know if scoring at the 50th percentile on Information at age 6 is a valid precursor of difficulties in later school achievement.

It is not clear how one should interpret the profile of scores. The authors do provide one contingency (a two-by-two matrix, which relates Independence to Information), but this is very limited. Also, the linking of the qualitative and quantitative scoring systems is nowhere described.

Test users will find no help from the manual in defining the types of interpretations that may be reached given a particular pattern of scores. In the end, and after much complicated scoring, the evaluator is left pretty much on his or her own when it comes time to reach a conclusion about a child. They would then need to rely rather strongly on intuitive clinical sense. From a practical as well as a technical viewpoint, this considerably reduces the potential usefulness of this device.

[315]
Repeatable Battery for the Assessment of Neuropsychological Status.

Purpose: Designed to measure "attention, language, visuospatial/constructional abilities, and immediate and delayed memory."
Population: Ages 20–89.
Publication Date: 1998.
Acronym: RBANS.
Scores, 18: Immediate Memory (List Learning, Short Memory, Total), Visuospatial/Constructional (Figure Copy, Line Orientation, Total), Language (Picture Naming, Semantic Fluency, Total), Attention (Digit Span, Coding, Total), Delayed Memory (List Recall, List Recognition, Story Memory, Figure Recall, Total), Total.
Administration: Individual.
Forms, 2: A, B.
Price Data, 1999: $120 per primary form kit including manual, record form A, stimulus book A, and coding scoring template A; $99 per alternative form kit including 25 record form B, stimulus book B, and coding scoring template B; $35 per 25 record forms (specify form); $65 per stimulus book (specify form); $10 per coding scoring template (specify form); $30 per manual.
Time: (20–30) minutes.
Author: Christopher Randolph.
Publisher: The Psychological Corporation.

Review of the Repeatable Battery for the Assessment of Neuropsychological Status by STEPHEN J. FREEMAN, Associate Professor of Counseling & Development, Department of Family Sciences, Texas Woman's University, Denton, TX:

The Repeatable Battery for the Assessment of Neuropsychological Status (RBANS) is intended to be used for the detection and characterization of dementia in the elderly or as a neuropsychological screening battery. The author's rationale for the test's development was that many dementia screening instruments are insensitive to mild impairment and their excessive length and item difficulty makes them inappropriate for older

populations; the RBANS is designed to bridge these gaps. The kit contains two forms of the test (Stimulus Booklet A & B) to allow for repeat assessment without interference from practice effect. The author intended the instrument to be useful across a wide range of individuals between the ages of 20 and 89 years of age in a variety of settings (hospitals, rehabilitation centers, nursing homes, etc.).

The assessment consists of 12 subtests divided into five domains: Immediate Memory, Visuospatial/Constructional, Language, Attention, and Delayed Memory. Eighteen scores are obtained, one for each subtest as well as an index score for each domain and a total scale score. RBANS yields index standard scores based on subtest raw score. Index scores have a mean of 100 and a standard deviation of 15. Individual test record booklets enable the examiner to record scores, percentile ranks, and confidence intervals.

A trained examiner can administer the RBANS in approximately 20–30 minutes. The test manual is well organized and contains information required to administer, score, and interpret the RBANS. Testing procedures are relatively easy to follow and the author states that a wide range of individuals with some formal graduate or professional training in assessment may administer and score the RBANS. However, competent interpretation of the results requires professional training in neuropsychology.

The standardized sample for the RBANS included 540 adults. The sample was stratified by gender, geographic region, educational levels, and ethnicity (White, African American, Hispanic, and other). The proportion is purported to be similar to that reported by the U.S. Census Bureau in 1995. The sample was divided into six age groups 20–39, 40–49, 50–59, 60–69, 70–79, and 80–89. Each age group consisted of 90 participants. It appears that a smaller interval (e.g., 5 years) and a larger sample would be more consistent with the goal of increased sensitivity to mild impairment. Additionally, given the percentages by ethnicity in the standardization sample, African Americans and Hispanics appear to be underrepresented. It has been reported that education has a significant influence on memory performance; therefore, practitioners using the RBANS would be better informed if more detailed educational breakdown of the standardization sample were provided. Finally, exclusionary criteria were listed in the manual because only normal (nonimpaired) participants were included in the sample; however, it is not clear how screening for impairment was accomplished.

Information on reliability estimates is somewhat terse. Little to no information was provided as to sample size, age, or other relevant characteristics. The manual states that for most subtests, reliability coefficients were calculated using individuals in the standardization sample. However, for the Line Orientation, Picture Naming, Semantic Fluency, and Delayed Memory List Recognition subtest, a sample group of clinical patients with various neurological diagnoses were used. Because no other meaningful information was provided, the coefficients, though acceptable, must be viewed skeptically. Standard error of measurement for the RBANS indices were also reported by age group; however, because SEMs are derived from the reliability coefficients, caution should be applied when interpreting this data. Stability coefficients for Form A of the RBANS indices were reported to range from .42 on Language to .77 on Attention and .85 for total score. Because these reliability coefficients vary greatly, serious caution is advised in using subtest scores lower reliability values as stand-alone diagnostic criteria. Alternate form reliability coefficients were provided and ranged from .39 for Language, .54 for Visuospatial/Construction, .56 for Immediate Memory, .59 for Delayed Memory, .78 for Attention, and .79 for total score. The low magnitudes of reliability coefficients for the alternate forms raised questions as to the time equivalence of the two forms.

Content validity was documented by selecting subtest items that were similar in nature to tasks contained in other clinical tests (e.g., Wechsler Adult Intelligence Scale—III, Wechsler Memory Scale—III, Boston Naming Test, Judgment of Line Orientation, and verbal fluency tests). Evidence supporting construct validity of the RBANS (convergent and divergent validity) was, as the author stated, very preliminary and not at all conclusive. Evidence supporting concurrent validity (e.g., comparing impaired participants' performance on the RBANS to their Rancho Levels) was conspicuously absent, as was any attempt to show ability to use the RBANS to discriminate clinically depressed individuals from those with dementia.

SUMMARY. The RBANS appears to be a collection of item types from various other tests frequently used to assess memory and cognitive function. This in itself raises an as-yet-unanswered question: Why use the RBANS instead of more traditional neuropsychological tests with items it mirrors? Given the problems with the standardization sample and the woeful lack of technical information demonstrating acceptable levels of reliability and validity, no support for the use of the RBANS can be made. The RBANS' lack of clear technical strength and meaningful difference (greater sensitivity) from other neuropsychological tests preclude its ability to accomplish its mission.

Review of the Repeatable Battery for the Assessment of Neuropsychological Status by TIMOTHY J. MAKATURA, Clinical Neuropsychologist and Assistant Professor, Department of Physical Medicine and Rehabilitation, University of Pittsburgh Medical Center, Pittsburgh, PA:

The Repeatable Battery for the Assessment of Neuropsychological Status (RBANS) is a recently developed battery of 12 subtests, designed to measure Attention, Language, Visuospatial/Constructional Abilities, and Immediate and Delayed Memory. This battery was originally developed to fill the need for a brief, comprehensive battery with measures that are known to be sensitive to dementia, especially mild dementia. This battery is also appropriate as a general neurospsychological screening battery with normative information for individuals 20–89 years. The specific uses outlined by the author include (a) as a stand-alone core battery for the detection and characterization of dementia in the elderly, (b) as a neuropsychological screening battery for use when lengthier standardized assessments are either impractical or inappropriate, and (c) for repeat evaluations when an alternate form is desirable in order to control for practice effects.

The 12 subtests that comprise the RBANS are (a) List Learning—a list of 10 semantically unrelated words is presented in four successive trials, with number of words recalled recorded for each trial; (b) Story Memory—a story with 12 critical items is presented in two successive trials with the number of critical items recalled recorded for each trial; (c) Figure Copy—copying of a figure with 10 critical components scored on accuracy of drawing and location; (d) Line Orientation—matching 10 pairs of angled lines to a standard presented as 13 lines in a semicircular, fanlike pattern; (e) Picture Naming—naming line drawings of 10 objects with a semantic cue if needed; (f) Semantic Fluency—generating words based on semantic category in a single 60-second trial; (g) Digit Span—repeating digits immediately after presentation; (h) Coding—writing numbers below their associated geometric figure in 90 seconds based on a legend at the top of the page; (i) List Recall—spontaneous recalling of the 10 words learned in the List Learning subtest; (j) List Recognition—identifying the 10 words learned in the List Learning subtest from a group of 20 words including 10 distractors; (k) Story Recall—spontaneous recalling from the Story Memory subtest; and (l) Figural Recall—spontaneous recalling of figure from the Figure Copy subtest. An alternative Form B is also available.

Raw scores from each of the subtests are used to determine standardized scores (index scores) in five domains (Immediate Memory, Visuospatial/Constructional, Language, Attention, Delayed Memory). These standard scores are provided for six different age groups with conversion tables conveniently located in the back of the stimulus book. Index scores from the five domains are also summed and converted to a standardized score (Total Scale score). Standard scores may then be converted to a percentile rank equivalent.

There are 90 adults in each of six age groups for a total of 540 individuals that make up the normative sample. This sample is considered to be representative of the adult population in the United States aged 20–89. This sample is matched to the most recent U.S. Census data on variables including age, sex, race/ethnicity, educational level, and geographic region. Standard exclusionary data including cognitive impairment, neurologic disease or insult, significant primary sensory loss, psychiatric history, history of substance use, and limited proficiency of English are noted.

Split-half reliability coefficients were calculated for each index by age group and these ranged from .75 to .90. Standard errors of measurement were also calculated for each index by age group and ranged from 4.69 to 7.55. Corrected test-retest reliability estimates for index scores on Form A were measured at an average 33–43-week interval on a group of 40 adults (Mean age 70.7, SD = 7.9) and ranged from .55 to .78 with a Total Scale reliability = .88. Corrected alternate form reliability estimates were measured on a group of 100

subjects after a 1–7-day interval and ranged from .46 to .80 with Total Scale reliability = .82. An interrater reliability estimate of .85 was calculated for the Figure Copy subtest and involved three raters blindly scoring 20 protocols.

The most obvious and compelling arguments for content validity of the RBANS are the recognizable and familiar tasks that make up this battery. The subtests are similar in style and format to those found in more frequently used tests including the Hopkins Verbal Learning Test (Brandt, 1991), Wechsler Adult Intelligence Scale—Revised (Wechsler, 1981), Wechsler Memory Scale—Revised (Wechsler, 1987), Boston Naming Test (Kaplan, Goodglass, & Weintraub, 1983), Judgement of Line Orientation (Benton, Hamsher, Varney, & Spreen, 1983), Rey Complex Figure (Rey, 1964), and the Controlled Oral Word Association Test (Spreen & Benton, 1977).

The evidence for construct validity is based on two lines of reasoning that involve intercorrelation and comparison studies. The intercorrelations between the RBANS index scores from the normative sample range from .28 to .63 and indicate relatively independent factors. Second, comparison studies involving correlations between the RBANS and external measures of general intellectual ability, memory, spatial processing, attention, and language/achievement typically range from .49 to .82. Specifically, the correlation between RBANS Total index score and WAIS-R Short Form Full Scale IQ = .78. Correlations between the RBANS index scores and scores from select measures of the WMS-R range from .22 to .69. The RBANS Visuospatial/Constructional Index correlates .62 with the Judgement of Line Orientation and .79 with the Rey Complex Figure Reproduction. The RBANS Attention index correlates .82 with the WMS-R Attention/Concentration index, .57 with WAIS-R Digit Symbol subtest, and .52 with the WAIS-R Arithmetic subtest. The RBANS Language index correlated .75 with the Boston Naming Test and .59 with the Controlled Oral Word Associations. This evidence is offered as preliminary rather than conclusive due to varied group characteristics and small sample sizes.

Interpretation guidelines are also provided within the manual as well as case studies that consider the typical pattern of performance associated with Alzheimer's Disease, early vascular dementia, post-anoxic injury, and screening for traumatic brain injury. This information is helpful in acquainting the clinician with this instrument.

SUMMARY. The RBANS is a welcome addition to measures of cognitive status. This battery does indeed fill an existing need for a brief, comprehensive measure of multiple neuropsychological domains. Although new, the RBANS has a familiar look and feel due to the subtests being derived from instruments that are well known in the fields of psychology and neuropsychology. The battery is also brief and practical with conversion tables conveniently located in the stimulus booklet. The RBANS does have some minor weaknesses including heightened sensitivity of index scores to single point raw score fluctuations, lack of standard scores for individual subtests, and a conversion process from raw to index scores that raises questions about the relative contribution of each subtest score. However, these issues as well as limited evidence for validity should be amended as investigators conduct further research using the RBANS.

REVIEWER'S REFERENCES

Rey, A. (1964). *L'Examen clinique en psychologie*. Paris: Press Universitaire de France.

Spreen, O., & Benton, A. L. (1977). Neurosensory Center Comprehensive Examination for Aphasia. Victoria, BC: University of Victoria Neuropsychology Laboratory.

Wechsler, D. (1981). Wechsler Adult Intelligence Scale—Revised. San Antonio, TX: The Psychological Corporation.

Benton, A. L., Hamsher, K. de S., Varney, N. R., & Spreen, O. (1983). Judgment of Line Orientation, Form H. New York: Oxford University Press.

Kaplan, E., Goodglass, H., & Weintraub, S. (1983). The Boston Naming Test (2nd ed.). Philadelphia: Lea & Febiger.

Wechsler, D. (1987). Wechsler Memory Scale—Revised. San Antonio, TX: The Psychological Corporation.

Brandt, J. (1991). The Hopkins Verbal Learning Test: Development of a new memory test with six equivalent forms. *Clinical Neuropsychologist, 5*(2), 125–142.

[316]
Revised Minnesota Paper Form Board Test, Second Edition.

Purpose: "Designed to measure aspects of mechanical ability requiring the capacity to visualize and manipulate objects in space."

Population: Grade 9 and over.

Publication Dates: 1934–1995.

Acronym: RMPFBT.

Scores: Total score only.

Administration: Group.

Forms, 4: Series AA, BB, MA, MB.

Price Data, 1999: $46 per examination kit including test booklets for 4 forms and manual ('95, 91 pages); $73.50 per 25 Form AA or BB test booklets for booklet scoring; $94 per 25 test booklets for Forms MA and MB for use with scannable or hand-scorable answer document; $7 per key for Forms AA and BB; $37 per key for hand scoring scannable answer document for

Forms MA and MB; $59.50 per 50 scannable answer documents for use with Form MA or MB; $36 per manual.

Foreign Language Edition: French Canadian edition of the RMPFBT is available; contact Institut de Recherches Psychologiques, Inc., 34 ouest rue Fleury, Montreal, Quebec H3L 1S9, Canada.

Time: 20(40) minutes.

Authors: Rensis Likert and W. H. Quasha.

Publisher: The Psychological Corporation.

Foreign Adaptations: Australian edition: 1981; revised edition prepared by J. Jenkinson; Australian Council for Education Research [Australia]; British norms supplement: 1978; Gil Nyfield, NFER-Nelson Publishing Co. [England].

Cross References: See T5:2217 (3 references) and T4:2262 (2 references); for a review by Paul W. Thayer, see 9:1045 (2 references); see also T3:2015 (19 references), T2:2266 (37 references), 7:1056 (19 references), and 6:1092 (16 references); for a review by D. W. McElwain, see 5:885 (29 references); for reviews by Clifford E. Jurgensen and Raymond A. Katzell, see 4:763 (38 references); for a review by Dewey B. Stuit, see 3:677 (48 references); for a review by Alec Rodger, see 2:1673 (9 references).

Review of the Revised Minnesota Paper Form Board Test, Second Edition by L. CAROLYN PEARSON, Professor of Education, University of West Florida, Pensacola, FL:

The Revised Minnesota Paper Form Board Test (RMPFBT) is a well-established measure of mechanical aptitude and is designed to assist in the selection of employees for jobs or training programs that require the capacity for spatial ability or the ability to visualize and manipulate objects in space. The instrument is typically used to predict performance in vocational/technical training settings and as a selection tool for mechanical/technical fields and similar occupations. In addition to updating the manual, revisions include a newly designed test booklet cover, newly designed scannable/hand-scorable answer sheets for the M series, and newly designed keys. Directions are printed in the test booklets in addition to being printed in the manual.

The RMPFBT is a speed (20-minute time limit) and power (item difficulty increases) test available in two series with alternate A and B forms: a machine-scorable version that is reusable and the traditional version in which the respondent marks in the booklet. The equivalence of the alternate forms has been established. The test is composed of 64 items that have the respondent match a geometric object to 1 of 5 possible rearrangements. Eight practice problems, more than adequate to explain the task, are provided. The administration and scoring procedures are explicit and the directions for the respondent are clear. The test is arranged in such a way as to make hand scoring easy.

Norming was previously done in representative regions across several educational levels and industrial occupations including utilities, manufacturing, and various vocational rehabilitation clients; applicants as well as employees were included. Instructions on how to use the tables are clear and cautions are indicated where appropriate. Separate tables are given for the hand- and machine-scored editions and the sample sizes are large and well defined. Data collected during 1993 and 1994 on over 3,000 adults in a variety of employment settings include information on gender and ethnicity. The authors state that the information is to be used primarily for research purposes and cautions on its use for selection purposes. There appear to be no ethnic biases and the authors state that recent studies have narrowed the gap on gender differences. There appears to be a slight age bias with younger respondents scoring higher than older respondents and slight educational differences with high school graduates scoring higher than nongraduates.

Reliability estimates for scores from the two versions appear to be more than adequate. Internal consistency coefficients, for the hand-scored A and B versions respectively, are .93 and .95 for split half, and .86 and .91 for alternate forms. Test-retest reliability was examined on the machine-scored version and coefficient ranged from .71 for delayed readministration to .85 for immediate readministration. (Interval for retest ranged from 0–88 months.) For alternate forms the standard error of measurement ranged from 3.1 to 4.5.

Extensive validation studies have been done on the RMPFBT over the years. The authors warn that users interested in content validity should establish that the job in question requires spatial ability. The preference may be to use a battery of instruments when the job is defined by several tasks that require different abilities. In terms of predictive validity, the test has been widely used to predict educational or occupational success and has been effective either alone or as part of a battery. The manual provides a large number of intercorrelations with criterion measures that usually included training course grades and supervisors' ratings. The highest ($r > .50$) intercorrelations were with course grades in machine design and detail drafting; general electrical, and military topography and graphics; grades and ratings of mechanical technique in dentistry; ratings of job proficiency/success in various aircraft plant occupations; and more recently, the previous years' science grade earned by college students enrolled in earth science courses. As for construct validity, early factor analytic studies during instrument development provide strong evidence for scores of the RMPFBT to be considered as valid measures of spatial ability; and divergent and convergent validity has been shown in a variety of settings. The instrument relates strongly to tests of both spatial and general intellectual ability and moderately with measures of mechanical, numerical, verbal, and clerical abilities. More recent studies provide further evidence of the spatial ability construct.

SUMMARY. In conclusion, the RMPFBT has proven over time to provide reliable and valid scores of spatial ability and is very useful in various mechanical/technical settings. The norming data have minority representation and the comprehensive manual now includes over 150 research references. Clear test administration and reporting procedures, along with newly designed keys and scan sheets, should do much to further increase the use of this test.

Review of the Revised Minnesota Paper Form Board Test, Second Edition by MICHAEL J. ROSZKOWSKI, Director, Institutional Research, La Salle University, Philadelphia, PA:

The Revised Minnesota Paper Form Board Test (RMPFBT) measures an aspect of mechanical skill known as spatial ability, namely, the visualization and manipulation of objects in space. A component of intelligence, this ability is considered necessary for mechanical, technical, engineering, and related occupations. The listed uses of the RMPFBT are employee selection, employee development, and evaluation of training and instruction. The RMPFBT is described as an aptitude rather than an achievement test (manual, p. 8), and training and experience are said to improve scores only slightly, so it is surprising that the manual indicates that the test can be used to assess the success of education programs teaching mechanical-spatial skills (p. 11). The test is related to years of education (median correlation equals .31), but it is proposed that ability probably accounts for both the higher scores and the higher levels of education, rather than that education increases the test scores (manual, p. 31).

The precursor of the current test, first published in the late 1920s, was revised into its present form in 1934 with two alternate forms, Series AA and Series BB, which had consumable test booklets that could only be hand scored. In 1941, reusable versions of the test, Series MA and Series MB, were developed. These forms, which can be either machine or hand scored, are identical to their two earlier counterparts, except that these newer forms do not contain a correction for guessing. All four forms of the test are currently in use. The RMPFBT manual was revised in 1970 and again in 1995. The 1995 manual (2nd edition) contains updated norms collected during 1993 and 1994. Other changes in the 1995 edition are cosmetic in nature: new test booklet covers, newly designed answer sheets and keys, and the inclusion of directions for administration with the test booklets.

The manual presents the most recent norms (i.e., 1993–1994) in the body of the document. Earlier norms, published in 1948 and 1970, are reported in appendices. The stated purpose of the older norms is research. However, the manual recommends that whenever possible, local norms should be used in lieu of the 1993–1994 norms as well. The advice is sound because the value of the new norms is limited.

The 1993–1994 norms are reported in terms of 18 groups totaling 3,138 individuals, consisting of eight industrial samples ($n = 1,841$) and clients from 10 vocational rehabilitation centers ($n = 1,297$). The manual indicates that the data for the sexes and various ethnic classifications were combined based on directives in the Civil Rights Act of 1991. The cited research on sex differences in performance on the RMPFBT indicates that older studies generally found a difference of about 1 point in favor of males, whereas newer studies fail to observe any differences. The conclusion is drawn that failure to find sex-related differences is because the RMPFBT is a measure of analytical spatial ability rather than pure spatial ability, so the often-observed sex differences in other tests of spatial ability do not occur on the RMPFBT. This explanation, however, fails to account for the ear-

lier studies. Research cited in the manual shows that age is negatively related to RMPFBT performance (median correlation of -.20), so one has to wonder whether age should be considered in the norms of this test.

Most of the norms for the industrial samples are on applicants rather than on incumbents. The eight industrial samples are identified in the manual by the type of industry and position: lineman/electrician applicants at an eastern utilities company, applicants for various positions at a utilities company, applicants at a plastics/metals manufacturer, applicants at a plastics/rubber manufacturer, applicants at a steel manufacturer, trade apprentices at a western municipality, and employees at a cabinet manufacturer.

The vocational rehabilitation clients are described in terms of the geographical location of the centers: three northeast, two west, two southwest, two north-central, and one southern. A set of norms is presented for each center. Because some of the norms are for Forms AA/BB and others are for Forms MA/MB, it is unclear how many vocational rehabilitation centers were actually involved. It may be that some of the centers collected data on both forms of the test.

Two tables report norms. One table deals with five industrial groups and seven rehabilitation centers, whereas the other table deals with three industrial groups and three vocational rehabilitation centers. The difference between these tables lies in the detail provided in the norms. Both tables list the sample size, mean, and standard deviation for each of the standardization samples. One table also reports percentiles by 23 bands (e.g., 60th to 64th); the other table reports the norms only by quartile. The rationale for reporting bands is stated to be that "any test score contains some degree of error" (manual, p. 24). The reason only quartiles are given for the groups is not stated explicitly, but appears to be based on the small sizes for these samples (under 100).

Most of the industrial samples consist of people applying for different types of positions at the same industrial site (e.g., plastics/metal manufacturer). It is questionable whether the different occupations at this site require the same degree of spatial ability. Therefore, strict reliance on these combined norms is unwise. It should be possible to combine some of the industrial samples, and thereby perhaps form a sample that would permit one to consider the performance of the different occupations. For example, both norm tables report norms based on applicants at a steel manufacturer. The sample in one table is based on 116 individuals and the other is based on 49 individuals. Both samples took the Series AA-BB forms of the test, so the separate norms are not justified because of form differences. Likewise, the data from the plastics/metals manufacturer ($n = 207$) and the plastics/rubber manufacturer ($n = 589$) could be consolidated, especially in view of the similar mean scores and standard deviations at both plants.

Similarly, one has to question the rationale for reporting separate norms for each of the rehabilitation centers instead of combining data from all the centers into one norm group. In general, the clients of the rehabilitation centers score close to 10 points lower than the industrial samples. The only noted differences between the various rehabilitation centers is geographical locale; it is questionable if differences on the RMPFBT should be expected on a regional basis. To obtain greater stability, it would have been more useful to pool the information from the different rehabilitation centers. Perhaps the samples would then be large enough to report the rehabilitation centers' norms by various client characteristics, most notably the client's occupation. As currently presented, the norms are on clients from various occupations consolidated into one norm for each rehabilitation center, which suffers from the same limitations as the consolidated industrial samples.

The evidence on the reliability and validity of the RMPFBT has changed only slightly from that available in the previous edition of the manual. The internal consistency reliability of the RMPFBT is high, as determined from various samples of undergraduates studied in the 1970s and 1980s. In a study based on female undergraduates, the internal consistency of Series AA was .85. Among engineering students, the split-half reliability for Series AA and Series BB was .93 and .95, respectively. In a third study, the KR-20 reliability estimate for the RMPFBT was .90.

In a study dated 1937, the alternate form reliability for Series AA-BB was reported to be .85 in a sample of college applicants. Four studies conducted in 1969 investigated the alternate form reliability of Series AA-BB and Series MA-MB using samples of high school and college students. The correlation coefficients ranged from .71 to .78. A more recent study based on two samples of engineering students reported alternate-form reliabilities of .86 for Series AA and .91 for Series BB.

Numerous temporal stability estimates exist for the RMPFBT. An early study of the test-retest reliability of the machine-scored version reported it as .85. The most impressive are longitudinal studies reported in the 1940s of children aged 10 to 14 who took Series AA over 4 years. The 1-year stability ranged from .79 to .90, with a median of .87. The 2-year test-retest correlations ranged from .80 to .86, with a median of .85. The mean 3-year test-retest correlation was .80 (range .77 to .82). Even after 4 years, the correlation between the two administrations remained high, .81. A study from the mid-1950s, also looking at long-term stability (average of 13.1 months between test and retest), was based on trade school students, and found a correlation of .71. Surprisingly, no studies are mentioned in the manual that have considered the correlation across the Series AA-BB and Series MA-MB (e.g., AA with MA, BB with MB).

The manual deals with the content, construct, and criterion-related aspects of the RMPFBT's validity. It indicates that content validity needs to be linked to a particular job through a job analysis at the local level. Construct validity evidence presented in the manual consists of studies showing differences in RMPFBT scores for groups that would be expected to differ in their mechanical-spatial abilities. Studies from the 1940s and 1950s are cited that show that mechanical draftsmen and engineering students scored higher than other occupational groups or the general population. Likewise, high school physics students scored higher than biology students. The more recent studies discussed in the manual under construct validity found that the test is related to speed of access to symbolic information and quality of mental representation of spatial data. Differences in performance have been linked to hemispheric activation and hormonal levels. The majority of the studies that consider the relationship of the RMPFBT to other tests are from the 1940s to 1970s. Only three studies from the 1980s are cited, and there are no studies from the 1990s.

The discussion of criterion-related validity includes studies that found the RMPFBT to be related to lip reading ability in hearing-impaired individuals, disciplinary problems in prisoners, artistic ability, grades in technical drawing and science courses, completion of mechanically oriented courses, recall of prose passages, and the solution of anagrams. In total, 45 validity studies involving the RMPFBT are reported. The correlations between the RMPFBT and school success range from .02 to .61, with a median correlation of .27. For job performance as the criterion, reported correlations range from .10 to .59, with a median of .32.

Approximately 57% of these criterion-related validity studies are from the 1940s, 12% are from the 1950s, and 26% date from the 1970s. There is only one study from the 1980s and none from the 1990s. The criteria used in these validity studies were primarily grade and/or instructor rating (63% of the studies), followed by supervisory ratings (25%) and salary (5%). The remaining studies (7%) used diverse criteria such as job level increases, objective measures of productivity, work samples, and years required to attain a management position. Because the RMPFBT is now marketed as a test for employee selection, it would be appropriate to see more studies involving personnel-type criteria.

SUMMARY. An examination of the latest release of the RMPFBT shows that the test's appearance has been improved by the noted cosmetic changes. The content of the test itself has not changed with the latest revision, so the psychometric properties of the instrument that were identified years ago continue to apply today. The reliability of the RMPFBT is strong and the validity of the test as a measure of spatial ability is without question. It is rather surprising, however, that the research on the RMPFBT is not continuing at the same pace as before and thus the major portion of the research base cited in support of the RMPFBT appears to be dated, even if it is not outmoded. The decision by the publisher to develop new norms for the test was appropriate, given the reported increases in cognitive ability test scores over the past 60 years (Neisser, 1998), but the usefulness of the new norms is questionable. The number of occupations for which the published norms apply is rather limited presently, so users will need to develop local norms to fully realize the potential of the RMPFBT.

REVIEWER'S REFERENCE

Neisser, U. (Ed.). (1998). *The rising curve: Long-term gains in IQ and related measures*. Washington, DC: The American Psychological Association.

Rey Auditory Verbal Learning Test: A Handbook.

Purpose: Designed to measure "verbal learning and memory."
Population: Ages 7–89.
Publication Date: 1996.
Acronym: RAVLT.
Scores, 3: Learning, Recall, Recognition.
Administration: Individual.
Price Data, 2001: $72.50 per complete kit including handbook (148 pages) and 25 record sheets and score summaries; $19.95 per 25 record sheets and score summaries; $54.50 per handbook.
Time: (15) minutes.
Author: Michael Schmidt.
Publisher: Western Psychological Services.
Cross References: See T5:2226 (42 references).

Review of the Rey Auditory Verbal Learning Test: A Handbook by KAREN MACKLER, School Psychologist, Lawrence Public Schools, Lawrence, NY:

The Rey Auditory Verbal Learning Test: A Handbook (RAVLT) is a handbook for a brief test of verbal learning utilizing a fixed order word list. The original list was created in French (Rey, 1941, 1958). Subsequent versions were translated into English and four other languages. The product is not a test. It is a handbook that contains results of various clinical studies as well as standard administration scoring procedures. Alternate test forms and supplementary scores and indexes are provided as well. Many reviews of studies involving the RAVLT were compiled and metanorms were developed. Information regarding which word list and procedure to use are provided within the handbook. The handbook is quite extensive and helpful in assisting the evaluator in determining which format to use with a particular individual or population.

The actual test comprises a 15-item list of words that is presented five times in the same order. Recall of the words in any order is counted after each trial. A delayed Recall task is given after a short interval of time (10–30 minutes). There is also a Recognition task. The one- or two-syllable words on the list are controlled for phonemic and semantic associations (Shapiro & Harrison, 1990). The words are of high imagery. The Recognition reading list is reported to be on a third-grade level (Binder, Villanueva, Howieson, & Moore, 1993).

The author states that the measure can be used to assess rote memorization, proactive and retroactive inhibition, retention, encoding versus retrieval, and subjective organization. Further elaboration is not provided. Administration of the test can be accomplished in 15 minutes. The test is easy to administer and directions are straightforward.

Norms for the measure are not as straightforward. The norms for ages 7 to 89 have been pulled together from many different studies, and as such, comparisons to these groups are limited, due to methodological differences. There has been no single comprehensive standardization study for the test. The original norms are almost 40 years old and specific to the French word list. More confusing is that administration procedures are different depending on the norms chosen. Many of the studies have small numbers of subjects or were conducted in Australia. Norms at some age levels are more complete than at others. Ceiling effects are noted for bright young people. There is only one choice for norms for children or the elderly (Mayo Older Americans Normative Studies [MOANS] for the RAVLT). For adults, several norms are available.

Scores are obtained for Learning trials, delayed Recall and for Recognition. Raw scores may be compared to normative means and standard deviations of either the metanorms or a particular reference group. Standard scores can be obtained by first calculating z-scores. The z-scores can also be converted to T-scores and/or normalized percentile scores.

Reliability and validity estimates also were obtained through several different studies. Test-retest reliability has been assessed using various alternative forms of the word lists. Overall, estimates are fair to good ranging from .12 to .86. Depending on the study, test-retest intervals ranged from 6 days to 3 years. Some data (see Geffen, Butterworth, & Geffen, 1994, and Uchiyama et al., 1995) suggest that scores for the last several learning trials are more stable than those for the initial trials. The reliability estimates for the recognition condition tend to be low, perhaps due to limited variability in many of the studies cited. Reliability scores for the initial trials are not that convincing, particularly because the studies are often done with newly created forms of the test. Comparisons between studies are nearly impossible.

Test validity was addressed in the same manner. Different studies are cited to substantiate the claim that the RAVLT does indeed measure verbal learning and memory. Content (face) validity is addressed in the handbook by the statement "it looks like a verbal learning test" (p. 48). No mention is made of any professionals other than the author addressing content validity of the measure.

Concurrent and criterion-related validity has been addressed by several factor analytic studies. Results of these studies indicate that the RAVLT scores load consistently with other verbal memory or verbal ability instruments. They do not load with nonverbal abilities such as motor or visuospatial skills. Highest correlations were with verbal memory measures.

Other studies are reported with the intent of using the RAVLT with patients with various brain lesions. Results indicate that the test is sensitive to brain disease. Many studies are described in detail to determine the ability of the RAVLT to discriminate between various clinical subpopulations. The RAVLT has been used with an extremely wide range of populations, such as individuals with language impairments, lupus, HIV, etc. Several of the studies found different performance based on group membership. For example, head trauma patients show normal primacy and recency, whereas patients with dementia show only a recency effect. The RAVLT has been shown to be sensitive to organic impairment, which would make this measure useful within a neuropsychological evaluation. Several investigators have looked at the internal structure of the RAVLT. Talley (1986) ran a factor analytic study using the RAVLT and the Digit Span (DS) subtest of the Wechsler Scales. He found that Trials I, II, and List B had strong loadings on short term memory, and Trials III, IV, V, and VI, and the delayed recall loaded on long-term memory, and the DS scores were on a separate factor. He concluded that the tasks on the RAVLT had stronger requirements on the control processes such as rehearsal, coding, and retrieval whereas Digit Span does not. Munson (1981) reported that Trial I is a measure of immediate auditory memory. Correlations with other memory span tasks were low, indicating that memory span tests are not interchangeable.

SUMMARY. Overall, the RAVLT is an easily administered measure of the ability of an individual to learn words over a period of five trials. A delayed recall task and a recognition task address storage and retrieval processes. Data exists to demonstrate that the test is sensitive to brain disease and can discriminate between normals and those with brain insult. If one is patient enough to locate the appropriate norms and the corresponding administration procedures, the test is appropriate to use within a neuropsychological battery.

REVIEWER'S REFERENCES

Rey, A. (1941). L'examen psychologique dans les cas d'encéphalopathie traumatique. *Archives de Psychologie, 28,* 286–340.

Rey, A. (1958). *L'examen clinique en psychologie* (pp. 141–193). Paris: Presses Universitaires de France.

Talley, J. L. (1986). Memory in learning disabled children: Digit span and the Rey auditory verbal learning test. *Archives of Clinical Neuropsychology, 1,* 315–322.

Munson, J. (1987). *Performance of adolescents on traditional measures of auditory-verbal learning and memory.* Unpublished data.

Shapiro, D. M., & Harrison, D. W. (1990). Alternate forms of the AVLT: A procedure and test of form equivalency. *Archives of Clinical Neuropsychology, 5,* 405–410.

Binder, L. M., Villanueva, M. R., Howieson, D., & Moore, R. T. (1993). The Rey AVLT recognition memory task measures motivational impairment after mild head trauma. *Archives of Clinical Neuropsychology, 8,* 137–147.

Geffen, G. M., Butterworth, P., & Geffen, L. B. (1994). Test-retest reliability of a new form of the Auditory Verbal Learning Test (AVLT). *Archives of Clinical Neuropsychology, 9,* 303–316.

Uchiyama, C. L., D'Elia, L. F., Dellinger, A. M., Becker, J. T., Selnes, O. A., Wesch, J. E., Chen, B. B., Satz, P., Van Gorp, W., & Miller, E. N. (1995). Alternate forms of the auditory-verbal learning test: Issues of test comparability, longitudinal reliability, and moderating demographic variables. *Archives of Clinical Neuropsychology, 10,* 133–145.

Review of the Rey Auditory and Verbal Learning Test: A Handbook by STEVEN R. SHAW, Lead School Psychologist, Department of Developmental Pediatrics, The Children's Hospital, Greenville, SC:

DESCRIPTION. The Rey Auditory and Verbal Learning Test: A Handbook (RAVLT) is a handbook for a brief test of verbal learning and memory. Administration is extremely simple. A 15-item word list is presented orally five times in the same order, and recall is assessed after each presentation. However, several variations have been developed over the years.

The *Rey Auditory and Verbal Learning Test: A Handbook,* published by Western Psychological Services, is not so much a test, but a comprehensive literature review and compilation of normative data of a classic neuropsychological tool. Since André Rey developed the RAVLT in 1941 there are well over 100 professional journal articles concerning this instrument. Moreover, the RAVLT has been translated into several languages and has multiple variations on administration. To have all of this information in one convenient location is a valuable contribution to neuropsychological assessment.

ADMINISTRATION AND SCORING. Administration of the RAVLT itself is not difficult. However, selecting which of the 19 variations of RAVLT administration is most appropriate is quite challenging. Variations of administration depend on list used, number of trials administered, interference word lists administered, whether patients are asked to recognize target words in a story or list, the length of delay between the last trial and a free recall trial, and the language in which the RAVLT list is to be administered.

The presentation of norms in the handbook is unique. Rather than a large-scale renorming of the RAVLT, normative data from 24 studies are presented. Studies use different variations of RAVLT administration and have different sample characteristics. Clinicians, therefore, have 24 different normative samples of varying quality and relevance—each with its own unique variation of administration of the RAVLT—from which to select. Normative data are presented stratified by age. For some age groups (i.e., children under 16 and adults over 70) there is only one set of norms (i.e., one applicable study), thus selection of norms is simple. However, for the general adult population there are nine different studies and nine different sets of norms and several variations in administration from which to choose. Each study is described in enough detail so that the appropriate normative data can be selected. For example, one sample is made up of inmates in a correctional institution, another of adults with depressive symptoms, another with spinal cord injuries, another with an Australian general population sample, and so on. Clinicians are not free to pick and choose whichever administration best suits their purpose. The clinician must select which of these studies is most appropriate for the current patient. The RAVLT needs to be administered in a manner consistent with the administration methods used to develop that specific set of normative data. Selecting appropriate norms and administrative variation is, and always has been, a challenge for clinicians using the RAVLT.

Another interesting approach and guide to interpreting these different normative samples is the use of metanorms. Pooled means and standard deviations from all studies were calculated. Then each study was compared to these weighted averages. This allows clinicians to decide if specific sample and administration procedures yield liberal or conservative means and standard deviations. Instructions are given for appropriate corrections to be made.

The RAVLT handbook contains a large number of stimulus sets, interference sets, recall paragraphs, and recall lists. Moreover, stimulus sets are presented in French and German. This allows clinicians to use a wide variety of variations on basic administration.

RELIABILITY AND VALIDITY. Evaluating the reliability and validity of scores from the RAVLT is challenging because there is no single RAVLT—there are 19 variations presented in the manual. There are over 100 studies using these variations. The author carefully reviews all of these data. Like interpretation of norms, evaluation of reliability and validity can be a bit daunting due to the variations of sample characteristics and administration procedures. There is compelling evidence that most variations of the RAVLT produce scores that have adequate reliability (reported as stability), construct validity, concurrent validity, and predictive validity. The primary weakness is that there are some variations of the RAVLT that have no reliability data and few validity studies. There are simply gaps in the literature. The value of having a single standardized administration becomes clear when evaluating the uneven reliability and validity data presented concerning the RAVLT. However, having all of these data in one place is a convenience.

CONCLUSION. The RAVLT has been and will continue to be an important component of neuropsychological assessment batteries. The RAVLT is quick to administer, simple to score, and allows experienced clinicians to gain a great deal of information on verbal learning, language, and memory in a short amount of time. Although having all of the relevant clinical information and norms in one place can be confusing, it is far more convenient than my current method of having several articles sloppily placed into a three-ring binder. Moreover, the author offers helpful tips on selecting appropriate administration procedures and norms. The production of a handbook for the RAVLT is not a novel contribution to neuropsychology. However, it makes André Rey's classic contribution to neuropsychology easier to use, more accessible, and more flexible than ever before.

Although a renorming of a standardized RAVLT might be more useful for many users (especially students and those unfamiliar with the RAVLT), it is unclear as to which administration procedure would be used for such a standardized RAVLT. At some point, a standardized and renormed RAVLT will be necessary if this neuropsychological instrument is to meet basic psychometric characteristics. This is a shortcoming

and a desire for an entirely new product. Despite these minor concerns, the *Rey Auditory and Verbal Learning Test: A Handbook,* a well-designed and comprehensive compilation of norms and validity studies, is a welcomed and useful step in the evolution of neuropsychological assessment.

[318]
Rey Complex Figure Test and Recognition Trial.

Purpose: Designed to "investigate visuospatial constructional ability and visual memory."
Population: Ages 18–89.
Publication Dates: 1995–1996.
Acronym: RCFT.
Scores, 9: Immediate Recall, Delayed Recall, Recognition Total Correct, Copy, Time to Copy, Recognition True Positives, Recognition False Positives, Recognition True Negatives, Recognition False Negatives.
Administration: Individual.
Price Data: Price information available from publisher for complete kit including manual ('95, 126 pages), 25 test booklets, stimulus card, and supplemental norms for children and adolescents ('96, 21 pages).
Time: (45) minutes, including a 30-minute delay interval.
Authors: John E. Meyers and Kelly R. Meyers.
Publisher: Psychological Assessment Resources, Inc.
Cross References: See T5:2227 (62 references).

Review of the Rey Complex Figure Test and Recognition Trial by D. ASHLEY COHEN, Clinical Neuropsychologist, CogniMetrix, San Jose, CA:

The Rey Complex Figure Test (RCFT) has appeared in various guises as a popular instrument in V.A. hospitals, academic neuropsychology training programs, rehabilitation facilities, and outpatient assessment offices. Its utility was apparent to many neuropsychologists (Kramer & Delis, 1998; Lynch, 1997) despite sometimes poorly reproduced and slightly varying versions of the stimulus figure, conflicting sets of administration and scoring instructions, differing times between the trials, and poor normative data, often requiring calculations and extrapolations. These factors almost completely precluded comparison of scores on ostensibly the same test, given in different facilities or regions, and contributed to unwanted variability in scores obtained from particular individuals. Data on older persons was virtually unavailable.

The present version of the RCFT addresses these shortcomings, and takes the concept from an error-variance-laden, rough approximation of an instrument with potential to a clean, well-constructed, modern neuropsychological test.

For those unfamiliar with the test in any of its extant forms, a line-drawing of a multipart geometric figure is shown, with the request to copy it exactly onto a separate paper. No mention is made of a memory task to come. Shortly following completion of the Copy trial, the subject is given a blank paper, and instructed to reproduce the same figure from memory. Thirty minutes after the Copy trial, the subject once again draws the figure. In the Meyers version (here reviewed), following the delayed recall, the subject is shown 24 smaller figures, half of which were part of the original stimulus, and is asked to mark the ones he or she has seen before.

The publisher lists the RCFT for use with individuals aged 6–89 years. A separate manual supplement is required to use the test with children and adolescents; this portion of the test is not discussed here as the publisher elected not to provide the children's manual for review. [Editor's Note: The publisher advises this was an oversight and provided the missing manual after the reviews were completed.]

IMPROVEMENTS AND UNIQUE FEATURES OF THE MEYERS AND MEYERS VERSION OF THE RCFT. The stimulus figure is provided with the test packet, and laminated to prevent deterioration. At many sites where the RCFT has been in use, it was customary to present the figure in "landscape" rather than "portrait" view. Examinees often gravitate to this orientation, as the figure is wider than it is tall. The manual states findings that the vertical presentation results in less inadvertent distortion of the figure by normal examinees.

The awkward practice of giving the examinee colored markers for doing the drawing, and having the examiner switch them at intervals, has been eliminated. As Meyers and Meyers observe, many neuropsychologically impaired individuals, or those with motor difficulties, are unduly distracted when drawing implements are exchanged. Examiners do not in practice switch colors reliably, and the process extends the administration time, which affects the time for copying, one of the important scores.

There were 601 subjects in the standardization sample in the 18–89-year age group, and 505 who were ages 6–17. All geographic regions of the U.S. and portions of Canada were included in the normative sample; both urban and rural areas were represented. A subset of the sample was selected to match year 2000 U.S. Census projections. The RCFT sample had slightly higher educational attainment than the U.S. population, although education was not found to be a factor in RCFT scores; neither was there an effect from gender. Age had by far the most significant influence on scores, and this version of the test provides normative data up to age 89 (the manual notes that relatively fewer of the oldest subjects are represented in the sample, however).

Because of the structure of the standardization sample, a given individual's score can be compared both to age-corrected scores, for purposes of diagnosis, and to the performance of the general adult population, when seeking to establish a level of performance in absolute terms.

Very precise scoring criteria, based on both placement of units of the figure, and accuracy in reproducing each unit, were developed empirically. The manual states experienced scorers do not need to use the detailed criteria for most protocols, and indeed they would be very time-consuming for everyday scoring. It is presumed, however, that the precise criteria were used in standardization, and the variability introduced hereby is unknown.

The Recognition Trial is an important addition to this test, enabling evaluation of the relative strengths of the processes of encoding, storage, and retrieval in a given subject. This trial is easy to administer, but recording and calculating the score is somewhat cumbersome. An additional feature of this trial is its potential utility in evaluating subjects suspected of questionable motivation; cut-off scores are suggested. Two types of errors are detailed, which are virtually never encountered in normals, extremely rarely seen in brain-injured patients, but are often found among malingerers.

Overall, strong reliability evidence was shown. Interrater reliability coefficients averaged .94. Test-retest reliability is a troublesome concept with this test, because once the examinee knows it is a memory test and has drawn the figure three times for the first administration, the situational demands change. Some of the obtained scores have a restricted range in normals, as well. Those portions of the test for which temporal stability is clinically meaningful yielded between .917 and 100% agreement in clinical rating or interpretation.

Good to excellent convergent and discriminant validities were found, using separate samples of both normal subjects and brain-injured patients. Construct validity was evaluated by comparing scores of the RCFT with the WAIS-R, and with related and unrelated neuropsychological tests, using both normal and brain-injured persons. As would be expected, the RCFT proved a strong measure of visuoconstructional ability and visuospatial memory.

Findings of a study were presented demonstrating the ability of the RCFT to discriminate among brain-injured patients, psychiatric patients, and healthy normal subjects. It was also found that the recognition trial provided incremental validity of 16.7%.

The authors present a "Profile Analysis" scheme similar, they state, to Roger Greene's (1991) codetype configuration analysis of the Minnesota Multiphasic Personality Inventory (MMPI). Five distinct patterns of scores were commonly found, and each pattern was associated with different recommendations for rehabilitation, as well as prognostic indicators for independence in activities of daily living.

GENERAL COMMENTS. In the manual, a brief historical summary of the RCFT is given, and research is cited on conditions and disorders with which the test has proven useful. Many helpful case illustrations, and detailed scoring examples, are provided. Overall, this version of the RCFT is easy to administer, and scoring, although still not simple, is much more likely to be accurate. Obtaining normative scores for a given protocol is efficient, and it is possible to compare the individual's score to both the general population, and to his or her appropriate age group, including elderly persons.

The newly developed Profile Analysis promises to increase clinical utility, and the Recognition Trial is a valuable addition to the test. It provides ability to locate where in the memory process the difficulty is occurring, and to measure the assistance, if any, obtained by provision of retrieval cues.

REVIEWER'S REFERENCES

Green, R. L. (1991). *The MMPI-2/MMPI: An interpretive manual.* New York: Allyn and Bacon.
Lynch, W. J. (1997). *Primary neuropsychological tests for use at the Brain Injury Rehabilitation Unit.* Palo Alto: Veterans' Affairs Medical Center.
Kramer, J. H., & Delis, D. C. (1998). Neuropsychological assessment of memory. In G. Goldstein, P. D. Nussbaum, & S. R. Beers (Eds.), *Neuropsychology* (pp. 333–356). New York: Plenum.

Review of the Rey Complex Figure Test and Recognition Trial by DEBORAH D. ROMAN, Assistant Professor and Director, Neuropsychology Lab, Departments of Physical Medicine and Rehabilitation and Neurosurgery, University of Minnesota, Minneapolis, MN:

The Rey Complex Figure Test (RCFT) has been around for over 50 years and has enjoyed popularity as a measure of constructional abilities and nonverbal memory. This version of the test uses the traditional figure without modification. The administration procedure has been standardized and a recognition trial has been added. Consistent with previously established scoring criteria, 18 design elements are scored for a total possible score of 36, based on the accuracy and placement of the elements. The current system provides more detailed scoring criteria that should enhance interrater reliability. Additionally, the authors provide the largest normative sample ever published for this test, enabling more accurate age comparisons.

There are four parts to the test administration. First, subjects copy the design from a model. Then it is redrawn from memory after a 3-minute delay and again after a 30-minute delay. Finally, in the recognition trial, RCFT design elements are selected from arrays of options (12 target details, 12 foils).

The normative sample consisted of 601 subjects who had been screened for learning disability, substance abuse, psychiatric disorders, and depression. Subjects were pooled from various sources including college students (134), families and friends of rehabilitation patients (74), and community dwellers enlisted from a variety of sources (393). Subjects ranged in age from 18 to 89. A subset of this sample ($n = 394$) was selected to mirror the U.S. population in terms of age. The manual contains a breakdown of the various RCFT score means and standard deviations across 14 age groups.

Polynomial regression analyses were conducted to determine the effects of age, gender, and education on RCFT scores. There was a significant quadratic effect for age on Copy and Time to Copy scores. There was a significant linear effect for age on all of the other RCFT variables. Gender and years of education were not significantly related to RCFT scores. Demographically corrected normative scores are provided in Appendix C and enable conversion of raw scores to percentiles and T-scores for the Immediate Recall, Delayed Recall, and Recognition scores. All other scores were divided into five ranges (with >16th percentile as the top range and ≤1st percentile as the lowest range).

To estimate interrater reliability the senior author and two trained psychometrists independently scored the same 15 protocols. Interrater reliability coefficients (Pearson product-moment correlations) ranged from .93 to .99, suggesting very good reliability among well-trained scorers.

Temporal reliability (average retest interval was 184 days) was assessed using 12 subjects drawn from the normative sample. Immediate Recall, Delayed Recall, and Recognition Total Correct test-retest coefficients were .759, .888, and .874, respectively. There were no significant differences across the two testings for mean scores of the remaining variables (Copy, Time to Copy, Recognition, True Positives, Recognition False Positives, Recognition True Negatives, and Recognition False Negatives).

Convergent and discriminant validity were assessed using the 601 normative subjects. Immediate and Delayed Recalls were highly correlated (.881). Lower, but still significant, positive correlations were noted between Recall and Recognition scores. Copy scores also correlated significantly with Recall scores. Convergent and discriminant validity were also assessed in a heterogeneous group of 100 brain-injured patients. Again, Immediate and Delayed Recall scores were highly correlated (.961). Copy scores correlated significantly with Immediate and Delayed Recalls. Overall, the intratest correlations were similar for the normal and brain-injured groups. Given the very high correlations between Immediate and Delayed recalls, it may be possible to abbreviate the test by giving only the Immediate Recall and excluding the Delayed Recall.

Construct validity was assessed by correlating RCFT scores with the Wechsler Adult Intelligence Scale—Revised (WAIS-R) and various neuropsychological measures. Using the brain-injured sample ($n = 100$), RCFT measures generally correlated more strongly with the WAIS-R Performance subtests than the Verbal subtests, as expected. Copy scores correlated with the Benton Visual Retention Test (BVRT), Hooper Visual Organization Test, and Trail Making Test (Part B). Immediate and Delayed RCFT recall correlated with the BVRT and Rey Auditory Verbal Learning Test. Language measures such as the Benton Sentence Repetition and Controlled Oral Word Association Test were not significantly correlated with any RCFT measure.

Factor analysis of the RCFT yielded a five-factor solution, which accounted for 98.4% of the variance. These factors were labeled visuospatial recall, visuospatial recognition, response bias, processing speed, and visuospatial constructional ability. The factor structure was very similar for the normal and brain-injured samples.

The RCFT was given to 30 brain-injured, 30 psychiatric, and 30 normal subjects. Analyses of variance revealed significant group differences for all RCFT variables. Post hoc analyses indicated that the brain-injured group scored significantly lower than the other two groups on the recall trials; the psychiatric group scored lower than the normal controls. For the other RCFT variables, the brain-injured group scored lower than the other groups and the psychiatric and normal groups did not differ from each other.

Discriminant function analysis was used to determine classification hit rates for the three groups. Using Copy and Time to Copy as the predictor variables, 58% of the subjects were correctly classified. Using Immediate Recall and Delayed Recall as the predictors, 61% were correctly classified. Finally, when using recall and recognition measures as predictors, 78% of the subjects were correctly classified. Overall, a larger number of psychiatric patients were misclassified. A substantial number of these patients were misclassified as brain injured. It may be that some of these patients had cerebral compromise. In any event, this test must be interpreted cautiously when used with psychiatric populations.

The clinical utility of the RCFT has been well established. It is a very useful measure of visuospatial processing abilities, constructional abilities, and nonverbal memory. The modifications made by these authors constitute significant improvements, which should enhance the usefulness of this measure. The more detailed scoring system should increase interrater reliability. The extended norms allow for better comparisons with age peers, including older adults. The addition of a recognition trial may prove especially useful in assessing neurobehavioral syndromes characterized by memory retrieval deficits (such as Parkinson's Disease and frontal lobe syndromes). In short, this is a valuable neuropsychological test.

The authors have demonstrated adequate test-retest and interrater reliability. The test scores also appear valid as a measure of brain dysfunction, as these scores have been shown to distinguish normals from brain-injured patients with a fairly high degree of accuracy. The extant literature suggests that the copy portion of the test is especially sensitive to parietal disease whereas recall scores are more sensitive to temporal disease. It remains to be seen whether the recognition trial developed by these authors is selectively sensitive to certain types of brain dysfunction, such as frontal lobe disease. Further studies with more homogeneous brain-injured populations are needed. It appears that many psychiatric patients score within the impaired range of this test, for reasons that are not yet clear. Again, studies with more homogeneous psychiatric populations are needed.

[**319**]

Reynell Developmental Language Scales III: The University of Reading Edition [British Edition].

Purpose: Developed for use by speech and language therapists in assessing children with suspected language problems.

Population: 15 months to 7 years.

Publication Dates: 1969–1997.

Acronym: RDLS III.

Scores: 2 scales; Comprehension Scale, Expressive Scale.

Administration: Individual.

Price Data, 1998: £375 per complete set including 35 record forms, manual ('97, 74 pages), and all stimulus items and pictures required for Comprehension and Expressive Scales; £42 per 35 record forms.

Time: (35–40) minutes

Authors: Susan Edwards, Paul Fletcher, Michael Garman, Arthur Hughes, Carolyn Letts, and Indra Sinka.

Publisher: NFER-Nelson Publishing Co., Ltd. [England].

Cross References: See T5:2228 (24 references) and T4:2271 (18 references); for reviews by Doris V. Allen and Diane Nelson Bryen of an earlier edition, see 9:1049 (6 references); see also T3:2018 (16 references); for reviews by Katharine G. Butler and Joel Stark, see 8:974 (3 references); see also T2:2025 (3 references).

Review of the Reynell Developmental Language Scales III: The University of Reading Edition [British Edition] by CAROL M. McGREGOR, Associate Professor of Education and Human Development, Brenau University, Gainesville, GA:

The third edition of the Reynell Developmental Language Scales (RDLS III) has changed its basic design from a developmental model to a measurement of structural and lexical properties in child language research while retaining the aim to evaluate the communicative component of language development. There has been significant revision for this edition with latter sections aimed at measuring metalinguistic skills. In so doing, validity may be compromised in that the authors acknowledge that cognition is a factor in these subtests. The RDLS III may be used by speech and language therapists as a diagnostic measure for children ages 1-6 to 7-0 to determine suspected language problems, provide broad therapy guidelines, and monitor progress. Other professionals could use it as a screening instrument. The tests is made up of two scales measuring comprehension and verbal expression. The Comprehension Scale requires verbal directions using toys and pictures as stimulus items. The Expressive Scale requires the child to deal with verbal directions and toys, pictures, and finger puppets in verbal responses. The test is to be used with English-speaking children and the authors caution that although it may be used with bilingual children, their scores cannot be compared with the norms developed.

TEST VALIDATION AND NORMING. In this present version of the RDLS, a development team assessed critical reviews written by speech and language therapists and used that input, drew information from clinical colleagues with experience and knowledge of language development, and conducted pretrials prior to formal pretesting. Trial versions were administered to 400 children using two equivalent versions. Items were then assessed with regard to discrimination index between item and total score; using the Rasch model, an item response analysis was carried out to identify items that did not fit; and facility values were set to provide an appropriate range of difficulty for each item. The test was then trimmed to 62 items in each scale.

The standardization used 1,074 children in England, Scotland, Wales, Northern Ireland, and the Republic of Ireland, with approximately equal numbers of gender representation. It appears a nonrandom selection process was used although the information is not available in the manual. Further documentation of participants according to socioeconomic status and educational background would be appropriate. A cross-validation was done using a smaller number of children in

Reading and Edinburgh with the Test of Reception of Grammar (Bishop, 1983) and the second version of the British Picture Vocabulary Test (Dunn, Dunn, Whetton, & Burley, 1997). Because neither of these tests purports to measure the same aspects of language as the RDLS III, a partial relationship would be expected. The correlational study used with the scores of children ages 4-0 to 7-0 ranged from .67 to .75, supporting the claim that the RDLS III has concurrent validity when compared to the above mentioned instruments. The RDLS III reports scores using standard scores, age equivalents, and percentiles.

RELIABILITY. The Kuder-Richardson split-half coefficient yielded an overall reliability of .97 on the Comprehension Scale and .96 on the Expressive scale. In reviewing the reliability coefficients, standard errors of measurement, and standard deviations by age, this test seems to have more integrity for those children between the ages of 3-0 and 5-11, particularly in regard to the Comprehension Scale. On the Comprehension Scale, the standard deviation for ages 1-6 to 3-0 is 13.75 around a mean of 24, which would make interpretation difficult. The reliability on the Comprehension Scale for children over age 6-0 is .44. All other reliability measures were within acceptable limits. With this age group, interrater reliability should have been tested. In comparing gender as a variable, means and standard deviations were compared. Girls scored approximately 2 points higher than boys on both the Comprehensive and Expressive scales. No statistical testing was done to determine the significance of the difference.

ADMINISTRATION. This test seems to have clear instructions regarding administration. Performance is to be measured using standard scores, age equivalents, and percentiles, all derived from raw scores. In age equivalence scores, one item may represent one month of age whereas for others, one may represent up to 6 months. The larger ratio scores appear mainly at the upper end of the Comprehension Scale. In general, items seem interesting, colorful, and developmentally appropriate. Several vocabulary terms are British in nature and would make the test items invalid for use with children not represented by the standardization group. Examples of such terms are *mummy* for a mother reference, *lorry* for a type of vehicle, *naughty* for misbehavior. Comprehension Scale directions are thorough and helpful for in-terpretation purposes. Items may only be given one time. Working with the younger children, in particular, who tend to have short attention, such a practice may be measuring sustained attention rather than language skills.

SUMMARY. The British Edition of the RDLS III seems to have been strengthened by the present revision. Skills being measured include a wider area of language forms than in previous editions of the test with good discussion of response expectations and some degree of interpretation. The test is usable by both speech and language therapists as well as those knowledgeable of language development in young children. The time for administration is of an appropriate length for the attention of younger children. Weaknesses include no interrater reliability, and limited theoretical basis in design and usability for use with children under age 3 and over age 6.

This continues to be one of the better language tests for use with young children. This version is standardized on British children and should only be used with that population.

REVIEWER'S REFERENCES

Bishop, D. (1993). TROG: Test for Reception of Grammar. Abingdom, UK: Thomas Leach.
Dunn, L. M., Dunn, L. M., Whetton, C., & Burley, J. (1997). British Picture Vocabulary Scale—Second Edition. Windsor, UK: NFER-NELSON.

[320]
Reynolds Depression Screening Inventory.

Purpose: Constructed as a "self-report measure of the severity of depressive symptoms."
Population: Ages 18–89.
Publication Date: 1998.
Acronym: RDSI.
Scores: Total score only.
Administration: Group or individual.
Price Data, 2000: $49 per introductory kit including manual (64 pages) and 25 booklets; $27 per 25 booklets; $26 per manual.
Time: (5–10) minutes.
Authors: William M. Reynolds and Kenneth A. Kobak.
Publisher: Psychological Assessment Resources, Inc.

Review of the Reynolds Depression Screening Inventory by MICHAEL H. CAMPBELL, Director of Residential Life, New College of University of South Florida at Sarasota, Sarasota, FL:

TEST COVERAGE AND USE. The Reynolds Depression Screening Inventory (RDSI) is a paper-and-pencil self-report measure based on the well-known Hamilton Depression Inventory (HDI; T5:1166), which in turn was adapted from the classic Hamilton Depression Rating Scale. The test was designed to provide a brief, convenient, and cost-effective screening for the severity of depressive symptoms. Items for the RDSI were drawn from the 32-item HDI and selected to provide broad coverage of the DSM-IV criteria for Major Depressive Disorder, as well as to maximize scale homogeneity. The authors make clear that the RDSI is not intended to function as a diagnostic or predictive instrument; rather, the test provides quantitative and qualitative information on current levels of depressive symptomatology. The test is appropriate for use with adult outpatients, whether or not they meet DSM-IV criteria for diagnosis of a depressive disorder.

NORMS AND TEST BIAS. The standardization sample for the RDSI consisted of 450 nonclient adults (ages 18–89) selected from a larger sample ($n = 531$) to provide balanced representation of gender and age groups. The authors also report norms from a psychiatric outpatient sample ($n = 324$), in which patients with Major Depressive Disorder ($n = 150$) were represented. Many of the analyses reported in the manual are based on the total development sample ($n = 855$).

The manual provides comprehensive descriptions and analyses of sample demographics. There was a significant effect of gender on RDSI scores, consistent with previous research demonstrating a slight trend for women to report greater depressive symptomatology. There were no significant main effects for age or ethnicity, and no significant age X gender or ethnicity X gender interaction effects. However, as the authors prudently note, ethnic minorities, especially Asians and Hispanics, had relatively small sample sizes; therefore, statistical power may be insufficient to detect ethnicity-related differences in scores.

ADMINISTRATION AND SCORING. The RDSI is clearly and elegantly designed. The test is easily administered in both individual and group formats and is sufficiently straightforward to be used by a wide variety of mental health professionals with appropriate training. The manual provides clear instructions for administration and scoring, which is readily accomplished by hand. Additionally, the manual includes procedures for prorating incomplete protocols and describes some simple validity checks based on usual or inconsistent response patterns. The RDSI also contains six critical items that merit follow-up when scored in the keyed direction.

The RDSI produces raw scores ranging from 0 to 63, although raw scores above 35 are rare. The manual provides tables for conversion of raw scores into T-scores and percentile ranks. Raw scores of 10 or below are not suggestive of clinical severity; scores from 11 to 15 suggest mild severity. A cutoff score of 16 identifies "a clinically relevant level of depressive symptoms" that warrants referral "for further evaluation and consideration of treatment" (professional manual, p. 15). The manual provides a detailed description of the cutoff score selection criteria: to maximize both hit rate and clinical sensitivity. In a study of the RDSI's ability to differentiate between participants with an existing diagnosis of Major Depressive Disorder and nonpatient controls, a score of 16 correctly classified 94.9% of persons overall and 95.3% of those with an existing diagnosis of Major Depression.

RELIABILITY. The reliability estimates of the RDSI appear excellent across a series of measures. Cronbach's alpha estimates of internal consistency were .93 for the total sample and .89 for the psychiatric outpatient sample, with minimal differences between genders. Test-retest reliability computed at approximately one-week intervals (using a sample of 190 adults retested after the initial data collection) yielded an overall correlation of .94. The authors also report correlations between individual items and total scale score for the total development sample. Correlations ranged from .44 to .83 (all but two were above .50), suggesting substantial homogeneity of item content, even though the RDSI taps a diverse group of depressive symptoms. Finally, the standard error of measurement is less than 3 points for both men and women, indicating a stability of measure that supports clinical use.

VALIDITY. The manual provides clear and comprehensive summaries of validational data. The descriptions of statistical and conceptual strategies for validation are very well written and well organized; the material should be broadly accessible, even to readers with relatively little training in quantitative methods. More importantly, the substance of these analyses is clear and convincing evidence of content, criterion-related, construct, and clinical validity.

The item selection procedures for the RDSI provide important evidence of content validity. The selection process ensured that items reflected mood, cognitive, somatic, neurovegetative, psychomotor, and interpersonal areas of symptomatology. The RDSI item content is tied to the diagnostic criteria of the DSM-IV; the instrument is therefore atheoretical in that content parallels the DSM's focus on symptom presentation rather than etiological explanation. Additionally, item validity can be implied from item homogeneity demonstrated by item-with-total-scale correlations, as noted above.

The authors' evaluation of criterion validity focuses on concurrent rather than predictive criteria, a choice defended on the grounds that the RDSI is designed to assess current levels of severity but not to predict the future course of depression. The manual presents strong evidence of concurrent validity based on correlations with a variety of criterion measures, including the Hamilton Depression Rating Scale (.93), the Beck Depression Inventory (.94), the Beck Hopelessness Scale (.80), the Adult Suicidal Ideation Questionnaire (.67), the Beck Anxiety Inventory (.71), the Rosenberg Self-Esteem Scale (-.71), and the Marlowe-Crowne Social Desirability Scale—Short Form (-.37). This is an impressive array of correlations with well-validated criterion instruments. Moreover, the choice of criterion instruments provides strong evidence of convergent and discriminant construct validity.

Further evidence of construct validity comes from factor analytic evaluation of the RDSI items. An initial principal components analysis using both orthogonal and oblique rotations yielded a consistent three-factor structure for the RDSI; the dimensions were depressed mood-demoralization, somatic complaints, and vegetative symptoms-fatigue. A second principal components analysis, restricted to data from psychiatric outpatients, yielded essentially the same factor structure.

The manual includes an interesting discussion of clinical efficacy or clinical validity. In addition to a detailed discussion of the issues of hit rate and sensitivity noted earlier, the authors demonstrate statistically significant differences in RDSI score among nonreferred adults, persons with Major Depressive Disorder, and persons with other psychiatric diagnoses; the authors term this type of analysis "contrasted groups validity."

SUMMARY. The RDSI provides a reliable, valid, and convenient short screening for severity of depressive symptoms in psychiatric outpatients.

The supporting materials are outstanding for their thorough documentation and clarity of expression, and the evidence of reliability and validity is compelling. Although the test probably does not provide much additional or qualitatively different clinical information relative to other instruments (e.g., Revised Hamilton Rating Scale for Depression [RHRSD; T5:1166], Beck Depression Inventory-II [BDI-II; 37], or Minnesota Multiphasic Personality Inventory-2 [MMPI-2; T5:1697], the RDSI is an excellent choice for clinicians who desire an efficient screening focused on depressive symptoms.

Review of the Reynolds Depression Screening Inventory by ROSEMARY FLANAGAN, Adjunct Associate Professor of Psychology, St. John's University, Jamaica, NY:

The Reynolds Depression Screening Inventory (RDSI) is an instrument in a series (e.g., Reynolds, 1986) of depression inventories. The manual is well written and appears useful for both researchers and practitioners. Standardization procedures and psychometric properties are carefully explained; illustrative case examples are provided. To the credit of the authors, sufficient data are reported in the manual, permitting test users to arrive at their own judgments about the RDSI. A literature search did not yield further information; therefore, this review is based on material in the manual, and a recent conference presentation (Reynolds, Flament, Masango, & Steele, 1999). The authors appear to have realized their stated goal of developing a measure of depression consistent with the diagnostic criteria for Major Depressive Disorder, according to the *Diagnostic and Statistical Manual of Mental Disorders* (DSM-IV; American Psychiatric Association, 1994).

Depression is a significant mental health problem in that surveys indicate (e.g., Kessler et al., 1994) prevalence rates as high as 10.3% for the general population. The RDSI is not intended for the diagnosis of depression, but rather, is to be used to provide an indication of the severity of the problem over the past 2 weeks. Items reflect the same domains that are covered on the Hamilton Depression Rating Scale (HDRS; Hamilton, 1960), with weighted response options for the items. The RDSI is similar in format to the Beck Depression Inventory (BDI; Beck, Steers, & Brown, 1987) in that each item is rated along a continuum, with higher scores indicative of greater depressive symptomatology. There are three to five response options for each item, stated in specific behavioral terms, similar to a structured interview. Administration and hand scoring can be accomplished in 10–15 minutes; there is no computer-scoring format. Scoring involves summing the numerical values assigned to the response options, with data reported as linear *T*=scores (*Mean* = 50; *SD* = 10) and percentiles. Responses to six critical items are also reviewed. These items address the following and its extent: whether the respondent is feeling depressed, the respondent's outlook, suicidal ideation, changes in interest and work performance, and general feelings about oneself. The RDSI is written at approximately a fifth-grade reading level, somewhat below the reading level of the BDI (eighth-grade). Similar to the BDI, this format is advantageous to practicing clinicians, as it can be administered and scored during an office visit, if necessary.

Norms were derived from a sample of 450 individuals who were matched for gender and age. A concern is that the sample is geographically limited, having been drawn from the Midwestern and Western United States. The racial-ethnic composition of the sample is 89.1% Caucasian, 4.5% African-American, 2.0% Asian, 3.3% Hispanic, and 1.1% Other. Approximately 72% of the individuals were between 25 and 64 years of age, with 14% in both the 18–24- and 65–89-year cohorts; the mean age of the participants was 43. Socioeconomic status varied from professionals to the unemployed; dwelling areas were urban, suburban, and rural. Data were collected on several additional samples that were used in subsequent analyses. The psychiatric sample was composed of 324 individuals, 150 of whom were diagnosed as having major depression, 123 had anxiety disorders, and 51 were diagnosed with other psychopathology. The demographic characteristics of this group were generally similar to the standardization sample. The mean scores for each group were such that the groups were collapsed into two groups: those with major depression and those with other psychopathology. An additional sample referred to as the total development sample was used for some analyses; its composition is demographically similar to the other samples used. It was composed of 855 individuals, approximately 62% had no DSM-IV (American Psychiatric Association, 1994) diagnosis. The remaining 38% comprised a group

with major depression and a group with other psychiatric problems.

Coefficient alpha for the total sample and the psychiatric sample was .933 and .898, respectively. Test-retest reliability at a 1-week interval was .944. These values are adequate for clinical decision making and research (Kaplan & Saccuzzo, 1997; Nunnally & Bernstein, 1994). The instrument appears to assess a sole construct, with scores demonstrating adequate stability.

Validity was examined in several ways: content, criterion-related, construct, and clinical (contrasted groups), and the efficiency, sensitivity, and diagnostic specificity of the RDSI cutoff score. Item-total correlations, reflecting content validity, are described as moderate to high, with approximately 25%–69% of the variance being explained for 16 of 19 items. Criterion-related validity was assessed by examining the sample correlation (r = .93) between an adapted version of the Hamilton Depression Rating Scale (HDRS; Reynolds & Kobak, 1995) and RDSI scores. The adapted form of the HDRS requires considerably less time to administer and is much less labor-intensive than the original HDRS (Hamilton, 1960), and is similar in format to the RDSI. Construct validity was evaluated by examining the relationship between the RDSI and several measures. Correlation with the Beck Depression Inventory (BDI; Beck, Steer, & Brown, 1987) was .94. Correlations with related constructs, such as suicide ideation, assessed by the Adult Suicidal Ideation Questionnaire (Reynolds, 1991) was .67. Correlation with the Rosenberg Self-Esteem Scale (Rosenberg, 1965) indicated an inverse relationship, as might be expected (-.71). Additional evidence of construct validity was provided as part of the validation of the Physical Self-Concept Scale (Reynolds, Flament, Masango, & Steele, 1999). The measure evaluates physical aspects of appearance, ability/skills, intelligence, health, and self-efficacy related to these same domains. A moderate relationship with the RDSI was demonstrated, accounting for 21% of the variance for a sample of community-based college students and adults.

Multiple regression analysis indicates that the RDSI measures depression as opposed to generalized psychological distress. This was substantiated in two analyses in which the beta weights for depression as assessed by the BDI and HDRS were .66 and .72, respectively. In contrast, beta weights ranged from -.22 to .18 for measures of hopelessness, suicide ideation, self-esteem, and anxiety. Factor analytic studies indicate that 58% of the variance in the total development sample is explained by a three-factor solution, corresponding to depressed mood, somatic complaints, and vegetative symptoms. The factors were extracted to provide evidence of validity, rather than to provide information about aspects of depression. It is made clear that the RDSI should not be the sole criterion used to diagnose depression, and that the factors should not be interpreted individually. This bears some similarity to the BDI.

The most critical validity evidence is the efficacy of the RDSI cutoff scores. Analyses were conducted to determine the level at which the combination of sensitivity (correct identification of those with major depression), specificity (correct identifications of those who do not have major depression), positive and negative predictive value (correct identifications), and hit rate (proportions of correct identifications) were optimized. Data are also presented on the strength of association (chi square, kappa coefficient) and the quantified clinical validity of the cutoff scores (phi coefficient). The cutoff score that is expected to result in optimal decision making is 16, substantiated by tabled data indicating four (sensitivity, hit rate, chi square, phi coefficient) indices at their peak; the remaining indices are acceptably high. This corresponds to the 96th percentile, or $T = .72$.

Should the score not be in the clinically significant range, the RDSI could be interpreted normatively. The item numbers of the six critical items are printed near the bottom of the front page of the protocol. Responses of "2" or higher on these items are clinically significant. Should an individual obtain scores of "3" or more on three critical items, further evaluation is indicated, irrespective of the total score.

SUMMARY. The data in the manual suggest that the RDSI should live up to the authors' claims. Psychometric properties are sound, despite a smaller norming sample than that used for the BDI. The level of detail in the manuals, particularly in the validity sections, exceeds that available in the BDI manual, and is an improvement. The RDSI is atheoretical; the BDI reflects Beck's theory (e.g., Beck, 1973). The strength of the RDSI may be that it is a technical advance. Nevertheless, the uses and properties of the RDSI are similar to the BDI. The need for a new instrument to assess depression in a brief, time-sensitive format is debatable. Researchers and practitioners may be less likely to utilize a new measure, given the existing data and large literature supporting the BDI. It is reasonable to expect that additional research is needed for the RDSI to become a commonly accepted alternative to the BDI.

REVIEWER'S REFERENCES

Hamilton, M. (1960). A rating scale for depression. *Journal of Neurology, Neurosurgery, and Psychiatry, 23*, 56–62.
Rosenberg, M. (1965). *Society and the adolescent self-image.* Princeton, NJ: Princeton University Press.
Beck, A. T. (1973). *Depression; Causes and treatment.* Philadelphia: University of Pennsylvania Press.
Reynolds, W. M. (1986). Reynolds Adolescent Depression Scale. Odessa, FL: Psychological Assessment Resources.
Beck, A. T., Steer, R. A., & Brown, G. K. (1987). *Beck Depression Inventory-II manual.* San Antonio, TX: Psychological Corporation.
Reynolds, W. M. (1991). *Adult Suicidal Ideation Questionnaire: Professional manual.* Odessa, FL: Psychological Assessment Resources.
American Psychiatric Association. (1994). *Diagnostic and statistical manual of mental disorders* (4th ed.). Washington, DC: Author.
Kessler, R. C., McGonagle, K. A., Zhao, S., Nelson, C. B., Hughes, M., Eshleman, S., Wittchen, H., & Kendler, K. S. (1994). Lifetime and 12-month prevalence of DSM-III-R psychiatric disorders in the United States: Results from the National Comorbidity Survey. *Archives of General Psychiatry, 51*, 8–19.
Nunnally, J. C., & Bernstein, I. H. (1994). *Psychometric theory* (3rd ed.). New York: McGraw-Hill.
Reynolds, W. M., & Kobak, K. A. (1995). Reliability and validity of the Hamilton Depression Rating Inventory: A paper and pencil version of the Hamilton Depression Rating Scale clinical interview. *Psychological Assessment, 7*, 472–483.
Kaplan, R. M., & Saccuzzo, D. (1997). *Psychological testing* (4th ed.). Pacific Grove, CA: Brooks-Cole.
Reynolds, W. M., Flament, J., Masango, S., & Steele, B. (1999, April). *Reliability and validity of the Physical Self-Concept Scale.* Paper presented at the annual convention of the American Educational Association, Montreal, Canada.

[321]
The Rivermead Behavioural Memory Test [Second Edition].

Purpose: "Developed to detect impairment of everyday memory functioning and to monitor change following treatment for memory difficulties."

Publication Dates: 1985–1991.

Acronym: RBMT.

Administration: Individual.

Price Data: Available from publisher.

Time: Administration time not reported.

Publisher: Thames Valley Test Company Ltd. [England].

a) THE RIVERMEAD BEHAVIOURAL MEMORY TEST.

Population: Brain-damaged persons, ages 11 to elderly adult.

Publication Dates: 1985–1991.

Scores, 2: Screening Score, Standardized Profile Score.

Comments: For multiple administrations with the same subject, four parallel versions available.

Authors: Barbara Wilson (test, manual, supplementary manual 2), Janet Cockburn (test, manual, supplementary manuals 2 and 3), Alan Baddely (test, manual, supplementary manual 2), Robert

Hiorns (supplementary manual 2), and Phillip T. Smith (supplementary manual 3).

b) THE RIVERMEAD BEHAVIOURAL MEMORY TEST FOR CHILDREN.

Population: Brain-damaged children, ages 5–10.

Publication Date: 1991.

Score: Standardized Profile Score.

Comments: Materials from adult version used for most subtests, but some additional materials needed.

Authors: Barbara A. Wilson (test and manual), Rebecca Ivani-Chalian (test and manual), Frances Aldrich (manual).

Cross References: See T5:2239 (35 references).

Review of the Rivermead Behavioural Memory Test [Second Edition] by ANTHONY M. PAOLO, Coordinator of Assessment and Evaluation, University of Kansas Medical Center, Kansas City, KS:

The Rivermead Behavioural Memory Test (RBMT) is not based upon any particular theoretical model of memory, rather it attempts to simulate the demands placed on memory by normal everyday life. It consists of 12 tasks that are analogues of everyday memory situations that may be problematic for persons with brain dysfunction. The tasks include remembering a person's first and last name, recalling a hidden belonging, remembering an appointment, face recognition, remembering a short story, picture recognition, remembering a new route, delivering a message, and answering typical orientation questions (i.e., date, place, etc.). The items for remembering a short story and new route have immediate and delayed recall components.

Interrrater reliability was excellent with 100% agreement between two raters for the scoring rules. Test-retest stability for the screening and profile scores was .78 and .85, respectively, for 118 patients tested twice. Performance on the second test administration was slightly better than the first. Although providing stability estimates is good practice, there is no information in the manual about which form(s) these coefficients were based on nor is there any information concerning the interval from test to retest. In addition, standard errors should be provided to allow users to be able to compute whether changes in RBMT scores reflect real change, rather than measurement error. The RBMT has four parallel forms that should reduce any meaningful practice effect that may occur with repeat testing. The correlations between Form A and Forms B and C are good and at least .80. The correlation between Forms A and

D is lower (.67). Considering this lower coefficient, the interscale correlations among all of the parallel forms should be provided.

The RBMT demonstrates moderate correlations (.20 to .63) with other memory tests including the Warrington Recognition Memory Test, digit span, Paired Associate Learning Test, and Corsi Block Span. These relationships suggest that the RBMT does assess memory functions tapped by other measures of memory, but is not entirely redundant with them. More importantly, the RBMT correlates highest (greater than .70 in absolute value) with the therapist ratings of memory lapses for persons with central nervous dysfunction and with self-reported memory problems. The latter findings suggest that the RBMT is tapping other aspects of memory abilities, presumably memory functions required for everyday tasks. In addition to the above validity information, persons with brain damage or dysfunction tend to score lower than normal controls. When the brain-damaged subjects were grouped by etiology (i.e., right CVA, left CVA, head injury, etc.), the RBMT was not very successful in distinguishing among them. Thus, the RBMT seems to be sensitive to general memory disruption, but not necessarily specific to any particular etiology. It is also important to note that, in general, the memory tasks seem relatively easy, suggesting that the RBMT may not be sensitive to mild forms of memory impairment. As such, the RBMT should not be used as a screening device for detecting persons with early or mild memory problems.

The initial standardization samples consisted of 188 healthy persons between the ages of 16 and 69 (mean age = 41.17) with an average IQ of 106 (range 68 to 136) and a patient sample composed of 113 men and 63 women ranging in age from 14 to 69 years (mean = 44.40). No information concerning the gender, racial, or educational make-up of the healthy group is provided. Additional standardization samples have been collected on elderly and preteenage groups. The community-dwelling elderly sample consists of 44 men and 75 women ranging in age from 70 to 94 years (mean = 80.49; *SD* = 5.22) and have an average educational level of 9.51 years. The preteen sample consists of 43 girls and 42 boys ranging from 11 to 14 years of age.

For persons 16 to 69 years of age, percentile tables are provided in the manual, but because over 50% of the patient group scored below the 5th percentile relative to the normal subjects, these tables provide very little meaningful information. For this reason, the authors provide cutoff scores for severity of memory impairment based upon their clinical experience. In addition, separate cutoff scores are provided for persons with expressive language difficulty and persons with perceptual problems, as these difficulties significantly impact RBMT performance. These distinct cutoff scores are presented only for persons 16 to 69 years of age.

Very little information is provided for the preteenage standardization group. Only means and standard deviations for the total group and cutoff points for children with below average intellectual functioning are provided. For the elderly sample, tables are provided that allow for an individual's profile score to be compared with that expected for a normal person of similar age and estimated premorbid IQ. No such tables are provided for persons younger than 70 years of age.

SUMMARY. The RBMT represents one of only a few tests currently available for the assessment of everyday memory functions. The tasks appear relevant for everyday living situations and the validity information supports the claim that the RBMT measures meaningful everyday memory functions. The availability of four parallel forms is good, especially in situations where repeat testing will be necessary. Unfortunately, not knowing the test-retest interval and the lack of standard errors limits the usefulness of retest comparisons. Although the standardization samples cover a wide age range, different interpretive procedures are provided for the young and the elderly groups. A consistent method for interpreting scores across all age groups would improve the usability of the RBMT. Overall, if one needs to assess everyday memory functions in persons with known brain dysfunction, the RBMT is a good choice, but the manual could be improved by including some additional psychometric information.

Review of the Rivermead Behavioural Memory Test [Second Edition] by GORAN WESTERGREN, Chief Psychologist, Department of Clinical Psychology, State Hospital, Halmstad, Sweden, and INGELA WESTERGREN, Neuropsychologist, Licensed Psychologist, Department of Clinical Psychology, State Hospital, Halmstad, Sweden:

The Rivermead Behavioural Memory Test (RBMT) covers a broad spectrum of memory functions and in so doing permits the identification of many different memory dysfunctions. The RBMT's focus is built around everyday memory problems. The strength one can find in strict standardized tests for laboratory settings has been successfully combined in an excellent way with simple, practical behavior measurements for memory disturbances. Consequently, in the construction of the test the authors have tried to achieve what is called "ecological validity." The RBMT assesses memory skills necessary for normal life. Thus it is not based on experimental data measuring the acquisition and retention or more or less abstract material that requires clinical judgment about practical consequences of the results. The type of reality-based functions the RBMT measures are things such as "if someone borrows something, then one must remember to get it back," "what must I remember when the bell rings," "orientation in time and space," "remember everyday information," "recognise people one has met," etc.

It is, then, a strength in the RBMT that, in comparison to more traditional tests such as the Wechsler Memory Test (416) and the Recognition Memory Test (T5:2193), the user obtain a direct understanding of which types of everyday problems memory-impaired people are likely to face.

The test is constructed so that it can also be used on patients with severe brain damage and others with limited endurance. This is often difficult to carry out with normal memory tests and memory questionnaires. For some clinical groups, such as patients with expressive aphasia and specific perceptual problems, the relevant test sections are specified. In contrast to many other memory tests, the RBMT can also help therapists to find memory functions in patients that are possible to treat.

There are four parallel versions of the RBMT, therefore making it usable both in longitudinal studies and in situations involving change from before and after interventions. In addition to an adult version (16 to 69 years), there is a version for brain-damaged children in the age group 5–10 years.

The strength of the test is also its weakness. By being fast and easily administered it can be a little superficial and give a coarse picture of possible memory dysfunctions. Therefore, it functions best as a fast and practical screening test. In most cases of brain damage, however, it is usually quite satisfactory to obtain general assessment of the memory dysfunctions and for this the RBMT is quite sufficient. If the therapist requires more detailed information, supplemental tests that measure more specific memory functions will be needed. Examples of clinical questions where the RBMT can be supplemented with other memory tests are given in the manual.

The RBMT has validity evidence for a group of brain-damaged patients (113 men and 63 women, mean age 44.40). The sample contained 60 head-injury patients, 34 suffering from a left CVA, 42 a right CVA, 13 subarachnoid hemorrhage, and 27 others. The latter included cerebral tumors removed, carbon monoxide poisoning patients, multiple sclerosis, etc. The control group consisted of 118 subjects aged between 16 and 69 years (mean 41.17) with a mean IQ of 106 (range 68–136). A supplement of norms for the elderly (70–94 years) is also provided.

The interrater reliability was estimated by having 40 subjects scored separately but simultaneously by two raters. There was 100% agreement between the raters for scoring procedures. Test-retest reliability (administration interval not specified) was .78 for the screening score and .85 for the profile score.

The RMBT is based on empirical facts of everyday memory problems rather than on a clear theory concerning the memory's localization and function. Despite this, scores from the RBMT show high correlations with other standard memory tests. It also has a high face validity in observations made by therapists as well as subjective ratings by patients and their relatives.

SUMMARY. The RBMT is well constructed with clear and easily read questionnaires and manuals. It is also easy to learn to administer. The resistance against laboratory tests that sometimes occurs in many patient groups can be avoided in this test. The results are also easy to communicate to nonpsychologists, partly because of the test's practically founded, descriptive character. The RBMT is a well-structured, easily administered, and excellent screening test for memory dysfunctions.

[322]
Roberts Apperception Test for Children [with new Interpretive Handbook].

Purpose: Constructed to "assess children's perceptions of common interpersonal situations."
Population: Ages 6–15.

Publication Dates: 1982–1994.
Acronym: RATC.
Scores, 13: 8 Adaptive Profile Scales (Reliance on Others, Support—Other, Support—Child, Limit Setting, Problem Identification, Resolution 1, Resolution 2, Resolution 3), 5 Clinical Profile Scales (Anxiety, Aggression, Depression, Rejection, Unresolved Problems), 3 Indicators (Atypical Responses, Maladaptive Outcome, Refusal), and 3 Supplemental Measures (Ego Functioning, Aggression, Levels of Projection).
Administration: Individual.
Price Data, 1999: $120 per kit including manual ('82, 129 pages), 1 set of pictures (does not include test pictures for black children), and 25 record booklets; $17.50 per 25 record booklets; $59.50 per test pictures; $59.50 per test pictures for black children; $46.50 per manual; $59.50 per interpretive handbook ('94, 270 pages).
Time: (20–30) minutes.
Authors: Dorothea S. McArthur and Glen E. Roberts.
Publisher: Western Psychological Services.
Cross References: See T5:2242 (8 references) and T4:2285 (5 references); for a review by Jacob O. Sines, see 9:1054.

Review of Roberts Apperception Test for Children by MERITH COSDEN, Professor of Counseling/Clinical/School Psychology, Graduate School of Education, University of California, Santa Barbara, CA:

The Roberts Apperception Test for Children (RATC) is a projective test in which children are asked to tell stories about a series of pictures. As with other picture-story tests, the 16 cards are designed to "pull" for certain types of responses, but are also ambiguous enough to allow respondents to insert themselves into the stories. The examiner uses the structure and thematic content of the stories to make inferences about the psychological functioning of the child. Although the RATC shares the strengths and weaknesses of this approach with other similar assessment tools, such as the Children's Apperception Test (CAT; Bellak & Bellak, 1949; T5:466), and the Thematic Apperception Test (TAT; Murray, 1943; T5:2749), it also differs from these picture-story tests in some significant ways. Unlike the TAT, the RATC was designed specifically for children. By using line drawings of people in common interpersonal situations, the RATC appeals to a wider age range of children than the CAT, which uses pictures of anthropomorphized animals. Finally, the RATC is distinct from most picture-story tests in that it provides standardized procedures for administering and scoring the test, with interpretation of scores based on their comparison to a normative sample of well-adjusted children.

Although the RATC was first published in 1982, frequent updates of the Manual and the development of an Interpretive Handbook reflect efforts to increase the standardized use of this tool. Both texts state that use of the RATC in an informal manner (e.g., administration of a few cards with a subjective content analysis) is not desirable if the RATC is to be an effective assessment tool. The authors promote the administration of all 16 cards, in order, following standardized instructions for questioning children as they tell their stories. Detailed scoring procedures are described, with examples provided from well-adjusted, as well as clinical, samples of children. Methods for interpreting scores are detailed, along with case examples of test interpretations for both well-adjusted and maladjusted children.

Three types of scales are described in the manual: Adaptive Scales, Clinical Scales, and Clinical Indicators. Development of the eight Adaptive Scales was based on the thematic material presented in the stories of the standardization sample. Scores reflect the children's demonstration of problem-solving skills in their stories. For example, Reliance on Others is scored when the character in a story reaches out for help, and Resolution 1, 2, or 3 is scored as a function of whether the story problem is resolved unrealistically or constructively. The five Clinical Scales, including Anxiety and Depression, are scored based on feelings reflected in the stories. The cumulative number of coded responses in each area is used to infer the child's strength or pathology. The three Clinical indicators, Atypical Response, Maladaptive Outcome, and Refusal occurred rarely in the standardization sample, and are thought to reflect clinical problems.

Normative data are reported on 200 children in three school districts in California. The sampling procedures were designed to select "well adjusted" students on which to standardize the test. Teachers were asked to nominate three or four children from their classes who met the following criteria: good peer relationships, coping skills, academic performance, and the absence of any obvious psychological or behavioral difficulties. After this screening, stratified random sampling was conducted to assure equal numbers of boys and girls at each age level. The children ranged in age from 6–15, and were collapsed into four age groups (6–7, 8–9, 10–12, and 13–15) for the normative tables. Although the manual reports that the children represent a cross-section of socioeconomic groups, specific data on this, and the ethnic composition of the sample, are not reported. Further, the year in which the standardization sample was obtained is not provided. The lack of information about ethnicity, socioeconomic status, and cohort, allows one to question the generalizability of results based on comparison to this sample.

The validity of the scale, and its scores, for assessing adaptive behavior and psychopathology, is questionable. In one set of unpublished studies described in the manual, scores on the Adaptive and Clinical Scales for the standardization sample of well-adjusted children are compared to scores obtained from a sample of 200 children seeking services at a Child Guidance Center. The demographic characteristics of the children at the Child Guidance Center are not provided. Global differences are found between groups for scores on most of these scales; that is, the well-adjusted children tend to score higher on the Adaptive Scales and lower on the Clinical Scales than the other group of children. In a second series of studies, scores on the supplementary measures (ego functioning, aggression, and levels of projection) are used to distinguish children with different types of problems. Although the studies provide some support for these scores as indicators of specific types of problems, they were obtained through a nonstandardized administration of the RATC and they are not part of the clinical scoring protocol recommended in the manual.

Support for the relationship between specific Adaptive and Clinical Scales and external referents is missing. For example, there is no evidence that scores of Reliance on Others reflect patterns of behavior that, in fact, demonstrate reliance on others. Without studies to validate these scales, there is little support for the need for the elaborate scoring system presented in the manual.

SUMMARY. Although the RATC is presented as a standardized projective test with scoring protocols that address children's strengths as well as psychopathology, there is not sufficient data to support its use for this purpose. Even though the manual was last updated in 1995, none of the references are more recent than 1980. The authors' efforts to create a standardized projective test for children is laudable, but more evidence is needed to support the utility of this test, and its scoring system, for assessing children's strengths and needs.

REVIEWER'S REFERENCES

Murray, H. A. (1943). *Thematic Apperception Test manual.* Cambridge, MA: Harvard University Press.
Bellak, L., & Bellak, S. S. (1949). Children's Apperception Test. New York: CPS, Inc.

Review of Roberts Apperception Test for Children by NIELS G. WALLER, Professor of Psychology and Human Development, Vanderbilt University, Nashville, TN:

The psychological assessment of children is arguably one of the most important functions of the practicing psychologist. It is also one of the most difficult. Language limitations may restrict the usefulness of entire classes of tests, such as self-report measures. Assessment via direct interviews presents its own problems because of the unreliability of the young child's memory reconstructions (Loftus, 1993; Pendergrast, 1995). For these and other reasons, many psychologists have included thematic apperception tests (TAT) in their standard diagnostic battery for children. At least 23 such tests have been developed for children since Murray (1943) introduced his classic set of TAT stimulus cards. Currently, only 12 of these are used regularly (Kroon, Goudena, & Rispens, 1998).

Roberts Apperception Test for Children (RATC) is an objectively scored TAT measure that was designed specifically for the psychological assessment of children and adolescents. After reviewing the stimulus cards, the test manual, and the recently published (1994) Interpretive Handbook, I wondered why anyone uses the RATC to formulate diagnostic impressions or to make clinical decisions. When conducting research, individuals are free to use any psychometric device they wish (after all, it is a free country). When functioning as a practicing psychologist, however, we have an ethical responsibility to use tests with demonstrated validity. Although the RATC has been marketed for more than 15 years, it still has no established validity for its intended purposes.

Sines (1985) presented a scholarly review of the RATC in the *Ninth Mental Measurements Yearbook.* Because the RATC and the test manual have not been updated in the 13 years since that review, Sines's pronouncements concerning the utility of the RATC are still valid. In summary, Sines bemoaned that, "when we examine the relations of the several objectively scored RATC variables to external criteria we can only be disappointed" (Sines, 1985, p. 1290).

One of the weaknesses of the RATC manual is its heavy reliance on unpublished doctoral dissertations. The manual cites numerous dissertations that found the RATC useful in the diagnosis of childhood problems. While preparing this review, I naively assumed that many of these studies would have found their way into print during the last 15 years, and I was intent on reading some of them. Before trekking to the library, I logged onto the computer and conducted a literature search with the keywords "Roberts Apperception Test" and "RATC." I located 23 references. All but two of these references were unpublished doctoral dissertations. I decided to stay in the office. One can only wonder why so few studies that use the RATC end up in refereed journals.

One of the putative strengths of the RATC is that the test includes a set of objective scoring rules. The new Interpretive Handbook, which includes additional scoring guidelines, also advocates a more impressionistic approach to scoring. For example, the Handbook notes that "The RATC's standard administration and scoring procedures and age norms are not intended to replace or eliminate subjective interpretation of a child's stories" (Interpretive Handbook, p. 2).

The Handbook offers a wide sampling of RATC protocols from so-called well-adjusted children. These normative responses are provided to help clinicians identify possibly deviant stories to the 16 RATC stimulus cards. Unfortunately, because we are told virtually nothing about the individuals who gave these responses, it is impossible to evaluate their usefulness in calibrating our internal standards. At the very least, one would expect a summary of the demographic characteristics of this group of well-adjusted individuals. For example, questions that come immediately to mind include the following: What percentage of the children are girls? What percentage is from urban areas? Does the sample include kids from different ethnic and/or racial groups? Do any of these demographic variables relate to group differences? The Handbook is conspicuously silent on these issues.

SUMMARY. Recent meta-analyses (Spangler, 1992) and empirical studies (Cramer & Block, 1998) conclude that TAT stories can be reliably and validly scored. Because neither the authors nor the users of the RATC publish their findings in refereed journals, it is impossible to evaluate the validity of scores from this instrument for their intended purposes. The recently published Interpretive Handbook is a cornucopia of clinical impressions and poorly organized material. For these reasons, clinicians would be well advised to avoid the RATC. Our children deserve better.

REVIEWER'S REFERENCES

Murray, H. A. (1943). *Thematic Apperception Test.* Cambridge, MA: Harvard University Press.

Sines, J. O. (1985). [Review of the Roberts Apperception Test for Children.] In J. V. Mitchell, Jr. (Ed.), *The ninth mental measurements yearbook* (pp. 1290–1291). Lincoln, NE: Buros Institute of Mental Measurements.

Spangler, W. D. (1992). Validity of questionnaire and TAT measures of need for achievement: Two meta-analyses. *Psychological Bulletin, 112,* 140–154.

Loftus, E. F. (1993). The reality of repressed memories. *American Psychologist, 48,* 518–537.

Pendergrast, M. (1995). *Victims of memory: Incest accusations and shattered lives.* Hinesberg, VT: Upper Access.

Cramer, P., & Block, J. (1998). Preschool antecedents of defense mechanism use in young adults: A longitudinal study. *Journal of Personality & Social Psychology, 74,* 159–169.

Kroon, N., Goudena, P. P., & Rispens, J. (1998). Thematic apperception tests for child and adolescent assessment: A practitioner's consumer guide. *Journal of Psychoeducational Assessment, 16,* 99–117.

[323]
Rorschach.

Purpose: A projective technique for clinical assessment and diagnosis.

Population: Ages 5 and over.

Publication Dates: 1921–1998.

Scores: Many variations of scoring and interpretation are in use with no single method generally accepted.

Administration: Individual.

Price Data, 1998: $75 per set of 10 plates; $17 per 100 recording sheets; $32 per set of 5 location charts; $66 per manual ('98, 228 pages).

Time: (20–30) minutes.

Comments: Variously referred to by such titles as Rorschach Method, Rorschach Test, Rorschach Psychodiagnostics; Rorschach Interpretation Assistance Program (RIAP 4): Version 4 for Windows (1985–1999) by John E. Exner, Irving B. Weiner, and PAR Staff designed to assist the clinical psychologist in scoring and interpreting Rorschach results is available from Psychological Assessment Resources, Inc.

Author: Hermann Rorschach.

Publisher: Hogrefe & Huber Publishers.

Cross References: See T5:2247 (136 references), T4:2292 (273 references), 9:1059 (79 references), and T3:2030 (155 references); for reviews by Richard H. Dana and Rolf A. Peterson, see 8:661 (360 references); see also T2:1499 (376 references); for reviews by Alvin G. Burstein, John F. Knutson, Charles C. McArthur, Albert I. Rabin, and Marvin Resnikoff, see 7:175 (455 references); see also P:470 (719 references); for reviews by Richard H. Dana, Leonard D. Eron, and Arthur R. Jensen, see 6:237 (734 references); for reviews by Samuel J. Beck, H. J. Eysenck, Raymond J. McCall, and Laurance F. Shaffer, see 5:154 (1078 references); for a review by Helen Sargent, see 4:117 (621 references); for reviews by Morris Krugman and J. R. Wittenborn, see 3:73 (452 references); see also 2:1246 (147 references).

Review of the Rorschach by ALLEN K. HESS, Professor and Department Head, Auburn University at Montgomery, Montgomery, AL, PETER ZACHAR, Associate Professor, Auburn University at Montgomery, Montgomery, AL, and JEFFREY KRAMER, Licensed Mental Health Counselor, Eyerly-Ball Community Mental Health Center, Des Moines, IA:

RORSCHACH. The test name itself evokes a host of responses. The term has entered the public's imagination as seen in TV and movies when psychological testing is mentioned, and when talk show hosts refer to an ambiguous situation as being like an inkblot. There is little doubt that Hermann Rorschach's variation of the child's game "Blotto," first published in September 1921, provides a rich set of responses for psychologists to interpret. Rorschach experimented with inkblots for 4 years; he died at age 37, within months of his book's publication, and never saw the further development of his "Psychodiagnostik."

THE RORSCHACH. There are 10 plates measuring 9 17/32 inches wide by 6 19/32 inches wide (24.6 centimeters by 17 centimeters) with an inkblot on each. Rorschach carefully crafted them to appear symmetrical. Five blots appear in black and white (Plates 1, 4, 5, 6, and 7); two appear in black, white, and red (Plates 2 and 3); and three are composed of pastel colors. The blots are presented to the respondent one at a time with the instruction to report: "What might this be?" If only one response is provided to the first blot, the examiner may encourage the person to see whether it looks like anything else. Consequently, there is often more than one response to each blot.

After the person provides a set of responses during Phase 1 or the "free association" stage, they are asked to revisit each of their responses to help the examiner understand what about the blot led them to see this response. Scoring a response involves coding aspects such as location (whether the whole blot, a common detail, or an unusual detail composed the response), whether the shape or the color or the appearance of movement determined the response, and the content of the response. Also, ancillary behavior, such as the respondent feeling the plate when reporting a fur skin, or the expression "Ugh" when reporting the percept of blood, contribute information to the Rorschach protocol that is interpreted by the examiner. These are the basics of the Rorschach, the story of which gets more complex and controversial as we proceed.

THE DEVELOPMENT OF THE ROR-SCHACH. Rorschach's "test" immediately excited others to experiment with this "technique." Subsequently, a number of psychologists developed Rorschach's rudimentary system for scoring responses. Complicating the story, various interpretive systems flowed from the scoring systems. Some saw the responses as products of perception; as indicators as to how a person structures and organizes the external world. Others took a more psychoanalytic path, seeing the responses as projective productions or symbolic manifestations of a person's internal world. And there were even some who, skilled at assessing how functioning has been compromised by brain injury, adapted the Rorschach for assessing "organicity."

The profusion of scoring and interpretive systems made for a richness in research efforts and clinical applications on the one hand, and for a virtual "Tower of Babel" on the other hand (Exner, 1969). Which system was best and whose interpretations were sound became the center of debate. Bitter controversies between proponents of different schools of scoring and interpretation erupted. This confusion and conflict led Exner (1974) to amalgamate the scoring and interpretive schema into what became the Comprehensive System, and to apply psychometrically sound procedures to the Rorschach.

THE POLITICS OF IT. The conflicts in the midcentury between users of the Rorschach were overshadowed to a great degree by the development of the empirically derived personality inventories. Rather than merely representing a different test procedure, the inkblots and the inventories represent wholly different ways of approaching psychology. Steeped in a more psychoanalytic theory the Rorschach came to represent a Freudian approach, whereas the Minnesota Multiphasic Personality Inventory (MMPI) purportedly represented a psychometric approach to psychology. The two tests represented nothing less than a culture clash, and a story that reaches into today's literature.

RELIABILITY. Tests with open-ended responses, that is, where a person does not simply select from choices a, b, c, or d, but comes up with their own production, must be subjectively scored. Thus the question arises as to the comparability of scores by various raters, termed interrater reliability. Finding evidence for Rorschach interrater reliability is not easy, in part because a plethora of Rorschach scoring categories are proposed and some are ill-defined. With respect to the Comprehensive System, it seems that trained scorers agree with expert scorers between 88% and 99% of the time when scoring the major variables. This indicates that different trained scorers can score protocols consistently.

Statistically sophisticated commentators disagree about what other kinds of reliability statistics should be computed (e.g., Cohen's kappa), and how to compute and evaluate that reliability. Mathematically complex arguments can be made for and against the Comprehensive System's average interrater reliability. On the one hand, Meyer (1997) shows that the average kappa value for chance-corrected reliability across studies is .86, a fine level of agreement. Yet Wood, Nezworksi, and Stejskal (1997) criticize various calculation errors, and wonder why Rorschach proponents need to use creative statistics rather than standard procedures. Acklin, McDowell, Verschell, and Chan (2000) demonstrate that the median interrater reliability of the Exner Comprehensive System is in the .80s.

Test-retest reliability, or the ability of a test to measure a trait that is supposed to be stable over time, is important. According to Exner's Volume 1 (1974), many variables in the Comprehensive System show reliability estimates at or above .70 at both 1-year and 3-year intervals. Those variables which Exner claims reflect state variables rather than trait variables, such as shading and inanimate movement, have low test-retest reliability as expected. Also, consistent with expectations, Exner and Weiner (1995) in Volume 3 show that the median test-retest reliability estimates of Comprehensive System with children is quite low, but the reliability estimates stabilize as participants reach later adolescence and their personalities begin to coalesce. Their point is that, in development, children are changing so rapidly that personality tests have to be taken as a measure of current state, rather than a measure of traits, which is reflected in the Rorschach. We can conclude that the test-retest reliability of the Comprehensive Systems is impressive.

VALIDITY. The touchstone for validity questions concerns whether inferences drawn from test scores are appropriate, meaningful, and useful. In addition to the traditional construct validity question as to whether the test scores support intended inferences, diagnostic assessments concern questions of incremental validity or whether a particular instrument provides added value vis-a-vis other available test instruments. Again, a simple answer eludes us for a number of reasons.

First, the Comprehensive System encourages interpretations based on the presence or absence of a single response, raising validity questions. Interpretations based on the presence or absence of one food or reflection or texture response are on shakier ground than interpretations based on summed responses across an entire protocol. Summed indices as Human Movement (M) or the Affective Ratio (Afr) should have higher validity.

Secondly, the purposes to which psychological test results are applied are so multifaceted, including intellectual, emotional, organic pathology, employment, and forensic questions. Each of these in turn are so complex that a single answer to the validity question is impossible.

Third, the different number of responses respondents give during administration of the Rorschach comprises the various Rorschach scoring categories. For example, the first response most people give tends to use the whole blot. As more responses are given, there will be fewer whole responses. Thus a person providing 16 responses will naturally tend to have more whole responses than a person who gives 33 responses, confounding research across subjects.

Fourth, a properly administered, scored, and interpreted Rorschach takes 3 or so hours of a trained psychologist's time in contrast to group-administered inventories. Consequently, Rorschach research is costly and will likely be based on fewer subjects, compromising statistical power, or the ability to detect significant relationships. With this in mind, let us summarize some of the validity research.

Meta-analyses by Atkinson (1986) and Parker, Hanson, and Hunsley (1988) provide support for the Rorschach. Garb, Florio, and Grove (1998) acknowledge that there may be some validity to scores from the Rorschach but not as strong as that shown for scores from the MMPI. Hiller, Rosenthal, Borenstein, Berry, and Brunell-Neulib (1999), correcting some of the problems in earlier meta-analyses, find the Rorschach indices to have a mean effect size of .26 and those of the MMPI to have a mean effect size of .37, both respectable for personality tests. This raises the question of whether the Rorschach is simply unnecessary or does provide incremental validity or added information otherwise unavailable.

Another way of approaching the validity question is to see what uses the proponents of the Rorschach admit as not being valid and what claims the opponents allow as sustainable. According to proponents, the Schizophrenia Index (SCZI) should not be used with children or gifted students; the Depression Index (DEPI) is not as good a measure of depression as is the MMPI or the Beck Depression Inventory because of its false negative rate; with low R and pure F, the Rorschach underidentifies aggressive people; and people can censor blatant sexual and aggressive themes in their responses on the Rorschach.

Opponents agree that the SCZI index is related to schizophrenic processes; that cognitive slippage indicators such as Deviant Verbalizations are related to schizophrenia and borderline personality; that the continuum of Form Quality is correlated with severity of psychopathology; and the oral dependence scale is related to dependent personality.

CONTENT ANALYSIS. The use of "content analysis" further complicates efforts to gather validity evidence for the Rorschach. Content analysis refers to at least five different approaches. The first addresses how the patient approaches the test situation. This ecological approach to assessment provides important information but is not an issue confined to the Rorschach. It is an advantage of the Rorschach tradition but not specific to the Rorschach test per se.

Klopfer, Ainsworth, Klopfer, & Holt (1954) advocated interpreting the sequence of responses to help see how a person copes with life events. That is, if a person is surprised by colors on Blot 7 and gives a poor response, but recovers to give a good follow-up response, then the inference was drawn that the person might have good coping resources. Cognitive psychologists might see sequence analysis, or viewing responses in context, as a part of practical and adaptive intelligence. Such contextual analysis is equally important to MMPI interpretation that takes into account peaks and valleys of a profile that could be lost with 2-point MMPI code type interpretations. Validating this type of process is not restricted to the Rorschach but extends to validity questions about the clinical-interpretive method.

Third, content analysis can refer to Exner scales such as the Isolation Index and sum of cooperative movement percepts which categorize contents such as "blood" and "botany" responses. These have been standardized and age-normed in Exner's Comprehensive system.

A fourth and related way content analysis is used is based on psychoanalytic symbolism begun by Rapaport, Gill, & Schafer (1946) and more recently by Lerner (1991). The Rapaport scales that Exner adapted, such scales as CONFAB and INCOM, tend to be difficult to learn. However, they are superceded in difficulty by attempts to analyze other psychoanalytic constructs such as symbiosis and autonomy, primary and secondary process thinking, and pre-oedipal defense mechanisms. Notwithstanding these difficulties, Hiller et al.'s meta-analysis (1999) found non-Exner content scales such as oral dependency, mutuality of autonomy, and primary process indices figured prominently in some of the studies with the highest effect sizes.

Finally, content analysis refers to the psychoanalytically based interpretations from which the term "projection" arises (i.e., the portraying on the blot of an inner theme of the patient). Interestingly, Exner minimizes the role of projection in the Comprehensive System. Weiner (1998) claims that projection can occur but sometimes a response such as "bat" to Blot 5 is not projective at all because Blot 5 does look like a bat.

Thematic analysis is high on drama and interpretive context but low on systematic rules by which we can eliminate rival hypotheses, and thus prone to abuse and wild interpretation. Furthermore, because thematic analysis requires both natural ability and experience, it is hard to teach. Clinicians have provided some suggestions, such as knowing what kinds of responses each card lends to elicit and paying attention to embellished responses, but it is not always easy to pick out what counts as a significant embellishment—especially when subtlety is involved. It is difficult to distinguish between a valid interpretation of thematic content and a clinical speculation.

These kinds of thematic interpretations are rich in hypothesis-generation but should be confirmed by other data the assessor learns about the person. However, if an interpretation must be confirmed by other information in order to be considered valid, the problem of incremental validity becomes an issue—what unique information is provided by thematic analysis? Those who favor content analysis claim that it can be an efficient method for gathering data, which is the primary justification for any kind of psychological assessment, especially in response to psychiatrists who claim that a clinical interview is sufficient.

Because the room for error in the form of inaccurate interpretations is so great, we cannot recommend widespread reliance on thematic analysis. Stories about what the increasingly rare master of thematic analysis can do should not be used to justify its general use. Thematic analysis can aid skilled interpreters in discovering important attributes of the person being tested, but those hypothesized attributes need to be justified independently, specifically either by other test data or by interview data.

As a test is defined as a standardized sample of behavior, the well-known qualities of the Rorschach plates allow us to see unusual responses that give a texture to the case. Just as an MMPI 2-point code type or a Wechsler profile require a skillful practitioner to see how that profile guides us in understanding the individual and his or her character, so the Rorschach protocol does not interpret itself. This will always be the case in the tension between nomothetic or general principles and idiographic description or the understanding of the single case; between prediction and control versus understanding or vehrstehen psychology.

RIAP: RORSCHACH COMPUTERIZED INTERPRETATION. Practicing clinicians should use the computer as an aid to the Comprehensive System. The latest version of the program developed by Psychological Assessment Resources, Inc. is called the Rorschach Interpretation Assistance Program 4 (RIAP4). It was published in 1999 and represents the first time the RIAP has been a Windows-based program.

Version 4.0 adds features such as interactive location charts that make it easier to score a protocol while typing in the responses, rather than first scoring a protocol and then typing in the responses. Unfortunately, the developers failed to include the scoring rules outlined in Exner's (1995) *A Rorschach Workbook* into the help features of the program—limiting its usefulness as a scoring tool. Although only trained examiners and not computer programs can score protocols, computer programs can help prevent common scoring errors. For example, if a certain developmental quality score requires a Z score, the computer will automatically enter the Z score, or force the examiner to choose among possible Z scores. Most importantly, the kinds of errors that occur in the tedious translation of individual scores into the more than 100 ratios, indices, and component scores on the Structural Summary sheet are eliminated because the program generates the Structural Summary sheet automatically. The point is that the computer program, in eliminating certain errors, should raise the reliability of scores from the test.

The interpretation aspect of the RIAP4 is an important time saver. In Exner's Volume 2, interpretation proceeds cluster by cluster. The book takes the reader through a systematic decision analysis within each cluster. For example, in the Controls cluster, if Adj D is -1, the book provides some suggestions about what the score might mean, and tells the reader what ratio or index to examine next. The computer program eliminates going through the book step by step by printing the relevant interpretive suggestions cluster by cluster in a systematic fashion. It also adjusts the norms based on reported age of the client. Experts will be able to read a Structural Summary more directly, but nonexperts can benefit from not having to plod through the book. One caution to consider is that students who begin using the program too early in their training may never learn for themselves what the scores really mean. As a matter of fact, even for more experienced users, it is not always easy to know to which specific numbers from the Structural Summary the hypotheses refer—especially when the Exner group adds new interpretations.

The reports generated by the RIAP4 are better looking than those generated by previous versions. The interpretive suggestions from the books have been improved both by relying less on "Exner jargon" and referring to persons rather than subjects. They provide more information about the implications of certain scores, and attempt to reframe some implications in a more positive light (i.e., the language is not as charged with pathological terms). Even though the phrasing of the report is less machine-like than in previous versions, the final product is still far too crude to be used as a basis of a professional report.

As is the case for most computer-generated psychological reports, each report offers too many statements for all of them to be valid. These interpretive summaries should be taken as guides or hypotheses: examiners are much better off learning to interpret the Structural Summary.

CONCLUSIONS. Three conclusions are clear: (a) the Rorschach, employed with the Comprehensive System, is a better personality test than its opponents are willing to acknowledge; (b) the Exner group exaggerates the virtues of its system; and (c) the Exner group does not acknowledge the surprisingly persistent virtues of traditional psychoanalytically oriented content analysis approaches.

Much of the controversy about the Rorschach intensified with the introduction of the clinical versus statistical prediction debate, and it is also where we will end this review. A recent meta-analysis by Grove, Zald, Lebow, Snitz, and Nelson (2000) offers some interesting facts about clinical versus statistical prediction. According to Grove et al., about half of the time clinical and statistical prediction are equally effective—they both work. Psychologists should understand that statistical prediction outperforms clinical prediction much more often than clinical prediction outperforms statistical prediction for the types of questions studied by the research reviewed by Grove et al. (2000). It would, however, be farcical to claim that statistical prediction is always better than clinical prediction, or that clinical prediction is not valid.

Along similar lines, many of the recent criticisms of the Rorschach should help Comprehensive System proponents improve research and interpretive fidelity regarding the Rorschach. But opponents confuse flaws with failures.

If we gave the following items on a test, what might we answer?: (a) Research is an ongoing enterprise; (b) The Rorschach generates much passion on all fronts; (c) Rorschach data are not similar to any other psychological data we are currently gathering and most likely tap a rich vein of material otherwise overlooked; (d) The research methodologies are not yet focusing on the way Rorschach data can be most useful; (e) As with most tests, some irresponsible practitioners may make wild interpretations with no appropriate data bases.

All the above are true. Consequently if a criterion for a useful theory is one that generates exciting research, then the Rorschach and the theories undergirding it certainly have hemeneutic validity or the ability to generate meaningful data. It is equally true that much work is yet to be done examining and gathering validity evidence for constructs and the interpretations drawn from them.

REVIEWER'S REFERENCES

Rapaport, D., Gill, M., & Schafer, R. (1946). *Diagnostic psychological testing.* Chicago: Year Book.

Klopfer, B., Ainsworth, M. D., Klopfer, W. G., & Holt, R. R. (1954). *Developments in the Rorschach technique I: Technique and theory.* New York: Harcourt, Brace, & World.

Exner, J. E. (1969). *The Rorschach systems.* New York: Grune & Stratton.

Exner, J. E. (1974). *The Rorschach: A comprehensive system* (volume 1). New York: Wiley.

Atkinson, L. (1988). The comparative validities of the Rorschach and MMPI. *Canadian Psychology, 27,* 238–347.

Parker, K. C. H., Hanson, R. K., & Hunsley, J. (1988). MMPI, Rorschach and WAIS: A meta-analytic comparison of reliability, stability, and validity. *Psychological Bulletin, 103,* 367–373.

Lerner, P. M. (1991). *Psychoanalytic theory and the Rorschach.* Hillsdale, NJ: The Analytic Press.

Exner, J. E. (1995). *A Rorschach workbook* (4th ed.). Asheville, NC: Rorschach Workshops.

Exner, J. E., & Weiner, I. B. (1995). *The Rorschach: A comprehensive system, assessment of children and adolescents* (vol. 3, 2nd ed.). New York: John Wiley & Sons.

Meyer, G. J. (1997). Thinking clearly about reliability: More critical corrections regarding the Rorschach Comprehensive System. *Psychological Assessment, 9,* 495–498.

Wood, J. W., Nezworski, M. T., & Stejskal, W. J. (1997). The reliability of the comprehensive system for the Rorschach: A comment on Meyer. *Psychological Assessment, 9,* 490–494.

Garb, H. N., Florio, C. M., & Grove, W. M. (1998). The validity of the Rorschach and the Minnesota Multiphasic Personality Inventory: Results from meta-analyses. *Psychological Science, 9,* 402–404.

Weiner, I. B. (1998). *Principles of Rorschach interpretation.* Mahwah, NJ: Lawrence Erlbaum.

Hiller, J. B., Rosenthal, R., Bornstein, R. F., Berry, D. T., & Brunell-Neuleib, S. (1999). A comparative meta-analysis of Rorschach and MMPI Validity. *Psychological Assessment 11,* 278–296.

Acklin, M. W., McDowell, C. J., Jr., Verschell, M. S., & Chan, D. (2000). Interobserver agreement, intraobserver reliability, and the Rorschach Comprehensive System. *Journal of Personality Assessment, 74,* 15–47.

Grove, W. M., Zald, D. H., Lebow, B. S., Snitz, B. E., & Nelson, C. (2000). Clinical versus mechanical prediction: A meta-analysis. *Psychological Assessment, 12,* 19–30.

[324]
Ross Information Processing Assessment—Geriatric.

Purpose: A clinical instrument designed to identify, describe, and quantify cognitive-linguistic deficits in the geriatric population following traumatic brain injury.

Population: Geriatric patients.

Publication Date: 1996.

Acronym: RIPA-G.

Scores, 12: Immediate Memory, Recent Memory, Temporal Orientation, Spatial Orientation, Orientation to Environment, Recall of General Information, Problem Solving and Abstract Reasoning, Organization of Information, Auditory Processing and Comprehension, Problem Solving and Concrete Reasoning, Naming Common Objects, Functional Oral Reading.

Administration: Individual.

Price Data, 1999: $198 per complete kit; $44 per examiner's manual (77 pages); $54 per 25 response record forms; $24 per 25 profile summary forms; $39 per picture book.

Time: (45–60) minutes.

Comments: 10 core subtests, 2 supplemental subtests.

Authors: Deborah Ross-Swain and Paul T. Fogle.

Publisher: PRO-ED.

Review of the Ross Information Processing Assessment—Geriatric by SURENDRA P. SINGH, Professor and Clinical Neuropsychologist, College of Education, University of South Florida, Tampa, FL:

The original Ross Information Processing Assessment (RIPA; Ross, 1986) was developed to assess "individuals' cognitive-linguistic deficits following traumatic brain injury (TBI)." According to the test developers the new Ross Information Processing Assessment—Geriatric (RIPA-F) is "a comprehensive, norm referenced, cognitive-linguistic battery" (manual, p. 4). The test is "designed to identify, describe, and quantify cognitive-linguistic deficits" (manual, p. 4). The test consists of 10 subtests, two supplemental subtests, and a record form with three subsections to include background, medical, RIPA-G test, and retest information.

The RIPA-G test developers have presented a strong test package without presenting equally strong validation data. The test package looks like a collection containing a psychometric instrument, a survey instrument, a health care management guide, a neuropsychological instrument, a clinical psychological behavior checklist, and a cognitive assessment. The test developers have made some exaggerated claims such as that "The RIPA-G provides information generally provided by more traditional and lengthy neuropsychological batteries" (manual, p. 43). The test developers did not produce any research including concurrent validity data in support of their claim. Due to the lack of substantive research and validation data, the test developers' expectations and claims that the test is comprehensive, and that the examiner will be able to assess complex neuropsychological and psychological phenomena, cannot be substantiated.

The test protocol directions, as presented, expect the examiner to record patient's responses to RIPA-G test items, and to observe and record confabulation, denial, delayed, error, irrelevant, perseveration, partially correct, repetition, self-corrected, and tangential behaviors. All this is to be accomplished during the test period lasting approximately 45 to 60 minutes. The guidelines and the examples provided to interpret diacritical scores are troubling. For example, the test manual provides some examples for scoring and interpreting diacritical scores such as to question "What would you do if you were not feeling well?" Response example: "I don't know, I can't figure it out." Suggested rating 1d (denial). Is it a denial or a possible confusion indicator? Another response example: "Tell the nurse, but she is always so busy that I hate to bother her." Suggested rating 2t (tangential). Is it a tangential or a possible psychosocial habitual response with some other clinical implications? Another response example: "I never get sick so I don't know." Suggested rating 1c (confabulation). Is it a confabulation response or a denial response? The test developers provided "Specific Instructions for the Use of Diacritical Scoring System" (manual, p. 29–31); however, the instructions as presented did not address the limitations in examples cited above.

The test manual contains some information in certain contexts that is unclear. For example, the test authors have cited three theories including Luria's neuroanatomical and processing theory in support of the test construct (manual, p. 5). However, the authors failed to mention that Luria's approach of assessment is different from the approach used in the current test. The authors attempt to establish the claims of validity by aligning the RIPA-G with information-processing theories including Luria's without clarifying that the test differs from Luria's pattern analysis theory, philosophy, and practice. The claim that the test measures cognitive functioning assessed by other standardized measures of cognitive functioning without any validation study and concurrent validation data is an extremely weak claim.

In all fairness, some parts of the battery that have adequate test construction, standardization, test administration procedures, test interpretation guidelines, and select disclaimer statements demonstrate potential. A test administrator is expected to have "formal training in assessment" (manual, p. 7). The testing procedures and directions for administering the test are clear. The manual contains some valuable information regarding common respiratory and circulatory medical problems resulting in neurological and communicative disorders in the elderly, resident assessment instrument and minimum data set, and a resource list of frequently used communication instruments. The theoretical rationale describing the concept of reliability and validity is defendable. The chapter on "Interpreting RIPA-G" is informative.

The test was standardized on 88 adults living in skilled nursing facilities. The testing sites were randomly chosen. The test yields three types of scores: raw scores, percentiles, and standard scores. The manual provides standard scores and percentiles for RIPA-G subtests, and conversion sums of standard scores to quotients. Reliability estimate measures, coefficients alpha (composite scores ranging from .88–.97), and *SEM*s (composite scores between 3–5) are within acceptable ranges. Attempts to establish the test validity were made by seeking professional reviews, by conducting item analysis, and by using construct validity analyses. The item discrimination, subtest interrelationships, and item validity coefficients fall within moderate range.

SUMMARY. The RIPA-G is a well-packaged assessment tool. The test needs validation studies to support its validation claims. The test in its present form should be used as a survey instrument with extreme caution. Anyone who attempts to interpret the test findings must be qualified both in speech pathology and neuropsychology. The test developers have set out for themselves to achieve so many goals to make their product politically correct and marketable that the test loses its core theme. Finally, the test users will have to differentiate between the test developers' varied goals and the instrument's differentiated limited professional use.

REVIEWER'S REFERENCE

Ross, D. (1986). Ross Information Processing Assessment. Austin, TX: PRO-ED.

Review of the Ross Information Processing Assessment—Geriatric by WILFRED G. VAN GORP, Professor of Psychology in Psychiatry, Director, Neuropsychology, New York Presbyterian Hospital—Cornell Medical Center Mental Health System, New York, NY:

The Ross Information Processing Assessment—Geriatric (RIPA-G) battery was designed to quantify and describe cognitive-linguistic deficits in geriatric patients. The battery has 10 subtests and 2 supplemental subtests measuring various cognitive or linguistic processes including memory, orientation, organization, problem solving, auditory processing, knowledge of general information, reading, and word finding. The RIPA-G is designed for and was standardized on a sample of geriatric patients residing in skilled nursing facilities. The test, according to the manual, takes approximately 45 to 60 minutes to administer with an additional 10 minutes for the two optional supplemental subtests. The manual states that the battery can be administered by "any professional" (p. v).

Although the authors are to be commended for attempting to develop a comprehensive battery of information and linguistic processing for cognitively impaired geriatric patients, a careful review of the construction, standardization, norming, reliability, and validity studies on the RIPA-G indicates that the test fails to meet many of the generally used criteria for adequate reliability and validity in order to warrant a strong recommendation for its use. Although the test manual (p. 4) states that the RIPA-G is a comprehensive, norm-referenced battery that can quantify and qualitatively describe different but interrelated cognitive or linguistic skills, a review of the normative data and validity studies does not support this contention. The test was normed on a total sample of only 88 residents of nursing homes residing in three states, who had a variety of diagnoses ranging from chronic obstructive pulmonary disease to Alzheimer's disease. Although the test was also normed on a sample of 50 normal control subjects, no data are provided on this sample in the test manual, and it is not clear how data from these subjects were used in the construction of the test.

A review of the 10 subtests and 2 supplemental subtests indicates that many of the subtests contain items that assess a mix of different linguistic and cognitive processes, all under one scale. For instance, the Immediate Memory Subtests assesses such components as immediate attention (Digit Span), as well as multiple-step commands that undoubtedly exceed a patient's primary memory abilities. Thus, attention and language comprehension are confused under one subtest labeled Immediate Memory. The Recent Memory Subtest assesses aspects of autobiographical memory (e.g., How many children do you have?) as well as other memory items reflecting more recently learned information. The Temporal Orientation Subtest confuses basic orientation (e.g., What year is it?) with more long held memory of our culture (e.g., What is a holiday in winter?) This type of confusion makes interpretation of scores on any individual subscale difficult. Indeed, the authors, in a chapter on test validity, report the data from a factor analysis (they do not indicate which factor analytic technique was used), which

indicated that all 12 subtests loaded on a single factor. This finding is in contrast to the authors' assertion that the test can adequately assist the clinician in quantifying a variety of different and distinct cognitive skills. Further, the very limited data on reliability and validity in the test manual must be interpreted with caution in that the normative sample included a total of only 88 individuals residing in nursing homes, and for whom very limited demographic data are presented in the manual. Further, almost no data on reliability are presented beyond a tale providing information on Cronbach's alpha for the various items within the subtests. No data were provided on interrater reliability or test-retest reliability for the RIPA-G. Validity was limited to essentially the factor analysis mentioned above as well as a review of the RIPA-G items by seven professionals (their disciplines are not listed) who rated each item for its degree of appropriateness. Despite obtaining these ratings on the RIPA-G items, no data were provided that indicated that any item was actually discarded or modified if it received a low acceptability rating by the reviewers.

Although the RIPA-G is based upon a noble intent and a critical need, given the increasing population of older adults, it appears that much work remains to be done regarding norming, reliability, and validity of this battery before the RIPA-G can be solidly recommended as a measure of choice for assessing a variety of cognitive and linguistic abilities in older adults.

[325]
Ross Information Processing Assessment, Second Edition.

Purpose: Designed to assess "cognitive-linguistic deficits following traumatic brain injury."
Population: Ages 15–90.
Publication Dates: 1986–1996.
Acronym: RIPA—2.
Scores, 20: 10 Subtest scores (Immediate Memory, Recent Memory, Temporal Orientation [Recent Memory, Remote Memory], Spatial Orientation, Orientation to Environment, Recall of General Information, Problem Solving and Abstract Reasoning, Organization, Auditory Processing and Retention); 10 Diacritical scores (Errors, Perseveration, Repeat Instructions/Stimulus, Denial/Refusal, Delayed Response, Confabulation, Partially Correct, Irrelevant, Tangential, Self-Corrected).
Administration: Individual.

Price Data, 1999: $114 per complete kit including manual ('96, 68 pages), 25 record forms, and 25 profile/summary forms in storage box; $44 per 25 record forms; $24 per 25 profile/summary forms; $49 per manual.
Time: (60) minutes.
Author: Deborah Ross-Swain.
Publisher: PRO-ED.
Cross References: See T4:2294; for a review of an earlier edition by Jonathan Ehrlich, see 11:337.

Review of the Ross Information Processing Assessment, Second Edition by STEPHEN R. HOOPER, Associate Professor of Psychiatry, University of North Carolina School of Medicine, Chapel Hill, NC:

The Ross Information Processing Assessment (RIPA-2) is the second edition of a battery of procedures originally published in 1986. The original purpose of this battery was to assist in the cognitive-linguistic assessment of individuals who had sustained a traumatic brain injury (TBI). The battery was designed to complement other assessment strategies, and suggested users included a wide variety of professionals. The manual noted that the original version of this test generated little in the way of research findings, and it was criticized because of its lack of adherence to psychometric standards. The current revision was developed "to create an instrument that meets the highest standards for a psychometrically sound test battery" (examiner's manual, p. 4).

The current version of the RIPA-2 remains relatively unchanged from the original version in terms of its content, administration format, interpretive guidelines, and general intent. An attempt is made to utilize both quantitative and qualitative findings in the clinical formulation of an individual patient. The RIPA-2 purportedly was based on several theories of information processing; however, the exact linkages to these theories were not described. In fact, given the cognitive-linguistic focus of this test battery, it would seem that the RIPA-2 only represents a small portion of these theories.

The manual and test protocol are straightforward and user-friendly. Detailed instructions for administration are provided in the manual and should facilitate an error-free administration. Scoring instructions are provided for the quantitative and qualitative indices. One of the unique facets of this test is its use of qualitative scoring. The manual refers to the qualitative observations as diacritical markings, and these are obtained for each subtest. These observations would have benefited from better operational criteria, but they are adequately described in the chapter on administration and scoring. Quantitative scoring is based on standard scores and percentile ranks for each of the 10 subtests. The profile summary form and the record form are user-friendly, and the manual contains clear examples for completing these forms.

Normative data for the RIPA-2 were developed from 126 individuals between the ages of 15 and 77 residing in nine states and who had sustained some type of TBI. Subject identification was achieved by using PRO-ED customer files to locate professionals who had purchased the test within a 2-year time frame. Subjects were included in the normative sample if (a) neurodiagnostic procedures showed diffuse bilateral brain injuries or no evidence of left hemisphere involvement, (b) there was no evidence of a dementing process (i.e., Alzheimer's Dementia), (c) they had attained a certain level of functioning following their injury (i.e., ≥ Level V on the Rancho Los Amigos Scale), and (d) English was their primary language. The manual noted that the sample was "representative of TBI cases relative to gender, area of residence (city/rural), geographic area, and ethnic background" (examiner's manual, p. 39); however, no data are provided in this regard. The manual does not provide any information pertaining to the distribution of age, race, gender, and socioeconomic status of the sample. There is no description of the types of head injuries represented, the severity of the initial injuries, premorbid levels of functioning, or the time interval between injury and time of testing. Given the description of the identification and inclusion criteria, one wonders if the sample was a heterogeneous group of individuals with neurological impairment as opposed to a heterogeneous group of individuals with TBI. The normative base as presented is quite inadequate, and likely will contribute to significant problems with interpretation of the findings. All of the raw scores for the normative sample were converted to standard scores and percentile ranks; however, it is not clear if the raw scores were normalized before these transformations were made.

In accordance with its overall mission for this revision, the internal consistency of the RIPA-2 appears to be satisfactory, with 9 out of the 10 scales showing alpha coefficients of at least .83 or higher. Only one subtest, Auditory Processing and

Retention, fell below that standard with an alpha coefficient of .67. The Standard Errors of Measurement were relatively small, suggesting good reliability of the scores. Interscorer reliability was quite high. No estimate of temporal stability was provided, although this may be difficult to determine with a population of individuals with TBI.

Estimates of content validity using experts and item-total correlations appear adequate. Despite these assertions, however, subtest-total test correlations are presented, and the specific item-total correlations are not provided. An inspection of individual items revealed most items to be verbal in nature, with no adaptations being suggested for patients experiencing problems with literal versus figurative language. For the memory items, homogeneous distractors abound, and these likely will present interference problems for many patients. Although these observations could be useful when working with patients with brain injuries, they are not accounted for in the current version of this battery. There is no discussion of item bias.

Also of concern was the high degree of subtest intercorrelations. Taken together with the principal components analysis, which was quite difficult to interpret given the extremely small subjects-to-variable ratio, these findings suggest the presence of one overall factor on the RIPA-2—not the 10 cognitive-linguistic domains as described. This was somewhat surprising given the multidimensionality of the information-processing theories upon which the RIPA-2 purportedly was based. The convergent and divergent validity of scores from the test with those from the Woodcock-Johnson Tests of Cognitive Abilities—Revised was difficult to determine without a priori hypotheses regarding the strength of the various associations reported. Finally, the RIPA-2 was not able to distinguish between individuals having mild versus severe TBI, although given that the analysis used the normative sample, this was not surprising. This finding also suggests that the severity dimensions suggested by the RIPA-2 remain unvalidated, and should not be used by clinicians outside of gaining a general clinical impression.

SUMMARY. The RIPA-2 is the second edition of a battery designed to assess cognitive-linguistic functions in older adolescents and adults with TBI. The sole purpose for the second edition was to improve its psychometric properties. Although it appears that additional information has been provided, the psychometric properties remain unclear. Scale reliabilities appear to meet current psychometric standards, but there are significant concerns about the overall validity of the test. The content validity was adequate, but individual items were questionable with respect to their impact on an individual's performance. Construct and criterion-related validity were problematic. The normative sample was quite small, apparently quite heterogeneous, and generally unrepresentative of the larger population of individuals with TBI. The RIPA-2 continues to evidence significant psychometric problems, and its use should be limited only to the most experienced clinicians who are familiar with its current psychometric properties.

[326]
Roswell-Chall Auditory Blending Test.

Purpose: "Developed to evaluate a student's ability to blend sounds to form words when the sounds are presented orally."

Population: Grades 1–4 and "older students with reading difficulties."

Publication Dates: 1963–1997.

Scores: Total score only.

Administration: Individual.

Price Data, 1999: $9.80 (6+ packets) or $14.70 (1–5 packets) per packet of 24 test forms; $3.50 (6+ copies) or $5.25 (1–5 copies) per manual of instructions ('95, 5 pages).

Time: Administration time not reported.

Comments: Oral administration; useful for judging the ease with which students will learn phonics.

Authors: Florence G. Rosewell and Jeanne S. Chall.

Publisher: Educators Publishing Service, Inc.

Cross References: See T5:2253 (2 references), T4:2296 (1 reference), and T2:1674 (7 references); for reviews by Ira E. Aaron and B. H. Von Roekel of an earlier edition, see 6:830 (2 references).

Review of the Roswell-Chall Auditory Blending Test by JOYCE R. McLARTY, Principal Research Associate, Workforce Development Division, ACT, Inc., Iowa City, IA:

The Roswell-Chall Auditory Blending Test comprises three sets of 10 words of increasing complexity that the examiner reads to each examinee. In reading, the examiner is instructed to separate the sounds and the examinee is instructed to try to put the word back together. Although subtotals are calculated for each set of 10 words, no separate interpretation of either the sets or the subscores is provided, and the very high internal consistency of the test (.96 in one reported study) suggests that only the total score should be considered in interpreting examinee performance.

Results of this test are used to identify examinees who may experience difficulty in learning phonics. Ability to learn phonics is described as resulting from a combination of maturation and specific instruction in phonemic awareness, auditory blending, segmentations, rhyming, and the like. The instructions for the Roswell-Chall test tell the examiner to "Give the sounds at the rate of about 1/2 second for each sound. Avoid inserting extraneous sounds at the end of each of the separate consonants. The separation between the sounds should be almost imperceptible. Try to enunciate the consonant sounds clearly and elongate the vowel sounds, especially the short vowels" (p. 1). It appears likely that examiners' abilities to follow these directions will vary, and that this variation may impact the examinee's ability to correctly respond to the words. Therefore, the same examiner should administer the test to all of the examinees in a given group if the scores of individuals are to be compared.

To help examiners determine whether examinees are ready to learn phonics, tables are provided for determining whether blending skills are adequate or inadequate based on the grade level of the examinee. For example, a correct response to 14 of the 30 words is considered to represent adequate blending skills through Grade 2 and inadequate blending skills thereafter. The cutoff scores for this table were arrived at by inspection of the scores of 26 students tested annually in Grades 1 through 4 and 25 severely retarded readers tested in Grades 3 through 5. Although these longitudinal data are helpful in documenting the relationship between auditory blending and grade level, no information about student characteristics, other than their reading skills, is provided to help test users determine comparability to their own students. These students appear to have been assessed in the early 1960s, and it is likely that characteristics of both students and reading instruction have changed since them.

In addition, these sample sizes are too small to provide assurance of generalizable data. Without a larger and more current sample, and without more extensive information about the examinees on which the norms are based, those using the test would be well advised to consider the cutoff scores for the adequate/inadequate determination as guidelines rather than established facts. This is especially the case where the test is being used with students who have diverse cultural or language backgrounds.

A 1988 study (Yopp, 1988) referenced in the Roswell-Chall Manual of Instructions provides data for a larger and more current sample of examinees ($N = 104$). In this study, examinees were administered 10 tests of phonemic awareness and one test of the rate at which they learned to decode novel words. Factor analysis using oblique rotation identified two factors that correlated .77. These factors accounted for 59% and 10% of the variance, respectively, and were identified as simple and compound phonemic awareness. The Roswell-Chall test loaded .84 on the first factor, and .001 on the second, indicating that it is a strong measure of simple phonemic awareness. The Roswell-Chall test also correlated .63 with the test of the subsequent rate of learning to read novel words, which is reasonably good.

The Yopp-Singer Test of Phoneme Segmentation is provided with permission to reproduce in *The Reading Teacher*, Vol. 49, No. 1, September 1995. The reviewer also found a copy of the test available on the internet, so readers may want to check there as well. This 22-item test had a reliability of .67 and loaded .89 on the first factor in the study cited above. Although somewhat less reliable, and lacking guidelines for score interpretation, this test may be a good alternative where high stakes decisions are not being made.

This reviewer found a relevant research paper by P. B. Gough, K. C. Larson, and H. Yopp, titled *The Structure of Phonemic Awareness* on the internet, as well as additional information on language instruction for young children. Readers may wish to investigate these resources.

SUMMARY. The Roswell-Chall Auditory Blending Test appears to be a sound measure of phonemic awareness with very high reliability and a good correlation with ability to read novel words. The cutoff scores given for distinguishing adequate from inadequate blending, however, are outdated and based on insufficient sample sizes. Those using this test would be well advised to develop their own standards for when an examinee is adequately prepared to begin learning phonics.

REVIEWER'S REFERENCE

Yopp, H. K. (1988). The validity and reliability of phonemic awareness tests. *Reading Research Quarterly, 23,* 159–177.

Review of the Roswell-Chall Auditory Blending Test by JANET NORRIS, Professor of Communication Disorders, Louisiana State University, Baton Rouge, LA:

The Roswell-Chall Auditory Blending Test was designed to evaluate a student's ability to blend sounds presented orally to form words. A table for interpretation of raw scores is provided but no norms are available. Sound blending is measured using three tasks. Part I measures the ability to blend two sounds (b-e), Part II measures the ability to blend onset and rime (c-ake), and Part II measures the ability to blend CVC words (m-a-p). The test is intended to identify children who are at-risk for learning phonics and therefore learning to read. It is reported to be appropriate to children in Grades 1 through 4 and for older students with reading difficulties.

The entire test is composed of 30 items, and although no time requirements are given, it should be completed easily in less than 15 minutes. The instructions are simple and no pictures, blocks, or other materials are required, rendering the test easy to use and administer. Raw scores are directly compared to a grade level criterion score. The manual is five pages in length.

However, the simplicity of the test is reflective of its limitations. A brief description of test tasks and opinions on the significance of test results is provided. For example, the predictive power of Part III for phonics readiness is discussed and recommended instructional approaches for children who do or do not perform well on this skill are provided. However, despite over 25 years of research and dozens of studies on phonological awareness skills like sound blending, no research support is provided for these claims. Only five references are cited, most of them old. The instructional approaches recommended also are old and not consistent with the recommendations of the report from the Committee of the National Research Council (Preventing Reading Difficulties in Young Children, Snow, Burns, & Griffin, 1998).

The assessment is limited to three sound blending tasks, representing a very limited view of phonological awareness skills and an even narrower view of developmental reading skills. Other tasks, such as phoneme or syllable deletion, awareness of same or different beginning and ending phonemes, sound segmentation, and rhyme are examples of other tasks shown to be indicative of the ability to manipulate the sound structure of words and are predictive of reading ability (Brady & Shankweiler, 1991). Many other abilities, such as vocabulary, syntactic proficiency, story grammar, general knowledge, and visual skills have been shown to be equally important to reading proficiency (Weintraub, 1992–1996). The limitations of the Roswell-Chall tasks as a predictive measure of reading are reflected in the correlations obtained between the Auditory Blending Total Scores and six tests of reading achievement. Most of these were low to moderate, in the .4 to .5 range, with only one correlation (out of 24) above a .6. Thus, the predictive validity is not strong and the construct validity is limited to a task that may be related to one aspect of reading (i.e., phonics), although even this was stated but not supported by data in the manual.

The reliability, established using a split-half procedure, was good, ranging from .86 to .93 for Grades 1 through 4 (26 children). This finding was supported by a study conducted by Yopp (1988) who obtained a reliability coefficient of .96 for her 104 kindergarten subjects.

The Roswell-Chall does not provide norms, but only a chart designed to interpret the Total Score for each grade level as either "Inadequate Blending" or "Adequate Blending." Although information is limited, this table appears to be derived from the performance of 26 children who were tested in Grade 1 and followed up in succeeding grades through Grade 4. No information is available on these subjects, such as age, geographic location, reading ability, intellectual ability, gender, and so forth. Thus, the population is far too small and homogeneous to establish the validity of the cutoff scores for "adequate" or "inadequate" blending, so at best they serve as guidelines. There are currently other instruments on the market that test similar skills, such as the Test of Phonological Awareness (Torgesen & Bryant, 1994; T5:2708) and the Test of Awareness of Language Segments (Sawyer, 1987; T5:2674) that are standardized on large representative samples of children and that do provide normative scores.

SUMMARY. In summary, the Roswell-Chall Auditory Blending Test measures a skill that is as popular in reading literature (i.e., phonemic awareness) as it was when the first edition was published in 1963. The 1997 version has not been updated in theory, research support, normative data, breadth of skills tested, or recommendations for intervention, so it is unclear why the instrument is being reissued with a new copyright date. Other instruments measuring similar skills may be better choices because of their stronger test construction and normative data.

REVIEWER'S REFERENCES

Sawyer, D. J. (1987). Test of Awareness of Language Segments. Austin, TX PRO-ED.

Yopp, H. K. (1988). The validity and reliability of phonemic awareness tests. *Reading Research Quarterly, 23,* 159–177.

Brady, S. A., & Shankweiler, D. P. (Eds.). (1991). *Phonological processes in literacy: A tribute to Isabelle Y. Liberman.* Hillsdale, NJ: Erlbaum Associates.

Weintraub, S. (Ed.). (1992–1996). *Annual summary of investigations relating to reading.* Newark, DE: International Reading Association.

Torgesen, J. K., & Bryant, B. R. (1994). Test of Phonological Awareness. Austin, TX: PRO-ED.

Snow, C. E., Burns, M. S., & Griffin, P. (1998). *Preventing reading difficulties in young children.* Washington, DC: National Research Council.

[327]
Roswell-Chall Diagnostic Reading Test of Word Analysis Skills.

Purpose: "Designed to evaluate the basic word analysis (decoding) and word recognition skills."
Population: Reading levels grades 1–4.
Publication Dates: 1956–1997.
Scores, 15: Words (High Frequency Words), Decoding Test (Consonant Sounds, Consonant Digraphs, Consonant Blends, Short Vowel Sounds, Short and Long Vowel Sounds, Rule of Silent e, Vowel Digraphs, Dipthongs and Vowels Controlled by r, Syllabication, Total), Letter Names (Naming Capital Letters, Naming Lower Case Letters), Encoding (Encoding Single Consonants, Encoding Regular Words).
Administration: Individual.
Forms, 2: A, B.
Price Data, 1999: $9.80 (6+ sets) or $14.70 (1–5) sets per 24 test forms (includes 12 each Form A and B); $4 (6+) or $6 (1–5) per manual of instructions ('97, 14 pages); $3.75 (6+) or $5.60 (1–5) per technical supplement ('97, 16 pages).
Time: (10) minutes.
Comments: Republication of 1978 version.
Authors: Florence G. Roswell and Jeanne S. Chall.
Publisher: Educators Publishing Service, Inc.
Cross References: For reviews by John Wills Lloyd and Ira E. Aaron of an earlier edition, see 9:1062 (1 reference); see also T3:2034 (3 references) and T2:1643 (2 references); for reviews by Ira E. Aaron and Albert Betts of an earlier edition, see 6:831 (1 reference); for a review by Byron H. Van Roekel of the original edition, see 5:667.

Review of the Roswell-Chall Diagnostic Reading Test of Word Analysis Skills by THOMAS P.

HOGAN, Professor of Psychology, University of Scranton, Scranton, PA:

The Roswell-Chall Diagnostic Reading Test of Word Analysis Skills is intended to measure work analysis and word recognition skills of persons reading at the grade 1–4 levels. The test contains a total of 169 items, yielding 15 scores (listed in the descriptive entry), some based on as few as 3 or 4 items. Previous editions of the test were published in 1956, 1959, and 1978.

The 1997 edition of the Roswell-Chall is a new edition only in the narrowest sense of the term. It has a new copyright date, a new publisher, several references in the introductory section of the Manual of Instructions to recent books about reading instruction, and a few minor, almost trivial changes in test format. In comparison with the previous, 1978 edition, there are no new items, no new norms, no new research studies regarding reliability or validity, and no changes to the Technical Supplement. The test stands essentially as it was almost 20 years ago.

The Ninth Mental Measurements Yearbook (9:1062) included two cogent, useful reviews of the 1978 Roswell-Chall, one by Lloyd (1985), another by Aaron (1985). These reviews may be consulted for descriptions of the subtests. Criticisms of the 1978 edition made in these reviews are equally applicable to the 1997 edition. These criticisms included: lack of data about relationships among subtests, failure to meet the "prescriptive" claim made in the manual, low reliability resulting in large standard errors of measurement for certain subtests, and lack of rationale for the criterion-referenced cut-points used for determining instructional needs. In addition to these criticisms, of course, one can now note that the data base for the test is quite thoroughly out-of-date.

SUMMARY. Reading specialists who may have developed a comfortable fund of experience with the 1978 edition can be assured that the "new" edition does not really supersede the older edition. Other than for that usage, there is not much to recommend the Roswell-Chall. Anyone looking for a diagnostic reading test can certainly find a better, more up-to-date test.

REVIEWER'S REFERENCES

Aaron, I. E. (1985). [Review of the Roswell-Chall Diagnostic Reading Test of Word Analysis Skills, Revised and Extended.] In J. V. Mitchell, Jr. (Ed.), *The ninth mental measurements yearbook* (pp. 1301–1302). Lincoln, NE: Buros Institute of Mental Measurements.

Lloyd, J. W. (1985). [Review of the Roswell-Chall Diagnostic Reading Test of Word Analysis Skills, Revised and Extended.] In J. V. Mitchell, Jr. (Ed.), *The ninth mental measurements yearbook* (pp. 1300–1301). Lincoln, NE: Buros Institute of Mental Measurements.

Rothwell Miller Values Blank.

Purpose: "Designed as a measure of work related values to be used primarily in career guidance, in conjunction with an occupational interests measure. Other applications include company selection (with school leavers or older basic level staff) and clinical and rehabilitation counseling."

Population: Ages 15 and older.

Publication Dates: 1968–1994.

Acronym: RMVB.

Scores, 5: Rewards, Interest, Security, Pride in Work, Autonomy.

Administration: Individual or group.

Price Data: Available from publisher.

Foreign Language Editions: French and Greek language editions available; Afrikaans, German, Hungarian, Icelandic, and Romanian editions in progress.

Time: [10–20] minutes.

Comments: Previously entitled Choosing a Career; developed as a complementary measure to be used with the Rothwell Miller Interest Blank (T5:2255).

Authors: J. W. Rothwell, K. M. Miller, and B. Tyler.

Publisher: Miller & Tyler, Ltd. [England].

Review of the Rothwell Miller Values Blank by JOHN S. GEISLER, Professor, College of Education, Western Michigan University, Kalamazoo, MI:

The Rothwell Miller Values Blank (RMVB), published in Great Britain in 1994 (and at that time entitled Choosing a Career), was designed to measure five constructs related to career choice: (a) Rewards, (b) Interests, (c) Security, (d) Pride in Work, and (e) Autonomy. These five constructs were advanced by Jack Rothwell, a career counselor in Australia. No other information on the rationale, background, or development of the instrument was provided. The five constructs became the names of the five RMVB scales. The instrument is designed to be used with other assessment tools, specifically, interest inventories, and, more specifically, the Rothwell Miller Interest Blank (Revised; T5:2255).

The RMVB is an ipsative instrument that consists of 50 statements arranged in 10 sets of five items each. Within each set respondents are asked to rank order the importance of each statement as it relates to their motivation when making a career choice. Therefore, the RMVB contains 10 Rewards statements, 10 Interest statements, etc. Each statement in each set is related to one of the five constructs being measured. The order of the statement/constructs differs in each set. There was no information given as to how judgments were made as to the match between statements and constructs.

The RMVB is hand scored. The five individual construct total scores are determined by summing the ranks (1 = High, 5 = Low) of each of the responses to the 10 statements associated with each construct (10 = High, 50 = Low). The protocol then calls for these five total scores to also be ranked (1 = High, 5 = Low). These total scores are then assigned a percentile based on a combination of gender and age norms. Summing the ranks requires an assumption that the ranks are parametric data. It could be argued that this procedure is not justified.

Reliability was examined by two methods: (a) internal consistency (computed by a Pearson product moment correlation coefficient, corrected by Spearman-Brown, between scores on the first half and scores on the second half of the test). Coefficients ranged from .67 to .85 ($N = 100$). (b) Test-retest coefficients ranged from .52 to .71 ($N = 68$) over a 4-month period. Both samples were composed of 16- and 17-year-old students. Most of the coefficients are in the questionable range and the samples are very small. Also, Pearson coefficients are based on parametric data. The scores on this instrument are rank-ordered (ordinal) data.

Validity evidence was gathered through (a) intercorrelations among the five CAC scales (range = -.6 to .07) and (b) correlations with each of the six scales of the Career Interests Test ($N = 13,500$ for both studies). No other validity data were reported.

Means and standard deviations for all five scales were reported on samples from England, Scotland, and Wales arranged by gender, age (15 to 50+ years), and years in school with sample sizes ranging from 59 to 15,955. The largest samples were in the lower age groupings (15–19 years of age). Again, computing means and standard deviations on ordinal data must be considered spurious. Raw score/decile conversions are available in 16 tables arranged by age and gender. Samples ranged from 59 to 8,665. The authors also report data indicating that there were statistically significant differences among mean gender scores for eight age groups across the five scales (40 age/scale samples). Student t tests were performed on the samples (no sizes reported) with significance at or less than .058 on 22 of the 40 samples.

Very little information was provided with respect to the norm groups. The size of the younger age groups was most adequate; however, the size of the adult samples was quite small. No data were reported on geographic distribution, income level, education (adults), socioeconomic level, employment, or other variables that would assist in determining the adequacy of the samples.

SUMMARY. Because of the lack of rationale and justification for the five scales, the dearth of adequate reliability and validity data, the questionable scoring methodology, the fact that the RMVB must be hand scored, the small size of the adult norm samples, and the lack of descriptive information on all norm groups, the instrument cannot be recommended for general use. The RMVB might have limited usefulness as an exploratory tool to generate career choice discussions with 15–19-year-olds; however, any other use would not be warranted.

Review of the Rothwell Miller Values Blank by WILLIAM I. SAUSER, JR., *Associate Dean and Professor, College of Business, Auburn University, Auburn, AL:*

"What do you want to be when you grow up?" This oft-asked childhood question takes on greater importance as one progresses through school and prepares to enter the workforce. Professional guidance counselors are frequently charged with helping high school students make vocational choices, and they depend on information gleaned from the students themselves to shape their guidance. The Rothwell Miller Values Blank is a straightforward, easily administered, written questionnaire designed to aid in the process of gaining useful information in an efficient manner from those seeking vocational guidance. It is intended as a companion piece to the Rothwell Miller Interest Blank (Revised; T5:2255), most recently reviewed by Harding (13:269) and Wilkinson (13:269).

The authors note that the Rothwell Miller Values Blank (RMVB), like its battery-mate the Rothwell Miller Interest Blank (RMIB), "emerged from Jack Rothwell's extensive practical experience as a careers counselor with the national vocational guidance service in Australia" (manual, p. 1). After working for years with the RMIB, Rothwell "decided that, before conducting a guidance interview, he would like (in addition to information about preferences among interest fields) to know the relative importance to the individual of five work-related values" (manual, p. 1). Thus was created the RMVB.

The blank itself consists of 50 statements that "refer to aspects of work or the work environment which can be important to choosing a career" (manual, p. 5). The statements are arranged in 10 sets of five items each, with one item in each set representing respectively the five values being measured (Rewards, Interest, Security, Pride in Work, Autonomy). The items are spiraled such that the five dimensions being measured are not obvious to the test taker. The test taker is to rank-order the statements within each set from highest (1) to lowest (5). These rank-order scores are summed across the 10 sets to produce summary scores for each of the five values. The authors note properly that this is an ipsative scale for which the primary interpretive value is to determine each individual's "comparative importance and strength of priority" (manual, p. 9) among the five values under consideration. Nonetheless, normative data are provided such that each individual's pattern of values can be compared with normative patterns for gender and age.

The manual makes no reference to the source of the 50 items, but they are clearly written and appear face valid with respect to the values they are intended to represent. Detailed administration and scoring instructions are provided in the test manual, as are guidelines for interpretation. This reviewer concurs with the authors' statement that "very limited information can be derived from using the results on their own to draw specific conclusions" (manual, p. 8). The blank results in: rank order scores that "summarise the individual's order of priorities among the five work values," category totals that "provide additional information ... as to the relative strength/consistency of the individual's priorities" and percentile scores that "enable comparison between the value pattern of a [*sic*] individual and that of a reference group drawn from his/her age group" (manual, p. 9).

Evidence documenting the psychometric quality of the RMVB is surprisingly weak. Only one study of 100 fifth formers (age 16/17) was used to derive the internal consistency reliability values for the subscales, which ranged from .67 (Security) to .85 (Rewards). Likewise, only one study of 68 fifth formers was employed to measure the (4-month) test-retest reliability of the subscales, which ranged from .52 (Autonomy) to .71 (Rewards). A much larger study (*N* = 3,500) was conducted to demonstrate the independence of the categories, with intercorrelations ranging from -.60 to +.07. The authors properly note that because the RMVB is an ipsative measure, "a high score on one scale must be balanced by low scores on other scales" (manual, p. 13). Data from the same sample (*N* = 13,500) were used to determine "concurrent validity," defined by the authors as significant intercorrelations (ranging from -.31 to +.36) between the RMVB subscale scores and those of a forced-choice questionnaire measuring preferences for each of six occupational fields.

The manual presents convincing evidence of gender differences on RMVB scores, so norms are tabulated by age and gender such that appropriate comparisons may be drawn. These norms "are based on the results of individuals who were assessed by the Morrisby Vocational Guidance Service during the 1992/93 school year" (manual, p. 17). Given that fact, and the changing nature of patterns of values over time among high school students noted by the authors (manual, p. 8), it is probably time to conduct another norming study of the RMVB. Such a study would provide an opportunity to conduct further research on the blank's reliability and validity as well.

How is the RMVB to be used? The authors suggest four possible ways (manual, p. 10): (a) as an aid to discussion within a career guidance interview or counseling session, (b) to generate discussion in a group organized within a school or careers guidance context, (c) as part of an assessment battery for educational or job selection, and (d) as a self-awareness exercise in personal counseling. This reviewer concurs that the RMVB might be useful for purposes (a), (b), and (d), particularly given the authors' recommendation that the RMVB be used only as a staring point for a deeper, more thorough interview with each student being counseled (manual, p. 8). Because the blank is easily faked and not a shred of evidence is presented documenting its predictive validity, this reviewer urges potential users not to make educational or job selection decisions based in whole or in part on the RMVB. The authors should remove this suggested use of the blank in future editions of the manual unless strong evidence of predictive validity is generated.

SUMMARY. The Rothwell Miller Values Blank is a straightforward measure of five career-related values that produce information found useful by vocational guidance counselors. It is easily administered (to individuals or groups) and scored, and can be completed by most high school students in 10 to 20 minutes. It is designed to be administered in a battery with the Rothwell Miller Interest Blank and provides limited information when used on its own. It appears useful as a "conversation starter" for individual vocational counseling sessions or group discussions in a vocational guidance context. Evidence for its psychometric quality is limited, and it should not be used as a basis for making critical educational or job selection decisions. The authors are urged to conduct more research with the RMVB and to renorm it using a broad sample of current high school students.

[329]
Sales Achievement Predictor.

Purpose: Constructed to assess "characteristics that are critical for success in sales."
Population: Adults.
Publication Date: 1995.
Acronym: Sales AP.
Scores, 21: Validity Scores (Inconsistent Responding, Self-Enhancing, Self-Critical), Special Scores (Sales Disposition, Initiative-Cold Calling, Sales Closing), Basic Domain Scores (Achievement, Motivation, Competitiveness, Goal Orientation, Planning, Initiative-General, Team Player, Managerial, Assertiveness, Personal Diplomacy, Extroversion, Cooperativeness, Relaxed Style, Patience, Self-Confidence).
Administration: Group.
Price Data, 1999: $175 per kit including manual (73 pages), 2 mail-in answer sheets, 2-use disk for on-site computer scoring, and 2 PC answer sheets; $45 per mail-in answer sheet; $50 per manual; $360 per 25-use computer disk (PC with Windows); $15 per 100 PC answer sheets; $39.50 per FAX service scoring.
Time: (20–25) minutes.
Comments: Microsoft Windows 3.1 or above required for computer scoring.
Authors: Jotham G. Friedland, Sander I. Marcus, and Harvey P. Mandel.
Publisher: Western Psychological Services.

Review of the Sales Achievement Predictor by GORDON C. BRUNER II, Associate Professor, Marketing Department, Director, Office of Scale Research, Southern Illinois University, Carbondale, IL:

The Sales Achievement Predictor, referred to as the Sales AP, was constructed in order to "assist in the selection, placement, and training of salespeople" (manual, p. 1). It is based upon a model that views achievement as being the product of many factors such as personality, work habits, and interpersonal style.

The instrument can be given as a paper-and-pencil test or taken on a PC. Several options for scoring the tests are offered. The manual seems to be clear in the instructions provided for administering the test as well as in interpreting the results. The authors indicated that multiple studies have shown little if any differences between groups based upon gender or ethnicity. Although fluency with English is needed, an assessment of readability level indicates the items are rather easy to read.

Estimates of internal consistency as well as one-year stability (test-retest) reliability were moderate to good for the 21 scales composing the instrument (ranging from .66 to .88 for internal consistency and .67 to .90 for test-retest).

However, the dimensionality of the various scales has not been established. This issue brings the reliability and validity into question if one accepts that dimensionality must be established first (Gerbing & Anderson, 1988). Putting that concern aside, the predictive validity might have been considered moderate to good had it not been based on disturbingly small samples (17 and 52). Further, the criterion in each case was a single item judgment made by sales managers about how salespeople met their expectations. The best that can be said is that about a quarter to a third of the variance of performance as determined by sales managers was predicted accurately by the Sales Disposition scale of the instrument.

Although convergent and discriminant validity were addressed in the manual, the evidence amounted to broad interpretation of correlation matrices. In fact, the naive reader would probably be overwhelmed by the quantity of data. Unfortunately, the manual fails to use theory to explain which correlations should be strong, which should not be strong, which should be positive, and which should be negative. Strong tests of relationships were not conducted (e.g., CFA, *SEM*). Even meager significance tests were missing from the correlation matrices that might assist in independently judging convergent and discriminant validity.

Maybe the most troublesome issue of the SalesAP has to do with its evidence related to content validity. The thoughtful reader wonders why we should expect these particular predictor variables to be associated with sales performance.

The authors repeatedly assure the reader that their "combined clinical and business experience" (manual, p. 13) provided them with the insight to know which variables are important. Disturbingly lacking is any connection between the model with which the authors appear to be working and the considerable scholarly literature that has accumulated over the years in sales. What is one to think when in the 60+ pages of the manual no literature is cited from the very field for which an instrument is designed (personal sales) nor is the model tested (using the contemporary sense of model testing) in a sales context? For example, there is strong evidence that not only are there different types of sales occupations but sales people pass through different stages over time, each with its own distinct activities (Cron & Slocum, 1986; Wotruba, 1991). It seems reasonable, therefore, that test developers would want to find a relationship between variables that predict performance per sales activity rather than for selling in general.

SUMMARY. A review of the performance literature has led experts in the field to conclude that "no general physical characteristics, mental abilities, or personality traits appear to be consistently related to sales aptitude and performance in all companies and selling situations" (Churchill, Ford, & Walker, 1997, p. 388). Instead, it is recommended that the tasks involved in a sales job be identified and then tests of those skills and abilities be utilized in the selection process. Given this, the best that one can say about the SalesAP is that it may be appropriate in some sales situations and not in others depending upon the degree to which the constructs being measured by the instrument are related to the job of interest.

REVIEWER'S REFERENCES

Cron, W. L., & Slocum, J. W., Jr. (1986, May). The influence of career stages on sales person's job attitudes, work perceptions, and performance. *Journal of Marketing Research, 23,* 119–129.

Gerbing, D. W., & Anderson, J. C. (1988, May). An updated paradigm for scale development incorporating unidimensionality and its assessment. *Journal of Marketing Research, 25,* 186–192.

Wotruba, T. R. (1991). The Evolution of Personal Selling. *Journal of Personal Selling and Sales Management, 11,* 1–12.

Churchill, G. A., Jr., Ford, N. M., & Walker, O. C., Jr. (1997). Sales force management. Chicago: Richard D. Irwin, Inc.

Review of the Sales Achievement Predictor by BRENT W. ROBERTS, *Assistant Professor of Psychology, University of Illinois at Urbana-Champaign, Champaign, IL.:*

The Sales Achievement Predictor (SalesAP) is designed to measure attributes associated with success in sales. The theory on which the SalesAP is based proposes that achievement at sales is determined by multiple factors, such as habits, interpersonal style, and personality, and thus the test takes a multidimensional approach to the assessment of sales success. A SalesAP test user receives scores on 15 Basic Domain scales, 3 Response Style scales, and an additional set of three scales meant specifically to predict success in sales. The SalesAP is a revised form of an unpublished test called the Motivation and Achievement Inventory (MAI). The MAI was originally developed to predict success in achievement-related settings. The primary difference between the SalesAP and the MAI is the addition of the three scales focusing on sales success. The SalesAP also includes interest scales that tap Holland's (1997) RIASEC (Realistic, Investigative, Artistic, Social, Enterprising, Conventional) model, but little or no information is provided on these scales in the manual.

The scales of the SalesAP are organized into six categories: (a) Sales Success, consisting of the Sales Disposition, Initiative-Cold Calling, and Sales Closing scales; (b) Motivation and Achievement, consisting of the Achievement, Motivation, Competitiveness, and Goal Orientation scales; (c) Work Strengths, consisting of the Planning, Initiative-General, Team Player, and Managerial scales; (d) Interpersonal Strengths, consisting of the Assertiveness, Personal Diplomacy, Extroversion, and Cooperativeness scales; and (e) Inner Resources, consisting of the Relaxed Style, Patience, and Self-Confidence scales. The sixth category, Response Style, is assessed via the inconsistent Responding, Self-Enhancing, and Self-Critical scales.

According to the manual the items for the SalesAP were written "based on the authors' years of professional experience in business and sales settings" (p. 23). The three Sales Success scales that warranted updating the MAI were developed from the existing item pool. It appears that the items for many scales were selected solely through a rational or logical approach. For example, the authors used their "combined clinical and business experience" (p. 13) to select items for the Cold Calling scale. For some scales, the authors claim to use criterion measures of sales success to help select scale items. Unfortunately, none of the item level evidence is presented supporting this empirical approach to scale development. In addition, the authors claim to use factor analytic techniques to define and refine scales, yet no factor analyses are reported.

The repeated claim that factor analysis was used to develop the SalesAP scales is ironic given the fact that the authors do not report a factor analysis of the SalesAP itself. Factor analysis can be a critical tool for understanding the construct validity of a test. Examination of the intercorrelations of the SalesAP scales would lead one to believe that there are fewer than 18 unique dimensions underlying the test. In fact, it would not be surprising to find that a factor analysis would not support the rational organization of scales into the five domains listed above. Of course, in the absence of a factor analysis all the reader can do is guess.

Convergent and discriminant validity were tested by correlating the SalesAP with the Sixteen Personality Factor Questionnaire (16PF; Cattell, 1986) and the Edwards Personal Preference Schedule (EPPS; Edwards, 1959). The magnitudes of the convergent validity coefficients were modest at best. The highest correlation across both tests was .66 and most convergent validity coefficients ranged from .20 to .45. The pattern of correlations supports the hypothesis that the SalesAP measures fewer than 18 constructs. Sixteen of the 18 SalesAP scales had substantive correlations with scales from the 16PF that measure extraversion (e.g., the Enthusiastic, Dominant, and Self-Doubting dimensions). A similar pattern of correlations was obtained on the EPPS.

The choice to use the 16PF and the EPPS to investigate the construct validity of the SalesAP is confusing. Several global personality measures that include "sales" subscales, such as the Hogan Personality Inventory (13:138) and the Jackson Personality Research Form (T4:2000) already exist. These instruments would have provided much better tests of convergent and discriminant validity than the 16PF or EPPS.

The fact that the majority of the SalesAP scales tap the extraversion domain can be seen as both a blessing and weakness of the test. On the positive side, many studies have shown that the extraversion domain is the most critical for success in sales. On the negative side, it appears that the SalesAP is measuring far fewer than 18 independent dimensions. Take for example the Sales Success scales, the primary focus of the SalesAP test. Because the Sales Success scale items are drawn from the existing item pool on the MAI, these three scales tend to correlate quite highly with several of the remaining 15 scales. For example, the Cold Calling scale is a "content-based subscore" (p. 27) of the Initiative scale, and is thus correlated above .90 with the Initiative scale. Both the Sales Disposition and Sales Closing scales correlate above .70 with several Domain scales. Although scale overlap is often misunderstood and too often criticized (see for example, Gough 1996 for an alternative viewpoint), a correlation above .90 presses the acceptable level of independence. One must ask whether the user of the SalesAP is getting much more than a multiscale assessment of extraversion.

Establishing the criterion-related validity of an instrument is the most important standard for a scale developed to be used in the work place. Thus, for the SalesAP, the ability to predict success in sales is paramount. To the test's credit, a large majority of the SalesAP scales correlated highly with supervisor ratings of sales performance in both concurrent and predictive studies and across several types of salespeople. One quizzical finding was that the best predictor of sales performance was often not one of the three Sales Success scales. In fact, across 12 supervisor ratings (four studies), scales from the other domains of the SalesAP met or exceeded the level of prediction of the three Sales Success scales in at least eight cases. It appears that interested consumers could use many of the SalesAP scales to predict sales success.

The SalesAP scales exhibit acceptable if not excellent levels of reliability. The internal consistency scales estimates ranged from .66 to .88, with most estimates exceeding .80. One-year test-retest reliability estimates were just as impressive, ranging from a low of .67 to a high of .90 with most estimates averaging around .80.

The normative information provided is sufficient. The authors describe the norm sample in detail; they also provide scale scores for gender, race, and different occupational groups such as salespeople, managers, and job applicants. The authors also provide detailed scale descriptions and case studies related to selection and development of sales people. The manual also contains information on scoring services and a sample report.

The SalesAP has several strengths. First, it appears to do a respectable job of predicting ratings of sales performance. However, it should be noted that none of the validity studies have been reported in peer-reviewed journals, so the quality of these studies is still unclear. Second, the scales show good levels of reliability. Finally, the manual

provides enough information for an informed consumer to judge the quality of the test in relation to other Sales performance predictors.

The primary weakness of the test is the false impression that it measures 18 distinct traits. Given the information in the test manual, the scales of the SalesAP fail to show adequate levels of construct validity. Furthermore, the addition of the three Sales performance scales adds little predictive utility over the original MAI scales. The lack of a factor analysis of the SalesAP scales is a second, related weakness of the test. Given the number of places that the authors invoke the use of factor analysis to develop specific scales, one would expect that an overall factor analysis of the SalesAP is feasible. A third flaw is the way the authors use the Response Style scales. Rather than using the scales to identify problematic protocols (e.g., people who may have lied), the authors argue that scale scores should be corrected for scores on the Response Style scales. To the contrary, numerous studies (e.g., Hough, 1998; Ones & Viswesvaran, 1998) have shown that correcting for "response style" does little or nothing to the validity of personality scales.

SUMMARY. Overall, the SalesAP appears to be useful for predicting sales success. Before the test can be endorsed, additional evidence for the convergent and discriminant validity of the test needs to be provided. One must also question, as has been questioned before (Camara, 1995), the need for another personality-based predictor of sales success. There are numerous tests in existence to do just that, many of which are embedded in more comprehensive instruments that will provide more complete descriptions of people.

REVIEWER'S REFERENCES
Edwards, A. L. (1959). The Edwards Personal Preference Schedule. San Antonio, TX: The Psychological Corporation.
Cattell, R. B. (1986). The Sixteen Personality Factor Questionnaire. Champaign, IL: Institute for Personality and Ability Testing.
Camara, W. J. (1995). Review of the Sales Personality Questionnaire. In J. C. Conoley & J. C. Impara (Eds.), The twelfth mental measurements yearbook (pp. 886-887). Lincoln, NE: Buros Institute of Mental Measurements.
Gough, H. (1996). The CPI manual. Palo Alto, CA: Consulting Psychologists Press.
Holland, J. L. (1997). Making vocational choices: A theory of vocational personalities and work environments. Odessa, FL: Psychological Assessment Resources, Inc.
Hough, L. M. (1998). Effects of intentional distortion in personality measurement and evaluation of suggested palliatives. Human Performance, 11, 209–244.
Ones, D. S., & Viswesvaran, C. (1998). The effects of social desirability and faking on personality and integrity assessment for personnel selection. Human Performance, 11, 245–270.

[330]

Sales Motivation Survey.

Purpose: Designed to assess the kinds of needs and values salespeople see as important considerations in making decisions about their work.

Population: Salespeople.
Publication Dates: 1972–1995.
Scores, 5: Basic Creative Comfort, Safety and Order, Belonging and Affiliation, Ego-Status, Actualization and Self-Expression.
Administration: Group.
Price Data, 1995: $7.95 per survey.
Time: Administration time is not reported.
Comments: Self-administered; self-scored.
Authors: Jay Hall and Norman J. Seim.
Publisher: Teleometrics International, Inc.

Review of the Sales Motivation Survey by LESLIE H. KRIEGER, Senior Consulting Psychologist, NCC Assessment Technologies, Jacksonville, FL:

[Editor's Note: This review is similar, and much of it is identical, to the review of the Incentives Management Index (173) by the same reviewer. This similarity in reviews is due to the similarity of the tests.]

The Sales Motivation Survey is a brief self-assessment that allows sales people to examine their motivational pattern and match that pattern to the level of need satisfaction available in a particular sales position. The Survey was designed in recognition of the fact that sales people who do not experience need satisfaction on the job often have lowered productivity and higher turnover. Both the individual sales person and the selling organization benefit when there is need congruency.

The needs assessed in the Sales Motivation Survey are those outlined in Maslow's Need Hierarchy Model onto which the authors overlay Herzberg's Hygiene-Motivator Theory. This theoretical amalgam results in two fundamental motivational types: Motivation Seekers who are motivated by the demands of the task and who have tolerance for poor environmental factors, and Maintenance Seekers who are motivated more by the nature of their environment. The Survey yields scores on each of the five Maslow need levels and an overall assessment of Motivation Seeker versus Maintenance Seeker style.

People unfamiliar with the theories of Maslow and Herzberg will find brief but quite insightful synopses of these models on the eight pages of the Survey booklet between the items themselves and the scoring grid. The authors provide concise definitions of each Maslow need level, linking these definitions to examples of actual sales motivation and behavior. They state their

underlying rationale for focusing on these models is to enable sales people to become aware of the operation of need systems and need conflict in order to better assess their own employment situation.

The assessment itself consists of 60 items, each of which contains the stem of a proposition about selling and two possible alternative conclusions or reactions to that proposition. The somewhat unusual format carries the following instructions:

> For each survey item, you have five points to distribute between two alternative reactions to the situation described. If A is completely characteristic and B is completely uncharacteristic, give 5 points to A and 0 points to B. If A is considerably characteristic and B is somewhat characteristic, give 4 points to A and 1 point to B. If A is only slightly more characteristic than B, give 3 points to A and 2 points to B. Each of the three combinations also may be reversed. (test booklet/manual, p. 2)

Responses are written directly into boxes coded for one of the five themes. The scoring consists of counting the number of points in the boxes for each of the themes and transposing those totals onto a large banded profile sheet. Normative bands on the profile sheet are derived from the responses of 409 sales people who are not further identified. No percentiles, standard scores, or other bases for score comparison are provided.

Although marketing materials from the publisher, Teleometrics, quote a research psychologist, "Reliability and validity studies on Teleometrics' materials were conducted within the stringent guidelines established by the American Psychological Association," repeated inquiries to the publisher confirmed that no such information was available for the Sales Motivation Survey. No test manual exists and there is no technical or psychometric documentation of any kind to support the design or use of the instrument.

SUMMARY. The complete absence of supporting psychometric data makes it impossible to recommend this attractively packaged assessment for anything other than a thought provoker or conversation starter on sales motivation issues. There appears to be no basis for its use in making decisions about sales career opportunities or performance management strategies.

Review of the Sales Motivation Survey by SHELDON ZEDECK, Chair and Professor of Psy-

chology, Department of Psychology, University of California, Berkeley, CA:

The Sales Motivation Survey (SMS) is a self-assessment instrument designed to help sales people assess the kinds of needs and values that they consider important in their work. It portends to provide information that will be helpful and meaningful regarding respondents' current and future success in sales. Sixty paired comparison items cover five need systems stemming from Maslow's Need Hierarchy Model and Herzberg's Hygiene-Motivator theory. The five needs are: (a) Basic Creature Comfort (concern with comfort, strain avoidance, pleasant working conditions, and environmental supports); (b) Safety and Order (concern with security and predictability); (c) Belonging and Affiliation (concern with social relationships and a preoccupation with being accepted as a member of a sales group); (d) Ego-Status (concern with achieving special status with the sales team and a desire for recognition); and (e) Actualization and Self-Expression (concern with testing personal potential and a preoccupation with challenge and opportunities to be creative). There are 24 statements for each need, with each statement paired with every other need a number of times so that each could be measured relative to the other four. The instrument is self-scored, with the advice that the respondent pay particular attention to the total constellation of needs rather than to only the strongest need. High scores on any need reflect those need systems that are *least* satisfied and which one should be most concerned about. If the high scores are associated with higher order needs (e.g., motivators), then the respondent is primed for using more mature behaviors and for making more constructive contributions to the organization's work, provided the organization can accommodate such opportunities. Higher scores on the lower order needs (e.g., hygiene factors) indicate the respondent is primed for dissatisfaction and a preoccupation with peripheral environmental factors that are not related to the work. The underlying practical rationale of the SMS is that by becoming aware of the operation of need systems and need conflict, the respondent is better able to assess his or her own situation and to engage in a self-development plan.

The 60 items and the 24 statements are clearly presented; the test is easily administered without any time frame. A chart is provided to allow the respondent to record his or her scores on a profile summary, which allows the respondent to interpret the pattern of scores.

The conceptual (construct) rationale and psychometric data for SMS are totally lacking. Though the items are purportedly based on Maslow's and Herzberg's research, there is no evidence presented regarding the construct validity of the five scores (needs). There is no evidence presented regarding the reliability of scores from the instrument. Likewise, there is no evidence presented regarding the relationship between scores on the SMS and other need scales, personality measures, or attitudinal (e.g., job satisfaction) and behavioral indices of work-related measures. Finally, the profile summary that is presented to the respondent indicates a band reflecting the average range of need scores from 409 salespeople. No data are provided with respect to the norm sample of 409; there is no description of gender, ethnicity, age, experience, success, etc. What is even more surprising is the fact that the test has been available since 1972 and revised in 1995, yet only 409 salespeople are used as the "norm."

SUMMARY. It is not clear why anyone would be interested in taking this instrument. There is no way to judge whether the instrument is worth the time to take. There is little guidance as to what to do with the results, much less what they mean in terms of future satisfaction or success. There is no prerequisite that there be discussion of the results with any professional; this situation could leave some respondents in a state of greater confusion or uncertainty than prior to taking the survey.

[331]
Sales Transaction Audit.

Purpose: Intended as an assessment of sales style and its impact on salesperson-customer transactions.
Population: Salespeople.
Publication Dates: 1972–1980.
Acronym: STA.
Scores, 3: Parent, Adult, Child.
Administration: Group.
Manual: No manual.
Price Data, 1997: $8.95 per test booklet.
Time: Administration time not reported.
Authors: Jay Hall and C. Leo Griffith.
Publisher: Teleometrics International.
Cross References: For a review by Stephen L. Cohen, see 8:1127.

Review of the Sales Transaction Audit by CHANTALE JEANRIE, Associate Professor, Measurement and Evaluation, Laval University, Quebec, Canada:

Reviewing the Sales Transaction Audit (STA) could have been a rather straightforward job. The fact that no information about the reliability or the validity of the STA is provided by the test's authors would be sufficient to impose a negative recommendation. However, because the STA could nevertheless appeal to some test users because of its apparent close connection with the specific behaviors of a selling job, it seems appropriate to review the instrument.

The general objective of the Sales Transaction Audit is to provide information about one's styles of interactions with different types of persons, in a sales context. Developed within the Transactional Analysis theory framework, a psychoanalytic theory that subdivides people's "subsystems" into three types—the Parent, the Adult, and the Child—the STA rests on the intuitively appealing assumption that effective selling will follow from the adoption of some effective transactional patterns. Therefore, the STA should permit the identification of effective salespeople and of transactional style deficiencies for which improvement should increase sales performance. A number of technical and conceptual deficiencies, however, lead this reviewer to believe that no such inferences can adequately be made from this test.

Because of its face validity, the content of the STA can be rather attractive. The test is composed of 18 situations made of a customer's question or assertion. For each situation, the respondent must distribute 5 points between three possible options, each representing either a Parent, Adult, or Child type of response. The test can be self-corrected, thus calling for clear and easy-to-follow directives. Not all directives are clear, however. The scoring of the Tension indices, meant to represent the percentage of one's transactions that will be characterized by either disruptive or constructive tensions, could easily lead to scoring mistakes. These indexes are calculated from scores that are circled or boxed on the scoring sheet. Circles and boxes are easy to localize but reporting them on the scoring sheet is made difficult by the arrangement by item, which is difficult to locate precisely on the responses column. The next step to calculate the Tension indices is

also complicated by a "formulae" that is presented without explanation or example. Whether the numbers provided must be divided or multiplied remains unclear and the unconventional visual expression of the formulae does not help to solve this problem. Of course, the implications of this lack of precise directives can have a dramatic impact on test scores.

Once the three main scores (Parent, Adult, Child) are computed, instructions and a Standard Scores table are given to transform raw scores into T scores. Transformation is easily completed. Details about the 307 individuals included in the normative sample are severely lacking, however. Although it is said that these individuals are from "a full range of sales organizations," more specific information regarding sales experience and performance, gender, and type of products sold would be essential to evaluate the population represented by these norms. The absence of such data should raise suspicion, and even more so because this is the second edition of the STA.

The interpretation guide provides an overview of the transactional analysis theory but it is doubtful that its content can genuinely be understood without further material or guidance. The content is explained well but is complex, and no developmental perspective is presented. Very few relations to the selling professions are made. The text mentions that "parallel-Adult" interactions might be the most productive but does not really explain how to "decode" the customer's way of entering a transaction nor how to modify one's habitual mode of transaction. In some regards, score explanations are also lacking. Although these indices should be important to assess the effectiveness of one's transactions, very little interpretative material is provided for the Tension indices, let alone any normative data that could serve to inform whether one uses disruptive or constructive transactions more or less than other salespeople. In addition, some details in the text may obscure score interpretation. For example, the "isolation" phenomenon is illustrated by an eloquent figure representing virtually impossible results given the Score summary plots on the scoring sheets. Also, although the explanations given for the "contamination" and "isolation" phenomena are expressed as T scores, the explanations of ideal score distributions are expressed in raw scores, and no mention is made of this difference. Serious misconceptions can result if the reader does not intuitively step from one type of score to the other.

Considered by this reviewer as a capital problem, the lack of information regarding the STA reliability and validity is without excuse. Because the response scale asks the test taker to distribute points among answers instead of choosing a particular option, the stability of the answers is at issue and thus requires that, at a minimum, an index of score stability be presented. Failure to provide such information should be considered as a major shortcoming. Still more serious are the deficiencies related to the expected demonstration of the scale validity. First, a quick note in the test directives threatens the validity of the scores interpretation. As a matter of fact, test takers are *invited* to fill out the test with a "fake-good" attitude, if desired. Although it is mentioned that results obtained should be interpreted in light of the option chosen, no other mention of this option is made anywhere. It is either assumed that "real" and "fake-good" answers are virtually identical, that faked or true response styles have the same impact on one's insights about his/her attitudes and behaviors, or that the test takers can spontaneously adapt the interpretation provided if they have chosen to "fake good." All these assumptions are weak, at best, and cannot stand without empirical support. More generally speaking, because the STA is developed to operationalize the transactional analysis theory, evidence of conceptual validity, documenting evidence of the link between the test and the measured construct, as well as evidence of the link between the construct and the context to which it is applied need to be provided. Neither of the two requirements are achieved. Although empirical relations with a selling behavior criteria would have been necessary to claim the appropriateness of the test to this specific context, either judgmental or empirical evidence that the items and answers of the STA are adequately linked to the Parent, Adult, and Child components would also be a necessary addition to this instrument before it should be used as proposed. In the absence of adequate and even minimal support for the inferences to be made from the Sales Transaction Audit test, it is legitimate to affirm that the test authors have failed in their responsibilities to provide tenable arguments about the quality and utility of the STA.

SUMMARY. After its second edition, the Sales Transaction Audit has yet to demonstrate its ability to reach its objectives. At this point, psychometric requirements are not met and technical shortcomings may even impede obtaining valid scores. As a consequence, it is this reviewer's opinion that the STA cannot be recommended for use, neither as a personnel selection device nor as a learning instrument aimed toward the development of more effective sales practices.

[332]
SAQ-Adult Probation III.

Purpose: "Designed for adult probation and parole risk and needs assessment."
Population: Adult probationers and parolees.
Publication Dates: 1985–1997.
Acronym: SAQ.
Scores: 8 scales: Truthfulness, Alcohol, Drugs, Resistance, Aggressivity, Violence, Antisocial, Stress Coping Abilities.
Administration: Group.
Price Data: Available from publisher.
Time: (30) minutes.
Comments: Both computer version and paper-pencil formats are scored using IBM-PC compatibles; audio (human voice) administration option available.
Author: Risk & Needs Assessment, Inc.
Publisher: Risk & Needs Assessment, Inc.
Cross Reference: For a review by Tony Toneatto, see 12:338.

Review of the SAQ—Adult Probation III by JONI R. HAYS, Senior Clinical Counselor and Adjunct Faculty School of Applied Health and Educational Psychology, Oklahoma State University, Stillwater, OK:

The SAQ, Version III, is a self-report and nondiagnostic instrument intended to assess substance abuse in mental health and criminal populations. The 165-item inventory contains true-false, Likert-type, and multiple-choice/blank-completion response formats. Version III incorporates separate scoring protocols and norms for men and women. The pencil/paper version is appropriate for individual and group administrations. Licensed user sites may administer the computerized version of the SAQ and obtain results "within 3 minutes of test completion" (An Inventory of Scientific Findings, p. ii).

Risks & Needs Assessment, Inc. chronicles development of the SAQ and summarizes more than two decades of research in a document entitled *The SAW Substance Abuse Questionnaire: An Inventory of Scientific Findings* (1996). Because of extensive use by State Departments of Correction (e.g., Missouri administered the SAQ to more than 10,000 inmates in 1996), substantial research with large sample sizes is available to current and potential users. This research supports consistently the statistical psychometric properties of the instrument.

The SAQ contains eight scales intended to measure constructs related to substance abuse treatment interventions. The Truthfulness scale purports to measure instrument validity and client truthfulness, defensiveness, and recalcitrance. According to SAQ documentation, Truthfulness scale scores below the 70th percentile suggest valid and accurate results; scores between the 70th and 89th percentile are, "Likely valid, but should be interpreted cautiously"; whereas scores above the 90th percentile are likely invalid and inaccurate. To yield more accurate results, other SAQ scale scores are adjusted based upon the index of client truthfulness.

The Alcohol scale is a measure of alcohol consumption (i.e., beer, wine, and other liquor) and alcohol-related problems. Independent of the Alcohol scale, the Drugs scale surveys drug use (i.e., marijuana, cocaine, crack, amphetamines, barbiturates, and heroin) and associated problems. The Antisocial scale offers information about client defensiveness, uncooperativeness, and resistance to intervention. Constructs measured by the Aggressivity scale include noncompliance, aggressiveness, and pushiness.

The Violence scale assesses client use of force to harm others or damage property. The Resistance scale measures antisocial, uncaring, hostile, disloyal, and unsociable behaviors. The Stress Coping scale provides information about client capacity to cope with stress and the relationship of stress to indices of mental health. In addition, the instrument incorporates information on alcohol and drug arrests, recent and current employment, and criminal history.

Users may find ambiguity in test publisher documentation about the role of client interviews. The SAQ Orientation and Training Manual describes the importance of structured interviews in gathering information on client motivation, attitude, outlook, bias, and perceptions. Other documentation characterizes the structured client interview as, "last sequence of multiple-choice items represent a concise structured interview" (An Inventory of Scientific Findings, p. 6).

A major strength of the SAQ lies in its multilingual (English and Spanish) and multimedia accessibility, allowing greater access for individuals with special needs. The SAQ and accompanying documentation offers a model of accessibility useful to test developers. Sensitivity to client confidentiality is demonstrated by an annual purge of client names from the SAQ research database maintained by the test publisher. The SAQ system offers flexibility to computerized users in the capacity to modify the SAQ for compliance with statutory or other requirements.

SUMMARY. The SAQ appears to be a sound instrument for assessing the treatment and intervention needs of criminal populations. Therefore, the SAQ may have limited applicability for other adult populations. The SAQ is user-friendly and offers substantial technical documentation for users. The computerized version, in particular, appears to be a flexible, efficient, and effective tool for client assessment.

REVIEWER'S REFERENCE

Behavior Data Systems, Ltd. (1996). *SAQ Substance Abuse Questionnaire: An inventory of scientific findings.* Phoenix, AZ: The author.

Review of the SAQ—Adult Probation III by ROBERT SPIES, Associate Director, Buros Institute of Mental Measurements, University of Nebraska—Lincoln, Lincoln, NE, and MARK COOPER, Training Specialist, Center on Children, Families & the Law, University of Nebraska—Lincoln, Lincoln, NE:

DESCRIPTION. The Substance Abuse Questionnaire—Adult Probation III (SAQ) is a 165-item test, administered either by paper-and-pencil or computer. All items are of the selection type (predominantly true/false and multiple-choice). Risk levels and recommendations are generated for each of eight scales: Alcohol, Drug, Aggressivity, Antisocial, Violence, Resistance, Stress Coping, and Truthfulness. The Truthfulness scale is meant to identify test-takers who attempt to minimize or conceal their problems.

Nonclinical staff can administer, score, and interpret the SAQ. Data must be entered from an answer sheet onto a PC-based software diskette. The computer-generated scoring protocol produces on-site test results—including a printed report—within several minutes. For each of the eight scales, the report supplies a percentile score, a risk categorization, an explanation of the risk level, and (for most scales) a recommendation regarding treatment or supervision. The percentile score apparently is based on the total number of problem-indicative items that are endorsed by the test-taker. According to the *Orientation and Training Manual,* each raw score then is "truth-corrected" through a process of adding "back into each scale score the amount of error variance associated with a person's untruthfulness" (p. 8). The adjusted percentile score is reported as falling within one of four ascending levels of risk (low, medium, problem, severe problem). The responsible staff person is expected to use information from the report, along with professional judgment, to identify the severity of risk and needs and to develop recommendations for intervention.

DEVELOPMENT. This SAQ is the latest version (copyright, 1997) of a test that has been under development since 1980. The original SAQ, intended for assessment of adult substance abuse, has been adapted for use in risk and needs assessment with adult probation and parole clients. Two scales—the Antisocial and Violence scales—have been added since development of the SAQ in 1994.

Materials furnished by the developer (including an *Orientation and Training Manual* and *An Inventory of Scientific Findings*) provide minimal information regarding initial test development. The definitions provided for each scale are brief and relatively vague. The constructs underlying several scales appear to overlap (e.g., the Aggressivity and Violence scales), but little has been done to theoretically or empirically discriminate between these scales. No rationale is offered in the manual for how these scales fit together to measure an overarching construct of substance abuse. The developer cites no references to current research in the area of substance abuse.

TECHNICAL. Information describing the norming process is vague. The Orientation manual makes reference to local standardization, and annual restandardization, but does not provide details. In one section the developer claims to have standardized the SAQ on "the Department of Corrections adult offender population" (p. 7). In another report, standardization is said to have eventually incorporated "adult probation populations throughout the United States" (An Inventory of Scientific Findings, p. 5). One might assume, based on the citing of SAQ research studies involving literally thousands of probationers that the recency and relevance of norms is beyond question. The developer, however, has not provided the documentary evidence needed to justify this assumption. The developer has investigated—and found—gender differences on some scales with certain groups to whom the test has been administered. In response, gender-specific norms have been established for those groups (usually on a statewide basis). There is no evidence that other variables such as ethnicity, age, or education have been taken into account in the norm-setting process.

The items selected for use in the test have several commonalities. Most items focus on personal behaviors, perceptions, thoughts, and attitudes and are linked in a direct and very obvious way to the content of associated scales (e.g., "I am concerned about my drinking," from the Alcohol scale). Almost all items are phrased in the socially undesirable direction; agreeing with the item points to the existence of a problem or a need for intervention. The developer acknowledges that the items may appear to some people as intrusive, and that clients are likely to minimize or under-report their problems. In the SAQ, the response to this concern has been the inclusion of the Truthfulness scale and calculation of "truth-corrected" scale scores. Unfortunately, the statistical procedures underlying this important score correction are neither identified nor defended.

Internal consistency for the individual subscales of the SAQ has been well-established by a large number of developer-conducted studies that report Cronbach alpha estimates generally in the .80s to .90s. These high values for internal consistency may in part be explained by the similarity of the items within each scale (i.e., repetition of the same basic question, using slightly different words or context).

Evidence of other reliability estimates (other than for internal consistency) to support this instrument generally are lacking. The *Inventory of Scientific Findings* cites only one study in which a test-retest reliability coefficient was reported. Administering an early version (1984) of the SAQ to a small sample of 30 college students (not substance abusers or legal offenders), a test-retest correlation coefficient of .71 was found across an interval of one week.

Evidence to support the validity of the SAQ is limited. Some concurrent validity evidence is presented, in the form of multiple studies showing modest correlations between some SAQ scales and subscales of the Minnesota Multiphasic Personality Inventory (MMPI). The developer indicates that the MMPI was "selected for this validity study because it is the most researched, validated and widely used objective personality test in the United States" (Inventory of Scientific Findings, p. 14). This explanation, however, does not suffice as a rationale for use of the MMPI to support concurrent validity; and no theoretical framework is provided about how the SAQ subscales relate to the personality constructs underlying the MMPI.

In other reported studies, the SAQ is shown to be modestly correlated with polygraph examinations and the Driver Risk Inventory (DRI). Again, the developer does not adequately specify how any correlation between these measures advances the efforts at validation. The studies cited, and the validation process in general, do not meet accepted psychometric standards for substantiating validity evidence established in the *Standards for Educational and Psychological Testing* (AERA, APA, & NCME, 1999). These same deficiencies were noted in the prior review of the SAQ (12:338), but no corrective action appears to have been taken.

COMMENTARY. The value of the SAQ as a measure of substance abuse severity with criminal justice populations seems to be compromised on a number of levels. First, the test lacks a clear focus. Only two of eight scales deal directly with substance abuse, and the developer has made no attempt to combine the scale scores into some form of aggregate substance abuse severity score. Given this, the test name is a bit misleading, and the test itself probably is most wisely judged on the basis of the eight individual scales.

Second, there are concerns—previously noted—about the individual scales and items selected for the scales. Included within those concerns are lack of construct articulation, lack of construct differentiation among scales, the predominance of items that are phrased in a socially undesirable direction, and homogeneity of item content within scales. Item phrasing and the bluntness of the items (e.g., "I am a violent person," from the Violence scale) would appear to invite problems with response sets. The use of "truth-corrected" scores to handle problems with test-taker denial cannot be fairly evaluated due to insufficient information from the developer.

Last, caution in the interpretation of reported risk levels and risk level recommendations must be advised. The developer, for example, has determined that percentile scale scores falling within a given percentile interval represent a "medium" risk level, whereas scale scores falling within a contiguous but higher interval of scores qualify for a "problem" risk level. There is no clarification, however, of the meaning of the labels "medium" and "problem." Further, there are no statements regarding how the two risk levels are to be discriminated from one another, and no identification of outcomes (or probabilities of outcomes) that are tied to the levels. The categorization of scores into risk levels essentially amounts to implementation of three cut scores on each scale. Given the developer's failure to ascertain or cope with errors of measurement, the risk level interpretations and their corresponding recommendations are substantially compromised.

SUMMARY. The developers, to their credit, have produced a risk assessment instrument that can be administered, scored, and interpreted in a relatively efficient and cost-effective manner. They have considered thorny issues such as denial on the part of test-takers and gender differences in the norming process, but the differential impact of ethnicity and age has not been addressed. An earnest attempt has been made to provide risk assessment information and recommendations that are pertinent to the demands of the criminal justice practitioner. On balance, however, the SAQ falls far short of the mark. Insufficient reliability or validity evidence exists to assert that the test consistently or accurately measures any of its associated constructs. There is continued doubt, in the words of the prior reviewer of the SAQ, that the test "conveys any useful information additional to simply asking the client if they have an alcohol-drug problem, if they are violent, and how they cope with stress" (Toneatto, 1995, p. 891). Readers seeking an alternative test for a substance abusing population may wish to consider tests such as the Substance Abuse Subtle Screening Inventory (SASSI; T5:2553).

REVIEWERS' REFERENCES

Toneatto, T. (1995). [Review of the SAQ—Adult Probation [Substance Abuse Questionnaire].] In J. C. Conoley & J. C. Impara (Eds.), *The twelfth mental measurements yearbook* (pp. 889–891). Lincoln, NE: Buros Institute of Mental Measurements.

American Educational Research Association, American Psychological Association, and National Council on Measurement in Education. (1999). *Standards for educational and psychological testing*. Washington, DC: American Educational Research Association.

[333]
Scale for Assessing Emotional Disturbance.

Purpose: Designed to assist in "the identification of children who qualify for the federal special education category of emotional disturbance."

Population: Students ages 5-0 to 18-11.

Publication Date: 1998.

Acronym: SAED.

Scores, 7: Inability to Learn, Relationship Problems, Inappropriate Behavior, Unhappiness or Depression, Physical Symptoms or Fears, Socially Maladjusted, Overall Competence.

Administration: Individual.

Price Data, 2001: $86 per complete kit.

Time: (10) minutes.

Comments: Should be "completed ... by teachers or other school personnel who have had substantial contact with the student."

Authors: Michael H. Epstein and Douglas Cullinan.

Publisher: PRO-ED.

Review of the Scale for Assessing Emotional Disturbance by SANDRA J. CARR, Certified School Psychologist, Harford County Public Schools, Bel Air, MD:

The Scale of Assessing Emotional Disturbance (SAED) is an instrument to aid in identifying children and adolescents, ages 5–18, who qualify for the special education category emotional disturbance (ED). The authors did a good job providing clarification of the definition of this disability. The SAED is based on the federal terminology and definition of emotional disturbance as presented in the Individuals with Disabilities Education Act of 1990. In order to qualify for ED, the federal definition includes five characteristics, of which one or more must be present over a long period of time and to a marked degree, that adversely affect educational performance. The SAED bases five of its subscales on these and terms them Inability to Learn, Relationship Problems, Inappropriate Behavior, Unhappiness or Depression, and Physical Symptoms or Fears. In addition, there are two subscales measuring Socially Maladjusted and Overall Competence.

The rationale for the SAED is very persuasive. It was developed based on characteristics determined from emotional disturbance (ED) literature, experiential knowledge of teachers and other practitioners, existing checklists, the federal definition of ED, and related publications. A list of 73 items (66 problems of emotion and behavior plus 7 competence items) was generated. In a study, 74 teachers completed scales on a modest number of students, ages 7 to 18, with ED (n = 369) and without ED (n = 386). One-way analyses of variance were significant for each item ($p<.0001$), indicating each item discriminated between the children with ED and those without ED. A factor analysis was also conducted on the 66 emotional and behavioral problem items with the students identified with ED. Five factors emerged, which were compared to the federal definition of ED. Item discrimination was next determined using the point biserial correlation technique. Those items with a value less than .3 were eliminated. The authors provide no specific data on this. In determining if the students' emotional and behavioral problems adversely affect the educational performance, a great deal of weight is given to just one item. As different raters will base their evaluations on their own personal experiences with the student, caution should be given for interpretation on a single question.

Two concurrent validity studies were conducted. Seven special education teachers completed the Teacher Report Form (TRF), a measure of emotional-behavioral problems and adaptive functioning, and the SAED on 61 students. Subscale scores and Total/Quotient scores correlations were all statistically significant. In the second study, the SAED and the Revised Behavior Problem Checklist (RBPC), a measure of emotional and behavioral problems, were completed by 12 special education teachers on 88 students with ED. All correlations were statistically significant.

To examine construct validity, the group identified as having emotional and behavioral disorders and the group not so identified were studied. T-tests were conducted on the seven subscales and the Quotient. Results indicate the differences were large enough to be statistically significant.

The SAED provides two sets of normative data. One is based on students not identified as having emotional disturbance (Non ED sample) and one on students diagnosed with emotional disturbance (ED sample). The standardization sample (Non ED sample) included 2,266 students ranging in age from 5-0 to 18-11 in 34 states. Characteristics such as gender, race, ethnicity, and family income were representative of the nation as a whole when compared with those reported in the Statistical Abstract of the United States (U.S. Bureau of the Census, 1990). The ED sample consisted of 1,371 students, ranging in age from

5-0 to 18-11. The authors did not state how or where these students were identified as ED.

Internal consistency reliability was computed using Cronbach's (1951) coefficient alpha method. All of the average coefficients for the subscales exceeded .75 and 6 of 16 exceeded .90. These indicate a reliable scale. The alphas for the five selected subgroups were also computed and were essentially the same as the average alphas, suggesting the SAED maintains its reliability level relative to the subgroups studied.

Time sampling was measured using the test-retest technique. Two studies were conducted of 53 and 33 students, both identified with ED, within a 2-week interval. The test-retest coefficient was .94 and .89 respectively, indicating adequate levels of reliability. Interrater reliability was measured on six pairs of special education teachers who independently rated 44 students identified with ED. The reliability coefficients for the subscales ranged between .51 to .84. For the SAED Quotient, the coefficient was .79. Even though interrater reliability is somewhat low, it is reasonably adequate considering the factors that can cause different raters to evaluate a student's emotional and behavioral tendencies differently. Scorer differences were measured from two staff persons in PRO-ED's research department independently scoring a set of 30 protocols randomly selected from the normative sample. The resulting coefficient was .99, suggesting a high scorer reliability.

Administration, scoring, and interpreting are quick and easy. In addition to raw scores, three kinds of normative scores were reported: percentile ranks, standard scores for the subscales, and a quotient representing overall emotional and behavior problems of the child rated. Scores can be graphically displayed, providing a visual presentation of the child's performance on the SAED. There are two norming samples each with three tables for a different age range: elementary, middle school, and high school age children.

The manual is clear and concise and very informative. It contains only a few errors, one being on page 27 under the heading "Overall Competence Subscale." It states "On the Overall Competence subscale, higher scores are considered deviant" and should read "... lower scores are considered deviant." The Inability to Learn subscale measures problems with school-related tasks. On the response form, Question 18 states "Listening and note-taking skills are weak." These are two separate skills and should have been listed separately.

SUMMARY. The SAED promises to be a practical and useful guide for determining the existence of the disabling condition emotional disturbance as defined by federal legislation and regulations. Although the identification decision must be reached from multiple assessments, the SAED is an objective measure that could provide important data about the emotional and behavioral problems of children and adolescents.

REVIEWER'S REFERENCES

Cronbach, L. J. (1951). Coefficient alpha and the internal structure of tests. *Psychometrika, 16,* 297–334.

U.S. Bureau of the Census. (1990). *Statistical abstract of the United States.* Washington, DC: Author.

Review of the Scale for Assessing Emotional Disturbance by GRETCHEN OWENS, Associate Professor of Child Study, St. Joseph's College, Patchogue, NY:

The Scale for Assessing Emotional Disturbance (SAED) was developed primarily to provide a standardized way for assessors to determine eligibility for special educational services by linking assessment directly to the federal definition of emotional disturbance. The authors also suggest that the SAED can be used for prereferral screening, to select goals for the IEP, and to document progress. To do this, a rater (usually the teacher, though the authors suggest that it may also be a parent or other adult who is familiar with the student's functioning) completes a total of 53 items measuring a student's competence in intellectual and academic functioning, extracurricular activities, peer support, family support for school, motivation, and personal hygiene; potentially problematic behaviors; and the rater's perception of how much the student's academic and extracurricular performance is adversely affected by his or her emotional and behavioral problems.

A trained examiner then sums the scores for the 7 items in the competence section, and for the 6–10 items in each of the five subscales in the problems section, to calculate an Overall Competence score and five problem scores: Inability to Learn, Relationship Problems, Inappropriate Behavior, Unhappiness or Depression, and Physical Symptoms or Fears. These five subscales represent the five characteristics in the federal definition of emotional disturbance, at least one of which must be present to a marked degree in order for a student to be eligible for special educational services. For students 12 years of age and older, a Socially Maladjusted score is also calculated to represent antisocial behaviors that violate legal or community standards but are supported and encouraged by a peer subgroup or gang.

Two separate sets of norms are provided, one based on a sample of 2,266 students, ages 5 to 18, not identified as having any emotional disturbance ("NonED"), the other from a sample of 1,371 students of the same age who were currently receiving special education services for emotional disorders ("ED"). The authors recommend that the NonED norms be used for screening and for making eligibility decisions, and the ED norms be used to assist in intervention planning, placement, and evaluating progress as a result of intervention. Extensive data indicate that the NonED standardization sample is roughly representative of the school-age population, using 1990 U.S. Census data. The ED normative group was selected to have "demographic characteristics that conform to what is known about school-age children who have been diagnosed with emotional disturbance" (examiner's manual, p. 26) (i.e., proportionately more male, more Black, and fewer Hispanic students).

Extensive reliability data are provided. Internal consistency (using Cronbach's alpha) was acceptable for most scales. The overall SAED quotients were over .90 for both samples at all age levels. Ninety percent of the coefficient alphas for subscales and quotients at 14 age levels were over .80 for the NonED group, with Inability to Learn and the overall Quotient over .90. Two subscales had insufficient reliability at some ages: Unhappiness/ Depression at ages 5 and 6, and Physical Symptoms/ Fears at ages 6–8 and 15–17. Among the ED sample, two subscales (Physical Symptoms/Fears and Overall Competence) failed to reach minimal levels of reliability at nearly all ages, and Socially Maladjusted was borderline. A breakdown by gender and race shows that the quotient and subscale reliabilities are roughly equal for all subgroups.

Test-retest reliability was generally good to excellent across two studies, with coefficients ranging from .84–.94 (1- to 2-week interval) for subscales and .89 to .94 for the overall problem quotients. Interrater reliability (based on ratings by six pairs of special education teachers working with the same students) was less acceptable. Correlations over .80 were obtained for Inappropriate

Behavior, Inability to Learn, Socially Maladjusted, and Overall Competence. Two subscales—Physical Symptoms/Fears and Unhappiness/Depression— were unacceptably low, at .51 and .61, respectively.

The section on content validity attests to the authors' thoroughness. They reviewed the professional literature, examined existing measurement devices, and analyzed the federal definition of ED, then wrote 85 items addressing children's emotional and behavioral problems and 9 competence items. These were later narrowed down via principal components analyses to a 66-item experimental version, which was completed by the norming sample. Items that did not load well on any factor, that were redundant, or that did not reach the .30 level in item-discrimination analyses were eliminated. This process resulted in the present 52-item scale. Studies of criterion-related validity compared the SAED to the Teacher Report Form (Achenbach, 1991a) and four subscales of the Revised Behavior Problem Checklist (Quay & Peterson, 1996). SAED Quotients correlated .80 with the TRF and .86 with the RBPC Total scores.

In support of construct validity, the authors note that they developed the subscales of the SAED empirically, using factor analysis, and from theoretically based items derived from their analyses of the federal definition of ED. They argue further for the construct validity of scores from the SAED by demonstrating that mean scores of groups of ED and NonED students differ significantly, with ED samples scoring about one standard deviation higher than the normal group on problem subscales and quotients, and one standard deviation lower on the Competence subscale. Unfortunately, the authors fail to spell out details regarding the scale's sensitivity and specificity. These numbers are key in determining whether the SAED is effective in achieving its stated goal of accurately identifying students with ED. This omission is particularly disquieting because of the authors' statement that a score at or above the 91st percentile on any of the problem subscales indicates a high likelihood of ED. This cutoff is considerably less stringent than the 95th–98th percentile recommended for other established rating scales. Any criterion that identifies 9% of all students on *each* of five subscales (even allowing for some children scoring high on more than one) is likely to result in cumulative prevalence rates of severe emotional disturbance that are considerably above the general estimates of 5%–10% of the school-age population.

The SAED possesses several strengths. First, the manual is clear and detailed, written for the everyday user of the test; in fact, the sections on psychometrics provide a good basic tutorial on the topic. The authors appropriately caution that this instrument is only one part of a complete assessment for ED, and they provide a section at the end of the SAED called "Key Questions" that can be used as the basis for an interview with the rater. These questions can help the examiner focus the rater on positive characteristics of the student. The authors also offer suggestions for using this information on the student's resources to develop recommendations, and the sample recommendations in the manual provide a good model.

Nonetheless, there are several problems with the current edition, some conceptual, some practical. Because the measure is structured around the federal definition of ED, it shares the same limitations as the definition. First, the definition is somewhat imprecise, and the authors have chosen interpretations with which some users will take issue, such as their contention that "inappropriate types of behavior and feelings in normal circumstances" refers only to aggressive and disruptive behaviors. Further, they have sidestepped the vagueness of the federal requirement that the ED be present "over a long period of time" by interpreting it as a requirement that *the rater* have known the student at least 2 months. This latter requirement was clearly not the intended meaning of the federal definition. Second, the federal category of "emotional disturbance" covers both emotional and behavioral disorders. In the SAED, as in the federal definition, behavioral problems tend to be neglected. Only one SAED subscale—Inappropriate Behavior—addresses behavioral problems, whereas three cover different types of emotional disorders. Third, it is arguable whether "an inability to learn which cannot be explained by intellectual, sensory, or health factors" should be part of the federal definition of emotional disturbance at all, as it better describes a learning disability.

A second set of problems has to do with the SAED items and rating system. Many of the items require the rater to make inferences—always a risky undertaking—about the student's thoughts or feelings ("fails to consider consequences of own acts," "has feelings of worthlessness," "has overly

sensitive feelings and emotions"). In addition, the ratings for items on the behavior problems subscales, rather than being based upon the frequency of observable behaviors, involve a subjective judgment that the behavior, feeling, or trait is *not a problem, mild problem, considerable problem,* or *severe problem.* Specific behavioral descriptions with a 4- or 5-point frequency rating from "seldom or never" through "more than once an hour" would provide greater objectivity. The one item assessing educational impact is also subjective and even more difficult to accurately rate, with its 6 scale points of *not adversely affected, affected to a slight extent, …to a moderate extent, …to a considerable extent, …to a severe extent,* or *…to an extreme extent.* Many teachers will find it hard to differentiate accurately between "considerable," "severe," and "extreme," but only the latter two scores are said to represent true educational need that qualifies the student for special educational services.

Another practical problem involves the organization of the manual. The "Administration and Scoring Procedures" and "Interpreting the Results" sections need some judicious editing and rearrangement. The background information presented in the "Overview" section is valuable, but frequently repetitive. A more succinct presentation would encourage the average user to read it in its entirety.

Another practical problem results from the authors' attempt to keep the summary/response form short and simple. They have therefore placed the Competence scale (on which a higher score indicates better functioning) next to the five problem subscales (on which a higher score indicates *worse* functioning), both in the norms table and on the profile of Standard Scores. It is likely that this will lead to confusion among some users of the test, especially in light of the error on page 27 stating that higher scores on the Overall Competence subscale are considered deviant. This is clearly inaccurate and contradicts page 20, where the authors state correctly that *low* scores on the competence subscale indicate problems.

The norms are problematic in other ways as well. First, even though the psychometric studies involved separate analyses for each year from ages 5 to 18, the norms tables are set up with students grouped into three excessively large age ranges: all children 5–11 (elementary age) in one norm group, 12- to 14-year-olds (middle school) in another,

15–18 (high school) in the third. Behaviors that are developmentally inappropriate for an 11-year-old may be quite common among 5-year-olds. Second, the authors state that the rater is usually a teacher, but also may be a parent, counselor, social worker, or close relative. However, only school personnel completed the scale in the normative sample. It is inappropriate to use the same norms for ratings from teachers (who have considerable experience with students of a given age) and those from parents (who, with a limited basis for comparison, have been shown in numerous studies to overidentify problem behaviors). The third—and most troubling—norms issue relates to the separate norms for ED and NonED samples, with no combined norm group. Because the NonED sample excluded any student with known emotional or behavioral problems, extreme care must be taken in using this scale as the authors recommend for eligibility decisions. A student who scores at the 91st percentile compared to this sample is scoring relatively high *for NonED children.* Looked at another way, if we follow the authors' recommended cutoff, 9% of the NonED children in the normative sample would have been considered to have an emotional disturbance on each of the five subscales, even though *none* of the students in that sample were so classified.

SUMMARY. The brevity and ease of scoring of the SAED will make it a tempting alternative to other behavior rating scales. The authors provide a clear, detailed, literature-based description of the theory and rationale behind the scale's development, and they have done a thorough job of validating their instrument. Its partial focus on a student's competencies and positive characteristics may aid in intervention planning. On the other hand, a couple of cautions are in order. Because the scale was normed only on school personnel, it should not be completed by a parent. It can provide a valuable view of a particular teacher's perceptions of the student, but due to the weak interrater agreement, it is highly advisable to have a second independent rater complete the scale as well. Finally, extreme caution should be taken in interpreting results, as it is highly debatable that all scores more than one standard deviation above the mean indicate emotional disturbance that warrants special educational services. Further discriminant validity studies clearly are needed.

According to the publisher, a strength-based parent scale—the Behavioral and Emotional Rating Scale—and a student self-rating scale are currently undergoing revision and data collection. Until these complementary components are available, examiners would do well to rely upon one of the more extensively investigated and comprehensive measures, such as the multi-axial Child Behavior Checklist (Achenbach, 1991b, 1992; T5:451).

REVIEWER'S REFERENCES
Achenbach, T. M. (1991a). *Manual for the Teacher's Report Form and 1991 profile.* Burlington: University of Vermont, Department of Psychiatry.
Achenbach, T. M. (1991b). *Manual for the Child Behavior Checklist/4–18 and 1991 profile.* Burlington: University of Vermont, Department of Psychiatry.
Quay, H. C., & Peterson, D. R. (1996). *Revised Behavior Problem Checklist: Professional manual.* Odessa, FL: Psychological Assessment Resources.

[334]
Scale of Marriage Problems: Revised.

Purpose: Designed to measure marital conflicts.
Population: Couples.
Publication Dates: 1975–1992.
Scores, 7: Problem-Solving, Childrearing, Relatives, Personal Care, Money, Outside Relationships, Total.
Administration: Group.
Price Data: Available from publisher.
Time: Administration time not reported.
Comments: Current edition now included in *Innovations in Clinical Practice: A Source Book* (Vol. II).
Authors: Clifford H. Swensen, Michele Killough Nelson, Jan Warner, and David Dunlap.
Publisher: Clifford H. Swensen.

Review of the Scale of Marriage Problems: Revised by CINDY CARLSON, Professor of Educational Psychology, University of Texas at Austin, Austin, TX:

The Scale of Marriage Problems: Revised is a 43-item measure of marital problems perceived by each spouse. The measure contains six subscales of problem domains derived from factor analysis. The revised scale contains the same items as the original scale published in 1975 (Swenson & Firoe, 1975, cited in Swensen, Nelson, Warner, & Dunlap, 1991). In the revised version the Likert response format has been expanded from three to five choices, and separate versions of the measure for husbands and wives are now available. Because items remain the same on the original and revised scale, the separate forms for husbands and wives appear to differ only in wording appropriate to the sex/marital role of the respondent. The scale has most frequently been used for providing direction to clinicians regarding areas in need of change in marriage counseling. Lack of adequate test validation data currently limits broader utility.

The structural properties of the test appear to be fairly good. The items have excellent face validity. All items used in the measure were marked as problematic for couples from both functional and dysfunctional marriages. Items are easy to comprehend and do not require a high reading level. Directions for scoring are simple and straightforward. Test-taking directions are also clear and normalize the existence of problems in all marriages. The measure is cost effective in that completion time is brief, and any answer sheet with spaces for a five-choice multiple-choice format may be used in conjunction with the measure. A major shortcoming is the lack of a test manual. Additionally, scoring interpretation guidelines are not based on actual data but rather appear to reflect the authors' clinical experience with the scale.

Normative data for the new version of the scale were based on a sample of 213 married people, most of whom were college educated and had been married an average of 18 years. Additional descriptive data were provided with a community sample of 60 couples seeking marriage counseling and a matched sample of 60 nondistressed couples. These test validation samples are relatively small. Moreover, the samples are neither adequately described nor are criteria for matching samples made explicit in Swensen et al., 1992. There are no data, for example, on socioeconomic status or ethnicity of the sample, and no data are provided on the range of ages, education levels, or marriage lengths of the sample. Based on the limited population data provided, the sample appears to be very homogeneous, and generalizability to different populations would not be warranted.

The psychometric properties of the revised scale have not, as yet, been adequately determined. Reliability estimates for internal consistency of the subscales range from .66 to .90, with a total scale alpha of .93. Reliability was reportedly enhanced with the use of separate spousal versions; however, reliability estimates for these subsamples are not provided by the authors. Test-retest reliability has not been published. The revised scale retains the original items and subscales that were determined using principal components factor analysis. No additional construct validation data are reported except that items on the revised scale are unrelated to social desirability (Dunlap, 1991, cited in Swensen et al., 1992). The revised scale discriminated significantly between a group of dysfunctional married couples seeking counseling and the matched nondistressed married couples group on all subscales as well as the total scale score. The measure did not find differences on marital problems between chronically ill and healthy older men. Thus, there is promising evidence of the discriminative validity of the revised scales in identifying troubled marriages. No predictive validity studies have been published. Nor have the revised scales been evaluated for sensitivity to change related to therapeutic intervention.

SUMMARY. The Scale of Marriage Problems: Revised, based on face validity and a single discriminant validity study, appears to have potential functional utility as a measure for screening dysfunctional marriages and for assisting clinicians in treatment planning. Functional clinical utility, as well as research utility, would be greatly enhanced with a test manual and additional studies documenting the technical properties (reliability, validity, and generalizability) of the measure to diverse populations. Until additional studies are completed in support of the psychometric properties of the measure, it should be used judiciously.

REVIEWER'S REFERENCE

Swensen, C. H., Nelson, M. K., Warner, J., & Dunlap, D. (1992). Scale of marriage problems: Revised. In L. VandeCreek, S. Knapp, & T. L. Jackson (Eds.), *Innovations in clinical practice: A source book* (vol. 11) (pp. 293–302). Sarasota, FL: Professional Resource Press.

Review of the Scale of Marriage Problems: Revised by DELORES D. WALCOTT, Assistant Professor, Counseling and Testing Center, Western Michigan University, Kalamazoo, MI:

In lieu of a manual the information provided for this review was taken from a book entitled, *Innovation in Clinical Practice: A Source Book* (vol. II), edited by VandeCreek, Knapp, and Jackson (1992). The scale under review was originally published in 1975 and republished in 1992. The Scale of Marriage Problems: Revised was designed to measure marital problems of dysfunctional couples. The scale is also useful as a diagnostic tool to evaluate specific items that husbands and wives cannot agree on, and it can indicate specific areas of trouble.

TEST DEVELOPMENT AND REVISION. The revised test comprises the same 43 items as the original scale. Unlike the original 3-point Likert scale, the revised scale uses a 5-point Likert scale for each item. In addition, two versions of the scale are provided, one for husbands and one for wives. These changes were made to improve the reliability of the scale. The original scale was derived from the marriage problems described by 35 dysfunctional married couples. Data were also obtained from a matched sample of 35 couples. One hundred items initially formed the scale, which was administered to the same sample. The data were factor analyzed using the principal components method, using a varimax rotation method that produced six main factors. Limited evidence concerning the results and a matrix of the results are provided. The revised Scale of Marriage Problems does not appear to be based on any particular model or theory.

USERS' QUALIFICATIONS, ADMINISTRATION, AND SCORING. In the documentation provided for the review, there was no statement regarding users' qualifications for either administration, scoring, or interpretation. In addition, the authors suggested that people from a wide variety of ages and educational backgrounds have no difficulty completing the scale. Specific details regarding user qualifications and to whom the test should be administered are needed.

The scale is easily administered making it an attractive choice. However, instructions for administering the scale, which are described in the Source Book, are limited and sketchy. Similarly, no formal answer sheet was provided. The authors suggested that any answer sheet with space for a five-choice answer can be used or answers may be marked on the test booklet.

The scales for both husband and wife are presented in the Source Book. It would be more appropriate to provide separate forms or have available for purchase separate forms. As indicated, the scores are derived by summing the items that comprise each scale. The scores are then compared to the normative or community scores. On the subscale on which one troubled married couple scores more than one standard deviation higher than the normative sample or the community sample, this indicates an area of serious marriage problems. The specific items on which husbands and wives disagree have been found to indicate specific areas of trouble within a marriage. Because most consumers are accustomed to conversion tables and charts when scoring, the authors might consider incorporating charts and scoring tables in their next publication.

SCALES AND NORMS. The authors indicated that the 43 items on the scale were empiri-

cally derived via factor analysis and yield six subscales: Problem-Solving, Decision Making, and the Goals of Marriage Scale; Childbearing and Home Labor Scale; Relatives and In-Laws Scale; Personal Care and Appearance Scale; Money Management Scale; and Outside Friendships and Expression of Affection Scale.

The normative sample for the revised version (1982) consisted of 213 married people, 102 men and 111 women. The normative sample was reasonably small making generalization problematic. It was noted that most of the samples consisted of husbands and wives married to each other, and that the spouses of a few of the people did not complete the scale. Their mean age was 42.06; average age when married was 23.9; and average length of marriage was 18.27 years. Most were college educated. Thus, the revised Scale of Marriage Problems is not representative of the general population but might be useful for couples seen at university and college counseling centers. One other source of concern is associated with there being no mention of ethnic background of couples nor allowance for couples who are in live-in relationships.

RELIABILITY. Reliability was estimated by Cronbach's alpha. Reportedly, reliabilities on each subscale for the revised version are higher than for the original version. However, reporting reliabilities alone, which typically varies from one group of test takers to another, is less informative. In the next publication the authors should include standard errors of measurement, confidence intervals, and/or other measures of estimates.

VALIDITY. The reviewer's major reservation is a question of validity. The authors indicated that for comparison purposes, matched samples of 60 married couples seeking marriage counseling were matched with 60 married couples from similar communities. The dysfunctional married couples scored significantly higher on all the subscales than the couples from the community. The community sample obtained scores that were approximately the same as those obtained by the normative sample. No differences in the scores were found between males and females. There were no other known studies provided for this review. Ideally, tests for clinical usage should undergo several types of validation study. Furthermore, data regarding ethnic background were omitted. Needed is a series of studies specifically designed to evaluate objectively the validity of scores from the revised version of the Scale of Marriage Problems.

SUMMARY. Although the Scale of Marriage Problems: Revised is available as a clinical tool and as a screening instrument, several cautions must be emphasized. Even though the Source Book cites references that suggest that the items on the scale are not influenced by social desirability, I strongly question this notion. It is a known fact that self-reporting is vulnerable to underreporting, distortions due to response style bias, inaccurate reporting, defensiveness, and denial. This is true with most self-reporting measures. Therefore, test users should proceed with caution when interpreting test results. Although self-reports have clear limitations, they have some validity related to standardization, economics, limited training required for administration, and administration time.

I recommend the revised version of the Scale of Marriage and Problems primarily as a research instrument; to use it in applied clinical work would be premature at this time. The authors frequently refer the reader to outside sources to gain crucial information that would have been better included in the text of the source book. Also, details to many of the studies presented as evidence of validation lack sufficient detail for proper evaluation of reliability, validity, and normative data. Furthermore, the authors should consider publishing a much needed manual that would provide enough information to help reduce the likelihood of misunderstanding or misuse of test data. The manual should be written to contemporary standards of completeness regarding test development, scoring, narrative information, and evidence of reliability and validity. Similarly, additional research on the reliability and validity of scores from the test using larger samples that include sufficient numbers in varying ethnic and educational background is needed. These concerns should be addressed in future publication of this scale. Perhaps using the scale as a quick screen, or as a way to elicit further information in an interview, may be appropriate.

REVIEWER'S REFERENCE

Swensen, C. H., Nelson, M. K., Warner, J., & Dunlap, D. (1992). Scale of Marriage Problems: Revised. In L. VandeCreek, S. Knapp, & T. L. Jackson (Eds.), *Innovation in clinical practice: A source book* (vol. II) (pp. 293-302). Sarasota, FL: Professional Resource Press.

[335]
Scales for Predicting Successful Inclusion.

Purpose: Designed to identify students with disabilities for potential for success in general education classes.
Population: Ages 5–18.
Publication Date: 1997.
Acronym: SPSI.
Scores: 4 scales: Work Habits, Coping Skills, Peer Relationships, Emotional Maturity.
Administration: Group.
Price Data, 1999: $79 per complete kit including manual (47 pages) and 50 summary/response forms; $39 per 50 summary/response forms; $42 per manual.
Time: (5–10) minutes.
Comments: Ratings by teachers, parents, and/or assistants.
Authors: James E. Gilliam and Kathleen S. McConnell.
Publisher: PRO-ED.

Review of the Scales for Predicting Successful Inclusion by DAVID GILLESPIE, Social Science Faculty, Detroit College of Business, Warren, MI:

The Scales for Predicting Successful Inclusion (SPSI) is designed to identify those students with disabilities, ages 5 through 18, who could be successful in a regular education environment. The instrument can also be used to identify school adjustment problems children may demonstrate. Results can furthermore be employed to identify intervention targets, assess changes as a result of intervention, and identify students appropriate for referral.

The SPSI attempts to assess behavior in four domains. These areas include Work Habits, Coping Skills, Peer Relationships, and Emotional Maturity. Work Habits focuses on a student's ability to follow directions, obey rules, and listen to instructions. The Coping Skills scale assesses a student's ability to deal with the conflict and stress that might result from interacting with others. The Peer Relations scale assesses a student's social skills. The Emotional Maturity section focuses on a student's perceived emotional adjustment.

The instrument consists of 60 behavioral descriptions and is to be completed by teachers or those familiar with a student's behavior in the classroom. The rater compares the behavior of a target child with the behavior of normally developing students of the same age. A 9-point Likert scale is used to quantify rater perceptions. Individuals who are familiar with the target child and normative functioning in the school setting can complete the rating scale in approximately 5 to 10 minutes.

There is no specialized training needed to administer or score the SPSI. In order to properly interpret the test results one should be familiar with basic measurement concepts. Although the manual states that teacher assistants and parents can complete the scale, the scale was normed based on the perceptions of teachers. Certainly, further research appears appropriate to support the reliability and validity of these scores when the scale is completed by parents.

Scoring is achieved by converting raw scores to standard scores and percentile ranks by using tables located in the Appendix. The sum of the standard scores for each the subscales is then converted into a measure of overall functioning referred to as the Successful Inclusion Quotient (SIQ). The SIQ has a mean of 100 and a standard deviation of 15. These scores can be plotted on the front of the Summary/Response Form. Students with school adjustment problems will have low scores suggesting a low probability of successful inclusion, whereas high scores are more likely to be achieved by those individuals who have a greater likelihood of being successful in inclusive settings. The manual also contains guidelines for interpreting SPSI standard scores. The authors underscore the importance of not using this instrument as the only means of assessment. Clearly, educational placement decisions should be made on the basis of information gained from multiple informants, including the student in question.

The SPSI was normed on a sample of 1,715 school-age children in the United States. Of this group, 50% had some form of disability (educational and/or behavioral). One-half (approximately 429) of this group were identified as Learning Disabled, 12% (approximately 102) were identified as having speech impairments, and 9% (approximately 77) were identified as mentally retarded.

Students employed in the normative sample were identified by general and special education teachers and principals. The educators themselves were respondents to a recruitment mailing conducted by the test authors. The names of 5,000 educators were randomly selected. Approximately 100 teachers and principals agreed to collect data. In addition, 27 educators known to the authors took part in the standardization sampling.

Test items were developed after reviewing the literature and other rating scales. A pool of 20 items was developed for each scale. Special and general education teachers, university professors, and test construction experts reviewed these items.

Content validity was studied by examining the relationship between the various items and the scale or portion of the SPSI it represents. Item discrimination studies strongly supported internal consistency with median item-to-scale correlations ranging from .85 to .91. Construct validity was also supported in relation to group differentiation and item performance.

Concurrent and criterion-related validity studies examined the relationship between the SPSI and the Conners' Teacher Rating Scales, Adjustment Scales for Children and Adolescents, and the Comprehensive Scales of Student Abilities. Typically, significant negative correlations were found between the various subscales of the SPSI and the comparative behavior rating scales.

Overall reliability evidence was found to lie within acceptable limits. Internal consistency for the full scale and for the subtests, based on Cronbach's alpha, fell within the range of .80s and .90s. These findings suggest that the items within the scale are homogeneous.

Two test-retest studies were conducted in order to investigate the stability of the SPSI scores over time. The first study consisted of 18 subjects with disabilities. The teachers rated the subjects on the SPSI at 1-week intervals. Correlation coefficients ranged from .63 to .98. In the second study all the correlation coefficients were greater than .60 and significantly different from zero at $p<.05$. Although these results provide strong evidence of test-retest reliability, further research to support this stability over greater periods of time is warranted. Interrater reliability was also estimated (correlation coefficients ranged from $r = .84-.94$).

There are many aspects of this scale that reflect sound test development practices. However, the most significant limitation focuses on its use in relation to children who present the greatest challenge to education in the general classroom setting or full inclusion. Although the standardization sample reflected the general distribution of children with specific forms of disabilities found in the educational setting, the vast majority of the children who were evaluated as part of the normative sample fell into categories that are normally considered to reflect relatively mild impairments. By contrast, the term full inclusion is usually reserved for an approach to the educational placement of more severely impaired children, such as those with some level of cognitive impairment or mental retardation, autism, or severe emotional disturbance. The standardization sample only included about 77 students who were identified as mentally retarded and no children identified as autistically impaired. As such, further research employing this scale in relation to this more significantly impacted group of students is recommended.

SUMMARY. The SPSI is a 60-item scale designed to identify the probability of a child's successful inclusion in a regular education setting based on their behaviors in particular target areas. It is designed to be completed by teachers who are familiar with the child who has a handicapping condition, based on their knowledge of the child's behavior compared to the functioning of normally developing children. Although parents and paraprofessionals can also complete it, data were not gained based on their perceptions and interrater reliability across teacher and parent perceptions was not examined at the time of scale development. Test results can also be employed to identify intervention targets and to chart progress over time. The principal weakness of the scale focuses on the relative lack of more significantly impacted students, such as those with some level of mental retardation, in the normative sample. Although these individuals were included in the norm group in a manner equal to their proportion in the national population, it is this group of students who are normally considered the target of inclusionary education. Students who had been identified as LD or speech and language impaired made up the greatest proportion of the special education population employed in the normative sample. Yet these students are already largely educated in general education settings in most school districts.

Review of the Scales for Predicting Successful Inclusion by JOSEPH R. MANDUCHI, Clinical Associate, Susquehanna Institute, Harrisburg, PA:

The Scales for Predicting Successful Inclusion (SPSI) is identified by the authors as a Norm referenced instrument for identifying students with disabilities for successful inclusion into general education. It is a 60-item instrument that contains four scales for rater estimates of Work habits, Coping Skills, Peer Relationships, and Emotional Maturity.

Each scale consists of 15 questions that are all behaviorally based. Each question is prefixed with the statement, "Compared to average students of the same age, rate the student in terms of …" (Protocol, p. 1), and then the item follows. Each item is scored on a 9-point Likert scale with ratings of Below, Average, and Above. Each rating is then subdivided into three numerical subratings that comprise the 9-point rating. Each scale then derives a "raw score," which is the sum for all ratings for the 15 questions of the scale. The raw scores are converted to a standard score between 1–20 (mean = 10, *SD* = 3) and subsequent percentile rankings. The sum of the scaled scores can be converted to a "Successful Inclusion Quotient" (SIQ), which is presented in customary fashion with a mean of 100 and a standard deviation of 15. Finally, the standard scores for the four SPSI scales can be converted to a probability rating for success in general education. The probability ratings are titled Extremely Probable, Highly Probable, Probable, Borderline, Unlikely, and Very Unlikely. The scores are easily interpreted by most professionals with only a casual knowledge of psychometrics and statistics.

Questions for each scale are presented in blocks of 15 questions. When rating questions about Coping Skills, for example, the rater answers all questions at one time. Therefore a mixing of the questions from the various scales is recommended.

The purpose of the test is to (a) identify specific problems in school adjustment, (b) identify strengths and weaknesses for intervention, (c) provide evidence of the need for referral to special education, (d) target goals for individualized education programs, (e) document progress, (f) provide evidence that students from special education are prepared for general education classes, and (g) to measure school adjustment skills and characteristics in research projects. Ostensibly this is all accomplished from the four scale scores, the Successful Inclusion Quotient, the Probability Ratings for Success, and the 60 rated questions. This seems ambitious.

The SPSI was normed on 1,715 school-aged children. The normative sample was collected by 100 experienced education professionals who taught students with disabilities as well as those without any known disability. The normative data did not yield differences based on age and as a result all students are scored and compared to the large norming sample. Conversion tables are provided for boys and girls both with and without known disabilities.

The test is a simple instrument with easy-to-understand questions and easy scoring procedures. It can be completed by most raters in less than 10 minutes. The test construction and administration practices may be somewhat biased because raters may have already made up their mind about the student's abilities. The SPSI seems more appropriate to be used by a rater who may have limited exposure to a student. Certainly exposure is required and therein may lie the source of rater bias. However, in the validity studies, there are high positive correlations for varying raters.

Reliability data are most impressive. Using Cronbach's alpha as an index for internal consistency, all values were above .95. The standard errors of measurement were low and ranged between .42 and .60. The data suggest that the SPSI is subject to little variability based on poor test construction. Correlation for stability over time (1-week interval) was high as well. Reliability evidence for the SPSI is strong.

The authors provide three sources of evidence for issues of validity. They provide data for content validity, criterion-related validity, and construct validity.

CONTENT VALIDITY. To assess content validity the authors calculated item to total correlations. For this procedure the scores for individual items are correlated with the scores obtained for the scale. The authors state that per Hammill, "item discrimination coefficients should be statistically significant at or beyond the .05 level and should reach or exceed .35 in magnitude" (p. 26). For the SPSI, the item to total coefficients were all at or above .8.

Every once in a while a test appears psychometrically too good. Based on these data, one is left with the notion that for each scale one and only one question needed to be asked. Given the simplistic nature of this test and the reliability and validity evidence, is this instrument of any more value than simply asking teachers, "Do you think this student is appropriate for inclusion in general education?"

CRITERION RELATED VALIDITY. The authors correlated data from the SPSI with the Conners' Teacher Rating Scales (CTRS), the Adjustment Scales for Children and Adolescents (ASCA), and the Comprehensive Scales of Stu-

dent Abilities (CSSA). For the CTRS the correlations for the SPSI Scales to the CTRS scores that suggest behavioral difficulties were broadly significant. The correlations were generally not significant for the Work habits and the Coping Skills scales of the SPSI when compared to the scales of the ASCA. Under the scales of Peer Relationships, Emotional Maturity, and the Successful Inclusion Quotient consistent significant findings are present. Finally, for the CSSA, all but a few correlations were significant. When CSSA scales were correlated with the SIQ_4 every correlation was significant at the .01 level.

CONSTRUCT VALIDITY. Three hypotheses were used to study construct validity. They were:

1. The various scales of the SPSI should be positively related to each other.
2. Scale items should strongly relate to the scale total score.
3. Scores on the SPSI should discriminate persons who are successful (i.e., receiving passing grades) from subjects who are not successful (receiving failing grades). (p. 29)

For the interrelation of SPSI scales (Hypothesis 1), all correlations were significant at the .01 level. The item to total correlations (Hypothesis 2) were discussed earlier in this review but once again were all of high positive value. For group differentiation data (Hypothesis 3), a multivariate ANOVA was utilized. For all groups significant predictive relationships were found.

SUMMARY. Psychometrically, the developers of the SPSI present strong statistical data for their instrument. This reviewer is left with the belief that its simplicity lies outside psychometric scrutiny. This measure seems to be constructed in such a way as to permit considerable rater bias. A standardized measure is by its nature developed to provide objective measurements. I do not believe the SPSI provides that benefit. The SPSI does have value. It provides a source of documentation for teachers and other school personnel to base their recommendations for inclusion, but these recommendations are probably already crystallized prior to completing the SPSI ratings.

[336]
Scales of Adult Independence, Language and Recall.

Purpose: By "assessing the domains of functional independence, language, and recall of adults with neurogenically based communication and cognitive disorders," the SAILR is "designed to differentiate between the communication and related deficits associated with stroke, dementia, and depression."

Population: Adults with dementia.
Publication Date: 1997.
Acronym: SAILR.
Scores, 8: Self-Care, Daily Living, Social Interaction, Client Interview, Word Retrieval, Sentence Comprehension, Paragraph Recall, Standard Score.
Administration: Individual.
Forms, 2: A, B.
Price Data, 1999: $189 per complete kit including examiner's manual (42 pages), stimulus manual (66 pages), 25 caretaker/relative interviews, and 25 record forms; $44 per examiner's manual; $44 per stimulus manual; $29 per 25 each of interview and record.
Time: Administration time varies.
Author: Barbara C. Sonies.
Publisher: PRO-ED.
[Editor's Note: The publisher advised in December 2000 that this test is now out of print.]

Review of the Scales of Adult Independence, Language and Recall by TIMOTHY J. MAKATURA, Clinical Neuropsychologist and Assistant Professor, Department of Physical Medicine and Rehabilitation, University of Pittsburgh Medical Center, Pittsburgh, PA:

The Scales of Adult Independence, Language and Recall (SAILR) were developed in response to assessment guidelines reported in a National Institutes of Health statement concerning the differential diagnosis of dementing diseases (NIH, 1987). This statement concluded that dementia is behavioral diagnosis and evaluation should include functional assessment, family history, standardized mental status examination, and reports from relatives, friends, and others. It was further recommended that the assessment should also be brief (10–30 minutes) and involve speech and language analysis to differentiate between complex language disorders and dementia. As a result, the Scales of Adult Independence, Language and Recall (SAILR) were developed to provide a systematic method to assess the domains of functional independence, language, and recall. The reported uses for the SAILR include (a) differentiating between communication and related deficits associated with stroke, dementia, and depression; (b) providing a baseline measure of a client's performance in the three specified areas; and (c) assisting professionals in responding to the client's

changing needs as well as in predicting future needs (manual, p. 3). All of these purposes are based on analysis of data from serial assessments with the instrument.

The five separate parts that comprise the SAILR are: (a) a 48-item Functional Independence Checklist that involves rating the level of independence for behaviors involved in self-care, daily living, and social interaction on a 4-point Likert scale; (b) a 17-item list of questions involving family, work history, education, and current status that are rated for accuracy on a 4-point Likert scale; (c) a 20-item Word Retrieval Task that requires naming line drawings of objects with each response rated for accuracy on a 4-point scale; (d) a 16-item Sentence Comprehension Task that requires evaluation of sentence length information with responses rated as correct or incorrect; and (e) a Paragraph Recall Task that involves recall of two individually presented paragraphs scored by number of items recalled. Alternate forms are provided for the Word Retrieval Sentence Comprehension, and Paragraph Recall subtests.

Raw scores, percentiles, and standard scores are derived for each subtest, components of functional independence (self-care, daily living, and social interaction), a composite of language/recall, and a total score. The standard scores have a Mean = 10 (*SD* = 3), which allows for easy comparison to other tests. Unfortunately, the table for converting subtest scores to percentile and standard scores in the SAILR manual (Table 3.2—SAILR Norms and Standard Errors of Measurement, p. 15) is misaligned and erroneously indicates that a standard score of 10 corresponds to a percentile rank of 63, raising questions about the accuracy of the entire table.

The SAILR was normed on a sample of 127 adults. The author readily admits this sample is not representative of elderly adults, does not reflect the proportionate occurrence of dementia in the population, and does not reflect the most recent U.S. Census data. This apparent convenience sample is predominantly female (76%), Caucasian (95%), and of medium income level. Educational levels are varied among less than 12 years (53%), 12 years (31%), and 16 years (16%). It is also reported that nearly all subjects lived in residential facilities.

Reported reliability estimates are generally within acceptable ranges. Coefficient alphas for subtests in samples of 29 to 116 adults range from

.74 to .95. Standard errors of measurement for these subtests range form 1.4 to 5.4. Test-retest reliability estimates in samples of 19 to 40 adults (tested an average of 94 days apart) range from .51 to .90. Reliability estimates for alternate forms of Word Retrieval, Sentence Comprehension, and Paragraph Recall are based on a sample of 20 adults (without counterbalancing) and are .95, .81, and .79, respectively.

The author attempts to justify content validity requirements with an argument based on the obvious relevance and representativeness of the target behaviors for each individual client (manual, p. 32). Evidence for criterion-related validity is not presented because of general difficulty in establishing clear criteria for dementia. Evidence for predictive validity includes means and standard deviations of raw data and the argument that subtest mean scores are consistently different among groups. However, plotting the means and standard deviations of the three groups demonstrates significant overlap among groups in nearly all subtests with little clear-cut distinctions.

Discriminant analyses results in 78% and 89% correct classification on Form A and B, respectively, when considering Dementia/No Dementia groups only. Correct classification nears 100% when behavioral observations are included in the analysis. Inclusion of the "Other" group in the analysis results in significant decrease to 55% and 75% correct classification on Forms A and B, respectively, even when including behavioral observations. Evidence for construct validity is provided indirectly with intercorrelations indicating relatively independent factors among subtests. The author does provide the cautionary statement that:

> although the SAILR measures were developed to measure the constructs implied by their labels, users should consider the data presented later in this chapter that supports the validity of the SAILR primarily as a measure of overall cognitive ability and general functional independence rather than more specific components that may be implied by the names of the tasks and sections of the Functional Independence Checklist. (manual, p. 28)

SUMMARY. The SAILR is a relatively new assessment tool that seems to have value as a structured interview and offers the particularly beneficial feature of side-by-side comparison of client and caregiver estimates of functional ability

on the record form. Apart from this feature, the SAILR seems to have little more to offer. Statistical studies indicate that the SAILR is accurate in differentiating between demented and nondemented subjects but lacks sensitivity to differentiate beyond this gross level. Further, the statistical information that is presented is based on a nonrepresentative normative sample. Evidence for validity of the SAILR is less than convincing. Although subtests do appear to have face validity, there is no evidence beyond the NIH consensus statement (NIH, 1987) that supports the choice of these subtests to fulfil the purposes of this test (including differentiating between cognitive and affective disturbances, providing an appropriate baseline to track cognitive changes, and assisting in responding to and predicting needs). Critical errors noted in the manual further limit the use of this instrument. Overall, the SAILR has a number of significant weaknesses that pervasively undermine its utility in a clinical setting. Further research is strongly recommended.

REVIEWER'S REFERENCE

National Institutes of Health. (1987, July). *NIH Consensus Development Conference Statement: Differential diagnosis of dementing diseases*, 6(11), 1–27.

Review of the Scales of Adult Independence, Language and Recall by RICHARD A. WANTZ, Associate Professor of Human Services, College of Education and Human Services, and Associate Clinical Professor of Psychiatry, School of Medicine, Wright State University, Dayton, OH, and BENJAMIN D. BARKER, Research and Clinical Associate, Dayton, OH:

TEST COVERAGE AND USE. The Scales of Adult Independence, Language and Recall (SAILR) provides a systematic method of assessing the domains of functional independence, language, and recall of individuals age 18 and older, suspected of having neurogenically based communication and cognitive disorders—stroke, dementia, and other neurogenic disorders associated with linguistic and/or cognitive impairments or decline. To increase the accuracy of diagnosis, the SAILR obtains input from the client, family, friends, care givers, and medical staff. The checklist may be readministered periodically to develop baseline observations to assist health care professionals in responding to the changing needs of the examinee. The author states that the SAILR may be used concurrently with other evaluations such as medical profiles. The instrument is not intended for those without impairment. The SAILR provides useful information regarding whether the client should consider assisted living.

APPROPRIATE SAMPLES FOR CHECKLIST VALIDATION AND NORMING. The checklist has adequate evidence of content and construct validity. The norm reference group appears inadequate, lacking in national, gender, and racial representation. The form used to collect data for the SAILR was prepared in 1990 and administered to 127 examinees over a period of one year. Fifty-five of the 127 examinees were retested within 4 months for a total of 182 total administrations. Nearly all examinees lived in nursing homes. The SAILR was administered by speech pathologists. One third of the subjects were between 70 and 80 years of age, most of the others were 80 or older. The maximum age was over 100. The sample contained more than three times more females than males.

Ninety-five percent of the examinees were white. Eighty-six percent reported middle class income levels. Of the original 127 examinees, 24% were reported by examiners to have some type of dementia. The SAILR standardization sample was constructed to include both normal elderly subjects and subjects with dementia and other health problems known to affect language, cognitive, and functional abilities. From the 127 examinees a single set of normative data was derived to exhibit the broad range of abilities.

According to the author, the population evaluated does not match the general population. Yet, she believes that these norms do reflect the specific populations found within institutional settings versus those who are self-sufficient or cared for by family members. Due to the small sample size of 127 and homogeneity of the pilot group, the norms may not be applicable to all regions of the United States. Additionally, if the norms had been based on adults with dependent and independent functioning as opposed to only those found in nursing homes, a broader range of functioning may have been revealed. Because only 127 examinees were evaluated and subgroups were not created or assessed, no information is available for subgroups or any group not matching the norming group characteristics.

RELIABILITY. The checklist demonstrated strong reliability with a small sample size. According to the author, the reliability of the final SAILR was examined using measures of internal consistency and test-retest reliability. Interitem consistency was computed using the Cronbach's alpha. Reliability ranged from .74 to .95. The author reports high reliability, but due to the make-up of the norming group, reliability estimates may be misleading and generalizability is limited.

PREDICTIVE VALIDITY. The author used the SAILR to classify the norming group into three sections: No dementia, Other (significant health problems), and Dementia. To examine the validity of scores from the SAILR the subjects were then assessed by independent criteria. Discriminant analysis revealed accuracy of classification ranging from 44% to 100% depending on type.

CONTENT VALIDITY. The SAILR evolved from the National Institutes of Health (NIP) Consensus Development Panel on Differential Diagnosis of Dementing Diseases' (NIH, 1987) guidelines for assessing patients who are suspected of having dementia or related disorders. The following is a condensed version of the guidelines cited by the author:

1. The client's history as related by the client and other family members.

2. Objective information provided by health care workers.

3. Short screening batteries.

4. Speech and language analysis.

5. Results from assessment of daily functioning.

CONSTRUCT VALIDITY. The purpose of the SAILR is to determine if the client has dementia and to chart the progression of the disease by repeated assessment. Dementia is a disease classified as a deteriorating condition where language and cognitive impairments affect daily living. The SAILR contains subsections to test each of these components. The hypothesis is that a normally functioning subject will exhibit skills in the above three domains. A lack of skills or a decline of previous skills may indicate dementia. If a patient has already been identified with dementia, repeated testing will show the progression of the disease.

TEST ADMINISTRATION. The SAILR is a straightforward test. All procedures are precisely stated and replicate the condition under which they were normed. Adequate information on how to give the checklists and the interview is provided.

TEST REPORTING. Appropriate scoring and interpretation guidelines are provided. The results are converted into normed scores such as percentile ranks.

TEST AND ITEM BIAS. The SAILR is designed to assess elderly white people who speak the English language and are suspected of having cognitive and linguistic impairment.

SUMMARY. The SAILR receives a "thumbs-up" rating worthy of use in clinical practice.

[337]
Scales of Independent Behavior—Revised.
Purpose: "Designed to measure functional independence and adaptive functioning in school, home, employment, and community settings."
Population: Infants to adults, with or without developmental disabilities.
Publication Dates: 1984–1997.
Acronym: SIB-R.
Scores, 24: Full Scale (Gross-Motor Skills, Fine Motor Skills, Social Interaction, Language Comprehension, Language Expression, Eating and Meal preparation, Toileting, Dressing, Personal Self-Care, Domestic Skills, Time and Punctuality, Money and Value, Work Skills, Home/Community Orientation), Problem Behavior Scale [optional] (hurtful to Self, Unusual or Repetitive habits, Withdrawal or Inattentive Behavior, Socially offensive Behavior, Uncooperative Behavior, Hurtful to Others, Destructive to property, Disruptive Behavior).
Administration: Individual.
Forms, 3: Comprehensive, Short Form, Early Development Form.
Price Data, 1999: $175 per kit including all test materials, 15 Full Scale Response Booklets, 5 Short Form Response Booklets, and 5 Early Development Form Response Booklets; $44.50 per 25 Full Scale Response Booklets; $28 per 25 Short Form Booklets; $28 per 25 Early Development Response Booklets; $34 per 25-item package (15 Full Scale, 5 Short Form, and 5 Early Development Booklets); $63 per comprehensive manual ('96, 287 pages); $79.50 per Interview Book.
Time: (60) minutes.
Comments: SIB-R in conjunction with the Woodcock-Johnson Psychoeducational Battery—Revised can be used as a comprehensive diagnostic system for measuring adaptive behavior, problem behavior, cognitive ability, language proficiency, and achievement; can be administered either via interview or checklist; short and early development forms available as part of test kit; computerized DOS-based scoring system available.
Authors: Robert H. Bruininks, Richard W. Woodcock, Richard F. Weatherman, and Bradley K. Hill.

Publisher: The Riverside Publishing Company.
Cross References: See T5:2299 (7 references) and T4:2335 (6 references); for reviews by Bonnie W. Camp and Louis J. Heifetz of the earlier version, see 10:321.

Review of the Scales of Independent Behavior—Revised by GLORIA MACCOW, School Psychologist, Guilford County Schools, Greensboro, NC:

The Scales of Independent Behavior—Revised (SIB-R) is similar in structure to its predecessor, the Scales of Independent Behavior (SIB). SIB-R is a comprehensive measure of adaptive and problem behaviors. Although no longer part of the Woodcock-Johnson Psycho-Educational Battery (WJ; T5:2901), WJ-R cognitive ability scores can still be compared to SIB-R adaptive behavior scores. The other parts measure cognitive ability, scholastic achievement, and a subject's preference for participating in scholastic or nonscholastic activities.

The SIB-R is administered individually to assess functional independence and adaptive functioning across settings—school, home, employment, and community. Information is obtained from an examinee's parents or caregivers and can be used to plan education and training activities and to plan and monitor service and support programs to enhance an individual's adaptive functioning. The SIB-R was designed for individual evaluation, individualized program planning, selection and placement, and to assess service needs. The instrument can be used for guidance, appraising skills gains, program evaluation and management, research, and psychometric training.

Compared to the SIB, which was designed to assess the adaptive behavior of individuals from 1 month to 40+ years, the SIB-R provides norms for individuals between 3 months and 80+ years. The SIB-R can be administered using the structured interview format common to the SIB, or using a "new" checklist procedure. The checklist procedure is recommended when the same respondent must assess several individuals, when the respondent is knowledgeable, or when an interview procedure is inconvenient or too time-consuming. No special qualifications are required to administer and score the SIB-R. However, a higher level of competency is required to evaluate and use the results. Practice exercises are provided in the manual and most examiners should be able to administer the SIB-R after completing the training sequence.

The SIB-R measures two broad constructs: the Adaptive Behavior Full Scale and the Problem Behavior Scale. Each consists of several subscales (see above). Different rating systems are used for the two constructs. The Adaptive Behavior items are rated based on the extent to which the individual does (or could do) a task completely, without help or supervision. At the low end of the scale, a score of 0 indicates the individual does the task never or rarely, even if asked. A score of 3 indicates the individual does the task very well, always or almost always, without being asked. The focus of the assessment, though, is on current level of performance or current capacity for performance. In his review of the SIB, Louis Heifetz (1989) described the interpretive difficulties inherent in a scoring system where "each point on the scale has multiple meanings" (p. 714). He indicated that adaptive functioning should describe what a person does on a regular basis, not only what the person is capable of doing. By rating individuals based on what they do or what they could do, the SIB-R (like the SIB) does not provide a clear picture of the person's skills and abilities.

The Problem Behavior categories are rated based on the frequency and severity of the behavior. The respondent indicates if the behavior occurs less than once a month (rating of 1) to 1 or more times an hour (rating of 5). In terms of the severity, the respondent indicates if the behavior is not serious or not a problem (rating of 0) to extremely serious or a critical problem (rating of 4). Because each of the scores has one meaning, the data from the Problem Behavior Scale are subject to less interpretive ambiguity than results from the Adaptive Behavior Scale.

Users can choose to administer individual subscales, cluster areas, the Full Scale, a Short Form screening measure, or a short measure of Early Development. The Early Development Form is used for young children and for individuals with developmental functioning levels below 8 years. The Short Form is used for individuals at any developmental level. Both of these forms require 15 to 20 minutes to complete. The Full Scale takes about 60 minutes to complete. The Short Form was adapted for use with individuals with visual impairments.

Professionals who have used the Woodcock-Johnson Psycho-Educational Battery (T5:2901) will be familiar with the scoring system of the SIB-R. Raw scores are computed and used to calculate cluster Relative Mastery Indexes, standard scores, percentile ranks, and adaptive behavior skills levels. Scoring of the SIB-R requires calculation of difference scores. Different tables are used to look up standard scores depending on whether the difference scores are positive or negative. Manual scoring of all parts of the Woodcock-Johnson can result in computational errors or in errors related to use of incorrect tables. To reduce the possibility of errors, users can purchase a computer scoring program. By entering the raw scores for all subscales administered, the SIB-R Scoring and Reporting Program generates all available scores, a full report, a summary report, and a narrative interpretive report. Reports can be exported to word processing programs for editing.

Norm-referenced scores describe relative levels of adaptive behavior, maladaptive behavior, and support needs. The support score is new for the SIB-R. It describes the amount of support required by an individual on a continuum ranging from Pervasive to Infrequent or No Support. The higher the score, the more independently the individual is functioning.

The SIB-R is based on the early development and standardization of the SIB. The item content was revised, additional norming data were collected, and the authors conducted additional technical studies and used advances in technical research procedures. The authors provide detailed information about the procedures used to select the items. The instrument was standardized on a sample of 2,182 individuals in 15 states and more than 60 communities throughout the United States. The group ranged in age from 3 months to 90 years and the authors used several stratification variables to achieve a sample representative of the United States population. The sample contains fewer adults than preschool and school-age individuals. The authors indicate that a smaller number of adults is required because changes in the abilities measured by the SIB-R are slower during the adult years than during the school-age years.

For adaptive behavior, median split-half reliabilities ranged from .88 to .98 for the four cluster and full scale scores. For the individual subscales, median split-half reliability coefficients (for all age levels) ranged from .70 to .88. For children with mental retardation, the split-half reliabilities were in the .90s for the clusters and subscales. Test-retest (4-week interval) reliabilities for children without disabilities ranged from .83 to .97 for the 14 subscales. For the clusters, the test-retest reliability (4-week interval) coefficients ranged from .96 to .97. The coefficients for the maladaptive behavior indexes were in the lower .80s.

There is discussion of interrater reliability, an important indicator for standardized rating scales. The studies reported evaluated similarities in scoring between independent examiners.

The authors report several studies as evidence of the construct validity of the SIB-R. Criterion-related validity is reported for the SIB-R and the WJ-R Broad Cognitive Ability Scores. For individuals without disabilities, correlations between adaptive behavior and cognitive ability were variable—.20s for 3- to 4-year-olds; .70s for 5- to 12-year-olds; and in the teens for adolescents and adults. The correlations were higher for individuals with disabilities.

SUMMARY. The Scales of Independent Behavior—Revised is a useful instrument for professionals who must determine the eligibility of individuals for educational and/or support services. It can be used alone or in conjunction with the Woodcock-Johnson Psychoeducational Battery. The reliability estimates of the Full Scale are good, the reliability estimates of the Short Form and the Early Development Form are questionable. The SIB-R allows professionals to identify the skills an individual performs, or could perform, and the degree of independence with which the skills are (or could be) performed. Also, it provides information about the problem behaviors that might interfere with independent functioning. Comparable instruments, such as the Vineland Adaptive Behavior Scales, typically assess adaptive behavior only. However, the Vineland assesses what an individual does and not just what the person could do. The authors identify as unique the fact that the SIB-R scores can be interpreted in light of the Broad Cognitive Ability cluster score. However, this feature becomes less appealing when users recognize that the construct validity of the Cognitive Ability cluster score is unsatisfactory (Sattler, 1992).

REVIEWER'S REFERENCES

Heifetz, L. J. (1989). [Review of the Scales of Independent Behavior.] In J. C. Conoley & J. J. Kramer (Eds.), *The tenth mental measurements yearbook* (pp. 713-718). Lincoln, NE: Buros Institute of mental Measurements.

Sattler, J. M. (1992). *Assessment of children: Revised and updated third edition.* San Diego: Jerome M. Sattler, Publisher, Inc.

Review of the Scales of Independent Behavior—Revised by LELAND C. ZLOMKE, Director of Psychological Services, OMNI Behavioral Health, Omaha, NE:

The Scales of Independent Behavior—Revised (SIB-R) is designed as a comprehensive measure of adaptive and problem behaviors. The scales primarily measure "functional independence and adaptive functioning in school, home, employment, and community settings" (manual, p. 1). The SIB-R is a revision of the Scales of Independent Behavior developed by the same authors and first published in 1984. The instrument is organized into three forms and a Problem Behavior Scale. The Early Development Form is composed of 40 items sampled from the SIB-R Full Scale. The Early Development Form is designed to assess children from early infancy through 6 years of age or older individuals with severe developmental disabilities. Administration time is reportedly approximately 15–20 minutes. The Short Form is composed of 40 items from SIB-R Full Scale. It is designed as a screening measure for individuals of all ages. Administration time is reported to be approximately 15–20 minutes. The SIB-R Full Scale is composed of 14 subscales (259 items) divided into four adaptive behavior clusters each composed of two or more subscales. The adaptive behavior clusters are: Motor Skills, Social Interaction and Communication Skills, Personal Living Skills, and Community Living Skills. The Problem Behavior Scale reviews eight areas of problem behavior across three maladaptive behavior indexes. The indexes are Internalized, Asocial, and Externalized. The SIB-R provides 11 types of scores for interpretation and worksheets/profiles to aid in program planning.

DESCRIPTION. The complete SIB-R consists of a Comprehensive Manual (287 pages) and an Interview Book. Protocols are provided for Early Development Form, Short Form, Short Form for the Visually Impaired, Individual Plan Recommendations for the Short Form, and a Response Booklet for the Full Scale Form. The protocols include the item Likert-type ratings, subscale summary scores, problem behavior item scores, Maladaptive Behavior Worksheet, Individual Plan Recommendations Worksheet, Test Scoring Tables, and Training Implications Profile. The SIB-R provides a computerized scoring and reporting program including and a manual.

ADMINISTRATION AND SCORING. Administration of the scales can take the form of a semistructured interview or a respondent check-list. Under an interview format, the page-by-page item presentation format has continued from the SIB 1984 edition. New to this revised edition is the protocol facilitating a respondent checklist as an administration format. Item scores on all adaptive behavior clusters and subscales are rated on a 0–3 Likert–type rating. The descriptors of the item rating range from "Never or rarely—even if asked" through "Does very well—without being asked." On each rating multiple meanings continue to be required. Those meanings include frequency of behavior, quality of performance of the skill, and initiative of the person to perform the task.

The intent of the scale was not, however, to simultaneously measure quality and frequency of performance. According to the instructions in the manual, "if the respondent has difficulty evaluating a task because it could be rated one way using quality of performance and another way using frequency of performance, the quality of an individual's performance should take precedence" (p. 34). Item scores are summed into subscale raw scores and corresponding age equivalent scores. Subscale raw scores are converted into cluster "W" scores and nine other scores can then be derived including standard scores, percentiles, Relative Mastery Indexes, Adaptive Behavior Skill Levels, Support Score, and several optional standard score scales.

The Behavior Problem Scale item scores are rated on two Likert-type scales. The descriptors for frequency range from "Never" through "1 or more times an hour" and the severity descriptors range from "Not serious; not a problem" through "Extremely serious; a critical problem." Item scores are corresponded to Part Scores and summed into one of the four Maladaptive Behavior Index Scores. These scores are plotted on a matrix showing the Maladaptive Behavior Index and one of the five corresponding levels of seriousness.

SCALE DEVELOPMENT. The authors have included in the Comprehensive Manual all pertinent data on test construction, standardization, and psychometrics for the SIB-R. The instrument includes refinements in the precise behavioral statements (items) on all scales. Overall 13 items from the original SIB were deleted and 46 new items were added. The Rasch analysis procedure was again used for item analysis and scaling. The authors added 418 new individuals to the SIB stratified norming sample. The addition of these stratified new individuals updated the sample to match 1990 U.S. census figures. Several analyses and special studies are reported to verify that excessive bias does not exist due to gender, race, and other common demographics.

RELIABILITY AND VALIDITY. The SIB-R Comprehensive Manual reports several studies supporting the Scales' reliability. Reliability coefficients for cluster scores were overwhelmingly above .8. Validity measures report favorable outcomes, most notably >.96 correlation with the SIB cluster scores for the Early Childhood and All Ages groups. The authors did not report validity measures that compare adaptive behaviors reported by informants on the SIB and adaptive behaviors routinely demonstrated by individuals and directly observed by examiners. This remains a key area of ambiguity when interpreting whether the SIB-R actually measures the adaptive behavior level typically displayed by individuals.

CRITIQUE. The SIB-R is a useful tool in rating the adaptive behavior of individuals across a wide range of ages and developmental levels. The materials provide direct and easy-to-understand administration and scoring instructions. Hand scoring to obtain standard scores can be a tedious task, very similar to the procedures required with the Woodcock-Johnson Psycho-Educational Battery—Revised (Woodcock & Johnson, 1990; T5:2901). The computer-scoring option is well designed and eliminates the cumbersome procedures that may lead to scoring errors. Unique and potentially useful additions, especially for the less experienced examiner, are the program planning questions at the end of each subscale. The responses to these questions and a review of items on the subscales themselves, when placed within the context provided in the Individual Plan Recommendations worksheet, should help organize the useful generation of annual goals/objectives for the individual.

The inclusion of the Problem Behavior Scale continues to be a strength of this instrument. However, the Problem Behavior Scale itself is an extremely limited sample of items and should only be used as a screening device that may point out areas for more in-depth examination.

SUMMARY. Overall, the SIB-R is a technically sound, well-developed instrument designed to measure an informant's impression of the adaptive behaviors demonstrated by an individual. A limitation continues due to the lack of the provision to measure skills through direct observation of the individual. Additions including a computer-scoring system and expanded information about psychometrics and administration of the instrument in the Comprehensive Manual are significant new strengths. These additions are major benefits to examiners in terms of both time efficiency and accuracy of administration and scoring.

In comparison to other measures of adaptive behavior, the SIB-R now sets the standard for ease of administration, construction, technical adequacy, scoring efficiency, and assistance with program planning. Examiners may find the Vineland (Sparrow, Balla, & Cichetti, 1984; T5:2813) and the AAMD Adaptive Behavior Scales—Residential and Community, Second Edition (Nihira, Leland, & Lambert, 1993; T5:1) to be more specific and useful if a specific skills-based review of items for program planning is a major expected outcome of the assessment.

REVIEWER'S REFERENCES

Sparrow, S. S., Balla, D. A., & Cicchetti, D. V. (1984). Vineland Adaptive Behavior Scales. Circle Pines, MN: American Guidance Services.
Woodcock, R. W., & Johnson, M. B. (1990). Woodcock-Johnson Psycho-Educational Battery—Revised. Chicago: Riverside Publishing.
Nihira, K., Leland, H., & Lambert, N. (1993). Adaptive Behavior Scale—Residential and Community (2nd ed.). Austin, TX: PRO-ED.

[338]
Schedule for Nonadaptive and Adaptive Personality.

Purpose: "Designed to assess trait dimensions in the domain of personality disorders."
Population: Ages 18 and older.
Publication Date: 1993.
Acronym: SNAP.
Scores: 34 scales: Trait (Mistrust, Manipulativeness, Aggression, Self-harm, Eccentric Perceptions, Dependency, Exhibitionism, Entitlement, Detachment, Impulsivity, Propriety, Workaholism), Temperament (Negative Temperament, Positive Temperament, Disinhibition), Diagnostic (Paranoid, Schizoid, Schizotypal, Antisocial, Borderline, Histrionic, Narcissistic, Avoidant, Dependent, Obsessive-Compulsive, Passive-Aggressive, Sadistic, Self-Defeating), Validity (Variable Response Inconsistency, True Response Inconsistency, Desirable Response Inconsistency, Deviance, Rare Virtues, Invalidity Index).
Administration: Individual or group.
Price Data, 2001: $55 per starter kit including 10 test booklets, 100 answer sheets, set of scoring keys, 25 profile forms, and manual for administration, scoring, and interpretation (92 pages); $10 per 10 test booklets; $15 per 100 answer sheets; $35 per set of 34 scoring keys; $5 per 25 profile forms (specify diagnostic scales or validity trait, and temperament scales); $15 per manual for administration, scoring, and interpretation; price data for scoring disks available from publisher.
Time: Administration time not reported.
Author: Lee Anna Clark.
Publisher: University of Minnesota Press, Test Division.
Cross References: See T5:2306 (1 reference) and T4:2341 (1 reference).

Review of the Schedule for Nonadaptive and Adaptive Personality by LIZANNE DeSTEFANO, Professor of Educational Psychology, University of Illinois at Urbana—Champaign, Champaign, IL, and DANIEL HECK, Research Associate, Horizon Research, Inc., Champaign, IL:

RATIONALE AND USES. The Schedule for Nonadaptive and Adaptive Personality (SNAP) is designed for use with both clinical and nonclinical populations for the assessment of personality traits and general temperaments related to personality disorders (specifically, DSM-III-R and DSM-IV Axis II personality disorders). The developer envisions three purposes for the SNAP: (a) to assess personality disorder pathologies in terms of specific personality traits, (b) to explore the relationships of specific personality traits and personality disorder diagnoses, and (c) to investigate the continuity of personality traits from the normal to the pathological range.

Two theoretical positions underlie the SNAP. First, the categorical scheme for representing Axis II personality disorders provides gross classifications that do not account for identifiable personality traits within each category nor for significant variations in traits within and across categories (see Frances & Widiger, 1986). Second, the relationship between normal and abnormal personality traits is not clear. Specifically, research has been inconclusive on the question of whether personality traits can be represented on a continuum from normal to pathological. The SNAP inventory provides an instrument for use both in research for testing these two theoretical propositions and in research grounded in these theoretical positions.

DESCRIPTION. The SNAP is a factor-analytically derived self-report inventory of 375 true-false items comprising 34 scales. The scales can be divided into four categories: 12 Trait scales, 3 Temperament scales, 13 Diagnostic scales, and 6 Validity scales. Some items overlap on two or more scales. The Temperament scales are available separately as the General Temperament Survey (Clark & Watson, 1990).

The SNAP scales and items were derived, revised, and selected in an extensive and rigorous multistage development procedure. Methods included expert (clinician and graduate student) synonym sorting of symptom descriptors of personality and related disorders and several administrations of preliminary versions of the inventory to college student and patient samples.

RELIABILITY. Alpha reliability coefficients, based on sufficiently large samples, for the Trait and Temperament scales are reported for college males, college females, adolescents, two male patient samples, and female patients. Several values fall below alpha = .70. For the Trait and Temperament scales, two had alpha reliability values less than .70 (Self-Esteem and Suicide Proneness). For the Diagnostic scales, across multiple samples, several revealed low alpha reliabilities. Out of the nine occurrences of low reliability values, four were for the Obsessive-Compulsive Personality Disorder scale.

Test-retest reliability values for the Trait and Temperament scales, also based on sufficiently large samples, are reported for college students at 1-month and 2-month intervals and for patients at a 1-week interval. All test-retest values except two exceed .70 with medians within samples near .80.

Scores from the SNAP appear to have acceptable levels of reliability. Reliability information is understandably not reported for the Validity scales. The lack of test-retest reliability information for the Diagnostic scales should be of concern for users intending to use these scales as measures of change over time.

VALIDITY. Validity evidence of scores from the SNAP scales began with the initial stage of development. Expert synonym sorting of symptom descriptors and subsequent analysis provided evidence supporting the need for the SNAP scales as specific measures of personality traits related to, but not redundant with, Axis II personality disorders. Moreover, these initial analyses supported the notion that adaptive and nonadaptive personality traits lay on a continuum.

The SNAP scales have been examined in relation to several existing self-report measures with college student samples and in relation to clinical determinations of personality disorders with patient samples. These investigations support the

concurrent and predictive validity of scores from the SNAP.

The Eysenck Personality Questionnaire (Eysenck & Eysenck, 1975) was used to assess the relationship of scores on the SNAP to a well-known three-factor assessment of personality. The three-factor model appears fairly consistent with the three temperament scales and relevant subscales of the SNAP. A number of five-factor assessments were used to assess the relationship of the SNAP to five-factor representations of personality. Correlational and factor analysis of the five-factor studies revealed a reasonable five-factor breakdown of the SNAP scales, although the "Openness" factor is not strongly represented in the SNAP.

Correlational analyses involving the SNAP and the PANAS-X Trait and State Mood scales with college student and patient samples revealed stronger and more consistent relationships to the Trait assessments than the State assessments.

Additional correlational analyses were performed with a college student sample for the Minnesota Multiphasic Personality Inventory—2 (MMPI-2) Standard Scales and Personality Disorder Scales (Morey, Waugh, & Blashfield, 1985). A number of SNAP and MMPI-2 scales were shown to have meaningful correlation suggesting some overlap in traits assessed, but some SNAP scales were essentially independent of MMPI-2 scales, suggesting that they assess some additional traits not covered on the MMPI-2.

Predictive validity of scores from the SNAP has been examined in comparison to personality disorder diagnoses based on both patient chart ratings and patient interviews. Correlations between SNAP Trait and Temperament scales and symptom ratings from patient charts were modest. The test developers note that lack of reliability in rating of symptoms from patient charts may explain these results, but further research is required.

Compared to diagnostic ratings based on patient interviews, the SNAP Trait and Temperament scales were generally consistent and logically predictable. The use of the SNAP to investigate relationships between personality traits and Axis II diagnoses appears justified and warranted.

The SNAP Diagnostic scales were also compared to diagnostic ratings based on patient interviews. Correlations in this case were modest (r = .36 to r = .85). The test developers note that these correlations mirror those reported between independent interview-based diagnostic ratings or between two self-report questionnaires. The Diagnostic scales appear usable in research but they should be interpreted with appropriate caution, as should any single source of evidence for clinical diagnoses.

Further validation studies for the SNAP, including longitudinal studies, are currently planned. Suggested additional studies that would enhance an understanding of the predictive validity of the SNAP scales include comparisons of SNAP scores to diagnostic ratings based on combinations of multiple sources of evidence.

The SNAP provides a valuable tool for identifying invalid protocols through its validity scales. Invalidity due to inconsistency, social desirability, deviance, and other patterns of response is assessed using these scales. Analyses using real and simulated data support the usefulness of these scales. Users should exercise extreme caution regarding decisions based on the Validity scales because unusual response patterns may in fact reflect serious disorders or cries for help rather than invalid responses.

NORMING. The SNAP Trait and Temperament scales and four of the six Validity scales have been normed separately for male ($n = 281$) and female ($n = 523$) college students. Due to their later development, the diagnostic scales and the remaining validity scales were normed on subsets of these samples ($n = 216$ and $n = 345$, respectively). All scoring conversions in the current version of the SNAP are based on college student norms.

Norming data for adult samples and adolescent samples (based on a revised version of the SNAP) are forthcoming. Interpretations of SNAP profiles on subjects in these populations should be made with caution until appropriate normative data become available. In particular, some results are reported that may suggest a unique factor structure of the trait and temperament scales for male patients.

ADMINISTRATION AND SCORING. The SNAP is appropriate for group or individual administration. Written and oral administration and response are considered appropriate, but evidence of consistent scale performance across formats is not provided. Conditions and instructions for administration are only very generally described; more specific instructions would be helpful. Due to the

number of items (375), considerable time should be provided for subjects to complete the inventory comfortably.

The test manual provides all information needed for scoring. The SNAP can be scored by hand or by computer. Additional materials to facilitate either method can be ordered. Scores are reported for each Validity, Trait, Temperament, and Diagnostic scale by T-scores representing item aggregates. Separate T-score results are provided for male and female subjects. Diagnostic scales can also be reported using a criterion method. Criteria for items representing symptoms and symptoms representing diagnostic categories are provided in the test manual.

The test manual also provides interpretive scale profiles. Trait and Temperament scales are interpretable at both extremes and the profiles afford descriptions for high and low scores. Interpretations for scores indicating invalidity of protocols via the Validity scales are also provided.

SUMMARY. The SNAP extends current assessments of personality traits from the normal range into the pathological range. The SNAP should be useful for researchers and clinicians examining a wide spectrum of personality traits, especially in relation to personality disorder diagnoses. The rigorous development procedures, reliability studies, and existing and planned validity studies are commendable and support the quality of the SNAP. Further norming data, which are forthcoming, are needed for adult samples.

REVIEWER'S REFERENCES

Eysenck, H. J., & Eysenck, S. B. G. (1975). *Eysenck Personality Questionnaire manual.* San Diego, CA: Educational and Industrial Testing Service.

Morey, L. C., Waugh, M. H., & Blashfield, R. K. (1985). MMPI scales for DSM-III personality disorders: Their derivation and correlates. *Journal of Personality Assessment, 49,* 245–251.

Frances, A. J., & Widiger, T. (1986). The classification of personality disorders: An overview of problems and solutions. In A. J. Frances & R. E. Hales (Eds.), *Psychiatry update: American Psychiatric Association Annual Review* (Vol. 5, pp. 240–257). Washington, DC: American Psychiatric Press.

Clark, L. A., & Watson, D. (1990). *General Temperament Survey.* Unpublished manuscript.

Review of the Schedule for Nonadaptive and Adaptive Personality by NIELS G. WALLER, Professor of Psychology and Human Development, Vanderbilt University, Nashville, TN:

The Schedule for Nonadaptive and Adaptive Personality (SNAP), by Lee Anna Clark, is one of a growing number of questionnaires for the assessment of maladaptive personality and the personality disorders. Among its peers (Chapman, Chapman, & Kwapil, 1995; Hyler & Rieder, 1987;

Livesley & Jackson, in press; Millon & Davis, 1997; Morey & Glutting, 1994; Morey, Waugh, & Blashfield, 1985), the SNAP is also one of the most promising questionnaires in its class.

The current version of the SNAP contains 375 dichotomously scored (true/false) items that are combined to form 6 validity scales, 12 factor analytically derived trait scales, 3 higher-order temperament scales, and 13 diagnostic scales for personality-disorder classification. Several features of these scales make the SNAP an attractive choice for clinical and research purposes. For instance, in contrast to other measures of maladaptive personality (e.g., Millon & Davis, 1997), the SNAP was designed to measure the lower-order personality traits and temperament dimensions that form the emotional and conative foundations of the personality disorders. It was not designed to generate Axis II diagnoses, although the 13 diagnostic scales of the SNAP can be effectively used for that purpose. The decision to focus on personality *dimensions* rather than personality disorders, or hypothetical types, was well thought out (Clark, Livesley, & Morey, 1997). Clark contends that the "investigation of whether and how personality traits combine to form discrete diagnostic categories will be most efficient when the component traits are well understood and can be assessed reliably and validly" (manual, p. 14). As a former musician who is interested in the valid identification of psychological types (Waller & Meehl, 1998), these words are music to my ears.

Measures of psychopathology often fail to provide adequate scales for the assessment of protocol validity. On this score the SNAP receives high marks—indeed, it sets new standards—because it offers a rich assortment of scales for the assessment of response sets, carelessness, deviance, and defensive responding. The SNAP Variable Response Consistency (VRIN) and True Response Consistency (TRIN) scales (Tellegen, 1988) were patterned after similar scales on the Multidimensional Personality Questionnaire (MPQ; Tellegen, in press) and the Minnesota Multiphasic Personality Scale—2 (MMPI-2; Butcher, Dahlstrom, Graham, Tellegen, & Kaemmer, 1989). The Desirable Response Inconsistency (DRIN), Rare Virtues (RV), and Deviance (DEV) scales were also modeled after MPQ and MMPI-2 validity scales. Importantly, Clark has performed extensive Monte Carlo work with the SNAP validity scales and she

has convincingly proved the usefulness of these scales for identifying various forms of distorted self-presentation and other sources of protocol invalidity.

The SNAP trait scales measure 12 constructs: (a) Mistrust, (b) Manipulativeness, (c) Aggression, (d) Self-harm, (e) Eccentric Perceptions, (f) Dependency, (g) Exhibitionism, (h) Entitlement, (i) Detachment, (j) Impulsivity, (k) Propriety, and (l) Workaholism. These factor analytically derived scales were carefully developed over numerous rounds of item writing, data collection and analysis, and item and scale revision. The care taken during the development of these scales has resulted in a set of measures with high internal consistency reliability (median alpha = .82) and test-retest stability in numerous samples (summarized in the SNAP manual). The trait scales also appear to measure their intended universes of content—that is, they show evidence of content validity. The items of the trait scales were written to reflect the content domains in "(1) all DSM-III personality-disorder criteria, (2) criteria from other conceptualizations of personality disorder, including psychopathy ... hysteroid dysphoria ... and other criterion sets for borderline personality disorder ... and (3) criteria from selected Axis I disorders (dysthymia, cyclothymia, and generalized anxiety disorder) that resemble personality disorders in important respects" (manual, p. 15). Clark (personal communication, July 18, 1998) is currently collecting data on a supplemental bank of 50 items that will bring the SNAP item pool more in line with DSM-IV criteria sets for the Axis II disorders.

Scores on the SNAP trait scales can be meaningfully combined to provide reliable measures of three higher-order personality dimensions with an emotional core: (a) Negative Temperament, (b) Positive Temperament, and (c) Disinhibition. These super factors are conceptually related to the Negative Emotionality, Positive Emotionality, and (-) Constraint dimensions of the MPQ (Tellegen, in press) and the Big Three—Extroversion, Neuroticism, and Conventionality—of the so-called Five Factor Model of normal range personality (Clark & Livesley, 1994; Clark, Vorhies, & McEwen, 1994).

Due to the conceptual diversity (some would say, confusion) within the personality disorders area, the construct validity of scores from the

SNAP is difficult to assess. It is not clear, for instance, whether we should require the SNAP (or any other inventory) to predict clinician-generated diagnoses when the psychometric foundation of the Axis II system is seriously being questioned (Clark, Livesley, & Morey, 1997). The SNAP manual summarizes evidence attesting to the convergent and discriminant validity of the SNAP higher- and lower-order trait and diagnostic scales. The manual reports between-inventory correlations with the MPQ (Tellegen, in press), the Eysenck Personality Questionnaire (Eysenck & Eysenck, 1975), the NEO (Costa & McCrae, 1985), the MMPI-2 standard scales (Butcher et al., 1989), the MMPI-2 Personality Disorder scales (Morey, Waugh, & Blashfield, 1985), and several other inventories. Unfortunately, the manual does not report the within-inventory correlations, and hence it is not possible to determine the amount of unique variance in the SNAP, nor is it possible to identify accurately traits that are not well captured by the SNAP scales. Clark has provided some additional information along these lines in recent publications (Clark, Vorhies, & McEwen, 1994; Clark, Livesley, Schroeder, & Irish, 1996) and this material will be incorporated into future updates of the SNAP manual (personal communication, July 22, 1998).

The SNAP manual provides a wealth of information that will allow clinicians and researchers to use the inventory in a responsible and ethical manner. The manual reports item composition and scoring keys for all scales as well as gender-specific scale means and standard deviations from a variety of samples (inpatients, outpatients, college students, and normal adolescents). It also reports gender specific linear T-score conversion tables for the validity, trait, temperament, and diagnostic scales. Inspection of these tables reveals several aspects of the SNAP that deserve attention in future questionnaire revisions. One aspect concerns the higher-order moments of the score distributions for several SNAP scales. Specifically, for many scales, the score distributions are highly skewed in nonclinical samples. Moreover, the degree of skewness varies considerably across scales. This feature limits the inferences that can be drawn from scale-by-scale comparisons because the same T-scores on different scales do not equal the same percentile scores, a problem that was recently redressed on the MMPI-2 by the intro-

duction of so-called uniform T-scores (Tellegen & Ben-Porath, 1992). Extending the "top" and "bottom" of several SNAP scales might ameliorate this problem. The maximum raw score on the Exhibition scale, for instance, is 16. Males from the college normative sample who endorsed 16 Exhibition items in the keyed direction received a T-score of only 67, a finding that suggests that a considerable portion of the sample received the maximum score. Thus, the ability of the SNAP to discriminate among individuals with high levels of Exhibitionism could be improved by adding more extreme Exhibition items. A different problem occurs on the Self-harm scale. Here we find that males from the normative group who endorsed zero Self-harm items received a T-score of only 41. It is unlikely that item revisions, additions, or deletions will generate normally distributed score distributions for a dimension of self-injurious behaviors (most healthy individuals do not want to hurt themselves!). Thus, with this and other scales with highly skewed score distributions, it may be more informative to report percentile scores rather than linear T-scores.

My overall impression of the SNAP is very positive. I completed the inventory in approximately 75 minutes. I found the scoring templates extremely easy to use. And my SNAP profile suggests that I am a workaholic with obsessive-compulsive tendencies (a finding that is corroborated by a peer-rating study conducted by my wife). According to the SNAP, I do not qualify for any Axis II diagnoses. This finding is not only personally comforting, it is noteworthy because other questionnaires of maladaptive personality (e.g., Millon & Davis, 1997) have a well-known tendency to overpathologize.

SUMMARY. The SNAP is a promising instrument that sets new standards for the psychometric assessment of maladaptive personality traits. If you are in the market for a comprehensive inventory for the assessment of nonadaptive and adaptive personality—an inventory with state-of-the-art validity scales—then I strongly recommend that you make a SNAP decision.

REVIEWER'S REFERENCES
Eysenck, H. J., & Eysenck, S. B. G. (1975). *Eysenck Personality Questionnaire manual*. San Diego: Education and Industrial Testing Service.

Costa, P. T., Jr., & McCrae, R. R. (1985). *The NEO Personality Inventory manual*. Odessa, FL: Psychological Assessment Resources.

Morey, L. C., Waugh, M. H., & Blashfield, R. K. (1985). MMPI scales for DSM-III personality disorders: Their derivation and correlates. *Journal of Personality Assessment, 49*, 245–251.

Hyler, S. E., & Rieder, R. O. (1987). PDQ-R: Personality Diagnostic Questionnaire—Revised. New York: New York State Psychiatric Institute.

Tellegen, A. (1988). The analysis of consistency in personality assessment. *Journal of Personality, 56,* 621–663.

Butcher, J. N., Dahlstrom, W. G., Graham, J. R., Tellegen, A., & Kaemmer, B. (1989). *MMPI-2 (Minnesota Multiphasic Personality Inventory—2): Manual for administration and scoring.* Minneapolis, MN: University of Minnesota Press.

Tellegen, A., & Ben-Porath, Y. S. (1992). The new uniform *T* scores for the MMPI-2: Rationale, derivation, and appraisal. *Psychological Assessment, 4,* 145–155.

Clark, L. A., & Livesley, W. J. (1994). Two approaches to identifying the dimensions of personality disorder: Convergence on the five-factor model. In P. T. Costa, Jr. & T. A. Widiger (Eds.), *Personality disorders and the five-factor model of personality* (pp. 261–277). Washington, DC: American Psychological Association.

Clark, L. A., Vorhies, L., & McEwen, J. L. (1994). Personality disorder symptomatology from the five-factor model perspective. In P. T. Costa, Jr. & T. A. Widiger (Eds.), Personality disorders and the five-factor model of personality (pp. 95–116). Washington, DC: American Psychological Associates.

Morey, L. C., & Glutting, J. H. (1994). The Personality Assessment Inventory and the measurement of normal and abnormal personality constructs. In S. Strack & M. Lorr (Eds.), *Differentiation of normal and abnormal personality* (pp. 402–420). New York: Springer.

Chapman, J. P., Chapman, L. J., & Kwapil, T. R. (1995). Scales for the measurement of schizotypy. In A. Raine, T. Lencz, & S. A. Mednick (Eds.), *Schizotypal personality* (pp. 79–106). New York: Cambridge University Press.

Clark, L. A., Livesley, W. J., Schroeder, M. L., & Irish, S. L. (1996). Convergence of two systems for assessing specific traits of personality disorder. *Psychological Assessment, 8,* 294–303.

Clark, L. A., Livesley, W. J., & Morey, L. (1997). Personality disorder assessment: The challenge of construct validity. *Journal of Personality Disorders, 11,* 205–231.

Millon, T., & Davis, R. D. (1997). The MCMI-III: Present and future directions. *Journal of Personality Assessment, 68,* 69–85.

Waller, N. G., & Meehl, P. E. (1998). *Multivariate taxometric procedures: Distinguishing types from continua.* Thousand Oaks, CA: SAGE.

Livesley, W. J., & Jackson, D. (in press). *Manual for the Dimensional Assessment of Personality Pathology—Basic Questionnaire.* Port Huron, MI: Sigma Press.

Tellegen, A. (in press). Multidimensional Personality Questionnaire. Minneapolis, MN: University of Minnesota Press.

[339]

School-Age Care Environment Rating Scale.

Purpose: Designed to assess the quality of center-based child care for school-aged children.

Population: Child care programs.

Publication Dates: 1980–1996.

Acronym: SACERS

Scores, 7: Space and Furnishings, Health and Safety, Activities, Interactions, Program Structure, Staff Development, Total.

Administration: Group.

Price Data, 1998: $10.95 per test booklet/manual ('96, 44 pages).

Time: (120) minutes.

Comments: An adaptation of the Early Childhood Environment Rating Scale (133); for use with center-based care (not family child care homes); respondents cue evaluators of the child-care environment; "Also includes a set of 6 supplementary items for centers that include children with special needs."

Authors: Thelma Harms, Ellen Vineberg Jacobs, and Donna Romano White.

Publisher: Teachers College Press.

Review of the School-Age Care Environment Rating Scale by PATRICIA B. KEITH, Assistant Professor, Psychology Department, University of South Carolina, Columbia, SC:

The School-Age Care Environment Rating Scale (SACERS) was designed as a self-evaluation instrument for agencies that provide before and after school care to children aged 5 through 12. The instrument will help administrators monitor and supervise classroom environments and programs in a structured, systematic, and perhaps even nonthreatening manner. The examiner is asked to make judgments regarding the classroom's space and furnishings, health and safety factors, classroom activities, program structures, and staff's professional skills/development.

Rather than imposing a specific program philosophy or orientation, the SACERS guides examiners in considering 49 developmentally appropriate classroom items for meeting the needs of children (with and without special needs). Much thought was put into the selection of the items. There is evidence that previous research, current evaluation tools, recognized professional standards, and common sense were employed in selecting the items for this short scale.

Items require examiners to use a 7-point measurement scale (1 through 7). The measurement scale is good; it provides four anchor points to guide in evaluating classroom environments (1 = *inadequate;* 3 = *minimal;* 5 = *good;* and 7 = *excellent).* This scale will assist examiners in measuring change in the physical, human interactional, and program components, either positive or negative, within the classroom. Yet, one is cautioned to make sure that teachers are not harshly judged with standards that they cannot change or have no control over. Often teachers can be put in a no-win situation. For example, teachers rarely have money to improve the physical surroundings in which their classroom operates. Also, teachers may not have control over class size or composition and children's needs that may vary from day to day.

Besides the instrument's items and scaling of items, the reliability and validity techniques used to measure the psychometric qualities of the instrument were appropriate. Reliability indices—internal consistency using Cronbach's alphas, interrater reliability using Kappa statistics—are within acceptable ranges. Cronbach's alphas are the following: Space and Furnishings = .76, Health and Safety = .82; Activities = .86; Interactions = .94; Program Structure = .67; Staff Development = .73; and Total Score = .95. Kappa statistics are: Space and Furnishings = .79; Health and Safety = .83; Activities = .86; Interactions = .82; Program Structure = .82; Staff Development = .91; and

Total Score = .83. And finally, interrater reliabilities using correlations are: Space and Furnishings = .87; Health and Safety = .95; Activities = .92; Interactions = .93; Program Structure = .99; Staff Development = .99; and Total Score = .96.

Validity indices—content validity using expert ratings and construct validity—are within good ranges too. Content validity determined using a 5-point scale (1 = *not important* to 5 = *very important*) had a mean rating of 4.5 to 5 on 91% of the items. Construct validity using correlations between total and subscale scores with staff training and staff-to-staff ratio are as follows: Space and Furnishings = .31; Health and Safety = -.40; Activities = -.39; Interactions = .29; Program Structure = .40; Staff Development = -.24; and Total Score = .29 and .30.

SUMMARY. The SACERS is an instrument that should be considered when an examiner is interested in monitoring and supervising before and after school programs for school-aged children.

Review of the School-Age Care Environment Rating Scale by HILLARY MICHAELS, Senior Research Scientist, CTB/McGraw-Hill, Monterey, CA:

OVERVIEW. The School-Age Care Environment Rating Scale (SACERS) is the latest edition of the childhood environment rating scales that aid program evaluation. It is intended for nonparental, center care settings for children between the ages of 5 and 12. Harms and associates have included this in their environmental rating scale series that also includes the Early Childhood Environment Rating Scale (133), the Family Day Care Rating Scale (T5:1009), and the Infant/Toddler Environment Rating Scale (T5:1264). To build the SACERS scales, the authors used the *Quality Criteria for School-Age Child Care Programs* (Albrecht, 1991), *Assessing School-Age Child Care Quality* (O'Connor, 1991), and the *Assessment Profile for Early Childhood Programs* (Abbott-Shim & Sibley, 1987) to guide scale development.

The SACERS consists of 43 items grouped into six subscales: Space and Furnishings, Health and Safety, Activities, Interactions, Program Structure, and Staff Development. An additional six items are included at the end of the scale for centers that accommodate students with special needs. The items and the scoring sheets are provided in the same booklet. Each item is rated on a 7-point scale. Descriptors and labels are only available for odd-numbered ratings. The value 1 is defined as inadequate; 3 is minimal; 5 is good; and 7 is excellent.

The SACERS includes a general training guide with a simple training activity. Also included are notes to aid raters with specific questions, referred to as "Notes for Clarification." The instructions review how points are administered. However, even-numbered scores may not have the same meaning across raters as these scores are defined as encompassing all of the lower category description and half or more of the next higher description.

ADMINISTRATION. The authors note that at least 2 hours are needed for an outside observer to use the SACERS at a site. Additional time will be necessary to interview the staff members. This time estimate infers complete familiarity with the criteria and a good use of the observer's time. In addition, staff interviews will most likely last longer than the 30 minutes estimated by the authors.

TECHNICAL ADEQUACY. Using the abbreviated information provided in the SACERS documentation, data for the reliability and validity of the scale were gathered from 24 after-school programs in the provinces of Quebec and Ontario, Canada. All rooms were rated by two observers. One observer rated all rooms. A second observer was drawn from a pool of five trained raters.

RELIABILITY. The reliability of the SACERS was estimated using three methods: Cronbach's alpha for internal scale consistency; kappa for interrater reliability (which corrects for chance agreement); and intraclass correlations for interrater reliability.

Cronbach's alpha for the subscales and total score are as follows: Space and Furnishings (alpha = .76), Health and Safety (alpha = .82), Activities (alpha = .86), Interactions (alpha = .94), Program Structure (alpha = .67), and Staff Development (alpha = .73). the Cronbach alpha for the total rating scale equaled .95.

Weighted kappas were used to determine interrater reliability. The kappas for the subscales and total score are as follows: Space and Furnishings (kappa = .79), Health and Safety (kappa = .83), Activities (kappa = .86), Interactions (kappa = .82), Program Structure (kappa = .82), and Staff Development (kappa = .91). The kappa for the total rating scale equaled .83.

The intraclass correlations could only be calculated using 13 of the 24 rooms as the calculation required the same two independent observers. The intraclass correlations for the subscales and total scale are as follows: Space and Furnishings (r = .87), Health and Safety (r = .95), Activities (r = .92), Interactions (r = .93), Program Structure (r = .99), and Staff Development (r = .99). The correlation for the total rating scale equaled .96.

The internal consistency of the Program Structure subscale is low. The alphas for the rest of the subscales and the entire scale are reasonable. The interrater reliability, using both the kappa and intraclass correlations, is high. This is not surprising using the pool of five trained raters with 13 of the 24 rooms rated by the same two raters. No reliability information is available on the six supplemental items for accommodated settings.

VALIDITY. Content validity was assessed using expert ratings for item importance. Nine experts from the United States and Canada were asked to rate each of the items on the SACERS using a 5-point scale (1 = *not important*, 5 = *very important*) to determine the importance of each item to the scale. The overall mean rating of the items was 4.8.

Construct validity evidence was gathered by correlating SACERS total and subscale scores with staff training and staff-to-child ratios. Staff training was estimated assigning a score between 0 and 5 to indicate the highest level of education attained. Staff training was found to have a moderate positive correlation with Space and Furnishings (r = .31), Interactions (r = .29), and program Structure (r = .40). Moderate negative correlations were obtained between staff-to-child ratios and Health and Safety (r = -.40), Activities (r = -.39), and Staff Development (r = -.24). The authors believe this represents good construct validity.

SUMMARY. Given that there is no information about the 24 Canadian settings, and the small pool of trained raters for the reliability studies, these data should be viewed cautiously. The reviewer requested a more extensive technical report from the publisher and authors, but it was unattainable. In addition, a reference to training tapes and/or slides about school-age programs was made for training purposes. No tape or slides were available from the publisher.

The SACERS provides a structured checklist that can be used as part of a program's self-evaluation and program planning. Even so, there is no information provided on score interpretation and use. Due to the limited information regarding technical adequacy, the use of this instrument for tracking or comparing programs should be cautiously considered.

REVIEWER'S REFERENCES

Abbott-Shim, M., & Sibley, A. (1987). *Assessment profile for early childhood programs: Manual administration.* Atlanta, GA: Quality Assist.
Albrecht, K. (1991). *Quality criteria for school-age childcare programs.* Alexandria, VA: Project Home Safe.
O'Connor, S. (1991). *Assessing school-age child care quality.* Unpublished manuscript, Wellesley College, School-Age Child Care Project, Wellesley, MA.

[340]
School Function Assessment.

Purpose: Designed to "measure a student's performance of functional tasks that support his or her participation in the academic and social aspects of an elementary school program."

Population: Grades K–6.

Publication Date: 1998.

Acronym: SFA.

Scores, 26: Participation, Task Supports (Physical Tasks Assistance, Physical Tasks Adaptations, Cognitive/Behavioral Tasks Assistance, Cognitive/Behavioral Tasks Adaptations), Activity Performance (Travel, Maintaining and Changing Positions, Recreational Movement, Manipulation with Movement, Using Materials, Setup and Cleanup, Eating and Drinking, Hygiene, Clothing Management, Up/Down Stairs, Written Work, Computer and Equipment Use, Functional Communication, Memory and Understanding, Following Social Conventions, Compliance with Adult Directives and School Rules, Task Behavior/Completion, Positive Interaction, Behavior Regulation, Personal Care Awareness, Safety).

Administration: Individual.

Price Data, 1999: $134 per complete kit including 25 record forms with 3 rating scale guides and User's manual (136 pages); $51.50 per 25 record forms with 3 rating scale guides.

Time: Administration time not reported.

Comments: Ratings to be completed by an educational and therapeutic professional who is familiar with the child's typical performance.

Authors: Wendy Coster, Theresa Deeney, Jane Haltiwanger, and Stephen Haley.

Publisher: Therapy Skills Builders—A Division of The Psychological Corporation.

Review of the School Function Assessment by WAYNE C. PIERSEL, *Licensed Psychologist, Heartspring, Wichita, KS:*

The assessment of school behavior has come under increasing scrutiny in both regular and special education. In particular, there has been an increased emphasis on practicality and functionality. In the special education arena, law and court decisions have increasingly stressed the treatment usefulness or applicability of assessment instruments and procedures. Not surprisingly, a number of new tests and procedures have been developed in an attempt to address this emphasis. The School Function Assessment is one such example.

According to the authors, the School Function Assessment (SFA) is intended to fit a niche that present assessment instruments and procedures (including adaptive behavior measures) do not address. The SFA is described as a criterion-referenced instrument and is intended to assess how individuals function in specific contexts and to provide directly useful information to assist in program planning and implementation. The authors define "School Function" as the "student's ability to perform important functional activities that support or enable participation in the academic and related social aspects of an educational program" (manual, p. 2). The authors acknowledge that school function assessment instruments and adaptive behavior scales overlap and have very similar content. The test authors state that the second purpose of the SFA is to examine behaviors most affected by physical impairments.

The SFA is divided into three parts. The first part is labeled "Participation" and is composed of one scale. This scale evaluates the student's participation in six major school activity settings. The second part is called "Task Supports." Task supports contains four scales. Two types of task supports, assistance and adaptation, are rated separately for physical tasks and cognitive/behavioral tasks. The third part is named "Activity Performance." This part consists of 21 scales. These 21 scales examine in detail the globally represented tasks presented in the second part.

PSYCHOMETRIC PROPERTIES. Review of the participants in the standardization sample suggests that (a) the sample was an adequate representation of urban, suburban, and rural participants; (b) gender and ethnicity were adequately sampled; and (c) age and grade were adequately represented. The authors also present a breakdown of participants by disability. This is a relatively unique and pleasant addition that is lacking in most other scales.

The internal consistency reliability coefficients range from .92 to .98 for each of the 27 scales. Test-retest (2-week interval) reliability coefficients on a sample of 29 participants range from .80 to .99. The magnitudes of the internal consistency and test-retest reliability estimates are quite adequate. It is important to note that no data are reported on the interrater agreement. This lack of an interrater agreement coefficient is a serious shortcoming.

There are no data on the scale structure of the SFA. Indeed, the only explanation and support provided for the selection and retention of items and the grouping of items on scales is that of expert opinion.

The user's manual is well organized, clearly written, and provides sufficient information regarding the development, standardization, and application to permit the potential user to make an informed decision regarding the merits of the instrument. The individual who completes the SFA protocol needs to be someone who is knowledgeable of the individual being evaluated. The directions for completing the observation rating form are clear and understandable. The authors provide a separate guide to assist raters in completing the observation rating scale. Once the observation rating scale is completed, the raw scores are transformed into "criterion scores" by using the appropriate table. Criterion scores are provided for two groupings of children: (a) kindergarten to third grade, and (b) fourth to sixth grade. After the criterion scores are computed for the individual, the user can determine which domains are furthest from the criterion score and focus on those domains for instruction. One can even place each of the individual items on a criterion profile to determine which specific activities or behaviors are in most need of assistance.

The SFA Record Form is well constructed and contains adequate instructions for the respondent who is completing the form. An accompanying Rating Scale Guide explains in detail how to complete the rating for each section of the record form. With the exception of Part 1 (Participation), which uses a 6-point scale, the remaining scales all use a 4-point scale. Examination of the items on the record form suggests that the specific items are well written with minimal ambiguity.

OVERALL UNIQUENESS AND DISTINCTIVENESS OF THE SCALE. The authors attempt to differentiate school function assessment and adaptive behavior assessment by stating that the two approaches differ in their purpose. The purpose of examining school function is to assess a student's ability to engage or do important functional activities that support or facilitate participation in academic and social aspects of education. The purpose of assessment of adaptive behavior assessment is to determine the effectiveness or degree with which an individual meets the community standard for age-appropriate behavior related to personal independence and social responsibility (Witt, Elliott, Kramer, & Gresham, 1994).

Careful examination of the SFA items strongly suggests that this is actually an adaptive behavior scale. For example, in Part III, the Hygiene Scale contains such items as "Dries hands (using any method)," "wipes nose," "cares for toileting needs in timely fashion," that strongly resemble items found on the Vineland Scales of Adaptive Behavior (T5:2813) or the Scales of Independent Behavior—Revised (337). The items on the scales of Travel, Using Materials, Setting and Cleanup, Eating and Drinking, Hygiene, Clothing Management, Functional Communication, and Memory and Understanding closely resemble items on adaptive behavior scales. The content of the dimensions strongly resembles the content of an adaptive behavior measure.

The authors assert that another advantage of the SFA is that the scores can be used for program planning. They also imply that the individual items can be utilized for precise targeting of skills that need to be addressed and suggest that available adaptive behavior measures providing normative data cannot be so used. This is an interesting assertion. Because the items are very similar, if one can use items from the SFA for selecting specific skills to be addressed one could obviously select items from one of the respective adaptive behavior scales to do the very same thing.

Adaptive behavior is defined as the ability of the individual to adapt and cope with his or her environment. In other words, when one measures adaptive behavior, one is theoretically measuring how one functions in a particular environment. For most purposes, the environment is defined as the community in which the individual lives (Lambert, Nihira, & Leland, 1993). The authors of the SFA talk about how an individual functions in particular environments. They note the criterion-referenced nature of the scale. They note that individual items can be utilized for planning pur-

poses and progress monitoring. With the exception of the criterion-referenced aspect and lack of norms, the SFA greatly resembles many available adaptive measures. This reviewer recommends that practitioners use existing measures of adaptive behavior such as the Vineland Adaptive Behavior Scales (T5:2813) or the Scales of Independent Behavior—Revised (337). Not only can one obtain normative data, it is also possible to examine the individual items for information about skills to target for instruction. The SFA is not sufficiently unique to warrant its use in addition to existing measures of adaptive behavior.

SUMMARY. In this reviewer's opinion, potential users would be better advised to stay with one of the adaptive behavior scales or select instruments that specifically target a defined area or function. The SFA does not provide any additional data not already provided by current adaptive behavior measures.

REVIEWER'S REFERENCES
Lambert, N., Nihira, K., & Leland, H. (1993). *Adaptive Behavior Scale—School* (2nd ed.). Austin, TX: PRO-ED.
Witt, J., Elliott, S., Kramer, J., & Gresham, F. (1994). *Assessment of children: Fundamental methods and practices.* Madison, WI: Brown & Benchmark.

Review of the School Function Assessment by WILLIAM D. SCHAFER, *Associate Professor of Measurement, Statistics, and Evaluation, University of Maryland, College Park, MD and State Director of Student Assessment, Maryland State Department of Education, Baltimore, MD:*

PURPOSE AND DESCRIPTION. The School Function Assessment (SFA) is designed to measure three aspects that affect how well a student performs functional tasks in elementary school programs. These comprise the three parts of the assessment (Part I) Participation as compared with peers in five types of activity settings (external travel, transitioning in school, eating, toileting, and free time) and either regular education or special education classroom settings; (Part II) Task Supports provided by the environment, either assistance or adaptations for either physical or cognitive tasks; and (Part III) degrees of specific Activity Performance for 12 physical tasks and for 9 cognitive/behavioral tasks. Additional rating opportunities exist for stairs, written work, and equipment use within Part II.

DEVELOPMENT. The developers began with 539 items that resulted from a survey of available literature. These were reviewed by 25 educators with various backgrounds to achieve a pilot version that was administered to a sample that included 102 students with broad demographic and impairment characteristics. Item-response theory (IRT) analyses were conducted to evaluate unidimensionality, spread of difficulty, and whether separate scales were needed for different subgroups. After modifications, a tryout version was administered to a broad range of 266 students with disabilities. The data were analyzed with further IRT analyses. Further revisions yielded the standardization version that was administered to a broad range of 363 students with disabilities and a similar group of 315 regular education students. Tables are given in the manual that support the consistency of the sample with the general United States population.

ADMINISTRATION. The SFA is to be completed by a person (or a group of collaborators) familiar with the typical performance of the student and of the student's age/grade peers. In addition, those who score and interpret the results are to be familiar with the specific test as well as standardized testing principles, education in general, and specific disabling conditions that affect the student. The manual estimates that a first-time assessment may take up to 2 hours to complete, which may be spread over as long as 2 or 3 weeks.

All ratings are completed according to behaviorally anchored scales. The distinctions between the levels of the scales appear crisp and easily applied. If in doubt, the manual supplies several examples of each score.

SCORING. Each scale is based on a raw score calculated by summing ratings across subtest items. Tables exist for translating the raw scores into scale scores and standard errors based on Rasch partial-credit model (IRT) analyses of the special-needs students in the standardization sample. The results may be displayed graphically using the score form. Different cutoff scores are provided for primary and intermediate grade levels. Two levels of interpretation are described, a "basic" one in which scores are compared with cutoffs, and an "advanced" one that is more clinical. The cutoff on each scale is the fifth percentile of the regular education students in the standardization sample.

The manual also describes the confidence-band approach (establishing a 1.96 *SEM* band around the scale score) for comparing two students or change in one student over time. This requires a difference of virtually four standard errors to be judged evidence of difference, a criterion many would feel is too stringent.

Item maps exist within the scales for further analyses. Each item map lists the items on the vertical axis; the horizontal axis is the range from zero to 100, interpreted as item difficulty (applied to rating score values). The available scores on the rating scale are listed in the body of the map according to their Rasch analysis locations. By drawing a vertical line at the student's score and error band limits and circling the student's ratings on the items, unusual item ratings are highlighted. This interesting analytic approach is well described in the manual but unfortunately is not supported on the record form.

RELIABILITY. Stability was studied through test-retest correlations for 29 students who exhibited several types of disabilities for a 2- to 4-week interval. Correlations ranged from .90 to .99 for the primary scales, with some of the optional scales as low as .80. Internal consistency estimates for a sample of 363 special education students ranged from .92 to .98.

VALIDITY. A series of analyses, essentially using data from the standardization sample, is described to support the validity of the SFA. Full descriptions of these studies should be available for review.

The manual does identify four hypotheses that the assessment should undergo to establish construct validity evidence. Some data are presented for each of these. But the amount of evidence is small and further validity studies are needed. Finally, because this is an individual assessment, studies that yield consequential evidence of validity would be valuable.

SUMMARY. The SFA is a well-developed instrument. It grows out of thoroughly described constructs and seems structurally consistent with the descriptions. Further, the scales and their recommended interpretations were constructed using a modern, item-response theory approach.

Distinctive use of the various scales on the SFA appears to be supported mostly by logical analyses. Except for a sketchily described factor analysis of Part III, there are no quantitative analyses reported that might have investigated their structure. Moreover, as the manual points out, study of potential biases introduced by different respondents would be valuable. Further research also will be needed to determine whether the levels at which data are reported on the SFA yield the best information for the decision making that the test is intended to support.

Although the scales comprising the parts were developed as related to each other, they are rated independently. The logical connections between them might have been incorporated into the ratings and the associated interpretation system recommended for practitioners. That might be another way that the structure of the tested constructs could be explored.

[341]
Scientific Orientation Test.

Purpose: "Designed to measure a range of affective outcomes for students of science or science-related subjects."
Population: Students in school years 5 to 12.
Publication Date: 1995.
Acronym: S.OR.T.
Scores, 4: Interest in Science, Scientific Attitude, Attitude to School Science, Total.
Administration: Group or individual.
Price Data, 1995: $120 per complete kit including manual (153 pages), 10 test booklets, and 10 response folios; $25 per 10 test booklets; $25 per 10 response folios; $75 per manual.
Time: (40) minutes.
Comments: Includes 5 subtests yielding 13 subscores; formerly titled A Test of Interests.
Author: G. Rex Meyer.
Publisher: GRM Educational Consultancy [Australia].

Review of the Scientific Orientation Test by BRUCE G. ROGERS, Professor of Educational Psychology, University of Northern Iowa, Cedar Falls, IA:

The Scientific Orientation Test (abbreviated in the manual as S.OR.T but, for ease of readability, abbreviated hereafter in this review as SORT) was designed to measure attitudes toward several science-related topics of students in grades 7 through 12. Because teachers and science educators frequently emphasize the value of positive orientations toward science as taught in the classrooms, there is a need for appropriate measuring instruments for assessing those attitudes. The SORT was constructed to address that need. For over 30 years, the SORT has been used in Australia, and more recently, has been used in several research projects in the United States. The author of the test is of the opinion that a wider use in the

schools would be of benefit to both students and teachers. This review therefore addresses some of the factors that might be considered by potential users of the SORT and also presents constructive analysis of the instrument and its application.

Evaluation refers to our like or dislike of a thing. The centrality of evaluation is mirrored in the SORT by the emphasis on asking the students what they most like to do or not like to do. Psychologists also emphasize that attitudes are learned from experience, not inherited. Accordingly, the SORT was conceptualized to assess changes in attitude as a student is exposed to science activities in the school curriculum.

The construct of attitude is perceived by psychologists as a distinct, but complex, psychological entity. By constructing a total, unified score from a set of subscores, the SORT conforms to this view. It is an instrument, therefore, that reflects a professional approach to attitude measurement and therefore is worthy of careful consideration.

DEVELOPMENT. About 40 years ago, a research project at the University of London focused on the development of affective constructs in the areas of science education. Tests were assembled to measure these constructs, which were eventually developed, about 1965 in Australia, as the SORT. The development of each of the subtests began with a review of the literature to generate initial concepts and ideas, followed by consultation with psychologists, science educators, and teachers. After the items were submitted to various panels of experts, they were pilot-tested with groups of students and the resulting item analysis data were used for item modification. The final scales were administered to representative groups, in the Sydney, Australia area, and norm tables were developed. Although the details of the procedures are not as fully explicated in the manual as might be desired, sufficient explanation is given to lead the reader to believe that the standard professional procedures for attitude scale development were followed.

However, in the intervening three decades since the inception of the SORT, new developments have occurred in both science education and attitude measurement. Whereas achievement tests are typically revised every decade, there is no evidence in the SORT manual that any revision has occurred subsequently with this instrument.

The test user today might expect that this attitude test would also have benefited if it had been revised during the subsequent years.

DESCRIPTION. Students are allowed 40 minutes to respond to a total of 170 items, presented in five subtests. Each item consists of a declarative sentence to be rated on a 5-point modified Likert-type scale. Three subtests measure scientific orientation, one subtest measures nonscientific interests, and a fifth subtest measures what the manual describes as "solving science problems by appeal to authority" (p. 23). These five areas can be further subdivided and combined to form a total of 18 scores. Instructions are given for creating several profiles to display the scores. The manual states that the function of the SORT is to "make available an easily administered battery of reliable and valid scales" (p. 13).

RELIABILITY. Evidence pertaining to the internal consistency of each of the subscales (called variables in the manuals) was obtained with the split-half method based on alternative items. These reliability indices had a median near .90, while the composite science orientation scales had reliabilities above that median. Test-retest reliability indices are also reported in the manual, with a median value for the 18 scales near .80. However, 16 of those values were based on a sample of 90 fifth grade students, tested across a 3-week interval, almost 40 years ago. Two of the values were based on a sample of 200 secondary students, over 30 years ago. Users of these tests could have more confidence in the reliability estimates if the data were available from larger samples and more recent administrations.

VALIDITY. As a check on "face" validity, the items were submitted to groups of teachers and other "criterion" groups (undefined in the manual), to obtain suggestions for rewording. Although this is a commendable procedure, it might be useful to also obtain comments from students when the test is revised in the future. Evidence for content validity was obtained by looking for agreement in judgments by judges. Although this is a desirable procedure, test users could have more confidence if there was an explanation of how phrases such as "high levels of agreement between judges" and "conceptually homogeneous as perceived by judges" (p. 66) should be interpreted by the reader of the manual. Without such an explanation, the reader is actually left with only the opinion of the author of the test. This reviewer hopes that these matters will be addressed in a future revision.

The results of several studies of criterion-related validity are presented in the manual. Test scores of students were compared with essay scores on their opinion of science courses; with their indication of what type of courses they would like to take the next year in school; with self-ratings, peer ratings, and teacher ratings on their interest in science; and with other science interest tests. The validity of the test is certainly enhanced by these type of studies. However, all of the studies were over 10 years old at the time the manual was published and the majority of them were over 20 years old. Newer studies are to be encouraged, and this reviewer suggests that they be done with a revised edition of the test.

Evidence for construct validity was presented primarily as correlations with scores from intelligence tests, achievement tests, other science attitude and interest tests, and nonscience attitude scales. Factor analysis studies were also reported. These are certainly commendable, but the comments made above about the recency of the criterion-related studies apply in the same manner to the construct-related evidence.

NORMS. The manual shows percentile norms for one group in Australia. It also lists means and standard deviations for five groups. The test user will need to examine these norm data carefully to decide to what extent they are current, relevant, and representative. The norms for the SORT are not as current as the norms for many achievement batteries. The Australian norm data were 15 years old when the manual was published and the other norm data were over 20 years old. Because major curriculum changes have been made in science education during the past several decades, the test user would find the norms of more value if they were current within the most recent decade of their intended use. The relevancy of the norms may also be problematical. How relevant are Australian norms to the populations of the other countries? Unfortunately, this question is not addressed in the manual, even though the author encourages the use of the test by teachers in other countries. If the test is revised, perhaps arrangements will be made to collect data relevant to other countries where the test might be used. At that time, the issue of representativeness will need to be addressed. How confident can the test user be that the norm sample was representative of the intended population? Unfortunately, there was no description of how the Australian sample was selected. Three grade levels were reported from boys and girls, but the procedure for selecting geographical areas, schools, and students within grades is not described in the manual.

USABILITY. How convenient will teachers find this test to administer, score, and interpret in actual classroom use? The manual recommends that the test be administered by a "neutral" person. It explains that the teacher is not a "neutral" person, but it does not explain who is a "neutral" person. Is another teacher a "neutral" person? It would be very useful if such questions were addressed in the manual. The instructions for administering do not contain a set of sentences to be read verbatim, but rather consist of a set of 14 statements to the teachers, such as "Tell pupils that the book consists of lots of statements ... Write the following scale on the board ... Say the scale over twice" (p. 19). When this reviewer had the instructions read aloud by a teacher, it took over 5 minutes. The test user must consider how many students might lose interest during that time.

The manual recommends that students be allowed 40 minutes to respond to the 170 items in the test, but also states that most students finish within 35 minutes which implies that the students are responding to each item in about 12 seconds. Test users will need to decide if they wish to encourage such quick judgments about attitudes. The entire administration procedure might be perceived by some teachers as being excessively time-consuming and therefore they may consider eliminating some of the subtests. This should be considered when the test is revised.

The directions for scoring begin by adding the votes to obtain 13 totals on the pages within the booklet, transferring these totals to the cover, followed by 4 additions, 1 division, and 2 subtractions. Then, using the tables of norms, these scores are to be converted into standard scores and percentiles. The norm tables are arranged by grouping the raw scores into intervals encompassing 8 points. For the other 7 points in any interval, the manual recommends interpolation. Over 200 words are devoted to describing the interpolation procedure, concluding with the sentence, "it is really simple and speedy" (p. 25). This reviewer does not consider interpolation in an 8-point interval to be either "simple" or "speedy." Furthermore, the manual explains that the relationship between raw scores and percentiles is nonlinear, yet linear interpolation is used within intervals as wide as 17 percentile points. For purposes of making comparisons, the manual recommends using standard scores, such a z-scores, but test users will also need to decide if they consider that computation to be "simple and speedy." In the opinion of this reviewer, the scoring procedures may be seen by many teachers as not being the best use of their time and thus they will be hesitant to use the instrument. The test user must again weigh the relative values of these activities.

When this test is revised, the authors might prioritize the type of decisions that teachers and pupils can make from the test and use that information to see if the test could be substantially reduced in length and time of administration. Because many schools now have, or plan to obtain, an optical scanner, it might be possible to arrange the items in a manner that the scanner could score the sheets. A computer program might be written to perform the score conversions, prepare profiles, and tabulate the results. This procedure is available for some other tests, and users might find it to be desirable for the SORT.

SUMMARY. The SORT is a set of attitude scales that were professionally constructed to assess interest in science. It reflects the state-of-the-art 30 to 40 years ago. Teachers will find the attitude constructs to be of value and students will find the items of interest as they respond. The results could, potentially, be of use to teachers in curriculum evaluation and to students in planning their courses of study. However, test users should be concerned that the test has not been revised in over 30 years, that there is a lack of supporting technical data, that the administration time is time-consuming, and that the scoring is labor intensive. The authors are urged to employ current technology and technical expertise to revise this instrument into one that teachers will find to be convenient to administer, score, and interpret. Until that occurs, this reviewer would urge caution in the adoption of this instrument.

Review of the Scientific Orientation Test by HERBERT C. RUDMAN, Professor Emeritus of Measurement and Quantitative Methods, Michigan State University, East Lansing, MI:

The Scientific Orientation Test (S.OR.T.) was first developed in Australia in the 1960s under the title of *A Test of Interests*. It was revised again in 1975 and new norms were established in the 1980s. A third modification was published in 1995. This "commercial" version carries the misnomer of a "test" of scientific interests. A test usually signifies a correct or incorrect response. A test is a measure of the application of cognitive factors or the level of a skill, but interests as used in the *Scientific Orientation Test* are affective variables that can be measured but not tested. One might measure the frequency of interests or their depth, but a survey of interests is not the same as a test nor is it necessarily a predictor of future interests or future vocational skills (Ebel & Frisbie, 1986; Mehrens & Lehmann, 1991).

The S.OR.T. has been designed primarily for students in the middle school grades of 7 to 10. The author claims that it can be used "with care" in the primary school grades of 5 and 6 as well as the senior high school grades of 11 and 12. Unfortunately, he fails to identify just what "care" means. He also claims that with slight modifications in wording it can be sued in "nonformal and informal educational programs and other (non-specified) programs which are approximately equivalent to the school years specified" (manual, p. 1). Even though the title of the S.OR.T. deals with interests and attitudes towards science, the test booklet includes measures in two nonscientific areas, Literature and Fine Art. This adds some confusion to interpreting assessment results obtained. The manual states that each of the nonscientific areas are "sufficiently valid and reliable in its own right to stand on its own" (p. 1). It is not clear, however, why these two areas are part of the S.OR.T. battery. Ostensibly they offer a contrast to scientific interests but this reviewer cannot see what contributions they make to contrasts between nonscientific and science intereests. It is unclear to what end the S.OR.T. will be used.

COMPONENTS OF THE S.OR.T. BATTERY. The Scientific Orientation Test consists of a test manual, a test booklet, and a response folio. The test battery is an independently published product of the GRM Consultancy located in New South Wales, Australia. The English language used is idiosyncratic to Australia and introduces a few words connected with the test booklet that may puzzle the reader (e.g., "You will be asked to give 4 votes to the statement with which you agree very strongly, 3 to the next most sensible ones, 2 to the next, 1 to those with which you least agree, and 0 to the ones with which you do not agree at all. ... Be sure to give some kind of vote to each"). Most readers will come to see that "votes" are ratings on a nominal scale.

The test manual is confusing. The manuscript is filled with ambiguities related to the content level of the S.OR.T., to its description of the ages of students that are appropriate for the administration of the test, and to its claims of validity, reliability, and concepts that normally could illustrate the purposes for which the test is being used. The material presented for this review needs considerable editing.

The manual that accompanies the test and its scoring folio was meant to explain the S.OR.T.'s purpose, its content, how to administer the test booklet, and to serve as a technical manual, but unfortunately, it goes off on tangents and loses its focus. Instead of focusing on the test itself, the manual centers on the research of other investigators who have studied phenomena that are not necessarily related to the S.OR.T. test booklet.

Under the section entitled, "Uses of the Test" the author introduces the user of the S.OR.T. to what he describes as a rationale for the test. However, the "rationale" is more of a traditional review of the cognitive psychology literature that has been studied over the past 50 years than it is a rationale for the use of the Scientific Orientation Test. Although the author cannot be faulted for such a review, he is not addressing the rationale for the development and use of the test. Thirty-eight pages into the manual one finds still another section entitled "Using the Test Results," which is a far better discussion of test use. This latter description lists 17 topics ranging from "Grouping Pupils" to "Facilitating Basic Research."

NUMBER OF SUBTESTS. The Scientific Orientation Test booklet contains five "subtests" or components. These are identified as "School Holidays," "Finding Out About Things," "Learning Things," "Talking Together," and "Talking About Science At School." The students are asked to respond to statements under each of the components and rate each statement from 4 to 0. The format of these subtests is confusing. A major error in the construction of the test booklet is that too much is packed into what is designed to be a hand-scored booklet. Each page has a series of abbreviations along the top of the page that represent descriptors of what is being measured. For example, under "School Holidays," the student is asked to place a rating on a line that is under one of the abbreviations. This will then give the person assigned to scoring the responses an indication of what is ostensibly being measured. If the student offers a rating on a statement "Write the story" his rating will appear under the abbreviation "L," which stands for Literature. The student does not know what L stands for but they do see that there is a space in which to enter their response. Only the person who scores the "test" knows what it means.

TEST ADMINISTRATION. Instructions for administering the S.OR.T. seem to be relatively clear and detailed. The test booklet is obviously designed for hand scoring. The directions seem primitive in light of the availability of computer scoring in all but the most underdeveloped parts of the world. Most assuredly Australia is not an underdeveloped nation. What follows are excerpts from "Directions for Administering" the Scientific Orientation Test.

"It is not recommended that the test be administered by the class teacher as this may cause some pupils to answer in a manner which they assume is expected by the teacher." "Space pupils as widely as possible. Issue test booklets but tell the class not to open them or start work until told to do so." "Tell the pupils, though, not to spend too much time thinking about each vote. Read a statement and vote on it quickly. Vote on each statement in turn and do not leave any unanswered." "Stress that results will not be used for grading but to help teachers give better lessons." "It is not necessary to insist on completion unless the results are to be used for individual analysis" (manual, p. 19). (This last statement is quite a contradiction to earlier directions.)

The last two pages of the test booklet are open-ended. The instructions on page 9 of the test booklet indicate to the test taker, "If you have time, use these two pages to write anything you would like to say about the science lessons in your school. You may write just a few lines or up to two pages according to the time you have left." The purpose served by these instructions is unclear to this reviewer.

The test manual is specific enough so that if a teacher, school administrator, or guidance coun-selor reads the supplied directions to those taking the test, the method for administering the test can be standardized. However, equally important is whether these directions have replicated the conditions under which the test was validated and normed. The Scientific Orientation Test appears to be a new test in name only. Its statistical descriptions utilize previous studies of its psychometric characteristics related to validity, reliability, and test construction. The research cited extends back more than 40 years. The various versions of this instrument were administered in four countries: England, Australia, Israel, and Bahrain.

DERIVATION OF AUSTRALIAN NORMS. S.OR.T. norms were gathered across three grade levels: 7th, 9th, and 11th. The norm sample consisted of 677 boys, and 640 girls for a total of 1,317 students. The students were not selected on a random base because classes remained intact. There appears to be no consideration given to randomizing a selection of schools from which the 50 classes could have been selected.

These norms were collected in mid year of 1980 in various areas of metropolitan Sydney. A remarkable jump in logic was made by the author when he observed that, "While the Australian norms were derived from only one city, evidence from international studies suggests that there are no significant differences between urban and rural groups or between geographic regions of a country" (p. 34). This singular observation is open for critical discussion. As one who has worked in schools abroad including the Middle East and Australia this reviewer finds this observation highly debatable.

A questionable practice in developing and using norms from which to draw conclusions is to be found on page 32 of the S.OR.T. manual. In discussing Australian norms for school years other than 7th, 9th, and 11th, the recommendation is made that grades 8, 10, and 12 use approximate norms by interpolation or extrapolation depending upon the level being approximated. The author does caution users to be careful in their generalizations.

DERIVATION OF BAHRAIN NORMS. Bahrain, we are told, is representative of the Arab States of Egypt, Iraq, Jordan, Kuwait, Libya, Oman, Qatar, Saudi Arabia, Sudan, Syria, and Yemen. The manual contains this generalization because the Arab states listed, ostensibly, have a common school structure, tend to follow the same or similar science curricula, and have a common culture and philosophy of education in relation to the teaching of science. Although all of the countries listed are Islamic in religion there are some considerable differences between Jordan, for example, and Saudi Arabia. The author draws generalizations from samples to populations too freely for this reviewer. Although it is likely that at some given point in time, sampling one Arab state or one city in a country might sound reasonable, generalizing from small samples to a population across decades, using data that ignore internal changes in a population over time, is a fundamental flaw in norm development.

TECHNICAL ASPECTS. The S.OR.T. manual describes the statistical analyses used to investigate the content, criterion-related, and construct validity of the test under review. Content validity is equated with "face" validity, which weakens the author's claims for content validity. A more substantive argument could have been made. From the beginning of the description of determining content validity, we can see what weakens the Scientific Orientation Test. In his desire to legitimize the bases of the "test" the author takes great pains to cite previous literature that is, at times, loosely linked to the content of the S.OR.T. booklet but does not deal directly with the S.OR.T. itself. As the manual states, "Content and 'face' validity are given credence … [by] relying heavily on the cumulative findings of previous research, including in most cases published and validated relevant affective tests" (p. 66).

It would appear from the full description of how content validity was determined for the S.OR.T., that a Q-sort technique was used with teachers and other members of criterion groups to identify certain concepts that were related to each area of scientific interest. A high level of agreement was found using a 1929 scaling procedure by Thurstone and Chave.

The techniques described for obtaining evidence of criterion-related validity are a particularly strong and positive approach to establishing validity of the S.OR.T. Thirteen different studies are described. A positive element in the manual's discussion of criterion-related validity is the treatment of relationships between specific variables that make up the S.OR.T. and more generalized concepts of Science interests.

Construct validity evidence was obtained through statistical analyses of eight construct studies

that used factor analysis, multiple regression, and discriminative analysis. As before, the discussion of construct validity leaned heavily upon studies of a variety of variables from differentiated studies not necessarily related or based upon the S.OR.T., and occurring at various periods in time. One would be hard-pressed to judge the excellence of the Scientific Orientation Test from the data reported in the test manual.

The manual reports reliability estimates by (a) split-half techniques using alternative items and (b) a Spearman Brown prophecy formula, (c) a test-retest estimate by a repeat testing 6-weeks later, and (d) Cronbach's alpha coefficient (an internal consistency measure).

The reliability estimates are reported by variables measured. The estimates are fragmented by year and by location. As an example, the split-half reliability estimate for "Science Orientation (variable 4.0)" is based on 200 randomly selected boys and girls in Forms 7, 9, and 11 in secondary schools in Sydney, Australia. This is contrasted with a test-retest at a 6-week interval. The estimates reported are given as split half (.968), and test-retest (.831). In the case of the example just cited, one cannot make much of a generalization about a scientific interest inventory under these conditions. Data are reported for different versions of the S.OR.T. (1959, 1965, 1985). This reviewer finds these data suspect because interests and attitudes are not always stable, and certainly they are not permanently fixed. Changing educational and social situations over time make disparate data of the kind described above not convincing.

The use of the reliability estimates is suspect, given the assumptions one would follow normally. It is essential to know the characteristics of the sample on which the reliability estimates were computed. The only characteristics identified in the descriptions given are gender, grade level, and location. Curriculums studied, science experiences in school, parental support, and the like are at least as important in the study of attitudes and interests, and in judging the reliability estimates computed. The use of coefficient alpha is most appropriate for personality measures, interest inventories, and other measures that are not scored for correct/incorrect responses. The use of Cronbach's coefficient alpha is mentioned in a review of a study conducted in Melbourne, Australia with 780 seventh graders. Unfortunately, this study had little to do with the development of the Scientific Orientation Test.

SUMMARY. The S.OR.T. is not representative of high-quality interest inventories usually reviewed in the *Mental Measurements Yearbook* series. The test manual reads more like a review of the literature in a doctoral dissertation than it does in (a) explaining how the interest inventory was developed, (b) the author's rationale for its use with students at various grade levels, (c) as a guide for administering the interest inventory, and (d) explaining other technical descriptions found in a test manual. The test manual as submitted for review only vaguely conforms to the *Standards for Educational and Psychological Testing* (AERA, APA, & NCME, 1985).

The overriding weakness of the S.OR.T. is that it overlooks the purposes that an interest inventory can serve. Scores derived from an administration of an inventory mean little if they are not interpreted correctly by a professional trained in the limitations of reported interests. Individual curiosities are rarely, if ever, stable. However, over time they can blossom into interests but even then they are not permanent. That being the case, the act of choosing vocations, or making advanced education choices based on interest inventory results is problematic.

This reviewer cannot recommend the Scientific Observation Test as it has been submitted. It needs severe editing and empirical use with a strong emphasis on currency of scientific concepts measured.

REVIEWER'S REFERENCES

American Educational Research Association, American Psychological Association, & National Council on Measurement in Education. (1985). *Standards for educational and psychological testing.* Washington, DC: American Psychological Association, Inc.

Ebel, R. L., & Frisbie, D. A. (1986). *Essentials of educational measurement* (4th ed.). Englewood Cliffs, NJ: Prentice-Hall.

Mehrens, W. A., & Lehmann, I. J. (1991). *Measurement and evaluation in education and psychology* (4th ed.). Fort Worth, TX: Holt, Rinehart and Winston, Inc.

[342]
Scorable Self-Care Evaluation (Revised).

Purpose: To assess clients' motivation and performance of self-care tasks and identify problems in basic living skills.

Population: Adolescent and adult occupational therapy clients.

Publication Date: 1993.

Acronym: SSCE.

Scores, 23: Subtasks divided among 4 subscales: Personal Care (Initial Appearance, Orientation, Hygiene, Communications, First Aid, Total), Housekeeping (Foods Selection, House Chores, Safety, Laundry, Total), Work and Leisure (Leisure Activity, Transportation, Job-Seeking Skills, Total), Financial Management (Making Change, Checking, Paying Personal Bills, Budgeting, Procurement of Supplemental Income, Source of Income, Total), Total Score.

Administration: Individual.

Price Data, 1999: $36 per manual (90 pages).

Time: (40–50) minutes.

Comments: Administrator must provide pencils, map of the local area, 16 3-inch cards, telephone book with yellow pages, and play money.

Authors: E. Nelson Clark and Mary Peters.

Publisher: Therapy Skill Builders—A Division of The Psychological Corporation.

Review of the Scorable Self-Care Evaluation (Revised) by ROBERT B. MILLER, Psychologist, Coordinator, Program Evaluation & Quality Improvement, Saginaw County Community Mental Health Center, Saginaw, MI:

TEST COVERAGE AND USE. The manual of the Scorable Self-Care Evaluation (Revised) (SSCE) states that the instrument is a "standardized self-care evaluation instrument designed to assess comprehensively and quantifiably the client's performance of self-care tasks" (manual, p. 1). Based on a review of the interpretations in the manual, the instrument appears to be an attempt to quantify a baseline assessment of self-help skills and to provide a means of the measurement of said constructs across interventions or treatment. This assessment device is primarily in use by occupational therapists and occupational therapy assistants.

The manual does not state age range or specifics regarding to whom the test can be administered. A preliminary standardization project was conducted on 67 persons ranging in age from 13–62. The sample was made up of students or adult volunteers from military families. No systematic sampling was conducted. There is no stratification by age, race, or educational attainment.

There is no evidence that stratification of subgroups by age, gender, ethnicity, educational attainment, or SES was conducted and clearly could not be conducted with the sample described.

There is no evidence in the manual of any attempt to consider neurodevelopmental theory within its design.

No item analysis was conducted and attempts to create an intercorrelation matrix for analysis were incorrectly designed. The insufficient variations of test scores suggest a lack of adequate score distribution. This may be due to limitations in size of the sample as well as individual subject similarity.

RELIABILITY. Pearson product moment correlations were determined across scores. No adequate measures of internal reliability are presented. There are no split-half reliability studies. Of particular concern, there is only one attempt to assess test-retest reliability, an important preliminary investigation in the development of measures of outcome. This was conducted on 10 subjects at a 60-day interval. The test-retest reliability coefficients ranged from .5 to 1.0. The sample size is so small that this should be interpreted with significant caution. The reliability studies described in the manual should be considered preliminary. Evidence is not sufficient to warrant decisions with this instrument's results alone. The sample for estimating reliability was chosen on availability and therefore is unlike a referred sample.

VALIDITY. There is not a clear statement of the universe of skills represented by the test. The instrument was designed to assess self-help with specific items believed to assess personal care, housekeeping, work and leisure, and financial management. The selection process for the items making up the instrument is not described. There is no evidence of attempts to assess construct validity of this instrument.

TEST ADMINISTRATION. The instrument's instructions are adequate. The administration procedures are the same as the conditions under which the test was validated and normed though some latitude in administration is allowed. It is unknown what effect this has upon results.

TEST REPORTING. Means and standard deviations are provided allowing for interpretation by persons with appropriate training and experience in the psychometric properties of measurement. Limited interpretations are provided in the manual.

TEST AND ITEM BIAS. There is no evidence of analysis of possible bias. Item selection procedures are not described. There is no evidence of analysis of differential validity across groups. There is no evidence of the assessment of persons who are non-English-speaking.

SUMMARY. The Scorable Self-Care Evaluation (Revised) (SSCE) is a measure intended to assess self-care skills for baseline occupational therapy assessment and across interventions and treatment. Although the attempt to design adequate measures of outcome is laudable, there is little evidence that this published instrument should be considered as meeting the minimum standard for use. The authors are to be praised for their effort to design a measure of outcome in the assessment of self-help skills and for consistently referring to limitations within their original work. However, until evidence of internal reliability, content validity, and construct validity is provided, professionals in need of measures of these constructs are encouraged to investigate the use of psychometrically sound measures of adaptive behavior.

Review of the Scorable Self-Care Evaluation (Revised) by STEVEN I. PFEIFFER, Adjunct Professor of Psychology and Education, and Executive Director, Duke University Talent Identification Program, Durham, NC:

The Scorable Self-Care Evaluation (SSCE) is a standardized evaluation scale designed to assess a client's level of self-care across four domains. The SSCE consists of 18 subtasks grouped into four subscales: Personal Care (Initial Appearance, Orientation, Hygiene, Communications, and First Aid), Housekeeping (Foods Selection, House Chores, Safety, and Laundry), Work and Leisure (Leisure Activity, Transportation, and Job-Seeking Skills), and Financial Management (Making Change, Checking, Paying Personal Bills, Budgeting, Procurement of Supplemental Income, and Source of Income). The SSCE takes approximately 45 minutes to administer and provides four subscale scores and a total score.

In the manual, the authors state three goals of the SSCE: to provide a baseline profile of functional self-care skills, to guide treatment and discharge planning, and to demonstrate treatment effectiveness. The instrument was developed based on a review of the literature and critique of nine of the more popular self-care scales. Great attention was paid to ensuring that the instrument had face validity and would support client motivation. Administration and scoring are straightforward, and the manual provides a list of suggested tasks for treatment planning.

Unfortunately, the SSCE has a host of psychometric weaknesses that greatly lessen its effectiveness in terms of its three stated goals. Very little information is provided on the standardization group, and it is therefore impossible to know who they represent. Second, the manual provides no information in support of the validity of scores from the SSCE. A user would not know, for example, whether the content of the SSCE adequately samples what others would consider the relevant skills in the self-care domain. Relatedly, the user would not know whether the SSCE provides similar scores to other self-care instruments or predicts relevant, extra-test client behavior. Third, the manual provides no guidance in how to interpret scores with regard to determining if a client has demonstrated appreciable improvement.

A final point bears mentioning. The authors use the labels "Functional" and "Dysfunctional" to demarcate the extreme two levels of performance on each of the four scales. It would be more accurate (as well as less pejorative) to relabel the scales in terms of level of functionality (perhaps providing a schema consistent with the new American Association of Mental Retardation [AAMR] definition of mental retardation that categorizes individuals in terms of their level of need for supportive services) (AAMR, 1992). "Dysfunctionality" implies something quite different from absence of or less-than-full expression of a skill.

The SSCE does have much to offer, however, as a research tool. The scores from the scale show fairly good reliability and the scale offers rather creative approaches to the measurement of self-care skills (e.g., having the person use an actual map to locate a street [Transportation subtask]). Considerable work still needs to be done, however, before the SSCE can be recommended for use with a client as a diagnostic, treatment planning, or outcome instrument.

REVIEWER'S REFERENCE

American Association on Mental Retardation. (1992). *Mental retardation: Definition, classification, and systems of supports.* Washington, DC: Author.

[343]
Selby MillSmith Values Indices.

Purpose: "A measure of personal values associated with work and the working environment."
Population: Adults.
Publication Dates: 1985–1991.
Administration: Individual or group.
Editions, 2: Management Values Index, Supervisory Values Index.
Price Data: Available from publisher.
Comments: Test may be paper-and-pencil or computer administered.
Author: Adrian W. Savage.
Publisher: Selby MillSmith [England].

a) MANAGEMENT VALUES INDEX.
Purpose: "For selection, assessment and training and development at managerial and senior levels within an organisation."
Population: Managers.
Acronym: MVI.
Scores, 27: Core Scales [Achievement Values (Work Ethic, Responsibility, Risk Taking, Task Orientation, Leadership, Activity, Need for Status, Self Esteem), Expertise Values (Need for Mental Challenge, Innovation, Analysis, Attention to Detail), Consolidation Values (Need for Stability, Need for Structure, Career Development), Interpersonal Values (Sociability, Inclusion, Personal Warmth, Tactfulness, Tolerance)], [Second Order Indices (Executive Index, Stability Index, Conscientiousness Index, Expert Orientation Index, Team Orientation Index, Empathy Index, Motivational Distortion Index)].
Time: (30–45) minutes.
b) SUPERVISORY VALUES INDEX.
Purpose: "For selection, assessment and training and development at supervisory and 'A' level standard."
Scores, 26: Core Scales [Achievement Values (Work Ethic, Responsibility, Risk Taking, Task Orientation, Leadership, Activity, Need for Status, Self Esteem), Expertise Values (Need for Mental Challenge, Innovation, Analysis, Attention to Detail), Consolidation Values (Need for Stability, Need for Structure, Career Development), Interpersonal Values (Sociability, Inclusion, Personal Warmth, Tactfulness, Tolerance)], Second Order Indices (Initiative Index, Team Orientation Index, Stability Index, Enquiry Index, Conscientiousness Index, Motivational Distortion Index).
Time: (30–45) minutes.

Review of the Selby MillSmith Values Indices by PETER MILES BERGER, Area Manager— Mental After Care Association, London, England:

The Management Values Index (MVI) and Supervisory Values Index (SVI) are intended to measure fundamental work-related attitudes and beliefs. The manual indicates that these instruments can be used for selection, training, and/or development at managerial or senior level. Each instrument contains 252 questions, each answered on a scale of 0 to 4. The instruments take approximately one-half hour to complete. Questionnaires have to be scored by computer, and the publisher supplies several PC-based scoring packages.

The instruments are available for interactive use on PCs. The interactive version was quite user friendly and appealing. The questions were stimulating and engaging, encouraging self-examination that seemed like a helpful, if unintended, outcome.

Of three available report formats I clearly preferred the briefer narrative report as it was most clear and incisive. The longer report differs from the briefer only in stating elaborate definitions for each scale. This information is particularly superfluous for scales falling in the average range.

Validity studies, reliability studies, and normative data were developed for the MVI using groups including managers, final year students, trainee airline pilots, and police inspectors. Of 1,158 norm group subjects, 319 are unclassified.

For the SVI, airline cabin crew, police superintendents, engineers, members of the fire brigade, and supervisors were used. Of 919 norm group subjects 337 are unclassified. These norm groups hardly represent the broad spectrum of different professions and trades. The norms offer a point of reference, rather than an authoritatively representative view; therefore, interpretation based on these norms should be cautious in the extreme. Workers will differ from these norms according to characteristics of each job.

The manual emphasizes the construct validity of scores from these instruments. No studies of predictive validity are presented, nor studies of performance against criteria. As a result, findings should be considered theoretical, rather than grounded in real life performance or behavior. This shortcoming undermines the author's proposal for use in selection or recruitment.

The manual details a conscientious effort to clearly define constructs articulating a wide range of work-related values. As a result, the user has little doubt about what is being measured. This documentation offers rationale for the face validity of the instruments.

The manual presents a number of studies testing concurrent validity by comparing results with The Myers-Briggs Type Indicator, the FIRO-B, The Jackson Personality Inventory, and the California Psychological Inventory. A number of strikingly significant correlations support construct validity. Findings offer evidence that the other instruments measure some factors in common with the MVI and SVI.

Reliability is examined solely through the alpha method. These coefficients are very acceptable, within the limits of the method. No impression of stability can be gained through the documentation. It would be interesting to know how stable work-related values are, and which values represent state or trait factors. Test-retest studies would reflect on the confidence that could be placed in findings.

The author makes a point of foregoing factor analytic methods for developing subscales. Subscales are devised by commonsense grouping. The result of eschewing a more rigorous factor-analytic approach is that boundaries between subscales seem fuzzy with single factors potentially contributing to several identified scales. The documentation surprisingly does not present a breakdown of which items are included in which scales. This vital information would allow users to better understand and evaluate the instruments.

More global "Second Order Scales" are produced by amalgamating several basic scales. Examples of these scales include "Executive Index," "Team Orientation Index," and others. These scales amplify the difficulties of intuitive rather than technical scale development. Scales contributing to the Second Order Scales can cancel each other out, so that these amalgamated scores can become nearly useless.

The impression of using and interpreting my personal results was that the scores mostly agreed with my self-perceptions. The report described me accurately in many respects. I felt that some of the narrative comments might be interpreted negatively by employers, to my disadvantage in selection.

I must raise several points of caution. The developers propose that the instrument be used for selection for employment. Use of these tests for selection does not seem appropriate, especially within an equal opportunities selection framework. No predictive validity is offered to indicate correlation between scale results and success in jobs. The tester-selector is asked to make an inductive leap from constructs to predicting job performance, and there appears to be no evidence to justify this proposed use. It may be tempting to recruiting employers to propose the desired profile for candidates, and select (or reject) candidates who meet (or do not meet) the hypothetical profile. This approach to using these test findings is speculative and creates fundamental unfairness in selection. My view is that these instruments should not be used for selection in recruitment or promotion.

Another important factor with these instruments is that they are comparatively expensive. The publishers require a license fee of approximately 500 pounds (700 USD) per year plus fees for each administration of 11 or 14 pounds (17 to 22 USD), with some discounts available. Thus, the instruments seem to be targeted for corporate use in organizations that can justify this level of expenditure for this type of information.

SUMMARY. Overall, these instruments were interesting to use. Results encouraged me to think more about values and my personal beliefs and conduct. Test consumers need to consider if these instruments justify their cost, or if perhaps other less costly instruments can be found to analyse an individual's values. After all, values are rather abstract constructs lending themselves to many different schemata, and there can be little argument about the relative merits of such schemata, as they are more in the eye of the beholder than grounded in any true life reality.

Frankly, I am troubled by the suggestion that these tests could be used in employee selection. Their use for that purpose, in absence of relevant predictive validity studies, seems indefensible. With an appreciation of these tests' limitations, organizations that can comfortably bear the cost may find these instruments useful in stimulating employees' self-examination, to facilitate team building and effective supervision, and for assisting employees to plan their future development and training needs.

Review of the Selby MillSmith Values Indices by GERALD R. SCHNECK, Professor of Rehabilitation Counseling, Mankato State University, Mankato, MN:

The Selby MillSmith Values Indices was developed by the authors in the United Kingdom for applied use in the "selection, assessment, training, development and employment or career counselling" of predominantly adults within employment settings. There are two versions of the Selby MillSmith Values Indices, those being the Management Values Index (MVI) and the Supervisory Values Index (SVI). The MVI "demands a level of knowledge of English broadly compatible with the ability to read a serious daily newspaper," whereas the SVI "uses simpler English, broadly compatible with a popular tabloid newspaper" (manual, p. 1). The MVI is designed to be used with "manage-

ment," "graduates and first year student" populations, whereas the SVI is intended for "people who may broadly be described as being of Supervisory level, or alternatively for school leavers of A-level standard" (manual, p. 1). The manual and user guide for the Selby MillSmith Values Indices provides a thoughtful discussion of the importance of values in the hierarchy of psychological constructs, particularly as they relate to beliefs and attitudes and to applications within the field of Human Resource Management.

Preliminary items for inclusion in the Values Indices instruments were developed through the guidance of the hypothetical framework of values and then administered to a sample of respondents. Items were excluded if they were ambiguous or unclear, with the remainder being weighted onto scales based on item-to-scale correlation. The scales were then checked on a cross-validated sample and split-half reliability coefficients were estimated using coefficient alpha. The authors state that this process resulted in the currently used scales owing their inclusion to: "(a) relevance to real-life; (b) evidence from the literature that those scales represent stable and widely recognised values; and (c) having had their relevance established statistically" (manual, p. 3). A combination of both "global" values and job-specific attitudes and preferences were ultimately included by the authors, to provide balance and relevance to the work situation, rather than to other life activities. The Values Indices scales have two formats: (a) item for response is placed into a context; and (b) presentation as single, context-free words. Responses made to items on the questionnaire are grouped and scored against 21 Core scales, which represent the basic value-structure of the subject, as measured by the instrument. In addition, Second Order scales are derived from combinations of scores on the Core scales. The MVI has six of these scales, whereas the SVI has five. Core and Second Order scales are as listed in the descriptive entry for this instrument.

Although both the MVI and SVI questionnaires are administered in a paper-pencil format, the scoring of the Values Indices is complex, requiring a licensed computer-scoring program (IBM PC or truly compatible machine only). Raw scores for each subject are converted to standardized score, specifically the STENS system (standard TENS). The manual provides a short explanation of each point in the STENS scale (ranging from 1 at the lowest to 10 at the highest) and appropriate manner of interpreting these scores, including various cautions regarding overinterpretation.

Comments within the manual addressed important issues surrounding instrument usage, such as: (a) strongly encouraging appropriate training of persons involved in administering, interpreting, and utilizing the instruments; and (b) providing one-on-one feedback to the subject, rather than only offering a written or diagrammatic summary that they might misunderstand. Manual appendices included extension reliability and other correlation data pertaining to the development of the Values Indices, normative data for Core and Second Order scales for total sample, and subsamples classified by primary occupational assignment (i.e., managers, first year students, trainee airline pilots and police inspectors for the MVI; airline cabin crew, police superintendents, engineers, supervisors, and fire brigade members for the SVI). Additional validation data were also provided in the Appendices, which included the principal correlations found between the Core scales of the Values Indices and each of the following tests: The Myers-Briggs Type Indicator; FIRO-B; Jackson Personality Inventory; and the California Psychology Inventory. Next, Core scales, which comprise the various Second Order scales or indices for the MVI and the SVI, were listed along with their related factor weightings. Finally, the weightings of each component scale of the MVI and SVI were listed along with their respective weightings, as they related to the Motivational Distortion Index for the Indices.

The review package provided by the test publisher also included sample computer-generated reports for both the MVI and SVI. The questionnaires and separate answer sheets for the MVI and SVI included the administration instructions for the test taker, which were not provided nor expanded upon anywhere within the manual and user guide that was provided for the administrator. Computer-generated reports provided both a Score Chart (list of the 20 Core scales with raw and sten scores, as well as a graphic representation of the scores) and a Full Narrative interpretation for each of the Core scales and summary paragraphs for each of the Second Order index scales. Either of these two choices in report formats can be requested from the test-scoring

program. No mention was made of whether the test user or administrator must key in actual item responses, raw or sten scores from the hand-corrected copy of each test, or if the questionnaire could be scanned into the program, thus saving time and effort. Review of narrative sample reports showed that the developers utilized gender references of he/his and she/her in an alternating format, leaving some discomfort on this reviewer's part with the manner in which the report spoke to an individual's specific results. Many other instruments that utilize computer scoring to generate a narrative report are able to incorporate the individual's name into the report to enhance personalization of results. Also, narrative discussion of individual results as compared to normative data emphasized "comparison to other UK (United Kingdom) supervisors" or "managers." This raises the point of the norm groups being taken from a rather limited range of supervisory and managerial occupations within the United Kingdom (although geographic or other demographic information was not provided to aid the reviewer in determining the actual representativeness of the norm groups, such as if they were taken from individuals only residing within England and/or the British Isles, or if the norm group(s) were also representative of other member countries).

The MVI and SCI may lend themselves to computer administration.

Selby MillSmith and other organizations have launched websites on the Internet that are designed to assist job seekers and employers in identifying qualified personnel for positions that are available within a particular organization. The Selby MillSmith *Inter-Work* (http://www.selbymillsmith.com/1ststep.htm) and Career Direct (http://www.careersdirect.com) websites are unique, in that they include an assessment capability for determining whether or not an individual is best suited for a particular type of occupation and work situation. Given the global nature of the Internet and the rapid acceleration of the number of websites that address employment listing and screening, the use of the MVI and SVI show tremendous potential to aid both employers and job seekers throughout the world, if the instrumentation that is used and its normative data facilitate application to other countries, participants, languages, and a wider array of occupational opportunities. This reviewer feels that although the Selby MillSmith Values Indices appears to provide important information about a relatively wide variety of values that appear to be appropriate to supervisory and managerial personnel, it does not fully explain the full range of this work behavior construct as evidenced by cross-validation data provided for the Myers-Briggs Type Indicator, FIRO-B, Jackson Personality Inventory, or the California Personality Inventory. Likewise, use of the results of instruments such as the MVI and SVI necessitate integration with other subject-linked information and measures of knowledge, skills, and abilities that are also relevant to successful career choices and human resource management activities. Current normative data do not provide any basis for the application of the MVI and SVI to populations located outside of the United Kingdom, other than by indirect and partial encouragement provided by the validation data included in the manual. Availability of alternative language format(s) are not addressed and it is therefore assumed that none are currently available.

SUMMARY. Although the manual and sample reports for the Selby MillSmith Values Indices (MVI and SVI) present a rather impressive package at first glance, this reviewer is of the opinion that other alternatives are currently available that would better address the issues raised. The publisher, Selby MillSmith, has indicated that the instruments and manual for the MVI and SVI are currently under revision, but these materials were not fully available at the time of this review. The aforementioned instruments reported in the validation studies for the MVI and SVI, in fact, would each be stronger choices for use in a package for employment assessment for persons not living in the United Kingdom. However, all of these and comparable instruments within this area of psychological tests and measures, need to be enhanced through better content analysis, particularly with the increasing demands for essential task representativeness and accuracy being placed on human resource operations with the implementation of the Americans With Disabilities Act and other efforts to overcome discriminatory practices in employment settings.

[344]
SELECT Associate Screening System.

Purpose: Designed to assist organizations in making effective employee selection decisions.

Publication Dates: 1995–1998.
Acronym: SELECT.
Administration: Individual or group.
Price Data, 1998: $189 per one-time purchase of Initial System including HASP key preloaded with units for 10–12 surveys, SELECT software, and user's guide ('98, 90 pages); $50 per additional HASPs for satellite sites; $12 or less per report.
Time: (20–45) minutes depending on survey.
Author: Bigby, Havis, & Associates, Inc.
Publisher: Bigby, Havis, & Associates, Inc.
Comments: A software platform that combines seven screening tools; computer administered, scored, and interpreted; reports include results, recommendations, and interview questions.

a) SELECT FOR CONVENIENCE STORES.
Purpose: Designed to "measure characteristics and abilities important in most convenience store jobs."
Population: Applicants for positions in convenience stores.
Scores, 3: Provides Overall Performance, Integrity, and Retail Math indices with recommended ranges; subscale results for Energy, Frustration Tolerance, Self-Control, Accommodation to Others, Acceptance of Diversity, Positive Service Attitude; also includes self-report of Counterproductive Work Behaviors, Willingness to Do Common C-Store Tasks.

b) SELECT FOR CUSTOMER SERVICE.
Purpose: Designed as an associate-level pre-employment test for positions in customer service.
Population: Job Applicants for customer service positions.
Scores, 2: Provides Overall Performance and Integrity indices with recommended ranges; subscale results for Energy, Frustration Tolerance, Accommodation to Others, Acceptance of Diversity, and Positive Service Attitude; optional modules available for Counterproductive Behaviors, Retail Math.

c) SELECT FOR HEALTH CARE.
Purpose: Designed to "measure characteristics important in most health care provider jobs."
Population: Applicants for health care positions.
Scores, 2: Provides Overall Performance and Integrity indices with recommended ranges; subscale results for Energy, Frustration Tolerance, Accommodation to Others, Acceptance of Diversity, Positive Service Attitude, Accountability, Rapport, Empathy, Multi-Tasking.

d) SELECT FOR PRODUCTION AND DISTRIBUTION.
Purpose: Designed to "measure characteristics important to team-oriented manufacturing and distribution jobs."

Population: Applicants for production and distribution positions.

Scores, 2: Provides Overall Performance and Integrity indices with recommended ranges; subscale results for Energy, Frustration Tolerance, Acceptance of Diversity, Self-Control, Acceptance of Structure, Productive Attitude; optional module is available for Counterproductive Behaviors.

e) SELECT FOR ADMINISTRATIVE SUPPORT.

Purpose: Designed "as a personality-based survey for measuring characteristics that have been found to predict job effectiveness in administrative or clerical positions."

Population: Applicants for administrative support positions.

Scores, 2: Provides Overall Performance and Integrity indices with recommended ranges; subscale results for Energy, Multi-Tasking, Attention to Detail, Self-Reliance, Task Focus, Interpersonal Insight, Criticism Tolerance, Acceptance of Diversity, Self-Control, Productive Attitude.

f) SELECT FOR PERSONAL SERVICES.

Purpose: Designed "as a personality-based survey for measuring characteristics that have been found to predict job effectiveness for those employed in personal-care-type positions."

Population: Applicants for personal services positions (i.e., hair stylists/photographers).

Scores, 2: Provides Overall Performance and Integrity indices with recommended ranges; subscale results for Energy, Frustration Tolerance, Accommodation to Others, Acceptance of Diversity, Social Comfort, Positive Service Attitude.

g) SELECT FOR CALL CENTERS—INBOUND SERVICE.

Purpose: Designed to help screen applicants for inbound service positions at call centers.

Population: Applicants for inbound sales positions at call centers.

Scores, 2: Provides Overall Performance and Integrity indices with recommended ranges; subscale results for Energy, Frustration Tolerance, Accommodation to Others, Acceptance of Diversity, Positive Service Attitude.

h) SELECT FOR CALL CENTERS—INBOUND SALES.

Purpose: Designed to help screen applicants for inbound sales positions at call centers.

Population: Applicants for inbound sales positions at call centers.

Scores, 2: Provides Overall Performance and Integrity indices with recommended ranges; subscale results for Energy, Frustration Tolerance, Accountability, Preference for Structure, Influence, Social Comfort, Productive Attitude.

i) SELECT FOR CALL CENTERS—OUTBOUND SALES.

Purpose: Designed to help screen applicants for outbound sales positions at call centers.

Population: Applicants for outbound sales positions at call centers.

Scores, 2: Provides Overall Performance and Integrity indices with recommended ranges; subscale results for Energy, Multi-Tasking Ability, Accountability, Assertiveness, Social Comfort, Diplomacy, Acceptance of Diversity, Frustration Tolerance, Criticism Tolerance, Productive Attitude.

Review of the SELECT Associate Screening System by JAMES T. AUSTIN, Research Specialist, Ohio State University, Columbus, OH:

Current personnel selection theory and practice is moving away from a strict reliance on cognitive ability measures toward including noncognitive characteristics (e.g., personality traits, vocational interests, and personal values). Ackerman (1997) provides one integrative approach toward the predictor domain. Such movement is believed to provide better prediction of an expanded performance domain (cf. Campbell, 1990). It is also possible that such attributes might provide better understanding and prediction of job performance in a service dominated economy. The SELECT battery of assessments (called "surveys") automates assessments for lower-level service and manufacturing jobs via technology (computer or paper-pencil format combined with a database application). Heavily weighted toward the noncognitive with 10 work-oriented personality traits (organized by seven job families at the "associate" level) and two optional modules for counterproductive behavior and retail math, the battery appears to be efficient. The system is installed via a set of installation diskettes with a security HASP that fits into a computer's parallel port. The testing process is then implemented as four easy steps: (a) Asking candidate to sign Informed Consent (which seems to waive the right to receive feedback), (b) administering an assessment in one of three formats (System PC, Survey diskette, paper-pencil), (c) importing or entering data, and (d) processing the report. The draft manual is organized into three sections that are entitled, "About SELECT," "Overview of the System," and "Surveys and Reports." In this review I consider the manual and the quality of the supporting evidence in turn.

MANUAL. The manual states in a footer that it is a draft and is dated 6-3-98. The first chapter, "About SELECT," defines the system as a screening assessment for seven job families and lists the 10 traits assessed. The next page contains a table summarizing validity evidence. This summary presents information on 10 samples, ranging in size from 52 nurses to 1,261 convenience store employees. For each sample, correlations between the Performance Index and Job Performance ratings and between the Integrity Index and Work Ethic ratings are provided. The range of validity coefficients for the Performance Index is from .26 to .47, and for the Integrity Index from .20 to .39. This table appears to be the only demonstration in the manual of support for the system.

Following the display of evidence are brief sections on the contents of SELECT reports, on candidates, and on the advantages of the system. The report provides information about the candidate and follows with scores for Random Response, Performance, and Integrity Indices, subscale "Flags," and Interview Suggestions. Two useful sections of the report are a Random Response "validity" score (valid or invalid profile) and Interview Suggestions for probing candidates on areas of weakness (i.e., "Flagged" subscale scores), which at least implies that the assessment is intended to be but one piece of information in the selection process. A problem with the suggested probes is that they represent a confirmatory strategy that focuses on the negative. It would be useful to suggest additional interview questions that would provide a converging perspective on strong points of the candidate as well.

The second chapter, "Overview of the System," contains straightforward installation instructions (single-user or network options) and subsequent sections on starting the program for the first occasion. Activation from a central location (password provision) is required to use the system. Most of the remainder of the first chapter contains information on operating the assessment and the database system. A section on troubleshooting concludes the chapter. There are helpful screen shots throughout that help the user to learn and work with the system.

The third and final chapter, "SELECT Surveys and Reports," works through most of the seven job family surveys in a standardized format. The subsections start with Customer Service and continue through Convenience Stores, Health Care, Production and Distribution, Administrative Support, and Personal Services, omitting only Call Center. The format for each subsection consists of answers to questions. The questions are: What is SELECT for Customer Services? Who is it for? What does it measure? (trait components of the Performance and Integrity Indexes, respectively, and either of the two Optional Modules) What information does it provide? What do the various indices mean? What does it mean when a subscale is flagged? How do I use the interview probes? How do I use the listing of undesirable responses? What is the positive response pattern? (apparently, impression management). In the optional modules, additional questions are: How do I use SELECT to make smart selection decisions? and Who should see the SELECT reports?

SUPPORTING EVIDENCE AND CONCLUSIONS. There is no description of the test development process. There is no literature review to support the utility of personality traits in selection or even to state why the 10 trait dimensions were chosen instead of the Big Five, Eysenck's Psychoticism-Extraversion-Neuroticism, or Cattell's source traits. The supporting evidence for this battery, although certainly not nonexistent, is not described in sufficient detail to permit any sort of evaluation. The provision of a single table of validity coefficients at the front of the manual is inadequate. It would be preferable to see several types of reliability estimates, tables of norms, and analyses of adverse impact. At a minimum, what is needed is far greater description of the samples, the procedures, and the results of these validity studies. The manual is incomplete (fails to include the Call Center job family survey) and seems almost to regard the job candidate as an adversary. I refer to the apparent requirement that an Informed Consent form be signed by the applicant before assessment. This form essentially waives the right of the candidate to her or his scores. The major reaction that I experienced with this system was the perception that it seems to be a "Ghost in the Machine" setup. The responses go in, various scoring rules are applied, and the report comes out. Everything is contained in the black box of the computer, but it is impossible to determine what is actually done.

SUMMARY. It is difficult to recommend this system based on the evidence available. Contrast the system under review with the PDI Employment Inventory (Paajanen, Hansen, & McLellan, 1993; PDI-EI; 278). The contrast, as it pertains to development and evaluation of the assessments, is like night and day.

REVIEWER'S REFERENCES

Campbell, J. P. (1990). Modeling the prediction problem in industrial and organizational psychology. In M. D. Dunnette & L. M. Hough (Eds.), *Handbook of industrial and organizational psychology* (2nd ed., Vol. 1, pp. 687–731). Palo Alto, CA: Consulting Psychologists Press.

Paajanen, G. E., Hansen, T. L., & McLellan, R. A. (1993). *PDI Employment Inventory and PDI Customer Service Inventory manual*. Minneapolis, MN: Personnel Decisions, Inc.

Ackerman, P. L. (1997). Personality, self-concept, interests, and intelligence: Which concept doesn't fit? *Journal of Personality, 65*, 171–204.

Review of the SELECT Associate Screening System by VICKI S. PACKMAN, Senior Assessment Analyst, SRP, Phoenix, AZ:

The SELECT Associate Screening System consists of seven computer surveys that measure work-oriented personality characteristics for positions in Customer Service, Convenience Stores, Health Care, Production & Distribution, Administrative Support, Personal Services, and Call Center environments. The software is easy to install and very user-friendly. The SELECT System software administers the tests, scores and interprets the test results, and prepares the reports.

The surveys vary in length from 96 items (Customer Service, Personal Services, and Call Center: Inbound Service) to 202 items (Call Center: Inbound & Outbound Sales). Retail Math (14 items) is offered as an option for the Customer Service and Convenience Store surveys. Counterproductive Behaviors (13 and 30 items) contains questions related to alcohol and drug use and dishonesty and theft. This module is offered as an option for the Customer Service, Production & Distribution, and Convenience Store surveys.

Instruments that attempt to measure honesty or integrity are often criticized because their items are considered to be intrusive. This reviewer did not find the test items on the SELECT surveys to be particularly intrusive or offensive. The overall impression is that the surveys are attempting to measure the candidates' view of themselves, others, and their code of conduct. Items randomly selected from the Convenience Store survey include "Most people do right rather than wrong only because of the fear of being caught"; "You believe you have to 'massage the truth' a little or tell small lies to get through life"; "You are well liked by everyone you know"; "Igno-rant people are a pain to deal with"; "Low pay can cause honest people to steal," and "People who always follow the rules don't get ahead." Candidates respond either "Agree" or "Disagree" to these questions.

Three indices, Random Response, Performance, and Integrity, are common to all seven surveys. The Random Response Index is a validity check to determine if the candidate is correctly reading the survey and sufficiently attending to the survey items. Examples of items for this index include: "You can read well enough to complete this survey," "Choose 'Disagree' as your response to this statement," and "For this item, please answer 'Disagree.'" This index is reported as either "Valid" or "Invalid."

The Performance Index is defined as a measure of the characteristics that differentiate good customer service providers from poor ones. This index is reported as a score with a scale that shows the score ranges for "Avoid," "Ok," and "Better." Candidates who score in the "Ok" and "Better" ranges are considered more likely to possess the traits required to perform well on the job.

The Integrity Index is defined as a measure of the candidate's attitudes that relate to personal integrity and productive work behaviors. This index is reported as a score with a scale that shows the score ranges for "Avoid," "Ok," and "Good." Candidates who score in the "Ok" and "Good" ranges are considered more likely to have a positive work ethic. Candidates who score in the "Avoid" range are considered more likely to tend to "get by" and not "give it their all" on the job.

The optional Retail Math Index is a measure of basic math skills. This index is reported as a score with a scale that shows the score ranges for "Needs Training" and "Ok." Candidates who score in the "Ok" range are considered to have the necessary skills to accurately make change, calculate sales tax and markdowns, and price merchandise.

The optional Counterproductive Behaviors module lists the Survey items that are answered in an undesirable way. The items listed relate to attitudes and behaviors regarding alcohol and drug usage, theft, and dishonesty. The User's Guide states that this information should be used to further investigate potential problem areas during the interview and through reference checks.

Each survey also contains 5 to 10 "subscales." The subscales comprising the seven surveys are:

Acceptance of Diversity, Acceptance of Others, Acceptance of Structure, Accommodation to Others, Accountability, Assertiveness, Counterproductive Behaviors, Criticism Tolerance, Diplomacy, Empathy, Frustration Tolerance, Influence, Interpersonal Insight, Multi-Tasking, Organizational Skills, Positive Service Attitude, Acceptance of Structure, Productive Attitude, Retail Math, Self-Control, Self-Reliance, Social Comfort, Energy, and Task Focus. Energy is the only subscale common to all seven surveys. The subscales are reported as either "Ok" or "Flagged." Interview Probes are questions that are provided to interviewers for flagged subscales. The responses to the probes allow the interviewer to determine if the candidate has developed strategies for compensating for a particular weakness. An example of a probe for a flagged Frustration Tolerance subscale is: "Ask her to describe those aspects of previous jobs which have frustrated or irritated her. Listen for responses that suggest a low frustration tolerance or a tendency to be easily disappointed or upset. Ask her how she deals with these" ("About SELECT," p. 43).

The User's Guide is easy to read and understand. It contains sections that explain test validation, define each index and subscale, describe each validation study, discuss the confidentiality of the reports, give detailed instructions on how to load and use the software, interpret the reports, and utilize the Interview Probes. The Guide does, however, lack attention to detail and appears to have been written in haste without a thorough proofreading. There is an unfinished sentence and paragraph on page 107. Page 115 states a level of significance of $p<.5$. These errors made this reviewer question how much time was spent writing the Guide, and whether the authors had formal training in psychometrics.

There are also discrepancies in the names of the dimensions or subscales measured by the surveys. Table 5, Select for Production & Distribution Dimensions, lists "Acceptance of Structure," whereas the production & Distribution Applicant Record Form lists "Accommodation of Structure." Table 6, Select for Administrative Support Dimensions, lists "Positive Attitude" and "Perceptive about People;" whereas the Administrative Support Applicant Record Form lists "Productive Attitude" and "Interpersonal Insight." "Task Focus" is listed on the Administrative Support Applicant Record Form as a Subscale but is not included in or defined by Table 6. "Social Restraint" is listed and defined on Table 6 but is not listed as a subscale on the Administrative Support Applicant Record Form. These discrepancies are unfortunate in a report that attempts to establish the validity of its surveys and could be easily corrected by a thorough proofreading.

The User's Guide fails to meet professional standards by reporting correlation coefficients that are higher than .05 (e.g., Tables 8, 36, & 44). This contradicts the *Uniform Guidelines on Employee Selection Procedures* (p. 14B; U.S. Equal Employment Opportunity Commission, 1978) and *The Principles for the Validation and Use of Personnel Selection Procedures* (p. 5c; Society for Industrial and Organizational Psychology, Inc., 1987). More importantly, it is also contrary to what is stated in the User's Guide "P value (probability value) indicates level of statistical significance—at a minimum this should be smaller than .05" (p. 95).

The data relating to validity are presented in insufficient detail to allow replicating any of the validation studies. Sixteen validation studies are referenced in the User's Guide and the chapter 4 addendum, Call Centers. However, sex and race are reported for only three of these studies. The job classifications of the validation samples are also described in vague terms. Examples of sample descriptions include "Key Patient Contact Positions," "Operators," "Store Associates," and "Incumbents." No data are presented on the tenure of the validation samples. This is disturbing as supervisory ratings of performance measures and attitudes are critical to 14 of the 16 validation studies. Finally, the actual statistical analyses conducted on the validation data are not identified. The User's Guide states "Statistical analyses, primarily correlations, were conducted to determine the best predictive set of items and scales" (p. 98). Again, the authors are too vague in reporting their research.

A final, yet major, criticism of the technical properties of the User's Guide is that not a single reference is made relating to the reliability of scores from the surveys. This omission does not meet the *Standards for Educational and Psychological Testing* (AERA, APA, & NCME, 1985).

SUMMARY. The SELECT Associate screening System holds promise but has some deficiencies that need to be corrected. This reviewer recommends a thorough proofreading of the Guide by someone trained in psychometrics, that the Guide not report validity coefficients that are significant at levels higher than <.05, that research be included that establishes the reliability of scores from the surveys, and that the validation samples and the research conducted are described in sufficient detail to allow replication.

REVIEWER'S REFERENCE

U.S. Equal Employment Opportunity Commission, U.S. Civil Service Commission, U.S. Department of Labor, & U.S. Department of Justice. (1978). *Uniform guidelines on employee selection procedures. Federal Register 43*(166), 38295–38309.

American Educational Research Association, American Psychological Association, & National Council on Measurement in Education. (1985). *Standards for educational and psychological testing.* Washington, DC: American Psychological Association, Inc.

Society for Industrial and Organizational Psychology, Inc. (1987). *Principles for the validation and use of personnel selection procedures* (3rd ed.). College Park, MD: Author.

[345]
Self-Directed Search, 4th Edition [Forms R, E, and CP].

Purpose: A vocational inventory designed to identify "a person's particular activities, competencies, and self-estimates compared with various occupational groups."
Population: Ages 12 and above.
Publication Dates: 1970–1997.
Acronym: SDS.
Scores, 6: Realistic, Investigative, Artistic, Social, Enterprising, Conventional.
Administration: Group.
Editions, 3: Form R (Regular), Form E (Easy), Form CP (Career Planning).
Price Data, 1998: $121 per kit (Form R) including manuals, 25 booklets and occupational finders, 25 "You and Your Career" booklets, 10 leisure activity finders, and 10 educational opportunities finders; $99 per kit (Form E) including manuals, 25 assessment booklets, 25 job finders, and 25 "You and Your Job" booklets; $125 per kit (Form CP) including manuals, 25 assessment booklets, 25 career options finders, and 25 exploring career options booklets; various combinations of components available in varied-priced kits; price information for additional versions and computer software available from publisher.
Foreign Language Editions: "Adaptations available in the following countries/continents: Australia, Canada, China, Finland, France, Greece, Guyana, Hungary, Indonesia, Israel, Italy, Japan, Netherlands, New Zealand, Nigeria, Norway, Poland, Portugal, Russia, Saudi Arabia, Slovenia, South Africa, South America, Spain, Switzerland"; English-Canadian, Spanish, Vietnamese, and Braille editions also available.
Time: (40–50) minutes.
Comments: Self-administered, -scored, and -interpreted; computer software available; based on the Holland typology of vocational preferences.

Authors: John L. Holland (test and manuals), Amy B. Powell (manuals), and Barbara A. Fritzsche (manuals).
Publisher: Psychological Assessment Resources, Inc.
Cross References: See T5:2360 (13 references); for reviews by Joseph C. Ciechalski and Esther E. Diamond of an earlier edition, see 13:281 (48 references); see also T4:2414 (23 references); for reviews by M. Harry Daniels and Caroline Manuele-Adkins, see 10:330 (19 references); for a review by Robert H. Dolliver, see 9:1098 (12 references); see also T3:2134 (55 references); for a review by John O. Crites and excerpted reviews by Fred Brown, Richard Seligman, Catherine C. Cutts, Robert H. Dolliver, and Robert N. Hanson, see 8:1022 (88 references); see also T2:2211 (1 reference).

Review of the Self-Directed Search: 4th Edition [Forms R, E, and CP] by MICHAEL B. BROWN, Associate Professor of Psychology, East Carolina University, Greenville, NC:

The Self-Directed Search (SDS) is a vocational interest inventory developed for use with adolescents and adults in a wide variety of situations. In schools, agencies, and human services programs the SDS can be used for career counseling and career education, whereas in business and industry it can be used for placement, job classification, and training. The inventory is self-administered, self-scored, and self-interpreted, and can be used to increase the number of persons that a counselor can serve, provide a career counseling experience for persons who cannot or will not access a counselor, or provide vocational assistance for persons whose need for vocational services is minimal. The SDS has a history of use with persons from a multitude of backgrounds and in a wide variety of settings. In addition, the SDS also provides an occupational organization system that can be used to organize career materials, guide in systematic occupational exploration, or classify jobs and positions. The SDS lends itself well to use in research in a number of areas. All versions are available in English, and some versions are available in French Canadian, Vietnamese, Spanish, and Braille. Many are also available in software format. The English versions are reviewed here.

The SDS is based on John Holland's theory of vocational choice, which posits that there are distinct vocational personality types and occupational environments. A match between an individual's characteristics and the requirements and demands of a job leads to increased vocational satisfaction. The SDS provides a description of a client's resemblance to one of six occupational personality types by providing an occupational code that indicates the three personality types that the person most closely resembles. Occupations are also described by a three-letter code by their resemblance to the six occupational environments. Clients use the information generated by the SDS to assess the congruence of their personality characteristics with the environments of jobs that they have or are considering. This is a well-researched system that has widespread popularity among career and vocational counselors and researchers.

MATERIALS. The materials are well designed, attractive, and professionally done. Three forms of the SDS are available, each consisting of an assessment booklet, a booklet describing occupations, and an interpretive guide. Form R is designed for use with high school and college students and adults. The 118 items require clients to rate their competencies and preferences for activities and occupations. Clients are directed through the scoring process that results in a three-letter code describing their occupational personality. The Occupations Finder is the companion booklet that describes over 1,300 occupations according to type and subtype, occupational code, and level of education required.

Form E is designed for students and adults with limited reading skills and is written at about the fourth grade level. There are 198 items that roughly parallel those of Form R. The scoring system is simplified and the resulting occupational code consists of only two types. The Jobs Finder booklet lists 800 occupations that generally require a high school education or less. You and Your Job is the interpretive booklet that provides an overview of the meaning of the assessment results and how to conduct a job search.

Form CP is an alternate version of Form R for use with professional-level employees and adults in transition. The Career Options Finder booklet supplies a description of over 1,300 occupations, primarily at the upper levels of educational requirements. A description of the theory of career exploration, the Holland system, and using the information provided by the assessment booklet and Career Options Finder is provided in The Exploring Career Options booklet.

MANUAL. Two manuals are provided for use with the SDS. The Professional User's Guide describes the materials, their theoretical underpinnings, and their application. Administration and scoring is briefly covered. There is a very useful section on interpretation that takes the interpretation to a higher level of sophistication than is usually appreciated. Many short cases are provided to assist the counselor in interpreting the SDS. The section on applying interpretive ideas in career assistance describes applications of the SDS to individual and group career counseling and the use of the materials with different age groups. A final section addresses some common questions and concerns about the SDS, its theoretical background, and diagnostic and intervention issues. There are norms tables for the scales, codes, congruence, differentiation, and consistency. A worksheet and an in-depth counselor self-test round out the User's Guide. The User's Guide is well written, relatively comprehensive, and provides plenty of information to enable a counselor to use and interpret the SDS.

The Technical Manual is a 104-page wealth of information about the development of the SDS, including reliability and validity information. A unique section discusses the "outcomes and effects" of the SDS—how using the SDS affects a person's career beliefs, feelings, and actions. A variety of studies are reviewed that examine the effects of using the SDS. There is also a discussion of the effect of demographic characteristics (such as age, sex, race) on the usefulness of the SDS. Numerous tables and an extensive reference list round out the Technical Manual. This is one of the better technical manuals in that it is detailed, informative, and of practical use to the counselor.

TECHNICAL CHARACTERISTICS. Form R is a revision of earlier versions of the SDS. The norm group consists of 2,602 students and working adults spread over 25 states and the District of Columbia. There were more females than males, and although the age ranged from 17 to 65 the mean age was 23.5 years of age. The norm group includes persons from a number of different racial backgrounds. Internal consistency coefficients ranged from .72 to .92 for the different scales, with coefficients from .90 to .94 for the summary scale. Test-retest reliability for a very small sample ($r = 73$) had reliability coefficients of .76 to .89 over 4 to 12 weeks. Validity is examined by reviewing summary scale intercorrelations and assuring that they fit the theoretical model. Also,

54.7% of the norm group had a match between their measured high-point code and one-letter aspirational code. Numerous other studies have examined the pattern of scores on the SDS and the Vocational Preference Inventory (a precursor to the SDS) and other characteristics of the respondents.

The norm group for Form E included 719 individuals from 15 to 72 years of age (mean age 24.5). The group includes high school students and graduates, community college students, and a smaller number of college students or graduates. The sample includes persons from a number of racial groups. Internal consistency reliability coefficients range from .94 to .96 for the summary scales and .81 to .92 for the section scales. Hit rates of aspiration and occupational code were 50.3% and 44.8% for adults and 55.1% for adolescents using aspirations.

Form CP was administered to 101 working adults from 19 to 61 years of age (mean age 34). The majority of the group had completed at least some college. Internal consistency reliability ranged from .87 to .93 for the summary scores and .69 to .87 for the section scales. Validity is examined by comparing the correlations between section and summary scale scores on Form CP to those on the 1985 version of Form R. The section scale correlations were all greater than .80 and the summary scale correlations were greater than .94. The occupational codes for half of the individuals were exactly the same for both forms, whereas almost two thirds had the first two-letter codes the same in any order.

OVERALL EVALUATION. The SDS is a sound vocational interest inventory that has a great deal of utility for a variety of career development applications. It has a long history of use and has many positive features. The manuals are detailed and well-written. The technical characteristics are very strong for Form R, although the other forms have more restricted norm groups. The SDS has a solid theoretical background and it has received considerable research study. The materials are attractive, easy to use, and comprehensive. The various forms meet the needs of a wide variety of persons with whom a counselor might work. The process of career exploration that is stimulated by the SDS is intuitively understandable and appealing to clients.

The major drawback to the SDS is that it does not provide evidence of predictive validity by having people complete the inventory and then follow up to establish how accurately the results matched a person's ultimate occupational choice and satisfaction. The SDS may also seem to oversimplify the process of career choice. Counselors who do not have a solid background in career counseling may underestimate the complexity of the career development process. Likewise, some clients will need the assistance of a counselor in order to understand their career situation and take proper action. The positive aspects of the SDS far outweigh its potential limitations.

[346]

Sensory Integration Inventory—Revised for Individuals with Developmental Disabilities.

Purpose: "Designed to screen for [occupational therapy] clients who might benefit from a sensory integration treatment approach."

Population: Developmentally disabled occupational therapy clients school aged to adults, including autism spectrum and PDD.

Publication Dates: 1990–1992.

Acronym: SI Inventory.

Scores: Item scores in each of 4 sections interpreted individually: Tactile, Vestibular, Proprioception, General Reactions.

Administration: Individual.

Price Data: Available from publisher.

Time: Administration time not reported.

Comments: A semistructured interview of a person who works/lives closely with the client (e.g., parent or therapeutic staff member); space also provided for qualitative comments.

Authors: Judith E. Reisman and Bonnie Hanschu.

Publisher: P.D.P. Press, Inc.

Review of the Sensory Integration Inventory—Revised for Individuals with Developmental Disabilities by WILLIAM VERDI, Manager of Employment Testing and Validation, Long Island Rail Road, Jamaica, NY:

The Sensory Integration Inventory for Individuals with Developmental Disabilities (herein indicated as the Inventory) is not a standardized test in the formal definition of a test. Users (therapists) are not able to use the Inventory to evaluate an individual's current level of disability or to make comparisons across individuals. Normative data or bench marking data are not provided nor would they be appropriate for this tool.

The Inventory is appropriate for use by therapists or therapeutic staff, who are familiar with both the client's medical history and Sensory Integration Dysfunction, in determining whether or not a patient is a good candidate for sensory integration treatment. The Inventory user guide defines "Sensory integration … as the ability of the central nervous system to organize and process input from different sensory channels to make an adaptive response" (user's guide, p. 2). It also states that about 30 minutes is required for therapeutic staff to complete the inventory.

The Inventory consists of 111 items covering four major areas: Tactile, Vestibular, Proprioception, and General Reactions. All, except for General Reactions, have subcategories. Tactile covers aspects of behavior that deal with the skin (touch, pressure, pain, and temperature), personal space issues, and how individuals obtain information from their skin. Tactile is broken down into: Dressing (10 items), Other Activities of Daily Living (2 items), Personal Space (2 items), Social (7 items), Self-Stimulatory Behaviors (8 items), and Self-Injurious Behaviors (6 items). Vestibular addresses the body's vestibular system (located within the inner ear), which detects information related to head acceleration and position. This is broken down into: Muscle Tone (4 items), Equilibrium Responses (5 items), Posture and Movement (10 items), Bilateral Coordination (3 items), Spatial Perception (5 items), Emotional Expression (4 items), and Self-Stimulatory Behaviors (7 items). Proprioception Items address the body's main sensorimotor functions: muscle tone, body image, and control of effort. Proprioceptors are housed within the musculatory system and are activated by bodily movement. Proprioception is broken down into: Muscle Tone (7 items), Motor Skills/Planning and Body Image (10 items), Self-Stimulatory Behaviors (8 items), and Self-Injurious Behaviors (4 items). General Reactions addresses behaviors not specifically within the domain of any specific sensory system, but that are influenced by changes affecting any one of the sensory systems. General Reaction contains 9 items. The Inventory's items attempt to list behaviors indicative of sensory integration disorders developed from a panel of experts. Each item is scored Yes or No (if the behavior has been observed or reported). Behavior must be "typical or characteristic of the client" (user's guide, p. 3). What constitutes "typical" or "characteristic" is left up to the user's professional judgment. So a familiarity with the client's medical history becomes essential. Raters are also required to indicate if a behavior is either "recent" or of

"long standing duration." The user's guide clearly differentiates what each term means. Occurrence of one or more behaviors is *not* indicative of possessing sensory integrative dysfunction. Users will need to look for patterns of consistent and sustained behavior when making a diagnosis.

One of the strengths of the Inventory is its ability to ensure that separate therapeutic staff are evaluating a client on a common metric. Separate staff can complete the Inventory either in unison or on separate occasions. Statistics of agreement or inter/intrarater reliability could be computed. The developers should have reported such statistics when they were creating the Inventory. Given the ease of use and focus upon observed behaviors, the Inventory could be a useful tool for therapists and other therapeutic staff. The Inventory allows for multiple therapists/therapeutic staff to evaluate a patient and can also serve as a basis for dialogue among therapeutic staff.

A second strength is the almost exhaustive definition provided for each behavior to be rated. Descriptions are lengthy and detailed so that separate raters can be assured what constitutes a specific behavior. Obviously care and time have been spent in creating the user's guide. Only future research and follow-up evaluation can tell the value of the inventory.

SUMMARY. The Sensory Integration Inventory can be a valuable instrument in helping a trained therapist/therapeutic staff to identify behaviors representative of a developmental disability. It should not be the only instrument, nor should it serve as the entire assessment for deciding if a developmental disability is present. The Inventory does serve a needed function and that is to help focus the therapist/therapeutic staff observational powers upon appropriate behaviors relevant in diagnosing developmental disorders.

[347]
Sentence Completion Series.

Purpose: Constructed as a "semiprojective method of gathering client information" for personality and psychodiagnostic assessment.
Population: Adolescents and adults.
Publication Dates: 1991–1992.
Acronym: SCS.
Scores: No scores.
Administration: Group.
Forms, 8: Adult, Adolescent, Family, Marriage, Parenting, Work, Illness, Aging.

Price Data, 1996: $69 per complete kit including manual and 15 of each form; $27 per 50 forms (specify Adult, Adolescent, Family, Marriage, Parenting, Work, Illness or Aging).

Time: [10–45] minutes.

Comments: Forms may be administered alone or in any combination.

Authors: Larry H. Brown and Michael A. Unger.

Publisher: Psychological Assessment Resources, Inc.

Review of the Sentence Completion Series by KEVIN L. MORELAND, Private Practice, Ft. Walton Beach, FL:

It is difficult to write a "test review" of the Sentence Completion Series because the components of the series are not "tests" as commonly conceived by psychologists, educators, and others who use tests. The "test" stimuli are standard and the "tests" are administered in a standardized fashion. However, there are no objective scoring schemes, nor are there normative, reliability, or validity data. Each of the eight forms comprises 50 sentence stems that can be combined into a priori "scales." Subjective suggestions concerning interpretation are also provided.

Three of the eight forms are broad ranging based on age. The adolescent-appropriate form offers sentence stems as short as "Dating ..." for the youngster to complete, and others as long as "Now that I am no longer a child ...." A typical stem is three or four words long. There are seven "scales" ranging from six to eight items in length: Goals, Self-Concept, Self-Esteem, Relations with Adults, Problems, Peer Relations, and Self-Control. This sentence completion form is a welcome addition to the clinician's armamentarium because unlike some of its predecessors, it deals directly with touchy but important issues such as sex, drugs, and alcohol.

Two other age-related members of the series deal with adulthood and aging. They are similar to, and have the same virtues as, the adolescent form.

The other five forms in the series are topical and can be used in combination with one of the age-related forms or with each other. They deal with the family, marriage, illness, parenting, and work. Many of these have few or no competitors in the literature and, thus, are especially welcome additions. Again, the stems tend to be short and appear to be easily read. Each form has six to eight a priori "scales," with the 50 items divided fairly evenly across them.

Interpretive suggestions include examining the general tone: defensiveness versus openness, concreteness versus abstractness, etc. Further suggestions include examining broad trends, using the a priori scales to identify narrow trends, and searching for dramatic responses. These are all good suggestions. One hopes the authors are trying to bring the most promising to psychometric fruition. For example, scoring each response for simple degree of pathology, as Rotter did with his Incomplete Sentences Blank (T5:2258), would permit psychometric interpretation of the forms. A score would permit verification of the composition of the a priori scales, examination of their reliability and validity, and the development of norms (cf. Lah, 1989). Nevertheless, because most incomplete sentence blanks are not formally scored, this series will no doubt prove very useful in any case.

REVIEWER'S REFERENCE

Lah, M. I. (1989). Sentence completion tests. In C. S. Newmark (Ed.), *Major psychological assessment instruments* (vol. II, pp. 133–163). Boston: Allyn & Bacon.

Review of the Sentence Completion Series by PAUL D. WERNER, Professor, California School of Professional Psychology, Alameda, CA:

The Sentence Completion Series (SCS) was designed to foster standardized collection of clinically relevant information from clients, in a focused manner and within a psychotherapeutic context, using the sentence completion method. It is composed of eight booklet forms (e.g., Adult, Marriage, Work), one or more of which may be administered to the client. Each booklet consists of 50 sentence completion stems, each of which is classified by the authors as pertaining to one of a number of thematic topic groups. The authors view the SCS not so much as an assessment device but as an extension of the clinical interview, promoting exploration of material to be pursued in psychotherapy. Responses to the sentence stems are to be considered clinically, as the SCS provides no summary scores or formal rules for integrating responses so as to yield inferences or interpretations.

Minimal documentation is available to provide a rationale for use of the SCS. A user's guide, amounting to approximately four and one-half pages of text, describes the SCS, informs the user about its background, and gives guidelines for administration and interpretation. Other than the user's guide, no publications or other documents have appeared concerning the SCS. In the context of this relative sparseness of information providing a foundation for use of the SCS, something of a leap of faith is required by those choosing to employ it.

The user's guide emphasizes the breadth and clinical relevance of the topic areas covered by the SCS sentence stems. Choice of the topic domains was based on the clinical judgment of the authors, augmented by input from nine other clinicians. Similarly, the authors derived the current set of sentence stems through a process of review and input from these same clinicians. This process has yielded topic groups and sentence stems that indeed, in a general sense, cover a variety of areas relevant to clinical work with a client. Clinical work in varied psychotherapeutic modalities, based on different theoretical understandings of psychopathology, might not benefit from identical topic lists or sentence stems. For this reason, the user's guide would have been improved by inclusion of the authors' views about therapeutic modalities with which the SCS, as currently constituted, might fit best, and those with which its topic areas and sentence stems might provide less useful information. Similarly, and more generally, I would have liked to see a discussion of linkages between the topics included and literature providing a rationale for coverage of particular areas and inclusion of particular topics in sentence stems in gathering information about clinical cases.

The user's guide provides no information about reliability of responses to the SCS, either from the perspective of consistency of clients' responses over time or from the perspective of internal consistency of responses within topic groups. Similarly, no information is presented concerning reliability or validity of interpretations based on the responses. This absence of attention to psychometric properties is consistent with the authors' view that the SCS is "not intended for use as a psychological test" (user's guide, p. 2). However, this sets the SCS outside of the mainstream of current assessment practice, and gives users little to fall back on, other than their own clinical judgment, in justifying their inferences based on SCS responses.

Adopting the authors' viewpoint, perhaps the SCS should be evaluated primarily as a standardized procedures for gathering information—in other words, as an extension of the clinical interview, rather than as a "mental measure." From this perspective, it offers a standard format for eliciting information from clinical clients, with attention to a number of clinically relevant domains. But is this a sufficient basis on which to recommend its use? For example, the clinician interested in tailoring sentence completion stimuli to his or her own modality, or to issues raised in early therapeutic sessions with a client, could, with some serious reflection, create a pool of sentence stems relevant to these aspects of his or her own practice. The SCS's developers have not convincingly demonstrated that the SCS substantially improves upon such an ad hoc procedure.

SUMMARY. If the undertaking of clinical assessment entails presentation of stimuli and the encoding of responses so as to provide implications of clinical usefulness, the strength of the SCS lies largely in its provision of standardized and differentiated sentence completion stimuli. Its major weakness is that it does not offer a psychometrically defensible procedure for deriving summary scores or inferences based upon responses to those stems.

[348]
ServiceFirst.

Purpose: Constructed to measure "customer service orientation or potential."

Population: Employees in service-oriented positions.

Publication Dates: 1990–1995.

Scores, 5: Active Customer Relations, Polite Customer Relations, Helpful Customer Relations, Personalized Customer Relations, Total.

Administration: Group.

Price Data, 1996: $25 per test kit including sample test booklet, sample answer sheet, test manual ('95, 47 pages), administration and scoring manual, and demonstration administration and scoring manual; $5 per administrator's manual; $3 per test booklet; scoring service $5 to $7.50 per applicant.

Time: (20) minutes.

Comments: Scoring is done via telephone by publisher or on site with a DOS-compatible disk; paper-and-pencil and computer administration.

Author: CORE Corporation.

Publisher: CORE Corporation.

Review of the ServiceFirst by MICHAEL B. BUNCH, Vice President, Measurement Incorporated, Durham, NC:

OVERVIEW. The 50-item ServiceFirst questionnaire contains 40 items keyed to four dimensions of customer service (Active, Polite, Helpful, and Personalized) in two formats (self-description and scenario) plus a 10-item lie scale. Scores include a summary evaluation of the candidate's employability (Highly Recommend, Recommend, Do Not Recommend). Initially applied to a sample of retail supermarket checkout personnel, the test has also been used with bank tellers, retail clerks, retail nursery employees, insurance company claim/service representatives, and employees in other industries.

DEVELOPMENT. The 52-page test manual gives a thorough and lucid description of each step of the development process, which included literature review, task analysis, focus group interviews, item writing and review, pilot testing, revision, and cross validation. The sections of the manual on the winnowing of the item pool and the subsequent reduction in the total number of dimensions to be assessed are particularly well written.

Factor analysis was used to refine the test. After the final four factors were identified, the 10 highest loading items for each factor were selected for the final form. The 10 lie scale items were added afterwards. Interestingly, the lie scale (consisting of statements such as "I am always happy") had a positive correlation with the criterion variable (supervisors' ratings).

PSYCHOMETRIC PROPERTIES. The final four highly intercorrelated scales may be summarized as follows: (a) Active—the ability to maintain a high energy level throughout the day and to perform numerous activities without tiring; (b) Polite—the ability to be courteous to customers at all times, using consideration and correct manners in dealing with others; (c) Helpful—the readiness to offer assistance to customers and serve them willingly; and (d) Personalized—the ability to make shopping a more familiar and personal experience for customers.

The test manual provides text and tables regarding estimates of reliability of individual scales and the total test. Alpha reliability coefficients for the four 10-item scales range from .57 to .87. The reliability coefficient for the total test was .87. Given the nature of the test, a test-retest reliability coefficient would have been useful, but its omission is not considered a serious flaw in the psychometric documentation of the test.

Means and standard deviations are also provided for each scale and total score, for the total population, and by race and sex. With regard to race and sex, the authors provide adverse impact data showing how different groups would be affected at different selection ratios. The five tables provided in the manual should be quite useful to anyone contemplating the use of a selection test in light of Uniform Guidelines on Employee Selection Procedures.

Information in the section of the manual describing the results of factor analyses constitutes evidence of construct validity. Concurrent and predictive validity evidence is based on correlations between this test and supervisor ratings or actual performance in a variety of settings.

EASE OF USE. The test manual is extremely well written. The questionnaire is printed on quality paper, is easy to read, and is uncluttered. Directions are quite clear. The administration and scoring manual not only provides step-by-step administration directions, it also gives some background and addresses several common questions about uses of the test. Directions for security, processing, and interpreting results are also provided. All are clear and concise. There is also a computer-based version, but it was not reviewed.

SUMMARY. ServiceFirst is well-designed, well-constructed test with solid psychometric properties. The publishers have done an excellent job in putting this test together. The population for whom it is intended is well defined; the purpose and design are well documented; and the results are easy to understand and use. Human resource managers in the service industry would do well to consider this test as an effective selection device.

Review of the ServiceFirst by MARY A. LEWIS, Director, Human Resources, Chlor-Alkali and Derivatives, PPG Industries, Inc., Pittsburgh, PA:

ServiceFirst is an untimed 50-item multiple-choice test designed to measure customer service orientation. It results in five measures, a Total score, and scores on four dimensions of customer service: Active Customer Relations, Polite Customer Relations, Helpful Customer Relations, and Personalized Customer Relations. It is offered as a tool to supplement existing hiring methods and also recommended as a prescreen. The administration and scoring guide does recommend that it be used with other information such as interviews, skill tests, application reviews, and reference checks. Hebrew, French, Spanish, and Swedish versions of the test are available.

The test can be administered and scored directly on the computer, or through the use of a test booklet and separate answer sheet. If the computer-scoring option is not used, the test can be scored through the use of a toll-free telephone scoring service or by mailing or faxing answer sheets to CORE Corporation. Scores on each of the four customer service dimensions can vary from 0 to 50, and the Total score is the sum of those four scores and can vary from 0 to 200. Each dimension score is reported as being high, moderate, or low, and definitions for the high and low categories are provided. For example, an individual high on Personalized Customer Relations is characterized as getting to know customers by name, addressing customers by name when known, taking an interest in customers' specific requests/needs, enjoying socializing with customers, and listening attentively to customers. An individual low on Personalized Customer Relations is described by the negative of the above statements. Although these dimension scores and bands and interpretations are given as part of the scoring process, they are described as being for informational purposes only. The administrator's guide recommends that the Total score be used for hiring decision. The total score is also categorized into three bands: highly recommend (described as very likely to succeed in customer service), recommend (highly likely to succeed), and do not recommend (less likely to succeed).

The ServiceFirst test manual describes its development and validation as a four-phase process. In the first phase, an extensive literature search was conducted for current research on customer service. From this review, several dimensions of customer service orientation were identified. The second phase of the process involved expanding on these dimensions through a job analysis. The position used in this phase of the study was the retail cashier/checker. A 102-item job analysis questionnaire was constructed and administered to 70 cashier trainees. The analysis of this questionnaire was used to provide a framework for the construction of the test, and focus groups of managers, employees, and customers were used to define specific employee behaviors that related to good or poor service. The results of these efforts led to five overall dimensions of customer service (the four dimensions that are scale scores and a fifth dimension, Consistent Customer Relations). Items were written to measure these dimensions using Self-Description (like

me/not like me), Forced Choice (choose which you would prefer to do), and Situational Judgment (likelihood to respond in the manner described) formats by a variety of test and subject matter experts. The items were pretested with a group of incumbent cashiers and refined into a pool of 293 items.

The third phase of the process was to develop, as a criterion measure, a performance appraisal that ultimately evaluated employees on the five customer service dimensions, and an overall rating of customer service performance.

The fourth phase was a concurrent validity study. Store managers were asked to complete appraisal on five to eight of their best and five to eight of their lowest performing employees. From these returned appraisals the top and bottom 22.5% were selected to take the prototype questionnaire and 867 (57.3%) did so. No information is provided on respondent/nonrespondent by top and bottom, although criterion means and standard deviations indicated that those returned averaged at the 75th percentile on the criterion; however, the criterion standard deviations ranged from 1.32 to 1.46 (on a 5-point scale) indicating reasonable variation in the criterion. This is an unusual sampling technique, preselecting the top and bottom of the performance distribution, and it is presented to counter concerns about restriction in range in a concurrent sample. I am not certain if that was accomplished and would have liked to see criterion means and standard deviations on the full sample as well as on the 867 who completed the questionnaire.

The 293 test items were reduced to 40 items based on univariate correlations of the items with the criterion scales. The 10 items that correlated highest with each scale were selected and the Consistent Customer relations scale was dropped. Scale scores were calculated by assigning a value from 1 to 5 for an item response and summing the responses. Scale means ranged from 32.99 to 38.94 with standard deviations ranging from 4.59 to 6.70. The Total score mean was 144.05 with a standard deviation of 17.45. Coefficient alpha reliability estimates for the scales ranged from .57 for Personalized Customer Relations to .87 for Active Customer Relations. The Total score had a coefficient alpha value of .87. Not surprisingly, all subscale scores and the Total score were significantly correlated with the criterion measures. A 10-item fake scale was included in the test; however, it is not scored, and the authors note that this scale also correlates highly with customer service, perhaps indicating that knowing what to fake is an important tool in dealing with the public. A subsequent construct validity study provides support that the instrument is measuring four customer service constructs.

Subsequent validation studies have been conducted with 12 different jobs and over 2,000 individuals, although the manual only details four studies, one for a retail nursery, two in telecommunications, and one for Swedish postal workers. These studies yielded consistent significant validity coefficients ranging from .16 to .30, with one exception. For technical jobs in telecommunications, the Total score was not significantly related to overall job performance, but was related to communication skills. The test manual also cites meta-analytical data to support the use of ServiceFirst and similar tests; however, as with all references in the manual, no detailed citation is provided.

The section on setting of cut scores is not easy to interpret. Although expectancy charts are provided that show five score ranges and the percent successful for each range, three cut scores are recommended. These score bands are described in terms of percent successful, but not in terms of percent applicants in the category. In addition, information about adverse impact is provided for the initial test development and validation study, but that information is not related to these cut scores. It is not clear whether or not there would be adverse impact due to use of these tests for the three cut score categories described. Although the manual indicates that ServiceFirst has less adverse impact than tests of general cognitive ability, no data are provided to support that statement. Of course, adverse impact is not the relevant question to be answered for this test. A valid test can have adverse impact and many valid and fair tests do. Although the issue of fairness has been well researched and understood for cognitive ability tests, the issue has not been resolved for customer service. More specific information and research on test fairness should be a next step.

SUMMARY. The ServiceFirst is a very promising tool to select individuals with a customer service orientation. It has a sound theoretical and empirical basis to build upon. It would appear that it is measuring skills that are important for those positions that must interact with the general public. I would recommend its use for a broad range of general customer service positions; however, its use for technical service positions may not be as helpful. More research and better information is needed on the distributions of the cut scores, and better information is needed about test fairness.

Severe Cognitive Impairment Profile.

Purpose: Designed to measure and monitor the cognitive performance of patients previously diagnosed with dementia.
Population: Severely demented patients.
Publication Dates: 1995–1998.
Acronym: SCIP.
Scores, 9: Comportment, Attention, Language, Memory, Motor, Conceptualization, Arithmetic, Visuospatial, Total.
Administration: Individual.
Price Data, 1998: $349 per complete kit including manual ('98, 67 pages), leather carrying case with secure lock, 25 record forms, and all other test materials.
Time: (30–45) minutes.
Author: Guerry M. Peavy.
Publisher: Psychological Assessment Resources, Inc.

Review of the Severe Cognitive Impairment Profile by JOAN C. BALLARD, Clinical Neuropsychologist, Associate Professor of Psychology, State University of New York College at Geneseo, Geneseo, NY:

The Severe Cognitive Impairment Profile (SCIP) was designed for use with severely demented patients for whom assessment has been limited by floor effects of most available dementia screening and evaluation instruments. The purposes of the SCIP include both clinical and research applications: (a) to assess cognitive functioning in severely demented patients; (b) to identify the patient's relative strengths and weaknesses as an aid in determining strategies to enhance communication and social interactions within clinical or institutional settings; (c) to serve as an outcome measure in clinical/pharmacological treatment trials; and (d) to serve as a research tool in producing neuropsychological profiles for patients near end stages of dementia.

The manual is well organized and clearly written. It includes a clear statement of the appropriate population for the test (adults aged 42 to 90 with previous diagnoses of severe dementia). The test is not validated for use with younger adults, adolescents, or children, although studies of children with Down's Syndrome are reportedly underway. Also clearly stated are user qualifications. Administration can be performed by anyone with training in psychological testing and appropriate supervision, although only doctoral level neuropsychologists or clinical psychologists should interpret results.

The SCIP kit includes all materials required for administration except a stopwatch, pen, and four U.S. coins. Objects such as cups and blocks are durable and easy to handle. Stimulus cards are sturdy and laminated, with large type for printed words and attention-getting colors and clear drawings for pictures. The leather carrying case is durable, although it may add unnecessarily to the cost of the kit. The record form is well designed and easy to use, although reference to the examiner's manual is required for administration of some subtests. Examiners should become very familiar with all procedures and materials before using the test in clinical evaluations. Fortunately, criteria for scoring items are clearly stated. Subtest scores are converted to scaled scores on a profile grid on the report form cover.

Content validity is evidenced by the inclusion of subtests assessing cognitive skills traditionally considered important. Many items are similar to those of traditional tests, but require lower levels of competence. For example, digit span is tested up to only four digits forward and two digits backward. Such procedures allow administering the entire test in a relatively brief time. Of note, some items represent improvements over existing tests. For example, the visual span subtest includes numbers on the backs of blocks, making the test substantially more examiner-friendly.

Studies reported in the manual provide evidence of both reliability and concurrent validity. In a sample of 41 previously diagnosed, severely demented older adults, as well as in the standardization sample of 92 adults with probable Alzheimer's Disease (AD), SCIP total scores were strongly correlated with summary scores on both the Dementia Rating Scale (DRS) and the Mini Mental State Examination (MMSE). In a subgroup of 23 patients from the former study, Spearman's rank correlations revealed excellent interrater reliability ($r > .95$) for the SCIP total and all subtests except Comportment ($r = .77$). Test-retest reliabilities at approximately 1-week intervals for 22 patients ranged from moderate correla-

tions for Motor ($r = .56$) and Comportment ($r = .62$) subtests, to the highest correlations for Language ($r = .90$), Attention ($r = .95$), and the SCIP totals ($r = .96$).

Additional validity information was provided by comparing subgroups of the standardization sample classified into severity levels based on SCIP total scores. Patients with total SCIP raw scores above 199 (60th percentile of the distribution) were classified as moderately severely impaired ($N = 29$). Very severe impairment was indicated by scores from 72 to 130 (17th to 29th percentile), and profound impairment was indicated by scores from 0 to 71 (below 16th percentile). Unfortunately, the number of patients in the last two categories was relative small ($N = 12$) in each subgroup). Nevertheless, these four subgroups differed in predictable directions on place of residence (home vs. institution), level of independence (determined by Pfeffer Outpatient Disability Scale), and overall functional impairment (determined by Clinical Dementia Rating), as well as on DRS and MMSE summary scores. Additional studies revealed significant relationships of SCIP total and subtest scores with post-mortem measures of brain weight, synapse counts, and neuritic plaque counts, as well as the ability of the SCIP to document decline in cognitive functioning over time.

The manual recommends a four-step process of interpretation for an individual patient's SCIP scores. First, the total SCIP score is compared to score ranges for the four severity levels of the standardization sample. The patient is thus categorized with moderately severe, severe, very severe, or profound impairment. Second, subtest scaled scores are examined to determine within-subject patterns relative to the entire standardization sample. Third, subtest scaled scores are compared to the profile produced by the corresponding severity group in the standardization sample. For example, the profile of a patient categorized based on total score as "severe" is compared to the mean profile of the "severe" group in the standardization sample. Individual subtests more than one standard deviation above the group mean are identified as relative strengths, whereas subtests more than one standard deviation below the group mean are labeled as relative weaknesses. Finally, the patient's capacity for activities of daily living (ADLs) and likelihood of psychiatric/behavioral problems are estimated from descriptions of the severity groups in the standardization sample.

The primary advantage of the SCIP is that it provides a range of scores for persons with low levels of cognitive functioning. This range of scores greatly reduces the problem of floor effects that result when other dementia instruments are used with severely demented patients, allowing meaningful comparisons both within- and between-subjects. Longitudinal studies have demonstrated that decline in cognitive functioning can be assessed with the SCIP, even for patients in the final year of life.

However, one important limitation of the SCIP is its inability to assess mild impairment. The manual provides no information on skew or kurtosis of the score distribution in the standardization sample. Inspection of the histogram suggests ceiling effects for the 92 "probable Alzheimer's" patients. Furthermore, scoring instructions indicate that even a perfect score of 245 on the SCIP total is classified as indicating "moderately severe impairment." It seems more reasonable to suggest that very high or perfect scores indicate a need for assessment with instruments more sensitive to individual differences within the mildly impaired range.

SUMMARY. The SCIP is a well-constructed instrument with adequate reliability and validity that will most likely prove very useful in both clinical and research settings for the assessment of cognitive functions in severely demented adults. Because of small subgroup sizes at the lower severity levels of the standardization sample, additional research is needed to support the descriptions of ADLs and behavioral characteristics of such patients. Patients who produce high or perfect scores on the SCIP should be evaluated with other instruments more appropriate for assessing mild cognitive impairment.

Review of the Severe Cognitive Impairment Profile by LAWRENCE J. RYAN, Core Faculty, The Graduate College of The Union Institute, Cincinnati, OH, and Vice President and Academic Dean, St. John's Seminary College, Camarillo, CA:

The Severe Cognitive Impairment Profile (SCIP) is an individually administered neuropsychological instrument specifically designed to assess the range of cognitive functions typically observed in severely demented patients. The SCIP does not pretend to diagnose dementia. It does purport to provide important descriptive and monitoring data regarding patients previously diagnosed with dementia. The instrument includes eight subtest areas including Comportment (behavior/appearance/communication/compliance), Attention, Language, Memory, Motor, Conceptualization, Arithmetic, and Visuospatial. The SCIP test materials are most attractive and durable and are compactly arranged in a sturdy brief case. The SCIP individual record booklet is clear and easy to follow including full instructions for administration as well as ample space for entering data in each of the clearly marked subtest areas. The accompanying manual is thorough and useful both in terms of the rationale and development of the instrument as well as with regard to the well-detailed normative data sections. Additionally, scoring standards are clearly detailed in the manual as are interpretive guides with descriptions of typical behaviors and case examples of patients with dementia at the levels of "Moderately Severe Impairment," "Severe Impairment," "Very Severe Impairment," and "Profound Impairment."

Validity and reliability data are extensive and convincing. The author reports consistently high correlation data between the SCIP and a number of other instruments that assess neurological impairment. The comparison data are drawn from comparisons with data from brief and functionally oriented instruments including The Physical Self Maintenance Scale (PSMS), The Pfeffer Outpatient Disability Scale (PODS), The Clinical Dementia Rating Scale (CDR; T5:776) and The Dementia Rating Scale (DRS). Although convergent validity data are impressive and representative of a solid research effort, no data are reported for more comprehensive instruments such as the Halstead Reitan (T5:1164), the Luria Nebraska (T5:1524), or even the Wechsler Adult Intelligence Scale—Third Edition (WAIS-III; 413).

The SCIP is a stimulating and enjoyable instrument to administer. Its materials and format have a Wechsler-like quality with bright and somewhat oversized stimuli cards and objects. The SCIP is paced similar to the Wechsler series. The entire battery takes about 45 minutes to administer. Even for very impaired individuals the nature of the items makes the administration a potentially enjoyable and highly interactive experience. Although the majority of the subtests and items are verbally oriented there are enough purely performance type items to make for a balanced and varied presentation. For the most part the items have excellent face validity.

The SCIP is obviously an instrument resulting from extensive development and research. The standardization sample of 92 impaired Alzheimer's disease patients is for the most part quite adequate. Because the sample was drawn from the San Diego, California area, one would assume that among other ethnic groups, the sample likely included at least some patients of Hispanic and Asian origins consistent with the population mix of that city. However, the manual makes no mention whatsoever of the ethnic composition of the sample. Nor does the manual address any issues regarding the accommodation of subjects for whom English may not be the primary language. The administration of the SCIP relies heavily on language and effective communication skills on the part of the examiner and the test subject. Although the author claims that the SCIP can be administered by any person with training in psychological testing, it is obviously an instrument that requires considerable clinical assessment acumen.

The SCIP is an instrument designed specifically for severely impaired individuals whose deficits are florid and no longer at the subtle level. In fact, the author claims that one of the most likely uses for the instrument will be repeated administrations as dementia patients approach death to monitor the level of functional impairment. For individuals with more subtle levels of neurological impairment, the instrument will be useless because of the very low difficulty level of the subtest items.

SUMMARY. The SCIP is an expertly developed and well-researched instrument that is likely to be useful in the clinical monitoring of cognitive functioning of patients with severe levels of dementia. The SCIP is a most attractive, engaging, and interactive instrument that will yield meaningful recommendations. Additionally, the SCIP has excellent potential as research instrument. It is a relatively quick and unobtrusive instrument that will produce minimal stress for the individual being assessed.

[350]
The Severity and Acuity of Psychiatric Illness Scales—Adult Version.

Purpose: Designed to assess the severity and acuity of psychiatric illness in adult mental health service recipients.
Population: Adults.
Publication Date: 1998.

Scores, 6: Severity (Complexity Indicator, Probability of Admission, Total), Acuity (Clinical Status, Nursing Status, Total).
Administration: Individual.
Price Data, 1999: $65 per starter kit including training manual (52 pages), 10 reusable Severity item booklets, 25 Severity scale rating sheets, 10 reusable Acuity item booklets, and 25 Acuity scale rating sheets; $15 per 10 Severity scale item booklets; $12.50 per 25 Severity scale rating sheets; $15 per 10 Acuity scale item booklets; $12.50 per 25 Acuity scale rating sheets; $17 per training manual.
Time: (5) minutes.
Comments: Computer versions available; two scales (Severity and Acuity) can be used separately or together; results to be used as an "integrated outcomes-management and decision-support system for assisting treatment decision-making"; ratings are done by caregivers about clients/patients.
Author: John S. Lyons.
Publisher: The Psychological Corporation.

Review of The Severity and Acuity of Psychiatric Illness Scales—Adult Version by MARK J. ATKINSON, Associate Professor of Psychiatry and Applied Psychology, University of Calgary, Calgary, Alberta, Canada:

The Severity and Acuity of Psychiatric Illness Scales consists of two components, a Severity rating scale and an Acuity rating scale. The Severity scale is a case descriptor and decision-support tool. The Acuity scale is an outcome measure associated with psychiatric and mental health interventions. Two versions are available, one for adults and one for children (5–18 years). Only the adult version is reviewed here. The adult scale takes raters 5–8 minutes to complete, and the training time requirements are 4–5 hours. The manual contains a good training package with clinical vignettes and master scoring keys to assess consistency of trainees.

Norming tables are provided for Inpatient and Partial Hospitalization Adult populations. Due to wide variation in case mix and service mandates across mental health jurisdictions, these norms should be used with caution. Similar questions should be asked of the inpatient norm group, which is not homogeneous with respect to patient condition (primarily patients with major depression). Again caution should be exercised when using the norms for normative comparisons of patients with less well represented psychiatric illness. In this respect, a breakdown of the norm group by diagnostic grouping would be particularly helpful, and could possibly avert comparison problems associated with differences in mental health policy and practice.

RELIABILITY OF SEVERITY MEASURES. The Total Raw Score on this scale provides an overview of the severity of a case. The Case Complexity Indicator is derived by the frequency of severity items rated over 1 on a 0–3 scale. A Probability of Admission Index Score is computed using items tapping suicide risk, danger to others, and the severity of psychiatric symptoms. The interrater reliability of the Severity Scale using ratings of patient charts is good, .83–.86 (weighted kappa). The reader, however, is left to assume that this range applies to both inpatient and partial hospitalization populations.

RELIABILITY OF ACUITY MEASURES. Raw subscale scores for the Clinical Status and the Nursing Status subscales are computed based on patient symptoms and need for medical assistance (respectively). The Total Acuity Raw Score is the sum of these two subscale scores. Raw scores are converted to T scores for normative comparison. The same caveats mentioned earlier apply when using these normative scores. The interrater reliability of the total Acuity Scale using patient charts by trained raters is moderate to high, .73–.84 (weighted kappa).

Cronbach's alphas for the Total Acuity Scale were also high, .81 for the Inpatient sample and .78 for the partial hospitalization sample. Estimates of internal consistency of the Probability of Admission Index, based on scores from the seven clinical status measures, were moderate and ranged from .70–.75 (Cronbach's alpha). The same estimates for the Nursing Status Subscale score (4 items) were good, with alphas of .63–.66. It should be noted here that internal consistency estimates for behavioral rating scales are typically lower than for scales that have been designed to measure unidimensional constructs.

VALIDITY. With respect to the face validity of item content, the scales are quite comprehensive and reflect clinically important aspects of patient conditions and treatment outcomes. There is some concern, however, that even though a family involvement rating is included, no items address the strength or level of other social involvements.

SEVERITY SCALE. The construct validity of the Severity Scale items has been examined using interview-based administration of the Geriatric Depression Scale (GDS), Hamilton Depression Rating Scale (HDRS), Brief Psychiatric Rating Scales (BPRS), Brief Cognitive Rating Scale (BCRS), and the Mini Mental State Exam (MMSE). Low to moderate convergence occurred between specific Severity Scale items and validation measures: Persistence of Symptoms (GDS = .20, HDRS = .19, BPRS = .21), Suicide Risk (GDS = .23, HDRS = .19), Severity of Symptoms (HDRS = .28, BPRS = .24, BCRS = .32), Danger to Others (BCRS = .17), Self-Care (BCRS = .46), Substance Abuse (BCRS = -.27), Medical Complications (HDRS = .23), and Motivation (BPRS = .15, BCRS = .33). The weak convergence is likely due to little variance on single items of the Severity Scale, as well as the heterogeneous inpatient case mix. As a result, these coefficients are acceptable. An unexplained observation is that MMSE scores were not significantly correlated with any severity scale items. Also missing were comparisons between scale items and various uniscale ratings of psychiatric conditions (e.g., Global Assessment of Functioning, Social and Occupational Functioning Assessment Scale, Clinical Global Impressions Scale).

The Severity Scale items are reported to discriminate between shorter and longer stay patients, primarily on the basis of suicide ratings, family involvement, and low motivation for treatment. Moreover, the scale has been shown to accurately predict hospital admissions 75% of the time, and those with appropriate admissions based on their scale and scores were shown to exhibit greater improvement than those scored as inappropriately admitted. Moreover, this scale appears to be able to make the important distinction between patient characteristics and treatment outcomes based on prediction of readmission rates.

ACUITY MEASURE. The construct validity of the Acuity Scale items has been examined using traditional interview-based clinical assessments: the Mini Mental State Exam (-.47), BPRS (.62), GDS (.27), and the HDRS (ns.) among older partial hospitalization patients. This scale has been used to examine patient outcomes, both retrospectively and prospectively. Issues of relapse-readmission and dual diagnosis have been successfully addressed using the substance abuse comorbidity item as fixed factors of study. The scales have been successfully used to explore the important relationships between readmission rates and the dual diagnosis. Missing are research findings with regard to medication compliance.

SUMMARY. The Severity and Acuity of Psychiatric Illness Scales, an outcomes-management and decision-support system, provides clinicians with a well-designed and useful set of clinical rating scales for assessing patient acuity and treatment-related outcomes. Materials for the training of raters are included. Careful attention should be given to the comparability between the diagnostic mix of service samples and those provided as normative reference samples. Information regarding the impact of patients' social context on symptomatology or outcome measures should be assessed concurrently.

Review of The Severity and Acuity of Psychiatric Illness Scales—Adult Version by ROGER A. BOOTHROYD, Associate Professor, Department of Mental Health Law and Policy, Louis de la Parte Florida Mental Health Institute, University of South Florida, Tampa, FL:

DESCRIPTION. The Severity and Acuity of Psychiatric Illness Scales—Adult Version "is an integrated outcomes-management and decision-support system for assisting treatment decision making and service delivery monitoring" (manual, p. 1). This individually administered measure was developed for use with adults to help determine their mental health service needs and their mental health status.

The Severity and Acuity of Psychiatric Illness Scales consists of two measures. The first is a 14-item Severity Scale intended to assist service providers in treatment planning. It consists of three subscales: Level of Care (4 items), Complications to Illness (4 items), and Complications to Treatment (6 items). Each item is rated using a 4-point Likert-type scale. Although the scale anchors differ for each item, they generally range from 0 (indicating no evidence of a problem) to 3 (denoting severe or profound problem). A fifth option is available to indicate if information is unavailable.

The second measure is a 15-item Acuity Scale. The Acuity Scale also consists of three subscales: Clinical Status (7 items), Nursing Status (4 items), and Additional Information (4 items). As with the Severity Scale, each item is also rated using a 4-point Likert-type scale and ranges from 0 (indicating no evidence of difficulty) to 3 (noting significant evidence). A fifth option is available to indicate if information is unavailable.

SCALE DEVELOPMENT. There is little specific information available on the scale development in the Severity and Acuity of Psychiatric Illness Scales manual. The author does indicate that a multi-stage development process was used and that the scales "were developed in parallel fashion" (manual, p. 43). The first stage involved a literature review related to decision making and outcomes in acute psychiatric services. This was followed by an unspecified number of focus groups with clinicians, the purpose of which was "to guide item selection and item definition development" (manual, p. 43). The next stage involved multisite pilot testing using retrospective chart reviews, followed by prospective testing during service delivery. The author notes that at each stage "modifications were made to ensure the clarity, efficiency, reliability, and validity" (manual, p. 43) but does not detail the scope or nature of these revisions.

ADMINISTRATION. A 4- to 5-hour training session is recommended for raters prior to using the Severity and Acuity of Psychiatric Illness Scales. An outline for the training and four scored practice vignettes are provided in the manual. Additionally, definitions are provided for each item and the rater is advised to use these when administering the scales. The author notes that items should be rated based "on contact with the patient or a review of the case files" (manual, p. 33) but provides no guidance regarding how familiar a rater should be with the client to ensure a reliable assessment is obtained. The Severity Scale can be completed using a semistructured interview format with the client. For each item to be rated, interview questions and prompts are provided in the manual.

SCORING. The Severity and Acuity Scales are manually scored although the manual indicates that a computerized version of both scales is available from the Psychological Corporation.

SEVERITY SCALE. Three different scores can be generated using the Severity Scale items although the author indicates that "it is generally not necessary to score this measure in a traditional manner" (manual, p. 33) given that the profile of item responses is intended to assist providers in the treatment planning process. The first score, a Total Raw Score, is calculated by summing the ratings across the 14 items. This score is intended to provide the rater with an overall index of the severity of the client's problems. The second score, a Complexity Score, can be generated by counting the number of items on which a client receives a rating of 2 or 3, the more severe ratings. The Complexity Score is intended to highlight the multiple areas in which a client is experiencing the greatest difficulties. A Probability of Admissions Index, the third score, can be obtained using the rating from three of the Severity Scale items found to be predictive of hospitalization: suicide risk, danger to others, and the severity of psychiatric symptoms. The author provides a probability table summarizing the likelihood of hospitalization for a person with various ratings on the three items. The table was constructed based on a logistic regression model developed on 254 consecutive hospital admissions and cross-validated on an unspecified number of managed care patients. One concern with the scoring procedures in the manual is that although an option is provided to note when information is not available to rate items, no instructions are provided on how to calculate or adjust these scores when necessary information is unavailable. Additionally, no directions are provided on the number of items that can be missing without compromising the measure's validity.

ACUITY SCALE. Three raw scores can be obtained from the Acuity Scale: a Clinical Status, Nursing Status, and Total Acuity score. The four Additional Information Scale items not included in the scoring are recommended for use as global markers of improvement. The Clinical Status and Nursing Status subscale scores are obtained by summing the ratings from the appropriate scale items. The Total Acuity Score is simply the sum of these two subscales scores. The raw scores are then converted to T scores using reference tables provided in the manual. Again, information is not provided on how to score the Acuity Scale when one or more items cannot be rated.

INTERPRETATION. Normative data are available for the Clinical Status and Nursing Status subscales and Total Acuity Scale. Norms are based on two small samples: 153 older adults (average age approximately 73 years old) in a partial hospitalization setting and 270 younger adults (average age approximately 31 years old) from an inpatient setting.

RELIABILITY. Two types of reliability estimates are provided: interrater and internal consis-

tency. Summaries of three retrospective file review studies are cited in which the interrater reliability of the Severity and Acuity of Psychiatric Illness Scales was assessed. Weighted kappa values ranged from .73 to .84 on the Acuity Scale and .83 to .86 on the Severity Scale indicating a sufficient level of agreement across independent raters. As previously noted, the manual includes four scored training vignettes that can be used to train raters and estimate interrater reliability.

Internal consistency reliability is provided for the Acuity Scale only, in the form of Cronbach alpha coefficients. The internal consistency estimates of the Clinical Status subscale were .70 and .75, and alphas on the Nursing Status subscale were .63 and .66. The internal consistency estimates for the Total Acuity Score were .78 and .81.

Validity.

SEVERITY SCALE. The construct validity of a preliminary version of the Severity Scale was assessed by examining the correlations between the Severity Scale items and five standard psychiatric assessments such as the Brief Psychiatric Rating Scale (BSRS) and Geriatric Depression Scale (GDS). The sample for this study was limited to 150 older adult inpatients. Of the 40 correlations between the eight Severity Scale items and the five standardized measures, 14 were significant, although most of these correlations were in the low to moderate range and some of the correlations seem to be in a counterintuitive direction.

The predictive validity of the Severity Scale is supported by the findings from four studies. Two of these studies examined inpatient psychiatric admissions and found that a predictive model developed using the Severity Scale items could correctly classify hospital admissions 75% of the time. Two other studies summarized in the manual focused on length of stay and found that items from the Severity Scale could "reliably distinguish" (p. 45) between brief- and long-term-stay psychiatric inpatients. Information on how well this model predicted length of stay is not provided in the manual and the definitions of brief and long-term stays differed across the two studies.

ACUITY SCALE. The construct validity of the Acuity Scale has been assessed by examining the correlations between the Total Acuity Score and the total scores on four frequently used standardized clinical assessments (i.e., Mini Mental State Exam [MMSE], Hamilton Depression Rating Scale [HDRS], BPRS, GDS). However, the corelations are based on a rather restrictive sample of 150 elderly inpatients. The Acuity Scale has a significant, moderate relationship with two global measures of symptomatology (i.e., .62 with BPRS and -.47 with MMSE) but a substantially weaker and in one case a near zero relationship with the two depression measures examined (.27 with GDS and .02 with HDRS).

The predictive validity of the Acuity Scale has been assessed both prospectively and retrospectively through the examination of patient outcomes following inpatient treatment (particularly readmission) and Acuity Scale scores. In general, the findings from the four studies reported in the manual indicate that readmission is more likely the result of poor aftercare rather than poor inpatient care and that inappropriate admissions, as based on the Severity scale ratings, result in poorer inpatient outcomes relative to appropriate admissions.

SUMMARY. The manual is well written and provides helpful information regarding the item definitions and the training of raters. Data on some forms of reliability and validity of the scales are provided in the manual and are clearly summarized. Like many more newly developed measures, the information available is limited in some areas. Stability estimates of reliability are not available. As previously noted, the scoring instructions do not indicate how to adjust scale scores when items cannot be rated, nor do they indicate how many items can be missing without affecting the scale's validity. The norms provided are based on small and rather restrictive subgroups of individuals. However, despite these concerns the Severity and Acuity of Psychiatric Illness Scales appear to be a promising set of clinician-rated measures that can be useful in both practice and research.

[351]
Sexual Adjustment Inventory.

Purpose: "Designed to identify sexually deviate and paraphiliac behavior."
Population: People accused or convicted of sexual offenses.
Publication Date: 1991.
Acronym: SAI.
Scores: 13 scales: Test Item Truthfulness, Sex Item Truthfulness, Sexual Adjustment, Child Molest, Sexual Assault, Exhibitionism, Incest, Alcohol, Drugs, Violence, Antisocial, Distress, Judgment.
Administration: Group.
Forms, 2: Adult, Juvenile.

Price Data: Available from publisher.
Time: (35–40) minutes.
Comments: Both computer version and paper-pencil format are scored using IBM-PC compatibles.
Author: Risk & Needs Assessment, Inc.
Publisher: Risk & Needs Assessment, Inc.

Review of the Sexual Adjustment Inventory by RICHARD F. FARMER, Associate Professor of Psychology, Idaho State University, Pocatello, ID:

The Sexual Adjustment Inventory (SAI) is a self-report measure "designed to identify sexually deviate and paraphiliac behavior in people accused or convicted of sexual offenses" (manual, p. 1), and is intended to supplement impressions gained from persons familiar with the respondent's sexual behavior or offenses (e.g., therapists), focused interview on the respondent's sexual adjustment, and available records. The SAI contains 214 items that belong to 13 subscales, and requires about 45 minutes to complete. Most of the items (84%) utilize a "true or false" format and the remaining require the respondent to choose among four response options. The SAI may be administered by computer or from a test booklet. Regardless of administration method, SAI protocols are scored and interpreted by a computer software program provided by the test publisher. No means are available for hand-scoring this measure. Potential users must be licensed by the test publisher.

The 13 subscales of the SAI assess content areas related to sexual deviance (i.e., sexual adjustment, pedophilia, sexual assault, exhibitionism, incest), as well as drug and alcohol abuse, proneness to physical violence, antisocial personality, psychological distress, and judgment. There are also two validity scales. The Test Item Truthfulness Scale purports to assess general test-taking defensiveness or deliberate falsification and the Sex Item Truthfulness Scale attempts to evaluate the degree of defensiveness or deception found in responses to sex-related questions. "Truth-corrected scores" for each of the 13 SAI scales are derived from these validity scale, although the manual does not clearly specify the methods used in the computation of adjusted scale scores.

Items initially selected for inclusion in the SAI were intuitively derived and subsequently administered to 14 pilot subjects described as patients of sex therapists. Those items that demonstrated the "best statistical properties" (unclear as to methods employed) were retained for inclusion in the inventory. Initial standardization work was subsequently conducted in 1991 on 11 of the 13 current scales with a sample of 358 (99% male, 92% White) convicted sex offenders, which resulted in some revisions in the inventory. Two other scales, the Antisocial and Violence Scales, were subsequently added in 1994.

Adjusted scale (or "truth-corrected") scores are interpreted in terms of percentile rankings referenced to a normative sample of sex offenders. These rankings, in turn, are interpreted in accordance with "risk ranges": 0 to 39th %ile = low risk, 40th to 69th %ile = medium risk, 70th to 89th %ile = problem risk, and 90th to 100th %ile = severe problem risk. Normative data (e.g., adjusted or unadjusted means, standard deviations) do not appear in the test manual, perhaps because the test is restandardized on a yearly basis. Data used in the restandardization process are collected by test users who, as part of the test use agreement, must mail to the test publisher used computer-scoring diskettes that contain respondents' responses.

The SAI computer-generated test report provides a graphic analysis of the respondent's percentile rankings across scales, as well as a brief description of the risk assessment associated with each of the individual scales and, if warranted, brief treatment recommendations. The test report does not provide an integrated summary based on an overall inventory profile, although it does provide a listing of noteworthy items endorsed across scales.

A supplement to the test manual ("Inventory of Scientific Findings") provides a summary of research performed on the SAI. In terms of reliability, several studies are reported that evaluated the internal consistency of the SAI scales. Alpha coefficients across studies generally ranged between .84 to .92 for each of the SAI scales, which is suggestive of good to excellent internal consistency. There are, however, no data presented on the test-retest reliability characteristics of the scales.

Data presented in support of the measure's validity are sparse and equivocal. Evidence in support of the two validity scales was evaluated by correlations that these scales had with the Minnesota Multiphasic Personality Inventory (MMPI) L and F scales as determined by responses from 205 convicted sex offenders. The SAI validity scales and MMPI were completed within the same 18-month period for all offenders, with most (89%) completing both instruments within one

year. The manual reports a correlation of .20 between the SAI Test Item Truthfulness Scale and the MMPI L Scale and a correlation of .33 between the SAI Sex Item Validity Scale and the MMPI F scale. However, the manual provides only a cursory delineation of the conceptual similarities between these SAI and MMPI scales; consequently, it is difficult to evaluate the claim that these relatively low correlations provide validation for the SAI validity scales. Furthermore, as these findings are the primary data that support the validity of the SAI validity scales, they challenge enthusiastic claims in the manual that adjusted scores "are more accurate than raw scores" and "reveal what the client is trying to hide" (p. 3).

Another study was conducted with 136 convicted sex offenders and 91 "normals" to evaluate the discriminant validity of one of the SAI subscales, the Sexual Adjustment Scale. The hypothesis that sexual offenders would endorse more deviant responses on this scale than normals was supported. However, the manual does not report how the normals were recruited. Similarly, there were some substantial differences in the subject composition of these two groups. For example, less than 1% of the offender sample versus 28.6% of normal sample were females. Similarly, the normal group was reported to be significantly younger and more educated. Despite an attempt by the test publisher to derive subsamples of normals and offenders matched on age and education (although not subject sex), it would seem that the "normal" group does not constitute an optimal comparison group to establish the discriminant validity of this scale.

In another supplement to the test manual ("Huttonsville Correctional Center West Virginia Summary Report"), data are presented for 51 sex offenders that showed good correspondence between the sample's distribution of risk categories for each of the 13 SAI scales when referenced to the inventory's national normative distribution. This limited finding suggests that the SAI national norms have some applicability to West Virginia sexual offenders. The only remaining evidence provided by the test publisher of the SAI's validity was done with 136 men convicted of sexual offenses who were receiving counseling. Fourteen sex therapists were reported to have rated the sex offenders "risk on behaviors measured by the SAI scales" ("Inventory of Scientific

Findings," p. 16) as either *low, medium,* or *severe problem.* No other information is provided about how therapists made these ratings, nor how these ratings were transformed into numerical values. Of the 11 correlations presented between SAI scales and therapist ratings, all but one (Judgment Scale) were statistically significant. However, 5 of the 11 correlations were less than .13, whereas the remaining 6 correlations ranged between .32 and .41. Of particular note were the correlations reported for the Test Item Truthfulness Scale and the Sex Item Truthfulness Scale, which were, respectively, .10 and .09. These findings further call into question the validity of these scales and the utility of adjusted scores in the interpretation of SAI scales.

SUMMARY. The SAI is presented as a measure of sexually deviant behavior among an offender population. Strengths of this measure include the breadth of domains the inventory attempts to assess, the apparent face validity of the item set (although the manual does not indicate the subscales to which items belong), and good to excellent internal consistency associated with each of the SAI subscales. However, limited or equivocal psychometric data on the validity of the SAI suggest caution in its use as an assessment device. Urgently needed are validity data that show some degree of correspondence between SAI scale scores and objective indices of respondents' behaviors, such as a documented history of or conviction for *specific* sexual offenses. Similarly, better controlled studies to evaluate the discriminant validity of the scales are required. Another area for investigation or comment is the need for separate norms for males and females. It is presently unclear how useful this measure is for a female population. In studies reported in the manual on the psychometric properties of the inventory where the sex of subjects was mentioned, sexual offender samples were either exclusively male or contained a very small minority of females (less than 7%). Finally, the test manual and supplements are poorly written, redundant, and omit important information related to the development and characteristics of the test.

Review of the Sexual Adjustment Inventory by SHEILA MEHTA, Associate Professor of Psychology, Auburn University at Montgomery, Montgomery, AL:

The Sexual Adjustment Inventory (SAI) is a 214-item true-false and multiple-choice, pencil-and-paper or computer inventory (for IBM PC compatible computers). Although there are two forms available for the SAI—adult and juvenile—it should be noted that this review is for the *adult form only.* The SAI can be used to screen sexual offenders, measuring the degree of severity of sexually deviant and paraphiliac behavior. Other related behaviors are also assessed: alcohol and drug use, judgment, antisocial behavior, violence, and distress. A nice feature of the SAI is that it assesses test-taking attitude, and thus, test-taking validity. Both the paper-and-pencil and the automated versions are scored by computer. The program automatically produces the report, performs risk classification, presents significant items, and prints a structured interview. Both versions are easy to administer, score, and interpret, and the directions are clear. No special training is needed to administer and score the test. Face validity is good, though some of the questions, given the nature of what is being assessed, may offend test takers.

Norms are available in the form of percentile scores. The standardization samples were convicted sex offenders. Although detailed demographic and inter-item reliability information is available, the test author includes no information about how the samples were chosen, participation rates, raw scores, and standardized scores. Information is available about subgroups that were included in the standardization samples but not about subgroup scores. Few women were in the original samples, so I would not recommend using the SAI with women. Ethnic minority populations were included but somewhat underrepresented, as were lower-education groups. The SAI database is analyzed annually, which means that the SAI is essentially standardized each year.

The only type of reliability addressed was inter-item reliability. The Cronbach coefficient alphas for each of the 13 SAI scales, drawn from close to a dozen studies, ranged from .80 to .92, indicating adequate internal consistency. Each SAI scale appears to measure consistently a particular characteristic.

The author seems to have carried out much research on the SAI. In terms of item development, it appears that a rational approach was used initially and then revisions were made based on empirical findings.

The author, on more than one occasion, states that within-test reliability measures to what extent a test with multiple scales assessing different factors measures each factor independently of other scales in the test. Although this statement can be true, it is not clear that the necessary analyses were conducted to warrant the author's claims of factor independence. In one study, 358 convicted sex offenders took the SAI; Cronbach alphas were computed for each of the SAI subscales. The results do demonstrate high inter-item congruency. The author's claims, however, that these results demonstrate that each SAI scale measure a *different* factor, and that each SAI scale is an *independent* measure of the trait it was designed to measure, are unfounded, given the information provided. If the subscale reliabilities were significantly greater than the correlations between the subscales or with the total SAI, then such a claim could be made. Another study was conducted on a sample of 165, wherein a within-subjects ANOVA was performed, apparently on each SAI scale. It is possible that the results of these two studies do provide evidence of the instrument's construct validity, but the information presented is insufficient to judge whether the author's claims are supported.

Another study appears to be an attempt to assess convergent validity of scores from the two SAI scales. It evaluated the relationships between the SAI Test Validity Scale (truthfulness while answering non-sex-related test items) and the Minnesota Multiphasic Personality Inventory (MMPI) L Scale, and the SAI Sex Validity Scale (truthfulness while answering obvious sex-related questions) and the MMPI F Scale. It should be noted that the MMPI was administered 12 to 18 months prior to the SAI administration. Although each SAI validity scale correlated with the corresponding MMPI validity scales in the expected direction, the strength of the relationships were weak (.197 with Test Validity Scale) to moderate (.332 with Sex Validity Scale). The results provide weak evidence of construct validity for scores from the instrument.

Another study provided evidence of criterion-related validity for another subscale, the Sexual Adjustment Scale, using the contrasted group method. Sex offender's scores on this subscale, which "measures sex adjustment and reflects the client's sexual satisfaction or dissatisfaction" (Inventory of Scientific Findings, p. 13) were compared with scores from a group of normals (indi-

viduals never charged with a sex offense). What is not clear, however, is whether the normals took the entire Sexual Adjustment Scale or just part of it. Leaving that question aside, the two groups' scores were significantly different from each other, suggesting that the scores on the subscale correlate with illegal sexual behavior. Thus the results of this study provide support for the construct validity of this particular subscale.

Evidence of criterion-related validity of 10 of the 13 subscales of the SAI comes from a study assessing the relationship between sex therapists' ratings and scores on 11 of the 13 SAI scales. (The Violence and Antisocial subscales were not assessed, and the Judgment subscale correlation was nonsignificant.) The correlations range from weak (.09) to moderate (.41), the average correlation being .23. The results of this study, though not strong, provided the best support for the construct validity of the scores from the SAI.

SUMMARY. In conclusion, the SAI is an instrument whose usefulness has yet to be fully established. It has demonstrated subscale inter-item consistency and preliminary support that its scores are related to external real-life criteria. Advantages of the SAI over other similar instruments are that it provides a comprehensive profile of sex and sex-related behaviors, includes two test-taking attitude scales, is relatively brief, and is easy to administer, score, and interpret.

[352]
SF—36 Health Survey.

Purpose: Designed as a "survey of general health concepts."

Population: Ages 14 and older.

Publication Dates: 1989–1993.

Acronym: SF-36.

Scores: 8 scales: Physical Functioning, Role-Physical, Bodily Pain, General Health, Vitality, Social Functioning, Role-Emotional, Mental Health.

Administration: Group.

Price Data: Available from publisher; administration and scoring software available from CogniSyst, Inc.

Time: Administration time not reported.

Author: John E. Ware, Jr.

Publisher: The Health Institute, New England Medical Center.

Cross References: See T5:2397 (1 reference).

Review of the SF-36 Health Survey by ASHRAF KAGEE, Postdoctoral Fellow, University of Pennsylvania, Philadelphia, PA:

INTRODUCTION. The SF-36 Health Survey is a structured-choice inventory that assesses general health concepts relevant to functional status and well-being and may be used for a large variety of research purposes including clinical practice, health policy evaluations, and general population surveys. Insofar as the scale is not specific to respondents' age, condition or disease, or treatment undergone, it may be said to be generic.

The SF-36 is highly practical and relatively unburdensome to respondents in that it may be self-administered by respondents usually in a short time period. Its versatility is reflected in the fact that it may be administered in a variety of settings, including a clinic or doctor's office, in the context of a telephone interview, as a mail-out/mail-back questionnaire, and as a face-to-face interview.

The key concepts assessed by the instrument are: Physical Functioning (10 items), Physical Role Functioning (4 items), Bodily Pain (2 items), General Health (5 items), Vitality (4 items) Social Functioning (2 items), Emotional Role (3 items), Mental Health (5 items), and Reported Health Transmission (1 item).

The recommended uses of the test are clearly stated and interpretations may be applied to a broad range of patient groups on whom it was normed. The test was constructed for self-administration by individuals age 14 and older and for use in clinical practice and research, health policy evaluations, and general population surveys.

ADMINISTRATION AND SCORING. Subjects are provided with a double-sided Scantron sheet containing all the items of the test and to which they are asked to respond by marking an oval representing their best choice. Following data entry, items and scales are scored in three steps: recoding the 10 items for which this is required, computing scale scores by summing raw scale scores, and transforming raw scale scores to a 0–100 scale. Scoring algorithms and computer software are available for these purposes. Scoring instructions are clearly described.

RELIABILITY. The samples used in the norming process cover a broad range of patients with various medical conditions. The reported reliability coefficients of the subtests arrived at by studies from the late-1980s to the present are generally above .70 for most sample groups (e.g., Garratt, Ruta, Abdulla, Buckingham, & Russell, 1993; Jenkinson, Coulter, & Wright, 1993; Bra-zier et al., 1992). These reliability coefficients are sufficiently high to warrant using the test for individual subjects. Reliability coefficient estimates were computed via three methods, test-retest reliability (intervals between 2 weeks and 6 months), internal consistency, and alternate form reliability.

NORMING. The sample on which the test was normed ($N = 2,474$) is highly representative of the intended population. A response rate of more than 89% was large enough to provide stable estimates. Moreover, the difficulty levels of the test provide an adequate basis for validating and norming the instrument and there were sufficient test-takers in each subgroup.

FACTOR ANALYSIS. Factor analysis of the SF-36 using principal components analysis revealed a two-factor solution representing the physical and mental dimensions of health and accounting for 82.4% of the reliable variance. This corresponds to the physical and mental dimensions of health that have been confirmed in previous studies (Hays & Stewart, 1990; Ware, Davies-Avery, & Brook, 1980). The questions regarding vitality and general health perceptions correlate moderately to substantially with each rotated principal component.

VALIDITY. Other psychometric properties of the SF-36 are good. Criterion validity of the SF-36 has been examined using conceptually related variables that provide empirical tests of each scale, such as ability to work, utilization of health care services and, in the case of mental health, other psychometric scales measuring psychopathology.

Correlations between the SF-36 subscales and scores on the general health dimension and between the SF-36 subscales and ratings of equality of life not specifically related to health were all significant in the positive direction, suggesting good convergent validity. Similarly, correlations between the Mental Health subscale and similar measures such as the General Health Rating Index (Read, Quinn, & Hoefer, 1987), Quality of Well-being Scale (Fryback et al., 1993), and the Physical Performance Test (Reuben & Siu, 1990) were positive, suggesting good convergent validity. On the other hand, divergent validity was demonstrated by strong negative correlations between the Physical Performance subscale and the Sickness Impact Profile (Weinberger et al., 1991; Katz, Larson, Phillips, & Liang, 1992).

SUMMARY. The SF-36 quickly and efficiently assesses health status and may be used for a variety of research purposes. The administration and scoring procedures are straightforward and easy to follow. The authors conscientiously used multiple procedures to assess and report reliability and validity data. Finally, the manual is readable and adequate enough to use the test.

REVIEWER'S REFERENCES

Ware, J. E., Davies-Avery, A., & Brook, R. H. (1980). *Analysis of relationships among health status measures.* Santa Monica, CA: Rand Corporation.

Read, J. L., Quin, R. J., & Hoefer, M. A. (1987). Measuring overall health: An evaluation of three important approaches. *Journal of Chronic Disease, 40*(Supp.), 75–215.

Hays, R. D., & Stewart, A. L. (1990). The structure of self-reported health in chronic disease patients. *Psychological Assessment: A Journal of Consulting and Clinical Psychology, 2,* 22–30.

Reuben, D. B., & Siu, A. L. (1990). An objective measure of physical function of elderly outpatients: The Physical Performance Test. *Journal of the American Geriatric Society, 38,* 1105–1112.

Weinberger, M., Samsa, G. P., Hanlon, J. T., Schmader, K., Doyle, M. E., Cowper, P. A., Utlech, K. M., Cohen, H. J., & Feussner, J. R. (1991). An evaluation of a brief health status measure in elderly veterans. *Journal of American Geriatric Society, 39*(7), 691–694.

Brazier, J. E., Harper, R., Jones, N. M. B., O'Cathain, A., Thomas, K. J., Usherwood, T., & Westlake, L. (1992). Validating the SF-36 Health Survey questionnaire: New outcome measure for primary care. *British Medical Journal, 305,* 160–164.

Katz, J. N., Larson, M. G., Phillips, C. B., Fossel, A. H., & Liang, M. H. (1992). Comparative measurement sensitivity of short and longer health status instruments. *Medical Care, 30*(10), 917–925.

Frybaek, D. G., Dorbach, F. J., Klein, R., Klein, B., Dorn, N., Peterson, K., & Martin, A. M. (1993). The Beaver Dam Health Outcomes Study. Initial catalog of health state quality factors. *Medical Decision Making, 13,* 89–102.

Garratt, A. M., Ruta, D. A., Abdalla, M. I., Buckingham, J. K., & Russell, I. T. (1993). The SF-36 Health Survey questionnaire: An outcome measure suitable for routine use within the NHS? *British Medical Journal, 306,* 1440–1444.

Jenkinson, C., Coulter, A., & Wright, L. (1993). The SF-36 Health Survey Questionnaire: Normative data from a large random sample of working age adults. *British Medical Journal, 306,* 1435–1440.

Review of the SF-36 Health Survey by NATHANIEL J. PALLONE, University Distinguished Professor (Psychology), Center of Alcohol Studies, Rutgers University, Piscataway, NJ, and JAMES J. HENNESSY, Professor, Graduate School of Education, Fordham University, New York, NY:

The SF-36 Health Status Survey is a self-report questionnaire for medical patients or prospective patients available in a variety of forms, ranging from (a) an interview schedule that actually contains 36 items, (b) a blacken-the-space, machine-scorable format that covers the same 36 aspects of health status but contains only 11 questions, and (c) a version that can be administered on a desktop PC. Neither of the latter two versions should require more than 10 minutes to complete. The instrument is the direct heir to the Medical Outcome Study surveys undertaken in the mid-1980s by Ware and other researchers at the New England Medical Center, in the first instance to attempt to differentiate respondents according to type of medical ailment and, in the second, to determine whether questionnaire responses might predict "use of medical resources."

In straightforward fashion, the instrument asks the respondent to assess the extent to which he or she is physically limited in each of what are increasingly called "activities of daily living" (ADLs) such as bathing, dressing, climbing stairs, housecleaning, etc., and whether impairment has increased or abated within the past month; typical level of physical pain during the past month; and how the respondent perceives his or her physical health absolutely and relatively on discrete 5-point scales. Parallel questions about "emotional problems" are interspersed. As is unfortunately typical in questionnaires that require highly subjective self-evaluations, neither positive nor negative anchor points are operationally defined, so that idiosyncratic variations are to be expected, perhaps most particularly in responses to items that seek to gauge emotional response to physical maladies. Emotional reactions to advancing osteoarthritis on the part of the warehouseman who lacks other marketable job skills may justifiably prove both more intense and more negative than those of the claims adjuster for an insurance company for whom the disease yields only minor impairments in job performance.

On the basis of factor analytic studies, responses to the 36 principal items are aggregated into discrete scores for eight scales: Physical Functioning, Role-Physical, Bodily Pain, General Health, with these four yielding a "summary measure" of physical health; and Vitality, Social Functioning, Role-Emotional, and Mental Health, with these four yielding (somewhat redundantly) a summary measure of mental health. Mental health professionals will justifiably complain that the items that purport to yield an index of psychological well-being constitute a woefully inadequate sample thereof. Indeed, the items on their face alone inquire primarily into emotional states *reactive to* the onset of physical illness and do not begin to probe ego-dystonic mental conditions. That these four items are then aggregated into a global self-assessment of mental health will strike most knowledgeable mental health professionals as a problem. The paranoid schizophrenic who is diagnosed with prostate cancer will, without doubt, respond to SF-36 items in ways that reveal depression, pessimism, and the like *with respect to his medical diagnosis*—but that *reactive mood* may reflect very little about his continuing psychosis, save perhaps in the case of the actively hallucinatory. Truth-in-labeling strictures alone suggest reconstruing what self-assessments the items now aggregated as a summary actually measure of mental health. In that process, some attention might profitably be given to the differentiation between Axis I and Axis II disorders and to Global Assessment of Functioning as enunciated in DSM-IV and its predecessors.

Reliability coefficients for the eight primary scales range from a low of .68 for Social Functioning to a high of .93 for Physical Functioning among nearly 2,500 subjects in the general population and from a low of .83 for Role-Emotional to a high of .93, once again for Physical Functioning, among nearly 3,500 subjects with documented physical ailments who had participated in the "parent" Medical Outcome Study surveys.

In the general population at least, scores from the instrument are more reliable in the physical than in the "mental health" scales. Validity coefficients are reported between scales on the SF-36 and membership in an array of medical diagnostic categories, including cardiovascular, neurological, musculo-skeletal, and gastrointestinal disorders. Coefficients between scales related to physical health tend to be stronger than those related to mental health, from which one might conclude either more accurate self-appraisal in the former than in the latter case or that emotional sequelae to physical ailments are substantially more variable and perhaps quite ipsative.

Its authors expect the instrument to be utilized to track, pre- and post-treatment, subjective assessments of physical functioning and emotional well-being among patients with medical disorders of varied sorts and, over time, to contribute to "guiding the efficient use of community resources and ... predicting more accurately the course of chronic disease" (manual, p. 10:1). In two very comprehensive manuals (of which the most recently published contains a useful discussion of effect size), norm tables are provided for subjects separated by gender and by age; for subjects whose medical ailments are chronic versus emergent; for patients diagnosed with a large array of medical disorders (including allergies, angina, arthritis, back pain, cancer, congestive heart failure, dermatitis, diabetes, hearing impairment, hypertension, lung disease, myocardial infarction, obstructive pulmonary disease, varicosities, vision impairment) or with combinations of disorders; and for changes over the space of a year for subjects with certain disorders.

To the extent that it codifies and standardizes against representative norm samples patient self-assessment data heretofore routinely gathered by physicians principally through free-form questioning or probing, the SF-36 may prove a valuable and relatively unobtrusive adjunct to clinical medical practice—provided only that the physician understands that the so-called "mental health" items and scale are inappropriately named and essentially limited in their applicability to the assessment of mood reactive to medical disorder.

SUMMARY. The SF-36 is a brief, unobtrusive device that situates a respondent's self-assessment of aspects of his or her physical health and emotional well-being (largely in response to recent or recently diagnosed changes in physical health) in relation to an array of normative data. Intended primarily for use with medical patients before and after treatment for particular disorders, by codifying information and providing a normative basis for the interpretation of patient self-assessments, it may provide a useful adjunct to clinical medical practice.

[353]
Shoplifting Inventory.

Purpose: "Designed to evaluate people charged or convicted of shoplifting."
Population: Shoplifting offenders.
Publication Date: 1995.
Acronym: SI.
Scores: 9 scales: Truthfulness, Entitlement, Shoplifting, Antisocial, Peer Pressure, Self-Esteem, Impulsiveness, Alcohol, Drugs.
Administration: Group.
Price Data: Available from publisher.
Time: (35) minutes.
Comments: Both computer version and paper-pencil format are scored on IBM-PC compatibles.
Author: Risk & Needs Assessment, Inc.
Publisher: Risk & Needs Assessment, Inc.

Review of the Shoplifting Inventory by G. GAGE KINGSBURY, Director of Research, Northwest Evaluation Association, Portland, OR:

The Shoplifting Inventory (SI) is a self-report inventory designed to delineate personality and behavioral characteristics of individuals who have been charged with or convicted of shoplifting. The SI can be administered in paper-and-pencil form, or with a PC-compatible computer. The expected time of administration is 35 minutes, although it is an untimed instrument.

The SI includes 137 true-false questions and 48 semantic differential items with five rating points. Answers to these questions are used to compute nine scale scores related to the individual's behavior and personality. These scales are named Truthfulness, Alcohol, Drugs, Antisocial, Shoplifting, Entitlement, Peer Pressure, Self-Esteem, and Impulsive.

The outcome of the SI is a computer-prepared profile that details the individual's percentile ranking on each of the nine scales and divides these into categories described as "Low Risk," "Medium Risk," "Problem Risk," or "Severe Problem Risk." This is accompanied by a narrative description of the meaning of the identified category for each scale.

When the inventory is administered via computer, results are available immediately following administration. When the inventory is administered in paper form, the individuals' responses are key-entered with an optional validity check. Results are then immediately available to be viewed on the computer screen or printed. A PC-compatible computer is required for key-entry and reporting.

RELIABILITY AND VALIDITY. Reliability and validity evidence for the SI is presented from a set of studies done from 1985 to the present. Because the SI includes several scales that were previously used in several other inventories, research presented includes some information for these scales as they appeared in the other inventories.

Internal consistency reliability information is presented for the individual scales from several studies. If we concentrate on only those studies that use the whole SI, we have four reliability studies that were conducted in 1997 with samples of convicted shoplifters with sample sizes of 107 to 378. Each of these studies indicated a fairly high degree of internal consistency reliability within each of the nine scales. Alpha coefficients ranged from .83 to .95, with a median of .87. The Entitlement scale consistently had the lowest internal consistency, with a median alpha of .84. The Self-Esteem scale consistently had the highest internal consistency, with a median alpha of .94. No evidence of test-retest reliability was presented.

No validity evidence was presented for the scale scores in the context of the SI, but some evidence of construct validity was presented in the form of correlations between individual scale scores (not in the context of the SI) and other external measures evaluating the same constructs. Evidence was presented for the Truthfulness, Self-Esteem, Alcohol, Aggressiveness, and Drug scales. Correlations ranged broadly, from a correlation of .11 between a counselor's rating of self-esteem and the Self-Esteem scale, to a correlation of .80 between the Alcohol scale and a court procedure used to estimate alcohol problems. Although the evidence is not always consistent, and is not based on the SI itself, there is some indication that these scales measure the construct that they are designed to measure.

The materials discuss Truth-Corrected scores and the advantages of their use. No information is given concerning how these scores are derived. In addition, no empirical information is given regarding changes in reliability or validity as a result of this correction. This seems to be a fairly serious oversight because the inventory uses these scores exclusively.

Another element that is missing from the support materials is a description of the norming sample that was used to create the percentile rankings that are used in scoring. This is another serious omission because the makeup of the norming group is critical to an understanding of the percentile values obtained by an individual taking the inventory.

STRENGTHS AND WEAKNESSES. The SI is designed to give information about the issues in a person's life that might contribute to shoplifting behavior. To achieve this goal, the SI needs to tap many different aspects of an individual's personality and behavior. The SI accomplishes this very nicely, including risk behaviors that might lead to shoplifting (such as drug and alcohol use), and personality and attitude variables that might allow someone to shoplift more easily (such as an attitude of entitlement). The SI is a fairly unique instrument in its comprehensive approach to identifying the issues that might have led an individual to shoplifting.

Results from the SI (with names removed) are also returned to the producers of the inventory. This is designed to allow additional empirical investigation of the SI as it is used in the field. This should facilitate reliability studies, and might facilitate additional validity studies if combined with other information about the individuals taking the inventory.

The SIU is straightforward to administer to individuals. The reading level seems appropriate, and the computer interface is fairly simple to use.

The ability to obtain instant reports should be very useful for counselors and others working with the individuals taking the inventory. The reports are also well designed and present the information from the inventory in a concise form.

The SI lacks guidelines for the use of the information once the report is produced. A consumer of the inventory would be likely to ask what they should do with the results, and this question is not addressed in the materials. Without this information, it is unclear how the counselor or the individual taking the inventory benefits from its use.

The SI was designed to work under a DOS computer-operating system, and as a result, it does not work smoothly under Windows. As an example, printing a report requires one to save the results to a file, open a second application, open the saved file, and then print the results. This is an awkward procedure, at best. The system is not available for Mac-OS or for LINUX operating systems.

While taking the inventory on the computer, I also ran into a few issues that would bother the person giving the inventory and the person taking it. The instructions for starting the inventory have the wrong program name. The application consistently told me I was entering invalid dates for the inventory. When taking the inventory, there was no way that I could find for an individual to change a response once it was given. This option would be useful because it would be expected that some individuals would make mistakes in taking the inventory, even if they were trying to answer truthfully.

SUMMARY. If an individual within the criminal justice system worked with shoplifters often, this inventory might provide some useful information concerning the behaviors and attitudes of the individual involved. On the other hand, no guidance is provided to indicate the appropriate treatment avenues, or even to discuss the attributes of common profiles. Without this information, the inventory is substantially less useful than it might be.

Review of the Shoplifting Inventory by KWONG-LIEM KARL KWAN, Assistant Professor, Counseling and Development, Purdue University, Lafayette, IN:

The Shoplifting Inventory (SI) is designed as a risk assessment and screening tool for shoplifting offenders. Along with the testing booklet, the reviewer also received (a) a one-sheet (two-sided) synopsis of the Inventory (dated 1995), (b) an SI Orientation and Training Manual (dated 1995), (c) an SI Computer Operating Guide and an SI Scoring Quick Reference (dated 1995), and (d) an SI computer-generated sample report (dated 1995). Empirical data of the SI were published in another document, "SI: An Inventory of Scientific Findings" (dated 1996), which was promptly sent to the reviewer after the initial contact. These loose documents should be compiled in a professional manual.

The SI consists of 185 items divided into two sections. The first section requires True-or-False responses to 137 items. The second section requires self-ratings on 49 pairs of antonyms on a 5-point scale with the ratings 1 and 5 = *Very Often*, 2 and 4 = *Often*, and 3 = *Can't Decide* for each pair. A sixth-grade reading level is required. Nine scale scores, corresponding to the Truthfulness, Entitlement, Shoplifting, Antisocial, Peer Pressure, Self-Esteem, Impulsiveness, Alcohol, and Drug scales, are yielded. Each scale score indicates a risk potential according to the percentile range in which the score is classified (Low Risk = 0 to 39th percentile; Medium Risk = 40th to 69th percentile; Problem Risk = 70th to 89th percentile; Severe Problem Risk = 90th to 100th percentile). The statistical and conceptual rationale for such classifications is not provided. Several significant items were included to augment interpretation of scale scores. The inventory can be administered by paper-and-pencil or by computer. The computer version was easy to use, with an accompanying instruction summary that was clearly and systematically written. Results can only be computer-scored using the vendor's computer diskette, which is also programmed to generate summary reports for up to 51 offenders. Used diskettes need to be returned so that stored data could contribute to the evolving database and restandardization of the instrument.

The Shoplifting Inventory is not purported to the theoretically based, which is reflected in the lack of a conceptual link among the nine scales. The multiple-scale approach attempts to capture various aspects of shoplifters' motivation, attitude, and behaviors. Scale items were selected, through consensual agreement and then statistical procedures, from an item pool generated by psychologists and criminal justice professionals. The field-based approach provides scientist-practitioner merit in these items' development. In general, items have face validity and reflect what the respective scales purport to measure. Five of the nine scales (i.e., Truthfulness Scale, Antisocial Scale, Self-Esteem Scale, Alcohol Scale, and Drug Scale) were incorporated from other forensic evaluation measures, including the Substance Abuse Questionnaire (SAQ), the Treatment Intervention Inventory (TII), and the Prison Inmate Inventory (PII). It is inconsistently stated that there is "some consensus" (in the two-page SI synopsis) and "little consensus" (in SI: An Inventory of Scientific Findings) about the characterological or personality differences common to shoplifters. Thus, it is not clear if SI items are constructed to conceptually represent commonality among shoplifters. Although the scales were sufficiently operationalized, the substantial overlap of these scales with other measures raise questions regarding the uniqueness of the construct assessed by the SI.

The Truthfulness Scale was designed as a "lie detector" and a scale-corrected measure; thus is a useful built-in system to minimize invalid results. Although the self-esteem characteristics, impulsiveness, and antisocial tendencies of shoplifters were briefly discussed, the conceptual rationales for including the Alcohol and Drug Scales were not provided. Beyond internal consistency data, no psychometric information of the Entitlement, Impulsiveness, and Shoplifting Scales were provided.

Research on the SI was reported in the document "SI: An Inventory of Empirical Findings." It is noted that the SI is a relatively new test, and that existing research was only on individual SI scales, not the *complete* SI. In this 1996 document, it is also stated that "research actually began in 1997 ... [and research] on the complete test began in 1996 and continues to the present" (p. 5). The PsycINFO computer database (1980–1998) was searched to locate references pertaining to the search terms "Shoplifting Inventory"; none could be identified. Empirical data of the reported Truthfulness, Alcohol, Drug, Antisocial, and Self-Esteem Scales were findings from concurrent validity studies of the SAQ, TII, or PII, but not for the SI. All statistics were reported in Pearson correlations and their significance levels. Although the years of these studies were quoted, no references were provided. In this 1996 document, several 1997 studies (no listed references) of the internal consistencies of the nine SI scales were reported using several samples of convicted shoplifters. Cronbach alphas ranged from .83 to .95; the Entitlement Scale consistently had the lowest alpha

coefficient, and the Self-Esteem Scale consistently had the highest alpha coefficient. Field samples (e.g., convicted shoplifters, DWI offenders, chemical dependency patients, probationers) were employed in these reported studies, which enhance the clinical relevance and applicability of findings.

SUMMARY. The SI is a developing instrument that combines existing and proposed scales. Studies of the psychometric properties of the *entire* instrument are needed. The convergent validity of the individual scales toward the purported construct assessed by the SI needs to be investigated. The overarching construct assessed by the entire SI and that assessed by the Shoplifting Scale need to be differentiated. Other statistical procedures (e.g., factor analysis) should be employed to explore item clusters and underlying scale structures. Normative data (e.g., score distributions across the nine scales), statistical procedures, and rationales that underlie the classification system, as well as items that constitute the respective scales, should be reported in a printed manual. The SI shares five scales with the PII and three scales with the SAQ and TII. Thus, the discriminant validity of these inventories, and the unique construct (and construct validity) of the SI, should be studied. Without a coherent conceptual or theoretical basis for assessment and the development of corresponding measures, the question of what constitutes a shoplifter profile remains.

[354]
Shortened Edinburgh Reading Test.

Purpose: Designed as a survey measure of children's reading skills in the upper primary school, and as a screening instrument to detect children who might need remedial help in reading.
Population: Ages 10-0 to 11-6.
Publication Date: 1985.
Scores, 5: Vocabulary, Syntax, Comprehension, Retention, General Reading Quotient.
Administration: Group.
Price Data, 1999: £13.99 per 20 test booklets; £12.99 per manual; £13.99 per specimen set.
Time: (40–45) minutes.
Authors: The Godfrey Thomson Unit, University of Edinburgh.
Publisher: Hodder & Stoughton [England].

Review of the Shortened Edinburgh Reading Test by DOUGLAS K. SMITH, Director of Programs in School Psychology, University of Albany—State University of New York, Albany, NY:

The Shortened Edinburgh Reading Test (SERT) is a group-administered reading test designed for students ages 10 years through 11 years, 6 months. There is no time limit for administration although one item is timed. The test consists of 75 items measuring Vocabulary (23 items), Structure (19 items), Reading Comprehension (25 items), and Retention of Significant Detail (8 items). The items were selected from the four stages of the Edinburgh Reading Tests, which were produced for the Bristol Child Health and Education Study. The items were selected by a team of reading specialists and other specialists involved in the Bristol Study.

The SERT was designed as a survey instrument with emphasis on students around age 10 who are lower achievers. In addition, it was designed to provide the classroom teacher with information that could be used in meeting the individual reading needs of students. A total score is provided as well as subtest scores. The total raw score is converted to a quotient indicating the relative standing of the student in comparison to others of the same age. Subtest scores are converted to standardized scores and are to be used in making comparisons with the child's own performance and not comparisons with other children. This allows for an examination of the child's strengths and weaknesses. This procedure can also be applied to the classroom as a whole.

Administration of the SERT is simple and straightforward. Previous experience in testing is not required and detailed instructions are provided for administration of the test. Verbatim instructions for the teacher to use are included. Specific scoring instructions are also provided. All items are scored either 0 or 1.

The Total Score is obtained by adding the subtest raw scores and converting the total to a "quotient," which is normally distributed with a mean of 100 and standard deviation of 15. The quotients range from 70 to 140. The authors indicate that the quotient is a measure of general reading performance at that particular point in time. Subtest scores are used to determine the student's individual profile of strengths and weaknesses *and not* to make comparisons with peers. Subtest raw scores are placed on a profile diagram for each subtest so that the placement of the subtest raw score corresponds to the standard score. Instructions for interpreting the profiles are provided on the profile sheet.

Items from each subtest are interspersed throughout the test. For example, the first 5 items are Vocabulary items, followed by 10 Structure (syntax and sequence) items. Vocabulary items fall into three categories. The first category requires the child to circle the word that represents the picture that is shown. Next, the child uses context to answer questions emphasizing a vocabulary word after reading a paragraph and to determine the meaning of a word in a sentence. The final set of items also emphasizes context by choosing phrases to substitute for underlined words in a paragraph. The Comprehension subtest emphasizes the understanding of what is read using pictures and written text. Both literal and inferential comprehension is measured. The Structure subtest consists of items measuring skills in syntax, sequence, and semantics. The Retention of Significant Details subtest measures short-term memory.

Standardization of the SERT is based on two samples of children during 1980–1981. The first sample consisted of 1,164 children in England, Scotland, and Wales randomly selected from the 16,000 national birthday sample of the British University Child Health and Education Study and the second sample was a local standardization with 1,234 children. No other details are provided about the two samples and their selection procedures.

Reliability data (from the national sample only) include the Kuder-Richardson internal consistency reliability indices. These values range from .95 for the total test and from .77 (Retention of Significant Details) to .89 (Comprehension) for the subtests. These values support the reliability of the instrument.

Validity data such as correlations with other measures are not provided. In terms of "face validity" some of the items are outdated and culture-specific. The Vocabulary subtest includes items that require reading of sentences and phrases that are usually not included in measures of vocabulary or word knowledge. Thus, comparisons of scores across tests would need to account for these differences. Although the rationale for each subtest is presented and has ample "face validity," there is a lack of documentation to support the inclusion of the skills measured by each subtest.

SUMMARY. The SERT is an easily administered group test of reading skills for students ages 10 years through 11 years, 6 months. Although some normative comparisons are possible, the instrument is best used in a diagnostic way to determine individual student strengths and weaknesses. Instructions for administering, scoring, and interpreting the test are clearly provided and suitable for use by classroom teachers.

There are a number of concerns with this instrument. The age range is very limited and the standardization data are 20 years old. In addition, some of the content of the test is outdated and culturally specific. Information regarding characteristics of the standardization sample are limited and do not meet current standards. Finally, the lack of validity studies is a major weakness. Although the SERT may provide useful diagnostic information, normative comparisons are not appropriate and the limited reliability and validity data preclude its use on a wide basis.

Review of the Shortened Edinburgh Reading Test by BETSY WATERMAN, Associate Professor, Counseling and Psychological Services Department, State University of New York at Oswego, Oswego, NY:

The Shortened Edinburgh Reading Test (SERT) was originally designed as a group-administered reading survey instrument for particular use with lower achievers between the ages of 10.0 and 11.6. The test authors suggest that the SERT may also be administered by a teacher (no particular psychological training is required for use of the test) in his or her classroom with results being used to identify the strengths and weaknesses of a child, select interventions and methods of instruction, and evaluate the success of instructional methods, particularly in reading.

The SERT is made up of items from each of the four stages of the Edinburgh Reading Test (T5:901). The shortened version (i.e., SERT) contains a total of 75 items that comprise four subtests—Vocabulary (23 items), Structure/Syntax (19 items), Reading Comprehension (25 items), and Retention of significant detail (8 items). The Vocabulary subtest is designed to test recognition of individual words in both isolation and context. The purpose of the Comprehension subtest is to measure both basic and inferential understanding of written text. The intent of the Structure subtest (called the Syntax subtest on the profile sheet) is to determine the ability of the child to sequence linguistic information (i.e., letters, words, phrases,

and clauses) including the use of syntactic and semantic clues. The Retention subtest is intended to measure the ability of the child to remember information he or she has read.

A single practice item is included at the beginning of some subtests but not in others. There are no instructions for the test administrator about how to proceed should an individual child within the group fail the practice item and it appears that the test simply proceeds whether a given child has been successful on the practice item or not.

Each individual child's test is hand scored against a key that is included in the manual. Scoring involves the awarding of 1 point for each correctly answered question. An easy-to-use table converts the total test raw score to a standard score with a mean of 100 and a standard deviation of 15. The conversion table is arranged in monthly intervals (i.e., 10.01, 10.02, etc.) and ranges from 10.01 to 11.06. Because of lack of sensitivity at the extremes, standard scores range from 70 to 140. Performance on subtests can be compared through the use of a "profile diagram" where each line on the diagram represents one Standard Error of Measure. Subtest scores that are 2 or more "steps" or Standard Error Units apart reflect strengths or weaknesses in specific subtest areas (i.e., Vocabulary, Structure, Comprehension, or Retention). The authors caution that the subtest scores are not intended for comparisons with other children and should be used only to compare a child with his or her own performance. A further caution is made related to scores on the Retention subtest. The extremely small sample of items (i.e., 8) requires that scores on this subtest must be 4 Standard Error Units higher or lower than other subtests before differences can be considered significant. Steps for interpreting class performance against the national mean and in terms of high and low achieving students within the same class are included in the manual.

A total of three standardization samples provided the basis for the development of the conversion tables. The first, a national sample, included a randomly selected group of 1,164 children born in the same week in England, Scotland, or Wales. The second and third groups represented a local sample made up of 1,234 and 836 students, respectively. Kuder-Richardson coefficients, based on data from the national sample, were reported at .95 for the whole test and ranged from .77 for the Retention subtest to .89 on the

Comprehension subtest. Subtest intercorrelations were generally quite high, ranging from .46 between Structure and Retention, to .75 between Vocabulary and Comprehension. No test-retest reliability studies were reported.

The standardization of subtests was also done on the national sample after removing all children who either answered all questions or no questions correctly on any of the subtests. A total of 812 children remained. In order to interpret the profile, "standard errors of the difference between scores were calculated, for each child, and averaged over the children involved" (manual, p. 22). No validation studies were reported in the manual.

The SERT is a group-administered reading achievement test that is a shortened version of the Edinburgh Reading Test (ERT). It is designed to measure four aspects of reading performance—Vocabulary, Structure, Comprehension, and Retention of material. The purpose of this test, according the SERT's authors, is to screen for possible problems in certain areas of reading achievement and to provide information to teachers that may help in designing instruction to students with specific reading difficulties.

Quite frankly, the strengths of this test appear few in number and the weaknesses, many. The SERT is generally easy to administer and easy to score. The inclusion of a test of memory seems good in concept but, unfortunately in this screening measure, is too limited in scope to give much reliable information. The "distracters" on the first vocabulary items appear well selected and may be sensitive to subtle types of reading errors (e.g., failure to read a whole word, use of shape of a word for decoding, or confusing words that are similar in sound). On the whole, however, the SERT is a screening measure for which utility is seriously limited. Some of the more mild problems associated with this instrument involve the assumption the authors of the manual make that users are familiar with the stages that are the basis for the "mother" instrument of the SERT (the ERT), the rather overstated purposes of the measure, the questionable suggestion of stopping some struggling children from continuing on a subtest while other children in the same class move ahead to other items, some sexist language evident in the manual, and occasional addition problems in the manual including an error in the scoring example.

More major concerns exist as they relate to the lack of validity and test-retest reliability studies conducted on this instrument. The small number of items and lack of adequate practice opportunities and feedback may well impact the reliability of scores from this instrument. This would appear to be particularly true for those students the measure intends to target—lower achievers. The results, then, could reflect difficulty with understanding what is wanted on a given set of questions rather than lack of reading ability, something that is clearly not an outcome that is desirable.

Several other issues related to this instrument also need to be raised. First, this instrument is not very sensitive at the lower end of the performance spectrum (i.e., the area of performance for the very group that is targeted). This is consistent with this reviewer's concern that many of the items on this instrument appeared too difficult for students with a significant reading disability. Results, then, would offer very little information that was specific enough to be helpful in designing interventions. Second, the extremely small number of items on the Retention subtest, a test that seems to be an important predictor of both reading and achievement ability in general, limits its usefulness here in very similar ways. Third is the question of generalizability of this instrument to other groups or geographic areas. No information was available related to the ethnic, racial, or ability level makeup of the samples. Some subtle language variations (particularly on Vocabulary items) may make the appropriateness of its use outside of England, Scotland, or Wales questionable. Fourth, the small age range for which this test was developed reduces the utility of this measure. A screening measure that is sensitive to reading problems earlier on in the development of this skill may be more useful to practitioners. It also seems very likely that some students in a given class would fall outside of the ages for which this test is designed, suggesting that not all students in a classroom could be included in the interpretation of classroom results. Finally, the intervention ideas suggested in the interpretation section of this test are too general to offer teachers or other educators much that would enhance the design of individualized programs.

SUMMARY. As a screening instrument for reading achievement, the SERT appears to offer little to educators. There are other methods and instruments that are more psychometrically sound, practical in their feedback, and more generalizable to different age, ability, ethnic, or racial groups. Curriculum-Based Measurement, for one, seems a better method for screening reading problems. It is quicker to administer and appears to offer more sensitive information about academic growth.

[355]
Silver Drawing Test of Cognition and Emotion [Third Edition Revised].

Purpose: Designed as a nonverbal measure of ability in three areas of cognition: sequential concepts, spatial concepts, and association and formation of concepts; and to screen for depression.

Population: Ages 5 and over.

Publication Dates: 1983–1998.

Acronym: SDT.

Scores, 5: Predictive Drawing, Drawing from Observation, Drawing from Imagination, Self-Image, Projection.

Administration: Individual or group.

Price Data, 1998: $10 per set of 10 test booklets, layout sheet, and scoring forms; $32 per manual ('96, 147 pages); $15 per manual entitled "Updating the Silver Drawing Test and Draw A Story Manuals" ('98, 32 pages).

Foreign Language Edition: Brazilian translation and standardization available.

Time: (12–15) minutes.

Comments: Revision of Silver Drawing Test of Cognitive Skills and Adjustment.

Author: Rawley Silver.

Publisher: Ablin Press Distributors.

Cross References: See T4:2462 (1 reference); for reviews of an earlier edition by Kevin D. Crehan and Annie W. Ward, see 11:362; for reviews of the original edition by Clinton I. Chase and David J. Mealor, see 10:333.

Review of the Silver Drawing Test of Cognition and Emotion [Third Edition Revised] by TERRY OVERTON, President, Learning and Behavioral Therapies, Inc., Farmville, VA:

DESCRIPTION AND PURPOSE. The Silver Drawing Test of Cognition and Emotion was designed to assess cognitive development and to screen for possible emotional problems in children and youth. The original concept of the test was to assess the cognitive and emotional problems in children with hearing impairments who were nonverbal. The test author states that hearing children use language concepts to label perceptions, organize experiences, and attempt to make sense of and control their worlds. The basic foundation of the theoretical base of this instrument is conceptualized in the writings of Piaget, Bruner, Arnheim, Torrance, and Sinclair-de-Zwart. The Silver Drawing Test focuses on assessing the child's spatial, conceptual, and sequential ability through structured and semistructured drawing tasks. The tasks include Predictive Drawing, Drawing from Observation, and Drawing from Imagination. Predictive Drawing measures sequential ability by asking the child to predict a sequence, to predict "horizontality," and to predict "verticality." This task presents stimuli for which the child is asked to draw what would happen under specific conditions, such as the liquid in a glass decreasing as it is consumed through a straw. Drawing from Observation is designed to measure concepts of space and spatial relationships between objects. Objects are placed within the environment in a standardized format and the child is required to draw the objects. Drawing from Imagination assesses the ability of the child to select content, combine content (visual stimuli), and represent ideas and feelings, or creativity. Drawing from Imagination is the task that the author states screens for emotional disturbance in children. This task presents visual stimuli: 15 pictures of people and objects, from which the child is asked to select 2 and is then asked to imagine something happening between the 2 pictures. The child is to then draw what they have imagined. Next, the child is requested to write a title or story for the drawing. Drawing from Imagination includes two sets of stimulus pictures, Form A and Form B.

ADMINISTRATION AND SCORING. According to the manual, the test can be administered without any prior training by a variety of professionals who work with children. The test is untimed but the author states administration usually takes from 12 to 15 minutes. The test may be administered in a group setting. Directions for arranging the stimuli are provided; however, the instructions for the examinee are not presented as standardized instructions but rather as a casual suggestion of what the examiner might say. The instructional format allows for the presentation of the test to nonhearing children and includes using pantomime or manual language as needed. Scoring takes 3 to 6 minutes according to the manual; however, the novice examiner would most likely be unable to complete the scoring within this time limit. The guidelines for scoring are provided as are examples of 1-to-5-point responses for Predictive Drawing. The predictive task is scored on predicting a sequence, predicting "horizontality," and predicting "verticality." Scoring criteria for Drawing by Observation are provided for horizontal or left-right relationships, vertical relationships, and front-back relationships or depth. The Drawing from Imagination subtest includes scoring for ability to select the content; ability to combine, or the form of the drawing; and the ability to represent, or creativity in form, content, title, or story. The Drawing from Imagination subtest scoring includes a projection scale for assessing the emotional content of responses on the dimensions of negative themes, moderately negative themes, neutral themes, moderately positive themes, and strongly positive themes. A self-image scale is also provided for the Drawing from Imagination subtest and includes criteria for scoring the drawing on morbid fantasy, ambiguous or ambivalent fantasy, pleasant fantasy, and wish-fulfilling fantasy.

TECHNICAL INFORMATION. The Silver Drawing Test provides no specific test construction information such as how the items were designed and selected on the basis of field trials or expert judges. The normative data are based on a sample of 624 children and adults. No substantial descriptive information is provided about the sample. The sample sizes by grade or age range from 16 tenth graders to 127 third graders. The adult group included 77 persons and there was no information provided in the table regarding the ages of the adults. The manual includes results from a variety of reliability and validity studies. Five interrater reliability studies were conducted. These studies compared scores from raters who were trained in the scoring methods and those from persons with no training. Various professions were represented across the studies. The largest number of tests scored in any of the interrater studies was 36. The interrater reliability coefficients ranged from .45 to .99 for the reliability of raters across tasks or subtests. One interrater reliability study is described that compared results from raters across the emotional content scale (n = .94) and the self-image scale (r = .74). This study compared results from five judges. Reliability studies include estimates of internal consistency reliability for the subtests and test-retest research. Two test-retest studies are included with sample

sizes of 12 students with learning disabilities and 10 third grade students (interval of approximately 1 month for both of the studies). These reliability coefficients ranged between .08 and .84.

The validity studies include research on discriminant validity of clinical samples, criterion-related validity studies, and evidence of construct validity through developmental changes. The conclusions from the validity studies are mixed and most of the research described involved studies using small sample sizes. The data are presented in an inconsistent format in the validity chapter. The manual includes a chapter of validity studies conducted from 1990–1995 ranging from gender comparison studies to studies on constructs such as aggression and attitude to comparison studies of scores from "deaf" and hearing children.

EVALUATION. The theoretical foundation of this instrument is intriguing and the author provides an interesting rationale. The author provides some evidence that this instrument may have the capability to measure the constructs that are purported to be measured. The test construction, standardization, and normative process lack a solid research base. The reliability and validity studies are based on very small samples and the author does not provide consistent information about the sample selection or the variables considered in selecting the samples (such as ages, socioeconomic status, geographic representation). The manual does not present the reliability and validity research studies in a consistent format and this results in extremely difficult interpretation for test consumers. The test instrument itself provides two sets of stimulus pictures for the Drawing from Imagination task; however, the author does not address the purpose of the two forms nor does the consumer know if these are equivalent forms. The scoring is fairly subjective and the examiner is not provided with diagnostic or interpretive information.

SUMMARY. In summary, the ideas proposed by the author are quite interesting and the concept of assessing nonverbal children, verbal children, and children in clinical populations in these areas is an excellent concept. This test may be able to assess the cognitive development of children on the dimensions proposed in the Predictive Drawing subtest in a manner not assessed by other instruments. The cognitive development areas assessed appear to have some validity as evidenced by the results of the validity studies included on developmental changes in samples. This aspect of the instrument deserves additional research. The test lacks the scientific rigor expected of an instrument designed to be used in the manner the author states.

Review of the Silver Drawing Test of Cognition and Emotion [Third Edition Revised] by JANET V. SMITH, Associate Professor of Psychology and Counseling, Pittsburg State University, Pittsburg, KS:

The Silver Drawing Test of Cognition and Emotion (SDT) is a revised version of the Silver Drawing Test of Cognitive and Creative Skills (1990), previously known in the original version as the Silver Drawing Test of Cognitive Skills and Adjustment (1983). Despite the name change, the third edition is essentially the same as the previous version of the test, with some improvements that attempt to address past criticisms of the test. According to the manual, the major changes from the earlier edition are: (a) addition of a second set of stimulus drawings; (b) addition of a new Self-Image scale; (c) two new chapters in the manual, one summarizing recent studies conducted on the SDT and one tying assessment to intervention techniques; (d) improvement of scoring guidelines; and (e) improvement of theoretical background and statistical analyses.

The SDT is designed for use with hearing- and/or language-impaired individuals, and is based on the premise that art can provide an effective medium for assessment of individuals with language deficiencies. The test can be used for examinees aged 5 years to adult, and provides measures of both cognitive and emotional functioning. The cognitive component is based on Piaget's concepts related to sequencing ability, space, and class inclusion. The emotional component is based on the assumptions of projective assessment. Previous versions of the test have been criticized for lack of adequate theory base. The third edition reports that the theoretical background has been expanded. However, certain aspects of the theoretical rationale for the test continue to be lacking and some references are rather dated.

There are three subtests to the SDT. Predictive Drawing involves asking subjects to draw predicted changes in appearance of objects and is designed to assess "ability to predict and represent horizontality, verticality, and sequential order" (manual, p. 10). Drawing from Observation involves presenting subjects with an array of simple objects and asking them to draw what they see. This subtest is designed to assess spatial relationships. Finally, Drawing from Imagination requires individuals to draw a picture of what they imagine happening between two subjects selected from a set of 15 stimulus drawings. This subtest is intended to assess functional grouping and relationships, as well as creativity. The Drawing from Imagination subtest is also the basis for the emotional component of the SDT, with the assumption that responses to this subtest will reveal attitudes toward self and others as well as facilitate early identification of depression. In addition, an individual's score for the new Self-Image scale is obtained from responses to this third subtest. Very little is said in the manual about the new scale but "it is theorized that the SDT Self-Image Scale can be useful in screening children and adults for depression or masked depression" (p. 20).

Administration of the test takes approximately 15 minutes, with an additional 3 to 6 minutes for scoring. Responses are scored on a 0- to 5-point scale. For the most part, scoring guidelines appear adequate, although it seems that there would still be room for subjectivity in scoring the emotional component of the test. Tables are provided to convert raw scores into T scores and percentile ranks. Normative data continue to be inadequate, with small, nonrepresentative samples. Data are pooled for males and females, which presents a problem given reported gender differences in subject responses. It is also troubling that the mean cognitive scores for some older age groups is lower than the mean for younger subjects, given the assumption that cognitive abilities should increase with age. No normative data are provided for the new Self-Image Scale.

Evidence for reliability of scores from the test is presented in the form of interscorer reliability as well as test-retest reliability. Although the manual for the third edition reports that "scoring guidelines have been tightened" (p. 1), there are no new data presented either in terms of interrater reliability or test-retest reliability. Previous criticisms of small, inadequate samples continue to be applicable. Reliability of scores from the SDT remains questionable.

Reviews of previous editions of the SDT also criticized the test for lack of adequate evidence of validity. The third edition of the SDT includes a new chapter entitled "1990–1996 Studies Showing Validity." The chapter reports findings from 11 different studies. However, 6 of the studies address gender and/or age differences in responses to the SDT, one study simply involves case examples, and another study involves comparing the stimulus drawings of the SDT with Silver's Draw a Story instrument in terms of likelihood to elicit negative responses. Unfortunately, the results of these studies contribute little to the establishment of validity of the scores from the SDT.

Of more importance in the new chapter are three studies that compare SDT scores of children with various disabilities to SDT scores of those without disabilities. However, these studies still fall short of establishing validity of scores from the test. It was predicted that scores from language- and/or hearing-impaired individuals should be equivalent to those from nonimpaired children in terms of spatial skills, but weaker in terms of verbal and sequencing skills. Overall, deaf children were found to have equivalent scores to nonimpaired children on most spatial tasks, except for lower scores on the Drawing from Observation subtest. No significant differences were found between the groups in terms of sequencing ability. In an expansion of this study, both of these groups of subjects scored higher on some spatial relationship tasks than did a group of learning-disabled students. In a third study, a small group of learning-disabled, dyslexic, and normal children in grades 3, 4, and 5 were administered both the California Achievement Test (CAT) and the SDT. The group of normal children had the highest mean scores on both the CAT and the SDT, followed by the learning-disabled group, with dyslexic students having the lowest mean scores on both instruments.

The last major change in the third edition of the SDT is a new chapter describing several art intervention techniques to remedy deficits identified by the SDT. The techniques appear to be potentially useful for art therapists in particular, but it is difficult to assess the effectiveness of these interventions as no evidence of validity is provided in the chapter, other than an illustrative case example.

SUMMARY. The underlying concept of using art to assess individuals with language difficulties is very appealing. The author appears to have responded to several criticisms of previous editions of the test. However, despite attempts to remedy serious deficits, psychometric properties of the test remain very weak. Overall, this reviewer concurs with reviews of previous editions of the SDT, concluding that this test should only be used for experimental purposes at this time, and cannot be recommended over other existing measures of cognitive and emotional abilities for hearing- and/or language-impaired individuals.

[356]
Singer-Loomis Type Deployment Inventory.

Purpose: Designed to assess "personality factors that may help an individual in self-understanding and in utilizing skills, talents, and abilities, so as to better deal with interactions between oneself and the environment."

Population: High school and college and adults.

Publication Dates: 1984–1997.

Acronym: SL-TDI.

Scores: Profile of 8 scores: Introverted, Extroverted for each of 4 functions (Thinking, Feeling, Sensing, Intuition), plus Extraversion, Introversion, Judging, Perceiving.

Administration: Group.

Price Data: Available from publisher.

Time: (30–40) minutes.

Comments: Self-report type profile based on Jung's typology; previous edition entitled Singer-Loomis Inventory of Personality.

Authors: June Singer, Mary Loomis, Elizabeth Kirkhart (revision), and Larry Kirkhart (revision).

Publisher: Moving Boundaries, Inc.

Cross References: For a review by Richard B. Stuart of the earlier edition, see 10:334 (1 reference).

Review of the Singer-Loomis Type Deployment Inventory by JONI R. HAYS, Senior Clinical Counselor and Adjunct Faculty School of Applied Health and Educational Psychology, Oklahoma State University, Stillwater, OK:

The Singer-Loomis Type Deployment Inventory (SL-TDI), the fourth revision of the Singer-Loomis Inventory of Personality (SLIP), is intended to measure empirically Carl Jung's constructs of personality and psychological type. Loyal to Jungian theory, the authors assert that the continuous response format of the SL-TDI embodies Jung's dynamic theory more accurately than the dichotomous response formats of other Jungian-influenced instruments (e.g., Myers-Briggs Type Indicator [251] and Gray-Wheelwright [1946] Jungian Type Survey).

To improve item content and structure, the authors incorporated comments and suggestions from Jungian colleagues. Beyond minor editorial revision, the SL-TDI uses 8 new scenarios combined with 12 scenarios from previous versions of the SLIP. Substantial changes in answer and scoring materials expand interpretive possibilities and usability of the SL-TDI. The 160-item SL-TDI is an untimed self-report measure of cognitive style in behavioral and environmental contexts. The instrument is not intended to assess aptitude, intelligence, or abnormality and is therefore indicated for use with psychologically healthy adults.

A preliminary statistical performance summary by SL-TDI collaborators, Kirkhart and Kirkhart (1999) reports greater statistical psychometric quality (evidence of reliability and validity) for the SL-TDI than for previous versions. A larger sample size and sharp increases in Cronbach's alpha on 14 of the 16 scale scores than the previous versions lend support to these preliminary conclusions. Likewise, data from preliminary factor analyses suggest higher construct validity for the eight Type Mode scales.

The SL-TDI asks respondents to indicate affinity for extraverted and introverted characteristics of thinking, feeling, sensing, and intuiting functions through judgment of their actual behavior in 20 situations (e.g., I am involved in a disagreement with a person I deeply respect. This person disapproves of what I want to do. I would …). Respondents use a 5-point Likert-type scale (i.e., Rarely, Occasionally, About Half, Usually, Almost Always) to rate their behavior on eight separate responses (e.g., worry about what might happen if I don't get my way) for each of the 20 scenarios.

The SL-TDI is available in self-scoring and prepaid computerized answer sheet formats. The self-scoring version includes a reusable test booklet and five-page answer sheet and scoring form for recording responses, scoring, and computing results. The answer document invites respondents to permit [by completing Part III: Bio Data (Optional)] the authors to incorporate their results into a research database. Part III queries respondent name (optional), age, sex, occupation, residence, marital status, ethnic background, and highest grade or degree, but omits reference to confidentiality, individual rights to informed consent, and database security. By including such a statement, the authors would enhance the ethos and integrity of their instrument. A four-page interpretive document, Understanding the Singer-Loomis Type Deployment Inventory™ (SL-TDI), offers a helpful description of Jungian theory, information about results, and strategies for growth.

Although the authors indicate use of the SL-TDI with high school, college, and other adult populations, some individuals may lack the cognitive or sensory capacity to read and understand the instrument and interpretive information. Likewise, unfamiliar jargon and complex terminology may hinder usability of the SL-TDI with some groups. Applicability to adult populations in general implies the need for thorough interpretation of results. The self-scoring process is somewhat laborious and complex. Although written directions are provided, the need for numerical calculation may increase the likelihood of respondent frustration and scoring errors. These challenges to SL-TDI usability parallel limitations evident in other measures of similar constructs (e.g., Myers-Briggs Type Indicator). The abstract nature of Jungian constructs may, however, preclude simplicity and universal accessibility. Concerns about respondent capacity for understanding are likely resolved by author classification of the instrument as a guarded, Level B instrument, which restricts use to trained professionals and qualified institutions.

The situational contexts of the SL-TDI personalize the testing experience and acknowledge diverse responses to real-life situations. The test booklet introduction and directions create a sense of freedom by dispelling notions of "right" and "wrong" answers. Beyond the meaning indicated by specific numerical quotients, the SL-TDI is a stimulus for self-awareness with application for enhancing decision making, communicating, leading, interacting, and living.

SUMMARY. The SL-TDI is an effective tool for facilitating growth, acknowledging strengths, and encouraging self-acceptance. The SL-TDI is superior to competing instruments in honoring unique and individual realities of respondents through use of a continuous response format and real-life scenarios. Human development, mental health, human resource, and other professionals may find the SL-TDI a useful tool for career development, relationship enhancement, psychotherapy, organizational effectiveness, and leadership development.

REVIEWER'S REFERENCES
Gray, H., & Wheelwright, J. B. (1946). Jung's psychological types; their frequency of occurence. *Journal of General psychology, 34*, 3–17.

Kirkhart, L., & Kirkhart, E. (1999). Statistical performance of the Singer-Loomis Type Deployment Inventory: An interim report. Gresham, OR: Moving Boundaries, Inc.

Review of the Singer-Loomis Type Deployment Inventory by KEVIN LANNING, Associate Professor of Psychology, Honors College of Florida Atlantic University, Jupiter, FL:

The Singer-Loomis Type Deployment Inventory (SL-TDI) is a revision of the Singer-Loomis Inventory of Personality (SLIP). Both the older SLIP and the current SL-TDI include a series of situations or scenarios. For the SL-TDI, the number of these situations has been increased from 15 to 20. For each of these situations, respondents are asked to rate eight items using a 5-point Likert scale. These items, when summed over the 20 situations, provide continuous scores on eight *type modes*. These type modes (e.g., Extraverted Thinking) are fusions of the two Jungian attitudes (Extraversion and Introversion) with the four type functions (Thinking, Feeling, Sensing, and Intuiting). The 20-item primary measures of type mode are combined to form 40-item composite measures of Thinking (i.e., Extraverted Thinking + Introverted Thinking), Feeling, Sensing, and Intuiting, as well as 80-item measures of Introversion, Extraversion, Judging, and Perceiving.

Documentation for the SL-TDI includes the Technical Manual for the Singer-Loomis Type Deployment Inventory, the Interpretive Guide for the Singer-Loomis Type Deployment Inventory, and Statistical Performance of the Singer-Loomis Type Deployment Inventory: An Interim Report. In addition, a Study Guide is available for those who participate in a qualifying program for potential SL-TDI users. Though the cover and title of the Technical Manual ostensibly describe the SL-TDI, this document appears to be a simple rebinding of the manual for the older SLIP.

CHANGES FROM THE PRIOR EDITION. For the SL-TDI, 8 of the 20 situations are new, and a number of the items were modified. The aim of these changes was to make the SL-TDI both more accessible and more valid for a broader range of socioeconomic levels. The Interim Report provides internal consistency estimates for the new scales of Version 4. For the 20-item primary scales, these range from .59 to .76. In most cases, these values are slightly higher than the corresponding figures reported for an earlier 20-item version of the SLIP. For two of the primary scales, Introverted Intuiting

and Extraverted Feeling, the increase in internal consistency was more substantial, with changes of .16 (to .73) and .14 (to .76), respectively. Additional evidence concerning the reliability of the SL-TDI comes from a forthcoming study that reports 2-week test-retest correlations averaging .72 for the primary scales and .77 for the composite measures (Arnau & Rosen, 2000). Unfortunately, there is no available evidence concerning the degree of correspondence between the new measures of the SL-TDI and the older measures of the SLIP.

VALIDITY. In an early study of the SLIP, response profiles of artists and psychotherapists were found to differ. Further, the nature of productions by artists was found to be meaningfully related to scores on the SLIP. Although there have been no studies of relations between the newer SL-TDI and nontest criteria, several studies have examined relations between the Singer-Loomis measures and other self-report measures of Jungian personality constructs. In the most recent of these, Arnau, Thompson, and Rosen (1999) found that bivariate correlations between the SL-TDI and like measures on the Personal Preferences Self Description Questionnaire (PPSDQ) were generally low. These results echo findings with the previous version of the Singer-Loomis measure. Karesh, Pieper, and Holland (1994) and MacDonald and Holland (1993) reported that the scales of the SLIP are only weakly related to corresponding scales of the Myers-Briggs Type Indicator (MBTI), and, further, that when 4-point "types" are constructed based on the SLIP, these do not correspond with MBTI typing at above-chance levels.

The lack of convergence between the SL-TDI/SLIP and these other measures, although troubling, is not in itself a fatal flaw, for although all are measures of Jungian constructs, the tests are based upon different assumptions. The most important of these is the "bipolarity assumption": On the MBTI and the PPSDQ, constructs such as Extraversion and Introversion form two poles of a common dimension, whereas on the SLIP and the SL-TDI they are measured as separate constructs. Although neither the SLIP Technical manual nor the SL-TDI Interim Report include correlation matrices describing relations among scales on the instruments, the studies cited above do present evidence relevant to bipolarity. Karesh et al. (1994) reported that partial correlations between opposing attitudes and functions on the SLIP ranged from

-.54 to -.75. Although these values are high, they do not approach unity. In two other studies, the Introversion measures of the SLIP (MacDonald & Holland, 1993) and the SL-TDI (Arnau et al., 1999) were found to be significantly correlated with measures of Neuroticism on the NEO-PI and NEO-FFI, respectively, whereas the Extraversion scales of the SLIP and SL-TDI were related to the NEO measures of Extraversion. Taken together, these studies suggest that the bipolarity assumption may be deserving of further empirical study and, in particular, that SL-TDI Introversion may be more closely associated with Neuroticism than with the negative pole of Extraversion.

SUMMARY. The internal consistency evidence suggests that the SL-TDI measures something, and the correlational evidence suggests that this is something different from that which is measured by the Myers-Briggs Type Indicator (251) and other Jungian personality inventories. Beyond this, there is little that is definitive that can be said about the SL-TDI. Without evidence of correspondence between the SL-TDI and the SLIP, the interscale correlation matrix, and some evidence of external validity, it is not clear what the SL-TDI does measure.

As many users are drawn towards Jungian constructs, it is likely that some will be drawn to measures other than the MBTI. As a consequence, the SL-TDI is likely to be widely used. But such use should be judicious. The SLIP was presented as an experimental measure, and the Technical manual includes the caveat that "there is not sufficient statistical evidence to make clinical or counseling judgments of individuals based on the SLIP classifications" (p. 2). This remains the case for the SL-TDI today.

REVIEWER'S REFERENCES

MacDonald, D. A., & Holland, C. J. (1993). Psychometric evaluation of the Singer-Loomis Inventory of Personality. *Journal of Analytical Psychology 38*, 303–320.
Karesh, D. M., Pieper, W., & Holland, C. L. (1994). Comparing the MBTI, the Jungian Type Survey, and the Singer-Loomis Inventory of Personality. *Journal of Psychological Type, 30*, 30–38.
Arnau, R. C., Thompson, B., & Rosen, D. H. (1999). Alternative measures of Jungian personality constructs. *Measurement and Evaluation in Counseling and Development, 32*, 90–104.
Arnau, R. C., & Rosen, D. H. (in press). Reliability and validity of scores from the Singer-Loomis Type Deployment Inventory. *Journal of Analytical Psychology.*

[357]

SIPOAS: Styles in Perception of Affect Scale.

Purpose: "Measures the preferred style in the awareness of, and response to, the minute changes in bodily feelings that lead to emotions and responses."

Population: Age 18 to adult.
Publication Date: 1995.
Acronym: SIPOAS.
Scores: 3 styles: BB (Based on Body), EE (Emphasis on Evaluation), LL (Looking to Logic).
Administration: Individual or group.
Price Data, 1996: $20 per 25 copies of questionnaire; $22.50 per complete research report (203 pages).
Time: [20–30] minutes.
Author: Michael Bernet.
Publisher: Institute for Somat Awareness.

Review of the SIPOAS: Styles in Perception of Affect Scale by BRIAN F. BOLTON, University Professor, Department of Rehabilitation Education and Research, University of Arkansas, Fayetteville, AR:

The Styles in Perception of Affect Scale (SIPOAS) is a self-report inventory designed to measure the construct known in the humanistic psychology literature as "Being in touch with one's feelings." Specifically, the SIPOAS purports to quantify three styles of perceiving one's emotions. Based on Body (BB) refers to integrated awareness of bodily feelings, Emphasis on Evaluation (EE) involves interpretation of feelings through introspection, and Looking to Logic (LL) assesses the use of reasoning to understand feelings.

Consistent with the author's theoretical and professional orientation, and supported by some research on the SIPOAS, a higher score on the BB scale is considered to be indicative of better mental health. The BB scale indicates whether respondents are sufficiently in touch with their feelings. Conversely, higher scores on the EE and LL scales reveal how the awareness of feelings is blocked. Participation in body and spiritual approaches to therapy is hypothesized to enhance the client's ability to attend to bodily feelings.

The author states that the SIPOAS is suitable for use in clinical, counseling, and human resource settings. Specific diagnostic applications suggested in psychology and medicine include depression, eating disorders, substance abuse, posttraumatic stress disorder, and career and family counseling. The author also offers training programs and workshops in the use of the SIPOAS.

The SIPOAS consists of 31 items that require respondents to choose among three alternatives. All 31 items are phrased in the first person, such as "When I feel frightened," followed by three alternatives, each representing one of the perceptual styles. An innovative forced-choice format gives respondents three options: Select one alternative and reject the other two (3, 0, 0); order the three alternatives from most to least preferable (2, 1, 0); or rate the three alternatives as equally preferable (1, 1, 1). This is accomplished by allocating 3 points to the alternatives in the patterns listed above.

Total scores are calculated for the three perceptual styles by summing the choice scores (3, 2, 1, 0) for the 31 alternatives that represent each style. The scoring process is facilitated by use of a tally sheet that incorporates the scoring key. The result is that respondents receive three raw scores that indicate *relative* preferences for the three perceptual styles. It is important to emphasize that the forced-choice response format guarantees that higher scores on one or two styles will necessarily be accompanied by lower scores on the other style(s).

There are no norms for the SIPOAS. The reason for this omission is that the instrument has not been administered to any broadly representative sample of respondents. Instead, members of a variety of organizations and populations were recruited for research purposes. For example, the three largest segments of the research sample were volunteers from the Association for Humanistic Psychology, the National Association of School Psychologists, and North American Mensa (the high IQ society). The majority of the approximately 1,000 research participants were college-educated professionals. Another indication of the nonrepresentativeness of the research sample is that one-half reported personal experience in some form of psychotherapy.

The SIPOAS is a revision of an earlier instrument called the Perception of Affect (POA) Profile. Development of the POA Profile began with 22 items taken from existing self-consciousness and self-awareness inventories and an equal number of items generated by graduate students. Several cycles of item analyses resulted in a 39-item version of the POA Profile that measured three perceptual styles named Propriocentric, Xenocentric/Vigilant, and Repressor. An interim version of the SIPOAS was created through further item revision and reconceptualization of the three styles. Continued refinement of the items produced the current version of the SIPOAS.

This sequence of progressive item revision and refinement, guided by the author's theoretical orientation and based on statistical analyses of the items, generated three homogenous scales that measure the SIPOAS perceptual styles. The average corrected item-scale correlations are: Based on Body (.45), Emphasis on Evaluation (.39), and Looking to Logic (.42). The internal consistency reliability coefficients for the three scales are .86, .81, and .84, respectively. Finally, the interscale correlations (-.51, -.62, and -.34) are artifacts of the forced-choice response format and do not provide any evidence about the "distinctiveness" of the three styles.

To clarify the trait validity of the three perceptual styles, the author conducted a comprehensive investigation of the relationship between the SIPOAS and selected scales from the NEO Personality Inventory and the Sixteen Personality Factor Questionnaire, the Toronto Alexithymia Scale, and several scales devised to measure body awareness, personal values, and experience in various forms of therapy. The correlational patterns generated detailed descriptions of the three styles. For example, individuals who score higher on Based on Body tend to be adaptable, mature, trusting, self-assured, and insightful. In contrast, high scorers on Emphasis on Evaluation are more likely to be apprehensive, angry, guilty, self-doubting, and suspicious. And respondents who score higher on Looking to Logic are typically impersonal, nondisclosing, unemotional, intellectually focused, and self-reliant. Correlations with gender, age, and affiliation were consistent with these characterizations.

There is no manual for the SIPOAS. The author's dissertation is offered as a substitute for a test manual. Because the 200-page dissertation contains much irrelevant, redundant, and speculative material, it is a major task for the reader to locate the necessary data about the SIPOAS. The test author is always responsible for providing essential information for the user of the instrument in a standard manual.

SUMMARY. The SIPOAS purports to measure three styles of perceiving emotions that have a variety of diagnostic applications in psychology and medicine. The self-report inventory is the product of a series of developmental analyses guided by a theoretical framework with origins in the human potential movement. The research evidence is generally supportive of the validity of the three perceptual styles. However, the SIPOAS should not be used for client assessment at this time because of the absence of appropriate norms and the lack of a published manual. When these deficiencies are addressed, the SIPOAS may be useful to practitioners who share the author's professional therapeutic orientation.

Review of the SIPOAS: Styles in Perception of Affect Scale by S. ALVIN LEUNG, Associate Professor, Department of Educational Psychology, The Chinese University of Hong Kong, Shatin, N. T., Hong Kong:

The Styles in Perception of Affect Scale (SIPOAS) was designed to measure the degree that a person is in touch with his/her feelings and emotions. The SIPOAS was developed and researched by the author through a doctoral dissertation project (Bernet, 1995). Currently, no test manual is available. The unpublished dissertation presents technical information about the construction of the instrument. A two-page brief description of the instrument and the meaning of the scores is also available for test users.

According to Bernet (1995), the SIPOAS is based on an earlier instrument called the "Perception of Affect" Profile developed by the same author. The SIPOAS has 31 items. For each item stem (e.g., "When I come up against a difficulty I find a solution by") there are three options from which to choose, and a test taker is given 3 points to allocate to the options, depending on the degree that each option describes the preference of the test taker. In other words, the test taker could give either 0, 1, 2, or 3 points to each of the three options as long as the cumulative total equals 3. This method of responding to the SIPOAS is somewhat complex and unusual, and test takers have to read the instructions very carefully to understand what is required. A "tally sheet" is available for test users to compute a total score for each of the three scales: Based on Body (BB), Looking to/for Logic (LL), and Emphasis on Evaluation (EE). According to the author, these scales represent three different personality styles related to "being in touch with one's feelings" (p. 49).

According to the two-page test description, persons with high BB scores (45 to 60) are in touch with their own emotions. They are emotionally healthy, insightful, and free of excessive worries and guilt. They are likely to have healthy personalities and good interpersonal relationships. A score of 25 or below in the BB scale is considered low and education in emotional awareness through therapy is recommended. Individuals with high EE scores (35 or higher) are out of touch with their own feelings and emotions. They are tense, easily discouraged, and overly sensitive to the opinions of others. Consequently their social and interpersonal skills are impaired. The author also suggested that high EE scores are associated with a lack of confidence in daily decision making. Individuals with high LL scores (40 or above) are logical, impersonal, and distant, and they rely on intellectualization and rationalization. They have little regard for emotions, and consequently they do not have adequate awareness of their emotional life. The author suggested that the BB scale should be used as an indicator of "being in touch with one's feelings" (p. 3), and the EE and LL scales indicate whether the blockage to awareness is due to an overreliance on logic, or having low confidence in one's inner processes.

Data on the SIPOAS (*N* = 997) were collected from participants through 10 different sources, including members of professional organizations (e.g., International Primal Society, National Association of School Psychologists) and a number of special settings (e.g., on display in practitioner's waiting room, computer bulletin board, and multicultural middle-class neighborhood). It was not clear how many copies of the instruments were sent out or the response rate. The sampling process was not systematic and the resultant normative sample was not representative of the general population. Several established instruments, including the NEO PI-R, Cattell's 16-PF (Fifth Edition), and the Toronto Alexithymia Scale, were administered to some of the participants in order to generate information related to the criterion validity of the SIPOAS. A number of so called "ad hoc measures," including a "Body-awareness scale," an "Emphasis on Intellect" scale, a "Personal Values and Attributes scale," and a "Practitioner's Checklist" were also administered to all or some of the participants. However, it was not clear which sample source completed these additional instruments.

Information on the reliability and validity for scores from the SIPOAS was summarized by the author (Bernet, 1995). The author suggested that the internal consistency of the scales was "well within accepted guidelines" (p. 68), but the alpha coefficients were not reported. The author instead reported split-half reliability coefficients for the BB, EE, and LL scales, which were .86, .81, and

.84, respectively. It is not clear how the items were divided into halves to perform this analysis. Test-retest reliability coefficients for the scales were not available. In terms of validity, the author claimed that the correlation between the SIPOAS and the other criterion measures (e.g., 16-PF) supported the validity of scores from the instrument. The results of the correlation analyses were used to generate interpretative ideas for the three SIPOAS scales. Similarly, the relationship between the SIPOAS scales and some of the criterion measures suggested that "being in touch with one's feelings" was related to mental health, therapy preference, and experience. In addition, factor analyses were computed on the scales. The results were only briefly reported, and it was not clear how the results were used to aid in the construction of scales and in the interpretation of scores.

The SIPOAS suffers from a number of limitations. First, the intercorrelations among the three scales are high. The correlation coefficients between the BB scale and the EE and LL scales were -.52 and -.62, indicating substantial overlapping between the scales. Such findings pose a challenge to the claim that these scales represent divergent personality styles. Second, with only limited normative information, it is risky to make decisions about what constitutes high and low scores. The cutoffs suggested by the author appeared to be quite arbitrary and were not based on sufficient research data. Third, the author developed a number of "ad hoc" scales and inventories (e.g., the Practitioner's Checklist) to serve as criterion variables for the SIPOAS. However, the validity of these scales and checklist have not been demonstrated. Finally, the author made a number of claims regarding the use of the SIPOAS in psychodiagnosis, different forms of psychotherapy, and medicine (Bernet, 1995, pp. 120–125). These claims, however, have not been substantiated through research.

SUMMARY. The SIPOAS appears to be an instrument that is at the beginning stage of development. Efforts should concentrate on refining the inventory and on accumulating research data to substantiate reliability and validity of the scores. At present, there are not enough research data on the reliability and validity to justify using the results in any psychotherapeutic or clinical settings. It is premature at this point to market and sell the instrument to professional and nonprofessional users, which the author is apparently doing.

The author promised in his two-page SIPOAS description that related books and materials are forthcoming, and that in-house training programs and seminars are available to train users on the use of this instrument and on heightening emotional awareness. The author should only consider marketing the instrument for professional use when sufficient data on reliability and validity are available, and when a comprehensive manual about the instrument is ready for test users to use as reference.

REVIEWER'S REFERENCE

Bernet, M. (1995). *Styles in the perception of affect and its relation to mental health.* Unpublished doctoral dissertation, The City University of New York.

[358]
SkillScan for Management Development.

Purpose: "A 360-degree diagnostic feedback tool that helps field managers understand how they can be more effective managers, and helps organizations understand the strengths and weaknesses of their managers."

Population: Sales managers.

Publication Date: 1994.

Scores: 8 Tasks: Staffing (Recruiting and Selecting), Training, Field Office Development, Administration, Performance Management (Supervision), Business Management, Sales Assistance, Management Development; 12 Behaviors: Communicating, Counseling, Planning, Delegating, Coordinating, Team Building, Supporting, Rewarding, Motivating, Networking, Monitoring, Problem Solving and Decision Making; 5 Personal Attributes: Ethics and Professionalism, Stress Tolerance, Achievement Motivation, Self Improvement, Other Orientation.

Administration: Individual or group.

Forms, 2: Form O (Assessment by Others) and Form S (Self-Assessment by the Manager).

Price Data, 1996: $110 per SkillScan kit including 1 Form S and 7 Form O questionnaires, instructions, and 8 postage-paid envelopes addressed to LIMRA; $3 per additional Form O questionnaire and envelope; $10 per manual (no publication date, 25 pages).

Time: Administration time not reported.

Comments: Replacement for the Management Development Profile (T4:1507); Manager development workshops available.

Authors: LIMRA International.

Publisher: LIMRA International.

Cross References: For a review by Richard M. Wolf of the Management Development Profile, see 12:225.

Review of the SkillScan for Management Development by KURT F. GEISINGER, Professor of Psychology and Academic Vice President, Le Moyne College, Syracuse, NY:

SkillScan for Management Development is an instrument developed and published by LIMRA International (Life Insurance Marketing and Research Association), a management research organization that works with the life insurance industry. This instrument replaces its predecessor, the Management Development Profile, an instrument that was also published by LIMRA International. This instrument suffers from many of the same problems identified in a previous review by Wolf (1995).

SkillScan is described in two documents produced by LIMRA International. One is entitled "Administrative Manual." This document contains much of the information that one would normally expect in a technical manual; it also provides considerable information about the use of SkillScan. The second is entitled "SkillScan for Management Development: Development Guide." This document is primarily a nontechnical user's guide; it does not include psychometric information per se. Both are reasonably clear and appropriate for their intentions.

The purposes of SkillScan are certain and well defined. The instrument is to be used for training purposes for first- or second-level managers within the life insurance industry or perhaps insurance more broadly defined. As will be described below based upon the nature of the research conducted in its development, the instrument should probably not be used outside of the insurance industry. The nature of the managerial training in which the use of the instrument is proposed is also carefully defined.

SkillScan is intended for management development and it is portrayed as a diagnostic tool for management to be used either by a manager seeking self-improvement or a manager working with a supervisor toward the same goal. The instrument is essentially an eight-page, machine-scorable questionnaire that is composed of three parts. The questions and responses both appear on the instrument. The first section of the instrument is perhaps the most important portion. This section of the inventory is entitled Management Tasks and Behaviors. It is composed of 104 survey-type statements to which respondents make ratings on a 1–7 scale. Each of these items is a behavior that is likely to be performed to an extent by lower- and mid-level managers within the insurance industry. An example of a behavior is "Demonstrate sales methods and procedures to new sales representatives." Each of these tasks or behaviors has been assigned to one of 25 dimensions as well. To each behavioral statement, respondents provide a 1–7 rating indicating the extent to which they engage in that behavior. Three anchors along the scale are provided, for 1, 4, and 7. One means "Never/Not at All"; three means "Some Extent/Average"; and seven means "Great Extent/Almost Always." The second part of the inventory carries the title: Importance Ratings. This section comes immediately after the first part. It provides a listing of 25 broader tasks and behaviors (examples of which would be Training or Motivating). Each task or behavior is defined in a brief sentence on the form itself. Respondents again make 1–7 ratings to ascribe the importance that they perceive for that area in their job. The descriptive words for the 1, 4, and 7 rating anchors are "Not Relevant," "Moderately Relevant," and "Absolutely Essential," respectively. The third section appears on the back page of the instrument booklet and asks eight questions about the nature of the assignment held by the responding manager (e.g., whether they work in the main office or a field office and how many people are supervised by the manager). The one optional question asks the respondent's gender.

The instrument is always completed by the manager him- or herself. Under normal circumstances, those who are directly supervised by the manager also complete the instrument. Subordinates assign ratings based on their perceptions of the manager's behavior. The manager's supervisor also will often complete the instrument based on his or her observations of the manager.

The publisher of the instrument scores the instrument and provides feedback sheets directly to the manager. Responding managers receive feedback from their responses; because the nature of the instrument is for diagnostic and developmental purposes, such feedback is essential. Feedback is provided primarily via two types of comparisons. The 104 management tasks and behaviors are grouped (via factor analysis as mentioned below) into the 25 dimensions found in the importance ratings section of the instrument. A manager may compare his or her ratings to norms that have been collected by the instrument's publisher. Because all of the 25 job dimensions are positive behaviors, it is better to be at or above the norms. The manager may also compare self-ratings to those assigned by the supervisor or the subordinates. Discrepancies between self-ratings and those provided by the supervisor or the subordinates are worthy of consideration from a developmental perspective. The feedback sheets provided by the instrument publisher are quite usefully done. For each of the 25 dimensions, the ratings of the manager, the supervisor, and the subordinates are placed in close proximity, one above the other. The ratings are given additional meaningfulness because the middle 50% of responses (from the norms for managers, supervisors, and subordinates) are banded. Thus, it is easy to identify visually whether the values are in the bottom 25%, the middle 50%, or the top 25%. In addition, actual raw score values of the ratings are provided along with the appropriate normative percentile. Hence, either graphic or numerical interpretation is possible. The Development guide provides excellent examples and case studies to provide practice in making interpretations, although more examples would be useful.

Materials provided by LIMRA International appear to make self-improvements a very direct process. Managers are encouraged to evaluate their own performance and to identify visible strengths, unacknowledged strengths (those that others believe that the manager has but about which the manager was not aware), visible weaknesses, and unacknowledged weaknesses. From the above, a manager can create an individual development profile. Excellent descriptive information is provided for each of the 25 dimensions. In the case of each dimension, instructional materials (such as books or videotapes) that a manager can use to attempt to improve his or her performance is provided. This last feature is rare and unusually valuable. Blank forms for engaging in these developmental behaviors are provided in the Development Manual.

Only one form of SkillScan is available. The lack of alternative forms is not a problem.

ANALYTIC INFORMATION. The development of this measure followed the construction of the Management Development Profile, which was based on a job analysis that is described only briefly in the manual. In that version, 101 management tasks, behaviors, and attributes were listed composing 18 factors. A second job analysis was performed in 1990 as part of the SkillScan development. Included in this job analysis were 1,757 managers from 22 companies. SkillScan was based upon a smaller analysis using 268 managers from 20 companies. These 268 managers were assessed as were over 1,650 supervisors and subordinates. This group of managers is reasonably well defined. They were first- (61%) and second-level (39%) managers with a median of approximately 10 years in management. All of the subordinates and supervisors worked with the manager for at least 6 months and the median respondent had worked with the manager for about 3 years.

The responses from the above group were subjected to factor analysis, although very little information regarding this analysis is provided. It is stated in the manual that because of the previous work, they intended to confirm their earlier findings. Wolf (1995) raised serious questions about the factor-analytic procedures employed with their previous instrument. They performed a procrustean rotation to their factor analysis to fit the proposed solution. Although such procedures are acceptable in some circumstances, it is surprising that they did not perform a more appropriate confirmatory factor analysis. They do report finding the 25 factors that were expected.

Two kinds of information are provided to assess the reliability of the instrument. First, internal consistency (presumably coefficient alpha, although no formula/approach is identified) results are provided. The results provided are quite acceptable, especially for dimensions with so few items (on average four items per dimension). The values range from .82 to .95, with a median value of .93.

The second form of traditional reliability information is interrater reliability information. Intraclass correlation coefficients are provided for each of the 25 dimensions; these coefficients provide the consistency of responses for each manager across the self, supervisor, and subordinate ratings. These values are much more modest than the internal consistency reliability coefficients noted above and range from .05 to .60. The coefficients for two of the dimensions, Supporting (.05) and Team Building (.26), are quite low but most of the others are perhaps moderate; the median coefficient is .44. The Administrative Manual describes the low to moderate level of these coefficients relative to the internal consistency coefficients as due to the different perspectives that supervisors, managers, and their subordinates have, and indeed, that many subordinates have due to their varying vantage points.

The above interrater reliability results border on concurrent validation information per se. Evaluations across 104 tasks and behaviors by managers, supervisors, and subordinates approximate a multimethod, multitrait matrix. Providing the information they have in such a matrix format would be most helpful. They do not, for example, provide the interrater agreement for the subordinates alone. They do not provide the specific levels of agreement between managers and their supervisors and between managers and their subordinates, the results of which are likely to be illuminating.

The Administrative Manual does not address validation per se. Essentially, it might be argued that they have provided some direct content validation evidence because they did perform a job analysis of the position of manager and items that remain on SkillScan and are clearly representative behaviors for the domain in question. The analyses performed and the results provided, however, do not permit a reader to assess the degree to which the entire domain has been completely and representatively sampled. Hence, no assessment of its content validity is possible.

It also would be difficult to argue that the measure is construct valid. The tasks and behaviors are not worded so as to be constructs as traditionally defined and few of the analyses appear to be oriented to demonstration of construct validation. It would have been useful if an appendix of the factor-analytic results could have been shared. It would be useful from an interpretative perspective to know the extent to which various tasks and behaviors loaded on the dimensions. Similarly, correlations among the 25 dimensions and, perhaps, even the 104 tasks and behaviors would be interesting.

Much of the usefulness of this measure relates to its use of norms. The entire norms sample, although reasonably well defined, is quite small. It appears, but is not stated directly in either manual, that the sample consists of over 250 managers and their supervisors and over 1,300 subordinates. In that these are the same numbers as were used in the factor-analytic research in the development of the measure, it is assumed that these two groups are in reality the same group, which is certainly fine. However, these sample sizes, especially those for the manager and supervisor groups, are too small, even for a measure with a use as specialized as for this instrument. The 1,300 sample for the subordinates is probably acceptable. One possible redeeming factor is that all of these individuals are appropriatly in the insurance industry. However, the lack of diversity necessitates the limitation of the instrument for use in this industry.

AN EVALUATION OF THIS INSTRUMENT. On its face, SkillScan appears to be a fine example of a management development inventory, especially as one that is intended for a distinct industry. It is somewhat unusual in that it has not been built primarily to represent a specific model of management. Its use would appear appropriate generally and has been very carefully described in the manual. The use of this instrument has been articulately described literally but the manual does not provide any research supporting its actual use. That is, no evidence documents that the instrument actually is able to meet effectively the needs for which it was developed. The job analysis and intraclass correlation research efforts appear mostly impressive, but an evaluation of its usefulness as a training aid also would be valuable. Frankly, it is difficult to be overly positive about any instrument for which there is so little validation research.

Perhaps the most impressive feature of this manual is the manner in which good and ethical testing practices are embedded in its administration and interpretation procedures. A few examples follow. It is stated that the measure should not be used to evaluate employees in any way. Specifically, that it should not be used in making promotion, bonus, or termination decisions is also explicitly stated. Excellent procedures are provided in terms of how the administration of the measure should be introduced; even sample letters are provided. Clear statements regarding who will have access to the results of the assessment are made early in the process. Confidentiality of the results is eased by the scoring of the instruments for all participants in the process at LIMRA's offices. (Individual postage-paid, addressed envelopes are provided to each respondent for this purpose.) Exemplary procedures are provide for identifying which subordinates should rate their supervisor and the principle is presented that a supervisor should not rate his or her subordinate manager if the supervisor is involved in helping the manager to plan for the manager's continuing development. At least three subordinates must respond on SkillScan before subordinate results are provided to the manager; otherwise, employee confidentiality would be lost.

In that subordinates may complete SkillScan wherever they choose causes the concern that individuals may work together in so doing. This procedural failing would make interrater reliability higher, but lose some of the independence of the process.

SUMMARY. SkillScan appears to have great potential. Its use in the insurance industry is likely. Its ongoing evaluation and validation is urgently needed.

REVIEWER'S REFERENCE

Wolf, R. (1995). [Review of the Management Development Profile.] In J. C. Conoley & J. C. Impara (Eds.), *The twelfth mental measurements yearbook* (p. 585). Lincoln, NE: Buros Institute of Mental Measurements.

Review of the SkillScan for Management Development by PATRICIA H. WHEELER, President and Principal Researcher, EREAPA Associates, Livermore, CA:

SkillScan for Management Development is described as "a diagnostic tool that helps field managers understand how they can be more effective managers, and helps organizations understand the strengths and weaknesses of their managers" (administrative manual, p. 1). It is composed of two tools, the "Self-Assessment by the Manager" and the "Assessment by Others." Comparing the results of the two tools, managers and organizations "can identify discrepancies between how they feel they're doing and how others see their performance" (p. 1). Both tools are in eight-page scannable booklets.

The "Self-Assessment by the Manager" consists of three parts. The first part has 104 statements of management tasks and behaviors for which the respondent marks to what extent the statement reflects his or her behavior. The second part has the 25 dimensions of tasks, behaviors, and attributes, and asks the respondent to rate how important that task or behavior is overall in successful job performance. The third part asks eight questions on background information and job context.

The "Assessment by Others" is to be completed by three to six employees and the manager's supervisor to help their "manager in his or her growth and development" (administrative manual, p. 1). Directions indicate that "The responses of individual subordinates will remain strictly confidential and will not be individually identified under any circumstances" (p. 1). Employees are provided with an envelope in which to mail the completed questionnaire directly to the publisher for scoring. No where does it ask for the employee's name. The questionnaire has two parts, corresponding to the first two parts of the "Self-Assessment by Manager," but instead of responding for one's self, the respondent answers on the basis of the extent to which the manager behaves in certain ways or considers various tasks as important or not.

On each of the two tools, respondents rate each item on a 7-point Likert-type scale. The 104 responses from the first part of each assessment tool are sorted into 25 dimensions. The second part of each tool has one item for each dimension. The eight Tasks are: Staffing (Recruiting and Selecting), Training, Performance Management, Business Management, Field Office Development, Administration, Sales Assistance, and Management Development. The 12 Behaviors are: Communicating, Counseling, Supporting, Delegating, Motivating, Rewarding, Team Building, Networking, Coordinating, Monitoring, Planning, and Problem Solving and Decision Making. The five Attributes are: Ethics and Professionalism, Stress Tolerance, Achievement Motivation, Self-Improvement, and Other Orientation.

The initial development of the instrument was done by a management committee of the publisher. The items then went through three rounds of pilot/field testing and factor analyses to arrive at the final set of items and the 25 dimensions. As a final step to gather technical and normative data, the tools were administered to 268 managers in insurance companies and to 262 supervisors and 1,391 subordinates of these managers. Based on this sample, the publisher confirmed the earlier factor analysis results, computed alpha reliabilities for each dimension, and calculated interrater reliabilities between managers and others. The dimension reliability estimates are all reported to be .82 or higher, whereas the interrater reliabilities, except for one that is very low (.05), fall in the range of .26 to .60.

The sample was also used to derive normative data. The Personal Feedback Report prepared for each manager provides the percentile rank for each dimension and shows, in graphic format, the range within which half of the 268 managers in the sample fell. There is no discussion of the appropriateness of generalizing from a sample of insurance company managers to sales managers in other businesses and industries. Also, it is easy to infer that what the normative sample does is what managers should be doing, which may not be a reasonable inference to make, either within the insurance industry or for other industries.

The Personal Feedback Report also provides a narrative summary of how the manager's self-ratings compared to those of the supervisor and the subordinates. Managers are provided with a Development Guide that contains a series of steps and guidelines for their use in preparing an Individual Development Plan. It starts with having them list five areas they feel are most important to their job performance. Next, it walks them through the Personal Feedback Report in a clear manner. Then, it gives a series of suggestions, including talking with the supervisor and exploring various ideas and strategies for growth and development. Additional resources available from the publisher are also listed in the Development Guide.

SUMMARY. It is clear that SkillScan for Management Development was designed for formative evaluation purposes, that is, for individual development and growth, as well as offering a composite profile of a company or office across several managers. It is made clear in the materials that SkillScan for Management Development is not to be used for administrative decisions, that is, summative evaluation. Keeping these limitations and purposes in mind, SkillScan for Management Development could be useful to individual managers who want to do some type of self-assessment and professional growth plan. Although it was designed for use by sales managers, many of the items could be useful to other types of managers as well.

[359]
Slosson Full-Range Intelligence Test.

Purpose: Constructed as a "quick estimate of general cognitive ability."
Population: Ages 5–21.
Publication Dates: 1988–1994.
Acronym: S-FRIT.
Scores, 8: General Cognition (Full-Range Intelligence Quotient, Rapid Cognitive Index, Best *g* Index), Cognitive Subdomains (Verbal Index, Abstract Index, Quantitative Index, Memory Index, Performance Index).
Administration: Individual.
Forms, 2: Item Profiles/Score Summaries Form, Brief Score Form.
Price Data, 1996: $115 per complete kit including examiner's manual ('94, 80 pages), normative/technical manual ('94, 93 pages), picture book, 50 motor response forms, 50 brief score forms, and 50 item pro-

files/score summaries: $20 per 50 forms (specify Motor response, brief score, or item profiles/score summaries); $26 per examiner's manual; $24 per normative/technical manual; $22 per picture book.
Time: (20–35) minutes.
Authors: Bob Algozzine, Ronald C. Eaves, Lester Mann, H. Robert Vance, and Steven W. Slosson (Brief Score Form).
Publisher: Slosson Educational Publications, Inc.

Review of the Slosson Full-Range Intelligence Test by GERALD S. HANNA, Professor of Education, Kansas State University, Manhattan, KS:

PURPOSE. Screening is a major suggested use of the Slosson Full-Range Intelligence Test (S-FRIT). Although there are circumstances in which one might reasonably use a quick, individually administered screening test, in this regard, I see only limited utility. If screening is sought for the general population, I would consider the convenience and economy of group instruments. If screening is used only for students who have been referred for suspected problems, I would wonder if the referral process itself had not served the screening function, thereby justifying more comprehensive assessment than a short screening test can offer.

In addition, the examiner's manual indicates that the S-FRIT is a quick, easily scored cognitive instrument intended to supplement the use of more extensive cognitive assessment instruments such as the Wechsler Intelligence Scale for Children, Third Edition (WISC-III), the Kaufman Assessment Battery for Children (K-ABC), and the Kaufman Adolescent and Adult Intelligence Test (KAIT) in assessing cognitive progress. In pursuit of this, the S-FRIT assesses cognition in ways similar to the Stanford-Binet Intelligence Scale, Fourth Edition (SB-IV). Several subscores are provided to help make tentative diagnoses of cognitive abilities, strengths, and weaknesses. By way of explanation of their purpose, the technical manual (p. 1) indicates:

> Though the … S-FRIT is a screening instrument, … [it can be used for] tentative diagnosis of intellectual strengths and weaknesses. It must be understood that … implementation must be considered as tentative, awaiting further confirmation by other diagnostic and remedial procedures. Many students will receive the S-FRIT for screening and it will be determined that they will not proceed through

further diagnostic evaluation. The techniques outlined in this Manual can be applied to these students to help them educationally.

The authors are to be commended for discouraging use of subscores on a short screening test for full-blown diagnosis. However, one is puzzled as to which students are to be helped educationally from the *tentative* diagnosis. Those for whom no further diagnostic evaluation is obtained? If so, both the method of confirmation and the need for diagnosis are obscure. Or those for whom the screening use of the S-FRIT leads to full diagnostic evaluation with more sophisticated procedures? If so, the tentative findings would seem to be of limited utility. Or those for whom one wishes to complement more sophisticated Wechsler or Kaufman tests with SB-IV type items? If so, the SB-IV itself might be more attractive than a short screening instrument.

TESTING MATERIALS AND ADMINISTRATION. Test materials are clear and well designed. Administration seems relatively easy and adequately standardized. Excellent use is made of color in aiding administration and scoring. Generally clear scoring criteria are very conveniently placed with the items in the manual.

Verbal items comprised about 36% of the test and were used as much for young children as for the older examinees. Item types included body parts, simple commands, verbal analogies, general information, verbal absurdities, explanation of sayings and proverbs, and vocabulary.

Performance items constitute 48% of the test and include, among others, counting, drawing shapes, picture completion, number and letter series, abstract figures, block counting (from printed materials), and a variety of quantitative items. Manipulatives are restricted to a few common objects (e.g., pencils and coins) and to drawings; this seems sensible for a screening instrument in that it keeps cost down, simplifies administration, and enhances mobility of testing materials.

Quite a few memory items require exact repetition of words, phrases, or sentences. Rote memory is also assessed with pictures, and digits forward and backward. The emphasis on memory—16% of the items—seemed a bit heavy.

Basals and ceilings are each established by eight-in-a-row criteria. It is interesting that the same basals and ceilings are used for all of the subscores, even though eight consecutive items

may contain as few as one or even zero items of a particular subpart. This would not seem justified, unless the subparts are intrinsically highly correlated. Otherwise, the use of common basals and ceilings would tend to artificially inflate correlations among the part scores.

I fret that examiners are provided no place to record examinees' responses; rather, they record only the score—1 or 0—for each item. Although most items could easily be scored during testing, there would surely be some for which one could profitably return at one's leisure to reconsider the scoring. Moreover, the absence of answers makes it difficult for scoring accuracy to be investigated, monitored, or improved.

SCORES. A variety of derived scores are provided. The General Cognitive Index is based on the conventional and sensible standard scores with $M = 100$ and $SD = 16$. Unfortunately, this index is labeled an IQ. This and the use of the word "intelligence" in the test's name do not help users to steer clear of the many misconceptions that attend these dated terms.

The four major cognitive subdomains have standard scores with $M = 50$ and $SD = 8$. The use of a standard deviation large enough to avoid introducing substantial grouping error, such as that found in Wechsler scales, is commendable.

THEORY, DEVELOPMENT, AND STANDARDIZATION. Item development is described only as being based on current cognitive assessment practices and theory. Theoretical foundations and rationale are not described.

In developing the test, 600 items were tried out on an unknown number of undescribed examinees and culled down to 355. These items were normed and then culled further to 252. Therefore, the norms appear to have been gathered under conditions of item order and item context that differ from those of the final version. This, of course, compromises their utility.

Overall, the description of sampling procedures for the norming sampling is meager. Field examiners were apparently instructed on how to sample and then were left to it. It seems possible that the adequacy of sampling among the examiners may have varied considerably.

A laudable feature of the technical manual is provision of comparative tables showing the sample of 1,509 in comparison with 1980 census data on a number of demographic characteristics.

RELIABILITY. In individually administered tests, there are four major sources of measurement error that are present in practice. Ideal reliability research would shed light on all of these sources of error.

Occasion Sampling Error. This was investigated with a test-retest study involving 14 children. Because the manual failed to report descriptive statistical data for this sample, the results are not interpretable.

Content Sampling Error. Reliability of the S-FRIT was investigated mainly by use of KR-20. However, a number of issues prevent the KR-20 data from being interpretable. First, the sample is not described; it may well have been the entire norming sample, but this is not made clear.

Second, if there is any sound rationale for the various subscores, then there would be more homogeneity of content within subscores than across subscores. Therefore, KR-20 would not be appropriate for the total score. Yet it is reported.

Third, internal consistency methods of estimating reliability, such as KR-20, are not appropriate for instruments having basal and ceiling levels because the double truncation inflates the results to an unknown extent.

Examiner Error. No data are presented on this topic.

Scoring Error. No data are presented on scoring error. In justice, it should be noted that, although unfortunate, the absence of these latter two kinds of reliability data is common among individually administered tests.

VALIDITY. The treatment of validity in the technical manual is disappointing. The terminology is, at best, of a pre-1985 vintage and it is not used in conventional ways. Empirical findings are reported rather meagerly, often without summary descriptive data. No data are provided that shed light on the statistical independence, or discriminant validity, of the several subscores.

Under the heading "Content Validity" is a description of S-FRIT content. Some data concerning the SB-IV are reviewed, but none reported for the S-FRIT.

A section on "Construct Validity" also provides description of kinds of test content, but no construct-related validity evidence for scores from the test. This, of course, is the place where data demonstrating the discriminant validity of the subscales would be expected.

Under "Concurrent Criterion Validity" are summaries of several studies. One group reports relationship of S-FRIT scores with those of other aptitude tests. In general the studies report impressive concurrent validity coefficients; however, the samples are very small and the accompanying data are reported rather haphazardly. For example, means and standard deviations of the samples are not reported in several studies. However, *SD*s are reported in a study in which the limited variability was used to explain the small correlation coefficient. Correction for restriction of range was used in another study for which *SD*s were not reported.

Another group of concurrent validity studies concerned special populations. Here too, the findings seem reasonable, yet the reporting omits essential important detail.

A methodological issue common to the above studies is the need for the examination of the S-FRIT and the other tests to be independent. That is, different examiners should administer the tests and they should not know each other's results until they are finished. As is typically the case in test manuals, no information was provided as to whether this condition was met.

Yet another group of validity studies reports correlation of S-FRIT scores with scores of achievement tests. Although the correlational findings seem adequate, they must be disregarded because descriptive data (*M*s and *SD*s) are not reported for the samples.

Missing, as mentioned above, is systematically presented information about the correlations among the several S-FRIT subscores. Without data suggesting some degree of statistical independence of the subscores, users cannot use them with confidence that they are not unduly redundant. Indirect data on this topic can be gleaned from three sources. First, Table 8 in the technical manual provides, for a sample lacking summary statistics, the intercorrelations among four basic S-FRIT subscores as well as the correlation between WISC-R Verbal and Performance IQs. The correlation between the two Wechsler scores was .71, that between pairs of the (much shorter, thus presumably less reliable) S-FRIT scores ranged from .77 to .90. Thus, there appears to be great redundancy among the S-FRIT subscores.

Second, in comparing the KR-20s for the subscores with that of the total score, one could not expect the KR-20 of the total to be as high as it is compared with those of the parts if the parts were not quite highly intercorrelated.

Third, a comparison in the norms tables of deviant status on the subscores and total scores reveals that it is not very much more unusual for people to be consistently deviant than to be occasionally deviant; this suggests that the subparts are highly correlated. Consequently, on the basis of the indirect data available, I believe the parts of the S-FRIT lack sufficient independence to warrant their use.

SUMMARY. The S-FRIT is a short, individually administered instrument offered for use in screening and in making tentative diagnoses. In those situations in which one wished an individually administered test for screening purposes, the S-FRIT seems quite serviceable. However, the absence of sound reliability information about the instrument precludes its being recommended for this purpose. Deficits including insufficient reliability information and the probability of poor discriminant validity among the subscales leave me unable to recommend the test for any diagnostic purposes, tentative or otherwise.

Review of the Slosson Full-Range Intelligence Test by GERALD TINDAL, Professor of Behavioral Research and Teaching, University of Oregon, Eugene, OR:

The Slosson Full-Range Intelligence Test (S-FRIT) is designed to screen students on intelligence and provide a tentative diagnosis of intellectual strengths and weaknesses. In reviewing the technical manual, the following perspectives and issues emerge.

ADMINISTRATION. The materials provided by the authors include the following: (a) an examiner's manual, (b) a picture book and a Motor Response Form (to be used with a subset of the problems listed in the examiner's manual), (c) Item Profile/Score Summaries Form, (d) a Brief Score Form, and (e) a technical manual, including a Slosson Classification Chart.

In the examiner's manual, directions are provided to obtain optimal performance from students. Examiners are provided explicit strategies for establishing rapport, annotating performance, establishing basal and ceiling levels (even when more than one is obtained), computing chronological age, establishing and maintaining an appropriate testing environment, managing students

who are reticent or recalcitrant, and reminding examiners of the importance of standard administration procedures (including prompts on items that should be timed, the use of scratch paper and pencil, and breaks in testing). The materials for administration are coordinated so that the examiner is provided verbatim directions on how to present each item and is cued when to present a figure in the Picture Book or to use the Motor Response Form.

When administering the test, the examiner records individual item responses as either correct or incorrect directly on either an Item Profiles/ Score Summaries Form or a Brief Score Form.

The Item Profiles/Score Summaries Form is composed of four major sections:

1 and 2. A cover sheet with basic summary performance information listed above demographic data.

3. Two pages of performance levels on the 252 items (with age levels listed at intervals of the cumulative list) for four subdomains and the Best g Index (BgI). Each of the items is color coded so that the examiner knows in which subdomain or BgI (some of which are precoded) to add the score. For each subdomain, the total number of items coded is cumulatively listed at the bottom of each column.

4. The last page consists of three sections: (a) recording of scores (for general cognition and the cognitive subdomains), (b) comparison of subdomain scores, and (c) score profiles. A supplementary mode of interpretation is provided with the two scores from the Abstract and the Quantitative Indices added together to form the Performance Index.

The Brief Score Form is color coded so that three major test results can be recorded: Verbal Index (VI), Performance Index (PI), and Memory Index (MI), with these three indices added to form the Full-Range Index (FRIQ).

The S-FRIT takes about 20–35 minutes to administer, though the Brief Form can be used with fewer items and the scores copied from the Profiles/Score Summaries Form. The test is relatively efficient in great part because a basal is used for the administrator to find the level in which the student answers eight successive items correctly and then proceeds until the examinee hits a ceiling in which eight items are successively failed. This approach, like other traditional intelligence tests, keeps the test oriented to those items most appropriate for the student.

SCORING AND INTERPRETATION. Three S-FRIT Scores are available from administration of this test: (a) the Full-Range (FRIQ), (b) Rapid Cognitive Index (RCI), and (c) Best g Index (BgI). These scores are based on the following items:

The Full-Range Intelligence Quotient (FRIQ) is based on the total test performance (all 252 items). The S-FRIT's General Cognitive Index (CGI) is composed of four subdomains, each with subtest scores: Verbal Index (VI) with 36% of the total items, Abstract Index (AI) with 25% of the total items, Quantitative Index (AI) with 23% of the total items, and Memory Index (MI) with 16% of the total items.

The Rapid Cognitive Index (RCI) provides a quick estimate of general cognitive ability based on approximately half the items in the full S-FRIT (134 of the 252). No subdomain analysis is available when administering the RCI.

There are two supplementary interpretations for the Best g Index (BgI) and Abstract/Quantitative Performance Index (PI). The BgI is based on those items that, regardless of the specific domains to which the items belong, correlate highest with the S-FRIT total score (with 181 items serving as the base for this index).

The directions include clear descriptions for obtaining any of these three indices as well as the subdomain scores and supplementary summaries. The examiner records the basal (including all items passed before it) and adds all items answered correctly until the ceiling. In cases of two basals, the examiner is directed to take the earlier one; in cases of two ceilings, the higher one is taken. The examiner is clearly directed which items fit into which domains and summary scores through the use of color-coded and "stippled" recording boxes on the response form.

When interpreting performance through the use of derived scores, the examiner is directed to a technical manual that includes a norms table providing standard scores. This table is clearly organized with the raw scores listed inside the table text and the standard score on the left side. Each page of the norms contains a 3-month interval of age and three major cognitive indices on the left side and the four subdomains on the right side. The normative tables provide well-scaled conversions from ages 5 years to 21 years, 11 months. A mean of 100 and a standard deviation of 16 are used for the CGI scores and a mean of 50 and a standard deviation of 8 are used for all subdomain scores. Separate tables also are provided for obtaining confidence intervals, standard errors of measurement, and statistically significant score differences between S-FRIT subtests at both the 85% and 95% levels of confidence. Finally, for the S-FRIT, a table is provided for obtaining standard score conversions to several other tests (Wechsler, General Aptitude Test Battery, and College Entrance Examination Board) and other metrics (z, T, normal curve equivalent scores, stanines, and percentile rank).

TECHNICAL ADEQUACY INFORMATION. The normative sample is composed of 1,509 children from 37 states, ages 5–21. This sample is generally consistent with the 1980 census data with several exceptions, all of which are detailed in the manual. For example, gender, ethnicity, parent education, region, and community size are included in the comparison between the population participating in the normative sample and base rate of individuals in the U.S. For the most part, some deviations exist between them; furthermore, the test user should be cautioned that the normative sample was tested 10 years ago and comparisons made to census data from 20 years ago.

The technical manual provides clearly displayed data on reliability and validity information for the S-FRIT, though most of the studies are somewhat dated (conducted a decade ago). Both internal consistency and test reliability data are presented.

Construct validity is presented by reference to two types of intelligence (g): Crystallized and Fluid, with quantitative reasoning and recall information also considered. The authors assert that g, global ability, is the "composite of abilities, especially verbal abilities, that enables an individual to learn and recall information, communicate with others, recognize likeness and differences, reason quantitatively, and to apply these abilities in solving unique problems and dealing effectively with the environment" (examiner's manual, p. 8). Crystallized intelligence is a product of native ability, culture, and life experiences. "Fluid intelligence is defined as a relation perceiving capacity which represents one's potential intelligence, independent of socialization and education" (p. 9). Quantitative reasoning is the ability to make numerical comparisons. Recall information is the ability to remember what has been learned.

The authors assert that the test measures both general intelligence and specific subdomains. In the technical manual, the items are cross-walked for each subdomain. As they note, however, the Verbal Index (VI) dominates with 90 of the 252 items coded in this area. In each of these descriptions, the authors provide labels for the types of problems and reference confirmatory factor analyses conducted over 15 years ago.

A series of concurrent criterion-validity studies has been summarized in which other measures of intelligence were administered concurrently with the S-FRIT. Most conclusions resulted from studies conducted by the second author in the late 1980s. Generally, the correlations have been high-moderate to high, and when not as high as expected, the authors described very plausible explanations (such as age restrictions leading to reduced variance, etc.).

TEST SUMMARY AND RECOMMENDATIONS. The authors present a test of intelligence that provides school psychologists and others interested in measuring ability with a quick screener. The manuals and materials are clearly organized with details explicitly listing how to administer the test and interpret performance. The test is loosely based on a theory of intelligence that incorporates both inherited and learned components of performance, though no attempt is made to fit the items into the constructs of crystallized or fluid intelligence. Rather, the items follow this orientation and only vaguely range from those that may be answered indirectly by inference (generalization or induction-deduction) or directly from experience (learning in and out of school). For example, several items require the examinee to visually reassemble a picture displayed in parts. Is this a component of crystallized or fluid intelligence; or is it a component of quantitative or recall information? In other items, the examinee is directed to repeat sentences or numbers, which clearly are part of recall information. In summary, the construct validity of the test is not substantive with depth; rather, it provides an organizing logic with thin data supporting it and fails to connect the items with summary constructs. The primary validity data comprise concurrent measures administered with the S-FRIT. Although the data consistently reveal reasonable correlations, an emphasis on decision making is lacking.

Several different summaries are presented, though some of them are questionable. For example, although the authors address the limitations of age equivalent scores, they assert that the scores are not inherently misleading but simply need to be used in the proper manner. And difference scores are presented among the various subdomains; yet they fail to mention that the reliability of difference scores is less than the reliability of the actual subdomain scores.

[360]
Smell Identification Test™ [Revised].

Purpose: Designed to measure an individual's ability to "identify a number of odorants at the suprathreshold level."

Population: People 5 years and up with suspected olfactory dysfunction.

Publication Dates: 1981–1995.

Acronym: SIT; UPSIT.

Scores: Total score only.

Administration: Individual.

Price Data, 1998: $169.50 per introductory/combination package including 50 Pocket Smell Tests, 3 Smell Identification Tests, administration manual ('95, 51 pages), and scoring keys; $26.95 per Smell Identification Test; $135 per Pocket Smell Test (75 Pocket Smell Tests); $12.95 per Cross-Cultural Smell Identification Test (must order at least 10); $19.50 per administration manual with scoring keys; $14.95 per Picture Identification Test; $3.50 per scoring key for Smell Identification Test, Picture Identification Test, or Cross-Cultural Smell Identification Test.

Time: [10-15] minutes.

Comments: A 40-item forced-choice questionnaire; also known as University of Pennsylvania Smell Identification Test; for use only by individuals "professionally engaged in the scientific or medical evaluation of smell function"; related versions include the Pocket Smell Test, the Cross-Cultural Smell Identification Test, and the Picture Identification Test (equivalent to the SIT except stimuli are pictures rather than odors).

Author: Richard L. Doty.

Publisher: Sensonics, Inc.

Cross References: See T5:2437 (4 references).

Review of the Smell Identification Test™ [Revised] by RALPH G. LEVERETT, Professor of Special and Regular Education, Union University, Jackson, TN:

DESCRIPTION. The Smell Identification Test (SIT) was developed to determine an individual's "smell function." Evaluation of olfactory ability is useful in identifying deficits related to a variety of physical and neurological disorders. Among those cited in the test manual were early-stage Alzheimer's disease, temporal lobe epilepsy, and Down's Syndrome. In addition, olfactory dysfunction may be an effect of alcoholism, smoking, and chemical exposure. In the latter instance, it is conceivable that documenting the loss of olfactory function might be useful in determining compensation related to actual or perceived negligence in a work setting.

The ability to detect odors has personal and occupational implications. The sense of smell has value for pleasure and safety. As related to pleasure, it is useful in enjoying perfumes, foods, and beverages. Its relationship to occupations may include the ability to formulate these items for the enjoyment of others or to detect odors that may signal danger.

The SIT provides employers with a tool for rapid assessment of the ability to detect a variety of "odorants." Those evaluated include odors related to pleasure and potential danger. The test facilitates the comparison of the skills of current and prospective employees. The developers of the SIT describe it as, "the most widely used quantitative olfactory test in the world, and ... the standard means for assessing the ability to smell in North America" (manual, p. 3).

ADVANTAGES OF THE CURRENT EDITION. The SIT has been administered to approximately 35,000 persons "in North America alone" (manual, p. 4). The current edition is the third revision of this test. It provides new data on "nearly" 4,000 men and women between the ages of 4 and 99 years. With these additions, the validity of the normative base is increased so that scores can be calculated "down to the 5th percentile in each 5-year age category" (manual, p. 4).

ADMINISTRATION. The SIT can be given in an industrial setting or mailed to the examinee for self-administration. An examiner is instructed to provide adequate information for the correct release of the odors and the scoring of responses. Test materials that are sent for self-administration should be accompanied by a cover letter clearly stating the procedure the examinee should follow.

The format is simple. Four booklets, each of which contains 10 brown panels or "labels" of encapsulated odorants, are provided in a packet with a pencil. The pencil is used to release the odor. A zigzag pattern drawn on the label is recommended. It is shown on the cover of the booklet. The pencil is also used to mark the

response on the test grid in each booklet. Booklets are designed with pages that contain the encapsulated label and a grid with four choices per item. Examinees are instructed to mark (release) the odor and to sniff the label immediately. The examinee is prompted by, "This odor smells most like ____" (manual, p. 5). A choice is to be marked even if no odor is detected.

The pages of the booklet are of varying width. As labels are sniffed and responses are marked, each successive page reveals a new label and the corresponding portion of the scoring grid. When all 10 labels have been sniffed, the entire scoring grid is revealed. Individual templates are provided in the test manual for scoring each of the four booklets. A total of 40 responses will be marked. Modification of instructions or length of testing is discussed for persons who have impairments or conditions of age that would make the typical testing format difficult. Examiners are encouraged to accommodate examinees with a variety of disorders.

The interpretation of the test results should be made in consideration of the examinee's general health, gender, and occupation. For example, a low score would likely be more significant for a chemist creating fragrances than for a secretary the same age in the same work setting. An individual's score will indicate any of several degrees of ability. Some of the score ranges are influenced by gender; as a result, some scores are irrespective of gender, and others are gender specific. The diagnostic categories are normosmia (normal ability to smell), mild microsmia, moderate microsmia, severe microsmia, total anosmia (total liability to smell), or probable malingering. The final category identifies examinees who deliberately create a low score, presumable for some form of compensation. The forced-choice format (four options) allows detection of malingerers. A person with total inability to smell should achieve a score of 10 out of 40 by chance. Those with scores of less than 10 would be suspects of malingering.

PSYCHOMETRIC ADEQUACY. The SIT is described as a measure of an individual's ability to detect odors. The 40 odors that comprise the test are familiar and are representative of pleasure and potential danger. Those in the latter category would vary depending on the context in which they are detected.

No discussion of the possible effects of consuming intensely flavored foods or beverages on test results was noted. Additionally, the presence of ambient odors in the workplace could conceivably influence test results. Although these factors may be negligible, it would have been of interest to address the possibility of their influence.

This test appears to have good face validity. The odorants are synthetic; however, they have remarkable similarity to the actual odors. Discussion of evidence of overall validity and reliability is minimal. Test-retest reliability estimates (6- or more month interval) is addressed in comparative detail and exceeds .90.

Discussion of the technical nature of the test is extended to test-retest diagnosis. The developers of the SIT are candid regarding the heuristic nature of the diagnostic categories. Borderline scores may change "boundaries" in the second administration. That is, a person might move from high mild to low moderate microsmia, in "most cases, however, [individuals] would be expected to remain within the same category" (manual, p. 7).

SUMMARY. This test has had wide use in industrial settings. It has apparently served its users satisfactorily, and the developers of the test have continued to add to the data base. Although limited in technical details, the SIT appears to be respected in what is apparently a small field of similar assessments. It was among 10 such tests reviewed by Doty and his colleagues (Doty, McKeown, Lee, & Shaman, 1996). Among their findings was that the reliability of olfactory tests was related to their length. The SIT has addressed that area in recommending that test administration be modified (including length) as needed to accommodate the needs of the examinees. This test has been described previously as the most widely used test of its kind, which is significant in a field of at least 10 similar assessments.

REVIEWER' REFERENCE

Doty, R. L., McKeown, D. A., Lee, W. W., & Shaman, P. (1996). A study of the test-retest reliability of ten olfactory tests. *Chemical Senses, 21*, 645–656.

[361]
Smit-Hand Articulation and Phonology Evaluation.

Purpose: Designed to assess a child's level of phonology.
Population: Ages 3–9.
Publication Date: 1997.
Acronym: SHAPE.
Scores, 11: Total, Weak Syllable Deletion, Final Consonant Deletion, Reduction of /lrw/ Clusters, Reduction of /s/ Clusters, Stopping of Initial Fricatives, Voicing of Initial Voiceless Obstruents, Fronting of Velars, Depalatalization, Gliding of Liquid Singletons, Vocalization of Liquids.
Administration: Individual.
Price Data, 2001: $$128 per kit including 10 record booklets, 10 autoscore answer forms, manual (63 pages), and 1 picture set; $29.50 per 10 record booklets; $16.50 per 10 autoscore forms; $35 per manual; $65 per picture set.
Time: (30) minutes.
Authors: Ann B. Smit and Linda Hand.
Publisher: Western Psychological Services.

Review of the Smit-Hand Articulation and Phonology Evaluation by DAVID P. HURFORD, Director of the Center for the Assessment and Remediation of Reading Difficulties and Professor of Psychology and Counseling, Pittsburg State University, Pittsburg, KS:

The Smit-Hand Articulation and Phonology Evaluation (SHAPE) is an instrument designed to assess the speech and phonological ability of children aged 3 to 9 years. The instrument is composed of 80 photographs depicting nouns that young children would be able to name. The items are arranged into semantic categories to increase the likelihood of producing the intended name. Embedded within the 80 items are the 108 targets that are evaluated by the SHAPE. The phonemes produced by the child are transcribed by circling either the correct form of the phoneme or an incorrect substitute from a list of likely incorrect substitutes. The transcription system decreases the time it takes to record the child's responses and increases accuracy. The authors suggest audiotaping the session to assist in transcription for children who have unintelligible speech. The SHAPE allows for independent analysis that is used to assess children with unintelligible speech or children who are very young. The independent analysis includes the Phonetic Inventory that is used to identify all of the phones produced by the child and the Syllable and Word Shape Inventory that is used to classify the complexity of the words the child produced. The SHAPE also provides a relational analysis that compares the child's phone production with that of adults.

The SHAPE was developed as an outgrowth of the need to have a knowledge base that was reflective of the current status of the age of acquisition norms. This instrument was also developed so that the child's phonology could be assessed as a self-contained language system without reference to adult norms. This allows speech-language pathologists to determine appropriate interventions for children who are not capable of producing intelligible speech. The SHAPE also affords relational analysis that compares the child's phonology with adult norms as optimally developed systems. The authors of the SHAPE used photographs to depict the target words. Harrington, Lux, and Higgins (1984) discovered that children are more likely to name photographs accurately than drawings. The authors of the SHAPE also argue that young children find photographs more interesting than drawings.

The SHAPE was standardized with two norming groups. The first was composed of 997 children from Iowa and Nebraska and did not exclude children who had speech and language disorders. The second group included 1,094 children, none of whom had speech and language disorders, and was constructed to reflect the demographic characteristics of the United States.

Reliability of scores from the SHAPE was evaluated by use of only one measure: interrater reliability. Pairs of speech-language pathologists assessed 26 children. One of the raters administered the SHAPE and transcribed the responses whereas the other rater simply transcribed the responses. Interrater reliability was quite high (.98).

Validity was examined by considering content validity, construct validity, and predictive validity. The SHAPE's content includes multiple exemplars of the speech sounds comprising English. A criticism of single-word instruments such as the SHAPE is that the data generated from such tests are not as representative of speech development as would occur from an analysis of conversational speech. The authors performed conversational analysis with several of the children in the norming group in addition to the data generated from the SHAPE. The authors indicated that the results were "about the same." However, the authors do not present means or p-values to substantiate their claims.

Construct validity was examined by comparing the results of the SHAPE with those of Templin (1957). The ages at which 75% of those assessed in a particular age group acquired specific consonant and consonant clusters for the SHAPE compared closely to those of Templin. However,

there were some minor differences between the two data sets. The authors explained these differences by pointing out that the targets from the earlier data set were transcribed with a broad phonemic rule whereas the SHAPE uses a narrow transcription. Because differences in methods could produce differences in results, this explanation is quite plausible.

Predictive validity was considered by comparing the SHAPE total scores of 69 children with known phonological disorders with those from the normative sample who did not have phonological disorders. The mean total score for each of the age groups of the individuals with phonological disorders averaged 2.31 standard deviations (with a range between 1.4 and 3.4 standard deviations) below that of the individuals without phonological disorders. Poor performance on the SHAPE is predictive of speech and language difficulties. Poor speech and language performance is highly predictive of the poor development of other language-based systems as well, including reading. The SHAPE has potential to not only identify children who are in need of speech and language interventions, but with the use of the independent and relational analyses it also has the ability to assist in the development of interventions geared to improve phonological processing abilities.

The manual is relatively user friendly. One exception concerns the section describing the Phonetic Inventory of the Independent Analysis. The manual indicates "enter each unique phone type or cluster that the child has produced, correctly or erroneously, as indicated on pages 5 and 12 of the form" (manual, p. 17). Even though this is exactly what should be done to complete the Phonetic Inventory correctly, further explanation would be quite helpful for the first-time user of the SHAPE. Providing explicit directions would help considerably. For example, in the manual a mock Phonetic Inventory was completed for the reader. There were seven instances in which the child produced the labiovelar glide /w/. The letter w is entered under Initial Position, Glides, and Labiovelar with "7" in parentheses [e.g., w(7)]. It would be helpful to indicate that the "7" reflects two appropriate uses of /w/ for "wing" and "watch" and five inappropriate uses of /w/ for "leaf," "lightning," "rope," "rainbow," and "earring." This is only a minor difficulty that upon correction might save the novice administrator of the SHAPE some frustration in figuring out the Phonetic Inventory. Finally, the manual includes an appendix that contains potential idiosyncratic processes, speech characteristics that are peculiar to children who are not developing speech and language skills appropriately. This appendix contains very useful information for identifying and specifying the speech patterns for such children.

SUMMARY. In conclusion, the SHAPE is a very thoroughly developed and useful instrument designed to assess the articulation and phonological production of children. It has acceptable psychometric properties and was constructed with items that are readily identifiable by young children.

REVIEWER'S REFERENCES

Templin, M. C. (1957). *Certain language skills in children* (Monograph Series No. 26). Minneapolis, MN: University of Minnesota, Institute of Child Welfare.
Harrington, J. F., Lux, L. L., & Higgins, R. L. (1984, November). *Identification of error types as related to stimuli in articulation tests.* Paper presented at the national convention of the American Speech-Language-Hearing Association, San Francisco, CA.

Review of the Smit-Hand Articulation and Phonology Evaluation by RALPH G. LEVERETT, Professor of Special and Regular Education, Union University, Jackson, TN:

DESCRIPTION. The Smit-Hand Articulation and Phonology Evaluation (SHAPE) measures speech and syllable production in young children, ages 3–9. Its primary purpose is to identify misarticulated sounds for early intervention. Analysis is two-fold: comparison of child to adult production and determination of the production features unique to the child.

TEST MATERIALS. The SHAPE consists of a spiral-bound set of 80 color photographs to elicit 108 target phonemes (individual consonants and consonant clusters) and four syllable patterns. All photographs depict single-syllable nouns. They were chosen to provide good exemplars of the stimuli and to be easily recognized by young children. A Record Booklet is utilized to record the child's speech productions. This information is transferred to an "AutoScore Form" for analysis. The Record Booklet provides cues to elicit productions. Procedures for the administration and scoring of the test are provided in a test manual that provides many useful tables for both analysis and intervention.

TEST ADMINISTRATION. The SHAPE is administered individually. The Record Booklet provides an introductory statement to elicit pro-

duction. Some statements introduce categories of words; others introduce a single item. A distinguishing feature of the SHAPE is its highly detailed, yet simplified scoring form. This format provides the benefits of narrow, or close, transcription without the tedious transcription itself. Narrow transcription allows the recording of pertinent details of a child's *actual* production rather than a single symbol that indicates only the sound produced. For example, in narrow transcription, a sound can be recorded as aspirated or as glottal stop. These are features that indicate *how* the sound was produced rather than just transcribing the sound alone. This information is especially beneficial in providing effective intervention.

The Record Booklet and AutoScore Form were designed to reduce the time required for testing and to provide detailed information for analysis and intervention. This was accomplished by listing typical phoneme substitutions for each target sound and error patterns for syllable production. These can be marked quickly rather than having to actually transcribe the sound or syllable pattern that is produced. A third feature provided for each target sound allows the examiner to identify whether the word containing the sound was produced spontaneously. A word that is not produced spontaneously may be elicited by direct imitation ("Say ____.") or by delayed imitation ("Is it ____ or ____?").

Although the AutoScore Form provides detailed analysis of testing, additional useful information is included in several tables in the test manual. In this manner, the manual serves as a valuable resource for developing intervention plans.

NORMS. The standardization of the SHAPE was conducted initially in Iowa and Nebraska on 997 children between the ages of 3.0 and 9.0 years. Due to the limitations of this sample, the second phase of standardization was conducted using a national sample of 1,094 children in four geographical areas. Children with known speech production problems were excluded. The ethnic and gender characteristics of the sample were similar to those for U.S. Census figures. The children in the national sample came from higher SES levels than are average for the United States in general. Norms are reported in 6-month intervals for the ages 3.0 to 9.0 years.

PSYCHOMETRIC ADEQUACY. The SHAPE is described as an instrument that measures a child's production of consonants, consonant clusters, and syllable production. Of the phonemes represented by the consonants and consonant clusters, production of all except y, ng, f, v, and voiced th as in "that" are assessed in two or more words in at least one position. Multiple exemplars are provided for many of the single phonemes and some of the consonant clusters. Four polysyllabic words representative of syllable patterns are assessed. Thus, content validity is generally adequate. The developers of the SHAPE address the concern that sounds are not evaluated in conversational speech by citing research by DuBois and Bernthal (1978) that suggests that errors in conversational speech may exceed those in single words.

In addressing construct validity, the scores from the SHAPE are compared to the data compiled by Templin (1957). The two measures "comport well," although there are some discrepancies that the authors suggest may be attributable to the difference in transcription. Whereas the SHAPE uses narrow transcription, the Templin study used broad transcription. The authors report that evidence in the predictive validity for scores from the SHAPE is good, identifying those children known to have articulation errors.

Interrater reliability was examined by assigning pairs of speech pathologists (SLPs) to transcribe a child's production. Although transcription is objective in its use of symbols, the interpretation of the actual production could conceivably vary slightly among SLPs. The SLPs were instructed to avoid discussing their results in any way. The result of their transcription showed a high correspondence between the two scores of (r = .98). This speaks well for the integrity that guided the development of the test.

SUMMARY. The SHAPE provides a comparatively rapid and highly detailed profile of a child's speech productions. Analysis allows comparison of the child's productions to an adult model as well as those unique to the child (diosyncratic processes). Speech-language pathologists trained to view misarticulated sounds as "articulation disorders" (substitutions, omissions, distortions, and additions) and those who view them as "phonological disorders" should be comfortable with the administration and interpretation of this instrument and its practical application.

REVIEWER'S REFERENCES
Templin, M. C. (1957). *Certain language skills in children* (Monograph Series No. 26). Minneapolis, MN: University of Minnesota, Institute of Child Welfare.
DuBois, E., & Bernthal, J. E. (1978). A comparison of three methods for obtaining articulatory responses. *Journal of Speech and Hearing Disorders*, 43, 295–305.

[362]
Social Competence and Behavior Evaluation, Preschool Edition.

Purpose: "Designed to assess patterns of social competence, affective expression, and adjustment difficulties."
Population: Children aged 30 months to 76 months.
Publication Date: 1995.
Acronym: SCBE.
Scores: 8 Basic scales (Depressive-Joyful, Anxious-Secure, Angry-Tolerant, Isolated-Integrated, Aggressive-Calm, Egotistical-Prosocial, Oppositional-Cooperative, Dependent-Autonomous); 4 Summary scales (Social Competence, Internalizing Problems, Externalizing Problems, General Adaptation).
Administration: Group.
Price Data, 1999: $75 per complete kit including 25 AutoScore™ forms and manual (67 pages); $33.50 per 25 AutoScore™ forms; $45 per manual.
Time: (15) minutes.
Comments: Ratings by teachers or other child care professionals.
Authors: Peter J. LaFreniere and Jean E. Dumas.
Publisher: Western Psychological Services.

Review of the Social Competence and Behavior Evaluation, Preschool Edition by RONALD A. MADLE, School Psychologist, Shikellamy School District, Sunbury, PA and Adjunct Associate Professor of School Psychology, Pennsylvania State University, University Park, PA:

TEST PURPOSE AND DESIGN. The Social Competence and Behavior Evaluation (Preschool Edition; SCBE)—previously known as the Preschool Socio-Affective Profile—is designed to "assess patterns of social competence, affective expression, and adjustment difficulties" (manual, p. 1). The authors indicate its function is to describe behavioral tendencies for the purposes of socialization and education rather than to classify children within diagnostic categories. The scale was formulated from a "developmental/adaptational perspective ... which emphasized the functional significance of affect in regulating social exchange" (p. 33). As such as it appears that the SCBE is more appropriately thought of as a personality instrument or measure of temperament than a typical behavior rating scale.

The SCBE provides eight basic scales and four summary scales. Each basic scale includes five items describing successful adjustment and five describing adjustment difficulties. Three basic scales describe the child's manner of emotional expression (Depressive-Joyful, Anxious-Secure, Angry-Tolerant), three describe social interactions with peers (Isolated-Integrated, Aggressive-Calm, Egotistical-Prosocial), and two describe teacher-child relations (Oppositional-Cooperative, Dependent-Autonomous). The four summary scales were developed based on statistical analyses and include Social Competence (40 items), Internalizing Problems (20 items), Externalizing Problems (20 items), and General Adaptation (all 80 items).

ADMINISTRATION, SCORING, AND INTERPRETATION. The SCBE is easy and straightforward to use. It comes as an AutoScore™ form that combines administration, scoring, and display of the score profile.

Completion of the 80 items should take a caregiver approximately 15 minutes, although considerable exposure to the child is needed before completing the ratings. Although many items are observable, numerous ones will require considerable interpretation and value judgments by the rater (e.g., using terms such as "takes pleasure," "enjoys," or "delights in playing"). All items are scored on a 6-point scale ranging from *Almost NEVER occurs* to *Almost ALWAYS occurs*. A number of items are "reversed" to minimize response sets by the rater.

Scoring takes about 10 minutes. Procedures for calculating raw scores for each scale are clearly specified in both the manual and on the scoring form. Raw scores are then converted to normalized *T*-scores by plotting them on the SCBE Profile. Although numerical *T*-scores are clearly noted on the Profile, actual percentiles are difficult to obtain and there is no table in the manual. Because the *T*-scores are normalized, percentiles could be obtained from standard tables; it would be useful to have this information in the manual. Completed scales are considered scorable if as many as seven items are left blank by substituting median values printed on the scoring form. This practice seems questionable because almost 10% of the items could have been left blank.

The manual presents extensive information on the interpretation of each scale, as well as nine detailed case studies describing the use of the scale in applied situations.

STANDARDIZATION. Early development of the SCBE was completed in Quebec with French-Canadian children and the manual details this work. The published scale was designed to make the measure available to the U.S. clinician and educator. The U.S. standardization sample consisted of 1,263 children between the ages of 30 and 78 months. They were selected from six sites in Indiana and Colorado. All respondents were preschool teachers and were overwhelmingly (95%) female. Only a small percentage (8.3%) of the sample was below age 4. Although the gender distribution of the children was good compared to 1991 U.S. Census data, the norm group oversamples low SES parents, although statistical simulation studies indicated this made no difference. The manual also states that the percentage of black children was "slightly above" the census distribution. The tabular breakdown, however, suggests considerable overrepresentation (20.6% versus 15%). Only separate norms for males and females are presented.

RELIABILITY. Estimates of interrater agreement and internal consistency are reported for each of the eight basic scales. The manual fails, however, to report reliability information on any of the four composites.

Interrater agreement was assessed only with the Indiana sample. Interrater agreement estimates were in the range of .72 to .89, similar to earlier Canadian results.

Internal consistency (coefficient alpha = .80 to .89) was reported across the Indiana and Colorado samples combined. No U.S. test-retest information is presented, although the Canadian information indicated estimates of 2-week test-retest reliability (.74–.87) and 6-month (.59–.70) stability for the eight subscales.

VALIDITY. Both construct and criterion validity research is reported. It is stated that content validity evidence is available in the manual, but it is not clear to what information this refers. Construct validity was examined primarily through independent factor analyses of the Colorado and Indiana samples. A relatively consistent factor structure, consisting of Internalizing Problems, Externalizing Problems, and Social Competence was obtained in each sample, as well as in the earlier Canadian research.

Convergent and discriminant validity were examined through correlation of the SCBE with the Achenbach Child Behavior Checklist (CBCL) for 177 of the French-Canadian children. Only the Internalizing and Externalizing dimensions were considered. Although convergent validity appears to be adequate for the scales, discriminant validity evidence was less convincing. For example, Internalizing Problems correlated equally well with the CBCL Internalizing and Externalizing scores.

Criterion validity was assessed in a study of 126 children in Montreal using peer sociometrics and direct observation criterion measures. The study primarily validated the social competence and anxious-withdrawn aspects of the scale. A subsequent chapter in the manual presents three additional studies that expand on the validity of scores from the scale. Each uses the "SCBE Typological Approach" (socially competent, anxious-withdrawn, angry-aggressive, or average). Although this system is described in the research in the manual, it is not a formal component of the published scale.

SUMMARY. The SCBE presents a promising approach to assessing preschool social and emotional characteristics. Its development, however, is incomplete and flawed and it cannot be recommended for use as other than a supplemental scale. The norm sample's quality is more typical of that seen in scales developed 10 or more years ago. Also, most development research stresses the basic scales and less information is available on more global composites or the typological approach used in some of the research. Other better developed measures such as the Achenbach Child Behavior Checklist (13:55) or the Behavior Assessment System for Children (13:34) are more rigorously developed and remain the instruments of choice.

Review of the Social Competence and Behavior Evaluation, Preschool Edition by G. MICHAEL POTEAT, Associate Professor of Psychology, East Carolina University, Greenville, NC:

The Social Competence and Behavior Evaluation, Preschool Edition (SCBE) is a rating scale designed to measure the social competence and affective, expressive, and adjustment difficulties in children from 30 to 78 months of age. The SCBE is a standardized and commercially published version of an earlier instrument—the Preschool Socio-Affective Profile (PSP)—designed to be completed by the student's teacher. Each item is a behavioral descriptor (e.g., Active, ready to play), which is rated as *Never* (1), *Sometimes* (2 or 3),

Often (4 or 5), or *Always* (6). The SCBE is described as providing (a) a standardized description of behavior, (b) a measure of social competence, (c) a differential assessment of emotional and behavioral problems, (d) data that are reliable and consistent, and (e) a method for evaluating changes that are functions of growth or treatment.

The 80 items are divided into eight basic scales (10 items each) and four summary scales. Three of the basic scales describe the child's typical or "characteristic" manner of emotional expression and are labeled using negative and positive poles: Depressive-Joyful, Anxious-Secure, and Angry-Tolerant. Three other basic scales are designed to describe social interactions with peers: Isolated-Integrated, Aggressive-Calm, and Egotistical-Prosocial. The last two scales are measures of teacher-child interactions: Oppositional-Cooperative and Dependent-Autonomous. Four summary scales are described as being developed on the basis of extensive statistical analysis and are labeled: Social Competence (based on 40 items), Internalizing Problems (20 items), and Externalizing Problems (20 items). The last summary scale is labeled General Adaptation and is based on all 80 items.

Scoring the SCBE is done by opening the score form, which employs carbon paper and then summing items following the printed directions. The raw scores are next transferred to the profile sheet, which has T-scores and percentile ranks. One side of the profile sheet has T-scores based on norms for boys and the other side has norms for girls. The instructions are clear and math checks are included to help reduce the number of scoring errors. Teachers should have no problem in obtaining the raw scores and transferring the raw scores to the profile sheet. The manual also contains a completed example of a form and profile sheet but the instructions on the form are satisfactory. All scales are constructed so that high T-scores are positive and low T-scores are indicative of problems. The T-scores are based on raw scores that have been transformed and normalized. T-scores of 63 or higher are indicative of good adjustment and T-scores of 37 or lower are interpreted as indicative of adjustment problems.

The technical and psychometric properties of the SCBE are overall very good. The initial version of the SCBE was published in French and preliminary data and psychometric properties are reported based on a sample of 979 French-Canadian preschool children. Based on the results obtained with the French version, the instrument was translated into English and standardized on a sample of 1,263 U.S. children at six sites in two states. The sample includes 631 girls and 632 boys from Colorado and Indiana who were enrolled in preschool classes. Modal age was 5 years (41.7%). Children aged 4 years (27.5%) and 6 years (22.5%) were also well represented but only 8.3% of the children were in the 3-year-old group. Age was significantly positively correlated with social competence and negatively correlated with behavioral problems, but the norms did not indicate any practically significant age differences. The magnitude of the correlation between age and the SCBE scales ranges from .09 to .32 with most of the correlation coefficients clustering around .20.

Comparison of the demographic characteristics of the normative sample to those of the U.S. show that children with less education and from Black families were overrepresented. Children from Hispanic families and children from families with some college or a college degree were underrepresented. The authors report the SES effects were relatively small and none of the correlations between SES and the SCBE were statistically significant. Significant differences were found between boys and girls using multiple *t*-tests with probability levels adjusted using Bonferroni's correction. Boys were found to have significantly more negative ratings than girls for Externalizing Problems and the four associated basic scales. Boys also had significantly less positive ratings on Social Competence and General Adaptation.

The reliability and internal consistency estimates for the SCBE are good. Interrater reliability estimates for the ratings of the 824 students in the Indiana sample were between .72 and .89. The internal consistency (using Cronbach's alpha) indices for the eight standard scales ranged from .80 to .89 in both the Indiana and Colorado samples.

Numerous data are presented to support the validity of the SCBE. Construct validity is evidenced in the factor structure of the SCBE, which demonstrates that the theoretical structure of the instrument (as a measure of social competence, externalizing problems, and internalizing problems) is supported by the data obtained in both the Indiana and the Colorado sample. Other evidence for the construct validity of the SCBE was obtained in a convergent and discriminant analysis comparing the SCBE with

the Child Behavior Checklist (CBCL; Edelbrock & Achenbach, 1984). The pattern of correlations between the scales of the SCBE and CBCL is supportive of the construct validity of the SCBE (e.g., the Anxiety scale of the CBCL had a high correlation with Internalizing Problems and a low correlation with Externalizing Problems on the SCBE).

Criterion-related validity was evaluated by comparing the SCBE with measures of peer sociometrics and direct observations of behavior. Based on a random sample of 126 children enrolled in preschool in the Montreal area, four groups were identified as socially competent (S-C), anxious-withdrawn (A-W), angry-aggressive (A-A), and average (AV). Analysis of variance demonstrated significant differences between the groups with the A-W children spending more time in noninteraction than the other groups, and the A-A group receiving significantly more peer rejection (negative peer nominations). The data are presented in some detail and were the basis for a publication (LaFreniere, Dumas, Capuano, & Dubeau, 1992). Additional information is presented on three other developmental and clinical studies using the SCBE, which are also indicative of the instrument's validity and utility.

In summary, the SCBE is a well-developed instrument with reasonably good psychometric properties. The test manual is well done with a great deal of technical information and details from a number of case studies. The manual contains information related to both research and clinical applications. Caution is advised in using the norms with 3-year-old children, and the limitations of the normative sample (the lack of geographical variation and the underrepresentation of children from higher SES families) should be noted. The SCBE is recommended for use as an aid in the identification of preschool children who have problems in the area of social competence and in research on children's social development. As the authors of the SCBE point out, the instrument should not be used as the sole basis for clinical identification but should be viewed as providing a basis for hypotheses about the behavior of individual children, which requires other collaboration.

REVIEWER'S REFERENCES

Edelbrock, C. S., & Achenbach, T. M. (1984). The teacher version of the child behavior profile: I. Boys aged 6–11. *Journal of Consulting and Clinical Child Psychology, 52,* 207–217.

LaFreniere, P. J., Dumas, J. R., Capuano, F., & Dubeau, D. (1992). The development of and validation of the preschool socioaffective profile. *Psychological Assessment: Journal of Consulting and Clinical Psychology, 4*(4), 442–450.

[363]
Social Phobia and Anxiety Inventory.

Purpose: Constructed for assessment of the "somatic, cognitive and behavioral aspects of social phobia."
Population: Ages 14 and older.
Publication Date: 1996.
Acronym: SPAI.
Scores, 3: Social Phobia, Agoraphobia, Difference.
Administration: Individual or group.
Price Data, 1999: $55 per complete kit including manual and 25 QuikScore™ forms; $30 per 25 QuikScore™ forms; $30 per manual; $33 per specimen set including manual and 3 QuikScore™ forms.
Time: (15) minutes.
Comments: Self-report.
Authors: Samuel M. Turner, Deborah C. Beidel, and Constance V. Dancu.
Publisher: Multi-Health Systems, Inc.

Review of the Social Phobia and Anxiety Inventory by GEORGE ENGELHARD, JR., Professor of Educational Studies, Emory University, Atlanta, GA:

The Social Phobia and Anxiety Inventory (SPAI) is a self-report instrument developed by Samuel M. Turner, Deborah C. Beidel, and Constance B. Dancu to measure individual differences in social phobia. Three scores are defined for each examinee: Social Phobia (SP) score, Agoraphobia (Ag) score, and Difference score (SP score minus the Ag score). Social phobia is defined as "a persistent fear of one or more social situations in which the person is exposed to possible scrutiny by others and fears that he or she will act in a way or show anxiety symptoms that will be humiliating or embarrassing" (American Psychiatric Association, 1994, p. 416). Agoraphobia is defined as "anxiety about, or avoidance of, places or situations from which escape might be difficult (or embarrassing) or which help may not be available in the event of having a Panic Attack or panic-like symptoms" (American Psychiatric Association, 1994, p. 393). The SPAI consists of 45 items designed to reflect how frequently (0 = *never* to 6 = *always*) an examinee experiences an anxious response to a variety of social situations. Clients taking the SPAI should have at least a sixth grade reading level, and individuals with lower reading levels should have the SPAI read to them. Thirty-two of the items are included in the Social Phobia scale and 13 items are included in the Agoraphobia scale.

SCORING. Even though all of the psychometric information is reported as if there are 45 items on the SPAI, the examinees actually rate themselves on 109 separate rating scales. This is because twenty-one of the items have subitems with nested ratings that refer to variations in the settings (e.g., anxiety in social situations when the examinee is with strangers, authority figures, opposite sex, or people in general) that lead to multiple ratings. Mean ratings are taken across these settings and treated as single items for the psychometric analyses that require item level data.

The guidelines for scoring are very straightforward, although the rationale for some of the steps is not clear. For example, several subscores are generated, averaged, divided by various weights, and rounded to the nearest whole number. Some of these steps are puzzling to say the least and should be explained in more detail. The manual recommends encouraging the examinees to complete all of the items, and recommends not scoring the SPAI if four or more items are omitted. A detailed appendix is provided for scoring the SPAI when less than four items are omitted.

It is curious that the authors do not provide a situation-specific score. Instead, the authors advocate clinical interpretation of examinee of the pattern of responses across items. There are sets of subitems that could be used to generate scores on anxiety in social situations with strangers, authority figures, opposite sex, and people in general. This summary information may be more helpful to clinicians than the examination of individual subitems recommended by the authors of the SPAI.

RELIABILITY. Based on an initial pool of 308 college students, the authors selected 182 students to calculate test-retest reliability coefficients over a 2-week period. The test-retest results were as follows: $r(173) = .85$ for the SP scores, $r(173) = .74$ for the Ag scores, and $r(173) = .86$ for the Difference scores. These correlation coefficients indicate that these scores are quite stable for these students.

Using the same sample, Cronbach's alpha was calculated to examine the internal consistency of the scales. Coefficient alpha for the SP scores was .96, and it was .85 for the Ag scores. These values are quite high, and provide support for the use of the scores for making decisions regarding individual clients. However, it is not clear how the use of means across sets of subitems affect the results of these internal consistency analyses. Coefficient alpha cannot be calculated for the Difference scores.

VALIDITY. An impressive amount of validity research has been conducted with the SPAI. These studies have included an examination of discriminant validity, external validity, concurrent validity, predictive validity, sensitivity to treatment effects, and convergent validity. It is curious to note that the correlation among the three scores on the SPAI is not reported in the manual. Most of the validity research provides reasonable support for the recommended uses of the SPAI.

The authors also report the results of several factor analyses of the SPAI. As expected with any sample-dependent statistical procedure, the factor structure of the SPAI varies across different groups. As was the case with coefficient alpha, it is unclear how the use of mean ratings for subitems that are nested within other items may influence the results of these factor analyses. Future work using factor analysis should be conducted using the 109 separate ratings collected from the examinee rather than averaging across subitems.

Another source of concern regarding the validity of the SPAI is due to the repetitive nature of some of the items. Many of the questions may appear to be redundant to the examinee, and this may lead to various types of response sets that would lower the validity of the inferences made on the basis of the SPAI scores.

Based on the results of several validity studies, the authors concluded that the Difference score (derived by subtracting the Ag score form the SP score) should be used. The authors claim that by "subtracting the agoraphobia from social phobia score (i.e., the Agoraphobia subscale serves as a suppressor variable), a purer measure of social phobia is provided (i.e., the Difference score)" (manual, p. 2). Potential users of the SPAI should be aware that there has been some debate in the literature regarding the use of these Difference scores. Perhaps a better approach would be to use a regression model to adjust the social phobia scores for individual differences in agoraphobia. An even better approach may be to recommend that the clinician examine client profiles with separate scores in order to sort out social phobia from agoraphobia. In any case, additional research is needed on the validity of the Difference subscale.

The authors should be complimented for providing some information regarding how the SPAI functions across several demographic groups related to gender, age, race, and ethnicity. All the sample sizes for these analyses are quite small, but the inclusion of this issue in the manual indicates a sensitivity on the part of the authors to the possibility that the meaning of the SPAI score may vary across various subgroups.

ADMINISTRATION/INTERPRETATION. Clear guidelines are provided for administering the SPAI. Throughout the technical manual the authors are very clear about how to interpret scores from the SPAI and stress the use of appropriate caution. An excellent section with eight case studies is provided in the technical manual illustrating how to interpret the SPAI scores in clinical settings.

SUMMARY. The development of the SPAI follows the recommendations of the *Standards for Educational and Psychological Testing* (American Educational Research Association, American Psychological Association, & National Council on Measurement in Education, 1985). A great deal of research effort has gone into documenting the validity of the SPAI scores for a variety of research and clinical uses. The authors have written an exemplary technical manual that could be used as a model for other developers of psychological inventories. In spite of some of the reservations raised in this review, such as the averaging of subitem ratings and the validity of the Difference score, the SPAI remains a sound choice for potential users who are seeking a scale to measure social phobia. The SPAI should be a very useful screening device in the hands of a skilled clinician.

Although not a criticism of the SPAI per se, the authors should consider using an item response theory model, such as the Rasch Measurement Model (RMM; Wright & Masters, 1982), to explore the psychometric quality of the SPAI. Briefly, the advantages of calibrating the SPAI items would be that the invariance of the scales can be explored—for example, it was clear that the factor analyses reported in the technical manual were sample-dependent, and produced different factor structures across different groups. The RMM has also been extended to provide information regarding how examinees use the categories provided to them on rating scales. This sort of information could be very useful in clinical discussions between clinician and client. It would also aid in the detection of response sets. A variable map that shows the location of the SPAI items calibrated onto a social phobia scale would also assist the clinician in interpreting SPAI scores. Model-data fit statistics would provide a wealth of diagnostic information to users that would be very helpful in stimulating clinical discussions with examinees.

REVIEWER'S REFERENCES

Wright, B. D., & Masters, G. (1982). *Rating scale analysis: Rasch measurement.* Chicago: MESA Press.

American Educational Research Association, American Psychological Association, & National Council on Measurement in Education. (1985). *Standards for educational and psychological testing.* Washington, DC: American Psychological Association, Inc.

American Psychiatric Association. (1994). *Diagnostic and statistical manual of mental disorders* (4th ed.). Washington, DC: Author.

Review of the Social Phobia and Anxiety Inventory by DELORES D. WALCOTT, Assistant Professor, Western Michigan University, Counseling and Testing Center, Kalamazoo, MI:

TEST DEVELOPMENT AND REVISION. The Social Phobia and Anxiety Inventory (SPAI) is a self-report inventory developed specifically to assess social phobia. The manual noted that the SPAI was developed to measure the severity of symptoms of social anxiety for adolescents and adults. The SPAI is intended to detect individuals who likely suffer from maladaptive social anxiety. The inventory is designed to assess the somatic, cognitive, and behavior symptoms of social phobia across a wide range of social situations and settings. It is made up of 45 statements to be rated on a 7-point Likert Scale.

MANUAL. The manual is impressive. I found it to be well organized and complete. It is divided into six chapters: Theoretical Rationale, Administration and Scoring, Interpretation, Case Studies, Scale Development and Psychometric Properties, and Concluding Comment. Each chapter contains enough information for a qualified user or reviewer of a test to evaluate the appropriateness and technical adequacy of the test.

USER QUALIFICATIONS, ADMINISTRATION, AND SCORING. User qualifications, administration, and scoring are clearly described in the manual. One area of concern pertains to using the SPAI Multi-Health Systems QuikScore™ form. This form contains scoring aids that were designed to make scoring rapid, while eliminating the potential for key error. Responses are transferred through to underlying pages where the administrator can follow steps for scoring. However, if the client fails to press hard and/or tries to erase a response after being told not to do so the scoring will become smudged and difficult to read. Other difficulties with the QuikScore™ form that may be problematic were the size of the font, the color of paper, and limited space between words and lines. These concerns can affect ease of reading, particularly for the visual challenged individual and many readers with minor visual impairments. Similarly, if the consumer separates the QuikScore™ form prematurely and attempts to place the form in correct order this can lead to a disaster.

SCALES AND NORMS. The SPAI is made up of 45 items, 32 items comprising a Social Phobia subscale and 13 items comprising an Agoraphobia subscale. Each item is rated on a 7-point Likert scale according to how frequently it is experienced. A confirmatory factor analysis was conducted with two separate samples using principal components analysis with varimax rotations. Factor analysis supports the division of the two subscale, SP and Ag.

Normative data were collected from the subjects ($n = 306$) who made up the samples in the reliability studies. The number of known ethnic minorities in the normative sample is extremely small. The number of minorities used in the normative sample is so small that to use this scale with minorities without some precaution would be unethical. Evidence is needed in order to judge whether the Social Phobia and Anxiety Inventory would yield different predictions among different minorities groups.

RELIABILITY. One-hundred eighty-two subjects participated in the test-retest study, 123 non-socially anxious and 59 socially anxious. Fifty-six of the 59 subjects designated as socially anxious were interviewed with the Anxiety Disorder Interview Schedule. Twenty-six percent of those interviewed were audiotaped and an interjudge reliability kappa of .81 was obtained. The 2-week test-retest reliability for total score was .86, was .85 for the SP subscale, and was .74 for the Ag subscale. In a study conducted by Herbert, Bellack, and Hope (1991), the SPAI was positively correlated with seven out of eight measures of social anxiety. Furthermore, the SPAI was positively correlated with subjective reports of anxiety. The SPAI has high test reliability estimates and reportedly good discriminative ability among patient groups and adequate evidence of concurrent and external validity. The SPAI was empirically derived and refined based upon its ability to differentiate between criterion groups of patients and nonclinical samples. Thus, it may lack acceptable external validity in that elevated subscale scores among nonpatient respondents cannot be assumed to reflect the same psychopathic patterns inferred to the patient group.

VALIDITY. There is a large body of research literature attesting to its score validity in a variety of contexts. The manual reported on several forms of validity studies: discriminant, external, concurrent, predictive, and convergent. Each type provided information on how well the SPAI measures the construct of interest. Likewise, the SPAI was cross-validated against other self-reports with both college students and treatment-seeking samples.

SUMMARY. I recommend the SPAI as an excellent test for assessing social phobia. The data reviewed in the manual demonstrated the reliability and validity properties of the SPAI. The discriminative ability of the SPAI in differentiating individuals with social phobia from other nonpatient and patient groups who also report symptoms of social anxiety is also noteworthy. Although the SPAI is available as a clinical tool and as a screening instrument, several cautions must be emphasized. It is a known fact that self-reporting is vulnerable to underreporting, distortions due to response style bias, inaccurate reporting, defensiveness, and denial. This is true with most self-reporting measures. Therefore, test users should proceed with caution when they are interpreting tests results. Although self-reports have clear limitations, they have some validity related to standardization and economics, and do not require a trained interviewer. Previous studies failed to address adequately the question of differential performance. Future studies on the SPAI or continued use of the SPAI should afford the opportunity to check for group differences and investigate whether or not these differences indicate test bias.

In closing, the original work with the SPAI focused on assessing adults. A child version, the SPAI-C, has recently been developed (Beidel, Turner, & Morris, 1995).

REVIEWER'S REFERENCES

Herbert, J. D., Bellack, A. S., & Hope, D. A. (1991). Concurrent validity of the Social Phobia and Anxiety Inventory. *Journal of Psychopathology and Behavioral Assessment, 13*, 357–368.

Beidel, D. C., Turner, S. A., & Morris, T. L. (1995). A new inventory to assess childhood social anxiety and phobia: The Social Phobia and Anxiety Inventory for Children. *Psychological Assessment, 7*, 73–79.

[364]
Spadafore Attention Deficit Hyperactivity Disorder Rating Scale.

Purpose: Designed "to examine the wide range of behaviors that are frequently associated with ADHD symptoms."

Population: Ages 5–19.

Publication Date: 1997.

Acronym: S-ADHD-RS.

Scores, 4: Impulsivity/Hyperactivity, Attention, Social Adjustment, ADHD Index.

Administration: Individual.

Price Data, 2001: $65 per test kit including 25 scoring protocols, 25 observation forms, 25 medication tracking forms, and manual (80 pages); $20 per 25 scoring protocols; $10 per 25 observation forms; $10 per 25 medication tracking forms; $22 per manual.

Time: Untimed.

Comments: Rating scale to be completed by classroom teachers about a child; also included in kit: behavioral observation form and medication monitoring form.

Authors: Gerald J. Spadafore and Sharon J. Spadafore.

Publisher: Academic Therapy Publications, Inc.

Review of the Spadafore Attention Deficit Hyperactivity Disorder Rating Scale by SCOTT T. MEIER, Associate Professor and Director of Training, Department of Counseling and Educational Psychology, SUNY Buffalo, Buffalo, NY:

Spadafore and Spadafore developed the Spadafore Attention Deficit Hyperactivity Disorder Rating Scale (S-ADHD-RS) to assist in quantifying the degree of severity of symptoms exhibited by children ages 6–19 suspected of possessing Attention Deficit Hyperactivity Disorder (ADHD). Using normative data classified by age and gender, the S-ADHD-RS helps to identify students whose ADHD interferes with their classroom performance. The S-ADHD-RS consists of two parts: a 50-item Behavior Rating Scale (BRS) and a 9-item ADHD Index.

Raters first complete the BRS. BRS scores are provided for 3 factors: Impulsivity/Hyperactivity (Factor I, composed of 20 items), Attention (Factor II, 22 items), and Social Adjustment (Factor III, 8 items). Using a 5-point Likert scale, raters complete such items as "Finds it difficult to pay attention," "Restless—always fidgeting," and "Anxious." It should be noted that classroom teachers are the preferred raters for both components of the S-ADHD-RS. The test manual recommends that teachers possess at least 5 weeks of interaction with ADHD students to be able to provide valid ratings. Teachers provide a summary rating of a child's behavior as opposed to ratings of a student in a particular occasion or class.

Completion of the 9-item ADHD Index follows BRS ratings. The ADHD Index requires 1-item ratings, on a 3-point scale, about the student's attention, hyperactivity, impulsivity, so-

cial skills, academics, noncompliance, self-concept, on-task performance during an academic
assignment, and a quantified evaluation of ADHD
symptoms (e.g., BRS factor scores for Impulsivity/
Hyperactivity or Attention). The noncompliant
item, for example, asks the rater to assess the
student's "Disregard for rules—defiant with peers
and teachers—disruptive and hard to manage" on
one of three response categories: (a) easy to manage and follows class rules, (b) at times shows signs
of misbehaving in class, or (c) ignores rules and is
difficult to control in class. The on-task performance rating may be completed with an included
ADHD Observation Form intended for observing
and recording the classroom performance of the
referred student and a comparison student. The
Form requires about 10 minutes and produces
scores in five categories (i.e., talk outs, out-of-seat,
physical response, passive, and acceptable behavior). The authors note that data about Index items
may be obtained from more than one person (e.g.,
multiple teachers familiar with the student).

As with the BRS Factor scores, the Index
items are summed and converted to a percentile
score based on age- and gender-based norms. A
Severity Scale provided with the S-ADHD-RS
then assists in interpretation of the Index and 3
BRS factor scores. The scale divides the quantitative scores into categories of severe, moderate,
mild, and not significant. The authors suggest that
Index scores with a percentile exceeding 90% (i.e.,
Moderate on the Severity Scale) should be regarded as indicative of ADHD and likely to require a formal intervention. No data are provided
supporting the use of the 90% percentile as a
threshold for ADHD. Spadafore and Spadafore
do note that test scores should be used in conjunction with clinical judgment before concluding that
an ADHD diagnosis is warranted.

The standardization procedure included administering items to 760 students ages 5–19 in 17
randomly selected states and 37 school districts.
Nearly equally split between boys (54%) and girls
(46%), students were predominantly White (78%,
compared to 14% African American), in regular
education classes (75%, compared to 13% in Special Education, 10% in Chapter 1, and 1% in
ADHD), in cities or suburbs above 20,000 persons (50%, compared to 38% rural), and had
fathers in white collar (36%), blue collar (34%),
and labor (25%) occupations. No data were pro-

vided about the number or characteristics of teachers who agreed or declined to participate in the
standardization study.

The BRS items were created by a review of
other ADHD instruments and then presented to
school psychologists, special education teachers,
administrators, and classroom teachers for review.
A factor analysis presumably conducted with the
standardization sample revealed 3 factors with
eigenvalues of 2 or greater that accounted for 73%
of the total variance. A similar procedure was
followed with ADHD Index items. The manual
provides means and standard deviations for each
factor and ADHD Index items grouped by age
and gender.

The manual also reports a pilot test of 50
previously identified ADHD students and 50 non-
ADHD students. The ADHD Index correctly
identified all 50 ADHD students and incorrectly
identified only 2 non-ADHD students as ADHD.
A second study of 185 students found comparable
hit rates. Test retest reliability for 92 students
with intervals of 2 weeks to 1 month found high
estimates for the ADHD Index (.88), Factor I
(.89), Factor II (.90), and Social Adjustment (.88).
Interrater reliability estimates for a sample of 17
students were lower: ADHD Index (.66), Factor I
(.87), Factor II (.74), and Social Adjustment (.64).

Spadafore and Spadafore indicate that the
ADHD Index is intended to provide a more
comprehensive picture of relevant symptoms. They
contrast the Index with use of Conners' (1990) 10
hyperactivity questions alone as diagnostic of
ADHD. Although they note that the Conners
approach has research support, Spadafore and
Spadafore provide no empirical evidence for their
use of content additional to hyperactivity. In contrast, the authors contend that BRS Factor I
(Hyperactivity/Impulsivity) or II (Attention) scores
may be employed as a screening tool for ADHD.
That is, if either Factor I or II scores fall below the
90th percentile, Spadafore and Spadafore indicate
the examiner may cease the assessment and conclude that ADHD is not a likely diagnosis. Scores
above the 90th percentile indicate that the assessment should continue with the ADHD Index.

Accompanying materials include the Medication Monitoring Form. The Form asks the rater
to evaluate ADHD symptoms, social interactions,
academic performance, classroom behavior, and
observable medication side effects. The authors

note the paradox that ADHD is diagnosed only by observation and rating scales, yet the treatment of choice is medication.

SUMMARY. Given the promising results of research examining the S-ADHD-RS's ability to discriminate ADHD students from others, this instrument would seem a useful complement to the more categorical approach of diagnosing ADHD as employed in the *DSM-IV* (American Psychiatric Association, 1994). Future research should address whether the comprehensive picture given by the S-ADHD-RS provides incremental validity in comparison to the DSM, other rating scales, and performance measures employed to diagnose students in this controversial domain (cf. Barkley, 1990; Fischer, Newby, & Gordon, 1995; Matier-Sharma, Perachio, Newcorn, & Sharma, 1995).

REVIEWER'S REFERENCES

Barkley, R. A. (1990). *Attention deficit-hyperactivity disorder: A handbook for diagnosis and treatment.* New York: Guilford.

Conners, C. K. (1990). *Conners' Rating Scales manual.* North Tonawanda, NY: Multi-Health Systems.

American Psychiatric Association. (1994). *Diagnostic and statistical manual of mental disorders* (4th ed.). Washington, DC: Author.

Fischer, M., Newby, R. F., & Gordon, M. (1995). Who are the false negatives on continuous performance tests? *Journal of Clinical Child Psychology, 24,* 427–433.

Matier-Sharma, K., Perachio, N., Newcorn, J. H., & Sharma, V. (1995). Differential diagnosis of ADHD: Are objective measures of attention, impulsivity, and activity level helpful? *Child Neuropsychology, 1,* 118–127.

Review of the Spadafore Attention Deficit Hyperactivity Disorder Rating Scale by JUDY OEHLER-STINNETT, Associate Professor, School of Applied Health and Educational Psychology, Oklahoma State University, Stillwater, OK:

The Spadafore Attention Deficit Hyperactivity Disorder Rating Scale (S-ADHD-RS) was developed to provide a quick procedure for identifying children with ADHD in schools. It includes a rating scale, an ADHD Index, an observation form, and a medication monitoring form. The authors surveyed other tests and professionals to determine items for the rating scale. For the ADHD Index, they also surveyed those who work with children with ADHD and the ADHD literature. However, for the 50-item rating scale, items are related to hyperactivity, impulsivity, attention, and some related social concerns. For the nine-item Index, there is one item each for attention, hyperactivity, impulsivity, social skills, academics, noncompliance, self-concept, the results of a 10-minute systematic observation, and results for the rating scale. This Index was developed so that a single means could be used for screening that would incorporate a wide range of ADHD symp-

toms with only one observation per area. As a result, a total percentile score is obtained for the Index, rather than a comprehensive interpretation of each area of concern.

The Medication Monitoring Scale contains ratings for behaviors organized differently than either the rating scale or the Index, making it difficult to use each of the measures for the pre-test-posttest intervention designs for which they were intended. Additionally, the introduction in the manual is exceptionally editorialized with few references to substantiate the authors' claims. The authors also contradict themselves, saying at one point that medication is overused and admonishing readers to conduct nonmedical interventions; then they say that medication therapy is effective and offer a protocol for medication monitoring only, rather than intervention monitoring.

Development of the rating scale did include some psychometric considerations. The 50 items were factor-analyzed, and three factors were retained. However, significant overlap is revealed in the factor loadings of items across factors. Therefore, the resulting subscales do not reflect distinct factors. In addition to overlap among impulsivity, hyperactivity, and attention, items for oppositional behavior, academic performance and attitude, and conduct problems are scattered throughout the Impulsivity/Hyperactivity and Attention factors. The Social Adjustment factor, which has only eight items, contains six items that load at least .30 on other factors. Items on this subscale also include depression, mood swings, and temper problems rather than simple social adjustment. Items such as "mean to other students," loads .57 on this factor but is included on Hyperactivity/Impulsivity.

The rating scale is described as being useful for children and adolescents ages 5–19. However, the norms include only 760 children, a very small sample for such a broad age range. Efforts were made to stratify the sample nationally. Norm tables are provided separately for gender and no general norms are reported. As the authors note, more boys exhibit ADHD symptoms. Utilizing separate norms makes it more likely that boys will be underidentified relative to the general population, and girls will be overidentified. For example, a girl age 5–7 who receives a raw score of 61 will be rated as significantly different from average; for a boy the same age to obtain a significantly different interpretation, he would have to obtain a raw score of 78. Only percentiles are reported rather than a standard score such as a *T*-score. Probably due to the difficulties of percentiles, some of the scores are extrapolated. Scoring is thus problematic, particularly in the upper ranges where discriminations need to be made. For example, for girls 5–7, a raw score anywhere from 65–100 (a third of the raw score range) yields the same percentile rank of 99!

Although the authors indicate the importance of using multimethods in other parts of the manual, in the interpretation section they give specific instructions utilizing percentile cutoffs for diagnosis of Severe (those they would assign an ADHD label), Moderate (those who need a formal treatment program but should not be labeled), Mild (require assistance from time to time), and Not Significant (teacher should be able to regulate behavior).

Test-retest and interrater reliability information are provided. Using a test-retest interval of 2 weeks to 1 month, coefficients ranging from .88 to .90 were obtained for 92 students. Although correlations in the .90s are preferable, these results do not preclude use of the test. Interrater reliability estimates were obtained for only 17 students, with results ranging from .64 to .87. The Hyperactivity/Impulsivity and Attention factors are the most reliable. No internal consistency data are reported other than factor loadings, which are discussed above. No standard error of measurement is reported. A quick calculation of the *SEM* for boys ages 8–10 on rating scale Factor 1 yields a mean of 54.2, a standard deviation of 23.9, and an *SEM* of 7.9. Overall, reliability data do not support that this scale can consistently diagnosis and measure treatment effects for ADHD.

The factor analysis is cited as support for the construct validity of the test; however, due to overlapping factor loadings, this support is weak. A study is reported in which the rating scale and the Index discriminated between generally diagnosed ADHD students and non-ADHD. Distinction of ADHD from other clinical groups is not reported. Validity of treatment effects for medication or other interventions is not reported for the rating scale, the Index of the Medication Monitoring Form.

SUMMARY. The inclusion of possible side effects on the medication monitoring form is an advantage of this test. Overall, however, this scale offers no advantages over currently available broadband behavior rating scales and those specific to

ADHD, such as the Behavior Assessment System for Children (40) and the Conners' Rating Scales—Revised (98). It may be useful to a clinician who is not trained in multidisciplinary multitrait/multimethod assessment and intervention. However, due to psychometric limitations, this use in the hands of a less knowledgeable person is not recommended.

[365]
SPAR Spelling and Reading Tests, Third Edition.

Purpose: Designed as a "group test of literacy."
Population: Ages 7-0 to 12-11 years.
Publication Dates: 1976–1998.
Acronym: SPAR.
Scores, 2: Reading Total Score, Spelling Total Score.
Administration: Group.
Parts, 2: Reading Test, Spelling Test.
Price Data, 1999: £5.99 per 20 For A or Form B; £8.99 per manual ('76, 32 pages) including photocopiable version of spelling test; £4.99 per scoring template (A or B); £9.99 per specimen set including 1 copy each of Test Forms A and B, and manual.
Time: 13 minutes for Spelling Test; (20–25) minutes for Reading Test.
Comments: Reading Test is available in parallel Forms (A and B); Spelling Test is created from three parallel banks of items found in the manual.
Author: Dennis Young.
Publisher: Hodder & Stoughton Educational [England].
Cross References: See T5:2467 (1 reference); for reviews by Cleborne D. Maddux and William R. Merz of the second edition, see 12:365 (2 references); see also T4:2520 (3 references); for reviews by J. Douglas Ayers of earlier editions of the Spelling Test and the Reading Test, see 8:76 and 8:742.

Review of the SPAR Spelling and Reading Tests, Third Edition by TIMOTHY Z. KEITH, Arthur L. & Lea R. Powell Professor of Psychology & Schooling, Alfred University, Alfred, NY:

The SPAR Spelling and Reading tests is a short, group-administered test of basic reading and spelling achievement for students in Year 3 (ages 7–8 years) in the United Kingdom. According to the author, it may also be used with older students with a suspected reading age of less than 9 years.

The SPAR is designed to be administered by teachers in a normal classroom setting; it takes about 20 minutes to set up and administer. The

Reading test includes 15 reading recognition items in which children choose one of four words that correspond to a picture, followed by 30 sentences in which children choose one of six words that complete the sentence. The later sentences are definitions (e.g., Rapid means _____). There are two forms of the Reading Test. The Spelling test follows a traditional format in which the word is read aloud by the examiner, used in a sentence, and repeated. There are three sets, or banks, of 40 words, and examiners are encouraged to mix and match words from different banks (e.g., Items 1 and 2 from Bank 1, Items 3 and 4 from Bank 3, and so on). Both tests are designed to increase in difficulty as the items progress. The Reading test has a scoring ceiling of 10 errors, even though in a group administration children would presumably attempt all items. The manual discusses several possible ceiling rules for the Spelling test, but the choice of whether to use any of them is apparently left to the examiner. Raw scores may be converted to age "quotients" (standard scores, $M = 100$, $SD = 15$), with separate tables for children ages 7-0 to 8-11 and those 9-0 to 12-11), or to age-equivalent scores.

The SPAR materials include a 32-page Teacher's Manual and answer sheets for Forms A and B of the reading test. Teachers are encouraged to provide numbered papers to children to complete the Spelling test.

Although the manual includes sections on construction and standardization, reliability, and validity, the discussion is quite general, with few details. The SPAR was standardized on an undefined group of 1,861 children ages 7-8 to 8-10 and 1,045 children ages 11-2 to 14-3 from "schools thought to be representative, as a group, of national [England and Wales] standards" (p. 27). Several supplemental procedures were used to extrapolate the norms beyond these ages. The manual reports a test/retest, alternate forms reliability estimate of .95, apparently for the reading test, with an unknown, but apparently short, time period. The manual also reports a reliability estimate of .94 for "randomly-chosen" spelling tests, but details are lacking. The section on validity rests primarily on verbal persuasion.

SUMMARY. The SPAR is a short, group-administered measure of reading and spelling achievement. The SPAR could provide useful information for teachers in the UK, but it is difficult to evaluate this possibility. More detail is needed concerning the development of the test and its items, the methods used to order items in the test, and rules and justification for discontinuation. A careful and explicit standardization is needed, across a wider age and grade range, and should be described in more detail. The technical quality of the scale needs to be assessed and described in detail. Without this additional information, the use of the SPAR should be limited to that of an informal assessment of UK Year 3 students' reading and spelling skills.

Review of the SPAR Spelling and Reading Tests, Third Edition by BRENDA A. STEVENS, School Psychologist, Indian Hill Exempted Village School District, Cincinnati, OH:

The SPAR Spelling and Reading Tests, Third Edition was created in England to assess the basic literacy skills of children from 7-0 to 12-11 years of age. It was designed to be a practical, efficient, cost effective, group-administered, norm-referenced measure. It was intended to be used with other short objective tests to provide "an overall view of attainments" and to "suggest what supplementary testing may be necessary" (manual, p. 4) for a student.

READING. The Reading test consists of two parts. The first part involves matching words and pictures. It contains 15 pictures with a list of four or five words printed next to each one. Using standardized directions for each item the student is asked to "put a ring around" the word that matches the picture. The second part uses a cloze format where the student is asked to complete a short sentence by choosing and circling the appropriate word from a selection of six words. The sentence completion format on the answer sheet seemed to be small and confusing especially for an instrument primarily designed for the developing younger reader. Unlike many reading inventories this instrument does not contain any reading comprehension passages because, as the manual explains, this test is "valid for children at earlier stages of reading development" (manual, p. 4).

No rules are given to help the examiner determine where students should start or end this Reading test. However, its total administration is expected to take 13 minutes. One overall Reading score is determined by counting and adding together the total number of correct word and sentence items. This score is then converted to a reading quotient and a reading age designed to help a teacher check impressions of abilities and to compare each student's performance to that of his or her age peers.

SPELLING. Each Spelling test consists of 40 words that are selected for the student by the examiner from a spelling bank of 120 words. Three-quarters of these words come from G. E. R. Burroughs's *A Study of the Vocabulary of Young Children* with other words coming from other sources. No answer sheets are provided for the Spelling test, and the test is administered in the traditional way: The examiner says the word, uses it in a sentence, and then says the word again.

MATERIALS. Test materials include a short manual that covers both the Reading and the Spelling tests and single-page answer sheets for the two alternate forms (Form A and Form B) of the Reading tests. The test manual devotes considerable attention to detailed descriptions of instructions for the administration, scoring, and interpretation of this test. Additionally, practical and specific ideas are provided about how to use test results for diagnostic and teaching purposes.

TECHNICAL CONSIDERATIONS. The information given about test construction and standardization is sparse. The tests were standardized in 1984–1986 on schools in England that were "thought to be representative, as a group, of national rather than local standards" (manual, p. 27). However, the criteria used to choose these schools and the information used to arrive at this conclusion were not supplied. The same population of almost 3,000 children was used as the standardization sample for both the Reading and Spelling tests. This sample of children ranged from 7-9 to 14-3 years of age. A smaller supplementary sample of children aged 6-8 to 7-10 was also used to make this instrument suitable for a younger population and to extend the Reading scores downward to age 7-0.

RELIABILITY. Test-retest reliability was calculated for 297 children using "a different form after a lapse of some days" (manual, p. 30). Under these conditions the correlation between scores was .95; this is an appropriate reliability coefficient for a standardized achievement test. Reliability was also estimated specifically for the Spelling test by looking at the "equivalence of randomly-chosen tests" (manual, p. 30). This refers to the different tests that can result when the 40 spelling words are selected by the examiner

from the Parallel Spelling Test bank. This technique produced a .94 coefficient of reliability.

VALIDITY. In presenting the case for content validity, the author indicates that reading is developmental and therefore defined differently depending upon the age of the reader. This test was designed to mirror the skills needed for the development of reading. It looks at skills from simple "single word reading (by means of picture-word matching)" (manual, p. 28) to knowledge of word meaning (comprehension). Support that scores from the graded word spelling test are valid is also made by claiming that its content includes a series of progressively more difficult tasks.

SUMMARY. The SPAR Spelling and Reading Tests are simple, quick, and economical assessments that could "ballpark" a child's beginning skills in the areas of reading and spelling. Strictly speaking, it is not standardized. The directions given during administration can vary. However, although it does have norms, characteristics of the standardization sample are not given. This instrument makes the attempt to be domain, criterion, and norm referenced but lacks convincing documentation to be any of these. Without strong evidence for its reliability and validity, this instrument should at best be used for screening or as a support for a teacher's initial impressions of a child's developing reading abilities.

[366]
Standardized Reading Inventory, Second Edition.

Purpose: "Designed primarily to assess children's independent, instructional, and frustration reading levels in word recognition and comprehension skills."
Population: Ages 6-0 to 14-6.
Publication Dates: 1986–1999.
Acronym: SCR-2.
Scores, 4: Passage, Comprehension, Word Accuracy, Vocabulary in Context, Reading Quotient.
Administration: Individual.
Forms, 2: A, B.
Price Data, 2001: $224 per complete kit including manual ('99, 134 pages), story book, 25 each Forms A and B vocabulary sheets, 25 each Forms A and B record booklets, and 50 profile scoring forms; $13 per 25 vocabulary sheets (specify form); $49 per 25 record booklets (specify form); $21 per 50 profile scoring forms; $36 per story book; $47 per examiner's manual.
Time: (30–90) minutes.
Comments: Second Edition is norm-referenced.
Author: Phyllis L. Newcomer.

Publisher: PRO-ED.
Cross References: For reviews by Kenneth W. Howell and Cleborne D. Maddux of the original edition, see 10:340.

Review of the Standardized Reading Inventory, Second Edition by ALAN SOLOMON, Research Associate, The School District of Philadelphia, Philadelphia, PA:

The Standardized Reading Inventory (SRI) is made up of five components: (a) Words In Isolation Checklist, (b) Passage Comprehension, (c) Word Recognition Accuracy, (d) Vocabulary in Context, and (e) Predictive Comprehension. According to the author, the SRI is designed to function as an informal reading inventory without its liabilities. These liabilities refer to the development of individual reading inventories by classroom teachers. Supposedly, classroom teachers have difficulty in finding appropriate reading passages.

There are two forms of the SRI with each including 10 reading passages. These passages range in reading level from preprimer to eighth grade. The first edition of the SRI was a criterion-referenced instrument. Norms were developed for the second edition and the author claims that this addition expands the test's diagnostic value. Because percentile ranks demonstrate status rather than knowledge, their use for this purpose is questionable.

Normative data were collected from 1,099 students who ranged in age from 6 to 14. The number of students at each age ranged from 60 to 197. These numbers may be sufficient for piloting the SRI in order to recognize and eliminate any problems linked to administration but are far below the numbers necessary for meaningful norming.

Eleven percent of the norm group students were categorized as disabled and the author should be recognized for including these individuals. Nationwide, the figure is 15%. However, the range of these disabilities varies tremendously and precluded a meaningful analysis.

The author computed three types of reliability estimates for the SRI—content sampling, time sampling (about 2 weeks), and interscorer differences. Reliability was high in the three categories but the number of scores used for time sampling and interscorer reliability was low, 30 third graders for time sampling and 30 tests for interscorer reliability.

The author examined content description, criterion prediction, and construct identification validity for scores from the SRI. She also studies the SRI's relationship to intelligence, group differentiation, interrelationships between the subtests, and item validity. For the most part, the author's work in this area was exceptional and should be used as a model for others. However, reporting the results of student performance on a norm-referenced-standardized achievement test and an earlier version of the SRI does not provide useful information.

SUMMARY. The SRI provides teachers with a useful assessment procedure in terms of presenting a series of passages designed to assess a student's reading ability efficiently. The procedures used to examine validity demonstrate this point. However, most teachers can construct, administer, and score meaningful informal reading inventories on their own. Therefore, there may not be a need to standardize this assessment procedure unless a school administrator dictates their use in a building or a district. It would be interesting to compare student performance on the SRI and an individual teacher's informal reading inventory.

Review of the Standardized Reading Inventory, Second Edition by BRENDA A. STEVENS, School Psychologist, Indian Hill Exempted Village School District, Cincinnati, OH:

The Standardized Reading Inventory, Second Edition (SRI-2) is somewhat unique among reading inventories, as it is generally an individually administered norm-referenced and criterion-referenced test. This allows a child's reading skill to be compared to his or her peers as well as to specific grade level material. Its format and administration are similar to that of many individually administered informal reading inventories as it assesses reading using word recognition and passage comprehension techniques. The SRI-2 has two forms (Form A and Form B), each one consisting of grade level word lists and reading passages. However, going beyond the first edition and the traditional reading inventory the second edition has added measures of vocabulary proficiency and predictive comprehension.

Designed much like a criterion-referenced reading measure, the original edition was standardized having specific administration procedures. Additionally, it used objective scoring criteria, guidelines for interpretation, and contained information about its reliability and validity. The second edition has added norms making it possible for a student's reading skills to be compared not only to specific criteria, but to his or her peers as well. The storybook and the profile/scoring form make the administration of this edition easier than before.

Students are asked to read words in isolation and passages of fictional text as well as to answer comprehension questions. Independent, instructional, and frustration levels for word recognition and comprehension are obtained. Reading performance is scored for word recognition and passage comprehension errors producing standard scores and percentile scores that can be converted to age and grade equivalents, and a reading quotient. The added supplemental vocabulary in context and predictive comprehension subtests may also be administered to help determine a student's ability to understand what they read.

MATERIALS. A revised and improved profile/scoring form allows other observational information having diagnostic value to be easily recorded. This includes different types of word recognition errors and irregularities (omissions, insertions, substitutions, reversals, repetitions, self-corrections, hesitations, and ignored punctuation), passage comprehension errors (factual, inferential, lexical, and predictive), and word attack skills. The manual is clearly written giving detailed administration procedures and scoring directions along with considerable technical information.

TECHNICAL CONSIDERATIONS. The SRI-2 was standardized using a sample of 1,099 children whose demographic characteristics were compared with 1997 census data. Even though overall there seems to be a good match, the norm group appears to be slightly overrepresented by white, middle income, northeasterners.

RELIABILITY. The test manual provides adequate support for internal consistency reliability using Cronbach's coefficient alpha; 80% of the alphas are at least .90. Test-retest reliability correlation coefficients are given for a small group ($n = 30$) of third grade on-level readers after 2 weeks. These coefficients range from .83 to .92 and are slightly better for Form B than for Form A. Data on alternate forms reliability for the same small group showed that all coefficients are above .80. A number of other studies also demonstrate adequate correlation coefficients for test-retest data, alternate forms, and consistent results for student reading level. Interscorer reliability results from more than one study show agreement ranging

from 90% to 97%. The content, time, and scorer reliability evidence presented for this edition indicates little overall test error and better documentation of the reliability of test results.

VALIDITY. The test manual presents considerable evidence for content, criterion, and construct validity. Evidence for content validity is presented in five ways by: (a) a description of the structure and content of the passages and comprehension questions, (b) a rationale and description of the development of the new subtests, (c) a description about the assignment of reading levels, (d) the results of item analysis procedures, and (e) a differential item functioning analysis.

The structure, organization, and complexity of text in the reading passages increase with each grade level. Each passage incorporates key words taken from and cited in at least two word lists from five popular basal reading series (Scott, Foresman Basics in Reading [1978], Houghton Mifflin Reading Series [1979], HBJ Bookmark Reading Program [1979], Macmillan Reading Series [1980], and Ginn Reading Series [1982]). The word list, comprehension passages, and questions used in this edition are the same as those used in the first edition 14 years ago.

Support for the assignment of reading levels appears to be adequate, as does the item analysis. However, the size of the dichotomous groups used to rule out bias is not given for the differential item functioning analysis. Moderate correlations between the reading test scores for small groups of students who have taken the SRI-2 and other reading tests are provided as evidence of criterion-prediction validity. Student test scores on the SRI-2 are correlated with the following tests: the reading section of the Stanford Achievement Test, the Reading Vocabulary subtest of the California Achievement Tests, Gray Oral Reading Tests—Third Edition Forms A & B, and the Grey Silent Reading Test.

Support for construct validity is given using correlation data by age for SRI-2 scores. Other support comes from the moderate correlation between the Otis-Lennon School Ability Test and SRI-2 scores. Additional strong support for construct validity is presented for using the SRI-2 to differentiate between capable and poor readers. The intercorrelations between the SRI-2 subtests and forms are also provided.

SUMMARY. Although the instrument remains fundamentally the same, the SRI-2 author has attempted to address and respond to a number of criticisms aimed at its first edition. Practically, the author has revised its format and clarified its administration procedures. As a criterion-referenced measure it now provides more information about a student's specific reading abilities, errors, vocabulary proficiency, and predictive comprehension skills. As a norm-referenced test it now provides a way to compare a student to his age and grade-level peers. In summary, this edition has taken a large step toward being a more frequently used and more valued reading inventory.

[367]
Stanford Writing Assessment Program, Third Edition.

Purpose: Provides for the direct assessment of written expression in four modes: Descriptive, Narrative, Expository, and Persuasive.
Population: Grades 3–12.
Publication Dates: 1982–1997.
Scores: 4 writing modes: Descriptive, Narrative, Expository, Persuasive.
Administration: Group.
Levels, 9: Primary 3, Intermediate 1, Intermediate 2, Intermediate 3, Advanced 1, Advanced 2, TASK 1, TASK 2, TASK 3.
Forms, 2: S, T (Form T is a secure form).
Price Data, 1999: $24 per 25 writing prompts, 25 response forms, and Directions for Administering (specify Descriptive, Narrative, Expository, or Persuasive); $7.50 per Directions for Administering (specify Descriptive, Narrative, Expository, or Persuasive); $9.75 per writing exam kit including 1 prompt each of Descriptive, Narrative, Expository and Persuasive, 1 Directions for Administering, 1 response form, and Reviewer's Edition; $61 per norms book; $19.25 per manual for interpreting ('97, 70 pages) (all forms and levels); scoring prices available from publisher.
Time: (50) minutes.
Comments: Holistic and analytic scoring available; computer scoring available; Form T is a secure form; Third edition provides information about student strengths and weaknesses, which can assist in instructional planning.
Authors: Harcourt Brace Educational Measurement—the educational testing division of The Psychological Corporation.
Publisher: Harcourt Brace Educational Measurement, a division of The Psychological Corporation.
Cross References: For reviews by Philip Nagy and Wayne H. Slater of an earlier edition, see 13:295.

Review of the Stanford Writing Assessment Program, Third Edition by LINDA CROCKER, Associate Dean, College of Education, University of Florida, Gainesville, FL:

The Stanford Writing Assessment Program is based upon a relatively conventional view that student writing assignments can be categorized into four modes: Descriptive, Narrative, Expository, or Persuasive. The assessment provides a series of pretested prompts, or topics, designed to elicit writing in these categories at each level. These prompts were developed with the intent of engaging students in a clearly specified writing task, administered under standardized conditions, that would be unambiguous, interesting, non-anxiety-producing, and scorable using a well-defined set of criteria.

The assessment is designed for administration in a 50-minute time period, allowing 40 minutes for writing and 10 minutes for activities such as planning the essay and final checking. Standardized features included instructions and topics that are read aloud by the administrator, an unscored page for making notes, four ruled pages for students to record their responses, a 10-minute warning so that students can begin their wrap-up and checking, and an editing checklist for use by the examinees to encourage proofreading of their written product. The editing checklist is read aloud to the examinees as part of the instructions. The instructions stress that this time period is not sufficient to obtain a polished product, but rather to gain a rough-draft response. Nevertheless, this time period may be a bit short to capture performance of students at upper grades who have been trained to spend considerable time in thinking and outlining before writing begins—or for those who tend to write much but then reorganize and edit their work.

As with any performance assessment, the critical part of the assessment lies in the scoring system or rubrics by which the examinee product is evaluated. The scoring scheme for the Stanford Writing Assessment provides for both holistic and analytic scoring. Holistic scoring is based on a 6-point scale. Two readings are recommended. The manual suggests that independent readers are ideal, but that the same reader may read on two separate occasions with a 2-day delay and masking the first score. The two scores are totaled yielding a possible score scale of 2–12 points. The general characteristics that comprise the holistic scoring features are organization, detailed clarification, attention to audience, and fluency.

Recognizing the developmental nature of writing, the scoring scheme is based on a concept of "Standards." There are four standards, each corresponding to a span of grade levels. For example, Standard I applies to Grade Levels 3.5–5.5 and the Primary 3, Intermediate level assessment; Standard II, to Grades 5.5–7.5 and the Intermediate 2,3 assessment; up to Standard IV from Grades 9.0–12.9 for the TASK 1,2,3. For each mode of writing there is a general description of characteristics of that form of writing. This is followed by some description of what writers at the level of a particular Standard typically generate. Finally, there is a separate scoring rubric for each Standard within each mode, providing a general description of the characteristics of a typical writing sample at each of the six score levels. Thus there are, for example, four holistic rubrics for descriptive writing—one for each Standard (or level).

Analytic scoring is intended to provide supplemental information about particular aspects of the student's writing. The scored features include ideas and development; word choice; organization, unity, and coherence; sentences and paragraphs; grammar and usage; and writing mechanics (e.g., punctuation, spelling, capitalization). Each feature is scored on a 4-point scale, using an analytic scoring rubric that provides a description of performance necessary to merit each level of performance. Again the concept of developmental Standards has been used to generate different rubrics for writers but only for three different levels.

Both holistic and analytic scoring services are available through the test publishing company. Nevertheless, the administration and interpretation manual provides information about the scoring process used at the assessment center that should enable local districts to obtain similar results by following the procedures described. The manual contains useful sections on dealing with unscorable papers, preparations for local scoring, use of anchor papers, steps in holistic and analytic scoring, and other scoring pointers. The manual also suggests that two raters scoring independently should be in agreement 75% of the time and within 1 point of agreement 95% of the time. An adjudication procedure is also suggested for instances when scores diverge by 2 or more points.

Scores available from the norms manual include scaled score, percentile rank, stanine, and NCE. The manual contains an excellent section explaining each type of score and demonstrating how to convert from raw score to equivalent scores on each score scale. The interpretation manual contains an illustrative group report, an individual student report, and a master list of results for group along with clear accompanying interpretations.

This standardized writing assessment program has been well assembled and empirically tested. Items and exercises were developed and reviewed by content experts, measurement experts, teachers, and a panel of minority educators. National item analysis tryouts provided for administration of each booklet to at least 500 students per grade level from 39 states (a total of 140,000 students). Approximately 250,000 students from more than 1,000 school districts participated in the national standardization study and an additional 80,000 in the form equating studies. For teachers, participation in administration and scoring of student exercises at the local level would be a powerful professional development experience in scoring writing assignments and in the instruction of these four writing modes.

Given the effort that has gone into assembling these exercises and supporting interpretive materials, it is disappointing that the materials on the Writing Assessment Program contained no information relating to interrater reliability, intrarater reliability, or estimates of variance components due to person x topic or person x mode effects from a generalizability study (e.g., Linn & Burton, 1994). Other forms of validity evidence commonly examined for writing assessments (e.g., Burger & Burger, 1994; Miller & Crocker, 1990; Roid, 1994) also were noteworthy in their absence.

SUMMARY. The exercises, norms, and supporting interpretive materials are useful, but potential users should be prepared to assemble additional validity and reliability information themselves for local samples before using these scores for important instructional decisions.

REVIEWER'S REFERENCES

Miller, M. D., & Crocker, L. (1990). Validation methods for direct writing assessment. *Applied Measurement in Education, 3,* 285–296.

Burger, S. E., & Burger, D. L. (1994). Determining the validity of performance-based assessment. *Educational Measurement: Issues & Practice, 13*(1), 9–15.

Linn, R. L., & Burton, E. (1994). Performance-based assessment: implications of task specificity. *Educational Measurement: Issues & Practice, 13*(1), 5–8, 15.

Roid, G. H. (1994). Patterns of writing skills derived from cluster analysis of direct-writing assessments. *Applied Measurement in Education, 7,* 159–170.

Review of the Stanford Writing Assessment Program, Third Edition by SHARON H. deFUR, Assistant Professor, School of Education, College of William and Mary, Williamsburg, VA:

The Third Edition of the Stanford Writing Assessment Program is a group-administered norm-referenced measurement of achievement for written expression, with norms for Grades 3–12 and one component of the Stanford 9 Tests of Achievement. Four types of writing may be assessed, holistically or analytically. This program offers a scoring service through Harcourt Brace Educational Measurement Center or a local scoring option with instructions for scoring.

This test was normed on 250,000 students across 1,000 school districts from 49 states and the District of Columbia. The sample was representative of the general school population across regions of the United States, socio-economic status, urbanicity, and ethnicity. Although the norming sample did include students with disabilities, the numbers of students included were not proportionate to the number of students identified within each disability area. Interestingly, there appeared to be a relative overrepresentation of students from nonpublic schools, particularly in the fall standardization sample (10.5% Catholic, 22.9% Private compared to 5.4% and 4.9%, respectively, in public school enrollment). Separate norms were developed for students who used a different response format than the response booklet.

Minimal technical data regarding reliability and validity were provided in the Multilevel Norms Manual or the Manual for Interpreting the Writing Assessment Program. A Technical Data Report was referenced that would presumably provide statistical analyses for these test evaluation elements. However, the test publishers detail the development of test content for all the Stanford 9 tests as an indication of the content and construct validity of test items. They describe the process as beginning with the identification of a national consensus curriculum through the analysis of major textbooks, state educational objectives, and the trends and directions in education according to major professional educational organizations. The test blueprints were then subjected to review by curriculum specialists and content experts. The publishers state that a national item analysis program determined the appropriateness of the item types and objectives, the difficulty and sensitivity of the items, the grade progression in difficulty, the effectiveness of the options, appropriate administration times, differential group performance on individual items, and the reactions of students

and teachers to the clarity, format, and content of the test materials (Stanford Multilevel Spring Norms Book, p. 9). All materials were reviewed by a panel of minority educators whose primary concern was to ensure that no bias or stereotyping existed within the items. One has to assume that the Writing Assessment Program was included in all stages of this detailed review, but no mention is made of it specifically in reference to these development steps.

The administration of the Stanford Writing Assessment Program is highly standardized with exact directions outlined for the administrator. It is intended to be group administered, although no group size minimum or maximum was named, so theoretically it could be individually administered as long as the standardized administration format was followed. Following a prompt (written and read orally), students are given 50 minutes to respond in writing. The prompt leads to one of four types of writing—descriptive, narrative, expository, or persuasive. It is not clearly defined how the decision is made as to which prompt to give, but one has to assume that this is a local school division assessment decision.

The uniqueness of the Stanford Writing Assessment Program as a group-administered norm-referenced test is twofold: one, writing samples can be evaluated either holistically or analytically or both, and two, there is an option of local scoring following the scoring rubrics provided in the Manual for Interpretation. The test publishers emphasize the developmental nature of writing and the need to recognize that the expectation for student writers should be one of "flawed excellence" and not perfection.

The option of adopting a holistic (focusing on overall quality of a student's writing) or analytical (examination of specific elements that contribute to writing achievement) evaluation offers test users a choice of report information based on the identified student or system diagnostic needs. The publishers describe a scoring process that promotes reliability of scores, either by assuring interrater reliability of two independent scorers (with a resolution scorer if scores are too discrepant) or assuring intrarater reliability of a single scorer who scores the same writing sample twice, with the first score masked (also using a resolution scorer if scores are inconsistent). Raw scores are converted to scaled scores; scaled scores can be converted to percentiles or stanines. This allows a comparison of performance of writing assessment test results to other Stanford academic test areas and a comparison to the normative population.

Although the manual provides rubrics for each of the writing types and scoring approaches, and even provides grade level standards to judge students at their developmental level, the local scoring option seems a bit formidable. There are "anchor papers" available that illustrate application of the scoring rubric that I think would be essential in establishing a local scoring program. Furthermore, written responses that have been scored through the Harcourt Brace Educational Measurement Center yield an assessment profile that offers detailed information about the student's performance. Theoretically, this same profile could be locally generated through the use of the Multi-level Norms Book, but there were no profile forms or report forms provided that would easily guide the local scorer through the completion of a similar assessment profile. Unfortunately, a quick cost benefit analysis might, in all probability, convince the local school division that centralized scoring might be more efficient. However, local scoring could serve a professional development purpose; the opportunity might be taken to instruct teachers in the use of rubrics for evaluating written work, as well as in establishing appropriate expectations for written expression for varying developmental levels.

SUMMARY. The Stanford Writing Assessment Program presents a thorough and convincing approach to the assessment of students' written expression achievement. Its extensive norm group offers a solid comparison base for grade level achievement and measuring student progress. The local scoring option is one that should benefit local districts, but the test publishers need to make the option more user friendly and offer more support through such avenues as inservice training, videos, samples, and scoring profile forms.

[368]
STAR Reading™.

Purpose: A computer-adaptive reading test and database designed "to quickly and accurately place students in books at the appropriate reading level."
Population: Grades 1–12.
Publication Dates: 1997–1998.
Scores: Total score only.
Administration: Individual.
Price Data, 1998: $1,499 per school license for up to 200 students, including administrator's manual (173 pages), 5 teacher's guides, norms/technical manual (94 pages), 1-year Expert Support Plan, and pre-test instruction kit; $399 per single-computer license, including administrator's manual, Quick Install card, 1-year Expert Support Plan, and pretest instruction kit.
Time: [10] minutes.
Comments: Provides grade equivalents, percentile scores, and instructional reading level; available for both Macintosh and IBM/Windows computers; can be repeated through school year to track growth at no extra cost.
Author: Advantage Learning Systems, Inc.
Publisher: Renaissance Learning, Inc.

Review of the STAR Reading by THERESA VOLPE-JOHNSTONE, Clinical and School Psychologist, Pleasanton, CA:

The STAR Reading is a computerized system developed to serve two purposes: (a) provide quick and accurate estimates of instructional reading levels (IRL), and (b) provide an estimate of students' reading levels compared to national norms. In doing so, this test purports to diagnose reading ability and help assess reading progress in 13 minutes or less with little administration effort. The test is dynamically scored using Item Response Theory through Adaptive Branching where the program weighs each answer provided by the student and presents the next question at an appropriate difficulty level. It is used primarily in the school setting and can yield valuable information at the teacher level in identifying children who need remediation/enrichment, at the principal level in obtaining class grade or year-to-year comparison, and at the district level for comparing data across schools, grades, or special student populations. The program may be installed on a Macintosh 68020 or an IBM-compatible 80386 with other provisions, such as space availability and installed memory. STAR Reading can be installed as a stand-alone program or placed on the network server (reviewer recommended) with a student capacity of 200 before necessitating the purchase of expansion codes in units of 50.

A sample size of 13,846 was used for pilot testing for content development and approximated the national school population well. Participation rates by grade were appropriate but ranged from 1,504 for Grade 8 to 573 for Grade 12. Item difficulty values provided an adequate basis for validating and norming the STAR Reading with sufficient variations in test scores. Normative data were subsequently based on a large sample (approximately 42,000), which was representative of the national population and balanced for demographics, SES, geographic region, and school type. In the development it is important to note that minority students typically scored lower than white grade peers with differences on the order of one-half to one standard deviation. This test should not be used with nonnative English speakers until English proficiency has been established. Special care was taken to minimize the influence of cultural factors including evaluating items for offensiveness. The normative data (percentile ranks and grade equivalents) are based on the unit-interval frequency distributions of the scaled scores of the students' first test. The data were weighted by demographic region and then by the type/size and SES of the school system. However, the tabled values indicated very minimal differences between weighted and unweighted scores.

In estimating reliability, measuring the internal-consistency of the STAR Reading was deemed inappropriate because it is a computer-adaptive test with many test forms. The authors chose test-retest estimation with alternative forms that were incorrectly stated as resulting in coefficients of stability and equivalence. This coefficient would be produced if there were relatively long periods of time separating administration. In this instance, "the median date of administration for the first test was April 25, 1996; the median date for the second test was April 30, 1996" (manual, p. 30), which suggests a coefficient of equivalence was obtained. This method was done to insure that no measurable growth in reading ability occurred between the two tests. Content-sampling would be a source of error, but given the method of content development, all individuals would be affected uniformly. Reliability estimates ranged from .85 to .95 for scaled scores, and from .79 to .91 for instructional reading levels (IRLs). Although there was consideration of practice effects, (a) the nature of adaptive branching would not allow for it, and (b) the retest scores were slightly lower than were the results of the first test, suggesting that practice was not an influencing factor. The standard errors of measurement (*SEM*) for the IRLs were impressive, with no more than a 1.1 grade level fluctuation due to chance across the grade span.

For the STAR Reading, it was sufficient to demonstrate content validity for the assessment of reading ability. The instrument appears to have strong content validity at least up to Grade 8. It was developed using 1995 updated vocabulary lists that were based on the Educational Development Laboratory's *A Revised Core Vocabulary* (1969), which the authors report is widely used in creating educational instruments. The STAR Reading correlated highly with at least three different, and common, reading tests spanning Grades 1 through 8. However, the coefficients were based on the STAR Reading versus older data by at least one year. There were too few comparisons with insufficient sample sizes to be considered as having established validity for Grades 9 through 12. The authors welcome additional data for validation purposes and continued supporting evidence is needed. The STAR Reading is prescriptive rather than predictive. It purports to measure growth based on external program implementation.

The STAR Reading makes use of instructional reading levels as a construct but validation was not conducted. It was simply defined as the "highest reading level at which the student can answer 80% or more of the items correctly" (manual, p. 45). Therefore, the STAR Reading does provide quick estimates of the IRLS but their accuracy may be questionable.

Administering the STAR Reading to replicate conditions used to demonstrate validity is a simple task. Directions come with easy-to-use transparencies for pretest instructions that can be taught to a class or one student at a time and can be administered up to five times per year. The STAR Reading comes with administrator, teacher, and pretest instruction guides that are all well-written, user-friendly manuals with excellent indices. This includes installing the program, setting up program preferences, working with lists of students, testing the students, and working with the various reports. The computer monitors the student progress item-by-item and guides the student toward completion without allowing frustration levels to be reached.

Results are reported through one, or all, of the program's 10 types of standard or customized reports for evaluating student test performance. Scores are delineated via the criterion-referenced Instructional Reading Level (IRL), and the norm-referenced Grade Equivalent (GE), Percentile Rank (PR), and Normal Curve Equivalent (NCE) scores.

Instructional Reading Levels indicate the reading level at which students can recognize words and understand instructional material with some assistance. The GE indicates the normal grade placement of students for whom a particular score is typical. Grade equivalents are not linear and therefore this is not an equal-interval scale. Caution should be taken in averaging GE scores across grades particularly when using the Summary Report. Percentile ranks show how an individual student's performance compares to same-grade peers. Normal Curve Equivalents act similarly to PRs but are based on an equal interval scale. The norm-referenced scores are based on the grade placement of the student at the time of the test. Therefore, it is crucial to use the correct grade placement values in order for the results to be accurate.

Two additional scores may be obtained: the Zone of Proximal Development (ZPD) and Diagnostic Codes, both derived from GEs. The ZPD defines the reading range from which students should be selecting books to achieve optimal reading growth without experiencing frustration. The Diagnostic Code ranges from 01 to 09 (the higher the GE, the higher the diagnostic code) and represents behavioral characteristics of readers at particular stages of development. These codes were not statistically validated. Scaled scores are available only on the Test Record Report, which generates results of every test taken during a specified time period for the student selected. Scaled scores range from 50 to 1,350 and are based on a Bayesian statistical model. Although scaled scores allow comparability among tests and were used to obtain PRs and NCEs, these scores were not clearly explained and are not easily interpreted.

Several assets were built into the STAR Reading. Each time the student takes a test, the program automatically begins just below the last tested reading level. The number of items presented reduces each time the student tests. Therefore, the STAR Reading does assess reading progress in 13 minutes or less. Teachers can group or sort students in characteristic ways. The program can be used in conjunction with, and may have been developed for, the Accelerated Reader™ to help match the right books for an individual's reading level. Program safeguards prevent unauthorized access to test content by program encryption, password protection, access levels, keydisk requirement, and test monitoring. The norming sample was of more than adequate size, and was sufficiently representative to establish appropriate norms and to provide evidence of students' reading ability from Grades 1 through 8.

SUMMARY. It seems that the STAR Reading was specifically developed to work well with Accelerated Reader. This is a shortcoming. If this program were not part of the curriculum, another type of organized reading program would need to be in place for this test to be useful. The results of the tests are based on grade placement and the ensuing reports are boilerplate—based on standard score and sequencing paradigms for the field of reading education that may not fit the profile of a student. Insufficient validity evidence is presented for 9th through 12th grades or for IRLs. This test has great potential but continued validation studies to support conclusions regarding the use of the STAR Reading for its entire intended purpose is needed.

Review of the STAR Reading by SANDRA WARD, Associate Professor of Education, The College of William and Mary, Williamsburg, VA:

The STAR Reading is an individually administered, computerized test of reading for Grades 1–12. The publishers state two main purposes of the STAR Reading: (a) to provide instructional reading levels, and (b) to compare reading levels to national norms. The test is not intended for use in promotion/placement decisions. The average completion time for the test is 7–8 minutes with an average of 30 items per administration. The computer input necessary for test completion is limited to four numeric keys, so necessary computer skills are minimized for examinees.

The items of the STAR Reading represent a vocabulary-in-context format that is similar to a cloze technique. Each item consists of a sentence with a missing word. The examinee must select the correct response for the missing word from three or four choices, within a 60- or 45-second time limit, depending on grade level. The correct response fits both the semantics and syntax of the sentence. Although the item format was chosen because success depends on comprehension of reading material, there is some concern regarding the artificial nature of the task. The presentation of only one sentence may not provide sufficient context for the reader. It appears that this instrument represents a measure of vocabulary development as well as reading comprehension.

In addition to careful writing, reviewing, and editing of items, an extensive item validation study included 13,846 students who were tested on a pool of 1,330 items. Although this sample matched national percentages for socioeconomic status and school type and enrollment, it was not representative for geographic region. The editing process included review of all items for possible gender and/or ethnic group bias; however, no statistical procedures were implemented. Final item selection was based on analyses of increased performance across grade levels, discrimination ability, reduced variability in item difficulty, and average response latency. The final selection resulted in a large item pool from which test items are selected. Consequently, the repetition of items in multiple administrations is minimized. A major advantage of the STAR Reading computer administration is the adaptive testing component. The program administers items of varying difficulty based on the students' responses, until a sufficient amount of data is gathered to obtain a reliable scaled score and indication of instructional level.

The STAR Reading was normed on 42,000 students from 171 schools. Sample sizes ranged from 326 in Grade 12 to 5,977 in Grade 5. The size of this sample is sufficient at every grade level. The variables controlled for in the standardization included geographic region, school system type, school system size, and socioeconomic status. The whole sample closely matched national characteristics on these variables; however, the representativeness at each grade level is not reported. Although school system location and instructional expenditures were not controlled for, the data on these variables closely matched national averages. With respect to ethnicity, only Hispanic students were underrepresented. The publishers noted that minority groups showed an average score between 1/2 to 1 standard deviation below the mean, which is consistent with other standardized tests of ability and achievement. The normative data for the test consist of percentile ranks and grade equivalents. Although scaled scores are discussed, the mean and standard deviation are not provided.

Average test-retest reliabilities are adequate for screening purposes and ranged from .79 to .91 with an average of 5 days between administrations. The publishers correctly acknowledge that the computer-adaptive testing restricts the methods for determining internal consistency reliability.

However, the publishers do not adequately explain how they determined item functioning in relation to item response theory. Although *SEM* estimates are provided, these are difficult to interpret because the standard score scale is not explained.

Data are provided to support concurrent and construct validity of test scores. Scores from the STAR Reading correlate sufficiently (.60 or higher) with scores from widely used standardized tests of reading ability across grade levels. Support for content validity is demonstrated through the purposeful approach in developing the instrument. Furthermore, STAR Reading scores increase with grade level, as would be expected for reading ability. It should be noted that the content validity is for a single item type that is highly dependent on vocabulary knowledge as well as reading comprehension. No evidence is presented for predictive validity; however, the publishers openly state that this test should not be used for placement or promotion decisions.

A proprietary Bayesian statistical model was used to convert scores to a common scale. Because the parameters and methodology of this model are not disclosed, it cannot be fully evaluated. Although scaled scores were reported to range from 50 to 1,350, no mean or standard deviation was reported. The norm-referenced score emphasized for interpretation is the grade equivalent. The publishers do an excellent job explaining the interpretation and pitfalls of grade equivalents. It is possible to convert scores to percentile ranks and normal curve equivalents. The instructional reading level is computed based on the level at which the examinee earned 80% proficiency. The program produces a Zone of Proximal Development score that is the readability level range from which students should select books to achieve optimally without frustration.

The Test Administrator's Manual and the Teacher's Guide are written in a straightforward and step-by-step manner. They assume minimal computer expertise and are very user-friendly. These manuals include information on program installation and a tutorial. Additionally, basic set-up, testing, and reporting procedures are outlined. Directions are brief with many examples, and they provide useful practical information. A number of different reports are available from the STAR Reading, depending on the type of information the examiner desires. These reports include Test

Activity Report, Growth Report, Summary Report, Test Record Report, and Diagnostic Report.

SUMMARY. The STAR Reading is a computerized measure of reading ability that produces grade equivalents and instructional reading levels. Directions for administration and scoring are straightforward and user-friendly. Although the standardization sample is adequate, the discussion of standard scores is confusing because the scale is never provided. The publishers provide excellent guidelines for the interpretation of grade equivalents. Specific information is provided to support the test's stability reliability and validity. A major concern regarding the use of the STAR Reading in establishing reading levels is its reliance on a single item type that represents an artificial reading task and depends heavily on vocabulary development. Consequently, this measure should be used as a screening device. Supplementary data on reading ability should be collected to support conclusions regarding reading level. The STAR Reading should not be used for the diagnosis of reading disabilities nor used for placement decisions.

[369]
START—Strategic Assessment of Readiness for Training.

Purpose: Designed to diagnose adult's learning strengths and weaknesses.
Population: Adults.
Publication Date: 1994.
Acronym: START.
Scores, 8: Anxiety, Attitude, Motivation, Concentration, Identifying Important Information, Knowledge Acquisition Strategies, Monitoring Learning, Time Management.
Administration: Group.
Price Data, 1996: $19.95 per user's manual (21 pages); $9.95 per assessment and learner's guide (volume discounts available).
Time: (15) minutes.
Comments: Self-administered; self-scored.
Authors: Claire E. Weinstein and David R. Palmer.
Publisher: H & H Publishing Company, Inc.

Review of START—Strategic Assessment of Readiness for Training by PHILLIP L. ACKERMAN, Professor of Psychology, Georgia Institute of Technology, Atlanta, GA:

The START is described by the authors as a "powerful assessment tool designed to diagnose adults' learning strengths and weaknesses and to provide prescriptive information and guidelines for both trainers and learners" (user's manual, p. 2). The authors state that the START is an outgrowth of the LASSI (Learning and Study Strategies Inventory), and was developed for human resource development specialists and trainers to assess adults in the workplace, to design remediation treatments, and to "modify and adapt instruction" (p. 14) in the workplace. They advise that the START "has excellent psychometric properties and is based on a model of strategic learning" (p. 2). The manual indicates that START is not designed for selection for employment "or as the sole criteria [*sic*] for participation in training opportunities" (p. 2). START is recommended for providing diagnostic feedback to employees/trainees, and as an aid to match training methods to trainee characteristics. There are no references in the manual to any research with the instrument or to the model that underlies the instrument.

RELIABILITY/VALIDITY. The only quantitative "reliability" data provided are actually measures of internal consistency (coefficient alpha), and these range from .65 to .87, but only two scales exceeded an alpha of .80, suggesting that most of the subscales are relatively heterogeneous. No aggregation of scale scores is recommended in the manual. No data are provided that indicate whether the START is capable of assessing the kinds of remediation-based changes that are mentioned as a purpose of the measure. Content validity was established by one survey of experts about a list of scales, and then a follow-up review by "more than 40 experts" of "more than 200 items" (p. 14). No criterion-related validity data are presented, either predictive or concurrent. No correlations between the scales of the START are presented with any other instruments. Minimal data are presented about the standardization sample, only a description of the sample as "226 persons enrolled in training programs at several different corporations" (p. 15). The only construct validity data presented are wholly inadequate for evaluation of the validity of the START. They consist of the intercorrelations of the eight scales, and a "factor analysis" that was a "principal components" analysis (obviously a confusion of the two different methods of analysis). Regardless, eight factors were extracted from the eight-variable correlation matrix, a fact that the authors regard as showing: "It is clear from this table that each scale loads on one and only one dimension" (p. 15). Such an analysis is completely uninformative, because it clearly violates a central tenet of factor analysis (that is, to represent a matrix of correlations by means of a smaller number of latent hypothetical factors). When eight factors are derived from eight variables, the result is a foregone conclusion, and not a property of the constructs. My own calculation of a factor analysis of the eight variables showed clearly that the largest number of defensible underlying factors was four (three by Kaiser's rule, and four by the Humphreys-Montanelli parallel analysis), and clearly demonstrated a lack of independence of the eight scales. Therefore, in the absence of any additional evidence, the only validation data presented in the manual suggest that the START should not be used to assess eight different constructs.

NORMS. Reported norms are inadequate to make judgments about which persons may appropriately take this test, such as education or experience background characteristics. No data describe gender or race ethnic group differences in scores. One of the more distressing aspects of the START is that discrepancies exist between the means and standard deviations shown for the norming sample (where scale means range from 22.04 to 29.18, and standard deviations range from 3.93 to 5.81), and the self-scoring graph for respondents to interpret their scores (which show "high scores" to be any scale score higher than 29, and "low scores" to be any score lower than 21). Thus, any respondent who obtains a mean score on the Attitude scale is told that they are "high" on this scale, and any respondent with a z-score of $-.22$ (corresponding to 41% of the norming sample) is told that they are "low" on "Time Management."

ADMINISTRATION/INTERPRETATION. Administration of the START is straightforward. The respondent is told that the measure is to be used to "provide you with valuable information about yourself" (p. 1); that the START "provides a list of suggestions for improving your skills" (p. 1); and that it "can be used by your trainers to help adapt their instruction" (p. 1). The START is self-scoring; the respondent tallies and then graphs the scale scores on another page (although the key for each scale is presented so participants can see the scheme while completing the form).

After completing the summation of scale scores, the rest of the test booklet is devoted to directions for interpreting the scale scores. There are separate recommendations for only low scores on each scale. Low Anxiety (where a low score indicates high anxiety) respondents are told that "You may want to think about why you are in the training program" (p. 14) or "you may want to use stress management techniques like muscle relaxation or mediation before each training session" (p. 14). Low Motivation respondents are told to "consider some of the actions suggested in the discussion of low Attitude Scale scores" (p. 15). Respondents who are low on Concentration are told to "get a good night's sleep before training sessions" (p. 16). Such recommendations are given without any documentation in the manual suggesting differential effectiveness with persons of different attributes, or whether the recommendations often take the form of Barnum statements, those that are clearly true, regardless of scale scores. (For example, imagine telling any trainee that he/she need *not* get a good night's sleep before training, regardless of score.)

The recommendations to the trainer are no better than those to the respondent. Trainers with a group of persons showing high levels of anxiety are told to "Check the level of difficulty of the course materials for the target population" (p. 9); for a group that is low in Attitude, trainers are told to "Try to create a supportive and friendly environment so that the trainees enjoy being there" (p. 10); and for those low on Identifying Important Information, trainers are told to "Make sure the instructional pace is not too fast for your participants" (p. 11).

SUMMARY. As a diagnostic instrument for trainees, a structured remediation plan for respondents, and a mechanism for trainers to tailor instruction for their trainees, this instrument has not demonstrated any of the characteristics that are concordant with standard guidelines. Both construct and criterion-related validity data are lacking, and the data that exist fail to support the assertions of the independence of the eight scales. The interpretations of scale scores are flawed by placing average or nearly average responses into high-score or low-score categories, without any diagnostic validation data to support such categorizations. The recommendations for both respondents and trainers are either not demonstrated to be supported by data of differential treatment effects, or are so general as to be self-evident or tautological.

Review of the START—Strategic Assessment of Readiness for Training by PATRICIA A. BACH-ELOR, Professor of Psychology, California State University at Long Beach, Long Beach, CA:

The Strategic Assessment of Readiness for Training (START) is designed as a self-administered and self-scored assessment of an adult's learning strengths and weaknesses. START is composed of eight scales that serve as a prescriptive and diagnostic measure that establishes a baseline, identifies areas of weaknesses and strengths, and thereby enables trainers to tailor instruction to create an effective and efficient learning environment. The transfer and extension of newly acquired ideas, knowledge, and skills beyond a specific learning or training experience may also be enhanced by the identification and targeting of a participant's responsiveness to a learning program. The eight scales, which assess key aspects of an adult's ability to benefit from training/education, are: *Anxiety* (degree of tension associated with performance in a learning environment), *Attitude* (level of commitment to training or value placed upon training), *Motivation* (acceptance of responsibility for active participation in training environment), *Concentration* (ability to focus and maintain attention on learning tasks or presentation of material), *Identifying Important Information* (ability to select and transfer important information), *Knowledge Acquisition Strategies* (ability to learn new information and skills), *Monitoring Learning* (degree to which learning is monitored/reviewed during learning program), and *Time Management* (ability to create and adhere to an effective schedule).

START is a self-administered, self-scored 56-item instrument. Most participants can complete the instrument in 15 minutes, although there is no time limit. The scores for each scale are derived by summing the responses to the seven items comprising each of the eight scales. This calculation is facilitated by a "scoring page" provided in the test manual. Also included is a graph grid with preprinted lines indicating the range of high scores (top 25%), middle scores (next 25%), and low scores (bottom 50%). These ranges of performance were not further detailed or justified. However, experts who were consulted agreed upon these designations (user's manual, p. 8). The plot of scale scores results in a visual presentation of the participant's responses and serves as a reference during the interpretative phase of the assessment.

Low or even middle scorers on any of the scales are referred to the corresponding "Suggestion" section. Each of the "Suggestion" sections interprets the scale, describes behaviors/attitudes that may lead to low scores, and offers strategies to improve performance. Learners, trainers, and/or program developers may design and modify instructional and learning environments to enhance learning readiness based on this knowledge. The language is upbeat, positively stated, and clearly articulated. The 10 to 16 suggestions per scale are appropriate and specific to producing an effective learning environment. The suggestions can be modified and tailored to a variety of learning situations and learners.

DEVELOPMENT. Thirty learning, adult education, and human resource development specialists generated the concept of nine scales in the initial version of the START. Psychometricians and learning specialists prepared 200 items, which were critically reviewed by 40 experts (half new to the START). These items were revised, pilot tested, and reanalyzed to produce 126 items, which were pilot tested and revised to 90 items. Thirty experts (two-thirds were among the earlier experts) reviewed and field tested this version of the START on trainees and participants in professional organizations, continuing education settings, manufacturing plants, and technical services. The current version of the START (56 items) is the result of these trials.

RELIABILITY. Evidence of the internal consistency reliability of the START was assessed by computing coefficient alpha indices for each scale. These coefficients were: *Anxiety* .87, *Attitude* .71, *Motivation* .65, *Concentration* .83, *Identifying Important Information* .75, *Knowledge Acquisition* .78, *Monitoring* .78, and *Time Management* .76. These seven-item scales can be considered to possess evidence of modest internal consistency reliability.

VALIDITY. The START manual does not contain a "Validity" section. However, content validity evidence can be inferred by the description of a series of reviews by experts in the fields of human learning, adult education, and resource development. The reported consensus of approximately 50 experts can be taken as sufficient evidence of the existence of content validity of the START scales. No attempt was made to address the construct validity of the START scales. The *Standards for Educational and Psychological Testing* (AERA, APA, & NCME, 1985) require such an investigation. In an otherwise carefully prepared manual, the assessment of such a critical psychometric quality was an obvious and glaring omission. Without an inquiry into the accuracy of the START scales, the usefulness of the instrument in practical applications is dubious.

NORMATIVE GROUPS. Unfortunately, no demographic or other information is provided about the adults who participated in the standardization sample. Without such information about the normative sample of the START, test users would be unable to evaluate if the test is appropriate for a specific application or to interpret performance with any confidence.

SUMMARY. The START consists of eight scales that assess an adult's learning strengths and weaknesses. It is a self-administered and self-scored prescriptive and diagnostic measure that may facilitate learners and trainers to modify an educational setting to enhance learning readiness. The user's manual of the START is a clearly articulated instructional guide that will benefit a variety of practitioners in the educational arena. The suggestions are relevant and appropriate for the stated target audience. Internal consistency estimates of the START scales reveal modest reliability; however, evidence is lacking regarding construct validity. The appropriateness of the use and interpretation of the START is questionable until such an assessment is presented to test users. The standardization sample needs to be described in detail. Additionally, normative and interpretative data are required before meaningful comparisons can be made. Test users cannot interpret scores or justify conclusions reached without such information.

REVIEWER'S REFERENCE

American Educational Research Association, American Psychological Association, & National Council on Measurement in Education. (1985). *Standards for educational and psychological testing.* Washington, DC: American Psychological Association, Inc.

[370]
State-Trait Anger Expression Inventory.

Purpose: Designed to measure "the experience and expression of anger."
Population: Ages 13 and up.
Publication Dates: 1979–1996.
Acronym: STAXI.
Scores, 8: State Anger, Trait Anger (Angry Temperament, Angry Reaction), Anger-in, Anger-out, Anger Control, Anger Expression.
Administration: Group or individual.
Editions, 2: Hand-scored, machine-scored.

Price Data, 1996: $74 per kit including manual ('96, 46 pages), 50 item booklets, and 50 rating sheets; $27 per manual; $29 per 50 item booklets; $29 per 50 rating sheets.
Time: (10–12) minutes.
Comments: Test forms are entitled Self-Rating Questionnaire; Self-rating; Form G recommended for large scale research.
Author: Charles D. Spielberger.
Publisher: Psychological Assessment Resources, Inc.
Cross References: See T5:2496 (6 references); for reviews by David J. Pittenger and Alan J. Raphael of the Revised Research Edition, see 13:296 (52 references); see also T4:2562 (12 references); for reviews by Bruce H. Biskin and Paul Retzlaff of the STAXI-Research Edition, see 11:379 (8 references).
[Editor's Note: These reviews are based on test materials received prior to 1999. The publisher advised in August 1999 that this test has been revised. The STAXI-2 will be reviewed in a future *MMY*.]

Review of the State-Trait Anger Expression Inventory by ROBERT J. DRUMMOND, Professor, Division of Educational Services and Research, University of North Florida, Jacksonville, FL:

The State-Trait Anger Expression Inventory (STAXI) is a 44-item inventory developed for two major purposes: first, to help assess components of anger that could be used in the assessment of normal and abnormal behavior, and second, to investigate the role of various components of anger to the development of medical conditions. Spielberger's construct of anger has two major components, state anger and trait anger. The STAXI consists of six scales and two subscales. The inventory has three parts: How I feel right now (10 items), How I generally feel (10 items), and When angry or furious (24 items). A 4-point Likert scale is utilized—*not at all* to *very much so* and *almost never* to *almost always.*

State Anger assesses the intensity of angry feelings the client has at a particular moment of time. Trait Anger, on the other hand, reflects the disposition of the individual to experience anger and is made up of two subscales, Angry Temperament and Angry Reaction. Anger-in measures how often the individual's anger is turned inside or suppressed. Anger-out taps anger directed toward other individuals and objects in the environment. Anger Control asks for the frequency the individual tries to control the expression of anger. Anger Expression measures the degree to which anger is expressed regardless of the direction of expression.

The STAXI can be administered to individuals age 13 through adulthood and is at the fifth grade reading level. The author presents norms for adolescents, college students, adults, and special populations. The average respondent takes from 10 to 12 minutes to complete the test. Scoring can be completed in 4 minutes or less. There are two versions of the STAXI, a handscorable version and a machine-scored version.

The STAXI has gone through elaborate validation proceedings and the manual presents considerable information of how the scale was developed, the conceptual issues, and the results of factor analysis. The STAXI has been compared to the Eysenck Personality Inventory and the State-Trait Personality Inventory. The STAXI has also been compared with physical correlates such as blood pressure. Alpha coefficients provide evidence of the reliability of the anger scales.

The red print on the test booklet and answer sheet make them harder to read. The layout of the test, however, is good. Overall, the manual is more of a scholarly treatise on the technical aspects of the test. Notably missing are several case studies to illustrate the use and interpretation of the test. The manual could present data to the clinician that would facilitate the interpretation and proper use of the test.

Although the author comments on age and gender differences, I would like to see ethnic and cultural group comparisons. Some evidence of the test-retest reliability would be helpful. It would also be useful to see comparisons with other scales from the Minnesota Multiphasic Personality Inventory (MMPI) so we could have more information on whether response set, faking, and social desirability affect the scores.

SUMMARY. The STAXI appears to be a well-developed measure of state and trait anger. The test is widely used as a research tool and can be a valuable clinical tool if the manual becomes more user friendly.

Review of the State-Trait Anger Expression Inventory by STEPHEN E. TROTTER, Associate Professor, Department of Educational & Counseling Psychology, University of the Pacific, Stockton, CA:

The recent revision of the State-Trait Anger Expression Scale (STAXI; 1996) represents a significant shift from its earlier stated use. Previously, the STAXI stated use was primarily as a research tool. Clinicians were instructed to be cautious in its use with clinical populations. The new version attempts to widen the potential pool of users by aiming more at the practitioner rather than the researcher. In addition, previous versions were consistent in suggesting that training in psychometrics was required. This seems somewhat softened in the new version, as training is required to interpret but not administer the instrument. This is in keeping with many checklists and self-report inventories on the market.

The instrument purports to measure the experience and expression of anger. It further divides these factors into state and trait anger. It also addresses patterns of overtly or covertly expressing anger. Finally, it attempts to measure the dimensions of control and frequency of anger expression.

The test comprises 44 items with responses rated from 1–4 along a consistent direction of *almost never* to *almost always*. It is helpful that Spielberger varied the polarity of the questions to make it less likely for respondents to autocorrelate their ratings. A fairly large number of items (9) need to be omitted before overall validity is compromised. However, on some scales the omission of one item will render it invalid. The items have a high degree of face validity, with the questions divided into three sections: How I feel right now, How I generally feel, When angry or furious. The majority of the questions are five words or less and reading level is referenced as the fifth grade. This should be well within the range of the majority of subjects 13 years of age and above for which the instrument is designed.

The STAXI is composed of two forms, HS (hand scored) and Form G (OCR Scored). The OCR format is returned to the publisher for scoring and is returned with percentiles and *t*-scores for each individual.

The manual is clearly written and provides guidelines for interpreting high scores. It is relatively brief, approximately 50 pages including references. It is divided into well-written sections addressing administration and interpretation, conceptual issues and scale development, validity studies, and current research. It is helpful that Spielberger provides the examiner information regarding the skewness of the distribution of scores that prevents it from discriminating between individuals with low scores. In addition, a thorough description of the normative sample is provided. The sample is composed of responses from more than 9,000 individuals. Separate norms are provided as a function of gender and further delineated by adolescent, college, or adult. The scores are transformed into T scores and percentiles.

The shortcomings of the STAXI appear to be centered on the norming sample. Issues of ethnicity and race raised in Pittenger's (1998) *MMY* review are very briefly addressed in the revision. Spielberger reports that approximately 18% of the high school norming population were Black (African-American). This suggests an overrepresentation based on the current census. In contrast the data for Hispanics are not reported, but rather referenced as a smaller proportion. The reader is left unaware of the representation, if any, for Asians and Native-Americans. Ethnicity and racial data are not provided for the remaining norms. This greatly limits their usage across ethnic and racial groups.

However, the largest threat to generalizability appears to be the use of approximately 2,000 individuals from the National Defense University. The reader is left uninformed as to differences in mean scores for these individuals in relationship to other adults in the norming population. This may be particularly problematic for adult male scores because 1,890 of the National Defense University pool were males. Therefore, the adult male normative group is largely composed of these individuals. Without reported comparative data this greatly limits the use with other males who are not members of this group. This flaw is continued in the college student normative group with 640 (600 males, 40 females) students selected from the United States Military Academy. The relatively low number of West Point females suggests that representation in the female normative group is less than 5%. In contrast West Point males represent approximately 45% of the college male group. Spielberger addresses this factor when he reports a 7-point higher score on S-Anger for Military Academy males when contrasted with urban undergraduate college males. He credits this with providing the impetus for reporting scores by gender. However, he notes that the scores are almost identical independent of gender for college students. Therefore, an alternative hypothesis might be that gender is not as large a factor as reported but rather that anger management and/or response style is reflected in career choice. This is also evident in differences between reported alpha coefficient estimates of internal consistency reliability as a function of college or Navy recruit membership.

The manual does an excellent job reporting factor loadings for the scales that support the construct of Anger-in and Anger-out as distinct styles. The manual is very thorough and provides an excellent and concise review of the literature associated with the STAXI and Anger Expression. It concludes with "Validity Studies and Current Research," which provides comparison data with the Minnesota Multiphasic Personality Inventory (MMPI), Eysenck Personality Questionnaire, and Buss-Durkee Hostility Inventory. The bulk of the research cited in the manual is dated and carries over from earlier editions. However, Anger-in scores were reported to correlate with blood pressure levels—finding that suggests a meaningful, real-world application for the STAXI in the treatment of elevated blood pressure levels.

SUMMARY. In closing the STAXI has much to offer the well-informed clinician. The reviewer's concerns center around the makeup of the normative group. Specifically, there appears to be an overrepresentation of military and allied individuals in both the college and adult normative group. In addition, the lack of data for Hispanic representation and the apparent absence of Native-Americans from the sample provide problematic. Moreover, the lack of a validity scale and the obvious intent of the items negate its use with populations that might be motivated to fake bad or good.

REVIEWER'S REFERENCE

Pittinger, D. J. (1998). [Review of the State-Trait Anger Expression Inventory, Revised Research Edition]. In J. C. Impara & B. S. Plake (Eds.), *The thirteenth mental measurements yearbook* (pp. 948–949). Lincoln, NE: Buros Institute of Mental Measurements.

[371]
Strength Deployment Inventory.

Purpose: Designed to assess "personal strengths in relating to others" under two conditions: when things are going well, and when there is conflict.
Population: Adults.
Publication Dates: 1973–1996.
Acronym: SDI®.
Scores: 7 Motivational Values Systems: (Altruistic-Nurturing, Assertive-Directing, Analytic-Autonomizing, Flexible-Cohering, Assertive-Nurturing, Judicious-Competing, Cautious-Supporting); 13 scores reflecting progression through stages of conflict.
Administration: Group or individual.
Price Data, 1999: $20 per Premier Edition including Standard Edition of the Strength Deployment

Inventory, interpretive charts, and 2 exercises; Portrait of Personal Strengths and Portrait of Overdone Strengths; $5 per either Portrait available separately: $9 per Standard Edition; $30 per manual ('96, 146 pages). **Foreign Language Editions:** Standard Edition available in French, German, and Spanish.
Time: (20–40) minutes for Premier Edition; (20–40) minutes per exercise.
Comments: Self-scorable; for corporate (e.g., team building), clinical (e.g., relationship counseling), and career development (e.g., outplacement and welfare-to-work) uses; Feedback Edition uses self-rating and ratings of a significant other person.
Author: Elias H. Porter.
Publisher: Personal Strengths Publishing, Inc.

Review of the Strength Deployment Inventory by FREDERICK T. L. LEONG, Professor of Psychology, The Ohio State University at Columbus, Columbus, OH:

The Strength Deployment Inventory (SDI) is based on the relationship awareness theory developed by Elias Porter. This theory can be summarized by four premises. The first premise is that behavior traits arise from the purposive strivings for gratification mediated by the concepts people form on how to obtain those gratifications. The second premise maintains that people are predictably uniform in their behavior when they are free, but they are predictably variable when they meet with obstructing conditions in the world. The third premise proposes that personal weakness is no more nor no less than the overdoing of a personal strength by an individual. The fourth and final premise is that the more clearly the concepts in personality theory approximate how one experiences oneself the more effectively they will serve as devices for self-discovery.

This theory is an amalgamation of the concepts and ideas from different psychological theorists such as Tolman, Fromm, Lewin, Erikson, and Rogers. The above premises form the bulk of this theory of relationship awareness. It is not so much an integration of the theorists cited (e.g., Tolman, Lewin, Rogers) but a selective borrowing of concepts from these theorists to form these underlying premises. In the final analysis, it seems less like a unified theory than a series of hypotheses about individual behavior (e.g., behavior is more variable under stress) based on some borrowed concepts.

This relationship awareness theory is translated by the Strength Deployment Inventory into a graphical representation represented by an inverted triangle. Different sections of the triangle represent different characteristics. For example, the northwest section of the triangle represents the Altruistic-Nurturing dimension. The northeast section of the triangle represents the Assertive-Directing dimension and the southern portion of the triangle represents the Analytic-Autonomizing dimension. Despite the fact that the theory resembles the circumplex model of personality developed by Leary (1957) and more recently researched by Wiggins (see Wiggins & Broughton, 1985), no attempts were made to link the relationship awareness theory to this circumplex model of personality that dates back to the 1950s. Furthermore, no evidence is presented in the test manual of studies conducted to validate this theory empirically. An interesting dimension to the theory is the notion that people change from one set of characteristics to another under stress. Yet, no empirical research is provided to demonstrate that this shift can be measured by the SDI. There is a very brief mention of a study of group leaders in a Catholic Diocese but no reference is provided for this study and almost no information is provided on the nature of the study and findings. In addition, no information was provided about the potential concurrent validity of the SDI (e.g., does the measure of Altruistic-Nurturing style correlate with similar established measures?) or the criterion-related validity (e.g., that the Analytic-Autonomizing style is correlated with psychological reactance). Without supporting research and considering the failure to link it to existing circumplex models, the current theory remains largely speculative.

In terms of the Inventory itself, the test manual presents an interesting proposition arguing that the Strength Deployment Inventory should not be viewed as a psychological test. Yet in the manual, the author proceeds to present reliability information and only proposes the idea that the Inventory should not be viewed as a test when discussing the validity of the instrument. Despite this proposition that the Inventory should not be viewed as a test, the author of the test manual proceeds to present various validity information. The quality of both the reliability and validity information remains suspect. When discussing test-retest reliability, the test manual refers to a Parson coefficient of correlation. It appears that the author has confused the Parson and the Pearson correlation. Furthermore, when estimating the validity of the Inventory using the concept of internal consistency, the author does not provide the typical Cronbach's alpha but instead presents differences between high and low scores using the chi-square method. In addition, none of the usual methods of assessing construct validity were undertaken for the current Inventory.

SUMMARY. In conclusion, given the weaknesses of the theory and the problems with the psychometric properties of the Strength Deployment Inventory, it cannot be recommended as a good test of personality or interpersonal behavior. Persons interested in assessing interpersonal behavior would have a better choice with the FIRO scales (Schulz, 1978) or the circumplex model proposed by Leary (1957) and assessed by Wiggins's Interpersonal Adjective Scales (see Wiggins & Broughton, 1985). An interesting dilemma presented by the author and later the developers of the SDI is their claim that the SDI is not a psychological test. This is a problematic proposition because it puts the reviewer in the bind of either accepting the author's proposition or rejecting it and evaluating it as a test. To do the latter would be to go against the claims of the author and yet we are expected to evaluate how well instruments have "lived up" to their authors' claims. My decision is to ignore the author's claim that the SDI is not a test and evaluate it as one.

REVIEWER'S REFERENCES

Leary, T. F. (1957). *Interpersonal diagnosis of personality: A functional theory and methodology for personality evaluation.* New York: Ronald.

Schulz, W. (1978). *FIRO awareness scales manual.* Palo Alto, CA: Consulting Psychologists Press.

Wiggins, J. S., & Broughton, R. (1985). The interpersonal circle: A structural model for the integration of personality research. In R. Hogan & W. H. Jones (Eds.). *Perspectives in personality: A research annual* (vol. 1, pp. 1–47). Greenwich, CT: JAI Press.

[372]
Stress Index for Parents of Adolescents.

Purpose: Designed to assess the level of stress in parents of adolescents.
Population: Parents of 11–19-year olds.
Publication Date: 1998.
Scores, 11: Adolescent Domain (Moodiness/Emotional Lability, Social Isolation/Withdrawal, Delinquency/Antisocial, Failure to Achieve or Perservere), Parent Domain (Life Restrictions, Relationship with Spouse/Partner, Social Alienation, Incompetence/Guilt), Adolescent-Parent Relationship Domain, Life Stressors, Total Parenting Stress.
Administration: Group or individual.

Price Data, 2000: $95 per introductory kit including 25 reusable item booklets, 25 hand-scorable answer sheet/profile forms, and professional manual (70 pages); $33 per 25 item booklets; $33 per 25 hand-scorable answer sheet/profile forms; $33 per professional manual.
Time: (20) minutes.
Authors: Peter L. Sheras, Richard R. Abidin, and Timothy R. Konold.
Publisher: Psychological Assessment Resources, Inc.

Review of the Stress Index for Parents of Adolescents by ELIZABETH L. JONES, Associate Professor of Psychology, Western Kentucky University, Bowling Green, KY:

The Stress Index for Parents of Adolescents (SIPA) is a 112-item self-report inventory developed to assess parenting stress in a way that (a) is sensitive to the developmental issues and behaviors of adolescents 11 to 19 years of age, (b) provides normative data for levels of stress experienced by parents of adolescents, and (c) measures change in stress levels of parents of adolescents over time. The SIPA is based on a multifactorial parenting stress model that includes child variables (Adolescent Domain, AD), parent variables (Parent Domain, PD), parent-child transactions (Adolescent-Parent Relationship Domain, APRD), and life stress events (Life Stressors, LS). The first two domains (AD and PD) each have four subscales with a total of 90 items that contribute to the Total Parenting Stress Score. These items are responded to on a 5-point rating scale ranging from *Strongly Agree* to *Strongly Disagree*. The last domain, Life Stressors (LS), is considered to be clinically relevant and important for interpretation of the Total Parenting Stress Score; however, the scores do not contribute to the Total Parenting Stress Score. This latter domain (LS) consists of 22 items that are responded to in a Yes/No format. Percentiles, T scores, and confidence intervals are provided for the raw scores on each subscale, domain, and the total score. The SIPA is designed to provide the interpretive ranges or categories of Within Normal Limits (below 85th percentile, Borderline (85th to 89th percentile), Clinically Significant (90th to 94th percentile), and Clinically Severe (95th to 100th percentile).

The SIPA materials include a manual, answer sheets, and a reusable item booklet. Administration and scoring are facilitated through the use of a carbonless response form with a reusable 4-page item booklet. The instructions are clear, concise, and easy to follow. The items are clearly worded and appear to be consistent with the espoused fifth grade reading level.

The SIPA manual is well organized and provides much of the information recommended for inclusion in test manuals by the *Standard for Educational and Psychological Testing* (AERA, APA, & NCME, 1985). However, although adequate information is available in most areas, there are some obvious omissions including: specifying the purpose of the instrument, providing a chart or listing of the items that compose each scale, providing confidence intervals for the percentiles (the recommended level of interpretation), and providing adequate empirical support for the accuracy and significance of the recommended interpretative ranges and the use of the measure to assess change in the construct over time.

NORMATIVE DATA. Normative data for this instrument are based on a sample of 778 parents configured to reflect the 1997 U.S. Census data. Caucasian and African American groups were slightly overrepresented whereas the "Other" ethnicity group was slightly underrepresented. The sample also overrepresents the higher education levels (vocational or some college and higher levels) over the levels of 9–12th grades and below. Mothers provided more ratings than fathers at the rate of 2:1. The manual provides statistical data to support that the gender of the parent and the age of the adolescent are not systematically related and thus, age-related norms are not necessary. Gender of the adolescent sample on which the ratings are based is composed of equivalent numbers of males and females. However, no investigation of the effects of gender of the adolescent on which the rating was based was conducted. This is a reasonable expectation and a glaring omission, given that gender of person being rated may influence ratings or be a significant predictor of certain types of behavior patterns (e.g., internalizing vs. externalizing) that may impact perceived parenting stress.

RELIABILITY. Internal consistency as measured by Cronbach's coefficient alpha indicates a high degree of internal consistency with coefficient alphas for subscales exceeding .80 and domains and Total Parenting Stress exceeding .91. Test-retest reliability (4-week, $n = 46$) is considered acceptable at the domain and total test level but not at the subscale level. Standard errors of measurement and confidence intervals for the raw scores indicate reasonable stability. Overall there are sufficient data to indicate consistent measurement at the domain and total score levels, the recommended levels for interpretation.

VALIDITY. Evidence of validity is provided through content, construct, convergent, and discriminant approaches. Content validity is documented through author review of the literature to determine variables associated with parenting stress, item refinement based on expert and parent review of items, and statistical refinement based on data from a field test version of the scale. Construct validity is addressed through principal component and maximum likelihood factor analyses, both exploratory factor analytic procedures. Factor analytic support is good as intercorrelations were strong for the three domains (AD, PD, and APRD) and their subscales. However, no evidence of confirmatory factor analyses is reported, which is curious given the attention to exploratory factor analytic techniques. Convergent validity is examined through correlating SIPA results with measures of child and family/parent behavior (e.g., Parenting Alliance Measure—PAM [previously called the Parenting Alliance Inventory—PAI]; Family Adaptability and Cohesion Evaluation Scales III—FACES III; Child Behavior Checklist—CBCL). Correlations revealed significant relationships between the SIPA domains and total score in the direction(s) expected or predicted. Stepwise regression analyses conducted on results of the PAI, Dyadic Adjustment Scale, and FACES III indicated that the PAI accounted for most of the variance of the SIPA domains. In this instance, parenting stress was most adequately predicted by the PAI, or by the quality of the parenting alliance.

Evidence of disciminant validity is provided by comparing group mean scores for several groups expected to differ in level of parenting stress (e.g., parent history of mental health services, history of adolescent delinquent behavior, clinical sample). In all groups, the clinically defined groups evidenced significantly higher SIPA scores. Support for the use of the clinical cutoff scores is weakly evident in examining the percentage of SIPA scores for adolescents in the clinical sample that fell within the Clinically Significant (90th to 94th percentile) and Clinically Severe (95th–100th percentile) ranges. The authors appropriately note that this evidence is limited and that a full investigation of the cutoff scores should include a nonclinical sample.

CONCLUSION. It is important to note that the authors provide no empirical information to substantiate two key areas cited as rationale for the scale's development: assessment of parenting stress that is more sensitive to adolescent issues and behaviors than existing measure of parenting stress and measurement of changes in stress levels of parents of adolescents over time. Other identified weaknesses include lack of thorough validation of the use of the cutoff levels for clinical significance, investigation of possible gender differences, lack of confidence intervals for percentile scores, and definition of the construct being measured. The SIPA holds promise; however, its clinical use should be limited to the normative information. Given further empirical support the SIPA holds good promise to be a useful measure for clinicians and researchers.

REVIEWER'S REFERENCE

American Educational Research Association, American Psychological Association, & National Council on Measurement in Education. (1985). *Standards for educational and psychological testing.* Washington, DC: American Psychological Association, Inc.

Review of the Stress Index for Parents of Adolescents by SUSAN M. SWEARER, Assistant Professor of School Psychology, University of Nebraska—Lincoln, Lincoln, NE:

The Stress Index for Parents of Adolescents (SIPA) is a 112-item self-report measure designed to identify stressful areas in parent-adolescent interactions. The SIPA is a developmentally sensitive upward extension of the Parenting Stress Index (PSI; T5:1889) and is designed to reflect multifactorial parenting stress models. It is standardized for use with parents of adolescents ages 11 to 19 years and can be used with biological, adoptive, or foster parents of either gender. The SIPA provides a comparison of normative levels of stress with high and low levels of stress. Thus, parents of adolescents who fall outside the normal range of stress can be identified. The SIPA also provides a longitudinal assessment of parenting stress that can be used for treatment outcome applications.

The SIPA yields scores on three domains: the Adolescent Domain (AD), a Parent Domain (PD), an Adolescent-Parent Relationship Domain (APRD), and a Life Stressors (LS) scale. A Total Parenting Stress (TS) score can be obtained by summing the three domains. The TS score reflects theoretical and empirical findings that stressors are additive. The TS score is a measure of the stress a parent experiences as a result of parenting a particular adolescent. The SIPA uses a 5-point response format (i.e., *Strongly Disagree* to *Strongly Agree*) for Items 1–90 and a yes-no format for Items 91–112. The AD and PD contain four subscales that will be described in detail below.

THE ADOLESCENT DOMAIN (AD). The 49-item Adolescent Domain measures the level of stress experienced by the parent as a result of characteristics of the adolescent such as mood and behavior. The four subscales include: (a) Moodiness/Emotional Lability (MEL), (b) Social Isolation/Withdrawal (ISO), (c) Delinquency/Antisocial (DEL), and (d) Failure to Achieve or Persevere (ACH).

THE PARENT DOMAIN (PD). The 34-item Parent Domain measures the level of stress experienced by the parent that is the result of juggling parenting with other life roles such as relationship with a partner, parenting competence, and social isolation. The four subscales include: (a) Life Restrictions (LFR), (b) Relationship with Spouse/Partner (REL), (c) Social Alienation (SOC), and (d) Incompetence/Guilt (INC).

THE ADOLESCENT-PARENT RELATIONSHIP DOMAIN (APRD). The 16-item Adolescent-Parent Relationship Domain measures the parent's perceived view of the adolescent-parent relationship. The scale is designed to assess the degree of communication and level of affection between parent and adolescent.

LIFE STRESSORS (LS). The 22-item Life Stressors scale assesses the number of stressful life events that the parent has experienced in the past year. Items are responded to in a yes-no format. The LS scale allows the level of parenting stress to be interpreted within the presence of external life stressors that can influence parenting stress.

Percentile scores are used to interpret the SIPA scores, with higher raw scores and percentile scores reflecting greater levels of parenting stress. Four levels of stress can be derived: (a) within normal limits (less than the 85th percentile), (b) borderline (85th to 89th percentile), (c) clinically significant (90th to 94th percentile), and (d) clinically severe (95th to 100th percentile).

Normative data from 778 parents of adolescents approximates the 1997 U.S. Census in terms of ethnicity, gender or parents and adolescents, and SES. SES is slightly higher in the SIPA normative sample than in the general population. The standardization sample was not randomized or stratified. The majority of the sample was Caucasian (approximately 79%), followed by African American (approximately 16%).

Reliability evidence of the SIPA is reported using internal consistency and test-retest reliability. Internal consistency reliabilities were computed on the norm group of 778 parents. Coefficient alphas for all subscales exceed .80. The Index of Total Parenting Stress (TS) has a coefficient alpha of 97. Test-retest reliability was computed from the scores of 46 parents who were asked to complete the SIPA approximately 4 weeks after the initial administration. Subscale coefficients ranged from .74 to .91. Test-retest reliability for the TS score was .93. No reliability information is reported for the Life Stress scale.

Validity data of the SIPA are reported in the manual. Convergent validity correlating the Parenting Alliance Inventory (PAI) (now called the Parenting Alliance Measure, PAM) and the SIPA scales suggests a significant negative correlation between the level of parenting stress and the parent's perception of his or her working relationship with the adolescent. Correlations are reported between the SIPA domains and the Achenbach Child Behavior Checklist (CBCL), the CRI (Coping Responses Inventory), the Personality Assessment screener (PAS), and the Family Adaptability and Cohesion Evaluation Scales III (FACES-III). Discriminant validity was conducted by investigating several groups of parents who were expected to differ in their levels of parenting stress. Parents from clinically defined groups (i.e., utilized mental health services or had an adolescent with mental health problems) had statistically significant higher scores on the SIPA than parents who were not from clinically defined groups.

Limitations of the SIPA include the fact that only high SIPA scores can be interpreted. Validity data on low SIPA scores are lacking and the authors note the importance of future research in determining the meaning of low SIPA scores (professional manual, p. 14). Data are reported on clinical groups (i.e., parents with adolescents diagnosed with Conduct Disorder, Oppositional Defiant Disorder, and Attention-Deficit/Hyperactivity Disorder). However, the clinical samples are too small to draw meaningful conclusions and the authors note that the presence of comorbidity confounds the results. The authors do not report the comorbidity results in the manual; however, they state that SIPA users should collect their own data and develop local norms for clinical groups (professional manual, p. 29). Additionally, items were not analyzed for possible bias, and differential validity across ethnic groups was not conducted. The SIPA should not be used with non-native speakers of English.

SUMMARY. Despite the aforementioned limitations, the SIPA is a useful self-report measure for assessing stress levels of parents of adolescents. As such, the SIPA represents an important upward extension from the Parenting Stress Index that is designed to reflect the unique developmental needs of parents of adolescents. The SIPA subscale scores can help clinicians target areas of treatment in parent-adolescent relationships. As with all self-report measures, the SIPA should be used as part of a multi-modal, multi-informant assessment process. Diagnostic decisions should not be based on one instrument alone. The SIPA can be used as a screening tool to identify parents who may be in need of parent training and/or professional services.

[373]
Structured Clinical Interview for DSM-IV Axis I Disorders: Clinician Version.

Purpose: Constructed as "a semistructured interview for making the major DSM-IV Axis I diagnoses."
Population: Psychiatric or general medical patients ages 18 or older.
Publication Date: 1997.
Acronym: SCID-CV.
Scores, 6: Mood Episodes, Psychotic Symptoms, Psychotic Disorders, Mood Disorders, Substance Use Disorders, Anxiety and Other Disorders.
Administration: Individual.
Price Data, 1998: $65 per complete kit including user's guide (138 pages), administration booklet (84 pages), and 5 score sheets; $21.95 per packet of 5 score sheets; $27.50 per user's guide; $24 per administration booklet.
Time: (45–90) minutes.
Comments: Shortened, clinician version of the Structured Clinical interview for DSM-IV Axis I Disorders: Research Version.
Authors: Michael B. First, Robert L. Spitzer, Miriam Gibbon, and Janet B. W. Williams.
Publisher: American Psychiatric Press, Inc.
Cross References: See T5:2519 (56 references).

Review of the Structured Clinical Interview for DSM-IV Axis I Disorders: Clinician Version by PAUL D. WERNER, Professor, California School of Professional Psychology, Alameda, CA:

The Structured Clinical Interview for DSM-IV Axis I Disorders: Clinician Version (SCID-CV) represents the confluence of two processes. The first is the process of refining the DSM itself, and the second is that of facilitating the use of DSM criteria by practicing clinicians.

The major innovation in DSM-IV is a shift from the use of experts' clinical judgment as a primary basis for specifying classifications and criteria to a more empirical approach entailing expert review of empirical literature, data re-analysis where appropriate, and field trials. It is unlikely that there could be any process for revising the DSM that would be greeted with universal acclaim, and the empirical review process leading to DSM-IV is not without limitations (e.g., as outlined by Frances, Mack, First, & Jones, 1995). However, because the new version of the DSM more solidly grounds psychodiagnostic classification in the empirical literature, it represents an important step forward. This is particularly the case with regard to the likely construct validity of the categorizations yielded by the SCID-CV.

Coinciding with the advent of the DSM-IV, the SCID-CV is offered in the hope of facilitating and improving the diagnostic activities of clinical practitioners. Although the SCID-CV user's guide describes the interview as "semi-structured" (p. 1), clinicians employing it will find it to be quite standardized (e.g., by providing the wording of questions to be asked). The user of the SCID-CV works with two booklets at once: (a) a reusable administration booklet, composed of over 80 pages of interview questions and associated diagnostic criteria, and (b) a single-use scoresheet (63 pages in length) for the case at hand. SCID-CV modules employ decision tree and "skip out" formats (in the latter, based on the answers obtained, the interviewer moves on to a question in another section).

In recognition of the complexity of the process of working with the SCID-CV, and of the need to foster standardized judgments about whether particular criteria have been met, the user's guide provides 32 pages of detailed instructions (including lists of "common pitfalls") for working with its modules. The developers emphasize the need for the user to get extensive practice in working through the materials, so that the SCID-CV's administration appears natural to the client and the diagnostic process flows easily. If users do not follow such steps, or do not benefit from them, rapport with the client, and consequently the client's engagement in the diagnostic process and the accuracy of his or her reports, may suffer. The user's guide provides very useful training materials in the form of six role-play cases and additional homework cases taken from the DSM-IV Casebook. Use of the accompanying training videotape is also recommended. All said, these materials, as well as the SCID-CV booklets themselves, may serve as useful training tools for neophyte mental health workers. They may also serve to remind experienced clinicians of the complete assessment required for a careful diagnostic work-up.

How good a job does the SCID-CV do of yielding reliable and valid categorizations of clinical cases? Evidence pertaining to the SCID-CV's interjudge reliability, for example, as summarized by Segal, Hersen, and Van Hasselt (1994) comes largely from work with the original SCID, conducted in clinical research settings, rather than from studies with the SCID-CV itself in front-line clinical practice. Thus, the obtained reliability coefficients, which have been predominantly encouraging, may not generalized to the SCID-CV's use in clinical practice. For this reason, the undertaking of reliability studies with the SCID-CV is strongly recommended.

As its developers point out, it is difficult to evaluate the SCID-CV with regard to the traditional reference point of concurrent validity because of the absence of a clear "gold standard" to serve as a criterion variable. Indeed, SCID-CV diagnoses, when formulated by experts and based on extensive information about clients, may themselves serve as such criteria. The two validity studies cited in the user's guide evaluated use of the SCID rather than the SCID-CV. Their results suggest that the SCID provided more valid diagnoses than did less structured clinical intake interviews. For example, in an unpublished report it was found that a psychiatric nurse's SCID-based diagnoses were more related to "expert-enhanced" SCID diagnoses (user's guide, p. 1) than were the clinician's diagnoses based on the unstructured interview. This result is not surprising, given that one version of the SCID would be expected to produce diagnoses paralleling those of another version. Further research is recommended, focusing on the SCID-CV in particular and using varied groups of clinical practitioners and clinical cases, as well as criterion diagnostic standards that others have accepted, such as the Research Diagnostic Criterion (RDC; Spitzer, Endicott, & Robins, 1978).

Because the SCID-CV is offered in the hope that it can be adopted as an element of actual-world clinical practice, its usability also must be considered. That is, even the most psychometrically sound diagnostic measure will be judged lacking if practicing clinicians find it awkward, cumbersome, and difficult to use. Yet this is how many clinicians might find the SCID-CV, especially when first attempting to employ it. Using it entails working with two large booklets that open flat and that must be kept side-by-side, moving back and forth rapidly between the two, and keeping track of one's place in each. Moreover, there is not a one-to-one correspondence between page locations of corresponding material in the two booklets, and the user must work through decision trees on the spot before determining whether to ask additional questions. Especially when jumps between items are indicated, the experience of the user is likely to be an awkward one, and this may translate into disengagement by the client who is faced with a clinician who is turning pages back and forth in two booklets as well as writing comments. One recommendation is that introductory comments should be provided to help the client understand why this process is necessary and to explain the ungraceful aspects. These could be read by the client or read aloud by the clinician.

Much of the awkwardness in using the SCID-CV arises from its thoroughness, and undoubtedly can be alleviated by extensive practice. However, more features need to be built into the SCID-CV booklets to aid the clinician. Currently, the authors label each item with its module code letter and item number, to help the user navigate simultaneously in both the administration booklet and the scoresheet. Additional coding (for example, using color coding or graphical symbols, or indicating at each jump the destination location in both the administration booklet and the scoresheet) might improve efficiency in use of the SCID-CV. Such changes might help clinical users reduce errors, improve rapport with clients during initial evaluation, and contribute to clients' engagement in the diagnostic process.

This having been said, it is difficult to envision how the complexities inherent in the two-booklet version of the SCID-CV can be handled

in a much more integrated fashion. A computerized version of the SCID-CV is apparently being developed, and it promises to expedite the information-gathering and diagnostic process. However, with such a system new questions arise, concerning how interposing a computer into the clinical/diagnostic interview will affect the validity of resulting classifications, to say nothing of clinical rapport.

SUMMARY. Standardization in the process of gathering and integrating diagnostic information is fundamental to responsible and consistent clinical practice. The authors of the SCID-CV are to be praised for their efforts at fostering these elements of practice. Their continued efforts are needed to facilitate and encourage adoption of this procedure by clinicians whose practice contexts necessitate determination of Axis I diagnoses. Clinicians who find use of the full interview awkward may nonetheless find it helpful to employ portions of it, in suggesting questions to ask clients and in corroborating suspected diagnoses.

REVIEWER'S REFERENCES

Spitzer, R. L., Endicott, J., & Robins, E. (1978). Research diagnostic criteria. *Archives of General Psychiatry, 35*, 773–782.

Segal, D. L., Hersen, M., & Van Hasselt, V. B. (1994). Reliability of the structured clinical interview for DSM-III-R: An evaluative review. *Comprehensive Psychiatry, 35*, 316–327.

Frances, A., Mack, A., First, M. B., & Jones, C. (1995). DSM-IV: Issues in development. *Psychiatric Annals, 25*, 15–19.

Review of the Structured Clinical Interview for DSM-IV Axis I Disorders: Clinician Version by THOMAS A. WIDIGER, Professor, Department of Psychology, University of Kentucky, Lexington, KY:

The Structured Clinical Interview for DSM-IV Axis I Disorders—Research Version (SCID-I; First, Gibbon, Spitzer, & Williams, 1996; 373) is perhaps the most frequently used semistructured interview in clinical research to diagnose the mental disorders included within the American Psychiatric Association's (APA) *Diagnostic and Statistical Manual of Mental Disorders* (DSM-IV; APA, 1994). The clinician version of this instrument (SCID-CV) was developed to facilitate obtaining of replicable and valid interview assessments of mental disorders within general clinical practice and to facilitate the generalizability of clinicians' diagnoses to those obtained in published research. The provision of relatively specific and explicit criteria sets for the diagnosis of mental disorders has improved substantially the obtaining of reliable and valid clinical diagnoses. However, this reliability and validity will occur in general clinical practice only if the criteria sets are assessed comprehensively and systematically. Semistructured interviews are the best means by which to ensure that diagnostic criteria sets are indeed being assessed in a manner that is replicable, objective, and valid (Rogers, 1995; Segal, 1997).

Many clinicians will find semistructured interviews to be constraining, impractical, and perhaps even superficial. Some clinicians will prefer to rely on the style and manner of interviewing they have developed through their own training and clinical experience (Westen, 1997). However, a substantial amount of research has indicated that unstructured clinical interviews are too often incomplete, unsystematic, and susceptible to idiosyncratic assumptions and expectations that undermine the validity of results from the assessments. Semistructured interviews are constraining, but it is precisely this constraint that ensures that the diagnostic criteria sets are indeed being thoroughly and objectively assessed. Even if a clinician prefers to rely upon his or her own judgments for a clinical diagnosis, this judgment will probably be best informed by a systematic and comprehensive assessment of the diagnostic criteria for the respective disorder. Semistructured interviews will be particularly useful when responding to assessment referrals or consultations or when an assessment might at some time in the future be critiqued or questioned. Minimally, clinicians will find the questions provided in the SCID-CV helpful in stimulating a consideration of additional ways to assess for the symptomatology of a particular mental disorder.

A limitation of the SCID-CV is that it does not cover all of the mental disorders in DSM-IV. Included within the SCID-CV are most of the mood, anxiety, psychotic, substance use, anxiety, and adjustment disorders. Not included (for example) are the eating, somatoform, dissociative, personality, social phobia, agoraphobia without a history of panic, or body dysmorphic disorders. Even important specifiers and subtypes for disorders that are covered have been excluded, such as the atypical features, seasonal pattern, and melancholic features of a major depressive disorder, the poor insight subtype for obsessive-compulsive disorder, and the physiological dependence subtype for substance dependence. The rationale for these exclusions was the effort to provide an interview that would not be experienced by clinicians as being too cumbersome, detailed, lengthy,

or complex (user's guide, p. 2). However, the failure to include these specifiers and subtypes undermines substantially the value of the SCID-CV, as these specifiers and subtypes will have important clinical implications. The authors might be expecting clinicians to administer routinely the entire interview as a means of screening for the presence of each of the disorders included therein. However, a more viable usage might be to administer only portions of the interview in order to document the provision of a systematic and comprehensive assessment of the disorders that are most likely to be present or the disorders that are the focus of a particular referral or consultation. The interview material for many of the excluded disorders and specifiers can be obtained, however, from the SCID-I (First et al., 1996); personality disorders are covered in the SCID-II (First, Gibbon, Spitzer, Williams, & Benjamin, 1997; 374). An additional alternative to the SCID-CV is to use a semistructured interview developed primarily for research purposes that is devoted to a particular mental disorder, such as the borderline personality, dissociative, or body dysmorphic disorders (Rogers, 1995; Segal, 1997).

No information is provided in the SCID-CV manual regarding the necessary qualifications for administering the SCID-CV, other than the presumption that the person is a "clinician." Prior training in diagnostic interviewing does appear to be necessary, along with a familiarity with DSM-IV (APA, 1994). A phone number is provided within the manual for a videotape training program. The manual can itself serve as a useful resource for commonly asked questions regarding the intention, application, or meaning of individual DSM-IV diagnostic criteria. The SCID-CV authors include the Text Editor for DSM-IV (Dr. First) and the Chair of the APA committees for DSM-III and DSM-III-R (Dr. Spitzer).

The manual is surprisingly weak in its presentation of data concerning the reliability and validity of the interview. This is due in part to the fact that there has been very little published research with the SCID-CV. However, there has been a substantial amount of published research with the SCID-I and the SCID-II that would be relevant to the reliability and validity of results from the SCID-CV (Rogers, 1995; Segal, 1997), yet there is only a cursory reference to just a few studies within the manual. The authors refer to an unpublished study by "Bascoe et al.," the specific findings (or even complete citation) for which are not provided. The authors appear to reject the need for validity data, indicating that "a gold standard for psychiatric diagnosis remains elusive" (user's guide, p. 46). It is indeed the case that diagnoses obtained through the administration of a semistructured interview are themselves often used as the criterion by which the validity of a self-report inventory is assessed. Nevertheless, the authors could have provided support for the construct validity of the SCID-I and SCID-II (if not the SCID-CV) through the substantial amount of research that has been conducted with these instruments. For example, research using the SCID-I that has supported the validity of the diagnosis of panic disorder by documenting its course, family history, or treatment responsivity would in turn also provide construct validity for the SCID-I assessment of this diagnosis.

The manual also fails to provide any normative data. This might be due in part to an assumption that assessments provided by any clinical interview are generally accepted at face value rather than being compared to a distribution of scores obtained from a normative sample. The assessments provided by a semistructured interview within a representative sample of the population are generally interpreted as providing the epidemiology of the disorder rather than providing the normative data for the interpretation of the interview. Nevertheless, it would still be useful for clinicians administering the SCID-CV within a particular clinical setting to be able to compare the results they obtained with those typically obtained in comparable settings.

Researchers and clinicians will generally obtain excellent interrater reliability in the administration and scoring of any particular semistructured interview within their clinical setting, but most interrater reliability studies have been confined largely to simply a test of the agreement in the scoring of respondents' answers to an administration of the interview. It is unclear whether the SCID-I, SCID-II, or SCID-CV is administered or even scored in a consistent manner across different research sites. The reliability and validity of any semistructured interview can depend substantially on the conscientiousness and perhaps even the skills of the interviewers at a particular site. Information concerning the reliability and validity of the SCID-CV could then be misleading, as the SCID-CV can be administered and scored in an unreliable and invalid manner even if it has been administered and scored validly many times before. It would then be informative for the authors of the SCID-CV to indicate what results should be obtained, or at least are typically obtained, within particular clinical settings.

SUMMARY. The value and importance of conducting systematic, comprehensive, and replicable interview assessments of the DSM-IV diagnostic criteria sets is becoming increasingly recognized, and many clinical training programs are now including the administration and scoring of semistructured interviews within their assessment curriculum. The SCID-CV would be an excellent addition to the assessment battery of any practicing clinician.

REVIEWER'S REFERENCES

American Psychiatric Association. (1994). *Diagnostic and statistical manual of mental disorders* (4th ed.). Washington, DC: American Psychiatric Association.
Rogers, R. (1995). *Diagnostic and structured interviewing: A handbook for psychologists.* Odessa, FL: Psychological Assessment Resources.
First, M. B., Gibbon, M., Spitzer, R. L., & Williams, J. B. W. (1996). *User's guide for the Structured Clinical Interview for DSM-IV Axis I Disorders—Research Version (SCID-I).* Washington, DC: American Psychiatric Press.
First, M. B., Gibbon, M., Spitzer, R. L., Williams, J. B. W., & Benjamin, L. S. (1997). *User's guide for the Structured Clinical interview for DSM-IV Axis II Personality Disorders (SCID-II).* Washington, DC: American Psychiatric Press.
Segal, D. L. (1997). Structured interviewing and DSM classification. In S. M. Turner & M. Hersen (Eds.), *Adult psychopathology and diagnosis* (3rd ed., pp. 24–57). NY: John Wiley & Sons.
Westen, D. (1997). Divergences between clinical and research methods for assessing personality disorders: Implications for research and the evolution of Axis II. *American Journal of Psychiatry, 154,* 895–903.

[374]

Structured Clinical Interview for DSM-IV Axis II Personality Disorders.

Purpose: Designed as "a semistructured diagnostic interview for assessing the 10 DSM-IV Axis II personality disorders as well as Depressive Personality Disorder and Passive-Aggressive Personality Disorder."
Population: Adults receiving psychiatric or general medical care.
Publication Date: 1997.
Acronym: SCID-II.
Scores, 13: Avoidant, Dependent, Obsessive-Compulsive, Passive-Aggressive, Depressive, Paranoid, Schizotypal, Schizoid, Histrionic, Narcissistic, Borderline, Antisocial, Not Otherwise Specified.
Administration: Individual.
Price Data, 1998: $46 per complete kit including user's guide and packet of 5 interviews and questionnaire; $21.95 per 5 interviews and questionnaires; $29.95 per user's guide.
Time: Administration time not reported.
Comments: Also includes optional, self-report SCID-II Personality Questionnaire.

Authors: Michael B. First, Miriam Gibbon, Robert L. Spitzer, Janet B. W. Williams, and Lorna Smith Benjamin.
Publisher: American Psychiatric Press, Inc.
Cross References: See T5:2520 (25 references).

Review of the Structured Clinical Interview for DSM-IV Axis II Personality Disorders by PAUL A. ARBISI, Minneapolis VA Medical Center, Assistant Professor Department of Psychiatry, and Assistant Clinical Professor Department of Psychology, University of Minnesota, Minneapolis, MN:

The Structured Clinical Interview for DSM-IV Axis II Personality Disorders (SCID-II) is a semistructured diagnostic interview for assessing the 10 *Diagnostic and Statistical Manual of Mental Disorders* (4th ed.; DSM-IV) personality disorders and Personality Disorder NOS. Two provisional personality disorders provided in DSM-IV for "further study"—Depressive Personality Disorder and Passive-Aggressive Personality Disorder—are also included in the SCID. The SCID-II was designed to provide DSM-IV Axis II diagnoses in both research and clinical settings. In clinical settings the SCID-II can be used in a number of ways. The clinician may use the SCID-II to confirm clinical impression. That is, after completing an unstructured clinical interview, the clinician may administer portions of the SCID to confirm and document one or more suspected Axis II disorders. Further, in a comprehensive, albeit time-consuming intake procedure, the entire SCID-II can be administered. Finally, the SCID-II can be used as a didactic device to improve the interviewing skills of students in the mental health professions.

Specifics of the instrument will be discussed, following several general issues that must be addressed prior to discussion of the merits of this semistructured interview. The first issue relates to the tautological nature of the validity data presented in the manual. That is, because the SCID-II is essentially a series of questions designed to elicit information regarding personality disorders based on the DSM-IV definition of a personality disorder, it is not surprising that the SCID-II agrees well with DSM-IV Axis II criteria. A more salient issue is that there are essentially no validity or reliability data presented in the manual nor are there currently any research studies contained in the literature directly related to the validity or reliability of this version of the SCID-II. The rather scant data that are reported in the manual

pertain to the previous *Diagnostic and Statistical Manual-III-Revised* (DSM-III-R) version of the SCID-II. Indeed, this is not directly acknowledged in the manual until the Reliability and Validity section (user's guide, p. 33). In fact, in a somewhat misleading manner, the second paragraph in the Introduction section of the manual states "The SCID-II has been used in three different types of studies" (user's guide, p. 1). The manual goes on to detail the types of studies where the "SCID-II" was used. These studies all used the DSM-III-R version of the SCID-II. This represents a particularly troubling and misleading lack of candor on the part of the authors because they later describe the alterations that occurred between the DSM-III-R version and the DSM-IV version of the SCID. After the publication of DSM-IV in 1994, the SCID-II was revised with many of the SCID-II questions reworded, "to make them more reflective of the subject's inner experience" (user's guide, p. 2). The final version of the revised SCID was published in 1997. Not only are the two versions not equivalent because the diagnostic criteria for several personality disorders changed between DSM-III-R and DSM-IV, but the questions were reworded to capture a different source of information. Therefore, to imply equivalency of the two versions is, at best, ingenuous.

The other issue involves the use of a categorical model rather than a dimensional model in DSM-IV for diagnosing personality disturbance. The issue of DSM's reliance on a categorical rather than a dimensional understanding of personality disorder has been the subject of discussion for some time (Widiger, 1993; Widiger & Costa, 1994). Recently, the finding of a stable structure of personality traits across clinical and nonclinical samples was interpreted as consistent with a dimensional classification of personality disorders (Livesley, Jang, & Vernon, 1998). Despite findings such as this, the DSM-IV and, in turn, SCID-II strictly adhere to a categorical diagnostic strategy despite the assertion to the contrary. The manual notes "SCID-II can be used to make Axis II diagnoses, either categorically (present or absent) or dimensionally (by noting the number of personality disorder criteria for each diagnosis that are coded '3')" (user's guide, p. 1). The implication that counting the number of symptoms present is somehow a dimensional approach is inaccurate. The finding of a significant residual heritability to lower order traits beyond that found for the broader traits drawn from higher in the hierarchy of personality suggests that specific symptoms may tap important molecular aspects of personality, but fail to tap the same higher-order dimensions within a particular disorder. Simply tallying up the symptoms will not necessarily lead to the accurate assessment of disorders of personality in any meaningful way (Livesley et al., 1998; Widiger & Costa, 1994).

All that being said, the SCID-II provides just what it says it provides: DSM-IV Axis II diagnosis for the following personality disorders: Avoidant, Dependent, Obsessive Compulsive, Passive Aggressive, Depressive, Paranoid, Schizotypal, Schizoid, Histrionic, Narcissistic, Borderline, Antisocial, and Personality NOS. Besides the manual and the interview itself, the material includes a SCID-II Personality Questionnaire. A computer-administered version of both the SCID-II Personality Questionnaire and the SCID-II interview is also available. The questionnaire is a self-report screening instrument designed to elicit behaviors that suggest the presence of a personality disorder and would therefore prompt the interviewer to administer the relevant portion of the SCID-II interview. The items on the questionnaire have a lower threshold than those contained on the interview. Indeed this strategy, as it relates to the DSM-III-R version of the SCID-II, results in lower false negative rates and increased predictive power (Jacobsberg, Perry, & Frances, 1995). For the time-conscious researcher, using the questionnaire provides a significant savings in time by allowing the interviewer to skip disorders where the subject has not endorsed a sufficient number of symptoms to warrant consideration of the disorder.

In general, the interview is well organized and easy to administer. It integrates the screening questionnaire in the probes (you've said that you ...) or phrases the probes in the present tense (do you ...). The interview also provides rule outs and a general description of the personality disorder prior to administering the symptom probes to fix, in the examiner's mind, what constitutes a particular personality disorder. Each question is tied to a symptom or sign of the particular personality disorder and is rated as ? = inadequate information, 1 = absent or false, 2 = subthreshold, and 3 = threshold or true. The interview encourages the examiner to elicit examples of behaviors to aid in

rating the presence or absence of a symptom. Finally, at the end of each personality disorder section are the criteria needed for the diagnosis of that particular personality disorder and a dichotomous rating as to the presence or absence of the disorder.

The manual is well written and clear. It systematically covers each question under each personality disorder by providing an item-by-item commentary explaining the intent of each question, offering examples of what constitutes an occurrence of the symptom, and explaining how the particular symptom may differ from other symptoms within the disorder. Additionally, the manual contains a case example accompanied by a completed SCID-II interview of the case. The manual has utility as a didactic tool for the instruction of mental health professionals in the assessment and diagnosis of DSM-IV personality disorders. Succinct and well-defined descriptions of each disorder as well as each symptom associated with the disorder are provided. This is an excellent place to start in teaching novice mental health professionals because it provides the paradigmatic DSM-IV definition of the disorder and offers rather well-constructed examples of what constitutes each symptom.

The manual provides suggestions for training in the use of the SCID-II. However, no guidelines are offered regarding the necessary level of training or general qualifications for use. A statement regarding user qualifications is required to meet Standard 5.4 of the *Standards for Educational and Psychological Testing* (American Educational Research Association, American Psychological Association, & National Council on Measurement in Education [Joint Committee], 1985). As mentioned previously, there are absolutely no data presented in the manual on the validity or reliability of the DSM-IV version of the SCID-II. Additionally, available evidence for the DSM-III-R version of the SCID indicates reliabilities varied greatly across disorders in clinical samples and were much lower for nonclinical samples. Indeed, even if the SCID had not been substantially altered between the two versions, extrapolation of reliability data from the DSM-III-R version to the DSM-IV is not warranted because the reported reliabilities are rather low and there is a complete lack of test-retest reliability for the DSM-III-R version (Rogers, 1995).

SUMMARY. Overall, the most recent version of the SCID-II would best be used as a research or didactic tool. In research settings individual investigators will have to establish both test-retest and interrater reliabilities for each personality disorder within the context of their sample. The lack of reliability and validity data for the current version of the SCID-II makes it difficult to develop an informed opinion with respect to the utility of the instrument in clinical practice. Additionally, a leap of faith is required with respect to the validity of the SCID because there are no data available to establish the concurrent validity of the instrument. As a tool for teaching DSM-IV-based diagnosis of personality disorder, the SCID-II shows great promise and stands out as a well-organized guide for the elicitation of symptoms compromising DSM-IV personality disorders. As far as the clinician is concerned, the SCID-II is best left in the lab or the classroom.

REVIEWER'S REFERENCES

American Educational Research Association, American Psychological Association, & National Council on Measurement in Education (Joint Committee). (1985). *Standards for educational and psychological testing.* Washington, DC: American Psychological Association, Inc.

Widiger, T. A. (1993). The DSM-III-R categorical personality disorder diagnoses: A critique and an alternative. *Psychological Inquiry, 4,* 75–90.

Widiger, T. A., & Costa. P. T. (1994). Personality and personality disorders. *Journal of Abnormal Psychology, 103,* 78–91.

Jacobsberg, L., Perry, S., & Frances, A. (1995). Diagnostic agreement between the SCID-II screening questionnaire and the personality disorder examination. *Journal of Personality Assessment, 65,* 428–433.

Rogers, R. (1995). *Diagnostic and structured interviewing: A handbook for psychologists.* Odessa, FL: Psychological Assessment Resources.

Livesley, W. J., Jang, K. L., & Vernon, P. A. (1998). Phenotypic and genetic structure of traits delineating personality disorder. *Archives of General Psychiatry, 55,* 941–948.

Review of the Structured Clinical Interview for DSM-IV Axis II Personality Disorders by SUZANNE G. MARTIN, Director of Needs Assessment, Charter Fairmount Behavioral Health System, Philadelphia, PA:

TEST COVERAGE & USE. The authors state that this test can be used for both research and clinical purposes. Although it is based on self-report, it does allow room for the clinician to respond with his or her observation of the patient's behavior during the interview. Where accurate diagnosis of Axis II disorder is necessary for either enrollment in research or for treatment planning, the SCID-II appears to provide an objective basis for diagnostic formulation. The SCID-II can also be used as a learning tool for students to improve interview skills by providing a sample of pertinent clinical questions to help make diagnostic decisions. In this respect, it appears it would be a useful tool for both graduate students and medical students in a training setting.

SAMPLES FOR TEST VALIDATION. No information is provided on test validation other than the fact that the test has been revised based on the changes in DSM-IV.

RELIABILITY. No data are available per the user's guide. Some clinical judgement is needed to differentiate between "true" and "subthreshold" responses and this may result in some variability in reliability.

PREDICTIVE VALIDITY. No data are available per the user's guide.

CONTENT VALIDITY. See above. Essentially, no guidance is provided for use of "Personality Disorder NOS."

TEST ADMINISTRATION. The test can be administered with a self-report completed by the patient (approximately 15 minutes) followed by a clinical interview (about 30 minutes depending on number of "yes" responses) or strictly by clinical interview. However, this latter procedure is very time-consuming for the clinician. Test instructions are provided; however, use of the test is not restricted to individuals trained in DSM-IV.

TEST REPORTING. Scoring is very clear and specific thresholds are specified for diagnosis consistent with DSM-IV criteria. No information is provided on reporting test results to patients or debriefing patients after the interview.

TEST AND ITEM BIAS. No information is provided on sample test groups. Some attempt is made to discriminate beliefs that are unique to the individual versus those shared by the majority of the individual's cultural group.

SUMMARY. Despite the lack of information provided regarding the reliability, validity, and field trials, the SCID-II appears to be a viable clinical and research tool for those trained in the use of diagnosis using the DSM-IV. The SCID-II offers an objective measure for pathology that is too frequently overlooked on Axis II or misdiagnosed because the same rigid diagnostic criteria applied to Axis I disorders are more casually used for personality disorders.

[375]
Student Styles Questionnaire™.

Purpose: "Designed to detect individual differences students display in their preferences, temperaments, and personal styles."
Population: Ages 8–13.
Publication Date: 1996.

Acronym: SSQ.

Scores, 8: Extroverted, Introverted, Practical, Imaginative, Thinking, Feeling, Organized, Flexible.

Administration: Group or individual.

Price Data, 1999: $80 per starter kit including manual (241 pages), classroom applications booklet, 5 Ready Score™ answer documents, and question booklet; $54 per 25 question booklets; $28.50 per 25 Ready Score™ answer documents; $15 per 25 record forms; $51 per manual; $15 per classroom applications booklet; $90.50 per microcomputer kit including 3.5-inch diskette, user's guide, and 25 record forms (Windows only).

Time: (30) minutes.

Authors: Thomas Oakland, Joseph Glutting, and Connie Horton.

Publisher: The Psychological Corporation.

Review of the Student Styles Questionnaire by GREGORY SCHRAW, *Associate Professor of Educational Psychology, University of Nebraska—Lincoln, Lincoln, NE:*

The Student Styles Questionnaire (SSQ) provides a measure of personal learning styles for students ages 8 through 17 using eight dimensions: Extroverted, Introverted, Practical, Imaginative, Thinking, Feeling, Organized, and Flexible. The SSQ is based on the assumption that preferred styles reflect a person's natural ability to learn.

The SSQ is accompanied by a 240-page manual that identifies four main uses. One is to match students' learning styles to teachers with similar styles. A second is to identify talented and gifted students. A third is to identify problem behaviors or students who may be at higher risk for problem behaviors. A fourth is to facilitate vocational counseling. Little information is given, however, about how the SSQ is interpreted to meet these purposes.

The SSQ is based on eight Jungian temperaments, including extraversion, introversion, sensing, intuiting, thinking, feeling, judging, and perceiving. A similar framework is used by the Myers-Briggs Type Indicator (MBTI; Myers & McCaulley, 1985; 251). Unfortunately, the manual does not provide information about Jungian psychology or how Jung's theory was used to construct the SSQ.

The SSQ includes 69 brief questions (e.g., When I have free time, I like to ...) followed by two alternatives. The test can be group or individually administered and requires approximately 15 to 30 minutes to complete. Each response is scored as a 1, 2, or 3 using a scoring key. Level 3 scores are weighted more heavily because they are more typical of idealized responses in each of the eight styles. Raw scores are computed for each style by adding individual responses.

The manual describes three separate interpretation strategies, one based on the eight basic styles, one based on four Keirseian styles, and one based on 16 style combinations. Separate 30- to 40-page chapters are devoted to each interpretative method in the test manual. Unfortunately, there is no explanation regarding which of the three interpretations is most valid.

Chapter 4 of the manual provides tips for interpreting the eight basic styles. Information is provided about the proportion of students who prefer that style, examples of typical family and social relationships, classroom applications designed to improve learning, suggestions for testing students with this preference, and a list of potential pitfalls (e.g., extroverted students act impulsively). Chapter 5 considers the four Keirseian combinations consisting of Practical-Organized, Practical-Flexible, Imaginative-Thinking, and Imaginative-Feeling. Chapter 6 considers each of the 16 mutually exclusive combinations that are possible from the eight basic styles (e.g., Extroverted, Practical, Feeling, Organized).

The SSQ has been standardized on a sample of 7,902 individuals, divided equally between males and females as well as each of the 10 age levels between the ages of 8 and 17. Approximately 70% were white, 15% Afro-American, and 10% Hispanic.

The manual provides limited information about the reliability and validity of scores from the SSQ. Norms are presented for four style scores (which do not correspond to those described in chapters 4, 5, and 6), including Extraverted-Introverted, Practical-Imaginative, Thinking-Feeling, and Organized-Flexible. Test-retest reliability at 7 months averaged .74. There is no information about the internal consistency of any of the scales.

The manual describes the SSQ's construct validity in more detail. The original instrument included 245 items that were reduced to 69 items in several standardization studies. The 69 items yielded four scores (i.e., Extraverted-Introverted, Practical-Imaginative, Thinking-Feeling, and Organized-Flexible) that were examined using exploratory factor analysis for validity. None of the four factors were highly intercorrelated, suggesting little redundancy among style scores.

Some criterion-related validity data are provided. For example, chapter 10 of the manual presents correlations between the four style scores and preferences for parties, quiet time, reading, and school activities. Information is included as well about program involvement (e.g., sports), activity preferences (e.g., art), and vocational choices (e.g., banker).

Convergent and divergent validity data compare the SSQ with a variety of other scales including the Myers-Briggs Type Indicator (Myers & McCaulley, 1985), Wechsler Intelligence Scale for Children—Third Edition (WISC-III; Wechsler, 1981), California Achievement Test (CAT; CTB/ McGraw-Hill, 1985), and the Values Inventory (VI; Oakland, 1990). Neither CAT nor WISC-R scores were correlated with the SSQ, suggesting that style preferences are independent of achievement and ability estimates. In contrast, style scores were correlated with the Helpfulness and Loyalty subscales of the VI. The Thinking-Feeling style score was negatively correlated with the VI, whereas the Organized-Flexible score was correlated positively. These findings indicate that students who prefer an organized style are more likely to be helpful. There were a number of significant correlations between SSQ scales and the MBTI in the expected direction.

The strengths of the SSQ include (a) easy administration and scoring, (b) convergent validity with the MBTI, and (c) a clearly written and informative manual. The instrument would be stronger, however, with a clear theoretical framework that explicates the relationship between Jung's work and the eight learning styles scores. As noted above, additional reliability data on the SSQ are needed.

There are two potential weaknesses with the SSQ. One is that the manual describes three rather different interpretation strategies based on 4, 8, or 16 style scores. Currently it is not clear whether these three strategies lead to the same conclusions. Differences in interpretation of the SSQ may adversely affect score validity. A second problem is the lack of a statistical relationship between the SSQ and achievement and ability scores. Presumably, understanding learning styles is important because a better match between students and teachers, or students and programs of study, may increase learning. The low correlations among the SSQ, CAT, and WISC-R belie this assumption.

SUMMARY. Overall, the SSQ provides a quick way to assess learning style preferences along eight dimensions. Debate continues as to whether the SSQ or MBTI measure stable preferences that are substantively related to important educational outcomes such as amount and depth of learning. SSQ scores should be used cautiously and combined with scores from similar tests whenever possible. Basing important educational decisions solely on the SSQ seems questionable.

REVIEWER'S REFERENCES

CTB/McGraw-Hill. (1985). California Achievement Tests. Monterey, CA: Author.
Myers, I. B., & McCaulley, M. H. (1985). Manual: A guide to the development and use of the Myers-Briggs Type Indicator. Palo Alto, CA: Consulting Psychologists Press.
Oakland, T. (1990). The Values Inventory. Austin, TX: Author.
Wechsler, D. (1991). Wechsler Intelligence Scale for Children—Third Edition. San Antonio, TX: The Psychological Corporation.

Review of the Student Styles Questionnaire by JAY R. STEWART, Assistant Professor and Director, Rehabilitation Counseling Program, Bowling Green State University, Bowling Green, OH:

GENERAL DESCRIPTION. The Student Styles Questionnaire (SSQ) is a self-report instrument designed to ascertain individual differences in students' preferences, temperaments, and personal styles. The primary use of the SSQ is to aid teachers in identifying student aptitudes and learning styles, promoting educational development, and exploring prevocational interests.

The SSQ contains 69 items, which refer to the respondent's behavior, reactions to various situations, and desired activities. Each item is a partial statement to be completed with a forced-choice completion format. All but one of the items refers directly to the respondent's desires, preferences, or behaviors. Each item was designed to measure an aspect of one of the four theoretical constructs described related to Jung's (1921/1972) typology of personal temperament described below. The SSQ, intended for children ages 8 through 17, has a reading level for students in third grade and above. The items describe common student activities with families, friends, and school settings.

ADMINISTRATION AND SCORING. The SSQ, as a paper-and-pencil test, can be administered individually or to large groups, depending on the children's ages, and takes about 30 minutes to complete. Additional test proctors can be used for large groups to help with appropriate test-taking behaviors. The test can be read by the student, or, when needed, by the test administrator. If needed, questionnaire words can be defined for students.

The SSQ can be hand or computer scored. For hand scoring, the answer sheet contains the scoring system. After the SSQ is completed, the item numerical scores (1–3) are entered in the appropriate boxes and tallied, producing preferred and nonpreferred learning styles. The nonpreferred are subtracted from the preferred learning styles and the difference scores are entered on a prevalence-based *T*-score graph, which produces a profile of learning styles. For computer scoring, the student enters SSQ answers directly onto a computer key entry form. The SSQ Interpretive Software produces an interpretive report from the entry form.

THEORETICAL AND TECHNICAL BACKGROUND. Those familiar with the Myers-Briggs Type Indicator (MBTI; 251) will recognized the SSQ's theoretical and technical origins. Carl Jung proposed psychological types as means of describing how individuals use the four functions—thinking, sensation, feeling, and intuition—combined with their tendencies on the Extroversion-Introversion continuum. Myers and Briggs (Myers & McCaulley, 1985) developed the MBTI to determine the direction and strength of a person's preference for Jung's functions. The SSQ was developed to measure the student learning styles (similar to Jung's functions), based on their dichotomous learning style scales of Extroverted-Introverted, Practical-Imaginative, Thinking-Feeling, and Organized-Flexible. The interaction among these styles is also determined. According to Oakland, Glutting, and Horton (the authors of the Student Styles Questionnaire), the dichotomous styles can be combined into 16 possible style combinations.

INTERPRETATION. SSQ results can be interpreted by three different methods. The first method is limited to determining learning preferences in each of the four dichotomous learning style scales. The other two determine a specific combination of styles: the Four Keirseian Combinations (Keirsey & Bates, 1984) and the Sixteen Style Combination, which is similar to the MBTI interpretation approach. The SSQ manual provides interpretations for each of the three methods, offering general characteristics, social and familial relationships, classroom applications, and potential pitfalls for each of the styles and style combinations.

TEST CHARACTERISTICS. Standard scores are based on a sample of 7,902 students ages 8–17 years. The sample was representative of ra-

cial, ethnic, gender, and region of residence for the United States (Stafford & Oakland, 1996b). Test-retest reliability with a 7-month interval between administrations averages .74 for the four scales. External validity was investigated through contrasted groups in vocational and activity preferences, resulting in highly significant differences between group SSQ scores. Understandably, the SSQ scores correlated highly with MBTI scores. The SSQ captured 30% of the total variability of the MBTI. The SSQ scores are similar among racial groups and age groups (Stafford & Oakland, 1996a).

CONCLUSION. The SSQ investigates important aspects of student learning styles. The questionnaire is easy to administer, score, and interpret, possibly making it a useful classroom activity for teachers attempting to improve learning environments and counselors trying to provide appropriate in-school interventions. However, more research is needed to confirm the usefulness of the instrument. There appears to be no controlled research in which the SSQ results are actually used to improve student performance. Additionally, the SSQ manual places a heavy emphasis on discovering the student's *preferred* learning style and accommodating the learning environment to that style. Myers and Myers (1980) suggested that balancing Jung's dominant with lesser-used functions is important so that each function is available for learning about and dealing with the environment. It seems appropriate the teachers also challenge their students to explore and strengthen their lesser-used functions. It appears that a number of common mental disorders, such as Attention Deficit Disorder, would skew the results of the SSQ. Finally, teachers and school counselors are cautioned not to use the SSQ as a replacement for proper referral and management of students with learning problems related to serious mental disorders.

REVIEWER'S REFERENCES

Jung, C. G. (1921/1972). Psychological types. In *Collected works* (vol. 6). Princeton, NJ: Princeton University Press.
Myers, I. B., & Myers, P. B. (1980). *Gifts differing.* Palo Alto, CA: Consulting Psychologists Press.
Keirsey, D., & Bates, M. (1984). *Please understand me: Character and temperament types* (4th ed.). Del Mar, CA: Gnosology Books.
Myers, I. B., & McCaulley, M. H. (1985). *Manual: A guide to the development and use of the Myers-Briggs Type Indicator.* Palo Alto, CA: Consulting Psychologists Press.
Stafford, M. E., & Oakland, T. D. (1996a). Racial-ethnic comparisons of temperament constructs for three age groups using the Student Styles Questionnaire. *Measurement and Evaluation in Counseling and Development, 29,* 100.
Stafford, M. E., & Oakland, T. D. (1996b). Validity of temperament constructs using the Student Styles Questionnaire: Comparison for three racial-ethnic groups. *Journal of Psychoeducational Assessment, 14,* 109–120.

Study Attitudes and Methods Survey [Revised Short Form].

Purpose: "Developed to measure non-cognitive factors associated with success in school."
Population: Junior high, high school, college.
Publication Dates: 1972–1985.
Acronym: SAMS.
Scores, 6: Academic Interest-Love of Learning, Academic Drive-Conformity, Study Methods, Study Anxiety, Manipulation, Alienation Toward Authority.
Administration: Group.
Price Data, 1998: $13.50 per 25 machine-scoring booklets and answer sheets [$47.50 per 100, $223.50 per 500]; $4.75 per 25 profile and interpretation guides (specify high school or college norms); $14.75 per set of hand-scoring keys; $7.75 per specimen set including test booklet, answer sheet, profile sheet, and manual ('88, 12 pages); $4 per manual.
Time: (20–25) minutes.
Authors: William B. Michael, Joan J. Michael, and Wayne S. Zimmerman.
Publisher: EdITS/Educational and Industrial Testing Service.
Cross References: See T5:2538 (1 reference), T4:2604 (6 references), and T3:2340 (2 references); for reviews by Allen Berger and John W. Lombard of an earlier edition, see 8:818 (6 references); see also T2:1766 (4 references).

Review of the Study Attitudes and Methods Survey [Revised Short Form] by ROBERT G. HARRINGTON, Professor, Department of Psychology & Research in Education, University of Kansas, Lawrence, KS:

The Study Attitudes and Methods Survey, 1985 Edition (SAMS Short Form) is a 90-item, Likert-type, self-report measure of attitudes toward school and associated study habits that the authors claim are associated with academic success in high school and college. The SAMS Survey can be administered either individually or on a group basis in 35 to 40 minutes according to the authors. The authors state that the SAMS can be used to identify students at risk for poor school performance due to ineffective study techniques or because of negative attitude toward school so that they might receive appropriate career counseling or strategies to overcome deficiencies in study skills. The authors suggest administering the SAMS at the beginning of the school year to identify students needing individual or group counseling.

The SAMS contains six factor dimensions with 15 items per factor scale. These factors include:

Academic Interest-Love of Learning—This factor is intended to measure the pleasure a student might gain in engaging in an academic activity. High scorers like writing papers, reading, solving problems, and doing library research. Low scorers may need the teacher to develop special assignments to improve interest and motivation.

Academic Drive-Conformity—This factor supposedly taps a student's persistence in academic task completion and conformity to rules and standards set by instructors. High scorers possess a very strong determination to succeed in academia by doing what their teachers require of them. Low scorers lack interest in meeting the standards and expectation of their teachers. It is suggested that sometimes clarification of teacher expectations on home assignments and on examinations can improve performance.

Study Methods—This factor tries to assess work habits conducive to academic success such as organization, planning, and time-management that might be used in taking examinations, meeting assignment requirements and deadlines, and in studying effectively. High scores are indicative of systematic and organized working habits useful in completing assignments and examinations efficiently. Low scores indicate a need to spend more time and effort in completing assignments and in achieving satisfactory grades. Remediations include instruction in study skills such as note taking, organization, writing skills, and in management of test anxiety.

Study Anxiety—This factor is meant to be sensitive to students who may lack self-confidence and exhibit performance anxiety that could interfere with effective study and test-taking skills. High scorers are very self-confident about their abilities to perform in school. Students scoring low on this scale are said to lack self-confidence and to have anxiety over meeting the standards set by themselves, teachers, and parents. It is suggested that one remediation for low scores might be an adjustment of goals to a more realistic level in keeping with the student's ability level.

Manipulation—This factor is designed to identify students who use power and influence to achieve academic goals rather than expending appropriate time at study and enjoying the intrinsic value of learning opportunity itself. Students scoring high on this scale tend to do their academic work without asking for special favors. Low scorers may tend to "con" a teacher into not having to meet course requirements. Students with a low score on this scale may need social skills training.

Alienation Toward Authority—This factor is developed to be sensitive to students who feel isolated or rejected and consequently defy the rules and regulations of the school or college. High scorers feel satisfied that the classroom rules and regulations are fair. Students scoring low tend to feel rejected and isolated, and may feel alone and not a part of the school environment. The authors advise that there may be a sense of pride in "beating the system" by trying to circumvent the rules. Feelings of alienation and rejection seem to interfere with work in school and in gaining success in interpersonal relationships. The authors advise that low scorers may need to "talk to blow off steam."

Students respond to each of the 90 items on the SAMS Short Form using a 4-point Likert-type response continuum in terms of the degree to which the activity described in the item is like the respondent. The response continuum ranges from, N-*Not at all like me, or different from me*; 1-*Seldom, or somewhat like me*; 2-*Frequently, or much like me*; and 3-*Almost always, or very much like me.*

Directions for administration of the SAMS appear on the cover of the test protocol but should be read by the test examiner in group administrations. Although the SAMS Short Form is untimed, it typically takes college students 20 minutes and high school students 25 minutes to complete the SAMS Survey. The authors of the SAMS state that the validity of the SAMS is "based on frank, accurate responses," but it is unclear how examiners can ensure that a respondent's answers are accurate and reliable given that there are no validity scales on the instrument with no opportunity to interview the subject about their written responses.

The SAMS items and response selections are printed in the SAMS Short Form machine scoring booklet for computer scoring using optical scanning on-site or by the publisher, EdITS. Alternatively, the test protocol may be hand scored using scoring stencil overlays. Because differential weights of 0, 1, 2, or 3 are assigned to responses,

the higher the raw score the more the activity represented by the items is like the examinee. A respondent's raw score for any one of the six factors may range between 0 and 45. The test developers admonish users to question the validity of test protocols in which 10 or more items have been omitted because the validity of the scores may be "questionable," but surely the validity of the scale is always in question when any of the items have been omitted. Scoring results are reported in *T*-scores and percentile rankings on a profile sheet for each of the six scales.

It is somewhat unclear what the qualifications of SAMS examiners must be but the examiner's manual persists in describing its use by counselors and teachers and claims that users must be trained in measurement theory and SAMS interpretation, but no specific qualifications for users are offered. The authors suggest that test results may be offered on an individual basis or in group sessions but given the confidentiality issues and the sensitivity of the contents of the test it is unlikely that group reporting could ever be undertaken ethically.

The strategy for interpretation is to plot raw scores on the SAMS profile sheets (High School or College) and to note the corresponding *T*-score and percentile rank. Each of the six SAMS factor scores has a mean *T*-score of 50 and a standard deviation of 10 but low and high scores are considered to be in the lower 25th percentile and upper 75th percentile respectively. The authors simply offer the following anecdotal bit of advice: "Profile patterns consistently above the mean suggest desirable habit and motivational characteristics. Low profiles are said to be indicative of problems in this area perhaps calling for individual counseling" (manual, p. 3).

The authors also advise that it is possible to compare the profile scores of an individual with those of others at the same educational level in their classroom. The more traits on which a student scores highly the more likely that they have the attitudes and skills helpful in achieving the best possible school marks. Several low scores are meant to suggest potential difficulties in learning and in adjusting to the requirements of the curriculum in that school. Attitudes represented by these low scores might account in part for failing grades and for disliking school. In general, high achieving students score best on the first three measured constructs (Academic Interest, Academic

Drive-Conformity, and Study Methods), whereas low achievers and "trouble makers," as described by the test authors, would be expected to score low on the last three scales (Student Anxiety, Manipulation, and Alienation). This finding makes good sense and has been corroborated by research by the authors in that two second-order factors exist that support these two, three-scale clusters (Michael & Bachelor, 1988).

The authors suggest that the SAMS may be used by a counselor in conjunction with an academic aptitude measure to evaluate a high school student's interest and motivation in pursuing a college education. They even suggest that it might be used in lieu of a college entrance examination or aptitude test but this practice would be ill-advised. Furthermore, the authors present no research that would support this practice. Because five of the six dimensions on the SAMS seem to be related to attitude, interest, temperament, and motivation toward study, and only one scale is directly related to study skills, the authors wrongfully have inferred that instruction in study skills is less important than these other attitudinal factors. Perhaps the authors of the SAMS Short Form need to conduct more research to create more items for scales that assess the many facets of study skills.

Items for the SAMS were developed based upon a review of the literature of student study methods and motivation as well as an informal analysis of student responses to personal interviews, written responses to open-ended questions on course evaluation forms, and from an analysis of a large set of items collected over a period of more than 20 years by William Michael (Michael & Reeder, 1952; Michael, Jones, & Trembly, 1959; Zimmerman, Michael, & Michael, 1970; Michael, Lee, Michael, Hooke, & Zimmerman, 1971). In addition, a number of unpublished correlational studies that distinguish high achieving from low achieving students are said to have been conducted but these data are not provided in the test manual. In 1985 the authors undertook to develop a shortened form of the original SAMS (Michael, Jones, & Trembly, 1959), which contained 150 test items. Using a principal components factor solution in two cross-validation studies that are not well described in the examiner's manual, the authors managed to reduce the length of the original SAMS Survey to 90 items resulting in what is now called the SAMS Short Form, 1985 Edition.

Norms for the SAMS Short Form for high school students are based upon scores from only four high schools (two in California, one in Oregon, and one in New Jersey). College norms are derived from only two colleges (a community college in a Los Angeles suburb and a state college in the Greater Los Angeles area). Although the authors hasten to add that this sparse data will be "supplemented over the next few years" (manual, p. 4), the current normative data contained in the examiner's manual are certainly not representative of the U.S. population and in no way represent the stratified random sample that would be most appropriate for this type of test.

Internal-consistency reliability estimates (coefficient alpha) for the six factors of the SAMS Short Form were reasonably high ranging between .76 and .90 with a median value of .87. Standard errors of measurement ranged between 2.5 and 3.6 with a median value close to 3.0, which is reasonable for a scale with a potential score range of 45 points. Unfortunately, no other reliabilities, such as test-reliability, are reported. This is a major shortcoming of the test. The authors offer evidence for the validity of the SAMS in three forms in the examiner's manual. First, the authors report one study of intercorrelations of the six factor scales of the SAMS Short Form for a sample of 588 tenth grade students in a suburban high school in the Greater Los Angeles area and a similar intercorrelational study for each of two samples: (a) a middle-class suburban Anglo group of 337 tenth and eleventh grade students; and (b) a middle-class rural Anglo group of 146 tenth and eleventh grade students. One other study was conducted on a sample of 181 community college students from the Greater Los Angeles area. Review of correlational matrices and factor solutions showed evidence for a relatively high degree of differential validity for the fourth, fifth and sixth factors of the SAMS that represent nonfacilitative dimensions of study attitudes, whereas the higher intercorrelations among the first three scales would indicate a tendency for them to define one dimension (Michael, Denny, Ireland-Galman, & Michael, 1985; Nadson, Michael, & Michael, 1988).

Only one study of 350 tenth grade students was reported to evaluate the criterion-related validity of the SAMS (Nadson, Michael, & Michael, 1988) with a standardized achievement test. The highest concurrent validity coefficient was statistically significant at the .01 level but showed a low correlation of only .34 between the Academic-Drive and Conformity factor scales and a standardized measure of computational skills. Previous studies of the original SAMS showed similarly low correlations with GKPA and school performance in college (Michael, Michael, & Zimmerman, 1972). The authors provide no data to support its use in making predictions about who will fare well in school based upon the SAMS Short Form results. The authors rely on old studies comparing the original SAMS with the COPES (Knapp & Knapp, 1977), the D-F Opinion Survey (Guilford, Christensen, & Bond, 1956), and the School Environment Preference Survey (SEPS) (Gordon, 1978) to show the concurrent validity relationship of the SAMS with other affective measures. Even though some of the correlations of the original SAMS are significant with some of the scales on these three instruments, those correlations are always low.

SUMMARY. The SAMS Short Form is a novel instrument that can be used to try to assess potentially important concepts of study attitudes and methods for learners needing counseling to decide what their academic futures should be. Unfortunately, the SAMS Short Form has not been developed based upon a nationally stratified random sample. Although there is some support for the factor structure of the instrument and the internal consistency of the instrument there is a dearth of research data to support the predictive validity and concurrent validity of scores from this instrument. Instruments addressing skills strengths and needs tend to fit into the current Zeitgeist of "positive psychology" but, unfortunately, the SAMS Short Form lacks the basic psychometric qualities required by the *Standards for Educational and Psychological Testing* (American Educational Research Association, American Psychological Association, & National Council on Measurement in Education, 1999) that would permit recommendation for its use at this time.

REVIEWER'S REFERENCES

Michael, W. B., & Reeder, D. E. (1952). The development and validation of a preliminary form of a study-habits inventory. *Educational and Psychological Measurement, 12,* 236–247.

Guilford, J. P., Christensen, P. R., & Bond, N. A., Jr. (1956). The DF Opinion Survey. Los Angeles: Sheridan Psychological.

Michael, W. B., Jones, R. A., & Trembly, W. A. (1959). The factored dimensions of a measure of motivation for college students. *Educational and Psychological Measurement, 19,* 667-671.

Zimmerman, W. S., Michael, J. J., & Michael, W. B. (1970). The factored dimensions of the Study Attitudes and Methods (Survey test—experimental form). *Educational and Psychological Measurement, 30,* 433–436.

Michael, W. B., Lee, Y. B., Michael, J. J., Hooke, O., & Zimmerman, W. A. (1971). A partial redefinition of the factorial structure of the Study Attitudes and Methods Survey (SAMS) test. *Educational and Psychological Measurement, 31,* 545–547.

Michael, W. B., Michael, J. J., & Zimmerman, W. S. (1972). Study Attitudes and Methods Survey (SAMS). San Diego, CA: EdITS.

Knapp, R. R., & Knapp, L. (1977). Career Orientation Placement and Evaluation Survey (COPES). San Diego, CA: EdITS.

Gordon, L. V. (1978). School Preference Survey (SEPS). San Diego, CA: EdITS.

Michael, W. B., Denny, B., Ireland-Galman, M., & Michael, J. J. (1985). The factorial validity of the Study Attitudes and Methods Scale (SAMS). *Educational and Psychological Measurement, 45,* 647–653.

Michael, W. B., & Bachelor, P. (1988). A comparison of the orthogonal and the oblique factor structures of correlation matrixes of individual items and composites of items (subtests) derived from a standardized affective measure. *Educational and Psychological Measurement, 48*(1), 93–103.

Nadson, J. S., Michael, W. B., & Michael, J. J. (1988). The factorial and concurrent validity of a revised form of the Study Attitudes and Methods Survey (SAMS). *Educational and Psychological Measurement, 48*(4), 969–994.

American Educational Research Association, American Psychological Association, & National Council on Measurement in Education. (1999). *Standards for educational and psychological testing.* Washington, DC: American Educational Research Association.

Review of the Study Attitudes and Methods Survey [Revised Short Form] by KENNETH A. KIEWRA, Professor of Educational Psychology, University of Nebraska—Lincoln, Lincoln, NE:

The original Study Attitudes and Methods Survey (SAMS) was published in 1972 and reviewed in *The Eighth Mental Measurements Yearbook* (Buros, 1978). The two reviewers criticized the SAMS on many levels and recommended against its use. The Survey was revised into a shorter form and that new edition was published in 1985. That shorter form actually contains the identical items of its predecessor and much of its supporting data still stem from the 1970s.

Because so little has changed, I raise many of the same criticisms voiced in the *Eighth MMY* and add several of my own. First, I provide a brief overview of the revised SAMS.

OVERVIEW. The SAMS' purpose is to measure noncognitive factors associated with school success (attitude, study habits, and motivation) in order to help identify and counsel students who might experience difficulty in high school or college.

The revised SAMS now contains 90 items that first appeared verbatim on the original 150-item version. The items are sorted into six scales: three representative of positive characteristics (Academic Interest, Academic Drive, and Study Methods) and three representative of negative characteristics (Study Anxiety, Manipulation, and Alienation Toward Authority). Students complete the SAMS by indicating whether each statement is "not at all like me, or different from me," "seldom, or somewhat like me," "frequently, or much like me," or "almost always, or very much like me."

The survey is group- or self-administered and takes about 20–25 minutes to complete. It is either machine scored or personally scored using an overlay stencil. Resulting scale scores are easily plotted on a profile sheet for interpretation.

CRITICISMS. Several criticisms are leveled against the SAMS pertaining to its composition, psychometric properties, and practical utility.

Composition. Regarding its composition, the survey is dated. The items used today were developed in the 1950s. Moreover, item development is tied neither to theory nor research. Instead, items represented students' interview statements or responses on course evaluation forms (presumably from the 1950s). Therefore, the items do not intentionally reflect any previous or contemporary theory relating to motivation or learning. Critical ideas and research findings related to attribution theory, self-efficacy, expertise, metacognition, information processing, problem solving, and studying, for example, are simply not represented in this survey. The omission of current research and theory is perhaps most obvious in the Study Methods scale where items often reflect vague or questionable practices. Although students are asked whether they review for tests, for example, no item probes *how* students review. Certain review practices, such as reciting or rewriting information, have proven ineffective but are actually considered positive behaviors in the SAMS. Meanwhile, certain key elements of academic success such as note taking, mnemonics, elaboration, and developing graphic organizers are never mentioned.

There are other problems with the SAMS items. As mentioned in previous reviews, some items seem redundant. As an example of the redundancy problem, note the similarity among the following items all probing test anxiety: (Item 4) "Examinations make me so nervous that I do not do nearly as well on them as I should." (Item 34) "I dread taking examinations even when I am reasonably well prepared." (Item 82) "I am anxious before an exam even when I have studied for it." Another item problem dating back to the original version is the uneven response categories. The four possible responses are associated with varying percentages. The first response ("not at all like me, or different from me") is chosen if it applies less than 5% of the time. The next three response categories have different and much larger ranges (i.e., 45%, 35%, and 15%, respectively). No rationale is provided for this uneven response distribution.

Psychometric Properties. Issues must also be raised regarding the SAMS psychometric properties. Regarding normative data, the test was normed for college students using only one community college (*n* = 181) and one state supported college (*n* = 179) both in Los Angeles. Including few students from only two public colleges in the same geographic region violates good norming procedures. Moreover, no mention is made about the grade level of the high school or college students participating or how they were selected.

Regarding reliability, each of the six scales showed good internal consistency (range .76–.90). High internal consistency, however, might be a byproduct of the item redundancy issue mentioned earlier. The SAMS also showed acceptable intercorrelations among scales. The three "positive" scales were appropriately intercorrelated. Similarly, the three "negative" scales were appropriately intercorrelated. Intercorrelations between the "positive" and "negative" scales were appropriately low or even negative. The concern is that test-retest reliability is not reported. Without this index, it is unwise to administer the SAMS pre-post and assume that performance changes are due to intervention.

Most of the validity data presented stem from the original 1972 version and therefore cannot confirm that the revised version meets its stated purpose. Only one study (completed with 350 tenth graders) examined the revised SAMS score validity and obtained "low validity coefficients for the SAMS factor scales" (manual, p. 10). In terms of criterion validity, SAMS scores are never correlated with scores on other study behavior inventories or with actual study behaviors.

Practical Utility. A final criticism involves the SAMS practical utility. The authors contend that it might be used as an entrance exam. This application is questionable given that the survey relies on self-report data that are easily faked. Moreover, there are no data linking performance on the SAMS to success beyond a single college course. The SAMS also has limited utility for clinical intervention. The authors offer vague or meaningless implications for students who score poorly on a SAMS scale, such as meeting with a counselor or teacher, spending more time on assignments, or resolving misunderstandings.

CONCLUSION. In conclusion, the "new" SAMS is not very new and is flawed in its composition, psychometric properties, and practical utility. It is still not recommended for use.

REVIEWER'S REFERENCE

Buros, O. K. (Ed.) (1978). *The eighth mental measurements yearbook.* Highland Park, NJ: The Gryphon Press.

[377]

Substance Abuse Life Circumstance Evaluation.

Purpose: "Designed to assess alcohol and drug use/abuse behavior, as well as the role that attitude and stress may play in this use/abuse."
Population: Adults.
Publication Date: 1988.
Acronym: SALCE.
Scores, 6: Test-Taking Attitude, Life Circumstance Evaluation, Drinking Evaluation Category, Alcohol Addiction Evaluation, Drug Use Evaluation, Summary Score.
Administration: Individual or group.
Manual: No manual.
Price Data, 1998: $4.50 per evaluation.
Time: (20) minutes.
Comments: Self-administered; computer scored, IBM compatible with either DOS or Windows required; provides both DSM-IV classification and ASAM patient placement criteria.
Author: ADE Incorporated.
Publisher: ADE Incorporated.

Review of the Substance Abuse Life Circumstance Evaluation by ANITA M. HUBLEY, Assistant Professor of Educational and Consulting Psychology, and Special Education, The University of British Columbia, Vancouver, British Columbia, Canada:

The Substance Abuse Life Circumstance Evaluation (SALCE) is a 98-item self-report inventory that assesses alcohol and drug use/abuse in adults as well as the role that attitude and stress play in this use/abuse. Results from the SALCE can be used to provide direction for an interview or to assist in decisions regarding initial level of intervention.

The SALCE is self-administered, but computer scored. The computer-scoring program produces information for six areas: (a) Test Taking Attitude (TTA), which acts as a validity measure and describes the respondent's attitude toward the test using one of six categories. This is an important measure whenever the behavior of interest is likely to be affected by a desire to avoid disapproval. It is disappointing, however, that no acknowledgement was given that the TTA subscale includes approximately 29 of the 33 Marlowe-Crowne Social Desirability Scale items. (b) Life Circumstance Evaluation (LCE) is a measure of life stress and instability and also indicates the type of impression the individual is attempting to portray of his or her life. Scores on LCE are divided into four categories. (c) Drinking Evaluation Category (DEC) consists of five categories and measures the respondent's self-report of behavioral, social, and clinical symptoms consistent with problem drinking and alcoholism. (d) Alcohol Addiction Evaluation (AAE) does not provide a score but simply indicates the degree to which the respondent identifies with symptoms of tolerance, loss of control, and withdrawal. (e) Drug Use Evaluation (DUE) classifies the respondent's drug use behavior into one of five categories and indicates whether addiction to drugs is indicated. (f) Summary Score combines the results of all of the subscores to reflect both "the individual's level of substance abuse ... [and] the relative level of ingrained behavior associated with his/her substance abuse" (SALCE computer-scoring demo). Along with each Summary Score are suggested DSM-IV classifications and a recommendation for type or level of intervention. It is not specified anywhere, however, exactly which items comprise each subscale, how the categories and descriptors for these subscales were derived or validated, or how the suggested level of intervention is determined. Such a lack of detail not only serves to "mystify" the assessment process for the test user (Butcher, 1994), but makes it nearly impossible for test users or evaluators to detect any errors that might exist in the algorithms used to determine subscale scores and interpretations (Most, 1987).

The computerized scoring program for the SALCE provides an easy-to-follow data entry system with plenty of instructions. ADE Inc. seems to acknowledge the human tendency to make data entry errors by requiring that all data be entered twice. If the entered responses to an item do not match, one is then cued to correct the discrepancy. The only problem with this system is that the initial row of data is visible on the screen while the data are being entered the second time and there is nothing to prevent the user from simply re-entering the data using the data on the screen rather than the raw data from the inventory. The computer instructions should be modified to remind users of the extremely common likelihood of making errors and the associated impact this has on test scores and interpretation.

In addition, the initial line of data should not be visible to the user when entering the data the second time.

Normative data for the SALCE are limited despite claims that the inventory is widely used. Norms are only available for TTA, LCE, and Summary Scores for male and female undergraduate students (Cannon, Childers, Allred, & Hines, 1992; Tolley, 1994). Further normative work needs to focus on large samples of (minority and non-minority) male and female inpatient and outpatient substance abusers, DWI offenders, and incarcerated individuals. In addition, norms for pregnant women users/abusers would be useful.

Very little reliability evidence for the SALCE has been provided. Cannon et al. (1992) examined test-retest reliability over a 2-week period in undergraduate students and reported reliabilities of .88 for TTA, .74 for LCE, and .82 for the Summary Score. There was 52.1% agreement over the 2 weeks for DEC category and 63.3% agreement for DUE category. Although the initial evidence is positive, further research is needed with other samples as noted above for the norms. No internal consistency data for the subscales appears to be available.

A small number of validity studies have been conducted using the SALCE. In a college sample, the SALCE correlated .45 with the Minnesota Multiphasic Personality Inventory-2 (MMPI-2) MacAndrew Scale (Wilson, Childers, Durham, Allred, & Hines, 1992) and .38 for men and .16 for women with the Common Alcohol Logistic—Revised (CAL-R; Wilson, Childers, Allred, & Durham, 1994). Both of these studies report a substantial number of low to moderate correlations between the MMPI-2 clinical scales and both the SALCE Summary Score and LCE. Work by Tolley (1994) shows some evidence for convergent and discriminant validity of SALCE Summary Scores using the California Personality Inventory—Revised (CPI-R) with college students, but not all of the correlational results fit the expected pattern. In a DUI offender sample, DEC category and counselor assessment of alcohol involvement were strongly related (gamma of .76; Siegal et al., no date). A document prepared by Marsteller, Falek, and Coltharp (no date) reports that the SALCE Summary Score was the best predictor of alcohol and drug DUI recidivism, followed by income, gender, marital status, employment status, age, and years of education.

Notably, the TTA subscale correlated .59 for men and .51 for women with the Good Impression subscale of the CPI-R and .43 for men and .40 for women with the Well-Being subscale of the CPI-R (Tolley, 1994). These moderate correlations with the CPI-R validity scales provide support for TTA as a measure of social desirability. However, ADE Inc. needs to clarify what role this subscale plays in the SALCE. Is TTA a validity (or bias) measure or is it a personality or situation-based characteristic?

SUMMARY. The SALCE is a fairly basic measure of alcohol and drug use/abuse. Although the measure has the advantage of including both alcohol and drug questions as well as items about "attitude" and stress in a single instrument, the SALCE is quite a bit longer than many other available measures (e.g., Drug Abuse Screening Test, DAST, T5:859; Michigan Alcoholism Screening Test, MAST, 232). Although the SALCE apparently has been in use since 1986, the normative data for the measure are inadequate; and both the reliability and validity evidence is too limited to support the widespread use of this measure. Future research needs to focus on larger and more diverse samples. Two additional problems with this measure include: (a) the lack of transparency in the scoring and interpretation of the subscales, and (b) the lack of published material in peer-reviewed and widely available outlets. All of the available material on this test consists of conference presentations, unpublished reports, and a Master's thesis. No manual is available. Given these limitations, readers would be wise to consider other measures with fewer items and more established psychometric properties such as the Alcohol Use Disorders Identification Test (AUDIT; Saunders, Aasland, Babor, De La Fuente, & Grant, 1993), TWEAK (Chan, Pristach, Welte, & Russell, 1993), DAST (Skinner, 1982), and MAST (Selzer, 1971).

REVIEWER'S REFERENCES

Marsteller, F. A., Falek, A., & Coltharp, J. C. (no date). *Summary of recent evaluation findings: Alcohol and drug DUI Risk Reduction Program.* Unpublished manuscript, Emory University.

Siegal, H. A., Fisher, J. H., Rapp, R. C., Cole, P. A., Wagner, J. H., Kelliher, C. W., & Kay, J. (no date). *Assessing driving under the influence offenders: Subgroups and classifications.* Unpublished manuscript, Wright State University.

Selzer, M. L. (1971). The Michigan Alcoholism Screening Test: The quest for a new diagnostics instrument. *American Journal of Psychiatry, 127,* 89–94.

Skinner, H. A. (1982). The Drug Abuse Screening Test. *Addictive Behaviors, 7,* 363–371.

Most, R. (1987). Levels of error in computerised psychological inventories. *Applied Psychology: An International Review, 36,* 375–383.

Mayer, J. E. (1988). The personality characteristics of adolescents who use and misuse alcohol. *Adolescence, 23,* 383–404.

Cannon, I. L., Childers, J. S., Allred, L. J., & Hines, L. L. (1992, March). *Reliability and concurrent validity of the SALCE and JASAE.* Symposium presentation at the 38th annual meeting of the Southeastern Psychological Association, Knoxville, TN.

Wilson, S. H., Childers, J. S., Durham, T. W., Allred, L. J., & Hines, L. L. (1992, March). *Correlations among the SALCE and MMPI-2 validity and clinical scales in a college student sample.* Symposium presentation at the 38th annual meeting of the Southeastern Psychological Association, Knoxville, TN.

Chan, A. W. K., Pristach, E. A., Welte, J. W., & Russell, M. (1993). Use of the TWEAK test in the screening of alcoholism/heavy drinking in three populations. *Alcoholism: Clinical and Experimental Research, 17,* 1188–1192.

Saunders, J. B., Aasland, O. G., Babor, T. F., De La Fuente, J. R., & Grant, M. (1993). Development of the Alcohol Use Disorders Identification Test (AUDIT): WHO collaborative project on early detection of persons with harmful alcohol consumption–II. *Addiction, 88,* 791–804.

Butcher, J. N. (1994). Psychological assessment by computer: Potential gains and problems to avoid. *Psychiatric Annals, 24,* 20–24.

Tolley, L. D. (1994). *Concurrent validity of the Substance Abuse/Life Circumstance Evaluation and the California Personality Inventory—Revised.* Unpublished Master's Thesis, East Carolina University.

Wilson, S., Childers, J., Allred, L., & Durham, T. (1994, April). *The CAL-R with the SALCE and MMPI-2 scales with college students.* Presentation at the Southeastern Psychological Association, New Orleans, LA.

[378]
Symptom Assessment—45 Questionnaire.

Purpose: Designed as a "brief yet comprehensive general assessment of psychiatric symptomalogy."

Population: Ages 13 and over, reading at the 6th grade level or higher.

Publication Dates: 1996–1998.

Acronym: SA-45.

Scores, 11: 9 subscales (Anxiety, Depression, Hostility, Interpersonal Sensitivity, Obsessive-Compulsive, Paranoid Ideation, Phobic Anxiety, Psychoticism, Somatization), 2 composite scores (Global Severity Index, Positive Symptom Total).

Administration: Group.

Price Data: Available from publisher.

Time: (10–15) minutes.

Comments: Derived from the original Symptom Checklist—90 (SCL-90; T5:2603); self-report inventory.

Author: Strategic Advantage, Inc. and Mark Maruish.

Publisher: Multi-Health Systems, Inc.

Review of the Symptom Assessment—45 Questionnaire by WILLIAM M. REYNOLDS, Professor, Department of Psychology, Humboldt State University, Arcata, CA:

The Symptom Assessment—45 Questionnaire (SA-45) is a shortened form of the original 90-item Symptom Checklist—90 (SCL-90; T5:2603), the latter originally developed by Derogatis, Lipman, and Covi (1973). The SA-45 consists of 45 items, each rated by the respondent on a 5-point scale ranging from *Not at all* to *Extremely* as to how much the symptom has bothered or caused distress over the past 7 days. The SA-45 consists of nine scales: Anxiety (ANX), Depression (DEP), Hostility (HOS), Interpersonal Sensitivity (INT), Obsessive-Compulsive (OC), Paranoid Ideation (PAR), Phobic Anxiety (PHO), Psychoticism (PSY), and Somatization (SOM), each scale consisting of 5 items. There are also two global scales, the Global Severity Index (GSI) and the Positive Symptom Total (PST).

The SA-45 is described as appropriate for ages 13 years and older, and requires a sixth grade reading level. Because a substantial proportion of adolescents read below this level, and 10 (22%) of the 45 items have readability levels of Grades 7.0 or higher (up to Grade Level 9.8), caution should be used in the application of this measure with adolescents below age 16 and those reading below grade level (as is the case with many adolescents referred for psychological problems).

The SA-45 was initially developed by analyzing data from the SCL-90 collected from an inpatient psychiatric sample of 1,519 adults and 866 adolescents using cluster analysis to produce nine 5-item subscales. The SA-45 represents a subset (half) of the items on the SCL-90 with the development based on persons who took the longer scale. Cluster analyses were then conducted with other inpatient and nonpatient samples to examine the consistency of initial results. Most of the items showed consistency with initial cluster analysis placement.

The SA-45 may be completed on a self-scoring paper-and-pencil answer sheet or using a separate computer program that provides for computer administration. Directions for scoring and interpretation of the SA-45 are provided in the manual, as are suggestions for use of the scale in treatment monitoring. Three case studies (all adults) are presented to illustrate interpretation of the SA-45. The manual also provides information on computer administration and scoring of the SA-45.

The manual does a competent job in reporting psychometric information on the SA-45. Norms for the SA-45 are provided as normalized *T*-scores and percentile ranks for several standardization samples including nonpatient and inpatient samples of adults and adolescents. Community sample norms are based on samples of 748 adult females and 328 adult males with a mean age of approximately 39 years. The adult sample was approximately 85% White, 5% African American, 3% Hispanic, 1% Asian, and 6% Other, drawn from the staff and family members of a large behavioral health care company. The adolescent normative sample consisted of 321 females and 293 males from a suburban high school in the Midwest. The mean age of the adolescent sample was approximately 16 years, with no age range provided. The adolescent sample was approximately 84% White, 12% Other, 2% Hispanic, 1% African American, and .5% Asian.

The age ranges of the adult and adolescent normative samples were not provided. This is somewhat problematic for understanding the representativeness of the samples. Because nonpatient adults were selected from employees and their family members, it is not known how many young adults ages 19 to 24 were included in the standardization sample as well as older adults ages 65 and above. Similarly, because the adolescent sample was selected from one high school, we can estimate that most youngsters were 15 to 17 years of age.

In addition to the nonpatient normative samples, the SA-45 manual also provides norms based on large samples of psychiatric inpatients, including over 10,000 adult males and females, and over 5,000 adolescent males and females tested at the time of admission to inpatient psychiatric settings operated by a large health care company. Age and ethnic information are provided for these samples. No other information is provided. It would be useful to know the psychiatric diagnoses, medical conditions, comorbidity, and other characteristics of the inpatient psychiatric normative sample given that the composition of this sample is important for interpretation of standard scores. Of greater utility would be well-defined norms based on outpatient groups, and normative information provided for specific disorder groups (e.g., Generalized Anxiety Disorder, Major Depressive Disorder, etc.). The author notes the utility of outpatient norms and in the manual suggests that such norms are being developed.

Reliability information is provided in the form of internal consistency (coefficient alpha) and test-retest reliability, the latter based on subsamples of nonpatient adults (n = 57) and adolescents (n = 64) using a 1- to 2-week retest interval. Internal consistency reliability coefficients for the nine subscales ranged from .74 to .87 (Median = .81) and .73 to .91 (Median = .86) for adult nonpatient and inpatient samples, respectively, and from .71 to .87 (Median = .79) and .74 to .90 (Median = .86) for adolescent nonpatient and inpatient samples, respectively. Internal consistency reliability for the GSI is not reported. Test-retest reliability was computed using raw scores and area T-scores, with generally consistent results obtained for both scores. Test-retest reliability coefficients (based on area T-scores) ranged from .49 to .84 (Median = .79, GSI = .84) and .54 to .83 (Median = .70, GSI = .73) for adult and adolescent samples, respectively. Relatively low test-retest reliability was found for subscales of Anxiety (.49) and Somatization (.63) with adults, and Anxiety (.54), Depression (.65), Hostility (.56), and Obsessive-Compulsive (.67) subscales with adolescents. The author provides scale mean scores for each assessment allowing for the evaluation of score changes over the retest interval. Test-retest reliability coefficients are also provided for adult and adolescent psychiatric inpatient samples using 1-week, 2-week, and 3-week retest intervals. The author also reports standard errors of measurement. In general, the test-retest reliability coefficients with the inpatient samples are low (for example, for adults 1-week test-retest coefficients range from .42 to .59) and it is difficult to disentangle treatment effects from measurement error in evaluating reliability.

In addition to the reliability results derived from the original development samples in which the SA-45 was extracted from the SCL-90 items, the author also presents internal consistency reliability for samples of adult inpatients (n = 4,000+) and nonpatients (n = 60), and adolescent nonpatients (n = 64), with median reliability coefficients of .86 (range = .74 to .90), .76 (range = .57 to .81), and .72 (range = .50 to .81), respectively. For the nonpatient adolescent sample the internal consistency reliability coefficients were .65 and lower for four (ANX, PAR, PHO, & PSY) of the SA-45 subscales.

Validity evidence for the SA-45 is provided in the form of construct validity, content validity, and criterion-related validity. Scale intercorrelations are presented, along with intercorrelations among SCL-90 and Brief Symptom Inventory (BSI; Derogatis, 1982, 1992, 1993) scales for comparison purposes. Raw score differences between inpatient and nonpatient samples of adult and adolescent males and females are provided as evidence of contrasted groups validity, along with data on the sensitivity and specificity of various GSI scores in classifying inpatients and nonpatients. Overall, moderate levels of sensitivity and specificity were found for adults with results somewhat higher for females than males, and results relatively poor for adolescents. Again, it would have been useful to know the diagnostic characteristics of the inpatient samples for assistance in interpreting the contrasted groups validity.

Criterion-related validity is presented by strong correlations between SA-45 scales and corresponding scales on the SCL-90 and BSI scales for the inpatient samples. Because the SA-45 is derived from the SCL-90, as are the BSI scales (35 of the 45 items on the SA-45 are also found on the BSI), strong correlations are to be expected and may be viewed as in part due to spuriousness given that the item correlation with itself is unity. The only external criterion validation evidence is the presentation of correlations between the SA-45 and the SF-12 (described as a short form of the SF-36 Health Survey by Ware, Kosinski, & Keller, 1995) and a self-report measure of health care utilization in a sample of 126 adults. Content validity is supported by item-total scale correlations.

There is little validity evidence for specific subscales on the SA-45 beyond differences between inpatients and nonpatients and similarities in subscale intercorrelations between the SA-45, BSI, and SCL-90, and there is limited evidence for the validity of the subscales for school-based adolescents. No evidence for discriminant validity is presented. The author does present data to show comparability of mean scores and cluster analysis results obtained for the SA-45 extracted from the SCL-90 in the adult psychiatric inpatient development sample, and another psychiatric inpatient sample (n = 3,000+) who were administered the stand-alone version of the SA-45, finding highly similar results.

SUMMARY. The SA-45 is a psychometrically sound screening measure, with greater support for its use with adults than adolescents. Additional evidence for validity would be useful, particularly with external validation measures (e.g., those other than the SCL-90 and BSI with which it shares substantial item overlap) and with outpatient samples.

The normative sample for nonpatient adults is sufficiently large, although more information on age characteristics of this sample is needed. The adolescent standardization sample is relatively small. This, in conjunction with the reading level of the items, relatively low reliability for a number of subscales, and limited validity evidence with this age group, suggests that the utility of the SA-45 is limited with adolescents.

It should be recognized that 5 items per scale does not provide for an in-depth evaluation of psychopathology, nor does the author claim this to be the case. The benefits of the SA-45 over the 53-item BSI, which shares 78% of the SA-45 items, appears to be somewhat limited, and for the most part, intercorrelations among subscales are similar for the two short forms. Users may wish to compare norms for the two measures, as well as other information if the decision is between these two scales. The availability of a computer administration and scoring program does enhance the utility of the SA-45 and the manual is well written and easy to understand.

REVIEWER'S REFERENCES

Derogatis, L. R., Lipman, R. S., & Covi, L. (1973). SCL-90: An outpatient psychiatric rating scale—preliminary report. *Psychopharmacology Bulletin, 9,* 13–27.

Derogatis, L. R., & Spencer, P. M. (1982). *The Brief Symptom Inventory (BSI) administration, scoring, and procedures manual—I.* Towson, MD: Clinical Psychometric Research.

Derogatis, L. R. (1992). *The Brief Symptom Inventory (BSI) administration, scoring, and procedures manual—II.* Towson, MD: Clinical Psychometric Research.

Derogatis, L. R. (1993). (BSI) *Brief Symptom Inventory administration, scoring, and procedures manual* (3rd ed.). Minneapolis: National Computer Systems.

Ware, J. E., Rosinski, M., & Keller, S. D. (1995). *SF-12: How to score the SF-12 Physical and Mental Health Summary scales* (2nd ed.). Boston: The Health Institute, New England Medical Center.

Review of the Symptom Assessment—45 Questionnaire by CHOCKALINGAM VISWESVARAN, Associate Professor, Florida International University, Miami, FL:

The Symptom Assessment—45 Questionnaire (SA-45) is a self-reported checklist comprising nine clusters of five items each. The instrument assesses nine symptom domain disorders as well as providing two indices of global distress. A 5-point Likert scale is used for ratings, with the respondents asked to indicate the extent to which each of the 45 problems had bothered them in the past 7 days (1 = *Not at all* to 5 = *Extremely*). The items were selected from the Symptom Checklist—90 (SCL—90; 9:1082) with the objective of providing a shorter version of the checklist. Another test with parallel intent as the SA-45 is the Brief Symptom Inventory (BSI; 10:35).

The scale development was based on a sample of 690 adult females, 829 adult males, 466 adolescent females (13–18 years), and 400 adolescent males. All (10 years of age or older), subjects were inpatients in private psychiatric hospitals who were administered the SCL—90. Across the four samples there were 12 Asian/Pacific Islanders, 108 Hispanics, 201 Blacks, and 14 Native Americans. Cluster analysis was used to develop the scales and a nine-cluster solution was forced with each cluster containing five items. Subsequent cluster analyses were performed on five samples: 1,307 adult inpatients, 736 adolescent inpatients, 994 adult and adolescent inpatients, 1,082 adult and adolescent inpatients, and 1,649 adult and adolescent nonpatients. No mention is made in the manual as to whether or not there was any overlap across the five samples.

Normative data using nonpatient samples are provided based on 748 adult females, 328 adult males, 321 adolescent females, and 293 adolescent males. Across the four nonpatient samples used for norming, there were 15 Asian/Pacific Islanders, 40 Hispanics, 65 Blacks, and 7 Native Americans. The nonpatient samples included employees of a national healthcare company and their family members along with 300 adolescents from a Midwestern suburban high school. It is not clear from the manual whether the employees were all in one geographical location or were a nationally representative sample. Normative data are also provided using inpatient samples based on SCL—90 data (rescored for the 45 items included in SA-45) from 5,317 adult females, 5,854 adult males, 2,889 adolescent females, and 2,331 adolescent males. Across these four inpatient samples, there were 59 Asian/Pacific Islanders, 499 Hispanics, 1,357 Blacks, and 337 Native Americans. The authors recommend the use of nonpatient norms in general. Area transformed T-scores are provided for the nine scale scores as well as for the two global indices.

Clear instructions are provided for the administration, scoring, and interpretation of responses. Guidelines are given for handling missing data as well as for detecting invalid responses. Illustrative case studies as well as instructions for using logistic regression estimates are provided. Also noted is the availability of computer administration and scoring. Unfortunately, empirical data on the cross-modal equivalence of test administrations have not been provided.

Test-retest and internal consistency reliability estimates are reported. Cronbach's alpha coefficients are reported for the nine subscales based on three adult samples administered the SCL—90 (from which the SA-45 scores were computed): 1,471 to 1,498 mental health or chemical dependency patients at intake and at treatment termination, 938 to 951 patients at intake and at 6 months after treatment termination, 1,077 to 1,085 nonpatients. Alpha coefficients were also reported on four adolescent samples: 827 to 858 mental

health or chemical dependency patients assessed with SCL—90 at intake and at termination, 598 to 605 patients at intake and at termination, 565 to 571 at intake and 6 months after treatment termination, and 610 to 619 nonpatients. Alpha coefficients were acceptable (.80s and .90s).

Test-retest reliability estimates are based on two small samples of 57 adult nonpatients and 64 adolescent nonpatients. A 2-week time interval was employed and the SA-45 (not the SCL—90) was administered to the two samples. Reliability estimates were reported for both raw and area T-scores. Stability estimates were acceptable (.70s and .80s) for all scales except for the Anxiety scale (.42). Further, the stability estimates were higher for adult samples when compared to adolescent samples. No major changes across the two administrations were found on the area T-score magnitudes. In addition, test-retest estimates of the SA-45 based on 1-, 2-, and 3-week intervals are also reported in the manual based on large samples of inpatients (500–4,200) who completed the SCL—90 (from which SA-45 scores were computed).

Intercorrelations among the nine scores in the SA-45 were compared with the intercorrelations from the SCL—90 (9:1082) and the BSI (10:35). Correlations with SCL—90 and BSI are high, suggesting good construct validity. However, given that the correlations with the SCL—90 are part-whole correlations, it is imperative that additional construct validity data are obtained. Item-total correlations, with the item response removed from the total score, were higher for most of the 45 items when compared to the correlation of that item with the total score on the eight other scales. Contrasted group validity analyses were undertaken by comparing the means and standard deviations of the 11 scores for patients at intake, treatment termination, follow-up, and for nonpatients. The pattern of means and standard deviations supports the construct validity of the measure.

Logistic regression estimates based on a subset of the nine scales are developed for different base rates. Again, SA-45 scores computed from responses to SCL—90 are relied upon. The manual presents this as evidence of predictive validity. More predictive validity evidence, especially the incremental validity over other comparable measures (e.g., BSI) should be examined. Content validity is claimed based on item-total correlations and a visual examination of the items. A more formal analysis based on panels of subject matter experts would be preferable. Also, the manual explicitly notes that it is not a comprehensive checklist of psychiatric disorders.

SUMMARY. Although the technical manual for the SA-45 presents impressive data, most of them were based on the SCL—90 responses. Analyses are presented, therefore, to check the comparability of the SA-45 scores obtained by rescoring the SCL—90 to the SA-45 scores obtained directly. Means, standard deviations, and item intercorrelations were shown to be comparable. However, covariance structure modeling should be used in future to test this equivalence. Similarly, factor loadings of the 45 items on the nine scales should be provided. Interscorer agreement (e.g., how do self-ratings correlate with ratings of others?) should be assessed both for the checklisting of 45 items as well as for the interpretations based on those responses. Item discrimination indices and item difficulty levels (in addition to item-total correlations) should be provided. Overall, despite limitations, the SA-45 is a potentially useful instrument for evaluating treatment effects and for large scale initial screening to flag psychiatric symptoms.

[379]
Symptom Scale—77.

Purpose: "Designed to reflect specific symptom changes ... capable of modification by psychotherapy or neuropharmacology."
Population: Adolescents and adults.
Publication Dates: 1992–1995.
Acronym: SS—77.
Scores: 10 scales: Somatic Complaints, Depression, Alcohol and Other Drug Abuse, Anxiety, Obsessive—Compulsive Symptoms, Panic Disorder Without and With Agoraphobia, Traumatic Stress, Minimization of Symptoms, Magnification of Symptoms, Guardedness Index.
Administration: Individual or group.
Price Data: Not available.
Time: (15–20) minutes.
Comments: Computer administration requires IBM-compatible with at least 4 MB RAM and 1.4 MB disk drive and mouse and Windows 3.1.
Author: Judith L. Johnson and William McCown.
Publisher: DocuTrac, Inc. [No reply from publisher; status unknown].

Review of the Symptom Scale—77 by HERBERT BISCHOFF, Licensed Psychologist, Psychology Resources, Anchorage, AK:

With the advent of managed care there has been a growing need for the quantification of clinical constructs that are typically viewed as being "qualitative" in nature. The Symptom Scale—77 (SS-77) attempts to do this by providing a 77-item questionnaire to be completed by an individual currently receiving some form of psychotherapy. The survey's intention is threefold: (a) to provide the therapist/clinician with an indication of current symptoms, (b) to demonstrate to third party payers progressive easement of symptoms thereby qualifying the need for current and possible further interventions, and (c) to provide a tracking device for a therapist/clinician to gain an overall estimate of the efficacy of specific techniques with certain populations. The first two goals are accomplished by relying on the client's self-reported measure of expressed symptom severity by taking the SS-77 at various times for an individual. The third goal is accomplished by compiling information from many respondents.

The SS-77 comes in a disk format and can be administered on-line or by a clinician. The format is user friendly and has options useful in printing reports and graphs. The scoring package provides the ability to access different reports for different administrations for comparison and then, as is recommended by the test author, a clinician/therapist can compile test results for all of their clientele to provide an overall indication of a particular practitioner's or agency's ability to successfully mitigate presenting symptoms. This can be done by selecting time frames and then asking the program to produce a summation of levels of symptoms.

However, if complications arise or there is a need to query the free help desk, the number provided in the test manual was no longer in service and no alternate was provided. Although the software is user friendly, the question is raised whether or not it is worth the risk with the inherent possibility of malfunction. Should this occur there are no immediate resources available to provide assistance.

A shortcoming of the SS-77, as with many self-report measures, is the 77-item survey's ability to accurately represent current self-reported symptoms. This is especially problematic when considering potential inherent limitations to insightfulness with certain clinical populations (e.g., delusional schizophrenics). However, the information may be helpful for a client who typically suffers from extreme variations of symptomatology by having them take the survey at various points during treatment providing valuable insight for them and their therapist/clinician. The symptom survey results may assist in the development of more proactive techniques and monitor the course of symptomatology (e.g., how levels of anxiety may be provoked/lessened by introducing various stimuli into the environment). Regardless of the intention of administering the SS-77, it still requires a fairly high level of insight, self-awareness, and intelligence.

Although the testing manual is written in an understandable format and the author has apparently taken into consideration the limitations of the manual, there is limited discussion regarding normative data. The author recommends individual clinicians compile their own normative data for their particular populations of interest and geographic area, with no way of comparing this information to other normative samples. Providing information to third party payers, demonstrating the need for continued interventions, or quantifying progress would have qualitative limitations.

Reliability is reported at acceptable levels using internal consistency indices. The author points out test-retest reliability is an inappropriate measure for this test, given the desired variance of levels of symptomatology from test to test. Test-retest reliability studies were conducted with individuals who were not currently in treatment and not excessively stressed. There was a high level of test-retest consistency found over a one-week interval suggesting the test's ability to detect real symptom change.

SUMMARY. In summation, the SS-77 is a 77-item survey intended to measure change in levels of symptoms chosen specifically because they are considered representative of "mainstream" symptomatology and considered treatable through typical psychotherapeutic or neuropharmacological techniques. The manual is well written, adequately covering evidence of score reliability. Problems with the SS-77 including lack of normative data and an assumption of insight needed to accurately self-report symptom severity. Also, there is a problem with the help desk number that was no longer in service with no available alternate.

Review of the Symptom Scale—77 by TONY TONEATTO, Scientist, Clinical, Social and Research Department, Addiction Research Foundation, Toronto, Ontario, Canada:

The Symptom Scale-77 (SS-77) is a 77-item test intended to screen for nonpsychotic psychiatric symptoms in psychiatric and medical patients. The SS-77 can be used to establish the need for treatment or indicate the need for a diagnostic assessment. The scale can also be used as a measure of baseline functioning to evaluate the effects of psychosocial and psychopharmacological interventions. One of the unique features of the SS-77 is the inclusion of symptoms that are potentially modifiable by treatment (psychological or medical). The authors of the SS-77 stress that the scale cannot be used to make psychiatric diagnoses, as a psychological test, or to supplant clinical judgment. The scale excludes symptoms that were either rare (e.g., hysterical paresis) or so common that they would routinely be observed by a clinician or self-reported by a patient (e.g., phobia). Instead, symptoms that are more subtle, difficult to self-report, or difficult to ascertain in a clinical interview by a clinician were selected. Norms for nonpatients and outpatients provide the user with direction on establishing the need for, and evaluate the result of, treatment. The manual author advises, however, that the regular user of the SS-77 should develop their own norms due to regional, ethnic, and cultural differences in symptom presentations.

The ease and rapidity with which the SS-77 can be administered make it useful for clinicians and researchers as prepurchased score sheets, computerized scoring, or mail-in services are not required.

The SS-77 consists of seven clusters of symptoms that correspond to commonly diagnosed psychiatric disorders: Somatic Complaints (8 items), Depression (10 items), Alcohol/Drug Abuse (8 items), Anxiety (10 items), Obsessive-Compulsive Symptoms (9 items), Panic Disorder without Agoraphobia (9 items) or with Agoraphobia (2 additional items), and Traumatic Stress (9 items). Three validity scales have also been included: Minimization of Symptoms (8 items), Magnification of Symptoms (6 items), and a Guardedness Index (2 items). The domain of the disorders they have defined does not include social phobia, a very common disorder, as well as hypomanic symptoms, which may frequently occur in mood disordered patients but are difficult to assess directly. An examination of the content of the clinical symptom scales reveals considerable symptom overlap. For example, the Somatic Complaints scale includes "feeling sick to my stomach" vs. "stomach problems"; the Alcohol/Drug Abuse scale includes "problems from alcohol or taking drugs" vs. "arguments with family or friends about my alcohol or drug use" and "feeling guilty about using drugs or drinking" vs. "feeling ashamed about using drugs or drinking"; the Anxiety Scale includes "feeling restless" vs. "feeling nervous" vs. "feeling anxious" vs. "feeling keyed up or edgy." In each of these examples, the symptoms are either very similar or potentially difficult for the patient to distinguish or discriminate. The discussion of the Guardedness Index, consisting of only two items, is accompanied by several recommendations on the interpretation of the scores; this appears to be premature given that no evidence on the reliability or validity of this subscale is provided.

A serious limitation of the SS-77 is the decision to use a Likert scale with ratings ranging from *not at all bothered* to *constantly bothered*. The choice of the label "bothered" is problematic as many symptoms may be clinically significant even if the patient is not "bothered" by them (e.g., "thoughts of hurting or killing myself," "fear of going outside alone," "fear of going crazy"). Because patients may not always understand, recognize, or have insight into the significance of symptoms, it would have been more appropriate to assess the presence or frequency of such symptoms and then to explore how bothersome or significant they were later. Furthermore, the effects of treatment cannot be unambiguously evaluated because symptoms that are less "bothersome" may not have necessarily diminished or disappeared.

The SS-77 manual reports good internal consistency reliability data for the nine subscales across several populations (e.g., normal college, geriatric, chronic pain) with about half of Cronbach alpha coefficients above .80. Test-retest reliability is judged to be an inappropriate reliability measure for the SS-77 as the symptoms may fluctuate rapidly. However, good test-retest reliability statistics for college students/adult nonstudents are reported (although they do not indicate the interval period between tests). Such data would have been useful to have for other populations as well, using brief intervals between administrations (e.g., 24 hours) in order to assess reliability of symptom report but not long enough to reflect treatment effects. One week test-retest data were presented

for four subscales (i.e., Somatic Complaints, Depression, Alcohol Abuse, Anxiety) that are identical to a previous version of the SS-77 were administered to nonpatients. Results showed poor to fair reliability (coefficients ranging from .60 to .77). Split-half reliability is estimated to be generally very good (generally above .80); unfortunately, however, the manual reports data combining clinical and nonclinical populations, making interpretation difficult.

The data for the validity of SS-77 scores are generally poor. Allusion to studies assessing criterion validity are made but no data are reported. Limited data for the concurrent validity of the Anxiety subscale are presented and almost none for the remaining subscales. Validity data for the validity subscales are again alluded to, but very little reported. It is noteworthy that no mention is made in the SS-77 manual of the Symptom Checklist-90 (Derogatis, 1983; T4:2674), a 90-item instrument with similar purposes and structure to the SS-77, especially measuring treatment-related clinical change. The Symptom Checklist-90 has considerably more sound psychometric data supporting its use. A briefer version of the instrument is also available; the 58-item Brief Symptom Inventory has also been shown to be a suitable instrument (Royse & Drude, 1984; T4:324). Future studies of the SS-77 should include concurrent validity evidence for these instruments. Furthermore, brief screening instruments for alcohol abuse, such as the Alcohol Use Disorders Identification Test (AUDIT; Saunders, Aasland, Babor, de la Fuente, & Grant, 1993; 15) have received considerable support and may be more effective as screening measures than the SS-77 Alcohol/Drug subscale.

At the present time, the SS-77 suffers from serious weaknesses (e.g., questionable content validity, limited validity data). Therefore, caution should be exercised when interpreting the scores from this measure. The existence of alternative, better established instruments should be used until the weaknesses noted above have been rectified.

REVIEWER'S REFERENCES

Derogatis, L. R. (1983). *SCL-90-R: Administration, scoring and procedures manual-II for the revised version and other instruments of the psychopathology rating scale series.* Baltimore, MD: Clinical Psychometrics Research.

Royse, D., & Drude, K. (1984). Screening drug abuse clients with the Brief Symptom Inventory. *The International Journal of the Addictions, 19,* 849–857.

Saunders, J. B., Aasland, O. G., Babor, T. F., de la Fuente, J. R., & Grant, M. (1993). Development of the Alcohol Use Disorders Identification Test (AUDIT): WHO collaborative project on early detection of persons with harmful alcohol consumption-II. *Addiction, 88,* 791–804.

Target Mathematics Tests.

Purpose: Designed "to provide achievement tests which reflect the content of the National Curriculum in Mathematics" in Great Britain.
Population: Levels 2–5, 2–6.
Publication Date: 1993.
Scores: Total score only.
Administration: Group.
Forms, 2: Test 4, Test 5.
Price Data, 1999: £8.50 per 20 test booklets (specify test); £7.99 per manual; £8.99 per specimen set.
Time: [30] minutes.
Author: D. Young.
Publisher: Hodder & Stoughton Educational [England].

Review of the Target Mathematics Tests by KEVIN D. CREHAN, Associate Professor of Educational Psychology, University of Nevada, Las Vegas, NV:

The Target Mathematics Tests are designed as norm-referenced measures of Britain's National Curriculum in Mathematics that was adopted in 1991. The two tests, Test 4 and Test 5, are targeted at the ends of Key Stage 1 and Key Stage 2 and are recommended for administration at the end of Years 4 and 5, respectively. The intent of the tests is to provide teachers with help in monitoring student progression through Key Stage 2 of the mathematics curriculum in order to identify individual and class weaknesses in a timely fashion.

Target Test 4 has 55 items presented on four pages. Most of the items are supply type but a few provide options from which the student may select. The first 30 items consist of a display of information (e.g., coins, clock face, diagrams, graphs) with the basis for answering supplied orally by the teacher. The oral presentation of the first 30 items is designed to discount the effect of reading difficulties in the assessment of mathematics achievement. The remaining 25 items are presented on the test booklet and the student is allowed 20 minutes to respond. Target Test 5 contains 50 items, all of which are presented on the four-page test booklet. Again, most of the items are supply type, but several items present options from which the student selects. Administration time is 30 minutes.

TECHNICAL CONSIDERATIONS. Test items, at least in part, were taken from the former Y Mathematics Series. There is no indication of other sources of test content. The manual states that the "validity is based on substantive rather than associative considerations" (p. 5). However, no indication of the basis for the substantive judgments is provided. That is, there is no mention of formal content validation procedures. No direct evidence of reliability is presented; however, the manual provides standard errors for the two tests obtained from reliability estimates derived from test-retest administrations within 10 days for sample sizes of 95 for Test 4 and 115 for Test 5. Based on the standard errors provided, the correlations of scores from the test-retest administrations would have been in the .96 range over the 10-day period.

SCORE INTERPRETATION. Age level norm tables, with 2-month intervals, are provided for each test. Test 4 age intervals go from 8 years-4 months to 10 years-3 months and the Test 5 intervals are from 9 years-4 months to 11 years-3 months. The norm data are based on samples from 18 schools of 359 males and 348 females for Year 4 and 370 males and 387 females for Year 5. The tables allow easy conversion of raw scores to age level "quotients" that appear to be normalized standard scores with a mean of 100 and standard deviation of 15 for each age interval. Standard errors for individual score interpretation are about 3 points or one-fifth of a standard deviation.

The manual suggests interpretation of results can be both norm-referenced, using the accompanying tables, and criterion-references, using raw scores. That is, a student's performance can be compared to his or her age peers or against the national curriculum standards. Additional suggested uses of the tests and test results may derive from teacher observations during scoring; that is, the teacher may informally identify points for further examination. The teacher is also directed to give special attention to differences in performance between orally presented and non-orally presented items as a check for the potential effect of poor reading ability.

OBSERVATIONS AND RECOMMENDATIONS. The Target Mathematics Tests should give the British teacher results that are useful as an aid to instructional decisions; however, the measures could easily be improved in both presentation and the provision of additional supporting interpretive information. There is some concern with the format, presentation, and arrangement of the individual items. For example, in some cases the student provides his or her answer as the solution to a problem and in other cases a separate answer space is provided. This inconsistency may cause difficulty in responding and scoring. Additionally, a few items could benefit from editing. For example, hand position in the clock face problems is ambiguous and caused this reviewer some pause in interpretation. Also, the ordering of items should be examined to place easier items of a type before more difficult items measuring similar content (e.g., the item asking the perimeter of a regular shape should be placed before the item asking the area of an irregular shape).

Given the effort needed to administer and hand score these tests, more in the way of suggested uses of results might be expected. For example, given the variety of content and the apparent broad range of item difficulties, subarea means and/or item difficulty data might be used to aid the teacher in diagnosing individual and class strengths and weaknesses both in a norm-referenced interpretation and for comparison to the national curriculum standards.

Finally, the choice to construct the norm tables using only normalized standard scores is questioned. Because the proposed prime user of these scores is the classroom teacher, norm tables presenting percentile rank conversion of raw scores may provide greater interpretive power.

SUMMARY. The Target Mathematics Tests have the potential for usefulness to the teacher in both norm-referenced and criterion-referenced interpretations. The usefulness of the tests could be expanded by the addition of item difficulty data and norm tables presenting percentile ranks.

Review of the Target Mathematics Tests by GERALD E. DeMAURO, *Coordinator of Assessment, New York State Education Department, Albany, NY:*

TEST COVERAGE AND USE. The Target Mathematics Tests 4 and 5 are designed to measure achievement of the National Curriculum of Great Britain in mathematics between the end of Key Stage 1 and Key Stage 2, Years 4 and 5. This is equivalent to American grades 4 and 5.

APPROPRIATE SAMPLES FOR TEST VALIDATION AND NORMING. The tests' normative samples were drawn from 18 schools. The Year 4 sample was composed of 707 children (359 boys and 348 girls) with an average age of 9 years

and 2.5 months. The Year 5 sample was composed of 757 children (370 boys and 387 girls), with an average age of 10 years and 2.5 months.

Quotients referenced to these samples are provided for Tests 4 and 5 based on a mean of 100 and standard deviation of 15. Test 4 has 54 possible scores and provides quotients for children in each of 12 two-month intervals ranging from 8-4 to 10-3, yielding 648 possible quotients. Test 5 has 49 possible scores and provides quotients in each of 12 two-month intervals, ranging from 9-4 to 11-3, yielding 588 possible quotient cells. The sizes of the normative samples suggest that these cells reflect considerable interpolations rather than observed performance throughout the ranges for all ages.

The author quite rightly states that raw scores are more helpful for the criterion-referenced interpretation of results. However, evidence of formal standard setting studies that reference performance to levels of competence is not presented.

CRITERION RELATED VALIDITY. The criterion of interest is achievement of the National Curriculum in mathematics. Formal validity data are not presented. Rather, the author states that the tests were designed in stages, beginning with *Y Mathematics Series* items and finalizing the item pool on the basis of the standardization trials. Scores of about 25 on Test 4 and 23 on Test 5 are held to be equivalent to Level 2 on the National Curriculum and the transitions between Levels 3 and 4, respectively.

CONTENT VALIDITY. Items on the two tests are proportionally distributed over four mathematics content areas and four and five ability levels, respectively. There do not appear to be sufficient items to provide reliable subscores related to these divisions.

The author states, "Since the tests are based on the content of the National Curriculum, the validity of the tests is based on substantive rather than associative consideration" (p. 5). Although these substantive considerations are vital to content validity, it would help readers evaluate their strength to present documentation of the expert judgments that support the substantive relationships between the curricular domain and the configuration of the tests. Analyses of 50 students at four ability levels in each year are said to confirm the appropriate item ability and discriminatory characteristics.

CONSTRUCT VALIDITY. Evidence is presented of attempts to purify the construct. Items are presented orally for 30 of the 55 items on Test 4 to avoid reading confounds. Cautions are raised that there may be common abilities that underlie both mathematics problem solving and reading comprehension.

TEST ADMINISTRATION. Test administration is completely specified, taking about 18 minutes for the orally administered section and 20 minutes for the read section of Test 4. Test 5, entirely read, takes 30 minutes to administer.

TEST REPORTING. As mentioned above, reporting may be in quotients or raw scores. Although there are recommended levels of performance, there is no indication of how these were determined. Interpretations seem to depend on achieving the average of the normative sample, and extreme performances are judged with reference to the performance of the normative sample rather than with reference to the probabilities that students possess certain knowledge or skills.

TEST AND ITEM BIAS. No information is reported on differential item functioning or differential test validity.

SUMMARY. The Target Mathematics Tests are referenced to specific portions of the National Curriculum of Great Britain in mathematics. They are undoubtedly reliable and useful for this purpose. The user would be aided with greater detail concerning the derivation of test specifications from the curriculum.

[381]

Taylor-Johnson Temperament Analysis [1996 Edition].

Purpose: Designed to "measure a number of … personality variables or attitudes and behavioral tendencies which influence personal, social, marital, parental, family, scholastic, and vocational adjustment."
Population: Ages 13 and up.
Publication Dates: 1941–1996.
Acronym: T-JTA.
Scores, 11: Nervous vs. Composed, Depressive vs. Light-Hearted, Active-Social vs. Quiet, Expressive-Responsive vs. Inhibited, Sympathetic vs. Indifferent, Subjective vs. Objective, Dominant vs. Submissive, Hostile vs. Tolerant, Self-Disciplined vs. Impulsive, Total, Attitude.
Administration: Group.
Forms, 4: Regular Edition (criss-cross and self-report forms); Form "S" for Adolescents (criss-cross and self-report).

Price Data, 1999: $236.50 per comprehensive kit (for handscoring); $92 per computer scoring package (for use with mail-in scoring service); $49 per secondary materials module; $85 per test manual; $36.50 per handbook.
Time: Untimed.
Comments: Can be used as a self-report questionnaire or as a tool for obtaining perceptions of another person (criss-cross form); Form S can be used with adolescents or with adults with poor reading skills; 1996 Edition based upon new norms.
Authors: Original edition by Roswell H. Johnson, revision by Robert M. Taylor, Lucile P. Morrison (manual), W. Lee Morrison (statistical consultant), and Richard C. Romoser (statistical consultant).
Publisher: Psychological Publications, Inc.
Cross References: For reviews by Jeffrey A. Jenkins and Barbara J. Kaplan of an earlier edition, see 13:315; see also T4:2690 (3 references); for reviews by Cathy W. Hall and Paul McReynolds, see 10:357; see also T3:2396 (1 reference) and T2:840 (3 references); for a review by Robert F. Stahmann, see 8:692 (18 references); for a review by Donald L. Mosher of an earlier edition, see 7:572 (1 reference); see also P:264 (3 references) and 6:130 (10 references); for a review by Albert Ellis of the original edition, see 4:62 (6 references); for a review by H. Meltzer of the original edition, see 3:57.

Review of the Taylor-Johnson Temperament Analysis [1996 Edition] by MICHAEL J. SPORAKOWSKI, Professor Emeritus of Human Development, Virginia Polytechnic Institute and State University, Blacksburg, VA:

The Taylor-Johnson Temperament Analysis (T-JTA) has a relatively long history tracing back to 1941 and the publication of its predecessor the Johnson Temperament Analysis (JTA), which was designed for general use in personality testing and premarital and marital counseling. The JTA had been used from 1941–1962 with over 70,000 individuals at The American Institute of Family Relations in California. An extensive revision process began in 1963, and in 1966 a wholly new instrument, the T-JTA, was published. The resulting 180-item measure has since been used to examine common personality variables and behavioral tendencies influencing a variety of personal, interpersonal, and scholastic/career factors and outcomes.

The T-JTA, through its graphical portrayals of personality, especially when used in its "criss-cross" scoring format, is useful in relationship counseling and educational applications. The instrument is not meant to be used in diagnosing clinical conditions or severe personality problems. It measures nine bipolar traits: Nervous vs. Composed; Depressive vs. Lighthearted; Active-social vs. Quiet; Expressive-responsive vs. Inhibited; Sympathetic vs. Indifferent; Subjective vs. Objective; Dominant vs. Submissive; Hostile vs. Tolerant; and, Self-disciplined vs. Impulsive. Several other scales are available when the computerized scoring service from the publisher is used: Overall Adjustment, Emotional Stability, Self-Esteem, Outgoing/Gregarious, Interpersonal Effectiveness, Alienating, Industrious/Persevering, and Persuasive/Influential. Detailed descriptions of all the scales are provided in the manual.

Trait patterns (e.g., Withdrawal Pattern—low scores on Active-Social/Quiet, Expressive-Responsive/Inhibited, and Subjective/Objective, along with a high score on Subjective/Objective) are also discussed with counseling-oriented discussions of their implications. Sections on the clinical use of the T-JTA, and The Report Booklet, a new tool for persons tested, published in 1996, are also included.

One of the more innovative parts of the T-JTA approach to assessment is the use of crisscross taking of the test and production of profiles. This could be done having an individual rate himself or herself and what he or she would like to be like. Or, in interpersonal relations, for example, the task would be to have individuals see how spouses see themselves and their partners. Comparisons on profile sheets are then made and used in counseling/enrichment discussions for better understanding relationships and where work might be done to improve upon them. Excellent discussions of this profiling and related utilizations are provided in the manual. I, personally, have found these techniques most helpful in some of the marriage and family counseling work I have done.

More than half of the 1996 manual is devoted to the research data attesting to the psychometric qualities of the T-JTA (e.g., evidence of reliabilities, validities, and comparisons with other instruments, and presenting the most recent, 1992, normative materials). Normative data are provided by gender for Adolescents, Young Adults, the General Adult population, and for Senior Adults. Cross-cross normative data are also included. What I found lacking was information related to unique cultural, socioeconomic, or educational groups, something that might be especially useful in our current world-of-diversity climate. This may be something the test-makers are beginning to address because they do present some information about a new version of the instrument, Secondary Edition (Form-S), written at the 5th grade reading level. Too, it would be helpful to have a generous listing of the references used in compiling these data and norms, and that represent the research, clinical, and educational usage of the instrument.

Even though this instrument has been with us for a fairly long period of time, and has had very positive contributions to make in a variety of areas, it still appears to be somewhere in the middle of its developmental process. I personally find the T-JTA helpful in relationship counseling and in family-life related educational endeavors. It has great potential for a variety of settings and practices, and it brings to us the solid beginnings of an instrument developed and used over a significant period of time.

Review of the Taylor-Johnson Temperament Analysis [1996 Edition] by STEPHEN E. TROTTER, Associate Professor, Department of Educational & Counseling Psychology, University of the Pacific, Stockton, CA:

The introduction to the 1996 revision of the Taylor-Johnson Temperament Analysis (T-JTA) manual provides an overview of its history dating back to its introduction in 1941 as the Johnson Temperament Analysis (JTA). The instrument has been revised extensively over the years and this version represents the newest permutation. The manual asserts that this most recent revision has resulted in a more modernized and statistically strengthened test.

The T-JTA consists of 180 items equally divided among what are described by the manual as nine bipolar traits. The manual defines each of the nine traits in a concise, but somewhat vague, fashion. In addition, a comment section provides the counselor with helpful information within the counseling context. The T-JTA may, also be computer scored and interpreted. Computer scoring provides additional scores that are unavailable when the instrument is hand scored. In addition, the T-JTA may utilize criss-cross ratings (self-ratings are contrasted with ratings of individual by significant other), a scoring option that appears to be an attractive and somewhat unique option for a purported personality test. The test is untimed and typically reported to take less than 45 minutes.

The T-JTA manual is extensive with a thorough description of the intent and construction of each scale. In addition, score patterns are addressed. These score patterns appear helpful in describing personality patterns and related behaviors. The physical construction, binding, and layout appear antiquated in relation to competing instruments. The light blue vinyl-covered three-ring binder appears less durable and effective than spiral or bound manuals. The multicolored 1992 norms do not add to the readability.

The interpretive language of the manual's text suggests to the reviewer that the instrument is aimed at a wide variety of professionals. This is portrayed as a strength, but in reality is a potential deficit. The measurement of personality is an extremely complex and difficult task requiring extensive theoretical and psychometric sophistication. The use of sten scores, a rarely used standard score form, rather than T-scores leads to difficulty in comparing scores across instruments.

The manual reports correlations between the T-JTA and both the Minnesota Multiphasic Personality Inventory (MMPI) and Sixteen Personality Factor Questionnaire (16PF). The MMPI and its revisions, the MMPI-2 (T5:1697) and MMPI-A (T5:1698; Butcher et al., 1992), are far superior instruments in a number of areas, including the following: overall construction, research base, norming (size and representation), administration options, and availability of continuing education. The same can be asserted for the less often used 16PF (Cattell, Cattell, & Cattell, 1993), an extremely well-crafted and referenced personality inventory.

The comparisons are based on the norms, which are no longer used in scoring. The validity and reliability data reported are from norms generated in 1996, 1977, and 1973. The current form of the test utilizes relatively recent 1992 norms. This suggests that a reasonable period of time has passed for updated data to have been generated and reported. The 1992 sample is described in relationship to geographical representation, which appears adequate. However, the Northeast U.S. is underrepresented; the T-JTA authors' home state of California represents 32.2% of the normative population. In addition, age representation is reported that indicates a number of uneven stratifications as a function of gender and age. For example, 79 males versus 119 females comprise the Age 17 group where there are 79 males versus

19 females in the Age 16 group. This greatly skews the representation percentages. The young adult, general adult, and senior adult norms appear less uneven. Previous editions of the *MMY* have raised concerns for the sample size for the 1992 norms (Jenkins, 1992), concerns that are shared by this reviewer. In addition, the norms fail to report ethnic and racial representation, an extremely egregious flaw, which greatly limits its use in a multicultural society.

SUMMARY. The aforementioned normative flaws and absence of supporting data for the 1992 norms suggest that the instrument would be best utilized as a tentative guide to creating areas of concern for counseling sessions rather than formulating any diagnostic categorization. This instrument appears greatly limited in its use when compared to better constructed and researched instruments, such as the following: MMPI-2, MMPI-A, and MACI (Millon Adolescent Clinical Inventory, T5:1685).

REVIEWER'S REFERENCES

Butcher, J. N., Williams, C. L., Graham, J. R., Archer, B. P., Tellegen, A., Ben-Porath, Y. S., & Kaemmer, B. (1992). *MMPI-A, Minnesota Multiphasic Personality Inventory—Adolescent: Manual for administration, scoring, and interpretation.* Minneapolis: University of Minnesota Press.
Cattell, R. B., Cattell, A. K. S., & Cattell, H. E. P. (1993). Sixteen Personality Factor Questionnaire, Fifth Edition. Champaign, IL: Institute for Personality and Ability Testing, Inc.
Jenkins, J. A. (1998). [Review of the Taylor-Johnson Temperament Analysis (1992 Edition)]. In J. C. Impara & B. S. Plake (Eds.), *The thirteenth mental measurements yearbook* (pp. 1000–1001). Lincoln, NE: Buros Institute of Mental Measurements.

[382]
Teacher Observation Scales for Identifying Children with Special Abilities.

Purpose: Designed as an assessment instrument for identifying gifted children, tailored to be culturally appropriate for use in New Zealand.
Population: Junior and middle primary school.
Publication Date: 1996.
Scores, 5: Learning Characteristics, Social Leadership Characteristics, Creative Thinking Characteristics, Self-Determination Characteristics, Motivational Characteristics.
Administration: Individual.
Price Data, 1996: NZ$12.50 per 20 observation scales; $12.50 per teacher's handbook (9 pages).
Time: Administration time not reported.
Authors: Don McAlpine and Neil Reid.
Publisher: New Zealand Council for Educational Research [New Zealand].

Review of the Teacher Observation Scales for Identifying Children with Special Abilities by IRA STUART KATZ, Clinical Psychologist, California

Department of Corrections, Salinas Valley State Prison, Soledad, CA, and Licensed Clinical Psychologist, Private Practice, Salinas, CA:

TEACHERS NEED TOOLS. Funds are not unlimited to assess and address the special needs of gifted children. School boards, parents, and the general public can be very critical about where and how education dollars are best spent for the greatest return on investment. The Teacher Observation Scales for Identifying Children with Special Abilities is designed as an instrument to identify gifted children tailored for use in New Zealand. Various methods have been utilized to assess giftedness ranging from scales for parents, teachers, peers, and students.

Teacher judgment continues to play a pivotal role in accurate assessment. Renzulli and Hartman (1971) addressed this need with a rating scale. The Scale for Rating Behavioural Characteristics of Superior Students (SRBCSS) has been widely used in the United States and elsewhere. The SRBCSS has not been effective for the needs of students and teachers in New Zealand. Three issues—composite scale statements, scale statement ambiguity, and lack of cultural relevance—were all not well addressed by the SRBCSS. Ultimately, with much empirical research effort, five scales emerged: Learning Characteristics, Social Leadership Characteristics, Creative Thinking Characteristics, Self-Determination Characteristics, and Motivational Characteristics. The Teacher Observation is a valuable assessment tool with some clear advantages and disadvantages.

SCALES. Advantages include the ease of use, clear language, focus of behavioral characteristics, scoring, and recognition of the unique traits incumbent with the gifted, or children with special abilities (CWSA). Despite some cultural nuances, the instrument appears to be culture-friendly and could be used beyond New Zealand with some minor modifications. A clinical and empirical advantage is its recognition of the psychological aspects of giftedness or special abilities. Ellen Winner (1996) in her wonderful contribution to the field, *Gifted Children: Myths and Realities*, provides insight on this unique population that is covered in the Teacher Observation Scales.

The authors of the scale, McAlpine and Reid, have given teachers a gift in identifying and working with children with special abilities. Combining the empirical research and clinical wisdom of Winner's work should be an adjunct for any teacher before using this scale or any other for this population. The Teacher Observation Scales Teacher's Handbook is a valuable tool that should be read and understood before any assessment. The handbook makes some valuable suggestions on utilization concerning timing and reliability of observations that should be followed scrupulously to increase empirical accuracy and effectiveness. Some of the suggestions are valuable for any teacher utilizing any tool.

Specifically, these suggestions include evidence to be familiar with the children (don't use the scales too soon in the school year), provide a wide range of learning experiences that encompass the behaviors measured in the scales, assess a small group of children (e.g., 4 or 5) concurrently over a brief period, record observations soon after events have highlighted a particular behavior, avoid the "halo" effect of allowing one or two "good" behaviors to affect ratings on other unrelated behaviors, and reassess from time to time because children change their behaviors as the result of new experiences.

Technical factors (validity and reliability) are well supported in the preliminary empirical data. Most striking here is the similarity with the SRBCSS validity research of a decade ago. Reliability evidence was less well grounded. The authors indicate accurately that intrarater reliability in the circumstances in which scales will be used makes little sense as a teacher's ratings will change based on the range of afforded observations. Hence, change, that is a *lack* of stability, is to be expected.

The authors close the handbook with some suggested curriculum models for the education of the CWSA and the integration of the Teacher Observation Scales.

SUMMARY. The Teacher Observation Scales for Identifying Children with Special Abilities is an assessment instrument with a future despite some preliminary limitations. It would be helpful to accelerate the process of closing the cultural diversity gap and put more emphasis of teacher development in future handbooks. Assessing the psychological aspects of giftedness should receive more treatment in future revisions of both the instrument and handbook. It can be hoped that the Educational Research and Development Center and New Zealand Council for Educational Research could combine the synergy of its counterparts and colleagues worldwide to better serve the needs of students, peers, teachers, and parents in our ever more culturally diverse and pluralistic world. The Teacher Observation Scales for Identifying Children with Special Abilities is on the vanguard of that needed change.

REVIEWER'S REFERENCES

Renzulli, J. S., & Hartman, R. K. (1971). Scales for rating behavioural characteristics of superior students. *Exceptional Children, 3,* 243–148.
Winner, E. (1996). *Gifted children: Myths and realities.* New York: Basic Books.

Review of the Teacher Observation Scales For Identifying Children With Special Abilities by KENNETH A. KIEWRA, Professor of Educational Psychology, University of Nebraska–Lincoln, Lincoln, NE:

This review focuses on the Teacher Observation Scales in terms of (a) purpose, (b) composition and development, (c) use (administration, scoring, and interpretation), and (d) technical information (validity and reliability).

PURPOSE. The Teacher Observation Scales are for screening and selecting talented students for inclusion in enriched or accelerated school programs. Although the scales are intended to offer a broader means for identifying talented students than conventional means such as intelligence testing, they are best used in conjunction with other identification methods.

COMPOSITION AND DEVELOPMENT. There are five Teacher Observation Scales: Learning Characteristics (13 items), Social Leadership Characteristics (12 items), Creative Thinking Characteristics (11 items), Self-Determination Characteristics (9 items), and Motivational Characteristics (8 items).

The scales were reportedly derived from the literature on gifted and talented, and then modified and confirmed through statistical techniques. The scales are not tied explicitly to any theoretical model of talent or intelligence such as Gardner's (1997) or Sternberg's (Sternberg & Kagan, 1986), and the literature base from which the scales were purportedly drawn is unspecified. Therefore there is reason to question the scales' conceptual basis. As such, the five scales seem arbitrary.

USE. The scales appear, on the surface, simple to administer. Teachers or school personnel simply mark a checklist showing the degree (*seldom, occasionally, often,* or *almost always*) to which a particular student demonstrates each of the 53 characteristics. At a deeper level, it might be difficult for a teacher to make certain student judgments such as: "easily grasps underlying prin-

ciples," "jumps stages in learning," "takes the initiative in social situations," "synthesises ideas from group members to formulate a plan of action," "enjoys speculation and thinking about the future," and "relates well to older children and adults and often prefers their company" (scoring booklet, pp. 2–5). Teachers obviously must first know their students well in varying situations before using the Teacher Observation Scales.

Another problem in administering the Teacher Observation Scales is the ambiguity associated with scale points ranging from "seldom" to "almost always." No operational definition is provided for these scale points and users might be hard pressed deciding whether a student engages in certain scale behaviors "occasionally" or "often."

Use of the Teacher Observation Scales is appropriate for students at all levels but is recommended for students at middle, primary, intermediate, and junior secondary levels. The Teacher Observation Scales are not to be used with all students. They are best used to select or confirm those few students being considered for gifted or accelerated programs.

The developers also recommend administering the Teacher Observation Scales to students who are "puzzling," "unknown," or "new to the school" (manual, p. 3). This recommendation though is at odds with the developers' recommendation to know the children well before administering the scales.

Scoring is done separately for each special ability scale. Scale scores are never combined to provide a general special ability score. Scoring is simple. For each scale, sum the responses marked "often" and multiply the sum by 3; sum the responses marked "almost always" and multiply the sum by 4. Then, add those two products to derive the total scale score.

Interpretation of scale scores is unclear. There are no national norms or predetermined cutoff scores for selection. Teachers are directed to "interpret scale scores in light of their particular circumstances and experience teaching children with special abilities" (manual, p. 4). Obviously, this directive offers little guidance. Consequently, test developers do offer tentative estimates of what they consider the upper ranges for selection.

Another concern in interpreting scores is that the scales are tipped in favor of quantity over quality. Because points are not earned for "occasionally" demonstrating a behavior, a student could conceivably write a single best selling novel and earn no points for the item "creates original stories."

TECHNICAL INFORMATION. The Teacher Observation Scales are problematic in some aspects of validity and reliability. In terms of validity, content validity has already been questioned. The scales are not tied to any existing model of talent or intelligence. Moreover, the scales do not reflect important aspects of talent such as hard work, time on task, and background knowledge. The Creative Thinking Scale, in particular, lacks validity. Creativity is an incremental process marked by small and predictable steps toward a solution (Weisberg, 1993) rather than the stereotypical characteristics found in the Creative Thinking Scale such as: "generates unusual insights" and "seeks unusual rather than conventional relationships" (scoring booklet, p. 4).

The Teacher Observation Scales also lack predictive and criterion validity. The predictive power is unknown because students selected into gifted programs through use of the Teacher Observation Scales have not been evaluated later in terms of actual success in their gifted programs or their talent areas. Similarly, criterion validity is lacking because there are only minimal data linking scale performance with performance on other established and related measures. For three of the five scales, there have been no attempts to establish criterion validity.

Regarding reliability, each of the five scales is internally consistent. This means that items within a scale generally measure the same attribute.

The test developers report consistently strong indices of interrater reliability. That is, pairs of teachers independently rate students similarly on the scales. Unfortunately, the numbers of teacher raters and students rated are unreported. The test developers themselves cast some doubt on the objective value of the Teacher Observation Scales. They state: "Over time, as teachers working together in schools moderate on another's interpretations of scale ratings …, it is anticipated that the degree of agreement will increase still further" (manual, p. 7).

SUMMARY. Although the Teacher Observation Scales are a convenient means for identifying exceptional students, they were not developed along any established or defensible theoretical model of intelligence or expertise. Once devel-

oped, there is not clear evidence that they measure what they purport to measure. Finally, their fundamental value is questionable given that teachers, in most cases, must first know a student well and recognize that student as exceptional before using the Teacher Observation Scales. Given the Teacher Observation Scales' subjective nature, it is possible teachers using the scales will find just what they intended to find.

REVIEWER'S REFERENCES

Sternberg, R. J., & Kagan, J. (1986). *Intelligence applied: Understanding and increasing your intellectual skills.* San Diego, CA: Harcourt Brace Jovanovich.
Weisberg, R. W. (1993). *Creativity: Beyond the myth of genius.* New York: W. H. Freeman.
Gardner, H. (1997). *Extraordinary minds: Portraits of exceptional individuals and an examination of our extraordinariness.* New York: Basic Books.

[383]

TerraNova.

Purpose: Constructed as a "comprehensive modular assessment series" of student achievement.
Population: Grades K–12.
Publication Date: 1997.
Administration: Group.
Levels, 12: 10, 11, 12, 13, 14, 15, 16, 17, 18, 19, 20, 21/22.
Price Data, 1997: $12.50 per practice activities (specify battery and level); $2.70 per directions for practice activities (specify battery and level); $25 per teacher's guide; $11.25 per additional test directions for teachers (specify battery and level); norms book available from publisher.
Foreign Language Edition: Available in English and in Spanish editions.
Time: Administration time varies by test and level.
Comments: Instruments may be administered alone or in any combination; revision of the Comprehensive Tests of Basic Skills, Fourth Edition (T5:665).
Author: CTB/McGraw-Hill.
Publisher: CTB/McGraw-Hill.
a) CTBS COMPLETE BATTERY AND COMPLETE BATTERY PLUS.
Population: Grades K–12.
Scores, 10: Complete Battery (Reading, Language Arts, Mathematics, Science, Social Studies), Complete Battery Plus (Word Analysis, Vocabulary, Language Mechanics, Spelling, Mathematics Computation).
Price Data: $115.50 per 30 Complete Battery consumable test booklets (specify level); $122 per 30 Complete Battery Plus consumable test booklets; $86 per 30 Complete Battery reusable test booklets (specify level); $92.50 per 30 Complete Battery Plus reusable test booklets (specify level); $30.75 per 50 reflective answer sheets (specify battery and level); $770 per 1,250 continuous for-

eign answer sheets (specify battery and level); $3.53 per student basic service scoring for Complete Battery; $3.80 per student basic service scoring for Complete Battery Plus.

b) CTBS BASIC BATTERY AND BASIC BATTERY PLUS.

Population: Grades K–12.

Scores, 8: Basic Battery (Reading, Language Arts, Mathematics), Basic Battery Plus (Word Analysis, Vocabulary, Language Mechanics, Spelling, Mathematics Computation).

Price Data: $108.15 per 30 Basic Battery consumable test booklets (specify level); $114.65 per 30 Basic Battery Plus consumable test booklets (specify level); $83.75 per 30 Basic Battery reusable test booklets (specify level); $90.25 per 30 Basic Battery Plus reusable test booklets (specify level); $30.75 per 50 reflective answer sheets (specify battery and level); $770 per 1,250 continuous form answer sheets (specify battery and level); $3.53 per student for Basic Battery basic service scoring; $3.80 per student for Basic Battery Plus basic service scoring.

c) CTBS SURVEY AND SURVEY PLUS.

Purpose: Designed as a norm-referenced measure of academic achievement.

Population: Grades 2–12.

Scores, 10: Survey (Reading, Language Arts, Mathematics, Science, Social Studies); Survey Plus (Word Analysis, Vocabulary, Language Mechanics, Spelling, Mathematics Computation).

Price Data: $103 per 30 Survey consumable test booklets (specify level); $109.50 per 30 Survey Plus consumable test booklets (specify level); $81.25 per 30 Survey reusable test booklets (specify level); $87.75 per 30 Survey Plus reusable test booklets (specify level); $30.75 per 50 reflective answer sheets (specify battery and level); $770 per 1,250 continuous form answer sheets (specify level); $3.37 per student for Survey basic service scoring; $3.64 per student for Survey Plus basic service scoring.

d) MULTIPLE ASSESSMENTS.

Purpose: Intended to assess academic achievement using "a combination of the selected-response items of the Survey edition and a section of constructed-response items that allow students to produce their own short and extended responses."

Population: Grades 1–12.

Scores, 5: Reading, Language Arts, Mathematics, Science, Social Studies.

Price Data: $125 per 30 consumable test booklets (specify level); $9.80 per student for basic service scoring.

e) SUPERA.

Purpose: Constructed as a "TerraNova Spanish edition."

Price Data: $13 per 30 practice activities (specify battery and level); $2.60 per directions for practice activities (specify battery and level); $24.25 per 30 locator tests (specify test and level); $21.50 per 50 locator answer sheets; $16.50 per SUPERA technical bulletin; $11.25 per SUPERA additional test directions for teachers (specify battery and level); $8.50 per locator manual.

1) *SUPERA Survey.*

Population: Grades 1–10.

Scores, 3: Reading, Language Arts, Mathematics.

Price Data: $103 per 30 consumable test booklets (specify level); $81.25 per 30 reusable test booklets (specify level); $30.75 per 50 answer sheets; $1,540 per 2,500 continuous feed answer sheets; $23.05 per 25 ScorEZE answer sheets; $2.83 per student for basic service scoring.

2) *SUPERA Multiple Assessments.*

Population: Grades 1–10.

Scores, 3: Reading, Language Arts, Mathematics.

Price Data: $87.50 per 30 consumable image-scorable test booklets (specify level); $6.35 per student for basic service scoring.

3) *SUPERA Plus.*

Population: Grades 1–10.

Scores, 5: Word Analysis, Language Mechanics, Vocabulary, Math Computation, Spelling.

Price Data: $30 per 30 test booklets (specify level); $30.75 per 50 answer sheets (specify regular or survey); $11.25 per manual (specify level).

Comments: Intended for use with either SUPERA Multiple Assessments or SUPERA Survey.

f) PERFORMANCE ASSESSMENTS.

Purpose: Constructed to "meet the needs of educators who wish to use context-based tasks or open-ended assessments."

Scores, 4: Communication Arts, Mathematics, Science, Social Studies.

Comments: Available only through contract with publisher; additional scores can be provided for broad competencies such as communication or problem solving.

Cross References: For information on the Comprehensive Tests of Basic Skills, see T5:665 (95 references); see also T4:623 (23 references); for reviews by Kenneth D. Hopkins and M. David Miller of the CTBS, see 11:81 (70 references); for reviews by Robert L. Linn and Lorrie A. Shepard of an earlier form, see 9:258 (29 references); see also T3:551 (59 references); for reviews by Warren G. Findley and Anthony J.

Nitko of an earlier edition, see 8:12 (13 references); see also T2:11 (1 reference); for reviews by J. Stanley Ahmann and Frederick G. Brown and excerpted reviews by Brooke B. Collison and Peter A. Taylor (rejoinder by Verna White) of Forms Q and R, see 7:9. For reviews of subtests of earlier editions, see 8:721 (1 review), 8:825 (1 review), 7:685 (1 review), 7:514 (2 reviews), and 7:778 (1 review).

Review of the TerraNova by JUDITH A. MONSAAS, Associate Professor of Education, North Georgia College and State University, Dahlonega, GA:

DESCRIPTION. The TerraNova comprises the revised versions of the Comprehensive Tests of Basic Skills with several optional packages including the CTBS Survey assessing Reading/Language Arts, Mathematics, Science, and Social Studies; the CTBS Complete Battery covering the same subjects but with more items per subject for more precise norms (according to the publisher) and for criterion-referenced test scores interpretations; and the CTBS Basic Battery, which only includes the Reading/Language Arts and Mathematics subtests. Each of these three Batteries has a Plus Version that includes supplemental tests in Word Analysis (Grades 1–3 only), Vocabulary, Language Mechanics, Spelling, and Mathematical Computation. The final set of assessments in the basic four subjects, called Multiple Assessments, includes a combination of the selected-response items from the Survey edition and constructed-response items, which allow students to produce their own responses. TerraNova Levels 10–22 cover Grades K–12. Additional testing materials, including performance assessments (reviewed in the *Thirteenth Mental Measurements Yearbook*), SUPERA, the Spanish edition, customized tests, and the CTB Writing Assessment (13:88) are available to supplement the TerraNova or as stand alone tests, but are not included in this review.

PURPOSE AND USES. The TerraNova, like other achievement test batteries, is designed to assess individual student learning in the basic subjects. When used in conjunction with other information, it can be used to assess individual and group status and change over time as well as provide information about the effectiveness of educational programs. The test results can be used to make comparisons with school, district, and national norm groups. Standardized achievement tests can provide important information for teachers about the knowledge and skills of their students and can be used for planning instruction based on analysis of individual student or class performance on educational objectives. The addition of performance standards to the TerraNova Batteries is helpful for schools and systems moving toward a standards-based curriculum framework. CTB/McGraw-Hill suggests that the TerraNova and other standardized achievement tests can assist in decision making in the following areas: evaluation of student progress, needs assessment, instructional program planning, curriculum analysis, program evaluation, class grouping, and administrative planning and direction. Given the multitude of assessment batteries and supplemental assessments, this claim appears to be quite supportable.

MANUALS AND OTHER ANCILLARY MATERIALS. Several manuals for test users and reviewers were provided with the TerraNova. The two most useful documents for test users are the Teacher's Guide and a separate guide for interpreting test scores and using test results. These are both well written and user friendly. The guide for interpreting test scores provides definitions and descriptions of the different score reporting methods and has a helpful section on appropriate uses of test data. This guide is relatively short and could be read or skimmed by conscientious test users to help them correctly use and interpret their students' test scores. The Teacher's Guide is a much more comprehensive description of the test content and purposes, the various score reporting profiles, and suggestions for communicating test scores to parents. In fact, there is a particularly useful question and answer section for parents embedded in the middle of the manual under the "Using Test Results" section that might be missed by someone not reading the lengthy manual carefully. The detailed description of the test development process, the content, the thinking skills framework, as well as comparisons with the CTBS/4 for previous users of the CTB tests are very useful for schools and districts attempting to determine the validity of the content for their particular curriculum and test use.

The tests are very engaging and user friendly, as well. The directions are clear and easy to follow and the tests are attractively packaged. According to the manuals, the tests were designed to look more like instructional materials than traditional achievement tests. To a certain extent, the test publishers were successful. Several test questions are linked to themes, which provide some continuity from item to item for students, making the test more closely resemble typical classroom material. Also, the constructed-response questions in the Multiple Assessments tests resemble instructional materials. Nonetheless, although these tests are attractive and more engaging than most achievement tests I have inspected, I doubt that students will forget that they are taking a test.

STANDARDIZATION AND NORMS. Norming of the TerraNova was completed in 1996 providing a relatively current set of national norms. The standardization sample was large and generally representative. Schools participating in the standardization completed a demographic survey and the results of the survey were compared to national demographic data. The norm group tended to have somewhat fewer minorities than the general population, but had more students on free and reduced-price lunch and more students from single-parent families. The final norms were, of course, weighted to reflect the national proportions. Thirty-four percent of the norm group were current users of the CAT/5 or CTBS/4, indicating that there was not an overrepresentation of CTB customers. The publishers did not specify how many schools and systems from the original sample declined to participate in the norming of the TerraNova. This information would have been helpful in evaluating the quality of the standardization sample.

A full complement of norms are available including local and national percentile ranks, normal curve equivalents, stanines, and grade equivalents. Developmental scale scores ranging from 0 to 999 span all the grade levels tested. This scoring method is especially useful for evaluating student change over time, but is not readily understandable to lay people (e.g., parents); the scores typically must be changed to derived scores such as percentiles to be useful to parents. The manuals clearly explain the benefits and limitations of each of these normative score reporting methods so that users can know when to use which method and why the various methods are used. A section on "Avoiding Misinterpretation" when using grade equivalents clearly explains the limited use of these scores and is clear on ways the scores should not be used. This disclaimer may not satisfy hard-core opponents of grade equivalents, but if teachers carefully read this section of the Teacher's Guide, they would be very circumspect in their use and interpretation of these scores.

CRITERION-REFERENCED INTERPRETATIONS. Two criterion-referenced reporting systems are provided for the TerraNova: an objectives mastery report and a performance level/standards report. The objectives mastery reports are similar to the criterion-referenced reports provided for most standardized test batteries in that students' levels of performance on subsets of objectives are provided. This is somewhat controversial, though common, because the number of items associated with each objective is sometimes too small for valid inferences regarding student performance on that objective. Also, items are typically not selected to determine mastery of the objectives, but to discriminate among students. The publishers provide an Objectives Performance Index (OPI), which is an estimate of the number of items that a student could be expected to answer correctly if there had been 100 such items for that objective. A Bayesian procedure, used to estimate the OPI, takes into account overall test performance as well as actual performance on a given objective, which serves to improve the reliability of the scores on the objectives. This procedure is an improvement on the "number correct" method considering the small number of items per objective. The score reports show student (class or district) performance on the objective using this 100-point index. The number of items used to assess the specific objectives is not provided on the score report, thus a user does not know if this index is based on the minimum of four items or considerably more. The number of items per objective would lead to more "truth in testing" and to more cautious interpretation of objectives with fewer items. Although it is possible that a test user may question how an OPI for a four-item objective is not divisible by four, it is also possible that a user might assume that an OPI of say, 79, was based on considerably more items than four. A somewhat questionable interpretation is the classification of OPI into mastery levels. An OPI of 75 and above is defined as Mastery, 50–74 as Partial Mastery, and 49 and below as Non-Mastery. These Mastery designations seem arbitrary. No standard-setting has been performed to indicate what experts (curriculum specialists, teachers) might consider mastery. If the average OPI is similar to the mean p-value the average child appears to be defined as having partial mastery of the grade level material because the average *p*-value per subtest ranges from about .50 to .70.

In addition to performance on the objectives, performance levels have been set that describe what a student can do in terms of the content across the grade spans: Grades 1–2 (primary), Grades 3–5 (elementary), Grades 6–8 (middle) and Grades 9–12 (high). Student performance is reported in terms of five Performance levels: Level 1 (Starting out or Step 1); Level 2 (Progressing); Level 3 (Nearing Proficiency); Level 4 (Proficient); and Level 5 (Advanced). Standard setting committees made up of curriculum experts and accomplished teachers set standards that included the setting of cut scores and development of performance level descriptors for each level of each subject. CTB used an IRT-based Bookmark Standard Setting procedure (Lewis, Mitzel, & Green, 1996) to set the cut scores for the TerraNova. For the Multiple Assessments, both the selected-response and constructed-response items are located on the same scale for developing performance standards. The procedure for setting the cut scores and performance descriptors is well-described and defensible. I wish that the procedure for defining Mastery levels using the OPI were as defensible, especially because that is the information schools are most likely to use in planning and evaluating instruction.

RELIABILITY. Reliability coefficients for the subtests and composite scores on the TerraNova were consistently high. KR-20 was used to estimate the reliability of the Survey Plus and the Complete Battery Plus and coefficient alpha was used to estimate the reliability of the Multiple Assessments. Reliability coefficients were computed separately for the fall and spring standardization samples. The reliability coefficients were consistently in the .80s and .90s. The only subtest demonstrating consistently lower coefficients was Spelling. Spelling also had consistently lower *p*-values indicating that it was more difficult. Slightly lower coefficients were also found at the lower grade levels (Grades 1 and 2) and for the fall standardization sample. Because the differences were slight and most testing is conducted in the spring, this coefficient discrepancy should not be of concern. It should be noted that the reliability coefficients for the Multiple Assessments were as consistently high as those of the other batteries.

Finally, interrater reliability studies were conducted on the constructed response items At selected grade levels (3, 6, and 8). The mean score points awarded by two raters were very close and the correlations were very high indicating high rater agreement. The technical manual reports that monitoring techniques are in place to ensure that interrater agreement and accuracy remain high.

VALIDITY. The process used to develop the test and ensure content validity was very thorough and clearly explained both in the Teacher's Manual and the Technical manual. Texts, basals, and numerous other publications, as well as standards developed by the states and the professional associations, were used in the development of the series. Frequent and thorough tryouts, reviews, and revisions were completed by a wide variety of classroom teachers and experts in the subject fields. Other data obtained included usability studies and sensitivity/bias reviews to ensure that the test materials were clear and appropriate and did not reflect possible bias in language, subject matter, or group membership. The *Dimensions of Thinking* (Marzano, et al., 1988) was used as a framework to ensure that the test reflected a full range of thinking skills. Tables for each test level show that the subtests assess a range of thinking skills. Not surprisingly, the Multiple Assessment battery has a greater number of items reflecting higher level thinking skills. Another feature that enhances the content validity of these tests is the thematic integration of subsets of items on the tests. This integration makes the tests more similar to materials to which students are exposed in the classroom and in their everyday lives.

Criterion-related validity studies were being planned at the time the various manuals were published. The publishers plan to correlate the TerraNova with the National Assessment of Educational Progress (NAEP), the Third International Mathematics and Science Study (TIMSS), and the SAT and ACT. Based on similar studies relating the California Achievement Tests with the SAT and ACT, the publishers expect strong relationships. These data are necessary to determine whether scores on this new test are related to other independent measures of achievement.

To support the construct validity of this test, the publishers cited the careful test development process to support the content validity and comprehensiveness of the test. A series of construct validity statements describe the skills, concepts, and processes measured in each of the subject areas. Detailed information on the subskills and objectives supports the content validity and further supports the construct validity of these tests. Convergent and discriminant validity evidence was supported by the correlations among the TerraNova subtests and total scores, and the subareas and total scores on the Test of Cognitive Skills, Second Edition. The pattern of correlations provides construct support for the TerraNova. Item review and item analysis were performed to support construct relevance and minimize construct irrelevance.

SUMMARY. The TerraNova is an innovative, well-developed set of achievement test batteries. The materials are all well constructed, attractive, and user friendly. The norming and score reporting methods are well developed. The performance standards development is state-of-the-art. My only serious reservation is with the mastery classifications for the criterion-referenced interpretations—the "cut scores" are arbitrarily defined. Although the Objectives Performance Index is technically sound and does increase the reliability of the criterion-referenced interpretations, these interpretations can still be misleading without reporting the number of items associated with each objective. Further, using technically sophisticated scaling methods and then using arbitrary, and possibly misleading, definitions of mastery, seems to be indefensible. Although I would caution teachers and schools to use the criterion-referenced scores carefully and devise their own mastery levels, in all other respects, this test is extremely well constructed. The content and construct validity evidence support the test and its appropriate uses in schools. The reliability evidence is strong as well. Planned criterion-related validity studies will likely provide additional validity support for these tests. As with all achievement tests, it is necessary that the users determine the extent to which the content of the TerraNova matches the curriculum in their schools.

REVIEWER'S REFERENCES

Marzano, R. J., Brandt, R. S., Hughes, C. S., Jones, B. F., Presseisen, B. Z., Rankin, S. C., & Suhor, C. (1988). *Dimensions of thinking: A framework for curriculum and instruction.* Alexandria, VA: The Association for Supervision and Curriculum Development.

Lewis, D. M., Mitzel, H. C., & Green, D. R. (1996, June). Standard setting: A bookmark approach. In D. R. Green (Chair), *IRT-based standard setting procedures utilizing behavioral anchoring.* Symposium conducted at the meeting of the Council of Chief State School Officers, National Conference on Large Scale Assessment, Phoenix, AZ.

Review of the TerraNova by ANTHONY J. NITKO, Professor, Department of Educational Psychology, University of Arizona, Tucson, AZ:

The TerraNova is the fifth revision of the Comprehensive Tests of Basic Skills (CTBS5). This edition's revisions to the established CTBS series are rather substantial. To understand this edition, it is first necessary to note that TerraNova is a general name for several overlapping, but distinct products, each tailored to specific purposes that potential users may have. Some understanding of the scope and purposes(s) of each of these products, in relation to individual assessment needs, is necessary to select the product that is appropriate.

ORGANIZATION OF THE TERRANOVA. The main products are the Survey Battery, Complete Battery, and Basic Battery. Each of these may be purchased with additional supplemental subtests. The word "Plus" is added to the preceding product titles when the supplemental tests are included.

The Survey Battery is a multiple-choice test. It has the fewest items per subtest. As a consequence of using a shorter test, the publisher correctly states that individual students' scores are somewhat less reliable. Thus, the publisher provides only norm-referenced information for individual students. However, curriculum-referenced information is provided at the class, school, and district levels. The Survey Battery includes subtests and scores for Reading/Language Arts, Mathematics, Science, and Social Studies. The Survey Battery Plus, contains additional subtests of Language Mechanics/Word Analysis, Vocabulary, Spelling, and Mathematics Computation. When the Survey Battery Plus product is used, composite scores are provided in reading, language, and mathematics that include the appropriate supplemental subtests.

The Complete Battery is a multiple-choice test also. To create the Complete Battery, the publisher used the items from the Survey Battery along with additional items. The consequences of lengthening the subtests are having more reliable individual student subtest scores and being able to report on each student's mastery of the objectives assessed within each subtest. These latter scores can be used to identify each student's strengths and needs within each curricular area assessed. The Complete Battery Plus includes the same supplemental subtests as were provided with the Survey Battery Plus. The composite scores the publisher reports include these supplements.

The Basic Battery is a multiple-choice test with sufficient reliability for individual student scores but only assesses reading and mathematics. It contains the same Reading/Language Arts and Mathematics subtests as the Complete Battery. The Basic Battery Plus includes the same set of supplemental subtests and also yields composite scores.

The Multiple Assessments Battery contains both multiple-choice and constructed-response items. It has the same subtests and multiple-choice items as the Survey Battery. At the end of each subtest, the publisher added short-response and extended-response items.

CHANGES AND NEW FEATURES. A distinguishing new feature of all the above-described TerraNova products is the way test items are organized within subtests. Items within each subtest are organized according to contextual themes, thus countering to some degree the often-heard criticism that standardized tests assess strictly decontextualized knowledge and skills. For example, a set of several mathematics items may be presented in the context of a neighborhood theme.

Within each subtest there are several themes. The themes are grade-appropriate so as to encourage students to engage and interact with the tests' materials. The publisher's studies of the impact of thematic graphical material concluded that there was no statistical difference in students' performance using illustrated and non-illustrated items. However, "below level" students liked the way the pages were designed, believed the illustrations helped them, and said when illustrations were present they knew more about the passages to be read.

VALIDITY AND USABILITY. The approach used to design and organize the TerraNova was thorough and careful. As is typical for better-developed standardized tests, the developers began with a thorough analysis of curriculum guides from around the country, of statements of national and state goals and standards, and of textbook series. Efforts were made to align the test content with the NAEP (National Assessment of Educational Progress) and NCTM (National Council of Teachers of Mathematics) frameworks. Teachers, curriculum experts, and other educators reviewed the test specifications and test materials for appropriateness, fairness, and accuracy. At the high school levels, attention was paid to school-to-career skills by requiring test items to assess students' abilities to apply knowledge to real-life situations.

In addition, the publisher conducted several usability studies to support the new test design and content, and the design of the reports available to a school district. Among the studies the publisher conducted were: impact of the graphical page design (referred to previously), readability of the background colors, clarity and usability of the directions to teachers, how students navigate their way through the test material, preferences students have for a specific test design, and verification of whether students responded to items using the processes that item developers intended them to use. Some of these studies were conducted in "cognitive lab" settings where under the watchful eyes of researchers and video cameras, individual students used their fingers to navigate test pages; talked aloud as they worked through the items; and expressed their concerns, confusions, and preferences. The results of these studies were used to improve test items, teachers' directions, and page designs.

There are important differences in the way earlier editions of the CTBS and TerraNova assess reading, language arts, mathematics, science, and social studies in the "non-Plus" subtests. The organization of the items into thematic context groups was discussed above. Beyond that, the subtests attempt to reflect recent developments in how each curriculum area teaches and integrates its unique base of knowledge, skills, and ability. For example, items from reading comprehension, language expression, vocabulary, and reference skills are intermixed within themes. Reading items tend to focus on comprehending the central message of the passage, and are sequenced systematically from lower level comprehension through extension, interpretation, and inference. Vocabulary items usually assess understanding the meaning of selected words in the context of the theme and passage reading. Items assessing language expression are similarly linked to the same passage or its thematic context. Passages are often extracted from published works and are presented in their original format. Unlike previous editions, the TerraNova reading passages tend to be realistically long.

To illustrate, consider one Reading/Language Arts section at Level 19 (Grade 9), Basic Battery. The thematic section begins with an approximately 520-word biographical sketch of an author, including the author's photograph. This is followed by four items: one reading comprehension and three about a related timeline printed on the page. Timeline items refer to events stemming from the author's biography. These are followed by an extended extract from one of the author's books (approximately 1,100 words). The extract is preceded by a paragraph introducing the material and setting the context. The extract is followed by six items assessing various aspects of comprehension and interpretation. Next, are two items assessing comprehension across both the extract and the biographical sketch. The next five items assess a student's language expression and usage, all within the theme of the author and the author's work. The material for applying language expression is a report written by a fictitious student about the author's book.

Mathematics, Science, and Social Studies subtests are comparably organized around applied themes with integrated skill assessment. In this manner, the publisher hopes to mirror the way language and reading are taught in schools.

You should note that the Plus subtests do not have the same organization and orientation as do the main batteries. They follow a more traditional presentation, using multiple-choice items to assess skills in isolation and without engaging themes.

A criticism of the CTBS4 was that no evidence was presented concerning the speededness of the test (Hopkins, 1992). In this edition, this shortcoming is corrected. The data presented show that typically fewer than 4% of the students fail to respond to the last multiple-choice item on the Survey Plus and the Complete Battery Plus. Data are not provided for the Multiple Assessments Battery in which constructed-response items are found. Experience in some large scale assessment programs indicates that students may respond less frequently to constructed-response items, not because the tests are speeded, but because students do not understand the question, think they cannot write a response that is worthy of full marks, or think the question requires too much writing. It would be useful for the publisher to explore these issues with the TerraNova. The item difficulty data for the constructed-response items show that there may be a tendency for them to be slightly more difficult than multiple-choice items, which is to be expected because students responding to multiple-choice items may answer correctly using partial knowledge and receive full credit. Whether this is a signal that there is not enough time to complete all constructed-response items cannot be ascertained from the data.

Throughout all the manuals and teacher's guides, the publisher addresses evidence of validity. Much of the evidence is provided in the technical publications. However, the bulk of the validity *argument* is presented in the Teacher's Guide to the TerraNova. Details are provided on the development procedures, the thinking skills frameworks, the rationales for the curriculum approaches taken, the proper interpretations and limitations of the scores, and the items' contents. A five-page appendix is devoted to an argument for the content validity of scores from the test. The publisher has provided one of the most complete discussions of validity currently available for standardized achievement batteries.

NORMS AND SCALES. The publisher provides fall, winter, and spring norms. Fall standardization included 71,366 students (Grades 1–12), and spring standardization included 100,650 students (K–12). Winter norms are generally interpolated, but over 8,000 students in Kindergarten and Grade 1 were sampled. The sample appears to be reasonably representative of the nation's students and not overrepresentative of former CTBS users. However, test users are urged to test in the spring or fall because empirical norms are available for late April and October, respectively.

The now-standard set of norm-referenced scores is provided: percentile ranks, normal curve equivalents, grade-equivalents, and stanines. The standard score scale, spanning all grades in a range of 0 to 999, is the main interpretive educational development growth scale. It is derived from an IRT item scaling in which multiple-choice and constructed-response items were scaled simultaneously using CTB/McGraw-Hill's proprietary software, PARDUX. This software uses marginal maximum likelihood implemented via the EM algorithm.

The norm-referenced scores and the IRT scoring (called "pattern scoring") are very well described in two excellent publications: the Teacher's Guide and *Beyond the Numbers*. Both publications should be read before using the test results. School principals, in particular, should not attempt to use the TerraNova unless they have studied both publications.

As with earlier editions of the CTBS, Anticipated Achievement Scores are provided when the Test of Cognitive Skills (TCS) is administered along with a TerraNova battery. These multiple-regression-based scores are a useful adjunct to other battery scores. They estimate what students of similar age, grade, and TCS score do on the average on each TerraNova subtest. However, the anticipated score should not be used as a goal or an "expectation." One should not expect a student to be "average" for his or her age and grade. It is inappropriate, also, based on these scores, to describe a student as an "overachiever" or "underachiever." One can say the student is above (or below) the average for his (her) age and grade.

CRITERION-REFERENCED INFORMATION. If the Complete or Basic Batteries are used, then each student can receive a score on each of the objectives the test measures. This score is called an Objective Performance Index (OPI). Each objective on which a score is reported is measured by at least four items. The score is an estimate of the percent of items for an objective that a student can answer correctly. The automated score report interprets the estimated percentage in this way: nonmastery (0–49%), partial mastery (50–74%), and mastery (75–100%). The hope is that teachers will use these scores to identify specific subject-matter objectives on which a student needs more instruction.

Objective-based information for the entire class (average OPI) is available for all three batteries. Average OPIs may help teachers plan instruction either for the current group or for next year's class.

Students' test results can also be reported as performance levels. Scores range from 1 to 5. The respective verbal labels are: Starting Out (or Step 1), Progressing, Nearing Proficiency, Proficient, and Advanced. This type of reporting mimics the way that the National Assessment of Educational Progress and several states report performance.

Performance levels were set using the Bookmark Standard Setting Procedure (Lewis, Mitzel, & Green, 1996). The standard errors for the cutscores resulting from this procedure seem reasonably small. Teachers and administrators are provided verbal description for each subject (reading, language arts, mathematics, science, and social studies) of the skills, knowledge, and concepts of which students at each performance level are supposed to be able to have reasonable mastery. These skills are described in the Performance Levels Handbook.

SUMMARY. The TerraNova is a technically well-built achievement test. It is one of the better batteries of its type. The new features of embedding items in thematic contexts, using more real-world item formats, and incorporating constructed-response items with the multiple-choice subtests seem to be educationally sound. The three versions (Survey, Complete, Basic), with their "Pluses," and the Multiple Assessment Battery have something to offer everyone, albeit as a confusing array on first blush. Teachers' materials are exceptionally well done and informative. The score reports that are available are also well done, having been, themselves, field tested. If the TerraNova's content and approach are a close fit to a school district's curriculum framework, it should be seriously considered for adoption. If this close match is not there, look elsewhere.

REVIEWER'S REFERENCES

Hopkins, K. D. (1992). [Review of the Comprehensive Tests of Basic Skills, Fourth Edition]. In J. J. Kramer & J. C. Conoley (Eds.), *The eleventh mental measurements yearbook* (pp. 215–217). Lincoln, NE: The Buros Institute of Mental Measurements.

Lewis, D. M., Mitzel, H. C., & Green, D. R. (1996, June). Standard setting: A bookmark approach. In D. R. Green (Chair), *IRT-based standard-setting procedures utilizing behavioral anchoring.* Symposium conducted at the meeting of the Council of Chief State School Officers National Conference on Large Scale Assessment, Phoenix, AZ.

[384]
Test for Auditory Comprehension of Language—Third Edition.

Purpose: Designed as a measure of receptive spoken vocabulary, grammar, and syntax.

Population: Ages 3-0 to 9-11.

Publication Dates: 1973–1999.

Acronym: TACL-3.

Scores, 4: Vocabulary, Grammatical Morphemes, Elaborated Phrases and Sentences, Total.

Administration: Individual.

Price Data, 2001: $254 per complete kit; $79 per manual (1999, 117 pages); $39 per Picture Book; $39 per 25 Profile/Examiner Record Booklets.

Time: (15–25) minutes.

Author: Elizabeth Carrow-Woolfolk.

Publisher: PRO-ED.

Cross References: See T5:2657 (37 references) and T4:2727 (20 references); for reviews by Nicholas W. Bankson and William O. Haynes of an earlier edition, see 10:363; see also T3:2472 (25 references); for reviews by John T. Hatten and Huberto Molina of an earlier edition, see 8:454 (6 references); see also T2:997A (2 references).

Review of the Test for Auditory Comprehension of Language—Third Edition by RAMASAMY MANIKAM, Clinical Faculty, University of Maryland School of Medicine, Baltimore, MD:

DESCRIPTION OF TEST. The Test for Auditory Comprehension of Language—Third Edition (TACL-3) was developed by the same author as its preceding versions. Therefore, the TACL-3 is very similar to their standardization and test structure, but with better all around improvement in psychometric properties and layout. The test was normed on 1,102 children with normal language ages 3-0 through 9-11. The test consists of 139 items grouped into three subtests (vocabulary, syntax, and grammar). Vocabulary measures the meanings of word classes; Syntax measures understanding of grammatical morphemes; and Elaborated Phrases and Sentences tests understanding of syntactically based word relations.

The test-kit includes a record booklet, an examiner's manual, and a picture book. The examiner reads the stimulus and the child is required to point to the picture that best represents the meaning of the word, phrase, or sentence (e.g., In Subtest I: Vocabulary section, Item 1: examiner reads aloud "Show me, cat," child will point to one of the three pictures of a fish, a dog, and a cat. This format is similar for Subtest II: Grammatical Morphemes, and Subtest III: Elaborated Sentences). Correct performance is scored a 1 and an incorrect performance is scored a 0. The instructions provided in the manual and test booklet are thorough and clear. As the child is required to use auditory discrimination the test should be administered in a quiet setting.

GENERAL EVALUATION. The TACL-3 is a very well-designed and studied instrument. The author has taken extraordinary steps to make this a useful instrument. The test is well validated. The manual and test material are well laid out with the size and colors of the pictures appealing to children. The TACL-3 should be given to children by a trained speech therapist, as proper speech and decoding are essential for administering and scoring this test. This test is highly recommended to address auditory comprehension and subsequent remedial planning.

Review of the Test for Auditory Comprehension of Language—Third Edition by CHRISTINE NOVAK, Clinical Assistant Professor, Division of Psychological and Quantitative Foundations, The University of Iowa, Iowa City, IA:

The Test for Auditory Comprehension of Language—Third Edition (TACL-3) assesses comprehension of language from the conceptual framework that poor comprehension can arise either due to a lack of association between linguistic forms and meaning or to problems processing language input (secondary to auditory acuity, discrimination, or memory deficits). The value of measuring comprehension as independent, yet related to expressive skill, lies in the assumption that such differences can be measured reliably and have meaningful implications for remediation. A great deal of care has been put into the development of the TACL-3 to demonstrate its usefulness in identifying auditory comprehension deficits.

A clear distinction is provided early in the description of the test regarding the nature of the content; rather than attempt to measure the full scope of skills required for a child to understand conversational language, the test focuses on limited, but well-defined content. Additionally, users are cautioned against relying on only one source of information when making important decisions about individuals. In other words, it is expected that the TACL-3 will be used in conjunction with other observations or test data to get a complete picture of the child's functioning.

For what it purports to do, the TACL-3 is a very reliable measure. Internal consistencies are reported for the Quotient and each of the three subtests by age; all are within the .90s except Vocabulary at ages 5 and 9 years (.89 and .84, respectively). Furthermore, the test shows consistency across various subgroups including gender, ethnicity, and disability. Some positive evidence is provided for stability; however, the sample is small and limited to second and third graders in an elementary school in Austin, Texas. Efforts were also directed at establishing interrater reliability for each of the subtests and the Quotient. Surprisingly, reliabilities for two of the subtests fell below .90; it is difficult to imagine how this might have occurred because the format of the test (multiple choice) leaves little room for judgment as to the accuracy of the response. Nevertheless, the Quotient is a robust index across age, gender, ethnicity, disability, time, and scorers.

The normative sample is stratified by age and generally represents the 1997 U.S. Census with the exception of fewer numbers from urban areas (55% vs. 75%) and more from rural areas (47% vs. 25%), which is most notable across the 5–9-year age span. Children with speech-language disorders and children with learning disabilities were included in the sample. The manual makes reference to the potential use of the TACL-3 with adults (p. 60); however, the norms extend only to age 9 years, 11 months and technical data only apply to use with children.

In looking at how the test functions across the age span, there is evidence of acceptable item discrimination and item difficulty. Vocabulary at age 9 is not as strong in discriminating between test-takers as the other subtests, which is consistent with its lower internal consistency estimates (for age 9, and for LD and ADHD students). Vocabulary also has more items with a significant index of bias (for blacks vs. non-blacks) than the other subtests except Elaborated Sentences (male vs. female). The manual indicates that due to potential bias, three items were discarded. It is unclear whether the items were from these two subtests or others.

Group differentiation was investigated as part of the validity studies. Males and females scored fairly consistently across subtests and Quotient. Hispanic Americans scored similarly to those with ADHD or LD, and African Americans scored somewhat lower (in terms of Quotient) though still within the normal range. If the difference for African Americans is considered slight, then the differences for LD and ADHD must also be considered so. Expectations of lower performance were borne out for children with delayed speech and language, hearing impairments, and mental retardation.

Further support for the validity of the test came from factor analysis (which demonstrated a single factor) and subtest intercorrelations (which showed that the subtests were related but not so strongly that each was not measuring a different aspect of comprehension). Additionally, the Vocabulary subtest from the TACL-3 was shown to correlate more highly with the Receptive than the Expressive Vocabulary subtest of the Comprehensive Receptive and Expressive Vocabulary Test. There were no current studies to support the claim that the TACL-3 is useful in predicting success in the early grades, although there were two studies reported using the 1973 version of the test, which showed correlations with reading and other achievement measures.

SUMMARY. The TACL-3 is easy to administer and score, and the addition of color pictures enhances its appeal. The manual is well-written and comprehensive, showing the exceptional care that went into the test's development. In sum, it appears to be a useful tool for identifying specific comprehension deficits in a wide range of children with sufficient reliability to allow progress monitoring. Program planning uses are limited to the areas delineated by the content.

[385]
Test for Creative Thinking—Drawing Production.

Purpose: "Meant to be a screening instrument which allows for a first rough, simple, and economic assessment of a person's creative potential."
Population: Age 4–adult.
Publication Date: 1996.
Acronym: TCT-DP.
Scores, 15: Continuations, Completions, New Elements, Connections Made with Lines, Connections that Contribute to a Theme, Boundary-Breaking Being Fragment—Dependent, Perspective, Humour/Affectivity/Emotionality/Expressive Power of the Drawing, Unconventionality A—Uncoventional Manipulation, Unconventionality B—Symbolic/Abstract/Fictional, Unconventionality C—Symbol-Figure-Combinations, Unconventionality D—Nonstereotypical Utilization of Given Fragments/Figures, Speed, Total.
Administration: Group.
Forms, 2: A, B.
Price Data: Available from publisher.
Time: (30) minutes.
Authors: Klaus K. Urban and Hans G. Jellen.
Publisher: SWETS Test Publishers [The Netherlands].

Review of the Test for Creative Thinking—Drawing Production by ALICE J. CORKILL, Associate Professor and Co-Director, Cognitive Interference Laboratory, University of Nevada, Las Vegas, NV:

The Test for Creative Thinking—Drawing Production is designed to serve as a culture-free (nonverbal) screening instrument for determining a person's creative potential. According to the authors, it is to be considered a first, rough estimate of creative potential. The test is appropriate for use with individuals ranging in age from 5 years through adulthood.

The authors' definition of creativity, based on their own work and the work of Amabile and Sternberg, is a compilation of both cognitive and personality components. The cognitive components are divergent thinking, general knowledge, and specific knowledge. The personality components are focusing and task commitment, motivation and motives, and tolerance of ambiguity. The authors' multidimensional approach to creativity is reflected by the scoring system designed for the test. The theoretical framework developed by the authors for this approach is compelling.

The test consists of an incomplete diagram—a 6.5 x 6.5-inch square with five picture fragments within the square and one picture fragment outside the square. The five fragments inside the square are a dot in the upper right corner, a semicircle in the upper left portion, an "s" shaped line in the lower right, a dashed line (similar to three hyphens) in the low-middle section of the diagram, and a 1 x 1-inch right angle in the right section about midway between the top and bottom lines of the 6.5 x 6.5-inch square (the right angle is oriented such that the angle appears in what would be the upper right portion of what could be seen as half a square). The single fragment outside the perimeter of the square is a small open square (the right side of the square is open). This fragment is located on the right side of the square about 1/3 of the way down from the top and about 1 inch to the right of the square's right edge.

Examinees are instructed to complete the incomplete drawing. Examinees are instructed that there are no wrong answers. Examinees are not given a time limit although after 15 minutes have passed they are instructed to finish their drawing. Examinees are encouraged to assign a title to their completed drawing. If examinees ask questions, the examiner is instructed to tell the examinees to "draw as you please." Further questioning is discouraged. Each examinee completes two incomplete drawings. Form A shows the incomplete drawing as described above. Form B shows the same figure as Form A; it is, however, rotated 180 degrees (upside-down).

Each completed diagram is assessed on 11 dimensions. These dimensions are: (a) Continuations, (b), Completions, (c) New Elements, (d) Connections Made with a Line, (e) Connections Made to Contribute to a Theme, (f) Boundary Breaking—Fragment Dependent, (g) Boundary Breaking—Fragment Independent, (h) Perspective, (i) Use of Humor, (j) Unconventionality, and (k) Speed. Each of these components is described below.

Continuations (a) includes the use of any of the six figure fragments in the completed drawing (e.g., using the single dot fragment as a bird's eye). Completions (b) includes adding points, lines, or

additional markings to the used fragments or connecting fragments (e.g., using the three dashed lines as the bottom of an animal's feet and using the semicircle as the bottom of the same animal's face). New Elements (c) includes use of any new symbol, figure, or element (e.g., a row of flowers or clouds or birds in a sky). Connections Made with a Line (d) includes any line that connects two continued fragments and another picture fragment or a new element in the drawing (e.g., rays of light from a sun that touch trees, house, flowers, and so forth). Connections Made to Contribute to a Theme (e) includes use of figure fragments or new elements that contribute to an overall picture theme (e.g., a completed picture is titled "funny car" and shows picture fragments used to create the pieces of the car). Boundary Breaking—Fragment Dependent (f) includes any use of the small open square outside the large square (e.g., the square is closed and attached to the larger square with a set of lines). Boundary Breaking—Fragment Independent (g) includes any picture element that extends beyond the boundaries of the large square (e.g., rays of light from a sun extend above the top line of the square). Perspective (h) includes an attempt to use three dimensions (e.g., two rows of flowers are drawn, one row behind the other). Use of Humor (i) includes any drawing that elicits a humorous response from the evaluator of the drawing or a drawing that shows affection or strong emotion (e.g., a drawing of a cartoon-like cat or a "funny car" that has eyes and a mouth). Unconventionality (j) includes unconventional manipulation of the material, use of abstract or fictional elements in the drawing, use of symbols or signs, and use of nonstereotypical or unconventional figures in the drawing (e.g., a drawing that includes speech bubbles that show what a character is thinking or saying). Speed (k) includes the assignment of additional points to a drawing if when scored it accumulated 25 points from the first IQ categories and the drawing was completed in less than 12 minutes.

The test manual includes more precise descriptions of each element and it also includes a set of 28 completed and scored drawings to which evaluators may refer when scoring. The scoring procedures are explained well and they are easy to follow. Achieving reasonable proficiency in scoring would not be difficult given the instructions and the examples in the test manual.

The test was normed on 2,519 Germans ranging in age from 4 to over 50 with roughly equal numbers of males (51%) and females (49%). The scores are broken into a seven-level classification system based on percentile ranks. The levels with labels are as follows: A—far below average—percentile ranks 0–10; B—below average—percentile ranks 11–25; C—average—percentile ranks 26–75; D—above average—percentile ranks 76–90; E—far above average—percentile ranks 91–97.5; F—extremely high above average—percentile ranks 97.5–100; and G—phenomenal—total score above upper limit of norm sample. A series of studies reported in the test manual indicate that the German norms are applicable to other European, Western, Australian, Asian, and African populations.

Estimates for interrater reliability are high (average = .93). Estimates for parallel forms reliability are somewhat less so (Hungarian population study: average parallel forms reliability = .70; small German sample: n = 57, parallel forms reliability = .70). Even so, the test appears to be reliable enough for a first, rough estimate of creative potential.

Evidence for construct validity is less straightforward. The test manual reports a validation study performed with verbally talented students in which scores on the Test for Creative Thinking, scores on a German verbal creativity test, and scores on a German intelligence-structure test were correlated. The correlations between the Test for Creative Thinking and these other two tests were significant, but low (.36 and .48 respectively but only for one group of students).

SUMMARY. The Test for Creative Thinking—Drawing Production is an instrument appropriate for a first, rough estimate of creative potential. The test is well documented, theoretically grounded, and adequately normed. Estimates of parallel forms reliability suggest the instrument scores are reasonably reliable. Estimates of interrater reliability indicate that the instrument may be scored satisfactorily by different evaluators. Evidence of construct validity is sadly lacking.

Review of the Test for Creative Thinking—Drawing Production by WILLIAM STEVE LANG, Associate Professor of Educational Measurement and Research, Department of Educational Measurement and Research, University of South Florida, St. Petersburg, FL:

The Test for Creative Thinking—Drawing Production (TCT-DP) is reported to be a figural measure of creative thinking, the purpose for which is primarily quick screening of creative potential for virtually all ages (5 to 95). The test is administered individually or in small groups and the administration time is usually less than 15 minutes. The test consists of incomplete figures that are used by the respondent to draw into a meaningful picture. The use of figures without a verbal component is an attempt to avoid cultural or language barriers. Additionally, the scoring system attempts to measure qualitative components of creativity (i.e., humor) and not just quantitative measures such as the counting of ideas produced (i.e., fluency).

The TCT-DP gives 14 subscores: Continuation, Completion, New Elements, Connections with a Line or Theme, Boundary Breaking with Dependent or Independent Fragments, Perspective, Humor and Affectivity, Unconventionality (4 types), and Speed. Specific verbal directions for administration are given. Scoring examples are provided and are clear. Some preliminary norms tables are provided, mostly from German populations (all European) that provide a T-score scale with classifications from Far Below Average through seven steps to Phenomenal. No English-speaking populations are included in the norms and one comparison study with Americans is reported, though the manual is unclear in its translation with regard to all the results.

Reliability studies are reported for interrater reliability, parallel test reliability, test-retest reliability, and differential reliability. Though some of the figures (.46 in one test-retest situation) are lower than generally obtained for achievement or intelligence tests, they are acceptable with projective tests of this nature.

Validity studies for the TCT-DP were generally lacking. The authors state, "It is difficult to answer the question of validity for our TCT-DP, since there are no other instruments which are directly comparable to it" (manual, p. 50). Therefore, the primary validity evidence is correlations with intelligence tests, admittedly a different construct than creativity. One useful study is reported in the manual reporting the correlation of the TCT-DP scores and teacher assessment of creativity. Most of the relationships reported in that study were positive and significant. The authors are in error to state there are no other similar instruments for validation studies. In fact, versions of the well-known Torrance Tests of Creative Thinking (Ball & Torrance, 1982; T5:2771) have a figural component, are scored on many similar criteria (Abstractness, Openness, Context, Combination/Synthesis [Gestalt], Breakthrough of Closure, Visual Perspective, Humor, Imagery, Feelings, Fantasy, and Movement), and would make an obvious choice for a criterion-related validity study.

The TCT-DP appears to be a potentially useful instrument for cross-cultural assessment of creative thinking. The authors make a compelling case for the use of figural items and construct validity. Unfortunately, the instrument needs much more work to produce useful norm tables and to evaluate predictive or concurrent validity. The lack of correlational evidence with well-established instruments for the measurement of creativity is a distinct weakness. The TCT-DP also does not clearly establish the usefulness of the instrument for the wide range of ages from 5 to 95. Most researchers would believe that using the same items for all persons would lead to a ceiling or floor effect, and the authors need to demonstrate that the traits measured would ever appear in some so young and similarly in elderly adults. Likewise, the same directions for all ages seems questionable and the burden is on the authors to verify that this is appropriate.

SUMMARY. In conclusion, the TCT-DP could be used currently for research or theoretical studies, but still lacks refinement for use in placement or diagnosis in applied settings. Its potential for cross-cultural measurement of creativity is a strength, but until better norms and validation studies are performed, more established measures of creative thinking would be a better choice.

REVIEWER'S REFERENCE

Ball, O. E., & Torrance, E. P. (1982). *Workbook for streamlined scoring of the figural forms of the Torrance Tests of Creative Thinking.* Bensenville, IL: Scholastic Testing Service.

[386]
Test of Articulation in Context.

Purpose: Designed to "examine a student's phonological abilities in the context of spontaneous conversation, and can be used to screen, predict change, diagnose and assess a student's phonological progress following treatment."
Population: Preschool through elementary-school-aged children.
Publication Date: 1998.
Acronym: TAC.

Scores, 4: Sound Production, Speech Mechanism, Intelligibility, Adverse Effect on Educational Performance.
Administration: Individual.
Price Data, 1999: $110 per kit including 25 reference forms, 4 laminated test boards, and manual (45 pages).
Time: Untimed.
Author: Teresa Lanphere.
Publisher: Imaginart International, Inc.

Review of the Test of Articulation in Context by THOMAS W. GUYETTE, Associate Professor, Marquette University, Milwaukee, WI:

The Test of Articulation in Context was designed to "examine a student's phonological abilities in a more naturalistic context and thereby provide the examiner with a more realistic picture of the child's true performance" (manual, p. 3). The author asserts that children may have the ability to correctly articulate the names of pictures at the single word level but may not be able to correctly articulate these same names when speaking in spontaneous conversation. The rationale is that when a speech pathologist uses a single word articulation test to evaluate a child's speech, there is a risk of underestimating the "true" severity of the child's problem (i.e., he may make errors in spontaneous conversation that do not show up on the single word articulation test). The author believes that this problem with sampling is significant and can be corrected if the speech sample is derived from spontaneous speech rather than single word naming.

The child's responses on the Test of Articulation in Context are elicited using a set of four pictures. Each picture is composed of a path with numerous scenes on either side of the path. As the child moves down the path, he or she is expected to name spontaneously the relevant items in the different scenes. In cases where the child does not name the relevant items, the examiner is allowed to cue and/or model the target response. The child will need to name a total of 86 pictures (67 words with single consonant targets and 19 words with consonant blend targets). After the picture descriptions, there is a short section where the examiner is instructed to test the stimulability of phonemes that were in error. This is followed by a section where the examiner records a spontaneous speech sample. I am not sure why this additional spontaneous sample is needed given that the utterances for the picture descriptions are intended to elicit responses spontaneously. Next there is a section where the examiner can identify common phonological processes present in the child's speech. Finally, the above information is used to fill out the Severity and Intelligibility Rating Scale.

The Test of Articulation in Context does not meet a number of important psychometric standards. For example, the author did not collect any normative data on the articulation responses. This is a significant deficiency. Instead of collecting responses from normal subjects in connected speech, the author presents us with a Developmental Sound Acquisition Chart adapted from an article by Eric Sander (1972) that was based primarily on data that were collected in 1931 and 1957. In these early studies, sounds were usually elicited by having children name single pictures rather than speak in connected speech. If these data were not collected using a connected speech sample, then they should not be used as a reference for data that were collected in connected speech. The author makes no attempt to assure the reader that these data are appropriate to use with data collected in connected speech.

The author does not provide the test user with information on the reliability of scores from the test. This is a significant omission because judgments of articulation errors are difficult to make reliably at the single word level and would likely be even more difficult to make in connected speech. Aside from the issue of judgment reliability, it would also be important to know if the test has adequate test-retest reliability.

The author does not provide the test user with information on test validity. The omission of these data leaves the user uncertain about how much confidence to place in the test results. Also, these data would be especially interesting because the implication of the test's rationale is that scores from this test should be more valid than those from a single word articulation test.

SUMMARY. This test lacks basic psychometric information. For example, the author did not collect data on normal children/adults to use as test norms. Data from previous studies (not associated with this test) are included as a substitute for the normative sample but these data do not appear to be appropriate. There are no reliability or validity data. In summary, this test has a thought-provoking rationale but I would not recommend it because of the absence of psychometric information.

Review of the Test of Articulation in Context by ROGER L. TOWNE, Associate Professor and Head, Department of Communication Disorders, Northern Michigan University, Marquette, MI:

The Test of Articulation in Context was developed to provide speech-language pathologists with a "systematic and comprehensive way to assess articulation skills in context" (manual, p. 3). Assessing children's articulation skills in context is desirable, as it has been shown that contextual assessment provides a more accurate measure of one's true phonological abilities, and will usually reveal more articulation errors than does testing at a single word level. Articulation in context traditionally has been evaluated using any sample of a child's speech. This task is typically rather time-consuming and often does not include a complete sampling of all consonants, vowels, and diphthongs. The Test of Articulation in Context purports to provide a more systematic means by which these phoneme productions can be sampled in context providing that a child is able and/or willing to perform at this level.

The test materials include an instruction manual, four colored-picture scenes used to elicit productions of specific phonemes, and a response form that is color coded to facilitate scoring a child's responses to the test. The task of the examiner is to elicit spontaneous utterances from a child that include words having targeted phonemes in the initial, medial, and final position. Ideally, this can be done by allowing the child to simply talk about what they see happening in the picture while providing minimal prompts such as "Tell me more," or "What else do you see happening?" If a child does not respond spontaneously then more specific prompts and cues can be given that include sentence completion and word repetition. At this level the child's responses are no longer "within context," thus diminishing the stated uniqueness of the test. Irrespective of their context, a child's production of targeted words and phonemes are transcribed on the response form and the level of cueing required is noted (i.e., spontaneous, questioning, or modeling). Phoneme production accuracy is then summarized on a developmental grid in order to determine the age appropriateness of the child's phoneme productions.

Because the test's targeted population includes school-age children, the author attempts to provide a means by which speech-language pathologists working in the public schools can document a student's eligibility for speech services and the need for intervention. This is facilitated in two ways: (a) by providing a means of summarizing test performance relative to age expectancies for sound competency, and (b) through a severity and intelligibility rating scale. Guidelines are provided in the examiner's manual on how to evaluate overall sound production, the child's speech mechanism, intelligibility, and adverse effects on educational performance relative to being normal, or having a mild delay, moderate delay, and/or severe delay. These are ultimately subjective measures that will likely need to be further supported by additional quantitative data in order to fully document a student's eligibility and special education needs.

The test itself was not normalized, but rather depends upon published developmental articulation milestones for comparison with the results. Nor were any reliability or validity assessments made. However, two field tests were completed prior to the development of the final and current test format. The first field test involved 12 examiners and 37 students; the second involved 39 examiners and 187 students. Average age of those students tested was 5 years, 9 months in the first field test and 6 years, 5 months in the second. Based on test results and evaluator feedback the author eliminated and replaced word stimuli deemed too difficult for younger children, modified the response form to make scoring and test interpretation easier, and had the picture scene stimuli redrawn to make stimulus presentation more user friendly. The author believes that the final version of the test is more enjoyable for the students and relatively easy for the speech-language pathologist to use.

SUMMARY. The Test of Articulation in Context presents another formal means of sampling a child's articulation performance. As the name suggests, the test does have the potential of eliciting targeted phonemes within the context of spontaneous speech and conversation. However, whether this is accomplished or not is dependent upon a child responding in sentence form to the test stimuli and the limited prompting of the examiner. If responses within context are inconsistent or nonattainable (e.g., the child only responding in single word utterances) then this test is little different from other articulation tests that focus on single word responses by design. Assessment of articulation within context must then be made through some other, perhaps more creative, means.

As a general test of a child's articulation, the Test of Articulation in Context appears to be appreciably no better or worse than other articulation tests currently used by professional speech-language pathologists. Whether the potential opportunity for sampling and assessing contextual articulation is a significant advantage will depend on the examiner's needs and purpose for administering the test. Ultimately, assessment of contextual articulation will likely still need to be accomplished through the analysis of a child's conversational speech.

[387]

Test of Children's Language: Assessing Aspects of Spoken Language, Reading, and Writing.

Purpose: "Designed to measure important aspects of spoken language, reading, and writing."

Population: Ages 5-0 to 8-11.

Publication Date: 1996.

Acronym: TOCL.

Scores, 11: 7 Component Scores (Spoken Language, Knowledge of Print, Word Recognition, Reading Comprehension, Writing Skills, Writing From Memory, Original Writing); 4 Combined Scores (Spoken Language Quotient; Reading Quotient, Writing Quotient; Total Language Quotient).

Administration: Individual.

Price Data, 1999: $139 per complete kit including manual (62 pages), "A Visit with Mr. Turtle" storybook, story picture sheet, 25 student workbooks, and 25 profile/examiner record forms in storage box; $39 per 25 student workbooks; $44 per 25 profile/examiner record forms; $44 per manual; $5 per storybook picture sheet; $12 per "A Visit with Mr. Turtle" storybook.

Time: (30–40) minutes.

Authors: Edna Barenbaum and Phyllis Newcomer.

Publisher: PRO-ED.

Review of the Test of Children's Language: Assessing Aspects of Spoken Language, Reading, and Writing by STEVE GRAHAM, Professor of Special Education, University of Maryland, College Park, MD:

The Test of Children's Language (TOCL) was developed to assess selected aspects of young children's spoken language, reading, and writing. According to the authors, the test is unusual in that it bridges the gap between traditional, standardized assessment and nontraditional, performance-based assessment, measuring the language skills of children between the ages of 5-0 and 8-11 using authentic and real-life tasks. The assessment of students' spoken language and reading skills is primarily conducted within the context of a storybook entitled *A Visit With Mr. Turtle*. The storybook is read to the child, with the examiner asking questions either before or after reading the material on a specific page. The only exception involves the last three printed pages of text that are read by the child if she or he is capable of doing so. Writing skills are assessed by asking the child to rewrite the story from memory, using the pictures from the storybook to facilitate recall, and by asking them to write letters, words, and a story about animal friends.

Although the use of the storybook provides an interesting and reasonably method for collecting a variety of information, it is unlikely that teachers will view this task as authentic or real-life. The story is constantly interrupted and parts of each page repeated as the examiner asks the student to carry out specific tasks, such as identifying the letters a specific sound makes, putting words together to form a sentence, and determining what a particular sentence means.

The TOCL can be administered in approximately 30 to 40 minutes, and the authors indicate that the test can be given in several sessions if the examiner decides that this is advisable. Administering the test across multiple sessions is likely to inflate estimates of the child's relative standing, however, especially on the task where the child is asked to rewrite the information in the storybook from memory. When the child is not administered this task immediately after the story is read, the examiner is directed to reread the storybook to the child. Rereading the story without the constant interruptions involved in the initial administration of the storybook tasks is likely to make the process of recalling information easier.

The authors are to be commended for indicating the type of children for which the TOCL is most appropriate, detailing the necessary qualifications for administering the test, and noting specific cautions that should be observed in interpreting the obtained scores. The TOCL is easy to administer and score, although examiners may experience some frustration when trying to determine the part of a word the child is pointing to when completing some of the items on the storybook task. The authors do, however, provide an alternative form of assessment for these items.

According to the authors, the TOCL can be used to determine students' relative standing in terms of their language and literacy skills, pinpoint individual strengths and weaknesses in these skills, identify children at-risk for failure in reading and writing, and document students' progress. Unfortunately, the developers of the TOCL do not present a strong or convincing case for each of these claims. For example, alternate forms of the test are not available and the instrument samples a relatively small range of behaviors in each of the domains tested, undermining the authors' contention that the test can be used to monitor student progress. Similarly, the only evidence to support the claim that the test is helpful in identifying children at-risk for failure in literacy were two small studies conducted by the authors. In the first study, TOCL scores of 43 kindergarten children identified by teachers as at-risk were lower than the scores of kindergarten students in the normative sample. In the second study, TOCL scores of 41 second grade students were related to final report card ratings in major subject areas. Additional research employing stronger outcome measures is needed before this instrument should be used as a device for identifying children at-risk for developing reading and writing difficulties.

Items for the TOCL were developed in response to a number of different theoretical positions concerning language and literacy development. Although the authors asked eight experts to classify items according to the content measured, they used a criterion of agreement barely better than chance to assign an item to a specific domain. There is also some question about the subclassifications given to some items. For instance, the authors indicated that some of the items on the test measure phonological awareness (an oral language skill). Instead, the items appear to assess the child's ability to produce an appropriate sound for an identified letter in a written word.

The initial pilot study for the TOCL involved a small number of participants—75 kindergarten through second grade children. Data form the pilot were used to make minor revisions in the instrument and it was then standardized on a relatively small sample of 908 children. The normative sample was reasonably representative of the population of children residing in the United States at the time of the 1990 census.

Overall, the reliability estimates for scores from the instrument appear adequate. Measures of internal consistency computed on the standardization sample were, in almost all instances, above .80 and often above .90. Although test-retest (with a 14–21 day interval) reliability coefficients were computed from a sample of only 45 children, they ranged from .82 to .98. The only exception involved the Reading Comprehension subtest for which the test-retest reliability coefficient was .77. It is important to note, however, that test-retest reliability coefficients were not available at different ages, and the authors failed to provide any information in intra- or interrater reliability.

It is possible that the TOCL is too easy for older children. There was very little difference in the test performance of 7- and 8-year-old children in the normative sample and the item analysis conducted by the authors on the test indicated that items measuring spoken language and reading were fairly easy for students at these ages. In contrast, results of the item analysis indicated that the criteria used to score two of the writing subtests, Writing From Memory (i.e., retelling the storybook) and Original Writing (writing a story about animal friends), are overly difficult for younger children— those who are 5 and 6 years of age.

Finally, the authors conducted several studies establishing that scores on the TOCL were related to other measures of early reading, language, and intelligence. They further provided evidence that students who typically have language-related problems scored lower on the TOCL than children in the normative sample. Unfortunately, these studies involved small numbers of children, and require replication before the authors of the TOCL can make a strong or convincing case regarding the validity for scores from the instrument. At this point, the TOCL appears to be best suited as a screening device for identifying young children who may benefit from additional testing in spoken language, reading, or writing.

Review of the Test of Children's Language: Assessing Aspects of Spoken Language, Reading, and Writing by RICHARD M. WOLF, Professor of Psychology and Education, Teachers College, Columbia University, New York, NY:

The Test of Children's Language (TOCL) is an individually administered test that measures proficiency in three areas of children's language: spoken language, reading, and writing. It is intended for use with children from age 5-0 to 8-11. It yields a number of scores in each area. A single score is obtained in the area of Spoken language, three scores in the area of reading (Knowledge of Print, Word Recognition, and Reading Comprehension), and three scores in writing (Writing Skills, Writing From Memory, and Original Writing). A total score can also be obtained. Administration time is estimated to be between 30 to 40 minutes and can be given in one or two testing periods. Much of the test material is based on a short book that is given to the student to read and answer questions. In addition, the student is asked to do some writing.

The testing situation is somewhat similar to a clinical interview. Detailed directions are provided to the examiner and a sheet for recording the student's answers is used. The recording sheet also contains the directions. An answer sheet is furnished the student. The testing situation attempts to combine elements of a conventional testing situation along with a whole language approach. The testing situation clearly depends heavily on the ability of the examiner to develop rapport with the student and to maintain a relaxed flow to the testing situation. Although no special training seems to be required, as the manual states, it seems that some experience in administering the test is needed in order to become proficient. Classroom teachers should be able to administer and score the test after a period of study and practice. Whether a classroom teacher would have the time to individually administer the test to some or all members of his or her class is open to question.

Raw scores are obtained for each subtest, which can then be converted to standard scores. These standard scores can then be aggregated into subscores for the three areas of language and, finally, into a total score. The total score can be expressed either as a quotient (really a standard score with a mean of 100 and a standard deviation of 15), an age equivalent, a percentile rank, or a stanine. It is also possible to obtain a total score based on from three to all seven subtests although this is questionable because it is not specified which three subtests are included in the derived total score.

Although the TOCL is intended for use with students from ages 5-0 to 8-11, the use of the test with 5-year-olds and 8-year-olds is questionable. Five-year-olds have usually had little formal instruction in reading, so testing at this age level is dubious. At the 8-year-old level, the tests show a distinct ceiling effect. For example, for 7-year-olds, the average percent correct for the test items ranges from .29 for Writing From Memory to .93 for Word Recognition with an average item difficulty of .71. At age 8, the average percent correct for the items ranges from .34 to .96 with an average item difficulty of .74. One would expect to see a much greater difference in the average item difficulties from age 7 to 8.

The TOCL was standardized on a sample of 908 students drawn from 15 states from around the country. The demographic characteristics of the standardization group fairly closely match characteristics of the U.S. population, based on the 1990 Census data. However, the number of students tested at each grade level varies from 136 at age 5 to 317 at age 7. Item analyses were carried out for each subtest at each age level. Median item difficulties increase substantially for each subtest at each age level except from age 7 to 8. Median discrimination indices appear to be acceptable. However, individual item difficulties and discrimination indices are not provided. The authors attempt to show that the tests do not exhibit any gender or racial bias by presenting correlations between delta values for gender and racial (white/ nonwhite groups). However, this merely shows that the items are of the same order of difficulty for the groups being studied. It says nothing about the actual item difficulties. One gender group could systematically score .50 higher than the other gender group on every item, for example, and the correlation would be +1.0.

Reliabilities of the subtests were estimated both by internal consistency and by test-retest. Internal consistency reliability estimates are generally above .80 with a number of tests yielding values above .90. A few subtests have internal consistency reliability values at some age levels between .73 and .77. Test-retest reliabilities (time interval ranged from 14 to 21 days) ranged from .77 for Reading Comprehension to .98 for Word Recognition. Most are .90 or higher. Clearly, the reliability scores from the tests is satisfactory. Validity information is provided in the form of correlations with other tests of reading and language ability. The correlations range from .56 (Writing From Memory vs. Reid, Hresko, & Hamill's Test of Early Reading Ability—2nd ed.) to .83 (Knowledge of Print vs. the same test). Total scores on the TOCL correlate .84 and .88 with other tests of reading ability and language ability. Evidence of construct validity inheres in increasing means with

age except for the fact that the means for 8-year-olds are only slightly higher than the means for 7-year-olds. Total scores on the TOCL correlate .86 with Wechsler Intelligence Scale for Children—Revised (WISC-R) total scores, but the analysis is based on only 33 second grade students. All subtests of the TOCL correlate significantly with WISC-R scores except for Writing From Memory and Original Writing.

In summary, the TOCL is an individually administered test based on a whole language concept and yields scores in spoken language, reading, and writing. Although intended for students from ages 5-0 to 8-11, it is probably best used with 6- and 7-year-olds. Testing time per student is from 30 to 40 minutes. The test items appear to have been carefully constructed and there is much testing of language in context. Reliability and validity information is generally acceptable. Whether teachers or other school personnel would want to administer such a labor intensive test is a question that can only be answered by prospective users.

[388]
Test of Early Language Development, Third Edition.

Purpose: Designed to measure the early development of spoken language in the areas of receptive and expressive language, syntax, and semantics.
Population: Ages 2-0 to 7-11.
Publication Dates: 1981–1999.
Acronym: TELD-3.
Scores, 3: Receptive Language, Expressive Language, Spoken Language Quotient.
Administration: Individual.
Forms, 2: A, B.
Price Data, 2001: $264 per complete kit; $74 per manual (1999, 159 pages); $64 per Picture Book; $39 each per Profile/Examiner Record booklet (Form A & Form B); $54 per manipulatives.
Time: (15–40) minutes.
Authors: Wayne P. Hresko, D. Kim Reid, and Donald D. Hammill.
Publisher: PRO-ED.
Cross References: See T5:2680 (19 references) and T4:2749 (6 references); for reviews by Javaid Kaiser and David A. Shapiro of an earlier edition, see 12:393 (4 references); for reviews by Janice Arnold Dole and Elizabeth M. Prather of an earlier edition, see 9:1250 (1 reference).

Review of the Test of Early Language Development, Third Edition by SHERWYN P.

MORREALE, *Associate Director, National Communication Association, Annandale, VA, and PHILIP A. BACKLUND, Professor of Speech Communication, Department of Communication, Central Washington University, Ellensburg, WA:*

The Test of Early Language Development (TELD) was first published in 1981 to meet the need for a quick, easily administered, oral language-screening test for young children. The original TELD was designed for use with children from 3 years of age to 7 years, 11 months. Items were selected that tested receptive and expressive aspects of language structures (i.e., syntax, morphology, and phonology) and meaningful language (i.e., semantics). A previous reviewer (Prather, 1985) noted that the test is most effective with 4-, 5-, and 6-year-old children but also has value at the 3- and 7-year age levels for identification of children who have difficulty in spoken language.

The TELD-3 has five purposes: (a) to identify those children who are significantly below their peers in early language development and thus may be candidates for early intervention, (b) to identify strengths and weaknesses of individual children, (c) to document children's progress as a consequence of early language intervention program, (d) to serve as a measure in research studying language development in young children, and (e) to accompany other assessment techniques.

Test authors have diligently responded to criticisms noted by previous reviewers (Dole, 1985; Essary, 1993; Hammill, Brown, & Bryant, 1989; Hammill, Brown, & Bryant, 1992; Shapiro, 1995) in developing the TELD-3. Issues addressed included division of items into Receptive Language and Expressive Language, development of standard scores, more effective coverage for children at the upper and lower age ranges, new studies supporting reliability and validity, increased normative data, more visually appealing pictures, more accurate wording, and clearer instructions for test administration.

The above information is presented in a well-designed manual. The examiner's manual begins with a clear rationale and overview for the TELD-3 that provides a reader unfamiliar with the test useful background information. The second chapter of the manual is relatively unique in that it provides information to consider before testing including eligibility criteria, examiner qualifications, testing time, scoring guidelines, and information basals and ceilings. The next two chapters provide administration and result interpretation procedures. Four chapters cover normative information, reliability, validity, and controlling for bias. Appendices include clear descriptions of how to convert scores into percentiles, age equivalents, standard scores, and other related information. The manual is effectively organized, written clearly, and contains the information necessary for administering the test and interpreting the results. The authors have done an excellent job in providing an effective and useful resource for the examiner.

Normative data were gathered on 2,217 children during 1990–1991 and 1996–1997 from four regions of the country representing 35 states. The data are organized by geographic area, gender, race, urban/rural, ethnicity, income, educational background of the parents, disability status, and age. The chapters on reliability, validity, and bias begin with a clear description of each concept, and then proceed to describe the studies used to support the claim for reliability and validity. The test evidences high reliability and excellent validity. The chapter on test bias describes methods the authors used to reduce bias and techniques the examiner might follow to further reduce the possibility of bias.

The test kit consists of an examiner's manual, a set of manipulatives, and a Profile/Examiner Record Booklet for each of Forms A and B, and a Picture Book for each form. The test kit is attractively packaged, clearly arranged, and easy to follow for an informed novice. The set of manipulatives is simple, colorful, and effective in their usefulness in testing children. The score sheets are visually appealing and arranged in such a way as to provide ease of scoring and usefulness of information.

The TELD-3 produces scores with a mean of 100 and a standard deviation of 15 for each subtest and the overall composite. Testing usually takes less than 30 minutes. As noted, the test kit provides two forms, A and B. Each form has two subtests (Receptive Language and Expressive Language). The Receptive Language subtest contains 37 items. For A has 24 semantic items and 13 syntax items, Form B has 25 semantic items and 12 syntax items. The items measure how well the child can understand spoken language. At the youngest level, information is requested from the parent or caregiver. The Expressive Language subtest is composed of 39 items. Form A has 22 semantic items and 17 syntax items; Form B has 24 semantic items and 15 syntax items.

SUMMARY. The TELD-3 is a useful instrument. It provides a usable and effective way of screening young children for potential problems. The scores resulting from the testing procedure given valuable analytical information for individual students and for groups. This instrument is a discriminating, dependable device that can be used routinely by a range of trained administrators without excessive demands on time or materials.

REVIEWER'S REFERENCES

Dole, J. A. (1985). [Review of the Test of Early Language Development.] In J. V. Mitchell, Jr. (Ed.), *The ninth mental measurements yearbook* (pp. 1557–1559). Lincoln, NE: Buros Institute of Mental Measurements.

Prather, E. M. (1985). [Review of the Test of Early Language Development.] In J. V. Mitchell, Jr. (Ed.), *The ninth mental measurements yearbook* (p. 1559). Lincoln, NE: Buros Institute of Mental Measurements.

Hammill, D. D., Brown, L., & Bryant, B. R. (1989). *A consumer's guide to tests in print.* Austin, TX: PRO-ED.

Hammill, D. D., Brown, L., & Bryant, B. R. (1992). *A consumer's guide to tests in print* (2ND Ed.). Austin, TX: PRO-ED.

Essary, C. (1993). Review of the Test of Early Language Development—2nd Edition (TELD-2). *Journal of Psychoeducational Assessment, 11,* 375–380.

Shapiro, D. A. (1995). [Review of the Test of Early Language Development, Second Edition.] In J. C. Conoley & J. C. Impara (Eds.), *The twelfth mental measurements yearbook* (pp. 1046–1048). Lincoln, NE: Buros Institute of Mental Measurements.

Review of the Test of Early Language Development, Third Edition by HOI K. SUEN, Professor of Educational Psychology, Pennsylvania State University, University Park, PA:

This is the third edition of the Test of Early Language Development (TELD-3), the first edition of which was published in 1981. The test is designed to assess receptive, expressive, and overall spoken language in children between 2 years and 7 years 11 months of age. The authors outlined five purposes of the TELD-3: (a) to identify candidates for early intervention, (b) to identify strengths and weaknesses of individuals, (c) to document progress in an intervention program, (d) to serve as a research tool in language development, and (e) to accompany other assessment techniques. The test consists of two subtests: one for the assessment of Receptive Language and the other for the assessment of Expressive Language. The changes in the third edition include using colored stimulus pictures and providing the manipulatives required to give the test, which were not provided in previous editions.

The TELD-3 is to be administered individually. There are two forms. Each form contains 37 items intended to assess Receptive Language and 39 items for Expressive Language. For each item, the child is given verbal instructions, shown a stimulus object, or shown a picture. The child is then asked to respond to a number of prompts for that item. The response is then scored. An example of an expressive language item is to show the child a picture card containing a number of pictures. The examiner points to the picture of the fireman and asks the child to tell the examiner about the picture. The child gets a point if the child mentions the fireman and describes the event depicted by the picture.

The test materials are professionally prepared and easy to use. The authors' explicit and detailed cautionary statements not to overinterpret the outcomes of the test are particularly ethical and commendable. Norming was based on a sample of 2,217 children in 35 states across the age categories. For scoring, linear standard scores (mean of 100 and standard deviation of 15), percentiles, and age equivalent scores are provided. Here again, the authors caution users in the use of age-equivalent scores. Score reliabilities have been estimated via a variety of classical approaches and all estimates are high with standard errors of measurement between 3 and 4 points on the linear standard score scale. The authors provide cogent evidence to support the validity of interpretation of the scores as indicators of early language development. Evidence reported includes the traditional content-related, criterion-related, and construct-related evidence. Additionally, DIF analysis results are reported and issues of clinical usefulness are explicitly addressed. Further, the authors report steps taken to safeguard against bias on the basis of race, gender, and disabilities. Overall, the psychometric analyses are thorough and impressive and the results are supportive of the appropriateness and meaningfulness of the inferences to be made from TELD-3.

In spite of their thoroughness and caution, the authors do appear to overreach on occasion. For example, they claim that the composite TELD-3 score is "the best single predictor of future language ability and school abilities influenced by language ability" (examiner's manual, p. 63). This appears to be an overstatement as there is no direct evidence to support such a claim. Also, whereas evidence to support interpretation is strong, evidence to support utility is rather weak. For example, the authors suggest that the TELD-3 can be used to identify candidates for early intervention, to identify individual strengths and weaknesses, and/or to document progress in program intervention. These are reasonable potential uses. However, the authors did not report any evidence to support the appropriateness of these particular uses. For example, there is no evidence, such as positive predictive power indices or over- or underreferral indices, to support its use for identification. There is also no evidence such as treatment validity or washback to support its use to identify strengths and weaknesses or to document progress in intervention. Given that appropriate test use is a shared responsibility between test developer and test users, individuals who wish to use the TELD-3 for these particular purposes should gather their own evidence to support these uses.

SUMMARY. There is cogent evidence that the scores of the TELD-3 are valid and unbiased indicators of early development in receptive, expressive, and overall spoken language. As such, it is appropriate to be used as a research tool in language development, as suggested by the authors. However, those who wish to use the TELD-3 to identify candidates for early intervention and to identify strengths and weaknesses of individuals, which were also suggested by the authors, will need to conduct their own studies to ascertain the appropriateness of such uses.

[389]
Test of Language Development—Intermediate, Third Edition.

Purpose: To determine strengths and weaknesses in language skills.
Population: Ages 8-0 to 12-11.
Publication Dates: 1977–1997.
Acronym: TOLD-I:3
Scores, 12: General Intelligence/Aptitude Quotient, Spoken Language Quotient (SLQ), Listening Quotient (LiQ), Speaking Quotient (SpA), Semantics Quotient (SeQ), Syntax Quotient (SyQ), Sentence Combining (SC), Picture Vocabulary (PV), Word Ordering (WO), Generals (GL), Grammatic Comprehension (GC), Malapropism (MP).
Administration: Individual
Price Data, 1999: $154 per complete kit.
Time: (30–60) minutes.
Comments: Primary edition also available.
Authors: Donald D. Hammill and Phyllis L. Newcomer.
Publisher: PRO-ED.
Cross References: See T5:2694 (27 references) and T4:2767 (7 references); for reviews by Rebecca McCauley and Kenneth G. Shipley of the TOLD-I:2,

see 11:436 (5 references). For a review by Doris V. Allen of an earlier version of the entire Test of Language Development, see 9:1261 (5 references).

Review of the Test of Language Development—Intermediate, Third Edition by DAVID P. HURFORD, Director of the Center for the Assessment and Remediation of Reading Difficulties and Professor of Psychology and Counseling, Pittsburg State University, Pittsburg, KS:

The Test of Language Development—Intermediate, Third Edition (TOLD-I:3) is to be used to measure the language skills of children between the ages of 8-0 and 12-11. The TOLD-I was originally developed to bridge the age gap between the Test of Language Development—Primary (TOLD-P), intended to examine the language development of children between the ages of 4-0 and 8-11 years, and the Test of Adolescent Language (TOAL), intended to examine the language development of children between the ages of 12-0 and 18-5 years. The age range for the TOLD-I:3 overlaps the age ranges for the TOLD-P and the TOAL. The revisions that resulted in the TOLD-I:3 occurred as a function of previous reviews. The TOLD-I:3 includes a new subtest, Picture Vocabulary, that replaced the Vocabulary subtest. The other subtests remain the same.

The TOLD-I:3 assesses overall spoken language, semantics, syntax, listening, and speaking. The test evaluates these skills with six subtests that produce five composite scores expressed as quotients. Although the TOLD-I:3 produces subtest scores, the authors recommend using the composite quotients. The description of each subtest in the order of their intended presentation is as follows. Sentence Combining measures the ability to combine two or more sentences into one complex or compound sentence while retaining all of the relevant information from the shorter sentences (e.g., I am big. I am tall. = I am big and tall.). Picture Vocabulary assesses the individual's ability to comprehend the meaning of two word phrases by pointing to a picture depicting the phrase. Word Ordering measures the ability to combine randomly presented words into meaningful sentences (e.g., big-am-I = I am big or Am I big?). Generals measures the ability to identify the similarities among three words (e.g., Monday, Tuesday, Wednesday). Grammatic Comprehension requires the individual to identify the word that has been used in an ungrammatical way (e.g.,

Me play ball). Malapropisms measures the ability to realize that a similar sounding word has been incorrectly substituted for another (.e.g., We should brush our feet every morning). All age groups begin with the first item on each subtest and proceed until ceiling. Each item is scored as 1 for correct and 0 for incorrect. Raw scores are simply the number of correct items per subtest that can be transformed into age equivalent scores, percentile ranks, and standard scores.

There are five composite scores, which are represented as quotients: spoken language (Spoken Language Quotient, SLQ), semantics (Semantics Quotient, SeQ), syntax (Syntax Quotient, SyQ), Listening (Listening Quotient, LiQ), and speaking (Speaking Quotient, SpQ). All six subtests are involved in the Spoken Language Quotient, which is the test's best indicator of a child's language ability. The Semantics Quotient is composed of the Picture Vocabulary, Generals, and Malapropisms subtests. The Syntax Quotient is composed of the Sentence Combining, Word Ordering, and Grammatic Comprehension subtests. The Listening Quotient is composed of the Picture Vocabulary, Grammatic Comprehension, and Malapropisms subtests. Finally, the Speaking Quotient is composed of the Sentence Combining, Word Ordering, and Generals subtests. The composite scores reflect the theoretical two-dimensional model that guided the design and construction of the test. The first dimension of the model includes the linguistic systems of reception (listening) and expression (speaking) and the second dimension of the model includes the linguistic features of syntax (the structure of the language) and semantics (the meaning associated with the language). The composite scores represent the various combinations of the two levels of the dimensions of the model: listening, speaking, semantics, and syntax. The Spoken Language Quotient reflects both dimensions and provides an overall evaluation of language ability. The composite quotients have a mean of 100 and standard deviations of 15 and easily converted from subtest standard score totals into quotients with the use of a table.

The TOLD-I:3 was normed with 779 children from 23 states. The norming sample closely approximated the U.S. Bureau of the Census information with regard to geographic area, gender, race, residence (urban vs. rural), ethnicity, family income, parents' educational attainment, age, and disability status (i.e., no disability, learning disability, speech-language disorder, mental retardation, other). The TOLD-I:3 provides standard scores with means of 10 and standard deviations of 3, age equivalents, and percentile ranks for the subtests, and, as mentioned above, quotients that have means of 100 and standard deviations of 15.

Reliability was examined with internal consistency and test-retest correlation coefficients. Cronbach's coefficient alphas for 8-, 9-, 10-, 11-, and 12-year-old participants ranged from .80 to .97 for the subtests (Mdn = .88). The coefficient alphas for the composites were considerably larger ranging from .92 to .96 (Mdn = .94). Coefficient alphas were generated for the subgroups within gender, ethnicity, and disability status which resulted in coefficients ranging from .70 to .97 for the subtests and .90 to .97 for the composites. Test-retest reliability coefficients ranged between .83 to .93 for the subtests and .94 and .96 for the composites. The test-retest study involved only 55 participants with the time between administrations of only one week. Interrater reliability was examined with the assistance of two staff personnel from PRO-ED's research department who scored 50 protocols chosen at random. Interrater reliability ranged from .94 to .97 on the subtests and .96 to .97 for the composites.

Validity was examined using content, criterion-related, and construct validity. The items for the subtests were created with the two-dimensional model described above as a guide. As a result, the items should reflect adequately the content they were purported to tap. To assess how closely the items represented the particular domains of interest, 71 individuals who had applied or theoretical experience in language were asked to rate the formats of the six subtests according to how closely they matched the two-dimensional model. The raters generally rated the subtests in a manner that was consistent with the model used to create the subtests. Criterion-related validity was assessed by correlating the subtest and composite scores on the TOLD-I:3 and the TOAL-3. The coefficients ranged from .58 to .86 for the subtests and .74 and .88 for the composites. The correlation coefficient between the Spoken Language Quotients for the TOLD-I:3 and the TOAL-3 was quite large (.85). No other tests were used to establish criterion-related validity.

Construct validity was evaluated by several approaches. If the TOLD-I:3 properly assessed language ability, subtest scores should increase with age as language skills develop. Positive correlation coefficients were reported for age and subtest scores that ranged between .32 to .47 on the various subtests. If scores from the TOLD-I:3 had construct validity, one would expect that disability groups (i.e., speech and language disabilities, learning disabilities, mental retardation, and attention-deficit/hyperactivity deficits) could be differentiated from nondisabled children. Although no results of statistical analyses were reported, the groups with disabilities had smaller standard score and composite means than the nondisabled group. Subtest correlation coefficients ranged from .38 to .63 indicating that the subtests are measuring a similar construct, language ability. The TOLD-I:3 composite scores were correlated with the Comprehensive Scales of Student Abilities (CSSA) test in a study examining 24 students. The correlation matrix included the five composites of the TOLD-I:3 and the five values (Verbal Thinking, Speech, Reading, Writing, and Mathematics) from the CSSA. Of the 25 coefficients, 17 were significant indicating that the TOLD-I:3 was related to school achievement. The subtest scores from the normative sample were also subjected to principal component analysis. The results indicated that all six subtests strongly loaded on a single factor. This factor accounted for 88% of the variance with loadings ranging from .59 to .79. It would have been interesting to see if the bidimensional model would have been supported by rotating the principal components solution. Rotating the principal components solution would allow one to determine if the resulting factors support the model used to build the TOLD-I:3.

To guard against test bias, the normative sample was diverse and representative of the U.S. population as reflected in the U.S. Bureau of Census information, which reduces the likelihood that a test will be biased. In addition, test bias was not indicated by the consistency of reliability and validity coefficients for the various ethnic and disability groups. Item response theory and Delta scores analyses were applied to the subgroups in the normative sample. Each approach suggested that bias was not present in the TOLD-I:3. Researchers have indicated that timed tests might underestimate the ability of certain groups. The

authors point out that none of the subtests are timed, as such, and that the test should not be biased in this regard.

The Record Booklet has sections for identifying information (e.g., name, gender, age, etc.), recording the scores (e.g., raw scores, standard scores, age equivalents, percentile ranks, and quotients), and score profiles (graphical display of the standard scores and quotients). The subtests along with their brief instructions are contained within the Record Booklet. There is a Comments section after the first subtest that should be used to record the disposition of the examinee, the environment of the examination, and other pertinent information. The examiner should realize that the Comments section refers to the entire test and not just the first subtest.

The TOLD-I:3 examiner's manual is well written, quite thorough, and informative. There are two points that need to be mentioned and further clarified. It is stated on page 5 that "No subtests were developed to measure the phonology feature. This is because children older than 6 or 7 usually have already incorporated successfully most phonological abilities into their language." Although this may be true for nondisabled children, it is most likely the case that individuals who will be assessed with this instrument will be suspected for language deficiencies. It has long been determined that children with language deficiencies are also likely to have phonological processing deficiencies as well. Assessing phonology would be a welcome addition to this test, particularly because one of its intended uses is to identify children who are experiencing learning and other language-related disabilities. On pages 29 and 30 a case sample is presented. The Spoken Language Quotient and an IQ score (Comprehensive Test of Nonverbal Intelligence) for this fictitious individual is 77 and 90, respectively. On page 30, the authors state "Comparison of Steve's SLQ (77) with his IQ (90) ... suggest that his poor language might be accounted for by low mental ability." Although Steve's SLQ is quite low (77, more than 1 standard deviation below the mean), his IQ is well within what most psychometricians would consider low average to average ability. Referring to an IQ score of 90 as low mental ability is not justified and certainly does not explain the relatively low Spoken Language Quotient.

SUMMARY. The TOLD-I:3 is a carefully constructed test of language ability to be used with children between 8-0 and 12-11 years of age. The theoretical framework that guided its creation is appropriate and item construction closely matched the framework. Reliability and validity seem to be well established, although in some cases the sample sizes of the studies were quite small. The TOLD-I:3 provides information concerning listening, speaking, semantics, and syntax abilities as well as an overall measurement of spoken language ability. This information is useful for the diagnosis of weaknesses and the planning of interventions.

Review of the Test of Language Development—Intermediate, Third Edition by PAT MIRENDA, Associate Professor, University of British Columbia, Vancouver, British Columbia, Canada:

The Test of Language Development—Intermediate, Third Edition (TOLD-I:3) is a 1997 revision of one of the most widespread measures of language skills of children between the ages of 8-0 and 12-11 who speak English and are not deaf or hard-of-hearing. Like its predecessor, the TOLD-I:3 requires approximately 1 hour to administer, and is meant to be used by examiners who have some formal training in assessment, including (ideally) supervised practice. The test manual is easy to read and well organized, and provides appropriate instructions to examiners with regard to test administration, scoring, and interpretation. It also contains an excellent, albeit brief, chapter that provides information about the usefulness and limitations of standardized tests in general, as well as resources related to language instruction and remediation.

The TOLD-I:3 measures both receptive (i.e., listening) and expressive (i.e., speaking) English language skills in each of two areas: semantics (the meaning of language) and syntax (the structure of language). With regard to semantics, the test includes subtests that measure the child's knowledge of picture vocabulary items, ability to identify malapropisms in spoken sentences, and ability to explain the similarities between three words spoken by the examiner. With regard to syntax, the test includes subtests related to the child's ability to recognize incorrect grammar in spoken sentences, to form one sentence from two or more spoken by the examiner, and to reorder a series of spoken words to form a complete sentence. Composite scores can also be calculated in each of five areas: semantics, syntax, listening, speaking, and spoken language overall.

The revision was undertaken to address some of the limitations of the previous version. In terms of the test items themselves, a new subtest, Picture Vocabulary, replaces Vocabulary from the previous edition; and children's names used in the test items were revised to reflect the current demographic makeup of U.S. schools. In addition, the rationale for the test has been updated to reflect current theories and research regarding oral communication.

The TOLD-I:3 was normed in 1996 on a sample of 779 persons in 23 states representing all regions of the U.S. Norming was done by 37 experienced examiners who were selected at random from a database of professionals who purchased the TOLD-I:2 within the previous 2 years. Characteristics of the normative sample were keyed to the 1990 U.S. Census data and are representative of the current U.S. population as well with regard to gender, race, ethnicity, family income, disabling conditions, and several other factors. Extensive demographic data for the sample are provided in the test manual. Normative data (percentiles and standard scores) are provided for each of the six subtests and five composite areas in an Appendix. Age equivalents are also provided, along with an appropriate note in the manual advising examiners to exercise caution when using such equivalents.

Content sampling error (i.e., internal consistency reliability) was evaluated using Cronbach's alpha as applied to five age intervals from the entire normative sample. All of the coefficients for the subtests exceeded .84, and all for the composites exceeded .90, indicating high degrees of internal reliability. In addition, alpha values for 11 selected demographic subgroups (including those related to gender, race, and various disabilities) within the normative sample are also reported. All but one exceeded .81, indicating that the TOLD-I:3 is about equally reliable for all subgroups investigated and contains little or no bias relative to those groups.

Test-retest reliability was measured with 55 fourth- fifth-, and sixth-grade students who attended regular classes in Texas, with a time lapse of one week between the two test administrations. Test-retest coefficients for all subtests were .83 or above, indicating that the test contains little or no time sampling error. Interscorer reliability was measured by having two individuals independently score a set of 50 completed protocols that were randomly selected from the normative sample.

The correlation coefficients were all .94 or above, indicating a high degree of scorer reliability for the test. Overall, scores from the TOLD-I:3 are highly reliable and show little evidence of significant test error when used as intended.

Content validity was established on the basis of the extant research and theoretical literature in the areas contained in the TOLD-I:3 and in other tests that measure the same constructs. In addition, 71 professionals who were "known to have a practical or theoretical interest in spoken language" (p. 59) read descriptions of the formats of the six subtests and rated them on two 9-point scales. On one scale, a low score indicated that the rater thought the test format was more a measure of semantics than syntax. On the other scale, a low score indicated that the test was seen as more a measure of listening than speaking. In general, the mean ratings provide support that the subtests were perceived by the experts to measure what they were intended to measure.

Quantitative evidence for content validity was measured using the point-biserial correlation technique to determine item discrimination. On the basis of the results, items that did not satisfy the item discrimination and item difficulty criteria were eliminated from the final version of the test. In the end, an item analysis was undertaken with the entire normative sample; the results indicated an acceptable degree of content validity. In addition, the Item Response Theory (IRT) approach was used to compare item performance between five demographic groups on the sample, including males/females, African Americans/non-African Americans, and learning-disabled/non-learning-disabled students. Only a few of the items (2.5–6.0%) were found to be potentially biased with regard to the groups studied. The Delta scores approach was applied to nine groups and the resulting correlation coefficients were generally .90 or above, with the exception of three scores of .82, .84, and .88. Together, these measures indicate that the test items contain little or no bias with regard to the groups investigated.

Criterion-related validity (i.e., predictive validity) was examined by correlating relevant TOLD-I:3 subtest scores with those from the Test of Adolescent and Adult Language—Third Edition (TOAL-3) (Hammill, Brown, Larsen, & Wiederholt, 1994). Both tests were administered to a group of 26 nondisabled fifth and sixth graders from Texas. Pearson product-moment coefficients were .58 or above for the selected subtests, indicating at least moderate correlations. In addition, five TOAL-3 composite score were correlated with 11 TOLD-I:3 variables, and the results indicated an overall correlation of .85. From these data, it appears that the TOLD-I:3 measures similar spoken language constructs to the TOAL-3.

Construct validity was measured in several ways, including calculations of (a) correlations between age and performance of the students in the normative sample on the subtests, (b) standard score means for 392 children with identified disabilities from the normative sample, (c) intercorrelations for the subtests for the entire normative sample, and (d) correlations between the TOLD-I:3 composite scores and school achievement scores as measured by the Comprehensive Scales of Student Abilities (CSSA) for a sample of 24 elementary-age students in Texas. Across all four of these measures, construct validity evidence was found to be well within the acceptable range. In addition, factor and item analyses provided additional evidence for a moderate to high degree of construct validity.

SUMMARY. The TOLD-I:3 is significantly improved from the previous versions, especially with regard to psychometric evidence that scores from the test are valid and reliable when used with a wide variety of demographic subgroups are well as with the general population. Examiners who read the manual thoroughly will be impressed with both its breadth and its depth, and with the extent to which it attempts to place the test in an appropriate theoretical and practical context.

REVIEWER'S REFERENCE

Hammill, D. D., Brown, V. L., Larsen, S. C., & Wiederholt, J. L. (1994). Test of Adolescent and Adult Language (3rd ed.). Austin, TX: PRO-ED.

[390]

Test of Language Development—Primary, Third Edition.

Purpose: To determine children's specific strengths and weaknesses in language skills.

Population: Ages 4-0 to 8-11.

Publication Dates: 1977–1997.

Acronym: TOLD-P:3.

Scores, 15: Subtests (Picture Vocabulary, Relational Vocabulary, Oral Vocabulary, Grammatic Understanding, Sentence Imitation, Grammatic Completion, Word Discrimination [Optional], Phoenemic Analysis [Optional], Word Articulation [Optional]); Composites

(Listening, Organizing, Speaking, Semantics, Syntax, Spoken Language).

Administration: Individual.

Parts, 2: Subtests, Composites.

Price Data, 1999: $218 per complete kit.

Time: (60) minutes.

Comments: Intermediate edition also available; orally administered; examiners need formal training in assessment; PRO-SCORE Computer Scoring System available for Macintosh, Windows, and DOS (1998).

Authors: Phyllis L. Newcomer and Donald D. Hammill.

Publisher: PRO-ED.

Cross References: See T5:2695 (72 references) and T4:2768 (21 references); for reviews by Linda Crocker and Carol E. Westby of a previous edition, see 11:437 (20 references).

Review of the Test of Language Development—Primary, Third Edition by RONALD A. MADLE, School Psychologist, Shikellamy School District, Sunbury, PA and Adjunct Associate Professor of School Psychology, Pennsylvania State University, University Park, PA:

TEST PURPOSE AND DESIGN. The purpose of the Test of Language Development—Primary, Third Edition (TOLD-P:3) is to provide reliable and valid scores for identifying English-speaking children who show significant delays in language proficiency. It also is intended to determine specific strengths and weaknesses in language development.

The TOLD-P:3 measures children's expressive and receptive competencies in major linguistic areas. The manual thoroughly discusses the constructs upon which the instrument is based. Specifically, it details the use of a two-dimensional conceptual model with linguistic features (Semantics, Syntax, and Phonology) on one dimension, and linguistic systems (Listening, Organizing, and Speaking) on the other. Although not all aspects of spoken language are assessed, the authors explicitly acknowledge this and suggest that some areas, such as pragmatics, are more appropriately assessed through informal methods rather than norm-referenced testing.

The most significant change in the TOLD-P:3 is the addition of integrating-mediating language to the systems measured. Two new subtests, Relational Vocabulary and Phonemic Analysis, were added to the existing Sentence Imitation task to accomplish this. The TOLD-P:3 also moves all phonological subtests from the core battery and now treats them as supplemental measures. This results in a clearer differentiation between the "language" and "speech" systems assessed by the test.

ADMINISTRATION AND SCORING. All materials are well constructed and durable. In keeping with trends in recently developed or revised tests, the pictures are now presented in full color rather than as black-and-white line drawings.

The time to administer the TOLD-P:3 core battery is estimated as 30 to 60 minutes. The supplemental phonology subtests take an additional 30 minutes. The administration and scoring procedures are presented clearly in the manual and should be followed easily by examiners with adequate preparation in individual assessment techniques. A complete discussion of issues such as testing of limits, interpretation, and local norms is included in the manual. Basal and ceiling procedures are followed easily with each subtest beginning at the first item and continuing until five consecutive items are failed.

Subtest raw scores are converted to standard scores (mean = 10; SD = 3) and percentiles. Although test users are advised not to employ them, age equivalents are also included, apparently as a concession to agencies that require them. In addition to the overall Spoken Language Quotient, five composites (mean = 100; SD = 15) are available. Two measure linguistic features (Semantics and Syntax) and three assess linguistic systems (Listening, Organizing, and Speaking). No composites are utilized for the phonological subtests.

STANDARDIZATION. The TOLD-P:3 was standardized on 1,000 children between the ages of 4 and 8, with all data collected in the spring of 1996. A significant criticism of the TOLD-P:2 was addressed with this renorming as the normative data previously had been aggregated across all earlier versions, resulting in some data being collected as early as 1976. The number of children at each age varies from 107 (age 4) to 258 (ages 7 and 8). Because standard score conversion tables use 6-month intervals, however, it is not clear how many children were used for each table. Information presented in the manual indicates the normative sample closely approximated the 1990 U.S. Census data on most demographic variables utilized, including geographic region, gender, race, rural versus urban status, ethnicity, educational attainment of parents, and disability status. Generally, the TOLD-P:3 standardization sample is quite appropriate. There was, however, a slight overrepresentation of lower income families.

RELIABILITY. The authors present reliability information covering each of the three primary sources of error variance: content sampling (internal consistency), time sampling (test-retest reliability), and scorer differences (interrater reliability). The internal consistency data for the TOLD-P:3 are comparable to those of major intelligence tests, typically the best developed of all measures. The internal consistency of the subtests is uniformly in the .80 to low .90 range, whereas composite data are in the low .90 range. The overall Spoken Language Composite internal consistency is .95 or higher across all ages. Data for each scale also are presented by gender, racial status, and disability with no meaningful variation being present across these variables. Although the associated standard errors of measurement are presented in the manual, there is no systematic method to note these on the record form. This is disappointing because most contemporary tests encourage consideration of this information by having spaces to record confidence intervals on the test booklet.

The test-retest reliability estimates for the TOLD-P:3 over a 4-month interval are somewhat lower, but quite acceptable, ranging from .81 to .92. Interrater reliability is reported to be uniformly high (.99) across all scales.

VALIDITY. Several validity studies are provided in the manual. Content validity was investigated qualitatively, through item reviews, as well as quantitatively by using classical item analysis and differential item functioning analysis. Generally, the results support a high degree of content validity, although there is limited item difficulty at ages 4 and 5. This is also evident by examining the subtest and composite floors at these ages. They do not meet Bracken's (1987) suggested criterion of at least two standard deviations below the mean until age 5 1/2. In fact, the minimum Spoken Language Quotient at age 4 is 85, only one standard deviation below the mean. This substantially compromises the authors' stated purpose of identifying children who show significant delays in language proficiency at these ages.

Criterion-related validity was examined by correlating scores from the TOLD-P:3 with those from the Bankson Language Test—Second Edition for 30 primary age students. Uniformly high correlations were found supporting convergent validity. There was limited support, however, for discriminant validity as scores from all subtests and composites correlated similarly with both the semantic and morphological/syntactic scales on the Bankson. More thorough validation studies would have been desirable, although the manual also contains a summary of research on the previous edition that has continuing relevance for the current version.

Construct validity was investigated through documentation of age differentiation, group differentiation, subtest interrelationships, factor analysis, and item validity. The factor analysis revealed all six core subtests loaded on a single factor rather than validating the theoretical structure of the test. This may, however, be due to "construct underrepresentation," a problem currently being dealt with in the area of intellectual assessment (cf. McGrew, 1997).

Several studies are also detailed documenting the absence of test bias for various dimensions such as gender and racial groups, responding to prior criticisms that the TOLD-P:2 included insufficient information about cultural fairness.

SUMMARY. The TOLD-P:3 represents a significant revision that has taken feedback from earlier test reviewers quite seriously. The manual summarized prior criticisms of the TOLD-P:2 and details how each has been addressed systematically in the current revision. Although a few shortcomings are present, the TOLD-P:3 remains one of the best developed and psychometrically sound measures of children's language available today. Special care should be taken, however, when using it with children below the age of 5 1/2 due to its limited floors. At these ages an alternative measure (e.g., Test of Early Language Development; 388) would be a better choice.

REVIEWER'S REFERENCES

Bracken, B. A. (1987). Limitations of preschool instruments and standards for minimal levels of technical adequacy. *Journal of Psychoeducational Assessment, 4,* 313–326.

McGrew, K. S. (1997). Analysis of the major intelligence batteries according to a proposed comprehensive Gf-Gc framework. In D. P. Flanagan, J. L. Genshaft, & P. L. Harrison (Eds.), *Contemporary intellectual assessment: Theories, tests, and issues* (pp. 151–179). New York: Guilford.

Review of the Test of Language Development— Primary, Third Edition by GABRIELLE STUTMAN, Private Practice, Westchester and Manhattan, NY:

The Test of Language Development—Primary, Third Edition (TOLD-P:3) is represented as the only comprehensive test of oral language abilities that uses a purely linguistic orientation. Its subtests were specifically designed to assess children's receptive and expressive spoken English language competence in the areas of semantics, syntax, and phonology. This third edition of a test originally published in 1977 is substantially improved from previous versions. Major improvements include two new subtests (Phonemic Analysis and Relational Vocabulary), a new composite score, "Organizing" (used to represent mediating processes between reception and expression), and new norms.

PURPOSE AND USE. The TOLD-P:3 is a standardized diagnostic tool that was developed to assess spoken English language. It is used to identify students who need special help, to document their strengths and weaknesses, monitor progress, and measure language for research studies.

The TOLD-P:3 uses a two-dimensional linguistic model that incorporates both linguistic components and linguistic systems of the English language. Three major component features of language are assessed: phonology (the 36 phonemic sounds of the English language), syntax (the morphological structure of English), and semantics (the relation between the spoken and the thought). The three organizing systems addressed are receptive systems (listening), integrating and mediating systems (organizing), and expressive systems (speaking). As each of these organizing systems are assessed via their related semantic, syntactic, and phonological subtests, a three-by-three matrix of linguistic ability is created. The three phonological subtests are supplemental and need not be administered. This two-dimensional organization of test components is very useful in pinpointing the source of linguistic strengths and weaknesses and structuring appropriate intervention.

The authors are clear and thorough in their rationale for and description of each of the subtests. The TOLD-P:3 appears appropriate for its intended population, practitioners, and uses.

ADMINISTRATION AND SCORING. The TOLD-P:3 is designed to be individually administered by a professional with graduate training in test characteristics and administration. The chapter devoted to test administration and scoring includes a section of instructions regarding motivation, the testing situation, etc., to guide the quality of administration. Testing materials have been updated and improved: The pictures are drawn in color and more contemporary names are used in the text. Some additional changes in the testing materials, however, would facilitate their use. The Picture Book would be easier to use if it was structured like an easel to be free standing. Tabs at the different sections would facilitate movement to the next subtest. Also the Record Booklet would be less awkward to use if the "correct response" column were adjacent to the "score" column, rather than at a maximum distance.

Although the instructions are precise, some practice and training should precede the use of this test, and those who are not specifically qualified to administer complex psychological tests should take extra precautions. Many of the subtests will be familiar to the experienced examiner. Scoring is objective for all subtests.

TOLD-P:3 raw subtest scores can be converted into percentiles, age equivalents, and standard scores (with a mean of 10 and a standard deviation of 3) for the subtests. One may compare the standard scores on the various subtests with each other and draw conclusions as to relative strengths and weaknesses of specific linguistic functions. To the authors' credit, strong warnings are issued against the use of age or grade equivalents, which are given only because of legal and administrative necessity. The composite scores are based on several subtests and are given in Quotients with a mean of 100 and a standard deviation of 15 in order to conform with the conventions of IQ testing. These Quotients indicate a child's ability relative to higher order categories. The Spoken Language Quotient (SLQ), calculated using all essential subtests, provides the most comprehensive measure of overall language ability. Comparisons among Quotients may also be made and are considered to be more reliable than comparisons among subtests, as they are based on more data. A sample case is also given to aid the formulation of interpretation and intervention. Because the scoring process is complex and time-consuming, an optional computer scoring/report program should be made available.

RELIABILITY AND VALIDITY. Sample selection procedures, demographic characteristics, reliability, and validity measures are fully documented. The authors have also given clear definitions and explanations of each type of reliability, validity, source of error variance, and the procedures used to gather the evidence.

Reliability was measured in terms of errors of content sampling (internal consistency coefficients), time sampling (4-month time lapse), and scorer differences. All content and time sampling coefficients were in the range of .80 to .90 except for the Word Discrimination subtest. Its time sampling coefficient was only .77, largely as a result of increased variance on the second testing. Scores of different scorers were correlated .99. The magnitude of these coefficients of reliability suggest that the TOLD-P:3 evidences a consistently high degree of reliability across all three types of test error. What the test lacks is a table of coefficients to partial out practice effects when retesting to assess intervention effectiveness.

Three types of validity—content, criterion-related, and construct validity—were investigated. The logical basis for content validity is given in the context of each subtest's derivation from longstanding approaches to the assessment of specific language abilities. Subtests that were changed in this new edition were extensively field tested. In addition, all new and revised subtests were subjected to a classical Item Analysis in which an item inclusion criteria of .3 or greater was used for point-biserial coefficients. Item difficulty analysis, although generally indicating sufficient dispersion, shows compression across the upper age categories for the phonemic subtests (Word Discrimination, Phonemic Analysis, and Word Articulation). Specifically, after about age 7 there is a ceiling effect such that only large age delays will be revealed. Although the authors state that these skills are mastered by that age, more difficult items (e.g., the use of nonsense syllables instead of meaningful words in the Word Discrimination subtest) might have revealed important developmental differences. Relational Vocabulary shows a floor effect for 4- and 5-year-olds.

Item and test bias were dealt with at length. Item bias was measured using the Item Response Theory (IRT) approach with the entire normative sample and a 3.5% level of potential bias was accepted. Test bias was carefully controlled through the use of a demographically representative sample with regard to gender, race, social class, and disability groups in the normative sample.

Criterion-related validity was assessed by correlating TOLD-P:3 scores with the Bankson Language Test—Second Edition (Bankson, 1990). All relevant correlations were significant beyond the .05 level. Strong and convincing evidence is presented for the construct validity through factor, correlational, and logical analysis. Problems with the phonemic scales are dealt with by assigning these tests a supplemental role and advising that they be interpreted strictly in terms of their individual contents.

NORMATIVE INFORMATION. The normative sample, comprising 1,000 children in 28 states, was tested in 1996. The characteristics of the sample with regard to geographic region, gender, race, residence, ethnicity, family income, educational attainment of parents, and disabling condition are representative of the Statistical Abstract of the United States (U.S. Bureau of the Census, 1990) for the school-aged population. Despite small sample size, the representation of population segments within each different age group, is preserved. However, the authors properly caution that, whenever possible, local norms should be developed and used.

SUMMARY. The TOLD-P:3 is substantially improved from earlier editions. As an evaluative and diagnostic tool it serves its stated purpose. It is also helpful in targeting general goals for remediation. Strengths of this test include objectivity of scoring, the three-by-three-matrix organization of test components useful in pinpointing the source of linguistic difficulties and structuring appropriate intervention, its strong historical and logical foundation, relative freedom from bias, acceptable subtest reliability (except for the Word Discrimination subtest), and generally good evidence of validity. Its weaknesses include unnecessarily awkward test materials, no option for computer scoring [Editor's Note: PRO-SCORE System for Macintosh, Windows, and DOS available 1998] , low ceilings on the phonemic measures, a high floor on the Relational Vocabulary subtest, and the lack of a table of test-retest coefficients that would enable the administrator to partial out practice effects when using the instrument to measure intervention effectiveness.

REVIEWER'S REFERENCES

Bankson, N. W. (1990). *Bankson Language Test* (2nd ed.). Austin, TX: PRO-ED.

U.S. Bureau of the Census. (1990). *Statistical abstract of the United States.* Washington, DC: Author.

[391]
Test of Mathematical Abilities for Gifted Students.

Purpose: "Designed to identify students who have talent or giftedness in mathematics."

Population: Ages 6–12.

Publication Date: 1998.

Acronym: TOMAGS.

Scores: Total score only.
Administration: Group or individual.
Levels, 2: Primary, Intermediate.
Price Data, 1999: $139 per complete kit including manual (53 pages), 25 each Primary Level and Intermediate Level student booklets, and 25 each Primary Level and Intermediate Level profile/scoring sheets; $39 per 25 student booklets (specify level); $14 per 25 profile/scoring sheets (specify level); $40 per manual.
Time: (30–60) minutes.
Authors: Gail R. Ryser and Susan K. Johnsen.
Publisher: PRO-ED.

Review of the Test of Mathematical Abilities for Gifted Students by ROBERT B. FRARY, Professor Emeritus, Virginia Polytechnic Institute and State University, Blacksburg, VA:

The Test of Mathematical Abilities for Gifted Students (TOMAGS) is composed of two forms, one for ages 6 through 9 and the other for ages 9 through 12. They are designed to evaluate mathematical talent with the purpose of identifying students with giftedness in mathematics. The tests can be administered individually or to groups. Responses to the test items are open-ended. However, scoring instructions provide essentially no leeway in determining correctness of responses. There is no time limit, but the examiner's manual accompanying the TOMAGS states that 30 to 60 minutes is usually sufficient.

The examiner's manual provides an extensive discussion of student characteristics associated with giftedness in mathematics and the problems encountered in identifying gifted children (pp. 2–4). The TOMAGS approach is characterized as responsive to these concerns. For example, "the test examines a sample of the child's ability to use flexibility in mathematical reasoning and transfer already learned mathematical knowledge to new situations" (examiner's manual, p. 4). This discussion ties in with a later discussion of content validity (examiner's manual, pp. 29–33), in which TOMAGS items are tied directly to content recommendations of the National Council of Teachers of Mathematics. In addition, this section provided a good description of how the items were developed, consistent with the characterization of giftedness.

The TOMAGS was normed using four separate samples, two for each level. For each level, one sample consisted of children previously identified as gifted and the other a general sample of children not so identified. However, the general samples no doubt included some children who would be considered gifted. Numbers in the samples ranged from 513 to 935. As tables in the examiner's manual attest, the samples were quite diverse with respect to a number of examinee characteristics, such as geographic locale, ethnicity, and socioeconomic status. Age and sex were distributed approximately uniformly. Norms are provided on a standardized scale with a mean of 100 and a standard deviation of 15. These scores are referred to as "quotients," which will, no doubt, lead to comparisons with IQ scores. Separate norms based on the gifted and general samples are provided with eight 6-month age strata for both the Primary and Intermediate tests. In addition, a table is provided for converting the quotients into percentile ranks. The examiner's manual provides an extensive discussion concerning application of the norms, providing appropriate caveats associated with use of test scores to make decisions about students.

Over the four norming samples, coefficient alpha reliability estimates ranged from .86 to .92. However, these values may be inflated (see discussion below). In addition to the content validity evidence noted in the preceding paragraph, the examiner's manual reports concurrent validity with respect to the Otis-Lennon School Ability Test (Total School Abilities Index), the CogAT Quantitative Battery score, and the Scholastic Achievement Test Mathematics score. Correlation coefficients ranged from .62 to .73. The examiner's manual also presents evidence of construct validity, noting factor-analytic results compatible with item content, high item discrimination coefficients, and strong differentiation between the gifted and general samples at both levels. The possibility of bias was addressed by statistical tests comparing item performance across males and females and across ethnic groups. No evidence was found to suggest performance differences by equally qualified examinees in any pair of groups.

DISCUSSION. The TOMAGS has some deficiencies of which the potential user should be aware:

Scoring. Hand scoring of the TOMAGS is tedious. Several of the items on both forms can be solved in multiple ways; hence, the scorer must be very alert and knowledgeable concerning the subject matter of the two forms. Future development of the TOMAGS might be directed toward development of machine-scorable but open-ended items, such as those now used in several admissions tests.

Item dependence. On both forms, but especially at the intermediate level, sets of items are dependent on each other (i.e., students are very likely to get all of the items in a set right or miss all of them). This characteristic leads to inflation of coefficient alpha. More important, it reduces the potential of the test to cover diverse subject matter by typing up examinee time on a single concept area that requires multiple responses.

Interpretation of norms. The provision of two sets of norms (for the gifted and general samples) may cause confusion, especially because both sets provide IQ-like quotients. Thus, a student might be found to have a rather high quotient in the norms for the general sample and a below-average quotient in the gifted norms. The same problem would result if the quotients were converted to percentile ranks, though the correct interpretation might be more obvious to users in that case. Because the general population is where one would seek students for mathematics programs for the gifted, it might make more sense to provide only the norms for the general population and use the scores attained by the gifted sample to interpret the level at which success might be likely in a program for the gifted.

Construction of norms. The 6-month age strata in the norms may be too fine, given the number of examinees on which each is based. The examiner's manual does not specify the number of cases for each stratum, but the numbers of examinees for each full age-year range from 91 to 228 with most between 100 and 170. Therefore, the quotients in a number of the norm strata may be based on fewer than 75 cases.

A search of various archives revealed no studies involving the TOMAGS. However, it is a relatively new test and, appropriately, its use should be a feature of various future research efforts in the identification of students gifted in mathematics.

SUMMARY. Despite the deficiencies noted above, the TOMAGS has many excellent qualities. If used circumspectly it should serve adequately for identification of students gifted in mathematics.

Review of the Test of Mathematical Abilities for Gifted Students by DELWYN L. HARNISCH, Professor of Curriculum and Instruction, University of Nebraska-Lincoln, Lincoln, NE:

The Test of Mathematical Abilities for Gifted Students (TOMAGS) is a standardized, norm-referenced test targeted to assess mathematical proficiency with children ranging in age from 6 to 12 years. The TOMAGS was introduced in 1998 and was designed to identify students (using a norm-referenced interpretation) who have talent or giftedness in mathematics. There are two levels of the test, a primary and an Intermediate level test. The Primary level is for children 6 through 9 years of age; the Intermediate level is for children 9 through 12 years of age. The TOMAGS is a test that can be group administered by teachers, counselors, and psychologists.

The TOMAGS was developed to assess problem-solving and reasoning abilities of students who are gifted in mathematics. In developing this test the authors sought to align the items to the National Council of Teachers of Mathematics (NCTM) standards. Currently mathematics education reformers encourage teachers to integrate the standards into their instruction. Therefore, this test helps address the need to match instruction with assessment.

The TOMAGS is a measure of math ability designed for use with students in the 6–12-year age group. The test is made up of open-ended questions presented in a problem-solving format. The Primary level of the test consists of 39 problems; the Intermediate level consists of 47 problems. The test was designed to estimate mathematical ability for children with problems that ask them to demonstrate their flexibility in mathematical reasoning and transfer to novel situations.

TEST DESCRIPTION. The principles used for selection of the items on the current forms include (a) alignment of items with the NCTM curriculum and evaluation standards, (b) attributes of good mathematical thinking, and (c) use of open-ended questions in problem-solving format. After several years of piloting mathematical items with students from gifted mathematics programs and with items grouped into booklets for grades 2 through 5, a set of items with positive discrimination for children gifted in mathematics was kept. In the spring of 1995 a pilot of the rewritten TOMAGS was conducted with 719 children, producing more evidence about the discrimination of the test with children identified as gifted in mathematics. After another pilot of the TOMAGS in spring of 1996 with two versions of the TOMAGS, additional items were added to complete the norming versions of the test to have 39 items for the Primary level and 52 items on the Intermediate level.

The TOMAGS Primary was aligned with the following number of items with six NCTM standards: number sense and numeration (8), concepts of whole number operations and whole number computation (5), geometry and spatial sense (6), measurement (7), statistics and probability (4), and patterns and relationships (8). The TOMAGS Intermediate was aligned with eight NCTM Curriculum standards in the following manner: number and number relationships (4), number systems and number theory (4), computation and estimation (4), patterns and functions (6), algebra (7), statistics and probability (7), geometry and spatial sense (11), and measurement (4). On the Intermediate level test the majority of open-ended questions test students' geometry skills. This test clearly lacks a sense of balance of items with each of the NCTM standards.

No item information is given about the difficulty of the items. Only item-discrimination information is provided for both levels of the test. A criterion of .3 was used for the item-discrimination index for the items that were kept on both levels of the test. This criterion was applied to the entire norming sample resulting in 39 items for the Primary level and 47 items for the Intermediate level. A summary of the median item discrimination indices reveals values on the Primary level test of .31 for the normal group and .44 for the gifted group. For the intermediate level test the median item-discrimination indices ranged from .31 for the gifted group to .33 for the normal group.

TEST ADMINISTRATION AND SCORING. The examiner's manual gives the instructions for administration and scoring of the TOMAGS. The requirements for the examiner are that they are familiar with the background and purpose of the instrument, are conversant with the psychometric properties of instrument and the general normative assessment procedures, are a practicing professional with test administration experience, and have a professional working knowledge and understanding for interpreting normative test data.

The TOMAGS has no set time limit for administration. General guidelines note that administration times may vary from 30 to 60 minutes. Most students, typically, will be able to finish in one testing session but additional sessions are allowed so the child can be evaluated under optimal circumstances. The administration of the TOMAGS Primary is targeted for children in Grade 1 through Grade 3. The TOMAGS Intermediate is targeted to children in Grade 4 through Grade 6. The children will each have their own test booklet, several pencils, and some scratchpaper at their desk. Basic demographic information is collected at the start of the test by asking the children to complete the information on the front of the test booklet. Children are encouraged to take as much time as needed to answer each problem on this test. Examiners are encouraged to walk around the room and to check with the students to make sure they understand the directions. Examiners are allowed to assist children who may have difficulty reading the test questions.

The scoring procedures are outlined with acceptable answers so that each problem is scored 1 for correct and 0 for incorrect response. Partial credit is not awarded on any of the problems. Several variations of completed student work are allowed that match the criteria for an acceptable response. The reading demands may be quite large for young students with developmental delay and thus requires the examiner to spend individual time to answer student questions. Allowing the examiner to read the test for those students who cannot read ensures that students are tested for their mathematical problem-solving abilities and not their speed or reading level.

The number of correct responses is examined for each student based on their respective age to give them a percentile and TOMAGS quotient compared with a normal and gifted population. The TOMAGS profile/scoring sheet allows for display of quotients from multiple sources to aid the decision maker in the assessment of the child's talent in mathematics. The authors recommend the use of the normal norming sample for making judgments on giftedness in mathematics. Scores of 125 or more on test quotients (centered at 100 with standard deviations of 15) are recommended as indicative of giftedness in mathematics.

NORMING. One standardization sample was used that included 935 students for the TOMAGS Primary and 637 for the TOMAGS Intermediate. Users can interpret TOMAGS scores with reasonable confidence as long as they keep in mind minor limitations of the norming sample. In general, the national norming sample is relatively small, compared to other national normed individual mathematical tests. The sampling frame and procedures resulted in final norming sample demographics that are compared with the 1990 U. S. Census demographics. For the Primary level the number of examinees in the Northeast seems a bit high and the number of examinees in the North Central a bit low. Information about participation and replacement of schools and students is not provided and no final information about number of students in suburban (only urban/rural provided) areas is included. The final norming sample varies from a low of 82 examinees at age 12 to a high of 310 at age 8. These small samples at the age level mean that when transforming the raw scores to percentiles based on age, these norms may be based on less than 50 examinees. Small samples of this size for norming samples are cause for concern about the representativeness of the data. Of particular note, 22% of the U.S. public school population is identified as rural and 44% (TOMAGS Primary) and 43% (TOMAGS Intermediate) of the norming sample is identified as rural.

The gifted normative sample (617 for TOMAGS Primary and 513 for Intermediate) reveals a similar pattern of overrepresentation in the rural area compared to the urban area. The geographic representation for the gifted normed sample is dramatically different from the U.S. population. For the TOMAGS Primary 72% of the sample from the South compared to 36% nationally. For the TOMAGS Intermediate the number of examinees in the South and North Central was a bit high and was a bit low in the West (9% in sample compared to 21% in population).

EVIDENCE FOR SCORE VALIDITY. Score reliability for the TOMAGS is incomplete but positive. As would be expected for a commercially produced test, most of the age- and group-based internal consistency (i.e., coefficient alpha) coefficients for total scores average at .84 or higher. Most of the coefficients are in the .81–.92 range. The standard error of measurement *SEM* for the TOMAGS score at the age- and group-based level varies from a low of 4.24 to a high of 6.53 with an average of 6.00 or lower. The publishers report confidence intervals and standard errors and provide details of how each is calculated. The publishers provide internal consistency measures for four selected subgroups within the two normative samples for both levels of the TOMAGS. The results are based on the total sample across all age groups within test levels and reveal similar measures of reliability. The test-retest reliabilities (time interval between 5 and 14 days) in studies of 30 children at each level were between .84 (TOMAGS Primary) and .94 (TOMAGS Intermediate). Correlations among scores assigned by two scorers in a special study conducted using 38 protocols for the TOMAGS Primary and 46 protocols from the TOMAGS Intermediate were high (.99). However, this evidence by itself is insufficient. It indicates that the scorers rank examinees similarly but does not indicate if any of the scorers scored accurately.

Some validity evidence for the TOMAGS is insufficient, but generally positive. The evidence on content validity, described earlier in the review, suggests a combination of positives (alignment with NCTM standards) and negatives (lack of balance of item representation across the standards). Construct validity evidence is not extensive. Comparison of student performance from normal and gifted groups was reported showing significant differences based on the TOMAGS at each age level. The publishers provide discriminate study results that show the contributions of the TOMAGS in maximally discriminating between normal and gifted groups as validity evidence. The factor analysis results reveal a multifactor structure with item loading shown by NCTM Standard. The authors should have shown the complete underlying complex factor structure for the resulting factor loadings. A confirmatory model should be shown to demonstrate the extent to which the NCTM Standard item alignment model is confirmed with the data. Bias studies were conducted by the authors using the Delta Scores approach and revealed that the TOMAGS items contain little or no bias for the groups studied.

SUMMARY. The results suggest a positive picture of the reliability and validity of TOMAGS scores for their intended uses. The norming procedures for the gifted sample are not well matched with the U.S. Census data by geographic region. In the next edition of this test the authors would do well to revise their sampling framework to correct this problem. The authors evidently recognize this and encourage the examiners to use the results from the normal normative sample when making their scoring interpretations.

The TOMAGS provides one source of evidence of giftedness in mathematics. The authors recommend the use of multiple tests to make this decision and have integrated that into their score profile. The means of allowing multiple sources of information should be encouraged when making decisions of giftedness. The TOMAGS should be used for the primary purpose of assessing talent in mathematics and not as a diagnostic tool.

The TOMAGS provides an indicator of giftedness in mathematics. This test utilizes the open-ended question format to tap mathematical problem-solving abilities. The problems encountered on this test represent problems for which children will have to use mathematical knowledge in novel situations. In some situations the students will be requested to construct new strategies to solve the problem on topics not taught formally in school. These problem types are capable of tapping the mathematical proficiencies targeted for this assessment and at the same time it has the potential to examine clinically the student's relative strengths and weaknesses (Harnisch, 1997; Nitko, 1996).

In closing, researchers in gifted education (Miller, 1990) have stressed the difference between mathematical giftedness and excelling in computation. Traditionally, tests for identifying the mathematically talented were heavily tilted to measuring students' computational abilities. Research does not indicate that this is a sign of giftedness. Students who are advanced in mathematical computations may be able to answer enough questions to score in the gifted range. Miller's definition of giftedness in mathematics focuses on identifying students who have an unusually high ability to understand mathematical ideas and to reason mathematically. The TOMAGS attempts to measure the problem-solving and reasoning abilities of students who are gifted in mathematics.

REVIEWER'S REFERENCES

Miller, R. C. (1990). *Discovering mathematical talent*. Reston, VA: Council for Exceptional Children. (ERIC Document Reproduction Service No. ED 321 487)
Nitko, A. J. (1996). *Educational assessment of students* (2nd ed.). Englewood Cliffs, NJ: Prentice-Hall, Inc.
Harnisch, D. L. (1997). Assessment linkages with instruction and professional staff development. In P. W. Thurston & J. G. Ward (Eds.), *Advances in educational administration* (vol. 5; pp. 145–164). Greenwich, CT: JAI Press Inc.

[392]
Test of Memory Malingering.

Purpose: To "assist neuropsychologists in discriminating between bona fide memory-impaired patients and malingerers."
Population: Ages 16 to 84.
Publication Date: 1996.
Acronym: TOMM.
Scores: Total score only.
Administration: Individual
Price Data, 1999: $95 per complete kit including manual (55 pages), 25 recording forms, and 1 set of stimulus booklets; $20 per 25 recording forms; $50 per set of 3 stimulus booklets; $35 per manual; $60 per Computer Program for Windows™ including user's manual, software manual, and 3 uses.
Time: (15) minutes.
Comments: Windows™ computer software available on CD or 3.5-inch disk to administer, score, and report results of TOMM.
Author: Tom N. Tombaugh.
Publisher: Multi-Health Systems, Inc.

Review of the Test of Memory Malingering by M. ALLAN COOPERSTEIN, Clinical Psychologist & Forensic Examiner, Independent Practice, Willow Grove, PA:

PROPOSED TEST USE. Medicolegal requirements for assessing malingering and other forms of dissimulation in cerebral, somatic, or psychological injuries, have created a need to assess the veracity and accuracy of patients' reports and efforts. The Test of Memory Malingering (TOMM) is designed to examine response bias, intentional faking, or exaggeration of symptoms. It is also necessary to assess whether a patient is exerting maximal effort in a test situation. The test should be neutral to neuropsychological deficits, enabling motivational differences to emerge without confounding brain dysfunctioning and motivation.

The TOMM, an item-recognition test for adults, is described as "a systematic method to assist neuropsychologists in discriminating between bona fide memory-impaired patients and malingerers" (manual, p. 1). Malingering is defined as "feigning illness or disability to escape work, excite sympathy, or gain compensation" (Stedman's, 1996). When assessment results may impact upon financial or emotional gain, the potential for malingering exists.

It has been demonstrated that traumatic brain injury (TBI) patients pursuing fiscal gain from their injuries may perform inconsistently when retested (Binder & Rohling, 1996; Reitan & Wolfson, 1997). Less than maximal effort may be exerted when financial and other incentives are present.

At first glance, the TOMM appears to be a psychometric tool for the assessment of memory. In fact, it provides a systematic protocol that enables neuropsychologists to discriminate between genuinely impaired patients and those exaggerating symptoms. The TOMM may complement neurological, neuropsychological, forensic, or disability batteries by providing an independent and reliable method of assessing systematic underperformance, using forced-choice visual recognition task that is easily passed by patients with severe brain injury.

TEST DEVELOPMENT AND RATIONALE. TOMM development is rooted in neuropsychology and cognitive psychology. It implements a recognition (specifically item recognition) paradigm as the means of detecting biased responding. It presents an apparent cognitive task with face validity and possessing a level of difficulty masking the actual test purpose. "Ideally, the stimulus materials used in any malingering test should create the impression that the test is relatively difficult, while in reality producing a test that is relatively easy. That is, the perceived difficulty of the task should exceed its actual difficulty" (manual, p. 9). Consequently, a forced-choice recognition process using drawings of ordinary objects is presented to the Examinee.

TEST FORM AND ADMINISTRATION. TOMM components include two trial stimulus booklets of 50 line-drawings each. There is a third booklet, the Retention test stimulus booklet, including 50 recognition panels of two drawings each. Administration of Parts 1 and 2 takes approximately 15 minutes. Retention, an optional trial, brings the complete administration to approximately 20 minutes.

The Examinee is given a brief, specific introduction, followed by a sample trial. After viewing the 50 pictures, he or she is shown recognition panels of two figures each and asked to select which figure they had seen earlier.

Upon completion of Trial 1, the second trial is completed. The third, or Retention, trial is optional. It is typically administered when Trial 2 results fall below chance. When it is administered, the Retention trial is given approximately 15 minutes later, after the Examinee is exposed to an interval involving nonvisual tests.

SCORING AND INTERPRETATION. Scoring is quite simple. All possible answers are presented on the scoring sheet and a check box is placed alongside. Chance dictates that an individual is capable of correctly identifying 50% of the pictures by guessing alone. Thus, a score of 25 represents the chance level.

Tombaugh reports that performance on the second trial is very high for non-malingerers, irrespective of age, neurological dysfunction, or psychological symptoms. Using the Trial 2 score as a reference point, scores lower than 45 on this trial or the Retention trial alert the examiner that the examinee is not exerting maximal effort and is likely to be malingering. The author cautions, however, that a score of 45 is viewed as a "guideline"—the likelihood that malingering exists with greater deviation from the normative baseline of specific diagnostic groups provided in the manual. As indicated above, the TOMM applies two decision rules: The first decision is based upon any performance that falls lower than chance; the second decision implements criterion-based norms from clinical samples.

NORMATIVE INFORMATION. The initial phase of normative testing originated with nonclinical subjects in two phases. During Phase 1, a preliminary, four-choice version of the TOMM was used. In the second, the format was modified to a two-choice test with Examiner feedback on response correctness. The results of the studies verified that test performance was not sensitive to age or education.

A validation study was conducted using a clinical population including examinees with no cognitive impairment, cognitive impairment, aphasia, TBI, and dementia. Performance of the first four groups was equivalent, although the accuracy of the dementia group was lower. However, with Trial 2, even the dementia group achieved 92% accuracy.

Statistical analysis demonstrated significant differences between groups. A comparison of learning and retention scores on a visual learning task and verbal learning task administered with the TOMM indicated that recognition performance measured by the TOMM was generally unrelated to free recall measure of visual and verbal learning. This was verified by low correlation coefficients (.20–.35) between the TOMM and other learning measures across trials. The lack of significant correlation between the TOMM and free recall scores demonstrates that the TOMM is generally insensitive to measures of learning and memory dysfunctions that were previously associated with a variety of neurological impairments.

Validation studies using simulated and "at-risk" malingerers were performed. In the first study, simulated malingerers role-played (without instructions) patients seeking compensation for TBI caused by a motor vehicle accident. The most convincing simulation would earn a reward of 50 dollars. Following a week of preparation, simulators were given a battery of neuropsychological tests, including the TOMM. Control subjects received the same test battery, but were requested to perform as well as they could and did not receive the scenario given to the experimental group.

Results effectively demonstrated no overlap between simulators and controls. All controls achieved a score of nearly 100% correct responses. Ninety-three percent of the simulators scored lower. When the Retention trial was added, the specificity of the results remained the same as test sensitivity reached 89%. The TOMM demonstrated a capacity to discriminate between Examinees who produced good effort (high specificity) and those who intentionally fake responses (low sensitivity). It also demonstrated a high face validity in being perceived by Examinees as a memory test.

In a validation study of patients at-risk for malingering (i.e., in which fiscal or other incentives were present), the TOMM was used with patients who suffered TBI. The experimental design compared litigating patients against a control group of nonlitigating patients. This study used four groups: TBI patients "not-at-risk" for malingering, TBI patients "at-risk," cognitively intact control subjects, and patient controls with significant focal neuropsychological impairment. All TBI patients had CT or MRI scans that were interpreted by radiologists as congruent with TBI. The risk of malingering was defined by pursuit of a personal injury suit, a disability petition, symptoms deviating from known neurologic diseases, or a combination of these.

Administered within the context of a neurological evaluation, the TOMM was identified as a memory test. Cognitively intact controls and patient controls achieved near perfect scores on all three trials. TBI patients considered "not-at-risk" for malingering performed at a slightly lower level on Trial 1 than either control group, but at comparable levels on the remaining trials. The "at-risk" TBI group achieved considerably lower scores. Statistical analysis verified that, in all three trials, scores from the "at-risk" TBI group were significantly lower than from other groups. The latter did not differ substantially from one another.

DISCUSSION. In assessing the TOMM, I administered it with the Structured Interview of

Reported Symptoms (SIRS; T5:2522), another instrument assessing response bias. In both cases, litigation was not a factor.

The first case involved a 49-year-old male—Mr. X—who received traumatic blows to the frontal region in a work-related accident. Neurophysiology demonstrated an abnormal EEG study with an epileptogenic focus in the left anterior temporal region. There were also episodes of violence and the presence of psychosis secondary to the head injury. The second case was a 46-year-old male—Mr. Y— who underwent a left anterior temporal lobectomy 10 years earlier and who was reported to become occasionally violent in domestic situations.

Presenting no obvious signs of psychosis, Mr. Y's scores on the SIRS all fell within the Honest range of responding; his TOMM results also demonstrated maximal effort. Although Mr. X's TOMM score indicated maximum effort, two of his eight SIRS scales fell into the Definite Feigning range and three more were within the Probable Feigning range.

In an attempt to understand the discrepancy, I suspect that the verbal questioning format of the SIRS elicited cognitively distorted responses from Mr. X related to the head injury and its secondary psychotic processes, which involved a form of dementia. Use of the SIRS alone would identify Mr. X as a malingerer, irrespective of his motivation. In assessing effort and response bias, recognition of the psychodynamics of the individual and his or her predispositions is mandatory or skewed interpretations may result.

SUMMARY. A valuable contribution towards understanding and identifying malingering, the TOMM's greatest value is that of a supplementary measure, set within a comprehensive assessment battery directed towards assessing neuropsychological functioning. Appropriately, the author cautions that "a diagnosis of malingering should never be advanced solely on the basis of the TOMM. Rather, it requires the same inferential processes and careful examination of all data involved in any clinical judgment" (manual, p. 22).

REVIEWER'S REFERENCES

Binder, L. M., & Rohling, M. L. (1996). Money matters: A meta-analytic review of the effects of financial incentives on recovery after closed-head injury. *American Journal of Psychiatry, 153*, 7–10.

Stedman's Medical Dictionary (26th ed.). (1996). Baltimore: Williams & Wilkins.

Reitan, R. M., & Wolfson, D. (1997). Consistency of neuropsychological test scores of head-injured subjects involved in litigation compared with head-injured subjects not involved in litigation: Development of the retest consistency index. *The Clinical Neuropsychologist, 11*, 69–76.

Review of the Test of Memory Malingering by ROMEO VITELLI, Staff Psychologist, Milbrook Correctional Centre, Millbrook, Ontario, Canada:

The Test of Memory Malingering (TOMM) "provides a systematic method to assist neuropsychologists in discriminating between bona fide memory-impaired patients and malingerers" (manual, p. 1). It was developed to provide professionals with a brief, self-contained, and well-normed test of feigned or exaggerated memory deficits. Its format consists of a 50-item recognition test with two learning trials and a retention trial. For each learning trial, the test-taker is presented with 50 line drawings (target pictures) of common objects for 3 seconds at 1-second intervals. The test-taker is then shown 50 recognition panels, one at a time, containing one of the previously administered target pictures and a new picture. A forced-choice format is used to require the test-taker to select the previously given target picture and the test-taker is given explicit feedback on response correctness for each of the 50 items. Although the same 50 pictures are used in each trial, the order is varied in the second learning trial. There is also an optional retention trial that may be given 15 minutes after the second recognition trial. The retention trial format is similar to the previous trials except that the target pictures are not re-administered. Although the author suggests that the two learning trials are usually sufficient to assess malingering, it is recommended that the retention trial be given to verify results. Full test (without retention trial) administration requires approximately 15 minutes.

SCORING AND INTERPRETATION. The TOMM is scored with one point being given for each item with a maximum possible score of 50. The possibility of malingering is determined by two decisions rules: (a) scoring lower than chance on any trial and (b) any score lower than 45 on the second trial or the retention test. It is suggested that the second rule be used as a guideline rather than a rigid cutoff. A caution is also given that a diagnosis of malingering should not be given based on TOMM performance alone and that evidence of intentionality and motivation should be based on other sources. Chapter 5 of the manual provides a good overview on the cautions involved with the diagnosis of malingering as well as a series of case studies to facilitate interpretation.

NORMS AND STANDARDIZATION. Information relating to norms and the standardiza- tion process is provided in chapter 3 of the manual. The TOMM was developed using a nonclinical sample of ($n = 475$) and a clinical sample ($n = 158$) to determine the sensitivity of the TOMM with respect to various types of organic syndromes (i.e., traumatic brain injury, aphasia, and dementia). It is of note that the TOMM was found to be relatively insensitive to age and educational history.

RELIABILITY AND VALIDITY. The manual provides little information as to reliability although additional sources (Spreen & Strauss, 1998) indicate high coefficient alpha reliabilities for each trial (.94–.95 range) but no information is available on other forms of reliability (i.e., test- retest reliability). There have been a number of validation studies of the TOMM as outlined in chapter 3 of the manual and later studies (Rees, Tombaugh, Gansler, & Moczynski, 1998). Initial normative studies with nonclinical samples found that perceived test difficulty was substantially greater than actual test performance indicating strong face validity, which is essential for a sensi- tive measure of poor effort on the part of the test- taker. Validation research was also done using a clinical sample composed of patients with primary diagnoses including aphasia, dementia, traumatic brain injury, and patients without cognitive im- pairments. Results indicated that performance in the No Cognitive Impairment, Cognitive Impair- ment, Aphasia, and Traumatic Brain Injury samples were analogous although performance for De- mentia patients was somewhat lower. Overall, the result indicated that the TOMM was relatively insensitive to various types of cognitive impair- ment although severity of impairment affects per- formance.

Performance on the TOMM was also com- pared to performance on several visual and verbal learning tests (Visual Reproduction subtest from the Wechsler Memory Scale—Revised [Wechsler, 1987]; and either the California Verbal learning Test [Delis, Kramer, Kaplan, & Ober, 1981] or the Word-List subtest from the Learning and Memory Battery [Schmidt & Tombaugh, 1995]). Analysis of the results showed only a modest correlation between the TOMM and the other learning measures (.2–.35 range) demonstrating the insensitivity of the TOMM to memory and learning impairments.

In a study of simulated malingering, the TOMM was administered as part of a battery of neuropsychological tests. Nonmalingering controls were found to score significantly higher than simulated malingerers on the TOMM (49.9 vs. 35.3 on the second trial) with virtually no overlap between the two groups indicating 100% specificity for controls and 93% sensitivity for simulate malingerers. In subject debriefing after the study, the TOMM was not distinguished from other tests as a test of malingering reflecting its high face validity.

In research into "at risk" malingerers, TOMM performance was contrasted between litigating and nonlitigating TBI patients, a group of patients with focal neuropsychological impairments, and a group of cognitively intact controls. Although nonlitigating TBI patients scored relatively poorly on the first trial alone, litigating TBI patients scored significantly lower than other groups on all three trials.

SUMMARY. The TOMM is a well-designed and useful measure of potential memory malingering which is insensitive to age, educational history, or type of cognitive impairment. There are some limitations, however, particularly in terms of limited information on the reliability of the TOMM. There is also a need for further validity research to investigate TOMM performance in factitious disordered and personality disordered populations. Specific concerns have also been raised about the vulnerability of the TOMM to psychological distress (i.e., anxiety and depression), which may artificially lower test performance (Spreen & Strauss, 1998). Despite these potential drawbacks, the TOMM appears to be a valuable tool for the detection of memory dissimulation.

REVIEWER'S REFERENCES

Delis, D. C., Kramer, J. H., Kaplan, E., & Ober, B. A. (1987). The California Verbal Learning Test: Research Edition, Adult Version. San Antonio, TX: The Psychological Corporation.
Wechsler, D. (1987). Manual for the Wechsler Memory Scale—Revised. San Antonio, TX: Psychological Corporation.
Schmidt, J. P., & Tombaugh, T. N. (1995). LAMB: Learning and Memory Battery. Toronto: Multi-Health Systems, Inc.
Rees, L. M., Tombaugh, T. N., Gansler, D. A., & Moczynski, N. P. (1998). Five validation experiments of the Test of Memory Malingering (TOMM). Psychological Assessment, 10, 10–20.
Spreen, O., & Strauss, E. (1998). Test of Memory Malingering (TOMM). In A Compendium of Neuropsychological Tests: Administration, norms, and commentary (2nd. ed.) (pp. 676–677). New York: Oxford University Press.

[393]
Test of Nonverbal Intelligence, Third Edition.

Purpose: "Developed to assess aptitude, intelligence, abstract reasoning, and problem solving in a completely language-free format."
Population: Ages 6-0 through 89-11.

Publication Dates: 1982–1997.
Acronym: TONI-3.
Scores: Total score only.
Administration: Individual.
Price Data, 1999: $229 per complete kit including manual ('97, 160 pages), picture book, and 50 each Form A and Form B answer booklets and record forms; $39 per 50 answer booklet and record forms (specify Form A or B); $96 per picture book; $59 per manual.
Time: (15–20) minutes.
Authors: Linda Brown, Rita J. Sherbenou, and Susan K. Johnson.
Publisher: PRO-ED.
Cross References: See T5:2704 (47 references) and T4:2775 (10 references); for reviews by Kevin K. Murphy and T. Steuart Watson of the Second Edition, see 11:439 (9 references); for reviews by Philip M. Clark and Samuel T. Mayo of the original edition, see 9:1266.

Review of the Test of Nonverbal Intelligence, Third Edition by JEFFREY A. ATLAS, Associate Clinical Professor (Psychiatry), Bronx Children's Psychiatric Center, Albert Einstein College of Medicine, Bronx, NY:

Tests of nonverbal intelligence are a critical part of mental health and educational workers' assessment tools in considering differential diagnostics, treatment and placement recommendations, and grade placement. Although tests such as the Peabody Picture Vocabulary Test (280), Goodenough-Harris Draw-A-Person Test (T5:1097), and Ravens Progressive Matrices (T5:2163), from which the Test of Nonverbal Intelligence (TONI) draws, have aided in nonverbal assessment, each suffers from various weaknesses ranging from oblique reliance upon verbal skills to outdated or constricted norms. It is unusual for a test to feature well-constructed norms while also making such minimal demands on the examinee such that nearly all populations except the blind may be evaluated for intelligence, viewed as the capacity to reason abstractly. The TONI-3 provides such a measure, which may be applied to the gifted, dyslexic, attention-deficit/hyperactive, learning-disabled, emotionally disturbed, and non-English-speaking groups (all having norms within the average range), while distinguishing such groups from mentally retarded individuals. In this manner, each group's particular handicapping conditions need not confound estimates of intelligence, which optimally could tailor educational and psychotherapeutic programming so as to maximize each person's potential in acting upon the world. Labels (or epithets) such as deaf-dumb, anachronistic yet still occasionally encountered, are reduced as we develop more sensitive means, such as the TONI-3, of recognizing and developing the potential of exceptional groups.

A limitation of the TONI-3, however, is the two-fold problem that special placement decisions do continue to be based primarily on Intellectual Quotient (IQ) scores derived from groundbreaking instruments, such as the Wechsler scales, and that the TONI-3 manual overstates the value of its concurrent validity. Correlations ranging from .53 to .63 between the TONI-3 and Wechsler Intelligence Scale for Children, Third Edition (WISC-III; the primary assessment instrument for the exceptional population served) are at best moderate (accounting for a little over one-third of the variability in scores) and based upon a small sample (of 34 students). Although this limitation is not insignificant, the TONI-3 is probably the best instrument we have in making some sort of comparison to the standard Wechsler scale when it cannot be validly administered due to sensory limitations of the subject. The authors of the TONI-3 are to be commended in presenting the instrument as a work-in-progress, to be revised with the accrual of data, despite validity and reliability estimates that already place it ahead of most "tests" on the market.

The TONI-3 is attractively packaged, with sturdy test plates featuring successively more difficult abstract design entries requiring indication by the subject of the logical complimentary or penultimate design. The manual is a model of historical background information, review of research, reflective consideration of limitations, and care of presentation, and is written in a manner accessible to psychometrically trained students and practitioners.

SUMMARY. The TONI-3 is best seen as a replacement intelligence test for individuals who do not speak English or who suffer sensory deficits. It correlates only moderately with the WISC-III and its pantomimic administration procedure, although as favorably "nonverbal" an administration procedure as one is likely to find, may render test administration to gifted or nonhandicapped students unnecessarily awkward. For those testing situations requiring minimal (mainstream) cultural interference or minimal dependence upon full sensory capacities of examinees, the TONI-3 is to be highly recommended.

Review of the Test of Nonverbal Intelligence, Third Edition by GERALD E. DeMAURO, Coordinator of Assessment, New York State Education Department, Albany, NY:

TEST COVERAGE AND USE. The third edition of the Test of Nonverbal Intelligence (TONI-3) is described as "a language-free measure of cognitive ability" (cover). It is preceded by the TONI and TONI-2 and is designed to assess aptitude of people from 5-0 to 85-11 years of age whose cognitive, linguistic, or motor skills would interfere with optimal performance on traditional intelligence measures. The authors believe the design and development of the test and its focus on problem solving makes its use particularly valid for a wide range of population groups. Specifically, Jensen's (1980) seven criteria for reducing the impact of language and culture served to guide the development of the two 45-item forms of the instrument.

SAMPLES FOR TEST VALIDATION AND NORMING. The TONI-3 was administered in 1995 to 2,060 individuals and again in 1996 to another 1,391 individuals, for a total of 3,451 examinees chosen to represent the United States population geographically, and by gender, community type, ethnicity and races, disabling condition, and socioeconomic status. The test provides deviation quotients for 23 age groups, demarcated by half years from 6-0 to 10-11, by whole years from 11-0 to 16-11, from 17-0 to 54-11, by 5-year intervals from 55-0 to 79-11 and from 80-0 to 89-11. The 46 raw scores yield 980 conversions to quotients (age intervals by raw scores). Within whole year intervals, the samples range from 54 (80-0 to 89-11) to 1,373 (17-0 to 59-11). The quotients are converted to percentile ranks with varying stability depending upon the size of the samples at the different score points and age groups.

Many validity studies are cited in the 1997 examiner's manual. Specific studies range in sample sizes from 16 (Brown, Sherbenou, & Johnsen, 1982) to item analysis based on the entire normative sample.

The normative data show a rise in mean raw scores over the age intervals up to the 17-0 to 54-11 interval. At 55-0 to 59-11, the means start dropping. Examinees in the 6-0 to 6-5 interval averaged only seven correct items of the 45, whereas examinees in the 17-0 to 54-11 interval averaged 31 correct items.

RELIABILITY. Coefficients alpha and standard errors of measurement (*SEM*s) were calculated for 20 age intervals, delineated by whole years until age 19 and by decades thereafter. The average coefficient for both forms was .93, and the ranges were .89 to .97. *SEM*s ranged from 3 to 5. Coefficients alpha were: .96 on both forms for males; .95 on both forms for females, Hispanic examinees, and for deaf examinees; .94 on both forms for African Americans and for learning-disabled examinees; and .92 on both forms for gifted examinees.

Alternate form correlations within the 20 age intervals ranged from .74 to .95, and test-retest correlations with a one-week separation ranged from .89 to .94 for both forms for 13-year-olds, 15-year-olds, and 19–40-years-olds. Rescoring of test protocols from the normative sample by staff members of PRO-ED's research department yielded .99 correlations for each form of the test, providing strong evidence of interrater reliability for trained scorers. The reliability studies support test-based decisions about individuals.

CRITERION-RELATED VALIDITY. Several small studies suggest that the convergence of TONI-3 scores with these other intelligence measures increases as their verbal demands decrease. For example, correlations for 19 students on Forms A and B were .57 and .51, respectively with the WAIS-R (Wechsler Adult Intelligence Scale—Revised) Verbal Scale but .75 and .76 with the WAIS-R Performance Scales.

These discriminant and convergent properties are less evident for younger examinees. Correlations for 34 seven- to 17-year-olds with the WISC-R (Wechsler Intelligence Scale for Children—Revised) Performance Scale were .56 and .58 for Forms A and B, respectively, whereas those with the WISC-R Verbal Scale were .59 and .53, respectively.

Median correlations of studies of the two earlier versions of the test demonstrate the same relationships, .52 with measure of general aptitude, .45 with measures of verbal aptitude, and .60 with measures of nonverbal aptitude. These correlations appear to be attenuated.

Taken in isolation, these studies contribute to the criterion-related evidence. Taken together, they elaborate the construct in terms of the test's discriminant and convergent properties. Purely from the perspective of criterion-related evidence, information about the types of decisions made about people of different ages and at different scoring ranges and empirical support for those decisions from other sources would be valuable to users.

CONTENT VALIDITY. The authors (Brown, Sherbenou, & Johnson) base their arguments for content validity on rationales for format and items, classical item analysis, and differential item functioning (DIF) analysis. The argument for content validity rests heavily on the fidelity of the test items to the domain. Therefore, evidence that the items are not biased supports the argument when success in the domain is equally likely for equally skilled examinees. The domain focuses on problem solving, and the format is abstract drawing, in light of logistical ease of administration and Jensen's (1980) criteria for language-free tests.

Originally, 307 items were reviewed by experts in psychology, testing, and nonverbal assessment. The 183 surviving items were field-tested, subjected to classical item analysis, and reduced to two parallel 50-item forms (TONI, in 1982). In 1990, the TONI-2 revision, 23 more difficult items were passed through the same screens, and 5 survivors were added to each form. These two forms were reduced to 45 items each on the basis of item analysis and bias analyses of the TONI-3 normative study.

Item analyses used criteria of point-biserial correlations of .33 or higher and p values ranging from .02 to .86 with a mean of .50. Forms were pre-equated on the bases of item p-values for the common normative sample.

DIF analyses employed IRT item characteristic curves and delta item difficulty correlations. Neither identified DIF problems in the surviving item pool related to gender, race, gifted status, or learning disabilities. The IRT approach utilizes hypothetical ability points, whereas the delta approach, without analysis of distance from the regression line of individual items, estimates whole test fairness.

CONSTRUCT VALIDITY. The authors base their construct validity argument on six types of evidence. First, the observed relationship of age to TONI-3 scores follows patterns observed on other intelligence measures. Second, they summarize studies relating TONI-3 scores to school achievement. Third, studies of the normative sample revealed that gifted examinees score highest, examinees with nonintellectual disabilities score lower than gifted examinees, and mentally retarded examinees score lowest. African-American examinees scored about a third of a standard deviation below the total sample, raising the question of culture-bound test content.

Fourth, a study by Vance, Hankins, and Reynolds (1988) is cited that indicates that the TONI-2 is as strong a predictor of the WISC-R Full Scale IQ as is the Quick Test (Ammons & Ammons, 1962). Fifth, exploratory factor analytic studies indicate a single strong factor (59% and 60% of the variance for the two forms, respectively after Promax rotation, and two weaker factors). Sixth, the median item point biserials by age group (medians of .49 for Form A and .50 for Form B) are presented as evidence of fidelity to the construct.

TEST ADMINISTRATION. The test administration procedures are clear and reasonable. They approximate those involved in the normative administration. Questions are nonverbal, and administrations may be curtailed when a ceiling is reached. Because items are arranged by difficulty, a criterion of three incorrect responses among five contiguous questions determines the ceiling. However, there is a provision for administering all 45 items. Three concerns arise under such conditions: (a) The ceiling criterion needs to be studied to assure that answers beyond ceiling are in fact guesses; (b) by not uniformly applying the ceiling criterion, some examinees may be credited with guessing whereas others are not; and (b) if the above concerns are without base, misfitting examinees may still be able to answer more difficult questions after failing earlier questions.

TEST REPORTING. TONI-3 information is summarized on the Answer and Record Form. The information provides quotient, reliability, and raw and percentile rank scores. Provisions are made for other information, some of which involves subjective interpretations of the examiner.

CONCLUSION. The TONI-3 offers much evidence to support its use. It would also be useful to examine differential validity for examinees of different degrees of verbal skills.

REVIEWER'S REFERENCES

Ammons, R. B., & Ammons, C. H. (1962). The Quick Test: Provisional manual. *Psychological Reports, 11,* 11–161.
Jenson, A. R. (1980). *Bias in mental testing.* New York: Free Press.
Brown, L., Sherbenou, R. J., & Johnsen, S. K. (1982). Test of Nonverbal Intelligence manual. Austin, TX: PRO-ED.
Vance, B., Hankins, N., & Reynolds, F. (1988). Prediction of Wechsler Intelligence Scale for Children—Revised Full Scale IQ from the Quick Test of Intelligence and the Test of Nonverbal Intelligence for a sample of referred children and youth. *Journal of Clinical Psychology, 44,* 793–794.

[394]
Test of Variables of Attention (Version 7.03).

Purpose: "Developed to assess attention and impulse control."

Population: Ages 4–80.
Publication Dates: 1988–1996.
Acronym: TOVA.
Administration: Individual.
Price Data: Available from publisher.
Time: (21.6) minutes.
Comments: Computer administered via separate or combined software; IBM and Macintosh versions available.
Authors: Lawrence M. Greenberg, Clifford L. Corman, and Carol L. Kindschi.
Publisher: Universal Attention Disorders, Inc.
  a) T.O.V.A. VISUAL.
    Scores, 3: Commission, Omission, Response Time Variability and Signal Detection.
  b) T.O.V.A. AUDITORY.
    Scores: Same as *a* above.
Cross References: See T5:2720 (2 references); for reviews by Rosa A. Hagin and Peter Della Bella and by Margot B. Stein of an earlier edition, see 13:336 (1 reference).

Review of the Test of Variables of Attention by SANDRA LOEW, Assistant Professor, Counselor Education, University of North Alabama, Florence, AL:

The Test of Variables of Attention (T.O.V.A.) is a continuous performance test using computerized visual and auditory stimuli to assess attention. It is administered individually and used in conjunction with a clinical history and other tests to diagnose and treat children and adults with attention deficits. In the Clinical Guide, the authors suggest six uses for the T.O.V.A.: (a) Assess attention in neuropsychological and neuropsychiatric evaluations, (b) screen for disorders of attention, (c) [use as] components in the diagnosis of disorders of attention, (d) predict medication response, (e) titrate dosage, and (f) monitor treatment over time. There is a screening version of the T.O.V.A. for use in schools that does not provide a diagnostic statement but suggests further evaluation if the results are not in the normal range.

The test kit comes with equipment for Macintosh or IBM-compatible computers and is easily installed. Hardware for computers without a soundcard is included for IBM-compatible computers; the auditory version of the test is not available for Macintosh systems. A specially designed highly accurate (+/- 1 msec) electronic microswitch is included to use in this non-language-based assessment. Because the visual stimuli are squares with a small square at the top or the bottom, there is no need to recognize numbers or letters, nor a need for right-left discrimination. The stimuli in the auditory version are two easily discriminated tones.

The test is designed to take 21.6 minutes, and one stimulus is presented for 100 msec every 2 seconds. Responses, nonresponses, and reaction times are automatically recorded through the microswitch, which eliminates examiner error.

The variables include errors of omission, errors of commission, response time, response time variability, d´ (d prime) score, ADHD score, anticipatories, and multiple responses. Errors of omission occur when a subject does not respond to a target when it is presented, and is considered to be a measure of inattention. Errors of commission occur when the test-taker incorrectly responds to a nontarget indicating impulsivity or disinhibition. The response time measures the processing time it takes for the test-taker to correctly respond to a target, and the response time variability measures the inconsistency in response times. The d´ score measures the ratio of the hit rate to the false alarm rate, determining the deterioration of performance over time. The ADHD score shows how similar the test performance is to an ADHD profile. An anticipatory response is recorded when the test-taker has pressed the microswitch within 200 msec of the appearance of the stimulus because that is essentially a "guess" that impacts the other scores. When the test-taker presses the microswitch more than once per stimulus, a multiple response is recorded. This test was intended to measure attentional and impulse control processes in the four areas of inattention or omissions, impulse control or commissions, response time, and response time variability for test-takers aged 4 years through adult.

Three manuals come with the testing kit and some information is repeated in each manual. The User's Manual clearly illustrates how to install the hardware and software and provides phone numbers for technical support. The user is shown how to copy files and merge files for more complete records. The T.O.V.A. will provide a report with specific behavior management techniques for each client after the test, and this manual provides the complete recommendations, which is helpful to the user in making selections. The manual also suggests putting each subject's file on a separate disc and keeping the disc in the paper file, which makes it easier to find and to send to other professionals. There should be no technical difficulty in using the T.O.V.A. because the instructions are so well written and illustrated.

The Professional Manual provides a history of continuous performance testing (CPT) and, more specifically, the T.O.V.A. There is a description of the variables and scoring of the test, and very clear administration directions. The T.O.V.A. was normed on 1,590 people ranging in age from 4 to 80+, with the 4- and 5-year-olds given a shortened version. The sample consisted of 882 females and 708 males, and 99% of the test-takers were Caucasian. This will certainly have an impact on the use of this test for racial/ethnic minorities. There was no information on the socioeconomic status of the individuals in the normative sample, therefore crucial information is missing that the user needs to determine if this test is an appropriate measure for a particular individual. The normative data presented are differentiated by gender and age, with age separated by 2-year intervals for the children and 10-year intervals for the adults. The children (n = 1,340) in the sample showed no deviant classroom behavior as defined by a score greater than 2 standard deviations on the Connors Parent-Teacher Questionnaire, Abbreviated form; were not currently using psychoactive medication; and were not receiving Special Education services. The adults (n = 250) in the sample were not currently using psychoactive medications; had no history of central nervous system disorders; and had no history of central nervous system injuries. All of the tests were administered in the morning with no distractions and the observer was present in the room. Each participant took the 3-minute practice test to be sure they understood the instructions and could use the microswitch. The T.O.V.A. is not an appropriate test for the visually impaired and the auditory test (T.O.V.A.-A) has been normed on only 2,551 children, aged 6 to 19 years. It has been found to be too difficult for children 4 and 5 years of age and it is currently being normed on adults.

The Clinical Guide explains the criteria for a diagnosis of ADHD and reminds the user that the T.O.V.A. is only one component to a comprehensive workup: "Nothing (not even the T.O.V.A.) replaces a detailed history" (p. 4). There is a 20% chance that any given T.O.V.A. will produce a false positive or a false negative result, which underscores the need to use other means of assessment in addition to the T.O.V.A. Additional information concerning validity is found in the Professional Manual, which cites a number of studies where significant differences in some of the variables were found between those diagnosed with attentional disorders and those in nondisordered control groups. The diagnoses were made by senior faculty level university psychiatrists or psychologists, independently of the test. Although the T.O.V.A. has high face validity, there is concern about the content validity of the instrument. Aside from the lack of clarity concerning validity, it is tiresome to have fragments of information in one manual and other information concerning the same topic in another.

There is a small section that addresses test-retest reliability (administration interval not provided), stating that there were no significant differences (paired t-test) in T.O.V.A. variables when the tests were readministered to 40 children with ADHD, 33 randomly selected normal children, and 24 normal adults. Elsewhere, it is stated that there are no appreciable practice effects. Because three of the suggested uses of the T.O.V.A. are prediction of medication response, titration of dosage, and monitoring treatment over time, it would be prudent to provide more information concerning test-retest reliability.

SUMMARY. The T.O.V.A. is a continuous performance test that could provide important information in the diagnosis and treatment of individuals with attentional disorders. It is only one component of a comprehensive workup, and should never be used alone to determine if an individual has attentional difficulties. The T.O.V.A. is easy to administer and is computer scored with hardware and software that is quickly installed. It may be particularly useful in determining the optimal dosage of medication, and to monitor treatment over time. Because there were few (1%) members of racial or ethnic minorities in the normative sample, it is not a useful measure for those populations. The manuals and computer printout provide useful information on appropriate interventions based on the outcome of the T.O.V.A. However, there are three manuals that come with the test and much of the information is repeated in at least two of the manuals. Consolidating them would lessen the redundancy, and make the manuals as easy to use as the test.

Review of the Test of Variables of Attention by SUSAN C. WHISTON, Professor, Department of Educational Psychology, University of Nevada, Las Vegas, NV, and HARRISON KANE, Assistant Professor, Department of Special Education, University of Nevada, Las Vegas, NV:

The Test of Variables of Attention (T.O.V.A.) is a set of standardized individually administered instruments designed to assess attention in children and adults. There are two assessments, the T.O.V.A. (visual version) and the T.O.V.A.-A (auditory version). Both instruments are computerized continuous performance tests (CPTs) that are designed to: (a) assess attention, (b) screen for disorders of attention, (c) assist in the diagnosis of attention disorders, (d) predict medication responses, (e) titrate medication dosage, and (f) monitor treatment over time. This review will focus on evaluating the T.O.V.A. instruments from a diagnostic and psychological interventions perspective.

In both the T.O.V.A. and the T.O.V.A.-A, individuals respond to a non-language-based stimuli using a standardized external microswitch. In the T.O.V.A., individuals distinguish between two geometric shapes, whereas in the T.O.V.A.-A the stimuli are two discernible tones. In both tests, the examinee presses the microswitch when the target stimulus is presented and refrains when the nontarget stimulus is provided. The visual test (T.O.V.A.) is available for both Macintosh and IBM/IBM-compatible computers, whereas the auditory test (T.O.V.A.-A) is only available for the IBM/IBM-compatible computers. The PC requirements are for a 286 processor or better, 1MB of available hard drive, and a parallel (printer) port. The T.O.V.A. tests require some hardware installation (e.g., microswitch, external speakers) that will vary depending on the computer being used. We had some difficulty installing the program using a comparatively new machine because the software programs appear somewhat outdated. For example, the software could not identify the sound card in the machine and, thus, required the installation of the Speaker Driver and external speakers. The programs require the use of MS-DOS (5.0 and up preferred) and the user needs to exit Windows and use MS-DOS mode. The continued use of MS-DOS for T.O.V.A. and T.O.V.A.-A can also cause printing problems, as many newer printers are no longer MS-DOS compatible. Users are provided with a phone number for technical support and, in our experience, these individuals were helpful in getting around outdated software problems.

The T.O.V.A. and the T.O.V.A.-A are designed to measure attention and impulse control in normal and clinical populations. There are two alternatives for scoring and interpretation: the Screening Version and the Clinical Version. The Screening Version includes information similar to that for the Clinical Version, but the printouts are formatted to reflect a screening focus as compared to a clinical diagnosis or treatment monitoring assessment. Purchasing scoring services is required, although there is an optional "self" report that provides qualified interpreters with raw data. There are nine variables used in interpretation, with the first five being of primary importance.

1. Errors of Omission (failure to respond to target stimuli) are considered a measure of inattention.

2. Errors of Commission (responding to nontarget stimuli) are considered to be a measure of impulsivity or disinhibition.

3. Response Time (time to respond correctly to the target) is designed to measure processing speed.

4. Response Time Variability (the standard deviation of the correct response times) is proposed to be the most important measure as those with attention deficits tend to stay focused at first but become less focused as the assessment progresses.

5. ADHD Score involves comparing the subject's performance to an identified ADHD sample's performance.

6. Post-Commission Response Time (average time the subject took after committing a commission error) is designed to differentiate between individuals with ADHD and children with conduct disorders.

7. Anticipatory Responses (responding to the stimuli before it can be differentiated) are considered one measure of test validity.

8. Multiple Responses (subject presses microswitch more than once) is considered a reflection of neurological status.

9. d´ or Response Sensitivity (ratio of the hit rate to false alarm rate) is designed to measure the rate of deterioration of performance over time.

The normative sample is not representative of minority populations with the majority (99%) of individuals tested being Caucasian. The generalizability of the sample is further compromised by geographic limitations, as both the children and adult samples consisted of individuals only from Minnesota. In order to be sensitive to developmental differences, there are year-by-year norms for each gender for children 4–19 years of age on the T.O.V.A. and 6–19 years of age for the T.O.V.A.-A. The normative group is considered representative of the normal population and children were excluded based on scores on a behavioral ratings scale, current use of psychoactive medications, or receiving Special Education services. There are a total of 1,911 children in the T.O.V.A. normative group and 2,551 children in the T.O.V.A. sample. The adult sample for the T.O.V.A., however, is not as large with only 250 subjects who are 20 years and older. There is no adult normative sample currently available for the T.O.V.A.-A Hence, clinicians making diagnostic decisions based on T.O.V.A. results from adults or children of diverse ethnic backgrounds need to consider the limitations of the current normative sample.

The authors of T.O.V.A. and T.O.V.A.-A claim that typical methods of calculating reliability (e.g., Cronbach alpha, split half) are a questionable estimate for timed tasks and instead used Pearson Product Moment correlations. For example, they correlated scores on Omission, Commission, Response time, Response Time Variability, and D Prime for Quarters 1 and 2, Quarters 3 and 4, and Quarter 1 with half 1 scores. The reliability estimates presented in the manual were all internal measures of consistency. There are some variations in coefficients depending on whether the analysis is over the first half of the assessment where the stimulus is presented infrequently or over the second half where the stimulus is presented frequently. Concerning the reliability of the T.O.V.A., the range for coefficients for Omission scores were from .72 to .93 (Professional manual, Version 7.0, 1996). The reliability estimates for Commission scores were from .71 to .96, whereas estimates for Response Time were .89 to .99. The range for reliability coefficients was similar for Response Time Variability (i.e., .70 to .94). The lowest reliability coefficients concerned D Prime, with correlations ranging from .52 to .99. T.O.V.A.-A reliability coefficients were similar to T.O.V.A. results, with the Omission range from .73 to .99. The range of correlations for Commission scores was from .71 to .97. The ranges for Response Time and Response Time Variability were .85 to .99 and .87 to .99, respectively. Once again, the coefficients were somewhat lower for D Prime scores with a range from .63 to .97. Although the magnitudes of the correlation coefficients are generally acceptable, the lack of data concerning test-retest coefficients is problematic, particularly because the instruments are designed for repeated measures to evaluate the effects of medications and other treatments. Hagin and Bella (1998), in an earlier review of the T.O.V.A., also noted the problematic nature of the lack of stability evidence and test-retest analyses.

The focus of the validation evidence presented concerns the T.O.V.A. and T.O.V.A.-A's abilities to differentiate ADHD subjects from the normal population. There is a beginning of validation evidence for the T.O.V.A., but the validity evidence for the T.O.V.A.-A is minimal. The validation evidence in the professional manual indicated that those in nonclinical settings (e.g., schools or work places) should use a cutoff point of 1.94 on the T.O.V.A. Using this cutoff point resulted in 72% of the ADHD subjects being correctly classified and 85% of the normals being correctly classified. The professional manual also cited a study performed using Receiver Operator Characteristic Analysis, which showed that 80% of both the ADHD subjects and normal subjects were correctly classified. The manual contains some preliminary evidence that supports the use of the T.O.V.A. in differential diagnostic decisions; however, this initial evidence only distinguishes between ADHD, Undifferentiated ADD, and Conduct Disordered. In addition, Forbes (1998) found that using a cutoff score of 1.5 standard deviations above the mean for any of the T.O.V.A. variables resulted in correctly identifying 80% of the sample with attention deficit disorders and 72% of the sample with other disorders. The validation evidence also included factor analytic results; however, we questioned the legitimacy of the factor analyses of scores based on the interdependency of the variables. Concerns about the factor analytic analysis are particularly noteworthy regarding the T.O.V.A.-A, as these results provided most of the validity evidence for the auditory version. Another concern regarding the validity information presented in the manual was the lack of evidence concerning the efficacy of the T.O.V.A. and T.O.V.A.-A in the titration of medication.

SUMMARY. The T.O.V.A. is one of the older and better known CPTs. The addition of the auditory assessment, the T.O.V.A.-A, complements and strengthens the T.O.V.A.'s assessment of attention deficits. These computerized, individually administered assessments are non-language-based, which may lessen the confounding effect of language processing skills on CPT performance (Forbes, 1998). Although both instruments have limitations, the authors have begun to develop potentially sound instruments that assess attention deficits. In the Clinical Guide, the authors (Greenberg & Kindschi) stress that neither the T.O.V.A. nor the T.O.V.A.-A should be used in isolation, but rather integrated into comprehensive evaluation that includes psycho-social history, behavioral ratings, observations, and other assessments. The use of multiple sources of information seems particularly important given the limitations noted in the validation evidence of the T.O.V.A. and the T.O.V.A.-A. In particular, the T.O.V.A.-A should be used cautiously because of the limited validity evidence and the lack of adult norms. The developers also should consider updating the software to make it more compatible with current hardware and technologies (e.g., Internet-based assessments).

REVIEWERS' REFERENCES
Forbes, G. B. (1998). Clinical utility of the Test of Variables of Attention (TOVA) in the diagnosis of attention-deficit/hyperactivity disorder. *Journal of Clinical Psychology, 54,* 461–476.
Hagin, R. A., & Bella, P. D. (1998). [Review of the Test of Variables of Attention.] In J. C. Impara & B. S. Plake (Eds.), *The thirteenth mental measurements yearbook* (pp. 1058–1060). Lincoln, NE: Buros Institute of Mental Measurements.

[395]
Test of Visual-Motor Integration.

Purpose: Constructed as "a standardized norm-referenced test of visual-motor integration."
Population: Ages 4 through 17.
Publication Date: 1996.
Acronym: TVMI.
Scores: Total score only.
Administration: Individual or group.
Price Data, 2001: $116 per complete kit including manual (75 pages) and 50 summary/response forms in storage box; $69 per 50 summary/response forms; $49 per manual.
Time: (20) minutes.
Authors: Donald D. Hammill, Nils A. Pearson, and Judith K. Voress.
Publisher: PRO-ED.
Cross References: See T5:2722 (1 reference).

Review of the Test of Visual-Motor Integration by DEBORAH ERICKSON, Director of Clinical Psychology, University of Sydney, Sydney, Australia:

The Test of Visual-Motor Integration (TVMI) is designed to assess "the ability to relate visual stimuli to motor responses in an accurate, appropriate manner" (p. 1). This is the definition given by the authors for visual-motor integration, which is also referred to as visual-motor association. The focus of this test is upon examining how a child interprets, organizes, and replicates the physical elements of a stimuli. Therefore, the TVMI test comprises 30 geometric figures administered to the child in an 11-page booklet with six figures in boxes on each page. The designs are to be copied by a child directly beneath the original picture. Depending upon the child's age, ability to reproduce the figures accurately, and speed of the child on a pencil/paper task, the test could take 15 to 30 minutes.

Copying visual figures has often been used as a reflection of how a child perceives a stimulus and examiners sometimes conclude that this assessment process predicts how a child will perceive other visual stimuli such as letters and numbers. Although numerous studies indicate a low correlation between visual-motor perception tests and school achievement tests, deficits in visual motor integration can interfere with the performance of important adaptive skills such as running, tracing, copying, writing, etc. Concluding that tests of visual-motor integration require considerable visual-perceptual ability and therefore yield valid information about an individual's perceptual abilities seems intuitively sensible. However, the authors of the TVMI have clearly articulated the cautions and the use of this test (and other acceptable tests like it such as the Developmental Test of Visual-Motor Integration [MVI; Beery, 1989; 119] and the Test of Visual-Motor Skills [TVMS; Gardner, 1986]). This reviewer would recommend that all beginning examiners (regardless of whether they use this test or the other tests mentioned) read pages 1–4 (introduction), 32–35 (interpretation action), and 46–48 (validity section) in the TVMI test manual for an excellent summary of cautions and uses of visual-motor tests.

The VMI and TVMS have been used successfully in the assessment process to document potential visual-motor difficulties in children and thereby develop effective intervention programs. The TVMI is a valuable addition to the options available for assessing visual-motor integration due to its excellent test development and construction. The normative sample and evidence for test reliability and validity is thoroughly explained and detailed with excellent reference to theory, other similar tests, and other types of assessment such as for intelligence and academic achievement.

The administration and scoring section is clear and easy to follow. The challenge, as with all visual-motor tests, is to score a student's drawing appropriately. The TVMI gives three examples of a 0-, 1-, 2-, and 3-point response for every stimulus. In addition, there is a description of each item gestalt with a general set of rubrics for all drawings. The interpretation section is clearly articulated with appropriate cautions and conclusions examined. Scores can be reported in age equivalents (with a section cautioning examiners about the problem with using age equivalents), percentiles, and standard scores.

In the standardization section, the authors detail the demographic characteristics of the sample and evidence that the sample is representative of the United States of America in regard to gender, residence, race, geographic region, ethnicity, family income, education level of parents, and age. The normative data were collected from 2,478 children residing in 13 states.

Reliability evidence, the extent to which test scores are due to real differences or to chance errors, is thoroughly described in the manual. Again, excellent cautions and explanations about reliability measures are given throughout the chapter on test reliability. Methods of evidencing reliability included content sampling, time sampling, and interscorer comparisons. The content sampling method reported with a Cronbach's coefficient alpha method for computing item correlations with each other yielded a mean alpha of .91. A coefficient of .80 is considered minimally acceptable and coefficients exceeding .90 are considered desirable. The time sampling method used to examine the extent to which test scores are consistent over time was measured using a test-retest technique yielding a 2-week stability correlation reported as .80. An interscorer comparison scoring 40 completed protocols yields a coefficient of .96. Overall, scores from the TVMI appear to be reliable.

The validity section is necessary to document that a test measures what it is supposed to measure. The TVMI manual examines content, criterion-related, and construct validity. Content validity is essential in the development of the items as this investigates the degree to which the test content covers a representative sample of the domain to be assessed. Selection of items was somewhat unclear in that a number of figures were taken from other visual-motor tests, without explanation as to why those particular figures were taken instead of other figures. Item analysis was performed with items satisfying the item discrimination criteria used and other less appropriate items deleted. In addition, an item bias method was performed to assure that all test items are fair for all groups represented in the normative sample. No item bias was evidenced through this statistical analysis. Criterion-related validity comparing another acceptable measure having similar purposes as the TVMI (concurrent validity) was reported. Criterion-related validity to predict the future performance of a student (predictive validity) was not reported. It would be an asset for the total validation section to eventually include predictive validity about this test. The concurrent validity of the TVMI was evidenced through the correlation of TVMI scores with the total scores of the Motor-Free Visual Perception Test (MVPT; Colarusso & Hammill, 1972) and the Developmental Test of Visual-Motor Integration (VMI; Beery, 1989). The coefficients were .67 and .95 respectively, which would be as expected. The TVMI correlates higher with the VMI because they both assess visual-motor integration through copying figures and the MVPT is a motor-reduced test. Construct validity examining the theoretical model upon which the test is based was described through articulation of five basic constructs about visual-motor integration.

SUMMARY. The TVMI is a valuable addition to the options available for the assessment of visual-motor perception. The TVMI can be used with confidence to screen for children with visual-motor integration problems. The challenge in assessing visual perception is discriminating between visual perception difficulties due to motoric involvement, sensory acuity deficits, and/or cognitive processing deficits. As cautioned in the manual, a comprehensive evaluation should include assessment of visual perception through tasks that require motor-involvement such as the TVMI and tests that do not require motor-involvement as well as a full assessment battery to examine cognitive processing aspects. Examiners should also be

sure that a referral to appropriate eye-care professionals (e.g., optometrists or ophthalmologists) indicates adequate sensory acuity. In addition, an authentic assessment process of observing a child in her or his own environment is necessary to support any diagnosis of a visual perception deficit. It is important to discern when a child is having difficulty in any facet of visual perception in order to plan the most appropriate special intervention program. In summary, the TVMI is an extremely well-constructed test with a clearly articulated manual and will be a welcome addition to the field when used appropriately for assessing visual-motor integration.

REVIEWER'S REFERENCES
Colarusso, R., & Hammill, D. D. (1972). Motor-Free Visual Perception Test. Novato, CA: Academic Therapy Publications.
Gardner, M. F. (1986). Test of Visual-Motor Skills. San Francisco: Psychological and Educational Publications.
Beery, K. (1989). Developmental Test of Visual-Motor Integration. Cleveland: Modern Curriculum Press.

[396]
Tests of Achievement and Proficiency, Forms K, L, and M.

Purpose: Designed to "provide a comprehensive and objective measure of students' progress in a high school curriculum."

Population: Grades 9–12.

Publication Dates: 1978–1996.

Acronym: TAP.

Forms, 3: K, L, M; 2 batteries: Complete and Survey.

Administration: Group.

Levels, 4: 15, 16, 17, 18.

Price Data, 1999: $17 per 25 practice test booklets including 1 directions for administration; $3 per practice test directions for administration; $7 per Preparing for Testing with the Tests of Achievement and Proficiency; $98 per 25 Form K or L Complete Battery reusable test booklets including 1 directions for administration; $12.50 per Forms K and L Complete Battery directions for administration; $98 per 25 Form K or L Survey Battery reusable test booklets including 1 directions for administration; $12.50 per Forms K and L Survey Battery directions for administration; $98 per 25 Form M Complete Battery reusable test booklets including 1 directions for administration; $12.50 per Form M Complete Battery directions for administration; $98 per 25 Form M Survey Battery reusable test booklets including 1 directions for administration; $12.50 per Form M Survey Battery directions for administration; $52 per 50 Forms K and 1 Listening Assessment answer documents including 1 directions for administration and score interpretation; $10 per Forms K and L Listening Assessment directions for administration and score interpretation; $44 per 50 Form M Listening Assessment answer documents including 1 directions of administration and score interpretation; $9.50 per Form M Listening Assessment directions for administration and score interpretation; $99 per Form K Complete Battery Braille Edition test, Braille administration notes, and supplement to the directions for administration; $118 per Form K Survey Battery Braille Edition test, Braille administration notes, and supplement to the direction for administration; $60 per Form K Complete Battery large-print edition including test booklet and general instructions for testing visually impaired students; $42 per Form K Survey Battery large-print edition including test booklet and general instructions for testing visually impaired students; $38 per 50 Forms K and L Complete Battery answer documents; $35 per 50 Forms K and L Survey Battery answer documents; $38 per 50 Form M Complete Battery answer documents; $35 per 50 Form M Survey Battery answer documents; $1,260 per 1,500 Forms K and L Complete Battery continuous-form answer documents; $1,260 per 1,500 Forms K and L Survey Battery continuous-form answer documents; $31 per 25 Form M Survey Battery easy-score answer documents including 1 class record folder; $25 per scoring key; $50 per Forms K and L Complete Battery scoring masks; $50 per Form M Complete Battery scoring masks; $44 per Complete Battery norms and score conversions booklet; $44 per Survey Battery norms and score conversions booklet; $47 per special norms booklets (large city, Catholic, high socioeconomic, international, or low socioeconomic); $120 per Forms K and L keyscore norm look-up software including program disk (3.5-inch) and user's guide; $6 per 5 class record folders (specify form); $9.50 per 25 student profile charts (specify form); $10 per 25 profile charts for averages; $16 per interpretive guide (Form M, '96, 140 pages; Forms K and L, '93, 149 pages) for teachers and counselors; $26 per interpretive guide for school administrators; $15 per 25 report to students and parents; $15 per 25 reporte para estudiantes y padres; $26 per content classifications with item norms booklets; $25 per Technical Summary 1.

Special Editions: Braille and large-print editions available.

Authors: Dale P. Scannell, Oscar M. Haugh, Brenda H. Loyd, and C. Frederick Risinger.

Publisher: Riverside Publishing.

a) COMPLETE BATTERY.

Scores, 15: Vocabulary, Reading Comprehension, Written Expression, Math Concepts and Problem Solving, Math Computation [optional], Social Studies, Science, Information Processing, Reading Total, Math Total, Core Total, Composite, plus Advance Skills Scores for reading, language, and mathematics.

Time: (255) minutes; (275) minutes with optional test.

b) SURVEY BATTERY.

Scores, 10: Reading (Vocabulary, Comprehension, Total), Written Expression, Math Concepts and Problem Solving, Math Computation [optional], Total, plus Advanced Skills Scores for reading, language, and mathematics.

Time: (90) minutes; (100) minutes with optional test.

Cross References: See T5:2735 (1 reference), T4:2810 (1 reference), and 11:445 (4 references); for a review by Elaine Clark of Forms G and H, see 10:375 (2 references); for reviews by John M. Keene, Jr. and James L. Wardrop of an earlier form, see 9:1282.

Review of the Tests of Achievement and Proficiency, Forms K, L, and M by SUSAN M. BROOKHART, Associate Professor, School of Education, Duquesne University, Pittsburgh, PA:

The Tests of Achievement and Proficiency (TAP) are part of the Riverside Integrated Assessment Program that also includes the Iowa Tests of Basic Skills (ITBS; T5:1318), the Iowa Tests of Educational Development (ITED; T5:1319), and the Cognitive Abilities Test (CogAT; T5:560). The ITBS measures basic skills for students in Grades K through 8, the ITED measures skills important for continued learning in adult life for students in Grades 9 through 12; the TAP measures skills commonly emphasized in the secondary school curriculum for students in Grades 9 through 12; and the CogAT measures cognitive abilities for students in Grades K through 12. The ITBS, ITED, and TAP were standardized and scaled in the same series of studies. Therefore, school districts that use the ITBS may use either the TAP or ITED for their secondary school students, depending on what kind of information they desire. A useful feature of this continuity is the availability of developmental standard scores (SS) on the same scale for all grades.

TESTS AND MATERIALS. Four levels (15 through 18) of Forms K, L, and M are available, for Grades 9 through 12, respectively. Two versions, a Complete Battery and a Survey Battery, are available. The Complete Battery takes more than twice as long to administer as the Survey Battery; the major difference is the inclusion of subtests in Science, Social Studies, and Information Processing (see the test description above for complete lists of the scores associated with each battery). The Complete Battery also composes a

Life Skills score based on a subset of the more practically oriented items, such as those dealing with extracting information from a newspaper or using mathematical reasoning in everyday life.

The booklets for the TAP student test batteries are well designed. The print is large, illustrations are clear, and two-color printing helps present the content well. There is plenty of white space, the pages are not cluttered, and page turns are in logical places. Practice tests for students follow the same format. Booklets for parents include sample test items.

Supporting materials for school personnel are also well designed. The manuals have been redesigned for Form K, L, and M in a manner that parallels the recent redesign of the ITBS manuals. Previous versions included both technical and administrative material in a daunting *Manual for School Administrators*. The present version includes two very helpful manuals, the *Interpretive Guide for School Administrators*, and the *Interpretive Guide for Teachers and Counselors*. These guides contain materials that would be useful for the kinds of tasks administrators, teachers, and counselors actually perform. One of the best features of these manuals is the inclusion in each of an extensive set of samples, explanations, and potential uses for each kind of score report. This reviewer recommends that schools and districts that use the TAP buy multiple copies of these interpretive guides and make them widely available to professional staff members, so as to maximize their use.

The technical data have been removed to a series of manuals, Technical Summary I, Technical Summary I Supplement, and Norms and Score Conversions with Technical Information for the various forms of the TAP. These technical manuals are well indexed and clear. A *Research Handbook*, in preparation, will complete the available technical information; its table of contents indicates that it will contain valuable information about TAP development, norming and scaling, reliability, and validity.

Both the Complete and Survey Batteries include a questionnaire asking students about future plans, current study habits, library use, and the like. In the sample tests provided to this reviewer, all forms of both batteries included this questionnaire only in Levels 17 and 18, for Grades 11 and 12. The manuals and accompanying materials implied that the questionnaires would be

available at all levels, and indeed "Questionnaire" was listed on the contents pages of the tests at Levels 15 and 16. The sample reports in the Interpretive Guides for both School Administrators and Teachers and Counselors include example questionnaire data from ninth graders taking Form 15. So the omission of the questionnaire in the test materials is curious.

Supplemental assessments in Listening and Writing are available, and the table of contents of the *Research Handbook* in preparation also refers to a Constructed Response Supplement for the TAP. These supplemental tests and their technical documentation were not provided for review. Therefore, this reviewer is not able to comment beyond noting that, assuming appropriate validity and reliability evidence, such supplements might provide useful information for some of the individual and group purposes of the TAP.

NORMS. The TAP Forms K and L were published in 1993, and TAP Form M was published in 1996. Norming data were obtained in 1992 and 1995 from well-described, nationally representative samples of schools. In the 1995 studies, Form M was equated to Form K, and 1995 norms were calculated for all three forms. Users may use either the 1992 or 1995 norms. Mathematics norms are calculated for students taking the tests both with and without calculators. Separate norms are available for fall, midyear, and spring administrations and for specific populations: Catholic/Private, Large City, International, High Socio-Economic Status, and Low Socio-Economic Status Schools. This reviewer encourages users to take advantage of this information, especially for purposes such as reviewing the effectiveness of school curriculum. This will require a little extra work on the part of school administrators, counselors, and teachers, because the individual and class score reports are printed with national percentile ranks.

The TAP yields a variety of scores and score reports. Norm-referenced and criterion-referenced scores are available. Reports can be prepared with various units of analysis in mind: for individuals, classes, and buildings. School norms are available for building level analyses. The *Interpretive Guide for School Administrators* includes a helpful section on Selecting Score Reports, suggesting which reports would be best for different purposes and different roles (e.g., teacher, principal). This reviewer recommends that users pay more attention to norm-referenced scores and interpretations than to criterion-referenced ones. Most of the design and statistical analysis for the TAP has been aimed at creating a state-of-the-art norm-referenced test, so that is what it should do best. Besides, the "criteria" for the criterion-referencing are general categories of items (e.g., "real numbers") and the subsets of items are relatively short. However, any of the scores or reports the TAP yields can be useful to educators if the information is matched to an intended purpose or decision, especially if used in combinations with additional appropriate sources of information.

VALIDITY. The publisher claims that TAP content has been selected to assess progress toward widely accepted secondary school curriculum goals. Content validity is carefully documented. For each form, items are classified according to content. Content categories include both simple knowledge and more complex cognitive activities such as making inferences or interpretations from written material. This reviewer spot-checked a sample of the items and agrees that they indeed tap the intended content and cognition categories. In addition to such logical and content review, a panel of experts reviewed the items for the appearance of bias.

The test manuals carefully and wisely point out, in several places, that the ultimate content validity review must rest with the school or district that uses that test. The information is available for school or district committees to review the item content for its coordination with valued local curriculum goals. Test users should exercise this responsibility before selecting the TAP. This reviewer agrees that content validity is of utmost importance for a test like the TAP.

Purposes for using TAP scores are listed as studying individual student and class strengths and weaknesses, studying student progress through the high school curriculum, planning instruction, selecting areas for remedial and enrichment activities, and revising courses of study and instructional activities (*Technical Summary I*, p. 32). These purposes, rephrased but essentially the same in meaning, are restated in the *Interpretive Guide for Teachers and Counselors* (p. 7) and in the *Interpretive Guide for School Administrators* (pp. 6–7). In these guides, three inappropriate purposes for using TAP scores are also listed (p. 7); "to judge the secondary school curriculum," "to encourage or discourage students from seeking formal education beyond high school," and "to steer students into certain career choices." It is not clear to this reviewer what the effective difference would be between "reviewing the overall effectiveness of the curriculum" or "revise courses of study and instructional activities," listed as appropriate purposes, and "to judge the secondary school curriculum" listed as an inappropriate purpose. In any case, some validity studies specifically targeted to the list of uses would strengthen the case for using the TAP for its intended purposes.

The publisher did provide some statistical evidence of construct validity in the *Manual for School Administrators* for Forms G and H, received by this reviewer with the publisher's note that this material will soon be updated and included in the new *Research Handbook* for Forms K, L, and M. This evidence included intercorrelations among standard scores for the TAP and correlations between TAP scores and CogAt scores, both of which featured expected patterns. For example, the correlation between CogAT Verbal scores and TAP Reading Comprehension scores is .78 or .79, compared with .69 or .70 with the TAP Mathematics score, whereas the opposite pattern obtains for the CogAT Quantitative score. As the reader can see, all of these correlations are high enough to suggest that a general academic achievement construct may underlie them. For a sample of four high schools, correlations of TAP scores with course grades, grade-point averages, and ACT and SAT scores are given. Correlations with grades are moderate as expected, higher for the relationships with other tests (ACT and SAT).

RELIABILITY. Reliability evidence is well reported in the TAP materials. All in all, the nature and quality of the reliability evidence presented is a strength of the TAP.

KR-20s and standard errors of measurement are reported for each form, level, and subscale. The KR-20 values are mostly between .85 and .95, with a few values above or below that range. The Mathematics Advanced Skills scale has consistently low KR-20 values, with many forms falling below .80. This may be explained by the difficulty of the test, where 10% to 20% of examinees, depending on the level and time of year, score below chance on this subtests; this is the only subtest reporting a consistent floor effect of this nature across forms and levels.

Several other kinds of statistical evidence for reliability are reported. Equivalent forms reliability estimates are given, based on data from a sample of examinees who took both the Complete and Survey Batteries. These values range from .52 to .97, with most falling in the .60 to .90 range for subtests and above .90 for the Math and Reading composites and total scores. Score-level standard errors of measurement are reported for standard scores. The reliabilities of differences among TAP scores are reported in the *Manual for School Administrators* for Forms G and H, in the material that the publisher claims will be updated soon for Forms K, L, and M.

SUMMARY. The TAP is a reliable indicator of basic academic skills commonly emphasized in the secondary school curriculum. It was normed and scaled on a nationally representative sample and provides information that, on the basis of the evidence presented in a wide array of manuals, is appropriate for the purposes of interpreting both individual and curricular strengths and weaknesses. The tests themselves are well designed; well-intentioned students should have no trouble understanding what is called for and doing their best.

In the opinion of this reviewer, the publisher has accomplished its intention with the redesigned manuals and companion materials. For Forms G and H, technical material was mixed with material for administrators in one manual. For Forms K, L, and M, separating the two has allowed for the presentation of more comprehensive technical material on the one hand and more useful, appropriately written material for administrators, teachers, and school counselors on the other. This reviewer encourages users of the TAP to take full advantage of all available material to reap for their schools and districts the maximum benefits of the information the TAP can provide because the scores themselves are only as good as the purposes they help users accomplish.

Review of the Tests of Achievement and Proficiency, Forms K, L, and M by DARRELL L. SABERS, Professor of Educational Psychology, University of Arizona, Tucson, AZ:

The Tests of Achievement and Proficiency (TAP), Forms K, L, and M, replace the earlier versions G and H. Forms K and L were published in 1993; Form M in 1996. These three forms make up the latest edition of TAP, which is part of the integrated assessment system of The Riverside Publishing Company that also includes the Iowa Tests of Basic Skills (ITBS; T5:1318), the Iowa Tests of Educational Development (ITED; T5:1319), and the Cognitive Abilities Test (CogAT; T5:560). Also available as part of this system are listening assessments, Iowa writing assessments, and performance assessments. Excluding the CogAT, the three achievement tests are also referred to as the Iowa Tests, although some documents referring to the integrated assessment system (also called Riverside 2000 assessment series) do not include information about the CogAT. A thorough review of the TAP requires examining material pertaining to the other aspects of the series; however, this review is intended to focus only on the TAP.

Forms K, L, and M of the TAP are published in two booklet formats: a Complete Battery and a Survey Battery. The Survey Battery consists of short tests (30 minutes each) in Reading, Written Expression, Math Concepts and Problem Solving, and Math Computation (optional). The Survey Battery is not comparable to the "basic battery" of previous forms; rather, the basic battery has been replaced by a scoring option (called the Core Battery), which consists of full-length Complete Battery tests in Reading, Language, and mathematics. The Core Battery is ignored in the rest of this review; the comments will apply to both the Complete and Survey Battery.

The TAP are multiple-choice tests intended to assess basic academic skills relevant to the curriculum for Grades 9–12. The authors make it clear that their definition of basic skills includes thinking skills necessary for academic success; thus the tests do not include an abundance of factual questions. The best evidence of the level of thinking required to answer the items can be obtained by the reader who "takes" the test personally. The potential user is encouraged to examine the content of the items in any achievement test prior to selection; such as examination provides better information than viewing the classification of item content. The exercise of taking the TAP should be an enjoyable one for the potential user, because the selections in the tests constitute interesting reading and the items are of very high quality. Item content information is contained in the booklet "Content Classifications with Item Norms" that describes the content and process intended to be measured by each item. Also in that booklet are *p*-values for each item for fall, midyear, and spring for the Complete and Survey Batteries. The *Interpretive Guide for Teachers and Counselors* provides an overview of the domain of the test and classifies the content and process of each item. One or more of these different ways to describe the relevance of the items should provide a user-friendly examination of the content. How well the collection of items in the tests represents a school's curriculum must be judged by local personnel.

Forms K, L, and M of the TAP continue the tradition of the TAP forms reviewed previously, and all of the praises and most of the cautions mentioned in those reviews (9:1282 & 10:375) apply to the new forms as well. Strengths include sound procedures for test development and standardization, well-written test materials that emphasize application of knowledge and skills rather than specific content, and clear presentation of information to the potential user. Although adequate technical data are available for the subtest and total scores, there are no adequate data to support the scores derived from items selected across subtests or for "criterion-referenced" scores. Any element deemed to be a shortcoming of the TAP is likely to be a shortcoming in any competing test battery.

One tradition the current forms continue is the multilevel nature of the TAP. Items from each level can be found in an adjacent level within a form, although separate booklets are provided for each grade. The advantage of the overlap is evident in the added amount of information available from students in adjacent grades who have taken the same items. The Survey Battery contains items found in the Complete Battery; this overlap should create no problem as there is not likely to be any user who would use both batteries for students at the same level.

The norms for the series were made more current by an advantageous combination of standardization sample data and information from users. Typically user norms are suspect, because users may differ systematically from schools in general. However, in the case of the TAP, norms that were originally obtained from a large, well-documented, carefully chosen national sample were adjusted based on the amount of change found in user norms. The assumption was made that the users do not differ substantially from the original sample in how much their students grow each year. If the tests were really used to modify and improve instruction, this assumption might be very questionable. Reviewers may disagree on the extent to which the above assumption is justified, but there should be agreement that the combination process is better than employing user norms (and it is unreasonable to expect a national standardization every few years). Potential users who worry about meeting psychometric assumptions will likely approve the traditional statistical techniques used in the development of the TAP.

The norms for the TAP are exemplary in that there are norms for many different populations and for school averages. The interpretation guides give a good explanation of the need for school norms and of the difference between building and system norms. Given the current misuse of pupil norms for reporting school standings that is prevalent in the press, this explanation might be helpful to school personnel presenting scores to the public.

Something new to the TAP is the way grade equivalents (GEs) are reported. The ITBS and TAP now use the decimal between the year and month; in this respect they report GEs like everyone else does. This improvement is relatively unimportant for the TAP because GEs are not useful at the high school level; perhaps it is another sign that there are becoming fewer differences among the major test batteries.

There is an abundance of validity information for the series, although it may not be easy to locate. Because TAP information is relevant to other tests, that information might be found in places where the potential TAP user would not look. In making most relevant information available to different user groups, the author teams have created many separate documents. How advantageous this proliferation of documents becomes will depend on the user; it is likely that what makes the TAP difficult to review comprehensively might also make it much easier for school personnel to use because each individual will read only those documents of interest. Because content is the most important category of validity evidence for an achievement test, examining the Content Classifications With Item Norms and taking the test will provide sufficient validity information to the user. After selecting the test, the user would be well advised to read the *Interpretive Guide for Teachers and Counselors*, which includes a good section on common misunderstandings about scores.

The *Interpretive Guide for Teachers and Counselors* suggests that a class average should be interpreted as the score for a typical student; this appears to misrepresent the meaning of the average (mean). Would a counselor use this wording with a student or parent who is familiar with the correct interpretation? The example on page 55 suggests that the typical student in the class would have the same pattern of scores as the class average, but there may be no student in the class who would have a pattern similar to that shown by the average scores. No evidence supporting this interpretation is found in the material reviewed. Granted this is a minor point, but misinterpretation of test scores is identified as a concern of the TAP authors.

The interpretive guides present clear descriptions of the many scores available for the TAP. There are clear directions for score conversions that should enhance users' understanding of the relationships among scores; these directions and score descriptions are found in enough documents to be easily accessible to individuals who read only the particular document intended for their use.

The massive amount of technical information includes data on longitudinal growth, floor and ceiling effects, and score level standard errors of measurement. The growth data provide a comparison of norm groups for the years 1985, 1988, and 1992 but do not relate to the stability of the TAP. Reliability data are extensive, with standard errors presented as raw scores or as standard scores, and internal consistency data provided for fall and spring testing. Higher order thinking items are expected to produce slightly lower reliability estimates than factual items, but there is ample evidence that the scores produced by the TAP continue to be highly reliable. Naturally, the Complete Battery is more reliable than the Survey Battery because each test is longer, and total scores are more reliable for the same reason.

SUMMARY. It is clear that the TAP are among the best of the high school testing batteries. A major complaint about all of the batteries is that the goal of improving instruction is not likely to be met because their content is not the content of high school courses—perhaps that is why no validity data are provided to support the major intended use of the batteries: To improve instruction. Supporters of the batteries can point to the items in the batteries and contend that the proficiencies measured by the tests are desirable

outcomes of schooling. The TAP will not satisfy those who want the content to be organized like high school courses, but may satisfy those who want academic proficiencies measured. No high school test battery is likely to be better, but one might be found that is different enough in content to satisfy potential users. The Riverside 2000 series contains one such competitor, the ITED—different, but not necessarily better. The TAP are an excellent choice for those schools looking for a norm-referenced achievement test battery.

[397]
Tiffany Control Scales.

Purpose: Designed to evaluate personality problems related to one's experience of control across different situations.

Population: Adolescents and adults.

Publication Dates: 1985–1999.

Acronym: TCS.

Scores, 16: Control from Self/Internal, Control over Self, Control over the Environment, Control from the Environment, Coping Index, Passive/Assertive/Aggressive Index, Extratensive/Intratensive Index, Repression, Expressive, Self-Directed, Non-Self-Directed, and 5 other measures.

Administration: Individual or group.

Editions, 2: Paper and pencil, computer administered.

Price Data, 1998: $12.50 per 25 paper and pencil tests; $695.95 per computer edition, unlimited use; $50 per limited use edition (5 uses); demo and sample report are free; $25 per test for mail-in scoring; $19.95 per manual ('99, 83 pages).

Time: [20] minutes for Standard TCS; varies when customized.

Comments: For research or clinical use or in employment screening; may be customized to fit examiner's needs; self-rating instrument; scoring and interpretation by computer.

Authors: Donald W. Tiffany and Phyllis G. Tiffany.

Publisher: Psychological Growth Associates, Inc.

Cross Reference: See T5:2759 (1 reference).

Review of the Tiffany Control Scales by BRIAN F. BOLTON, University Professor, Department of Rehabilitation Education and Research, University of Arkansas, Fayetteville, AR:

The Tiffany Control Scales (TCS) is a self-report inventory designed to measure various aspects of experienced control. The authors' concept of control is described as the subjectively experienced operations that actuate, regulate, or inhibit an individual's psychological functioning. Three features of the authors' Experienced Control Theory are that it is phenomenologically oriented, concerned with intrapersonal and interpersonal life events, and addresses self-directed and non-self-directed determinants of behavior.

The authors state that the TCS may be used to evaluate personality problems in the area of control across any situations in any culture. The inventory may be administered in paper-and-pencil format or via computer. The computer version generates a two-page narrative report followed by 10 pages of scores and profiles. The TCS report is advertised as a supplement to traditional personality assessment in diagnosing problems in the area of situational control. Suggested applications include individual counseling, marital counseling, and drug abuse counseling.

The TCS operationalizes a two-facet model of experienced control. The two facets are locus and direction. Control may have an *internal* or an *external* locus and may be experienced *over* something or *from* something. Combining these two binary facets produces a four-fold typology of experienced control, which subsumes biological drives (from internal), self-control (over internal), environmental pressures (from external), and environmental mastery (over external).

Each of the four components of experienced control is applied to eight standard situations: work, school, opposite sex, same sex, community, home, other people, and self-in general. The 32 self-rating items that comprise the TCS are of the form, "indicate the amount of control you feel (from or over) (internal or external) pressures when (in specified situation)." The response format requires a judgment of magnitude ranging from 1 (low) to 10 (high). Twelve preliminary questions ascertain features of the respondent's life circumstances, such as marital status, employment, education, living arrangements, religion, and "worst problems" (e.g., smoking, sex, anger, gambling, etc.).

The TCS is scored on 18 scales: four components of experienced control, three indices that are algebraic combinations of the four components (coping, assertiveness, and outgoingness), eight combinations of two components (internal, external, expressor, repressor, self-directed, non-self-directed, extratensive, and intratensive), experienced control total, response bias, and chemical dependency. The computer report generates composite scores for the scales and then disaggregates the scores for the eight situations, presenting this detailed information as profiles using the T-score metric.

The T-scores are calculated using a norm group of 2,650 nonpsychiatric respondents described by the authors as being primarily drawn from the Midwest. No information is given about how the normative sample was selected, nor is a demographic description of the sample provided. The best guess is that the norm group was assembled by combining samples from various research projects conducted over a period of 20 years. The T-scores are based on the gender and age segment of the norm group appropriate for the respondent.

The two-page TCS computer-generated narrative provides brief personality interpretations for three indices (coping, assertiveness, and outgoingness) and slightly longer interpretations for the respondent's profile and component types. Twenty-seven profile types were developed by dividing the scores on the three indices into low, middle, and high categories and listing all 27 possible combinations. Eighty-one component types are generated following the same procedure using the four components of experienced control. The only explanation the authors give about the development of the narrative personality interpretations is that they were carefully worked out in a clinical setting with thousands of patients, experiments, and other tests over many years.

This statement is undoubtedly true, because the TCS has its origins in the senior author's dissertation, which was completed more than 30 years ago. Furthermore, the bibliography lists approximately 75 articles, reports, papers, unpublished manuscripts, and theses dated from 1966 to 1995 that report research using the instrument. Because the findings of these studies are not systematically reviewed and summarized in the manual, there is no basis for evaluating the evidence pertaining to the validity of scores from the TCS. Moreover, there is no empirical foundation to support the clinical personality interpretations printed in the computer-generated report.

Only limited evidence concerning the reliability of the TCS is provided in the interpretative guide. Retest (2-week interval) and internal consistency coefficients for the total score are in the low .70s and low .80s. But, these data are irrelevant, because the experienced control total score is not interpreted. Retest reliabilities for the four component scores are typically in the .50s and low .60s. No reliability data are given for the three indices or the two types, the scores that are the focus of the clinical personality interpretations in the narrative report. Finally, the few studies cited in the validity section of the interpretative guide do not support the use of the instrument.

The manual for the computer version of the TCS and the accompanying interpretative guide are not well organized, the writing style is poor, and much essential information is omitted. These problems are unfortunate because they make a fair evaluation of some 30 years of work by the authors a difficult task.

SUMMARY. The TCS purports to measure several aspects of experienced control useful in a variety of counseling applications. The self-report inventory operationalizes a four-fold typology of control posited by the authors. The modest reliability and validity evidence does not support the reporting of 18 scale scores, which are distributed across eight life situations. The explanation of how the narrative personality interpretations were written is inadequate. The development of the norm group is not explained, nor are its characteristics described. The manual and interpretive guide do not present basic information needed by users of the instrument. The TCS should not be used for client assessment until these deficiencies are addressed.

[398]
Time Use Analyzer.

Purpose: Designed to "clarify the importance of using time effectively in various aspects of life."
Population: Adults.
Publication Dates: 1981–1990.
Scores: 2 scores (Typicalness, Dissatisfaction) for 8 areas: Work, Sleep, Personal, Personal/Family, Community, Family/Home, Education/Development, Recreation/Hobbies.
Administration: Group.
Price Data, 1999: $38.50 per complete kit including manual ('90, 8 pages), and 10 inventories; $24.50 per 10 inventories; $16.50 per manual.
Time: (5–10) minutes.
Comments: May be used alone or in combination with the Time Perception Inventory (T5:2761) and the Time Problems Inventory (T5:2762).
Author: Albert A. Canfield.
Publisher: Western Psychological Services.

Review of the Time Use Analyzer by JoELLEN V. CARLSON, Measurement and Training Consultant, Washington, DC:

The Time Use Analyzer is a self-assessment instrument for which the major purpose, as stated in the Time Use Analyzer manual, is to "clarify the importance of using time effectively in various aspects of life" (p. 1). However, although some audiences may find this instrument helpful in systematically generating an inventory of their use of time, the lack of critical information about the characteristics of the scale seriously limits general usability of the instrument.

The instrument presents brief descriptions of eight areas of time use, and the respondent indicates feelings about his or her time use in each of the areas. The areas include Work, Sleep, Personal Hygiene, Personal/Family Business, Community/Church, Family/Home, Education/Development, and Recreation/Hobbies. The response requested is to complete the phrase, "In this area, I would like to spend" with one of five scale points ranging from "a lot less time" to "a lot more time." The "Typicalness" score is derived from this scale. The second task is to choose the three of these areas that are most important and rank them in relative importance; from this task the "Dissatisfaction" score is derived.

The Typicalness score is derived by weighting the response to each item by the percentage of people in the "normative group" who gave that response. The author suggests that the higher the individual's response, the more like the "normative group" the individual is. The Dissatisfaction score is said to reflect "the general level of satisfaction with the way that time is being used" (manual, p. 2).

The Time Use Analyzer manual fails to present needed information and contains a number of unsupported generalizations and conclusions. Of particular concern about this instrument are the lack of information available to support the reliability, validity, scoring and reporting processes, and the lack of cautions against the most likely misinterpretations that could be made from the use of this instrument.

The only information provided about the "normative group" is that it "consisted of 283 managers and educators. This sample was more than 90% male, mostly between the ages of 30 and 45" (manual, p. 4). This information is clearly inadequate for any valid interpretation of the two "scores" yielded by the instrument. To consider this number of a mix of two groups of individuals as a reference group does not meet even minimal standards for norms. Important unanswered questions include, but are not limited to:

How many managers? How many educators?

What kinds of managers? What kinds of educators? What are their occupational and professional roles?

What are the important characteristics of the individuals in this group relative to time use, such as level of employment, stage in career, household structure, household demands for time, and others?

Who is likely to find results for a group that is 90% male useful for comparison?

Are the managers a homogeneous group in their own right? Are the educators?

These and other unanswered questions about the composition of this "group," as well as the small group size considered to indicate norms, makes any comparisons for individuals using scores from the instrument very tenuous. Inexcusably, there are no cautions or qualifications about interpretation of the scores.

The manual provides no quantitative information about reliability or validity of the scores yielded by the instrument. The only information that even comes close to describing technical characteristics of the scales is anecdotal information gathered by the author. The concerns expressed above about the "normative group" makes even this information of little value to potential users of the Time Use Analyzer.

The manual contains a number of statements relating to interpretation of scores, such as, "The data presented confirm the notion that satisfaction and importance are often poorly related" (p. 1), and "Such discussions direct respondents to examine the differences between importance and satisfaction and generally produce considerable insight into the effective use of time" (p. 2). Absolutely no data or research studies are cited in support of these types of statements. The potential user is expected to take the author's word for the reliability and validity of the suggested interpretations.

SUMMARY. All things considered, this instrument cannot be suggested for use by professionals in its present state. Until such time as limitations like those referred to above are rectified, the Time Use Analyzer can be recommended only for experimental or research purposes.

Review of the Time Use Analyzer by JIM C. FORTUNE, Professor of Educational Research and Evaluation, Virginia Tech University, Blacksburg, VA:

PURPOSE. The Time Use Analyzer is a device that is used to introduce the concept of time management by getting an individual to think about their relative feelings concerning their time use. Chris Gruber, Director of Research and Development for Western Psychological Services, the distributor of the instrument stated in an e-mail to me, "Our catalog description of the Time Use Analyzer begins 'This simple exercise ... allows individuals to determine how "typical" they are in their use of time.' It is not a test, an inventory, or in any sense a formally presented instrument. It is basically an ice-breaking exercise for business or educational management consultants to use informally when they conduct team-building interventions" (personal communication, May 23, 1998).

DESCRIPTION. The instrument is a self-report type instrument which asks the respondent to mark eight areas of time use individually on a 5-point scale. The scale ranges across five options in spending time: I would like to spend: a lot less time, a little less time, nor more or no less time, a little more time, and a lot more time. The eight areas are: work, sleep, personal hygiene, personal/family business, community/church, family/home, education/development, and recreation/hobbies. After marking the eight categories the respondent is asked to rank the three most important of these eight areas. Two scores are developed from the responses, a Typicalness score and a Dissatisfaction score. Both scores permit one to compare their responses to a norm group. The instrument takes about 10 minutes to complete.

RATIONALE. The Time Use Analyzer is used to make participants think about their time use, about what they consider important in their life activity, and their satisfaction with the distribution of their time use. The eight areas of time use cover the gambit of life activity. An individual can use the instrument to develop feedback, but a time management workshop context appears necessary to maximize potential utility.

TECHNICAL INFORMATION. The manual reports a minimum of technical information. Included in the manual is a description of the norm group, which was made up of 283 managers and educators. This group was reported to be about

90% male and mostly between the ages of 30 and 45. The manual provided background of the instrument, scoring and profiling information, and instructions to interpret the profile. No information was provided on evidence related to reliability.

EVALUATION. The instrument does have potential to get a group thinking in a similar manner about their individual use of time. We do not see any potential for the instrument with regard to its use to measure or to provide feedback. Acceptable reliability evidence would have to be gathered for it to be used in either of these two ways.

[399]
Toddler and Infant Motor Evaluation.

Purpose: Designed to be used for "diagnostic, comprehensive assessment of children who are suspected to have motor delays or deviations, the development of appropriate remediation programs, and treatment efficacy research."
Population: Ages 4 months to 3.5 years.
Publication Date: 1994.
Acronym: TIME: Version 1.0.
Scores: 5 Primary Subtests: Mobility, Stability, Motor Organization, Social-Emotional, Functional Performance; 3 Clinical Subtests: Quality Rating, Component Analysis Rating, Atypical Positions.
Administration: Individual.
Price Data, 1999: $395 per complete kit including manual (324 pages), 10 record forms, timer, rattle, 2 balls, squeak toy, toy car, 3 containers, toy telephone, 2 shoelaces, 6 blocks, and nylon tote bag; $35 per 10 record forms; $125 per manual.
Time: (15–40) minutes.
Comments: Diagnostic assessment tool designed to be used by licensed/highly trained physical and occupational therapists, or appropriately trained adaptive physical educators, special education teachers, or others with expertise in the motor domain; administered utilizing a partnership between parent(s) or caretaker(s) and a trained examiner.
Authors: Lucy J. Miller and Gale H. Roid.
Publisher: Therapy Skill Builders—A Division of The Psychological Corporation.

Review of the Toddler and Infant Motor Evaluation by LARRY M. BOLEN, Professor and School Psychology Trainer, East Carolina University, Greenville, NC:

The Toddler and Infant Motor Evaluation (T.I.M.E.) is purported to be a comprehensive assessment of motor ability for children 4 months to 3.5 years of age. The intent was to develop an instrument useful in the diagnostic assessment, treatment planning, and treatment efficacy research of very young children. The test is administered by observing a parent or caregiver interacting/playing with the child. Prompting by the examiner to elicit specific motor abilities allows for the measurement of movement in five positions: supine, prone, sit, quadruped, and stand positions.

The T.I.M.E. manual, for the most part, could serve as a model for test developers to emulate. Detailed explanations for all aspects of test development, item content, standardization, and psychometric properties are presented. The authors identify in the Preface the one major concern potential test users may have: "While waiting for sufficient funding to complete a large-scale national standardization … [the] … issue became whether to publish The T.I.M.E.™ or await large-scale funding" (p. xv). The decision was made to use volunteer testers and decrease standardization from a target number of 100 boys and 100 girls in each age group to a minimum of 30 boys and 30 girls. Therefore, in that sense, the T.I.M.E. may be viewed as an experimental test even though there was extensive attention to construct and content development between 1986 and 1993.

The test is not intended for the novice user. Extensive familiarity with motor development and assessment expertise is required. The test is expected to be used by occupational and physical therapists and other professionals with specific skill in motor assessment. Two competency levels are involved: Administration of the five primary scales is straightforward and should be adequately accomplished by professionals with, at least, moderate training. The three clinical scales, however, require advanced training and comprehensive training and knowledge are required.

Item development began in 1986 at the Developmental Disabilities Research Symposium in Boston. A panel of 12 pediatric occupational therapists reviewed the related literature and existing motor assessments for infants and toddlers. A table of specifications for the measurement of motor development in infants and toddlers was developed encompassing four subdomains: neurological foundations, stability, mobility, and motor organization. The relative importance of each was rated in each of the age groups from birth through 3.5 years. The initial item pool was field tested by the same 12 clinicians ($n = 100$ children, 10 in each age group). Data analyses were completed and changes in procedure and items incorporated.

Two additional pilot testings were completed in 1988. The final try-out edition occurred in 1989 with 25 pediatric occupational and physical therapists, all with 10 or more years of experience, testing an average of 15 to 16 children each (total n = 390). There were 257 children included without motor delays and 133 with motor delays distributed across 10 age groups. Gender was evenly distributed (52% female) with 89% White, 6% Black, and 4% Hispanic. Geographically, 41% of the sample was from the East, 21% West, 15% South, 14% Central, and 8% Canadian.

The final edition of the T.I.M.E. was developed by having a methodical review by a panel of seven national subject matter experts who refined the table of specifications and construct definitions during a 3-day symposium. Additionally, the validity of each item was discussed and changes made to improve interrater reliability.

The final standardization was begun in 1992. The sample (n = 731) was divided into 10 age groups: four groups of 3 months each in the 0–12 month age span, three groups of 4 months each in the 13–24-month age span, and three groups of 6 months each in the 25–42-month age span. A team of 75 volunteer testers evaluated a randomly selected sample, stratified by race/ethnicity, gender, socioeconomic status, and age, based on the 1990 U.S. Census Bureau demographic statistics. The sample consisted of two groups of children: those with motor delays and those without motor delays. Children classified as "at-risk," however, were not included. These included children whose birth weight was below 1000 grams or who were premature by less than 32 weeks as well as those who were environmentally "at-risk" (extreme poverty, parental substance abuse, etc.). The samples were taken from 10 states: California, Oklahoma, Kansas, Colorado, Texas, Ohio, New York, New Jersey, and Pennsylvania.

Raw score conversions to age-based standard scores are provided for the five primary scales, with a mean of 10 and a SD of 3. Corresponding percentile ranks and a standard score for corrected age are also provided. Cutoff score points of -1.5 SDs are suggested for classification accuracy. That is, using scaled scores of 5 or 6 or lower to denote motor impairment decreases false positive significantly compared to using a 1.0 SD cutoff.

Item stability (n = 33) was examined for retest-retest and internal (alpha) consistency, and for interrater reliability (n = 34). Test-retest was completed by the participating examiner testing the same child within a period of 1 to 3 weeks. Test-retest coefficients were computed across age groups and across group inclusion (i.e., 91% of the children included were without motor delays whereas 9% included in the test-retest sample had motor delays). Thus, the reliabilities reported for each of the subdomains may be spuriously high (all coefficients ranged from .965 to .998) due to the dichotomous nature of the sample. Internal consistency estimates were calculated using Cronbach's alpha. Generally, these reliability estimates were computed on a sample of children without motor delays except for Stability and Atypical Total where the sample was a mix of children with and without delays. Within each test subdomain, alpha values ranged from .79 to .93 for the 0–6-month age group; .88 to .97 for the 7–12-month age group; .79 to .96 for the 13–24-month age group; and .72 to .96 for the 25–42-month age group. Interrater reliability was examined by having a second examiner unobtrusively observe and independently score a child during the same test session. Several pairs of examiner-observers participated. Consistency between the pairs resulted in correlations of .90 or higher.

Validity indices were assessed in four ways: content validity; construct validity denoted by differentiating age/developmental trends and factor analysis; discriminant validation; and classification accuracy. The authors' utilization of expert subject matter specialists to develop specification tables, to develop items, and the various item validity reviews suggests excellent content validity for the five primary subdomains.

Construct validity was investigated by examining the age trend of increasing performance or mastery across items as a function of increase in age for each of the subdomains. This pattern is identifiable, on the standardization sample of 731 children without motor delays, for the Mobility subdomain until the 19–21-month age group. Here, only 2 points separate this group from the 22–24-month age group performance. Similarly, only 1 point separated the 25–28-month age group from the 29–32-month age group; and the 37–42-month age group actually scored lower than the 33–36-month age group. Additional construct validity was studied using factor analysis and unidimensionality was concluded. Limited data are presented, however, and the authors' conclusion that the various methods of factoring support their construct claim requires additional documentation.

Discriminant validity studies were reported on a sample of 153 children with motor delays (20 more than the 133 previously indicated as comprising this sample) compared to the 731 children without motor delay. Significant differences were obtained for all subdomain comparisons, levels of motor organization, and clinical scales except for Atypical age, Reactivity, and Social/Emotional age. However, none of the comparisons report sample sizes, post-hoc follow-up tests of the four levels of age, or alpha error rate adjustments.

Classification analysis was completed for the Mobility, Stability, and Atypical Positions subtests total score. Data suggest a high degree of accuracy for identifying children correctly as with or without motor delay. False positives were highest for Mobility (11.8%) scores if one standard deviation was used as the cutoff point. The rate decreases to 6.2% when the recommended -1.5 *SD* cutoff point is used.

The test equipment is remarkably limited in scope and size. Toy cars, a small and large ball, toy telephone, rattle, a squeaky toy, blocks, a timer, and containers make up the majority of items furnished in the test kit. The examiner supplies items such as masking tape, cereal pieces, pencils, and a blanket (if the test surface is cold). The record form is simultaneously complex and extremely comprehensive. One glance, and it becomes apparent the degree of training and knowledge necessary to adequately administer and prompt while observing the child's motor behavior, score, and interpret the various test subdomains. The manual does include detailed, but easy to follow, testing procedures and guidelines, pictorials of motor actions, and a glossary of terms and definitions. Moreover, an appendix provides description of positions for the Mobility, Component Analysis, and Atypical Positions subtests clarifying testing for supine, side, prone, quadruped, bear, squat, sit, support, transition stand, kneel, and run/walk positions.

In sum, the T.I.M.E. has evidence of good face validity. National standardization should be a primary goal for the test authors. The knowledgeable professional should be able to use the test effectively. Considerably more research is needed at the infant level to determine the T.I.M.E.'s usefulness and sensitivity in differentiating motor delays versus normal fluctuation in development se-

quence. Moreover, the utility of the test for treatment planning, and treatment efficacy has yet to be determined. The authors indicate continued ongoing research in a variety of movement areas. As an experimental instrument, the test has promise.

Review of the Toddler and Infant Motor Evaluation by WILLIAM R. MERZ, SR., FPPR, Professor-School Psychology Training Program, California State University, Sacramento, CA:

The Toddler and Infant Motor Evaluation (T.I.M.E.) is a new diagnostic assessment that evaluates motor proficiencies and difficulties of children from 4 months to 3.5 years. It uses parent-elicited responses from children allowing qualified professionals to obtain accurate quantitative and qualitative observations of children's motor skills. This standardized instrument includes eight subtests for observing a child's motor development; these subtests are divided into two types: (a) Primary Subtests that include: Mobility—the ability to move one's body in space; Stability—the dynamic and discrete balance of muscles; Motor Organization—the ability to perform unique motor skills requiring visual and spatial skills, balance and complex sequential motor abilities, also called praxis and sequencing; Social/Emotional Abilities—ratings of behaviors observed during the test session (i.e., state, activity level, emotionality, reactivity, temperament, interaction level, and attention span); Functional Performance—adaptive skills such as feeding, dressing, toileting, grooming, self-management and mastery, relationships and interactions, and functioning in the community; and (b) Clinical Subtests that include: Quality Rating—detailed descriptions in tone, reflex integration, balance, balance between flexion and extension; Component Analysis—completed separately for each of seven positions and for transitions between positions; and Atypical Positions—atypical movement patterns.

The authors categorize the scales into three groups: Screening Instruments, Comprehensive Assessments, and Diagnostic Assessments. They are administered through a partnership between a parent or caregiver and a trained examiner. The examiner must be familiar with motor development, with assessing motor development, and have formal training in administering the T.I.M.E. Usually occupational or physical therapists administer this test but, according to the authors, appropriately trained educators, medical professionals, and mental health professionals may use it, too.

The authors demonstrate through their review of research on motor performance that there is a need for a diagnostic motor assessment that measures quality of movement in young children, is sensitive to small changes in motor performance, and has documented evidence of reliability and validity. Assessing the quality of movement is the focus of this instrument. The authors developed a taxonomy to define quality of movement and identified a set of measurable constructs to assess it. In the process, quality of movement was defined in objective, measurable terms based on constructs defined by experts.

Different levels of performance are determined by briefly observing the child or asking the parent for input. The authors identify a general order of subtest administration. The observations on which scoring is based include free-play as well as structured subtests. There are screening and assessment subtests. Observations can be quite confusing if an assessor is not familiar with the development of movement and the subtle observations of that development. For the five primary subtests, raw scores are converted to scaled scores that range from 1 to 19. Scaled scores can be converted to percentile ranks. There are clinical scores for out-of-age-range, atypical mobility patterns, and Motor Organization subtest growth. There are rules for obtaining total raw scores, the most complicated of which is for the Mobility subtest.

The Motor Organization subtest lends itself to traditional item analysis methodology including p-values, item-total correlations, item intercorrelations, discrimination indices, and correlation of items with age in months, along with Rasch item analysis. The Social/Emotional Abilities subtest consists of 20 Likert-type items that were examined for statistically significant age trends across five age groups. Other internal psychometric properties such as item-total correlations and factor structure are examined, as well. Performance on tasks making up the Functional Performance subtest and the Atypical Positions subtest was examined with analysis of variance for differences between delayed and not delayed groups as well as for difference among age categories.

The T.I.M.E. was developed carefully from 1986 through its release in 1994. A grant from the American Occupational Therapy Foundation funded the Pilot I study. On the basis of findings of Pilot I, a revised test was administered by 18 pediatric occupational and physical therapists in Colorado. In this Pilot II study approximately 150 children were assessed; some of the children experienced delays and deviations and some did not. In 1989 a try-out edition was used to accumulate item data on 390 children. Twenty-five pediatric occupational and physical therapists participated in training in standardized test administration and scoring and in methods of random, stratified sampling before assessing children. Results of this try-out yielded a new taxonomy as well as tried items that were incorporated into the T.I.M.E. Pilot III study.

Norming was completed during 1992 and 1993. A team of 75 trained and closely supervised testers was recruited. A sample of children was randomly selected and stratified by race/ethnicity, gender, parents' education, and age based on 1990 U.S. Census statistics. Children without delays and deviations as well as children with delays and deviations were included. The sample included 875 children between the ages of 3 and 42 months.

Interrater, internal consistency, and test-retest reliabilities were computed. Coefficient alpha for internal consistency reliabilities ranged from .72 to .97. Test-retest (1- to 3-week interval) reliabilities ranged from .965 to .998 and interrater reliabilities ranged from .897 to .996.

Investigations supporting validity include content-related evidence, construct-related evidence, and criterion-related evidence. The three studies that included expert panels give evidence that the content applies to the construct being assessed. Age trends and factor analysis give evidence that the T.I.M.E. functions as one would hypothesize it should. Means increase with age, and factor analysis yields evidence of unidimensionality for the Motor Organization subtest. Factor analysis of the Social/Emotional subtest shows that items load onto three factors as one would expect, and this finding held across three different factoring methods. Criterion-related evidence of validity includes discriminant validity studies that show the T.I.M.E. discriminated between groups of children with motor delays and those without motor delays. Classification accuracy studies yield excellent rates of accurate identification.

SUMMARY. The information gathered is important for early intervention with young children under IDEA (federal Special Education law and regulation) and Section 504 (Vocational Rehabilitation provisions applied to those with disabilities). The data generated evaluate a child's level of function, help develop appropriate interventions, and can evaluate the efficacy of those interventions. The instrument is not easy to administer unless the examiner is very familiar with motor function and development and has been trained to administer the T.I.M.E. Collaborating with parents as partners in evaluating a child's function requires the examiner to have excellent people skills. It is essential that the examiner elicit the desired behaviors by directing the parent's work with the child, observe astutely, and be very familiar with the test. The examiner must record observations accurately in order to interpret the data collected and translate the data into appropriate remedial activities or efficacious accommodations. The disadvantage here is that these are skills beyond the experiences of most educators and mental health professionals. Also, physicians may not have the time to administer, record, and interpret the information much less to develop appropriate intervention strategies.

Devising this instrument is an important step toward objective assessment of motor development. It is one of the few norm-referenced tests that targets younger children. With "child find" provisions of IDEA, having such an instrument becomes even more important. The T.I.M.E. provides objective, standardized, norm-referenced assessment of young children's motor development. The device is built on a sound developmental base and has had input from specialists and practitioners in the area of children's motor and movement development.

[400]
Transition Planning Inventory.

Purpose: To identify and plan for the comprehensive transition needs of students.
Population: High school and middle school students with disabilities who need future planning.
Publication Date: 1997.
Acronym: TPI.
Scores: Ratings in 9 areas: Employment, Further Education/Training, Daily Living, Leisure Activities, Community Participation, Health, Self-Determination, Communication, Interpersonal Relationships.
Administration: Individual or group.
Forms, 4: Student, Home, School, Profile and Further Assessment Recommendations.
Price Data, 1999: $126 per complete kit; $35 per Administration and Resource Guide (232 pages), $24 per 25 Profile and Further Assessment Recommenda-

tions Forms; $24 per 25 School Forms; $24 per 25 Home Forms; $24 per 25 Student Forms; $24 per 25 Spanish Home Forms.
Foreign Language Edition: Spanish version of Home Form available.
Time: Administration time not reported.
Authors: Gary M. Clark and James R. Patton.
Publisher: PRO-ED.

Review of the Transition Planning Inventory by ROBERT K. GABLE, Professor of Educational Psychology, and Associate Director, Bureau of Educational Research and Service, University of Connecticut, Storrs, CT:

The Transition Planning Inventory (TPI) addresses the area of transition of adolescents from school to adult living. Although it can be used for any student, it is most appropriate for students needing special and/or related services. Consistent with the Individuals with Disabilities Education Act of 1990 (IDEA), the TPI addresses four critical transition planning areas (i.e., instruction, community experience, employment, and post-school goals).

The TPI contains 46 transition-planning statements reflecting the nine planning areas listed earlier in the descriptive entry. Each area is assessed by three or more items regarding knowledge, skills, or behaviors associated with successful adjustment in the respective area.

Ratings and written comments are obtained from the student, the student's parents or guardians, and one or more school professionals using one of four forms. While maintaining parallel item content across the forms, appropriate modifications in the item wording are included on the Student, Home, and School forms based upon the respondent groups. Ratings are obtained using a 6-point Likert scale with end-point anchors of *Strongly Disagree* (0) and *Strongly Agree* (5); *Not Appropriate* (NA) and *Don't Know* (DK) options are also provided. The scale appears appropriate for this type of survey; the completion instructions are clearly presented. Overall, the layout of the survey foldout is well done.

The Profile and Further Assessment Recommendations Form includes sections for recording the results of other assessment, student preferences and interests, and likely postschool setting(s). In addition, a profile section is included for recording the ratings obtained from the School, Home, and Student forms.

ADMINISTRATION. Well-written, specific directions are provided for administering the Student and Home forms using three options as deemed appropriate: independent self-administration, guided self-administration, or oral administration. A suggested self-administration time of 15–20 minutes, and oral administration time of 20–30 minutes seem appropriate. Teachers or school personnel can complete the School form in 15–20 minutes. Completion of the entire Profile and Further Assessment Recommendations form would most likely take at least one hour.

VALIDITY. Comprehensive and appropriate evidence is offered in support of content validity. A literature review on follow-up studies, adult adjustment of persons with disabilities, and transition needs was conducted; references are provided. Expert judges (direct service personnel in schools, individuals in higher education or special education) reviewed the items in relation to transition planning needs. Limited correlational evidence is presented to support the concurrent validity aspect of criterion-related validity. Based on the proposed nine dimensions assessed by the TPI, it is surprising that the authors have not reported any confirmatory factor analytic evidence of construct validity. Given the alpha reliabilities to be discussed in the next section of this review, it appears the TPI Teacher, Parent, and Student data could fit the proposed model. Without such empirical support for construct validity called for in the *Standards for Educational and Psychological Testing* (AERA, APA, & NCME, 1985), the meaningfulness of the TPI score interpretations could be in question. The authors should report the results of these analyses on existing and future data sets. We do note that the DK and NA response options mentioned earlier will reduce the numbers of complete sets of data desired for these analyses.

RELIABILITY. Impressive alpha internal consistency and stability reliabilities are reported. Average alpha reliabilities across 329 school-based personnel, 227 parents, and 288 students (grade level not identified) ranged from .70 to .94 for the nine planning areas. The students rated had been identified as having a learning disability or mental retardation. Stability reliabilities based on a small sample of 36 students averaged from .70 to .98 across the three survey forms; the time interval between testing was not identified.

SCORING AND SCORE INTERPRETATION. A comprehensive, well-done section is included regarding interpretation and use of results in transition planning. As noted by the authors, "The comprehensive gathering of information about a student's transition needs does not ensure that these needs will be addressed" (manual, p. 26). The TPI manual provides valuable information for "moving from assessment to planning" (p. 28). Included are sections regarding interpreting transition needs data using TPI forms provided, further needs assessment instrument references, individualized transition planning goals, and turning plans into action. Three well-done case studies illustrating completed TPI surveys and forms are presented. Users will find these materials quite useful.

SUMMARY. The TPI is a well-developed and comprehensive set of materials for needs assessment and transition planning for high school students with disabilities. In addition to the assessment materials, the TPI manual is an excellent transition planning resource with over 140 appendix pages devoted to such topics as: planning notes, additional interpretive case studies, resources for professionals and parents, transition goals, and developing a transition portfolio. Overall, the TPI represents a well-designed and delivered set of materials. Future development efforts should be focused on providing empirical evidence of construct validity to support meaningful score interpretations.

REVIEWER'S REFERENCE

American Educational Research Association, American Psychological Association, & National Council on Measurement in Education. (1985). *Standards for educational and psychological testing.* Washington, DC: American Psychological Association, Inc.

Review of the Transition Planning Inventory by ROSEMARY E. SUTTON, Professor of Education, and THERESA A. QUIGNEY, Assistant Professor, Cleveland State University, Cleveland, OH:

The Individual Educational Plans (IEPs) of all students with disabilities aged 14 and older must address educational needs and/or services to assist the transition from school to post-school activities (Individuals with Disabilities Education Act, 1997). The Transition Planning Inventory (TPI) was designed to help the IEP team develop an individual transition plan by assessing students' strengths, weaknesses, preferences, and interests.

The focus of the inventory is 46 transition planning statements categorized into nine areas:

Employment, Further Education/Training, Daily Living, Leisure Activities, Community Participation, Health, Self-Determination, Communication, and Interpersonal Relationships. These statements indicate the current level of competence of the student and occur on each of three forms: Student, Home, and School. For example, the item on the Student form is "I know how to get a job," whereas on the School form the equivalent item is "Knows how to get a job."

The format of the three forms is consistent: a 6-point Likert scale for the 46 transition planning statements; a brief checklist on likely post-school settings; and an area for open-ended comments. In addition, there is a section on the Student form entitled "Student Preferences and Interests" with items such as "Where do you plan to live after high school?" (p. 5) and "What type of friendships do you plan on having?" (p. 6). The TPI also includes a "Profile and Further Assessment Recommendations Form," which allows the test administrator to summarize and display the data from the three previously described forms, and to identify planning strategies.

ADMINISTRATION. The Student, School, and Home forms are designed to be completed independently. However, the manual contains extensive instructions for guided self-administration and oral administration for the Home and Student forms. These instructions, according to the authors, are not intended to be prescriptive, but should be considered as a guide to enhance understanding and elicit appropriate responses. Ensuring that students and parents understand the items is more important than standardized instructions as the TPI is not norm-referenced.

The detailed instructions for nonindependent administration are a strength of the TPI. They allow test administrators to use the instrument with a broad range of students with disabilities. However, the need for such detailed instructions is particularly great because the directions and the wording of the items are often complex and vague. For example, "I know how to use a variety of services and resources successfully" (p. 2), and "I have the work habits and attitudes for keeping a job and being promoted—with or without special help" (p. 1). Field testing of the instrument raised this and other issues. The authors state that, "Self-administration of the TPI for students and parents should be offered selectively" (manual, p. 15). In

addition, they discuss other concerns and provide recommendations to address these.

RELIABILITY AND VALIDITY. The authors provide two types of reliability data. An internal consistency index, Cronbach's alpha, was calculated for the three forms (school personnel, parents, and students) and ranged from .70 to .95, with the majority of indices over .80. These data are based on three groups, Learning Disabled (LD), Mentally Retarded (MR), and "Total." Unfortunately the authors do not state who comprises the total group. Nor do they provide the sample size or demographic information about the three groups. The second type of reliability evidence provided by the authors, test-retest, was based on 36 students in Kansas. The indices ranged from .70 to .98. The authors do not state what interval occurred between the test and retest.

The omission of descriptive information about the sample and test-retest interval is puzzling because detailed reliability index tables are provided. It is also surprising that only two disability groups, LD and MR, were included in the reliability studies because the manual states that this instrument is designed for all students with disabilities.

The authors provide both content and concurrent validity evidence. Two aspects of content validity are examined. First, the authors provide a rationale for the format of the TPI by critiquing other related instruments. Second, they describe the process of developing and narrowing the item pool through a review of the literature and expert judgments. Concurrent validity evidence was derived from 48 students who had previously been administered the Weschler Intelligence Scale for Children—Third Edition (WISC-III) (Weschler, 1991) and the Vineland Adaptive Behavior Scales (Harrison, 1985). The actual correlations between the TPI and these two measures are not provided. The authors argue that many of the correlations are not statistically significant because the sample size is small and yet they conclude that, "The limited data available suggest that the TPI is valid with regard to concurrent validity" (p. 76). We disagree for two reasons. First, the WISC-III is an inappropriate criterion as it is not directly related to transition planning assessment. The authors should compare scores on the TPI with other currently available transition skills assessments. Second, the statistical data on concurrent validity are inadequate. The authors admit that more valid ity data are needed but it is disappointing that they did not provide these in this edition of the TPI.

SUMMARY. The TPI has a number of strengths. It systematically addresses critical transition areas required by the Individual With Disabilities Education Act (1990) by including data from nine domains and input from three raters: student, parent, school personnel. It provides a framework to assist the IEP team link the assessment data to IEP goals and activities. The manual contains a wealth of supplemental materials including case studies, suggested transition goal statements, and additional forms. Although the goal to develop an inventory for all students with disabilities is laudable, it created some problems related to format, item wording, and administration. The authors do provide two types of reliability evidence but the sample size and composition are limited. The validity information is weak. The concept of the TPI is very good and the need for such a planning inventory is great. We hope that the authors continue to refine this instrument and collect more reliability and validity data.

REVIEWERS' REFERENCES

Harrison, P. (1985). *Vineland Adaptive Behavior Scales: Classroom Edition manual.* Circle Pines, MN: American Guidance Service.
Weschler, D. (1991). Weschler Intelligence Scale for Children—Third Edition. San Antonio: Psychological Corporation.
Individuals with Disabilities Education Act of 1990. P.L. 101–476, 101st Congress, 20 U.S.C. §1401 *et seq.*
Individuals with Disabilities Education Act Amendments of 1997, P.L. 105–17, 105th Congress.

[401]
Transition-to-Work Inventory: A Job Placement System for Workers with Severe disAbilities.

Purpose: "Designed to assist employers, supported employment counselors, and other transition professionals in identifying the best match between the skills of an individual with disabilities and the requirements of the job."
Population: Individuals with severe disabilities.
Publication Dates: 1995–1996.
Acronym: TWI™.
Scores, 3: Job Analysis Rating, Worker Analysis Rating, Difference Score.
Administration: Individual.
Parts, 2: Job Analysis Scale, Worker Analysis Scale.
Price Data, 1999: $86.50 per starter kit including user and accommodation manual, 10 job analysis booklets, 25 worker analysis booklets, and 25 profile sheets; $29 per 25 worker analysis booklets; $15 per 10 job analysis booklets; $14 per individual profile sheets; $52 per manual and accommodation guide ('96, 102 pages).

Time: (30–35) minutes per scale.
Comments: Ratings by transition professionals.
Authors: Lee Friedman, Carl Cameron, and Jennifer Fletcher.
Publisher: The Psychological Corporation.

Review of the Transition-to-Work Inventory: A Job Placement System for Workers with Severe disAbilities by CHANTALE JEANRIE, Industrial/Organizational Psychologist, Associate Professor of Measurement and Evaluation, Department of "Fondements et pratiques en éducation," Faculty of Education, Laval University, Quebec, Canada:

The general objectives of the Transition-to-Work Inventory (TWI) scales are to assess the job-related challenges imposed by an individual's disabilities and evaluate worker-job fit across diverse jobs. Using two different scales, the "job analysis" and "worker analysis" scales, this instrument intends to serve as a job placement system for workers with severe disabilities, and to help in determining accommodation/job redesign needs of an individual in respect to particular positions. Although the demonstration of psychometric qualities of this instrument is not fully convincing yet, the efforts put on the development and the validation of the TWI warrant its use, for the time being, if employed as cautiously as required by a relatively new measurement device.

SCORES. Two different scales are provided. The job analysis (JA) scale serves to indicate the likelihood of occurrence of a number of activities or working conditions for a specific job. The worker analysis (WA) scale is used to indicate the extent to which the worker is capable of performing each of the activities or working conditions. Each is to be rated separately by more than one assessor. Both averaged scores are used to calculate a difference score. When the difference shows that the job demands outweigh the individual's abilities by a score of 1.5 or more, the item is categorized as a target item, indicating that accommodation, redesign, or training might be required to insure a better worker-job fit.

RELIABILITY. Interraters and test-retest analyses were conducted to assess the reliability of scores from the two scales. Results are presented in a nontechnical language accessible to users with a limited psychometric background but too laconic for those readers more familiar with this domain. For example, the authors state that the interrater data were severely influenced by range restriction

(User's Manual and Accommodation Guide, p. 26) and that, consequently, it is more appropriate to present the median of the obtained correlations instead of their range. Although this choice could be justified, its rigor would be more easily defended by the addition of a technical appendix containing the descriptive statistics for each item of the two scales.

Interrater agreement and test-retest reliability coefficients were presented for both scales. Interrater statistics are calculated from 32 (JA) and 47 (WA) pairs of raters. Median correlations reach $r = .81$ for the former scale and $r = .75$ for the latter. Whether these reliability coefficients are sufficient cannot really be stated without additional data. Both medians reach an acceptable level, but an authors' remark suggests that at least some of the coefficients are, indeed, much lower.

A statistic called "percent agreement," which refers to "the proportion of items for which the difference between the ratings of two raters was one-point or less discrepant," is included in the user's manual (p. 26). These values are very high (98% and 97%) but do not bring much comfort to this reviewer. A one-point discrepancy between two raters represents a discrepancy of 20%, which is not meaningless. An index of agreement based on corrected percentage of perfect matches between ratings would have been more stringent but more informative.

Finally, the authors also present test-retest reliability coefficients, using the correlation and "percentage of agreement" formats. Median test-retest correlation coefficient for JA (administration intervals = 2 weeks) is low ($r = .60$) but, as mentioned by the authors themselves, these statistics were calculated from very small samples and should therefore be considered preliminary only. The stability coefficients obtained on the WA were based on a larger sample and reached a median of $r = .73$, which is satisfying but perhaps lower than would be expected because ratings were done 2 weeks apart only, by "the job coach ... with whom the worker interacted most often" (User's Manual and Accommodation Guide, p. 26).

VALIDITY. Content and criterion validity of the JA and WA scales are analyzed. Again, explanations are accessible and nontechnical although more difficult to understand than those provided in the reliability chapter. The section related to content validity contains no specification table nor any other domain definition and the test user is left with only the option to go back to the Development section (p. 15) and decide whether or not the steps followed were likely to enhance content validity. It is this reviewer's opinion that care has been taken to provide a sound measure of the common area of work-related problems for workers with severe disabilities but, again, details are lacking.

The criterion validity of the TWI is studied using two different criteria: "success" and "confidence" scales. The success scale represents "the extent to which the worker successfully completed each task in terms of quantity and quality of performance." The confidence scale represents "the degree of confidence in the worker's ability to perform each job task in a competitive work environment" (p. 32). The rationale for the use of the latter original criterion is not discussed and is, at least, puzzling. In addition, because results obtained on this criterion are very close to those obtained with the classical success criterion, the use of this criterion appears pointless.

The authors claim that "results indicate that the TWI consistently identified as problem areas work activities and conditions that caused performance problems for the individuals in the study" (p. 35). This statement appears largely overstated. Results obtained are weak in many regards. The validity coefficients obtained are low (corrected: $r = .27$ to $r = .34$) and they are corrected for the unreliability of the TWI, which is inappropriate in such a situation (SIOP, 1987). In addition, the authors cite Barrick and Mount (1991) to mention that corrected coefficients of $r = .20$ and more are predictive and useful, without considering that these last authors were linking personality scales (and not job or worker's behaviors ratings) to job performance data.

The biggest problem encountered in the validity study, however, comes from the fact that the predictors used to predict job performance are not ratings from the scales. The three chosen predictors are indicators of the importance, for the job, of the items where the worker abilities are estimated to be less than what is required by the job. The rationale for these predictors is very indirect, it does not take into account the size of the discrepancy between the two ratings and introduces an additional judgmental source of variance without providing any information about its accuracy.

SUMMARY. The Transition-to-Work Inventory seems to have been developed cautiously, with obvious concerns for content validity. The serious flaws found in the criterion-validity study presented do not weaken the quality of the instrument but question the relevance of the study itself and leave wide open the search for evidence of criterion validity. From this perspective, there is enough information, at this moment, to believe that the TWI can usefully serve its intended purpose but the evidence of reliability and validity provided should still be considered preliminary. However, without more detailed information and further studies, the psychometric support existing will soon become inadequate.

REVIEWER'S REFERENCES

Society for Industrial and Organizational Psychology, Inc. (1987). *Principles for the validation and use of personnel selection procedures* (3rd ed.). College Park, MD: Author.

Barrick, M. R., & Mount, M. K. (1991). The big five personality dimensions and job performance: A meta-analysis. *Personnel Psychology, 44,* 1–26.

Review of the Transition-to-Work Inventory: A Job Placement System for Workers with Severe disAbilities by ERICH P. PRIEN, Professor of Industrial Psychology (Retired) and President, Performance Management Press, Memphis, TN:

The Transition-to-Work Inventory (TWI) is a comprehensive, very basic and concrete system designed to perform an essential function. The TWI is more than a set of forms; it constitutes an integrated system to identify, define, and solve a problem at the individual level.

The TWI system begins with the identification of an individual who is challenged or limited by an individual difference condition or characteristic. The individual difference characteristic may arise from a variety of dynamic sources but the essential result is a limitation in the individual's capacity or competency to function. This outcome is by definition a problem that warrants or demands an analysis and evaluation in order to understand the characteristic, limitation, or deficiency. Only then can constructive action be taken to alleviate or remedy the problem in order to place the individual in the most appropriate environment to capitalize on their individual talents and resources.

The TWI system is focused on the total spectrum of potential disabilities and addresses each of the components in operational terms. However, the focus is on that segment of the population otherwise identified as "marginal manpower," "challenged," or "disabled." For the most part, these individuals constitute the forgotten, overlooked, or ignored persons in our society, who are, however, "philosophically" entitled to participate in our society. In the past, intervention has been piece-meal and generally uncoordinated, at least in terms of being guided by a comprehensive and integrated conceptual plan.

The TWI system is based on and incorporates an adaptation of existing methods and procedures. The TWI manual describes the measurement base for defining the job and competency characteristics keyed to the feasible measurement properties. Conventionally, these are the tasks and knowledge, skills and abilities, and other characteristics. Then the focus shifts to the individual, again using the same methods and procedures to derive a diagnostic and evaluative frame of reference to guide actions. The action is a constructive intervention to, first, alleviate or remedy the problem and then move toward continual individual development or placement.

The TWI is a content-oriented measurement procedure based on operationally defined measurement dimensions. The structure of the instrument is based on a thematic analysis of critical incident data produced by 50 supported employment counselors (subject matter experts). The content domain was revised and refined to yield 81 behavioral items and further processed to define 16 activity categories based on a thematic classification reflecting functional competency.

The measurement procedure is represented by two primary metric scales defined as: "likelihood of occurrence" of the activity named and "likelihood of ability to perform" the activity. Thus, the measurement is based on two questions for each of the 81 items that constitute the TWI. The final step in the assessment consisted of calculating a difference score as the outcome of the "likelihood of occurrence" ratings and the "likelihood of ability to perform" (p. 9) ratings. Thus, the measurement operation is simply the categorized difference score. Interpretation of the difference score profile is limited to those target items that constitute the supported employment counselors (the assessment SMEs) view as essential.

In this respect, the TWI is an idiosyncratic measurement procedure and thus the interpretation of results is problematic. However, if all goes well, the results can be productively used in designing accommodations in the workplace.

Evaluation of the TWI as a measurement procedure is, at best, nonconventional. The basic metric is a single dimension using two judgments with a calculated difference score, which is a unique (idiosyncratic) application activity.

The first issue of evaluation is reliability of scores from the instrument. This was addressed by calculating correlations between raters representing a range of subject (job incumbents) performance. For the job rating, the reliability estimates (one dimension) were in the range of .81 to .98 depending on the strategy. When evaluating the same scale/different judgment in terms of worker analysis and evaluation, the reliability estimates were comparable (.75, .97). Test-retest estimates (administration interval = 2 weeks) were similar and the overall evaluation indicates that the instrument (two scales—one metric) produces usable results.

The subject of validity of the ratings is an altogether different issue. Estimates of validity, which range from .19 to .34, are somewhat difficult to derive from the report because several measurement operations are used with the option of some form of "correction" for the specific and unique content of the rating measurement. At face value, the TWI appears to yield results that are related to a practical outcome. However, the interpretation of the value of the measurement is essentially in the content of the procedure combined with the application of results at the individual case level, which is best described as an idiosyncratic assessment procedure.

SUMMARY. There are several points worth noting regarding the quality and utility of the TWI:

1. The taxonomy of behavioral dimensions is ultimately pragmatic.

2. The measurement metrics are conventional.

3. The measurement operation (two scales) is questionable.

4. The outcome measure (which reflects a difference score) is problematic.

5. The interpretation of the results, although unique, is essentially irrelevant because the value of the instrument (method and procedure) is embedded in the interpretation methodology.

6. The TWI, although conceptually linked to the job content domain, does not capitalize on the extensive and available relevant measurement history.

7. The TWI is not conceptually linked to the underlying individual difference content domain.

8. Although the TWI content is obviously very pragmatic, the results of measurement do not lead to increased or enhanced understanding of the results of measurement or interpretation.

Overall, even though the system operation is impressive, it is superficial and warrants—actually, demands—improvements. Some recommendations are as follows:

1. The job analysis should be enhanced through meaningful linkage to the PAQ, the Fleishman F-JAS scales, or the PMP taxonomy and scales (Prien & Hughes, 1993).

2. The job analysis operations should be enhanced to provide a separate scale for individual difference measurement using a core of basic constructs similar to the ETS model.

3. The measurement structure should be enhanced to provide for a range of talent/competency beyond the limits of marginal manpower/challenged/disabled persons. Some of those persons in these categories may be quite talented and capable of filling potentially high value jobs.

REVIEWER'S REFERENCE

Prien, E. P., & Hughes, G. L. (1993). Job analysis and ADA compliance. A workshop presented at the 1993 Society for Industrial and Organizational Psychology, San Francisco, CA.

[402]
Trauma Symptom Inventory.

Purpose: Designed for the "evaluation of acute and chronic traumatic symptomatology."

Population: Ages 18 and older.

Publication Date: 1995.

Acronym: TSI.

Scores, 13: Validity Scales (Response Level, Atypical Response, Inconsistent Response); Clinical Scales (Anxious Arousal, Depression, Anger/Irritability, Intrusive Experiences, Defensive Avoidance, Dissociation, Sexual Concerns, Dysfunctional Sexual Behavior, Impaired Self-Reference, Tension Reduction Behavior).

Administration: Group.

Price Data, 1996: $110 per complete kit including manual (67 pages), 10 item booklets, 25 hand-scorable answer sheets, and 25 each of male and female profile forms; $22 per 10 reusable item booklets; $29 per 25 hand-scorable answer sheets; $21 per 25 profile forms (specify male or female); $33 per manual.

Time: (20) minutes.

Comments: Computer scoring system available from publisher.

Author: John Briere.

Publisher: Psychological Assessment Resources, Inc.

Cross References: See T5:2782 (3 references).

Review of the Trauma Symptom Inventory by EPHREM FERNANDEZ, Associate Professor of Clinical Psychology, Southern Methodist University, Dallas, TX:

Psychological features of trauma are often elusive and misdiagnosed and thus in need of standardized psychometric assessment through tests like the Trauma Symptom Inventory (TSI). This is a paper-and-pencil test with 100 items describing trauma-related symptoms that are to be rated on a 4-point scale of frequency of occurrence over the preceding 6 months. Ten symptom domains are assessed: Anxious Arousal, Depression, Anger/Irritability, Intrusive Experiences, Defensive Avoidance, Dissociation, Sexual Concerns, Dysfunctional Sexual Behavior, Impaired Self-Reference, and Tension Reduction Behavior. Unlike many of its rival tests, the TSI possesses built-in validity scales to detect underendorsement, overendorsement, and inconsistent responding to items. The test is worded at the fifth- to seventh-grade reading level and takes about 20 minutes to complete.

It should be noted at the outset that the test does not ask about what may have triggered the trauma. In effect, the various symptoms can be endorsed independently of any traumatic event. This makes it difficult to justify diagnoses of Posttraumatic Stress Disorder (PTSD) or Acute Stress Disorder (ASD) both of which require the actual experience or witnessing of an event involving actual or threatened death or serious injury or threat to the physical integrity of oneself or others (American Psychiatric Association, 1994). Implicitly, the TSI takes a response perspective of trauma while ignoring the stimulus. This limitation may have been avoided by simply wording the items as reactions to a traumatic event as in the Impact of Event Scale (Horowitz, Wilner, & Alvarez, 1979) rather than as "loose symptoms" unconnected to any precipitating event. Alternatively, the utility of the TSI in diagnosing and quantifying trauma can be assured when collateral sources of information are used to confirm the existence of a trigger event.

Related to the above comment, a definition of trauma seems to be missing in the manual. Given their relatively recent entry into psychiatric nosology, labels such as PTSD and ASD also need to be explained in relation to the TSI. Also, how does trauma differ from the so-called major life events? A brief clarification of these concepts in the introduction of the manual would guide the researcher or clinician in choosing the most appropriate test for the problem in question.

Of the 10 clinical scales, 2 (Sexual Concerns or SC and Dysfunctional Sexual Behavior or DSB) are primarily relevant to one particular type of trauma—that associated with rape and sexual abuse. On Page 38 of the manual, the author acknowledges that victims of sexual trauma might be expected to have higher scores on these scales. A related possibility is that those with nonsexual trauma are likely to have lower scores on these two scales and therefore lower scores on the test as a whole even though their actual degree of trauma (due to whatever event) may be no less. Because rape and sexual molestation are more prevalent among women, this may also explain the higher mean TSI scores for women as compared to men. In short, trauma of a sexual nature may be the concern of many people today but it is only one of several types (including but not limited to combat, industrial accidents, and natural disasters), and it certainly does not define conditions like PTSD or ASD despite its relevance to subpopulations in this area of enquiry. Quite likely, the SC and DSB scales are vestiges of the forerunner of the TSI: the Trauma Symptom Checklist (TSC; Briere & Runtz, 1989; Elliott & Briere, 1992). The TSC had been designed primarily to assess sequelae of sexual abuse. On the other hand, the TSI is supposed to be a general test of trauma symptoms.

One scale that did exist in the TSC but was surprisingly dropped from the TSI is "sleep disturbance." Persistent difficulty falling or staying asleep is one of the indications of heightened arousal in PTSD sufferers. Another co-occurring problem, though not among the formal DSM criteria for PTSD, is substance abuse. Many trauma victims resort to medication and legal and illicit drugs to sleep or counteract hyperarousal or just distract themselves from intrusive cognitions. Like depression, anxiety and irritability, sleep disturbance and substance abuse are not definitive of trauma but they are part of the broad symptomatology and hence worthy of assessment.

Moving beyond issues of content validity, the psychometrics of the TSI surpass those of the TSC and many of the other existing tests of trauma-related symptoms. In constructing the TSI, a study of 279 university students was conducted to refine 100 items out of an initial pool of 182 statements. A second study administered these items to 404 females and 66 males from clinical settings, and a third study obtained data from 3,659 U.S. Navy recruits divided almost equally between males and females. These three studies revealed mean clinical scale internal consistency reliability estimates of .84, .87, and .85 respectively. A final stratified random sample of 836 subjects representing all geographical units of the U.S. was used to generate norms. This revealed significant intercorrelations among all the clinical scales. Discriminant function analyses showed TSI *T* scores to be significantly associated with interpersonal violence or natural disasters in adults or children. TSI scores showed reasonable concurrent validity with similar scales from the Brief Symptom Inventory (Derogatis & Spencer, 1982) and the PTSD scale of the Symptom Checklist-90-Revised (Saunders, Arata, & Kilpatrick, 1990). Moreover, for females, the TSI exceeded the SCL (Symptom Checklist) and the IES (Impact of Event Scale) in identification of distress due to victimization. An optimally weighted combination of TSI scales correctly predicted 24 of 26 PTSD positive cases and 385 of 423 PTSD negative cases. When the subject also reported a traumatic event in his or her life, the TSI's accuracy increased to 96% true-positive and 91% true-negative prediction.

Concurrent and discriminant validity evidence was presented for TSI validity scales with the exception of the INC scale intended to measure inconsistent responding. The INC scale consists of pairs of items that are expected to be answered alike. Closer scrutiny reveals that there are also other items similar in meaning to the paired items. For example, Item 14 ("not feeling happy") is part of the same INC pair as Item 17 ("feeling depressed") but also reads much the same as Item 7 ("sadness"); Item 8 ("flashbacks" or sudden memories or images of upsetting things) is not only similar to its INC partner Item 62 ("suddenly remembering something upsetting from your past") but also to Item 66 ("suddenly being reminded of something bad"). This means that the items fall short of capturing the complexity of the phenomenon under investigation thus deflating the content validity of the test with the probable result of inflating the measures of internal consistency.

On a final matter of format, the TSI symptoms are rated on a 4-point frequency scale with reference to the 6-month time period prior to test-taking. This could be qualified by measures of symptom intensity and duration too. Furthermore, expanding the time frame beyond 6 months might also add to the clinical picture; it could pose some problems of recall but may be particularly appropriate for delayed onset PTSD.

SUMMARY. The TSI addresses an important need in the assessment of psychological symptoms of trauma. It is a very fine example of the process of test construction and refinement. Data available so far attest to its overall psychometric soundness. It goes beyond its rivals by including validity scales to detect random or biased responding and also including critical items for identifying issues worthy of crisis intervention or follow-up evaluation. The author of the instrument is careful to temper his advocacy of the test with concluding remarks about the complex nature of PTSD and ASD and the recommendation to use a battery of standardized tests along with a face-to-face interview when assessing these conditions.

REVIEWER'S REFERENCES

Horowitz, M., Wilner, N., & Alvarez, W. (1979). Impact of Event Scale: A measure of subjective stress. *Psychosomatic Medicine, 41,* 209–218.
Derogatis, L. R., & Spencer, P. M. (1982). *The Brief Symptom Inventory administration, scoring, and procedures.* Baltimore: Clinical Psychometric Research Institute.
Briere, J., & Runtz, M. (1989). The Trauma Symptom Checklist (TSC-33): Early data on a new scale. *Journal of Interpersonal Violence, 4,* 151–163.
Saunders, B. E., Arata, C. M., & Kilpatrick, D. G. (1990). Development of a crime-related Post-Traumatic Stress Disorder scale for women within the Symptom Checklist-90-Revised. *Journal of Traumatic Stress, 3,* 267–277.
Elliott, D. M., & Briere, J. (1992). Sexual abuse trauma among professional women: Validating the Trauma Symptom Checklist-40 (TSC-40). *Child Abuse and Neglect, 16,* 391–398.
American Psychiatric Association. (1994). *Diagnostic and statistical manual of mental disorders* (4th ed.). Washington, DC: American Psychiatric Association.

Review of the Trauma Symptom Inventory by JACK E. GEBART-EAGLEMONT, *Lecturer in Psychology, Swinburne University of Technology, Hawthorn, Victoria, Australia:*

The Trauma Symptom Inventory (TSI) is a 100-item self-report instrument that measures symptoms of Posttraumatic Stress Disorder (PTSD) and Acute Stress Disorder (ASD). The clinical scales assess the following groups of symptoms: (a) posttraumatic hyperarousal or "anxious arousal" (jumpiness, tension); (b) depressive symptomatology or "depression" (sadness, hopelessness); (c) irritable affect or anger (angry cognitions and behavior); (d) intrusive experiences (flashbacks, nightmares); (e) posttraumatic defensive avoidance (cognitive and behavioral); (f) dissociative symptomatology (depersonalization, derealization, numbing); (g) sexual distress (dissatisfaction, dysfunction, unwanted sexual thoughts); (h) dysfunctional sexual behavior (promiscuity, risky or potentially harmful sexual behaviors, sex performed to accomplish nonsexual goals); (i) impaired self-reference (identity confusion, low self-esteem); and (j) tension reduction (self-mutilation, angry outbursts, manipulative behaviors). The TSI includes also three validity scales that measure level of dissimulation, atypical response style, and inconsistent response style.

The TSI kit includes the manual, reusable item-booklet, hand-scorable answer sheet, and profile forms. The materials are professionally presented and the administration of the test is uncomplicated and well explained. The scoring and profiling procedures using the normative tables are clear and easy to follow. The manual is written in a transparent, succinct style, and adequately presents all information needed by the user, such as interpretation, normative data, and information related to the development and validation of the test.

TEST DEVELOPMENT. The construction of the TSI followed the objective of measuring the multidimensional diagnostic aspects of posttraumatic stress. The recent form of the test is based mainly on the Trauma Symptom Checklist (Briere & Runtz, 1989), oriented towards measurement of the typical posttraumatic domains. The initial version containing 182 items was tested with 279 university students and 370 clinical subjects to demonstrate its psychometric properties. After deletion of the redundant or poorly performing items, the resulting final version contained 100 items. The psychometric properties of this version were assessed using several different groups of subjects (including both normal and clinical samples).

NORMATIVE DATA. The normative sample ($N = 836$) was obtained using mail sampling methodologies (a stratified and random sample). The sample's demographic distributions approximately correspond to the 1990 U.S. Census distribution of sex, ethnic group, age, marital and employment status, education, and state of residence. The T-scores for each scale were computed for four groups (sex X age condition). The age grouping classifies ages 55 years and above as "Older." The manual also contains normative tables for U.S. Navy recruits (male and female).

RELIABILITY. The psychometric properties of the TSI were analyzed using four samples (standardization sample, $N = 828$; university students, $N = 279$; clinical sample, $N = 370$; Navy recruits, $N = 3,659$). The student and clinical samples were characterized by a gender imbalance (the majority of the subjects were females). Internal consistency of the TSI scales was estimated using alpha reliability coefficients. All clinical scales demonstrated respectable levels of internal consistency across the four validation studies: Anxious Arousal from .82 to .87; Depression from .87 to .91; Anger/Irritability from .88 to .90; Intrusive Experience from .87 to .90; Defensive Avoidance from .87 to .90; Dissociation from .82 to .88; Sexual Concerns from .80 to .89; Dysfunctional Sexual Behavior from .77 to .89; Impaired Self-Reference from .85 to .88; and Tension Reduction Behavior from .69 to .76. The average alpha coefficient for all clinical scales and across studies was above .85. Reliability of the control scales was reported for only two studies. The alpha coefficients were .75 in both studies for the Atypical Response scale, .80 and .78 for the Response Level, .51 and .55 for the Inconsistent Response scale. It should be noted that the low alpha coefficients for the IR do not discredit this scale, which by definition reflects low consistency among the responses of some participants. The manual does not provide any data concerning test-retest reliability.

FACTOR STRUCTURE. The factor structure of the TSI is not clear. Exploratory factor analysis (the extraction and rotation methods were not reported) resulted in one large factor (explaining from 62% to 67% of variance in two studies), and one small factor (explaining from 9% to 12% of variance). The first factor may be interpreted as general distress, as it loads on all clinical scales except for Sexual Concerns and Dysfunctional Sexual Behavior. The second factor represents sexual distress (it loads very strongly on Dysfunctional Sexual Behavior and strongly on Sexual Concerns). Some scales (Impaired Self-Reference and Tension Reduction) are shared by both factors. The attempt at confirmatory factor analysis presented in the manual was ill-conceived. The three-factor model, computed using the EQS program (Bentler, 1992) to "fit" the instrument's structure into "current trauma theory" is conceptually wrong; the proposed components Trauma and Dysphoria were correlated at $r = .95$, which clearly indicates that they constitute one factor. The efforts to force the instrument's structure into a three-factor model were in fact not necessary because the TSI is merely a standardized and quantified symptom checklist, and such instruments are not expected to demonstrate clear second-order factor structures. Another part of the problem is that the analysis attempted to factor analyze clinical scales (item packets) instead of items. This represents a second-order factor-analytic approach, which is based on an assumption that the primary scales represent genuine and moderately correlated factors. The assumption that the primary scales themselves are factor-analytically sound (i.e., self-contained and non-overlapping) was probably not met, and this must subsequently result in the poor structures obtained from the second-order factor analyses. A feasible latent variable approach to such data would be first to form the clinical scales by factor-analyzing all items, and then try a second-order analysis of these factorial scales.

VALIDITY. Data concerning convergent validity of the TSI are presented in the manual. Some correlation coefficients between the TSI scales and the Brief Symptom Inventory (BSI; Derogatis & Spencer; 1982) dimensions indicated a high level of convergent validity of at least three scales: Anxious Arousal ($r = .75$ with BSI-Anxiety), Anger/Irritability ($r = .77$ with BSI-Hostility), and Depression ($r = .82$ with BSI-Depression). The other TSI scales demonstrated a rather diffuse pattern of correlating with all BSI scales, which indicates that they measure rather general psychological distress. This indicates a potential problem of considerably limited evidence of discriminant validity. A similar pattern, albeit to a somewhat lesser extent, was present in correlations between the TSI scales and the scales of two other instruments measuring posttraumatic stress: the Impact of Event Scale (IES; Horowitz, Wilner, & Alvarez; 1979) and the Symptom Checklist (SCL). Incremental validity was assessed using sequential entry regressions, with Impact of Event Scale, Symptom Checklist, and Brief Symptom Inventory as primary predictors of a dichotomous variable "interpersonal trauma" versus "no interpersonal trauma" based on self-reported history of childhood and/or adult victimization. For male subjects, the TSI failed to contribute significantly more variance than was accounted for already by any of the three above-mentioned instruments. For female subjects, significant incremental validity was demonstrated in the cases of the IES and the BSI (as the initial entry). These data raise the possible question of gender specificity of the TSI items. Criterion validity of the TSI scales was

tested using analysis of variance (ANOVA) and discriminant function analysis (DFA). The results of analysis of variance indicated significant differences between all scale means for trauma positive versus trauma negative cases in the standardization sample ($N = 449$). The DFA reclassification resulted in 92% true positive classifications and 91% true negative classifications using joint scoring procedures involving IES and SCL as taxonomical criteria. The reclassification results were increased to 96% true positive using a diagnosis augmented by an additional criterion of a past traumatic experience at some point in the subject's life. It should be noted that some of the scales (Anger/Irritability, Sexual Concerns, Dysfunctional Sexual Behavior, Impaired Self-Reference, and Tension Reduction) also differentiated significantly between positive versus negative diagnosis of Borderline Personality Disorder, and the resulting DFA reclassification achieved 88% positive (Personality Disorder) diagnoses. These results again indicate a possible problem with discriminant validity of at least some elements of the TSI; the ability of the test to discriminate between Posttraumatic Stress and Personality Disorder appears to be doubtful. This problem should be further investigated by DFA analyses of PTSD cases versus BPD cases; the reported analyses differentiated merely between "No Dx" and "Yes Dx" for these two types of psychopathology separately, without any attempt to differentiate between them.

CONTROL SCALES. The TSI has three short (10 items each) control scales: Atypical Response (ATR), Response Level (RL), and Inconsistent Response (INC). The correlations between these validity scales and the control scales of the Personality Assessment Inventory (PAI; Morey; 1991) and Minnesota Multiphasic Personality Inventory-2 (MMPI-2) were in the expected directions, although they were moderate. For example, the ATR scores demonstrated correlation coefficients of .52 with the PAI-Negative Impression Management, and .50 with the MMPI-2 F scale. The RL scores correlated .46 and .36 with the MMPI-2 K and L scales respectively. The scores of the RL scale correlated -.33 with the PAI-Negative Impression Management, and .50 with the PAI Positive Impression Management. The distributions of scores of the validity scales are presented in the TSI manual and demonstrate the high discriminatory value of the ATR scale and the good discriminatory value of the RL scale. Discrimination provided by the scores of the INC scale was moderate, although still psychometrically useful. Overall, the TSI control scales performed their functions moderately well. They assess the level of dissimulation, the unusual responding set that may indicate simulation, and the random (neglectful) responding set.

Discriminatory power of validity scales is of paramount importance for an instrument such as the TSI, as the diagnostic opinions concerning posttraumatic stress may be used in legal proceedings involving litigation and compensation, as well as by prosecution teams in some specific criminal cases (e.g., rape, assault, sexual harassment, violent victimization). The use of the PTSD diagnostic data by defense teams in criminal cases is also likely (e.g., violent involvements of war veterans, criminal negligence attributable to psychopathology, sexual crimes committed by abuse victims). In such cases, it would be prudent to augment diagnostic validity, possibly using MMPI 2 control scores.

SUMMARY. The TSI scales demonstrated high internal consistency and good convergent validity, but somewhat lower discriminant validity. Although the level of diagnostic differentiation between the positive and negative (known) PTSD cases is high, the diffuse patterns of correlations with other measures of general distress and positive identification of cases of personality disorders by some of the subscales indicate that the instrument should be used with care, and not be the sole basis of clinical, and particularly forensic, evaluation. The TSI data should be integrated with the results of other diagnostic instruments measuring the broad psychopathological spectrum, especially in forensic evaluations. It is advisable to use the TSI in conjunction with at least one measure of general psychopathology (such as the MMPI-2), which would provide useful multiphasic and differential diagnostic information. Moreover, because the method of simulation detection implemented by the TSI is considerably weaker than its dissimulation control scale, and both are quite short (10 items each), some specialized instruments measuring simulation should also be used in conjunction with forensic application of the TSI in order to eliminate deception and malingering as a diagnostic possibility. Another possible weak point is related to indications of the gender-specificity of the TSI items that suggest that the scale performs better with females.

The strong points of the TSI are: (a) the clinically clear, internally consistent organization and quantification of diagnostic information useful in assessment of the known clinical PTSD cases; (b) the incorporation of critical items, indicating potential risks and clinical problems presented by the patient; and (c) satisfactory levels of convergent validity, which makes the TSI useful in situations not requiring differential diagnostic decisions.

REVIEWER'S REFERENCES

Horowitz, M., Wilner, N., & Alvarez, W. (1979). Impact of Event Scale: A measure of subjective stress. *Psychosomatic Medicine, 41,* 209–218.
Derogatis, L. R., & Spencer, P. M. (1982). *The Brief Symptom Inventory (BSI): Administration, scoring, and procedures manual-I.* Baltimore: Clinical Psychometric Research Institute.
Briere, J., & Runtz, M. (1989). The Trauma Symptom Checklist (TSC-33): Early data on a new scale. *Journal of Interpersonal Violence, 4,* 151–163.
Morey, L. C. (1991). *Personality Assessment Inventory professional manual.* Odessa, FL: Psychological Assessment Resources.
Bentler, P. M. (1992). *EQS Structural Equations Program manual.* Los Angeles: BMDP Statistical Software.

[403]
Treatment Intervention Inventory.

Purpose: Designed for intake, referral and post-treatment comparisons of adult counseling clients.
Population: Ages 12–18; Adult counseling clients.
Publication Dates: 1991–1997.
Acronym: TII; TII-J.
Scores, 9: Truthfulness, Anxiety, Depression, Self-Esteem, Distress, Family, Alcohol, Drug, Stress Coping Abilities.
Administration: Group.
Levels, 2: Adult, Juvenile.
Price Data: Available from publisher.
Time: (35) minutes Adult; (25–30) minutes Juvenile.
Comments: "A computerized, self-report assessment"; administration by paper and pencil or by computer; computer scored.
Author: Behavior Data Systems Ltd.
Publisher: Behavior Data Systems Ltd.

Review of the Treatment Intervention Inventory by JANICE G. MURDOCH, Professor of Psychology, Clemson University, Clemson, SC:

The Treatment Intervention Inventory (TII) is intended as a brief assessment device for measuring change over treatment. According to the manual, it can be used to document need for treatment and to judge appropriateness for treatment, as well as assessing improvement during treatment. Thus, one potential purpose of the test is to provide data to insurance providers to demonstrate treatment effectiveness.

Although the TII is administered in a paper-and-pencil format, all scoring is done with a computer program. The computer program also stores data on scored tests, so that a database can be developed. This feature would allow for easy development of local norms for the measure.

The TII manual and "Inventory of Scientific Findings" are vague and poorly written. No references are given, suggesting that none of the studies done on the TII have been published in refereed journals. No authors' names are mentioned. A literature search turned up no mention of the TII. The only information available about the TII appears to be what is given out by the publishers. This information is incomplete and unsatisfying.

The manual indicates that the TII was developed "empirically" from a large item pool. No specific information is given for selection criteria for items. The authors report that items from other tests were used, but do not reveal which other tests. No normative information is provided.

Internal consistency reliability estimates for the nine scale scores as given in the "Inventory of Scientific Findings" are all above .80, indicating that each of the scales is measuring a single construct consistently. Cronbach's alphas are provided for two groups of outpatients and two groups of inpatients. Although the TII is intended to be given as a before and after measure, no information is given on test-retest reliability.

VALIDITY. The most impressive validity information provided for TII scales is concurrent validity with other measures. Concurrent validity estimates range from .72 for the Truthfulness Scale (with the MMPI Lie Scale) to .17 for the Alcohol Scale (with the MacAndrew Alcoholism Scale). Low to moderate correlations (.17 to .62) are reported for the other scales with MMPI scales and other measures. Most attention is paid in the manual to the validity of the Stress Coping Abilities Scale and the Alcohol and Drug scales, which overall appear to have good concurrent validity. The authors accept any statistically significant correlation as evidence of validity and do not address the variance unaccounted for by the relationship between TII scores and other measures.

The TII manual does not address the particular difficulties of assessing change. There is no discussion of the reliability of the TII over time, or of the sensitivity of the measure for detecting changes. No studies were reported illustrating the use of the TII for measuring treatment outcome. The nine scales of the TII cover a range of issue areas, but it is not clear how or why these particular areas were chosen. Each scale appears to be a global measure of the concept; therefore, it is not clear how helpful the measure would be for detecting treatment-related changes in functioning for clients with specific problems.

SUMMARY. The TII is a brief instrument intended for determining appropriate referral and for assessing change over the course of treatment. Its strengths are that it is quickly administered and has a built-in capacity for development of a database. Also, the subscales have demonstrated good internal consistency reliability and some subscales have good concurrent validity with established measures. Weaknesses of the TII include lack of information on test-retest reliability and lack of information on sensitivity of the TII to change as a result of treatment. The manual is poorly written and lacks detail. The TII should be used cautiously until more data are available to confirm the reliability and validity uses of its scores.

Review of the Treatment Intervention Inventory by LINDA J. ZIMMERMAN, Clinical/School Psychologist, Private Practice, Pittsburgh, PA:

The Treatment Intervention Inventory (TII) was designed for use in clinical settings. Changes in health care systems over the past decade, particularly in mental health and chemical dependency counseling agencies, have directed an emphasis on accurate problem identification and documented treatment intervention. Decisions regarding interventions, changes in patient status, continuation of treatment, and provider accountability are subject to review. The authors assert that the TII was developed to help meet those needs. Specifically, the TII was designed for intake, referral, and post treatment comparisons of adult populations (a juvenile format is available). The authors suggest that the TII "enables staff to compare patient's opinions with empirically based objective measures of client problems and need" (manual, p. 1). However, they acknowledge no diagnosis or decision should be based solely on the test results.

There was no traditional manual for this instrument; however, there was a detailed computer operating guide and a summary of scientific findings. Although the computer operating guide presented information and instructions that appeared easy to follow, I was unable to activate the test demonstration diskette using the prompts and commands indicated in the instructions. Therefore, I will address only the written material that was provided to me and cannot speak to the ease or difficulty of using the computer administration, supervisor data entry, or retrieval of the report.

The TII can be administered in paper-and-pencil test booklet format or on the computer. The assessment instrument contains 195 items and can be completed in 35 minutes. Within minutes, a computer-generated report can be available onsite. The eight scales are presented in a profile utilizing percentiles for easy and quick interpretation. Descriptive narratives for each scale provide more in depth information regarding the client's responses. Significant test items that were endorsed by the client are identified and may assist in understanding the client's situation. The report format is concise and user friendly. However, there was no specific information provided indicating how the report is developed, nor was there indication of appropriate studies supporting the report data and subsequent interpretations.

In the summary of scientific findings, the TII was described as having been researched and normed on inpatient and outpatient treatment and counseling populations. Although this measure refers to use in mental health and chemical dependency populations, it seems to be mostly dedicated to chemical dependency treatment. Certainly mental health issues can impact chemical use issues and this measure seems to be based on this premise for the most part. There was little evidence to support that this instrument would be helpful in the general clinical population.

There were several studies cited designating this instrument as psychometrically sound. The validity studies compared the various scales on the TII to similar scales of other measures. Although the results of these studies were supportive, it was often difficult to follow the reading and interpretation of the study due to abbreviations, acronyms, and lack of information identifying the other measures. It would have been helpful to have fully identified the comparative measures that had been used in a separate section, indicating their purpose and reasons for comparisons. The comparative instruments were reported to be psychometrically sound, but again little identifying information was provided.

There were four reliability studies discussed in the summary and scores from this instrument were considered to be reliable. The populations involved were described as outpatient or inpatient,

but it was unclear as to whether they were in the general clinical population or substance abuse population. There were numerous breakdowns of identifying categories of the participants, including gender, race, educational level, age, marital status, and employment information. Only one of the four studies recognized a significant population of minorities. For the most part, the studies included Caucasian males and thus it would be difficult to generalize the results to the general clinical population due to the risk of biased information. The TII does allow for continued research through the data collection on the diskettes, which must be returned to the authors on an annual basis. There is a method for erasing confidential identifying information of the patient prior to returning the diskette. Although this method of data collection is helpful to continuing research, it is not necessarily conducive to casual use by small agencies or sole proprietors. Credit is given for unused portions of the diskette.

SUMMARY. This instrument is viewed as an important endeavor for current clinical health care treatment needs and documentation. Although there were positive characteristics of this instrument, such as the clinical report format, there were also numerous issues that restrict me from recommending this instrument for use. The lack of a formal organized manual limited the ease of identifying pertinent information in a timely and user-friendly manner. Further, there needs to be additional research that would support the psychometric quality of this measure. The authors appear to have developed an important tool that could be improved upon and better defined in several areas.

[404]
Universal Nonverbal Intelligence Test.

Purpose: "Designed to provide a more fair measure of the general intelligence and cognitive abilities of children and adolescents ... who may be disadvantaged by traditional verbal and language-loaded measures."
Population: Ages 5–17.
Publication Date: 1998.
Acronym: UNIT.
Scores, 11: Symbolic Memory, Cube Design, Spatial Memory, Analogic Reasoning, Object Memory, Mazes, Memory Quotient, Reasoning Quotient, Symbolic Quotient, Nonsymbolic Quotient, Full Scale IQ.
Administration: Individual.
Forms: Abbreviated Battery, Standard Battery, Extended Battery.

Price Data, 2001: $460 per complete kit including examiner's manual (334 pages), stimulus book 1 & 2, 16 response chips, response grid, 9 cubes, response mat, 10 symbolic memory cards, 25 record forms, 25 mazes response booklets, black pencil, red pencil, administration at a glance, and canvas carrying case; $35 per 25 record forms; $17 per 25 abbreviated record forms; $39 per 25 mazes response booklets; $67 per manual.

Time: (10–15) minutes, Abbreviated Battery; (30) minutes, Standard Battery; (45) minutes, Extended Battery.

Authors: Bruce A. Bracken and R. Steve McCallum.

Publisher: Riverside Publishing.

Review of the Universal Nonverbal Intelligence Test by DEBORAH L. BANDALOS, Associate Professor, Department of Educational Psychology, University of Nebraska—Lincoln, Lincoln, NE:

The Universal Nonverbal intelligence Test (UNIT) is an individually administered, completely nonverbal instrument designed to measure "the general intelligence and cognitive abilities of children and adolescents from ages 5 years through 17 years who may be disadvantaged by traditional verbal and language-loaded measures" (manual, p. 1). The UNIT was designed to provide an accurate assessment of intellectual functioning for children and adolescents for whom traditional language-loaded measures may not be appropriate due to speech, language, or hearing impairments, differences in cultural background, or certain psychiatric disorders.

The UNIT consists of six subtests: Symbolic Memory, Cube Design, Spatial Memory, Analogic Reasoning, Object Memory, and Mazes. These subtests were designed to measure two components of intelligence: memory, assessed by the Symbolic Memory, Spatial Memory, and Object Memory subtests, and reasoning, assessed by the Cube Design, Analogic Reasoning, and Mazes subtests. Although the measures are administered nonverbally and include no actual words, the authors of the UNIT characterize the Symbolic Memory, Analogic Reasoning, and Object Memory subtests as *verbally mediated.* By this they mean that, because the objects presented in these subtests are concrete representations of things such as animals or people, they can be *mentally* labeled and organized by examinees. Material on the other three subtests consists of more abstract figures and geometric shapes that are not as amenable to verbal labeling. Another dimension along which

the six subtests can be categorized is therefore as symbolic, including the verbally mediated subtests, and nonsymbolic, encompassing the Cube Design, Spatial Memory, and Mazes subtests. The examiner may choose from three administration options: the Extended Battery, which includes all six subtests; the Standard Battery, which includes the first four subtests listed; or the Abbreviated Battery which includes the first two subtests. The Standard Battery is intended as the most frequently administered option, whereas the Abbreviated Battery is appropriate only for initial screening. The Extended Battery is intended to be used for "more in-depth diagnostic assessments" (manual, p. 2), according to the authors.

The theoretical foundation for the UNIT is based on the conceptualization of intelligence as a superordinate general ability factor (g) that encompasses two subordinate factors of associative ability, or memory, and cognitive ability, or reasoning. The items included in the UNIT were identified through a review of the literature and modified or adapted for nonverbal administration.

The manual states that the memory subtests of the UNIT provide a more comprehensive measure of memory processes than those of the Wechsler and Stanford-Binet scales because they require both verbal mediation and motoric responses. However, the extent to which the requirement for motoric responses (i.e., pointing to the correct answer) increases the *cognitive* complexity of the tasks is not clear. UNIT memory items differ on at least three dimensions (e.g., color, type of object, number, location, or sequence), making the tasks more complex and thus potentially more difficult than those on other instruments. The reasoning subtests contain item types that are more similar to those found on traditional verbally administered instruments, but differ in their nonverbal administration format. These tasks include analogies, block design tasks, progressive matrices, and mazes.

NORMS. The UNIT was standardized on a carefully chosen, nationally representative sample of 2,100 children aged 5 years, 0 months to 17 years, 11 months, and 30 days. The sample was stratified on the following variables: gender, race, Hispanic origin, region, parental educational attainment, community setting, classroom placement (regular or special education), special education services received (learning disability, speech and language impairments, serious emotional disturbance, mental retardation, giftedness, English as a second language and bilingual education, and regular education). Similarity of the sample to the 1995 U.S. Census data on the first five of these variables is remarkably close. Although the norm group is impressive in this regard, separate norms for specific groups would be an extremely useful future addition to the normative data. Because the authors state that the UNIT can be validly used with deaf or hearing impaired, mentally retarded, seriously emotionally disturbed, and speech and language impaired individuals, separate norms for these groups, although admittedly difficult to obtain, would provide a valuable frame of reference within which to interpret their scores.

SCORING OPTIONS. Scoring options include raw and scaled scores for each subtest. Scaled scores were developed for each full year age group based on conversion of percentile ranks. Standard scores are also computed for each of the following scales: Memory, Reasoning, Symbolic, Nonsymbolic, and Full Scale, by adding together the appropriate subtests and converting these sums to scores having means of 100 and standard deviations of 15, based on percentile ranks within each age group. Test-age equivalents are also available for all subscales, which can be interpreted as the level of performance of an average child at that age. Tables are given to determine whether differences between pairs of subtest or scale scores should be considered statistically significant.

RELIABILITY. Estimates of internal consistency for the subtests and scales using corrected split-half correlations are reported for each age group as well as for a clinical/exceptional sample. It should be noted that this may not be appropriate for the Cube Design and Mazes subtests, which are speeded. Coefficients for these subtests may be inflated for this reason. For the standardization sample, reliability estimates for the full scale range from .84 to .94 for the Abbreviated Battery, from .89 to .95 for the Standard Battery, and from .91 to .94 for the Extended Battery, with the majority of the coefficients in the higher end of each range. Not surprisingly, reliability estimates for younger children tend to be slightly lower than those for older children. The estimates for the clinical/exceptional sample are slightly higher at .96, .98, and .98 for the Abbreviated, Standard, and Extended Batteries, respectively.

Subtest reliabilities were somewhat lower, as would be expected. Averaged across all ages, these ranged from .64 for the Mazes subtest to .91 for Cube Design. For the scale scores, coefficients were in the high .80s to low .90s for both the Standard and Extended Batteries. Test retest reliability was estimated over a 3-week time interval for a sample of 197 children. After correction for restriction of range, these coefficients range from .78 to .91 for the Standard and Extended Battery full scale scores; values for the Abbreviated Battery are only slightly lower, ranging from .74 to .89. Again, these values tend to increase with age. Values for the Object Memory and Mazes subtests were in the .50s and .60s for all ages, but values for the other subtests were quite acceptable overall. It should also be noted that the UNIT subtests have very adequate floors and ceilings, making them appropriate for assessing both extremely low and high ability examinees.

VALIDITY. Given that the UNIT was first published in 1998, an impressive amount of validity evidence is presented in the manual. Factor analyses indicate that the subtests cluster into a memory and a reasoning factor, as expected. Confirmatory factor analytic methods were used to test three models: a one-factor model, a two-factor memory/reasoning factor, and a two-factor symbolic/nonsymbolic factor. The two-factor memory/reasoning factor was found to fit the data best, confirming the structure hypothesized by the test's authors. Evidence of concurrent validity was presented through correlations of the UNIT with the Wechsler Intelligence Scale for Children—Third Edition (WISC-III), the Woodcock-Johnson Psycho-Educational Battery—Revised (WJ-R), the Kaufman Brief Intelligence Test (K-BIT), and the Test of Nonverbal Intelligence—Second Edition (TONI-2), among others. Although these studies were based on small samples of children, the evidence obtained from them is generally supportive of the validity of the UNIT as a measure of intelligence that shares considerable variance with these commonly used scales. For example, correlations between the WISC-III and UNIT full scale scores were generally in the mid to high .80s (corrected for attenuation) for samples of learning disabled, mentally retarded, gifted, and Native American children. Average scores on the two instruments were extremely close for the first and last sample, but differed for the mentally retarded and gifted sample in predictable ways. Because the

UNIT was specifically developed to have reduced dependence on verbal skills in which mentally retarded examinees are typically deficient, scores from this sample were higher on the UNIT than on the WISC-III. Intellectually gifted students, on the other hand, tend to have stronger verbal than performance skills and thus scored lower on the UNIT, which emphasizes the latter type of skill.

Correlations of the UNIT with measures of academic achievement such as the Tests of Achievement of the WJ-R, the Spanish form of the Woodcock Language Proficiency Battery—Revised (WLPB-R), the Wechsler Individual Achievement Test (WIAT), and the Peabody Individual Achievement Test—Revised (PIAT-R) were presented as evidence of predictive validity. The studies presented were based on small sample sizes, and it was not clear whether the UNIT and achievement scores had been obtained concurrently, or whether the achievement scores were obtained after some time interval. More description of the procedures would have been helpful. These correlations were typically much lower than those of the UNIT with other measures of intelligence, and varied somewhat widely across the different studies. For example, correlations between the UNIT Standard Battery full scale scores and the WJ-R Broad Knowledge scale were .51, .56, and .66 for samples of learning disabled, mentally retarded, and intellectually gifted students, respectively. However, the highest correlations of the UNIT with WLPB-R subscales were .55 and .10 for samples of Bilingual Education and ESL students.

No studies of the validity of the UNIT for predicting school grades or classroom achievement are presented. This type of evidence would be a useful addition to the data on the UNIT. Evidence is presented to show that this measure is able to accurately identify and classify mentally retarded and learning disabled students, but it is relatively less successful in identifying intellectually gifted students.

FAIRNESS. Because the UNIT was designed to provide a fair assessment of intelligence for individuals differing in cultural background as well as for those with hearing impairments, language disabilities, and learning disabilities, great care was taken in its development to avoid or eliminate sources of bias. The development of test content focused on item formats that were thought to be least culturally influenced, and item fairness was assessed by various methods including indices of differential item functioning. Group comparisons indicate no significant differences in performance based on gender and smaller differences for African-American, Hispanic, and Native American children than those that have been reported for other tests of intelligence. In addition, the UNIT was found to be equally reliable for members of different gender and ethnic groups.

PRACTICAL CONSIDERATIONS. Administration times as reported by the authors are 15 minutes for the Abbreviated, and 30 and 45 minutes, respectively, for the Standard and Extended Batteries. The manual provides detailed instructions for scoring along with information on score interpretation. The authors indicate that the inclusion of varied stimulus formats both within and across subtests results in a test that is more interesting to examinees. However, it should also be pointed out that switching between stimuli within a subtest may be confusing for some children. Finally, the proscription of any verbalization may be frustrating when examinees are able to verbalize responses.

SUMMARY. The UNIT provides a much-needed means of obtaining reliable and valid assessments of intelligence for children with a wide array of disabilities who cannot be tested accurately with existing instruments. It is a carefully developed instrument with excellent reliability and impressive evidence of validity for use as a supplement to or substitute for more traditional measures such as the WISC-III. Although additional validity evidence based on larger groups, as well as studies of predictive validity for school grades or other classroom achievement measures would be desirable, the evidence presented in the manual is both appropriate and convincing.

[405]

University Residence Environment Scale [Revised].

Purpose: Designed to "assess the social climate of university student living groups."
Population: University students and staff.
Publication Dates: 1974–1988.
Acronym: URES.
Scores, 10: Involvement, Emotional Support, Independence, Traditional Social Orientation, Competition, Academic Achievement, Intellectuality, Order and Organization, Student Influence, Innovation.
Administration: Group.

Forms, 4: Real (R), Ideal (I), Expectations (E), Short (S).

Price Data, 1997: $25 per sampler set including manual, test booklet (Forms R, I, E, and S), scoring key, and profile sheet; $90 per permission set.

Time: Administration time not reported.

Comments: Part of the Social Climate Scales (T5:2445).

Author: Rudolf H. Moos.

Publisher: Mind Garden, Inc.

Cross References: See T4:2865 (8 references) and T3:2534 (3 references); for reviews by Fred H. Borgen and James V. Mitchell, Jr. of an earlier edition, see 8:700 (12 references).

Review of the University Residence Environment Scale [Revised] by BARBARA A. ROTHLISBERG, Professor of Psychology in Educational Psychology, Ball State University, Muncie, IN:

The University Residence Environment Scale, second edition (URES) is one of Moos and Associates' 10 Social Climate Scales. The second edition is less a revision of the basic instrument than it is an expansion of the manual to include information about the URES' utility for program and research applications. Although Moses (1992) explains that the URES was devised in line with a three-category social ecological model derived from Murray, the theoretical justification for the construction and analysis of the URES is not provided in the manual. In fact, little information is offered for the scale's focus other than to state that the URES assesses the "social climate of university student living groups" (manual, p. 5). It is said to address the student-student, student-staff, and organizational structure of student living units.

The URES has four forms, three of which are derivatives of the fourth, the Real Form (Form R). Form R can measure student and staff views of the *current* living group and is made up of 100 items said to assess 10 subscales with a true-false response format. The ideal Form (Form I) adjusts the wording of the same set of 100 items to ask the respondent's view of an ideal living situation—what the ideal setting *will* include. The Expectations Form (Form E) items mirror those of Form I but include different instructions. Form E asks the respondent to answer questions about the living situation they are about to enter and what they anticipate will be their real experience. A Short Form (Form S) includes the first 40 items of Form R and gives a quick overview of student residential climate.

The 10 subscales (9 or 10 scorable items each) are variously referred to as evaluating three domains, dimensions, or categories of social climate. Relationship, which is designed to measure student involvement and supportive relationships among the students, is assessed by Involvement and Emotional Support subscales. Personal Growth/Goal Orientation, which is meant to highlight personal, social, and academic maturation, is made up of subscales Independence, Traditional Social Orientation, Competition, Academic Achievement, and Intellectuality. Finally, System Maintenance and Change, which assesses the orderliness and influence that students have or feel they have, is characterized by Order and Organization, Student Influence, and Innovation subscales. Although the reviewer expected that these dimensions suggested an underlying factor structure that supported the assignment of subscales to the three domains, this was not the case. Instead, items were chosen for inclusion on the 10 subscales to maximize high item-subscale correlations but minimize subscale intercorrelations. Whereas reference is made to the three dimensions, the 10 subscales are discussed as independent scores. Thus, raw scores can be converted into standard scores for the 10 subscales; there are no domain scores or a total score provided.

The items, plus a form requesting some basic demographic information, are available in test booklet form. Responses can be transferred to a separate answer sheet for scoring. A scoring key is used to assign a point per correct answer, either true or false. Six of the subscales have total raw scores of 10 and four subscales have total raw scores of 9: there appear to be four filler items on Forms R, I, and E. Scoring keys for Forms R, I, and E are identical. Conversion tables are provided in the manual to translate raw scores into standard scores for both group mean raw and individual raw scores.

Normative information on any of the scales is limited at best with no justification given for the choice of procedures employed. The anchor scale, Form R, was reportedly normed on "168 living group units representing a wide range of residence halls from 16 colleges and universities in the United States" (manual, p. 10). Subscale means and standard deviations are provided for the total group, yet there is no accounting of the total sample size or its demographic characteristics.

Likewise, the subscale standard deviations are tabled for a sample of 505 individuals presumably from the normative sample but without accompanying mean raw scores. Different sets of living groups or individual students are reported as normative samples for the other forms with no explanation as to why some forms are listed as group data and some as student data. Additionally, although purportedly developed for staff development and applications, no specific information was given that highlighted the meaning of scores for staff members.

Perhaps the least understood element of the URES for the reviewer is the assignment of points for "correct" scores on the URES. There seems to be an underlying and unexplained assumption that an "average" score exists for college-aged students for their opinions on personal involvement, academic achievement, and the other areas of social climate assessed by the URES. Likewise, the manual indicates that item selection for the subscales was conducted to offer "maximum item discrimination among living groups" (manual, p. 14). These decisions in scale construction suggest that the author had some preconceived notion that there are minimum acceptable values for social climate constructs and that distinct profiles of climate dimensions exist for different social groupings. Without further conceptual or theoretical explanation, this attempt at standardizing ratings of social climate would seem difficult to support psychometrically.

Given the difficulties with the aspects of normative scoring of behavioral observations for groups and a paucity of information about the representativeness of normative sampling, discussion of reliability and validity for the URES remains speculative. Data provided for reliability refers only to Form R. Internal consistency coefficients suggest that the subscales measure discrete aspects of social behavior/climate, whereas test-retest reliability offers moderate to high levels of association between subscale scores for 1- to 4-week periods. Validity is less clear. Mention is made of content and face validity and the formulation of items based on specific constructs. Concurrent validity was described as established because interviews and feedback questionnaires provided to students and staff in selected living groups generally established the agreement of URES scores with these other measures of student perceptions. Studies mentioned in the clinical and research sections of the manual also were used as support for the validity of the URES.

SUMMARY. In general, the 10 subscales of social climate on the URES afford an interesting method of viewing the social connections and concerns of college students in residential settings. Taken as a snapshot of the diversity of student perceptions of lifestyle, the measure (particularly Form R) may hold some value in residential planning. However, the clinical profiling of groups based on standard scoring of behavioral or social climate variables should be undertaken with caution. The choice of norming the measure in terms of correctness of response and maximum discrimination of living groups does not appear to suit the variables or the underlying questions asked. Likewise, the undescribed and varying nature of the normative samples used for different scales does not allow prospective users a clear sense of the groups to which they are comparing their students. If used, investigators would be well served by developing local norms for the measure and recognizing that the standard scores may only provide a common point along a measurement scale, not an accurate perception of specific clinical or behavioral groups who systematically vary on aspects of social climate.

REVIEWER'S REFERENCE

Moses, J. A., Jr. (1992) [Review of the University Residence Environment Scale]. In D. J. Keyser & R. C. Swetland (Eds.), *Test critiques* (Vol. 9) (pp. 625–642). Austin: PRO-ED.

Review of the University Residence Environment Scale [Revised] by THERESA G. SISKIND, Assessment Coordinator, South Carolina Education Oversight Committee, Columbia, SC:

The University Residence Environment Scale (URES), 1 of 10 social climate scales authored by Rudolph Moos and originally published in 1974, is somewhat unique among extant college and university adjustment scales in that its primary unit of analysis is "living groups" rather than individuals. Although there are other measures of group functioning developed by various authors, this scale appears to be the only one specifically focused on residences in a higher education setting. In short, the URES measures the "personality" of college and university residences.

Like the other social climate scales developed by Moos and coauthors during the early 1970s, the URES is theoretically grounded on environmental press, a term attributed to Murray in 1938, connoting the influence of environment on human behavior. There are three dimensions common to all of the scales: relationship, personal development, and system maintenance/change. Depending upon the environment studied, the components of each dimension may vary. For the URES, 10 subscales represent the components of the three dimensions. These dimensions, subscales, and illustrative items (Smail, DeYoung, & Moos, 1974) are: (a) Relationship (Involvement [Inv]): "In this house there is a strong feeling of belongingness"; (b) Relationship (Emotional Support [S]): "People here are concerned with helping and supporting one another"; (c) Personal Growth (Independence [Ind]): "Behaving properly in social situations is not considered important here"; (d) Personal Growth (Traditional Social Orientation [TSO]): "Dating is a recurring topic of conversation around here"; (e) Personal Growth (Competition [C]): "Around here discussions frequently turn into verbal duels"; (f) Personal Growth {Academic Achievement [AA]): "Most people here consider studies as very important in college"; (g) Personal Growth (Intellectuality [Int]): "People around here talk a lot about political and social issues"; (h) System Maintenance and System Change (Order and Organization [OO]): "House procedures here are well established"; (i) System Maintenance and System Change (Student Influence [SI]): "Students enforce house rules here"; and (j) System Maintenance and Change (Innovation [Inn]): "New approaches to things are often tried here."

The URES is a straightforward, easily administered scale composed of 100 true-false items in the Real (R), Ideal (I), and Expectations (E) forms. A Short Form (S) extracts the first 40 items of Form R. Forms R and S measure resident and staff views about the living environment as it is perceived to be at present. Forms I and E are adapted from Form R and items have been reworded slightly to reflect resident and staff perceptions of an ideal living environment (I) and expectations (E) about the future living environment (as for entering freshmen). The same scoring key is used for all three forms. Administration of combinations of Forms R, I, and E allow for comparative study as in contrasting the expected living environment with the actual living environment.

Despite some minor discrepancies between the manual and an early paper describing scale development (Smail, DeYoung, & Moos, 1974), item development appears to have followed a careful iterative process by which items were initially derived through a review of the literature and other scales, and discussions with appropriate groups of people. The item pool was winnowed by the authors, who categorized the items according to the theoretical framework they associated with social climate. The resulting 238 (or 278, depending on source) item form was reduced to 140 (or 150) items after a trial utilizing 13 dormitories. This form, composed of highly discriminating items that did not correlate with a social desirability scale, was administered to students in 74 residences. Subscales were reconfigured after three trials. The criteria for the final Form R included "high item-subscale correlations, low to moderate correlations among subscales, and maximum item discrimination among living groups" (manual, p. 14).

Reliability data report item-subscale correlations for 505 students and range from .44 for Innovation to .62 for Involvement with a mean of .52. KR-20s for 13 living groups were calculated using average within-living group variances and range from .77 (Independence, Competition, Innovation) to .88 (Involvement) with a mean of .82. Although details are omitted in the manual, these data appear to be drawn from the original samples used for development.

Stability estimates were calculated for intervals of 1 and 4 weeks, respectively, with a sample of 83 students from one women's dormitory and one men's dormitory. Mean stability estimates based on student data are .72 and .68, respectively. Intraclass correlations over the same time period were .96 and .86 for the men's dormitory and .96 and .98 for the women's dormitory. The manual does not report when these studies were conducted.

Subscale intercorrelations vary widely from .62 to -.40. Moos indicates an average correlation of "around .20" (manual, p. 15). He describes the subscales as "distinct though somewhat related" (manual, p. 15) although the correlation of .62 between Involvement and Emotional Support may be more than just moderate. Moos reports that a factor analysis conducted by Waldman, Crouse, and Corazzini in 1982 supported the 10 subscales.

Additional validity evidence is alluded to in general reports of discrimination between living groups. A number of research studies conducted with the URES lend support to the construct validity; a table summarizing such findings might make it more easily discernible.

The manual provides some detail about the normative sample including the number of living groups, the number of universities, the type of university (public and private), and other details. Unfortunately, omissions include details about the timeframe in which the samples were drawn, the size of the colleges and universities, and the geographic location. In lieu of including these data in future documentation, however, some revision and renorming might be reconsidered. In the quarter century since the scale was first published, there has been some change in students that might be reflected in their perceptions about residence life.

The scale appears dated in a couple of ways. Items are administered in a booklet and responses are circled, ostensibly for hand scoring. Administrators interested in machine scoring must transcribe responses onto a separate document. For ease of scoring, both by hand and by machine, scannable or self-scoring "bubble" forms might be preferable.

The reference in items to "the house" appears limiting as well as dated. In recent years, "traditional social orientation" may have given way to "social orientation." These presumptions should be put to an empirical test along with the norms and factor structure.

The URES is easy to administer and score. A single score point is assigned to each item if it is the keyed response. Points are summed within subscales, averaged for the residence unit, and converted to scale scores (*T*-scores) utilizing a set of simple tables. When scores are displayed as profiles, they have particular utility for the clinician, the evaluator, the researcher, or the college/university housing staff. In the manual, Moos reviews ways in which profiles can be utilized. A stronger, more meaningful presentation of the same data is given in various journal articles that actually display and discuss the profiles.

SUMMARY. Moos has authored or coauthored 10 social climate scales in all and 18 different scales during the period from 1974–1994. The URES reflects his expertise in the construction of scales and the measurement of social climate. Furthermore, the URES fills a niche. It would be unfortunate if this useful tool were to fall into disuse simply because it had become outmoded or because of a perception that it had.

REVIEWER'S REFERENCE

Smail, M. M. P., DeYoung, A. J., & Moos, R. H. (1974). The University Residence Environment Scale: A method for describing university student living groups. *Journal of College Student Personnel, 15*(5), 357–365.

[406]
Validity Indicator Profile.

Purpose: "Designed to … evaluate an individual's motivation and effort during cognitive testing."
Population: Ages 18–69.
Publication Date: 1997.
Acronym: VIP.
Scores, 2: Nonverbal Subtest Response Style, Verbal Subtest Response Style.
Administration: Individual.
Price Data, 2000: $32 per test booklet; $18 per 25 answer sheets; $35 per manual; $16 per interpretive report (MICROTEST Q™ scoring); $18 per interpretive report (mail-in scoring); $8.50 per profile report (MICROTEST Q™); $10.50 per profile report (mail-in scoring); $100 per preview package including manual, test booklet, 3 answer sheets, and 3 interpretive reports (specify MICROTEST Q™ scoring or mail-in scoring); quantity discounts available for the reports.
Time: (30) minutes.
Comments: Instrument must be scored by computer.
Author: Richard I. Frederick.
Publisher: NCS (Minnetonka).

Review of the Validity Indicator Profile by JACK E. GEBART-EAGLEMONT, Lecturer in Psychology, Swinburne University of Technology, Hawthorn, Victoria, Australia:

The Validity Indicator Profile (VIP) is defined as "a measure of malingering" (manual, p. 1), "a general assessment of response style" (p. 2), useful "in identifying when the results of cognitive or neuropsychological testing may be invalid" (p. 2). Detection of malingering, faking, and deception in neuropsychological evaluation is of paramount importance, considering the alarming data concerning compromised psychological evaluation used in legal proceedings (manual, p. 7) involving workers' compensation cases (50%), personal injury (75%), and disability claims (20%). The objective approach to the identification of invalid response styles offered by the VIP uses the paradigm based on consistency of responses to cognitive tasks presenting increasing levels of difficulty. Such tasks involve two measurable aspects: motivation and effort. The theoretical premise of the VIP is that a person who attempts to fake a cognitive test will try hard (high effort) to obtain a poor result (motivation to fail). Therefore, a valid response style is characterized by motivation to excel and high effort (Compliant Response Style). Invalid response styles are defined as Careless (low effort, motivation to excel), Irrelevant (low effort, motivation to fail), and Malingered (high effort, motivation to fail).

The VIP materials are professional in format and presentation, and consist of a manual, reusable test booklet, and computer-scorable response sheets (mail-in or MICROTEST type). The manual is written in a clear, succinct style and provides information about development of the VIP, descriptions of concepts and measures, psychometric characteristics of scores from the VIP and their interpretation, as well as several case studies. The VIP must be computer-scored. The computer program produces an interpretive report that may then be used for diagnostic or forensic purposes. The items are similar to typical tasks used in intelligence measurement; there are 100 matrices-type items (Nonverbal Subtest) and 78 two-choices word similarity items (Verbal Subtest). The VIP provides two types of indicators: measures of response consistency, and measures derived from performance curve analysis. The measures of response consistency include Consistency Ratio (index of the extent to which an individual correctly answers items of comparable difficulty), Norm Conformity Index (response consistency in comparison to the average response pattern of a normative group), and Individual Consistency Index (response consistency across five parallel sets of items). The performance curve shape analysis involves computation of Curvature (nonlinear regression equation predicting performance from item difficulty), and utilizes the fact that the curves of compliant test takers have a distinct shape. Other measures based on performance curve analysis include Slope (best linear fit), Point of Entry (the first running mean of 10 easiest items), Peak Performance Interval (number of consecutive running means that have a value of 1.0), Sector 1 Distance (curve sector between the point of entry and a running mean of .8), Sector 2 Distance (transition sector, between Sector 1 and a running mean of .5), Sector 3 Distance (the random sector, running means around .5), Tail Score (responses to the eight "unusual," nonobvious verbal items), and Sector 1 Residual (the extent to which running means in Sector 1 deviate from

perfect performance). The two interaction measures (Score by Correlation and Slope by Consistency Ratio) are included "because of their high efficiency in discriminating between compliant and noncompliant individuals" (manual, p. 20). Classification of test performance as "valid" or "invalid" is a categorical decision, based on a number of rule violations (i.e., indices exceeding critical conditions defined by the cutoff scores), separately for the Verbal and Nonverbal subtests. Violation of two or more of the rules results in an "invalid" categorization of the result for a given subtest. Although many of the indices used by the VIP are complex, scoring procedures are fully computerized and the algorithm provides categorical diagnoses (valid vs. invalid) for the Verbal and the Nonverbal tests. The software also produces values for all validity indices and a narrative report, illustrated by performance curves (diagrammed together with the expected curves for comparisons).

TEST DEVELOPMENT. The Nonverbal items of the VIP were adapted from the Test of Nonverbal Intelligence (Brown, Sherbenou, & Johnsen, 1982). The verbal items come from a study by Frederick, Sarfaty, Johnston, and Powel (1994), which used a college student population. In the development phase, the test was administered to clinical participants (N = 104) and to nonclinical participants (N = 944). The nonclinical group was then divided into three groups: "honest normals" (N = 336), "naive malingering" (N = 330), and "informed malingering" (N = 139). Both malingering groups were instructed to fake cognitive impairment, and the "informed malingering" groups was also additionally coached in strategies to avoid detection. Some case records were also randomly computer-generated to simulate the careless responding style. The clinical participants were classified as compliant or noncompliant on the basis of three screening tests of malingering (Lezak, 1995) and clinician ratings. The validity indicators were then calibrated to provide 90% correct congruent classifications (positive-positive with the a priori classification described above). The cross-validation phase involved comparisons of results obtained from the following groups: honest normals (N = 100), coached normals (N = 52), brain injured (N = 61), suspected malingerers (N = 49), and persons with mental retardation (N = 40). The VIP results were cross-tabulated against the results of four screening devices: Portland

Digit Recognition Test, Rey Memory Test, Word Recognition Test, and Dot Counting Test. The resulting contingency tables were statistically analyzed using the kappa coefficients, which indicated a moderate level of concordance. The congruent classifications ranged from 69% to 73%.

NORMATIVE DATA. The statistics obtained from the normative sample are based on over 350 participants (100 honest normals, 61 brain-injury patients, 52 coached normals, 49 suspected malingerers, 50 random respondents, and 40 persons with mental retardation). The means and standard deviations for all these groups, and the final descriptive statistics for the resulting diagnostic groups (valid vs. invalid) are tabulated in the manual. The honest normals were overrepresented in this sample, and the number of malingerers appears rather small, considering the purpose of the test.

RELIABILITY. Internal consistency models are not entirely applicable for assessing the reliability of the VIP because the item-total correlations should theoretically differ between compliant and noncompliant groups. Some attempt at internal consistency evaluation was made by cross-tabulation of the Verbal versus Nonverbal subscale classifications, which resulted in 86% of congruent "valid" classification, and in 85% of congruent "invalid" classification. The resulting kappa coefficient of concordance was .70, which indicates an acceptable level of reliability. Test-retest reliability was not properly assessed; the sample used in the test-retest situation did not include malingerers (only 49 honest normals; manual, pp. 32–33). Such a design is at odds with the diagnostic purpose of the VIP. The test should be able to provide a reliable test-retest reclassification of invalid response styles, at least in terms of broad categories (careless, irrelevant, malingered); the mere (and trivial) reclassification of honest normals is not indicative of test-retest stability of a measure of malingering, as the critical and primary task of differential diagnosis of response styles was not involved.

VALIDITY. The reported comparisons with other measures of malingering are based on cross-tabulations of dichotomous classifications (valid vs. invalid styles) with the validating instruments (Portland Digital Recognition Test, Rey Memory Test, Word Recognition Test, and Dot Counting Test). The 2 X 2 classifications achieved typically about 70% of congruent taxonomy (ranging from 69% to 73%). The overall diagnostic efficiency of the VIP seems to be skewed toward sensitivity (comparably high percentage of correct diagnosis of invalid response style) at the cost of specificity (somewhat higher percentages of misdiagnoses of valid response styles as invalid) in comparison with the validating devices.

SUMMARY. The VIP offers an objective measurement of a construct that is insufficiently addressed by traditional psychometric instruments, and that is of great importance to forensic psychology. The theory and conceptual background of this test are sound and based on well-documented and substantial empirical premises. It seems that the VIP's score reliability needs to be more extensively investigated using a more refined approach; the mere Verbal versus Nonverbal consistency approach was too crude, and the test-retest evaluation was conceptually irrelevant to the objective of the test (only the honest respondents were used); test-retest reliability should be investigated using coached participants. The diagnostic value of the VIP possibly could be enhanced also by reliability indices obtained from testing with a parallel form of the test. The validity indices of the VIP are promising, and the scores from the instrument overall show sufficient psychometric quality to be included in test batteries used for forensic psychological assessment purposes. The overall diagnostic efficiency of the VIP is biased toward higher sensitivity (high detection rates) at the cost of specificity, which leads to higher percentages of misdiagnoses of valid response styles as invalid (false positive), in comparison with traditional malingering detection methods. This would suggest that a conservative and cautious diagnostic approach using a multi-test battery should be recommended, especially in forensic cases. A diagnostic strategy relying on the VIP as a sole instrument in assessment of malingering should be avoided. Finally, it appears that the VIP needs further validation studies, as the original validation sample was small, and oversaturated with honest normals. At the present stage, the VIP can be described as a very promising instrument with great potential for further development.

REVIEWER'S REFERENCES

Brown, L., Sherbenou, R. J., & Johnsen, S. K. (1982). Test of Nonverbal Intelligence: A language-free measure of cognitive ability. Austin, TX: PRO-ED.

Frederick, R. I., Sarfaty, S. D., Johnston, J. D., & Powel, J. (1994). Validation of a detector of response bias on a forced-choice test of nonverbal ability. *Neuropsychology, 8,* 118–125.

Lezak, M. D. (1995). *Neuropsychological assessment.* New York: Oxford.

Review of the Validity Indicator Profile by STEPHEN H. IVENS, Vice President, Touchstone Applied Science Associates, Brewster, NY:

The Validity Indicator Profile (VIP) was designed to provide a clinician with an objective measure of an individual's motivation and effort during cognitive testing. As a measure of malingering and other response styles in individuals between the ages of 18 and 69, the instrument is not recommended for individuals with a history of documented mental retardation or severe cognitive impairment. The primary users of the VIP are forensic and clinical psychologists and neuropsychologists.

The VIP contains separate Verbal and Nonverbal subtests. The Verbal subtest consists of 78 multiple-choice vocabulary items, each with two response alternatives. The Nonverbal subtest contains 100 picture puzzles. Respondents must select one of two puzzle pieces that best completes the puzzle. The Nonverbal subtest was derived from the Test of Nonverbal Intelligence and first published as the Forced-Choice Test of Nonverbal Ability. Both subtests are forced-choice measures and respondents are specifically instructed to respond to all items.

Administration procedures are thorough and easy to follow. The VIP can be individually or group administered, and the Verbal and Nonverbal subtests are untimed. Respondents typically need about 30 minutes to complete both subtests using a separate machine-scorable answer document. The items on each subtest are presented in a random order of difficulty. In scoring, however, these items are rearranged in order of empirical difficulty and running means are calculated across each set of either 9 or 10 items. The first running mean, therefore, represents the respondent's performance on the 10 easiest items on the subtest. Running means can range in value from 1.0, for respondents who answer all of the items in the set correctly, to 0.0, for respondents who answer all items in the set incorrectly. A total of 69 running means are generated for the Verbal subtest and 91 for the Nonverbal. Plotting these running means yields a performance curve for the respondent on each subtest. Due to the complexity of the scoring, users have the option of using a computer program obtained from the publisher or returning the answer sheets to the publisher for central scoring.

The respondent's performance is not compared to a normative group, but rather to his or her own abilities. The performance curve displays the relationship between the respondent's motivation and effort. A respondent who is motivated to do well and demonstrates high effort, for example, generates a performance curve that has a distinct shape. On the easiest items, the performance curve is high and stable. This is followed by a drop in the performance curve as the difficulty of the items approaches the respondent's level of ability. The last section of the performance curve, where the difficulty of the items is beyond the ability of the respondent, hovers around .5—the expected value for random guessing on two alternative, forced-choice items. Although the drop-off point for the performance curve varies as a function of ability, the shape of the curve remains essentially the same for all motivated respondents with a high effort to succeed.

Combining the two dimensions, motivation and effort, results in four distinct response styles: compliant, careless, irrelevant, and malingered. A compliant response style is characterized by high effort to perform well and the performance curve for the compliant respondent shows cooperation with the testing procedures. For the compliant test-taker, there is a high probability that the performance is an accurate representation of ability. At the other extreme, respondents with a malingered response style have performance curves that demonstrate a high effort to perform poorly. On a two-alternative, forced-choice measure, it requires the same amount of motivation and effort to perform poorly as it does to perform well. For these respondents, the performance curve on the easiest items is quite low, which is an indication that they tried to feign cognitive deficits.

SUMMARY. The Validity Indicator Profile manual is an excellent publication. It documents the fact that conceptually the instrument is as deceptively elegant as it is intuitively simple. The theory and rationale underlying the development of the VIP are described in detail. The psychometric characteristics of the VIP are sufficient to justify the use of the instrument for its intended purposes. All users of the VIP should be thoroughly familiar with the thorough discussion of score interpretation, which includes a number of helpful case studies. Finally, the manual repeatedly and appropriately cautions users that clinical judgment remains a requirement in the interpretation of VIP results. In this regard, users must actively evaluate their conclusions about the motivation of test takers to do their best in psychological evaluations by reviewing all of the evidence for and against their conclusions.

The VIP appears to be an excellent clinical instrument for objectively evaluating an individual's motivation and effort during cognitive testing.

[407]
Victoria Symptom Validity Test.

Purpose: "Designed to provide evidence that can help to confirm or disconfirm the validity of an examinee's reported cognitive impairments."
Population: Ages 18 and over.
Publication Date: 1997.
Acronym: VSVT.
Scores, 6: Total Items Correct, Easy Items Correct, Difficult Items Correct, Easy Items Response Latency, Difficult Items Response Latency, Right-Left Preference.
Administration: Individual.
Price Data, 1998: $399 per kit including 3.5-inch disk (unlimited uses) and professional manual (93 pages); $149 per introductory kit including program disk, 3.5-inch disk (10 uses), and professional manual; $99 per 25-use disk; $149 per 50-use disk; $35 per professional manual.
Time: Administration time not reported.
Comments: Requires IBM of compatible personal computer (80386 required; Pentium recommended) with MS Windows 3.11 or Windows 95; computer administered, scored, and interpreted.
Authors: Daniel Slick, Grace Hopp, Esther Strauss, and Garrie B. Thompson.
Publisher: Psychological Assessment Resources, Inc.

Review of the Victoria Symptom Validity Test by STEPHEN J. FREEMAN, Associate Professor of Counseling & Development, Department of Family Sciences, Texas Woman's University, Denton, TX:

The Victoria Symptom Validity Test (VSVT) is a test of memory designed to provide evidence to help confirm or refute the validity of an examinee's reported neuropsychological impairments. The VSVT material consists of a manual and software. Software allows for computer administration, scoring, and generation of a written report (including binomial probability estimates) and an interpretative classification diagnostic label of valid, questionable, or invalid. The test was developed for use with adult populations 18 years of age and older. The authors intended the instrument to be useful in assessing forensic patients or those seeking financial compensation for central nervous system impairments secondary to mid-to-

moderate head injury, toxic exposure, electric shock, and other trauma.

The assessment is computer administered and includes a total of 48 items, presented in three blocks of 16 items each. In each block a single five-digit number (study number) is presented on the computer screen, followed by a retention interval (blank screen), and finally the examinee is presented with two five-digit numbers, the study number and a foil. The examinee is then asked to choose the number he or she saw in the study trial. The method is repeated for each block of 16 items. The retention interval is 5 seconds for the first block, 10 seconds for the second, and 15 seconds for the third. Standardized instructions include the examinee being told that they are taking a test of memory that requires concentration and that people with memory problems often find this test difficult. Prior to the presentation of the second and third blocks, examinees are told they may find the next items more difficult. The VSVT presents items within each block that appear to be either easy or difficult; however, the authors report no significant difference in performance with increases in retention interval or between easy and difficult items. Scores on the VSVT are reported for total items correct, easy items correct, difficult items correct, easy item response latency, difficult item latency, and right-left preference.

Any trained examiner with a background in psychological testing and a working knowledge of personal computers can administer this test. Clinical interpretation of the VSVT, according to the manual, requires professional training and expertise in both clinical psychology and neuropsychology. Deception of the respondent is a necessary part of many tests that are designed to detect malingering; the VSVT is no exception. The authors acknowledge ethical dilemma in which clinical necessity must be balanced against potential harm to the respondent. They state that "clearly it is the user's ethical responsibility to thoroughly explore alternative explanations when a respondents performance is in the questionable or invalid range" (manual, p. 10).

The manual states that standardized normative data were not required for the VSVT because interpretation was predominately guided by binomial probability. This is unacceptable for the following reasons: A theoretical distribution, like the binomial distribution, is based on logic and mathematics rather than observation and may not reflect what would actually happen. For the probability figures obtained from the theoretical distribution to be an accurate predictor of actual events they must be shown to be similar to an empirical distribution. Data from four research groups were reported; however, these data were extremely weak due to the relatively limited sample size.

Internal consistency reliability estimates are reported for Easy items, Difficult Items, and Total Items. Coefficient alphas for the Easy Items were .82, Difficult Items .87, and Total Items .89. Test-retest reliability estimates were obtained on 31 control group participants (14-day interval) and 28 patient group participants (median interval of 31 days; 1–550-day range). The patient group coefficients were .83 for Easy Items Correct, .78 for Difficult Items Correct, .84 for Total items Correct, .56 for Easy Item Response Latency, and .84 for Difficult Item Response Latency. The control participants' reliability coefficients were stated to be moderate; however, no coefficients were reported for the Easy, Difficult, or Total Items Correct because of reported inaccuracies resulting from range restriction. Control group coefficients for Easy Item Response Latency was .54 and for Difficult Item Response Latency was .53.

Evidence supporting construct validity was offered through correlations between VSVT scores and selected neuropsychological tests (divergent validity). Validity coefficients reported were acceptable; however, the small sample sizes limit the generalizability of these findings. Moderate correlations demonstrating convergent validity were also reported; nonetheless, the small sample size ($n = 9$) negated this endorsement. Findings reported for predictive validity suffer similarly due to inadequate sample sizes.

Criticism can be made regarding the lack of norm-referenced data to support binomial probability estimates. There have also been relatively few studies of the reliability and validity of scores from the VSVT. The sample size of the reported validity studies severely limits the overall support and generalizability of these findings. However, the VSVT does warrant further research in order to continue its development and to document its validity as a clinical diagnostic tool. The potential diagnostic usefulness and forensic clinical utility of the VSVT will be contingent on the outcome of this research. Until such supportive research is

forthcoming, clinical forensic use of the VSVT is not recommended.

Review of the Victoria Symptom Validity Test by LINDA J. ZIMMERMAN, Clinical/School Psychologist, Private Practice, Pittsburgh, PA:

The Victoria Symptom Validity Test (VSVT) is a computerized test that is most frequently used in forensic settings or to assess those seeking financial compensation for central nervous system (CNS) impairment secondary to mild-to-moderate head injury, toxic exposure, electric shock, or other trauma. The VSVT uses a two-alternative, forced-choice paradigm to assess symptom validity and has been developed and validated for use with adults 18 years and older. The two-alternative forced-choice paradigm is similar to other tests that assess malingering or exaggerated memory impairment. It is intended to provide evidence that can support or counter the validity of an examinee's reported cognitive impairments.

The authors provided an in-depth and user-friendly manual that clearly discussed administration, scoring, interpretation, psychometric properties, and limitations. The explanation of rationale and methods is thorough and can be quite helpful to a new user in developing an understanding of the instrument. Scoring procedures and interpretation are discussed at length and give the reader an opportunity to comprehend thoroughly the many aspects of assessment in this area, as well as this instrument in particular.

The administration of this test is documented on the disk as well as in the manual and is quite easy to follow. The administration is time efficient and a report can be generated immediately upon completion of the test. The report format is very good in displaying the respondent's performance as pertinent to several areas and in comparing the results to the normative data. Graphs exhibiting the items correct and the mean response latency are helpful for a quick reference and can be printed with the report. Limitations of the instrument are identified in the manual and also on the first page of the report. The authors took great caution to alert the evaluator to the importance of understanding the issues at hand and making valid judgments when interpreting the results.

As far as the instructions for use of the software, the installation and uninstallation were clearly explained. A novice computer user could understand the installation procedures, administration process, and how to uninstall if necessary. The program automatically calculates the client's age using the test date and the date of birth of the client. There is an option to purchase a disk with unlimited uses for a higher fee or a disk with a specific number of uses less expensive. If the latter is purchased, the program alerts the examiner as to the number of uses remaining on the disk after each test administration and scoring.

Psychometric characteristics were thoroughly explained and documented. Internal consistency reliability indicated that the VSVT test items were homogeneous. Test-retest reliability calculations suggested that as a whole, classifications remained stable over time. However, differences were noted in one of the classifications in the Compensation-Seeking Control Group and the results were sufficiently defined. Validity studies included those measuring divergent, convergent, and predictive validity. Results and limitations of generalizability, when so indicated, were thoroughly discussed. Tests used for comparisons in the studies were clearly identified and tables illustrated the information very clearly.

SUMMARY. Overall, I was quite pleased with this test and believe it would be very helpful to clinicians working in the field of assessing cognitive impairments and CNS dysfunction. The test itself is easy to administer and the necessary supporting documents provide a wealth of information to the clinician in an easy-to-understand format. The test appears to be psychometrically sound with limitations identified and explained. The VSVT could be a beneficial tool in a battery of assessment techniques when one is attempting to differentiate between actual impairments and feigning or malingering.

[408]
Vineland Social-Emotional Early Childhood Scales.

Purpose: Designed to assess the social and emotional functioning of young children.
Population: Birth to age 5-11.
Publication Date: 1998.
Acronym: SEEC.
Scores, 4: Interpersonal Relationships, Play and Leisure Time, Coping Skills, Composite.
Administration: Individual.
Price Data, 1999: $54.95 per complete kit; $24.95 per 25 record forms; $199.95 for reporting software (Early Childhood Assessment ASSIST).

Foreign Language Edition: Spanish edition available.
Time: (15–25) minutes.
Comments: Administered as a structured oral interview; interviewee should be the person with the most knowledge of the child's social and emotional functioning (e.g., parent, grandparent, legal guardian).
Authors: Sara S. Sparrow, David A. Balla, and Dominic V. Cicchetti.
Publisher: American Guidance Service, Inc.

Review of the Vineland Social-Emotional Early Childhood Scales by JOSEPH C. KUSH, Associate Professor and Coordinator School Psychology Program, Duquesne University, Pittsburgh, PA:

The Vineland Social-Emotional Early Childhood Scales (Vineland SEEC Scales) is a newly developed instrument designed to assess the social and emotional functioning of children from birth through 5 years 11 months of age. The Vineland SEEC Scales are a subset of items from the Socialization Domain of the Vineland Adaptive Behavior Scales, Expanded Form (T5:2813) and the Vineland SEEC is designed to be individually administered through a semistructured interview with a respondent who is familiar with the child's behavior. The test consists of three scales: Interpersonal Relationships, Play and Leisure Time, and Coping Skills that combine to yield a Social-Emotional Composite score.

The Interpersonal Relationships Scale consists of 44 items that describe the child's ability to communicate in social contexts, establish and maintain friendships, and appropriately recognize and express emotions. The Play and Leisure Time scale also consists of 44 items and is designed to assess how the child plays with toys, constructs make-believe activities, and plays and shares with other children. The 34 items of the Coping Skills Scale assess the child's ability to use manners, follow rules, engage in impulse control, and manage feelings. As indicated in the Vineland SEEC Scales manual, because the Social-Emotional Composite score is derived from all 122 items of the scale it will be the most statistically reliable score and will provide a comprehensive estimate of the child's level of personal and social sufficiency.

The Vineland SEEC Scales kit contains the test manual and a Record Form and Profile Booklet. Total administration time is approximately 15 to 25 minutes. Computerized scoring and interpretation are also available for both Windows and

Macintosh platforms. The Vineland SEEC Scales manual is a comprehensive guidebook that contains directions for administration, scoring, and interpretation as well as technical information regarding the standardization procedures and psychometric properties of the instrument. The manual also includes an appendix containing a reproducible master of a Report to Parents that can be used to summarize assessment results. Both English and Spanish language versions of the Parent Report are included in the appendix. The Record Form and Profile Booklet allows the examiner to record the child's responses and includes a Program Planning Profile designed to graphically display the child's strengths and weaknesses and identify possible educational or clinical interventions.

As indicated previously, the Vineland SEEC Scales are a subset of items taken from the Socialization domain of the Vineland Adaptive Behavior Scale (ABS). Following an extensive pilot testing program and national item tryout, the Vineland ABS was standardized in the early 1980s at 35 sites in 24 states. The Vineland ABS was standardized on a nationally representative sample of 3,000 individuals from birth through 18 years 11 months of age. The sample was selected to match 1980 U.S. Census characteristics for age, gender, community size, geographic region, parent education, and ethnic classification. Ethnic status was defined as African American, Hispanic, White, and Other (including Native American, Aleut Eskimos, Asian, and Pacific Islanders). From this total, 1,200 children from birth through 5 years 11 months were included, representing the age range of the Vineland SEEC Scales. To prevent possible biasing, 58% of these subjects aged 3-0 through 5-11 were enrolled in preschool or school programs, a figure approximating U.S. Department of Education data from 1982. Data from these 1,200 subjects were then used to create standard scores, percentile ranks, stanines, and age equivalents.

The test manual includes a well-written section describing the methods for administering and scoring the Vineland SEEC Scales. Interviewer characteristics are identified as including professionals with a graduate degree and specific training in early childhood assessment and interpretation. Respondent characteristics are also delineated in careful detail. The manual also indicates that normative data on multiple respondents are not available. Additional information on preparing for the administration of the instrument and suggestions for establishing rapport are included in an easy-to-read format, with guidelines that do not use technical language and are free of jargon. Guidelines for the actual administration are also well detailed in an organized and intuitive manner. Scoring criteria are carefully detailed, as is the process of obtaining raw scores and derived scores. Numerous examples and figures are also provided as a supplement to the step-by-step administration and scoring procedures as well as for the completion of the Program Planning Profile. An additional section on interpretation and case studies is equally informative and carefully written. This section includes a review of basic psychometric principles including appropriate cautions ("A disadvantage of stanines is that they are overly sensitive to standard score values occurring at the break between two adjacent stanines"), as well as practical, applied information ("The chief advantage of percentile ranks is that they are easily understood," manual, pp. 65–67). Case interpretation is also provided, together with a section on how to best use the Vineland SEEC Scales with other instruments. The section concludes with several case studies that illustrate an interpretation of the results of the Vineland SEEC Scales when they are administered as part of a battery of tests.

Information on the reliability of the Vineland SEEC Scales is also presented in a clear and comprehensive manner. Internal consistency levels are adequate, with median values of the Interpersonal Relationships, Play and Leisure Time, and Coping Skills Scales ranging from .80 to .87. the internal reliability coefficients of the Scale Composite, across six age groups, range from .89 to .97 with a median value of .93. Resulting standard errors of measurement are also reported across six age groups for each of the three component scales and the composite. Specifically, mean standard errors of measurement include values of 5.8 for Interpersonal Relationships, 6.4 for Play and Leisure Time, 5.2 for Coping Skills, and 3.9 for the Vineland SEEC Scales Composite. Test-retest reliability coefficients are also reported following re-administration of the scale after a 2- to 4-week interval (mean interval of 17 days). Adequate stability is also well documented with the vast majority of the component scale and composite score test-retest correlations falling between .71 and .79. Only the Coping Skills scale, for the age group 0-6 to 2-1, yielded an unacceptable stability coefficient ($r = .54$) and the manual appropriately cautions examiners that "Use of this scale with very young children or children with low abilities is not recommended" (p. 86). Additional information is also provided in the manual regarding the test-retest reliability of the Vineland SEEC Scales when different interviewers administer the instrument. In this instance parents or caregivers of 160 individuals were interviewed twice by two different interviewers (with a mean interval of 8 days). Resulting stability coefficients dropped substantially yielding test-retest correlations of .47 for Interpersonal Relationships, .47 for Play and Leisure Time, .60 for Coping Skills, and .50 for the Composite score. Although these lowered coefficients are noted in the manual, the implications of this finding are not fully explained nor are suggestions for improving interrater reliability through activities such as workshops on scoring rubrics as part of clinical staff development or inservice training.

Finally, the manual concludes with a section describing the validity evidence for the Vineland SEEC Scales. Reflecting perhaps the weakest part of the manual, only one paragraph is devoted to a description of the construct validity evidence of the scale. Data are provided, for only one age group, describing a principal factor analysis with varimax rotation. Results indicated a somewhat unexpected four-factor solution; however, the manual makes no attempt to explain the significance of the "extra" factor. Equally surprising is the lack of explanation for why data for only one age group are presented and whether additional analyses (e.g., confirmatory analyses) were performed. Data describing the convergent and criterion validity of the Vineland SEEC Scales are presented in a somewhat more clear and comprehensive manner. Moderate correlations are presented relating the Vineland SEEC Scales to other developmental scales (e.g., Battelle Developmental Inventory; Scales of Independent Behavior) as well as to additional measures of social-emotional behavior, receptive vocabulary, and cognitive ability. Empirical research examining the concurrent and predictive validity of the Vineland SEEC Scales is relatively well outlined for children with normal development and for children from clinical populations.

SUMMARY. The Vineland SEEC Scales appears to be a useful instrument for assessing the social and emotional behaviors of young children. The Scales have many desirable features: The standardization process was comprehensive, the instrument is easy to administer and score, and the concurrent and predictive validity with other developmental scales is quite acceptable. Given the expected fluctuation in developmental scores, because by definition developmental growth is expected across time, the test-retest reliability estimates for the Vineland SEEC Scales are quite adequate. However, the significantly lower coefficients for interrater reliability of the scale underscore the importance of familiarity with child development by different examiners who are likely to assess the same child, as well as their familiarity with the administration and scoring rubrics of the scale. There are, additionally, some unanswered questions about the construct validity of the scale and it remains unclear exactly how many constructs are being measured by the Vineland SEEC Scales as well as whether or not these constructs are stable across developmental levels.

The scales are well suited for both clinical and educational settings to assist in the screening and early identification of developmental delays and to chart developmental progress. As indicated in the manual, however, the Vineland SEEC Scales must be combined with other sources of psychoeducational assessment data when making diagnostic decisions. Additional research is also required to more adequately determine the clinical utility and benefits of the scale over and above the more comprehensive Socialization Domain of the Vineland Adaptive Scales (Expanded Form) from which it was derived.

Review of the Vineland Social-Emotional Early Childhood Scales by DONALD LEE STOVALL, Associate Professor, Department of Counseling & School Psychology, University of Wisconsin—River Falls, River Falls, WI:

The Vineland Social-Emotional Early Childhood Scales (Vineland SEEC) is designed to assess the social and emotional functioning of children from birth through 5 years, 11 months. The Vineland SEEC is a semistructured interview given to a child's parent, caregiver, or a person who is familiar with the child's behavior. The Vineland SEEC is designed to be used in settings that provide services to preschool-age children. These settings include Head Start programs, early childhood intervention programs, and special education programs where developmental delay is a concern. The Vineland SEEC is intended to be used to assist in the evaluation of a child's social or emotional functioning where developmental delays in such areas could affect a child's growth. As stated by the authors, an Individualized Education Plan (IEP), or Individualized Family Service Plan (IFSP), require understanding of the skills necessary for social sufficiency. The Vineland SEEC is presented as a means to assess a child's social skills that could contribute to independent functioning. Additionally, the Vineland SEEC is promoted as a means to monitor a child's development. Norms are provided at 1-month intervals from birth to age 2, and at 2-month intervals from age 2 through 5 years, 11 months. Finally, the Vineland SEEC has application as a research tool involving relationships between social-emotional development and cognitive skills, or in documenting the effects of intervention as a pre- and post-intervention measure. The Vineland SEEC could also be used in longitudinal studies that involve assessing the development of a child's social or emotional skills.

The Vineland SEEC is constructed along three scales. These scales are labeled Interpersonal Relationships, Play and Leisure, and Coping Skills. A Composite Scale provides an overall summary of the child's social-emotional development. Within each scale are several items that assess a specific category of behaviors. These items are termed "clusters." These clusters are arranged in a developmental sequence from lowest to highest level of difficulty. The examiner begins with the cluster of items associated with the child's chronological age. Basal and ceiling rules apply. The manual provides examples of how they are to be followed.

The Interpersonal Relationships scale on the Vineland SEEC involves clusters such as the child's ability to respond to familiar people, engage in cooperative activities, or initiate social communication. The Play and Leisure scale involves the child's ability to demonstrate an interest in his or her environment, play with toys, or engage in pretend play. The Coping Skills scale assesses the child's ability to follow rules, control his or her impulses, or demonstrate responsible behavior.

Graduate level education and training are necessary to administer, score, and interpret the Vineland SEEC. Persons who use the Vineland SEEC should also have a background in child development. The Vineland is a semistructured interview that presents certain challenges to the examiner. The examiner needs to be very familiar with the instrument and the types of skills assessed. As stated in the manual, the examiner needs to establish rapport with the respondent. The interviewer does not read test items, or allow the respondent to read test items. The interviewer asks open-ended questions designed to elicit responses. Probes that clarify information given by the respondent may follow these open-ended questions. One challenge with a semistructured interview format is the potential to get off-task with open-ended questions. This requires an ability on the part of the examiner to monitor appropriately the course of the interview. A benefit of a semistructured format is that the tone of the interview is more conversational, which could assist in the rapport-building process with the respondent. The examiner controls the scoring. The use of this method of the examiner assigning a score based upon the interview is thought by the test developers to be an important strategy to reduce score bias. The respondent remains unaware of the significance of points assigned to their description of the child's performance.

The examiner provides a score for each item within each scale completed. A specific scoring criterion is used, based upon a range of points from 0 to 2. A score of 0 is given when the child "never performs" the behavior in question. A score of 1 is given when the child "sometimes or partially" performs the behavior. A score of 2 is given when the child "usually" performs the behavior. Additional scores of DK for "Don't Know" or N for "No opportunity" can also be given in certain situations. The authors provide an appendix that presents each item and examples of scored items. Although helpful, on some items it is difficult to determine the difference between a score of 2 (usually performs), and a score of 1 (sometimes or partially performs the behavior). In most of the examples given, differentiation between a 2-point response and a 0-point response is given.

The Vineland SEEC yields a standard score with a mean of 100 and a standard deviation of 15. In addition to use of standard scores, the examiner may also compute percentile ranks. The examiner may select a confidence band based upon 90 or 95%. It is also possible for the examiner to compute age equivalent scores for the child assessed.

The descriptive categories that are used are "High," "Moderately High," "Adequate," "Moderately Low," and "Low." A Program Planning Profile is also available. The Program Planning Profile allows the examiner to determine a child's strengths or weaknesses by comparing a child's score to other children the same age.

STANDARDIZATION. The Vineland SEEC is derived from the Vineland Adaptive Behavior Scales (Vineland ABS; Sparrow, Balla, & Cichetti, 1984; T5:2813). Within the Vineland SEEC manual, the initial information about development and standardization refers to procedures used for the Vineland ABS. As stated in the Vineland SEEC manual, "Vineland SEEC Scales items are a subset of the items in the Socialization Domain of the Vineland ABS" (Vineland SEEC manual, p. 12). Items from the Vineland ABS were reviewed and selected for inclusion in the Vineland SEEC. Items or skills that did not apply to preschool age populations were not used. It is important to note that the Vineland ABS was developed based upon 1980 census data. As a derivative, the norms from the Vineland SEEC are also based upon modifications of the norms from the Vineland ABS 1980 norms data. Statistical procedures were employed to create the standard scores for the Vineland SEEC. There have been questions raised about the norms of the Vineland ABS (Silverstein, 1986). The age of the norm sample from which the Vineland SEEC was derived is a concern, as those norms are almost two decades old.

Caution should be exercised by the professional using the Vineland SEEC when evaluating validity evidence from the manual. In the discussion about different approaches to assessing validity contained in the manual for the Vineland SEEC, the statement is made "Much of the evidence cited in the following sections is based upon studies using the Socialization Domain of the Vineland ABS Survey Form or Expanded Form." This evidence is "generalized to the Vineland SEEC" (Vineland SEEC manual, p. 91). Clearly, validity studies of the Vineland SEEC as a separate instrument are needed. Information about the reliability of the Vineland SEEC should also be collected independently from studies that employed the Vineland ABS.

SUMMARY. The Vineland SEEC is presented as a means to assess the social-emotional development of children from birth through age 5 years 11 months. It is a semistructured interview designed to be used in the assessment of children in early childhood programs, or those referred for special education programs. It can also be used as a research tool involving interventions with young children, or to follow the growth of young children. The administrator of the Vineland should have training in assessment, and have competency in child development. The Vineland SEEC is derived from the Vineland Adaptive Behavior Scales, with norms based on 1980 U.S. Census data. This creates some concerns due to the age of the norms and the use of statistical procedures to create a separate instrument. Additionally, validity information reported in the manual is based upon the Vineland ABS, rather than the Vineland SEEC as a separate instrument. Some administrators may be challenged to differentiate between a 2-point response, and a 1-point response for some items.

REVIEWER'S REFERENCES

Sparrow, S. S., Balla, D. A., & Cicchetti, D. V. (1984). Vineland Adaptive Behavior Scales. Circle Pines, MN: American Guidance Service.
Silverstein, A. B. (1986). Nonstandard scores on the Vineland Adaptive Behavior Scales: A cautionary note. *American Journal of Mental Deficiency, 91,* 1–4.

[409]
Vocational Decision-Making Interview—Revised.

Purpose: Constructed as a structured interview process to assist persons who have disabilities in making vocational decisions.

Population: Disabled individuals who need to make vocational decisions.

Publication Date: 1993.

Acronym: VDMI-R.

Scores, 4: Decision-Making Readiness, Employment Readiness, Self-Appraisal, Total.

Administration: Individual.

Price Data: Available from publisher.

Time: (20–40) minutes.

Comments: Structured interview administered by vocational rehabilitation workers.

Authors: Thomas Czerlinsky and Shirley K. Chandler.

Publisher: JIST Works, Inc.

Review of the Vocational Decision-Making Interview—Revised by KAREN T. CAREY, Professor of Psychology, California State University, Fresno, Fresno, CA:

The Vocational Decision-Making Interview—Revised (VDMI-R) is a 54-item individually administered, structured interview composed of three scales: Decision-Making Readiness, Employment Readiness, and Self-Appraisal. The Decision-Making Readiness Scale is composed of 17 questions that address readiness to make vocational decisions; the Employment Readiness Scale is composed of 11 questions that examine the desire to obtain work and external influences that can affect motivation; and the Self-Appraisal Scale contains 23 questions designed to address knowledge and self-appraisal including interests and abilities. The sum of the three scales results in a Total Scale score. There are also 3 open-ended summary items.

Items are scored Yes (Y), Not Sure (NS), and No (N). "Yes" items receive a score of 1 and "NS" and "N" items receive scores of 0. Each item consists of a closed-ended question (e.g., "Are there any specific jobs you have been thinking about?") and following a response by the interviewee, a follow-up open-ended question is asked for each item (e.g., "Name three jobs you have been thinking about").

The norm group consisted of 592 to 690 individuals with disabilities including mental retardation, learning disabilities, physical or sensory disabilities, traumatic head injury, and severe/chronic mental illness. A total of 592 subjects were included for the Total score, 666 for Decision-Making Readiness, 690 for Employment Readiness, and 593 for Self-Appraisal. The authors reported no significant score differences between the various samples; however, no information is given in the manual regarding the number of persons from each disability category included in the sample. There is also no information provided related to the age or sex of subjects. Several research studies are provided in the manual to support evidence of reliability and validity. Unfortunately, the information provided is general in nature and the two reliability studies that are reported give coefficients that are less than adequate for individual decision making.

Percentiles, T-scores, and cumulative percentages are obtained and the authors state that it is up to the individual interviewer to determine whether a score on any scale indicates a significant problem. They do recommend that any score falling one standard deviation below the mean be considered indicative of a possible problem. Should such a problem be noted, individual program planning should be provided to the individual. A profile sheet is provided in the protocol to conduct further analyses of subcategories for each scale if needed. Subscales for each scale include: Opportunities and Requirements, Tasks and Duties, Rewards and Punishers, Acquisition of Information, and Skills in Choosing for the Decision-Making Readiness scale; Coercion, Lack of Reinforcement, Economics, and Mobility for the Employment Readiness scale; and Needs, Beliefs and Interests, Abilities, Personality, Success in Previous Choices, Responsibility/Control, and Anxiety/Fear of Decision-Making for the Self-Appraisal scale. Each of the subscales consists of only two or three items. The authors state that such analyses need not be conducted with every individual but only when very specific information is needed.

SUMMARY. The VDMI-R items have good face validity, but the scale lacks necessary technical information including age and sex of subjects and adequate reliability and validity coefficients. Thus, the scale should not be used for individual decision-making purposes until these problems have been addressed.

Review of the Vocational Decision-Making Interview—Revised by DONALD W. TIFFANY, Director, Psychological Growth Associates, Inc., Lawrence, KS:

The Vocational Decision-Making Interview—Revised (VDMI-R) is a structured interview, not a test, and is designed to be administered verbally (fourth grade reading level). It can be administered to individuals with a variety of disabilities. There are three scales with 54 questions. These questions refer to (a) Vocational Decision-Making Readiness (17 questions; Opportunities and Requirements, Tasks and Duties, Rewards and Punishers, Acquisition of Information, and Skills in Choosing) (e.g., "Are there any specific jobs you have been thinking about?"); (b) areas of difficulty or Employment Readiness (11 questions; General, Coercion, Lack of Reinforcement, Economics, and Mobility) (e.g., "Would you let others decide which jobs you should take?"); (c) developing vocational plans that meet the needs of the individuals with whom they work based on Self-Appraisal (23 questions; Needs, Beliefs and Interests, Abilities, Personality, Success in Previous Choices, Responsibility/Control, and Anxiety/Fear of Decision-Making) (e.g., "Are there certain types of jobs you would not take because of your beliefs and values?"); and (d) three summary questions.

Applications of the VDMI-R are in general counseling and guidance, development of appropriate Individualized Education Plans, Individualized Transition Plans, or individualized Written Rehabilitation Plans. The VDMI-R is a "useful mechanism for assessing individual vocational decision-making skills prior to focusing efforts on development of these plans" (manual, p. 10). The VDMI-R is useful for vocational evaluation to determine individual training strategies in identified problem areas, and determining group characteristics for individuals with special needs and for developing specialized group programs. Finally, the VDMI-R can be used to further enhance the ongoing program development.

Sampling ranges from residential to sheltered workshops. Reliability studies reported in 1994 (Chandler & Czerlinsky, 1994) show internal consistency estimates of the three subscales range from .62 to .84. Test-retest reliability coefficients ranged from .62 to .80. Using a sample of students from several special education settings, the test-retest from 2 weeks to 9 months ranged from .55 to .87 with "no drop in reliability as the test-retest intervals increased" (manual, p. 6).

Discriminant, content, and predictive validity supported the authors' claims that the content areas of the VDMI-R adequately measured the vocational decision-making problems of persons with disabilities.

The administration of the VDMI-R requires interviewers to work with interviewees on a one-to-one basis. The interview generally lasts from 20–40 minutes and there are no "right" or "wrong" answers. The VDMI-R is designed for use "with individuals who need to make vocational decisions and who have the intellectual capacity needed to make such decisions, either independently or with assistance from various support professionals" (manual, p. 15). It is not limited to a specific disability group, but would be considered inappropriate to use with individuals who lack appropriate cognitive skills to participate in the interview process. Qualified interviewers should be trained in interviewing techniques and have knowledge of the "world of work, the career development process, and the vocational preparation and needs of individuals with various disabilities" (manual, p. 15). The majority of the questions require a "Yes," "Not Sure," or "No" response. On the answer sheet, the left half of each page contains the actual questions, and some of the questions on the right half of the page contain open-ended prompts. The size of the norming sample ranged from 592 to 690 individuals. The raw scores are converted to T-scores and percentiles. A T score below one standard deviation (40 or less) "could be considered indicative of a possible problem which may require some form of assistance" (manual, p. 20). It is not clear what a T score of 60 or more would mean. Clearly marked norm tables in the back of the manual provide the raw score, T score, cumulative percent, and the percent of each score.

This reviewer's experience is more in psychometrics, evidence for which the VDMI-R lacks; however, the VDMI-R serves a very different purpose and appears to fill a gap in a much-needed area. Standardizing performance outcomes on individuals with a variety of disabilities would be a monumental task. These authors have captured a simplistic model allowing for a profile of a diverse group of individuals, in a difficult to evaluate domain, for a population who frequently cannot respond to many assessment instruments. Admittedly, the summary profile would not be cast in hard science; however, the information gleamed from the structured interview would serve many of the stated purposes. Vocational decision making is still an art form, particularly when persons with many different disabilities are included in a rapidly changing work world. The VDMI-R at least gives the painter the brush, canvas, and some important varieties of paint to work with, which does not exist without this structured interview. Rehabilitative organizations would be well equipped to learn this technique for use with their clients, which, of course, means interview training of the staff. I would assume that the VDMI-R will continue to be researched so the current norms may be expanded and broken out by disabilities and more specifically linked to special rehabilitative problems. This reviewer feels that the current test is a big net thrown out to catch as many types of disabilities as possible. Some sorting out should be a future goal. Such direction is a natural progression with an innovative technique such as the VDMI-R.

REVIEWER'S REFERENCE

Chandler, S. K., & Czerlinsky, T. (1994). Vocational Decision-Making Interview—Revised: Assessing the vocational decision-making of individuals with disabilities. *Assessment in Rehabilitation and Exceptionality, 1,* 111–124.

Vocational Integration Index.

Purpose: Constructed "to determine how integrated a person with a disability will be with nondisabled co-workers in a given work setting."

Population: Professionals or paraprofessionals who are responsible for providing employment services for persons with disabilities.

Publication Date: 1992.

Acronym: VII.

Scores, 4: Company Indicators, Work Area Indicators, Employee Indicators, Benefit Indicators.

Administration: Group.

Price Data: Not available.

Time: [30] minutes.

Authors: Wendy S. Parent, John Kregel, and Paul Wehman.

Publisher: PRO-ED, Inc.

a) JOB SCALE.

Purpose: Designed "for assessing how integrated a particular job is."

b) CONSUMER SCALE.

Purpose: Designed "for assessing the level of integration experienced by an employee with a disability."

[Editor's Note: The publisher advised in February 1999 that this test is now out of print.]

Review of the Vocational Integration Index by RICHARD HARDING, Director of Research, Kenexa Corporation, Lincoln, NE:

The Vocational Integration Index (VII) is designed to help supported employment specialists and professionals assist their clients in making better decisions about the work setting. The overall goal is to provide these professionals with information about work environments so that placement decisions on people with severe disabilities can be made in a more appropriate manner. The issue is the degree to which the person with the disability is integrated into the work setting. The authors indicate utilizing the VII will help professionals and the disabled person to choose "jobs that are socially compatible and personally satisfying" (manual, p. 5). It can also be used after job placement to determine the level of the individual's integration so that interventions can be planned to maximize the disabled person's chances for success in the work environment.

The VII is composed of two scales of 32 items each. The Job Scale describes the physical and social characteristics of a work environment and its relationship to integration of the disabled worker. This scale can be utilized in a preemployment setting to assist the supported employment specialist in helping his or her client make a better job decision. The Consumer Scale measures the level of integration already experienced by an employee with a disability in a work environment.

In both the Job and Consumer Scales are four subscales called (a) Company Indicators, (b) Work Area Indicators, (c) Employee Indicators, and (d) Benefit Indicators. Each subscale is composed of eight items with five response choices. The Company Indicators subscale measures operational and administrative procedures, policies, and other types of employee support programs available in the company. The Work Area indicator subscale provides information on work schedules, physical environment, supervisor and departmental policies, and specifics around the work area. The Employee Indicator subscale measures workday activities, social interactions, and more of the interpersonal relationship to be expected in the work environment. The Benefit Indicator subscale provides information on wages, raises, benefits, vacation time, etc.

Each of the subscales can range from a score of 8 to 40, as each question uses a 5-point scale. Response categories range from "1" being the least desirable situation or response to "5" being the most positive or desirable. This is one problem with the VII; in an attempt to score the instrument, assumptions are made about the relative desirability or positiveness of issues to which direction every organization should work. In fact, the scores on the subscales have to be a perfect 40 (value 5 x 8 questions) for there to be no problems, according to the manual. For example, under the Work Area subscale, one of the questions is, "Does an employee in this position work in physical proximity to coworkers?" (manual, p. 10). A "5" response is listed as employees continuously work side-by-side compared to a "1" response where employees work in an isolated area where there are no other employees. There are other similar issues within the VII, but it seems as if the type of work being considered should be taken into account. The work itself may dictate that employees cannot interact or work side-by-side with one another. Yet, one must also take into account the desirability for a disabled person to have those opportunities for social interaction and that, if one were to answer "1" to this particular question, no value of good or bad is ascribed to that answer; rather, it is a fact of the job and position and therefore a disabled person may need to consider other job settings or positions.

Psychometrically, the validation efforts have been extremely sound. The very detailed manual provides information on validity and reliability. Validity was first studied using six experts in the field of supported employment. They were asked to review the draft instrument and address 10 questions regarding face validity, comprehensiveness, clarity, etc. From their comments, items were reworded as well as the instructions to administer the instrument.

A pilot study was then conducted from nine geographically dispersed states. In all, a total of 36 employment specialists were asked to identify two individuals they had as clients. Of these individuals one was labeled as "most integrated" and one as "least integrated." This was an extreme groups approach that is quite acceptable. From the data supplied by these 36 employment specialists and 72 actual clients, the VII underwent a revision in which items were added, deleted, and combined.

The next validity effort involved a concurrent validity study where 32 programs from 19 different states participated. Complete data were obtained on 121 matched pairs or 242 clients. Once again, each employment specialist was asked to indicate two clients who were most integrated in their present position compared to two who were least integrated. These employment specialists were asked to make these designations prior to receiving information on the VII. Results revealed that the items on the VII provided excellent discrimination between the most integrated and least integrated clients. On the Consumer Scale, all 32 items were statistically significant with regard to differences between most and least integrated clients. On the Job Scale, 26 of the 32 successfully differentiated between most and least integrated. Furthermore, a discrimination function analysis was done where the Consumer Scale successfully and correctly classified 97.5% of the most integrated group compared to 88.3% of the least integrated group. For the Job Scale, the discriminant function analysis successfully classified 97.5% in the most integrated group compared to 80.2% in the least integrated group.

Construct validity was studied from an internal consistency point of view. Cronbach's alpha revealed reliability estimates for subscales from .66 to .80. The Company Indicators subscale on both the Job and Consumer Scales had reliabilities of .68 and .66 respectively. Work Area Indicators had .80 and .79 reliability estimates for the Job and Consumer Scales respectively. The Employee Indicator area had .87 and .88 for Job and Consumer Scale reliability estimates, and for Benefit Indicators, it was .83 and .80 respectively.

The authors also did a study of interrater agreement and report a proportion of agreement for each of the subscales and the total scales scores. These ranged from .89 to .91.

The manual is very detailed and specific on helping the reader understand why the VII was developed, providing an adequate description of the VII, demonstrating the efforts made to document the reliability and validity of scores from the VII as well as administration and scoring protocols. Additionally, several case study examples are presented. This helps the professional to have some confidence that he or she can reliably make the observations, score the items, and interpret the identified areas of need.

SUMMARY. The VII has much to recommend it for use by supported employment professionals. The methodology used to develop it is psychometrically sound and very acceptable. The manual is detailed and provides a great amount of information on supportive employment, utilization, and interpretation of the index of the VII, and practice in scoring. It would seem the next area of research would document the utility of the VII in helping professionals better place disabled individuals and helping organizations provide a more positive work environment for disabled individuals.

[411]
Vulpe Assessment Battery—Revised.

Purpose: Designed as "a comprehensive, process-oriented, criterion-referenced assessment that emphasizes children's functional abilities."

Population: Children functioning between full term birth to six years of age.

Publication Date: 1994.

Acronym: VAB-R.

Scores: 8 scales: Basic Senses and Functions, Gross Motor, Fine Motor, Language, Cognitive Processes and Specific Concepts, Adaptive Behaviors, Activities of Daily Living, Environmental Assessment.

Administration: Individual or group.

Price Data, 1994: $65 per complete kit including manual ('94, 480 pages) and 50 record sheets; $12 per 50 record sheets.

Time: Administration time not reported.
Comments: Ratings by person familiar with the child.
Author: Shirley German Vulpe.
Publisher: Slosson Educational Publications, Inc.

Review of the Vulpe Assessment Battery—Revised by THERESA GRAHAM, Assistant Professor of Educational Psychology, University of Nebraska-Lincoln, Lincoln, NE:

The Vulpe Assessment Battery—Revised (VAB-R) is a comprehensive developmental assessment battery for children with special needs from birth through 6 years of age. As a criterion-referenced test, it is intended to provide an overview of children's strengths and weaknesses for enhancing programming and intervention. The VAB-R purports that it can be used with children with a variety of developmental disabilities. The VAB-R includes three sections: Assessment of Basic Senses and Functions of the central nervous system, Assessment of Six Domains of Developmental Behaviors (Gross Motor, Fine Motor, Language, Cognitive Processes, Adaptive Behaviors, and Activities of Daily Living), and Assessment of the Environment. The six domains include 60 skill sequences. The individual activities (over 1,300 activities) were developed through examination of relevant literature. The activities are organized according to domain, skill sequence, and age. For each activity, a description of the equipment needed and directions are provided. In addition, the supporting references and cross referencing to other skills are noted. The VAB-R can be individually tailored to the specific needs of the child. It can be administered in multiple settings and different materials can be used to elicit the same developmental skill.

The scoring system consists of the Vulpe Performance Analysis Scale (VPAS), Task/Activity Analysis, and Information Processing Analysis. The VPAS uses a 7-point scale for evaluating a child's performance in terms of type of assistance (if any) needed by the child to perform the task. This continuum system provides the examiner with a much better picture of the child's abilities than a dichotomous "yes"/"no" assessment of performance. Task/Activity Analysis considers aspects of the child's abilities that may inhibit the child's performance of a particular activity. Information Processing Analysis requires the examiner to consider the activities in terms of input, integration, and output.

Although there are many strengths to the VAB-R (e.g., the focus on intervention, appreciation of the family, and a dynamic approach to assessment; flexibility in administration; the variety of activities provided; the literature-based activities; cross-referencing of activities; etc.), there are a number of weaknesses. Flexibility in administration and variety of activities may make administration difficult for examiners with less skilled backgrounds. Making appropriate modifications within a testing situation may be a difficult task for individuals who have not had extensive training.

Scoring of the VAB-R may be difficult for both experienced and inexperienced examiners. First, although the VPAS is unique in its evaluation approach, it may be problematic in that it may be an inappropriate technique for certain activities. For example, how does an examiner provide physical assistance for verbal tasks? Also, the VPAS may be influenced by the examiner. Given the focus on flexibility and adaptation, an examiner may be more likely to provide assistance when it may not be needed. The Information Processing Analysis might be difficult given the paucity of the description of what the examiner is supposed to do. In addition, it is not clear how it differs from the Task/Activity Analysis and what additional information it provides.

In terms of reliability, three studies were described. Although the studies indicated interrater agreement rates between 87%–95%, there may be weaknesses in the studies that may limit their usefulness. For example, none of the studies provided much, if any, information regarding the children used in the studies (e.g., age, developmental abilities) or information about the raters and their training (although in the present version a training packet for examiners to use is provided). In addition, none of the samples were very large, which may limit the generalizability of the findings across evaluators and children. Finally, little information was provided regarding on what the percent agreements were based. Given the types of interpretations that hinge on the VPAS scoring, one-point disagreements may be very meaningful.

Bias, content validity, curriculum validity, and concurrent validity were each discussed. The author claimed that there is no unsystematic error bias citing that the VAB-R has been used by various disciplines and in a variety of settings and countries. The reliability of scores was also cited as evidence of lack of bias. However, the concerns raised earlier concerning the studies used to assess reliability still apply. The author stated that the inherent flexibility of the VAB-R reduces possible bias that may occur with children with atypical development. However, in both cases of bias, no studies were reported.

Content validity was considered by examining various sources, including relevant psychological and educational literature, and professionals, and child development experts, to assess validity of the placement of items in each domain and the placement of items at various age levels. Curriculum validity was examined by comparing the six domains and the 60 skill sequences to typical early child curricula. The VAB-R was seen as similar to the developmental tasks attended to in preschools and to the developmental sequences used in treatment activities.

Only one study was reported to examine concurrent validity. This study examined the concurrent validity of the gross motor items from the Vulpe Second Edition and the Peabody Developmental Scales. No other items were examined. In addition, very little information was given regarding the sample used. For example, was the test better suited for children with physical disabilities? Thus, it is difficult to assess the concurrent validity of the test for other domains included in the VAB-R or for particular populations.

SUMMARY. The goal of the VAB-R is "to enable appropriate early intervention in the child's life as soon as possible, to support families in the difficult task of raising a special child and to help children learn to the maximum of their endowed abilities" (p. xiii, VAB-R manual). Although the information regarding validity and reliability is weak and the preparation for and administration of the VAB-R may be somewhat burdensome, the VAB-R meets its goal of providing a comprehensive view of a child with special needs. The flexibility in administration is well suited to tap the "best" performance of these children, and the information gained will provide caregivers with a better sense of the child's strengths and weaknesses in order to create appropriate environments to best meet the child's needs.

Review of the Vulpe Assessment Battery—Revised by DIANE J. SAWYER, Murfree Professor of Dyslexic Studies, Middle Tennessee State University, Murfreesboro, TN:

DESCRIPTION. The Vulpe Assessment Battery—Revised is the third edition of this test. Originally published in 1969, it is intended for use with individuals who evidence atypical development related to medical or social conditions that affect developmental potential. It may be used with individuals functioning between full-term birth to 6 years of age regardless of one's chronological age. The authors indicate that the test is appropriate for all children regardless of disabling condition, sex, or cultural background (manual, p. 1). They also indicate that it may be used by any responsible person who knows the child well or who was trained in child development. Further, the authors indicate that the battery may be administered to individuals or to groups of children and that it may be used in multiple settings where the child spends time. For example, it may be used at home, in a hospital, or in a school setting.

The Vulpe Assessment Battery—Revised is made up of six subscales: Gross Motor skills, Fine Motor skills, Language, Cognitive Processes and Specific Concepts, Adaptive Behaviors, and Activities of Daily Living. Each scale is composed of observable activities. These activities are arranged according to developmental expectations from 0–1 month through age 6 years. Each activity may be interpreted into a scale-score devised by the authors. This score is intended to quantify observations of behaviors observed or elicited. The 7-point scale ranges from 1, indicating that the child shows no interest in the activity, to 7, indicating that the child can demonstrate the ability to successfully transfer performance of a task to unfamiliar situations (such as a test situation) as well as to other tasks demanding equal skills in different forms and contexts (manual, p. 28). Two other assessments are also included in this battery: the Basic Senses and Functions Assessment and the Assessment of the Environment. The former addresses issues with visual acuity, auditory acuity, the sense of smell and touch, as well as various aspects of growth and fine motor development. Assessment of the Environment offers questions to raise and discuss with the caretakers responsible for the child being assessed. Questions address the adequacy of the environment, the degree of stimulation available within the environment, the degree of psychological support available in the environment, and the degrees to which the environment adapts to the needs of the child.

These last two assessments yield comments and interpretations that are not subsequently quantified. All of the developmental assessment scales are arranged hierarchically by the age at which an activity is expected to be developmentally appropriate. For each age (e.g., 0–1 month) activities to be elicited or observed are described, the equipment and directions for eliciting or observing the behavior are listed, and the 7-point scale used to transform the behavior observed into a quantitative index is provided. Space for comments is also provided on the record sheet. A total of 1,014 items appeared in the six main assessment scales. Entry into the assessment is determined by the examiner based upon personal observation and/or discussions with one or more of the caregivers.

Another component of these scales is the Special Scales section. There are Special Scales presented for gross motor, fine motor, functional tests, and analysis of posture and mobility. These special scales include items drawn from the primary developmental scales that specifically address particular subsets of behavior specific to each scale. This reviewer could find no discussion of these special scales that would assist in understanding when they should be used and how these special scales relate to the primary scales in the battery.

An interesting feature of the assessment battery is the assessment references. The authors have indexed each activity in the battery to professional references that support the importance of that activity in scaling an individual's development. References include assessment tools, professional journal articles, text references, and instructional guides, as well as government documents.

The battery includes three appendices. The first details a study of interrater reliability for applying the 7-point Performance Analysis Scale. The second offers illustrations of how to scale behavior, including a sample developmental report for a young child (22 months) and one for an older individual (23 years). Illustrations are also provided for home-based programs for various individuals, individualized education plans, an individual program progress plan, and daily and weekly classroom schedules. Appendix 3 details the application of the performance analysis scale as it is applied to some of the assessment items. Authors state that this scale may be used to teach a task or to enhance performance on a task by attending to a sequence of steps for gaining a child's attention

or to manipulating the task, or the environment, to improve task performance (manual, p. 16). In this way, the authors indicate that the assessment is directly linked to subsequent instruction as well as to subsequent evaluation of progress.

RELIABILITY. Estimates of reliability are based upon two elements. The first is the number of items in the battery. Authors cite references that indicate that the greater the number of items used to make an assessment of a child's functioning in a particular area, the more likely it is that the assessment will reflect the actual ability of the child (manual, p. 67). Secondly, the authors indicate that three studies of interrater reliability have been conducted. They report interrater agreement ranging from 87%–95% and interrater reliability coefficients reported for two studies range from .74–.94. These studies involved five and eight children, respectively, with various developmental handicaps. No scores are reported for interrater reliability in studies of group administration. Neither does the manual clearly indicate how a group administration might be managed. Further, in two studies for which details are provided, only professionally prepared individuals were involved in administering the battery. However, the authors state that anyone who is familiar with the child may reasonably administer this battery. It is not clear how a parent or daycare provider would be supported in evaluating the outcome of the assessment even if the tasks could be adequately presented and recorded.

VALIDITY. The authors offer little evidence of validity. They claim content validity and reference a report that evaluated face validity of the second edition. The authors also claim concurrent validity, based upon a study conducted on the second edition comparing the gross motor scales with the Peabody Developmental Scales gross motor scales. No other evidence of test validity is provided. The authors do claim, however, that extensive field testing has removed any unclear measurement descriptions (manual, p. 69) and thereby has essentially eliminated the source of unsystematic error, which might be associated with poorly described measures. They further indicate that the potential impact of a child's handicapping condition or of differing cultural experiences on the assessment of the child's development is addressed directly in the administration of this battery. Examiners are required to modify directions to the child, performance expectations, testing materials, as well as sources of information to assure that the child's full scope of abilities may be observed and recorded.

SUMMARY. The Vulpe Assessment Battery—Revised is a comprehensive but cumbersome tool developed for the assessment of development among individuals with medical or sociocultural limitations that might impede development. No evidence is provided to document that this tool effectively distinguishes between individuals who experience typical development and those who evidence atypical development in any one or combination of domains assessed by this battery. The primary utility of this battery would appear to be in identifying the particular state or stage of development an individual has achieved when that individual has already been identified as evidencing delays in development. This battery might then identify entry points for intervention within specific domains.

The authors provide little direction for interpreting the battery results into a plan of intervention. One page (p. 31) offers suggestions for things to consider in designing a program. These include such global recommendations as, "what is the basal age at which the child accomplishes tasks without assistance within any given skill area?" "Is there a particular type of assistance that helps the child perform most often?" The authors also refer users of the battery to Appendix 2 for sample report formats prepared by the authors. These samples support the impression that highly trained professionals should administer, interpret, and develop intervention plans based upon the Vulpe Assessment Battery. It is not likely that parents or other caregivers could effectively administer, interpret, and build intervention plans of the sort provided, without a great deal of guidance and support. A statement by the authors seems to underscore this reality. "Admittedly, the flexibility and choices inherent in the VAB-R are a challenge and can be considered very complex for persons with limited experience and knowledge" (p. 36).

In the hand of skilled professionals, it may be that the Vulpe Assessment Battery—Revised can accomplish the purpose for which it was developed.

[412]
WAIS-R NI.

Purpose: Constructed as a "process approach to neuropsychological assessment of cognitive functions."
Population: Ages 16–74.

Publication Date: 1991.
Scores, 14: Verbal (Information, Comprehension, Arithmetic, Similarities, Digit Span, Vocabulary, Total), Performance (Digit Symbol, Picture Completion, Block Design, Picture Arrangement, Object Assembly, Total), Total.
Administration: Individual.
Price Data, 1999: $418 per complete kit including manual (153 pages), stimulus booklet, sentence arrangement booklet, 25 response booklets, 25 record forms, 3 puzzles/boxes, spatial span board, object assembly layout shield, and 3 Koh's blocks; $1,050 per combination kit including WAIS-R NI complete kit, WAIS-R complete set and attaché case; $23.50 per 25 digit symbol response booklets; $84.50 per 25 record forms.
Time: Administration time varies by number of supplemental subtests administered.
Comments: It is necessary to have the Wechsler Adult Intelligence Scale—Revised (WAIS-R; T4:2937) complete set in order to administer WAIS-R NI.
Authors: Edith Kaplan, Deborah Fein, Robin Morris, and Dean C. Delis.
Publisher: The Psychological Corporation.

Review of the WAIS-R NI by KEITH HATTRUP, Associate Professor of Psychology, San Diego State University, San Diego, CA:

The WAIS-R as a Neuropsychological Instrument is an adaptation of the WAIS-R (Wechsler Adult Intelligence Scale—Revised; 9:1348) designed to facilitate a process-based approach to the assessment of neuropsychological functioning. The WAIS-R NI is designed to be used in conjunction with the WAIS-R, with modifications to subtest administration and scoring. The WAIS-R NI materials include the manual; a stimulus booklet that includes new stimuli for the Information, Vocabulary, Block Design, Arithmetic, Comprehension, and Similarities multiple-choice subtests; additional stimuli for the Object Assembly and Block Designs subtests; and stimuli for three new subtests, the Sentences Arrangement, Symbol Copy, and Spatial Span subtests. The WAIS-R NI is designed for use by professionals who are trained in the use of the WAIS-R, and who wish to use the procedures outlined in the manual to facilitate understanding of the possible neuropsychological functioning of examinees.

The WAIS-R NI represents an attempt to modify a widely used standardized battery of cognitive ability tests to provide a more in-depth analysis of the possible cognitive and neuropsychological processes underlying test performance. As noted in the manual, traditional approaches to cognitive assessment, such as the WAIS-R, yield only a single score for each subtest. Traditional scoring methods fail to address the cognitive processes leading to the production of a response, and focus instead on the response outcome itself. As a consequence, examinees with differing cognitive impairments may receive the same subtest score even though they may use different processes in achieving the same score. The WAIS-R NI is designed to provide a process-based approach to assessment that may be used to facilitate diagnoses about possible neurological or sensory disorders. The test is based on the notion that specific neurological disorders reveal themselves in the pattern of behavior observed across the subtests. The goals of the WAIS-R NI are highly commendable, and the authors have done a reasonable job developing procedures to facilitate systematic and objective scoring of the processes leading to the production of test responses.

A significant challenge of developing a process-based approach to psychological assessment is developing standardized test protocols and procedures for reliable scoring of behavior. The WAIS-R NI accomplishes this by providing detailed information about subtest administration and scoring, thereby facilitating a systematic approach to the documentation of qualitative aspects of test performance. For most of the subtests, the manual describes modifications of the standard WAIS-R administration procedures designed to elicit additional information relevant to possible neurological functions. For example, it is recommended that standard discontinue rules not be followed on most subtests to permit observation of examinees' problem-solving behavior. For other subtests, new administration procedures are provided in addition to the standard WAIS-R procedures. The level of detail provided about the administration of the subtests contributes to the usefulness of the WAIS-R NI as a standardized process-based method of assessment.

The manual also describes methods of scoring each of the subtests. Although the focus of the WAIS-R NI is on the processes leading to the production of test responses, standard administration and scoring procedures can be followed for most subtests. This permits the derivation of an IQ score that may be used when comparing scores

with the normative data provided with the WAIS-R. However, given that changes in test administration may affect test scores, users must exercise caution when attempting to derive a scaled IQ score then implementing any of the adaptations of the standard WAIS-R protocol.

Methods for scoring the subtests to permit an assessment of the processes underlying performance are also described in the manual. These methods focus primarily on an analysis of the types of errors made during performance on the subtests. For example, a measure of Intratest Scatter can be calculated for most subtests, indicating the extent to which an examinee's responses are inconsistent across subtest items that are graded in difficulty. The manual also describes procedures for recording behaviors during test administration and then using the patterns of errors specific to each subtest to develop hypotheses about possible neuropsychological and sensory disorders. Many of these patterns of errors and their clinical significance have been empirically demonstrated in the studies cited in the manual. However, in general, the hypotheses described in the manual about the implications of specific patterns of errors for possible neurological problems are not based on empirical validation using the WAIS-R NI. The manual provides appropriate cautions about the interpretation of behaviors and scores observed on the subtests. In particular, test users are urged to consider the entire pattern of responses across the subtests, along with other clinical and diagnostic information, when developing hypotheses about neuropsychological deficits.

The most significant weaknesses of the WAIS-R NI include the lack of normative information about process-based scores, and the lack of information supporting the reliability and validity of the scores. Norms are provided for Intratest Scatter based on the WAIS-R standardization sample; however, their relevance to the specific types of neurological diagnoses described in the manual is unclear. There is a significant need for normative data on each of the subtest scores, including the behavioral observations scored during test performance. Research is needed to assess the reliability of subtest scores across raters and time. Finally, there is a significant need for the development of a cumulative body of research on the validity of the new subtest scores used in the WAIS-R NI. Until additional supporting validation evidence is provided, the WAIS-R NI cannot be recommended as a stand-alone assessment battery for the purposes of diagnosing neurological problems. However, one of the most significant strengths of the WAIS-R NI is the level of detail provided in the manual about hypothesized relationships between patterns of behavior on each of the subtests and specific neurological impairments. The manual should stimulate considerable research designed to explore the hypothesized linkages between neurological processes and test performance.

SUMMARY. The WAIS-R NI is a battery of tests designed to facilitate the identification of neuropsychological impairments among examinees. The test is based on a process-based approach to assessment that focuses on the cognitive processes and behaviors leading to the production of test responses. The goals of the test are significant and important, and represent advanced thinking about the role of standardized testing in psychological assessment. The most significant strengths of the test include the level of detail provided in the manual about hypothesized relationships between process-based observations and neurological functioning, including appropriate cautions to test users about the tentative nature of many of the hypothesized interpretations provided in the manual. Much more information about the reliability, criterion-related validity, and norms for the measure are needed to guide test users in selecting this test and interpreting scores. Until additional psychometric evidence is made available, the measure can only be recommended for applications in which psychometric issues are secondary, such as in the development and exploration of hypotheses about the relationships between observed behaviors and neurological functioning. It is hoped that the WAIS-R NI will stimulate additional research about underlying processes leading to test responses, including their neurological significance.

Review of the WAIS-R NI by DAVID C. S. RICHARD, Clinical Coordinator, Assistant Professor, Psychology, Southwest Missouri State University, Springfield, MO:

The WAIS-R as a Neuropsychological Instrument (WAIS-R NI) is an adaptation of the WAIS-R so that it can be readily administered to neurologically impaired individuals. The purpose of the instrument is to retain and take advantage of the rich history associated with the Wechsler Scales while facilitating process-oriented assessment.

Process-oriented assessment emphasizes the qualitative aspects of behavior during a test session. Historically, tests of cognitive abilities that were developed from a classic psychometric model emphasized single scores or scale scores because the purpose of these tests is largely to rank order, or sort, individual cases relative to the performance of a standardization sample (i.e., nomothetic analysis) and to the mean of one's own performance (i.e., ipsative analysis). However, this type of approach is of marginal utility to the neuropsychologist assessing brain function in neurologically impaired individuals. First, raw scores and scaled scores shed little light on the genesis of neurological dysfunction. Neurological impairments with diverse etiologies may yield similar score patterns. Second, aggregating scores from individual items into a subtest raw score implicitly assumes homogeneity of item content (and task demands) across items. This assumption is suspect, however, for any test that requires the use of diverse cognitive abilities and/or problem-solving strategies across items. Third, neuropsychologists are often more interested in *how* an individual solves a problem than the scoring of the item. In the Piagetian tradition, the authors of the WAIS-R NI advocate understanding cognitive dysfunction through a careful examination of problem-solving errors.

Throughout the WAIS-R NI, administration of the parent instrument has been modified to facilitate systematic documentation of the "qualitative aspects of performance" (manual, 1991, p. 2). For example, the time limit is not observed on Picture Completion, Picture Arrangement, Arithmetic, and Object Assembly. Discontinuation rules are eschewed or left to the examiner's judgment across most of the subtests. A stimulus booklet is presented for several subtests and items have been revised to a multiple-choice format making it easier for aphasic patients or patients with other retrieval problems to select rather than vocalize an answer. Extra blocks are presented for Block Design and a modified booklet includes pictures of the designs that have grid overlays. A response booklet has been included for Arithmetic, two versions of Digit Symbol, and Symbol Copy. A Spatial Span subtest, similar to that included in the WMS-III, is also included. Finally, the WAIS-R NI provides a revised record form that facilitates detailed qualitative recording of an individual's responses.

WAIS-R NI PSYCHOMETRIC INFORMA-TION. A significant shortcoming of the WAIS-R NI is that the authors have not reported any meaningful psychometric information. The appendix includes numerous tables detailing intrasubtest scatter for the various subtests based upon the performance of the WAIS-R standardization sample. However, intrasubtests scatter statistics for the WAIS-R NI are not included. Intrasubtest scatter statistics derived from the WAIS-R may not be meaningfully applied to WAIS-R NI results because the administration guidelines and test stimuli are considerably different. In fact, I was unable to find any reference tables in the appendix that reported patient performance on the WAIS-R NI. As Slick, Hopp, Strauss, and Fox (1996) noted, there is a pressing need for comprehensive WAIS-R NI normative data. Calculating WAIS-R NI scaled scores using WAIS-R norms is not justified. Relatedly, basing clinical judgment of cognitive functioning on tables derived from the WAIS-R (e.g., intrasubtest scatter) is not justified and may lead to erroneous inferences and treatment recommendations. Mercer et al. (1998) recently reported supplemental WAIS-R NI norms. However, their sample was very small and was only a first step in addressing this issue.

The WAIS-R NI also does not include any statistics pertaining to the reliability or validity of the modified subtest scores. Because the net effect of the administration modifications in many instances is to change a subtest from a speeded test to a power test, especially with the Performance Scale subtests, it is reasonable to assume that the reliability of the subtest scores would be affected as well. In addition, given that the WAIS-R NI will be primarily used with patients recovering from neurological injury, one might also wish to consider the temporal stability of the test at different postmorbid intervals. For example, individuals with mild closed-head injuries may improve rapidly within a 2-week period and evidence significantly better performance upon retesting. Low retest correlations would most likely reflect the instrument's sensitivity to clinical change rather than measurement instability. The WAIS-R NI, however, includes no data related to the temporal stability of the instrument in those populations where it is most likely to be used.

An implicit assumption made by the WAIS-R NI authors is that process-oriented assessment will lead to better diagnostic efficiency and "more sophisticated interpretations of an examinee's WAIS-R responses" (manual, p. 107). As a result, numerous additional indexes are calculated using the WAIS-R NI record form. For example, the Digits Forward and Digits Backward record form includes several alternative ways of recording recall errors. The Picture Arrangement record form includes columns for raw scatter, whether or not the individual exceeded the time limit, and sequencing errors. Block Design similarly includes numerous additional entries. A reasonable question to ask, however, is whether the effort results in demonstrable improvement in clinical diagnostic decision making (i.e., incremental validity). The WAIS-R NI manual does not provide any evidence that the use of the WAIS-R NI, as opposed to the WAIS-R, results in greater diagnostic efficiency. In addition, one would also be interested in the utility of the clinical signs the WAIS-R NI is attempting to detect. Are the clinical signs observed in test behavior reliably associated with performance outside of the test in meaningful activities? How much better is the WAIS-R NI at detecting meaningful signs compared to the WAIS-R? What is the rationale for calculating a raw error index and why is it useful? The question, of course, is whether the increase in observation and recording complexity results in the generation of assessment heuristics and clinical hypotheses that may be meaningfully incorporated into the patient's treatment plan. Simply providing the means for observing additional signs and calculating new scores does not speak to their utility or importance and many examiners may begin to wonder whether the greater recording required by the WAIS-R NI necessarily translates into a better understanding of the patient's cognitive functioning.

DISCUSSION. A significant issue in the utilization of the WAIS-R NI is the degree to which altering administration procedures affects raw scores and, consequently, scaled scores. The authors state in a footnote that the effect of administration modifications is "probably minimal" (manual, p. 4). However, no data are presented to support this claim and results from other researchers suggest that the administration modifications may not yield equivalent results. For example, Slick et al. (1996) found in 20 university students that a significant minority of subjects received lower scores on some multiple-choice items than they did when the items were administered with the WAIS-R using traditional instructional sets. However, Troester, Fields, Paolo, and Koller (1996) found that scores from the WAIS-R NI multiple-choice versions of the Vocabulary and Information subtests were not significantly different from scores derived from a traditional WAIS-R administration. At the very least, additional studies are required to show which subtests may be most affected by the administration rules changes, which modifications are most likely to impact scores, and which populations (e.g., traumatic brain injury, dementia, etc.) would most likely receive higher or lower scaled scores as a result of the changes.

How the WAIS-R NI will fare now that the WAIS-III has been published is another question. Given the well-known phenomenon that test norms become outdated over time (Flynn, 1983, 1984), scores derived from an instrument using older norms are more likely to be inflated than scores derived from newer instruments. This criticism is, of course, mediated by the process-oriented nature of the WAIS-R NI, which deemphasizes scaled scores and IQs in favor of qualitative analysis. A second criticism, however, is not as easy to dismiss. The WAIS-R's norms extended only to age 74. Although the WAIS-R NI authors advocate examining intrasubtest scatter for meaningful diagnostic clues, scatter norms are provided only to the ceiling age of the WAIS-R and only using WAIS-R, not WAIS-R NI, data. Neuropsychological examiners testing septo- and octagenerians will have little or no help evaluating scatter scores with these individuals. Of course, the WAIS-III includes norms to age 89 as well as a more contemporary standardization sample.

One other concern involves the content validity of the WAIS-R NI. An instrument is only content valid in the context of the purposes for which it was developed (Haynes, Richard, & Kubany, 1995). The WAIS-R was primarily designed to assess intellectual functioning in intact adults. Even though it has been a staple of the neuropsychological battery for many years, it was never conceptualized as primarily a neuropsychological instrument. It is not clear that the WAIS-R NI provides clinically useful information in a way that (a) comprehensively addresses neuropsychological functioning and (b) does so more efficiently than other neuropsychological instruments. Most neuropsychologists will be disappointed to find that the WAIS-R NI does only a marginally

better job of assessing short-term memory than the WAIS-R. Although the Spatial Span subtest is included, there is no equivalent to the WAIS-III (415) Letter-Number Sequencing subtest or the Wechsler Memory Scale—III (WMS-III; 416) visual memory subtests. The WAIS-R NI remains a poor cousin to these other instruments with regard to memory assessment.

Certainly the most problematic issue associated with the WAIS-R NI is the fact it has not been normed or assessed for its equivalence to the WAIS-R administration using a large sample. The authors may be correct that the modifications have "minimal" impact on scores. However, only empirical data, and not speculation, will truly resolve this question. The potential ramifications are clear when one considers that the WAIS-R NI could likely be used as part of disability claim evaluations or in other forensic contexts. Scaled scores could very well change as a result of the WAIS-R NI stimulus presentation modifications. It remains to be shown empirically whether this is the case. However, the claim made by the authors that any effects are "minimal" is not justified at this point.

SUMMARY. The WAIS-R NI is a laudable effort to encourage process-oriented assessment of cognitive functions. However, the manual does not address many important issues regarding the basic psychometric properties of the WAIS-R NI. The administration and item modifications have not been meaningfully examined and reliance on WAIS-R normative data for interpretation of WAIS-R NI results is not justified. The manual does not provide rationale for the plethora of indexes and additional scores that the examiner must calculate. An effort to examine the criterion-related validity of the additional indexes should be undertaken. Finally, the incremental validity of the WAIS-R NI has yet to be established and many examiners may wonder whether the WAIS-R NI is the best instrument available for the assessment of a broad range of neurological functions.

REVIEWER'S REFERENCES

Flynn, J. R. (1983). Now the great augmentation of the American IQ. *Nature,* 301, 655.

Flynn, J. R. (1984). The mean IQ of Americans: Massive gains from 1932 to 1978. *Psychological Bulletin, 94,* 29–51.

Haynes, S. N., Richard, D. C., & Kubany, E. S. (1995). Content validity in psychological assessment: A functional approach to concepts and methods. *Psychological Assessment, 7,* 238–247.

Slick, D., Hopp, G., Strauss, E., & Fox, D. (1996). Effects of prior testing with the WAIS-R NI on subsequent retest with the WAIS-R. *Archives of Clinical Neuropsychology, 11,* 123–130.

Troester, A. I., Fields, J. A., Paolo, A. M., & Koller, W. C. (1996). Performance of individuals with Parkinson's disease on the vocabulary and information subtests of the WAIS-R as a neuropsychological instrument. *Journal of Clinical Neuropsychology, 2,* 215–223.

Mercer, W. N., Harrell, E. H., Miller, D. C., Childs, H. W., Rockers, D. M., & Deldotto, J. E. (1998). Performance of healthy adults versus individuals with brain injuries on the supplemental measures of the WAIS-R NI. *Brain Injury, 12,* 753–758.

[413]
Ward Atmosphere Scale (Third Edition).

Purpose: Designed to evaluate treatment program social climates in health care settings.

Population: Patients and staff members.

Publication Dates: 1974–1996.

Acronym: WAS.

Scores, 10: Involvement, Support, Spontaneity, Autonomy, Practical Orientation, Personal Problems Orientation, Anger and Aggression, Order and Organization, Program Clarity, Staff Control.

Administration: Group.

Forms, 3: Real, Ideal, Expectations.

Price Data, 1998: $100 per permission set including sampler set plus permission to reproduce up to 200 copies of the instrument; $25 per sampler set including manual ('96, 73 pages), questionnaire/answer sheet, and scoring directions.

Foreign Language Editions: Translations available in Danish, Dutch, Finnish, French, German, Hebrew, Italian, Norwegian, Spanish, and Swedish.

Time: Administration time not reported.

Comments: Used to describe, plan for, and monitor change or improvements in treatment programs by examining patient and staff social climate perceptions.

Author: Rudolph H. Moos.

Publisher: Mind Garden, Inc.

Cross References: See T%:2850 (3 references), T4:2925 (17 references), and T3:2587 (16 references); for a review by Earl S. Taulbee of an earlier edition, see 8:706 (31 references). For a review of the Social Climate Scales, see 8:681.

Review of the Ward Atmosphere Scale (Third Edition) by RONALD A. BERK, Professor of Biostatistics and Measurement, School of Nursing, Johns Hopkins University, Baltimore, MD:

The Ward Atmosphere Scale (WAS), originally published in 1974, has a third edition manual, but not a revised scale. There is no indication in the 1996 revision of the manual that any changes have been made in any of the Forms (R, I, E, or S). This manual, however, includes extensive new information on the use of the WAS in clinical, consulting, and program evaluation applications, and an update and expanded review of research applications.

The WAS consists of 10 Social Climate Scales (or subscales) with 10 items each, clustered into three sets of dimensions or domains. The Relationship dimensions are composed of the Involvement, Support, and Spontaneity subscales; the Personal Growth dimensions contain the Autonomy, Practical Orientation, Personal Problems Orientation, and Anger and Aggression subscales; and the System Maintenance dimensions include the Order and Organization, Program Clarity, and Staff Control subscales.

There are three different forms of the total scale that are completed by patients and/or staff members in psychiatric and substance abuse treatment programs. Form R (the Real Form) measures patients' and staff members' views of their current program, for example, "Patients often criticize or joke about the staff." Form I (the Ideal Form) presents the same 100 statements as Form R, but uses future tense to assess preferences about what the ideal treatment program would be like, for example, "Patients will often criticize or joke about the staff." Form E (the Expectations Form) is identical to Form I, except that it asks patients what they expect the program they are about to enter will be like. These three forms contain 100 statements each, answerable in a true-false format. There is also Form S, which is a short-form version of Form R with only 40 items.

CONTENT SPECIFICATIONS. The specifications or blueprint from which the WAS was built consists of only a list of the subscales under the dimensions identified above, with one-line descriptions of the 10 subscales. The manual states that "Our focus was on relatively broad constructs ... that assess key aspects of treatment programs. As knowledge about broad constructs accumulates, we may be able to define and assess more specific constructs" (p. 25). Despite the 22 years of research and applications of the WAS reported in this latest edition of the manual, there are no detailed definitions of what the subscales measure.

ITEM DEVELOPMENT. An item pool of 206 items was developed on the basis of structured interviews with patients and staff, observations of a representative sample of programs, and analyses of sources about various treatment programs. These items were administered to patients and staff in 14 programs. A subset of 130 items was then selected. No criteria for selection were given. These items were then administered in 160 psychiatric programs in the United States and Canada. There is no information on how or why this sample of programs was selected. A final set of 100 items was chosen for Form R according to two criteria: (a) No more than 80% of the respondents should answer an item true or false, and (b) the item should correlate more highly with its own subscale than with any other. Three other criteria related to the subscale structure were considered: (a) Each subscale should have a nearly equal balance of true and false items, (b) the subscales should have low to moderate intercorrelations, and (c) each subscale should discriminate significantly among treatment programs.

These procedures were followed for only Form R. The other forms were just adapted from Form R by changing the tense of the verb in each statement. The short version of R, Form S, was built by selecting 4 of the 10 items from each subscale. The manual does not indicate any systematic content or technical criteria for the selection of these 40 items.

The validity of rating scale items is a function of the information available to the respondents upon which to base their opinions. In Form R, patients are asked to evaluate their own treatment program by rating program characteristics as true or false. The characteristics describe what patients, doctors, nurses, and staff do in the program. Is an individual patient in a position to know how all patients and staff behave and perform? He or she can certainly evaluate how his or her own doctor or nurse and some staff members and patients behave. For example, how valid is a single patient's answer to the following: "Doctors have very little time to encourage patients"; "If a patient's medicine is changed, a nurse or doctor always explains why"; "Patients are strongly encouraged to plan for the future"; "Staff sometimes argue openly with each other." The majority of the 100 statements follow this pattern. Patients' impressions about their program may be drawn from incomplete or unrepresentative information or misinformation about how everybody else performs.

The dichotomous response options of true-false to those statements is another limitation of the scale. The author of the manual argues for this format "because of its simplicity. A true-false format obtains as much information as multipoint formats, and it avoids problems stemming from personal styles" (p. 35). Although it is simple to answer, it can oversimplify what is being measured. The use of four or five anchors measuring the intensity or frequency with which each statement characterizes a patient's treatment program

provides more information. It is sensitive to a continuum of behavior observed in the program rather than just whether or not it exists. Future editions of the scale and research should test different multipoint anchors.

ADMINISTRATION AND SCORING. Administration and scoring are clear and simple. Raw scores are computed in an efficient, straightforward manner. Tables are provided for converting raw scores into standard scores for Forms R and S only. The type and characteristics of the standard scores as well as the method for their derivation are not identified in the manual. They appear to be T-scores with a mean of 50 and standard deviation of 10. There are no conversion tables for Forms I or E.

STANDARDIZATION AND NORMS. Patient and staff means and standard deviations are provided for American and British normative samples for the subscales on Forms R, I, and S. The Form R norms are based on 160 programs in 44 hospitals in 16 states for a total of 3,575 patients and 1,958 staff. The British sample was composed of 36 programs in eight hospitals with 450 patients and 290 staff. Form I norms consisted of 2,364 patients and 897 staff in 68 treatment programs. Unfortunately, the manual does not report the dates for these norms, the sampling designs and methods, population sizes, patient and staff participation and nonresponse rates, and detailed clinical and sociodemographic descriptions of the norm samples selected. Individual and program standard score comparisons are meaningless without this information.

RELIABILITY. Internal consistency reliability estimates using Kuder-Richardson Formula 20 for Form R ranged from .55 to .65 for six subscales and .75 to .78 for four others in a patient sample of 46 programs randomly selected from presumably the normative sample of 160 programs. Neither the sampling procedures nor descriptions of the programs upon which the estimates were calculated are reported in the manual. Coefficients for the staff members' responses were slightly higher, .60 to .70 for six subscales and .74 to .82 for the remainder. Considering the fact that these estimates are based on 10 dichotomous-item subscales, they are adequate for program evaluation decisions and research comparing programs. Individual patient or staff subscale scores should be interpreted with caution and account for the relatively large standard errors of measurement of 2.54 to 3.50 score points on the 10-point scale. One-week test-retest reliability coefficients based on a sample of only 42 patients ranged from .68 to .79, similar to the higher K-R20 estimates noted above. Test-retest profile stability estimates computed from very small patient and staff samples from one to seven programs were in the .70 to .76 ranges for 1 month to 3 years 4 months. All of the K-R20 and retest coefficients were consistently moderate and warrant caution when interpreting individual patient profiles.

Intraclass profile correlations were computed for Form S, the 40-item short-form of Form R, using 10 Form R and 10 Form S standard scores for a sample of 28 university hospital programs. Most of the coefficients exceeded .80 for both patients' and staff members' scores. This is inadequate evidence to support the similarity of the two forms. Equivalence or parallel-forms reliability coefficients between the forms would have been much more informative.

Kuder-Richardson Formula 20 coefficients were also computed for Form I based on a sample of 20 programs. They ranged from .71 to .88 for the 10 subscales. Profile stability coefficients for 6- to 12-month intervals were .78 for patients and .82 for staff. No Form E reliability estimates were reported in the manual.

VALIDITY. As noted previously, only minimal specifications are provided to describe the constructs being measured. The content validity of the majority of the items on the patient scales (Forms R and S) is questionable insofar as a patient's ratings of how other patients, doctors, nurses, and staff behave and perform in the treatment program may be uninformed or misleading. Although one can argue that patients' true-false answers give a "global impression," that impression may still be inaccurate compared to "actual practices."

The three-dimension, 10-subscale structure of the WAS has no theoretical rationale or definitive empirical foundation. The construct-validity evidence presented in the manual consists of a subscale intercorrelation matrix and brief descriptions of four factor analytic studies and a discriminative validity study analyzing between-program differences. This evidence is only given for Form R.

First, the subscale intercorrelatins produce an empirically ambiguous three-dimension structure. Several of the WAS subscales (Support, Autonomy, Practical Orientation, Anger and Aggression, Program Clarity) have higher correlations with subscales in the other two dimensions than with those within their respective dimensions. This overlap occurs in both the patient and staff samples. In fact, the highest correlations in the matrix are between Support and Program Clarity ($r = .49$) subscales from the Relationship and System Maintenance dimensions, respectively, for the patient sample, and between Support and Practical Orientation and Program Clarity ($r = .50$) subscales from the three different dimensions, for the staff subscale. The Anger and Aggression and Staff Control subscales share less than 7% of their total variance with any of the other subscales, including those in their respective dimensions.

Second, the factor analysis studies of the WAS conducted between 1977 and 1984 yielded inconsistent factor solutions for the a priori dimensions and subscale structure. The inability to explain empirically the constructs measured by the WAS weakens the meaning and usefulness of the scale.

Third, discriminative validity evidence is reported in the form of program comparison studies. The results of one study presented in the manual indicate that "a substantial proportion of the subscale variance is accounted for by variations among programs" (p. 34). However, there is no description of the samples of programs, patients, and staff, or criteria for their selection to furnish meaning for the program differences.

Beyond the preceding evidence of validity, there is a review of several research applications and validity studies, the findings of which the author claims "support the construct, concurrent, and predictive validity of the WAS" (p. 39). This claim is unsubstantiated by the evidence presented. The abstracted studies provide descriptive information of a variety of treatment programs and relationships between program variables and patient outcomes. No clear evidence of controlled validity studies and appropriate indices, such as validity coefficients and standard errors of estimate, were reported.

SUMMARY. The WAS is a convenient, easy-to-administer, quick-scoring tool that has been widely used in clinical settings and in program evaluation to describe treatment programs, contrast patients' and staff members' views of a program, and compare actual with preferred programs. According to the latest edition of the manual, the scale remains unchanged since 1974. Despite the evidence of psychometric characteristics presented in the manual, there are serious omissions in methodology and interpretation that render the tool less useful than the manual leads the user to believe. For example, score interpretation is restricted by the lack of descriptive information on the normative samples and dates of the studies; reliability coefficients limit score use to research and program applications rather than individual interpretation; and there is a sparsity of well-designed, controlled validity studies to furnish empirical support for the content and constructs measured and specific uses and inferences drawn from the scores.

Review of the Ward Atmosphere Scale (Third Edition) by MARY ANNE BUNDA, Professor, Educational Leadership, Western Michigan University, Kalamazoo, MI:

The Ward Atmosphere Scale (WAS) battery of forms and approaches has a long history of use, both nationally and internationally. Originally designed by Moos (1974), the structure of the instrument has changed little across the three editions. In fact, it is unclear whether any significant change has taken place since the original version of the instrument. The response format is simply answering true or false to a series of 100 questions for the typical form or 40 questions for the short form. The forms of the instrument allow the patients and staff to report the actual conditions, the ideal conditions, or their expectations (Aubry, Bradley, Siddique, & LeBlanc, 1996). In each case, 10 scores are reported. Although the development procedures attempted to secure independence of the 10 scales, moderate to small intercorrelations are reported in both the patient and staff populations. Factor analysis of the instrument yielded three factors (Squier, 1994) that confirmed the presumed relationship among the scores (i.e., the first three scores involve relationships, the next four scores involve personal development and treatment, and the last three scores concern system maintenance).

The manual reports both internal consistency and test-retest reliability indices. The K-R 20 indices range from .55 to .78 with a mean of .66 for patients. Test-retest coefficients are presented at the scale level for a one-week interval with a mean of .75. However, additional indices are presented over a wide variety of time intervals with

profile average coefficients. The one-week interval is reported with a .92 coefficient for patients. Intervals of less than one year tend to have averages in the .7 range for patient data and in the .8 range for the staff data. Beyond one year, the coefficients are similar for the patients, but higher for the staff. These coefficients signal no problems when the scale is used in the description or evaluation of a program. However, the manual suggests that individual patient profiles might be compared to the aggregate profile for an organization. The indices of reliability may not be strong enough to sustain an analysis of difference scores at the individual level. Individual score interpretation may be additionally hampered by the norms presented in the manual. The size of the norm population is relatively small for both the American and British groups. Standard scores are presented in the *T* scale, which may not be as helpful as percentiles for the scores that have highly skewed distributions.

The validity of this instrument is increasingly enhanced by its use both nationally and internationally (e.g., Burti, Glick, & Tansella, 1990). Approximately five new uses of the instrument appeared annually during the 1990s, resulting in an evidence file for the instrument of well over 200 uses. Content validity of the instrument was enhanced by item construction and selection procedures that ensured variance and by the systematic use of expert judges. The norms indicate systematically higher scores by staff over patients. The stability of the interpretations have been repeated in the literature a number of times (e.g., Steiner, Marx, & Walton, 1991). The construct validity of the instrument has been examined through a variety of sources of evidence. The instrument has detected differences in perceptions after planned change activities (Smith, Gross, & Roberts, 1996). It can differentiate between different types of wards (BootsMiller et al., 1997). It also was shown to be sensitive to differences created by an intervention (Hansen & Slevin, 1996). The breadth of evidence allows for rich interpretations of the information. Clearly, this instrument provides a valuable tool to the evaluation community in the health professions.

SUMMARY. Although the reliability of the individual scales is not strong enough to be used as a decision-making tool for individuals, this instrument clearly has strong technical quality. It has produced evidence for valid inferences in a wide variety of settings. Health care evaluators can interpret individual findings against a strong evidence file.

REVIEWER'S REFERENCES

Moos, R. H. (1974). *Evaluating treatment environments: A social ecological approach.* New York: John Wiley & Sons.

Burti, L., Glick, I. D., & Tansella, M. ('1990). Measuring the treatment environment of a psychiatric ward and a community mental health center after the Italian reform. *Community Mental Health Journal, 26,* 193–204.

Steiner, H., Marx, L., & Walton, C. (1991). The ward atmosphere of a child psychosomatic unit: A ten-year follow-up. *General Hospital Psychiatry, 13,* 246–252.

Squier, R. W. (1994). The relationship between ward atmosphere and staff attitude to treatment in psychiatric in-patient units. *British Journal of Medical Psychology, 67,* 319–331.

Aubry, T., Bradley, L., Siddique, C. M., & LeBlanc, A. (1996). Program development in an acute in-patient psychiatric unit. *Journal of Mental Health, 5,* 507–514.

Hansen, J. T., & Slevin, C. (1996). The implementation of therapeutic community principles in acute care psychiatric hospital settings: An empirical analysis and recommendations to clinicians. *Journal of Clinical Psychology, 52,* 673–678.

Smith, J., Gross, C., & Roberts, J. (1996). The evolution of a therapeutic environment for patients with long-term mental illness as measured by the Ward Atmosphere Scale. *Journal of Mental Health, 5,* 349–360.

BootsMiller, B. J., Davidson, W. S., II, Luke, D. A., Mowbray, C. T., Ribisl, K. M., & Herman, S. E. (1997). Social climate differences in a large psychiatric hospital: Staff and client observations. *Journal of Community Psychology, 25,* 325–336.

[414]
Wechsler Abbreviated Scale of Intelligence.

Purpose: Designed as a "short and reliable measure of intelligence."

Population: Ages 6–89.

Publication Date: 1999.

Acronym: WASI.

Administration: Individual.

Price Data, 1999: $185 per complete kit; $30 per 25 record forms; $108 per 100 record forms; $75 per stimulus book; $59 per manual.

Author: The Psychological Corporation.

Publisher: The Psychological Corporation.

a) TWO SUBTEST FORM.

Scores, 3: Verbal (Vocabulary), Performance (Matrix Reasoning), Full Scale IQ.

Time: (15) minutes.

b) FOUR SUBTEST FORM.

Scores, 7: Verbal (Vocabulary, Similarities), Performance (Block Design, Matrix Reasoning), Verbal IQ, Performance IQ, Full Scale IQ.

Time: (30) minutes.

Review of the Wechsler Abbreviated Scale of Intelligence by TIMOTHY Z. KEITH, Arthur L. & Lea R. Powell Professor of Psychology & Schooling, Alfred University, Alfred, NY:

The Wechsler Abbreviated Scale of Intelligence (WASI) is a short (two to four subtests), individually administered test of intelligence for children and adults ages 6 through 89. In addition to assessing general, or Full Scale, intelligence, the WASI is also designed to provide estimates of

Verbal and Performance intelligence consistent with other Wechsler tests.

As noted in the WASI manual, short, easy-to-administer individual tests of intelligence are often needed in school, clinical, hospital, and other settings. Popular choices for such brief intelligence tests are shortened versions of longer tests, especially of the Wechsler Scales. There are numerous such short forms, however, with variations in reliability, validity, and utility. In addition, such short forms are not independently normed. The WASI was designed to alleviate these shortcomings, and to provide a consistent, well-normed, and technically adequate brief measure of intelligence. According to the manual, the WASI is appropriate for screening, estimating IQ when a full evaluation is not possible, reevaluations when time is limited, research estimates of IQ, and other situations when a more comprehensive evaluation is not needed or not possible.

The WASI may be thought of a short-form version of a combination of the popular Wechsler Intelligence Scale for Children—Third Edition (WISC-III; T5:2862) and the Wechsler Adult Intelligence Scale—Third Edition (WAIS-III; 415). As such, the subtests will be familiar to anyone familiar with these instruments. The Vocabulary subtest includes 38 standard oral vocabulary items in which the examinee defines words presented orally and visually. In addition, the Vocabulary subtest includes four items (the first four) in which the examinee names pictures. For Block Design examinees use red and white blocks to build geometric designs modeled (three items) by the examiner, or shown in two dimensions in the stimulus booklet. The Similarities test includes 22 verbal items in which the examinee must explain the similarity between two words or concepts. The four easiest items use a pictorial presentation in which examinees must pick one of four pictures that is most similar to three initial pictures. Matrix Reasoning uses a standard progressive matrix design in which the examinee must pick one design (out of five) that completes a set of designs in which one design is missing. One less common aspect of administration is that the WASI tests include stop points, items at which one stops testing, depending on the examinee's age. All four of the subtests may be administered in about 30 minutes, according to the manual, or a two-subtest version (Vocabulary and Matrix Reasoning) may be administered in about 15 minutes.

For all subtests, raw scores are converted to T scores. If the two-subtest version of the WASI is administered, the sum of these T scores may be converted into a Full Scale IQ. If all four subtests are administered, Verbal, Performance, and Full Scale Scores may be calculated. All IQs have a mean of 100 and a standard deviation of 15. If the four-subtest version of the WASI is administered, the manual also provides tables for estimating likely ranges of WISC-III or WAIS-III scores; both 68% and 90% confidence intervals are provided.

The primary WASI materials include the manual, an easel that includes items from each of the subtests, the blocks used for Block Design, and the individual test records; the materials fit into a small, cloth attaché. The manual is generally well-organized and complete, with considerable information about the purpose and development of the scale, test administration and scoring, and reliability and validity. The only disappointment is the section on interpretation, which seems out of place (in the chapter with reliability and validity estimates) and skimpy. On the other hand, it seems likely that many users of the WASI will already be well-versed in interpretation of Wechsler tests.

The manual provides considerable detail concerning the development of the WASI. The subtests were chosen based on research with the WISC-III and WAIS-III. The subtests used were chosen because they were good measures of general intelligence, measured verbal and nonverbal (Performance) skills, were thought to measure both fluid and crystallized intelligence, and measured a variety of specific abilities. With the possible exception of the measurement of fluid intelligence, it appears that these goals were accomplished. Although the subtests used are similar to their counterparts on the other Wechsler Scales, all new items were developed for the WASI. The development, tryout, and final selection or deletion of items appears to have been expertly conducted.

The WASI was standardized on a national sample of 2,245 children and adults, ages 6 through 89. As would be expected, more narrow age ranges were studied for children than for adults. The exclusionary criteria (e.g., insufficient English language proficiency, color blindness, etc.) are well explained in the manual. With few exceptions, the standardization sample appears to be representative of the U.S. population based on sex, racial and ethnic group, socioeconomic status (education level), and geographic region.

A fair amount of information concerning reliability and validity of the WASI is presented in the manual. Corrected split-half reliabilities are presented for all tests and composites for all age levels, and most appear quite acceptable, ranging from .81 to .98 for the subtests, and .92 to .98 for the IQs. These internal consistency reliability estimates were slightly higher for adults than for children. Stability (test-retest with administration intervals of 2 to 12 weeks) coefficients are presented for 222 members of the normative sample, spread equally across the age levels. Test-retest coefficients appear adequate for the composite scores, and ranged from .83 (FSIQ-2, Ages 6–11) to .95 (FSIQ-4, Ages 12–16); almost all were above .85. Most stability coefficients for the subtests were in the high .70s to high .80s.

There is also considerable information concerning the validity of the WASI for its intended purposes, including correlations with other tests, and exploratory and confirmatory factor analyses. As expected, the correlations between same-named subtests and scales on the WASI and WAIS-III were moderate to high (.66–.88 for subtests; .76–.92 for IQs). Likewise, it appears that the WASI IQs are capable of predicting achievement, as measured by the Wechsler Individual Achievement Test (WIAT; T5:2861). The exploratory factor analyses were cleverly conducted. Because the WASI only includes four subtests, and supposedly measures two latent factors, two joint factor analyses were conducted with the WISC-III and the WAIS-III. For each, the WASI subtests were substituted for the same-named subtest from the other battery. For both the WASI/WISC-III and the WASI/WAIS-III analyses, Vocabulary and Similarities loaded on a clear Verbal factor and Block Design and Matrix Reasoning loaded on a Perceptual Organization factor. The confirmatory factor analyses were conducted using only the four WASI subtests, but showed, at each age level, that a two factor Verbal/Performance structure fit the standardization data better than did a one factor model. Finally, a series of clinical studies reported in the manual suggests that the WASI behaves as would be expected for a measure of intelligence when used to assess a variety of exceptional samples.

Although the validity information reported is generally supportive of the WASI, it is incomplete. The correlations between the WASI and the WISC-III and WAIS-III should report *all* correlations, not just those between same-named tests. Indeed, for these studies and the WASI/WIAT study, the full correlation matrices should be reported. The exploratory factor analyses used Promax rotation, the factor correlation matrices should be reported. Likewise, the confirmatory analyses should report factor correlations and factor loadings for the two factor solutions. Finally, confirmatory analyses using the WASI/WISC-III and WASI/WAIS-III data would be very instructive.

In a sense, the biggest strength of the WASI— its connection to the other Wechsler Scales—is also a chief limitation. There is little effort to connect the tests and scales of the WASI to anything beyond the Wechsler dichotomy, including all other tests or any modern theory of intelligence. There are references to *Gf-Gc* theory in the manual, but this is to an outdated version of the theory, not its modern counterpart or to its integration into the three-stratum theory of intelligence. Furthermore, there is no effort to establish, beyond citation of a few references, whether the tests used on the WASI in fact measure crystallized and fluid intelligence. In essence, the WASI manual demonstrates that the test measures something similar to that measured by the other Wechsler scales, without recognizing that it is still not entirely clear what those other scales measure.

SUMMARY. The Wechsler Abbreviated Scale of Intelligence is an individually administered brief test of intelligence for children and adults ages 6 through adulthood. It is closely tied to both the Wechsler Intelligence Scale for Children—III (T5:2862) and the Wechsler Adult Intelligence Scale—III (415). The test appears to be well standardized, and to have adequate reliability and validity for the uses suggested in the manual. The ability to estimate scores on the other Wechsler Scales will be a major advantage to those who wish to use it as a screening, reevaluation, or research device. Interpretation beyond the Full Scale IQ should be cautious, however, until further evidence of the validity and meaning of the Verbal and Performance scores is published.

Review of the Wechsler Abbreviated Scale of Intelligence by CEDERICK O. LINDSKOG, Professor, and JANET V. SMITH, Associate Professor, Psychology and Counseling, Pittsburg State University, Pittsburg, KS:

The Wechsler Abbreviated Scale of Intelligence (WASI) is designed as a short, reliable, individually administered test of intelligence for ages 6 to 89. It is intended for use in clinical, psychoeducational, and research settings to provide an estimate of intellectual functioning when a more in-depth intellectual functioning assessment is not necessary or is impractical.

The test materials are well designed, and the manual is very organized and easy to follow. In many respects the WASI is similar to the Wechsler Adult Intelligence Scale—Third Edition (WAIS-III; 415), and the Wechsler Intelligence Scale for Children—Third Edition (WISC-III; T5:2862), which makes it very easy to use for those examiners familiar with these Wechsler tests. The WASI consists of four subtests: Vocabulary, Block Design, Similarities, and Matrix Reasoning. These subtests have the same format as their WAIS-III/WISC-III counterparts. However, item content is different, reducing practice effects if it is later necessary to do more extensive testing using the WAIS-III or WISC-III. Examiners have the option of administering all four subtests, which takes approximately 30 minutes and yields a Verbal IQ score, a Performance IQ score, and a Full Scale IQ score. Alternatively, examiners can administer only the Vocabulary and Block Design subtests in 15 minutes or less, to obtain a full Scale IQ score. If only two subtests are administered, it is not possible to obtain Verbal and Performance IQ scores. The four subtests were selected because of their high loading on general intellectual functioning and other psychometric properties, as well as their coverage of a wide range of cognitive skills.

The WASI manual provides comprehensive documentation of very acceptable psychometric properties. The WASI is a nationally standardized test, with normative data based on 1,100 children and 1,145 adults. The normative sample consists of equal number of males and females and is representative of 1997 census data in terms of race/ethnicity, educational level, and geographic region. The manual provides tables to convert raw scores into standard scores. In addition, test age equivalents are provided for children. At the subtest level, raw scores are converted to T scores rather than the usual scaled subtest scores used with the WAIS-III/WISC-III. The manual provides the rationale that the use of T scores allows for a greater range of score points, making it easier to differentiate among ability levels. Although this score conversion is theoretically appropriate, for ease of use it may have been desirable to keep consistency with the WAIS-III/WISC-III and use standard scales scores with a mean of 10, as the WASI is so similar to these Wechsler tests in most other aspects. At the IQ score level, scores have a traditional mean of 100 and standard deviation of 15, with a range from 50 to 160. It all four subtests are administered, it is also possible to obtain estimates of WAIS-III/WISC-III IQ scores. Score interpretation is highly consistent with the WAIS-III/WISC-III.

The manual provides data for both internal consistency and test-retest reliability. For the adult sample, split-half reliability coefficients (corrected using the Spearman-Brown formula) range from .84 to .98 for subtests scores, and from .92 to .98 for the IQ scores. For children, these values range from .81 to .96 at the subtest level, and from .92–.97 at the IQ score level. Data for test-retest reliability are based on 222 participants with a testing interval of 2 to 12 weeks. For adults, test-retest reliability coefficients range from .79 to .90 for subtest scores, and from .87 to .92 for IQ scores. For children, these values range from .73 to .86 at the subtest level, and from .85 to .93 at the IQ score level. The average standard error of measurement ranges from 2.38 to 3.13 for the adult sample and from 2.94 to 3.99 for the children's sample.

In terms of validity, scores on the WASI are highly correlated with scores on the WAIS-III/WISC-III. Based on a sample of 248 adults, correlations between the WASI and the WAIS-III range from .66 to .88 for subtest scores, and from .84 to .92 for IQ scores. Similarly, for a nonclinical sample of 176 children, correlations between the WASI and the WISC-III range from .69 to .74 for subtest scores, and from .76 to .87 for IQ scores. In addition, factor analyses and intercorrelations of subtest scores and IQ scores support construct validity of the test. Furthermore, the manual provides evidence that the WASI provides accurate score estimates for previously identified clinical groups, including mentally retarded and gifted students.

SUMMARY. The WASI is not intended as a replacement for the WAIS-III or WISC-III, and if an in-depth intellectual evaluation were needed, the WAIS-III or WISC-III would still be the recommended Wechsler test. However, as a quick estimate of intellectual functioning, the WASI is an excellent instrument. In the opinion of this reviewer, the psychometric qualities and usefulness of the WASI far exceeds those of other existing brief measures of intelligence, and the WASI would be the recommended instrument when a quick and accurate estimate of general intellectual functioning is needed.

[415]
Wechsler Adult Intelligence Scale—Third Edition.

Purpose: Designed to assess the intellectual ability of adults.

Population: Ages 16–89.

Publication Dates: 1939–1997.

Acronym: WAIS-III.

Scores, 22: Verbal (Vocabulary, Similarities, Arithmetic, Digit Span, Information, Comprehension, Letter-Number Sequencing, Total), Performance (Picture Completion, Digit Symbol-Coding, Block Design, Matrix Reasoning, Picture Arrangement, Symbol Search, Object Assembly, Mazes, Total), Verbal Comprehension Index, Perceptual Organization Index, Working Memory Index, Processing Speed Index, Total.

Administration: Individual.

Price Data, 1999: $682.50 per complete set in attaché case; $625 per complete set in box; $35 per 25 response books; $134 per 100 response books; $68.50 per 25 response forms; $263.50 per 100 response forms; $73.50 per administration and scoring manual ('97, 217 pages); $42 per technical manual ('97, 370 pages).

Time: (60–90) minutes.

Author: David Wechsler.

Publisher: The Psychological Corporation.

Cross References: See T5:2860 (1422 references) and T4:2937 (1131 references); for reviews by Alan S. Kaufman and Joseph D. Matarazzo of the revised edition, see 9:1348 (291 references), T3:2598 (576 references), 8:230 (351 references), and T2:529 (178 references); for reviews by Alvin G. Burstein and Howard B. Lyman of the original edition, see 7:429 (538 references); see also 6:538 (180 references); for reviews by Nancy Bayley and Wilson H. Guertin, see 5:414 (42 references).

Review of the Wechsler Adult Intelligence Scale—Third Edition by ALLEN K. HESS, Distinguished Research Professor and Department Head, Department of Psychology, Auburn University at Montgomery, Montgomery, AL:

When planning concerts during his later years Frank Sinatra lamented that if he sang his classic ballads, the audience would complain that he had done nothing new in years. If he sang new songs, the audience would complain that they were disappointed because they came to hear their old favorites. Such a dilemma confronts those who revise a classic test such as the Wechsler Adult Intelligence Scale. Let us examine some of the constancies and changes in the WAIS-III.

During the last three decades, the Cohen (1952a, 1952b, 1957a, 1957b) factor scores became a major alternative to the traditional Wechsler dichotomy of Verbal (VIQ) and Performance (PIQ) intelligence quotients and are finally incorporated into the structure of the new WAIS. The WAIS-III is composed of a core of 9 subtests: Picture Completion (PC), Vocabulary (V), Digit Symbol—Coding (CD), Similarities (S), Block Design (BD), Arithmetic (A), Matrix Reasoning (MR), Digit Span (DS), and Information (I). The examiner who wishes to determine the traditional VIQ, PIQ, and Full Scale intelligence quotient (FSIQ) can administer the Picture Arrangement (PA) and Comprehension (C) subtests in addition to the core 9 and determine these quotients on the basis of the 11 subtests. If the examiner wants to determine the new index scores [Verbal Orientation Index (VOI), Perceptual Organization Index (POI), Working Memory Index (WMI), and Processing Speed Index (PSI)] based on the Cohen factors, the Symbol Search (SS) and Letter-Number Sequencing (LN) subtests are given in addition to the 9 core subtests. To determine both the traditional and factor quotients, the examiner needs to administer 13 subtests. The Object Assembly (OA) is now optional unless one needs to substitute it for a "spoiled" performance subtest. The OA is still the best measure of perceptual-organization and worth administering. The administration manual claims that the whole battery takes about 80 minutes to administer, though this examiner finds his colleagues and students take longer when carefully administering the WAIS-III.

The WAIS-III technical manual documents how the mental processes that underlie the subtest scores, the index scores, and the intelligence quotients articulate with the language, theory, and research of information processing models. The WAIS-III technical manual is a model of how a test manual should be composed. It reviews the theoretical rationale and the extensive procedures and data upon which the WAIS-III is constructed and has but one typographical error (p. 174, a PSI should read POI). It would help the reader if future printings of the 350-page manual included a subject index.

A number of changes mark the WAIS-III. In addition to the inclusion of the index scores, the SS, LN, and MR subtests are new subtests. The SS subtest measures processing speed by using 60 items that include a pair of symbols and a set of five symbols to the right of the pair. The examinee is to mark whether or not either of the target pair of symbols appears in the search set. This subtest can replace a "spoiled" CD administration in calculating the PIQ. The LN subtest measures working memory and attention by having the examinee listen to a set of numbers and letters, then recomposing them so the examinee repeats back the numbers in ascending order and then the letters in alphabetical order. The LN can substitute for a "spoiled" administration of the DS in determining the VIQ. The MR measures nonverbal untimed abstract reasoning by having the examinee point to the one of five responses that would complete the incomplete stimulus target. The OA was dropped from the required sets of subtests because the developers determined the MR has a higher split-half reliability, the MR is easier and quicker to administer, the MR is a better measure of nonverbal, fluid reasoning, and the MR draws less on the ability to respond quickly so perceptual-organization is not confounded with processing speed.

The WAIS-III is paired with the revised and embellished Wechsler Memory Scale-III (WMS-III; 416). The two tests share subtest LN, which was standardized on the WMS-III using a weighted sample of 1,250, not the WAIS-III sample of 2,450. More central, the conceptual link regarding memory processes is well-stated in the technical manual that the two tests share. Though the manual presents the WAIS-III data then the WMS-III data in each of the chapters' sections, one can easily parse the sections in order to learn either the WAIS-III or the WMS-III with little interference by material about the other test. However, the pairing will encourage professors to teach both instruments to graduate students. Given the necessity to examine memory for geriatric, forensic, and neuropsychiatric purposes, this is a positive development.

The WAIS-III retained some 68% of the WAIS-R items in their original or slightly modified form but revamped the others based on datedness, clinical utility, content relevance, and psychometric considerations. Artwork was updated. The timed nature of some subtests was de-emphasized so processing speed would not confound other attributes measured by the subtests. Because performance speed is important, there are still timed aspects of the WAIS-III, and the clinician should note the examinee's functioning under time pressure. Those familiar with the Stanford-Binet (T5:2485) will find a similarity with the WAIS-III as the new test also uses the reverse sequence procedure in determining the basal level for the subtests; that is, if a certain number of items are missed in the beginning of a subtest, the examiner administers the easier items until a success criterion (basal level) is reached, then testing proceeds forward (through the harder items) until a ceiling level is ascertained.

The WAIS-III extends the intelligence quotient band from 45 to 155 points. The new standardization sample carefully matches 1995 census data with respect to gender, socioeconomic status, race and ethnicity, educational attainment, and geographical residence. It is stratified for 13 age bands, extending the WAIS-III's applicability to people from 16 to 89 years of age.

RELIABILITIES. Evidence suggests that the subtests are reliable. Test-retest reliabilities, based on 2- to 12-week spans (mean = 34.6 days), range from the .70s (OA, DS, LN, PA, MR, C, and BD) to the .80s (SS, PC, S, CD, and A) to the .90s (V and I). The VIQ, PIQ, and FSIQ have stability coefficients in the low .90s and the indexes range from the .80s to the .90s, again demonstrating excellent stability. The manual notes a gain of about a half subscale point for the subtests, of about 3 points for the intelligence quotients, and of about 5 points for the indexes due to the practice effect upon retesting. The technical manual claims the simple and objective scoring criteria lead to high interscorer agreement as shown by .95 (V), .92 (S), and .91 (C) coefficients. Whether this agreement is achieved by examiners in general remains to be determined.

VALIDITY. The technical manual claims the three foci of the WAIS-III are to help assess psychoeducational disability, neuropsychiatric and organic dysfunction, and giftedness. In keeping with the intended purposes of the WAIS-III, studies are presented that show how groups of people with neurological disorders (Alzheimer's, Huntington's, and Parkinson's diseases; temporal lobe epilepsy; traumatic brain injury; and Korsakoff's syndrome) are portrayed on the WAIS-III. Then a study is presented on how a schizophrenic group functions on the WAIS-III. Finally, people with psychoeducational and developmental disorders (mental retardation, attention-deficit/hyperactivity, learning disorders, and deaf and hearing impaired) are depicted on the WAIS-III. The descriptions of the disorders are of the highest caliber. The data support the differences expected in people with their respective disorders, lending credence to the validity of the WAIS-III. The technical manual presents an impressive array of studies supporting the construct validity of the WAIS-III.

The WAIS-III was examined for content coverage and relevance. It covers well the traditional views of intellectual functioning. However, the newer focus on emotional intelligence, or what used to be called social intelligence on tests such as the Vineland, is not directly assessed. Of course, the competent clinician has plenty of opportunities to observe the examinee over the varied WAIS-III materials and in the social exchange that occurs over the course of the testing in order to estimate emotional intelligence.

The factorial analyses presented are elegant and support the four factor or index model. The conceptual validity of the WAIS-III includes its articulation with the WISC-III. The WAIS-III VIQ (.88), PIQ (.78), FSIQ (.88), and index scores correlate well with their WISC-III counterparts. Also, the WAIS-III correlates .88 with the Stanford-Binet-IV. Compelling evidence on the concordance of WAIS-III scores with measures of cognitive ability, attention, memory, language, fine motor speed and dexterity, spatial processing, and executive functioning provide convergent and construct validity evidence. Research needs to be done to see the degree to which the subtests and indexes are saturated with fluid or crystallized intelligence. Little in the way of discriminant validity is presented, but given the scope of the construct "intelligence," its inclusion of so many attributes, and its relationship to so many outcome variables, conceiving attributes that diverge from intelligence presents a challenge. Still discriminant validity needs to be ascertained.

FUTURE CONCERNS. A number of research questions are posed by the WAIS-III. Interscorer reliability of clinicians not trained by the WAIS-III team need to be determined. The test-retest reliabilities and practice effects over different interims are unknown. Even though there is a bounty of outcome research (i.e., future educational and economic success) concerning measures of intelligence, studies specific to the WAIS-III, and especially the new index scores, need to be conducted. Disciminant validity needs to be determined. The technical manual provides group differences data that support convergent validity but do not provide validation for using the WAIS-III for classification purposes. If the WAIS-III will be used for classification then studies concerning its classification efficiency, or hits and misses, must be conducted. Determination of test reliability and validity should be made independent of the Wechsler research team in order to provide ecological validity of the WAIS-III.

Despite the administration manual admonishing against using short forms of the WAIS-III for specialized purposes, it seems inevitable in this era of "cost containment" that the full and careful examination of the individual may be sacrificed. Also, the length of the WAIS-III may impel some to abbreviate the WAIS-III. Any such short cuts vitiate the validity of using the standardization tables, especially with respect to the intelligence quotients and the index scores. Using short forms may constitute poor practice unless compelling reasons force their use and norms are developed for any derived summary or "estimated" subtest, index, or intelligence quotient scores.

SUMMARY. There is no way to overstate the importance of the role of intelligence in the history of psychology, in the success of individuals in society, and in the assessment of people. William James and his contemporaries saw psychology through a prism of affective, cognitive, and conative domains.

The study of individual differences is marked by Galton's landmark 1893 work, which was followed by Binet's development of a measure to assess the ability of Parisian children to succeed in school. During World War I, Wechsler worked with Spearman and Pearson (Matarazzo, 1979). Subsequently Wechsler was awarded a fellowship allowing him to study in Paris with Lapique and Pieron and to meet Simon and Janet. Thus was Wechsler steeped in the best of the British psychometric tradition as well as the French experimental and clinical methods; both influences heavily mark the initial and all subsequent Wechsler

scales. About 30 years after the development of the Binet-Simon scales, David Wechsler was faced with trying to assess the strengths and weaknesses of patients at New York's Bellevue Hospital, leading him to develop the Wechsler-Bellevue scales.

Both aspects of cognition, the general laws of learning and information processing and the differences in the individual's capacities, are central in the person's ability to adapt and adjust to the world—in a Darwinian sense, to survive and master life's tasks. In the century preceding Darwin, John Locke expressed the view that the learning process and the individual's capacities and limitations must be brought into harmony:

> He, therefore, that is about children should well study their natures and aptitudes, and see, by often trials, what turn they easily take; and what becomes them; observe what their native stock is, how it may be improved, and what it is fit for; He should consider, what they want; whether they be capable of having it wrought into them by industry, and incorporated there by practice; and whether it be worthwhile to endeavor it. For in many cases, all that we can do, or should aim at, is to make the best of what nature has given; to prevent the vices and faults to which such a constitution is most inclined, and give it all the advantages it is capable of. Everyone's natural genius should be carried as far as it could, but to attempt the putting another upon him, will be but labor in vain; and what is so plaister'd on, will at best fit but untowardly, and have always hanging to it the ungracefulness of constraint and affectation. (Traxler, Jacobs, Selover, & Townsend, 1953, p. 1)

In their pursuits to assess children and adults, both Binet and Wechsler proved to be sensitive clinicians in composing their tests to be vehicles by which the tester interacted with the testee. The rich array of tasks allowed the clinician to develop a sense of the person both globally and with specific regard to strengths and deficits, both intellectually and with respect to how the capacities and inabilities fit in the totality of the person.

The WAIS-III retains the best features of the classic WAIS-R, and it incorporates the Cohen factor scores and an information processing orientation in its linkage to the WMS-III. The WAIS-III accomplishes what Frank Sinatra aimed for in his artistic performance—the blending of the beloved classics with the best of contemporary developments. Similarly, the psychometric excellence of the WAIS-III blended with the continuing emphasis on the rich clinical material that makes a psychological examination a portrait of a person would delight David Wechsler. John Locke, too, would be encouraged in that we might be approaching a nexus between optimally matching the needs and abilities of the people we test with learning regimens and employment that make capital of each person's "natural genius."

REVIEWER'S REFERENCES

Cohen, J. (1952a). A factor-analytically based rational for the Wechsler-Bellevue. *Journal of Consulting Psychology, 16,* 272–277.

Cohen, J. (1952b). Factors underlying Wechsler-Bellevue performance of three neuropsychiatric groups. *Journal of Abnormal and Social Psychology, 47,* 359–365.

Traxler, A. E., Jacobs, R., Selover, M., & Townsend, A. (1953). *Introduction to testing and the use of test results in public schools.* New York: Harper & Brothers.

Cohen, J. (1957a). The factorial structure of the WAIS between early adulthood and old age. *Journal of Consulting Psychology, 21,* 283–290.

Cohen, J. (1957b). A factor-analytically based rationale for the Wechsler Adult Intelligence Scale. *Journal of Consulting Psychology, 21,* 451–457.

Matarazzo, J. D. (1972). *Wechsler's measurement and appraisal of adult intelligence* (5th ed.). Baltimore, MD: Williams & Wilkins.

Review of the Wechsler Adult Intelligence Scale—Third Edition by BRUCE G. ROGERS, Professor of Educational Psychology, University of Northern Iowa, Cedar Falls, IA:

The Wechsler Adult Intelligence Scale formally began in 1939 as the Wechsler-Bellevue Intelligence Scale. At that time, it set a precedent by incorporating both verbal and performance scores into a composite intelligence score. Although new, it reflected David Wechsler's experience of administering intelligence tests during World War I to those who had failed the group tests as he observed how these individuals performed on a variety of tasks that were individually administered. Through his practical experiences and his studies under James Cattell, Edward L. Thorndike, Charles Spearman, and others, he came to envision intelligence both as a unitary concept (the *g* factor of Spearman) and as a composite of distinct abilities (as espoused by Thorndike) and he merged those two concepts into a theory that many psychologists and educators have found acceptable. Wechsler's definition of intelligence, now over 50 years old, is still regarded as an eloquent description because it emphasizes the ability to act with a purpose in mind, to think in a logical manner, and to interact with the current environment. Or, as some would say, to use common sense!

This third revision of the scale, completed after Wechsler's death, reflects this strong theoretical tradition and builds on it by attempting to incorporate the latest theoretical concepts and emerging technical procedures such as confirmatory factor analysis and item response theory. The developers of the WAIS-III sought to retain the original structure while updating the norms, extending the age range (ages 16 through 89), and modifying the items both from theoretical and aesthetic perspectives. The WAIS-R has been the most used individually administered test of intelligence for adults and this revision will likely continue that acceptance by professionals.

DESCRIPTIONS. The WAIS-III consists of 14 subtests that yield two sets of summary scores. First, there are the traditional Verbal, Performance, and Full Scale scores. Second, there are four index scales, based on more refined domains of cognitive functioning, which are labeled Verbal Comprehension, Perceptual Organization, Working Memory, and Processing Speed. The first set is likely to be of most frequent use in educational settings, and the second set is more likely to be interpreted in clinical settings. However, all administrators of the test will find both sets of scores to be of complementary use.

Although the overlap between the items on the WAIS-R and WAIS-III is considerable, many revisions have been made for this edition. The artwork shows both more color and reflection of diversity in gender and minorities. The wording of the items has also been addressed to reflect the gradual evolution of language patterns in adult society. New items were added to both the floors and ceilings (i.e., easy and hard items) to obtain more accurate measures at those extremes. The Object Assembly tests was made optional and replaced by a new Matrix Reasoning test that places more emphasis on fluid reasoning and abstract mental operations. Details of the subtest revisions have been described in the manual, so that users of the WAIS-R can make comparisons between it and the WAIS-III.

Overall, the revisions are positive improvements. However, this reviewer feels that some of the artwork may potentially contribute to irrelevant variance in the scores. Attention to detail may be interpreted in different ways. For example, suppose that an item showed a picture of a venetian blind with one slat missing. Gestalt theory suggests that our mind will see a pattern and fill in the empty space. Is that to be counted toward intelligence or against it? It appears to be the latter in this scale. In the real world, sometimes it is important to focus upon overall patterns and ignore details whereas at other times minor details are very important. The administrator will need to keep the examinee focused upon the concept being tested in order to insure that the resulting scores can be properly interpreted. In one example of a picture of a pair of shoes, this reviewer found differences other than the keyed response. The administrator may be faced with the problem of how to score a response in such a situation. The authors may want to consider examining the artwork very carefully with the intent of reducing the possibility of ambiguities.

PURPOSES AND USES. The term "intelligence" has accrued many meanings in our society, as seen in any dictionary. The authors of this test have attempted to reflect the views given by Wechsler, thus emphasizing a multitude of verbal and nonverbal skills. Accordingly, the test is appropriate for the purpose of educational planning and placement with older adolescents and adults of any age. Although group-administered tests are most commonly used for this purpose, decisions of special education placement sometimes necessitate an individually administered test for persons of low cognitive ability. Similarly, at the other extremity, superior cognitive ability is one of the components of "giftedness" and thus evaluations of it typically include an assessment of intelligence. Toward this type of application, the test ceiling has been raised to 155 to improve the reliability of the scores for high achieving adolescents and adults. Another purpose of the test is the diagnosis of the extent to which neurological and psychiatric disorders may affect mental functioning. When used in the context of interviews and other psychological measures, this instrument can add an important dimension to this diagnosis. In addition to its applied uses in these contexts, it can also be appropriately used in research studies of the relationships among hypothetical constructs.

It is important to emphasize that because of the test's complexities, examiners should have received professional training and experience in its use. Although the test publisher attempts to insure that the test is made available only to qualified applicants, the successful implementation of that policy is dependent upon the ethical and professional behavior of the potential users. For those with professional experience in the use of the WAIS-R, the transition to the WAIS-III will be straightforward because the differences are clearly described in the manuals.

VALIDITY. Traditionally, the degree to which any test measures what it purports to measure is emphasized throughout the professional literature as the most important aspect of a test. In recent years, this aspect has been explicated with an emphasis upon the defensibility of the interpretations of the test scores. The appropriateness of the interpretations of the WAIS-III scores is evaluated with both empirical and theoretical rationales. Thus, in one sense, validity can be viewed as a very subjective procedure, but its objectivity increases as professionals in the field communicate, confer, and concur on the interpretation of the evidence that is presented.

EVIDENCE SUPPORTING CONTENT VALIDITY. The content of this intelligence test should focus on cognitive functions that are considered important for persons aged 16–89 years. To ensure this, the authors state that they conducted literature reviews to identify problems with the WAIS-R. Several consultants, including school psychologists and clinical psychologists, examined the items for content coverage, potential biases, and theoretical relevance. An advisory panel of appropriate experts was formed to review and critique all of the procedures of test development. Even though these are most desirable procedures, the reader must accept the word of the authors of the technical manual as to what was actually done. In the appendix, the names of the reviewers and consultants are listed. Although there were undoubtedly differences of opinion within this group, most readers are likely to assume that each of the reviewers and consultants agreed that the test was constructed in a professional manner or else they would have declined to have their name associated with it.

EVIDENCE FOR CRITERION-RELATED VALIDITY. This evidence consists of the correlations of the test with other measures. Although there is not a specific criterion, there are measures that purportedly tap intellectual ability and it is this set of correlations that is presented in the technical manual as evidence. When the subtests of the WAIS-III were correlated with the corresponding subtests of the WAIS-R, the median value was about .80; when correlated with the corresponding subtests of the Wechsler Intelligence Scale for Children—Third Edition (WISC-III), the median value was about .75. When compared with the Stanford-Binet, the correlation of the composite scores was .88. When compared with an academic achievement test, all of the subtests on the achievement test were predicted best by the verbal intelligence score. There appears to be considerable evidence that the test scores will predict appropriate criterion measures with reasonable accuracy.

EVIDENCE FOR CONSTRUCT VALIDITY. Both exploratory and confirmatory factor analyses yielded results that can be interpreted as consistent with the hypothesized four-factor hierarchical model corresponding to the four Index scores that combine to form the *g*-factor. Factor analysis within age bands was reasonably consistent, although the 75 through 89 year age band results appeared not as consistent as those of the other age bands. Some have asked if the factorial composition has been fully resolved, and the answer is no. A more fruitful question may be to ask if the four-factor hierarchical model is useful in interpreting the results, and the answer to that question is yes. The four-factor approach also appears to be fruitful in suggesting avenues for further research. The traditional two-factor hierarchical model appears to be the one for which the data most often will be first interpreted, followed by further examination of the four-factor model. The evidence for convergent and divergent construct validity shows reasonable support for the two-factor hierarchical model, although the results could be interpreted as showing that the full scale score is more heavily loaded with the verbal component than with the perceptual component. The technical manual does not evaluate the convergent and divergent construct validity for the four-factor model, but that may be a fruitful avenue for further research. Also contributing to the evidence supporting construct validity are correlations with other measures that are theoretically related to intelligence, such as the Standard Progressive Matrices, the Wechsler Memory Scale, and the Boston Naming Test. These correlations lend support for the full-scale score, and for the two-factor model to a lesser degree.

EVIDENCE FOR CLINICAL VALIDITY. Data from clinical groups with various mental disorders such as Alzheimer's Disease, Parkinson's Disease, and Mental Retardation were analyzed. As was expected, the scores of persons with these types of disorders were, on the average, lower than those in the standardization sample, thus suggesting that the WAIS-III may be found to be a useful tool when used in conjunction with other clinically appropriate procedures. Studies in this area are very problematical, because of the challenge of obtaining a reasonably randomly drawn representative sample of the special groups. However, the authors were aware of these limitations, and their interpretations are presented with the necessary precautions. Those who expect a definitive connection between intelligence measures and mental disorders are likely to be disappointed with the WAIS-III, but those who employ it in conjunction with other measures are more likely to find it to be a useful supplement.

EVIDENCE FOR BIAS REDUCTION. According to the technical manual, considerable attention was directed toward the detection of item bias, including formal reviews by appropriate experts and item analysis based on both the traditional Mantel-Haenszel bias analysis and item response theory (IRT). The use of these contemporary methodologies is exemplary and would be further enhanced if examples of some of the statistical results were presented in the manual for perusal by the interested reader.

RELIABILITY. To assess the internal consistency of scores from the WAIS-III, each subtest was analyzed with the split-half estimation procedure. The reader with a strong technical background will likely understand why this procedure was used in preference to the widely used Kuder-Richardson Formula 20, but an explanation of it would be appropriate in the technical manual, as that manual will be consulted by many persons who may not fully understand how adapting the test to the ability level of the respondent affects this decision. Subtest reliability estimates are quite high, with the median about .85. The Verbal, Performance, and Full Scale have values above .90, as do three of the Index scores. Furthermore, the values are consistent across all of the age groups, 16 through 89. Stability coefficients were also obtained, most with a time span of approximately one month, and showed results similar to those found with the internal consistency indices.

Estimates of the standard error of measurement are also provided for each subscale by age group. These values are used to create tables in the administration manual wherein the scaled scores are converted to confidence intervals. For the middle of the Full Scale, the standard error is about two points. At the extremes, a confidence interval is not symmetric around the estimated score, reflecting the regression toward the mean. The authors are to be commended for the improvement in clarity of interpretation that derives from this procedure. Users would be wise to always report the results in terms of these confidence intervals and treat the single score as a step in the procedure of generating the confidence interval. This emphasis on the interpretation of scores in the context of the estimated error is again reflected in the tables that show observed differences between the Intelligence scores and the Index scores, to address the question "Is the observed difference larger than what would be expected by the chance error in the scores?" The tables show the minimum value for the difference to be statistically significant at the .05 and .15 level. Even though this is a commendable procedure, it might be useful, in the future, to consider reporting them at the .05 and .10 level, corresponding to the levels reported for the confidence intervals. As an alternative, this information could also be reported as confidence intervals. Again, it is important to avoid interpreting a difference score until some probability estimate can be made concerning the error involved.

NORMS AND SCORES. The sampling plan for the standardization sample was carefully constructed to attain a representative sample of adults stratified on age, sex, race/ethnicity, education level, and geographic region using the then current census data (corrected for 1995). Marketing research firms were employed to recruit participants, who were paid a fee for their participation. Although the actual sampling procedure was not strictly mathematically random, the results do indicate that the national sample was reasonably close to approximating the census data on the stratified variables.

A variety of scores is offered by the WAIS-III, for use in different settings. The subtest raw scores are converted to standardized scale scores, which are then summed and adjusted by age group to form the Verbal, Performance, and Full Scale scores. In a similar manner, the Index scores were formed. A commendable improvement in the third edition of this test is the transformation of the scores based on age-appropriate norms. Without this transformation, older adults are likely to show a decline in mental functioning when compared to a younger group. When interpreting the scores from the WAIS-III, the new appropriate norm reference group is the particular age group rather than the previously used reference group aged 20–34, or adults combined from all age groups. As for the proper interpretations of the names of the 14 subtests, the three intelligence scores and the four index scores, very good explanations are given in the two manuals. These explanations are written at a level at which it is assumed that the reader has had appropriate professional training and for that audience, the explanations are a good review of what was learned in that training.

Tables are given to convert Intelligence scores and Index scores to confidence intervals and percentile ranks. This conversion of the intelligence scores to confidence intervals is a most desirable procedure; however, no conversion was done for the percentile ranks. To help the administrator do that using the data in the tables, directions would be helpful. Although the procedure is straightforward, it is, nevertheless, a tedious task because it involves the construction of a nonsymmetric interval in many cases. Because it is "traditional knowledge" that intelligence scores have a mean of 100, most of the adult population knows whether or not a given intelligence score is above or below the mean. However, an understanding of the standard deviation on the normal curve is not "traditional knowledge," so most of the adult population will find it a challenge to give further interpretation to a given intelligence score. Therefore, the reporting of percentile ranks is a commendable feature for this test, because those test scores can be readily explained to almost all adults.

The labeling of the normalized intelligence scores as "IQ" scores appears to this reviewer to give a misleading connotation. The acronym "IQ" was derived from Intelligence Quotient, namely, the quotient of the "mental age" and the chronological age. The authors of the manuals carefully explain why the concept of mental age is not used with this test and why deviation scores are to be preferred to quotient scores. But then the term "deviation IQ" is used, which appears to be self-contradictory because there is not a quotient of two scores. Authors of other tests have adopted terminology that avoids the word "quotient" and this reviewer would be pleased if the term IQ would not be used in the technical literature or in the popular literature.

MANUALS AND MATERIALS. The supporting material for the test is divided into two manuals, one for administration and scoring, and the other for technical materials. The administration manual is spiral bound in crackback covers for ease of frequent use. Both manuals are printed in readable format that does not detract from the content being presented. The test materials, including pictures and puzzle-type pieces, appear to be of high professional quality that will endure repeated use. Because the test is certainly not inexpensive, administrators can reasonably expect it to remain in good condition for use with many subjects.

SUMMARY. The WAIS-III is the oldest and most frequently used intelligence scale for individual administration to adults. It is composed of a set of 14 subtests that have been improved with extensive research while maintaining the historical continuity. Reviewers of the two previous editions have made criticisms and suggestions that have been addressed by the authors, and the changes appear to result in improvements for those practitioners and researchers who use the test. The scores from the test are reliable enough to be used in all of the designated age ranges and the validity evidence gives confidence that the test scores measure those intellectual constructs that it purports to measure. Psychologists in educational institutions will find it to be a useful tool for assessing those persons who are not adequately evaluated with group intelligence tests. Clinicians and clinical researchers will probably continue to employ the test as their primary instrument for assessing adult intelligence. The manuals are written in a clear, readable manner for those with proper training. Although there are areas in which the manuals could be improved, they provide more information than the manuals of most other tests. The WAIS-III gives promise of continuing the evolutionary trend toward improved measurement. Those who are looking for a revision with major changes, such as a multiplicity of factors, will not find it here, although the verbal and performance scores have been supplemented with more refined index scores. Those users who are looking for an improved interpretation of a parsimonious approach toward intelligence testing will find this in the WAIS-III.

[416]
Wechsler Memory Scale III.

Purpose: Designed to "provide a detailed assessment of clinically relevant aspects of memory functioning" using both auditory and visual stimulus.

Population: Ages 16–89 years.

Publication Dates: 1945–1997.

Acronym: WMS-III.

Scores, 22: Six primary subtests yielding 10 scores (Logical Memory I, Logical Memory II, Verbal Paired Associates I, Verbal Paired Associates II, Letter-Numbering Sequencing, Faces I, Faces II, Family Pictures I, Family Pictures II, Spatial Span); five optional subtests yielding 6 scores (Information and Orientation, Word Lists I, Word Lists II, Mental Control, Visual Reproduction I, Visual Reproduction II); Five Supplemental Scores (Recall Total, Recognition Total, Copy Total, Discrimination Total, Percent Retention).

Administration: Individual.

Price Data: Available from publisher.

Time: (30–35) minutes for primary subtests.

Comments: "When used in conjunction with the WAIS-III, it is possible to compute ability-memory difference scores"; WAIS-III/WMS-III Writer interpretive report software available for use with IBM or compatible PC with at least 486 processor.

Author: David Wechsler.

Publisher: The Psychological Corporation.

Cross References: See T5:2863 (431 references) and T4:2940 (117 references); for reviews of an earlier edition by E. Scott Huebner and Robert C. Reinehr, see 11:465 (166 references); see also 9:1355 (49 references); T3:2607 (96 references); 8:250 (36 references); T2:592 (70 references), and 6:561 (9 references); for reviews of the original version by Ivan Norma Mensh and Joseph Newman, see 4:364 (6 references); for a review by Kate Levine Kogan, see 3:302 (3 references).

Review of the Wechsler Memory Scale III by RIK CARL D'AMATO, Professor and Director of Training Programs in School Psychology and Neuropsychology Laboratory, M. Lucile Harrison Professor of Excellence, University of Northern Colorado, Greeley, CO:

Historically, memory is an area with a rich history. Memory was evaluated in patients as early as 1900 (Hess & D'Amato, 1998). Perhaps its long history is related to the importance of memory for everyday functioning. Without memory one cannot read, write, or leave one's home. Driving, eating, and thinking all require the use of a variety of memory-related functions. Memory and learning are also closely related. The importance of memory has long been recognized by Wechsler who published the Wechsler Memory Scale in

1945 (Wechsler, 1945). The scale was revised in 1987, Wechsler Memory Scale—Revised (Wechsler, 1987), and the current version was issued in 1997, Wechsler Memory Scale III (WMS-III; Wechsler, 1997). Most authors seem to agree that the different versions of the Wechsler Memory Scale are the most popular memory instruments in use today (Elwood, 1993). The WMS-III is an individually administered instrument with a rationally derived theoretical base. Such a foundation is typical of most instruments developed by Wechsler. The WMS-III is significantly improved from earlier versions. The manual details information concerning improved norms, revised and clearer scoring rules, new subtests for measuring delayed recall of information, deletion of some older less useful subtests, extended floors, redesigned materials, and the addition of some new subtests (WMS-III technical manual).

Scoring and report writing software is also available and seems quite useful and promising (Wechsler Adult Intelligence Scale-III—Wechsler Memory Scale-III Writer, 1999). The Writer program allows one to interpret results and generate four types of reports: Interpretive, Clinical, Client, and Statistical. But this program, like the manual, covers both the Wechsler Intelligence Test and the Memory Scale. The idea of allowing one to use both instruments with a single client, to measure intelligence and memory in tandem (from the same normative base), is quite appealing. But in reality, the clumsiness of the manuals and computer programs makes the idea fall far short. It is difficult to find information pertaining to a single measure in the technical manual and thus it becomes quite user *un*friendly.

Interestingly, most if not all of the previous criticisms of the earlier versions of the test (e.g., low reliabilities, large standard errors of measurement) have been positively dealt with in the revision of the WMS-III (Elwood, 1991; Huebner, 1992). These changes make the WMS-III surprisingly versatile, comprehensive, and relevant.

For years, concern has been voiced regarding the lack of an appropriate standardization sample for all previous versions of the Wechsler Memory Scale (Heiby, 1987; Huebner, 1992). The standardization sample was quadrupled and currently includes 1,250 individuals ranging in age from 16 to 89. This sample represents a vital age extension (now including more elderly clients) and sampling

of individuals from all age ranges—another consequential improvement because currently no interpolated norms are used. The overall sample was divided into 13 age groups with 100 participants in most groups—except the older two age groups were each composed of 75 participants. Using the typical format, the sample was stratified according to age, race/ethnicity, and education in an effort to mirror the U.S. Census population (WMS-III technical manual). This standardization sample is substantially improved from the previous version of the measure.

The factor structure of the WMS-III changes across age groups. Specifically, the age group of 16 to 29 years has a 3-factor structure and the age groups of 30 to 89 years have a 5-factor structure. Thus, one must certainly be cautious and careful when interpreting index scores at different age levels. Although such factor structure changes are common with some measures (e.g., Kaufman Assessment Battery for Children; T5:1379) they make appropriate interpretation difficult at best. They also indicate the questionable nature of the overall format of the test.

Extensive information concerning the validity of the measure can be found in the manual. Although much is supportive of the current measure, many of the intercorrelations of WMS-III primary subtests for all age ranges were very low (e.g., .14, .13, .18). Even though these intercorrelations indicate that the measure may evaluate distinctly different abilities, when considered in light of the unsteady and shifting theoretical and empirical base of the instrument, they are another area of concern.

The WMS-III average reliabilities for the subtest scores of the Primary Indexes across age groups ranged from .74 to .93, with a .81 median reliability. The Primary Index reliabilities across ages ranged from .74 to .93 with a .87 median reliability. The reliabilities for the supplemental subtest scores were somewhat lower but similar. In general, most reliabilities on the WMS-III seemed acceptable to excellent and greatly improved in comparison to the WMS-R.

TEST ORGANIZATION. The most striking change in the WMS-III is the increase in the number of indexes. The older version offered five indexes; the measure now includes eight Primary Indexes (Auditory Immediate, Auditory Delayed, Visual Immediate, Visual Delayed, Immediate Memory, Auditory Recognition Delayed, General Memory, and Working Memory), and four supplementary Auditory Process Composites (Single-Trial Learning, Learning Slope, Retention, and Retrieval). The Primary Indexes are offered as the primary scores used to evaluate memory functioning, whereas the Auditory process Composites are viewed as optional to evaluate auditory functions. Nevertheless the Auditory Process Composites may be necessary (and even critical) for untangling complex memory disturbances. All four seem to simplify the clinical utility of the measure.

Index nomenclature was changed to be more consistent with the field in which verbal labels can be used to code nonverbal materials. Thus, the focus was on the modality of presentation rather than on the index content in isolation. Moreover, the label *auditory* is now used instead of *verbal*. The old Attention/Concentration Index was renamed the Working Memory Index to more accurately portray new content items that have shifted from relatively low-level attentional tasks to high-level working memory tasks.

TEST CONTENT. Significant and very appropriate changes have also been made in the content of the test items. Three new subtests have been added to the primary battery. New subtests entitled Faces I & II and Family Pictures I & II now contribute to the visual/nonverbal memory domain. A Letter-Number Sequencing subtest is also new and contributes to the working memory domain. The subtests of Logical Memory I & II, Verbal Paired Associates I & II, and Spatial Span were retained and can be found in the Primary Subtests. Three additional subtests were retained in the battery and are optional (Visual Reproduction I & II, Mental Control, and Information and Orientation).

The method of calculating several of the WMS-III Index scores has also changed in this updated measure. The old WMS-R Verbal Memory index is similar to the WMS-III Auditory Immediate Index and the WMS-R Visual Memory Index is similar to the WMS-III Visual Immediate Index. A great deal of detailed information regarding the grouping of subtests in the measure is presented in the manual and is not considered here. One of the many highlights of the manual is its presentation of how and why the measure has changed. In this area the manual is a model of organization, detail, and completeness. The new protocol is easy to follow and the Discrepancy Analysis Page is extremely beneficial. Testing materials are also colorful, portable, and seem well designed. Subtests include:

INFORMATION AND ORIENTATION. This optional subtest can help the examiner determine if the subject has the prerequisite skills necessary to be validly evaluated. The subtest covers historical, autobiographical, and informational questions.

LOGICAL MEMORY I & II. This subtest is retained from earlier versions but includes a new story and revised administration and scoring procedures. This subtest continues to evaluate learning and memory of auditorily presented conceptual material through the recall of stories and related information.

VERBAL PAIRED ASSOCIATES I & II. This subtest measures verbal learning and auditory memory using word-pair lists. Changes have included the replacement of overlearned or easily acquired word associations.

WORD LISTS I & II. This new optional subtest evaluates learning and immediate recall ability. A list-learning format is used with an interference trial.

FACES I & II. This new subtest was included to more comprehensively cover right hemisphere deficits. The subtest evaluates memory weaknesses or visually presented material deficits through the identification of target faces.

FAMILY PICTURES I & II. This new subtests considers the subject's ability to recall objects, events, and people. It is seen as a measure of verbal encoded memory. This area is advocated as critical when evaluating subgroups (e.g., schizophrenics) that may display difficulties in spatial location and content (WMS-III manual, p. 201).

VISUAL REPRODUCTION I & II. This optional visual reproduction subtest allows the consideration and comparison of delayed recall and recognition. Two new design cards have been added. This subtest was used in the WMS and in the WMS-R. Recognition, discrimination, and reproduction are all included.

LETTER-NUMBER SEQUENCING. This new measure of auditory working memory is offered as a task sensitive to neurocognitive disorders. Subjects must remember numbers and letters and then reorganize them.

SPATIAL SPAN. Using a three-dimensional board, this subtest is similar to Digit Span but considers visual information instead of auditory information. This subtest evaluates the subject's ability to hold and use a visual-spatial sequence in working memory.

DIGIT SPAN. This optional subtest considers together the information gathered from digit span forward and digit span backwards. This *summation* is problematic and is a great disappointment because the manual details the importance of considering information from the forward and backward sections separately.

MENTAL CONTROL. The content of this previously used subtest has been expanded and the scoring has changed. The subtest continues to measure the retrieval of overlearned information and the ability to mentally process and integrate such information.

SUMMARY. The WMS-III seems improved in a variety of ways. The normative sample is larger and more representative than previous versions of the test. Item content and coverage also seem more focused, but also expanded, and the test appears more user friendly, with subtests easier to administer and index scores easier to understand. The instrument also is colorful, easy to use, and interesting and challenging for subjects. Psychometrically, the test also seems significantly refined but low reliabilities and an unsteady factoral base continue to be areas of concern. However, the improvements noted make the WMS-III the test of choice when evaluating memory and learning with adolescents and/or adults.

REVIEWER'S REFERENCES

Wechsler, D. (1945). The Wechsler Memory Scale. New York: Psychological Corporation.

Heiby, E. M. (1987). Wechsler Memory Scale. In D. J. Keyser & R. C. Sweetland (Eds.), *Test critiques compendium: Reviews of major tests from the Test Critiques series* (pp. 560–567). Kansas City, MO: Test Corporation of America/Westport Pubs.

Wechsler, D. (1987). The Wechsler Memory Scale—Revised. San Antonio, TX: Psychological Corporation.

Elwood, R. W. (1991). The Wechsler Memory Scale—Revised: Psychometric characteristics and clinical application. *Neuropsychology Review, 2*, 179–201.

Huebner, E. S. (1992). Review of the Wechsler Memory Scale—Revised. In J. J. Kramer & J. C. Conoley (Eds.), *The eleventh mental measurements yearbook* (pp. 1023–1024). Lincoln, NE: Buros Institute of Mental Measurements.

Elwood, R. W. (1993). Delayed recall on the Wechsler Memory Scale—Revised: The factor structure revisited. *Journal of Clinical Psychology, 49*, 854–859.

Wechsler, D. (1997). The Wechsler Memory Scale III. San Antonio, TX: Psychological Corporation.

Hess, R., & D'Amato, R. C. (1998). Assessment of memory, learning, and special aptitudes. In A. S. Bellack & M. Hersen (Series Eds.), & C. R. Reynolds (Vol. Ed.), *Comprehensive clinical psychology: Vol. 3. Assessment* (pp. 239–265). Oxford, England: Pergamon-Elsevier Science.

Wechsler Adult Intelligence Scale-III Wechsler Memory Scale-III Writer User's Guide. (1999). San Antonio, TX: Psychological Corporation.

Review of the Wechsler Memory Scale III by CECIL R. REYNOLDS, *Professor of Educational Psychology, Professor of Neuroscience, Distinguished Research Scholar, Texas A&M University, College Station, TX:*

The Wechsler Memory Scale III (WMS-III) is the third incarnation of the original WMS, first published in 1945. The first revision, published in 1987 as the WMS-R, improved upon the archaic format of the original, its limited norms, narrow view of memory, and problematic scaling. Many problems remained and the WMS-R was staunchly criticized (e.g., Leonberger, Nicks, Larrabbee, & Goldfader, 1992; Loring, 1989). The changes made in going from WMS to WMS-R did little to close the conceptual gap between the pragmatic 1945 representation of memory in the original battery and the richness of the context of neuropsychological and cognitive research on memory and the memory process so evident by the 1980s. This is not true of the WMS-III. The WMS-III represents major conceptual and psychometric improvements over the WMS-R, so much so that there is indeed little similarity now between the original 1945 scale and its 1997 version. The WMS-III is more akin to a new test than a revision of an old favorite. There is little transfer of training between the WMS-R and WMS-III, and, given the complexity of administration and scoring, administrators will need to devote a significant amount of time to learning the new scale.

SCALE ORGANIZATION AND MATERIALS. The WMS-III contains 6 primary subtests and 5 optional subtests; however, 6 of these subtests have an immediate and a delayed administration, yielding a total of 17 subtests. The manual estimates administration time at 30–35 minutes but experience suggests 45–60 minutes is more realistic.

The primary subtests must be administered in their immediate and delayed format to obtain some eight index scores: Auditory Immediate, Visual Immediate, Immediate Memory, Auditory Delayed, Visual Delayed, Auditory Recognition Delayed, General Memory, and Working Memory. If the optional subtests are administered, Indexes for Recall, Recognition, Copy, Discrimination, and Percent Retention can be calculated.

The organization of the scales and the layout of the protocols are confusing initially but easily learned in several administrations of the WMS-III, although all of the copying back and forth of scores is awkward and bound to produce clerical errors. The materials, beyond the record form, are well designed, reflect current society, and have an air of sophistication lacking from prior versions.

STANDARDIZATION. The WMS-III standardization sample consists of 1,250 persons ranging in age from 16 years to 89 years. The sample was stratified on the basis of age, sex, race/ethnicity, educational level, and geographic region. Appropriate age-bands were used with 100 persons per group except for the 80–84 and 85–89-year-old groups containing 75 persons per group. The sample overlapped with the Wechsler Adult Intelligence Scale—Third Edition (WAIS-III) standardization sample, aiding score interpretation when both instruments are used. Traditionally, The Psychological Corporation provides the best of standardization samples for its individually administered tests, and the WMS-III sample is no exception.

ITEM SELECTION AND CONTENT. On a prima facie basis the test appears to have appropriate content. The manual discusses briefly the use of focus groups and consultants to determine the appropriateness of the items and whether there was any objectional content in the items. There is some carryover of content from WMS-R, but it is remarkable how little is actually revealed concerning the item analyses. Even the WMS-III technical manual is largely silent on what item statistics were derived and how they were used.

There is no discussion of analyses of item or other content-bias questions with regard to gender, race, or ethnicity. In today's Zeigeist, the absence of empirical studies of content bias of the test items is inexcusable and represents a serious drawback to use of the test with ethnic minorities (e.g., see Camilli & Shepard, 1994; Reynolds, in press). There is considerable literature on this topic, and test manuals must address the potential for cultural item bias from an objective, statistical basis. There are comments in the technical reports on the test that cause one to suspect some form of study of differential item functioning was conducted, but none is reported.

SCALING. In general, the WMS-III scaling is quite appropriate but again more details concerning smoothing methods and other scaling issues would have been helpful, especially in the technical manual. The WMS-III subtests (for the first time in the WMS series) yield age-corrected deviation scaled scores set to a mean of 10 and a standard deviation of 3. This is a much appreciated change. The various index scores are scaled to a mean of 100 and standard deviation of 15, and each index score is an equally weighted composite of its component subtests. Scaled scores are provided as age-corrected and by reference-group scaling for the core 20–34-year-old age group.

Why reference-group scaling is provided is not clear, especially because the technical manual notes that such scaling often leads to interpretive errors on other Wechsler Scales (see WMS-II technical manual, p. 40) along with acknowledging other problems of reference group scaling (e.g., Kaufman, Reynolds, & McLean, 1989). All of the scores were normalized and smoothed using a combination of objective and subjective methods that go largely undescribed.

RELIABILITY AND VALIDITY. The WMS-III manuals provide for more extensive data concerning the reliability and validity of WMS-III scores than any of its predecessors. The overall internal consistency reliability of WMS-III scores at the subtest and the index levels is good (subtest scores average about .81 and indexes about .87) but not outstanding relative to other comprehensive memory scales. Stability coefficients range from .62 to .82 across subtests over about one month.

Validity data are extensive and exceptionally thorough, surpassing any other versions of the scale in breadth and depth of presentation. There is good evidence of convergent and divergent validity of scores and their interpretations as reflections of memory are supported strongly. However, the correlation of .68 between the WMS-III working memory index and the WAIS-III full scale IQ is uncomfortably large. A strong general memory factor is evident that is more aligned with IQ than is desirable in a memory battery intended for differential diagnosis of memory-specific problems. This correlation of .68 is very close to the correlations (.70–.80) often seen between measures of intelligence. However, the studies of various clinical samples represented in the technical manual do show promise as the correlations are lower in these samples (although restriction of range is evident in most of the clinical samples, spuriously attenuating these r values). Despite these concerns (which could have been addressed by a conjoint WAIS-III/WMS-III series of exploratory and confirmatory factor analyses; also see Larrabee, 1999), the WMS-III validity evidence supports the use of the scale as an assessment of important memory factors among the cultural majority group at adult ages in the U.S.A.

Conspicuously absent are needed studies of the cultural test bias hypothesis with WMS-III scores by race/ethnic group and by gender. Studies of cross-cultural differences in construct and criterion-related validity are absent. The WMS-III cannot be recommended for use with ethnic minorities without extreme caution. Studies demonstrating any differences in mean level of performance and in patterns of performance across race, ethnicity, and gender are also needed, and are absolutely crucial when the scale is used to assess or to infer brain injury or dysfunction. Data for such studies as suggested in this paragraph were developed during the standardization of the WMS-III and for other validity studies. Why this research has not been done or reported is not known, but it would be quite useful in application of the WMS-III to minority groups in the U.S.A.

Another curious feature of the WMS-III is the continuing need to sum forward and backward recall on Digit Span to obtain a scaled score. The technical manual acknowledges that forward and backward Digit Span measure different constructs and there is considerable evidence in the empirical literature that these scores should not be combined (e.g., Reynolds, 1997). Yet, the examiner is not allowed to compute separate scaled scores for forward and for backward recall. This is simple enough to provide and should have been done.

SUMMARY AND CONCLUSIONS. The WMS-III represents a major advance over previous versions of the scale. Many improvements have been made to the scale and the current manuals are also superior to any previously provided. The publisher is to be congratulated for improving the scale to this extent. Several aspects of improvement were neglected. Data are available to remedy these concerns, and it is hoped they will be published. Needed information primarily concerns cross-cultural validity and studies of item bias across race, ethnicity, and gender; levels and patterns of performance across these same groups; and separate scaled scores for forward and for backward recall. Additionally, a series of joint exploratory and confirmatory factor analyses of the WMS-III and the WAIS-III would be helpful in understanding how to use these scales in combination. Additional information on scaling and related psychometric issues should be provided as well. Nevertheless, the many improvements made in the WMS-III make it the leading instrument for assessment of memory function in adults at this point.

REVIEWER'S REFERENCES

Kaufman, A. S., Reynolds, C. R., & McLean, J. (1989). Age and WAIS-R intelligence in a national sample of adults in the 20 to 74 age range: A cross-sectional analysis with educational level controlled. *Intelligence, 13,* 235–253.

Loring, D. W. (1989). The Wechsler Memory Scale—Revised; or the Wechsler Memory Scale—revisited? *The Clinical Neuropsychologist, 3,* 59–69.

Leonberger, F. T., Nicks, S. D., Larrabee, G. J., & Goldfader, P. R. (1992). Factor structure of the Wechsler Memory Scale—Revised within a comprehensive neuropsychological battery. *Neuropsychology, 6,* 239–249.

Camilli, G., & Shepard, L. A. (1994). *Methods for identifying biased test items.* Thousand Oaks, CA: Sage.

Reynolds, C. R. (1997). Forward and backward memory span should not be combined for clinical analysis. *Archives of Clinical Neuropsychology, 12,* 29–40.

Larrabee, G. J. (1999). Review of the Wechsler Memory Scale—III. *Archives of Clinical Neuropsychology, 14,* 473–477.

Reynolds, C. R. (in press). Methods for detecting and evaluating cultural bias in neuropsychological tests. In E. Fletcher-Janzen, T. Strickland, & C. R. Reynolds (Eds.), *Handbook of cross-cultural neuropsychology.* New York: Plenum Press.

[417]
Weinberg Depression Scale for Children and Adolescents.

Purpose: Designed to detect depression in children and adolescents.

Population: Children and adolescents with at least a 4th grade reading level.

Publication Dates: 1987–1998.

Acronym: WDSCA.

Scores: Total score only.

Administration: Individual.

Price Data, 1999: $94 per complete kit; $39 per examiner's manual ('98, 40 pages); $29 per 50 summary sheets; $29 per 50 student response sheets.

Time: (5) minutes.

Comments: Normed on children diagnosed with major depression, ages 7 to 18; a self-report measure; WDSCA items based in part on the DSM-IV criteria.

Authors: Warren A. Weinberg, Caryn R. Harper, and Graham J. Emslie.

Publisher: PRO-ED.

Review of the Weinberg Depression Scale for Children and Adolescents by SANDRA J. CARR, Certified School Psychologist, Harford County Public Schools, Bel Air, MD:

The Weinberg Depression Scale for Children and Adolescents (WDSCA) is a self-report measure of depression in children and adolescents with at least a fourth grade reading level. It consists of 56 items pertaining to dysphoric mood, self-deprecatory ideation, agitation, sleep disturbance, change in school performance, diminished socialization, change in attitude toward school, somatic complaint, loss of usual energy, and unusual change in appetite or weight. This 10-symptom criterion followed Kraepelin's (1921) depression symptomatology of manic-depressive disease, with modifications based on studies of depression in children and adolescents. The WDSCA claims to be consistent with the Feighner Criteria (Feighner et al., 1972), the Research Diagnostic Criteria (RDC; Spitzer, Endicott, & Robins, 1978) and the *Diagnostic and Statistical*

Manual of Mental Disorders (DSM-III, DSM-III:R, DSM-IV; American Psychiatric Association, 1980, 1987, 1994) criteria for depression.

To determine item discrimination, an item analysis was performed. The WDSCA median item discrimination coefficients were computed for the two standardization groups. The nonreferred normal sample ($M = .3795$) and the referred with Major Depressive Disorder (MDD) sample ($M = .4527$) provide some limited quantitative evidence of content validity.

Because of the widespread use of the DSM-IV in recognizing depressive spectrum illness, two scoring options are presented: the DSM-IV criteria, containing 9 major symptoms, and the Weinberg Criteria containing 10 major symptoms, including a somatic symptom category. Concurrent validity was investigated using the DSM-IV criteria and the Beck Depression Inventory (BDI). In one study, 758 adolescents were either identified or not as depressed by using the Weinberg kCriteria and by the DSM-IV criteria. An American Psychiatric Association (APA, 1994) 2 x 2 contingency table was constructed and a phi was computed. The phi coefficient was .87, suggesting a strong relationship and evidence of criteria-referenced validity. A second study consisted of 1,224 adolescents, aged 13–20 years, who were administered the WDSCA and the BDI. The scores were correlated using a Pearson Product-Moment correlation. The resulting coefficient was .6881, showing concurrent criterion-related validity evidence.

The WDSCA was studied in over 5,000 referred children and adolescents, in two large normal (nonreferred) populations of 9th–12th grades with 96% participation (3,292 students in a large metropolitan school district and 1,298 students in a rural mid-sized school district) and two research studies of depressed adolescents and children comparing treatment with specific medication versus placebo. It was normed on three large samples of children and adolescents, two of nonreferred "normal" children and one sample of children who had been identified with Major Depressive Disorder (MDD). The standardization sample was composed of 1,224 nonreferred children, aged 13.0–18.11. This sample was representative in terms of gender, ethnicity, and race with the United States Bureau of the Census 1990. The referred sample consisted of 245 students, aged 7.0–18.11, referred to the Children's Medical Center in Dallas, and all diagnosed with MDD.

The two groups were studied as a way of examining construct validity. The nonreferred group of children and adolescents had a mean standard score of 9.57 and the referred group with MDD had a mean standard score of 20.34. The results of the *t*-tests indicate that differences are large enough to be statistically significant.

Cronbach's coefficient alpha method was used to estimate the internal consistency reliability of the items within the test. For the nonreferred normal group, the coefficient alpha was .89 and for the group referred with major depressive disorder it was .93, both within the acceptable range. The standard error of measurement for the nonreferred normal group was 4.90, and for the group referred with Major Depressive Disorder (MDD), the *SEM* was 3.97. Time sampling was measured using the test-retest technique. One hundred thirteen students referred with MDD were administered the WDSCA on two occasions in a 2-week time period. The test-retest coefficient was .76, which is adequate for self-rated measures. To measure scorer differences, two staff persons in PRO-ED's research department scored 30 completed protocols randomly selected from the normative sample of children and adolescents aged 9–17 years. The resulting coefficient was .99, providing convincing evidence that supports the test's scorer reliability.

Two sets of norms can be used. One normative sample, the nonreferred normal sample, is a representative sample of U.S. school-aged adolescents. The second group, the referred sample, is of U.S. school-aged children and adolescents referred with MDD. This set of norms may be most helpful in testing for intervention or treatment needs. Two kinds of normative scores are reported: percentile ranks and standard scores. The WDSCA can be given in most settings—clinical, school, or home.

The manual is not without errors. On page 10, last paragraph, it should read "55% ... rated themselves as *more* depressed," instead of *less*. On page 19, first paragraph, it should read "Depression Scale for Children and *Adolescents*," instead of *Adults*. On page 25, last paragraph, it should read "1 to 1 1/2 standard deviations *higher* than the nonreferred group," instead of *lower*. On page 26, last paragraph, the hypothesis should read that all children and adolescents would have lower depression scores in the final treatment phase than from the initial evaluation phase. Instead it reads "lower depression scores from the initial evaluation phase than they did in the final treatment phase," which makes little sense. [Editor's Note: The publisher confirms that the first printing had several errors but that these have been corrected in subsequent printings.] Scoring is also somewhat confusing when using the Summary Sheet. Part I explains the criteria for depression; however, only A and C are needed as B is the criteria for a particular category. A brief description of each symptom on the form would have been helpful.

SUMMARY. Overall, the WDSCA, which claims to be the only criteria-referenced self-administered form for depression, may prove to be a valuable tool to detect depression in children and adolescents. The ease of administration and scoring makes the WDSCA a quick screening for depression, as well as a measure of the effectiveness of treatment.

REVIEWER'S REFERENCES

Kraepelin, E. (1921). *Manic-depressive insanity and paranoia.* Edinburgh: E & S Livingston.

Feighner, J. P., Robbins, E., Guze, S. P., Woodruff, R. A., Jr., Winokur, G., & Munoz, R. (1972). Diagnostic criteria for use in psychiatric research. *Archives of General Psychiatry, 26,* 57–63.

Spitzer, R. L., Endicott, S., & Robins, E. (1978). Research diagnostic criteria: Rationale and reliability, *Archives of General Psychiatry, 35,* 773–782.

American Psychiatric Association. (1980). *Diagnostic and statistical manual of mental disorders* (3rd ed.). Washington, DC: Author.

American Psychiatric Association. (1987). *Diagnostic and statistical manual of mental disorders* (3rd ed. Rev.). Washington, DC: Author.

American Psychiatric Association. (1994). *Diagnostic and statistical manual of mental disorders* (4th ed.). Washington, DC: Author.

Review of the Weinberg Depression Scale for Children and Adolescents by RADHIKA KRISHNAMURTHY, Associate Professor, School of Psychology, Florida Institute of Technology, Melbourne, FL:

The ubiquity of depression as a symptomatic condition has cast considerable clinical and research attention on this disorder and prompted numerous investigations of the similarities and differences between childhood and adult depression. This extensive interest has partially manifested in the development of a plethora of depression measures. Child and adolescent depression measures range in methodology from structured diagnostic schedules to adjective checklists, self-report inventories, and parent report and teacher report checklists. Among this abundance of depression scales, the Weinburg Depression Scale for Children and Adolescents (WDSCA) has been proffered as an option that is built upon a sound understanding of childhood depression.

The WDSCA is constructed from the bedrock of the modified Weinberg Criteria for depression, which are more elaborate and developmentally sensitive than standard psychiatric diagnostic (DSM-IV) criteria. It is essentially a 56-item, self-report instrument that requires "yes" or "no" responses to a series of questions relating to dysphoric mood, somatic concerns, disruption in school work and social relationships, negative self-perceptions, and various behavioral, attitudinal, and cognitive changes. It is easy to administer, brief, and quite straightforward in instructions. Test items have face validity for the assessment of children as several items deal with children's experiences (e.g., going to school, fighting, talking back to adults). The test manual indicates a fourth-grade reading requirement; in fact, a lower age limit is not proposed, suggesting that the requisite reading ability is the only consideration for administering this scale (and even that can be circumvented by the provision that items can be read to the child). Scoring is accomplished rather easily be adding positive responses for 50 items, excluding 5 items that are unrelated to depression. Normative comparisons are possible by transforming raw scores into standard scores and percentiles, with separate norms provided for normal adolescents and depressed children and adolescents. The summary sheet enables use of both Weinberg and DSM-IV criteria for diagnostic assessment. Both methods evaluate expressed and symptomatic manifestations of depression and also direct attention to the child's responses to selected "critical" items.

Norming of the WDSCA appears to have been done painstakingly over the course of a decade, which followed an earlier protracted period of item selection research. The reasons for this lengthy process are unclear, particularly when the standardization sample appears to have been drawn solely from the city of Dallas, Texas. The depressed sample was obtained from a single treatment center, whereas the source of the normal sample is not indicated in the test manual. Although the standardization sample is sufficiently large and matches 1990 U.S. Census data, it is by no means representative of the national population. Additional problems with the sample include the fact that the normal (nonreferred) sample comprises only adolescents whereas the depressed (referred) sample encompasses the 7-to-18-year age group. It would follow, then, that the norms based on the nonreferred group are only applicable to adolescents, and that children younger than 7 years of age should not be evaluated with the WDSCA.

The WDSCA manual furnishes data indicating adequate internal consistency and test-retest reliability and acceptable Standard Errors of Measurement. Interscorer reliability data are also provided, which is quite unusual and unnecessary for a self-report test with standardized scoring procedures. Validity findings include item analysis results demonstrating the discriminative power of items which, however, were based on the normative samples and require replication in independent samples. Evidence of concurrent validity with the Beck Depression Inventory, although adequate, is insufficient. Convergence with other child and adolescent measures such as the Children's Depression Inventory (Kovacs, 1985; T5:472) or the Reynolds Adolescent Depression Scale (Reynolds, 1987; T5:2230) would have been more appropriate. Most depression scales lack evidence of adequate discriminant validity, a feature that seems to be shared by the WDSCA. As a matter of fact, the manual offers *no* information on this form of validity. Demonstrations of test sensitivity and specificity with regard to depression diagnosis are also lacking.

The two major limitations of the WDSCA are as follows: (a) There is no convincing evidence that this scale represents an improvement over existing depression scales. The WDSCA has not been compared with other child/adolescent depression scales to examine how it holds up. Moreover, although the Weinberg criteria appears to represent children's depressive features more distinctly than the DSM-IV criteria do, the strong coefficient of agreement between the two sets of criteria suggest that they are not markedly different when used for diagnostic purposes. (b) Use of a single scale for children and adolescents may be problematic. Previous research (e.g., Achenbach & Edelbrock, 1983) has indicated that depression symptoms tend to vary as a function of age and gender. This issue requires further investigation.

SUMMARY. The WDSCA is a measure that appears to have been developed with considerable sensitivity to the construct definition of depression in children and adolescents and a methodical process of test development and validation. The test is relatively inexpensive, easy to use, and test materials are satisfactory. However, the application of this scale for children and adolescents alike is questionable based on developmental considerations as well as age limitations of the normative sample. Moreover, in the vast expanse of depression scales, this measure does not have a clear advantage. Confidence in the use of this measure will depend largely on evidence of discriminant validity, diagnostic classification accuracy, and invariance in item endorsement for the depiction of depression between early childhood and late adolescence.

REVIEWER'S REFERENCES
Achenbach, T. M., & Edelbrock, C. (1983). *Manual for the Child Behavior Checklist and Revised Child Behavior Profile.* Burlington, VT: University of Vermont, Dept. of Psychiatry.
Kovacs, M. (1985). The Children's Depression Inventory (CDI). *Psychopharmacology Bulletin, 21,* 995–998.
Reynolds, W. M. (1987). *Reynolds Adolescent Depression Scale professional manual.* Odessa, FL: Psychological Assessment Resources.

[418]
Wide Range Assessment of Visual Motor Abilities.

Purpose: A standardized assessment of visual-motor, visual-spatial, and fine motor skills.
Population: Ages 3–17 years.
Publication Date: 1995.
Acronym: WRAVMA.
Scores, 4: Fine Motor, Visual-Spatial, Visual-Motor, Visual-Motor Integration Composite.
Administration: Individual.
Price Data, 1998: $40 per manual (151 pages); $48 per 25 drawing or matching forms; $40 per 25 examiner record forms; $50 per pegboard with pegs; $12 per pencil and marker resupply pack; $38 per soft attaché case.
Time: (15–30) minutes; (5–10) minutes per subtest.
Comments: Best results when "integrated with data from other standardized tests and clinical observations"; test should be interpreted by "those with graduate or equivalent professional training in cognitive assessment."
Authors: Wayne Adams and David Sheslow.
Publisher: Wide Range, Inc.

Review of the Wide Range Assessment of Visual Motor Abilities by LINDA K. BUNKER, Professor of Human Services, University of Virginia, Charlottesville, VA:

The Wide Range Assessment of Visual Motor Abilities (WRAVMA) consists of three subtests for Visual-Motor (Drawing), Visual-Spatial (Matching), and Fine Motor (Pegboard) abilities for 3–17-year-olds. The authors, Wayne Adams and David Sheslow, suggest that these moderately related components should be assessed together in order to provide a comparison of a child's visual-spatial and fine motor skills with his or her visual-motor abilities.

The three subtests of the WRAVMA were chosen because of their importance in school success. For example, a case is made for the fact that many visual motor difficulties experienced by children are the result of the inadequacy of spatial skills, motor skills, or the integration of the two. By using the tests either independently or in combination, it may be possible to assess more adequately the integrated skills of a child, compared to the usual single-dimension instruments.

The Visual-Motor test is essentially a drawing test that presents designs to be copied by the children. The designs are arranged in a developmental order, with instructions that children continue to copy each item until three consecutive items are failed. Evaluation criteria for each design are presented on the examiner form for ease of administration and dichotomous scoring (either all criteria are present = 1 point; or if any one aspect is missing it is scored a failure). Only the first attempt at copying is scored and the examiner must attend to the subtle differences in criteria between such words as "clearly" versus "generally" or "mostly" in assessing the child's output.

The Visual-Spatial test is a matching exercise that presents a test item and then asks children to select which of four options "goes best" with the target figure. Successful matches require skills such as orientation, perspective, rotation, and size discrimination, and are not dependent on fine motor skills to manipulate objects. The child responds by merely pointing or touching a marker to the match. Scoring criteria are provided on the examiner form and a child continues until he or she misses six items within a series of eight. When a child selects a correct match, the examiner's guidelines indicate that the child should be praised; if an error occurs, the child is told "No, that's not right. See, it is this one [pointing to the correct alternative]" (manual, p. 40). This guideline for providing feedback is a welcome addition to this assessment battery.

The Fine Motor test involves having a child insert as many pegs in the pegboard as possible within 90 seconds. The primary score is determined with the dominant hand (the preferred writing or drawing hand), but assessment is encouraged with both hands. Norms are provided for both hands based on raw scores, and are said to be important to "Quantifying possible compromise resulting from insults such as peripheral nerve damage, unilateral frontal brain injury or hemiplegia" (manual, p. 5). Unfortunately, little information is provided about the interpretation of the pegboard performance in terms of any neurological or visual-motor dysfunction.

Each subtest is individually scored and a composite WRAVMA score can also be computed. Standard scores are provided for each test that may be combined to create the composite score. The composite score should, however, be carefully evaluated because it is derived by summing the standard scores of the Drawing, Matching, and Pegboard Tests. With no weighting of the three tests, the possibility for misleading averages (when one test is particularly high and another low) should be carefully evaluated. There is also a place on the examiner form to graphically compare the results from the three tests.

Test materials for all three subtests are attractively presented and conveniently structured for ease of administration and transport. The test booklets for drawing and matching are well organized and easy to utilize. The pegs for the Fine Motor test are conveniently stored within the waffled surface pegboard itself, and all materials are located in a convenient canvas carrying case.

The testing guidelines are clear and concise. The authors briefly review concepts of good test administration and provide reference for novice testers or experienced examiners who may wish a review of techniques and procedures. Several cautions are also provided, particularly as they apply to children with ADHD (Attention Deficit/Hyperactivity Disorders) or with visual impairments.

In testing the children, each subtest begins on an item that corresponds with the chronological age of the child. For example, in the Matching test, children 7 years and up start on Item 6. Several case studies are presented to help the clinician integrate the scores on the WRAVMA with other assessments. These cases also give some suggested recommendations for each child, but little supporting evidence is provided about the validity of these recommendations.

The WRAVMA was standardized using a stratified sample of 2,282 children from ages 3–17. The model controlled for age, gender, ethnicity, regional residence, and socioeconomic level. Extensive tables of data and item statistics are provided in the manual, which clearly represents careful attention to sampling. For example, item separation reliability coefficients are provided that were derived from a Rasch analysis, and the authors suggest that this provides "strong support that the respective tests are defining clear variables for the total sample and each age group" (manual, p. 125). Similarly, person separation statistics are provided to justify the ability of the test to differentiate among samples of persons.

In scoring the WRAVMA, raw scores are converted to standard scores by using the data tables that provide 6-month increments for children ages 3–12; 6-months, and 1-year increments for children 13 and above. The authors reported no gender differences so scores are not differentiated by male versus female. This is somewhat surprising given the prevalence of evidence in other research reports about gender differences in spatial awareness and drawing. The justification given was that item bias was avoided by carefully selecting the figures so as to guarantee that the tests were not unfair to one group versus another.

Psychometric properties of reliability and validity are reported in several ways. Person separation reliability coefficients are presented for the Drawing and Matching tests for each age group and for the total sample. This measure of internal consistency indicated $r = .93$ for the Drawing test and $r = .95$ for the Matching tests. The authors also suggest that the item separation reliability index presents adequate evidence for content validity, though this does not seem compelling justification. Split-half and coefficient alphas are also reported for each age group, ranging from .63 to .90. Interrater reliability is also provided for three examiners, but this, of course, should be re-established in each testing environment.

The case for construct validity is based on seven assumptions including the developmental nature of the WRAVMA, intercorrelations of the WRAVMA, WRAVMA relationship with cognitive ability and academic achievement, and Rasch properties of WRAVMA. In addition, the authors suggest that the WRAVMA provides important information not provided in other standardized instruments such as Wechsler Intelligence Scale for Children—3 (WISC-III) or Wide Range Achievement Test—3 (WRAT3) and support that by presenting factor analysis data. The seventh assumption relates to concurrent validity in terms of how the WRAVMA relates to similar tests.

Correlational data are provided for the Drawing test with the Developmental Test of Visual Motor Integration (VMI: $r = .76$), for the Matching test with the Motor-Free Visual Perception Test (MVP: $r = .54$), and for the Pegboard test (dominant, nondominant hand) with the Grooved Pegboard Test (GPT) (dominant hand $r = .35$; nondominant hand $r = .39$, respectively). The latter correlations should be cautiously interpreted because the GPT does not have adequate norming of its own, and thus the comparisons are tenuous.

The Visual-Spatial skills test (Matching) was reported to be highly correlated with traditional spatial skill tests such as the WISC-III Block Design ($r = .61$). This needs to be interpreted with caution because a child has only four choices for a match, yielding a 25% chance occurrence of matches. The authors suggest that increasing the choices beyond four would tax the attention of young children, especially those with attention deficit-hyperactivity disorders. Although that is true for the young children or those with ADHD, it may be insufficient justification for not increasing the choices (and thus more rigorously examining validity) for older children.

SUMMARY. The WRAVMA is a convenient test of drawing, matching, and pegboard abilities that shows evidence of validity and reliability of test scores. The authors clearly invite other researchers to test the WRAVMA and encourage collaboration in the further exploration of its psychometric properties. The extent to which the instrument "provides a basis for explanations of otherwise puzzling, but not uncommon occurrences such as a kindergartner whose block building skills are quite adequate but who cannot write well, the child who has trouble copying from the blackboard but performs well on puzzle construction tasks, or the teen who can draw single designs or write individual spelling words well enough, but who shows an obvious deficit in writing a page of text" (manual, p. 3) seems unsubstantiated. It is clearly an efficient and economical battery to assess three particular abilities, but it does not provide much explanatory information or information about recommendations after the three abilities are assessed.

Review of the Wide Range Assessment of Visual Motor Abilities by KEITH F. WIDAMAN, Professor of Psychology, University of California at Davis, Davis, CA:

The Wide Range Assessment of Visual Motor Abilities (WRAVMA) is a measure of visual-motor and visual-spatial skills for children and adolescents between the ages of 3 and 17 years. Visual-motor and visual-spatial skills are important in the diagnosis of children with learning problems, to determine whether problems in this domain are responsible for levels of academic performance that are inconsistent with a child's intelligence. Moreover, the skills assessed by the WRAVMA appear to underlie one major subtype of learning disability, one based on visual and sensory-motor deficits.

DESCRIPTION. The WRAVMA is divided into three tests. The first is the Drawing Test, which assesses visual-motor skills. The Drawing Test consists of 24 items that are arranged in order of increasing difficulty. Some items require the subject to complete simple pictures that have omitted parts; other items ask the subject to copy simple two-dimensional designs, more complex two-dimensional objects with multiple parts, or complex objects with three dimensional perspective.

The second test is the Matching Test, a measure of visual-spatial skills. The Matching Test contains 46 items, once again arranged in order of increasing difficulty. Each item on this test consists of a standard figure and four alternative figures, and the subject selects the correct alternative. The items on this test appear to be a mixture of several types of items. On some items, the correct alternative is precisely the same as the standard, and distractors are completely different from the standard. On other items, one part of the standard figure is missing, and the respondent must select the alternative that correctly completes the standard. Still other items seem like items from the Matching Familiar Figures Test, with all four alternatives being very similar to the standard except for minor details. In addition, on some items, the correct alternative is in the same orientation as the standard, whereas other items require two-dimensional rotations, mirror reflections, or three-dimensional rotations in order to match the correct alternative with the standard. Thus, items on this test appear to assess a mixture of different spatial skills, so the total score on this test probably represents individual differences on a general spatial skills dimension.

The third test is the Pegboard Test, indexing fine motor skills. The Pegboard Test consists of a board with eight rows of 10 holes, and the subject must place as many pegs as possible in the holes within 90 seconds. The test is administered twice, once with the preferred hand and once with the nonpreferred hand.

ADMINISTRATION. The WRAVMA was designed to be administered individually, but the Drawing and Matching Tests are designed to be group administered as well. Because only one pegboard is included and no physical record of performance on the Pegboard Test is available unless a tester writes the number of pegs placed, the Pegboard Test must be administered individually. Total testing time for the three-test battery is 14–24 minutes. Testing time during individual administration would be less than under group administration, given stopping criteria for the Drawing and Matching Tests that may be invoked during individual administration.

SCORING. The raw score on each test is the number of items answered correctly. The raw score may be converted to a standard score, with mean of 100 and standard deviation of 15, using nicely formatted conversion tables. Conversion tables are presented for each half-year between 3 and 13 years (e.g., 3.0–3.5 years, 3.5–3.11 years) and then for one-year intervals through 17 years. After obtaining the standard scores on the three tests, one may sum these three standard scores and then obtain an overall standard score from a final conversion table.

The standardization sample consisted of a national sample of 2,282 children and adolescents between the ages of 3 and 17 years, a sample approximately evenly divided between males and females. The sample was selected by stratifying on ethnicity and region of residence, and information is provided on socioeconomic status. In general the standardization sample appears representative of the U.S. population. The sample size of 2,282 seems reasonably large. However, because there are 25 age groups, the average age sample contained only 90 subjects, which is on the small size for establishing normative scores based on percentiles.

RELIABILITY. For the Drawing and Matching Tests, results of Rasch modeling are presented. Here, indices of item separation, person separation, and the standard error of measurement (*SEM*) are listed. The person separation measures are akin to traditional internal consistency reliability coefficients, which average .81 (range .71–.86) for the Drawing Test, and average .81 (range .65–.90) for the Matching Test. Coefficient alphas average .75 (range .63–.82) for the Drawing Test and .81 (range .65–.89) for the Matching Test. Split-half coefficients average .81 (range .69–.89) for the Drawing Test and .84 (range .68–92) for the Matching Test. Test-retest reliabilities, over an average 6-week interval, ranged from .82 to .89 for the three tests. Item bias by gender and ethnic status is not a problem, with correlations of item difficulties over .99 for all inter-group comparisons. Also, interrater reliabilities for the Drawing Test are .96 or higher.

The reliability coefficients exhibit one interesting, troubling trend: For the Drawing Test, reliabilities are rather low at the youngest age levels, but then increase to higher levels at the oldest age levels. The Matching Test shows the opposite trend, with quite high levels of reliability at the youngest age levels, and lower levels of reliability at the oldest age levels. Perhaps floor effects on the Drawing Test and ceiling effects on the Matching Test account for these contrasting trends in reliability. Moreover, reliabilities on all tests are good, but sufficiently low that the precision of scores for an individual is modest. The standard error of measurement (*SEM*) ranges from about 5.0 to 9.0, depending on the age and reliability coefficient used. At best, the 95% confidence interval around a true score (or the true score ± twice the *SEM*), is an interval of about ± 10 points, a 20-point range; at worst, the 95% confidence interval is an interval of ± 18 points, a 36-point range.

VALIDITY. Several analyses related to validity for the WRAVMA tests are presented. Raw scores on all three tests correlate highly with age (range .74–.80). The correlations among the three tests are moderate, averaging between .28 and .38, which suggest the three tests assess different aspects of visual, motor, and spatial skill. The three tests have moderate correlations with intelligence, shown by correlations ranging from .13 to .61 with subtests of the Wechsler Intelligence Scale for Children—3 (WISC-III). The composite WRAVMA score is correlated .62 with Full Scale WISC-III IQ. The three WRAVMA tests also correlated moderately with academic achievement, with correlations between .31 and .46 with subtests of the Wide Range Achievement Test 3 (WRAT3). A principal component analysis of the tests from the WRAVMA, WISC-III, and WRAT3 led to a six-component structure. However, little detail regarding this analysis is provided, and certain anomalous results are reported. For example, each of the WRAVMA tests defined a different factor,

questioning the validity of the WRAVMA composite score; and, given the varimax rotation, all three WRAVMA components are independent of the intelligence and achievement components, conflicting with prior discussions of moderate correlations with these domains. Thus, the analysis is of limited utility. Finally, concurrent validity for the WRAVMA tests was strong for the Drawing Test (*r* = .76 with the Developmental Test of Visual Motor Integration), moderate for the Matching Test (*r* = .54 with the Motor-Free Visual Perception Test), and low for the Pegboard Test (*r* = .39 with the Grooved Pegboard Test).

SUMMARY. The WRAVMA is a quick and easy-to-administer battery assessing visual-motor and visual-spatial skills of children and adolescents. The WRAVMA consists of three tests that have good reliability and reasonable validity, but users should be aware that individuals might score rather differently upon retest. However, few alternative batteries assessing visual-motor and visual-spatial skills exist, and the WRAVMA is well standardized. As a result, the WRAVMA appears to be a useful new device for investigating whether deficiencies in visual-motor and visual-spatial skills underlie discrepancies between intelligence and achievement.

[419]
The Wiesen Test of Mechanical Aptitude.

Purpose: Designed to measure mechanical aptitude for purpose of personnel selection.
Population: Applicants (18 years and older) for jobs requiring mechanical aptitude.
Publication Dates: 1997–1999.
Acronym: WTMA.
Scores, 12: Total Score and 11 research scores: Basic Machines, Movement of Simple and Complex Objects, Center of Gravity and Gravity, Basic Electricity/Electronics, Transfer of Heat, Basic Physical Properties of Matter and Materials, Miscellaneous, Academic, Kitchen Objects, Non-Kitchen Objects, Other Everyday Objects.
Administration: Group.
Price Data: Available from publisher.
Time: (30) minutes.
Comments: A 60-item multiple-choice objective test.
Author: Joel P. Wiesen.
Publisher: Psychological Assessment Resources, Inc.

Review of The Wiesen Test of Mechanical Aptitude by JOHN M. ENGER, Professor of Education, Barry University, Miami Shores, FL:

The Wiesen Test of Mechanical Aptitude (WTMA) is designed to measure one's propensity towards mechanical aptitude, which is defined as the ability to learn about mechanical objects and physical and mechanical principles. Using the WTMA, mechanical ability is measured by one's familiarity with everyday physical objects, their function, and their appearance. According to Wiesen, the test author, the development of this instrument was prompted by need, because other tests on the market were outdated, biased, and lacked desired psychometric rigor.

The WTMA is a 60-item, three-option multiple-choice test; the score is the number of correct responses. There are seven or eight items for each of eight mechanical content subscales: machines, movement, gravity/center of gravity, electricity/electronics, heat, physical properties of materials, miscellaneous, and academic. For each subscale, a set of seven or eight items depicts three commonplace occurrences (kitchen, household, and everyday). The WTMA is written at a sixth-grade reading level.

Recently, Psychological Assessment Resources, Inc. took over the publishing of the WTMA. The presentation is more appealing than the earlier edition; the format and content are similar to the previous publication. The test has a 30-minute time limit with most test takers completing the test within 20 minutes.

Overall, the items appear relatively easy. However, the normative data indicate an overall mean of 41.8 (70% correct) with standard deviation 5.69. The primary normative sample consisted of 1,817 industrial job applicants and incumbents. There does not appear to be a ceiling effect and the distribution of scores for the normative sample appears to be fairly widespread.

The reported coefficient alpha internal consistency reliability estimate of the WTMA is very high ($r = .97$). The 11 subscale reliability estimates range from $r = .55$ to $r = .92$ (averaging $r = .81$).

The author and publisher addressed validity issues for the WTMA in a number of ways consistent with recommendations for test development and validation (AERA, APA, & NCME, 1985). First, the test was constructed to measure mechanical aptitude in eight identified content areas where items were presented in three commonplace domains. This was done to try to make the instrument independent of specialized learning about mechanics. Specialized learning would generally be more job-related or school-related.

The WTMA compared favorably to other measures, including mechanical aptitude tests, other aptitude assessments, and general knowledge tests in areas such as reading and arithmetic. There was a close alignment ($r = .80$) of WTMA scores with a related instrument, the Bennett Mechanical Comprehension Test (Bennett, 1969).

Several job-related studies were conducted with employees in industries who were in positions identified as requiring a "mechanical aptitude." The WTMA scores were correlated with criterion variables such as supervisor evaluations, training performance, and job performance. Although reliability estimates for the various measures generally were very favorable, the criterion-related validity coefficients were quite modest.

As reported in the manual, an impetus in the development of the WTMA was to address the shortcomings of other mechanical aptitude measures on the market. Much concern was raised on gender and ethnicity differences produced by earlier tests of mechanical aptitude. The WTMA does not alleviate those concerns; there are still marked differences in mechanical aptitude scores when results are contrasted by gender and by ethnicity. In the test manual a recommendation is made for using selected groupings of subscale scores—this needs to be investigated. Perhaps, more research needs to be reported on these recommendations before this becomes a viable option for the user.

SUMMARY. The WTMA is a welcome attempt to measure mechanical aptitude to aid decisions on employment in positions requiring skill in operating machinery and performing related functions. However, for the WTMA to be used for a specific hiring purpose, research should be done to assess the relationship between WTMA scores and employee performance measures for that position.

REVIEWER'S REFERENCES

Bennett, G. K. (1969). Bennett Mechanical Comprehension Test. San Antonio, TX: The Psychological Corporation.
American Educational Research Association, American Psychological Association, & National Council on Measurement in Education. (1985). *Standards for educational and psychological testing.* Washington, DC: American Psychological Association, Inc.

Review of The Wiesen Test of Mechanical Aptitude by NAMBURY S. RAJU, Distinguished Professor, Institute of Psychology, Illinois Institute of Technology, Chicago, IL:

The Wiesen Test of Mechanical Aptitude (WTMA) consists of 60 multiple-choice items, with three options per item, and the content for these items reflects "common everyday objects and events" (manual, p. 1). The items are classified in two ways: Principles (8) and Objects (3). The eight broad classes of mechanical/physical principles are: Basic Machines, Movement, Gravity and Center of Gravity, Electricity/Electronics, Heat, Physical Properties of Materials, Miscellaneous, and Academic. There are 7 or 8 items in each of the principle categories. The three Object categories, reflecting where the objects involved in the items are likely to be found, are: Kitchen, Household, and Everyday. Each Object category contains 20 items. The WTMA is designed for both machine and hand scoring. The test is timed, with a 30-minute time limit.

The WTMA was designed to be a purer measure of mechanical aptitude with test content that is up-to-date, bias-free, and less reliant on academic training and specific job experience than the current, commercially available tests of mechanical aptitude. Twelve different scores are reported for the WTMA: one overall score, eight Principle scores, and three Object scores. All scores are reported as percent correct.

RELIABILITY. The technical manual reports internal consistency estimates of reliability for the 12 scores. The reported reliability estimate for the total is .82. The Object scale reliabilities are .47, .62, and .66 for the Kitchen, Household, and Everyday objects, respectively. The reliabilities for the Principle scales vary from a low of .22 for Heat to a high of .54 for Miscellaneous. These reliability estimates are based on an industrial sample of 1,082 subjects, representing both incumbents and applicants from eight different companies/organizations. Even though brief descriptions of the eight companies included in the reliability analysis are given in the technical manual, it is difficult to assess how well this sample represents the world of work in which mechanical aptitude is relevant. No test-retest or parallel-form reliability estimates are provided. Also unavailable are the item p-values and item-test correlations.

The reliability estimate for the total score appears to be acceptable. The same, however, cannot be said of the reliabilities for the Object and Principle part scores. The use of part scores at an individual level, especially in personnel selection, should be discouraged. At the group level, these part scores may have some psychometric utility.

VALIDITY. The technical manual presents various types of data for assessing the validity of the WTMA. One study shows that the correlation between the WTMA total scores of 95 carpet manufacturing machine operators and their supervisors' evaluations was .24, which was statistically significant. This was the only study mentioned in the technical manual as evidence of criterion-related validity. As the technical manual notes, more studies are certainly needed in this regard.

The construct validity of the WTMA was assessed by correlating it with some of the known measures of mechanical aptitude. Correlations with the SRA, FIT, and Bennett tests ranged from a low of .21 for the FIT tests to a high of .80 for the Bennett test, with the SRA tests falling in the middle. These correlations appear to support the construct validity of the WTMA. A careful review of the item content appears to show that the items indeed measure mechanical aptitude and do not appear to depend on the knowledge gained in the classroom or on the job. In this sense, it appears that one of the goals guiding the development of the WTMA was achieved.

ADVERSE IMPACT. The technical manual addresses the question of adverse impact with empirical data from several sources. In general, there does appear to be adverse impact in the sense of males scoring higher on the WTMA than females and Whites performing better than the Blacks and Hispanics. In the reliability sample, the male-female difference (expressed as effect size) was -.43, the White-Black difference was -1.13 and the White-Hispanic difference was -.59. Similar differences were also found with other samples as shown in the technical manual. Furthermore, these substantial effect sizes appear to be similar to those reported for other tests of mechanical aptitude.

An effect size is defined as the mean difference divided by the pooled standard deviation. The pooled standard deviation is defined as the square-root of the weighted average of the two variances. The technical manual defines the pooled standard deviation as the simple average of the two standard deviations, and this definition is inconsistent with the professionally accepted standard.

NORMS. Two sets of norms are available for the WTMA: Industrial and Educational. In both cases, percentile scores are available only for the total score. The industrial sample is identical to the reliability sample of 1,817 cases. The educational sample consisted of 221 mostly undergraduate students in introductory psychology classes. The sample size for the educational sample appears to be much too small for developing reliable normative data. It is difficult to assess the representativeness of these samples.

SUMMARY. The WTMA is a new psychometric instrument designed to measure mechanical aptitude. The total score reliability estimate is good, but the part score reliabilities are quite low. The content and construct validity evidence appears to be acceptable, and there is a definite need for more work in terms of criterion-related validity. In view of the reported adverse impact data, a differential item functioning (DIF) analysis is strongly recommended, separately for females and male, Blacks and Whites, and Hispanics and Whites. A factor analysis of the 60 items is also recommended to gain a better understanding of the underlying structure of this new measure of mechanical aptitude.

[420]
Wisconsin Card Sorting Test, Revised and Expanded.

Purpose: "Developed ... as a measure of abstract reasoning among normal adult populations" and "has increasingly been employed as a clinical neuropsychological instrument."

Population: Ages 6.5–89.

Publication Dates: 1981–1993.

Acronym: WCST.

Scores, 11: Number of Trials Administered, Total Number Correct, Total Number of Errors, Perseverative Responses, Perseverative Errors, Nonperseverative Errors, Conceptual Level Responses, Number of Categories Completed, Trials to Complete First Category, Failure to Maintain Set, Learning to Learn.

Administration: Individual.

Price Data: Price information available from publisher for complete kit including manual ('93, 234 pages), 2 decks of cards, and 25 record booklets; price information also available from publisher for computer version.

Time: (20–30) minutes.

Comments: Additional materials necessary for testing include a pen or pencil and a clipboard.

Authors: Robert K. Heaton, Gordon J. Chelune, Jack L. Talley, Gary G. Kay, and Glenn Curtiss.

Publisher: Psychological Assessment Resources, Inc.

Cross References: See T5:2892 (309 references) and T4:2967 (96 references); for reviews by Byron Egeland and Robert P. Markley of an earlier edition, see 9:1372 (11 references).

Review of the Wisconsin Card Sorting Test, Revised and Expanded by ELAINE CLARK, Professor of Educational Psychology, University of Utah, Salt Lake City, UT:

The Wisconsin Card Sorting Test (WCST) was originally published in 1981 and was intended as a measure of abstract reasoning and ability to shift cognitive strategies when faced with changing stimuli. In as much as the WCST requires strategic planning, organized searching, and the use of environmental feedback to shift strategies to solve problems, it has been considered to be a measure of "executive function." The WCST is one of the most widely used tests in neuropsychology and is likely to be used more since some useful revisions in 1993. For one, age and education corrections were provided for the normative sample of adults 20 years and older. Secondly, normative data have been expanded to include individuals from the age of 6.5 through 89. Finally, the authors developed a computer-administered version of the test. The primary focus of this review, however, is on the manually administered version of the WCST.

ADMINISTRATION AND SCORING. The WCST still consists of four stimulus cards and two sets of 64 response cards that depict four forms (circle, crosses, triangles, and stars), four colors (red, yellow, blue, and green), and four numbers (one, two, three, and four). Adequate performance on the test requires that the examinee determine the correct sorting principle and maintain that set across changing stimulus conditions. Failure to maintain the set or perseveration on an older, and ineffective, principle is taken into consideration in the scoring. The procedures for administering the test are standardized, and the same instructions are considered adequate for children and adults. The authors, however, suggest that examiners introduce the test as a "game" to young children.

Four stimulus cards are placed in front of the examinee in a specific order from left to right. Examinees are then given the first deck of 64 cards and asked to match each of the cards with one of the four stimulus cards that they think it matches. Feedback is provided by the examiner as to whether the examinee's response is correct or incorrect. Although instructions can be repeated, no other information is given that might help examinees figure out the correct matching principle. After 10 consecutive correct matches to color, the sorting principle shifts to number. The test is then repeated in the same order (color, form, and number) using the remaining response cards. The examiner records the examinee's response on a record booklet. The record booklet is clearly printed, and, for the most part, self-explanatory. The responses that examinees give, however, need to be considered on three dimensions (i.e., correct and incorrect, ambiguous and unambiguous, and perseverative and nonperseverative). These dimensions are described thoroughly in the manual. The test is not timed and examinees can pace themselves as they wish.

According to the manual, the test can be administered by "any trained person with a background in psychological testing" (p. 3). Clinical interpretation of the test, however, is said to require "professional training and expertise in clinical psychology and/or neuropsychology ... and a clear understanding of brain-behavior relationships and the medical and psychological factors that affect them" (p. 4). Potential test users are warned, and rightfully so, that the procedures used to administer, record, and score the test need to be carefully studied and mastered before using the WCST clinically. Although Heaton and his colleagues have provided about as comprehensive an instructional manual as possible, some of the scoring is difficult. This is especially true of the rules for scoring perseverative response and error scores. Fortunately, the authors have provided in the manual sample protocols to illustrate difficult scoring situations (e.g., discriminating ambiguous from unambiguous errors in order to score perseverations). Although with practice scoring can be mastered, it is time-consuming. For novice examiners the time it takes to score the test is likely to be estimated in hours, not minutes. To give the test, however, even the novice can be finished in 20 or 30 minutes (excluding the amount of time needed to reorder the response cards for each administration). The computer version of the WCST provides an immediate solution to the scoring problem. It is unclear, however, how comparable the computer-generated scores are to those obtained through the manual administration. As with any computer-administered test there are potential drawbacks. For one, examinees who need this type of test are

often uncomfortable with unfamiliar tasks, in particular, computers. Experience with computer testing has also shown that some examinees get confused during the test. For example, some examinees have difficulty keeping track of what they are matching to, that is, mistakenly matching to the bottom row of response cards instead of the top row of stimulus cards. Examinees with reduced vision may also find the computer version more difficult to see. Of course, this often depends on the size and quality of the monitor displaying the stimuli.

NORMATIVE DATA. The revised WCST was normed on a group of 899 "normal" subjects between the ages 6 years, 6 months and 89 years, 11 months. The 899 subjects were drawn from six distinct samples. For example, one group of 150 subjects was described as being in the original WCST manual and normative study published in 1991 by Heaton and his colleagues, whereas another was a group of 124 commercial airline pilots participating in a study of computerized neuropsychological testing. Given a lack of information on the consistency of administration and scoring procedures, it is unclear how reliable and valid these normative data are. It is also unclear how representative these data are for examinees living in various geographic regions, and of various socioeconomic and racial/ethnic backgrounds. According to the manual, the majority of subjects in the norming groups were selected from the southeastern and southwestern/Rocky Mountain regions of the United States. Data pertaining to race were reported in only one sample, a group of 379 children from an urban setting in the southeast. No race data were provided for the remaining subjects, and no socioeconomic data were included for any subjects. Gender data were provided, and for the most part, evenly distributed. Age and education data were also provided; however, the mean age of the child and adolescent samples was not given.

The mean age of the 384 adult subjects (i.e., 20 years and older) was noted to be 49.89 with a standard deviation (*SD*) of 17.94. The data were compared to the 1995 census data and showed an underrepresentation of younger adults, and an overrepresentation of older adults. This, however, does not mean that all groups of older adults are adequately represented in the norming sample. In fact, only four subjects comprise the 85 years and older group. The mean adult education level given was 14.95 (*SD* of 2.97). Comparing this with the 1987 U.S. Census data (the most recent education data available at the time) showed that the WCST sample education mean was 3 years higher. Although it would have been preferred to equate on education, the analyses of the normative data showed that the demographic variable with the greatest relationship to WCST performance was age. According to regression analyses, performance on the WCST steadily increases from 6.5 through about 19 years of age. Performance remains stable from the 20s through the 50s, after which time it begins to decline. The data indicate that individuals with higher levels of education perform better on the WCST.

RELIABILITY AND VALIDITY. Reliability data reported in the manual pertain to interscorer and intrascorer agreement for the child/adolescent and adult samples, and generalizability coefficients and standard error of measurement values for the child and adolescent data only. The interscorer and intrascorer reliability studies reported in the manual were conducted with 30 adult psychiatric inpatients. The first study used experienced clinicians and showed a range of interscorer reliability between .88 and .93 and a range of intrascorer coefficients between .91 to .96. Coefficients found for novice examiners were also adequate (i.e., coefficients ranged from .75 to .97 for both inter- and intrascorer data). Similar data were obtained for a sample of children and adolescents. With the exception of the Learning to Learn score, interscorer coefficients ranged from .90 to 1.00 (the Learning to Learn coefficient was .66). Intrascorer coefficients for the same set of data ranged from .83 to 1.00.

Generalizability coefficients intended to assess fidelity of measurement (i.e., how well the instrument measures a subject's true score) were calculated for the child and adolescent data only. Generalizability coefficients for 46 subjects ranged from .39 to .72, and averaged .57 (a coefficient of .60 or higher is considered to be indicative of "very good" scale reliability). Standard errors of measurement (*SEM*) were also calculated for the child and adolescent "reliability sample." These data are provided in the manual for each of the WCST standard scores (i.e., scores with a mean of 100 and *SD* of 15). Because the sample was "normal", further data are needed to determine what the *SEM*s would be for a clinical group of children and adolescents, as well as for a clinical and normal group of adults.

A number of validity studies, in particular, correlational and discriminant function analyses, were described in the manual. The data from these studies support the use of the WCST for a variety of neurological and psychological problems, and with a variety of populations. Studies of adults with closed head injuries, demyelinating diseases, seizure disorders, and schizophrenia, and children with traumatic brain injuries (TBI), seizures, learning disabilities (LD), and attention deficit hyperactivity disorders (ADHD) indicate that the WCST may be useful in assessing "executive functions" in these groups. Although some correlational data have shown that the WCST is sensitive to frontal lesions, data provided in the manual and in the research literature suggest that the WCST is also sensitive to dysfunction in other areas of the brain.

TEST SCORE INTERPRETATION. Raw scores from 9 of the 13 WCST variables can be converted to *T* scores, standard scores (mean of 100 and *SD* of 15), and percentile ranks. The other remaining WCST variables (i.e., the Number of Categories Completed, Trials to Complete the First Category, Failure to Maintain set, and Learning to Learn) can only be converted to percentile ranks. Appendix D of the manual provides data that have been demographically corrected for age and education. Demographic corrections are provided for each decade of life from 6 years, 6 months through 89 years, 11 months (with the exception of only a half decade being represented for children between ages 6 years, 6 months and 7 years). Categories of educational attainment, however, begin at age 20. These categories include 8 years of education or less, 9 to 11, 12, 13–15, 16 to 17 years of education, and greater than or equal to 18 years of education. These data allow examiners to compare an examinee's score with those of individuals who are similar in age and from similar educational backgrounds.

Examiners may also compare an adult examinee's score with the general adult population. These data represent the U.S. Census age-matched adult sample. Base rate data are also provided for examiners who wish to assess the likelihood that an examinee's score is more similar to a clinical (i.e., neurologically impaired) population than a normal (non-neurologically impaired) one. The "normal" sample was represented by data from the normative group, whereas the clinical sample consisted of subjects who had frontal,

frontal plus (i.e., focal lesions involving frontal and nonfrontal areas), diffuse damage, and nonfrontal brain lesions. Base rate data for the diagnostic categories, TBI, seizure disorder, ADHD, and LD, are also provided in Appendix E for comparative purposes.

SUMMARY. The WCST has essentially remained unchanged since its publication in 1981. The test's normative data, however, have been expanded to include children as young as 6 years, 6 months and adults as old as 89. Although the small number of adults in the 85 and older category makes it difficult to interpret test scores for this age group, the authors should be commended for their recognition of the need to include these individuals in normative studies of this type. The authors also demonstrate a recognition for the need of base rate information to compare an individual score and draw conclusions about impairment. These data are conveniently provided in the manual so that comparisons can be made between an examinee's WCST scores and those of "nonimpaired" or normal individuals with those of individuals with known neurologic impairments and psychological/behavioral problems (e.g., ADHD).

It is not surprising to find that Heaton and his colleagues have also included demographically corrected normative data to compare an examinee's test scores. These scores were intended to allow comparisons of an examinee's score to that of individuals of similar age and educational background. These norms, however, were obtained by combining test scores of control subjects involved in six different studies. Little information was found in the manual about the subjects or procedures used to collect the data. Demographic information important in interpreting test scores (e.g., racial/ethnic and socioeconomic background) is missing. Knowing so little about the normative sample makes it somewhat difficult for test users to interpret any differences they find between their examinees and the normative group. Although it is recognized that conducting large normative studies is extremely expensive, equating procedures such as those used by educational test publishers need to be considered. "Equating" the normative data of the WCST with those of similar tests (e.g., tests of reasoning) may provide more convincing support for the test norms.

The WCST has enjoyed a long history of use in neuropsychological research and clinical practice. The 1993 revisions of the test are likely to insure that it retains its place. Although investigations with the WCST indicate that it does not have sufficient specificity to warrant its use as a frontal lobe sign (i.e., it is also sensitive to nonfrontal lesions), it has been shown to be particularly sensitive to frontal lesions and useful as a measure of "executive function." Whether the number and/or complexity of hypotheses needed to solve the sorting problem of color, form, and number is sufficient for higher functioning individuals, however, needs to be further evaluated. As a measure of executive function, the WCST provides information that many other executive function measures do not, even those that are considered more conceptually complex. Rather than generating a total or cutoff score to determine success or failure on the tasks, the WCST yields scores that help one to understand how well a person conceptualizes the problem of the card sort (i.e., how efficiently they learn) and how flexibly they shift strategies to solve the problem. These features are likely to insure that the WCST continues to be one of the most frequently used tests for "executive" skill.

Review of the Wisconsin Card Sorting Test, Revised and Expanded by DEBORAH D. ROMAN, Assistant Professor and Director, Neuropsychology Lab, Departments of Physical Medicine and Rehabilitation and Neurosurgery, University of Minnesota, Minneapolis, MN:

The manual for the Wisconsin Card Sorting Test (WCST) provides extended norms and some new research findings for this popular test. The scoring system is unchanged relative to the system proposed by Heaton (1981), though scoring criteria are described in greater detail and illustrated with numerous examples.

The normative sample is composed of 899 normal subjects including 453 children and adolescents. Subjects ranged in age from 6.5 to 89 years. To correct for irregularities in the distribution of scores, continuous norming was used to derive norms for a census-matched sample of the entire normative group. Regression analysis showed a significant quadratic effect for age on all WCST variables. Scores improved with age between ages 6.5 and 19 and then tended to be stable throughout most of adulthood. Performance declines after age 60. Gender was not significantly related to performance.

The WCST yields a number of scores measuring different aspects of problem solving including the efficiency with which hypotheses are generated and tested and the extent to which defective strategies are abandoned and revised. The advantage of these various scores is that it enables the examiner to determine more specifically the nature of executive deficits. The disadvantage is that it makes for a complex scoring system. The test is time-consuming to score and would take practice to master. Studies are cited indicating acceptable levels for inter- and intrascorer reliability estimates.

Reliability was further evaluated through a study design based on Cronbach's generalizability theory (Cronbach, Glaser, Nanda, & Rajaratnam, 1972). Subjects were 46 children and adolescents tested twice over the span of a month. Based on a single test administration, generalizability coefficients ranged from .39 to .72, with a mean of .57 and median of .60. Previous authors had suggested that coefficients of .60 or better are considered good. Using this criteria, most of the WCST scores showed good reliability evidence. Scores for the Percent Perseverative Responses and Percent Perseverative Errors had lower reliability estimates. Standard errors of measurement are provided for most WCST scores, but only for this subsample.

There seems to be ample evidence that the WCST scores are valid measures of executive abilities and provide a sensitive measure of brain dysfunction. Defective WCST performance has been observed in organic disorders characterized by executive dysfunction, such as schizophrenia and Parkinson's disease. Poor WCST performance has also been reported in children with Attention Deficit Disorder.

Accordingly, the WCST has come to be regarded as a frontal lobe test and has been used as such in the context of neuropsychological evaluations. But given the complexities of the task, it is unclear whether it is selectively sensitive to frontal lobe disease. In this regard the literature is mixed. In one of the earliest neuropsychological studies, Milner (1963) reported significantly lower card sort performance in epilepsy patients with focal frontal lobe disease. Since then, some studies have confirmed these results (Heaton, 1981) and others have refuted them (Anderson, Damasio, Jones, & Tranel, 1991; Grafman, Jones, & Salazar, 1990). The authors caution against using the WCST in isolation to diagnose frontal lobe dysfunction.

In reaching decisions about focal brain disease, the WCST should be used in conjunction with other neuropsychological measures and clinical observations. Because the ecological validity of scores from the test has not been established, it is not possible to predict the kinds of problems low scorers are apt to have in the real world. Further studies are needed to determine the effects of practice on test performance, as neuropsychological measures are commonly given repeatedly in assessing conditions that may be progressive or reversible.

The WCST is one of only a small handful of executive tests. Of these it is one of the best normed and most extensively researched measures. It can be used with both children and adults. These factors, combined with good reliability and acceptable validity, make it one of the best executive measures available. Despite its imperfect specificity as a frontal lobe test, it has a well-deserved place in the neuropsychological battery.

REVIEWER'S REFERENCES

Milner, B. (1963). Effects of different brain lesions on card sorting. *Archives of Neurology, 9,* 90–100.
Cronbach, L. J., Gleser, G. C., Nanda, H., & Rajaratnam, N. (1972). *The dependability of behavioral measurements.* New York: Wiley.
Heaton, R. K. (1981). *A manual for the Wisconsin Card Sorting Test.* Odessa, FL: Psychological Assessment Resources.
Grafman, J., Jones, B., & Salazar, A. (1990). Wisconsin Card Sorting Test performance based on location and size of neuroanatomical lesion in Vietnam veterans with penetrating head injury. *Perceptual and Motor Skills, 71,* 1120–1122.
Anderson, S. W., Damasio, H., Jones, R. D., & Tranel, D. (1991). Wisconsin Card Sorting Test performance as a measure of frontal lobe damage. *Journal of Clinical and Experimental Neuropsychology, 13,* 909–922.

[421]
Wonderlic Personnel Test and Scholastic Level Exam.

Purpose: Designed to be used by businesses and schools to measure general cognitive ability in order to determine "how easily individuals can be trained, how well they can adjust and solve problems on the job, and how well satisfied they are likely to be with the demands of the job."

Population: Ages 15 and up.

Publication Dates: 1937–1998.

Acronym: WPS and SLE.

Scores: Total score only.

Administration: Individual or group.

Forms: 6 alternate forms of the WPT, and 4 alternate forms of the SLE.

Price Data, 2000: $1.80 per test.

Foreign Language and Special Editions: Canadian, Swedish, French, Spanish, Tagalog, Vietnamese, German, Chinese, Portuguese, Japanese, Korean, Russian, large print, Braille, and audio editions.

Time: 12 minutes.

Comments: Computer-administered version available; alternate forms exist to reduce risk of retesting with identical form.
Author: Charles Wonderlic.
Publisher: Wonderlic, Inc.
Cross References: See T5:2899 (20 references) and T4:2972 (11 references); for a review by Marcia J. Belcher of an earlier edition, see 11:475 (10 references); for reviews by Frank L. Schmidt and Lyle F. Schoenfeldt, see 9:1385 (8 references); see also T3:2638 (24 references), and T2:482 (10 references); for reviews by Robert C. Droege and John P. Foley, Jr., see 7:401 (28 references); for reviews by N. M. Downie and Marvin D. Dunnette, see 6:513 (17 references); see also 5:400 (59 references); for reviews by H. E. Brogden, Charles D. Flory, and Irving Lorge, see 3:269 (7 references); see also 2:1415 (2 references).

Review of the Wonderlic Personnel Test and Scholastic Level Exam by KURT F. GEISINGER, Professor of Psychology and Academic Vice President, Le Moyne College, Syracuse, NY:

Various forms of essentially the same test are known as the Wonderlic Personnel Test (WPT) and the Scholastic Level Exam. The WPT in particular has a long history of use in employment settings, both personnel offices of companies and employment agencies. It was originally adapted from the Otis Self-Administering Tests of Mental Ability in 1938. It is not clear the extent to which the Scholastic Level Exam has gained usage in education, although it is employed by educational institutions to determine eligibility for federal financial aid and under the "opportunity to learn"/"ability to benefit" criterion. Both employment and educational forms are essentially brief tests of general intelligence/general cognitive ability. The tests are composed of 50 multiple-choice or short-answer questions that are administered in 12 minutes. The test is rather highly speeded. Although it is also now available in a computer-administered version, it is primarily administered in a two-page, bifold test format. A test taker places one's name and certain demographic information on the cover of the test, opens the test, and all 50 items are in the interior of this two-page instrument. The test has been faulted previously for small print and it continues to suffer from this problem, except in the computerized version. Although the test is called self-administering, it is clear that its administration needs to be proctored, for both cheating and test security reasons. An individual's test score is simply the number of correct answers with no correction for guessing.

Until the use of the WPT was challenged in several highly visible court cases (Griggs vs. Duke Power, Albermarle vs. Moody), it enjoyed wide industrial use in making hiring decisions. It is very brief, its administration does not require a trained examiner, and it can be easily scored by the use of a key. Certainly, the above aspects are some of the reasons for its popularity and longevity.

The test is intended as a general measure of intelligence, although that word is infrequently used in the manual. There are a variety of items present in the instrument: vocabulary, sentence rearrangement, sentence parallelism, number series, analysis of geometric figures, logic, arithmetic problem-solving, and interpretation of proverbs, for example. The manual states that the items are written at a sixth-grade reading level and that little specific knowledge is needed: basic math, how to tell time, the days of the week, months of the year, U.S. monetary units, measures and weights. Although the manual reports that the test does not measure achievement per se, obviously substantial general knowledge is involved, including vocabulary and other aspects of developed abilities; some aspects, such as the interpretation of proverbs, appear surprisingly culturally loaded. The items are arranged by their level of difficulty, with the easiest items falling at the beginning of the test.

Most tests of general mental ability involve both speed and power. Speed is clearly more important on the WPT than it is on most tests of this type. Murphy (1984) addressed the speededness factor on this test and its impact on specific candidates. Few candidates (less than 1%) generally even attempt the last 10 items on the test. The speededness of the instrument is likely to affect adversely those who are older, who have various kinds of disabilities, and those for whom English (or whatever language the instrument in which the test is administered) is not their primary language. Only if significant speededness on a job or in an educational experience is critical, does this fairly extreme level of speededness make sense. The manual provides score adjustments for age due to the speededness. For example, it is recommended that those between 40 and 49 years old receive two raw score points added to their score to balance the speededness factor. One other adjustment is provided for other factors that might influence a test taker's ability to take the test quickly; the manual states that if a test taker answers many questions correctly given a limited number of items attempted, a "misassessment" may be diagnosed. To rectify this problem, another form of the WPT may be given in an untimed fashion, with 6 points subtracted from the resulting score. No justification for this computation is provided.

There are at least 10 forms of the WPT, including four identified as Scholastic Level Exam forms. In addition, large-print, Braille, and audiotape forms of the test are available for individuals with disabilities.

ANALYTIC INFORMATION. Because of the extensive history and use of this instrument, the validation and related data supporting its use is voluminous. Predictive validity coefficients are provided for a number of job families (e.g., supervisory positions) and these coefficients are in the range of .22–.67. In addition, the construct validity of the instrument is also nicely addressed; its correlations with instruments such as the WAIS Full Scale IQ and the General Aptitude Test Battery's "Aptitude G" (for general mental ability or intelligence) are high—in the range of .70–.92. (Corrections of various types have undoubtedly been applied to the above correlation coefficients.) Although there may be a selection bias due to the fact that most of the studies cited were published, such indices indeed suggest that the instrument is a reasonably valid test of general developed ability, especially given its short length. Given the relatively unsophisticated users of the measure, however, this reviewer nevertheless questions the inclusion in the manual of a table that permits one to convert WPT scores to WAIS IQ scores. A caution relates to what is apparently at least a moderate correlation between scores on this measure and educational level. Tables in the test manual document the substantial relationship between average test scores and education levels; at increasing educational levels, average test scores rise. Although evidence is provided in the manual documenting higher evidence of criterion-related validity for tests like the Wonderlic over educational level, studying the incremental validity of a test such as this one over more easily accessible information is always desirable.

The reliability of the instrument has been likewise subjected to much, generally successful, evaluation. The manual reports test-retest coefficients of .82–.94 and longitudinal coefficients as high as .94, although the times between testings are not provided. The range of alternate-forms reliability coefficients is provided as .73–.95 and the Kuder-Richardson-20 formula is listed as .88 (with no range provided). One must be careful with some of the estimates of test reliability provided in the manual, however, especially because many of the earlier values (and even some of the recent ones) are listed as split-half-type internal consistency coefficients. Split-half reliability coefficients are normally unacceptable for speeded tests because they provide somewhat inaccurate, higher estimates of the reliability of a measure. Communication with the test publisher over this point led to a statement from them that in this analysis, the test was administered in an untimed fashion, and, therefore, the split-half reliability estimate is appropriate. Because the measure is not normally given in an untimed fashion, users should generally not give this estimate of reliability significant interpretive weight. However, the research cited in the manual reports the test as having been administered "under standard conditions," in which case, the coefficients are not appropriate.

A section on test fairness is provided in the manual. It suggests that the test has been found to be fair and appropriate for use in employment settings. Schoenfeldt's (1985) review of the instrument effectively considers these issues, as noted below. One of the norms tables in the user's manual provides mean and median values, respectively, for whites (22.76 and 23), African-Americans (16.20 and 16), and Hispanic-Americans (17.26 and 17). Such differences are likely to yield problems in employment settings that are potentially litigious or where diversity of the workforce is valued.

The normative data afforded in the manual are voluminous and outstanding. Norms are provided for the adult working population, high school graduates, college graduates, by positions applied for, by sex, by age and education, by race/ethnic background, and by test forms. One must be certain, however, that the norms that one is using are current. Some of the norms provided include data that are more dated than would be preferred. Because of differences across some of the test forms, conversion of scores from one form to another may involve adding or subtracting a point or two.

AN EVALUATION OF THIS INSTRUMENT. Because of the large number of forms available, retesting of candidates is relatively easy to accomplish. In many instances, such availability is a significant advantage. Because of its brevity, it has great applicability for research and other settings where estimates of general mental ability are needed.

The importance of general intelligence or general mental ability has been widely considered in the past two decades. Schmidt (1985), one of the strongest proponents of general cognitive ability measures, stated in his review of this measure that "reliable measures of general mental ability such as the WPT are indeed valid in varying degree for predicting performance on all jobs" (p. 1756). He believed all other concerns about the measure were minor. Schoenfeldt (1985) softened Schmidt's conclusions somewhat and stated:

> A major concern potential users would have to consider is the adverse impact this test could have on protected groups. The *Uniform Guidelines on Employee Selection* (Section 3-B) state that 'where two or more selection procedures are available which serve the user's legitimate interest in efficient and trustworthy workmanship ... the user should use the procedure which has been demonstrated to have the lesser adverse impact.' In most situations, the WPT will have greater adverse impact, and thus present problems in the applications for which it is intended. (p. 158).

Several past reviewers of this instrument have had problems with suggested passing scores for different occupations that are provided in the manual. In general, these scores have been set close to the median score of applicants for each occupation. The most recent manual also reports that they have been set using ratings of job complexity taken from the *Dictionary of Occupational Titles:* The more complex the job, the higher the suggested passing score. Although the setting of passing scores on examinations is hardly the most elegant and most empirically based aspect of psychometric science, providing passing scores with such limited information of the specifics of the actual test use is probably not advisable. Murphy (1984) also argued that the test may be too difficult for screening uneducated individuals for unskilled jobs.

Forms of this test are available in 11 languages other than English: Chinese, German, French, Japanese, Korean, Portuguese, Russian, Spanish, Swedish, Tagalog, and Vietnamese. There are also English versions intended for use in Australia and the United Kingdom. The manual only addresses a few issues related to the Spanish translation. Except for the Spanish language version,

little information is provided regarding the quality of these translations, and the translations other than the Spanish adaptation should be used with great caution, preferably in conjunction with local validation studies performed using the specific language form. Extensive norming of the Spanish form has been performed, but a statement in the manual, "it is reasonable to conclude that these forms are indeed equivalent" (p. 44) is perhaps an overstatement in the absence of an appropriate equating study. They do appear to be parallel forms, however. What has been done to establish equivalence is certainly questionable. In that the reliability coefficients, though acceptable, were found to be lower for the Spanish forms—the only forms for which data are provided—it should not be assumed that the forms or the scores resulting from them are comparable (Geisinger, 1994).

Within the past decade, the WPT and the Scholastic Level Exam have become available via computer administration. Two studies have been performed to document the equivalence of both methods of test administration (Equivalence and validity study, 1993; Hensley & Morris, 1992). Such preliminary research does document equivalent scores from both approaches. The authors of the reports also state that individuals, who were students in both instances, preferred the computer administration to paper-and-pencil format. Perhaps not all test takers who are applicants for positions for which the WPT is used would find taking this test on a computer as comfortable as they may have traditionally taken the paper-and-pencil version due to their reduced familiarity with computers. Such reluctance will likely decline over time.

To describe reliability and its impact on test interpretation to readers who may not be technically sophisticated. The manual provides a number of the test translation/adaptation rules that are required for successfully adapting tests from one language to the other. They mention considering differences of directly translated words across languages, for example, and the necessity of evaluating translated items for cultural nuances. From data provided in the manual, however, it is not clear how successful the test authors were in translating versions of this highly successful English language test. Because relatively more work appears to have been performed on the Spanish form, its use is probably appropriate. Use of the other translated forms should be in light of the cautions noted above related both to the lack of detail regarding their development and the apparent absence of validation data.

SUMMARY. Although it is clear that the test can be administered and scored by an individual with little technical knowledge, it is not clear that it can be interpreted by such an individual. Some interpretative material in the manual is overly simplistic. Even though they provide good suggestions in some places (e.g., "All employment tests should be used in conjunction with other job-related qualifications. All test scores should be used with confidentiality," user's manual, p. 2), they also provide tables permitting one to convert scores from the Wonderlic to Full Scale WAIS scores. Clearly, many who could administer and score this instrument are not qualified either to interpret intelligence quotients or to consider the differences between a 12-minute group test and a more clinically appropriate individually administered measure. The instrument should only be considered to produce a very rough estimate of intelligence. More attention to test interpretation for the audience that uses the test in future manuals would be positively received.

REVIEWER'S REFERENCES

Murphy, K. R. (1984). The Wonderlic Personnel test. In D. J. Keyser & R. C. Sweetland (Eds.), *Test critiques: Volume I* (pp. 769–775). Kansas City: Test Corporation of America.

Schmidt, F. L. (1985). [Review of Wonderlic Personnel Test.] In J. V. Mitchell, Jr. (Ed.), *The ninth mental measurements yearbook* (pp. 1755–1757). Lincoln, NE: Buros Institute of Mental Measurements.

Schoenfeldt, L. F. (1985) [Review of Wonderlic Personnel Test.] In J. V. Mitchell, Jr. (Ed.), *The ninth mental measurements yearbook* (pp. 1757–1758). Lincoln, NE: Buros Institute of Mental Measurements.

Hensley, A. C., & Morris, T. R. (1992). *A comparison of computer and paper media in psychological testing* (AFIT/GIR/LSR/92S-22). Master's thesis presented to the faculty of the School of Systems and Logistics of the Air Force Institute of Technology, Air University, Wright-Patterson Air Force Base, Ohio.

Equivalence and validity study for the Scholastic Level Exam—Personal Computer version. Unpublished manuscript.

Geisinger, K. F. (1994). Cross-cultural normative assessment: Translation and adaptation issues influencing the normative interpretation of assessment instruments. *Psychological Assessment, 6,* 304–312.

Review of the Wonderlic Personnel Test and Scholastic Level Exam by GREGORY SCHRAW, Associate Professor of Educational Psychology, University of Nebraska—Lincoln, Lincoln, NE:

The Wonderlic Personnel Test (WPT) and Scholastic Level Exam (SLE) is a norm-referenced test of general cognitive ability used to evaluate new job applicants (WPT) and college students (SLE). The test purports to measure general intelligence, or "g," which provides insight into how easily individuals can be trained and how well they adjust in work and school settings. Thus the Wonderlic measures potential to learn, rather than how well that potential is utilized.

The Wonderlic was first published in 1937. There is no information in the test manual regarding how much the test has changed since its inception, nor is there information about the frequency and scope of periodic revisions. Initial development of the Wonderlic, as well as current interpretation, reflect a strong psychometric orientation typical of Charles Spearman (Spearman, 1923) and, more recently, Arthur Jensen (Jensen, 1980). Both of these theorists presume the existence of "g," a general intelligence factor, that is heritable and unchangeable. More recent theories of intelligence question this monolithic worldview, but especially the work of Robert Sternberg (1988) and Howard Gardner (1983). Sternberg emphasizes changeable adaption skills such as selection and shaping that enable one to improve one's intelligence. In contrast, Gardner emphasizes the role of eight autonomous intelligence "modules" that each perform a specific intellectual function. Both theories question whether a general intellectual factor exists and, if it does, whether it can be measured reliably and validly with a 50-item instrument (see Carroll, 1993, for an extended review). None of these concerns are addressed in the test manual.

There are 12 alternate forms of the WPT and four forms of the SLE. Each version of the Wonderlic test includes 50 items, which must be completed within 12 minutes. Items cover a number of cognitive domains, including number comparisons, number series, analysis of geometric figures, story problems, and word comparisons. These tests closely resemble a cluster of tests identified in the Radex model developed by Marshalek, Lohman, and Snow (1983), which includes the Raven Progressive Matrices Test (Raven, 1962), verbal and geometric analogies, letter and number series, and arithmetic operations. Carpenter, Just, and Shell (1990) provide a detailed analysis of these tests and what they measure.

Both paper-and-pencil and computer forms of the WPT are available. The test is proctored by an expert, though completed entirely by the examinee. Individual and group administrations of the tests are permitted. The manual includes a number of suggestions for optimizing the effectiveness of test sessions. Guidelines for scoring and retesting individuals are included as well.

The final score consists of the number of correct responses. The manual includes information for adjusting the scores of examinees over the age of 29, as well as methods for equating timed and untimed versions of the test. The manual also provides cut scores by job type and occupational domain and guidelines for test interpretation.

Extensive information is available regarding the reliability and validity of the Wonderlic. Reliability has been measured in numerous studies. Test-retest and internal consistency estimates typically approach .90. Evidence of construct and predictive validity are provided as well. Regarding construct validity, the WPT correlates with the WAIS-R (Weschler Adult Intelligence Scale—Revised) in excess of .90 and with the GATB (General Aptitude Test Battery) in excess of .70. In contrast, the WPT is uncorrelated with a wide variety of personality assessment measures. Regarding predictive validity, higher scores on the WPT are related to higher levels of educational and occupational success.

The strengths of the WPT are many: (a) it has a proven 50-year track record, (b) it repeatedly demonstrates a high positive correlation with other measures of intellectual ability such as the WAIS-R, (c) there is ample empirical evidence of sufficient reliability, and (d) the available data support the claim of one underlying general ability factor. Considering the WPT can be administered in 12 minutes, it probably is the best quick-administration instrument available.

But the Wonderlic is not without its weaknesses. One is that it conceptualizes intelligence in a way that is challenged by many contemporary theorists who view intelligence as socially constructed and changeable. The WPT seems to be at odds with this view, but fails to address these highly important issues explicitly. A second concern is the test's length and ease of administration. One wonders whether it is possible to measure a lifetime of intellectual attainment with a 12-minute, 50-item test! The WPT might best be thought of as an approximate benchmark of a person's true intellectual ability. A third concern is that the WPT, and most other ability tests, fail to consider the role of motivation. This is important given experiments that have shown that students' beliefs about their intelligence are better predictors of classroom behavior than measured intelligence itself (Dweck & Leggett, 1988).

SUMMARY. Overall, the WPT appears to be a good measure of general ability that approximates true intellectual ability. Important decisions regarding a student's educational or occupational future should be based on multiple measures that incorporate detailed assessments of multiple abilities. If one relies solely on the WPT, its results should be used to make large-grain rather than fine-grain decisions.

REVIEWER'S REFERENCES

Spearman, C. (1923). *The nature of intelligence and the principles of cognition.* London: McMillan.
Raven, J. C. (1962). Advanced Progressive Matrices, Set II. London: H. K. Lewis. (Distributed in the United States by the Psychological Corporation, San Antonio, Texas)
Jensen, A. R. (1980). *Bias in mental testing.* New York: Free Press.
Gardner, H. (1983). *Frames of mind: The theory of multiple intelligences.* New York: Basic Books.
Marshalek, B., Lohman, D. F., & Snow, R. E. (1983). The complexity continuum in the radex and hierarchical models of intelligence. *Intelligence, 7,* 107–127.
Dweck, C. S., & Leggett, E. S. (1988). A social-cognitive approach to motivation and personality. *Psychological Review, 95,* 256–273.
Sternberg, R. J. (1988). *The triarchic mind: A new theory of human intelligence.* New York: Penguin Books.
Carpenter, P. A., Just, M. A., & Shell, P. (1990). What one intelligence test measures: A theoretical account of the processing in the Raven Progressive Matrices Test. *Psychological Review, 97,* 404–431.
Brody, N. (1992). *Intelligence* (2nd ed.). San Diego: Academic Press.
Carroll, J. B. (1993). *Human cognitive abilities: A survey of factor-analytic studies.* Cambridge, England: Cambridge University Press.

[422]
Woodcock Diagnostic Reading Battery.

Purpose: "Provides a diagnostic test that assesses reading achievement and important related abilities."
Population: Ages 4–95.
Publication Date: 1997.
Acronym: WDRB.
Scores, 17: Letter-Word Identification, Word Attack, Reading Vocabulary, Passive Comprehension, Incomplete Words, Sound Blending, Oral Vocabulary, Listening Comprehension, Memory for Sentences, Visual Matching, Total Reading, Broad Reading, Basic Reading Skills, Reading Comprehension, Phonological Awareness, Oral Comprehension, Reading Aptitude.
Administration: Individual.
Price Data, 1999: $273 per complete kit; $37 per 25 recording forms; $45 per examiner's manual (152 pages); $40 per norms manual (161 pages); $175 per scoring and interpretation program (Windows or Macintosh).
Time: (60) minutes; (20–25) minutes for four reading achievement tests only.
Comments: Battery comprises selected tests from the Woodcock-Johnson Psycho-Educational Battery—Revised (T5:2901); for educational, clinical, or research purposes; optional to use any combination of the subtests that are relevant to individual subjects.
Author: Richard W. Woodcock.
Publisher: The Riverside Publishing Company.

Review of the Woodcock Diagnostic Reading Battery by D. JOE OLMI, Associate Professor, Department of Psychology, The University of Southern Mississippi, Hattiesburg, MS:

The Woodcock Diagnostic Reading Battery (WDRB) is a selection of several tests from parts of the Woodcock-Johnson Psycho-Educational Battery—Revised (WJ-R; T5:2901; Tests of Achievement and Tests of Cognitive Ability; Standard and Supplemental Batteries). Four (Reading) tests were selected from the Tests of Achievement (Letter-Word Identification, Word Attack, Passage Comprehension, and Reading Vocabulary) and six (Related Abilities Tests) from the Tests of Cognitive Ability (Incomplete Words, Sound Blending, Memory for Sentences, Oral Vocabulary, Visual Matching, and Listening Comprehension). The WDRB is designed to assess reading-related areas including Total Reading (Broad Reading, Basic Reading Skills, and Reading Comprehension), Phonological Awareness, Oral Comprehension, and Reading Aptitude in individuals from ages 4 through 90+. The test kit contains an easel test book, an examiner's manual, a manual of norm tables, test records, and an audio test tape. There exists a computer-scoring and report-writing program (Scoring and Interpretive Program for the Woodcock Diagnostic Reading Battery) for the WDRB, but it was not made available for this review. One is likely to be very familiar with the WDRB's predecessor, the WJ-R. For Cumming's (1995) and Lee and Stefany's (1995) extensive reviews of the WJ-R, refer to the *Twelfth Mental Measurements Yearbook*.

The WDRB is described as "a comprehensive set of individually administered tests that measures important dimensions of reading achievement and closely related abilities" (p. 1). Although the reading tests are designed to assess aspects of reading, the related abilities tests are predicated on the Horn-Cattell Gf-Gc theory of intellectual processing. Similar to its predecessor, the WDRB is not designed to be administered in its entirety, but rather the user should determine which tests are applicable to the referral question(s) and select accordingly. Administration of all 10 tests of the WDRB should take approximately 60 minutes, but administration of the reading tests of the battery should take approximately 20–25 minutes. The easel format of the WDRB is essentially the same as that of the WJ-R, thereby making administration easy for anyone familiar with the format.

The test record is a direct descendant of the test records of the WJ-R in appearance and raw score conversion. W scores, standard errors of measurement, age equivalents, grade equivalents, test or cluster difference scores, relative proficiency indexes, (extended) standard scores, and percentile ranks are derived from the raw score conversion. The examiner is advised to calculate only the derived scores necessary for the examiner's intended purposes. It is not necessary to calculate all transformations of the raw score. As with the WJ-R, the hand scoring of a protocol can be a daunting task for the novice examiner. Much practice is needed to become proficient in managing the manipulation of the norm tables and scoring the protocol, so as to reduce the potential for error. One is well advised to purchase the computer-scoring package. If it is similar to the scoring package for the WJ-R, it is well worth the cost.

Examiner qualifications require base knowledge of psychometrics and appropriate training in administration and interpretation of the battery. An examiner training sequence and training materials are contained in the examiner's manual and should be beneficial to those who are unfamiliar with the testing procedures and the protocol of the WDRB or the WJ-R.

Normative data were derived from a sample of 6,026 individuals ranging from ages 4 to 95 who were administered all tests, although normative tables begin for children 2 years of age. Subjects included preschoolers not enrolled in kindergarten, a K–12 school-aged sample, a college/university sample, and an adult nonschool sample 14 to over 90 years of age. Normative data were gathered from subjects from the "100 geographically diverse communities obtained during the standardization of the WJ-R" (p. 57) and prescribed to match as closely as possible data from the 1980 U.S. Census. Sampling variables included region of U.S., community size, gender, race, Hispanic versus non-Hispanic, public versus private funding of college/university, education level of adults, occupational or employment status of adults, and occupation of adults. Continuous-year norming procedures were employed, and data were gathered from September 1986 to August 1988.

Psychometric support is more than adequate with internal consistency reliability coefficients ranging from .78 to .94 for all tests in the battery. The average median internal consistency reliability coefficient for the achievement tests was .92, and the average median coefficient for the cognitive tests was .84. Reliabilities were consistently in the mid-.90s for the clusters (ranging from .90 for phonological awareness to .98 for total reading).

Limited information is presented in the manual regarding content validity of items of the WDRB, other than item selection based on "item validity studies as well as expert opinion" (p. 66). However, the author provides references to other sources for more information about content validity. Concurrent validity evidence using correlations of the WDRB areas and the Peabody Individual Achievement Test (PIAT) total reading score ranged from .45 for Phonological Awareness and .88 for Basic Reading Skills. Correlations ranged from .53 for Phonological Awareness to .75 for Oral Vocabulary and Reading Aptitude when compared to the Wechsler Intelligence Scale for Children—Revised. Additional validity data are available comparing the WDRB to the BASIS, the Kaufman Assessment Battery for Children, the Kaufman Test of Educational Achievement, the PIAT, the Wide Range Achievement Test, the Stanford-Binet Intelligence Test—Fourth Edition, the Mini-Battery of Achievement, and the WJ-R (Cognitive Ability). Intercorrelations among tests of the WDRB and cluster intercorrelations provide support for construct validity of the instrument.

SUMMARY. In conclusion, the WDRB appears as a "marketing spinoff" of the WJ-R with limited rationale for use by the author or publisher. This reviewer can hardly generate a reason for its use in light of access to the WJ-R. Although the WDRB can provide useful information, has a sound psychometric foundation, and is rather easy to administer, use of the WJ-R is advised and would likely occur in day-to-day assessment situations.

REVIEWER'S REFERENCES

Cummings, J. A. (1995). [Review of the Woodcock-Johnson Psycho-Educational Battery—Revised]. In J. C. Conoley & J. C. Impara (Eds.), *The twelfth mental measurements yearbook* (pp. 1113–1116). Lincoln, NE: Buros Institute of Mental Measurements.
Lee, S. W., & Stefany, E. F. (1995). [Review of the Woodcock-Johnson Psycho-Educational Battery—Revised]. In J. C. Conoley & J. C. Impara (Eds.), *The twelfth mental measurements yearbook* (pp. 1116–1117). Lincoln, NE: Buros Institute of Mental Measurements.

Review of the Woodcock Diagnostic Reading Battery by HERBERT C. RUDMAN, Professor Emeritus of Measurement and Quantitative Methods, Michigan State University, East Lansing, MI:

The Woodcock Diagnostic Reading Battery (WDRB) is in one sense, a new, clinically administered diagnostic tool, and in another sense it is a specialized application of several other versions of the Woodcock-Johnson Psycho-Educational Battery—Revised (WJ-R; T5:2901). The present WJ-R was first published in 1977 and underwent major revisions in 1989 and 1990. The latest revision of the Woodcock-Johnson Psycho-Educational Battery—Revised consists of two major components: The Woodcock-Johnson Tests of Cognitive Ability (WJ-R COG) and the Woodcock-Johnson Tests of Achievement (WJ-R ACH). The latter test, the WJ-R ACH, consists of two parallel forms, A and B. The WDRB is the latest addition to the family of tests developed by the authors of the series.

The Woodcock-Johnson Diagnostic Reading Battery (WDRB) consists of 10 tests, all of which are available in the Woodcock-Johnson Psycho-Educational Battery—Revised. Because these tests were distributed among four different test books of the WJ-R, it became difficult for reading specialists to locate and use the full range of tests needed in their work with students and other clients. The solution was to develop the WDRB by including the 10 tests that were available in the Woodcock-Johnson Psycho-Educational Battery—Revised, but focused on the diagnosis of reading and listening skills.

TEST CONTENT OF THE WDRB. The subtests of the Woodcock-Johnson Diagnostic Reading Battery consist of Letter-Word Identification, Word Attack, Reading Vocabulary, Passage Comprehension, Incomplete Words, Sound Blending, Oral Vocabulary, Listening Comprehension, Memory for Sentences, and Visual Matching. These 10 subtests can be combined into seven clusters of achievement in reading abilities and aptitudes: Total Reading Clusters, Broad Reading Cluster, Basic Reading Skills Cluster, Reading Comprehension Cluster, Phonological Awareness Cluster, Oral Comprehension Cluster, and Reading Aptitude Cluster.

TEST COMPONENTS OF THE WDRB. The diagnostic reading battery consists of several components: an easel test book, an examiner's manual, a norms manual, a test record, and an audio tape used to administer four of the subtests dealing with Incomplete Words, Sound Blending, Listening Comprehension, and Memory for Sentences.

Although one could argue that the WDRB and the WJ-R seem to be clones of each other, those who have used both batteries could attest that the distillation of the WJ-R into the WDRB improves the uses made of the latter. This reviewer believes that what the authors have done is to make a portion of the WJ-R more useful to those who need a comprehensive tool for diagnosing strengths and weaknesses in reading that will help focus on the treatment of reading, which undergirds so much of the formal education of students.

As noted earlier, the WDRB contains 10 tests, which can be found in their entirety in the WJ-R. But the WJ-R also contains tests of other program areas not found in the WDRB (e.g., Calculation, Applied Problems, Science, Social Studies, Humanities, Spelling, Handwriting, and the like). Because the internal structures of the two batteries are similar, the absence of these curricular areas also includes the absence of Broad Mathematics, and Broad Mathematics Skills. When one compares the uses of the WDRB and its family member the WJ-R, as described in the manuals accompanying them, the similarity of the two batteries is remarkably the same. Both identify their uses as diagnosis, determination of an aptitude/achievement discrepancy in reading (or in the case of the WJ-R, psychoeducational discrepancies), planning individual programs, guidance, assessing growth, research, and psychometric training. The more this reviewer reads the manuals accompanying the WDRB and the WJ-R, the more he sees the "cloning" of the two tests. Detailed descriptions of how these two tests can be used are strikingly the same. In fact, the two descriptions of use are mainly "boiler plate" (common text). Manuals written for group-administered achievement test batteries that cover multiple grade levels utilize much the same type of "boiler plate" descriptions. The common text, the common norm data, and the common internal organization used in the examiner's manuals shared emphasize that the WDRB is a condensed version of the WJ-R, and more useful to those who are reading specialists and researchers.

NORM DEVELOPMENT. The examiner's manual accompanying the WDRB states that "Normative data for the WDRB are a subset of the data gathered from subjects in over 100 geographically diverse U.S. communities obtained during the standardization of the WJ-R" (p. 57).

The total norm population for the WDRB was 6,026. Of this number, a preschool sample of ages 4 to 5 years (not enrolled in kindergarten) contained 372 subjects, a kindergarten through 12th grade sample contained 3,245 students, a college/university sample consisted of 916 students, and the adult nonschool sample (age 14 to more than 90 years of age and not enrolled in high school or college) consisted of 1,493 subjects.

Given the nature of the wide range of age characteristics, the authors wisely chose to use continuous-year norms. These norms include age and grade equivalents, percentile ranks, and standard scores. Norm data for the school-age sample were gathered continuously from September 1986 to April 1988. Higher education data were collected from September 1987 to March 1988. The adult nonschool norms were collected from January 1987 to August 1988. This approach to norms differs from many group-administered standardized achievement tests that are based on data gathered at Fall, Winter, and Spring points in the school year and interpolated for intermediate times.

These samples were selected within a stratified random research design. Ten specific community and subject variables compared within the design matrix reflected 1980 census data, supplemented by "later data."

The 10 sampling variables included Census Region, Community Size, Gender, Race, Hispanic/Non-Hispanic, Funding Sources of College/University, Type of College/University, Education Level Reached by Adults, Occupational Status of Adults, and Occupation of Adults. The author weighted the variables and compared them to the characteristics of the U.S. population. This yielded a close approximation to the national distribution.

VALIDITY. The WDRB's validity is discussed through an analysis of content, concurrent (or criterion-related), and construct validity. Item analysis research is commonly described in manuals that accompany achievement and other cognitively oriented standardized tests. Item analysis studies are an important source of data used to justify a claim for content validity. There is a generalized discussion of content validity in the examiner's manual accompanying the WDRB. The authors acknowledge that "Content validity is the extent to which the content of a test represents the domain that it is designed to measure" (p. 65). This important observation is not addressed, however, with specific information about the domains and the items that sample them. How was item content determined? Was it through an analysis of instructional materials used in the schools at the appropriate grade levels? It is clear, from the metrics used for interpreting test results, that the author of these tests was sensitive to school-related contexts given the grade-equivalent scores used.

The reader of the examiner's manual is referred to Chapter 2 for more extensive information about the content of the WDRB. Each of the 10 subtests are listed along with descriptions of the reading functions addressed but these descriptions do not contain information about the sources from which the items were drawn. What this reviewer would have appreciated, in addition to these descriptions, would have been quantitative data that indicated the difficulties of the items rather than the range of reliability indices that were given. Reliability data indicate the consistency of responses to the items, but not their difficulty.

The examiner's manual (again in general terms) describes the selection of items through "validity studies as well as expert opinion" (p. 66). Who served as experts? What qualifications did they possess? Was "expert" opinion interpreted to also mean the written standards of learned societies? No specific information is given.

Concurrent (or criterion-related) validity is expressed more specifically than is content validity. Detailed studies for grades 3, 3/4, and 10/11 are given across several criterion measures, and correlation coefficients are used to indicate the relationship between the WDRB and other clinically administered standardized tests (e.g., the Stanford-Binet Intelligence Scale—Fourth Edition, Peabody Individual Achievement Test (PIA), the Wechsler Intelligence Scale for Children—Revised (WISC-R), and the WJ-R.

The author is to be commended for the clarity of the tables used to document the concurrent validity of the WDRB. The author calls attention to the WDRB's Broad Reading correlation with the criterion measures that were used for comparison purposes. The coefficients ranged from .43 to .91. The author states "A review of the correlations across the three age groups provides strong support for the concurrent validity of the WDRB Broad Reading score" (p. 68). This reviewer respectfully disagrees with that statement. Most of the correlations between the WDRB and the criterion measures fall below what might be considered as acceptable levels of predictive indices of an individual's test performance (rs range from .26 to .97).

Construct validity evidence is expressed primarily as cluster intercorrelation coefficients. As noted earlier in this review, there is a strong similarity among the Woodcock family of tests. A review of one family test member, good or bad, can usually be found in another Woodcock test as well. This concept of a core test that serves as a template for other tests can be very useful but also counterproductive. There are strong points to this system of test development but also dangers of repeating weaknesses found by external reviewers over a long period of time. For example, one reviewer of the Woodcock Language Proficiency Battery—Revised (WLPB-R) made this observation of the use of criterion measures to establish concurrent validity of the WLPB-R: "Regretfully, the samples used were very small (less than 100). I would be remiss if I did not compliment Woodcock for drawing the user's attention to the above average restricted range of the $3^{rd}/4^{th}$ and $10^{th}/11^{th}$ grade samples noting that generalizations to a more representative population should be made with caution … even with this caveat, the very low intercorrelations could not be increased to a respectable range" (Lehmann, 1995).

RELIABILITY. Reliability of the subtests in the WDRB has been estimated through internal consistency procedures as well as by test-retest techniques. Internal consistency is estimated by split-half procedures and corrected for length through the use of the Spearman-Brown formula. Length of the test has a bearing on reliability, as does the interval between testing sessions. Estimates of reliability differ depending upon the sources of error considered. The interweaving of tests, as discussed earlier in this review, using norms that are 10 years old makes one cautious about interpreting the reliability estimates of the 10 subtests of the WDRB. However, the author describes a repeated measures study of the WJ-R. "The study was designed to allow a systematic accounting of the components of test reliability, test stability, trait change and trait stability … based on a sample of 504 subjects age 5 to 95 years, who were readministered the norming version of the WJ-R at a widely different sampling of times between tests. … Several of the tests are components of the WDRB" (p. 64).

A surprising picture of the stability of traits estimated over time was shown by this study. An analysis of internal consistency, test stability, trait stability, and test-retest variance help mitigate for this reviewer skepticism about the "template" approach that Woodcock and his colleagues have taken since 1977. The most stable traits noted were Letter-Word Identification (.936) and Passage Comprehension (.909). The traits estimated to have the greatest fluctuation in scores were Listening Comprehension (.778) and Incomplete Words (.787).

SCORING AIDS FOR THE WDRB. A recent addition to the Woodcock Diagnostic Reading Battery is a computer program that can be used to generate test scores and narrative reports that are remarkable for their comprehensiveness and detail. The Scoring and Interpretive Program can be used with several other related tests in the Woodcock family of tests. It was designed for use with the Woodcock Diagnostic Reading Battery, but can also be used with the corresponding reading ability and reading achievement tests from the WJ-R and the Spanish version, Bateriá Woodcock-Muñoz—Revisada (T5:264).

The computer program can generate four reports: (a) a data report for the individual including name, gender, date of testing, birthdate (which automatically generates age of the individual in years and months), raw scores on the 10 tests of the WDRB, behavioral observations during testing, and name of the examiner; (b) a table of scores with derived scores that are norm-based for either chronological age or grade equivalent, cluster data, discrepancy scores in aptitude and achievement, and other statistical data; (c) a detailed and comprehensive computer-generated narrative report that describes the tests administered to the individual (described by name), reading achievement, aptitude/achievement discrepancies, contributing factors to the individual's achievement based on cluster scores, as well as the likelihood of future reading performance, and (d) a summary report.

The narrative reports are remarkably smooth and do not read as most computer generated narratives normally do. After working with the Scoring and Interpretive Program for the WDRB, I would recommend this program to all users of the WDRB who have experience working with PCs and a Microsoft platform, versions 3.1 or Windows95.

SUMMARY. The Woodcock series has come a long way in the company of other clinically administered measures. It has its faults, as I have indicated in this review, but it also has its strengths. It has developed into a high-quality instrument and its authors have shown sensitivity to its users and those who have reviewed the various test batteries comprising the series. I would recommend the Woodcock Diagnostic Reading Battery for its psychometric qualities and its sensitivity to reading diagnosti-

cians and other specialists. I would, especially, recommend that the Scoring and Interpretive program for the WDRB be used over the hand-scoring method—a method that is complicated, complex, and prone to clerical errors.

REVIEWER'S REFERENCE

Lehmann, I. J. (1995). [Review of the Woodcock Language Proficiency Battery]. In J. C. Conoley & J. C. Impara (Eds.), *The twelfth mental measurements yearbook* (pp. 1118–1119). Lincoln, NE: Buros Institute of Mental Measurements.

[423]
Woodcock Reading Mastery Tests—Revised [1998 Normative Update].

Purpose: To measure "several important aspects of reading ability."

Population: Kindergarten through adult.

Publication Dates: 1973–1998.

Scores, 11: Readiness Cluster (Visual-Auditory Learning, Letter Identification, Total), Basic Skills Cluster (Word Identification, Word Attack, Total), Reading Comprehension Cluster (Word Comprehension, Passage Comprehension, Total), Total Reading—Full Scale, Total Reading—Short Scale, plus a Supplementary Letter Checklist.

Administration: Individual.

Forms, 2: G, H (includes Reading Achievement tests only).

Price Data, 1999: $314.95 per Form G and Form H combined kit including Form G and Form H test books, 25 each of test records, sample Form G & H summary record form, pronunciation guide cassette, sample report to parents, and examiner's manual ('98, 214 pages); $234.95 per Form G complete kit including materials in combined kit for Form G only; $229.95 per Form H complete kit including materials in combined kit for Form H only; $39.95 per 25 test records (specify Form G or Form H); $23.95 per 25 Form G and H summary record forms; $19.95 per 25 reports to parents; $199.95 per ASSIST scoring software (specify IBM PC/XT/AT, PS/2, and compatibles of Apple IIc, enhanced IIe, and IIGS).

Time: (40–45) minutes for entire battery; (15) minutes for Short Scale.

Comments: Test same as 1987 edition but with 1998 norms for grades K–12 and ages 5–22.

Author: Richard W. Woodcock.

Publisher: American Guidance Service, Inc.

Cross References: See T5:2905 (123 references) and T4:2976 (34 references); for reviews by Robert B. Cooter, Jr. and Richard M. Jaeger, see 10:391 (38 references); see also T3:2641 (17 references); for reviews by Carol Anne Dwyer and J. Jaap Tuinman, and excerpted reviews by Alex Bannatyne, Richard L. Allington, Cherry Houck (with Larry A. Harris), and Barton B. Proger of the 1973 edition, see 8:779 (7 references).

Review of the Woodcock Reading Mastery Tests—Revised [1998 Normative Update] by LINDA CROCKER, Associate Dean, College of Education, University of Florida, Gainesville, FL:

The Woodcock Reading Mastery Tests-Revised [1998 Normative Update] (NU) Edition (WRMT-R) differs from the 1987 edition only in updated norms. These were derived from a new data collection design implemented in 1995–1996. Because the revised test has been previously reviewed (Cooter, 1989; Jaeger, 1989), this commentary is restricted to the normative update.

The norming study involved a nationwide sample of over 3,000 examinees from 129 sites in 40 states. Examinees were students in Grades K–12 or young adults, stratified by gender, race, parental education, and geographic region to reflect U.S. demographic distributions. The numbers at each grade level ranged from 204–295 from Grades 12–K, respectively. This posed a challenge to the developers' goal of maintaining nationally representative samples at each grade level. For example, 22.7% of the 4th graders were from the Northeast, but only 4.1% of the 9th graders resided in that area. Similarly, at 10th grade, the sample was 11.1% African American and 12.4% Hispanic; but at 6th grade, 18.5% African American and 9.7% Hispanic. Students were included from gifted (2.3%) and special education classes (10.8%), but their distribution across grade levels is not specified. In addition, the proportions tested in fall and spring varied over grade level and demographic subgroup. Finally, as noted below, different groups of examinees took different subtests, and the number of cases taking the subtests varied.

The norming study design was complex. Four different individually administered achievement batteries developed by different authors were taken by overlapping samples. Five broad achievement domains were covered to some degree by these batteries: word reading, reading comprehension, mathematics computation, mathematics applications, and spelling. Only three subtests of the WRMT-R matched any of these domains: Passage Comprehension (matched to the domain of reading comprehension) and Letter Identification and Word Identification (matched to the word-reading domain). Each examinee in the norm sample took at least one complete test battery plus at least one subtest from another battery. Approximately one-fifth of the norm sample took the WRMT-R as an intact battery.

Examinee ability scores on Letter Identification, Word Identification, and Passage Comprehension were estimated for over 2,000 examinees on a common ability scale for all batteries using a single Rasch linking and scaling, employing the BIGSTEPS program (Linacre & Wright, 1994). Linking samples were used to scale the item difficulties from various subtests in a domain to a common scale. Every examinee who took a subtest in that domain received an estimated ability score for the domain. Examinee scores on the Letter Identification, Word-Identification, and Passage Comprehension subtests were converted to domain scores, prior to conversion to various norm scores. The numbers of examinees in the linking samples varied and were less than the overall norming sample (e.g., 378 for word reading and 96 for reading comprehension). Separate norms for the Visual-Auditory Learning, Word Attack, and Word Comprehension subtests were established using raw scores, because these subtests did not match the cross-battery domain. The normative samples for these tests were $n = 1,309$, 751, and 721 cases, respectively.

Norm tables are provided to convert raw scores into W scores, grade-equivalents, and age-equivalents. The 10th, 50th, and 90th percentile points were estimated empirically. The percentile rank points at the other intervals were extrapolated. Percentile ranks and standard scores were based on the discrepancy between the examinee's score and the median value of the reference group at intervals of one-tenth of a year for Grades K–16.9, or to the month for ages 5-0 to 18-11. After age 19, one-year intervals were used. A W-value of 500 represents a score at the median at the beginning of Grade 5 in the new reference group. It is commendable that *SEM* values are reported for multiple score scale points. The case studies provided in the manual as aids to score interpretation have not changed from the previous version reviewed, but are helpful guides.

Comparison of performance on the previous and current norms suggests that, for most grade levels, students in the below-average range earn a higher percentile and a standard score on the NU norm than would be obtained by converting the equivalent raw score to those scales using norm tables of the previous edition. For example, a student who scored at the 40th percentile, using the old norm, could actually answer fewer items correctly in retesting with the same test, but remain at the 40th percentile rank, using the new norms. This should give users pause in testing situations where the WRMT-R is used for re-assessment of students in special programs.

Validity data in the form of correlations to other external measures and split-half reliability estimates are from the previous normative scores, not for the current norm sample. Extrapolating these data to support use of present scores seems risky. Another validity issue has been created by the norming/equating design itself. The calibration of item and ability estimates from a collection of assorted subtests from different batteries, based on the assumption of a single underlying trait or ability for broader achievement domains, operationally defined by multiple tests, raises questions about the essence of the trait being assessed. Obviously, traditional approaches to establish content representation aspects of validity by inspection of test content from a single battery would no longer be applicable. This raises the questions of whether these scores represent a more general performance domain than is inferred from examination of these test items or whether this trait is readily amenable to specific curricular or instructional intervention.

SUMMARY. Adequacy of test norms is typically evaluated on characteristics such as recency, representativeness, relevance, and clarity of interpretive materials. The WRMT-R (NU) edition should receive "high marks" for recency and clarity. With respect to representativeness and relevance, however, users should exercise due caution and critical judgment in terms of test fit to their local populations and content domains of interest. In attempting to economize by using the same norm-study participants for multiple batteries, the developers have introduced issues of context effects as well as serious scaling/equating issues. Finally, the fact that validity and reliability data presented in the manual do not apply to the current norm sample should discourage use of this test when making individual decisions affecting examinee diagnosis or placement.

REVIEWER'S REFERENCES

Cooter, R. B., Jr. (1989). [Review of the Woodcock Reading Mastery Tests—Revised]. In J. C. Conoley & J. J. Kramer (Eds.), *The tenth mental measurements yearbook* (pp. 910–913). Lincoln, NE: Buros Institute of Mental Measurements.
Jaeger, R. M. (1989). [Review of the Woodcock Reading Mastery Tests—Revised]. In J. C. Conoley & J. J. Kramer (Eds.), *The tenth mental measurements yearbook* (pp. 913–916). Lincoln, NE: Buros Institute of Mental Measurements.
Linacre, J. M., & Wright, B. D. (1994). *A user's guide to BIGSTEPS Rasch-Model computer program. (Version 2.4).* Chicago: MEGA Press.

Review of the Woodcock Reading Mastery Tests—Revised [1998 Normative Update] by

MILDRED MURRAY-WARD, Professor of Education, California Lutheran University, Thousand Oaks, CA:

The 1998 Woodcock Reading Mastery Tests—Revised (WRMT-R/NU) is an update of the 1987 test, a major revision of the 1973 test. The 1998 edition involves a new norming procedure, instructional and diagnostic profiles, and part score tables. The 1998 test and manual are virtually identical to the 1987 version; only the norms have been updated.

The use claims include: clinical diagnosis; creating IEPs; selection and placement; guidance for students, understanding reading achievement strengths and weaknesses; measuring gains; program evaluation and research. The WRMT-R/NU is a comprehensive reading assessment, including six tests, many score forms, diagnostic procedures, and profiles.

No review of the WRMT-R would be complete without acknowledgment of the test's long history and the fact that it has been previously reviewed twice in the *Eighth Mental Measurements Yearbook* (1978) and the *Tenth Mental Measurements Yearbook* (1989). Because of its history, the developer began the 1998 examiner's manual with a discussion of this version of the test as compared to previous editions. In the 1998 edition, content, items, score forms and groupings, the system of recording and analyzing errors, and the computerized scoring packages have been maintained. All of these features have been previously reviewed by Cooter (1989) and Jaeger (1989).

Because the WRMT-R/NU is not a complete revision, it still does not address a number of validity and interpretation problems cited in previous reviews. First, the content domain is not described. The words in Word Identification are presented in isolation and chosen for their increasing rarity in usage. The author appears more interested in Word Attack because the examinees respond to the words without having experience with them. Word Attack is a nonsense word exercise, and Word Comprehension seems to be a reasoning test. These criticisms were noted in the *Eighth* and *Tenth MMYs*.

A problem in previous editions was that no sources or rationale for the selection of certain words or skills in any test were supplied. In Word Identification, the criteria for selecting words (except their apparent rarity in usage) are not provided. In Word Comprehension, the words are sorted by domains (i.e., general reading, science-mathematics), but no information on the sources of the words and their grade level appropriateness is offered.

Finally, the author continues to describe patterns of achievement across the scales for differential diagnosis and predictions of future performance. However, this edition, as with previous ones, provides no validity information for these uses.

In examining the new information in the WRMT-R/NU manual, the procedures appear to be rigorous. Creating norms on several tests at one time is an innovative idea that is certainly economical. These provide some interesting psychometric possibilities, but present some new issues. First, the NU norms seem to restrict, rather than maintain or expand the interpretive value of the test. While adhering to the U.S. Census figures available at the time, the sample is much smaller than the 1987 one, a reduction of approximately 57%. Furthermore, the types of students also changed, in that the 18–22-year-old group were not all in college (less than 40%) as was the case for many of the 1987 group. In addition, no adults older than 22 years of age were included in the new norming studies. Finally, even though the author did locate persons in most of the 50 states, he did not include persons from many of the major cities.

Second, norming procedures are somewhat unclear. The rationale for combining norming procedures for the six tests in the NU norms is never explained. One reason may be that the author was attempting to create domains similar to ones found on traditional group achievement tests, because the domain titles are nearly exactly the titles used in such group tests. But no item intercorrelations were presented. Another possible, less acceptable, reason is that subjects for the other instruments were simply available.

The Rasch procedures used in norming are also difficult to follow. For example, the author states that the item difficulties for the Letter and Word Recognition for K–1 children had larger gaps than for other persons in the group. No information is provided on how these gaps were determined to be so large as to require removal of scores of these children from the rest of the group. More seriously, it is not clear how well that removal improved the overall range of difficulties. Even though a curriculum-based explanation for this gap was given, it is suggested by this reviewer

that other causes such as a poor match to the overall domain are possible and should have been explored. Furthermore, the norms tables for Word and Letter Identification for K–1 students are not separated from other scores, but are presented as part of the continuum of development in these two tests.

Finally, three interpretation issues arise. First, the use of the norms generated from the smaller norm sample means that interpretations are limited. Children from large metropolitan areas have few persons to whom their scores may be compared. The failure to include college students (only 37% of the new norm group were in 2-year or 4-year college programs) in the 18–22-year-old group and no persons 23 years and older makes the new norms of questionable value. The 1987 data are now well over 10 years old, and the presence of new and old norms in the same manual and norms tables is misleading at best.

Second, scores for special education students should be used cautiously. Although the author did include special education and gifted students in the norm sample, matching their prevalence in the general population, their actual numbers are quite small. In addition, there are still no predictive validity studies to validate the WRMT-R/NU with this population; a serious omission because this test is frequently used in placement and re-evaluation.

Furthermore, the author states that comparisons of old and new norm data clearly show a pattern of lower performances *and* higher standard and percentile scores of lower achievers. This effect could result in overestimation of students' reading levels. Thus, students might not receive appropriate services or services may be terminated prematurely. Interestingly, there are no cautions to examiners to readjust score referents to account for these changes.

Finally, the problem with domain definition mentioned earlier makes the WRMT-R/NU difficult to interpret. Certainly, the new validity studies involving other measures of reading could help to create a domain that is more analogous to traditional views of reading. However, this information is not provided. It should also be remembered that no changes have been made in test skills or items, and there is no stipulation that the other measures clarify the meaning of the WRMT-R/NU scores.

SUMMARY. In conclusion, the WRMT-R/NU is a limited norms update. The test still contains many test items and scores, but does not address problems identified by previous reviewers. Furthermore, the renorming has narrowed the utility of the test. Therefore, the WRMT-R/NU should be used in conjunction with other measures of reading. Results should not be overinterpreted. The examiner should also be very cautious in using the test with a wide range of age groups. If these cautions are observed, the test may be useful in helping estimate reading achievement.

REVIEWER'S REFERENCES

Cooter, R. B. (1989). [Review of the Woodcock Reading Mastery Tests—Revised.] In J. C. Conoley & J. J. Kramer (Eds.), *The tenth mental measurements yearbook* (pp. 910–913). Lincoln, NE: Buros Institute of Mental Measurements.

Jaeger, R. M. (1989). [Review of the Woodcock Reading Mastery Tests—Revised.] In J. C. Conoley & J. J. Kramer (Eds.), *The tenth mental measurements yearbook* (pp. 913–916). Lincoln, NE: Buros Institute of Mental Measurements.

[424]
The Word Memory Test.

Purpose: Designed for symptom validity testing—detecting malingering and feigning in comparison to cases of true brain injury and amnesia.
Population: Adults.
Publication Dates: 1995–1996.
Acronym: WMT.
Scores, 5: Immediate Recognition, Delayed Recognition, Multiple Choice, Paired Associates, Free Recall.
Administration: Individual.
Forms, 2: Oral, Computerized.
Price Data, 1996: $300 per complete test including copyable administration forms and unlimited administration/scoring disk; $25 per manual ('96, 132 pages).
Time: (15) minutes.
Comments: Computerized form (C-WMT) self-administered.
Authors: Paul Green, Kevin Astner, and Lyle M. Allen.
Publisher: CogniSyst, Inc.

Review of the Word Memory Test by M. ALLAN COOPERSTEIN, Clinical Psychologist, Disability & Forensic Examiner, Independent Practice, Willow Grove, PA:

PROPOSED TEST USE. The Word Memory Test (WMT) is a symptom validity test embedded within symptom and ability batteries in psychological, vocational, disability, and neuropsychological testing to detect feigning or symptom exaggeration. Its development is based on the assumption that "instruments designed to assess mental *ability* cannot be used reliably to detect malingering, and that some instruments intended to assess exaggeration inadvertently require too much subject ability and therefore lack sufficient discriminative power" (user's guide, p. vii).

TEST RATIONALE AND DEVELOPMENT. Rogers, Harrell, and Liff (1993) report that strategies using performance curves appeared to have the greatest promise in identifying potential malingerers. Nies and Sweet's (1994) review indicate that those who feign and malinger demonstrate behaviors associated with (a) lower verbal learning and recall testing scores, (b) unexpectedly low scores on recognition memory testing, (c) inconsistent performance on tests of similar abilities, (d) inconsistencies within the same test or from test to retest, and (e) lower scores on symptom validity tests, falling at or below chance level.

Paul Green proposed the assessment of patient effort employing forced-choice recognition of simple words. Collaborating with Lyle Allen, codeveloper of the Computerized Assessment of Response Bias (CARB), this target word list was expanded to include 40 words grouped into hard and easy linked pairs. The lengthy list increased face validity, but early studies showed that neurological and severe traumatic brain injury (STBI) patients still recognized over 90% of the words. Surprisingly, 30-minute delayed recognition was undiminished in STBIs, but proved a most sensitive measure of exaggeration. The WMT was refined and additional memory ability subtests were devised and perfected, measures of response consistency were added, and the test was fully computerized. Subsequent work focused largely on the computerized version. The test was initially examined using STBI and neurological patients, who became the authors' comparison groups of choice. The WMT was also cross-validated against CARB performance in a larger population of compensation-related disability claimants carrying various diagnoses. Comparisons were also made with other effort measures, such as Warrington's Recognition Memory Test, Rey's 15-item test, Millis' criteria for the CVLT, and the 21-item test. More recently, the TOMM, the Tenhula-Sweet method for evaluating effort on the Category Test, and the CVLT logit method of Millis have been studied. Asked to defeat the test, highly educated people (mainly psychologists) failed, possibly due to (a) the deceptive ease of recognition measures, (b) the invisibility of the consistency measure being undetectable, and (c) rapid administration of multiple subtests, making it difficult to maintain track of one's responses.

The core WMT database to date consists of 900 subjects of various diagnoses claiming compensation. It has been supplemented by a parallel series of 850 cases and other samples providing information from independent sources about diverse populations such as mentally handicapped people and patients with fibromyalgia and other chronic pain syndromes.

TEST FORMS AND ADMINISTRATION. Oral and computerized test administrations are available. The authors recognize that differences are sometimes found between the standard computerized and oral administrations. Results from these modes of administration were analyzed and determined to be virtually identical, although caution is suggested when interpreting computerized administrations using oral data. Cutoff levels for displaying effort measures differ between the two forms; therefore, each should be analyzed separately.

The total WMT test time is given as approximately 15 minutes. Two learning trials are presented followed by Immediate Recognition. Immediate and Delayed Word Recognition are similar and objectively easy to take, with visual (or auditory) presentation of 40 undemanding spoken word pairs. Following a 30-minute delay, the Delayed Recognition trial is administered, accompanied by foil words. Although appearing to be a test of spontaneous recall, the WMT actually taps recognition memory.

SCORING AND INTERPRETATION. Scoring is accomplished easily by computer. The WMT is scored immediately, with results available on screen, printed, or sent to a text file. The data compare the patient's performance to control populations of patients with severe traumatic brain injury. Z scores and associated probability values are provided for blocks of items. Normative comparisons are made with the performance of other groups of subjects.

A number of later studies have replicated and extended these findings in independent investigations, confirming that poor overall WMT performance is related to symptom exaggeration or incomplete effort, whereas performance is not related to ability, age, sex, educational level, or the subject's IQ. When CARB performance is added to the WMT, discriminative power is enhanced.

DISCUSSION. SVTs have tended largely to employ forced-choice formats (e.g., Frederick, 1997; Tombaugh, 1996) evaluating validity but not abilities. The WMT appears to assess cognitive ability, but is criterion-referenced and constructed specifically to quantitatively measure test-taking attitude, effort, and response bias. In addition, four subtests (Multiple Choice, Paired Associates, Delayed Free Recall, and Free Recall) tap verbal memory.

Sloping gradients of difficulty found within the WMT subtests are such that preceding words are easier than subsequent words. Despite this, normal individuals and patients who apply effort can score beyond the 90% level. Difficulty slopes provided by separate WMT subtests make it difficult to falsify, and appear able to identify inconsistent biasing strategies. This is facilitated by comparing the contour of the individual's performance curve to normal individuals and patients with or without genuine memory impairment using established base rates for feigning, malingering, and symptom exaggeration (as high as 75% in some clinical populations).

Despite the accuracy of the WMT, the authors caution that multiple measures of response bias are still needed. The ultimate determination of malingering must be based on overall clinical evaluation (Frederick, Sarfaty, Johnston, & Powel, 1994).

As SVT research progresses, it is hoped that the accretion of knowledge will lead towards more sophisticated classification schema on the basis of motivation and effort and not a crude Honest versus Malingering dichotomy.

SUMMARY. The WMT blends well within a battery of cognitive or other symptom validity measures. In addition, it provides the options of administering actual memory measures including Multiple Choice, Paired Associates subtest, Free Recall, and Delayed Free Recall. Differing from other symptom validity tests, these subtests lend further confidence to the battery, enabling the examiner to enhance basic information and provide supplementary data for discrimination when borderline efforts result, reducing errors in classification. Accordingly, the WMT is a tool with considerable flexibility and ease of use that may be used to replace or supplement other SVT measures. To the authors' credit, they continue an active research program to refine it, requesting willing consumers to submit data from their administrations to refine those already in CogniSyst's database.

REVIEWER'S REFERENCES

Rogers, R., Harrell, E. H., & Liff, C. (1993). Feigning neuropsychological impairment: A critical review of methodological and clinical considerations. *Clinical Psychology Review, 3*(3), 255–274.

Frederick, R. I., Sarfaty, S. D., Johnston, J. D., & Powel, J. (1994). Validation of a detector of response bias on a forced-choice test of nonverbal ability. *Neuropsychology, 8*(1), 118–125.

Nies, K. J., & Sweet, J. J. (1994). Neuropsychological assessment and malingering: A critical review of past and present strategies. *Archives of Clinical Neuropsychology, 9*(6), 501–552.

Tombaugh, T. N. (1996). Test of Memory Malingering. Toronto: Multi-Health Systems.

Frederick, R. I. (1997). *Validity indicator profile manual.* Minneapolis: National Computer Systems, Inc.

Review of the Word Memory Test by MICHAEL P. GAMACHE, Clinical Assistant Professor of Psychology, Department of Neurology, University of South Florida, College of Medicine, Tampa, FL:

TEST COVERAGE AND USE. The Word Memory Test (WMT) is designed as a measure of verbal memory allowing for the simultaneous assessment of response bias. It is intended for use primarily in forensic settings in the context of a comprehensive assessment of cognitive functioning, but where high base-rates of malingering, feigning, or deception may be the norm. These would specifically include cases involving a high potential for secondary gain such as personal injury litigation, worker's compensation, Social Security disability claims, and the assessment of competency and sanity in criminal matters. The test is appropriate for adults who allege to be suffering from cognitive impairment secondary to disease or injury of the brain. The authors do not identify specific demographic characteristics of appropriate subjects.

The authors emphasize that the design and interpretation of the WMT (for assessment of response bias, but not verbal memory) are intended to be independent of actual cognitive ability. In fact, they state that in contrast to other tests of response bias and malingering, such as "symptom validity" tests, they created the WMT with the objective of obtaining a high rate of correct responses (greater than or equal to 90% correct) even among patients with "severe" brain injury. Scores from a sample of "severe" brain injury subjects did exceed 90% correct for measures of immediate recall, delayed recall, and recall consistency.

The authors do not identify the appropriate age range for this test. The mean age of the subjects in the "clinical study of 159 compensation claimants" was 38.3 years (*SD* +/- 11.0). They do not report the range of age in the manual. Age and education may affect results; consequently, the WMT may not be appropriate for use with the elderly or with adolescents (although the authors assert that the WMT is unrelated to level of education and age). If the test is administered to patients with particularly limited education, the results should be interpreted cautiously. The test is inappropriate for use with patients where (a) English is a second language or (b) the use of an interpreter is necessary.

SIZE AND REPRESENTATIVENESS OF SAMPLE FOR VALIDATION AND NORMING. The test manual reports two validation studies, a preliminary validation study involving 58 consecutive referrals to a private practice in Edmonton, Alberta, and a second validation study involving 159 consecutive referrals to the same private practice. Only 50.9% of this sample was referred for, or diagnosed with, neurological disease, with the remainder composed of orthopaedic injuries, psychiatric, chronic fatigue, chronic pain, and heterogeneous diagnoses. It is not clear from the manual whether there is overlap of subjects between the two studies. Additional data collection is described as "ongoing." Separate data are presented for normal controls (*N* = 21) who were obtained from an entirely different site, presumably tested by different examiners, and who are not to be comparable to the clinical sample in terms of education.

The authors make a large number of subset comparisons using small sample sizes, including comparisons based on severity of brain injury, type of neuropathology, and diagnostic subgroup. They also offer data on comparisons between WMT results and the results of the study subjects on other measures of response bias, and other measures of verbal memory. The comparisons are well intended and potentially important, but clearly exceed the limits imposed by the small and possibly unrepresentative sample sizes. The biggest weakness is that none of these data have been published or subjected to peer review.

RELIABILITY. The reliability data of this test are sparse. From the secondary validation study, the authors report an "internal reliability" coefficient of .89 between immediate and delayed recall measures. They offer the conclusion, without supporting data, that alternate form (oral versus computerized administration) reliability results show that "the two forms of the test appear to be identical."

VALIDITY. The validity of scores from tests purported to measure response bias or malingering have been routinely criticized as methodologically weak due to the absence of adequate criterion measures. The WMT is no exception. In many studies, patients with financial incentive are assumed to be malingering, or at least to have a major incentive for response bias, and are compared with patients who have no financial incentive (nonlitigation or litigation resolved). Unfortunately, all 159 of the subjects included in the WMT validation study would meet this external criterion for malingering in that all of them were involved in compensation claims at the time of testing.

Construct validity evidence is offered in the form of comparative data for the WMT versus another measure of response bias, specifically the Computerized Assessment of Response Bias (published by the same company), and versus response bias indicators from genuine tests of memory (e.g., California Verbal Learning Test, CVLT; Warrington Recognition Memory Test). The authors also argue that the genuine memory portions of the WMT have been validated against the CVLT, with subtest correlations between the two instruments ranging from .49 to .73.

TEST ADMINISTRATION. The WMT comes in both oral administration and computerized administration forms. The computerized form is a DOS program operated within a proprietary CogShell environment for IBM-compatible computers only. It requires 580K of free DOS memory (a fairly demanding requirement). DOS 6.2 is recommended. The authors indicate that the program can be operated under Windows or Windows 95. Installation is straightforward, though not bug free. The program loaded and operated adequately, and the CogShell program was intuitively straightforward, but operation and administration of the test were somewhat cumbersome, resulting in the occasional error message, with the need for frequent reentry of protective passwords. There were on-screen prompts to move the monitor from the subject's view, without prior warning.

The manual is lengthy (130 pages) and not well organized or indexed. For those not already familiar with computer administration of tests, 8 to 10 practice administrations or more may be necessary to become comfortable with administration. Otherwise, the computer WMT offers all the usual advantages and disadvantages of computerized neuropsychological testing, and is a much more efficient means of administration and scoring than the oral version. Computerized scoring of the oral version is also available. Face validity, in terms of disguising the intended purpose of the test by creating the appearance of a test of memory,

is good, and is distinctly better than most forms of symptom validity testing.

TEST REPORTING. An interpretive report is easily initiated from the CogShell menu. It can be printed, viewed on screen, or saved to file. The printing and viewing function worked adequately. Common word processing programs did not recognize a report file as a readable or convertible file, which complicates the use of this test on laptop computers. The report is a mix of elaborate statistical data and significance tests, together with narrative conclusions. The data are confusing and poorly organized. The narrative conclusions are brief, elegant, and informative, but concern only the response bias indicators, offering no interpretation for verbal memory performance as touted in the advertising and manual. The interpretation of response bias is determined by cutoff scores on each of three measures: immediate recall, delayed recall, and immediate recall/delayed recall consistency. Response bias classification is based on the total number of cutoff scores exceeded, and ranged from Type 1—"unbiased responder who appears to be making a genuine effort" to Type 4—"very strong evidence of response bias is evident" (manual, p. 48).

TEST BIAS. There are insufficient normative data to determine test bias. The clinical validation sample was 60% female and apparently was composed exclusively of Canadians.

SUMMARY. Tests to detect malingering and deception are becoming an increasingly important component of the psychological and neuropsychological test battery, especially in forensic matters. The accuracy of diagnosis and assessment can be increased, and the risks of false positive errors in assessing malingering can be offset, by using multiple measures of response bias. In fact, the failure to incorporate such measures may now constitute negligent practice in forensic matters where estimates of 25% to 50% or more of the patients referred for assessment may be engaging in some exaggeration of symptoms. The WMT is a well-reasoned, logically constructed measure that deserves consideration for inclusion in the test battery of competent clinicians. It should not be used as a stand-alone instrument. It is very much in need of additional validation, normative data, peer review, streamlined documentation, and software refinement, but it holds promise as an effective tool for the assessment of response bias in neuropsychological populations.

Word Recognition and Phonic Skills.

Purpose: "Designed to give the teacher two assessments of a child's word recognition ability."

Population: Ages 5.0 to 8.6.

Publication Date: 1994.

Acronym: WRaPS.

Scores: Word Recognition.

Administration: Group.

Price Data, 1999: £9.99 per 20 test booklets; £10.50 per diagnostic scoring template; £9.99 per manual (31 pages); £10.99 per specimen set including one copy of test form and manual.

Time: (30) minutes.

Authors: Clifford Carver and David Moseley.

Publisher: Hodder & Stoughton Educational [England].

Cross References: See T5:2910 (1 reference).

Review of the Word Recognition and Phonics Skills by ROBERT G. HARRINGTON, Professor, Department of Psychology and Research in Education, University of Kansas, Lawrence, KS:

Word recognition and phonics are two very important skills in learning to decode and comprehend reading. The Word Recognition and Phonics Skills test (WRaPS) was designed to assess children's developing word recognition and phonic skills during the early part of the spring semester of "Year 1" or "Year 2" according to the English educational system of grades. This timeline would be equivalent in the U.S. to the spring of kindergarten or first grade. The WRaPS was published and "normed" in England.

The WRaPS comes in a six-page test booklet composed of 50 items and takes between 15 and 30 minutes to administer. Each item consists of rows of five or six "words," some of which are real words and some of which are not. The examiner's manual instructs the examiner to read a word to the examinee and then to repeat the word in the context of a sentence or a phrase which is also provided. The task for the examinee is to "puzzle out" the right word from the five or six choices provided for each item using either word recognition skills or phonics skills. One example might be the word, "LOOK," which is then used in a sentence, "LOOK at the words." After hearing the examiner say the word and use it in a sentence the examinee must underline the word, "LOOK" from the several options that, in this case, include "lake," "look," "like," "book," and "kool" in the test booklet.

To be successful, the examinee must either recognize the correct spelling of the target word or must consider the alternatives carefully and select one using phonics skills. This presentation of items is different from other word recognition tests in that each word is presented within a structured group of alternatives and children are to select the right word from the list rather than use their word recognition and phonics skills to "read" the word presented to them as is done on the Reading Test (i.e., word recognition test) contained on the Wide Range Achievement Test-III (WRAT-III; T5:2879). With the approach used in the WRaPS, children must distinguish between letters with confusing names and/or shapes, they must decide on directionality of word attack, they must deal with long-term memory for words they think they recognize, and finally they must try to "sound out" using phonics to pronounce the sounds made by the letters represented in the words.

The philosophy of these authors and the WRaPS is that reading is an interplay of visual, auditory, and linguistic factors. Their beliefs about how children learn to read and why the WRaPS word recognition and phonics test must have distracters can be best summed up in the authors' own words contained in the examiner's manual:

> The perceptions of sound elements (or phonological awareness) is not just a matter of hearing (although it is certainly affected by hearing loss). It progresses from a basic awareness of differences in initial sound and in syllable structure to an awareness of rhyming endings and then to a precise identification of phonemes even in the longest words. If the task becomes to complex, similar sounds will be confused or sound elements will be omitted or guessed at. Similarly, visual perception is not just a matter of visual acuity, but involves the coordination of eye movements, the discrimination of distinctive features, pattern-recognition, naming and memory. In word-recognition, letter shape and orientation are important, as well as direction attack and memory for sequential patterns. (pp. 17–18)

Items on the WRaPS are arranged in increasing order of difficulty but generally all children are expected to attempt all 50 items regardless of prior performance. Unfortunately, there are no basal or ceiling rules provided so examiners must be judicious in making sure that they do not frustrate children experiencing test anxiety. The test is intended for children between 5 and 8 years of age and may be individually or group administered. The authors recommend that when the WRaPS is used as a group measure it can be employed for large-scale assessments to identify early reading problems, as part of a school record to evaluate progress in early reading skills, as part of a diagnostic teaching regimen to evaluate miscues in phonics, to assess the progress of older slow readers, and for research purposes. It is recommended that younger children should be tested in smaller groups with an assistant in the testing room to make sure that the children know how to respond, that they are not losing their places, and that they are on the right items. A teacher assistant would most assuredly be mandatory.

After the WRaPS is completed it is scored by crediting the child with one "mark" for each word correctly underlined resulting in the WRaPS raw score ranging from 0 to 50. This raw score can be converted to an age-equivalent score and a "stage level score." The authors suggest that they have identified 10 stages of development of word recognition and phonics from ages 5 to 8 years. For example, it is stated that at Stages 1–2 common single-consonant sounds and the easiest vowels (a and o) come to be correctly identified if they are in the initial position in the spoken word, whereas in Stages 9–10 the child can successfully recognize words with double initial consonants. The authors state that these "stages" are based on "a great deal of research" (manual, p. 18) but they provide no research data to substantiate this statement. As for the age scores, it is doubtful that these age scores would have much value to a potential examiner because in addition to the psychometric problems inherent in the interpretation of age-equivalent scores the WRaPS Test makes no allowance for early preschool reading experiences that a subject might have had and that could affect that age-equivalent score up or down.

The results of the WRaPS Test are designed to show the child's overall level of ability in word recognition and phonics in the form of a total score of correct responses. In addition, a profile of strengths and weaknesses in word recognition and phonics is provided supposedly diagnosing problems associated with the number of consonant graphemes incorrect, number of vowel graphemes incorrect, number of letter orders incorrect, or reading problems associated with the shortening

of words (i.e., fewer letters, e.g., "wenty" for "twenty"). Determination of the error type depends upon the results of an error analysis of "miscues" conducted by the examiner by referring to a page within the examiner's manual that designates which items are tapping knowledge of consonants, knowledge of vowels, letter order and directional attack, and significance of word shortening.

When raw scores are below 40, it is recommended examiners refer to a "Table of Miscue Norms" to make a determination as to whether the number of miscues within each type places the child in the "strong," "average," or "weak" range compared to other readers at that age and stage. Once again, the authors provide absolutely no research information about how and under what stratification specifications these "norms" were derived. Once a determination has been made about the nature of the miscues in terms of consonants, vowels, letter order, and shortening of words using the WRaPS Profile, and once the stage at which the child is recognizing words is determined the examiner is next directed to the examiner's manual for a few pages of suggestions for teaching interventions. Rather cryptic and short suggestions for modifying teaching activities are described on only six pages of the examiner's manual for each of the four types of miscues identified as well as for word analysis and word-building activities. Unfortunately, no treatment validity data are provided as evidence for the validity of these treatments. Consequently, it is impossible to determine the efficacy of these suggested reading interventions.

Items on the WRaPS apparently were derived from a battery of 300 test items that appeared on the original Word Recognition Test (Carver, 1970) used to investigate aural (sound) and visual factors in word recognition. Presumably every item in the larger battery was statistically analyzed before final item selection, intercorrelations, and factorial analyses were conducted. A scant synoptic review is provided in Appendix 1 of the examiner's manual and shows that 148 children participated in the original 1970 battery tryout that included 90 items. No information is provided about where this sample came from and how the original 300-item instrument was reduced to only 90 items now.

As a crude measure of total test difficulty the authors offer only a frequency distribution of the number of subjects scoring within various total raw score ranges. To assess item difficulty, a similarly simple "facility" statistic is offered in which the authors compute the total percentage of the whole sample of children answering each item correctly. For example, an item with 20% facility would be "difficult," whereas one with 90% facility would be "easy." Using this technique the authors report that the items are "generally" in order of increasing difficulty, but that the main body of items was selected to reflect a level of ability around the age of 6 to 6 1/2 years. Even though this 6- to 6 1/2-year age range for most items may be "the crucial area of the early stages of word recognition, and the area where accurate information is most needed" (manual, p. 16), the test is surely made more difficult for struggling readers in the 5-year-old age range. To determine the discrimination of each item the authors simply created a chart showing how each item in successive order of increasing word difficulty discriminates the more able from the less able word recognizers. Surely, item response theory (IRT) could have been applied to these data to more appropriately analyze the same statistical questions more rigorously.

No standard scores are provided for the WRaPS and no standard errors of measurement are provided either. Nevertheless, in discussing the reliability of the WRaPS the authors state that "great confidence can be placed in the accuracy of obtained raw scores. The true score will almost certainly be within plus or minus one point of the obtained score" (manual, p. 26). No statistical evidence is provided to substantiate such a statement.

As some support for the validity of the final version of the WRaPS the authors cite in the examiner's manual a correlation between the Schonell Reading test age-equivalent scores of 79 children with the age-equivalent scores of the full 50-item final version of the WRaPS Test to be r = .90. In another study from the examiner's manual the authors indicate that a correlation between the WRaPS and the Burt Reading Test scores for 168 children who participated in the validation study was reported to be r = .82. In yet a third study of 440 children between 5-3 and 8-4 years of age, conducted in 1993 in seven schools in the United Kingdom, a correlation of r = .87 was found between the WRaPS and the Young Group Reading Test. The problem with all three of these so-called validation studies is that none of the samples

in any of these studies is adequately described and the validity of the comparison tests are never discussed.

SUMMARY. The WRaPS is an interesting test of early word recognition and phonics skills that uses a unique method for testing these skills by asking the child to visually "recognize" or "sound out" the right word from a set of distracters containing a variety of "miscues." The statistical methods used to determine the reliability and validity of this test were overly simplified and lacked necessary information to fully evaluate their psychometric qualities. In addition, the instructional strategies that are recommended are unverified. There are absolutely no case studies on the use and application of this instrument with children with varying types of reading problems. Finally, the examiner's manual is woefully lacking in content not the least of which is the lack of any bibliographic references. The goal of creating an assessment tool that would easily assess early word recognition and phonics skills for individuals or groups of young children is laudable. But for the reasons stated above, examiners are best directed to investigate curriculum-based measures for assessing the constructs of word-recognition and phonics within a young child's own curriculum from which they are being taught.

REVIEWER'S REFERENCE

Carver, C. (1970). *Manual of instructions, Word Recognition Test*. London: Hodder & Stoughton Educational.

Review of the Word Recognition and Phonic Skills by JOYCE R. McLARTY, Principal Research Associate, Workforce Development Division, ACT, Inc., Iowa City, IA:

The Word Recognition and Phonic Skills test (WRaPS) covers word recognition "from the earliest stages of letter knowledge to a level normally achieved by the age of 8" (manual, p. 6). The test is designed to be administered to an individual or group of children as young as 4 to 5 years. The booklet includes five pages of test items with 10 items per page. Each item appears as a single row with the key word in a group of five or six alternatives, requiring the child either to recognize the correct spelling of the target word or to pay very careful attention to the phonic elements.

The child is to underline the correct word in each row. To help the examiner ensure that examinees are on the correct page and row, pages in the answer booklet have a number of stars at the top to represent the page number, and rows on each page are clearly numbered. Despite its careful design, the test booklet appears to be difficult for a very young child or one "at the earliest stages of letter knowledge" (manual, p. 6) to use. It is likely that examinees with very weak reading skills will need close supervision or individual assessment.

The examiner is to first say the word the examinee is to locate, then use the word in a phrase provided as part of the test, and finally repeat the word. Example: "The word is ... CAT ... A cat chases mice ... Find cat ..." (manual, p. 8). This test was developed in England, and users in the United States will find many of the suggested phrases to be inappropriate. For example, the word "WIG" is associated with a judge wearing a wig. The word "APPLE" is associated with pie and custard. Test users in the United States should review the phrases in advance of the test and modify them, as necessary, so that they will be familiar to the examinees. It is not clear what impact changing the phrases will have on the established norms of the test. However, it is clear that failing to change the phrases to something that will help examinees to recognize the words would result in an even greater negative impact on the accuracy of the test scores.

It is not appropriate to change the words themselves, even though some of them may be less familiar to children in the United States than to children in England (e.g., KETTLE). This is because each test question is keyed to one of four specific types of error: consonant grapheme, vowel grapheme, order of letters, and shortening. Both total scores and subscores based on these categories are interpreted using tables found in the manual to indicate stages of phonetic skills development.

Standardization was based on a sample of 148 children: the full reading range of children ages 6 and 7, the lower half of the reading range for children ages 7 to 9, and remedial classes of students ages 7, 8, and 9. The authors caution that age norms are of limited value until the age of about 6 1/2 because so much depends on the extent and quality of preschool instruction. Norms were built on the assumption of steady linear growth in word recognition, and are most applicable for spring testing, especially for younger children. Stages of word recognition and grade equivalent norms are best interpreted as general descriptive information rather than as standards.

In studies apparently conducted in 1993, the overall test had an internal consistency reliability estimate of .98, which is extremely high, and also high correlations with a variety of word recognition and reading tests. Reliability and validity data for the subscores were not reported, although it is reasonable to expect that both reliability and validity coefficients would be lower for them due to the smaller numbers of test items.

The manual includes a section on interpreting the diagnostic profile and offers suggestions for teaching. These should be quite useful to teachers needing to provide support to student who have not yet mastered some of these skills.

The authors suggest that each child be asked to draw a person on the inside of the cover page. They suggest that "The drawing can be carried out at the end of the Test as a relaxing reward. It gives a rough indication of the child's motor or visuo-motor ability" (manual, p. 7). Test users should be aware that "draw-a-person" is a well-known projective technique used to analyze a number of personality and other psychological variables. For this reason, it may be inappropriate to give children directions to "draw a person" unless the teacher has the appropriate qualifications to administer and interpret this information and parental permissions are obtained.

SUMMARY. The WRaPS test appears to be a properly developed test of word recognition and phonics that would be more appropriate to use in England than in the United States, although a number of modifications can be made to improve the appropriateness for the United States. In general, and especially if modifications are made in the test, the score interpretation information should be considered to be general guidelines rather than standards.

[426]
The Work Experience Survey.

Purpose: Designed as a "structured interview protocol for identifying barriers (and possible solutions) to career maintenance" for a disabled person.
Population: "Individuals with disabilities who are either employed or about to begin employment."
Publication Date: 1995.
Acronym: WES.
Scores: Not scored.
Administration: Individual.
Price Data, 1998: $7.50 per 50 surveys; $5 per manual (59 pages).
Time: (30–60) minutes.

Comments: Administered in a face-to-face or telephone interview.
Authors: Richard T. Roessler (survey and manual), Cheryl A. Reed (manual), and Phillip D. Rumrill (manual).
Publisher: The National Center on Employment & Disability.

Review of The Work Experience Survey by ALBERT M. BUGAJ, Associate Professor of Psychology, University of Wisconsin—Marinette, Marinette, WI:

The Work Experience Survey (WES) is a structured interview protocol that enables people with disabilities to direct their own accommodation planning (manual, p. 1). Accommodation planning is intended to reduce or remove barriers to access to job sites and/or to productivity. The WES is meant to be administered by a rehabilitation professional, either face-to-face or by telephone. It consists of sections assessing respondent background information, job accessibility, essential job functions, job mastery, job satisfaction, and concludes with development of the accommodation plan. It also provides a framework for accommodation planning. However, strong evidence is lacking that it is statistically reliable and valid.

Although some sections of the WES are entirely new (those on assessing accessibility and developing the accommodation plan), others are based on previous tests. The checklist for assessing essential functions is based on the RehabMatch (Greenwood, Johnson, Wilson, & Schriner, 1988) and the scale for assessing job mastery is based on items selected from the Career Mastery Inventory (Crites, 1990). However, as adaptations forming integral parts of a new test, any evidence of measures of validity and reliability for scores from these tests would not be completely applicable to the WES. These scales, along with a scale for assessing job satisfaction based on Dawis and Lofquist's (1984) theory of work adjustment, bolster the theoretical basis of the WES.

Both the "job mastery scale" and the job satisfaction scale have high interitem consistency (coefficients alpha = .74 and .78, respectively). However, the nature of the subject pool used in determining these estimates of reliability is not found in the manual. Further, the manual provides no other indices of reliability, such as test-retest reliability.

Limited data regarding the validity of scores from the WES are also presented in the manual. The data reported are taken from a 1995 study by Roessler and Rumrill that examined the relationship of perceived work site barriers to job mastery and satisfaction for employed people with multiple sclerosis. Thirty-four of the subjects were interviewed face-to-face using the WES, and the remaining 16 were interviewed by phone. Unfortunately, there is no indication in the manual or the paper (Roessler & Rumrill, 1995) as to whether separate analyses were performed to determine if there were significant differences in results related to the different means of test administration.

The data available in the manual speak somewhat to the internal validity of the WES. Namely, the total number of perceived barriers to accessibility and performance of essential job functions correlated significantly with the number of problems in job mastery ($r = .34$, $p < .01$). Further, participants who experienced more barriers tended to report lower levels of job satisfaction ($r = -.50$, $p < .01$). These results are as would be expected, given the theoretical basis of the WES presented in the manual.

Despite the results of Roessler and Rumrill's (1995) study discussed in the WES manual, questions still exist about the validity of scores from the instrument. First, the study was performed on a limited group of subjects. Roessler and Rumrill (1995) report the 50 subjects were primarily white (96%). As previously mentioned, all suffered from multiple sclerosis. Thus, whether the results can be generalized to other groups is questionable. Data are also lacking regarding criterion-related validity. For example, there are no data available examining the correlation of scores from the WES to already existing tests of job satisfaction. Also, no data are presented regarding changes in job satisfaction and adaptation over time, as a result of the accommodation planning the WES is meant to guide.

SUMMARY. Because of limited data available concerning the technical quality (validity and reliability) of scores from the WES, it can only be recommended with reservations. It should be treated as a guide and framework to accommodation planning until data regarding criterion-related validity are available. Until that time, perhaps its greatest usefulness would be for those interested in performing research in the area of accommodation planning, using the WES for purposes of construct validation.

REVIEWER'S REFERENCES

Dawis, R. V., & Lofquist, L. H. (1984). *A psychological theory of work adjustment: An individual differences model and its applications.* Minneapolis, MN: University of Minnesota Press.

Greenwood, R., Johnson, V., Wilson, J., & Schriner, K. (1988). RehabMatch. Fayetteville, AR: Arkansas Research & Training Center in Vocational Rehabilitation.

Crites, J. (1990). *The Career Mastery Inventory.* Boulder, CO: Crites Career Consultants.

Roessler, R. T., & Rumrill, P. D., Jr. (1995). The relationship of perceived work site barriers to job mastery and job satisfaction for employed people with multiple sclerosis. *Rehabilitation Counseling Bulletin, 39,* 2–14.

Review of The Work Experience Survey by LAWRENCE H. CROSS, Professor of Educational Research and Evaluation, Virginia Polytechnic Institute, Blacksburg, VA:

The Work Experience Survey (WES) is an interview schedule designed for use with disabled workers or potential workers. As the subtitle suggests, it is "A structured interview for identifying barriers to career maintenance" (manual, p. 1). The manual suggests that the interview can be conducted person to person (preferably) or by phone in 30 to 60 minutes. The Service Provider's Guide describes the instrument and provides suggestions for its use. It also contains information about its use with a sample of 50 employed adults with multiple sclerosis (MS), 34 of whom were interviewed in person and the rest by telephone. The interview schedule is arranged in six sections, each presented on a separate page of the instrument. Instead of arranging the pages in a booklet, the instrument is printed on a single large sheet (19-inch X 22-inch) and folded much like a birthday card. I found this foldout format awkward when I used it to interview a person with MS as preparation for this review. A brief description of the six sections follows.

DESCRIPTION OF THE WES. The first section focuses on background information, including the nature of the disability and the current employment situation. The second section, labeled "Accessibility," provides a checklist of 20 potential problems disabled persons may experience in getting to, from, or around on the job. Listed are such items as parking, seating/tables, lighting, and temperature. Space is provided to record (a) accessibility problems that may exist but are not listed and (b) solutions to two of the most important accessibility problems. If this instrument is to be used to formulate an accommodation plan, it might also be useful to inquire about barriers for which the employer has already made accommodations.

The third section, labeled "Essential Job Functions," provides a checklist of 68 job functions or conditions that may pose a problem. These job functions are grouped under the following six subheadings: Physical Abilities, Cognitive Abilities, Task-Related Abilities, Social Abilities, Working Conditions, and Company Policies. Space is provided at the bottom of the page to record two job modifications that would be most helpful.

The fourth section, labeled "Job Mastery," provides a checklist of tasks that may pose a concern for the person's success on the job. Items for this checklist were adapted with permission from The Career Mastery Inventory by Crites (1990). Four items (tasks) are listed under each of the following headings: Getting the job done, Fitting into the workforce, Learning the ropes, Getting along with others, Getting ahead, and Planning the next career step. There is also space to "Describe one solution to each of your two most important job mastery concerns" (p. 12). The Service Provider's Guide suggests that the items of this checklist form a scale and reports an internal consistency reliability coefficient of .74, presumable based on the sample of 50 adults with MS. However, the manual does not suggest that users should compute a score for this scale, so this coefficient has no relevance to service providers. The modest size of this coefficient reflects the diversity of the concerns listed and suggests that the "scale" may not be unidimensional.

The fifth section, labeled "Satisfaction" provides another checklist of sorts. The words "In my job ..." appear at the top of the checklist followed by 20 statements adapted from the Minnesota Theory of Work Adjustment by Dawis and Lofquist (1984). Space also is provided to describe two ways the job could be made more personally satisfying. Although most statements flow directly from the introductory clause, some are clumsy (*In my job* my pay compares well with that of other workers), and others do not work well at all (*In my job* my job gives me a feeling of satisfaction). Instead of an agree/disagree response scale, the response options are: Too Little, About Right, Too Much. Although these options are appropriate for some of the items (e.g., I do things that make use of my abilities), they are logically inconsistent for other items (e.g., The job provides for steady employment). The manual suggests the following problematic advice: "It is helpful to remind participants that the answers 'too little' or 'too much' are negative answers" (p. 17). A coefficient alpha reliability estimate of .78 is reported for these items, but once again there is no suggestion in the user's guide to sum responses to these items to produce a job satisfaction score.

The final section, labeled "Developing an Accommodation Plan," provides space to list the three most significant barriers to success on the job. For each barrier the respondent is to identify a possible solution and people or resources that could help. To call the limited amount of information requested in this section an accommodation plan is a bit of an exaggeration, in my opinion.

SUPPORTING EVIDENCE. The rationale offered is that "barrier reduction is related to increased job mastery and increased job satisfaction .... Increased job mastery and job satisfaction improve the probability of job retention" (p. 22). The manual suggests that this rationale is based on relationships established by research. Although this rationale is intuitively appealing, it cannot be supported by the research reported or cited in the manual. The only outside references offered in support of this rational are those mentioned above by Crites (1990) and Dawis and Lofquist (1984). Another article written by the author of the WES (Roessler & Rumrill, 1995) is also listed in support of the rationale. Judging by the title of that article, in all likelihood, it presents the same analysis of data as that described in the WES manual. Specifically, among the sample of 50 adults with MS, the number of perceived barriers correlated .34 with the number of job mastery concerns checked, and -.50 with levels of job satisfaction reported. Although the reduction of barriers may result in higher levels of job satisfaction and a greater sense of job mastery, such a causal assertion cannot be supported by correlational evidence alone, even if the coefficients were impressively high. Not even correlational evidence is offered to link job satisfaction and job mastery with job retention.

The manual also asserts that, by completing the WES with a rehabilitation professional, disabled people will gain a sense of self-determination and empowerment as they "participate in the identification and implementation of their own on-the-job accommodation strategies" (p. 5). Perhaps, but simply completing the WES can be considered only a first step toward implementation of any "accommodation plan." Although information obtained from the WES may provide new insights to the disabled person, and may facilitate negotiation of reasonable accommodations with employers, no evidence is offered to support such assertions.

CONCLUSION. Despite inconsistent wording in the section concerning job satisfaction and the dearth of empirical evidence to support the rationale and uses suggested for the WES, it may prove worthwhile nonetheless. The WES certainly can be used as a mechanism for structuring a productive conversation with a disabled person about his or her work situation. Whether or not use of the WES will result in a reduction in barriers and an enhanced sense of job mastery, job satisfaction, or job retention for the person interviewed is an open question.

REVIEWER'S REFERENCES
Dawis, R. V., & Lofquist, L. H. (1984). *A psychological theory of work adjustment: An individual differences model and its applications.* Minneapolis, MN: University of Minnesota Press.
Crites, J. (1990). The Career Mastery Inventory. Boulder, CO: Crites Career Consultants.
Roessler, R. T., & Rumrill, P. D., Jr. (1995). The relationship of perceived work site barriers to job mastery and job satisfaction for employed people with multiple sclerosis. *Rehabilitation Counseling Bulletin, 39,* 2–14.

[427]
Work Readiness Profile.

Purpose: "Developed as a tool for the initial descriptive assessment of individuals with disabilities."

Population: Older adolescents and adults with disabilities.

Publication Date: 1995.

Scores, 14: Physical effectiveness (Health, Travel, Movement, Fine Motor Skills, Gross Motor Skills and Strength, Total Average), Personal effectiveness (Social and Interpersonal, Work Adjustment, Communication Effectiveness, Abilities and Skills, Literacy and Numeracy, Total Average), Hearing, Vision.

Administration: Group.

Price Data, 1995: $75 per set including manual (64 pages), 10 answer books, 10 group record forms, and 10 individual record forms; $15 per 10 answer books; $6 per 10 group record forms; $6 per 10 individual record forms; $45 per manual.

Time: (10–15) minutes.

Comments: Self-administered or ratings by informant.

Author: Helga A. H. Rowe.

Publisher: Australian Council for Educational Research Ltd. [Australia].

Review of the Work Readiness Profile by JEAN POWELL KIRNAN, Associate Professor of Psychology, The College of New Jersey, Ewing, NJ:

[The reviewer wishes to acknowledge the contributions of Monica Chlupsa. Her careful research and thoughtful insights contributed greatly to this review.]

The Work Readiness Profile is designed as a quick measure of the work effectiveness of differentially abled adolescents and adults who are entering or reentering the workforce. The instrument provides measures of physical, personal, and sensory effectiveness with a focus on the client's abilities and level of support needed to function properly in a work environment. The focus on abilities and strengths, rather than disabilities and weaknesses, is refreshing and fits in well with the spirit of the Americans with Disabilities Act of 1990.

There are three methods of administration: (a) self-administration, (b) completion by an informant who knows the client very well, or (c) ratings obtained by the test administrator during an interview(s) with the client or informant(s). The form of administration suggested for use varies depending upon the client's ability level, although self-report is preferred.

With the exception of the recommendation to administer this test in a quiet environment, free of interruptions, there were no special instructions given regarding the setting. Test materials include a well-written test manual, a 17-page answer booklet that contains both the test statements and an answer column to mark responses, an Individual Record Form, and a Group Record Form. The Work Readiness Profile has no set time limit, but is estimated to require about 10 to 15 minutes.

The instrument consists of 12 separate sections each measuring a different factor. Arithmetic averages of specific factors are calculated to derive the summary scores of Physical Effectiveness (Health, Travel, Movement, Fine Motor Skills, and Gross Motor Skills), and Personal Effectiveness (Social and Interpersonal, Work Adjustment, Communication Effectiveness, Abilities and Skills, and Literacy and Numeracy). There are separate factor scores for Hearing and Vision and an overall Summary Score that is the average of all 12 factors.

Each section contains statements that the rater is required to answer as true (applicable to the client's present condition), not true (nonapplicable to the client's present condition), or 0 (the rater does not know). Although the "0" option can only be used in the informant or interview mode of administration, the instructions for informant administration fail to mention its use. Additionally, it is unclear how a "0" response is scored.

Score ranges vary from section to section, but the higher the score, the more capable the individual is in that area. For example, scores for Vision can range from 4 to 6, whereas scores for Communication can range from 1 to 8. This varia-tion in score range leads to differential weightings of the factors when one derives the summary scores for Personal Effectiveness, Physical Effectiveness, and overall Summary. This may be intentional on the part of the test author, yet no documentation was provided to explain or justify this.

The differential starting and ending points for the various factors may be confusing to the respondent. For six of the factors, one is to begin at the highest rating; whereas for the other six one begins responding at Level 5. These are marked in the answer book with an arrow and instructions. After responding to the statements at the starting point, the respondent either proceeds down the page to statements representing a lower rating of the factor, up the page to statements representing a higher rating of the factor, or considers him/herself finished and moves on to the next factor. The decision of how to proceed depends on whether this particular factor begins at the highest level or Level 5, and if the respondent answers "true" to all statements at a rating level. It seems unwise to burden the respondent with the responsibility of deciding when a factor is complete. Such knowledge might also influence their responses.

Another troublesome aspect of the scoring is the possible occurrence of what the author terms "patchy performance," defined as when one cannot assign a rating for a client because they do not answer "true" for all the statements at any one level. Fortunately, the author suggests that this is rare for if it were to occur with any frequency, it would suggest that the statements are not grouped properly and/or that the linear ordering of the ratings does not reflect a corresponding increase in the factor.

Factor scores are transcribed onto the Individual Record Form and then graphed to determine the aspect(s) of the work environment that will require support. Factors with a score of 6 or greater are interpreted as strengths and those rated 4 or less are indicative of work areas that will require some level of intervention and/or support. Suggestions for the level and type of support needed can be derived from this form, interpretive guidelines in the manual, and case studies.

The development of the Work Readiness Profile should be better documented in the test manual. Although various groups of subject matter experts and service providers were consulted in the initial stages of test development, it is unclear how critical decisions were made in the final stage.

Further documentation of how items were selected/deleted, why factors vary in score range, and how the ratings were assigned to each item is needed.

These gaps in information about the development of the instrument are also reflected in the description of the normative sample, which is lacking. It is specifically stated in the test manual that the client is compared with people in the general population; indeed, a score of 6 is considered "average" on all factors. Yet, a specific normative group is never defined.

The test manual presents evidence of validity through a series of factor analytic studies with four distinct samples varying in terms of presence of disability, type of disability, and employment status. The 12 variables loaded similarly in the studies producing four factors of Work Readiness, Health and Physical Effectiveness, Hearing, and Vision. These findings provide initial support for the construct validity of the Work Readiness Profile.

An adequate demonstration of construct validity, however, calls for an accumulation of evidence through a variety of techniques. The authors are encouraged to continue research along these lines. For example, a comparison of mean scores on the factors between a known disabled population and a nondisabled population would be useful. Similarly, pre/post measures of work readiness with the intervention of a training program should show an increase in scores. Although these are not stand-alone validation techniques, such studies would add to the "accumulation of evidence" that constitutes construct validity.

The author specifically cites the purpose of the Work Readiness Profile as one of describing and not predicting performance. However, it seems reasonable to expect that clients scoring low on the Work Readiness Profile would take longer to learn a job, have difficulty reaching acceptable production levels, and express less satisfaction in the workplace relative to high scorers or low scorers receiving adequate support. Again, evidence of this type would support the test's validity.

Very good reliability measures were obtained for scores on the Work Readiness Profile utilizing two techniques: test-retest and interrater reliability. Test-retest reliability coefficients ranging from .74 to 1.00 were obtained for the 12 factors utilizing the total sample with no obvious major disabilities tested over an 11-day interval. An additional measure of "agreement rate" was calculated

for this data and is a percentage determined from number of observations agreed upon. The agreement rate for the 12 factors ranged from 71% to 100%. In both analyses the majority of the factors showed agreement or correlation above 80% or .80, respectively. It would be interesting to demonstrate test-retest reliability in a sample of disabled subjects.

Interrater reliability is critical for this instrument as it may be completed by an informant rather than by the clients themselves. Although the sample size was very small, excellent interrater reliability for total sample was demonstrated with correlations ranging from .89 to 1.00 and agreement ratings ranging from 69% to 100%.

A few minor editorial details should be addressed. These include modification of wording to better fit a U.S. population, consistency in the use of italics in the behavioral statements, and correction of inconsistencies between the Individual Record Form and the answer booklet. Also, the administration should be completely standardized by eliminating the optional section in the verbal instructions and enforcing a precise order of the questions in the interview mode of administration.

To summarize, the Work Readiness Profile represents a good "first attempt" at the measure of work effectiveness in a differentially abled population. The manual and record forms are clearly written and easy to understand with a much-needed emphasis on what the individual can do rather than on what they are lacking. Noted discrepancies and editorial errors should be corrected. Similarly, more detail on the development and normative sample need to be provided. Future research should aim at providing additional evidence of validity. To the credit of the author, she points out that the instrument is in the early stages of development. This reviewer looks forward to continued research and revision of the Work Readiness Profile.

Review of the Work Readiness Profile by S. ALVIN LEUNG, Associate Professor, Department of Educational Psychology, The Chinese University of Hong Kong, Shatin, N.T., Hong Kong:

The Work Readiness Profile was developed to assess individuals with disabilities on their readiness to engage in work or employment. According to Rowe, the author, this instrument was designed to provide descriptive information on how a person functions within his/her environment, and to highlight personal strengths rather than deficiencies. The objective was to describe current characteristics and behavior, instead of predicting long-term future behavior. The Work Readiness Profile was intended for adolescents and adults with a range of disabilities, including people with intellectual, physical, and multiple disabilities.

The manual of the Work Readiness Profile briefly described how the instrument was developed. The process appeared to be systematic. Initially, a number of factors related to the work performance of disabled individuals were identified through literature search and consultation with professionals. A set of items related to each factor was then written. A "multidiscipline panel" of experts and service providers then reviewed these items. It was not clear, however, who these experts were in terms of training, education, and actual experiences. The number of factors and items were eventually reduced after several trials of the instrument. The nature and procedures of the trials were not clearly described in the manual. The process resulted in a Work Readiness Profile that has 12 factors or scales, which were: Health (H), Hearing (D), Vision (V), Travel (T), Movement (M), Fine Motor Skills (MF), Gross Motor Skills and Strength (MS), Social and Interpersonal Skills (SI), Work Adjustment (WA), Communication Effectiveness (C), Abilities and Skills (AS), and Literacy and Numeracy (LN).

An important feature of the Work Readiness Profile is that respondents are asked to rate themselves or a target person by comparing with people in the general population. The belief is that the identification of handicaps could help organizations determine what supports are needed for disabled workers and job applicants so as to facilitate their work adjustment. A criterion-referenced approach was used in the design of items and factors. Items in each factor were arranged to reflect progressive levels of behavior competence. The higher the level, the higher the degree of competence a person has achieved in relation to the required skill area. Of the 12 factors, 6 factors (the MS, SI, WA, C, AS, and LN scales) have eight competency levels (1–8). The V factor has three competency levels (4–6), the D factor has four competency levels (3–6), the H factor has five competency levels (2–6), and the T, MF, and M factors each have six competency levels (1–6). Three of the 12 factors (the H, D, and V scales) have a single item at each competency level, and

other factors have multiple items at each competency level. The varying structures of the factors could be confusing for test-takers and users.

Items are written using behavior terms, and respondents are asked to indicate whether each item is "true" or "not true" in describing themselves or a target person. A respondent's score on each factor is the highest level in which a "true" response is given to all the items at that level. For five factors, respondents are asked to start at the highest level, and if the answer is "true," the highest level would be their score. For other factors, respondents are asked to start at Level 5, and they move up or down depending on whether or not their answers to all items at that level are in the "true" direction. For all the factors, a score of 6 or above reflects competencies of individuals without disabilities. The 12 factors are arranged into three clusters, which are Physical Effectiveness, Personal Effectiveness, and Sensory Effectiveness. An average score for each cluster, as well as an average score for all the 12 factors, is also computed. Overall, the method of scoring is somewhat complex because the number of competency levels for each factor is not the same. The instructions for test administration are somewhat complex, particularly for individuals who might have some intellectual disabilities. Also, these instructions are printed in the manual, and they are not printed on the text booklet. Printing the instructions on the text booklet is important, especially for individuals with disabilities.

The Work Readiness Profile could be completed in about 10–15 minutes. A person could rate himself/herself directly. A service provider could rate a client through an interview or through information provided by an informant. Test scores are arranged and summarized using a profile form. An organization could also aggregate and summarize test scores for a group of individuals and plot their average scores using a group profile form. Both the individual and group profile forms are well designed, which should facilitate the process of test interpretation.

Information regarding reliability and validity is summarized in the manual. The average test-retest (11 days) reliability coefficient for the 12 factors is .89, and the range of the coefficients is between .74 and 1.0. The average test-retest agreement rate for the 12 factors is 90%, and the range is between 71% and 100%. The average interrater reliability coefficient for the 12 factors is .95, and the range of coefficients is between .89 and 1.0. The average interrater agreement rate for the 12 factors is 85%, with a range between 69% and 100%. The levels of test-retest reliability and interrater reliability appear to be adequate.

The manual of the Work Readiness Profile reported five studies that were done to investigate the validity of scores from the instrument. The five studies were actually five factor analyses of the 12 scores using different samples. The author claimed that the findings supported the existence of a Work Readiness factor as well as a Physical Effectiveness factor across different samples. The factor analysis procedure suffered from two major limitations. First, the five studies used overlapping samples of participants with and without disabilities. For example, the 229 intellectually disabled participants whose responses were used in the first factor analysis were also included in the second study focusing on people with disabilities. Also, the fifth factor analysis consisted of participants examined in Study 1, 2, and 4. One could argue that similar structures were found across studies because overlapping samples were used. Separate factor analyses on independent samples should be performed if the author would like to show that the factor structure across samples was similar. Second, the sample size used in Study 3 was too small ($N = 57$). A bigger sample should be used to ensure that the resultant factor structure is valid and stable.

More research work should be done to examine the validity of the Work Readiness Profile. A more vigorous approach to factor analysis is only one way to examine the validity of scores from the instrument. If the goal intention of the instrument were to help disabled individuals to identify strengths that could be used in an occupational setting, some form of predictive validation would be necessary. Rowe insisted that the purpose of the Work Readiness Profile is to describe and not to predict. However, if the scores of this test cannot accurately predict work-related competencies at least in the short term, the test scores would not be useful to test takers or organizations that are using the data. Moreover, the test scores were expected to "predict" the degree of support a disabled worker might need in a work setting. Consequently, I believe that evidence on the predictive and concurrent validity of scores from the instrument is important and necessary.

The Work Readiness Profile suffers from three other limitations. First, a group form is available and group data could be computed. However, there is no information on how to use the group data, and on the validity of using group data. Second, the manual suggested that informants could be used as sources of information about a disabled person. Test interpretation based on informants without actually meeting a target client is quite risky. Finally, the utility of the aggregated scores (Physical Effectiveness and Personal Effectiveness) and the total score should be more clearly explained in the manual. The validity of these aggregated scores should be examined through research work.

SUMMARY. Overall, the Work Readiness Profile is a carefully designed instrument that could provide useful information for practitioners and employers about the status of disabled individuals in relation to their work competencies and potential. The manual is concisely written and well designed to help test users understand the construction and use of the test. At this point, the amount of research evidence to support the validity of scores from the instrument is inadequate. Consequently, practitioners are advised to use the instrument and interpret the test scores with caution.

[428]
Worker Rehabilitation Questionnaire.

Purpose: Designed to suggest "alternative occupations for vocational rehabilitation clients."
Population: Vocational rehabilitation clients.
Publication Dates: 1984–1989.
Acronym: WRQ.
Scores: 15 areas: Making Decisions/Communicating/Having Responsibility, Operating Vehicles, Using Machines/Tools/Instruments, Performing Physical Activities, Operating Keyboard and Office Equipment, Monitoring and/or Controlling Equipment and/or Processes, Working Under Uncomfortable Conditions, Working with Art/Decor/Entertainment, Performing Supervisory Duties, Performing Estimating Activities, Processing Written Information, Working with Buyers/Customers/Salespersons, Working Under Hazardous Conditions, Performing Paced and/or Repetitive Activities, Catering/Serving/Smelling/Tasting.
Administration: Individual.
Price Data: Available from publisher.
Time: Administration time not reported.
Comments: Ratings by rehabilitation counselor or self-ratings; based upon the Position Analysis Questionnaire (T5:2016).
Authors: David D. Robinson (manual), Robert C. Mecham (test), Alma F. Harris (test), E. J. McCormick (test), and P. R. Jeanneret (test).
Publisher: Consulting Psychologists Press, Inc.

Review of the Worker Rehabilitation Questionnaire by ALBERT M. BUGAJ, Associate Professor of Psychology, University of Wisconsin—Marinette, Marinette, WI:

The Worker Rehabilitation Questionnaire (WRQ) is a "computer-assisted system for suggesting alternative occupations for vocational rehabilitation clients" (manual, p. 1). The WRQ is a specialized extension of the Position Analysis Questionnaire (PAQ; T5:2016). As such, the two tests share many similar characteristics.

The PAQ consists of 187 "job elements" that characterize "generic" human behaviors and work situations. These behaviors include using measuring devices, working in high temperatures, supervising others, and so forth. They are meant to be *worker-oriented* rather than *job-oriented*. Worker-oriented behaviors apply to a wide range of jobs on an across-the-board basis, rather than to specific jobs. The PAQ matches the characteristics of an individual with a range of potential jobs, based on the jobs' generic requirements. Although the PAQ is intended for the general population, the WRQ is intended for use with vocational rehabilitation clients. Computer packages score both the PAQ and WRQ.

Directions for the WRQ require a 12th grade reading level. It is intended to be administered by a rehabilitation counselor or other professional examiner, although self-ratings are possible under certain circumstances (e.g., clients with a high degree of maturity).

In administering the WRQ, the client is rated on 150 job elements on 6-point scales. The counselor would rate, for example, the ability of the client to perform repetitive activities, using a zero to indicate the client could take no part in such activities, up to a six, indicating the client could take an extensive part in such activities. Limits on up to a dozen items can be set to prevent the program from listing occupations on the output report beyond the client's capabilities. Thus, if the client lacks a high school education or GED, the item rating the client's education level can be used to prevent occupations requiring such an educational level from being reported as potential job choices. As an option, the client's General Aptitude Test Battery Score, or its equivalent, can be entered.

The WRQ results report how closely the client's capabilities match the characteristics of specific occupations listed in the PAQ database.

The report first indicates the percentage of occupations rejected due to the limits set. Next, potential matches, as well as false positives (matches that should be eliminated due to lack of experience, lack of such positions in the local economy, etc.) are listed. Among the remaining wealth of data supplied from the PAQ database are the prospects for employment opening in the occupations listed (taken from the *Occupational Outlook Handbook* of the U.S. Department of Labor), expected average incomes derived from census data, and the match between the client's aptitude and that required in the occupation (excellent, good, fair, or poor). Matches are considered potential, as the job listed might not be available in the client's community, or the client might not have the *specific* education required for the job.

Jobs rejected during the computer analysis of the WRQ are also listed. The program allows the user to check for *false negatives* that may result when item limits were set too stringently in an objective statistically based manner.

The statistical principle used in determining the match between client characteristics and specific jobs is *maximum likelihood estimation.* PAQ job data were factor analyzed using principal components analysis, resulting in 15 factors. The WRQ computer program calculates factor scores based on client data, and matches these to job data by minimizing the sums of the squared differences between client factor scores and job factor scores. Occupations with low sum of squared difference scores receive high ratings in the WRQ report. Although the 15 factors derived from the analysis, and their constituent items, are reported in an appendix of the manual, it should be noted that statistical data such as factor loadings or communalities are not reported. Conclusions as to the adequacy of the factor analysis are thus difficult to make.

There are also minimal statistical data regarding the reliability and validity of the WRQ in the manual. Reliability data are based on only 36 cases. Without providing coefficients, the manual reports that interrater reliability is low when performed by friends or family members of the client. Test-retest reliabilities are reported for psychologists in private practice and occupational therapists ($r = .84$), rehabilitation clients ($r = .60$), and parents, friends, and other concerned adults ($r = .32$). However, the exact interval between testings is not reported. The manual does state both interrater and test-retest reliabilities can be assessed using the WRQ software, so these measures should be fairly easy to assess.

The WRQ appears to have high content validity, being closely linked to the PAQ, which has an almost 30-year history of use. However, the predictive validity of the WRQ is at present unknown; as the manual points-out, evidence of the success of individuals placed in jobs on the basis of the WRQ will not be known until some time in the future. Criterion-related validity is also lacking, the manual stating it would be desirable to compare a set of WRQ ratings with actual performance tests of handicapped clients.

To their credit, the authors of the WRQ do not present the questionnaire as something that it is not—a stand-alone test of vocational rehabilitation client abilities. It is rather presented as a part of an approach to counseling involving medical, cognitive, and interest testing, and the like. Care is also taken in the manual to discuss how the results of the WRQ should be presented to the client.

The authors of the WRQ manual further recognize that much work needs to be done collecting reliability and validity data. Various research questions are posed for prospective users of the WRQ. Commendably, the manual ends with the statements "user feedback is needed to help" (the authors) "improve the system" (manual, p. 30).

SUMMARY. As an integral part of a comprehensive approach to counseling vocational rehabilitation patients, the WRQ should prove useful to professionals. However, it cannot be looked upon as a test to be used apart from the comprehensive approach presented in the manual. Professionals who adopt the WRQ must also be aware that data on the reliability and validity still need to be collected.

Review of the Worker Rehabilitation Questionnaire by BRUCE THOMPSON, Professor and Distinguished Research Scholar, Department of Educational Psychology, Texas A&M University, and Adjunct Professor of Community Medicine, Baylor College of Medicine, College Station, TX:

According to the manual, the Worker Rehabilitation Questionnaire (WRQ) is "a computer-assisted system for suggesting alternative occupations for vocational rehabilitation clients" (p. 1). The WRQ is intended to help counselors work with clients in identifying new occupations, given skills and interests, following an injury or illness.

The manual notes that "one of the highest priorities in vocational rehabilitation is to evaluate a new client's physical and psychological capabilities and tolerances" (p. 1). Other tasks include taking an employment history, assessing vocational interests, and identifying potentially transferable skills.

The WRQ's objective is to identify roughly a half-dozen potential occupations for further exploration with clients. The manual clearly communicates that WRQ results are intended only to provide a framework for counseling with clients, and not to identify a single definitive job choice. Nor is the WRQ intended for use as a forensic tool for estimating lost wages resulting from an injury or illness. The WRQ output includes potential occupations organized by the *Dictionary of Occupational Titles* (DOT) codes, typical wage rates, required education for each occupation, and projections of related occupational demand changes over the next decade.

The WRQ is generally completed by the rehabilitation counselor, and not by the client. However, the manual recommends that the WRQ be completed in the client's presence. Most of the job elements are rated on a 6-point scale, but some responses also set "limits" that the program uses to screen out any occupation requiring a higher skill rating (i.e., 0 to 5) than that assigned to the client (e.g., a "1").

In short, the WRQ is a career-counseling measure grounded in the trait-and-factor approach to personnel selection. This approach has a long tradition, but potential users also may wish to consider other counseling frameworks as well.

Specifically, the WRQ invokes a matching strategy based on 15 jobs-dimensions identified as statistical factors in prior research. Examples of these factors are "operating vehicles," "performing physical activities," and "catering, serving, smelling, or tasting." As our economy continues to change during the information age, one might question whether these 15 dimensions continue to be the correct dimensions characterizing job activities.

RELIABILITY AND VALIDITY. In some locations the manual describes reliability and validity as if they were properties of tests (p. 27), rather than of scores and particular uses of scores (cf. Thompson & Vacha-Haase, 2000; Wilkinson & The APA Task Force on Statistical Inference, 2000). The manual notes that reliability evidence is "quite limited" (p. 27), perhaps because WRQ data are available for only 36 cases. Test-retest reliability coefficients (administration interval not given) for scores are reported to be .84 for counselor-completed protocols, .60 for client-completed, and .32 for protocols completed by "other concerned adults." It is not clear whether each coefficient involved the same 36 cases, or mutually exclusive subsets of these 36 cases.

The author of the manual suggests that two sorts of validity evidence should be evaluated as regards scores on the measure. First, it is suggested that content validity is very relevant. However, no direct content validity evidence is presented. Second, it is suggested that construct validity evidence is important.

However, the construct validity evidence presented involved merely a generic reference to prior research with the Position Analysis Questionnaire (PAQ), a precursor to the WRQ. It is noted that "the validity of the PAQ [sic] as a job analysis instrument has been well established through research and by its widespread use" (manual, p. 28).

Of course, widespread use is not direct evidence of validity. For example, in some areas of inquiry the field has tended to use most often exactly those measures yielding scores with the least psychometric integrity (Garbarino, 1998).

SUMMARY. If viewed as a framework within which rehabilitation counselors may discuss skills and interests with clients, the WRQ may be useful for skilled and experienced counselors. The WRQ would help skilled counselors organize and integrate information. Nevertheless, as the manual itself notes, "Many questions remain unanswered that only further research can answer" (p. 30).

REVIEWER'S REFERENCES

Garbarino, J. (1998). Comparisons of the constructs and psychometric properties of selected measures of adult attachment. *Measurement and Evaluation in Counseling and Development, 31,* 28–45.

Thompson, B., & Vacha-Haase, T. (2000). Psychometrics *is* datametrics: The test is not reliable. *Educational and Psychological Measurement, 60,* 174–195.

Wilkinson, L., & The APA Task Force on Statistical Inference. (1999). Statistical methods in psychology journals: Guidelines and explanations. *American Psychologist, 54,* 594–604. [reprint available through the APA Home Page: http://www.apa.org/journals/amp/amp548594.html]

[429]
Working—Assessing Skills, Habits, and Style.

Purpose: "Designed to assess personal habits, skills, and styles that are associated with a positive work ethic."

Population: High school and college students and potential employees.

Publication Date: 1996.

Scores: 9 competencies: Taking Responsibility, Working in Teams, Persisting, Having A Sense of Quality, Life-Long Learning, Adapting to Change, Problem Solving, Information Processing, Systems Thinking.

Administration: Group.

Price Data, 1996: $4 each for 1–49 instruments, $3.50 each for 50–499; $3 each for 500–1999; $2.50 each for 2000–4999; $2 each for 5000+; technical and applications manuals available upon request (price information available from publisher); user's manual free with each order.

Time: (30–35) minutes.

Comments: Inventory for self-rating; can be self-administered and self-scored.

Authors: Curtis Miles (test and user's manual) and Phyllis Grummon (test, user's manual, and technical manual), and Karen M. Maduschke (technical manual).

Publisher: H & H Publishing Co., Inc.

Review of Working—Assessing Skills, Habits, and Style by WAYNE CAMARA, Executive Director of Research & Development, The College Board, New York, NY:

Working is a self-assessment designed to address nine broad-based competencies associated with high-performance workplaces and based on findings of the Secretary's Commission on Achieving Necessary Skills (SCANS) (1992, Department of Labor). The workplace skills framework proposed by SCANS and others goes beyond the basic skills in reading, writing, and mathematics. Thinking skills and competencies in understanding systems, technology, resource allocation, teamwork, and acquisition/analysis of information are viewed as essential for jobs in an increasingly competitive, technologically sophisticated, global economy (Linn, p. 1996).

This self-assessment is designed for use as a counseling or career/job planning tool for students planning to enter the workforce, or adults first entering or re-entering the workforce. It is described as a "launching pad for discussion, instruction, application, planning … the basis of seminars, counseling sessions, classes, orientations" (manual, p. 4). It provides information to the test taker, which may also be of use to teachers, trainers, and others when used as part of a group exercise in a counseling or learning situation.

Working includes a user's manual that briefly describes the directions for administration, scoring, and the development of the instrument. The publisher also provides a modest technical document that provides an overview of results from field testing and a description of the scales, a test booklet, and an optional applications manual describing possible uses for the instrument. Working is part of a series of products marketed by H&H Publishing Company labeled "the mindful workforce portfolio" designed for transitioning from school to entry level work.

Working's nine competencies provide a framework of broad applied learning competencies that are not targeted to specific jobs or groups of occupations. The competencies are not skilled based in the traditional sense of job analyses and personnel selection, but rather broader enabling skills and productive work behavior. Working's competencies appear to tap aspects of three of the five SCANS competencies (interpersonal skills, information, and systems, but not resources and technology) and two of three foundation skills (thinking skills and personal qualities, but not basic skills). Together these nine competencies include broad thinking and reasoning skills, as well as positive work behaviors and productive predispositions that together are believed to be transferable across high performance workplaces. The nine competencies include:

1. Solving Problems—interest and skill in using systematic problem solving methods with complex problems.

2. Information Processing—managing one's learning and using multiple strategies when learning.

3. Thinking in Terms of Systems—understanding the relationship among parts in a system and effects of actions within a system.

4. Adapting to Change—comfort with frequent or major changes in one's environment.

5. Having a Sense of Quality—understanding of how exceeding expectations can help one succeed (e.g., "more than expected" vs. "just enough").

6. Interest in Life Long Learning—interest in engaging in learning across a variety of settings.

7. Working in Teams—degree to which one is comfortable working in teams and using skills associated with effective teamwork.

8. Persistence—willingness to expend time and effort to ensure that what is started is completed.

9. Taking Responsibility—Desire to take personal responsibility for task completion. (Technical manual, pp. 2–7)

The nine scales were developed through a content validation process that began with a re-view of the surveys of workplace skills and a review by a panel of experts. No empirical evidence is provided (e.g., correlations of items across scales) to support the reporting of nine separate subscores and it is likely that subscores across several of these scales are highly related.

The scales and items are more appropriately considered a self-reporting of interests, attitudes, or self-perceptions about competencies rather than a cognitive measure of these competencies. This is a critical distinction for potential users to understand. As a self-report instrument, Working resembles personality, attitude, or career interest inventories rather than objective skill assessments. Items on the test further reinforce this distinction: I like working in teams (Working in Teams Scale); I follow through on things no matter what it takes (Persisting Scale); When learning something, I think carefully about the very best way to tackle it (Information Processing Scale); I know how to get things done in a system or an organization (Thinking in Terms of a System Scale).

Working provides a measure of individuals' perceived and self-reported interests and understanding of these competencies, not objective competency profiles. This distinction is made quite clear in all material on the test. The authors are very cautious in describing what the test does and how it can be appropriately used, yet potential users must understand this distinction. Working is not designed for individual decision making such as with hiring, job placement, or performance appraisals.

A field test with a longer 85-item draft instrument was conducted with students at 13 community colleges and 4-year institutions across geographic regions, resulting in a final sample of 640 students completing the items. About two-thirds of these students were freshmen, 17% were sophomores, 3% were high school seniors, and the remaining 4% were upper-class college students. Over half of the participants in the field test were 18–19 years of age, with an additional 30% between the ages 20—29. Seventy percent of students worked at least part-time and about half of those had worked for 5 years or more. English teachers were recruited at each site to administer the test.

The final instrument is composed of 50 items that are answered using a 5-point scale. Individuals read each statement and circle one of five statements that best described (or fits) them: (e) Almost always like me, (d) Quite a bit like me,

(c) Moderately like me, (b) Occasionally like me, and (a) Almost never like me. The 50 items are each scored for only one of the nine competencies, resulting in nine separate scale scores. Each scale has only four to six items, a relatively small number of items to produce a reliable subscore. Coefficient alphas for the longer field test instrument ranged from .52 to .75 across the nine scales. The median coefficient alpha was .59, however, final reliability for the shorter final instrument is not reported. Coefficients in the .5 range have marginal reliability and the reliability of the final 50-item test will likely be lower. This level of reliability may be adequate for initiating discussions of career exploration and interest but insufficient for many other uses.

The instructions note, "remember that this is not a 'test'—there are no right answers. Merely *your* answers based on *your* personality" (test booklet, p. 2). Administration time is estimated at 10–20 minutes. The instructions are simple and clear. The items are printed on pressure-sensitive pages so responses are recorded on the scoring sheet used to compute each subscore. The scoring sheet assigns values of 1–5 to each response and also indicates which items correspond to each of the nine scales. Scale scores are computed by copying the circled value for each item into a box placed under the appropriate column corresponding to the scales. The test taker then adds the total points achieved on those items in each scale. Scores for 16 reverse-coded items are inverted on the score sheet so that more positive responses always result in more points. Score scales range form 6–30 points for the six-item scales and 4–20 points for the four-item scales. The final step in scoring is to convert the scale score for the nine competencies to a percentile score on profile charts. Two additional pressure-sensitive pages are provided for this task and the test taker is instructed to remove these pages from the booklet prior to testing (this is presumably required so that marks will not go through all four pages). Two profile charts are provided—one for the test taker and one for the administrator. Again, all directions for scoring the instrument are quite clear and examples are very helpful. Most secondary students and young adults should be able to complete this instrument independently.

Working is a norm-referenced instrument where scale scores and percentiles are based on responses from up to 566 students completing each scale in the field test and also providing criterion data. However, the manual does not provide adequate explanations of how criterion data were determined and criteria were used to generate these scores.

Working is described as a "diagnostic and prescriptive instrument" (user's manual, p. 1). This description is questionable because more than a profile among subtest scores is required to provide diagnostic value. The only materials discussing interpretation simply note that higher scores are better. There is no prescriptive information, rather all test takers are told "you can improve yourself in any or all of the nine areas. Build on your strengths; improve those areas where you already score well. Find ways to improve on any scores that are lower than you would like" (test booklet, p. 9).

There is limited evidence of validity for the instrument at this time. Students completing the field test were asked for two types of data that served as criteria for the validity study and were also used to determine the scale and percentile scores: (a) self-reported GPA and (b) years of work experience. There are problems with these criteria. First, years of work experience is related to age and is not a convincing indicator of high skills in the workplace. Second, difficulties in using grades as a criteria are summarized in Camara (1998), but are more problematic with an instrument such as Working where there is no evidence that success in traditional college courses is a sufficiently credible and valid predictor for work place skills such as adapting to change, working in teams, and life-long learning, which may not be factored into college grades. About 560 students provided criterion data. Results illustrate 14 of 18 correlations were statistically significant ($p<.01$) but that 5 of 9 scales have correlations of .20 or higher with work experience (Taking Responsibility, Persisting, A Sense of Quality, Life-Long Learning, and Adapting to Change) and 3 of 9 scales have a moderate correlation with GPA (Taking Responsibility, Persisting, and A sense of Quality). Working in Teams was not significantly related to work experience or GPA. The authors attempted to collect additional criterion data from teachers and work supervisors. English teachers returned completed assessments of Working for 98 students. Student and teacher perceptions correlated between .11 and .33 across the scales, yet English teachers may interact with students for less than 45 hours in a typical college course and it is questionable the extent that they could provide objective and valid evaluations of students on several of these competencies. The authors emphasize that although no single line of validation evidence may be overly convincing, together, data from teacher and students ratings provide a lien of convergent validity for the instrument.

SUMMARY. Working is a self-assessment designed to measure nine competency areas that are associated with high-performance workplaces. In general, there is insufficient evidence in the literature linking the skills and competencies prescribed by SCANS and other state and national efforts to high performance workplaces or job success and satisfaction. Despite this void in the research, some employers and policymakers continue to define such broad-based competencies as essential for future workplaces. Even though there is insufficient empirical basis supporting these skill frameworks, Working does attempt to meet a need for educators and employers who believe in the common foundation of generic and broad-based competencies. It appears to be the first assessment designed to address SCANS-like competencies and may be useful for providing students and entry-level workers with a profile of their self-perceived competencies and interests. The instrument is easy to administer, score, and interpret. The authors are quite open in emphasizing the instrument's use for initiating discussions, career explorations and guidance, and not for any high stakes purposes. The reliability and independence of the separate scales are often questionable, and additional items may be needed in nine separate scales are to be reported. Additional validation evidence is also required as are more appropriate criteria for validation studies. Ultimately, employer ratings may be the only defensible criteria in measuring competencies associated with high-performance workplaces. College GPA, teacher ratings, and years of experience do not provide the type of qualitative evidence or have a conceptual link to the types of competencies instruments such as Working attempt to measure.

REVIEWER'S REFERENCES

Secretary's Commission on Achieving Necessary Skills. (1992). *Learning a living: A blueprint for high performance: A SCANS report for America 2000.* Washington, DC: U.S. Department of Labor.
Linn, R. L. (1996). Work readiness assessment: Questions of validity. In L. B. Resnick & J. G. Wirt (Eds.), *Linking school and work* (pp. 249–266). San Francisco: Jossey-Bass Publishers.
Camara, W. (1998). *High school grading policies.* Research Notes (RN-04) New York, NY: College Board.

Review of Working—Assessing Skills, Habits, and Style by JOYCE MEIKAMP, Associate Professor

of Special Education, Marshall University Graduate College, South Charleston, WV:

NATURE AND USES. Working—Assessing Skills, habits, and Style (Working) is a self-administered and scored inventory for either individuals or groups. It was designed to be used for both diagnostic and prescriptive purposes, purportedly tapping workplace skills beyond academic competencies and technical skills. Its intent was to be a simple, inexpensive way to measure competencies that may be necessary for productive and rewarding employment into the 21st Century in the United States.

Reportedly employers describe successful employees as individuals who can do more than perform specific job tasks. They have skills that are essential and transferable across workplace settings. Based on the Secretary's Commission on Achieving Necessary Skills (SCANS) Report released by the United States Department of Labor, Working taps nine transferable workplace skills. In addition to working in teams, orientation to learning, problem solving and decision making abilities, and the ability to adapt to change, these skills include persisting and taking personal responsibility for task completion. Working also addresses focusing on work quality and understanding how an individual's work fits into the overall goals of the organization.

The nine scales that comprise Working assess each of nine constructs via 50 statements. Subjects are asked to record their responses, using a 5-point Likert scale, directly beside each of the statements in the Working inventory booklet. A unique feature of the booklet is that it has pressure sensitive pages corresponding to the scoring page for ease in scoring. Raw scores generated from the nine scales are each converted to percentile ranks.

According to the authors, Working is a diagnostic tool that can be used to identify relative strengths and weaknesses. Results are to be used to develop individual plans for intervention or as a counseling tool.

DEVELOPMENT AND STANDARDIZATION. Based upon review of the literature and national and state level surveys, skill areas most critical to employers were identified. As a result, a matrix of 24 potential competencies was given to a panel of experts for review. From this review, 24 competencies were collapsed into the nine Working scale areas and then the items were developed. No mention was made in the technical manual as to how these competencies were "collapsed." Apparently only review rather than statistical procedures was utilized.

Items were pilot tested and reviewed by psychometricians. Items correlating with social desirability were eliminated. The technical manual only alludes to this correlation and does not specify the exact statistical procedures performed nor results.

Standardization procedures for Working are cause for concern. For example, no mention is made of the total number of students initially administered Working. The authors make note that a number of student participants did not take the assignment seriously and completed it in a haphazard manner. As such, 640 student responses were usable.

Moreover, the sample was not randomly stratified for age, gender, race, geographic region, work experience, or community setting. Although Working's target population is supposed to include high school students, none were used in standardization. Participants were from 13 institutions, consisting of community, technical, and 4-year colleges. These institutions were recruited via the Internet and personal contact. In fact, of the 13 institutions participating, nine were community colleges.

RELIABILITY AND VALIDITY. Alpha coefficients for each of the scales ranged from .52 to .75. However, no other measures of reliability were reported.

Relative to content validity, rater judgments were used. However, in the technical manual no mention was made about their relevant training, experience, or qualifications.

Convergent validity relating teachers' perceptions of strengths and weaknesses of students and the students' performances on Working was investigated for 98 of the students' self-assessments. Pearson r correlations ranged from .11 to .33. Adapting to Change was not significantly correlated with the teachers' perceptions. Working scale correlations were also reported for work experience and grade-point average. Work experience did not correlate significantly with Working in Teams. In addition, grade-point average correlated significantly with six of the nine scales. The authors cited these patterns of correlations as supportive of convergent and divergent validity.

INTERPRETATION HAZARDS. Although the rationale supporting Working seems to have merit, given the limited research cited in the technical manual, results must be interpreted with caution.

Until additional research is conducted relative to construct and criterion validity, Working results can be interpreted within the constraints of relative strengths and weaknesses for only the nine scales. Due to the very limited research to date, one cannot make assumptions as to how Working results may generalize to future workplace success.

SUMMARY. Working is a self-administered and scored inventory to assess relative strengths and weaknesses on nine scales related to workplace competencies other than academic/technical skills. Although the premise supporting Working may be worthwhile, due to technical limitations results should be interpreted with caution.

[430]
Young Adult Behavior Checklist and Young Adult Self-Report.

Purpose: "Designed to provide standardized descriptions of behavior, feelings, thoughts, and competencies."

Publication Date: 1997.

Scores, 11: Anxious/Depressed, Withdrawn, Somatic Complaints, Thought Problems, Attention Problems, Intrusive, Aggressive Behavior, Delinquent Behavior, Internalizing, Externalizing, Total.

Administration: Group.

Price Data, 1997: $10 per 25 test booklets (specify instrument); $10 per 25 profiles for hand scoring (specify instrument); $25 per manual (217 pages); $7 per template for hand scoring (specify instrument); $220 for computer program scoring.

Authors Thomas M. Achenbach.

Publisher: Child Behavior Checklist.

a) YOUNG ADULT BEHAVIOR CHECKLIST.
Population: Young Adults.
Acronym: YABCL.
Time: (10–15) minutes.
Comments: Ratings by parents.
b) YOUNG ADULT SELF-REPORT.
Population: Ages 18–30.
Acronym: YASR.
Time: (15–20) minutes.

Review of the Young Adult Behavior Checklist and Young Adult Self-Report by PATTI L. HARRISON, Professor of School Psychology and Assistant Dean of the Graduate School, The University of Alabama, Tuscaloosa, AL:

The Young Adult Self-Report (YASR) and Young Adult Behavior Checklist (YABCL) are designed to provide an assessment of the problem behaviors and competencies of adults aged 18–30 years. The YASR is self-administered by young adults, and the YABCL is completed by parents and other adults who know the young adult, although users are cautioned that norms are based on parent reports only. The YASR and YABCL represent an upward extension of instruments developed by the same author, including the Child Behavior Checklist/4–18 (CBCL; Achenbach, 1991a; T5:451), Teacher's Report Form (TRF; Achenbach, 1991b; T5:451), Youth Self-Report (YSR; Achenbach, 1991c; T5:451), and Semistructured Clinical Interview for Children and Adolescents (McConaughy & Achenbach, 1994; T5:451). The YASR, YABCL, and other instruments use an empirical paradigm based on statistical procedures for deriving taxonomic groupings of specific problem behaviors and evidence that the problem behaviors distinguish among people with and without mental problems.

CONTENT AND SCORING. The Problem Scales are the major components of the YASR and YABCL. Most of the 116 YASR problem behavior items have counterparts in the 113 YABCL problem behavior items. Each problem behavior item of the YASR and YABCL is scored by the respondent on a 3-point scale of 0, 1, or 2 to indicate if the behavior is *not true, somewhat or sometimes true,* or *very true or often true* for the young adult over the past 6 months.

The problem behavior items form three global scales (Total problems, Internalizing, and Externalizing) and eight syndromes scales. The Anxious/Depressed and Withdrawn syndrome scales comprise the Internalizing global scale, and the Intrusive, Aggressive Behavior, and Delinquent Behavior syndrome scales comprise the Externalizing global scale. Somatic Complaints, Thought Problems, and Attention Problems are not categorized on the Internalizing or Externalizing global scales, but are included in the Total problems scale. Each syndrome scale has 7–17 items. In addition, 35 items on the YASR and 25 items on the YABCL are not included on a syndrome scale or the Internalizing or Externalizing global scales, but are included on the Total Problems scale.

The YASR, but not the YABCL, includes brief Adaptive Functioning and Substance Use scales. Five scales of Adaptive Functioning (Friends, Education, Job, Family, Spouse) include 3–7 items each; a mean Adaptive Functioning Score also is provided. The three Substance Use scales (Tobacco, Alcohol, and Drugs) have one item each, and a mean Substance use score is provided. A criticism of the CBCL (Doll, 1998; Furlong, 1998) was the incomplete measurement of the strengths and competence of children and adolescents. The young adult extensions also place very little emphasis on adaptive functioning.

The raw scores for the three global scales and eight syndrome scales are converted to normalized T scores, based on the scores of normative samples for each gender. The T scores were normalized to result in comparable percentile ranks across the eight syndrome scales. Because large percentages of the normative sample obtained scores of 0 and 1 on the syndrome scales, a minimum T score of 50 (raw scores at the 50th percentile or lower) was set for the syndrome scales. The T scores for most syndromes have a maximum of 100. The normative sample exhibited more variability in the raw scores for the three global Problem Scales, and T scores for global scales range from 20–100. The T scores for the Adaptive Functioning and Substance Use Scales of the YASR were developed in a similar manner. Higher T scores on the problem Scale and Substance Use Scales indicate poorer functioning, and higher T scores on the Adaptive Functioning Scales indicate better functioning.

Profiles allow professionals to graph the scores from the YASR and YABCL and identify the percentile rank and a "normal," "borderline," and "clinical" category for each score. For the eight problem syndromes, T scores below 67 (percentile ranks below 95) are classified in the normal range. T scores between 67 and 70 (percentile ranks 95–98) fall in the borderline range, and T scores greater than 70 (percentile ranks greater than 98) form the clinical range. For the Total Problems, Internalizing, and Externalizing Scales, T scores of 60 (82nd percentile) and 63 (90th percentile) were selected to demarcate the normal, borderline, and clinical categories. Similar profiling systems are used with the Adaptive Functioning and Substance Use Scales of the YASR. The author indicates that the selection of T-scores to demarcate the categories was based on discrimination of scores for referred and nonreferred samples, but recommends that other cutoffs be tested for their effectiveness. The author cautions professionals to use the scores and the normal, borderline, and clinical categories as estimates, an important caution given that a difference of only 2–3 raw score points differentiates the clinical and normal categories for some syndromes.

Scoring and profiling the YASR and YABCL can be accomplished by hand or with a computer-scoring program. Because the hand scoring is tedious and prone to clerical errors, professionals are encouraged to use the computer-scoring program. A similar recommendation was made for the CBCL (Doll, 1998; Furlong, 1998).

TECHNICAL DATA. The YASR and YABCL have a wealth of supporting data from numerous pilot, normative, reliability, and validity studies, and comprehensive descriptions of these studies fill most of the manual. Similarly, the empirical base of the CBCL has been identified as its major strength (Doll, 1998; Furlong, 1998). Development of the YASR and YABCL began with a generation of large pools of items, and items were deleted and modified during testing of five successive pilot editions with young adults and their parents. The eight syndromes were derived using principal components analysis by gender with data from large samples of clinically referred and nonreferred young adults. The Internalizing-Externalizing groups were formed using principal factor analyses with the same samples.

T scores for the YASR and YABCL are based on normative samples of nonreferred young adults. The 575 females and 484 males for the YASR and 553 females and 521 males for the YABCL were selected from a national representative sample. Although the manual does not include national percentages with which to compare the sample demographics, the normative samples appear to be fairly comparable to the U.S. population. The sample appears to be somewhat underrepresented in the lower SES group, with only 18% of the sample falling in the lower SES.

Large, matched samples of nonreferred and referred young adults were used in reliability studies. Test-retest reliability studies with a one-week interval yielded generally acceptable correlations for the YASR (mean $r = .84$, Total Problems $r = .89$, Mean Adaptive scale $r = .82$) and YABCL (mean $r = .87$, Total Problems $r = .93$), although some syndromes had correlations in the .60s and .70s. Long-term stability studies resulted in a mean correlation of .58 for the YASR, over an average of 39 months, and a mean correlation of .60 for the YABCL, over an average of 44 months. Internal consistency analyses yielded alphas primarily in the .70s and .80s for the syndrome scales, .88–.95 for Internalizing and Externalizing, and .96–.97 for the Total Problems scales. Alpha coefficients are not reported for the Adaptive Functioning scales of the YASR; the Adaptive Functioning scales have fewer items than the Problems scales, which not only affects the computation of alpha coefficients but also suggests that the Adaptive Functioning scales should have limited use only. The reliability data suggest that the Total Problems scale provides the most reliable measure and that individual syndrome scales and Adaptive Functioning scales should be interpreted cautiously.

The author emphasizes the importance of cross-informant ratings and provides data in the manual to support the cross-information approach. Reliability studies found an average correlation of .60 between mothers and mothers on the YABCL and .42 between informants on the YASR and YABCL. The author also provides a method for using a cross-informant approach in the interpretation of scores for an individual. The computer-scoring program provides cross-informant Q correlations between item, syndrome, and global scores, if the YASR and YABCL are administered to several informants, and compares the Q correlations to typical correlations of a reference sample.

A variety of validity studies for the YASR and YABCL report differences between referred and nonreferred samples. The author supports content validity with the finding that, with one exception, all items were scored significantly higher for referred than nonreferred individuals; however, most items had small effect sizes. Several studies investigated criterion-related validity. All problem syndromes and global scores were significantly different for referred and nonreferred samples, although multiple regression analyses suggested referral status generally accounted for small amounts of variance in scores. Other analyses found that proportions of referred subjects significantly exceeded nonreferred subjects who scored in the clinical range. These analyses suggested that the largest proportion of subjects would be correctly classified on the YASR according to a combination of the Total Problems, Mean Adaptive Functioning, and Mean Substance Use scores (67% accuracy) and the Total Problems score of the CBCL (71% accuracy). This accuracy in classification was not improved substantially as a result of a series of discriminant analyses of items and individual syndromes. Another analysis reported that Total Problems *T*-scores in the clinical range had a 74%–82% probability of being from referred samples.

Construct validity studies investigated the relationship between the YASR and YABCL and other measures of psychopathology. Studies found significant longitudinal relationships between the CBCL and YSR and later YABCL and YASR scores for American and Dutch samples. Other studies found significant relationships between the YASR syndrome scores and some DSM diagnostic constructs for American and Dutch samples. Dutch studies indicated that the YASR discriminated between referred and nonreferred samples as well as or better than other adult measures of psychopathology. A Turkish study found significant correlations between the YASR and Minnesota Multiphasic Personality Inventory—2 (MMPI-2). Although there are only a few construct validity studies presented in the manual and limited support for using the YASR and YABCL in identifying psychopathology, it is anticipated that many additional construct validity studies will be conducted by the author and other researchers, as has been done with the CBCL.

APPLICATIONS. Although the manual for the YASR and YABCL provides a detailed analysis of technical data, a major disappointment is that the manual is not directed to the clinical user. The limited information about scoring, interpretation, and use of the instrument by practitioners has been a weakness also cited for the children and youth versions (Doll, 1998; Furlong, 1998). Most of the limited information for everyday, clinical use is in an appendix on hand scoring and a chapter with answers to common questions or is embedded in technical chapters. For example, a brief description of the hand-scored and computer-scored profiles and a sample profile are in the same chapter as the description of the principal components analysis for deriving syndromes and data about the normative sample. A sample printout and description of cross-informant comparison for a person are in the chapter on reliability. A clinician will not find a chapter with detailed, comprehensive, sequential presentation of sample case studies and recommendations for interpretation.

Although the author describes practical uses in a brief chapter, the chapter is limited to a general, vague, and unsupported discussion of the use of the instrument in managed care, fee-for-service, and forensic contexts. The author suggests several uses of the instruments, including using individual items to select targets for treatment and using the instruments for pretreatment and outcome assessment, that were not investigated or supported by validity studies summarized in the manual. Similarly, the chapter includes a table relating YASR and YABCL syndromes to DSM-IV disorders; although a validity study did investigate the relationship between syndromes and DSM classification, the table is not consistent with the results of the validity study reported in the manual. Fortunately, the author does include a chapter outlining needed research studies to support these practical applications of the instruments.

SUMMARY. The strength and weakness of the YASR and YABCL are similar to those for the children and adolescent versions: The comprehensive empirical foundation is far stronger than translation of research into clinical use. The development and research for the YASR and YABCL can serve as a model for comprehensive test development procedures and reliability and validity investigations for new instruments. The technical data support that scores from the instruments have adequate reliability and validity to distinguish between referred and nonreferred samples, although studies suggest that users should rely on the Total Problems score and have limited interpretation of the individual problem syndrome and Adaptive Functioning scores. The manual includes only a few investigations of construct validity, but the author provides guidelines for future research to support different uses of the instruments.

The clinician will be disappointed by the lack of information in the manual to guide the everyday use of the instrument with clients experiencing problems and with the general, vague, and unsupported suggestions for the practical settings in which the instrument may be used. The clinician will appreciate the research data that comprise most of the manual, but also would have appreciated chapters dedicated to case studies and guidelines for interpretation of scores. It is strongly recommended that the author develop future manuals with far greater emphasis on the needs of practitioners in clinical settings.

REVIEWER'S REFERENCES

Achenbach, T. M. (1991a). *Manual for the Child Behavior Checklist/4–18 and 1991 Profile.* Burlington, VT: University of Vermont Department of Psychiatry.
Achenbach, T. M. (1991b). *Manual for the Teacher's Report Form and 1991 Profile.* Burlington, VT: University of Vermont Department of Psychiatry.
Achenbach, T. M. (1991c). *Manual for the Youth Self-Report and 1991 Profile.* Burlington, VT: University of Vermont Department of Psychiatry.

McConaughy, S. H., & Achenbach, T. M. (1994). *Manual for the Semistructured Clinical Interview for Children and Adolescents.* Burlington, VT: University of Vermont Department of Psychiatry.

Doll, B. (1998). [Review of the Child Behavior Checklist.] In J. C. Impara & B. S. Plake (Eds.), *The thirteenth mental measurements yearbook* (pp. 217–220). Lincoln, NE: Buros Institute of Mental Measurements.

Furlong, M. J. (1998). [Review of the Child Behavior Checklist.] In J. C. Impara & B. S. Plake (Eds.), *The thirteenth mental measurements yearbook* (pp. 220–224). Lincoln, NE: Buros Institute of Mental Measurements.

Review of the Young Adult Behavior Checklist and Young Adult Self-Report by JONATHAN SANDOVAL, Professor, Division of Education, University of California, Davis, Davis, CA:

This paired set of self-reports and other-reports of problems experienced by young adults is an extension of the author's earlier work with children and adolescents. These initially developed measures—The Child Behavior Checklist (T5:451), the Teacher's Report Form (T5:451), and the Youth Self-Report (T5:451)—have been widely adopted for use in schools, clinics, and research studies. It seems reasonable to extend them to an older population of young adults. In so doing, the author breaks new ground in developing instruments explicitly for this age group, which includes many students in college.

The manual for the test is really a short text on the research and theory that have been done to develop the concepts of internalizing and externalizing symptoms of behavior. The manual is dense with information. An unusual amount of detail about the test development efforts may be found in the manual, and the reader in a hurry may be overwhelmed or frustrated, although others will appreciate the thoroughness of this approach. The author has used the statistical techniques of principal component analysis, analysis of variance, regression analysis, and discriminant analysis to construct and validate the measures. We should look forward to the application of other modern techniques such as structural equation modeling to examine the latent traits that may underlie these scales.

The intent of the Young Adult Self-Report (YASR) and the Young Adult Behavior Checklist (YABCL) is to identify behavioral and emotional problems of young adults and discriminate between those individuals who are considered relatively normal and those who are considered maladaptively deviant. The items on the two scales overlap in content to a large extent. The measures yield normalized T scores and percentiles by gender in relationship to a representative U.S. norm group. The reports and ratings produce eight scales, two composites (internalizing and externalizing), and a Total Problems score. In addition, the YASR contains items related to adaptive functioning with friends, family, education, job, and spouse. These items combine into an adaptive scale. Some of these adaptive scales may not be relevant to a particular individual, such as the spouse scale for someone unmarried, and need not be administered. The YASR also has items related to alcohol, drug, and tobacco use, which combine into a substance use scale. The YABCL does not include these or other items thought to be unreliably observed by parents or other adults who know the subject well. In addition, the manual contains information about the prevalence rate of each item, inasmuch as they are discrete problems such as "Self-conscious," "Nausea," and "Brags" that may need to be followed up. The percent reporting each problem is listed by gender and by referral status. Absent from the measures is a social desirability scale or a lie scale. We have little information about the extent to which informants may be minimizing problems or faking problems. Although useful, such scales would add to the length of the measures. The author recommends that extreme scores be considered carefully in light of other information about the informant.

The reporting forms for the scales are simple and laid out in a straightforward manner. There is limited space available for the respondent to elaborate or to list additional concerns. The problems listed, on their face, seem to be appropriate to this age group. The items, however, are general in nature and subject to interpretation. A strength of the scales is the inclusion of items related to Attention Deficit Hyperactivity Disorder, Oppositional Defiant Disorder, and Conduct Disorder, items often missing from scales designed for older adults.

The norms for the scales were obtained from the same subjects used in norming previous measures developed by the author. There was some attrition in the sample over time, and one can speculate that this factor may have biased the norms as being conservative, in that more unstable individuals may have been lost over time.

The norm sample consisted of over 1,200 individuals across the country, from different ethnicities and different socioeconomic statuses, who did not report receiving mental health or substance abuse treatment, who did not report being suicidal or having experienced a traumatic event, or who had not been incarcerated during the previous year. Those who did *report* receiving clinical services were retained in the "referred" sample along with others who had been obtained from clinical settings. This referred sample, used extensively in the validation of the scale, is not described in any detail, although further description of what kind of services they sought would have been informative. The lack of information about this clinical sample is a serious omission. Undoubtedly they are a heterogeneous group. The norm sample is also referred to as the "nonreferred sample" (manual, pp. 41, 86). They are somewhat representative of the nation but underrepresent the western region of the country and the Latino population, to some degree. More seriously, they underrepresent the lower socioeconomic status group, a population from which a larger number of problems may come.

Test-retest stability over one week is good, ranging from .72 for Thought Problems to .89 for Total Problems and Anxious/Depressed on the YASR. Values for the special Substance Use scale reached .92. Many of the coefficients are in the low .90s for the YABCL with the glaring exceptions of Somatic Complaints and Thought Problems (.43 and .64, respectively), which reflects the difficulty in observing these phenomena by others. Longer term stability coefficients over 3 years are lower, but the same patterns are present. The correlations of scores average around .60 over this relatively long interval.

Internal consistency reliability measures are also quite good, with the Cronbach alpha statistic for the main scores of Internalizing and Externalizing on both measures averaging around .90 and the Total Problems score equaling .96. Here too, the reliabilities for Thought Problems are lowest, ranging from .56 to .77. The user should be most concerned about the reliability of this score.

Interrater reliability on the YABCL is fairly good. The manual reports an average correlation of .60 between the ratings of mothers and fathers. The correlations across the YABCL and YASR are in the .4 range, which is not unusual for the agreement between a self-report and another's report. The lowest correlation, not unexpectedly, is on the scale Thought Disorders. An interesting feature of the computer scoring program for the scales is the side-by-side listing of ratings of each item by different informants as well as the Q correlations between the self-report and up to five informants on the YABCL.

The validity evidence for the two scales is based on the history of the utility of the items in the author's and other's previous work, the ability of the items to discriminate between the referred and nonreferred individuals in the large sample used for test development and norming, and correlations with previous status and other measures. The evidence presented is persuasive that the measures can discriminate between referred and nonreferred populations, and that there is consistency between younger adjustment status and older in both U.S. and Dutch populations. Little evidence is available on the extent to which these measures correlate with other conventional measures of problem behaviors in adults, although the manual reports encouraging findings in U.S., Dutch, and Turkish samples. It will be important for more studies to be done on the concurrent validity of the scale, although it is likely to do as good a job as any in predicting future difficulties with the law or future mental health needs.

It would also be useful to have support for the validity of the scale by the performance of carefully diagnosed groups of young adults with aggressive behavior, depression, emotional disturbance, somatic complaints, etc. This kind of validation will be necessary for clinical applications of the scales.

Many of the criticisms that have been leveled at Achenbach's other measures have applicability to the YABCL and the YASR (Drotar, Stein, & Perrin, 1995). The measures may have limited sensitivity in detecting less serious and subtle problems and changes in problem behavior below the threshold for disturbance. The assessment of adaptive functioning and substance use may be limited in scope, and there may be problems in interpreting data on clients who are culturally, ethnically, or economically diverse. Nevertheless, because of the focus on the young adult population, these measures deserve serious consideration for use in screening and research.

SUMMARY. In summary, the YASR and YABCL are a well-designed and potentially useful set of measures for the assessment and identification of young adults with emotional disturbances and behavioral disorders. By combining information from two sources and comparing them, it is possible to have a richer picture of an individual's functioning than just from one measure alone. Those familiar and comfortable with the author's previous work will welcome the availability of these new measures.

REVIEWER'S REFERENCE

Drotar, D., Stein, R. E. K., & Perrin, E. C. (1995). Methodological issues in using the Child Behavior Checklist and its related instruments in clinical child psychology research. *Journal of Clinical Child Psychology, 24,* 184–192.

APPENDIX

TESTS LACKING SUFFICIENT TECHNICAL DOCUMENTATION FOR REVIEW

Effective with this publication (14th MMY), an additional criterion has been added for tests reviewed in The Mental Measurements Yearbook. Only those tests for which at least minimal technical or test development information is provided are now reviewed. This list includes the names of the new and revised tests received since publication of the 13th MMY that are lacking this documentation. The publishers have been advised that these tests do not meet our review criteria.

[431]
Ability Explorer.
Publisher: Riverside Publishing.

[432]
Analytical Thinking Test.
Publisher: Training House, Inc..

[433]
Ann Arbor Learning Inventory [1996 Edition].
Publisher: Academic Therapy Publications.

[434]
The ANSER System-Aggregate Neurobehavioral Student Health and Educational Review [Revised 1997].
Publisher: Educators Publishing Service, Inc.

[435]
The Assertiveness Skills Inventory.
Publisher: Millard J. Bienvenu, Northwest Publications.

[436]
Attention Disorders in Children: School-Based Assessment, Diagnosis, and Treatment.
Publisher: Western Psychological Services.

[437]
Barsch Learning Style Inventory.
Publisher: Academic Therapy Publications.

[438]
The Bricklin/Elliot Child Custody Evaluation.
Publisher: Village Publishing.

[439]
Career Occupational Preference System, Interest Inventory, Form R.
Publisher: EdITS/Educational and Industrial Testing Service.

[440]
Career Occupational Preference System, Intermediate Inventory.
Publisher: EdITS/Educational and Industrial Testing Service.

[441]
Child Abuse/Husband Abuse/Wife Abuse.
Publisher: Diagnostic Specialists, Inc.

[442]
Coaching Effectiveness Survey.
Publisher: International LearningWorks®.

[443]
Coaching Skills Inventory.
Publisher: Jossey-Bass/Pfeiffer.

[444]
Colored Overlay Assessment Kit.
Publisher: National Reading Styles Institute, Inc.

[445]
Comprehensive Affair Worksheets.
Publisher: Diagnostic Specialists, Inc.

[446]
Comprehensive Assessment of Reading Strategies.
Publisher: Curriculum Associates, Inc.

[447]
Comprehensive Sex History.
Publisher: Diagnostic Specialists, Inc.

[448]
Comprehensive Spouse's Worksheets.
Publisher: Diagnostic Specialists, Inc.

[449]
Conners-March Developmental Questionnaire.
Publisher: Multi-Health Systems, Inc.

[450]
COPSystem Picture Inventory of Careers.
Publisher: EdITS/Educational and Industrial Testing Service.

[451]
CTB Kindergarten–Grade 1 Assessment Activities.
Publisher: CTB/McGraw-Hill.

[452]
CTB Performance Assessment.
Publisher: CTB/McGraw-Hill.

[453]
Developing the Leader Within.
Publisher: Mind Garden, Inc.

[454]
A Developmental Assessment for Individuals with Severe Disabilities, Second Edition.
Publisher: PRO-ED.

[455]
Dissociative Features Profile.
Publisher: The Sidran Foundation.

[456]
Early Language Skills Checklist.
Publisher: Hodder & Stoughton Educational [England].

[457]
Employability Development Plan.
Publisher: JIST Works, Inc.

[458]
Employee Involvement Status Survey.
Publisher: Training House, Inc.

[459]
English as a Second Language Oral Assessment, Second Edition.
Publisher: Literacy Volunteers of America, Inc.

[460]
Enneagram Personality Portraits Inventory and Profile.
Publisher: Jossey-Bass/Pfeiffer.

[461]
Evaluating Courses for Inclusion of New Scholarship on Women.
Publisher: Association of American Colleges and Universities.

[462]
Evaluating Diversity Training.
Publisher: Jossey-Bass/Pfeiffer.

[463]
Examination for the Certificate of Competency in English.
Publisher: English Language Institute, University of Michigan.

[464]
Examination for the Certificate of Proficiency in English.
Publisher: English Language Institute, University of Michigan.

[465]
Flex Style Negotiating.
Publisher: Human Resource Development Press.

[466]
GAINS: A Pre-test and Post-test for Measuring Career Development Competency Progress.
Publisher: Wintergreen/Orchard House, Inc.

[467]
Goyer Organization of Ideas Test, Form S (Revised).
Publisher: Robert S. Goyer (the author).

[468]
Humanics National Child Assessment Form [Revised].
Publisher: Humanics Learning.

[469]
The Influence Styles Inventory.
Publisher: Human Resource Development Press.

[470]
Instructional Skills Assessment.
Publisher: Training House, Inc.

[471]
Interest Explorer.
Publisher: Riverside Publishing.

[472]
Interpersonal Style Questionnaire.
Publisher: Sopris West.

[473]
Jail Inmate Inventory.
Publisher: Risk & Needs Assessment, Inc.

[474]
Job Interactions Inventory.
Publisher: Personal Strengths Publishing.

[475]
Jungian Type Survey: The Gray-Wheelwrights Test (16th Revision).
Publisher: C. G. Jung Institute of San Francisco.

[476]
Just-in-Time Training Assessment Instrument.
Publisher: Human Resource Development Press.

[477]
The LAW-PSI Adult Life History Questionnaire.
Publisher: California Counseling Centers.

[478]
The LAW-PSI Child/Adolescent Life History Questionnaire.
Publisher: California Counseling Centers.

[479]
The LAW-PSI Sexual History Questionnaire.
Publisher: California Counseling Centers.

[480]
Leading Edge Portrait.
Publisher: Consulting Psychologists Press, Inc.

[481]
Learning-Style Inventory, Revised Scoring.
Publisher: Hay/McBer.

[482]
Making Work Teams Work.
Publisher: Training House, Inc.

[483]
Management of Differences Inventory.
Publisher: The Center for Management Effectiveness.

[484]
Management Situation Checklist.
Publisher: Hay/McBer.

[485]
Managerial Competency Questionnaire.
Publisher: Hay/McBer.

[486]
Measures in Post Traumatic Stress Disorder: A Practitioner's Guide.
Publisher: NFER-Nelson Publishing Co., Ltd. [England].

[487]
Mentoring Skills Assessment.
Publisher: Mind Garden, Inc.

[488]
Mobile Vocational Evaluation.
Publisher: Hester Evaluation Systems, Inc.

[489]
Multifactor Leadership Questionnaire for Teams.
Publisher: Mind Garden, Inc.

[490]
Nims Observation Checklist.
Publisher: Village Publishing.

[491]
O'Brien Vocabulary Placement Test.
Publisher: Educational Activities, Inc.

[492]
Observation of Type Preference.
Publisher: International LearningWorks®.

[493]
Organizational Behavior Profile.
Publisher: Jossey-Bass/Pfeiffer.

[494]
Parents' Observation of Study Behaviors Survey.
Publisher: The Cambridge Stratford Study Skills Institute.

[495]
Pediatric Early Elementary Examination— II [Revised].
Publisher: Educators Publishing Service, Inc.

[496]
The People Process.
Publisher: Jossey-Bass/Pfeiffer.

[497]
Personal Values Inventory [Personal Strengths Publishing].
Publisher: Personal Strengths Publishing.

[498]
Portrait of Overdone Strengths.
Publisher: Personal Strengths Publishing.

[499]
Portrait of Personal Strengths.
Publisher: Personal Strengths Publishing.

[500]
Productivity Profile.
Publisher: Training House, Inc.

[501]
Quality Culture Assessment.
Publisher: Teleometrics International.

[502]
Revised Pre-Reading Screening Procedures.
Publisher: Educators Publishing Service, Inc.

[503]
Risk Taking Inventory & Guide.
Publisher: The Center for Management Effectiveness.

[504]
Riverside Performance Assessment Series.
Publisher: Riverside Publishing.

[505]
Sales Competency Inventory.
Publisher: Hay/McBer.

[506]
Sales Effectiveness Survey.
Publisher: International LearningWorks®.

[507]
Sales Relations Survey.
Publisher: Teleometrics International.

[508]
SCL-90-Analogue.
Publisher: NCS [Minnetonka].

[509]
The Self-Esteem Inventory.
Publisher: Millard J. Bienvenu, Northwest Publications.

[510]
Speech Evaluation of the Patient with a Tracheostomy Tube.
Publisher: Imaginart International, Inc.

[511]
The Stanton Profile.
Publisher: Pinkerton Services Group.

[512]
Strategic Decision Making Inventory.
Publisher: The Center for Management Effectiveness.

[513]
Survey of Influence Effectiveness.
Publisher: International LearningWorks®.

[514]
Survey of Student Assessment of Study Behaviors.
Publisher: The Cambridge Stratford Study Skills Institute.

[515]
Teaching Resource and Assessment of Critical Skills.
Publisher: Program Development Associates.

[516]
Team Competency Assessment.
Publisher: Human Resource Development Press.

[517]
Test of Creativity.
Publisher: Training House, Inc.

[518]
Troubled Talk Test.
Publisher: International Society for General Semantics.

[519]
The Uncritical Inference Test.
Publisher: International Society for General Semantics.

[520]
Values Preference Indicator.
Publisher: Consulting Resource Group International, Inc.

[521]
Wife's or Husband's Marriage Questions.
Publisher: Diagnostic Specialists, Inc.

[522]
Word Finding Referral Checklist.
Publisher: PRO-ED.

[523]
Word Identification Scale.
Publisher: Academic Therapy Publications.

[524]
Work Keys Assessments.
Publisher: ACT, Inc.

TESTS TO BE REVIEWED FOR THE FIFTEENTH MENTAL MEASUREMENTS YEARBOOK

By the time each new Mental Measurements Yearbook *reaches publication, the staff at the Buros Institute have already collected many new and revised tests destined to be reviewed in the next* Mental Measurements Yearbook. *Following is a list of tests that meet the review criteria and that will be reviewed, along with additional tests published and received in the next year, in the* Fifteenth Mental Measurements Yearbook.

ACER Test of Employment Entry Mathematics
Ackerman-Banks Neuropsychological Rehabilitation Battery
ADHD Rating Scale–IV
ADHD Symptom Checklist–4
Adolescent Psychopathology Scale—Short Form
Adolescent Symptom Inventory-4
The Affective Perceptions Inventory/Primary Level [2000 Revision]
Apraxia Battery for Adults, Second Edition
Asperger Syndrome Diagnostic Scale
Assessment for Persons Profoundly or Severely Impaired
Assessment of Language-Related Functional Activities
Attitudes Towards Guns and Violence Questionnaire
The Autistic Continuum: An Assessment and Intervention Schedule

BarOn Emotional Quotient Inventory: Youth Version
Basic Number Diagnostic Test [1996 Edition]
Basic Number Screening Test [1996 Edition]
Basic Skills Locater Test
Behavior Rating Inventory of Executive Function
Behavioral Objective Sequence
Boston Qualitative Scoring System for the Rey-Osterrieth Complex Figure
Brief Test of Attention
Brief Visuospatial Memory Test—Revised
British Ability Scales: Second Edition

Career Transitions Inventory
Child Symptom Inventory 4
Children's Interview for Psychiatric Syndromes
Children's Inventory of Anger
Cognitive Distortion Scales

College Student Inventory [part of the Retention Management System]

Color Trails Test

Comprehensive Assessment of Spoken Language

Comprehensive Test of Phonological Processing

The Computer Category Test

Computerized Lifestyle Assessment

Conners' Adult ADHD Rating Scales

Coping Inventory for Stressful Situations [Revised]

Coping Scale for Adults

Coping With Health Injuries and Problems

d2 Test of Attention

DCS—A Visual Learning and Memory Test for Neuropsychological Assessment

Developmental Readiness Scale—Revised

Devereux Early Childhood Assessment

Diagnostic English Language Tests

Diagnostic Reading Record, Second Edition

The Discipline Index

Everstine Trauma Response Index

Experience and Background Inventory (Form S)

Expressive One-Word Picture Vocabulary Test [Revised]

Family System Test

Firefighter Learning Simulation

Firefighter Selection Test [Revised]

Fluharty Preschool Speech and Language Screening Test—Second Edition

Functional Fitness Assessment for Adults over 60 Years, Second Edition

Goldman Fristoe Test of Articulation—Second Edition

Graded Arithmetic-Mathematics Test

Gray Silent Reading Tests

H.R.R. Pseudoisochromatic Plates for Detecting, Classifying and Estimating the Degree of Defective Color Vision

HCR-20: Assessing Risk for Violence

Health and Daily Living Form, Second Edition

The Hospital Anxiety and Depression Scale with the Irritability-Depression-Anxiety Scale and The Leeds Situational Anxiety Scale

IDEA Feedback for Department Chairs

Illinois Test of Psycholinguistic Abilities, Third Edition

Illness Behaviour Questionnaire, Third Edition

Infant Index

Interference Learning Test

International Personality Disorder Examination

Job Stress Survey

Level of Service Inventory—Revised: Screening Version

Manifestation of Symptomatology Scale

The Maroondah Assessment Profile for Problem Gambling

Matching Assistive Technology & Child

Miller Common Sense Scale

Miller Depression Scale

Miller Emotional Maturity Scale

Miller Getting Along With People Scale

Miller Happiness Scale

Miller Love Scale

Miller Marriage Satisfaction Scale

Miller Motivation Scale

Miller Psychological Independence Scale

Miller Self-Concept Scale

Miller Stress Scale

Morrisby Profile

Multidimensional Anxiety Questionnaire

Multidimensional Aptitude Battery-II

Multimedia Learning Styles

Neale Analysis of Reading Ability, 3rd Edition [Australian Standardisation]

Observational Assessment of Temperament

The Parenthood Questionnaire

Parenting Alliance Measure

Paulhus Deception Scales: Balanced Inventory of Desirable Responding—7

Peabody Developmental Motor Scale—Second Edition

Perceptual Speed (Identical Forms)

Personal Outlook Inventory

Phonemic-Awareness Skills Screening

Phonological Assessment Battery [Standardised Edition]

The Phonological Awareness Skills Program Test

Post-Assault Traumatic Brain Injury Interview and Checklist

Pre-Kindergarten Screen

Pre-LAS 2000

Progressive Achievement Tests in Mathematics—Revised

PSYPERCEPT-170

Reading and Arithmetic Indexes

Reading-Level Indicator

Reading Progress Tests

Receptive One-Word Picture Vocabulary Test [Revised]

Rehabilitation Checklist

Ross Information Processing Assessment—Primary

Ruff Figural Fluency Test

Ruff-Light Trail Learning Test

The Scenotest: A Practical Technique for Understanding Unconscious Problems and Personality Structure

The Schedule of Growing Skills: Second Edition

Screening Assessment for Gifted Elementary and Middle School Students, Second Edition

Screening Test for Developmental Apraxia of Speech—Second Edition

Search Institute Profiles of Student Life: Attitudes and Behaviors

Secondary Screening Profiles

The Self-Perceptions Inventory [1999 Revision]

Service Animal Adaptive Intervention Assessment

Sexual Violence Risk-20

16PF Select

Social Adjustment Scale—Self Report

Social Phobia & Anxiety Inventory for Children

Space Relations (Paper Puzzles)

Spanish/English Reading Comprehension Test [Revised]

Spatial Awareness Skills Program Test

Spousal Assault Risk Assessment Guide

SRA Sales Aptitude Test

STAR Math™

State-Trait Anger Expression Inventory-2

Stoelting Brief Nonverbal Intelligence Test

Stress in General Scale

Stress Profile

Structured Interview for the Five-Factor Model of Personality

Student Behavior Survey

The Substance Abuse Subtle Screening Inventory-3

Supervisory Behavior Description Questionnaire

TD (Tardive Dyskinesia) Monitor

Teacher Performance Assessment

Teamwork-KSA Test

Test for the Reception of Grammar

Test of Gross Motor Development—Second Edition

Test of Interpersonal Competence for Employment

Test of Word Finding, Second Edition

Test of Word Reading Efficiency

Test of Written Spelling, Fourth Edition

Transition Competence Battery for Deaf and Hard of Hearing Adolescents and Young Adults

Trauma Symptom Checklist for Children

Useful Field of View

Visual Analog Mood Scales

Wagner Enneagram Personality Style Scales

Who Am I?

Wide Range Intelligence Test

Wisconsin Card Sorting Test—64 Card Version

Work Potential Profile

Worley's ID Profile

Young Children's Achievement Test

Youth's Inventory-4

CONTRIBUTING TEST REVIEWERS

PHILLIP L. ACKERMAN, Professor of Psychology, Georgia Institute of Technology, Atlanta, GA

EUGENE V. AIDMAN, Lecturer in Psychology, School of Behavioural & Social Sciences & Humanities, University of Ballarat, Victoria, Australia

MARK A. ALBANESE, Professor, Preventive Medicine and Director, Medical Education Research and Development, University of Wisconsin—Madison, Madison, WI

JULIE A. ALLISON, Associate Professor of Psychology, Pittsburg State University, Pittsburg, KS

JOHN O. ANDERSON, Professor, Faculty of Education, University of Victoria, Victoria, British Columbia, Canada

PAUL A. ARBISI, Minneapolis VA Medical Center, Assistant Professor Department of Psychiatry and Assistant Clinical Professor Department of Psychology, University of Minnesota, Minneapolis, MN

RAOUL A. ARREOLA, Professor and Director of Educational Evaluation and Development, The University of Tennessee Health Science Center, Memphis, TN

PHILIP ASH, Director, Ash, Blackstone and Cates, Blacksburg, VA

MARK. J. ATKINSON, Associate Professor of Psychiatry and Applied Psychology, University of Calgary, Calgary, Alberta, Canada

JEFFREY A. ATLAS, Associate Clinical Professor (Psychiatry), Bronx Children's Psychiatric Center, Albert Einstein College of Medicine, Bronx, NY

JAMES T. AUSTIN, Research Specialist, Ohio State University, Columbus, OH

STEPHEN N. AXFORD, Psychologist, Pueblo School District No. Sixty, Pueblo, CO, and University of Phoenix, Colorado Springs, CO

GLEN P. AYLWARD, Professor of Pediatrics, Psychiatry and Behavioral and Social Sciences, Southern Illinois University School of Medicine, Springfield, IL

PATRICIA A. BACHELOR, Professor of Psychology, California State University at Long Beach, Long Beach, CA

PHILIP A. BACKLUND, Professor of Speech Communication, Department of Communication, Central Washington University, Ellensburg, WA

THERESA M. BAHNS, Licensed Psychologist, Heartspring, Wichita, KS

SHERRY K. BAIN, Associate Professor, Department of Educational Psychology, University of Tennessee, Knoxville, TN

JOAN C. BALLARD, Clinical Neuropsychologist, Associate Professor of Psychology, State University of New York College at Geneseo, Geneseo, NY

DEBORAH L. BANDALOS, Associate Professor, Department of Educational Psychology, University of Nebraska—Lincoln, Lincoln, NE

BENJAMIN D. BARKER, Research and Clinical Associate, Wright State University, Dayton, OH

LAURA L. B. BARNES, Associate Professor of Educational Research and Evaluation, School of Education Studies, Oklahoma State University—Tulsa, Tulsa, OK

JANET BARNES-FARRELL, Associate Professor of Psychology, University of Connecticut, Storrs, CT

JAMES K. BENISH, School Psychologist, Helena Public Schools, Adjunct Professor of Special Education, Carroll College, Helena, MT

PETER MILES BERGER, Area Manager—Mental After Care Association, London, England

RONALD A. BERK, Professor of Biostatistics and Measurement, School of Nursing, Johns Hopkins University, Baltimore, MD

FRANK M. BERNT, Associate Professor, Health Services Department, St. Joseph's University, Philadelphia, PA

FREDERICK BESSAI, Professor of Education, University of Regina, Regina, Saskatchewan, Canada

HERBERT BISCHOFF, Licensed Psychologist, Psychology Resources, Anchorage, AK

LISA BISCHOFF, Associate Professor, School of Education, Indiana State University, Terre Haute, IN

LARRY M. BOLEN, Professor and School Psychology Trainer, East Carolina University, Greenville, NC

NANCY B. BOLOGNA, Clinical Assistant Professor of Psychiatry, Louisiana State University Medical Center, and Program Director, Touro Senior Day Center, New Orleans, LA

BRIAN F. BOLTON, University Professor, Department of Rehabilitation Education and Research, University of Arkansas, Fayetteville, AR

ROGER A. BOOTHROYD, Associate Professor, Department of Mental Health Law and Policy, Louis de la Parte Florida Mental Health Institute, University of South Florida, Tampa, FL

GREGORY J. BOYLE, Professor of Psychology, Bond University, Gold Coast, Queensland, and Visiting Professor, Department of Psychiatry, University of Queensland, Royal Brisbane Hospital, Hesston, Australia

JEFFERY P. BRADEN, Professor, School Psychology Program, Department of Educational Psychology, University of Wisconsin-Madison, Madison, WI

SUSAN M. BROOKHART, Associate Professor, School of Education, Duquesne University, Pittsburgh, PA

LYNN L. BROWN, Assistant Professor, Northern Arizona University, Phoenix, AZ

MICHAEL B. BROWN, Associate Professor of Psychology, East Carolina University, Greenville, NC

RIC BROWN, Associate Vice President, Research, Graduate and Extended Programs, California State University, Sacramento, Sacramento, CA

ROBERT BROWN, Carl A. Happold Distinguished Professor of Educational Psychology Emeritus, University of Nebraska—Lincoln, and Senior Associate, Aspen Professional Development Associates, Lincoln, NE

GORDON C. BRUNER II, Associate Professor, Marketing Department, Director, Office of Scale Research, Southern Illinois University, Carbondale, IL

ALBERT M. BUGAJ, Associate Professor of Psychology, University of Wisconsin—Marinette, Marinette, WI

MICHAEL B. BUNCH, Vice President, Measurement Incorporated, Durham, NC

MARY ANNE BUNDA, Professor, Educational Leadership, Western Michigan University, Kalamazoo, MI

LINDA K. BUNKER, Professor of Human Services, University of Virginia, Charlottesville, VA

MATTHEW BURNS, Assistant Professor of School Psychology, Central Michigan University, Mt. Pleasant, MI

CAROLYN M. CALLAHAN, Professor of Educational Leadership, Foundations, and Policy, Curry School of Education, University of Virginia, Charlottesville, VA

WAYNE CAMARA, Executive Director of Research & Development, The College Board, New York, NY

MICHAEL H. CAMPBELL, Director of Residential Life, New College of University of South Florida at Sarasota, Sarasota, FL

GARY L. CANIVEZ, Assistant Professor of Psychology, Eastern Illinois University, Charleston, IL

KAREN T. CAREY, Professor of Psychology, California State University, Fresno, CA

CINDY CARLSON, Professor of Educational Psychology, University of Texas at Austin, Austin, TX

JANET F. CARLSON, Professor of Counseling and Psychological Services, Associate Dean School of Education, Oswego State University, Oswego, NY

JoELLEN V. CARLSON, Measurement and Training Consultant, Washington, DC

C. DALE CARPENTER, Professor of Special Education, Western Carolina University, Cullowhee, NC

SANDRA J. CARR, Certified School Psychologist, Harford County Public Schools, Bel Air, MD

JOHN C. CARUSO, Assistant Professor of Psychology, University of Montana, Missoula, MT

TONY CELLUCCI, Associate Professor and Director of Psychology Training Clinic, Department of Psychology, Idaho State University, Pocatello, ID

MARY MATHAI CHITTOORAN, UC Foundation Assistant Professor of School Psychology, The University of Tennessee at Chattanooga, Chattanooga, TN

JAMES P. CHOCA, Director of Doctoral Studies, School of Psychology, Roosevelt University, Chicago, IL

ROBERT CHRISTOPHER, President, International Mental Health Network, Ltd., Poway, CA

JOSEPH C. CIECHALSKI, Professor of Counselor and Adult Education, East Carolina University, Greenville, NC

GREGORY J. CIZEK, Associate Professor of Educational Measurement and Evaluation, University of North Carolina, Chapel Hill, NC

ELAINE CLARK, Professor of Educational Psychology, University of Utah, Salt Lake City, UT

ASHLEY COHEN, Clinical Neuropsychologist, CogniMetrix, San Jose, CA

LIBBY G. COHEN, Professor of Special Education, University of Southern Maine, Gorham, ME

SANFORD J. COHN, Professor, Division of Curriculum and Instruction, Arizona State University, Tempe, AZ

THEODORE COLADARCI, Professor of Education, University of Maine, Orono, ME

CAROL COLLINS, Family Counseling and Research Center, Caldwell, ID

JANE CLOSE CONOLEY, Dean, College of Education, Texas A&M University, College Station, TX

COLIN COOPER, Senior Lecturer, School of Psychology, The Queen's University, Belfast, United Kingdom

MARK COOPER, Training Specialist, Center on Children, Families & the Law, University of Nebraska—Lincoln, Lincoln, NE

M. ALLAN COOPERSTEIN, Clinical Psychologist, Disability & Forensic Examiner, Independent Practice, Willow Grove, PA

ALICE J. CORKILL, Associate Professor and Co-Director, Cognitive Interference Laboratory, University of Nevada, Las Vegas, NV

MERITH COSDEN, Professor of Counseling/Clinical/School Psychology, Graduate School of Education, University of California, Santa Barbara, CA

ANDREW A. COX, Professor of Counseling and Psychology, Troy State University, Phenix City, AL

KEVIN D. CREHAN, Associate Professor of Educational Psychology, University of Nevada—Las Vegas, Las Vegas, NV

LINDA CROCKER, Associate Dean, College of Education, University of Florida, Gainesville, FL

LAWRENCE H. CROSS, Professor of Educational Research and Evaluation, Virginia Polytechnic Institute, Blacksburg, VA

THOMAS J. CULLEN, JR., Clinical Psychologist, Cullen Psychological Services, P.C., Fairless Hills, PA

JACK A. CUMMINGS, Professor and Chair, Department of Counseling and Educational Psychology, Indiana University, Bloomington, IN

RHODA CUMMINGS, Professor of Educational Psychology and Human Growth and Development, University of Nevada, Reno, NV

RIK CARL D'AMATO, Professor and Director, Programs in School Psychology, the Neuropsychology Laboratory, and the Center for Collaborative Research in Education (CCoRE), and M. Lucille Harrison Professor of Excellence, Division of Professional Psychology, University of Northern Colorado, Greeley, CO

AYRES D'COSTA, Associate Professor of Education, The Ohio State University, Columbus, OH

MARK H. DANIEL, Associate Director of Development, American Guidance Service, Circle Pines, MN

STEPHEN F. DAVIS, Professor of Psychology, Emporia State University, Emporia, KS

GARY J. DEAN, Associate Professor, Department of Adult and Community Education, Indiana University of Pennsylvania, Indiana, PA

RAYMOND S. DEAN, Director, Neuropsychology Laboratory, Ball State University, Muncie, IN

R. J. DE AYALA, Associate Professor of Educational Psychology, University of Nebraska—Lincoln, Lincoln, NE

SHARON H. deFUR, Assistant Professor, School of Education, College of William and Mary, Williamsburg, VA

CONNIE KUBO DELLA-PIANA, Director of Evaluation, Model Institutions for Excellence and the Partnership for Excellence in Teacher Education, The University of Texas at El Paso, El Paso, TX

GERALD E. DeMAURO, Coordinator of Assessment, New York State Education Department, Albany, NY

LIZANNE DeSTEFANO, Professor of Educational Psychology, University of Illinois at Urbana—Champaign, Champaign, IL

JOSEPH O. PREWITT DIAZ, School Psychologist, Chester Upland School District, Chester, PA

JAMES CLYDE DiPERNA, Assistant Professor, School Psychology Program, Lehigh University, Bethlehem, PA

FAITH GUNNING-DIXON, Research Assistant, Psychology Department, The University of Memphis, Memphis, TN

BETH DOLL, Associate Professor of Educational Psychology, University of Nebraska-Lincoln, Lincoln, NE

GEORGE DOMINO, Professor of Psychology, University of Arizona, Tucson, AZ

E. THOMAS DOWD, Professor of Psychology, Kent State University, Kent, OH

LEE DROEGEMUELLER, Professor of Education, University of West Florida, Pensacola, FL

ROBERT J. DRUMMOND, Professor, Division of Educational Services and Research, University of North Florida, Jacksonville, FL

ROBERT W. ELLIOTT, Director, Aviation Psychology Center, Los Angeles, CA

BRIAN ENGDAHL, Counseling Psychologist, U.S. Department of Veterans Affairs Medical Center, and Clinical Associate Professor, Department of Psychology, University of Minnesota, Minneapolis, MN

GEORGE ENGELHARD, JR., Professor of Educational Studies, Emory University, Atlanta, GA

JOHN M. ENGER, Professor of Education, Barry University, Miami Shores, FL

DEBORAH ERICKSON, Director of Clinical Psychology, University of Sydney, Sydney, Australia

JENNIFER J. FAGER, Assistant Professor, Teaching, Learning, and Leadership, Western Michigan University, Kalamazoo, MI

DOREEN WARD FAIRBANK, Associate Professor of Psychology, Meredith College, Raleigh, NC

RICHARD F. FARMER, Associate Professor of Psychology, Idaho State University, Pocatello, ID

WILTRUD FASSBINDER, Doctoral Student, Department of Communication Science and Disorders, University of Pittsburgh, Pittsburgh, PA

EPHREM FERNANDEZ, Associate Professor of Clinical Psychology, Southern Methodist University, Dallas, TX

F. FELICIA FERRARA, Assistant Professor, College of Behavioral Sciences, The University of Sarasota, Sarasota, FL

TRENTON R. FERRO, Associate Professor of Adult and Community Education, Indiana University of Pennsylvania, Indiana, PA

MAYNARD D. FILTER, Professor of Speech-Language Pathology, James Madison University, Harrisonburg, VA

CORINE FITZPATRICK, Associate Professor of Counseling Psychology, Manhattan College, Riverdale, NY

ROBERT FITZPATRICK, Consulting Psychologist, Cranberry Township, PA

ROSEMARY FLANAGAN, Adjunct Associate Professor of Psychology, St. John's University, Jamaica, NY

JOHN W. FLEENOR, Director of Knowledge Management, Center for Creative Leadership, Greensboro, NC

JANET H. FONTAINE, Associate Professor of Counseling, Indiana University of Pennsylvania, Indiana, PA

JIM C. FORTUNE, Professor of Educational Research and Evaluation, Virginia Tech University, Blacksburg, VA

GLEN FOX, Clinical Psychologist, Occupational Psychology Services, Sevenoaks, Kent, England

MARY LOU BRYANT FRANK, Professor and Department Head of Psychology, North Georgia College & State University, Dahlonega, GA

ROBERT B. FRARY, Professor Emeritus, Virginia Polytechnic Institute and State University, Blacksburg, VA

RICHARD I. FREDERICK, Staff Psychologist, U.S. Medical Center for Federal Prisoners, Springfield, MO

STEPHEN J. FREEMAN, Associate Professor of Counseling & Development, Department of Family Sciences, Texas Woman's University, Denton, TX

PATRICIA K. FREITAG, Assistant Professor of Education Research, The George Washington University, Washington, DC

SOLOMON M. FULERO, Chair, Department of Psychology, Sinclair College, Dayton, OH

MICHAEL FURLONG, Professor, School Psychology Program, University of California, Santa Barbara, Graduate School of Education, Santa Barbara, CA

ROBERT K. GABLE, Professor of Educational Psychology, and Associate Director, Bureau of Educational Research and Service, University of Connecticut, Storrs, CT

ROBERT K. GABLE, Professor of Educational Psychology, and Associate Director, Bureau of Educational Research and Service, University of Connecticut, Storrs, CT

MICHAEL P. GAMACHE, Clinical Assistant Professor of Psychology, Department of Neurology, University of South Florida, College of Medicine, Tampa, FL

RONALD J. GANELLEN, Director, Neuropsychology Service, Michael Reese Hospital and Medical Center, and Associate Professor, Northwestern Medical School, Chicago, IL

ALAN GARFINKEL, Professor of Spanish and Education, Purdue University, Department of Foreign Languages and Literatures, West Lafayette, IN

JACK E. GEBART-EAGLEMONT, Lecturer in Psychology, Swinburne University of Technology, Hawthorn, Victoria, Australia

KURT F. GEISINGER, Professor of Psychology and Academic Vice President, Le Moyne College, Syracuse, NY

JOHN S. GEISLER, Professor, College of Education, Western Michigan University, Kalamazoo, MI

GLENN B. GELMAN, Executive Director, Northern Illinois Counseling Associates, P.C., Arlington Heights, IL, and Adjunct Professor of Psychology, Roosevelt University, Schaumburg, IL

DAVID GILLESPIE, Social Science Faculty, Detroit College of Business, Warren, MI

HUGH W. GLENN, Educational Consultant, Kohut Psychiatric Medical Group, San Bernardino, CA

BERT A. GOLDMAN, Professor of Education, Curriculum and Instruction, School of Education, University of North Carolina at Greensboro, Greensboro, NC

EDWARD E. GOTTS, Chief Psychologist, Madison State Hospital, Madison, IN

STEVE GRAHAM, Professor of Special Education, University of Maryland, College Park, MD

THERESA GRAHAM, Assistant Professor of Educational Psychology, University of Nebraska-Lincoln, Lincoln, NE

FELICE J. GREEN, Professor of Education, University of North Alabama, Florence, AL

J. JEFFREY GRILL, Professor and Chair, Special Education Department, Athens State University, Athens, AL

ROBERT M. GUION, Distinguished University Professor Emeritus, Bowling Green State University, Bowling Green, OH

TERRY B. GUTKIN, Professor of Educational Psychology, University of Nebraska—Lincoln, Lincoln, NE

THOMAS W. GUYETTE, Associate Professor, Marquette University, Milwaukee, WI

ROBERT R. HACCOUN, Professor and Chair, I-O Psychology, Université de Montréal, Montreal, Quebec, Canada

GENEVA D. HAERTEL, Senior Educational Researcher, SRI International, Menlo Park, CA

GERALD S. HANNA, Professor of Education, Kansas State University, Manhattan, KS

WILLIAM E. HANSON, Assistant Professor, Department of Educational Psychology, University of Nebraska—Lincoln, Lincoln, NE

RICHARD HARDING, Director of Research, Kanexa Corporation, Lincoln, NE

DELWYN L. HARNISCH, Professor of Curriculum and Instruction, University of Nebraska-Lincoln, Lincoln, NE

DENNIS C. HARPER, Professor of Pediatrics and Rehabilitation, College of Medicine, University of Iowa, Iowa City, IA

ROBERT G. HARRINGTON, Professor, Department of Psychology and Research in Education, University of Kansas, Lawrence, KS

PATTI L. HARRISON, Professor of School Psychology and Assistant Dean of the Graduate School, The University of Alabama, Tuscaloosa, AL

MICHAEL HARWELL, Professor, Research Methodology, University of Minnesota—Twin Cities, Minneapolis, MN

KEITH HATTRUP, Associate Professor of Psychology, San Diego State University, San Diego, CA

THEODORE L. HAYES, Research Analyst, U.S. Immigration and Naturalization Service, Washington, DC

SANDRA D. HAYNES, Assistant Professor, Department of Human Services, The Metropolitan State College of Denver, Denver, CO

JONI R. HAYS, Senior Clinical Counselor and Adjunct Faculty School of Applied Health and Educational Psychology, Oklahoma State University, Stillwater, OK

DANIEL HECK, Research Associate, Horizon Research, Inc., Champaign, IL

CARLEN HENINGTON, Associate Professor of Educational Psychology, Mississippi State University, Starkville, MS

MARTHA E. HENNEN, Consultant, The Pittman McLenagan Group, L.C., Bethesda, MD

JAMES J. HENNESSY, Professor, Graduate School of Education, Fordham University, New York, NY

ALLEN K. HESS, Distinguished Research Professor and Department Head, Department of Psychology, Auburn University at Montgomery, Montgomery, AL

SCOTT KRISTIAN HILL, Co-Director, Neuropsychology Laboratory, Ball State University, Muncie, IN

THOMAS P. HOGAN, Professor of Psychology, University of Scranton, Scranton, PA

CANDICE HAAS HOLLINGSEAD, Assistant Professor, Department of Special Education, Minnesota State University, Mankato, MN

STEPHEN R. HOOPER, Associate Professor of Psychiatry, University of North Carolina School of Medicine, Chapel Hill, NC

ANITA M. HUBLEY, Assistant Professor of Educational and Consulting Psychology, and Special Education, The University of British Columbia, Vancouver, British Columbia, Canada

E. SCOTT HUEBNER, Professor of Psychology, University of South Carolina, Columbia, SC

DAVID P. HURFORD, Director of the Center for the Assessment and Remediation of Reading Difficulties and Professor of Psychology and Counseling, Pittsburg State University, Pittsburg, KS

CARLOS INCHAURRALDE, Professor of Linguistics and Psychologist, University of Zaragoza, Zaragoza, Spain

CARL ISENHART, Coordinator, Addictive Disorders Section, VA Medical Center, Minneapolis, MN

STEPHEN H. IVENS, Vice President, Touchstone Applied Science Associates, Brewster, NY

CHANTALE JEANRIE, Associate Professor, Measurement and Evaluation, Laval University, Quebec, Canada

JEFFREY A. JENKINS, Assistant Professor, Roger Williams University, Bristol, RI

JILL ANN JENKINS, Psychologist on Sabbatical, Barcelona, Spain

RICHARD W. JOHNSON, Adjunct Professor of Counseling Psychology and Associate Director Emeritus of Counseling & Consultation Services, University Health Services, University of Wisconsin—Madison, Madison, WI

CHRISTINA FINLEY JONES, School Psychologist, Battle Ground School District, Battle Ground, WA

ELIZABETH L. JONES, Associate Professor of Psychology, Western Kentucky University, Bowling Green, KY

KEVIN M. JONES, Assistant Professor, University of Cincinnati, Cincinnati, OH

SAMUEL JUNI, Professor, Department of Applied Psychology, New York University, New York, NY

ASHRAF KAGEE, Postdoctoral Fellow, University of Pennsylvania, Philadelphia, PA

R. W. KAMPHAUS, Professor, Department of Educational Psychology, The University of Georgia, Athens, GA

HARRISON KANE, Assistant Professor, Department of Special Education, University of Nevada—Las Vegas, Las Vegas, NV

MICHAEL KANE, Professor, Department of Kinesiology, University of Wisconsin, Madison, WI

DAVID M. KAPLAN, Professor and Director of the Graduate Program in Counseling, Alfred University, Alfred, NY

IRA STUART KATZ, Clinical Psychologist, California Department of Corrections, Salinas Valley State Prison, Soledad, CA, and Licensed Clinical Psychologist, Private Practice, Salinas, CA

ALAN S. KAUFMAN, Clinical Professor of Psychology, Yale University School of Medicine, New Haven, CT

NADEEN L. KAUFMAN, Lecturer, Clinical Faculty, Yale University School of Medicine, New Haven, CT

MICHAEL G. KAVAN, Associate Dean for Student Affairs and Associate Professor of Family Practice, Creighton University School of Medicine, Omaha, NE

PATRICIA B. KEITH, Assistant Professor, Psychology Department, University of South Carolina, Columbia, SC

TIMOTHY Z. KEITH, Arthur L. & Lea R. Powell Professor of Psychology & Schooling, Alfred University, Alfred, NY

HAROLD R. KELLER, Professor and Chair, Department of Educational Psychology, University of Nebraska—Lincoln, Lincoln, NE

MARY LOU KELLEY, Professor of Psychology, Louisiana State University, Baton Rouge, LA

CAROL E. KESSLER, Assistant Professor of Education, Chestnut Hill College, Philadelphia, PA, and Adjunct Professor of Special Education, West Chester University, West Chester, PA

SANDRA M. KETROW, Professor of Communication Studies, University of Rhode Island, Kingston, RI

KENNETH A. KIEWRA, Professor of Educational Psychology, University of Nebraska—Lincoln, Lincoln, NE

ERNEST KIMMEL, Executive Director, Office of Public Leadership, Educational Testing Service, Princeton, NJ

G. GAGE KINGSBURY, Director of Research, Northwest Evaluation Association, Portland, OR

JEAN POWELL KIRNAN, Associate Professor of Psychology, The College of New Jersey, Ewing, NJ

HELEN KITCHENS, Associate Professor, Troy State University—Montgomery, Montgomery, AL

BEVERLY M. KLECKER, Assistant Professor, Department of Administration, Counseling, and Educational Studies, College of Education, Eastern Kentucky University, Richmond, KY

HOWARD M. KNOFF, Professor of School Psychology, University of South Florida, Tampa, FL

TIMOTHY R. KONOLD, Assistant Professor of Education, University of Virginia, Charlottesville, VA

JEFFREY KRAMER, Licensed Mental Health Counselor, Eyerly-Ball Community Mental Health Center, Des Moines, IA

JOHN H. KRANZLER, Professor of Educational Psychology, College of Education, University of Florida, Gainesville, FL

LESLIE H. KRIEGER, Senior Consulting Psychologist, NCC Assessment Technologies, Jacksonville, FL

RADHIKA KRISHNAMURTHY, Associate Professor, School of Psychology, Florida Institute of Technology, Melbourne, FL

SALLY KUHLENSCHMIDT, Associate Professor of Psychology, Western Kentucky University

JOSEPH C. KUSH, Associate Professor and Coordinator School Psychology Program, Duquesne University, Pittsburgh, PA

KWONG-LIEM KARL KWAN, Assistant Professor, Counseling and Development, Purdue University, Lafayette, IN

MATTHEW E. LAMBERT, Research Neuropsychologist, Neurology Research Education Center at St. Mary Hospital, Lubbock, TX

WILLIAM STEVE LANG, Associate Professor of Educational Measurement and Research, Department of Educational Measurement and Research, University of South Florida, St. Petersburg, FL

AIMÉE LANGLOIS, Professor, Department of Child Development, Humboldt State University, Arcata, CA

KEVIN LANNING, Associate Professor of Psychology, Honors College of Florida Atlantic University, Jupiter, FL

CYNTHIA A. LARSON-DAUGHERTY, Adjunct Professor, Psychology Department, Towson University, Towson, MD, and Director of Training & Development, Federal Reserve Bank, Baltimore, MD

JOSEPH G. LAW, JR., Associate Professor of Behavioral Studies and Educational Technology, University of South Alabama, Mobile, AL

ROBERT A. LEARK, Associate Professor, Psychology Department, Pacific Christian College, Fullerton, CA

STEVEN B. LEDER, Professor, Department of Surgery, Section of Otolaryngology, Yale University School of Medicine, New Haven, CT

FREDERICK T. L. LEONG, Professor of Psychology, The Ohio State University at Columbus, Columbus, OH

S. ALVIN LEUNG, Associate Professor, Department of Educational Psychology, The Chinese University of Hong Kong, Shatin, N.T., Hong Kong

RALPH G. LEVERETT, Professor of Special and Regular Education, Union University, Jackson, TN

MARY A. LEWIS, Director, Human Resources, Chlor-Alkali and Derivatives, PPG Industries, Inc., Pittsburgh, PA

NEIL P. LEWIS, Management Psychologist, Marietta, GA

STEVEN J. LINDNER, Executive Director, Industrial/Organizational Psychologist, The WorkPlace Group, Inc., Morristown, NJ

CEDERICK O. LINDSKOG, Professor, Department of Psychology and Counseling, Pittsburg State University, Pittsburg, KS

MARIA PRENDES LINTEL, Psychologist, The Wellness Center, Lincoln, NE

HOWARD A. LLOYD, Neuropsychologist, Hawaii State Hospital, Kaneohe, HI

SANDRA LOEW, Assistant Professor, Counselor Education, University of North Alabama, Florence, AL

CHARLES J. LONG, Professor of Psychology, Psychology Department, The University of Memphis, Memphis, TN

EMILIA C. LOPEZ, Assistant Professor, Queens College, City University of New York, Flushing, NY

JERRY M. LOWE, Associate Professor of Educational Leadership, Sam Houston State University, Huntsville, TX

LESLIE EASTMAN LUKIN, Assessment Specialist, Lincoln Public Schools/ESU 18, Lincoln, NE

GLORIA MACCOW, School Psychologist, Guilford County Schools, Greensboro, NC

JOHN MacDONALD, School Psychologist, North Kitsap School District, Poulsbo, WA

KAREN MACKLER, School Psychologist, Lawrence Public Schools, Lawrence, NY

CLEBORNE D. MADDUX, Professor of Educational Psychology and Information Technology in Education, University of Nevada, Reno, NV

RONALD A. MADLE, School Psychologist, Shikellamy School District, Sunbury, PA and Adjunct Associate Professor of School Psychology, Pennsylvania State University, University Park, PA

TIMOTHY J. MAKATURA, Clinical Neuropsychologist and Assistant Professor, Department of Physical Medicine and Rehabilitation, University of Pittsburgh Medical Center, Pittsburgh, PA

KORESSA KUTSICK MALCOLM, School Psychologist, Augusta County School Board, Fishersville, VA

SUSAN J. MALLER, Associate Professor of Educational Psychology, Purdue University, West Lafayette, IN

MARGARET E. MALONE, Language Testing Specialist, Peace Corps, Washington, DC

JAY A. MANCINI, Professor of Human Development, Virginia Polytechnic Institute & State University, Blacksburg, VA

JOSEPH R. MANDUCHI, Clinical Associate, Susquehanna Institute, Harrisburg, PA

KENNETH J. MANGES, Director, Kenneth J. Manges & Associates, Inc., Cincinnati, OH

RAMASAMY MANIKAM, Clinical Faculty, University of Maryland School of Medicine, Baltimore, MD

GREGORY J. MARCHANT, Associate Professor, Educational Psychology, Ball State University, Muncie, IN

GARY L. MARCO, Consultant, Chapin, SC

HOWARD MARGOLIS, Professor of Educational and Community Programs, Queens College of the City University of New York, Flushing, NY

SUZANNE G. MARTIN, Director of Needs Assessment, Charter Fairmount Behavioral Health System, Philadelphia, PA

WILLIAM E. MARTIN, JR., Professor of Educational Psychology, Northern Arizona University, Flagstaff, AZ

PAUL MASTRANGELO, Associate Professor, Division of Applied Psychology and Quantitative Methods, University of Baltimore, Baltimore, MD

KEVIN J. McCARTHY, Assistant Clinical Professor of Psychiatry, Louisiana State University, Health Sciences Center, Department of Psychiatry, New Orleans, LA

REBECCA McCAULEY, Associate Professor, Communication Sciences, University of Vermont, Burlington, VT

ANDREW A. McCONNEY, Associate Research Professor, Teaching Research Division, Western Oregon University, Monmouth, OR

RICHARD J. McCOWAN, Professor Emeritus and Director, Research and Evaluation, Center for Development of Human Services, State College at Buffalo, Buffalo, NY

SHEILA C. McCOWAN, Doctoral Candidate in Counseling Psychology, State University of New York at Buffalo, Buffalo, NY

MERILEE McCURDY, Pediatric Psychology Intern, Munroe-Meyer Institute for Genetics and Rehabilitation, University of Nebraska Medical Center, Omaha, NE

CAROL M. McGREGOR, Associate Professor of Education, School of Education and Human Development, Brenau University, Gainesville, GA

THOMAS McKNIGHT, Psychologist, Private Practice, Spokane, WA

JOYCE R. McLARTY, Principal Research Associate, Workforce Development Division, ACT, Inc., Iowa City, IA

McLellMARY J. McLELLAN, Associate Professor, Northern Arizona University, Flagstaff, AZ

MALCOLM R. McNEIL, Professor and Chair, Department of Communication Science and Disorders, University of Pittsburgh, Pittsburgh, PA

MARIA DEL R. MEDINA-DIAZ, Associate Professor, Department of Graduate Studies, University of Puerto Rico, Rio Piedras, PR

SHEILA MEHTA, Associate Professor of Psychology, Auburn University at Montgomery, Montgomery, AL

SCOTT T. MEIER, Associate Professor and Director of Training, Department of Counseling and Educational Psychology, SUNY Buffalo, Buffalo, NY

JOYCE MEIKAMP, Associate Professor of Special Education, Marshall University Graduate College, South Charleston, WV

PETER F. MERENDA, Professor Emeritus of Psychology and Statistics, University of Rhode Island, Kingston, RI

WILLIAM R. MERZ, SR., Professor—School Psychology Training Program, California State University, Sacramento, CA

HILLARY MICHAELS, Senior Research Scientist, CTB/McGraw-Hill, Monterey, CA:

DANIEL C. MILLER, Associate Professor of Psychology, Texas Woman's University, Denton, TX

M. DAVID MILLER, Professor, University of Florida, Gainesville, FL

ROBERT B. MILLER, Psychologist, Coordinator, Program Evaluation & Quality Improvement, Saginaw County Community Mental Health Center, Saginaw, MI

ROBERT J. MILLER, Professor of Special Education, Minnesota State University, Mankato, Mankato, MN

JOHN A. MILLS, Professor, Counseling and Student Development, Indiana University of Pennsylvania, Indiana, PA

PAT MIRENDA, Associate Professor, University of British Columbia, Vancouver, British Columbia, Canada

CAROLYN MITCHELL-PERSON, Associate Professor of Communication Disorders, Southern University, Baton Rouge, LA

JUDITH A. MONSAAS, Associate Professor of Education, North Georgia College and State University, Dahlonega, GA

PAMILLA MORALES, Senior Lecturer, Bolton Institute, Bolton, Lancashire, England

KEVIN L. MORELAND, Psychologist, Private Practice, Ft. Walton Beach, FL

CLAUDIA J. MORNER, Professor and University Librarian, University of New Hampshire, Durham, NH

SHERWYN P. MORREALE, Associate Director, National Communication Association, Annandale, VA

ROBERT G. MORWOOD, Professor of Education, and Assistant Director, Point Loma Nazarene University, Pasadena, CA

PAUL M. MUCHINSKY, Joseph M. Bryan Distinguished Professor of Business, The University of North Carolina at Greensboro, Greensboro, NC

JANICE W. MURDOCH, Professor of Psychology, Clemson University, Clemson, SC

MILDRED MURRAY-WARD, Professor of Education, School of Education, California Lutheran University, Thousand Oaks, CA

SCOTT A. NAPOLITANO, Adjunct Assistant Professor, Department of Educational Psychology, University of Nebraska–Lincoln, Lincoln, NE, and Pediatric Neuropsychologist, Lincoln Pediatric Group, Lincoln, NE

WENDY NAUMANN, Assistant Professor, Department of Psychology, University of Memphis, Memphis, TN

LEAH M. NELLIS, Assistant Professor of Educational Psychology, Northern Arizona University, Flagstaff, AZ

JEAN NEWMAN, Assistant Professor of Educational Psychology, University of South Alabama, Mobile, AL

ANTHONY J. NITKO, Professor, Department of Educational Psychology, University of Arizona, Tucson, AZ

JANET NORRIS, Professor of Communication Disorders, Louisiana State University, Baton Rouge, LA

CHRISTINE NOVAK, Clinical Assistant Professor, Division of Psychological and Quantitative Foundations, The University of Iowa, Iowa City, IA

JUDY OEHLER-STINNETT, Associate Professor, School of Applied Health and Educational Psychology, Oklahoma State University, Stillwater, OK

BILLY T. OGLETREE, Associate Professor, Communication Disorders Program, Western Carolina University, Cullowhee, NC

STEPHEN OLEJNIK, Professor of Educational Psychology, University of Georgia, Athens, GA

D. JOE OLMI, Associate Professor, Department of Psychology, The University of Southern Mississippi, Hattiesburg, MS

DENIZ S. ONES, Hellervik Professor of Industrial-Organizational Psychology, Department of Psychology, University of Minnesota, Minneapolis, MN

TERRY OVERTON, President, Learning and Behavioral Therapies, Inc., Farmville, VA

STEVEN V. OWEN, Senior Biostatistician, Department of Preventive Medicine and Community Health, University of Texas Medical Branch, Galveston, TX

GRETCHEN OWENS, Associate Professor of Child Study, St. Joseph's College, Patchogue, NY

ABBOT PACKARD, Instructor, Educational Psychology and Foundations, University of Northern Iowa, Cedar Falls, IA

VICKI S. PACKMAN, Senior Assessment Analyst, SRP, Phoenix, AZ

KATHLEEN D. PAGET, Director of Research and Evaluation, The Center for Child and Family Studies, College of Social Work, University of South Carolina, Columbia, SC

NATHANIEL J. PALLONE, University Distinguished Professor (Psychology), Center of Alcohol Studies, Rutgers University, Piscataway, NJ

ANTHONY W. PAOLITTO, Assistant Professor, School Psychology Program, Ohio State University, Columbus, OH

ANTHONY M. PAOLO, Coordinator of Assessment and Evaluation, University of Kansas Medical Center, Kansas City, KS

ILA PARASNIS, Associate Professor, Department of Applied Language and Cognition Research, National Technical Institute for the Deaf, Rochester Institute of Technology, Rochester, NY

RENEE PAVELSKI, Doctoral Candidate, Counseling, Clinical, School Psychology Program, University of California, Santa Barbara, Graduate School of Education, Santa Barbara, CA

L. CAROLYN PEARSON, Professor of Education, University of West Florida, Pensacola, FL

CAROLYN MITCHELL PERSON, Associate Professor of Urban and Ethnic Communication Disorders, Southern University, Baton Rouge, LA

CHARLES A. PETERSON, Staff Clinical Psychologist, Department of Veterans Affairs, Minneapolis Medical Center, and Associate Clinical Professor of Psychology, University of Minnesota, Minneapolis, MN

FRANCISCA ESTEBAN PETERSON, School Psychologist, Lincoln Public Schools, Lincoln, NE

STEVEN I. PFEIFFER, Adjunct Professor of Psychology and Education, and Executive Director, Duke University Talent Identification Program, Durham, NC

WAYNE C. PIERSEL, Licensed Psychologist, Heartspring, Wichita, KS

DAVID J. PITTENGER, Associate Professor of Psychology, The University of Tennessee at Chattanooga, Chattanooga, TN

JOHN POGGIO, Professor of Psychology and Research in Education, School of Education, University of Kansas, Lawrence, KS

MARK POPE, Associate Professor, Division of Counseling, University of Missouri–St. Louis, St. Louis, MO

JULIA Y. PORTER, Assistant Professor of Counselor Education, Mississippi State University, Meridian, MS

G. MICHAEL POTEAT, Associate Professor of Psychology, East Carolina University, Greenville, NC

SHEILA PRATT, Assistant Professor of Communication Science & Disorders, University of Pittsburgh, Pittsburgh, PA

ERICH P. PRIEN, Professor of Industrial Psychology (Retired) and President, Performance Management Press, Memphis, TN

KRISTIN O. PRIEN, Assistant Professor of Management, Christian Brothers University, Memphis, TN

THERESA A. QUIGNEY, Assistant Professor, Cleveland State University, Cleveland, OH

NAMBURY S. RAJU, Distinguished Professor, Institute of Psychology, Illinois Institute of Technology, Chicago, IL

BIKKAR S. RANDHAWA, Professor of Educational Psychology, University of Saskatchewan, Saskatoon, Canada

ALAN J. RAPHAEL, President, International Assessment Systems, Inc., Miami, FL

JAMES C. REED, Chief Psychologist, St. Luke's Hospital, New Bedford, MA

JEFF REESE, Psychology Intern, Texas Tech University, Lubbock, TX

ROBERT C. REINEHR, Professor of Psychology, Southwestern University, Georgetown, TX

PAUL RETZLAFF, Professor, Psychology Department, University of Northern Colorado, Greeley, CO

CECIL R. REYNOLDS, Professor of Educational Psychology, Professor of Neuroscience, Distinguished Research Scholar, Texas A&M University, College Station, TX

WILLIAM M. REYNOLDS, Professor, Department of Psychology, Humboldt State University, Arcata, CA

DAVID C. S. RICHARD, Clinical Coordinator, Assistant Professor, Psychology, Southwest Missouri State University, Springfield, MO

ROGER A. RICHARDS, Consultant, Office of Certification and Credentialing, Massachusetts Department of Education, Malden, MA

MICHELE L. RIES, Research Assistant, Psychology Department, The University of Memphis, Memphis, TN

BRENT W. ROBERTS, Assistant Professor of Psychology, University of Illinois at Urbana—Champaign, Champaign, IL

MARK W. ROBERTS, Professor of Psychology, Idaho State University, Pocatello, ID

BRUCE G. ROGERS, Professor of Educational Psychology, University of Northern Iowa, Cedar Falls, IA

CYNTHIA A. ROHRBECK, Associate Professor of Psychology, The George Washington University, Washington, DC

DEBORAH D. ROMAN, Assistant Professor and Director, Neuropsychology Lab, Departments of Physical Medicine and Rehabilitation and Neurosurgery, University of Minnesota, Minneapolis, MN

MICHAEL J. ROSZKOWSKI, Director, Institutional Research, La Salle University, Philadelphia, PA

BARBARA A. ROTHLISBERG, Professor of Psychology in Educational Psychology, Ball State University, Muncie, IN

MARY ROZNOWSKI, Associate Professor of Psychology, Ohio State University, Columbus, OH

HERBERT C. RUDMAN, Professor Emeritus of Measurement and Quantitative Methods, Michigan State University, East Lansing, MI

MICHAEL LEE RUSSELL, Commander, 47th Combat Support Hospital, Fort Lewis, WA

LAWRENCE J. RYAN, Core Faculty, The Graduate College of The Union Institute, Cincinnati, OH, and Vice President and Academic Dean, St. John's Seminary College, Camarillo, CA

DARRELL L. SABERS, Professor of Educational Psychology, University of Arizona, Tucson, AZ

SALVADOR HECTOR OCHOA, Associate Professor, Department of Educational Psychology, Texas A&M University, College Station, TX

VINCENT J. SAMAR, Associate Professor, Department of Applied Language and Cognition Research, National Technical Institute for the Deaf, Rochester Institute of Technology, Rochester, NY

JONATHAN SANDOVAL, Professor of Education, Division of Education, University of California, Davis, Davis, CA

ELEANOR E. SANFORD, Director of Technical Research, MetaMetrics, Inc., Durham, NC

WILLIAM I. SAUSER, JR., Associate Dean and Professor, College of Business, Auburn University, Auburn, AL

DIANE J. SAWYER, Murfree Professor of Dyslexic Studies, Middle Tennessee State University, Murfreesboro, TN

WILLIAM D. SCHAFER, Associate Professor of Measurement, Statistics, and Evaluation, University of Maryland, College Park, MD and State Director of Student Assessment, Maryland State Department of Education, Baltimore, MD

GERALD R. SCHNECK, Professor of Rehabilitation Counseling, Mankato State University, Mankato, MN

RICHARD V. SCHOWENGERDT, Assistant Professor of Psychology and Counseling, Pittsburg State University, Pittsburg, KS, and School Psychologist, Olathe, KS

GREGORY SCHRAW, Associate Professor of Educational Psychology, University of Nebraska—Lincoln, Lincoln, NE

GENE SCHWARTING, Assistant Professor, Department of Education/Special Education, Fontbonne College, St. Louis, MO

TIMOTHY SHANAHAN, Professor of Urban Education, University of Illinois at Chicago, Chicago, IL

STEVEN R. SHAW, Lead School Psychologist, Department of Developmental Pediatrics, The Children's Hospital, Greenville, SC

EUGENE P. SHEEHAN, Professor of Psychology, University of Northern Colorado, Greeley, CO

MARK D. SHRIVER, Assistant Professor of Pediatrics, Munroe-Meyer Institute for Genetics and Rehabilitation, University of Nebraska Medical Center, Omaha, NE

MARK E. SIBICKY, Associate Professor of Psychology, Marietta College, Marietta, OH

SURENDRA P. SINGH, Professor and Clinical Neuropsychologist, College of Education, University of South Florida, Tampa, FL

DOROTHY M. SINGLETON, Associate Professor of Education, Winston-Salem State University, Winston-Salem, NC

THERESA G. SISKIND, Assessment Coordinator, South Carolina Education Oversight Committee, Columbia, SC

WAYNE H. SLATER, Associate Professor, Department of Curriculum and Instruction, University of Maryland, College Park, MD

DOUGLAS K. SMITH, Director of Programs in School Psychology, University at Albany—State University of New York, Albany, NY

EVERETT V. SMITH JR., Assistant Professor of Educational Psychology, University of Illinois, Chicago, IL

JANET V. SMITH, Associate Professor, Department of Psychology and Counseling, Pittsburg State University, Pittsburg, KS

JEFFREY K. SMITH, Professor of Educational Psychology, Rutgers, the State University of New Jersey, New Brunswick, NJ

LISA F. SMITH, Assistant Professor, Psychology Department, Kean University, Union, NJ

KATHARINE SNYDER, Assistant Professor of Psychology, Shepherd College, Shepherdstown, WV

ALAN SOLOMON, Research Associate, The School District of Philadelphia, Philadelphia, PA

RHONDA H. SOLOMON, Psychologist, Los Angeles Unified School District, Los Angeles, CA

JANET E. SPECTOR, Assistant Professor of Education and Human Development, University of Maine, Orono, ME

LORAINE J. SPENCINER, Professor of Special Education, University of Maine at Farmington, Farmington, ME

ROBERT SPIES, Associate Director, Buros Institute of Mental Measurements, University of Nebraska—Lincoln, Lincoln, NE

STEPHEN A. SPILLANE, Learning Specialist/Educational Consultant, Centerville, MA

MICHAEL J. SPORAKOWSKI, Professor Emeritus of Human Development, Virginia Polytechnic Institute and State University, Blacksburg, VA

STEVEN A. STAHL, Professor of Reading Education, The University of Georgia, Athens, GA

GARY J. STAINBACK, Senior Psychologist I, Developmental Evaluation Clinic, East Carolina University School of Medicine, Department of Pediatrics, Greenville, NC

CHARLES W. STANSFIELD, President, Second Language Testing, Inc., N. Bethesda, MD

MARGOT B. STEIN, Clinical Assistant Professor of Psychiatry, UNC School of Medicine, Director of Training, Center for the Study of Development and Learning, University of North Carolina at Chapel Hill, Chapel Hill, NC

STEPHANIE STEIN, Professor of Psychology, Central Washington University, Ellensburg, WA

BRENDA A. STEVENS, School Psychologist, Indian Hill Exempted Village School District, Cincinnati, OH

JAY R. STEWART, Assistant Professor and Director, Rehabilitation Counseling Program, Bowling Green State University, Bowling Green, OH

TERRY A. STINNETT, Associate Professor, School Psychology Programs, Oklahoma State University, Stillwater, OK

DONALD LEE STOVALL, Associate Professor of Counseling & School Psychology, University of Wisconsin—River Falls, River Falls, WI

GABRIELLE STUTMAN, Private Practice, Westchester and Manhattan, NY

HOI K. SUEN, Professor of Educational Psychology, Pennsylvania State University, University Park, PA

NORMAN D. SUNDBERG, Professor Emeritus, Department of Psychology, University of Oregon, Eugene, OR

ROSEMARY E. SUTTON, Professor of Education, Cleveland State University, Cleveland, OH

JODY L. SWARTZ-KULSTAD, Assistant Professor of Counselor Education, University of Wisconsin—Superior, Superior, WI

SUSAN M. SWEARER, Assistant Professor of School Psychology, University of Nebraska—Lincoln, Lincoln, NE

MARK E. SWERDLIK, Professor of Psychology, Illinois State University, Normal, IL

BRUCE THOMPSON, Professor and Distinguished Research Scholar, Department of Educational Psychology, Texas A&M University, and Adjunct Professor of Community Medicine, Baylor College of Medicine, College Station, TX

DONALD THOMPSON, Dean and Professor of Counseling and Psychology, Troy State University Montgomery, Montgomery, AL

GEORGE C. THORNTON III, Professor of Psychology, Colorado State University, Fort Collins, CO

DONALD W. TIFFANY, Director, Psychological Growth Associates, Inc., Lawrence, KS

GERALD TINDAL, Professor of Behavioral Research and Teaching, University of Oregon, Eugene, OR

WILLIAM C. TIRRE, Senior Research Psychologist, Air Force Research Laboratory, Brooks Air Force Base, TX

RUTH E. TOMES, Associate Professor, Early Childhood Education, Northeastern State University—Tulsa, Tulsa, OK

TONY TONEATTO, Scientist, Clinical, Social and Research Department, Addiction Research Foundation, Toronto, Ontario, Canada

ROGER L. TOWNE, Associate Professor and Head, Department of Communication Disorders, Northern Michigan University, Marquette, MI

ROSS E. TRAUB, Professor, Department of Curriculum, Teaching and Learning, The Ontario Institute for Studies in Education, the University of Toronto, Toronto, Ontario, Canada

MICHAEL S. TREVISAN, Assistant Professor, Department of Educational Leadership and Counseling Psychology, Washington State University, Pullman, WA

STEPHEN E. TROTTER, Associate Professor, Department of Educational & Counseling Psychology, University of the Pacific, Stockton, CA

SUSANA URBINA, Professor of Psychology, University of North Florida, Jacksonville, FL

JOHN J. VACCA, Certified School Psychologist, Assistant Professor of Special Education, Advisor, Graduate Program in Early Intervention, Loyola College, Baltimore, MD

WILFRED G. VAN GORP, Professor of Psychology in Psychiatry, Director, Neuropsychology, New York Hospital—Cornell Medical Center Mental Health System, New York, NY

JAMES P. VAN HANEGHAN, Associate Professor, Department of Behavioral Studies and Educational Technology, University of South Alabama, Mobile, AL

GABRIELE van LINGEN, Professor of Educational Studies, Leadership and Counseling, Murray State University, Murray, KY

MOLLY L. VANDUSER, Alfred University, Alfred, NY

WILLIAM VERDI, Manager Employment Testing and Validation, Long Island Railroad, Middle Village, NY

JAN VISSER, Assistant Professor of Kinesiology, Pennsylvania State University, State College, PA

CHOCKALINGAM VISWESVARAN, Associate Professor, Florida International University, Miami, FL

ROMEO VITELLI, Staff Psychologist, Milbrook Correctional Centre, Milbrook, Ontario, Canada

THERESA VOLPE-JOHNSTONE, Clinical and School Psychologist, Pleasanton, CA

DELORES D. WALCOTT, Assistant Professor, Western Michigan University, Counseling and Testing Center, Kalamazoo, MI

WILLIAM J. WALDRON, Administrator, Employee Testing & Assessment, TECO Energy, Inc., Tampa, FL

ROBERT WALL, Professor of Reading, Special Education and Instructional Technology, Towson State University, Towson, MD

NIELS G. WALLER, Professor of Psychology and Human Development, Vanderbilt University, Nashville, TN

SANDRA J. WANNER, Professor of Education and Director of Special Education, University of Mary Hardin-Baylor, Belton, TX

RICHARD A. WANTZ, Associate Professor of Human Services, College of Education and Human Services, and Associate Clinical Professor of Psychiatry, School of Medicine, Wright State University, Dayton, OH

ANNIE W. WARD, Emeritus Professor, University of South Florida, Daytona Beach, FL

SANDRA WARD, Associate Professor of Education, The College of William and Mary, Williamsburg, VA

OREST EUGENE WASYLIW, Director of Adult Clinical Psychology, Isaac Ray Center, Rush-Presbyterian—St. Luke's Medical Center, Chicago, IL

BETSY WATERMAN, Associate Professor, Counseling and Psychological Services Department, State University of New York at Oswego, Oswego, NY

T. STEUART WATSON, Professor of Counselor Education/Educational Psychology, Mississippi State University, Starkville, MS

TERRI L. WEAVER, Assistant Professor of Psychology, Saint Louis University, St. Louis, MO

PAUL D. WERNER, Professor, California School of Professional Psychology, Alameda, CA

GORAN WESTERGREN, Chief Psychologist, Department of Clinical Psychology, State Hospital, Halmstad, Sweden

INGELA WESTERGREN, Neuropsychologist and Licensed Psychologist, Department of Clinical Psychology, State Hospital, Halmstad, Sweden

PATRICIA H. WHEELER, President and Principal Researcher, EREAPA Associates, Livermore, CA

SUSAN C. WHISTON, Professor, Department of Educational Psychology, University of Nevada—Las Vegas, Las Vegas, NV

KEITH F. WIDAMAN, Professor of Psychology, University of California at Davis, Davis, CA

THOMAS A. WIDIGER, Professor, Department of Psychology, University of Kentucky, Lexington, KY

MARTIN J. WIESE, Licensed Psychologist/Certified School Psychologist, Lincoln Public Schools, Lincoln, NE

WILLIAM K. WILKINSON, Consulting Psychologist, Boleybeg, Barna, County Galway, Ireland

HILDA WING, Personnel Psychologist, Federal Aviation Administration, Washington, DC

CARRIE L. WINTEROWD, Assistant Professor of Counseling Psychology, College of Education, Oklahoma State University, Stillwater, OK

DAVID L. WODRICH, Director of Psychological Assessment Services, Phoenix Children's Hospital, Phoenix, AZ

RICHARD M. WOLF, Professor of Psychology and Education, Teachers College, Columbia University, New York, NY

JAMES A. WOLLACK, Assistant Scientist, Department of Testing & Evaluation, University of Wisconsin—Madison, Madison, WI

CLAUDIA R. WRIGHT, Professor, Educational Psychology, California State University, Long Beach, Long Beach, CA

DANIEL L. YAZAK, Assistant Professor of Counseling and Human Services, Montana State University—Billings, Billings, MT

JOHN W. YOUNG, Associate Professor of Educational Statistics and Measurement, Rutgers University, New Brunswick, NJ

JAMES YSSELDYKE, Birkmaier Professor of Educational Leadership, University of Minnesota, Minneapolis, MN

PETER ZACHAR, Associate Professor, Auburn University at Montgomery, Montgomery, AL

SHELDON ZEDECK, Chair and Professor of Psychology, Department of Psychology, University of California, Berkeley, CA

MICHAEL J. ZICKAR, Assistant Professor of Industrial-Organizational Psychology, Bowling Green State University, Bowling Green, OH

LINDA J. ZIMMERMAN, Clinical/School Psychologist, Private Practice, Pittsburgh, PA

LELAND C. ZLOMKE, Director of Psychological Services, OMNI Behavioral Health, Omaha, NE

INDEX OF TITLES

This title index lists all the tests included in The Fourteenth Mental Measurements Yearbook. *Citations are to test entry numbers, not to pages (e.g., 54 refers to test 54 and not page 54). (Test numbers along with test titles are indicated in the running heads at the top of each page, whereas page numbers, used only in the Table of Contents but not in the indexes, appear at the bottom of each page.) Superseded titles are listed with cross references to current titles, and alternative titles are also cross referenced.*

Many tests in this volume were previously listed in Tests in Print V *(1999) and* The Supplement to the Thirteenth Mental Measurements Yearbook *(1999). An* (N) *appearing immediately after a test number indicates tha the test is a new, recently published test, and/or that it has not appeared before in any Buros Institute publication other than* Tests in Print V *or* The Supplement to the Thirteenth Mental Measurements Yearbook. *An* (R) *indicates that the test has been revised or supplemented since last included in a Buros publication.*

INDEX OF ACRONYMS

This Index of Acronyms refers the reader to the appropriate test in The Fourteenth Mental Measurements Yearbook. *In some cases tests are better known by their acronyms than by their full titles, and this index can be of substantial help to the person who knows the former but not the latter. Acronyms are only listed if the author or publisher has made substantial use of the acronym in referring to the test, or if the test is widely known by the acronym. A few acronyms are registered trademarks (e.g., SAT); where this is known to us, only the test with the registered trademark is referenced. There is some danger in the overuse of acronyms, but this index, like all other indexes in this work, is provided to make the task of identifying a test as easy as possible. All numbers refer to test numbers, not page numbers.*

AAA: Assessment of Adaptive Areas, 25
AAC: Adolescent Apperception Cards, 7
A-ADDES: Adult Attention Deficit Disorders Evaluation Scale, 10
ABES: Adaptive Behavior Evaluation Scale, Revised, 4
ACDI: ACDI-Corrections Version and Corrections Version II, 2
ACE: Analyzing the Communication Environment, 16
ACTeRS: AD/HD Comprehensive Teacher's Rating Scale, Second Edition [1998 Revision], 5
ADDES: Attention Deficit Disorders Evaluation Scale, Second Edition, 27
ADDES-S: The Attention Deficit Disorders Evaluation Scale Secondary-Age Student, 28
A-DES: Adolescent Dissociative Experiences Scale, 8
ADHDT: Attention-Deficit/Hyperactivity Disorder Test, 30
ADSA: Attention-Deficit Scales for Adults, 29
AIA: Ashland Interest Assessment, 20
A-LAS®: Adult Language Assessment Scales, 11
AMP: Achievement Motivation Profile, 3
AMTC: Assessing Motivation to Communicate, 23
API: Adult Personality Inventory [Revised], 12
Aprenda 2: Aprenda®: La prueba de logros en español— Segunda edición, 18
APS: Adolescent Psychopathology Scale, 9
APSIP: Assessment of Parenting Skills: Infant and Preschooler, 26
AROE: Adult Rating of Oral English, 13

ASCA: Adjustment Scales for Children and Adolescents, 6
ASQ: Ages and Stages Questionnaires, 14
ASSESS: ASSESS Personality Battery [Expert System Version 5.X], 21
ATD PA: Matching Person and Technology, 221
AUDIT: Alcohol Use Disorders Identification Test, 15

BADS: Behavioural Assessment of the Dysexecutive Syndrome, 43
BAI: Braille Assessment Inventory, 49
BarOn EQ-i: BarOn Emotional Quotient Inventory, 32
BASC: Behavior Assessment System for Children [Revised], 40
BASC Monitor for ADHD: BASC Monitor for ADHD, 33
BBCS-R: Bracken Basic Concept Scale—Revised, 48
BCT: The Booklet Category Test, Second Edition, 47
BDI-II: Beck Depression Inventory—II, 37
BDS: Behavior Dimensions Scale, 41
BED: Bedside Evaluation of Dysphagia, 38
BERS: Behavioral and Emotional Rating Scale: A Strength-Based Approach to Assessment, 42
BEST-2: Bedside Evaluation Screening Test, Second Edition, 39
BHI: Battery for Health Improvement, 36
BNCE: Brief Neuropsychological Cognitive Examination, 50

CLASSIFIED SUBJECT INDEX

The Classified Subject Index classifies all tests included in The Mental Measurements Yearbook *into 18 major categories: Achievement, Behavior Assessment, Developmental, Education, English and Language, Fine Arts, Foreign Languages, Intelligence and General Aptitude, Mathematics, Miscellaneous, Neuropsychological, Personality, Reading, Science, Sensory-Motor, Social Studies, Speech and Hearing, and Vocations. This Classified Subject Index for the tests reviewed in* The Fourteenth Mental Measurements Yearbook *includes tests in 16 of the 18 available categories. (The categories of Fine Arts and Social Studies have no representative tests in this volume.) Each category appears in alphabetical order and tests are ordered alphabetically within each category. Each test entry includes test title, population for which the test is intended, and the test entry number in* The Fourteenth Mental Measurements Yearbook. *All numbers refer to test numbers, not to page numbers. Brief suggestions for the use of this index are presented in the introduction and definitions of the categories are provided at the beginning of this index.*

Achievement

Tests that measure acquired knowledge across school subject content areas. Included here are test batteries that measure multiple content areas and individual subject areas not having separate classification categories. (Note: Some batteries include both achievement and aptitude subtests. Such batteries may be classified under the categories of either Achievement or Intelligence and Aptitude depending upon the principal content area.)

See also Fine Arts, Intelligence and General Aptitude, Mathematics, Reading, Science, and Social Studies.

Behavior Assessment

Tests that measure general or specific behavior within educational, vocational, community, or home settings. Included here are checklists, rating scales, and surveys that measure observer's interpretations of behavior in relation to adaptive or social skills, functional skills, and appropriateness or dysfunction within settings/situations.

Developmental

Tests that are designed to assess skills or emerging skills (such as number concepts, conservation, memory, fine motor, gross motor, communication, letter recognition, social competence) of young children (0-7 years) or tests that are designed to assess such skills in severely or profoundly disabled school-aged individuals. Included here are early screeners, developmental surveys/profiles, kindergarten or school readiness tests, early learning profiles, infant development scales, tests of play behavior, social acceptance/social skills; and preschool psychoeducational batteries. Content-specific screeners, such as those assessing readiness, are classified by content area (e.g., Reading).

See also Neuropsychological and Sensory-Motor.

Education

General education-related tests, including measures of instructional/school environment, effective schools/teaching, study skills and strategies, learning styles and strategies, school attitudes, educational programs/curriculae, interest inventories, and educational leadership.

Specific content area tests (i.e., science, mathematics, social studies, etc.) are listed by their content area.

English and Language

Tests that measure skills in using or understanding the English language in spoken or written form. Included here are tests of language proficiency, applied literacy, language comprehension/development/proficiency, English skills/proficiency, communication skills, listening comprehension, linguistics, and receptive/expressive vocabulary. (Tests designed to measure the mechanics of speaking or communicating are classified under the category Speech and Hearing.)

Fine Arts

Tests that measure knowledge, skills, abilities, attitudes, and interests within the various areas of fine and performing arts. Included here are tests of aptitude, achievement, creativity/talent/giftedness specific to the Fine Arts area, and tests of aesthetic judgment.

Foreign Languages

Tests that measure competencies and readiness in reading, comprehending, and speaking a language other than English.

Intelligence and General Aptitude

Tests that measure general acquired knowledge, aptitudes, or cognitive ability and those that assess specific aspects of these general categories. Included here are tests of critical thinking skills, nonverbal/verbal reasoning, cognitive abilities/processing, learning potential/aptitude/efficiency, logical reasoning, abstract thinking, creative thinking/creativity; entrance exams and academic admissions tests.

Mathematics

Tests that measure competencies and attitudes in any of the various areas of mathematics (e.g., algebra, geometry, calculus) and those related to general mathematics achievement/proficiency. (Note: Included here are tests that assess personality or affective variables related to mathematics.)

Miscellaneous

Tests that cannot be sorted into any of the current MMY categories as listed and defined above. Included here are tests of handwriting, ethics and morality, religion, driving and safety, health and physical education, environment (e.g., classroom environment, family environment), custody decisions, substance abuse, and addictions. See also Personality.

Neuropsychological

Tests that measure neurological functioning or brain-behavior relationships either generally or in relation to specific areas of functioning. Included here are neuropsychological test batteries, questionnaires, and screening tests. Also included are tests that measure memory impairment, various disorders or decline associated with dementia, brain/head injury, visual attention, digit recognition, finger tapping, laterality, aphasia, and behavior (associated with organic brain dysfunction or brain injury).

See also Developmental, Intelligence and General Aptitude, Sensory-Motor, and Speech and Hearing.

Personality

Tests that measure individuals' ways of thinking, behaving, and functioning within family and society. Included here are projective and apperception tests, needs inventories, anxiety/depression scales; tests assessing substance use/abuse (or propensity for abuse), risk taking behavior, general mental health, emotional intelligence, self-image/-concept/-esteem, empathy, suicidal ideation, schizophrenia, depression/hopelessness, abuse, coping skills/stress, eating disorders, grief, decision-making, racial attitudes; general motivation, attributions, perceptions; adjustment, parenting styles, and marital issues/satisfaction.

For content-specific tests, see subject area categories (e.g., math efficacy instruments are located in Mathematics). Some areas, such as substance abuse, are cross-referenced with the Personality category.

Reading

Tests that measure competencies and attitudes within the broadly defined area of reading. Included here are reading inventories, tests of reading achievement and aptitude, reading readiness/early reading ability, reading comprehension, reading decoding, and oral reading. (Note: Included here are tests that assess personality or affective variables related to reading.)

Science

Tests that measure competencies and attitudes within any of the various areas of science (e.g., biology, chemistry, physics), and those related to general science achievement/proficiency. (Note: Included here are tests that assess personality or affective variables related to science.)

Sensory-Motor

Tests that are general or specific measures of any or all of the five senses and those that assess fine or gross motor skills. Included here are tests of manual dexterity, perceptual skills, visual-motor skills, perceptual-motor skills, movement and posture, laterality preference, sensory integration, motor development, color blindness/discrimination, visual perception/organization, and visual acuity. See also the categories Neuropsychological and Speech and Hearing.

Social Studies

Tests that measure competencies and attitudes within the broadly defined area of social studies. Included here are tests related to economics, sociology, history, geography, and political science, and those related to general social studies achievement/proficiency. (Note: Also included here are tests that assess personality or affective variables related to social studies.)

Speech and Hearing

Tests that measure the mechanics of speaking or hearing the spoken word. Included here are tests of articulation, voice fluency, stuttering, speech sound perception/discrimination, auditory discrimination/comprehension, audiometry, deafness, and hearing loss/impairment. See also Developmental, English and Language, Neuropsychological, and Sensory-Motor.

Vocations

Tests that measure employee skills, behaviors, attitudes, values, and perceptions relative to jobs, employment, and the work place or organizational environment. Included here are tests of management skill/style/competence, leader behavior, careers (development, exploration, attitudes); job- or work-related selection/admission/entrance tests; tests of work adjustment, team or group processes/communication/effectiveness, employability, vocational/occupational interests, employee aptitudes/competencies, and organizational climate.

See also Intelligence and General Aptitude, and Personality and also specific content area categories (e.g., Mathematics, Reading).

ACHIEVEMENT

Aprenda®: La prueba de logros en español—Segunda edición; Grades K.5–12.9; 18

BRIGANCE® Diagnostic Comprehensive Inventory of Basic Skills, Revised; Ages 5–13; 51

BRIGANCE® Diagnostic Life Skills Inventory; Grades 2–8; 53

Canadian Achievement Survey Tests for Adults; Adults; 61

Closed High School Placement Test; Eighth grade students; 80

Curriculum Frameworks Assessment System; Students in grades 1–12 from the California public school districts; 108

Evaluation of Basic Skills; Ages 3 to 18; 142

Hammill Multiability Achievement Test; Ages 7-0 to 17-11; 159

High School Placement Test-Open Edition; Eighth grade students; 166

Kaufman Test of Educational Achievement [1998 Normative Update]; Grades 1 through 12, ages 6–22; 191

Metropolitan Performance Assessment: Integrated Performance Tasks; Ages 4-4 to 6-3; ages 5-5 to 7-0; 230

Monitoring Basic Skills Progress—Second Edition; Grades 1–7; 238

Peabody Individual Achievement Test—Revised [1998 Normative Update]; Grades K–12; 279

TerraNova; Grades K–12; 383

Tests of Achievement and Proficiency, Forms K, L, and M; Grades 9–12; 396

BEHAVIOR ASSESSMENT

AD/HD Comprehensive Teacher's Rating Scale, Second Edition [1998 Revision]; Grades K–adult; 5

Adaptive Behavior Evaluation Scale, Revised; Ages 5-0 to 18-0; 4

Adjustment Scales for Children and Adolescents; Ages 5–17; 6

Adult Attention Deficit Disorders Evaluation Scale; Adults; 10

Assessment of Adaptive Areas; Ages 3–60+ years; 25

Attention Deficit Disorders Evaluation Scale, Second Edition; Ages 3–20 years, ages 4–19 years; 27

The Attention Deficit Disorders Evaluation Scale Secondary-Age Student; Ages 11.5–19; 28

Attention-Deficit Scales for Adults; Adults; 29

Attention-Deficit/Hyperactivity Disorder Test; Ages 3–23; 30

BASC Monitor for ADHD; Ages 4–18; 33

Behavior Assessment System for Children [Revised]; Ages 2 1/2–18; 40

Behavior Dimensions Scale; Ages 3–19; 41

Behavioral and Emotional Rating Scale: A Strength-Based Approach to Assessment; Ages 5-0 to 18-11; 42

DEVELOPMENTAL

EDUCATION

ENGLISH AND LANGUAGE

FOREIGN LANGUAGES

INTELLIGENCE AND GENERAL APTITUDE

MATHEMATICS

MISCELLANEOUS

NEUROPSYCHOLOGICAL

PERSONALITY

READING

Basic Reading Inventory, Seventh Edition; Pre-primer through grade 12, grades 3–12; 34

Burns/Roe Informal Reading Inventory: Preprimer to Twelfth Grade, Fifth Edition; Beginning readers–grade 12; 56

Degrees of Reading Power [Revised]; Grades 1–12; 111

Dyslexia Screening Instrument; Grades 1–12, ages 6–21; 130

Group Reading Test, Fourth Edition; Ages 6:4 to 8:11 and less able children 8:0 to 11:11; 158

Reading Comprehension Battery for Aphasia, Second Edition; Pre-adolescent to geriatric aphasic people; 308

Reading Evaluation Adult Diagnosis, Fifth Edition; Illiterate adult students; 309

Roswell-Chall Diagnostic Reading Test of Word Analysis Skills, Revised and Extended; Reading levels grades 1–4; 327

Shortened Edinburgh Reading Test; Ages 10-0 to 11-6; 354

SPAR Spelling and Reading Tests, Third Edition; Ages 7-0 to 12-11 years; 365

Standardized Reading Inventory, Second Edition; Ages 6-0 to 14-6; 366

STAR Reading™; Grades 1–12; 368

Woodcock Diagnostic Reading Battery; Ages 4–95; 422

Woodcock Reading Mastery Tests—Revised [1998 Normative Update]; Kindergarten through adult; 423

Word Recognition and Phonic Skills; Ages 5.0 to 8.6; 425

SCIENCE

Scientific Orientation Test; Students in school years 5 to 12; 341

SENSORY-MOTOR

Developmental Test of Visual-Motor Integration, 4th Edition, Revised; Ages 3-0 to 17-11; 119

Dysphagia Evaluation Protocol; Adult patients; 131

Gibson Spiral Maze, Second Edition; Children and adults; 155

Infant/Toddler Symptom Checklist; 7–30 months; 178

Kent Visual Perception Test; Ages 5–11; 193

McDowell Vision Screening Kit; Birth to age 21; 226

The McGill Pain Questionnaire; People in pain; 227

Motor-Free Visual Perception Test—Revised; Ages 4–11, adults; 241

Motor-Free Visual Perception Test—Vertical; People with brain injuries; 242

Sensory Integration Inventory—Revised for Individuals with Developmental Disabilities; Developmentally disabled occupational therapy clients school aged to adults; 346

Test of Visual-Motor Integration; Ages 4–17; 395

Wide Range Assessment of Visual Motor Abilities; Ages 3–17 years; 418

SPEECH AND HEARING

The Apraxia Profile: A Descriptive Assessment Tool for Children; Ages 3–13; 17

Assessing and Teaching Phonological Knowledge; Young children; 22

Bedside Evaluation of Dysphagia; Adults neurologically impaired; 38

Communication Activities of Daily Living, Second Edition; Aphasic adults; 84

Communication Profile: A Functional Skills Survey; Elderly adults; 85

Cooper Assessment for Stuttering Syndromes; Ages 3–13 years, Adolescents and adults age 13 and over; 103

VOCATIONS

PUBLISHERS DIRECTORY
AND INDEX

This directory and index gives the names and test entry numbers of all publishers represented in The Fourteenth Mental Measurements Yearbook. *Current addresses are listed for all publishers for which this is known. Those publishers for which a current address is not available are listed as "Address Unknown." This directory and index also provides telephone and FAX numbers and email and Web addresses for those publishers who responded to our request for this information. Please note that all test numbers refer to test entry numbers, not page numbers. Publishers are an important source of information about catalogs, specimen sets, price changes, test revisions, and many other matters.*

Ablin Press Distributors
700 John Ringling Blvd., #1603
Sarasota, FL 34236-1504
Telephone: 941-361-7521
FAX: 941-361-7521
Tests: 355

Academic Therapy Publications
20 Commercial Boulevard
Novato,CA 94949-6191
Telephone: 800-422-7249
FAX: 415-883-3720
E-mail: atp@aol.com
Web URL: www.atpub.com
Tests: 126, 241, 242, 306, 310, 364, 433, 437, 523

Thomas M. Achenbach, Ph.D.
Child Behavior Checklist
University Medical Education Associates
1 South Prospect Street, Room 6434
Burlington, VT 05401-3456
Telephone: 802-656-8313
FAX: 802-656-2602
E-mail: checklist@uvm.edu
Web URL: checklist.uvm.edu
Tests: 67, 430

ACT, Inc.
2201 N. Dodge Street
P.O. Box 168
Iowa City, IA 52243-0168
Telephone: 319-337-1000
FAX: 319-339-3021
Web URL: www.act.org
Tests: 524

ADE Incorporated
P.O. Box 660
Clarkston, MI 48347
Tests: 190, 253, 377

AJA Associates
c/o Marchman Psychology
720 South Dubuque
Iowa City, IA 52240
Tests: 249

American Guidance Service, Inc.
4201 Woodland Road
Circle Pines, MN 55014-1796
Telephone: 800-328-2560
FAX: 612-786-5603
E-mail: agsmail@agsnet
Web URL: www.agsnet.com
Tests: 33, 40, 116, 143, 191, 194, 244, 266, 267, 279, 289, 408, 423

The American Occupational Therapy Association, Inc.
4720 Montgomery Lane
Bethesda, MD 20814-3425
Tests: 199

American Psychiatrics Press, Inc.
1400 K Street, NW — Suite 1101
Washington, DC 20005
Tests: 373, 374

Assessment Systems Corporation
2233 University Avenue, Suite 200
St. Paul, MN   55114-1629
Telephone: 651-647-9220
FAX: 651-647-0412
E-mail: info@assess.com
Web URL: www.assess.com
Tests: 236

Association of American Colleges and Universities
1818 "R" Street, NW
Washington, DC 20009
Telephone: 202-387-3760
FAX: 202-265-9532
E-mail: pubs_desk@aacu.nw.dc.us
Web URL: www.aacu-edu.org
Tests: 461

Australian Council for Educational Research Ltd.
19 Prospect Hill Road
Private Bag 55
Camberwell, Victoria 3124
Australia
Tests: 22, 222, 427

Thomas F. Babor
Department of Community Medicine
University of Connecticut
Farmington, CT 06030-1910
FAX: 860-679-2374
E-mail: babor@nso.uchc.edu
Tests: 15

Ballard & Tighe Publishers
480 Atlas Street
Brea, CA 92821
Tests: 171

Behavior Data Systems, Ltd.
P.O. Box 44256
Phoenix, AZ 85064-4256
Tests: 127, 403

Behavior Science Systems, Inc.
P.O. Box 580274
Minneapolis, MN 55458
Telephone: 612-929-6220
FAX: 612-920-4925
Tests: 71, 176

Behavioral-Developmental Initiatives
14636 North 55th Street
Scottsdale, AZ 85254
Telephone: 800-405-2313
FAX: 602-494-2688
E-mail: BDI@TEMPERAMENT.COM
Web URL: www.b-di.com
Tests: 68

Nancy E. Betz, Ph.D.
2758 Kensington Place, West
Columbus, OH 43202
Tests: 62

Millard J. Bienvenu, Ph.D.
Northwest Publications
710 Watson Drive
Natchitoches, LA 71457
Telephone: (318) 352-5313
Tests: 435, 509

Bigby, Havis, & Associates, Inc.
12750 Merit Drive, Suite 660
Dallas, TX 75251
Telephone: 972-233-6055
FAX: 972-233-3154
E-mail: kcapelle@bigby.com
Web URL: www.bigby.com
Tests: 21, 344

BrainTrain
727 Twin Ridge Lane
Richmond, VA 23235
Telephone: 804-320-0105
FAX: 804-320-0242
E-mail: ginger@braintrain-online.com
Tests: 180

Brookes Publishing Co., Inc.
P.O. Box 10624
Baltimore, MD 21285-0624
Tests: 14

Brunner/Mazel, Inc.
1900 Frost Road, Suite 101
Bristol, PA 19007-1598
Tests: 29

California Counseling Centers
22797 Barton Road, Suite 200
Grand Terrace, CA 92324
Tests: 477, 478, 479

The Cambridge Stratford Study Skills Institute
8560 Main Street
Williamsville, NY 14221
Tests: 494, 514

Cambridge University Press
110 Midland Avenue
Port Chester, NY 10573-4930
Telephone: 800-872-7423
FAX: 914-937-4712
Tests: 255

Canadian Test Centre
Educational Assessment Services
85 Citizen Court, Suites 7 & 8
Markham, Ontario L6G 1A8
Canada
Tests: 61

The CATI Corporation
10 East Costilla
Colorado Springs, CO 80903
Tests: 102

Center for Applied Linguistics
1118 - 22nd Street, NW
Washington, DC 20037
Tests: 163

Center for Creative Leadership
One Leadership Place
P.O. Box 26300
Greensboro, NC 27438-6300
Tests: 195, 299

The Center for Management Effectiveness
P.O. Box 1202
Pacific Palisades, CA 90272
Telephone: 310-459-6052
FAX: 310-459-9307
E-mail: kindlerCME@aol.com
Tests: 286, 483, 503, 512

Center for the Study of Higher Education
The University of Memphis
Memphis, TN 38152
Tests: 87

Centre for Addiction and Mental Health
Marketing Services
33 Russell Street
Toronto, Ontario M5S 2S1
Canada
Tests: 128, 186

Centreville School
6201 Kennett Pike
Wilmington, DE 19807
Telephone: 302-571-0230
FAX: 302-571-0270
E-mail: language@del.net
Tests: 314

Vicentita M. Cervera, Ed.D.
13 Miller Street
San Francisco Del Monte
Quezon City 1105, Philippines
Telephone: 411-2673
FAX: 371-6490
E-mail: vcervera@skyinet.net
Tests: 148

Checkmate Plus, Ltd.
P.O. Box 696
Stony Brook, NY 11790-0696
Telephone: 800-779-4292
FAX: 516-360-3432
E-mail: inpo@checkmateplus.com
Web URL: www.checkmateplus.com
Tests: 134

Child Welfare League of America, Inc.
Publications Department
440 First Street, NW — Suite #310
Washington, DC 20001-2085
Telephone: 202-638-2952
FAX: 202-638-4004
E-mail: sgretchen@cwla.org
Web URL: www.cwla.org
Tests: 144

The Clark Wilson Group, Inc.
4900 Nautilus Court N., Suite 220
Boulder, CO 80301-3242
Tests: 298

Clinical Psychometric Research, Inc.
P.O. Box 619
Riderwood, MD 21139
Telephone: 800-245-0277 and 410-321-6165
FAX: 410-321-6341
E-mail: mdero@aol.com
Web URL: derogatis-tests.com
Tests: 112

CogniSyst, Inc.
3937 Nottaway Road
Durham, NC 27707
Tests: 95, 272, 352, 424

Cogscreen LLC
5021 Seminary Road, Suite 110
Alexandria, VA 22311
Tests: 83

Communication Skill Builders—A Division of the Psychological Corporation
555 Academic Court
San Antonio, TX 78204-9941
Telephone: 800-211-8378

FAX: 800-232-1223
Web URL: www.hbtpc.com
Tests: 16, 17, 129, 189

Consulting Psychologists Press, Inc.
3803 East Bayshore Road
P.O. Box 10096
Palo Alto, CA 94303
Telephone: 800-624-1765
FAX: 650-969-8608
Web URL: www.cpp-db.com
Tests: 63, 146, 251, 428, 480

Consulting Resource Group International, Inc.
#386 - 200 West Third Street
Sumas, WA 98295-8000
Tests: 520

CORE Corporation
Pleasant Hill Executive Park
391 Taylor Blvd., Suite 110
Pleasant Hill, CA 94523-2275
Tests: 348

CTB/McGraw-Hill
20 Ryan Ranch Road
Monterey, CA 93940-5703
Tests: 11, 108, 383, 451, 452

Curriculum Associates, Inc.
153 Rangeway Road
P.O. Box 2001
North Billerica, MA 01862-0901
Telephone: 800-225-0248
FAX: 800-366-1158
E-mail: cainfo@curriculumassociates.com
Web URL: www.curriculumassociates.com
Tests: 51, 52, 53, 446

Department of Research Assessment and Training
1051 Riverside Drive, Unit 123
New York, NY 10032
Telephone: 212-543-5536
FAX: 212-543-5386
Tests: 140, 303

Development Associates, Inc.
1730 North Lynn Street
Arlington, VA 22209-2023
Telephone: 703-276-0677
FAX: 703-276-0432
E-mail: TSTEPHENSON@DEVASSOC1.COM
Web URL: WWW.DEVASSOC1.COM
Tests: 13

Developmental Therapy Institute, Inc.
P.O. Box 5153
Athens, GA 30604-5153

Telephone: 706-369-5689
FAX: 706-369-5690
E-mail: mmwood@arches.uga.edu
Web URL: www.uga.edu/dttp
Tests: 118

Diagnostic Counseling Services, Inc.
P.O. Box 6178
Kokomo, IN 46904-6178
Tests: 245

Diagnostic Specialists, Inc.
1170 North 660 West
Orem, UT 84057
Telephone: 801-225-7698
Tests: 441, 445, 447, 448, 521

Docutrac, Inc.
1330 North King Street
Wilmington, DE 19801
Tests: 379

Ed & Psych Associates
2071 South Atherton Street, Suite 900
State College, PA 16801
Telephone: 814-235-9115
FAX: 814-235-9115
Tests: 6

EdITS/Educational and Industrial Testing Service
P.O. Box 7234
San Diego, CA 92167
Telephone: 800-416-1666 or 619-222-1666
FAX: 619-226-1666
E-mail: edits@k-online.com
Web URL: www.edits.net
Tests: 65, 285, 376, 439, 440, 450

Educational Activities, Inc.
ATTN: Rose Falco
1937 Grand Avenue
Baldwin, NY 11510
Telephone: 800-645-3739
FAX: 516-379-7429
E-mail: LEARN@EDACT.COM
Web URL: WWW.EDACT.COM
Tests: 19, 209, 491

Educational Testing Service
Publication Order Services
P.O. Box 6736
Princeton, NJ 08541-6736
Telephone: 609-921-9000
FAX: 609-734-5410
Web URL: www.ets.org
Tests: 94

Educators Publishing Service, Inc.
31 Smith Place
Cambridge, MA 02138-1089
Telephone: 800-225-5750
FAX: 617-547-0412
E-mail: cps@epsbooks.com
Web URL: www.epsbooks.com
Tests: 151, 282, 326, 327, 434, 495, 502

Ellsworth & Vandermeer Press, Ltd.
4405 Scenic Drive
Nashville, TN 37204
Telephone: 615-386-0061
FAX: 615-386-0346
E-mail: evpress@edge.net
Web URL: edge.net/~evpress
Tests: 277

English Language Institute
University of Michigan
3021 N. University Building
1205 North University Avenue
Ann Arbor, MI 48109-1057
Telephone: 734-764-2416
FAX: 734-763-0369
E-mail: melabelium@umich.edu
Web URL: www.lsa.umich.edu/eli/testing.html
Tests: 233, 463, 464

Enhanced Performance Systems, Inc.
1010 University Avenue, Suite 265
San Diego, CA 92103
Telephone: 619-497—0156
FAX: 619-497-0820
E-mail: sagal@enhanced-performance.com
Web URL: www.enhanced-performance.com
Tests: 31

Enrichment Press
5441 SW Macadam Avenue, #206
Portland, OR 97201
Tests: 293

GB Software LLC
4607 Perham Road
Corona del Mar, CA 92625
Tests: 300

Ruth M. Geiman, Ph.D.
1217 Ironwood Drive
Fairborn, OH 45324
Telephone: 937-754-3981
E-mail: drgeiman@worldnet.att.net
Tests: 154

Gerontology Center
College of Health and Human Development
The Pennsylvania State University
105 Henderson Building South
University Park, PA 16802-6500
Telephone: 814-865-1710
FAX: 814-863-9423
E-mail: GERO@psu.edu
Web URL: geron.psu.edu
Tests: 229

Golden Educational Center
857 Lake Blvd.
Redding, CA 96003
Tests: 181

Robert S. Goyer
Department of Communication
Arizona State University
Tempe, AZ 85287
Tests: 467

GRM Educational Consultancy
P.O. Box 154
Beecroft, New South Wales 2119
Australia
Telephone: 61-2-9484-1598
FAX: 61-2-9875-3638
Tests: 341

H & H Publishing Co., Inc.
1231 Kapp Drive
Clearwater, FL 33765
Telephone: 800-366-4079
FAX: 727-442-2195
E-mail: hhservice@hhpublishing.com
Web URL: www.hhpublishing.com
Tests: 283, 369, 429

Harcourt Brace Educational Measurement
555 Academic Court
San Antonio, TX 78204-2498
Telephone: 800-211-8378
FAX: 800-232-1223
E-mail: CUSTOMER_SERVICE2@HBTPC.COM
Web URL: WWW.HBEM.COM
Tests: 18, 252, 271, 367

Hawthorne Educational Services, Inc.
800 Gray Oak Drive
Columbia, MO 65201
Telephone: 800-542-1673
FAX: 800-442-9509
Tests: 4, 10, 27, 28, 41, 49, 132, 156, 207

Hay/McBer
Training Resources Group
116 Huntington Avenue
Boston, MA 02116
Telephone: 800-729-8074
FAX: 617-927-5060
E-mail: TRG_McBer@haygroup.com
Web URL: trgmcber.haygroup.com
Tests: 481, 484, 485, 505

The Health Institute
New England Medical Center #345
750 Washington Street
Boston, MA 02111
Tests: 352

Herrmann International
794 Buffalo Creek Road
Lake Lure, NC 28746
Tests: 165

Hester Evaluation Systems, Inc.
2410 SW Granthurst Avenue
Topeka, KS 66611-1274
Telephone: 800-832-3825
FAX: 785-357-4041
E-mail: hester@inlandnet.net
Tests: 488

High/Scope Educational Research Foundation
600 North River Street
Ypsilanti, MI 48198-2898
Telephone: 734-485-2000
FAX: 734-485-0704
E-mail: info@highscope.org
Web URL: www.highscope.org
Tests: 167

Hodder & Stoughton Educational
Hodder Headline PLC
338 Euston Road
London NW1 3BH
England
Telephone: 0171 873 6000
FAX: 0171 873 6024
E-mail: chas.knight@hodder.co.uk
Tests: 150, 155, 157, 158, 222, 275, 354, 365, 380, 425, 456

Hogan Assessment Systems, Inc.
P.O. Box 521176
Tulsa, OK 74152
Telephone: 918-749-0632
FAX: 918-749-0635
E-mail: aferg@webzone.net
Web URL: www.hoganassessments.com
Tests: 168, 240

Hogrefe & Huber Publishers
P.O. Box 2487
Kirkland, WA 98083
Telephone: 800-228-3749
FAX: 425-823-8324
E-mail: HH@HHPUB.COM
Web URL: WWW.HHPUB.COM
Tests: 323

Houghton Mifflin Company
222 Berkeley Street
Boston, MA 02116-3764
Tests: 56

Human Resource Development Press
22 Amherst Road
Amherst, MA 01002–9709
Telephone: 800-822-2801
FAX: 413-253-3490
E-mail: marketing@hrdpress.com
Web URL: www.hrdpress.com
Tests: 70, 88, 96, 114, 124, 202, 225, 269, 270, 284, 465, 469, 476, 516

Human Sciences Research Council
Private Bag X41
Pretoria 0001, South Africa
Telephone: +(27) 12 - 302-2166
FAX: +(27) 12 - 302-2994
E-mail: DJFM@silwane.hsrc.ac.za
Tests: 274

Humanics Learning
P.O. Box 7400
Atlanta, GA 30357-0400
Telephone: 404-874-2176
FAX: 404-874-1976
E-mail: humanics@mindspring.com
Tests: 468

IDEA Center
Kansas State University
1615 Anderson Avenue
Manhattan, KS 66502-4073
Telephone: 785-532-5970
FAX: 785-532-5637
E-mail: IDEA@KSU.EDU
Web URL: WWW.IDEA.KSU.EDU
Tests: 172

Imaginart International, Inc.
307 Arizona Street
Bisbee, AZ 85603
Telephone: 520-432-5741
FAX: 520-432-5134
E-mail: IMAGINART@AOL.COM
Tests: 38, 386, 510

Insight Institute, Inc.
7205 NW Waukomis Drive
Kansas City, MO 64151
Telephone: 800-861-4769
FAX: 816-587-7198
E-mail: handleyp@aol.com
Tests: 179

The Institute for Matching Person & Technology, Inc.
486 Lake Road
Webster, NY 14580
Telephone: 716-671-3461
FAX: 716-671-3461
E-mail: impt97@aol.com
Web URL: members.aol.com/IMPT97/Mpt.html
Tests: 221

Institute for Somat Awareness
Michael Bernet, Ph.D.
1270 North Avenue, Suite 1-P
New Rochelle, NY 10804
Telephone: 914-633-1789
FAX: 914-633-3152
E-mail: mBernet@aol.com
Tests: 357

International Assessment Network
7600 France Avenue South, Suite #550
Minneapolis, MN 55435-5939
Tests: 218

International Association for the Study of Pain
909 NE 43rd Street, Suite 306
Seattle, WA 98105-6020
FAX: 206-547-6409
E-mail: IASP@LOCKE.HS.WASHINGTON.EDU
Web URL: www.halcyon.com/iasp
Tests: 227

International Learningworks®
1130 Main Avenue
P.O. Box 1310
Durango, CO 81302
Telephone: 800-344-0451
FAX: 970-385-7804
E-mail: learning@lorenet.com
Web URL: INTLLEARNINGWORKS.COM
Tests: 215, 442, 492, 506, 513

International Society for General Semantics
P.O. Box 728
Concord, CA 94522
Telephone: 925-798-0311
FAX: 925-798-0312
E-mail: ISGS@A.CRL.COM
Web URL: generalsemantics.com
Tests: 518, 519

International Training Consultants, Inc.
P.O. Box 35613
Richmond, VA 23235-0613
Tests: 210

JIST Works, Inc.
720 North Park Avenue
Indianapolis, IN 46202-3431
Telephone: 800-648-5478
FAX: 800-547-8329
E-mail: jistworks@aol.com
Web URL: www.jist.com
Tests: 409, 457

Jossey-Bass/Pfeiffer
350 Sansome, 5th Floor
San Francisco, CA 94104
Tests: 24, 44, 86, 185, 203, 204, 208, 213, 214, 443,
    460, 462, 493, 496

C. G. Jung Institute of San Francisco
2040 Gough Street
San Francisco, CA 94109
Tests: 475

Kendall/Hunt Publishing Company
4050 Westmark Drive
P.O. Box 1840
Dubuque, IA 52004-1840
Telephone: 800-228-0810
FAX: 800-772-9165
E-mail: orders@kendallhunt.com
Web URL: WWW.KENDALLHUNT.COM
Tests: 34

Dr. Donald L. Kirkpatrick
1920 Hawthorne Drive
Elm Grove, WI 53122
Telephone: 414-784-8348
FAX: 414-784-7994
Tests: 197

Kolbe Corp
3421 N. 44th Street
Phoenix, AZ 85018
Telephone: 602-840-9770
FAX: 602-952-2706
E-mail: info@kolbe.com
Web URL: www.kolbe.com
Tests: 200

Life Innovations, Inc.
P.O. Box 190
Minneapolis, MN 55440-0190
Telephone: 651-635-0511
FAX: 651-635-0716
E-mail: dolson@lifeinnovation.com
Web URL: lifeinnovation.com
Tests: 295

LIMRA International
P.O. Box 208
Hartford, CT 06141-0208
Tests: 358

Literacy Volunteers of America
635 James Street
Syracuse, NY 13203
Telephone: 315-472-0001
FAX: 315-472-0002
E-mail: lvanat@aol.com
Web URL: www.literacyvolunteers.org
Tests: 309, 459

MetriTech, Inc.
4106 Fieldstone Road
Champaign, IL 61821
Telephone: 800-747-4868
FAX: 217-398-5798
E-mail: mtinfo@metritech.com
Web URL: www.metritech.com
Tests: 5, 12

Miller & Tyler Limited
Psychological Assessment and Counselling
96 Greenway
London N20 8EJ
England
Telephone: 44-181-445-7463
FAX: 44-181-445-0143
Tests: 328

Mind Garden, Inc.
1690 Woodside Road, Suite #202
Redwood City, CA 94061
Telephone: 650-261-3500
FAX: 650-261-3505
E-mail: info@mindgarden.com
Tests: 59, 79, 106, 152, 223, 248, 258, 264, 302, 3134, 405, 413, 453, 487, 489

Modern Curriculum Press
4350 Equity Drive
Columbus, OH 43216
Tests: 119

Monaco & Associates
4125 Gage Center Drive, Suite 204
Topeka, KS 66604
Tests: 239

Moving Boundaries
1375 SW Blaine Court
Gresham, OR 97080
Telephone: 888-661-4433
FAX: 503-661-5304
E-mail: info@movingboundaries.com
Tests: 356

Multi-Health Systems, Inc.
908 Niagara Falls Blvd.
North Tonawanda, NY 14120-2060
Telephone: 416-424-1700
FAX: 416-424-1736
E-mail: CUSTOMERSERVICE@MHS.COM
Web URL: www.mhs.com
Tests: 32, 69, 78, 97, 98, 104, 110, 145, 147, 162, 169, 188, 205, 212, 246, 363, 378, 392, 449

Multiple Intelligences Research and Consulting, Inc.
1316 South Lincoln Street
Kent, OH 44240
Telephone: 330-673-8024
FAX: 330-673-8810
E-mail: sbranton@kent.edu
Web URL: www.angelfire.com/OH/THEMIDAS
Tests: 234

National Association of Secondary School Principals
P.O. Box 3250
1904 Association Drive
Reston, VA 22091-1598
Telephone: 800-253-7746 and 703-860-0200
FAX: 703-476-5432
E-mail: nassp@nassp.org
Web URL: www.nassp.org
Tests: 90

The National Center on Employment & Disability
P.O. Box 1358
Hot Springs, AR 71902
Tests: 426

National Clearinghouse of Rehabilitation Training Materials
5202 N. Richmond Hill Drive
Oklahoma State University
Stillwater, OK 74078-4080
Tests: 265

National Communication Association
5101 Backlick Road, Bldg. E
Annandale, VA 22003
Telephone: 703-750-0533
Web URL: www.natcom.org
Tests: 23, 89, 101

National Reading Styles Institute, Inc.
P.O. Box 737
Syosset, NY 11791-0737
Tests: 444

NCS [Minnetonka]
Sales Department
5605 Green Circle Drive
Minnetonka, MN 55343
Tests: 36, 60, 107, 153, 236, 273, 294, 304, 406, 508

New Standards, Inc.
8441 Wayzata Blvd., Suite 105
Minneapolis, MN 55426-1349
Telephone: 800-755-6299
FAX: 612-797-9993
E-mail: tjk@newstandards.com
Tests: 311

New Zealand Council for Educational Research
Education House West
178-182 Willis Street
Box 3237
Wellington 6000
Tests: 382

NFER-Nelson Publishing Co., Ltd.
Darville House
2 Oxford Road East
Windsor, Berkshire SL4 1DF
England
Tests: 319, 486

Norland Software
P.O. Box 84499
Los Angeles, CA 90073-0499
Telephone: 310-202-1832
FAX: 310-202-9431
E-mail: emiller@ucla.edu
Web URL: www.calcaprt.com
Tests: 58

Northern California Neurobehavioral Group, Inc.
909 Hyde Street, Suite #620
San Francisco, CA 94109-4835
Telephone: 415-922-5858
FAX: 415-922-5849
Tests: 81

Occupational Research Centre
"Highlands" Gravel Path
Berkhamsted, Hertfordshire HP4 2PQ
United Kingdom
Tests: 198

E. R. Oetting, Ph.D.
Psychology Department
Colorado State University
Fort Collins, CO 80523
Telephone: 970-491-1615
FAX: 970-491-0527
E-mail: goetting@lamar.colostate.edu
Tests: 262

P.D.P. Press, Inc.
12015 North July Avenue
Hugo, MN 55038
Telephone: 651-439-1638

FAX: 651-351-7361
E-mail: PRODEUPRY@AOL.COM
Web URL: MEMBERS.AOL.COM/PRODEUPRYL
Tests: 346

Personal Strengths Publishing
P.O. Box 2605
Carlsbad, CA 92018-2605
Telephone: 800-624-7347
FAX: 760-730-7368
E-mail: mail@PersonalStrengths.com
Web URL: www.PersonalStrengths.com
Tests: 371, 474, 497, 498, 499

Personnel Decisions, Inc.
2000 Plaza VII Tower
45 South Seventh Street
Minneapolis, MN 55402-1608
Tests: 278

Pinkerton Services Group
6100 Fairview Road, Suite 900
Charlotte, NC 28210-3277
Telephone: 800-528-5745
FAX: 704-554-1806
Web URL: www.pinkertons.com
Tests: 511

Preschool Skills Test
c/o Carol Lepera
P.O. Box 1246
Greenwood, IN 46142
Telephone: 317-881-7606
Tests: 296

PRO-ED
8700 Shoal Creek Blvd.
Austin, TX 78757-6897
Telephone: 800-897-3202
FAX: 512-451-8542
E-mail: proedrd2@aol.com
Web URL: WWW.PROEDINC.COM
Tests: 25, 30, 35, 39, 42, 84, 93, 113, 115, 117, 159,
160, 183, 193, 196, 201, 206, 238, 268, 291, 308,
324, 325, 333, 335, 336, 366, 384, 387, 388, 389,
390, 391, 393, 395, 400, 410, 417, 454, 522

Program Development Associates
P.O. Box 2038
Syracuse, NY 13220-2038
Telephone: 800-543-2119
FAX: 315-452-0710
E-mail: pdassoc@servtech.com
Web URL: www.PDAssoc.com
Tests: 515

Psychological Assessment Resources, Inc.
P.O. Box 998
Odessa, FL 33556-9908
Telephone: 800-331-8378
FAX: 800-727-9329
Web URL: www.parinc.com
Tests: 9, 47, 66, 72, 82, 100, 105, 122, 138, 182, 184,
247, 254, 260, 287, 288, 289, 301, 318, 320, 345,
347, 349, 370, 372, 402, 407, 419, 420

The Psychological Corporation
555 Academic Court
San Antonio, TX 78204-2498
Telephone: 800-211-8378
FAX: 800-232-1223
E-mail: customer_servicce@HBTPC.com
Web URL: www.HBEM.com
Tests: 37, 48, 54, 55, 57, 73, 75, 76, 85, 103, 120, 130,
149, 174, 177, 230, 231, 243, 256, 276, 307, 315,
316, 350, 375, 401, 412, 414, 415, 416

Psychological Growth Associates
Products Division
3813 Tiffany Drive
Lawrence, KS 66049
Telephone: 785-841-1141
FAX: 785-749-2190
E-mail: 73204.303@compuserve. com
Tests: 397

Psychological Publications, Inc.
P.O. Box 3577
Thousand Oaks, CA 91359-0577
Telephone: 800-345-8378
FAX: 805-373-1753
E-mail: TJTA@aol.com
Web URL: www.TJTA.com
Tests: 381

Psychological Services, Inc.
100 West Broadway, Suite #1100
Glendale, CA 91210
Telephone: 818-244-0033
FAX: 818-247-7223
Web URL: www.psionline.com
Tests: 137, 292

Rebus, Inc.
P.O. Box 4479
Ann Arbor, MI 48106-4479
Telephone: 800-435-3085
FAX: 734-665-4728
E-mail: MAIL@REBUSINC.COM
Web URL: WWW.REBUSINC.COM
Tests: 135

Renaissance Learning, Inc.
P.O. Box 8036
2911 Peach Street
Wisconsin Rapids, WI 54495-8036
Telephone: 800-338-4204
FAX: 715-424-4242
E-mail: answers@advlearn.com
Web URL: www.advlearn.com
Tests: 368

Research for Better Schools, Inc.
444 North Third Street
Philadelphia, PA 19123-4107
Telephone: 215-574-9300
FAX: 215-574-0133
E-mail: maguire@rbs.org
Web URL: www.rbs.org
Tests: 123

Risk & Needs Assessment, Inc.
P.O. Box 44828
Phoenix, AZ 85064-4828
Tests: 2, 125, 297, 332, 351, 353, 473

Riverside Publishing
425 Spring Lake Drive
Itasca, IL 60143-2079
Telephone: 800-323-9540
FAX: 630-467-7192
Web URL: WWW.RIVERPUB.COM
Tests: 46, 109, 224, 337, 396, 404, 422, 431, 471, 504

Scholastic Testing Service, Inc.
480 Meyer Road
Bensenville, IL 60106-1617
Tests: 80, 91, 166, 228

Search Institute
700 South 3rd Street, Suite 210
Minneapolis, MN 55415-1138
Telephone: 800-888-7828
FAX: 612-376-8956
Web URL: www.search-institute.org
Tests: 235

Selby MillSmith, Ltd.
30 Circus Mews
Bath BA1 2PW
United Kingdom
Telephone: +44 1225-446655
FAX: +44 1225-446643
E-mail: Info@SelbyMillSmith.com
Web URL: www.SelbyMillSmith.com
Tests: 139, 261, 343

Melvin Selzer, M.D.
6967 Paseo Laredo
La Jolla, CA 92037
Telephone: 619-459-1035
Tests: 232

Sensonics, Inc.
P.O. Box 112
Haddon Heights, NJ 08035
Telephone: 609-547-7702
FAX: 609-547-5665
Web URL: www.smelltest.com
Tests: 360

The Sidran Foundation
2328 West Joppa Road, Suite 15
Lutherville, MD 21093
Telephone: 410-825-8888
FAX: 410-337-0747
E-mail: sidran@sidran.org
Web URL: www.sidran.org
Tests: 8, 455

Sigma Assessment Systems, inc.
511 Fort Street, Suite 435
P.O. Box 610984
Port Huron, MI 48061-0984
Telephone: 800-265-1285
FAX: 800-361-9411
E-mail: SIGMA@sigmaassessmentsystems.com
Web URL: www.sigmaassessmentsystems.com
Tests: 20, 187

Slosson Educational Publications, Inc.
P.O. Box 280
East Aurora, NY 14052-0280
Tests: 359, 411

Sopris West
4093 Specialty Place
Longmont, CO 85040
Telephone: 800-547-6747
FAX: 303-776-5934
E-mail: WWW.SOPRISWEST.COM
Tests: 136, 472

Stoelting Co.
Oakwood Center
620 Wheat Lane
Wood Dale, IL 60191
Telephone: 630-860-9700
FAX: 630-860-9775
E-mail: psychtests@stoeltingco.com
Web URL: www.stoeltingco.com/tests
Tests: 211

Clifford R. Swensen
Department of Psychological Sciences
Purdue University
1364 Psychological Sciences Building
West Lafayette, IN 47907-1364
Telephone: 765-496-6977
FAX: 765-496-2670
E-mail: cswensen@psych.purdue.edu
Tests: 334

Swets Test Publishers
P.O. Box 820
2160 Sz Lisse
The Netherlands
Telephone: +31 252 435375
FAX: +31 252 435671
E-mail: STP@SWETS.NL
Web URL: WWW.SWETS.NL/
Tests: 385

Teachers College Press
Teachers College
Columbia University
525 W. 120th Street, Box 303
New York, NY 10027
Telephone: 212-678-3929
FAX: 212-678-4149
E-mail: puciatc@exchange.tc.columbia.edu
Web URL: www.tc.columbia.edu
Tests: 133, 399

Teleometrics International
1755 Woodstead Court
The Woodlands, TX 77380-0964
Tests: 173, 290, 305, 330, 331, 501, 507

Thames Valley Test Company, Ltd.
7-9 The Green
Flempton
Bury St. Edmunds, Suffolk IP28 6EL
England
Telephone: +44 1284 728608
FAX: +44 1284 728166
E-mail: TVTC@MSN.COM
Web URL: www.tvtc.com
Tests: 43, 321

Therapy Skill Builders—A Division of The Psycho-
    logical Corporation
555 Academic Court
San Antonio, TX 78204-2498
Telephone: 800-211-8378
FAX: 800-232-1223
Web URL: www.hbtpc.com
Tests: 77, 99, 131, 175, 178, 263, 340, 342, 399

Touchstone Applied Science Associates (TASA), Inc.
4 Hardscrabble Heights
P.O. Box 382
Brewster, NY 10509-0382
Web URL: WWW.TASA.COM
Tests: 111

Training House, Inc.
22 Amherst Road
Pelham, Ma 01002-9745
Telephone: 609-452-1505
FAX: 609-452-2790
E-mail: training@traininghouse.com
Web URL: www.traininghouse.com
Tests: 432, 458, 470, 482, 500, 517

Trust Tutoring
912 Thayer Avenue, Suite #205
Silver Spring, MD 20910
Telephone: 301-589-0733 or 800-301-3131
FAX: 301-589-0733 *51
E-mail: HAVIS@EROLS.COM
Web URL: WWW.WDN.COM/TRUST
Tests: 142

Universal Attention Disorders, Inc.
4281 Katella Avenue, #215
Los Alamitos, CA 90720
Telephone: 800-729-2886
FAX: 714-229-8782
E-mail: info@tovatest.com
Web URL: www.tovatest.com
Tests: 394

University of Maryland
University Counseling Center
Shoemaker Hall
College Park, MD 20742
Tests: 259

University of Minnesota Press
Test Division
Mill Place, Suite 290
111 Third Avenue South
Minneapolis, MN 55401-2520
Telephone: 612-627-1963
FAX: 612-627-1980
Web URL: www.upress.umn.edu/tests
Tests: 338

Village Publishing
73 Valley Drive
Furlong, PA 18925
Tests: 1, 26, 438, 490

Vine Publishing, Ltd.
10 Elgin Rd.
Bournemouth BH4 9NL
United Kingdom
Telephone: 011-44-1202-761766
FAX: 011-44-1202-761766
Tests: 312

Virtual Knowledge
200 Highland Avenue
Needham, MA 02194
Tests: 64

Otto Weininger
Ontario Institute for Studies in Education
The University of Toronto
252 Bloor Street West
Toronto, Ontario M5S 1V6
Canada
Telephone: 416-929-2348
FAX: 416-929-3440
Tests: 121

Western Psychological Services
12031 Wilshire Blvd.
Los Angeles, CA 90025-1251
Telephone: 310-478-2061
FAX: 310-478-7838
Tests: 3, 7, 45, 50, 74, 161, 170, 192, 216, 219, 220, 226, 250, 257, 317, 322, 329, 361, 362, 398, 436

Wide Range, Inc.
P.O. Box 3410
Wilmington, DE 19804-0250
Tests: 418

Wintergreen/Orchard House, Inc.
425 Spring Lake Drive
Itasca, IL 60143-2076
Tests: 466

Wonderlic, Inc.
1795 N. Butterfield Road
Libertyville, IL 60048-1238
Telephone: 800-323-3742
FAX: 847-680-9492
E-mail: testingservices@wonderlic.com
Web URL: www.wonderlic.com
Tests: 92, 141, 164, 421

World Health Organization
[Address Unknown]
Switzerland
Tests: 15

INDEX OF NAMES

This index indicates whether a citation refers to authorship of a test, a test review, or a reviewer's reference for a specific test. Numbers refer to test entries, not to pages. The abbreviations and numbers following the names may be interpreted as follows: "test, 73" indicates authorship of test 73; "rev, 86" indicates authorship of a review of test 86; "ref, 45" indicates a reference in one of the "Reviewer's References" sections for test 45. Names mentioned in cross references are also indexed.

SCORE INDEX

This Score Index lists all the scores, in alphabetical order, for all the tests included in The Fourteenth Mental Measurements Yearbook. *Because test scores can be regarded as operational definitions of the variable measured, sometimes the scores provide better leads to what a test actually measures than the test title or other available information. The Score Index is very detailed, and the reader should keep in mind that a given variable (or concept) of interest may be defined in several different ways. Thus the reader should look up these several possible alternative definitions before drawing final conclusions about whether tests measuring a particular variable of interest can be located in this volume. If the kind of score sought is located in a particular test or tests, the reader should then read the test descriptive information carefully to determine whether the test(s) in which the score is found is (are) consistent with reader purpose. Used wisely, the Score Index can be another useful resource in locating the right score in the right test. As usual, all numbers in the index are test numbers, not page numbers.*